# DICTIONARY

# OF CANADIAN

# BIOGRAPHY

## INDEX

VOLUMES I TO XII
1000 TO 1900

UNIVERSITY OF TORONTO PRESS
Toronto   Buffalo   London

© University of Toronto Press and
Les Presses de l'université Laval, 1991
Printed in Canada

ISBN 0-8020-3464-0 (regular edition)

**Canadian Cataloguing in Publication Data**
Main entry under title:

Dictionary of Canadian biography: index, volumes I to XII, 1000 to 1900

Regular ed.
Supplement to: Dictionary of Canadian biography.
Regular ed.
Issued also in French.
ISBN 0-8020-3464-0

1. Dictionary of Canadian biography – Indexes.
2. Canada – Biography – Indexes.

FC25.D52 1991      920.071      C90-095482-5
F1005.D52 1991

# Contents

# Introduction

The *Index, volumes I to XII* fulfils a hope on the part of the *Dictionary of Canadian biography/Dictionnaire biographique du Canada* to offer to users, both specialists and general readers, a cumulative index when it had published a continuous series of volumes up to 1900. This series was completed with the publication of volume XII in the spring of 1990. The 12 volumes contain the biographies of 6,520 persons who died or flourished up to and including the year 1900. A list of the volumes and the periods covered is provided on page 2.

This cumulative *Index* is in two parts. The first provides a list of Subjects of Biographies, arranged alphabetically. The chronological arrangement of volumes according to death dates has had important benefits for the DCB/DBC because it has made possible insights into social groups and concerns of different periods. But readers do not carry death dates in their memories and 12 volumes present a challenge in locating biographies. The *Index* answers this need and also allows a general overview of the contents of the whole series.

The second part of the *Index*, the Cumulative Nominal Index, brings together the names of all individuals mentioned in the 6,520 biographies. It is a vast web of references and cross-references which stretches across the volumes.

Preparation of the *Index* has been made possible through the generous grant of the Social Sciences and Humanities Research Council of Canada for work on the DCB/DBC project in 1985–90 and also by the timely and welcome assistance of a grant in 1990 from the Ministry of Culture and Communications of the Province of Ontario.

FRANCESS G. HALPENNY

JEAN HAMELIN

# SUBJECTS OF BIOGRAPHIES

# Subjects of Biographies

Dates are provided in this list of subjects in order to identify the volume in which a biography may be found. In a few cases a biography does not appear in the appropriate volume and the location of the entry is given. When a death date was determined after the publication of an entry, the correct date is provided.

Individuals are listed only under the name used for the entry of the biography and variants are not included. Indigenous people, for example, are usually entered under their names in their native tongue. As a result, when trying to locate biographies, readers should also consult the Cumulative Nominal Index where names are fully cross-referenced.

ABBADIE de Saint-Castin, Bernard-Anselme d', Baron de Saint-Castin (1689–1720)

Abbadie de Saint-Castin, Jean-Vincent d', Baron de Saint-Castin (1652–1707)

Abbadie de Saint-Castin, Joseph d', Baron de Saint-Castin (fl. 1720–46)

Abbott, Job (1845–96)

Abbott, Sir John Joseph Caldwell (1821–93)

Abbott, Joseph (d. 1862)

Abbott, Wilson Ruffin (1801–76)

Abercrombie, James (1732–75)

Abercromby, James (1706–81)

Abishabis (d. 1843)

Abraham, John (fl. 1672–89)

Abrams, William (d. 1844)

A-ca-oo-mah-ca-ye (d. 1859 or 1860)

Acheson, Archibald, 2nd Earl of Gosford (1776–1849)

Achintre, Auguste (1834–86)

Acoutsina (fl. 1717–19)

Adams, John (fl. 1710–45)

Adams, Joseph (d. 1737)

Adams, Mary Electa (1823–98)

Adamson, William Agar (1800–68)

Addison, Robert (1754–1829)

Adhémar, Jean-Baptiste (d. 1754)

Adhémar, Jean-Baptiste-Amable (1736–1800)

Adhémar, *dit* Saint-Martin, Toussaint-Antoine (1740–1804)

Adhémar de Lantagnac, Gaspard (1681–1756)

Adhémar de Saint-Martin, Antoine (d. 1714)

Aernoutsz, Jurriaen (fl. 1674)

Agariata (fl. 1666)

Agnew, Stair (d. 1821)

Agrain, Jean-Antoine d', Comte d'Agrain (d. 1722)

Agramonte, Juan de (fl. 1511)

Ahatsistari (d. 1642)

Aide-Créquy, Jean-Antoine (1749–80)

Aigron, *dit* Lamothe, Pierre (fl. 1660–85)

Aikins, William Thomas (1827–97)

Ailleboust, Charles-Joseph d' (d. 1761)

Ailleboust d'Argenteuil, Pierre d' (1659–1711)

Ailleboust de Cerry, Philippe-Marie d' (1702–87)

Ailleboust de Coulonge et d'Argentenay, Louis d' (d. 1660)

Ailleboust de La Madeleine, François-Jean-Daniel d' (1702–93)

Ailleboust de Manthet, Nicolas d' (d. 1709)

Ailleboust de Périgny, Paul d' (d. 1746)

Ailleboust Des Muceaux, Charles-Joseph d' (d. 1700)

Ailleboust Des Muceaux, Jean-Baptiste d' (1666–1730)

Ainse, Sarah (Montour; Maxwell; Willson) (d. *c.* 1823)

Ainslie, George Robert (1776–1839)

Ainslie, Thomas (1729–1806)

Ainsse, Joseph-Louis (1744–1802)

Aird, James (d. 1819)

Aisance, John (d. 1847)

Aitken, Alexander (d. 1799)

Akins, Thomas Beamish (1809–91)

Akomápis, Nicholas (fl. 1778–80)

Alavoine, Charles (d. 1764)

Albanel, Charles (d. 1696)

Alberni, Pedro de (1747–1802)

Albro, John (1764–1839)

Alcalá-Galiano, Dionisio (1762–1805)

Alden, John (d. 1701/2)

Alder, Robert (1796–1873)

Aldridge, Christopher (d. 1745/46)

Aldridge, Christopher (d. 1760)

Alexander, James Lynne (1801–79)

Alexander, Robert (1822–84)

Alexander, William, Earl of Stirling (d. 1640)

Alexander, Sir William (d. 1638)

Aleyrac, Jean-Baptiste d' (1737–96)

Allain, Jean-Baptiste (1739–1812)

Allamand, Jeanne-Charlotte (Berczy) (1760–1839)

Allan, Ebenezer (1752–1813)

Allan, Sir Hugh (1810–82)

Allan, John (1747–1805)

Allan, Peter John (1825–48)
Allan, William (d. 1853)
Allanson, John (d. 1853)
Allard, Ovid (1817–74)
Allard de Sainte-Marie, Jean-Joseph d' (d. 1730)
Allard de Sainte-Marie, Philippe-Joseph d'
  (d. 1778)
Allart, Germain (1618–85)
Allcock, Henry (d. 1808)
Allemand, Pierre (d. 1691)
Allen, Sir John Campbell (1817–98)
Allenou de Lavillangevin, René-Jean (d. 1753)
Allet, Antoine d' (fl. 1657–93)
Alleyn, Charles Joseph (1817–90)
Alline, Henry (1748–84)
Allison, Charles Frederick (1795–1858)
Allouez, Claude (1622–89)
Allsopp, George (d. 1805)
Allsopp, George Waters (d. 1837)
Almon, Mather Byles (1796–1871)
Almon, William Bruce (1787–1840)
Almon, William James (1755–1817)
Aloigny, Charles-Henri d', Marquis de La Groye
  (d. 1714)
Alquier de Servian, Jean d' (fl. 1710–61)
Alsop, Robert (1814–71)
Alston, Edward Graham (1832–72)
Amantacha (d. c. 1636)
Ameau, dit Saint-Séverin, Séverin (1620–1715)
Amherst, Elizabeth Frances (Hale) (1774–1826)
Amherst, Jeffery, 1st Baron Amherst (1717/18–97)
Amiot, Charles (1636–69)
Amiot, Jean (d. 1648)
Amiot, Jean-Baptiste (fl. 1720–63)
Amiot, Jean-Baptiste (1717–69)
Amiot, Laurent (1764–1839)
Amiot, Noël-Laurent (1793–1845)
Amiot, dit Villeneuve, Mathieu (d. 1688)
Amiot de Vincelotte, Charles-Joseph (1665–1735)
Amyot, Guillaume (1843–96)
Anadabijou (fl. 1603–11)
Anandamoakin (fl. 1756–72)
Anderson, Alexander Caulfield (1814–84)
Anderson, David (1814–85)
Anderson, James (1812–67)
Anderson, John (fl. 1850–62)
Anderson, Robert (1803–96)
Anderson, Samuel (1839–81)
Anderson, Thomas (d. 1696)
Anderson, Thomas Brown (1796–1873)
Anderson, Thomas Gummersall (1779–1875)
Anderson, William James (1812–73)
Andigné de Grandfontaine, Hector d' (d. 1696)
André, Alexis (1832–93)
André, Louis (1631–1715)
André de Leigne, Louise-Catherine (Hertel de
  Rouville) (1709–66)

André de Leigne, Pierre (1663–1748)
Andrews, Israel de Wolfe (1813–71)
Andrews, Samuel (1737–1818)
Angeac, François-Gabriel d' (1708–82)
Angers, François-Réal (1812–60)
Angibault, dit Champdoré, Pierre (fl. 1604–8)
Anglin, Timothy Warren (1822–96)
Ango Des Maizerets, Louis (1636–1721)
Angwin, Maria Louisa (1849–98)
Annand, William (1808–87)
Annaotaha (d. 1660)
Annenraes (d. 1654)
Ansley, Amos (d. 1837)
Anspach, Lewis Amadeus (1770–1823)
Anthony, Gabriel (d. 1846)
Antrobus, Edmund William Romer (1795–1852)
Antrobus, John (d. 1820)
Aouenano (fl. 1699–1701)
Api-kai-ees (d. 1897)
Aplin, Joseph (d. 1804)
Appleton, Thomas (fl. 1818–35)
Aprendestiguy de Martignon, Martin d'
  (fl. 1656–86)
Apthorp, Alexander (d. c. 1720)
Aradgi (fl. 1700–2)
Arbuthnot, Mariot (1711–94)
Archambault, Paul-Loup (1787–1858)
Archambault, Pierre-Urgel (1812–71)
Archambeault, Louis (1814–90)
Archibald, Sir Adams George (1814–92)
Archibald, Charles Dickson (1802–68)
Archibald, Sir Edward Mortimer (1810–84)
Archibald, Samuel George William (1777–1846)
Archibald, Thomas Dickson (1813–90)
Argall, Sir Samuel (d. 1626)
Arimph, Jean-Baptiste (fl. 1776–78)
Armour, Rebecca Agatha (Thompson) (1845–91)
Armour, Robert (1781–1857)
Arms, William (1794–1853)
Armstrong, Sir Alexander (1818–99)
Armstrong, George (1821–88)
Armstrong, James Rogers (1787–1873)
Armstrong, James Sherrard (1821–88)
Armstrong, John Belmer (d. 1892)
Armstrong, Lawrence (1664–1739)
Armstrong, Sir Richard (d. 1854)
Arnaud, Jean-Charles d' (fl. 1722–52)
Arnaud, Marie-Marguerite-Daniel, named
  Saint-Arsène (1699–1764)
Arnold, Benedict (1741/42–1801)
Arnold, Oliver (1755–1834)
Arnold, William (fl. 1713–16)
Arnold, William (1804–57)
Arnoldi, Daniel (1774–1849)
Arnoldi, Michael (1763–1807)
Arnoldi, Phebe named de Sainte-Angèle (Diehl)
  (1767–1825)

Arnoux, André (d. 1760)
Arraud, Jacques-Victor (1805–78)
Arrigrand, Gratien d', Sieur de La Majour
    (b. 1684, d. in or after 1754)
Arsac de Ternay, Charles-Henri-Louis d'
    (1723– 80)
Arsenault, Joseph-Octave (1828–97)
Arthur, Sir George (1784–1854)
Ash, John (d. 1886)
Ashe, Edward David (d. 1895)
Askin, John (1739–1815)
Askin, John Baptist (1788–1869)
Assiginack, Jean-Baptiste (d. 1866)
Assikinack, Francis (1824–63)
Asticou (fl. 1608–16)
Atecouando (fl. 1701–26)
Atecouando (fl. 1749–57)
Atiatoharongwen (d. 1814)
Atironta (fl. 1615)
Atironta (d. 1650)
Atironta (d. 1672)
Atkinson, George (d. 1792)
Atkinson, George (1777–1830)
Atwater, Edwin (1808–74)
Auber, Claude (d. 1694)
Aubert, Pierre (1814–90)
Aubert, Thomas (fl. 1508)
Aubert de Gaspé, Ignace-Philippe (1714–87)
Aubert de Gaspé, Philippe-Joseph (1786–1871)
Aubert de Gaspé, Pierre-Ignace (1758–1823)
Aubert de La Chesnaye, Charles (1632–1702)
Aubert de La Chesnaye, François (d. 1725)
Aubert de La Chesnaye, Louis (1690–1745)
Aubery, Joseph (1673–1756)
Aubin, Napoléon (1812–90)
Aubry, Nicolas (fl. 1604–11)
Auchagah (fl. 1729)
Auclair, Joseph (1813–87)
Audouart, *dit* Saint-Germain, Guillaume
    (fl. 1648–63)
Auffray, Charles-Dominique (1794–1837)
Augé, Étienne (d. 1780)
Auger de Subercase, Daniel d' (1661–1732)
Auld, William (fl. 1790–1830)
Auldjo, Alexander (1758–1821)
Auldjo, George (1790–1846)
Aulneau, Jean-Pierre (1705–36)
Aumasson de Courville, Louis-Léonard, known
    as Sieur de Courville (fl. 1723–82)
Aumond, Joseph-Ignace (1810–79)
Auoindaon (fl. 1623)
Austin, Sir Horatio Thomas (1801–65)
Austin, James (1813–97)
Avaugour, Louis d' (1669–1732)
Aveneau, Claude (1650–1711)
Aw-gee-nah (fl. 1771–1821)
Aylen, Peter (1799–1868)

Aylwin, Thomas (d. 1791)
Aylwin, Thomas Cushing (1806–71)
Ayre, William (d. 1855)

BABBITT, John (1845–89)
Babey, Peter Paul Toney (fl. 1849–55)
Babie, Jacques (d. 1688)
Babineau, François-Xavier (1825–90)
Baby, Charles-François-Xavier (1794–1864)
Baby, François (1733–1820)
Baby, François (1768–1852)
Baby, James (1763–1833)
Baby, *dit* Dupéront, Jacques (d. 1789)
Bachand, Pierre (1835–78)
Back, Sir George (1796–1878)
Baddeley, Frederick Henry (1794–1879)
Badeaux, Jean-Baptiste (1741–96)
Badeaux, Joseph (1777–1835)
Badelard, Philippe-Louis-François (1728–1802)
Badgley, Francis (1767–1841)
Badgley, Francis (1807–63)
Badgley, William (1801–88)
Baffin, William (d. 1622)
Bagg, Stanley Clark (1820–73)
Bagnall, James (d. 1855)
Bagot, Sir Charles (1781–1843)
Baile, Joseph-Alexandre (1801–88)
Bailey, Jacob (1731–1808)
Baillairgé, François (1759–1830)
Baillairgé, Jean (1726–1805)
Baillairgé, Louis de Gonzague (1808–96)
Baillairgé, Pierre-Florent (1761–1812)
Baillairgé, Thomas (1791–1859)
Baillargeon, Charles-François (1798–1870)
Baillie, Thomas (1796–1863)
Baillie Hamilton, Ker (1804–89)
Baillif, Claude (d. *c.* 1698)
Bailloquet, Pierre (1613–92)
Bailly, Guillaume (d. 1696)
Bailly, Joseph (1774–1835)
Bailly, *dit* Lafleur, François (d. 1690)
Bailly de Messein, Charles-François (1740–94)
Bain, Francis (1842–94)
Baird, Edmond (1802–59)
Baird, John (1795–1858)
Baird, Nicol Hugh (1796–1849)
Baird, William Teel (d. 1897)
Baker, Charles (1743–1835)
Baker, Hugh Cossart (1818–59)
Baker, Loran Ellis (1831–99)
Baldwin, Augustus Warren (1776–1866)
Baldwin, Connell James (1777–1861)
Baldwin, Robert (1804–58)
Baldwin, William Henry (1827–94)
Baldwin, William Warren (1775–1844)
Baley, Henry (d. 1701)
Balfour, James (1731–1809)

5

Balfour, William Douglas (1851–96)
Ball, Ingram (1752–1807)
Ballantyne, Robert Michael (1825–94)
Ballenden, John (d. 1856)
Bamford, Stephen (1770–1848)
Bangs, Nathan (1778–1862)
Banks, Sir Joseph (1742/43–1820)
Bannatyne, Andrew Graham Ballenden (1829–89)
Bannerman, Sir Alexander (1788–1864)
Baptist, George (1808–75)
Baraga, Frederic (1797–1868)
Barbel, Jacques (d. 1740)
Barbel, Marie-Anne (Fornel) (1704–93)
Barber, George Anthony (1802–74)
Barber, Polly (Scovill) (1803–98)
Barbier, Louis-Marie-Raphaël (1792–1852)
Barbier, Marie, named de l'Assomption (d. 1739)
Barclay, George (d. 1857)
Barclay, John (1795–1826)
Barclay, Robert Heriot (1786–1837)
Barclay, Thomas Henry (1753–1830)
Bardy, Pierre-Martial (1797–1869)
Barker, Edward John (1799–1884)
Barker, William (d. 1894)
Barkley, Charles William (1759–1832)
Barlow, Robert (1813–83)
Barlow, Thomas (1788–1844)
Barnard, Édouard-André (1835–98)
Barnard, Francis Jones (1829–89)
Barnard, John (1681–1770)
Barnes, John (d. 1810)
Barnes, Richard (1805–46)
Barnston, George (d. 1883)
Barnston, James (1831–58)
Barolet, Claude (d. 1761)
Barr, Robert (1831–97)
Barrat, Claude (fl. 1681–1711)
Barrett, Alfred (d. 1849)
Barrett, Michael (1816–87)
Barrie, Sir Robert (1774–1841)
Barrin de La Galissonière, Roland-Michel, Marquis de La Galissonière (1693–1756)
Barry, James (1795–1865)
Barry, John Alexander (d. 1872)
Barry, Robert (d. 1843)
Barsalou, Jean-Baptiste (1706–76)
Barsalou, Joseph (1822–97)
Barss, John (1778–1851)
Barss, Joseph (1776–1824)
Barthe, Georges-Isidore (1834–1900)
Barthe, Joseph-Guillaume (1816–93)
Barthélemy (fl. 1687)
Barthélemy, Michel (1638–1706)
Bartlett, William Henry (1809–54)
Basquet, Pierre (fl. 1841–52)
Basset, David (d. 1724)
Basset, Jean (d. 1715)

Basset Des Lauriers, Bénigne (d. 1699)
Basset Du Tartre, Vincent (fl. 1665–68)
Bastarache, *dit* Basque, Michel (1730–1820)
Bastide, John Henry (fl. 1711–70)
Bâtard, Étienne (fl. 1750–53)
Bates, Walter (1760–1842)
Batiscan (fl. 1610–29)
Batt, Isaac (d. 1791)
Baudeau, Pierre (1643–1708)
Baudoin, Gervais (1686–1752)
Baudoin, Jean (d. 1698)
Baudouin, Gervais (d. 1700)
Baudouin, Michel (1691–1768)
Baudrand, Fleury (1811–53)
Baudry, Marie-Victoire, named de la Croix (1782–1846)
Baudry, *dit* Des Butes, Guillaume (1657–1732)
Baudry, *dit* Saint-Martin, Jean-Baptiste (d. 1755)
Baudry de Lamarche, Jacques (fl. 1676–1738)
Baugy, Louis-Henri de, known as Chevalier de Baugy (d. 1720)
Bauzhi-geezhig-waeshikum (d. 1841 or 1842)
Baveux, Jean-Claude-Léonard (1796–1865)
Bayard, Robert (1788–1868)
Bayfield, Henry Wolsey (1795–1885)
Bayly, Charles (fl. 1630–80)
Bayne, Daniel (d. 1769)
Bayne, John (1806–59)
Baynes, Sir Robert Lambert (1796–1869)
Bazalgette, John (1784–1868)
Bazil, Louis (1695–1752)
Bazire, Charles (1624–77)
Beach, Thomas Billis (1841–94)
Beale, Anthony (d. 1731)
Beamer, Jacob R. (fl. 1837–47)
Bean, John (fl. 1751–57)
Beardsley, Bartholomew Crannell (1775–1855)
Beardsley, John (1732–1809)
Beare, James (fl. 1577–85)
Beasley, Richard (1761–1842)
Beatson, Patrick (1758–1800)
Beatty, William (1835–98)
Beaty, James (1798–1892)
Beaubien, Joseph-Octave (1824–77)
Beaubien, Marguerite (1797–1848)
Beaubien, Pierre (1796–1881)
Beaubois, Nicolas-Ignace de (1689–1770)
Beauchemin, Charles-Odilon (1822–87)
Beaudry, Jean-Louis (1809–86)
Beaudry, Joseph-Ubalde (1816–76)
Beauharnois de Beaumont et de Villechauve, Claude de (1674–1738)
Beauharnois de La Boische, Charles de, Marquis de Beauharnois (d. 1749)
Beauharnois de La Chaussaye, François de, Baron de Beauville (d. 1746)
Beaulieu, François (1771–1872)

Beaumont, William Rawlins (1803–75)
Beaussier de Lisle, Louis-Joseph (d. 1765)
Beauvais, *dit* Saint-James, René (1785–1837)
Beaven, James (1801–75)
Bécart de Granville et de Fonville, Charles (d. 1703)
Bécart de Granville et de Fonville, Paul (1695–1754)
Becher, Henry Corry Rowley (1817–85)
Becket, John C. (1810–79)
Beckwith, John Adolphus (1800–80)
Beckwith, John Charles (1789–1862)
Beckwith, Julia Catherine (Hart) (1796–1867)
Beckwith, Sir Thomas Sydney (1772–1831)
Becquet, Romain (d. 1682)
Bédard, Elzéar (1799–1849)
Bédard, Jean-Baptiste (1761–1818)
Bédard, Jean-Charles (1766–1825)
Bédard, Joseph-Isidore (1806–33)
Bédard, Pierre-Stanislas (1762–1829)
Bédard, Thomas-Laurent (1747–95)
Beddome, Henry Septimus (d. 1881)
Bedout, Jacques (1751–1818)
Bedson, Samuel Lawrence (1842–91)
Beechey, Frederick William (1796–1856)
Beers, William George (1841–1900)
Begbie, Sir Matthew Baillie (1819–94)
Begg, Alexander (1839–97)
Bégon de La Cour, Claude-Michel (1683–1748)
Bégon de La Picardière, Michel (1667–1747)
Begourat (fl. 1603)
Bélanger, Alexis (1808–68)
Bélanger, François-Xavier (1833–82)
Bélanger, Horace (1836–92)
Belcher, Andrew (1763–1841)
Belcher, Benjamin (1743–1802)
Belcher, Clement Horton (1801–69)
Belcher, Sir Edward (1799–1877)
Belcher, Jonathan (1710–76)
Belford, Charles (1837–80)
Bell, Andrew (1803–56)
Bell, Andrew (fl. 1827–63)
Bell, Herbert (1818–76)
Bell, Hugh (1780–1860)
Bell, James (d. 1814)
Bell, John (1788–1855)
Bell, John (d. 1868)
Bell, Joshua (d. 1863)
Bell, Mathew (d. 1849)
Bell, Robert (1821–73)
Bell, Robert (1808–94)
Bell, William (1806–44)
Bell, William (1780–1857)
Belleau, Sir Narcisse-Fortunat (1808–94)
Bellecourt, George-Antoine (1803–74)
Bellenger, Étienne (fl. 1580–84)
Bellenger, Joseph-Marie (1788–1856)

Bellerose, Joseph-Hyacinthe (1820–99)
Bellet, François (1750–1827)
Bellingham, Sydney Robert (1808–1900)
Bellot, Joseph-René (1826–53)
Bellot, *dit* Lafontaine (fl. 1664–67)
Belvèze, Paul-Henry de (1801–75)
Beman, Elisha (1760–1821)
Bemister, John (1815–92)
Bénard, Michel (fl. 1733–60)
Bendixen, Fanny (d. 1899)
Benedict, Roswell Gardinier (1815–59)
Benjamin, Alfred David (1848–1900)
Benjamin, George (1799–1864)
Bennett, Charles James Fox (1793–1883)
Bennett, George (d. 1880)
Bennett, Thomas (d. 1872)
Bennett, William (d. 1857)
Benning, Clement Pitt (1785–1865)
Benoist, Antoine-Gabriel-François (1715–76)
Benoît, Olivier-David (1837–97)
Benoît, Pierre (d. 1786)
Benoît, *dit* Livernois, Jules-Isaïe (1830–65)
Benson, William John Chapman (d. 1850)
Benson, William Thomas (1824–85)
Bentley, Elijah (fl. 1799–1814)
Bentley, John (d. 1813)
Bentom, Clark (d. *c.* 1820)
Berbudeau, Jean-Gabriel (1709–92)
Berczy, Charles Albert (1794–1858)
Berczy, William (d. 1813)
Berczy, William Bent (1791–1873)
Berger, Jean (fl. 1704–9)
Bergier, Clerbaud (fl. 1680–85)
Bergier, Marc (d. 1707)
Bergin, Darby (1826–96)
Berkeley, Sir George Cranfield (1753–1818)
Berley, George (d. *c.* 1720)
Bermen, Laurent (fl. 1647–49)
Bermen de La Martinière, Claude de (1636–1719)
Bermen de La Martinière, Claude-Antoine de (1700–61)
Bernard, Aldis (d. 1876)
Bernard, Hewitt (1825–93)
Bernard, Noël (fl. 1781–1801)
Bernard, Philip (fl. 1786)
Bernard de La Rivière, Hilaire (d. 1729)
Bernier, Benoît-François (1720–99)
Bernières, Henri de (d. 1700)
Berry, Sir John (1635–89/90)
Berry, Jonathan (1787–1878)
Berthelet, Antoine-Olivier (1798–1872)
Berthelet, Pierre (1746–1830)
Berthelot, Amable (1777–1847)
Berthelot, Hector (1842–95)
Berthelot Dartigny, Michel-Amable (1738–1815)
Berthier, Isaac (1638–1708)
Berthon, George Theodore (1806–92)

Bertier, Michel (1695–1740)
Berton, George Frederick Street (1808–40)
Bertram, George Hope (1847–1900)
Bertrand, Charles (1824–96)
Bertrand, Joseph-Laurent (1741–1813)
Beschefer, Thierry (1630–1711)
Besnard, *dit* Carignant, Jean-Louis (1743–91)
Besserer, Louis-Théodore (1785–1861)
Best, George (d. 1583/84)
Best, George (d. 1829)
Bethune, Alexander Neil (1800–79)
Bethune, Angus (1783–1858)
Bethune, Donald (1802–69)
Bethune, James Gray (1793–1841)
Bethune, John (1751–1815)
Bethune, John (1791–1872)
Bethune, Norman (1822–92)
Bethune, Robert Henry (1836–95)
Bétournay, Louis (1825–79)
Bettridge, William Craddock (1791–1879)
Betzner, Samuel D. (1771–1856)
Bevan, William (fl. 1723–37)
Biard, Pierre (d. 1622)
Bibaud, François-Maximilien (1823–87)
Bibaud, Michel (1782–1857)
Bibb, Henry Walton (1815–54)
Bidwell, Barnabas (1763–1833)
Bidwell, Marshall Spring (1799–1872)
Biencourt de Poutrincourt et de Saint-Just, Jean de (1557–1615)
Biencourt de Saint-Just, Charles de (d. 1623 or 1624)
Bigault d'Aubreville, Louis-Nicolas-Emmanuel de (fl. 1791–1828)
Bigot, François (d. 1708)
Bigot, François (d. 1778)
Bigot, Jacques (1651–1711)
Bigot, Vincent (1649–1720)
Bigsby, John Jeremiah (1792–1881)
Bill, Ingraham Ebenezer (1805–91)
Billaudèle, Pierre-Louis (1796–1869)
Billings, Elkanah (1820–76)
Billings, Joseph (d. 1806)
Binney, Hibbert (1819–87)
Binney, Jonathan (1723/24–1807)
Binney, Stephen (1805–72)
Binns, Charles (d. 1847)
Birchall, Reginald (1866–90)
Bird, Curtis James (d. 1876)
Bird, James (d. 1856)
Bird, James (d. 1892)
Bird, Thomas (d. 1739)
Birdsall, Richard (1799–1852)
Birrell, John (1815–75)
Bisaillon, Peter (d. 1742)
Bishop, Nathaniel (d. 1723)
Bisshopp, Cecil (1783–1813)

Bissot, François-Joseph (1673–1737)
Bissot de Vinsenne, François-Marie (1700–36)
Bissot de Vinsenne, Jean-Baptiste (1668–1719)
Bizard, Jacques (1642–92)
Bjarni Herjólfsson (fl. 986)
Black, Edward (1793–1845)
Black, George (d. 1854)
Black, Henry (1798–1873)
Black, James (1797–1886)
Black, John (fl. 1786–1819)
Black, John (d. 1823)
Black, John (1817–79)
Black, John (1818–82)
Black, Martin Gay (1786–1861)
Black, Samuel (d. 1841)
Black, William (1760–1834)
Black, William (1771–1866)
Blackadar, Hugh William (1808–63)
Blackburn, Josiah (1823–90)
Blackman, Charles (d. 1853)
Blackwood, John (d. 1819)
Blackwood, Thomas (1773–1842)
Blaiklock, Henry Musgrave (1790–1843)
Blain de Saint-Aubin, Emmanuel-Marie (1833–83)
Blais, Michel (d. 1783)
Blaise Des Bergères de Rigauville, Nicolas (1679–1739)
Blaise Des Bergères de Rigauville, Raymond (1655–1711)
Blake, Charles (1746–1810)
Blake, Dominick Edward (1806–59)
Blake, William Hume (1809–70)
Blake, William Rufus (1802–63)
Blanchard, Guillaume (1650–1716)
Blanchard, Hiram (1820–74)
Blanchard, Jotham (1800–39)
Blanchard, Tranquille (d. 1843)
Blanchet, Augustin-Magloire (1797–1887)
Blanchet, François (1776–1830)
Blanchet, Jean (1795–1857)
Blanchet, Joseph-Godric (1829–90)
Bland, Henry Flesher (1818–98)
Bland, John (fl. 1790–1825)
Blanshard, Richard (1817–94)
Bleakley, Josiah (d. 1822)
Blinkhorn, Thomas (1806–56)
Bliss, Henry (1797–1873)
Bliss, John Murray (1771–1834)
Bliss, Jonathan (1742–1822)
Bliss, William Blowers (1795–1874)
Blondeau, Maurice-Régis (1734–1809)
Blowers, Sampson Salter (1741/42–1842)
Bochart de Champigny, Jean, Sieur de Noroy et de Verneuil (d. 1720)
Bodega y Quadra, Juan Francisco de la (d. 1794)
Boiret, Urbain (1731–74)
Bois, Louis-Édouard (1813–89)

Boisdon, Jacques (fl. 1648)
Boispineau, Jean-Jard (1689–1744)
Boisseau, Josias (fl. 1679–81)
Boisseau, Nicolas (1700–71)
Boisseau, Nicolas-Gaspard (1726–1804)
Boisseau, Nicolas-Gaspard (1765–1842)
Boivin, François (d. 1675 or 1676)
Bolvin, Gilles (d. 1766)
Bonami, *dit* Lespérance, Alexis (1796–1890)
Bonamour, Jean de (fl. 1669–72)
Bond, George (d. 1852)
Bond, Joseph Norman (1758–1830)
Bond, William (fl. 1672–91)
Bonfoy, Hugh (d. 1762)
Bonhomme, *dit* Beaupré, Noël (1684–1755)
Bonnécamps, Joseph-Pierre de (d. 1790)
Bonne de Missègle, Louis de (d. 1760)
Bonnemere, Florent (1600–83)
Bonner, John (d. 1725/26)
Bonnycastle, Sir Richard Henry (1791–1847)
Booker, Alfred (1800–57)
Booker, Alfred (1824–71)
Boomer, Michael (1810–88)
Booth, Joshua (d. 1813)
Boquet, Charles (fl. 1657–81)
Borden, Harold Lothrop (1876–1900)
Borneuf, Joseph (1762–1819)
Boscawen, Edward (1711–61)
Boschenry de Drucour, Augustin de (d. 1762)
Bossu, *dit* Lyonnais, Pierre-Jacques, named Brother Félix (1770–1803)
Boston, John (1786–1862)
Bostwick, John (1780–1849)
Botsford, Amos (1744/45–1812)
Botsford, Amos Edwin (1804–94)
Botsford, Bliss (1813–90)
Botsford, William (1773–1864)
Bouat, François-Marie (d. 1726)
Bouc, Charles-Jean-Baptiste (1766–1832)
Boucault, Nicolas-Gaspard (fl. 1719–55)
Boucault de Godefus, Gilbert (fl. 1729–56)
Bouchard, Arthur (1845–96)
Bouchard, Étienne (d. 1676)
Boucher, Cyrille (1834–65)
Boucher, François (1730–1816)
Boucher, Geneviève, named de Saint-Pierre (1676–1766)
Boucher, Jean-Baptiste (1763–1839)
Boucher, Pierre (d. 1717)
Boucher, Pierre-Jérôme (d. 1753)
Boucher-Belleville, Jean-Philippe (1800–74)
Boucher de Boucherville, Pierre (1689–1767)
Boucher de Boucherville, René-Amable (1735–1812)
Boucher de Boucherville, Thomas-René-Verchères (1784–1857)
Boucher de Grandpré, Lambert (d. 1699)

Boucher de La Bruère, Pierre-Claude (d. 1871)
Boucher de La Perrière, René (1668–1742)
Boucher de Montbrun, Jean (d. 1742)
Boucher de Niverville, Jean-Baptiste (1673–1748)
Boucher de Niverville, Joseph (1715–1804)
Boucher de Niverville, Louis-Charles (1825–69)
Boucherville, Georges de (1814–94)
Bouchette, Jean-Baptiste (1736–1804)
Bouchette, Joseph (1774–1841)
Bouchette, Robert-Shore-Milnes (1805–79)
Boudreau, Cécile (Pitre; Pellerin) (d. 1811)
Bougainville, Louis-Antoine de, Comte de Bougainville (1729–1811)
Bouillet de La Chassaigne, Jean (1645–1733)
Boulanger, Clément (1790–1868)
Boulduc, Louis (d. between 1699 and 1701)
Bouler, Robert (d. 1734)
Boullard, Étienne (1658–1733)
Boullé, Eustache (fl. 1618–38)
Boullé, Hélène, named de Saint-Augustin (Champlain) (1598–1654)
Boullongne, Marie-Barbe de (Ailleboust de Coulogne et d'Argentenay) (d. 1685)
Boulton, Charles Arkoll (1841–99)
Boulton, D'Arcy (1759–1834)
Boulton, D'Arcy (1825–75)
Boulton, George Strange (1797–1869)
Boulton, Henry John (1790–1870)
Boulton, William Henry (1812–74)
Bourassa, François (1813–98)
Bourassa, *dit* La Ronde, René (d. 1778)
Bourchier, Hugh Plunkett (d. 1862)
Bourdages, Louis (1764–1835)
Bourdages, Raymond (d. 1787)
Bourdon, Anne, named de Sainte-Agnès (1644–1711)
Bourdon, Jacques (d. 1724)
Bourdon, Jean, known as Monsieur de Saint-Jean or Sieur de Saint-François (d. 1668)
Bourdon, Marguerite, named de Saint-Jean-Baptiste (1642–1706)
Bourdon d'Autray, Jacques (1652–88)
Bourdon de Dombourg, Jean-François (1647–90)
Bourdon de Dombourg, Jean-François (b. 1720, d. in or after 1789)
Bourdon de Romainville, Jean (b. 1627, d. in or after 1654)
Bourg, Abraham (b. 1662, d. in or after 1727)
Bourg, Joseph-Mathurin (1744–97)
Bourg, *dit* Belle–Humeur, Alexandre (1671–1760)
Bourgeau, Eugène (1813–77)
Bourgeau, Victor (1809–88)
Bourgeois, Jacques (d. 1701)
Bourgeoys, Marguerite, named du Saint-Sacrement (1620–1700)
Bourget, Ignace (1799–1885)
Bourinot, John (1814–84)

9

Bourlamaque, François-Charles de (1716–64)
Bourne, Adolphus (1795–1886)
Bourne, John Gervas Hutchinson (d. 1845)
Bourneuf, François-Lambert (1787–1871)
Boutet de Saint-Martin, Martin (d. 1683?)
Bouthillier, Jean-Antoine (1782–1835)
Boutillier, Thomas (1797–1861)
Boutroue d'Aubigny, Claude de (1620–80)
Bouvart, Martin (1637–1705)
Bovell, James (1817–80)
Bowen, Edward (1780–1866)
Bowes, John George (d. 1864)
Bowles, George John (1837–87)
Bowman, James (d. 1787)
Bowman, James (1793–1842)
Bowring, Benjamin (d. 1846)
Bowring, Charles R. (1840–90)
Boxer, Edward (1784–1855)
Boyd, John (1823–80)
Boyd, John (1826–93)
Boyer, Louis (1795–1870)
Boyle, Alexander (1771–1854)
Boys, Henry (1775–1868)
Bradford, Richard (1752–1817)
Bradford, William (1823–92)
Bradley, Thomas (fl. 1484–1505)
Bradstreet, John (1714–74)
Brandeau, Esther (fl. 1738–39)
Bras-de-fer de Chateaufort, Marc-Antoine
   (fl. 1635–38)
Brass, William (d. 1837)
Brassard, Louis-Marie (1726–1800)
Brassard, Louis-Moïse (1800–77)
Brassard Deschenaux, Charles-Joseph (1752–1832)
Brassard Deschenaux, Joseph (1722–93)
Brasseur de Bourbourg, Charles-Étienne (1814–74)
Brassier, Gabriel-Jean (1729–98)
Braun, Antoine-Nicolas (1815–85)
Brauneis, Jean-Chrysostome (1814–71)
Brauneis, John Chrisostomus (d. 1832)
Bray, Émile-Frédéric de (1829–79)
Bréard, Jacques-Michel (d. 1775)
Brébeuf, Jean de (1593–1649)
Brecken, John (1800–47)
Bréhant de Galinée, René de (d. 1678)
Brehaut, Pierre (1764–1817)
Bréhaut Delisle, Achille de (fl. 1636–42)
Breithaupt, Ezra Carl (1866–97)
Breland, Pascal (1811–96)
Brenan, Daniel (1796–1876)
Brendan, Saint (d. c. 578)
Brennan, James (1812–66)
Brennan, Margaret, named Sister Teresa
   (1831–87)
Brenton, Edward Brabazon (1763–1845)
Brenton, James (1736–1806)
Breslay, René-Charles de (1658–1735)

Bressani, François-Joseph (1612–72)
Bresse, Guillaume (1833–92)
Brew, Chartres (1815–70)
Brewse, John (d. 1785)
Breynton, John (d. 1799)
Briand, Jean-Olivier (1715–94)
Bricault de Valmur, Louis-Frédéric (d. 1738)
Brice, Mme de (fl. 1644–52)
Bridgar, John (fl. 1678–87)
Bridge, Thomas Finch Hobday (1807–56)
Bridges, Timothy (fl. 1702–8)
Bridgland, James William (1817–80)
Brien, Jean-Baptiste-Henri (1816–41)
Brigeac, Claude de (d. 1661)
Brisay de Denonville, Jacques-René de, Marquis de
   Denonville (1637–1710)
Brisebois, Éphrem-A. (1850–90)
Bristow, William (b. 1808, d. in or after 1868)
Bro, Jean-Baptiste (1743–1824)
Brock, Sir Isaac (1769–1812)
Broke, Sir Philip Bowes Vere (1776–1841)
Bromley, Walter (d. 1838)
Bronson, Henry Franklin (1817–89)
Brooke, John (d. 1789)
Brooking, Robert (1813–93)
Brooking, Thomas Holdsworth (d. 1869)
Brossard, Jean-François (1654–1716)
Brossard, Urbain (1633–1710)
Brossard, dit Beausoleil, Joseph (1702–65)
Brouse, George (1790–1860)
Brouse, William Henry (1824–81)
Brousseau, Léger (1826–90)
Brown, Andrew (1763–1834)
Brown, Corydon Partlow (1848–91)
Brown, Frederick (d. 1838)
Brown, George (1818–80)
Brown, James (1776–1845)
Brown, James (1790–1870)
Brown, Michael Septimus (1818–86)
Brown, Paola (fl. 1828–52)
Brown, Peter (d. 1845)
Brown, Peter (1784–1863)
Brown, Robert (1842–95)
Brown, Robert Christopher Lundin (d. 1876)
Brown, Thomas Storrow (1803–88)
Brown, William (d. 1789)
Browne, Frances (Stewart) (1794–1872)
Browne, George (1811–85)
Browne, John James (1837–93)
Browne, Timothy (d. 1855)
Bruce, James, 8th Earl of Elgin and 12th Earl of
   Kincardine (1811–63)
Bruce, John (d. 1866)
Bruce, John (1837–93)
Bruce, Robert George (d. 1779)
Bruff, Charles Oliver (1735–1817)
Brûlé, Étienne (d. c. 1633)

Bruneau, François-Jacques (1809–65)
Bruneau, François-Pierre (1799–1851)
Bruneau, Pierre (1761–1820)
Brunel, Alfred (1818–87)
Brunet, Alexandre-Auguste (1816–66)
Brunet, Louis-Ovide (1826–76)
Brunet, Wilfrid-Étienne (1832–99)
Brunet, *dit* La Sablonnière, Jean (1687–1753)
Brunet, *dit* L'Estang, Véronique, named Sainte-
 Rose (1726–1810)
Brush, George (1793–1883)
Bruslé, Michel (1673–1724)
Bruyas, Jacques (1635–1712)
Bruyère, Élisabeth (1818–76)
Bruyères, John (d. before 1787)
Bruyeres, Ralph Henry (d. 1814)
Brydges, Charles John (1827–89)
Brymer, Alexander (d. 1822)
Bryson, George (1813–1900)
Buade, Louis de, Comte de Frontenac et de Palluau
 (1622–98)
Buchan, David (b. 1780, d. in or after 1838)
Buchanan, Alexander (1798–1851)
Buchanan, Alexander Carlisle (1808–68)
Buchanan, Isaac (1810–83)
Buchanan, Peter (1805–60)
Buck, Walter M. (1826–81)
Buckland, George (1804–85)
Budd, Henry (d. 1875)
Buell, Andrew Norton (1798–1880)
Buell, William (1751–1832)
Buell, William (1792–1862)
Buisson de Saint-Cosme, Jean-François (d. 1712)
Buisson de Saint-Cosme, Jean-François (1667–
 1706)
Bulger, Andrew H. (1789–1858)
Bulkeley, Richard (1717–1800)
Bull, George Perkins (1795–1847)
Buller, Sir Arthur William (1808–69)
Buller, Charles (1806–48)
Bulley, Samuel (d. between 1806 and 1809)
Bullock, William (1797–1874)
Bulteau, Guillaume (1666–1716)
Bunbury, Joseph (fl. 1773–1802)
Bunn, John (d. 1861)
Bunn, Thomas (1830–75)
Bunning, Maria, named Sister Mary Martha
 (1824–68)
Buntin, Alexander (1822–93)
Bunting, Christopher William (1837–96)
Bunting, William Franklin (1825–97)
Burbidge, John (d. 1812)
Burch, John (1741–97)
Bureau, Pierre (1771–1836)
Burgess, Alexander Mackinnon (1850–98)
Burgoyne, John (1722–92)
Burke, Edmund (fl. 1785–1801)

Burke, Edmund (1753–1820)
Burley, Cornelius Albertson (d. 1830)
Burn, William (1758–1804)
Burn, William John (1851–96)
Burn, William Scott (1797–1851)
Burnaby, Robert (1828–78)
Burnet, David (d. 1853)
Burnham, Zacheus (1777–1857)
Burns, Alexander (1834–1900)
Burns, John (d. 1822)
Burns, Kennedy Francis (1842–95)
Burns, Robert (1789–1869)
Burns, Robert Easton (1805–63)
Burns, William (d. 1829)
Burpe, David (1752–1845)
Burpee, Isaac (1825–85)
Burpee, Richard E. (1810–53)
Burr, Rowland (1798–1865)
Burrage, Robert Raby (1794–1864)
Burrows, John (1789–1848)
Burstall, John (d. 1896)
Burtis, William Richard Mulharen (1818–82)
Burton, Sir Francis Nathaniel (1766–1832)
Burton, John (1760–1838)
Burton, Ralph (1724–68)
Burwell, Adam Hood (1790–1849)
Burwell, Mahlon (1783–1846)
Busby, Thomas (1735–98)
Bushby, Arthur Thomas (1835–75)
Bushell, John (d. 1761)
Butcher, Mark (1814–83)
Buteux, Jacques (1599–1652)
Butler, John (d. 1791)
Butler, John (d. 1796)
Butler (Dight), John Butler (d. 1834)
Butler, Walter (1752–81)
Button, Sir Thomas (d. 1634)
By, John (1779–1836)
Byers, Peter, known as Black Peter (d. 1815)
Byles, Mather (1734/35–1814)
Bylot, Robert (fl. 1610–16)
Byng, John (d. 1757)
Byron, John (1723–86)
Byssot de La Rivière, François (d. 1673)

CABAZIÉ, Pierre (d. 1715)
Cabot, John (d. *c.* 1498)
Cabot, Sebastian (d. 1557)
Caddy, John Herbert (1801–83)
Cadet, Joseph-Michel (1719–81)
Cadieux, Louis-Marie (1785–1838)
Cadot, Jean-Baptiste (fl. 1723–1803)
Cadotte, Joseph (fl. 1814–22)
Cadron, Marie-Rosalie, named de la Nativité (Jetté)
 (1794–1864)
Caën, Émery de (fl. 1603–33)
Caën, Guillaume de (fl. 1619–43)

11

Cagenquarichten (fl. 1699–1726)

Cahideuc, Emmanuel-Auguste de, Comte Dubois de La Motte (1683–1764)

Cailly, François-Joseph (fl. 1700–62)

Caldicott, Thomas Ford (1803–69)

Caldwell, Billy (d. 1841)

Caldwell, Francis Xavier (1792–1851)

Caldwell, Henry (d. 1810)

Caldwell, James (d. 1815)

Caldwell, Sir John (d. 1842)

Caldwell, William (d. 1822)

Caldwell, William (1782–1833)

Caldwell, William Bletterman (d. 1882)

Caleff, John (1726–1812)

Callbeck, Phillips (d. 1790)

Callet, Luc (1715–67)

Callière, Louis-Hector de (1648–1703)

Callihoo, Louis (fl. 1819–45)

Calonne, Jacques-Ladislas-Joseph de (1743–1822)

Calvarin, Goulven (d. 1719)

Calvert, George, 1st Baron Baltimore (d. 1632)

Calvin, Dileno Dexter (1798–1884)

Cambridge, John (1748–1831)

Cameron, Æneas (d. 1822)

Cameron, Alexander (1827–93)

Cameron, Angus (d. 1876)

Cameron, David (1804–72)

Cameron, Duncan (d. 1848)

Cameron, George Frederick (1854–85)

Cameron, John (1820–88)

Cameron, John Dugald (d. 1857)

Cameron, John Hillyard (1817–76)

Cameron, Malcolm (1808–76)

Cameron, Malcolm Colin (1831–98)

Cameron, Sir Matthew Crooks (1822–87)

Cameron, Sir Roderick William (1823–1900)

Campbell, Alexander (d. 1854)

Campbell, Sir Alexander (d. 1892)

Campbell, Andrew (fl. 1892–95)

Campbell, Sir Archibald (1769–1843)

Campbell, Archibald (1790–1862)

Campbell, Colin (fl. 1699–1710)

Campbell, Sir Colin (1776–1847)

Campbell, Colin (1822–81)

Campbell, Donald (d. 1763)

Campbell, Sir Donald (1800–50)

Campbell, Dugald (d. 1810)

Campbell, Duncan (1818–86)

Campbell, George William (1810–82)

Campbell, James (fl. 1806–17)

Campbell, John (1721–95)

Campbell, John Saxton (d. 1855)

Campbell, Patrick (fl. *c.* 1765–1823)

Campbell, Robert (1808–94)

Campbell, Robert (1826–98)

Campbell, Rollo (1803–71)

Campbell, Stewart (1812–85)

Campbell, Thomas Edmund (d. 1872)

Campbell, Lord William (d. 1778)

Campbell, Sir William (1758–1834)

Campion, Étienne-Charles (1737–95)

Campot, Jacques (d. 1751)

Canac, *dit* Marquis, Pierre (1780–1850)

Canning, Francis (1851–99)

Cannon, Edward (d. 1814)

Cannon, John (d. 1833)

Cannon, Mary (d. 1827)

Cantin, Augustin (1809–93)

Capitanal (d. 1634)

Capreol, Frederick Chase (1803–86)

Carbonariis, Giovanni Antonio de (fl. 1489–98)

Cardenau, Bernard (b. 1723, fl. 1751–64)

Cardero, Manuel José Antonio (b. 1766, d. in or after 1810)

Cardinal, Joseph-Narcisse (1808–38)

Carey, Daniel (1829–90)

Carey, John (1780–1851)

Carheil, Étienne de (1633–1726)

Carigouan (d. 1634)

Carleton, Guy, 1st Baron Dorchester (1724–1808)

Carleton, Thomas (d. 1817)

Carmichael, James (1788–1860)

Carmichael, John Edward (d. 1828)

Caron, Charles (1768–1853)

Caron, Édouard (1830–1900)

Caron, René-Édouard (1800–76)

Caron, Thomas (1819–78)

Carpenter, Philip Pearsall (1819–77)

Carpentier, Bonaventure (1716–78)

Carpmael, Charles (1846–94)

Carrall, Robert William Weir (1837–79)

Carrefour de La Pelouze, Pierre-Joseph (1738–1808)

Carrerot, André (d. 1749)

Carrerot, Philippe (d. 1745)

Carrerot, Pierre (d. 1732)

Carrier, Charles William (1839–87)

Carrier, Michel (1805–59)

Carroll, John Saltkill (1809–84)

Carson, William (d. 1843)

Carter, Sir Frederic Bowker Terrington (1819–1900)

Carter, Sir James (1805–78)

Carter, Robert (1791–1872)

Cartier, Claude (d. 1855)

Cartier, Sir George-Étienne (1814–73)

Cartier, Jacques (1491–1557)

Cartier, Jacques (1750–1814)

Cartier, Toussaint, known as "the hermit of Saint-Barnabé" (d. 1767)

Cartwright, George (1739/40–1819)

Cartwright, John Solomon (1804–45)

Cartwright, Richard (1759–1815)

Carvell, Jedediah Slason (1832–94)
Cary, George Hunter (1832–66)
Cary, George Marcus (1795–1858)
Cary, Lucius Bentinck, 10th Viscount Falkland (1803–84)
Cary, Thomas (1751–1823)
Cary, Thomas (1797–1869)
Casault, Louis-Adolphe (1832–76)
Casault, Louis-Jacques (1808–62)
Casavant, Joseph (1807–74)
Case, William (1780–1855)
Casey, William Redmond (d. 1846)
Casgrain, Charles-Eusèbe (1800–48)
Casgrain, Pierre (1771–1828)
Casot, Jean-Joseph (1728–1800)
Cassegrain, Olivier-Arthur (d. 1868)
Cassels, Robert (1815–82)
Cassidy, Francis (1827–73)
Cassiet, Pierre (1727–1809)
Cassils, William (1832–91)
Castaing, Pierre-Antoine (d. 1799)
Castanet, Jean-Baptiste-Marie (1766–98)
Castle, John Harvard (1830–90)
Catalogne, Gédéon (de) (1662–1729)
Catalogne, Joseph de (1694–1735)
Cathcart, Charles Murray, 2nd Earl Cathcart (1783–1859)
Cauchon, Joseph-Édouard (1816–85)
Caughey, James (1810–91)
Caulfeild, Thomas (d. 1716/17)
Caumont, Pierre de (d. 1694)
Cavelier, Jean (1636–1722)
Cavelier de La Salle, René-Robert (1643–87)
Cawdell, James Martin (d. 1842)
Cawthra, Joseph (1759–1842)
Cawthra, William (1801–80)
Cayley, William (1807–90)
Cazeau, Charles-Félix (1807–81)
Cazeau, François (d. 1815)
Cazeneuve, Louis-Joseph-Charles (1795–1856)
Cazes, Charles de (1808–67)
Céloron, Marie-Catherine-Françoise (1744–1809)
Céloron de Blainville, Jean-Baptiste (d. 1735)
Céloron de Blainville, Pierre-Joseph (1693–1759)
Céré de La Colombière, Marie-Julie-Marguerite, named Sister Mance (1807–76)
Cerré, Jean–Gabriel (1734–1805)
Chabanel, Noël (1613–49)
Chabert, Joseph (1831–94)
Chabert de Cogolin, Joseph-Bernard de, Marquis de Chabert (1724–1805)
Chabert de Joncaire, Louis-Thomas (d. 1739)
Chabert de Joncaire, Philippe-Thomas (fl. 1707–66)
Chabert de Joncaire de Clausonne, Daniel-Marie (d. 1771)
Chaboillez, Augustin (1773–1834)

Chaboillez, Charles (1772–1812)
Chaboillez, Charles-Jean-Baptiste (1736–1808)
Chaboillez, Louis (1766–1813)
Chabot, Jean (1806–60)
Chabot, Julien (1801–64)
Chaboulié, Charles (d. 1708)
Chabrand Delisle, David (1730–94)
Chachagouesse (fl. 1674–1712)
Chadwick, Charles Eli (1818–96)
Chaffey, Samuel (1793–1827)
Chaigneau, Léonard (1663–1711)
Chaloux, Marie-Esther, named de Saint-Joseph (d. 1839)
Chambalon, Louis (d. 1716)
Chamberlain, Theophilus (1737–1824)
Chambly, Jacques de (d. 1687)
Champagneur, Étienne (1808–82)
Champflour, François de (fl. 1636–49)
Champion, Gabriel (1748–1808)
Champion de Cicé, Louis-Armand (1648–1727)
Champlain, Samuel de (d. 1635)
Champy, Gélase (1657–1738)
Chandler, Edmund Leavens (1829–80)
Chandler, Edward Barron (1800–80)
Chandler, James Watson (1801–70)
Chandler, Kenelm (d. 1803)
Chandler, Kenelm Conor (1773–1850)
Chandler, Samuel (1791–1866)
Chandler, William (1804–56)
Chandonnet, Thomas-Aimé (1834–81)
Chanter, Thomas Burnard (1797–1874)
Chapais, Jean-Charles (1811–85)
Chaperon, John (1825–51)
Chapleau, Sir Joseph-Adolphe (1840–98)
Chapoton, Jean-Baptiste (d. 1760)
Chappell, Benjamin (1740/41–1825)
Chappell, Edward (1792–1861)
Charbonnel, Armand-François-Marie de (1802–91)
Chardon, Jean-Baptiste (1671–1743)
Charest, Étienne (1718–83)
Charest, Zéphirin (1813–76)
Charité (fl. 1628–29)
Charland, Louis (1772–1813)
Charlevoix, Pierre-François-Xavier de (1682–1761)
Charly Saint-Ange, Jean-Baptiste (1668–1728)
Charly Saint-Ange, Louis (b. 1703, d. 1767 or 1768)
Charly Saint-Ange, Marie-Catherine, named du Saint-Sacrement (1666–1719)
Charon de la Barre, François (1654–1719)
Charron, Amable (1785–1844)
Charron de La Barre, Claude (d. 1687)
Chartier, Étienne (1798–1853)
Chartier, Louis (1633–60)
Chartier, Michel (d. 1750)
Chartier de Lotbinière, Eustache (1688–1749)

Chartier de Lotbinière, Eustache (b. 1716, d. in or after 1785)
Chartier de Lotbinière, Louis-Théandre (fl. 1641–80)
Chartier de Lotbinière, Michel, Marquis de Lotbinière (1723–98)
Chartier de Lotbinière, Michel-Eustache-Gaspard-Alain (1748–1822)
Chartier de Lotbinière, René-Louis (d. 1709)
Chartrand, Vincent (1795–1863)
Chase, Henry Pahtahquahong (1818–1900)
Chasseur, Pierre (1783–1842)
Chassin de Thierry, François-Nicolas de (d. 1755)
Chastellain, Pierre (1606–84)
Chatelain, Nicolas (d. 1892)
Chauchetière, Claude (1645–1709)
Chaudière Noire (d. 1697)
Chaudillon, Antoine (1643–1707)
Chaumonot, Pierre-Joseph-Marie (1611–93)
Chaumont, Alexandre de (d. 1710)
Chaussegros de Léry, Alexandre-René (1818–80)
Chaussegros de Léry, Charles-Étienne (1774–1842)
Chaussegros de Léry, Charles-Joseph (1800–64)
Chaussegros de Léry, Gaspard-Joseph (1682–1756)
Chaussegros de Léry, Gaspard-Joseph (1721–97)
Chaussegros de Léry, Louis-René (1762–1832)
Chauveau, Pierre-Joseph-Olivier (1820–90)
Chauvigny, Marie-Madeleine de (Gruel de La Peltrie) (1603–71)
Chauvin de La Pierre, Pierre (fl. 1603–11)
Chauvin de Tonnetuit, Pierre de (d. 1603)
Chauvreulx, Claude-Jean-Baptiste (d. c. 1760)
Chavigny Lachevrotière, François de (1650–1725)
Chazelle, Jean-Pierre (1789–1845)
Chefdostel, Thomas (fl. 1597–1603)
Chejauk (fl. 1761–1804)
Chénier, Jean-Olivier (1806–37)
Chenneque, Martin (d. 1825)
Cherououny (d. 1627)
Cherrier, Côme-Séraphin (1798–1885)
Cherrier, François (1745–1809)
Cherrier, François-Pierre (d. 1793)
Chesley, Solomon Yeomans (1796–1880)
Cheval, dit Saint-Jacques, dit Chevalier, Jacques-Joseph (d. 1757)
Chevalier, Henri-Émile (1828–79)
Chevalier, Jean-Baptiste (d. 1746 or 1747)
Chevalier, Jean-Charles (1694–1760)
Chevalier, dit Beauchêne, Robert (1686–1731)
Chew, Joseph (d. 1798)
Chewett, James Grant (1793–1862)
Chewett, William (1753–1849)
Chewett, William Cameron (1828–97)
Chèze, François (1683–1740)
Chichikatelo (d. 1701)

Chicoisneau, Jean-Baptiste-Jacques (1737–1818)
Chihwatenha (d. 1640)
Child, Marcus (1792–1859)
Chingouessi (fl. 1695–1701)
Chinic, Guillaume-Eugène (1818–89)
Chinic, Martin (1770–1836)
Chiniquy, Charles (1809–99)
Chipman, Eliza Ann (Chipman) (1807–53)
Chipman, Samuel (1790–1891)
Chipman, Ward (1754–1824)
Chipman, Ward (1787–1851)
Chipman, William Allen (1757–1845)
Chipman, William Henry (1807–70)
Chisholm, George King (1814–74)
Chisholm, William (1788–1842)
Chisholme, David (1796–1842)
Cholenec, Pierre (1641–1723)
Chomedey de Maisonneuve, Paul de (1612–76)
Chomina (fl. 1618–29)
Chouart Des Groseilliers, Médard (fl. 1618–84)
Christian, Washington (d. 1850)
Christie, Alexander (1792–1872)
Christie, Alexander James (1787–1843)
Christie, David (1818–80)
Christie, Gabriel (1722–99)
Christie, Robert (1787–1856)
Christie, William Joseph (1824–99)
Christie, William Mellis (1829–1900)
Christie, William Plenderleath (1780–1845)
Chubb, Henry (1787–1855)
Church, Benjamin (1639–1717/18)
Church, John (1757–1839)
Church, Levi Ruggles (1836–92)
Churchill, Ezra A. (1804–74)
Cimon, Simon-Xavier (1829–87)
Ciquard, François (1754–1824)
Cirier, Antoine (1718–98)
Clairambault d'Aigremont, François (d. 1728)
Claparède, Jean (fl. 1714–58)
Clare, James Robert (1827–67)
Clark, Alexander (1818–98)
Clark, Duncan (d. 1808)
Clark, George (d. 1759)
Clark, James (fl. 1790–1807)
Clark, Robert (d. 1794)
Clark, Robert (1744–1823)
Clark, Thomas (d. 1835)
Clarke, Sir Alured (d. 1832)
Clarke, Henry Joseph (1833–89)
Clarke, James Paton (d. 1877)
Clarke, John (1781–1852)
Clarke, Lawrence (1832–90)
Clarke, Richard (fl. 1572–96)
Clarke, Septimus D. (1787–1859)
Clarkson, Thomas (1802–74)
Claude, Joseph (d. 1796)
Claus, Christian Daniel (1727–87)

14

Claus, William (1765–1826)
Claverie, Pierre (1719–56)
Cleary, James Vincent (1828–98)
Clément Du Vuault de Valrennes, Philippe (1647–1707)
Clemo, Ebenezer (d. *c.* 1860)
Clench, Joseph Brant (d. 1857)
Clench, Ralfe (d. 1828)
Clerk, George Edward (1815–75)
Clerke, Charles (1741–79)
Cleveland, Aaron (1715–57)
Clinch, John (1748/49–1819)
Clindinning, Robert Wilson (1815–98)
Clinton, George (d. 1761)
Clitherow, John (1782–1852)
Clopper, Henry George (1792–1838)
Closse, Raphaël-Lambert (d. 1662)
Clouet, Michel (1770–1836)
Cloutier, Zacharie (d. 1677)
Coates, Richard (1778–1868)
Coats, William (d. 1752)
Cobb, Silvanus (1709/10–62)
Cobbett, William (1763–1835)
Cobbie, Walsall (fl. 1676–82)
Cochran, Andrew William (d. 1849)
Cochran, James (1802–77)
Cochran, James Cuppaidge (1798–1880)
Cochran, William (d. 1833)
Cochrane, Henry (d. 1898)
Cochrane, John (d. 1850)
Cochrane, John James (d. 1867)
Cochrane, Sir Thomas John (1789–1872)
Cochrane, William (1831–98)
Cockburn, Sir Francis (1780–1868)
Cockburn, James (1819–83)
Cockburn, James Pattison (1779–1847)
Cocking, Matthew (1743–99)
Cockran, William (d. 1865)
Cockrell, Richard (d. 1829)
Codd, Donald (d. 1896)
Codner, Samuel (d. 1858)
Coffin, Sir Isaac (1759–1839)
Coffin, John (1729–1808)
Coffin, John (d. 1838)
Coffin, Nathaniel (1766–1846)
Coffin, Thomas (1762–1841)
Coffin, Thomas (1817–90)
Coffin, Thomas Aston (1754–1810)
Coffin, William Foster (1808–78)
Coghlan, Jeremiah (fl. 1756–88)
Cogswell, Henry Hezekiah (1776–1854)
Cogswell, Isabella Binney (1819–74)
Cohen, Jacob Raphael (d. 1811)
Colborne, John, 1st Baron Seaton (1778–1863)
Colby, Moses French (1795–1863)
Colclough, Cæsar (1764–1822)
Cole, John (d. 1799)

Colebrooke, Sir William MacBean George (1787–1870)
Colen, Joseph (d. 1818)
Coles, George (1810–75)
Colin, Michel (d. 1616)
Collard, Frederick John Martin (d. 1848)
Collet, Charles-Ange (b. 1721, d. in or after 1801)
Collet, Mathieu-Benoît (d. 1727)
Collier, Sir George (1738–95)
Collier, John (d. 1769)
Collins, Enos (1774–1871)
Collins, Francis (d. 1834)
Collins, James Patrick (d. 1847)
Collins, John (fl. 1706–20)
Collins, John (d. 1795)
Collins, Joseph Edmund (1855–92)
Collinson, Sir Richard (1811–83)
Collver, Jabez (1731–1818)
Colnett, James (d. 1806)
Colston, William (fl. 1610–12)
Coltman, William Bacheler (d. 1826)
Colvile, Eden (1819–93)
Colvill, Alexander, 7th Baron Colvill (1717/18–70)
Comeau, Anselm-François (1793–1867)
Côme de Mantes (fl. 1632–58)
Comingo, Bruin Romkes (1723–1820)
Comingo, Joseph Brown (1784–1821)
Compain, Marie-Louise, named Saint-Augustin (1747–1819)
Compain, Pierre-Joseph (1740–1806)
Condo, Francis (d. 1837)
Conefroy, Pierre (1752–1816)
Conger, Wilson Seymour (1804–64)
Conilleau, Charles (1811–79)
Connell, Charles (1809–73)
Connolly, Suzanne (d. 1862)
Connolly, Thomas Louis (1814–76)
Connolly, William (d. 1848)
Connon, Thomas (1832–99)
Connor, George Skeffington (1810–63)
Conroy, George (1832–78)
Conroy, Nicholas (1816–79)
Constantin, Justinien (1716–60)
Constantin, Nicolas-Bernardin (1664–1730)
Constantin, Pierre (fl. 1696–1750)
Conway, Honoria, named Mother Mary Vincent (1815–92)
Cook, James (1728–79)
Cook, James William (1820–75)
Cook, John (1805–92)
Cook, William Francis (1796–1862)
Cook, William Hemmings (d. 1846)
Cooke, Thomas (1792–1870)
Cooney, Robert (1800–70)
Cooper, James (b. 1821, d. in or after 1879)
Cooper, James Barrett (1811–88)
Cooper, William (d. 1840)

15

Cooper, William (1786–1867)
Cope, Henry (d. 1742)
Cope, Jean-Baptiste (fl. 1750–58)
Copp, William Walter (1826–94)
Coquart, Claude-Godefroy (1706–65)
Corbin, André (d. 1777)
Corbin, David (d. 1755)
Corby, Henry (1806–81)
Cordner, John (1816–94)
Cormack, William Eppes (1796–1868)
Cormier, Pierre (1734–1818)
Cornish, Francis Evans (1831–78)
Cornish, George (d. 1895)
Cornwallis, Edward (1712/13–76)
Corolère, Jean (fl. 1750–52)
Coron, Charles-François (1704–67)
Corpron, Jean (fl. 1755–65)
Corrigan, Robert (d. 1855)
Corriveau, Marie-Josephte, known as La Corriveau
  (Bouchard; Dodier) (1733–63)
Corte-Real, Gaspar (d. c. 1501)
Corte-Real, Miguel (d. c. 1502)
Cosby, Alexander (d. 1742)
Cossit, Ranna (1744–1815)
Coster, George (1794–1859)
Côté, Cyrille-Hector-Octave (1809–50)
Coté, Joseph-Olivier (1820–82)
Cotté, Gabriel (d. 1795)
Cotter, James Laurence (1839–89)
Cotton, Barthélemy (1692–1780)
Cotton, Charles Caleb (1775–1848)
Cotton, Michel (b. 1700, d. in or after 1747)
Couagne, Charles de (1651–1706)
Couagne, Jean-Baptiste de (1687–1740)
Couagne, Jean-Baptiste de (d. 1800)
Couagne, Michel de (1727–89)
Couagne, René de (d. 1767)
Couagne, Thérèse de (Poulin de Francheville)
  (1697–1764)
Couc, Elizabeth(?) (La Chenette, Techenet;
  Montour) (d. c. 1750)
Coughlan, Laurence (d. c. 1784)
Couillard, Antoine-Gaspard (1789–1847)
Couillard de Lespinay, Guillaume (d. 1663)
Couillard de Lespinay, Jean-Baptiste (d. 1735)
Couillard de Lespinay, Louis (1629–78)
Couillard de Lespinay, Louis (d. 1728)
Couillard-Déprés, Emmanuel (1792–1853)
Coulon de Villiers, François (1712–94)
Coulon de Villiers, Louis (1710–57)
Coulon de Villiers, Nicolas-Antoine (1683–1733)
Coulon de Villiers, Nicolas-Antoine (1708–50)
Coulon de Villiers de Jumonville, Joseph (1718–
  54)
Counter, John (1799–1862)
Couper, William (fl. 1860–86)
Courreaud de La Coste, Pierre (d. 1779)

Courseron, Gilbert (fl. 1621)
Coursol, Charles-Joseph (1819–88)
Coutlée, Thérèse-Geneviève (1742–1821)
Couture, George (1824–87)
Couture, Guillaume (d. 1701)
Couturier, dit Les Bourguignon, Pierre (d. 1715)
Couvert, Michel-Germain de (1653–1715)
Coventry, George (1793–1870)
Coverdale, William (1801–65)
Covert, John (d. 1843)
Cowan, Agnes (1839–93)
Cowdell, Thomas Daniel (1769–1833)
Cowley, Abraham (1816–87)
Cox, Nicholas (d. 1794)
Cox, Ross (1793–1853)
Cox, William George (d. 1878)
Coy, Amasa (1757–1838)
Coy, Mary (Morris; Bradley) (1771–1859)
Craig, Sir James Henry (1748–1812)
Craig, John (1804–54)
Craigie, John (d. 1813)
Craigie, William (d. 1863)
Cramahé, Hector Theophilus (1720–88)
Cramp, John Mockett (1796–1881)
Cramp, Thomas (1827–85)
Crandall, Joseph (d. 1858)
Crandall, Reuben (1767–1853)
Crane, Samuel (1794–1858)
Crane, William (1785–1853)
Crate, William Frederick (d. 1871)
Crawford, Alexander (1786–1828)
Crawford, George (1793–1870)
Crawford, Isabella Valancy (1850–87)
Crawford, John Willoughby (1817–75)
Crawley, Edmund Albern (1799–1888)
Creedon, Marianne, named Mother Mary Francis
  (1811–55)
Creelman, Samuel (1808–91)
Creighton, John (1721–1807)
Creighton, John (1817–85)
Creighton, Letitia (Youmans) (1827–96)
Crémazie, Jacques (1810–72)
Crémazie, Octave (1827–79)
Crespel, Emmanuel (1703–75)
Crespieul, François de (1639–1702)
Cressé, Pierre-Michel (1758–1819)
Cresswell, Samuel Gurney (1827–67)
Crevier, Joseph-Alexandre (1824–89)
Crevier de Saint-François, Jean (1642–93)
Crisafy, Antoine de, Marquis de Crisafy
  (d. 1709)
Crisafy, Thomas (d. 1696)
Croft, Henry Holmes (1820–83)
Croft, Thomas (1442–88)
Crofton, John ffolliott (1800–85)
Croke, Sir Alexander (1758–1842)
Croke, Nicholas (d. 1850)

16

Cronan, Daniel (1807–92)
Cronyn, Benjamin (1802–71)
Crooks, Adam (1827–85)
Crooks, James (1778–1860)
Crooks, Ramsay (1787–1859)
Crookshank, George (1773–1859)
Crosskill, John (1740–1826)
Crosskill, John Henry (1817–57)
Crout, Henry (fl. 1612–17)
Crowdy, James (1794–1867)
Crowe, Josias (d. 1714)
Crowne, William (1617–82)
Crozier, St George Baron Le Poer (1814–92)
Cruickshank, Robert (d. 1809)
Cruse, Thomas (fl. 1634–77)
Crusoe, Robinson (d. 1755)
Crysler, John (1770–1852)
Cubit, George (d. 1850)
Cudlip, John Waterbury (d. 1885)
Cugnet, François-Étienne (1688–1751)
Cugnet, François-Joseph (1720–89)
Cuillerier, Marie-Anne-Véronique (1680–1751)
Cuillerier, René (d. c. 1712)
Cull, Henry (1753–1833)
Cull, James (d. 1849)
Cull, William (fl. 1792–1823)
Cumberland, Frederic William (1820–81)
Cumings, Archibald (fl. 1698–1726)
Cumming, Cuthbert (1787–1870)
Cunard, Joseph (1799–1865)
Cunard, Sir Samuel (1787–1865)
Cunnabell, William (1808–68)
Cunningham, John (1575–1651)
Cunningham, Robert (1836–74)
Cuny Dauterive, Philippe-Antoine de (1709–79)
Cuoq, Jean-André (1821–98)
Curatteau, Jean-Baptiste (1729–90)
Curot, Marie-Louise, named de Saint-Martin (1716–88)
Currie, Donald (d. 1880)
Currier, Joseph Merrill (1820–84)
Curtis, James (d. 1819)
Curtis, Sir Roger (1746–1816)
Cushing, Lemuel (1806–75)
Cusson, Jean (d. 1718)
Cuthbert, James (d. 1798)
Cuthbert, Ross (1776–1861)
Cuthbert, William (1795–1854)
Cutler, Thomas (1752–1837)
Cuvillier, Austin (1779–1849)
Cuyler, Abraham Cornelius (1742–1810)

DABLON, Claude (d. 1697)
Daccarrette, Michel (d. 1745)
Daccarrette, Michel (1730–67)
Dadson, Ebenezer William (1845–1900)
Dagneau Douville, Alexandre (1698–1774)

Dagneau Douville de Quindre, Louis-Césaire (d. 1767)
Daine, François (d. 1770)
Dallas, Alexander Grant (1816–82)
Dalmas, Antoine (1636–93)
Dalrymple, George R. (d. 1851)
Dalton, Charles (1786–1859)
Dalton, John (d. 1869)
Dalton, Thomas (1782–1840)
Daly, Sir Dominick (1798–1868)
Daly, John Corry Wilson (1796–1878)
Daly, Thomas Mayne (1827–85)
Damours de Chauffours, Louis (d. 1708)
Damours de Chauffours, Mathieu (1618–95)
Damours de Clignancour, René (fl. 1660–1710)
Damours de Freneuse, Mathieu (d. 1696)
Dandonneau, dit Lajeunesse, Pierre (d. 1702)
Daneau de Muy, Charlotte, named de Sainte-Hélène (1694–1759)
Daneau de Muy, Jacques-Pierre (d. 1758)
Daneau de Muy, Nicolas (1651–1708)
Danforth, Asa (b. 1768, d. in or after 1821)
Dangé, François (fl. 1662–63)
Daniel, Antoine (1601–48)
Daniel, Charles (d. 1661)
Daniel, Thomas Wilder (1818–92)
Daniélou, Jean-Pierre (1696–1744)
Danks, Benoni (d. 1776)
Danré de Blanzy, Louis-Claude (fl. 1710–70)
Daoust, Charles (1825–68)
Darby, Nicholas (d. 1785)
Dargent, Joseph (1712–47)
Darling, Sir Charles Henry (1809–70)
Darling, John (1769–1825)
Darling, William (1819–85)
Dart, Elizabeth (Eynon) (1792–1857)
Darveau, Jean-Édouard (1816–44)
Darveau, Louis-Michel (1833–75)
Dasilva, dit Portugais, Nicolas (1698–1761)
Daudin, Henri (d. 1756)
Daulé, Jean-Denis (1766–1852)
Daumont de Saint-Lusson, Simon-François (fl. 1663–77)
Dauphin de La Forest, François (d. 1714)
Dauphin de Montorgueil (d. 1694)
Davanne, Marguerite, named de Saint-Louis de Gonzague (1719–1802)
Davers, Sir Robert (d. 1763)
David, Claude (1621–87)
David, David (1764–1824)
David, Eleazar David (1811–87)
David, Ferdinand (1824–83)
David, Jacques (d. 1726)
Davidson, Alexander (1794–1856)
Davidson, Arthur (1743–1807)
Davidson, William (d. 1790)
Davie, Alexander Edmund Batson (1847–89)

17

Davie, Allison (1796–1836)
Davie, Theodore (1852–98)
Davies, Thomas (d. 1812)
Davion, Albert (d. 1726)
Davis, John (d. 1605)
Davis, John (1802–75)
Davis, Joseph (fl. 1692–1715)
Davis, Marie-Anne, named de Saint-Benoît
    (d. 1749)
Davis, Mathilda (d. 1873)
Davis, Robert (d. 1838)
Davis, Samuel (1834–95)
Davis, Silvanus (d. 1703)
Davison, Edward Doran (1819–94)
Davison, George (d. 1799)
Davost, Ambroise (1586–1643)
Dawson, Sir John William (1820–99)
Day, Charles Dewey (1806–84)
Day, John (d. 1775)
Day, Samuel Stearns (1808–71)
Dazemard de Lusignan, Paul-Louis (1691–1764)
Dearin, John Joseph (d. 1890)
Deas, John Sullivan (d. 1880)
Dease, Ellen, named Mother Teresa (1820–89)
Dease, John (d. 1801)
Dease, Peter Warren (1788–1863)
Déat, Antoine (1696–1761)
Debartzch, Pierre-Dominique (1782–1846)
de Blaquière, Peter Boyle (1783–1860)
DeBlois, George Wastie (1824–86)
Deblois, Joseph-François (1797–1860)
Deblois, Sarah (Deblois) (1753–1827)
Deblois, Stephen Wastie (1780–1844)
De Bonne, Pierre-Amable (1758–1816)
Decoigne, François (fl. 1798–1818)
Decoigne, Pierre-Théophile (1808–39)
De Cosmos, Amor (1825–97)
Decoste, Jean-Baptiste (1703–78)
DeCow, John (1766–1855)
DeGaugreben, Friedrich (d. 1822)
Degeay, Jacques (1717–74)
Deguire, *dit* Desrosiers, Joseph (1704–89)
Deguise, *dit* Flamand, Girard-Guillaume (d. 1752)
Deguise, *dit* Flamand, Jacques (1697–1780)
De Haven, Edwin Jesse (1816–65)
Deighton, John (1830–75)
Dejean, Philippe (b. 1736, d. in or after 1809)
Dejordy de Villebon, Charles-René (d. 1761)
Dekanahwideh [volume I]
Delaborde, Jean (d. 1754)
Delagrave, Cyrille (1812–77)
DeLancey, James (1746–1804)
Delaney, John (1811–83)
Delaney, Patrick (1829–74)
Delaunay, Charles (1648–1737)
DeLaune, William (d. 1761)
Déléage, Jean-François-Régis (1821–84)

Delesdernier, Moses (d. 1811)
Delezenne, Ignace-François (d. 1790)
Delezenne, Marie-Catherine (Pélissier; Sales
    Laterrière) (1755–1831)
Delhalle, Constantin (d. 1706)
Delisle, Alexandre-Maurice (d. 1880)
De Lisle, Augustin (1802–65)
De Lisle, Jean (d. 1814)
De Lisle, Jean-Guillaume (d. 1819)
Delorme, Charles-Simon (1769–1837)
Delort, Guillaume (d. before 1749)
Delvecchio, Thomas (1758–1826)
Démaray, Pierre-Paul (1798–1854)
Demasduwit (d. 1820)
Demers, Jérôme (1774–1853)
Demers, Louis (1732–1813)
Demers, Modeste (1809–71)
De Mille, James (d. 1880)
Demosny, Jean (1643–87)
Denaut, Pierre (1743–1806)
Dénéchau, Claude (1768–1836)
Dénéchaud, Jacques (1728–1810)
Denis, Pierre (fl. 1837–41)
Denis de Saint-Simon, Antoine-Charles (1734–85)
Denison, Avery (d. 1826)
Denison, Frederick Charles (1846–96)
Denison, George Taylor (1816–73)
Denison, Robert (1697–1765)
Denke, Christian Frederick (1775–1838)
Dennis, John (1758–1832)
Dennis, John Stoughton (1820–85)
Denoon, Hugh (1762–1836)
Denson, Henry Denny (d. 1780)
Dent, John Charles (1841–88)
Denys, Jean (fl. 1506)
Denys, Joseph (1657–1736)
Denys, Nicolas (1598–1688)
Denys de Bonaventure, Simon-Pierre (1659–1711)
Denys de Bonnaventure, Claude-Élisabeth
    (1701–60)
Denys de Fronsac, Richard (d. 1691)
Denys de La Ronde, Louis (1675–1741)
Denys de La Ronde, Pierre (1631–1708)
Denys de La Trinité, Simon (b. 1599, d. between
    1678 and 1680)
Denys de Saint-Simon, Charles-Paul (1688–1748)
Denys de Saint-Simon, Paul (1649–1731)
Denys de Vitré, Charles (1645–1703)
Denys de Vitré, Théodose-Matthieu (d. 1775)
Depéret, Élie (1691–1757)
De Peyster, Abraham (1753–98)
DePeyster, Arent Schuyler (1736–1822)
Derbishire, Stewart (b. 1794 or 1795, d. 1863)
Dermer, Thomas (d. 1621)
Derome, François-Magloire (1821–80)
Derré de Gand, François (d. 1641)
Desandrouins, Jean-Nicolas (1729–92)

Desautels, Joseph (1814–81)
Desbarats, George-Édouard (1838–93)
Desbarats, George-Paschal (1808–64)
Desbarats, Pierre-Édouard (1764–1828)
DesBarres, Joseph Frederick Wallet (1721–1824)
Des Brisay, Albert (1795–1857)
DesBrisay, Mather Byles (1828–1900)
Desbrisay, Theophilus (1754–1823)
Desbrisay, Thomas (d. 1819)
Deschamps, Isaac (d. 1801)
Deschamps de Boishébert, Henri-Louis (1679–1736)
Deschamps de Boishébert et de Raffetot, Charles (1727–97)
Deschamps de La Bouteillerie, Jean-Baptiste-François (d. 1703)
Deschenaux, Pierre-Louis (1759–1802)
Deschênes, Georges-Honoré (1841–92)
Deschevery, *dit* Maisonbasse, Jean-Baptiste (d. 1744 or 1745)
Descouts, Martin (fl. 1682–1745)
Desdames, Thierry (fl. 1622–46)
Desdevens de Glandons, Maurice (b. 1742, d. in or after 1799)
Deserontyon, John (d. 1811)
Des Friches de Meneval, Louis-Alexandre (fl. 1687–1703)
Deshayes, Jean (d. 1706)
Des Herbiers de La Ralière, Charles (d. 1752)
Désilets, Aimé (1826–60)
Desilets, Luc (1831–88)
Desjardins, François-Xavier (d. 1867)
Desjardins, Peter (1775–1827)
Desjardins, Philippe-Jean-Louis (1753–1833)
Desjardins, *dit* Desplantes, Louis-Joseph (1766–1848)
Desjordy de Cabanac, Joseph (1657–1713)
Desjordy Moreau de Cabanac, François (1666–1726)
Des Landes, Joseph (1691–1742)
Deslongrais, Nicolas (fl. 1734–58)
De Smet, Pierre-Jean (1801–73)
de Sola, Abraham (1825–82)
Despard, John (1745–1829)
Desportes, Hélène (Hébert; Morin) (d. 1675)
Desrivières, François (1764–1830)
Des Rivières, Rodolphe (1812–47)
Desrochers, Urbain (1781–1860)
Desroches, Charles (fl. 1816–26)
Dessailliant, *dit* Richeterre, Michel (fl. 1701–23)
Dessane, Marie-Hippolyte-Antoine (1826–73)
Dessaulles, Jean (1766–1835)
Dessaulles, Louis-Antoine (1818–95)
Dethunes, Exupère (d. 1692)
Devau, *dit* Retor, Claude (d. 1784)
Devine, Thomas (d. 1888)
Devisme, Léopold (1816–1900)

Devlin, Bernard (1824–80)
Dewar, Edward Henry (1812–62)
De Witt, Jacob (1785–1859)
Déziel, Joseph-David (1806–82)
Diamond, Abraham (1828–80)
Dibblee, Frederick (1753–1826)
Dick, Robert (1814–90)
Dick, Thomas (1809–74)
Dickens, Francis Jeffrey (1844–86)
Dickerson, Silas Horton (1799–1857)
Dickie, John Barnhill (1829–86)
Dickinson, Moss Kent (1822–97)
Dickson, James (fl. 1835–37)
Dickson, John Robinson (1819–82)
Dickson, Robert (d. 1823)
Dickson, Samuel (1810–70)
Dickson, Thomas (d. 1825)
Dickson, Thomas (1791–1855)
Dickson, William (1769–1846)
Dièreville (fl. 1699–1711)
Dieskau, Jean-Armand, Baron de Dieskau (1701–67)
Digé, Jean (d. 1813)
Dimock, Joseph (1768–1846)
Dimock, Shubael (1707–81)
Dinning, Henry (d. 1884)
Dionne, Amable (1781–1852)
Disbrow, Noah (1772–1853)
Disney, Richard Randolph (1830–91)
Dixon, Charles (1730/31–1817)
Dixon, George (fl. 1776–91)
Dixon, William (d. 1873)
Dizy, *dit* Montplaisir, Marguerite (Desbrieux) (fl. 1663–1730)
Dizy, *dit* Montplaisir, Michel-Ignace (d. 1723)
Dizy de Montplaisir, Pierre (d. 1761)
Doak, Robert (1785–1857)
Doan, Joshua Gwillen (1811–39)
Dobbs, Harriet (Cartwright) (1808–87)
Dobie, Richard (d. 1805)
Dodd, Archibald Charles (d. 1831)
Dodd, Charles (d. 1860)
Dodd, Edmund Murray (1797–1876)
Doel, John (1790–1871)
Doggett, John (1723/24–72)
Doherty, Patrick J. (1838–72)
Dolbeau, Jean (1586–1652)
Dolebeau, Jean (1608–43)
Dollard, Patrick (1804–68)
Dollard, William (d. 1851)
Dollard Des Ormeaux, Adam (1635–60)
Dollier de Casson, François (1636–1701)
Donegani, John Anthony (1798–1868)
Donkin, John George (1853–90)
Donlevy, Charles (d. 1858)
Donnacona (d. *c.* 1593)
Donnelly, James (1816–80)

Doolittle, Lucius (1800–62)
Doreil, André (fl. 1749–59)
Dorion, Sir Antoine-Aimé (1818–91)
Dorion, Eugène-Philippe (1830–72)
Dorion, Jacques (d. 1877)
Dorion, Jean-Baptiste-Éric (1826–66)
Dorion, Pierre-Antoine (d. 1850)
Dorion, Vincislas-Paul-Wilfrid (1827–78)
Dorland, Thomas (1759–1832)
Dormer, Henry Edward (1844–66)
Dorrill, Richard (d. 1762)
Dorval, Marie-Louise, named Sainte-Élisabeth
    (1794–1866)
Dorwin, Jedediah Hubbell (1792–1883)
Dosquet, Pierre-Herman (1691–1777)
Douay, Anastase (fl. 1684–99)
Doublet, François (d. before 1678)
Doucet, Amable (1737–1806)
Doucet, André (1782–1824)
Doucet, Nicolas-Benjamin (1781–1858)
Doucet, Pierre (b. 1750, d. in or after 1799)
Doucett, John (d. 1726)
Dougall, James (1810–88)
Dougall, John (1808–86)
Douglas, Sir Charles (d. 1789)
Douglas, David (1799–1834)
Douglas, François-Prosper, Chevalier de Douglas
    (1725–81)
Douglas, George (1825–94)
Douglas, George Mellis (d. 1864)
Douglas, Sir Howard (1776–1861)
Douglas, James (d. 1803)
Douglas, James (1789–1854)
Douglas, Sir James (1803–77)
Douglas, James (1800–86)
Douglas, Thomas, Baron Daer and Shortcleuch,
    5th Earl of Selkirk (1771–1820)
Douse, William (1800–64)
Doutre, Gonzalve (1842–80)
Doutre, Joseph (1825–86)
Dow, William (1800–68)
Dowd, Patrick (d. 1891)
Downing, John (fl. 1647–82)
Downing, William (d. 1681)
Downs, Andrew (1811–92)
Doyle, Sir Charles Hastings (1804–83)
Doyle, Laurence O'Connor (1804–64)
Doyle, Patrick (1777–1857)
Drachart, Christian Larsen (1711–78)
Drake, Sir Bernard (d. 1586)
Drake, Sir Francis (d. 1595/96)
Drake, Francis William (d. 1788 or 1789)
Drapeau, Joseph (1752–1810)
Drapeau, Stanislas (1821–93)
Draper, Francis Collier (1837–94)
Draper, Thomas (fl. 1670–81)
Draper, William Henry (1801–77)

Drew, Andrew (1792–1878)
Driard, Sosthenes Maximilian (1819–73)
Drolet, Charles (1795–1873)
Drouin, Pierre (1810–60)
Drouin, Robert (1607–85)
Drué, Juconde (b. 1664, d. in or after 1726)
Druillettes, Gabriel (1610–81)
Druillon de Macé, Pierre-Jacques (d. 1780)
Drummond, Sir Gordon (1772–1854)
Drummond, Lewis Thomas (1813–82)
Drummond, Robert (1791–1834)
Drummond, Thomas (d. 1835)
Duberger, Jean-Baptiste (1767–1821)
Dubois Berthelot de Beaucours, Josué (d. 1750)
Dubois Davaugour, Pierre (d. 1664)
Dubois de Cocreaumont et de Saint-Maurice,
    Jean-Baptiste (fl. 1665–66)
Dubok (fl. 1645–46)
Dubord, Hippolyte (1801–72)
Du Bos, Nicolas (d. 1699)
Dubreil de Pontbriand, Henri-Marie (1708–60)
Dubreuil, Jean-Étienne (d. 1734)
Du Calvet, Pierre (1735–86)
Duchaîne, Amable-Daniel (1774–1853)
Ducharme, Charles-Joseph (1786–1853)
Ducharme, Dominique (1765–1853)
Ducharme, Jean-Marie (1723–1807)
Ducharme, Laurent (fl. 1723–87)
Du Chesne, Adrien (fl. 1631–56)
Duchesneau de La Doussinière et d'Ambault,
    Jacques (d. 1696)
Duckworth, Sir John Thomas (1747/48–1817)
Duder, Edwin (d. 1881)
Dudevant, Arnauld-Germain (b. 1751, d. c.
    1798)
Dudley, William (1686–1743)
Dudouyt, Jean (d. 1688)
Duffin, Simon (d. 1900)
Duffy, James W. (d. 1860)
Dufour, dit Bona, Joseph (1744–1829)
Dufournel, Louis-Gaspard (1662–1757)
Dufresne, Jacques (1844–96)
Dufresne, Nicolas (1789–1863)
Dufrost de La Jemerais, Christophe (1708–36)
Dufrost de Lajemmerais, Marie-Marguerite
    (Youville) (1701–71)
Dugal, Olivier (1796–1829)
Dugas, Joseph (1714–79)
Dugas, Joseph (d. 1823)
Dugay, Jacques (d. 1727)
Duggan, George (1812–76)
Du Gua de Monts, Pierre (d. 1628)
Dugué de Boisbriand, Michel-Sidrac (d. 1688)
Dugué de Boisbriand, Pierre (1675–1736)
Duhamel, Georges (1855–92)
Duhamel, Joseph (1834–94)
Du Jaunay, Pierre (d. 1780)

Du Laurent, Christophe-Hilarion (d. 1760)
Dulongpré, Louis (d. 1843)
Dumaresq, Perry (1788–1839)
Dumas, Alexandre (d. 1802)
Dumas, Jean-Daniel (1721–94)
Dumas Saint-Martin, Jean (1725–94)
Dumouchelle, Jean-Baptiste (1784–1844)
Dumoulin, Jean-Gaspard (1832–60)
Dumoulin, Pierre-Benjamin (d. 1856)
Dumoulin, Sévère (1793–1853)
Dun, John (1763–1803)
Duncan, Charles (fl. 1786–92)
Duncan, Henry (d. 1814)
Duncan, James D. (1806–81)
Duncan, Richard (d. 1819)
Duncanson, Robert Stuart (d. 1872)
Duncombe, Charles (1792–1867)
Dundas, George (1819–80)
Dunière, Louis (1723–1806)
Dunkin, Christopher (1812–81)
Dunlop, James (1757–1815)
Dunlop, Robert Graham (1790–1841)
Dunlop, William, known as Tiger Dunlop
   (1792–1848)
Dunn, John Henry (d. 1854)
Dunn, Oscar (1845–85)
Dunn, Thomas (1729–1818)
Dunn, Timothy Hibbard (1816–98)
Dunsmuir, Robert (1825–89)
Duparc, Jean-Baptiste (1676–1742)
Du Peron, François (1610–65)
Du Perron, Thalour (d. 1663)
Dupleix Silvain, Jean-Baptiste (b. 1721, d. in or
   after 1796)
Duplessis, Marguerite (fl. 1726–40)
Duplessis, Pacifique (d. 1619)
Du Plessis-Bochart, Charles (fl. 1633–36)
Dupont, Siméon (1671–1732)
Dupont de Neuville, Nicolas (d. 1716)
Du Pont de Renon, Michel (d. 1719)
Du Pont Duchambon, Louis (d. 1775)
Du Pont Duchambon de Vergor, Louis (b. 1713, d.
   in or after 1775)
Du Pont Duvivier, François (1676–1714)
Du Pont Duvivier, François (1705–76)
Du Pont Duvivier, Joseph (d. 1760) [volume IV
   appendix]
Duprac, Jean-Robert (d. 1726)
Dupré, François (d. 1720)
Dupuis, Nazaire (1843–76)
Dupuy, Claude-Thomas (1678–1738)
Dupuy, Jean-Baptiste (1804–79)
Dupuy, Zacharie (d. 1676)
Dupuy de Lisloye, Paul (d. 1713)
Duquesne de Menneville, Ange, Marquis Duquesne
   (d. 1778)
Duquet, Joseph (1815–38)

Duquet de La Chesnaye, Pierre (1643–87)
Durand, James (1775–1833)
Durand, Justinien (d. 1746 or 1748)
Durand de La Garenne (d. 1715)
Durell, Philip (1707–66)
Duret de Chevry de La Boulaye, Charles
   (fl. 1677–90)
Durie, William Smith (1813–85)
Durieu, Paul (1830–99)
Durnford, Elias Walker (1774–1850)
Durocher, Eulalie (Mélanie), named Mother
   Marie-Rose (1811–49)
Durocher, Flavien (1800–76)
Durocher, Joseph (1706–56)
Dussaus, Marie-Angélique (1737–1809)
Du Thet, Gilbert (d. 1613)
Dutisné, Claude-Charles (d. 1730)
Duval, Charles (b. 1758, d. in or after 1828)
Duval, Edmund Hillyer (1805–79)
Duval, Jean (d. 1608)
Du Val, Peter (1767–1851)
Duvernay, Ludger (1799–1852)
DuVernet, Henry Abraham (1787–1843)
Dyas, Thomas Winning (1845–99)

EAGAR, William (d. 1839)
Eagleson, John (fl. 1765–90)
Earle, Sylvester Zobieski (1822–88)
Early, May Agnes (Fleming) (1840–80)
Eastman, Daniel Ward (1778–1865)
Easton, Peter (fl. 1610–20)
Easton, Robert (d. 1831)
Eaststaff, Thomas George William (d. 1854)
Eaton, Wyatt (1849–96)
Eby, Benjamin (1785–1853)
Eccles, Henry (1817–63)
Echevete, Matias de (d. 1599)
Ecuier, Charles (d. 1820)
Eda'nsa (d. 1894)
Eddy, Jonathan (1726/27–1804)
Edgar, Sir James David (1841–99)
Edgcombe, Leonard (d. 1696)
Edmonds, Henry Valentine (1837–97)
Edmundson, William Graham (d. 1852)
Edson, Allan Aaron (1846–88)
Edward Augustus, Duke of Kent and Strathearn
   (1767–1820)
Edwards, Edward (d. 1816)
Edwards, Richard (d. 1795)
Eenoolooapik (d. 1847)
Egan, John (1811–57)
Egushwa (fl. 1730–1800)
Eirikr Thorvaldsson (fl. 982-85)
Eirikr *upsi* Gnupsson (d. 1146)
Elder, William (1784–1848)
Elder, William (1822–83)
Élie, Jacques (d. 1710)

21

Eliot, Hugh (fl. 1480–1510)
Eliza y Reventa, Francisco de (1759–1825)
Ellice, Alexander (d. 1805)
Ellice, Edward (1783–1863)
Ellice, Robert (1747–90)
Elliot, Adam (d. 1878)
Elliot, Robert (fl. 1740–65)
Elliot, William (1812–93)
Elliott, Andrew Charles (d. 1889)
Elliott, Matthew (d. 1814)
Ellis, John (d. 1877)
Ellis, William (1780–1837)
Ellis, William (1774–1855)
Elmsley, John (1762–1805)
Elmsley, John (1801–63)
Elwyn, Thomas (d. 1888)
Emerson, Thomas (d. 1843)
Emery-Coderre, Joseph (1813–88)
Émond, Pierre (1738–1808)
Énault de Barbaucannes, Philippe (b. 1651,
    d. in or after 1708)
End, William (d. 1872)
England, Richard G. (d. 1812)
Enjalran, Jean (1639–1718)
Enslin, Christian (1800–56)
Entremont, Benoni d' (d. 1841)
Entremont, Simon d' (1788–1886)
Erad, Johann Burghard (d. 1757)
Erb, Abraham (1772–1830)
Erhardt, John Christian (d. 1752)
Erlandson, Erland (d. 1875)
Ermatinger, Charles Oakes (1776–1833)
Ermatinger, Edward (1797–1876)
Ermatinger, Frederick William (d. 1827)
Ermatinger, Frederick William (1811–69)
Ermatinger, Lawrence (d. 1789)
Erouachy (fl. 1618–29)
Espérance (fl. 1628–29)
Espiet de Pensens, Jacques d' (d. 1737)
Esson, Henry (d. 1853)
Esson, John (d. 1863)
Estcourt, James Bucknall Bucknall (1802–55)
Estèbe, Guillaume (b. 1701, d. in or after 1779)
Esten, James Christie Palmer (1805–64)
Estienne Du Bourgué de Clérin, Denis d' (d. 1719)
Estimauville, Jean-Baptiste-Philippe-Charles d'
    (1750–1823)
Estimauville, Joséphine-Éléonore d' (Taché;
    Clément) (1816–93)
Estimauville, Robert-Anne d' (1754–1831)
Estourmel, Constantin-Louis d' (1691–1765)
Etter, Benjamin (1763–1827)
Evans, Ephraim (1803–92)
Evans, Francis (1801–58)
Evans, James (1801–46)
Evans, John (1816–79)
Evans, Thomas (1777–1863)

Evans, William (1786–1857)
Évanturel, François (1821–91)
Evison, Robert (fl. 1746–49)
Ewart, James Bell (d. 1853)
Ewart, John (1788–1856)
Ewer, Thomas Anthony (d. 1833)
Eynard, Marie-Germain-Émile (1824–73)
Eynon, John Hicks (1801–88)
Eyre, William (d. 1765)

FABRE, Édouard-Charles (1827–96)
Fabre, Édouard-Raymond (1799–1854)
Fafard, Léon-Adélard (1850–85)
Fafard, Théogène (1855–90)
Fagundes, João Alvares (fl. 1521)
Fahey, James A. (d. 1888)
Faillon, Étienne-Michel (1799–1870)
Fairbanks, Charles Rufus (1790–1841)
Fairbanks, Samuel Prescott (1795–1882)
Fairbrother, Anne (Hill) (d. 1896)
Fairfield, William (d. 1816)
Fairweather, Charles Henry (1826–94)
Falardeau, Antoine-Sébastien (1822–89)
Falcon, Pierre (1793–1876)
Falkingham, Edward (d. 1757)
Fanning, David (1755–1825)
Fanning, Edmund (1739–1818)
Faraud, Henri (1823–90)
Farewell, Abram (1812–88)
Fargues, Thomas (1777–1847)
Faribault, Barthélemy (1728–1801)
Faribault, Georges-Barthélemi (1789–1866)
Faribault, Jean-Baptiste (1775–1860)
Faribault, Joseph-Édouard (1773–1859)
Farrar, George Whitefield (1812–81)
Farrell, John (1820–73)
Fassio, Gerome (d. 1851)
Faucher de Saint-Maurice, Narcisse-Henri-Édouard
    (1844–97)
Fauquier, Frederick Dawson (d. 1881)
Fautoux, Léon (d. 1748)
Fauvel, William Le Boutillier (1850–97)
Feild, Edward (1801–76)
Felton, William Bowman (1782–1837)
Felton, William Locker Pickmore (1812–77)
Feltz, Charles-Elemy-Joseph-Alexandre-Ferdinand
    (d. 1776)
Fenelon, Maurice (1834–97)
Fenerty, Charles (1821–92)
Fenety, George Edward (1812–99)
Fenouillet, Émile de (1807–59)
Fenwick, George Edgeworth (1825–94)
Ferguson, Bartemas (d. 1832)
Ferguson, Robert (1768–1851)
Ferguson, Thomas Roberts (1818–79)
Fergusson, Adam (1783–1862)
Fergusson Blair, Adam Johnston (1815–67)

Ferland, Jean-Baptiste-Antoine (1805–65)
Fernandes, João (fl. 1486–1505)
Ferrar, Constance (fl. 1629)
Ferrer Maldonado, Lorenzo (d. 1625)
Ferres, James Moir (1813–70)
Ferrie, Adam (1813–49)
Ferrie, Adam (1777–1863)
Ferrie, Colin Campbell (d. 1856)
Ferrier, James (1800–88)
Fézeret, René (d. 1720)
Fidler, Peter (1769–1822)
Field, Eleakim (fl. 1831–35)
Field, Elizabeth (Jones; Carey) (1804–90)
Field, Robert (d. 1819)
Fife, David (1805–77)
Filiastre, Luc (1646–1721)
Fillion, Michel (d. 1689)
Fillis, John (d. 1792)
Finlay, Hugh (d. 1801)
Finlay, Jacques-Raphaël (d. 1828)
Finlay, William (d. 1834)
Finlayson, Duncan (d. 1862)
Finlayson, Margaret (Haberkorn; Pabst), known as
 Margaret Bloomer and Margaret Mather (1859–
 98)
Finlayson, Nicol (d. 1877)
Finlayson, Roderick (1818–92)
Firth, William (1768–1838)
Fisbach, Marie, named Marie du Sacré-Cœur (Roy)
 (1806–85)
Fiset, Louis (1797–1867)
Fisher, Charles (1808–80)
Fisher, Duncan (d. 1820)
Fisher, Finlay (d. 1819)
Fisher, Sir George Bulteel (1764–1834)
Fisher, James (d. 1822)
Fisher, John Charlton (1794–1849)
Fisher, Peter (1782–1848)
Fisher, Richard (fl. 1593)
Fisher, Thomas (1792–1874)
Fisher, Wilford (1786–1868)
Fitzgerald, David (1813–94)
FitzGibbon, James (1780–1863)
FitzRoy, Sir Charles Augustus (1796–1858)
Fléché, Jessé (d. 1611?)
Fleming, John (d. 1832)
Fleming, John Arnot (1835–76)
Fleming, Michael Anthony (d. 1850)
Fleming, Peter (fl. 1815–52)
Flemish Bastard (fl. 1650–87)
Fletcher, Edward Taylor (1817–97)
Fletcher, Henry Charles (1833–79)
Fletcher, John (d. 1697)
Fletcher, John (d. 1844)
Fletcher, Robert (fl. 1766–85)
Fleury de La Gorgendière, Joseph de (1676–1755)
Fleury Deschambault, Jacques de (1672–98)

Fleury Deschambault, Jacques-Alexis de (d. 1715)
Fleury Deschambault, Joseph (1709–84)
Flint, Billa (1805–94)
Floquet, Pierre-René (1716–82)
Floyd, Henry, known as Black Harry (d. 1830)
Foi (fl. 1628)
Foley, Michael Hamilton (1820–70)
Fontbonne, Marie-Antoinette, named Sister
 Delphine (1813–56)
Fonte, Bartholomew de (fl. 1640)
Fonteneau, Jean, known as Jean Alphonse
 (1484–1544)
Forant, Isaac-Louis de (d. 1740)
Forbes, Charles John (1786–1862)
Forbes, Sir Francis (1784–1841)
Forbes, John (1707–59)
Forbin-Janson, Charles-Auguste-Marie-Joseph de
 (1785–1844)
Fordyce, John (d. 1751)
Foreman, James (1763–1854)
Forestier, Antoine (1646–1717)
Forestier, Antoine-Bertrand (1687–1742)
Forestier, Marie, named de Saint-Bonaventure-de-
 Jésus (d. 1698)
Foretier, Marie-Amable (Viger) (1778–1854)
Foretier, Pierre (1738–1815)
Forget, Antoine (1672–1749)
Forget Duverger, Jacques-François (fl. 1753–64)
Forgues, Michel (1811–82)
Forman, James (1795–1871)
Fornel, Joachim (b. 1697, d. in or after 1753)
Fornel, Louis (d. 1745)
Forrester, Alexander (1805–69)
Forrester, Andrew (fl. 1629–33)
Forrester, Thomas (d. 1841)
Forsyth, James Bell (1802–69)
Forsyth, John (d. 1837)
Forsyth, Joseph (d. 1813)
Forsyth, William (d. 1814)
Forsyth, William (1771–1841)
Fortier, Michel (1709–76)
Fortier, Narcisse-Charles (1800–59)
Fortin, Pierre-Étienne (1823–88)
Forton, Michel (1754–1817)
Foster, Asa Belknap (1817–77)
Foster, Colley Lyons Lucas (1778–1843)
Foster, Eliza Lanesford (Cushing) (1794–1886)
Foster, Sewell (1792–1868)
Foster, William Alexander (1840–88)
Fotherby, Charles (d. 1720)
Fothergill, Charles (1782–1840)
Foucault, François (1690–1766)
Foucault, Nicolas (d. 1702)
Foucault, Simon (Pierre) (1699–1744)
Foucher (fl. 1626–29)
Foucher, François (1699–1770)
Foulis, Robert (1796–1866)

Foureur, *dit* Champagne, Louis (1720–89)
Fournier, Charles-Vincent (1771–1839)
Fournier, Télesphore (1823–96)
Fowell, William Newton (1803–68)
Fowler, Daniel (1810–94)
Fox, John C. (1832–68)
Fox, Luke (1586–1635)
Franchère, Gabriel (1786–1863)
Francheville, Pierre (d. 1713)
Francklin, Michael (1733–82)
François, Claude, known as Brother Luc (1614–85)
Franklin, Sir John (1786–1847)
Franklin, Lumley (d. 1873)
Franks, Jacob (d. 1840)
Franquelin, Jean-Baptiste-Louis (fl. 1671–1712)
Franquet, Louis (d. 1768)
Fraser, Alexander (d. 1799)
Fraser, Alexander (1786–1853)
Fraser, Christopher Finlay (1839–94)
Fraser, Donald (d. 1897)
Fraser, Donald Allan (1793–1845)
Fraser, James (d. 1822)
Fraser, James Daniel Bain (1807–69)
Fraser, John (d. 1803)
Fraser, John Arthur (1838–98)
Fraser, John James (1829–96)
Fraser, Malcolm (1733–1815)
Fraser, Peter (1765–1840)
Fraser, Richard Duncan (d. 1857)
Fraser, Simon (1776–1862)
Fraser, Thomas (1749–1821)
Fraser, William (d. 1851)
Frasse de Plainval, Louis (d. 1890)
Frémin, Jacques (1628–91)
Frémiot, Nicolas-Marie-Joseph (1818–54)
Frémont, Charles-Jacques (1806–62)
French, Charles (d. 1828)
French, John (d. 1687)
French, John (1843–85)
Friel, Henry James (1823–69)
Frobisher, Benjamin (d. 1787)
Frobisher, Benjamin Joseph (1782–1821)
Frobisher, Joseph (1740–1810)
Frobisher, Sir Martin (d. 1594)
Frost, James (d. 1803)
Frothingham, John (1788–1870)
Fry, Henry (1826–96)
Fuca, Juan de (1536–1602)
Fulford, Francis (1803–68)
Fullartine, John (d. 1738)
Fuller, Thomas (1823–98)
Fuller, Thomas Brock (1810–84)
Fuller, Thomas Horace (d. 1861)
Fulton, James (1739–1826)
Fulton, John (1837–87)
Fulton, Stephen (1810–70)

Futvoye, George (1808–91)
Fyfe, Robert Alexander (1816–78)

GABOURY, Marie-Anne (Lagimonière) (1780–1875)
Gadbois, Albine, named Marie de Bonsecours (1830–74)
Gadois, Pierre (1632–1714)
Gadois, *dit* Mauger, Jacques (d. 1750)
Gadoys, Pierre (d. 1667)
Gage, James (1774–1854)
Gage, Thomas (d. 1787)
Gaggin, John Boles (d. 1867)
Gagnon, Antoine (1785–1849)
Gagnon, Ferdinand (1849–86)
Gagnon, Lucien (1793–1842)
Gagnon, Mathurin (1606–90)
Gaillard, Guillaume (d. 1729)
Gaillard, Mathieu (fl. 1683–94)
Galaup, Jean-François de, Comte de Lapérouse (1741–88)
Gale, Alexander (d. 1854)
Gale, Samuel (1747–1826)
Gale, Samuel (1783–1865)
Galiffet de Caffin, François de (1666–1746)
Gallant, Xavier, known as Pinquin (d. 1813)
Gallard, Charlotte (1648–1725)
Galleran, Guillaume (d. 1636)
Gallop, William (d. 1804)
Galt, Sir Alexander Tilloch (1817–93)
Galt, John (1779–1839)
Gamache, Louis (fl. 1808–52)
Gambier, James, 1st Baron Gambier (1756–1833)
Gamble, John William (1799–1873)
Gamble, William (1805–81)
Gamelain de La Fontaine, Michel (b. 1640, d. *c.* 1676)
Gamelin, Ignace (1663–1739)
Gamelin, Ignace (1698–1771)
Gamelin, Pierre (1789–1856)
Gamelin, Pierre-Joseph (1736–96)
Gamelin Maugras, Pierre (1697–1757)
Gandeacteua (d. 1673)
Ganet, François (d. 1747)
Gannes de Falaise, Louis de (1658–1714)
Gannes de Falaise, Michel de (d. 1752)
Garakontié (d. 1677 or 1678)
Garden, George (d. 1828)
Gargot de La Rochette, Nicolas (1619–64)
Garland, Charles (1730–1810)
Garland, George (d. 1833)
Garland, Thomas (fl. 1678–87)
Garneau, François-Xavier (1809–66)
Garnier, Charles (d. 1649)
Garnier, Constant (1816–94)
Garnier, John Hutchison (1823–98)
Garnier, Julien (1643–1730)

Garreau, Léonard (d. 1656)
Garreau, *dit* Saint-Onge, Pierre (1722–95)
Garrettson, Freeborn (1752–1827)
Garry, Nicholas (d. 1856)
Garvie, William (1837–72)
Gaschet, René (d. 1744)
Gascoin, Léocadie, named Marie des Sept-Douleurs (1818–1900)
Gastineau Duplessis, Jean-Baptiste (1611–1750)
Gates, Horatio (1777–1834)
Gatien, Félix (1776–1844)
Gatty, Juliana Horatia (Ewing) (1841–85)
Gaudais-Dupont, Louis (fl. 1663)
Gaudé, Françoise (1671–1751)
Gaudet, Joseph (1818–82)
Gaudron de Chevremont, Charles-René (b. 1702, d. before 1745)
Gaufin, Valérien (1699–1759)
Gaukel, Friedrich (1785–1853)
Gaulin, Antoine (1674–1740)
Gaulin, Rémi (1787–1857)
Gault, Mathew Hamilton (1822–87)
Gaultier, Jean-François (1708–56)
Gaultier de Comporté, Philippe (1641–87)
Gaultier de La Vérendrye, Jean-Baptiste (1713–36)
Gaultier de La Vérendrye, Louis-Joseph (1717–61)
Gaultier de La Vérendrye et de Boumois, Pierre (1714–55)
Gaultier de Varennes, Jacques-René (d. 1757)
Gaultier de Varennes, Jean-Baptiste (1677–1726)
Gaultier de Varennes, René (d. 1689)
Gaultier de Varennes et de La Vérendrye, Pierre (1685–1749)
Gaultier Du Tremblay, François (1715–94)
Gauthier, Amable (1792–1873)
Gauthier, Félix-Odilon (1808–76)
Gauthier, Marie-Angèle, named Sister Marie-Angèle (1828–98)
Gautier, Nicolas (1731–1810)
Gautier, *dit* Bellair, Joseph-Nicolas (1689–1752)
Gautron, *dit* Larochelle, Siméon (1808–59)
Gauvreau, Ferdinand-Edmond (1806–75)
Gauvreau, Louis (1761–1822)
Gauvreau, Pierre (1813–84)
Gawèhe (d. 1766)
Gay, James (1810–91)
Gay, Robert-Michel (1663–1725)
Gay Desenclaves, Jean-Baptiste de (b. 1702, d. in or after 1764)
Geddie, John (d. 1843)
Geddie, John (1815–72)
Gélinas, Évariste (1840–73)
Gell, Molly Ann (Thomas) (fl. 1807–22)
Genaple de Bellefonds, François (d. 1709)
Gendron, François (1618–88)
Gendron, Pierre-Samuel (d. 1889)

Geoffrion, Christophe-Alphonse (1843–99)
Geoffrion, Félix (1832–94)
Geoffroy, Louis (d. 1707)
George, David (d. 1810)
George, James (1800–70)
Georgemé, Séraphin (d. 1705)
Gérin, Elzéar (1843–87)
Gérin-Lajoie, Antoine (1824–82)
Germain, Césaire (1808–74)
Germain, Charles (1707–79)
Germain, Joseph-Louis (1633–1722)
Gerrard, Samuel (1767–1857)
Gerrish, Benjamin (1717–72)
Gerrish, Joseph (1709–74)
Gerrish, Moses (1744–1830)
Gervais, Gualbert (1844–88)
Gervaise, Louis (1708–63)
Gesner, Abraham (1797–1864)
Geyer, George (fl. 1672–97)
Giard, Antoine (b. 1682, d. 1746 or 1747)
Giard, Louis (1809–87)
Gibault, Pierre (d. 1802)
Gibb, Benaiah (1755–1826)
Gibb, James (1799–1858)
Gibbons, Richard (d. 1794)
Gibbons, Simon Thomas (d. 1896)
Gibbons, William (fl. 1612–14)
Gibbs, Thomas Nicholson (1821–83)
Gibson, David (1804–64)
Gibsone, Sir John (1637–1717)
Gidney, Angus Morrison (1803–82)
Giffard, Marie-Françoise, named Marie de Saint-Ignace (1634–57)
Giffard de Moncel, Robert (1587–1668)
Gilbert, Sir Humphrey (d. 1583)
Gilchrist, Frederick Charles (1859–96)
Gilchrist, John (1792–1859)
Gildersleeve, Henry (1785–1851)
Gildersleeve, Overton Smith (1825–64)
Gilkison, David (d. 1851)
Gilkison, William (1777–1833)
Gill, Ignace (1808–65)
Gill, Joseph-Louis, known as Magouaouidombaouit (1719–98)
Gill, Michael (d. 1720)
Gillam, Benjamin (1662/63–1706)
Gillam, Zachariah (1636–82)
Gillespie, George (1771–1842)
Gillespie, Robert (1785–1863)
Gillmore, George (d. 1811)
Gilmore, Thomas (d. 1773)
Gilmour, Allan (1775–1849)
Gilmour, Allan (1805–84)
Gilmour, Allan (1816–95)
Gilmour, John (1812–77)
Gilpin, John Bernard (1810–92)
Gingras, Édouard (1806–57)

Gingras, Léon (1808–60)
Gingras, Louis (1796–1866)
Girard, Jacques(?) (d. 1782)
Girard, Marc-Amable (1822–92)
Girod, Amury (d. 1837)
Girouard, Antoine (1762–1832)
Girouard, Gilbert-Anselme (1846–85)
Girouard, Jean-Joseph (1794–1855)
Giroux, André-Raphaël (1815–69)
Girroir, Hubert (1825–84)
Girty, Simon (1741–1818)
Gisborne, Frederic Newton (1824–92)
Givins, James (d. 1846)
Glackemeyer, Frederick (1759–1836)
Glackmeyer, Louis-Édouard (1793–1881)
Gladman, George (1800–63)
Gladwin, Henry (d. 1791)
Glandelet, Charles de (1645–1725)
Glapion, Augustin-Louis de (1719–90)
Glasgow, George (d. 1820)
Glasier, Beamsley Perkins (d. 1784)
Glasier, John (1809–94)
Gledhill, Samuel (b. 1677, d. 1735 or 1736)
Glen, Thomas (1796–1887)
Glenie, James (1750–1817)
Glenn, John (1833–86)
Glikhikan (d. 1782)
Globensky, Hortense (Prévost) (1804–73)
Globensky, Maximilien (1793–1866)
Glode, Charles (d. 1852)
Glode, Gabriel (fl. 1842–57)
Gloria, Jean (d. 1665)
Glover, Sir John Hawley (1829–85)
Gobin, Jean (1646–1703)
Godefroy, Jean-Paul (d. c. 1668)
Godefroy de Linctot, Daniel-Maurice (d. c. 1783)
Godefroy de Lintot, Jean (d. 1681)
Godefroy de Lintot, Michel (d. 1709)
Godefroy de Normanville, Thomas (d. 1652)
Godefroy de Saint-Paul, Jean-Amador (d. 1730)
Godefroy de Tonnancour, Charles-Antoine
  (1698–1757)
Godefroy de Tonnancour, Charles-Antoine
  (1755–98)
Godefroy de Tonnancour, Joseph-Marie (1750–
  1834)
Godrefoy de Tonnancour, Léonard (1793–1867)
Godefroy de Tonnancour, Louis-Joseph (d. 1784)
Godefroy de Tonnancour, René (d. 1738)
Godefroy de Vieuxpont, Jacques (d. 1661)
Godefroy de Vieuxpont, Joseph (b. 1645, d. c. 1716)
Godet, Rolland (fl. 1651–53)
Godet Des Maretz, Claude de (d. c. 1627)
Godin, *dit* Bellefontaine, *dit* Beauséjour, Joseph (b.
  1697, d. in or after 1774)
Goessman, John (1786–1841)
Goff, Fade (1780–1836)

Goffe, Edmund (d. 1740)
Goguet, Denis (1704–78)
Gohin, Pierre-André, Comte de Montreuil (b. 1722,
  d. in or after 1793)
Goldie, Thomas (1850–92)
Goldsmith, Oliver (1794–1861)
Goldthwait, Benjamin (1704–61)
Gomes, Estevão (d. 1538)
Gonish, Peter (fl. 1841–46)
Gonsales, João (fl. 1501–3)
Good, James (d. 1889)
Gooderham, William (1790–1881)
Gooderham, William (1824–89)
Goodfellow, James (1828–98)
Goodhue, George Jervis (1799–1870)
Gordon, Andrew Robertson (1851–93)
Gordon, Edward John (1791–1870)
Gordon, George Nicol (1822–61)
Gordon, Lord Gordon (d. 1874)
Gordon, James Douglas (1832–72)
Gordon, John (1792–1869)
Gordon, John (1828–82)
Gore, Sir Charles Stephen (1793–1869)
Gore, Francis (1769–1852)
Goreham, Joseph (1725–90)
Gorham, John (1709–51)
Gorrell, James (d. c. 1769)
Gorst, Thomas (fl. 1668–87)
Gosse, Philip Henry (1810–88)
Gosselin, Clément (1747–1816)
Gosselin, Jean-Baptiste (d. 1749)
Gosselin, Léon (1801–42)
Gosselin, Scholastique (1806–76)
Gossip, William (1809–89)
Gotteville de Belile, Robert-David (fl. 1696–1724)
Goudie, John (1775–1824)
Gouentagrandi (fl. 1689–1738)
Gould, Joseph (1808–86)
Goulet, Elzéar (1836–70)
Goupil, René (1608–42)
Gourdeau de Beaulieu et de La Grossardière,
  Jacques (d. 1720)
Gourlay, Robert Fleming (1778–1863)
Goutin, François-Marie de (d. 1752)
Goutin, Mathieu de (d. 1714)
Gow, Peter (1818–86)
Gowan, Ogle Robert (1803–76)
Gowan, Robert (d. 1879)
Gower, Sir Erasmus (1742–1814)
Goyer, Olivier (1663–1721)
Grace, Thomas, named Father James (1755–1827)
Graham, Aaron (d. 1818)
Graham, Andrew (d. 1815)
Graham, Hugh (1758–1829)
Graham, James Elliot (1847–99)
Graham, John Hamilton (1826–99)
Grandmaison, Éléonore de (Boudier de Beauregard;

Chavigny de Berchereau; Gourdeau de Beaulieu; Cailhault de La Tesserie) (d. 1692)
Grant, Alexander (1734–1813)
Grant, Colin P. (d. 1839)
Grant, Cuthbert (d. 1799)
Grant, Cuthbert (d. 1854)
Grant, James (fl. 1777–99)
Grant, Peter (d. 1848)
Grant, Walter Colquhoun (1822–61)
Grant, William (1744–1805)
Grant, William (1743–1810)
Grant, Sir William (1752–1832)
Grasett, Henry James (1808–82)
Grass, Michael (d. 1813)
Grasset de Saint-Sauveur, André (1724–94)
Gravé de La Rive, Henri-François (1730–1802)
Gravé Du Pont, François (fl. 1599–1629)
Gravé Du Pont, Robert (d. 1621)
Gravelet, Jean-François, known as Charles Blondin (1824–97)
Graves, Thomas, 1st Baron Graves (1725–1802)
Gravier, Jacques (1651–1708)
Gray, Benjamin Gerrish (1768–1854)
Gray, Edward William (1742–1810)
Gray, John (d. 1829)
Gray, John Hamilton (1811–87)
Gray, John Hamilton (1814–89)
Gray, John William Dering (1797–1868)
Gray, Ralph (d. 1813)
Gray, Robert (1755–1806)
Gray, Robert (d. 1828)
Gray, Robert Isaac Dey (d. 1804)
Graydon, John (d. 1726)
Gray Lock (fl. 1675–1740)
Grece, Charles Frederick (d. 1844)
Greeley, Horace (1811–72)
Green, Anson (1801–79)
Green, Bartholomew (1699–1751)
Green, Benjamin (1713–72)
Green, Francis (1742–1809)
Green, George Everitt (1880–95)
Green, James (d. 1835)
Green, William (1787–1832)
Green, William (fl. 1783–1833)
Greenwood, William (d. 1824)
Gregory, John (d. 1817)
Gregory, John (1806–61)
Grey, William (1819–72)
Greysolon de La Tourette, Claude (fl. 1683–1716)
Greysolon Dulhut, Daniel (d. 1710)
Gridley, Richard (1710/11–96)
Griebel, Ferdinand (d. 1858)
Grieve, Walter (d. 1887)
Griffin, Jane (Franklin, Lady Franklin) (1792–1875)
Griffin, William Henry (1812–1900)
Griffith, John (fl. 1825–47)
Grigor, William (1798–1857)

Grillot de Poilly, François-Claude-Victor (1726–61)
Grimington, Michael (d. 1710)
Grimington, Michael (fl. 1698–1719)
Grisé, Antoine (1728–85)
Grollier, Pierre-Henri (1826–64)
Groston de Saint-Ange, Robert (fl. 1692–1738)
Groston de Saint-Ange et de Bellerive, Louis (d. 1774)
Gschwind, John Frederick Traugott (d. 1827)
Gueguen, Joseph (1741–1825)
Guen, Hamon (1687–1761)
Guenet, Marie, named de Saint-Ignace (1610–46)
Guernon, *dit* Belleville, François (d. 1817)
Guerout, Pierre (1751–1830)
Guesdron, Julien (1667–1735)
Gugy, Bartholomew Conrad Augustus (1796–1876)
Gugy, Conrad (d. 1786)
Gugy, Louis (1770–1840)
Guiboche, Louis (d. before 1860)
Guibord, Joseph (1809–69)
Guichart, Vincent-Fleuri (1729–93)
Guignas, Michel (1681–1752)
Guigues, Joseph-Bruno (1805–74)
Guillemot, *dit* Du Plessis-Kerbodot, Guillaume (d. 1652)
Guillet, Louis (1788–1868)
Guillet de Chaumont, Nicolas-Auguste (d. 1765)
Guillimin, Charles (1676–1739)
Guillimin, Guillaume (1713–71)
Guillimin, Marie-Françoise, named de Saint-Antoine (1720–89)
Guillot, *dit* Larose, François (b. 1727, d. before 1785)
Guillouet d'Orvilliers, Claude (1668–1728)
Guillouet d'Orvilliers, Rémy (d. 1713)
Guion, François (b. 1666, d. *c.* 1701)
Guitet, Claude (d. 1802)
Guiton de Monrepos, Jacques-Joseph (fl. 1740–64)
Guitté, Pierre-Joseph (fl. 1846–67)
Gunn, Donald (1797–1878)
Gunn, Isabel (fl. 1806–9)
Gurnett, George (d. 1861)
Gurney, Edward (1817–84)
Guy, Étienne (1774–1820)
Guy, John (d. *c.* 1629)
Guy, Louis (1768–1850)
Guy, Nicholas (fl. 1612–31)
Guy, Pierre (1701–48)
Guy, Pierre (1738–1812)
Guyart, Marie, named de l'Incarnation (Martin) (1599–1672)
Guyart de Fleury, Jean-Baptiste (fl. 1740–61)
Guyon, Jean (1659–87)
Guyon, Louise (Thibault; Damours de Freneuse) (fl. 1668–1711) [volume III appendix]
Guyon Du Buisson, Jean (d. 1663)
Guyon Du Duisson, Jean (1619–94)

27

Guyotte, Étienne (d. 1701)
Gwillim, Elizabeth Posthuma (Simcoe) (d. 1850)
Gwynne, William Charles (1806–75)
Gyles, John (d. 1755)
Gzowski, Sir Casimir Stanislaus (1813–98)

HACHÉ, Juste (1823–95)
Haché-Gallant, Michel (d. 1737)
Hackett, Nelson (fl. 1840–42)
Haenke, Tadeo (1761–1817)
Hagan, Michael (d. 1896)
Hagarty, Sir John Hawkins (1816–1900)
Hagerman, Christopher Alexander (1792–1847)
Haimard, Pierre (1674–1724)
Haldane, John (d. 1857)
Haldimand, Sir Frederick (1718–91) [volumes IV and V]
Haldimand, Peter Frederick (d. 1765)
Hale, Edward (1800–75)
Hale, Horatio Emmons (1817–96)
Hale, Jeffery (1803–64)
Hale, John (1765–1838)
Hale, Robert (1702/3–67)
Halhead, Edward (fl. 1749–52)
Haliburton, Susanna Lucy Anne (Weldon) (d. 1899)
Haliburton, Thomas Chandler (1796–1865)
Haliburton, William Hersey Otis (1767–1829)
Halkett (Wedderburn), John (1768–1852)
Hall, Archibald (1812–68)
Hall, Charles Francis (1821–71)
Hall, George Benson (1780–1821)
Hall, George Benson (1810–76)
Hall, James (d. 1612)
Hall, Sir Robert (d. 1818)
Hall, William (1767–1854)
Halliburton, Sir Brenton (d. 1860)
Haly, Sir William O'Grady (1810–78)
Hamare de La Borde, Jean-Baptiste-Julien (b. 1693, d. in or after 1729)
Hamel, André-Rémi (1788–1840)
Hamel, Théophile (1817–70)
Hamelin de Bourgchemin et de L'Hermitière, Jacques-François (b. 1664, d. before 1698)
Hamilton, Alexander (1790–1839)
Hamilton, Andrew (fl. 1688–89)
Hamilton, Sir Charles (1767–1849)
Hamilton, George (1788–1836)
Hamilton, George (1781–1839)
Hamilton, Henry (d. 1796)
Hamilton, James (1810–96)
Hamilton, John (1802–82)
Hamilton, John (1827–88)
Hamilton, Otho (d. 1770)
Hamilton, Peter Stevens (1826–93)
Hamilton, Robert (1753–1809)
Hamilton, Robert Douglas (1783–1857)

Hamilton, William (1810–80)
Hamm, Albert (1860–91)
Hamond, Sir Andrew Snape (1738–1828)
Handasyde, Thomas (d. 1712)
Handfield, John (fl. 1719/20–60)
Hanington, William (d. 1838)
Hanna, James (d. 1787)
Hanna, James G. (d. 1807)
Hanna, James Godfrey (d. 1851)
Hannan, Michael (1821–82)
Hanrahan, Edmund (1802–75)
Hans Hendrik (d. 1889)
Hantraye, Claude (d. 1777)
Harding, Francis Pym (d. 1875)
Harding, Harris (1761–1854)
Harding, Thomas (d. 1854)
Hardisty, Richard Charles (d. 1889)
Hardisty, William Lucas (d. 1881)
Hardy, Sir Charles (d. 1780)
Hardy, Elias (d. 1798)
Hardy, George (d. in or after 1803)
Hargrave, James (1798–1865)
Hargrave, Joseph James (1841–94)
Harley, John (1800–75)
Harman, Samuel Bickerton (1819–92)
Harmon, Daniel Williams (1778–1843)
Harper, Charles (1800–55)
Harper, Jerome (1826–74)
Harries, John (1763–1810)
Harrington, Joanna, named Sister Mary Benedicta (1845–95)
Harriott, John Edward (1797–1866)
Harris, Alexander (1805–74)
Harris, Frederick Warren (1823–63)
Harris, James Stanley (1803–88)
Harris, John (1739–1802)
Harris, John (1841–87)
Harris, John Leonard (1833–98)
Harris, Joseph (1835–99)
Harris, Joseph Hemington (1800–81)
Harris, Michael Spurr (1804–66)
Harris, Robert William (d. 1861)
Harris, Thomas Dennie (1803–73)
Harrison, Edward (d. 1794)
Harrison, John (fl. 1710–21)
Harrison, Mark Robert (1819–94)
Harrison, Robert Alexander (1833–78)
Harrison, Samuel Bealey (1802–67)
Hart, Aaron (d. 1800)
Hart, Aaron Ezekiel (1803–57)
Hart, Adolphus Mordecai (1814–79)
Hart, Benjamin (1779–1855)
Hart, Ezekiel (1770–1843)
Hart, Marmaduke (d. 1829)
Hart, Moses (1768–1852)
Hart, Samuel (d. 1810)
Hart, Theodore (1816–87)

Hartman, Joseph (1821–59)
Hartshorne, Lawrence (1755–1822)
Hartt, Charles Frederick (1840–78)
Harvard, William Martin (d. 1857)
Harvey, Alexander (1827–86)
Harvey, Sir John (1778–1852)
Harwood, Robert Unwin (1798–1863)
Haskins, James (d. 1845)
Hassall, Thomas (d. 1844)
Haswell, Robert (1768–1801)
Haszard, James Douglas (1797–1875)
Hatheway, Calvin Luther (1786–1866)
Hatheway, George Luther (1813–72)
Hatt, Richard (1769–1819)
Havard de Beaufort, François-Charles, known
  as L'Avocat (fl. 1737–42)
Haven, Jens (1724–96)
Haviland, Thomas Heath (d. 1867)
Haviland, Thomas Heath (1822–95)
Haviland, William (1718–84)
Havy, François (1709–66)
Hawke, Anthony Bewden (d. 1867)
Hawkeridge, William (fl. 1610–31)
Hawkins, Alfred (d. 1854)
Hawkins, Ernest (1802–68)
Hawley, William Fitz (1804–55)
Haws, John (d. 1858)
Hay, Lord Charles (d. 1760)
Hay, Charles (fl. 1770–83)
Hay, Jehu (d. 1785)
Hay, Robert (1808–90)
Hay, William (1818–88)
Hayes, Edward (d. c. 1613)
Hayes, Isaac Israel (1832–81)
Hayes, Moses Judah (1799–1861)
Hayman, Robert (d. 1629)
Haynes, John Carmichael (1831–88)
Haythorne, Robert Poore (1815–91)
Hazen, Moses (1733–1803)
Hazen, Robert Leonard (1808–74)
Hazen, William (1738–1814)
Hazeur, François (d. 1708)
Hazeur, Jean-François (d. 1733)
Hazeur, Joseph-Thierry (1680–1757)
Hazeur de L'Orme, Pierre (1682–1771)
Hazlewood, Samuel (1822–78)
Head, Sir Edmund Walker (1805–68)
Head, Sir Francis Bond (1793–1875)
Head, Samuel (d. 1837)
Hearn, John (d. 1894)
Hearne, Samuel (1745–92)
Heath, John (d. 1874)
Heaviside, Mary (Love, Lady Love) (fl. 1825–66)
Heavysege, Charles (1816–76)
Hébert, Étienne (1736–1823)
Hébert, Guillemette (Couillard de Lespinay) (d.
  1684)

Hébert, Jean-François (1763–1831)
Hébert, Joseph (b. 1636, d. 1661 or 1662)
Hébert, Louis (d. 1627)
Hébert, Nicolas-Tolentin (1810–88)
Heck, Samuel (1771–1841)
Heer, Louis-Chrétien de (b. 1760, d. before 1808)
Heintzman, Theodor August (1817–99)
Helliwell, Thomas (d. 1862)
Henday, Anthony (fl. 1750–62)
Henderson, Alexander (1824–87)
Henderson, Andrew (d. 1869)
Hendery, Robert (1814–97)
Heney, Hugues (1789–1844)
Hennepin, Louis (b. 1626, d. c. 1705)
Henry, Alexander (d. 1814)
Henry, Alexander (1739–1824)
Henry, Anthony (1734–1800)
Henry, Edme (1760–1841)
Henry, John (d. 1853)
Henry, Robert (d. 1859)
Henry, Walter (1791–1860)
Henry, William Alexander (1816–88)
Hensley, Joseph (1824–94)
Henson, Josiah (1789–1883)
Hepburn, John (1794–1864)
Herbert, Mary Eliza (1829–72)
Herbert, Sarah (1824–46)
Herbomez, Louis-Joseph d' (1822–90)
Herchmer, William Macauley (1844–92)
Heriot, Frederick George (1786–1843)
Heriot, George (1759–1839)
Heron, Patrick (fl. 1709–52)
Heron, Samuel (b. 1770, d. 1817 or 1818)
Herring, John (1818–96)
Herron, William (1784–1838)
Hertel de La Fresnière, Jacques (d. 1651)
Hertel de La Fresnière, Joseph-François (d. 1722)
Hertel de La Fresnière, Zacharie-François (d. 1752)
Hertel de Moncours, Pierre (1687–1739)
Hertel de Rouville, Jean-Baptiste (1668–1722)
Hertel de Rouville, Jean-Baptiste-Melchior
  (1748–1817)
Hertel de Rouville, Jean-Baptiste-René (1789–
  1859)
Hertel de Rouville, René-Ovide (1720–92)
Hertel de Saint-François, Étienne (1734–60)
Hertel de Saint-François, Joseph-Hippolyte
  (1738–81)
Hervieux, Louis-François (1711–48)
Heustis, Daniel D. (b. 1806, d. in or after 1846)
Hewett, Edward Osborne (1835–97)
Hey, William (d. 1797)
Hibbard, Ashley (1827–86)
Hibbard, Jedediah (1740–1809)
Hiché, Henry (d. 1758)
Hicks, John (1715–90)
Hicks, William Henry (d. 1899)

29

Hickson, Sir Joseph (1830–97)
Higgins, David (d. 1783)
Higginson, Sir James Macaulay (1805–85)
Hildrith, Isaac (1741–1807)
Hill, Charles (d. 1825)
Hill, Henry George (d. 1882)
Hill, John (d. 1735)
Hill, John (d. 1841)
Hill, Philip Carteret (1821–94)
Hill, Samuel (b. 1668, d. c. 1732)
Hill, Sir Stephen John (1809–91)
Hill, Thomas (1807–60)
Hill, William (fl. 1634–38)
Hillaire de La Rochette, Alexandre-Robert (d')
    (fl. 1755–72)
Hillier, George (d. 1840)
Hills, George (1816–95)
Hilton, John (d. 1866)
Hilton, Winthrop (d. 1710)
Hilyard, Thomas (1810–73)
Hincks, Sir Francis (1807–85)
Hincks, William (1794–1871)
Hind, William George Richardson (1833–89)
Hindenlang, Charles (1810–39)
Hinton, William (d. c. 1688)
Hiriberry, Joannis de (fl. 1718–22)
Hobby, Sir Charles (d. 1715)
Hobson, Benjamin (d. c. 1832)
Hocquart, Gilles (1694–1783)
Hodder, Edward Mulberry (1810–78)
Hodges, James (1814–79)
Hodgson, John (fl. 1774–1828)
Hodgson, Robert (d. 1811)
Hodgson, Sir Robert (1798–1880)
Hodiesne, Gervais (1692–1764)
Hoerner, Olympe (Tanner) (1807–54)
Hoffmann, Matthias Francis (d. 1851)
Hogan, John Sheridan (d. 1859)
Hogg, James (1800–66)
Hogg, Simon Jackson (1845–87)
Hogsett, Aaron (d. 1858)
Hogsett, George James (1820–69)
Holbrook, James (d. 1846)
Holdsworth, Arthur (1668–1726)
Holl, John Myrie (1802–69)
Holland, Anthony Henry (1785–1830)
Holland, John Frederick (d. 1845)
Holland, Samuel Johannes (1728–1801)
Holloway, John (1743/44–1826)
Holman, James Henry (1824–91)
Holman, Sarah (Dalton) (d. 1888)
Holmes, Andrew Fernando (1797–1860)
Holmes, Benjamin (1794–1865)
Holmes, Charles (d. 1761)
Holmes, Elkanah (1744–1832)
Holmes, John (1799–1852)
Holmes, John (1789–1876)

Holmes, William (d. 1792)
Holmes, William (d. 1834)
Holton, Luther Hamilton (1817–80)
Homer, John (1781–1836)
Honatteniate (d. 1650)
Honeyman, David (1817–89)
Honorat, Jean-Baptiste (1799–1862)
Hood, Robert (d. 1821)
Hooper, Edmund John Glyn (1818–89)
Hooper, John (1791–1869)
Hope, Adam (1813–82)
Hope, Henry (d. 1789)
Hopkins, Caleb (d. 1880)
Hopkins, Samuel (fl. 1715–31)
Hopper, Arthur (1784–1872)
Hopper, John Elisha Peck (1841–95)
Hoppner, Henry Parkyns (1795–1833)
Hopson, Peregrine Thomas (d. 1759)
Horan, Edward John (1817–75)
Horden, John (1828–93)
Hore, Richard (fl. 1536–40)
Horetzky, Charles George (1838–1900)
Horn, Kate M. (Buckland) (d. 1896)
Horne, Robert Charles (d. 1845)
Horné, dit Laneuville, Jacques de (1664–1730)
Hornor, Thomas (1767–1834)
Hotsinoñhyahta? (fl. 1748–74)
Houde, Frédéric (1847–84)
Houdet, Antoine-Jacques (1763–1826)
Houdin, Jean-Michel, known as Father Potentien
    (b. 1706, d. c. 1766)
Houghton, Charles Frederick (1839–98)
Houliston, George Baillie (d. 1891)
How, Deborah (Cottnam) (d. 1806)
How, Edward (d. 1750)
How, Henry (1828–79)
Howard, Henry (1815–87)
Howard, James Scott (1798–1866)
Howard, John George (1803–90)
Howard, Joseph (d. 1797)
Howard, Peter (d. 1843)
Howard, Robert Palmer (1823–89)
Howatt, Cornelius (1810–95)
Howe, Alexander (1749–1813)
Howe, John (1754–1835)
Howe, Joseph (1804–73)
Howison, John (1797–1859)
Howland, William Holmes (1844–93)
Howley, Thomas (d. 1889)
Howorth, William (d. 1881)
Howse, Joseph (d. 1852)
Hoyle, Robert (1781–1857)
Hoyles, Sir Hugh William (1814–88)
Hoyles, Newman Wright (1777–1840)
Huault de Montmagny, Charles (d. c. 1653)
Hubbard, Hester Ann (Case) (d. 1831)
Hubert, Jean-François (1739–97)

Hubert, Louis-Édouard (1766–1842)
Hudon, Hyacinthe (1792–1847)
Hudon, Victor (1812–97)
Hudson, Henry (d. c. 1611)
Hudson, John (d. c. 1611)
Huet, Paul (d. 1665)
Huet de La Valinière, Pierre (d. 1806)
Hughes, Sir Richard (d. 1812)
Huguet, Joseph (1725–83)
Huguet, *dit* Latour, Pierre (1749–1817)
Humbert, Stephen (d. 1849)
Hume, Catherine Honoria (Blake) (d. 1886)
Humphreys, James (1748/49–1810)
Humphreys, James Dodsley (d. 1877)
Humphreys, Thomas Basil (1840–90)
Hunkajuka (d. 1873)
Hunt, Charles (1820–71)
Hunt, James (1779–1847)
Hunt, Thomas Sterry (1826–92)
Hunter, Charles (1808–39)
Hunter, James (1817–82)
Hunter, Sir Martin (1757–1846)
Hunter, Peter (d. 1805)
Hunter-Duvar, John (1821–99)
Huntington, Herbert (1799–1851)
Huntington, Lucius Seth (1827–86)
Huntley, Sir Henry Vere (1795–1864)
Huot, François (1756–1822)
Huot, Hector-Simon (1803–46)
Huot, Marie-Catherine, named Sainte-Madeleine (1791–1869)
Huot, Marie-Françoise, named Sainte-Gertrude (1795–1850)
Huppé, *dit* Lagroix, Joseph (b. 1696, d. in or after 1776)
Hurd, Samuel Proudfoot (1793–1853)
Hurlburt, Thomas (1808–73)
Hurteau, Isidore (1815–79)
Huston, James (1820–54)
Hutchings, Richard (d. 1808)
Hutchins, Thomas (d. 1790)
Hutchinson, Robert (1802–66)
Hutton, James Scott (1833–91)
Hutton, Samuel (1845–94)
Hutton, William (1801–61)
Huyghue, Samuel Douglass Smith (1816–91)
Hwistesmetxē'qEn (fl. 1793–1859)
Hyatt, Gilbert (d. 1823)
Hyman, Ellis Walton (1813–78)
Hyman, William (1807–82)

IFFLAND, Anthony von (1798–1876)
Ignace de Paris (d. 1662)
Imbault, Maurice (b. 1686, d. in or after 1759)
Imbert, Bertrand (1714–75)
Imbert, Jacques (d. 1765)
Ingersoll, Laura (Secord) (1775–1868)

Inglis, Charles (1734–1816)
Inglis, John (1777–1850)
Ingram, David (fl. 1568–83)
Inkster, John (1799–1874)
Iredell, Abraham (1751–1806)
Ironside, George (d. 1831)
Ironside, George (d. 1863)
Iroquet (fl. 1609–15)
Irumberry de Salaberry, Charles-Michel d' (1778–1829)
Irumberry de Salaberry, Charles-René-Léonidas d' (1820–82)
Irumberry de Salaberry, Édouard-Alphonse d' (1792–1812)
Irumberry de Salaberry, Ignace-Michel-Louis-Antoine d' (1752–1828)
Irvine, George (1826–97)
Irvine, James (1766–1829)
Irving, Paulus Æmilius (1714–96)
Irving, William (1816–72)
Irwin, Marie, named de la Conception (1626–87)
Irwin, Thomas (d. 1847)
Isabeau, Michel-Philippe (d. c. 1724)
Isadore (d. 1894)
Isapo-muxika (d. 1890)
Isbister, Alexander Kennedy (1822–83)
Isbister, Joseph (d. 1771)
Isbister, William (fl. 1739–51)
Isham, Charles Thomas (d. 1814)
Isham, James (d. 1761)
Ives, William Bullock (1841–99)

JACAU de Fiedmont, Louis-Thomas (d. 1788)
Jack, William Brydone (1817–86)
Jackman, William (1837–77)
Jackson, Edward (1799–1872)
Jackson, James (d. 1851)
Jackson, John (d. 1717)
Jackson, John Mills (d. 1836)
Jackson, Sir Richard Downes (1777–1845)
Jacob, Edwin (d. 1868)
Jacob, Étienne (fl. 1665–1726)
Jacobs, Ferdinand (d. 1783)
Jacobs, Samuel (d. 1786)
Jacquelin, Françoise-Marie (Saint-Étienne de La Tour) (1602–45)
Jacques, John (1804–86)
Jacquet, François (fl. 1731–77)
Jacquies, Adolphe (d. 1860)
Jacquiés, *dit* Leblond, Jean (b. 1688, d. in or after 1724)
Jacquin, *dit* Philibert, Nicolas (1700–48)
Jacrau, Joseph-André-Mathurin (d. 1772)
Jacson, Antoine (d. 1803)
Jadis, Charles Newland Godfrey (b. 1730, d. in or after 1788)
Jago, John (b. 1684, d. in or after 1724)

Jalobert, Macé (fl. 1528–55)
James, Philip (d. 1851)
James, Thomas (d. *c.* 1635)
Jameson, Richard Willis (1851–99)
Jameson, Robert Sympson (d. 1854)
Jamet, Denis (d. 1625)
Jamet, John (d. 1763)
Jamot, Jean-François (1828–86)
Janson, *dit* Lapalme, Dominique (1701–62)
Janvrin, John (1762–1835)
Jardine, Robert (1812–66)
Jarret de Verchères, Marie-Madeleine (Tarieu de La Pérade) (1678–1747)
Jarret de Verchères, Pierre (d. 1708)
Jarvis, Edward (d. *c.* 1800)
Jarvis, Edward James (1788–1852)
Jarvis, George Stephen Benjamin (1797–1878)
Jarvis, Munson (1742–1825)
Jarvis, Samuel Peters (1792–1857)
Jarvis, William (1756–1817)
Jarvis, William Botsford (1799–1864)
Jautard, Valentin (d. 1787)
Jay, John (d. 1528)
Jeanneau, Étienne (d. 1743)
Jeanson, Guillaume (b. 1721, d. in or after 1777)
Jeantot, Jean (d. 1748)
Jebb, Sir Joshua (1793–1863)
Jeffers, Wellington (1814–96)
Jeffery, Joseph (1829–94)
Jeffery, Thomas Nickleson (1782–1847)
Jehin-Prume, Frantz (1839–99)
Jenkins, John (1813–98)
Jenkins, William (1779–1843)
Jennings, Amelia Clotilda (d. 1895)
Jennings, John (1814–76)
Jérémie, *dit* Lamontagne, Catherine (Aubuchon; Lepallieur de Laferté) (d. 1744)
Jérémie, *dit* Lamontagne, Nicolas (d. 1732)
Jérémie, *dit* Lamontagne, Noël (d. between 1694 and 1697)
Jervois, Sir William Francis Drummond (1821–97)
Jessen, Dettlieb Christopher (1730–1814)
Jessup, Edward (1735–1816)
Jewitt, John Rodgers (1783–1821)
Joannès de Chacornacle (1672–1707)
Job, Thomas Bulley (1806–78)
Jobin, André (1786–1853)
Joe (fl. 1771–89)
Joe, Sylvester (fl. 1822)
Jogues, Isaac (1607–46)
John, Noel (fl. 1821–41)
Johnson, Sir Francis Godschall (1817–94)
Johnson, George (1564–1605)
Johnson, George Henry Martin (1816–84)
Johnson, Guy (d. 1788)
Johnson, Sir John (1741–1830)
Johnson, John (1792–1886)

Johnson, John Mercer (1818–68)
Johnson, Theresa Mary (Gowanlock) (d. 1899)
Johnson, Sir William (d. 1774)
Johnson, William Arthur (1816–80)
Johnston, Alexander (d. 1778)
Johnston, George Moir (1817–77)
Johnston, Hugh (1756–1829)
Johnston, Hugh (1790–1850)
Johnston, James (d. 1800)
Johnston, James (d. 1849)
Johnston, James Finlay Weir (1796–1855)
Johnston, James William (1792–1873)
Johnston, John (1762–1828)
Johnston, William (d. 1828)
Johnston, William (1782–1870)
Johnston, William (1848–85)
Johnstone, James, known as Chevalier de Johnstone (b. 1719, d. in or after 1791)
Johnstone, Walter (fl. 1795–1824)
Joliette, Barthélemy (1789–1850)
Jolliet, Louis (d. 1700)
Jolliet de Mingan, Jean-Baptiste (d. between 1732 and 1735)
Jones, Augustus (d. 1836)
Jones, Caleb (d. 1816)
Jones, Charles (1781–1840)
Jones, David Thomas (d. 1844)
Jones, Ephraim (1750–1812)
Jones, Henry (fl. 1725–50)
Jones, Henry (1776–1852)
Jones, James (1742–1805)
Jones, John (1737–1800)
Jones, John (d. 1818)
Jones, John (d. 1823)
Jones, John (1798–1847)
Jones, Jonas (1791–1848)
Jones, Oliver (1821–99)
Jones, Peter (Kahkewaquonaby) (1802–56)
Jones, Robert (1778–1859)
Jones, Solomon (d. 1822)
Jones, Thomas Mercer (1795–1868)
Jordan, Jacob (1741–96)
Joseph, Abraham (1815–86)
Joseph, Henry (d. 1832)
Joseph, John (d. 1851)
Joseph, Judah George (1798–1857)
Jourdain, Charles (b. 1734, d. in or after 1823)
Jourdain, *dit* Labrosse, Paul-Raymond (d. 1769)
Joybert de Soulanges et de Marson, Louise-Élisabeth de (Rigaud de Vaudreuil, Marquise de Vaudreuil) (1673–1740)
Joybert de Soulanges et de Marson, Pierre de (d. 1678)
Juchereau de La Ferté, Denis-Joseph (d. 1709)
Juchereau de La Ferté, Jean (d. 1685)
Juchereau de La Ferté, Jeanne-Françoise, named de Saint-Ignace (1650–1723)

Juchereau de Maur, Jean (d. 1672)
Juchereau de Maur, Paul-Augustin (1658–1714)
Juchereau de Saint-Denis, Charlotte-Françoise,
  known as Comtesse de Saint-Laurent (Viennay-
  Pachot; Dauphin de la Forest) (d. 1732)
Juchereau de Saint-Denis, Louis (1616–1744)
Juchereau de Saint-Denis, Nicolas (d. 1692)
Juchereau de Saint-Denys, Charles (1655–1703)
Juchereau Des Chatelets, Noël (d. 1648)
Juchereau Duchesnay, Antoine (1740–1806)
Juchereau Duchesnay, Antoine-Louis (1767–
  1825)
Juchereau Duchesnay, Elzéar-Henri (1809–71)
Juchereau Duchesnay, Henri-Jules (1845–87)
Juchereau Duchesnay, Ignace (1658–1715)
Juchereau Duchesnay, Jean-Baptiste (1779–1833)
Juchereau Duchesnay, Marie-Joseph, named de
  l'Enfant-Jésus (1699–1760)
Juchereau Duchesnay, Michel-Louis (1785–1838)
Jukes, Joseph Beete (1811–69)
Julien, John (fl. 1779–1805)
Juneau, Félix-Emmanuel (1816–86)
Juneau, Laurent-Salomon (1793–1856)

KAGHSWAGHTANIUNT (d. c. 1762)
Kahgegagahbowh (1818–69)
Kaieñʔkwaahtoñ (d. 1786)
Kain, William (1809–30)
Kakȣenthiony (d. 1756)
Kallihirua (d. 1856)
Kalm, Pehr (1716–79)
Kamīyistowesit (d. 1889)
Kane, Elisha Kent (1820–57)
Kane, Paul (1810–71)
Kanon, Jacques (fl. 1756–61)
Kapapamahchakwew (d. 1885)
Kāpeyakwāskonam (d. 1886)
Karaghtadie (d. 1759)
Katzmann, Mary Jane (Lawson) (1828–90)
Kavanagh, Laurence (1764–1830)
Kay, Thomas (1810–63)
Kayahsotaʔ (fl. 1725–94)
Keats, Sir Richard Goodwin (1757–1834)
Keefer, George (1773–1858)
Keefer, Jacob (1800–74)
Keefer, Samuel (1811–90)
Keen, William (d. 1754)
Keir, John (d. 1858)
Keith, Alexander (1795–1873)
Keith, George (1779–1859)
Keith, James (1782–1851)
Kellett, Sir Henry (1806–75)
Kellogg, Joseph (1691–1756)
Kelly, Francis (1803–79)
Kelly, Jean-Baptiste (1783–1854)
Kelly, Michael John (d. 1890)
Kelly, William Moore (1827–88)

Kelsey, Henry (d. 1724)
Kemble, William (1781–1845)
Kemp, Alexander Ferrie (1822–84)
Kempt, Sir James (d. 1854)
Kempthorne, Thomas (d. 1736)
Kendall, Edward Nicholas (1800–45)
Kendrick, John (d. 1794)
Kennedy, Sir Arthur Edward (1809–83)
Kennedy, William (1814–90)
Kennedy, William Nassau (1839–85)
Kenny, Sir Edward (1800–91)
Kent, John (1805–72)
Kent, Robert John (1835–93)
Kenwendeshon (d. 1834)
Ker, Robert (1824–79)
Kerby, James (1785–1854)
Kérouac, Léon (1805–80)
Kerr, James (1765–1846)
Kerr, James Hooper (1828–77)
Kerr, Robert (d. 1824)
Kerr, William Johnson (1787–1845)
Kerrivan, Peter [volume IV]
Kerry, John (1825–96)
Ketchum, Henry George Clopper (1839–96)
Ketchum, Jesse (1782–1867)
Ketchum, Seneca (1772–1850)
Keveny, Owen (d. 1816)
Kezhegowinninne (d. 1889)
Kiala (fl. 1733–34)
Kidd, Adam (d. 1831)
Kielley, Edward (d. 1855)
Kierzkowski, Alexandre-Édouard (1816–70)
Kilborn, Charles (1758–1834)
Kilby, Thomas (1699–1746)
Killaly, Hamilton Hartley (1800–74)
Killam, Thomas (1802–68)
Kilpatrick, Robert (d. 1741)
Kimber, René (1762–1841)
Kimber, Timothée (1797–1852)
Kineubenae (fl. 1797–1812)
King, Boston (d. 1802)
King, Edward Hammond (1832–61)
King, Edwin Henry (1828–96)
King, George (d. 1867)
King, James (1750–84)
King, James (1848–1900)
King, John Mark (1829–99)
King, Richard (d. 1876)
King, William (1812–95)
King, William Henry (1833–59)
Kingminguse (fl. 1776–92)
Kingsford, William (1819–98)
Kingston, George Templeman (1816–86)
Kinnear, David (d. 1862)
Kinnear, William Boyd (1796–1868)
Kinongé (fl. 1660–1713)
Kinousaki (d. 1752)

Kiotseaeton (fl. 1645–46)
Kirby, Ann (Macaulay) (d. 1850)
Kirby, John (1772–1846)
Kirke, Sir David (d. 1654)
Kirke, Sir Lewis (d. before 1683)
Kirke, Thomas (fl. 1628–42)
Kirkpatrick, Sir George Airey (1841–99)
Kirkpatrick, Thomas (1805–70)
Kirwan, Miss, named Sister Mary Bernard (1797–1857)
Kisensik (fl. 1756–60)
Kitchi-manito-waya (d. 1897)
Kittson, Norman Wolfred (1814–88)
Kittson, William (d. 1841)
Kiwisānce (d. probably 1886)
Klatsassin (d. 1864)
Klingensmith, Peter, known as White Peter (d. 1855 or 1856)
Knaut, Philip Augustus (1716–81)
Kneller, Henry (d. 1776)
Knight, James (d. c. 1720)
Knight, John (d. 1606)
Knight, Richard (1788–1860)
Knowlton, Paul Holland (1787–1863)
Knox, John (d. 1778)
Koenig, Edmond-Victor de, Baron von Koenig (1753–1833)
Kohlmeister, Benjamin Gottlieb (1756–1844)
Kondiaronk (d. 1701)
Koñwatsiˀtsiaiéñni (d. 1796)
Kough, Patrick (d. 1863)
Koutaoiliboe (fl. 1700–12)
Koyah (d. 1795)
Kribs, Louis P. (1857–98)
Krieghoff, Cornelius (1815–72)
Kukatosi-poka (d. 1889)
ˀKwah (d. 1840)

LABADIE, Louis (1765–1824)
Labatt, John Kinder (1803–66)
Labelle, François-Xavier-Antoine (1833–91)
Labelle, Jean-Baptiste (1825–98)
Labelle, Ludger (d. 1867)
Laberge, Charles (1827–74)
Labillois, Charles-Marie (1793–1868)
Laborde, Jean (1710–81)
Labrèche-Viger, Louis (1824–72)
La Bretonnière, Jacques-Quintin de (1689–1754)
Labrie, Jacques (1784–1831)
La Brosse, Jean-Baptiste de (1724–82)
La Cetière, Florent de (d. 1728)
La Chasse, Pierre de (d. 1749)
La Colle (fl. 1736–42)
La Colombière, Joseph de (1651–1723)
Lacombe, Patrice (1807–63)
La Corne, Louis de, known as the Chevalier de La Corne (1703–61)

La Corne, Luc de, known as Chaptes de La Corne or La Corne Saint-Luc (d. 1784)
La Corne de Chaptes, Jean-Louis de (1666–1732)
La Corne de Chaptes, Joseph-Marie de (d. 1779)
La Corne de Chaptes, Marie-Madeleine de, named du Saint-Sacrement (1700–62)
La Corne Dubreuil, François-Josué de (1710–53)
Lacoste, Louis (1798–1878)
Lacoste, Louis-René (1823–54)
La Court de Pré-Ravillon et de Granpré (fl. 1591)
Lacroix, Hubert-Joseph (1743–1821)
La Croix, Hubert-Joseph de (1703–60)
Lacroix, Janvier-Domptail (1778–1856)
La Croix de Chevrières de Saint-Vallier, Jean-Baptiste de (1653–1727)
Ladan, Adrien (1647–1722)
La Faye, Louis-François de (1657–1729)
Lafitau, Joseph-François (d. 1746)
Laflamme, Toussaint-Antoine-Rodolphe (1827–93)
Laflèche, Louis-François (1818–98)
La Fontaine, Sir Louis-Hippolyte (1807–64)
Lafontaine de Belcour, Jacques de (1704–65)
Laforce, René-Hippolyte (1728–1802)
La Forest, Marc-Antoine de (d. 1738)
Laframboise, Maurice (1821–82)
Lafrance, François-Xavier-Stanislas (1814–67)
La France, Joseph (fl. 1723–42)
La Frenaye, François de (1677–1705)
La Frenaye de Brucy, Antoine de (d. 1684)
Lagarde, Pierre-Paul-François de (1729–84)
Lagier, Lucien-Antoine (1814–74)
Lagimonière, Jean-Baptiste (1778–1855)
Lagorce, Charles-Irénée (1813–64)
La Goudalie, Charles de (d. c. 1753)
Lagrené, Pierre de (1659–1736)
Lagueux, Louis (1793–1832)
Lahaille, Jean-Baptiste (1750–1809)
Laidlaw, George (1828–89)
Laird, Alexander (1797–1873)
Laird, Alexander (1830–96)
Lajoüe, François de (d. c. 1719)
Lajus, François (1721–99)
Lajus, Jordain (1673–1742)
La Lande, Jean de (d. 1646)
Lalemant, Charles (1587–1674)
Lalemant, Gabriel (1610–49)
Lalemant, Jérôme (1593–1673)
La Maisonfort Du Boisdecourt, Alexandre de, Marquis de La Maisonfort (fl. 1699–1752)
Lamaletie, Jean-André (fl. 1718–74)
La Marche, Dominique de (d. 1738)
Lamarre, dit Bélisle, Henri (d. 1740)
Lamb, Henry (d. 1841)
Lambert, Eustache (d. 1673)
Lambert, John (fl. 1806–16)
Lambert, Patrick (d. 1816)
Lambert, dit Saint-Paul, Paul (1691–1749)

34

Lambert Dumont, Nicolas-Eustache (1767–1835)
Lamberville, Jacques de (1641–1710)
Lamberville, Jean de (1633–1714)
Lambly, John Robert (1799–1863)
Lambton, John George, 1st Earl of Durham
   (1792–1840)
Lamorinie, Jean-Baptiste de (fl. 1705–64)
Lamothe, Joseph-Maurice (1781–1827)
La Motte de Lucière, Dominique (1636–1700)
Lamotte de Saint-Paul, Pierre (fl. 1665–70)
Lampman, Archibald (1861–99)
Lancaster, Joseph (1778–1838)
Lanctôt, Magloire (1823–77)
Lanctot, Médéric (1838–77)
Land, Robert (1772–1867)
Landmann, George Thomas (1780–1854)
Landon, Simple (1641–1712)
Landriaux, Louis-Nicolas (d. 1788)
Landrième Des Bordes, Jean-Marie (1712–78)
Landron, Jean-François (b. 1686, d. between 1756
   and 1760)
Landry, Alexis (d. 1798)
Landry, Amand (1805–77)
Landry, Jean-Étienne (1815–84)
Lane, Ambrose (d. 1853)
Lane, Daniel (d. 1686 or 1687)
Lane, Henry Bowyer Joseph (1817–78) [volume
   VIII]
Lane, Richard (d. 1877)
Lang, George (d. 1881)
Langevin, Antoine (1802–57)
Langevin, Edmond (1824–89)
Langevin, Jean (1821–92)
Langford, Edward Edwards (1809–95)
Langford, James Irwin (d. 1847)
Langhorn, John (d. 1817)
Langlois, Marie-Thérèse, named de Saint-Jean-
   Baptiste (1684–1743)
Langlois, Noël (d. 1684)
Langlois, *dit* Germain, Augustin-René (1770–1852)
Langman, Edward (1716–84)
Langoissieux, Charles (d. 1645)
Langton, Anne (1804–93)
Langton, John (1808–94)
Languedoc, François (1790–1840)
Lannelongue, Jean-Baptiste (1712–68)
Lanouguère, Thomas de (1644–78)
Lanoullier de Boisclerc, Jean-Eustache (d. 1750)
Lanoullier de Boisclerc, Nicolas (d. 1756)
La Place, Louis-Hyacinthe de (1673–1737)
La Place, Simon-Gérard de (d. 1699)
La Poippe (d. 1684)
Laporte de Lalanne, Jean de (fl. 1720–58)
La Porte de Louvigny, Louis de (d. 1725)
La Ralde, Raymond de (fl. 1621–32)
Larcher, Nicolas (1722–88)
Lareau, Edmond (1848–90)

Largillier, Jacques, known as Le Castor (d. 1714)
La Ribourde, Gabriel de (d. 1680)
La Richardie, Armand de (1686–1758)
Larkin, George (d. 1703 or 1704)
Larkin, John (1801–58)
Larkin, Patrick Joseph (1829–1900)
La Roche Daillon, Joseph de (d. 1656)
La Roche de Mesgouez, Troilus de, Marquis de La
   Roche-Mesgouez (d. 1606)
La Rochefoucauld, François-Alexandre-Frédéric de,
   Duc de La Rochefoucauld-Liancourt, Duc
   d'Estissac (1747–1827)
La Rochefoucauld de Roye, Jean-Baptiste-Louis-
   Frédéric de, Marquis de Roucy, Duc d'Anville
   (1709–46)
Larochelle, Louis-Napoléon (1834–90)
La Rocque, Charles (1809–75)
Larocque, François-Antoine (1784–1869)
Larocque, Joseph (d. 1866)
La Rocque, Joseph (1808–87)
La Rocque de Roberval, Jean-François de (d. 1560)
Larocque de Rochbrune, Alphonse-Barnabé
   (1823–93)
La Roque, Marguerite de (fl. 1536)
Lartigue, Jean-Jacques (1777–1840)
Lartigue, Joseph (d. 1743)
Larue, Auguste (1814–1900)
La Rue, François-Alexandre-Hubert (1833–81)
Larue, François-Xavier (d. 1855)
Larue, Guillaume de (d. 1717)
La Salle, Nicolas de (d. 1710)
Lascaris d'Urfé, François-Saturnin (1641–1701)
Lascelles, Horace Douglas (1835–69)
Latham, Robert (d. 1713)
Latouche MacCarthy, Charles (1706–65)
Latour, Bertrand de (1701–80)
La Tourasse, Charles, known as Chevalier
   (d. 1696)
Lauder, Abram William (1834–84)
Laumet, *dit* de Lamothe Cadillac, Antoine
   (1658–1730)
Laure, Pierre-Michel (1688–1738)
Laurent, Paul (fl. 1753–63)
Laurin, Joseph (1811–88)
Lauson, Gilles (1631–87)
Lauson, Jean de (d. 1666)
Lauson, Jean de (d. 1661)
Lauson de Charny, Charles de (fl. 1652–89)
Lauverjat, Étienne (1679–1761)
Lauzon, Pierre de (d. 1742)
Laval, François de (1623–1708)
Lavallée, Calixa (1842–91)
Laver, Augustus (1834–98)
Laverdière, Charles-Honoré (1826–73)
Lavigne, Azarie (1841–90)
Lavigueur, Célestin (1831–85)
Laviolette (fl. 1634–36)

Laviolette, Godefroy (1826–95)
Laviolette, Pierre (1794–1854)
Law, Robert (d. 1874)
Lawrason, Lawrence (1803–82)
Lawrence, Alexander (1788–1843)
Lawrence, Charles (d. 1760)
Lawrence, Joseph Wilson (1818–92)
Lawrence, William Dawson (1817–86)
Lawson, Alexander (1815–95)
Lawson, David (d. in or after 1803)
Lawson, George (1827–95)
Lawson, William (d. 1848)
Lawson, William (1793–1875)
Leach, William Turnbull (1805–86)
Leahey, Richard Henry (d. 1889)
Leake, Sir John (1656–1720)
Leavitt, Thomas (d. 1850)
Le Baillif, Georges (fl. 1620–25)
Lebeau, Claude (fl. 1724–31)
Le Ber, Jacques (d. 1706)
Le Ber, Jeanne (1662–1714)
Le Ber, Pierre (d. 1707)
Leblanc, Augustin (1799–1882)
Leblanc, Charles-André (1816–77)
Le Blanc, Étienne (d. 1831)
Leblanc, Étienne (1839–97)
Le Blanc, Pierre (d. 1799)
Leblanc, *dit* Le Maigre, Joseph (1697–1772)
  [volumes III and IV]
Leblanc de Marconnay, Hyacinthe-Poirier (1794–
  1868)
Leblond de Latour, Jacques (1671–1715)
Le Borgne, Emmanuel (1610–75)
Le Borgne de Belle-Isle, Alexandre (d. *c.* 1693)
Le Boutillier, David (b. 1811, d. probably in 1854)
Le Boutillier, John (1797–1872)
Le Breton, John (d. 1848)
Lebrun de Duplessis, Jean-Baptiste (d. 1807)
Le Caron, Joseph (d. 1632)
Lechasseur, Jean (d. 1713)
Leclerc, Jean-Baptiste (d. 1739)
Leclerc, Michel (1762–1813)
Leclerc, Nazaire (1820–83)
Le Clercq, Chrestien (b. 1641, d. in or after 1700)
Leclère, Pierre-Édouard (1798–1866)
Le Comte Dupré, Georges-Hippolyte, known as
  Saint-Georges Dupré (fl. 1738–97)
Le Comte Dupré, Jean-Baptiste (d. 1765)
Le Comte Dupré, Jean-Baptiste (1731–1820)
Le Conte Dupré, Louis (1654–1715)
Le Coq, Robert (d. 1650)
Le Coq de la Saussaye, René (fl. 1612–13)
Le Courtois, François-Gabriel (1763–1828)
Le Courtois de Surlaville, Michel (fl. 1714–96)
Le Coutre de Bourville, François (fl. 1690–1744)
Le Creux Du Breuil, Nicolas (fl. 1632–52)
Ledingham, John (1846–97)

Le Dorz, Bénin (fl. 1718–36)
Ledru, Jean-Antoine (b. 1752, d. in or after 1794)
Leduc, Anne-Françoise, named Saint-Joseph
  (1664–1750)
Lee, Fitzroy Henry (1698/99–1750)
Lee, Samuel (1756–1805)
Lee, William Henry (1799–1878)
Leech, Peter John (d. 1899)
Leeming, Ralph (1788–1872)
Lees, John (d. 1807)
Lefebvre, Camille (1831–95)
Lefebvre, Jean (1714–60)
Lefebvre, Thomas (d. 1715?)
Lefebvre, *dit* Laciseraye, Michel (1654–1708)
Lefebvre Angers, Marie-Angélique, named Saint-
  Simon (1710–66)
Lefebvre de Bellefeuille, François (1708–80)
Lefebvre de Bellefeuille, Jean-François (b. 1670,
  d. *c.* 1744)
Lefebvre de Bellefeuille, Louis-Charles (1795–
  1838)
Le Febvre de La Barre, Joseph-Antoine (1622–88)
Lefebvre Duplessis Faber, François (1689–1762)
Le Fevre, François (d. 1718)
Lefferty, John Johnston (d. 1842)
Lefrançois, Charles (d. 1829)
Lefroy, Sir John Henry (1817–90)
Legacé, Josette (Work) (d. 1896)
Legaic, Paul (d. 1894)
Le Gallais, Wellmein William (d. 1869)
Legardeur de Beauvais, René (d. 1742)
Le Gardeur de Courtemanche, Augustin
  (1663–1717)
Legardeur de Croisille, Charles (1677–1749)
Legardeur de Croisille et de Montesson, Joseph-
  Michel (d. *c.* 1776)
Legardeur de Repentigny, Jean-Baptiste
  (1632–1709)
Legardeur de Repentigny, Louis (1721–86)
Legardeur de Repentigny, Marie-Jeanne-Madeleine,
  named de Sainte-Agathe (d. 1739)
Legardeur de Repentigny, Pierre (d. 1648)
Legardeur de Repentigny, Pierre (1657–1736)
Legardeur de Repentigny, Pierre-Jean-Baptiste-
  François-Xavier (1719–76)
Legardeur de Saint-Pierre, Jacques (1701–55)
Legardeur de Saint-Pierre, Jean-Paul (b. 1661,
  d. 1722 or 1723)
Legardeur de Tilly, Charles (d. 1695)
Legardeur de Tilly, Jean-Baptiste (1698–1757)
Legardeur de Tilly, Pierre-Noël (d. 1720)
Légaré, Antoine (1799–1873)
Légaré, Joseph (1795–1855)
Léger de La Grange, Jean (b. 1663, d. *c.* 1736)
Legge, Charles (1829–81)
Legge, Francis (d. 1783)
Le Gouès de Sourdeval, Sébastien (1657–1710)

Le Guerne, François (1725–89)

Leifr *heppni* Eiriksson (d. *c.* 1020)

Leigh, Charles (1572–1605)

Leigh, John (d. 1823)

Leitch, William (1814–64)

Leith, James (1777–1838)

Lejamtel, François (1757–1835)

LeJeune, Marie-Henriette (Comeau; Lejeune, *dit* Briard; Ross) (d. 1860)

Le Jeune, Olivier (d. 1654)

Le Jeune, Paul (1591–1664)

Le Loutre, Jean-Louis (1709–72)

Lemaire, Félix-Hyacinthe (1808–79)

Lemaire, Marie-Marguerite (1769–1838)

Le Maistre, Francis (d. 1805)

Le Maistre, Jacques (d. 1661)

Lemaître, *dit* Jugon, François (b. 1707, d. *c.* 1751)

Le Marchand de Lignery, Constant (d. 1731)

Le Marchand de Lignery, François-Marie (1703–59)

Le Marchant, Sir John Gaspard (1803–74)

Le Mercier, François-Joseph (1604–90)

Le Mercier, François-Marc-Antoine (b. 1722, d. *c.* 1798)

LeMesurier, Henry (1791–1861)

Lemieux, François-Xavier (1811–64)

Lemire, Jean (1626–85)

Lemoine, *dit* Monière, Alexis (1680–1754)

Lemoine Despins, Jacques-Joseph (1719–87)

Lemoine Despins, Marguerite-Thérèse (1722–92)

Le Moyne, Simon (1604–65)

Le Moyne de Bienville, François (1666–91)

Le Moyne de Bienville, Jean-Baptiste (d. 1767)

Le Moyne de Châteauguay, Louis (1676–94)

Le Moyne de Longueuil, Charles, Baron de Longueuil (d. 1729)

Le Moyne de Longueuil, Charles, Baron de Longueuil (1687–1755)

Le Moyne de Longueuil, Joseph-Dominique-Emmanuel (1738–1807)

Le Moyne de Longueuil, Marie-Charles-Joseph, Baronne de Longueuil (Grant) (1756–1841)

Le Moyne de Longueuil, Paul-Joseph, known as Chevalier de Longueuil (1701–78)

Le Moyne de Longueuil et de Châteauguay, Charles (1626–85)

Le Moyne de Maricourt, Paul (1663–1704)

Le Moyne de Martigny et de La Trinité, Jean-Baptiste (d. 1709)

Le Moyne de Sainte-Hélène, Jacques (1659–90)

Le Moyne de Saint-Marie, Marguerite, named du Saint-Esprit (1664–1746)

Le Moyne de Serigny et de Loire, Joseph (d. 1734)

Le Moyne d'Iberville et d'Ardillières, Pierre (d. 1706)

Leneuf de La Poterie, Jacques (b. 1606, d. in or after 1685)

Leneuf de La Vallière et de Beaubassin, Alexandre (1666–1712)

Leneuf de La Vallière et de Beaubassin, Michel (d. 1705)

Leneuf de La Vallière et de Beaubassin, Michel (d. 1740)

Leneuf Du Hérisson, Michel (d. *c.* 1672)

Lennox, Charles, 4th Duke of Richmond and Lennox (1764–1819)

Lenoir, *dit* Rolland, François (d. 1707)

Lenoir, *dit* Rolland, Joseph (1822–61)

Le Normant de Mézy, Jacques-Ange (d. 1741)

Le Normant de Mézy, Sébastien-François-Ange (1702–91)

Leonard, Elijah (1787–1855)

Leonard, Elijah (1814–91)

Leonard, George (1742–1826)

Léonard de Chartres (d. 1654)

LePage, John (1812–86)

Lepage de Sainte-Claire, Louis (1690–1762)

Lepallieur de Laferté, Michel (d. 1733)

Le Pape Du Lescöat, Jean-Gabriel-Marie (1689–1733)

Le Pesant (fl. 1703–12)

Le Picard Du Mesnil de Norrey, Jacques (d. 1713)

Lépine, Jean-Baptiste (fl. 1869–71)

Lépine, Maxime (d. 1897)

Le Poupet de La Boularderie, Antoine (1705–71)

Le Poupet de La Boularderie, Louis-Simon (d. 1738)

Le Prévost, Pierre-Gabriel (d. 1756)

Le Prévost Duquesnel, Jean-Baptiste-Louis (d. 1744)

Leprohon, Jean-Lukin (1822–1900)

Leprohon, Joseph-Onésime (1789–1844)

Le Rouge, Jean (1639–1712)

Leroux, Laurent (1759–1855)

Le Roux, Thomas-François (1730–94)

Leroux, Valentin (1642–1708)

Le Roy, Henri (1639–1708)

Leroy, Pierre-Auguste (b. 1846, d. in or after 1886)

Le Roy de La Potherie, *dit* Bacqueville de La Potherie, Claude-Charles (1633–1736)

Le Roy Desmarest, Claude-Joseph (d. 1737)

Le Saulnier, Candide-Michel (1758–1830)

Lescarbot, Marc (d. 1642)

Lesieur-Désaulniers, Isaac-Stanislas (1811–68)

Lesieur-Désaulniers, Louis-Léon (1823–96)

Leslie, James (1786–1873)

L'Espérance, Charles-Gabriel-Sébastien de, Baron de L'Espérance (1725–91)

L'Espérance, Charles-Léopold-Ébérard de (d. 1738)

Lesperance, John (1835–91)

Lespérance, Pierre (1819–82)

Lespinay, Jean-Michel de (d. 1721)

Lessard, Étienne de (1623–1703)

Lessel, Arthur C. (d. 1895)

Lesslie, James (1802–85)

Lestage, Pierre de (1682–1743)

Lester, Benjamin (1724–1802)
Lester, Robert (d. 1807)
Lestringant de Saint-Martin, Alexandre-Joseph
(d. 1722)
Le Sueur, Jacques-François (d. 1760)
Le Sueur, Jean, known as Abbé de Saint-Sauveur
(d. 1668)
Le Sueur, Pierre (d. 1704)
Le Sueur, Pierre (1684–1752)
Le Tac, Xiste (d. 1718)
Letardif, Olivier (d. 1665)
Letellier de Saint-Just, Luc (1820–81)
Letendre, *dit* Batoche, Jean-Baptiste (b. 1762,
d. in or after 1827)
Létourneau, Jean-Charles (1775–1838)
Lett, Benjamin (1813–58)
Levasseur, François-Noël (d. 1794)
Levasseur, Louis (1671–1748)
Levasseur, Michel (fl. 1699–1709)
Levasseur, Noël (1680–1740)
Levasseur, Pierre-Noël (1690–1770)
Levasseur, René-Nicolas (d. 1784)
Levasseur, *dit* Delor, Jean-Baptiste-Antoine
(d. 1775)
Levasseur, *dit* Lavigne, Jean (1622–86)
Levasseur, *dit* L'Espérance, Pierre (b. 1629,
d. in or after 1681)
Le Vasseur Borgia, Joseph (1773–1839)
Levasseur de Neré, Jacques (d. in or after 1723)
Léveillé, Mathieu (d. 1743)
Leverett, John (1616–78/79)
Le Verrier de Rousson, François (d. 1732)
Le Verrier de Rousson, Louis (b. 1705, d. in or after
1789)
LeVesconte, Isaac (1822–79)
Lévesque, Charles-François (1817–59)
Lévesque, François (1732–87)
Lévesque, Guillaume (1819–56)
Le Vieux de Hauteville, Nicolas (fl. 1651–58)
Lévis, François de, Duc de Lévis (1719–87)
Levrault de Langis Montegron, Jean-Baptiste
(d. 1760)
Lewellin, John Lewellin (d. 1857)
Lewin, James Davies (1812–1900)
Lewis, Asahel Bradley (d. 1833)
Lewis, John Bower (1817–74)
Lewis, Martha Hamm (Peters) (1831–92)
Lewis, William (fl. 1777–87)
Leys, John (d. 1846)
L'Hermitte, Jacques (d. 1725)
Lichtenstein, Elizabeth (Johnston) (1764–1848)
Liddell, Thomas (1800–80)
Liébert, Philippe (1733–1804)
Liégeois, Jean (d. 1655)
Liénard de Beaujeu, Daniel-Hyacinthe-Marie
(1711–55)
Liénard de Beaujeu, Louis (1683–1750)

Liénard de Beaujeu de Villemonde, Louis
(1716–1802)
Liette, Pierre-Charles de (fl. 1687–1721)
Light, Alexander Luders (1822–94)
Lillie, Adam (1803–69)
Lilly, George (d. 1846)
Lind, Henry (1805–70)
Lindsay, Sir James Alexander (1815–74)
Lindsay, William (d. 1834)
Linton, John James Edmonstoune (1804–69)
Litchfield, John Palmer (1808–68)
Little, James (1803–83)
Little, Otis (b. 1711/12, d. *c.* 1754)
Little, Philip Francis (1824–97)
Livingston, John (1680–1719/20)
Livingston, John (1837–94)
Livingston, Samuel Henry Harkwood (1831–97)
Livius, Peter (1739–95)
Lloyd, Jesse (1786–1838)
Lloyd, Thomas (d. 1710)
Lobley, Joseph Albert (1840–89)
Lockerby, Elizabeth Newell (Bacon) (1831–84)
Lockman, Leonard (d. 1769)
Lockwood, Anthony (d. 1854 or 1855)
Loedel, Henry Nicholas Christopher (d. 1830)
Logan, Alexander (1841–94)
Logan, Robert (1773–1866)
Logan, Sir William Edmond (1798–1875)
Lola, Noel (d. before 1861)
Lola, Peter (fl. 1837–52)
Lolo, Jean-Baptiste (1798–1868)
Lombard de Combles, Jean-Claude-Henri de
(1719–56)
Lom d'Arce, Louis-Armand de, Baron de Lahontan
(b. 1666, d. before 1716)
Lomeron, David (b. 1591, d. in or after 1636)
Long, John (fl. 1768–91)
Longland, John (d. 1757)
Longley, Avard (1823–84)
Longley, George (d. 1842)
Longley, Lydia named Sainte-Madeleine
(1674–1758)
Longmoor, Robert (fl. 1771–1812)
Longmore, George (d. 1811)
Longworth, Francis (1766–1843)
Longworth, Francis (1807–83)
Longworth, John (1814–85)
Loppinot, Jean-Chrysostome (fl. 1699–1712)
Loranger, Thomas-Jean-Jacques (1823–85)
Lord, John Keast (1818–72)
Lord, William Warren (1798–1890)
Lorimier, Chevalier de (1803–39)
Lorimier, Claude-Nicolas-Guillaume de
(1744–1825)
Lorimier, Jean-Baptiste de (d. 1845)
Lorimier de La Rivière, Claude-Nicolas de (d. 1770)
Lorimier de La Rivière, Guillaume de (d. 1709)

Loring, Joshua (1716–81)
Loring, Robert Roberts (d. 1848)
Lorit, *dit* Gargot, François (d. 1702)
Losee, William (1757–1832)
Lossing, Peter (1761–1833)
Lottridge, John (d. 1763)
Louet, Jean-Claude (1681–1739)
Lount, Samuel (1791–1838)
Lovell, John (1810–93)
Lovett, Phineas (1745–1828)
Lowell, Robert Traill Spence (1816–91)
Loyard, Jean-Baptiste (1678–1731)
Lozeau, Jean-Baptiste (d. *c.* 1745)
Luard, Richard George Amherst (1827–91)
Lucas, Francis (d. 1770)
Lucas, Richard (fl. 1678–86)
Ludlow, Gabriel George (1736–1808)
Ludlow, George Duncan (1734–1808)
Lugger, Robert (1793–1837)
Lugrin, George Kilman (d. 1835)
Lundrigan, James (d. *c.* 1863) [volume VI]
Lunn, William (1796–1886)
Lupien, *dit* Baron, Pierre (d. 1744)
Lusher, Robert Langham (d. 1849)
Lyall, William (1811–90)
Lydall, William (fl. 1674–92)
Lÿdius, John Hendricks (d. 1791)
Lyman, Benjamin (1810–78)
Lymburner, Adam (d. 1836)
Lynch, John (1798–1884)
Lynch, John Joseph (1816–88)
Lynd, David (d. 1802)
Lyon, George (1790–1851)
Lyon, James (1735–94)
Lyon de Saint-Ferréol, Jean (b. 1692, d. in or after 1744)
Lyonne, Martin de (1614–61)

MABANE, Adam (d. 1792)
Mabey, Paul (d. 1863)
Macallum, Archibald (1824–79)
Macallum, John (1806–49)
M'Alpine, John (1748–1827)
Macard, Charles (1656–1732)
Macarmick, William (d. 1815)
McArthur, Alexander (1843–87)
McArthur, Alexander (1839–95)
McAskill, Angus (1825–63)
Macaulay, Angus (1759–1827)
Macaulay, James (1759–1822)
Macaulay, Sir James Buchanan (1793–1859)
Macaulay, John (1792–1857)
Macaulay, John Simcoe (1791–1855)
Macaulay, Robert (1744–1800)
Macaulay, William (1794–1874)
Macaulay, Zachary (d. 1821)
McBeath, George (d. 1812)

McBeath, Robert (1805–86)
Macbeth, George (1825–70)
MacBraire, James (1760–1832)
McBride, Edward William (d. 1834)
McCall, Duncan (1769–1832)
McCallum, James (d. 1825)
McCann, Rosanna, named Sister Mary Basilia (1811–70)
McCarthy, D'Alton (1836–98)
McCarthy, James Owen (d. 1835)
McCarthy, Jeremiah (d. 1828)
McCarty, Charles Justin (d. *c.* 1790)
McCarty, Richard (d. 1781)
McCaul, John (1807–87)
McCawley, George (1802–78)
McClearn, Matthew (1802–65)
McCliesh, Thomas (fl. 1698–1746)
McClure, Leonard (1835–67)
McClure, Sir Robert John Le Mesurier (1807–73)
McClure, William (1803–71)
M'Coll, Duncan (1754–1830)
MacColl, Evan (1808–98)
McConville, John (d. 1849)
McCord, Andrew Taylor (1805–81)
McCord, Thomas (1750–1824)
McCord, William King (1803–58)
McCormick, Robert (1800–90)
McCormick, William (1784–1840)
McCoubrey, John Williams (1806–79)
McCrea, Robert Barlow (1823–97)
McCulloch, Thomas (1776–1843)
McCully, Jonathan (1809–77)
McCurdy, James MacGregor (1830–86)
McDermot, Andrew (1790–1881)
MacDhòmhnaill 'Ic Iain, Iain (John MacDonald) (1795–1853)
McDonald, Alexander (d. 1834)
McDonald, Angus (d. 1887)
McDonald, Angus (1830–89)
McDonald, Archibald (1790–1853)
Macdonald, Bernard Donald (1797–1859)
McDonald, Charles (1784–1826)
McDonald, Donald (1795–1854)
McDonald, Donald (1783–1867)
McDonald, Donald (d. 1879)
McDonald, Edmund Mortimer (1825–74)
Macdonald, Edward C. (d. 1889)
McDonald, Francis John (1815–1900)
MacDonald, James (1736–85)
McDonald, John (1770–1828)
McDonald, John (1787–1860)
McDonald, John (d. 1874)
Macdonald, John (1824–90)
Macdonald, Sir John Alexander (1815–91)
Macdonald, John Sandfield (1812–72)
Macdonald, John Small (d. 1849)
Macdonald, Ranald (1824–94)

Macdonald, Ronald (1797–1854)
MacDonald, William Peter (1771–1847)
Macdonald (Sandfield), Donald Alexander
(1817–96)
McDonald of Garth, John (d. 1866)
MacDonald of Glenaladale, Helen (MacDonald)
(d. *c.* 1803)
MacDonald of Glenaladale, John (1742–1810)
MacDonell, Alexander (fl. 1813–28)
McDonell, Alexander (1762–1840)
MacDonell, Alexander (1782–1841)
McDonell, Alexander (1786–1861)
McDonell, Allan (d. 1859)
Macdonell, Allan (1808–88)
Macdonell, Archibald (d. 1830)
MacDonell, Donald Aeneas (1794–1879)
Macdonell, George Richard John (d. 1870)
Macdonell, Sir James (d. 1857)
MacDonell, Jean-François-Marie-Joseph
(1799–1866)
McDonell, John (1768–1850)
Macdonell, Miles (d. 1828)
McDonell (Aberchalder), Hugh (d. 1833)
McDonell (Aberchalder), John (d. 1809)
McDonell (Collachie), Alexander (1762–1842)
Macdonell (Collachie), Angus (d. 1804)
Macdonell (Greenfield), Alexander (1782–1835)
Macdonell (Greenfield), Donald (1778–1861)
Macdonell (Greenfield), John (1785–1812)
MacDonell of Scothouse, Alexander (d. 1803)
Macdonnell, Daniel James (1843–96)
MacDonnell, Sir Richard Graves (1814–81)
MacDonnell, Robert Lea (1818–78)
McDouall, Robert (1774–1848)
Macdougall, Alan (1842–97)
McDougall, Alexander (d. 1821)
MacDougall, Dugald Lorn (1811–85)
McDougall, Duncan (d. 1818)
McDougall, George Millward (1821–76)
McDougall, John (d. 1892)
McDougall, John (1805–70)
McDougall, John Lorn (1800–60)
MacDougall, Sir Patrick Leonard (1819–94)
McDowall, Robert (1768–1841)
McDowell, Eugene Addison (1845–93)
Macé, Catherine (1616–98)
McEachen, Emanuel (d. 1875)
MacEachern, Angus Bernard (1759–1835)
Macfarlane, James (d. 1847)
McGarvey, Owen (d. 1897)
McGee, Thomas D'Arcy (1825–68)
Macgeorge, Robert Jackson (1808–84)
MacGhillEathain, Iain (1787–1848)
McGill, James (1744–1813)
McGill, John (1752–1834)
McGill (McCutcheon), Peter (1789–1860)
McGill, Robert (1798–1856)

McGillivray, Alexander (1801–62)
McGillivray, Donald (1857–1900)
McGillivray, Duncan (d. 1808)
McGillivray, Simon (d. 1840)
McGillivray, William (1764–1825)
McGillivray (Dalcrombie), John (d. 1855)
McGray, Asa (1780–1843)
McGreevy, Thomas (1825–97)
MacGregor, James Drummond (1759–1830)
McGregor, John (d. 1828)
MacGregor, John (1797–1857)
Machar, John (d. 1863)
McInnes, Donald (d. 1900)
McIntosh, John (b. 1777, d. 1845 or 1846)
McIntosh, John (1796–1853)
McIntyre, Alexander (1841–92)
McIntyre, Duncan (1834–94)
McIntyre, Peter (1818–91)
Mack, Theophilus (1820–81)
MacKay, Alexander (d. 1811)
McKay, Angus (b. 1836, d. in or after 1897)
Mackay, Donald (1753–1833)
McKay, James (1828–79)
Mackay, John (fl. 1785–87)
McKay, John (d. 1810)
McKay, John Richards (d. 1877)
Mackay, Joseph (1810–81)
Mackay, Joseph William (1829–1900)
Mackay, Robert Walter Stuart (d. 1854)
McKay, Smith (1817–89)
McKay, Thomas (1792–1855)
McKay, William (1772–1832)
McKeagney, Henry (1796–1856)
McKeagney, James Charles (1815–79)
McKeand, Alfred (1849–87)
Mackechnie, Stuart Easton (d. 1853)
McKee, Alexander (d. 1799)
McKee, Thomas (d. 1814)
McKellar, Archibald (1816–94)
McKellar, John (1833–1900)
Mackellar, Patrick (1717–78)
McKenney, Henry (d. 1886)
Mackenzie, Sir Alexander (1764–1820)
McKenzie, Alexander (d. 1830)
Mackenzie, Alexander (1822–92)
McKenzie, Charles (d. 1855)
McKenzie, Donald (1783–1851)
Mackenzie, George (1795–1834)
McKenzie, George Rogers (1798–1876)
McKenzie, Henry (d. 1832)
McKenzie, James (d. 1832)
McKenzie, James (d. 1849)
McKenzie, James (1788–1859)
McKenzie, John (1790–1855)
MacKenzie, John George Delhoste (1822–73)
MacKenzie, Kenneth (d. 1816)
McKenzie, Kenneth (1811–74)

McKenzie, Nancy (McTavish; Le Blanc)
  (Matooskie) (d. 1851)
Mackenzie, Roderick (d. 1844)
McKenzie, Roderick (d. 1859)
Mackenzie, William Lyon (1795–1861)
McKiernan, Charles, known as Joe Beef (d. 1889)
Mackieson, John (1795–1885)
McKindlay, John (d. 1833)
MacKinlay, Andrew (1800–67)
MacKinnon, Colin Francis (1810–79)
McKinnon, Ranald (1737–1805)
McKinnon, William (d. 1811)
McKinnon, William Charles (1828–62)
MacKintosh, John (1790–1881)
MacKintosh, William (d. 1842)
Mackintosh of Mackintosh, Angus, 26th Chief of
  Clan Chattan and 25th Chief of Clan Mackintosh
  (1755–1833)
McKnight, Alexander (1826–94)
McLachlan, Alexander (1817–96)
McLachlin, Daniel (1810–72)
McLane, David (d. 1797)
Maclaren, James (1818–92)
McLaren, Neil (1766–1844)
McLaren, William Paterson (1810–66)
Maclean, Allan (1725–98)
McLean, Allan (1855–81)
McLean, Archibald (d. 1830)
McLean, Archibald (1791–1865)
McLean, Donald (1805–64)
MacLean, Donald Charles (1786–1873)
Maclean, Duncan (1799–1859)
McLean, Francis (d. 1781)
McLean, John (1828–86)
McLean, John (d. 1890)
MacLean, Malcolm Alexander (1844–95)
McLean, Neil (d. 1795)
McLean, Neil (1759–1832)
MacLean, Peter (1800–68)
Maclear, Thomas (1815–98)
McLearn, Richard (1804–60)
McLeay, James Franklin (1864–1900)
McLelan, Archibald Woodbury (1824–90)
McLelan, Gloud Wilson (1796–1858)
McLennan, Hugh (1825–99)
MacLennan, John (1797–1852)
McLeod, Alexander (1796–1871)
McLeod, Alexander Roderick (d. 1840)
McLeod, Angus Jonas (1861–1900)
M'Leod, Donald (1779–1879)
McLeod, Donald (1846–94)
McLeod, Ezekiel (1812–67)
Macleod, James Farquharson (d. 1894)
McLeod, John (1788–1849)
McLeod, John M. (b. 1795, fl. 1816–42)
McLeod, Norman (1780–1866)
MacLeod, Normand (d. 1796)

McLeod, Peter (d. 1852)
McLeod, Sarah (Ballenden) (1818–53)
McLoughlin, John (1784–1857)
McLoughlin, Marie-Louise, named de Saint-Henri
  (1780–1846)
McMahon, John Baptist (b. 1796, d. in or after 1840)
McMahon, Patrick (1796–1851)
McMartin, Alexander (1788–1853)
McMaster, William (1811–87)
MacMhannain, Calum Bàn (fl. 1803)
McMicken, Gilbert (1813–91)
McMicking, Thomas (1829–66)
McMillan, Archibald (1762–1832)
McMillan, James (d. 1858)
McMillan, John (1816–86)
McMillan, Joseph C. (1836–89)
McMurray, Thomas (b. 1831, d. in or after 1884)
McMurray, William (1810–94)
McMurrich, John (1804–83)
MacNab, Sir Allan Napier (1798–1862)
McNab, Archibald, 17th Chief of Clan Macnab
  (d. 1860)
McNabb, Colin (d. 1810)
McNabb, James (d. 1820)
McNeill, William Henry (1801–75)
Macnider, Adam Lymburner (1778–1840)
McNiff, Patrick (d. 1803)
McNutt, Alexander (b. 1725, d. *c*. 1811)
McPhelim, Francis (1811–66)
Macpherson, Sir David Lewis (1818–96)
Macpherson, Donald (d. 1829)
McPherson, John (1817–45)
McQueen, Thomas (1803–61)
McQuesten, Calvin (1801–85)
McSpiritt, Francis (1836–95)
McSwiney, Edward (fl. 1812–15)
Mactaggart, John (1791–1830)
McTavish, Donald (d. 1814)
Mactavish, Dugald (1817–71)
McTavish, John George (d. 1847)
Mactavish, Letitia (Hargrave) (1813–54)
McTavish, Simon (d. 1804)
Mactavish, William (1815–70)
McVicar, Kate (d. 1886)
McVicar, Robert (d. 1864)
McVicar, Victoria (d. 1899)
Madjeckewiss (fl. 1763–1805)
Madoc (fl. 1170)
Madran, Jean-Marie (1783–1857)
Madry, Jean (d. 1669)
Magnan, Pierre (d. 1627)
Magon de Terlaye, François-Auguste (1724–77)
Magowan, Peter (d. 1810)
Maguire, John (1810–80)
Maguire, Thomas (1776–1854)
Maheut, Louis (d. 1683)
Mailhot, Nicolas-François (d. 1834)

41

Maillard, Pierre (d. 1762)
Maillet, Marie (1610–77)
Maillou, Benjamin-Nicolas (1753–1810)
Maillou, *dit* Desmoulins, Jean-Baptiste (1668–1753)
Mailloux, Alexis (1801–77)
Mainwaring, Sir Henry (1587–1653)
Maisonnat, Marie-Madeleine (Winniett) (b. 1695, d. in or after 1770)
Maisonnat, *dit* Baptiste, Pierre (b. 1663, d. in or after 1714)
Maitland, Sir Peregrine (1777–1854)
Makheabichtichiou (d. 1640 or 1641)
Malapart, André (fl. 1629–49)
Malaspina, Alejandro (1754–1810)
Malcolm, Eliakim (1801–74)
Malepart de Beaucourt, François (1740–94)
Malepart de Grand Maison, *dit* Beaucour, Paul (d. 1756)
Maleray de Noiré de La Mollerie, Jacques (1657–1704)
Malherbe, François (1627–96)
Malherbe, François (1768–1832)
Malhiot, Charles-Christophe (1808–74)
Malhiot, Édouard-Élisée (d. 1875)
Malhiot, François (1733–1808)
Malhiot, François-Xavier (1781–1854)
Malhiot, Jean-François (1692–1756)
Malie, Joseph (fl. 1841–46)
Mallet, Denis (d. 1704)
Mallet, Marie-Anne-Marcelle (1805–71)
Mallet, Pierre-Antoine (b. 1700, d. in or after 1751)
Mallory, Benajah (d. 1853)
Man, James (d. 1820)
Manach, Jean (d. 1766)
Manahan, Anthony (d. 1849)
Mance, Jeanne (d. 1673)
Mangeant, *dit* Saint-Germain, François (fl. 1713–44)
Manitougatche (d. 1634)
Mann, Gother (1747–1830)
Mann, John (1798–1891)
Manners-Sutton, John Henry Thomas, 3rd Viscount Canterbury (1814–77)
Manning, Edward (1766–1851)
Manseau, Antoine (1787–1866)
Manson, Donald (1796–1880)
Maranda, Jean-Baptiste (1803–50)
March, John (1658–1712)
Marchand, Étienne (1707–74)
Marchand, Félix-Gabriel (1832–1900)
Marchand, Gabriel (1780–1852)
Marchand, Jean-Baptiste (1760–1825)
Marchand, Louis (1800–81)
Marchesseault, Siméon (1806–55)
Marchildon, Thomas (1805–58)
Marchinton, Philip (d. 1808)

Marcol, Gabriel (1692–1755)
Marcot, Marguerite-Magdelaine (La Framboise) (1780–1846)
Marcoux, Joseph (Tharoniakanere) (1791–1855)
Marcoux, Pierre (1757–1809)
Maréchal, Louis-Delphis-Adolphe (1824–92)
Marest, Joseph-Jacques (1653–1725)
Marest, Pierre-Gabriel (1662–1714)
Mareuil, Jacques de (fl. 1693–94)
Mareuil, Pierre de (1672–1742)
Margane de Batilly, François-Marie (1672–1704)
Margane de Lavaltrie, François (1685–1750)
Margane de Lavaltrie, Pierre-Paul (1743–1810)
Marguerie de La Haye, Francois (d. 1648)
Mariauchau d'Esgly, François (d. 1730)
Mariauchau d'Esgly, François-Louis (d. 1736)
Mariauchau d'Esgly, Louis-Philippe (1710–88)
Marie (d. 1759)
Marie-Joseph-Angélique (d. 1734)
Marin de La Malgue, Charles-Paul (1633–1713)
Marin de La Malgue, Joseph (d. 1774)
Marin de La Malgue, Paul (d. 1753)
Marin de La Perrière, Claude (d. 1752)
Marion, Salomon (1782–1830)
Markland, George Herchmer (d. 1862)
Markland, Thomas (1757–1840)
Markle, Abraham (1770–1826)
Marks, Thomas (1834–1900)
Marling, Alexander (1832–90)
Marot, Bernard (fl. 1610–50)
Marquette, Jacques (1637–75)
Marrant, John (1755–91)
Marryat, Frederick (1792–1848)
Marsden, Joshua (1777–1837)
Marsh, John (d. 1688/89)
Marshall, John George (1786–1880)
Marshall, John Joseph (1807–70)
Marshall, Joseph (d. 1847)
Marshall de Brett Maréchal, Joseph, Baron d'Avray (1811–71)
Marsolet de Saint-Aignan, Nicolas (d. 1677)
Marsters, Richard Upham (1787–1845)
Marston, Benjamin (1730–92)
Martel, Pierre (1801–91)
Martel, Pierre-Michel (1719–89)
Martel, Raymond (1663–1708)
Martel de Belleville, Jean-Urbain (b. 1708, d. in or before 1764)
Martel de Brouague, François (b. 1692, d. *c.* 1761)
Martel de Magos, Jean (d. 1729)
Marten, Humphrey (d. before 1792)
Martin, Abraham, known as L'Écossais or Maître Abraham (1589–1664)
Martin, Barthélemy (fl. 1749–65)
Martin, Charles-Amador (1648–1711)
Martin, Christopher (fl. 1661–78)
Martin, Félix (1804–86)

Martin, George (d. 1724)
Martin, George (Shononhsé:se') (1767–1853)
Martin, John Wills (fl. 1816–43)
Martin, Mathieu (fl. 1689–1724)
Martin de Lino, Antoine (1690–1733)
Martin de Lino, Jean-François (1686–1721)
Martin de Lino, Mathieu-François (1657–1731)
Martineau, Jérôme (1750–1809)
Martinet, *dit* Bonami, Louis (1764–1848)
Martinet de Fonblanche, Jean (1645–1701)
Martínez Fernández y Martínez de la Sierra, Esteban
  José (1742–98)
Mascarene, Paul (d. 1760)
Mascle de Saint-Julhien, Jean (1693–1759)
Maseres, Francis (1731–1824)
Maskepetoon (d. 1869)
Mason, John (1586–1635)
Massé, Énemond (1575–1646)
Massey, Daniel (1798–1856)
Massey, Hart Almerrin (1823–96)
Massey, Samuel (1817–97)
Masson, Francis (1741–1805)
Masson, Isidore-Édouard-Candide (1826–75)
Masson, Joseph (1791–1847)
Masson, Luc-Hyacinthe (1811–80)
Masson, Marc-Damase (1805–78)
Massow, Friederike Charlotte Louise von (Riedesel,
  Frelin zu Eisenbach) (1746–1808)
Massue, Louis-Joseph (1786–1869)
Mather, John B. (d. 1892)
Matheson, Roderick (1793–1873)
Mathevet, Jean-Claude (1717–81)
Mathews, David (d. 1800)
Mathews, Robert (d. 1814)
Mathieson, Alexander (1795–1870)
Mathison, John Augustus (1781–1868)
Matonabbee (d. 1782)
Matthews, John (d. 1832)
Matthews, Peter (d. 1838)
Maturin, Edmund (d. 1891)
Maufils, Marie-Madeleine, named de Saint-Louis
  (d. 1702)
Maugenest, Germain (d. 1792)
Mauger, Joshua (d. 1788)
Maugue, Claude (d. 1696)
Maugue-Garreau, Marie-Josèphe, named de
  l'Assomption (d. 1785)
Maumousseau, Françoise (1657–1704)
Maupassant, Eustache (d. 1692)
Maurault, Joseph-Pierre-Anselme (1819–70)
Maurès de Malartic, Anne-Joseph-Hippolyte de,
  Comte de Malartic (1730–1800)
Maurin, François (fl. 1756–65)
May, Henry (fl. 1591–94)
Mayerhoffer, Vincent Philip (1784–1859)
Mayrand, Étienne (1776–1872)
Meagher, Thomas (d. 1837)

Meares, John (d. 1809)
Mecham, George Frederick (1828–58)
Mechtler, Guillaume-Joseph (d. 1833)
Medcalf, Francis Henry (1803–80)
Medley, John (1804–92)
Meilleur, Jean-Baptiste (1796–1878)
Mein, Susan (Sibbald) (1783–1866)
Mékaisto (d. 1900)
Melançon, Marie-Vénérande, named de Sainte-
  Claire (1754–1817)
Melanson, Charles (b. 1643, d. before 1700)
Membertou (d. 1611)
Membré, Zénobe (1645–89)
Ménage, Pierre (d. 1715)
Ménard, René (b. 1605, d. *c.* 1661)
Menou d'Aulnay, Charles de (d. 1650)
Menut, Alexandre (d. *c.* 1805)
Menzies, Archibald (d. 1842)
Menzies, George (d. 1847)
Mercer, Alexander Cavalié (1783–1868)
Mercer, Andrew (d. 1871)
Mercier, Antoine (1817–75)
Mercier, Honoré (1840–94)
Mercier, Jean-François (b. 1699, d. 1769 or
  1770)
Mercier, Jean-Pierre (1694–1753)
Mercure, Louis (1753–1816)
Meredith, Edmund Allen (1817–99)
Meriel, Henri-Antoine (1661–1713)
Merlac, André-Louis de (fl. 1667–98)
Merle, Jacques, named Father Vincent de Paul
  (1768–1853)
Mermet, Jean (1664–1716)
Merrick, John (d. 1829)
Merrill, Horace (1809–83)
Merritt, Nehemiah (1770–1842)
Merritt, Thomas (1759–1842)
Merritt, William Hamilton (1793–1862)
Merry, Ralph (1753–1825)
Mésaiger, Charles-Michel (d. 1766)
Mesplet, Fleury (1734–94)
Messamouet (fl. 1604–7)
Messier, Martine (Primot) (b. 1607, d. in or after
  1672)
Messier, *dit* Saint-Michel, Michel (1640–1725)
Metcalf, William George (1847–85)
Metcalfe, Charles Theophilus, 1st Baron Metcalfe
  (1785–1846)
Metherall, Francis (1791–1875)
Méthot, François-Xavier (1796–1853)
Méthot, Michel-Édouard (1826–92)
Meulles, Jacques de (d. 1703)
Meuse, Andrew James (fl. 1821–50)
Meyers, John Walden (1745/46–1821)
Mézière, Henry-Antoine (d. in or after 1819)
Michaux, André (1746–1803)
Michel, Sir John (1804–86)

Michel de Villebois de La Rouvillière, Honoré (1702–52)

Michikinakoua (d. 1812)

Michipichy (fl. 1695–1706)

Middleton, Christopher (d. 1770)

Middleton, Sir Frederick Dobson (1825–98)

Middleton, Robert (1810–74)

Miertsching, Johann August (1817–75)

Migeon de Branssat, Jean-Baptiste (1636–93)

Migeon de Branssat, Marie-Anne, named de la Nativité (d. 1771)

Migeon de La Gauchetière, Daniel (d. 1746)

Mignault, Pierre-Marie (1784–1868)

Mikak (d. 1795)

Mikinak (d. 1755)

Milbanke, Mark (d. 1805)

Miles, Abner (d. 1806)

Miles, Edward Madan (1835–66)

Miles, Elijah (1753–1831)

Miles, Frederick William (d. 1842)

Miles, Henry Hopper (1818–95)

Miles, Stephen (1789–1870)

Milette, Alexis (1793–1869)

Millar, James (d. 1838)

Miller, Hugh (1818–98)

Miller, James Andrews (1839–86)

Miller, John Classon (1836–84)

Miller, Linus Wilson (1817–80)

Millet, Pierre (1635–1708)

Millidge, Thomas (d. 1816)

Millidge, Thomas (1776–1838)

Millier, Hilaire (1823–89)

Milloy, Duncan (1825–71)

Mills, Joseph Langley (d. 1832)

Mills, Samuel Sylvester (1806–74)

Mills, Sir Thomas (d. 1793)

Milly, François (d. before 1749)

Milner, Christopher (1787–1877)

Milnes, Sir Robert Shore (d. 1837)

Mīmīy (d. 1884)

Minahikosis (d. 1885)

Miniac, Jean-Pierre de (d. 1771)

Minns, William (d. 1827)

Minweweh (d. 1770)

Miristou (d. 1628)

Miscomote (d. 1721)

Miscouaky (fl. 1700–13)

Missenden, Samuel (fl. 1685–88)

Mistahimaskwa (d. 1888)

Mitchell, David (d. 1832)

Mitchell, George (d. 1755)

Mitchell, James (1843–97)

Mitchell, Peter (1824–99)

Mitchell, Thomas (fl. 1743–51)

Mius d'Entremont, Philippe, Baron de Pobomcoup (d. 1700 or 1701)

Miville, Pierre, known as Le Suisse (d. 1669)

Moffatt, George (1787–1865)

Moffatt, Lewis (d. 1892)

Mog (d. 1724)

Mohier, Gervais (1599–1662)

Mohr, Sigismund (1827–93)

Moir, William Church (1822–96)

Moireau, Claude (d. 1703)

Molesworth, Thomas Nepean (1824–79)

Molony, Belinda, named Sister Mary Xavier (1781–1865)

Molson, Anne (Molson) (1824–99)

Molson, John (1763–1836)

Molson, John (1787–1860)

Molson, Thomas (1791–1863)

Molson, William (1793–1875)

Molt, Théodore-Frédéric (d. 1856)

Monbeton de Brouillan, Jacques-François de (1651–1705)

Monbeton de Brouillan, dit Saint-Ovide, Joseph de (1676–1755)

Monck, Charles Stanley, 4th Viscount Monck (1819–94)

Monckton, Robert (1726–82)

Moncoq, Michel (1827–56)

Mondelet, Charles-Elzéar (1801–76)

Mondelet, Dominique (d. 1802)

Mondelet, Dominique (1799–1863)

Mondelet, Jean-Marie (d. 1843)

Monic, Joseph de (d. 1707)

Monk, Henry Wentworth (1827–96)

Monk, James (d. 1768)

Monk, Sir James (1745/46–1826)

Monk, Maria (1816–49)

Monro, Alexander (1813–96)

Monro, David (d. 1834)

Monro, George (1801–78)

Monroe, Moses (1842–95)

Monseignat, Charles de (d. 1718)

Montcalm, Louis-Joseph de, Marquis de Montcalm (1712–59)

Montferrand, dit Favre, Joseph (1802–64)

Montgenet, Thérèse-Bernardine, Comtesse de Montgenet, known as Mme de Saint-Laurent (1760–1830)

Montgolfier, Étienne (1712–91)

Montgomery, Donald (1848–90)

Montgomery, John (1800–67)

Montgomery, John (d. 1879)

Montgomery, Richard (1736–75)

Montgomery, William (1765–1800)

Montigny, François de (1669–1742)

Montminy, Théophile (1842–99)

Montmollin, David-François de (d. 1803)

Montour, Nicholas (1756–1808)

Montresor, John (1736–99)

Monts, Sieur de (fl. 1662)

Moodie, John Wedderburn Dunbar (1797–1869)

Moody, James (d. 1809)
Moody, John (d. 1736)
Moody, Richard Clement (1813–87)
Moody, Samuel (1675/76–1747)
Moody, Sewell Prescott (d. 1875)
Moor, William (d. 1765)
Moore, Dennis (1817–87)
Moore, Frances (Brooke) (d. 1789)
Moore, John Warren (1812–93)
Moore, Philip Henry (1799–1880)
Moore, Thomas (fl. 1671–1713)
Moore, William (fl. 1779–98)
Moorsom, William Scarth (1804–63)
Morand, Paul (d. 1854)
Moreau, Edme (fl. 1706–47)
Moreau, Hippolyte (1815–80)
Moreau, Jean-Baptiste (d. 1770)
Moreau de Brésoles, Judith (1620–87)
Morehouse, Daniel (1758–1835)
Morel, Thomas (1636–87)
Morel de La Durantaye, Olivier (1640–1716)
Moreton, Julian (1825–1900)
Morgan, Henry (1819–93)
Morgann, Maurice (1726–1802)
Morillon Du Bourg (d. 1670)
Morin, Achille (1815–98)
Morin, Augustin-Norbert (1803–65)
Morin, Germain (d. 1702)
Morin, Louis-Siméon (1831–79)
Morin, Marie (1649–1730)
Morin de Fonfay, Jean-Baptiste (fl. 1737–93)
Morpain, Pierre (d. 1749)
Morrill, Simeon (1793–1871)
Morrin, Joseph (1794–1861)
Morris, Alexander (1826–89)
Morris, Charles (1711–81)
Morris, Charles (1731–1802)
Morris, Charles (1759–1831)
Morris, Edward (1813–87)
Morris, Frederick William (d. 1867)
Morris, James (1798–1865)
Morris, James Rainstorpe (d. 1809)
Morris, Maria Frances Ann (Miller) (1813–75)
Morris, Patrick (d. 1849)
Morris, William (1786–1858)
Morrison, Angus (1822–82)
Morrison, Daniel (1826–70)
Morrison, Joseph Curran (1816–85)
Morrison, Joseph Wanton (1783–1826)
Morrison, Thomas David (d. 1856)
Morrison, Thomas Fletcher (1808–86)
Morse, Robert (1743/44–1818)
Mortimer, Edward (d. 1819)
Mortimer, George (1784–1844)
Morton, Catharine (McLellan) (1837–92)
Morton, George Elkana (1811–92)
Morton, James (1808–64)

Morton, Silvanus (1805–87)
Moschell, Johann Adam (1795–1849)
Moss, Thomas (1836–81)
Motin, Jeanne (Menou d'Aulnay; Saint-Étienne de La Tour) (d. c. 1666)
Mott, Jacob S. (d. 1814)
Motton, Robert (d. 1898)
Mouat, William Alexander (1821–71)
Mouchy, Nicolas de (fl. 1663–72)
Mouet de Langlade, Charles-Michel (d. c. 1800)
Moulton, Ebenezer (1709–83)
Moulton, Jeremiah (1688–1765)
Mounier, François (d. 1769)
Mounier, Jean-Mathieu (fl. 1715–74)
Mount, Roswell (1797–1834)
Mountain, George Jehoshaphat (1789–1863)
Mountain, Jacob (1749–1825)
Mountain, Jacob George (1818–56)
Mountain, Jehosaphat (1745–1817)
Mousseau, Joseph-Alfred (1838–86)
Mowat, John (1791–1860)
Mowat, John Bower (1825–1900)
Mowat, Thomas (1859–91)
Moyen, Jean (1828–99)
Moziño Losada Suárez de Figueroa, José Mariano (d. 1820)
Muir, Adam Charles (d. 1829)
Muir, Andrew (d. 1859)
Muir, John (1799–1883)
Muiron, David-Bernard (1684–1761)
Mulkins, Hannibal (d. 1877)
Mullins, Rosanna Eleanora (Leprohon) (1829–79)
Mullock, John Thomas (1807–69)
Mulvany, Charles Pelham (1835–85)
Munk, Jens Eriksen (1579–1628)
Munn, Alexander (1766–1812)
Munn, John (1788–1859)
Munn, John (1807–79)
Munn, Robert Stewart (1829–94)
Munro, George (1825–96)
Munro, Hector (1807–88)
Munro, Hugh (d. 1846)
Munro, John (1728–1800)
Munson, Mrs Letitia (fl. 1882)
Muquinna (d. 1795)
Muquinna (fl. 1786–1817)
Murchie, James (1813–1900)
Murdoch, Beamish (1800–76)
Murdoch, William (1800–66)
Mure, John (d. 1823)
Murphy, Anna Brownell (Jameson) (1794–1860)
Murphy, Michael (1826–68)
Murray, Alexander (d. 1762)
Murray, Alexander (1810–84)
Murray, Alexander Hunter (d. 1874)
Murray, Anne (Powell) (1755–1849)
Murray, Sir George (1772–1846)

Murray, George (1825–88)
Murray, Hugh (1836–74)
Murray, James (d. 1794)
Murray, John (d. 1824)
Murray, Louisa Annie (1818–94)
Murray, Robert (d. 1853)
Murray, Walter (d. 1772)
Musgrave, Sir Anthony (1828–88)
Musquakie (d. 1864)
Myatt, Joseph (d. 1730)
Myeerah (fl. 1805–16)
Myers, Samuel H. (1838–87)

NAFZIGER, Christian (1776–1836)
Nahnebahwequay (1824–65)
Nairn, Stephen (1838–1900)
Nairne, John (1731–1802)
Napier, Duncan Campbell (d. 1865)
Napper, James (d. 1737)
Natawista (d. 1893)
Natos-api (d. 1897)
Natte, *dit* Marseille, Jean-Sébastien (1734–1803)
Nau, Louis (b. 1799, d. in or after 1843)
Nau, Luc-François (1703–53)
Navarre, Robert (d. 1791)
Navières, Joseph (1709–56)
Nawahjegezhegwabe (1786–1863)
Ne-can-nete (d. 1897)
Nédélec, Jean-Marie (1834–96)
Need, Thomas (1808–95)
Needham, William Hayden (1810–74)
Neelon, Sylvester (1825–97)
Negabamat (d. 1666)
Neilson, John (1776–1848)
Neilson, Samuel (1771–93)
Neilson, Samuel (1800–37)
Nelles, Abram (1805–84)
Nelles, Robert (1761–1842)
Nelles, Samuel Sobieski (1823–87)
Nelson, George (1786–1859)
Nelson, Hugh (1830–93)
Nelson, John (1654–1734)
Nelson, Robert (1794–1873)
Nelson, William (1750–1834)
Nelson, Wolfred (1791–1863)
Nepean, Nicholas (d. 1823)
Nesbitt, William (d. 1784)
Nescambiouit (d. 1727)
Neveu, Jean-Baptiste (d. 1754)
Nevins, Archibald (1782–1812)
Nevins, James (1821–93)
Newbigging, James (d. 1838)
Newman, Robert (d. 1803)
Newman, William Herman (1829–94)
Newton, John (d. 1750)
Nichol, Robert (d. 1824)
Nicholas of Lynne (fl. 1360)

Nicholson, Francis (1655–1727/28)
Nickinson, John (1808–64)
Nicollet de Belleborne, Jean (d. 1642)
Nicolls, Jasper Hume (1818–77)
Niles, William E. (1799–1873)
Nisbet, James (1823–74)
Nisbet, Thomas (d. 1850)
Nissowaquet (d. 1797)
Nixon, John (d. 1692)
Noad, Henry John (1812–70)
Noad, Joseph (d. 1873)
Nobili, John (1812–56)
Noble, Arthur (d. 1746/47)
Noble, Seth (1743–1807)
Nodogawerrimet (d. 1765)
Noël, Jacques (fl. 1585–88)
Noël, Marie-Geneviève (Drapeau) (1766–1829)
Nolan Lamarque, Charles (1694–1754)
Nolin, Jean-Baptiste (d. 1826)
Nooth, John Mervin (d. 1828)
Nordbeck, Peter (1789–1861)
Nordheimer, Abraham (1816–62)
Norman, Nathan (1809–83)
Normand, François (1779–1854)
Normandin, Daniel (d. 1729)
Normant Du Faradon, Louis (1681–1759)
Noro (fl. 1700–1)
Norquay, John (1841–89)
Norris, Sir John (d. 1749)
Northup, Jeremiah (1816–79)
Norton, John (fl. 1784–1825)
Norton, Moses (d. 1773)
Norton, Richard (1701–41)
Notman, William (1826–91)
Nouchet, Joseph (1690–1750)
Nouchet, Joseph-Étienne (1724–58)
Nouë, Anne de (1587–1646)
Nouvel, Henri (d. 1701 or 1702)
Noyelles de Fleurimont, Nicolas-Joseph de (1695–1761)
Noyon, Jacques de (1668–1745)
Noyrot, Philibert (1592–1629)
Nugent, John (d. 1880)
Nugent, John Valentine (1796–1874)
Nugent, Richard (1815–58)
Nutt, John (fl. 1620–32)
Nutting, James Walton (d. 1870)

OAKES, Forrest (d. 1783)
Oakley, Alfred (d. 1883)
O'Beirne, Eugene Francis (d. in or after 1864)
O'Brien, Dennis (1792–1865)
O'Brien, Edward George (d. 1875)
O'Brien, John (1790–1855)
O'Brien, John Daniel O'Connell (1831–91)
O'Brien, Laurence (1792–1870)
O'Brien, Lucius James (1797–1870)

O'Brien, Lucius Richard (1832–99)
O'Callaghan, Edmund Bailey (d. 1880)
O'Connor, John (1824–87)
O'Connor, William Joseph (1862–92)
Odelin, Jacques (1789–1841)
Odell, Jonathan (1737–1818)
Odell, William Franklin (1774–1844)
Odell, William Hunter (1811–91)
Odet d'Orsonnens, Thomas-Edmond d' (1818–92)
Odin, Henriette (Feller) (1800–68)
O'Donel, James Louis (d. 1811)
O'Donnell, James (1774–1830)
O'Donoghue, William Bernard (1843–78)
Ogden, Charles Richard (1791–1866)
Ogden, Peter Skene (d. 1854)
Ogenheratarihiens (d. 1687)
Ogilvie, James (d. 1813)
Ogilvie, John (1724–74)
Ogilvie, William Watson (1835–1900)
Ogilvy, John (d. 1819)
Ogimauh-binaessih (1764–1828)
O'Grady, Standish (fl. 1807–45)
O'Grady, William John (d. 1840)
O'Hara, Edward (d. 1833)
O'Hara, Felix (d. 1805)
O'Hara, Walter (d. 1874)
O'Hea, Timothy (1846–74)
Ohonsiowanne (fl. 1699–1704)
Ohquandageghte (fl. 1757–73)
Ohtowaʔkéhson (d. 1837)
Oille, George Nicholas (1817–83)
Oionhaton (fl. 1628–55)
Olabaratz, Jean d' (1727–1808)
Olabaratz, Joannis-Galand d' (d. 1778)
O'Leary, Henry (1832–97)
Oliva, Frédéric-Guillaume (d. 1796)
Oliver, Adam (1823–82)
Olivier, Abel (d. 1768)
Olivier, *dit* Le Picard, Marc-Antoine (fl. 1688–96)
Olivier de Vézin, Pierre-François (b. 1707, d. in or after 1776)
O'Meara, Frederick Augustus (1814–88)
Onasakenrat, Joseph (1845–81)
Ondaaiondiont (d. 1649)
O'Neill, John (1834–78)
O'Neill, Terence Joseph (1802–72)
Onistah-sokaksin (d. 1873 or 1874)
Onista'poka (d. 1897)
Ononwarogo (d. 1764)
Ooligbuck (d. 1852)
Oppenheimer, David (1834–97)
O'Reilly, Gerald (1806–61)
O'Reilly, Hugh (d. 1859)
O'Reilly, James (1823–75)
Orillat, Jean (1733–79)
Orkney, James (1760–1832)
Orontony (fl. 1739–50)

Orr, Wesley Fletcher (1831–98)
Osborn, Sir Danvers (1715–53)
Osborn, Elizabeth (Myrick; Paine; Doane) (1715–98)
Osborn, Henry (d. 1771)
Osborn, Mary (London) (d. 1801)
Osborn, Sherard (1822–75)
Osgood, Thaddeus (1775–1852)
Osgoode, William (1754–1824)
Osler, Featherstone Lake (1805–95)
Ossaye, Frédéric-M.-F. (fl. 1851–63)
Ostell, John (1813–92)
O'Sullivan, Dennis Ambrose (1848–92)
O'Sullivan, Michael (d. 1839)
Otreouti (fl. 1659–88)
Ottrowana (fl. 1746–74)
Ouachala (fl. 1716–27)
Ouagimou (fl. 1604–10)
Ouenemek (fl. 1695–1717)
Ougier, Peter (d. 1803)
Ouimet, André (1808–53)
Oumasasikweie (d. *c.* 1636)
Ounanguissé (fl. 1695–1716)
Ourehouare (d. 1698)
Outlaw, John (d. between 1696 and 1698)
Outoutagan (fl. 1698–1712)
Overholser, Jacob (d. 1815)
Owen, David (d. 1829)
Owen, William (1737–78)
Owen, William Fitz William (1774–1857)
Oxenden, Ashton (1808–92)
Ozon, Potentien (d. 1705)

PACAUD, Édouard-Louis (1815–89)
Pacaud, Philippe-Napoléon (1812–84)
Pack, Robert (1786–1860)
Padanuques, Jacques (d. 1744)
Pagan, Robert (1750–1821)
Pagan, William (1744–1819)
Pagé, *dit* Carcy, Jacques (1682–1742)
Pahtahsega (d. 1890)
Paillard, Léonard, known as Le Poitevin (1647–1729)
Pain, Félix (1668–1741)
Painchaud, Alexis (1792–1858)
Painchaud, Charles-François (1782–1838)
Painchaud, Joseph (b. 1819, d. probably in 1855)
Painchaud, Joseph (1787–1871)
Paine, William (1750–1833)
Painter, John (d. 1815)
Palliser, Sir Hugh (1722/23–96)
Palliser, John (1817–87)
Palmer, Edward (1809–89)
Palmer, Henry Spencer (1838–93)
Palmer, James Bardin (d. 1833)
Pambrun, Pierre-Chrysologue (1792–1841)
Pampalon, Alfred (1867–96)

Pandosy, Charles (1824–91)
Panet, Bernard-Claude (1753–1833)
Panet, Bonaventure (1765–1846)
Panet, Jacques (1754–1834)
Panet, Jean-Antoine (1751–1815)
Panet, Jean-Claude (d. 1778)
Panet, Philippe (1791–1855)
Panet, Pierre (1731–1804)
Panet, Pierre-Louis (1761–1812)
Panet, Pierre-Louis (1800–70)
Pangman, Peter (1744–1819)
Panneton, Charles-Marie (d. 1890)
Panounias (d. 1607)
Panton, George (d. 1810)
Papin, Joseph (1825–62)
Papineau, Denis-Benjamin (1789–1854)
Papineau, Joseph (1752–1841)
Papineau, Louis-Joseph (1786–1871)
Papineau, *dit* Montigny, Samuel (d. 1737)
Pâquet, Anselme-Honoré (1830–91)
Pâquet, Benjamin (1832–1900)
Paquet, Joseph-Marie (1804–69)
Paquet, Marie-Anne, named de Saint-Olivier (1755–1831)
Paquet, *dit* Lavallée, André (1799–1860)
Paquin, Jacques (1791–1847)
Paradis, Jean (b. 1658, d. before 1725)
Paradis, Roland (d. 1754)
Parant, Antoine (1785–1855)
Parant, Joseph (1796–1856)
Parat, Antoine (d. 1696)
Pardee, Timothy Blair (1830–89)
Paré, Hubert (1803–69)
Paré, Joseph-Octave (1814–78)
Parent, Étienne (1802–74)
Parent, Louis-François (1778–1850)
Parent, Marie-Geneviève, named de Saint-François d'Assise (1740–1804)
Paris, Bernard (1708–60)
Parisien, Norbert (d. 1870)
Parke, Ephraim Jones (1823–99)
Parke, Thomas (1793–1864)
Parker, Neville (1798–1869)
Parker, Robert (1796–1865)
Parker, Snow (1760–1843)
Parkhurst, Anthony (fl. 1561–83)
Parkin, Edward (1791–1844)
Parkin, John Buckworth (1816–75)
Parkman, Francis (1823–93)
Parks, William (b. 1800, d. in or after 1870)
Parmenius, Stephanus (d. 1583)
Parmentier, Jean (1494–1529)
Parr, John (1725–91)
Parry, Sir William Edward (1790–1855)
Parsons, Robert John (d. 1883)
Partelow, John Richard (1796–1865)
Pascaud, Antoine (d. 1717)

Pascaud, Antoine (1729–86)
Paskwāw (d. 1889)
Pasquine (fl. 1681–88)
Pastedechouan (d. 1636)
Pastour de Costebelle, Philippe (1661–1717)
Paterson, John (1805–56)
Paterson, Peter (1807–83)
Paton, Andrew (1833–92)
Patoulet, Jean-Baptiste (d. 1695)
Patrick, William (1810–83)
Pattee, David (1778–1851)
Patterson, George (1824–97)
Patterson, Peter (1768–1851)
Patterson, Robert (1732–1808)
Patterson, Robert J. (1809–84)
Patterson, Walter (d. 1798)
Patterson, William Jeffrey (1815–86)
Pattin, John (d. 1754)
Paul, Mary Christianne (Morris) (d. 1886)
Paumart, Jean (1583–1648)
Pawling, Benjamin (d. 1818)
Payen de Noyan, Marie-Catherine, named de Saint-Alexis (d. 1818)
Payen de Noyan, Pierre (1663–1707)
Payen de Noyan, Pierre-Benoît (d. 1765)
Payen de Noyan et de Chavoy, Pierre-Jacques (1695–1771)
Payne, Samuel (b. 1696, d. in or after 1732)
Payzant, John (1749–1834)
Peabody, Francis (1760–1841)
Peachey, James (d. 1797)
Péan, Michel-Jean-Hugues (d. 1782)
Péan de Livaudière, Jacques-Hugues (1682–1747)
Pearkes, George (1826–71)
Pearson, Bartholomew (fl. 1612–34)
Peaseley, William (b. 1714, d. in or after 1756)
Pécaudy de Contrecœur, Antoine (1596–1688)
Pécaudy de Contrecœur, Claude-Pierre (1705–75)
Pécaudy de Contrecœur, François-Antoine (d. 1743)
Pedley, Charles (1820–72)
Peel, Paul (1860–92)
Peemeecheekag (d. 1891)
Peenaquim (d. 1869)
Peers, Henry Newsham (1821–64)
Peguis (d. 1864)
Peiras, Jean-Baptiste de (d. 1701)
Pélerin, Ambroise (1656–1708)
Pélissier, Christophe (b. 1728, d. before 1800)
Pellegrin, Gabriel (1713–88)
Pelletier, Didace (1657–99)
Peltier, Hector (1822–78)
Peltier, Orphir (1825–54)
Peltier, Toussaint (1792–1854)
Pemberton, Joseph Despard (1821–93)
Peminuit Paul, Jacques-Pierre (1800–95)
Peminuit Paul, Louis-Benjamin (1755–1843)
Pemoussa (d. 1716 or 1717)

Pennefather, Richard Theodore (d. 1865)
Pennisseaut, Louis (b. 1724, d. in or after 1771)
Pennoyer, Jesse (1760–1825)
Penny, Edward Goff (1820–81)
Penny, William (1809–92)
Pépin, Joseph (d. 1842)
Pepperrell, William (d. 1733/34)
Pepperrell, Sir William (1696–1759)
Peré, Jean (fl. 1660–99)
Pérez Hernández, Juan Josef (d. 1775)
Périnault, Joseph (1732–1814)
Perkins, Simeon (1734/35–1812)
Perley, Israel (1738–1813)
Perley, Moses Henry (1804–62)
Perley, William Goodhue (1820–90)
Peronne de Mazé, Louis (fl. 1661–65)
Peronne Dumesnil, Jean (d. before 1667)
Pérot, Gilles (d. 1680)
Perrault, Charles-Norbert (1793–1832)
Perrault, François (d. 1745)
Perrault, Jacques, known as Perrault l'ainé
    (1718–75)
Perrault, Jacques-Nicolas (1750–1812)
Perrault, Jean-Baptiste (1761–1844)
Perrault, Joseph-François (1753–1844)
Perrault, Joseph-Julien (1826–66)
Perrault, Julien (d. 1647)
Perrault, Louis (1807–66)
Perrault, Olivier (1773–1827)
Perrault, Paul (d. 1765)
Perré, Henri (d. 1890)
Perreault, Hyacinthe (1654–1700)
Perrey, Sylvain-Éphrem (d. 1887)
Perrin, Antoine (d. c. 1738)
Perrot, François-Marie (1644–91)
Perrot, Nicolas (d. 1717)
Perrot de Rizy, Pierre (1672–1740)
Perry, George Hugo (1817–88)
Perry, Peter (1792–1851)
Perry, Stanislaus Francis (1823–98)
Perthuis, Charles (1664–1722)
Perthuis, Jean-Baptiste-Ignace (b. 1716,
    d. in or after 1767)
Perthuis, Joseph (1714–82)
Peters, Benjamin Lester (1790–1852)
Peters, Charles Jeffery (1773–1848)
Peters, Hannah (Jarvis) (1763–1845)
Peters, James Horsfield (d. 1891)
Peters, Joseph (1729–1800)
Peters, Thomas (d. 1792)
Peters, William Birdseye (1774–1822)
Peterson, Heinrich Wilhelm (1793–1859)
Petit, Jean (1663–1720)
Petit, Louis (1629–1709)
Petit, Pierre (d. 1737)
Petitclair, Pierre (1813–60)
Petit de Levilliers, Charles (d. 1714)

Petitpas, Barthélemy (1687–1747)
Petitpas, Claude (d. before 1733)
Pettit, Nathaniel (1724–1803)
Pettrequin, Jean (d. 1764)
Peuvret de Gaudarville, Alexandre (d. 1702)
Peuvret Demesnu, Jean-Baptiste (1632–97)
Peyton, John (1749–1829)
Pézard de La Tousche Champlain, Étienne (b. 1624,
    d. c. 1696)
Phelan, Patrick (1795–1857)
Philippe de Hautmesnil de Mandeville, François (d.
    1728)
Philippon, Joseph-Antoine (1789–1832)
Philipps, Erasmus James (1705–60)
Philipps, John (d. 1801)
Philipps, Richard (d. 1750)
Philips, Henry Joseph (b. 1811, fl. 1845–50)
Philips, James (d. 1838)
Phillips, Alfred Moore (1847–96)
Phipps, George Augustus Constantine, 3rd Earl of
    Mulgrave and 2nd Marquess of Normanby
    (1819–90)
Phipps, Thomas (fl. 1679–86)
Phips, Sir William (1650/51–94/95)
Phlem, dit Yvon, Yves (d. 1749)
Piat, Irénée (1594–1674)
Picard, Louis-Alexandre (d. 1799)
Picard Destroismaisons, Thomas-Ferruce (1796–
    1866)
Pichard, Amable (d. 1819)
Pichon, Thomas (1700–81)
Pichot de Querdisien Trémais, Charles-François (d.
    1784)
Pickard, Humphrey (1813–90)
Pickard, John (1824–83)
Pickmore, Francis (d. 1818)
Picoté de Belestre, François-Marie (1716–93)
Picoté de Belestre, Pierre (d. 1679)
Picotte, Louis (d. 1827)
Picquet, François (1708–81)
Pienovi, Angelo (d. 1845)
Pierpoint, Richard (fl. 1779–1838)
Pierre (d. 1747)
Pierron, Jean (1631–1700)
Piers, Temple Foster (1783–1860)
Pieskaret (d. 1647)
Pigarouich (fl. 1639–44)
Pigeon, François-Xavier (1778–1838)
Pijart, Claude (1600–83)
Pijart, Pierre (1608–76)
Pilgrim, Robert (d. 1750)
Pilkington, Robert (1765–1834)
Pillard, Louis (d. 1768)
Pilote, François (1811–86)
Pilotte, Angelique (fl. 1815–18)
Pim, Bedford Clapperton Trevelyan (1826–86)
Pinard, Louis (d. 1695)

Pinaud, Nicolas (d. 1722)
Pinguet de Vaucour, Jacques-Nicolas (1692–1749)
Pinhey, Hamnett Kirkes (1784–1857)
Pinsent, Robert John (1797–1876)
Pinsent, Sir Robert John (1834–93)
Pinson, Andrew (d. 1810)
Pinsonaut, Paul-Théophile (1780–1832)
Pinsoneault, Pierre-Adolphe (1815–83)
Piot de Langloiserie, Charles-Gaspard (d. 1715)
Piot de Langloiserie, Marie-Marguerite, named
    Saint-Hippolyte (1702–81)
Pītikwahanapiwīyin (d. 1886)
Piuze, Liveright (1754–1813)
Plamondon, Antoine (1804–95)
Plamondon, Louis (1785–1828)
Plamondon, Marc-Aurèle (1823–1900)
Plantavit de Lapause de Margon, Jean-Guillaume
    (1721–1804)
Plante, Charles (1680–1744)
Planté, Joseph-Bernard (1768–1826)
Plaw, John (d. 1820)
Playter, George Frederick (d. 1866)
Plessis, Joseph-Octave (1763–1825)
Plessy, dit Bélair, Jean-Louis (1678–1743)
Plumb, Josiah Burr (1816–88)
Point, Nicolas (1799–1868)
Polette, Antoine (1807–87)
Pollard, Richard (1753–1824)
Pollet, Arnould-Balthazar (1702–56)
Pollet de La Combe-Pocatière, François (d. 1672)
Pommereau, Jean-Baptiste (1702–42)
Pommier, Hugues (d. 1686)
Poncet de La Rivière, Joseph-Antoine (1610–75)
Poncin, Claude (1725–1811)
Pond, Peter (1739/40–1807)
Ponekeosh (d. 1891)
Pontiac (d. 1769)
Poor, John Alfred (1808–71)
Pope, James Colledge (1826–85)
Pope, John Henry (1819–89)
Pope, Joseph (1803–95)
Pope, William Henry (1825–79)
Porlier, Pierre-Antoine (1725–89)
Porteous, Andrew (d. 1849)
Porteous, Thomas (1765–1830)
Porter, Charles (d. 1864)
Porter, James (1812–74)
Portlock, Nathaniel (d. 1817)
Post, Jordan (1767–1845)
Pote, William (b. 1718, d. in or after 1752)
Pothier, Toussaint (1771–1845)
Potier, Pierre-Philippe (d. 1781)
Potier Dubuisson, Robert (1682–1744)
Potot de Montbeillard, Fiacre-François (1723–78)
Pottier, Jean-Baptiste (d. 1711)
Potts, Jerry (d. 1896)
Potts, John (d. 1764)

Pouchot, Pierre (1712–69)
Pouget, Jean-Baptiste-Noël (1745–1818)
Poulain, Guillaume (d. 1623)
Poulet, Georges-François, known as Monsieur
    Dupont (fl. 1714–18)
Poulin, Pierre (b. 1684, d. in or after 1744)
Poulin de Courval, François-Louis (1728–69)
Poulin de Courval, Jean-Baptiste (1657–1727)
Poulin de Courval, Louis-Jean (1696–1743)
Poulin de Courval Cressé, Louis-Pierre (1728–64)
Poulin de Francheville, François (1692–1733)
Poulin de La Fontaine, Maurice (d. between 1670
    and 1676)
Pourroy de Lauberivière, François-Louis de
    (1711–40)
Poutré, Félix (1814–85)
Powell, Anne (1787–1822)
Powell, Charles Stuart (d. 1811)
Powell, Grant (d. 1838)
Powell, William Dummer (1755–1834)
Power, John (d. 1823)
Power, Michael (1804–47)
Power, Michael Joseph (1834–95)
Power, Patrick (1815–81)
Power, Richard (d. 1681)
Power, Thomas Joseph (1830–93)
Powlis, George (b. 1812. d. in or after 1852)
Pownall, Sir George (1755–1834)
Pozer, Christian Henry (1835–84)
Pozer, George (1752–1848)
Prat, Jean-Baptiste (1812–76)
Prat, Louis (1662–1726)
Pratt, Charles (d. 1888)
Preissac de Bonneau, Louis de (b. 1724,
    d. in or after 1789)
Prendergast, James Luke (1800–95)
Prescott, Charles Ramage (1772–1859)
Prescott, Sir Henry (1783–1874)
Prescott, Robert (d. 1815)
Pressart, Colomban-Sébastien (1723–77)
Pressé, Hyacinthe-Olivier (fl. 1735–46)
Preston, Richard (d. 1861) [volume VIII appendix]
Prevost, Sir George (1767–1816)
Prévost, Martin (d. 1691)
Prévost, Oscar (1845–95)
Prevost de La Croix, Jacques (1715–91)
Price, Benjamin (d. 1768)
Price, Evan John (1840–99)
Price, James Hervey (1797–1882)
Price, William (1789–1867)
Price, William Evan (1827–80)
Primeau, Louis (fl. 1749–1800)
Prince, Jean-Charles (1804–60)
Prince, John (1796–1870)
Pring, Daniel (d. 1846)
Pringle, Robert (d. 1793)
Pringle, William Allen (1841–96)

Pritchard, Azariah (d. *c.* 1830)
Pritchard, John (1777–1856)
Procter, Henry (d. 1822)
Proudfoot, William (1788–1851)
Proudfoot, William (fl. 1817–66)
Proulx, Jean-Baptiste (1793–1856)
Proulx, Jean-Baptiste (1808–81)
Proulx, Louis (1751–1838)
Proulx, Louis (1804–71)
Prouville, Alexandre de, Marquis de Tracy (d. 1670)
Provancher, Léon (1820–92)
Provencher, Joseph-Alfred-Norbert (1843–87)
Provencher, Joseph-Norbert (1787–1853)
Provost, François (1638–1702)
Pruden, John Peter (d. 1868)
Prud'homme, Louis (d. 1671)
Pryor, Henry (1808–92)
Pryor, John (1805–92)
Pryor, William (1775–1859)
Pryor, William (1801–84)
Puisaye, Joseph-Geneviève de, Comte de Puisaye (1755–1827)
Puiseaux, Pierre de (d. *c.* 1647)
Pullen, William John Samuel (1813–87)
Punshon, William Morley (1824–81)
Purcell, James (fl. 1841–58)
Purdy, William (1769–1847)
Purss, John (1732–1803)
Purvis, George (b. 1842, d. in or after 1894)
Purvis, Nancy (d. 1839)
Pushee, Nathan (1758–1838)
Putnam, William (d. 1838)
Pyke, George (1775–1851)
Pyke, John George (d. 1828)
Pynne, William (fl. 1689–1713)

QUEN, Jean de (d. 1659)
Quentin, Claude (1597–1676)
Quentin, Jacques (1572–1647)
Quéré de Tréguron, Maurice (d. 1754)
Quertier, Édouard (1796–1872)
Quesnel, Frédéric-Auguste (1785–1866)
Quesnel, Joseph (1746–1809)
Quesnel, Jules-Maurice (1786–1842)
Quesneville, Jean (d. 1701)
Quetton St George, Laurent (1771–1821)
Quévillon, Louis (1749–1823)
Quiblier, Joseph-Vincent (1796–1852)
Quinan, John Joseph (1834–70)
Quiniard, *dit* Duplessis, Antoine-Olivier (d. 1738)
Quintal, Augustin (1683–1776)
Quirk, John (1783–1853)
Quirouet, François (1776–1844)

RABY, Augustin (d. 1782)
Raby, Augustin-Jérôme (1745–1822)
Racine, Antoine (1822–93)

Racine, Dominique (1828–88)
Radcliff, Thomas (1794–1841)
Radenhurst, Thomas Mabon (1803–54)
Radisson, Pierre-Esprit (d. 1710)
Rae, Ann Cuthbert (Knight; Fleming) (1788–1860)
Rae, John (1796–1872)
Rae, John (1813–93)
Raffeix, Pierre (1635–1724)
Rageot, Gilles (d. 1692)
Rageot de Saint-Luc, Charles (d. 1702)
Rageot de Saint-Luc, Nicolas (d. 1703)
Ragueneau, Paul (1608–80)
Raimbault, Jean (1770–1841)
Raimbault, Pierre (1671–1740)
Raimbault de Piedmont, Joseph-Charles (1693–1737)
Raisin, Marie (d. 1691)
Raizenne, Marie, named Saint-Ignace (1735–1811)
Raizenne, Marie-Clotilde, named Marie de l'Incarnation (1766–1829)
Rale, Sébastien (1657–1724)
Ralluau, Jean (fl. 1604–15)
Ramage, John (d. 1802)
Rambau, Alfred-Xavier (1810–56)
Ramezay, Claude de (1659–1724)
Ramezay, Jean-Baptiste-Nicolas-Roch de (1708–77)
Ramezay, Louise de (1705–76)
Ramezay, Marie-Charlotte de, named de Saint-Claude de la Croix (1697–1767)
Ramsay, David (fl. 1758–1810)
Ramsay, George, 9th Earl of Dalhousie (1770–1838)
Ramsay, Thomas Kennedy (1826–86)
Rand, Silas Tertius (1810–89)
Rand, Theodore Harding (1835–1900)
Randal, Robert (d. 1834)
Randal, Stephen (1804–41)
Randin, Hugues (b. 1628, d. *c.* 1680)
Rankin, Alexander (1788–1852)
Rankin, Arthur (1816–93)
Rankin, Coun Douly (d. 1852)
Rankin, John (fl. 1741–48)
Rankin, Robert (1801–70)
Rankin, William (d. 1837)
Ransonnet, Sylvestre-François-Michel (fl. 1726–43)
Ranvoyzé, Étienne (1776–1826)
Ranvoyzé, François (1739–1819)
Rastel de Rocheblave, Pierre de (1773–1840)
Rastell, John (fl. 1510–40)
Rastrick, Frederick James (d. 1897)
Rattier, Jean (d. 1703)
Rattray, William Jordan (1835–83)
Raudot, Antoine-Denis (1679–1737)
Raudot, Jacques (1638–1728)
Raymbaut, Charles (1602–42)

Raymond, Jean-Baptiste (1757–1825)
Raymond, Jean-Louis de, Comte de Raymond
(d. 1771)
Raymond, Jean-Moïse (1787–1843)
Raymond, Joseph-Sabin (1810–87)
Rayner, John (fl. 1661–62)
Razilly, Isaac de (1587–1635)
Read, John Landon (d. 1857)
Ready, John (d. 1845)
Réaume, Charles (1743–1813)
Reboul, Louis-Étienne-Delille (1827–77)
Récher, Jean-Félix (1724–68)
Record, Charles B. (1817–90)
Redpath, John (1796–1869)
Rees, William (d. 1874)
Reeve, William Albert (1842–94)
Reeves, John (1752–1829)
Regnard Duplessis, Georges (d. 1714)
Regnard Duplessis, Marie-Andrée, named de Sainte-
Hélène (1687–1760)
Regnard Duplessis de Morampont, Charles-Denis (b.
1704, d. in or after 1759)
Regnaud, François-Joseph-Victor (1799–1872)
Reid, Hugo (1809–72)
Reid, James Murray (1802–68)
Reiffenstein, John Christopher (d. 1840)
Reilly, Edward (d. 1872)
Rémy, Pierre (1636–1726)
Rémy de Courcelle, Daniel de (1626–98)
Renaud, Jean (d. 1794)
Renaud, Jean-Baptiste (1816–84)
Renaud, Louis (1818–78)
Renaud, *dit* Cannard, Pierre (d. 1774)
Renaud d'Avène de Desmeloizes, François-Marie
(d. 1699)
Renaud d'Avène Des Méloizes, Angélique (Péan)
(1722–92)
Renaud d'Avène Des Méloizes, Nicolas (1729–
1803)
Renaud d'Avène Des Méloizes, Nicolas-Marie
(1696–1743)
Renaud Dubuisson, Jacques-Charles (1666–1739)
Renaud Dubuisson, Louis-Jacques-Charles (b. 1709,
d. *c.* 1765)
Rendell, Stephen (1819–93)
Render, Thomas (fl. 1729–34)
René, Patrice (1667–1742)
Renfrew, George Richard (1831–97)
Resche, Pierre-Joseph (1695–1770)
Révol, Pierre (d. 1759)
Reynard, Alexis (1828–75)
Rézé, Joseph-Pierre (1814–99)
Rhoades, John (fl. 1674–76)
Riall, Sir Phineas (1775–1850)
Rice, Jacob (1683–1728)
Rice, Samuel Dwight (1815–84)
Richard, Louis-Eusèbe (1817–76)

Richard, *dit* Lafleur, Guillaume (1641–90)
Richards, Sir George Henry (d. 1896)
Richards, Jackson John (1787–1847)
Richards, Michael (1673–1722)
Richards, William (d. 1811)
Richards, Sir William Buell (1815–89)
Richardson, Edward Mallcott (b. 1839, d. in or after
1865)
Richardson, Hugh (1784–1870)
Richardson, James (d. 1832)
Richardson, James (1791–1875)
Richardson, James (1810–83)
Richardson, James (1819–92)
Richardson, John (d. 1831)
Richardson, John (1796–1852)
Richardson, Sir John (1787–1865)
Richardson, Samuel (d. 1843)
Richey, Matthew (1803–83)
Ridley, Thomas (1799–1879)
Ridout, George (1791–1871)
Ridout, George Percival (1807–73)
Ridout, Joseph Davis (1809–84)
Ridout, Lionel Augustus Clark (1817–59)
Ridout, Samuel Smith (1778–1855)
Ridout, Thomas (1754–1829)
Ridout, Thomas Gibbs (1792–1861)
Riel, Louis (1817–64)
Riel, Louis (1844–85)
Rieutord, Jean-Baptiste (d. 1818)
Rigaud de Vaudreuil, François-Pierre de (1703–79)
Rigaud de Vaudreuil, Joseph-Hyacinthe de
(1706–64)
Rigaud de Vaudreuil, Louis-Philippe de, Marquis de
Vaudreuil (1691–1763)
Rigaud de Vaudreuil, Philippe de, Marquis de
Vaudreuil (d. 1725)
Rigaud de Vaudreuil de Cavagnial, Pierre de,
Marquis de Vaudreuil (1698–1778)
Rindisbacher, Peter (1806–34)
Rine, David Isaac Kirwin (1835–82)
Rintoul, William (1797–1851)
Riordon, John (d. 1884)
Ritchie, John (d. 1790)
Ritchie, John William (1808–90)
Ritchie, Thomas (1777–1852)
Ritchie, William (1804–56)
Ritchie, Sir William Johnston (1813–92)
Rivard, Sévère (1834–88)
Riverin, Denis (d. 1717)
Riverin, Joseph (1699–1756)
Rivet Cavelier, Pierre (d. 1721)
Roaf, John (1801–62)
Robb, James (1815–61)
Robert, Antoine-Bernardin (1757–1826)
Robert, Clément (d. 1730 or 1736)
Roberts, Benjamin (fl. 1758–75)
Roberts, Charles (d. 1816)

Roberts, Lewis (1596–1641)
Robertson, Alexander Rocke (1841–81)
Robertson, Andrew (1815–80)
Robertson, Andrew (1827–90)
Robertson, Charles (d. 1763)
Robertson, Colin (1783–1842)
Robertson, Daniel (d. 1810)
Robertson, James (1747–1816)
Robertson, James (1831–1900)
Robertson, John (1799–1876)
Robertson, Joseph Gibb (1820–99)
Robertson, Margaret Murray (d. 1897)
Robertson, Thomas Jaffray (1805–66)
Robertson, William (d. 1806)
Robertson, William (1784–1844)
Robertson-Ross, Patrick (1828–83)
Robichaux, Jean-Baptiste (d. 1808)
Robichaux, Louis (1704–80)
Robichaux, Otho (1742–1824)
Robichaux, Vénérande (1753–1839)
Robie, Simon Bradstreet (1770–1858)
Robin, Charles (d. 1824)
Robinau de Bécancour, Pierre, Baron de Portneuf (1654–1729)
Robinau de Bécancour, René, Baron de Portneuf (d. 1699)
Robinau de Neuvillette, Daniel (d. 1702)
Robinau de Portneuf, Philippe-René (d. 1759)
Robinau de Portneuf, Pierre (1708–61)
Robinau de Portneuf, René (1659–1726)
Robinau de Villebon, Joseph (1655–1700)
Robinson, Sir Bryan (1808–87)
Robinson, Christopher (1763–98)
Robinson, Hezekiah (1791–1851)
Robinson, John (1762–1828)
Robinson, Sir John Beverley (1791–1863)
Robinson, John Beverley (1820–96)
Robinson, Joseph (d. 1807)
Robinson, Joseph Hiram (1807–96)
Robinson, Peter (1785–1838)
Robinson, Sir Robert (d. 1705)
Robinson, William Benjamin (1797–1873)
Robinson, Sir William Cleaver Francis (1834–97)
Robitaille, Olivier (1811–96)
Robitaille, Théodore (1834–97)
Roblin, David (1812–63)
Roblin, John P. (1799–1874)
Roblot, Louis, known as Brother Aidant (1796–1866)
Robson, John (1824–92)
Robson, Joseph (fl. 1733–63)
Robutel de La Noue, Zacharie (1665–1733)
Rocbert de La Morandière, Étienne (b. 1668, d. 1753 or 1754)
Rocbert de La Morandière, Marie-Élisabeth (Bégon de La Cour) (1696–1755)
Roche, John Knatchbull (1817–59)

Rochette, Cléophas (d. 1895)
Rochfort, John (d. 1865)
Rodier, Charles-Séraphin (1797–1876)
Rodier, Charles-Séraphin (1818–90)
Rodier, Édouard-Étienne (1804–40)
Rodrigue, Antoine (1722–89)
Rodrigue, Jean-Baptiste (d. 1733)
Roe, Walter (d. 1801)
Roebuck, John Arthur (1802–79)
Roger, Charles (1819–89) [volume X]
Roger, Guillaume (1632–1702)
Rogers, Albert Bowman (1829–89)
Rogers, David McGregor (1772–1824)
Rogers, Robert (1731–95)
Rogers, Thomas (d. 1853)
Rogers, William Henry (d. 1894)
Rolette, Joseph (1820–71)
Rolland, Jean-Baptiste (1815–88)
Rolland, Jean-Roch (1785–1862)
Rollet, Marie (Hébert; Hubou) (d. 1649)
Rollin, Paul (1789–1855)
Rollo, Andrew, 5th Baron Rollo (1703–65)
Rollo, James (d. 1820)
Rolph, John (1793–1870)
Rolph, Thomas (d. 1858)
Roma, Jean-Pierre (fl. 1715–57)
Romain, François (1768–1832)
Romieux, Pierre (fl. 1659–75)
Rondeau, Jacques-Philippe-Urbain (d. c. 1749)
Roope, John (d. 1719)
Roque, Jacques-Guillaume (1761–1840)
Roquemont de Brison, Claude (d. 1628)
Rose, George Maclean (1829–98)
Rose, Sir John (1820–88)
Roseboom, Johannes (d. 1745)
Ross, Alexander (1783–1856)
Ross, Alexander Milton (1832–97)
Ross, Bernard Rogan (1827–74)
Ross, David Alexander (1819–97)
Ross, Dunbar (d. 1865)
Ross, Duncan (d. 1834)
Ross, Flora Amelia (Hubbs) (1842–97)
Ross, George McLeod (1804–55)
Ross, Hugh (d. 1858)
Ross, James (1835–71)
Ross, James (1811–86)
Ross, Sir James Clark (1800–62)
Ross, James Gibb (1819–88)
Ross, John (fl. 1762–89)
Ross, Sir John (1777–1856)
Ross, John (1818–71)
Ross, Malchom (d. 1799)
Ross, Sally (d. 1884)
Rottenburg, Francis de, Baron de Rottenburg (1757–1832)
Rottermund, Édouard-Sylvestre de, Count de Rottermund (d. 1859)

Roubaud, Pierre-Joseph-Antoine (b. 1724, d. in or after 1789)
Roubel, William (fl. 1801–39) [volume VII]
Rouer d'Artigny, Louis (1667–1744)
Rouer de Villeray, Benjamin (1701–60)
Rouer de Villeray, Louis (1629–1700)
Rouer de Villeray et de La Cardonnière, Augustin (d. 1711)
Rouffio, Joseph (b. 1730, d. in or after 1764)
Rouillard, Ambroise (1693–1768)
Roupe, Jean-Baptiste (1782–1854)
Rous, John (d. 1760)
Rousseau, Dominique (1755–1825)
Rousseau de Villejouin, Gabriel (1709–81)
Rousseaux St John, John Baptist (1758–1812)
Roussel, Timothée (d. 1700)
Rousselot, Benjamin-Victor (1823–89)
Roussy, Louis (1812–80)
Routh, Sir Randolph Isham (1782–1858)
Routh, Richard (d. 1801)
Roux, Jean-Henry-Auguste (1760–1831)
Row, William Bickford (1786–1865)
Rowan, Sir William (1789–1879)
Rowand, John (d. 1854)
Rowley, Thomas (fl. 1612–28)
Rowsell, Henry (1807–90)
Roy, Joseph (d. 1856)
Roy, Louis (1771–99)
Roy, Louis-David (1807–80)
Roy, Marguerite, named de la Conception (1674–1749)
Roy, Narsise (1765–1814)
Roy, Thomas (d. 1842)
Roy, *dit* Châtellerault, Michel (1649–1709)
Roy-Audy, Jean-Baptiste (b. 1778, d. *c.* 1848)
Roybon d'Allonne, Madeleine de (d. 1718)
Roy Portelance, Louis (1764–1838)
Rubidge, Charles (1787–1873)
Rubidge, Frederick Preston (1806–97)
Ruckle, Barbara (Heck) (1734–1804)
Rudolf, William (1791–1859)
Ruette d'Auteuil, Denis-Joseph (1617–79)
Ruette d'Auteuil de Monceaux, François-Madeleine-Fortuné (d. 1737)
Rundle, Robert Terrill (1811–96)
Russell, Andrew (1804–88)
Russell, Elizabeth (1754–1822)
Russell, Joseph (1786–1855)
Russell, Peter (1733–1808)
Rut, John (fl. 1512–28)
Ruttan, Henry (1792–1871)
Ryan, Henry (1775–1833)
Ryan, Hugh (1832–99)
Ryan, James A. (d. 1896) [volumes X and XII]
Ryan, John (d. 1847)
Ryan, John B. (1792–1863)
Ryan, Thomas (1804–89)

Ryerse, Amelia (Harris) (1798–1882)
Ryerse, Samuel (1752–1812)
Ryerson, Egerton (1803–82)
Ryerson, George (d. 1882)
Ryerson, John (1800–78)
Ryerson, William (1797–1872)
Rykert, George (1797–1857)
Ryland, Herman Witsius (d. 1838)
Rymal, Joseph (1821–1900)

Sabatier, Antoine (d. 1747)
Sabatier, William (d. 1826)
Sabine, Sir Edward (1788–1883)
Sabrevois, Jacques-Charles de (d. 1727)
Sabrevois de Bleury, Clément de (d. 1781)
Sabrevois de Bleury, Clément-Charles (1798–1862)
Saccardy, Vincent (1691)
Saffray de Mézy, Augustin de (d. 1665)
Sagard, Gabriel (fl. 1614–36)
Sagean, Mathieu (fl. 1700–11)
Saguima (fl. 1707–12)
Sahneuti (d. 1900)
Sahonwagy (fl. 1753–87)
Saillant, Jean-Antoine (1720–76)
Sailly, Louis-Arthus de (d. 1668)
Saint-Aubin, Ambroise (d. 1780)
Saint-Aubin, Joseph-Thomas (d. 1821)
Saint-Clair, Pierre de (d. 1736)
Saint-Étienne de La Tour, Agathe de (Bradstreet; Campbell) (b. 1690, d. in or after 1743)
Saint-Étienne de La Tour, Charles de (1593–1666)
Saint-Étienne de La Tour, Charles de (d. 1731)
Saint-Étienne de La Tour, Claude de (fl. 1609–36)
Saint-Germain, Jean-Baptiste (1788–1863)
St Jean, Pierre (1833–1900)
St Leger, Barrimore Matthew (d. 1789)
Saint-Ours, Charles de (1753–1834)
Saint-Ours, François-Xavier de (1717–59)
Saint-Ours, Pierre de (1640–1724)
Saint-Ours Deschaillons, Jean-Baptiste de (1669–1747)
Saint-Pé, Jean-Baptiste de (1686–1770)
Saint-Père, Agathe de (Legardeur de Repentigny) (b. 1657, d. 1747 or 1748)
Saint-Père, Jean de (d. 1657)
Salaberry, Melchior-Alphonse de (1813–67)
Sales Laterrière, Marc-Pascal de (1792–1872)
Sales Laterrière, Pierre de (d. 1815)
Sales Laterrière, Pierre-Jean de (1789–1834)
Salignac de La Mothe-Fénelon, François de (1641–79)
Sallaberry, Michel de (1704–68)
Salter, Malachy (d. 1781)
Salusbury, John (1707–62)
Sampson, James (1789–1861)
Samson, James Hunter (d. 1836)
Samuel, Lewis (1827–87)

Sanborn, John Sewell (1819–77)
Sandom, Williams (d. 1858)
Sanford, Esbon (1645/46–82)
Sanford, William Eli (1838–99)
Sangster, Charles (1822–93)
Sanguinet, Simon (1733–90)
Sarcel de (Du) Prévert, Jean (d. 1622)
Sargent, John (1750–1824)
Sarrazin, Michel (1659–1734)
Sarrebource de Pontleroy, Nicolas (1717–1802)
Sasseville, François (1797–1864)
Sattin, Antoine (1767–1836)
Sauguaaram (fl. 1724–51)
Saul, Thomas (fl. 1750–60)
Saunders, Sir Charles (d. 1775)
Saunders, John (1754–1834)
Saunders, John Simcoe (1795–1878)
Saurel, Pierre de (1628–82)
Sauvageau, Charles (d. 1849)
Savage, Arthur (fl. 1720–31)
Savage, John (1740–1826)
Savage, Thomas (d. 1705)
Savary, Charles (1845–89)
Saveuse de Beaujeu, Georges-René, Comte de
 Beaujeu (1810–65)
Saveuse de Beaujeu, Jacques-Philippe (d. 1832)
Savignon (fl. 1610–11)
Savonnières de La Troche, Marie de, named de
 Saint-Joseph (de Saint-Bernard) (1616–52)
Sawtelle, Jemima (Phipps; Howe; Tute) (d.
 1805)
Sawyer, William (1820–89)
Sayer, John (d. 1818)
Sayer, Pierre-Guillaume (d. in or after 1849)
Sayre, James (1761–1849)
Sayward, Mary, named Marie-des-Anges
 (1681–1717)
Scales, Caroline (Hoyt), known as Caroline Miskel
 and Caroline Miskel-Hoyt (1873–98)
Scallan, Thomas (d. 1830)
Scallon, Édouard (1813–64)
Scatchamisse (d. 1712)
Scatcherd, Thomas (1823–76)
Schank, John (d. 1823)
Schindler, Joseph (d. 1792)
Schneider, Joseph (1772–1843)
Schoultz, Nils von (1807–38)
Schultz, Sir John Christian (1840–96)
Schurman, William (d. 1819)
Schuyler, Johannes (1668–1747)
Schuyler, Peter (1657–1723/24)
Schuyler, Peter (1710–62)
Schwartz, Otto William (1715–85)
Schwatka, Frederick (1849–92)
Scobie, Hugh (1811–53)
Scoble, John (b. 1799, d. in or after 1867)
Scolvus, John (fl. 1476)

Scott, Alfred Henry (d. 1872)
Scott, Christopher (d. 1833)
Scott, George (d. 1767)
Scott, John (b. 1816, d. 1864 or 1865)
Scott, Jonathan (1744–1819)
Scott, Jonathan (1803–80)
Scott, Joseph (d. 1800)
Scott, Patrick J. (1848–99)
Scott, Thomas (d. 1810)
Scott, Thomas (d. 1824)
Scott, Thomas (d. 1870)
Scott, Thomas Charles Heslop (d. 1813)
Scott, Thomas Seaton (1826–95)
Scott, William Henry (1799–1851)
Scriven, Joseph Medlicott (1819–86)
Scroggs, John (fl. 1718–24)
Seaman, Amos Peck (1788–1864)
Seccombe, John (1708–92)
Secord, David (1759–1844)
Secoudon (d. before 1616)
Sedgwick, Robert (1611–56)
Seely, Alexander McLeod (1812–82)
Seely, Caleb (1787–1869)
Seely, Joseph (b. 1786, d. in or after 1814)
Sefton, Henry Francis (d. 1892)
Seghers, Charles John (1839–86)
Segipt (fl. 1629–32)
Séguin, François-Hyacinthe (1787–1847)
Selby, George (d. 1835)
Selby, Prideaux (d. 1813)
Selee, Peet (1766–1844)
Sellar, Thomas (1828–67)
Semple, Robert (1777–1816)
Senécal, Louis-Adélard (1829–87)
Senet, dit Laliberté, Nicolas (d. 1732)
Senezergues de La Rodde, Étienne-Guillaume
 de (1709–59)
Sergeant, Henry (fl. 1683–89)
Serreau de Saint-Aubin, Jean (1621–1705)
Serres, Alexandre (d. 1812)
Sevestre, Charles (d. 1657)
Sewell, Jonathan (d. 1839)
Sewell, Stephen (d. 1832)
Sexton, John Ponsonby (1808–80)
Seymour, Frederick (1820–69)
Shadd, Mary Ann Camberton (Cary) (1823–93)
Shade, Absalom (d. 1862)
Shah-wun-dais (d. 1875)
Shakóye:wa:tha? (d. 1830)
Shanly, Charles Dawson (1811–75)
Shanly, Francis (1820–82)
Shanly, Walter (1817–99)
Shannon, Samuel Leonard (1816–95)
Sharples, John (1814–76)
Shaw, Æneas (d. 1814)
Shaw, Angus (d. 1832)
Shaw, Emily Elizabeth (Beavan) (fl. 1838–45)

Shaw, James (1798–1878)
Shaw, William (fl. 1759–89)
Shawanakiskie (fl. 1813–26)
Shawnadithit (d. 1829)
Shea, Henry (d. 1830)
Shea, William Richard (1813–44)
Sheaffe, Sir Roger Hale (1763–1851)
Shedden, John (1825–73)
Shenston, Thomas Strahan (1822–95)
Shepard, Joseph (d. 1837)
Shepard, Thomas (fl. 1668–81)
Shepherd, James (d. 1822)
Sheppard, William (1784–1867)
Sherbrooke, Sir John Coape (d. 1830)
Sherwood, Adiel (1779–1874)
Sherwood, Henry (1807–55)
Sherwood, Levius Peters (1777–1850)
Shibley, Schuyler (1820–90)
Shiels, Andrew (1793–1879)
Shirreff, Charles (1768–1847)
Shives, Robert (d. 1879)
Shore, George (d. 1851)
Shorey, Hollis (1823–93)
Short, Edward (1806–71)
Short, Richard (fl. 1754–66)
Short, Robert Quirk (d. 1827)
Shortland, Peter Frederick (1815–88)
Shortt, Jonathan (1809–67)
Shuldham, Molyneux, 1st Baron Shuldham (d. 1798)
Sibley, Joseph (d. 1862)
Sicotte, Louis-Victor (1812–89)
Signay, Joseph (1778–1850)
Sigogne, Jean-Mandé (1763–1844)
Si'k-okskitsis (d. 1897)
Silly, Jean-Baptiste de (fl. 1728–30)
Silver, Mary (1694–1740)
Silvy, Antoine (1638–1711)
Simard, Georges-Honoré (1817–73)
Simcoe, John Graves (1752–1806)
Simms, James (1779–1863)
Simms, Sophia (Dalton) (d. 1859)
Simon de Longpré, Marie-Catherine de, named de Saint-Augustin (1632–68)
Simonds, Charles (1783–1859)
Simonds, James (1735–1831)
Simonds, Richard (1789–1836)
Simonet d'Abergemont, Jacques (d. 1742)
Simonnet, François (1701–78)
Simpson, Æmilius (1792–1831)
Simpson, Alexander (b. 1811, d. in or after 1845)
Simpson, Frances Ramsay (Simpson, Lady Simpson) (d. 1853)
Simpson, Sir George (d. 1860)
Simpson, Isobel Graham (Finlayson) (1811–90)
Simpson, John (1788–1873)
Simpson, John (1807–78)
Simpson, John (1812–85)

Simpson, Melancthon (d. 1899)
Simpson, Robert (1834–97)
Sincennes, Jacques-Félix (1818–76)
Sinclair, James (1811–56)
Sinclair, Patrick (1736–1820)
Sinclair, William (d. 1868)
Singleton, George (d. 1789)
Siveright, John (1779–1856)
Skakel, Alexander (1776–1846)
Skanudharoua, named Geneviève-Agnès de Tous-les-Saints (1642–57)
Skead, James (1817–84)
Skeffington, George (fl. 1700–29)
Skerrett, John (d. 1813)
Skerry, John (1763–1838)
Skinner, Robert Pringle (1786–1816)
Skinner, Thomas (1759–1818)
Skirving, Catherine Seaton (Ewart) (1818–97)
Skrimsher, Samuel (d. 1755)
Slade, John (1719–92)
Slade, Thomas (d. 1816)
Sleigh, Burrows Willcocks Arthur (1821–69)
Small, James Edward (1798–1869)
Small, John (d. 1831)
Smallwood, Charles (1812–73)
Smart, Thomas (d. 1722)
Smart, William (1788–1876)
Smiley, Robert Reid (1817–55)
Smith, Sir Albert James (1822–83)
Smith, Alexander (d. 1892)
Smith, Alexander Mortimer (1818–95)
Smith, Bennett (1808–86)
Smith, Charles Douglass (d. 1855)
Smith, Charles-Gustave (1826–96)
Smith, Sir David William (1764–1837)
Smith, Francis (fl. 1737–47)
Smith, Sir Henry (1812–68)
Smith, Henry William (1826–90)
Smith, Hollis (1800–63)
Smith, James (fl. 1708–15)
Smith, James (1806–68)
Smith, James (1820–88)
Smith, John (1801–51)
Smith, John (d. 1881)
Smith, Joseph (d. 1765)
Smith, Michael (b. 1776, d. in or after 1816)
Smith, Peter (1752–1826)
Smith, Philander (1796–1870)
Smith, Richard (1783–1868)
Smith, Samuel (1756–1826)
Smith, Sidney (1823–89)
Smith, Titus (1768–1850)
Smith, William (1728–93)
Smith, William (fl. 1784–1803)
Smith, William (1769–1847)
Smith, William (1821–97)
Smith, William Henry (fl. 1843–73)

Smith, William Osborne (d. 1887)
Smithe, William (1842–87)
Smithsend, Nicholas (fl. 1685–98)
Smithsend, Richard (fl. 1685–91)
Smithurst, John (1807–67)
Smyth, George Stracey (1767–1823)
Smyth, Sir James Carmichael (1779–1838)
Smyth, John (d. 1852)
Smyth, Wyllys (fl. 1832–33)
Smythe, Sir Hervey (1734–1811)
Snorri Thorfinnsson (b. c. 1005–13)
Snow, John Allan (1824–88)
Solomon, William (1777–1857)
Solomons, Levy (1730–92)
Somerville, Alexander (1811–85)
Somerville, James (1775–1837)
Somerville, James (d. 1852)
Somerville, Martin (d. 1856)
Sorbier de Villars, François (1720–88)
Sotai-na (d. 1878)
Souart, Gabriel (d. 1691)
Soubras, Pierre-Auguste de (d. 1725)
Soulard, Auguste (1819–52)
Soulerin, Jean-Mathieu (1807–79)
Soullard, Jean (1642–1710)
Soumande, Louis (1652–1706)
Soumande, Louise, named de Saint-Augustin
    (1664–1708)
Sou-neh-hoo-way (d. 1838)
Soupiran, Simon (1670–1724)
Soupiran, Simon (1704–64)
Souste, André (d. 1776)
Southack, Cyprian (1662–1745)
Southcott, James Thomas (1824–98)
Sovereene, Henry (d. 1832)
Sower, Christopher (1754–99)
Spagniolini, Jean-Fernand (1704–64)
Spark, Alexander (1762–1819)
Sparks, Nicholas (1794–1862)
Spence, Robert (1811–68)
Spence, Thomas (d. 1881)
Spence, Thomas (1832–1900)
Spencer, Aubrey George (1795–1872)
Spencer, Hazelton (1757–1813)
Spencer, James (1812–63)
Spike, James (1807–79)
Spilsbury, Francis Brockell (1784–1830)
Spragg, Joseph (1775–1848)
Spragge, John Godfrey (1806–84)
Sprott, John (1780–1869)
Sproule, George (d. 1817)
Sproule, Robert Auchmuty (d. 1845)
Spurrell, George (d. 1770)
Stabb, Henry Hunt (1812–92)
Staines, Robert John (d. 1854)
Stairs, William Machin (1789–1865)
Stamp, Edward (1814–72)

Stanser, Robert (1760–1828)
Stanton, Robert (1794–1866)
Stark, Mark Young (1799–1866)
Starnes, Henry (1816–96)
Starr, John Leander (1802–85)
Staunton, Richard (fl. 1694–1741)
Stayeghtha (d. 1813)
Stayner, Thomas Allen (1788–1868)
Steele, Elmes Yelverton (1781–1865)
Steeves, William Henry (1814–73)
Steinhauer, Henry Bird (d. 1884)
Stephens, Harrison (1801–81)
Stephenson, Eleazer Williams (1798–1867)
Stephenson, John (1796–1842)
Sterling, James (fl. 1759–83)
Steven, Andrew (d. 1861)
Stevens, Abel (d. 1825 or 1826)
Stevens, Brooke Bridges (d. 1834)
Stevens, Paul (1830–81)
Stevenson, David Barker (1801–59)
Stevenson, James (1813–94)
Stevenson, John (1812–84)
Stewart, Alexander (1794–1865)
Stewart, Charles (d. 1813)
Stewart, Charles James (1775–1837)
Stewart, Donald Alexander (1851–97)
Stewart, James, 4th Lord Ochiltree (d. 1659)
Stewart, James Green (1825–81)
Stewart, John (d. 1834)
Stewart, John (1773–1858)
Stewart, John (d. 1880)
Stewart, John (1812–91)
Stewart, John Cunningham (1839–88)
Stewart, Peter (1725–1805)
Stewart, Thomas Alexander (1786–1847)
Stewart, William (d. 1856)
Stimson, Elam (1792–1869)
Stinson, Joseph (d. 1862)
Stirling, David (1822–87)
Stisted, Sir Henry William (1817–75)
Stobo, Robert (1726–70)
Stone, Joel (1749–1833)
Stone, Thomas (1852–97)
Storm, William George (1826–92)
Story, George Philliskirk (1853–94)
Stourton, Erasmus (1603–58)
Stout, Richard (d. 1820)
Strachan, James McGill (1808–70)
Strachan, John (1778–1867)
Strange, James Charles Stuart (1753–1840)
Strange, Sir Thomas Andrew Lumisden (1756–
    1841)
Street, George Frederick (1787–1855)
Street, John Ambrose Sharman (1795–1865)
Street, Samuel (1753–1815)
Street, Samuel (1775–1844)
Street, Samuel Denny (1752–1830)

Street, Thomas (d. 1805)
Street, Thomas Clark (d. 1872)
Strickland, Catharine Parr (Traill) (1802–99)
Strickland, Samuel (1804–67)
Strickland, Susanna (Moodie) (1803–85)
Strobridge, James Gordon (1788–1833)
Strouds, Gilles William (d. 1757)
Stuart, Andrew (1785–1840)
Stuart, Sir Andrew (1812–91)
Stuart, Charles (1783–1865)
Stuart, George Okill (1776–1862)
Stuart, George Okill (1807–84)
Stuart, Sir James (1780–1853)
Stuart, John (1740/41–1811)
Stuart, John (1780–1847)
Stuart, John (1813–82)
Stuart, William (d. 1719)
Studholme, Gilfred (1740–92)
Stutsman, Enos (1826–74)
Suckling, George (fl. 1752–80)
Suève, Edmond de (d. 1707)
Sullivan, Daniel (d. 1887)
Sullivan, Edward (1832–99)
Sullivan, Robert Baldwin (1802–53)
Sullivan, Timothy (d. 1749)
Sureau, *dit* Blondin, Esther, named Mother
    Marie-Anne (1809–90)
Suria, Tomás de (1761–1835)
Sutherland, Daniel (d. 1832)
Sutherland, George (fl. 1774–99)
Sutherland, James (d. 1797)
Sutherland, Murdoch (d. 1858)
Sutherland, Patrick (d. *c.* 1766)
Sutherland, Thomas Jefferson (d. 1852)
Suzor, François-Michel (1756–1810)
Suzor, Louis-Timothée (1834–66)
Swabey, William (1789–1872)
Swan (fl. 1715–19)
Swan, Anna Haining (Bates) (1846–88)
Swanton, Robert (d. 1765)
Swatana (d. 1748)
Swayne, Hugh (d. 1836)
Swayze, Isaac (1751–1828)
Sweetman, Pierce (d. 1841)
Swift, Henry (1848–91)
Switzer, Martin (1778–1852)
Syme, James (1832–81)
Symes, George Burns (1803–63)
Szalatnay, Márk (d. 1875)

TABARET, Joseph-Henri (1828–86)
Tabeau, Pierre-Antoine (1782–1835)
Taché, Alexandre-Antonin (1823–94)
Taché, Sir Étienne-Paschal (1795–1865)
Taché, Jean (1698–1768)
Taché, Joseph-Charles (1820–94)
Taché, Pascal (1757–1830)

Taffanel de La Jonquière, Jacques-Pierre de,
    Marquis de La Jonquière (1685–1752)
Tailhandier, *dit* La Beaume, Marien (b. 1665,
    d. 1738 or 1739)
Talbot, Edward Allen (d. 1839)
Talbot, Jacques (1678–1756)
Talbot, John (1797–1874)
Talbot, Richard (1772–1853)
Talbot, Thomas (1771–1853)
Talon, Jean (d. 1694)
Tanaghrisson (d. 1754)
Tanfield, Sir Francis (b. 1565, d. in or after 1630)
Tanner, John (d. in or after 1846)
Tanswell, James (d. 1819)
Tantouin de La Touche, Louis (d. 1722)
Taondechoren (fl. 1640–77)
Taratouan (d. 1637)
Tarbell, John (b. 1695, d. in or after 1740)
Tareha (fl. 1691–95)
Tarieu de La Naudière, Charles-François (1710–76)
Tarieu de Lanaudière, Charles-Louis (1743–1811)
Tarieu de Lanaudière, Xavier-Roch (1771–1813)
Tarride Duhaget, Robert (d. 1757)
Taschereau, Elzéar-Alexandre (1820–98)
Taschereau, Gabriel-Elzéar (1745–1809)
Taschereau, Jean-Thomas (1778–1832)
Taschereau, Jean-Thomas (1814–93)
Taschereau, Joseph-André (1806–67)
Taschereau, Marie-Anne-Louise, named de Saint-
    François-Xavier (1743–1825)
Taschereau, Thomas-Jacques (1680–1749)
Taschereau, Thomas-Pierre-Joseph (1775–1826)
Tasker, Patrick (1823–60)
Tassé, Joseph (1848–95)
Tassie, William (1815–86)
Ta-tanka I-yotank (d. 1890)
Tatanka-najin (d. 1870)
Tattannoeuck (d. 1834)
Taverner, William (d. 1768)
Tavernier, Émilie (Gamelin) (1800–51)
Taylor, Alexander (d. 1811)
Taylor, Henry (fl. 1799–1859)
Taylor, Henry (1841–93)
Taylor, James (1761–1834)
Taylor, James (d. 1856)
Taylor, James Wickes (1819–93)
Taylor, John (1809–71)
Taylor, John Fennings (1817–82)
Taylor, William (d. 1834)
Taylor, William (1803–76)
Taylor, William Henry (1820–73)
Taylour, Joseph (d. 1734)
Tazewell, Samuel Oliver (fl. 1820–38)
Tecumseh (d. 1813)
Teganissorens (fl. 1682–1721)
Tehorenhaegnon (fl. 1628–37)
Tehowagherengaraghkwen (fl. 1776–1834)

Teiorhéñhsere? (d. 1780)
Tekakwitha, Kateri (1656–80)
Tekanoet (fl. 1680–1701)
Tekarihogen (d. 1830)
Tekarihogen (1794–1832)
Tekarihoken (fl. 1726–28)
Tekawiroñte (d. 1777)
Telfer, Walter (1800–57)
Tellier, Rémi-Joseph (1796–1866)
Temple, Sir Thomas (1613/14–74)
Tenskwatawa (d. 1836)
Teouatiron (d. 1640 or 1641)
Terrill, Timothy Lee (1815–79)
Terriot, Pierre (d. 1725)
Terroux, Jacques (fl. 1725–77) [volumes III and IV]
Tessier, François-Xavier (1799–1835)
Tessier, Ulric-Joseph (1817–92)
Tessier, *dit* Lavigne, Paul (1701–73)
Tessouat (fl. 1603–13)
Tessouat (d. 1636)
Tessouat (d. 1654)
Testard de La Forest, Gabriel (1661–97)
Testard de Montigny, Casimir-Amable (1787–1863)
Testard de Montigny, Jacques (1663–1737)
Testard de Montigny, Jean-Baptiste-Philippe
    (1724–86)
Testard Louvigny de Montigny, Jean-Baptiste-Pierre
    (1750–1813)
Testu de La Richardière, Richard (1681–1741)
Tétreau, Hubert-Joseph (1803–77)
Tétro, Jean-Baptiste (d. before 1730)
Têtu, Charles-Hilaire (1802–63)
Têtu, Cléophée, named Thérèse de Jésus (1824–91)
Teyohaqueande (fl. 1756–83)
Thain, Thomas (d. 1832)
Thanadelthur (d. 1717)
Thaumur de La Source, Dominique-Antoine-René
    (d. 1731)
Thavenet, Jean-Baptiste (1763–1844)
Thavenet, Marguerite de (Hertel de La Fresnière)
    (1646–1708)
Thayendanegea (d. 1807)
Theller, Edward Alexander (1804–59)
Thériault, Lévite (1837–96)
Thevet, André (1502–90)
Theyanoguin (d. 1755)
Thibaudeau, Isidore (1819–93)
Thibaudeau, Joseph-Élie (1822–78)
Thibault, Jean-Baptiste (1810–79)
Thibault, Norbert, named Brother Oliver Julian
    (1840–81)
Thibodeau, Simon (d. 1819)
Thiboult, Thomas (d. 1724)
Thirkill, Lancelot (fl. 1498–1501)
Thom, Adam (1802–90)
Thom, Alexander (1775–1845)
Thomas, Jean (fl. 1635)

Thomas, John (d. 1822)
Thomas, Sophia (Mason) (1822–61)
Thomas, Thomas (d. 1828)
Thomas, William (d. 1860)
Thompson, David (1770–1857)
Thompson, David (d. 1868)
Thompson, Edward (fl. 1725–49)
Thompson, Hannah Maynard (Pickard) (1812–44)
Thompson, James (1733–1830)
Thompson, John Sparrow (1795–1867)
Thompson, Sir John Sparrow David (1845–94)
Thompson, Joseph (fl. 1674–79)
Thompson, Joshua Spencer (1828–80)
Thompson, Mary (b. 1801, d. in or after 1824)
Thompson, Samuel (1810–86)
Thompson, Thomas (1803–68)
Thompson, Toler (d. 1846)
Thompson, William (1786–1860)
Thomson, Charles Edward Poulett, 1st Baron
    Sydenham (1799–1841)
Thomson, Edward William (1794–1865)
Thomson, Hugh Christopher (1791–1834)
Thomson, John (1808–84)
Thomson, Samuel Robert (1825–80)
Thomson, William Alexander (1816–78)
Thorburn, Alexander Gillan (1836–94)
Thorfinnr *karlsefni* Thordarson (fl. 1000–20)
Thorn, Jonathan (1779–1811)
Thorne, Benjamin (1794–1848)
Thorne, Robert (d. 1519)
Thorne, Robert (1492–1532)
Thorpe, Robert (d. 1836)
Thresher, George Godsell (1780–1857)
Thubières de Levy de Queylus, Gabriel (1612–77)
Thurgar, John Venner (1797–1880)
Thurston, David (fl. 1859–89)
Thury, Louis-Pierre (d. 1699)
Tiarks, Johann Ludwig (1789–1837)
Tibaudeau, Pierre (1631–1704)
Tibierge (fl. 1695–1703)
Tibierge, Marie-Catherine, named de Saint-Joachim
    (1681–1757)
Tiedemann, Hermann Otto (1821–91)
Tielen, Jean (1824–97)
Tiffany, Gideon (1774–1854)
Tiffany, Silvester (1759–1811)
Tilley, Sir Samuel Leonard (1818–96)
Tillson, George (1782–1864)
Tisquantum (d. 1622)
Tisserant de Moncharvaux, Jean-Baptiste-
    François (d. 1767)
Tobin, James (d. 1838)
Tobin, James William (d. 1881)
Tobin, John (1810–69)
Tocque, Philip (1814–99)
Tod, James (d. 1816)
Tod, John (1794–1882)

Todd, Alpheus (1821–84)
Todd, Isaac (d. 1819)
Todd, Jacob Hunter (1827–99)
Todd, Robert Clow (d. 1866)
Todd, William (d. 1851)
Todd, William (1803–73)
Togouiroui (d. 1690)
Toler, Joseph (fl. 1831–42)
Tolmie, William Fraser (1812–86)
Tomah, Francis (fl. 1813–50)
Tomah, Pierre (fl. 1775–80)
Tomah, Pierre, known as Governor Tomah
    (fl. 1759–1827)
Tomison, William (d. 1829)
Tonatakout (fl. 1700–34)
Tonge, Grizelda Elizabeth Cottnam (d. 1825)
Tonge, William Cottnam (1764–1832)
Tonge, Winckworth (1727/28–92)
Tonsahoten (d. 1688)
Tonty, Alphonse (de), Baron de Paludy (d. 1727)
Tonty, Henri (de) (d. 1704)
Tonty de Liette, Charles-Henri-Joseph de (1697–
    1749)
Toosey, Philip (d. 1797)
Topp, Alexander (1814–79)
Torrance, David (1805–76)
Torrance, John (1786–1870)
Totiri (fl. 1642–46)
Tourangeau, Adolphe (1831–94)
Tournois, Jean-Baptiste (b. 1710, d. in or after
    1761)
Toussaint, François-Xavier (1821–95)
Townsend, Isaac (d. 1765)
Townsend, John (1819–92)
Townsend, William H. (1812–73)
Townshend, George, 4th Viscount and 1st Marquess
    Townshend (1723/24–1807)
Townshend, William (d. 1816)
Tracey, Daniel (d. 1832)
Trahan, Grégoire, known as Gregory Strahan (d.
    1811)
Tredwell, Nathaniel Hazard (1768–1855)
Tremain, Richard (1774–1854)
Tremblay, Henri-Jean (1664–1740) [volume III
    appendix]
Tremblay, Pierre-Alexis (1827–79)
Tremblay, dit Picoté, Alexis (1787–1859)
Tremlett, Thomas (d. 1830)
Trestler, Jean-Joseph (d. 1813)
Trevanion, Sir Nicholas (d. 1737)
Treworgie, John (fl. 1635–60)
Triaud, Louis-Hubert (1790–1836)
Troop, Jacob Valentine (1809–81)
Trotain, dit Saint-Seürin, François (d. 1731)
Trotter, Thomas (1781–1855)
Trottier, Marguerite, named Saint-Joseph (1678–
    1744)

Trottier Desauniers, Pierre (b. 1700, d. in or after
    1755)
Trottier Desrivières Beaubien, Eustache-Ignace
    (1761–1816)
Trottier Dufy Desauniers, Thomas-Ignace (d. 1777)
Trouvé, Claude (d. 1704)
Troy, Edward (d. 1872)
Troyer, John (1753–1842)
Troyes, Pierre de, known as Chevalier de Troyes (d.
    1688)
Trudeau, Romuald (1802–88)
Trudeau, Toussaint (1826–93)
Trudel, François-Xavier-Anselme (1838–90)
Trullier, dit Lacombe, Jacques (d. 1821)
Truscott, George (d. 1851)
Truteau, Alexis-Frédéric (1808–72)
Tubbee, Okah (fl. 1830–56)
Tucker, Richard Alexander (1784–1868)
Tuckett, George Elias (1835–1900)
Tuglavina (d. 1798)
Tupper, Charles (1794–1881)
Turc de Castelveyre, Louis, named Brother Chrétien
    (1687–1755)
Turcotte, Joseph-Édouard (1808–64)
Turcotte, Louis-Philippe (1842–78)
Turgeon, Louis (1762–1827)
Turgeon, Pierre-Flavien (1787–1867)
Turnbull, William Wallace (1828–99)
Turner, William (1743–1804)
Turnor, Philip (d. 1799 or 1800)
Tutty, William (d. 1754)
Tuyll van Serooskerken, Vincent Gildemeester van,
    Baron van Tuyll van Serooskerken (1812–60)
Twining, John Thomas (1793–1860)
Twiss, William (1745–1827)
Tyng, Edward (fl. 1680–91)
Tyng, Edward (1683–1755)

UMFREVILLE, Edward (fl. 1771–89)
Uniacke, James Boyle (d. 1858)
Uniacke, Norman Fitzgerald (d. 1846)
Uniacke, Richard John (1753–1830)
Uniacke, Richard John (1789–1834)
Uniacke, Robert Fitzgerald (d. 1870)
Upham, Joshua (1741–1808)
Usborne, Henry (d. 1840)

VACHON, Paul (d. 1703)
Vachon, Paul (1656–1729)
Vachon de Belmont, François (1645–1732)
Vail, Edwin Arnold (1817–85)
Vaillant de Gueslis, François (1646–1718)
Valade, Marie-Louise, named Mother Valade
    (1808–61)
Valentine, William (1798–1849)
Valin, Pierre-Vincent (1827–97)
Vallée, François-Madeleine (fl. 1710–42)

Vallette de Chévigny, Médard-Gabriel (fl. 1712–54)
Vallier, François-Elzéar (1707–47)
Vallières de Saint-Réal, Joseph-Rémi (1787–1847)
Valois, Michel-François (1801–69)
Valois, Narcisse (1811–80)
Van Buskirk, Jacob (1760–1834)
Van Cortlandt, Edward (1805–75)
Vancouver, George (1757–98)
Vandusen, Conrad (1801–78)
Vane, George (d. 1722)
Van Egmond, Anthony Jacob William Gysbert (1775–1838)
Vanfelson, George (1784–1856)
VanKoughnet, Philip (d. 1873)
VanKoughnet, Philip Michael Matthew Scott (1822–69)
Van Norman, Joseph (1796–1888)
Varin, *dit* La Pistole, Jacques (d. 1791)
Varin de La Marre, Jean-Victor (b. 1699, d. before 1786)
Varlet, Dominique-Marie (1678–1742)
Vassal de Monviel, François (1759–1843)
Vattemare, Nicolas-Marie-Alexandre (1796–1864)
Vaughan, David (fl. 1713–19)
Vaughan, George (1676–1724)
Vaughan, Sir William (1575–1641)
Vaughan, William (1703–46)
Vauquelin, Jean (1728–72)
Vavasour, Henry William (d. 1851)
Vavasour, Mervin (1821–66)
Veney, Anderson (d. 1894)
Véniard de Bourgmond, Étienne de (fl. 1695–1725)
Vennor, Henry George (1840–84)
Verey, George (d. 1881)
Verner, Hugh (fl. 1678–97)
Véron de Grandmesnil, Étienne (1649–1721)
Véron de Grandmesnil, Étienne (1679–1743)
Véronneau, Agathe (1707–64)
Verrazzano, Giovanni da (d. *c.* 1528)
Verreau, Barthélemy (1678–1718)
Verrier, Étienne (1683–1747)
Verrier, Louis-Guillaume (1690–1758)
Verville, Jean-François de (d. 1729)
Vetch, Samuel (1668–1732)
Veyssière, Leger-Jean-Baptiste-Noël, named Father Emmanuel (1728–1800)
Vézina, Charles (1685–1755)
Vézina, François (1818–82)
Viau, Charles-Théodore (1843–98)
Viau, Pierre (1784–1849)
Vickery, Ann (Robins) (d. 1853)
Viel, Nicolas (d. 1625)
Viennay-Pachot, François (d. 1698)
Vienne, François-Joseph de (d. *c.* 1775)
Vieth, Adolphus Christoph (1754–1835)
Viets, Roger (1738–1811)
Viger, Bonaventure (1804–77)

Viger, Denis (1741–1805)
Viger, Denis-Benjamin (1774–1861)
Viger, Jacques (1787–1858)
Viger, Louis-Michel (1785–1855)
Vignal, Guillaume (d. 1661)
Vignau, Nicolas de (fl. 1611–13)
Vilermaula, Louis-Michel de (d. 1757 or 1758)
Villain, Jean-Baptiste (fl. 1666–70)
Villedonné, Étienne de (d. 1726)
Villeneuve, Robert de (fl. 1685–92)
Villes, Jean-Marie de (1670–1720)
Villieu, Claude-Sébastien de (fl. 1690–1705)
Villieu, Sébastien de (1693–1715)
Vimont, Barthélemy (1594–1667)
Vincent (fl. 1740–45)
Vincent, Charles (1828–90)
Vincent, John (1764–1848)
Vincent, Nicolas (1769–1844)
Vincent, Robert (d. 1765)
Vincent, Sarah Anne (Curzon) (1833–98)
Vincent, Thomas (d. 1832)
Vincent, Zacharie (1815–86)
Vining, Pamelia Sarah (Yule) (1826–97)
Vivant, Laurent (d. 1860)
Volant de Radisson, Étienne (d. 1735)
Volant de Saint-Claude, Claude (1654–1719)
Volant de Saint-Claude, Pierre (1654–1710)
Vondenvelden, William (d. 1809)
Vondy, John (d. 1847)
Vossnack, Emil (1839–85)
Voyer, Antoine (1782–1858)
Voyer, Jacques (1771–1843)
Voyer, Ludger-Napoléon (1842–76)
Voyer d'Argenson, Pierre de (d. *c.* 1709)
Vuil, Daniel (d. 1661)

WABAKININE (d. 1796)
Wabbicommicot (d. 1768)
Waddell, John (1810–78)
Waddens, Jean-Étienne (d. 1782)
Waddington, Alfred Penderell (1801–72)
Wade, Robert (d. 1849)
Waggoner, Rowland (d. 1740)
Wagner, James Theodore (1837–96)
Wahpasha (probably d. before 1805)
Wait, Benjamin (1813–95)
Wakefield, Edward Gibbon (1796–1862)
Waldegrave, William, 1st Baron Radstock (1753–1825)
Waldo, Samuel (1695–1759)
Waldron, John (b. 1744, d. in or after 1818)
Wales, William (d. 1798)
Walker, Alexander (1764–1831)
Walker, Hiram (1816–99)
Walker, Sir Hovenden (d. 1725 or 1728)
Walker, Nehemiah (fl. 1670–87)
Walker, Richard (fl. 1637–80)

Walker, Thomas (d. 1788)
Walker, Thomas (d. 1812)
Walker, William (d. 1792)
Walker, William (1797–1844)
Wallace, Michael (d. 1831)
Wallace, William (1820–87)
Wallbridge, Lewis (1816–87)
Waller, Jocelyn (d. 1828)
Walley, John (1644–1711/12)
Wallis, Sir Provo William Parry (1791–1892)
Walsh, Aquila (1823–85)
Walsh, John (1830–98)
Walsh, Kyran (d. 1868)
Walsh, William (1804–58)
Wanzer, Richard Mott (d. 1900)
Wapinesiw (fl. 1755–72)
Wappisis (d. 1755)
Warburton, George Drought (1816–57)
Ward, Edmund (1787–1853)
Ward, James (d. 1891)
Ward, John (1753–1846)
Ward, Richard (fl. 1698–1720)
Ward, Samuel Ringgold (1817–66)
Warren, John (d. 1813)
Warren, Sir John Borlase (1753–1822)
Warren, John Henry (d. 1885)
Warren, Sir Peter (d. 1752)
Washburn, Ebenezer (1756–1826)
Washburn, Simon Ebenezer (d. 1837)
Washington, John (fl. 1719–24)
Wasson (fl. 1763–76)
Waterman, Zenas (1789–1869)
Waterous, Charles Horatio (1814–92)
Watson, Sir Brook (1735/36–1807)
Watson, Charles (1714–57)
Watson, James Craig (1838–79)
Watson, Samuel James (d. 1881)
Watson, William (d. 1867)
Watteville, Louis de (1776–1836)
Watts, Richard (1688–1739/40)
Waugh, Wellwood (1741–1824)
Wawatam (fl. 1762–64)
Waxaway (fl. 1694–1710)
Waymouth, George (fl. 1601–12)
Webb, James (d. 1761)
Webb, William Hoste (1820–90)
Webber, George (fl. 1851–57)
Webber, John (1751–93)
Weber, Anna (1814–88)
Webster, Joseph Harding (d. 1868)
Webster, William Bennett (1798–1861)
Wedderburn, Alexander (d. 1843)
Weekes, William (d. 1806)
Weeks, Otto Schwartz (1830–92)
Welch, Thomas (1742–1816)
Weld, Isaac (1774–1856)
Weld, William (1824–91)

Weller, William (1799–1863)
Wells, James Edward (1836–98)
Wells, Joseph (1773–1853)
Wells, William Benjamin (1809–81)
Welsford, Augustus Frederick (1811–55)
Wenemouet (d. 1730)
Wenger, Johannes (d. 1827)
Wenman, Richard (d. 1781)
Wentworth, John (d. c. 1820)
Wentworth, Sir John (1737–1820)
Wentworth, Thomas Hanford (1781–1849)
Wentworth-Fitzwilliam, William, Viscount
    Milton (1839–77)
West, John (1778–1845)
West, John Conrade (1786–1858)
Westbrook, Andrew (1771–1835)
Westphal, Sir George Augustus Alexander
    (1785–1875)
Wetherald, William (1820–98)
Wetherall, Sir George Augustus (1788–1868)
Wetmore, Andrew Rainsford (1820–92)
Wetmore, George Ludlow (1795–1821)
Wetmore, Thomas (1767–1828)
Weyapiersenwah (d. c. 1810)
Whale, Robert (d. 1887)
Wheelwright, Esther named de l'Enfant-Jésus
    (1696–1780)
Whelan, Edward (1824–67)
Whelan, Patrick James (d. 1869)
Whetstone, Sir William (d. 1711)
Whitaker, George (1811–82)
Whitbourne, Sir Richard (fl. 1579–1628)
White, Andrew (d. 1832)
White, Edward (1822–72)
White, Edward (1811–86)
White, George Harlow (d. 1887)
White, Gideon (1753–1833)
White, John (fl. 1577–93)
White, John (d. 1800)
White, John Henry (d. 1843)
White, Joseph (1799–1870)
White, Richard (fl. 1726–49)
White, Thomas (fl. 1719–56)
White, Thomas (1830–88)
Whitman, Abraham (1761–1854)
Whitmore, Edward (d. 1761)
Whittemore, Ezekiel Francis (1818–59)
Whitworth-Aylmer, Matthew, 5th Baron Aylmer
    (1775–1850)
Whyte, James Matthew (d. 1843)
Widder, Frederick (1801–65)
Widmer, Christopher (1780–1858)
Wiebe, Gerhard (1827–1900)
Wier, Benjamin (1805–68)
Wigate, John (fl. 1741–46)
Wightman, Joseph (1806–87)
Wikaskokiseyin (d. 1877)

Wikinanish (fl. 1788–93)
Wilcocke, Samuel Hull (d. 1833)
Wilkes, Henry (1805–86)
Wilkes, Robert (1832–80)
Wilkie, Daniel (d. 1851)
Wilkie, William (fl. 1820)
Wilkins, Harriett Annie (1829–88)
Wilkins, John (fl. 1748–75)
Wilkins, Lewis Morris (d. 1848)
Wilkins, Lewis Morris (1801–85)
Wilkins, Martin Isaac (1804–81)
Wilkinson, John (1804–71)
Willan, John Henry (1826–88)
Willard, Abijah (1724–89)
Willard, Samuel (1766–1833)
Willcocks, Joseph (1773–1814)
Willcocks, William (1735/36–1813)
Williams, Arthur Trefusis Heneage (1837–85)
Williams, Eleazer (Onwarenhiiaki) (1788–1858)
Williams, Eunice (1696–1785)
Williams, Griffith (d. 1790)
Williams, James (fl. 1803–15)
Williams, James Miller (1818–90)
Williams, James William (d. 1892)
Williams, Jenkin (d. 1819)
Williams, John (fl. 1711–18)
Williams, John (1664–1729)
Williams, John Æthuruld (1817–89)
Williams, Richard (d. 1856)
Williams, Thomas (d. 1848)
Williams, William (d. 1837)
Williams, Sir William Fenwick (1800–83)
Williamson, George (d. 1781)
Williamson, James (1806–95)
Willis, Edward (1835–91)
Willis, John Robert (1825–76)
Willis, John Walpole (1793–1877)
Willis, Michael (1798–1879)
Willis, Robert (1785–1865)
Willoughby, Mark (d. 1847)
Willoughby, Thomas (b. 1593, d. in or after 1621)
Wills, Frank (d. 1857)
Willson, David (1778–1866)
Willson, Hugh Bowlby (1813–80)
Willson, John (1776–1860)
Wilmot, John McNeil (d. 1847)
Wilmot, Lemuel Allan (1809–78)
Wilmot, Montagu (d. 1766)
Wilmot, Robert Duncan (1809–91)
Wilmot, Samuel (1822–99)
Wilson, Sir Adam (1814–91)
Wilson, Charles (1808–77)
Wilson, Sir Daniel (1816–92)
Wilson, James Crocket (1841–99)
Wilson, John (1807–69)
Wilson, William Mercer (1813–75)
Windham, Sir Charles Ash (1810–70)

Wingfield, Alexander Hamilton (1828–96)
Winniett, James (d. 1849)
Winniett, William (d. 1741)
Winniett, Sir William Robert Wolseley
  (1793–1850)
Winninnewaycappo (d. 1799)
Winslow, Edward (1746/47–1815)
Winslow, John (1703–74)
Winslow, Joshua (1726/27–1801)
Winton, Henry (1817–66)
Winton, Henry David (1793–1855)
Wisner, Jesse Oldfield (1811–97)
Wiswall, John (1731–1812)
Withall, William John (1814–98)
Withrow, John Jacob (1833–1900)
Wix, Edward (1802–66)
Wolfe, James (1727–59)
Wolhaupter, Benjamin (1800–57)
Wolhaupter, John (d. 1839)
Wood, Alexander (1772–1844)
Wood, Charles (1790–1847)
Wood, Edmund Burke (d. 1882)
Wood, Enoch (d. 1888)
Wood, John Fisher (d. 1899)
Wood, Robert (1792–1847)
Wood, Samuel Simpson (1795–1868)
Wood, Thomas (1711–78)
Wood, Thomas (1815–98)
Woodman, Elijah Crocker (1797–1847)
Woods, Joseph (1813–71)
Woolford, John Elliott (1778–1866)
Woolsey, John William (1767–1853)
Wooster, Hezekiah Calvin (1771–98)
Work, John (d. 1861)
Workman, Joseph (1805–94)
Workman, Thomas (1813–89)
Workman, William (1807–78)
Worrell, Charles (d. 1858)
Worsley, Miller (1791–1835)
Worthington, Edward Dagge (1820–95)
Worts, James Gooderham (1818–82)
Wowurna (fl. 1670–1738)
Wright, Alonzo (1821–94)
Wright, Amos (1809–86)
Wright, Charles (1782–1828)
Wright, Fanny Amelia (Bayfield) (d. 1891)
Wright, George (1752–1819)
Wright, George (1779–1842)
Wright, George (1810–87)
Wright, Gustavus Blinn (1830–98)
Wright, Philemon (1760–1839)
Wright, Thomas (d. 1812)
Wright, William (d. 1878)
Wroth, Robert (d. c. 1735)
Wugk, Charles-Désiré-Joseph, known as Charles
  Sabatier (1819–62)
Wurtele, Josias (1760–1831)

Wyatt, Charles Burton (d. 1840)
Wyet, Sylvester (fl. 1594)
Wynne, Edward (fl. 1621–26)

YALE, James Murray (d. 1871)
Yates, Horatio (1821–82)
Yeo, James (1789–1868)
Yeo, Sir James Lucas (1782–1818)
Yonge, James (1646/47–1721)
York, Jack (fl. 1800)
You de La Découverte, Pierre (1658–1718)
Young, Sir Aretas William (d. 1835)
Young, David (1848–87)
Young, George Paxton (1818–89)
Young, George Renny (1802–53)
Young, James (fl. 1688–93)
Young, John (d. 1819)
Young, John (d. 1825)
Young, John (1773–1837)

Young, John (1808–73)
Young, John (1811–78)
Young, John, 1st Baron Lisgar (1807–76)
Young, Joseph-Marie (1820–97)
Young, Plomer (1787–1863)
Young, Thomas (fl. 1634–40)
Young, Thomas (d. 1860)
Young, Thomas Ainslie (1797–1860)
Young, Sir William (1799–1887)
Young, Sir William Alexander George (d. 1885)
Youville, Charles-Marie-Madeleine d' (1729–90)

ZEISBERGER, David (1721–1808)
Zeno, Antonio (d. c. 1403)
Zeno, Nicolò (d. c. 1402)
Zheewegonab (fl. 1780–1805)
Zimmerman, Samuel (1815–57)
Zouberbuhler, Sebastian (d. 1773)

# CUMULATIVE NOMINAL INDEX

## In preparation

# Cumulative Nominal Index

Included in the index are the names of persons mentioned in volumes I to XII. They are listed by their family names, with first names and titles following. Wives are entered under their maiden name with their married name (or names) in parentheses. Persons who appear in incomplete citations in the text are fully identified when possible. Titles, nicknames, pseudonyms, variant spellings, and married, religious, and stage names are fully cross-referenced. Numerals in bold face indicate the pages on which a biography appears.

A full explanation of the DCB/DBC editorial practices is found in the Editorial Notes of each volume.

An asterisk indicates that the person so identified will probably receive a biography in a volume yet to be completed. A death date or last floruit date constitutes a reference for the reader to the volume in which the biography will be found.

This index incorporates the results of continuing research at the DCB/DBC; the form and content of names have thus been made consistent for the published volumes and with volumes in progress.

AAOUANDIO. *See* Le Maistre, Jacques

Aaron. *See* Kanonraron

Aasance, VII, 11

Abancourt. *See also* Jolliet

Abancourt, Marie d' (Jollyet; Guillot; Prévost), I, 392, 554

Abbadie, Jean-Jacques-Blaise d', III, 527

Abbadie de Saint-Castin, Bernard-Anselme d', Baron de Saint-Castin, II, xxxvii, **3–4**, 5, 7, 37, 38, 177, 238, 289, 437, 452; III, xxxix, 3, 330

Abbadie de Saint-Castin, Brigitte d', II, 4

Abbadie de Saint-Castin, Isabeau d', Baronne de Saint-Castin. *See* Béarn-Bonasse

Abbadie de Saint-Castin, Jean-Jacques d', Baron de Saint-Castin (father), II, 4

Abbadie de Saint-Castin, Jean-Jacques d', Baron de Saint-Castin, II, 4, 5

Abbadie de Saint-Castin, Jean-Pierre d', II, 7

Abbadie de Saint-Castin, Jean-Vincent d', Baron de Saint-Castin, I, 63, 185, 510, 577, 649; II, xxxvii, 3, **4–7**, 145, 167, 177, 182, 394, 440, 480, 494, 579, 605, 626, 654; III, xxxix, 3; IV, xviii

Abbadie de Saint-Castin, Joseph d', Baron de Saint-Castin, II, 7, 669; III, xxxii, **3**, 359

Abbadie de Saint-Castin, Louise d', II, 4

Abbadie de Saint-Castin, Marie d' (Labaig), II, 4, 7

Abbadie de Saint-Castin, Marie-Anselme d', Baronne de Saint-Castin (Bourbon), II, 4; III, 3

Abbadie de Saint-Castin, Marie-Charlotte d', Baronne de Saint-Castin. *See* Damours de Chauffours

Abbadie de Saint-Castin, Marie-Josephe (Anastasie) d' (Le Borgne de Belle-Isle), II, 7; III, 567

Abbadie de Saint-Castin, Marie-Mathilde d', Baronne de Saint-Castin. *See* Pidianske

Abbadie de Saint-Castin, Thérèse d' (Mius d'Entremont), II, 7

Abbadie de Saint-Castin, Ursule d' (Damours de Freneuse), II, 7

Abbot, George, I, 678

Abbot, Jonas, V, 422

Abbott, Anderson Ruffin, X, 3

Abbott, Arthur, XII, 6

Abbott, Edward, IV, 321, 322; V, 147

Abbott, Elizabeth (Baby), VI, 21

Abbott, Elizabeth Caroline (Alston), X, 9

Abbott, Elizabeth L. *See* Noyes

Abbott, Ellen. *See* Toyer

Abbott, Frances (Baby), VIII, 33

Abbott, Harriet. *See* Bradford

Abbott, Harriet, XII, 6

Abbott, Harry Braithwaite IX, 4; XI, 557; XII, 5, 964

Abbott, Henry, XII, 5

Abbott, Isabella (mother of JOSEPH), IX, 3

Abbott, Job, XII, **3–4**

Abbott, John Bethune, XII, 5, 6

Abbott, Sir John Joseph Caldwell, IX, 3, 4, 274; X, 123, 136; XI, 6, 7, 12, 381, 556, 609, 706; XII, **4–9**, 35, 90, 181, 246, 477, 502, 583, 636, 685, 726, 1045, 1046

Abbott, Jonas, X, 531

Abbott, Joseph, IX, 3

Abbott, Joseph, V, 107; VI, 528; VII, 381; IX, **3–4**; XII, 4

Abbott, Mary Martha. *See* Bethune

Abbott, Nathan B., XII, 3

Abbott, William (brother of JOSEPH), VI, 528; VII, 682; IX, 3

Abbott, William (son of Sir JOHN JOSEPH CALDWELL), XII, 6

Abbott, Wilson Ruffin, X, **3**

Abdy, Matthew, IV, 705

Abeel, Catalina (Mathews), IV, 522

Abel, Olivier. *See* Olivier, Abel

Abell, Edward, VIII, 532; IX, 155

Aberchalder. *See* Macdonell; MacDonell; McDonell

Abercrombie, James, IV, **3–4**, 98

Abercromby, Alexander, IV, 4

Abercromby, Helen. *See* Meldrum

Abercromby, James (brother of Sir Ralph), IV, 4

Abercromby, James (son of JAMES), IV, 4

Abercromby, James, III, xxv, xxviii, xxix, 85, 273, 462, 535, 588, 591; IV, 3, **4–5**, 22, 23, 34, 85, 115, 117, 129, 174, 211, 278, 297, 335, 395, 396, 460, 479, 503, 531, 606, 634, 642, 670, 679, 680, 694, 793; V, 40, 163, 295, 681, 803, 888; VI, 717

Abercromby, Jemmy, IV, 4

Abercromby, Mary. *See* Duff

Abercromby, Sir Ralph, IV, 4; V, 110, 776; VIII, 458

Aberdeen, Earl of. *See* Hamilton-Gordon

Aberdeen and Temair, Marchioness of. *See* Marjoribanks

Aberdeen and Temair, Marquess of. *See* Hamilton-Gordon

Abergemont. *See* Simonet
Aberli, Johann Ludwig, IV, 762
Abernethy, George, VIII, 662; X, 427, 486
Abernethy, John, IX, 308; X, 38, 691; XI, 271
Abishabis, VII, **3–4**
Abraham. *See also* Maskepetoon
Abraham, VI, 350
Abraham, Apolline (Lefebvre), X, 613
Abraham (Abram), Chapman, IV, 332, 718, 719
Abraham, John, I, **39**, 107, 329, 493, 529; II, 265
Abraham, Mary, I, 39
Abraham, Miriam (Franklin), X, 295
Abraham, Robert, VIII, 22, 694
Abram. *See* Abraham
Abrams, Mary Ann (Thomson), XI, 878
Abrams, Sarah. *See* Trigholon
Abrams, William, VII, **4–5**; VIII, 737, 740; X, 333
A-ca-oo-mah-ca-ye (Ac ko mok ki, Ak ko mock ki,
    A'kow-muk-ai, Old Swan) (probably grandfather of A-
    CA-OO-MAH-CA-YE), VIII, 3
A-ca-oo-mah-ca-ye (Ac ko mok ki, Ak ko mock ki,
    A'kow-muk-ai, Feathers, Old Swan) (uncle or father of
    A-CA-OO-MAH-CA-YE), VIII, 3
A-ca-oo-mah-ca-ye, VI, 250; VIII, **3–4**
Acaret. *See* Daccarette
Accault, Michel, II, 278, 281, 635
Accolti, Michael, VIII, 654
Achallader. *See* Campbell
Achard, Charles, II, 127
Aché de Serquigny, Anne-Antoine, Comte d'Aché, IV, 131
Acheson, Archibald, 2nd Earl of Gosford, VI, 575; VII,
    **5–9**, 61, 147, 148, 160, 180, 190, 236, 247, 283, 300,
    345, 346, 354, 360, 361, 489, 490, 513, 550, 624, 770,
    771, 789, 818, 908; VIII, xxiv, xxxii, 18, 22, 147, 207,
    209, 210, 260, 261, 367, 407, 433, 434, 465, 586, 619,
    712, 729, 730, 758, 792, 893, 907, 939; IX, 73, 142, 143,
    286, 441, 594, 650, 696; X, 11, 132, 163, 343, 440, 499,
    555, 574, 582; XI, 84, 874; XII, 88
Acheson, Arthur, 1st Earl of Gosford, VII, 5
Acheson, Mary, Countess of Gosford. *See* Sparrow
Acheson, Millicent, Countess of Gosford. *See* Pole
Achiendassé. *See* Lalemant, Jérôme
Achim, André, VI, 626
Achinaga, II, 263
Achintre, Anne-Marie. *See* Duprey
Achintre, Auguste, XI, **3–4**, 177, 218, 809; XII, 90, 504,
    693
Achintre, Guillaume-Auguste, XI, 3
Achintre, Joseph, XI, 3
Ackler, Mary (Forsyth), VII, 311
Ackmobish. *See* Akomápis
Ac ko mok ki. *See* A-ca-oo-mah-ca-ye
Acosta, José de, III, 337
Acoutsina (Acountsina), II, **7–10**, 384
Acqueville, Baron d'. *See* Bernières
Acqueville, Baronne d'. *See* Le Breton
Acroid, Stephen, VII, 102, 103
Actodin, I, 501
Acton, Anna (Warburton), VIII, 921
Adair, Christian (Ross), VIII, 770
Adair, Sir Frederick, X, 433
Adam, I, 559
Adam, Alexander, VII, 400

Adam, Sir Frederick, IX, 138
Adam*, Graeme Mercer (1839–1912), XII, 97, 572, 573,
    923
Adam, James, V, 424
Adam, Jean (Wilson), IX, 843
Adam, Joseph, XII, 276
Adam, Robert, V, 424
Adames. *See* Adams
Adams, Anne Maria (Fulford), IX, 289
Adams, Augusta Minerva, XII, 10
Adams, Avis (mother of JOHN), III, 3
Adams, Betsy Almira (Hurlburt), X, 372
Adams, Beulah (Carroll), XI, 153
Adams, Catherine Jane (Mack), XI, 559
Adams, Clarissa (Gates), VI, 277
Adams, Clement, I, 158
Adams, Dorothea (Crysler), VIII, 194
Adams, Elias Smith, XI, 559
Adams, Elizabeth (Monk), VI, 511
Adams, Ezra, X, 372
Adams*, Frank Dawson (1859–1942), XI, 49
Adams, George, XI, 363
Adams, George F., IX, 832
Adams, Helen (Blair; Boomer), XI, 89
Adams, James, II, 54
Adams, Jane Wilson (Walsh), XI, 909
Adams, John (father of JOHN), III, 3
Adams, John (officer), II, 644
Adams, John (U.S. president), IV, 715; V, 15; VII, 86
Adams, John, III, **3–4**, 143, 437, 517
Adams, Joseph, II, **10**, 62, 65, 492, 493, 563; III, 415, 661
Adams, Joshua, XI, 671
Adams, Katherine (mother of JOSEPH), II, 10
Adams, Levi, V, 800
Adams, Maria. *See* Hubbard
Adams, Maria (Macallum), X, 451
Adams, Mary. *See* Wyer
Adams, Mary (aunt), II, 10
Adams, Mary (Ferguson), VIII, 292
Adams, Mary Electa, VIII, 15; XI, 729; XII, **9–10**
Adams, Michael, XII, 339
Adams, Robert, IV, 153
Adams, Robert Chamblet, XII, 866
Adams, Rufus, XII, 9
Adams, Samuel (brother-in-law of Kennedy Francis
    BURNS), XII, 143
Adams, Samuel (politician), IV, 715
Adams, Sarah (Willis), XII, 1103
Adams, Thomas (artisan), VII, 654
Adams, Thomas (partner of George RYKERT), VIII, 785
Adams, Sir Thomas, III, 411
Adams, William, II, 10
Adams, Zachariah, XII, 1103
Adamson, James Agar, IX, 4
Adamson, Peter, VIII, 188
Adamson, Sarah. *See* Walsh
Adamson, William Agar, IX, **4–5**
Addeawando. *See* Atecouando (fl. 1701–26)
Addie, G., XII, 902
Addie, George, XII, 902
Addie, William, XII, 902
Addington, Baron. *See* Hubbard

Addington, Henry, 1st Viscount Sidmouth, V, 674, 758;
  VII, 547
Addison, Anne Agnes (Crofton), XI, 219
Addison, Ellinor. *See* Parkinson
Addison, John, VI, 3
Addison, Joseph, IV, 553; VII, 417
Addison, Mary. *See* Atkinson
Addison, Rebecca. *See* Plummer
Addison, Robert, V, 279, 519, 640, 724, 810, 841; VI, **3–6**,
  148, 373, 406, 488, 545, 552, 579; VIII, 276; X, 436
Addison, Thomas, X, 83
Adeawanadon (Adeawando). *See* Atecouando (fl. 1701–26)
Adelbertus, Brother. *See* Lesage
Adems. *See* Adams
Adet, Pierre-Auguste, VI, 700
Adhasatah. *See* Togouiroui
Adhémar, Catherine. *See* Lepallieur de Laferté
Adhémar, Catherine. *See* Moreau
Adhémar, Cécile. *See* Gasche
Adhémar, Geneviève. *See* Blondeau
Adhémar, Geneviève (Truillier, *dit* Lacombe), IX, 439
Adhémar, Jacques, VI, 795
Adhémar, Jean-Baptiste, II, 11, 164; III, **4–5**, 271; IV, 5,
  34, 200, 270; V, 3
Adhémar, Jean-Baptiste-Amable, IV, **5–8**, 543; V, 3, 90,
  241, 380; VI, 145, 494
Adhémar, Marguerite. *See* Lemoine Despins
Adhémar, Marie-Madeleine. *See* Trestler
Adhémar, Michel, II, 11
Adhémar, Patrice, V, 828
Adhémar, *dit* Saint-Martin, Marie (Tessier, *dit* Lavigne),
  IV, 732
Adhémar, *dit* Saint-Martin, Toussaint-Antoine (Martin), V,
  **3–4**
Adhémar de Lantagnac, Anne. *See* Rigaud de Vaudreuil
Adhémar de Lantagnac, Anne (La Barre), III, 5
Adhémar de Lantagnac, Antoine, III, 5
Adhémar de Lantagnac, Gaspard, II, 465, 565, 571; III, **5**,
  550; V, 97
Adhémar de Lantagnac, Geneviève-Françoise. *See* Martin
  de Lino
Adhémar de Lantagnac, Jeanne-Antoinette. *See* Truchi
Adhémar de Lantagnac, Pierre, II, 565; III, 5
Adhémar de Lantagnac, Pierre-Gaspard-Antoine, III, 5
Adhémar de Saint-Martin, Antoine, II, xxiv, **10–12**, 133,
  135, 160, 190, 196, 422, 458; III, 4, 505
Adhémar de Saint-Martin, Geneviève. *See* Sageot
Adhémar de Saint-Martin, Marie. *See* Sédilot
Adhémar de Saint-Martin, Michelle. *See* Cusson
Adiawonda. *See* Atecouando (fl. 1701–26)
Adié, Count d'. *See* Jadis
Adie, Mr (teacher), IX, 497
Adlam, Charlotte (Dickson), VII, 250
Admyrauld, Pierre-Gabriel, IV, 433
Adolphus Frederick, Duke of Cambridge, VI, 724
Adonwentishon. *See* Ohtowaʔkéhson
Adoucourt. *See* Souart
Adrawanah. *See* Ottrowana
Adriansdatter, Katherine (Munk), I, 514
Adye, Maria (Buchan), VII, 114
Aenon, I, 133
Aëoptahon. *See* Atironta (d. 1650)
Aernoutsz, Jurriaen, I, 25, **39–40**, 185, 399, 573

Affleck*, Annie Emma (Thompson, Lady Thompson)
  (1845–1913), IX, 787; XII, 610, 943, 1039, 1040, 1041,
  1042, 1046, 1047
Agar, Dorothy (Ash), XI, 33
Agariata, I, **40–41**, 308, 556
Agashawa. *See* Egushwa
Agassiz, Jean Louis Rodolphe, IX, 660; X, 338, 360; XI,
  509; XII, 233
Agate, Maria (Cramp), XI, 209
Agathas. *See* Mith-coo-coo-man E'Squaw
Agathas (Aggathas). *See* Wash-e-soo E'Squaw
Agathe, I, 523
Agemantan. *See* Argimault
Aggathas (Agathas) (mother of William KENNEDY), XI,
  445, 470
Agibicocoua, VIII, 830
Agmabesh. *See* Akomápis
Agnello, I, 317
Agnew, John, VI, 6
Agnew, Sophia Winifred (wife of STAIR), VI, 6
Agnew, Stair, V, 94, 160, 456; VI, **6–7**, 139, 757; VII, 331
Agnew, Teresa (mother of STAIR), 6
Agona, I, 168, 169, 276
Agonstot, II, 624, 634
Agoriata. *See* Agariata
Agrain, Jean-Antoine d', Comte d'Agrain, II, **12**
Agrain du Mazel, Jugues d', II, 12
Agramonte, Juan de, I, **41**
Aguesseau, Henri-François d', III, 491, 639
Aguesseau, Jean-Baptiste-Paulin d', III, 639
Aguiguida, II, 646
Aharathanha. *See* Koska, Stanislas
Ahatsistari, I, **41–42**, 344, 388, 523; II, 157
Ahdohwahgeseon. *See* Ohtowaʔkéhson
Ahier, Francis, XI, 440
Ahier, Gédéon, VIII, 675
Ahier, Victoire. *See* Painchaud
Ahinsistan. *See* Pastedechouan
Ah je juk. *See* Chejauk
Ahrens, Jacob, XII, 157
Ahuntsic, I, 661
Ahweyneyonh, VI, 703
Ahyonwaeghs (Ahyouwaeghs). *See* Tekarihogen (John
  Brant)
Aiandacé, I, 637
Aidant, Brother. *See* Roblot
Aide-Créquy, Jean-Antoine, IV, **8–10**
Aide-Créquy, Louis, IV, 8
Aide-Créquy, Marie-Hélène. *See* Lefebvre
Aigremont. *See* Clairambault
Aigron, Marie. *See* Daquin
Aigron, Pierre, I, 42
Aigron, *dit* Lamothe, Marie-Madeleine. *See* Doucet
Aigron, *dit* Lamothe (La Motte), Nicolas, II, 454
Aigron, *dit* Lamothe, Pierre, I, **42**, 666; II, 367, 454
Aiguillon, Duc d'. *See* Vignerot
Aiguillon, Duchesse d'. *See* Vignerot
Aiken, Sarah (Gilchrist), VIII, 324
Aikenhead, James, XI, 736
Aikins*, James Cox (1823–1904), XI, 645, 646; XII, 11,
  43, 95, 383, 706
Aikins, Louisa Adelia. *See* Piper
Aikins, Lydia Ann. *See* Piper

Aikins, Mary Jane (Graham), XII, 383
Aikins, William Thomas, VIII, 934; XII, **10–13**, 976
Aikman, Hannah (Ryerson), XI, 783
Ailleboust, Antoine d', I, 42
Ailleboust, Catherine d', I, 43
Ailleboust, Charles d', I, 42
Ailleboust, Charles-Joseph d', III, **5–7**, 236; IV, 644, 656
Ailleboust, Dorothée d'. *See* Manthet d' Argentenay
Ailleboust, Françoise-Charlotte d'. *See* Alavoine
Ailleboust, Jean d', I, 42
Ailleboust, Marie-Charlotte d' (Estimauville de Beau-mouchel), VI, 239, 240
Ailleboust, Marie-Josephte d'. *See* Bertrand
Ailleboust, Marie-Thérèse. *See* Juchereau Duchesnay
Ailleboust, Suzanne d'. *See* Hotman
Ailleboust d'Argenteuil, Jean d', II, 451
Ailleboust d'Argenteuil, Louis d', IV, 10
Ailleboust d'Argenteuil, Louise-Charlotte d' (Margane de Lavaltrie), V, 578
Ailleboust d'Argenteuil, Marie-Louise d'. *See* Denys de La Ronde
Ailleboust d'Argenteuil, Pierre d', II, **12–13**, 168, 284, 324, 415; III, 5, 7; IV, 10
Ailleboust de Cerry, Marie-Madeleine d'. *See* Chéron
Ailleboust de Cerry, Philippe-Marie d', IV, **10–11**, 620
Ailleboust de Coulonge et d'Argentenay, Louis d', I, **42–47**, 60, 79, 110, 112, 128, 217, 218, 219, 230, 231, 339, 340, 344, 349, 353, 373, 412, 431, 447, 453, 473, 480, 494, 511, 538, 580, 606, 645, 662; II, xvi, 83, 426, 489, 639
Ailleboust de Coulonge et d'Argentenay, Marie-Barbe d'. *See* Boullongne
Ailleboust de La Boulasserie, Jean-Baptiste-Alphonse d', IV, 11
Ailleboust de La Madeleine, Catherine d', named de la Visitation, V, 186
Ailleboust de La Madeleine, François-Jean-Daniel d', IV, **11–12**
Ailleboust de La Madeleine, Marie-Charlotte d'. *See* Godefroy de Linctot
Ailleboust de La Madeleine et de Coulonge, Louis d', II, 67
Ailleboust de La Madeleine et de Coulonge, Nicolas d', I, 43, 45, 47
Ailleboust de Manthet, Catherine-Angélique d' (Wilson), X, 715
Ailleboust de Manthet, Françoise d'. *See* Denys de La Ronde
Ailleboust de Manthet, Louise-Catherine d' (Charly Saint-Ange; Payen de Noyan et de Chavoy), II, 131; III, 110; IV, 612
Ailleboust de Manthet, Louise-Catherine d' (Charly Saint-Ange; Payen de Noyan et de Chavoy), V, 661
Ailleboust de Manthet, Madeleine d' (Jarret de Verchères; Levrault de Langis Montegron), III, 399
Ailleboust de Manthet, Nicolas d', I, 466; II, **13–14**, 131, 284, 383, 392, 406, 523, 546, 581, 603
Ailleboust de Manthet, Pierre-Joseph d', IV, 11
Ailleboust de Périgny, Ignace-René d', IV, 11
Ailleboust de Périgny, Madeleine-Louise d'. *See* Margane de Lavaltrie
Ailleboust de Périgny, Paul d', II, 284; III, **7**
Ailleboust de Périgny, Thérèse d' (Hertel de Moncours), II, 284; III, 7

Ailleboust de Saint-Vilmé, Hector-Pierre d', III, 6; IV, 10
Ailleboust Des Muceaux, Anne d'. *See* Le Picard
Ailleboust Des Muceaux, Catherine d'. *See* Legardeur de Repentigny
Ailleboust Des Muceaux, Catherine d' (Daneau de Muy), II, 168
Ailleboust Des Muceaux, Charles-Joseph d', I, 44, 45, **47**, 219, 447, 508, 592, 600; II, 12, 13, 14, 92, 421; III, 7
Ailleboust Des Muceaux, Félicité d' (Guillet de Chaumont), III, 270
Ailleboust Des Muceaux, Jean-Baptiste d', II, **14**, 159, 284; III, 270; IV, 11
Ailleboust Des Muceaux, Nicolas-Marie d', IV, 11
Ailly. *See* Albert
Aimard, Gustave. *See* Gloux, Olivier
Ainse. *See also* Ainsse
Ainse, Sarah (Montour; Maxwell; Willson), V, 602, 722; VI, **7–9**
Ainsley, Mary Ann (Mouat), X, 535
Ainslie, Charles, XII, 885
Ainslie, Christian. *See* Rutherford
Ainslie, Christian (Christianna) (Young), V, 6, 879, 881, 882; VI, 367, 423; VIII, 962
Ainslie, Elizabeth. *See* Martin
Ainslie, Elizabeth. *See* Williamson
Ainslie, Elizabeth, Lady Ainslie. *See* Gray
Ainslie, George Robert, V, 780; VI, 214; VII, **9–11**; VIII, 459
Ainslie, Gilbert (father of THOMAS), V, 4
Ainslie, Gilbert (office holder), VI, 801
Ainslie, Gilbert (son of THOMAS), V, 6, 879
Ainslie, John, V, 4
Ainslie, Mary. *See* Potts
Ainslie, Sir Philip, VII, 9
Ainslie, Sophia Charlotte. *See* Nevile
Ainslie, Thomas, IV, 74, 550, 570, 791; V, **4–7**, 191, 745, 746, 879; VIII, 962
Ainsse, Charlotte. *See* Vigneau
Ainsse, Charlotte-Henriette (De Lisle), IX, 200
Ainsse, Constante. *See* Chevalier
Ainsse, Françoise (Duchesnois), VII, 345
Ainsse, Joseph (grandfather), V, 7
Ainsse, Joseph, V, 9; VII, 345, 347, 622; IX, 200
Ainsse, Joseph-Louis, IV, 241; V, **7–9**, 229, 760; VI, 8, 188, 318; VII, 622
Ainsse, Marie-Thérèse. *See* Bondy
Ainsse, Zoé (Nichols; Girod), VII, 345, 346
Ainsworth, George Jennings, XII, 1132
Ainsworth, Henry, I, 391
Ainsworth, John C., XII, 1132
Aird, George, V, 10; VII, 328
Aird, James, V, 8, **9–10**, 835; VI, 210, 211; VII, 328, 329
Aird, John, VII, 575
Aird, Margaret (Anderson), V, 10
Aird, Rosina (Macnider), VII, 575
Airey, Julius, VIII, 860
Airey, Richard, Lord Airey, VIII, 275, 860; IX, 475, 644
Airth, Elizabeth (Cook), XII, 210
Airy, Sir George Biddell, VIII, 102; XI, 447
Aisance, John, VII, 11
Aisance, John, VII, **11–12**; IX, 9; X, 12
Aitchison, Isobel (Isabella) (Proudfoot), VIII, 715
Aitken, Alexander, IV, **12–13**; VII, 919

Aitken, Catherine (mother of ALEXANDER), IV, 12
Aitken, David, IV, 12
Aitken, Janet (Wilson), XII, 1109
Aitken, Sophia (Rintoul), VIII, 750
Aiton, William, V, 56, 580
Aix de La Chaise, François d', II, 330, 369, 371
Ajac, Baron d'. See Lévis
Ajac, Baronne d'. See Maguelonne
Ajetance (Ajetans), James, IX, 593
Akaitcho, VII, 324; IX, 658
Aka-kitsipimi-otas (Many Spotted Horses), X, 560
Akamih-kayi (Big Swan), IX, 537; XI, 443; XII, 779
Akay-nehka-simi (Many Names), XI, 442
Akins, Margaret Ott. See Beamish
Akins (Akin), Thomas, XII, 13
Akins, Thomas Beamish, IV, xxvi; VI, 322, 500, 622; VII, 88; IX, 187, 600; XII, **13–17**, 35, 537, 825
Ak ko mock ki (A'kow-muk-ai). See A-ca-oo-mah-ca-ye
Akomápis, Nicholas, IV, **13**; V, 435; VI, 678
Akwirente, Joseph. See Onasakenrat, Joseph
Akwirente, Lazare, XI, 655
Alain, Marie (Labelle), XII, 503
Alard. See also Allard
Alard, Madeleine (Troyes), I, 653
Alardyce, Margaret (MacKinlay), IX, 510
Alary, Pierre, V, 51
Alary, Siméon, XII, 848, 850
Alavoine, Charles, III, 7
Alavoine, Charles, II, 48; III, 6, **7–8**, 430
Alavoine, Françoise-Charlotte (Ailleboust; Guyon, Marquise de Diziers), III, 6
Alavoine, Marie-Anne. See Lefebvre, *dit* Laciseraye
Alavoine, Marie-Françoise (Chevalier), III, 121
Alavoine, Marie-Thérèse. See Macard
Albanel, Charles, I, 35, **47–50**, 83, 108, 226, 227, 244, 282, 396, 402, 558, 625, 629; II, xxxiv, 161, 179, 347, 537
Albany, Duke of. See Leopold George Duncan Albert
Albarade, Jean d', V, 591
Albemarle, Countess of. See MacNab
Albemarle, Duke of. See Monk
Albemarle, Earl of. See Keppel
Alberni, Pedro de, V, **10–11**, 12, 399, 411, 571, 615; VI, 233
Albert, Prince Consort of Great Britain and Ireland, IX, 711; X, 448
Albert, George Dallas, VIII, 476
Albert, Guillaume, I, 256
Albert, Marie-Louise (Demosny), I, 256
Albert, Thomas, VIII, 488
Albert d'Ailly, Honoré d', Duc de Chaulnes, II, 27
Albery, James, XII, 623
Albon. See Lefèvre
Albro, Elizabeth Margaret. See Dupuy
Albro, Elizabeth Margaret. See Vandergrift
Albro, Jane. See Cole
Albro, John, VII, 12
Albro, John, VII, **12–13**
Albro, Samuel (father), VII, 12
Albro, Samuel, VII, 12
Alby, Comte d'. See Sartine
Alcalá-Galiano, Antonia (Alcalá-Galiano), V, 11
Alcalá-Galiano, Dionisio, IV, 745; V, **11–12**, 140, 141, 571, 615; VI, 234

Alcalá-Galiano Pareja y Valera de la Serna, Antonio, V, 11
Alcock, Margaret (Hargrave), IX, 366
Alcorn, Annie Elizabeth (Macdonald), XI, 551
Alden, Elizabeth. See Phillips
Alden, Elizabeth (wife of JOHN), II, 15
Alden, John, II, 14
Alden, John, I, 576, 654; II, **14–15**, 177, 494; III, 7, 596
Alden, Priscilla. See Mullens
Alden, William, I, 576, 654; II, 14
Alder, Robert, VII, 45, 276, 277, 522; VIII, 216, 361, 372, 373, 478; X, **3–5**, 640; XI, 660, 733, 734, 935; XII, 931
Alder, Thomas, V, 526
Alderman, Isaac W., X, 486
Aldridge, Christopher, III, 10
Aldridge, Christopher (d. 1745/46), II, 668; III, **8–9**, 10, 297
Aldridge, Christopher (d. 1760), III, **9–10**, 324
Aldridge, Martha (wife of CHRISTOPHER, d. 1760), III, 10
Aldridge, Mary (Bradstreet; Bradstreet), IV, 83
Aleman, Lazaro. See Noremberguer
Alembert. See Le Rond
Alençon, François-Hercule, Duc d'Alençon, I, 229
Alenza y Nieto, Leonardo, X, 410
Alès de Corbet, Louise d' (Brisay de Denonville), II, 98
Alexander I, Emperor of Russia, VI, 803
Alexander II, Emperor of Russia, XI, 932
Alexander VII, I, 111, 645
Alexander, Elizabeth. See Newell
Alexander, Emilia. See Nelles
Alexander, Sir James Edward, VII, 91, 262; VIII, 588; IX, 5, 596; X, 52
Alexander, James Lynne, X, **5**
Alexander, Janet, Countess of Stirling. See Erskine
Alexander, Jean (Hay), XI, 391
Alexander, Jessie (Roberts), XII, 668, 948
Alexander*, Richard Henry (1844–1915), XII, 666
Alexander, Robert, XI, **4–5**
Alexander, William, XI, 4
Alexander, William, Earl of Stirling, I, 25, **50–54**, 55, 242, 311, 407, 497, 597, 605, 613, 636; III, 653; IV, xvii
Alexander, Sir William, I, 25, 53, **54–55**, 311, 405, 499, 593, 597, 605, 613
Alexandra, Princess of Denmark (Alexandra, Queen Consort of Great Britain and Ireland), XII, 436, 831
Alexandre, Victoire (Marchildon), VIII, 617
Alexis (Chilcotin chief), IX, 713
Alexis (messenger of WENEMOUET), II, 665
Aleyrac, Jean-Baptiste d', IV, **14**
Aleyrac, Jeanne-Marie d'. See Vernhes
Aleyrac, Noé d', IV, 14
Alfaro, Maria Concepsion d' (Allsopp), VII, 15
Alfonse, Jean. See Fonteneau, Jean
Alfonse, Valentine (Fonteneau), I, 309
Alfonso, Don, Duke of San Jaime, X, 542
Alfonso XII, King of Spain, X, 542
Alford, George, VII, 708, 709
Alford, Hannah. See Pozer
Alfred Ernest Albert, Duke of Edinburgh and Duke of Saxe-Coburg and Gotha, X, 625
Alger, Cyrus, IX, 175
Alger, Francis, IX, 308
Algimou, III, 358
Algimou, Louis Francis, VII, 437

Aliecte, Antoine, I, 167
Aliecte, Guillaume, I, 167
Aliés, Joseph, IV, 125
Aliomet, Isabelle (Prud'homme), I, 557
Alix, Marguerite (Boullé), I, 109, 110
Allain, Angélique (Bureau), VII, 119
Allain, Jean-Baptiste, V, 12–13, 181, 458; VI, 393; VII, 197
Allain, Jeanne. See De Lille
Allain, Louis, II, 198; III, 254
Allain, Marguerite. See Bourg
Allain, Marie (Gautier, dit Bellair), III, 254; V, 338
Allain, Michel, VII, 752
Allain, Pierre, V, 12
Allaire*, Jean-Baptiste-Arthur (1866–1943), IV, 87
Allaire, Marie, V, 331
Allaire, Marie-Louise (Testard de Montigny), IX, 782
Allamand, Jean-Emmanuel, VII, 13
Allamand, Jeanne-Charlotte (Berczy), V, 70; VII, 13–14; VIII, 83; X, 50
Allamand, Judith-Henriette-Françoise. See David
Allan. See also Allen; Havelock-Allan
Allan, Aaron, V, 14
Allan, Agnes (Graham), VI, 293
Allan, Agnes (Ledingham), XII, 543
Allan, Alexander (father of Sir HUGH), XI, 5
Allan, Alexander (father of WILLIAM), VIII, 4
Allan*, Andrew (1822–1901), IX, 224; X, 726; XI, 5, 6, 8, 10, 11, 380, 755, 758; XII, 21, 62, 63, 249
Allan, Bryce, XI, 6
Allan, Charles, XI, 335
Allan, Colin, VII, 14
Allan, Ebenezer, VI, 117
Allan, Ebenezer, V, 13–15, 749, 846; VI, 177, 490, 808; VIII, 608, 887
Allan, Elizabeth (cousin of John MUNN), VIII, 649
Allan, Elizabeth (daughter of WILLIAM), VIII, 11
Allan, Elizabeth (Pyke), VI, 621; VIII, 726
Allan, Francis, VIII, 587
Allan, George William, VIII, 11, 12, 486; X, 392, 393; XI, 150, 509, 877; XII, 101, 680, 1110
Allan, Sir Hugh, VII, 611; VIII, 815; IX, 183, 224, 281, 390, 773; X, 18, 102, 123, 150, 293, 294, 501, 651, 657, 724, 725, 726; XI, 5–15, 46, 121, 140, 211, 315, 380, 438, 464, 511, 556, 767, 781, 812, 814; XII, 5, 6, 21, 35, 62, 73, 88, 90, 134, 152, 167, 168, 465, 502, 571, 602, 603, 604, 623, 628, 629, 632, 635, 636, 649, 685, 964, 986, 987, 1057
Allan*, Sir Hugh Montagu (1860–1951), XI, 11
Allan, Isabella. See Maxwell
Allan, Isabella (Hill), VI, 319
Allan, James, XI, 5, 6
Allan, Jane. See Gibbon
Allan, Jean. See Crawford
Allan, John, IV, 13, 30, 79, 81, 196, 275, 693, 723, 736; V, 15–17, 257, 295, 296, 416, 465, 627; VI, 304, 363, 621, 678, 718, 774
Allan, John B., XII, 498
Allan, Leah Tyrer. See Gamble
Allan, Louisa Matilda. See Robinson
Allan, Lucy. See Chapman
Allan, Margaret. See Mowatt
Allan, Margaret. See Sinclair

Allan, Mary. See Gregory
Allan, Mary. See Patton
Allan, Matilda Caroline, Lady Allan. See Smith
Allan, Peter John, VII, 14
Allan, Sally. See Kyen-da-nent
Allan (Allen), Thomas, XI, 385, 386
Allan, William, V, 15
Allan, William, V, 65, 285, 366, 549, 643, 750, 753, 755; VI, 416, 623; VII, 75, 175, 208, 229, 261, 315, 338, 418, 459, 702, 756, 834, 919, 920; VIII, 4–13, 29, 191, 253, 255, 282, 338, 517, 519, 520, 521, 697, 709, 760, 795, 847, 848, 860, 896; IX, 49, 399, 400, 416, 497, 524, 535, 647, 662, 836, 837; X, 299; XII, 680
Allanby, William, IV, 607, 608; V, 825
Allanson, Elizabeth (wife of JOHN), VIII, 13
Allanson, John, VIII, 13–15; XII, 667
Allard, Euphémie (Chiniquy), XII, 189
Allard, Geneviève (Jékimbert), VII, 468
Allard, Joseph-Frédéric, IX, 207
Allard, Justine (wife of OVID), X, 6
Allard, Louise-Joséphine (Irumberry de Salaberry), XI, 441
Allard, Marie-Antoinette (Demers; Rambau), VIII, 736
Allard, Ovid, X, 5–6, 720
Allard, Thomas, IV, 203
Allard de Sainte-Marie, Monsieur, known as Chevalier de Sainte-Marie (brother of PHILIPPE-JOSEPH), IV, 15
Allard de Sainte-Marie, Angélique d'. See Carrerot
Allard de Sainte-Marie, Jean-Joseph d', II, 15, 336; IV, 14
Allard de Sainte-Marie, Jeanne d'. See Jacau
Allard de Sainte-Marie, Marie-Anne d'. See Tour
Allard de Sainte-Marie, Philippe-Joseph d', II, 15; IV, 14–16, 62, 248, 382
Allart, Germain (Théodore), I, 55, 313, 420, 439; II, 344, 345
Allchechaque. See Chejauk
Allcock, Hannah (wife of HENRY), V, 17
Allcock, Henry, V, 17
Allcock, Henry, V, 17–19, 292, 304, 420, 440, 441, 453, 519, 639, 845, 854, 855, 881; VI, 52, 79, 416, 452, 513, 608, 609, 613, 656, 698, 721; VII, 785, 812; VIII, 337
Allcock, Mary. See Askin
Allde, John, I, 670
Allègre, Marguerite d' (Lascaris, Marquise d'Urfé et de Baugé), II, 349
Alleine, Joseph, III, 470
Allemagne, Antoinette d' (La Corne), II, 327
Allemand, Claude, I, 56
Allemand, Louise. See Douaire de Bondy
Allemand, Marie. See Mandet
Allemand, Pierre, I, 56, 653; II, 526
Allemewi (Salomon), IV, 26, 27
Allen. See also Allan; Allyn
Allen, Mr (Orangeman), X, 528
Allen, Aaron, VI, 537
Allen, Abigail (Belcher), IV, 50; VII, 62
Allen, Abigail (Bissell; Williams), II, 667
Allen, Ann. See Blair
Allen, Ann. See Cunard
Allen, Ann (Gillmore), V, 343
Allen, Anne (Coster), VIII, 171
Allen, Charles Grant Blairfindie, XII, 776
Allen, Charles William, IX, 457
Allen, Edward, IV, 556; V, 66

Allen, Edward Carter, VI, 537
Allen, Elizabeth. *See* Saul
Allen, Elizabeth (Heath), X, 345
Allen, Elizabeth (Iffland), X, 376
Allen, Esther (Talbot), VIII, 855
Allen, Ethan, IV, 120, 130, 427, 545, 546, 694, 759; V, 29, 167
Allen, Florence. *See* Townsend
Allen, George, IX, 822
Allen, George Lyttleton, IX, 45; X, 121, 313
Allen, George Nickleson, IV, 713; V, 764
Allen, Ira, VI, 574, 641
Allen, Isaac, IV, 55; V, 35, 158, 349, 456; VI, 138, 142; XII, 17
Allen*, James (1843–1918), XII, 708
Allen, Jean (Chipman), VII, 177
Allen, Joanna (Brinley; Archibald), VII, 21, 23
Allen, John (father of Sir JOHN CAMPBELL), IX, 766; XII, 17
Allen, John (officer), VIII, 802
Allen, Sir John Campbell, X, 288, 679; XI, 688, 830; XII, 17–20, 338, 898
Allen, Joseph Antisell, XII, 776
Allen, L. L., VIII, 899
Allen, Margaret Austen, Lady Allen. *See* Drury
Allen, Mary (Hardisty), XI, 384
Allen, Mary (Jones), V, 456
Allen, Mary (Stayner), IX, 742
Allen, Richard, XII, 259
Allen, Sarah (Killam), IX, 424
Allen, Thomas, II, 667
Allen, William (author), IV, 416; V, 803
Allen, William (scientist), VI, 551; VII, 481
Allen, William (ship's captain), I, 641; II, 266, 394
Allen, William (whaling captain), X, 328
Allen, William Cox, IX, 588
Allenou de Grandchamp, Marie, IV, 95
Allenou de Lavillangevin, René-Jean, III, 10–12, 193, 259, 546; IV, 95, 429
Allet, Antoine d', I, 56–57, 220, 612, 644
Alley, John, IX, 729
Alley, Thomas, XI, 137
Alleyn, Charles Joseph, X, 20; XI, 15–16, 774, 861; XII, 1068
Alleyn, Margaret. *See* O'Donovan
Alleyn, Richard Israël, XI, 15
Alleyn, Zoé. *See* Aubert de Gaspé
Alliés, Geneviève (Amyot de Vincelotte; Marcoux), V, 577
Alliés, Marie-Geneviève (Couillard), IV, 71
Allin. *See* Allan
Alline, Henry, IV, 16–20, 217, 343, 705; V, 665, 744; VI, 63, 64, 67, 131, 171, 275, 276, 573, 574; VII, 120, 215, 252, 562, 915; VIII, 177, 179, 610, 611, 612; XI, 153, 923
Alline, Mary (Payzant), VI, 573
Alline, Rebecca. *See* Clark
Alline, William, IV, 16
Allion, Marie (Rousselot), XI, 776
Allison, Alexander, VI, 297
Allison, Ann (Bell), VIII, 73
Allison, Charles Frederick, VII, 854; VIII, 15–16, 183, 216; XI, 687; XII, 966
Allison, David, VII, 272

Allison, Elizabeth (Bennett), VIII, 82
Allison, Emily (Cudlip), XI, 223
Allison, James, VIII, 15
Allison, John C., VIII, 183
Allison, John Fall, XI, 395
Allison, Joseph, VI, 38; VII, 491; VIII, 73, 710; IX, 175, 176, 710; X, 188, 189, 551; XII, 436
Allison, Margaret. *See* Hutchinson
Allison, Mary Arabella. *See* Cogswell
Allison, Milcah. *See* Trueman
Allison, Nancy (Shannon), XII, 966
Allison, Rebecca (Crane), VIII, 183
Allison, Susanne (Aubert de Gaspé), VI, 16; IX, 702; X, 18
Allison, Thérèse. *See* Baby
Allison, Thomas, X, 18
Allison, William Henry, XI, 502
Allman, George James, XII, 232
Allmon. *See* Almon
Allom, Thomas, VII, 195
Allonne. *See* Roybon
Allouez, Claude, I, 14, 457–58, 121, 244, 249, 492, 626; II, 347, 501, 517, 607
Allport, Sir James Joseph, XII, 432
Allsopp, Adélaïde (Saint-Georges), VII, 15
Allsopp, Anna Marie. *See* Bondfield
Allsopp, Ann Maria, VII, 15
Allsopp, Carleton, V, 22; VII, 14, 15
Allsopp, George, IV, 104, 190, 323, 369, 379, 385, 399, 538, 554, 570, 618; V, 19–23, 44, 142, 164, 215, 289, 290, 317, 368, 369, 370, 371, 372, 426, 427, 602, 816, 843; VI, 49, 424; VII, 14, 15, 523; VIII, 201
Allsopp, George Alfred, VII, 15
Allsopp, George Waters, V, 22, 23; VI, 206, 750, 752; VII, 14–15, 373, 461; VIII, 154; XI, 547
Allsopp, James, V, 22; VII, 15
Allsopp, John, V, 22; VII, 14
Allsopp, Maria Concepcion. *See* Alfaro
Allsopp, Robert, V, 22; VII, 15
Allsopp, William, V, 22
Allumapees, III, 607
Allyn (Allen), Elizabeth (Gorham), III, 260
Almain, Élisabeth-Simone. *See* Lajus
Almighty Voice. *See* Kitchi-manito-waya
Almodóvar del Río, Duke of. *See* Luján
Almon, Amelia Elizabeth (Johnston), VII, 16; X, 383
Almon, Amelia Rebecca (Ritchie), XI, 754
Almon, James, V, 23
Almon, Laleah Peyton. *See* Johnston
Almon, Mather Byles, VII, 16, 63; VIII, 417, 905; IX, 181, 184; X, 6–8, 73, 189, 232, 293, 365, 385; XI, 155
Almon, Rebecca. *See* Byles
Almon, Ruth. *See* Hollywood
Almon, Sophia. *See* Pryor
Almon, William Bruce, V, 23; VII, 16, 391, 491; VIII, 398; IX, 573; XI, 754
Almon, William James, V, 23–24, 128, 187, 297; VII, 16; X, 6
Almon*, William Johnston (1816–1901), VII, 16; IX, 281; XI, 754
Aloigny, Charles-Henri d', Marquis de La Groye, I, 85; II, 15–16, 304, 507, 533; III, 410
Aloigny, Charlotte d', Marquise de La Groye. *See* Chasteigner

Aloigny, Geneviève d', Marquise de La Groye. *See* Macard
Aloigny, Louis d', Marquis de La Groye, II, 15
Aloperca. *See* Laborde
Alquier de Servian, Jean d', III, **12**, 86; IV, 480
Alsop, Mrs (wife of Robert, of England), IX, 591
Alsop, Richard, VI, 351
Alsop, Robert (probably father of ROBERT), VIII, 165
Alsop, Robert (of England), IX, 591
Alsop, Robert, X, **8–9**
Alston, Anna Maria. *See* Tuzo
Alston, Anne Charlotte. *See* Oxenden
Alston, Edward Graham, IX, 114, 428; X, **9–10**, 112, 113, 587
Alston, Elizabeth Caroline. *See* Abbott
Alston, George, X, 9
Althorp, Viscount. *See* Spencer
Altman, Henry Joseph, VIII, 446
Altrocchi, Julia. *See* Cooley
Altsdorf, Mr (artist), XI, 913
Alvarado, Juan Bautista, X, 240
Alves, Maria da Purïfecacao (Boys), IX, 79
Alvord, Clarence Walworth, V, 175
Alward, Robert, I, 369
Alymph. *See* Arimph
Amable, Sister. *See* Dorion, Marie-Céphise
Amadeo I, King of Spain, X, 542
Amantacha, I, **58–59**, 247
Amaraguened, III, 266
Amaugère, Geneviève (Bourdon), I, 114
Ambault. *See* Duchesneau
Amboise. *See also* Bergeron
Amboise, Michel d', I, 424
Ambroise (Ambroise Bear, Ambroise Pier, Ambroise Var). *See* Saint-Aubin, Ambroise
Ambroise, Father, IV, 134
Ambrose*, Robert Steele (1824–1908), XII, 1116
Ameau, Françoise. *See* Remogis
Ameau, Jean, II, 16
Ameau, Marguerite (Godefroy de Tonnancour), II, 253; III, 259; IV, 304
Ameau, *dit* Saint-Séverin, Madeleine. *See* Baudoin
Ameau, *dit* Saint-Séverin, Séverin, I, 327, 550, 575, 579; II, xvi, xvii, **16–17**, 253, 282, 382, 528
Amelote, Denis, IX, 18
Amelotte, Marguerite (Chartier), I, 202
Ames*, Alfred Ernest (1866–1934), XII, 973
Ames, Amelia (Riordon), XI, 753
Ames, Ezra, V, 811
Ames, Fisher, VI, 76
Amesbury, Joseph, X, 350
Amey, Ella (Cameron), XI, 141
Amherst, Elizabeth. *See* Kerrill
Amherst, Elizabeth. *See* Patterson
Amherst, Elizabeth, Baroness Amherst. *See* Cary
Amherst, Elizabeth Frances (Hale), VI, **9**; VII, 372; IX, 347; X, 326
Amherst, Jane, Lady Amherst. *See* Dalison
Amherst, Jeffery (father of JEFFERY), IV, 20
Amherst, Jeffery (son of JEFFERY), IV, 25
Amherst, Jeffery, 1st Baron Amherst, III, xxii, xxv, xxvi, xxix, xxxviii, xli, 10, 33, 71, 72, 73, 86, 87, 89, 167, 209, 211, 215, 230, 256, 268, 283, 320, 332, 364, 365, 371, 409, 467, 479, 480, 501, 509, 526, 527, 528, 529, 536,

558, 565, 588, 589, 601, 605, 654, 663, 666, 667, 668, 669, 671, 704; IV, xxvii, xxxiii, xxxiv, xxxv, 3, 4, 5, **20–26**, 31, 53, 79, 85, 93, 96, 109, 115, 117, 162, 211, 228, 279, 280, 297, 298, 299, 308, 314, 331, 335, 368, 380, 393, 396, 401, 408, 415, 421, 431, 481, 487, 491, 500, 541, 542, 545, 552, 569, 570, 571, 586, 587, 588, 595, 606, 637, 646, 670, 672, 673, 680, 685, 686, 700, 722, 730, 734, 737, 768, 772, 773, 783, 793; V, 104, 134, 163, 172, 182, 227, 253, 339, 348, 363, 384, 415, 454, 478, 479, 528, 545, 650, 681, 690, 719, 747, 759, 794, 803, 823, 888; VI, 227, 316, 484; VII, 614, 690; IX, 743
Amherst, Sackville, IV, 25
Amherst, William, III, 132; IV, 24, 26, 31, 223, 598; V, 338, 381, 430; VI, 9
Amherst, William Pitt, 1st Earl Amherst, IV, 26; VI, 329; IX, 347; X, 326, 701
Amhurst, Edward, III, 277
Amiconti, Sieur (officer), II, 523
Amiot, Anne. *See* Convent
Amiot, Augustin, III, 12
Amiot, Basile, VII, 876
Amiot, Catherine. *See* Mouet de Mora
Amiot, Charles, I, **59–60**, 250, 387; II, 17, 155, 159, 500
Amiot, Françoise (Gaulin), VIII, 316
Amiot, Geneviève. *See* Chavigny de Berchereau
Amiot, Geneviève (Delagrave), X, 217
Amiot, Jean, VII, 16
Amiot, Jean, I, **60**, 490
Amiot, Jean-Baptiste, V, 26
Amiot, Jean-Baptiste (fl. 1720–63), III, **12–13**; IV, 241
Amiot, Jean-Baptiste (1717–69), III, **13–14**; IV, 123, 263, 729; V, 667, 703
Amiot, Jean-Nicolas, IV, 702; V, 329; VI, 230, 584; VII, 16
Amiot, Laurent, III, 346; IV, 206; V, 218, 329, 437, 708, 709; VI, 28, 557; VII, **16–18**, 233; VIII, 638; IX, 701, 702; XI, 514, 515
Amiot, Louise. *See* Bazin
Amiot, Marguerite. *See* Levasseur, *dit* Borgia
Amiot, Marie-Anne. *See* Cadet
Amiot, Marie-Anne (wife of JEAN-BAPTISTE, fl. 1720–63), III, 12
Amiot, Marie-Anne (Perrault), III, 13; V, 667
Amiot, Marie-Louise. *See* Chrestien
Amiot, Marie-Madeleine (Barbel), II, 43
Amiot, Michel-Auguste, VII, 876
Amiot, Noël-Laurent, VII, 16, **18–20**, 209, 411
Amiot, Philippe, I, 59, 60
Amiot, Pierre (father of JEAN-BAPTISTE, 1717–69), III, 13; IV, 123
Amiot, Pierre (politician), VIII, 605
Amiot, Rosalie (Plamondon), VI, 584
Amiot, Thomas, VIII, 495
Amiot, *dit* Villeneuve, Charles, I, 61
Amiot, *dit* Villeneuve, Étienne, IV, 35
Amiot, *dit* Villeneuve, Marie. *See* Miville
Amiot, *dit* Villeneuve, Marie-Anne (Aumasson de Courville), IV, 35
Amiot, *dit* Villeneuve, Marie-Catherine (Maillou, *dit* Desmoulins), III, 420
Amiot, *dit* Villeneuve, Mathieu, I, **60–61**, 250
Amiot de Lincourt, Étienne, II, 508

Amiot de Vincelotte, Charles-Joseph, I, 60; II, **17–18**, 114, 142, 155, 452, 520, 567; III, 177, 682

Amiot de Vincelotte, Marie-Gabrielle. *See* Philippe de Hautmesnil de Marigny

Amiotte, Monsieur (companion of Louis-Joseph GAULTIER de La Vérendrye), III, 242

Amiot-Villeneuve, Gertrude (Garneau), IX, 297

Amirault, Catherine-Josephe (Blanchard), VII, 85

Amirault, Marguerite (Mius d'Entremont, Baronne de Pobomcoup), VII, 275

Amirault, Marie-Gertrude (Comeau), IX, 148

Amiscouecan. *See* Chomina

Amitak, VII, 271

Ammann, Jacob, VII, 641

Amours. *See* Damours

Ampère, Jean-Jacques, IX, 302

Amundsen*, Roald (1872–1928), VII, 327; XI, 199; XII, 879

Amussat, Jean, X, 38

Amy, XII, 289

Amy, Anne (Le Boutillier), VIII, 493

Amyot. *See also* Amiot

Amyot, Georges-Élie, XII, 127

Amyot, Guillaume, XI, 115; XII, **20–21**, 581

Amyot, Guillaume-Eusèbe, XII, 20

Amyot, Louise. *See* Gosselin

Amyot, Marguerite-Alice-Gertrude. *See* Pennée

Amyot, Thomas, VI, 615; VII, 769, 770, 771; IX, 189, 191

Amyot de Vincelotte, Geneviève. *See* Alliés

Anaclet, Brother. *See* Constantin

Anadabijou, I, **61**, 86, 508, 638

Anandamoakin, IV, **26–27**

Anapā, IV, 567

Anatoha (Kanakonme), Thomas, VII, 137

Ance, V, 9

Anceau, Anne, named de Sainte-Thérèse, IV, 535

Andehoua (Jean-Armand), I, 637, 638

Andersen, Hans Christian, X, 112; XI, 333

Anderson, Mrs. *See* Marsden

Anderson, Miss (Norton), VI, 550

Anderson, Alexander Caulfield, VII, 809; VIII, 654; IX, 5, 625; XI, **16–18**; XII, 768

Anderson, Andrew, V, 23

Anderson, Ann. *See* Graham

Anderson, Ann. *See* Richardson

Anderson, Anthony (merchant), VI, 582; VIII, 359

Anderson, Anthony (partisan of William Lyon MACKENZIE), IX, 503

Anderson, Archibald (father of DAVID), XI, 18

Anderson, Archibald (father of ROBERT), XII, 21

Anderson, C. E., VIII, 163

Anderson, David, VII, 253; VIII, 855

Anderson, David, VII, 455, 526; VIII, 574, 767; IX, 136, 579, 732; X, 109, 324, 629, 673, 674; XI, **18–20**, 64, 79, 208, 436, 437, 643, 653; XII, 446

Anderson, Deliverance. *See* Butts

Anderson, Duncan, VIII, 586

Anderson, Sir Edmund, I, 280

Anderson, Eliza. *See* Birnie

Anderson, Elizabeth (Jacobs), XI, 660

Anderson, Elizabeth (Mitchell), VI, 508

Anderson, Elizabeth Ann. *See* Hamilton

Anderson, Elizabeth Magdalene (Forsyth), X, 10

Anderson, Eliza Charlotte. *See* Simpson

Anderson, Gustavus Alexander, X, 12

Anderson, James, XII, 737

Anderson, James, IX, **5–6**; XI, 16, 384, 854, 855; XII, 155, 156

Anderson, John (merchant), IV, 273

Anderson, John (settler), VI, 6

Anderson, John, VII, 365; IX, **6–7**, 513, 677, 705; XII, 400

Anderson, Joseph (justice of the peace), VIII, 583

Anderson, Joseph (office holder), V, 549

Anderson, Louisa Dorothea. *See* Brown

Anderson, Margaret. *See* Aird

Anderson, Margaret. *See* McKenzie

Anderson, Margaret, VIII, 574

Anderson, Margaret (Robins), IX, 315

Anderson, Margaret Beatrice (Burgess), XII, 140

Anderson, Marie-Reine (Faribault), IX, 249

Anderson, Mary (Navarro), XII, 316

Anderson, Murray, XII, 939

Anderson, Osborne Perry, XII, 961

Anderson, Robert, IX, 5; XI, 16; XII, 68

Anderson, Robert, IX, 224; XI, 6, 8; XII, **21–22**

Anderson, Samuel (father of SAMUEL), XI, 20

Anderson, Samuel (father of THOMAS GUMMERSALL), X, 11

Anderson, Samuel, XI, **20–22**; XII, 892

Anderson, Sarah Ann (Bliss), VII, 86; X, 72, 73

Anderson, Thomas, X, 362

Anderson, Thomas, I, **61**; II, 454

Anderson, Thomas Brown, VIII, 749; IX, 290; X, **10–11**; XII, 486

Anderson, Thomas Gummersall, V, 10; VI, 510; VII, 11, 328, 329; VIII, 287, 309, 831; IX, 9, 11, 407, 589, 627; X, **11–13**, 269, 623; XI, 653, 715

Anderson, William, XI, 64

Anderson, William James, X, **13–14**

Andigné de Grandfontaine, Anne d', I, 62

Andigné de Grandfontaine, Gaston d', I, 62

Andigné de Grandfontaine, Hector d', I, 62

Andigné de Grandfontaine, Hector d', I, **61–64**, 185, 398, 435, 436, 510, 637, 667; II, 5, 88, 532

Andigné de La Chaise, Jeanne-Françoise d' (Cahideuc, Comtesse Dubois de La Motte), III, 92

Andioura, I, 429

André, IV, 375

André, Alexis, XI, 746, 748; XII, **22–23**, 554

André, Annette. *See* Guevel

André, Balthazar, III, 545

André, Édouard, X, 82

André, François, III, 14

André, Guesnou, XII, 22

André, John, IV, 721; V, 34, 629; VII, 894

André, Louis, I, 50; II, **18**; III, 104

André, Marie. *See* Turin

André de Leigne, Anne-Catherine, III, 15

André de Leigne, Claude. *See* Fredin

André de Leigne, Jeanne (Lanoullier de Boisclerc), III, 14, 15, 352

André de Leigne, Louise-Catherine (Hertel de Rouville), II, 286; III, **14**, 15, 285; IV, 343; V, 421

André de Leigne, Pierre, II, 155; III, **14–16**, 44, 75, 160, 340, 352, 398, 519; IV, 344

Andresy, Sieur d' (officer), II, 507
Andrew, Jane (Harris), XII, 413
Andrew, John Albion, X, 15
Andrewes, William, I, 334
Andrews, Mrs. *See* Shade
Andrews, Abigail. *See* Tyler
Andrews, Angelique (Givins), VII, 347
Andrews, Anne (Whitaker), XI, 916
Andrews, Catherine (Wurtele), VI, 819
Andrews, Elizabeth (Chipman), VIII, 148
Andrews, Hannah Ann. *See* Shelton
Andrews, Henry Ogden, VIII, 110, 916
Andrews, Israel de Wolfe, X, **14–15**
Andrews, James K., IX, 717
Andrews, Margaret (Morrill), X, 534
Andrews, Samuel, V, 24
Andrews, Samuel, V, **24–26**, 59, 135; VI, 301, 563
Andrews, Sarah (Burns), XII, 142
Andrews, Thomas, XII, 142
Andriani, Paolo, Count Andriani, V, 563; VI, 357
Andros, Sir Edmund, I, 537, 573, 654; II, xxxix, 6, 103, 182, 494, 496; III, 470
Angalook, VII, 271
Angeac, François-Gabriel d', III, 211, 418, 538; IV, **27–29**, 79, 122, 153, 175, 223, 240, 470, 598, 678, 783; V, 339; VI, 304
Angeac, Gabriel d', IV, 27
Angeac, Geneviève d'. *See* Lefebvre de Bellefeuille
Angeac, Marguerite d'. *See* Bertrand
Angel*, James (1838–1918), XII, 543, 544
Angélique (wife of Roderick McKENZIE), VIII, 562
Angélique-Denise, III, 399
Angélique de Sainte-Agnès. *See* Tibierge
Angélique de Saint-Joseph. *See* Hayot
Angélique de Saint-Martin. *See* Viger
Angelis, Filippo de, XI, 250
Angers. *See also* Lefebvre
Angers*, Sir Auguste-Réal (1838–1919), VIII, 17; X, 25; XI, 520; XII, 180, 277, 695, 726, 1046
Angers, François, VIII, 16
Angers, François-Réal, VII, 776; VIII, **16–17**
Angers, Geneviève (Blondeau), V, 89
Angers, Louise. *See* Panet
Angers, Louise-Adèle. *See* Taschereau
Angers, Marie-Anne-Madeleine, named Marie de Saint-Vincent de Paul, XI, 318
Angers, Marie-Desanges. *See* Larue
Angers, Pierre, III, 75, 76
Angerville, Moufle d', IV, 68
Anghiera. *See* Martire
Angibault, *dit* Champdoré, Pierre, I, **64**, 69, 72, 189, 292, 293, 564
Angilliers. *See* Largillier
Anglebert. *See* Poitevin
Anglesey, Earl of. *See* Villiers
Anglesey, Marquess of. *See* Paget
Anglin, Arthur Whyte, XII, 28
Anglin, Ellen. *See* McTavish
Anglin, Francis, XII, 23
Anglin*, Francis Alexander (1865–1933), XII, 28, 811
Anglin, Joanna. *See* Warren
Anglin, Margaret. *See* O'Regan
Anglin, Mary Margaret (Hull), XII, 28

Anglin, Timothy Warren, XI, 134, 350, 578, 830; XII, 18, **23–28**, 122, 144, 607, 1055, 1105
Ango, Jean, I, 72, 532
Ango de La Mothe, Monsieur (lawyer), II, 18
Ango Des Maizerets, Louis, I, 92, 291, 506; II, **18–20**, 207, 238, 240, 248, 329, 629, 655; III, 684
Angulo. *See* Flórez
Angus*, Richard Bladworth (1831–1922), XII, 248, 288
Angus, Susan (Keith), VIII, 455
Angwin, Louisa Emma. *See* Gill
Angwin, Maria Louisa, XII, **28–29**
Angwin, Thomas, XII, 28
Anjou, Duc d'. *See* Philip V
Anjoult, Anne (Lefebvre), II, 382
Ann. *See* Nancy
Anna (wife of GLIKHIKAN), IV, 302
Annahotaha. *See* Annaotaha
Annance, *dit* Kadnèche, Jacques-Joseph, VIII, 78
Annand, Emily. *See* Cuff
Annand, James, XI, 22
Annand, Jane. *See* Russell
Annand, Martha. *See* Tupper
Annand, William, XI, 22
Annand, William, VIII, 160, 417, 657, 958; IX, 537, 786, 840; X, 177, 367, 385, 395, 457, 539, 685; XI, **22–25**, 197, 262, 279, 347, 348, 399, 710, 835, 927, 933; XII, 32, 250, 437, 766, 880
Annaotaha, I, **64–65**, 267, 272
Anne, Princess of Spain (Anne, Queen of France), I, 129, 324, 328, 348, 389, 484; II, 360, 363
Anne, Queen of Great Britain and Ireland, II, 3, 123, 232, 233, 286, 289, 319, 332, 339, 373, 475, 487, 497, 498, 511, 603, 661, 666; III, 111, 428, 623; IV, xxi; V, 803
Anne de Saint-Bernard. *See* Le Cointre
Anne de Sainte-Agnès. *See* Bourdon
Anne de Sainte-Thérèse. *See* Anceau
Annenraes, I, **65–66**, 524
Annesley. *See* Ansley
Anneville, Gabrielle d' (Lagrange; Bernard de La Rivière), II, 59
Annis, Elizabeth (Farewell), XI, 311
Annssoet, III, 654
Anoghsoktea (Isaac Hill), V, 255, 256, 809
Anonchiara. *See* Du Peron, François
Anondounoakom. *See* Anandamoakin
Anotaha. *See* Annaotaha
Anꝶennen. *See* Daniel, Antoine
Ansley, Amos, VII, 20
Ansley, Amos, VII, **20**, 124
Ansley, Christina. *See* McMichael
Ansley, Harriet Kirkpatrick. *See* Henderson
Anson. *See also* Enneson
Anson, Adelbert John Robert, XII, 141
Anson, George, 1st Baron Anson, III, 6, 610, 657, 658; IV, 15, 122, 382, 699, 701, 702
Anspach, Isaac Salomon, VI, 9
Anspach, Jean-Louis, VI, 9
Anspach, Jeanne-Marie. *See* Audibert
Anspach, Lewis Amadeus, V, 275; VI, **9–11**, 244; X, 588; XII, 589
Anssart, Louis-Modeste, XI, 351
Anstruther, Jane (Strange, Lady Strange), 831
Antaïok. *See* Amiot, Jean

Anthoine, Dom, I, 167
Anthony, Gabriel, VII, **20–21**
Anticosti. *See* Jolliet
Antill, Edward, IV, 215; V, 414
Antill, Harriet (Blake; Panet), V, 88
Antin, Marquis d'. *See* Pardaillan
Anton, Christiana (Cary, Viscountess Falkland), XI, 155
Antonelli, Giacomo, XI, 172
Antonelli, Leonardo, IV, 43, 372
Antonio, Dom, I, 228
Antrobus, Catharine Esther. *See* Brehaut
Antrobus, Catherine Betsey Isabella. *See* Cuthbert
Antrobus, Edmund William Romer, V, 27; VIII, **17–19**
Antrobus, John, IV, 330; V, **26–27**, 283, 576; VIII, 17
Antrobus, William D., XII, 11, 1129
Anu'tsis-tsis-aki (Pretty Wolverine Woman), XII, 970
Anville, Duc d'. *See* La Rochefoucauld
Anville, Duchesse d'. *See* La Rochefoucauld
Anwyl, William, III, 634, 635
Aoghyatonghsera, Neggen (Margaret) (Brant), V, 804
Aonetta (Marie), I, 212
Aongote. *See* Williams, Eunice
Aontamsati, I, 65; II, 624
Aouandoie, I, 73
Aouenano, II, xxxix, **20**, 21, 323, 502, 631; III, xl
Aouschik. *See* Hotchig
Apānas, IV, 768
Apaschiskoos (Apaschaskoos, Little Bear), XI, 460
Apawakaasi, X, 662
Api-kai-ees, XII, **29–30**
Apistchi-koimas. *See* Wikaskokiseyin
Aplin, John, V, 27
Aplin, Joseph, V, **27–28**, 239, 263, 309, 310, 311, 425, 516, 568, 569, 717, 778, 779, 826, 847; VI, 107, 108; VII, 407
Apolline de Sainte-Angèle. *See* Arnoldi
Apostolos Valerianos. *See* Fuca, Juan de
App-Griffith, Julia Howard (Bovell), X, 83
Appledore, Margaret (Holland), VI, 321
Appleton, Elizabeth (probably wife of THOMAS), VI, 12
Appleton, Rebecca (Brown), XI, 116
Appleton, T., VI, 12
Appleton, Tapple, VI, 12
Appleton, Teavill C., VI, 12
Appleton, Thomas, VI, 12
Appleton, Thomas, VI, **11–12**; VII, 702, 822; IX, 423; X, 91
Applewaite, Sarah (Bovell), X, 83
Aprendestiguy, Jeanne d'. *See* Saint-Étienne de La Tour
Aprendestiguy, Joanis d', I, 66
Aprendestiguy, Marianne d' (Bourgeois), I, 67
Aprendestiguy de Martignon, Martin d', I, 25, 63, **66–67**, 595
April, Nance. *See* Shawnawdithit
Apsley, Baron. *See* Bathurst
Apthorp, Alexander, II, **20–21**
Apthorp, Charles, III, 33
Apthorp, Charles Ward, V, 374
Aque-Noch-Quah, V, 593
Aquinas. *See* Thomas
Aquipaguetin, II, 279
Arabin, Eliza. *See* Mountain
Aradgi, II, xxxvi, 20, **21**, 502, 631
Arago, François, VIII, 240, 867

Arbalestre de Melun, Élisabeth (Sarrebource de Pontleroy), V, 738
Arblay, Frances d'. *See* Burney
Arble, Mr (clergyman), XII, 322
Arboulin, Marie-Françoise d' (Bougainville), V, 102
Arbour, Marie (Dufresne), IX, 227
Arbuckle, Isabel (Maclear), XII, 667
Arbuckle, John, XI, 549
Arbuthnot, Mariot, IV, **29–30**, 80, 111, 161, 275, 708; V, 382, 434; VII, 196
Arce. *See* Lom
Archambault. *See also* Archambeault; Guibord
Archambault, Alexandre, XI, 26
Archambault, Anne (Chauvin), I, 557
Archambault, Catherine. *See* Raimondvert
Archambault, Cyrille, XII, 277
Archambault, Françoise. *See* Toureault
Archambault, Georgine (Bruneau; Taillon), X, 16
Archambault, Jacques (father-in-law of Gilles LAUSON), I, 427, 463; X, 15
Archambault, Jacques (father of LOUIS), XI, 25
Archambault, Jean-Baptiste, VIII, 19
Archambault, Jean-Marie-Ignace, VII, 267
Archambault, Jeanne (Lamarre, *dit* Bélisle), II, 340
Archambault, Joséphine. *See* Beaupré
Archambault*, Joseph-Papin (1880–1966), IX, 615, 862
Archambault, Laurent, VIII, 209
Archambault, Louis, X, 16
Archambault, Louise. *See* Poulin
Archambault, Louis-Misaël, XII, 254
Archambault, Madeleine. *See* Bruguière
Archambault, Marie (Baudry; Jobin), VIII, 433
Archambault, Marie (Lauson), I, 427
Archambault, Marie-Angélique. *See* Hachin, *dit* Baron
Archambault, Marie-Louise. *See* Papin
Archambault, Marie-Marguerite (Bardy), IX, 32
Archambault, Paul-Loup, VII, 501, 721; VIII, **19–21**, 727; X, 604; XI, 864; XII, 698
Archambault, Pierre-Amable, VIII, 500; X, 15
Archambault, Pierre-Urgel, X, **15–16**; XI, 26
Archambault, Pierre-Victor, IX, 533
Archambault, Urgel, VI, 786
Archambeault, Éloïse. *See* Roy
Archambeault, Horace, XI, 25, 27
Archambeault, Joseph-Alfred, XI, 25
Archambeault, Louis, IX, 614; X, 15; XI, **25–27**, 352; XII, 57
Archambeault, Marguerite-Élisabeth. *See* Dugal
Archambeault*, Urgel-Eugène (1834–1904), X, 16
Archbold, George, VII, 827; X, 163
Archer, Joseph, XII, 626
Archibald, Sir Adams George, VII, 540; IX, 330; X, 148, 387, 439, 457, 458, 474, 702; XI, 46, 192, 193, 546, 610, 612, 643, 742, 743, 755, 947; XII, 13, 15, 16, **30–36**, 132, 244, 369, 370, 371, 405, 477, 602, 641, 678, 951, 952, 954, 983, 1007, 1008, 1030, 1092
Archibald, Bridget. *See* Walker
Archibald, Charles Dickson, VII, 21, 535; IX, **7–8**; XI, 28, 486
Archibald, Charles William, IX, 7
Archibald, David (father of THOMAS DICKSON), XI, 29
Archibald, David (grandfather of SAMUEL GEORGE WILLIAM), VII, 21

Archibald, David (police inspector), XII, 454
Archibald, Sir Edward Mortimer, VII, 23, 508; IX, 7, 195, 695; XI, **27–29**, 44, 761; XII, 375
Archibald, Elizabeth. *See* Dickson
Archibald, Elizabeth. *See* Hughes
Archibald, Elizabeth (Archibald), XII, 30
Archibald, Elizabeth (Taylor), VI, 755
Archibald, Elizabeth Archibald. *See* Burnyeat
Archibald, Joanna. *See* Allen
Archibald, John Sprott, XI, 489
Archibald, Katherine Elizabeth. *See* Richardson
Archibald, Maria Louisa. *See* Goudge
Archibald, Mary (Campbell), VIII, 122
Archibald, Olivia. *See* Dickson
Archibald, Rachel. *See* Todd
Archibald, Raymond Clare, IX, 27
Archibald, Sampson Salter Blowers, XI, 29
Archibald, Samuel (father of Sir ADAMS GEORGE), XII, 30
Archibald, Samuel (father of SAMUEL GEORGE WILLIAM), VII, 21
Archibald, Samuel George, XI, 29
Archibald, Samuel George William, V, 854; VI, 307, 786, 792, 807; VII, **21–25**, 108, 142, 531, 532, 535, 742, 875, 910, 934; VIII, 222, 355, 428, 603, 752; IX, 7; X, 539; XI, 28, 431
Archibald, Susan. *See* Corbett
Archibald, Sir Thomas Dickson, IX, 7; XI, **29–30**
Arcos, Duke of. *See* Ponce de León
Ardesoif, Marianne (Sproule), VII, 823
Ardie. *See* Hardy
Ardillières. *See* Le Moyne
Ardilliers, François-Paul, IV, 77
Ardouin, Jeanne (Badeaux), IV, 40
Arentson. *See* Aernoutsz
Arévalo. *See* Sánchez
Argall, Emmeline (Sanford), XII, 939
Argall, Mary. *See* Scott
Argall, Richard, I, 67
Argall, Sir Samuel, I, 24, 53, **67–69**, 95, 98, 101, 299, 441, 470, 498, 560, 592, 596
Argenson. *See* Voyer
Argenson, Comte d'. *See* Voyer
Argentenay. *See* Ailleboust; Manthet
Argenteuil. *See* Ailleboust
Argimault (Agemantan), Joseph, III, 418
Argo, George, VIII, 126
Argoll. *See* Argall
Argyll, Duchess of. *See* Bellenden; Louise Caroline Alberta
Argyll, Duke of. *See* Campbell
Argyll, Earl of. *See* Campbell
Ariail, Marie-Anne (Quertier), X, 604
Arimph, Jean-Baptiste, IV, **30**
Arioo. *See* Chastellain, Pierre
Ariosto, Ludovico, VII, 603
Aristotle, XII, 250
Arlens. *See* Preissac
Arles, Henri d'. *See* Beaudé, Henri
Armand, Henriette (Brunet; Bellerose), XII, 87
Armand, Joseph-François, XI, 404; XII, 87
Armand, *dit* Chartrand, Joseph, VII, 479; X, 527
Armand, *dit* Flamme, François, XII, 87
Armault, Camille (Waggaman), X, 462

Armes, Polly (Barber), XII, 54
Armistead, Anne (Croke), VII, 216
Armitinger. *See* Ermatinger
Armour, Andrew Harvie, VIII, 22, 23
Armour, Annie G. (Chase), XII, 186
Armour, Elizabeth. *See* Harvie
Armour, Hugh, VIII, 21
Armour, Jean. *See* Shaw
Armour, John Douglas, XII, 101
Armour, Joseph, XII, 36
Armour, Margaret. *See* Hazlett
Armour, Rebecca Agatha (Thompson), XII, **36–37**
Armour, Robert (father of ROBERT), VIII, 21
Armour, Robert (son of ROBERT), VIII, 22, 23; IX, 429
Armour, Robert, VI, 238; VII, 134; VIII, **21–23**, 785
Armour, Shaw, VIII, 21
Arms, John, II, 285
Arms, Mercy (mother of WILLIAM), VIII, 23
Arms, Miranda. *See* Haven
Arms, William, VIII, 23
Arms, William, VIII, **23–24**
Armstrong, Alexander, XII, 37
Armstrong, Sir Alexander, X, 397; XI, 544; XII, **37–39**
Armstrong, Ann (Pruden), IX, 648
Armstrong, Anna Maria B. (Livingston), XII, 566
Armstrong, Bertie, XII, 39
Armstrong, Charles Logie, XI, 31
Armstrong, Charles Newhouse, XII, 726
Armstrong, Charlotte. *See* Simpson
Armstrong, David, XII, 39
Armstrong, Eleanor (Beatty), X, 16
Armstrong, Elizabeth. *See* Champion
Armstrong, Emma Champion (Roberts), VIII, 24
Armstrong, George (correspondent of Eliza Ann CHIP-MAN), VIII, 149
Armstrong, George (father of GEORGE), XI, 30
Armstrong, George, XI, **30–31**
Armstrong, Hannah. *See* Dougall
Armstrong, James Rogers, X, 16
Armstrong, James Rogers, X, **16**, 262, 331; XI, 357
Armstrong, James Sherrard, XI, **31–32**; XII, 94, 95, 828
Armstrong, Janet. *See* Scott
Armstrong, Janet (Richardson), XII, 893
Armstrong, Jeanett (Oliver), XI, 651
Armstrong, John (father of JAMES ROGERS), X, 16
Armstrong, John (politician), VIII, 609, 795
Armstrong, John (printer), XI, 580, 648
Armstrong, John Belmer, XII, **39**
Armstrong, Lawrence, II, **21–24**, 93, 96, 97, 199, 219, 238, 275, 462, 591, 643, 663, 670; III, 4, 8, 9, 83, 84, 120, 143, 144, 256, 276, 277, 287, 297, 343, 426, 427, 437, 439, 453, 500, 514, 516, 517, 596, 665; IV, xxii, xxv, 305, 453, 454
Armstrong, Margaret. *See* Dryden
Armstrong, Margaret. *See* Longmoore
Armstrong, Margaret Ray (Wightman), XI, 922
Armstrong, Marie-Anne-Charlotte. *See* Olivier
Armstrong, Marjory. *See* Ferguson
Armstrong, Mary. *See* Rogers
Armstrong, Mary (Ryerson), X, 16, 262; XI, 783
Armstrong, Phoebe Anne (Duggan), X, 16, 262
Armstrong, Richard, VIII, 24
Armstrong, Sir Richard, VIII, **24–25**, 164

Armstrong, Robert (businessman), VII, 594
Armstrong, Robert (father of JOHN BELMER), XII, 39
Armstrong, Sarah Ann (Radcliff), VII, 719
Armstrong, Sarah Anne (Beaty), XII, 71
Armstrong, William (nephew of GEORGE), XI, 31
Armstrong, William (shoemaker), XII, 71
Armstrong*, William (1822–1914), XII, 394
Armstrong, William James, X, 128
Arnald (Arnall). *See* Arnold
Arnaud, Bertrand, II, 175
Arnaud, Charles (husband of Marie Willis), II, 520
Arnaud, Charles (Oblate), XI, 514
Arnaud, Constance (Cazes), IX, 122
Arnaud, Jean, II, 195; III, 17
Arnaud, Jean-Charles d', III, **16–17**, 47, 492
Arnaud, Marie. *See* Truteau
Arnaud, Marie. *See* Willis
Arnaud, Marie-Charlotte (Potier Dubuisson), III, 533
Arnaud, Marie-Marguerite-Daniel, named Saint-Arsène, III,
**17–18**, 630; IV, 638
Arnaud, Olive (Huet de La Valinière), V, 431
Arnauld, Antoine, known as le Grand Arnauld, II, 249
Arnauld, Henri, I, 512
Arnauld, Madeleine (Sabatier), III, 575
Arnett, Margaret (MacLeod), VIII, 590
Arnold, Benedict, V, 28
Arnold, Benedict, IV, 114, 120, 142, 215, 223, 270, 329,
494, 503, 545, 547, 548, 549, 552, 759, 791; V, 16,
**28–36**, 64, 118, 130, 147, 167, 277, 413, 414, 481, 492,
588, 604, 629, 754; VI, 16, 75, 76, 138, 239, 262, 298,
401, 403, 788; VII, 894; X, 13; XII, 37
Arnold, Charlotte. *See* Wiggins
Arnold, Charlotte Hannah (Vail), XI, 896
Arnold, Ellen. *See* Boyle
Arnold, Hannah. *See* Waterman
Arnold, Hannah, V, 35
Arnold, Henry, V, 35
Arnold, Horatio Nelson, VI, 13
Arnold, Joseph, VI, 282
Arnold, Margaret. *See* Mansfield
Arnold, Margaret. *See* Shippen
Arnold, Maria Charlotte. *See* O'Hara
Arnold, Mary. *See* Holyoke
Arnold, Mary (Jarvis), VI, 349; VIII, 428
Arnold, Mary Antoinette (Castle), XI, 157
Arnold, Matthew, XII, 516, 517
Arnold, Nathan, VI, 12
Arnold, Oliver, VI, **12–14**, 139, 209, 282; VII, 109, 198,
902; XI, 896
Arnold, Prudence. *See* Denison
Arnold, Richard, V, 35
Arnold, Samuel Edwin, VI, 13
Arnold, William, II, **24–25**
Arnold, William, VIII, **25–26**
Arnoldi, Aurelia Felicite (McCord), VII, 27; VIII, 524
Arnoldi, Caroline Matilda (Gillespie), VII, 27
Arnoldi, Charles, V, 37, 218; VI, 14
Arnoldi, Daniel, VII, **25–27**, 119, 594, 824; VIII, 403, 404,
524; IX, 16, 396, 572; X, 544; XI, 58, 302
Arnoldi, Élisabeth. *See* Franchère
Arnoldi, Élisabeth (Holmes), VII, 26; IX, 396
Arnoldi, François-Cornelius-Thomas, VII, 26; IX, 16, 17
Arnoldi, Louise Priscille (Furniss), VII, 27

Arnoldi, Michael, IV, 206; V, **36–37**, 218, 708, 727; VI,
14; VII, 25
Arnoldi, Peter (father), V, 36; VI, 14; VII, 25
Arnoldi, Peter, IV, 206; V, 37, 218
Arnoldi, Phebe (rebaptized Apolline), named de
Sainte-Angèle (Diehl), V, 36; VI, **14–15**; VII, 25
Arnoldi, Philipina Maria. *See* Horn
Arnot, Christian (Reid), X, 611
Arnot, Elizabeth (Fleming), X, 291
Arnoulet, Jacqueline (Le Poupet de Saint-Aubin), II, 417
Arnoult, Maître (former notary), IV, 127
Arnouville. *See* Machault
Arnoux, Alexandre, III, 18
Arnoux, André, III, **18–20**, 35
Arnoux, Blaise, III, 19
Arnoux, Charlotte. *See* Soupiran
Arnoux, Joseph, III, 19, 292
Arnoux, Lucresse. *See* Masson
Arnoux, Suzanne. *See* Levret
Aroas, III, 320
Arosen (François-Xavier), IV, 770
Arouet, François-Marie (Voltaire), II, 444; III, 92, 104,
108, 283; IV, 44, 92, 234, 391, 544; V, 165, 232, 248,
372, 486, 668, 701; VI, 85, 764; VII, 209, 430, 503, 603,
645, 675, 677; X, 164; XI, 36
Arpentigny. *See* Aprendestiguy
Arran, Countess of. *See* Stewart; Underwood
Arran, Earl of. *See* Butler; Gore; Stewart
Arraud, Augustin, X, 16
Arraud, Jacques-Victor, X, **16–17**; XI, 96
Arraud, Marguerite. *See* Florence
Arrigrand, Gratien d', Sieur de La Majour, II, 220; III, **20**,
234, 235, 456, 478, 479
Arrigrand, Jean-Jacques d', III, 20
Arrigrand, Marguerite d'. *See* Auger de Subercase
Arrowsmith, Aaron, IV, 742; V, 198; VI, 250, 464; VIII, 3,
414
Arsac, Charles-François d', Marquis de Ternay, IV, 31
Arsac, Louise d', Marquise de Ternay. *See* Lefebvre de
Laubrière
Arsac de Ternay, Charles-Henri-Louis d', III, 132, 538; IV,
xxvii, 24, **30–32**, 53, 163, 223, 282, 448, 513, 733; V,
381, 491; VI, 193
Arsenault. *See also* Arseneaux
Arsenault, Anne (Nanon) (Gueguen), VI, 304
Arsenault*, Aubin-Edmond (1870–1968), XII, 40
Arsenault, Bibienne. *See* Poirier
Arsenault, François, VI, 304
Arsenault, Gertrude. *See* Gaudet
Arsenault, Joseph-Félix, XII, 40
Arsenault, Joseph-Octave, XII, **39–41**, 837
Arsenault, Mélème, XII, 39
Arsenault, Pierre, IV, xx
Arseneau, Geneviève (Compain), V, 201
Arseneau, Louise (Dugas), IV, 239, 240
Arseneaux (Arsenault), Marguerite (Painchaud), VIII, 675
Artaguiette Diron, Bernard d', III, 383
Artaguiette Diron, Jean-Baptiste-Martin d', II, 349; III, 380
Artaguiette d'Itouralde, Pierre d', II, xxviii, 67, 215, 216,
267, 457, 523; III, xxxiii, 47, 108, 383, 626, 627; IV, li
Artaud, Euphrasie (Pinsonnault), VI, 584
Arteaga, Ignacio de, IV, 73
Arthur, Catherine. *See* Cornish

Arthur, Eliza Ann (Fenety), XII, 313
Arthur, Elizabeth Orde Usher, Lady Arthur. *See* Smith
Arthur, Sir George, VII, 56, 253, 317, 326, 365, 370, 371, 372, 405, 406, 409, 460, 478, 495, 519, 550, 551, 665, 756, 795, 857, 859, 860; VIII, 11, **26–31**, 48, 84, 125, 254, 255, 303, 305, 311, 431, 444, 445, 502, 512, 520, 521, 522, 523, 524, 535, 539, 587, 708, 709, 778, 788, 798, 847, 848, 855, 871, 927, 932, 946; IX, 49, 79, 165, 201, 241, 252, 278, 369, 370, 399, 535, 566, 644, 675, 761, 794, 837, 858; X, 63, 259, 311, 334, 403, 639; XI, 787; XII, 681, 1079
Arthur, John, VIII, 26
Arthur, Julia. *See* Lewis, Ida
Arthur* William Patrick Albert, Duke of Connaught and Strathearn (1850–1942), XI, 453; XII, 677, 788, 789
Artigny. *See* Berthelot; Rouer
Artois, Comte d'. *See* Charles X
Artz, Mary Ann (Willis), X, 704
Arundel, Earl of. *See* Howard
Arundel, Laura (Macdonell), IX, 485
Arundell, Thomas, 1st Baron Arundell, I, 667
Asbury, Francis, V, 728; VI, 64, 65, 67, 276, 404, 405, 430, 672; VII, 44, 587
Ascanse. *See* Aisance
Ascumbuit. *See* Nescambiouit
Asenragéhaon (Jeanne), I, 610
Asfeld, Marquis d'. *See* Bidal
Ash, Adelaide Anne Amelia. *See* Veulle
Ash, Almira (Gibbs), XI, 346
Ash, Anna (Pack), VIII, 673
Ash, Annie Freer, XI, 33
Ash, Dorothy. *See* Agar
Ash, John, IX, 115; X, 479; XI, **32–33**, 291; XII, 929
Ash, William, XI, 32
Ashbridge, Mrs Sarah, V, 419
Ashbridge, Sarah (Heron), V, 419
Ashburton, Baron. *See* Baring; Dunning
Ashe, Edward David, XII, **41–42**
Ashe, Marcella. *See* Percy
Ashe, William Austin, XII, 42
Ashmore, Sarah (Bryant; Richardson), VI, 638; X, 615
Ashton, Jane (Bromley), VII, 107
Ashworth, Ann (Helliwell), IX, 387
Ashworth, Caldwell, XI, 575
Askin, Alice. *See* Rea
Askin, Catherine (Robertson; Hamilton), V, 39, 402, 405, 718; VII, 375, 378
Askin, Charles (son of JOHN), V, 39
Askin, Charles (uncle of Alexander HAMILTON and George HAMILTON, 1788–1836), VII, 375
Askin, Elisa. *See* Van Allen
Askin, James, V, 37
Askin, John, V, 38, 39, 178, 548, 553, 714; VI, 72, 210, 236, 340; VII, 329, 849; VIII, 161, 831; IX, 8
Askin, John, IV, 592, 680, 778; V, 3, 14, 15, 17, **37–39**, 129, 168, 178, 179, 306, 364, 365, 366, 367, 402, 403, 404, 495, 527, 528, 529, 536, 552, 553, 565, 718, 722, 750, 760, 815, 818, 819, 820, 821, 822, 841; VI, 8, 148, 189, 308, 318, 462, 473, 509, 539, 550, 600, 601, 628; VII, 57, 309, 735, 812, 813, 814; VIII, 743, 744; IX, 8
Askin, John Baptist, VII, 127, 234; VIII, 476; IX, **8–9**
Askin, Madelaine (Richardson), V, 39; VIII, 743, 744
Askin, Marie-Archange. *See* Barthe

Askin, Mary (Allcock), V, 17
Askin, Thérèse (McKee), V, 39, 536
Aspden, Thomas, XI, 69
Assacambuit. *See* Nescambiouit
Assakis. *See* Nonosecash
Assekinack. *See* Assiginack
Asselin, Léon, VIII, 284
Asselin, Louis-Napoléon, X, 226
Asselin, Malvina. *See* Derome
Assendasé, Pierre, II, 107
Asshehurst, Thomas, I, 302, 343, 386
Assheton, Susanna (Humphreys), V, 438
Assichqua, II, 20
Assiginack. *See also* Assikinack
Assiginack, Jean-Baptiste, VII, 11; VIII, 831; IX, **9–10**; XI, 714
Assiginack, Theresa Catherine. *See* Kebeshkamokwe
Assigny. *See* Le Moyne
Assikinack, Francis, IX, 9, **10–11**
Assikinock. *See* Assiginack
Assiniboine, L. *See* Battenotte, Louis
Assomption. *See* Barbier; Maugue-Garreau
Assour, Marie (Byssot Du Hommée), I, 145
Assup, IV, 774
Assurowlaway. *See* Waxaway
Asticou, I, **69–70**, 101, 526
Astohkomi. *See* Isapo-muxika
Astohkomi (Shot Close, Frank Red Crow), XII, 718, 719
Aston, Sir Arthur, I, 672
Aston, Salusbury (Haviland), IV, 334
Astor, John Jacob, V, 318, 418, 526, 528, 529, 533, 544, 559, 562, 635, 813, 822; VI, 148, 210, 211, 236, 286, 318, 357, 358, 447, 455, 623, 643, 665; VII, 687, 702, 706, 736; VIII, 158, 175, 190, 557, 768, 881; IX, 279, 280
Atarhea. *See* Tareha
Atawenta, III, 615
Atayataghronghta, Louis. *See* Atiatoharongwen
Atchamissey. *See* Scatchamisse
Atcheson, Robert S., xxxviii, VIII, 111
Atecouando, II, xxxviii, **25–26**, 543; III, 21, 23
Atecouando, II, 26; III, **20–21**, 24
Atetkouanon. *See* Pastedechouan
Athasata. *See* Togouiroui
Atherton, Charles, X, 404
Athiconando. *See* Atecouando (fl. 1701–26)
Athlone, Earl of. *See* Ginkel
Athol, Margaret. *See* Dechman
Atholl, Earl of. *See* Stewart
Athurnando. *See* Atecounado (fl. 1701–26)
Atia?tawì?tshera?. *See* Anandamoakin
Atiatoharongwen, V, **39–41**, 809; VII, 911; VIII, 939
Atic. *See* Chomina
Atikuapi, Josephte (McLeod), VIII, 570, 571
Atironta (fl. 1615), I, **70**
Atironta (d. 1650), I, **70–71**, 128
Atironta (d. 1672), I, **71–72**
Atkin, Eva. *See* Dawson
Atkin, Marie-Anne (Racine; Sauvageau), VII, 774
Atkins, Elizabeth (Kenwrick), IV, 410
Atkins, Francis Alexander, VII, 917
Atkins, Martha (Gray), V, 388
Atkinson, Abraham Fuller, IX, 719

Atkinson, Ann (Lawson), X, 434
Atkinson, Elizabeth (Harris), X, 334
Atkinson, Frances Deering. *See* Wentworth
Atkinson, George, IV, **32–33**; V, 451; VI, 15
Atkinson, George, IV, 33; V, 526; VI, **15–16**, 767, 795
Atkinson, Harriet (West), VII, 900
Atkinson, Henry (merchant), XII, 145, 1072
Atkinson, Henry (timber contractor), VII, 470
Atkinson, Isabella (Gledhill), II, 249
Atkinson, Mary (Addison), VI, 3
Atkinson, Matilda (Gamble), X, 299
Atkinson, Theodore, V, 848
Atontinon, Marrie-Barbe, I, 118
Atotarho, I, 253, 254
Atquandadeghte. *See* Ohquandageghte
Atseouatagon. *See* Vincent, Christine
Attacked Toward Home. *See* Axkyahp-say-pi
Atterwana. *See* Ottrowana
Attickasish, III, 286
Attwood, James Henry, VII, 228
Atwater, Albert, X, 17
Atwater, Albert William, XII, 173, 197
Atwater, Caleb, V, 797
Atwater, Edwin, X, **17–18**; XI, 211, 380
Atwater, Linus, X, 17
Atwater, Lucy Huntington. *See* Greene
Atwell, Mary (Small), VI, 721
Atwood, Anne Traill Fotheringhame. *See* Traill
Atwood, Mary (Homer), VII, 416
Au, Chevalier d'. *See* Jolliet, Jean-Pierre
Auber, Anne (Baudouin), I, 80; II, 286; III, 35, 36
Auber, Claude, I, **72**, 80; II, 228, 582; III, 201
Auber, Élisabeth (Chesné; Franquelin), II, 228
Auber, Félix, I, 72
Auber, Geneviève (Roberge), II, 520
Auber, Jacqueline. *See* Lucas
Auber, Jacques, I, **72**
Auber, Marguerite (Doublet), I, 277
Auber, Marguerite (Grouvel; Fillion), I, 305
Auber, Marie. *See* Le Boucher
Auberi. *See* Aubery
Aubert, Anne, II, 26
Aubert, François, II, 129
Aubert, Jacques, II, 26
Aubert, Jean-Joseph-Louis-Pierre, XI, 33
Aubert, Laure-Modeste. *See* Castellan
Aubert, Louis, II, 27
Aubert, Louis-François, II, 509, 575; III, 352
Aubert, Marie. *See* Goupy
Aubert, Marie (Milly), III, 451
Aubert, Pierre, II, 666
Aubert, Pierre, VIII, 722; X, 322; XI, **33–34**, 310; XII, 1003
Aubert, Thomas, I, 22, **72**, 658, 660
Aubert de Courserac, Marie-Anne (Savigny; Boschenry de Drucour), III, 72, 73
Aubert de Gaspé, Adélaïde (Saveuse de Beaujeu), IX, 702; X, 20
Aubert de Gaspé, Antoine-Thomas, VI, 16
Aubert de Gaspé, Atala (Hudon), X, 20
Aubert de Gaspé, Catherine. *See* Tarieu de Lanaudière
Aubert de Gaspé, Charlotte-Elmire (Stuart), X, 20; XII, 999
Aubert de Gaspé, Geneviève (Bailly de Messein), VI, 29

Aubert de Gaspé, Ignace-Philippe, IV, **33–34**; VI, 16, 29; VII, 89, 502; X, 18
Aubert de Gaspé, Madeleine-Angélique. *See* Legardeur de Tilly
Aubert de Gaspé, Marie-Anne. *See* Coulon de Villiers
Aubert de Gaspé, Philippe-Ignace-François, X, 19, 20
Aubert de Gaspé, Philippe-Joseph, II, 33, 58; III, 143, 677; IV, 34, 589, 590; V, 498, 622, 793; VI, 16, 59, 119, 120, 290, 300, 680, 681; VII, 168, 213, 332, 504, 505, 591, 785, 787, 790, 876, 877, 881; IX, 702, 774; X, 13, **18–23**; XI, 15, 37, 87, 531; XII, 247, 558, 999
Aubert de Gaspé, Philomène, X, 20
Aubert de Gaspé, Pierre, II, 33; IV, 33; X, 18
Aubert de Gaspé, Pierre-Ignace, IV, 34; V, 44; VI, **16–17**; X, 18
Aubert de Gaspé, Susanne. *See* Allison
Aubert de Gaspé, Susanne (Power), X, 20
Aubert de Gaspé, Thomas, X, 20
Aubert de Gaspé, Wilhelmine-Anaïs (Fraser), X, 20
Aubert de Gaspé, Zélie (Borne), X, 20
Aubert de Gaspé, Zoé (Alleyn), X, 20; XI, 15
Aubert de La Chesnaye, Anne-Ursule. *See* Denys de La Ronde
Aubert de La Chesnaye, Catherine (Galiffet de Caffin), III, 233
Aubert de La Chesnaye, Catherine-Gertrude. *See* Couillard de Lespinay
Aubert de La Chesnaye, Charles, II, 33
Aubert de La Chesnaye, Charles, I, 21, 56, 84, 85, 104, 105, 178, 200, 224, 227, 289, 338, 387, 393, 396, 397, 400, 444, 445, 538, 602; II, 14, **26–34**, 43, 138, 174, 178, 190, 251, 261, 263, 273, 275, 276, 375, 381, 387, 391, 448, 459, 464, 488, 509, 522, 523, 526, 538, 657; III, 21, 22, 192, 233, 493; IV, 33; V, 108; X, 18
Aubert de La Chesnaye, François, II, 32, 33, **34–35**, 305; III, 22; IV, 265; V, 288
Aubert de La Chesnaye, Françoise (Le Moyne de Maricourt; Dubois Berthelot de Beaucours), II, 405; III, 192
Aubert de La Chesnaye, Ignace-François, III, 21, 22; V, 288
Aubert de La Chesnaye, Louis, II, 33; III, **21–23**
Aubert de La Chesnaye, Marie-Angélique. *See* Denys de La Ronde
Aubert de La Chesnaye, Marie-Angélique (Goutin), III, 264; IV, 41
Aubert de La Chesnaye, Marie-Anne-Josette. *See* Lestringant de Saint-Martin
Aubert de La Chesnaye, Marie-Charlotte, named de Saint-Michel, III, 369
Aubert de La Chesnaye, Marie-Louise. *See* Juchereau de La Ferté
Aubert de La Chesnaye, Marie-Thérèse. *See* La Lande Gayon
Aubert de La Chesnaye, Marie-Ursule (Le Marchand de Lignery; Feltz), IV, 265
Aubert Duforillon, Barbe. *See* Leneuf de La Vallière et de Beaubassin
Aubert Duforillon, Louis, II, 33, 587; III, 21, 22, 291
Aubery, Joseph, II, 25, 26, 447, 495, 665; III, 21, **23–25**, 395; IV, 424
Aubigné, Françoise d', Marquise de Maintenon, I, 631; II, 98, 132, 330, 483
Aubigny. *See* Boutroue

Aubigny, Duke of. *See* Lennox

Aubin, Élisabeth. *See* Escuyer

Aubin, Marie-Luce-Émilie. *See* Sauvageau

Aubin, Michel, II, 639

Aubin, Napoléon (Aimé-Nicolas), VII, 775, 776; VIII, 290, 420, 423, 495, 496, 537, 834, 962; IX, 33, 300, 805; X, 20, 213; XI, **34–37**, 178, 179; XII, 269, 300, 324, 846, 847, 1032

Aubin, Pierre-Louis-Charles, XI, 34

Aubin-Delisle, Marie-Françoise (Gatien), VII, 340

Aubreville. *See* Bigault

Aubrey, Elizabeth Ann. *See* Monk

Aubrey, Thomas, V, 348

Aubry. *See also* Aubery

Aubry, Ambroise, VIII, 218

Aubry, Auguste-Eugène, IX, 119, 120; X, 542

Aubry, Charles, II, 208

Aubry, Charles-Philippe, III, 87, 531

Aubry, Élisabeth (Dupuy), II, 207, 208

Aubry, Jacques-Charles, II, 208

Aubry, Joseph, IX, 118

Aubry, Laurent, VIII, 19

Aubry, Nicolas, I, 64, **72**, 192, 292

Aubuchon, Catherine. *See* Jérémie, *dit* Lamontagne

Aubuchon, Jacques, II, 296, 413; III, 314

Aubuchon, Jean, II, 11

Aubuchon, Marie-Anne (Chorel de Saint-Romain, *dit* d'Orvilliers), II, 267

Aubuchon, *dit* Lespérance, Catherine (Fabre, *dit* Laperrière), V, 736

Aubuchon, *dit* L'Espérance, Marguerite (Courreaud de La Coste), IV, 178

Aubuchon, *dit* L'Espérance, Marie-Joseph (Jourdain, *dit* Labrosse), 366

Aubussargues. *See* Vergese

Aubusson. *See* Du Verger

Aubut, Marie-Anne (Piuze), V, 676

Auchagah, II, **35**; III, 248

Auchechaque. *See* Chejauk

Aucher, Anne (Gilbert), I, 331

Auchinleck, Gilbert, V, 800; VIII, 188; IX, 407; XI, 558

Auchmuty, Elinor Isabella (Fisher), VII, 286

Auchmuty, Samuel, V, 59, 445, 786

Au-Ciel. *See* Ogenheratarihiens

Auckland, Earl of. *See* Eden

Auclair, Élie-Joseph-Arthur, VII, 150; X, 431

Auclair, Étienne, XI, 37

Auclair, Joseph, VI, 487, 488

Auclair, Joseph, X, 603; XI, **37–39**

Auclair, Marie-Jeanne. *See* Blondeau

Auclair, Narcisse, V, 218, 727

Aucoin, Marie-Josette (Jeanson), IV, 392

Audet*, Francis-Joseph (1867–1943), IV, 232, 398, 698; V, 183, 395, 429, 530, 572, 577; VI, 433; VII, 69, 150, 703; X, 503; XI, 27, 903

Audet, Isidore-François-Octave, XI, 496

Audet, Louis-Philippe, VI, 206, 483; XI, 182

Audet, Nicodème, XI, 492

Audet de Piercotte de Bailleul, Marguerite (Lajus), IV, 432

Audette, Rodolphe, XII, 1038

Audette, *dit* Lapointe, Marie-Josette (Jacobs; Rieutord), IV, 385; V, 713

Audette, *dit* Lapointe, Théotiste (Huston), VIII, 419

Audi. *See* Roi

Audibert, Jeanne-Marie (Anspach), VI, 9

Audiepvre, Michel, I, 167

Audin. *See* Daudin

Audivert, *dit* Romain. *See also* Romain

Audivert, *dit* Romain, Anne. *See* Ledroit, *dit* Perche

Audivert, *dit* Romain, François, VI, 658

Audoire, Marguerite (Morpain), III, 474

Audouart, *dit* Saint-Germain, Guillaume, I, **73**, 91, 224, 298, 430, 538; II, xvi, 91

Audrie, Jean-Baptiste, VII, 167

Audrie, Marie-Geneviève (Charron), VII, 167

Audubon, John James, VII, 320, 442, 540; IX, 660, 722, 850; XI, 55, 418; XII, 268, 778

Audy. *See also* Roy-Audy

Audy, Pierre, VII, 761

Auffray, Charles, VII, 27

Auffray, Charles-Dominique, VII, **27–28**

Auffray, Charles-Victor, VII, 28

Auffray, Jeanne. *See* Cantin

Auffray, Jeanne-Mathurine, VII, 27

Auffray, Nathalie. *See* Bourgeois

Auffray, Victor, VII, 27

Augé. *See also* Dangé; Lemaître-Augé

Augé, Antoinette. *See* Barabé

Augé, Étienne, IV, **34–35**, 530; V, 394, 703

Augé, François, IV, 732

Augé, Jeanne (Digé), V, 256

Augé, Louis, IV, 34

Augé, Louise-Françoise. *See* Dalgueuil, *dit* Labrèche

Augé, Marie-Josephte (Séguin), VII, 781

Augé, Marie-Louise (Dejean), V, 237

Augé, Michel, IV, 35

Auger. *See also* Dangé

Auger, Agathe. *See* Roy

Auger, *dit* Le Baron, Jean, I, 109

Auger de Marillac, Charles-François, IV, 14

Auger de Subercase, Daniel d', II, 3, 4, 15, **35–39**, 117, 118, 120, 177, 180, 187, 206, 214, 258, 285, 350, 411, 434, 437, 445, 452, 461, 482, 487, 495, 497, 510, 511, 534, 583, 588, 609, 618, 626, 651, 654; III, 20, 22, 177, 190, 207, 234, 247, 264, 290, 436, 474, 505, 552, 682

Auger de Subercase, Marguerite d' (Arrigrand), III, 20

Auger de Subercase, Marie-Anne d'. *See* Du Bourget

Aughneeta, XI, 655

Augier, Daniel, IV, 678

Augier, *dit* Desjardins, Christophe, I, 267

Augooshaway. *See* Egushwa

Auguel, *dit* Le Picard Du Guay, Antoine, II, 278, 281

August, John. *See* John August

Augusta of Saxe-Gotha (Augusta, Princess of Wales), IV, 536

Augustin, Father. *See* Lestrange

Augustine of Hippo, XII, 250

Augustus. *See* Tattannoeuck

Augustus Frederick, Duke of Sussex, VII, 481; VIII, 927

Auld, Agnes (Longworth), VII, 511; XI, 526, 528

Auld, Jane (Charles), VI, 18

Auld, John Allan, XII, 52

Auld, Mary (Taite), VI, 18

Auld, Robert, VI, 18

Auld, Wilberforce, VI, 18

Auld, William, VI, 18

Auld, William, VI, **17–18**, 250, 251, 321, 443, 767, 795; VII, 206, 748; VIII, 546

Auldjo, Alexander, V, 133, 259, 320, 461; VI, **18–20**, 271, 272, 433, 471, 476; VII, 28, 525

Auldjo, Eweretta Jane. *See* Richardson

Auldjo, George, VII, 28

Auldjo, George, IV, 48; VI, 19, 272; VII, **28–29**, 381, 717

Auldjo, Helen. *See* Richardson

Auldjo, John (father), VI, 18

Auldjo, John, VI, 18

Auldjo, Louis, X, 10

Auldjo, Margaret. *See* McKenzie

Auldjo, Susan. *See* Beauvais

Aulnay. *See* Menou

Aulneau (Aulneau de La Touche), Jean-Pierre, II, **39–40**, 239; III, 46, 137, 241, 251, 361; IV, 240

Aulneau (Aulneau de La Touche), Michel, II, 40

Aulquoy, Ambroise d' (Thomelin), I, 213

Aulte, Catherine, V, 198

Aumale, Duc d'. *See* Lorraine

Aumasson de Courville, Charles-Léonard, IV, 36

Aumasson de Courville, Claude, IV, 35

Aumasson de Courville, Judith. *See* Chevreau

Aumasson de Courville, Louis-Léonard, known as Sieur de Courville, III, 124; IV, **35–36**, 249, 250, 251, 425, 455, 457, 621, 660; VII, 190, 818

Aumasson de Courville, Marie-Anne. *See* Amiot, *dit* Villeneuve

Aumon. *See also* Aumond

Aumon, Euphrosine. *See* Robichaud

Aumon, Ignace, X, 23

Aumond, Charles, X, 23

Aumond, Jane. *See* Cumming

Aumond, Joseph-Ignace, VIII, 268, 269; X, **23–24**; XI, 682; XII, 937

Aumur, François, VI, 59

Aunois, Jeanne (Lefebvre), II, 382

Auoindaon, I, **73**

Aupetit, Anne (Cazeau), V, 173

Aureil. *See* Doreil

Aussillon de Sauveterre, Paul d', I, 423, 424

Austen, Eliza (Richardson), IX, 656

Austen, George W., IX, 311

Austen, Henry, IX, 738, 739

Austen, Jane, VII, 817; XI, 783

Austen, John H., IX, 311

Austen, Mary. *See* Ede

Austin*, Albert William (1857–1934), XII, 44, 45

Austin, Ann Eliza. *See* Hawkins

Austin, Benjamin Fish, XII, 708

Austin, Elizabeth. *See* Gooch

Austin, Elizabeth (Hill), II, 287

Austin, George, XI, 685

Austin, Sir Horatio Thomas, VII, 327; VIII, 447, 448, 623, 624, 773; IX, **11–13**; X, 29, 408, 561, 562, 563; XI, 198, 199; XII, 835, 836

Austin, James, XI, 449, 575; XII, **42–45**, 107, 108

Austin, John Marks, XII, 42

Austin, Nicholas, VI, 501

Austin, Samuel, II, 287

Austin, Susan. *See* Bright

Austin, William, XI, 685

Austria, Archduke of. *See* Maximilian

Austria, Princess of. *See* Maria Carolina; Marie-Antoinette

Austria, Anne of. *See* Anne

Auterive. *See* Cuny

Auteuil. *See* Ruette

Autray. *See* Bourdon

Auvergne. *See also* La Tour

Auvergne, Mary Anne Charlotte d' (Prescott), X, 600

Aux (Eau) de Jolliet, Pierre d', II, 441, 602

Auxillon. *See* Aussillon

Auzon, Françoise, IV, 235

Avamy, Jeanne (Viennay-Pachot), I, 661; II, 305

Avaray, Comte d'. *See* Bésiade

Avaugour, Louis d', II, **40–41**; III, 23, 336

Avène. *See* Renaud

Aveneau, Claude, II, **41**, 144, 347, 468, 501; III, 103

Averill, J. Ketchum, IX, 551

Averne, Comte d', II, 485

Avery, Benjamin Parke, IX, 280

Avet Forel, Gabrielle (Desdevens de Glandons), IV, 215

Avisse, Marie-Jeanne (Trefflé, *dit* Rottot; Soupiran), III, 596

Avocat, L'. *See* Havard de Beaufort, François-Charles

Avray. *See* Marshall

Avray, Baron d'. *See* Marshall

Aw-gee-nah, V, 538; VI, **20**

Awanano (Awenano). *See* Aouenano

Awanwest. *See* Hawawes

Awenemwet. *See* Wenemouet

Axkyahp-say-pi (Attacked Toward Home), XI, 442

Ayagon, VIII, 653

Ayala, Pedro de, I, 147, 148, 149, 150, 151

Aycrigg, John Hurst, VII, 918

Aycrigg, Mary Payne (Wolhaupter), VII, 918; VIII, 951

Aycrigg, Rachael. *See* Lydekker

Ayen, Comte d'. *See* Noailles

Ayen, Duc d'. *See* Noailles

Ayer, Dolly (Chandler), X, 156

Ayer, Thomas, II, 285

Ayers, Thomas Henry, XII, 1115

Āyimisīs (Imasees), XI, 261, 599, 600; XII, 478

Aylen, Eleanor. *See* Thomson

Aylen, John, XII, 197

Aylen, Peter, IX, 14; XII, 197

Aylen, Peter, VII, 382, 445, 446, 796; VIII, 839; IX, **13–14**

Aylmer, Baron. *See* Whitworth-Aylmer

Aylmer, Baroness. *See* Call

Aylmer, Catherine, Baroness Aylmer. *See* Whitworth

Aylmer, Lady Catherine (Plunket; Warren), III, 654

Aylmer, Elizabeth (Norris), III, 488

Aylmer, Henry, 4th Baron Aylmer, VII, 904

Aylmer, Matthew, 1st Baron Aylmer, III, 488, 655

Aylwin, Ann. *See* Blake

Aylwin, Charles, IX, 773

Aylwin, Charles-Félix, IX, 598

Aylwin, Eliza Margaret. *See* Felton

Aylwin, Louise-Catherine. *See* Connolly

Aylwin, Lucy. *See* Cushing

Aylwin, Margaret Nelson. *See* Hanna

Aylwin, Thomas (father of THOMAS CUSHING), X, 24

Aylwin, Thomas (partner of Austin CUVILLIER), VII, 224

Aylwin, Thomas, IV, **37–38**, 725; V, 283; VI, 492
Aylwin, Thomas Cushing, IV, 38; VI, 585; VII, 32, 158, 836; VIII, 137, 497, 678, 938; IX, 56, 83, 191, 290, 444; X, **24**, 134, 219, 548, 653; XI, 178, 179; XII, 66
Ayolas, Juan de, I, 342, 343
Ayotte, Pierre, IV, 71; V, 358
Ayre, William, VIII, **31–32**
Ayres. *See also* Eyre
Ayres, Dr, X, 349
Ayscough, Augusta Anne (Cockburn, Lady Cockburn), IX, 132

BABBITT, Frances Maria. *See* Nealon
Babbitt, George Nealon, XI, 39
Babbitt, John, XI, **39**
Babbitt, Margaret. *See* Turnbull
Babbitt, Samuel Wellington, XI, 39
Babel*, Louis (1829–1912), IX, 864; X, 737
Babey, Peter Paul Toney, VIII, **32–33**
Babie, Isabeau. *See* Robin
Babie, Jacques, I, **74**; II, 11
Babie, Jeanne. *See* Dandonneau, *dit* Lajeunesse
Babie, Jeanne (Dazemard de Lusignan), III, 168
Babie, Raymond, I, 74
Babin, Jean-Marie, VII, 167
Babin, Marie-Anastasie (Charron), VII, 167
Babin, Marie-Josephte (Hébert), VI, 315
Babin, Marie-Madeleine (Le Blanc), IV, 441
Babineau, François-Xavier, XI, **39–40**
Babineau, Joseph (father of FRANÇOIS-XAVIER), XI, 39
Babineau, Joseph (silversmith), VII, 18
Babineau, Joseph-Auguste, XI, 40
Babineau, Nathalie. *See* Le Blanc
Babonneau, Renée, II, 490
Baby, Mlle (fiancée of Laurent QUETTON St George), VI, 624
Baby, Alice (Caron, Lady Caron), IX, 16
Baby, Antoine, IV, 38; V, 41, 42
Baby, Archange (Ross Lewen; Cannon), VI, 120
Baby, Charles, VII, 364
Baby, Charles-François-Xavier, V, 217; VII, 166; IX, **14–16**
Baby, Charles T., XI, 649
Baby, Clothilde. *See* Pinsoneaut
Baby, Eliza Anne (Casgrain), VII, 161
Baby, Elizabeth. *See* Abbott
Baby, Frances. *See* Abbott
Baby, Francis, VIII, 119
Baby, François, V, 45
Baby, François, I, 74; IV, xxxix, 38, 39, 72, 146, 147, 197, 324, 344, 495, 549; V, **41–46**, 149, 164, 165, 289, 290, 396, 398, 484, 492, 577, 736, 794, 863; VI, 383, 392, 486, 576, 700; VII, 687, 771, 884; VIII, 33, 937, 962; IX, 14
Baby, François, V, 366, 449; VI, 22, 120, 628, 809; VII, 200, 661; VIII, **33–35**, 120; XI, 268
Baby*, François-Louis-Georges (1832–1906), IV, 799; IX, 868; X, 738; XI, 624; XII, 821
Baby, James, IV, 39, 778; V, 44, 365, 536, 722; VI, **21–22**, 32, 266, 416, 612, 723; VII, 161, 662; VIII, 33, 281, 511, 517; XI, 268
Baby, Joseph, IX, 15
Baby, Josephte (Perrault), VII, 687

Baby, Louis, IV, 38; V, 41
Baby, Marguerite (Selby), VI, 700
Baby, Marie-Anne. *See* Tarieu de Lanaudière
Baby, Marie-Louise (Irumberry de Salaberry), XI, 441
Baby, Mary Frances. *See* Réaume
Baby, Michel-Guillaume, IX, 16
Baby, Monique-Ursule (Young), VIII, 962
Baby, Raymond, IV, 38; V, 41; VII, 687
Baby, Susanne (Dougall), XI, 268
Baby, Suzanne (Caldwell), VI, 101; VII, 132; VIII, 119
Baby, Thérèse. *See* Le Comte Dupré
Baby, Thérèse (Allison), X, 18
Baby, Véronique (Corbin), IV, 167
Baby, *dit* Dupéront, Jacques, I, 74; IV, **38–40**; V, 41, 42, 44, 396, 721, 852; VI, 21, 101, 607; VII, 687, 688; VIII, 33, 119
Baby, *dit* Dupéront, Susanne. *See* Réaume, *dit* La Croix
Baby-Chenneville, Angélique (Chaboillez), V, 180; VI, 125
Baby de Ranville, Jacques, IV, 38
Bacelet, *dit* Casirtan (Cassista), Françoise (Gamache), VIII, 312
Bach, Johann Sebastian, XII, 471
Bachaddelebat, Marie (Druillon), IV, 226
Bachand, Delphine. *See* Dufort
Bachand, Joseph, X, 24
Bachand, Josephte. *See* Fontaine
Bachand, Marie-Louise. *See* Marchand
Bachand, Pierre, X, **24–26**, 420; XI, 480; XII, 324, 693, 694, 721
Bachand, *dit* Vertefeuille, Joseph, IV, 151
Bache, Alexander Dallas, XI, 509
Bachelerie, Marguerite (Moyen), XII, 769
Bacholtz, Mr (piano-key maker), XII, 422
Back, Ann (mother of Sir GEORGE), X, 26
Back, Sir George, VI, 218, 328, 754; VII, 324, 325, 390, 570; VIII, 772; IX, 6, 197, 198, 389, 658, 659; X, **26–29**, 406, 407, 408, 454
Back, John, X, 26
Back, Theodosia Elizabeth. *See* Hammond
Backhouse, John, V, 734; VIII, 607
Backus, Abigail (Perkins), V, 664
Backwell, William, VIII, 483
Bacon, Miss (friend of William BURN), V, 126
Bacon, Christiana (Medley), VIII, 942; XII, 713
Bacon, David, VI, 509
Bacon, Elizabeth Newell. *See* Lockerby
Bacon, Francis, Viscount St Albans, XII, 1100
Bâcon, François, X, 345
Bacon, Hiram, XI, 524
Bacon, John, VIII, 942
Bacon, Louise (Constantin), III, 134
Bâcon, Madeleine, named de la Résurrection, II, 93
Bacon, Nathaniel, III, xxiv
Bacon, Rebecca (Watson), X, 698
Bacon, Sarah (Phillips), XII, 842
Bacquet, Jean-Baptiste-Édouard, VIII, 495; IX, 463; X, 134, 201, 301
Bacqueville. *See* Le Roy
Bad Arrow. *See* Manachoos
Bad Bird. *See* Madjeckewiss
Baddeley, Frederick Henry, VII, 197, 747, 837; VIII, 385, 520; X, **29–31**

Baddeley, Susan. *See* Green
Badden, Margaret (McKenzie), VI, 469
Badeau, Fabien, III, 138
Badeau, Madelaine (Secord), VII, 780
Badeaux, Antoine-Isidore, IV, 40; V, 603; VI, 22; VII, 644
Badeaux, Catherine. *See* Loisy
Badeaux, Charles, IV, 40
Badeaux, Geneviève. *See* Berthelot
Badeaux, Jacques, IV, 40
Badeaux, Jean-Baptiste, IV, **40–41**, 109, 304, 320, 547; VI, 22
Badeaux, Jeanne. *See* Ardouin
Badeaux, Joseph, IV, 40, 332; V, 76; VI, **22–24**, 50, 289, 634; VII, 388; VIII, 231, 364, 368
Badeaux, Joseph-Michel, VII, 388
Badeaux, Marguerite. *See* Bolvin
Badeaux, Marguerite. *See* Dumont
Badeaux, Marguerite. *See* Pratte
Badel, Antoine, V, 417
Badel, Marie-Angélique (Heer), V, 417
Badelard, Bernard, V, 649
Badelard, Esther. *See* Bruyer
Badelard, Louise-Philippe (Panet), V, 46, 648; VIII, 677
Badelard, Louise-Suzanne, V, 46
Badelard, Marie-Charlotte. *See* Guillimin
Badelard, Philippe-Louis-François, IV, 82, 106; V, **46–47**, 329, 330, 501, 648, 788; VI, 258, 379
Badelard, Philippe-Martin, V, 46
Badger, Daniel D., VIII, 876
Badgley, Mr (possible bankrupt), VII, 30
Badgley, Charles Howard, X, 382
Badgley, Elizabeth. *See* Lilly
Badgley, Elizabeth (Molson) VII, 30; X, 518, 525; XI, 40; XII, 748
Badgley, Elizabeth Wallace. *See* Taylor
Badgley, Francis, V, 259, 260, 283, 376, 566; VI, 365, 469; VII, **29–30**; IX, 16; X, 518; XI, 40
Badgley, Francis, VII, 30; IX, **16–17**, 358; XI, 40, 58, 302; XII, 106
Badgley, James, VI, 365; VII, 30
Badgley, John Thompson, VII, 620; X, 518, 519
Badgley, Sidney Rose, XII, 704, 708
Badgley, William, VII, 30, 478, 810; VIII, 800; IX, 16, 119, 290, 554, 779; X, 219, 257, 326, 418, 518, 642, 724; XI, **40–42**, 609; XII, 5, 888
Badon, Clémence de (La Motte), I, 415
Baffin, Mrs (wife of WILLIAM), I, 75
Baffin, William, I, 5, 20, **74–75**, 144, 145, 252, 360, 378; VIII, 771, 772; IX, 691
Bagg, Abner, XI, 267
Bagg, Catharine. *See* Mitcheson
Bagg, Mary Ann. *See* Clark
Bagg*, Robert Stanley (1848–1912), X, 32
Bagg, Stanley, VI, 783, 812; VII, 26, 226, 482, 751; VIII, 631, 918, 919; IX, 288, 554; X, 31, 526; XI, 117
Bagg, Stanley Clark, X, **31–32**
Bagnall, Anna Matilda. *See* Gardiner
Bagnall, Caroline Charlotte Augusta (Baker), VIII, 37
Bagnall, Elizabeth. *See* Whitehouse
Bagnall, James, VI, 414, 566, 568; VII, 189; VIII, **35–38**, 741; X, 339

Bagnall, Jane (Cooper), XI, 201
Bagnall, Samuel (father), VIII, 35
Bagnall, Samuel, VIII, 36
Bagnall, Samuel James, VIII, 37
Bagot. *See also* Howard
Bagot, Sir Charles, VII, 11, **30–33**, 158, 306, 364, 441, 579, 604, 795, 880, 917; VIII, xxv, xxviii, xxxiii, 50, 51, 255, 332, 432, 445, 521, 571, 727, 745, 764, 765, 786, 799, 839, 848, 849, 912, 933; IX, 190, 238, 266, 285, 301, 371, 372, 444, 445, 458, 520, 524, 569, 600, 700, 725, 728, 741, 761, 775, 796, 815, 818; X, 39, 254, 255, 311, 325, 403, 404, 462, 506, 527, 583; XI, 35, 188, 218, 238, 281, 405, 408, 409, 540, 631, 713; XII, 391
Bagot, Elizabeth Louisa, Baroness Bagot. *See* St John
Bagot, Jean, II, 18, 359, 360
Bagot, Mary Charlotte Anne, Lady Bagot. *See* Wellesley-Pole
Bagot, William, 1st Baron Bagot, VII, 30
Bagshawe, Catherina. *See* Stratham
Baguleughe, Elizabeth (Pearson), I, 535
Baile, Joseph-Alexandre, VIII, 490, 728; IX, 246; XI, **42–43**, 273, 777
Bailey, Captain, I, 383
Bailey, Ann (Emerson), VII, 274
Bailey, Charles, XII, 61
Bailey, David, V, 47
Bailey (Baley), Deborah (Dimock), VII, 252
Bailey, Elizabeth Pierce (Lambly), IX, 454
Bailey, Henry W., XII, 137
Bailey, Jacob, IV, 94, 504, 763; V, **47–48**, 430, 871; VI, 169, 171, 363
Bailey, John, VII, 363
Bailey*, Loring Woart (1839–1925), IX, 667; X, 338; XI, 39, 447
Bailey, Mary. *See* Hodgkins
Bailey, Mary (Fairbrother), XII, 305
Bailey, Percis (Persis) Maria (Pope), XI, 705
Bailey, Philip James, XII, 945
Bailey, Sally. *See* Weeks
Bailey, Thomas Henry, VI, 169
Bailey, William Whitman, XI, 39
Baillairgé*, Charles (1826–1906), V, 50; VIII, 40; IX, 120, 318, 863; X, 603, 735; XI, 337, 505; XII, 47, 345, 534, 627
Baillairgé, Flavien, VIII, 213
Baillairgé, François, IV, 9; V, 49, 50, 51, 61, 139, 140, 193, 305, 329, 452, 708; VI, **24–29**, 119, 223, 367, 570; VII, 17, 18, 95, 255, 761, 870; VIII, 38, 330, 655
Baillairgé, François-Xavier, XII, 47
Baillairgé*, George-Frédéric-Théophile (1824–1909), V, 48; VIII, 38, 40; XII, 47
Baillairgé, Jean, V, 48
Baillairgé, Jean, V, **48–51**, 305, 452; VI, 24, 25, 26; VII, 168; VIII, 38, 330, 333; XII, 45
Baillairgé, Jeanne. *See* Bourdois
Baillairgé, Josephte. *See* Boutin
Baillairgé, Louis de Gonzague, VII, 592; X, 132, 162; XII, **45–47**
Baillairgé, Marie-Anne (Girouard), VIII, 330, 331
Baillairgé, Marie-Félicité, VIII, 202
Baillairgé, Marie-Louise. *See* Cureux, *dit* Saint-Germain
Baillairgé, Marie-Louise. *See* Parent

Baillairgé, Pierre, V, 48
Baillairgé, Pierre-Florent, V, 49, 50, **51–52**, 61, 305; VI, 27, 367; VII, 168, 761; VIII, 40, 202, 330; XII, 45
Baillairgé, Thomas, I, 76, 77; II, 200; V, 50, 51, 305; VI, 24, 26, 28, 119, 554; VIII, **38–41**, 213, 581, 655, 680, 681; IX, 120, 317, 318, 552, 799; XI, 92, 337, 506
Baillargeon, Anne (Dugay), II, 203
Baillargeon, Catherine (Bigot), II, 63
Baillargeon, Charles-François, I, 356; VII, 427, 886, 887; VIII, 676; IX, **17–21**, 118, 121, 255, 642, 799, 800; X, 251, 429, 489, 493, 576, 603; XI, 40, 109, 167, 170, 171, 175, 258, 487, 507, 694; XII, 818, 819, 847, 1017, 1018, 1019, 1020
Baillargeon, Étienne, IX, 19; XII, 818
Baillargeon, François, IX, 17
Baillargeon, Marie-Louise. See Langlois, dit Saint-Jean
Bailleul. See Audet
Baillie, Charles, VI, 768
Baillie, Elizabeth. See Hall
Baillie, Elizabeth. See Odell
Baillie, George, VIII, xxxii; IX, 21, 24
Baillie, Helena. See Douglas
Baillie, James Little, VII, 320, 321
Baillie, Jane (Douglas, Lady Douglas), IV, 223
Baillie, Mary Hamilton (Begbie), XII, 77
Baillie, Thomas, VI, 74, 685, 686, 687; VII, 140, 291, 444, 637, 658, 659, 691, 692, 807; VIII, xxxii, 157, 377, 378, 418, 738, 803, 807, 808, 841, 842; IX, **21–24**, 53, 147, 171, 221, 399; X, 41, 158, 315, 644, 703, 710; XII, 752, 797
Baillie, William, IX, 21, 24
Baillie-Grohman, William, XI, 840
Baillie Hamilton, Charles, XI, 43
Baillie Hamilton, Charlotte. See Home
Baillie Hamilton, Emma. See Blair
Baillie Hamilton, Ker, VIII, 104; IX, 195, 196; XI, **43–44**, 243, 432, 881; XII, 439, 564
Baillif, Catherine. See Sainctar
Baillif, Claude, I, **75–77**, 460, 536, 664; II, 338, 418, 467; III, 419
Bailloquet, Pierre, I, **78**, 282, 345; II, 174
Bailly, Alexis, VI, 29, 30
Bailly, Angelique. See Bead-way-way
Bailly, Catherine Margaret (Comingo), V, 199
Bailly, Georges-Frédéric, III, 474
Bailly, Guillaume, I, **78**; II, 46
Bailly, Jane (Jeanne) Margaret (Comingo), VI, 168
Bailly, Joseph, VI, **29–30**, 664, 667
Bailly, Lucie-Anne. See Faribault
Bailly, Marie. See Fonteneau
Bailly, Marie. See Lefevre
Bailly, Robertus de, I, 659
Bailly, dit Lafleur, François, I, 78; II, 105
Bailly de Messein, Anne. See Bonhomme
Bailly de Messein, Anne. See Marsain
Bailly de Messein, Charles-François, IV, **41–44**, 72, 80, 89, 372, 373, 374, 469, 676, 698, 799; V, 58, 150, 179, 186, 246, 449, 459, 667; VI, 29, 85, 228, 774
Bailly de Messein, Félicité-Élisabeth (Le Moyne de Martigny), IV, 43
Bailly de Messein, François-Augustin, IV, 41; V, 829
Bailly de Messein, Geneviève. See Aubert de Gaspé
Bailly de Messein, Marie-Anne. See Goutin

Bailly de Messein, Marie-Appolline (Trottier Desrivières Beaubien), V, 829; VII, 688
Bailly de Messein, Michel (ancestor of CHARLES-FRANÇOIS), IV, 41
Bailly de Messein, Michel (father of Joseph BAILLY), VI, 29
Bailly de Messein, Nicolas, IV, 41
Baily. See Bayly
Bain, Caroline. See Clark
Bain, Charles, VII, 917
Bain, Ellen. See Dockendorff
Bain, Francis, XII, **47–49**
Bain*, James (1842–1908), XII, 663
Bain, John, X, 336
Bain, William, XII, 47
Bainbridge, John, IX, 176; VII, 654; X, 71
Bainbrigge, Philip John, XI, 137
Baine, Walter, XI, 376
Baines, Elizabeth (By), VII, 128
Baines, Mary Catherine (Draper), XII, 273
Baionas, Rachel Relind (Strouds), III, 602
Baird, Anne. See Robinson
Baird, Annie. See Diggin
Baird, Charles, VII, 33
Baird, Charlotte (Gordon, Lady Haddo), IX, 326
Baird, Edmond, VIII, **41–42**; IX, 390
Baird, Elizabeth Therese. See Fisher
Baird, Emmaline Edmond (Ryckman), VIII, 42
Baird, Freeman, VIII, 855, 856
Baird, George Husband, VII, 723
Baird, Hugh, VII, 33
Baird, James, VIII, 41; IX, 390
Baird*, James (1828–1915), XII, 844
Baird, James George, XI, 159
Baird, Jane. See Keirnan
Baird, John, VI, 506; VIII, **42–43**; XII, 49
Baird, Lydia (Talbot), VII, 842; VIII, 855; X, 671
Baird, Margaret. See Burnthwaite
Baird, Mary. See White
Baird, Nicol Hugh, VI, 813; VII, **33–35**, 122, 223, 712; VIII, 117, 534; X, 403, 404; XII, 930
Baird, Robert, XI, 924
Baird, Sarah Ann. See Shea
Baird, Spencer Fullerton, XII, 269, 368, 868
Baird, Susan. See Teel
Baird, William, VIII, 41, 42
Baird, William Teel, VII, 274, 330; VIII, 42, 509; XII, **49–50**
Baker, Miss (Simpson), X, 656
Baker, Abigail (Fairfield), V, 307
Baker, Ann. See Barron
Baker, Ann. See Cole
Baker, Blanche (Davie), XII, 227
Baker, Caroline Charlotte Augusta. See Bagnall
Baker, Cephas, X, 511
Baker, Charles, XI, 864
Baker, Charles, VI, **30–31**
Baker, Delina. See Kenney
Baker, Mrs Dorinda (Dorine), V, 389
Baker, Edgar Crow, XII, 806
Baker, Edward, IV, 30
Baker (Littlehales), Sir Edward Baker, V, 519
Baker, Elizabeth (Peters), VII, 690

Baker, Ellis, XII, 50
Baker, Emma. *See* Wyatt
Baker, Frances Isabella. *See* Farish
Baker, George William (father), VIII, 43
Baker, George William, VIII, 44
Baker, Hugh Cossart, VIII, **43–45**; IX, 512
Baker, J. S., V, 689
Baker, James, XII, 466, 919
Baker, John (agent of John HILL, d. 1841), VII, 406
Baker, John (defendant), VII, 331; IX, 220
Baker, John (merchant), XII, 1121
Baker, John (of Newfoundland), IV, 784
Baker, John (son of Mrs Dorinda Baker), V, 389
Baker, John Carpenter, XI, 296; XII, 287
Baker, Loran Ellis, XII, **50–51**
Baker, Mary Eliza. *See* Bond
Baker, Mary Isabel. *See* Creighton
Baker, Olive (Hornor), VI, 330
Baker, Samuel (creditor of John YOUNG, d. 1819) V, 879, 881
Baker, Samuel (provisioner), III, 585
Baker, Sarah. *See* Mallory
Baker, Simon, V, 389
Baker, Sophia (Girouard), XI, 350
Baker, Susannah. *See* Rice
Baker, William (father of CHARLES), VI, 30
Baker, William (merchant), III, 585, 586
Baker, William (son of CHARLES), VI, 31
Balcarres, Earl of. *See* Lindsay
Balch, A. P., VIII, 965
Balcomb. *See* Bolscomb
Baldwin, Alice, VII, 36
Baldwin, Annie Jane. *See* Lee
Baldwin, Augusta Elizabeth. *See* Sullivan
Baldwin, Augusta Elizabeth (Ross), VIII, 58; X, 632
Baldwin, Augusta Mary Melissa. *See* Jackson
Baldwin, Augustus Warren, VII, 42, 439; VIII, 11, 29, 847, 848; IX, **24–25**, 400, 535, 542
Baldwin, Barbara. *See* Spread
Baldwin, Barbara (Sullivan), VIII, 58, 845
Baldwin, Connell James, VII, 661; IX, **25–26**
Baldwin, David, V, 681
Baldwin, Elizabeth. *See* MacDougall
Baldwin, Esther (McQuesten), XI, 583
Baldwin, George R., XII, 86
Baldwin, Henry (friend of James HASKINS), VII, 389, 390
Baldwin, Henry (grandfather of WILLIAM HENRY), XII, 51
Baldwin, Henry (son of WILLIAM WARREN), VII, 36; VIII, 45
Baldwin, Henry (uncle of WILLIAM HENRY), XII, 51
Baldwin, Henry Porter, XI, 10
Baldwin, Herbert, IX, 25
Baldwin, Isabella. *See* Gilley
Baldwin, James, IX, 25
Baldwin, John Spread, VI, 624; VII, 506, 716, 717; VIII, 8, 846; IX, 24, 647, 661, 745
Baldwin, Margaret Phœbe. *See* Willcocks
Baldwin, Mary. *See* O'Connell
Baldwin, Mary. *See* Sprague
Baldwin, Mary (Sherwood), X, 651
Baldwin*, Maurice Scollard (1836–1904), X, 209
Baldwin, Patrick (Peter), XII, 51
Baldwin, Peter, XII, 52

Baldwin, Phoebe. *See* Willcocks
Baldwin, Phœbe Maria, VIII, 58
Baldwin, Quetton St George, VIII, 45
Baldwin, Robert (grandfather of ROBERT), VI, 721; VII, 35, 36; IX, 24
Baldwin, Robert (son of ROBERT), VIII, 47, 58, 290
Baldwin, Robert, VI, 12, 45, 165, 188, 468; VII, 32, 35, 36, 37, 39, 40, 41, 42, 43, 44, 158, 162, 163, 164, 227, 442, 460, 479, 550, 580, 604, 605, 606, 607, 638, 652, 664, 747, 756, 772, 773, 858, 860, 861, 896; VIII, 7, 22, 29, 30, **45–59**, 125, 135, 137, 138, 148, 203, 205, 230, 253, 254, 255, 256, 303, 370, 392, 427, 513, 523, 550, 553, 587, 602, 641, 643, 668, 687, 696, 698, 733, 790, 799, 846, 847, 848, 849, 850, 916, 926, 932, 933, 934, 959; IX, 24, 25, 55, 56, 58, 59, 71, 74, 83, 90, 100, 109, 139, 151, 190, 191, 211, 212, 230, 238, 244, 257, 267, 287, 323, 344, 346, 370, 371, 372, 373, 396, 411, 444, 445, 448, 449, 463, 469, 486, 490, 498, 501, 505, 506, 524, 525, 547, 575, 596, 635, 644, 645, 650, 661, 677, 680, 684, 685, 686, 687, 688, 690, 700, 702, 724, 725, 728, 735, 740, 741, 744, 762, 775, 776, 796, 804, 815, 819; X, 24, 62, 80, 81, 92, 93, 94, 95, 109, 110, 119, 124, 125, 126, 127, 132, 133, 134, 143, 160, 169, 254, 255, 256, 257, 263, 299, 311, 312, 325, 343, 358, 359, 364, 365, 380, 398, 440, 442, 462, 463, 465, 466, 468, 512, 515, 584, 610, 618, 622, 623, 632, 642, 705, 706, 708, 714; XI, 35, 41, 60, 98, 127, 132, 150, 160, 179, 180, 206, 238, 273, 281, 282, 286, 405, 407, 408, 409, 410, 411, 412, 413, 415, 517, 518, 541, 618, 640, 680, 698, 713, 714, 730, 786, 825, 845, 908, 914, 927; XII, 43, 71, 146, 349, 473, 593, 967, 1107, 1130
Baldwin, William Augustus, VIII, 58; IX, 25; XII, 672
Baldwin, William Henry, VIII, 93; XI, 264; XII, **51–52**
Baldwin, William Warren, V, 521, 858, 860; VI, 4, 57, 79, 407, 416, 543, 544, 624, 647, 670; VII, **35–44**, 286, 367, 368, 378, 442, 457, 459, 479, 716, 753, 860, 865, 896; VIII, 6, 7, 45, 46, 48, 281, 602, 642, 643, 697, 733, 846, 847, 885, 932; IX, 24, 100, 139, 230, 513, 520, 684, 685, 686, 724, 789, 790; X, 61, 344, 618, 705; XI, 407, 517; XII, 43, 672
Baldwin, William Willcocks, VIII, 58
Baldwyn, William Devereux, VIII, 25
Balenden, Eliza (Bannatyne), VIII, 60; XI, 44
Baley. *See also* Bailey
Baley, Henry, I, 308, 611; II, **41–42**, 203, 231, 266, 267, 311, 319, 395, 406, 407
Baley, Judith (wife of HENRY), II, 42
Balfour, Ann. *See* Emray
Balfour, David, XII, 52
Balfour, George, III, 71
Balfour, Henry, III, 262
Balfour, James, V, **52–53**, 492
Balfour, Janet. *See* Douglas
Balfour, John, VIII, 790
Balfour, John Hutton, VIII, 62; XII, 539, 540, 541, 542
Balfour, Josephine. *See* Brodhead
Balfour, Katherine Jane (Ellice), IX, 238
Balfour, William Douglas, XII, **52–53**
Balkwill, John, IX, 436
Balkwill, William, IX, 436
Ball, Sir Alexander John, V, 53
Ball, Anna. *See* Coutts
Ball, Mrs Betsy, V, 678

Ball, Catherine (Carleton; Skelton), V, 141, 155
Ball, Emma Wilder (Dyas), XII, 286
Ball, Henry Maynard, IX, 82; XI, 845; XII, 450
Ball, Ingram, IV, 523; V, **53–54**, 204, 634, 766; VI, 213, 535
Ball, John (official), X, 81; XI, 662
Ball, John (preacher), IV, 515, 627; V, 341
Ball, Joseph (nephew of John PLAW), V, 678
Ball, Joseph (surveyor general), XI, 940
Ball, Margaret. *See* Childs
Ball, Mary. *See* Dickerson
Ball, Robert, V, 53
Ball, Victoria (Ramage), V, 705
Ballaine, Esther Maria (Marshall), IX, 536
Ballaine, John, VII, 589; IX, 536
Ballantyne, Alexander, XII, 53
Ballantyne, Anne Randall Scott. *See* Grant
Ballantyne, Duncan Stephen, VIII, 571
Ballantyne, James, XII, 53
Ballantyne, Jane Dickson. *See* Grant
Ballantyne, Robert Michael, XII, **53–54**, 334, 876
Ballard, Hannah (Moulton), III, 476
Ballard, Michael, V, 491
Ballenden, Anne Christie (McMurray), VIII, 573
Ballenden, Elizabeth. *See* Gray
Ballenden, Frances Isobel Simpson, VIII, 574
Ballenden, Harriet (McKay), X, 475
Ballenden, John, VI, 17; VIII, 59, 412
Ballenden, John, VII, 777; VIII, **59–60**, 573, 574, 815; IX, 136, 663; X, 390; XI, 17, 139, 875; XII, 206
Ballenden, Sarah. *See* McLeod
Ballerini, Girolamo Pietro, XII, 819
Ballock, Jane (Wilmot), X, 710
Ballou, William T., XII, 784
Balls, Jemima Harris (Wetherald), XII, 1095
Balmer, Jennette Elizabeth (Cochrane), XII, 201
Balmes, Jaime Luciano, XII, 501
Balneavis, Jane (Pringle), IV, 647
Baltimore, Baron. *See* Calvert
Baltimore, Baroness. *See* Mynne
Balzac, Honoré de, X, 410; XI, 82, 181
Balzaretti, Émilie (Blanchet), XI, 85
Balzaretti, Giovanni Domenico, VIII, 495
Bamford, Abigail. *See* Kirk
Bamford, Jane (wife of STEPHEN), VII, 44
Bamford, Margaret, VII, 44
Bamford, Stephen, VII, **44–45**
Bancker. *See* Banker
Bancroft, Charles, VI, 277, 279
Bancroft, Elizabeth Ann (Clement), XII, 322
Bancroft, George, IX, 250
Bancroft, Hubert Howe, XI, 18, 887, 888
Bancroft, Mary. *See* Foster
Bangs, Chauncey Ward, XII, 937
Bangs, Lemuel, IX, 26
Bangs, Mary. *See* Bolton
Bangs, Nathan, IV, 777; VI, 336, 670, 671, 674, 675; VII, 451; VIII, 132, 309; IX, **26–27**; XI, 317
Bangs, Rebecca. *See* Keeler
Banker (Bancker), Evert, III, 56
Bankhead, Charles, VII, 250
Banks, Dorothea, Lady Banks. *See* Weston-Hugessen
Banks, James, X, 49

Banks, Sir Joseph, IV, 156, 218, 536, 601, 747, 762; V, **54–56**, 71, 166, 167, 502, 581; VI, 317, 549, 550; VII, 414, 599, 830, 865; VIII, 771; IX, 160, 658
Banks, Maud Mary (Burn), XII, 141
Banks, Sarah. *See* Bate
Banks, William, V, 54
Bannatyne, Andrew Graham Ballenden, VIII, 574; XI, **44–47**, 52, 79, 325, 538, 546, 743, 842; XII, 82, 132, 280, 370
Bannatyne, Annie. *See* McDermot
Bannatyne, Eliza. *See* Balenden
Bannatyne, James, XI, 44
Bannatyne, Laurenda (Black), XI, 79
Bannatyne, Mary (Stark), IX, 741
Bannerman, Captain, III, 136
Bannerman, Sir Alexander, VII, 146; VIII, 485, 531, 532, 564, 863; IX, **27–31**, 192, 375, 393, 395, 403, 583, 584, 585, 606, 846; X, 141, 184, 185, 331, 352, 400, 588; XI, 243, 432, 465, 527, 615, 665, 881, 910; XII, 91, 162, 319, 425, 565, 589, 862
Bannerman, James, V, 560, 561
Bannerman, Margaret, Lady Bannerman. *See* Gordon
Bannerman, Thomas (father), IX, 27
Bannerman, Thomas, IX, 27
Bapst, Jean, XI, 109
Baptist (Battiste) (Jesuit novice), VIII, 654
Baptist, Alexander, X, 33, 34; XII, 451
Baptist, George, IX, 488; X, **32–34**, 490; XII, 451
Baptist, Helen Oliver (McDougall), X, 34
Baptist, Isabella. *See* Cockburn
Baptist, Isabella (Houliston), X, 34; XII, 451
Baptist, Jane (Mackay), X, 34
Baptist, John, X, 33
Baptist, Margaret (Pentland), X, 34
Baptist, Phillis (Dean), X, 34
Baptiste. *See also* Maisonnat
Baptiste, Jean, III, 452
Baquette, *dit* Lamontagne, Marie (Paquet, *dit* Lavallée), VIII, 680
Bar (Barre), François (de). *See* Bigot, François (d. 1778)
Bar, Marguerite (Messier), II, 469
Barabé, Antoinette (Augé), IV, 34
Baraga, Frederic, VIII, 308; IX, **31–32**
Baraga, Johann Nepomuc, IX, 31
Baraga, Maria Katharina Josefa. *See* Jenčič
Barbarin, Arsène-Louis, IX, 632
Barbaucannes. *See* Énault
Barbe, Élisabeth (Hazeur), II, 276
Barbe, Jeanne. *See* Girardin
Barbé, Jeanne (Villain), I, 663
Barbe, Sylvain, II, 276
Barbeau, Edmond-Julien, XII, 248
Barbeau, François, V, 622
Barbeau, Joseph, V, 622
Barbeau, Louis, VII, 395
Barbeau, Marie-Anne (Gauvreau), X, 302
Barbeau, Marie-Louise. *See* Fluette
Barbeau*, Marius (1883–1969), VI, 231; X, 412, 413; XII, 105, 552
Barbeau, *dit* Lucault, Barbe. *See* Poisson
Barbeau, *dit* Lucault, Léonard, I, 230; II, 164
Barbeau, *dit* Lucault, Marie (Cuillerier), II, 164; III, 155
Barbée. *See* Barbet

Barbel, Catherine. *See* Provost
Barbel, Charles, II, 42
Barbel, Jacques, II, xxiii, xxiv, **42–44**, 58, 256, 325, 521; III, 78, 224, 299, 498, 642; IV, 44, 263
Barbel, Jacques-François, IV, 678
Barbel, Louise-Renée. *See* Toupin
Barbel, Marie-Anne. *See* Le Picard
Barbel, Marie-Anne (Fornel), III, 154, 224, 282; IV, **44–45**, 66, 386; V, 277, 576
Barbel, Marie-Madeleine. *See* Amiot
Barbequière, Jeanne (Dudevant), IV, 234
Barbequière, Louis-Hyacinthe, IV, 234
Barber, Anna, X, 34
Barber, Asahel, XII, 54
Barber, George Anthony, X, **34–35**, 599; XII, 101
Barber, Jonathan, XI, 286
Barber, Lucinda. *See* Shortiss
Barber, Mary (Dunkin), XI, 286
Barber, Polly. *See* Armes
Barber, Polly (Scovill), XII, **54–55**
Barber, William, XI, 153
Barbet (Barbée), Marie-Charlotte (Michaux), V, 592
Barbeyrac, Adèle de (Quetton de St Georges), VI, 622
Barbier, Catherine. *See* La Vau
Barbier, Elizabeth. *See* Cairns
Barbier, Elizabeth. *See* Walker
Barbier, Gilbert, known as Le Minime, I, 230; II, 44
Barbier, Josephte. *See* Tellier
Barbier, Jules, XII, 316, 471, 533
Barbier, Louis-Marie-Raphaël, VII, 527; VIII, **60–61**; XII, 257
Barbier, Marie, named de l'Assomption, I, 117; II, **44–45**, 132, 249, 378; III, 385; IV, 529
Barbier, Raphaël, VIII, 60
Barbocant. *See* Énault
Barbour, Margaret Nelson. *See* Brown
Barbreck. *See* Campbell
Barbu. *See* Kamīyistowesit
Barçalo. *See* Barsalou
Barcelo, Jacob, X, 438
Barcelo, Luce. *See* Dorion
Barcelo, Luce (Lemaire), X, 438
Barcelos, Pedro de, I, 234, 305
Barclay, Agnes. *See* Cosser
Barclay, Anthony, VIII, 882
Barclay, Archibald, VIII, 580, 818
Barclay, George, VIII, 61
Barclay, George, VII, 596; VIII, **61**
Barclay, Henry (clergyman), III, 323; IV, 586
Barclay, Henry (father of THOMAS HENRY), VI, 33
Barclay, Janet. *See* Tullis
Barclay, John (clergyman), IX, 461; XII, 616
Barclay, John (merchant), IV, 286
Barclay, John (professor), XI, 271
Barclay, John, VI, **31–33**, 480; VII, 45, 370; VIII, 645; IX, 495
Barclay, Margaret (Wood), VII, 919
Barclay, Mary. *See* Rutgers
Barclay, Peter, VI, 31; VII, 45
Barclay, Robert (brewer), VI, 551, 552, 553
Barclay, Robert (merchant), IV, 286
Barclay, Robert Heriot, V, 696, 748, 799, 875, 876; VI, 309, 617, 661, 803, 817; VII, **45–47**, 709; VIII, 100

Barclay, Susan. *See* DeLancey
Barclay, Thomas Henry, IV, 604; V, 106, 574, 874; VI, **33–36**, 142, 790; VII, 87, 866; VIII, 274, 752
Barclay, William, VIII, 61
Bárdarson. *See* Herjólfr; Ivar
Bardin, Étienne, Baron de Bardin, IX, 772
Bardin, Susanna (Palmer), VI, 565
Bardou, Anselme (Ignace), I, 55, 312, 420; II, 344
Bardy, Jules-Édouard, IX, 204
Bardy, Louise. *See* Cochy, *dit* Lacouture
Bardy, Marie-Marguerite. *See* Archambault
Bardy, Marie-Soulange. *See* Lefebvre
Bardy, Marie-Virginie-Célina (Valin), IX, 32; XII, 1071
Bardy, Mathieu, IX, 32
Bardy, Pierre, IX, 32
Bardy, Pierre-Martial, VII, 61; IX, **32–33**; XI, 484; XII, 1072
Barelli, John, VII, 542
Barette, Guillaume, IV, 720
Barford, Mary (Mortimer), VII, 634, 635
Bargus, Thomas, IX, 138
Barham, Baron. *See* Middleton; Noel
Barham, Richard Harris, IX, 350
Bariac, Marguerite (Berthier), II, 59
Baring, Alexander, 1st Baron Ashburton, VIII, 157, 401; X, 483
Barker. *See also* Berker
Barker, Abraham, VIII, 836
Barker, Andrew, I, 74
Barker, Bethiah (Johnson; Winslow), IV, 774
Barker, Edward John, VI, 220; VIII, 24, 552, 761; XI, **47–49**; XII, 990
Barker, Elizabeth. *See* Phillips
Barker, Elizabeth Mary (Collyer; wife of WILLIAM), XII, 55, 56
Barker, Ellen. *See* Griffiths
Barker, Emma Eliza (Driver), XII, 55
Barker*, Sir Frederick Eustache (1838–1915), XII, 341
Barker, Hannah (Noble), V, 627
Barker, Jacob, IV, 389; VII, 120
Barker, Jane. *See* Brighton
Barker, Jane. *See* Young
Barker, John (brother-in-law of Robert HAYMAN), I, 365
Barker, John (uncle of EDWARD JOHN), XI, 48
Barker, Joseph, V, 627
Barker, Llewellys Franklin, XII, 384
Barker, Margaret. *See* Greenwood
Barker, Mary Spafford (Smith; Coy), VII, 215
Barker, Nancy (Tillson), IX, 789
Barker, Phoebe (Stevenson), VIII, 836
Barker, Robert, VI, 257
Barker, Samuel, XII, 55
Barker, William, XI, 47
Barker, William, XII, **55–56**
Barkley, Charles, VI, 36
Barkley, Charles William, IV, 498; VI, **36–37**
Barkley, Frances Hornby. *See* Trevor
Barley (Barlow). *See* Berley
Barlow*, Alfred Ernest (1861–1914), XI, 50
Barlow, Bradley, XI, 813
Barlow, Eliza Hoosse. *See* Morris
Barlow, Ezekiel (father), VII, 47

Barlow, Ezekiel, VII, 47
Barlow, John Rigney, XI, 50
Barlow, Richard, IV, 300
Barlow, Robert, XI, **49–50**
Barlow, Roger, I, 156
Barlow, Scott, XI, 49, 50
Barlow, Thomas, VII, 47
Barlow, Thomas, VII, **47–48**
Barlow, William, VI, 696, 697
Barnabé. *See* Martin
Barnabo, Alessandro, IX, 343; X, 251; XI, 694; XII, 1017, 1018
Barnaby, Eliza Irene (Rand), XII, 879
Barnaby, Thomas, VII, 204
Barnard, Alice (Mara), XI, 50
Barnard, Amélie. *See* Chapais
Barnard, Anna. *See* Woodbury
Barnard, Anne (Fox), I, 311
Barnard, Catherine. *See* Telfer
Barnard, Edmund, XI, 755; XII, 57
Barnard, Édouard-André, X, 15; XII, **57–60**, 758
Barnard, Edward, XI, 657; XII, 57, 66
Barnard, Ellen. *See* Stillman
Barnard, Esther. *See* Travis
Barnard, Francis Jones, XI, **50–52**; XII, 784
Barnard*, Sir Frank Stillman (1856–1936), XI, 50, 51
Barnard*, George Henry (1868–1954), XI, 50
Barnard, Isaac Jones, XI, 50
Barnard, John (deacon), III, 26
Barnard, John (father of JOHN), III, 25
Barnard, John, III, **25–26**
Barnard, Margaret. *See* Berkley
Barnard, Margaret. *See* Whitney
Barnard, Mathilde. *See* Blondin
Barnard, Sarah (Burwell), VII, 124
Barnard, W. S., XI, 285
Barnard, William, IV, 501
Barnardo, Thomas John, XII, 387
Barnes, Eliza (Case), VI, 336; VIII, 132, 133
Barnes, Elizabeth (Coffin), VII, 196, 198
Barnes, Eunice Alice. *See* Morris
Barnes, Hannah. *See* Butler
Barnes, Isabella. *See* Johnson
Barnes, Jane, V, 560; IX, 482
Barnes, John, V, **56–57**, 747
Barnes, Lawrence, XII, 258
Barnes, Mary Ann (Smith), XII, 975
Barnes, Richard, VII, **48–49**; VIII, 380; XI, 673
Barnes, William, VII, 48
Barnes, William M., XI, 4
Barnet. *See also* Carrihogo
Barnet, Elizabeth (MacLaren), XII, 664
Barnet, Jane (Munro), XI, 628
Barnhill, Rebecca (Dickie), XI, 262
Barnley, George, VII, 3, 4, 276; XII, 446, 931, 932
Barnoin, François de, I, 478
Barnsfare, Adam, IV, 548; V, 191
Barnston, Alexander, XII, 613
Barnston, Ellen. *See* Matthews
Barnston, George, VI, 219, 648; VII, 3; VIII, 61, 574; IX, 170; XI, 45, **52–53**; XII, 53, 198
Barnston, James, VIII, **61–62**, 405; XI, 52; XII, 540
Barnston, Johnston George Hillbride, XII, 613

Barnston, Maria Anne. *See* McDonald
Barnum, Phineas Taylor, IX, 475; XI, 865; XII, 386
Barolet, Claude, II, 129; III, 26, 35, 194; IV, 602
Barolet, Françoise. *See* Dumontier
Barolet, Françoise (Bedout), III, 26; V, 61
Barolet, Marie. *See* Dauteuil
Barolet, Marie-Louise (Panet), III, 26; IV, 602; V, 648; VI, 569, 571
Barolet, Pierre, III, 26
Barolette. *See* Papin
Baron. *See also* Hachin; Lupien
Baron, Le. *See* Le Baron
Baron, Catherine. *See* Hubert
Baron, Thomas, V, 322; VIII, 301
Barr, Elizabeth Wilkinson. *See* Tarbotton
Barr, Harriet. *See* Mallinson
Barr, Henry, XI, 146
Barr, John, XII, 62
Barr, Margaret (Lawrence), VII, 491
Barr, Margaret Robinson (Gwynne; Poor), X, 590
Barr, Robert, XII, **60–62**
Barr*, Robert (1850–1912), XII, 213
Barramollach, Mary Macalpine (Macallum), X, 451
Barrande, Joachim, X, 65
Barras, Pierre, XI, 208
Barrat, Barbe (Nouchet), III, 490
Barrat, Claude, II, **45**
Barrat, Jeanne. *See* Quisence
Barre, Sieur de (brother-in-law of François BIGOT, d. 1778), IV, 70
Barré, Charlotte, named de Saint-Ignace, I, 43, 208, 217, 230
Barré, Isaac, III, 672; IV, 571; V, 145
Barrell, John, IV, 291, 292
Barrell, Joseph, IV, 411; V, 387, 410, 411
Barrère, Rosalie (Maugenest), IV, 524
Barret, Norbert, IX, 64
Barrett, Alfred, VII, **49–50**; X, 404
Barrett, Elizabeth (Browning), VIII, 651
Barrett, Ellen. *See* McCallum
Barrett, Frances. *See* Scott
Barrett, J. T., XI, 116
Barrett*, John Kelly (b. 1850, d. in or after 1911), XII, 1012
Barrett, Mary (O'Connor), XI, 649
Barrett, Mary Ann Elizabeth. *See* Molson
Barrett, Michael, XI, 53
Barrett, Michael, XI, **53–54**; XII, 10, 11
Barrett, Robert G., XII, 43
Barrett, William, VIII, 969
Barrett, Wilson (William Henry), XII, 668, 669
Barrette, Marie-Josephte (Viau), VII, 885
Barrie, Dorothea. *See* Gardner
Barrie, Julia Wharton, Lady Barrie. *See* Ingilby
Barrie, Robert, VII, 50
Barrie, Sir Robert, VII, **50–52**, 214, 368, 410, 458, 747
Barrière, Marie (Lannelongue), III, 349
Barrin de La Galissonière, Catherine. *See* Bégon
Barrin de La Galissonière, Marie-Catherine-Antoinette, Marquise de La Galissonière. *See* Lauson
Barrin de La Galissonière, Roland, III, 26, 57
Barrin de La Galissonière, Roland-Michel, Marquis de La Galissonière, II, 595; III, 22, **26–32**, 49, 57, 92, 99,

231, 253, 261, 320, 322, 375, 401, 554, 564, 570, 610, 628, 675, 678, 680; IV, 63, 76, 143, 145, 147, 169, 187, 226, 256, 289, 365, 407, 449, 456, 633, 636, 661, 666; V, 176
Barrington, Charles, VIII, 824
Barrington, Daines, V, 221
Barrington, John, III, 295
Barrington, Samuel, V, 220, 221
Barrington, William Wildman, 2nd Viscount Barrington, IV, xxxvii
Barrois. *See* Lothman
Barron. *See also* Lupien
Barron, Ann (Baker), VI, 30
Barron, Catherine-Charlotte. *See* Saveuse de Beaujeu
Barron, Edward, VI, 30
Barron, Frederick William, XII, 514
Barron, Hughes E., IX, 61
Barron, Thomas, V, 322; VII, 746
Barrow, Henry, I, 390
Barrow, Isabella (Hicks), XII, 431
Barrow, Sir John, VII, 115, 323, 324; VIII, 671, 683, 771, 772, 773, 774; IX, 161; XI, 544
Barroy, Anna, II, 376
Barruel, Augustin de, IV, 502
Barry, Alexander, VII, 52
Barry, Sir Charles, XI, 225; XII, 885
Barry, David, VI, 166
Barry, Sir David, X, 660
Barry, Eliza J. *See* Mercier
Barry, James, IX, 33
Barry, James, IX, **33–34**; XI, 148
Barry, John (agent of John HILL, d. 1841), VII, 406
Barry, John (clergyman), VIII, 67
Barry, John (father of ROBERT), VII, 52
Barry, John Alexander, VI, 62; VII, 52, 416; IX, 710; X, **35–36**
Barry, Mary. *See* Black
Barry, Mary. *See* Jessop
Barry, P. J. S., IX, 294
Barry, Robert, VII, **52–53**; X, 35
Barry, Sophia. *See* Pernette
Barry, Thomas, V, 724
Barry, Thomas F., XII, 954, 955
Barsalou, Arthur, XII, 62
Barsalou, Élisabeth. *See* Urtebise
Barsalou, Érasme, XII, 63
Barsalou, François, VIII, 471
Barsalou, Geneviève. *See* Bouchard, *dit* Dorval
Barsalou, Gérard, II, 173; III, 88, 270, 523; IV, 46
Barsalou, Hector, XII, 63
Barsalou, Jean-Baptiste, III, 88, 270; IV, **45–46**
Barsalou, Jean-François, IV, 46; V, 322
Barsalou, Joseph (brother of JEAN-BAPTISTE), IV, 46
Barsalou, Joseph (father of JOSEPH), XII, 62
Barsalou, Joseph (great-nephew of JEAN-BAPTISTE), IV, 46
Barsalou, Joseph, XII, **62–64**
Barsalou, Julie-Adèle. *See* Gravel
Barsalou, Marie. *See* Beaupré
Barsalou, Marie-Catherine. *See* Legras
Barsalou, Marie-Jeanne. *See* Becquet
Barsalou, Maurice, XII, 63
Barss, Edward Collins, VIII, 63

Barss, Elizabeth. *See* Crowell
Barss, Hannah, VI, 412
Barss, James, VI, 37; VIII, 62
Barss, John, VI, 37; VII, 681; VIII, **62–63**
Barss, Joseph, VI, 37; VII, 681; VIII, 62
Barss, Joseph, VI, **37–38**; VII, 217; VIII, 62; IX, 710
Barss, Olivia. *See* DeWolf
Barss, Rebecca. *See* Gammon
Barss, Sarah. *See* Collins
Bartaud, Anne (Bouillet de La Chassaigne), II, 87
Barthe, Charles, IV, 204
Barthe*, Émilie (Lavergne) (d. 1930), XII, 65
Barthe, Georges-Isidore, VIII, 458; X, 505; XI, 12, 811; XII, **64–65**, 67, 297, 451
Barthe, Jean-Baptiste, V, 129; VII, 735
Barthe, Joseph, XII, 64, 65
Barthe, Joseph-Guillaume, VII, 502, 836, 880, 881; VIII, 262, 420, 493, 736; IX, 614, 805; X, 337, 555, 581; XI, 27, 36, 37, 343, 657; XII, 64, **65–68**, 846
Barthe, Joséphine-Charlotte. *See* Meilleur
Barthe, Louise-Adélaïde. *See* Pacaud
Barthe, Louise-Françoise. *See* Poisset
Barthe, Marie-Archange (Askin), V, 39
Barthe, Marie-Louise-Esther. *See* Tapin
Barthe, René, XII, 65, 451
Barthe, Thaddée-Alexis, XII, 64, 65
Barthe, Thérèse (Grant), V, 363, 366, 367
Barthélemy, I, **79**; II, 124
Barthélemy, Michel, I, 126, 127, 647; II, **45–46**, 191, 241
Bartholdy. *See* Mendelssohn-Bartholdy
Bartholomy, Néron, V, 385
Bartlet, Smith, VII, 228, 229
Bartlett, Ann (mother of WILLIAM HENRY), VIII, 63
Bartlett, James, XII, 3
Bartlett*, John (1839–1927), XII, 123
Bartlett, John Sherren, VII, 286
Bartlett, Margaret (Taylor), VI, 755
Bartlett, Richard, VI, 755
Bartlett, Susanna. *See* Moon
Bartlett, William, VIII, 63
Bartlett, William Henry, VIII, **63–65**; IX, 850
Bartolozzi, Francesco, IV, 763; V, 382
Barton, Ann (Hayes), XI, 393
Barton, Françoise-Marthe (Chevalier), III, 121
Barton, Joseph, V, 669
Barton, Margaret (Cronyn), X, 205
Barton, Thomas, IV, 731
Bartram, John, III, 335, 606, 607; IV, 407
Bartzsch (Bartzch, de Bartzch, Debartzch), Dominicus, VII, 235
Bartzsch, Thérèse. *See* Filiau, *dit* Dubois
Barwick, John, VII, 863
Barwis, Thomas Shepard, XII, 864
Basaline, Elizabeth (Mackellar), IV, 500
Basing. *See* Paulet
Basque. *See also* Bastarache
Basque, John, X, 446
Basquet, Pierre (Peter Basket), VII, 204, 579; VIII, **65–66**
Basset, Bonaventure, I, 80
Basset, Catherine. *See* Gaudreau
Basset, David, I, 530; II, **46–47**
Basset, Jean, I, 79
Basset, Jean, II, **47**; III, 284

Basset, Marie. *See* Laverdure

Basset Des Lauriers, Bénigne, I, **79**, 80, 201, 225, 230, 266, 273, 465, 498, 557; II, xvi, xvii, 111, 192, 276, 377, 469, 470

Basset Des Lauriers, Jeanne. *See* Vauvilliers

Basset Du Tartre, Vincent, I, **79–80**

Bastarache, Jean-Baptiste, V, 57

Bastarache, Pierre, V, 57, 58

Bastarache, *dit* Basque, Marguerite. *See* Gaudet

Bastarache, *dit* Basque, Michel, V, **57–58**

Bastarache, *dit* Le Basque, Marguerite. *See* Forest

Bastarache, *dit* Le Basque, Pierre, V, 57

Bastard, Hélène (Révol), III, 554

Bastide, John Henry, III, **32–34**, 507, 532, 645; IV, 93, 314, 500; VI, 193

Bastien. *See* Rocan

Bastien-Lepage, Jules, XII, 287, 831

Bastille. *See* Le Breton-Bastille

Batailler, Angélique. *See* Roy

Batailler, Catherine (Paradis), II, 508

Batailler, Pierre, II, 508

Bâtard, Étienne (Anthony), III, **34–35**, 136, 298

Bâtard Flamand. *See* Flemish Bastard

Batchelor, George, IX, 193, 211

Bate, Gerardine (Macpherson), VIII, 649, 651

Bate, Sarah (Banks), V, 54

Bateman-Hanbury, Elizabeth Augusta (Warburton; Rushout, Baroness Northwick), VIII, 921

Bateman-Hanbury, William, 1st Baron Bateman, VIII, 921

Bates, Abigail. *See* Lyon

Bates, Ann (Herbert), VII, 396

Bates, Anna Haining. *See* Swan

Bates, Joanna (Dibblee), VI, 208

Bates, John, VII, 53

Bates, Joseph, XI, 516

Bates, Lucy (Martin; Smith; wife of WALTER), VII, 53

Bates, Martin Van Buren, XI, 865, 866

Bates, Sarah. *See* Bostwick

Bates, Walter, VII, **53–54**, 691

Bath, Tamar (Troop), XI, 888

Bathgate, Robert, XII, 39

Bathurst, Henry, X, 663

Bathurst, Henry, 1st Baron Apsley and 2nd Earl Bathurst, IV, 350; V, 479

Bathurst, Henry, 3rd Earl Bathurst, V, 268, 489, 490, 672, 673, 674, 882; VI, 32, 97, 98, 115, 117, 122, 126, 149, 163, 167, 196, 214, 359, 371, 410, 507, 513, 514, 527, 538, 542, 543, 567, 593, 594, 595, 596, 597, 613, 668, 692, 693, 706, 714, 715, 716, 724, 725, 726, 732, 744, 770, 801; VII, 10, 134, 152, 153, 189, 281, 286, 302, 304, 486, 546, 547, 548, 647, 724, 728, 729, 730, 741, 742, 743, 786, 787, 789, 843, 865, 878, 889, 913; VIII, xxiv, xxvii, xxviii, xxxii, 124, 165, 337, 340, 351, 460, 506, 507, 575, 576, 585, 596, 598, 599, 660, 706, 795, 813, 824, 826, 827, 844, 856, 859, 860; IX, 21, 133, 160, 174, 220, 221, 637, 669, 671, 672, 673, 757; X, 71

Batilly. *See* Margane

Batiscan (Batisquan), I, **80**, 222

Batoche. *See* Letendre

Batoni, Pompeo, III, 166

Batt, Isaac, III, 304, 595; IV, **46–48**, 156, 160; V, 450, 500

Batt, Sarah. *See* Fowler

Batt, Thomas, IV, 309, 723; V, 296

Battenotte, Louis, known as L'Assiniboine, X, 699, 700

Batteux, Charles, VI, 650

Batts, Elizabeth (Cook), IV, 163

Bau. *See* Ruau

Baubee. *See* Babie

Baucher, *dit* Morency, Sophie (Taché), IX, 775

Baudart de Vaudésir, Claude, Baron de Sainte-James, III, 142, 442; IV, 353

Baudeau, Pierre, II, **47–48**, 416, 594

Baudet, Marie-Anne (Desjardins de Lapérière), VI, 200; VII, 246

Baudin, Madeleine (Cugnet), III, 151

Baudin, Nicolas, V, 105, 593

Baudoin. *See also* Baudouin

Baudoin, Charles-Louis, III, 35

Baudoin, Françoise (Blais), IV, 71

Baudoin, Gervais, I, 81; III, **35**, 36

Baudoin, Jean, I, **80**, 577; II, 626; IV, xxiii

Baudoin, Madeleine (Ameau, *dit* Saint-Séverin), II, 16

Baudoin, Marie-Agathe (Martel), IV, 517

Baudoin, Marie-Thérèse. *See* Guyon Fresnay

Baudoin, Marthe. *See* Marcoux

Baudoin, Marthe (Pélissier), IV, 618

Baudouin, Anne. *See* Auber

Baudouin, Gervais, I, 80

Baudouin, Gervais, I, **80–81**; II, 286; III, 35, 36, 237, 344; IV, 618

Baudouin, Jeanne. *See* Desrues

Baudouin, Louis, III, 35

Baudouin, Marie-Anne. *See* Roussel

Baudouin, Marie-Anne (Hertel de Rouville), II, 286; III, 15, 35; IV, 343

Baudouin, Marie-Jeanne (Dizy, *dit* Montplaisir), II, 190

Baudouin, Marie-Madeleine (Lucas Dontigny; Dizy de Montplaisir), III, 187

Baudouin, Michel, I, 81; III, 35, **36**

Baudouin, René, II, 190; III, 187

Baudrand, Fleury, VIII, **66–67**; IX, 397

Baudrand, Jean-Fleury, VIII, 66

Baudrand, Madelaine. *See* Faure

Baudre, Julien, VIII, 66; XII, 187

Baudry. *See also* Beaudry

Baudry, Anne (Lefebvre de Bellefeuille), III, 372; IV, 445

Baudry, Catherine (Milly), III, 451

Baudry, Élisabeth. *See* Truteau

Baudry, Françoise (Rondeau), III, 567, 568

Baudry, Jean-Baptiste, II, 48

Baudry, Jeanne. *See* Mechin

Baudry, Louis, VIII, 433

Baudry, Madeleine (Puybarau de Maisonneuve; Tailhandier, *dit* La Beaume), II, 617

Baudry, Marie. *See* Archambault

Baudry, Marie-Joseph (Jobin), VIII, 433

Baudry, Marie-Victoire, named de la Croix, VII, **54**

Baudry, Pierre, III, 451

Baudry, Toussaint (father of MARIE-VICTOIRE), VII, 54

Baudry, Toussaint (partner of Nicolas PERROT), II, 517

Baudry, *dit* Des Butes, Claude-Charles, III, 37

Baudry, *dit* Des Butes, Guillaume, II, **48**; III, 36

Baudry, *dit* Des Butes, Jean, III, 37

Baudry, *dit* Des Butes, Jeanne. *See* Soullard
Baudry, *dit* Des Butes, René, III, 37
Baudry, *dit* Des Butes, Urbain, III, 37
Baudry, *dit* Desbuttes, *dit* Saint-Martin, Mary Archange (Mackintosh), VI, 473
Baudry, *dit* La Marche, Jeanne (Dugay), II, 202
Baudry, *dit* La Marche, Madeleine. *See* Boucher
Baudry, *dit* La Marche, Urbain, II, 48, 202; III, 37
Baudry, *dit* Saint-Martin (Baudry Desbuttes, Baudry Soulard), Jean-Baptiste, III, **36–37**
Baudry, *dit* Saint-Martin, Marie-Louise. *See* Doyon
Baudry de Lamarche, Jacques, II, **48**, 632
Bauffremont, Marquise de. *See* Courtenay
Bauffremont, Joseph de, Prince de Listenois, III, 93
Baugé, Marquis de. *See* Lascaris
Baudry, Marquise de. *See* Allègre
Baugé, Jeanne de (Le Royer de La Dauversière), I, 214
Baugy, Guillaume de, II, 48
Baugy, Louis-Henri de, known as Chevalier de Baugy, I, 178, 444; II, **48–49**, 488, 634
Baulos, Marie-Anne (Pascaud), IV, 605
Bauman, Joseph, VI, 235
Baussy. *See* Lambert
Bautron, Marie (Ouimet), VIII, 667
Bauvais, Jean-Baptiste, VII, 60
Bauvais, Marianne. *See* Lancto
Baüyn, Bonaventure, V, 680
Bauzhi-geezhig-waeshikum, VII, **54–55**, 871
Bavaria, Elector of. *See* Maximilian II Emanuel
Baveux, Jean-Claude, IX, 34
Baveux, Jean-Claude-Léonard, known as Jean-Claude Léonard, IX, **34**, 342; XII, 282
Baveux, Marie-Catherine. *See* Lefranc
Bavin, Thomas, I, 333
Bavis, Jean, I, 74
Bawerk. *See* Böhm-Bawerk
Baxter, Alexander, VI, 317
Baxter, Amelia (McMurray), XII, 680
Baxter, Eliza Jane (Sawyer), XI, 802
Baxter, Helen (Ferguson; McIntosh), VIII, 550
Baxter, Isabel (Mackenzie), VIII, 550; IX, 497
Baxter, Jane (McMurray), XI, 580
Baxter, Jemima Nicolina (King), XII, 491
Baxter, Joseph, II, 543, 668
Bayard, Edwin, IX, 35
Bayard, Frances Catherine. *See* Robertson
Bayard, Gertrude (Kemble), IV, 279
Bayard, Pierre-Terrail, IX, 35
Bayard, Robert, IX, **35**, 339
Bayard, Robertson, X, 679
Bayard, Samuel Vetch, VII, 587; IX, 35
Bayard, William, IX, 35
Baye de La Giraudière (La Girodière), Charles, I, 257
Bayer. *See also* Boyer
Bayer, Justina Sophia (Clark), V, 187
Bayfield, Eliza. *See* Petit
Bayfield, Fanny Amelia. *See* Wright
Bayfield, Henry Wolsey, VI, 193; VII, 51; VIII, 670, 900; XI, **54–57**, 799; XII, 962, 1130, 1131
Bayfield, John Wolsey, XI, 54
Bayle. *See also* Baile
Bayle, Mariette (Durieux), XII, 281
Bayley (Bayly). *See also* Baley

Bayley, Elizabeth Ann, named Mother Seton (Seton), VIII, 865; IX, 476
Bayly, Miss (Mansel, Lady Mansel; St Leger), IV, 694
Bayly, Charles, I, 39, 47, 49, 50, **81–84**, 107, 129, 226, 328, 337, 343, 396, 477, 518, 519, 553, 657, 666; II, 49, 487, 537
Bayly, Eliza Walters (Carter), XII, 161
Bayly, Fanny (Spilsbury), VI, 730
Bayly, Hannah (wife of CHARLES), I, 83, 84
Bayne, Daniel, III, **37–38**; IV, 194, 195, 599; VI, 89
Bayne, John, III, 38
Bayne, John, VIII, **67–69**, 716, 751, 829; IX, 742
Bayne, Kenneth, VIII, 67
Bayne, Margaret. *See* Hay
Bayne, William, V, 277
Baynes, Edith (Collins; mother of Sir ROBERT LAMBERT), IX, 35
Baynes, Edward, VI, 342, 557; VII, 897; IX, 264
Baynes, Frances, Lady Baynes. *See* Denman
Baynes, Sir Robert Lambert, IX, **35–36**; X, 244, 245; XII, 892
Baynes, Thomas, IX, 35
Bazaine, Achille, XII, 849
Bazalgette, Herbert Sawyer, IX, 37
Bazalgette, John, IX, **36–37**
Bazalgette, John Van Norden, IX, 37
Bazalgette, Louis, IX, 36
Bazalgette, Sarah Crawford Magdalen (wife of JOHN), IX, 36
Bazán. *See* Valdés
Bazette, Elizabeth (Dunn), VIII, 251
Bazil, Charlotte. *See* Duroy
Bazil, Louis, III, 38
Bazil, Louis, II, 43; III, **38–39**, 224, 281
Bazil, Marie-Madeleine. *See* Moreau
Bazin, Catherine (Gill), IX, 315
Bazin, François, XII, 532
Bazin, Louise (Amiot), III, 13
Bazin, Marie-Angélique (Berthelot Dartigny), V, 74; VII, 71
Bazin, Marie-Louise-Élizabeth (Taschereau), V, 793; VI, 750, 752
Bazin, Nicolas, XII, 846
Bazin, Pierre, V, 74
Bazire, Charles, I, 84
Bazire, Charles, I, **84–85**, 114, 238, 326; II, 16, 28, 29, 31, 174, 178, 375, 448, 533
Bazire, Geneviève. *See* Macard
Bazire, Jean, I, 84
Bazire, Jeanne. *See* Le Borgne
Bazire, Marie (Gaultier de Comporté), I, 84, 326; II, 576
Beach, Eleanor (Morrill), X, 534
Beach, John Joseph Billis, XII, 68
Beach, Maria. *See* Passmore
Beach, Nancy (Dibblee), VI, 208
Beach, Thomas Billis, X, 559; XII, **68–69**, 677, 678
Beaconsfield, Earl of. *See* Disraeli
Beadle, Irwin, XII, 771
Bead-way-way (Angelique McGulpin) (Bailly), VI, 29
Beaglehole, John Cawte, IV, 167, 746
Beale, Anthony, II, 10, **49–52**, 65, 232, 266, 311, 312, 313, 314, 319, 474, 602; III, 414, 415, 489
Beale, Frances, II, 51

Beale, Joanna (wife of ANTHONY), II, 51
Beale, Mary (wife of ANTHONY), II, 50
Beall, Joshua, III, 261
Beals, Experience (Gidney), XI, 347
Beamer. *See also* Beemer
Beamer, David, VII, 56
Beamer, Jacob R., VII, **55–56**, 405, 460; VIII, 27; X, 514; XII, 1079
Beamer, Joseph, VII, 55
Beamer (Beemer), Margaret (Burley), VI, 91
Beamer, Mary (mother of JACOB R.), VII, 55
Beamer, Mary (wife of JACOB R.), VII, 55
Beamish, Elizabeth (Murdoch), X, 539
Beamish, Harriet Jane Ott, X, 539
Beamish, Margaret Ott (Akins), XII, 13
Beamish, Thomas Ott, X, 539
Bean, John, III, **39**
Bean, Joseph, II, 664
Beanlands, Sophia Theresa. *See* Pemberton
Bear. *See* Le Pesant
Bear, Ambroise. *See* Saint-Aubin, Ambroise
Bear Back Bone, XII, 970
Bear Child. *See* Potts, Jerry
Beardmore, Charles, VIII, 646; X, 535
Beardsley, Anna (wife of JOHN), 59
Beardsley, Bartholomew Crannell, V, 60, 643, 673; VI, 247; VII, 369, 497; VIII, **69–70**
Beardsley, Catharine. *See* Brooks
Beardsley, Charles Edwin, VIII, 69
Beardsley, Gertrude. *See* Crannell
Beardsley, Hannah (Dibblee), V, 60
Beardsley, Horace Homer, VIII, 70
Beardsley, John, V, 58
Beardsley, John, V, 24, **58–60**; VIII, 69
Beardsley, John Davis, V, 60
Beardsley, Keziah. *See* Wheeler
Beardsley, Mary. *See* Jenkins
Beardsley, Samuel, IV, 108
Beardsley, Sylvia. *See* Punderson
Beardy. *See also* Kamīyistowesit
Beardy, James, XI, 436
Beare, James, I, **85–86**, 317
Bear Ghost. *See* Isapo-muxika; Kyi-i-staah
Béarn-Bonasse, Isabeau de (Abbadie de Saint-Castin, Baronne de Saint-Castin), II, 4
Bears, Nathan, IX, 481
Beasley, Catherine Priscilla (Ferrie), VIII, 293
Beasley, Henrietta. *See* Springer
Beasley, Henry, VII, 56
Beasley, Joanne (Cartwright), V, 167
Beasley, Maria. *See* Noble
Beasley, Richard, V, 440, 669, 724, 841; VI, 230, 722; VII, 37, **56–59**, 251, 378, 466, 475; VIII, 86, 87, 265, 293, 708, 945
Beasly, Jane (Lovell), XII, 569
Beaton. *See also* Bethune
Beaton, A. S., VIII, 526
Beaton, David, V, 101
Beaton, Eleanor (Bridgland), X, 90
Beaton, Elizabeth. *See* Bruce
Beatson, John (father), IV, 48
Beatson, John, IV, 48, 49; V, 617
Beatson, Patrick, IV, **48–49**; V, 283; XII, 51

Beatson, William, IV, 48, 49; V, 617
Beattie, John, XII, 745
Beattie, Mary (Easton), VI, 232
Beattie, William, VIII, 63, 64
Beatty, Eleanor. *See* Armstrong
Beatty, Frances. *See* Hughes
Beatty*, Henry (1834–1914), XII, 971
Beatty, Isabella Eliza. *See* Bowes
Beatty, James Hughes, XII, 69, 70
Beatty, John, X, 16
Beatty, William, XII, 69
Beatty, William, XII, **69–70**
Beatty*, William Henry (1835–1912), XI, 938
Beaty, James, XII, 71
Beaty, James, IX, 576; X, 43, 313; XI, 920; XII, 11, **71–74**, 292, 976
Beaty, John, XII, 71
Beaty, Robert (grandfather), XII, 71
Beaty, Robert, XII, 73
Beaty, Sarah Anne. *See* Armstrong
Beau*, Henri (1863–1949), XII, 171
Beaubassin. *See* Hertel; Leneuf
Beaubien. *See also* Cuillerier; Desrivières-Beaubien; Trottier
Beaubien, Alexis, VII, 59
Beaubien, Benjamin, VI, 126, 204; VII, 666; IX, 728; XII, 118
Beaubien, Caroline-Alix (Frémont), X, 37
Beaubien, Catherine-Élisabeth-Aglaé. *See* Chenet
Beaubien, Elizabeth. *See* Manseau
Beaubien, Jacques-Télesphore-Cléophas, XII, 937
Beaubien, Jean-Louis (clergyman), VI, 448; X, 36
Beaubien, Jean-Louis (father of PIERRE), XI, 57
Beaubien, Joseph-Octave, X, **36–37**
Beaubien, Louis, X, 36
Beaubien*, Louis (1837–1915), IX, 64; XI, 7, 8, 13, 58, 320; XII, 59, 60, 457
Beaubien, Marguerite. *See* Durocher
Beaubien, Marguerite, VII, **59–60**, 500; X, 107
Beaubien, Marie-Jeanne. *See* Manseau
Beaubien, Marie-Justine. *See* Casgrain
Beaubien, Pierre, VII, 25, 26; VIII, 210; IX, 555; X, 589; XI, **57–58**, 303
Beaubois, Nicolas-Ignace de, II, 41, 646; III, **39–41**, 382
Beauceron. *See* Riday-Beauceron; Ridday
Beauchamp, Viscount. *See* Seymour
Beauchamp, Angélique (Réaume), V, 710
Beauchamp, Élizabeth (Roy), VIII, 781
Beauché, *dit* Morency, Magdeleine (Tremblay), VIII, 892
Beauchemin. *See also* Picart
Beauchemin, André, XII, 132
Beauchemin, Charles-Odilon, XI, **58–59**; XII, 573
Beauchemin, Jean-Baptiste, XII, 132
Beauchemin, Joseph-Odilon, XI, 59
Beauchemin, Louise. *See* Valois
Beauchemin, Marie-Julie (Larocque de Rochbrune), XII, 530
Beauchêne. *See* Chevalier
Beauchesne, Arthur, XII, 180
Beauchesne, Pierre-Clovis, XII, 521
Beauclerk, Elizabeth Catherine, Duchess of St Albans. *See* Gubbins

Beauclerk, Laura Maria Theresa (Wentworth-Fitzwilliam, Lady Milton), X, 699
Beauclerk, Vere, 1st Baron Vere, III, 126, 323, 324; IV, 594, 595
Beaucour; Beaucourt. *See* Malepart
Beaucours. *See* Dubois
Beaudé*, Henri (Henri d'Arles) (1870–1930), X, 87
Beaudéduit, Alexandre-René, IV, 28
Beaudet, Élisée, XI, 774
Beaudet, Louis, IX, 120; XI, 83
Beaudet, Marie-Anne-Mathilde (Dunn), XI, 288
Beaudin, Marie-Catherine. *See* Vallée
Beaudin, Pierre, VIII, 500
Beaudoin, Marie-Angèle (Maranda), VII, 581
Beaudrieau, J.-Guillaume, X, 492
Beaudry. *See also* Baudry
Beaudry, Caroline (Beaudry), X, 37
Beaudry, Desanges (Benoît, *dit* Livernois), IX, 47
Beaudry, Félicité. *See* Dubreuil
Beaudry, Jean-Baptiste, XI, 59
Beaudry, Jean-Louis, VIII, 667; X, 219, 625, 717; XI, **59–62**, 235, 336, 756, 763
Beaudry, Joseph-Ubalde, X, 37
Beaudry, Joseph-Ubalde, X, **37–38**, 59, 135, 434, 533, 620; XI, 103, 250, 253, 721
Beaudry, Louis, X, 37
Beaudry, Marguerite (Pillard), III, 521
Beaudry, Marie-Anne. *See* Bogennes
Beaudry, Marie-Anne (Vinet), IX, 616
Beaudry, Marie-Josephte (Papineau), VII, 673
Beaudry, Pierre, VIII, 240
Beaudry, Pierre-J., VIII, 504
Beaudry, Pierre-Janvier, X, 37
Beaudry, Prudent, XI, 59
Beaudry, Thérèse. *See* Vallée
Beauffremont, Marquise de. *See* Courtenay
Beaufort. *See also* Havard
Beaufort, Duc de. *See* Bourbon
Beaufort, Monsieur (steward), II, 116
Beaufort, Daniel Augustus, X, 104
Beaufort, Sir Francis, IX, 659; X, 42; XI, 198, 199, 544
Beaugny (Beaunier), Éléonore-Jeanne de (Le Poupet de La Boularderie), IV, 468
Beaugrand*, Honoré (1848–1906), VII, 514; XI, 62, 186, 330, 480; XII, 99, 308, 362, 530, 722, 723
Beaugrand, Simon, V, 436, 727
Beauharnais de Miramion, Marie de. *See* Bonneau de Rubelles
Beauharnois, Marquise de. *See* Pays
Beauharnois, Anne de (Phélypeaux de Pontchartrain), III, 51
Beauharnois, Claude-Charles de, III, 47
Beauharnois de Beaumont, Claude de, II, 52
Beauharnois de Beaumont et de Villechauve, Claude de, II, **52–53**; III, 42, 50
Beauharnois de Beaumont et de Villechauve, Renée de. *See* Hardouineau
Beauharnois de Beauville, Guillaume de, II, 52
Beauharnois de La Boische, Charles de, Marquis de Beauharnois, II, 35, 52, 66, 91, 126, 147, 156, 209, 210, 211, 239, 253, 269, 284, 301, 316, 317, 327, 333, 346, 358, 389, 390, 433, 457, 503, 520, 530, 531, 580, 632, 665; III, 7, 13, 14, 15, 16, 24, 26, 27, 38, **41–51**, 52, 56, 57, 74, 75, 81, 99, 107, 114, 115, 117, 118, 119, 135, 150, 153, 154, 161, 162, 168, 178, 179, 202, 203, 223, 234, 238, 239, 240, 242, 246, 249, 250, 251, 252, 253, 284, 312, 328, 339, 340, 341, 349, 351, 352, 353, 354, 355, 359, 374, 375, 384, 412, 422, 431, 434, 450, 451, 482, 486, 491, 492, 495, 550, 551, 563, 569, 570, 579, 584, 585, 603, 604, 612, 617, 621, 623, 631, 646, 647, 650, 675; IV, 11, 56, 76, 143, 153, 177, 220, 221, 236, 265, 284, 289, 305, 318, 319, 355, 356, 358, 360, 361, 362, 363, 364, 376, 424, 425, 440, 458, 463, 464, 465, 488, 601, 611, 612, 617, 633, 636, 651, 663, 666, 667, 728, 783; V, 791
Beauharnois de La Boische, François de, II, 52; III, 41, 51
Beauharnois de La Boische, Jeanne-Élisabeth de (Bégon de La Picardière), II, 52; III, 51, 57, 61
Beauharnois de La Boische, Marguerite-Françoise de. *See* Pyvart de Chastullé
Beauharnois de La Boische, Renée de, Marquise de Beauharnois. *See* Pays
Beauharnois de La Boische et de La Chaussée, François de, III, 50
Beauharnois de La Boische et de La Chaussée, Marie-Anne de. *See* Pyvart de Chastullé
Beauharnois de La Chaussaye, Anne de, Baronne de Beauville. *See* Desgrez
Beauharnois de La Chaussaye, François de, Baron de Beauville, II, 39, 52, 70, 74, 147, 155, 190, 201, 226, 374, 387, 409, 410, 426, 448, 484, 488, 509, 521, 555, 557, 578, 604; III, 42, **51–54**, 57, 433, 512; IV, 355
Beauharnois de Villechauve, François de, II, 52
Beaujeu. *See also* Le Gallois; Liénard; Saveuse
Beaujeu, Monongahéla de, IX, 703
Beaujot, Jean, I, 311
Beaujour. *See* Delestre
Beaulac. *See* Hertel
Beaulieu. *See also* Gourdeau; Hudon-Beaulieu; Le Gay; Sarrebource
Beaulieu, Étienne, X, 38
Beaulieu, François, X, **38**
Beaulieu, Jacques, X, 38
Beaulieu, Jean-Baptiste, IX, 123
Beaumanoir. *See* Duclos
Beaumarchais. *See* Caron
Beaumarchais, Sieur de. *See* Juchereau de Saint-Denys, Charles
Beaumont. *See also* Beauharnois; Couillard
Beaumont, Elizabeth (Broke), VII, 106
Beaumont, Henry, XII, 131
Beaumont, Marie-Barbe de. *See* Le Prince
Beaumont, William, XI, 414
Beaumont, William Rawlins, VIII, 749, 869, 933, 934; IX, 707; X, **38–39**
Beaumouchel. *See* Estimauville
Beaune (Bône), Marie-Anne (Cirier), IV, 151
Beaunier. *See* Beaugny
Beaupoil, Jean de, Marquis de Saint-Aulaire, VI, 619, 620
Beaupré. *See also* Bonhomme
Beaupré, Baron de. *See* Choiseul
Beaupré, Vicomte de. *See* Des Granches
Beaupré, Benjamin, VII, 757
Beaupré, Élise (Rodier), VII, 757
Beaupré, Joséphine (Archambault), X, 16

Beaupré, Julie. *See* Mercier
Beaupré, Marie (Barsalou), XII, 62
Beaupré, Marie-Darie (Martel), XII, 699
Beaupré, Marie-Louise (Confoulan; Masson), X, 500
Beauregard. *See also* Boudier; Jarret
Beauregard, Barthélemy de, I, 533; II, 182
Beaurivage. *See* Rageot
Beauséjour. *See* Godin
Beausoleil. *See also* Brossard; Rousseau
Beausoleil, Célestin, X, 545
Beausoleil*, Cléophas (1845–1904), XI, 891, 893; XII, 722, 724
Beaussier, Claire. *See* Portanier
Beaussier, Louis, III, 54
Beaussier de Lisle, Louise-Françoise. *See* Jouenne de Lorière
Beaussier de Lisle, Louis-Joseph, III, **54–55**, 293
Beauvais. *See also* Legardeur
Beauvais, Étiennette (Pottier), II, 528
Beauvais, Susan (Auldjo), VII, 28
Beauvais, *dit* Saint-James, René, VI, 227, 626; VII, **60–61**, 685, 686; VIII, 38, 763; IX, 126
Beauval. *See* Durand
Beauville. *See* Beauharnois
Beauville, Baron de. *See* Beauharnois
Beauville, Baronne de. *See* Desgrez
Beauvillier, Paul de, Duc de Saint-Aignan, II, 104
Beauvoir Du Roure de Combalet, Marie-Madeleine de. *See* Vignerot
Beavan, Emily Elizabeth. *See* Shaw
Beavan, Frederick William Cadwallader, VII, 792
Beaven, Elizabeth Speed. *See* Frowd
Beaven, James, VIII, 95; X, **39–40**, 270; XI, 942
Beaven, Mary (mother of JAMES), X, 39
Beaven*, Robert (1836–1920), X, 40; XI, 33, 435, 840; XII, 240
Beaven, Samuel, X, 39
Beaver, Herbert, X, 240; XII, 441
Beawando. *See* Atecouando (fl. 1701–26)
Bebee, Amasa, VIII, 206, 207
Bécancour. *See* Robinau
Bécart de Granville, Jean-Baptiste, II, 53
Bécart de Granville, Louis, II, 53
Bécart de Granville, Marie-Anne. *See* Macard
Bécart de Granville, Pierre (father), I, 387; II, 53, 213, 296, 410, 532, 533; III, 55
Bécart de Granville, Pierre, III, 55
Bécart de Granville et de Fonville, Charles, II, **53**, 410; III, 55
Bécart de Granville et de Fonville, Paul, III, **55–56**, 374
Bécasseau, Gabrielle (Gobin), II, 251, 522
Béchard, Auguste, XI, 903
Béchard, Rémi, XI, 175
Becher, Alexander, XI, 62
Becher, Caroline. *See* Street
Becher, Frances. *See* Scott
Becher, Henry Corry Rowley, VIII, 749; IX, 323, 324, 475; XI, **62–63**
Becher, Sarah Evanson. *See* Leonard
Bechourat. *See* Begourat
Bechtel, Jacob, VIII, 86, 87
Beck. *See also* Beke

Beck, Adam, VIII, 447
Beck*, Sir Adam (1857–1925), X, 375; XII, 1095
Beck, Pierre, X, 53
Beck, Thomas, VII, 508, 597, 598, 629; VIII, 469
Beck, William, X, 716
Becket, John C., X, **40–41**, 129, 672; XII, 921
Beckett, Jane (Fife), X, 283
Beckwith, Ann. *See* Jouett
Beckwith, Anne Susanne Caroline. *See* Valle
Beckwith, Clementina, Lady Beckwith. *See* Loughnan
Beckwith, George, V, 705
Beckwith, Harry, X, 41
Beckwith, John (father of JOHN CHARLES), IX, 37
Beckwith, John (father of Sir THOMAS SYDNEY), VI, 38
Beckwith, John Adolphus, X, **41–42**
Beckwith, John Charles, VIII, 465; IX, **37–38**
Beckwith, Julia Catherine (Hart), VI, 772; VII, 725; IX, **38–39**, 254
Beckwith, Julie-Louise. *See* Lebrun de Duplessis
Beckwith, Marie Ann. *See* Berton
Beckwith, Mary. *See* Halliburton
Beckwith, Nehemiah, V, 35; IX, 38; X, 41
Beckwith, Rebecca (Smith), XI, 827
Beckwith, Sir Thomas Sydney, VI, **38–39**; IX, 37, 133
Beckx, Pierre, XI, 109
Becquet, Anne. *See* Vasse
Becquet, Jean, III, 98
Becquet, Julien, I, 86
Becquet, Marie. *See* Pellerin
Becquet, Marie-Jeanne (Barsalou), IV, 46
Becquet, Romain, I, 85, **86**, 106; II, 242, 448
Becquet, Romaine. *See* Boudet
Bédard, Antoine, VI, 126, 392; XII, 874
Bédard, Delphine (Dufresne), XII, 275
Bédard, Elzéar, VI, 49, 681; VII, 7, 8, 9, **61–62**, 72, 191, 430, 880; VIII, 137, 141, 489, 678, 907; IX, 32, 261, 299, 485, 486, 539, 682, 683, 696, 775, 795; X, 132, 574, 580, 581, 582; XI, 623
Bédard, François-Zoël, VI, 40, 49
Bédard, Hélène (Ellen McEnes) (Berthelot), VII, 62
Bédard, Isaac, VI, 41
Bédard, Jacques, II, 88; VI, 41
Bédard, Jean-Baptiste, V, **60–61**; VI, 125, 367; VII, 462
Bédard, Jean-Charles, VII, 885
Bédard, Jean-Charles, V, 212; VI, **39–40**, 332; VII, 94, 759
Bédard, Joseph, VI, 41, 86, 126; VII, 393, 485; VIII, 693; IX, 807
Bédard, Joseph-Édouard, XII, 46
Bédard, Joseph-Isidore, VI, **40–41**, 49; IX, 299
Bédard, Julie-Henriette. *See* Marett
Bédard, Luce. *See* Lajus
Bédard, Madeleine. *See* Daigle
Bédard, Marie-Angélique. *See* Fiset
Bédard, Marie-Anne. *See* Toupin
Bédard, Marie-Anne (Évanturel), XII, 298
Bédard, Marie-Josephte. *See* Thibault
Bédard, Pierre, IX, 63
Bédard, Pierre-Hospice, VI, 49
Bédard, Pierre-Laurent, IV, 42, 638
Bédard, Pierre-Stanislas, VI, 39, 41
Bédard, Pierre-Stanislas, IV, 432; V, 207, 208, 210, 211, 212, 233, 234, 460, 580, 651, 695, 792, 828, 881; VI,

40, **41–49**, 50, 68, 80, 81, 82, 225, 241, 242, 347, 392, 546, 577, 586, 591, 645, 750; VII, 41, 61, 504, 645, 647, 676, 688, 689, 786, 836, 872, 878, 879; VIII, 141, 214, 388, 693, 843; IX, 299, 807, 808, 809, 810, 811, 814; X, 566, 567, 568, 571
Bédard, Sélina (Giroux), IX, 318
Bédard, Théophile-Pierre, XI, 115, 490
Bédard, Thomas (brother of PIERRE-STANISLAS), VI, 41
Bédard, Thomas (father of JEAN-BAPTISTE and THOMAS-LAURENT), IV, 49; V, 60
Bédard, Thomas-Laurent, IV, **49–50**, 477, 511; V, 60; VI, 24, 650; VII, 17
Beddé, Gilles de, I, 474
Beddoes, Thomas, VII, 477
Beddome, Frances. See Omand
Beddome, Henry Septimus, XI, **63–64**
Beddome, William, XI, 63
Bedford, Duke of. See Russell
Bedini, Cajetan, VIII, 911; XI, 285
Bédos de Celles, François de, X, 153
Bedouin, Marie (Hamel), VII, 373
Bedout, Françoise. See Barolet
Bedout, Jacques, III, 26; V, **61–63**
Bedout, Jean-Antoine, III, 26, 300; V, 61
Bedout, Jeanne. See Lafont
Bedout, Marie-Jeanne. See Daigre
Bedson, Florence A. See Frankfort
Bedson, Jemima Alexandrina. See Murray
Bedson, Samuel A., XII, 74
Bedson, Samuel Lawrence, XII, **74–75**, 735
Beebe, Maria M. (Gzowski, Lady Gzowski), XII, 389, 390, 391
Beecham, John, VII, 277
Beecher, Harriet Elizabeth (Stowe), VII, 396; IX, 390; X, 44, 653; XI, 401; XII, 667, 788
Beecher, Henry Ward, XI, 348
Beechey, Charlotte. See Stapleton
Beechey*, Frances Anne (Hopkins) (1838–1918), VIII, 70
Beechey, Frederick William, VI, 330; VII, 325; VIII, **70–72**; IX, 197, 198, 659; X, 27, 42, 407; XI, 198
Beechey, Henry William, VIII, 71, 72
Beechey, Phyllis Ann, Lady Beechey. See Jessup
Beechey, Sir William, V, 587; VI, 517, 518; VIII, 70
Beedy, Josiah Crosby, XI, 51
Beek. See also Beke
Beek, John Gerbrand, VI, 285
Beemer. See also Beamer
Beemer, Horace Jansen, XI, 774
Beemer, Jacob, VII, 56
Beemer, Joseph, VIII, 180
Beemer, Julia. See Smith
Beemer (Beamer), Mary (Sovereene), VI, 729
Beer, Elizabeth Jane (Jones), XII, 479
Beer, Henry, XII, 417
Beer, Jakob Liebmann Meyer (Giacomo Meyerbeer), XII, 471
Beers, Isabella. See Hope
Beers, James Crawford, XII, 75
Beers, Mary E. See Hope
Beers, William George, XII, **75–77**
Beete, Sophia (Jukes), IX, 417
Beethoven, Ludwig van, VIII, 634; X, 229; XII, 223, 471
Beeton, Ann (Blinkhorn), VIII, 97

Beevin. See Bevan
Beevor, Sarah (Bigsby), XI, 72
Begbie, Mary Hamilton. See Baillie
Begbie, Sir Matthew Baillie, IX, 82, 433; X, 112, 113, 116, 245, 678; XI, 236, 604, 605, 757, 951; XII, **77–81**, 92, 227, 523, 914
Begbie, Thomas Stirling, XII, 77
Begg, Alexander, XII, 81
Begg, Alexander, IX, 617; X, 629, 645, 669; XI, 45, 47, 539, 563, 842; XII, **81–84**, 132, 690, 922, 939, 983
Begg*, Alexander (1825–1905), XII, 84, 918
Begg, Katherine Glenn Macaulay Rae. See Hamilton
Begg, Magnus, XII, 779
Begg, May. See Urquhart
Begg, William Proudfoot, XII, 663
Bégin, Auguste, IX, 123
Bégin, Charles (clergyman), IX, 783
Bégin, Charles (politician), V, 278
Bégin, Louise (Lagueux), VI, 384
Bégin, Louis-Jacques, VI, 762, 763
Bégin*, Louis-Nazaire (1840–1925), XI, 485, 486; XII, 46, 511, 819, 820, 821, 1020, 1023, 1024, 1050, 1066
Begley, Mary (Brennan), XI, 110
Begley, Thomas A., IX, 288; X, 404
Bégon, Catherine (Barrin de La Galissonière), III, 26, 57
Bégon, Catherine (Lafon de La Duye), III, 62
Bégon, François, III, 60
Bégon, Jeanne-Élisabeth (Lorgeril), III, 62; IV, 517
Bégon, Marie-Madeleine, III, 62
Bégon, Marie-Rose, III, 62
Bégon, Marie-Thérèse, III, 62
Bégon, Michel (great-grandfather), II, 470
Bégon, Michel, III, 62
Bégon, Scipion-Jérôme, III, 57, 59, 60, 62
Bégon de La Cour, Claude-Michel, II, xxi; III, 43, **56**, 57, 62, 445, 563, 564, 579; IV, 661
Bégon de La Cour, Claude-Michel-Jérôme, III, 56, 564
Bégon de La Cour, Marie-Catherine-Élisabeth (Michel de Villebois de La Rouvillière), III, 56, 445, 563, 564
Bégon de La Cour, Marie-Élisabeth. See Rocbert de La Morandière
Bégon de La Picardière, Mlle (Meulles), II, 472
Bégon de La Picardière, Jeanne-Élisabeth. See Beauharnois de La Boische
Bégon de La Picardière, Jeanne-Élisabeth, II, 460
Bégon de La Picardière, Madeleine. See Druillon
Bégon de La Picardière, Michel, II, 188, 197, 422, 470, 589; III, 51, 53, 56, 57
Bégon de La Picardière, Michel, II, 11, 25, 42, 43, 52, 56, 57, 58, 60, 77, 81, 92, 125, 135, 147, 150, 156, 171, 188, 208, 235, 273, 292, 299, 337, 402, 413, 416, 417, 447, 460, 463, 492, 508, 516, 519, 528, 535, 541, 543, 559, 561, 571, 598, 604, 649; III, 4, 5, 23, 26, 29, 51, 56, **57–63**, 69, 74, 77, 112, 113, 138, 153, 159, 161, 217, 224, 225, 227, 299, 305, 313, 353, 360, 419, 420, 445, 512, 520, 553, 563, 564, 567, 632, 633, 637; IV, 41, 356, 449, 720
Be-gou-ais (Be-gwa-is). See Peguis
Begourat, I, 61, **86**
Behzer, Traugott Leberecht. See Piuze, Liveright
Beikie, John, V, 521; VI, 498; VII, 545
Béique, Caroline-Angélina. See Dessaulles
Béique*, Frédéric-Ligori (1845–1933), XII, 256, 720

Beke (Beck, Beek), Margaret S. (Jones), V, 457
Bélair. *See also* Dalpech; Plessis-Bélair; Plessy
Bélair, Ann. *See* Fraser
Bélair, Louis, V, 269, 270, 271; VI, 546
Belamy, Pierre de, III, 389
Béland, Angélique (Bolvin), III, 68
Béland, Euphrosine (Caron), X, 136
Béland, Pierre, VIII, 108
Bélanger, Alexis, IX, 514
Bélanger, Alexis, IX, **39–40**; XII, 356, 357
Bélanger, Alfred, XII, 1133
Bélanger, Ann. *See* Fraser
Bélanger, Catherine (Lespérance), XI, 514
Bélanger, Charles, II, 440
Bélanger, Édouard, XII, 84
Bélanger, F.-S.-A., IX, 690
Bélanger, Ferdinand, XI, 507
Bélanger, François, VII, 134
Bélanger, François-Xavier, XI, **64–65**
Bélanger, Geneviève-Luce. *See* Robitaille
Bélanger, Horace, XII, **84–85**
Bélanger, Jean, VII, 709
Bélanger, Jean-Baptiste (clergyman), VI, 287; VII, 656
Bélanger, Jean-Baptiste (farmer), VII, 173
Bélanger, Joseph, VIII, 77
Bélanger, Louis, XI, 623
Bélanger, Louis-Charles, XII, 904
Bélanger, Louise (Marcoux), V, 231
Bélanger, Marguerite (Couillard de Lespinay), II, 156
Bélanger, Marguerite (Levasseur), III, 396
Bélanger, Marie-Catherine. *See* Manisson, *dit* Philibert
Bélanger, Marie-Marthe. *See* Talbot
Bélanger, Marie-Sophie. *See* Casgrain
Bélanger, Marthe (Souhet; Soupiran), II, 613; III, 595
Bélanger, Narcisse, VIII, 329
Bélanger, Philippe, IV, 629
Bélanger, Pierre, IX, 39
Bélanger, Rosalie. *See* Marion
Bélanger, Vitaline. *See* Fontaine
Belcher, Abigail. *See* Allen
Belcher, Andrew, V, 423, 872; VI, 90; VII, **62–64**; X, 7, 42
Belcher, Benjamin (father of BENJAMIN), V, 63
Belcher, Benjamin (father of CLEMENT HORTON), IX, 40
Belcher, Benjamin (grandfather of CLEMENT HORTON), IX, 40
Belcher, Benjamin, V, **63**, 122
Belcher, Clement Horton, V, 63; IX, **40–41**
Belcher, Diana. *See* Jolliffe
Belcher, Sir Edward, VII, 64, 326; VIII, 80, 449, 624, 625; IX, 167, 659; X, **42–43**, 89, 396, 407, 455, 562, 563; XI, 198, 200, 543, 691, 692, 718; XII, 38, 892
Belcher, James (boxer), VII, 317
Belcher, James (ship's captain), II, 267; III, 414
Belcher, Jonathan (father of JONATHAN), II, 254, 669; III, 274, 437, 584, 635; IV, 50
Belcher, Jonathan (great-uncle of Mather BYLES), V, 127
Belcher, Jonathan, III, 130, 174, 363, 364, 365, 366, 418, 650, 651, 664; IV, xxvii, **50–54**, 56, 110, 240, 258, 267, 273, 274, 291, 292, 313, 414, 528, 561, 562, 695, 723, 764; V, 63, 81, 554, 555; VII, 62; X, 42
Belcher, Mary. *See* Partridge
Belcher, Mary (Vaughan), II, 644

Belcher, Mary Ann. *See* Geyer
Belcher, Mary Jane. *See* Starr
Belcher, Percy, XII, 671
Belcher, Sarah. *See* Post
Belcher, Sarah. *See* Starr
Belcher, Thomas, VII, 317
Belcour. *See* Lafontaine
Belcourt. *See also* Bellecourt
Belcourt, Adélaïde (Glenn), XI, 354
Belcourt, François-Onésime, VIII, 769
Belcourt*, Napoléon-Antoine (1860–1932), XII, 938
Belden, Howard Raymond, XII, 794
Belden, Reuben Booth, XII, 794
Belding, Albert Martin, XII, 1048
Belding, Priscilla (Whittemore), VIII, 930
Beleau, Marie-Louise (Gauvreau), VI, 280
Belestre. *See* Picoté
Bélestre-MacDonell. *See* MacDonell
Belet. *See* Blet
Belford, Alexander, X, 43, 44
Belford, Alexander Beaty, XII, 923
Belford, Charles, X, **43–44**; XI, 920; XII, 73, 604, 923
Belford, Jennie. *See* Thomas
Belford, Robert J., X, 43, 44
Belford, Robert James, XII, 923
Belile. *See* Gotteville
Belin, Madeleine (Le Febvre de La Barre), I, 442
Bélisle. *See* Lamarre
Belisle, Alexandre, XI, 330
Belisle, Augustin, VI, 447
Belisle, Mary Charlotte. *See* McDougall
Belknap, Jeremy, V, 741; VI, 87, 88
Belknap, S. K., X, 293
Belknap, Sally (Foster), IX, 276; X, 293
Bell, Alexander (father of JOSHUA), IX, 43, 44
Bell, Alexander (probably son of JAMES), V, 64
Bell, Alexander (shoemaker), IX, 44
Bell, Alexander D., IX, 273
Bell*, Alexander Graham (1847–1922), X, 102; XI, 39, 452; XII, 746
Bell, Andrew (father of WILLIAM, 1780–1857), VIII, 76
Bell, Andrew (teacher), VII, 481, 822
Bell, Andrew, VIII, **72–73**, 77, 751
Bell, Andrew, IX, **41–42**, 303, 305; X, 446; XII, 570
Bell, Ann. *See* Allison
Bell, Ann. *See* Cross
Bell, Ann. *See* MacKenzie
Bell, Ann (Forsyth), V, 325
Bell, Ann (Irvine), XII, 464
Bell, Bryan, VII, 68
Bell, Catherine. *See* Wallace
Bell, Christian. *See* Dalziel
Bell, David (merchant), VIII, 559
Bell, David (son of MATHEW), VII, 68
Bell, Eliza. *See* Thomson
Bell, Elizabeth. *See* Lain
Bell, Elizabeth. *See* Notman
Bell, Elizabeth (Bonar; Burns), IX, 104
Bell, Elizabeth (Bond), VI, 76
Bell, Eliza Jane Erskine (Church), XII, 196
Bell, Emmeline Sedate. *See* Jones
Bell, Frances (Forsyth), IX, 273
Bell, Frances (Lawson), X, 434

Bell, George, VIII, 77; XII, 767
Bell, Sir George, XII, 196
Bell, Helen. *See* Howatt
Bell, Henry, VII, 921
Bell, Herbert, X, **44–45**
Bell, Hugh, VII, 270, 279; VIII, **73–75**, 193
Bell, James (cousin of William VALENTINE), VII, 875
Bell, James (father of MATHEW), VII, 64
Bell, James (son of MATHEW), VII, 67
Bell, James, V, **63–64**, 414
Bell, Jane. *See* Bowness
Bell, Jane (Clarke), XI, 194
Bell, Jane (Howatt), XII, 452
Bell, Jane (Montmollin), V, 600
Bell, Jane Lambert. *See* Heartz
Bell, John (brother of WILLIAM, 1806–44), VII, 69
Bell, John (lawyer), X, 632
Bell, John (merchant), X, 721
Bell, John (shipbuilder), VI, 546
Bell, John, VII, 220; VIII, **75–76**, 477
Bell, John, VII, 327; VIII, 663; IX, **42–43**; XI, 194, 445; XII, 877
Bell, John George, IX, 287; X, 45
Bell, John Howatt, XII, 453
Bell, Joshua, IX, 43
Bell, Joshua, IX, **43–44**
Bell, Luther Vose, VIII, 74
Bell, Margaret. *See* Christie
Bell, Margaret. *See* Shaw
Bell, Margaret, V, 64
Bell, Margaret (mother of MATHEW), VII, 64
Bell, Margaret Waugh. *See* Buckham
Bell, Maria. *See* Miller
Bell, Marie-Luce-Eugénie. *See* Patry
Bell, Mary. *See* Black
Bell, Mary Ann (wife of JOHN, 1788–1855), VIII, 75
Bell, Mathew, IV, 198; V, 182, 214, 484, 566, 738; VI, 23, 96, 424, 417, 515, 516; VII, **64–69**, 381, 387, 465, 730, 771, 880; VIII, 18, 115, 123, 368, 370, 837, 838; IX, 273; XII, 464
Bell, Nancy. *See* Dease
Bell, Peter Warren, IX, 43
Bell, Robert (father of JOHN), VIII, 75
Bell, Robert (father of ROBERT), X, 45
Bell, Robert (politician), XI, 537
Bell, Robert (son of WILLIAM, 1780–1857), VIII, 733
Bell, Robert, VIII, 759, 840; IX, 287; X, **45–46**, 147, 645; XI, 161, 171; XII, 353
Bell, Robert, VII, 69; XII, **85–86**
Bell*, Robert (1841–1917), VIII, 73; X, 445; XI, 50; XII, 383, 541, 542
Bell, Samuel (brother of JOSHUA), IX, 43
Bell, Samuel (father of HUGH), VIII, 73
Bell, Samuel (son of HUGH), VIII, 73
Bell, Sarah (mother of JOHN), VIII, 75
Bell, Thomas (brother of JOSHUA), IX, 43, 44
Bell, Thomas (officer), III, 173, 668, 670, 672, 673; V, 767
Bell, William (lawyer), XII, 196
Bell, William (merchant), VIII, 559
Bell, William (son of HUGH), VIII, 73
Bell, William (son of JAMES), V, 64
Bell, William, VII, **69–70**; VIII, 77; XII, 85

Bell, William, VI, 232; VII, 69, 852; VIII, 72, 73, **76–77**, 534, 733, 828, 829; X, 660; XII, 85
Bell, William Cairns, XI, 652
Bell, Winthrop Pickard, XII, 251
Bellair. *See* Gautier
Bellanger, Monsieur (guardian), VIII, 940
Bellanger, Françoise (Gamelain), I, 321
Bellarmino, Roberto, VII, 886
Belle, Joseph-Achille-A., XI, 70
Belleau, Gabriel, XII, 86
Belleau, Louise (Boucher-Belleville), X, 75
Belleau, Marie-Reine-Josephte, Lady Belleau. *See* Gauvreau
Belleau, Marie-Renée. *See* Hamel
Belleau, Sir Narcisse-Fortunat, VI, 280; VII, 169; IX, 360, 778; X, 135, 147, 148; XI, 161, 162, 183, 557, 623, 774, 920; XII, **86–87**, 118, 197, 270
Belleau, René-Gabriel, XI, 203
Belleau, *dit* La Rose, Michel, III, 424
Belleborne. *See* Nicollet
Bellecour (Bellecourt). *See* Lafontaine
Bellecourt. *See also* Pouteret
Bellecourt, Antoine, X, 46
Bellecourt, George-Antoine, VII, 232, 777; VIII, 308, 529, 721, 722; IX, 663; X, **46–48**; XI, 34, 310; XII, 1003
Bellecourt, Josephte. *See* Lemire
Bellefeuille. *See also* Lefebvre
Bellefeuille, Henry, VI, 666
Bellefonds. *See* Genaple
Bellefonds, Marquis de. *See* Gigault
Bellefontaine. *See also* Fortin; Godin
Bellefontaine, Marie-Anne (Chaloux), VII, 164
Belle-Humeur. *See* Bourg
Bellehumeur. *See* Monet
Belle-Isle. *See* Le Borgne; Lefebvre
Belle-Isle, Duc de. *See* Fouquet
Bellejambe, Jeanne (Jacob), II, 294
Bellemare, Alphonse, XII, 504
Bellemare, Antoine-Narcisse, XII, 301
Bellemare, Raphaël, VIII, 260; X, 304; XI, 341
Bellenden, Mary (Campbell, Duchess of Argyll), IV, 131
Bellenger, Étienne, I, **87–89**, 421
Bellenger, Joseph-Marie, VII, 19, 448; VIII, **77–79**
Bellenger, Narcisse, XII, 270
Bellenoix. *See* Le Maître-Bellenoix
Bellenoy, Thérèse (Brehaut; Sheppard), V, 107
Bellerive. *See* Crevier; Groston
Bellerose. *See also* Jourdain
Bellerose, Geneviève-Sophie. *See* Lemaître, *dit* Lottinville
Bellerose, Henriette. *See* Armand
Bellerose, Joseph-Hyacinthe, X, 533; XII, **87–88**
Bellerose, Michel-Hyacinthe, XII, 87
Bellet, Cécile. *See* Flamme
Bellet, François, VI, 49
Bellet, François, VI, **49–51**; VII, 372
Bellet, Marie-Anne. *See* Réaume
Bellet, Marie-Honoré. *See* Fournier
Bellet, Mary. *See* Robinson
Belleville. *See* Boucher; Boucher-Belleville; Gauchet; Guernon; Martel
Bellevue. *See* Pinguet
Bellevue, Antoinette de. *See* Dolebeau

Bellew, Anne. *See* Tasker
Bellew, Frank Henry Temple, X, 649
Bellew, Henry, V, 847
Belley, Louise (Josephte) (Du Boishué, *dit* Berland), XII, 124
Bellin, Jacques-Nicolas, III, 105, 108
Bellinger. *See* Bellenger
Bellingham, Sir Allan, XII, 88
Bellingham, Arabella. *See* Holmes
Bellingham, Elizabeth, Lady Bellingham. *See* Walls
Bellingham, Sydney Robert, VI, 327; X, 219, 220; XII, 7, **88–91**, 569, 571, 572, 573
Bellini, Vincenzo, XII, 503
Bellinzani, Francesco, II, 31
Belliveau, François, XII, 159
Belliveau, Marguerite (Bourgeois), II, 94
Bellmore, Anne (Harrison), XII, 414
Bellois, Cornelis (Corneille) de, I, 291, 294
Bellomont, Earl of. *See* Coote
Belloni, J., XI, 813
Bellot, Adélaïde-Estelle. *See* Laurent
Bellot, Charlotte-Marguerite. *See* Ramezay
Bellot, Étienne-Susanne-Zacharie-Brumaire, VIII, 79
Bellot, Joseph-René, VIII, **79–81**; IX, 199, 389, 390; X, 89, 90; XI, 470, 471
Bellot, *dit* Lafontaine, I, **89**
Bellows, Abel, VI, 277
Bell-Smith*, Frederic Marlett (1846–1923), XII, 795
Belmont. *See* Vachon
Belrieux de Virazel, Marie-Anne de (Chateigner de Cramahé et Des Rochers), IV, 787
Belt of Wampum. *See* Kaghswaghtaniunt
Belugard. *See* Dupin
Belvèze, Antoine-Jean-François de, X, 48
Belvèze, Marie-Joséphe-Jeanne. *See* Garrigues de Saint-Fauste
Belvèze, Paul-Henry de, IX, 250, 302; X, **48–49**; XI, 181
Belyea, Miss (Hutton), XII, 461
Belzunce, Armand de, Vicomte de Belzunce, IV, 307
Beman, Eli, VI, 51, 52
Beman, Elisha, VI, **51–52**, 604; VII, 753; X, 622
Beman, Esther. *See* Sayre
Beman, Joel, VI, 51
Beman, Susan (Boulton), X, 78
Bemer. *See* Beamer
Bemister, Ann. *See* Howell
Bemister, George, XII, 249
Bemister, Jane. *See* Taylor
Bemister, John, X, 8; XI, 433; XII, **91–92**
Bemister, William Willis, XII, 91
Bémont. *See* Du Saussay
Bénac, Rose (Poutré), XI, 708
Benar, Nuel. *See* Bernard, Noël
Benar, Sunum, V, 74
Bénard, Louis, III, 63
Bénard, Marie. *See* Guy
Bénard, Marie-Germaine-Eustache. *See* Lanoullier de Boisclerc
Benard, Marie-Josephe, V, 293
Bénard, Michel, III, **63–64**, 353
Bénard, *dit* Carignan, Amable (Charron), VII, 167
Bénard, *dit* Carignan, Catherine (Spagniolini), III, 598
Bénard, *dit* Carignan, Joseph, III, 598

Benbow, John, II, 260, 666
Bender, Anna Matilda Louisa. *See* Heintzman
Bender, François-Xavier, V, 294
Bender, Karl (Charles), XII, 422
Bender, Mary Elizabeth Alexowina (Muir), VI, 529
Bendixen, Fanny, XII, **92–93**
Bendixen, Louis A., XII, 92
Benedict XIV, III, 192, 416
Benedict, Daniel Davis, VIII, 81
Benedict, David, VIII, 613
Benedict, Elizabeth. *See* Smith
Benedict, Lewis, VIII, 81
Benedict, Phoebe. *See* Hedges
Benedict, Roswell Gardinier, VIII, **81–82**, 964, 965, 966
Benet, Marie-Anne (Lamaletie), IV, 433
Benett, Charlotte. *See* Jones
Benfield, Mary (Steele), IX, 743
Bengough*, John Wilson (1851–1923), XII, 607
Benham, Beacher, VIII, 785, 786
Benham, John B., VI, 335
Benincasa. *See* Mannucci-Benincasa
Benjamin (father of HANS HENDRIK), XI, 382
Benjamin (son of MASKEPETOON), XII, 932
Benjamin, Alfred David, XI, 801
Benjamin, Alfred David, XII, **93–94**
Benjamin, David, XII, 93
Benjamin, Esther. *See* Solomon
Benjamin, Frank D., XI, 801; XII, 93
Benjamin, George, IX, **44–46**; X, 80, 121, 312, 313, 314
Benjamin, J., VIII, 41
Benjamin, Rosetta. *See* Levy
Benne, Monsieur de (commissioner), I, 419
Bennet, Cornelius, V, 804
Bennet, Stephen, I, 450
Bennett, Mrs (Grant; wife of WILLIAM), VIII, 82
Bennett, Adolphus B., XII, 1090, 1091
Bennett, Anne. *See* Hopson
Bennett, Bertha (Botsford), V, 94
Bennett, Catherine Rose (Brousseau), XI, 115
Bennett, Charles James Fox, VIII, 381, 863; IX, 159, 604, 605; X, 8, 50, 716; XI, **65–69**, 108, 239, 354, 376, 561, 762, 881, 910; XII, 92, 163, 164, 310, 311, 440, 482, 543, 844, 860, 956
Bennett, Charlotte (Record), XI, 726
Bennett, Elizabeth. *See* Allison
Bennett, George, X, **49**, 103
Bennett, Isabella. *See* Sheppard
Bennett, John, IV, 690
Bennett, Joseph, II, 668; III, 436
Bennett, Leah (mother of CHARLES JAMES FOX and THOMAS), X, 50; XI, 65
Bennett, Mary Ann (Smith), XI, 837
Bennett, Samuel, IV, 139
Bennett, Sophia. *See* Sargent
Bennett, Thomas (father of CHARLES JAMES FOX and THOMAS), X, 50; XI, 65
Bennett, Thomas (officer), VI, 189
Bennett, Thomas, VII, 154; VIII, 233, 863; X, **49–50**, 600; XI, 65, 66, 68
Bennett, William, X, 617
Bennett, William, VI, 65, 66, 671, 672; VII, 424, 587; VIII, **82–83**
Benning, Clement Pitt, VIII, 950; IX, **46–47**

Benning, Elizabeth (Cantin), XII, 158
Benning, James, X, 723; XII, 62
Benning, Susan. *See* Penny
Benoist, Antoine-Gabriel-François, III, 94, 408; IV, **54–55**, 192, 637
Benoist, Claude, IV, 204
Benoist, Françoise. *See* Trevet
Benoist, Gabriel, IV, 54
Benoist, Geneviève (Dupleix Silvain), IV, 245, 246
Benoist, Joseph, II, 60; III, 603; IV, 265
Benoist, Marie-Louise. *See* Le Ber de Senneville
Benoît, Jacques, II, 517
Benoît, Mathilde. *See* Thouin
Benoît, Olivier-David, XII, **94**
Benoît, Pierre, IV, **55**; VI, 139
Benoît, Ursule (McCarty), IV, 495
Benoît, *dit* Livernois. *See also* Livernois
Benoît, *dit* Livernois, Amable, IX, 47
Benoît, *dit* Livernois, Desanges. *See* Beaudry
Benoît, *dit* Livernois, Élise. *See* L'Hérault, *dit* L'Heureux
Benoît, *dit* Livernois, Jules-Isaïe, IX, **47–48**; XII, 247
Benoît, *dit* Marquet, Pierre-Salomon, IX, 126
Benson, Alicia Fenton. *See* Russell
Benson, Ann (Dickson), XI, 263
Benson, Augusta. *See* Neelon
Benson, Charles Otis, X, 561
Benson, Dorothy. *See* Braithwaite
Benson, Egbert, V, 809
Benson, George Frederick, XI, 69
Benson, Helen. *See* Wilson
Benson, Robert, XI, 69
Benson, Thomas, VII, 71
Benson, Thomas Starling, VII, 873, 874
Benson, William John Chapman, VII, **70–71**
Benson, William Thomas, XI, **69–70**; XII, 964
Benson, Willis A., VII, 71; XII, 279
Bentham, Jeremy, VI, 495; VII, 645, 855; X, 626
Bentinck. *See also* Cavendish
Bentinck, Charlotte Frances (Milnes, Lady Milnes), VII, 613, 616
Bentinck, William, 1st Earl of Portland, VII, 613
Bentley, Benjamin, V, 66
Bentley, Catherine (wife of JOHN), V, 66, 67
Bentley, Deborah. *See* McKay
Bentley, Elijah, V, **64–66**, 749; VI, 324, 489, 734; VIII, 5, 61, 180, 608
Bentley, Ira, V, 65, 66
Bentley, John, V, **66–68**
Bentley, Margaret (Hutton; wife of JOHN), V, 68
Bentley, Mary Colley (Gill; wife of JOHN), V, 67
Bentley, Prudence (Webster), IX, 825
Bentley, Reuben, V, 65
Bentley, Richard, VII, 338; IX, 352; XI, 859, 860, 861; XII, 463
Bentley, Thomas, IV, 369
Bently, Samuel, V, 64, 65, 66
Bentom, Clark, V, **68–70**, 768, 769; VI, 528; VII, 464; VIII, 648
Benton, Rhoda Anne (Ellis), X, 270
Benton, Thomas Hart, IX, 279
Benwell, F., XI, 77
Benwell, Frederick Cornwallis, XI, 77, 78
Benyovszky, Móric, Count de Benyovszky, IV, 513

Béranger, Pierre-Jean de, VII, 98
Bérard, *dit* Lépine, Jean-Baptiste, X, 481; XII, 554
Bérard, *dit* Lépine, Julia. *See* Henry
Berbudeau, Monsieur (surgeon), IV, 56
Berbudeau, Jean, IV, 56
Berbudeau, Jean-Gabriel, IV, **55–56**
Berbudeau, Marie-Anne. *See* Duvivier
Berbudeau, Marie-Gervaise. *See* Paris
Berbudeau, Marie-Reine (Texier de La Touche), IV, 56
Berchenbos, Catherine (Lafitau), III, 334
Berchereau. *See* Chavigny
Berczy, Albert-Guillaume. *See* Berczy, William
Berczy, Ann Eliza. *See* Finch
Berczy, Charles Albert, V, 70; VI, 745; VII, 13, 179; VIII, **83–85**; IX, 399; XI, 676
Berczy, Jeanne-Charlotte. *See* Allamand
Berczy, Louise-Amélie. *See* Panet
Berczy, William, V, **70–72**, 114, 417, 419, 420, 428, 440, 448, 496, 596, 597, 614, 731, 755, 757, 781, 811; VI, 177, 223, 260, 270, 296, 299, 374, 549, 550, 559, 560, 745; VII, 13, 98, 255, 892; VIII, 10, 83, 592, 911, 952; X, 50
Berczy, William Bent, V, 70, 72; VI, 745; VII, 13; VIII, 83; X, **50–51**
Berenhardt, Jeanne-Catherine de (La Salle), II, 349
Berens, Henry Hulse, IX, 261
Berens, Joseph, VI, 441; VIII, 660
Beresford, Caroline (Gore), VIII, 336
Beresford, Sir John Poo, VII, 257
Beresford, Marianne Catherine Emily (Windham), IX, 844
Beresford, William, IV, 218
Berey Des Essarts, Félix (Charles), IV, 43, 231; V, 570; VI, 85; VII, 591, 592; XII, 46
Bergeaux, Anne-Marie. *See* Gautier, *dit* Bellair
Berger, Le. *See* Honatteniate
Berger, Charles, IV, 532
Berger, Éléonore. *See* Montalan
Berger, Jean, II, **54**
Berger, Jean-Claude, II, 54
Berger, Marie-Françoise. *See* Storer, Rachel
Bergereau, Marie (Hudon), VII, 423
Bergeron, Dominique, II, 235
Bergeron, Louise-Catherine. *See* Denys de Saint-Simon
Bergeron, Marie-Anne (Landron), III, 347
Bergeron, Pierre, I, 409
Bergeron d'Amboise, Marie-Anne (Godin, *dit* Bellefontaine, *dit* Beauséjour), IV, 305
Bergeron d'Amboise, Michel, IV, 305
Berges. *See* Renaud d'Avène
Bergevin, Célestin, X, 148
Bergevin, Marie-Joseph (Clouet), VII, 188
Bergevin, *dit* Langevin, François, VIII, 637
Bergevin, *dit* Langevin, Marie-Anne. *See* Dufresne
Bergevin, *dit* Langevin, Rose-Louise (Lagueux), VI, 384
Bergier, Clerbaud, I, **89–90**, 258, 260, 298, 542; II, 408, 410, 630
Bergier, Jean-Jacques, II, 55
Bergier, Marc, II, **54–56**, 110, 227, 468; III, 639, 640
Bergier, Nicolas, VII, 886
Bergier Deshormeaux (Des Ormeaux), Monsieur (son of Clerbaud BERGIER), I, 90; II, 408
Bergin, Darby, XII, **94–97**, 633
Bergin, John, XII, 95, 97

Bergin, Mary. *See* Flanagan

Bergin, William, VII, 662, 896; IX, 265; XII, 94

Berhouague. *See* Martel

Bériault, Élisabeth (Simonet), III, 592

Bérichon. *See* Laurent

Beridge (Berridge), Frances (Gladwin), IV, 297

Bérin, Marguerite (Daumont de Saint-Lusson), I, 249, 250

Bering, Vitus Jonassen, IV, 165, 166

Bériot, Charles-Auguste de, VIII, 347

Berk, Anna Maria. *See* Walton

Berkeley, Augustus, 4th Earl of Berkeley, V, 72

Berkeley, Elizabeth, Countess Berkeley. *See* Drax

Berkeley, Emilia Charlotte, Lady Berkeley. *See* Lennox

Berkeley, Frances (Byron, Baroness Byron; Hay), IV, 121

Berkeley, Sir George Cranfield, V, **72–73**, 861; VI, 781; VIII, 338

Berkeley, Sir George Henry Frederick, V, 73

Berkeley, Georgiana Mary (Seymour, Lady Seymour), XII, 474

Berker (Barker), Mercy (Millidge), V, 598; VII, 612

Berkley, Margaret (Barnard; Buell), VI, 90

Berland. *See* Breland; Du Boishué

Berley, George, II, 56

Berley, George, II, **56**, 319, 320, 644

Berlinguet*, François-Xavier (1830–1916), VIII, 40; X, 603; XII, 280

Berlinguet, Louis-Thomas, VI, 227; VII, 685; VIII, 40; IX, 318

Berlise. *See* Faure

Bermen, Laurent, I, **90–91**; II, xv

Bermen de La Martinière, Anne de. *See* Després

Bermen de La Martinière, Claude de, I, 39, 56, 107, 329, 430, 529, 581, 611; II, **56–58**, 325, 607; III, 59, 60, 64, 113

Bermen de La Martinière, Claude-Antoine de, II, 57; III, **64–65**, 627

Bermen de La Martinière, Françoise de. *See* Juchereau

Bermen de La Martinière, Hannah de. *See* Parsons

Bermen de La Martinière, Jean-Baptiste de, II, 57

Bermen de La Martinière, Jeanne-Françoise de, named de Sainte-Hélène, II, 57

Bermen de La Martinière, Louis de, II, 56

Bermen de La Martinière, Marie de. *See* Molin

Bermen de La Martinière, Marie-Anne de. *See* Cailleteau

Bernal, Esther (Crawley), XI, 214

Bernard. *See also* Carrihogo

Bernard, Lieutenant, X, 706

Bernard, Agnes Elizabeth. *See* Lally

Bernard, Aldis, X, **51–52**

Bernard, André, I, 383

Bernard, Antoinette (wife of NOËL), V, 74

Bernard, Sir Francis, IV, 292; VI, 74

Bernard, Hannah (Goffe), II, 254

Bernard, Henriette Rosine (Sarah Bernhardt), XII, 316, 831

Bernard, Hewitt, XII, **97–98**, 593, 599, 601, 604, 605, 729

Bernard, J. D., X, 23

Bernard, Jean-Baptiste, V, 74

Bernard, Jean-Dominique, VII, 595; VIII, 259

Bernard, Jean-Frédéric, II, 297

Bernard, John, V, 690

Bernard, Louis, V, 73, 74

Bernard, Madeleine (Cotin, *dit* Dugal), VI, 226

Bernard, Madeleine de (Chabert), V, 176

Bernard, Marie, V, 74

Bernard, Marie (Landry), II, 625

Bernard, Marie-Joseph. *See* Daveine

Bernard, Marie-Madeleine, V, 74

Bernard*, Mary Agnes (Fitzgibbon) (1862–1933), XII, 584

Bernard, Mary Webb. *See* Meredith

Bernard, Noël (Neville), V, **73–74**

Bernard, Philip, IV, **56–57**

Bernard, Pierre-Joseph, IV, 123

Bernard, Renée (Dargent), III, 164

Bernard, Richard Barrett, XII, 578

Bernard, Rosalie-Victoire (Prévost), XII, 862

Bernard, Sarah. *See* Couch

Bernard*, Susan Agnes (Macdonald, Baroness Macdonald) (1836–1920), XII, 73, 97, 98, 591, 604, 605, 606, 610, 611

Bernard, Theodora. *See* Foulkes

Bernard, Thomas James, XII, 97

Bernard, Zacharie, V, 74

Bernard de La Rivière, Gabrielle. *See* Anneville

Bernard de La Rivière, Hilaire, I, 76; II, xxiii, **58–59**, 338, 467

Bernard de La Rivière, Marguerite. *See* Gillet

Bernard de La Rivière, Marie-Madeleine. *See* Voyer

Bernardin de Saint-Pierre, Henri, VII, 645, 675

Bernatchez, Nazaire, XII, 758

Bernera. *See* MacLeod

Berners, Bridget (Vancouver), IV, 744

Berney, Michael, VII, 292

Bernhardt, Sarah. *See* Bernard, Henriette Rosine

Bernier, Adélaïde (Guillet, *dit* Tourangeau), XII, 1064

Bernier, Benoît-François (Joseph-Pierre), III, 19, 188; IV, **57–58**

Bernier, Cécile, IX, 362

Bernier, François, IV, 57

Bernier, Jeane. *See* Villain

Bernier*, Joseph-Elzéar (1852–1934), X, 397

Bernier, Marie. *See* Malen

Bernier, Mathurin, I, 663

Bernier, Michel-Esdras, XII, 720

Bernier, Philippe, III, 227

Bernières, Henri de, I, **91–92**, 291, 355; II, 19, 207, 303, 329; III, 683

Bernières, Jourdaine de, I, 91

Bernières, Madeleine de, Baronne d'Acqueville. *See* Le Breton

Bernières, Pierre de, Baron d'Acqueville, I, 91

Bernières de Louvigny, Jean de, I, 91, 208, 291, 587; II, 18, 360

Bernini, Giovanni Lorenzo, II, 71

Bernis, Monsieur de (friend of François BIGOT, d. 1778), IV, 69

Bernon, Anne (Lavergne), II, 524

Bernou, Claude, I, 174, 175, 179; II, 538, 589

Bernstorff, America von, Countess von Bernstorff. *See* Riedesel

Berrichon. *See* Bottier

Berridge. *See* Beridge

Berrin, Marguerite (Bouin), I, 250

Berruyer, Élisabeth (Petit de Levilliers), II, 523

Berry. *See also* Morillonnet
Berry, Duc de. *See* Bourbon; France, Charles de
Berry, Duchesse de. *See* Caroline
Berry, Ann (Clark), IV, 152
Berry, Deborah. *See* Bootman
Berry, Sir John, I, 24, **92–93**, 278, 370
Berry, Jonathan, X, **52**
Berry, Marie. *See* Mars
Berry, Mary (wife of JONATHAN), X, 52
Berry, Paul, III, 168
Berry, Thomas, X, 52
Berry, Walter (officer), IV, 352
Berry, Walter (sheriff), VI, 107
Berryer, Nicolas-René, Comte de La Ferrière, III, 257, 467; IV, 68, 69, 187, 312, 422, 616, 632, 670, 673; V, 103, 104
Bersalou. *See* Barsalou
Bersolles, Yves-Augustin, IV, 421
Berson, *dit* Chatillon, Antoine, II, 294
Bertaut, Anne-Catherine de. *See* Pastour de Costebelle
Bertaut, Jacques de, II, 512
Berteau, Catherine (Pascaud), II, 508
Berthé de La Joubardière, Gabriel de, II, 412
Berthelet, Amélia (Larocque), IX, 456; X, 53
Berthelet, Anne. *See* Boullard
Berthelet, Antoine-Olivier, VI, 52; VIII, 864; IX, 111, 208, 456; X, **52–53**
Berthelet, Cécile (O'Sullivan), VII, 666
Berthelet, Charlotte. *See* Guy
Berthelet, François, VI, 52
Berthelet, Françoise. *See* Meloche
Berthelet, Henry, VI, 52
Berthelet, Joachim, V, 242
Berthelet, Marguerite. *See* Viger
Berthelet, Marie-Angélique. *See* Chaboillez
Berthelet, Pierre, VI, **52–53**; VII, 666; X, 52
Berthelet, Radegonde (De Lisle), V, 242
Berthelette, Catherine. *See* Vallée
Berthelette, Nicolas, V, 394
Berthelot. *See also* Dubois
Berthelot, Adèle (La Fontaine, Lady La Fontaine), VII, 73; VIII, 332; IX, 440, 445, 450
Berthelot, Alexis, VII, 258
Berthelot, Amable, VII, 73
Berthelot, Amable, V, 75, 649; VI, 23, 546, 634, 802; VII, **71–73**, 373, 643, 878; VIII, 489, 907; IX, 261, 299, 300, 440, 441; X, 337
Berthelot, Caroline-Anne (Bouchette), X, 78
Berthelot, Charles, III, 554; V, 74; VII, 72
Berthelot, Charlotte-Archange. *See* Mézière
Berthelot, Émélie (Girouard), V, 51; VII, 174; VIII, 332, 333
Berthelot, François, Comte de Jouy et de Saint-Laurent, I, 661; II, 235, 305, 639
Berthelot, Geneviève (Badeaux), V, 76; VI, 22
Berthelot, Hector, VI, 52; VII, 619; XII, **98–100**
Berthelot, Hélène. *See* Bédard
Berthelot, Jane. *See* Mason
Berthelot, Joseph-Amable (judge), VII, 62; IX, 78, 441, 442, 444, 449; X, 37, 143, 434
Berthelot, Joseph-Amable (notary), VII, 172; VIII, 331, 332
Berthelot, Joséphine (Faucher de Saint-Maurice), XII, 308

Berthelot, Louis-Flavien, XII, 98
Berthelot, Marie-Louise (Planté), VI, 585
Berthelot, Michel, V, 76; VI, 483; VII, 65, 689
Berthelot, Thérèse. *See* Roussel
Berthelot Dartigny, Marie-Angélique. *See* Bazin
Berthelot Dartigny, Michel-Amable, IV, 89, 185; V, **74–76**, 234, 508, 649, 650, 878; VI, 23, 346, 586; VII, 71, 72, 169
Berthet, Marie-Philippe (Picquet), IV, 637
Berthiaume, Jean-Baptiste, VIII, 243
Berthiaume, Jean-Jacques, IV, 8, 43
Berthiaume, Moïse, IX, 552
Berthiaume\*, Trefflé (1848–1915), XII, 180, 181, 1026
Berthier, Alexandre, II, 59, 60, 69
Berthier, Isaac (Alexandre), I, 494, 556, 565, 602; II, **59–60**, 155, 295
Berthier, Marguerite. *See* Bariac
Berthier, Marie. *See* Legardeur de Tilly
Berthier, Marie-Françoise. *See* Viennay-Pachot
Berthier, Michel, III, 165
Berthier, Pierre, II, 59
Berthon, Clare Elizabeth. *See* La Haye
Berthon, Frances-Desirée. *See* Maugenet
Berthon, George Theodore, VI, 560; XII, **100–3**
Berthon, Marie-Zélie. *See* Boisseau
Berthon, René-Théodore, XII, 100
Bertier, Antoine, II, 60
Bertier, Antoinette. *See* Cochon
Bertier, Ferdinand de, VII, 304
Bertier, Marie-Anne. *See* Denys de Saint-Simon
Bertier, Michel, II, **60**, 151; III, 67, 518; IV, 203, 265
Bertin, Louis, IV, 56
Bertin, Louise, V, 192
Berton, Abigail Louisa (Pullen), XI, 718
Berton, Ann Frances. *See* Street
Berton, Delia. *See* Hooke
Berton, George Duncan, VI, 741; VII, 73
Berton, George Frederick Street, VII, **73–74**; VIII, 152; XII, 797
Berton, James, VII, 330
Berton, Maria (Fraser), VII, 330
Berton, Marie Ann (Beckwith), X, 41
Bertram, Alexander, XII, 103
Bertram, Christina. *See* Murray
Bertram, George Hope, XII, **103–4**
Bertram, Hugh, XII, 103
Bertram\*, John (1837–1904), XII, 103
Bertram, John H., XII, 103, 104
Bertrand, Apolline. *See* Saindon
Bertrand, Arthémise. *See* Dionne
Bertrand, Charles, VIII, 419
Bertrand, Charles, XII, **104–6**, 251, 252
Bertrand, Charles-Georges, XII, 105
Bertrand, Elizabeth (Mitchell), VI, 509, 510; VII, 582
Bertrand, Éphrem-Réginald, XII, 99
Bertrand, Esther (Montferrand, *dit* Favre), IX, 563, 564
Bertrand, François, II, 411
Bertrand, Jacques, V, 76
Bertrand, Jean-Baptiste, XII, 280
Bertrand, Jeanne. *See* Giraudin
Bertrand, Joseph-Laurent, V, **76–77**; VI, 594; VII, 486
Bertrand, Julie, named Marie de Saint-Basile, XII, 359
Bertrand (Bertrend), Laurent, IV, 384

Bertrand, Louis (employee of John McDOUGALL), IX, 487
Bertrand, Louis (father of CHARLES), XII, 104
Bertrand, Louis-Achille, XII, 104
Bertrand, Marguerite (Angeac), IV, 27
Bertrand, Marie. *See* Hamel
Bertrand, Marie-Josephe (Paulet), XI, 698
Bertrand, Marie-Josephte (Rousseau de Villejouin; Aille-boust), III, 6, 368; IV, 688
Bertrand, Marie-Louise. *See* Dumouchel
Bertrand, Marie-Thérèse. *See* Dulignon
Bertrand, Pierre, II, 282
Bertrand, Renée (Leneuf de La Vallière et de Beaubassin), II, 411; II, 454; IV, 689
Bertrand, Thomas, II, 57, 561
Bertrand de Latour, Louis. *See* Latour, Bertrand de
Bertrend. *See* Bertrand
Bérulle, Pierre de, I, 115
Berwick, Duke of. *See* Fitz-James
Berzelius, Jöns Jacob, Baron Berzelius, VIII, 435
Besaillion. *See* Bisaillon
Beschefer, Thierry, I, 50, 108, 345, 445; II, **61–62**, 343
Besferer, Johann Theodor, known as Jean-Théodore Besserer, IX, 48
Bésiade, Antoine-Louis-François de, Comte d'Avaray, VI, 620
Besnard. *See also* Bénard
Besnard, Jacques, II, 83
Besnard, Jeanne (Gadois), II, 234; III, 232
Besnard, T. P., IX, 597, 598
Besnard, *dit* Bourjoly, René, II, 234
Besnard, *dit* Carignant, Charlotte. *See* Brebion
Besnard, *dit* Carignant, Félicité. *See* Pillet
Besnard, *dit* Carignant, Jean-Baptiste, IV, 58
Besnard, *dit* Carignant, Jean-Louis, IV, **58–59**, 485, 547; V, 4, 272, 843
Besnard, *dit* Carignant, Marie-Joseph. *See* Gervaise
Besnard, *dit* Saint-André, Jacques, II, 168
Besné. *See* Du Chaffault
Besouat. *See* Tessouat (fl. 1603–13)
Bessabes, I, 69, 529
Bessborough, Earl of. *See* Ponsonby
Besse, Édouard, IX, 552
Bessels, Emil, X, 328
Besserer, Angèle. *See* Rhéaume
Besserer, Jean-Théodore. *See* Besferer, Johann Theodor
Besserer, Louis-Théodore, VII, 188, 427; VIII, 839, 907; IX, **48**, 299, 300
Besserer, Margaret. *See* Cameron
Besserer, Marie-Anne. *See* Giroux
Bessette, Michel-Adrien, XI, 438
Bessonett, Daniel, VI, 242
Bessonett, Elizabeth, XII, 786
Bessonett, Joanna. *See* Stairs
Bessonett, John Stayner, XI, 116
Bessonett, Mary (Etter), VI, 242
Best, Elizabeth. *See* Stanser
Best, Elizabeth (Ritchie), VIII, 752
Best, George, I, 5, 85, **93–94**, 153, 316, 317, 318, 670
Best, George, VI, **53–54**, 431, 757; VII, 187, 434; VIII, 171, 172, 345, 346
Best, Hannah (Gosse), XI, 363
Best, John, VII, 138
Best, William, V, 63

Bestland, William, VI, 155
Béthune, Chevalier de, II, 270
Béthune, Comtesse de. *See* Pollet de La Combe-Pocatière
Bethune, Alexander Neil, V, 79; VI, 528; VII, 75, 467; VIII, 85, 117, 187, 390, 485, 623; IX, 49, 205, 292, 760, 762, 763, 764, 848; X, 12, **53–57**, 121, 206, 207, 381, 477; XI, 313, 314, 327, 368, 523, 639, 654, 917; XII, 107, 681, 751, 808
Bethune, Angus, V, 77
Bethune, Angus, V, 79, 526; VI, 468; VII, 566, 913; VIII, **85–86**, 176, 314, 390, 454, 576; X, 53; XII, 106, 680
Bethune, Ann (McKenzie), VI, 468
Béthune, Armand de, II, 399
Bethune, Cecilia (Wilkinson; Kirby), V, 79; VII, 469
Bethune*, Charles James Stewart (1838–1932), X, 53; XI, 364; XII, 108
Bethune, Christian. *See* Campbell
Bethune, Christine (Farrand; Henry), VIII, 390
Bethune, Donald, V, 79; VII, 75, 369; VIII, 85, 326; IX, **48–50**, 241, 657; XI, 378
Bethune, Elizabeth. *See* Hallowell
Bethune, Helen. *See* King
Bethune*, Henry Norman (1890–1939), V, 79; XII, 106
Bethune, James Gray, V, 79; VI, 773; VII, **74–76**, 214; VIII, 7, 85, 117, 390, 391; IX, 49; X, 53
Bethune, Jane Eliza. *See* Crooks
Bethune, Jane Frances. *See* Ewart
Bethune, Janet. *See* Smith
Bethune, Janet Ann. *See* Nicolson
Bethune, John, IV, 757; V, **77–79**, 280, 320, 520, 770; VI, 468, 822; VII, 74, 469, 820; VIII, 85, 560, 882; IX, 48, 232; X, 53, 57
Bethune, John, V, 79; VI, 364, 528, 734, 735; VII, 358, 412, 751; VIII, 85, 768; IX, 3, 49, 289, 290, 291, 333, 580, 719, 756, 848; X, 53, **57–58**; XI, 503, 533, 914; XII, 4, 5
Béthune, Louis de, Comte de Béthune, II, 399
Bethune, Louisa. *See* McKenzie
Béthune, Marguerite-Louise-Suzanne de (Gramont, Comtesse de Guiche), II, 440
Béthune, Marie-Armande de, II, 399
Béthune, Marie-Thérèse de, Comtesse de Béthune. *See* Pollet de La Combe-Pocatière
Bethune, Martha. *See* Covert
Bethune, Mary Martha (Abbott), XII, 4, 5
Béthune, Maximilien I de, Baron de Rosny, Duc de Sully, I, 293
Bethune, Norman, VI, 318; VII, 75; IX, 49
Bethune, Norman, VIII, 86; XI, 328; XII, 11, **106–7**
Bethune, Robert Henry, X, 53; XII, 43, **107–8**
Bethune, Strachan, IX, 290, 292; X, 58; XI, 286, 721; XII, 4
Bethune, Véronique. *See* Waddens
Bétournay, Archange. *See* Vincent
Bétournay, Louis, X, **58–59**, 143
Bétournay, Marie. *See* Mercil
Bétournay, Pierre, X, 59
Bétourné, Marguerite (Leclerc), V, 480
Bétourné, *dit* La Violette, Adrien, X, 59
Bétourné, *dit* La Violette, Marie. *See* Deshaies
Bettesworth, Lady Hannah Althea. *See* Grey
Bettez, Jacob, IV, 37
Bettridge, Mary. *See* Hounsfield

Bettridge, William, X, 60
Bettridge, William Craddock, VIII, 205; X, **59–60**, 206
Betts, Edward Ladd, X, 591
Betts, Ephraim Wheeler, VIII, 225
Between the Logs. *See* Tau-yau-ro-too-yau
Betzner, David, VIII, 87
Betzner, Elizabeth. *See* Brech
Betzner, Maria. *See* Detweiler
Betzner (Bezner), Samuel, VIII, 86
Betzner, Samuel D., VI, 235; VII, 778; VIII, **86–87**
Bevan, Sophia (Mountain; Feild), VIII, 644; X, 278; XII, 364
Bevan, William, II, 62, 10, 492, 563
Beverly, Robert, II, 498
Bewick, Thomas, VII, 317, 320; VIII, 13, 14
Beyigishiqueshkam. *See* Bauzhi-geezhig-waeshikum
Bezeau, Marguerite (Decoigne), VII, 238
Bezeau, Michel-Charles, V, 77
Bezellon. *See* Bisaillon
Bezner. *See* Betzner
Biard, Jean, I, 94
Biard, Jeanne. *See* Cluzel
Biard, Pierre, I, 67, 68, 69, **94–96**, 97, 98, 100, 101, 165, 299, 307, 347, 441, 442, 456, 470, 498, 500, 560, 604
Bibaud, Adèle, XI, 71
Bibaud, Cécile-Clémence. *See* Fresne
Bibaud, Élizabeth. *See* Delisle
Bibaud, François-Maximilien, III, 80; IV, 208, 510; VII, 423, 503, 505; VIII, 88, 318, 845, 911; IX, 64, 250, 303, 615; XI, **70–72**, 891; XII, 720
Bibaud, Jean-Gaspard, VIII, 88; XI, 217, 303
Bibaud, Michel, V, 243, 702; VI, 242, 381; VII, 61, 72, 236, 448, 818; VIII, 79, **87–89**, 240, 290, 911; IX, 250, 255, 279, 300, 303; X, 505; XI, 70, 489; XII, 495, 570
Bibaud, Michel-Ange, VIII, 87
Bibaud, Pierre, VIII, 88
Bibaud, Victoria, XI, 71
Bibb, Henry Walton, VII, 365; VIII, **89–90**; IX, 6, 821; XII, 492, 960
Bibb, James, VIII, 89
Bibb, Malinda (wife of HENRY WALTON), VIII, 89
Bibb, Mary Elizabeth. *See* Miles
Bibb, Milldred. *See* Jackson
Bibeau, Angèle (Chandonnais), XI, 174
Bibron (Biberon) de Ctorméry, Marthe-Françoise (Puisaye, Marquise de La Coudrelle), VI, 618
Bica, Philippe (Massé), I, 497
Bichat, Marie-François-Xavier, VI, 763; X, 236
Bickerstaff, Margaret Ann (Cronyn), X, 206
Bickersteth, Edward, VI, 328
Bickett, Joseph, XII, 483
Bickford, William, IX, 694
Bickley, Francis Price, XII, 939
Bidal, Abbé, II, 443
Bidal, Claude-François, Marquis d'Asfeld, II, 648; III, 118, 644
Bidaut, Michelle (Brossard), II, 105
Bideau, *dit* Portugal, Marie-Madeleine (Iffland; Edelston), X, 375
Bidgood, Thomas, XI, 692
Bidoux de Lartigue, Monsieur (associate of Jean-François LA ROCQUE de Roberval), I, 423
Bidwell, Adonijah, VI, 54

Bidwell, Barnabas, V, 308; VI, **54–59**, 331, 543, 544, 657, 772, 805; VII, 38, 178, 230, 367, 378, 458, 795; VIII, 34, 125, 187, 514, 515, 598, 599, 639, 689; IX, 551, 670, 671, 673; X, 60, 706
Bidwell, Clara. *See* Willcox
Bidwell, Jemima. *See* Devotion
Bidwell, Marshall Spring, VI, 57, 58, 331, 467, 468, 543, 762, 772; VII, 40, 41, 42, 158, 230, 367, 370, 379, 445, 457, 458, 497, 550, 664; VIII, 28, 34, 46, 47, 51, 54, 125, 253, 598, 599, 642, 643, 695, 696, 697, 698, 946; IX, 139, 231, 360, 498, 504, 671, 673, 680, 684, 685, 686, 724, 740; X, **60–64**, 109, 124, 343, 344, 573, 619, 624, 705; XI, 787, 853, 914; XII, 925
Bidwell, Mary. *See* Gray
Bielby, Sarah (Reeve), XII, 887
Bielby, Sarah Theresa (Reeve), XII, 887
Bielke, Sten Carl, Baron Bielke, IV, 406
Biencourt, Charles de, I, 96
Biencourt, Florimond de, I, 96
Biencourt, Jacques de (uncle), I, 96
Biencourt, Jacques de, I, 96, 99
Biencourt, Jeanne de. *See* Salazar
Biencourt, Jeanne de, I, 96
Biencourt, Louis de, I, 96
Biencourt de Poutrincourt, Claude de. *See* Pajot
Biencourt de Saint-Just, Charles de, I, 25, 51, 67, 69, 94, 95, 97, 98, **99–102**, 293, 299, 307, 347, 470, 471, 476, 501, 592; IV, xix
Biencourt de Poutrincourt et de Saint-Just, Jean de, I, 28, 64, 67, 94, 95, **96–99**, 100, 101, 110, 189, 292, 293, 294, 299, 300, 307, 347, 367, 441, 469, 470, 476, 495, 500, 501, 507, 526, 527, 564, 592, 596, 604; IV, xix, xx
Bienvenu; Bienvenue. *See* Fontaine
Bienville. *See* Le Moyne
Bier, Anne de (La Cetière), II, 325
Bierce, L. V., VII, 253, 715
Bierne (Byrne), Abbé, III, 566
Bierstadt, Albert, XII, 794
Bièvre. *See* Suzor
Bigaouet. *See* Thomas
Big Arrow (Joe Crawford), VI, 552
Bigault d'Aubreville, Catherine de. *See* Ribenzki
Bigault d'Aubreville, Emmanuel-Xavier de, VI, 59
Bigault d'Aubreville, Louis-Nicolas-Emmanuel de, VI, **59–60**, 433
Big Bear. *See* Mistahimaskwa
Big Child. *See* Mistawāsis
Bigeau, Marie-Joseph. *See* Dumouchel
Bigelow, Catherine Scollay (Parkman), XII, 823, 824
Bigelow, L. C., XI, 379
Bigelow, Levi, XI, 229, 589
Bigelow, Lucius, VI, 399
Biggar, Charles Robert Webster, XI, 221
Biggar, Herbert, X, 641
Biggar, Mary (Macallum), X, 451
Biggar, William, VIII, 609
Big Mouth. *See* Otreouti
Bignell, Emily Sarah (Widmer), VIII, 931
Bignon, Jean-Paul, II, 595, 599
Bigot, Bonaventure, IV, 59
Bigot, Catherine. *See* Baillargeon
Bigot, Étienne, IV, 59
Bigot, François, II, **62–63**

Bigot, François, II, xxi, 225, 226; III, 6, 8, 18, 19, 75, 76, 78, 98, 118, 124, 137, 138, 141, 154, 160, 161, 169, 182, 188, 193, 195, 196, 198, 199, 225, 228, 231, 236, 237, 243, 255, 256, 271, 272, 291, 292, 300, 305, 321, 354, 355, 385, 389, 392, 409, 416, 425, 433, 441, 456, 461, 466, 468, 487, 494, 510, 511, 524, 537, 540, 551, 557, 561, 563, 564, 576, 611, 612, 644, 676, 677, 680; IV, 36, 45, 56, **59–71**, 76, 88, 91, 92, 124, 125, 145, 148, 187, 192, 202, 205, 206, 214, 236, 237, 247, 248, 249, 250, 252, 253, 254, 256, 257, 263, 264, 271, 286, 306, 312, 335, 344, 353, 364, 420, 421, 432, 435, 449, 456, 459, 460, 466, 512, 514, 517, 558, 588, 614, 615, 616, 620, 621, 623, 624, 629, 632, 639, 643, 644, 645, 646, 659, 660, 668, 670, 672, 673, 678, 691, 692, 720, 729, 750, 755; V, 88, 104, 164, 276, 638, 652, 711; VI, 84; IX, 301; XII, 825
Bigot, Jacques, II, 5, **63–64**, 542; III, 24, 168
Bigot, Joseph-Amable, IV, 60
Bigot, Louis, IV, 59, 60
Bigot, Louis-Amable, IV, 59, 60
Bigot, Louis-Joseph, IV, 60
Bigot, Marguerite. *See* Lombard
Bigot, Marie. *See* Bouchard d'Orval
Bigot, Marie. *See* Renard
Bigot, Marie, II, 62
Bigot, Marie-Louise (Brulart de Sillery), IV, 59
Bigot, Vincent, II, 63, **64–65**, 95, 664; III, 104, 329; IV, 764, 765
Bigot, *dit* Dorval, Alexis, V, 736
Bigot, *dit* Lamothe, François, II, 62
Bigot, *dit* Lamothe, Marguerite. *See* Drapeau
Bigsby, Jacob, XI, 72
Bigsby, John Jeremiah, VI, 646; VII, 732; VIII, 866; IX, 769; XI, **72–73**; XII, 232, 233
Bigsby, Sarah. *See* Beevor
Big Snake. *See* Omoxesisixany
Big Swan. *See* Akamih-kayi; Omukaiee
Bill, Asahel, XII, 108
Bill, Caleb Rand, XII, 108
Bill, Ingraham Ebenezer, VII, 177, 272; VIII, 179, 567; XI, 215; XII, **108–10**, 872
Bill, Isabella. *See* Lyons
Bill, Mary. *See* Rand
Bill, Mary, XII, 109
Bill, Susan L. (Dove; wife of INGRAHAM EBENEZER), XII, 108
Billaudèle, Catherine. *See* François
Billaudèle, Pierre-Louis, VIII, 731; IX, **50–52**, 246; XI, 42
Billeron, *dit* Lafatigue, Jeanne. *See* Dalgueuil, *dit* Labrèche
Billinger, William, V, 127
Billings, Bradish, X, 64
Billings, Ekaterina. *See* Pestel
Billings, Eliza. *See* Moore
Billings, Elizabeth (Fairfield), V, 307
Billings, Elkanah, X, **64–66**, 361, 446, 447, 448; XI, 73, 218; XII, 233
Billings, Helen Walker. *See* Wilson
Billings, John, XII, 1069, 1070
Billings, Joseph, IV, 744; V, **79–81**
Billings, Lamira. *See* Dow
Billingsley, Frederick, XII, 145
Billington, Ray Allen, VII, 626
Billion, Louis-Léon, XII, 769

Billopp, Catherine (Black), VI, 61
Billopp, Christopher, IV, 327; V, 349; VI, 61, 143, 799; VIII, 507, 806; IX, 53, 622
Billopp, Jane (Black), IX, 53
Billopp, Mary (Willis), IX, 841
Billouart de Kerlérec, Louis, III, 36, 531; IV, 667
Billuart, Charles-René, VII, 886
Billy, Godefroy de, I, 469
Billy, Guillaume, II, 499
Billy, Madeleine. *See* Normandin
Bilodeau, Jean, III, 518, 519
Bilodeau, Léocadie, IX, 359
Bilodeau, Louis, XII, 126
Bilodeau, Marie. *See* McNeil
Bilodeau, Marie. *See* Turgeon
Bilodeau, Marie-Esther (Garneau), IX, 297
Bilodeau, Michel, IX, 362
Bindon, Louisa Anna (Stuart), XI, 862
Binessie (Pinessie), XI, 939
Bineteau (Binneteau), Julien, II, 55, 109, 110, 454
Bingay, George, VI, 77
Bingay, Jacob, VI, 793
Bingay, John, VI, 793
Bingay, Mary, VI, 793
Bingay, Thomas, VI, 793
Bingham, A. R., XII, 894
Bingham, Abel, VII, 845
Bingham, Abner, VIII, 614
Bingham, Amanda (Marchand), VIII, 614
Bingham, James, VI, 324
Bingham, Marie-Charlotte. *See* Chartier de Lotbinière
Bingham, William, VI, 133
Bingle, Maria Jane. *See* Waddell
Bingle, Samuel, VII, 650
Binks, Emma (Somerville), XI, 843
Binneteau. *See* Bineteau
Binney, Emily. *See* Pryor
Binney, Hannah Adams. *See* Newton
Binney, Hannah Harriet (Hill), XII, 435, 436
Binney, Henrietta Amelia. *See* Stout
Binney, Hibbert, V, 781; IX, 601; XI, 73; XII, 872
Binney, Hibbert, VII, 436; VIII, 357; IX, 338, 339, 801; X, 8, 73, 110, 178; XI, **73–77**, 754; XII, 364, 436, 712, 797, 1061
Binney, Hibbert Newton, V, 82, 216; X, 66, 539; XI, 155
Binney, Jonathan, IV, 110, 111, 116, 199, 273, 275, 291, 450, 451, 581; V, **81–82**; VI, 395; XI, 73
Binney, Lucy. *See* Creighton
Binney, Margaret. *See* Miller
Binney, Martha. *See* Hall
Binney, Mary. *See* Bliss
Binney, Stephen, X, **66–67**; XII, 436
Binney, Stephen Hall, V, 82
Binney, Stephen Newton, VII, 63
Binney, Thomas, V, 81
Binns, Charles, VII, **76–77**; VIII, 827
Binns, Elizabeth. *See* Clarke
Binot, Marie-Louise (Coron), III, 141
Birch. *See also* Burch
Birch, Sir Arthur Nonus, IX, 712, 714, 716; XI, 395; XII, 450
Birch, Phœbe Ann (Usborne), VII, 874
Birch, Samuel, V, 468

Birchall, Florence. *See* Stevenson
Birchall, Joseph, XI, 77
Birchall, Reginald, XI, **77–78**
Birchall, Thomas William, VIII, 9; XI, 332
Bird, Annabella. *See* Ross
Bird, Catherine (Swabey), X, 669
Bird, Curtis James, VIII, 91; IX, 330; X, **67–68**, 631; XI, 64
Bird, Edward Joseph, IX, 659; XI, 799
Bird, Elizabeth (Sinclair), VIII, 820
Bird, Eliza Margaret (Griffen), VIII, 91
Bird, Frances. *See* Ross
Bird, Henry, IV, 260, 410, 499; V, 301, 345, 346; VI, 101, 153, 189; VII, 527
Bird, James, V, 531; VI, 17, 100, 466, 767; VII, 455, 526, 749; VIII, **90–91**, 158, 159, 350, 412, 413, 414, 574, 660, 766, 767, 820; IX, 260, 648; X, 67; XII, 110
Bird, James, VIII, 91, 819; XII, **110–11**, 932
Bird, Joseph (father), V, 785
Bird, Joseph, V, 785
Bird, Mary. *See* Lowman
Bird, Mary. *See* Street
Bird, Mary (Lowman; wife of JAMES, d. 1856), VII, 455, 526; VIII, 91
Bird, Thomas, XI, 546
Bird, Thomas, II, 51, **65**, 658; III, 489
Bird, Thomas Street, V, 785
Birdsall, Charlotte Jane. *See* Everett
Birdsall, Elizabeth. *See* Burnham
Birdsall, Elizabeth. *See* Canby
Birdsall, Francis, VIII, 91
Birdsall, Richard, VII, 754; VIII, **91–92**, 116
Birdsall, Samuel, VI, 178
Birdsall, William, VIII, 92
Birdseye, Mary (Peters), VI, 578
Birkett, William, X, 721
Birney, James Gillespie, IX, 704
Birney, Joseph, IX, 455
Birnie, Alexander, VII, 351; VIII, 443
Birnie, Eleanor (Davidson), V, 224
Birnie, Eliza (Anderson), XI, 17
Birnie, George, VII, 351
Birnie, James, XI, 17
Birnie, Samuel, IV, 403; V, 684
Biron, François-Xavier, IX, 315
Biron, Pierre, II, 160
Birrell, Eliza. *See* Thompson
Birrell, Elizabeth (Hyman), X, 68
Birrell, George Sunley, X, 68
Birrell, John, X, **68**; XI, 423
Birrell, Maria Louisa. *See* Sunley
Birrell, Ralph, X, 68
Birstone, Catherine, XI, 882
Bisaillon, Catherine-Charlotte. *See* Saveuse de Beaujeu
Bisaillon, Louise. *See* Dublay
Bisaillon, Martha. *See* Coombe
Bisaillon, Michel, III, 65
Bisaillon, Peter, III, **65–66**; IV, 173
Bisaillon, Richard, III, 65
Bisaillon, Suzanne-Marie. *See* Fortin
Biscaret, Jean, V, 172, 719
Biscoe, Catherine Mary (Hewett), XII, 429
Bishop. *See also* Bisshopp

Bishop, Abraham John, VII, 424
Bishop, Amelia (Dickson), VIII, 222
Bishop, Annie (Creighton), XII, 219
Bishop, Charles, IV, 420, 569; V, 618
Bishop, Nathaniel, II, 51, **65**, 492; III, 489
Bishop, Rebecca (Stone), VI, 738
Bishop, Robert, XI, 236; XII, 227
Bishoppe. *See* Bisshopp
Bisse, Martha (Wright), V, 872
Bissell, Abigail. *See* Allen
Bisset, Miss (Thom), XI, 874
Bisset, Elizabeth (Thom), XI, 874
Bissett, James, VIII, 210
Bissett, Mary (Jackson), II, 293
Bissett, Mary (Tiedemann), XII, 1049
Bisshopp, Cecil, V, **82–83**; VI, 541; VII, 92; VIII, 794; XII, 476
Bisshopp, Cecil, 12th Baron Zouche, V, 83
Bisshopp, Charlotte Barbara. *See* Townshend
Bisshopp, Harriet Anne, Baroness Zouche. *See* Southwell
Bisshopp, Lucy (Johnson), XII, 476
Bisson. *See also* Buisson
Bisson, Élie-Hercule, XII, 1026
Bisson, Julienne (Demosny), I, 256
Bissonnette, Isaïe, XII, 693
Bissot. *See also* Byssot
Bissot, Charles-François, I, 146; II, 66, 256, 300
Bissot, Charlotte (Lafontaine de Belcour), III, 339; IV, 315
Bissot, Claire-Françoise (Jolliet), I, 146, 395, 396; II, 66, 68, 300
Bissot, François-Joseph, II, **65–66**, 256, 300; III, 339; IV, 315
Bissot, Geneviève (Maheut), I, 480; II, 168
Bissot, Jeanne (Clément Du Vuault de Valrennes), II, 148
Bissot, Louise (Margane de Lavaltrie), II, 455; III, 429
Bissot, Marie. *See* Lambert Dumont
Bissot, Marie (Porlier; Gourdeau de Beaulieu et de La Grossardière), II, 256
Bissot de Vincenne (Vinsenne), Marie-Louise (Boisseau), IV, 75
Bissot de Vinsenne, François-Marie, I, 146; II, xxviii, **66–68**, 216, 436, 563, 632; III, 258; IV, 315
Bissot de Vinsenne, Jean-Baptiste, I, 146; II, 66, **68**, 128, 569; IV, 75
Bissot de Vinsenne, Marguerite. *See* Forestier
Bissot de Vinsenne, Marie. *See* Longpré
Bitterman, Sarah (Spragg), VII, 821; XI, 845
Bizaillon. *See* Bisaillon
Bizard, David, I, 102
Bizard, Guillemette. *See* Robert
Bizard, Jacques, I, **102–3**, 231, 540, 600; II, 70, 401, 526, 527, 563
Bizard, Jeanne-Cécile. *See* Closse
Bizard, Louise (Renaud), II, 563
Bjarni Herjólfsson, I, **103–4**, 448
Blache, François, V, 436; VI, 487
Blache, René, V, 218
Blachford, Baron. *See* Rogers
Blachford, Anne (Thom), XI, 874
Blachford, Christabella (Curtis), V, 220
Black, Colonel, IX, 768
Black, Angélique. *See* Cameron
Black, Archibald, XII, 963

Black, Catherine. *See* Billopp
Black, Edmund, XII, 52
Black, Edward, VI, 105, 260; VII, **77–78**, 575, 701; VIII, 21, 272, 273, 310, 545; IX, 257
Black, Elizabeth. *See* Stocks
Black, Elizabeth (Wilmot), X, 710
Black, Elizabeth McCullough. *See* Craw
Black, Emma (Strickland), IX, 768
Black, Frances. *See* Smith
Black, George, VIII, 93, 124; XII, 51
Black, George, VI, 291; VIII, **92–93**, 123, 648; IX, 179; XI, 264; XII, 51, 52
Black, Henrietta. *See* Ross
Black, Henry (merchant), V, 85; VI, 290; VII, 873
Black, Henry (treasurer), XII, 553
Black, Henry, VII, 836, 837; VIII, 116, 323, 692, 938; IX, 538; X, **68–69**, 282; XI, 408, 862; XII, 1000, 1024
Black, Isabella (MacGhillEathain), VII, 559
Black, James (brother of JOHN, 1818–82), XI, 79
Black, James (father of EDWARD), VII, 77
Black, James (father of HENRY), X, 68
Black, James, XI, **78–79**; XII, 71
Black, Jane. *See* Billopp
Black, Jane. *See* Gilley
Black, Jane. *See* McMun
Black, Jane. *See* Rawson
Black, Jane (Goudie), VI, 289
Black, Janet. *See* Campbell
Black, John (father of JAMES), XI, 78
Black, John (father of SAMUEL), VII, 78
Black, John, IV, 501, 502; V, **83–85**, 878, 879; VI, 289, 512; VII, 767
Black, John, V, 328, 646, 647; VI, **60–62**, 355, 697; VII, 343; VIII, 903; IX, 53, 175
Black, John, VIII, 574; X, **69–70**, 629, 646; XI, 739, 740, 741; XII, 82, 1007, 1030
Black, John, VIII, 767, 768; IX, 106, 472; X, 549; XI, 19, **79–80**, 540, 571, 776
Black, Laurenda. *See* Bannatyne
Black, Lois. *See* Humphrey
Black, Lydia (Davis), III, 168
Black, Margaret. *See* Christie
Black, Margaret. *See* Halliday
Black, Margaret (mother of HENRY), X, 68
Black, Martha (Calkin; wife of WILLIAM, 1760–1834), VI, 62
Black, Martin Gay, VI, 62; IX, **52–53**, 175; X, 189
Black, Mary. *See* Gay
Black, Mary. *See* Leith
Black, Mary (Barry), VI, 62; X, 35
Black, Mary (Bell), VII, 69; VIII, 72, 76; XII, 85
Black, Mary (McGeorge; wife of JOHN, d. 1823), VI, 61
Black, R. Delamere, VII, 320
Black, Rosina Jane (Uniacke), VI, 61; VIII, 903
Black, Samuel, VI, 62
Black, Samuel, VI, 250, 251, 437; VII, **78–79**, 564, 571, 749, 913; VIII, 413, 421, 660; IX, 197, 456, 473; XI, 882
Black, Sarah Elizabeth (Fulton), IX, 294
Black, Thomas, VII, 899
Black, Wilhemina. *See* MacMillan
Black, William (father of JOHN, fl. 1786–1819), V, 83
Black, William (father of JOHN, 1818–82), XI, 79
Black, William (father of WILLIAM, 1760–1834), VI, 62

Black, William, IV, 19, 258; V, 468, 469, 573, 664, 665, 871; VI, **62–68**, 131, 170, 243, 275, 276, 430, 672; VII, 52, 424, 587; VIII, 82, 83, 177, 216; IX, 52; X, 35, 710; XI, 406, 734
Black, William, V, 646, 647; VI, 60, 563, 725; VII, 140, 331, 612, 807, 899, 916; VIII, 98, 102, 224; IX, **53–54**
Black, William Anderson, VI, 62, 243
Blackadar, Amy (mother of HUGH WILLIAM), IX, 54
Blackadar, Hugh, IX, 54
Blackadar, Hugh William, VI, 322; VII, 541; VIII, 922; IX, **54–55**; XII, 859
Blackadar, Mary. *See* Sharpless
Blackadar, Sophia. *See* Coleman
Blackaller, Joanna (Yonge), II, 670
Blackaller, Nicholas, II, 670
Black Bear. *See* Kyiyo-siksinum
Blackbird. *See* Assiginack, Jean-Baptiste; Mkedepenase; Siginakee
Blackburn, Augustin, V, 621
Blackburn, Emma Jane. *See* Dallimore
Blackburn, Hugh, V, 331
Blackburn, John (brother of JOSIAH), XI, 80
Blackburn, John (father of JOSIAH), XI, 80
Blackburn, John (merchant), IV, 676; V, 364
Blackburn, Josiah, IX, 267; X, 464; XI, **80–82**, 928
Blackburn, Mary. *See* Nairne
Blackburn, Robert, XI, 682
Blackburn, Sarah. *See* Smith
Blackburn, Stephen, XI, 80
Blackburn, Victoria Grace, XI, 80
Black Cauldron. *See* Chaudière Noire
Black Dick. *See* Pierpoint, Richard
Blackeby, Alfred H., X, 32
Blackeye, XI, 17
Blackhall, James Gordon Canning, XII, 397
Black Harry. *See* Floyd, Henry
Black Hawk, VIII, 446
Black Jack. *See* Byers, John
Blacklandt, Martin van, II, 279
Blackler, Ann (Duder), XI, 284
Blackler, George, VIII, 673
Blacklock, Ann (Tanswell), V, 789, 790
Blackman, Charles, VII, 99; VIII, **94–95**, 104; XI, 44
Blackman, Julia. *See* Williams
Blackman, Thomas John Mark Willoughby, VIII, 94
Blackney, John, VII, 841
Black Peter. *See* Byers, Peter
Blacksnake. *See* Thaonawyuthe
Black Snake Man. *See* Omoxesisixany
Blackstock*, George Tate (1857–1921), XI, 78
Blackstone, Sir William, IV, 184, 186; V, 165, 372, 486, 855; VI, 46, 557, 790; VII, 35, 457, 458, 645, 675, 785; VIII, 515, 957; X, 540; XI, 70, 784, 786; XII, 887
Blackwell, Elizabeth, XII, 28
Blackwell, Emily, XII, 28
Blackwell, George, IX, 178
Blackwood, Arthur Johnstone, VIII, xxxiii, 565; XII, 815
Blackwood*, Frederick Temple Hamilton-Temple, 1st Marquis of Dufferin and Ava (1826–1902), IX, 707; X, 148, 292, 330, 729; XI, 194, 261, 300, 368, 458, 520, 731, 744, 760, 884; XII, 75, 150, 265, 271, 347, 367, 395, 430, 579, 599, 603, 650, 652, 653, 655, 656, 657, 658, 679, 794, 899

Blackwood, Hariot Georgina, Marchioness of Dufferin and Ava. *See* Hamilton
Blackwood, Jane. *See* Holmes
Blackwood, John (brother of THOMAS), VII, 79
Blackwood, John (son of JOHN), V, 87
Blackwood, John, V, 27, **85–88**, 95, 182, 211, 270, 493, 494, 769, 816; VI, 336, 531; VII, 79, 311, 504
Blackwood, Margaret. *See* Grant
Blackwood, Thomas, V, 528; VI, 180, 204, 285, 644; VII, 58, 59, **79–80**, 310
Blackwood, William, VII, 336, 338, 539
Black Wood Ashes. *See* Si'k-okskitsis
Blagden, Anne (Prescott), VIII, 709
Blaignier, Marie-Suzanne (Meilleur), X, 504
Blaikie, John M., VIII, 568; XI, 572
Blaiklock, Caroline Cecilia. *See* Price
Blaiklock, Catherine (wife of HENRY MUSGRAVE), VII, 80
Blaiklock, Elizabeth. *See* Harris
Blaiklock, George, VII, 80, 81
Blaiklock, Henry Musgrave, VII, **80–81**; VIII, 39; XI, 118
Blaiklock, John, VII, 80
Blaiklock, Mary. *See* Morris
Blaiklock, Musgrave, VII, 80
Blain, Marie (Brunet), IX, 96
Blain de Saint-Aubin, Charles, XI, 82
Blain de Saint-Aubin, Charlotte-Euphémie. *See* Rhéaume
Blain de Saint-Aubin, Emmanuel-Marie, X, 229; XI, **82–84**, 912; XII, 558
Blain de Saint-Aubin, Emmanuelle-Sophie-Jeanne. *See* Delamarre
Blaine, Alexander, V, 301
Blaine, James Gillespie, XII, 150, 610
Blainville. *See* Céloron
Blair. *See also* Fergusson; Johnston
Blair, Adam Johnston Fergusson, X, 725
Blair, Andrew, V, 349, 351
Blair*, Andrew George (1844–1907), XI, 298, 299, 897; XII, 340, 341, 739, 740, 1103
Blair, Ann (Allen), XII, 17
Blair, Emma (Baillie Hamilton), XI, 43
Blair, Helen. *See* Adams
Blair, Isabella (Shiels), X, 652
Blair, Janet (McKenzie), X, 477
Blair, Marcus, VII, 917
Blair, Rebecca (DePeyster), VI, 188, 190
Blair, Robert (father-in-law of Arent Schuyler DEPEYSTER), VI, 188
Blair, Robert (of Glasgow), I, 54
Blais, André-Albert, XII, 522
Blais, Françoise. *See* Baudoin
Blais, Françoise (Casault), IX, 116; X, 152
Blais, Jean-Baptiste, V, 165
Blais, Joseph, IV, 71
Blais, Louis, IV, 72
Blais, Louis-Eugène, XII, 1072
Blais, Marguerite, named de Saint-Pierre, IV, 72
Blais, Marie-Françoise. *See* Lizot
Blais, Marie-Joseph, named de Saint-Michel, IV, 72
Blais, Michel, IV, 72
Blais, Michel, IV, **71–72**; V, 499; VI, 768, 769
Blais, Pierre (father), IV, 71
Blais, Pierre, IV, 71
Blais de Surlaville. *See* Le Courtois

Blaise Des Bergères, Jean, II, 69
Blaise Des Bergères, Marie. *See* Boucher
Blaise Des Bergères de Rigauville, Anne. *See* Richard de Goigni
Blaise Des Bergères de Rigauville, Charles-Régis, II, 69; IV, 96
Blaise Des Bergères de Rigauville, Jean-Baptiste-Marie, II, 69; IV, xliii, 547; V, 143
Blaise Des Bergères de Rigauville, Jeanne-Cécile. *See* Closse
Blaise Des Bergères de Rigauville, Marguerite. *See* Vauvril de Blason
Blaise Des Bergères de Rigauville, Marie-Françoise. *See* Viennay-Pachot
Blaise Des Bergères de Rigauville, Marie-Joseph (Denys de Vitré), II, 70; IV, 209
Blaise Des Bergères de Rigauville, Nicolas, II, **68–69**, 70; III, 80, 208, 394, 450
Blaise Des Bergères de Rigauville, Raymond, I, 103, 231; II, 68, **69–71**, 162, 186, 441; III, 372
Blake, Alice (Croke, Lady Croke), VII, 216
Blake, Ann (Aylwin), X, 24
Blake, Anne Margaret. *See* Hume
Blake, Caroline. *See* Placide
Blake, Catherine Honoria. *See* Hume
Blake, Charles, IV, 82; V, 46, **88–89**, 318, 584; VI, 258, 402, 699; VII, 25, 704
Blake, Charlotte. *See* Herring
Blake, Dominick Edward, VIII, 95; IX, 55; X, 206
Blake, Dominick Edward, VIII, **95–96**; IX, 55; X, 206; XI, 434
Blake*, Edward (1833–1912), IX, 55, 56, 292, 324; X, 102, 123, 206, 441, 467, 468; XI, 135, 145, 146, 193, 221, 229, 233, 247, 300, 324, 367, 368, 399, 410, 434, 497, 537, 541, 608, 622, 648, 743, 783, 792, 793, 820, 832, 921, 928, 934; XII, 27, 28, 137, 144, 151, 291, 292, 325, 331, 453, 497, 602, 607, 609, 614, 644, 649, 650, 651, 653, 655, 656, 658, 659, 722, 898, 934, 1044, 1087, 1130
Blake, Frances Mary, X, 206
Blake, Frances Mary (Flood), XI, 570
Blake, Harriet. *See* Antill
Blake, Joanna Harriet (Burke; Daly), IX, 189
Blake, John, V, 88
Blake, Joseph Henry, 1st Baron Wallscourt, IX, 189
Blake*, Kathleen (Willis; Watkins; Coleman) (1863–1915), XII, 137
Blake, Louisa. *See* Jones
Blake, Margaret. *See* Cronyn
Blake, Maria Elizabeth (Hoskin; Burrows), VII, 121, 122
Blake, Mary. *See* Sunderland
Blake, Mary Jane (Talbot), X, 671
Blake, Rebecca. *See* Cronyn
Blake*, Samuel Hume (1835–1914), IX, 55; X, 206, 258, 510; XI, 368, 434; XII, 454, 455, 606
Blake, Sarah (Gridley), IV, 314
Blake, Sophia (Cronyn), X, 206; XI, 434
Blake, Wilhelmina (Brough), X, 206
Blake, William (father of WILLIAM RUFUS), IX, 60
Blake, William (poet), IV, 19
Blake, William Hume, VII, 896; VIII, 53, 95, 426, 427, 587, 698, 849; IX, **55–60**, 109, 151, 244, 245; X, 24, 206, 529; XI, 427, 434, 616, 617, 619

Blake, William Rufus, IX, **60–61**
Blakeney, William, Lord Blakeney, III, 33; IV, 335
Blakey, Robert, VIII, 25
Blakiston, Thomas Wright, X, 81; XI, 662, 663
Blakow-Coneehaw, XII, 289
Blanc, Antoine, IX, 636; XII, 183
Blanc, Jean-Joseph-Charles-Louis, IX, 395; X, 166, 585
Blanchard, Agapit, VII, 86
Blanchard, Catherine-Josephe. *See* Amirault
Blanchard, Eliza. *See* Cantrell
Blanchard, Flavien-R., XI, 438
Blanchard, François-Benjamin, XI, 116, 117
Blanchard, George Augustus, XII, 250
Blanchard, Guillaume, II, **71**, 105, 629, 654
Blanchard, Hiram, X, **70–71**, 457; XI, 279, 619; XII, 436
Blanchard, Huguette. *See* Gougeon
Blanchard, Jane Walker (Waddell), X, 696
Blanchard, Jean, II, 71
Blanchard, Jonathan, VII, 81; X, 70
Blanchard, Joseph-Henri, IV, xxii
Blanchard, Jotham, VII, 81
Blanchard, Jotham, VII, 23, **81–85**, 535; VIII, 222; X, 70
Blanchard, Madeleine (Richard), II, 105
Blanchard, Margaret (Spears; wife of JOTHAM), VII, 81, 83
Blanchard, Marie-Anne (Thibodeau), V, 812, 813
Blanchard, Marie-Modeste. *See* Robichaux
Blanchard, Marin, X, 47
Blanchard, Nancy (Waddell), X, 695
Blanchard, Olivier, VII, 85
Blanchard, Radegonde. *See* Lambert
Blanchard, Sarah. *See* Goggins
Blanchard*, Théotime (1846–1911), XII, 397, 398
Blanchard, Tranquille, VII, 86
Blanchard, Tranquille, VII, **85–86**
Blanchard, William, VI, 483
Blanchard, *dit* Raynaud, Marie-Charlotte (Gingras), IX, 317
Blanchet, Augustin, VIII, 20
Blanchet, Augustin-Magloire, VIII, 317, 318; XI, **84–85**; XII, 282
Blanchet, Catherine-Henriette. *See* Juchereau Duchesnay
Blanchet, Émilie. *See* Balzaretti
Blanchet, François, V, 211, 212; VI, 42, 43, 47, 48, 50, **68–70**, 82, 259, 326, 381, 392, 576, 750, 762, 787; VII, 168, 504; VIII, 96, 141, 154, 388; X, 566, 580
Blanchet, François-Norbert, VII, 672, 762, 836; VIII, 561, 580, 722, 723; X, 221, 227; XI, 84, 402, 805; XII, 282
Blanchet, Hilarion, VIII, 97
Blanchet, Jean, XI, 87
Blanchet, Jean, VII, 169, 427; VIII, **96–97**, 682, 907; IX, 119, 286; XI, 85, 484, 861
Blanchet, Jean-Baptiste, VI, 68
Blanchet, Joseph, VIII, 96
Blanchet, Joseph-Godric, IX, 463; X, 163; XI, **85–86**, 491, 492
Blanchet, Louis, XI, 85
Blanchet, Marie. *See* Sédilot
Blanchet, Marie-Euphrosine. *See* Cloutier
Blanchet, Marie-Geneviève. *See* Destroismaisons
Blanchet, Marie-Marguerite. *See* Fontaine
Blanchet, Pierre, X, 165, 252; XI, 274
Blanchet, René, II, 11

Blancheteau, Jeanne-Catherine (Doreil), III, 187
Blanchette, Josette (Kérouac), X, 401
Blanchette, Marie-Rose (Blanchette), XI, 84
Blanchette, Pierre, XI, 84
Blanchon, Anne. *See* Convent
Blanchon, Marie-Charlotte (Carpentier), IV, 133
Bland, Anthony, XII, 111
Bland, Charles Edward, XII, 111
Bland, Emma. *See* Levell
Bland, Henry Flesher, XII, **111–13**
Bland, John, VI, **70–72**, 372, 580; VII, 302
Bland, John Bayley, VI, 71; XI, 880
Bland, Martha. *See* Flesher
Bland*, Salem Goldworth (1859–1950), XII, 111
Bland, Sarah (wife of JOHN), VI, 70
Blaney, Charlotte (Somerville), VII, 820
Blanshard, Emily. *See* Hyde
Blanshard, Richard, VIII, 97, 646, 836; IX, 337; X, 196, 241, 243; XI, 882; XII, **113–14**, 522
Blanshard, Thomas Henry, XII, 113
Blanzy. *See* Danré
Blaquiere. *See* de Blaquiere
Blarye, *dit* Titailt, Monsieur (murderer), I, 425
Blas, Hernando, I, 157
Blasdell, Julius Caesar, XII, 367
Blasdell, Nathaniel Sherrald, XII, 258, 367
Blaskowitz, Charles, V, 611
Blason. *See* Vauvril
Blatch, George, VIII, 157
Blathwayt, William, II, 279
Blaut. *See* Bleau
Blawbek. *See* Cagenquarichten
Blay. *See* Blais
Bleakley, John, VIII, 110
Bleakley, Josiah, VI, **72–73**, 665; VII, 342, 702
Bleakley, Margaret. *See* McCord
Bleau, Catherine (Carrier), VIII, 129
Bleau (Blaut), Charlotte (Harper), VIII, 363
Bleecker, John James. *See* Flint, John James Bleecker
Bleeker (Bleecker), Elizabeth (Powell), VII, 704
Bleeker, Lucretia (Finkle), VIII, 325, 326
Blenkinsop, George, VIII, 646; XI, 627
Blenshel, Isabel (Purse), V, 699
Blessington, Countess of. *See* Power
Blessington, Earl of. *See* Gardiner
Blet (Belet, Blette), Jeanne (Deguire, *dit* Desrosiers), IV, 201
Bleury. *See also* Sabrevois
Bleury, Marguerite-Émilie (Boucherville), XII, 117
Blevins, John, XI, 649
Blewbeck. *See* Cagenquaritchen
Bligh, William, I, 378; V, 55, 686; VIII, 204
Blinkhorn, Ann. *See* Beeton
Blinkhorn, Ann (mother of THOMAS), VIII, 97
Blinkhorn, Thomas, VIII, 97
Blinkhorn, Thomas, VIII, **97–98**, 836; X, 196, 242
Bliss, Daniel, V, 350, 831; VI, 73; VII, 915; X, 709
Bliss, E. W., VIII, 204
Bliss, Elizabeth Ann (Odell), X, 73; XII, 797
Bliss, Elizabeth Murray (Johnston), VII, 444
Bliss, George, XI, 770
Bliss, George Pidgeon, VI, 73, 74, 810; IX, 22; X, 710
Bliss, Hannah (Wilmot), X, 709

Bliss, Henry, VI, 76, 143, 810; VII, 88, 654, 658, 684; VIII, xxvi, xxviii, 355, 631, 802; X, **71–72**, 644
Bliss, Isabella. *See* Murray
Bliss, John Murray, V, 456, 831; VI, **73–74**, 75, 139, 143, 726, 740, 810; VII, 444, 916; IX, 620; XII, 19
Bliss, John Worthington, VI, 76
Bliss, Jonathan, V, 35, 94, 157, 350, 416, 456, 630; VI, 73, **74–76**, 137, 138, 139, 140, 141, 142, 685, 740, 811; VII, 658, 691, 783; VIII, 428; IX, 62; X, 71, 72; XII, 797
Bliss, Lewis, VI, 76; X, 73
Bliss, Louisa (Kelly), X, 73
Bliss, Luke, VI, 74
Bliss, Mary. *See* Worthington
Bliss, Mary (Binney), X, 73; XI, 76
Bliss, Mercy. *See* Ely
Bliss, Philip, VII, 219
Bliss, Sarah. *See* Wetmore
Bliss, Sarah Ann. *See* Anderson
Bliss, Sarah Green. *See* Upham
Bliss, William Blowers, VI, 76; VII, 82, 88, 278, 492; VIII, 355; X, 7, 71, **72–73**, 395; XI, 76, 372; XII, 797, 870
Blizard, Sir William, VIII, 96; IX, 572
Blodget, Lorin, XII, 1029
Blodget, Samuel, V, 415; VI, 718
Bloem, Maria (Gijben), VII, 882
Blomfield, Charles James, X, 278, 663
Blondeau, Angélique (Cotté), IV, 171; VII, 500; VIII, 301
Blondeau, Catherine (Lamothe), VI, 387
Blondeau, Catherine-Apolline (Godefroy de Linctot), IV, 302
Blondeau, François, V, 89
Blondeau, Geneviève. *See* Angers
Blondeau, Geneviève (Adhémar), V, 3
Blondeau, Isabelle (Isabeau) (Phélypeaux de Villesavin), I, 484
Blondeau, Jean-Baptiste (father of MAURICE-RÉGIS), V, 89
Blondeau, Jean-Baptiste (fur trader), VI, 317
Blondeau, Joseph, V, 89
Blondeau, Joseph-Barthélemy, IV, 366; V, 602
Blondeau, Marie-Jeanne (Auclair), XI, 37
Blondeau, Marie-Josephe. *See* Le Pellé Lahaye
Blondeau, Marie-Madeleine (Legardeur; Céloron de Blainville), III, 99
Blondeau, Maurice, V, 89
Blondeau, Maurice-Régis, IV, 171, 277; V, **89–90**, 241, 242, 511, 528, 662, 663, 700, 701, 818, 819; VI, 387, 664; IX, 649
Blondeau, Nicolas, IV, 592
Blondeau, Suzanne (Hertel de Saint-François), III, 289; IV, 347
Blondeau, Suzanne-Amable (Chénier), VII, 172
Blondeau, Thomas, V, 89
Blondel, Jacques-François, VI, 26; VIII, 39, 213
Blondin. *See also* Sureau
Blondin, Charles. *See* Gravelet, Jean-François
Blondin, Joseph, IV, 331
Blondin, Mathilde (Barnard), XII, 57
Bloomer, Margaret. *See* Finlayson, Margaret
Bloomfield, Anna C. (Lawrence), XII, 536
Bloor, Elizabeth (Morrison), XI, 617
Bloor, Joseph, IX, 411
Blouin, Jean-Baptiste, XII, 1050
Blowers, John, VII, 86

Blowers, Sampson Salter, IV, 737; V, 35, 94, 446, 630, 698, 854; VI, 75, 137, 157, 519, 520, 790; VII, 23, **86–89**, 218, 531, 832, 933; VIII, 167, 354, 355, 356; X, 72, 73; XI, 944; XII, 797
Blowers, Sarah. *See* Kent
Blowers, Sarah. *See* Salter
Blue Jacket. *See also* Weyapiersenwah
Blue Jacket, George, V, 852
Blue Jacket, Jim, V, 852
Blue Jacket, Mary (Lacelle), V, 852
Blue Jacket, Nancy (Stewart), V, 852
Blumhart, Octavie. *See* Senécal
Blumhart, William, XI, 809, 812; XII, 180
Blundell, James, X, 350
Blundeville, Thomas, I, 678
Blyth, Mary Ann (Webb; Howland), XII, 453
Blythe, Martha (Estimauville), VI, 240
Blythe, William, XI, 69
Boas*, Franz (1858–1942), XII, 401, 402, 403
Boak, Robert, IX, 243
Bobbeie, Peter. *See* Babey, Peter Paul Toney
Bobbie. *See* Eenoolooapik
Bobé, Jean, III, 248
Bocall, Stevande, I, 306, 671, 672
Bochart. *See also* Du Plessis-Bochart
Bochart, Guillaume, II, 72
Bochart, Jean, II, 72
Bochart de Champigny, Jean (father), II, 72
Bochart de Champigny, Jean, II, 71
Bochart de Champigny, Jean, Sieur de Noroy et de Verneuil, I, 56, 103, 114, 138, 141, 239, 299, 320, 338, 398, 488, 528, 577, 582, 664; II, 16, 17, 32, 53, 58, 70, **71–80**, 86, 100, 102, 110, 114, 115, 120, 129, 133, 137, 148, 149, 162, 185, 195, 213, 214, 228, 229, 230, 338, 340, 346, 353 371, 383, 401, 404, 410, 413, 427, 432, 440, 450, 456, 458, 464, 466, 473, 483, 486, 488, 491, 513, 524, 539, 540, 561, 566, 568, 576, 580, 586, 594, 596, 598, 617, 618, 655; III, 7, 15, 22, 190, 233, 237, 309, 310, 311, 372, 396, 563
Bochart de Champigny, Marie. *See* Boivin
Bochart de Champigny, Marie (Prouville), I, 554
Bochart de Champigny, Marie-Madeleine. *See* Chaspoux
Bochsa, Charles Nicholas, VIII, 746
Bocquet, Marie-Jeanne (Lanoullier de Boisclerc), III, 352
Bocquet, Simple, II, 173, 174
Boddington, John, IV, 93
Bodeau, Mme (of Paris), I, 610
Bodega, Francisca de Mollineda de la. *See* Mollineda
Bodega y de las Llanas, Tomás de la, IV, 72
Bodega y Quadra, Juan Francisco de la, IV, **72–74**, 568, 746; V, 11, 387, 411, 615; VI, 743; VII, 599
Boden (Bowden), Ann (Burrows), VII, 121
Bodichon, Barbara Leigh. *See* Smith
Bodley, Richard D., X, 647
Bodoin, Louis, V, 269
Bodquín. *See* Flórez
Body, Charles William Edmund, XI, 917
Boehler, Valentine, XII, 157
Böhm-Bawerk, Eugen von, X, 608
Boehme, Jacob, IV, 19
Boerhaave, Hermann, II, 595
Boerstler, Charles, VII, 516; IX, 264, 406
Bœsson, Jacques-Ange, III, 612

Boeve, Jacobus, I, 369
Boganientim, II, 646
Bogart, M. W., XII, 972
Bogennes, Marie-Anne (Beaudry), XI, 59
Bogert, John, VIII, 797
Boggs, Ann (Fulton), VI, 268
Boggs, Charles, VIII, 891; X, 395
Boggs, Elizabeth Mary (Pryor), XII, 871
Boggs, Henry, IX, 182, 184
Boggs, Mary (Tremain), VIII, 891
Boggs, Thomas, VI, 313, 314
Bogle, Janet (Howison), VIII, 409
Bogue, Christian (Hope), XI, 422
Bogue, David, IX, 467
Bohle, Charles-David, V, 218; VI, 664
Bohle, Peter, V, 218; XII, 424
Boieldieu, Adrien, XII, 532, 533
Boies, Thomas, VIII, 738
Boileau, Emmélie (Kimber), VIII, 471
Boileau, Marguerite (Serreau de Saint-Aubin), II, 604
Boileau, René, VIII, 471
Boileau, *dit* Boileau-Despréaux, Nicolas, V, 486, 701, 702; VIII, 88
Boilleau. *See* Gauldrée-Boilleau
Boin, Esther (Rolland), XI, 765
Boire, Agnès (Lanctôt), X, 420
Boiret, Denis, IV, 75
Boiret, René, IV, 74
Boiret, Urbain, IV, **74–75**, 387, 643; V, 379
Bois, Firmin, XI, 86
Bois, Geneviève (Parant), VIII, 681, 682
Bois, Louis-Édouard, IV, 493, 801; VI, 597, 598, 599; VII, 255, 502; IX, 250, 255, 862; X, 507; XI, **86–88**, 172, 182
Bois, Marie-Anne. *See* Boissonnault
Boisberthelot. *See* Dubois
Boisbriand. *See* Dugué
Boisbuisson. *See* Boucher
Boisclerc. *See* Lanoullier
Boisdale. *See* MacDonald
Boisdon, Jacques, I, **104**
Boisguibert. *See* Le Verrier
Boishébert. *See* Deschamps
Boismenay, Marie (Simonnet), IV, 708
Boismorel. *See* Petit
Boispineau, Charles, I, 108; III, 67
Boispineau, Jean-Jard, I, 108; II, 35, **66–67**, 518
Boisseau, Angélique (Rolland), IX, 682
Boisseau, Antoine, VIII, 761
Boisseau, Catherine. *See* Gaspé
Boisseau, Catherine (Létourneau), VII, 502, 503
Boisseau, Claire. *See* Jolliette
Boisseau, Ignace-Gaspard, VII, 503
Boisseau, Josias, I, **104–6**, 290, 396, 397, 541; II, 29, 483
Boisseau, Marguerite. *See* Gérin
Boisseau, Marguerite-Angélique (Lambert Dumont), VI, 385
Boisseau, Marie. *See* Colombier
Boisseau, Marie-Anne. *See* Pagé, *dit* Carcy
Boisseau, Marie-Louise. *See* Bissot de Vincenne
Boisseau, Marie-Zélie (Berthon), XII, 100
Boisseau, Nicolas, IV, **75–76**, 263, 601, 692; V, 90; VI, 385

Boisseau, Nicolas-Gaspard, IV, 75, 692; V, **90–91**, 492, 507, 654, 816; VII, 89
Boisseau, Nicolas-Gaspard, V, 91, 580; VII, **89–90**, 502
Boisseau, Pierre (father of NICOLAS), IV, 75
Boisseau, Pierre (merchant), IX, 538
Boisseau, Thérèse. *See* Couillard
Boisseau, *dit* Cognac, Jacques, I, 267, 273
Boissel, Marguerite (Bouchard), I, 109
Boissemances. *See* Dufrost
Boissi, Charles de, VII, 51
Boissier, Edmond, X, 82
Boissières, Catherine (Perrin), II, 516
Boissonnault, François, XI, 86, 87
Boissonnault, Joseph-Marie, VII, 340
Boissonnault, Marie-Anne (Bois), XI, 86
Boissy, Madeleine (Pellegrin), IV, 620
Boisvert. *See* Joubin-Boisvert; Rapine
Boit, John, IV, 420; V, 387, 388
Boiton de Fougères, Augustin, VI, 623
Boivin, Anne (Lauson), I, 427
Boivin, Charles, I, 106
Boivin, François, I, **106**
Boivin, Guillaume, I, 106
Boivin, Léopoldine (Mercier), XII, 719, 720
Boivin, Marie (Bochart de Champigny), II, 71, 323
Boivin, Marie-Angélique (Paradis), III, 500
Boivin, Pierre, I, 106
Boivin, Thiennette. *See* Fafard
Bolduc, Aurélie-Rosalie (Chaperon), VIII, 139
Bolduc, Henri, VIII, 139
Bolduc, Jean-Baptiste-Zacharie, X, 221; XI, 104; XII, 820
Bolduc, Marie-Françoise (Corriveau), III, 142
Bolduc, Marie-Louise (Gautron), VIII, 319
Bolduc, Mary. *See* Travers
Bolingbroke, Viscount. *See* St John
Bolívar, Simón, VII, 344, 482; VIII, 852
Bollan, William, III, 108, 326
Bolles, Mary Anne Frances (Stimson), IX, 748
Bolles, Susan (Stimson), IX, 748
Bolman, Jane. *See* Brimner
Bolon, Andrew J., XII, 817
Bolper, Marie-Louise (Quiniard, *dit* Duplessis), II, 534
Bolscomb (Balcomb), Rachel (Harris), XI, 385
Bolt, Elizabeth (Wills), VIII, 941
Bolton. *See also* Paulet
Bolton, Duchess of. *See* Lowther
Bolton, Daniel, VIII, 743
Bolton, Mary (Bangs), IX, 26
Bolton, Mason, V, 676, 805, 895
Bolvin, Angélique. *See* Béland
Bolvin, Claire. *See* Jutras
Bolvin, Gilles, II, 200; III, **67–68**; IV, 40, 201, 649; V, 497; VI, 22; VIII, 655
Bolvin, Jean-Baptiste, III, 68
Bolvin, Jean-François, III, 67
Bolvin, Marguerite (Badeaux), IV, 40; VI, 22
Bolvin, Marie-Anne. *See* Isabeau
Bolvin, Marie-Marguerite. *See* Lamarque
Bomer, Louis, IV, 619
Bomoseen, II, 25, 452, 475, 476, 654, 664
Bona. *See* Dufour
Bonacina, Joseph-Maximilien, IX, 208
Bonald, Guillaume-Sylvain de, X, 580; XI, 218

Bonald, Louis-Gabriel-Ambroise, Vicomte de Bonald, VI, 85; VIII, 212; IX, 466; X, 579; XII, 501
Bonald, Mathilde-Sabine de. *See* Parent
Bonami. *See also* Martinet
Bonami, *dit* Lespérance, Alexis, XI, **88–89**
Bonami, *dit* L'Espérance, Marguerite. *See* Gouin
Bonami, *dit* Lespérance, Marguerite. *See* Guernon
Bonami, *dit* L'Espérance, Pierre, XI, 88
Bonamour, Jean de, I, **106–7**
Bonaparte, Charles-Louis-Napoléon. *See* Napoleon III
Bonaparte, Elizabeth. *See* Patterson
Bonaparte, Jérôme (Jérôme, King of Westphalia), V, 660; VI, 642
Bonaparte, Joseph (Joseph, King of Naples; Joseph, King of Spain), V, 616
Bonaparte, Lucien, VII, 51
Bonaparte, Napoléon. *See* Napoleon I
Bonar, Elizabeth. *See* Bell
Bonaventure. *See also* Denys
Bonaventure, Brother, I, 386
Bonaventure, François, IV, 134
Bond, Captain, III, 380
Bond, Anne (Ritchie), VIII, 752
Bond, Elizabeth. *See* Bell
Bond, Frank, XI, 556
Bond, George, VIII, **98**, 224
Bond, James, VI, 76
Bond, James P., VI, 77
Bond, Joseph Norman, VI, **76–77**; VIII, 752
Bond, Mary (mother of JOSEPH NORMAN), VI, 76
Bond, Mary Eliza (Baker), XII, 50
Bond, Norman, VI, 77
Bond*, Sir Robert (1857–1927), XII, 482
Bond, Susan, I, 107
Bond, William, VIII, 165, 166
Bond, William, I, **107**, 361, 493, 529, 657; II, 265
Bond*, William Bennett (1815–1906), VII, 914; IX, 291; X, 138; XI, 503, 557; XII, 431, 573, 711, 814, 1001
Bond, William Cranch, XII, 41
Bondfield, Acklam, V, 21
Bondfield, Anna Marie (Allsopp), IV, 554; V, 20; VII, 14
Bondfield, John, V, 21, 385
Bondfield, John Taylor, IV, 104, 654; V, 20
Bondy. *See also* Douaire
Bondy, Marie-Thérèse (Ainsse; Godefroy), V, 7
Bône. *See* Beaune
Bone, Henry, IX, 543
Bonekeosh. *See* Ponekeosh
Bonemant, Émile, XI, 813
Bonenfant, Charlotte (Têtu), IX, 783
Boneval. *See* Benoît
Bonfield, James, VIII, 269
Bonfils, Marguerite de (Galiffet d'Honon), III, 233
Bonfin, Richard-François, IV, 507
Bonfoy, Hugh, III, **68–69**, 189; IV, 226
Bonga, Jean, V, 715
Bonga, Marie-Jeanne (wife of Jean), V, 715
Bonham, Francis Robert, XII, 292
Bonhomme, Anne (Minet; Bailly de Messein), IV, 41
Bonhomme, Jeanne (Thaumur de La Source), II, 628
Bonhomme, *dit* Beaupré, Agnès. *See* Morin
Bonhomme, *dit* Beaupré, Félicité. *See* Hamel
Bonhomme, *dit* Beaupré, Ignace, III, 69

Bonhomme, *dit* Beaupré, Noël, III, **69**, 617
Boniface, François, II, 61
Bonin, Joseph, VII, 447
Bonnafoux. *See* Bonnefoux
Bonnault, Claude de, VII, 238
Bonnaventure. *See* Denys
Bonneau. *See also* Preissac
Bonneau de La Varenne, Roger de, I, 573
Bonneau de Rubelles, Marie (Beauharnais de Miramion), I, 117
Bonnécamps, Anne de. *See* Muerel
Bonnécamps, Joseph-Pierre de, III, 31, 100, 538, 540, 678; IV, **76–77**, 298, 620
Bonnécamps, Nicolas de, IV, 76
Bonne de Missègle, Louis de, III, **69–70**; V, 128, 230, 487
Bonne de Missègle, Louise de. *See* Prud'homme
Bonne de Missègle, Louis-Joseph de, III, 69
Bonne de Missègle, Marie de. *See* Villeneuve
Bonnefoux (Bonnafoux), Monsieur (merchant), VII, 411, 412
Bonnefoy, Madeleine de (Sarrazin), II, 593
Bonnegrâce, Marie-Anne (Pellegrin), IV, 619
Bonnel, Marie (Turc de Castelveyre), III, 632
Bonnell, Elizabeth (Tonge), VI, 777, 778
Bonnemere, Florent, I, **107–8**
Bonnenfant, Marie-Marguerite (Casgrain), VI, 124; VII, 161
Bonner, Eleanor. *See* Pritchard
Bonner, Elizabeth (Lancaster), VII, 481
Bonner, Jane, II, 81
Bonner, John, II, 81
Bonner, John, II, **80–81**, 287
Bonner, Mary. *See* Clark
Bonner, Samuel, VIII, 632
Bonnerme, Monsieur (surgeon), I, 190, 300
Bonnes, Catherine de (Taffanel de La Jonquière), III, 609
Bonnet, Claire-Sophie (Mille), VIII, 291
Bonnet, Jane (Schurman), V, 742
Bonnet, Jeanne (Richard), I, 473
Bonnet, Joseph, V, 95
Bonneville, Benjamin-Louis-Eulalie de, VII, 672
Bonneville, Judith (Lemieux), IX, 463
Bonnot de Condillac, Étienne, VII, 645
Bonnot de Mably, Gabriel, VI, 85; VII, 675
Bonnycastle, Bridget. *See* Johnstone
Bonnycastle, Frances, Lady Bonnycastle. *See* Johnstone
Bonnycastle, John, VII, 90
Bonnycastle, Sir Richard Henry, VI, 10; VII, **90–92**, 99, 297, 315, 760, 761, 846; VIII, 381, 551; X, 30, 178, 601; XII, 526
Bonrepaus. *See* Dusson
Bonsall, Amos, VIII, 449
Bontein, Helen McKellar (Howe), V, 430
Bontemps, Sieur de (ship's captain), I, 348; II, 82
Bontemps, Jean, III, 422
Bontine. *See also* Buntin
Bontine, Alexander, XII, 135
Bontine, Isabel. *See* McLeod
Bonwah. *See* Benoît
Booker, Alfred, VIII, **98–99**; X, 73
Booker, Alfred, VIII, 99; X, **73–75**, 558; XI, 245, 295, 843; XII, 244, 622, 673, 1055
Booker, Ann (Gardner; wife of ALFRED, 1800–57), VIII, 98

Booker, Sophia. *See* Varnham
Booker, Theophorus, VIII, 99
Boomer, George (father of MICHAEL), XI, 89
Boomer, George (lawyer), IX, 151
Boomer, Harriet Ann. *See* Mills
Boomer, Helen. *See* Adams
Boomer, Isabella Jemima. *See* Davidson
Boomer, Mary. *See* Knox
Boomer, Michael, XI, **89–90**
Boone, Henriette (Marett), IX, 539
Boone, Henry, V, 283, 322
Booth, Benjamin, V, 91
Booth, Edwin Thomas, XII, 622
Booth, Sir Felix, VIII, 772, 773
Booth, Sir George, I, 369
Booth*, John Rudolphus (1826–1925), VIII, 269; XI, 682; XII, 70, 615
Booth, John Wilkes, XII, 449
Booth, Joshua, V, **91–92**, 170, 550, 772
Booth, Junius Brutus, VII, 110; XII, 414
Booth, Margaret. *See* Fraser
Booth, Mary (Richardson), IX, 658, 659
Bootman, Deborah (Berry; Greenwood), VI, 302
Boott, Francis, IX, 658; X, 82
Boquet, Charles, I, **108**, 315, 547, 635, 651; II, 61
Borck, Julianna Sophia Amelia von (Peterson), VIII, 700
Borda. *See* Laborde
Borden*, Sir Frederick William (1847–1917), XII, 97, 114, 115, 941
Borden, Harold Lothrop, XII, **114–15**
Borden, Julia Maude. *See* Clarke
Borden*, Sir Robert Laird (1854–1937), XI, 399, 755, 804; XII, 114, 422
Boré, Étienne, III, 36
Borgia. *See also* Levasseur; Le Vasseur
Borgia, Louis, VII, 176
Borgne de l'Île, Le. *See* Tessouat (d. 1636)
Borland, John, II, 497
Borne, Louis-Eusébe, X, 20
Borne, Michel, VI, 281
Borne, Zélie. *See* Aubert de Gaspé
Borne, Zélie-Angélique (Loranger), XI, 531
Borneuf, Joseph, V, **92–93**, 480; VI, 397
Borneuf, Marie-Madeleine. *See* Degrès
Borneuf, Pierre, V, 92
Borough, Stephen, I, 158
Borough, William, I, 333
Borrel, Joseph, V, 436
Borrel, Théophile-Marie-Louise (Bray), X, 89
Borry de Grandmaison, Laurent, II, 295
Borsalou. *See* Barsalou
Borthwick, Hugh J., IX, 306
Borthwick*, John Douglas (1832–1912), VII, 235; VIII, 470; IX, 78; X, 614; XI, 117, 118; XII, 89, 571, 573
Bory, Gabriel de, III, 31
Boscawen, Charlotte. *See* Godfrey
Boscawen, Edward, III, xxv, **70–71**, 72, 73, 92, 121, 131, 209, 210, 268, 293, 362, 363, 606, 666, 667; IV, xxvi, 21, 22, 327, 661, 668, 751; V, 172, 273, 274, 339, 393, 510, 719
Boscawen, Frances. *See* Evelyn-Glanville
Boscawen, George Evelyn, 3rd Viscount Falmouth, V, 510
Boscawen, Hugh, 1st Viscount Falmouth, III, 70

Boschenry, Jean-Louis de, Baron de Drucourt, III, 71
Boschenry, Marie-Louise de, Baronne de Drucourt. *See* Godard
Boschenry de Drucour, Augustin de, III, xix, xxvii, 6, 55, **71–74**, 230, 231, 268, 417, 440, 570, 667; IV, 22, 214, 250, 644, 645, 646, 656, 673, 751
Boschenry de Drucour, Marie-Anne de. *See* Aubert de Courserac
Boschet de Saint-Martin, François, III, 156
Boschet de Saint-Martin, Marie-Charlotte (Morin de Fonfay), IV, 558
Boschette (Brusquet), Suzanne (Dupuy), II, 213
Bossac, Baron de. *See* Peschart
Bossac, Baronne de. *See* Dollier de Casson
Bossange, Gustave, X, 203
Bossange, Hector, VIII, 283, 679; X, 203; XII, 301
Bossange, Julie. *See* Fabre
Bossange, Martin, VII, 487; VIII, 283
Bossé, François-Xavier, XII, 520
Bossé, Joseph-Noël, VIII, 834; XI, 492; XII, 247
Bossé, Lucianne (Lucie-Anne) (Desbarats), XII, 247, 248, 249
Bossé, Ovide, VIII, 140
Bossu, Catherine. *See* Jean
Bossu, Jean-Bernard, III, 443
Bossu, Jean-Michel-Jacques, V, 93
Bossu, *dit* Lyonnais, Joseph, XII, 503
Bossu, *dit* Lyonnais, Pierre-Jacques, named Brother Félix, V, **93–94**; VII, 591; VIII, 211, 212
Bossuet, Jacques-Bénigne, I, 488; II, 259, 330; IV, 92; V, 165; VIII, 283; IX, 18; X, 579, 580, 585
Boston, Isabella. *See* Stewart
Boston, John, IX, **61–62**; XI, 556, 557
Boston, Lucy (MacDougall), XI, 556, 557
Boston, Margaret. *See* Walker
Boston, Thomas, IX, 61
Bostonais. *See* Pangman, Peter
Bostwick, David Augustus, X, 653
Bostwick, Gesie. *See* Burghardt
Bostwick, Gideon, VII, 92
Bostwick, Henry (fur trader), IV, 369; V, 8, 129; VI, 316
Bostwick, Henry (militia officer), VI, 331; VII, 92
Bostwick, John, VI, 497; VII, **92–93**, 127; VIII, 860
Bostwick, Mary. *See* Ryerson
Bostwick, Polly (wife of JOHN), VII, 92
Bostwick, Sarah (Bates), VII, 53
Boswell, Arthur Radcliffe, XII, 244, 1119
Boswell, Edward Jukes, X, 206
Boswell, George Morss, IX, 49
Boswell, James, V, 166, 803, 805, 811; VIII, 741
Boswell, Jane Georgina (Rubidge), XII, 930
Bosworth, Newton, X, 627; XI, 285
Botha, Louis, XII, 115
Botsford, Amos, V, **94–95**, 160, 258, 353, 354, 416, 607, 831, 867; VI, 7, 655, 740; VII, 806; VIII, 139; IX, 62; X, 157; XI, 90; XII, 115
Botsford, Amos Edwin, VIII, 216; IX, 63; X, 67; XII, **115–17**
Botsford, Bertha. *See* Bennett
Botsford, Blair, IX, 63
Botsford, Bliss, IX, 63; X, 66; XI, **90–91**; XII, 116, 607, 1097
Botsford, Charles, XII, 972

Botsford, Chipman, IX, 63
Botsford, George, XII, 1097, 1098
Botsford, Gideon, V, 94
Botsford, Hazen, IX, 63
Botsford, Hester (Viets), V, 832
Botsford, Jane. *See* Chapman
Botsford, LeBaron, IX, 63, 339
Botsford, Mary Anne (Simpson), XII, 972
Botsford, Mary Arabella. *See* Cogswell
Botsford, Sarah. *See* Chandler
Botsford, Sarah Ann (Hazen), X, 341
Botsford, Sarah Lowell. *See* Hazen
Botsford, William, V, 94, 416, 456; VI, 75, 138, 139, 395,
    727, 740, 810; VII, 412, 692, 854; VIII, 139, 151, 428;
    IX, **62–63**; X, 157, 271, 341; XI, 90; XII, 115
Bott, Elizabeth. *See* LeVallée
Bott, Peter, XII, 1117
Botterell, John Henderson, XII, 126
Bottier, *dit* Berrichon, Nicolas, IV, 252
Bottum, Sarah (Sherwood), VII, 795
Bouat, Abraham, I, 416; II, 81, 509
Bouat, Agathe. *See* Legardeur de Repentigny
Bouat, François-Marie, II, **81–82**, 381, 604; III, 159, 169,
    390, 539
Bouat, Jean-Marie, II, 160
Bouat, Louise-Jeanne (Daine), III, 159
Bouat, Madeleine. *See* Lambert Dumont
Bouat, Madeleine-Marguerite (Dazemard de Lusignan), III,
    169
Bouat, Marguerite. *See* Névellet
Bouat, Marguerite (Pascaud), II, 81, 269, 509; III, 393
Bouat, Thérèse (Poulin de Courval; Gannes de Falaise;
    Jautard), III, 63, 539; IV, 391
Bouate, Jean-Baptiste, VIII, 480
Bouate, Marie-Anne (Lacroix), VIII, 480
Bouate, Marie-Céleste. *See* Foucher
Bouc, Archange. *See* Lepage
Bouc, Charles-Jean-Baptiste, V, 234, 395, 840; VI, **77–78**
Bouc, Louis, VI, 77, 78
Bouc, Marie-Angélique. *See* Comparé
Boucault, Françoise-Anne. *See* Devene
Boucault, Marguerite. *See* Buirette
Boucault, Nicolas-Gaspard, III, 74, 77
Boucault, Nicolas-Gaspard, II, xxiv, 151; III, 64, **74–77**,
    78, 135, 226, 291, 299; IV, 319, 360
Boucault de Godefus, Gilbert, III, 75, **77–78**, 500; IV, 271,
    386
Boucault de Godefus, Marie-Madeleine. *See* Lajoüe
Bouchard, Arthur, XII, **117**
Bouchard, Charles, III, 142
Bouchard, Étienne, I, **108–9**, 201
Bouchard, Félicité. *See* Lebel
Bouchard, Marguerite. *See* Boissel
Bouchard, Marie-Josephte. *See* Corriveau
Bouchard, Mathieu, XII, 117
Bouchard, *dit* Dorval, Geneviève (Forestier; Barsalou), IV,
    46
Bouchard, *dit* Lavallée, André, IX, 782
Bouchard d'Orval, Marie (Bigot), II, 63
Bouchard d'Orval, Marie-Antoinette. *See* Chouart Des
    Grosseilliers
Boucheau. *See* Pouchot
Boucher. *See also* Boucherville

Boucher, Monsieur (merchant), I, 89
Boucher, Adélard-Joseph, X, 31; XII, 977
Boucher, Charles-Auguste, IX, 213
Boucher, Cyrille, IX, **63–66**, 437, 816; X, 542; XI, 623;
    XII, 254
Boucher, Élisabeth (Guion), II, 271
Boucher, Félicité. *See* Roy
Boucher, Florence. *See* Gareman
Boucher, François (clergyman), XI, 396
Boucher, François (father-in-law of Antoine CHAUDILLON),
    II, 140
Boucher, François (father of FRANÇOIS), V, 95
Boucher, François (seigneur), XI, 31
Boucher, François (violinist), XII, 472
Boucher, François, V, **95–96**, 334, 482; VI, 50, 135, 289,
    400; VIII, 101
Boucher, François-Claude, V, 164
Boucher, François-Firmin, VII, 795; VIII, 343
Boucher, François-Xavier, IX, 63
Boucher, Frédéric, IX, 640
Boucher, Gaspard, I, 330; II, 82, 83
Boucher, Geneviève, named de Saint-Pierre, III, **78–79**
Boucher, Jean-Baptiste, IV, 639; VI, 592; VII, **93–95**, 341,
    645; X, 76
Boucher, Jeanne. *See* Crevier
Boucher, Jeanne (Sabrevois), II, 86, 589; IV, 690
Boucher, Jonathan, V, 628
Boucher, Joseph, V, 588
Boucher, Josephte. *See* Kanhopitsa
Boucher, Julienne (Chapais), XI, 175
Boucher, Léocadie (Nelson; Lacombe), IX, 439
Boucher, Louis-Michel, V, 95
Boucher, Lucie-Angélique. *See* Cotté
Boucher, Madeleine (Baudry, *dit* La Marche), II, 48, 82,
    83
Boucher, Madeleine (Legardeur de Tilly), II, 387
Boucher, Marguerite (Daneau de Muy), II, 168; III, 161,
    162
Boucher, Marguerite (Riel, *dit* L'Irlande), IX, 663
Boucher, Marguerite (Toupin), II, 82
Boucher, Marguerite-Madeleine. *See* Goutin
Boucher, Marie (Blaise Des Bergères), II, 69
Boucher, Marie (Chaudillon), II, 140
Boucher, Marie (Gaultier de Varennes), I, 327; II, 85, 202,
    240; III, 245, 246, 247; IV, 234
Boucher, Marie (La Fond), II, 82, 83; III, 629
Boucher, Marie-Anne. *See* Martel
Boucher, Marie-Joseph. *See* Tremblay
Boucher, Marie-Madeleine. *See* Ouebadinskoue
Boucher, Marin, I, 330
Boucher, Nicolas, II, 82
Boucher, Nicole. *See* Lemer
Boucher, Philippe, II, 523
Boucher, Pierre, V, 95
Boucher, Pierre, I, 32, 45, 109, 123, 172, 200, 238, 283,
    327, 349, 354, 404, 468, 511, 512, 543, 579, 619; II, xvi,
    xvii, 16, 61, 62, **82–87**, 92, 168, 189, 202, 240, 387, 433,
    540, 589, 597, 599, 624; III, 78, 80, 81, 82, 83, 161, 247,
    629; IV, 234; VIII, 100; IX, 66, 696; X, 18
Boucher, Pierre-François, IV, 69, 127
Boucher, Pierre-Jérôme, II, 154, 648; III, **79–80**, 229, 575,
    644
Boucher, Renée (Paris), III, 501

Boucher, *dit* Belleville, Jean-Baptiste (father of Jean-Baptiste BOUCHER), VII, 93
Boucher, *dit* Belleville, Jean-Baptiste (stonemason), III, 220, 234; IV, 203, 659
Boucher, *dit* Belleville, Marie. *See* Martin
Boucher, *dit* Boisbuisson, Louis-Marin, I, 619
Boucher-Belleville, Jean-Philippe, VII, 173, 236, 247, 248, 345, 346; VIII, 471, 616; X, **75–76**, 576
Boucher-Belleville, Louise. *See* Belleau
Boucher-Belleville, Marguerite. *See* Porlier
Boucher-Belleville, Pierre, X, 75
Boucher* de Boucherville, Sir Charles-Eugène (1822–1915), X, 25, 26, 218, 438; XI, 27, 185, 345, 480, 492, 520, 531, 625, 920; XII, 88, 90, 118, 175, 176, 181, 197, 421, 464, 655, 694, 721, 726, 903, 1046
Boucher de Boucherville, Charles-Marie, V, 96
Boucher de Boucherville, Charlotte. *See* Denys de La Trinité
Boucher de Boucherville, Charlotte (Perrault), IV, 623; V, 667; VI, 577; VII, 687
Boucher de Boucherville, Claire-Françoise (Pommereau; Legardeur de Croisille et de Montesson), III, 339, 525; IV, 109, 447
Boucher de Boucherville, Joséphine. *See* Proulx
Boucher de Boucherville, Madeleine. *See* Raimbault de Saint-Blaint
Boucher de Boucherville, Madeleine-Charlotte (Chaussegros de Léry), V, 96; VI, 133
Boucher de Boucherville, Marguerite. *See* Raimbault
Boucher de Boucherville, Marie-Marguerite (La Corne), IV, 427
Boucher de Boucherville, Pierre, II, 617; III, 80, 525
Boucher de Boucherville, Pierre, II, 542; III, **80–81**, 269; IV, 427, 623; V, 96, 667
Boucher de Boucherville, René-Amable, IV, 346; V, **96–97**; VI, 133, 239; VIII, 100
Boucher de Boucherville, Thomas-René-Verchères, V, 96; VIII, **99–101**
Boucher de Boucherville et de Montarville, Charles, II, 296
Boucher de Boucherville et de Montarville, Françoise. *See* Bourot
Boucher de Grandpré, Geneviève (Hertel de Chambly; Simonet d'Abergemont), III, 592
Boucher de Grandpré, Lambert, I, **109**; II, 70; III, 592
Boucher de Grandpré, Marguerite. *See* Vauvril de Blason
Boucher de Grosbois, Charlotte (Mondelet), VII, 622; IX, 559; X, 526
Boucher de La Broquerie. *See* Labroquerie
Boucher de La Bruère. *See also* Labruère
Boucher de La Bruère, Charlotte (Trottier Desrivières Beaubien), V, 829
Boucher de la Bruère (La Bruyère), Françoise (Le Mercier), IV, 458
Boucher de La Bruère, Julie-Aurélie (Pacaud), XI, 658
Boucher de La Bruère, Marie-Hippolyte. *See* La Broquerie
Boucher de La Bruère, Marie-Julie. *See* Weilbrenner
Boucher de La Bruère, Montarville, VIII, 617
Boucher* de La Bruère, Pierre (1837–1917), X, 77; XII, 720, 725
Boucher de La Bruère, Pierre-Claude, VIII, 712; X, **76–77**; XI, 659
Boucher de La Bruère, Pierre-René, VII, 883, 884

Boucher de La Bruère, René, V, 248, 829; VIII, 108, 479; X, 76
Boucher* de La Bruère, René-Montarville (1867–1943), X, 736
Boucher de la Bruère de Montarville, Françoise (Taschereau), VI, 752; IX, 779
Boucher de La Bruère de Montarville, Joseph, V, 165
Boucher de La Perrière. *See also* Laperière
Boucher de La Perrière, Charlotte (Vassal de Monviel; Boucher de La Bruère), VII, 883
Boucher de La Perrière, Françoise. *See* Malhiot
Boucher de La Perrière, François-Clément, III, 81; IV, 142
Boucher de La Perrière, Joseph, X, 490
Boucher de La Perrière, Julie (Malhiot), X, 490
Boucher de La Perrière, Marie-Madeleine (Pécaudy de Contrecœur), III, 81; IV, 618
Boucher de La Perrière, René, II, 201; III, 44, 80, **81–82**, 103, 269; IV, 618
Boucher de Montbrun, François, III, 82
Boucher de Montbrun, Françoise. *See* Godefroy de Saint-Paul
Boucher de Montbrun, Françoise, named Saint-Placide, III, 630
Boucher de Montbrun, Françoise-Claire. *See* Charest
Boucher de Montbrun, Jacques-Timothée, IV, 303
Boucher de Montbrun, Jean, III, **82**
Boucher de Montbrun, Jean-Baptiste, III, 82
Boucher de Montbrun, Madeleine. *See* Godefroy de Saint-Paul
Boucher de Montbrun, René, III, 82
Boucher de Montizambert, Jacques, II, 433
Boucher de Niverville, Éliza. *See* Lafond
Boucher de Niverville, Françoise (Spagniolini), III, 598
Boucher de Niverville, Jean-Baptiste, IV, 150; V, 98; VIII, 655
Boucher de Niverville, Jean-Baptiste, III, **82–83**, 598; IV, 690; V, 97
Boucher de Niverville, Joseph, III, 83, 375, 429; IV, 332, 634; V, 26, **97–100**, 216, 217, 225
Boucher de Niverville, Joseph-Michel, IX, 66
Boucher de Niverville, Josephte. *See* Laviolette
Boucher de Niverville, Louis-Charles, VIII, 247; IX, **66–67**, 487
Boucher de Niverville, Marguerite-Thérèse. *See* Hertel de La Fresnière
Boucher de Niverville, Marie-Josephte. *See* Chastelain
Boucher de Niverville, Marie-Josephte. *See* Châtelin
Boucher de Niverville, Marie-Marguerite (Marchand), VI, 485
Boucher de Niverville de Montisambert, Louis, IV, 653
Boucher de Niverville (Nebourvele) Grandpré, François, IV, 214, 240; V, 97, 98
Boucher de Niverville Montizambert, Pierre-Louis, V, 98
Boucherville. *See also* Boucher; Verchères
Boucherville, Georges de, VIII, 668; IX, 440; XII, **117–19**
Boucherville, Louise de. *See* Gregory
Boucherville, Marguerite-Émilie de. *See* Bleury
Boucherville, Pierre de, V, 96; VII, 397; XI, 274; XII, 117
Bouchet. *See* Bouchette
Bouchette, Adélaïde. *See* Chaboillez
Bouchette, Caroline-Anne. *See* Berthelot
Bouchette, Clara. *See* Lindsay

Bouchette, Jean-Baptiste, IV, 547; V, 99, **100–2**, 699, 791, 877; VI, 695; VII, 95
Bouchette, Joseph, VII, 97; XII, 321
Bouchette, Joseph, V, 61, 72, 101, 179, 183, 228, 235, 428, 460, 835, 879, 880; VI, 69, 84, 119, 224, 240, 339, 383, 386, 423, 428, 477, 585, 681, 749; VII, **95–98**, 134, 168, 283, 658, 702, 771, 836, 837, 865, 877; VIII, 108, 223, 274, 585, 911; IX, 387; X, 30, 32, 77
Bouchette, Luce (Rolette), V, 101
Bouchette (Bouchet), Marc, V, 100
Bouchette, Marie-Angélique. *See* Duhamel
Bouchette, Marie-Louise-Adélaïde. *See* Chaboillez
Bouchette, Marie-Thérèse. *See* Grenet
Bouchette, Mary Ann. *See* Gardner
Bouchette*, Robert-Errol (1863–1912), X, 78, 586
Bouchette, Robert-Shore-Milnes, VII, 97, 248, 427, 836; VIII, 471, 617, 938; IX, 699; X, **77–78**, 260, 546
Bouchette, Samuel-Louis, VI, 585
Bouchy, Pierre-Henri, X, 228; XII, 731, 732
Boucicault, Dion, XII, 572, 622
Boucicaut, Aristide, XII, 761
Boudeau. *See* Baudeau
Boudet, Anne (Du Calvet), IV, 227
Boudet, Romaine (Becquet), I, 86
Boudier de Beauregard, Antoine, I, 344
Boudier de Beauregard, Éléonore. *See* Grandmaison
Boudon, Henri-Marie, II, 360
Boudor, Jean, II, 160, 453
Boudor, Marguerite. *See* Seigneuret
Boudreau, Cécile (Pitre; Pellerin), V, **102**
Boudria, Élisabeth. *See* Saint-Denis
Boudria, J.-B., VII, 149
Boudrias, Rachel (Couillard), VIII, 479
Boudrot. *See also* Boudreau
Boudrot, Abraham, I, 427
Boudrot, Charles, V, 102
Boudrot, Élisabeth (Le Blanc), IV, 441
Boudrot, François, III, 97
Boudrot, Marguerite. *See* Bourgeois
Boudrot, Marguerite (Bourg), III, 83
Boudrot, Marie-Josephe. *See* Landry
Bouette, Jeanne (Roussel), I, 583
Bougainville, Jean-Pierre de, IV, 755
Bougainville, Louis-Antoine de, Comte de Bougainville, III, 86, 293, 328, 408, 459, 464, 466, 535, 560, 671, 672; IV, 54, 68, 76, 207, 208, 214, 335, 479, 507, 588, 620, 646, 670, 671, 672, 691, 754, 755; V, **102–6**, 462, 738, 739, 824
Bougainville, Marie-Françoise de. *See* Arboulin
Bougainville, Marie-Joséphine de. *See* Longchamps-Montendre
Bougainville, Pierre-Yves de, V, 102
Bouge, Ange, known as La Corruble, I, 203; II, 243
Bougret Dufort, Marguerite (Bourgy; Simonnet), IV, 709
Bouillet, Claude, II, 88
Bouillet de La Chassaigne, Anne. *See* Bartaud
Bouillet de La Chassaigne, Gaudefroy, II, 87
Bouillet de La Chassaigne, Jean, II, **87–88**, 125, 603; III, 60, 191; IV, 663
Bouillet de La Chassaigne, Marie-Anne. *See* Le Moyne de Longueuil
Bouillon, Duc de. *See* La Marck
Bouin, Julien, I, 250

Bouin, Marguerite. *See* Berrin
Bouin, *dit* Dufresne, Geneviève (Gagnon), VII, 332
Boujonnier, Florent, II, 83
Boulanger. *See also* Le Boulanger; Lefebvre
Boulanger, Bernard-Joseph, IV, 539
Boulanger, Clément, VII, 171; IX, **67–68**, 781; XI, 588
Boulanger, Damase, VIII, 572
Boulanger, Marguerite. *See* Receveur
Boulanger, Pierre, IX, 67
Boulay. *See* Boullet; Talon
Boulay, Marquise de. *See* Molé
Boulduc, Élisabeth. *See* Hubert
Boulduc, Gilette. *See* Pijart
Boulduc, Louis, II, xxiv, **88–89**, 213
Boulduc, Louise, II, 89
Boulduc, Pierre, II, 88
Bouler, Robert, II, 295, **89–90**
Bouliane, Modeste (Tremblay, *dit* Picoté), VIII, 892
Boulic, Marie-Renée, named de la Nativité, II, 303
Boullard, Anne (Berthelet), VI, 52
Boullard, Étienne, II, **90–91**, 211, 587; III, 15, 45, 114, 201, 202, 240, 330, 522, 553, 646
Boullé, Eustache, I, **109–10**, 193, 195, 200, 311, 495, 509
Boullé, Hélène, named de Saint-Augustin (Champlain), I, 109, **110**, 161, 190
Boullé, Marguerite. *See* Alix
Boullé, Nicolas, I, 109, 110
Boullet (Boulay), Captain, I, 110
Boullongne, Eustache de. *See* Quéan
Boullongne, Florentin de, I, 43, 110
Boullongne, Louis de, IX, 361
Boullongne, Marie-Barbe de (Ailleboust de Coulonge et d'Argentenay), I, 43, 44, 47, **110–11**, 113, 204, 206, 217, 230, 412, 612; II, 605, 639; III, 548
Boullongne, Philippine-Gertrude de, named de Saint-Dominique, I, 43, 44, 111, 217, 230
Boullot, Pierre, IV, 678
Boult, Anne (Hincks), X, 349; XI, 406
Boultbee, Alfred, XI, 582
Boulton, Anna Maria. *See* Walton
Boulton, Augusta. *See* Latter
Boulton, Charles Arkoll, IX, 617, 618, 708; XI, 571, 740, 929; XII, **119–20**, 203, 752, 951
Boulton, D'Arcy, VI, 80; VII, 753; IX, 346, 647, 745; X, 79
Boulton, D'Arcy, V, 521, 559, 734; VI, **78–80**, 116, 118, 630, 631, 656, 770; VII, 285, 369, 438, 617, 920, 929; VIII, 5, 180, 511, 515; IX, 68, 69, 519, 668, 669, 673; X, 78, 79; XI, 165
Boulton, D'Arcy, X, **78–79**; XII, 119, 578
Boulton, D'Arcy Edward, VIII, 391, 486, 555; XI, 196; XII, 119
Boulton, Eliza. *See* Jones
Boulton, Elizabeth. *See* Forster
Boulton, Elizabeth (Boulton), IX, 68
Boulton, Elizabeth (Cameron), X, 118
Boulton, Emily. *See* Heath
Boulton, Emma Robinson (Cayley), XI, 165
Boulton, George Strange, VII, 34, 75, 319; VIII, 391, 486; IX, 44, **68**, 69; X, 79, 253; XII, 781
Boulton, Harriette Elizabeth. *See* Dixon
Boulton, Henry (father), VI, 78
Boulton, Henry, VI, 79

Boulton, Henry John, V, 458, 673; VI, 79, 80, 164, 369, 497, 630, 631, 633; VII, 40, 42, 98, 99, 113, 154, 155, 207, 230, 294, 295, 296, 315, 319, 369, 370, 494, 507, 631, 632, 662, 793, 834; VIII, 6, 53, 55, 56, 69, 233, 234, 246, 252, 337, 403, 426, 431, 468, 469, 511, 512, 521, 733, 797, 846, 847, 850, 877, 950; IX, 68, **69–72**, 108, 168, 329, 499, 500, 501, 520, 670, 674, 721, 724; X, 79, 118, 180, 310, 359, 433, 553, 600, 601, 656, 687, 688, 705; XI, 28, 412, 427, 552, 673, 760; XII, 101

Boulton, Mrs Irma, VII, 662

Boulton, James, VIII, 486, 733; IX, 233; X, 78, 441

Boulton, John George, XI, 57

Boulton, Louisa Charlotte. *See* Corbett

Boulton, Mary. *See* Preston

Boulton, Matthew, V, 55; VIII, 630

Boulton, Sarah Ann. *See* Robinson

Boulton, Susan. *See* Beman

Boulton, William Henry, VIII, 52, 282, 486, 801; IX, 72, 346, 542, 689; X, **79–81**, 119, 121, 619; XI, 143, 144, 228; XII, 101, 907, 1108

Boumois. *See* Gaultier

Bound, John, IV, 565

Bouquet, Henry, III, xxvi, 219, 529, 530; IV, 24, 25, 38, 85, 86, 297, 347, 408, 409; V, 301, 714, 887, 888, 889, 902

Bouquin, Claude, I, 361; II, 189

Bourassa, Alfred, XII, 120

Bourassa, Augustin-Médard, IX, 398

Bourassa, Azélie. *See* Papineau

Bourassa, François, XII, 120

Bourassa, François, XII, **120–21**, 692

Bourassa, Geneviève. *See* Patenaude

Bourassa, Gustave, XI, 182

Bourassa*, Henri (1868–1952), XII, 120, 727, 938

Bourassa, Joseph, VII, 137; XII, 1004

Bourassa*, Napoléon (1827–1916), VII, 697; IX, 364, 450; X, 577; XI, 309, 716; XII, 120, 170, 171, 789

Bourassa, Sophie. *See* Trahan

Bourassa, *dit* La Ronde, Agnès. *See* Gagné

Bourassa, *dit* La Ronde, Charlotte-Ambroisine (Mouet de Langlade), IV, 78, 563

Bourassa, *dit* La Ronde, François, IV, 77

Bourassa, *dit* La Ronde, Ignace, IV, 78

Bourassa, *dit* La Ronde, Marie. *See* Le Ber

Bourassa, *dit* La Ronde, Marie-Catherine. *See* Leriger de La Plante

Bourassa, *dit* La Ronde, René, IV, 78

Bourassa, *dit* La Ronde, René, III, 205; IV, **77–78**, 563

Bourbeau, Désiré-Olivier, XI, 112

Bourbeau, Marie-Angèle (Drapeau), XII, 269

Bourbon. *See also* Alfonso; Carlos

Bourbon, Duc de. *See* Condé

Bourbon, Caroline de, Duchesse de Berry. *See* Caroline

Bourbon, César de, Duc de Vendôme, I, 129, 434, 436, 514

Bourbon, Charles de, I, 87, 88, 89, 421

Bourbon, Charles de, Comte de Soissons, I, 186, 191, 294

Bourbon, François de, Duc de Beaufort, II, 98

Bourbon, François de, Duc de Montpensier, I, 421

Bourbon, Louis-Alexandre de, Comte de Toulouse, II, 273, 417, 425, 648; III, 74, 105, 106, 108, 118, 345

Bourbon, Louis-François de, Prince de Conti, IV, 477, 558

Bourbon, Louis-Jean-Marie de, Duc de Penthièvre, III, 108, 118

Bourbon, Louis-Joseph de, Prince de Condé, IV, 344, 481; VI, 59

Bourbon, Marie-Anselme de. *See* Abbadie de Saint- Castin

Bourbon, Marie-Louise de (Orléans, Duchesse de Montpensier), IX, 854

Bourbonnais, Avila-Gonzalve, XII, 277

Bourbonnière. *See* Gaudry

Bourbourg. *See* Brasseur

Bourchier, Mrs. *See* Macnamara

Bourchier, Hugh Plunkett, IX, **72–73**

Bourchier, John, IX, 72

Bourchier, Sir Thomas, IX, 72

Bourcier, Françoise (Chartier), I, 202

Bourdages, Esther. *See* Leblanc

Bourdages, Louis, IV, 79; V, 165, 269, 813; VI, 42, 48, 50, 68, **80–83**, 207, 384, 433; VII, 61, 119, 226, 236, 374, 878, 879; VIII, 155, 175, 213, 248, 491, 681, 711, 717; IX, 360, 441, 485, 795, 810, 811; X, 554, 567, 569, 574; XI, 623

Bourdages, Louise-Catherine. *See* Soupiran

Bourdages, Louise-Esther (Couillard-Després), VIII, 175

Bourdages, Marie-Anne. *See* Chevalier

Bourdages, Marie-Antoinette (Dubord; Chinic), VII, 176; X, 261

Bourdages, Pierre, IV, 78

Bourdages, Raymond, IV, **78–79**; VI, 80

Bourdaloue, Louis, VIII, 283

Bourdois, Jeanne (Baillairgé), V, 48

Bourdon, Anne. *See* Gasnier

Bourdon, Anne, named de Sainte-Agnès, I, 112, 113, 430; II, **91–92**

Bourdon, Geneviève. *See* Amaugère

Bourdon, Geneviève, named Marie de Saint-Joseph, I, 113; II, 92

Bourdon, Jacqueline. *See* Potel

Bourdon, Jacques, II, **92**

Bourdon, Jean, II, 92

Bourdon, Jean (known as Monsieur de Saint-Jean or Sieur de Saint-François), I, 45, 49, 106, **111–13**, 114, 202, 204, 227, 339, 340, 344, 353, 359, 371, 372, 373, 389, 396, 397, 404, 430, 472, 480, 523, 538, 580, 584, 585, 587, 588, 589; II, xvii, 82, 91, 92, 137

Bourdon, Marguerite. *See* Legris

Bourdon, Marguerite, named de Saint-Jean-Baptiste, I, 113; II, **92–93**, 613

Bourdon, Marie. *See* Ménard

Bourdon, Marie, named de Sainte-Thérèse-de-Jésus, I, 113; II, 92

Bourdon, Marie (Gloria), I, 339

Bourdon, Nicolas, I, 114

Bourdon d'Autray, Jacques, I, 111, **113–14**, 178; II, 672

Bourdon de Dombourg, Jean-François, I, 112, 113, **114**; II, 176, 205, 347

Bourdon de Dombourg, Jean-François, III, 417, 425; IV, **79–80**; V, 339; VI, 228

Bourdon de Dombourg, Jeanne. *See* Jannière

Bourdon de Dombourg, Marguerite. *See* Gautier, *dit* Bellair

Bourdon de Dombourg et de La Pinaudière, Jean- François, IV, 79

Bourdon de Dombourg et de La Pinaudière, Madeleine. *See* Poirel

Bourdon de Romainville, Catherine, I, 114

Bourdon de Romainville, Jean, I, **114–15**, 257

Bourdon de Romainville, Madeleine. *See* Daguerre
Bourduceau, Anne-Françoise (Sailly), I, 592
Bourduceau, Médéric, I, 592
Bourg, Abraham, II, 23, **93–94**
Bourg, Anne. *See* Hébert
Bourg, Antoine, II, 93
Bourg, Antoinette. *See* Landry
Bourg, Brigitte. *See* Martin
Bourg, François, III, 83
Bourg, Isabelle (Dugas), VI, 227
Bourg, Joseph-Mathurin, IV, 13, **80–82**, 136, 153, 423, 436, 444, 469, 470, 511, 736; V, 458, 587, 687; VI, 86, 228; VII, 246, 801
Bourg, Madeleine (Maisonnat; Le Blanc), II, 449; III, 421, 665
Bourg, Marguerite. *See* Boudrot
Bourg, Marguerite (Allain), III, 254
Bourg, Marie. *See* Brun
Bourg, Marie-Anne (Leclère), IX, 459
Bourg, Michel, IV, 80
Bourg, Rosalie (Prince), VIII, 711
Bourg, *dit* Belle-Humeur, Alexandre, II, 23; III, **83–84**, 366, 421, 427; IV, 80, 441
Bourg, *dit* Belle-Humeur, Anne (Leblanc, *dit* Le Maigre), III, 366; IV, 441
Bourg, *dit* Belle-Humeur, Marguerite. *See* Melanson, *dit* La Verdure
Bourgchemin. *See* Hamelin
Bourgeau, Delphine. *See* Viau
Bourgeau, Delphine-Denise. *See* Perrault
Bourgeau, Edwidge. *See* Vaillant
Bourgeau, Eugène, X, **81–82**; XI, 662; XII, 194
Bourgeau, Victor, XI, 92
Bourgeau, Victor, VI, 554; VII, 697; VIII, 763; IX, 552; XI, **91–94**, 506, 588
Bourgeau, Victor-Henri, X, 657
Bourgeault, Bazile, XI, 91
Bourgeault, Marie. *See* Lavoie
Bourgeaux, Françoise. *See* Missilier
Bourgeaux, Jacques, X, 81
Bourgeois, Anne. *See* Dugas
Bourgeois, Anne (Caissy), III, 426
Bourgeois, Charles, II, 94
Bourgeois, Élizabeth (Leménager), VII, 28
Bourgeois, Germain, II, 94
Bourgeois, Guillaume, I, 67; II, 93, 94
Bourgeois, Jacques, II, 94
Bourgeois, Jacques (Jacob), I, 67, 510; II, **94**, 410, 449; IV, xx
Bourgeois, Jean-Baptiste, X, 25; XI, 479, 624
Bourgeois, Jeanne. *See* Trahan
Bourgeois, Jeanne (Robichaux), IV, 676; VI, 651; VII, 752
Bourgeois, Louis-Thomas, XI, 494
Bourgeois, Madeleine. *See* Dugas
Bourgeois, Marguerite. *See* Belliveau
Bourgeois, Marguerite (Boudrot; Mirande; Maisonnat), II, 449
Bourgeois, Marianne. *See* Aprendestiguy
Bourgeois, Marie (Leblanc), III, 366; IV, 441
Bourgeois, Nathalie (Auffray), VII, 28
Bourgeois de Boynes, Pierre-Étienne, IV, 70
Bourgeoys, Abraham, I, 115
Bourgeoys, Anne, I, 115

Bourgeoys, Guillemette. *See* Garnier
Bourgeoys, Marguerite, named du Saint-Sacrement, I, 31, **115–19**, 213, 220, 231, 344, 453, 486, 487, 564, 598; II, 44, 47, 132, 222, 233, 249, 376, 377, 601; III, 332, 385, 386, 407, 580, 629, 630; IV, 638; VII, 54, 431; IX, 216, 217, 247, 248; XII, 1002
Bourget, Claude, II, 159; XI, 94
Bourget, Élisabeth (Jacquet), IV, 386
Bourget, Ignace, VII, 8, 19, 54, 59, 171, 264, 267, 268, 306, 423, 431, 449, 487, 488, 490, 496, 624, 644, 677, 679, 680, 705, 799, 800, 887, 940; VIII, 20, 66, 141, 145, 146, 214, 241, 243, 244, 261, 262, 318, 333, 457, 458, 490, 595, 619, 703, 704, 711, 712, 713, 722, 730, 731, 777, 792, 864, 865, 912, 974; IX, 18, 19, 20, 50, 51, 64, 67, 96, 111, 117, 194, 211, 228, 249, 343, 397, 402, 447, 450, 452, 453, 466, 533, 549, 615, 617, 681, 698, 781, 799, 802, 805, 861; X, 17, 52, 107, 148, 151, 154, 165, 175, 176, 193, 237, 250, 251, 252, 266, 281, 315, 322, 416, 417, 421, 422, 429, 430, 527, 532, 578, 589, 689, 715, 733; XI, 13, 34, 42, 43, 58, 70, 71, 93, **94–105**, 109, 110, 167, 168, 169, 170, 171, 173, 184, 185, 187, 188, 235, 249, 250, 251, 253, 270, 273, 274, 275, 276, 277, 303, 424, 493, 494, 588, 692, 693, 694, 695, 725, 726, 744, 746, 755, 776, 777, 782, 865, 890, 892, 893, 894, 895, 955; XII, 57, 90, 173, 190, 191, 192, 214, 249, 255, 267, 301, 302, 303, 304, 305, 354, 360, 501, 506, 509, 511, 546, 573, 692, 697, 698, 732, 788, 809, 819, 820, 821, 875, 891, 1003, 1017, 1018, 1020, 1021, 1133, 1137
Bourget, Marie. *See* Couture
Bourget, Pierre (father), XI, 94
Bourget, Pierre, XI, 94
Bourget, Thérèse. *See* Paradis
Bourgina, Hélène (Gaschet), III, 237
Bourgine, Hilaire, II, 11
Bourgmond. *See* Véniard
Bourgogne, Duc de. *See* Louis de France
Bourgoin, Mr (judge), XII, 99
Bourgonnière de Hauteville, Barthélemy-François, II, 116, 483
Bourguignon. *See also* Guichard; Janot
Bourguignon, Isaac, XII, 692
Bourgy, Léger, IV, 709
Bourgy, Marguerite. *See* Bougret Dufort
Bourinot, John, XI, **105–6**
Bourinot*, Sir John George (1836–1902), VII, 231, 589; X, 413; XI, 106, 724, 755, 871, 884; XII, 152, 236, 516
Bourinot, Margaret Jane. *See* Marshall
Bourinot, Marshall, XI, 106
Bourjoly. *See* Besnard
Bourk; Bourke. *See also* Burke
Bourke, John Palmer, VIII, 537
Bourlamaque, François-Charles de, III, 12, 19, **84–87**, 243, 259, 459, 467, 535, 565, 591; IV, 23, 211, 347, 382, 427, 479, 588, 729; V, 164, 638, 677, 739
Bourlamaque, Jean-François de, III, 84
Bourlet, Nicolas, II, 33, 273, 464, 465, 508
Bourloton, Charlotte (Spagniolini), III, 598
Bourn, George, XI, 403
Bourne, Adolphus, VII, 70, 823; XI, **106–7**
Bourne, Elizabeth (wife of JOHN GERVAS HUTCHINSON), VII, 98
Bourne, Elizabeth J. (Gault), XI, 335

Bourne, George, III, 305; VII, 194, 625
Bourne, John, VII, 98
Bourne, John Gervas Hutchinson, VII, **98–100**; VIII, 234, 380, 382, 950; IX, 169; XI, 761
Bourne, Ruth Elizabeth (mother of JOHN GERVAS HUTCHINSON), VII, 98
Bourneuf, François, X, 83
Bourneuf, François-Lambert, V, 261; VII, 895; X, **83**
Bourneuf, Marie. See Doucet
Bourneuf, Michelle. See Énolle
Bournicat, Marie (Degeay), IV, 200
Bouron, Henri, IV, 270; V, 652
Bourond, Marie-Louise (Landriaux), IV, 434
Bourot, Françoise (Chaviteau; Jérémie, dit Lamontagne; Boucher de Boucherville et de Montarville), II, 296, 298
Bourque, Louis-Quentin, VII, 805
Bourque, Marguerite (Trahan), V, 827
Bourret, Alexis, VIII, 694
Bourret, François-Emmanuel, V, 207, 495; VI, 397, 398, 526; VII, 720
Bourret, Henriette. See Peltier
Bourret, Joseph, VIII, 693; XI, 58, 70
Bourret, Louis-Alexis, VII, 581
Boursier, Joseph, I, 461
Boursois, Marie-Nicole (Point), IX, 636
Bourville. See Le Coutre
Boussat, Jean, I, 108
Boussin, Simon, VII, 746; VIII, 490
Bouteiller. See Bouthellier
Boutet de Saint-Martin, Catherine. See Soulage
Boutet de Saint-Martin, Catherine (Phélippeaux; Soullard), II, 612
Boutet de Saint-Martin, Marie, I, 119
Boutet de Saint-Martin, Martin, I, **119**, 359; II, 17, 227, 228, 508, 612
Bouteville, Geneviève (Peuvret de Gaudarville), II, 525
Bouthellier (Bouteiller), Magdeleine (Rollin), VIII, 762
Bouthier, François, IV, 653
Bouthier, Françoise. See Denys de La Ronde
Bouthier, Guillaume, II, 14
Bouthillier. See also Boutillier
Bouthillier, Angèlique. See Lemaire Saint-Germain
Bouthillier, Anne-Elmire (Rastel de Rocheblave), VII, 735
Bouthillier, C.-E.-E., X, 422
Bouthillier, Claire. See Parent
Bouthillier, François, VI, 664
Bouthillier, Jean (father-in-law of Pierre-Louis PANET), IX, 613
Bouthillier, Jean (father-in-law of Pierre de RASTEL de Rocheblave), VII, 737
Bouthillier, Jean-Antoine, VI, **83–84**
Bouthillier, Léonard, VII, 595
Bouthillier, Louise-Clorinthe (Panet), IX, 613
Bouthillier, Louis-Tancrède, IX, 697
Bouthillier, Pierre (father of JEAN-ANTOINE), VI, 84
Bouthillier, Pierre (partner of Joseph QUESNEL), V, 701
Bouthillier, Tancrède, VII, 580
Bouthillier, Véronique (Moquin; Lefebvre), XII, 546
Boutilier, Monsieur (of France), I, 503
Boutillac, Jean de, I, 424
Boutillier, Mrs (mother-in-law of Constant GARNIER), XII, 356
Boutillier, Anne-Françoise. See Normand

Boutillier, Eugénie. See Papineau
Boutillier, Guillaume, IX, 73
Boutillier, Thomas, VIII, 175, 712; IX, **73–74**; X, 545; XI, 822; XII, 253
Boutin, Charles-Robert, IV, 632
Boutin, Josephte (Baillairgé), VI, 24; VIII, 38
Boutin, Renée (Taschereau de Sapaillé), III, 616
Boutineau, Susannah (Francklin), IV, 272
Boutonne, Josette (Boyer), IX, 77
Boutroue, Mlle de (daughter of CLAUDE), I, 322
Boutroue d'Aubigny, Claude de, I, **119–20**, 322, 326, 534, 571, 624; II, xix, 166
Boutroue d'Aubigny, Marie de. See Lescot
Boutwell, Hester. See Crooks
Bouvart, Martin (Samuel), II, **94–95**, 245, 331, 332
Bouveret. See Dagnan-Bouveret
Bouvier (Boyer), Monsieur (trader), I, 382
Bouvier, Jean-Baptiste, XI, 99; XII, 359
Bouvier, Michel, I, 78; II, 105
Bouvot de Chevilly, François, I, 213
Bouvot de Chevilly, Jacqueline. See Chomedey
Bove, Monsieur (fur trader), IV, 160
Bovell, James, VIII, 96, 442; X, 39, **83–85**, 350, 351, 381, 382; XI, 54, 916; XII, 11, 106, 383
Bovell, John, X, 83
Bovell, Julia Howard. See App-Griffith
Bovell, Sarah. See Applewaite
Boves, Charles de, I, 386, 417
Bovey*, Henry Taylor (1852–1912), IX, 655
Bow, Agnes (Robertson), XI, 757
Bowden. See also Boden
Bowden, Elizabeth (Harbidge), VII, 902
Bowdoin, James, V, 238
Bowell*, Sir Mackenzie (1823–1917), X, 121, 136; XI, 203, 232, 422, 744, 909; XII, 88, 294, 322, 323, 457, 467, 585, 606, 703, 704, 706, 837, 952, 1043, 1046, 1047, 1120
Bowen, Augustus, XI, 55
Bowen, Charlotte Louise Caldwell (Buchanan), IX, 97
Bowen, Edward, VI, 120; VII, 785, 872, 876; VIII, 17, 154, 843; IX, **74–76**, 97, 568; X, 326, 337; XII, 1024
Bowen, Edward Henry, IX, 74
Bowen, Eliza. See Davidson
Bowen, Eliza Cecilia (Hale), X, 326
Bowen, George Frederick, XII, 349
Bowen, William D., VIII, 609
Bower, Elizabeth (MacBraire), VI, 417, 418
Bower, Helen Fletcher (Murray), XI, 630
Bower, James, VI, 418
Bower, Jane (Yates), XI, 940
Bower, Janet (Mowat), VIII, 644
Bower, Joseph, VI, 418
Bowers, Amelia (Sabrevois de Bleury), IX, 696
Bowes, Ann. See Hall
Bowes, Emily (Gosse), XI, 363
Bowes, Isabella Eliza (Beatty), XII, 69
Bowes, John, IX, 54
Bowes, John George, VIII, 230, 256; IX, **76–77**, 506; X, 119, 224, 503, 620; XI, 150, 322, 413, 414, 618; XII, 69, 71, 72, 907, 1108
Bowes, Margaret (Foster), XI, 322
Bowes, Mary (Sayre), VII, 777
Bowes, Patrick, XI, 310

Bowes, Robert H., XI, 324
Bowes-Lyon, Mary Isabella (Willis), X, 705, 706
Bowes-Lyon, Thomas, 11th Earl of Strathmore, X, 705
Bowie, Barbara (Graham), V, 363
Bowie, William, VI, 792, 810; VII, 22, 237
Bowker, John, V, 672; VII, 376
Bowlby, David Sovereign, XII, 124
Bowlby, Elizabeth (Willson), VIII, 945; X, 708
Bowler. See Bouler
Bowles, George, VIII, 678
Bowles, George John, XI, **107–8**
Bowles, Isabella. See Patterson
Bowles, John, XI, 107
Bowles, Margaret. See Cochrane
Bowley, William, V, 27, 219, 310, 568, 778, 825; VI, 107, 108, 110; VII, 406, 407
Bowman, Amelia Martha (Christie), VII, 184
Bowman, Baxter, IX, 562, 563; XII, 664
Bowman, Charles (businessman), XI, 824, 825
Bowman, Charles (clergyman), X, 453
Bowman, James, IV, **82–83**, 511; V, 88, 788; VI, 699
Bowman, James, VII, **100–1**, 573; X, 389, 390; XII, 414, 845
Bowman, Julia M. See Chew
Bowman, Whitney, IV, 82
Bown, Harriet. See Stout
Bown*, Walter Robert (d. 1903), XII, 950, 952, 953
Bowness, Jane (Bell), X, 44
Bowring, Benjamin, VII, **101–2**; XI, 108
Bowring, Charles R., VII, 102; XI, **108–9**, 911; XII, 754
Bowring, Charles Tricks, VII, 101, 102; XI, 108
Bowring, Charlotte. See Price
Bowring*, Sir Edgar Rennie (1858–1943), XI, 108
Bowring, Edward, VII, 101
Bowring, Harriet. See Harvey
Bowring, Henry Price, VII, 101
Bowring, John, XI, 108
Bowring, Laura. See Warren
Bowring, Nathaniel, VII, 101
Bowring, Susannah. See White
Bowring, William, VII, 101
Bowron, George J., XII, 444
Bowron, William, VIII, 415
Bowyer, Henry, V, 442
Boxer, Edward, VII, 71, 441; VIII, **101–2**, 135; X, 404
Boxer, Elizabeth (first wife of EDWARD), VIII, 102
Boxer, Elizabeth (second wife of EDWARD), VIII, 102
Boxer, James, VIII, 101
Boxer, Kitty (mother of EDWARD), VIII, 101
Boy, Michel-Philibert, II, 190
Boyat, Jeanne-Marie (Le Roy), II, 424
Boyce, Rebecca (Thompson), IX, 787
Boyd*, Alfred (d. 1909), XI, 643, 742; XII, 33, 369, 370
Boyd, Amelia Janetta (Emslie; Haviland), IX, 376
Boyd, Andrew, XII, 136
Boyd, Angus, X, 86
Boyd, Ann. See MacDonald
Boyd, Anna Maria (Jarvis), VIII, 428
Boyd, Annie E. See Jones
Boyd, Cornelia Jane (Boyle), VIII, 102
Boyd, George, XII, 136
Boyd, James, XII, 121
Boyd, John (brother-in-law of Alexander BOYLE), VIII, 103

Boyd, John (father-in-law of Alexander BOYLE), VIII, 102, 428
Boyd, John (father of JOHN, d. 1880), X, 85
Boyd, John, X, **85–86**
Boyd, John, XII, **121–22**, 226, 341, 537, 566, 1059
Boyd*, Sir John Alexander (1837–1916), VII, 315
Boyd, John Parker, VI, 521
Boyd, Letitia (Kinnear), IX, 430
Boyd, Margaret E. See Lynn
Boyd, Mossom, XII, 527, 782
Boyd, Mary. See MacDonald
Boyd, Robert, X, 660
Boyd, Sir Robert, V, 206
Boyer. See also Bouvier
Boyer, Charles, IV, 262, 585; V, 534, 656
Boyer, Daniel, I, 193, 194, 291
Boyer, Élisabeth. See Mathieu, dit Laramée
Boyer, François, IX, 77
Boyer, Françoise (Denaut), V, 245
Boyer, Henry, VI, 500
Boyer, Jean-Baptiste, VII, 232
Boyer, Josette. See Boutonne
Boyer, Louis (doctor), X, 589; XI, 303
Boyer, Louis (nephew of LOUIS), IX, 78
Boyer, Louis, IX, **77–79**; XI, 235
Boyer, Louis-Alphonse, IX, 78
Boyer, Marie (Gervaise), III, 257
Boyer, Marie-Aurélie. See Mignault
Boyer, Robert F., XI, 727
Boyer (Bayer), Sarah (Merrick), VI, 500
Boyer, dit Quintal, Olive (David), XI, 235
Boyle, Alexander, VI, 725; VIII, **102–3**, 428
Boyle, Bridget (Whelan), IX, 835
Boyle, Catherine. See Twite
Boyle, Cornelia Jane. See Boyd
Boyle*, David (1842–1911), XII, 663
Boyle, Donald, IX, 835
Boyle, Ellen (Arnold), VIII, 25
Boyle, Henry, Earl of Shannon, II, 461
Boyle, John, IV, 267
Boyle, Mary Anne (Todd), IX, 792
Boyle*, Patrick (1832–1901), XI, 307, 537; XII, 925, 1086
Boyle, Robert, I, 385
Boyles, Hannah, IV, 778
Boyles, Mary (Powell), VII, 638
Boynes. See Bourgeois
Boyrie, Marie (Madeleine) de (Dauger), II, 35
Boys, Henry, VIII, 927; IX, **79–80**; XII, 1123
Boys, Jane. See Fuller
Boys, Maria da Purifecacao. See Alves
Boys, William, IX, 79
Boysdale. See MacDonald
Boyvinet, Gilles de, I, 468, 582; II, 193, 380
Brackett, Ada Josephine (Schwatka), XII, 954
Braco, Baron. See Duff
Bradbury, Judith (Moody), III, 470
Bradbury, Mary Kent (Hart), XI, 389
Braddock, Edward, II, 660; III, xvii, xxiv, xxv, 89, 149, 161, 185, 186, 214, 218, 219, 306, 320, 362, 378, 401, 496, 508, 526, 600; IV, 84, 207, 257, 278, 281, 302, 395, 408, 500, 552, 563, 668, 733; V, 40, 729, 730; VI, 30
Bradford, Hannah. See Kempton
Bradford, Harriet (Abbott), V, 107; IX, 4; XII, 4

Bradford, Mary. *See* Breed
Bradford, Melvin, XII, 122
Bradford, Richard, V, 106
Bradford, Richard, V, **106–7**, 716; VI, 525; IX, 3, 4
Bradford, Sarah. *See* Jefferey
Bradford, Susanna. *See* Cole
Bradford, William (Pilgrim father), I, 392; V, 865
Bradford, William (printer), V, 438
Bradford, William, XI, 393; XII, **122–23**
Bradlaugh, Charles, XII, 866, 867
Bradley, Amy (Lewis), VI, 399
Bradley, Arthur Granville, V, 152
Bradley, E. D., VIII, 852
Bradley, Emma Catherine (Snow), XI, 841
Bradley, Katherine (Parkin), X, 587
Bradley, Leverit, VIII, 176
Bradley, Lucina (Massey), VIII, 621; XII, 700
Bradley, Mary. *See* Coy
Bradley, Mary (Moor), III, 471
Bradley, Thomas, VIII, 26
Bradley, Thomas, I, **120**, 150, 164, 641
Bradshaw, Blanche (Holman), XI, 419
Bradshaw, Mary (McBride), VI, 420
Bradshaw, Sarah (Oxenden), XII, 812
Bradstreet, Agathe. *See* Saint-Étienne de La Tour
Bradstreet, Edward, II, 590; IV, 83
Bradstreet, John (Jean-Baptiste), II, 590; III, xxv, xxviii, xxxviii, 10, 102, 373, 409, 495, 507, 530, 641, 652; IV, xix, 4, **83–87**, 117, 297, 347, 552, 587, 612, 670, 734, 762; V, 253, 739, 759, 804; VI, 317
Bradstreet, Mary. *See* Aldridge
Bradstreet, Mary (Robie), VIII, 754
Bradstreet, Simon (brother of JOHN), II, 590; IV, 83
Bradstreet, Simon (governor), II, 410; VIII, 754
Bradt, Andrew, IX, 455
Bradt, Catalyntje, known as Catharine Bratt (Butler), IV, 117, 120
Brady, Crosbie, VIII, 759
Brady, James, VIII, 532
Brady, Jane Sarah (Curtis, Lady Curtis), V, 220
Brady, Matthew, V, 220
Bragelonne, Claude, II, 440
Bragg, Sir James, I, 605
Braidwood, Thomas, V, 390
Braille, Louis, XI, 777
Braine, John C., XI, 373
Brainerd, David, III, 607
Braithwaite, Dorothy (Benson), XI, 69
Braithwaite, John, VIII, 773, 774
Braithwaite, Joseph, VII, 682, 827; X, 5; XI, 326; XII, 348
Bramley, James Irvine, X, 217
Bramley, Julia Elizabeth (Gould; Ridout), XI, 225, 735
Bramley, Matilda Ann (Ridout), IX, 661; XI, 225
Bramley, Wilmot Mary (Cumberland), XI, 225
Bramston, James Yorke, VII, 294
Brandeau, David, II, 95
Brandeau, Esther, II, **95–96**
Brandisi, Joseph, XI, 419
Brandon, John Raphael, XII, 343
Brandon, Joshua Arthur, XII, 343
Brannan, Catharine Phoebe (Wolhaupter), VIII, 951
Branner, John Casper, X, 338
Branquais, Jeanne (Quiniard), II, 534

Branscombe, William, IV, 712
Bransfield, Margaret (Prendergast), XII, 861
Branssat (Bransac). *See* Migeon
Brant. *See also* Carrihogo; Sa Ga Yeath Qua Pieth Tow
Brant, Catharine. *See* Ohtowaʔkéhson
Brant, Catharine (John), V, 804
Brant, Charlotte (Smith), IV, 416; V, 803
Brant, Christiana. *See* Kayatontye
Brant, Christiana (Hill), V, 804; VI, 373
Brant, Elizabeth (Kerr), V, 804, 811; VI, 374, 375, 760; VII, 466, 666
Brant, Isaac, V, 804, 809
Brant, Jacob, V, 804
Brant, John. *See* Tekarihogen (1794–1832)
Brant, Joseph. *See also* Thayendanegea
Brant, Joseph, IV, 416; V, 803, 804
Brant, Margaret (Powless), V, 804; VIII, 708
Brant, Mary. *See* Koñwatsiʔtsiaiéñni
Brant, Mary (Hill), V, 804
Brant, Neggen. *See* Aoghyatonghsera
Brant, Nicholas, IV, 692
Brant, Susanna (wife of THAYENDANEGEA), V, 804
Brant's Joseph. *See* Thayendanegea
Bras Croche. *See* Maskepetoon
Bras-de-fer de Chateaufort, Marc-Antoine, I, **120–21**, 127, 372, 454
Brasen, Christoph, IV, 334
Brash, Mr (merchant), VI, 400
Brass, David, VI, 146, 147; VII, 102
Brass, Elizabeth (wife of WILLIAM), VII, 102
Brass, Mary Magdalen. *See* Mattice
Brass, William, VII, **102–3**, 460; XII, 592
Brassard, Dorothée (Ménage), II, 467
Brassard, Jean-Baptiste (father of LOUIS-MARIE), IV, 87
Brassard, Jean-Baptiste (father of LOUIS-MOÏSE), X, 86
Brassard, Louis-Marie, IV, **87**; V, 216, 217, 253; VII, 711; X, 86
Brassard, Louis-Moïse, VII, 267; X, **86**
Brassard, Marie-Anne (Proulx), VII, 711
Brassard, Marie-Françoise. *See* Huppé, *dit* Lagroix
Brassard, Marie-Josephte. *See* Manseau
Brassard, Pierre, V, 217
Brassard, Thomas-Léandre, X, 86
Brassard Deschenaux. *See also* Deschenaux
Brassard Deschenaux, Charles, IV, 88
Brassard Deschenaux, Charles-Joseph, IV, 89; V, 47; VI, **84–85**, 584, 590; XII, 861
Brassard Deschenaux, Joseph, IV, 69, **87–89**, 125; V, 252, 576, 711; VI, 84, 404
Brassard Deschenaux, Madeleine. *See* Vallée
Brassard Deschenaux, Marie-Joseph. *See* Hébert
Brassard Deschenaux, Marie-Madeleine-Claire (Lorimier), VI, 404
Brassard Deschenaux, Suzanne-Élisabeth. *See* Filion
Brasseur de Bourbourg, Charles-Étienne, VII, 800; VIII, 912; IX, 255; X, **86–88**; XI, 96, 490; XII, 731
Brasseuse. *See* Des Friches
Brassey, Thomas, X, 591, 725; XII, 494
Brassier, Gabriel-Jean, IV, **89–90**, 272, 544; V, 92, 294, 432, 480, 524, 680, 701; VI, 485, 486, 668
Brassier, Jacques, I, 267
Bratt, Catharine. *See* Bradt, Catalyntje
Brault, Marguerite (Chevalier), VI, 185

Braun, Antoine-Nicolas, XI, 109
Braun, Antoine-Nicolas, VIII, 143; X, 493; XI, 104, **109–10**; XII, 1021
Braun, Antoine-Théodore, IV, 318; V, 480
Braun, Frederick, XII, 1068
Braun, Marguerite-Victoire. *See* Simonet
Brauneis, Christine. *See* Hudson
Brauneis, Franz Benedikt, VI, 85
Brauneis, Jean-Chrysostome, VI, 85; VIII, 635; X, **88–89**
Brauneis, Jeanet. *See* Johnson
Brauneis, John Chrisostomus, VI, **85–86**; VII, 774; VIII, 635; X, 88
Brauneis, Katharina (mother of JOHN CHRISOSTOMUS), VI, 85
Bray, Achille-Hector-Camille de, X, 89
Bray, Émile-Frédéric de, X, **89–90**
Bray, Loetitia-Constance-Marie de. *See* Le Bléis
Bray, Margery (Pepperrell), II, 516; III, 505
Bray, Théophile-Marie-Louise de. *See* Borrel
Brazil, William, XII, 157
Breachin, Mary (Dadson), XII, 224
Breadalbane, Marquis of. *See* Campbell
Breakenridge, David, VI, 673
Breakenridge, Jennet (Read), VIII, 743
Breakenridge, John, IX, 108
Breakey, Hans Denaston, XII, 488
Breakey, John, XII, 488
Bréanainn. *See* Brendan
Bréard, Jacques, IV, 91
Bréard, Jacques-Michel, III, 124; IV, 66, 67, **90–92**, 128, 263, 264, 435, 474, 517, 614, 615, 750
Bréard, Jean-Jacques, IV, 92
Bréard, Marcellin-Nicolas, IV, 91
Bréard, Marie. *See* Chasseriau
Bréard, Marie-Anne. *See* Marcellin
Bréaux, Brigitte. *See* Martin
Breaux, Marie (Brun), II, 93
Bréaux, Séraphin, VI, 86
Brébeuf, Georges de, I, 121
Brébeuf, Jean de, I, 9, 31, 60, 64, 73, **121–26**, 130, 203, 205, 206, 219, 247, 253, 281, 369, 388, 390, 411, 413, 414, 420, 458, 459, 460, 461, 483, 521, 522, 527, 549, 561, 562, 609, 610, 639, 661; II, 82; XI, 186
Brébeuf, Nicolas de, I, 121
Brebion, Charlotte (Besnard, *dit* Carignant), IV, 58
Brebner*, John Bartlet (1895–1957), IV, xvii, xxii, xxvi, 30, 199, 273, 450, 528, 562, 696; V, 109, 554; VI, 88; XII, 15
Brech, Elizabeth (Betzner), VIII, 86
Brechin, Elizabeth (West), VIII, 928
Bréchon, Victor, VII, 412
Breck, Marion Maria (Calvin), XI, 139
Brecken, Anna Matilda (McDonald), VIII, 531, 533
Brecken*, Frederick de St-Croix (1828–1903), VII, 103; X, 613; XI, 703
Brecken, Jane Rebecca (Haviland), IX, 376; XII, 414
Brecken, John, V, 424
Brecken, John, VI, 821; VII, **103–4**
Brecken, Margaret Leah. *See* St Croix
Brecken, Matilda. *See* Robinson
Brecken, Matilda (Mackieson), XI, 566
Brecken, Ralph, V, 720; VI, 162; VII, 103; XI, 566
Breçon, Monsieur de (engineer), III, 229

Breed, Mary (Bradford), XII, 122
Breen, Sarah (Van Buskirk), VI, 793
Brega, Solomon, VII, 116; VIII, 822
Bréguier-Saint-Pierre, Jean-Baptiste, VIII, 864
Bréhant, Mathurin de, I, 126
Bréhant de Galinée, René de, I, 35, **126–27**, 173, 174, 248, 393, 572, 625, 647; II, 191, 192, 517
Brehaut, Catharine Esther (Antrobus), VIII, 17
Brehaut, Marie. *See* Todevin
Brehaut, Pierre, V, 107
Brehaut, Pierre, V, 84, **107–8**, 283, 637; VI, 578; VIII, 17, 937
Brehaut, Thérèse. *See* Bellenoy
Bréhaut, William-Henry, X, 219
Bréhaut Delisle, Achille (Antoine-Louis?) de, I, 121, **127–28**, 372, 446; II, xv
Brehm, Anna Dorothea (Vieth), VI, 794
Brehm, Dietrich, IV, 39; V, 894
Brehm, Georg Philipp, VI, 794
Breithaupt, Catharine. *See* Hailer
Breithaupt, Ezra Carl, XII, **123–24**
Breithaupt, John Christian, XII, 124
Breithaupt, Louis, XII, 123
Breithaupt, Louis Jacob, XII, 124
Breithaupt, Melvina Emilia, XII, 124
Breithaupt, William Henry, XII, 124
Brekenmacher, François (Jean-Melchior), I, 312
Breland, Alexandre, XII, 124
Breland, Maria. *See* Grant
Breland, Pascal, VIII, 344; XI, 193, 610, 738; XII, **124–25**, 370
Breland, Patrice, XII, 124
Bremmer, Jacob, VII, 56
Bremnar, John S., XI, 201
Bremner, Alexander, XI, 376
Bremner, Charles, XII, 75, 735
Bremner, Elizabeth (Stewart), IX, 746
Bremond, Marie-Thérèse (Honorat), IX, 397
Brenan, Daniel, IX, 28; X, **90**
Brenan, Justin, VIII, 744, 747
Brenan, Margaret (wife of DANIEL), X, 90
Brenchley, Elizabeth Bowles (Gamble), XI, 332
Brendan, Saint, I, **675**
Brennan, Catharine (Phelan), VIII, 702
Brennan, James, IX, **80–81**
Brennan, Margaret, named Sister Teresa, VIII, 299; XI, **110–11**
Brennan, Mary. *See* Begley
Brennan, Michael, XI, 110
Brennan, Thomas, XII, 861
Brent, J. W., X, 450
Brent, Marie. *See* Houghton
Brenton, Catherine. *See* Taylor
Brenton, Edward Brabazon, V, 108, 697; VII, **104–5**, 507, 768
Brenton, Elizabeth. *See* Russell
Brenton, Frances. *See* Cranston
Brenton, Jahleel, V, 108
Brenton, James, IV, 111, 112, 581, 604, 696; V, 63, **108–9**, 251, 431, 574; VI, 34; VII, 87, 104, 831; VIII, 354
Brenton, Mary (Gerrish), IV, 292
Brenton, Rebecca. *See* Scott
Brenton, Susannah (Halliburton), VIII, 354

123

Brereton, John, I, 364
Bresdin, Rodolphe, XII, 170
Breslay, René-Charles de, II, 23, 24, 46, **96–97**, 195, 524; III, 181, 517, 584
Brésoles. *See* Moreau
Bressani, François-Joseph, I, 59, 71, 124, **128–29**, 389, 549; XI, 588
Bresse, Charles, XII, 126
Bresse, Guillaume, XII, **126–27**
Bresse, Olivier, XII, 127
Bresse, Marie. *See* Rocheleau
Bretherton, James, V, 844
Brethous, Jeanne. *See* Picot
Brethous, Léon, III, 157; IV, 245
Brétigny. *See* Poncet de La Rivière
Bretonvilliers. *See* Le Rageois
Brett. *See also* Marshall
Brett, John Watkins, XII, 374, 375
Brett, Robert Henry, VIII, 930; X, 702
Brew, Chartres, IX, **81–83**, 433, 712, 713; X, 698; XI, 301, 394, 607
Brew, Tomkins, IX, 81
Brewer, Christina Henrietta. *See* Rose
Brewer, Emma (Hunt), X, 372
Brewer, S., VI, 499
Brewse, John, IV, **92–93**, 559, 737
Brewse, Mary (wife of JOHN), IV, 92
Brewse, Mary (Kesterman), IV, 93
Brewster, Benjamin, VIII, 219, 220
Brewster, Sir David, XI, 446
Breynton, Elizabeth (wife of JOHN), IV, 94
Breynton, John, IV, 93
Breynton, John, III, 133, 635, 651; IV, 29, **93–94**, 258, 292, 451, 625, 764, 775, 776; V, 128, 430, 746; VI, 276, 731
Breynton, Mary. *See* Cradock
Briand. *See also* Triaud
Briand, Mlle (Gaubert), IV, 95
Briand, Catherine-Anne-Marie, IV, 95, 98, 102
Briand, François, IV, 95
Briand, Jean-Joseph, IV, 95
Briand, Jeanne. *See* Burel
Briand, Jeanne. *See* Desbois
Briand, Jean-Olivier, II, 200; III, 36, 193, 197, 199, 547, 549; IV, xlii, 6, 7, 8, 9, 41, 42, 43, 49, 80, 81, **94–103**, 109, 134, 135, 141, 142, 188, 189, 201, 205, 270, 271, 286, 287, 296, 298, 299, 305, 370, 371, 372, 373, 388, 423, 425, 430, 469, 497, 509, 510, 511, 543, 544, 549, 571, 572, 639, 642, 686, 720, 752, 753, 779, 788, 789, 798; V, 46, 49, 76, 92, 118, 143, 146, 185, 196, 201, 202, 224, 241, 245, 246, 294, 305, 342, 343, 379, 380, 432, 433, 452, 471, 481, 569, 570, 658, 667, 687, 704; VI, 16, 85, 145, 184, 379, 492, 527, 569, 571, 572, 586, 587, 592, 650, 752; VII, 165, 514; XI, 87
Briand, Yves, IV, 95
Briant, Marie (Normandin), II, 499
Briard. *See also* Lejeune
Briard, Francis, VII, 86
Briault, Antoine, IV, 265
Bricault de Valmur, Louis-Frédéric, II, **97**, 447, 530; III, 146, 153; IV, 284, 356
Brice, Mme de, I, **129**, 380, 434, 514
Brice de Sainte-Croix, Monsieur de (son of Mme de BRICE), I, 129, 434, 514

Bricker, Catharine (Eby), VIII, 265
Bricker, Samuel, VIII, 265
Brickwood, John, IV, 403
Bricquet, Marie-Alexandrine (Herbomez), XI, 401
Briderie. *See* Romanet
Bridgar, John, I, 39, 56, 83, **129–30**, 227, 337, 338, 518, 528, 601, 696; II, 247, 391, 538
Bridge, Samuel Southby, VII, 575
Bridge, Sarah Christiana. *See* Dunscombe
Bridge, Thomas (father of THOMAS FINCH HOBDAY), VIII, 103
Bridge, Thomas (relative of Malachy SALTER), IV, 696
Bridge, Thomas Finch Hobday, VIII, 94, **103–4**, 644; IX, 695, 847
Bridgeman, William, XII, 441
Bridges, Edith (Patterson), XI, 677
Bridges, George, XII, 997
Bridges, MacDonald, XII, 306
Bridges, Rosalie. *See* Hill
Bridges, Timothy, II, **97–98**, 293, 438, 486, 487
Bridgewater, Earl of. *See* Egerton
Bridgland, Eleanor. *See* Beaton
Bridgland, James W., X, 90
Bridgland, James William, X, **90–91**
Bridgland, Maria. *See* Dennis
Bridgland, Martha Anne. *See* Jones
Bridgman, John Wesley, XI, 683
Bridou, Marie (Noyelles), III, 491
Brien, Jean-Baptiste-Henri, VII, **105–6**
Brien, *dit* Dérocher (Desrochers). *See also* Desrochers
Brien, *dit* Dérocher, Jessé, VIII, 218
Brien, *dit* Dérocher, Joseph, VIII, 218
Brien, *dit* Dérocher, Marguerite. *See* Rive
Brien-Desrochers, Louise (Leblanc), X, 434
Brienne, Henri de, Comte de Conflans, III, 556
Brière (Brilliere), Louis, VI, 364
Briet, Louise (La Bazanière), II, 424
Brigeac, Claude de, I, **130**, 274, 662; II, 164
Briggs, Henry, I, 311, 312
Briggs, Jacob, VII, 371
Briggs*, William (1836–1922), XII, 664, 999, 1077
Brigham, Abigail. *See* Wright
Brigham, Moses, V, 14; VIII, 887, 888
Brigham, Thomas, VII, 928
Bright, John, IX, 591
Bright, Margaret (Gooderham), XI, 360
Bright, Richard, X, 83
Bright, Sarah (Worts), XI, 360, 937
Bright, Susan (Austin), XII, 42
Brighton, Jane (Barker), XII, 55
Brightwen, Eliza (Gosse), XI, 363
Brijat. *See* Brigeac
Brill, Hannah (Lossing), VI, 406
Brilliere. *See* Brière
Brimner, Jane (Knaut; Bolman), IV, 414
Brims, Christina (Keith), X, 395
Brin, Ursule (Céré de La Colombière), X, 156
Brind'amour. *See* Taton
Brinley, Joanna. *See* Allen
Brinley, William Birch, VII, 21
Brinon, Marie de (Chauvin de Tonnetuit), I, 209
Brinton, Daniel Garrison, XII, 401, 403
Briot, Noel, VII, 352

Brisac. *See* Brigeac

Brisacier, Jacques de, II, 248

Brisay. *See also* La Cour

Brisay, François de, II, 98

Brisay, Marie de. *See* Hémard

Brisay de Denonville, Catherine de, Marquise de Denonville. *See* Courtin de Tangeux

Brisay de Denonville, Jacqueline de. *See* Orléans

Brisay de Denonville, Jacques de, II, 98

Brisay de Denonville, Jacques-René de, Marquis de Denonville, I, 56, 103, 109, 112, 114, 119, 137, 138, 204, 239, 295, 308, 320, 327, 397, 446, 463, 465, 488, 523, 526, 528, 537, 572, 582, 650, 653, 664; II, xxxi, 6, 13, 15, 32, 49, 57, 60, 62, 63, 69, 72, 73, 86, 88, 89, **98–105**, 113, 124, 137, 148, 162, 168, 169, 182, 185, 186, 195, 202, 213, 214, 218, 228, 229, 237, 252, 254, 261, 263, 269, 270, 282, 284, 295, 302, 303, 304, 321, 341, 343, 344, 345, 371, 380, 385, 386, 391, 401, 403, 406, 410, 440, 472, 473, 478, 488, 491, 518, 532, 533, 539, 566, 576, 583, 586, 592, 594, 620, 635, 636, 643; III, 65, 82, 109, 373, 548; IX, 256

Brisay de Denonville, Louise de. *See* Alès de Corbet

Brisay de Denonville, Pierre de, II, 98

Brisay de Denonville, Pierre de, Vicomte de Montbazillac, II, 98

Brisay d'Huillé, Charles de, II, 98

Brisbane, Albert, X, 315

Brisco, Arthur, XI, 663

Briscoe, Charles Joseph, VI, 122

Brisebois, Adelle. *See* Malcouronne

Brisebois, Éphrem-A., XI, **111–12**, 354; XII, 673

Brisebois, Henriette. *See* Piette

Brisebois, Joseph, XI, 111

Brison. *See* Roquemont

Brisset, Gervais, III, 173

Brisson, Mathurin-Jacques, VIII, 212

Bristol, Earl of. *See* Hervey

Bristow, William, VII, 836; IX, **83–84**; X, 130, 723; XI, 117

Brittain, John, VI, 333

Brittain, Mary Ann (O'Leary), XII, 801

Brittlebank, W., XI, 326

Britton, Byron Moffatt, XI, 140; XII, 887

Britton, John, VIII, 63

Bro, Jean-Baptiste, IV, 80; VI, **86–87**

Brochard, Françoise (Chapeleau), XII, 172

Brochet, Le. *See* Kinongé

Brock, Daniel de Lisle, IX, 138

Brock, Elizabeth. *See* de Lisle

Brock, Irving, V, 111

Brock, Sir Isaac, V, 14, 72, 83, **109–15**, 191, 518, 521, 522, 643, 695, 697, 714, 748, 769, 775, 782, 798, 800, 857, 858; VI, 5, 94, 114, 148, 190, 210, 229, 286, 299, 309, 375, 463, 465, 489, 530, 539, 540, 541, 551, 609, 617, 638, 808; VII, 92, 161, 175, 212, 348, 397, 452, 469, 472, 497, 517, 545, 602, 703, 704, 753, 794, 852, 904; VIII, 100, 112, 431, 465, 467, 485, 608, 620, 793, 794, 796, 830, 866, 875, 960; IX, 8, 138, 245, 264, 484, 485, 668, 754, 788; X, 181, 329; XI, 326, 795; XII, 102, 946, 1076

Brock*, Isaac (1829–1911), XI, 75, 89

Brock, John (father), V, 109

Brock, John, V, 109, 110

Brock, William, V, 111

Brodeur, Catherine (Geoffrion), XII, 362, 363

Brodeur, Eusèbe, X, 153

Brodeur, Louis, VII, 670

Brodeur, Lucie (Lavigne), XI, 499

Brodeur, Marie-Anne (Sénécal), XI, 806

Brodhead, Daniel, IV, 410; VIII, 476

Brodhead, John Romeyn, IX, 250

Brodhead, Josephine (Balfour), XII, 52

Brodie, Alexander Anderson, XI, 397, 398

Brodie, Ann (Hixon), XII, 432

Brodie, George, XI, 397

Brodie, Margaret (Grant), IX, 336

Brodie, Margaret (McKellar), XII, 645

Brodie, William, IX, 336

Brodribb, John Henry. *See* Irving, Sir Henry

Broeffle, John Ludwig, IX, 232

Broke, Elizabeth. *See* Beaumont

Broke, Philip Bowes, VII, 106

Broke, Sir Philip Bowes Vere, VI, 508, 713; VII, **106–7**; XII, 1082

Broke, Sarah Louisa, Lady Broke. *See* Middleton

Broken Arm. *See* Maskepetoon

Bromley, Ann. *See* DeLancey

Bromley, Jane. *See* Ashton

Bromley, Jane (mother of WALTER), VII, 107

Bromley, Robert, VII, 107

Bromley, Stephen, VII, 107

Bromley, Susanna (Ready), VII, 740

Bromley, Walter, VI, 14, 282, 731; VII, **107–10**, 218, 219, 433, 482, 530, 609, 684, 722; VIII, 300, 626; IX, 37, 350; XII, 221

Brompton, Richard, IV, 702

Brondel, Jean-Baptiste, XI, 805

Brongniart, Adolphe-Théodore, X, 106

Bronsdon, Joseph Russell, X, 130

Bronson, Alvah, XI, 112

Bronson, Editha Eliza. *See* Pierce

Bronson, Erskine Henry, XI, 113

Bronson, Henry Franklin, XI, **112–13**, 590, 682, 826

Bronson, Sarah. *See* Tinker

Brontë, Charlotte (Nicholls), XII, 570

Brooke, Elizabeth (MacNab), IX, 519

Brooke, Frances. *See* Moore

Brooke, Frances Mingay (Mountain), VIII, 644

Brooke, John, III, 296; IV, **103–5**, 399, 553, 554, 555, 753; V, 600, 601, 620; VI, 492

Brooke, Sir John, I, 311

Brooke, John Moore, IV, 555

Brooker, Lydia. *See* Peabody

Brookes, Elizabeth. *See* Lawrear

Brooking, Elizabeth (wife of ROBERT), XII, 127

Brooking, Frances. *See* Mclea

Brooking, George Thomas, IX, 84

Brooking, Hannah. *See* Channel

Brooking, Jane (Young), VIII, 956

Brooking, Marmaduke Hart, IX, 84

Brooking, Robert, XII, **127–28**

Brooking, Selina (Robinson), XI, 760

Brooking, Thomas, IX, 84

Brooking, Thomas Holdsworth, VI, 312; VIII, 956; IX, **84–86**, 179

Brooks, Alphonse, XII, 933

Brooks, Catharine (Beardsley), V, 59
Brooks, Cornelia Eleanor (Robertson), V, 718
Brooks, Edward Towle, X, 643
Brooks, Eleanor Hall (Sanborn), X, 641
Brooks, Eliza Wilson (Thresher), VIII, 886
Brooks, Henry, VIII, 449
Brooks, Honoria (Dillon), VIII, 886
Brooks, J. W., IX, 134
Brooks, J. Wallis, VIII, 886
Brooks, John, IX, 771
Brooks, Joseph, XI, 722
Brooks, Lucy (Stuart), IX, 771; XI, 861
Brooks, Samuel, VIII, 221; IX, 727; X, 641; XII, 348, 349, 350
Brooks, Samuel M., XI, 867
Brooks, Thankful (Cossit), V, 204
Brooks, William, XII, 349
Broom, Louisa (Pinsent), X, 589; XII, 843
Broquerie. See Labroquerie
Brossard, Agnès. See Tibaudeau
Brossard, Alexandre, III, 87
Brossard, Catherine. See Richard
Brossard, Catherine (Sareau), II, 105
Brossard, Jean-François, II, 105; III, 87
Brossard, Madeleine (Campot), II, 105
Brossard, Marguerite. See Tibaudeau
Brossard, Mathurin, II, 105
Brossard, Michelle. See Bidaut
Brossard, Pierre, II, 105
Brossard, Urbain, I, 78; II, 105–6
Brossard, Urbaine. See Hodiau
Brossard, dit Beausoleil, Agnès. See Thibodeau
Brossard, dit Beausoleil, Alexandre, II, 105
Brossard, dit Beausoleil, Joseph, II, 105; III, 87–88; IV, xxv, 541
Brosseau, Charlotte. See Roy
Brosseau, Pierre, II, 521
Brosseau, Toussaint, VIII, 667
Brouague. See Martel
Broudou, Louise-Éléonore (Galaup, Comtesse de Lapérouse), IV, 282
Brouet, Ambroise, I, 461
Brough, Charles Crosbie, X, 206; XI, 653, 714, 715
Brough, Katherine Jane (Parker; O'Brien), XII, 792
Brough, Wilhelmina. See Blake
Brougham, Henry Peter, 1st Baron Brougham and Vaux, VI, 481; VII, 84, 118, 477, 478, 479, 480; VIII, 756; IX, 335, 818; X, 260, 342, 514; XI, 875; XII, 1079
Brougham, John, IX, 597
Broughton, Baron. See Hobhouse
Broughton, Mary (Glover), XI, 355
Broughton, William Robert, V, 12
Brouilhet. See Drouilhet
Brouillan. See also Monbeton
Brouillan, Isabeau de, II, 478
Brouillet, Jean-Baptiste-Abraham, XI, 85
Brouillette, Benoît, VII, 687
Broun, Christian (Ramsay, Countess of Dalhousie), VII, 722, 723, 725, 732, 733; IX, 38, 718
Broun, Sir Richard, IX, 567
Brouse, Abigail Ann (Patrick), VIII, 105; XI, 676
Brouse, Catherine. See Carman
Brouse, Eliza (mother of GEORGE), VIII, 104

Brouse, Frances Amelia. See Jones
Brouse, George, VIII, 104–5; XI, 677
Brouse, George William, VIII, 105
Brouse, Guy Carleton, VIII, 105
Brouse, Jacob, XI, 114
Brouse, Nancy. See Parlow
Brouse, Peter (father), VIII, 104
Brouse, Peter, VIII, 105
Brouse, William Henry, IX, 166; XI, 114, 818; XII, 964
Broussais, François, VI, 763
Broussard. See Brossard
Brousse. See also Bruce
Brousse (Bruce), Marie, VIII, 591
Brousseau, Catherine Rose. See Bennett
Brousseau, François, IX, 486
Brousseau, Georgiana. See Garneau
Brousseau, Jean-Baptiste, VIII, 394; XI, 114
Brousseau*, Jean-Docile (1825–1908), X, 676; XI, 115; XII, 270
Brousseau, Léger, XI, 115
Brousseau, Léger (Joseph), XI, 114–16; XII, 270, 271, 272
Brousseau, Marie-Anne-Charlotte. See Hertel de Rouville
Brousseau, Marie-Louise (Nau, dit Labry), VI, 381
Brousseau, Nathalie. See Doré
Brousseau, dit Lafleur de Verchères, Marie-Françoise (Globensky), IX, 320; X, 306
Browallius, Johan, IV, 406
Brower, Mary (Munro), IV, 566
Brown. See also Browne; Johnstone-Brown; Radcliffe-Brown
Brown, Mr. See Comingo, Bruin Romkes
Brown, Colonel, XI, 797
Brown*, Adam (1826–1926), IX, 511; XI, 915; XII, 126
Brown, Agnes (Sawyer), XI, 802
Brown, Alba, VIII, 23
Brown, Alexander (baker), XII, 195
Brown, Alexander (professor), XI, 528, 664
Brown, Alexander (shepherd), V, 126
Brown, Alexander D., XII, 543
Brown, Alfred, XII, 620, 621
Brown, Andrew, VIII, 832
Brown, Andrew, IV, xxx, 560; V, 58, 240; VI, 87–89, 651; VII, 832; XII, 14, 15, 17
Brown, Angélique (Pacaud), XI, 656, 658
Brown (Lebrun), Ann (Graham), XII, 383
Brown, Ann (Short), X, 654
Brown, Anne. See Nelson
Brown, Annie (Cunningham), X, 210
Brown, Annie (Hamilton), XII, 405
Brown, Arthur, IV, 570
Brown, Caroline (Cook), IX, 151
Brown, Catherine. See Cameron
Brown, Catherine Edith (Sandeman), X, 101
Brown, Charles, V, 298; VII, 111
Brown, Colin, XI, 547
Brown, Corydon Partlow, XI, 646; XII, 128–29
Brown, D. L., VII, 110
Brown, Daniel. See Cranstoun
Brown, Deborah. See Marsters
Brown, Ebenezer, XI, 300
Brown*, Edward Killoran (1905–51), XII, 518
Brown, Edward Lothrop, IX, 426
Brown, Elizabeth (Chipman), VI, 135

Brown, Emma. *See* Davidson
Brown, Frederick, VII, **110–11**
Brown, George (contractor), XII, 933
Brown, George (oarsman), XII, 407, 408
Brown, George, VIII, 53, 56, 57, 58, 161, 170, 230, 371, 402, 698, 789, 791, 817, 837, 872; IX, 45, 77, 83, 84, 88, 105, 106, 109, 149, 151, 194, 233, 252, 253, 267, 268, 288, 383, 384, 463, 492, 506, 507, 508, 524, 525, 576, 587, 614, 700, 705, 711, 726, 727, 735, 737, 742, 776, 777, 778; X, 45, 49, 79, 80, 81, **91–103**, 120, 122, 126, 127, 128, 144, 146, 169, 170, 171, 175, 200, 230, 258, 277, 304, 313, 356, 357, 359, 364, 415, 422, 463, 464, 465, 466, 467, 468, 469, 470, 503, 598, 623, 624, 630, 632, 637, 641, 642, 645, 656, 667, 671, 672, 676, 703, 707, 725; XI, 81, 82, 129, 144, 145, 160, 163, 167, 170, 176, 247, 275, 283, 347, 366, 374, 410, 411, 412, 413, 414, 416, 438, 439, 471, 481, 497, 518, 519, 530, 537, 552, 573, 574, 579, 581, 582, 610, 617, 619, 622, 669, 677, 681, 706, 714, 737, 783, 788, 792, 822, 823, 853, 877, 908, 932, 934, 939; XII, 11, 71, 73, 86, 131, 137, 146, 151, 153, 200, 202, 240, 254, 262, 263, 286, 291, 292, 330, 351, 352, 353, 489, 492, 494, 583, 586, 594, 595, 596, 597, 598, 609, 643, 644, 645, 648, 649, 651, 652, 654, 655, 658, 659, 676, 720, 738, 750, 793, 884, 907, 976, 983, 1054, 1059, 1108, 1123
Brown, George Mackenzie, X, 101
Brown, George Stayley, XI, 303
Brown, Henriette (Guibord), IX, 343; X, 154, 527, 689; XI, 777; XII, 505
Brown, Henry B., XII, 466
Brown, Henry Barlow, XI, 116
Brown, Hester. *See* Livingstone
Brown, Hugh William, VII, 420
Brown, Isabel (Neilson), IV, 580; VII, 644
Brown, Isabella. *See* Forrest
Brown, Jacob Jennings, VIII, 237, 238, 239; IX, 415
Brown, James (brother-in-law of Frédéric-Eugène Globensky), IX, 458
Brown, James (contractor), XII, 933
Brown, James (convicted murderer), VIII, 401, 402; XI, 618
Brown, James (father of JAMES, 1790–1870), IX, 86
Brown, James (father of PETER, 1784–1863), IX, 88
Brown, James (labour activist), XI, 346
Brown, James (mill builder), VII, 695
Brown, James (politician), X, 230; XI, 203
Brown, James (professor), IX, 752, 753, 754, 755
Brown, James, V, 87, 211, 298; VII, **111–12**, 644; VIII, 331, 791
Brown, James, VIII, 435, 436; IX, **86–88**, 340, 409; X, 286; XI, 828; XII, 232
Brown, James C., IX, 705
Brown, Jane. *See* Hughes
Brown, Jane (Porter; Pushee), VII, 714
Brown, Jane (Wilson), X, 715
Brown, Janet. *See* Douglas
Brown, Janet (Dick), XI, 259
Brown, Jean. *See* Lyon
Brown, Jennie. *See* Davidson
Brown, Joanna. *See* Stairs
Brown, John (abolitionist), IX, 769; XII, 925, 961
Brown, John (American officer), V, 34, 64
Brown, John (British officer), IV, 675

Brown, John (father of WILLIAM), IV, 105
Brown, John (hotel owner), VII, 313, 314
Brown, John (mechanic), XI, 547
Brown, John (merchant), XII, 886
Brown, John (of Londonderry, N.S.), VI, 294, 458, 459, 659
Brown, John (of Scotland), VI, 293
Brown, John (politician), IX, 44
Brown, John (shipowner), VII, 707
Brown, John Gordon, IX, 88; X, 93, 97, 102; XI, 554
Brown, John T., XI, 682
Brown, Jonah, VII, 695
Brown, Joseph Cameron, XI, 466
Brown, Kristiane Augusta Maria Eleonora. *See* Rudmose
Brown, Lemuel, VII, 698
Brown, Louisa Dorothea (Anderson), XI, 20
Brown, Lucretia (Hoyles), VII, 420; XI, 431
Brown, Lydia Marion (Young), XI, 941
Brown, Margaret (Crawford), IX, 166; X, 200
Brown, Margaret Nelson (Barbour), X, 99
Brown, Marianne. *See* Mackenzie
Brown, Mary. *See* Clark
Brown, Mary. *See* Grant
Brown, Mary. *See* McCarthy
Brown, Mary. *See* Ogilvie
Brown, Mary (Cawthra), VII, 163
Brown, Mary (Peabody), VII, 683
Brown, Mather, V, 128
Brown, Michael Septimus, VII, 589; IX, 599; XI, **116**; XII, 787
Brown, Nicholson William, XI, 312
Brown, Paola, VI, 262; VIII, **105–6**
Brown, Pattison (Somerville), VIII, 832
Brown, Paul, VII, 795
Brown, Peter, VIII, 368
Brown, Peter, VII, **112–14**, 155; VIII, 469
Brown, Peter, IX, **88–89**, 105; X, 91, 92, 93; XII, 200, 643
Brown, Peter Johnston, XI, 652
Brown, Prudence (Hartt), X, 338
Brown, Rebecca. *See* Appleton
Brown, Richard (engineer), IX, 730, 731
Brown, Richard (father of ANDREW), VI, 87
Brown, Robert (botanist), VI, 218
Brown, Robert (father of ROBERT CHRISTOPHER LUNDIN), X, 103
Brown, Robert (librarian), V, 55
Brown, Robert (loyalist), VIII, 509
Brown, Robert, IX, 656; X, 9; XI, 468; XII, **129–30**
Brown, Robert Christopher Lundin, IX, 432, 433; X, **103–4**
Brown, Russell Searle, VIII, 897
Brown, Salome (Philips), VII, 695
Brown, Sarah. *See* Sharman
Brown, Sophia. *See* de Camp
Brown, Sophia (Minns), VI, 508
Brown, Thomas (father of ROBERT), XII, 129
Brown, Thomas (watchmaker), XI, 116
Brown, Thomas Storrow, VI, 180; VII, 160, 247, 347, 509, 758; VIII, 219, 616, 703, 730; IX, 84, 485, 502, 826, 827; X, 574; XI, **116–17**; XII, 456
Brown, William (chief trader), VII, 205
Brown, William (father of CORYDON PARTLOW), XII, 128
Brown, William (father of MICHAEL SEPTIMUS), XI, 116
Brown, William (manufacturer), XI, 403

Brown, William (neighbour of Bartholomew Conrad Augustus GUGY), X, 321
Brown, William (partner of JAMES ROBERTSON), XII, 901
Brown, William (professor), XI, 454
Brown, William, IV, **105–7**, 184, 186, 295, 392, 393, 423, 424, 533, 534, 557, 580, 689; V, 224, 298, 834; VII, 644, 650
Brown, William Marsters, VII, 589
Browne, Miss (Wix), IX, 846
Browne, Agnes Dunlop. *See* Hay
Browne, Anna Maria. *See* Jameson
Browne, Anna Maria. *See* Noble
Browne, Catherine. *See* Winthrop
Browne, Elizabeth (Rogers), IV, 679
Browne, Felicia Dorothea (Hemans), VI, 728; VII, 792
Browne, Fitzjames, XI, 119
Browne, Frances (Stewart), VII, 829; VIII, 92; X, **104–5**, 453; XII, 525, 782, 997, 998, 999
Browne, Francis, X, 104
Browne, George, XI, 119
Browne, George, V, 678; VII, 159; VIII, 39, 645, 762; IX, 165; XI, **117–20**; XII, 131
Browne, Goodlatte Richardson, XI, 336; XII, 626
Browne, Helen. *See* Kissock
Browne, James, XI, 864
Browne, John Cave, VIII, 166
Browne, John James, XI, 119; XII, **130–31**, 813
Browne, Maurice, I, 229, 334, 531, 532
Browne, Oliver. *See* Brunel, Olivier
Browne, Richard, I, 380
Browne, Selina Cave (Codner), VIII, 166
Browne, Sophia (Forbes), IX, 268
Browne, T. H., XII, 131
Browne, Thomas, V, 785
Browne, Thomas Richardson, XI, 119
Browne, Timothy, VI, 693; VII, 297; VIII, **106–8**, 246
Brownel, Oliver. *See* Brunel, Olivier
Brownell, John, VI, 79
Brownell, Peleg Franklin, XII, 367
Browning, Arthur, X, 701
Browning, Elizabeth. *See* Barrett
Browning, Robert, VIII, 651; XII, 516
Brownson, Anna (Sherwood), X, 651
Brownson, Orestes Augustus, IX, 302; X, 175, 361
Browse, George, VII, 70
Brubacher, Mary (Eby), VIII, 265
Bruce. *See also* Brewse; Brousse; Cumming-Bruce
Bruce, Mr (father of ROBERT GEORGE), IV, 107
Bruce, Angélique. *See* Gaudry
Bruce, Archibald, VI, 457
Bruce, Elizabeth. *See* Oswald
Bruce, Elizabeth (Beatson), IV, 48
Bruce, Elizabeth Mary, Countess of Elgin and Kincardine. *See* Cumming-Bruce
Bruce, George, XII, 201
Bruce, Isabella (Keith), VIII, 453, 454
Bruce, James, 8th Earl of Elgin and 12th Earl of Kincardine, VII, 601; VIII, xxv, 18, 30, 52, 53, 54, 55, 109, 136, 205, 230, 249, 304, 383, 445, 495, 528, 679, 800, 822, 840, 850, 867, 916, 959; IX, 6, 8, 11, 45, 56, 83, **89–93**, 118, 191, 195, 238, 257, 287, 289, 302, 329, 378, 382, 383, 446, 447, 448, 449, 450, 525, 547, 570, 642, 677, 688, 690, 764; X, 14, 79, 93, 119, 131, 133, 144,
159, 257, 311, 312, 389, 392, 409, 411, 412, 415, 463, 464, 502, 512, 536, 548, 563, 622, 634, 642, 691, 707, 724; XI, 41, 156, 166, 167, 220, 274, 341, 410, 412, 414, 677, 789, 791, 883, 905; XII, 350, 351, 492, 612, 1109
Bruce, Jessy (Chaboillez), V, 177
Bruce, John, VII, 617, 618; VIII, 630; X, 517
Bruce, John, IX, **93–94**
Bruce, John, XI, 193, 738, 739; XII, **131–33**
Bruce, Joseph, VIII, 645
Bruce, Margaret. *See* Hay
Bruce, Marguerite. *See* Desrosiers
Bruce, Mary Louisa, Countess of Elgin and Kincardine. *See* Lambton
Bruce, Pierre, XII, 132
Bruce, Robert, VIII, 163
Bruce, Robert George, IV, **107–8**
Bruce, Thomas, 7th Earl of Elgin and 11th Earl of Kincardine, IX, 89
Bruce, William (army doctor), IX, 229
Bruce, William (fur trader), V, 602
Bruce, William (trader), III, 452
Bruce, William (physician), V, 23
Bruchési*, Paul (1855–1939), XII, 192, 305, 511, 696
Brucy. *See* La Frenaye
Brünnow, Franz Friedrich Ernst, X, 698, 699
Bruère. *See* Boucher
Bruere, Frances (Tucker), IX, 794
Bruere, Mary Todd (Tucker), IX, 794
Bruff, Charles Oliver, V, **115–16**
Bruff, James Earle (father), V, 115
Bruff, James Earle, V, 115
Bruff, Mary. *See* Letellier
Bruff, Peter Schuyler, V, 116
Bruguier. *See also* Bruyère
Bruguier, Charles, X, 107
Bruguier, Jean-Baptiste, X, 107
Bruguier, Sophie. *See* Mercier
Bruguière, Madeleine (Archambault), X, 15
Bruillard, Philibert de, VIII, 66
Bruix, Eustache, V, 62
Brulart de Sillery, Madeleine (Faure), I, 484
Brulart de Sillery, Marie-Louise. *See* Bigot
Brulart de Sillery, Nicolas, I, 484
Brulart de Sillery, Noël, I, 263, 470, 484, 516, 565
Brulé. *See also* Bruslé
Brûlé, Étienne, I, 16, 59, **130–33**, 190, 191, 192, 196, 381, 493, 494, 516, 590, 603, 639; II, xl
Brulotte, Malvina (Rochette), XII, 920
Brun. *See also* Malte-Brun
Brun, Marie. *See* Breaux
Brun, Marie (Bourg), II, 93
Brun, Vincent, II, 93
Brunatti, Anne-Marie (Rottenburg), VI, 660
Brundage, Elizabeth (Purdy), VII, 712
Bruneau, Antoine, IX, 94
Bruneau, Athanase, IX, 94
Bruneau, François-Jacques, VIII, 721; IX, **94–96**
Bruneau, François-Pierre, VIII, **108–9**, 800; XI, 71
Bruneau, François-Xavier, VIII, 108
Bruneau, Georgine. *See* Archambault
Bruneau, Jean-Casimir, VIII, 108, 109
Bruneau, Julie (Papineau), V, 116; VI, 591; VII, 879; VIII, 145; IX, 94; X, 567, 577; XII, 253, 846

Bruneau, Marguerite. *See* Harrison
Bruneau, Marie-Anne. *See* Robitaille
Bruneau, Marie-Élizabeth. *See* Morin, *dit* Chêneverd
Bruneau, Olivier-Théophile, VIII, 109; XI, 302
Bruneau, Pierre, V, 108, **116–17**, 817; VI, 533; VII, 468, 484; X, 567
Bruneau, Pierre-Guillaume, V, 116
Bruneau, René-Olivier, V, 116
Bruneau, Théophile, V, 117; VIII, 108; X, 576
Bruneau, Thérèse. *See* Leblanc
Brunel. *See also* Brunet
Brunel, Alfred, XI, **120**; XII, 72
Brunel, Isambard Kingdom, XI, 121
Brunel, Olivier, known as Oliver Brown (Brownel), I, 408
Brunelle, Laura (Doutre), X, 249
Brunelle, Louis-Joseph-Onésime, XII, 451
Brunet, Alexandre-Auguste, IX, **96–97**; X, 419
Brunet, Antoine, XI, 379, 380
Brunet, Cécile-Adélaïde. *See* Lagueux
Brunet, Georges-Henri, XII, 133
Brunet, Henriette. *See* Armand
Brunet, Jean-Baptiste, IX, 96
Brunet (Brunnet), Jean-Jacques, IV, 136
Brunet, Jean-Olivier, VI, 50; VIII, 675; X, 105; XII, 133
Brunet, Louis-Ovide, X, **105–7**, 361; XI, 107; XII, 247, 541, 542, 769, 868
Brunet, Marie. *See* Blain
Brunet, Marie (Roy), X, 635
Brunet, Marie-Reine (Rousseau, *dit* Saint-Jean), V, 723
Brunet, Mathieu, II, 63
Brunet (Brunel), *dit* La Sablonnière, Jean, III, 88
Brunet, Michel, XII, 87
Brunet, Victoria. *See* Duberger
Brunet, Wilfrid-Étienne, XII, **133–34**
Brunet, Wilfrid-Jean-Baptiste, XII, 133
Brunet, *dit* La Sablonnière, Jean, III, **88**
Brunet, *dit* La Sablonnière, Louise. *See* Maugue
Brunet, *dit* La Sablonnière, Marie-Madeleine. *See* Richaume
Brunet, *dit* L'Estang, Jean, V, 117
Brunet, *dit* L'Estang, Marguerite. *See* Dubois
Brunet, *dit* L'Estang, Véronique, named Sainte-Rose, V, **117–18**, 703
Brunlees, Sir James, XII, 562
Brunnet. *See* Brunet
Brunskill, Carrie (Clarkson), X, 174
Brunskill, Thomas, X, 174
Brunswick, Duke of. *See* Ferdinand; Karl Wilhelm Ferdinand
Brunswick, Princess of. *See* Caroline Amelia Elizabeth
Brunton, William Y., XII, 469
Brush, Alathea. *See* Frink
Brush, Alicia (Sampson), IX, 699
Brush, Eliza Maria. *See* Seymour
Brush, Elkanah, XI, 120
Brush, George, XI, **120–21**
Brush, George S., XI, 121
Brush, Nellie (Rogers), XI, 764
Bruslart, Louis-Philogène, Marquis de Puysieux, IV, 401
Bruslé, Michel, II, **106**
Bruslon. *See* Gaultier
Brusquet. *See* Boschette
Brutelles. *See* L'Héritier

Bruyas, Jacques, I, 321, 635, 651; II, 20, **106–8**, 114, 126, 237, 341, 404, 410, 621, 631; III, 335, 337
Bruyer, Esther (Badelard), V, 46
Bruyere. *See also* Bruyères
Bruyère, Élisabeth, VII, 59; VIII, 703; X, **107–8**, 323, 691; XI, 96; XII, 937, 977
Bruyère, Jean-Baptiste, XII, 1036
Bruyère, Jean-Marie, XI, 694, 695; XII, 1084
Bruyeres, Anne-Françoise (Pothier), IV, 109; VII, 703
Bruyères, Catherine-Élisabeth. *See* Pommereau
Bruyeres, Janet. *See* Dunbar
Bruyères, Jeanne-Marie-Catherine (Kennelly; O'Sullivan), IV, 109; VII, 667
Bruyères, John, III, 525; IV, **108–9**, 316, 447; V, 118; VII, 667
Bruyères, Marguerite (Burton), IV, 109
Bruyeres, Ralph Henry, IV, 109; V, **118–19**; VI, 182, 223, 484; VII, 703; VIII, 483
Bry, Catherine (Pennisseaut), IV, 621
Bryan, Mary (By), VII, 128
Bryan (Bryant), Needham, VI, 245
Bryant, John E., XI, 869
Bryant, Sarah. *See* Ashmore
Bryant, William Cullen, XII, 288, 925, 946, 948
Bryce*, George (1844–1931), XI, 80, 539; XII, 83
Bryce, James, XII, 491
Bryce, John D., XI, 581
Bryden, Janet (Jack), XI, 446
Bryden*, John (1831–1915), XI, 292, 293
Brydges, Charles John, VIII, 81, 823, 964; IX, 274, 369; X, 725; XI, 7, 69, **121–25**, 128, 132, 211, 226, 910, 915, 934; XII, 280, 394, 432, 607, 685, 686, 687
Brydges, Letitia Grace. *See* Henderson
Brymer, Alexander, IV, 111; V, 281; VI, **89–90**; VII, 62, 63
Brymer, Harriet. *See* Parr
Brymer, William, III, 37, 38; IV, 194, 195, 599; VI, 89, 90
Brymner*, Douglas (1823–1902), III, 695; IV, 232, 502; V, 610, 611; VIII, 341; IX, 873; XII, 16, 495, 737
Brymner*, William (1855–1925), XII, 288, 337, 830
Bryson, George, XII, 134
Bryson, George, XI, 522; XII, **134–35**, 197, 1130
Bryson, James, XII, 134
Bryson, Jane. *See* Cochrane
Bryson, John, XII, 134
Bryson, Robina. *See* Cobb
Bryson, Thomas, XII, 134
Bryzelius, Paulus, III, 474
Buache de La Neuville, Philippe, I, 676, 677
Buade, Anne de, Comtesse de Frontenac et de Palluau. *See* La Grange
Buade, Anne de, Comtesse de Frontenac et de Palluau. *See* Phélypeaux de Pontchartrain
Buade, Antoine de, I, 134
Buade, François-Louis de, I, 134, 142; II, 259
Buade, Henri de, Comte de Frontenac et de Palluau, I, 133, 134
Buade, Louis de, Comte de Frontenac et de Palluau, I, 32, 35, 40, 47, 49, 83, 84, 102, 104, 105, 106, 109, **133–42**, 174, 175, 177, 178, 185, 201, 204, 226, 238, 239, 245, 250, 286, 287, 288, 289, 290, 291, 295, 297, 309, 320, 323, 326, 327, 340, 361, 398, 399, 400, 402, 410, 417, 420, 439, 440, 443, 444, 448, 464, 466, 488, 489, 498, 499, 502, 528, 534, 535, 539, 540, 541, 544, 545, 565,

572, 573, 575, 576, 578, 581, 582, 583, 584, 585, 599, 600, 602, 613, 620, 622, 627, 632, 634, 650; II, xix, xxxi, 5, 6, 11, 12, 13, 15, 16, 17, 29, 31, 34, 36, 47, 48, 57, 59, 60, 61, 68, 70, 72, 73, 74, 75, 76, 77, 78, 80, 88, 89, 99, 103, 107, 113, 114, 118, 119, 120, 137, 142, 144, 148, 149, 153, 155, 162, 168, 169, 170, 172, 175, 178, 183, 184, 185, 186, 190, 193, 194, 202, 203, 205, 222, 224, 228, 229, 230, 242, 243, 248, 249, 253, 255, 258, 259, 262, 263, 264, 269, 276, 282, 283, 286, 295, 302, 303, 317, 320, 321, 322, 326, 327, 330, 335, 338, 343, 344, 345, 346, 350, 352, 353, 354, 369, 370, 375, 380, 383, 385, 386, 392, 393, 398, 401, 403, 404, 408, 409, 410, 412, 416, 418, 419, 420, 421, 425, 426, 427, 432, 441, 442, 446, 449, 450, 451, 456, 458, 459, 464, 470, 474, 483, 488, 491, 501, 504, 505, 507, 513, 514, 517, 518, 519, 523, 524, 525, 526, 532, 538, 540, 542, 545, 561, 566, 567, 573, 576, 578, 579, 580, 582, 585, 586, 588, 591, 592, 593, 594, 601, 602, 603, 618, 620, 621, 626, 631, 635, 654, 672; III, 7, 22, 44, 82, 83, 190, 233, 247, 308, 311, 344, 373, 446, 505, 578, 587; IV, xvii, 655; VII, 238; XI, 490; XII, 825

Bubear, George, XII, 408

Bucareli y Ursúa, Antonio Maria, IV, 165, 622, 623

Buchan, David, V, 243, 244, 275, 672; VI, 71, 176, 372, 393, 409, 410, 706, 707, 708; VII, **114–16**, 152, 301, 303, 323, 377, 507, 628; VIII, 70, 683, 771; IX, 389; X, 26

Buchan, Maria. *See* Adye

Buchanan, Agnes. *See* Jarvie

Buchanan, Agnes Jane (Marks), XII, 698

Buchanan, Alexander, VII, 394; VIII, **109–10**, 938; IX, 610, 728; X, 181, 624; XI, 286; XII, 89, 118, 476

Buchanan, Alexander Carlisle, VIII, 581; IX, 97

Buchanan, Alexander Carlisle, VI, 376; VIII, 109; IX, **97–98**, 377; X, 231

Buchanan, Arthur William Patrick, VII, 893

Buchanan, Charlotte Louise Caldwell. *See* Bowen

Buchanan, Dugald, VI, 459

Buchanan, Elizabeth. *See* Clarke

Buchanan, Flora. *See* MacLeod

Buchanan, George (clergyman), VIII, 828

Buchanan, George (preceptor), I, 50

Buchanan, George Carlo Vidua, VIII, 110

Buchanan, Isaac, VII, 164, 606, 860; VIII, 44, 81, 110, 111, 255, 294, 789, 790, 798, 823, 932, 965, 966; IX, 105, 368, 369, 504, 512, 575, 576, 577, 662, 745; X, 68, 74, 528, 559, 619, 721; XI, 13, 122, **125–31**, 423, 617, 618, 676, 774, 907; XII, 631, 884, 886, 1088

Buchanan, James (father of ALEXANDER CARLISLE), VI, 376; VII, 460; VIII, 109; IX, 97, 837; X, 14, 552

Buchanan, James (son of ISAAC), XI, 130

Buchanan, John, VIII, 109

Buchanan, Lillias (Campbell), VII, 145

Buchanan, Lucy. *See* Richardson

Buchanan, Malcolm Bàn. *See* MacMhannain, Calum Bàn

Buchanan, Margaret (Buchanan), VIII, 110; XI, 125

Buchanan, Mary Ann (Buchanan), VIII, 109

Buchanan, Peter (father of ISAAC and PETER), VIII, 110; XI, 125

Buchanan, Peter (son of ISAAC), XI, 127

Buchanan, Peter, VIII, xxv, 10, 81, **110–11**, 280, 965; IX, 368, 369, 525, 526, 662; X, 720; XI, 122, 126, 128, 130, 423

Buchanan, Robert, VIII, 559

Buchanan, Robert Stewart, IX, 97

Buchanan, Thomas, I, 50

Buchez, Philippe-Joseph-Benjamin, X, 585

Buchon, Joseph-Maximilien, X, 410

Buck. *See also* Burch

Buck, Miss (Saunders, Lady Saunders), IV, 699

Buck, Cynthia (Herring), XII, 428

Buck, Eunice (Stevens), VI, 732

Buck, James, IV, 699

Buck, John. *See* Skanawati

Buck, Walter M., XI, **131–32**

Bucke*, Richard Maurice (1837–1902), XI, 591; XII, 1073, 1074

Buckham, Margaret Waugh (Hawley; Bell), X, 45

Buckingham, Duke of. *See* Grenville; Villiers

Buckingham, Marquess of. *See* Grenville

Buckingham, William, VIII, 768; X, 629; XII, 648, 651, 657, 659

Buckingham and Chandos, Duke of. *See* Grenville

Buckinghamshire, Earl of. *See* Hobart

Buckland, Amelia (wife of GEORGE), XI, 132

Buckland, Francis Trevelyan, X, 449

Buckland, George, VIII, 267; XI, **132–33**

Buckland, John Wellington, VIII, 897; XII, 448, 449

Buckland, Kate M. *See* Horn

Buckland, William, VIII, 866; XI, 72

Buckley, Patrick, IX, 835

Buckton, C., IV, 613

Budai Parmenius István. *See* Parmenius

Buday Fleury, Charlotte de (Loustelneau), II, 179

Budd, Betsy. *See* Work

Budd, Elizabeth (DeMill), X, 223

Budd, Elizabeth Jane (Cochrane), XII, 200, 201

Budd, Henry (clergyman), VII, 900

Budd, Henry (son of HENRY), X, 109

Budd, Henry, VII, 232, 499, 901; IX, 732; X, **108–9**; XI, 436; XII, 201

Budden, Mrs. *See* Fisher

Budden, Agnes Elizabeth (King), XII, 485

Budden, John, X, 409, 412

Buddington, James, X, 43, 396

Budé, Jacques de, V, 893

Budemon. *See* Derivon

Budgell, Elizabeth (Graves), V, 380

Budington, Sydney O., X, 327, 328

Bueil, Honorat de, I, 421

Buell, A. K., IX, 232

Buell, Andrew Norton, VII, 420; VIII, 797; IX, 99, 575; X, **109–10**, 310, 311, 631; XI, 730; XII, 146

Buell, Ann Eliza. *See* Thorp

Buell, Calcina. *See* Richards

Buell, Calcina Medora (Cameron), XII, 146, 147

Buell, Catherine. *See* Dockstader

Buell, Deborah. *See* Dockstader

Buell, Margaret. *See* Berkley

Buell, Martha. *See* Naughton

Buell, Mary-Ann Angelica. *See* Story

Buell, Mercy. *See* Peters

Buell, Phoebe (Richards), XI, 732

Buell, Sarah Josepha (Hale), XII, 400

Buell, Timothy, VI, 90

Buell, William, VI, **90–91**; VII, 419, 452; IX, 99; X, 109

Buell, William, VI, 91, 262; VII, 420, 453, 458, 459, 695; VIII, 50, 305, 426; IX, **98–100**; X, 109, 631; XI, 730; XII, 85
Buffalo, V, 419
Buffalo Bill. *See* Cody, William Frederick
Buffon, Comte de. *See* Leclerc
Bufi. *See* Buti
Buffum, Ruth (Walker), XII, 1079
Bugaret, Catherine (La Tourasse), I, 427
Bugaret, Catherine (Petitpas), II, 524
Bugbee, Anna (Holmes), VIII, 405
Buhl, Anna Maria (Ermatinger), IV, 262
Buies*, Arthur (1840–1901), IX, 213; XI, 99, 489; XII, 256, 471, 502
Buil, Friar, I, 150
Buirette, Marguerite (Boucault), III, 74
Buisset, Luc, I, 438, 501; II, 278, 421
Buisson, Gervais, II, 108
Buisson, Marie. *See* Lereau
Buisson, Paul, I, 352
Buisson, *dit* Saint-Cosme, Michel, II, 109
Buisson, *dit* Saint-Cosme, Suzanne. *See* Delicérasse
Buisson de Saint-Cosme, Jean-François (d. 1712), II, **108–9**, 240
Buisson de Saint-Cosme, Jean-François (1667–1706), II, 55, 108, **109–10**, 171; III, 469, 522
Buisson de Saint-Cosme, Marie-Françoise, named de Saint-Pierre, II, 109
Buisson de Saint-Cosme, Michel, II, 55, 108, 109
Bujeau, Amand, III, 427
Bulger, Alicia (wife of ANDREW H.), VIII, 113
Bulger, Andrew H., VI, 210, 438, 648, 649, 768, 818; VIII, **111–13**, 159, 352, 721
Bulger, Catherine. *See* Foran
Bulger, John, VIII, 111
Bulkeley, Elizabeth, Lady Bulkeley. *See* Freke
Bulkeley, James Michael Freke, IV, 111, 112
Bulkeley, John, IV, 111
Bulkeley, Sir Lawrence, IV, 109
Bulkeley, Mary. *See* Burgess
Bulkeley, Mary. *See* Rous
Bulkeley, Peter, V, 628
Bulkeley, Richard, III, 91, 365, 573; IV, **109–13**, 258, 342, 703; V, 108, 121, 251; VI, 193, 778
Bull, Captain, V, 15
Bull, Bartholomew (Bartley), XI, 357
Bull, Dorothea. *See* Burland
Bull, Edward Claxton, VIII, 178
Bull, Eleanor (Good), XI, 357
Bull, George Perkins, VII, **116–17**, 358; VIII, 822; X, 309, 312, 313, 314
Bull, Harcourt Burland, VII, 117
Bull, Joseph, VII, 116
Bull, Mary J. (Kerr), X, 402
Bull, Richard, VII, 116
Bull Collar. *See* Peenaquim
Bullen, Charles, VIII, 506
Bullen, Emily Cecilia (Tobin), XI, 880
Bullen, Frances (Morris), VII, 626, 633
Bullen, William, XI, 880
Buller, Annie. *See* Templar
Buller, Sir Arthur William, VII, 67, 117; VIII, 730, 769; IX, **100–2**, 798; X, 505; XI, 286

Buller, Barbara Isabella. *See* Kirkpatrick
Buller, Catherine (Macarmick), V, 510
Buller, Charles, VII, 117; IX, 100
Buller, Charles, VII, 31, 41, **117–19**, 478; VIII, xxiii, 416, 691, 730; IX, 100, 441, 814, 818; X, 7, 142; XI, 874, 945
Buller, Rebecca (Watson), III, 659
Buller, Susannah Catherine (Duckworth, Lady Duckworth), V, 273
Buller, William, V, 273
Bulley, Joanna. *See* Wood
Bulley, John, V, 119
Bulley, Samuel, V, 120
Bulley, Samuel, V, **119–20**; XII, 888
Bulley, Sarah (Job), X, 381
Bulley, Thomas, V, 120; XII, 888
Bulley, William Wilking, V, 120
Bullingbrooke, Edward, IV, 50
Bullion, Angélique de. *See* Faure de Berlise
Bullion, Claude de, I, 484
Bullock, Artemissa (Ives), XII, 466
Bullock, Mary. *See* Clinch
Bullock, Mary Elizabeth. *See* Clinch
Bullock, Richard (father), VIII, 794
Bullock, Richard, VII, 103; X, 557
Bullock, William, V, 190; X, **110–11**, 454; XI, 75, 76
Bulmer, Henry, XI, 62, 758
Bulmer*, John Thomas (b. 1845 or 1846, d. 1901), XII, 15
Bulmer, Mary Ann (Sales Laterrière), VI, 680
Bulpit, James, VIII, 83
Bulteau, Guillaume, II, **110–11**
Bulwer, William Henry Lytton Earle, 1st Baron Dalling and Bulwer, X, 724
Bulwer-Lytton, Edward George Earle Lytton, 1st Baron Lytton, VII, 119; IX, 81, 114, 511; X, 112, 196, 244; XI, 299, 603, 604
Bunbury, Sir Henry Edward, VI, 713; XII, 316, 449, 922
Bunbury, Joseph, V, **120–21**
Bunbury, Thomas, V, 348
Bunel, Louis, IX, 148
Bunn, Catherine. *See* Thomas
Bunn, Frances (Harriott), IX, 367
Bunn, Isabella. *See* Clouston
Bunn, John, XI, 384
Bunn, John, VIII, 766, 767, 889; IX, **102–3**, 367, 530; X, 67, 111, 215; XI, 436, 876; XII, 641
Bunn, Mary (McKay), XII, 641
Bunn, Phoebe. *See* Sinclair
Bunn, Rachel. *See* Harriott
Bunn, Sarah. *See* McNab
Bunn, Thomas, IX, 102; XII, 641
Bunn, Thomas, IX, 102; X, **111**; XI, 739, 740, 842
Bunning, Ellen (mother of MARIA), IX, 103
Bunning, Maria, named Sister Mary Martha, VIII, 299; IX, **103–4**, 325; XI, 110
Bunning, Wileum, IX, 103
Bunoz, Émile-Marie, XII, 284
Bunster, Arthur, XII, 242
Bunt. *See* Hotsinoñhyahta?
Buntin, Alexander, XII, 136
Buntin, Alexander, XII, **135–37**, 571
Buntin, Isabella. *See* McLaren
Buntin, James, XII, 135
Bunting, Christopher William, XII, **137–39**, 286

Bunting, Elizabeth. *See* Giraud
Bunting, Frederick, XII, 157
Bunting, Jane. *See* Crowe
Bunting, Joshua, XII, 139
Bunting, Mary Elizabeth. *See* Ellis
Bunting, William, XII, 137
Bunting, William Franklin, XII, **139–40**
Bunyan, John, I, 378; XII, 997
Burbage, Bridget (Jackman), X, 378
Burbidge, Elizabeth (wife of JOHN), V, 121
Burbidge*, George Wheelock (1847–1908), XI, 748; XII, 1043, 1045
Burbidge, John, V, 63, **121–22**
Burbidge, Rebecca. *See* Dudley
Burch, John, VII, 833
Burch, John, IV, **113**; V, 402
Burch, John Edgar, XII, 115
Burch, Martha (Ramsey; wife of JOHN), IV, 113
Burchett, Elizabeth (Hardy, Lady Hardy), IV, 326
Burchett, Josiah, II, 661
Burchill, George, VIII, 783, 784; X, 333
Burdett-Coutts, Angela Georgina, Baroness Burdett-Coutts, XI, 314; XII, 441
Burdick, James, XII, 92
Bureau, Angélique. *See* Allain
Bureau, Geneviève. *See* Gilbert
Bureau, Geneviève (Dorion), VII, 254; IX, 210; X, 236; XII, 260
Bureau, Jacques-Olivier, IX, 78
Bureau, Jean-Baptiste, VII, 119
Bureau, Napoléon, VIII, 217; IX, 66; X, 237, 238; XII, 64
Bureau, Pierre, IX, 210
Bureau, Pierre, VI, 634; VII, **119–20**, 254; VIII, 18, 128; XII, 260
Burel, Gilbert, I, 121
Burel, Jacquette. *See* Quémar
Burel, Jeanne (Briand), IV, 95
Burel, Mathurin, IV, 95
Burges, Frances Anne (Head), X, 342
Burges, Mary Anne, VII, 362, 363
Burgess, Agnes (Hall), IX, 357
Burgess, Alexander Mackinnon, XI, 748; XII, **140–41**
Burgess, Ann. *See* Davidson
Burgess, John, XII, 140
Burgess, Margaret Beatrice. *See* Anderson
Burgess, Mary (Bulkeley), IV, 110
Burgess, Rachel (Churchill), X, 172
Burghardt, Gesie (Bostwick), VII, 92
Burghley, Baron. *See* Cecil
Burgo, Marcel, VIII, 591
Burgoyne, Anna Maria. *See* Burnestone
Burgoyne, Lady Charlotte. *See* Stanley
Burgoyne, John, IV, 113
Burgoyne, John, IV, 3, **113–15**, 118, 121, 130, 155, 375, 395, 403, 427, 428, 442, 503, 549, 564, 603, 694, 771, 792; V, 32, 33, 34, 40, 64, 88, 96, 146, 147, 148, 181, 206, 222, 231, 254, 282, 306, 307, 319, 321, 343, 347, 422, 454, 457, 548, 567, 575, 582, 583, 772, 791, 890, 891; VI, 77, 90, 146, 150, 153, 188, 264, 298, 320, 337, 345, 363, 374, 403, 411, 502, 695, 733, 788, 804; VII, 186, 911; IX, 282
Burgoyne, Sir John Fox, X, 402, 406; XI, 468; XII, 41, 475
Burke, Annie (Simpson), XI, 825

Burke, Edmund, IV, 90, 335, 413, 701; V, 145; VI, 55, 57, 85, 94, 646; VII, 645; VIII, 306; IX, 352, 354, 355; X, 314; XII, 525
Burke, Edmund (fl. 1785–1801), V, **122–23**, 124, 408, 459, 632; VII, 841
Burke, Edmund (1753–1820), IV, 43, 445; V, **123–25**, 181, 306, 494, 524, 695; VI, 158, 217, 293, 406, 448, 449, 595, 650, 691, 731; VII, 355, 530, 551, 552, 705, 803, 804, 805, 811; VIII, 33, 64, 592, 626; IX, 548
Burke*, Edmund (1850–1919), XII, 973
Burke, Eliza (Howley), XI, 429
Burke, George Thew, VIII, 510
Burke, Joanna Harriet. *See* Blake
Burke, John (brother-in-law of John SIMPSON, 1812–85), XI, 825
Burke, John (lawyer), IV, 414
Burke, John (merchant), XII, 143
Burke, Patrick, X, 559
Burke, Sarah (Simpson), XI, 825
Burke, Sarah M. (Fraser), XII, 329, 330
Burke, Thomas K., VI, 692, 693
Burke, William, VII, 591
Burkholder, Benjamin, VIII, 271
Burkholder, Mabel Grace, VII, 733
Burlamaqui, Jean-Jacques, VII, 675
Burland, Benjamin, VIII, 210
Burland, Dorothea (Bull), VII, 116
Burland, George Bull, XII, 248
Burley, Cornelius Albertson, VI, **91–93**
Burley, Margaret. *See* Beamer
Burley, Sally. *See* King
Burley, William, VI, 91
Burls, Anne (Cramp), XI, 209, 211
Burn, Mrs (wife of WILLIAM SCOTT), VIII, 114
Burn, David (estate assignee), VIII, 113
Burn, David (father of WILLIAM SCOTT), VIII, 113
Burn, Eliza (Stisted), X, 667
Burn, Helen. *See* Scott
Burn, Maud Mary. *See* Banks
Burn, Thomas, IX, 488
Burn, William, V, **125–27**; VII, 554
Burn, William John, XII, **141–42**
Burn, William Lewis, XII, 141
Burn, William Scott, VIII, **113–15**
Burnaby, Andrew, III, 587
Burnaby, Robert, IX, 115; X, **111–12**
Burnaby, Sarah. *See* Meares
Burnaby, Thomas, X, 111
Burnard, Elizabeth (Chanter), X, 161
Burnard, Thomas, VIII, 270; IX, 856; X, 161
Burnestone, Anna Maria (Burgoyne), IV, 113
Burnet (Burnett), Mary (Schank), VI, 694
Burnet, David, III, **115–16**, 323
Burnet, James, V, 781
Burnet, Mary (Keir), VIII, 451
Burnet, Mary Ann. *See* Forsyth
Burnet, Peter, VIII, 115
Burnet, William, II, 87, 209, 572, 603, 625; III, 43
Burnett. *See also* Burnet
Burnett, David, XII, 489
Burnett, Emily. *See* Krieghoff
Burnett, Hamilton, X, 413
Burnett, James, XI, 556

Burnett, Thomas, VI, 19
Burnett, William, VI, 72
Burnett, Sir William, XI, 544
Burney, Charles, X, 663
Burney, Frances (Arblay), IV, 555, 763; VIII, 46
Burney, James, V, 80
Burnham, Achsah (Ermatinger), X, 273
Burnham, Asa (father), VIII, 116
Burnham, Asa, VIII, 116
Burnham, Elizabeth. *See* Choate
Burnham, Elizabeth. *See* Cutler
Burnham, Elizabeth (Birdsall), VIII, 91
Burnham, Mark (uncle), VIII, 324
Burnham, Mark, VIII, 117
Burnham, Zacheus, VII, 75; VIII, 92, **116–18**, 324, 519; X, 273
Burns, Alexander, XII, **142–43**
Burns, Ann. *See* Ryan
Burns, Ann. *See* Tod
Burns, Anne Flora. *See* Taylor
Burns, Britannia. *See* Warton
Burns, David (office holder), V, 389, 520; VII, 36; VIII, 749
Burns, David (potter), XII, 157
Burns, Elizabeth. *See* Bell
Burns, Elizabeth. *See* McAdam
Burns, George (brother of ROBERT), IX, 105
Burns, George (clergyman), VI, 355, 460; VII, 491
Burns, George (father-in-law of Robert GRAY, d. 1828), VI, 298; XI, 369
Burns, George (merchant), IX, 180, 181, 182, 183, 185
Burns, George (officer), VI, 95
Burns, Grizzell. *See* Ferrier
Burns, Harriet. *See* McKenna
Burns, James (father of ALEXANDER), XII, 142
Burns, James (merchant), IX, 180
Burns, Jane (mother of ROBERT EASTON), VI, 93; IX, 108
Burns, Janet. *See* Orr
Burns, John (clergyman), VI, 233; VII, 77; VIII, 220; IX, 539
Burns, John (father of ROBERT), IX, 104
Burns, John, V, 279; VI, **93–95**; IX, 108, 232, 544
Burns, Kennedy Francis, XII, 27, **143–44**, 339
Burns, Lewis, VII, 203
Burns, Mary (Gray), VI, 298; VIII, 428; XI, 369
Burns, Patrick (brother of KENNEDY FRANCIS), XII, 143
Burns, Patrick (rioter), XI, 863
Burns, Phoebe Maria (Fanning), V, 309
Burns, Robert, VI, 190; VII, 601; VIII, 503; IX, 353, 658; X, 653; XI, 949; XII, 474, 475, 588, 661, 662, 945, 1116
Burns, Robert, VII, 532, 533, 538; VIII, 68, 570, 767; IX, **104–8**, 742; X, 442; XI, 467; XII, 492
Burns, Robert Easton, VI, 93; VIII, 53, 473, 927; IX, 57, 79, **108–9**, 244, 804; XII, 1123
Burns, Sarah. *See* Andrews
Burns, Thomas B., VI, 93
Burns, Thomas E., XII, 143
Burns, Walter, XI, 770
Burns, William, V, 566, 746; VI, **95–97**, 424; VIII, 952
Burnside, Alexander, VIII, 86
Burnthwaite, Margaret (Baird), VII, 33
Burnyeat, Elizabeth Archibald (Archibald), XII, 30
Burnyeat, John, XII, 30

Burnyeat, Maria Louisa. *See* Goudge
Burpe, David, VII, 121
Burpe, David, VI, 504; VII, **120–21**
Burpe, Edward, VII, 120
Burpe, Elizabeth. *See* Gallishan
Burpe, Jeremiah, VII, 120
Burpe, Jonathan, VII, 120
Burpe, Mary. *See* Saunders
Burpee, Charles, XI, 134
Burpee, Egerton Ryerson, XI, 134
Burpee, Esther. *See* Gallop
Burpee, Frederick, XI, 133
Burpee, Henrietta. *See* Robertson
Burpee, Hephziba (Pickard), XI, 688
Burpee, Isaac, XI, 133
Burpee, Isaac, XI, **133–35**, 224, 298, 350; XII, 651, 785
Burpee, Laleah. *See* Johnston
Burpee*, Lawrence Johnston (1873–1946), IV, 555; X, 346, 347
Burpee, Mary (Pickard), XI, 687
Burpee, Phoebe. *See* Coban
Burpee, Richard E., VIII, **118–19**, 613
Burpee, Thomas, VIII, 118
Burr, Aaron, V, 72; VI, 55, 177
Burr, Elizabeth. *See* Cleever
Burr, Grace Hubbard (Plumb), XI, 697
Burr, Hester. *See* Lamoreaux
Burr, Rachel (Goodhue), IX, 323
Burr, Rheuben, IX, 109
Burr, Rowland, IX, **109–10**
Burrage, Elizabeth. *See* Chapman
Burrage, Robert, IX, 110
Burrage, Robert Raby, VII, 809; VIII, 937; IX, **110–11**
Burrell, Frances Julia (Percy, Duchess of Northumberland), VI, 552
Burritt, Read, XI, 914
Burritt, Stephen, V, 457
Burroughs. *See also* Burrowes
Burroughs, Edward, XII, 86
Burroughs, Louisa (Strange, Lady Strange), VII, 831
Burroughs, Stephen, VI, 592; VIII, 406
Burrow, Genevieve (Macaulay), VI, 416
Burrow, James, IV, 389
Burrowes (Burroughs), Sarah (Fauquier), XI, 313, 314
Burrows, Ann. *See* Boden
Burrows, Charles Acton, XII, 129
Burrows, Elizabeth (Honey), VII, 121
Burrows, John, VII, **121–22**, 129; IX, 733, 734
Burrows, Maria Elizabeth. *See* Blake
Burry. *See also* Bury
Burry, William, XII, 620
Burstall, Edward, XII, 144, 145, 531
Burstall, Fanny Bell. *See* Forsyth
Burstall, Henry, XII, 144, 145
Burstall, John, XI, 774; XII, **144–46**
Burstall, John Forsyth, XII, 146
Burstall, William, XII, 144
Burt*, Alfred Leroy (1888–1970), IV, 279, 321, 336, 350; V, 147, 152, 585
Burt, Frederick, IX, 550
Burt, Silas Wright, VIII, 81
Burtch, Jane (Mount; Corlis), VI, 521
Burthen, Sophia (Pooley), VII, 666

Burtis, John, IX, 744
Burtis, William Richard Mulharen, XI, **135–36**
Burton. *See also* Christie; Conyngham
Burton, Arundel Charlotte (Whitaker), XI, 916
Burton, Clarence Monroe, III, 706; IV, 817; V, 237
Burton, Elizabeth. *See* Clements
Burton, Sir Francis Nathaniel, V, 96; VI, **97–98**, 119, 326, 597, 645, 802; VII, 189, 225, 729, 770, 771, 787, 788, 789, 878; VIII, 461; IX, 189, 190, 812
Burton, Sir George William, XI, 915
Burton, Harriet (Menzies), VII, 600
Burton, Jack. *See* Anderson, John
Burton, John, VII, **122–24**, 272, 434; VIII, 968; XII, 872
Burton, Joseph Netterville, X, 667
Burton, Margaret, III, 90
Burton, Marguerite. *See* Bruyères
Burton, Maria (Stisted), X, 667
Burton, Marie. *See* Tomlin
Burton, Mary (wife of JOHN), VII, 122
Burton, Mary (Hutton), XII, 460, 461
Burton, Moses, IX, 6
Burton, Nathaniel, VI, 629, 630
Burton, Ralph, III, **88–90**, 525, 541, 669; IV, xxxiii, xxxv, 85, 108, 109, 188, 279, 290, 300, 316, 331, 369, 379, 491, 570, 572, 685, 787, 793, 794; V, 142, 181, 272, 823, 888, 889
Burton, Sir Richard Francis, X, 667
Burton, Robert, III, 89
Burton, Sarah (Clitherow), VIII, 164
Burton, Valentina Letitia. *See* Lawless
Burton, William, X, 360
Burwash*, Nathanael (1839–1918), IV, 495; XI, 641, 794; XII, 10, 169, 993
Burwell, Adam, VII, 124, 125
Burwell, Adam Hood, VI, 612; VII, **124–25**, 543; XII, 570, 1130
Burwell, Alexander, VII, 126
Burwell, Edward, VII, 126
Burwell, Hannibal, VII, 126
Burwell, Hercules, VII, 126
Burwell, Isaac Brock, VII, 126
Burwell, John, VII, 126, 127
Burwell, John Walpole, VII, 126
Burwell, Leonidas, VII, 126, 127
Burwell, Mahlon, VI, 57, 91, 92, 399, 400, 497, 521, 522, 612; VII, 58, 92, 124, **125–28**, 337, 715; VIII, 608, 858, 860
Burwell, Sarah. *See* Barnard
Burwell, Sarah. *See* Haun
Burwell, Sarah. *See* Veal
Bury, Viscount. *See* Keppel
Bury, Viscountess. *See* MacNab
Bury (Burry), Anne de (Talon), I, 614
Busby, Henrietta Jane Cater (Smith), XII, 978
Busby, Thomas, IV, 116
Busby, Thomas, IV, **115–16**
Bush, Sally (Mallory), VIII, 606
Bush, Sarah. *See* Mallory
Bushby, Agnes. *See* Douglas
Bushby, Anne Sarah. *See* Stedman
Bushby, Arthur Thomas, X, **112–14**, 247; XI, 394, 395
Bushby, Joseph, X, 112

Bushel, John, III, 90
Bushel, Rebecca. *See* Parker
Bushell, Elizabeth. *See* Strowbridge
Bushell, John, III, **90–91**, 267, 404; IV, 342, 343
Bushnan, John, X, 27
Bushnell, Charles Ira, V, 605
Bussell, Margaret (McClure), X, 455
Bustin, Alice Elizabeth (Metcalf), XI, 590
Butcher, Catherine. *See* Hooper
Butcher, Margaret. *See* Chappell
Butcher, Mark, XI, **136–37**
Butcher, Patience (mother of MARK), XI, 136
Butcher, William, XI, 136
Bute, Earl of. *See* Stuart
Buteau, Félix, IX, 118
Buteau, Flore (Turcotte), IX, 796
Buteau, François, IX, 796
Buteux, Jacques, I, 106, **142–43**, 214, 287, 341, 432, 453, 481, 549, 551, 558, 566, 640; II, 158
Buteux, Jean, I, 142
Buti (Bufi), Catherine (Delvecchio), VI, 185
Butler, Andrew, IV, 119; V, 781
Butler, Benjamin Franklin, XII, 418
Butler, Catalyntje. *See* Bradt
Butler, Lady Charlotte (Cornwallis, Baroness Cornwallis), IV, 168
Butler, Deborah. *See* Dennison
Butler, Edward Kent Strathearn, VI, 99
Butler, Elizabeth. *See* Molyneux
Butler, Elizabeth (Dight), VI, 98
Butler, Frances (Harrison), X, 336
Butler, Hannah (Barnes), VII, 48
Butler, Jean, III, 58, 59, 60, 228
Butler, John (agent), V, 407
Butler, John (bishop), IV, 511
Butler, John (d. 1791), IV, 53, 111, **116–17**, 131, 199, 266, 273, 275, 450, 526, 527, 528, 529, 696; V, 82, 257, 607, 843; VI, 98
Butler, John (d. 1796), IV, 113, **117–20**, 121, 155, 394, 405, 417, 731, 735; V, 14, 15, 121, 147, 168, 229, 254, 439, 454, 517, 660, 661, 669, 781, 805, 841, 894, 900; VI, 152, 153, 488; VII, 665, 697; VIII, 194
Butler (Dight), John Butler, IV, 529; VI, **98–99**, 313
Butler, Joseph, XII, 112
Butler, Melinda Burgess. *See* Morden
Butler, Philip, IV, 393, 409, 410, 411, 711; VII, 115, 152, 507, 628; VIII, 234; IX, 682
Butler, Rachel (Morris), VII, 48
Butler, Rachel (Wall; wife of JOHN, d. 1791), IV, 116
Butler, Richard, 1st Earl of Arran, IV, 168
Butler, Robert, II, 520
Butler, Samuel (poet), V, 48
Butler, Samuel (writer), X, 334
Butler, Thomas, IV, 117
Butler, Walter, IV, 117
Butler, Walter, IV, 117, 118, **120–21**, 683; V, 517, 788, 805
Butler, William, VIII, 555
Butler*, Sir William Francis (1838–1910), VIII, 4; IX, 624; XI, 195; XII, 132, 194
Butson, John, XII, 56
Butt, Elizabeth (Felton), VII, 281
Buttar, William, IV, 384

Butterfield, Isaac, VI, 403
Butterfield, William, VIII, 943; XII, 714
Butters, Mr (daguerreotypist), VII, 900
Butterworth, Joseph, VII, 634
Butterworth, Mary (Haven), IV, 333
Button, Barbara. *See* Merrick
Button, Margaret. *See* Lewis
Button, Mary. *See* Rice
Button, Miles (grandfather), I, 144
Button, Miles, I, 144
Button, Thomas, II, 123
Button, Sir Thomas, I, 20, 74, **144–45**, 312, 329, 362, 378, 515
Button Chief. *See* Natose-Onista
Butts, Deliverance (Anderson), X, 11
Butts, Robert, III, 634
Butts, Thomas, I, 371
Buxton, Sir Thomas Fowell, VIII, 670, 968
Buydens, Marie-Jeanne (De Smet), X, 226
By, Elizabeth. *See* Baines
By, Esther. *See* March
By, George, VII, 128
By, John, V, 106; VI, 127, 220, 221, 223, 224, 481, 482, 485, 812; VII, 33, 90, 122, **128–31**, 183, 266, 268, 494, 726, 820; VIII, 552, 583, 840; IX, 412, 485, 734; XI, 766
By, Mary. *See* Bryan
Byam, Christiana Elizabeth (Musgrave), XI, 634
Byers, Amelia (mother of PETER), V, 127
Byers, John, known as Black Jack, V, 127
Byers, Peter, known as Black Peter, V, **127**
Byers, Sancho, V, 127
Byles, Anna. *See* Noyes
Byles, John Barnard, XI, 129
Byles, Katherine, V, 128
Byles, Mary, V, 128
Byles, Mather, V, 127
Byles, Mather, V, 23, **127–28**, 250, 430, 705; VII, 16; X, 6; XII, 250
Byles, Rebecca. *See* Walter
Byles, Rebecca (Almon), V, 23, 24, 430; VII, 16; X, 6
Byles, Sarah. *See* Lyde
Byles, Susanna. *See* Lawlor
Bylot, Robert, I, 20, 74, 75, 144, **145**, 329, 374, 376, 377, 378
Byng, George, 1st Viscount Torrington, II, 316, 609; III, 91, 496
Byng, John, III, 31, 70, **91–92**, 209, 293, 496, 629; IV, 171; V, 730
Byng, Margaret, Viscountess Torrington. *See* Masters
Byng, Sarah (Osborn), III, 496
Byrne. *See also* Bierne
Byrne, Mary Anne (Colclough), VI, 160
Byrne, Michael, V, 229
Byrne, Rebecca (Hart), V, 409, 410
Byrne, Thomas, IX, 393
Byrne, William (artisan), IV, 763
Byrne, William (clergyman), VII, 171
Byrns, Bridget (Doherty), X, 233
Byron, Frances, Baroness Byron. *See* Berkeley
Byron, George Gordon, 6th Baron Byron, IV, 122; VI, 375, 376, 646; VII, 14, 82, 337, 734; VIII, 386, 744, 853; XII, 460, 516, 823, 945
Byron, John, IV, 122

Byron, John, III, xxv, 132; IV, 28, 80, **121–23**, 155, 158, 176, 195, 282, 600, 707; V, 52, 359, 369, 382
Byron, Sophia. *See* Trevannion
Byron, William, 4th Baron Byron, IV, 121
Byrsarius, Torquatus, II, 98
Byssot. *See also* Bissot
Byssot de La Rivière, François, I, **145–46**, 395, 447, 480, 620, 622; II, 65, 68, 158, 159, 256; IV, 182; V, 288
Byssot de La Rivière, Marie. *See* Couillard
Byssot Du Hommée, Jean, I, 145
Byssot Du Hommée, Marie. *See* Assour
Bythesea, John, X, 406

CAAMAÑO, Jacinto, VI, 233
Caamaño, Saturnina Norberta (Eliza), VI, 233
Caballero, Fernán, XI, 848
Cabanac. *See* Desjordy
Cabané, Pierre, VI, 666
Cabanel, Alexandre, IX, 359
Cabarrus, Dominique, IV, 421
Cabart de Villermont, Esprit de, II, 62, 589, 633
Cabazié, Delphine. *See* Desbordes
Cabazié, Jeanne. *See* Guiberge
Cabazié, Pierre, II, 111
Cabazié, Pierre, II, **111**
Cabot, Catalina. *See* Medrano
Cabot, Elizabeth, I, 158
Cabot, John, I, 19, 21, 22, 41, 120, **146–52**, 153, 154, 164, 166, 171, 234, 240, 304, 316, 333, 386, 641, 643
Cabot, Juana (Joanna) (wife of SEBASTIAN), I, 158
Cabot, Lewis (Louis, Ludovico), I, 147
Cabot, Sancio, I, 147
Cabot, Sebastian, I, 19, 21, 146, 147, 148, 149, 151, **152–58**, 316, 375, 378, 565, 643
Caboto. *See also* Cabot
Caboto, Giulio, I, 146
Caboto, Mattea, I, 146
Caboto, Piero, I, 146
Cabrara, Father, III, 204
Caché, Marguerite (Perrault), III, 509
Cachointioni. *See* Kakouenthiony
Cachupín. *See* Vélez
Cadart, Nicolas, II, 244
Caddy, Douglas T., XI, 138
Caddy, Edward C., XI, 138
Caddy, Georgiana. *See* Hamilton
Caddy, Hannah. *See* Godard
Caddy, John Herbert, XI, **137–38**; XII, 327
Caddy, John Thomas, XI, 137
Cadet. *See also* Robichaux
Cadet, Le. *See* Chomina
Cadet, Angélique. *See* Fortier
Cadet, Angélique (Rossay), IV, 124
Cadet, Augustin, III, 571; IV, 123
Cadet, Françoise (Esprit de Vantelon), IV, 124
Cadet (Caddé), François-Joseph, IV, 123
Cadet, Joseph, III, 156
Cadet, Joseph-Michel, III, 19, 76, 124, 141, 321, 322, 435, 441, 477, 510, 537; IV, 5, 64, 66, 67, 69, 88, 92, **123–28**, 263, 312, 378, 433, 435, 461, 572, 612, 615, 621, 632, 660; V, 90, 131, 368
Cadet, Louise (Rouffio), III, 571, 572; IV, 123
Cadet, Marie-Anne (Amiot), III, 13; IV, 123

Cadet, Marie-Joseph. *See* Daveine
Cadet, Marie-Joseph (Vignau), IV, 123
Cadet, Michel, III, 569
Cadet, Michel-François, IV, 123
Cadet Deschamps, Joseph, IV, 124
Cadieu, Charles, I, 585
Cadieu de Courville, Charles, II, 30
Cadieux, Henriette (Lorimier), VII, 512, 513, 514
Cadieux, Jean-Marie, VII, 512
Cadieux, Louis, VII, 131
Cadieux, Louis-Marie, VI, 597, 598; VII, **131–32**, 670;
    VIII, 78, 259, 302, 317
Cadieux, Madeleine. *See* Serre
Cadieux, Marie-Anne (Quévillon; Chabot), VI, 625
Cadieux, Rose, VII, 132
Cadillac. *See* Laumet
Cadman, Harriet. *See* Smith
Cadogan, Sir William, II, 513
Cadot. *See also* Cadotte
Cadot, Athanasie (wife of JEAN-BAPTISTE), V, 129, 130
Cadot, Jean-Baptiste, V, 129, 130, 177, 178; VIII, 454
Cadot, Jean-Baptiste, IV, 675; V, 90, **128–30**, 242, 568,
    682, 715, 741; VI, 99, 317, 357
Cadot, Jean-François, V, 128
Cadot, Joseph-Marie, V, 130
Cadot, Marie. *See* Mouet
Cadot, Marie-Josephe. *See* Proteau
Cadot, Michel, V, 129, 130
Cadotte, Joseph, VI, **99–101**, 167, 665
Cadotte (Cadot), Marie-Charlotte (Valade), IX, 802
Cadron, Marie-Rosalie, named de la Nativité (Jetté), IX,
    **111–12**; XI, 96
Cadron, *dit* Saint-Pierre, Antoine, IX, 111
Cadron, *dit* Saint-Pierre, Rosalie. *See* Roy, *dit* Desjardins
Cadsedan-hiunt. *See* Kaghswaghtaniunt
Caën, Émery de, I, 30, 58, **159**, 160, 161, 194, 195, 197,
    211, 266, 296, 297, 405, 407, 411, 419, 441, 473, 479,
    533, 546
Caën, Ézéchiel de, I, 159, 160
Caën, Guillaume de, I, 159, 419
Caën, Guillaume de, I, 30, 110, **159–62**, 194, 247, 266,
    346, 368, 411, 419, 433, 473, 521
Caën, Hélène de, I, 161
Caën, Marie de. *See* Langlois
Caën, Marie de. *See* Sores
Caën, Marie de, I, 161
Caën, Suzanne de. *See* Petit
Caesar, Julius, I, 89
Caffin. *See* Galiffet
Caffrey, Mary Theresa (McGee), IX, 490
Cagenquarichten, II, xxxix, **111–12**; III, xl
Caghswoughtiooni. *See* Kakouenthiony
Cahbeach, John, IX, 419
Cahideuc, Emmanuel-Auguste de, Comte Dubois de La
    Motte, III, 55, 70, 72, **92–93**, 358; IV, 282, 327, 699
Cahideuc, Gilonne-Charlotte de, Comtesse Dubois de La
    Motte. *See* Langan
Cahideuc, Jean-François de, Comte Dubois de La Motte,
    III, 92
Cahideuc, Jeanne-Françoise de, Comtesse Dubois de La
    Motte. *See* Andigné de La Chaise
Cahiheue, Louis, VII, 137
Cahoon, Benjamin Parker, VI, 252, 253; VIII, 120, 121

Cahouet, Marie-Anne. *See* Maisonnat, *dit* Baptiste
Caigin, Marie-Anne. *See* Noguet
Cailhault de La Tesserie, Éléonore de. *See* Grandmaison
Cailhault de La Tesserie, Jacques de, I, 285, 344, 345, 537,
    589; II, 61
Cailhe (Caille), Michel, II, 129, 143, 196
Caillé, Jean, II, 467
Cailleteau, Françoise (Denys de Fronsac; Rey Gaillard), I,
    260; II, 106
Cailleteau, Marie-Anne (Bermen de La Martinière), II, 57;
    III, 64
Cailleux, Françoise de (Dollier de Casson), II, 190
Cailly, Anne-Marie. *See* Volant
Cailly, François-Joseph, II, 424; III, **93–94**, 392
Cailly, Jean-Christophore, III, 93
Cailly, Marie-Salomé. *See* Duvallier
Cain. *See* Cane
Cair, John, I, 150
Caird, Edward, XI, 943
Caird, John, XII, 616
Caird, Sir James, IX, 405
Caird, William R., XI, 797
Cairns, Alexander, VIII, 60
Cairns, Catherine (Cuthbert), IV, 190; V, 26; IX, 187
Cairns, Elizabeth (Barbier), VIII, 60
Cairns, Hugh McCalmont, 1st Earl Cairns, IX, 114; XII, 77
Cairns, William, IX, 310; XI, 91
Caissie (Casey), Pélagie (Landry), X, 426
Caissy, Anne. *See* Bourgeois
Caissy (Keissis), Marguerite (Mangeant), III, 426
Caissy, *dit* Roger, Jean, III, 426
Calanne, Monsieur de (friend of Pierre de RIGAUD de
    Vaudreuil de Cavagnial), IV, 669
Calder, John, XII, 631
Calder, Newman Fletcher, XII, 275
Calder, Sir Robert, VIII, 787
Calder, Sarah Jane (Duffin), XII, 275
Caldicott, Joseph, IX, 112
Caldicott, Nancy (mother of THOMAS FORD), IX, 112
Caldicott, Samuel, IX, 112
Caldicott, Thomas Ford, IX, **112–13**; XII, 225
Caldwell, Mr (merchant), VII, 176
Caldwell, Alexander, V, 133
Caldwell, Amelia (Mary), V, 133
Caldwell, Ann. *See* Hamilton
Caldwell, Ann, V, 132
Caldwell, Anne, Lady Caldwell. *See* French
Caldwell, Antoinette (Morin), XII, 762
Caldwell, Billy, V, 798; VI, 101, 103, 340; VII, **132–33**;
    VIII, 120
Caldwell, Boyd, XI, 846
Caldwell, Catherine (Riall), VII, 744
Caldwell, Daniel, XI, 727
Caldwell, Francis Xavier, VI, 102, 253; VIII, **119–21**
Caldwell, George, VI, 104
Caldwell, Henry, IV, 146, 150, 493, 538, 548, 554, 753; V,
    30, 31, 44, 57, 84, **130–33**, 149, 191, 215, 331, 371, 428,
    460, 486, 502, 566, 600, 602, 621, 745, 768, 769, 864,
    870, 879, 892; VI, 296, 423, 427, 615, 688; VII, 133,
    134, 136, 176, 380; VIII, 690; IX, 74
Caldwell, Sir Henry John, V, 132; VII, 134, 135, 136; XII,
    104
Caldwell, James, V, 177, 285

Caldwell, James, V, **133–34**; VIII, 353
Caldwell, Jane, Lady Caldwell. *See* Davidson
Caldwell, Jane (Sewell), VI, 700, 702
Caldwell, Jane Douglass. *See* Sweeny
Caldwell, Jean. *See* Wilson
Caldwell, John, IX, 640
Caldwell, Sir John, V, 130
Caldwell, Sir John, V, 132, 768; VI, 267, 281, 750; VII, 70,
  **133–37**, 225, 373, 484, 728, 789, 879; VIII, 123, 319,
  690, 803; IX, 75, 179, 671; X, 32; XI, 379
Caldwell, Louisa. *See* Melvin
Caldwell, Louisa, V, 133
Caldwell, Mary Frances. *See* Réaume
Caldwell, Prudence (Richardson), VII, 747
Caldwell, Rebecka (mother of WILLIAM, d. 1822), VI, 101
Caldwell, Samuel, XI, 679
Caldwell, Suzanne. *See* Baby
Caldwell, Thomas. *See also* Caldwell, Billy
Caldwell, Thomas, VI, 102
Caldwell, William (father of WILLIAM, d. 1822), VI, 101
Caldwell, William (mayor), XI, 679
Caldwell, William (son of FRANCIS XAVIER), VIII, 120
Caldwell, William (son of WILLIAM, d. 1822), VI, 102
Caldwell, William (d. 1822), V, 302, 517, 805; VI, **101–4**,
  153, 189, 340; VII, 132, 527; VIII, 119, 795
Caldwell, William (1782–1833), VI, **104–5**; VII, 25, 667,
  751, 824; VIII, 404
Caldwell, William Bletterman, VIII, 574, 767; IX, 102,
  136, 732; X, 47, 168; XI, **138–39**, 220, 546, 875; XII,
  206, 477
Calef, Margaret. *See* Staniford
Calef, Robert, V, 134
Caleff, Dorothy. *See* Jewett
Caleff, John, V, **134–35**, 336; VI, 562
Caleff, Margaret. *See* Rogers
Calehue. *See* Callihoo
Calf of Many Colours. *See* Natchookoneck
Calf Old Woman, XII, 779
Calf Rising in Sight. *See* Peenaquim
Calf Shirt. *See* Onistah-sokaksin
Calf Tail, XII, 802
Calhoun, Thomas, V, 902
Calignon, Jeanne de (Saint-Ours), II, 592
Calihoo, Felix, VII, 137
Calihue, Louis, VII, 137
Calistrois. *See* Callihoo
Calkin, Martha. *See* Black
Call, Mr (harbour inspector), VII, 760
Call, Sir John, VII, 904
Call, Louisa Anne (Whitworth-Aylmer, Baroness Aylmer),
  VII, 100, 194, 904, 905, 908; VIII, 124
Callahan, John, VII, 833
Callan, James, X, 557
Callan, Mary, X, 557
Callbeck, Ann. *See* Coffin
Callbeck, Phillips, IV, **128–29**, 353, 608, 609, 610, 708; V,
  27, 219, 220, 250, 309, 515, 568, 717, 777, 778, 825,
  873; VI, 131, 197, 736
Callendar, Alexander, III, 634
Callender, Mr (painter), V, 844
Callender-Campbell, Mary (O'Brien), IX, 606; X, 554
Callet, Donat-Nicolas, III, 94
Callet, Luc (baptized Léonard-Philibert), III, **94–95**

Callicum, IV, 568; V, 411; VI, 234
Callière, Louis-Hector de, I, 103, 138, 139, 140, 204, 540,
  541, 581, 583, 634; II, xxi, xxx, xxxi, 15, 16, 17, 20, 53,
  70, 74, 77, 79, 80, 87, 102, 103, 108, 110, **112–17**, 119,
  130, 133, 140, 143, 144, 148, 155, 156, 162, 168, 175,
  180, 186, 218, 220, 237, 300, 322, 323, 330, 336, 338,
  346, 353, 354, 383, 386, 387, 402, 404, 410, 411, 416,
  423, 428, 433, 446, 450, 451, 456, 459, 466, 474, 483,
  499, 500, 502, 504, 505, 507, 519, 527, 532, 533, 566,
  567, 573, 580, 587, 593, 598, 603, 618, 621, 631, 642,
  665; III, xxxv, 53, 147, 310, 433, 611; IV, liii, 662
Callières, François de, II, 112, 114, 116, 567
Callières, Jacques de, II, 112
Callières, Jehan de, II, 112
Callières, Madeleine de. *See* Potier de Courcy
Callières, Perrette de. *See* Du Fort
Callihoo, John, VII, 137
Callihoo, Josephte. *See* Patenaude
Callihoo, Louis, VII, **137**
Callihoo, Marie. *See* Patenaude
Callihoo (Calistrois), Michel, VII, 137
Calloway, William, X, 511
Calmonotius. *See* Chaumonot
Calonne, Anne-Henriette de. *See* Franqueville
Calonne, Charles-Alexandre de, V, 671; VI, 105, 106
Calonne, Jacques-Ladislas-Joseph de, V, 181, 671; VI,
  **105–7**, 448, 573; VII, 655; XI, 684
Calonne, Louis-Joseph-Dominique de, VI, 105
Caloosà. *See* Kallihirua
Calquieres, Marie (Dumas), IV, 243
Calvarin, Goulven, II, **117**, 628; III, 442, 443, 640
Calvé, Joseph, V, 273, 760
Calvert, Alice. *See* Crosland
Calvert, Anne, Baroness Baltimore. *See* Mynne
Calvert, Calista (Haws), VIII, 386
Calvert, Cecilius, 2nd Baron Baltimore, I, 163, 369, 406; II,
  580; VI, 314
Calvert, Frederick, 7th Baron Baltimore, IV, 84
Calvert, George, 1st Baron Baltimore, I, 23, **162–63**, 365,
  369, 405, 406, 419, 522, 567, 614, 653, 655, 672
Calvert, Jane, Baroness Baltimore (wife of GEORGE), I, 162
Calvert, Leonard (grandfather), I, 162
Calvert, Leonard, I, 163; VI, 314
Calvert, Richard, VIII, 387
Calvet, Pierre, IV, 227
Calvin, Abigail. *See* Chipman
Calvin, Catherine. *See* Wilkinson
Calvin, Dileno Dexter, VIII, 326; IX, 162, 274; XI, **139–41**,
  820; XII, 278, 279
Calvin, Harriet. *See* Webb
Calvin, Marion Maria. *See* Breck
Calvin, Sandford Jenks, XI, 139
Calvonotti. *See* Chaumonot
Camagne, Benoîte (Malepart de Beaucourt; Franchère), IV,
  507
Camagne, Joseph-Gaëtan, IV, 507
Camanne, Charles-Étienne, III, 420
Camaret, Marie, I, 197
Cambie, Jean (Major; Hamilton), XI, 381
Cambridge, Duke of. *See* Adolphus Frederick; George
  William Frederick Charles
Cambridge, Earl of. *See* Hamilton
Cambridge, Artemas, VI, 109

Cambridge, John, IV, 152, 609; V, 27, 219, 310, 568, 679, 778, 825, 826, 848; VI, **107–10**, 568, 818; VII, 406, 407, 924; VIII, 505, 954; IX, 179

Cambridge, Lemuel, VI, 109; VII, 924, 925; X, 161

Cambridge, Lydia (Wright), VI, 818

Cambridge, Mary. *See* Winchester

Cambridge, Phebe (Wright), VII, 924; XI, 939

Cambridge, Sarah Caroline (Gray), XI, 369

Camden, Earl of. *See* Pratt

Camden, Earl and Marquess. *See* Pratt

Camelford, Baron. *See* Pitt

Camerlique, II, 7, 8, 9

Cameron. *See also* Household

Cameron, Miss (Fraser), VI, 262

Cameron, Æneas, VI, **110–11**, 446; VIII, 538; X, 114, 115

Cameron, Alexander (father of ÆNEAS), VI, 110

Cameron, Alexander (father of DUNCAN), VII, 137

Cameron, Alexander (merchant), VI, 477

Cameron, Alexander, XII, **146–47**

Cameron, Allan, XII, 146

Cameron, Amelia (McDonald), VI, 435; VIII, 533

Cameron, Angélique (Black), VII, 79

Cameron, Angus (father of JOHN), XI, 142

Cameron, Angus (father of JOHN HILLYARD), X, 118

Cameron, Angus (father of MALCOLM), X, 124

Cameron, Angus (nephew of ANGUS), VIII, 538

Cameron, Angus, VI, 111; VII, 578; VIII, 537, 538, 821; X, **114–15**

Cameron, Ann (Taylor), VI, 756

Cameron, Anne Fleming. *See* Leavenworth

Cameron, Calcina Medora. *See* Buell

Cameron, Cariboo. *See* Cameron, John

Cameron, Catharine. *See* Lyon

Cameron, Catharine. *See* Wechikiwekapawiqua

Cameron, Catharine (McDougall), VIII, 539, 540

Cameron, Catherine (Gillespie; Brown), IX, 86

Cameron, Cecilia Eliza. *See* Douglas

Cameron, Cecilia Eliza Cowan (Young), X, 117; XI, 949

Cameron, Charles John, XI, 142

Cameron, Charlotte, VI, 555

Cameron, Charlotte Ross. *See* Wedd

Cameron, Christina. *See* McGregor

Cameron, Christina Adelaide. *See* Wood

Cameron, David, VIII, 97, 836; IX, 428, 457, 853; X, **115–18**, 196, 242; XI, 949; XII, 523, 833

Cameron, Donald Roderick, XI, 21

Cameron, Duncan, V, 65, 113, 453, 521, 522, 750; VI, 476; VIII, 5, 6, 431; IX, 788

Cameron, Duncan, IV, 727; V, 544, 742; VI, 443, 445, 665; VII, **137–39**, 498, 749; VIII, 304, 342, 583, 653, 714, 820; X, 607; XII, 149

Cameron, Edith Rebecca (Doughty), X, 115

Cameron, Elizabeth. *See* Boulton

Cameron, Elizabeth. *See* Morison

Cameron, Elizabeth (McKenzie), VIII, 558

Cameron, Elizabeth (McTavish), VII, 578

Cameron, Elizabeth (O'Hara), VI, 556

Cameron, Ella. *See* Amey

Cameron, Ellen. *See* Mallet

Cameron, Euphemia. *See* McGregor

Cameron, George A., XII, 167

Cameron, George Frederick, XI, **141–42**; XII, 515

Cameron, Grace. *See* Grant

Cameron, Hector, XI, 621

Cameron, Hector Charles, V, 56

Cameron, Isabella. *See* McDougal

Cameron, Isabella (Darling), IX, 195

Cameron, James (father of ANGUS), X, 114

Cameron, James (nephew of ANGUS), X, 114

Cameron, James Grant, XI, 141

Cameron, Janet. *See* Farquharson

Cameron, Jessie. *See* Sutherland

Cameron, Jessie H. *See* McLean

Cameron, John. *See also* Ogimauh-binaessih

Cameron, John (brother of MALCOLM), X, 124

Cameron, John (financier), XI, 150

Cameron, John (Indian Department employee), VI, 555

Cameron, John (king's printer), VI, 420

Cameron, John (police chief), XI, 112

Cameron, John, XI, **142–43**

Cameron*, John (d. 1910), X, 480; XII, 509, 640, 1040, 1041, 1042

Cameron, John Dugald, VI, 442, 445; VII, 138, 526; VIII, **121–22**, 350, 391, 527, 576, 813; IX, 722

Cameron, John Hillyard, VIII, 52, 170, 171, 473, 513, 800, 964, 966; IX, 45, 292, 751, 835; X, **118–24**, 125, 257, 312, 314, 336, 515, 561, 620; XI, 12, 144, 845, 877, 880; XII, 89, 151, 291, 409, 578, 595, 599, 601, 607, 907, 1108

Cameron, John McAlpine, XI, 143

Cameron, Kenneth, VIII, 847

Cameron, Malcolm, VII, 70, 852, 860; VIII, 35, 49, 52, 55, 269, 587, 733, 931; IX, 202, 469, 479, 506, 528, 529, 688, 706; X, 95, 119, **124–29**, 169, 246, 359; XI, 150, 166, 167, 233, 347, 411, 518, 789, 853; XII, 146, 147, 247, 588, 648

Cameron, Malcolm Colin, XII, **147–49**

Cameron, Margaret. *See* McDonell

Cameron, Margaret. *See* McLeod

Cameron, Margaret, VIII, 122

Cameron, Margaret (Besserer), IX, 48

Cameron, Margaret (McDonell), VI, 111; VIII, 538

Cameron, Margaret (McMillan), VI, 475

Cameron, Margaret (McMillan), VIII, 583

Cameron, Margaret Sophia. *See* Groves

Cameron, Mary (MacColl), XII, 588

Cameron, Mary Ann. *See* Cumming

Cameron, Sir Matthew Crooks, X, 79, 468, 504; XI, **143–46**, 166, 221, 366, 614, 650; XII, 151, 598

Cameron, Nancy. *See* Foy

Cameron, Ranald, VIII, 121

Cameron, Sir Roderick William, VII, 139; X, 607, 608; XII, **149–50**

Cameron, Simon, XII, 150

Cameron, Stephen, VI, 756

Cameron*, William Bleasdell (1862–1951), XI, 460, 599, 600; XII, 478

Camier, Abbé, VIII, 212

Camoin, Élisabeth-Charlotte (Forestier), III, 220

Camp, John, XI, 629

Campagna, Charles, III, 292

Campagna, Marguerite. *See* Lareau

Campagna, Simon, III, 559

Campan, Gabriel, I, 213

Campau. *See* Campot

Campbel, John, X, 129
Campbel, Nelly. *See* Smith
Campbell. *See also* Callender-Campbell
Campbell, Mrs. *See* Stewart
Campbell, Agathe. *See* Saint-Étienne de La Tour
Campbell, Alexander (duellist), III, 590
Campbell, Alexander (father-in-law of Joseph POPE), XII, 856
Campbell, Alexander (father of Sir WILLIAM), VI, 113
Campbell, Alexander (politician), XII, 31
Campbell, Alexander (religious spokesman), XI, 78
Campbell, Alexander (son of DUGALD), V, 135
Campbell, Alexander, VIII, **122–23**, 222, 770
Campbell, Sir Alexander, VIII, 837; IX, 431, 680; X, 459; XI, 216, 422, 579, 592, 593, 650, 698, 820, 846, 909; XII, 95, 98, **150–54**, 497, 515, 540, 592, 602, 605, 606, 607, 610, 611, 612, 615, 672, 673, 729, 856, 886, 946, 1042, 1043
Campbell, Andrew, XII, **154–55**
Campbell, Angus, VII, 145
Campbell, Ann (Radenhurst), VIII, 732
Campbell, Annabella (Stuart), V, 776
Campbell, Ann Cordelia (Schoultz), VII, 779
Campbell, Anne (Murray), X, 541
Campbell, Archibald (commissioner), XI, 20, 21; XII, 892
Campbell, Archibald (father of ARCHIBALD), IX, 113, 718
Campbell, Archibald (father of Sir ARCHIBALD), VII, 139
Campbell, Archibald (father of JOHN SAXTON), VIII, 123
Campbell, Archibald (officer), VII, 450
Campbell, Archibald (son of ALEXANDER, d. 1854), VIII, 123
Campbell, Archibald (son of Sir ALEXANDER), XII, 515
Campbell, Archibald, VII, 709, 790, 891; VIII, 123, 495, 701, 702; IX, **113–14**, 217, 298, 363, 718; XI, 353
Campbell, Sir Archibald, VI, 686; VII, 48, **139–42**, 144, 291, 658, 692, 807, 899, 915, 916; VIII, xxiv, 151, 183, 184, 377, 384, 465, 495, 783, 802, 807, 808, 841, 868; IX, 22, 23, 53, 220, 620; X, 710; XII, 797
Campbell, Archibald, 7th Earl of Argyll, I, 50
Campbell, Bertie (wife of ANDREW), XII, 154, 155
Campbell, Bruce, X, 131
Campbell, Caroline Eliza, Lady Campbell. *See* Plomer
Campbell, Catherine (mother of GEORGE WILLIAM), XI, 148
Campbell, Catherine (Gibb), VI, 284
Campbell, Charles J., X, 121, 651
Campbell, Charles James, XII, 150, 152, 153, 602, 604
Campbell, Charlotte. *See* Saxton
Campbell, Charlotte Saxton (Douglas), IX, 217
Campbell, Christian (Bethune), V, 77
Campbell, Christina (McAskill), IX, 474
Campbell, Clarence Thomas, IX, 324, 618
Campbell, Colin (architect), VIII, 39
Campbell, Colin (father-in-law of Sir Brook WATSON), V, 844
Campbell, Colin (father of COLIN, 1822–81), XI, 146
Campbell, Colin (HBC post chief), VIII, 820; X, 541
Campbell, Colin (officer), XII, 734
Campbell, Colin (of St Andrews, N.B.), IV, 769; V, 337; VII, 657; IX, 62
Campbell, Colin, II, **117–18**, 165, 293, 351, 583
Campbell, Sir Colin, VII, 24, **142–45**, 269, 391, 535, 858; VIII, xxiv, 31, 74, 378, 379, 416, 603, 710, 757, 892,

904, 956; IX, 52, 180, 226, 747; X, 364, 384, 534; XI, 146, 155, 308, 847, 925, 945; XII, 966
Campbell, Colin, XI, **146–47**
Campbell, Colin, 1st Baron Clyde, IX, 844; XII, 733
Campbell, Colin Cole, XII, 157
Campbell*, Colin H. (1859–1914), XII, 490
Campbell, Coll, V, 221
Campbell, David, VIII, 123
Campbell, Donald, V, 101
Campbell, Donald, III, **95–96**, 167, 258, 320, 526, 528; IV, 761
Campbell, Sir Donald, VII, **145–46**; VIII, 485, 564; IX, 375, 403, 830; X, 90, 184; XI, 665; XII, 857
Campbell, Donald Alexander, XII, 368
Campbell, Dugald, VIII, 324
Campbell, Dugald, V, **135–38**, 159, 161, 355, 456, 774; VI, 7, 112, 474, 740; VIII, 802
Campbell, Duncan, VIII, 178
Campbell, Duncan, III, 439; VI, 88; XI, **147–48**
Campbell, Eliza (Pope), XII, 855
Campbell, Elizabeth. *See* Murray
Campbell, Elizabeth. *See* Steel
Campbell, Elizabeth (Esson), VIII, 272
Campbell, Elizabeth Amelia (Robertson), VII, 750
Campbell, Elleonora C. *See* Stirling
Campbell*, Francis Wayland (1837–1905), X, 130; XII, 315
Campbell, Lord Frederick, VI, 736
Campbell, George (politician), XII, 583
Campbell, George (professor), V, 768
Campbell, George (shipowner), XII, 783
Campbell, George Douglas, XI, 147
Campbell, George Douglas, 8th Duke of Argyll, IX, 143
Campbell, George Montgomery, XI, 447
Campbell, George William, IX, 34; XI, **148–49**, 428, 533; XII, 315
Campbell, Georgina Fredrica Locke, Lady Campbell. *See* Sandwith
Campbell, Georgina McIntosh. *See* Richardson
Campbell, Hannah, Lady Campbell. *See* Hadley
Campbell, Harriet (Sheppard), IX, 718
Campbell, Helen, Lady Campbell. *See* Macdonald of Garth
Campbell, Helen (Watson, Lady Watson), V, 844
Campbell, Henriette-Julie. *See* Juchereau Duchesnay
Campbell, Hugh, II, 590
Campbell, Isabella (Fulton), XI, 328
Campbell, Isabella (Sutherland), VIII, 850
Campbell, J., VIII, 320
Campbell, J. B., XI, 64
Campbell, J. M., IX, 106
Campbell, Jacobina. *See* Drummond
Campbell, James (brother of ALEXANDER, d. 1854), VIII, 122
Campbell, James (editor), XII, 571
Campbell, James (father of Sir ALEXANDER), XII, 150
Campbell, James (merchant), II, 117, 118, 316; III, 618
Campbell, James (officer), V, 747
Campbell, Sir James, III, 218
Campbell, James, V, **138–39**, 373, 472; VII, 357, 358
Campbell, Jane. *See* Hamilton
Campbell, Jane, Lady Campbell. *See* Hendon
Campbell, Janet. *See* Purvis
Campbell, Janet (Black), XI, 78

Campbell, Janet (Murchie), XII, 773
Campbell, John (blacksmith), VIII, 587
Campbell, John (clergyman), XII, 829
Campbell, John (governor), IV, 159, 260, 402; V, 122, 361, 595, 632; VI, 244
Campbell, John (major-general), IV, 707; V, 136, 157, 158
Campbell, John (merchant), IX, 489
Campbell, John (painter), IX, 850
Campbell, John (politician), XI, 621
Campbell, John (son of COLIN, 1822–81), XI, 147
Campbell, John (son of STEWART), XI, 149
Campbell, John, IV, 117, **129–31**, 149, 150, 155, 294, 394, 427, 547, 612, 634, 759; V, 895; VI, 152, 403, 463
Campbell*, John (1840–1904), X, 40; XII, 660
Campbell, John, 2nd Duke of Argyll, II, 250
Campbell, John, 4th Duke of Argyll, IV, 131, 571
Campbell, John, 5th Duke of Argyll, IV, 130
Campbell, John, 4th Earl of Loudoun, III, xxv, xxvi, xxix, 72, 89, 218, 283, 295, 364, 460, 573, 586; IV, 3, 4, 21, 57, 84, 85, 115, 278, 282, 297, 308, 314, 326, 335, 396, 415, 478, 487, 552, 772, 775; V, 134, 425, 888
Campbell, John, 2nd Marquis of Breadalbane, IX, 162
Campbell, John C., XI, 147
Campbell, John Dilworth, XII, 157
Campbell*, John Douglas Sutherland, Marquess of Lorne and 9th Duke of Argyll (1845–1914), III, 722; IX, 903; XI, 6, 195, 355, 459, 500, 643, 696, 884; XII, 236, 309, 427, 533, 534, 568, 576, 588, 632, 703, 733, 793, 794, 795, 899, 1114
Campbell, John Duncan, VI, 267; VIII, 390
Campbell, John Saxton, VII, 64, 426; VIII, 93, **123–24**; IX, 179; XII, 51
Campbell, Lavinia. See Scatcherd
Campbell, Lillias. See Buchanan
Campbell, Louise Caroline Alberta, Marchioness of Lorne and Duchess of Argyll. See Louise Caroline Alberta
Campbell, Margaret. See Dillworth
Campbell, Margaret. See Henderson
Campbell, Margaret. See Hutchison
Campbell, Margaret. See Small
Campbell, Margaret (Fulton), VI, 268
Campbell, Margaret Glen (Rae), XII, 876
Campbell, Maria. See Taylor
Campbell, Marie-Anne. See La Corne
Campbell, Martha Hopkins (Davison), XII, 229
Campbell, Mary. See Archibald
Campbell, Mary. See Stewart
Campbell, Mary, Duchess of Argyll. See Bellenden
Campbell, Mary (Craigie), IX, 165
Campbell, Mary (McDonald), XI, 548
Campbell, Mary (Maclean), IV, 503
Campbell, Mary (Ridout), VI, 647; IX, 661; X, 618
Campbell, Mary (Sinclair), VIII, 820
Campbell, Mary Ann (Loring), VII, 517
Campbell, Mary Carne. See Vivian
Campbell, Patrick, V, 135, 136, 137, 506, 549, 646, 707; VI, 6, **111–13**, 154, 264, 373, 396, 474, 505, 563; VII, 57, 665; XII, 692
Campbell, Peter Colin, X, 442; XII, 767
Campbell, Phoebe Ann. See Seely
Campbell, Rachel (Ferrie), VII, 284; VIII, 293; IX, 259
Campbell, Robert (father of GEORGE WILLIAM), XI, 148
Campbell, Robert (officer), XII, 576

Campbell, Robert (partner of Robert CLARK, d. 1794), IV, 607; VI, 130
Campbell, Robert (1808–94), IX, 5, 42; XI, 384, 854, 855; XII, **155–56**
Campbell, Robert (1826–98), XII, **156–57**
Campbell, Robert Francis, VII, 260
Campbell, Robert Wesley, XII, 157
Campbell, Rollo, IX, 41, 83; X, 41, **129–30**
Campbell, Sarah. See Izard
Campbell, Sarah (Sleigh), IX, 723
Campbell, Stewart, IX, 295, 426; XI, **149**
Campbell, Susannah. See Poole
Campbell, Thomas, VI, 481, 728, 762; VIII, 386, 924; IX, 299
Campbell, Thomas Edmund, VII, 859; VIII, 163, 394; IX, 11; X, **130–31**, 164
Campbell, William (brother of ALEXANDER, d. 1854), VIII, 122
Campbell, William (father of ALEXANDER, d. 1854), VIII, 122
Campbell, William (brother of ROBERT, 1826–98), XII, 156
Campbell, William (HBC officer), XII, 832
Campbell, William (master of Thomas PETERS), IV, 626
Campbell, William (mayor), V, 504, 647; VI, 355
Campbell, William (officer), V, 121
Campbell, Lord William, IV, 41, 110, 116, **131–32**, 266, 274, 313, 450, 528, 561, 596, 737; V, 199, 215, 720
Campbell, Sir William, V, 557, 558, 559, 643, 672, 673, 674; VI, 79, **113–19**, 203, 535, 538, 611, 612, 631, 632, 706, 729, 770, 773; VII, 40, 224, 367, 368, 369, 517, 751; VIII, 5, 46, 69, 305, 511, 602, 708; IX, 674; X, 705, 706
Campbell, William M., IX, 587
Campbell*, William Wilfred (1861–1918), XII, 515, 516, 1111
Campbell of Achallader, Colina (Campbell of Melfort), VII, 142
Campbell of Achallader, John, VII, 142
Campbell of Barbreck, John, VI, 429
Campbell of Kildalloig, John, V, 776
Campbell of Melfort, Colina. See Campbell of Achallader
Campbell of Melfort, John, VII, 142
Campeau, Marguerite (Dulongpré), VII, 254, 256
Campeau, Michel-Archange (Mézière), V, 590
Campion, Étienne-Charles, IV, **132–33**, 233; V, 9, 178, 259, 260, 377; VI, 316; VII, 735; VIII, 320
Campion, Madeleine. See Gautier
Campion, Marie-Josephte. See Maillet
Campion, dit Labonté, Charlotte. See Pepin
Campion, dit Labonté, Étienne, IV, 132
Campofranco, Princess of. See Caroline
Campot, Catherine. See Paulo
Campot, Étienne, II, 105, 106; III, 96
Campot, François, II, 106
Campot, Jacques, III, 96
Campot, Jeanne-Cécile. See Catin
Campot, Madeleine. See Brossard
Camus (Le Camus), Claude (Charron de La Barre), I, 200, 201; II, 132
Canac, Angélique. See Pepin
Canac (Canac, dit Marquis), Jean, VII, 146
Canac, dit Marquis. See also Marquis
Canac, dit Marquis, Marie-Salomé. See Michaud

Canac, *dit* Marquis, Pierre, VII, **146–47**; X, 605; XI, 519
Canaghquiesa (Kanaghgwasea), IV, 691
Canby, Amelia (Disbrow), VIII, 224
Canby, Benjamin, VI, 178, 629, 630; VII, 375
Canby, Elizabeth (Birdsall; Darling), VI, 178
Canchy de Lerole, Louis de, I, 40, 308; II, 61
Candler, John, IX, 821
Candolle, Augustin-Pyramus de, V, 616
Cane (Cain), Elizabeth (Rochfort), IX, 682
Cane, James, VIII, 960
Caner, Henry, V, 128
Canfield, Anna (Hyatt), VI, 337
Cannan, H. H., XI, 122
Cannard. *See* Renaud
Cannehoot (Cannehouet). *See* Tekanoet
Cannematchie, V, 885
Canniff*, William (1830–1910), V, 307; VII, 418; VIII, 934; IX, 607; X, 610
Canning, Francis, XII, **157–58**
Canning, George, V, 286; VII, 31, 337, 510; IX, 221; X, 398
Canning, Hannah. *See* Donnelly
Canning, Mrs Olive, XII, 365
Cannon. *See also* Kanon
Cannon, Ambrose, V, 139; VI, 119
Cannon, Angèle. *See* Grihaut, *dit* Larivière
Cannon, Archange. *See* Baby
Cannon, Edward, V, 51, **139–40**; VI, 119, 482, 627
Cannon, Eleanore (Horan), X, 360
Cannon, Helena. *See* Murphy
Cannon, John, V, 139, 140; VI, **119–21**, 482; VII, 373, 879; VIII, 581
Cannon, Laurence, V, 139; VI, 119, 482
Cannon*, Lawrence Arthur Dumoulin (1877–1939), XI, 658
Cannon, Lawrence John, XII, 854
Cannon, Martin, V, 61
Cannon, Mary, V, 204; VI, **121–22**, 192, 194, 196, 197, 806, 807
Canon. *See* Kanon
Canot, Claude-Joseph-Marie, II, 531
Canterbury, Viscount. *See* Manners-Sutton
Canterbury, Viscountess. *See* Denison; Tompson
Cantin, Augustin, VIII, 559; XI, 121; XII, **158–59**
Cantin, Catherine. *See* Defoie
Cantin, Charles-Albert, XII, 159
Cantin, Elizabeth. *See* Benning
Cantin, Guillaume, XII, 158
Cantin, Jeanne (Auffray), VII, 28
Cantino, Alberto, I, 235
Cantray. *See* Dallas
Cantrell, Eliza (Blanchard), X, 70
Capaccini, Francesco, VII, 294, 295
Capdeviolle, Marie de (Catalougne), II, 120
Capeau, Antoinette (Mesplet), IV, 532
Capel, Antoine, IV, 5; VI, 145
Capelli, Fiametta (da Verrazzano), I, 657
Capineseweet, XI, 875
Capitanal, I, **163–64**
Capon, Peter, II, 123
Capponi. *See* Mannucci-Benincasa
Capreol, Mrs. *See* Skyring
Capreol, Fanny (mother of FREDERICK CHASE), XI, 150

Capreol, Frederick Chase, VIII, 10; X, 80; XI, **150–51**; XII, 72, 907
Capreol, Thomas, XI, 150
Capron, Hiram, IX, 789, 790; XI, 898
Captain Bull. *See* Bull
Captain Dick. *See* Pierpoint, Richard
Captain Douglas. *See* Eda'nsa
Captain Jecob. *See* Winninnewaycappo
Captain John. *See* Deserontyon, John; Nagiscoig; Ogimauh-binaessih
Captain Joseph. *See* Wowurna
Captain Louis. *See* Wahawanulet
Captain Pipe. *See* Konieschguanokee
Captain Swan. *See* Swan
Captain Tinnewabano. *See* Tinnewabano
Captured the Gun Inside. *See* Mékaisto
Caradec, Zacharie, IV, 466
Carayon, Auguste (Augustin), IX, 325
Carbery, Earl of. *See* Vaughan
Carbery, James Joseph, XII, 333
Carbonariis, Giovanni Antonio de, I, 150, **164**
Carbonneau, Charles-Alphonse, XII, 324
Carbonnel, Jean, IV, 125
Carbouere. *See* Rocques
Carcaud, Daniel, VIII, 494
Carcy. *See* Pagé
Cardenat, Monsieur de (painter), I, 359
Cardeneau, Bernard, III, **96–97**
Cardeneau, Marie-Anne. *See* Guérin
Cardero, Antonia Romero de. *See* Romero
Cardero, Gregoria Rosalia de la Vega de. *See* Vega
Cardero, Manuel José Antonio, V, 12, **140–41**, 571; VI, 743
Cardero, Salvador Dieguez, V, 140
Cardin, Marguerite (Chastelain), III, 8, 430
Cardin, Maurice, I, 553
Cardin, *dit* Loiseau, Marie-Madeleine (Letendre), VI, 398
Cardinal, Eugénie. *See* Saint-Germain
Cardinal, Joseph, VII, 147
Cardinal, Joseph-Narcisse, VII, **147–51**, 264, 265; VIII, 364, 365; XI, 623
Cardinal, Marguerite (Cardinal), VII, 147
Cardinal, Pierre, IV, 591
Cardwell, Edward, 1st Viscount Cardwell, IX, 712, 713, 716, 845; X, 265, 443, 444; XI, 634, 830, 932, 933; XII, 622, 1055
Carew. *See also* Pole
Carew (Hallowell), Sir Benjamin, IX, 239
Carey, Daniel, XI, **151–52**
Carey, Elizabeth. *See* Field
Carey, Eustace, VIII, 99
Carey, Henry Charles, XI, 129
Carey, John, XI, 316, 317
Carey, John, VI, 164, 728; VIII, **124–26**
Carey, John Francis Xavier, XI, 152
Carey, Margaret (wife of JOHN), VIII, 124
Carey, Mary. *See* Murphy
Carey, Mary (Le Marchant), X, 438
Carey, Michel, XI, 716
Carey, Richard, VIII, 907
Carey, William, XI, 753
Carfrae, Thomas, IX, 345

Carheil, Étienne de, I, 322, 331; II, **118–19**, 237, 353, 453, 501; III, 355, 446
Carigan, Mary (Kent), XII, 482
Carignan. *See* Bénard
Carignant. *See* Besnard
Carigouan, I, 6, **164–65**, 533
Carion. *See also* Dufresnoy
Carion, Monsieur de (confidant of François-Marie PERROT), I, 600
Caritat, Marie-Jean-Antoine-Nicolas de, Marquis de Condorcet, VII, 645; X, 585
Carle, Anne (Clinton), III, 126
Carleill, Christopher, I, 333, 336, 363, 364
Carlet de la Rozière, Marie-Claude (Potot de Montbeillard), IV, 641
Carle Tom. *See* Gélinas, Évariste
Carleton, Anne, V, 161
Carleton, Catherine. *See* Ball
Carleton, Christopher (grandfather), V, 141, 155
Carleton, Christopher, V, 584, 745, 896
Carleton, Emma, V, 161
Carleton, Guy, 1st Baron Dorchester, II, 69; III, 102, 154, 172, 478, 541, 609, 669, 670; IV, xxxvii, xxxviii, xli, xlii, xliii, xliv, xlv, xlvi, xlvii, xlviii, 6, 12, 25, 37, 41, 42, 50, 58, 72, 80, 82, 86, 98, 101, 102, 104, 106, 107, 114, 117, 118, 120, 130, 131, 135, 138, 139, 144, 146, 147, 149, 150, 154, 155, 162, 171, 179, 183, 184, 185, 188, 190, 198, 201, 202, 215, 228, 229, 231, 233, 234, 269, 271, 276, 281, 282, 298, 299, 304, 320, 321, 324, 327, 328, 330, 344, 345, 346, 347, 349, 350, 367, 371, 372, 373, 374, 375, 379, 380, 388, 399, 400, 415, 427, 428, 432, 436, 442, 445, 477, 484, 485, 491, 492, 493, 503, 510, 513, 530, 538, 544, 546, 547, 548, 549, 550, 556, 564, 570, 573, 577, 579, 592, 602, 604, 618, 619, 634, 635, 643, 697, 698, 715, 716, 717, 725, 729, 738, 739, 752, 753, 759, 787, 788, 790, 791, 793, 794; V, 5, 6, 19, 20, 21, 22, 26, 30, 31, 32, 33, 42, 43, 44, 46, 87, 88, 94, 98, 99, 100, 101, 121, 124, 130, 132, 133, 136, **141–55**, 157, 158, 161, 162, 180, 182, 185, 186, 191, 192, 224, 225, 229, 230, 232, 237, 238, 241, 242, 246, 254, 260, 271, 282, 289, 290, 300, 316, 317, 318, 324, 331, 334, 351, 364, 369, 371, 378, 383, 393, 398, 413, 414, 427, 432, 439, 442, 445, 454, 455, 457, 468, 470, 471, 478, 479, 482, 485, 486, 487, 493, 494, 499, 507, 509, 518, 528, 552, 553, 576, 577, 578, 585, 588, 594, 600, 601, 606, 607, 621, 630, 637, 650, 652, 653, 663, 669, 684, 690, 691, 699, 717, 718, 721, 736, 745, 752, 754, 756, 757, 759, 767, 781, 789, 790, 791, 794, 802, 807, 808, 809, 816, 831, 834, 841, 843, 844, 863, 864, 866, 878, 889, 890, 891, 892, 897, 901; VI, 8, 16, 18, 21, 81, 128, 132, 133, 136, 137, 150, 151, 152, 239, 258, 269, 295, 298, 299, 313, 317, 357, 363, 374, 387, 389, 401, 403, 404, 439, 452, 484, 491, 492, 493, 494, 495, 511, 512, 523, 524, 525, 537, 548, 559, 606, 607, 608, 615, 616, 647, 679, 695, 700, 712, 715, 788; VII, 87, 89, 196, 357, 522, 523, 524, 674, 766, 777, 783, 817, 889; VIII, 605
Carleton, Hannah. *See* Van Horn
Carleton, Henrietta Anne (Pigott-Carleton; Leir), V, 152
Carleton, Maria, Baroness Dorchester. *See* Howard
Carleton, Thomas, IV, 136, 150, 211, 229, 328, 329, 436, 483, 603, 627; V, 25, 56, 60, 136, **155–63**, 347, 348, 349, 350, 351, 352, 353, 354, 355, 356, 357, 504, 505,

506, 507, 589, 590, 630, 631, 646, 733, 763, 774, 831, 868; VI, 7, 75, 112, 137, 141, 142, 143, 145, 155, 246, 356, 431, 474, 504, 563, 564, 654, 684, 719, 724, 726, 740, 741, 756; VII, 121, 198, 274, 289, 331, 428, 429, 764; VIII, xxiv, 805; IX, 38, 850; X, 341
Carleton, William, V, 161
Carli, Bernardo, I, 658, 659
Carlié, Marie (Fézeret), II, 221
Carlier, Anne (Du Saussay de Bémont), I, 583
Carling*, Sir John (1828–1911), IX, 323; X, 375; XI, 63, 81, 145; XII, 554, 707, 1046, 1094
Carlisle, Earl of. *See* Howard
Carlisle, Sir Anthony, X, 691
Carlos, Don, Count of Molina, XI, 481
Carlos, Don, Duke of Madrid, X, 542
Carlton, Jane (Cochin), IV, 156
Carlyle, Jane Baillie. *See* Welsh
Carlyle, Mary (McMartin), VIII, 582
Carlyle, Thomas, VII, 117, 118; IX, 27
Carman*, Albert (1833–1917), V, 729; X, 616, 617; XI, 931; XII, 169, 707
Carman, Ann. *See* Sharman
Carman, Catherine (Brouse), VIII, 104
Carman, Mary (Rushmore; Losee), VI, 405
Carman, William, VI, 741; VIII, 738, 739
Carman*, William Bliss (1861–1929), V, 800; VI, 741; VII, 14; X, 498; XI, 448; 205, 213, 513, 517, 518, 714, 947
Carmel-Levasseur, Louise (Viger), X, 694
Carmichael, Ann (mother of JAMES), VIII, 126
Carmichael, Christian. *See* McKenzie
Carmichael, Frederica Ubrica Charletta Caterina. *See* Smith
Carmichael, Hester (Haynes), XI, 394
Carmichael, Hugh, IX, 689
Carmichael, Humphrey Henry, VIII, 832
Carmichael, James (clergyman), X, 207; XII, 1000
Carmichael, James (father of JAMES), VIII, 126
Carmichael, James (sergeant), VIII, 126
Carmichael, James, VIII, **126–28**; X, 476
Carmichael*, James William (1819–1903), VIII, 127; IX, 427; X, 476
Carmichael, John Edward, VI, **122–23**, 737; VIII, 444, 484, 531, 547, 824, 825, 826; IX, 474
Carmichael, John Robert, VIII, 127
Carmichael, John Wilson, XII, 791
Carnarvon, Earl of. *See* Herbert
Carnegie, Andrew, XII, 1095
Carnegie, James, 9th Earl of Southesk, X, 473; XI, 195; XII, 194, 878
Caro, Gregorio, I, 156
Caroline, Princess of the Two Sicilies (Bourbon, Duchesse de Berry; Lucchesi-Palli, Princess of Campofranco), VI, 201; XII, 182
Caroline Amelia Elizabeth, Princess of Brunswick (Caroline Amelia Elizabeth, Princess of Wales), VIII, 823
Carolus-Duran. *See* Durand, Charles
Caron*, Sir Adolphe-Philippe (1843–1908), IX, 16; X, 136; XI, 83, 697, 747, 750; XII, 5, 96, 179, 180, 246, 293, 576, 610, 733, 734, 735, 736, 940, 1010, 1027, 1037, 1043, 1047
Caron, Alexis, IV, 502; V, 792; VI, 223
Caron, Alice, Lady Caron. *See* Baby

Caron, Antoine, IX, 452
Caron, Antoinette (Du Bos), I, 286
Caron, Augustin, X, 131
Caron, Barthélemy, VIII, 128
Caron, Charles, VIII, 18, **128–29**; XII, 160
Caron, Charles-François, VIII, 128; X, 107
Caron, Corine (Fitzpatrick), X, 136
Caron, Édouard, XII, **159–60**
Caron, Élisabeth. *See* Lessard
Caron, Euphrosine. *See* Béland
Caron, Ferdinand, XII, 159
Caron, François (brother of CHARLES), VIII, 128; XII, 160
Caron, François (father of ÉDOUARD), XII, 159
Caron, François (habitant), III, 227
Caron, François (surgeon's aide), I, 109
Caron*, Ivanhoë (1875–1941), VI, 599, 828; VII, 940; XII, 1138
Caron, Louis, X, 136
Caron, Marguerite (Maillou, *dit* Desmoulins), III, 346, 420
Caron, Marie. *See* Crevet
Caron, Marie-Anne (Paré; Hotesse; Foretier), V, 321
Caron, Marie-Françoise. *See* Rivard
Caron, Marie-Françoise, named de Saint-Charles, VIII, 128
Caron, Marie-Henriette. *See* Coulombe
Caron, Marie-Joséphine (Taschereau), X, 136; XII, 1024
Caron, Marie-Josephte. *See* Parent
Caron, Marie-Louise. *See* Lemaître-Augé
Caron, Marie-Vénérande-Joséphine. *See* Deblois
Caron, Michel (father of CHARLES), VIII, 128
Caron, Michel (politician), VI, 515; VIII, 128
Caron, Nicolas, III, 429
Caron, Nicolas-François, named Brother Pacifique, III, 292; IX, 680
Caron, René-Édouard, VII, 7, 61, 62, 280, 373, 430, 606, 836, 858; VIII, 52, 138, 497, 800, 849, 907; IX, 190, 261, 362, 445, 449, 538, 570, 571, 645, 774, 779; X, **131–36**, 145, 217, 256, 580, 690; XI, 166, 170, 179, 238, 480, 520, 721, 861; XII, 45, 46, 270, 299, 324, 1024, 1037
Caron, Robert, I, 417
Caron, Thomas, X, **136–37**
Caron, Victoire (Gérin-Lajoie), VIII, 128
Caron, Vital, III, 429
Caron de Beaumarchais, Pierre-Augustin, V, 233; VI, 106
Caront. *See* Caron
Carpenter, Alexander, XI, 377
Carpenter, Anna. *See* Penn
Carpenter, Etta (Dinning), XI, 264
Carpenter, Henry, X, 648
Carpenter, Henry Bernard, XII, 961
Carpenter, Land, X, 137
Carpenter, Minna. *See* Meyer
Carpenter, Philip Herbert, XII, 233, 234
Carpenter, Philip Pearsall, X, **137–38**; XII, 710
Carpentier, Bonaventure (Étienne), IV, **133–34**
Carpentier, Claude, V, 432
Carpentier, Étienne, IV, 133
Carpentier, Jeanne. *See* Toussaint
Carpentier, Marie-Charlotte. *See* Blanchon
Carpmael, Charles, XI, 475; XII, **160–61**, 236, 382
Carpmael, Julia. *See* McKenzie
Carpmael, Sarah. *See* Pitt
Carpmael, William, 160

Carqueville, Josepha (Porteous), VII, 700
Carr, Mary Rowe (Pickard), XI, 687
Carr, Miriam (Reiffenstein), VII, 743
Carr, Sarah (Fanning), VI, 245, 246
Carr, Ursula Sarah (Harris), X, 334
Carracci, Annibale, VI, 25
Carrall, Elizabeth Amelia. *See* Macdonald
Carrall, James, X, 138
Carrall, Jane (mother of ROBERT WILLIAM WEIR), X, 138
Carrall, Robert William Weir, X, **138–40**; XI, 635, 636, 697; XII, 372, 915
Carre, Jane (Knox), IV, 416
Carré de Luzançay, Nicolas-Philippe, II, 596
Carrefour de La Pelouze, Abraham, V, 163
Carrefour de La Pelouze, Gabrielle-Marie. *See* Vernas
Carrefour de La Pelouze, Pierre-Joseph, V, **163–64**
Carrel, Louis, II, 29
Carrell, James, XII, 746
Carreño, Alberto M., V, 616
Carrerot, André, II, 119; III, 76, **97–98**, 173, 389; IV, 247, 249, 252, 305, 420, 558, 644, 645
Carrerot, Angélique (Allard de Sainte-Marie), IV, 14
Carrerot, Barbe-Blanche (Du Pont Duchambon Dumaine), IV, 249
Carrerot, Françoise-Ovide (Delort), II, 119; III, 173
Carrerot, Louise (Godefroy de Tonnancour), IV, 303, 305; VI, 288
Carrerot, Marguerite-Thérèse (Prevost de La Croix), IV, 644
Carrerot, Marie. *See* Picq
Carrerot, Marie-Anne (La Salle de Sertrouville), II, 119; III, 235
Carrerot, Marie-Josephte. *See* Chéron
Carrerot, Marie-Thérèse. *See* Gaultier
Carrerot, Philippe, II, 119; III, 76, 97, **98**, 172, 389; IV, 14, 60
Carrerot, Pierre, II, **119–20**; III, 97, 98, 173, 387
Carrier, Antoine, XII, 745
Carrier, Catherine. *See* Bleau
Carrier, Charles-Henri, XI, 153
Carrier, Charles William, XI, **152–53**, 774
Carrier, Charlotte (Thibault), X, 676
Carrier, Henriette (Carrier), XI, 152
Carrier, Ignace, XI, 152
Carrier, Jean-Baptiste, X, 346
Carrier, Louis, XI, 152, 207
Carrier, Marie-Louise. *See* Dallaire
Carrier, Michel, VIII, 129
Carrier, Michel, VII, 322; VIII, **129–30**
Carrier, Pierre, XI, 258
Carrier, Suzanne (Chabot), IX, 123
Carrière, Joseph, IX, 51
Carrières, Louis de, IX, 18
Carrihogo (News Carrier, Barnet, Bernard, Brant), V, 803
Carrington, Frederick Hamilton, VI, 409, 693; VIII, 94, 103, 947
Carrington, Isura (Macfarlane), VII, 558
Carritt, Edward, XII, 30
Carroll. *See also* Carrall
Carroll, Beulah. *See* Adams
Carroll, Charles, IV, 270, 549, 759; V, 31
Carroll, Charles Ingersoll, IX, 233
Carroll, Joanna, named Sister Mary Josephine, XII, 411

Carroll, John (bishop), IV, 270, 371, 445; V, 186, 343, 434; VI, 145; VII, 746
Carroll, John (clergyman), VI, 450, 691; VIII, 306, 307
Carroll, John D., IX, 656
Carroll, John Saltkill, VI, 266, 336, 405, 671, 675; VIII, 105, 310, 372, 422, 423; IX, 635, 736; X, 536, 646, 692; XI, **153–54**, 734, 784, 785, 794; XII, 169
Carroll, Joseph, XI, 153
Carroll, Margaret (Perry), XII, 836
Carroll, Mary (Hannan), XI, 381
Carroll, Molly. *See* Rideout
Carroll, Nancy (Manning), VIII, 610
Carroll, Peter, VII, 126
Carruthers, Ann (Laird), XII, 512, 513
Carruthers, George, XII, 135
Carruthers, J. J., IX, 467; XI, 924
Carruthers, John (explorer), II, 319
Carruthers, John (merchant), VIII, 645
Carruthers, Michael, VIII, 738; IX, 171
Carson, Esther (wife of WILLIAM), VII, 151
Carson, Jessy (Job), X, 381
Carson, Margaret. *See* Clachertie
Carson, Samuel (grandfather), VII, 151
Carson, Samuel, VII, 154, 155; VIII, 468, 469
Carson, William, V, 274, 275; VI, 71, 163, 372, 410, 708, 711; VII, 113, 114, **151–56**, 220, 293, 296, 303, 421, 507, 508, 590, 629, 631, 632, 633, 765, 793; VIII, 233, 234, 381, 403, 467, 468, 469, 470, 947, 948, 951; IX, 71, 85, 168, 435, 436, 605, 682, 694; X, 50, 179, 381, 551, 553, 601, 687; XI, 673, 674, 760
Carswell, Jane Elizabeth (Sexton), X, 647
Carter, Anne. *See* Hutchings
Carter, Anne. *See* Weston
Carter, Anne (Hunter-Duvar), XII, 458
Carter, C., IX, 594
Carter, Christopher (creditor of John ANTROBUS), V, 27
Carter, Christopher (inventor), V, 519
Carter, Edward, X, 229; XII, 173, 197
Carter, Elizabeth (Field), XI, 316
Carter, Eliza Walters. *See* Bayly
Carter, Emma. *See* Wellbeloved
Carter, Sir Frederic Bowker Terrington, IX, 393, 606, 846; X, 8, 141, 399, 716; XI, 4, 67, 68, 239, 354, 355, 356, 430, 431, 433, 634, 762, 881, 910; XII, 91, 92, **161–65**, 310, 311, 381, 439, 440, 482, 600, 770, 844, 889, 956
Carter, James, X, 140
Carter, Sir James, VII, 74, 413, 692; VIII, 151, 174, 394; IX, 146, 382, 619, 620; X, **140–41**, 286, 713; XII, 18, 20
Carter, John, XII, 483
Carter, John Bonham, X, 140
Carter, John W., XI, 648
Carter, Margaret Spencer. *See* Coster
Carter, Mary Ann Elizabeth. *See* Miller
Carter, Mary Elizabeth Henrietta (Mondelet), X, 526
Carter, Peter Weston, X, 50; XII, 161
Carter, Robert (businessman), IX, 181
Carter, Robert (justice of the peace), IV, 784
Carter, Robert, IX, 694; X, **141**; XI, 433; XII, 161
Carter, Sydney. *See* Livingstone
Carter, William (father), X, 141
Carter, William, X, 141; XII, 161
Carteret (Thynne), Henry Frederick, 1st Baron Carteret, V, 315, 316, 317

Carteret, John, 2nd Baron Carteret and 1st Earl Granville, III, 283, 405
Carthew, Arthur, VIII, 486
Carthew, John, VII, 747; X, 30
Cartier, Angélique. *See* Sarasin Depelteau
Cartier, Anne (wife of CLAUDE), VIII, 130
Cartier, Bonaventure, III, 134
Cartier, Catherine. *See* Des Granches
Cartier, Catherine (Gagnon), VII, 333
Cartier, Cécile. *See* Gervaise
Cartier, Cécile (Hubert), V, 164; VII, 422
Cartier, Claude, VIII, **130–31**
Cartier, François-Damien, X, 142, 143
Cartier, Sir George-Étienne, IV, 403; V, 164; VII, 422, 513; VIII, 138, 231, 260, 262, 286, 402, 736; IX, 45, 64, 65, 74, 122, 193, 208, 211, 243, 267, 274, 328, 383, 384, 437, 438, 447, 449, 463, 485, 492, 560, 573, 588, 735, 775, 777, 795, 845; X, 37, 59, 97, 98, 99, 100, 120, 121, 122, 123, 128, 131, 134, **142–52**, 155, 170, 220, 235, 258, 282, 293, 294, 304, 356, 361, 418, 422, 423, 424, 425, 429, 430, 434, 435, 464, 465, 466, 468, 481, 499, 533, 614, 632, 642, 654, 690, 725, 726, 727; XI, 6, 7, 10, 11, 12, 13, 16, 26, 27, 42, 46, 70, 83, 103, 104, 144, 157, 161, 163, 166, 170, 171, 176, 180, 182, 183, 184, 185, 188, 192, 193, 196, 206, 238, 252, 273, 283, 334, 336, 352, 379, 438, 442, 480, 530, 624, 625, 690, 722, 731, 738, 741, 742, 743, 759, 760, 763, 767, 821, 822, 823, 831, 837, 877, 880, 920, 932; XII, 6, 32, 33, 35, 86, 87, 89, 99, 152, 171, 173, 174, 175, 182, 197, 244, 262, 263, 301, 347, 349, 351, 352, 353, 355, 369, 370, 424, 456, 477, 494, 504, 594, 595, 596, 597, 598, 600, 601, 602, 603, 610, 629, 678, 720, 737, 862, 907, 951, 957, 986, 987, 1006, 1007, 1008, 1017, 1025, 1027, 1054, 1056, 1068
Cartier, Henry, X, 142
Cartier, Hortense, X, 151
Cartier, Hortense, Lady Cartier. *See* Fabre
Cartier, Jacques (father of Sir GEORGE-ÉTIENNE), V, 164, 165; VII, 225; X, 142
Cartier, Jacques, I, 7, 11, 19, 21, 22, 27, **165–72**, 188, 191, 275, 276, 301, 371, 372, 384, 409, 423, 424, 426, 432, 469, 500, 520, 553, 557, 612, 659, 680; II, xxxi, 8; III, xxxv, 99, 248; VII, 169; IX, 249, 250, 256, 301, 360; X, 142, 166; XI, 186; XII, 235, 402, 424
Cartier, Jacques, IV, 403; V, **164–65**; VI, 305; VII, 422; X, 142
Cartier, Jeanne (Noël), I, 520
Cartier, Joseph (brother of JACQUES, 1750–1814), V, 164; VI, 82, 689
Cartier, Joseph (nephew of JACQUES, 1750–1814), V, 165
Cartier, Joseph (partner of Pierre GAULTIER de Varennes et de La Vérendrye), III, 250
Cartier, Joséphine, X, 151
Cartier, Louise (Raimond), XI, 725
Cartier, Marguerite. *See* Paradis
Cartier, Marie-Régis (Levasseur, *dit* Delor), IV, 475
Cartier, Reine-Victoria, X, 151
Cartier, René (navigator), IV, 475
Cartier, René (seigneur), IV, 326, 709
Cartier, Toussaint, known as "the hermit of Saint-Barnabé," III, **98–99**, 572
Cartier, William C., VIII, 131
Cartier, *dit* L'Angevin, Jacques, V, 164; X, 142

Cartier, *dit* L'Angevin, Marguerite. *See* Mongeon
Cartland, Elizabeth. *See* Denson
Cartland, George, IV, 208
Cartwright, Anne (Cartwright), V, 165
Cartwright, Edmund, V, 166
Cartwright, Edward, V, 333
Cartwright, Elizabeth (Robison), V, 168
Cartwright, George, V, 166
Cartwright, George, III, 411; IV, 158, 159, 195, 600, 712; V, 55, **165–67**, 221, 576, 577, 641, 675, 784; VI, 707; VII, 522
Cartwright, Sir George, I, 226, 337
Cartwright, Hannah, V, 171
Cartwright, Harriet. *See* Dobbs
Cartwright, James, V, 171; VI, 300
Cartwright, Joanne. *See* Beasley
Cartwright, John (brother of GEORGE), IV, 413, 600; V, 55, 166, 167, 243, 784; VI, 707
Cartwright, John (clergyman), I, 667
Cartwright, John Robison, XII, 1073
Cartwright, John Solomon, V, 172; VI, 416, 467; VII, 102, **156–60**, 371, 460, 606, 857; VIII, 8, 520, 522, 697, 760, 786, 799; IX, 274, 471, 520, 523, 524; X, 30, 254; XI, 118
Cartwright, Magdalen. *See* Secord
Cartwright, Mary Magdalen (Dobbs), V, 172
Cartwright, Richard (father of RICHARD), IV, 120; V, 167, 168
Cartwright, Richard (son of RICHARD), V, 171
Cartwright, Richard, IV, 494, 495, 777; V, 17, 38, 92, **167–72**, 189, 304, 326, 402, 404, 442, 443, 492, 494, 519, 550, 718, 724, 757, 765, 772, 781, 819, 821, 841; VI, 147, 209, 215, 216, 296, 364, 452, 503, 531, 558, 559, 608, 610, 619, 638, 657, 722, 804, 805; VII, 57, 156, 159, 250, 309, 310, 375, 439, 524, 583; VIII, 606, 607, 608, 937; IX, 550, 551, 752; XI, 265
Cartwright*, Sir Richard John (1835–1912), V, 172; X, 122, 441; XI, 196, 265, 421, 422, 610, 683, 697, 698, 770, 820, 853; XII, 6, 8, 103, 151, 153, 438, 497, 583, 586, 630, 651, 652, 654, 657, 658, 686, 737, 1046, 1057
Cartwright, Robert David, V, 172; VII, 157; VIII, 760; IX, 496; XI, 265
Cartwright, Sarah Hayter. *See* Macaulay
Cartwright, Stephen, V, 171
Cartwright, Thomas Robison, V, 172
Cartwright, William, V, 165
Carufel. *See* Sicard
Carundawana (Robert Hunter), III, 147
Carvell, Alice Caroline. *See* Hanford
Carvell, Isabella. *See* Henderson
Carvell, Isabella (Gough; Mitchell), XII, 740
Carvell, Jacob (father), XII, 166
Carvell, Jacob, XII, 166
Carvell, Jedediah Slason, XI, 699; XII, **166–67**, 740
Carvell, Lewis, 166
Carver, Jonathan, III, 452; IV, 681; V, 682, 684, 821
Carver, William, VIII, 368
Carvosso, Benjamin, XII, 931
Carvosso, Grace (Rundle), XII, 931
Carvosso, William, XII, 931
Cary. *See also* Kerry
Cary, Amelia, Viscountess Falkland. *See* FitzClarence
Cary, Anne Eliza (wife of GEORGE MARCUS), VIII, 131

Cary, Charles John, 9th Viscount Falkland, XI, 155, 308
Cary, Christiana, Viscountess Falkland. *See* Anton
Cary, Elizabeth. *See* Malins
Cary, Elizabeth (Amherst, Baroness Amherst), IV, 26
Cary, Elizabeth Catherine, Viscountess Falkland. *See* Gubbins
Cary, Eliza Heath Ellen. *See* Noyes
Cary, Ellen. *See* Martin
Cary, George, IV, 26
Cary, George Hunter, IX, **114–15**, 428; XI, 950; XII, 239, 523
Cary, George Marcus, VIII, **131–32**, 767
Cary, George Thomas, IX, 116; XI, 928
Cary, Henry, 1st Viscount Falkland, I, 365, 632, 655, 669
Cary, Jane. *See* Oliver
Cary, Joseph, VI, 123, 124; VIII, 353; IX, 116
Cary, Lucius Bentinck, 10th Viscount Falkland, VII, 21, 24, 144, 308, 442, 610, 685, 804, 858; VIII, 74, 168, 193, 194, 334, 382, 417, 657, 757, 904, 905, 957; IX, 177, 349, 747, 748, 786; X, 7, 66, 232, 365, 385; XI, **155–56**, 398, 847, 945, 946; XII, 268
Cary, Mary Ann. *See* Dorion
Cary, Mary Ann Camberton. *See* Shadd
Cary, Thomas, IX, 699
Cary, Thomas, IV, 106, 107; V, 225; VI, **123–24**, 191, 642; VII, 768; IX, 115
Cary, Thomas, VI, 123, 124, 191, 392; VII, 287, 462; VIII, 408; IX, **115–16**, 202
Cary, Thomas Fauntleroy, XII, 960
Cary, William Henry, IX, 114
Casault, Flavien-Édouard, VII, 503
Casault, Françoise. *See* Blais
Casault, Jean-Baptiste, IX, 116
Casault, Julie-Cimodecée. *See* Cauchon
Casault, Louis, IX, 116; X, 152
Casault, Louis-Adolphe, X, **152**
Casault, Louis-Jacques, VII, 341; VIII, 215, 406, 682; IX, 19, **116–21**, 255, 317, 361, 362; X, 152, 432; XI, 102; XII, 324, 519, 732, 1016, 1017, 1025
Casault*, Sir Louis-Napoléon (1822–1908), X, 152, 488; XII, 303, 324, 521
Casault, Luce-Gertrude. *See* Drapeau
Casault, Thomas, VI, 749
Casavant, Antoine, X, 26
Casavant, Claver, X, 153
Casavant, Dominique, X, 152
Casavant, Jean-Baptiste, XII, 455, 456
Casavant, Joseph, VIII, 243; X, 26, **152–53**, 428; XII, 532
Casavant, Marie-Desanges. *See* Coderre
Casavant, Marie-Olive. *See* Sicard de Carufel
Casavant, Samuel, X, 153
Case, Eliza. *See* Barnes
Case, Eliza Jane. *See* Hurlburt
Case, George, VIII, 132
Case, Hester Ann. *See* Hubbard
Case, Roxana (Randal), VII, 733
Case, William, VI, 335, 336, 373, 670, 672, 673, 674, 675, 758; VII, 276, 455; VIII, **132–34**, 309, 422, 440, 441, 898; IX, 27, 750; X, 471, 647, 648; XI, 154, 660, 796, 848; XII, 186
Casewell, J. D., XI, 135
Casey. *See also* Caissie
Casey, Samuel, VI, 56

Casey, Willet, V, 857; X, 548

Casey, William Redmond, VII, **160**; X, 403

Casgrain. *See also* Cassegrain

Casgrain, Charles-Eusèbe, VI, 125, 749; VII, **61**, 161; X, 580

Casgrain, Eliza Anne. *See* Baby

Casgrain, Henri-Raymond, XII, 96

Casgrain*, Henri-Raymond (1831–1904), III, 34, 166, 185, 256, 468, 553; VII, 161; IX, 47, 48, 256, 303, 304, 305, 306, 542; X, 19, 22, 203, 204, 205, 433; XI, 83, 115, 249, 310, 342, 343, 495, 589, 873; XII, 14, 15, 17, 247, 271, 309, 824, 825, 1023

Casgrain, Jean, VI, 124

Casgrain, Luce (Panet), VI, 125; VIII, 677

Casgrain, Marguerite. *See* Cazeau

Casgrain, Marie-Hortense. *See* Dionne

Casgrain, Marie-Justine (Maguire; Beaubien), VI, 125; XI, 57

Casgrain, Marie-Marguerite. *See* Bonnenfant

Casgrain, Marie-Sophie (Letellier de Saint-Just; Bélanger), VI, 125; XI, 519; XII, 84

Casgrain, Olivier-Eugène, VI, 125; VIII, 223; IX, 121

Casgrain, Philippe-Baby, XI, 178, 519

Casgrain, Pierre, V, 668; VI, **124–25**, 422, 423; VII, 161, 877; VIII, 223; IX, 783; XI, 57; XII, 84

Casgrain, Pierre-Thomas, VI, 125; IX, 640, 783; X, 605

Casgrain*, Thomas Chase (1852–1916), XI, 748; XII, 211, 727

Casirtan. *See* Bacelet

Caslon, William (father), IV, 105, 295

Caslon, William, IV, 556

Casot, Jacques, IV, 134

Casot, Jean-Joseph, IV, **134–35**, 298, 299; V, 90, 247; VI, 23, 712; VII, 65; VIII, 201; IX, 67; XI, 110

Casot, Jeanne. *See* Dauvin

Cass, Lewis, VI, 358, 809; VII, 849; IX, 805; X, 548

Cassady, Henry, VII, 102; VIII, 762; XII, 150

Cassady, Patrick, XI, 863

Cassaignolles, Blaise, III, 156; IV, 253

Cassegrain. *See also* Casgrain

Cassegrain, Félixine. *See* Hamel

Cassegrain, Olivier-Arthur, IX, **121–22**

Casselle, Laurence (Vallée), III, 636

Casselman, Sarah (Cook), X, 195

Cassels*, Hamilton (1854–1925), XI, 157, 233

Cassels, Janet. *See* Scougall

Cassels, Mary Gibbens. *See* MacNab

Cassels, Richard Scougall, XI, 157

Cassels, Robert, XI, 157; XII, 898

Cassels, Robert, VIII, 9; IX, 578, 662; XI, **156–57**, 557, 676; XII, 486

Cassels, Walter Gibson, XI, 156

Cassels*, Sir Walter Gibson Pringle (1845–1923), XI, 157

Cassera. *See* Castera

Cassidy, Francis, X, 153

Cassidy, Francis, X, 51, **153–55**, 435; XI, 100, 289, 891, 893

Cassidy, Henry, IX, 700

Cassidy, John, VI, 425, 426

Cassidy, Mary. *See* McPharlane

Cassiet, Jeanne. *See* Dangoumau

Cassiet, Pierre, V, 172

Cassiet, Pierre, IV, 456; V, **172–73**, 719

Cassils, Agnes Simpson. *See* Hossack

Cassils, Charles, XII, 167

Cassils, Jane Allan (McIntyre), XII, 635

Cassils, John, XII, 167

Cassils, Margaret. *See* Murray

Cassils, William, XII, **167–68**

Cassista. *See* Bacelet

Casson. *See* Dollier

Cassoni, Ida (Vossnack), XI, 906

Casswettune. *See* Kakouenthiony

Castagnac de Pontarion, Jean-Marie, III, 677

Castaing, Antoine, IV, 135

Castaing, Charlotte-Isabelle. *See* Chevalier

Castaing, Isabau. *See* Sareillier

Castaing, Jean, IV, 135

Castaing, Pierre-Antoine, IV, **135–36**

Castaing, Rose (Rodrigue), IV, 135, 136

Castaing, Willobe. *See* King

Castanet, Jean-Baptiste-Marie, IV, 81, **136–37**; V, 493; VI, 391; VII, 246, 340; VIII, 201

Casteel, Anthony, III, 34, 136, 137, 358

Castel, Françoise-Jeanne, Comtesse de Saint-Pierre, Marquise de Crèvecœur et de Kerfily. *See* Kerven

Castel, Louis-Hyacinthe, Comte de Saint-Pierre, Marquis de Crèvecœur et de Kerfily, II, 35, 96, 120, 219, 254, 255; III, 156, 175, 178, 532, 567

Castellan, Laure-Modeste (Aubert), XI, 33

Castellane. *See* Lauris

Castelli, Joseph-Marie, IV, 97

Castelveyre. *See* Turc

Castera (de Cassera), Saubade (Imbert), IV, 378

Castille, Marie (Olivier), III, 494

Castille, Pierre de, I, 470

Castle, John Harvard, XI, **157–59**, 577; XII, 882

Castle, Mary Antoinette. *See* Arnold

Castle, Robert, XI, 157

Castle Leathers. *See* Mackintosh

Castlemaine, Countess of. *See* Villiers

Castlereagh, Viscount. *See* Stewart

Castonguay, Émile (Bernard Dufebvre), IV, 104; VII, 173

Castonguay, Jean-Baptiste, IX, 459

Castonguay, Josephte (Leclère), IX, 459

Castonguay, Marie-Louise (Lemaire), VII, 499

Castor, Le. *See* Largillier, Jacques

Castries, Marquis de. *See* La Croix

Castro, Isabel de (Corte-Real), I, 236

Caswell, Alexis, VIII, 567; X, 384

Caswell, Edward S., XII, 358

Caswell*, Edward Samuel (1861–1938), XI, 804

Caswell, Henry, X, 536

Caswell, John, VII, 102, 103

Cataldo, Joseph Mary, XI, 806

Caswell, Thomas J., XII, 759

Caswell, W., XII, 275

Catalogne, Élisabeth de (Gannes de Falaise), III, 235

Catalogne, Gédéon (de), II, 31, 63, 86, **120–22**, 154, 195, 196, 254, 327, 491, 592; III, 117, 191, 234, 235, 505, 649

Catalogne, Joseph de, II, 120, **122**

Catalogne, Louis-François-Gédéon de, II, 122

Catalogne, Marie-Anne de. *See* Lemire

Catalogne, Marie-Charlotte de. *See* Renaud Dubuisson

Catalon, Catherine (Foucault), III, 225

Catalougne. *See also* Catalogne
Catalougne, Gédéon (father), II, 120
Catalougne, Gédéon, II, 120
Catalougne, Marie. *See* Capdeviolle
Catchamisse. *See* Scatchamisse
Catenach, John, VI, 259
Catharine. *See also* Ohtowaʔkéhson
Catharine, VI, 759
Cathcart, Charles Murray, 2nd Earl Cathcart, VII, 441, 607, 914; VIII, 52, **134–36**, 320, 775; IX, 434; X, 255, 405
Cathcart, Elizabeth, Countess Cathcart. *See* Elliot
Cathcart, Sir George, VIII, 539, 778; XII, 493
Cathcart, Henrietta, Countess Cathcart. *See* Mather
Cathcart, Robert (St John's Island merchant), IV, 352
Cathcart, Robert (York merchant), XI, 574
Cathcart, William Schaw, 1st Earl Cathcart, VIII, 134
Catherine. *See also* Gandeacteua; Karighwaycagh
Catherine (daughter of TOTIRI), I, 652
Catherine (Iroquois), II, 595
Catherine (wife of ATIRONTA (d. 1650)), I, 71
Catherine, Grand Duchess of Russia, XII, 471
Catherine, Princess of Portugal (Catherine of Braganza) (Catherine, Queen of England, Scotland, and Ireland), X, 342
Catherine II, Empress of Russia, V, 80
Catherine de Médicis, Queen of France, I, 367, 421, 680
Catherwood, Frederick, XI, 138
Catignon, Charles, II, 133
Catin, Henri, II, 446
Catin, Jeanne-Cécile (Campot), III, 96
Catlin, George, V, 800, 811; VI, 649; VII, 353, 849; IX, 537; X, 390, 392
Cato, IV, 764
Caton. *See* Dupuis
Cator, John Bertie, IX, 12
Cats, Jacob, II, 279
Cattanach, Margaret Anne (MacLean), XII, 666
Cattermole, William, VII, 221
Cattley, George W., X, 404
Cattoonaluté, Charlotte (Ermatinger), VI, 236, 237
Cauchois, Madeleine (Curot), IV, 189
Cauchon, Emma. *See* Lemoine
Cauchon, Joseph, XI, 164
Cauchon, Joseph-Ange, XI, 159
Cauchon, Joseph-Édouard, VIII, 138, 291, 420, 497, 628, 629; IX, 210, 274, 444, 447, 449, 463, 525, 650, 776, 779; X, 24, 152, 203, 213, 361, 418, 632, 723; XI, 37, **159–65**, 179, 180, 181, 183, 184, 256, 272, 274, 281, 287, 288, 325, 480, 487, 496, 513, 520, 624, 644, 675, 698, 768, 774, 775, 822; XII, 86, 87, 90, 174, 270, 280, 324, 372, 471, 528, 627, 628, 651, 652, 846, 847, 848, 864, 1017, 1064, 1065
Cauchon, Joséphine (Gaudreau), XI, 164
Cauchon, Julie. *See* Lemieux
Cauchon, Julie-Cimodecée (Casault), X, 152
Cauchon, Marguerite. *See* Valée
Cauchon, Marie-Louise. *See* Nolan
Cauchon, Nolan, XI, 164, 165
Cauchon, Théotiste (Cauchon, *dit* Laverdière), X, 432
Cauchon, *dit* Laverdière. *See also* Laverdière
Cauchon, *dit* Laverdière, Charles, X, 432
Cauchon, *dit* Laverdière, Théotiste. *See* Cauchon
Caughey, James, XII, 142, **168–70**

Caulet, Isidore, II, 381
Caulfeild, Anne. *See* Margetson
Caulfeild, Thomas, II, 22, **122–23**, 198, 289, 498, 651, 667, 668; III, 208, 439, 516, 665; IV, xxi
Caulfeild, William, 2nd Viscount Charlemont, II, 122
Caulfield, Alexander, XI, 16
Caulfield, Susan, IV, 115
Caulincourt, Marie de (Lespinay), I, 425
Caumont, Pierre de, I, **172**
Caupemartissue Winnekee, IV, 726
Causabon, *dit* Didier, Élizabeth (St Jean), XII, 937
Cavagnial. *See* Rigaud
Cavanagh. *See* Kavanagh
Cavelier. *See also* Rivet
Cavelier, Dr, V, 248
Cavelier, Catherine. *See* Geest
Cavelier, Colette (Le Ber), II, 374
Cavelier, Jean, I, 172; II, 123
Cavelier, Jean, I, 79, 180, 183; II, **123–24**, 441, 443
Cavelier, Louise-Anne. *See* Du Souchet
Cavelier, Perrette (Godefroy), I, 340
Cavelier, Pierre, II, 124, 576
Cavelier de La Salle, René-Robert, I, 35, 79, 113, 126, 136, **172–84**, 226, 248, 289, 290, 379, 415, 420, 438, 440, 444, 446, 464, 501, 502, 557, 572, 573, 600, 625, 653; II, xxviii, xxxii, 29, 31, 48, 49, 76, 123, 124, 133, 169, 170, 173, 190, 191, 197, 203, 228, 230, 262, 263, 264, 270, 278, 280, 281, 328, 343, 348, 349, 374, 375, 380, 396, 397, 441, 443, 483, 488, 517, 537, 538, 584, 585, 589, 631, 633, 634, 635, 636, 672; III, xxxiv, xxxvi, xl, 65, 106, 380, 469, 558; IV, lii, lvi; V, 759; VI, 403; XII, 824, 825
Caven, John, X, 612
Caven*, William (1830–1904), XII, 489, 581, 582, 617
Cavendish, Henry, VIII, 866
Cavendish, Lord John, V, 145
Cavendish, Thomas, I, 252
Cavendish Bentinck, Lord William, VII, 5, 281, 603
Cavendish Bentinck, William Henry, 3rd Duke of Portland, IV, 522, 767; V, 28, 35, 121, 149, 152, 160, 161, 186, 279, 303, 354, 388, 440, 510, 634, 655, 850; VI, 173, 270, 331, 535, 559, 790; VII, 613, 614, 767
Cavendish Bentinck, William John Arthur Charles James, 6th Duke of Portland, XI, 771
Caverly, Sarah (Hills; M'Alpine), VI, 411
Cavilhe, Louis, IV, 89; V, 242, 727
Cawdell, James, VII, 161
Cawdell, James Martin, VII, **161–63**
Cawdell, Sarah. *See* Martin
Cawthra, Henry, VII, 163
Cawthra, John, VII, 163, 519; X, 622
Cawthra, Joseph, VII, **163–64**; X, 155
Cawthra, Mary. *See* Brown
Cawthra, Mary. *See* Turnpenny
Cawthra, Sarah Ellen. *See* Crowther
Cawthra, William, VII, 163, 164; X, **155**; XI, 360, 938; XII, 993
Caxton, William, XII, 16
Caya, Louis, XI, 811
Cayley, Emma Robinson. *See* Boulton
Cayley, Harriet. *See* Raikes
Cayley, John, XI, 165
Cayley, William, VII, 262; VIII, 540, 800; IX, 49, 525,

528, 529, 607, 655; X, 128, 134, 257, 405; XI, 144, **165–67**, 228, 410, 575; XII, 351, 528, 594, 596

Cazalès, E., VI, 174

Cazeau, Anne. *See* Aupetit

Cazeau, Charles-Félix, VIII, 138, 302, 722; IX, 20, 800; X, 87, 176, 604; XI, 96, 115, **167–73**, 184, 657; XII, 324, 1018

Cazeau, Clément, XI, 457

Cazeau, François, V, **173–74**, 893; VI, 663

Cazeau, Geneviève. *See* Chabot

Cazeau, Jean-Baptiste (father of CHARLES-FÉLIX), XI, 167

Cazeau, Jean-Baptiste (politician), VII, 719

Cazeau, Léonard, V, 173

Cazeau, Marguerite. *See* Vallée

Cazeau, Marguerite (Casgrain), VI, 124

Cazeau, Vincent, XI, 170

Cazelet, Marie-Angélique (Lenoir, *dit* Rolland), IX, 464

Cazeneuve, Charlotte. *See* Cormier

Cazeneuve, Esther. *See* Daguilhe

Cazeneuve, François-Joseph, VIII, 241

Cazeneuve, Louis-Amable, VIII, 136

Cazeneuve, Louis-Joseph-Charles, VIII, **136–37**; X, 266, 505

Cazes, Charles de, IX, 122

Cazes, Charles de, IX, **122**; XI, 912

Cazes, Constance de. *See* Arnaud

Cazes*, Paul de (1840–1913), IX, 122; XII, 719, 720

Cébet, Étienne, IV, 127

Cecil, Robert, 1st Earl of Salisbury, I, 162, 364, 365

Cecil, William, 1st Baron Burghley, I, 306, 362, 363, 364, 391, 409, 450, 671; V, 54

Cécile, I, 523

Cécile, Joseph-Étienne, XI, 684

Cécile de Sainte-Croix, I, 353

Cecilia. *See* Natoukwabekwe

Célerier, *dit* Roch, Marie-Anne (Guibord, *dit* Archambault), IX, 343

Céleste. *See* Ogenheratarihiens

Cèllere, Giulio, Count of Cèllere, I, 187, 658

Celles. *See* Bédos; Duclos

Celles Duclos, Barbe. *See* Poisson

Celles Duclos, Gabriel, II, 221

Céloron, Antoine, II, 125

Céloron, Catherine, II, 125

Céloron, Marie. *See* Rémy

Céloron, Marie-Catherine-Françoise, V, **174**

Céloron, Marie-Madeleine, V, 174

Céloron de Blainville, Catherine. *See* Eury de La Pérelle

Céloron de Blainville, Geneviève. *See* Damours de Chauffours

Céloron de Blainville, Geneviève-Gertrude. *See* Legardeur de Tilly

Céloron de Blainville, Hélène. *See* Picoté de Belestre

Céloron de Blainville, Hélène (Saint-Ours), II, 125; III, 577

Céloron de Blainville, Jean-Baptiste, I, 410; II, 88, **124–25**, 336, 527; III, 99

Céloron de Blainville, Marie-Anne-Thérèse (Nolan Lamarque), VI, 383

Céloron de Blainville, Marie-Madeleine. *See* Blondeau

Céloron de Blainville, Pierre-Joseph, III, 100

Céloron de Blainville, Pierre-Joseph, II, 125; III, xlii, 12, 28, 31, **99–101**, 158, 162, 373, 383, 384, 526, 611, 623;

IV, 76, 77, 145, 213, 241, 256, 463, 512, 563, 582, 617, 633, 666; V, 98, 174

Céloron de Blainville, Suzanne. *See* Piot de Langloiserie

Celsius, Anders, IV, 406

Cénas, Joseph-François, XI, 493

Cendre Chaude. *See* Ogenheratarihiens

Cérat, Pierre, IX, 437

Céré, Charlotte (Marchand), XI, 585

Céré, François, XI, 585

Céré, Henriette, named Mother Marie-Madeleine, VII, 267

Céré de La Colombière, François, X, 155

Céré de La Colombière, Marie-Julie-Marguerite, named Sister Mance, X, **155–56**

Céré de La Colombière, Ursule. *See* Brin

Ceredo, Paul, IX, 772

Cerré, Catherine. *See* Giard

Cerré, Jean-Gabriel, IV, 303, 592; V, **174–75**, 654, 663

Cerré, Marie-Anne (Panet), V, 653, 654; IX, 613

Cerré, Marie-Thérèse (Chouteau), V, 175

Cerré, Paschal, V, 175

Cerry (Cery, Cerry d'Argenteuil). *See* Ailleboust

Certain, André, I, 504

César, II, 457

Césarée, Brother, III, 208

Cézanne, Paul, XII, 328

Chabanel, Noël, I, **184–85**, 412, 414

Chabert, François, XII, 170

Chabert, Jeanne de, I, 213

Chabert, Joseph, X, 600; XI, 218; XII, **170–71**

Chabert, Joseph-François de, V, 176

Chabert, Madeleine de. *See* Bernard

Chabert, Marguerite. *See* Thomassin

Chabert de Cogolin, Hélène-Marguerite-Barbe de, Marquise de Chabert. *See* Tascher

Chabert de Cogolin, Joseph-Bernard de, Marquis de Chabert, III, 31; V, **175–77**

Chabert de Joncaire, Antoine-Marie, II, 125

Chabert de Joncaire, Gabrielle. *See* Hardi

Chabert de Joncaire, Louis-Thomas, II, xxxix, 20, 114, **125–27**, 323, 404, 553, 567, 572, 623, 631; III, xxxvi, xl, 43, 101, 105, 320; IV, 137, 187

Chabert de Joncaire, Madeleine. *See* Renaud Dubuisson

Chabert de Joncaire, Madeleine-Thérèse (Cuny Dauterive), IV, 187

Chabert de Joncaire, Marie-Madeleine. *See* Le Gay de Beaulieu

Chabert de Joncaire, Philippe-Thomas, II, 127, 436; III, **101–2**, 401, 611, 613; IV, 137; V, 98

Chabert de Joncaire de Clausonne, Daniel-Marie, II, 125, 127; II, 101; IV, **137–38**, 187, 595; V, 143

Chabert de Joncaire de Clausonne, Marguerite-Élisabeth-Ursule. *See* Rocbert de La Morandière

Chaboillez. *See also* Chaboulié

Chaboillez, Adélaïde (Bouchette), V, 179; VII, 95

Chaboillez, Angélique. *See* Baby-Chenneville

Chaboillez, Augustin, VI, 39, **125–27**, 597; VII, 131, 486, 488, 500, 667, 699, 728, 877; IX, 698

Chaboillez, Charles, II, 127; III, 122; V, 178

Chaboillez, Charles, V, **177–78**, 179, 535; VI, 267; VII, 565, 736; VIII, 537, 556

Chaboillez, Charles-Jean-Baptiste, II, 127; IV, 58, 592; V, 177, **178–79**, 180, 333, 527, 564, 566; VII, 95, 565

Chaboillez, Jessy. *See* Bruce

Chaboillez, Louis, II, 127; IV, 188, 698; V, **180**, 636; VI, 285; VII, 622; VIII, 313; IX, 459
Chaboillez, Louis-Joseph, IV, 58; V, 180; VI, 125
Chaboillez, Marguerite. *See* Conefroy
Chaboillez, Marguerite. *See* Larchevêque
Chaboillez, Marie-Angélique (Berthelet), X, 53
Chaboillez, Marie-Anne. *See* Chevalier
Chaboillez, Marie-Anne (Parent), V, 436
Chaboillez, Marie-Charlotte-Domitille (Doëy), V, 178
Chaboillez, Marie-Louise-Adélaïde (Bouchette), X, 77
Chaboillez, Marie-Marguerite (McTavish; Plenderleath), V, 179, 566; VII, 595
Chaboillez, Pierre-Louis, IV, 592; V, 178; VIII, 500
Chaboillez, Rachel (Marie-Louise) (Mackenzie), V, 179; VII, 565
Chabot, Basile, VIII, 137
Chabot, Cécile (Têtu), XII, 1033
Chabot, François (father-in-law of Louis QUÉVILLON), VI, 625
Chabot, François (father of JULIEN), IX, 122
Chabot, François (militiaman), IV, 548
Chabot, Geneviève (Cazeau), XI, 167
Chabot, Hortense. *See* Hamel
Chabot, Jean, VIII, **137–38**, 497, 676; X, 134, 217, 591; XI, 861
Chabot, Josephte. *See* Prévost
Chabot, Julien, IX, **122–23**
Chabot*, Julien (1834–1914), IX, 123
Chabot, Laurent, IX, 123
Chabot, Marie-Anne. *See* Cadieux
Chabot, Marie-Françoise. *See* Pépin, *dit* Lachance
Chabot, Marie-Joseph (Rousseau, *dit* Beausoleil), VI, 663
Chabot, Philippe de, I, 660
Chabot, Suzanne. *See* Carrier
Chaboulié, Angélique. *See* Dandonneau Du Sablé
Chaboulié, Charles, II, **127–28**, 430
Chaboulié, Jean, II, 127
Chaboulié, Marie. *See* Le Hour
Chabrand, David, IV, 138
Chabrand, Marguerite. *See* Roussel
Chabrand Delisle, David, III, 296; IV, 104, **138–40**, 753, 754; V, 78, 321, 333, 369, 527, 600, 602, 663, 786; VI, 822; VII, 200
Chabrand Delisle, Margaret. *See* Henry
Chabrat, Jeanne (Gougeon), II, 71
Chachagouesse (Chachagwessiou, Chachagouache, Chachagonache, Chachagonesse), II, **128**, 435
Chacornacle (Chacornac, Chacornade). *See* Joannès
Chacornacle, Baron de. *See* Joannès
Chadwick, Benjamin, XII, 171
Chadwick, Charles Eli, XII, **171–72**
Chadwick, Sir Edwin, XI, 430
Chadwick, Eli, XII, 171
Chadwick, Elizabeth. *See* Keefer
Chadwick, Filinda, VII, 102
Chadwick, Jane. *See* McCartney
Chadwick, Lydia F. (Child), VIII, 147
Chadwick, Margaret. *See* Weal
Chaffers, N. C., XII, 456
Chaffey, Benjamin (father), VI, 127
Chaffey, Benjamin, VI, 127
Chaffey, Elswood, VIII, 930
Chaffey, Mary Ann. *See* Poole

Chaffey, Samuel, VI, **127–28**
Chaffey, Samuel Benjamin, VI, 127
Chaffey, Sarah (mother of SAMUEL), VI, 127
Chagny, André, IV, 637
Chaigneau, Léonard, II, **128–29**
Chalain. *See* Fouquet
Chalet, François, IV, 360
Chalette, Blandine (Chazelle), VII, 170
Chalifour, Paul, I, 460
Chalifoux, Theresa (Robertson), VII, 748
Chaline, Jean-Daniel, I, 311, 593, 597
Challe. *See* Delhalle
Challoner, Richard, VII, 94
Challoner, Sir Thomas, I, 530
Chalmers, Alexander Jekyll, VI, 684
Chalmers, Arianna Margaretta Jekyll (Saunders), VI, 683, 684; X, 643
Chalmers, Sir David Patrick, XII, 381
Chalmers, Elizabeth. *See* Mackenzie
Chalmers, George (author), V, 149
Chalmers, George (businessman), XII, 1107
Chalmers, James (grandfather of John Simcoe SAUNDERS), VI, 683; X, 644
Chalmers, James (son-in-law of J. F. W. DESBARRES), VI, 196
Chalmers, Jane (Wilson), XII, 1107
Chalmers, Thomas, IX, 105, 270, 752; X, 667; XII, 210, 211, 489, 492, 659
Chalmette. *See also* Martin
Chalmette, Antoinette (Martin de Lino), II, 464
Chalmette, Jean-François, II, 276, 464
Chaloner, Mary (Hale), VII, 372
Chaloux, Jean-Baptiste, VII, 164
Chaloux, Louis, IX, 699
Chaloux, Marie-Anne. *See* Bellefontaine
Chaloux, Marie-Esther, named de Saint-Joseph, VII, **164–65**
Chalus. *See also* Lechtier; Raudot
Chalus, Jean-Louis de, Vicomte de Chalus, VI, 619, 620
Chalus, René-Augustin de, Comte de Chalus, VI, 619, 623
Chamard, Louise (Forton), V, 329
Chambalon, Geneviève. *See* Roussel
Chambalon, Louis, II, 129
Chambalon, Louis, I, 583; II, 32, 116, **129–30**, 138, 201, 235, 256, 382, 413, 447, 533; III, 26, 291, 647
Chambalon, Marie. *See* Prieur
Chambalon, Marie-Anne. *See* Pinguet
Chambellan, François, III, 144, 181
Chambellé, Perrine de (Dugué de La Boulardière), I, 295
Chamberlain, Adelaide Augusta (Miller), XI, 594
Chamberlain, Alexander Francis, XII, 403
Chamberlain, Anne. *See* Merriman
Chamberlain, Brown, VIII, 789
Chamberlain, Editha. *See* White
Chamberlain, Ephraim, VI, 128
Chamberlain, Joseph, IX, 355; XII, 1043
Chamberlain, Lamira. *See* Humphraville
Chamberlain*, Theodore F. (1838–1927), XII, 1073, 1074
Chamberlain, Theophilus, V, 423, 431, 804; VI, **128–30**; VIII, 159
Chamberland, Catherine (Chartier), III, 111, 112
Chamberland, Jean-Baptiste (carpenter), VI, 482
Chamberland, Jean-Baptiste (merchant), VIII, 359

Chamberland, Marie-Marguerite (Jacson), V, 451

Chamberlayne, Cassandra Agnes (Hamilton, Lady Hamilton), VII, 376

Chamberlen, Elizabeth (Walker), II, 658

Chamberlen, Peter, II, 658

Chamberlin, Agnes Dunbar. *See* Moodie

Chamberlin, Brown, IX, 258; X, 532; XI, 920

Chamberlin, Hannah (Luard), XII, 575

Chamberlin, John Brown, IX, 276

Chamberlin, Wright, VII, 374; VIII, 147

Chambers, Alicia. *See* Westphal

Chambers, Charles, VIII, 17

Chambers, Coote M., IX, 428

Chambers, Mary Anne (Kennedy), XI, 471

Chambers, Robert (assemblyman), XI, 633

Chambers, Robert (mayor), VIII, 17

Chambers, Robert (teacher), VII, 928

Chambers, Robert William, IV, 397

Chamblain. *See* Volant

Chambly. *See also* Hertel

Chambly, Jacques de, I, 40, 63, **185**, 399, 556; II, 4, 5, 284, 629

Chambly, Louise de. *See* Laulne

Chambly, Philippe de, I, 185

Chambrois, Edmée (Imbert), III, 299

Chamfort, Sébastien-Roch-Nicolas (Nicolas de Chamfort), VII, 90

Chamilly de Lorimier, Charles, XI, 530

Champagne. *See* Foureur; Laplante; Macard; Malherbe

Champagneur, Étienne, VII, 449; IX, 534; XI, **173–74**

Champaigne. *See* Champion

Champdoré. *See* Angibault

Champernowne, Katherine (Gilbert), I, 331

Champflour, Bertrand de, I, 186

Champflour, Étienne de, III, 633

Champflour, François de, I, **186**, 370, 403, 489, 548, 640; II, xv, 158

Champigny. *See also* Bochart

Champigny, Marie de (Lebrun de Duplessis), V, 478

Champion (Champaigne), Captain, I, 380

Champion, Anne. *See* Cordon

Champion, Elizabeth (Armstrong), VIII, 24

Champion, Gabriel, V, 13, **180–81**, 458

Champion, Gilles, V, 180

Champion, Marie (Muiron), III, 478

Champion, Pierre, I, 563

Champion de Cicé, Charles, II, 130

Champion de Cicé, Judith. *See* Thévin

Champion de Cicé, Louis-Armand, II, **130**

Champlain. *See also* Dupéré; Pezard

Champlain, Anthoine de, I, 186

Champlain, Hélène de. *See* Boullé

Champlain, Marguerite de. *See* Le Roy

Champlain, Samuel de, I, 7, 10, 11, 12, 13, 16, 27, 28, 29, 34, 35, 36, 53, 59, 61, 64, 70, 72, 76, 80, 86, 87, 96, 99, 100, 101, 109, 110, 120, 121, 122, 123, 125, 127, 130, 131, 132, 143, 159, 160, 161, 163, 164, **186–99**, 200, 208, 209, 211, 222, 236, 237, 238, 253, 262, 263, 265, 283, 292, 293, 294, 297, 300, 302, 303, 307, 311, 339, 340, 341, 342, 345, 346, 347, 366, 367, 368, 372, 373, 381, 382, 386, 405, 406, 407, 411, 424, 428, 432, 433, 436, 437, 452, 454, 470, 471, 473, 479, 482, 487, 488, 493, 494, 495, 500, 501, 507, 508, 509, 511, 516, 517, 526, 529, 557, 558, 564, 565, 567, 568, 569, 570, 578, 579, 591, 593, 602, 603, 604, 613, 615, 638, 639, 659, 662, 663, 680; II, xv, xxxv, 86, 363, 367, 429; III, 250; V, 874; VI, 35, 563; VII, 213; IX, 203, 256, 301, 360; X, 432; XI, 86; XII, 271, 728

Champoux, Marie (Déziel, *dit* Labrèche), XI, 257

Champvallon. *See* Harlay

Champy, Gélase, II, **130–31**

Champy Desclouzeaux, Hubert (de), II, 589

Chance, Hannah. *See* Foulkes

Chance, James, XI, 654

Chancellor, Richard, I, 158

Chandler, Amanda Jane. *See* Darling

Chandler, Amos Henry, XI, 628

Chandler, Ann. *See* McKelsey

Chandler, Charles Henry, VIII, 138; X, 157

Chandler, Charlotte. *See* Dunière

Chandler, Daniel, X, 156

Chandler, Dolly. *See* Ayer

Chandler, Edmund Leavens, X, **156–57**

Chandler, Edward Barron, VII, 141, 445; VIII, 15, 139, 174, 216, 738, 806, 807, 808, 809, 810; IX, 8, 22, 123, 146, 147, 381, 382, 414, 622, 623, 631, 766, 767; X, 67, **157–61**, 285, 315, 341, 495, 543, 666, 682, 711, 712; XI, 375, 412, 827, 829; XII, 115, 377, 683, 896, 1096, 1106

Chandler, Elizabeth. *See* Rice

Chandler, Elizabeth (Wright), VII, 926

Chandler, Hannah. *See* Chapin

Chandler, Horace Mitchell, X, 156

Chandler, James Watson, VIII, 139; IX, **123–24**, 431; X, 286

Chandler, Jane. *See* Grant

Chandler, Joseph, IX, 124

Chandler, Joshua (grandfather), VIII, 139; X, 157

Chandler, Joshua, VIII, 139

Chandler, Julia. *See* Hatheway

Chandler, Kenelm, IV, 738; V, **181–83**, 284, 745, 817; VII, 165

Chandler, Kenelm Conor, V, 182, 217; VI, 428; VII, **165–67**; VIII, 717

Chandler, Lydia. *See* Hawkins

Chandler, Lydia. *See* Leavens

Chandler, Mary (Upham), V, 831; X, 157

Chandler, Nathaniel, V, 181

Chandler, Phoebe. *See* Millidge

Chandler, Ruth Roach. *See* Smith

Chandler, Samuel, IX, 123; X, 157

Chandler, Samuel, VII, 56, 405; VIII, 27; IX, **124–25**; XII, 1079

Chandler, Sarah (Botsford), V, 94; IX, 63; X, 157

Chandler, Sarah (Paine), VI, 563

Chandler, Susan. *See* Watson

Chandler, Thomas, V, 181

Chandler, Thomas Bradbury, IV, 485; V, 657

Chandler, William, VIII, **138–39**

Chandonnais, Angèle. *See* Bibeau

Chandonnais, Joseph, XI, 175

Chandonnet, Thomas-Aimé, XI, **174–75**

Chanel, Marguerite (Hoerner), VIII, 396

Changing Feathers. *See* Penagashea

Changouessi (Changouessy, Changouossy). *See* Chingouessi

Chanmazart, Pierre, III, 165

Channal, Elizabeth (M'Coll), VI, 429, 430
Channel, Hannah (Brooking), IX, 84
Chantal. *See* Rabutin-Chantal
Chanter, Elizabeth. *See* Burnard
Chanter, Isabella. *See* Scott
Chanter, Moses, X, 161
Chanter, Robert Campbell, X, 161
Chanter, Thomas Burnard, VII, 408; VIII, 270; IX, 375, 376, 856; X, **161**
Chantler, Elizabeth (McDougall), X, 471
Chaouerindamaguetch. *See* Boullongne, Marie-Barbe de
Chapais, Amélie (Barnard), XII, 58
Chapais, François, XI, 175
Chapais, Georgina. *See* Dionne
Chapais, Jean, XI, 175
Chapais, Jean-Charles (father of JEAN-CHARLES), VI, 749; X, 605; XI, 175, 176
Chapais, Jean-Charles, VIII, 223, 938; IX, 776; X, 418; XI, 170, **175–77**, 519, 520, 554, 690; XII, 58, 556, 913
Chapais*, Jean-Charles (1850–1926), XI, 175; XII, 758
Chapais (Chapet), Julie (Hudon), XII, 455
Chapais, Julienne. *See* Boucher
Chapais*, Sir Thomas (1858–1946), IV, 183; VII, 61; VIII, 248, 679, 843; IX, 143, 775; X, 133; XI, 115, 175; XII, 58, 60, 262, 296
Chap de La Corne. *See* La Corne, Luc de
Chapeau, Madeleine (Levasseur), III, 397
Chapel, Mr (slave owner), V, 340
Chapeleau, Françoise. *See* Brochard
Chapeleau, Jean (father), XII, 172
Chapeleau, Jean, XII, 172
Chapeleau, Jeanne. *See* Gagnon
Chapelier, Marie (Drouin), I, 281
Chaperon, Aurélie-Rosalie. *See* Bolduc
Chaperon, Constance. *See* Simard
Chaperon, John, VIII, **139–40**
Chaperon, Marguerite (Girouard; Trudel), VI, 286
Chaperon, Michel, VIII, 139
Chapet. *See* Chapais
Chapin, Clarissa (Stephenson), IX, 744
Chapin, Cyrenius, VI, 324
Chapin, Hannah (Chandler), IX, 124
Chapleau, Henri, XII, 172
Chapleau, Sir Joseph-Adolphe, IX, 437, 438; XI, 7, 27, 184, 192, 208, 309, 374, 521, 623, 624, 625, 626, 744, 746, 750, 774, 812, 813, 815, 893, 894; XII, 8, 87, **172–82**, 197, 272, 276, 451, 456, 464, 465, 501, 510, 558, 607, 610, 611, 629, 694, 696, 721, 722, 723, 799, 862, 903, 904, 913, 1010, 1011, 1023, 1027, 1043, 1046, 1065, 1120
Chapleau, Marie-Louise. *See* King
Chapleau, Philomène, XII, 172
Chapleau, Pierre, XII, 172
Chapleau, Zoé. *See* Sigouin
Chapman, Edward Henry, VII, 70
Chapman*, Edward John (1821–1904), VIII, 775; X, 446; XI, 541
Chapman, Elizabeth (Burrage), IX, 110
Chapman, Frances Mary (French), XI, 326
Chapman, Francis, IX, 557
Chapman, Sir Frederick Edward, XII, 430
Chapman, George, V, 406
Chapman, Henry (merchant), X, 724; XI, 781

Chapman, Henry (printer), VII, 339
Chapman, Henry Samuel, X, 567
Chapman, James, VIII, 325
Chapman, Jane (Botsford), XI, 90
Chapman, John (brewer), IX, 557
Chapman, John (clergyman), XI, 19
Chapman, John, known as Johnny Appleseed, VII, 563
Chapman, John Summerfield, XII, 555
Chapman, Lucy (Allan), V, 15
Chapman, Richard, VIII, 270
Chapman, William, III, 528
Chapman, William B., XII, 745
Chapoton, André, III, 102
Chapoton, Anne. *See* Lassaigne
Chapoton, Jean-Baptiste, III, **102–3**
Chapoton, Marguerite. *See* Estève
Chapouin. *See* Garnier
Chappell, Benjamin, IV, 152; VI, **130–32**
Chappell, Edward, IX, **125–26**; XII, 589
Chappell, Elizabeth. *See* Wood
Chappell, Elizabeth (wife of BENJAMIN), VI, 130, 131
Chappell, John, XI, 501
Chappell, Margaret (Butcher), XI, 136
Chappell, Mary (Monro), XII, 753
Chappell, Rachel (mother of BENJAMIN), VI, 130
Chappell, Richard, VI, 130
Chappell, William, VI, 130, 131
Chappuis. *See* Joram
Chaptes. *See* La Corne
Chaptes (Chapt) de La Corne. *See* La Corne, Luc de
Charbonneau, Marie (Trudel), IX, 200
Charbonneau, Napoléon, XI, 891
Charbonneaux, Joseph, VI, 231
Charbonnel, Armand-François-Marie de, VII, 706; VIII, 230, 299, 491, 636, 637; IX, 26, 103, 325, 781; X, 323, 662; XI, 111, 240, 275, 449, 450, 536, 693, 694, 903, 904; XII, **182–85**, 267, 594, 1077, 1083
Charbonnel, Félix-Louis de, Comte de Charbonnel, XII, 183
Charbonnel, Jean-Baptiste de, Comte de Charbonnel, XII, 182
Charbonnel, Marie-Claudine de, Comtesse de Charbonnel. *See* Pradier
Charbonner, Marie-Madeleine (Lenoir, *dit* Rolland), II, 413
Charcoal. *See* Si'k-okskitsis
Chardon, Jean-Baptiste, II, 455, 501; II, 81, **103**
Chardon, Mathias, VII, 886
Chardon, Rosalie-Renée (Gascoin), XII, 359
Chardon de Tressonville, Jacques de, I, 87
Chardon Duranquet. *See* Duranquet
Charencey, Henry de, X, 88
Charest, Anne-Thérèse. *See* Duroy
Charest, Antoine, X, 161
Charest, Catherine (Trottier Desauniers), III, 631; IV, 739
Charest, Étienne (father of ÉTIENNE), II, 131, 561; III, 631; IV, 140
Charest, Étienne (grandfather of ÉTIENNE), I, 620; III, 82, 433
Charest, Étienne, III, 631; IV, **140–41**, 298, 432, 739; V, 368, 481
Charest, Françoise-Claire (Boucher de Montbrun), III, 82
Charest, Joseph, III, 165

Charest (Dufy Charest), Joseph, III, 631, 632; IV, 141; V, 481

Charest, Marguerite. *See* Trottier Desauniers

Charest, Marie-Anne. *See* Marchand

Charest, Marie-Catherine. *See* Trottier Desauniers

Charest, Marie-Charlotte (Martel de Brouague; Le Gardeur de Courtemanche), II, 8, 9, 383, 384, 458, 459; III, 134, 429, 433, 434

Charest, Thérèse (Charly Saint-Ange), II, 131

Charest, Zéphirin, IX, 216; X, **161–62**, 267; XI, 37

Charité, I, 196, **199–200**, 237, 366, 452, 494

Charland, Alexis, V, 183

Charland, Louis, V, **183–84**, 834; VI, 223, 428; VII, 240; VIII, 909

Charland, Marie. *See* Poulin

Charland, Marie-Joseph. *See* Fearson

Charland, Sarah. *See* Jones

Charland, Thomas-Marie, XI, 88

Charlebois, Marguerite (Ducharme), VIII, 241

Charlemont, Viscount. *See* Caulfeild

Charles. *See also* Ondaaiondiont

Charles, Captain, I, 451

Charles I, King of England, Scotland, and Ireland, I, 50, 51, 52, 53, 54, 81, 163, 311, 369, 384, 405, 406, 407, 419, 605, 613, 655, 673; IV, xix

Charles II, King of England, Scotland, and Ireland, I, 62, 82, 226, 241, 242, 337, 369, 406, 407, 436, 481, 513, 604, 636, 637; II, 391, 537, 580, 650; III, 369, 596; IV, xvii; VIII, 297, 649; X, 696

Charles II, King of France, II, 98

Charles II, King of Spain and Sicily, II, 115

Charles III, Duke of Parma, XI, 309

Charles III, King of Spain, IV, 568

Charles IV, King of Spain, IV, 73

Charles V, Holy Roman Emperor, I, 27, 155, 156, 157, 158, 168, 342, 423

Charles V, King of France, III, 703

Charles VI, Holy Roman Emperor, III, 609

Charles VI, King of France, I, 202

Charles VII, King of France, I, 107, 287

Charles IX, King of France, I, 96, 573

Charles X, King of France, VI, 619; VII, 305; VIII, 619; XII, 414, 845, 850, 1102

Charles, the Young Pretender, III, 27, 91, 357, 497, 666; IV, 400, 503; V, 514; VII, 544, 830; VIII, 585; IX, 480, 495

Charles Albert, King of Sardinia, IX, 38

Charles Emmanuel I, Duke of Savoy, I, 300, 301

Charles, Elizabeth (Macallum), VII, 526

Charles, Jane. *See* Auld

Charles, John, VII, 526

Charles, Lucy (Lucille, Lucinda) (Harris), X, 335

Charles, Margaret. *See* Macallum

Charles, Margaret (McLean), XI, 569

Charles*, William (1831–1903), XII, 641

Charlesworth*, Hector Willoughby (1872–1945), XI, 753, 754; XII, 317, 329, 499, 668, 669, 924, 948, 949

Charleton, Ann (Hervey), XI, 389

Charlevoix, Antoinette de. *See* Forestier

Charlevoix, François de, III, 104

Charlevoix, Pierre-François-Xavier de, I, 45, 76, 100, 112, 183, 239, 267, 355, 357, 424, 440, 455, 466, 471, 492, 522, 523, 545, 633, 635, 649, 650; II, 116, 118, 119, 168, 173, 182, 218, 255, 256, 267, 270, 283, 297, 387, 423, 436, 448, 453, 495, 504, 505, 536, 544, 554, 566, 577, 581, 596, 600, 606, 627; III, 81, **103–10**, 184, 248, 249, 308, 309, 310, 315, 330, 335, 337, 395, 443, 444, 627; IV, 500; VI, 382; VII, 401, 818; VIII, 64, 88, 352; IX, 200, 250, 360; XI, 851

Charlier, Monsieur (notary), IV, 69

Charlot Kaské, III, 530

Charlotte. *See* Cameron, Charlotte

Charlotte Augusta, Princess of Wales (Charlotte Augusta, Princess of Saxe-Coburg-Saalfeld), VI, 240, 517; VIII, 649

Charlotte de Sainte-Hélène. *See* Daneau de Muy

Charlotte de Saint-Ignace. *See* Barré

Charlotte Elizabeth, Princess Palatine, II, 401

Charlotte Sophia, Princess of Mecklenburg-Strelitz (Charlotte, Queen of Great Britain and Ireland), V, 297; VIII, 336, 649

Charlton, Edward, IV, 133

Charlton*, John (1829–1910), XII, 577, 583, 934, 1046

Charlton, Richard, VIII, 816

Charly, Jacques, III, 220

Charly, Louis, III, 220

Charly, *dit* Saint-Ange, André, II, 131, 132

Charly, *dit* Saint-Ange, Marie. *See* Dumesnil

Charly Saint-Ange, Jacques, II, 131; III, 110, 111; IV, 141

Charly Saint-Ange, Jean-Baptiste, II, **131–32**; III, 110; IV, 612

Charly Saint-Ange, Jean-Baptiste-François, II, 131; III, 110

Charly Saint-Ange, Louis, II, 131; III, **110–11**, 178, 179, 631; IV, 356, 360; V, 368, 369

Charly Saint-Ange, Louise-Catherine. *See* Ailleboust de Manthet

Charly Saint-Ange, Marie-Catherine, named du Saint-Sacrement, I, 117; II, **132**

Charly Saint-Ange, Marie-Charlotte. *See* Le Conte Dupré

Charly Saint-Ange, Thérèse. *See* Charest

Charly Saint-Ange, Ursule. *See* Godefroy de Tonnancour

Charnisay. *See* Menou

Charnock, John, IV, 595

Charny. *See* Lauson

Charon. *See also* Charron

Charon, Geneviève (Pijart), I, 549

Charon de La Barre, François, II, 48, 127, **132–35**, 195, 377, 378, 556; III, 292, 299, 314, 407, 493, 612, 632, 633; IV, 236, 237, 708, 720

Charpentier, Brother, III, 208

Charpentier, Monsieur (of Placentia, Nfld), II, 119

Charpentier, Marie. *See* Picq

Charrière, Marie-Thérèse-Augustine (Vincent), XI, 903

Charron, Amable. *See* Bénard, *dit* Carignan

Charron, Amable, VI, 626; VII, **167–68**

Charron, Charles, VII, 167

Charron, Jean-Jacques, Marquis de Menars, II, 472

Charron, Marguerite. *See* Hogue

Charron, Marie. *See* Pélerin

Charron, Marie (Colbert), III, 57

Charron, Marie-Anastasie. *See* Babin

Charron, Marie-Archange (Labadie), VI, 380

Charron, Marie-Geneviève. *See* Audrie

Charron de La Barre, Claude. *See* Camus

Charron de La Barre, Claude, I, **200–1**, 478, 588, 589; II, 27, 132, 133

Charron de La Barre, Élisabeth. *See* Damours de Chauf-fours

Charry, Jean-Antoine, Marquis Desgouttes, III, 55, 72, 268

Charters, Alice (Thompson), VII, 854

Charters, Ann (Simonds), VII, 806

Chartier, Alain, I, 202; II, 137

Chartier, Anne. *See* Destroismaisons

Chartier, Catherine. *See* Chamberland

Chartier, Charles, III, 112

Chartier, Étienne, VII, 105, 210, 345, 346, 412, 513, 582; VIII, **140–46**, 317, 915; IX, 814; X, 545, 567, 574, 575, 576, 602; XI, 94, 483

Chartier, Françoise. *See* Bourcier

Chartier, Jean, IV, 654

Chartier, Jean-Baptiste, VIII, 140

Chartier, Jeanne. *See* Chartré; Grondin

Chartier, Joseph, I, 202

Chartier, Louis, I, 109, **201**

Chartier, Marguerite. *See* Amelotte

Chartier, Marie. *See* Lenoir; Magné

Chartier, Marie-Geneviève. *See* Picard Destroismaisons

Chartier, Marie-Josephte (Hubert), VII, 421

Chartier, Martin, III, 65, 66

Chartier, Michel, III, 111

Chartier, Michel, II, 146; III, **111–12**

Chartier, Peter, III, 66, 162

Chartier, Philippe, I, 202

Chartier, Pierre, VIII, 142

Chartier, René (chaplain), I, 202, 662

Chartier, René (of Lachine), I, 452

Chartier de La Broquerie, Louis, I, 201

Chartier de Lotbinière, Angélique (Martin de Lino; Renaud d'Avène Des Méloizes), II, 463, 465; III, 112, 550; IV, 659; V, 711

Chartier de Lotbinière, Clément, I, 202

Chartier de Lotbinière, Élisabeth. *See* Damours

Chartier de Lotbinière, Eustache (son of EUSTACHE, 1688–1749), III, 115; IV, 142

Chartier de Lotbinière, Eustache, II, 90, 91, 211, 457, 463; III, 45, **112–15**, 240, 491, 648; IV, 141, 142, 143, 221, 440, 539

Chartier de Lotbinière, Eustache (baptized François-Louis), III, 115; IV, **141–43**; V, 432

Chartier de Lotbinière, Françoise. *See* Jachée

Chartier de Lotbinière, Josette. *See* Tonnancour

Chartier de Lotbinière, Julie-Christine (Joly), VI, 133

Chartier de Lotbinière, Louise (De Bonne; MacKay), IV, 143; V, 231

Chartier de Lotbinière, Louise, named de Saint-Eustache, III, 115

Chartier de Lotbinière, Louise-Madeleine, Marquise de Lotbinière. *See* Chaussegros de Léry

Chartier de Lotbinière, Louise-Philippe (Mariauchau d'Esgly), II, 457; III, 112; IV, 510

Chartier de Lotbinière, Louis-Théandre, I, 112, **201–3**, 245, 399, 588, 589, 617, 629; II, xvi, xix, xxiii, 136, 243, 301; III, 112

Chartier de Lotbinière, Marie-Charlotte (Bingham), VI, 133

Chartier de Lotbinière, Marie-Françoise. *See* Renaud d'Avène de Desmeloizes

Chartier de Lotbinière, Marie-Françoise (Joybert de Soulanges et de Marson), I, 202, 203, 399, 400; II, 301

Chartier de Lotbinière, Marie-Françoise (Juchereau Duchesnay), III, 115; V, 462

Chartier de Lotbinière, Marie-Louise (Denys de La Ronde), III, 110, 175, 176, 177, 179

Chartier de Lotbinière, Marie-Louise-Josephte (Harwood), VI, 133; IX, 373

Chartier de Lotbinière, Marie-Madeleine. *See* Lambert

Chartier de Lotbinière, Mary Charlotte. *See* Munro

Chartier de Lotbinière, Michel, Marquis de Lotbinière, II, 52; III, 31, 113, 115, 119; IV, 142, **143–45**, 364; V, 42, 231, 300, 462, 652, 738, 739; VI, 132, 493, 690

Chartier de Lotbinière, Michel-Eustache-Gaspard-Alain, IV, 143, 185, 591; V, 96, 99, 207, 231, 232, 233, 650; VI, **132–33**, 690; VII, 622; IX, 360, 373

Chartier de Lotbinière, Pierre-Alain, III, 112, 113

Chartier de Lotbinière, René-Louis, I, 202; II, xxi, xxii, xxiv, **135–39**, 213, 457, 463, 465, 520, 526, 561, 587; III, 112, 176, 420, 550

Chartier de Lotbinière, René-Pierre, I, 202; II, 136

Chartier de Lotbinière, Valentin (baptized Antoine), III, 112, 113

Charton, François, I, 121

Charton, Nicolas, I, 48

Chartrain, Noël, II, 303

Chartrand. *See also* Armand

Chartrand, Marie-Charlotte. *See* Labelle

Chartrand, Toussaint, IX, 127

Chartrand, Vincent, IX, 126

Chartrand, Vincent, IX, **126–27**

Chartré, Jeanne (Chartier), III, 112

Chartroux, Madeleine (La Salle), II, 349

Chase, Annie G. *See* Armour

Chase, Elizabeth. *See* Lawrear

Chase, Henry Pahtahquahong, XII, **186–87**

Chase, Rebecca M. (Wells), XII, 1094

Chase, Salmon Portland, XII, 1029

Chase, Samuel, IV, 270, 549, 759; V, 31, 629

Chase, Wellington, XII, 792

Chasle, Catherine. *See* Fol

Chasle, Claude (father), I, 255

Chasle, Claude, III, 350

Chasle, Marie-Anne (Gouze; Perthuis), IV, 624

Chasle, Marie-Marguerite. *See* Duroy

Chasley (Chassley, Chesley), All Saints, X, 163

Chasley, Lené. *See* Yeomans

Chaspoux, Marie-Madeleine de, Dame de Verneuil et Du Plessis-Savari (Bochart de Champigny), II, 71; III, 22

Chassagne. *See* Bouillet

Chassebœuf, Constantin-François, Comte de Volney, V, 594

Chasseriau, Marie (Bréard), IV, 92

Chasseur, Marie-Anne, VI, 534

Chasseur, Pierre, VI, 69, 186; VII, **168–69**, 427; X, 505

Chassin, Charlotte de. *See* Thyerry

Chassin, Marie-Agnès (Tisserant de Moncharvaux), III, 626

Chassin, Nicolas de, III, 115

Chassin de Thierry, François-Nicolas de, III, **115–16**, 645

Chassin de Thierry, Marie-Josephte de. *See* Rousseau de Souvigny

Chassley. *See* Chasley

Chaste, Aymar de, I, 27, 188, 209, 210, 346

Chasteigner, Charlotte de (Aloigny, Marquise de La Groye), II, 15

Chastelain, Marguerite. *See* Cardin

Chastelain, Marie-Josephte (Boucher de Niverville), III, 8, 430

Chastelard, Henri de, Marquis de Salières, I, 286, 555, 570, 602; II, 11, 412

Chastellain, Pierre, I, 125, **203–4**, 324; II, 613

Chastellaine. *See* Chatelain

Chastullé. *See* Pyvart

Chatchmaid, William, I, 350

Chateaubriand, François-René, Vicomte de Chateaubriand, II, 444; III, 24, 108; VII, 671; VIII, 329, 330; IX, 193; X, 166; XI, 273, 725; XII, 118

Chateaufort. *See* Bras-de-Fer

Châteauguay. *See* Le Moyne

Châteauneuf. *See* Meneux

Chateauverdun, Marie de (Rigaud de Vaudreuil, Baronne de Vaudreuil), II, 565

Chateauvert, Victor, XI, 728

Châteauvieux. *See* Gamelin

Chateigner de Cramahé et Des Rochers, Hector-François, IV, 787

Chateigner de Cramahé et Des Rochers, Marie-Anne. *See* Belrieux de Virazel

Châtel, Edmée, I, 116

Chatelain, Nicolas, XII, **187–88**

Châtelet, Florent-Louis-Marie du, Comte et Duc du Châtelet-Lomont, V, 791

Châtelin, Marie-Josephte (Boucher de Niverville), V, 97

Châtellerault. *See* Roy

Chatellereaux, Marie-Anne (Parent), V, 658

Chatham, Earl of. *See* Pitt

Chatillon. *See* Berson; Godin; Mignot

Châtillon, Maréchal de. *See* Coligny, Gaspard I de

Chatillonnet. *See* Sauvage

Chaton de La Jannaye, Étienne, I, 520

Chauchetière, Claude, I, 651; II, 107, **139–40**

Chaudière Noire, I, **204–5**

Chaudillon, Antoine, II, **140–41**

Chaudillon, Antoinette. *See* Tin

Chaudillon, Claude, II, 140

Chaudillon, Marie. *See* Boucher

Chaudron. *See* Le Page

Chaudrue, Jean, V, 276

Chauffours. *See* Damours

Chaufour, Jean-Baptiste, IV, 376

Chaulnes, Duc de. *See* Albert

Chaumeaux. *See* Citoys

Chaumier, Catherine. *See* Nafrechoux

Chaumine. *See* Tessier

Chaumonot, Pierre-Joseph-Marie, I, 111, 121, 123, 124, **205–7**, 244, 269, 271, 273, 345, 415, 461, 523, 563, 612, 633, 665; II, 82, 94, 160, 536, 540, 643; III, 337

Chaumont. *See also* Guillet

Chaumont, Alexandre de, II, 141

Chaumont, Alexandre de, I, 554; II, **141**

Chaumont, Isabelle de. *See* Du Bois Des Cours

Chauncey, Eliza Touzou (Tocque), XII, 1060

Chauncey, Isaac, V, 696, 875, 876; VI, 479, 520; VII, 888; VIII, 794; IX, 414, 415, 754

Chauniers. *See* Sabourin

Chaüosé. *See* Le Mercier, François-Joseph

Chauret. *See also* Choret

Chauret, Joseph, VI, 582

Chaussat, Armand-Joseph, V, 49

Chaussegros, Anne. *See* Vidalle

Chaussegros, Gaspard, III, 116

Chaussegros de Léry, Alexandre-André-Victor, V, 270; VII, 213

Chaussegros de Léry, Alexandre-René, IX, 127, 128; X, **162–63**; XI, 491

Chaussegros de Léry, Catherine (Saveuse de Beaujeu), VI, 690; IX, 702

Chaussegros de Léry, Catherine-Charlotte-Élise. *See* Couillard

Chaussegros de Léry, Charles-Étienne, V, 75; VI, 134; VII, **169–70**; IX, 127; X, 162

Chaussegros de Léry, Charles-Joseph, IX, **127–28**

Chaussegros de Léry, François-Joseph, Vicomte de Léry, III, xxii; IV, 435; VI, 133; VII, 170

Chaussegros de Léry, Gaspard-Joseph, I, 76; II, xxi, 202, 209, 431, 432, 434, 515, 593; III, 47, 79, 115, **116–19**, 191, 194, 229, 231, 241, 307, 420, 534, 610, 631; IV, 143, 145, 174, 203, 435, 448, 474; V, 49, 738, 739

Chaussegros de Léry, Gaspard-Joseph, III, xxii, 28, 31, 116, 118, 162, 171, 222, 408, 434, 451, 459, 613; IV, xliii, 89, **145–47**, 150, 395, 464, 651, 733; V, 60, 75, 143, 481, 794; VI, 132, 133, 690; VII, 169, 213; IX, 702

Chaussegros de Léry, Gaspard-Roch-George, VI, 133

Chaussegros de Léry, Josephte. *See* Fraser

Chaussegros de Léry, Josephte-Antoinette, named de Sainte-Marie, IV, 203

Chaussegros de Léry, Louise. *See* Martel de Brouague

Chaussegros de Léry, Louise-Madeleine (Chartier de Lotbinière, Marquise de Lotbinière), III, 115, 119; IV, 143, 144; V, 231; VI, 132, 690

Chaussegros de Léry, Louis-René, V, 97, 270; VI, **133–34**, 690, 787; VII, 235; VIII, 100; IX, 613

Chaussegros de Léry, Madeleine-Charlotte. *See* Boucher de Boucherville

Chaussegros de Léry, Marie-Angélique (Couillard), VII, 213

Chaussegros de Léry, Marie-Gilles (Landriève Des Bordes), IV, 435

Chaussegros de Léry, Marie-Madeleine-Régis (Legardeur de Repentigny), III, 119; IV, 448

Chaussegros de Léry, Marie-Renée. *See* Legardeur de Beauvais

Chaussegros de Léry, Mary. *See* O'Hara

Chaussegros* de Léry, William-Henri-Brouague (1851–1914), X, 162

Chausson, Marie-Élisabeth, III, 552

Chauveau, Alexandre, XI, 181

Chauveau, Annette, XI, 181

Chauveau, Éliza, named Sainte-Florine, XI, 185

Chauveau, Flore, XI, 185

Chauveau, François, I, 214

Chauveau, Henriette (Glendonwyn), XI, 185

Chauveau, Marie-Charlotte. *See* Lavallée

Chauveau, Marie-Louise. *See* Roy

Chauveau, Marie-Louise-Flore. *See* Masse

Chauveau, Olympe, XI, 181

Chauveau, Pierre (cooper), XI, 177

Chauveau, Pierre (son of PIERRE-JOSEPH-OLIVIER), XI, 181, 345

Chauveau, Pierre-Charles, XI, 177

Chauveau, Pierre-Joseph-Olivier, VII, 373; VIII, 137, 215, 277, 291, 407, 408, 420, 497, 691, 775, 834, 835; IX, 194, 201, 212, 213, 303, 304, 305, 306, 612, 774, 805; X, 16, 36, 148, 203, 218, 401, 415, 418, 508, 542, 635; XI, 26, 27, 42, 83, 160, 170, **177–87**, 287, 334, 338, 342, 345, 457, 480, 496, 519, 690, 893; XII, 86, 134, 174, 175, 236, 249, 271, 299, 300, 324, 385, 421, 431, 464, 558, 693, 1006, 1012, 1013, 1066
Chauveaux, Catherine (Raby), VI, 626
Chauveaux, Charles, V, 242; VI, 650; VII, 93
Chauveton, Urbain, I, 154
Chauvieux. *See* Chauvreulx
Chauvigny, Jeanne. *See* Du Bouchet
Chauvigny, Marie-Madeleine de (Gruel de La Peltrie), I, 43, 205, **207–8**, 215, 217, 230, 352, 354, 373, 457, 483, 485, 552, 604, 640, 665; IV, 535
Chauvigny et de Vaubougon, Guillaume de, I, 207, 208
Chauvin, Anne. *See* Archambault
Chauvin, François, I, 209
Chauvin, Jean, X, 413
Chauvin, Marc, IX, 210
Chauvin, Marie (Noyon), III, 493
Chauvin, Marie-Marthe (Lupien, *dit* Baron), III, 412
Chauvin, Michel, I, 557
Chauvin, Pierre, II, 105
Chauvin de La Pierre, Pierre, I, 80, 190, **208–9**
Chauvin de Tonnetuit, Jeanne de. *See* Mallemouche
Chauvin de Tonnetuit, Madeleine de, I, 210
Chauvin de Tonnetuit, Marie de. *See* Brinon
Chauvin de Tonnetuit, Pierre de, I, 27, 208, **209–10**, 291, 345, 422, 601
Chauvreulx, Claude-Jean-Baptiste, II, 513; III, **119–21**, 166, 256, 257; IV, xxv, 296
Chavagnac, Louis-Henri de, Comte de Chavagnac, II, 398
Chavenault, Marie-Françoise (Levasseur de Neré), II, 432
Chaverlange, Antoine de, I, 474
Chaverlange, Jeanne de (Levasseur, *dit* L'Espérance), I, 474
Chaverlange, Marthe de. *See* Guérin
Chavigny, Élisabeth de (Landron), III, 347
Chavigny de Berchereau, Éléonore de. *See* Grandmaison
Chavigny de Berchereau, François de, I, 56, 344, 345; II, 141, 223; III, 379
Chavigny de Berchereau, Geneviève de (Amiot; Couillard de Lespinay), I, 59; II, 17, 155
Chavigny de Berchereau, Madeleine de (Lemoine), II, 236; III, 379
Chavigny de Berchereau, Marguerite de (Douaire de Bondy; Fleury Deschambault), I, 309, 418; II, 223, 224, 433; III, 216
Chavigny de La Chevrotière, Monsieur (notary), XI, 353
Chavigny Lachevrotière, Antoinette de. *See* Poussans
Chavigny Lachevrotière, François de, II, 142
Chavigny Lachevrotière, François de, I, 345, 394; II, **141–42**
Chavigny Lachevrotière, Geneviève de. *See* Guion Desprez
Chavigny Lachevrotière, Louise de, II, 142
Chavin. *See* Chauvin
Chaviteau, Françoise. *See* Bourot
Chaviteau, Jean, II, 298
Chavoy. *See* Payen
Chawchinahaw, IV, 339
Chazel, Guillaume, II, 208; III, 62

Chazelle, Blandine. *See* Chalette
Chazelle, Jean-Pierre, VII, **170–71**, 706; VIII, 490; IX, 67; XI, 95, 96, 588; XII, 724
Chazelle, Pierre, VII, 170
Chazy, Lieutenant, I, 40, 308; II, 159
Cheadle, Walter Butler, IX, 94, 296, 473, 602, 603; X, 198, 699, 700; XII, 642
Chearnley, William, VIII, 33; XI, 679
Cheatle, Mary (Stinson), IX, 749
Chedékki, IX, 433
Chef de la Pluie. *See* Sotai-na
Chefdostel, Thomas, I, **210**, 421, 422
Chejauk, V, **184–85**
Chelmsford, Baron. *See* Thesiger
Chenard de La Giraudais, François, III, xxv, 606; IV, 28, 80, 207, 208; V, 105
Chenery, Hannah (Peters), IV, 624
Chenet, Antoine, X, 36
Chenet, Catherine-Élisabeth-Aglaé (Beaubien), X, 36
Chenet Dubreuil, Pierre, II, 182, 459, 521, 522
Chêneverd. *See* Morin
Cheney, Harriet Vaughan. *See* Foster
Cheney, Ida. *See* Lewis
Cheney, Mary Youngs (Greeley), X, 316
Chénier, Cécile. *See* Morel
Chénier, Félix, VII, 174
Chénier, François, VII, 172
Chénier, Jean-Olivier, VI, 382; VII, 26, **171–74**, 346, 422, 513, 586, 679, 757; VIII, 144, 245, 330, 332, 470, 471, 792; IX, 203, 827; X, 307, 499; XII, 303
Chénier, Suzanne-Amable. *See* Blondeau
Chénier, Victor (father), VII, 172
Chénier, Victor, VII, 174
Chénier, Zéphirine. *See* Labrie
Cheniqui. *See* Chinic
Cheniquy, Charles, XII, 189
Cheniquy, Marie-Reine. *See* Perrault
Chenneque, Élizabeth. *See* Pelerin
Chenneque, Marie-Louise. *See* Grenete
Chenneque, Martin, V, 95; VI, **134–35**, 483; VII, 176; XI, 189
Chenneque, Susanne. *See* Rollete
Chennequi (Chennequy). *See* Chenneque
Chennequy, Marie (Malherbe), VI, 483
Chenneville. *See* Baby-Chenneville
Chenughiyata. *See* Hotsinoñhyahta?
Chéron, Charles, III, 75, 429, 602; IV, 11
Chéron, Marguerite (Trottier Desauniers), III, 631
Chéron, Marie-Josephte (Carrerot), III, 97
Chéron, Marie-Madeleine (Ailleboust de Cerry), IV, 10
Chéron, Marie-Ursule, named des Anges, IV, 189
Chéron, Martin, II, 66; III, 631
Cherououny, I, **210–11**, 302, 303, 479
Cherrier, A.-Benjamin, XI, 979
Cherrier, Benjamin-Hyacinthe-Martin, IV, 148; V, 186; VII, 485
Cherrier, Côme-Séraphin, IV, 148; V, 186, 702; VI, 783; VII, 606; VIII, 284, 694, 909, 914; IX, 458, 649, 651, 813, 816; X, 37, 52, 194, 237, 298, 417, 527, 533, 625; XI, 103, **187–89**, 206, 249, 821; XII, 253, 260, 261
Cherrier, François, IV, 147
Cherrier, François, IV, 148, 592, 639; V, **185–86**, 200, 704, 833; VI, 286, 589; VII, 422, 486, 850; VIII, 456; IX, 548

Cherrier, François-Pierre, IV, **147–49**, 270; V, 185, 833; VII, 485, 674; IX, 807
Cherrier, Georges-Hippolyte, X, 164; XI, 181, 979
Cherrier, Joseph-Marie, IV, 148; XI, 187
Cherrier, Joseph-Marie-Simon, IV, 148
Cherrier, Marguerite (Godefroy de Tonnancour), IX, 321
Cherrier, Marie. *See* Dubuc
Cherrier, Marie-Charlotte (Larthigue), IV, 148; VII, 485
Cherrier, Marie-Josephte. *See* Gaté
Cherrier, Mélanie. *See* Quesnel
Cherrier, Périne-Charles (Viger), IV, 148; V, 833; IX, 807
Cherrier, Rosalie (Papineau), IV, 148; VII, 674; VIII, 678; X, 564
Cherrier, Séraphin, IV, 148; V, 186
Cherriman*, John Bradford (1823–1908), XI, 475; XII, 656
Cherubini, Luigi, X, 221
Chesley. *See also* Chasley
Chesley, Margaret Ann. *See* Vankoughnet
Chesley, Solomon Yeomans, VIII, 619; X, **163–64**
Chesné, Élisabeth. *See* Auber
Chesne, *dit* Labutte, Pierre, III, 528
Chesneau, Anne. *See* Lalande
Chesneau, Guillaume, I, 287
Chesnel, Judith (Du Gua de Monts), I, 291
Chesney, Francis Rawdon, VIII, 274
Chesser, John, VII, 111
Chessus, IX, 433
Chesterfield, Earl of. *See* Stanhope
Chettle, John, IX, 749
Chetwood, Elizabeth (Hamilton), VII, 379
Cheval, Geneviève. *See* Leduc
Cheval, Gilette. *See* Nève
Cheval, Marie-Renée. *See* Cousineau
Cheval, Thomas, III, 121
Cheval, *dit* Saint-Jacques, *dit* Chevalier, Jacques-Joseph, III, **121**
Chevalier. *See also* La Tourasse
Chevalier, Monsieur (of Port-Royal), I, 564
Chevalier, Angélique (De Lisle), V, 241
Chevalier, Catherine (Noyon), I, 250
Chevalier, Charlotte-Isabelle (Castaing), IV, 135
Chevalier, Constante (Ainsse), V, 7
Chevalier, Françoise-Marthe. *See* Barton
Chevalier, Henri-Émile, VIII, 160, 161; IX, 194, 464, 612, 615; X, **164–67**, 237
Chevalier, Jacques, II, 142; V, 249
Chevalier, Jean, II, 142
Chevalier, Jean-Baptiste, IV, 659
Chevalier, Jean-Baptiste, III, **121–22**; IV, 78; V, 7, 179
Chevalier, Jean-Charles, III, **122**
Chevalier, Jeanne. *See* Vilain
Chevalier, Joseph (father of JEAN-BAPTISTE), III, 121
Chevalier, Joseph (of Trois-Rivières), III, 430; IV, 331
Chevalier, Louis, III, 223
Chevalier, Louise (Rézé), XII, 891
Chevalier, Louise (Roy), II, 584
Chevalier, Marguerite. *See* Brault
Chevalier, Marie (L'Hermitte), II, 434
Chevalier, Marie-Anne (Bourdages), IV, 78
Chevalier, Marie-Anne (Chaboillez), III, 122; V, 178
Chevalier, Marie-Anne (Dubreuil), II, 201
Chevalier, Marie-Françoise. *See* Alavoine
Chevalier, Michel, VI, 185

Chevalier, Paul, II, 142
Chevalier, Pierre, II, 133
Chevalier, Sophronie. *See* Rouvier
Chevalier, Sulpice-Guillaume (Paul Gavarni), VIII, 13
Chevalier, Thérèse (Delvecchio), VI, 185
Chevalier, *dit* Beauchêne, Robert, II, **142–43**
Chevallier. *See also* Courselle
Chevallier, Louis-Thérèse, III, 122; V, 7, 8
Chevallier, Marie-Madeleine. *See* Réaume
Chevenaux. *See* Chauvreulx
Chevert, François de, V, 103
Cheverus. *See* Lefebvre
Chevigny. *See* Choiseul-Chevigny
Chévigny. *See* Vallette
Chevilly. *See* Bouvot
Chevreau, Judith de (Aumasson de Courville), IV, 35
Chevremont. *See* Gaudron
Chevrier, Pierre, Baron de Fancamp, I, 214, 215; III, 395
Chevrières. *See* La Croix
Chevry. *See also* Duret
Chevry, Marquis de, IV, xxiv
Chew, John, IV, 149; V, 121
Chew, Joseph, IV, **149**; V, 147
Chew, Julia M. (Bowman), VII, 100
Chew, William Johnson, IV, 149
Chewett, Mrs (wife of Alexander), IX, 645
Chewett, Alexander, IX, 645
Chewett, Isabella. *See* Macdonell
Chewett, James Grant, VII, 178, 712, 846; VIII, 419; IX, **128–29**, 657; XII, 188, 667
Chewett, Maria Susan. *See* Ranney
Chewett, Martha Smith. *See* Robison
Chewett, William, V, 519; VI, 406, 647; VII, 95, 126, **174–76**, 207, 350, 747, 846, 929; VIII, 5, 418, 749, 750, 795; IX, 128; XII, 188
Chewett, William Cameron, IX, 128; XII, **188–89**, 212, 667
Chèze, François, II, **143**; III, 603
Chiasson, Agnès (Gaudet), V, 203
Chiasson, Anne (Gallant), V, 335
Chiasson, Marie (Poirier), XI, 684
Chicagou, II, 646
Chichikatelo (Chichicato), II, xxxiii, **143–44**
Chicoine. *See* Chicoyne
Chicoisneau, Guillaume, V, 186
Chiçoisneau, Hélène. *See* Gaulthier
Chicoisneau, Jean-Baptiste-Jacques, V, **186–87**, 680; VI, 84, 332; VII, 759, 773; VIII, 239
Chicot, Jean, I, 463; XI, 821
Chicou, *dit* Duvert, Pierre, V, 248
Chicoux-Duvert, Hélène-Flavie (Drolet; Renaud), X, 614
Chicoyne*, Jérôme-Adolphe (1844–1910), XI, 331
Chicoyneau, Catherine (La Maisonfort Du Boisdecourt, Marquise de La Maisonfort), III, 345
Chief Cobbeyall. *See* Glode, Gabriel
Chief Joseph. *See* Onasakenrat, Joseph
Chief Moon. *See* Nina-kisoom
Chihwatenha (Chihouatenha, Chihouatenhoua), I, **211–12**, 344, 388, 523
Chiksika, VII, 847
Child, Mr (commercial agent), V, 784
Child, Isabella (Coffin), V, 190; VII, 199, 200
Child, Lydia F. *See* Chadwick
Child, Marcus, VII, 374; VIII, **147–48**, 221; IX, 144

Child, Susannah (Sheaffe), VIII, 793
Childs, John, VII, 709
Childs, Margaret (Ball), V, 53
Childs, Mary (Lavigueur), XI, 500
Childs, S., VIII, 347
Chillihetza, XI, 568
Chillis, Isabella (Disbrow), VIII, 224
Chinard, Gilbert, III, 337
Chineque. *See* Chenneque
Chingouessi, II, xxxvii, **144**
Chinic, Eugène-Philéas-Nowlan, XI, 189, 190
Chinic, Guillaume-Eugène, VII, 176; VIII, 629; XI,
    **189–91**, 264, 901, 902; XII, 1035
Chinic, Joseph-Martin (father), VII, 176
Chinic, Joseph-Martin, VII, 176; XI, 189
Chinic, Julie. *See* Measam
Chinic, Julienne-Claire. *See* Enouille, *dit* Lanois
Chinic, Marie-Anne-Claire. *See* Leblond
Chinic, Marie-Antoinette. *See* Bourdages
Chinic, Martin, V, 84, 270; VI, 134, 483; VII, **176–77**, 718;
    XI, 189
Chiniquy, Charles, IV, 43l; VI, 134; VII, 267; VIII, 223;
    IX, 96, 153, 292, 361, 421, 466; X, 86, 374, 419, 488,
    604; XI, 99, 173, 175, 467, 565, 655; XII, **189–93**, 270,
    846
Chiniquy, Euphémie. *See* Allard
Chinn, Edward, IV, 369, 592; V, 20, 142
Chinn, John, IV, 369; V, 129; VI, 317
Chinnequy. *See* Chinic
Chinoniata. *See* Hotsinoñhyahta⁊
Chiohoarerha. *See* Chihwatenha
Chipman. *See also* Shaw Chipman
Chipman, Abigail (Calvin), XI, 139
Chipman, Alice Starr (Tilley, Lady Tilley), XII, 1051, 1056
Chipman, Ann. *See* Osborn
Chipman, Eliza (Quirk), VIII, 731
Chipman, Eliza Ann (Chipman), VIII, **148–49**
Chipman, Elizabeth. *See* Andrews
Chipman, Elizabeth. *See* Brown
Chipman, Elizabeth. *See* Gesner
Chipman, Elizabeth. *See* Hazen
Chipman, Elizabeth. *See* Wright
Chipman, Elizabeth (Gray), VI, 142
Chipman, Handley, VII, 177
Chipman, Holmes, VIII, 148
Chipman, Isaac, XI, 209
Chipman, Isaac Logan, VIII, 149; XII, 230
Chipman, Jared Ingersoll, VIII, 752
Chipman, Jean. *See* Allen
Chipman, Jessie W. *See* Hardy
Chipman, John (brother of WILLIAM ALLEN), VII, 177
Chipman, John (father of WARD, 1754–1824), VI, 135, 136
Chipman, Laura Edith (Howland), XII, 453
Chipman, Leverett DeVeber, IX, 130
Chipman, Mary. *See* Dickey
Chipman, Mary Frances (Howard), XI, 428
Chipman, Samuel, VII, 177; XII, **193–94**
Chipman, Sophia Araminta. *See* Cogswell
Chipman, Thomas Handley, IV, 19; VI, 276, 574; VII, 177;
    VIII, 611; XII, 109
Chipman, Ward, IV, 55, 329, 516, 723, 769; V, 35, 156,
    157, 161, 390, 416, 456, 504, 505, 506, 630, 867, 874;
    VI, 35, 60, 73, 75, 76, **135–45**, 283, 356, 563, 685, 700,

726, 727, 740, 811, 813; VII, 74, 87, 657, 658, 691, 783;
    VIII, xxiv, 69, 149, 150, 274, 507, 806; IX, 622; XII, 19,
    536
Chipman, Ward, VI, 73, 74, 135, 138, 140, 142, 143, 810;
    VII, 658, 691, 692; VIII, 98, **149–54**, 428, 841; IX, 146,
    382, 399, 619, 620; X, 140, 712; XII, 17, 20, 536
Chipman, William, VII, 177; VIII, 148; IX, 129
Chipman, William Allen, IX, 129
Chipman, William Allen, VII, **177**; XII, 193
Chipman, William Henry, VII, 177; IX, **129–30**
Chiquet, Monsieur (carpenter), III, 139
Chiquot (Cicotte), Zacharie, III, 529
Chirat, Élisabeth (Mercier), X, 510
Chirouse, Eugène-Casimir (uncle), XII, 282
Chirouse, Eugène-Casimir, XII, 284
Chisholm, Adeline. *See* Davies
Chisholm, Æneas, VIII, 306
Chisholm, Alexander, VII, 549; VIII, 583
Chisholm, Archibald, IX, 788
Chisholm, Barbara. *See* McKenzie
Chisholm, George (father), VII, 178
Chisholm, George, VII, 179
Chisholm, George King, VII, 179; X, **167**
Chisholm, Helena (Grant), VII, 355
Chisholm, Hiram, VIII, 749; XI, 501
Chisholm, Isabella. *See* Land
Chisholm, Jane (Fraser), VIII, 306
Chisholm, John (bishop), VII, 355, 551; VIII, 306
Chisholm, John (collector of customs), VIII, 310
Chisholm, John (uncle of WILLIAM), VII, 178
Chisholm, John Alexander, VII, 179
Chisholm*, Sir Joseph Andrew (1863–1950), IX, 787
Chisholm, Louisa Latham (Neelon), XII, 782, 783
Chisholm, Mary (MacDonell), VII, 551
Chisholm, Rebecca. *See* Silverthorn
Chisholm, Robert Kerr, VII, 179
Chisholm, Selina. *See* Lee
Chisholm, William, VII, 355
Chisholm, William, VII, **177–79**; VIII, 186, 310, 855; IX,
    128, 657, 718; X, 167
Chisholme, David, VII, **179–81**, 183, 907; VIII, 22
Chisholme, Rachel Cuthbert. *See* Robertson
Chittenden, Newton Henry, XII, 290
Chittick, Victor Lovitt Oakes, VI, 307, 308; IX, 353, 354,
    355
Chitty, Joseph, VIII, 428; X, 644
Chkoudun. *See* Secoudon
Chlapowski, Jadwiga. *See* Opid
Choate, Elizabeth (Burnham), VIII, 116
Choate, Thomas, VIII, 324
Chocarne, Bernard, X, 431
Choderlos de Laclos, Pierre, VII, 90
Choiseul, Étienne-François, Duc de Choiseul, II, 270; III,
    xvi, 86, 97, 142, 300, 442, 538, 601; IV, 31, 56, 68, 69,
    207, 257, 457, 481, 602, 621, 634, 646, 660, 673, 734,
    739, 752; V, 104, 105
Choiseul, François-Joseph de, Baron de Beaupré, known as
    Comte de Choiseul, III, 474, 475
Choiseul-Chevigny, César-Gabriel de, Duc de Praslin, IV,
    646, 657
Choisser, Jean, IV, 748
Cholenec, Pierre, I, 635; II, **144–45**; III, 649
Chôlet, Marie-Charles (Gauthier), XII, 360

Cholmondeley, Harriet (Lambton), VII, 476, 477
Cholmondeley, Robert, IV, 103
Chomedey, Hierosme de, I, 213
Chomedey, Jacqueline de (Bouvot de Chevilly), I, 213
Chomedey, Louis de, I, 212
Chomedey, Louise de, named de Sainte-Marie, I, 115, 213, 220
Chomedey, Marie de. See Thomelin
Chomedey, Odard de, I, 213
Chomedey de Maisonneuve, Paul de, I, 32, 43, 44, 45, 46, 47, 109, 115, 130, 200, 208, **212–22**, 230, 231, 266, 273, 284, 297, 310, 319, 330, 344, 373, 412, 427, 430, 447, 453, 457, 464, 485, 486, 487, 540, 543, 547, 548, 557, 558, 598, 640, 648; II, xv, 131, 193, 234, 375, 376, 469, 490; III, 692; IX, 617, 864; X, 736
Chomel, Sieur (doctor), III, 676
Chomina, I, 80, **222–23**, 302, 509, 516, 578, 639
Chomonot. See Chaumonot
Choné, Jean-Pierre, VII, 171, 706; VIII, 308; IX, 408
Choquet, Marie-Louise (Masson), X, 499
Choquette*, Charles-Philippe (1856–1947), VIII, 711; X, 421
Choquette, Delphine (Rivard), XI, 755
Chorel de Saint-Romain, Edmond, III, 311, 312
Chorel de Saint-Romain, dit d'Orvilliers, Élisabeth (Groston de Saint-Ange), II, 267
Chorel de Saint-Romain, dit d'Orvilliers, François, II, 267, 616; III, 311
Chorel de Saint-Romain, dit d'Orvilliers, Madeleine (Lefebvre Duplessis Faber), III, 372
Chorel de Saint-Romain, dit d'Orvilliers, Marie-Anne. See Aubuchon
Chorel de Saint-Romain, dit d'Orvilliers, Marie-Madeleine (Gadois, dit Mauger), III, 232
Chorel de Saint-Romain, dit d'Orvilliers, Marie-Marguerite (Lorimier de La Rivière), II, 445; III, 408
Chorel de Saint-Romain, dit d'Orvilliers, Marie-Renée (Le Picard Du Mesnil de Norrey), II, 416, 520
Chorest, Jean-Baptiste, III, 272
Choret (Chauret), Élisabeth (Paquet), VI, 572
Chotard, Jean-Baptiste, II, 516
Chotard, Marie-Anne (Perrin), II, 516
Chotard, Marie-Catherine. See Fortin
Chou, Juan, I, 263
Chouart, Marie. See Poirier
Chouart, Médard, I, 223
Chouart Des Groseilliers, Hélène. See Martin
Chouart Des Groseilliers, Jean-Baptiste, I, 39, 223, 227; II, 538, 539, 647
Chouart Des Groseilliers, Marguerite. See Hayet
Chouart Des Groseilliers, Marguerite, I, 223, 228
Chouart Des Groseilliers, Marie-Anne, I, 223
Chouart Des Groseilliers, Marie-Antoinette (Jalot; Bouchard d'Orval), I, 223; II, 647
Chouart Des Groseilliers, Médard, I, 223
Chouart Des Groseilliers, Médard, I, 16, 20, 39, 48, 49, 50, 56, 82, 83, 129, **223–28**, 250, 271, 282, 337, 338, 385, 397, 429, 464, 495, 518, 528, 578, 602, 607, 625; II, 298, 391, 501, 535, 536, 537, 538, 647
Chouinard, Monsieur (attorney), XII, 745
Chouinard, Élizabeth (Dease), IX, 198
Chouinard*, Honoré-Julien-Jean-Baptiste (1850–1928), X, 205; XI, 457

Chouinard, Jean-Marie, V, 359
Chouly, Philippe-Claude-Auguste de, Marquis de Permangle, VI, 516, 517
Choumin. See Chomina
Chouteau, Auguste, V, 175, 820; VI, 72
Chouteau, Marie-Thérèse. See Cerré
Chrestien, Father. See Le Clercq
Chrestien, Marie-Louise (Amiot), VII, 16
Chrestienne, Marie-Madeleine. See Ouebadinskoue
Chrétien, Brother. See Turc de Castelveyre, Louis
Chrétien, Jean, II, 179
Chrétien, Louis, XI, 173
Chrétien, Marie-Charlotte (Denys de Vitré), II, 179
Christe, Marie (Garnier), XII, 356
Christian (Mohawk), II, 477
Christian (servant), II, 486, 487
Christian I, King of Denmark, Norway, and Sweden, I, 679
Christian IV, King of Denmark and Norway, I, 243, 360, 514, 515
Christian, Ann (wife of WASHINGTON), VII, 181
Christian, Washington, VII, **181–82**; VIII, 99
Christie. See also Christie Burton
Christie, Mr (officer), VI, 629
Christie, Mr (teacher), V, 321
Christie, Alexander (father of ALEXANDER JAMES), VII, 182
Christie, Alexander (grandson of ALEXANDER), X, 167
Christie, Alexander (son of ALEXANDER), X, 167
Christie, Alexander (son of ALEXANDER JAMES), VII, 182
Christie, Alexander, VI, 766; VIII, 454, 573, 585, 819; IX, 530; X, 69, **167–68**; XI, 219, 220, 546, 875; XII, 194
Christie, Alexander James, VI, 481; VII, 179, **182–84**, 445, 927; VIII, 707, 839; IX, 287, 497
Christie, Amelia Martha. See Bowman
Christie, Ann. See Thomas
Christie, Catherine. See Napier
Christie, Catherine (Robertson), IV, 151; V, 716
Christie, David, IX, 507; X, **168–71**; XI, 939; XII, 967
Christie, Gabriel, IV, 151
Christie, Gabriel, IV, 146, **149–51**, 269, 278, 464, 570, 612, 691; V, 63, 164, 331, 413, 414, 716; VI, 296, 629; VII, 184, 395
Christie, George, IV, 151
Christie, Isabella. See Turnbull
Christie, James (employee of John HILL), VII, 408
Christie, James (father of GABRIEL), IV, 150
Christie, James (father of ROBERT), VIII, 154
Christie, James (son of GABRIEL), IV, 151
Christie, Jane. See Grant
Christie, Jane. See Turner
Christie, Janet. See McIntosh
Christie, John, XII, 195
Christie, Margaret. See Telfer
Christie, Margaret (Bell), V, 63
Christie, Margaret (Black), X, 69
Christie, Mary. See Sinclair
Christie, Mary Jane. See McMullen
Christie, Monique-Olivier. See Doucet
Christie, Robert, X, 168
Christie, Robert, VI, 40, 241, 401, 750; VII, 135, 374, 461, 462, 613, 618, 879; VIII, **154–56**, 196, 207, 471; IX, 143, 300, 303, 329, 560; X, 418, 627; XII, 65, 495, 570
Christie, Robert Jaffray, XII, 196

Christie, Sarah. *See* Stevenson
Christie, Sarah (Tunstall), IV, 151
Christie, Thomas, VII, 442; VIII, 715; X, 168
Christie, Thomas A., VII, 183
Christie, William, IV, 151; V, 63
Christie, William Joseph, XII, 195
Christie, William Joseph, X, 167; XI, 383, 595, 612, 663;
  XII, **194–95**
Christie, William Mellis, XII, 103, **195–96**
Christie, William Plenderleath, IV, 151; VII, **184–86**, 914;
  IX, 291, 719; X, 163
Christie Burton, Napier, IV, 150, 151; VII, 184, 185, 333,
  395
Christison, Sir Robert, IX, 606, 607
Christmas, Anne (Vaughan), I, 656
Christmas, Benjamin, XI, 723
Christmas, John, I, 656
Christmas, Joseph Stibbs, XII, 322
Christopher, John, V, 626
Christopher, Thomas, VII, 591
Christy Ann. *See* Paul, Mary Christianne
Chrystal, William, VII, 649
Chubb, George James, VIII, 157
Chubb, Henry, V, 613; VI, 408, 409; VII, 289, 899; VIII,
  **156–58**; IX, 391, 399
Chubb, Henry John, VIII, 156
Chubb, Jane. *See* Lugrin
Chubb, John, VIII, 156
Chubb, Mary (mother of HENRY), VIII, 156
Chubb, Pascoe, II, 394
Chubb, Thomas, VIII, 157
Chubbee, William. *See* Tubbee, Okah
Chubbock, Laura (McMicking), IX, 517
Chudleigh, Sir John, I, 669
Church, Adaline (Merrill), XI, 589
Church, Alice. *See* Southworth
Church, Basil Rorison, XII, 197
Church, Benjamin, I, 26, 427, 577; II, **145–46**, 177, 287,
  382, 409, 410, 480, 481, 605, 638; III, 111, 112, 273,
  596
Church, Catherine (Shufelt), VII, 186
Church, Elizabeth. *See* Shufelt
Church, Elizabeth. *See* Warren
Church, Eliza Jane Erskine. *See* Bell
Church, Frederick Edwin, XII, 123
Church, Henry, VII, 186
Church, John, VII, 186
Church, John, VII, **186–87**
Church, Jonathan Mills, XII, 196
Church, Levi Ruggles, XI, 920; XII, 173, **196–97**, 903
Church, Mary Isabella (Moir), XII, 747
Church, Peter Howard, XII, 196
Church, Richard, II, 145
Church, Richard, XII, 196
Church, Sir Richard, X, 59
Church, Sylvia Comstock. *See* Coller
Church, Thomas, II, 146
Church, Tryphena. *See* Huntington
Churchill. *See also* Spencer-Churchill
Churchill, Ann. *See* Davidson
Churchill, Arabella (Godfrey), III, 70
Churchill, Charles, V, 629
Churchill, Chatham Horace, XI, 591

Churchill, Elizabeth. *See* Trefry
Churchill, Ezra, X, 171
Churchill, Ezra A., X, **171–72**, 551
Churchill, George, X, 172
Churchill, John, X, 172
Churchill, John, 1st Duke of Marlborough, I, 493; II, 21,
  265, 286, 287, 351, 513, 659; III, xxvii, 70, 135; IV, 26;
  V, 166, 486; X, 663
Churchill, Louise Anne (Michel), XI, 591
Churchill, Rachel. *See* Burgess
Churchill, Sarah, Duchess of Marlborough. *See* Jennings
Churchward, William, VIII, 949
Churchyard, Thomas, I, 335
Churiau, Catherine, II, 95
Cibber, Colley, V, 689
Cicaterri, Charles, VIII, 243
Cicé. *See* Champion
Cicero, VI, 84
Cicot. *See also* Sicotte
Cicot, Marguerite. *See* Gauthier, *dit* Saint-Germain
Cicot, Toussaint, XI, 821
Cicotte. *See* Chiquot
Cimère, Marie-Josephte (Ecuier), V, 294
Cimon, Cléophe, XI, 690
Cimon, Marie-Claire. *See* Garon
Cimon, Simon, XI, 192
Cimon, Simon-Xavier, XI, **191–92**
Cincinnatus, XII, 935
Cinq-Mars. *See also* Viau
Cinq-Mars, Marquis de. *See* Coiffier de Ruzé
Cinq-Mars, Ernest-E., XII, 99
Cinq-Mars, François, X, 75; XI, 302
Ciquard. *See also* Roussel
Ciquard, François, IV, 5; VI, **145–46**; VII, 678
Cirier, Antoine, IV, **151–52**; V, 392, 393, 497
Cirier, Marguerite. *See* Desroches
Cirier, Marie-Anne. *See* Beaune
Cirier, Marie-Joseph. *See* Lenoir
Cirier, Martin, IV, 151
Citoys de Chaumeaux, François, II, 143
Clachertie, Margaret (Carson), VII, 151
Clairambault, Charles, II, 146
Clairambault, Claude, II, 146
Clairambault, Nicolas, II, 146
Clairambault, Pierre, II, 146
Clairambault d'Aigremont, François, II, xxii, xxiii, 13, 135,
  **146–48**, 354, 355, 415, 475, 484, 505, 547, 559, 569,
  606, 618, 632, 645; III, 74, 220, 499
Clairaut, Alexis, V, 102
Claire. *See* Petit-Claire
Clameron, Marie (Poncin), V, 680
Clan Ay, Chief of. *See* Shaw
Clan Chattan, Chief of. *See* Mackintosh
Clan Macdonald of Glengarry, Chief of. *See* Macdonell
Clan Macdonell of Glengarry, Chief of. *See* Macdonell
Clan Mackintosh, Chief of. *See* Mackintosh
Clan Menzies, Chief of. *See* Menzies
Clan Tavish, Chief of. *See* Mactavish
Clanwilliam, Countess of. *See* Sarney
Claparède, Jacques, III, 123
Claparède, Jean, III, **123**
Claparède, Marie. *See* Guy
Claparède, Marie-Josephe. *See* Seigneur

Claparède, Renée. *See* Grosse
Claparède, Renée, III, 123
Claparet. *See* Claparède
Clapham, John Greaves (father), IX, 690
Clapham, John Greaves, VII, 280, 709
Clapp, Lucy (Creighton), V, 215
Clapp, William W., VI, 321
Clappison, David C., XII, 143
Clare, James Robert, IX, **130–31**
Clare, John K., XI, 80
Clare, Margaret. *See* Sinclair
Clare, Stephen, IX, 130
Clare, William H., X, 450
Clareau. *See* Pratt
Clarence and St Andrews, Duke of. *See* William IV
Clarendon, Earl of. *See* Hyde; Villiers
Claret, Charles-Pierre, Comte de Fleurieu, I, 280
Clarina, Baron. *See* Massey
Clark. *See also* Clarke
Clark, A. M., VIII, 524
Clark, Alexander, XII, **197–98**
Clark*, Andrew Hill (d. 1975), IV, xxiii, xxvi, xxxi, 559; VII, 814
Clark, Ann. *See* Berry
Clark, Benjamin, V, 642, 643, 644
Clark, Betsy. *See* Lamphier
Clark, Caroline (Bain), XII, 47
Clark, Christian (Ross), IX, 691
Clark*, Daniel (1835–1912), XI, 591, 748, 749
Clark, Duncan, V, 24, **187–88**
Clark, Elizabeth. *See* Hare
Clark, Elizabeth (mother of Robert HALE), III, 274
Clark, Elizabeth (wife of ROBERT, d. 1794), IV, 152
Clark, Elizabeth (wife of Robert HALE), III, 274
Clark, Festus, VI, 278
Clark, George, III, **123–24**
Clark, George Rogers, IV, 303, 322, 324, 337, 564; V, 3, 8, 175, 238, 342, 567, 806; VI, 101, 189; VII, 688, 735
Clark, Helen Matilda (Wilmot), XII, 1106
Clark, Henry James, XII, 188, 212, 213
Clark, Isabella (Macdonald), XII, 591, 592
Clark, Isobel. *See* Ketchum
Clark, James, V, 188
Clark, James, IV, 505; V, **188–89**; VI, 147, 609; VII, 36
Clark, Jane. *See* Mortimer
Clark, Jemima. *See* Mason
Clark, John (clergyman), XII, 186
Clark, John (innkeeper), IV, 608
Clark, John (of Aberdeen, Scotland), X, 683
Clark, John (partner of Enos COLLINS), X, 189
Clark, John (partner of Edward MORTIMER), V, 611
Clark, John (politician), V, 188; VII, 497; VIII, 208
Clark, Julius Taylor, IX, 420
Clark, Justina Sophia. *See* Bayer
Clark, Lovell Crosby, XII, 587
Clark, Margaret (Coffin), X, 182
Clark, Mary (mother of ROBERT, d. 1794), IV, 152
Clark, Mary (Bonner), II, 81
Clark, Mary (Brown), IV, 105
Clark, Mary (Clindinning), XII, 200
Clark, Mary (Dundas), X, 264
Clark, Mary Ann (Bagg), X, 31
Clark, Mary Margaret. *See* Kerr

Clark, Peter, V, 188
Clark, Rebecca (Alline), IV, 16
Clark, Robert, IV, 129, **152–53**, 606, 608, 609; V, 407, 873; VI, 107, 130
Clark, Robert, IV, 495; V, 169, 188; VI, **146–47**
Clark, Samuel, VI, 147
Clark, Thomas, V, 403, 405, 549, 672, 673, 674, 841; VI, 4, 5, 22, **147–50**, 153, 212, 229, 286, 375, 462, 475, 531, 539, 543, 629, 630, 631, 632, 633; VII, 38, 250, 251, 312, 314, 315, 470, 555, 833, 834, 835, 920; VIII, 10, 185, 186, 252, 279, 281, 465; IX, 331, 332, 333, 670; X, 668
Clark, William (clergyman), V, 832
Clark, William (explorer), V, 9, 418, 419; VIII, 3, 556, 661, 881; IX, 455
Clark, Wotherton, IV, 152
Clarke. *See also* Clark; Clerke
Clarke, Adam, XI, 785, 786
Clarke, Sir Alured, IV, 43, 130; V, 151, 206, 318, 372, 433, 479, 552, 705, 724; VI, **150–51**, 338, 380, 397, 501, 640, 650, 816
Clarke, Sir Andrew, XII, 430
Clarke, Ann. *See* Hynes
Clarke, Ann. *See* Waldorf
Clarke, Ann (Hicks), IV, 350
Clarke, Anne. *See* Powell
Clarke, Catherine. *See* McKay
Clarke, Charles, VI, 150
Clarke*, Charles (1826–1909), IX, 576; X, 169, 464; XI, 367, 518, 590
Clarke*, Charles Kirk (1857–1924), XI, 591; XII, 1126
Clarke, Cyrus S., XI, 706
Clarke, Edward, VIII, 934
Clarke*, Edward Frederick (1850–1905), XI, 580; XII, 455
Clarke, Elizabeth. *See* Mitton
Clarke, Elizabeth (Binns), VII, 76
Clarke, Elizabeth (Buchanan), IX, 97
Clarke, Elizabeth (Tyng), I, 654; III, 635
Clarke, Emma (Metcalf), XI, 590
Clarke, Francis, XI, 192
Clarke, Helen. *See* Fullerton
Clarke, Henry James, X, 148
Clarke, Henry Joseph, XI, **192–94**, 611, 644, 743, 935; XII, 33, 369, 370
Clarke, Hugh Archibald, X, 173
Clarke, Isaac Winslow, V, 138; VI, 606, 620; VII, 357; IX, 610
Clarke, Isabella Elizabeth (Gamble), X, 299; XI, 332
Clarke, James, X, 44
Clarke, James B., XI, 324
Clarke, James Paton, IX, 600; X, **172–73**; XI, 541, 558
Clarke, Jane. *See* Bell
Clarke, Jane. *See* Mullins
Clarke, Jane (Dorion), X, 236
Clarke, Jane Isabella (Smith), VI, 722
Clarke, Job Bennet, IV, 627
Clarke (Clerke), John (Brownist), I, 390, 391, 392
Clarke, John (trader), IV, 33
Clarke, John, VI, 20, 767; VII, 567, 568, 749, 838, 913; VIII, 85, 112, **158–59**, 175, 538, 546, 557, 721, 813; X, 719, 720
Clarke, John T., XI, 122
Clarke, Josephte. *See* Kanhopitsa

Clarke, Julia Maude (Borden), XII, 114
Clarke, Lawrence, X, 276
Clarke, Lawrence, XI, **194–95**, 571
Clarke, Margaret (Rubidge), X, 635
Clarke, Maria Merrick (Sinclair; wife of HENRY JOSEPH), XI, 193
Clarke, Marianne. *See* Trustler
Clarke, Mary, VIII, 589
Clarke, Peter, I, 407
Clarke, Peter Hall, XI, 29
Clarke, Rebecca (Williams), XI, 930
Clarke, Richard, I, **228–30**, 334, 335, 363, 532
Clarke, Richard Marshall, VIII, 783
Clarke, Richard Samuel (loyalist), V, 25
Clarke, Richard Samuel (sheriff), XII, 560
Clarke, Robert, IX, 599
Clarke, Samuel, V, 837
Clarke, Sarah (Sprott), IX, 738
Clarke, Sarah Ann (Lewin), XII, 560
Clarke, Septimus D., VIII, **159–60**, 969
Clarke, Simon, VIII, 158
Clarke, Sophia Jacobina. *See* Spence
Clarke, Susan (Ogden), IX, 610
Clarke, Thaddeus, I, 654
Clarke, William F., XI, 133
Clarkson, Benjamin Reid, X, 174
Clarkson, Carrie. *See* Brunskill
Clarkson, Edward Roper Curzon, X, 174
Clarkson, Elizabeth. *See* Farnham
Clarkson, Elizabeth (mother of THOMAS), X, 173
Clarkson, John (father of THOMAS), X, 173
Clarkson, John (officer), IV, 111, 604, 627, 628; V, 341, 469; VI, 313, 800; VII, 814
Clarkson, John Brunskill, X, 174
Clarkson, Robert Guy, known as Tommy Dodd, X, 174
Clarkson, Sarah. *See* Helliwell
Clarkson, Thomas, IV, 627
Clarkson, Thomas, IX, 657; X, **173–74**; XI, 553
Clarry, Lewis Frederick, XI, 804
Clatsoppe, Marguerite. *See* Kil-a-ko-tah
Claude. *See also* Glode
Claude, Appoline (Fafard), XI, 306
Claude, Joseph, IV, **153–54**, 180; VII, 204
Claudius Clavus. *See* Swart
Claus, Adam Frederic, IV, 154
Claus, Ann. *See* Johnson
Claus, Anna Dorothea (mother of CHRISTIAN DANIEL), IV, 154
Claus, Catherine. *See* Jordan
Claus, Christian Daniel, III, 409, 452; IV, 59, 105, 117, 118, 119, 120, 130, 139, 149, **154–55**, 368, 393, 394, 396, 397, 416, 417, 586, 587, 613, 692, 753; V, 147, 229, 254, 256, 260, 272, 600, 804, 843, 895; VI, 151, 353
Claus, John, VI, 761
Claus, William, IV, 155; V, 256, 365, 467, 536, 673, 724, 749, 797, 810, 842; VI, 4, 102, 103, **151–53**, 331, 340, 550, 551, 552, 703, 761; VII, 57, 466, 496, 848, 849; VIII, 161, 252, 620; IX, 334
Clausewitz, Karl von, IX, 772
Clausonne. *See* Chabert
Claver, Peter, XII, 250
Claverie, Jean, III, 124

Claverie, Jeanne. *See* La Barthe
Claverie, Marie-Anne. *See* Dupéré
Claverie, Pierre, III, **124–25**, 141, 142; IV, 66, 125, 264, 755
Clavering, Caroline (Warren, Lady Warren), VI, 802
Clavering, Sir John, VII, 428
Clay, Henry, IX, 415
Clay*, Henry Clay (1843–1938), XII, 708
Clay, John, X, 103
Claye, Cécile (Michaux), V, 592
Clayton, George, VII, 50
Clayton, Harriet Middleton (Douglas; Peterson), VIII, 700
Clayton, John Middleton, VIII, 700
Cleak, James, XII, 322
Cleary, Andrew V., VII, 403, 404
Cleary, James Vincent, XI, 536; XII, **198–200**, 332, 333, 1087
Cleary, Margaret. *See* O'Brien
Cleary, Thomas, XII, 198
Cleaskina, IV, 325
Cleaveland. *See also* Cleveland
Cleaveland, William H., VI, 334
Cleever, Elizabeth (Burr), IX, 109
Cleeves, William, III, 618, 619
Cleff, Monsieur (painter), VII, 697
Cleghorn, Suzan (Douglas), IX, 218
Cleghorn, William, XII, 152
Cleland, James, XI, 804
Cleland, John, IV, 631
Clemens, Samuel Langhorne (Mark Twain), X, 44, 223
Clément. *See also* Proulx
Clement X, III, 11, 546
Clement XI, II, 332
Clement XII, IV, 220
Clement XIII, IV, 99, 543; V, 173
Clement XIV, IV, 510; VII, 889
Clément, Catherine (La Croix), III, 334
Clément, Charlotte (Séguin), VII, 781
Clement, Elizabeth Ann. *See* Bancroft
Clément (Vincent), Jacquette (Jeanneau), III, 313
Clément, Joséphine-Éléonore. *See* Estimauville
Clément, Léon-Charles, XII, 297
Clément, Marguerite (Plamondon), XII, 853
Clément, Marie (Vézina), III, 648
Clement, Phoebe Sawyer (Flint), XII, 321
Clément Du Vuault de Monceaux, Anne. *See* Gasnier
Clément Du Vuault de Monceaux, Claire-Françoise (Ruette d'Auteuil), I, 585; II, 585
Clément Du Vuault de Monceaux, Jean, I, 113, 585
Clément Du Vuault de Valrennes, Jeanne. *See* Bissot
Clément Du Vuault de Valrennes, Philippe, II, 13, 103, **148–49**, 168, 269, 386, 603
Clements, Eleanor (Parr), IV, 603
Clements, Elizabeth (Conyngham (Burton), Baroness Conyngham), VI, 97
Clemo, Ebenezer, VIII, **160–61**; XII, 570
Clench, Mrs (wife of F. S.), X, 390
Clench, Caroline, VIII, 162
Clench, Elizabeth. *See* Johnson
Clench, Esther Serena Joseph. *See* Leon
Clench, F. S., X, 389
Clench, Hannah. *See* Vernon

161

Clench, Harriet (Kane), X, 393
Clench, Holcroft, VIII, 163
Clench, Joseph Brant, VI, 154, 400; VII, 127; VIII, **161–63**, 620
Clench, Leon Moses, VIII, 163
Clench, Ralfe, V, 279, 405, 520, 549, 782, 842, 845, 856; VI, **153–54**, 746; VII, 251; VIII, 161
Clench, Robert, VI, 153
Clench, Victorine Leon (Cornish), VIII, 162; X, 198
Clendinning, Mary. *See* Fife
Clendinning, Robert W., XII, 200
Clensmith, Peter. *See* Peter, John
Clérel de Tocqueville, Charles-Alexis-Henri, VII, 582, 714; VIII, 921; X, 573
Clérin. *See* Estienne; Desvoges
Clerk. *See also* Clerke
Clerk, Sir George, X, 174, 175
Clerk, George Edward, X, **174–76**; XI, 170
Clerk, Harriet Bousfield. *See* Molson
Clerk, Jean-Pio-Robert, X, 176
Clerk, Marie. *See* Law
Clerk, Marie-Louise-Élisabeth. *See* Dupuis
Clerk, William, I, 386
Clerke, Charles, IV, 73, **155–56**, 165, 412
Clermont, Comte de. *See* Orléans
Cléron d'Haussonville, Joseph-Louis-Bernard de, Comte d'Haussonville, IV, 31, 32
Cleveland, V, 258
Cleveland, Duchess of. *See* Villiers
Cleveland, Aaron, III, 125
Cleveland, Aaron, III, **125–26**; IV, 527
Cleveland, Abigail. *See* Waters
Cleveland, Chester B., X, 642
Cleveland, Sarah. *See* Rudduck
Cleveland, Stephen Grover, III, 126; XII, 1030
Cleveland, Susannah. *See* Porter
Cleveland, William, IX, 176, 177
Clevett (Cleverley), Ann, IV, 701
Cliff, Millie (Kribs), XII, 499
Clignancour. *See* Damours
Clinch. *See also* Clench
Clinch, Hannah. *See* Hart
Clinch, John, V, 190
Clinch, John, V, **189–90**, 785; VI, 77, 274, 393; VIII, 483; X, 110
Clinch, Joseph Hart, V, 190
Clinch, Mary Elizabeth (Bullock), V, 190; X, 110
Clinch, Thomas, V, 189
Clindinning, David, XII, 200
Clindinning, Jane. *See* McLean
Clindinning, Mary. *See* Clark
Clindinning, Robert Wilson, XII, **200**
Cline. *See also* Clyne
Cline, F. C., IX, 279
Cline, Margaret (Morris), XI, 608
Clingersmith (Clinglesmith). *See also* Klingensmith
Clingersmith, Eliza, VIII, 477
Clingersmith, John, VIII, 477
Clinglesmith, Philip, VIII, 476
Clinton, Anne. *See* Carle
Clinton, DeWitt, VIII, 516, 517
Clinton, Francis Fiennes, 6th Earl of Lincoln, III, 126
Clinton, George, V, 896

Clinton, George, II, 251; III, 49, 101, **126–27**, 324, 327, 365, 588, 623; IV, 173, 595
Clinton, Sir Henry, III, 127; IV, 3, 504, 682; V, 34, 148, 222, 604, 629, 730, 831, 866, 890, 891, 893, 896; VI, 299
Clinton, Henry Pelham Fiennes Pelham, 5th Duke of Newcastle-under-Lyme, IX, 30, 183, 238, 383, 385, 409, 591, 712, 715, 716; X, 116, 117, 121, 122, 128, 146, 246, 264, 265, 289, 465, 588, 595, 596, 630, 666; XI, 43, 44, 432, 548, 606, 607, 634, 686, 829, 949, 950; XII, 406, 809, 815, 1054, 1084
Clinton, James, IV, 121; V, 895
Clinton, Lucy Mary (Roddam), III, 127
Clinton, Susan. *See* Penniston
Clitherow, Anne. *See* Jodrell
Clitherow, Christopher, VIII, 163
Clitherow, Sir Christopher, VIII, 163
Clitherow, James, VIII, 164
Clitherow, John, VII, 149, 264, 514; VIII, 24, **163–64**, 539
Clitherow, John Christie, VIII, 164
Clitherow, Millicent. *See* Pole
Clitherow, Sarah. *See* Burton
Clive, Robert, 1st Baron Clive, III, 659; IV, 114; V, 166
Clober. *See* Dunlop; McGregor
Clocher, Marie-Joseph (Roupe), VIII, 776
Clodoré (Closdoré), Jean de, I, 443
Cloncurry, Baron. *See* Lawless
Clopper, Garret, VII, 187
Clopper, Henry George, VI, 810; VII, **187–88**; VIII, 805, 842; X, 314
Clopper, Lucy Anne (Simonds), VIII, 805
Clopper, Mary Ann. *See* Ketchum
Clopper, Penelope. *See* Miller
Cloran, Henry Joseph, XII, 276
Closdoré. *See* Clodoré
Closse, Cécile. *See* Delafosse
Closse, Élisabeth. *See* Moyen Des Granges
Closse, Élisabeth, I, 231, 266
Closse, Jean, I, 230
Closse, Jeanne-Cécile (Bizard; Blaise Des Bergères de Rigauville), I, 103, 231; II, 70
Closse, Raphaël-Lambert, I, 103, 219, **230–32**, 266, 271, 274, 297, 463; II, 70, 105; III, 580
Closson, Joseph, II, 285
Cloud, Daniel, V, 557, 558
Clouet, Madame (house owner), VIII, 962
Clouet, Joseph-Marie, VII, 188
Clouet, Josephte (Huot), VII, 430
Clouet, Josephte (Parent), X, 576
Clouet, Louise (Simard), X, 654
Clouet, Marie-Joseph. *See* Bergevin
Clouet, Marie-Josephte. *See* Lalime
Clouet, Michel, VI, 337, 546; VII, **188–89**, 430; X, 580, 654
Clough, Sarah (Wells), XI, 914
Clouston, Anne Rose (Pelly), VIII, 574
Clouston, Isabella (Bunn), X, 111
Clouston, James, VI, 15; X, 284
Clouston, Robert, VIII, 574; XI, 775
Cloutier, Anne (Drouin), I, 232, 281, 330
Cloutier, Gabriel, XII, 554
Cloutier, Louise (Marguerie; Mignot, *dit* Chatillon; Mataut), I, 490

Cloutier, Madeleine. *See* Esmard
Cloutier, Marie-Euphrosine (Blanchet), VIII, 96
Cloutier, Marie-Françoise (Létourneau), VII, 502
Cloutier, Xainte. *See* Dupont
Cloutier, Zacharie, I, 473
Cloutier, Zacharie, I, **232**, 330, 359, 490; II, 158, 205
Cloux, Isaac, IX, 608
Clow, Alice (Alison) (Todd), IX, 791
Clowes, George, V, 760
Clowes, Samuel, VI, 481; VII, 453; VIII, 785
Clut*, Isidore (1832–1903), X, 275, 614; XI, 311
Cluzel, Jeanne de (Biard), I, 94
Clyde, Baron. *See* Campbell
Clyne (Cline, Klein), Margaret (Rousseaux St John), V, 724
Cnoyen, James, I, 678
Coade, Anne Catherine (Gossip), XI, 364
Coade, John Charles, VIII, 193; XI, 365
Coady, Richard Theodore, XII, 410
Coape. *See* Sherbrooke
Coape (Sherbrooke), Sarah. *See* Sherbrooke
Coate, Samuel, VII, 557
Coates, Dorothy. *See* Reynolds
Coates, Isabella. *See* Smith
Coates, John, IV, 524
Coates, Richard, IX, 131
Coates, Richard, IX, **131–32**, 842
Coates, Susanna (Dixon), V, 257
Coats, Mary. *See* McCliesh
Coats, William, III, 123, **127–28**, 407, 415, 449, 454, 489
Coatsworth, Emerson, XII, 992
Coban, Phoebe (Burpee), XI, 133
Cobb, Elisha, III, 128
Cobb, Elizabeth. *See* Rider
Cobb, Elizabeth (Eddy), V, 295
Cobb, Elizabeth (Forbes), IX, 268
Cobb, Jabez, III, 129
Cobb, Lydia. *See* Rider
Cobb, Robina (Bryson), XII, 134
Cobb, Silvanus, III, **128–30**, 572; IV, 193, 219
Cobbett, Ann. *See* Vincent
Cobbett, Anne. *See* Reid
Cobbett, George, VI, 154
Cobbett, William, VI, **154–56**; IX, 330
Cobbeyall. *See* Glode, Gabriel
Cobbie, Diana (Hall), I, 233
Cobbie, Eliza (mother of WALSALL), I, 233
Cobbie, Walsall, I, **232–33**
Cobbold, Mary (Dodd), VIII, 226
Cobden, Richard, XI, 843
Cobreth, William, I, 667
Coccola, Nicolas, XII, 283
Cochin. *See also* Cocking
Cochin, Jane. *See* Carlton
Cochin, Louis, XI, 697
Cochin, Richard, IV, 156
Cochon, Antoinette (Bertier), II, 60
Cochon, Jean, XI, 159
Cochon, Jehan, XI, 159
Cochran, Andrew William, V, 697; VI, 158, 645; VII, **189–92**, 726, 727, 728, 729, 731, 733, 740, 768, 769, 786, 879; VIII, 36, 155; IX, 250; X, 178

Cochran, Anna Mathilda. *See* Power
Cochran, Arthur McNutt, XI, 620
Cochran, Catherine. *See* Walsh
Cochran (Cochrane), Elizabeth (Inglis), VII, 432
Cochran, Elizabeth (Morris), VIII, 639; XI, 609
Cochran, Emily (Northup), X, 551
Cochran, Houstoun. *See* Thomson
Cochran, James, V, 494
Cochran, James, X, **176–77**
Cochran, James Cuppaidge, VI, 158; VII, 932; IX, 574; X, **177–78**; XI, 75
Cochran, Magdalen. *See* Kerr
Cochran, Mary (Wright), V, 872
Cochran, Rebecca. *See* Cuppaidge
Cochran, Thomas, V, 389, 494; VI, 319
Cochran, William, V, 494; VI, 319
Cochran, William, V, 124, 872; VI, **156–58**, 242, 333, 731; VII, 88, 189, 530, 723; VIII, 155, 459, 573, 811; IX, 637, 638; X, 177
Cochrane, Miss (McKeand), XI, 562
Cochrane, Sir Alexander Forrester Inglis, V, 314; VI, 782, 803; VIII, 506; X, 178
Cochrane, Andrew, VI, 156
Cochrane, David, VII, 192
Cochrane, Sir Edward O., VIII, 672
Cochrane, Elizabeth. *See* Paton
Cochrane, Elizabeth Jane. *See* Budd
Cochrane, Henry, XII, **200–1**
Cochrane, Hugh, XII, 93
Cochrane, James (father), VII, 192
Cochrane, James, VII, 192
Cochrane, Jane (Bryson), XII, 134
Cochrane, Jennette Elizabeth. *See* Balmer
Cochrane, John, IV, 185; V, 284, 863; VI, 511, 606
Cochrane, John, VII, **192–93**, 706
Cochrane, John Bray, XII, 430
Cochrane, John James, IX, **132**
Cochrane, Mrs Leonie Fanny, XII, 92
Cochrane, Margaret (Bowles), XI, 107
Cochrane, Maria. *See* Shaw
Cochrane, Mary. *See* Gowler
Cochrane, Mary. *See* McMillan
Cochrane, Mary, X, 180
Cochrane, Mary Neilson. *See* Houston
Cochrane, Mathilda. *See* Ross
Cochrane*, Matthew Henry (1823–1903), XII, 167
Cochrane, Susannah, Countess of Dundonald. *See* Hamilton
Cochrane, Thomas (judge), V, 220
Cochrane, Thomas (son of William COCKRAN), IX, 134, 136; XI, 20
Cochrane, Thomas, 10th Earl of Dundonald, VI, 445; IX, 310, 312
Cochrane, Thomas B. H., XII, 991
Cochrane, Sir Thomas John, VI, 692, 693; VII, 104, 153, 154, 293, 294, 421, 507, 628, 630, 631; VIII, 103, 171, 467; IX, 70, 167, 168, 436, 721, 794; X, **178–80**, 433, 553, 600, 601, 687; XI, 28, 66, 355, 760
Cochrane, William, XII, 201
Cochrane, William, XII, **201–3**, 617, 1091
Cochy, *dit* Lacouture, Louise (Bardy), IX, 32
Cock, Daniel, V, 344; VI, 294, 457, 458, 461
Cock, Elizabeth (Davie), VII, 233

Cock, Frances (Copp), XII, 212
Cockan. *See* Cocking
Cockburn, Alicia, Lady Cockburn. *See* Sandys
Cockburn, Augusta Anne, Lady Cockburn. *See* Ayscough
Cockburn, Elizabeth (Procter), VI, 616
Cockburn, Elizabeth Johanna. *See* Vansittart
Cockburn, Sir Francis, V, 72; VII, 852; VIII, 856; IX, **132–34**
Cockburn, Sir George, VI, 38; VII, 51; IX, 278, 658; X, 701
Cockburn*, George Ralph Richardson (1834–1912), XII, 993
Cockburn, Isabella (Baptist), X, 34
Cockburn, Isabella Susan. *See* Patterson
Cockburn, James (father of JAMES), XI, 195
Cockburn, James (surgeon), IX, 572
Cockburn, Sir James (brother of Sir FRANCIS), VIII, 922
Cockburn, Sir James (father of Sir FRANCIS), IX, 132
Cockburn, Sir James (grandfather of JAMES PATTISON), VII, 193
Cockburn, James, X, 123; XI, **195–97**, 768, 838
Cockburn, James Pattison, III, 305; V, 228; VII, **193–96**, 316, 402; VIII, 64, 124; XI, 137
Cockburn, John, VII, 193
Cockburn, Mary (Cockburn), VII, 193
Cockburn, Sarah. *See* Turnbull
Cockeye. *See* Questach
Cocking, Mary. *See* Mith-coo-coo-man E'Squaw
Cocking, Matthew, IV, 47, **156–58**, 277, 341, 384, 647, 760; V, 129, 363, 450, 682; VI, 317, 775; VII, 206
Cockran, Ann (wife of WILLIAM), IX, 134
Cockran, William, VII, 454, 455, 902; VIII, xxx, 721, 767; IX, **134–37**, 732, 733, 784; X, 108; XI, 19, 20, 208, 209, 712
Cockrell, Mary. *See* Stewart
Cockrell, Richard, V, 846; VI, **158–60**, 230, 247, 747, 760; VIII, 887, 945; IX, 544
Cockshutt*, Ignatius (1812–1901), XII, 968, 1090, 1091
Cockshutt, James G., XII, 1091
Cocoran, Margaret. *See* Flood
Cocoran (Corcoran), Timothy, X, 176
Cocreaumont. *See* Dubois
Codd, Alfred, XII, 204
Codd, Alfred Arthur, XII, 204
Codd, Charles Edward, XII, 203
Codd, Donald, XII, **203–4**
Codd, Sarah (wife of DONALD), XII, 204
Codde, Pierre, II, 279
Coderre. *See also* Emery-Coderre
Coderre, Marc, XI, 302
Coderre, Marie-Angélique. *See* Desgranges
Coderre, Marie-Desanges (Casavant), X, 152
Codman, Richard, IV, 273
Codman, Stephen, VII, 573
Codner, Daniel, V, 119; VIII, 164
Codner, Joan (mother of SAMUEL), VIII, 164
Codner, John, IV, 159
Codner, Samuel, VI, 692; VII, 914; VIII, **164–67**
Codner, Selina Cave. *See* Browne
Codner, Susan Grace (Wilson), X, 716
Codrington, Christopher, II, 659
Cody*, Henry John (1868–1951), XI, 869
Cody*, Hiram Alfred (1872–1948), XII, 376

Cody, William Frederick (Buffalo Bill), XII, 788
Coëtnempren de Kersaint, Guy-François de, III, 356
Coeuret, Claude-Audet, IV, 645
Coffin, Adeline (Coffin), XI, 197
Coffin, Ann. *See* Mathews
Coffin, Ann (mother of JOHN), V, 190
Coffin, Ann (Callbeck), IV, 128; V, 220, 515
Coffin, Elizabeth. *See* Barnes
Coffin, Elizabeth Browne. *See* Greenly
Coffin, Sir Isaac, V, 13, 281; VI, 348; VII, **196–97**, 198; VIII, 675; IX, 39
Coffin, Isabella. *See* Child
Coffin, James (brother of THOMAS, 1817–90), XI, 197
Coffin, James (son of JOHN, 1729–1808), V, 191
Coffin, John (son of JOHN, 1729–1808), V, 191
Coffin, John, IV, 548; V, 31, 182, **190–92**, 214, 370, 509; VII, 198, 199, 200; VIII, 793; X, 180
Coffin, John, IV, 301, 328; V, 137, 354, 504, 505; VI, 14, 139; VII, **197–99**; VIII, 741; IX, 610, 619
Coffin, Louisa, V, 192
Coffin, Margaret. *See* Clark
Coffin, Margaret. *See* Homer
Coffin, Margaret (Sheaffe, Lady Sheaffe), V, 191; VIII, 793
Coffin, Marguerite. *See* Godefroy de Tonnancour
Coffin, Marie-Louise, V, 192
Coffin, Mary (mother of THOMAS ASTON), V, 192
Coffin, Mary Aston Augusta (Ogden), IX, 610
Coffin, Nathaniel, VII, 196, 198
Coffin, Nathaniel, V, 191; VI, 338, 574; VII, 58, **199–200**, 314, 316; VIII, 119; X, 557
Coffin, Sarah. *See* Doane
Coffin, Sarah, V, 192
Coffin, Susannah (Grant; Craigie), V, 191, 214
Coffin, Thomas (father of THOMAS, 1817–90), XI, 197
Coffin, Thomas (son of WILLIAM FOSTER), X, 182
Coffin, Thomas, V, 191, 214, 291, 372, 603; VI, 23, 289, 588, 717; VII, 65, 199, **200–2**, 387; VIII, 366; X, 181
Coffin, Thomas, XI, **197–98**, 710; XII, 651
Coffin, Thomas Aston, V, **192–93**, 486, 508, 705, 844; VII, 372, 638
Coffin, William (father of JOHN, 1729–1808), V, 190
Coffin, William (father of THOMAS ASTON), V, 192
Coffin, William (son of JOHN, 1729–1808), V, 191
Coffin, William Craigie Holmes, VII, 201
Coffin, William Foster, V, 191; VII, 545; VIII, 393, 938; IX, 61, 406; X, **180–82**, 529
Coffre, Monsieur (soldier), III, 139, 140
Coggeshall, William Turner, XII, 1076
Coghill, Sophia Cramer (Doyle, Lady Doyle), XI, 278
Coghlan, James, IX, 719
Coghlan, Jeremiah, III, 411, 412; IV, **158–60**, 712, 713, 714; V, 166, 491, 783
Coghlan, Joanna (wife of JEREMIAH), IV, 158
Cognac. *See* Boisseau
Cogolin (Cogollin). *See* Chabert
Cogswell, Abigail (Dayton; Stone), VI, 738, 739
Cogswell, Ann (Morton), XII, 764
Cogswell, Charles, XII, 407
Cogswell, Henry Hezekiah, VI, 800; VII, 492, 867; VIII, **167–69**, 460, 724; IX, 175, 176; X, 182, 189; XI, 74, 847; XII, 436, 764
Cogswell, Isabella. *See* Ellis

Cogswell, Isabella Binney, VIII, 169; X, **182**
Cogswell, James, XI, 944
Cogswell, James Colquhoun, VIII, 169, 656
Cogswell, Leander, XII, 764
Cogswell, Lydia. *See* Huntington
Cogswell, Mary Arabella (Allison; Botsford), XII, 115
Cogswell, Mason, VIII, 167
Cogswell, Sophia Araminta (Chipman), IX, 129
Cogswell, William, VII, 435; X, 182
Cohen, Abraham Haim, V, 194
Cohen, Jacob Raphael, IV, 719; V, **193–94**; VI, 179; VII, 328; VIII, 366
Cohen, Rebecca. *See* Luria
Coiffier de Ruzé, Henri, Marquis de Cinq-Mars, II, 656
Coigne. *See* Couagne; Decoigne
Coigny, Duc de. *See* Franquetot
Coindat, Marguerite (La Colombière), II, 326
Coke, Lady Anne Amelia, Countess of Leicester. *See* Keppel
Coke, D'Ewes, V, 492, 725, 726; VI, 636, 637, 784
Coke, Edward Thomas, IX, 850
Coke, Thomas, V, 573; VI, 64, 65, 66, 275; VII, 587; VIII, 371
Colbert, Charles, Marquis de Croissy, I, 513
Colbert, Jean-Baptiste, I, 25, 33, 34, 49, 63, 74, 115, 116, 120, 127, 135, 136, 137, 185, 227, 283, 284, 285, 287, 315, 326, 327, 396, 410, 418, 442, 443, 499, 534, 541, 555, 556, 565, 571, 581, 587, 589, 600, 615, 616, 617, 618, 619, 620, 621, 622, 623, 624, 627, 628, 629, 630, 648; II, xviii, 28, 59, 76, 80, 85, 86, 100, 115, 184, 262, 295, 350, 366, 368, 369, 400, 470, 538, 585, 586, 628; III, xvii, 57, 701, 702; IV, 354, 355
Colbert, Jean-Baptiste, Marquis de Seignelay, I, 56, 119, 138, 179, 181, 250, 289, 290, 443, 446, 448, 526, 537, 586; II, 57, 63, 86, 99, 104, 124, 147, 184, 197, 253, 261, 262, 263, 344, 371, 401, 442, 470, 471, 472, 473, 533, 539, 577, 583
Colbert, Marie. *See* Charron
Colbert de Terron, Charles, I, 62, 418, 419, 443, 534, 621, 627
Colborne, Cordelia Anne. *See* Garstin
Colborne, Elizabeth, Baroness Seaton. *See* Yonge
Colborne, James, IX, 138
Colborne, John, 1st Baron Seaton, VI, 12, 91, 165, 407, 425, 426, 467, 522, 628, 633, 742, 761, 773; VII, 8, 9, 11, 33, 62, 91, 100, 116, 143, 149, 150, 173, 176, 180, 183, 214, 222, 227, 259, 260, 264, 315, 319, 334, 346, 351, 354, 361, 369, 370, 372, 411, 412, 439, 440, 445, 459, 478, 497, 513, 514, 548, 549, 585, 635, 640, 660, 661, 662, 664, 703, 755, 756, 822, 846, 856, 860, 861, 880, 907, 917; VIII, xxiv, xxxiv, 7, 8, 27, 28, 29, 47, 109, 113, 117, 120, 162, 163, 164, 253, 274, 276, 288, 303, 332, 365, 418, 419, 431, 437, 464, 465, 514, 518, 519, 539, 586, 602, 603, 604, 615, 619, 622, 640, 678, 696, 727, 729, 730, 778, 845, 896, 926, 932, 933; IX, 24, 69, 72, 75, 99, 127, **137–44**, 190, 201, 240, 265, 266, 269, 315, 320, 328, 345, 377, 378, 386, 434, 448, 498, 499, 500, 502, 520, 522, 523, 534, 535, 540, 554, 589, 610, 674, 682, 683, 685, 741, 759, 760, 790, 814, 826, 827, 848, 857; X, 12, 61, 130, 181, 206, 233, 260, 269, 307, 310, 342, 343, 344, 521, 531, 546, 582, 606, 634, 636, 655, 693; XI, 84, 234, 387, 388, 427, 653, 713, 786; XII, 88, 89, 680, 681, 762

Colborne, Samuel, IX, 137
Colburn, Henry, VII, 91, 338; VIII, 744
Colby, Charles Carroll, IX, 145; XII, 610
Colby*, Charles William (1867–1955), XII, 826
Colby, Lemira. *See* Strong
Colby, Moses French, VIII, 147; IX, **144–45**
Colby, Ruth. *See* French
Colby, Samuel, IX, 144
Colclough, Adam, VI, 160
Colclough, Cæsar, V, 220, 335, 474, 678, 776, 861; VI, 109, **160–64**, 196, 298, 414, 566, 567, 614, 662, 663, 785; VII, 301; VIII, 429, 741, 824
Colclough, Mary Anne. *See* Byrne
Colclough, Susan. *See* Leech
Colcord, Harry, XII, 387
Colden, Cadwallader, II, 619, 622, 623; III, 126; IV, 427; V, 506, 646; VI, 375, 552; VII, 450
Colden, Elizabeth (De Lancey), V, 239
Coldwell, Jemima. *See* Ross
Coldwell*, William (1834–1907), VIII, 768; X, 210, 629; XII, 950
Cole, Ann (Baker), VIII, 43
Cole, Sir Henry, VII, 117
Cole, Jane (Albro), VII, 12
Cole, John, IV, **160**, 366; V, 363, 656, 682
Cole, John Ambler, X, 332
Cole, Samuel, VI, 244
Cole, Susanna (Bradford), V, 106
Cole, Timothy, XII, 288
Colebrook, Colin C., XII, 498, 499
Colebrooke, Mrs. *See* Grant
Colebrooke, Emma Sophia (Colebrooke, Lady Colebrooke), IX, 145
Colebrooke, Frances Elizabeth (Reade), IX, 146
Colebrooke, Paulet Welbore, IX, 145
Colebrooke, Sir William MacBean George, VII, 445, 659, 692, 899; VIII, xxiv, 65, 151, 152, 153, 173, 293, 378, 803, 809, 841, 842; IX, 23, **145–48**, 309, 340, 341, 381, 439, 452, 619, 622, 623, 628, 629, 665, 766, 767; X, 158, 271, 341, 644, 711; XI, 799; XII, 17, 714, 896
Coleman, Anne (Young), X, 721
Coleman*, Arthur Philemon (1852–1939), VII, 760
Coleman, James (missionary), VIII, 309
Coleman, James (partner of Henry Franklin BRONSON), XI, 113
Coleman, John, II, 288
Coleman, Kathleen. *See* Blake
Coleman, Louisa (Diamond), X, 230
Coleman, Lucius, XII, 10
Coleman, Maggie (Motton), XII, 765
Coleman, Seth, V, 608
Coleman, Sophia (Blackadar), IX, 54
Coleman, Thomas, V, 551
Coleman, William J., X, 176
Colen, Joseph, IV, 726, 727; V, **194–95**, 451; VI, 767, 776; VIII, 411, 413, 878, 879
Colen, Thomas, VIII, 411
Colenso, John William, X, 208
Coleridge, Hartley, VIII, 426
Coleridge, Sir John Taylor, XII, 713
Coleridge, Samuel Taylor, I, 385; V, 167; VIII, 426; IX, 89; XII, 460, 516
Coles, Edward, II, 265

Coles, George, VII, 145, 146; VIII, 198, 539, 564, 566; IX, 28, 158, 183, 191, 192, 375, 395, 401, 403, 830, 831, 832, 833, 857; X, **182–88**, 264, 265, 352, 397, 419, 594, 598, 612, 670; XI, 369, 370, 528, 532, 567, 665, 666, 669, 700, 704, 922, 940; XII, 40, 319, 415, 416, 418, 425, 426, 512, 638, 639, 837, 857

Coles, James, X, 182

Coles, Mercy. *See* Haine

Coles, Sarah. *See* Tally

Coligny, Gaspard I de, known as Maréchal de Châtillon, II, 98

Coligny, Gaspard II de, known as Amiral de Coligny, I, 27

Colin, Françoise (Gaultier), III, 675

Colin, Michel, I, **233**, 265

Coll. *See* Maclean

Collachie. *See* Macdonell; McDonell

Collard, Frederick John Martin, VII, **202–3**

Collas, Marguerite-Angélique (Olabaratz), V, 638

Colledge, Lucy (Pope), X, 593; XI, 699; XII, 855

Collégien. *See* Saillant

Coller, Sylvia Comstock (Church), XII, 196

Collet. *See also* Callet

Collet, Anne (Raisin), I, 564

Collet, Antoinette. *See* Thomé

Collet, Benoît, II, 149

Collet, Charles-Ange, III, 94, 553; IV, 430; V, **195–96**; VI, 588

Collet, Claude, V, 195

Collet, Élisabeth. *See* Denys de Saint-Simon

Collet, Hippolyte, III, 94

Collet, Marguerite. *See* Fauché

Collet, Marie (Lemaitre, *dit* Jugon; Frémont), III, 377

Collet, Mathieu, II, 151

Collet, Mathieu-Benoît, II, xxv, **149–52**, 449, 523; III, 74, 83, 299, 352, 576, 646, 647

Colletet, Guillaume, I, 469

Colleton, Sir Peter, I, 519

Colley, Mary (Fisher), X, 290

Collier, Christiana, Lady Collier. *See* Gwyn

Collier, Cordelia (Murray), IV, 569

Collier, Elizabeth, Lady Collier. *See* Fryer

Collier, Elizabeth (Southworth), II, 145

Collier, George, IV, 160

Collier, Sir George, IV, **160–61**, 504, 693; V, 16, 296; VII, 413

Collier, John, III, **130–31**, 363; IV, 53, 527, 562, 724

Collier, Julia Maria (Jones), VIII, 437

Collier Pendu, Le. *See* Kaghswaghtaniunt

Collins, Ann. *See* Moore

Collins, Benajah, VII, 681

Collins, Bill, VIII, 919

Collins, Catharine (Ramage), V, 705

Collins, Charles W., V, 590

Collins, Charlotte Amelia (Eaton), XII, 287

Collins, Edith. *See* Baynes

Collins, Edward, II, 152

Collins, Eleanor. *See* O'Reiley

Collins, Enos, VI, 37, 38; VII, 83, 84, 533, 867; VIII, 62, 167, 168, 169, 183, 710; IX, 52, 175, 176, 710; X, **188–90**; XI, 847

Collins, Francis, VI, **164–66**, 248, 265, 266, 609, 742, 773, 802; VII, 39, 318, 369, 379, 409, 418, 548, 662, 664,

795; VIII, 69, 124, 125, 602, 608, 642, 846, 946; IX, 69, 139, 497, 498, 509, 673, 674, 683, 724; X, 705; XII, 436, 480

Collins, Gertrude Anna. *See* Murphy

Collins, Hallet, IV, 259; IX, 710; X, 188

Collins, Isabella. *See* Hughes

Collins, James Patrick, VII, **203–4**, 891

Collins, John (brother of FRANCIS), VI, 165

Collins, John (playwright), V, 689

Collins, John (prisoner), VII, 360

Collins, John, II, **152–53**, 163, 164, 534, 619

Collins, John, IV, 12, 153, 154, **161–62**, 447, 574, 613; V, 146, 149, 426, 428, 519, 552, 892; VI, 147, 484, 615; VII, 175, 450, 866

Collins, Joseph Edmund, XII, **204–6**, 515, 923

Collins, Margaret. *See* Halliburton

Collins, Margaret (wife of JOHN, d. 1795), IV, 162

Collins, Martha (Cronyn), X, 206

Collins, Margaretta Rhoda (Hill), XII, 435

Collins, Mary. *See* Quin

Collins, Mary (Rankin), IV, 162

Collins, Patrick (father of JAMES PATRICK), VII, 203

Collins, Patrick (Oblate), XII, 283

Collins, Philip Edward, XI, 54, 55

Collins, Phoebe (Seely), IX, 710

Collins, Rhoda. *See* Peek

Collins, Richard, VII, 873; VIII, 689

Collins, Sarah (Barss), VIII, 62

Collins, Sophia Augusta. *See* Pernette

Collins, William Joseph, XII, 204

Collins, William Wilkie, X, 269; XII, 572, 922

Collinson, John, XI, 198

Collinson, Sir Richard, VIII, 101; X, 396, 405, 454; XI, **198–201**; XII, 38

Collinson, Thomas Bernard, XI, 201

Collison, William Henry, XII, 441

Collnett, James (father), V, 197

Collnett, James, V, 197, 387

Collnett, Sarah (wife of James, father), V, 197

Collver. *See also* Culver

Collver, Anna (wife of JABEZ), V, 196

Collver, Freelove. *See* Lamb

Collver, Jabez, V, **196–97**; VI, 729; IX, 232

Collver, John, V, 196

Collyer, Elizabeth Mary. *See* Barker

Collyer, Joanne (Hughes, Lady Hughes), V, 434

Colnett, Elizabeth Caroline, V, 198

Colnett, James, IV, 218, 244, 245, 411, 520, 568, 767; V, **197–99**, 387, 571, 586; VI, 36, 234; VII, 599

Coloma, Carlos, I, 187

Colombet, Antoinette de (Rigaud de Vaudreuil), II, 566, 571

Colombier. *See also* Pouteret

Colombier, Marie (Boisseau), I, 104

Colonel Louis. *See* Atiatoharongwen

Colquhoun, Agnes (Trent; Fergusson), IX, 251

Colquhoun, Janet (Smith), XI, 838

Colquhoun, Patrick, V, 219

Colson, Nicolas, I, 109

Colston, Elizabeth. *See* Gittens

Colston, William, I, 233

Colston, William, I, **233–34**, 350

Coltman, John, VI, 166

Coltman, William Bacheler, V, 268; VI, 100, **166–68**, 255, 445, 446; VII, 300, 373, 498, 877, 878; VIII, 343, 690
Colton, Hiram, XII, 134
Coltrin, Elizabeth. *See* Keefer
Columbus, Christopher, I, 12, 21, 147, 148, 150, 155, 157, 234, 303, 657, 658, 677, 678
Colven, Catherine (Waugh), VI, 806
Colvile (Wedderburn), Andrew, V, 266; VI, 17, 438, 441, 446, 767; VII, 454, 748, 900, 913; VIII, 112, 113, 351, 375, 714, 812, 817; IX, 179, 234, 472; X, 115, 478; XI, 824; XII, 206
Colvile, Anne. *See* Maxwell
Colvile, Eden, VIII, 574, 767, 817, 889; IX, 95, 102, 338; X, 69; XI, 45, 139, 626, 627, 876; XII, **206–7**
Colvile, Mary Louisa. *See* Eden
Colvill, Alexander, 7th Baron Colvill, III, **131–33**, 209, 210, 606; IV, 31, 163, 223, 481, 701; V, 381; VI, 193
Colvill, Charles, III, 133
Colvill, Elizabeth, Baroness Colvill. *See* Erskine
Colvill, Elizabeth, Baroness Colvill. *See* Johnston
Colvill, James Alexander, III, 133
Colvill, John, 6th Baron Colvill, III, 131
Colvill, Sophia, III, 133
Colville. *See also* Colvill
Colville, John, VIII, 191
Colville, John Mark Alexander, 4th Viscount Colville, III, 133
Colwell, Elizabeth (Ryerse), V, 732
Combalet. *See* Beauvoir
Combalot, Théodore, IX, 466
Combe, Abram, VIII, 437
Combe, William, V, 541, 542
Combes (Combles). *See* Lombard
Comcomly, V, 419, 526; VIII, 526; XII, 612
Comeau, Anselm-François, IX, **148–49**
Comeau, Félicité. *See* Le Blanc
Comeau, François, IX, 148
Comeau, François (Maza), IX, 148
Comeau, Joseph, VIII, 498
Comeau, Marguerite. *See* Melanson
Comeau, Marie-Gertrude. *See* Amirault
Comeau, Marie-Henriette. *See* LeJeune
Côme de Mantes, I, **234**, 434
Comhommon. *See* Onedahauet
Comingo, Bruin Romkes, IV, 490, 705; V, **199–200**; VI, 168, 169, 294; VII, 636
Comingo, Catherine Margaret. *See* Bailly
Comingo, Ebjen (Eljen, Fruche) (wife of BRUIN ROMKES), V, 199
Comingo, Elizabeth Brown, VI, 169
Comingo, Elizabeth Winslow. *See* Reynolds
Comingo, J. Brown, VI, 169
Comingo, Jane Catherine, VI, 169
Comingo, Jane Margaret. *See* Bailly
Comingo, Joseph, VI, 169
Comingo, Joseph Brown, VI, **168–69**
Comingo, Renée. *See* Des Camps
Comingo, Romkes, VI, 168
Commeau, Pierre, IV, xx
Commis, VIII, 653
Compain, Geneviève. *See* Arseneau
Compain, Marie-Louise, named Saint-Augustin, V, 186, **200–1**, 704; VII, 54

Compain, Pierre-Joseph, IV, 265; V, 200, **201–2**, 501, 502; VI, 549, 589
Compain, *dit* L'Espérance, Françoise. *See* Vacher
Compain, *dit* L'Espérance, Pierre, V, 200, 201
Comparé, Marie-Angélique (Bouc), VI, 77
Comporté. *See* Gaultier
Compton, Charlotte, Baroness Ferrers (Townshend, Viscountess Townshend), V, 824
Comstock, William Henry, XII, 1120
Comte, Benjamin, IV, 591
Comte, Benjamin-Godfroi, XI, 235
Comte, Isidore-Auguste-Marie-François-Xavier, X, 586
Comtois. *See* Dextreme; Joram
Conant, Sylvanus, V, 744
Conception. *See* Roy
Conck. *See* Cooke
Condé, Prince de. *See* Bourbon
Condé, Princesse de. *See* Montmorency
Condé, Henri II, Prince de, I, 42, 98, 186, 187, 191, 192, 193, 194, 294, 386
Condé, Louis II, Prince de, known as Le Grand Condé, I, 225, 283, 561, 563; II, 85, 262, 545
Condé, Louis-Henri, Prince de, Duc de Bourbon, II, 646
Condillac. *See* Bonnot
Condo, Francis, IV, 154; VII, 204, 579
Condon, William, XI, 398
Condon, William, XII, 31
Condorcet, Marquis de. *See* Caritat
Condren, Charles de, I, 115, 208
Conefroy, Marguerite (Chaboillez), V, 180
Conefroy, Marie-Josette. *See* Métivier
Conefroy, Pierre, V, 97, **202–3**, 247, 248; VI, 85, 287
Conefroy, Robert, V, 202
Coney, Mr (of Newfoundland), I, 93
Conflans, Comte de. *See also* Brienne
Conflans, Hubert de, Comte de Conflans, IV, 282
Confoulan, Marie-Louise. *See* Beaupré
Congdon, Ann (Duder), XI, 284
Conger, Elizabeth. *See* Seymour
Conger, Peter, IX, 149
Conger, Wilson Seymour, VII, 214; IX, **149**; X, 389
Congreve, Sir William, IV, 773
Conigon de Cangé, Charles, I, 257
Conilleau, Charles, X, **190**
Conke. *See* Cooke
Conley, Peter, XII, 407, 408
Conlin, Bernard (William Jermyn Florence), IX, 597
Conlon, John, XII, 783
Conmee*, James (1848–1913), XII, 333
Connacher, Marjory (Ferguson), VIII, 292
Connaught and Strathearn, Duke of. *See* Arthur William Patrick Albert
Conneequese, IV, 339
Connell, Ann. *See* Fisher
Connell, Charles, X, 190
Connell, Charles, VII, 291; VIII, 70; X, **190–91**, 287; XI, 578
Connell, Mary. *See* Palmer
Connell, William, VIII, 178
Connelly, Rosanna (Mullins), X, 536
Conner, John (soldier), III, 136, 137
Conner, John (teacher), VI, 159

Connolly, Amelia (Douglas, Lady Douglas), IX, 150; X, 239, 247, 248; XI, 866
Connolly, Ann (Lynch), XI, 535
Connolly, John (clergyman), XII, 1086
Connolly, John (son of WILLIAM), VII, 206; IX, 150
Connolly, Joseph, XII, 199, 1085
Connolly, Julia. See Woolrich
Connolly, Louise-Catherine (Aylwin), X, 24
Connolly, Mary Ellen (Tremblay), X, 686
Connolly, Michael (businessman), XII, 629
Connolly, Michael (Patriote), VIII, 582; IX, 695, 795
Connolly, Nicholas Knight (Karrol), XII, 629, 630
Connolly, Suzanne, VII, 205, 206; IX, **149–51**
Connolly, Thomas Louis, VIII, 920; IX, 616, 651, 791, 833; X, **191–93**, 476; XI, 76, 280, 351, 381, 399, 709, 710; XII, 32, 208, 209, 222, 397, 411, 480, 481, 548, 637, 638, 880, 1039, 1040
Connolly, William, VII, **204–6**, 564, 672; VIII, 454; IX, 149, 150, 197; X, 239
Connon, Ann. See Findlay
Connon, Mrs E., XII, 208
Connon, Jean. See Keith
Connon, John Robert, XII, 207
Connon, Robert, XII, 207
Connon, Thomas, XII, **207–8**
Connor, Eliza. See Hume
Connor, George Skeffington, IX, 55, **151**; XI, 617; XII, 492
Connor, Ralph. See Gordon, Charles William
Connor, Thomas, V, 742
Conolly, John, XII, 985
Conor, Elizabeth, V, 183; VII, 165
Conott (Connott), Sarah (Heron), V, 420
Conroy, Catherine. See McDonald
Conroy, Christine. See Le Herron
Conroy, George, X, **193–94**, 488; XI, 42, 43, 104, 163, 188, 251, 252, 253, 451, 514; XII, 303, 521, 652, 820, 1022, 1086
Conroy*, James Gervé (1836–1915), XII, 381, 860
Conroy, James Herron, X, 195
Conroy, Nicholas, X, **194–95**; XI, 664
Conroy, Thomas, X, 194
Consalvi, Ercole, VI, 596
Consigny, Antoine-Pierre-Louis, X, 75, 576
Constable, John, VI, 256, 257; XII, 326, 328
Constables, Jane Gabrielle (Sandom), VIII, 787
Constant, Benjamin, XII, 831
Constantin, Denis, III, 134
Constantin, Guillaume, III, 134
Constantin, Jean-Baptiste, IX, 126; X, 305
Constantin, Jeanne. See Masse
Constantin, Justinien (Louis-Alexandre), III, **133–34**
Constantin, Louis, named Brother Anaclet, IX, 681
Constantin, Louise. See Bacon
Constantin, Marguerite-Suzanne. See Guyon Durouvray
Constantin, Nicolas-Bernardin, II, **153**, 173
Constantin, Pierre, II, 8, 276, 384; III, 75, **134–35**, 226: IV, 91
Contant*, Alexis (1859–1918), X, 734
Contant, Élisabeth (Tranchant), III, 398, 399
Contant, dit Lafranchise, Nicolas, III, 398, 399
Contarini, Gasparo, I, 148, 153, 155, 157
Contarini, Marcantonio, I, 153
Conti, Prince de. See Bourbon

Contrecœur. See Pécaudy
Contremine, dit Jolicœur, Louise (Gingras), VIII, 328
Convent, Anne (Amiot; Maheu; Blanchon), I, 59, 60
Converse, Charles Crozart, XI, 804
Converse, John K., VIII, 634
Conway, Eleanor. See McCarthy
Conway, Henry Seymour, IV, 759; V, 142, 148, 149
Conway, Honoria, named Mother Mary Vincent, XII, **208–10**
Conway, Margaret (Donnelly), XII, 208
Conway, Margaret (Ryan), XII, 932
Conway, Michael, XII, 208
Conwell, Henry, VIII, 144
Conybeare, William Daniel, X, 445
Conyngham, Elizabeth, Baroness Conyngham. See Clements
Conyngham, Elizabeth, Marchioness Conyngham. See Denison
Conyngham (Burton), Francis Pierpont, 2nd Baron Conyngham, VI, 97
Conyngham, Williams, IV, 399, 414, 570
Cook. See also Koch
Cook, Ann (Smith), VI, 722
Cook, Benjamin, IX, 151
Cook, Caroline. See Brown
Cook, Charlotte (Spence), XII, 982
Cook, Christopher, X, 282
Cook, Eliza. See Cunningham
Cook, Elizabeth. See Airth
Cook, Elizabeth. See Batts
Cook, Elizabeth (mother of WILLIAM HEMMINGS), VII, 206
Cook, Ephraim, III, 364, 457; IV, 526
Cook, George, X, 195
Cook, George J., X, 195
Cook, Grace. See Pace
Cook, Hermon Henry, X, 195; XII, 578, 579
Cook, Hiram, IX, 162; XI, 140; XII, 278, 279
Cook, James, IV, 163
Cook, James, III, 133, 210; IV, lv, 28, 73, 156, **162–67**, 217, 218, 223, 283, 325, 340, 341, 411, 412, 413, 519, 567, 568, 569, 599, 600, 601, 622, 700, 744, 746, 758, 762, 763; V, 55, 80, 107, 197, 274, 381, 387, 425, 538, 539, 570, 580, 684, 686, 773, 837; VI, 36, 193, 797; VII, 830, 831; VIII, 70, 672, 686; XI, 55
Cook, James William, X, **195–96**; XII, 577
Cook, Jean, VI, 666
Cook, John (father of JOHN), XII, 210
Cook, John (father of WILLIAM HEMMINGS), VII, 206
Cook, John (uncle of JAMES WILLIAM), X, 195
Cook (Van Keugh), John, X, 195
Cook, John, VIII, 68, 751, 938; IX, 461; XII, **210–12**, 617
Cook, John L., X, 195
Cook, Joseph (catechist), IX, 135; XII, 200
Cook, Joseph (son of WILLIAM HEMMINGS), VII, 206
Cook, Louis. See Atiatoharongwen
Cook, Marion. See Wilson
Cook, Mary. See Mith-coo-coo-man E'Squaw
Cook, Philomela. See Hull
Cook, Richard, X, 337
Cook, Sarah. See Casselman
Cook, Simon Sephrenus, X, 195
Cook, William Francis, IX, **151–52**

Cook, William Hemmings, V, 194; VII, **206–7**; VIII, 411, 413, 766
Cooke, Anna Brown (Pinsent), XII, 843
Cooke, Elizabeth (Hoby, Lady Hoby; Russell, Lady Russell), I, 362
Cooke, Eliza M. (Pope), XII, 855
Cooke, Isabelle. *See* Guay
Cooke, Jay, XII, 685, 1030
Cooke, John Thomas, IX, 152
Cooke, Martha (Wilkes), X, 702
Cooke (Conck, Conke), Mary (Kieffer; Teeter), VIII, 450
Cooke, Samuel, VII, 657
Cooke, Thomas, VII, 35
Cooke, Thomas, VII, 574, 752; VIII, 129, 130, 241, 718; IX, **152–54**, 541; X, 137; XI, 170, 171, 251; XII, 508, 509
Cooke, Valentine, XI, 809, 811; XII, 628
Cooke, William Bernard, VII, 193, 195
Cookson, James, VI, 13
Cooley, Julia (Altrocchi), VI, 30
Cooley, Mary (Hatt), V, 411
Coombe, Martha (Bisaillon), III, 65
Coombes, Joseph, XII, 1039
Coombs, Henry, XII, 469
Coon, Peter, IX, 230
Cooney, Robert, VII, 52, 291; IX, **154–55**; XI, 135
Cooney, Susan Catherine. *See* Shaw
Cooper, Ann. *See* Skeet
Cooper, Ann (wife of WILLIAM), VII, 207
Cooper, Anthony Ashley, 1st Earl of Shaftesbury, I, 519
Cooper, Sir Astley Paston, VI, 680; VIII, 96; IX, 308; X, 83, 610; XI, 271, 543
Cooper, Elizabeth (Thompson), XI, 877
Cooper, Frances (Thompson), VI, 769
Cooper, H. G., XI, 929
Cooper, Henry, XI, 202
Cooper, Isabella. *See* Watson
Cooper, James (businessman), XII, 3
Cooper, James (father of JAMES BARRETT), XI, 201
Cooper, James (shoe factory owner), XI, 837
Cooper, James (son of JAMES BARRETT), XI, 202
Cooper, James, VIII, 97, 835, 836; X, 116, **196–97**, 216, 241, 242, 243; XI, 882; XII, 114, 523
Cooper, James Barrett, VIII, 563; X, 211, 339; XI, **201–2**; XII, 319
Cooper, James Fenimore, VII, 339; IX, 420; X, 166; XII, 823
Cooper, Jane. *See* Bagnall
Cooper, John Montgomery, VII, 4
Cooper, John W., IX, 157
Cooper, Margaret (McGarvey), XII, 624
Cooper, Myles, V, 630, 657
Cooper, Oscar, IX, 157
Cooper, Phoebe (Martin), VII, 590
Cooper, Richard John, VIII, 39; XI, 336
Cooper, Robert, X, 459
Cooper, Sarah. *See* Glover
Cooper, Thomas (Chartist), XI, 935
Cooper, Thomas (son of WILLIAM, d. 1840), VII, 208
Cooper, William, V, 597; VII, **207–8**, 652; VIII, 522
Cooper, William, VI, 821; VII, 76, 437, 542, 925; VIII, 37, 198, 296, 375, 376, 377, 531, 563, 742; IX, **155–58**, 223,

375, 394, 400, 857; X, 419; XI, 370, 526, 567, 666; XII, 415, 416, 856
Coopman, François, IX, 255
Coote, Sir Eyre, VII, 316
Coote, Isaac, XI, 808
Coote, Richard, 1st Earl of Bellomont, II, 46, 108, 114, 404, 410, 450, 591, 603, 622; III, 493
Cope, Henry, III, **135–36**, 665
Cope, Jane. *See* Patteshall
Cope, Jean-Baptiste, III, 34, **136–37**, 294, 298
Cope, Joseph, III, 136
Copernicus, Nicolaus, VIII, 214
Copley, Ellen, VI, 560
Copley, Sir Godfrey, III, 449
Copley, John Singleton, IV, 292, 553; V, 844
Copley, John Singleton, 1st Baron Lyndhurst, IX, 611
Copp, Mr (businessman), VIII, 758
Copp, Caroline Ann. *See* Thomas
Copp, Frances. *See* Cock
Copp, William (grandfather), XII, 212
Copp, William, XII, 213
Copp, William Walter, VIII, 790; XII, 188, **212–13**, 667, 923
Copt (Coptk). *See* Cope
Copway, Elizabeth. *See* Howell
Copway, George. *See* Kahgegagahbowh
Copway, John, IX, 419
Coquart, Claude-Godefroy, II, 296, 608; III, **137–38**, 197, 252; IV, 241, 423
Coram, Joseph, XI, 298
Corbarboineau, Anne de (Péan), III, 503
Corbet. *See also* Alès
Corbet, Elizabeth (Durell), III, 208
Corbett, Mrs Abigail, X, 307
Corbett*, Griffith Owen (fl. 1851–1904), X, 630; XI, 19, 20, 437
Corbett, Ichabod, XI, 754
Corbett, Louisa Charlotte (Boulton), X, 78
Corbett, Susan (Archibald), XI, 29
Corbin, André, IV, 167
Corbin, André, IV, **167–68**
Corbin, Charlotte. *See* Rainville
Corbin, David, III, 138
Corbin, David, III, **138–39**
Corbin, Étienne, III, 138, 139
Corbin, Geneviève. *See* Gariépy
Corbin, James, IX, 749
Corbin, Jean-Baptiste, VIII, 937
Corbin, Joseph-Marie, III, 138, 139
Corbin, Louise. *See* Petit
Corbin, Madeleine (Laforce), V, 470
Corbin, Marie. *See* Parent
Corbin, Marie-Angélique (Sauvageau), VII, 774
Corbin, Marie-Jeanne. *See* Faveron
Corbin, Véronique. *See* Baby
Corby, Alma. *See* Williams
Corby, Edward, XI, 203
Corby, George, XI, 203
Corby, Henry, XI, 203
Corby, Henry, XI, **202–3**
Corby, Isabel. *See* Metcalfe
Corby, James, XI, 202
Corby, John. *See also* Howard, John George

Corby, John, XI, 426
Corby, Matilda. *See* Williams
Corby, Sarah (mother of John George HOWARD), XI, 426
Corbyn, W., XII, 448
Corcelles. *See* Motin
Corcoran. *See also* Cocoran
Corcoran, Thomas, VII, 4
Cordé, Catherine de (Legardeur de Tilly), I, 446, 447
Cordis, Mary (Haswell), V, 410
Cordner, Caroline Hall. *See* Parkman
Cordner, John, XII, 213
Cordner, John, VII, 160; VIII, 424; X, 357; XI, 937; XII, **213–15**, 922
Cordner, Mary. *See* Neilson
Cordon, Anne (Champion), V, 180
Coré, Catherine (Decoste), IV, 200
Corey, Hannah (Jones), XII, 479
Corlis, Jane. *See* Burtch
Cormack, Alexander, IX, 158
Cormack, William, VIII, 293; IX, 258
Cormack, William Eppes, V, 244; VI, 351, 352, 707, 708; VII, 404; IX, **158–62**, 418; X, 419; XI, 632
Corméry. *See* Bibron
Cormier, Anne. *See* Gaudet
Cormier, Anne (Haché-Gallant), II, 272
Cormier, Cécile. *See* Thibodeau
Cormier, Charles, X, 615
Cormier, Charlotte (Cazeneuve), VIII, 136
Cormier, Clément, XII, 550
Cormier, Émélie (Marchessaut), VIII, 616
Cormier, François, V, 203
Cormier, Jacques, V, 203
Cormier, Jean, IV, 436
Cormier, Marie. *See* Terriot
Cormier, Pierre (carpenter), VI, 306
Cormier, Pierre (father of PIERRE), V, 203
Cormier, Pierre, V, **203–4**
Cormier, Robert, VIII, 616
Cormier, Suzanne (Haché), XII, 397
Cormier, *dit* Malouin, François, VIII, 136
Cornabat, Jeanne (Jamot), XI, 449
Cornbury, Lord. *See* Hyde, Edward
Corneille, Pierre, XI, 341
Corneillier, *dit* Grandchamp, Marguerite (Vallières; Munday), VII, 876
Cornelius*, Julius (1825–1916), XII, 786
Cornell, Joseph, VI, 733
Cornet, Marguerite de (Monic), II, 482
Corning, Erastus, VIII, 81
Corning, Sophia (Killam), IX, 425
Cornish, Catherine (Arthur), VIII, 26
Cornish, Francis Evans, VIII, 162; X, **197–98**; XI, 63, 193, 325, 611; XII, 679, 952
Cornish, George, IX, 468; XII, **215–17**
Cornish, Hubert Kestell, XII, 713, 717
Cornish, Martha. *See* Harvey
Cornish, Victorine Leon. *See* Clench
Cornish, William King, X, 197
Cornplanter. *See* Kaiũtwahʔkũ
Cornud, Angélique-Louise (Papineau), VIII, 678
Cornut (Cornutus), Jacques-Philippe, II, 596; III, 108, 678; X, 106
Cornwall, Clement Francis, X, 139; XI, 568

Cornwall, John, VII, 527
Cornwall, Mary (McCormick), VII, 527
Cornwallis, Charles, 4th Baron Cornwallis, IV, 168
Cornwallis, Charles, 2nd Earl and 1st Marquess Cornwallis, IV, 121, 694; V, 53, 134, 227, 657, 730; VI, 33, 77, 202, 245, 246, 429; VII, 428
Cornwallis, Charlotte, Baroness Cornwallis. *See* Butler
Cornwallis, Edward, III, 120, 125, 128, 130, 212, 261, 298, 343, 361, 362, 404, 405, 417, 439, 457, 473, 514, 517, 518, 573, 583, 585, 634, 666; IV, xxiv, xxv, 51, 92, 93, 110, 112, **168–71**, 249, 296, 312, 414, 455, 526, 559, 581, 703, 775; V, 215, 239, 250; VI, 621; VIII, 704; XII, 268, 275
Cornwallis, Frederick, IV, 168
Cornwallis, Mary. *See* Townshend
Cornwallis, Sir William, V, 359
Cornwell, Frances (Miles), VI, 504
Corolère, Christophe, III, 139
Corolère, Françoise. *See* Laurent
Corolère, Jean, III, **139–40**
Corolère, Marie. *See* Dorollaire
Coron, Angélique-Françoise. *See* Roland
Coron, Charles-François, III, **140–41**
Coron, François, III, 140
Coron, Marie. *See* Cyr
Coron, Marie-Louise. *See* Binot
Coron, Victoire (Jendon), III, 141
Corporon, Isabelle (Johnson), IV, 392
Corpron, Charles, III, 141
Corpron, Jean, III, **141–42**; IV, 66, 125, 127, 435, 517
Corpron, Marie. *See* Gabriel
Corpron, Marie. *See* Roy
Corps, Mary (Dixon), V, 257
Corrigal, Jacob, IV, 774; V, 185; VIII, 391
Corrigan, Catherine. *See* Mortin
Corrigan, Grace. *See* McNult
Corrigan, Henrietta, VIII, 171
Corrigan, Patrick, VIII, 169, 170, 171
Corrigan, Robert, VIII, 171
Corrigan, Robert, VIII, **169–71**; X, 120
Corrigan, William, VIII, 171
Corrivault, Marguerite (Maheut), I, 479
Corriveau, Joseph (father of MARIE-JOSEPHTE), III, 142, 143; IV, 299
Corriveau, Joseph (of Saint-Vallier, Que.), III, 142
Corriveau, Marie-Françoise. *See* Bolduc
Corriveau, Marie-Josephte, known as La Corriveau (Bouchard; Dodier), III, **142–43**; IV, 299, 692; X, 21
Corruble, La. *See* Bouge, Ange
Corry (Curray, Currie), Thomas, IV, 47, 160, 277, 761; V, 818
Corsane, Elizabeth (Ross), VIII, 770
Cort, John, IV, 195, 196; V, 465
Corte-Real, Gaspar, I, 19, 21, 151, 166, 171, **234–36**, 304
Corte-Real, Isabel. *See* Castro
Corte-Real, João Vaz, I, 234, 236
Corte-Real, Miguel, I, 19, 21, 166, 171, 234, 235, **236**
Corte-Real, Vasco Añes, I, 236
Corvaisier, Charles, III, 613
Corwin, George, I, 242
Cosa, Juan de la, I, 148, 149, 150, 151, 304
Cosby, Alexander, III, 143

Cosby, Alexander, II, 23, 663; III, 4, **143–44**, 421, 426, 437, 517, 518, 665
Cosby, Anne. *See* Winniett
Cosby, Elizabeth. *See* L'Estrange
Cosby, Elizabeth (Philipps), III, 143, 518
Cosby, Philipps, III, 144
Cosby, William, III, 144
Cosford, Mary Ann (Hartman), VIII, 370
Cosgrove, Owen, XII, 273
Cosineau de Mareuil, Jacques-Théodore. *See* Mareuil, Jacques de
Cosme, Father, IV, xxiii
Cosnier, Marie (Denys de La Thibaudière), I, 256, 261
Cosser, Agnes (Barclay), VII, 45
Cossit, Ranna, VII, 10
Cossit, Ranna, IV, 522, 523; V, 53, **204–5**, 446, 546, 634, 766; VI, 77, 203, 213, 535
Cossit, Thankful. *See* Brooks
Cossitt, Phoebe. *See* Hillyer
Cossitt, Rene, V, 204
Cosson, Ernest, X, 82
Coste, François, IX, 204
Coste, Madeleine (Petitpas), III, 512
Coste (Costa), Mathieu de, I, 452
Costé, Michel, I, 87
Costebelle. *See* Pastour
Costello, Joseph H., IX, 720
Coster, Anne. *See* Allen
Coster, Charles, VIII, 174
Coster, Charles G., VII, 413
Coster, Eleanor. *See* Hansard
Coster, Ellen (Robb), IX, 665
Coster, Emily (Wills), VIII, 941
Coster, Frederick, VI, 54; VIII, 172, 345; IX, 339
Coster, George, VI, 54; VII, 413, 434; VIII, **171–74**, 345, 346, 941; IX, 339, 665, 847; XII, 714, 716
Coster, George Nathaniel, VIII, 171
Coster, Gerritje (Roseboom), III, 568
Coster, Margaret Spencer (Carter), X, 140
Coster, Nathaniel, VIII, 173
Coster, *dit* Coster de Saint-Victor, Jean-Baptiste, VI, 619, 620
Costigan*, John (1835–1916), X, 230, 557; XI, 624, 832; XII, 549, 607, 721, 881, 980, 1034, 1035, 1120
Costin, Brigid (Little), XII, 563
Costin, Thomas, V, 590
Coswentannea. *See* Kaghswaghtaniunt
Côté. *See also* Cotté
Côté, Anne. *See* Martin
Côté, Antoine, VII, 646
Côté*, Augustin (1818–1904), IX, 302, 303; X, 203, 213; XI, 88, 159; XII, 270
Côté, Charles, VII, 208
Côté, Cyrille-Hector-Octave, VII, 19, 105, **208–11**, 239, 334, 411, 479, 484, 513, 515, 757, 758, 759; VIII, 144, 145, 285, 313, 606, 616; IX, 73, 610, 814; X, 491, 545, 546, 574, 576, 633; XI, 60; XII, 761
Coté, Gabriel. *See* Mīmīy
Côté, Georges, XII, 126
Côté, Jean, I, 495
Côté, Joseph-Amable, XII, 126
Coté, Joseph-Olivier, XI, **203–4**
Côté, Louis, XII, 126

Côté, Louise-Charlotte. *See* Sasseville
Côté, Magloire, XII, 126
Côté, Margaret Yelloby. *See* Jobson
Côté, Marie (Manseau), IX, 533
Côté, Marie-Geneviève (Gabriel; Levasseur), IV, 471
Côté, Marie-Joseph (Hébert), VI, 315
Coté, Marie-Julie-Léocadie. *See* Leprohon
Coté, Narcisse-Omer, XI, 204; XII, 842
Côté, Olivier, XI, 203
Côté, Rose. *See* Duhamel
Coté, Simone (Soumande), II, 275, 612, 613
Côté, Victoire (Morin), XII, 761
Cotentin, *dit* Lavallée, Guillaume, II, 16
Cotes, Sara Jeannette. *See* Duncan
Cotesworth, Charles, II, 231, 266
Cotin, Dugal, VI, 226
Cotin (Cottin), *dit* Dugal, Louis, VI, 226
Cotin, *dit* Dugal, Madeleine. *See* Bernard
Cotman, John Sell, VII, 193; XII, 326
Coton, Pierre, I, 97, 100, 121, 498
Cottard, Claude, III, 566
Cotté. *See also* Kotte
Cotté, Agathe. *See* Roy-Desjardins
Cotté, Angélique. *See* Blondeau
Cotté, Gabriel, IV, **171–72**, 403; V, 90, 376, 663; VI, 382; VII, 138, 500, 716; VIII, 301; IX, 455; XI, 479
Cotté, Honoré, XII, 248
Cotté, Josette (Quesnel), VII, 716
Cotté (Côté), Lucie-Angélique (Boucher; Laframboise), IV, 172; XI, 479
Cotté, Marianne, IV, 171
Cotté, Marie-Catherine-Émilie (Larocque), IV, 172; IX, 455
Cotté, Marie-Claude. *See* Levasseur
Cotté, Marie-Josephte (Quesnel), IV, 172
Cotté, Nicolas, IV, 171
Cotté, Pierre-Gabriel, IV, 172; VI, 664
Cotter, Agnes. *See* Kilgour
Cotter, Frances Symington. *See* Ironside
Cotter, George Sackville, XI, 204
Cotter, James Laurence, XI, **204–5**
Cotterell, William, III, 137, 365; IV, 110
Cotterill, Agnes (Storm), XII, 991
Cottin. *See also* Cotin
Cottin, *dit* Dugal, Marianne (Morin), IX, 568
Cottnam, Deborah. *See* How
Cottnam, George, IV, 199
Cottnam, Grizelda Elizabeth, V, 430
Cottnam, Henrietta Maria (Day), IV, 199
Cottnam, Margaret Ramsey (Scott), IV, 704
Cottnam, Martha Grace (Tonge), IV, 736; V, 430; VI, 777, 778
Cottnam, Samuel, V, 430
Cotton. *See also* Couton
Cotton, Ann. *See* Lemoine
Cotton, Barthélemy, II, 520; III, 550; IV, **172–73**, 376; V, 249, 699
Cotton, Caleb, VII, 211
Cotton, Charles Caleb, V, 106; VI, 526; VII, 186, **211–12**, 825
Cotton, Drusilla. *See* Pettis
Cotton, Françoise. *See* Gagnon
Cotton, Hester (Salusbury), III, 583

Cotton, Jean-François, IV, 173
Cotton, John, XII, 499
Cotton, Marguerite, IV, 173
Cotton, Marie. *See* Willis
Cotton, Michel, III, **144–45**, 181, 346, 348; IV, 173
Cotton, Richard, VIII, 425
Cotton, Sir Robert, III, 583
Cotton*, William Lawson (1848–1928), IX, 828; XI, 704
Cottrell, Sophia (Lefroy), XI, 508
Couagne. *See also* Decoigne
Couagne, Anne de. *See* Mars
Couagne, Charles de, II, 153
Couagne, Charles, de, II, **153–54**, 413, 526, 529; III, 145, 146, 379, 493; VII, 238
Couagne, Charles-René de, III, 145
Couagne, François-Marie de, III, 333; IV, 268
Couagne, Jean-Baptiste de, II, 121, 153, **154**, 285, 339, 648; III, 79, 229, 236, 644; IV, 174; VII, 238
Couagne, Jean-Baptiste de, III, 146, 652; IV, **173–74**
Couagne, Jean-François de, II, 154
Couagne, Jeanne de. *See* Loppinot
Couagne, Louise de. *See* Pothier
Couagne, Marguerite-Madeleine de. *See* Gannes de Falaise
Couagne, Marie de. *See* Gaudé
Couagne, Marie-Anne de. *See* Hubert de Lacroix
Couagne, Marie-Josephte de (Lemoine, *dit* Monière), III, 379
Couagne, Michel de, II, 154; III, 229; IV, 28, **174–75**
Couagne, René de, III, 145
Couagne, René de, II, 153; III, **145–46**, 351; IV, 173; V, 662
Couagne, Renée de. *See* Greffière
Couagne, Thérèse de (Poulin de Francheville), II, 153, 529; III, **146–47**, 537
Couc, Elizabeth, II, 505, 645; III, **147–48**, 607; V, 602
Couc, *dit* Lafleur, Marie. *See* Miteouamegoukoue
Couc, *dit* Lafleur, Pierre, III, 147; V, 602
Couch, Sarah (Bernard), X, 51
Couche, Edward, VI, 541
Couche, John Rodolph, VI, 369, 370
Couche, Rebecca. *See* Smith
Coucher, Elizabeth Seeley (Steele), IX, 743
Coucher, Robert, VII, 917
Couc Montour, Jean (John), III, 147
Couc Montour, Louis, III, 147
Couèche, La. *See* Le Blanc, Madeleine
Coughlan, Ann (Harley), X, 333
Coughlan, Betsey, IV, 176
Coughlan, Daniel, VIII, 467
Coughlan, Laurence, IV, **175–77**, 402; V, 52; VI, 10
Cougle, Frances Charlotte (Vail), XI, 896
Couillard, André, IV, 424
Couillard, Antoine, VIII, 479
Couillard, Antoine-Gaspard, VII, **212–13**
Couillard, Catherine-Charlotte-Élise (Chaussegros de Léry), X, 162
Couillard, Élisabeth. *See* Vesins
Couillard, Élisabeth-Simone. *See* Lajus
Couillard, Geneviève (Denys Du Tartre), II, 176
Couillard, Guillaume, I, 236
Couillard, Jacques, VIII, 174
Couillard, Jean-Baptiste, IV, 71; VII, 213
Couillard, Jean-Baptiste-Alexandre, X, 435

Couillard, Joseph, III, 560
Couillard, Louis, V, 91
Couillard, Louise (Letardif), I, 473
Couillard, Marguerite. *See* Wilson
Couillard, Marie (Byssot de La Rivière; Lalande de Gayon), I, 145, 146, 395, 661; II, 65, 68
Couillard, Marie-Angélique. *See* Chaussegros de Léry
Couillard, Marie-Angélique-Flore. *See* Wilson
Couillard, Marie-Françoise (Turgeon), VI, 787
Couillard, Marie-Geneviève. *See* Alliés
Couillard, Nicolas, I, 366, 367
Couillard, Rachel. *See* Boudrias
Couillard, Thérèse (Boisseau), 91
Couillard de Beaumont, Charles, IV, 71
Couillard de Beaumont, Charles-Marie, III, 69
Couillard de Beaumont, Charles-Thomas, II, 159
Couillard de Beaumont, Louise. *See* Couture
Couillard de Lespinay, Catherine-Gertrude (Aubert de La Chesnaye), II, 33
Couillard de Lespinay, Élisabeth (Guyon Du Buisson), I, 359, 366
Couillard de Lespinay, Geneviève. *See* Chavigny de Berchereau
Couillard de Lespinay, Geneviève. *See* Desprez
Couillard de Lespinay, Guillaume, I, 366
Couillard de Lespinay, Guillaume, I, 109, 145, 200, **236–37**, 287, 359, 366, 452, 473, 517, 578; II, 33, 213, 448; VII, 213; VIII, 174
Couillard de Lespinay, Guillemette. *See* Hébert
Couillard de Lespinay, Jacques, I, 161; II, 155
Couillard de Lespinay, Jean-Baptiste, II, xxiv, 17, **154–55**; III, 15, 74, 569
Couillard de Lespinay, Jeanne (Dupuy de Lisloye), II, 213
Couillard de Lespinay, Louis, I, 48, **237–38**, 420, 430; II, 155, 213
Couillard de Lespinay, Louis, II, **155–56**, 256
Couillard de Lespinay, Louise. *See* Nolin
Couillard de Lespinay, Marguerite. *See* Bélanger
Couillard de Lespinay, Marguerite (Nicollet de Belleborne; Macard), I, 84, 369, 517; II, 16, 181, 448
Couillard de Lespinay, Marie. *See* Fortin
Couillard de Lespinay, Marie. *See* Vandry
Couillard Des Islets, Catherine (Dambourgès; Oliva), IV, 589
Couillard Des Islets, Louis, IV, 589; V, 654
Couillard-Després*, Azarie (1876–1939), IX, 424; XI, 595
Couillard-Després, Emmanuel, VIII, 174
Couillard-Després, Emmanuel, VIII, **174–75**
Couillard-Després, Emmanuel-Louis-Rémi, VIII, 175
Couillard-Després, Jacques, VI, 281
Couillard-Després, Jean-Baptiste, VIII, 174
Couillard-Després, Joseph-François, VII, 503
Couillard-Després, Louise-Esther. *See* Bourdages
Couillard-Després, Marie-Françoise. *See* Robichaud
Couillaud. *See* La Roque
Coulanges. *See* Petit
Coulaud (Couleau), Catherine (Courreaud de La Coste), IV, 178
Coulman, Ann (Ross, Lady Ross), IX, 693, 694
Coulogne. *See* Robin
Coulombe, Marguerite (Pilote), XI, 689
Coulombe, Marie-Henriette (Caron), XII, 159
Coulon, Marie (Guernon), V, 392

Coulon de Villiers, Angélique. *See* Jarret de Verchères

Coulon de Villiers, Élisabeth. *See* Groston de Saint-Ange

Coulon de Villiers, François, II, 267; IV, **177–78**

Coulon de Villiers, Jumonville, IV, 178

Coulon de Villiers, Louis, II, 156; III, **148–49**, 150, 151, 320, 502; IV, 33, 177, 257, 459, 617; V, 96, 486

Coulon de Villiers, Louise. *See* La Fosse

Coulon de Villiers, Madeleine-Marie-Anne. *See* Tarieu de La Pérade

Coulon de Villiers, Marie (Dagneau Douville), IV, 192

Coulon de Villiers, Marie-Amable. *See* Prud'homme

Coulon de Villiers, Marie-Anne (Aubert de Gaspé), IV, 33, 34; VI, 16

Coulon de Villiers, Marie-Geneviève. *See* Énault de Livaudais

Coulon de Villiers, Marie-Madeleine. *See* Marin

Coulon de Villiers, Marie-Madeleine (Regnard Duplessis; Marin de La Perrière; Damours Des Plaines), II, 156; III, 432

Coulon de Villiers, Nicolas-Antoine, II, **156**, 284, 316, 317; III, 46, 148, 149, 150, 432, 491; IV, 33, 177, 192

Coulon de Villiers, Nicolas-Antoine, III, 49, 87, **149–50**, 260, 331, 378, 432, 484, 676; IV, 177, 459, 512, 559, 651

Coulon de Villiers, Raoul-Guillaume, II, 156

Coulon de Villiers de Jumonville, Joseph, II, 156; III, 148, **150–51**, 376, 600, 614; IV, 33, 34, 177, 178, 227, 459, 647; V, 96, 470, 486

Coulon de Villiers de Jumonville, Marie-Anne- Marguerite. *See* Soumande

Coulonge. *See* Ailleboust

Coulson, Sarah Ann (Verey), XI, 900

Counter, Hannah. *See* Roode

Counter, John, IX, 162

Counter, John, VIII, 326, 760; IX, **162–63**, 314; XI, 140; XII, 278

Counter, Susannah (mother of JOHN), IX, 162

Coupeaux, François, V, 813

Couper, Sir George, VII, 478; VIII, 603

Couper, William, XI, 65, 107, **205–6**; XII, 868

Courault, *dit* La Coste, Angélique (Lupien, *dit* Baron), III, 412

Courbet, Jean-Désiré-Gustave, X, 410

Courcelle (Courcelles). *See* Rémy

Courcelles. *See* Motin

Courcillon, Louis de, Abbé de Dangeau, II, 589

Courcy. *See also* Potier

Courcy, Henry de, VIII, 911, 940; X, 87; XI, 172

Courier, Joseph, III, 443

Cournoyer. *See also* Hertel

Cournoyer, Élisabeth de (Pascaud), IV, 605

Courpont, Monsieur de (member of Compagnie des Cent-Associés), I, 297

Courraud Lacoste, Louise (Pothier), VII, 702

Courreaud de La Coste, Catherine. *See* Coulaud

Courreaud de La Coste, Élie, IV, 178

Courreaud de La Coste, Marguerite. *See* Aubuchon, *dit* L'Espérance

Courreaud de La Coste, Marie-Anne. *See* Massé

Courreaud de La Coste, Marie-Josephte (Estimauville), VI, 239

Courreaud de La Coste, Marin, IV, 179

Courreaud de La Coste, Pierre, II, 614; IV, **178–79**, 732

Courselle, *dit* Chevallier, Joseph, VI, 812

Courserac. *See* Aubert

Courseron, Gilbert, I, **238**

Coursier, Catherine (Genaple), II, 241

Coursol, Charles-Joseph, IX, 437, 438, 450, 651, 728; X, 219, 422; XI, **206–7**; XII, 5, 68, 597

Coursol (Coursolles), Charlotte (Jones), V, 456; VII, 452, 456

Coursol, Émilie-Hélène-Henriette. *See* Taché

Coursol, Mélanie. *See* Quesnel

Coursol, Michel, IX, 649; XI, 187, 206

Coursolle, Jean-Marie, V, 572

Coursolles. *See* Coursol

Court, James, VIII, 396; IX, 105; X, 672

Courtade, Suzanne (Masclé), III, 440

Court de La Bruyère, Claude-Élisée de, III, 27, 557, 609, 610; IV, 256

Courtemanche. *See* Legardeur; Le Gardeur

Courtenay, Princesse de, Marquise de Bauffremont (Beauffremont), IV, 469

Courthiau, Marie-Anne (La Forest), II, 336

Courthiau, Pierre-Noël, III, 394; V, 312

Courtin, Michel, II, 238

Courtin de Tangeux, Catherine (Brisay de Denonville, Marquise de Denonville), II, 98, 99

Courtin de Tangeux, Germain, II, 98

Courtney*, John Mortimer (1838–1920), XII, 1057

Courtois, Jacques, VI, 390

Courtois, Louise (Duberger, *dit* Sanschagrin), VI, 223

Courtois, Marguerite. *See* Le Ménager

Courtois, Maurice, IV, 509

Courval. *See* Cressé; Poulin

Courville. *See* Aumasson; Cadieu

Courville, Sieur de. *See* Aumasson de Courville, Louis-Léonard

Cousineau, Marie-Renée (Cheval), III, 121

Coussez, Captain, I, 422

Coussirat, Daniel, XI, 37

Coustan, Madeleine (Sarrebource Pontleroy de Beaulieu), V, 738

Cousture. *See* Couture

Coutant, Marie-Joseph (Tanswell), V, 790

Coutelais. *See* Coutlée

Couteron, Louise-Élisabeth (Deschevery, *dit* Maisonbasse), III, 181, 182

Coutlée, Thérèse-Geneviève, IV, 462; V, 293; VI, **169–70**; VII, 499, 774

Coutlée, *dit* Marcheterre, Geneviève. *See* Labrosse

Coutlée (Coutelais), *dit* Marcheterre, Louis, VI, 169

Couton. *See also* Cotton

Couton, Barthélemy, III, 144; IV, 172

Couton, Jeanne. *See* Le Rouge

Coutré, Marquis de, II, 77

Couttes. *See* Le Fascheux

Coutts. *See also* Burdett-Coutts

Coutts, Anna (Ball), V, 53

Coutts, Katherine B., V, 800

Couture, Anastasie. *See* Lefebvre, *dit* Boulanger

Couture, Anne. *See* Esmard

Couture, Geneviève. *See* Jelly

Couture, George, XI, **207–8**

Couture, Guillaume, II, 157

Couture, Guillaume, I, 42, 60, 124, 145, 227, 282, 298,

344, 387, 388, 396, 403, 404, 523; II, **157–59**, 635; XI, 94, 207
Couture*, Guillaume (1851–1915), XII, 471, 472, 504, 533
Couture, Ignace (father), XI, 207
Couture, Ignace, XI, 207
Couture, Jean, I, 79; II, 635
Couture, Joseph-Alphonse, XII, 758
Couture, Louise (Couillard de Beaumont), II, 159
Couture, Louis-Édouard, XI, 207, 259
Couture, Madeleine. See Mallet
Couture, Marguerite (Marsolet), II, 159
Couture, Marie. See Roy
Couture, Marie, XI, 258
Couture, Marie (Vézier; Bourget), II, 159; XI, 94
Couture, Peter, IV, 613
Couture de La Cressonnière, Joseph-Oger, II, 159
Couturier, Jean, II, 530; III, 119, 192, 256, 486; IV, 89, 237, 542; V, 432
Couturier, Marie. See Guillier
Couturier, Michel, II, 159
Couturier, dit Le Bourguignon, Jeanne-Charlotte (Janson, dit Lapalme), II, 160; III, 307
Couturier, dit Le Bourguignon, Marguerite. See Payet
Couturier, dit Le Bourguignon, Marie-Joseph (Janson, dit Lapalme), II, 160; III, 307
Couturier, dit Le Bourguignon, Michel-Étienne, IV, 204
Couturier, dit Le Bourguignon, Pierre, II, **159–60**, 546; III, 307; IV, 732
Couvay, Jean, VI, 26
Couvert, Michel-Germain de, II, **160–61**, 337
Couvillon. See Quévillon
Couvret, Joseph-Victor, VI, 547
Couvret, Marie-Angélique (Nolin), VI, 547
Couvret, Marie-Louise (Favre, dit Montferrand), IX, 561
Couvreur, Jeanne (Soullard), II, 612
Coux, Anne de. See Du Pont Duchambon de Mézillac
Coux, Louis de, IV, 248
Coventry, Elizabeth. See Thornbarrow
Coventry, George, V, 419; IX, **163–64**, 547
Coverdale, Catherine. See Delmage
Coverdale, Christopher, IX, 164
Coverdale, Frances (Creighton), XI, 216
Coverdale, William, VIII, 761; IX, **164–65**; XI, 216, 266
Coverdale, William Miles, IX, 165
Covernton, Charles William, XI, 329, 591
Covert, Caroline (Moffatt), XII, 744
Covert, Elizabeth (wife of JOHN), VII, 214
Covert, Frederick Peechy, VII, 215
Covert, Henry, VII, 214, 215
Covert, John, VII, 75, 200, **213–15**; IX, 44; X, 253
Covert, Martha (Bethune), VII, 74
Cowan, Agnes, XII, **217**
Cowan, Cecilia Eliza. See Douglas
Cowan, Elizabeth. See Hastie
Cowan, Harriett (Molt), VIII, 635
Cowan, Harriette. See Sinclair
Cowan, Janet, XII, 217
Cowan, John, XII, 217
Cowan, Mahlon K., XII, 1073
Cowan, Malcolm, VIII, 280; X, 708
Cowan, William, VII, 645, 649, 650; VIII, 408
Cowans, John R., XII, 1002
Cowans*, Mary (McDougall) (d. 1901), XII, 620

Cowans, Robert, XII, 620, 621
Cowdell, Margaret (wife of THOMAS DANIEL), VI, 170
Cowdell, Samuel, VI, 170
Cowdell, Thomas Daniel, VI, 65, **170–72**; VII, 425
Cowessess. See Kiwisānce
Cowhoe, George. See Ga'wu
Cowie, Mary (Harris), XII, 412
Cowin, Sarah (Quirk), VIII, 731
Cowley, Abraham, VII, 232; XI, **208–9**; XII, 201
Cowley, Arabella. See Sainsbury
Cowley, Mary (mother of ABRAHAM), XI, 208
Cowley, Robert, XI, 208
Cowper, William, VIII, 924
Cox, Ann (Eakins), XII, 10
Cox, Charles, X, 198
Cox, Christiana (Christina) Lætitia (Longmore), V, 501
Cox, David, XII, 326
Cox, Deborah (wife of NICHOLAS), IV, 179
Cox, Hannah. See Cumming
Cox, Jacob, VI, 554
Cox, James, VI, 793
Cox, John Henry, IV, 325
Cox, Margaret. See Thorpe
Cox, Nicholas, IV, 153, **179–80**; V, 485, 501, 502, 503, 637; VI, 653; VII, 204
Cox, Ross, V, 419, 526, 560, 814; VI, 321; VII, 206; VIII, 85, 158, **175–76**, 660, 768; IX, 279
Cox, Samuel, VIII, 175
Cox, Sarah (Young, Lady Young), VI, 820
Cox, Sophia Elizabeth. See Webb
Cox, Thomas, VI, 157; IX, 637
Cox, Thomas W., XII, 444
Cox, William (captain), I, 334, 335, 363
Cox, William (nephew of Thomas SLADE), V, 764
Cox, William George, IX, 81, 82, 433, 473, 514, 712, 713; X, **198–99**; XI, 394
Coxe, Daniel, III, 65
Coxon, Jane (Shirreff), VII, 796
Coy, Ama. See Titus
Coy, Amasa, VII, **215–16**, 916; VIII, 176
Coy, Asa, VII, 216
Coy, Elizabeth. See Holly
Coy (McCoy), J. Edward, VII, 215; VIII, 176
Coy, Mary (Morris; Bradley), VII, 215; VIII, **176–77**
Coy, Mary Spafford. See Barker
Coya (Coyour). See Koyah
Coye. See Coy
Coyne*, James Henry (1849–1942), VIII, 861
Coyne, Margaret Jane (Phillips), XII, 842
Cozens, Charles, VII, 112, 590; VIII, 477
Cozer, Françoise-Marie (Guichart), IV, 317
Cracroft, Sophia, VIII, 80; X, 27, 29, 247, 319, 320, 748
Cradock, Mary (Gerrish; Breynton), IV, 94, 292
Cragg, James, II, 288
Craig, Charlotte (wife of JOHN), VIII, 177
Craig, George, XI, 390
Craig, Gerald Marquis, VII, 929
Craig, Hew, V, 205
Craig, James, VIII, 588
Craig, Sir James Henry, V, 13, 18, 51, 85, 86, 87, 111, 119, 138, 161, 165, **205–14**, 215, 225, 235, 236, 286, 291, 292, 386, 461, 489, 651, 693, 694, 695, 696, 697, 753, 769, 796, 797, 828, 829, 881; VI, 43, 47, 50, 68, 69, 82,

187, 223, 242, 245, 260, 299, 347, 367, 378, 383, 387, 388, 392, 416, 433, 477, 513, 527, 533, 577, 585, 586, 594, 642, 645, 646, 701, 715, 750; VII, 65, 94, 133, 165, 349, 358, 359, 388, 422, 503, 504, 524, 545, 613, 614, 616, 622, 646, 673, 676, 768, 769, 770, 771, 786, 817, 836, 872, 884, 908; VIII, xxiv, 26, 155, 236, 337, 338, 388, 389, 458, 491, 839, 843, 914; IX, 75, 115, 187, 188, 302, 808, 809, 814; X, 580

Craig, John, XI, 599, 696
Craig, John, VIII, **177–78**; IX, 345
Craig, Laurent-David, VII, 388
Craig, Mathilda, VIII, 177
Craig, Thomas, XI, 335
Craigie, Anna Cecilia (Mills), VI, 505
Craigie, John, V, 214
Craigie, John, IV, 493; V, 61, 191, 192, **214–15**, 291, 326, 442, 485, 495, 496, 794; VI, 166, 267, 299, 452, 505, 586; VII, 201, 380, 401
Craigie, Mary. *See* Campbell
Craigie, May. *See* Ness
Craigie, Susannah. *See* Coffin
Craigie, Susannah Christiana (Hamilton), VII, 380; XI, 379
Craigie, William, IX, 165
Craigie, William, IX, **165–66**; X, 607
Cramahé. *See also* Chateigner
Cramahé, Hector Theophilus, III, 111, 142; IV, xxxviii, xxxix, xlvi, xlvii, 100, 107, 109, 189, 229, 323, 484, 503, 538, 547, 550, 570, 575, 618, 739, **787–93**; V, 44, 132, 142, 144, 146, 289, 481, 508, 706, 889, 892, 895; VI, 295
Cramahé, Margaret (wife of HECTOR THEOPHILUS), IV, 793
Cramer, Charles, V, 838, 839
Cramer, Christy, IV, 703
Cramolet, Captain, I, 64
Cramp, Anne. *See* Burls
Cramp, John Mockett, VII, 253; X, 130, 295; XI, **209–10**, 211, 215; XII, 109
Cramp, Maria. *See* Agate
Cramp, Marianne. *See* Dunn
Cramp, Rebecca. *See* Gouger
Cramp, Thomas, XI, 209
Cramp, Thomas, X, 683, 724; XI, 209, **211–12**, 557, 758
Crampe, Charlotte Augustina (O'Callaghan), X, 555
Crampporn, Jane (Yonge), II, 672
Crampporn, Thomas, II, 672
Crampton, Sir John Fiennes Twisleton, X, 14
Crandall, Joseph, VII, 610, 916; VIII, **179–80**, 227, 360, 361
Crandall, Julia. *See* Smith
Crandall, Laban, VIII, 180
Crandall, Lida. *See* Mace
Crandall, Martha. *See* Hopper
Crandall, Mercy. *See* Vaughan
Crandall, Molly. *See* Seein
Crandall, Reuben, V, 65; VIII, **180–81**
Crandall, Webber, VIII, 179
Crane. *See also* Chejauk; Tarhe
Crane, Miss (McKinnon), IX, 511
Crane, Eliza. *See* Wood
Crane, Eunice (wife of SAMUEL), VIII, 181
Crane, Jonathan, V, 63; VIII, 183
Crane, Mary. *See* Myarwikishigoqua

Crane, Philip, VIII, 107
Crane, Rebecca. *See* Allison
Crane, Rebecca (Starr), XI, 679
Crane, Robert E., IX, 511
Crane, Samuel, VIII, **181–83**, 836; XII, 682
Crane, Susannah. *See* Dixon
Crane, Thomas, VIII, 183
Crane, William, VIII, 183
Crane, William, VII, 140, 141; VIII, 15, **183–84**, 807, 808; X, 426, 710
Crane, William Henry, XI, 419
Cranmer, Thomas, VIII, 521
Crannell, Bartholomew, VIII, 69
Crannell, Gertrude (Beardsley), V, 59; VIII, 69
Cranston, Frances (Brenton), V, 108
Cranston, Samuel, V, 108
Cranstoun, Daniel (wife of Andrew BROWN), VI, 87
Crapanoz. *See* Vachon
Crapaut. *See* Chomina
Crash, Susanna (Wakefield), IX, 817
Crasset, Jean, III, 104
Craston, William, I, 450, 451
Crate, Sarah (wife of WILLIAM FREDERICK), X, 199
Crate, William Frederick, X, **199–200**
Crathern, Thomas, XII, 483
Craufurd, Robert, X, 634
Crausee, Miss von (Massow), V, 582
Craw, Elizabeth McCullough (Black), VII, 77
Crawford, Earl of. *See* Lindsay
Crawford, Alexander, VI, **172–73**
Crawford, Anne E. (Keefer), XI, 463
Crawford, Caroline. *See* Sherwood
Crawford, Edward Patrick, IX, 167
Crawford, Emma Naomi, XI, 212, 213
Crawford, George, IX, **166–67**, 788; X, 200, 631, 632; XI, 114, 162, 463
Crawford, George Gillespie, VII, 652
Crawford, Helen. *See* Sherwood
Crawford, Isabella Valancy, XI, **212–14**; XII, 516
Crawford, James (physician), VII, 26
Crawford, James (son of GEORGE), IX, 167; X, 200
Crawford, Jane. *See* MacLaren
Crawford, Jane. *See* Munse
Crawford, Jean (Allan), XI, 5
Crawford, Jessie. *See* Mitchell
Crawford, Joe. *See* Big Arrow
Crawford, John (brother of GEORGE), IX, 166
Crawford, John (businessman), XII, 43
Crawford, John (nephew of Adam LYMBURNER), VII, 523
Crawford, John Irwin, XI, 213
Crawford, John Willoughby, VIII, 587; IX, 166, 167; X, 171, **200–1**, 561; XI, 150; XII, 273, 399, 976
Crawford, Lewis, VI, 509
Crawford, Margaret. *See* Brown
Crawford, Margaret (Ross), X, 632
Crawford, Margaret Ann (Westbrook), VI, 808
Crawford, Patrick, IX, 166
Crawford, Stephen, XI, 212
Crawford, Stephen Dennis, XI, 212
Crawford, Stephen Walter, XI, 212, 213
Crawford, Sydney. *See* Scott
Crawford, William (ancestor of ISABELLA VALANCY), XI, 212

Crawford, William (soldier), V, 302, 345, 346; VI, 101, 153, 189
Crawley, Edmund Albern, VII, 123, 252, 272, 536; VIII, 567, 568, 612, 613, 656, 968; X, 384, 385; XI, 210, **214–16**, 896; XII, 109, 872
Crawley, Elizabeth. *See* Johnston
Crawley, Esther. *See* Bernal
Crawley, Julia Amelia. *See* Wilby
Crawley, Thomas H., VII, 10; XI, 214
Crawley, Thomas Henry, XI, 215
Crean, Johanna (Kenny), XII, 480
Crease*, Sir Henry Pering Pellew (1825–1905), IX, 114, 296; X, 112; XI, 568, 635; XII, 227
Crebassa, John George, XII, 64
Creed, Eliza (McCully), X, 457
Creedon, Ellen (mother of MARIANNE), VIII, 184
Creedon, Ellen Maria (Nugent), VIII, 184; X, 552
Creedon, John, VIII, 184
Creedon, Marianne, named Mother Mary Francis, VII, 298; VIII, **184–85**
Creelman*, Adam Rutherford (1849–1916), XII, 586
Creelman, Elizabeth Elliott. *See* Ellis
Creelman, Hannah. *See* Tupper
Creelman, Isabella (Ross), VI, 659, 660; XI, 772
Creelman, John Ernest, XII, 218
Creelman, Samuel, XI, 620; XII, **217–19**
Creelman, William, XII, 217
Creen, Thomas, VI, 93; XI, 326
Cregan, McMahon, XII, 484
Creighten, Christian (Christen) (Fisher), V, 319
Creighton, Annie. *See* Bishop
Creighton, David (editor), XII, 581, 583
Creighton, David (of Pictou, N.S.), XI, 926
Creighton*, Donald Grant (1902–79), V, 153, 288; XII, 587, 612
Creighton, Elizabeth (Robie), VIII, 754
Creighton, Frances. *See* Coverdale
Creighton, Hugh, XI, 216
Creighton, James Moore, XI, 216
Creighton, John (father of LETITIA), XII, 219, 573
Creighton, John (son of JOHN, 1721–1807), V, 216
Creighton, John, IV, 780; V, **215–16**; VI, 310; VII, 910
Creighton, John, XI, **216–17**; XII, 599, 945, 946
Creighton, Joseph, V, 216
Creighton, Letitia (Youmans), XII, **219–21**
Creighton, Lucy. *See* Clapp
Creighton, Lucy (Binney), V, 216; X, 66
Creighton, Maria (wife of JOHN, 1721–1807), V, 215
Creighton, Mary. *See* Young
Creighton, Mary Isabel (Baker), XII, 50
Creighton, Sarah (Wilkins), V, 216; VII, 910; XI, 925, 926
Crémazie, Jacques, X, 201, 202
Crémazie, Jacques, VIII, 291, 573; IX, 119; X, **201–2**, 203, 218, 418; XII, 888
Crémazie, Joseph, VI, 84; VIII, 489; X, 202; XII, 270
Crémazie, Louis, X, 202
Crémazie, Marie-Anne. *See* Miville
Crémazie, Octave (Claude-Joseph-Olivier), VI, 84; VII, 592; VIII, 291, 408, 489, 503; IX, 465, 855; X, 21, 105, 201, **202–5**, 229; XI, 83, 172, 181, 342, 484, 495, 873, 902; XII, 270
Crénier, Louis-Alexandre, V, 680
Crépeaux, Geneviève (Gosselin), V, 358

Crépin, François, X, 82
Créquy. *See* Aide-Créquy
Crespel, Emmanuel (Jacques-Philippe), II, 390; IV, **180–82**
Crespel, Louis, XI, 88
Crespel, Louise-Thérèse. *See* Devienne
Crespel, Sébastien, IV, 180
Crespi, Juan, IV, 623
Crespieul, François de, I, 49, 396, 483; II, 61, **161–62**, 296, 357, 501, 607
Crespieul, Jean de, II, 161
Crespieul, Marguerite de. *See* Théry
Crespin, Antoine, III, 203
Crespin, Jean, III, 182; IV, 263
Cressé. *See also* Poulin
Cressé, Louise (Dumoulin), V, 216; VIII, 248, 249
Cressé, Louise (Poulin de Courval), II, 529; III, 539
Cressé, Luc-Michel, VII, 166
Cressé, Marguerite. *See* Denys
Cressé, Marie-Victoire. *See* Fafard Laframboise
Cressé, Michel, II, 529; V, 216
Cressé, Pierre-Joseph, VIII, 221
Cressé, Pierre-Michel, III, 540; V, **216–17**, 377; VI, 428; VIII, 248, 249; IX, 14, 15
Cressé de Courval. *See* Poulin de Courval Cressé
Cresson, Ezra Townsend, XI, 65
Cresswell, Francis, IX, 167
Cresswell, Rachel Elizabeth. *See* Fry
Cresswell, Samuel Gurney, IX, **167–68**
Cresswell, William Nichol, XII, 327
Creste, Jeanne (Juchereau), I, 401, 402
Crète, Marie-Louise (Desbarats), VI, 191
Crevant, Louis de, Duc d'Humières, II, 401
Crèvecœur, Marquis de. *See* Castel
Crèvecœur, Marquise de. *See* Kerven
Crevel de Moranget, Monsieur (nephew of René-Robert CAVELIER de La Salle), I, 182, 183; II, 197
Crevet, Marie (Caron; Langlois), I, 417
Crevier, Christophe, I, 475; II, 86; VIII, 258
Crevier, Édouard-Joseph, VI, 288; XI, 217
Crevier, François-Xavier, VII, 711
Crevier, Jeanne. *See* Énard
Crevier, Jeanne (Boucher), I, 109; II, 86; III, 78, 81, 82, 83
Crevier, Joseph, I, 239
Crevier, Joseph-Alexandre, XI, 3, **217–18**, 496
Crevier, Joseph-Antoine, VII, 711
Crevier, Louis, I, 239; II, 283
Crevier, Marguerite (Fournier; Gamelain de La Fontaine; Renou, *dit* La Chapelle; Groston de Saint-Ange), I, 321; II, 236, 267; IV, 315
Crevier, Marie (Gastineau Duplessis), III, 237
Crevier, Pierre-Jérémie, VIII, 243
Crevier, William, XI, 756
Crevier, Zoé-Henriette. *See* Picard, *dit* Destroismaisons
Crevier, *dit* Bellerive, Frédéric-François, XI, 217
Crevier, *dit* Bellerive, Joseph, VI, 486; VII, 661, 662, 663, 736; VIII, 34
Crevier, *dit* Bellerive, Louise. *See* Rocheleau
Crevier, *dit* Duvernay, Marie-Anne-Julie (Fortin), XI, 320
Crevier, *dit* La Meslée, Christophe, I, 238
Crevier Décheneaux, Marguerite (De Saulles), VI, 206, 207
Crevier Décheneaux, Marie-Anne (Simon, *dit* Delorme), VI, 207
Crevier de Saint-François, Jean, I, **238–39**, 321, 369

Crevier de Saint-François, Marguerite. *See* Hertel de La Fresnière
Crevier Descheneaux, Geneviève (Proulx), VII, 711; VIII, 716
Crevier Duvernay, Jacques, VIII, 258
Crevier Duvernay, Jean-Baptiste, III, 493
Crevier Duvernay, Joseph, VIII, 258
Crevier Duvernay, Marie-Anne-Julie. *See* Rocbert de La Morandière
Crevier Duvernay, Pierre, VIII, 258
Crevier Duverné (Duvernay), Jean-Baptiste, VIII, 258
Crey, Élisée, II, 130
Crichton, Ann (McKay), VIII, 552
Crichton, John, XII, 136
Cridge, Edward, XII, 61, 79, 81, 441, 442
Crignon, Pierre, I, 235, 532
Crillon, Édouard, Comte de. *See* Soubiran
Cringan*, Alexander Thom (1860–1931), XII, 959
Crinnon, Peter Francis, XII, 1084
Crippen, Lucy (Pennoyer), VI, 574
Cripps*, Eleanor Eliza (Kennedy) (1825–1913), XI, 470
Crisaci (Crisacy, Crisasy). *See* Crisafy
Crisafy, Antoine de, Marquis de Crisafy, I, 239; II, 15, 70, **162–63**, 186, 203, 303, 485, 533
Crisafy, Françoise de. *See* Grimaldi
Crisafy, Marie-Claire de, Marquise de Crisafy. *See* Ruette d'Auteuil
Crisafy, Mathieu de, II, 162
Crisafy, Thomas, I, **239**; II, 70, 162, 523; III, 310
Crisp, Delivrance (Longley), III, 407
Critcherson, George B., XII, 123
Croates, Margaret (MacDonnell), X, 470
Crochet, Le. *See* Kiotseaeton
Crocker, Charles, XI, 292
Crocker, Lydia (Woodman), VII, 923
Crocker, Nancy. *See* Homer
Crocker, Samuel Eastman, VIII, 394
Crockery Old Man. *See* Natos-api
Crocket, Elizabeth (Wilson), XII, 1114
Croft, Henry Holmes, VII, 32; VIII, 57, 473, 775, 776; XI, **218–19**
Croft, Mary. *See* Shaw
Croft, Thomas, I, 19, 21, 147, **239–40**, 386
Croft, William (father of HENRY HOLMES), XI, 218
Croft, William (father of THOMAS), I, 239
Crofton, Anne Agnes. *See* Addison
Crofton, Frances. *See* ffolliott
Crofton, Henry, XI, 219
Crofton, John ffolliott, X, 168; XI, **219–20**, 546
Crofton, Louisa (Maitland), VIII, 596
Crofton, Sir Walter, XII, 731
Crofts, Henry O., XII, 909
Croghan, George (Indian agent), III, 49, 323, 495, 502, 526, 530, 614; IV, 395, 408, 409, 499; V, 804; VII, 665
Croghan, George (officer), VI, 809
Croisille. *See* Legardeur
Croissy, Marquis de. *See* Colbert
Croix. *See* Baudry
Croizille. *See* Legardeur
Crokatt, Charles, IV, 330
Croke, Alexander, VII, 216
Croke, Sir Alexander, V, 108, 109, 446, 694; VI, 90, 99, 157, 333; VII, 63, 87, 88, 107, **216–20**, 530, 910; VIII, 257, 755; IX, 173
Croke, Alice, Lady Croke. *See* Blake
Croke, Anne. *See* Armistead
Croke, Mary. *See* Flynn
Croke, Nicholas, VII, **220**
Croker, John Wilson, VI, 803; VIII, 683, 772
Cromartie, Charlotte Louisa (Newman), XII, 786
Cromartie, John (HBC employee), III, 124
Cromartie, John (HBC officer), VII, 3
Cromarty, Earl of. *See* Mackenzie
Cromberger. *See* Noremberguer
Crombie, Alexander, XI, 736
Crombie, Catherine Eliza (MacKenzie), X, 477
Crombie, Ernestus, X, 200
Crombie, Marcus C., X, 477
Cromwell, James Oliver, VI, 64, 275, 276
Cromwell, Oliver, I, 242, 406, 407, 474, 595, 604, 605, 636, 652; IV, xvii; XII, 1109, 1122
Cromwell, Thomas, I, 566
Cronan, Daniel, XII, 221
Cronan, Daniel, VII, 107; XII, **221–22**
Cronan, John, XII, 221
Cronan, Mary. *See* McCarthy
Cronan, William, XII, 221
Cronk, Sarah (Green), VI, 300
Cronyn, Benjamin, X, 206
Cronyn, Benjamin, VIII, 95, 276, 715, 749; IX, 55, 151, 205, 292, 323, 378, 763; X, 55, 59, 60, 84, 121, **205–10**, 270; XI, 368, 570, 916, 917; XII, 681, 1000
Cronyn, Margaret. *See* Barton
Cronyn, Margaret (Blake), X, 206
Cronyn, Margaret Ann. *See* Bickerstaff
Cronyn, Martha. *See* Collins
Cronyn, Mary Elizabeth. *See* Dixon
Cronyn, Mary G. *See* Goodhue
Cronyn, Rebecca (Blake), X, 206
Cronyn, Robert, VIII, 870
Cronyn, Sophia. *See* Blake
Cronyn, Thomas, X, 205
Cronyn, Verschoyle, X, 206
Crook, Olivia (Hill), XII, 306
Crooke, Margaret (Inglis), V, 444; VII, 432
Crooked Arm. *See* Maskepetoon
Crooked Back. *See* Namo-pisi
Crooked Legs, XII, 780
Crooks, Adam, VIII, 187; IX, 246, 292; X, 509; XI, 145, **220–23**, 537, 541, 587, 621; XII, 151, 332, 1086, 1087
Crooks, Emily Anne. *See* Evans
Crooks, Francis, VIII, 185
Crooks, Hester (Boutwell), VIII, 191
Crooks, James, V, 189, 405, 639, 643, 673, 725, 842, 846; VI, 149, 199, 200; VII, 28, 833, 835; VIII, **185–90**, 279, 327, 519; IX, 718; X, 53; XI, 220
Crooks, Jane. *See* Cummings
Crooks, Jane Eliza (Bethune), VIII, 187; X, 53; XII, 107
Crooks, John, VI, 248, 421; VII, 835
Crooks, Margaret. *See* Ramsay
Crooks, Marianne Pelagie Emilie. *See* Pratte
Crooks, Mary Margaret (Ewart), VIII, 279
Crooks, Mathew, VII, 28
Crooks, Ramsay, V, 526; VI, 358; VII, 582; VIII, **190–91**, 557; IX, 280; X, 628

Crooks, Robert P., IX, 804
Crooks, William (brother of JAMES), V, 189, 725; VIII, 185
Crooks, William (father of JAMES), VII, 28, 835; VIII, 185, 190
Crooks, William (politician), VII, 497
Crookshank, Andrew, VI, 169
Crookshank, Catherine. *See* Norris
Crookshank, Catherine (Heward), VIII, 192
Crookshank, Catherine (McGill), VI, 451; VIII, 191
Crookshank, George (father of GEORGE), VIII, 191
Crookshank, George (son of GEORGE), VIII, 192
Crookshank, George, VI, 416, 451, 452; VII, 162, 920; VIII, 6, 10, **191–92**, 251
Crookshank, Rachel (Macaulay, Lady Macaulay), VI, 415; VIII, 191
Crookshank, Robert William, VII, 444; VIII, 192
Crookshank, Sarah Susanna. *See* Lambert
Crop Eared Wolf. *See* Makoyi-Opistoki
Crosby, Ann (O'Donel), V, 631
Crosby, Anne (Currier), XI, 229
Crosby, Elisha Oscar, X, 587
Crosby*, Thomas (1840–1914), X, 701
Croscombe, William, VII, 45
Croskill. *See* Crosskill
Crosland, Alice (Calvert), I, 162
Crosland, John, I, 162
Crosley, Henry, VIII, 706
Crosman, A., VI, 728
Cross, Ann (Bell), VIII, 73
Cross, Martha (Steeves), X, 665
Cross, Sarah Mary (Hill), II, 287
Crossen, Mary, XII, 10
Crosskill, Catherine Charlotte. *See* Weeks
Crosskill, Charlotte. *See* Fillis
Crosskill, Frances. *See* Gidney
Crosskill, Henry, VIII, 192
Crosskill, John, VI, **173–74**; VII, 272; VIII, 193, 732
Crosskill, John Henry, VII, 576; VIII, **192–94**, 656; XI, 135; XII, 765
Crosskill, Sarah Ann. *See* McIntosh
Crossley*, Hugh Thomas (1850–1934), XII, 707
Crossley, Phoebe (Lloyd), VII, 508
Crossman, William, X, 406
Croswell, Sherman, VIII, 436
Crotty, Mary. *See* Meagher
Croucher, Mary (Truscott), VIII, 895
Crouckeshanks, Alexander, V, 217
Crout, Henry, I, 233, **240–41**, 670, 671
Crow, Mary (O'Neill), X, 558
Crow, Robert, II, 493
Crowdy, Caroline Augusta. *See* Dunscombe
Crowdy, Elizabeth Sarah. *See* Stout
Crowdy, James, V, 781; VII, 156; VIII, 382; IX, **168–69**, 195, 605; XI, 29, 761
Crowe, Jane (Bunting), XII, 137
Crowe, Josias, II, 152, **163–64**, 534, 636
Crowell, Elizabeth (Barss), VI, 37; VIII, 62
Crowell, Thomas, VII, 562
Crowfoot. *See also* Isapo-muxika
Crowfoot, XI, 443
Crown. *See* Crowne
Crowne, Agnes. *See* Mackworth
Crowne, John, I, 241, 242

Crowne, William, I, 25, **241–42**, 434, 435, 595, 605, 636; IV, xxiv
Crowther, James, X, 155
Crowther, Sarah Ellen (Cawthra), X, 155
Crozat, Antoine, II, 203, 355, 356, 425; III, 380
Crozier, Francis Rawdon Moira, VII, 327; X, 29
Crozier, Isabella. *See* Deacon
Crozier, John Albert Gordon, XII, 222
Crozier*, Leif Newry Fitzroy (1846–1901), XI, 195, 261, 479, 596, 598, 599, 747, 870; XII, 222, 223, 427, 608, 734, 1009
Crozier, St George Baron Le Poer, IX, 600; XII, **222–23**
Crozier, Thomas, X, 587
Crozier, Thomas Charles, XII, 222
Cruger. *See* Kruger
Cruickshank, Ann (Kay; wife of ROBERT), V, 218
Cruickshank, Elizabeth (Webster), V, 218
Cruickshank, James F., XII, 785
Cruickshank, Robert, IV, 206, 629, 702, 748; V, 36, 37, **217–19**, 437, 595, 614, 708, 727, 728; VII, 17
Cruikshank, Ann (Roger), X, 627
Cruikshank*, Ernest Alexander (1853–1939), V, 759, 800; VI, 545
Cruikshank, John, VIII, 645; X, 118
Cruse, Thomas, I, **242–43**
Crusoe, Robinson, III, **151**
Crusson, *dit* Pilote, François, I, 267
Cruzat, Francisco, IV, 303
Cryn. *See* Togouiroui
Crynssen, Abraham, I, 443
Crysler, Dorothea. *See* Adams
Crysler, Dorothy. *See* Meyers
Crysler (Krausler), John (Johannes), VIII, 194
Crysler, John, VI, 521, 532; VIII, **194–95**, 304
Crysler, John Pliny, VIII, 195; IX, 858
Crysler, Nancy. *See* Finkle
Crysler, Nancy. *See* Loucks
Cuadra. *See* Bodega
Cubit, George, VII, **220–21**; VIII, 75, 76, 477
Cubitt, Thomas, XI, 119
Cucurron, *dit* Sicard, Roch-Ambroise, VIII, 536
Cudlip, Emily. *See* Allison
Cudlip, John, XI, 223
Cudlip, John Waterbury, XI, **223–25**; XII, 1097
Cudlip, Rebecca. *See* Waterbury
Cuff, Emily (Annand), XI, 22
Cugnet, Mme (of Quebec), IV, 127
Cugnet, Antoine, IV, 182
Cugnet, François-Étienne, II, 530; III, 16, 48, 146, **151–55**, 159, 224, 237, 340, 353, 490, 538, 592, 608, 617, 647; IV, 45, 64, 66, 167, 182, 264, 284, 344, 358, 359, 360, 361, 362, 590; V, 252, 498; VII, 68
Cugnet, François-Joseph, III, 154; IV, xlv, 105, 146, **182–87**, 315, 349, 388, 602; V, 43, 144, 252, 253, 606, 794, 863; VI, 27, 493
Cugnet, Gilles-Louis, III, 154; IV, 182, 185, 430; V, 196
Cugnet, Jacques-François, IV, 182, 184, 185; V, 482, 792; VII, 169
Cugnet, Jean (Jean-Baptiste), III, 151; IV, 182
Cugnet, Jean-Baptiste (uncle), III, 152; IV, 182
Cugnet, Jean-Baptiste, III, 154
Cugnet, Louise-Charlotte (Liénard de Beaujeu de Villemonde), III, 16; V, 462, 498

Cugnet, Louise-Madeleine. *See* Dusautoy
Cugnet, Madeleine. *See* Baudin
Cugnet, Marie-Angélique. *See* Le Comte Dupré
Cugnet, Marie-Josephte. *See* Lafontaine de Belcour
Cugnet, Thomas-Marie, III, 154, 647; IV, 182, 185; V, 368
Cuillerier, Angélique (Porlier), IV, 638
Cuillerier, Julien, II, 164
Cuillerier, Julienne. *See* Faifeu
Cuillerier, Marie. *See* Barbeau, *dit* Lucault
Cuillerier, Marie-Anne-Véronique, III, **155–56**, 238
Cuillerier, René, I, 130, 598, 662; II, **164–65**; III, 155
Cuillerier, *dit* Beaubien, Angélique (Sterling), IV, 722
Cuillerier, *dit* Beaubien, Antoine, III, 528
Cuillerier, *dit* Beaubien, Marie-Catherine. *See* Trottier Desruisseaux
Culbertson, Mrs. *See* Medicine Snake Woman
Culbertson, Alexander, IX, 623, 624; XII, 778
Cull, Elizabeth. *See* McMillan
Cull, George, VI, 175
Cull, George Irwin, VI, 174
Cull, Henry, VI, **174–75**, 377, 706, 708; VII, 767
Cull, James, VII, **221–23**, 760, 863
Cull, Louis, VI, 174
Cull, Mary (wife of WILLIAM), VI, 175
Cull, Sarah (wife of JAMES), VII, 221
Cull, William, IV, 714; VI, **175–76**, 271, 323, 580; VII, 377
Cullen, Dr, VI, 801
Cullen, Ann. *See* Skeet
Cullen, Elizabeth. *See* Willis
Cullen, John, VIII, 761
Cullen, Paul, X, 191, 193; XII, 860, 861
Cullen, Sarah (Parkin), VII, 681; X, 587
Cullen, William (father-in-law of James Barrett COOPER), XI, 201
Cullen, William (of London, England), V, 260
Cullimore, Grace (Spike), X, 664
Culshaw, Alice (Swift), XII, 1001
Culver. *See also* Collver
Culver, Anne (Sovereen), VI, 729
Culver (Collver), Nathan, V, 197
Cumberland, Captain, X, 593
Cumberland, Duke of. *See* Ernest Augustus; William Augustus
Cumberland, Caroline (Ridout), XI, 225, 735
Cumberland, Frederic Barlow, XI, 225, 227
Cumberland, Frederic William, VIII, 486, 761, 872, 876, 943, 944, 961; XI, 167, **225–29**, 482, 618, 736; XII, 344, 394, 809, 885, 908, 962, 991, 992, 994
Cumberland, Richard, V, 689
Cumberland, Thomas, XI, 225
Cumberland, Wilmot Mary. *See* Bramley
Cumberlege, S. A., IV, 578
Cumings, Archibald, II, 118, **165**, 316, 583, 610, 611, 643
Cummer, Rebecca (Harris), XII, 413
Cumming, Alexander, XII, 338
Cumming, Cuthbert, IX, **169–70**
Cumming, Hannah (Cox), VIII, 175
Cumming, Jane. *See* McMurray
Cumming, Jane (Aumond), X, 23
Cumming, John, VI, 722
Cumming, Margaret (Jennings), X, 380
Cumming, Martha (Fraser), XII, 338

Cumming, Mary Ann (Cameron), XII, 149
Cumming-Bruce, Elizabeth Mary (Bruce, Countess of Elgin and Kincardine), IX, 89
Cummings, Caroline. *See* Street
Cummings, Jane (Crooks), VIII, 185; XI, 220
Cummings, Samuel, V, 94
Cummings, Thomas, VI, 18; VIII, 185
Cummins, Elizabeth (Murray), XI, 632
Cumshewa, IV, 420
Cunard, Abraham, IX, 170, 172, 174
Cunard, Ann (Allen), IX, 180
Cunard, Edward (uncle), IX, 174, 177, 181, 182, 223; XI, 664
Cunard, Edward, IX, 173, 178, 181, 182, 184; XII, 838, 839
Cunard, Elizabeth, IX, 183
Cunard, Henry, VIII, 737; IX, 170, 174, 177, 179
Cunard, Jane (Francklyn), IX, 173, 182, 185
Cunard, John, IX, 174
Cunard, Joseph, VII, 5, 637, 683, 684, 691; VIII, 737, 738, 739, 740, 783, 809; IX, 22, 154, **170–72**, 174, 177, 178, 179, 181, 182, 184, 438, 452, 766; X, 158; XII, 838
Cunard, Margaret. *See* Murphy
Cunard, Mary. *See* Peters
Cunard, Mary (Peters), XII, 838
Cunard, Sir Samuel, VI, 110; VII, 64, 84, 237, 691, 867; VIII, 93, 167, 168, 169, 193, 400, 956; IX, 86, 170, 171, **172–86**, 223, 325, 731; X, 185, 187, 189, 308, 596; XI, 5, 241, 567, 666, 701, 847; XII, 436, 765, 838, 839, 840, 966
Cunard, Susan. *See* Duffus
Cunard, Thomas, IX, 174
Cunard, William (uncle), IX, 174
Cunard, William, IX, 173, 182, 184
Cundall, Robert, X, 352
Cunnabell, Jacob Sparling, VII, 81; IX, 186
Cunnabell, John, IX, 186
Cunnabell, Margaret. *See* Dechman
Cunnabell, Nancy. *See* Leonard
Cunnabell, William, IX, **186–87**
Cunningham, Annie. *See* Brown
Cunningham, Archibald, V, 402
Cunningham, Barbara. *See* Newlands
Cunningham, Eliza (Cook), IX, 151
Cunningham, Emily. *See* Woodman
Cunningham, James, XII, 367
Cunningham, John (father of ROBERT), X, 210
Cunningham, John (interpreter), XII, 932
Cunningham, John (politician), VII, 589
Cunningham, John, I, **243**, 360, 408
Cunningham, John P., IX, 128
Cunningham, Patrick, IX, 239
Cunningham, Richard W., VII, 272
Cunningham, Robert, X, **210–11**; XI, 46, 644
Cunningham, William, XII, 659
Cuny, Élisabeth. *See* Dupont
Cuny, Philippe-Antoine, IV, 187
Cuny Dauterive, Madeleine-Thérèse de. *See* Chabert de Joncaire
Cuny Dauterive, Philippe-Antoine de, IV, **187**
Cuoq, Jean-André, V, 480; IX, 421; XII, **223–24**, 570
Cuoq, Jean-Pierre, XII, 223
Cuoq, Marie-Rosalie. *See* Delholme

179

Cuppaidge, Rebecca (Cochran), VI, 156; VII, 189; X, 177
Curatteau, Claude, IV, 188
Curatteau, Jean-Baptiste, IV, 90, **187–89**; V, 51, 143, 164, 241, 242, 294; VI, 485, 586; VII, 673
Curatteau, Jeanne. *See* Fonteneau
Curatteau, Pierre (father), IV, 187
Curatteau, Pierre, IV, 188
Curatteau, René, IV, 188
Curaux. *See* Curot
Curchot, Jacques, IV, 303, 304
Cureux, Marguerite (Dumas), V, 276
Cureux, *dit* Saint-Germain, Marie-Anne (Fortier), IV, 271
Cureux, *dit* Saint-Germain, Marie-Louise (Baillairgé), V, 51; XII, 45
Curie, Henriette-Edwige, Baronne de L'Espérance (Sandersleben), II, 424
Curie, Richard, II, 424
Curie, Sébastienne, Baronne de L' Espérance (Sifert), II, 424
Curler, Arent van, I, 308
Curot, Josette (Guy), VII, 360
Curot, Madeleine. *See* Cauchois
Curot, Marie-Louise, named de Saint-Martin, IV, **189–90**
Curot, Martin, IV, 189
Curran, James Watson, XII, 499
Curran, Mary (Morrison), XI, 615, 617
Curray (Currie). *See* Corry
Currer, Alice, XII, 524, 526
Currer, Ellen (Langton), XII, 523, 524, 526, 527
Currey, William Samuel, V, 443
Currie, Donald, X, **211**; XI, 202
Currie, John, XI, 565; XII, 147, 660
Currie, William, X, 85
Currier, Anne. *See* Crosby
Currier, Christina. *See* Wilson
Currier, Ezekiel, XI, 229
Currier, Hannah. *See* Wright
Currier, Joseph Merrill, VIII, 552; X, 23, 441; XI, **229–30**, 590, 682; XII, 258, 664, 937, 938
Currier, Nathaniel, VIII, 959, 961
Curry, Charles, X, 656
Curry, James, XII, 147
Curry, John, XII, 147
Curry, Mary Rebecca (Wilkinson), X, 703
Curtain, Alice (Pedley), X, 587
Curtis, Mr (of Newfoundland), V, 244
Curtis, Anne Jeanette (Miller), X, 514
Curtis, Christabella. *See* Blachford
Curtis, Elizabeth. *See* Lawson
Curtis, James. *See also* Bird, James
Curtis, James, V, **219–20**, 263, 335, 477; VI, 162, 566, 663, 736, 785; VIII, 547
Curtis, Jane Sarah, Lady Curtis. *See* Brady
Curtis, Sir Lucius, V, 221
Curtis, Mary (Haythorne), XII, 418
Curtis, Mary (Loring), IV, 486
Curtis, Roger (grandfather), V, 220
Curtis, Roger, V, 221
Curtis, Sir Roger, IV, 708; V, **220–22**
Curtis, Thomas, V, 407, 777
Curtius, Charles, IV, 384; V, 315
Curtius, Marie-Anne-Joseph (Trestler), V, 827
Curwen, John, XII, 959

Curzon, Robert, XII, 1075
Curzon, Sarah Anne. *See* Vincent
Cusack, James William, IX, 611
Cushing, Caleb, VIII, 448; XI, 768
Cushing, Catherine. *See* Hutchins
Cushing, Eliza Lanesford. *See* Foster
Cushing, Elmer, VI, 186, 700, 701, 816; X, 211
Cushing, Frederick, XI, 321
Cushing, Job, X, 211
Cushing, Lemuel, X, 212
Cushing, Lemuel, X, **211–12**
Cushing, Lucy (Aylwin), IV, 37
Cushing, Matthew, X, 211
Cushing, Sarah. *See* Rice
Cushman, Charlotte Saunders, XII, 448
Cushman, Eliza. *See* Moore
Cushman, Josiah, X, 290
Cusson, Catherine, IV, 235
Cusson, Jacqueline. *See* Pépin
Cusson, Jean, II, 166
Cusson, Jean, II, xix, 11, **165–66**; III, 4
Cusson, Marie. *See* Foubert
Cusson, Marie-Joseph (Périnau), V, 662
Cusson, Michelle (Adhémar de Saint-Martin), II, 11; III, 4
Cussy, Geneviève (Paradis), III, 500
Custer, George Armstrong, XI, 869
Cuthbert, Alexander (grandfather), IV, 190
Cuthbert, Alexander, IV, 191; V, 312, 687
Cuthbert, Ann (Thornton), VIII, 197
Cuthbert, Beatrix (Cuthbert), IV, 190
Cuthbert, Catherine. *See* Cairns
Cuthbert, Catherine Betsey Isabella (Antrobus), V, 26; VIII, 17
Cuthbert, Christiana. *See* Montgomery
Cuthbert, Édouard-Octavien, XII, 818
Cuthbert, Emily. *See* Rush
Cuthbert, James, IV, 191; V, 636; VI, 634; VII, 527, 717; XI, 88
Cuthbert, James, IV, **190–91**, 379, 579; V, 21, 26, 142, 312, 313, 432, 579, 636, 687; VI, 416, 417, 769; VIII, 17; IX, 187
Cuthbert, Margaret. *See* Mackenzie
Cuthbert, Margaret (Rae), VIII, 734; X, 605
Cuthbert, Rebecca. *See* Stockton
Cuthbert, Robert, VIII, 196
Cuthbert, Ross, IV, 191; V, 209, 210; VI, 392; VII, 645; VIII, 60, 890; IX, **187–88**
Cuthbert, William, VIII, **195–97**
Cutler, Elizabeth. *See* Goldsbury
Cutler, Elizabeth (Burnham), VIII, 116
Cutler, Robert Molleson, VII, 589; VIII, 782
Cutler, Sarah. *See* Reade
Cutler, Thomas, VII, 223
Cutler, Thomas, VI, 113; VII, **223–24**, 589, 933; IX, 152
Cut Nose. *See* Saswaypew
Cut-Nosed Chief. *See* Peguis
Cutt, Margaret (Vaughan), II, 644
Cuttan (Cutten), Josiah, V, 639
Cutting Woman. *See* Sisoyaki
Cuvier, Anne-Catherine (Vallet Des Barres), VI, 192
Cuvier, Frédéric, III, 679
Cuvier, Georges, Baron Cuvier, IX, 660; X, 65; XI, 72
Cuvillier, Angélique. *See* Miot, *dit* Girard

Cuvillier, Angélique-G. (Symes), IX, 772
Cuvillier, Augustin, VII, 224
Cuvillier, Austin (Augustin), VI, 281, 381, 701, 802; VII, 135, 148, **224–28**, 393, 482, 489, 647, 650, 717, 739, 770; VIII, xxvii, 21, 284, 433, 480, 781; IX, 360, 456, 560, 569, 644, 650, 773, 810, 811; X, 219, 421; XI, 59, 237, 315; XII, 62
Cuvillier, Marie-Angélique (Delisle), X, 219
Cuvillier, Marie-Claire. *See* Perrault
Cuvillon. *See* Quévillon
Cuyler, Abraham, III, 528, 529
Cuyler, Abraham Cornelius, IV, 293, 522 ; V, 204, **222–23**, 510, 545, 552, 766; VI, 194, 195
Cuyler, Catalyntje. *See* Schuyler
Cuyler, Cornelius, V, 222
Cuyler, Jane Elizabeth. *See* Glen
Cygne, Le. *See* Onasakenrat, Joseph
Cyr (Sire), Félicité (Robichaux), V, 719
Cyr, Marie (Coron), III, 140, 141
Cyr, Narcisse, IX, 610; X, 165
Cyrier. *See* Cirier
Czerny, Karl, VIII, 634

DABIN, Josette (Kimber), VIII, 470
Dablon, Claude, I, 48, 49, 58, 205, 206, 207, **244**, 282, 393, 394, 395, 396, 445, 461, 491, 492, 523; II, 61, 62, 158, 218, 347, 501, 517, 536; III, xxix; IV, lvi
Daccarrette, Catherine. *See* Gonillon
Daccarrette, Catherine (Lagoanere), III, 156
Daccarrette, Jacques (father), III, 156
Daccarrette, Jacques, III, 156
Daccarrette, Jeanne. *See* Gonillon
Daccarrette, Joannis, III, 156
Daccarrette, Marguerite. *See* La Borde
Daccarrette, Marie. *See* Gastaignol
Daccarrette, Marie-Charlotte (Leneuf de Beaubassin), III, 157
Daccarrette, Michel (d. 1745), II, 220; III, **156–57**, 350, 452, 532; IV, 245, 253
Daccarrette, Michel (1730–67), III, **157–58**; IV, 421, 422, 645
Dache, Jacques, II, 513
Da Costa. *See* Norris
Dadavant, Madeleine (Roblot), IX, 680
Dadson, Ebenezer William, XII, **224–26**, 1094
Dadson, Julia Elizabeth. *See* French
Dadson, Mary. *See* Breachin
Dadson, Stephen, XII, 224, 225
Daer and Shortcleuch, Baron. *See* Douglas
Daer and Shortcleuch, Baroness. *See* Wedderburn
Dagenais, Louis, VIII, 243, 244
Daggart. *See* Dykert
Dagge, Mary (Worthington), XII, 1128
Dagnan-Bouveret, Pascal-Adolphe-Jean, XII, 287
Dagnau de Quindre de La Picanier, Guillaume- François, III, 159
Dagneau Douville, Alexandre, IV, 54, **191–92**
Dagneau Douville, Alexandre-René, IV, 192
Dagneau Douville, Marie. *See* Coulon de Villiers
Dagneau Douville, Marie. *See* Lamy
Dagneau Douville, Michel, III, 158; IV, 191
Dagneau Douville de Lamothe, Guillaume, III, 159; IV, 192

Dagneau Douville de La Saussaye, Philippe, IV, 192
Dagneau Douville de Quindre, Archange (Maurin), III, 441
Dagneau Douville de Quindre, Françoise-Marie-Anne. *See* Picoté de Belestre
Dagneau Douville de Quindre, Louis-Césaire, III, **158–59**, 432, 441; IV, 192
Dagron-Richer, L., XI, 802
Daguerre, Louis-Jacques-Mandé, VII, 875
Daguerre, Madeleine (Bourdon de Romainville), I, 114
Daguilhe, Esther (Cazeneuve), VIII, 136
Daguilhe, Joseph, VIII, 136
Dagworthy, John, III, 261
Dahon, Laurens-Alexandre, IV, 124
Daigle, Madeleine (Bédard), V, 60
Daigle, Marie-Charles (Giard), XI, 345
Daignault, Angélique (Vandandaigue, *dit* Gadbois), X, 297
Daigre, Jacques, II, 549
Daigre, Marie-Jeanne (Bedout), V, 61
Daillon. *See* La Roche
Daine, Angélique. *See* Pagé
Daine, Antoinette. *See* Pelletier
Daine, François, III, 15, 64, 139, **159–61**, 203, 226, 272, 291, 340, 505, 608; IV, 66, 75, 264, 602, 614
Daine, Jacques (father), III, 159
Daine, Jacques, III, 159
Daine, Louise. *See* Pécaudy de Contrecœur
Daine, Louise-Jeanne. *See* Bouat
Daine, Marius-Basile, III, 159
Daine, Nicolas, III, 159
Dakeyne, Mary (Gladwin), IV, 297
Dalaire (Dallaire), Étienne, XI, 207, 498
Dalaire, Marie-Louise (Laurin), XI, 152, 498
Dalard. *See* Allard
Dalciat, Marie-Louise (Petit-Claire; Huguet, *dit* Latour), V, 437
Dalcrombie. *See* MacGillivray; McGillivray
Dale, David, V, 69
Dalgueuil (Delguiel), *dit* Labrèche, Jeanne (Billeron, *dit* Lafatigue), IV, 34
Dalgueuil (Delguiel), *dit* Labrèche, Louise-Françoise (Augé), IV, 34
Dalhousie, Countess. *See* Broun; Glene
Dalhousie, Earl of. *See* Maule Ramsay; Ramsay
Dalison, Jane (Amherst, Lady Amherst), IV, 25
Dallaire, Marie-Louise (Carrier), XI, 152
Dallas, Alexander Grant, VIII, 818; IX, 518, 530, 714, 853; X, 244, 247, 478; XI, **230–31**, 476, 540, 563; XII, 194, 334, 335
Dallas, Alister Grant, XI, 231
Dallas, Helena. *See* Grant
Dallas, Jane. *See* Douglas
Dallas, John, XI, 230
Dallas, Margaret (Linton), IX, 469
Dallas, Margaret Johnston (O'Meara), XI, 653
Dallas, Murdoch, XI, 230
Dallas, Sarah (Macarthur), XI, 538
Dallas of Cantray, Agnes (Mackintosh), VI, 473
Dallas of Cantray, Anne (Shaw), V, 752
Dallest, Marguerite-Joséphine-Marie (Pandosy), XII, 817
Dalley, Edwin, VIII, 822
Dalley, Henry, VII, 93
Dallimore, Emma Jane (Blackburn), XI, 80
Dalling, Sir John, III, 12; IV, 779

Dalling and Bulwer, Baron. *See* Bulwer
Dalmas, Antoine, I, **244–45**; II, 161
Dalpech, *dit* Bélair, Marie (Guernon, *dit* Belleville), V, 392
Dalquier. *See* Alquier
Dalrymple, Alexander, IV, 218, 244, 245, 325, 340, 741; V, 541, 684
Dalrymple, Christian (Skakel), VII, 809
Dalrymple, Eliza. *See* Webster
Dalrymple, George R., VIII, **197–98**, 376; XII, 856
Dalton, Adelaide Annabella (Young), X, 729
Dalton, Charles, VII, 292, 295; VIII, **198–200**, 475; IX, 188
Dalton, Emma (Wilson, Lady Wilson), XII, 1107
Dalton, James T., XI, 419
Dalton, John, VIII, 199; IX, **188–89**, 393, 582
Dalton, Rebecca. *See* Watson
Dalton, Robert Gladstone, VIII, 804
Dalton, Sarah. *See* Holman
Dalton, Sarah. *See* Pratt
Dalton, Sophia. *See* Simms
Dalton, Thomas, VI, 165, 470, 772; VII, **228–31**, 368, 543, 548, 600, 846; VIII, 251, 515, 602, 804; IX, 509, 557; XI, 785; XII, 1107
Dalton, William (father), VII, 228
Dalton, William, VII, 228
Dalton, William Henry, VIII, 804
Daly, Caroline Maria, Lady Daly. *See* Gore
Daly, Charles, VIII, 959
Daly, Charles Patrick, XI, 393
Daly, Dominick, IX, 189
Daly, Sir Dominick, VI, 120; VII, 32, 180, 478, 605, 606, 607; VIII, 51, 256, 565, 582, 775, 800, 804; IX, **189–93**, 370, 371, 372, 415, 459, 690, 725, 796, 818, 819; X, 93, 255, 256, 404, 670; XI, 118, 247, 281, 405, 409, 555, 666; XII, 89
Daly, Helen McLaren. *See* Ferguson
Daly, Joanna Harriet. *See* Blake
Daly, John Augustin, XII, 316, 948
Daly, John Corry Wilson, IX, 469; X, **212–13**; XI, 231
Daly, John Porter, X, 610
Daly, Leonora. *See* Mayne
Daly, Sir Malachy Bowes, IX, 192; XII, 51
Daly, Thomas Mayne, X, 213; XI, **231–32**
Daly*, Thomas Mayne (1852–1911), X, 213; XI, 231
Dalyell (Dalzell), James, III, 528, 529; IV, 297, 308, 680
Dalzell, Alexander, IX, 195
Dalziel, Christian (Bell), VIII, 72
Damboise, Jeanne (Deschevery), III, 181
Dambourgès, Catherine. *See* Couillard Des Islets
Dambourgès, François, IV, 386, 548; V, 654, 816; XI, 87
Dame, Auguste-Frédéric, XII, 159
Dame, George, IV, 304; V, 584
Damestoye, Bernard, III, 157
Damien, Geneviève (Légaré), VIII, 494
Damienne (servant), I, 426
Damour, Pierre, X, 492
Damours, Charlotte (Raimbault), II, 542
Damours, Élisabeth. *See* Tessier
Damours, Élisabeth (Chartier de Lotbinière), I, 202, 245; II, 136
Damours, Jean, I, 245
Damours, Louis, I, 245
Damours de Chauffours, Élisabeth (Charron de La Barre), I, 201; II, 133

Damours de Chauffours, Geneviève (Céloron de Blainville), II, 125, 442
Damours de Chauffours, Louis, I, 245, 246; II, 3, **166–67**, 271, 626; III, 273, 474, 681
Damours de Chauffours, Marguerite. *See* Guyon
Damours de Chauffours, Marguerite (Testard de Montigny), II, 627
Damours de Chauffours, Marie. *See* Marsolet de Saint-Aignan
Damours de Chauffours, Marie (Villedonné), II, 653
Damours de Chauffours, Marie-Charlotte (Abbadie de Saint-Castin, Baronne de Saint-Castin), II, 3, 4
Damours de Chauffours, Marie-Joseph (Morpain), III, 474
Damours de Chauffours, Mathieu, I, 137, 201, 202, **245**, 289, 587, 588, 589; II, xvii, 125, 166, 167, 442, 588, 653; III, 681
Damours de Clignancour, Françoise-Charlotte. *See* Legardeur de Tilly
Damours de Clignancour, Louis-Mathieu, III, 178, 233
Damours de Clignancour, Mathieu-Benjamin, IV, 375
Damours de Clignancour, René, I, 245; II, 166, **167–68**, 626
Damours de Freneuse, Antoine, III, 681
Damours de Freneuse, Joseph, IV, 181
Damours de Freneuse, Louis, II, 7
Damours de Freneuse, Louise. *See* Guyon
Damours de Freneuse, Mathieu, I, **245–46**, 577; II, 166, 271, 626; III, 111, 552, 681
Damours de Freneuse, Ursule. *See* Abbadie de Saint-Castin
Damours de Louvières, Louis, II, 633
Damours de Louvières, Marie-Françoise (Raymond), VI, 634
Damours de Plaines, Bernard, I, 245
Damours Des Plaines, Joseph, III, 432
Damours Des Plaines, Marie-Madeleine. *See* Coulon de Villiers
Dana, James Dwight, XII, 233, 457
Danao. *See* David
Dance, Nathaniel, IV, 601
Dancereau, Marie-Josephte. *See* Privée
Dandane Danseville de L'Étendard, Marie-Anne. *See* Dupéré
Dandane Danseville de L'Étendard, Nicolas-Antoine, III, 125
Dandin. *See* Daudin
Dandonneau, Isabelle. *See* Fain
Dandonneau, Jacques, II, 168
Dandonneau, Périnne (Lamarre, *dit* Bélisle), II, 340
Dandonneau, *dit* Lajeunesse, Françoise. *See* Jobin
Dandonneau, *dit* Lajeunesse, Jeanne (Babie), I, 74
Dandonneau, *dit* Lajeunesse, Pierre, I, 74; II, **168**
Dandonneau Du Sablé, Angélique (Chaboulié), II, 127
Dandonneau Du Sablé, Louis, II, 168; III, 247
Dandonneau Du Sablé, Marguerite. *See* Sabrevois de Bleury
Dandonneau Du Sablé, Marie-Anne (Gaultier de Varennes et de La Vérendrye), II, 168, 239; III, 241, 244, 247, 252; IV, 288
Dandonneau Du Sablé, Marie-Louise (Robinau de Portneuf), III, 560
Dandridge, Martha (Washington), V, 313

Dandurand, Albert, XI, 424
Dandurand, Françoise (Daoust), IX, 193
Dandurand, Louise (Duquet), VII, 264
Dandurand, Marie-Jovite. *See* Descombes-Porcheron
Dandurand*, Raoul (1861–1942), XI, 275, 276, 277; XII, 695, 696
Dandurand, Roger-François, VIII, 209
Dandurand, *dit* Marcheterre, Élisabeth (Doutre), X, 249; XI, 272
Daneau, Catherine. *See* Driot
Daneau, Jacques, II, 168
Daneau de Muy, Catherine. *See* Ailleboust Des Muceaux
Daneau de Muy, Charlotte, named de Sainte-Hélène, III, **161**
Daneau de Muy, Jacques-Pierre, II, 168; III, **161–63**, 601; IV, 634
Daneau de Muy, Louise-Geneviève. *See* Ruette d'Auteuil
Daneau de Muy, Marguerite. *See* Boucher
Daneau de Muy, Marguerite (Robinau de Portneuf), II, 580; III, 559, 560
Daneau de Muy, Nicolas, II, **168–69**, 395, 416, 504, 580, 588, 603, 617; III, 161, 162, 380, 505
Danford, Jacob, V, 817
Danforth, Asa, VI, 176
Danforth, Asa, VI, 160, **176–78**
Danforth, Hannah. *See* Wheeler
Danforth, Olive. *See* Langdon
Dangé, François, I, **246**
Dangeac. *See also* Angeac
Dangeac, Gabriel, II, 424
Dangeac, Marguerite (L'Espérance), II, 424; IV, 470
Dangeau. *See* Courcillon
Dangoumau (Dengomau), Jeanne (Cassiet), V, 172
Danguel Lamarche, Jacques, III, 165
Daniel. *See also* Garakontié
Daniel (miner), I, 334
Daniel (servant), III, 425
Daniel, André, I, 247
Daniel, Antoine, I, 247
Daniel, Antoine, I, 70, 122, 124, 125, 128, 206, **246–47**, 252, 253, 388, 414, 461, 633, 637, 638, 639
Daniel, Catherine. *See* Quevillon
Daniel, Charles, I, 25, 53, **247–48**, 252, 261, 305, 482, 521, 567, 613, 665
Daniel, François (author), IV, 344; XI, 490
Daniel, François (brother of CHARLES), I, 247
Daniel, Hannah Maria. *See* Lancaster
Daniel, Louisa Sophia. *See* Jordan
Daniel, Marguerite. *See* Martin
Daniel, Thomas, XII, 121, 226
Daniel, Thomas Wilder, XII, 121, **226–27**
Daniel, Wilder, XII, 226
Daniell, James, XI, 80
Daniélou, Jean-Pierre, III, **163**; IV, 289
Daniels, Lucinda (Miles), IX, 550
Danio. *See* Noyon
Danjaique. *See* Angeac
Danks, Benoni, IV, **192–94**
Danks, Lucy (wife of BENONI), IV, 193
Danks, Mary. *See* Morris
Danks, Rebecca. *See* Rust
Danks, Robert, IV, 192
Danré de Blanzy, Charles, III, 163

Danré de Blanzy, Louis-Claude, II, 92; III, 121, **163–64**, 211; IV, 270, 621, 720; V, 652
Danré de Blanzy, Suzanne. *See* Estienne Du Bourgué de Clérin
Danré de Blanzy, Suzanne. *See* Morillon
Dansereau, Almaïde (Geoffrion), XII, 363
Dansereau, Charles, X, 575
Dansereau*, Clément-Arthur (1844–1918), X, 374; XI, 624, 802, 812; XII, 172, 175, 179, 180, 465, 722, 903, 1026
Dansereau, Cordélie. *See* Hurteau
Dansereau, Delphine (Senécal), XI, 806
Dansereau, Joseph, XI, 806, 807; XII, 363
Danseville. *See* Dandane
Danson, Thomas, VII, 113
Danton. *See* Michel
Daoust, Adélina (Tassé), XII, 1025
Daoust, Angèle. *See* Doutre
Daoust, Charles, IX, 193
Daoust, Charles, IX, **193–95**, 211; X, 237, 249, 304, 415, 421; XI, 99, 273, 275; XII, 1025
Daoust, Charles-Roger, IX, 195
Daoust, Françoise. *See* Dandurand
Daoust, Roger, IX, 193
Daprandesteguy. *See* Aprendestiguy
Daquin, Marie (Aigron), I, 42
Darboy, Georges, XI, 339
Darby. *See also* Derby
Darby, Catherine (Gurnett), IX, 346
Darby, George, III, 189; IV, 226
Darby, Hatty. *See* Vanacott
Darby, Joseph, XII, 368
Darby, Mary, known as Perdita (Robinson), IV, 195
Darby, Nicholas, III, 411; IV, **194–95**, 536, 712; V, 166, 675
Darby, Suzan (Pennefather), IX, 627
Darce. *See* Lom
Darche, Noël, VIII, 618
Darcy, Mary (O'Brien), VIII, 658
D'Arcy, Robert, 4th Earl of Holderness, III, 364, 502; IV, 422
Dardaine, Françoise (Olivier), I, 524
Daret (Dazé), Françoise (Pinaud), II, 526
Dargent, François, III, 164
Dargent, Joseph, III, **164–65**
Dargent, Renée. *See* Bernard
Darguinarat, Joannis, III, 157
Darivière. *See* Bernard
Darles, Sieur (laboureur), II, 134
Darles, François, III, 633; IV, 720
Darles de Lignières, Monsieur (inventor), IV, 187
Darling, Amanda Jane (Chandler; Patten), X, 156
Darling, Andrew, XI, 232
Darling, Sir Charles Henry, IX, 28, 29, **195–96**; X, 141, 495; XI, 44, 66; XII, 564
Darling, Elizabeth. *See* Canby
Darling, Elizabeth Isabella Caroline, Lady Darling. *See* Salter
Darling*, Frank (1850–1923), XII, 794
Darling, Henry Charles, VII, 348; VIII, 162; IX, 195
Darling, Henry W., XI, 576
Darling, Isabella. *See* Cameron
Darling, James, XI, 232

Darling, John, VI, **178–79**
Darling, Joseph, VI, 178
Darling, Mary. *See* Davidson
Darling, Mary. *See* Street
Darling, Sir Ralph, IX, 195
Darling, Thomas J., XI, 232
Darling, William, XI, 232, 233
Darling, William, XI, **232–34**, 336
Darling, William Stewart, XI, 917
Darmeville. *See* Olivier
Darnaud (Darnault). *See* Arnaud
Darontal. *See* Atironta (fl. 1615)
Darouet, Simon, IV, 331
Darrigrand. *See* Arrigrand
Darris, Marie-Charlotte. *See* Sajos
Darris, Pierre, V, 257
Darroch, Duncan, VII, 743
Darrow, John L., IX, 477
Darrow, Sophia (McClearn), IX, 477
Dart, Elizabeth (Eynon), VIII, **200–1**, 425, 908; XI, 304
Dart, John, XI, 75
Dartigny. *See* Berthelot
Dartmouth, Baron. *See* Legge
Dartmouth, Earl of. *See* Legge
Darveau, Charles, VII, 231
Darveau, Grégoire, X, 213
Darveau, Henriette. *See* Giguère
Darveau, Jean-Édouard, VII, **231–33**; VIII, 722
Darveau, Louis-Michel, VIII, 702; IX, 303, 306; X, 204, **213–14**; XI, 177, 343
Darveau, Marguerite-Marie. *See* Roi, *dit* Audi
Darveau, Marie. *See* Simpson
Darwin, Charles Robert, VIII, 867; IX, 660; X, 65, 84, 350, 713; XI, 418, 640; XII, 234, 328, 541, 660, 865, 869, 879, 1111, 1114
Dashwood, Anne (Stewart, Countess of Galloway), VII, 825
Dashwood, Francis, 15th Baron Le Despencer, V, 315
Dasilva, Dominique, III, 165
Dasilva, Jeanne. *See* Greslon Laviolette
Dasilva, Pedro, III, 165
Dasilva, *dit* Portugais, Élisabeth. *See* Laisné
Dasilva, *dit* Portugais, Marie-Gabrielle. *See* La Roche
Dasilva, *dit* Portugais, Nicolas, III, **165**, 420; IV, 263
Dassemat. *See* Dazemard
Dasylva, Héloïse-Euphémie (Emery-Coderre), XI, 302
Datte, Nicolas, III, 613
Daudet, Jean, XI, 694
Daudin, Henri, III, 120, **165–66**, 257; V, 172
Dauger, Jean (father), II, 35
Dauger, Jean, II, 35
Dauger, Jourdain, II, 35
Dauger, Marie. *See* Boyrie
Daulac (Daulat). *See* Dollard
Daulé, Firmin, VIII, 201
Daulé, Jean-Denis, IV, 136; VI, 391; VII, 246; VIII, **201–2**, 593
Daulé, Marie-Madeleine. *See* Mireux
Daulier Des Landes, André, II, 381; III, 390
Daumont de Saint-Lusson, Jean-Baptiste, I, 250
Daumont de Saint-Lusson, Magdeleine, I, 249
Daumont de Saint-Lusson, Marguerite. *See* Bérin
Daumont de Saint-Lussion, Marguerite. *See* La Verge

Daumont de Saint-Lusson, Simon-François, I, 35, 57, 63, 127, 226, **248–50**, 345, 393, 394, 572, 625, 626; II, 141, 347, 517, 537
Daunais, Amable, VII, 412, 514; X, 527
Daunais, Josephte (Girard), XII, 369
Daunet, Gertrude (Senet), II, 604
Dauphin, Charles, VIII, 218
Dauphinais, François-Xavier, XII, 132
Dauphin de La Forest, Charlotte-Françoise. *See* Juchereau de Saint-Denis
Dauphin de La Forest, François, I, 178, 661; II, 76, **169–70**, 270, 305, 306, 355, 435, 562, 588, 634, 636
Dauphin de Montorgueuil, I, **250**, 299
Dauphine, Caroline (Smith; Lessel), XII, 559
Dauterive. *See* Cuny
Dauteuil, Marie (Barolet), III, 26
Dauth, Rose de Lima, X, 510
Dauvergne, Anne (Robin), VI, 652
Dauvin, Jeanne (Casot), IV, 134
Dauzet, Marguerite (Taché), III, 608
Davanne, Louis, V, 223
Davanne, Marguerite. *See* Germain
Davanne, Marguerite, named de Saint-Louis de Gonzague, V, **223–24**
Davaugour. *See* Dubois
Daveine, Gabriel, IV, 123
Daveine (Davenne, Davesne), Marie-Joseph (Cadet; Bernard), IV, 123
Daveluy, Paul-Édouard, VII, 623
Daveluy, Pierre-Léandre, VIII, 218
Daveluy, *dit* Larose, François-Xavier, VII, 256
Davène de Fontaine, Monsieur (château owner), I, 424
Davenport, Addington, III, 200
Davenport, E. Montagu, IX, 143, 328
Davenport, Edward Loomis, XII, 448
Davenport, Elizabeth (Dudley), III, 200
Davenport, Lewis, VII, 364
Davenport, Lydia (Dickinson), XII, 257
Davenport, Sarah. *See* Underhill
Davenport, Thomas, XII, 1090
Daverne, Joseph, VII, 852
Davers, Sir Charles, III, 167
Davers, Sir Jermyn, III, 166
Davers, Margaretta, Lady Davers. *See* Green
Davers, Sir Robert, III, **166–67**, 528, 559; VI, 317
Davesne. *See* Daveine
David (Danao) (privateer), III, 497
David, Aaron Hart, IV, 104, 105, 366; VII, 825; XI, 234
David, Abigail (Hayes), IX, 379
David, Albert, III, 34; IV, 458
David, Catharine. *See* Joseph
David, Cécile. *See* Poitras
David, Claude, I, 225, **250–51**
David, David, V, 193; VI, **179–81**, 204, 358, 623, 665; VII, 329; VIII, 366
David, David-Fleury, XI, 235
David, Eleazar David, VIII, 363; XI, **234–35**
David, Eliza Locke. *See* Walker
David, Félicien, IX, 632
David, Ferdinand, VIII, 347
David, Ferdinand, XI, 61, **235–36**, 755; XII, 63
David, Frances Michael (Hart), XI, 389
David, Jacques, II, **170–71**; III, 316

David, Jacques-Louis, XII, 100, 101
David, Judith-Henriette-Françoise (Allamand), VII, 13
David*, Laurent-Olivier (1840–1926), VI, 599; VII, 149, 150, 173, 513, 514, 515, 881; VIII, 283, 435, 470, 471, 616, 667, 668; IX, 65, 193, 321, 437, 438, 615, 633; X, 153, 154, 155, 176, 237, 238, 415, 421, 422, 425, 499, 533, 544, 547; XI, 100, 159, 277, 289, 530, 531, 623, 624, 823; XII, 173, 248, 249, 276, 301, 309, 477, 506, 533, 725
David, Lazarus, IV, 332, 385; VI, 179
David, Louis, IX, 362; XII, 850
David, Marie. See Montet
David, Marie-Louise. See Normandin, dit Le Sauvage
David, Marie-Madeleine (Lagier), X, 419
David, Moses, VI, 179
David, Moses Samuel, VIII, 363; XI, 234
David, Olive. See Boyer, dit Quintal
David, Paul, II, 170
David, Phebe. See Samuel
David, Phoebe (Hart), VIII, 363
David, Samuel, VI, 179, 629; VIII, 363; XI, 234
David, Sarah. See Hart
David, Sophia (Joseph), VI, 366; XI, 455
David, Sophie. See Homier
David, Suzanne. See Noyon
Davidge, William Pleater, XII, 448
David of Schoharie, XII, 402
Davids, Walter Charles, VII, 764
Davidson. See also Davison
Davidson, Mr (printer), VI, 248
Davidson, Alexander, VIII, **202–4**
Davidson, Ann (Burgess), XII, 140
Davidson, Ann (Churchill), X, 171
Davidson, Arthur, IV, 295; V, 99, **224–26**, 492, 817; VI, 86, 465; VII, 783
Davidson, David, X, 10; XI, 556; XII, 485
Davidson, Eleanor. See Birnie
Davidson, Eliza (Bowen), IX, 74
Davidson, Eliza (McKay), V, 224; VI, 465
Davidson, Elliott, IX, 270
Davidson, Emma (Brown), XII, 128
Davidson, Helen (Jardine), IX, 409
Davidson, Hugh, III, 583; IV, 170
Davidson, Isabella Jemima (Shade; Boomer), IX, 716; XI, 89
Davidson, James (doctor), IV, 82, 295; IX, 74
Davidson, James (health official), IX, 439
Davidson, James Alexander, VIII, 203
Davidson, Jane. See Fraser
Davidson, Jane (Caldwell), VII, 133
Davidson, Jane (Ross), V, 224
Davidson, Jennie (Brown), XII, 128
Davidson, John (brother-in-law of Edward BOWEN), IX, 75, 133
Davidson, John (brother-in-law of Sir John CALDWELL), VII, 134, 135, 136
Davidson, John (crown lands commissioner), VII, 382; VIII, 858
Davidson, John (Lachine Canal commissioner), X, 404
Davidson, John (mess steward), VIII, 574; XI, 139
Davidson, John (nephew of Sir John CALDWELL), VII, 135
Davidson, John (politician), VII, 331
Davidson, Joseph, XI, 652

Davidson, Margaret Tweddale (Forrester), IX, 270
Davidson, Mary (wife of ALEXANDER), VIII, 202
Davidson, Mary (Darling), XI, 232
Davidson, Sarah. See Nevers
Davidson, Thomas (businessman), XI, 556
Davidson, Thomas (father of ALEXANDER), VIII, 202
Davidson, Walter (grandfather), V, 224
Davidson, Walter, IV, 276; V, 224, 225
Davidson, William, IV, 195
Davidson, William, IV, **195–97**, 328; V, 328, 350, 416, 465, 795; VI, 263
Davie, Alexander Edmund Batson, XI, **236–37**, 293; XII, 227, 916, 1063
Davie, Allison, VII, 233
Davie, Allison, VII, **233–34**; VIII, 559
Davie, Anne Collard. See Waldron
Davie, Blanche. See Baker
Davie, Constance Langford. See Skinner
Davie, Elizabeth. See Cock
Davie, Elizabeth Johnson. See Taylor
Davie*, George Taylor (1828–1907), VII, 233, 234; VIII, 647; XI, 190
Davie, John Chapman (father), XI, 236; XII, 227
Davie, John Chapman, XII, 1063
Davie, Mary Alice. See Yorke
Davie, Sarah Holmes. See Todd
Davie, Theodore, XII, **227–28**, 1063
Davie, William, VII, 233
Davies. See also Davis
Davies*, Adeline (Chisholm; Foster, Lady Foster) (d. 1919), XII, 220, 610
Davies, Anne (Owen), VI, 560
Davies, Benjamin, X, 473; XII, 841
Davies, Charles Lennox, XII, 286
Davies, David, V, 226
Davies, George (merchant), VII, 380; VIII, 631; X, 519
Davies, George (partner of John MOLSON, 1787–1860) VII, 620
Davies, George Crew, VII, 620; VIII, 631; X, 519
Davies*, Sir Louis Henry (1845–1924), X, 195, 679; XI, 242, 601, 703; XII, 340, 417, 512, 513, 639, 1045
Davies, Mary (wife of THOMAS), V, 226
Davies, Richard, VI, 810
Davies, Robert, X, 672
Davies, Thomas, III, 592; V, **226–28**, 767; VII, 402
Davies*, William (1831–1921), XI, 576
Davies, William Henry Allan, XI, 557, 569
Davignon, Joseph-François, VII, 25; VIII, 209, 210, 471; X, 429, 545, 694; XI, 585
Daviler, Augustin-Charles, VIII, 213
Davin*, Nicholas Flood (1843–1901), IX, 607; X, 49; XI, 724; XII, 91, 340, 668
Davion, Albert, II, **171**, 227, 331; III, 469, 639
Davis, David, XII, 228
Davis*, Delos Rogest (1846–1915), XII, 53, 1073
Davis, Donald Watson, XI, 384
Davis, Elizabeth. See Robertson
Davis, Elizabeth (Thorburn), XII, 1048
Davis, Faith. See Fulford
Davis, Frances (Hopkins; Tiffany), V, 814
Davis, George, IV, 175
Davis (Davies), George, VII, 134; VIII, 21
Davis, Hugh (father), VII, 234

Davis, Hugh, VII, 235
Davis, Isaac, III, 168
Davis, John, X, 215
Davis, John, I, 20, 75, **251–52**, 336, 360, 375, 377, 378, 397, 676; VII, 271; XII, 835
Davis, John, VI, 63; VIII, 360, 361; X, **214–15**
Davis, Joseph, II, 56, **171–72**, 232, 267, 319, 662
Davis, Kate, XI, 819
Davis, Lydia. *See* Black
Davis, Marie-Anne (Sarah), named de Saint-Benoît, III, **167–68**
Davis, Marie-Anne, named de Sainte-Cécile, II, 65
Davis, Mary (Gage), VIII, 309
Davis, Mathilda, X, **215**
Davis, Minnie. *See* Falk
Davis*, Sir Mortimer Barnett (1864–1928), XII, 228
Davis, Nancy, X, 215
Davis (Davies), Richard, X, 214
Davis, Robert, VII, **234–35**
Davis*, Robert Atkinson (1841–1903), X, 474; XI, 539, 644; XII, 83, 370, 371, 372
Davis, Rosina (wife of ROBERT), VII, 234
Davis, Samuel, XII, **228–29**
Davis, Samuel H., XI, 400
Davis, Sarah. *See* Davis, Marie-Anne
Davis, Silvanus, II, 145, **172**, 579
Davis, Susanna. *See* Francklin
Davis, Susannah (Powlis), VIII, 708
Davis, Theodore, V, 716
Davis, Thomas. *See* Tehowagherengaraghkwen
Davis, Thomas Osborne, IX, 494
Davis, William, XI, 864
Davison, Alexander (father), IV, 197
Davison, Alexander, IV, 197, 198, 317, 320, 324; V, 22, 43, 71, 181, 182, 277, 289, 483, 484, 718; VI, 296, 515; VII, 64, 65, 66
Davison, Desiah. *See* Mack
Davison, Dorothy. *See* Neal
Davison, Edward Doran, XII, **229–30**
Davison, Eleanor. *See* Doran
Davison, George, IV, **197–99**, 324, 538; V, 43, 132, 289, 371, 484; VI, 417, 515, 516; VII, 64, 65
Davison, Martha Hopkins. *See* Campbell
Davison, Samuel, XII, 229
Davost, Ambroise, I, 122, 125, **252–53**, 388
D'Avray. *See* Marshall
Davy, Sir Humphry, VII, 930
Davy, Sophia (Meyers), VI, 502
Davys. *See also* Davis
Davys, Samuel, IV, 194, 195
Dawbeny, Oliver, I, 371
Dawe, William, VI, 410; VII, 377
Dawes, William, V, 341
Dawson, Mrs (wife of John), XII, 893
Dawson, Æneas McDonell, XI, 84
Dawson, Andrew, XII, 858
Dawson, Anna Lois (Harrington), XII, 236, 237
Dawson, Eva (Atkin), XII, 237
Dawson*, George Mercer (1849–1901), VI, 220; XI, 21, 73, 732, 887, 888, 899; XII, 233, 237, 402
Dawson, Grace Annie. *See* Lockhart
Dawson, James, XII, 230
Dawson, James Cosmo, XII, 233

Dawson, John, XII, 893
Dawson, John T., X, 512
Dawson, Sir John William, V, 529, 530; VIII, 32, 62; IX, 87, 270, 271, 309, 383, 409, 666; X, 131, 137, 338, 446, 447, 704; XI, 53, 73, 238, 255, 420, 503, 561, 899; XII, 48, 211, 213, 216, **230–37**, 288, 431, 541, 571, 748, 749, 829, 869, 926, 1114
Dawson, Margaret Ann Young, Lady Dawson. *See* Mercer
Dawson, Mary. *See* Rankine
Dawson, Mary (Hamilton), IV, 321
Dawson, Mary Jane (Fry), XII, 342
Dawson, Rankine, XII, 237
Dawson, Robert, XII, 474
Dawson*, Samuel Edward (1833–1916), X, 346; XII, 923
Dawson*, Simon James (1818–1902), IX, 319, 804; X, 342; XI, 441, 553, 612, 662, 716, 737, 841, 842, 939; XII, 1006
Dawson, William Bell, XII, 237
Dawson, William McDonell, IX, 486
Day, Barbara. *See* Lyon
Day, Charles Dewey, VII, 62, 149, 514, 914; VIII, 269, 848; IX, 571; X, 135, 620; XI, 184, **237–39**, 281, 408, 721, 766; XII, 232, 476, 684
Day, Forshaw, XII, 792
Day, George, IV, 199
Day, Henrietta Maria. *See* Cottnam
Day, Ithmar Hubbell, XI, 237
Day, Jeremiah, X, 215
Day, John (captain), IX, 478
Day, John (merchant), I, 21, 148, 149, 150, 240, 302, 643
Day, John, IV, 116, **199**, 451, 581, 704
Day, John James, VIII, 525; X, 625
Day, Laura. *See* Dewey
Day, Maria Margaret. *See* Holmes
Day, Nathaniel (office holder), V, 214, 584
Day, Nathaniel (plenipotentiary), V, 737
Day, Roxanna (Richardson), XII, 893
Day, Samuel Stearns, X, **215–16**
Day, Sarah (Mercer; wife of JOHN), IV, 199
Day, Thomas, XII, 996
Dayfoot, Philo Warner, VIII, 99
Dayley, James, VI, 796
Dayton, Abia (Mallory), VIII, 606
Dayton, Abigail. *See* Cogswell
Dayton, Abraham, VI, 738; VIII, 606
Dazé. *See* Daret
Dazemard de Lusignan, Jeanne. *See* Babie
Dazemard de Lusignan, Louis-Antoine, III, 169
Dazemard de Lusignan, Madeleine-Marguerite. *See* Bouat
Dazemard de Lusignan, Paul-Louis, III, 168
Dazemard de Lusignan, Paul-Louis, III, 31, 64, **168–69**
Deacon, Isabella (Crozier), XII, 222
Deacon, J. A., XI, 418
Deacon, William Arthur, XII, 361
Dean, Cyrus, XI, 651
Dean, Eunice (Waterman), IX, 821
Dean, Hannah (De Witt), VIII, 219
Dean, James, X, 33, 34
Dean, Phillis. *See* Baptist
Dean, Sarah (Farrar; Tiffany), V, 814; VIII, 887
Dean, T. A., VII, 45
Dean, William Warren, X, 230
Deanaghrison. *See* Tanaghrisson

Deane, Joseph, III, 132, 133, 606
Deane*, Richard Burton (1848–1930), XI, 479
Deane-Drummond, Sophia Theresa. *See* Pemberton
Dearborn, Henry, V, 66, 113, 695; VII, 889, 912; VIII, 191, 794
Dearin, Bessie Josephine Stanislaus. *See* Furlong
Dearin, Catherine (wife of JOHN JOSEPH), XI, 239
Dearin, Elizabeth. *See* King
Dearin, George, XI, 239
Dearin, John Joseph, XI, **239–40**; XII, 956
Dearin, William, XI, 239
Deas, Fanny. *See* Harris
Deas, John Sullivan, X, **216–17**
Dease, Anne. *See* Johnson
Dease, Anne. *See* Nugent
Dease, Élizabeth. *See* Chouinard
Dease, Ellen, named Mother Teresa, VII, 706; VIII, 299, 704; XI, **240–41**; XII, 183
Dease, Jane. *See* French
Dease, John, IV, 119; V, 8, 9, **228–30**; IX, 196
Dease, John Warren, IX, 197, 851
Dease, Lawrence Joseph, VIII, 307, 664, 665
Dease, Nancy (Bell), IX, 42
Dease, Oliver, XI, 240
Dease, Peter Warren, V, 228; VII, 205, 326; VIII, 538, 661, 663, 815; IX, 42, **196–99**; X, 407; XII, 155, 876, 877, 878
Dease, Richard, V, 228
Dease, William, XI, 738
Déat, Antoine, III, 169
Déat, Antoine, III, **169–70**; IV, 236
Déat, Catherine. *See* Metayer
D'Eath, Elizabeth (How), III, 297
Debartzch. *See also* Bartzsch
Debartzch, Caroline (Monk), VII, 236
Debartzch, Cordelia (Rottermund, Comtesse de Rottermund), VII, 236; VIII, 774; IX, 424
Debartzch, Dominique, VII, 235, 666, 711
Debartzch, Elmire (Drummond), VII, 236; XI, 282
Debartzch, Josette. *See* Saint-Ours
Debartzch, Louise (Kierzkowski), VII, 236; IX, 424
Debartzch, Marie-Josephte. *See* Simon, *dit* Delorme
Debartzch, Pierre-Dominique, V, 695; VI, 48, 82, 207, 287, 680; VII, 7, 227, **235–37**, 247, 345, 354, 361; VIII, 284, 735, 736, 774; IX, 424; X, 75; XI, 282; XII, 255
Debelius, Domine, II, 108
Debigaré, *dit* Lebasque, Agathe (Romain), VI, 658
Debin, Élisabeth (Deschamps), II, 181
de Blaquiere, Eleanor, Lady de Blaquiere. *See* Dobson
de Blaquière, Eliza. *See* O'Brien
de Blaquière, Eliza. *See* Roper
de Blaquiere, Henry, VIII, 965
de Blaquiere, John, 1st Baron de Blaquiere, VIII, 204
de Blaquiere, John, 2nd Baron de Blaquiere, VIII, 204
de Blaquiere, Lucianne, Baroness De Blaquiere. *See* Desbarats
de Blaquière, Peter Boyle, VIII, 29, 188, **204–6**; IX, 690
de Blaquiere, William, 6th Baron de Blaquiere, VIII, 204; XII, 249
Deblois, Ann Maria, VI, 181
Deblois, Claire. *See* Parent
Deblois, Elizabeth. *See* Jenkins
Deblois, François, VIII, 206

Deblois, François-Xavier, VIII, 206, 207
Deblois, George, VI, 181; VII, 237
Deblois, George Wastie, IX, 183; XI, **241–42**, 703
Deblois, Gilbert, VI, 181
Deblois, Jane Catherine. *See* Witham
Deblois, Joseph, X, 136
Deblois, Joseph-François, VIII, **206–7**
Deblois, Lewis, VI, 181
Deblois, Louis, VI, 181
Deblois, Lydia, VI, 181
Deblois, Marie-Geneviève. *See* Létourneau
Deblois, Marie-Vénérande. *See* Ranvoyzé
Deblois, Marie-Vénérande-Joséphine (Caron), IX, 363; X, 136
Deblois, Sarah (Deblois), VI, **181–82**; VII, 237
DeBlois, Sarah Frances. *See* Haviland
Deblois, Stephen, VI, 181
Deblois, Stephen Wastie, VI, 181; VII, **237–38**, 308; IX, 181, 183; X, 539; XI, 241
Deblois, William Minet, VI, 181; VII, 237
Debonnaire, Susanna Selina Sophia (Smith; Metcalfe, Lady Metcalfe), VII, 603
De Bonne, François, Duc de Lesdiguières, V, 230
De Bonne, Louise. *See* Chartier de Lotbinière
De Bonne, Louise-Élizabeth. *See* Marcoux
De Bonne, Pierre-Amable, V, 87, 96, 207, 208, 210, 211, 226, **230–36**, 243, 385, 386, 464, 487, 650, 651, 654, 696, 701, 828, 878, 881; VI, 42, 132, 226, 344, 381, 512, 533, 559, 578, 750; VII, 242, 255, 688, 689, 690, 769, 784, 872; VIII, 491
Debray. *See* Bray
Debrier, Anne-Marie (Le Normant de Mézy), III, 386; IV, 465
Debrisay, Bonna (Thorp), VII, 864
Debuire, Marie-Marguerite (Hantraye), IV, 326
DeBurgo. *See* Burke
Decaisne, Joseph, X, 106
De Camp, Maria Theresa (Marie Thérèse) (Kemble), VII, 110
De Camp, Sophia (Brown), VII, 110
De Camp, Vincent, VII, 110; IX, 60
Decanesora. *See* Teganissorens
Decaraffe, Jean-Baptiste, IV, 206
Decarrihoga. *See* Tekarihogen (d. 1830)
DeCarteret, Peter, X, 440
Decatur, Stephen, V, 813
De Celles. *See* Duclos
DeCew. *See also* DeCow
DeCew, Edmund, VIII, 208
DeCew, John, VIII, 208
DeCew, Robert, VIII, 208
DeCew, William, VIII, 208
D'echambault (Déchambault). *See* Fleury
Dechamps, Victor-Auguste, X, 542
Decharnay, Marie-Louise (Magnan; Taché), VI, 749
Dechart (Duhart), Catherine (Laborde), IV, 420
Dechêne. *See* Miville
Décheneaux. *See* Crevier
Dechennequi. *See* Chenneque
Decheuraineville, Marie (Lamy), II, 458
Decheverry, Bernard, IV, 253, 421
Dechinique. *See* Chenneque; Chinic
Dechman, Margaret (Athol; Cunnabell), IX, 186

Decker, Elizabeth (Oille), XI, 650
Decker, Sarah (Westbrook), VI, 808
Decoigne, François, V, **236–37**; VII, 749
Decoigne, Louis, VII, 238
Decoigne, Louis-Mars, VII, 238, 239
Decoigne, Marguerite. *See* Bezeau
Decoigne, Mary. *See* McCabe
Decoigne, Olivier, VII, 238, 239
Decoigne, Pierre-Théophile, VII, **238–39**; VIII, 504; XII, 762
De Cosmos, Amor, IX, 114, 479, 480, 714, 715, 716; X, 116, 117, 196, 246, 697; XI, 33, 435, 469, 605, 635, 839, 950; XII, 78, 79, **237–43**, 523, 784, 833, 916, 919, 1049
Decoste, Catherine. *See* Coré
Decoste, Jean-Baptiste, IV, **200**
Decoste, Jean-Christophe, IV, 200
Decoste, Louis, IV, 200
Decoste, Marie-Joseph. *See* Dumouchel
Decoste, Marie-Renée. *See* Marchand
DeCou. *See also* DeCow
De Cou, Anne (Odell), V, 628; VII, 657
De Couagne. *See* Decoigne
De Courcey, R., VIII, 474
Decous (Decoust). *See* Descouts
Decousse, Bernard, V, 727
DeCow, Catherine. *See* Docksteder
DeCow, Jacob, VIII, 208
DeCow, John, VIII, **207–9**, 450; IX, 264, 406
Decrès, Denis, Duc Decrès, V, 62
Decwando. *See* Atecouando (fl. 1749–57)
Dee, John, I, 148, 302, 316, 332, 333, 336, 643, 677, 678
Deerfoot. *See* Api-kai-ees; Ha-ga-sa-do-ni
Dees, Robert, V, 139
Defoe, Daniel, IV, 711; VI, 351; VII, 53; XII, 996
Defoie, Catherine (Cantin), XII, 158
De Forest, Sarah (Washburn), VI, 804; VII, 896
Defosse, Anne (Le Conte), II, 381
Defoy, Anne-Marie-Angélique (Suzor), IX, 771
Defoy, Charles-Maxime, XI, 901
Deganawidah. *See* Dekanahwideh
DeGaugreben, Friedrich, VI, **182–83**
Degawehe. *See* Gawèhe
Degeay, Henri, IV, 200
Degeay, Jacques, IV, **200–1**; V, 432; VI, 86; VIII, 591
Degeay, Marie. *See* Bournicat
Degonnor, Nicolas, III, 81, 249, 269, 355; IV, 270
Degoutin (De Goutin, Degoutins). *See* Goutin
De Grassi, A., X, 405
Degrès, Marie-Madeleine (Borneuf), V, 92
De Guerne. *See* Le Guerne
Deguire, Jean, IV, 732
Deguire, Jean-Baptiste, VIII, 19
Deguire, Marie-Josephte (Waddens), IV, 757
Deguire, *dit* Desrosiers, Angélique. *See* Pepin
Deguire, *dit* Desrosiers, Jeanne. *See* Blet
Deguire, *dit* Desrosiers, Joseph, IV, **201–2**; V, 143
Deguire, *dit* Desrosiers, Marie (Leverrier), IV, 202
Deguire, *dit* Desrosiers, Pierre, IV, 201
Deguise, François-Joseph, VI, 126, 288; VII, 656, 761
Deguise, Marie-Émilie (Viau), XII, 1074
Deguise, *dit* Flamand, Élisabeth. *See* Laisné, *dit* Laliberté
Deguise, *dit* Flamand, Élisabeth (Falardeau), IV, 203

Deguise, *dit* Flamand, François (son of GIRARD-GUILLAUME), III, 170
Deguise, *dit* Flamand, François (son of JACQUES), IV, 203
Deguise, *dit* Flamand, Girard-Guillaume, III, **170**, 420; IV, 202, 659; XI, 336
Deguise, *dit* Flamand, Guillaume, III, 170; IV, 202; XI, 336
Deguise, *dit* Flamand, Jacques, III, 170; IV, **202–4**, 659
Deguise, *dit* Flamand, Marie-Anne. *See* Morin
Deguise, *dit* Flamand, Marie-Anne. *See* Rouillard
Deguise, *dit* Flamand, Marie-Françoise. *See* Jourdain, Bellerose
Deguise, *dit* Flamand, Thérèse. *See* Rinfret, *dit* Malouin
De Haven, Edwin Jesse, VII, 326; VIII, 448, 623; IX, **199–200**; XI, 470
De Haven, Maria. *See* McKeever
De Haven, Mary. *See* Norris Da Costa
De Haven, William, IX, 199
Dehorné. *See* Horné
Deian. *See* Dejean
Deiaquande. *See* Teyohaqueande
Deighton, Emma (sister-in-law of JOHN), X, 217
Deighton, John, X, **217**
Deighton, Thomas, X, 217
Déjarlais, Archange (Picotte), VI, 581
Dejean, Jeanne. *See* Rocques de Carbouere
Dejean, Josette. *See* Larchevêque
Dejean, Marie-Louise. *See* Augé
Dejean, Philippe, V, 237
Dejean, Philippe, IV, 321, 702, 722; V, **237–38**
Dejean, Théotiste. *See* Saint-Cosme
Dejordy. *See also* Desjordy
Dejordy de Villebon, Catherine. *See* Trottier Desrivières
Dejordy de Villebon, Charles-René, III, **170–71**, 243
Dekanahwideh, I, 7, **253–55**; II, xxix; III, xli; IV, lvii
Dekarihokenh. *See* Tekarihogen
De Kay, Helena (Gilder), XII, 288
De la Beche, Sir Henry Thomas, X, 445; XI, 631
Delaborde, Jean, III, **172**
Delacroix, Eugène, IX, 362
Delafaye. *See* La Faye
Delafield, Joseph, XI, 72
Delafontaine. *See* Lafontaine
Delafosse, Cécile (Closse), I, 230
Delagarde. *See* Lagarde
Delage, Maître (notary), IV, 127
Delage, François-Xavier, VIII, 302
Delage, *dit* Lavigueur, Jean, XI, 500
Delage, *dit* Lavigueur, Marguerite. *See* Douglass
Delagrave, Cyrille, X, **217–18**
Delagrave, François, VIII, 359; X, 217
Delagrave, Geneviève. *See* Amiot
Delagrave, Louise. *See* Mason
Delagrave, Louise (Provencher), XI, 716
Delain, Marie (Papineau), II, 507
Delamarre, Emmanuelle-Sophie-Jeanne (Blain de Saint-Aubin), XI, 82
DeLancey, Ann (Bromley), VII, 107
De Lancey, Elizabeth. *See* Colden
DeLancey, James, III, 126, 497, 655
DeLancey, James, V, **238–39**; VI, 404; VII, 107
DeLancey, Martha. *See* Tippett
De Lancey, Oliver, V, 604
De Lancey, Peter, V, 238

DeLancey, Stephen (grandfather), III, 394, 655
De Lancey, Stephen (cousin), IV, 675; V, 239
DeLancey, Stephen, V, 552
DeLancey, Susan (Barclay), VI, 33
DeLancey, Susannah (Warren), III, 655
Deland, Marie (Menut), V, 588
Delaney, Edward Magdalene Joseph, XI, 243
Delaney, Elizabeth. *See* Troy
Delaney, John, XI, 306
Delaney, John, X, 688; XI, **242–43**, 431
Delaney, John Joseph, XI, 243
Delaney, Mary Ann. *See* Kennedy
Delaney, Patrick, X, 688
Delaney, Patrick, X, **218–19**
Delaney, Mrs Theresa, XI, 306, 460; XII, 478
Delannes, Pierre, IV, 124
Delany, Martin Robinson, XII, 961
De La Rue, Warren, XII, 41
Delatre, Emily Louisa (Sullivan; Hincks, Lady Hincks), VIII, 846; XI, 406
Delatre, Philip Chesneau, VIII, 846
Delaunay, Anne (Maillou, *dit* Desmoulins), III, 419
Delaunay, Charles, II, **173**, 264; III, 88, 523; IV, 46
Delaunay, Françoise. *See* Pinguet
Delaunay, Louis, V, 77
Delaunay, Marie-Anne. *See* Legras
Delaunay, Marie-Joseph (Lenoir, *dit* Rolland), II, 173
Delaunay, Pierre, II, 173
DeLaune, Henry, III, 172
DeLaune, Lucy (mother of WILLIAM), III, 173
DeLaune, William, III, **172–73**, 669, 672
Delavall, Ann (Milbanke, Lady Milbanke), V, 595
Delavall, Edward, V, 595
De La Vigne, Marie. *See* Lefevre
De La Warr, Baron. *See* West
Deléage, François, XI, 243
Deléage, Jean-François-Régis, XI, **243–44**
Deléage, Jeanne. *See* Romeyer
Delegal, Catherine (Lightenstone), VII, 506
Delesdernier, Eleanor. *See* Pritchard
Delesdernier, Gideon, V, 239, 240
Delesdernier, Judith. *See* Martin
Delesdernier, Lewis Frederick, V, 240
Delesdernier, Martha Maria (Uniacke), VI, 789, 792; VII, 872; VIII, 903; IX, 801
Delesdernier, Moses, IV, xxix; V, **239–41**; VI, 789
Delesdernier, Sophie (Uniacke), VII, 872
Delesderniers, John Mark Crank, IV, 516; IX, 203
Delesderniers, Mary (Desjardins), IX, 203
Delesnerac, Marguerite (Monseignat), II, 483
Delestrade, Anne (Desroches), VI, 206
Delestre, Alonié, I, 267
Delestre, *dit* Beaujour, Pierre, III, 165
Delezenne, Ignace-François, IV, **204–7**, 619, 629, 748; V, 218, 707, 708, 709, 710, 736, 737; VI, 183, 184, 231
Delezenne, Joseph-Christophe, IV, 205; V, 709
Delezenne, Marie-Catherine. *See* Janson, *dit* Lapalme
Delezenne, Marie-Catherine (Pélissier; Sales Laterrière), IV, 205, 618, 619; V, 708, 735, 736, 737, 738; VI, **183–85**, 680; X, 431
Delezenne, Marie-Christine. *See* Jacquemart
Delezenne, Martin, IV, 204
Delezenne, Michel-Mathieu, IV, 205; V, 736, 737; VI, 184

Delfosse, Maurice, XI, 832; XII, 1040
Delguiel. *See* Dalgueuil
Delhalle, Constantin, II, **173–74**, 414, 475, 505, 645; III, 355
Delholme, Marie-Rosalie (Cuoq), XII, 223
Delicérasse, Suzanne (Buisson, *dit* Saint-Cosme), II, 109
Deliette. *See* Liette; Tonty
Delille, Jacques, IX, 465
De Lille, Jeanne (Allain), V, 12
Delique, Charles-François, IV, 748; V, 727
Delisle. *See also* Aubin-Delisle; Bréhaut; Chabrand
Delisle, Alexandre-Maurice, VII, 858; IX, 650, 699; X, **219–21**, 522, 717; XI, 188; XII, 89, 1115
De Lisle, Angélique. *See* Chevalier
De Lisle, Ann. *See* Denton
Delisle, Antoine, V, 727
De Lisle, Augustin, V, 241; IX, **200–1**; XI, 217
Delisle, Benjamin (constable), VI, 434
Delisle, Benjamin (merchant), IX, 396
Delisle, Charles-Alexandre, X, 220
De Lisle, Charlotte-Henriette. *See* Ainsse
Delisle, Claude, III, 248
Delisle, Élizabeth (Bibaud), VIII, 87; XI, 70
De Lisle, Elizabeth (Brock), V, 109
Delisle, Émilie (Thibaudeau), X, 675; XII, 1036
Delisle, Françoise (Toupin, *dit* Dussault; Raby), IV, 650; VI, 626
Delisle, Frédéric, V, 218
Delisle, Guillaume, II, 428, 653; III, 248
De Lisle, Henriette. *See* Trudel
Delisle, Jean, XII, 197
De Lisle, Jean, IV, 6, 7, 189, 543; V, **241–42**, 380, 398, 663; VI, 494; VII, 673, 674; IX, 200
De Lisle, Jean-Guillaume, V, 241
De Lisle, Jean-Guillaume, IV, 534; V, 180, 211, 233, 241, **242–43**, 701; VII, 255
De Lisle, John (Jean-Baptiste), VI, 666; X, 219
Delisle, Joseph, VIII, 87
Delisle, Joseph-Nicolas, I, 677; IV, 76, 77, 82
Delisle, Marie-Angélique. *See* Cuvillier
De Lisle, Marie-Anne. *See* Rousseau
De Lisle, Marie-Louise. *See* Heer
De Lisle, Mary. *See* Robinson
Delisle, Maurice-Nolan, X, 220
Delisle, Michel-Charles, X, 219
De Lisle, Pierre-Guillaume, V, 417
De Lisle, Radegonde. *See* Berthelet
De Lisle, Suzanne. *See* Lacroix-Mézière
Delisle, Thérèse (Larue), VIII, 491
Delisle, William, VI, 487
Dellius, Godfrey, II, 474, 603; III, 622
Delmage, Catherine (Coverdale), IX, 164
De Lolme, Jean-Louis, VI, 46
Delong, Catherine (Vanderburg; Lossing), VI, 406
Delong, Peter, VI, 406
Delongrais. *See* Deslongrais
Delor. *See* Levasseur
Delord. *See* Delort
Delorme. *See also* Hénault; Simon
Delorme, Monsieur (fur trader), V, 533
Delorme, Catherine. *See* Roy
Delorme, Charles-Simon, VII, 239
Delorme, Charles-Simon, VII, **239–41**, 762

Delorme, Joseph, IX, 330
Delorme, Joseph-Victor, VIII, 87
Delorme, Louis, IX, 344, 345
Delorme, Marianne-Josette (Dénéchau), VII, 241
Delorme, Marie (Pigeon), VII, 698
Delorme, Marie-Marguerite. *See* Dufresne
De L'Orme, Philibert, III, 419; VI, 27
Delorme, Pierre, XI, 742; XII, 372
Delort, Barbe. *See* Leneuf de La Vallière et de Beaubassin
Delort, Françoise-Ovide. *See* Carterot
Delort, Guillaume, III, 173, 174
Delort, Guillaume, II, 119; III, 97, **173–74**; IV, 433
Delort, Jacques, III, 173
Delort, Louis, II, 119; III, 173, 174
Delort, Marie-Charlotte. *See* Gaultier
Delort, Michel, III, 173
Delort, Philippe, III, 173
Delort, Suzanne. *See* Despenan
Delpech, Jacques-Mathieu, VI, 763
Delphine, Sister. *See* Fontbonne
Delvecchio, Catherine. *See* Buti
Delvecchio, Marie-Christine (Leblanc), VI, 186
Delvecchio, Pierre, VI, 185
Delvecchio, Pierre (Pietro), VI, 185
Del Vecchio, Rosita (Rosa) (Jehin-Prume), XII, 471, 533
Delvecchio, Thérèse. *See* Chevalier
Delvecchio, Thomas, VI, **185–86**
Démaray, Marie-Jovite. *See* Descombes-Porcheron
Démaray, Pierre-Octave, VIII, 210
Démaray, Pierre-Paul, VII, 264; VIII, **209–10**, 471; X, 429, 694; XI, 585; XII, 88, 120
Démarest, Louise. *See* Patrie
Démarest, Pierre, VIII, 209
Demarquay, Pierre, named Brother Euverte, IX, 681
Demasduwit, V, **243–44**; VI, 392, 393, 580, 706, 708, 709; VII, 115, 377; VIII, 924; IX, 161
Demay, André, II, 273
Demay de Termont, Charles-Gilbert, IV, 99
Demers, Alexis (brother of LOUIS), VIII, 211
Demers, Alexis (doctor), V, 245; VIII, 736
Demers, François-Xavier, VII, 423
Demers, Geneviève. *See* Loignon
Demers, Hermine (Fournier), XII, 323
Demers, Jean, VIII, 211
Demers, Jean-Baptiste (father of JÉRÔME), VIII, 210
Demers, Jean-Baptiste (scrutineer), VII, 133
Demers, Jérôme, V, 245; VI, 26, 202, 597, 650; VII, 280, 341, 655, 721, 892; VIII, 38, 39, **210–15**, 407, 408, 595, 681, 682; IX, 117, 120, 465, 466; X, 488; XI, 177; XII, 846, 847, 1016
Demers, Louis, V, 244
Demers, Louis (baptized Jean), V, **244–45**; VI, 588; VII, 591; VIII, 211
Demers, Marie-Antoinette. *See* Allard
Demers, Michel, X, 221
Demers, Modeste, VII, 672; VIII, 561, 654, 677, 722; X, **221–22**, 227; XI, 173, 402, 805; XII, 282, 360, 398, 819, 847
Demers, Rosalie. *See* Foucher
Demers, Thérèse. *See* Gagnon
Demers, *dit* Dumé, Françoise (Ducharme), V, 272
Demers Dessermont, Marie-Catherine, IV, 235
Demers Monfort, Catherine. *See* Thunay, *dit* Dufresne

Demers Monfort, François, III, 295
Demesi. *See* Le Normant
Demesnu. *See* Peuvret
Demeule, Joseph-Étienne, IV, 42
DeMill, Elisha Budd, X, 223
DeMill, Elizabeth. *See* Budd
DeMill, Nathan Smith, X, 223
De Mille, Elizabeth Ann. *See* Pryor
De Mille, James, X, **223–24**, 269; XI, 210
Deming, Hannah (Gridley), IV, 313
Deminiac. *See* Miniac
Demoiselle, La. *See* Memeskia
Demontézon, Fortuné, XI, 588
Demontreau, A., II, 164
Demosny, Catherine. *See* Fol
Demosny, Catherine (Lamarre, *dit* Bélisle), II, 340
Demosny, Jean, I, 256
Demosny, Jean, I, 249, **255–56**, 550, 583; II, 340
Demosny, Julienne. *See* Bisson
Demosny, Marie. *See* Filleul
Demosny, Marie-Louise. *See* Albert
Demosny, Paul, I, 255
Dempsey, Mr (merchant), VII, 248
Dempsey, Laurence, IX, 604
Dempsey, Mary Ann, VII, 102
Denaut, André, V, 245
Denaut, Archange (Raymond), VII, 739
Denaut, Françoise. *See* Boyer
Denaut, Marguerite (Quesnel), IX, 650
Denaut, Marguerite-Amable, V, 217, 248
Denaut, Pierre, IV, 135, 374, 436, 799; V, 77, 93, 123, 186, 203, 217, 224, **245–48**, 292, 294, 374, 380, 471, 494, 516, 524, 525, 659, 671, 680, 687, 688, 691; VI, 106, 125, 145, 170, 216, 383, 403, 448, 524, 587, 588, 589, 593, 620, 668, 669, 700; VII, 321, 340, 486, 545, 615, 699, 720, 767, 784, 788, 798, 801, 802, 850; VIII, 201, 214, 240, 592, 776; XI, 87
Denbigh, Earl of. *See* Feilding
Dencke, Jeremiah, VII, 243
Dencke, Sara. *See* Test
Deneau, Anne. *See* Morin
Deneau, René, II, 447
Dénéchau, Adélaïde. *See* Gauvreau
Dénéchau, Claude, V, 249, 651; VI, 280, 287; VII, **241–43**, 300; VIII, 690; X, 431; XII, 323, 911
Dénéchau, Marianne-Josette. *See* Delorme
Dénéchaud, Angélique. *See* Gastonguay
Dénéchaud, Antoinette. *See* Lubet
Dénéchaud, Charles-Denis, V, 249; VII, 241, 242, 677
Dénéchaud, Eulalie-Antoinette (Sales Laterrière), IX, 360, 362; X, 431
Dénéchaud, Jacques, V, **248–49**, 699; VII, 224, 241
Dénéchaud, Pierre (grandfather), V, 248
Dénéchaud, Pierre, V, 249; VII, 241
Dénéchaud, Zoé-Louise (Robitaille), XII, 911
Dengomau. *See* Dangoumau
Denham, Euphemia (Telfer), VIII, 869
Deniau-Destaillis, Joseph, II, 11
Deniger, Florence (Viau, *dit* Cinq-Mars), XII, 1074
Denis. *See also* Denys
Denis, Aurélie (Devisme), XII, 257
Denis, Françoise (Outlaw), I, 529
Denis, Jean, II, 582

Denis, Marie-Anne (Forgues), XI, 319
Denis, Marie-Gabrielle, named de l'Annonciation, II, 93, 613
Denis, Michel, III, 307
Denis, Paul, XI, 891
Denis, Pierre, VII, **243**
Denis, Pierre-François, named Brother Denis, III, 292; IX, 680
Denis de Saint-Simon, Antoine-Charles, IV, **207–8**; V, 104
Denison, Avery, VI, **186–87**
Denison, Deborah. *See* Griswold
Denison, Egerton Edmund Augustus, XII, 245
Denison, Elisha, VI, 186
Denison, Elizabeth (Conyngham, Marchioness Conyngham), VI, 98
Denison, Esther Borden. *See* Lippincott
Denison, Eunice. *See* Williams
Denison, Eunice, VI, 187
Denison, Frederick Charles, XI, 472, 473; XII, 117, **243–46**, 704
Denison, George Taylor (father of GEORGE TAYLOR), IX, 345; X, 224; XI, 871
Denison, George Taylor, X, 74, **224–25**; XI, 245; XII, 243
Denison*, George Taylor (1839–1925), X, 224, 225; XI, 249, 322, 323, 324, 368, 741, 743, 916; XII, 244, 246, 558, 950, 951
Denison, Joanna. *See* Stanton
Denison, John, V, 326; VII, 207; X, 224
Denison, John Williams, VI, 187
Denison, Julia Abigail. *See* Macklem
Denison, Keturah. *See* Minor
Denison, Lucy Maria Charlotte (Manners-Sutton, Viscountess Canterbury), X, 494
Denison, Malvina, VI, 187
Denison, Mary Anne. *See* Dewson
Denison, Mary Elizabeth (Taylor), XI, 871
Denison*, Merrill (1893–1975), XI, 387; XII, 709
Denison, Prudence. *See* Sherman
Denison, Prudence (Arnold), VI, 13
Denison, Richard Lippincott, X, 225; XII, 244
Denison, Robert, III, 174
Denison, Robert, III, **174–75**; IV, 217, 351
Denison, Robert Brittain, X, 225; XII, 344
Denison, Simeon Minor, VI, 187
Denison, Sir William Thomas, VIII, 297
Denke, Anna Maria. *See* Heckedorn
Denke, Christian Frederick, VII, **243–44**
Denke, Maria. *See* Steiner
Denman, Frances (Baynes, Lady Baynes), IX, 35
Denman, Thomas, 1st Baron Denman, VII, 98; IX, 35
Denmark, Prince of. *See* George
Denmark, Princess of. *See* Alexandra
Dennett, Elizabeth (Todd), VIII, 888, 889
Dennis, Henry, VI, 187
Dennis, Jane Gray (Mulkins), X, 536
Dennis, John, VI, **187–88**; X, 615; XI, 244
Dennis, John Stoughton, VI, 188
Dennis, John Stoughton, XI, 246
Dennis, John Stoughton, VI, 188; VIII, 898, 960; IX, 549; X, 74, 91, 282, 558; XI, 45, **244–46**, 738, 739, 740, 842; XII, 69, 119, 125, 187, 203, 204, 854, 855, 950, 1009
Dennis, Joseph, XI, 244
Dennis, Maria (Bridgland), X, 91

Dennis, Martha. *See* Lynn
Dennis, Martha (McLaney; wife of JOHN), VI, 187
Dennis, Mary. *See* Stoughton
Dennis, Mary Charlotte. *See* Munro
Dennis, Paul, VI, 132
Dennis, Rebecca (Richardson), X, 615
Dennis, Sarah Maria. *See* Oliver
Dennison, Deborah (Ely; Butler), IV, 117
Denniston, John, V, 287
Dennistoun, James Frederick, XII, 782
Dennistoun, Robert, XII, 782
Denny, Sir Cecil Edward, XII, 802
Denny, Plato, IV, 597
Denny, William, VIII, 648
Denonville. *See* Brisay; Hémard
Denonville, Marquis de. *See* Brisay
Denonville, Marquise de. *See* Courtin de Tangeux
Denoon, Catherine. *See* Fraser
Denoon, David, VII, 244
Denoon, Hugh, VII, 84, **244–46**
Denoon, Mary. *See* Inglis
Denroche, Edward, X, 536
Denson, Edith (wife of HENRY DENNY), IV, 208
Denson, Elizabeth (Cartland), IV, 208
Denson, Henry Denny, IV, 17, 29, **208–9**, 217, 451
Dent, Catherine. *See* Mawson
Dent, Elsie. *See* McIntosh
Dent, John, XI, 246
Dent, John Charles, VI, 22, 165; VII, 313, 418, 861; VIII, 340, 848, 850; IX, 72, 230, 335, 509, 576, 686, 689, 724; X, 120, 169, 181, 565, 705; XI, 144, **246–49**, 415; XII, 142, 143, 593
Denter, J. G., IX, 179
Denton, Ann (De Lisle), V, 241, 242
Denton, Frances Diana (Wetherall), IX, 826
Denton, Sarah (Toosey), IV, 738
Dentremont. *See* Entremont
Denys. *See also* Denis
Denys, Jean, I, 22, **256**
Denys, Jean-Baptiste, XI, 671
Denys, Joseph (Jacques), I, 536; II, 110, 130, 131, **174–76**, 178, 222, 223, 245, 294, 419, 429, 506; III, 233
Denys, Louis-Jean, IV, 732
Denys, Marguerite. *See* Lafite
Denys, Marguerite (Cressé), II, 529
Denys, Marguerite (Forsayth), I, 258
Denys, Marie (Leneuf de La Vallière et de Beaubassin), I, 258; II, 236, 408, 409, 411, 654
Denys, Nicolas, I, 25, 32, 66, 89, 90, 114, **256–59**, 260, 261, 277, 383, 433, 434, 476, 503, 505, 514, 568, 595, 597, 621; II, 178, 217, 408, 409; III, 108
Denys de Bonaventure, Jeanne. *See* Jannière
Denys de Bonaventure, Simon-Pierre, I, 114, 246, 576, 654; II, 14, 37, **176–78**, 206, 257, 449, 450, 481; III, 175, 176, 499, 500, 552, 681, 682; IV, 10
Denys de Bonnaventure, Claude-Élisabeth, II, 17; III, **175–76**, 183, 236, 264, 268; IV, 56, 79, 239, 688; V, 339
Denys de Bonnaventure, Louise. *See* Denys de La Ronde
Denys de Fronsac, Anne. *See* Parabego
Denys de Fronsac, Françoise. *See* Cailleteau
Denys de Fronsac, Louis, I, 261
Denys de Fronsac, Marie-Anne (Merçan), I, 260; II, 477

Denys de Fronsac, Nicolas, I, 260
Denys de Fronsac, Richard, I, 90, 258, **259–61**, 649; II, 106, 178, 217, 256, 409, 477; IV, 195
Denys de La Ronde, Anne-Ursule (Aubert de La Chesnaye), II, 34; III, 22
Denys de La Ronde, Catherine. *See* Leneuf de La Poterie
Denys de La Ronde, Françoise (Bouthier; Ailleboust de Manthet), II, 14
Denys de La Ronde, Louis, II, 17, 123, 154, 198, 203, 219, 254, 285, 339, 411, 452, 498, 511, 668; III, 22, 47, 110, 175, **176–80**, 208, 374, 436, 454, 475; IV, 358, 359
Denys de La Ronde, Louise (Denys de Bonnaventure), III, 175
Denys de La Ronde, Marguerite-Renée (Lanouguère; Fleury Deschambault), I, 418; II, 224; III, 311, 312
Denys de La Ronde, Marie-Angélique (Aubert de La Chesnaye), II, 33; III, 21, 22, 192, 233
Denys de La Ronde, Marie-Charlotte (Ramezay), II, 545, 548, 606; III, 543; IV, 41, 650, 653, 690
Denys de La Ronde, Marie-Louise. *See* Chartier de Lotbinière
Denys de La Ronde, Marie-Louise (Ailleboust d'Argenteuil), II, 12; III, 5; IV, 10
Denys de La Ronde, Philippe, III, 179
Denys de La Ronde, Pierre, I, 85, 260, 418; II, 12, 28, 33, 34, 131, 174, 176, **178–79**, 224, 545; III, 176
Denys de La Ronde, Pierre-François-Paul, III, 179
Denys de La Thibaudière, Jacques, I, 256, 261
Denys de La Thibaudière, Marie. *See* Cosnier
Denys de La Trinité, Barbe (Pécaudy de Contrecœur; Gannes de Falaise), I, 535; II, 236; III, 505
Denys de La Trinité, Charlotte (Dupas; Boucher de Boucherville), III, 80
Denys de La Trinité, Françoise. *See* Du Tartre
Denys de La Trinité, Françoise (Leneuf de La Vallière et de Beaubassin), II, 409
Denys de La Trinité, Jeanne. *See* Dubreuil
Denys de La Trinité, Simon, I, 257, **261–62**, 514, 535, 589; II, 174, 176, 178, 179, 236, 409; III, 178
Denys de Saint-Pierre, Simon-Pierre, II, 176
Denys de Saint-Simon, Charles-Paul, II, 179; III, 180, 549, 551; IV, 207
Denys de Saint-Simon, Élisabeth (Collet), II, 151
Denys de Saint-Simon, Louise-Catherine (Bergeron; Gaillard), II, 235
Denys de Saint-Simon, Marie-Anne (Bertier), II, 60, 151
Denys de Saint-Simon, Marie-Joseph. *See* Prat
Denys de Saint-Simon, Marie-Madeleine. *See* Peiras
Denys de Saint-Simon, Paul, I, 35, 49, 226, 396, 625; II, 60, 151, **179**, 514, 520, 537; III, 180; IV, 209
Denys de Vitré, Catherine. *See* Loustelneau
Denys de Vitré, Charles, II, 32, 78, 137, **179–80**, 276, 295, 448
Denys de Vitré, Guillaume-Emmanuel-Théodose, IV, 209
Denys de Vitré, John, IV, 210
Denys de Vitré, Marie-Anne-Noële, V, 323
Denys de Vitré, Marie-Charlotte. *See* Chrétien
Denys de Vitré, Marie-Gabrielle (Descayrac de L'Autheur), II, 179
Denys de Vitré, Marie-Joseph. *See* Blaise Des Bergères de Rigauville
Denys de Vitré, Marie-Thérèse. *See* Juchereau Duchesnay
Denys de Vitré, Mathieu-Théodore, V, 323

Denys de Vitré, Théodose-Matthieu, IV, **209–10**, 650; VI, 134
Denys Du Tartre, Geneviève. *See* Couillard
Denys Du Tartre, Pierre, II, 176
Deowando. *See* Atecouando (fl. 1749–57)
Depelteau. *See* Sarasin
Depéret, Elie, III, **180–81**
Depéret, Jean, III, 180
Depéret, Valère. *See* Limousin
DePeyster, Abraham, VI, 188
De Peyster, Abraham, IV, **210–11**; VI, 188, 350
DePeyster, Arent Schuyler, IV, 233, 302, 303, 337, 369, 496; V, 8, 9, 38, 39, 567, 568, 682, 710, 760, 836, 884; VI, 8, **188–91**, 509
De Peyster, Catherine. *See* Livingston
DePeyster, Cornelia. *See* Schuyler
De Peyster, James (Jacobus), IV, 210
DePeyster, John Watts, VI, 190
DePeyster, Pierre Guillaume, VI, 188
DePeyster, Rebecca. *See* Blair
De Peyster, Sarah. *See* Reade
Depin, Joseph, IV, 202
De Pue, Sarah (Van Norman), XI, 897
Deray, Françoise (Rieutord), V, 712
Derbishire, Ann. *See* Masterton
Derbishire, Philip, IX, 201
Derbishire, Stewart, VII, 184, 287, 446, 860; VIII, 587, 745, 815, 839; IX, **201–2**, 203, 204, 734, 741, 814; XI, 874, 920; XII, 247
Derby, Earl of. *See* Stanley
Derby (Darby), Benjamin, VII, 383
Derby (Darby), Mary (Hanington), VII, 383
Derbyshire, Daniel, VI, 733
Derenzy, Elizabeth. *See* Selby
Dering, Ann (Monk), III, 457; VI, 511
Dering, Sir Edward, II, 309
Derivon de Budemon, Marie. *See* Gaudé
Derivon de Budemon, Pierre, II, 153; III, 146
Dermer, Thomas, I, **262**, 650
Dérocher. *See* Brien; Desrochers
Derome, Éléonore. *See* Pagé
Derome, François, X, 225
Derome, François-Magloire, VII, 776; VIII, 420, 834, 835; X, **225–26**; XI, 494; XII, 67
Derome, Léon, XII, 532, 533
Derome, Malvina. *See* Langevin
Derome, Malvina (Asselin), X, 226
Derome, Marie-Bénigne (Gaudron de Chevremont), III, 239
Derome, Théotiste. *See* Labadie
Derosiers. *See* Deguire
Derré de Gand, François, I, **262–63**, 297, 637; II, xv
Derry, Margaret. *See* Geddes
Déry, Maurice, II, 111
Desagondensta. *See* Jones, Peter
Desandrouins, Benoît-Nicolas, IV, 211
Desandrouins, Jean-Nicolas, III, xix, 406, 534, 536, 606; IV, **211–12**; V, 739
Desandrouins, Marie-Scholastique. *See* Hallot
Des Assises. *See* La Grive
De Saulles, Jean-Pierre, VI, 206
De Saulles, Marguerite. *See* Crevier Décheneaux
Désaulniers. *See* Lesieur-Désaulniers

Desaulniers*, Gonzalve (1863–1934), XII, 272
Desauniers. *See also* Trottier
Desauniers, Marguerite, III, 47, 611, 627
Desauniers, Marie-Anne, III, 47, 611, 627
Desauniers, Marie-Madeleine, III, 47, 611, 627
Desautels, Joseph, XI, 249
Desautels, Joseph, X, 689; XI, **249–51**; XII, 509, 798, 1022
Desautels, Joseph-Marie, IV, 533, 534
Desautels, Madeleine. *See* Fréchette
Desbarats, Cécile, XII, 249
Desbarats, Charles-Henri-Hullet, XII, 250
Desbarats, Charlotte. *See* Selby
Desbarats, Charlotte-Louise (Perrault), VI, 192, 576
Desbarats, Édouard-Olivier, VI, 84, 192
Desbarats, Édouard-Stanislas-Cirice, XII, 250
Desbarats, George-Édouard, VI, 84, 192; IX, 203; XI, 3, 71, 623, 843; XII, **246–50**, 558, 789
Desbarats, George-Joseph, XII, 250
Desbarats, George-Paschal, VI, 192; VII, 287, 703; VIII, 223, 938; IX, 116, **202–3**, 204, 741; X, 22, 128; XII, 246, 247, 248
Desbarats, Hélène (Pemberton), VI, 192
Desbarats, Henriette. *See* Dionne
Desbarats, Jean-Robert-Alexandre, XII, 249
Desbarats, Jessé-Louise. *See* Pothier
Desbarats, Joseph, VI, 191
Desbarats, Josette. *See* Voyer
Desbarats, Louise-Sophie (Fisher), VI, 192
Desbarats, Lucianne. *See* Bossé
Desbarats, Lucianne (de Blaquiere, Baroness de Blaquiere), XII, 249
Desbarats, Marie-Louise. *See* Crète
Desbarats, Pierre-Édouard, IV, 107, 303; V, 139, 834; VI, 84, 123, 124, **191–92**, 391, 392, 576; VII, 287, 462, 645, 892; IX, 202
Desbarats, Sophie (Pemberton), VI, 192
Desbarats, William-Amable, VI, 192; XII, 248, 250
Des Barres. *See* Vallet
DesBarres, Amelia, VI, 121, 196
DesBarres, Augustus Wallet, VII, 99; IX, 721, 794; X, 179
Desbarres, François. *See* Bigot, François (d. 1778)
DesBarres, James Luttrell, VII, 925
DesBarres, Joseph Frederick Wallet, III, 133, 620; IV, 208, 292, 293, 522, 603, 613; V, 204, 222, 223, 335, 427, 430, 510, 516, 569, 607, 766, 773, 776, 780, 826, 862, 874, 887; VI, 31, 109, 121, 122, 161, 162, 163, **192–97**, 203, 213, 298, 359, 413, 414, 565, 566, 567, 568, 662, 663, 737, 785, 806, 807; VII, 352, 362, 414; VIII, 35, 122, 802, 824, 954; IX, 709; XI, 55, 664
DesBarres, William Frederick, X, 70
Des Bergères. *See also* Blaise
Des Bergères de Rigauville, Charles-Régis, VI, 344
Desbois, Jeanne (Briand), IV, 95
Desbois, Olivier, IV, 95
Des Bordes. *See also* Landrière
Desbordes, Sieur (plenipotentiary), II, 491
Desbordes, Delphine (Cabazié), II, 111
Desbordes, Marie (Migeon), I, 508
Des Bordes Landrière, Gabriel-Alexis, IV, 435
Des Bordes Landrière, Marguerite. *See* Mercier
Desbrieux, François, II, 189
Desbrieux, Jean, II, 186, 189, 616

Desbrieux, Marguerite. *See* Dizy, *dit* Montplaisir
DesBrisay, Ada A. *See* Harley
Des Brisay, Albert, VIII, 177, **215–17**; XI, 687; XII, 116
Desbrisay, Ellen. *See* Landers
DesBrisay, Helen (Pope), X, 593
DesBrisay, Lestock, XI, 828
DesBrisay, Lucretia Bourdette. *See* Woodward
DesBrisay, Magdalen. *See* Vergese d'Aubussargues
Desbrisay, Margaret. *See* Stewart
Desbrisay, Margaret (St Croix), VII, 103
Des Brisay, Margaret B. *See* McLeod
Desbrisay, Mary (Stewart), V, 775
DesBrisay, Mather Byles, XII, **250–51**
DesBrisay, Theophilus (grandson of THOMAS), V, 250; VI, 738
DesBrisay, Theophilus (great-grandson of THOMAS), V, 250; VIII, 954; X, 593, 594
DesBrisay (La Cour de Brisay), Theophilus (Samuel-Théophile de) (father of THOMAS), V, 249
Desbrisay, Theophilus, V, 250, 263, 775, 777; VI, 65, 131, **197–98**, 736; VIII, 215, 825
Desbrisay, Thomas, IV, 129, 353, 608, 609, 610; V, 128, 219, **249–50**, 263, 569, 775, 777, 778, 826; VI, 122, 197; VII, 103; VIII, 824; XII, 250
DesBrisay, Thomas Belcher, XII, 250
Des Butes (Desbutes); Desbuttes. *See* Baudry
Des Camps, Renée (Comingo), V, 199
Descaris, Jean-Baptiste, IV, 732
Descaris, Jeanne. *See* Lefebvre
Descaris, Marie-Joseph (Martinet), VII, 591
Des Cars. *See* Pérusse
Descartes, René, VII, 656; VIII, 212
Descary, Gabriel, IV, 178
Descary, Louise (Maugenest), IV, 524
Descayrac de L'Autheur, Marie-Gabrielle. *See* Denys de Vitré
Desceliers, Pierre, I, 170
Deschaillons. *See* Saint-Ours
Deschambault. *See* Fleury
Deschamps. *See also* Cadet; Éno
Deschamps, Anne (Mangeant), III, 426
Deschamps, Élisabeth. *See* Debin
Deschamps, George, V, 251
Des Champs, Guillaume, I, 293
Deschamps, Isaac, IV, 110, 111, 116, 526, 528, 604; V, 63, 109, **250–52**, 431, 574; VI, 34, 87; VII, 87, 104, 831
Deschamps, Jean, II, 181
Deschamps, Sarah. *See* Ellis
Deschamps de Boishébert, Charlotte (Saint-Ours), VI, 679
Deschamps de Boishébert, Claude-Louis, II, 181
Deschamps de Boishébert, Henri-Louis, II, **180–81**, 409; III, 65, 102; IV, 212, 654, 728; V, 668
Deschamps de Boishébert, Louise-Geneviève. *See* Ramezay
Deschamps de Boishébert, Louise-Geneviève (Tarieu de La Naudière), IV, 728, 729; V, 791
Deschamps de Boishébert et de Raffetot, Charles, II, 181; III, 28, 29, 87, 128, 183, 358, 417, 573, 610; IV, 78, 79, 125, 169, **212–15**, 290, 305, 392, 447, 453, 614, 616, 688, 729; V, 102, 451, 668
Deschamps de Boishébert et de Raffetot, Charlotte-Élisabeth-Antoinette (Deschamps de Boishébert et de Raffetot), IV, 212

Deschamps de Fellière, Marie-Anne (Vallette de Chévigny), III, 637

Deschamps de La Bouteillerie, Catherine-Gertrude. *See* Macard

Deschamps de La Bouteillerie, Charles-Joseph, II, 181

Deschamps de La Bouteillerie, Jean-Baptiste-François, II, 180, **181**; V, 668

Deschamps de La Bouteillerie, Jeanne-Marguerite. *See* Le Chevalier

Des Chatelets. *See* Juchereau

Deschenaux. *See also* Brassard

Deschenaux, Geneviève. *See* Dumon

Deschenaux, Marie-Joseph. *See* Perrault

Deschenaux (Brassard Deschenaux), Pierre-Louis, IV, 89; V, 84, **252–53**, 289, 290, 792; VII, 709; VIII, 491

Descheneaux. *See* Crevier

Deschênes, Georges-Honoré, XII, 105, **251–52**

Deschênes, Suzanne. *See* Michaud

Deschevery, Jean, III, 181

Deschevery, Jeanne. *See* Damboise

Deschevery, *dit* Maisonbasse, Jean-Baptiste, III, **181–82**, 346, 499

Deschevery, *dit* Maisonbasse, Louise-Élisabeth. *See* Couteron

Deschevery, *dit* Maisonbasse, Marie-Françoise, III, 181

Desclaux, Pierre, IV, 124, 125, 126, 127

Desclouzeaux. *See* Champy

Descombes. *See also* Lombard; Métayer-Descombes

Descombes, Pierre, XII, 1065

Descombes-Porcheron, Marie-Jovite (Dandurand; Démaray), VIII, 209

Descoteaux, Angèle (Houde), XI, 424

Descouando. *See* Atecouando (fl. 1749–57)

Des Cours. *See* Du Bois

Descouts, Martin, III, **182**; IV, 56

Desdames, Thierry, I, **263–64**, 266, 579

Desdevens de Glandons, Gabrielle. *See* Avet Forel

Desdevens de Glandons, Joseph, IV, 215

Desdevens de Glandons, Marie-Thérèse. *See* Mathon

Desdevens de Glandons, Maurice, IV, **215–16**; V, 146

Desenclaves. *See* Gay

Deserontyon, John, IV, liv; V, **253–56**, 806, 810; VI, 550

Deserontyon, Peter John, V, 255

Des Essarts. *See* Berey

De Sève, Alfred, XII, 472

Desève, Charlotte (Leheup, *dit* Latulippe; Huguet, *dit* Latour), V, 435

Desève, François-Xavier, VII, 173, 679

Desève, Jean-Baptiste, V, 437

Desferières Renaud, Sieur (merchant), III, 135

Desfonds, Bazile, V, 322

Des Fontaines. *See* Leduc

Des Forges. *See* Robin

Desforges, Anne-Céleste (Foureur), IV, 272

Des Forges, Marie. *See* Viel

Des Friches de Brasseuse, Artus, II, 182

Des Friches de Meneval, Louis-Alexandre, I, 426, 436, 533, 542, 544, 576, 578; II, **182–84**, 257, 352, 522, 578, 638

Desgagnés, Joseph, VI, 226

Desgagnés, Louis, VIII, 893

Desgagnés, Olive. *See* Gagné

Desglis (Desgly). *See* Mariauchau

Desgoutins. *See* Goutin

Desgouttes, Marquis. *See* Charry

Des Granches, Alizon (Jalobert), I, 384

Des Granches, Antoine, I, 167

Des Granches, Catherine (Cartier), I, 167, 170

Des Granches, Guyon, Vicomte de Beaupré, I, 169

Des Granches, Jacques, I, 170

Des Granges. *See also* Lanoullier; Moyen

Desgranges, Marie-Angélique (Coderre), XI, 302

Des Granges de Mauprée, Alixe. *See* La Feuillée

Des Granges de Mauprée, Louis, I, 415

Desgrez, Anne. *See* Hugot

Desgrez, Anne (Beauharnois de La Chaussaye, Baronne de Beauville), III, 51

Desgrez, François, III, 51

Des Groseilliers. *See* Chouart

Deshaies, Marie (Bétourné, *dit* La Violette), X, 59

Deshaies-Gendron, Claude, I, 328, 550

Deshayes, Catherine, known as La Voisin (Monvoisin), III, 143

Deshayes, Jean, I, 56; II, **184–85**, 230; III, 620

Desherbert de Lapointe, Joseph-Simon, IV, 252, 263, 433

Des Herbiers, Antoine-Auguste, Marquis de L'Étenduère, III, 183

Des Herbiers, Armand, III, 182

Des Herbiers, Henri-François, Marquis de L'Étenduère, III, 27, 182, 183, 557; IV, 699

Des Herbiers, Marie-Olive (Des Herbiers de La Ralière), III, 183

Des Herbiers de La Ralière, Charles, III, 30, **182–84**, 294, 570; IV, 254, 454, 455, 655

Deshormeaux. *See* Bergier

Desilets. *See also* Desrosiers

Désilets. *See also* Huard

Désilets, Aimé, VIII, **217**

Desilets, Alfred, XI, 252, 253

Désilets, Alphonse, VIII, 16

Désilets, Élize. *See* Dumont

Désilets, François, XI, 251

Desilets, Gédéon, XI, 252

Désilets, Isidore, VIII, 217

Désilets, Joseph-Octave, X, 533

Désilets, Louis-Eusèbe, VIII, 217; IX, 66

Desilets, Luc, XI, **251–53**; XII, 303, 509, 510, 820, 1023

Désilets, Marguerite. *See* Hébert

Désilets, Marie. *See* Morasse

Desilets, Pierre, XI, 252

Des Islets. *See* Couillard

Desjardins. *See also* Augier; Roy; Roy-Desjardins

Desjardins*, Alphonse (1841–1912), XII, 62

Desjardins*, Alphonse (1854–1920), X, 47; XI, 744, 813, 891, 893, 902; XII, 725

Desjardins, Alselme, IX, 203

Desjardins, Fabien, IX, 203, 204

Desjardins, François-Xavier, IX, **203–4**

Desjardins, Joseph, IX, 203

Desjardins*, Louis-Édouard (1837–1919), XII, 799

Desjardins, Madeleine, named du Sacré-Cœur, XII, 1034

Desjardins, Marie-Josephte. *See* Prévost

Desjardins, Mary. *See* Delesderniers

Desjardins, Paul, IX, 862

Desjardins, Peter, VI, **198–200**, 229, 230; VII, 178, 379; VIII, 687, 946

Desjardins, Philippe-Jean-Louis, I, 314; IV, 90, 136; V, 380, 494, 659; VI, 85, **200–2**, 398, 596, 598, 752; VII, 246, 256, 321, 573, 761; VIII, 456, 494, 592; XII, 845

Desjardins, Valère, IX, 863

Desjardins, Virginie. *See* Laviolette

Desjardins, *dit* Desplantes, Louis-Joseph, IV, 81, 136, 137; V, 659; VI, 201, 202, 391; VII, **246–47**, 721, 752, 869, 870; VIII, 201; IX, 359; XII, 845

Desjardins de Lapérière, Jacques, VI, 200; VII, 246

Desjardins de Lapérière, Marie-Anne. *See* Baudet

Desjardins Du Val, Monsieur (agent), I, 383, 503, 504

Desjarlais. *See* Jarlais

Desjean de Pointis, Jean-Bernard-Louis, III, 488

Desjordy. *See also* Dejordy

Desjordy de Cabanac, François, I, 361; II, 633

Desjordy de Cabanac, Joseph, II, **185–86**, 580

Desjordy de Cabanac, Madeleine. *See* Pézard de La Tousche

Desjordy de Cabanac, Melchior, II, 185, 186

Desjordy Moreau de Cabanac, Anne. *See* Nolan

Desjordy Moreau de Cabanac, François, I, 361; II, 185, **186–87**, 189, 190; III, 171

Desjordy Moreau de Cabanac, Louise-Catherine. *See* Robinau de Bécancour

Des Landes. *See also* Daulier

Deslandes, Jean, II, 105, 159

Des Landes, Joseph, III, 108, **184**; VIII, 212

Deslandes, Marie-Josephe. *See* Le Pellé Lahaye

Deslandes, Marie-Josephte (Quesnel), V, 700; VII, 716; IX, 649

Deslandes, Pierre-Louis, V, 89

Des Lauriers. *See* Basset

Deslauriers. *See* Le Cavelier; Normandeau

Desliettes. *See* Liette; Tonty

Desloges, Anne (Guenet), I, 347

Deslongrais, Nicolas, III, **184–85**

Desmaisons, Gabriel, III, 519

Des Maizerets. *See* Ango

Desmarais. *See also* Godet

Desmarais, Monsieur (fur trader), VII, 356

Desmarais, Abraham, VII, 149

Desmarais, Innocent, I, 264

Desmarais, Madelaine (Grant), VIII, 341

Desmarais, Michel, III, 518

Desmarais, Odilon, XII, 721

Desmarais, Paul, III, 519

Desmarest. *See* Le Roy; Pinet

Desmarets, Monsieur (artist), I, 313

Desmarets, Monsieur (relation of Jean-Pierre ROMA), III, 566

Desmarets, Jean-Baptiste-François, Marquis de Maillebois, IV, 181

Des Maretz (Desmarets). *See* Godet

Desmarteau, Narcisse-Birtz, XI, 586

Desmazures, Adam-Charles-Gustave, IX, 247

Desmeloizes; Des Méloizes. *See* Renaud

De Smet, Josse, X, 226

De Smet, Marie-Jeanne. *See* Buydens

De Smet, Pierre-Jean, VIII, 654, 780; IX, 366, 636; X, 221, **226–28**, 391; XII, 110

Desmottes, Marie-Anne (Moncoq), VIII, 636

Desmoulins. *See* Maillou

Des Muceaux. *See* Ailleboust

Desnoyers, Elmire. *See* Leblanc

Desnoyers, Mathias-Charles, X, 435

de Sola, Abraham, VI, 366; X, 337; XI, **253–56**; XII, 570

de Sola, Clarence I., XI, 255

de Sola, David Aaron, XI, 254

de Sola, Esther. *See* Joseph

de Sola, Meldola, XI, 255

de Sola, Rebecca. *See* Meldola

Des Ormeaux. *See* Bergier; Dollard; Hazeur

Despard, Green, VI, 624

Despard, Harriet Anne. *See* Hesketh

Despard, John, IV, 523; V, 53, 205, 546, 766, 780; VI, 113, 114, **202–4**, 213, 535, 536, 537, 538; VII, 10

Despard, William, VI, 202

Despeiroux (Desperoux). *See* Lestage

Despenan, Suzanne (Delort), III, 173

Despiaube, Catherine (Olabaratz), IV, 589; V, 638

Despins. *See* Lefaivre; Lemoine

Des Plaines. *See* Damours

Desplantes. *See* Desjardins

Des Porques, Anne (Liébert), V, 497

Desportes, Françoise. *See* Langlois

Desportes, Hélène (Hébert; Morin), I, **264**, 367, 495; II, 489

Desportes, Pierre, I, 233, 264, 495

Desportes de Lignères, Pierre, I, 248, 264

Despréaux. *See* Boileau-Despréaux

Després. *See also* Couillard-Després; Guyon; Le Loutre

Després, Anne (Lauson; Bermen de La Martinière), I, 428, 430; II, 56, 57

Després, Étiennette (Guillemot), I, 349

Després, *dit* Disséré (Dicere), Marie-Reine (Gamache), VIII, 311

Desprez. *See also* Guion; Guyon

Desprez (Després), Geneviève (Couillard de Lespinay), I, 237; II, 60, 155, 213; VIII, 174

Desquairac (Desquerac). *See* Escairac

Des Reaux, Marie (Léger), II, 387

Desrivières; Des Rivières. *See also* Trottier

Desrivières, Monsieur (of Montreal), V, 705

Des Rivières, Adélard-Isidore, VII, 247, 248

Desrivières, François, V, 133, 527, 528, 529; VI, **204–5**, 424; VII, 58, 79, 310, 827

Desrivières, Henri, VIII, 108

Desrivières, Hypolite, IV, 592

Desrivières, James McGill, V, 527, 529; VI, 204; VII, 827

Desrivières, Marguerite-Thérèse. *See* Trottier Desrivières Beaubien

Des Rivières, Rodolphe, VII, **247–49**, 478; VIII, 471, 616, 617, 667; XI, 117

Desrivières-Beaubien. *See also* Trottier Desrivières Beaubien

Desrivières-Beaubien, Édouard, V, 829

Desrivières-Beaubien, Henri, V, 829

Desrochers. *See also* Brien-Desrochers

Des Rochers. *See* Chateigner

Desrochers, Benjamin, XII, 732

Desrochers, Louis-Auguste, VII, 174

Desrochers, Marie-Josephte. *See* Rocan, *dit* Bastien

Desrochers, Marie-Xavier (Méthot), XII, 731

Desrochers, Pierre-Urbain, VIII, 218

Desrochers, Urbain, V, 497; VI, 626; VIII, **217–19**, 456

Desrochers, Vital, V, 570; VIII, 218

Desrochers, Zéphirine. *See* Labrie

Desrochers, Zoé, VIII, 218
Desroches. *See also* Tinon-Desroches
Desroches, Anne. *See* Delestrade
Desroches, Charles, VI, 206
Desroches, Charles, VI, **206;** VII, 15
Desroches, Jean, II, 517
Desroches, Marguerite (Cirier), IV, 151
Desroches, Nathalie. *See* Marcotte
Des Roches Duplesy, Charlotte (Monbeton de Brouillan), III, 454
Desrosiers. *See also* Deguire; Jutras
Desrosiers, Anne. *See* Leneuf Du Hérisson
Desrosiers, Antoine, I, 468; XI, 251
Desrosiers, Hersélie (Mousseau), XI, 622
Desrosiers, Jean-Baptiste, XI, 480
Desrosiers, Marguerite (Bruce), XII, 132
Desrosiers, *dit* Desilets, Jean-Baptiste, XI, 251
Desrues, Jeanne (Baudouin), I, 80
Des Ruisseaux; Desruisseaux. *See* Trottier
Desruisseaux, Félix, VIII, 196
Dessailliant, *dit* Richeterre, Michel, II, **187–88**, 613
Dessane, Irma. *See* Trunel de La Croix-Nord
Dessane, Louis, X, 228
Dessane, Marie. *See* Maurel
Dessane, Marie-Hippolyte-Antoine, VII, 349; VIII, 347, 635; X, **228–29**; XI, 82, 500; XII, 977
Dessaulles*, Caroline-Angélina (Béique) (1852–1946), VI, 208; XII, 252
Dessaulles, Catherine-Zéphirine. *See* Thompson
Dessaulles, Georges-Casimir, VI, 208; XI, 479, 480
Dessaulles*, Henriette (Saint-Jacques) (1860–1946), VI, 208
Dessaulles, Jean, VI, 50, **206–8**, 287, 428; VII, 256, 574, 676; VIII, 711; IX, 74; X, 153; XI, 479; XII, 252, 1033
Dessaulles, Louis-Antoine, VI, 207, 208; VIII, 262; IX, 74, 193, 194, 211, 215, 243, 343, 466; X, 154, 165, 213, 237 250, 304, 315, 316, 429, 430; XI, 98, 101, 102, 105, 160, 273, 275, 289, 479, 494, 507, 659, 725; XII, **252–57**, 260, 261, 505, 506, 719, 720
Dessaulles, Marguerite-Anne. *See* Waddens
Dessaulles, Marie-Rosalie. *See* Papineau
Dessaulles, Rosalie (Laframboise), VI, 208; XI, 479
Dessermont. *See* Demers
Destaillis. *See* Deniau-Destaillis
Destailly, Sieur (expedition member), III, 83
D'Este, Sir Augustus Frederick, VIII, 441; IX, 266
Des Touches. *See* Peronne
Destroismaisons. *See also* Picard
Destroismaisons, Anne (Chartier), III, 112
Destroismaisons, Marie-Geneviève (Blanchet), VI, 68
Destroyer. *See* Peguis
Des Vœux, Charlotte Jane (Windham), IX, 844
Des Vœux*, Sir George William (1834–1909), XI, 31; XII, 311
Desvoges de Clérin, Françoise (Estienne Du Bourgué), II, 220
Désy, Joseph-Édouard, XII, 46, 47
Détailleur, Joseph, IV, 82
Dethunes, Exupère, I, **264–65**, 438, 439; II, 174, 420, 429, 430
Detlor, Elizabeth (Dunham), VI, 405
Detlor, George Hill, VI, 56, 772; VII, 158; VIII, 697
Detweiler, Maria (Betzner), VIII, 86

Deupet, Louisa (Mallet), III, 423
Devarenne. *See* Gaultier
Devau, Benoît, IV, **216**
Devau, Marie. *See* Potier
Devau, *dit* Retor, Claude, IV, **216**
Devau, *dit* Retor, Marie-Madeleine. *See* Gendron
De Veaux, Samuel, VII, 312
De Veber, Gabriel, VI, 504
DeVeber, Leverett, IX, 129
Devene, Françoise-Anne (Boucault), III, 74, 77
Devennes, Gilles, I, 109; II, 105
De Vere, William Aubrey, 9th Duke of St Albans, XI, 155
Devereux, Nicholas, VI, 244, 691; VII, 292
Device. *See* Davis
Devienne, Louise-Thérèse (Crespel), IV, 180
Devin, Sieur (engineer), II, 525
De Vine, George Frederick, XII, 1116
Devine, James Arthur, XI, 256
Devine, Jane. *See* Molloy
Devine, Patrick Kevin, XI, 67, 376
Devine, Thomas, XI, **256–57**
Devisme, Aurélie. *See* Denis
Devisme, Geneviève-Adélaïde-Albertine. *See* Helluin
Devisme, J., XII, 738
Devisme, Léopold, XII, **257**
Devisme, Pierre-Louis-Fleur, XII, 257
Devitt, Barnabas, VI, 235
Devlin, Anna Eliza. *See* Hickey
Devlin, Bernard, IX, 493; X, **229–30**; XII, 89
Devlin, Catherine. *See* Mellany
Devlin, Charles, X, 229
Devlin, Owen, X, 229
Devon, Earl of. *See* Alexander
Devos, Frederick, V, 902
Devotion, Jemima (Bidwell), VI, 54
Devotion, Rachel (Kellogg), III, 325
Dewando. *See* Atecouando (fl. 1749–57)
Dewar, Miss (Foulis), IX, 277
Dewar, Amy (wife of EDWARD HENRY), IX, 204
Dewar, Andrew, XI, 856
Dewar, Caroline. *See* Elliott
Dewar, Edward Henry, IX, **204–5**; XI, 916
Dewar, John, IX, 204
Dewar, Maria (mother of EDWARD HENRY), IX, 204
Dewart*, Edward Hartley (1828–1903), XII, 570, 662, 663, 704, 946, 1076, 1077
Dewdney*, Edgar (1835–1916), XI, 355, 444, 462, 477, 598, 599, 600, 746, 870, 921; XII, 23, 30, 140, 201, 608, 611, 674, 688, 718
Dewey, Elizabeth (Ingersoll), IX, 405
Dewey, Laura (Day), XI, 237
Dewey, Lucretia (Harmon), VII, 385
De Wint, Peter, XII, 326
De Winton, Francis Walter, X, 405
De Witt, Hannah. *See* Dean
De Witt, Henry, VIII, 219
De Witt, Jabez, VIII, 219
De Witt, Jabez Dean, X, 518
De Witt, Jacob, VI, 278, 783; VII, 240, 482; VIII, **219–20**, 284, 369, 667, 781, 915, 916; IX, 397, 430; X, 591; XI, 116; XII, 262, 809
De Witt, Sophronia. *See* Frary
De Witt, Tjerck Claessen, VIII, 219

Dewolf, Edward, VIII, 63
DeWolf, Elisha, VI, 37
DeWolf, James Ratchford, IX, 710
DeWolf, Olivia (Barss), VI, 37
DeWolf, Rachel Otis (Fraser), VI, 262
DeWolf, Thomas Andrew Strange, X, 7
DeWolfe, Mary Louisa (Moore), XII, 759
Dewson, Mary Anne (Denison), X, 224; XII, 243
Dextreme, *dit* Comtois, Pierre, IV, 336
Deyohninhohhakarawenh. *See* Theyanoguin
Dézery. *See* Latour-Dézery
Dézéry Latour, Charles, VI, 666
Déziel, Joseph-David, IX, 123, 361; XI, **257–59**; XII, 1019
Déziel, *dit* Labrèche, Gabriel, XI, 257
Déziel, *dit* Labrèche, Marie. *See* Champoux
Dhiarse (Dihars, Hiarse), Jeanne (Lartigue), II, 381; III, 357
Diamond, Abraham, X, **230**
Diamond, Elizabeth. *See* Jeffers
Diamond, John, X, 230
Diamond, Louisa. *See* Coleman
Diamond, Wellington Jeffers, X, 230
Diaquande. *See* Teyohaqueande
Díaz de Solís, Jean, I, 155
Dibble, Abigail (Jessup), V, 454
Dibblee (Diblee), Ebenezer, VI, 208
Dibblee, Frederick, V, 73, 74; VI, **208–9**, 678, 774; VII, 53, 243; VIII, 509
Dibblee, Fyler, VI, 208
Dibblee, George Jarvis, VII, 74; XII, 1096
Dibblee, Hannah. *See* Beardsley
Dibblee, Joanna. *See* Bates
Dibblee, John, VIII, 509
Dibblee, Nancy. *See* Beach
Dicere. *See* Després
Dick, A., V, 811
Dick, Alexander, XI, 260
Dick, James (captain), X, 231
Dick, James (father of ROBERT), XI, 259
Dick, Janet. *See* Brown
Dick, John (agent), III, 212
Dick, John (captain), X, 306
Dick, Mary. *See* Muir
Dick, Robert, XI, **259–61**; XII, 922
Dick, Thomas, IX, 49; X, **230–31**; XI, 554; XII, 198
Dick, William, XI, 259, 260
Dickens, Catherine. *See* Hogarth
Dickens, Charles, V, 725; VI, 108; VII, 287, 441; VIII, 173, 744; IX, 83, 352, 355; XI, 261; XII, 570
Dickens, Francis Jeffrey, XI, **261–62**, 599
Dickerson, Mary. *See* Price
Dickerson, Mary (Ball), V, 53
Dickerson, Silas Horton, VI, 802; VII, 300; VIII, **221–22**
Dickey, Arthur Rupert, XII, 1120
Dickey, Mary (Chipman), IX, 129
Dickey, Robert Barry, XI, 754, 755, 926; XII, 95
Dickie, Ellen. *See* Putnam
Dickie, Harriet. *See* Dickson
Dickie, Isaac Patton, XI, 262
Dickie, James, XI, 263
Dickie, John Barnhill, XI, **262–63**; XII, 437
Dickie, Rebecca. *See* Barnhill
Dickinson, Anson, VI, 344
Dickinson, Barnabas, XII, 257

Dickinson, Charles M., XII, 75
Dickinson, Elizabeth Mary. *See* Trigge
Dickinson, H., IX, 825
Dickinson, Lydia. *See* Davenport
Dickinson, Moss Kent, XI, 229; XII, **257–59**, 664
Dickinson, Sarah (Lane; Kellogg), III, 324
Dickinson, Temperance (Odell), V, 628
Dickinson, Tertullus, IV, 327, 328
Dickonson, Mary (Worsley), VI, 817
Dickson, Miss (Mercer), IX, 543
Dickson, Sir Alexander, VII, 257; IX, 543
Dickson, Amelia. *See* Bishop
Dickson, Ann. *See* Benson
Dickson, Anne, XI, 263
Dickson, Archange. *See* Grant
Dickson, Charles, VIII, 222
Dickson*, Charles Rea (1858–1938), XI, 263
Dickson, Charles W., XI, 29
Dickson, Charlotte. *See* Adlam
Dickson, Sir Collingwood, XI, 932
Dickson, David, XI, 263
Dickson, Eliza. *See* Wilkinson
Dickson, Elizabeth (Archibald), VII, 21; IX, 7; XI, 28
Dickson, Frances Elizabeth Hartwell (Vavasour), IX, 806
Dickson, George D., X, 230
Dickson, Harriet (Dickie), XI, 262
Dickson, Helen. *See* To-to-win
Dickson, Helen. *See* Wight
Dickson, Isabella. *See* Robinson
Dickson, James, VIII, 249
Dickson, James, VII, **249–50**, 570; VIII, 579; X, 276
Dickson, Jean (Hunter, Lady Hunter), V, 630, 631; VII, 428, 429
Dickson, Jessie (Murray), VIII, 651
Dickson, John, VI, 209, 211; VII, 250
Dickson, John Robinson, IX, 462; XI, **263–64**, 591, 941; XII, 12, 990
Dickson, Olivia (Archibald), XI, 29
Dickson, Robert, VIII, 222
Dickson, Robert, V, 9, 10, 403, 714, 799; VI, 29, 148, **209–11**, 509, 531, 542, 547, 643, 665, 722; VII, 251, 328; VIII, 112, 190, 287
Dickson, Samuel, IX, **205–6**
Dickson, Sarah Ann. *See* Patterson
Dickson, Thomas, V, 258, 355
Dickson, Thomas, V, 403, 549, 642, 643, 842; VI, 4, 209, **211–12**, 248, 489, 539, 541; VII, 251, 833
Dickson, Thomas, VII, 21, 81; VIII, 123, **222**, 770
Dickson, Walter, VII, 834
Dickson, Walter Hamilton, VIII, 800
Dickson, William (agent), VII, 834
Dickson, William (brother of THOMAS, 1791–1855) VIII, 222
Dickson, William, V, 403, 520, 549, 639, 782, 841, 842, 845; VI, 4, 5, 93, 148, 149, 209, 211, 475, 539, 630, 631, 746; VII, 38, **250–52**, 312, 314; VIII, 185, 340; IX, 313, 332, 333, 334, 335, 670, 717
Diderot, Denis, II, 444; V, 202; VI, 85, 764; VII, 645
Didier. *See also* Causabon
Didier, Marie-Jeanne (Frémiot), VIII, 308
Didot. *See* Firmin-Didot
Didsbury, Jane. *See* Hopper
Diehl, John Justus, IV, 703; V, 36, 484; VI, 14

Diehl, Peter, V, 37, 88; VI, 14, 416
Diehl, Phebe. *See* Arnoldi
Dielle, Paul, IV, 40, 331
Diemert, Christine (Wagner), XII, 1077
Dière, *dit* Maréchal, Geneviève. *See* Saint-Denis
Dière, *dit* Maréchal, Louis, XII, 697
Dières, Guyon, II, 188
Dières, Jacques, II, 188
Dières, Jacques-Christophe, II, 188
Dières, Pierre, II, 188
Dièreville, I, 577, 649; II, **188–89**, 597; IV, xx
Dièreville, Jehan, II, 188
Dies, Jane (Nelson), VI, 537; VIII, 652; IX, 593; X, 544
Diesbach, Comte de, IV, 70
Diescaret. *See* Pieskaret
Dieskau, Jean-Armand, Baron de Dieskau, III, xix, 18, 21, 174, **185–86**, 188, 214, 322, 376, 409, 458, 459, 623, 624; IV, 57, 67, 224, 307, 353, 395, 426, 459, 642, 668, 669; V, 98, 393, 677
Dietz, George, X, 530; XI, 50; XII, 784
Dietz, Marie Susanne Elizabeth (Van Egmond), VII, 882
Digby, Robert, V, 148
Digby, Sarah. *See* Moore
Digby, William, V, 152
Digé, Geneviève (Pelletier), V, 257
Digé, Jacques, V, 256
Digé, Jean, V, 256
Digé, Jean, V, **256–57**, 654
Digé, Jeanne. *See* Augé
Digé, Marie-Charlotte. *See* Sajos
Digé, Véronique. *See* Lévêque
Digges, Sir Dudley, I, 374, 377
Diggin, Annie (Baird), VIII, 42; XII, 49
Diggle, Wadham Neston, XI, 291, 292
Diggs, Seneca T. P., IX, 6
Dight. *See also* Butler
Dight, Elizabeth. *See* Butler
Dight, Joshua, VI, 98
Dighton, Robert, V, 844
Digoine Du Palais, Camille de, II, 479
Dihars. *See* Dhiarse
Dijean. *See* Dejean
Dill, George, XI, 306, 460
Dill, Harry P., XII, 361
Dillon, Honoria. *See* Brooks
Dillon, John, VIII, 886
Dillon, Peter, IV, 283
Dillworth, Margaret (Campbell), XII, 156
Dimock, Abigail. *See* Doane
Dimock, Betsy (Dimock), VII, 252
Dimock, Betsy (Knowles; Tupper), XI, 895
Dimock, Daniel, IV, 217; VII, 252
Dimock, Deborah. *See* Bailey
Dimock, Eunice. *See* Marsh
Dimock, George, VIII, 566
Dimock, Ichabod, XI, 834
Dimock, Joseph, IV, 217; VI, 276; VII, 123, **252–53**, 272, 562; VIII, 179, 361, 611
Dimock, Percilla. *See* Hovey
Dimock, Sarah. *See* Knowlton
Dimock, Shubael, XI, 834
Dimock, Shubael, IV, **216–17**; VII, 252
Dimock (Dimmick), Timothy, IV, 216

Dimsdale, Thomas, Baron Dimsdale, IX, 163
Dinan, *dit* Saint-Étienne, Pierre, III, 258
Dingle, Mr (of Newfoundland), VI, 10
Dinning, Etta. *See* Carpenter
Dinning, Henry, VIII, 559; XI, **264–65**; XII, 51, 52, 342
Dinning, Isabella. *See* Gilley
Dinning, James, XI, 264; XII, 51
Dinning, William, XII, 52
Dinwiddie, Mary (Stuart), V, 785
Dinwiddie, Robert, III, 375, 376, 600; IV, 227
Dion, Charles (photographer), VIII, 918
Dion, Charles (teacher), XI, 457; XII, 269
Dion, Claude, III, 142
Dion, Marie-Louise (Gendron), XI, 337
Dionne, Alexandre, VIII, 222
Dionne, Amable, VI, 125, 369, 749; VII, 61, 147, 161, 670, 763; VIII, **222–24**; IX, 203, 359, 362; XI, 176; XII, 189, 246, 1024
Dionne, Arthémise (Bertrand), XII, 104
Dionne, Benjamin, XII, 104
Dionne, Caroline (Têtu), IX, 362
Dionne, Catherine. *See* Perreault
Dionne, Charles-Eusèbe, XI, 65
Dionne, Georgina (Chapais), XI, 175, 176; XII, 58
Dionne, Germain, V, 358
Dionne, Henriette (Desbarats), IX, 203; XII, 246
Dionne, Louise-Adèle (Taschereau), XII, 1024
Dionne, Magdelaine. *See* Michaud
Dionne, Marie (Gosselin), V, 358
Dionne, Marie-Hortense (Casgrain), IX, 121
Dionne*, Narcisse-Eutrope (1848–1917), VI, 40; VII, 62; X, 433; XI, 115, 484; XII, 758
Dionne, Pascal-Amable, IX, 121
Diron. *See* Artaguiette
Dirop, Saturnin, II, 382
Disbrow, Amelia. *See* Canby
Disbrow, Caroline Amelia (Jack), VIII, 224; XI, 446
Disbrow, Isabella. *See* Chillis
Disbrow, Noah, VII, 654; VIII, **224**
Discombe, Reece, IV, 283
Disney, Daniel, IV, 759; V, 98
Disney, Henry, XII, 259
Disney, Rebecca (mother of RICHARD RANDOLPH), XII, 259
Disney, Richard Randolph, XII, **259–60**
Disney, Sarah Elizabeth (wife of RICHARD RANDOLPH; Jones), XII, 259
Disraeli, Benjamin, 1st Earl of Beaconsfield, X, 140; XII, 326, 328, 437, 600, 604
Disséré. *See* Després
Disy. *See* Dizy
Diutz, Judith (Koopman), XI, 585
Diverny, *dit* Saint-Germain, Charles, IV, 205, 629
Dix, Dorothea Lynde, VIII, 74, 75; XII, 575, 985
Dix, Elizabeth (Kelsey), II, 313, 314
Dix, John Adams, VIII, 53
Dixon, Alexander, X, 231
Dixon, Alfred, VIII, 784
Dixon, Charles, V, 257
Dixon, Charles, V, 94, **257–58**; VII, 854
Dixon, Clara. *See* Rowsell
Dixon, Elizabeth Jane (Irving), X, 378
Dixon, Esther. *See* O'Dwyer

Dixon, G. W., X, 389
Dixon, George, IV, 166, **217–19**, 244, 245, 325, 419, 498, 499, 744; V, 586, 686
Dixon, Harriette Elizabeth (Boulton; Smith), X, 79
Dixon, Janet (McMurrich), XI, 581
Dixon, John, VIII, 476
Dixon, Mary. *See* Corps
Dixon, Mary Elizabeth (Cronyn; Wilson), X, 716
Dixon, Matthew Charles, VI, 183
Dixon, Susanna. *See* Coates
Dixon, Susannah (Crane), VIII, 183
Dixon, Thomas, V, 355
Dixon, Thomas C., IX, 844
Dixon, William, IX, 98, 377; X, **231–32**
Dizet, Pierre, III, 621
Diziers, Marquise de. *See* Alavoine
Dizy, *dit* Montplaisir, Charles, II, 190
Dizy, *dit* Montplaisir, Élisabeth (Hamelin de Bourgchemin et de L'Hermitière), I, 360
Dizy, *dit* Montplaisir, Marguerite (Desbrieux), I, 361; II, 186, **189–90**
Dizy, *dit* Montplaisir, Marie. *See* Drouillet
Dizy, *dit* Montplaisir, Marie-Jeanne. *See* Baudouin
Dizy, *dit* Montplaisir, Michel-Ignace, II, 189, **190**; III, 187
Dizy, *dit* Montplaisir, Pierre, I, 360; II, 189, 190; III, 187
Dizy de Montplaisir, Marguerite, named de Saint-Pierre, III, 187
Dizy de Montplaisir, Marie-Madeleine. *See* Baudouin
Dizy de Montplaisir, Pierre, II, 190; III, **187**
Doak, Agnes (mother of ROBERT), VIII, 224
Doak, James (brother of ROBERT), VIII, 225
Doak, James (printer), VIII, 394, 395; X, 140
Doak, James Andrew, VIII, 225
Doak, Jean. *See* Kirkland
Doak, Robert, VIII, 224
Doak, Robert, VIII, **224–26**
Doan, Ebenezer, IX, 842
Doan, Fanny. *See* Milard
Doan, Joel P., VII, 253, 254
Doan, Jonathan, VII, 253
Doan, Joshua Gwillen, VII, **253–54**; VIII, 27, 162, 798, 855
Doane, Abigail (Dimock), IV, 216
Doane, Edmund, IV, 593, 594
Doane, Elizabeth. *See* Osborn
Doane, Sarah (Coffin), XI, 197
Dobbins, Daniel, VII, 46
Dobbs, Alexander Thomas, V, 172
Dobbs, Arthur, I, 677; II, xxviii, 314, 493, 604; III, xxxiii, 302, 303, 342, 447, 448, 449, 471, 472, 482, 483, 489, 544, 561, 562, 594, 624, 662, 663; IV, 680
Dobbs, Conway Edward, XI, 265
Dobbs, Francis William, XI, 266
Dobbs, Harriet (Cartwright), XI, **265–66**
Dobbs, Maria Sophia (mother of HARRIET), XI, 265
Dobbs, Mary Magdalen. *See* Cartwright
Dobbs, Olivia (Higginson), XI, 404, 405
Dobie, Ann (Mitchell), XII, 739
Dobie, Richard, IV, 58, 277, 311, 330, 485, 757; V, **258–61**, 320, 376, 391, 745; VI, 18, 110, 111, 254, 446, 471, 472; VII, 30, 523, 735; VIII, 320
Dobie, Sophia (Robertson), X, 620
Doble, Arthur, VIII, 425

Dobson, Eleanor (de Blaquiere, Lady de Blaquiere), VIII, 204
Dobson, Harriet. *See* Parr
Dobson, Margaret (Euart), VIII, 280
Dochert (Dochart), Janet (MacGregor), VI, 457
Dockendorff, Ellen (Bain), XII, 47
Dockstader, Catherine (Buell), IX, 99
Dockstader, Deborah (Buell), IX, 99
Docksteder, Catherine (DeCow), VIII, 208
Dodd, Ann (Pinson), V, 674
Dodd, Archibald Charles, IV, 523; V, 53, 205, 546; VI, 113, 203, **212–14**, 535, 792; VII, 10, 839; X, 232
Dodd, Bridget (wife of ARCHIBALD CHARLES), VI, 212
Dodd, Caroline Maria. *See* Ritchie
Dodd, Charles, VIII, **226–27**, 561, 579, 646
Dodd, Edmund Murray, VI, 214, 370; IX, 748; X, **232–33**; XI, 926
Dodd, Grace. *See* McTavish
Dodd, Jane. *See* Lynd
Dodd, John Beck, VIII, 226
Dodd, Mary. *See* Cobbold
Dodd, Mary Ann Sarah. *See* Weeks
Dodd, Murray, VI, 214
Dodd, Robert, V, 687
Dodd, Ross, VIII, 886
Dodd, Susannah. *See* Gibbons
Dodd, Thomas, V, 509
Dodd, Tommy. *See* Clarkson, Robert Guy
Dodds, Edward King, XII, 843
Dodds, James, X, 306
Dodds, Margaret (Goodfellow), XII, 379
Dodge, Anson Greene Phelps, XI, 594; XII, 70
Dodge, William Wallin, VII, 427; VIII, 853, 871; X, 260, 346
Dodier, Louis, III, 142
Dodier, Marie-Josephte. *See* Corriveau
Dodier, Sébastien, I, 468
Dods. *See* Dodd
Dodsley, Robert, V, 298; VII, 645
Dodun, Charles-Gaspard, II, 646; III, 382
Doel, Hannah. *See* Huntly
Doel, John, VI, 770; VIII, 178, 643; IX, 423, 502; X, **233**, 529; XI, 713, 714
Doëy, Marie-Charlotte-Domitille. *See* Chaboillez
Doggett, Abigail. *See* House
Doggett, Ebenezer, IV, 219
Doggett, Elizabeth. *See* Rickard
Doggett, John, IV, **219–20**
Doggett, Samuel, IV, 219
Doherty, Bridget. *See* Byrns
Doherty, Marcus, X, 219
Doherty, Patrick, X, 233
Doherty, Patrick J., X, **233–34**
Doige, Thomas, VII, 30, 618; VIII, 551
Doiron, Jérôme, X, 47
Dolabarats. *See* Olabaratz
Dolabaratz, Jean, IV, 588
Dolbeau. *See also* Dolebeau
Dolbeau, Jean, I, 233, **265–66**, 385, 437, 590
Dolbec, Joseph-Romain, III, 227
Dolbec, Romain, IV, 124
Dolci, Carlo, XI, 309
Dolebeau, Antoinette (Bellevue), I, 484

Dolebeau, Charles, I, 484
Dolebeau, Jean, I, **266**, 477, 483
Dolebeau, Nicolas, I, 483
Dolebeau, Simon, I, 483
Dollard, Anastasia. *See* Dunphy
Dollard, Michael, VIII, 227
Dollard, Patrick, VIII, 318; IX, **206–7**
Dollard, William, VI, 450; VII, 333; VIII, **227–28**, 317, 529, 591; IX, 154, 339, 616; X, 191
Dollard Des Ormeaux, Adam, I, 11, 32, 40, 65, 201, 225, **266–75**, 463, 547, 612, 633; II, 193, 469, 656; XI, 851
Dollier de Casson, Mlle (Peschart, Baronne de Bossac), II, 194, 272
Dollier de Casson, Charles, II, 190
Dollier de Casson, François, I, 35, 78, 126, 173, 174, 180, 213, 215, 217, 219, 220, 230, 231, 248, 266, 269, 270, 273, 274, 319, 393, 410, 416, 439, 483, 484, 485, 486, 540, 547, 556, 558, 572, 598, 599, 613, 625, 647; II, 11, 45, 96, 111, 124, 128, 133, **190–97**, 222, 223, 241, 245, 272, 326, 376, 594, 638, 642; III, 221, 469, 542; IX, 51; XI, 851
Dollier de Casson, Françoise. *See* Cailleux
Dollier de Casson, Julienne-Angélique, named de Jésus Pâtissant, II, 191
Dolobarats. *See* Olabaratz
Dolphyn, William, I, 371
Dolsealwhite, Henry, VIII, 494
Dolsen, Charles, IX, 528
Dolsen, John, XII, 643
Dolu, Jean-Jacques, I, 160, 194, 433
Domagaya, I, 11, 166, 167, 168, 275, 276
Dombourg. *See* Bourdon
Domenichino, VI, 25
Domerque, Sieur (soldier), II, 603
Domingué Meyracq, Laurent de, IV, 644
Dominguez de Mendoza, Maria Josefa (Suria), VI, 742
Dominic, Joseph, VII, 352, 353
Dominique, Brother. *See* French, Charles
Domitilde (Villeneuve; Mouet de Langlade), IV, 563
Domville*, James (1842–1921), XI, 134; XII, 1058
Don, George, VI, 221
Don, Sir George, VIII, 26
Donaldson, Alison (Kerby), VIII, 465
Donaldson, James, IX, 180
Donaldson, Lauchlan, VII, 915; VIII, 224; IX, 263; XII, 307
Donaldson, Mary (Honeyman), XI, 420
Donaldson, William, V, 349
Donay, Armand, III, 221, 612
Donay, Euphrasine (Roland), XI, 765
Donck, Adriaen van der, I, 525
Done. *See* Doan
Donegana, Giuseppe, IX, 207
Donegani, Giuseppe, VI, 185; IX, 207
Donegani, John Anthony, VI, 585; VII, 134; VIII, 918; IX, **207–9**; X, 52
Donegani, Joseph (brother of JOHN ANTHONY), IX, 207, 208
Donegani, Joseph (father of JOHN ANTHONY), IX, 207
Donegani, Joseph (uncle of JOHN ANTHONY), IX, 207
Donegani, Rosalie-Louise-Geneviève. *See* Plamondon
Donegani, Thérèse (Donegani), IX, 207
Donegani, William, IX, 207

Donellan, John, VII, 894
Doney, Jean-Marie, IX, 465
Dongan, Thomas, I, 444, 445, 526; II, 61, 69, 101, 184, 343, 344, 585, 643; III, 568
Donge, Comtesse de, III, 16
Donizetti, Gaetano, VIII, 347; XII, 223, 503
Don Jacque. *See* Angeac
Donkin, Arthur Scott, XI, 266
Donkin, John George, XI, **266–67**, 600
Donkin, Mary. *See* Moor
Donkley, John, V, 359
Donlevy, Charles, VII, 664; VIII, 12, **228–31**, 704
Donlevy, Mary. *See* Walsh
Donlevy, Patrick, VIII, 228
Donnacona, I, 11, 166, 167, 168, 169, **275–77**
Donnelly, Charles Francis, XII, 209
Donnelly, Ellen F. (Kent), XII, 482
Donnelly, Hannah (Canning), XII, 157
Donnelly, Hugh, XII, 208
Donnelly, J. J., X, 556
Donnelly, James, X, **234–35**; XII, 1086
Donnelly, Johannah. *See* Magee
Donnelly, Margaret. *See* Conway
Donnelly, Norah. *See* Kennedy
Donnelly, Rosanna, named Sister Mary Vincentia, XII, 209
Donnelly, William, X, 234, 235
Donnelly*, William J. S. (1844–1914), XII, 311, 755, 956, 957
Donovan, John, VIII, 749
Donovan, Sarah (Elliott), V, 303
Dontaille, Anne-Madeleine (Lacroix), III, 334; VI, 382
Dontenwill, Augustin, XII, 284
Dontigny. *See* Lucas
Doodebewshet, VI, 706
Doohan (Droohan), Bridget (Kelly), XI, 465
Doolittle, Clarissa Goss. *See* Lawrence
Doolittle, Jesse, IX, 209
Doolittle, Lucius, IX, **209–10**; XI, 523
Doolittle, Mary (Stevens), VI, 732
Doran, Catherine, XII, 229
Doran, Eleanor (Davison), XII, 229
Doran (Dorin), Hannah (McIntosh), VII, 563
Doran, John (father-in-law of John HEARN), XII, 420
Doran, John (justice of the peace), XII, 397
Doran, Mary (Hearn), XII, 420
Doran, William, XI, 851
Dorchester, Baron. *See* Carleton
Dorchester, Baroness. *See* Howard
Doré, Gustave, XII, 271
Doré, Nathalie (Brousseau), XI, 115
Doreil, André (Jean-Baptiste), III, 18, 19, 186, **187–89**, 300, 463, 464; IV, 57, 68, 307, 308, 353, 513, 514, 616, 669, 670; V, 677
Doreil, Jeanne-Catherine. *See* Blancheteau
Doreil, Marguerite-Charlotte-Baptistine. *See* Pontevès
Doreil, Philippe, III, 187
Dores. *See* Shaw
Dorfeuille, Pierre, I, 361
Dorin. *See* Doran
Dorion, Mme. *See* Trestler
Dorion, Sir Antoine-Aimé, V, 828; VII, 254; VIII, 402, 775; IX, 65, 151, 210, 211, 213, 214, 215, 253, 267, 268, 383, 384, 397, 430, 463, 492, 576, 614, 727, 776, 777;

X, 37, 96, 97, 99, 101, 128, 144, 145, 146, 147, 210, 213, 236, 237, 238, 258, 355, 356, 357, 415, 465, 466, 467, 533, 548, 600, 625, 632, 642, 643, 676, 724, 725; XI, 81, 170, 176, 187, 275, 283, 411, 438, 480, 520, 530, 624, 681, 822, 823, 908; XII, 62, 86, 98, 151, 254, **260–65**, 299, 325, 351, 362, 363, 487, 505, 649, 651, 656, 693, 720, 721, 853, 1037, 1054, 1108

Dorion, Barbe. *See* Trudelle
Dorion, Catherine-Louise. *See* Lovell
Dorion, Célina, X, 236
Dorion, Charles, X, 236
Dorion, Eugène-Philippe, X, **235–36**
Dorion, Eugénie (Duclos de Celles), X, 236
Dorion, Eulalie (Geoffrion), XII, 260, 362
Dorion, François-Edmond, IX, 210, 211, 214; X, 236, 237
Dorion, Geneviève. *See* Bureau
Dorion, Henriette-Amélie. *See* Saint-Ours
Dorion, Hercule, IX, 210, 211, 213; X, 236; XII, 260
Dorion, Iphigénie. *See* Trestler
Dorion, Jacques, X, 235, **236**
Dorion, Jane. *See* Clarke
Dorion, Jean-Baptiste-Éric, VII, 254; VIII, 617; IX, 193, **210–15**, 315, 344, 345, 614, 727; X, 130, 236, 237, 252, 304, 415, 512, 615; XI, 98, 170, 287, 339, 623, 624, 659, 810; XII, 260, 264, 270, 505, 853, 1013
Dorion, Joseph, IX, 210
Dorion, Joseph-Adolphe, X, 236
Dorion, Joséphine (Pampalon), XII, 816
Dorion, Louis-Eugène, IX, 210; X, 236; XII, 260
Dorion, Luce (Barcelo), X, 438
Dorion, Marie. *See* Panet
Dorion, Marie Abby Victoria. *See* Hays
Dorion, Marie-Céphise, named Sister Amable, VII, 254; X, 236
Dorion, Mary Ann (Cary), IX, 115
Dorion, Noël, VII, 254
Dorion, Peter, IX, 115
Dorion, Pierre (ancestor of JEAN-BAPTISTE-ÉRIC), IX, 210
Dorion, Pierre (father of JACQUES), X, 236
Dorion, Pierre-Antoine, VII, **254**; IX, 210; X, 236; XII, 260, 507
Dorion, Pierre-Nérée, IX, 210, 211; X, 236; XI, 811; XII, 260
Dorion, Vincislas-Paul-Wilfrid, VII, 254; X, 37, **236–38**; XI, 187; XII, 260, 261
Dorland, Alley. *See* Gow
Dorland, Philip, VI, 215
Dorland, Samuel, VI, 214
Dorland, Thomas, V, 550, 772, 857; VI, **214–16**, 406, 656, 804, 805; VII, 419
Dorland, Willet Casey, VIII, 837
Dorman, Mary Elizabeth (Pearkes), X, 587
Dormer, Elizabeth Anne, Lady Dormer. *See* Tichborne
Dormer, Henry Edward, IX, **215–16**
Dormer, Sir James Charlemagne, IX, 215
Dormer, Joseph Thaddeus, 11th Baron Dormer, IX, 215
Dormicourt. *See* Huart
Dornan, J. O., IX, 164
Dornelos (Dorvelos), Juan de, I, 41
Dornon, Marianne. *See* Lafontaine
Dorollaire, Marie (Corolère), III, 139
Dorothy de Saint-Joseph. *See* Jeryan
Dorrill, Elizabeth (wife of RICHARD), III, 189

Dorrill, Richard, III, **189**; IV, 259; V, 337, 632
Dorset, Duke of. *See* Sackville
Dorval. *See also* Bigot; Bouchard
Dorval, Élisabeth. *See* Godbout
Dorval, François, IX, 216
Dorval, Marie-Élize (Jobin), VIII, 433
Dorval, Marie-Louise, named Sainte-Élisabeth, IX, **216–17**; X, 480
Dorval, Marie-Louise-Adeline (Odet d'Orsonnens), XII, 798
Dorval, Pierre-Férréol, IX, 615; X, 15
Dorvelos. *See* Dornelos
Dorwin, Canfield, XI, 268
Dorwin, Isabella. *See* Williamson
Dorwin, Jedediah Hubbell, VII, 612, 621; XI, **267–68**, 850
Dorwin, Lewis, XI, 268
Dorwin, Mary. *See* Hubbell
Dorwin, Philo, XI, 267
Dosque, Bernard-Sylvestre, IV, 497
Dosquet, Anne-Jeanne. *See* Goffar
Dosquet, Laurent, IV, 220
Dosquet, Pierre-Herman, II, 135, 530, 542; III, 40, 41, 47, 114, 115, 119, 122, 169, 193, 194, 196, 202, 223, 263, 284, 292, 319, 349, 361, 386, 390, 413, 426, 470, 480, 481, 487, 544, 545, 557, 574, 575, 630, 638; IV, **220–22**, 356, 387, 429, 440, 491, 509, 510, 535, 538, 539, 654; V, 4; VII, 64; IX, 718; XI, 87
Dosta. *See* Hosta
Dostaler, Pierre-Eustache, XII, 818
Dostyne, Louis van der, II, 279
Doty, James, X, 661
Doty, John, IV, 139, 753; V, 27, 139, 600, 747; VII, 825; IX, 610, 728
Douaire Bondy, Clotilde-Héloïse (Sincennes), X, 657
Douaire de Bondy, Cécile. *See* Gosselin
Douaire de Bondy, Charles-Dominique, IV, 265
Douaire de Bondy, Louise (Allemand; Pinaud), I, 56; II, 526
Douaire de Bondy, Marguerite. *See* Chavigny de Berchereau
Douaire de Bondy, Thomas, II, 223
Douay, Anastase, I, 180, 182, 183; II, **197**, 441
Doublet, François, I, 277
Doublet, François, I, **277**
Doublet, Jean-François, I, 277
Doublet, Madeleine. *See* Fontaine
Doublet, Marguerite. *See* Auber
Doucet, Father, XII, 1009
Doucet, Amable, V, **261–62**; VI, 228; VII, 803
Doucet, André, VI, **216–18**, 588; VII, 798, 801, 802
Doucet, Charles, VIII, 231
Doucet, Charles-Odilon, XII, 64
Doucet, Eugénie (Middleton, Lady Middleton), XII, 733
Doucet, François, IV, 222, 441; V, 261
Doucet, Françoise (Raimbault), VII, 720
Doucet, Jean, VI, 216; VIII, 231
Doucet, Jeanne (Marie) (Dubreuil; Loppinot), II, 445
Doucet, Madeleine (Magdalene) (Gallant), V, 335
Doucet, Magdeleine. *See* Mirau
Doucet, Marguerite. *See* Petitot, *dit* Saint-Sceine
Doucet, Marie (Bourneuf), X, 83
Doucet, Marie (Doucet), V, 261
Doucet, Marie-Antoinette (Parant), VIII, 682

Doucet, Marie-Euphrosine. *See* Kimber
Doucet, Marie-Gertrude. *See* Gaudet
Doucet, Marie-Josèphe. *See* Robichaud
Doucet, Marie-Madeleine (Aigron, *dit* Lamothe), I, 42
Doucet, Marie-Marguerite. *See* Le Blanc
Doucet, Monique-Olivier (Christie), VII, 618; VIII, 154
Doucet, Nicolas-Benjamin, VI, 22, 216, 217; VIII, **231–33**, 479; XII, 570
Doucet, Olivier, IV, 222
Doucet, Pierre, V, 261
Doucet, Pierre, IV, xxix, **222–23**, 441; V, 261; VI, 228; VIII, 232; IX, 208
Doucet, Théodore, XII, 733
Doucet de La Verdure, Germain, II, 94; VIII, 231
Doucett, Honoria, II, 199
Doucett, Isabella, II, 199
Doucett, John, II, 22, 96, **198–99**, 668; III, 143, 208, 436, 512, 515, 516, 517, 518
Dougall, Agnes Rebecca (Stevenson), VIII, 836
Dougall, Elizabeth. *See* O'Neill
Dougall, Elizabeth. *See* Redpath
Dougall, Francis James, XI, 269
Dougall, Hannah (Armstrong), X, 16
Dougall, James, VI, 253; VIII, 34; X, 372; XI, **268–70**
Dougall, Jane Eleanor (Jeffers), XII, 468
Dougall, John (father of JOHN), XI, 268, 270
Dougall, John (son of JAMES), XI, 269
Dougall, John, IX, 655; X, 41, 175, 672, 715; XI, 268, **270–71**, 564
Dougall, John Redpath, XI, 270
Dougall, Margaret. *See* Yool
Dougall, Susanne. *See* Baby
Dougall, William, X, 16
Dougherty, Catherine (Houde), XI, 425
Doughty*, Sir Arthur George (1860–1936), III, 257; IV, xlv, 416
Doughty, Edith Rebecca. *See* Cameron
Douglas. *See also* Hamilton
Douglas, Captain. *See* Eda'nsa
Douglas, Agnes (Bushby), X, 113, 247
Douglas, Alexander, X, 238
Douglas, Alice (Good; Wiederhold), X, 247
Douglas, Amelia, Lady Douglas. *See* Connolly
Douglas, Anne, Lady Douglas. *See* Dundas
Douglas, Anthony Gilbert, VII, 67; VIII, 240
Douglas, Campbell Mellis, XII, 96
Douglas, Cecilia (Helmcken), X, 247
Douglas, Cecilia Eliza (Cowan; Cameron), X, 115, 117, 238, 240, 243
Douglas, Charles, Comte de Douglas, IV, 224
Douglas, Sir Charles, III, 132; IV, 28, **223–24**, 549; V, 31, 33, 36, 100, 281, 381, 686; VI, 694; IX, 218
Douglas, Charles-Luc, IV, 224
Douglas, Charlotte. *See* La Corne
Douglas, Charlotte Saxton. *See* Campbell
Douglas, David, VI, 424
Douglas, David, VI, **218–20**, 222, 254; VII, 599; VIII, 528; XI, 53
Douglas, Dunbar James, 6th Earl of Selkirk, VII, 735; VIII, 742; IX, 179, 223
Douglas, Elizabeth. *See* Ferguson
Douglas, Frances Harriet (Wentworth-Fitzwilliam, Lady Fitzwilliam), X, 699

Douglas, François-Prosper, Chevalier de Douglas, IV, **224–25**, 242
Douglas, George (father of JAMES, 1800–86), IX, 217; XI, 271
Douglas, George (son of JAMES, 1800–86), XI, 272
Douglas, George, XII, **265–66**
Douglas, George Mellis, VIII, 581; IX, **217–18**; XI, 271
Douglas, Hannah. *See* Williams
Douglas, Harriet Middleton. *See* Clayton
Douglas, Helen (Hall, Lady Hall), V, 861
Douglas, Helena (Baillie), IX, 218
Douglas, Sir Howard, IV, 223; V, 691; VI, 53, 54, 73, 74, 143, 685, 686, 726, 774, 811; VII, 198, 331, 654, 658, 691, 806, 807, 899; VIII, xxxii, 103, 151, 153, 172, 275, 345, 346, 418, 507, 802, 806, 807, 841, 842; IX, 21, 22, 53, **218–22**, 408, 409, 620, 849, 850; X, 72, 271, 495; XII, 37
Douglas, Hugh R., VIII, 233
Douglas, James, III, 210
Douglas, James, 4th Earl of Morton, IV, 224
Douglas, James, IV, 551; V, 28, 220, **262–64**, 311, 424, 478, 516, 569, 779, 826, 848
Douglas, James, VII, 296, 633; VIII, **233–34**, 948; IX, 605; XI, 673; XII, 563
Douglas, Sir James, VII, 475, 672; VIII, 97, 226, 578, 580, 662, 816, 835, 836; IX, 36, 81, 82, 114, 115, 132 150, 295, 296, 327, 337, 338, 428, 479, 625, 712, 713, 714, 715, 716, 852, 853, 854; X, 6, 112, 113, 115, 116, 117, 128, 196, 198, 221, 222, **238–49**, 391, 426, 478, 486, 487, 552, 587, 665, 678, 697, 701, 720; XI, 7, 33, 50, 52, 80, 230, 231, 299, 300, 301, 394, 468, 603, 604, 605, 606, 607, 627, 756, 866, 882, 886, 888, 949, 950, 951; XII, 61, 77, 78, 79, 80, 113, 114, 238, 240, 289, 318, 334, 335, 441, 450, 523, 642, 815, 833, 892, 914, 918, 1062, 1131
Douglas, James, VII, 650; VIII, 559, 676; IX, 128, 217, 286, 572; X, 13, 376, 563, 564; XI, **271–72**, 484; XII, 189, 314, 1128
Douglas*, James (1837–1918), XI, 272; XII, 458
Douglas, James William, X, 247, 248; XI, 301
Douglas, Jane, Lady Douglas. *See* Baillie
Douglas, Jane (Dallas), X, 247; XI, 230
Douglas, Jane, Lady Douglas (Stewart), IV, 401
Douglas, Jane Hamilton, X, 238
Douglas, Janet (Balfour), XII, 52
Douglas, Janet (Brown), IX, 86
Douglas, Jean. *See* Drummond
Douglas, Jean, Baroness Daer and Shortcleuch, Countess of Selkirk. *See* Wedderburn
Douglas, Jessie. *See* Hamilton
Douglas, John (brother of JAMES, d. 1803), V, 262
Douglas, John (editor), IV, 167, 341, 412
Douglas, John (father of DAVID), VI, 218
Douglas, John (father of GEORGE), XII, 265
Douglas, John (father of JAMES, d. 1803), V, 262
Douglas, John (father of JAMES, 1789–1854), VIII, 233
Douglas, John (father of Sir JAMES), X, 238
Douglas, John (politician), X, 403
Douglas, John Erskine, IX, 24
Douglas, Lady Katherine (Halkett), V, 266, 269; VIII, 351
Douglas, Louis-Archambaud, Comte de Douglas, IV, 224
Douglas, Lydia. *See* Schimmelpinck
Douglas, Maria Bolton. *See* Pearson

Douglas, Marie-Anne, Comtesse de Douglas. *See* Lilia
Douglas, Martha (Harris), X, 247; XII, 335
Douglas, Mary. *See* Hood
Douglas, Mary. *See* Mellis
Douglas, Sir Neill, X, 238
Douglas, Robert, VIII, 452
Douglas, Sarah. *See* Hunter
Douglas, Sarah, Lady Douglas. *See* Wood
Douglas, Suzan. *See* Cleghorn
Douglas, Thomas, VII, 769
Douglas, Thomas, Baron Daer and Schortcleuch, 5th Earl
   of Selkirk, IV, 551; V, 125, 126, 195, 237, **264–69**, 309,
   440, 465, 466, 516, 518, 529, 531, 533, 542, 544, 547,
   591, 636, 657, 701, 734, 751, 776, 821, 860, 861, 862,
   879; VI, 17, 100, 109, 148, 161, 162, 167, 195, 211, 236,
   251, 264, 267, 272, 357, 358, 359, 362, 413, 414, 415,
   436, 437, 438, 441, 442, 443, 444, 445, 455, 456, 464,
   466, 469, 472, 533, 534, 547, 566, 612, 644, 648, 663,
   665, 705, 759, 767, 814; VII, 138, 207, 251, 408, 498,
   517, 553, 554, 555, 561, 564, 570, 571, 667, 671, 736,
   748, 749, 750, 811, 845, 900, 901, 920; VIII, 112, 113,
   121, 250, 342, 343, 351, 352, 396, 413, 443, 482, 527,
   537, 546, 569, 575, 607, 714, 719, 720, 721, 767, 812,
   845, 888, 954; IX, 134, 223, 234, 285, 297, 456, 472,
   482, 531, 532, 553, 626, 669, 670, 755; X, 276, 297,
   324, 469; XI, 18, 539, 545; XII, 1003
Douglas, Waitsill. *See* Haszard
Douglas, William, V, 586; XII, 289
Douglas, William James, XII, 137, 286
Douglass, Frederick, IX, 821
Douglass, Marguerite (Delage, *dit* Lavigueur), XI, 500
Douglass, William (author), III, 200
Douglass, William (merchant), XI, 59
Douhet de Larivière, *dit* de L'Étang, Marie-Jeanne. *See*
   Jarret de Verchères
Douillet, Emanuel, X, 116
Doull, John, IX, 587; X, 176; XI, 405
Douniol, Charles, X, 87
Dourado. *See* Vaz
Douse, Esther. *See* Young
Douse, William, VII, 202, 735; VIII, 742; IX, **222–23**; X,
   183, 184; XI, 665
Doussin, René, I, 267, 273
Doussineau, Gillette (Gendron), I, 328
Doutre, Adolphe, XI, 276
Doutre, Agnès (Lanctot), X, 422, 425
Doutre, Angèle (Daoust), IX, 193
Doutre, Angéline. *See* Varin
Doutre, Élisabeth. *See* Dandurand, *dit* Marcheterre
Doutre, François, X, 249; XI, 272
Doutre, Gonzalve, IX, 194; X, **249–53**, 422; XI, 72, 275,
   490, 491; XII, 5, 255, 303
Doutre, Harriet. *See* Greene
Doutre, Jean-Baptiste, X, 249; XI, 275
Doutre, Joseph, VIII, 284, 285; IX, 193, 194, 211, 440,
   464, 614, 615; X, 154, 219, 252, 417, 421, 422, 613; XI,
   37, 102, **272–78**, 494; XII, 5, 260, 261, 505, 506, 853
Doutre, Laura. *See* Brunelle
Doutre, Léon, X, 422
Douville. *See also* Dagneau; Jérémie
Douville, Joseph-Antoine-Irénée, IV, 87; X, 137
Dovan, Earl of. *See* Alexander
Dove, Susan L. *See* Bill

Dover, Baron. *See* Yorke
Dow, Andrew, IX, 224
Dow, Catherine (Hickson, Lady Hickson), XII, 432, 435
Dow, Helen (Miller), XII, 738
Dow, James, VI, 180
Dow, Lamira (Billings), X, 64
Dow, William, IX, **223–24**, 773, 793, 823; X, 524, 723; XI,
   5, 12, 557
Dowd, Mary. *See* McDonald
Dowd, Patrick, XII, 267
Dowd, Patrick, VIII, 731; XII, 215, **266–68**, 1084
Dowie, Alexander, IX, 553
Dowie, George, XII, 426
Dowie, James, VIII, 541, 542; IX, 639, 640, 641; XII,
   863
Dowie, Kenneth, VIII, 541; IX, 639; XII, 863
Dowling, Sir James, VII, 301
Down, Ann. *See* Eynon
Downer, Samuel, IX, 311
Downie, George, V, 696, 876; VII, 710
Downing, Andrew Jackson, VIII, 943
Downing, John, I, 278
Downing, John, I, 24, 93, **277–78**
Downing, William, I, **277–78**, 370
Downman, John, V, 615; VI, 257, 529
Downs, Andrew, XII, **268–69**
Downs, Elizabeth. *See* Plum
Downs, Mary Elizabeth. *See* Matthews
Downs, Mathilda E. *See* Muhlig
Downs, Robert, XII, 268
Downsley, Anne (Shaw), X, 650
Dowse, Relief (Gill), II, 246
Dowse, Thomas, I, 417
Dowset. *See* Doucet
Doxater, Susannah, VIII, 708
Doyle, Bridget. *See* O'Connor
Doyle, Sir Charles Hastings, IX, 845; X, 73, 332, 443; XI,
   **278–81**, 555, 927, 933; XII, 35, 481, 786
Doyle, Sir Charles William, XI, 278
Doyle, Edmond, VII, 404
Doyle, James H., IX, 233
Doyle, James Warren, VIII, 107
Doyle, Sir John, IX, 138
Doyle, John Sidney, XI, 48
Doyle, Julia (Leahey), XI, 504
Doyle, Laurence, IX, 233
Doyle, Laurence O'Connor, VII, 24, 804, 811, 867; VIII,
   348, 904, 906; IX, **224–27**, 350, 791; XI, 22, 945
Doyle, Mary (wife of PATRICK), VIII, 234
Doyle, Patrick, VII, 629, 631, 632, 633, 634; VIII, 233,
   **234–35**
Doyle, Patrick Adam, IX, 70
Doyle, Sarah Ann. *See* Driscoll
Doyle, Sophia Cramer, Lady Doyle. *See* Coghill
Doyon, Marie-Louise (Baudry, *dit* Saint-Martin), III, 37
Doyon, Nicolas, III, 37
Drachart, Christian Larsen, IV, liii, **225**, 334, 536, 537,
   599; V, 54, 829
Drage, Theodorus Swaine, known as Charles Swaine, I,
   677; III, 502
Drake. *See also* Tyrwhitt-Drake
Drake, Sir Bernard, I, 23, **278–80**, 364, 668
Drake, Edwin Laurentine, XI, 930

Drake, Sir Francis, I, 278, **280**, 318, 336, 362, 364, 378; IV, 226
Drake, Sir Francis Henry, IV, 226
Drake, Francis William, IV, **226**; V, 596
Drake, George, I, 306, 672
Drake, Gertrude, Lady Drake. *See* Fortescue
Drake, Hugh, I, 278
Drake, John, I, 280
Drake, Miriam (Swayze), VI, 746
Drake, Samuel, III, 497
Drapeau, Caroline. *See* Drolet
Drapeau, Charles, V, 271
Drapeau, Jean-Baptiste, XII, 269
Drapeau, Joseph, V, 165, **269–72**, 278, 301, 580; VI, 383, 546; XII, 296, 1032
Drapeau, Luce-Gertrude (Casault), VI, 546
Drapeau, Marguerite (Bigot, *dit* Lamothe), II, 62
Drapeau, Marie-Angèle. *See* Bourbeau
Drapeau, Marie-Geneviève. *See* Noël
Drapeau, Marie-Joseph. *See* Huard
Drapeau, Marie-Joseph (Estimauville), XII, 296
Drapeau, Pierre, V, 269
Drapeau, Stanislas, VII, 592; VIII, 419; X, 202, 582; XI, 115; XII, 86, **269–73**
Draper, Augusta. *See* White
Draper, Chester, XI, 366
Draper, Elsie (Routh; wife of FRANCIS COLLIER), XII, 273
Draper, Francis Collier, XII, **273–75**
Draper, Henry, X, 253
Draper, John, III, 267
Draper, Louisa Anne (Gildersleeve), IX, 314
Draper, Lyman Copeland, IV, 416; V, 803, 812
Draper, Margaret. *See* Green
Draper, Mary. *See* White
Draper, Mary Catherine. *See* Baines
Draper, Thomas, I, **280–81**, 324; II, 264
Draper, Thomas Fraser, XII, 364, 365
Draper, Sir William, IV, 577
Draper, William George, X, 258
Draper, William Henry, VI, 425, 467, 468; VII, 32, 102, 158, 262, 364, 370, 371, 606, 607, 760, 795, 833, 857, 858, 859, 880; VIII, 29, 50, 52, 135, 137, 188, 254, 262, 303, 513, 587, 641, 679, 709, 790, 799, 800, 822, 848, 849, 932; IX, 7, 56, 58, 71, 90, 91, 191, 262, 314, 324, 370, 371, 372, 445, 482, 513, 523, 524, 525, 526, 535, 546, 570, 575, 611, 645, 650, 697, 724, 726, 728, 762, 776, 779, 815; X, 60, 80, 93, 118, 119, 125, 133, 136, 173, **253–59**, 311, 312, 442, 462, 463, 502, 622, 668; XI, 41, 127, 166, 179, 286, 368, 378, 409, 410, 501, 712, 731, 778, 787, 788, 789, 791, 927; XII, 101, 273, 322, 400, 593, 1108
Drax, Elizabeth (Berkeley, Countess Berkeley), V, 72
Drayson, Maria Caroline (Richardson), VIII, 743, 744
Drayson, William, VIII, 744
Dreuillettes. *See* Druillettes
Drever, Mary Isabella (Macleod), XII, 672, 673, 674
Drew, Andrew, VII, 586; VIII, 205, 431, 709, 788; IX, 163, 241, 523; X, **259–60**, 482; XI, 631
Drew, Gruzzel (Tutty), III, 634
Drew, John (captain), I, 667
Drew, John (father of ANDREW), X, 259
Drew, Mary. *See* Henderson
Drew, Mary (mother of ANDREW), X, 259

Drewry. *See* Drury
Driard, Sosthenes Maximilian, X, **260**
Dricoll, Mr (teacher), X, 282
Drinkwater, John, XI, 840
Driot, Catherine (Daneau), II, 168
Driscoll, Henry Peard, XII, 476
Driscoll, John Campbell, VII, 527
Driscoll, Sarah Ann (Doyle), IX, 225
Driver, Emma Eliza. *See* Barker
Drolet, Angélique. *See* Hill
Drolet, Antonio, VI, 124
Drolet, Caroline (Drapeau), XII, 270
Drolet, Charles, X, 260
Drolet, Charles, VII, 427; VIII, 871, 893, 907; X, 77, **260–61**, 346
Drolet, Charles-Joseph-René, X, 614
Drolet*, François-Xavier (d. 1913), XII, 920
Drolet, Gustave-Adolphe, XI, 3, 235, 755; XII, 277
Drolet, Hector-Antoine, IX, 616
Drolet, Hélène-Flavie. *See* Chicoux-Duvert
Drolet, Joseph-Toussaint, XI, 345
Drolet, Laure (Thibaudeau), XII, 1036, 1037
Drolet, Lucille (Giard), XI, 345
Drolet, Marguerite. *See* Quirouet
Drolet, Marie-Anne (Thibodeau), V, 812
Drolet, Pierre-Olivier, XII, 272
Droohan. *See* Doohan
Drouard, Robert, II, 520, 597
Drouet de Richerville, Jean, IV, 332
Drouet de Richerville, Joseph, II, 67
Drouilhet (Brouilhet), Gratien, III, 124, 441; IV, 66, 125, 621
Drouillet (Drouillettes). *See* Druillettes
Drouillet (Drouillard), Marie (Dizy, *dit* Montplaisir), II, 189, 190; III, 187
Drouin, Angélique (Painchaud; Laviolette), VII, 668; VIII, 675; X, 563
Drouin, Anne. *See* Cloutier
Drouin, François, VIII, 235
Drouin, Marie. *See* Chapelier
Drouin, Marie. *See* Dubois
Drouin, Marie. *See* Paquet
Drouin, Marie-Louise. *See* Fraise
Drouin, Pierre, VIII, 235
Drouin, Pierre, VIII, **235–36**
Drouin, Robert, I, 281
Drouin, Robert, I, 232, **281**, 330
Droz, Adelgonde Humbert (McKenzie), VIII, 558
Drucour (Drucourt). *See* Boschenry
Drucour, Chevalier de. *See* Boschenry de Drucour, Augustin de
Drucourt, Baron de. *See* Boschenry
Drucourt, Baronne de. *See* Godard
Drué, Juconde, I, 312; II, **199–200**, 451; IV, 649
Druillettes, Gabriel, I, 49, 59, 244, **281–82**, 340, 379, 396, 402, 491, 498, 516, 558; II, 18, 158, 517
Druillon, Madeleine (Bégon de La Picardière), III, 56, 57
Druillon, Marie. *See* Bachaddelebat
Druillon, Pierre-Jacques, IV, 226
Druillon de Macé, Marie-Anne. *See* Petit de Thoizy
Druillon de Macé, Pierre-Jacques, IV, **226–27**
Drum, William, VIII, 559; XII, 889
Drummond. *See also* Deane-Drummond; Hay-Drummond

Drummond, Andrew (businessman), VIII, 645

Drummond, Andrew (father of ROBERT), VI, 220

Drummond*, Andrew Thomas (1843–1923), XII, 540, 541

Drummond, Anne. *See* Dundas

Drummond, Charles, XI, 282

Drummond, Donald, V, 135; VI, 474

Drummond, Elmire. *See* Debartzch

Drummond*, Sir George Alexander (1829–1910), IX, 654, 655; X, 725; XI, 286

Drummond, George Edward, XII, 621

Drummond, Sir Gordon, IV, 487; V, 66, 107, 114, 117, 267, 550, 558, 559, 643, 644, 749, 876; VI, 103, 115, 125, 182, 212, 267, 272, 343, 489, 521, 541, 542, 657, 661, 818; VII, 316, 366, 397, 402, 517, 518, 545, 640, 744, 745, 769, 889, 898; VIII, 34, 112, 155, **236–39**, 313, 466, 750, 802, 843; IX, 245, 412, 669, 756; XI, 798

Drummond, Henrietta Martha (Hamilton, Lady Hamilton), V, 244; VII, 376

Drummond, Henry (author), XII, 112, 438, 439

Drummond, Henry (husand of Anne Douglas), VII, 830

Drummond, Jacobina (Campbell), V, 135

Drummond, James (brother of THOMAS), VI, 221

Drummond, James (father of James Drummond Mac-Gregor), VI, 457

Drummond, James, 5th Earl of Perth, VI, 457

Drummond, James D., VIII, 247

Drummond, Jane (Redpath), IX, 655; XII, 846

Drummond, Jean. *See* Newton

Drummond, Jean (Douglas), VI, 218

Drummond, John, IV, 403; V, 214, 745

Drummond, Lewis (grandfather), XI, 281

Drummond, Lewis, XI, 282

Drummond, Lewis Thomas, VII, 149, 150, 236, 264, 265, 411, 514, 606; VIII, 138, 364, 365, 775; IX, 193, 276, 434, 443, 449, 463; X, 131, 203, 219, 418, 522, 632, 715, 723, 724; XI, 6, 181, 273, **281–83**, 409, 438, 529, 623, 822; XII, 254, 261, 505

Drummond, Margaret. *See* Gentle

Drummond, Margaret, Lady Drummond. *See* Russell

Drummond, Mary (Fulford), IX, 289

Drummond, Peter, V, 282; VI, 264; VIII, 483

Drummond, Robert, VI, **220–1**, 470, 481, 812; VII, 130, 927; VIII, 326; IX, 577

Drummond, Susan (McLean), V, 135; VI, 474

Drummond, Thomas, VI, 218, **221–22**; VII, 599; IX, 658, 660

Drummond, Thomas Joseph, XII, 621

Drummond of Hawthornden, William, I, 51

Drummond of Megginch, Catherine. *See* Oliphant of Rossie

Drummond of Megginch, Colin, IV, 402, 403, 618; V, 289, VIII, 236

Drury, Miss (Huntley, Lady Huntley), IX, 401

Drury*, Ernest Charles (1878–1968), XI, 804

Drury, Margaret Austen (Allen, Lady Allen), XII, 17

Drury (Drewry), Thomas, X, 389

Dryden, Agnes (Porter), X, 599

Dryden, John, V, 629

Dryden, Margaret (Armstrong), XII, 39

Drysdale, Alica Murray (Stewart), X, 667

Drysdale, John, V, 617

Duaime. *See* Le Maître

Duane, Mary Ann (Lowell), XII, 574

Du Bellineau, Catherine (Petit), II, 521

Duberger, Geneviève. *See* Langlais

Duberger, Georges, XII, 847

Duberger, Jean-Baptiste, VI, 224

Duberger, Jean-Baptiste, V, 834; VI, **223–24**, 269, 427; VII, 128; XII, 133

Duberger, Mary. *See* Plumby

Duberger, Victoria (Brunet), XII, 133

Duberger, *dit* Sanschagrin, Jean-Baptiste, VI, 223

Duberger, *dit* Sanschagrin, Louise. *See* Courtois

Dubergès, Jean-Bernard, V, 736

Dubergès, Marie-Magdelaine (Ornelin; McCarthy), VI, 426

Du Boccage, Joseph, III, 566

Dubocq, Laurent, I, 286

Dubocq, Marie-Félix. *See* Marie-Félix

Dubocq, Michelle. *See* Mars

Duboct. *See* Dubok

Du Bog, Jacques, I, 167

Dubois. *See also* Filiau

Dubois, Monsieur (officer), III, 464

Dubois, Anne (Lemort; Pécaudy de Contrecœur), I, 535

Dubois, Baptiste, VII, 387

Dubois, Donatien, II, 374

Dubois, Elizabeth (Solomon), VIII, 830

Dubois, Émile, VII, 174

Dubois, Guillaume, II, 288, 588

Dubois, Jacques, I, 550

Dubois, Jean-Baptiste (Alphonse), XII, 472

Dubois, Jeanne (Hertel de Rouville), II, 286

Dubois, John, VII, 705

Dubois, Joséphine (Lacoste), X, 417

Dubois, Marguerite (Brunet, *dit* L'Estang), V, 117

Dubois, Marguerite (Rolette), X, 628

Dubois, Marie (Drouin), I, 281

Dubois, Pierre-Cyrille-Adolphe, VIII, 140

Dubois Berthelot, Jacques-Hyacinthe, III, 189

Dubois Berthelot, Péronelle. *See* Magnan

Dubois Berthelot de Beaucours, Gabrielle-Françoise. *See* Aubert de la Chesnaye

Dubois Berthelot de Beaucours, Georges-François, III, 192

Dubois Berthelot de Beaucours, Josué, II, 36, 58, 121, 160, 180, 186, 255, 269, 337, 338, 432, 545, 649; III, 24, **189–92**, 331, 384, 445, 575, 630, 650; IV, 41, 663

Duboiscuvier, Louise (La Brosse), IV, 423

Dubois Davaugour, Pierre, I, 32, 146, 200, 202, **282–85**, 305, 325, 387, 402, 494, 537, 538, 563, 587, 647; II, 85, 86, 136, 158, 178, 365, 367

Dubois de Cocreaumont et de Saint-Maurice, Jean-Baptiste, I, **285–86**

Du Boisdecourt. *See* La Maisonfort

Dubois de La Milletière, Honoré, III, 102

Dubois de La Motte, Comte. *See* Cahideuc

Dubois de La Motte, Comtesse. *See* Andigné de La Chaise; Langan

Du Bois Des Cours, Adrien, II, 141

Du Bois Des Cours, Isabelle (Chaumont), II, 141

Dubois d'Esgriseilles, Jean-Baptiste, I, 285

Du Bois Duclos, Jean-Baptiste, II, 355

Du Boishué, *dit* Berland, Louise. *See* Belley

Du Boishué, *dit* Berland, Pierre, XII, 124

Dubok, I, **286**

Dubord, Alexis, X, 423, 424

Dubord, Bridget. *See* Furlong

Dubord, Hippolyte, VIII, 682; X, **261–62**
Dubord, Louis, VII, 176; X, 261
Dubord, Marie-Antoinette. *See* Bourdages
Du Bos, Antoinette. *See* Caron
Du Bos, Nicolas, I, 286
Du Bos, Nicolas, I, **286**
Du Bouchet, Jeanne (Chauvigny), I, 207
Du Bouëxic, Luc-Urbain, Comte de Guichen, III, 55
Du Bourg. *See* Morillon
Du Bourget, Marie-Anne (Auger de Subercase), II, 39
Du Bourgué. *See* Estienne
Dubreil, Angélique-Sylvie, Comtesse de Pontbriand. *See*
    Marot de La Garaye
Dubreil, Joseph-Yves, Comte de Pontbriand, III, 192
Dubreil de Pontbriand, Henri-Marie, III, 10, 11, 36, 50,
    103, 120, 122, 134, 137, **192–99**, 223, 246, 256, 259,
    263, 279, 285, 296, 314, 416, 435, 486, 487, 538, 546,
    547, 559, 580, 617, 625, 628, 638, 643; IV, 64, 87, 95,
    96, 97, 141, 142, 151, 201, 220, 236, 237, 256, 287, 289,
    295, 304, 319, 370, 387, 429, 430, 452, 453, 457, 458,
    509, 521, 536, 539, 542, 572, 645, 752, 779; V, 48, 195,
    276, 379, 432; VI, 573; XI, 87
Dubreuil. *See also* Chenet; La Corne
Du Breuil. *See* Le Creux
Dubreuil, Monsieur (judge), II, 445
Dubreuil, Catherine. *See* Lemarinier
Dubreuil, Félicité (Beaudry), X, 37
Dubreuil, Jean, II, 201
Dubreuil, Jean-Étienne, II, 129, **201**; III, 77, 144
Dubreuil, Jeanne. *See* Doucet
Dubreuil, Jeanne (Denys de La Trinité), I, 261; II, 178
Dubreuil, Marguerite. *See* Legardeur
Dubreuil, Marie-Anne. *See* Chevalier
Dubreuil, Marie-Jeanne. *See* Routier
Dubuc, Henriette (Polette), XI, 698
Dubuc, Jean-Baptiste, XI, 698
Dubuc*, Sir Joseph (1840–1914), X, 210; XI, 46, 164, 743,
    744; XII, 369, 370, 371, 372, 1008
Dubuc, Marie (Cherrier), IV, 148; V, 185
Dubuc, Marie-Angélique (Pillard), III, 521
Dubuc, Michel (churchwarden), IV, 148
Dubuc, Michel (mason), II, 105
Dubuc, Pierre, II, 526
Du Buisson. *See* Guyon; Poitiers
Dubuisson. *See* Potier; Renaud
Dubuque, Julien, VIII, 287
Duburon. *See also* Feré
Duburon, Joseph, IV, 203
Du Calvet, Anne. *See* Boudet
Du Calvet, Guy, IV, 231
Du Calvet, Marie-Louise. *See* Jussaume, *dit* Saint-Pierre
Du Calvet, Pierre, IV, 230
Du Calvet, Pierre (John), IV, 231
Du Calvet, Pierre, IV, xliv, 7, **227–32**, 336, 344, 436, 492,
    493, 534, 687, 759, 791; V, 21, 58, 75, 144, 398, 484,
    649, 892, 893; VI, 492, 494, 606; XI, 489
Ducas, Catherine (Martinet), II, 465
Ducasse, Jean-Baptiste, II, 260, 666
Ducasse, Marthe (La Rochefoucauld, Marquise de Roye),
    III, 356
Du Chaffault, Louis-Charles, Comte Du Chaffault de
    Besné, IV, 282; V, 62
Du Chaigneau. *See* Chaigneau

Duchaîne, Amable-Daniel, VIII, **239–41**
Duchaîne, Jean-Baptiste, VIII, 239
Duchaîne, Marie. *See* Paquin
Duchaîne, Pierre, VIII, 241
Duchambon. *See* Du Pont
Duchanquette, Rita-Élizabeth (Lespérance), XII, 557
Ducharme, Agathe. *See* Lorimier
Ducharme, Catherine (Roy), III, 574
Ducharme, Charles-Joseph, VI, 589, 593; VIII, **241–44**,
    458, 480, 481; X, 153; XI, 94
Ducharme, Dominique (cousin of DOMINIQUE), VIII, 245
Ducharme, Dominique (father of CHARLES-JOSEPH), VIII,
    241, 245
Ducharme, Dominique (musician), IX, 855; XI, 671
Ducharme, Dominique (François), IV, 592; V, 273; VI,
    404; VII, 466, 516; VIII, **244–46**, 540; IX, 264, 406
Ducharme, Françoise. *See* Demers, *dit* Dumé
Ducharme, Jean-Marie, IV, 58, 592; V, **272–73**, 394, 567,
    760; VIII, 244
Ducharme, Joseph (grandfather), V, 272
Ducharme, Joseph, VIII, 245
Ducharme, Julien, III, 144
Ducharme, Laurent, IV, **233**; V, 273
Ducharme, Louis (grandfather), IV, 233
Ducharme, Louis, IV, 268
Ducharme, Marguerite. *See* Charlebois
Ducharme, Marguerite. *See* Métivier
Ducharme, Marie. *See* Picard
Ducharme, Marie-Angélique. *See* Roy, *dit* Portelance
Ducharme, Paul, V, 273; VIII, 245
Ducharme, Pierre, I, 452
Ducharme, Thérèse. *See* Trottier
Du Chartran. *See* Gaudais
Duchartre, Pierre-Étienne-Simon, X, 105
Duchatelet, Marie (Potier), IV, 640
Duché, Mlle (Henry), VIII, 387
Duché, Jean-Baptiste, II, 425
Ducheneau, *dit* Sanregret, Marguerite (Natte, *dit*
    Marseille), V, 622
Duchesnay. *See also* Juchereau
Duchesnay, Louise (Gugy), X, 322
Duchesne. *See also* Du Quesne
Du Chesne. *See also* Le Ber
Du Chesne, Adrien, I, **287**, 463, 495
Du Chesne, Judith (Le Moyne), I, 287, 463
Duchesne, Léonard, I, 264; II, 278
Duchesneau, W., XII, 746
Duchesneau de La Doussinière et d'Ambault, Monsieur
    (son of JACQUES), I, 105, 137
Duchesneau de La Doussinière et d'Ambault, Jacques, I,
    103, 104, 105, 136, 177, 179, 203, 238, 245, **287–90**,
    340, 345, 396, 397, 399, 438, 445, 448, 464, 537, 553,
    565, 575, 581, 582; II, 29, 72, 88, 137, 194, 252, 253,
    262, 263, 335, 369, 370, 409, 412, 470, 532, 533, 574,
    575, 576, 585, 586, 616, 647
Duchesnois, Eugène-Napoléon, VII, 239, 345, 346; XI, 117
Duchesnois, Françoise. *See* Ainsse
Duchouquet. *See also* Lefebvre; Lefebvre-Duchouquet
Duchouquet, Charlotte (Dumoulin), V, 329
Duck, George (civil servant), XII, 688
Duck, George (lawyer), X, 119
Duck, Simeon, XII, 916
Duckett, Donalda. *See* Dunn

Duckworth, Anne. *See* Wallis

Duckworth, Henry, V, 273

Duckworth, Sir John Thomas, V, **273–76**; VI, 71, 176, 372, 419, 708; VII, 114, 152, 421, 765; VIII, 264

Duckworth, Sarah. *See* Johnson

Duckworth, Susannah Catherine, Lady Duckworth. *See* Buller

Duclaux. *See also* Pouget

Duclaux, Antoine, IX, 228

Duclos. *See also* Celles; Dubois

Duclos, *dit* Saint-Front, Jean-Baptiste, III, 140

Duclos de Beaumanoir, Sieur (soldier), II, 185

Duclos* de Celles, Alfred (1843–1925), VIII, 409; X, 236; XI, 159, 342, 343; XII, 181, 308, 325, 1027

Duclos de Celles, Eugénie. *See* Dorion

Du Cloux, Catherine (Dutisné), II, 215

Du Coigne. *See* Couagne; Decoigne

Ducondu, Jean, V, 479

Ducondu, Mathilde (Scallon), IX, 704

Du Cosnier. *See* Michelet

Du Coudray. *See* Le Borgne

Ducourday Feuillet, Monsieur (dancing master), III, 172

Du Creux, François, I, 523; II, 429

Ducros, *dit* Laterreur, Marguerite, V, 331

Du Daugnon, Comte. *See* Foucault

Duder, Ann. *See* Blackler

Duder, Ann. *See* Congdon

Duder, Arthur, XI, 284

Duder, Edwin, XI, **284**; XII, 974

Duder, Edwin John, XI, 284

Duder, Mary Elizabeth. *See* Edgar

Duder, Thomas, XI, 284

Dudevant, Arnauld-Germain, IV, **233–34**; V, 146, 471; VII, 17

Dudevant, Aurore, Baronne Dudevant. *See* Dupin

Dudevant, Jacques, IV, 234

Dudevant, Jeanne. *See* Barbequière

Dudevoir, Claude, II, 105

Dudley, Ambrose, Earl of Warwick, I, 316

Dudley, Ann (Hilton), II, 287

Dudley, Anne, Countess of Warwick. *See* Russell

Dudley, Elizabeth. *See* Davenport

Dudley, Henry, VIII, 943

Dudley, Joseph, I, 654; II, 38, 145, 285, 289, 437, 452, 480, 495, 511, 543, 606, 651, 664, 667; III, 178, 200; IV, 764

Dudley, Paul, III, 325

Dudley, Rebecca. *See* Tyng

Dudley, Rebecca (Gerrish; Burbidge), IV, 290; V, 121

Dudley, Thomas, II, 287

Dudley, William, III, **200–1**, 587

Dudley, William, 1st Earl of Dudley, IX, 731

Dudman, Elizabeth Gale (Killam), IX, 425

Dudouyt, Jean, I, 89, 92, 105, 249, **290–91**, 359, 506; II, 19, 29, 244, 369, 638; III, 683

Du Faradon. *See* Legrand; Normant

Du Fau, Abbé, III, 417

Dufaux, François, II, 640

Dufaux, François-Xavier, VI, 486

Du Fay, Polycarpe, I, 590

Dufebvre, Bernard. *See* Castonguay, Émile

Duff, Alexander, V, 750

Duff, Ann Theresa (McMicken), XII, 675

Duff, Charles, XII, 19

Duff, John, XII, 945

Duff, Mary (Abercromby), IV, 4

Duff, Robert, IV, 437, 708

Duff, William, 1st Earl Fife, Baron Braco, IV, 4

Dufferin and Ava, Marchioness of. *See* Hamilton

Dufferin and Ava, Marquis of. *See* Blackwood

Duffield, William Henry, XII, 939

Duffin, Sarah Jane. *See* Calder

Duffin, Simon, XII, **275**

Duffus, John, IX, 181

Duffus, Susan (Cunard), IX, 172

Duffus, William, VI, 243; IX, 174

Duffy, James, VIII, 114

Duffy, James W., VII, 292, 294, 295, 590, 591; VIII, 107, 198, **246–47**

Duffy, John, XI, 91

Duffy, Peter, XI, 91

Dufloc, Catherine (Petit), II, 521

Duforillon. *See* Aubert

Dufort. *See also* Bougret

Dufort, Delphine (Bachand), X, 25

Du Fort, Perrette (Callières), II, 112

Dufort, Théophile, VII, 411; VIII, 283, 489

Dufour, Bonaventure, VI, 224

Dufour, Joseph (cousin of Joseph DUFOUR, *dit* Bona), VI, 226

Dufour, Joseph (inspector), VI, 226

Dufour, Joseph (of Île aux Coudres), VI, 226

Dufour, Joseph (uncle of Joseph DUFOUR, *dit* Bona), VI, 226

Dufour, Joseph (voyageur), VI, 226

Dufour, *dit* Bona, Charlotte. *See* Tremblay

Dufour, *dit* Bona, Élisabeth. *See* Tremblay

Dufour, *dit* Bona, Joseph, VI, **224–26**

Dufour, *dit* Latour, Joseph, VI, 226

Dufournel, Guillaume, III, 201

Dufournel, Louis-Gaspard, II, 90, 200, 367, 587; III, **201–3**

Dufresne. *See also* Bouin; Rivard; Rivard-Dufresne; Thunay

Dufresne, Monsieur (captive), I, 130, 662

Dufresne, Alexandre, X, 430; XI, 480

Dufresne, Claire (Normand), VIII, 655

Dufresne, Delphine. *See* Bédard

Dufresne, Éléonore. *See* Perrault

Dufresne, François, VII, 239

Dufresne, Jacques (captive), II, 164

Dufresne, Jacques (father of JACQUES), XII, 275

Dufresne, Jacques, XII, **275–76**

Dufresne, Jean-Baptiste, III, 140

Dufresne, Louis, IX, 227

Dufresne, Marie. *See* Arbour

Dufresne, Marie-Agathe-Élodie (Gérin), XI, 338

Dufresne, Marie-Anne (Bergevin, *dit* Langevin; Morand), VIII, 637

Dufresne, Marie-Marguerite (Delorme), VII, 239

Dufresne, Marie-Michelle (Rastel de Rocheblave), VII, 735

Dufresne, Mélodie, named Mother Marie-Agnès, VII, 267

Dufresne, Nicolas, IV, 268

Dufresne, Nicolas, V, 480; VII, 488; VIII, 729; IX, **227–28**

Dufresne, Roger, X, 589

Dufresne, Toussaint, named Brother Jean-Baptiste, IX, 681

Dufresnoy Carion, Jeanne (Le Moyne de Sainte-Hélène; Monic), I, 466; II, 482

Dufresnoy Carion, Philippe, II, 105
Dufrost, Charles. *See* Youville, Charles-Marie-Madeleine d'
Dufrost de Boissemances, Christophe, II, 202
Dufrost de Boissemances, Marguerite. *See* La Forest de La Gemerais
Dufrost de La Gemerais, Charles, IV, 234
Dufrost de La Gemerais, François-Christophe, I, 204; II, 201, 202; III, 234, 247, 603; IV, 234
Dufrost de La Gemerais, Joseph, IV, 234, 509
Dufrost de La Gemerais, Marie-Clémence (Gamelin Maugras), III, 234; IV, 235
Dufrost de La Gemerais, Marie-Louise (Gamelin), IV, 235, 283
Dufrost de La Gemerais, Marie-Renée. *See* Gaultier de Varennes
Dufrost de La Jemerais, Christophe, II, **201–2**, 239; III, 241, 244, 245, 247, 249, 250, 251, 444; IV, 234
Dufrost de Lajemmerais, Marie-Marguerite (Youville), II, 110, 135, 202, 378, 414, 673; III, 195, 314, 385, 486, 604, 643, 691; IV, **234–39**, 265, 283, 434, 462, 508, 779, 780, 799; V, 241, 293, 498, 680; VI, 169, 170, 627; VII, 774; IX, 247; X, 492, 493, 735
Dufy. *See* Trottier
Dufy Charest. *See* Charest
Dugal. *See also* Cotin; Cottin
Dugal, Félicité-Zoë. *See* Séguin
Dugal, François, VI, 226, 227; VII, 60
Dugal, Léandre, XII, 1072
Dugal, Marguerite-Élisabeth (Archambeault), XI, 25
Dugal, Marguerite-Hortense. *See* Limoges
Dugal, Marie-Louise (Rivard, *dit* Loranger), XI, 529
Dugal, Olivier, VI, **226–27**
Dugard, Robert, III, 281, 282
Dugardin, L., I, 487
Dugas, Abraham, IV, xx
Dugas, Adolphe, VII, 411; XII, 276
Dugas, Agnès (Thibodeau), III, 87
Dugas, Anne (Bourgeois), II, 94
Dugas*, Georges (1833–1928), XI, 842; XII, 950
Dugas, Isabelle. *See* Bourg
Dugas, Isabelle, VI, 228
Dugas, Joseph (father of JOSEPH, d. 1823), III, 97; IV, 239
Dugas, Joseph (son of JOSEPH, d. 1823), VI, 228
Dugas, Joseph, IV, **239–40**, 252
Dugas, Joseph, VI, **227–28**
Dugas, Louise. *See* Arseneau
Dugas, Madeleine (Bourgeois), II, 94
Dugas, Marguerite. *See* Leblanc
Dugas, Marguerite. *See* Richard
Dugas, Marie (Melanson), I, 500
Dugas, Marie-Catherine-Cordélia (Duhamel), XII, 276
Dugas, Marie-Josephte. *See* Robichaud
Dugas, Pierre, VI, 227
Dugas, Victoire (Reynard), X, 614
Dugast, Jean-Baptiste, II, 294, 523
Dugay, Anne. *See* Baillargeon
Dugay, Catherine. *See* Laubret
Dugay, Jacques, II, **202–3**
Dugay, Jeanne. *See* Baudry, *dit* La Marche
Dugay, Michel, II, 202
Dugey Rozoy de Mannereuil, Charles, II, 380

Duggan, George, X, 262
Duggan, George, VII, 896; VIII, 347; IX, 25, 56, 346; X, 16, **262–63**, 299; XII, 191, 399
Duggan, John (bishop), XII, 191
Duggan, John (father of GEORGE), X, 262
Duggan, John (lawyer), VIII, 162; IX, 108; X, 262; XI, 501
Duggan, Mary (mother of GEORGE), X, 262
Duggan, Philip, XI, 673
Duggan, Phoebe Anne. *See* Armstrong
Duglas, Bishop, I, 469
Du Gousset, Jeanne (Provost), II, 532
Dugré, Adélard, XII, 512
Dugré, Alexandre, V, 603
Du Gua, Claire. *See* Goumard
Du Gua, Guy, I, 291
Du Gua de Monts, Judith. *See* Chesnel
Du Gua de Monts, Pierre, I, 23, 28, 69, 72, 95, 96, 98, 99, 186, 188, 189, 190, 191, 197, 209, **291–95**, 300, 346, 367, 422, 452, 469, 470, 495, 500, 526, 527, 529, 564, 565, 601, 603, 604; IV, xvii, xix, xx; V, 874; VI, 563
Du Guay. *See* Auguel; Le Guet
Duguay. *See also* Dugay
Duguay, Joseph-Nestor, XI, 811
Duguay, Josephte (Tremblay), X, 685
Duguay, Louis-Eugène, XI, 252
Duguay, Marie-Jeanne (Dulongpré), VII, 254
Duguay-Trouin, René, III, 42, 92, 609
Dugué, Louis-Rémy, II, 521
Dugué de Boisbriand, Charlotte (Petit), II, 521
Dugué de Boisbriand, Jean-Sidrac, II, 527
Dugué de Boisbriand, Marie. *See* Moyen Des Granges
Dugué de Boisbriand, Marie-Thérèse (Piot de Langloiserie), II, 527; IV, 638
Dugué de Boisbriand, Michel-Sidrac, I, **295**, 308; II, 203, 521, 527; IV, 638
Dugué de Boisbriand, Pierre, I, 308; II, **203–4**, 215, 216
Dugué de La Boulardière, Perrine. *See* Chambellé
Dugué de La Boulardière, Pierre, I, 295
Duguen, Pélagie-Jeanne-Marguerite (Quesnel), V, 700
Du Guesclin. *See* Lefebvre
Duhaget. *See* Tarride
Duhamel, Alphonsine. *See* Masson
Duhamel, Domitille. *See* Mousseau
Duhamel, Georges, XII, **276–77**, 502, 724
Duhamel, Joseph, XII, 277
Duhamel, Joseph, XII, **277**
Duhamel*, Joseph Thomas (1841–1909), XI, 868
Duhamel, Julien, V, 100
Duhamel, Louise (Hurteau), X, 373
Duhamel, Marie-Angélique (Bouchette), V, 100; VII, 95
Duhamel, Marie-Catherine-Cordélia. *See* Dugas
Duhamel, Rose (Côté), VII, 208
Duhamel, Théotiste. *See* Ostilly
Duhamel, Toussaint, XII, 276
Duhamel Du Monceau, Henri-Louis, III, 30, 77, 675, 677, 678, 679, 680
Duhart. *See* Dechart
Duhaut, Dominique, I, 182, 183
Duhaut, Pierre, I, 182, 183; II, 197
Du Heaume, Emma (Fauvel), XII, 309
Du Hérisson. *See* Leneuf
Du Hommée. *See* Byssot
Du Houssaye, Alliette (Morel de La Durantaye), II, 488

Du Jardin, Monsieur (merchant), I, 100
Du Jardin, Marie (Le Mercier), I, 458
Du Jaunay, Pierre, III, 12, 306, 347; IV, **240–42**; V, 8, 129
Du Laurent, Christophe-Hilarion, III, 160, 194, **203–4**, 647; IV, 88
Du Lescöat. *See* Le Pape
Dulhut. *See* Greysolon
Dulignon, Marie-Thérèse (Bertrand), V, 76
Dullard. *See* Dollard
Dulongpré, Louis (father of LOUIS), VII, 254
Dulongpré, Louis (son of LOUIS), VII, 255
Dulongpré, Louis, V, 51, 71, 243, 417, 437, 529, 701; VI, 169, 223, 570; VII, **254–57**, 688; VIII, 592; IX, 131
Dulongpré, Marguerite. *See* Campeau
Dulongpré, Marie-Jeanne. *See* Duguay
Dulude. *See* Huet
Du Luth. *See* Greysolon
Dumaine. *See* Du Pont
Dumais, Émile, XI, 506
Dumanoir. *See* Faucon
Du Marché, Charles, I, 214, 453
Dumaresq, Guillé, VII, 257
Dumaresq*, James Charles Philip (1840–1906), XII, 340
Dumaresq, Jersua. *See* Perry
Dumaresq, John, VII, 257
Dumaresq, Louisa W. *See* Newton
Dumaresq, Mary. *See* Stewart
Dumaresq, Perry, VII, **257–58**
Dumaresq, Perry John Newton, VII, 257
Dumaresq, Philippe (Philip), VII, 257
Dumas, Alexandre, XI, 82; XII, 669
Dumas, Alexandre, III, 555; IV, 205, 243, 618, 619; V, 74, 271, **276–79**, 289, 315, 470, 484, 736, 737; VI, 183
Dumas, Anne. *See* Martin
Dumas, Antoine-Libéral, IV, 244, 752; V, 276
Dumas, Catherine. *See* Lee
Dumas, François (husband of Marie Montmainier), II, 42
Dumas, François (partner of Olivier BUSSE), XII, 127
Dumas, Jean, V, 276
Dumas, Jean-Baptiste, VIII, 775
Dumas, Jean-Daniel, III, xxiv, 378, 402, 465, 496, 526, 578; IV, 224, **242–43**, 302, 408, 476, 531, 563, 633, 672; V, 276, 487
Dumas, Marguerite. *See* Cureux
Dumas, Marie. *See* Calquieres
Dumas, Marie. *See* Favar
Dumas, Marie. *See* Montmainier
Dumas, Marie-Françoise. *See* Fornel
Dumas, Marie-Joseph. *See* La Roche
Dumas, Marie-Josephte-Caroline (Masson), X, 499
Dumas, Michel (farm instructor), XI, 461, 748
Dumas, Michel (nephew of Jean DUMAS Saint-Martin), IV, 244
Dumas, Norbert, XI, 273, 821
Dumas, Pierre (father of Jean DUMAS Saint-Martin), IV, 243
Dumas, Pierre (trader), V, 817
Dumas, Samuel (father of JEAN-DANIEL), IV, 242
Dumas, Samuel (merchant), VIII, 359
Dumas Saint-Martin, Jean, III, 555; IV, 228, 232, **243–44**, 403, 618; V, 241, 276, 277, 289
Dumas Saint-Martin, Madeleine. *See* Morisseau
Dumble, David William, XI, 471

Dumé. *See* Demers
Dumergue, François, IV, 200
Du Mesnil. *See* Le Picard; Letélaud
Dumesnil. *See also* Peronne
Dumesnil, Marie (Charly, *dit* Saint-Ange), II, 131, 132
Dumeyniou, Étienne, VI, 471
Dummer, Shubael, III, 476
Dummer, William, II, 665; III, 43, 200, 265, 506, 584, 587; VI, 605
Dummier, Mr (victim), II, 601
Dumon, Geneviève (Deschenaux), V, 252
Du Monceau. *See* Duhamel
Dumons. *See* Monts
Dumont. *See also* Lambert
Du Mont. *See* Thier
Dumont, Élize (Désilets), VIII, 217
Dumont, Elmire (Laviolette), VIII, 492; XII, 535
Dumont*, Gabriel (1838–1906), VIII, 344; XI, 195, 461, 597, 598, 745, 746, 747, 748; XII, 23, 275, 554, 608, 734, 735, 1009
Dumont, Julie. *See* Valière
Dumont, Julie (Leblanc), X, 435
Dumont, Julie-Victoire (Rodier), VII, 757
Dumont, Louise-Élisabeth (Turgeon), IX, 797
Dumont, Marguerite (Badeaux), VI, 22
Dumont, Philippe, X, 435
Dumont d'Urville, Jules-Sébastien-César, IV, 283
Dumontet, *dit* Lagrandeur, Jean-Baptiste, III, 210
Dumontier, Baptiste, V, 576
Dumontier, François, II, 304
Dumontier, Françoise (Barolet), III, 26
Du Mortier, Madeleine (Roussel), I, 583
Dumouchel, Camille, VII, 259
Dumouchel, Félicité. *See* Girouard
Dumouchel, Hercule, VII, 259
Dumouchel, Ignace, VIII, 332
Dumouchel, Léandre, IX, 782; X, 499
Dumouchel, Marie-Joseph (Bigeau; Decoste), IV, 200
Dumouchel, Marie-Louise (Bertrand), V, 76
Dumouchelle, Jean-Baptiste, VII, **258–59**, 345, 346; VIII, 144, 331, 332, 791
Dumouchelle, Joseph, VII, 105
Dumouchelle, Louis-Vital, VII, 258
Dumouchelle, Magdeleine. *See* Goyau
Dumouchelle, Victoire. *See* Félix
Dumoulin, Monsieur (apprentice), III, 144
Dumoulin, Monsieur (servant), I, 302, 509
Dumoulin, Alida. *See* Pacaud
Dumoulin, Anne-Hermine (Pacaud), XI, 656
Dumoulin, Charles, VIII, 249
Dumoulin, Charlotte. *See* Duchouquet
Dumoulin, François, VIII, 248, 249
Dumoulin, Françoise (Pacaud), XI, 656
Dumoulin, Hermine. *See* Rieutord
Dumoulin, Jean-Emmanuel, VIII, 209, 248, 249
Dumoulin, Jean-Gaspard, VIII, **247–48**, 249
DuMoulin*, John Philip (1834–1911), X, 207; XI, 314; XII, 1000
Dumoulin, Louise. *See* Cressé
Dumoulin, Louis-François, VIII, 248
Dumoulin, Marguerite (Stuart), VII, 835; XII, 999
Dumoulin, Pantaléon-Benjamin, VIII, 249
Dumoulin, Philippe-Benjamin, VIII, 248

Dumoulin, Pierre-Benjamin, VIII, 217, 247, **248–49**, 250, 259; X, 526
Dumoulin, Sévère, VII, 517, 571, 736, 901; VIII, 248, **249–51**, 352, 719, 720, 721; XI, 657, 808
Dumoulin*, Sévère (1829–1910), VIII, 249; XI, 341
Dun, James, V, 279
Dun, John, V, **279–80**, 639; VI, 93
Dunbar, David, II, 669; III, 453
Dunbar, Sir George, VIII, 907; IX, 806
Dunbar, Hugh, VIII, 452
Dunbar, Janet (Bruyeres), IV, 109; V, 118
Dunbar, Louisa (Vavasour), VIII, 907; IX, 806
Dunbar, Marie-Josèphe (Selby), VI, 699
Dunbar, Thérèse-Josèphe. *See* Fleury Deschambault
Dunbar, Thomas, IV, 281
Dunbar, William, IV, 269; V, 118; VI, 699
Duncan, XII, 289
Duncan, A. H., VIII, 922
Duncan, Adam, 1st Viscount Duncan, V, 280
Duncan, Andrew, XII, 857
Duncan, Arthur, V, 281
Duncan, Caroline Benedict. *See* Power
Duncan, Charles, IV, 218, **244–45**, 419; V, 197, 500, 586
Duncan, David, VI, 102
Duncan, Frances (Ludlow) (mother of Gabriel George and George Duncan LUDLOW), V, 503, 505
Duncan, Frances (Ludlow) (wife of George Duncan LUDLOW), V, 505
Duncan, Henry, V, 281
Duncan, Henry, IV, 223; V, 187, **280–81**, 435; VII, 196, 197
Duncan, Isabella (Twisden), V, 281
Duncan, James, X, 211; XI, 702
Duncan, James D., VIII, 64; IX, 792; X, 412; XI, 106, **284–86**, 296, 417
Duncan, John (father of RICHARD), IV, 261, 722; V, 281, 282, 299
Duncan, John (of Newport, N.S.), XI, 834
Duncan, John (theologian), XII, 659
Duncan, Maria. *See* March
Duncan, Mary. *See* French
Duncan, Mary. *See* Wright
Duncan, Mary Tufton (Dundas), X, 264
Duncan, Richard, V, 279, **281–83**, 285, 518; VI, 264
Duncan*, Sara Jeannette (Cotes) (1862–1922), XI, 921
Duncan, Thomas, IX, 752
Duncan*, William (1832–1918), IX, 714, 716; XI, 236, 301; XII, 79, 284, 441, 442, 551, 552
Duncannon, Baron. *See* Ponsonby
Duncanson, Robert Stuart, X, **263–64**; XI, 296; XII, 789
Duncombe, Charles, VI, 331, 407; VII, 56, 92, 234, 253, 467, 923; VIII, 162, 276, 855, 933; IX, 9, **228–32**, 522, 683; X, 489; XI, 713, 914; XII, 1078, 1123, 1124
Duncombe, David, IX, 228
Duncombe, Elijah, IX, 228
Duncombe, Lucy. *See* Millard
Duncombe, Nancy. *See* Haines
Duncombe, Rhoda. *See* Tyrrell
Duncombe, Thomas, IX, 228
Dundas. *See also* Saunders
Dundas, Anne (Douglas, Lady Douglas), VI, 54; IX, 218, 849, 850
Dundas, Anne (Drummond; Strange), VII, 830

Dundas, Charlotte Anna (Mountain; Lefroy, Lady Lefroy), XI, 508
Dundas, Sir David, VIII, 458
Dundas, George, X, **264–65**, 352, 595, 612; XI, 548, 549
Dundas, Henry, 1st Viscount Melville, IV, 627, 717; V, 131, 149, 152, 159, 160, 262, 318, 351, 452, 730, 758; VI, 151, 397, 525, 607, 636, 637, 721; VII, 343, 524, 731, 811, 831; VIII, xxvii, xxx
Dundas, Henry, 3rd Viscount Melville, VII, 779; VIII, 788; IX, 278, 858
Dundas, James, X, 264
Dundas, Mary. *See* Clark
Dundas, Mary Tufton. *See* Duncan
Dundas Saunders, Robert, 2nd Viscount Melville, VIII, 684, 771; IX, 306
Dundonald, Countess of. *See* Hamilton
Dundonald, Earl of. *See* Cochrane
Dunham, Aileen, VI, 45
Dunham, Darius, VI, 405
Dunham, Elizabeth. *See* Detlor
Dunham, Sarah (Jones), VI, 363
Dunière, Charlotte (Chandler), V, 182; VII, 165
Dunière, Élisabeth. *See* Trefflé, *dit* Rottot
Dunière, Geneviève (Wills), V, 603
Dunière, Louis, III, 509; V, 283
Dunière, Louis, IV, 48, 49; V, 67, 107, 182, 233, **283–84**, 470, 566, 575, 576, 577, 650, 653; VI, 305; VII, 30, 673
Dunière, Louis-François, V, 283
Dunière, Marguerite. *See* Durand
Dunière, Marguerite (Panet), VII, 673
Dunière, Marie-Anne (Marcoux), V, 576; VII, 673
Dunk, George Montagu, 2nd Earl of Halifax, III, 90, 129, 340, 361, 362, 363, 365, 366, 496, 497, 583, 663, 664; IV, xxxv, xxxvi, xxxviii, xl, xli, xliii, 168, 228, 559, 571, 686, 787
Dunkin, Christopher, VII, 914; IX, 100, 214, 727; XI, 161, 187, 238, **286–88**, 721; XII, 4, 7, 406, 464, 903
Dunkin, Martha. *See* Hemming
Dunkin, Mary. *See* Barber
Dunkin, Summerhays, XI, 286
Dunlap, James Trites, XII, 479
Dunlap, William, V, 705, 706; VII, 255
Dunlop, Alexander (brother of JAMES), V, 284, 286
Dunlop, Alexander (father of ROBERT GRAHAM and WILLIAM), VII, 259, 260
Dunlop, David, V, 284
Dunlop, James, V, 287
Dunlop, James, V, **284–87**, 646, 828; VI, 60, 180, 254, 417, 471, 531; VII, 224, 309, 343, 920
Dunlop, Jane (Ogilvy; Robertson), V, 635, 718
Dunlop, Janet. *See* Graham
Dunlop, Janet Graham, VII, 262
Dunlop, John, VII, 262
Dunlop, Louisa. *See* McColl
Dunlop, Mary (Hay), XI, 390
Dunlop, Robert, V, 284, 286
Dunlop, Robert Graham, VII, **259–60**, 261, 262, 263, 883
Dunlop (Dunlap), William, IV, 105, 294, 392
Dunlop, William, known as Tiger Dunlop, VI, 481; VII, 100, 158, 259, **260–64**, 319, 337, 364, 446, 847, 882; VIII, 238, 358; IX, 416, 687, 751, 768, 837; X, 334, 536
Dunlop of Clober, Alexander, V, 284, 287
Dunlop of Garnkirk, James, V, 286

Dunmore, Earl of. *See* Murray
Dunmore, John B., XII, 123
Dunn. *See also* Dun
Dunn, Mr (husband of Mary Page), VII, 780
Dunn, Alexander Roberts, VIII, 256
Dunn, Andrew Hunter, XII, 630, 1101
Dunn, Charles (father), XI, 288; XII, 277
Dunn, Charles, XII, 277, 278
Dunn, Charles Edward, XI, 31; XII, 278, 279
Dunn, Charlotte. *See* Roberts
Dunn, Donalda (Duckett), XI, 289
Dunn, Elizabeth. *See* Bazette
Dunn, Emmeline (Zimmerman), VIII, 963
Dunn, Henriette. *See* Guichaud
Dunn*, Sir James Hamet (d. 1956), XII, 773
Dunn, John, IX, 263
Dunn, John Charles, VIII, 251
Dunn, John Henry, VI, 148; VII, 32, 42, 164, 664, 756, 833; VIII, xxvi, 6, 8, 9, 11, 29, 30, 47, 191, **251–57**, 451, 520, 643, 798, 849, 895, 896, 897, 898, 926, 932; IX, 502, 545, 647, 685; X, 62, 79, 343, 528, 529, 619; XI, 127, 409
Dunn, Logie Henry, XII, 279, 280
Dunn, Margaret. *See* Turner
Dunn, Marianne (Cramp), XI, 211
Dunn, Marie-Anne-Mathilde. *See* Beaudet
Dunn, Marie-Mathilde. *See* Leblanc
Dunn, Mary. *See* Hibbard
Dunn, Mary. *See* Page
Dunn, Mary Ann (Ogilvie-Grant), VIII, 251
Dunn, Oscar, IX, 65; X, 415, 416, 417, 430, 435; XI, 273, **288–90**, 345; XII, 249, 278
Dunn, Peter, VIII, 729
Dunn, Rebecca. *See* Logie
Dunn, Robert, V, 290; VII, 280
Dunn, Sophie-Louise. *See* Juchereau Duchesnay
Dunn, Stuart Hunter, XII, 279, 281
Dunn, Thomas (brewer), IX, 223, 224
Dunn, Thomas (paymaster), V, 289
Dunn, Thomas (son of THOMAS), V, 290; VII, 280
Dunn, Thomas, III, 541; IV, 37, 197, 243, 324, 538, 570, 602, 618, 716, 788, 790, 791; V, 18, 43, 44, 69, 100, 108, 111, 138, 142, 146, 150, 191, 214, 215, 224, 226, 234, 277, **287–93**, 332, 368, 369, 370, 371, 373, 374, 422, 460, 492, 493, 494, 496, 576, 637, 694, 745, 746, 793, 794, 840, 843, 863; VI, 384, 392, 524, 574, 587, 588; VII, 65, 201, 280, 380, 523, 613, 615, 767, 768, 784, 825; VIII, 914, 937
Dunn, Timothy Hibbard, VII, 71; VIII, 963; XII, **277–81**, 864
Dunn, William (cashier), XII, 988
Dunn, William (soldier), V, 290; VII, 280
Dunn, William E., XII, 994
Dunn, William Oscar, XI, 273, 288, 289; XII, 278
Dunning, John, 1st Baron Ashburton, V, 145
Dunoon. *See* Denoon
Dunphy, Anastasia (Dollard), VIII, 227
Dunscombe, Caroline Augusta (Crowdy), IX, 169
Dunscombe, John, VIII, 103; IX, 169
Dunscombe, Sarah Christiana (Bridge), VIII, 103
Dunsford, Lydia (Langton), XII, 526, 527
Dunsmuir, Alexander, XI, 291
Dunsmuir, James, XI, 290

Dunsmuir*, James (1851–1920), XI, 291, 292, 293
Dunsmuir, Joan Olive. *See* White
Dunsmuir, Marion (Houghton), XII, 449, 450
Dunsmuir, Robert, IX, 457; XI, **290–94**, 301, 637, 638, 840; XII, 450, 916, 919
Du Palais. *See* Digoine
Dupanloup, Félix, IX, 63, 64; XI, 182, 339; XII, 59, 819
Du Parc. *See* Godet
Duparc, Jean-Baptiste, II, 448; III, 24, **204–5**, 330, 361, 427
Duparc, Jeanne. *See* Meur
Duparc de Tenanguer, Claude, III, 204
Dupas, Charlotte. *See* Denys de La Trinité
Dupasquier, Abram, V, 239
Du Paty (Patés), Jean, II, 449
Dupaul, Pierre, IV, 320
Dupeer, Susannah, IV, 583
Dupéré, Marie-Anne (Claverie; Dandane Danseville de L'Étendard), III, 125
Dupéré, *dit* Champlain, Jean-Baptiste-François-Xavier, III, 125; IV, 206; V, 436; VI, 231
Dupéré, *dit* Champlain, Magdeleine. *See* Huguet
Duperié (Duperier), Anne. *See* Le Borgne de Belle-Isle
Duperié (Duperier), Jean, II, 582
Du Peron, François, I, 48, 205, 206, 217, **295–96**, 461, 602
Du Peron, Joseph-Imbert, I, 295, 296, 523
Dupéront (Dupéron, Duperron). *See* Baby
Du Perron, Thalour, I, 25, 89, **296**, 323
Dupin, Aurore, (Dudevant, Baronne Dudevant) (George Sand), X, 410; XI, 82
Dupin, Pierre, X, 33
Dupin de Belugard, Jean-Baptiste, IV, 458
Duplaix, Catherine. *See* Gonillon
Duplaix (Duplex Silvain), Claude, IV, 245
Dupleix, Joseph-François, IV, 126
Dupleix Silvain, Geneviève. *See* Benoist
Dupleix Silvain, Jean-Baptiste, IV, 28, **245–46**, 678
Duplessis. *See also* Gastineau; Guillon-Duplessis; Lebrun; Lefebvre; Quiniard; Radisson; Regnard; Robereau; Robreau; Sirois; Sirois-Duplessis
Du Plessis. *See also* Vignerot
Du Plessis, Armand-Jean (Cardinal de Richelieu), I, 29, 53, 115, 121, 124, 129, 159, 160, 161, 186, 195, 196, 203, 248, 261, 297, 372, 427, 428, 471, 482, 484, 504, 521, 567, 568, 579, 593, 615, 642; II, xv, 72, 228, 656
Du Plessis, Charles, Duc de Liancourt, I, 98
Du Plessis, Jeanne, Marquise de Liancourt, Duchesse de La Roche-Guyon. *See* Schomberg
Duplessis, Madeleine, IV, 591
Duplessis (Gastineau Duplessis; Radisson, *dit* Duplessis), Marguerite, III, **205**
Du Plessis, Marie (Pastour de Costebelle), II, 509
Duplessis*, Maurice Le Noblet (1890–1959), XII, 511
Duplessis, Pacifique, I, 108, **296**, 368, 379, 385, 552, 590
Du Plessis-Bochart, Charles, I, 159, **296–97**, 349, 527, 633; II, 82
Du Plessis de Liancourt, Antoinette. *See* Pons
Duplessis de Mornay, Louis-François, II, 333; III, 40, 41, 114, 193, 284, 319, 545, 638, 640; IV, 220, 221; XI, 87
Du Plessis-Kerbodot. *See* Guillemot
Du Plessis-Savari. *See* Chaspoux
Duplesy. *See* Des Roches
Duplex. *See* Duplaix

Du Ponceau. *See also* Favry
Du Ponceau, Peter Stephen, V, 885
Dupont. *See also* Gaudais-Dupont
Du Pont. *See also* Gravé
Dupont, Monsieur. *See* Poulet, Georges-François
Dupont, Charles-Vinceslas, VIII, 836
Dupont, Élisabeth (Cuny), IV, 187
Dupont, Étienne-Claude, IV, 69
Dupont, Guillaume, III, 165
Dupont, Jean, II, 204
Dupont, Jeanne. *See* Gaudais
Dupont, Marie. *See* Gauchet
Dupont, Siméon, II, **204**
Dupont, Xainte (Cloutier), I, 232
Dupont, *dit* Printemps, Jean, III, 422
Dupont de Gourville, Michel, IV, 61, 252, 253, 255, 466, 783
Dupont de Neuville, Françoise-Thérèse (Renaud d'Avène de Desmeloizes), I, 572; II, 205; III, 112, 550
Dupont de Neuville, Marie-Madeleine (Le Moyne de Maricourt), II, 205, 404; III, 407
Dupont de Neuville, Nicolas, I, 114, 232, 325, 572; II, **204–5**, 369, 387, 404, 463; III, 112, 550
Du Pont de Renon, Anne. *See* Goutin
Du Pont de Renon, Anne-Claire (L'Espérance), IV, 470
Du Pont de Renon, Michel, II, **205**; IV, 246, 251, 470
Du Pont de Renon, Philippe-Michel, IV, 247
Du Pont Duchambon, Charles-François-Ferdinand, IV, 249
Du Pont Duchambon, François, IV, 247, 248
Du Pont Duchambon, Jean-Baptiste-Ange, IV, 248
Du Pont Duchambon, Jeanne. *See* Mius d'Entremont de Pobomcoup
Du Pont Duchambon, Louis, II, 205, 220; III, 116, 236, 368, 393, 475, 508, 533, 615, 644, 645, 656; IV, 15, 29, 60, 62, 239, **246–49**, 251, 252, 254, 688, 783
Du Pont Duchambon, Marguerite-Josephe. *See* Rodrigue
Du Pont Duchambon, Marie-Anne. *See* Roma
Du Pont Duchambon de Mézillac, Anne (Coux), IV, 248
Du Pont Duchambon de Vergor, Joseph, IV, 251
Du Pont Duchambon de Vergor, Louis, III, 72, 547, 570, 588, 672; IV, xxv, 29, 36, 60, 247, 248, **249–51**, 452, 457, 541, 631; V, 104
Du Pont Duchambon de Vergor, Marie-Joseph. *See* Riverin
Du Pont Duchambon Dumaine, Barbe-Blanche. *See* Carrerot
Du Pont Duchambon Dumaine, Mathieu, IV, 248, 249
Du Pont Duvivier, Anne-Marie, II, 206
Du Pont Duvivier, François, II, **205–6**; III, 499, 552; IV, 246, 251, 783
Du Pont Duvivier, François, II, 206; III, 84, 175, 176, 236, 255, 260, 277, 287, 297, 366, 392, 438, 456, 475, 507; IV, xxiv, 29, 60, 61, 62, 239, 247, 249, **251–55**, 454, 466, 588, 676, 783
Du Pont Duvivier, Hugues, II, 205; IV, 246
Du Pont Duvivier, Joseph, II, 206; III, 567; IV, 247, 251, 255, **783–84**
Du Pont Duvivier, Joseph-Michel, II, 206
Du Pont Duvivier, Louis, II, 206
Du Pont Duvivier, Marie. *See* Hérauld de Gourville
Du Pont Duvivier, Marie. *See* Mius d'Entremont de Pobomcoup
Du Pont Duvivier, Marie-Joseph, II, 206

Du Pont Duvivier, Marie-Josephe. *See* Gautier, *dit* Bellair
Du Pont Duvivier, Marie-Josephe. *See* Le Borgne de Belle-Isle
Du Pont Duvivier de Gourville, Michel, II, 206; III, 570
Du Pont de Gourville, Michel, IV, 61, 252, 253, 255, 466, 783
Dupont-Gravé; Du Pont-Gravé. *See* Gravé Du Pont
Duport, Frances (Suckling), IV, 724
Duport, John, IV, 128, 267; V, 777, 873
Du Poyet. *See* Girault
Duprac, Françoise. *See* Lamoureux
Duprac, Jacques, II, 206
Duprac, Jean-Robert, II, **206**, 639
Duprac, Marguerite. *See* Vachon
Duprac, Noël, II, 206
Duprat, Jean, X, 599
Du Pratz (Duprat). *See* Le Page
Dupré. *See also* Le Comte; Le Conte; Saint-Georges
Dupré, Monsieur (merchant), IV, 148
Dupré, Anne de (Preissac), IV, 642
Dupré, François, I, 488; II, **206–7**; III, 546
Dupré, Hector-Edmond, XI, 190
Dupré, Philippe, II, 207
Dupré de Saint-Maur, Nicolas, IV, 55
Du Prévert. *See* Sarcel
Duprey, Anne-Marie (Achintre), XI, 3
Dupuis, Alphonsine. *See* Saint-Onge
Dupuis (Dupuy), Anastasie (Landry), X, 426
Dupuis, Euphrasie. *See* Richard
Dupuis, Jean, II, 517
Dupuis, Joseph, X, 265
Dupuis*, Joseph-Nazaire-Odilon (1871–1941), X, 265
Dupuis, Louis, IX, 487, 488
Dupuis, Marguerite (Thibodeau), VI, 651
Dupuis, Marie-Louise-Élisabeth (Clerk), X, 175
Dupuis*, Nathan Fellowes (1836–1917), IX, 461; XII, 926, 1102
Dupuis, Nazaire, X, **265–66**
Dupuis, *dit* Caton, Marie (Wood), VII, 923
Dupuy, Claude, II, 207, 208
Dupuy, Claude-Thomas, II, 90, 91, 147, 151, **207–13**, 235, 277, 334, 433, 449, 520, 535, 548, 577, 597, 606; III, 15, 26, 44, 45, 46, 48, 62, 114, 118, 153, 178, 182, 204, 225, 226, 227, 240, 291, 299, 330, 352, 353, 410, 420, 499, 553, 569, 603, 616, 620, 621; IV, 355, 356, 359, 488
Dupuy, Élisabeth. *See* Aubry
Dupuy, Elizabeth Margaret (Albro), VII, 12
Dupuy, Étienne, II, 207, 208
Dupuy, Françoise. *See* Richard
Dupuy, Henry, VIII, 7
Dupuy, Jacques, II, 207
Dupuy, Jean-Baptiste, VII, 496; X, **266–67**
Dupuy, Jeanne. *See* Fauvenel
Dupuy, Jeanne. *See* Groisard
Dupuy, Jean-Patrice, IV, 69
Dupuy, Joseph, X, 266
Dupuy, Louise (Milly; Laborde), IV, 420
Dupuy, Marie (Orillat), IV, 591
Dupuy, Marie-Madeleine. *See* Lefouyn
Dupuy, Simon, II, 285, 437, 606
Dupuy, Suzanne. *See* Boschette
Dupuy, Suzanne (Petit), II, 521
Dupuy, Zacharie, I, 102, **297–98**, 416

Dupuy de La Grandrive, Thomas, II, 208
Dupuy de Lisloye, Jeanne. *See* Couillard de Lespinay
Dupuy de Lisloye, Paul, II, xxiv, **213–14**, 303
Dupuy de Lisloye, Simon, II, 213
Dupuytren, Guillaume, VI, 764; VIII, 96; X, 236
Duquerny, Jeanne (Lomeron), I, 476
Du Quesne, Captain, III, 164
Du Quesne (Duchesne), Monsieur (merchant), I, 100
Duquesne, Abraham (father of ANGE), IV, 255
Duquesne, Abraham (partner of Nicolas DENYS), I, 257
Duquesne, Jacob, I, 257
Duquesne, Ursule-Thérèse. *See* Possel
Duquesne de Menneville, Ange, Marquis Duquesne, III,
    xxiv, 72, 76, 100, 118, 119, 148, 149, 162, 243, 385,
    431, 432, 435, 628; IV, 213, **255–58**, 426, 447, 457, 459,
    514, 563, 595, 605, 614, 617, 621, 636, 656, 667, 691,
    733; V, 272, 276, 312
Duquesnel. *See* Le Prévost
Du Quesnoy. *See* Talon
Duquet, Catherine. *See* Gauthier
Duquet*, Cyrille (1841–1922), XI, 496, 515; XII, 746, 747
Duquet, Denis, I, 298
Duquet, Françoise (Madry; Morel de La Durantaye), I, 479;
    II, 235, 488; III, 60
Duquet, Joseph (clergyman), VIII, 243
Duquet, Joseph (father of JOSEPH), VII, 264
Duquet, Joseph, VII, 149, 150, **264–65**; VIII, 244, 364; XI,
    623
Duquet, Joseph-Norbert, XII, 299
Duquet, Louise. *See* Dandurand
Duquet de La Chesnaye, Anne. *See* Lamarre
Duquet de La Chesnaye, Pierre, I, 73, **298**, 305, 474, 479,
    537; II, 88, 136, 158, 418
Duquette, Geneviève, X, 614
Duran. *See* Carolus-Duran
Durand, Asher Brown, VI, 344
Durand, Catherine (Roque), VII, 759
Durand, Charles (Carolus-Duran), XI, 671
Durand, Charles Morrison, VI, 198, 230, 728; VII, 44, 365,
    734; VIII, 12, 854; XI, 864
Durand, Françoise-Élizabeth (Roux), VI, 667
Durand, James, VI, 230; IX, 520, 521, 718, 735; X, 359
Durand, James, VI, 160, 198, **228–30**, 247, 490, 544, 629,
    631, 728; VII, 378, 379, 833; VIII, 339, 945
Durand, Jean, I, 91
Durand, Jeanne (Feré Duburon), IV, 306
Durand, Justinien, II, 45, 238; III, **207–8**, 240, 516, 552
Durand, Kezia. *See* Morrison
Durand, Laura B., VIII, 106
Durand, Laurent, IV, 533
Durand, Marguerite (Dunière), V, 283
Durand, Marie-Anne (Marchand), IV, 509
Durand, Pierre, II, 63
Durand, Servant, V, 276
Durand de Beauval, Monsieur (receiver), II, 215
Durand de La Garenne, II, **214–15**, 336, 482
Durand de Villegaignon, Nicolas, I, 469, 679
Durang, John, IV, 557
Du Ranquet (Chardon Duranquet), Dominique, VIII, 636;
    IX, 31
Durant, William, VI, 408; VII, 764, 765; VIII, 156
Durantal. *See* Atironta (fl. 1615)
Duras, Duc de. *See* Durfort

D'Urban, Sir Benjamin, VI, 820, 821
Durell, Mrs. *See* Skey
Durell, Mrs (Taylor; wife of PHILIP), III, 208
Durell, David, VI, 274
Durell, Elizabeth. *See* Corbet
Durell, John, III, 208
Durell, Madeline. *See* Saumarez
Durell, Philip, III, 71, 132, 133, **208–10**, 507, 573, 669; IV,
    163, 209, 210, 650, 699, 700
Durell, Thomas, II, 199; III, 208; IV, 169
Duret, Louise (Rageot), I, 560
Duret de Chevry, Charles-François, Marquis de Villeneuve,
    I, 89, 298, 436; II, 182, 183, 257
Duret de Chevry de La Boulaye, Charles, I, 90, **298–99**
Durette, François-Xavier, VIII, 614
Du Revest. *See* Noble
Durfee, Amos, VIII, 871; IX, 241; X, 482
Durfort, Jacques-Henri de, Duc de Duras, III, 14
Durham, Countess of. *See* Grey
Durham, Earl of. *See* Lambton
Durham, Margaret (Strange), VII, 830
Durie, Anna (wife of WILLIAM SMITH), XI, 294
Durie, Helena. *See* Lee
Durie, William H., XI, 294
Durie, William Smith, XI, **294–95**
Durieu, Paul, XI, 402; XII, **281–85**, 817
Durieux, Blaise, XII, 281
Durieux, Mariette. *See* Bayle
Durkee, Martha (Hebbard), V, 422
Durling, Mary (McLelan), VIII, 568
Durnford, Andrew, VII, 266
Durnford, Elias, VII, 265
Durnford, Elias Walker, VII, **265–67**; X, 30
Durnford, Jane Sophia. *See* Mann
Durnford, Philip, VII, 266
Durnford, Rebecca. *See* Walker
Durocher, Alexis-Basile, VIII, 240, 776
Durocher, Eulalie (Mélanie), named Mother Marie-Rose,
    VII, **267–68**; IX, 361; XI, 96
Durocher, Eusèbe, VII, 267; IX, 96
Durocher, Flavien, VII, 267; IX, 398; X, **267–68**, 532; XI,
    169, 170; XII, 223
Durocher, Geneviève (Durocher), VII, 267; X, 267
Durocher, Jean-Baptiste-Amable, IV, 534; V, 285, 370,
    663, 821; X, 567
Durocher, Joseph, III, 210
Durocher, Joseph, III, **210–11**
Durocher, Laurent, VI, 600
Durocher, Marguerite. *See* Gaudé
Durocher, Marguerite. *See* Le Roy
Durocher, Marguerite (Beaubien), VII, 59
Durocher, Marie-Louise-Catherine. *See* Juillet
Durocher, Olivier (father), VII, 267
Durocher, Olivier, VII, 267; X, 267
Durocher, Séraphine, named Sainte-Cécile, VII, 267
Durocher, Théophile, VII, 267
Durocher, Vital, XII, 846
Durondu, Zoë (Pannetion), XI, 671
Durosoy, Geneviève, I, 117
Du Roure. *See* Beauvoir
Durouvray. *See* Guyon
Duroy, Anne-Thérèse (Charest), IV, 140
Duroy, Charlotte (Bazil), III, 38, 224

Duroy, Marie-Marguerite (Chasle; Lanoullier de Boisclerc), III, 350

Durrell, Thomas, VIII, 268

Duruy, Victor, XI, 182, 186

Du Sablé. *See* Dandonneau

Dusablé, Marie (Germain), X, 305

Dusaultoir. *See* Dusautoy

Du Saussay de Bémont, Anne. *See* Carlier

Du Saussay de Bémont, Jacques, I, 583

Du Saussay de Bémont, Marie-Anne (Rouer de Villeray), I, 583

Dusautoy (Dusaultoir), Charles, III, 152

Dusautoy, Henri, III, 35

Dusautoy (Dusaultoir), Louise-Madeleine (Cugnet), III, 152; IV, 182; V, 252, 253

Dusautoy, Marie-Anne. *See* Roussel

Du Sicquet d'Esmainville, Françoise (Le Roy de La Potherie de Bacqueville), II, 421

Du Sillar, Marguerite (Le Marchand de Lignery), II, 389

Du Souchet, Louise-Anne (Cavelier), II, 576

Dusourdy. *See* Landriaux

Dussau, Joseph, V, 249

Dussault. *See also* Toupin

Dussault, David, VIII, 40

Dussaus, Jean, V, 293

Dussaus, Marie-Angélique. *See* Huard

Dussaus, Marie-Angélique, V, **293**

Dussaut, Geneviève (Noël), VI, 546

Dusson de Bonrepaus, François, II, 280, 443, 444

Dussy, Chevalier, II, 555, 560

Dustan, George Gordon, XII, 1058

Dutalmé, Pierre-Paul, VI, 81

Du Tartre. *See also* Basset; Denys

Du Tartre, Françoise (Denys de La Trinité), I, 261; II, 176, 179, 236

Du Tartre (de Tard), *dit* La Verdure, Jean, II, 47

Dutast, Captain, II, 440

Dutch Bastard. *See* Flemish Bastard

Dutcher, Frederick R., XI, 898

Duteau, *dit* Grandpré, Sophie (Mousseau), XI, 622

Duteau, *dit* Tourville, Charles, II, 190

Du Thet, Gilbert, I, 68, 95, 98, 100, 101, **299**, 441, 470, 560

Du Tillet. *See* Hélie

Du Tilly. *See also* Testu

Du Tilly, Captain, II, 511

Dutisné, Catherine. *See* Du Cloux

Dutisné, Charles, II, 216

Dutisné, Claude-Charles, II, 215

Dutisné, Claude-Charles, II, xxix, xxxvii, **215–16**, 646; III, xxxiii, xxxix

Dutisné, Louis-Marie-Charles, II, 67, 216

Dutisné, Louis-Marie-Joseph, II, 216

Dutisné, Marguerite. *See* Margane de Lavaltrie

Dutisné, Marie-Anne. *See* Gaultier de Comporté

Du Tremblay. *See also* Gaultier

Du Tremblay, François-Joseph, named Father Joseph, I, 428

Du Val. *See also* Desjardins

Duval. *See also* Thuot

Duval, Miss (teacher), XII, 561

Du Val, Amice, VIII, 257

Duval, Anne (Polette), XI, 698

Duval, Catherine (Horné), II, 292

Duval, Charles, IV, 206; V, 436, 708; VI, **230–31**, 663

Duval, Clarice (Pacaud), XI, 658

Duval, Edmund Hillyer, X, **268**; XII, 561

Du Val, Elizabeth. *See* Hubert

Duval, Elizabeth. *See* Wood

Duval, Françoise-Élisabeth. *See* Panneton

Duval, Jacques, VI, 230

Du Val, Jean, VIII, 257

Duval, Jean, I, 190, **299–300**, 346

Duval, Jean-François-Joseph, VII, 879; VIII, 155, 170, 907; IX, 261, 262; X, 120; XI, 168, 698

Du Val, John, VIII, 258

Duval, Joseph, V, 577

Duval, Lizette (Elizabeth) (Harmon), VII, 385

Duval, Louis-de-Gonzague, XII, 66

Duval, Louis-Zéphirin, IX, 487

Duval, Magdelaine. *See* You

Du Val, Marie. *See* Piton

Du Val, Nicholas, VIII, 257

Duval, Nicolas, I, 271

Duval, Peter, X, 268

Du Val, Peter, VIII, 207, **257–58**

Du Val, Peter John, VIII, 257, 258

Duval, Pierre, VI, 230

Duval, Sarah. *See* Turner

Duvallier, Marie-Salomé (Cailly), III, 93

Duvar. *See* Hunter-Duvar

Du Vault. *See* Clément

Duvergé, Bertrand, IV, 378

Duverger. *See also* Forget

Duverger, Élisabeth (Rocbert de La Morandière), III, 563

Du Verger d'Aubusson, Marie-Jeanne. *See* Jarret de Verchères

Du Vergier. *See* Véniard

Duvernay. *See also* Crevier; Crevier Duverné

Duvernay, Franklin, VIII, 262

Duvernay, Louis-Napoléon, VIII, 262; X, 374; XI, 339; XII, 1025

Duvernay, Ludger, VI, 379, 392, 783, 802; VII, 131, 208, 334, 353, 411, 512, 515, 737, 757, 758, 771, 781, 789; VIII, 20, 143, 144, 248, **258–63**, 285, 605, 635, 667, 726, 736, 911, 914; IX, 43, 73, 440, 444, 485, 486, 554, 568, 633, 695, 696, 811; X, 75, 374, 491, 492, 526, 546, 567, 568, 576, 577, 581; XI, 37, 60, 187, 320, 339, 531, 657, 821; XII, 66, 261

Duvernay, Ludger-Denis, VIII, 263; XII, 1025

Duvernay, Marie-Adèle-Victorine (Pelletier), VIII, 262

Duvernay, Marie-Reine-Joséphine (Glackmeyer), VIII, 262

Duvernay, Reine. *See* Harnois

Duverné. *See* Crevier

DuVernet, Abraham, VII, 268

DuVernet, Frances Eliza (Gibbons), XII, 363

DuVernet*, Frederick Herbert (1860–1924), XII, 364

DuVernet (DuVernet Grosset Muirhead), Henry Abraham, VII, **268–69**

DuVernet (DuVernet Grosset Muirhead), Martha Maria Iqualin. *See* Van Kemper

DuVernet, Miriam. *See* Grosset Muirhead

Duvert. *See* Chicou; Chicoux-Duvert

Du Vignau, Captain, II, 590

Duvilleray, Hypolithe, VI, 49

Duvivier. *See also* Du Pont

Duvivier, Adrienne (Hébert; Le Cavelier), II, 226

Duvivier, Marie-Anne (Berbudeau), IV, 56
Duvoisin, Jean-Baptiste, VIII, 212
Du Vuault (Vault). *See* Clement
Duyckinck, Evert Augustus, VIII, 744
Dwerniki, General, XII, 390
Dyaderowane. *See* Ottrowana
Dyas, Bessie Emma Mathilda (MacLean), XII, 287
Dyas, Ellen. *See* Warren
Dyas, Emma Wilder. *See* Ball
Dyas, John, XII, 285
Dyas, John Joseph, XII, 286, 287
Dyas, Thomas Winning, XII, **285–87**
Dyas, William Jacob, XII, 287
Dyce, William, IV, 569
Dyck, Agatha (Wiebe), XII, 1098
Dyck, Elizabeth (Wiebe), XII, 1098
Dyckhuyse, Swantie (Schuyler), III, 587
Dyer, Edward, I, 531
Dyer, Hannah (Winslow), V, 865
Dyer, Luther, IX, 744
Dyer, Matilda (Hilyard), X, 349
Dygart, Eleanor (Putnam), VII, 715
Dyke, James, VII, 873; VIII, 689
Dyke, Joseph, VII, 510
Dykert (Daggart), Gertrude (Niles), X, 549
Dymond, Joseph, IV, 758
Dynevor, Baron. *See* Rice
Dyonnet, Edmond, XII, 170
Dysan. *See* Dejean
Dysart, Earl of. *See* Murray
Dyson, Anne (Philipps), III, 514
Dyson, William, XII, 361

EADIE, Annie (Workman), XI, 936
Eadie, Elizabeth (Trotter), VIII, 894
Eadie, John, XI, 936
Eagan, Catherine (Herbert), VII, 396; X, 348
Eagar, Maria. *See* Saunders
Eagar, William, VII, 269
Eagar, William, VII, **269–70**
Eagles, Horatio, IX, 311
Eagleson, John, IV, **258–59**; V, 446, 869; VII, 391
Eagleson, Peter, IX, 835
Eagleson, Sophia Augusta. *See* Pernette
Eagleson, Sophia Augusta (Head), VII, 391
Eakins, Ann. *See* Cox
Eakins, James, XII, 10
Eakins, Thomas, XII, 830
Earle, Catherine McGill. *See* Otty
Earle, Maria. *See* Hughson
Earle, Sylvester Zobieski, IX, 87, 340; XI, 295
Earle, Sylvester Zobieski, XI, **295–96**; XII, 307, 1057
Earle, William, XII, 245
Earls, John, XI, 864
Early, Bernard, X, 268
Early, Mary (mother of MAY AGNES), X, 268
Early, May Agnes (Fleming), X, 44, **268–69**
Easson. *See also* Esson
Easson, Avis Phillips (Gray), IX, 338
Easson, Robert, VIII, 272
Eastaff. *See* Eaststaff
Eastburn, Robert, III, 588
Easthope, Ann (McGillivray), VII, 561

Easthope, Sir John, VII, 562
Eastlake, Sir Charles Lock, VIII, 651; XII, 625
Eastlake, Elizabeth, Lady Eastlake. *See* Rigby
Eastman, Bridget (Lowe; wife of DANIEL WARD), IX, 232
Eastman, Daniel Ward, IX, **232–33**
Eastman, Elizabeth. *See* Hopkins
Eastman, Margaret. *See* Merritt
Eastman, Polly. *See* Owen
Eastman, Tilton, IX, 232
Easton, Eliza Margaret (Leach), XI, 502
Easton, Mary. *See* Beattie
Easton, Nellie. *See* Thomson
Easton, Peter, I, 24, 240, **300–1**, 350, 481, 668
Easton, Robert, VI, **231–33**; VII, 77, 442, 820; VIII, 77; IX, 108; X, 660
Easton, William, VI, 231
Eaststaff, Elizabeth (wife of THOMAS GEORGE WILLIAM), VIII, 264
Eaststaff, Thomas George William, V, 274; VIII, **264–65**
Eastwood, James, XII, 787
Eastwood, John, VIII, 266, 278
Eaton, Amos, X, 504
Eaton*, Arthur Wentworth Hamilton (1849–1937), VII, 507
Eaton, Charlotte Amelia. *See* Collins
Eaton, Constance Laure. *See* Papelard
Eaton, Emeline Augusta (Rand), XII, 879
Eaton, George, IX, 40
Eaton*, Sir John Craig (1876–1922), XII, 973
Eaton, Jonathan Wyatt, XII, 287
Eaton, Joseph Oriel, XII, 287
Eaton, Mary. *See* Smith
Eaton*, Timothy (1834–1907), XI, 551; XII, 972, 973
Eaton, Wyatt, XII, **287–89**
Eau. *See* Aux
Eaume. *See* Reaume
Eberts, Effie (Robertson), XI, 756
Eberts, Margaret Bruce (Robertson), XI, 756
Ebey, Isaac N., VIII, 226
Ebierbing, Joe. *See* Ipilkvik
Eby, Barbara (Schneider), VII, 778
Eby, Benjamin, VI, 235; VII, 778; VIII, 87, **265–66**, 271, 316, 701
Eby, Catharine. *See* Bricker
Eby, Christian (grandfather), VIII, 265
Eby, Christian, VIII, 265
Eby, Heinrich, VIII, 271, 701
Eby, Magdalena. *See* Erb
Eby, Mary. *See* Brubacher
Eby, Peter, VIII, 265
Eby, William, XII, 157
Eccles, Anna (Lewis), X, 441
Eccles, Elizabeth (mother of HENRY), IX, 233
Eccles, Henry, IX, **233**
Eccles, Hugh, IX, 233
Eccles, Jane. *See* Lelièvre
Eccles, Samuel, IX, 436
Eccles, William, IX, 233
Echenic, Marie d'. *See* Urcudoy
Echenic, Martin d', VI, 134
Echevete, Matias de, I, **301**
Échon. *See* Brébeuf, Jean de; Chaumonot, Pierre-Joseph-Marie

Eckart, Jonathan, VI, 819
Eckart, Margaret Roberts (Hanna), VIII, 359
Eckermann, Johann Peter, VIII, 651
Eckford, Henry, VI, 290
Ecossais, L'. *See* Martin, Abraham
Ecuier, Charles, V, **294–95**; VIII, 129, 406
Ecuier, Jean, V, 294
Ecuier, Marie-Josephte. *See* Cimère
Ecuyer, Benjamin, VI, 427
Eda'nsa, XII, **289–91**
Eddis, Eden Upton, VII, 599
Eddy, Eleazar, V, 295
Eddy, Elizabeth. *See* Cobb
Eddy*, Ezra Butler (d. 1906), XI, 113; XII, 258, 1130
Eddy, Jonathan, IV, 13, 29, 161, 193, 258, 309, 451, 562,
    693, 723, 736; V, 15, 16, 240, 257, 258, **295–96**, 416,
    627, 666; VI, 30, 242, 678, 718, 790; VII, 120, 215
Eddy, Mary. *See* Ware
Ede, Mary (Austen; Howe), VI, 333; X, 362
Edelston, Marie-Madeleine. *See* Bideau, *dit* Portugal
Eden, George, 3rd Earl of Auckland, VII, 855
Eden, Horatia Katharine Frances. *See* Gatty
Eden, Mary Louisa (Colvile (Wedderburn)), XII, 206
Eden, Richard, I, 153, 154, 155
Eden, Robert, X, 278
Edensa (Edensaw; Edenshaw, Albert Edward). *See* Eda'nsa
Edenshaw, Charlie. *See* Tahaygen
Edenshaw, Henry, XII, 289
Eder de La Fontanelle, Guy, I, 186
Edewancho. *See* Atecouando (fl. 1701–26)
Edgar, George, XII, 316
Edgar, Grace Matilda. *See* Fleming
Edgar, James, XII, 291
Edgar, Sir James David, XII, **291–94**, 653, 657
Edgar, Mary Elizabeth (Duder), XI, 284
Edgar, Matilda, Lady Edgar. *See* Ridout
Edgar*, Oscar Pelham (1871–1948), XII, 291
Edgar, William, V, 511, 560, 561; VI, 318
Edgcombe, Leonard, I, **301–2**; II, 42, 265, 266
Edge, William, VII, 736; VIII, 250, 719
Edgerton, Julius, XII, 1090
Edgeworth, Maria, XII, 996
Edgeworth de Firmont, Henry Essex, VIII, 909
Edghill, John Cox, XI, 76
Edinburgh, Duke of. *See* Alfred Ernest Albert
Edinsa (Edinso). *See also* Eda'nsa
Edinsa, XII, 289
Edison, Thomas Alva, XI, 39, 496; XII, 289
Edmond, Janet (Logan), X, 444
Edmonds, Henry Valentine, XII, **294–95**
Edmonds, Jane Fortune. *See* Kemp
Edmonds, Matilda. *See* Humphries
Edmonds, William, XII, 294
Edmondson, Jonathan, XII, 1060
Edmonstone, William, VII, lvi, 611; IX, 224, 540; XI, 5, 315
Edmundson, James, VIII, 266
Edmundson, Margaret. *See* Graham
Edmundson, William Graham, VIII, **266–68**, 278; XI, 132
Édouin, Charles, II, 187
Edowishcosh, IX, 10
Edridge, Henry, VI, 529
Edson, Allan Aaron, XI, **296–97**; XII, 287, 288, 793
Edson, Calvin, VI, 483

Edson, Elvira. *See* Gilmore
Edson, Hiram, XI, 296
Edson, Mary. *See* Stewart
Edward III, King of England, I, 678
Edward IV, King of England, I, 239
Edward VI, King of England and Ireland, I, 157, 158
Edward VII, King of Great Britain and Ireland, VIII, 818,
    961; IX, 26, 87, 275, 344, 385, 406, 407, 464, 512, 627,
    726, 777, 855; X, 31, 74, 121, 145, 146, 220, 319, 351,
    529, 625, 668, 726; XI, 228, 294, 590, 606, 679, 686,
    762, 767, 771, 797, 866, 948; XII, 75, 86, 186, 268, 290,
    350, 386, 387, 406, 409, 436, 444, 669, 677, 788, 963,
    983, 1001, 1084
Edward, Catherine (Munn), V, 616
Edward Augustus, Duke of Kent and Strathearn, IV, 43,
    147, 190, 523, 718; V, 24, 45, 84, 85, 87, 93, 101, 108,
    119, 122, 136, 159, 160, 161, 187, 188, 192, 205,
    **296–98**, 318, 354, 356, 366, 372, 405, 425, 431, 439,
    449, 504, 508, 541, 605, 608, 622, 634, 635, 649, 689,
    690, 691, 763, 789, 849, 851, 872, 880; VI, 89, 96, 99,
    140, 155, 160, 173, 201, 202, 243, 256, 257, 325, 341,
    343, 345, 346, 380, 408, 412, 445, 501, 516, 517, 518,
    535, 536, 548, 549, 556, 587, 608, 650, 723, 769, 779,
    781; VII, 96, 104, 107, 241, 242, 349, 372, 401, 414,
    503, 543, 783, 787, 817, 918, 923; VIII, 286, 354, 483;
    IX, 172, 245; X, 13; XI, 931; XII, 312
Edwards. *See also* Noel
Edwards, Charity (Goldthwait), III, 259
Edwards, Edward, IV, 689; V, **298–99**, 383, 821; VI, 642,
    744; VII, 111, 112, 768
Edwards, George, III, 302
Edwards, Henry, II, 534
Edwards, John Thomas, XI, 568
Edwards, Jonathan, V, 729, 744; IX, 233; XI, 584
Edwards, Mary Ann, V, 401
Edwards, Richard, IV, 159, **259–60**, 402, 437, 648; V, 52,
    361
Edwards, Thomas, II, 117
Edwards*, William Cameron (1844–1921), XII, 258
Edwards, William Henry, XI, 108; XII, 868
Edy, John William, VI, 256
Eenoolooapik, VII, **270–71**; XII, 835
Effingham, Earl of. *See* Howard
Egan, Anne Margaret. *See* Gibson
Egan, John, VIII, **268–70**, 821, 840; IX, 462; X, 23; XI,
    414
Egan, Michael P., VII, 353
Egan, William, V, 632
Egede, Hans, I, 252
Egerton, John, 2nd Earl of Bridgewater, II, 496
Eghohund, IV, 27
Egmont, Earl of. *See* Perceval
Egremon, John, II, 265
Egremont, Earl of. *See* Wyndham
Egushwa, IV, lvi, **260**; V, 710; VI, 8
Ehlers, Gustav, XII, 379
Ehrenkrock, Johann Gustav von, VII, 348
Ehrentraut, Christine Dorothea (Tiarks), VII, 865
Ehrhard. *See* Erad
Eichwald, Carl Eduard von, X, 65
Eirikr *upsi* Gnupsson, I, **675–76**
Eirikr Thorvaldsson, I, 17, 103, 448, 612, 642, 643, **676**
Eisenbach, Freiherr zu. *See* Riedesel

Eisenbach, Frelin zu. *See* Massow
Elden, Apphia (Woodman), VII, 923
Elder, Elizabeth. *See* Fraile
Elder, John, VII, 272
Elder, Matthew, VII, 273
Elder, Rebecca. *See* Jenkins
Elder, Samuel, VII, 272
Elder, William, VII, 272
Elder, William, VI, 172; VII, **271–73**, 713
Elder, William, IX, 621; XI, **297–99**; XII, 339, 566
Eldon, Earl of. *See* Scott
Elgee, Jane (McClure), X, 454
Elgee, Jane Francisca (Wilde, Lady Wilde), IX, 494
Elgin, Countess of. *See* Cumming-Bruce; Lambton
Elgin, Earl of. *See* Bruce
Elibank, Baron. *See* Murray
Éliçagaray. *See* Renau
Élie. *See also* Hélie
Élie, Jacques, II, **216–17**, 549
Élie, Marie-Joseph. *See* Maréchal
Eliot, George. *See* Evans, Mary Ann
Eliot, Hugh, I, 21, 148, **302**, 343, 386, 643
Eliot, John, VIII, 411
Eliot, Sir John, I, 522
Eliott. *See* Eliot
Élisabeth (wife of Pierre YOU de La Découverte), I, 573; II, 673
Eliza, Saturnina Norberta Caamaño de. *See* Caamaño
Elizabeth (wife of James BIRD), VIII, 91
Elizabeth I, Queen of England and Ireland, I, 93, 229, 279, 331, 333, 365, 566, 667, 678
Eliza y Reventa, Francisco de, IV, 520, 568; V, 10, 11, 12, 198, 411, 615; VI, **233–35**
Ellegood, Jacob, VI, 683, 684
Ellegood, Mary. *See* Saunders
Ellery, Elizabeth (Hawkins), VIII, 385
Ellice, Alexander, IV, 39, 144, 261, 403; V, 270, 282, **299–301**, 326, 333, 494, 511; VI, 108, 110, 639, 640, 641; VII, 201, 309; IX, 234
Ellice, Ann. *See* Russell
Ellice, Lady Anne Amelia. *See* Keppel
Ellice, Edward, VII, 105; IX, 237, 238, 239, 814; X, 470
Ellice, Edward, V, 86, 300, 301, 531, 822, 848; VI, 533, 641, 644, 645, 646, 801, 815; VII, 29, 105, 261, 311, 478, 513, 561, 562, 838, 856; VIII, xxvi, 10, 85, 322, 365, 812, 815, 817, 845; IX, **233–39**, 315, 384, 415, 416, 441, 442, 482, 484, 671, 818; X, 546; XI, 45, 312, 766; XII, 348, 878
Ellice, Lady Hannah Althea. *See* Grey
Ellice, James, IV, 261; V, 299
Ellice, Katherine Jane. *See* Balfour
Ellice, Robert, IV, **261–62**; V, 299, 300, 512; VI, 102, 639, 640; VII, 309
Ellice, Russell, VIII, 543
Ellice of Knockleith, Mary. *See* Simpson of Gartly
Ellice of Knockleith, William, IV, 261; V, 299
Ellicott, Andrew, VII, 866
Elligood, Anne (Elmsly), V, 303
Elliot, Adam, X, 269
Elliot, Adam, VII, 467; X, 12, **269–70**; XI, 451, 452, 639, 653
Elliot, Charlotte. *See* Racey
Elliot, Elizabeth (Cathcart, Countess Cathcart), VIII, 135

Elliot, Elizabeth (Vaughan), II, 644; III, 641
Elliot, Eliza Beulah. *See* Howells
Elliot*, Gilbert John Murray Kynynmond, Viscount Melgund and 4th Earl of Minto (1845–1914), XI, 326, 884; XII, 245, 669, 735
Elliot, Howard, XII, 296
Elliot, John (governor), IV, 784; V, 123, 359, 361, 632; VI, 244
Elliot, John (partner of Sylvester Neelon), XII, 783
Elliot, Margaret. *See* Little
Elliot, Mary. *See* Oliphant
Elliot, Robert, III, **211–12**; IV, 28, 80
Elliot*, Robert Watt (1835–1905), XII, 296
Elliot, Sir Thomas Frederick, VI, 821; VII, 6; VIII, xxxii, xxxiii, xxxiv; X, 567
Elliot, William, X, 450; XII, **296**, 738
Elliot-Murray-Kynynmound, Gilbert, 2nd Earl of Minto, VIII, xxxii
Elliott, Abner, IX, 591
Elliott, Alexander, V, 302, 303
Elliott, Andrew, V, 730
Elliott, Andrew Charles, XI, 236, **299–301**, 435, 805, 840; XII, 242, 650
Elliott, Caroline (Dewar), IX, 204
Elliott, Francis Gore, V, 303
Elliott, James Sutton, IX, 734
Elliott, Jane (Pardee), XI, 671
Elliott, John (father of ANDREW CHARLES), XI, 299
Elliott, John (witness of Louis BOYER), IX, 78
Elliott, Mary (wife of ANDREW CHARLES), XI, 299
Elliott, Matthew, V, 303
Elliott, Matthew, IV, 302, 499, 777; V, **301–3**, 306, 345, 449, 535, 536, 750, 797, 798, 799, 884; VI, 101, 102, 340; VII, 132; VIII, 119, 337; IX, 9, 407
Elliott, Robert Herriot Barclay, V, 303
Elliott, Sarah. *See* Donovan
Elliott, Thomas, I, 242, 636, 637
Ellis, Anne. *See* Jarvis
Ellis, Edward (brother-in-law of Thomas KILBY), III, 326
Ellis, Edward (landowner), XI, 307
Ellis, Elizabeth Elliott (Creelman), XII, 217
Ellis, Frances Elizabeth (Grey), X, 318
Ellis, Henry, I, 677; III, 303, 472, 562, 664; IV, 51; V, 20, 555
Ellis, Isabella (Cogswell), VIII, 167; X, 182
Ellis, James, XI, 502
Ellis, James Spencer, XII, 866, 867
Ellis, John, V, 228
Ellis, John, VIII, 347; X, **270**; XI, 541
Ellis*, John Valentine (1835–1913), XII, 1103
Ellis, Margaret (Mein), IX, 542
Ellis, Margery (McCord), VI, 432
Ellis, Mary. *See* Handford
Ellis, Mary Elizabeth (Bunting), XII, 137
Ellis, Rhoda Anne. *See* Benton
Ellis, Robert, VIII, 270
Ellis, Roswell Albert, VIII, 758
Ellis, Sarah (Deschamps), V, 250, 252
Ellis, Sarah (Kilby), III, 326
Ellis, Thomas (sailor), I, 318
Ellis, Thomas (settler), XI, 395
Ellis, Welbore, 1st Baron Mendip, IV, 336, 571; V, 870
Ellis, William, XI, 778

Ellis, William, VII, 220, **273–74**; VIII, 75
Ellis, William, VIII, **270–71**; IX, 856
Ellis, William Henry, XI, 674
Ells, Margaret, V, 851
Ells, Robert Wheelock, IX, 309
Ellyot. *See* Eliot
Elmsley, Anne Gee (Macaulay), VIII, 522
Elmsley, Charlotte. *See* Sherwood
Elmsley, John, IV, 12; V, 17, 18, 188, 226, **303–4**, 389, 440, 453, 731, 732, 815, 841, 846, 864; VI, 452, 513, 558, 578, 600, 608, 609, 611, 721; VII, 175, 373, 812, 813, 814, 920; VIII, 522; IX, 239
Elmsley, John, V, 303; VI, 467, 468; VII, 543; VIII, 11, 299, 522, 695, 797, 847, 896; IX, 49, 103, **239–42**, 535; X, 662; XI, 110, 111, 407, 903; XII, 183, 1084
Elmsley, Mary. *See* Hallowell
Elmsley, Remigius, XI, 537
Elmslie, George, VIII, 327
Elmsly (Elmslie), Alexander, V, 303
Elmsly, Anne. *See* Elligood
Elmsly (Elmslie), Peter, V, 303
Elphinston, James, V, 628
Elphinstone, George Keith, 1st Viscount Keith, V, 206
Elphinstone Fleeming, Charles, VIII, 787
Elrington, Elisabeth Golding (Marshall), X, 497
Elsdale, Mary (Molson), VII, 616
Elsdale, Samuel, VII, 617
Elskwatawa. *See* Tenskwatawa
Elson, John, XII, 1061
Elwyn, Rebecca. *See* McNeill
Elwyn, Thomas, XI, 301
Elwyn, Thomas, IX, 81; X, 112; XI, **301–2**, 394; XII, 545
Ely, Deborah. *See* Dennison
Ely, Ezra Stiles, IX, 551
Ely, Mercy (Bliss), VI, 74
Elyot. *See also* Eliot
Elyot, Richard, I, 371
Embito. *See* Ruis-Embito
Embury, Catherine (Fisher), V, 320
Embury, Margaret (Ruckle), V, 728
Embury, Philip, V, 320, 728
Eméric, Amélie (Smith), XII, 976
Emerson, Ann. *See* Bailey
Emerson, George Henry (grandfather), XI, 47; XII, 564
Emerson, George Henry, XII, 755, 756
Emerson, Hugh Alexander, XI, 761
Emerson, Ralph Waldo, III, 471; X, 537; XII, 288, 925, 927
Emerson, Rebecca (wife of THOMAS), VII, 274
Emerson, Thomas, **274–75**; VIII, 507
Émery. *See also* Particelli
Emery, Christiana (Nairne), V, 620; VII, 569
Émery, Jacques-André, IV, 90, 544; VI, 145, 396, 668
Emery, Ruhama. *See* Rich
Emery-Coderre, Héloïse-Euphémie. *See* Dasylva
Émery-Coderre, Joseph, IX, 17; XI, **302–3**; XII, 66, 530, 799, 926
Emich Charles, Prince of Leiningen, V, 298
Emmanuel, Father. *See* Veyssière, Leger-Jean-Baptiste-Noël
Emmerling, George, XI, 562; XII, 983
Emmerson*, Henry Robert (1853–1914), XII, 340
Émond, Françoise. *See* Navarre
Émond, Pierre, V, 304

Émond, Pierre, V, 51, **304–6**, 452, 659
Émonnot, Catherine (Mance), I, 483
Emory, Jane. *See* McBride
Empey, Eve (VanKoughnet), X, 693
Emray, Ann (Balfour), V, 52
Emslie, Amelia Janetta. *See* Boyd
Énard, Jeanne (Crevier), I, 238; II, 86
Énault de Barbaucannes, Philippe, I, 260; II, **217**
Énault de Livaudais, Marie-Geneviève (Fontenelle; Coulon de Villiers), IV, 177
End, Lucy. *See* Morse
End, William, VII, 637; VIII, 292, 808; X, **270–72**; XI, 90
Endemare, Georges d', I, 388
Endicot, John, I, 241
Enemikeese. *See* Vandusen, Conrad
Engel, Jacob, VI, 807
Engels, Friedrich, X, 670
England, Anne. *See* O'Brien
England, John, VIII, 144, 307
England, Margaret Hickman (Herkimer; Shaw; Leeming), XI, 326
England, Mary O'Brien (Fuller), XI, 326
England, Poole, V, 307
England, Sir Richard, V, 307
England, Richard G., V, **306–7**, 365, 552, 802, 852; VI, 21, 102, 103
Engleheart, Sir John Gardner Dillman, XII, 809
English, Caleb E., XI, 322
English, John, VI, 322; VIII, 922; IX, 54; XII, 859
English, Thomas, V, 678
English Chief. *See* Aw-gee-nah
Enjalran, Jean, II, 61, **217–18**, 383
Enmegahbowh (John Johnson), IX, 419, 421
Enneson (Anson), Sara (Sabourin), VI, 627
Enniskillen, Earl of. *See* Willoughby
Éno, *dit* Deschamps, Joséphine (Meilleur), X, 505
Énolle, Michelle (Bourneuf), X, 83
Enouille, *dit* Lanois, Julienne-Claire (Chinic), VII, 176
Enright, Cornelius T., XII, 796
Enslin, Christian, VIII, **271–72**, 701
Enslin, Julia (wife of CHRISTIAN), VIII, 271
Entheaume, Samuel, II, 223
Entremont. *See also* Mius
Entremont, Anne-Marguerite d'. *See* Pothier
Entremont, Benoni d', V, 545; VII, **275**; XI, 303
Entremont, Élisabeth d'. *See* Thériault
Entremont, Elizabeth d'. *See* Larkin
Entremont, Simon d', VIII, 275; XI, **303–4**
Épée, Charles-Michel de l', X, 298
Épernon, Duc d'. *See* Nogaret
Eppes, Abigail (Routh), V, 725; VIII, 777
Eppes, William (father-in-law of Richard ROUTH), V, 725
Eppes, William (grandfather of William Eppes CORMACK), IX, 158
Eppes, William Isham, VI, 311
Erad, Johann Burghard, III, **212**, 405
Éraque, Monsieur d' (commandant), II, 428
Érard, Sébastien, XII, 422
Erasmus, IV, 175
Erasmus*, Peter (1833–1931), XI, 849
Erasmus York. *See* Kallihirua
Erb, Abraham, VI, **235–36**; VIII, 265
Erb, Christian, VI, 235

Erb, Daniel, VI, 235; VIII, 265
Erb, Jacob, VI, 235; VII, 351, 641
Erb, John, VI, 235
Erb, Magdalena (Erb; Eby), VI, 235; VIII, 265
Erb, Maria. *See* Scherch
Erhardt, John Christian, III, **212–13**
Eric, Bishop. *See* Eiríkr *upsi* Gnupsson
Eric the Red. *See* Eiríkr Thorvaldsson
Erlan, Anne. *See* Kilgallen
Erlandson, Erland, X, **272–73**, 284; XI, 569, 570
Ermatinger, Lieutenant, X, 694
Ermatinger, Achsah. *See* Burnham
Ermatinger, Anna Maria. *See* Buhl
Ermatinger, Caroline-Élisa. *See* Juchereau Duchesnay
Ermatinger, Charles Oakes, VI, 237; VIII, 209; IX, 242, 243
Ermatinger, Charles Oakes, IV, 263; VI, **236–37**, 238, 254, 547; IX, 242; X, 273
Ermatinger, Charles Oakes Zaccheus, VII, 126; VIII, 861
Ermatinger, Charlotte. *See* Cattoonaluté
Ermatinger, Edward, VII, 93, 126; VIII, 117, 527, 861, 967; IX, 475, 852, 854; X, **273–74**; XI, 882; XII, 550, 612
Ermatinger, Francis, VII, 672; X, 273, 486
Ermatinger, Frederick William, IV, 263; V, 285, 383, 384, 614; VI, 179, 236, **237–39**, 254, 499; VII, 619; VIII, 389, 631; IX, 242; XII, 676
Ermatinger, Frederick William, VI, 237; IX, **242–43**; XI, 850
Ermatinger, George, VI, 179
Ermatinger, Jemima. *See* Oakes
Ermatinger, Laurenz, IV, 262
Ermatinger, Lawrence, IV, **262–63**, 330, 585; V, 258, 382, 383; VI, 236, 237; X, 273
Ermatinger, Lawrence Edward, IV, 263; VI, 237; X, 273
Ermon. *See* Ormond
Ernest Augustus, King of Hanover (Ernest Augustus, Duke of Cumberland), VIII, 857; X, 121, 309
Ernestine, XI, 382
Ernette, Victor, XII, 846
Ernst, Heinrich Wilhelm, VIII, 347
Ernst, Johann Jakob, VIII, 271
Erouachy (Eroachi), I, 211, 222, **302–3**, 479, 509
Erskine. *See also* Askin
Erskine, Alexander, 5th Earl of Kellie, III, 131
Erskine, David Montagu, VI, 333
Erskine, Ebenezer, VI, 457; VII, 529; VIII, 451; XII, 489
Erskine, Lady Elizabeth (Macfarlane; Colvill, Baroness Colvill), III, 131
Erskine, Janet (Alexander, Countess of Stirling), I, 50
Erskine, John, 3rd Earl of Mar, I, 50
Erskine, John, 23rd Earl of Mar, V, 37
Erskine, Louisa, Lady Erskine. *See* Paget
Erskine, Margaret (Woolford), IX, 849, 850
Erskine, Sir William, I, 50
Erskine of Torriehouse, Sir James, VII, 640
Erxleben, C. A. (Miertsching), X, 513
Escairac (Desquairac, Desquerac), Pierre d', II, 410, 603
Escande. *See* Poursin-Escande
Eschaux, Bertrand d', I, 352
Eschlemann, Elizabeth (Wenger), VI, 807
Escourre, Pierre, IV, 124
Escuyer, Élisabeth (Aubin), XI, 34
Esdaile, John, IX, 555, 558

Esdaile, Robert, V, 320; IX, 558
Esgly (Esglis). *See* Mariauchau
Esgriseilles. *See* Dubois
Esmainville. *See* Du Sicquet
Esmanville, Father d', I, 180
Esmard, Anne (Couture), II, 158, 159
Esmard (Esmart), Barbe (Michel; Letardif), I, 473; II, 158
Esmard, Madeleine (Cloutier), II, 158
Esmond, Marie-Anne, II, 141
Esnault. *See also* Énault
Esnault, Marie (Pichon), IV, 630
Esneval. *See* Leroux
Espagnoli. *See* Spagniolini
Espérance, I, 196, **199–200**, 237, 366, 452, 494
Espiet, Jean-Georges d', II, 220
Espiet de La Plagne, Pierre-Paul d', II, 220; IV, 783
Espiet de Pensens, Jacques d', II, 123, **218–20**, 339, 412, 498, 668; III, 20, 173, 178, 436, 532, 533, 566, 615; IV, 15, 247
Espiet de Pensens, Jean d', II, 220
Espinay de Saint-Luc, François d', Marquis de Saint-Luc, I, 133
Espinay de Saint-Luc, Timoléon d', Marquis de Saint-Luc, I, 133
Espinosa y Tello, José, V, 140
Esprit, Marie-Louise (Guillet de Chaumont), III, 269
Esprit de Vantelon, François, IV, 124
Esprit de Vantelon, Françoise. *See* Cadet
Esprit Errant. *See* Kapapamahchakwew
Esquairac. *See* Escairac
Esrouachit. *See* Erouachy
Essens. *See* Aisance
Essling, Prince d'. *See* Masséna
Esson, Adam, IX, 243
Esson, Campbell Sweeny, VIII, 272
Esson, Charles (father), IX, 243
Esson, Charles, IX, 243
Esson, Elizabeth. *See* Campbell
Esson, Elizabeth. *See* Whyte
Esson, Harriet Ann. *See* Leonard
Esson, Henry, VI, 105, 478; VII, 77, 575, 701, 821, 887; VIII, 21, 68, **272–73**, 310, 666; X, 606; XI, 467; XII, 986
Esson, Henry Robert, VIII, 272
Esson, Jean (Gale), VIII, 310
Esson, John, VII, 492; IX, **243–44**
Esson, Maria. *See* Sweeny
Esson, William, IX, 243
Est, *dit* Condeau, François. *See* Condo, Francis
Estaing, Jean-Baptiste-Charles (Charles-Henri) d', Comte d'Estaing, IV, 122, 153, 282; V, 105, 173, 176, 893; VI, 271; VII, 255
Estcourt, Caroline. *See* Pole Carew
Estcourt, Eleanor. *See* Sutton
Estcourt, James Bucknall Bucknall, VIII, **273–76**; XII, 463
Estcourt, Thomas Grimstone Bucknall, VIII, 273
Este, Rinaldo d', Prince of Este, II, 144
Estèbe, Arnaud (Armand), IV, 263
Estèbe, Élisabeth. *See* Garde
Estèbe, Élisabeth-Cécile. *See* Thibierge
Estèbe, Guillaume, III, 124, 125, 160, 165, 300, 433, 524, 593; IV, 66, 67, 91, 209, **263–64**, 271, 361, 433, 447, 615, 750, 755
Esten, Ann Frederica. *See* Hutchison

Esten, Ester. *See* Palmer
Esten, James Christie, IX, 244
Esten, James Christie Palmer, VIII, 426, 427; IX, 57, **244–45**
Estève, Marguerite (Chapoton), III, 102
Estienne Du Bourgué, Denis d', II, 220
Estienne Du Bourgué, Françoise d'. *See* Desvoges de Clérin
Estienne Du Bourgué de Clérin, Denis d', II, **220–21**, 673; III, 164; IV, 720
Estienne Du Bourgué de Clérin, Jeanne d'. *See* Le Selle
Estienne Du Bourgué de Clérin, Marie-Louise d' (Souste), IV, 720
Estienne Du Bourgué de Clérin, Suzanne d' (Danré de Blanzy), III, 164
Estimauville, Jean-Baptiste-Philippe d', VI, 239; XII, 296
Estimauville, Jean-Baptiste-Philippe-Charles d', V, 61; VI, **239–40**, 658, 753; IX, 683
Estimauville, Joséphine-Éléonore d' (Taché; Clément), VIII, 457; XII, 65, **296–97**
Estimauville, Marguerite d' (Rolland), IX, 362, 683
Estimauville, Marie-Joseph d'. *See* Drapeau
Estimauville, Marie-Josephte d'. *See* Courreaud de La Coste
Estimauville, Martha d'. *See* Blythe
Estimauville, Robert-Anne d', VI, 239, **240–42**, 658, 659; VII, 80, 769; VIII, 154
Estimauville de Beaumouchel, Jean-Baptiste-Philippe d', VI, 239, 240
Estimauville de Beaumouchel, Marie-Charlotte d'. *See* Ailleboust
Estissac, Duc d'. *See* La Rochefoucauld; La Rochefoucauld de Roye
Estissac, Duchesse d'. *See* Lannion; La Rochefoucauld
Estourmel, Constantin-Louis d', III, **213–14**, 356, 610; IV, 454
Estourmel, Louis d', Marquis d'Estourmel, III, 213
Estourmel, Marie-Aimée d', Marquise d'Estourmel. *See* Hautefort de Montignac
Estrades, Godefroi-Louis, Comte d'Estrades, I, 185, 284, 554, 587
Estrées, Jean d', I, 443; II, 538
Estrées, Lucie-Félicité d', Duchesse d'Estrées. *See* Noailles
Etches, Richard Cadman, V, 686
Etherington, George, III, 13, 262, 306; IV, 233, 241, 564; V, 7, 567
Éthier, Joseph-Arthur-Calixte, VII, 174
Étienne. *See also* Annaotaha; Petit-Étienne; Pigarouich; Totiri
Étienne, Claude, I, 223, 495
Étienne, Hélène. *See* Martin
Étioles. *See* Le Normant
Étouat, I, 516
Etter, Benjamin, VI, **242–43**
Etter, Benjamin B., VI, 242
Etter, Margaret Elizabeth. *See* Tidmarsh
Etter, Mary. *See* Bessonett
Etter, Peter (father), VI, 242
Etter, Peter, VI, 242
Etter, Sarah. *See* Holmes
Ettwein, John, V, 884
Euart. *See also* Ewart
Euart, Margaret. *See* Dobson

Euart, William, VIII, 280
Euclid, XII, 961
Eudes, Jean, II, 303
Eugene. *See* Huyghe, Samuel Douglass Smith
Eugénie, Empress of the French. *See* Montijo
Eury de La Pérelle, Catherine (Céloron de Blainville), III, 99; V, 174
Eury de La Pérelle, Jean-François, II, 339
Eustache. *See* Ahatsistari
Eutizi, Rosa (Nobili), VIII, 654
Euverte, Brother. *See* Demarquay
Evans, Ann. *See* Thomas
Evans, Benjamin, IX, 474
Evans, Catherine. *See* Jones
Evans, Catherine (Morrin), IX, 572
Evans, Catherine Maria (Hellmuth), IX, 246
Evans, Charlotte. *See* Shaw
Evans, Edward, XI, 432, 762
Evans, Emily Anne (Crooks), IX, 246; XI, 220
Evans, Ephraim, VII, 276; VIII, 216, 372, 373; IX, 736; X, 616, 701; XI, 729; XII, **297–98**
Evans, Eugenia Clarissa (McLean), VII, 277; XI, 569
Evans, Francis, VIII, 276
Evans, Francis, VI, 717; VIII, **276–77**
Evans, Francis Armstrong, VIII, 221
Evans, Sir George de Lacy, VIII, 745; IX, 81, 201
Evans, Geraint Nantglyn Davies, VI, 197
Evans, Harriet Lawrence. *See* Ogden
Evans, James, VII, 275; XII, 297
Evans, James, VII, 3, 55, **275–78**, 390; IX, 419, 732, 750, 784; X, 4, 373; XI, 436, 509, 569, 660, 849, 886; XII, 128, 297, 446, 931
Evans, Jane. *See* Stephens
Evans, John (commodore), IV, 161, 471
Evans, John (shipbuilder), VIII, 270
Evans, John, X, **274–75**
Evans, John J., X, 335
Evans, Lewis, VIII, 607
Evans, Maria Sophia. *See* Lewis
Evans, Martha (Evans), X, 274
Evans, Martha (Owen), VIII, 668
Evans, Mary (mother of EPHRAIM), XII, 297
Evans, Mary (mother of JAMES), VII, 275
Evans, Mary (Jenkins), XII, 472
Evans, Mary (Price), IX, 638
Evans, Mary Ann (Marian) (George Eliot), XII, 776
Evans, Mary Blithe. *See* Smith
Evans, Mary E. *See* Gunn
Evans, Onesimus, VII, 364
Evans, Richard, IX, 245
Evans, Richard John, IX, 246
Evans, Samuel, X, 10
Evans, Selina. *See* Wood
Evans, Simon, IV, 759
Evans, Taliesin, X, 274
Evans, Thomas, X, 10
Evans, Thomas, V, 113; VIII, 276, 794; IX, **245–46**, 292; XI, 220
Evans, W. L., VIII, 568
Evans, William (partner of Thomas Brown ANDERSON), X, 10
Evans, William (son-in-law of François-Marie PICOTÉ de Belestre), IV, 634

Evans, William (son of WILLIAM), VIII, 277
Evans, William, VII, 345, 347; VIII, 266, **277–79**; IX, 612
Evans, William B., VIII, 277
Évanturel, François, XII, 298
Évanturel, François, VIII, 291; IX, 771; X, 203, 213; XII, **298–300**, 1065
Évanturel, Louise-Jeanne-Eugénie. *See* Huot
Évanturel, Marie-Anne. *See* Bédard
Évanturel, Sophie (Suzor), IX, 771
Evarts, William Maxwell, X, 63
Evatt, Jane (McLaren), IX, 511
Eveleth, Sarah (Glasier), IV, 299
Evelin, Robert, I, 673
Evelyn-Glanville, Frances (Boscawen), III, 70
Everest, Olivia (Porteous), VI, 602
Everett, Alexander Hill, X, 606
Everett, Charlotte Jane (Birdsall), VIII, 91
Everett, Mary (Wallbridge), XI, 908
Everill, Elizabeth. *See* Phillips
Everitt, Mary Ann (Haskins), VII, 389
Evertsen, Cornelis, I, 196
Evison, Robert, III, **214**, 520
Ewart, Catherine Seaton. *See* Skirving
Ewart*, David (1843–1921), XII, 346
Ewart, George, VIII, 282
Ewart, James Bell, VIII, 280
Ewart, James Bell, VI, 253; VIII, **279–80**, 687; XII, 107
Ewart, Jane. *See* Wilson
Ewart, Jane (Mowat, Lady Mowat), VIII, 282; XII, 973
Ewart, Jane Emily (Steele), XII, 974
Ewart, Jane Frances (Bethune), XII, 107
Ewart, John, VIII, 282
Ewart, John, VII, 37, 843; VIII, **280–82**, 485, 596, 750, 959, 960; IX, 618
Ewart*, John Skirving (1849–1933), VIII, 282; XII, 585, 974
Ewart, Louise E. (Henderson), XII, 974
Ewart, Mary Margaret. *See* Crooks
Ewart, Thomas, X, 359; XII, 973
Ewen*, Alexander (1832–1907), XII, 768, 1063
Ewer. *See also* Yore
Ewer, Catherine (mother of THOMAS ANTHONY), VI, 243
Ewer, John, VI, 243
Ewer, Thomas Anthony, V, 632; VI, **243–45**, 691; VII, 292, 403; VIII, 198
Ewing, Alexander, XI, 333
Ewing, Calvin, XI, 638
Ewing, Janet (Mathieson), IX, 539
Ewing, Juliana Horatia. *See* Gatty
Exmouth, Viscount. *See* Pellew
Eymard, Jean, III, 272
Eynard, Jacques, X, 275
Eynard, Marie-Anne-Agathe. *See* Lévêque
Eynard, Marie-Germain-Émile, X, **275–76**
Eynon, Ann (Down; wife of JOHN HICKS), XI, 304
Eynon, Elizabeth. *See* Dart
Eynon, John Hicks, VIII, 200, 425, 908; XI, **304–5**
Eyquem de Montaigne, Michel, III, 334
Eyre, Sir William, XI, 759
Eyre, William, III, **214–15**; IV, 299

FABER (Fabert). *See* Lefebvre
Faber, John, III, 624

Fabre. *See also* Sales Laterrière
Fabre, Monsieur (probably father of Pierre de SALES Laterrière), V, 735
Fabre, Édouard-Charles, VII, 174; VIII, 286; X, 151, 252, 658; XI, 104, 110, 424, 894; XII, **300–5**, 359, 362, 371, 502, 573, 698, 799, 821, 1022
Fabre, Édouard-Raymond, VI, 784; VII, 148, 208, 226, 247, 512, 513, 757; VIII, 137, 259, 262, **282–86**, 408, 667, 668, 694, 730, 781, 914, 915; IX, 448, 596, 614, 633, 814; X, 52, 151, 236, 554, 555, 575; XI, 188, 273, 275, 659, 821; XII, 254, 260, 261, 300, 301
Fabre*, Hector (1834–1910), VII, 514; VIII, 286; X, 151, 154, 262, 304; XI, 71, 100, 184, 338, 343, 722, 814; XII, 179, 262, 299, 1065
Fabre, Hortense (Cartier, Lady Cartier), VIII, 286; X, 151; XII, 301
Fabre, Josephte (Trudel), VIII, 282
Fabre, Julie (Bossange), VIII, 282, 283; XII, 301
Fabre, Luce. *See* Perrault
Fabre, Marie-Anne. *See* Lamontagne
Fabre, Pierre, VIII, 282
Fabre, Raymond, VIII, 282
Fabre, Sophie (Gravel), VIII, 282, 283
Fabre, *dit* Laperrière, Catherine. *See* Aubuchon, *dit* Lespérance
Fabre, *dit* Laperrière, Henri-Marie-Paschal (Pascal Rustan), V, 277, 735, 736
Fabre Surveyer, Édouard, V, 37, 530, 577; VII, 69
Fabry de La Bruyère, André, III, 424
Fabus, Michel-Henri, IV, 422
Fabvre, Bonaventure, II, 161
Facile, Brother. *See* Rabut, Benoît
Fadette. *See* Dessaulles, Henriette
Faerrie, James, IX, 258
Faerrie, Jean. *See* Robertson
Fafard, Abel, XI, 306
Fafard, Ambroise, XI, 873
Fafard, Anna-Séphora. *See* Germain
Fafard, Appoline. *See* Claude
Fafard, Charles, XI, 305
Fafard, Jean, II, 488
Fafard, Léon-Adélard, XI, **305–6**, 460; XII, 478
Fafard, Norbert (father), XI, 306
Fafard, Norbert, XI, 306
Fafard, Tersile. *See* Olivier
Fafard, Théogène, XI, **306–7**
Fafard, Thiennette (Boivin), I, 106
Fafard, *dit* Laframboise, Marguerite (Grant), V, 376
Fafard de La Framboise, Jean-Baptiste, III, 541
Fafard Laframboise, Marie-Victoire (Cressé), V, 216
Fagot, Marie-Madeleine (Jourdain, *dit* Labrosse), III, 316
Fagundes, João Alvares, I, 21, 166, 171, **303–4**, 422
Faguy, François-Xavier, XII, 46
Fahey, F., XI, 307
Fahey, James A., XI, **307–8**
Faifeu, Julienne (Cuillerier), II, 164
Faillon, Claire. *See* Raoûx
Faillon, Étienne-Michel, III, 629, 692; VIII, 911; IX, 51, 228, **246–49**, 255, 256, 448, 450; XI, 489, 490, 776, 821, 851; XII, 223
Faillon, Jacques-Michel, IX, 246
Fain, Isabelle (Dandonneau), II, 168
Fainante, Monsieur (NWC employee), V, 564

Fairbanks, Anne. *See* Prescott

Fairbanks, Catherine, VII, 280

Fairbanks, Charles Rufus, VII, 25, 82, 84, 189, **278–80**, 532, 933; VIII, 36; IX, 225; X, 383, 551; XI, 308, 944

Fairbanks, Charlotte Ann. *See* Newton

Fairbanks, Constance, XI, 463

Fairbanks, Joseph, IV, 704

Fairbanks, Rufus (brother-in-law of Charles Ramage PRESCOTT), VIII, 709

Fairbanks, Rufus (father of CHARLES RUFUS and SAMUEL PRESCOTT), VII, 278; XI, 308

Fairbanks, Samuel Prescott, VII, 278; VIII, 74, 382; XI, **308–9**, 944

Fairbanks, Sarah Elizabeth. *See* Lawson

Fairbanks, William B., VIII, 183

Fairborne, Sir Stafford, II, 290, 373, 564

Fairbrother, Anne (Amelia) (Hill), XII, **305–6**

Fairbrother, Mary. *See* Bailey

Fairbrother, Robert, XII, 305

Fairchild*, George Moore (1854–1912), X, 413

Fairchild, Jemima (McCall), VI, 421

Fairfield, Abigail. *See* Baker

Fairfield, Benjamin, V, 307, 308

Fairfield, Clarissa. *See* Fulton

Fairfield, Elizabeth. *See* Billings

Fairfield, John, VIII, 379

Fairfield, Stephen, V, 307, 308

Fairfield, William, V, 307

Fairfield, William, V, **307–8**; VII, 558

Fairholme, Caroline, XI, 664

Fairholme, William, XI, 661

Fairly, Marion (Veitch), II, 650

Fairweather, Charles Henry, XII, **306–8**

Fairweather, James, XII, 306

Fairweather, Lucille H. *See* Hall

Fairweather, Margaret R. *See* Robertson

Fairweather, Martha. *See* Humbert

Faithfull, Emily, VIII, 651

Falaise (Falaize). *See* Gannes

Falardeau, Antoine-Sébastien, IX, 113, 298, 792; XI, **309–10**; XII, 848

Falardeau, Caterina. *See* Mannucci-Benincasa

Falardeau, Édouard-Sébastien, XI, 905

Falardeau, Élisabeth. *See* Deguise, *dit* Flamand

Falardeau, Isabelle. *See* Savard

Falardeau, Joseph (father of ANTOINE-SÉBASTIEN), XI, 309

Falardeau, Joseph (son-in-law of Jacques DEGUISE, *dit* Flamand), IV, 203

Falardeau, Marie. *See* Vincent

Falcon, Mary. *See* Grant

Falcon, Pierre, V, 535; X, 276

Falcon, Pierre, IV, 310; VII, 250; X, **276–77**

Falconbridge*, John Delatre (1875–1968), XII, 887

Falconer, Henrietta (Roebuck), X, 626

Falconer, Margaret Malissa (McIntyre), XII, 634

Falconer, Thomas, IV, 300

Falconer, William, VI, 320

Falcoz, Mathieu, III, 422

Falk, Minnie (Davis), XII, 228

Falkiner, Sir Charles Leslie, XII, 1082

Falkingham, Edward, III, 216

Falkingham, Edward, II, 25, 316; III, 126, **215–16**

Falkland, Viscount. *See* Cary

Falkland, Viscountess. *See* Anton; FitzClarence; Gubbins

Falkner, Joseph-Pascal, XII, 263

Fallon*, Michael Francis (1867–1931), IX, 215

Falloux, Frédéric, Comte de Falloux, XI, 339; XII, 819

Falmouth, Viscount. *See* Boscawen

Fancamp, Baron de. *See* Chevrier

Fane, Anne (Michel), XI, 591

Fane, Lady Cecilia Georgiana, X, 593; XI, 241

Fane, Sir Henry, XI, 591

Fane, John, 10th Earl of Westmorland, VI, 359, 567; VII, 439

Faneuil, Mr (father or uncle of Peter), II, 482

Faneuil, Peter, II, 482; III, 326; IV, 253, 273

Fanning, David, VI, 245

Fanning, David, VI, **245–47**

Fanning, Edmund, IV, 129, 551, 610; V, 27, 28, 219, 250, 262, 263, **308–12**, 424, 425, 431, 478, 515, 516, 568, 569, 717, 720, 775, 778, 779, 825, 826, 847, 848, 866; VI, 65, 107, 108, 161, 195, 297, 298, 413, 565, 682, 736, 737; VII, 406, 407, 864; VIII, 35; XI, 369

Fanning, Hannah. *See* Smith

Fanning, James, V, 308

Fanning, Phoebe Maria. *See* Burns

Fanning, Sarah. *See* Carr

Far, Walter, I, 578; II, 318

Faraday, Michael, VIII, 867; IX, 162, 277, 309; XI, 218

Faraud, François-Xavier, XI, 310

Faraud, Henri, IX, 342; X, 275, 614; XI, **310–11**; XII, 170, 1004, 1005, 1006

Faraud, Madeleine. *See* Faurye

Farcy, Ambroise de, VI, 620, 623

Farewell, Abram, XI, **311–12**, 346, 347

Farewell, Acheus Moody, XI, 311

Farewell, Caroline. *See* Stone

Farewell, Elizabeth. *See* Annis

Fargis, James, IX, 717

Fargues, Henriette. *See* Guichaud

Fargues, Jean, V, 290

Fargues, Pierre, V, 287, 290, 492, 601; VII, 280

Fargues, Thomas, V, 290, 291; VI, 326, 597; VII, **280–81**, 650; VIII, 682

Faribault, Adolphe, VIII, 288

Faribault, Alexander, VIII, 287

Faribault, Aurélie (Saint-Ours; Viger), VIII, 288, 916

Faribault, Barthélemi, IX, 249

Faribault, Barthélemy, V, 817

Faribault, Barthélemy, V, 271, **312–13**, 817; VIII, 286, 287

Faribault, Bernard, V, 312

Faribault, Catherine (Jolliet; Pétrimoulx), VII, 446

Faribault, Catherine-Antoine. *See* Véronneau

Faribault, Emily (Fowler), VIII, 287

Faribault, Geneviève. *See* Fauteux

Faribault, Georges-Barthélemi, V, 330, 649; VI, 40, 84, 585; VII, 72; VIII, 594; IX, **249–51**, 261, 301, 303, 359, 360, 450; X, 21; XI, 588

Faribault, Georgina-Mathilde (Hamel), IX, 249, 359

Faribault, Jacques-Eugène, VIII, 288

Faribault, Jean-Baptiste, VI, 29; VIII, **286–87**

Faribault, Jean-Marie, VIII, 288

Faribault, Joseph-Édouard, V, 313; VII, 447; VIII, 286, **287–89**, 331, 501, 916

Faribault, Lucie-Anne (Bailly), VI, 29

Faribault, Madelaine. *See* Hamon

Faribault, Marie-Anne-Élisabeth. *See* Poudret
Faribault, Marie-Julie. *See* Planté
Faribault, Marie-Reine. *See* Anderson
Faribault, Narcisse, VIII, 288
Faribault, Norbert, VIII, 288
Faribault, Pelagie. *See* Hince
Farington, Joseph, VI, 257
Farish, Frances Isabella (Baker), XII, 50
Farley, Alfred M., XII, 62
Farley, Anne (Scatcherd), X, 644
Farmar, Hugh Hovell, VII, 35
Farmer, Ferdinand. *See* Steinmeyer, Ferdinand
Farmer, Marguerite. *See* Power
Farmer, William, XII, 1129
Farmer, William A., XI, 193
Farnham, Charles Haight, XII, 827
Farnham, Elizabeth (Clarkson), X, 174
Farquharson, Agnes Campbell (Schultz, Lady Schultz), XII, 949, 954
Farquharson, Janet (Cameron), X, 114
Farr, Robert, VII, 207
Farr, Timothy J., X, 450
Farrain, Charles, VI, 712
Farrand, Christine. *See* Bethune
Farrand, J. W., IX, 550
Farrar. *See also* Ferrar
Farrar, Alma. *See* Lawrence
Farrar, Ebenezer Lawrence (uncle), XI, 312
Farrar, Ebenezer Lawrence, XI, 312
Farrar, George Henry, XI, 312
Farrar, George Whitefield, XI, **312–13**, 550, 551
Farrar, Isaac Brown, XI, 312
Farrar, Jacob, XI, 312
Farrar, Sarah. *See* Dean
Farrar, Sophia Adams. *See* Winslow
Farrell*, Edward (1842–1901), XII, 438
Farrell, James, X, 277
Farrell, Joan. *See* Patterson
Farrell, John, VIII, 318, 704; IX, 31, 104, 325; X, **277–78**, 662; XII, 183
Farrell, Margaret (Kavanagh), VI, 370
Farrell, Patrick, X, 234
Farrell, Paul, VII, 840
Farrer*, Edward (1850–1916), XI, 307; XII, 138, 585, 610
Farries, Charlotte. *See* Robertson
Farries, Francis Wallace, XI, 468
Farries, John, V, 716
Farrington, Harvey, XII, 171
Farwell, Abel, X, 371
Farwell, Arthur Stanhope, IX, 115
Fassett, Jonathan, VII, 926
Fassio, Eugenio, VIII, 289, 290, 291
Fassio, Gerome, VII, 790; VIII, **289–91**, 495; XI, 309
Fastray, Basile, VIII, 66; IX, 397
Father of Many Children. *See also* Onista'poka; Stoókyatosi
Father of Many Children, XII, 803
Fauché, Marguerite (Collet), V, 195
Faucher, Catherine-Henriette. *See* Mercier
Faucher, Édouard, IX, 362
Faucher, Geneviève-Françoise (Lefebvre Angers), III, 371
Faucher, Marie-Josephte (Planté), VI, 585
Faucher, Marie-Louise (Philippon), VI, 581

Faucher, Narcisse-Constantin, XII, 308
Faucher, *dit* Saint-Maurice, Léonard, XII, 308
Faucher de Saint-Maurice, Joséphine. *See* Berthelot
Faucher de Saint-Maurice, Narcisse-Henri-Édouard, X, 163, 432; XI, 83, 490, 852; XII, 236, 271, **308–9**, 725
Fauchois, Michel, II, 378
Faucon, Antoine, IV, 521
Faucon Dumanoir, Marie (Payen de Noyan), III, 502
Faucrolle (Foucrelle), Françoise (La Porte), II, 345
Faulkner, Elizabeth. *See* Trefry
Faulkner, Hannah (Morrison), XI, 619
Fauquier, Frederick Dawson, X, 56; XI, **313–15**, 450; XII, 1001
Fauquier, Sarah. *See* Burrowes
Fauquier, Thomas, XI, 313
Faure, Madelaine (Baudrand), VIII, 66
Faure, Madeleine. *See* Brulart de Sillery
Faure de Berlise, Angélique (Bullion), I, 220, 484, 485, 486; II, 491
Faure de Berlise, Guichard, I, 484
Faurye, Madeleine (Faraud), XI, 310
Faustin, Élisabeth (Le Coutre de Bourville), III, 367
Fauteux, Ægidius, III, 603; IV, 34, 36, 107, 698, 755; V, 735; VII, 150, 248; VIII, 470, 471, 616, 668, 736, 915; IX, 43; X, 41, 418; XI, 709
Fauteux, Geneviève (Hénault; Faribault), VIII, 288
Fauteux, Héva. *See* Mercier
Fauteux, Joseph-Noël, IV, 376
Fautoux, Sieur (ship's captain), III, 124
Fautoux, Georges, III, 216
Fautoux, Léon, III, **216**, 281, 357, 501
Fautoux, Marie. *See* Meyracq
Fautoux, Marie-Madeleine. *See* Lartigue
Fauvault, Jeanne (Le Prévost), III, 391
Fauvel, Emma. *See* Du Heaume
Fauvel, George Philip, XII, 310
Fauvel, Henriette-Marie. *See* Le Boutillier
Fauvel, John, VIII, 257; XII, 309
Fauvel, John Bertram, XII, 310
Fauvel, Louise (Léger), II, 387
Fauvel, William Le Boutillier, XII, **309–10**
Fauvenel, Jeanne (Dupuy), I, 297
Favar, Marie (Dumas), V, 276
Favell, John, V, 534
Favell, Mary (McKay), V, 534; X, 475
Faveron, Marie-Jeanne (Corbin), III, 138
Favery, Marie (Legardeur de Repentigny), I, 447, 637; II, 385
Favre. *See also* Montferrand
Favre, René, I, 105
Favre, *dit* Montferrand, François, IX, 562
Favre, *dit* Montferrand, François-Joseph, IX, 561
Favre, *dit* Montferrand, Marie-Louise. *See* Couvret
Favry Du Ponceau, Anne-Marie (Martel de Brouague), III, 434
Fawcett, Edgar, X, 260
Fawson, Jones, VI, 173
Fay, Claude, VI, 669; VII, 746; VIII, 730, 736, 864
Fay, Marie-Victor-Nicolas, Marquis de Latour-Maubourg, VII, 486
Fayard, Augustin, XI, 173
Fayard, Joseph, IX, 453
Faye, Anne de (Mars), II, 301

Faye, Claude de (Gallard), II, 235
Fearson, Marie-Joseph (Charland), V, 183
Feathers. *See* A-ca-oo-mah-ca-ye
Featherstonhaugh, George W., VIII, 379
Fébronie, Sister. *See* Fontbonne
Féderbe, Louis-Laurent de, Comte de Maudave, IV, 752
Fee, William G., XII, 584
Feild, Edward, IV, 438; VIII, 94, 104, 380, 447, 644, 725; IX, 30, 379, 460, 468, 469, 582, 584, 695; X, **278–81**, 318, 663; XI, 43, 44, 66, 74, 391, 392, 431, 432, 433, 762; XII, 364, 574, 575, 590, 759, 760
Feild, James, X, 278
Feild, Sophia. *See* Bevan
Feilde, Matthew Smithers, VI, 526; IX, 578
Feilding, Basil, 2nd Earl of Denbigh, I, 241
Feitten, Magdeleine (Tröstler), V, 827
Féligonde. *See* Pélissier
Félix, Brother. *See* Bossu, *dit* Lyonnais
Félix, Jeanne (Léger), II, 387
Félix, Marie-Louise (Girouard), VIII, 331
Félix, Maurice-Joseph, VII, 258; VIII, 331
Félix, Victoire (Dumouchelle), VII, 258
Fell, Charles Kinsey, VIII, 785
Fellenberg, Philipp Emanuel von, VII, 344; X, 497
Feller, François-Xavier de, VII, 886
Feller, Henriette. *See* Odin
Feller, Louis, IX, 608
Fellière. *See* Deschamps
Fellowes (Lyon), George Byron, VIII, 510
Fellows (Fellowes), Annie Starr (Shannon), XII, 966
Fellows, Catherine (Troop), XI, 888
Fels. *See* Feltz
Felt, Joseph Barlow, III, 707
Felton, Anna Maria. *See* Valls
Felton, Charles Bridgeman, VII, 281, 282
Felton, Clara. *See* Lloyd
Felton, Elizabeth. *See* Butt
Felton, Eliza Margaret (Aylwin), X, 24
Felton, John (father), VII, 281
Felton, John, VII, 281; VIII, 221
Felton, William Bowman, VII, 191, **281–84**, 797; VIII, 147; X, 282
Felton, William Hughes, X, 282
Felton, William Locker Pickmore, VII, 281, 283, 836; IX, 614; X, 249, **281–82**; XII, 352
Feltz, Cécile. *See* Gosselin
Feltz, Charles-Elemy-Joseph-Alexandre-Ferdinand, IV, **264–65**, 434; V, 201
Feltz, Elemy-Victor, IV, 264
Feltz, Marie-Ursule. *See* Aubert de La Chesnaye
Feltz, Marie-Ursule. *See* Mouthe
Felx. *See* Feltz
Fénelon. *See also* La Mothe-Fénelon
Fénelon, Abbé de. *See* Salignac de La Mothe-Fénelon, François de
Fenelon, Ellen. *See* Kitchen
Fenelon, Maurice, XI, 466; XII, **310–11**, 755, 956
Fenerty, Ann. *See* Hamilton
Fenerty, Charles, XII, **311–13**
Fenerty, Elizabeth. *See* Lawson
Fenerty, James, XII, 311
Fenerty, Mary. *See* Hall
Fenerty, William, XII, 313

Fenety, Mrs. *See* Wallace
Fenety, Eliza Ann. *See* Arthur
Fenety, George Edward, VII, 107, 601; VIII, 193, 868; IX, 148, 622, 623; X, 271, 287, 543, 711, 712; XI, 372, 375; XII, 307, **313–14**, 537, 566, 895, 896, 897, 1051, 1103
Fenety, William, XII, 313
Fenlon, Walter Welsh, VIII, 552, 583
Fenouillet, Émile de, VIII, **291–92**
Fenton, Edward, I, 317
Fenton, Elizabeth (McLearn), VIII, 566
Fenton, John, X, 199
Fenwick, Alexander Greig, XII, 314
Fenwick, Augusta Julia (Winniett, Lady Winniett), VII, 918
Fenwick, Benedict Joseph, II, 544; VIII, 406
Fenwick, Eliza Charlotte. *See* Hertel
Fenwick, George Edgeworth, XII, **314–16**, 1128, 1129
Fenwick, Joseph, XII, 314
Fenwick, Margaret Elizabeth. *See* Greig
Fenwick, William, VII, 918
Ferchaud, Laurent, I, 593
Ferchault de Réaumur, René-Antoine, II, 595, 599; III, 675, 678, 679, 680
Fercourt. *See* Perrot
Ferdinand, Duke of Brunswick, V, 166, 584
Ferdinand I, King of the Two Sicilies (Ferdinand IV of Naples), V, 400; X, 59, 497
Ferdinand II, King of Aragon and Sicily, I, 41, 147, 154, 155, 241
Ferdinand VII, King of Spain, VII, 543
Féré, Émery, VII, 173
Féré, Jean-Baptiste, VI, 386
Fereday, Elizabeth (Smith), IX, 730
Fereday, Samuel, IX, 730
Feré Duburon, Jean-Joseph, II, 274; IV, 123, 306
Feré Duburon, Jeanne. *See* Durand
Feré Duburon, Louise-Élisabeth (Goguet), IV, 123, 306
Fergus, James, XI, 353
Ferguson, Mrs (wife of BARTEMAS), VI, 248
Ferguson, Adam, VIII, 292
Ferguson, Agnes (Gow), XI, 366
Ferguson, Alexander, VIII, 292
Ferguson*, Alexander Hugh (1853–1911), XII, 1095
Ferguson, Andrew, X, 282
Ferguson, Ann (MacIntosh), VIII, 549
Ferguson, Archibald, XI, 271
Ferguson, Bartemas, V, 661; VI, 92, 159, 230, **247–49**, 421, 543, 579, 747; VII, 37, 251, 369; VIII, 69, 945, 946; IX, 334
Ferguson, Catherine (Scott), VIII, 791
Ferguson, David, VIII, 550
Ferguson, Elizabeth (Douglas), XI, 271
Ferguson, Emily. *See* Gowan
Ferguson, Frances Jane. *See* Gowan
Ferguson, Francis, VIII, 737
Ferguson, Frederick, IX, 149
Ferguson, George Richard, VII, 235
Ferguson, Helen. *See* Baxter
Ferguson, Helen (Rankin), VIII, 736; IX, 652
Ferguson, Helen McLaren (Daly), XI, 231
Ferguson, Henry, V, 556
Ferguson, Isabella (Gregory), V, 391
Ferguson, Israel, IV, 710

Ferguson, John (editor), VIII, 613, 656; IX, 601; XII, 872
Ferguson, John (office holder), V, 256
Ferguson, Margaret. *See* Hill
Ferguson, Marjory. *See* Connacher
Ferguson, Marjory (Margery) (Armstrong), XI, 31
Ferguson, Martha (Pennoyer), VI, 574
Ferguson, Mary. *See* Adams
Ferguson, Nancy (Singleton), IV, 710
Ferguson, Patrick, IV, 211; V, 733
Ferguson, Rebecca (Hall), IX, 357
Ferguson, Robert, VII, 204, 258, 637; VIII, **292–93**; X, 271
Ferguson, Sir Samuel, IX, 494
Ferguson, Thomas Roberts, X, 78, **282–83**, 313, 623
Ferguson, William, IX, 726; XI, 533
Ferguson, William H., XII, 1120
Fergusson, Adam, VII, 312, 833; VIII, 188, 266; IX, 83, 106, **251–52**, 253, 575; XI, 132, 133
Fergusson, Agnes. *See* Colquhoun
Fergusson*, Charles Bruce (1911–78), XII, 268
Fergusson, Jemima. *See* Johnston Blair
Fergusson, Jessie. *See* Tower
Fergusson, Mary, X, 670
Fergusson, Neil, IX, 251
Fergusson, Robert Colquhoun, IX, 252
Fergusson Blair, Adam Johnston, IX, **252–54**; XII, 151, 154
Ferland, Antoine, IX, 254
Ferland, Élizabeth. *See* Lebrun de Duplessis
Ferland, Jean-Baptiste-Antoine, VI, 593, 599; VIII, 79, 217, 312; IX, 38, 117, 118, 120, 121, 201, 250, **254–57**, 303, 305, 800; X, 13, 87, 105, 203, 432; XI, 83, 172, 341, 342, 489, 588, 851; XII, 507, 737
Fernald, Merritt Lyndon, X, 106
Fernandes, Francisco, I, 228, 229, 302, 304, 343
Fernandes, João, I, 19, 21, 153, 234, **304–5**, 343
Fernández. *See* Martínez
Fernandez, Simon, I, 332, 333
Férolles, Marquis de. *See* La Ville
Ferrand, Élisabeth-Françoise. *See* Levasseur
Ferrand, Laurent-René, IV, 354
Ferrant, Marguerite (Verrier), III, 643
Ferrar, Constance, I, 248, **305**, 613
Ferrara, Francesco, X, 608
Ferrer Maldonado, Lorenzo, I, **676–77**; V, 571
Ferrers, Baroness. *See* Compton
Ferres, James Moir, VII, 77; IX, 144, **257–58**, 430; X, 321; XI, 680
Ferres, Sarah. *See* Robertson
Ferrie, Adam (son of ADAM, 1777–1863), IX, 259
Ferrie, Adam, VII, **284–85**; VIII, 293, 294
Ferrie, Adam, VII, 284; VIII, 293, 295; IX, **258–60**; XII, 214
Ferrie, Catherine Priscilla. *See* Beasley
Ferrie, Colin Campbell, VI, 470; VII, 178, 284, 909; VIII, **293–95**; IX, 258, 259, 746
Ferrie, Grace (Kemp), XI, 467
Ferrie, James, VII, 284
Ferrie, Jane. *See* Kinsey
Ferrie, John, VIII, 295
Ferrie, Rachel. *See* Campbell
Ferrie, Robert, VII, 284, 285; VIII, 294, 295
Ferrier, Andrew, IX, 106

Ferrier, George Davies, XI, 315
Ferrier, Grizzell (Burns), IX, 104
Ferrier, James, XI, 315, 316
Ferrier, James, VIII, 815; IX, 422, 793; X, 522, 524, 725; XI, **315–16**, 556; XII, 232, 265, 434, 435, 1000
Ferrier, Margaret Watson (Torrance), XI, 316
Ferrier, Mary. *See* Todd
Ferris, John Horatio, V, 88
Ferris, Lena. *See* Swayze
Ferron, François, VIII, 128
Ferry, Jules, XI, 345
Ferry, William, VII, 582
Feti (Fetti), Domenico, XII, 846
Fettes, James, XII, 492
Feuille, La. *See* Wahpasha
Feuillet. *See* Ducourday
Feuillon, Michel, I, 305
Feuquières, Marquis de. *See* Pas
Fevret de Fontette, Charles-Marie, II, 422
Fézeret, Claude, II, 221
Fézeret, Marie. *See* Carlié
Fézeret, Marie. *See* Philippe
Fézeret, Marie-Joseph (Marie-Rose) (Thiersant), II, 221
Fézeret, René, I, 663; II, **221**
Fézeret, Suzanne. *See* Guillebaut
ffolliott, Frances (Crofton), XI, 219
fforbes. *See* Forbes
ffraser. *See* Fraser
Fichet, Monsieur (millionaire), XI, 814
Fidalgo, Salvador, V, 12, 80; VI, 233
Fiddler, Jack. *See* Maisaninnine
Fiddler, Joseph. *See* Pesequan
Fidler, James (father of PETER), VI, 249
Fidler, James (HBC employee), II, 233
Fidler, Mary (mother of PETER), VI, 249
Fidler, Peter, IV, 160, 310, 684, 741; V, 236, 684; VI, 17, **249–52**, 443, 776; VII, 78, 138, 564, 913; VIII, 3, 90, 343, 350, 412, 537, 660, 879
Fidler, Sally (Williams), VII, 913
Fidler, T. Claxton, XII, 562
Fiedmont. *See* Jacau
Field, Charles, XI, 316
Field, Cyrus West, XII, 375
Field, Eleakim, VI, **252–53**; VIII, 120
Field, Elizabeth. *See* Carter
Field, Elizabeth (Jones; Carey), VIII, 309, 439, 441, 442, 443; IX, 590; XI, **316–17**
Field, Emeline, VII, 779
Field, Jeanie Lucinda (Musgrave, Lady Musgrave), XI, 634, 636
Field, Matthew, XII, 375
Field, Robert, V, 24, **313–14**, 612; VI, 169, 500, 716; VII, 63, 875, 876
Fielding*, William Stevens (1848–1929), XI, 573; XII, 103, 859, 1092
Fiennes, Marquis de. *See* Fontanieu
Fiennes, William, 1st Viscount Saye and Sele, I, 435, 636
Fife, Earl. *See* Duff
Fife, Agnes. *See* Hutchinson
Fife, David, X, **283–84**; XII, 225
Fife, Jane. *See* Beckett
Fife, John, X, 283
Fife, Mary (Clendinning), XII, 200

Figueroa. *See* Moziño

Filiastre, Luc, II, 110, 130, 204, **221–23**, 421

Filiatreault*, Aristide (1851–1913), XII, 304

Filiau, *dit* Dubois, François, IV, 272; VII, 235

Filiau, *dit* Dubois, Jean-Baptiste, IV, 272

Filiau, *dit* Dubois, Marie-Amable (Orillat), IV, 591

Filiau, *dit* Dubois, Thérèse (Bartzsch), VII, 235

Filion, Adèle. *See* Liénard de Beaujeu de Villemonde

Filion, Suzanne-Élisabeth (Brassard Deschenaux), IV, 89

Filleul, Esther Elizabeth (Janvrin), VI, 347

Filleul, Marie (Demosny), I, 255

Fillion, André, I, 305

Fillion, Antoine, I, 305

Fillion, Antoinette, I, 305

Fillion, Françoise (Ranvoyzé), VI, 633

Fillion, Gabrielle. *See* Senler

Fillion, Jean, I, 305

Fillion, Joseph, IV, 659

Fillion, Marguerite. *See* Auber

Fillion, Michel, I, **305–6**, 589; II, xvi

Fillis, Charlotte (Crosskill), VI, 173

Fillis, Elizabeth. *See* Stoddard

Fillis, John (father of JOHN), IV, 266

Fillis, John (son of JOHN), IV, 267

Fillis, John, IV, 116, 131, **266–67**, 526, 527, 528, 696; VI, 173, 500; VIII, 192

Fillis, Sarah. *See* Rudduck

Fillon, François, I, 536

Fillon, Michel, I, 305

Filmer, Sir Robert, V, 628

Filteau, Gérard, VII, 247, 703

Filteau, Jacques-Richard, VII, 18

Fin, Louis, I, 221

Finch, Ann Eliza (Berczy), VIII, 83

Finch, Daniel, 8th Earl of Winchelsea, III, 131

Findlater, Andrew, VIII, 408

Findlay, Ann (Connon), XII, 207

Findlay, Helen R., XII, 388

Findlayson, Elizabeth (Strachan), IX, 752

Finkle, Henry, VIII, 325, 326

Finkle, Lucretia. *See* Bleeker

Finkle, Nancy (Crysler), VIII, 194

Finkle, Sarah (Gildersleeve), VIII, 325; IX, 314

Finlay, Charles, V, 746

Finlay, Elizabeth. *See* Grant

Finlay, George, V, 746

Finlay, Hamilton, V, 746

Finlay, Hugh, IV, 323, 324, 570, 716, 794; V, 21, 44, 146, 150, 165, 278, **314–19**, 427, 484, 503, 552, 692, 745, 746, 774, 794, 817, 821; VI, 254, 269, 380, 531, 615; VII, 401, 402, 767

Finlay, Jacques-Raphaël, VI, **253–54**

Finlay, James (father), V, 390, 537, 682; VI, 72, 253, 254

Finlay, James, V, 260; VI, 180, 254; VII, 224

Finlay, Jane (Walker), V, 839

Finlay, John, V, 543; VIII, 158

Finlay, Kirkman, VII, 336

Finlay, Mary. *See* Phillips

Finlay, Robert, V, 314

Finlay, Susanna. *See* Parkins

Finlay, William, VI, **254–56**, 534; VIII, 321

Finlayson, Alexander, XII, 317

Finlayson, Ann. *See* Mather

Finlayson, Anne Jane (Keith), XII, 318

Finlayson, Duncan, VIII, 577, 589, 811; IX, **260–61**, 852; X, 284, 484; XI, 546, 824; XII, 53, 317

Finlayson, Elizabeth. *See* Kennedy

Finlayson, Isobel Graham. *See* Simpson

Finlayson, John, XII, 316

Finlayson, Margaret (Haberkorn; Pabst), known as Margaret Bloomer and Margaret Mather, XII, **316–17**

Finlayson, Mary. *See* Morrison

Finlayson, Nicol, VI, 754; VIII, 663; IX, 260; X, 272, **284**; XII, 54, 317

Finlayson, Roderick, VIII, 836; IX, 327, 852, 853; X, 242; XII, **317–18**, 642

Finlayson, Sarah. *See* Work

Finley, Eleanor Elizabeth. *See* Smith

Finney, Charles Grandison, IX, 769

Finnis, Robert, VI, 803

Finucane, Andrew, V, 158

Finucane, Bryan, IV, 328, 562; V, 109, 251; VI, 34, 138, 395

Fiott, Nicholas, IV, 176

Firmin-Didot, Ambroise, II, 422

Firmont. *See* Edgeworth

Firth, Anne. *See* Watts

Firth, Elizabeth (mother of WILLIAM), VII, 285

Firth, Lucy Rosalind Proctor, VII, 286

Firth, William, VII, 36, 37, 285

Firth, William, V, 521; VI, 79, 656; VII, 161, **285–86**; VIII, 339, 431; IX, 512

Fisbach, Marie, named du Sacré-Cœur (Roy), IX, 799; X, 603; XI, **318–19**

Fisbacht, Charles, XI, 318

Fisbacht, Marie-Geneviève. *See* Nadeau

Fiset, Jean-Baptiste-Romuald, XII, 521

Fiset, Louis, IX, **261–62**

Fiset, Louis-Joseph-Cyprien, IX, 262

Fiset, Marie-Angélique (Bédard), IV, 49; V, 60

Fiset, Mary. *See* Powers

Fiset, Pierre (father of LOUIS), IX, 261

Fiset, Pierre (Oblate), IX, 398

Fiset, Ursule. *See* Maufet

Fish, Elizabeth (Foster), X, 293

Fish, Hamilton, X, 102; XI, 768, 769; XII, 601, 654

Fisher, Mr (officer), VI, 257

Fisher, Mrs (Budden; King; wife of Duncan, son of DUNCAN), V, 320

Fisher, Alexander (brother of DUNCAN), V, 319, 321

Fisher, Alexander (cousin of DUNCAN), V, 319, 321

Fisher, Alexander (father-in-law of Thomas KIRKPATRICK), V, 92, 772; IX, 431

Fisher, Alexandre-Pierre, XII, 554

Fisher, Amelia. *See* Hatfield

Fisher, Ann (Connell), VII, 291; X, 191

Fisher, Anne (Hagerman), VII, 365

Fisher, Anne (Leverett), I, 474

Fisher, Annie Connell (Parkin, Lady Parkin), VII, 291

Fisher, Benjamin, VI, 256, 257

Fisher, Catherine. *See* Embury

Fisher, Catherine (Shepard), VII, 794

Fisher, Charles, VI, 757; VII, 74, 291; VIII, 809, 810, 842, 868; IX, 86, 87, 123, 381, 382, 392, 413, 431, 515, 516, 527, 623, 631; X, 140, 158, 159, 191, 271, **284–90**, 494, 495, 666, 682, 710, 711, 712, 713; XI, 224, 373, 375,

578, 688, 689, 828, 829, 830, 831; XII, 24, 26, 313, 338, 741, 896, 897, 1052, 1053, 1105
Fisher, Christian. *See* Creighten
Fisher, Christine (Monro), X, 528
Fisher, Cuthbert, IV, 93
Fisher, Duncan (father of DUNCAN), V, 319
Fisher, Duncan (lawyer), IX, 728
Fisher, Duncan (son of DUNCAN), V, 320
Fisher, Duncan, V, **319–21**, 770; VI, 822, 823; VII, 820; IX, 792; XI, 533
Fisher, Edwin Colley, X, 290
Fisher, Elinor Isabella. *See* Auchmuty
Fisher, Elizabeth. *See* Laurens
Fisher, Elizabeth. *See* Rawlings
Fisher, Elizabeth (Torrance), V, 320; IX, 792
Fisher, Elizabeth Therese (Baird), VI, 29
Fisher, Esther. *See* Foster
Fisher, Finlay, V, 319, **321**
Fisher, Frederic Horatio, VI, 192
Fisher, Sir George Bulteel, VI, **256–58**; VII, 401
Fisher, Helen (Kirkpatrick), IX, 431; XII, 496
Fisher, Henry, VII, 291; X, 287, 628
Fisher, Irving, X, 608
Fisher, Isabella (Munn), X, 538
Fisher, James, V, 319, 321
Fisher, James, IV, 107, 493, 589; VI, 68, 224, **258–59**, 325, 326, 416, 586; V, 6, 318, 331, 493, 494, 495, 496, 501, 502, 817; VIII, 575; X, 385, 563
Fisher, Jane M. Paulette (Fraser), XII, 338
Fisher, Jannet (Hick), V, 320
Fisher, John (brother of DUNCAN), V, 319, 320, 321
Fisher, John (brother of GEORGE BULTEEL), VI, 256
Fisher, John (cousin of Calvin MCQUESTEN), XI, 376, 583
Fisher, John (father of GEORGE BULTEEL), VI, 256
Fisher, John (father of THOMAS), X, 290
Fisher, John (politician), VI, 783
Fisher, John Arbuthnot, 1st Baron Fisher, X, 397
Fisher, John Charlton, VI, 802; VII, **286–88**, 462, 463, 645, 649, 837; VIII, 385
Fisher, Lewis, VII, 288
Fisher, Lewis Peter, VII, 291
Fisher, Louise-Sophie. *See* Desbarats
Fisher, Margaret (Hutchison; Lunn), V, 320; XI, 533
Fisher, Margaret (McQuesten), XI, 583
Fisher, Mary. *See* Colley
Fisher, Mary (Valentine; wife of PETER), VII, 291
Fisher, Mary Barbra. *See* Till
Fisher, Nancy (Mackenzie), V, 320
Fisher, Peter, X, 284
Fisher, Peter, VII, **288–91**; VIII, 157; XI, 135
Fisher, Richard, I, **306–7**, 364, 409, 450, 671, 672
Fisher, Robert, I, 306
Fisher, Sarah. *See* Sykes
Fisher, Sarah Elizabeth. *See* Ingalls
Fisher, Sarah Maria. *See* Thomson
Fisher, Susanna. *See* Williams
Fisher, Susannah Stephens. *See* Williams
Fisher, Thomas, X, **290–91**; XI, 332
Fisher, Turner, IX, 262
Fisher, Wilford, IX, **262–64**
Fisher, William, VII, 291
Fisk, James, XII, 532
Fisk, Wilbur, XI, 687

Fitch, John Charles, XII, 993
Fitzbach. *See* Fisbach
FitzClarence, Lady Amelia (Cary, Viscountess Falkland), XI, 155
FitzClarence, Lady Mary (Fox), VII, 23
Fitzgerald, Mrs. *See* Schank
Fitzgerald, Alexander, VII, 403
Fitzgerald, Anne. *See* Minnitt
Fitzgerald, Charity Christina. *See* Purdon
Fitzgerald, David, XI, 202, 549; XII, **318–20**
Fitzgerald, Delia. *See* Hooke
Fitzgerald, Edward, XI, 144
Fitzgerald, Lord Edward, IV, 159
Fitzgerald, Eliza Ann (Monk), XII, 751
Fitzgerald, Gerald, 11th Earl of Kildare, I, 168
Fitzgerald, James Fitzmaurice, I, 421
FitzGerald, John, Knight of Glin, IX, 264
Fitzgerald, Mary (Longworth), VII, 511
Fitzgerald, Norman, IX, 568
Fitzgerald, Pamela. *See* Simms
Fitzgerald, Thomas, IX, 72
Fitzgerald, William, XII, 318
FitzGibbon, Agnes Dunbar. *See* Moodie
FitzGibbon, Garrett (Gerald), IX, 264
FitzGibbon, James, V, 539, 760; VII, 200, 260, 754, 889, 896; VIII, 208, 245, 445, 650, 651, 707, 885; IX, 127, **264–67**, 313, 346, 406, 407, 500, 513, 522; X, 118, 344, 557
FitzGibbon, Margaret (Washburn), VII, 896
FitzGibbon, Mary. *See* Haley
FitzGibbon, Mary. *See* Widenham
Fitzgibbon, Mary Agnes. *See* Bernard
FitzGibbon, Mary Agnes, XII, 999, 1076
Fitzhenry, Thomas, XII, 1083, 1084
Fitzherbert, Jonas, VII, 10
Fitz-James, James Stuart, Duke of Berwick, III, 458
Fitzmaurice. *See* Petty-Fitzmaurice
Fitzpatrick, Ambrose, VI, 244; VIII, 107
Fitzpatrick*, Sir Charles (1853–1942), X, 136; XI, 748, 749; XII, 695
Fitzpatrick, Corine. *See* Caron
Fitzpatrick, John Bernard, X, 87
FitzRandolph, Phebe. *See* Tupper
FitzRandolph, Robert, VIII, 731
Fitzroy, Augustus Henry, 3rd Duke of Grafton, V, 142; VIII, 295
FitzRoy, Lord Charles, VIII, 295
FitzRoy, Sir Charles Augustus, VI, 821; VII, 103, 437, 542, 858, 925; VIII, 198, **295–97**, 377, 429, 485, 531, 742, 954; IX, 157, 179, 223, 394, 857; XII, 856
Fitzroy, Lady Charlotte (Lee, Countess of Lichfield), III, 369
FitzRoy, Frances. *See* Mundy
FitzRoy, Margaret Gordon, Lady FitzRoy. *See* Milligan
FitzRoy, Mary, Lady FitzRoy. *See* Lennox
Fitzsimmins, Mary Ann (Leviston), XII, 567
Fitzsimons, Ellen (McKenzie), VII, 564, 565
Fitzsimons, Thomas, VII, 564
Fitzwilliam. *See also* Wentworth-Fitzwilliam
Fitzwilliam, Lady. *See* Douglas
Fitzwilliam, William, 4th Earl Fitzwilliam, V, 851
Flaget, Benoît-Joseph, VII, 170, 171, 489; IX, 636
Flamand (Flamant). *See* Deguise

Flame. *See* Phlem
Flamme. *See also* Armand
Flamme, Cécile (Bellet), VI, 50
Flanagan, Mary (Bergin), XII, 94
Flannery*, William (1830–1901), XII, 1085
Flat Button, IV, 260
Flavelle*, Sir John Wesley (1858–1939), XII, 973
Fléché, Jessé, I, 95, 97, 99, **307**, 500, 501
Flèche, Une. *See* Kāpeyakwāskonam
Fleming, Mrs (wife of Sampson), V, 39
Fleming, Andrew Greig, X, 291
Fleming, Ann Cuthbert. *See* Rae
Fleming, Atwell, XII, 924
Fleming, Charles, X, 499
Fleming, Daniel, VI, 259
Fleming, Elizabeth. *See* Arnot
Fleming, Frank, XII, 447
Fleming, Grace Matilda (Edgar), XII, 291
Fleming, James (alleged murderer), IX, 151
Fleming, James (merchant), VIII, 734; X, 606
Fleming, Janet (Gourlay), IX, 330
Fleming, John, VI, **259–61**, 278, 584, 668; VII, 809; VIII, 542, 734; X, 606
Fleming, John Arnot, X, **291**
Fleming, John Ramsay, VIII, 734
Fleming, Margaret. *See* McHardy
Fleming, Martin, VII, 292
Fleming, Mary, VI, 670
Fleming, Mary, named Mother Gertrude, XI, 240
Fleming, Mary Stewart (Mackenzie), XII, 647
Fleming, May Agnes. *See* Early
Fleming, Michael Anthony, VI, 693, 694; VII, 153, 154, 220, **292–300**, 404, 631, 633; VIII, 107, 184, 185, 198, 199, 233, 235, 246, 247, 380, 474, 475, 725, 948, 949, 950, 951; IX, 70, 71, 435, 556, 557, 582, 583, 605, 819; X, 180, 279, 398, 399, 553, 600, 601, 687, 688; XI, 376, 673; XII, 563, 860
Fleming*, Oscar Ernest (1861–1944), XII, 202, 294, 333, 584
Fleming, Peter, VIII, **297–98**
Fleming*, Robert John (1854–1925), XII, 454
Fleming, Robert M., XII, 605
Fleming, Sampson, V, 39
Fleming*, Sir Sandford (1827–1915), VIII, 14, 960, 961; IX, 575, 804; X, 291, 466, 630; XI, 123, 124, 132, 195, 228, 354, 632, 663, 764, 855; XII, 164, 213, 247, 249, 280, 367, 447, 448, 495, 496, 562, 653, 729, 933, 999
Fleming, William John, X, 269
Flemish Bastard, I, 7, 40, 41, **307–8**, 325, 555, 556, 602
Flemme. *See* Phlem
Flemming, Patrick, VII, 923
Flemming, Rachel (Motton), XII, 765
Flemming, William, IX, 7
Flesche, Jossé. *See* Fléché, Jessé
Flesher, Martha (Bland), XII, 111
Fletcher, Alexander, IV, 129; V, 219, 309
Fletcher, Anna (Gschwind), VI, 303
Fletcher, Benjamin, I, 634
Fletcher, Edward Charles, X, 291
Fletcher, Edward Taylor, VIII, 494, 495; XI, 336; XII, **320–21**
Fletcher, Ellen Mary. *See* Shore
Fletcher, Frances. *See* Marsham

Fletcher, Harriet. *See* Marsham
Fletcher, Henrietta Amelia. *See* Lindsay
Fletcher, Henry Charles, X, **291–92**; XII, 430
Fletcher, Isabella (Morrison), XI, 619
Fletcher*, James (1852–1908), XI, 108; XII, 998
Fletcher, James Hayden, IX, 828, 833; X, 211
Fletcher, John, XII, 320
Fletcher, John, I, **308–9**, 611; II, 266
Fletcher, John, VI, 167, 168; VII, **300–1**, 498, 907; VIII, 221
Fletcher, John William, VI, 336
Fletcher, Margaret Brown (Morrison), XI, 619
Fletcher, Mary (wife of JOHN, d. 1697), I, 308
Fletcher, Mary (Richardson), IX, 658, 659
Fletcher, Pendleton, II, 54
Fletcher, Sir Richard, V, 450
Fletcher, Robert, IV, 51, **267–68**, 342, 343
Fletcher, Silas, VII, 404; IX, 502
Flett, George, VIII, 768; X, 549, 550; XI, 776
Flett, Mary. *See* Ross
Flett, Peter, XII, 832
Fleuche (Fleuchy). *See* Fléché
Fleuriau, Charles-Jean-Baptiste de, Comte de Morville, III, 106; IV, 60
Fleurieu, Comte de. *See* Claret
Fleurimont. *See* Noyelle; Noyelles
Fleurimont, Baron de. *See* Noyelles
Fleury. *See also* Buday; Guyart
Fleury, André-Hercule de, II, 530, 551; III, 40, 192, 196; IV, 355, 358
Fleury, Charles (captain), I, 68, 299, 441
Fleury, Charles (clergyman), XII, 1000
Fleury, Jacques, II, 223
Fleury, Jean, II, 424
Fleury, Madeleine (Jacson), V, 451
Fleury, Perrine. *See* Gabar
Fleury de La Gorgendière, Charlotte de (Marin de La Malgue), IV, 512
Fleury de La Gorgendière, Claire de. *See* Jolliet
Fleury de La Gorgendière, Joseph de, II, 66, 224; III, 62, **216–18**, 300, 333, 339, 616, 617, 621; IV, 268, 512, 661, 739; VI, 751
Fleury de La Gorgendière, Louise de (Rigaud de Vaudreuil), IV, 661
Fleury de La Gorgendière, Marie-Claire de (Taschereau), III, 616, 617; V, 793; VI, 751
Fleury de La Gorgendière, Marie-Louise (Juchereau Duchesnay), VI, 368; X, 388
Fleury de La Gorgendière, Marie-Thomas de (Trottier Dufy Desauniers), IV, 739
Fleury de La Janière, Simon-Thomas de, II, 224; III, 217
Fleury Deschambault, Catherine. *See* Véron de Grand-mesnil
Fleury Deschambault, Charles de, II, 224, 654; III, 217
Fleury Deschambault, Jacques de, I, **309**; II, 224
Fleury Deschambault, Jacques-Alexis de, I, 309, 344, 418; II, 81, **223–24**, 433; III, 216, 311; IV, 268
Fleury Deschambault, Jeanne-Charlotte de (Le Verrier de Rousson; Rigaud de Vaudreuil de Cavagnial, Marquise de Vaudreuil), I, 345; II, 224, 433; IV, 286, 476, 663; V, 741
Fleury Deschambault, Joseph, III, 217, 243; IV, **268–70**; V, 143, 413, 794; VI, 699; VII, 500

Fleury Deschambault, Louis-Joseph de, V, 374; VI, 345; VII, 622; X, 544
Fleury Deschambault, Marguerite de. *See* Chavigny de Berchereau
Fleury Deschambault, Marguerite-Renée de. *See* Denys de La Ronde
Fleury Deschambault, Marie-Anne-Catherine (Le Moyne de Longueuil, Baronne de Longueuil; Grant), IV, 268; V, 288, 369; VII, 500
Fleury Deschambault, Thérèse-Josèphe (Dunbar), IV, 269
Fleutelot, François, Marquis de Rompré, II, 162, 499
Flibot, Jean, II, 273
Flieger, J., V, 872
Flinders, Matthew, V, 55; VII, 323; VIII, 669
Flint, Billa, XII, 321
Flint, Billa, XI, 853, 908; XII, **321–23**, 469
Flint, G. H., X, 346
Flint, John James Bleecker (John James Bleecker), XII, 321
Flint, Phoebe. *See* Wells
Flint, Phoebe Sawyer. *See* Clement
Flood, Eliza. *See* Saunders
Flood, Eliza (Parsons), XI, 673
Flood, Frances Mary. *See* Blake
Flood, Kathleen Wilhelmina (McLean), XI, 570
Flood, Margaret (Cocoran), X, 176
Flood, Richard, XI, 570, 653
Floquet, Pierre-René, IV, **270–71**, 544; V, 369, 414, 432
Florence, Chevalier de, II, 4
Florence, Marguerite (Arraud), X, 16
Florence, Pierre, V, 668
Florence, Thérèse-Esther. *See* Hausman, *dit* Ménager
Florence, William Jermyn. *See* Conlin, Bernard
Flores. *See* Valdés
Flórez Maldonado Martínez de Angulo y Bodquín, Manuel Antonio, IV, 519, 520; V, 197, 198
Florin (Florentin), Jean, I, 658
Flowerdew, Edward, I, 280
Flowers, Dudley, VII, 239
Floyd, Mr (slaveowner), VI, 262
Floyd, Henry, known as Black Harry, VI, **261–62**
Fluet, Catherine (Laurin), XI, 498
Fluet, Louis-Joseph, VII, 661, 662, 663; VIII, 34
Fluette, Marie-Louise (Barbeau; Natte, *dit* Marseille), V, 622
Flulin, Auguste, VII, 27
Flynn*, Edmund James (1847–1927), XI, 192, 320; XII, 181
Flynn, Edmund Power, XII, 880, 881
Flynn, Mary (Croke), VII, 220
Fogarty, Richard, VII, 597
Fogget, James, VI, 15
Foi, I, **199–200**
Foissey, Marie (Simonet d'Abergemont), III, 592
Foisy, François-Théodule, XI, 208
Foisy, Marie-Charlotte (Marion), VI, 487
Foisy, Marie-Thaïs (Proulx), XI, 714
Foix, Comte de. *See* Gaston III
Foix, Germaine de (Germaine, Queen of Aragon and Sicily), I, 120
Fol, Catherine (Demosny; Chasle), I, 249, 255
Foley, James William, IX, 836
Foley, Katherine (wife of MICHAEL HAMILTON), IX, 267
Foley, Mary (Morris), VII, 626

Foley, Michael Hamilton, IX, 253, **267–68;** X, 465, 466; XI, 230; XII, 595, 644
Foley, Thomas, VII, 627
Follett, Thomas, VII, 420
Follin, Nicolas, I, 621
Folsom, C. W., IX, 294
Fonblanche. *See* Martinet; Quesnel
Fond, Anne de. *See* Manet
Fond, Jean de, II, 581
Fonds, Jean de. *See* Rodrigue, Jean-Baptiste
Fondville. *See* Rouillard
Fonfay. *See* Morin
Fontaine. *See also* Davène
Fontaine, Jacques, I, 277
Fontaine, Josephte (Bachand), X, 24
Fontaine, Jules. *See* Crémazie, Octave
Fontaine, Madeleine (Doublet), I, 277
Fontaine, Marguerite (Picart, *dit* Beauchemin), XI, 59
Fontaine, Marie-Marguerite (Blanchet), XI, 85
Fontaine, Raphaël-Ernest, IX, 344, 345; XII, 719
Fontaine, Vitaline (Bélanger), XI, 64
Fontaine, *dit* Bienvenu, Pierre, III, 311
Fontaine, *dit* Bienvenue, Marie-Josephte (Ménard, *dit* La Fontaine), IX, 440
Fontana, Francesco, VI, 596
Fontanieu, Gaspard-Moïse-Augustin de, Marquis de Fiennes, IV, 353
Fontanille, Monsieur de (husband of Marie-Marguerite Lemoine, *dit* Monière), IV, 622
Fontanille, Marie-Marguerite de. *See* Lemoine, *dit* Monière
Fontarabie, Pierre, I, 143
Fontbonne, Antoinette, named Sister Fébronie, VIII, 299
Fontbonne, Claude, VIII, 298
Fontbonne, Jacques, VIII, 299
Fontbonne, Jeanne, named Mother Saint-Jean, VIII, 299
Fontbonne, Marie-Antoinette, named Sister Delphine, VIII, **298–99**; IX, 103; XI, 111; XII, 183
Fontbonne, Marie-Françoise. *See* Pleynet
Fonte, Bartholomew de, I, 676, **677**; IV, 165, 746
Fontenay. *See* Prévost
Fonteneau, Jean, known as Jean Alfonse, I, **309**, 423, 680
Fonteneau, Jeanne (Curatteau), IV, 187
Fonteneau, Jérémie, I, 78
Fonteneau, Marie (Bailly), I, 78
Fonteneau, Valentine. *See* Alfonse
Fontenelle. *See also* Le Bovier
Fontenelle, Marie-Geneviève. *See* Énault de Livaudais
Fontette. *See* Fevret
Fonville. *See* Bécart
Foote, Phylina (Jones; Smart), X, 659
Foote, S. B., IX, 577
Footner, William, XI, 92, 629
Foran, Catherine (Bulger), VIII, 111
Forant, Isaac-Louis de, II, **224–26**; III, 17, 18, 256, 368, 392, 456, 557, 630; IV, 15, 60, 253
Forant, Job de, II, 224
Forant, Marguerite de, II, 255; III, 630
Forbes, Alexander, V, 486
Forbes, Amelia Sophia, Lady Forbes. *See* Grant
Forbes, Charles, Comte de Montalembert, X, 580; XI, 96, 175, 182, 339, 725; XII, 819
Forbes, Charles John, IX, **268–70**
Forbes, Eliza (Holton), X, 354

Forbes, Elizabeth. *See* Cobb
Forbes, Elizabeth. *See* Graham
Forbes, Euphemia (Garden), VI, 271
Forbes, Francis, VII, 301
Forbes, Sir Francis, VI, 410, 411, 614; VII, 152, **301–4**, 377
Forbes, Geneviève (Grant), V, 376
Forbes, James (surgeon), VII, 182, 183
Forbes, James (uncle of Charles FOTHERGILL), VII, 317
Forbes, John, III, 218
Forbes, John, III, **218–19**, 261, 283, 378, 526, 558; IV, 4, 177, 408, 670; V, 545; VI, 30
Forbes, John Colin, XII, 795
Forbes, Margaret (Lockerby), XI, 524
Forbes, Marianne Elizabeth (Peters), VII, 690
Forbes, Mary. *See* Tucker
Forbes, Mary (MacDonald), VIII, 525
Forbes, Mary Anne (Fothergill), VII, 317
Forbes, Robert, IX, 268
Forbes, Sophia. *See* Browne
Forbin, Claude de, Comte de Forbin, III, 42, 609
Forbin-Janson, Charles-Auguste-Marie-Joseph de, VII, **304–7**; VIII, 261, 290, 703, 712, 730; IX, 34, 153, 228, 681, 698, 798, 805; X, 220, 419, 421, 604, 689; XI, 95, 97; XII, 189
Forbin-Janson, Cornélie-Henriette-Sophie-Louise-Hortense-Gabrielle de, Comtesse de Forbin-Janson. *See* Galléan
Forbin-Janson, Michel-Palamède de, Comte de Forbin-Janson, VII, 304
Forcade, Pierre de, II, 270; IV, 358
Forcade, Ezelia (Morton), XI, 620
Ford, John (architect), VIII, 281
Ford, John (ship's captain), I, 301; II, 265
Ford, Mary Elizabeth (Jones), VII, 456
Ford, Polly (wife of MICHIKINAKOUA), V, 593
Ford, Thomas, III, 323
Ford, William, XI, 426
Fordyce, John, III, **219–20**, 504
Forel. *See* Avet
Foreman, Catherine Louisa (Grigor), VIII, 348
Foreman, James, VI, 181; VIII, **299–301**, 348, 929; X, 292
Foreman, John, VIII, 299
Foreman, Margaret Ann. *See* Richardson
Foreman, Mary. *See* Gardner
Foremost Man. *See* Ne-can-nete
Forest, George, VIII, 140
Forest, Marguerite (Bastarache, *dit* Le Basque), V, 57
Forest, William D., VI, 265, 266
Forester, Cecil Scott, VI, 803
Forestier. *See also* Fortier
Forestier, Antoine, II, 68, **226**, 465; III, 220
Forestier, Antoine-Bertrand, II, 226; III, **220–21**
Forestier, Antoinette (Charlevoix), III, 104
Forestier, Élisabeth (Istre), III, 220
Forestier, Élisabeth-Charlotte. *See* Camoin
Forestier, Françoise. *See* Ricard
Forestier, Geneviève. *See* Bouchard, *dit* Dorval
Forestier, Jean, II, 226
Forestier, Jean-Baptiste, III, 220
Forestier, Marguerite (Bissot de Vinsenne), II, 66, 68; III, 69

Forestier, Marie, named de Saint-Bonaventure-de-Jésus, I, **310**, 347, 353, 609, 611
Forestier, Marie-Madeleine. *See* Le Cavelier
Forestier, Marie-Madeleine (Poulin de Courval), II, 529
Forestier, Pierre, IV, 46
Forêt, Adélaïde (Tabaret), XI, 867
Foretier. *See also* Forestier
Foretier, Catherine. *See* Hubert
Foretier, Étienne, V, 322
Foretier, Jacques, V, 321, 322
Foretier, Marie-Amable (Viger), VII, 703, 836, 879; VIII, **301–2**; IX, 807
Foretier, Marie-Anne. *See* Caron
Foretier, Pierre, IV, 58, 140, 592; V, 241, 259, **321–25**, 662, 663, 833; VI, 204; VII, 703; VIII, 301; IX, 807
Foretier, Thérèse. *See* Legrand
Forget*, Amédée-Emmanuel (1847–1923), XI, 746
Forget, Anastase, X, 266
Forget, Antoine, III, **221**, 612
Forget, Louis-Joseph, XI, 814
Forget Duverger, Jacques-François, III, **221–22**, 442; IV, 390; V, 342
Forgie, Helen (Shaw), X, 650
Forgues, Marie. *See* Paquet
Forgues, Marie-Anne. *See* Denis
Forgues, Michel, XI, 319
Forgues, Michel, IX, 118; XI, **319–20**
Forgues, Simon, VIII, 235
Fork. *See* Nissowaquet
Forman, James, VIII, 300; X, 7, **292–93**; XI, 486
Forman, James R., XI, 717
Forman, John, VIII, 416
Fornel, Anne-Thérèse. *See* Levasseur
Fornel, Jean, III, 222, 224
Fornel, Joachim, II, 328, 381; III, **222–24**, 284, 285, 553; IV, 44
Fornel, Louis, III, 38, 154, 205, 222, **224–25**, 226, 280, 281, 282; IV, 44, 45, 66; V, 277, 576
Fornel, Marie-Anne. *See* Barbel
Fornel, Marie-Françoise (Meignot; Dumas), V, 277
Forneri, James, XI, 541
Forrest, Catherine (Munro), XII, 771
Forrest, Charles, V, 723
Forrest, Isabella (Brown), VI, 87
Forrest, Jane (Jenkins), VII, 442
Forrest*, John (1842–1920), XI, 773; XII, 772
Forrest, John, 1st Baron Forrest, XI, 884; XII, 911
Forrest, Robert, V, 320; VI, 232, 472, 823; VII, 820
Forrestall, Ann (Kenny, Lady Kenny), XII, 480
Forrestall, Margaret. *See* Hendricken
Forrester, Alexander, VII, 307
Forrester, Alexander, IX, **270–73**, 785; X, 362, 534; XII, 879, 880
Forrester, Andrew, I, **310–11**, 568, 593
Forrester, Elizabeth. *See* Martin
Forrester, Margaret Tweddale. *See* Davidson
Forrester, Mary (mother of THOMAS), VII, 307
Forrester, Thomas, VII, 22, **307–9**; VIII, 160, 417
Forsayth, James, I, 258
Forsayth, Marguerite. *See* Denys
Forstall, Juliet (Sweetman), VII, 840, 841
Forster, Christopher Henry, III, 179
Forster, Elizabeth (Boulton), VI, 78; IX, 68, 69

Forster, George, V, 32; VI, 403
Forster, Johann Reinhold, V, 362
Forster, John Adam, III, 179
Forster*, John Wycliffe Lowes (1850–1938), VII, 277; VIII, 427; XII, 102
Forster, William, III, 87
Forsyth, Alexander (merchant), V, 299
Forsyth, Alexander (pharmacist), XII, 764
Forsyth, Alice. *See* Robins
Forsyth, Ann. *See* Bell
Forsyth, Charles Codrington, VIII, 624
Forsyth, Elizabeth Magdalene. *See* Anderson
Forsyth, Emma Kirby (Pardee), XI, 671
Forsyth, Fanny Bell (Burstall), XII, 144
Forsyth, Frances. *See* Bell
Forsyth, George, V, 189, 262, 402, 405, 841; VIII, 4
Forsyth, James (father of WILLIAM, 1771–1841), VII, 311
Forsyth, James (uncle of JAMES BELL), IX, 273
Forsyth, James Bell, V, 325, 617; VII, 157, 311; VIII, 115, 269, 691; IX, **273–76**, 774; XI, 140, 774; XII, 144, 279
Forsyth, Jane (wife of WILLIAM, 1771–1841), VII, 311
Forsyth, Jane Prescott (Gregory), V, 391; VII, 311
Forsyth, Jean. *See* Phyn
Forsyth, John, IV, 261; V, 101, 287, 300, 325, 326, 391; VI, 72, 204, 238, 639, 644, 764; VII, 29, **309–11**; VIII, 4, 321, 350; IX, 179, 273
Forsyth, John Blackwood, VII, 311
Forsyth, Joseph, IV, 494; V, 92, 168, 170, **325–27**, 402; VI, 722, 772; VII, 309, 311, 366, 919, 920; VIII, 514; IX, 273
Forsyth, Joseph Bell, X, 10
Forsyth, Margaret. *See* Grant
Forsyth, Mary. *See* Ackler
Forsyth, Mary (mother of WILLIAM, 1771–1841), VII, 311
Forsyth, Mary Ann (Burnet), VIII, 115
Forsyth, Nelson, VII, 315
Forsyth, Robert, VII, 132
Forsyth, Thomas (brother of JOSEPH), V, 259, 325, 512; VI, 664, 666; VII, 132, 309
Forsyth, Thomas (son of WILLIAM, d. 1814), V, 328
Forsyth, Thomas (uncle of JAMES BELL), IX, 273; X, 10
Forsyth, William (clergyman), XII, 764
Forsyth, William (father of JOHN and JOSEPH), V, 325; VII, 309
Forsyth, William (fur trader), IV, 506
Forsyth, William, IV, 197; V, 299, **327–29**, 350, 410, 608, 646; VI, 60, 90, 262, 263, 313; VIII, 300; IX, 175
Forsyth, William, VI, 266; VII, 39, 200, **311–16**, 369, 410, 834; VIII, 602; XII, 386
Forsyth Grant, William, VII, 311
Fort, Claude, IV, 124
Fortel. *See* Robert
Fortelle. *See* Robinau
Fortescue, Gertrude (Drake, Lady Drake), I, 278
Fortescue, Sir John William, I, 546; IV, 26; VII, 139
Fortier. *See also* Forestier
Fortier, Angelique (Hall), VI, 308; X, 329
Fortier, Angélique. *See* Manseau
Fortier, Angélique (Cadet), IV, 123
Fortier, Charles, VI, 623
Fortier (Forestier), Étienne, III, 472
Fortier, François (merchant), VIII, 302
Fortier, François (physician), V, 676

Fortier (Forestier), Françoise (Moreau), III, 472
Fortier*, Jean-Marie (fl. 1888–1917), XII, 228
Fortier, Joseph-Octave, VIII, 408
Fortier, Julie-Louise. *See* Taschereau
Fortier, Justine (Toussaint), XII, 1065
Fortier, Marie. *See* Poulin
Fortier, Marie-Anne. *See* Cureux, *dit* Saint-Germain
Fortier, Marie-Josephte (Turcotte), X, 690
Fortier, Michel, IV, 123, 271
Fortier, Michel, IV, **271–72**
Fortier, Moïse, XI, 716
Fortier, Narcisse-Charles, VI, 593; VIII, **302**; XI, 168; XII, 1066
Fortier, Pierre-Michel, IV, 271
Fortier, Thérèse (Heney), VII, 393
Fortier, Thomas, X, 576; XI, 657
Fortin, Monsieur (settler), I, 116
Fortin, Jean-Baptiste, VII, 503
Fortin, Jean-Marie, V, 651; VII, 698
Fortin, Louise. *See* Sommillard
Fortin, Marie (Couillard de Lespinay), II, 156
Fortin, Marie-Anne-Julie. *See* Crevier, *dit* Duvernay
Fortin, Marie-Catherine (Chotard), II, 516
Fortin, Pierre, XI, 320
Fortin, Pierre-Étienne, XI, **320–21**
Fortin, Suzanne-Marie (Bisaillon), XI, 320
Fortin, *dit* Bellefontaine, Julien, I, 432
Forton, Jean (father), V, 329
Forton, Jean, V, 329
Forton, Louise. *See* Chamard
Forton, Michel, IV, 702; V, **329**; VI, 557; VII, 17
Fortune, Joseph, VIII, 688
Fortune, Nancy. *See* Hatfield
Fortune, William, VIII, 868
Foseler, Hannah Rachel (West), VIII, 928
Foss, Christopher Vaughan, VIII, 574; IX, 136; XI, 139, 875; XII, 206
Fossambault. *See* Nau
Foster, Adeline, Lady Foster. *See* Davies
Foster, Alice (LePage), XI, 512
Foster, Asa Belknap, IX, 276; X, **293–94**; XI, 283, 438, 439; XII, 635, 636
Foster, Augustus John, V, 113
Foster, Colley Lyons Lucas, VII, 199, **316–17**, 518; IX, 372, 522, 523, 858; X, 104
Foster, Elizabeth. *See* Fish
Foster, Elizabeth. *See* Kirkpatrick
Foster, Eliza Lanesford (Cushing), XI, **321–22**; XII, 570, 776
Foster, Ellen. *See* Humphreys
Foster, Esther (Fisher), IX, 262
Foster*, Sir George Eulas (1847–1931), XI, 448; XII, 314, 383, 610, 612, 706, 1047, 1120
Foster, Hannah. *See* Webster
Foster, Harriet Vaughan (Cheney), XI, 321; XII, 570
Foster, Henry, IX, 11; XI, 198
Foster, Hiram Sewell, IX, 276; XI, 438
Foster, J. Noble, IX, 185
Foster, James, XI, 322
Foster, James C., XII, 933
Foster, John (father of ELIZA LANESFORD), XI, 320
Foster, John (neighbour of William KAIN), VI, 369
Foster, Margaret. *See* Bowes

Foster, Margaret (Withrow), XII, 1118
Foster, Mary. *See* Morrison
Foster, Mary (Punshon), XI, 719
Foster, Mary (Whitman; Bancroft), VIII, 929
Foster, Mercy (Piers), VIII, 704
Foster, Myles Birket, XII, 793
Foster, Patience. *See* Freeman
Foster, Patty. *See* Wilkings
Foster, Sally. *See* Belknap
Foster, Samuel (father of SEWELL), IX, 276
Foster, Samuel (neighbour of William KAIN), VI, 369
Foster, Samuel Willard, IX, 276; X, 157
Foster, Sewell, IX, **276–77**; X, 293
Foster, Thankful (Moore), XII, 759
Foster, Thomas, IV, 219
Foster, William Alexander, XI, **322–25**, 621; XII, 951
Foster, William Hershall (Herschel), IX, 276
Fotherby, Charles, II, **226–27**, 637
Fothergill, Charles, VI, 164, 265, 498, 604, 612, 633, 770, 771; VII, 162, 312, **317–21**, 417, 418, 664; VIII, 125, 602; IX, 346, 497; X, 5; XI, 877; XII, 200, 526
Fothergill, Charles Forbes, VII, 320
Fothergill, Charlotte. *See* Nevins
Fothergill, Eliza. *See* Richardson
Fothergill, John (uncle), VII, 317
Fothergill, John, VII, 317
Fothergill, Mary Anne. *See* Forbes
Fothergill, Samuel, VII, 317
Fothersall, Ann (Williams), IV, 771
Foubert, Marie (Cusson), II, 166
Foucault, Catherine. *See* Catalon
Foucault, Catherine. *See* Nafrechoux
Foucault, Catherine. *See* Sabourin, *dit* Chauniers
Foucault, Eusèbe, III, 225
Foucault, François, III, 227
Foucault, François, III, 75, 135, **225–27**, 300, 400, 491, 525, 539, 647; IV, 318, 359, 360, 361, 433; V, 315
Foucault, Françoise (Poulin de Courval), III, 538, 539
Foucault, Louise-Catherine (Nouchet), III, 226, 491
Foucault, Marie-Claude-Geneviève (Guillimin), III, 226; IV, 318
Foucault, Marie-Thérèse (Lamaletie), III, 226; IV, 433
Foucault, Michelle-Élisabeth (Liénard de Beaujeu), III, 400
Foucault, Nicolas, I, 361; II, 186, 189, 190, **227**; III, 380
Foucault, Nicolas-Denis, III, 226
Foucault, Simon (Pierre), III, **227**
Foucault de Saint-Germain-Beaupré, Louis de, Comte Du Daugnon, I, 324
Foucher, Monsieur, I, **311**
Foucher, Antoine, III, 141; IV, 534; V, 602
Foucher, Charlotte-Élisabeth. *See* Goubert
Foucher, François, III, 228
Foucher, François, III, **227–28**, 279; IV, 11, 356
Foucher, Jacques, III, 227
Foucher, Louis-Charles, IV, 345, 346; V, 207, 322, 434, 591; VI, 383, 385; VII, 72, 225, 235, 387, 388, 393, 485, 614, 769; VIII, 366, 480; IX, 568, 807
Foucher, Marie-Bernadine. *See* Lebé
Foucher, Marie-Céleste (Bouate), VIII, 480
Foucher, Marie-Joseph. *See* Le Gardeur de Courtemanche
Foucher, Marie-Léocadie (Heney), VII, 393
Foucher, Marie-Madeleine-Françoise (Panet), IV, 601; V, 652

Foucher, Rosalie (Demers), X, 221
Foucher de Labrador, Charles, III, 228
Foucquet. *See* Fouquet
Foucrelle. *See* Faucrolle
Fougeray, Monsieur (companion of Samuel de CHAMPLAIN), I, 293
Fougères. *See* Boiton
Fouilleuse, Louise de (Prouville, Marquise de Tracy), I, 557
Foulis, Mrs. *See* Dewar
Foulis, Andrew, IX, 277
Foulis, Elizabeth. *See* Leatham
Foulis, Robert, IX, **277**
Foulkes, Hannah (Chance), XI, 654
Foulkes, Sarah (Lancaster), VII, 481
Foulkes, Theodora (Bernard), XII, 97
Fount, William de la, I, 239, 240
Fouquet, Charles-Louis-Auguste, Duc de Belle-Isle, III, 458; IV, 307, 670
Fouquet, Léon, XII, 284
Fouquet (Foucquet), Nicolas, I, 296, 323
Fouquet de Chalain, Christophe, I, 257
Fourche, La. *See* Nissowaquet
Foureur, Anne-Céleste. *See* Desforges
Foureur, Charlotte (Rousseau), IV, 272; VI, 663, 666
Foureur, Pierre, IV, 272
Foureur, *dit* Champagne, Catherine. *See* Guertin
Foureur, *dit* Champagne, Jean-Louis, IV, 151, 272; V, 392, 833; VI, 499; VII, 255
Foureur, *dit* Champagne, Louis, IV, **272**; VI, 663
Foureur, *dit* Champagne, Pierre, IV, 272; V, 436, 727; VI, 230, 663; VII, 255
Fourier, François-Marie-Charles, VIII, 438; X, 315, 585
Fourier, Louis, IV, 200
Fourier, Pierre, I, 115, 118
Fourmond, Vital, XI, 746, 748
Fournel. *See also* Fornel
Fournel, Jean, III, 569
Fournerie de Vézon, Joseph, V, 714
Fournerie de Vézon, Marie-Louise. *See* Réaume
Fournier, Adrienne, XII, 325
Fournier, Catherine (Roussel), I, 583
Fournier, Charles-Godfroid, XII, 913
Fournier, Charles-Vincent, VII, **321–23**, 678; VIII, 129
Fournier, Flavie (Smith), XI, 836
Fournier, Françoise. *See* Hébert
Fournier, Geneviève (Henry), VII, 394
Fournier, Guillaume (son-in-law of Hélène DESPORTES), I, 264
Fournier, Guillaume (father of TÉLESPHORE), XII, 323
Fournier, Hermine. *See* Demers
Fournier, Joseph (mason), VII, 240
Fournier, Joseph (merchant), IV, 329
Fournier, Louise (Gendron), XI, 337
Fournier, Marguerite. *See* Crevier
Fournier, Marie-Anne. *See* Peguy
Fournier, Marie-Archange. *See* Morin
Fournier, Marie-Honoré (Bellet), VI, 50
Fournier, Pierre, IV, 386
Fournier, Pierre-Laurent, VII, 321
Fournier, Rosalie (Picard Destroismaisons), IX, 633
Fournier, Télesphore, VIII, 834; XI, 160, 178; XII, **323–26**, 651, 655, 693, 853

Fournier, Thomas, VIII, 40; IX, 318; XII, 847
Fournier, *dit* Préfontaine, Joseph-Raymond, XI, 211, 766
Fowell, John Digby, IX, 277
Fowell, Sarah. *See* Knowling
Fowell, Theana. *See* Holland
Fowell, William Newton, VII, 34; VIII, 788, 789; IX, **277–78**
Fowle, Daniel, III, 91
Fowler, Charles, VIII, 959
Fowler, Daniel, XII, 326
Fowler, Daniel, XII, 101, **326–29**, 776
Fowler, Elizabeth. *See* Gale
Fowler, Emily. *See* Faribault
Fowler, Mary Ann. *See* Pope
Fowler, Mary Ann (King), IX, 429
Fowler, Orson Squire, VI, 93
Fowler, Pamelia (Herring), XII, 428
Fowler, Reginald, XII, 327
Fowler, Sarah (Batt), IV, 46, 47
Fowler, Thomas, VII, 312, 313
Fowler, William, IX, 709
Fox, Anne. *See* Barnard
Fox, Anne (Todd), XII, 1062
Fox, Charles James, IV, 350; V, 145, 849, 867, 898; VI, 137; VII, 35, 151, 524; X, 573
Fox, Elizabeth (Laver), XII, 534
Fox, George, I, 81, 82, 84
Fox, Henry, 1st Baron Holland, IV, 57, 606
Fox, Henry Edward, V, 156, 630, 867, 868; VI, 137, 820; IX, 137
Fox, Henry Stephen, VII, 412; VIII, 27
Fox, Sir James, XII, 484
Fox, John C., IX, **278–79**
Fox, Joseph, VII, 481
Fox, Luke, I, 20, 144, **311–12**, 329, 362, 375, 384, 668
Fox, Margaret, VIII, 449, 450
Fox, Mary. *See* FitzClarence
Fox, Richard, I, 311
Fox, Samuel, VI, 811
Fox, Theophilus, V, 502
Foxcroft, John, V, 315
Foxcroft, Samuel, I, 499
Foxe. *See* Fox
Foy, Edward, V, 584
Foy, Elizabeth (Southack), III, 596
Foy, Hannah. *See* Van Horn
Foy*, James Joseph (1847–1916), XII, 333
Foy, Lewis, VII, 213
Foy, Nancy (Cameron), XI, 143
Foy, Nathaniel, V, 161
Foy, Patrick, XII, 42
Fraile, Elizabeth (Elder), VII, 271
Fraise, Marie-Louise (Drouin), VIII, 235
Fraisses de Long, Antoine, V, 276
France, Charles de, Duc de Berry, II, 98, 104, 301, 618; IV, 663
Franchère, Benoîte. *See* Camagne
Franchère, Charlotte (Prince; wife of GABRIEL), IX, 280
Franchère, Élisabeth (Arnoldi), VII, 25; IX, 396
Franchère, Félicité. *See* Morin
Franchère, Gabriel, IV, 508; VII, 622; IX, 279
Franchère, Gabriel, IV, 508; V, 236, 237, 419, 533, 534,

814; VI, 236, 547, 665; VII, 512, 622; VIII, 158, 176, 540, 557, 768; IX, **279–80**; X, 414
Franchère, Marie-Victorine-Cordélia (Irumberry de Salaberry), XI, 441
Franchère, Rose (Laberge), X, 414
Franchère, Sophie. *See* Routhier
Franchère, Timothée, IX, 699; XI, 585
Francheville. *See also* Poulin; Terrier
Francheville, Pierre, I, 393; II, **227–28**, 460
Franchi, Alessandro, XI, 104; XII, 820, 1020, 1022
Francis. *See also* Leblanc, *dit* Latour, François
Francis, Mr (of England), I, 370
Francis, Mary (Yeo), IX, 855
Francis, Samuel, II, 293
Francis, Toma. *See* Tomah, Francis
Francis, W. W., VII, 825
Francis de Sales, I, 91; II, 34; VIII, 283; XII, 861
Franck, César, X, 228
Francklin, Edith. *See* Nicholson
Francklin, Elizabeth Gould (Uniacke), IX, 801
Francklin, George Germaine Sackville, IV, 502
Francklin, James Boutineau, IV, 781
Francklin, Michael, IV, 272
Francklin, Michael, IV, 13, 29, 80, 111, 116, 131, 132, 258, **272–76**, 291, 292, 300, 308, 313, 352, 450, 502, 504, 528, 561, 696, 723, 736, 781; V, 16, 81, 240, 251, 257, 409, 416, 435, 465, 556, 607, 608, 843; VI, 193, 228, 307, 678, 718, 774; VII, 384; IX, 801
Francklin, Susanna (Davis; Haliburton), VI, 307
Francklin, Susannah. *See* Boutineau
Francklyn, Jane. *See* Cunard
François (son of OUMASASIKWEIE), I, 527
François, Father (French priest), II, 8
François, Father (Recollet), III, 369
François, Mlle (Havy), III, 282
François I, King of France, I, 27, 126, 165, 166, 168, 309, 384, 423, 424, 658, 659, 660; III, 703
François, Catherine (Billaudèle), IX, 50
François, Jeanne (Le Borgne), I, 435
François, Laurent, VIII, 283
François, Luc (baptized Claude), I, 55, **312–15**, 359, 420; II, 199, 200, 344; V, 497
François, Mathieu, I, 312
François, Perrette. *See* Prieur
François, *dit* Saint-François, Joseph, IV, 386
François-Marie de Paris (Sieur Marie), I, 505
François-Xavier. *See also* Arosen; Tonsahoten
François-Xavier, II, 665
François-Xavier, Father. *See* Kaiser
Frankfort, Florence A. (Bedson), XII, 74
Franklin. *See also* Franklyn
Franklin, Miss (Sleigh), IX, 723
Franklin, Benjamin, I, 255; III, 125; IV, 105, 230, 270, 407, 532, 549, 759; V, 31, 315, 316; VI, 548; VII, 537; VIII, 240, 262; X, 335
Franklin, Edward, X, 295
Franklin, Eleanor Anne. *See* Porden
Franklin, Eleanor Isabella (Gell), VIII, 447
Franklin, Hannah. *See* Weekes
Franklin, Jane, Lady Franklin. *See* Griffin
Franklin, Sir John, I, 20, 375, 378; VI, 218, 221, 222, 327, 328, 329, 437, 648, 753, 754; VII, 64, 115, **323–28**, 405, 463, 902, 912; VIII, 70, 71, 79, 80, 85, 447, 448, 623,

624, 663, 685, 686, 773; IX, 6, 12, 43, 167, 197, 198, 199, 389, 390, 532, 648, 658, 659, 660, 693; X, 26, 27, 28, 29, 38, 42, 89, 319, 320, 327, 328, 396, 397, 407, 408, 453, 454, 513, 514, 561, 562, 748; XI, 55, 199, 200, 382, 384, 393, 436, 470, 471, 543, 544, 691, 718, 854; XII, 38, 122, 524, 668, 835, 877, 878, 892, 954, 955, 1079
Franklin, Lewis, X, 294
Franklin, Lumley, X, 113, **294–95**
Franklin, Miriam. *See* Abraham
Franklin, Selim, X, 295
Franklin, Thomas, V, 647
Franklin, William, V, 438, 628, 629, 657; VI, 562, 781; VII, 657
Franklin, Willingham, VII, 323
Franklyn. *See also* Francklin
Franklyn (Franklin), Mary (Montgomery), IV, 545
Franklyn, William Hayles, X, 199
Frank Red Crow. *See* Astohkomi
Franks, Abraham, IV, 332
Franks, Appollonia (mother of JACOB), VII, 328
Franks, Charles William, XI, 950
Franks, David Salisbury, IV, 332
Franks, Jacob (John), V, 9; VI, 365; VII, **328–29**; VIII, 245; X, 12
Franks, John (father of JACOB), VII, 328
Franks, John (of Montreal), IV, 332
Franks, Mary. *See* Solomons
Franks, Rachel (Lawe), VII, 328
Franks, Rebecca (Kemble), VII, 462
Franks, Rebecca (Solomons), IV, 718
Franks, Thérèse. *See* Gère, *dit* Larose
Franquelin, Élisabeth. *See* Auber
Franquelin, Élisabeth (Lemieux), II, 230
Franquelin, Jean-Baptiste-Louis, I, 119, 537, 664; II, **228–31**, 352, 427, 594, 599
Franquelin, Marie-Anne (Quesnel), II, 230
Franquet, Jean-Baptiste, III, 228
Franquet, Louis, III, 24, 79, 80, 117, 118, 183, **228–32**, 255, 267, 268, 440, 699, 700; IV, 64, 68, 174, 304, 344, 645, 656, 657; V, 738
Franquet, Marie-Marguerite. *See* Romby
Franquetot, François de, Duc de Coigny, IV, 477
Franqueville, Anne-Henriette de (Calonne), VI, 105
Fransoni, Giacomo Filippo, VII, 295, 296, 297; VIII, 307, 318; IX, 18; X, 53
Fransoni, Luigi, X, 479
Franzini, Marino Miguel, VIII, 669
Frary, Sophronia (De Witt), VIII, 219
Fraser, Miss (Needham), X, 543
Fraser, Mrs. *See* Cameron
Fraser, Mrs (grandmother of JOHN ARTHUR), XII, 335
Fraser, Agnes. *See* Maxwell
Fraser, Alexander (apprentice), V, 437; VIII, 638
Fraser, Alexander (Chambly merchant), V, 877
Fraser, Alexander (commander), IV, 130, 146, 418
Fraser, Alexander (father of DONALD ALLAN), VII, 329
Fraser, Alexander (father of JAMES), VI, 262
Fraser, Alexander (fur trader), IV, 685; VIII, 546, 575, 880
Fraser, Alexander (Halifax merchant), VI, 263
Fraser, Alexander (judge), V, 772
Fraser, Alexander (office holder), V, 132, 317, 318, 374, 427; VI, 615
Fraser, Alexander (officer), III, 525, 530

Fraser, Alexander (of Grenada), V, 349
Fraser, Alexander (of Quebec), VI, 27
Fraser, Alexander (seigneur), VII, 96
Fraser, Alexander, IV, **276**; V, 224, 225
Fraser, Alexander, VIII, 188, **302–4**, 547, 583; X, 462, 463; XII, 613
Fraser*, Alexander (1860–1936), XII, 13, 589
Fraser, Angélique (McLoughlin), VII, 573; VIII, 575
Fraser, Ann. *See* Hudson
Fraser, Ann. *See* McDonell
Fraser, Ann (Bélanger; Bélair), V, 331
Fraser, Anne Maria. *See* Sayer
Fraser, Catharine. *See* Grant
Fraser, Catherine. *See* Macdonell
Fraser, Catherine. *See* McKay
Fraser, Catherine (Denoon), VII, 245
Fraser, Catherine (Macdonald), XII, 613
Fraser, Catherine Isabella. *See* Maclean
Fraser, Christiana. *See* MacKay
Fraser, Christina (Holmes), X, 353
Fraser, Christopher Finlay, XII, **329–34**, 1120
Fraser, Cornelia. *See* Munro
Fraser, Daniel, IX, 280
Fraser, Daniel R., XII, 671
Fraser, Donald, V, 330
Fraser, Donald, IX, 656; XI, 231, 467; XII, **334–35**
Fraser, Donald Allan, VI, 660; VII, **329–30**, 532, 533, 536, 636; VIII, 569, 570, 770
Fraser, Lady Elizabeth, Lady Lovat. *See* Stewart
Fraser, Helen, XII, 365
Fraser, Hugh, XII, 6
Fraser, Isaac, VI, 56; VII, 580
Fraser, Isabella. *See* Grant
Fraser, Isabella. *See* Maclean
Fraser, Isabella. *See* Warren
Fraser, James (father of PETER), VII, 330
Fraser, James (partner of Pierre de RASTEL de Rocheblave), VII, 735
Fraser, James, V, 58, 795; VI, 112, **262–63**; VII, 331; IX, 175, 328
Fraser, James A., XII, 1092
Fraser, James Daniel Bain, IX, **280–82**
Fraser, James DeWolf, IX, 154
Fraser, Jane. *See* Chisholm
Fraser, Jane. *See* McCord
Fraser, Jane (Davidson), IV, 276; V, 224
Fraser, Jane M. Paulette. *See* Fisher
Fraser, Janet. *See* McIntosh
Fraser, Janet (McKenzie), VIII, 560
Fraser, Jean. *See* Rose
Fraser, John (agent), XII, 348
Fraser, John (apprentice), VII, 25
Fraser, John (brother of JAMES DANIEL BAIN), IX, 281
Fraser, John (brother of RICHARD DUNCAN), VIII, 305
Fraser, John (businessman), V, 283, 333, 562, 563, 564, 565
Fraser, John (cousin of Simon MCTAVISH), VI, 454
Fraser, John (father of JOHN ARTHUR), XII, 335
Fraser, John (father of JOHN JAMES), XII, 338
Fraser, John (father of WILLIAM), VIII, 306
Fraser, John (lawyer), V, 861
Fraser, John (Mohawk chief), XII, 401
Fraser, John (notary), VIII, 606

Fraser, John (partner of JAMES), VI, 263
Fraser, John (second cousin of Simon MCGILLIVRAY), VII, 561
Fraser, John (shipbuilder), XII, 785
Fraser, John (shipyard owner), VIII, 783; XI, 834
Fraser, John (son of THOMAS), VI, 265
Fraser, John (teacher), XII, 661, 662, 663
Fraser, John (uncle of Simon FRASER), IV, 229, 269, 345, 346, 492, 570, 574, 602, 634, 759; V, 142, 146, 149, 150, 216, 225, 232, 599, 839, 892; VI, 295, 606; VII, 169; IX, 282; X, 162
Fraser, John, V, 46, **329–30**; VIII, 936; IX, 249
Fraser, John Arthur, XII, 207, 327, 328, **335–38**, 789, 790, 793, 794
Fraser, John James, XI, 298; XII, 19, **338–42**
Fraser, John Malcolm, V, 331
Fraser, John S., XII, 329
Fraser, Joseph (partner of Claude DÉNÉCHAU), VII, 241
Fraser, Joseph (son of MALCOLM), V, 331
Fraser, Josephte (Chaussegros de Léry), VII, 169; IX, 127; X, 162
Fraser, Luke, VII, 400
Fraser, Malcolm (merchant), V, 713
Fraser, Malcolm (son of Malcolm, merchant), V, 99
Fraser, Malcolm, IV, 107, 150, 548, 574; V, 131, **330–31**, 620; VI, 225, 557; VII, 573; VIII, 575; X, 22
Fraser, Margaret, IV, 276
Fraser, Margaret (Booth), V, 91
Fraser, Margaret (Fraser), XII, 338
Fraser, Margaret (Kelly), XI, 466
Fraser, Maria. *See* Berton
Fraser, Marjory (Tolmie), XI, 885
Fraser, Martha. *See* Cumming
Fraser, Mary. *See* MacBean
Fraser, Mary. *See* MacDonell
Fraser, Mary. *See* McDonell
Fraser, Mary Ann. *See* Lafayette
Fraser, Mary Ann (McNabb), V, 550
Fraser, Maxwell D., XII, 470
Fraser, Paul, VIII, 303, 422; IX, 513, 514
Fraser, Peter, VI, 356, 474; VII, **330–32**; VIII, 509
Fraser, Rachel Otis. *See* DeWolf
Fraser, Richard Duncan, VI, 265; VII, 459; VIII, **304–6**; IX, 333
Fraser, Robert Grant, IX, 281
Fraser, Robert Peden, IX, 281
Fraser, Sarah M. *See* Burke
Fraser, Sarah Rachel (Gore, Lady Gore), IX, 328
Fraser, Simon (father of SIMON), IX, 282
Fraser, Simon (father of Simon, partner of John YOUNG, d. 1819), V, 64, 713, 816, 817, 877
Fraser, Simon (merchant), V, 816
Fraser, Simon (officer), IV, 190
Fraser, Simon (partner of John YOUNG, d. 1819), V, 270, 877, 879; VI, 556
Fraser, Simon (son of MALCOLM), V, 331
Fraser, Simon (uncle of John MCLOUGHLIN), VIII, 575
Fraser, Simon, V, 531, 541; VI, 436, 466; VII, 385, 716, 837, 838; VIII, 303, 453, 527, 546; IX, **282–86**; X, 720
Fraser, Susan. *See* Moulton
Fraser, Thomas, XI, 258
Fraser, Thomas, V, 282; VI, **263–65**, 475; VII, 251; VIII, 304

Fraser, Thomas Roderick, IX, 281
Fraser, Wilhelmine-Anaïs. *See* Aubert de Gaspé
Fraser, William (brother of SIMON), IX, 282
Fraser, William (brother of THOMAS), VI, 264
Fraser, William (father of THOMAS), VI, 263
Fraser, William (lawyer), XI, 925
Fraser, William (Métis captain), VIII, 342
Fraser, William (son-in-law of Philippe-Joseph AUBERT de Gaspé), X, 20
Fraser, William (son of MALCOLM), V, 331
Fraser, William (son of THOMAS), VI, 264
Fraser, William, VI, 449, 450, 691; VII, 355, 551, 552, 581, 582, 805, 934; VIII, 247, **306–8**, 554, 627, 664, 665, 894, 919, 920; XI, 351; XII, 548
Fraser, William Lewis, XII, 287, 337, 789
Frasse, Louis, Vicomte de Plainval, X, 59
Frasse de Plainval, Louis, XI, **325–26**
Frasse de Plainval, May Susee. *See* Van Nostrand
Fraysse, Françoise (Veyssières), IV, 752
Frayssinous, Denis, Comte de Frayssinous, VI, 201; VIII, 212
Frazer. *See also* Fraser
Frazer, Jean (Paterson), VIII, 686; XI, 675
Fréchette, E.-R., VIII, 537
Fréchette, Jean-Baptiste, VII, 61, 430, 650; VIII, 537, 962; IX, 262, 299; X, 580, 582, 583; XI, 159; XII, 269
Fréchette*, Louis (1839–1908), III, 148; V, 130; VII, 514; IX, 121, 465; X, 203; XI, 83, 218, 352, 659, 709, 852; XII, 67, 271, 309, 471, 472, 725, 853
Fréchette, Madeleine (Desautels), XI, 249
Fréchette, Marie-Louise (St Jean), XII, 937
Fréchette, Pierre, VIII, 590
Fréchette, R., VII, 762
Frederick II, King of Prussia, IV, 67; V, 166, 582, 791; VI, 240, 679
Frederick, Lucy (Young), X, 728
Frederick Augustus, Duke of York, IV, 25; V, 110, 206, 346, 356, 488, 802; VI, 560, 713, 789; VII, 744; VIII, 26, 336; IX, 485, 730, 731; XI, 947
Frederick Louis, Prince of Wales, III, 658
Fredette, Jean-Baptiste, VII, 239
Fredin, Claude. *See also* Robin
Fredin, Claude (André de Leigne), III, 14
Fredin, Gabriel, III, 14
Fredin, Jean, II, 133, 377; III, 15, 407
Freed, Augustus Toplady, XI, 32
Freeman, Abigail (Street), VI, 740; VIII, 840; IX, 766
Freeman, Alma Hopkins (Lewis), VI, 399
Freeman, Anne (Grant), V, 260
Freeman, Edward Augustus, XII, 582
Freeman, Elisha, IV, 219
Freeman, Elkanah, VI, 412
Freeman, Experience (Waterman), IX, 821
Freeman, John, VI, 37
Freeman, Joseph, V, 817; IX, 477, 710; X, 36
Freeman, Patience (Foster; Waterman), IX, 821
Freeman, Samuel Black, IX, 6; XI, 934
Freeman, Thomas Birch, XII, 127
Freer, Noah, VI, 96, 309; VII, 619; VIII, 369; IX, 179; X, 518
Frégault*, Guy (1918–77), IV, xxv, 61, 68, 71, 355, 634, 660, 674; VIII, 88
Freiligrath, Hermann Ferdinand, IX, 420, 421

Freke, Elizabeth (Bulkeley, Lady Bulkeley), IV, 109
Frémin, Jacques, I, 48, 108, **315**, 445, 461, 547, 635, 650;
   II, 61, 341, 540; III, 335
Frémiot, Joseph, VIII, 308
Frémiot, Marie-Jeanne. *See* Didier
Frémiot, Nicolas-Marie-Joseph, VIII, **308–9**, 636
Frémont, Caroline-Alix. *See* Beaubien
Frémont, Cécile. *See* Panet
Frémont, Charles-Jacques, VIII, 682; IX, 32, 119, **286–87**,
   572; X, 376; XI, 272, 484; XII, 911
Frémont, Charles-Pierre, IX, 286
Frémont, Charlotte. *See* Voyer
Frémont, Jean-Louis, III, 377; IV, 303
Frémont, Jules-Joseph-Taschereau, X, 37
Frémont, Marie. *See* Collet
Frémont, Reine (Godefroy de Tonnancour), IV, 303
French, Anne (Caldwell, Lady Caldwell), V, 130
French, Arthur, V, 640
French, C. A., XII, 466
French, Charles, VI, **265–67**
French, Charles, named Brother Dominique, VI, 528
French, Edwin C., XI, 807
French, Frances Mary. *See* Chapman
French*, Sir George Arthur (1841–1921), XI, 326; XII, 23,
   673, 674, 858
French, Isabella. *See* Hamilton
French, James, VI, 474
French, Jane (mother of CHARLES), VI, 265
French, Jane (Dease), V, 228; IX, 196
French, John (father of CHARLES), VI, 265
French, John (father of JOHN, 1843–85), XI, 326
French, John, I, **315**, 605
French, John, XI, **326**; XII, 735
French, Julia Elizabeth (Dadson), XII, 225
French, Lawrence, I, 315
French, Margaret, III, 147
French, Mary (Duncan), V, 280
French, Prudence (McLean), VI, 473
French, Ruth (Colby), IX, 144
French, T. B., VI, 599; IX, 257
Frenchwoman (wife of Billy CALDWELL), VII, 132
Frenel, Joseph-Antoine de, II, 632
Frenel, Marie-Anne de. *See* La Marque
Freneuse. *See* Damours
Fresnay. *See* Guyon
Fresne, Cécile-Clémence (Bibaud), VIII, 87
Fresnoy, Marquis de, IV, 622
Fresnoy, Agathe-Louise de (Renaud d'Avène Des
   Méloizes), V, 711
Fresnoy, Marie-Marguerite de. *See* Lemoine, *dit* Monière
Fressel, Jeanne (Jacob), II, 294
Frey, Philip, VII, 450
Freydis, I, 449, 643
Friand. *See* Triaud
Frichet, Charles, IV, 502; VI, 560
Frichet, Jean-Baptiste, V, 185
Friday, III, 151
Friedel, Ignace, V, 248
Friedrich I, Duke of Württemberg, I, 632
Friel, Charles, IX, 287
Friel, Henry James, IX, **287–88**; X, 45; XI, 685
Friel, Mary Anne. *See* O'Connor
Friend. *See* Triaud

Frigon, Joseph-Georges-Antoine, VIII, 217
Frink, Alathea (Brush), XI, 120
Frisbie, Levi, VII, 911
Frisbie, Levi, VII, 911
Frisius, Gemma, I, 154, 679
Frith, Elizabeth (Ryland), VII, 766
Frith, Jane (Jeffers), XII, 468
Frizzell, Richard, VII, 863
Frobisher, Alexander, VII, 776
Frobisher, Benjamin, IV, 262, **276–78**, 532; V, 90, 178,
   179, 258, 331, 332, 512, 528, 561, 562, 563, 564, 602,
   818; VI, 267
Frobisher, Benjamin Joseph, V, 291, 333; VI, **267–68**; VII,
   201, 205, 567, 762; VIII, 159
Frobisher, Bernard, I, 316
Frobisher, Charlotte. *See* Jobert
Frobisher, Dorothy (Widmerpole; wife of Sir MARTIN), I,
   318
Frobisher, Isabel (wife of Sir MARTIN), I, 318
Frobisher, Isabella. *See* Grant
Frobisher, James Joseph, VI, 268
Frobisher, Joseph, IV, 276; V, 331
Frobisher, Joseph, IV, 47, 133, 139, 276, 277, 278, 647; V,
   8, 90, 129, 134, 177, 178, 214, 215, 218, 258, 291, 301,
   **331–34**, 391, 495, 500, 512, 528, 561, 562, 564, 565,
   566, 592, 602, 614, 636, 682, 715, 818, 820, 822; VI,
   204, 267, 285, 296, 317, 318, 433, 454, 455, 456, 471,
   499, 640, 700, 743, 744; VII, 30, 79, 201, 737, 825; VIII,
   575
Frobisher, Josette (Sayer), VII, 776
Frobisher, Sir Martin, I, 19, 85, 86, 93, 94, 153, **316–19**,
   332, 375, 385, 607, 669, 670, 677, 679, 680; IV, liii; X,
   327; XI, 200; XII, 835
Frobisher, Nathaniel, VI, 267
Frobisher, Peter, I, 318
Frobisher, Rachel. *See* Hargrave
Frobisher, Rachel-Charlotte (O'Brien), VI, 499
Frobisher, Thomas, IV, 276; V, 129, 331, 332, 500, 682,
   683, 685; VI, 267, 317
Fromenteau, Louis, V, 225
Fromont, *dit* La Bouille, Thomas, I, 167, 169
Fronsac. *See* Denys
Frontenac, Comte de. *See* Buade
Frontenac, Comtesse de. *See* La Grange; Phélypeaux de
   Pontchartrain
Frontigny, Catherine (Mourongeau), III, 78
Frontigny, Marie-Madeleine. *See* Lajoüe
Frontigny, Pierre, III, 77
Front Man. *See* Ne-can-nete
Froschauer, Christoph, VII, 778
Frost, Ebenezer, XII, 701
Frost, James, V, 95, **334–35**, 386; VI, 135; VIII, 101
Frost, Jeremiah, V, 545
Frost, John, IV, 565; V, 545
Frost, Phoebe. *See* Wallen
Frothingham, John (father of JOHN), IX, 288
Frothingham, John (son of JOHN), IX, 289
Frothingham, John, VIII, 631; IX, **288–89**; X, 335, 717; XI,
   899, 936
Frothingham, Joseph May, IX, 288
Frothingham, Louisa Goddard (Molson), IX, 289
Frothingham, Martha (mother of JOHN), IX, 288
Frotté, Monsieur (ship's commander), I, 423
Froude, James Anthony, XII, 112

Frowd, Elizabeth Speed (Beaven), X, 40
Frowd, John Speed, X, 40
Froyer de La Baronnière, Jeanne (La Roche Daillon), I, 420
Fruing, William, VIII, 493
Fry, Charlotte Augusta. *See* Goss
Fry, Edward Carey, XII, 342
Fry, Elizabeth. *See* Gurney
Fry, George, XII, 342
Fry, Henry, XII, 343
Fry, Henry, XII, **342–43**, 1089
Fry, Jane (Macleod), XII, 672
Fry, John S., XII, 280
Fry, Mary Jane. *See* Dawson
Fry, Rachel Elizabeth (Cresswell), IX, 167
Frye, Joseph, III, 87, 129
Fryer, Elizabeth (Collier, Lady Collier), IV, 160
Fryer, Mary (Massey), XII, 710
Fryer, William, VIII, 673, 674
Fryfogel, Sebastian, VII, 882; X, 213
Fubbister, John; Fubbister, Mary. *See* Gunn, Isabel
Fuca, Juan de, I, 676, **677**; IV, 165, 244, 746; VI, 36
Fudger, Harris Henry, XII, 973
Fulford, Andrew, I, 278
Fulford, Anne Maria. *See* Adams
Fulford, Baldwin, IX, 289
Fulford, Faith (Davis), I, 251
Fulford, Francis, IX, 246, **289–93**, 378, 558, 579, 581; X, 58, 548; XI, 503, 872; XII, 431, 573, 788, 789, 813, 1100
Fulford, Sir John, I, 251
Fulford, Mary. *See* Drummond
Fullartine, John, II, 49, 50, 51, **231–33**, 266, 311, 312, 319, 492; III, 414
Fuller, Amos, IV, 351
Fuller, Andrew, V, 557, 558
Fuller, Caroline Anne. *See* Green
Fuller, Charles, XII, 188, 213
Fuller, Cynthia. *See* Street
Fuller, Elizabeth (McQuesten), XI, 583
Fuller, Frank, XI, 806
Fuller, Hyacinth Huden, IX, 293
Fuller, James Canning, XI, 400
Fuller, Jane (Boys), IX, 79
Fuller, John, IX, 293
Fuller, Margaret. *See* Lanigan
Fuller, Mary. *See* Oakley
Fuller, Mary. *See* Tiley
Fuller, Mary O'Brien. *See* England
Fuller, Robert, X, 172
Fuller, Sarah Margaret (Ossoli, Marchioness Ossoli), VII, 582
Fuller, Thomas, XII, 343
Fuller, Thomas, VIII, 872, 944; XI, 464; XII, **343–46**, 534, 535, 627, 930, 958
Fuller, Thomas Brock, VII, 835; X, 55, 56; XI, **326–28**, 917; XII, 681
Fuller, Thomas Horace, IX, **293–94**
Fuller, Thomas Richard, XI, 326
Fuller, Thomas William, XII, 346
Fuller, William Henry, XII, 623, 624
Fullertine (Fullerton). *See* Fullartine
Fullerton, Helen (Clarke), X, 172
Fullerton, Jane (Stirling), XI, 856

Fullerton, Maria (Goodhue), IX, 323
Fulton, Alexander Thomson, XII, 44
Fulton, Allison, IX, 294
Fulton, Ann. *See* Boggs
Fulton, Clarissa (Fairfield), V, 307
Fulton, Isabella. *See* Campbell
Fulton, James, V, 612; VI, **268**, 780
Fulton, John, VI, 268
Fulton, John, XI, **328–29**
Fulton, Joseph, V, 656
Fulton, Julia Ann. *See* Heustis
Fulton, Margaret. *See* Campbell
Fulton, Robert (engineer), VI, 355; VII, 617, 618
Fulton, Robert (oarsman), XII, 461, 462
Fulton, Sarah Elizabeth. *See* Black
Fulton, Stephen, IX, **294–95**, 426
Fulton, Thomas, IX, 294
Fulton, William (grandfather), IX, 294
Fulton, William, IX, 294
Funcken, Eugene, X, 277
Funcken, Louis G. F. H., X, 277
Furey, Charles, IX, 393, 820; XI, 433
Furey, George, IX, 584, 585
Furlong, Bessie Josephine Stanislaus (Dearin), XI, 239
Furlong, Bridget (Dubord), X, 262
Furmage, Mary (Lewin), XII, 560
Furnell, William, VI, 274
Furness, Frank, XII, 131
Furniss, Albert, VII, 27, 594; VIII, 84; XI, 315; XII, 72, 809
Furniss, Louise Priscille. *See* Arnoldi
Fuseli, Henry, VII, 91
Fustel, Charles, II, 451
Futcher, Thomas Barnes, XII, 384
Futvoye, Catherine Hedwige. *See* Lozeau
Futvoye, George, XII, **346–48**
Futvoye, Isaac Booth, XII, 347
Fyfe, Elizabeth (Rose), XI, 766
Fyfe, Jane. *See* Thomson
Fyfe, Rebecca S. *See* Kendall
Fyfe, Robert Alexander, IX, 113; X, **295–96**; XI, 158, 576, 577; XII, 1076, 1094

GABAR, Perrine (Fleury), II, 223
Gaboto, Antonio, I, 304
Gaboury (Gabourie), Charles, X, 296
Gaboury, Marguerite (Gingras), VIII, 328, 329
Gaboury, Marie-Anne. *See* Tessier
Gaboury, Marie-Anne (Lagimonière), VI, 398; VIII, 481; IX, 626, 663; X, **296–97**; XI, 736
Gabriel, VI, 352
Gabriel, Gilles, IV, 471
Gabriel, Jacques, III, 235
Gabriel, Marie (Corpron), III, 141
Gabriel, Marie-Geneviève. *See* Côté
Gabrielle, Suzanne de (Robutel de La Noue), II, 581
Gadbois. *See also* Vandandaigue
Gadbois, Albine, named Marie de Bonsecours, X, **297–99**
Gadbois, Azilda, X, 298
Gadbois, Malvina, X, 298
Gadbois, Philomène, X, 298
Gaden, George, VI, 311
Gadiou, Jean-Baptiste, VI, 49

Gadiou, Marie-Anne. *See* Réaume

Gadois, Jeanne. *See* Besnard

Gadois, Jeanne-Françoise (Hattanville), II, 234

Gadois, Marie. *See* Pontonnier

Gadois, Pierre, I, 319; II, **233–34**; III, 232

Gadois, *dit* Mauger, Jacques, II, 234; III, 181, **232–33**; IV, 204, 748

Gadois, *dit* Mauger, Marie-Madeleine. *See* Chorel de Saint-Romain, *dit* d'Orvilliers

Gadoys, Françoise (Godé), I, 319

Gadoys, Jean-Baptiste, I, 319; II, 234

Gadoys, Louise. *See* Mauger

Gadoys, Pierre, I, 218, **319**, 464, 557; II, 233; III, 232

Gadoys, Roberte (Prud'homme; Verrier), I, 319, 557; II, 466

Gage, Andrew, VIII, 309

Gage, Benedicta Maria Theresa, Viscountess Gage. *See* Hall

Gage, James, VII, 451; VIII, 309

Gage, James, VII, 451; VIII, **309–10**

Gage, James Philipse, VIII, 310

Gage, Margaret. *See* Kemble

Gage, Mary. *See* Davis

Gage, Mary. *See* Jones

Gage, Thomas, III, xxvii, 89, 141, 145, 292, 333, 367, 410, 495; IV, xxxiii, xxxv, xxxvii, xxxix, 3, 17, 36, 85, 86, 114, 138, 148, 188, 266, **278–82**, 297, 300, 331, 337, 369, 375, 393, 396, 435, 451, 503, 506, 546, 570, 572, 575, 582, 587, 606, 675, 680, 681, 709, 720, 734, 768, 787, 793, 794; V, 146, 147, 282, 312, 389, 413, 457, 478, 479, 706, 741, 831, 865, 871, 888, 889, 890, 891; VI, 89, 136, 316, 332, 682, 739

Gage, Thomas, 1st Viscount Gage, IV, 278

Gage, William, VIII, 309

Gage*, Sir William James (1849–1921), XII, 571, 707, 923

Gagen, Robert Ford, XII, 329, 336

Gaggin, John Boles, IX, **295–96**

Gaghswaghtaniunt. *See* Kaghswaghtaniunt

Gagné, Agnès (Bourassa, *dit* La Ronde), IV, 77

Gagné, Louis, IX, 200

Gagné, Olive (Desgagnés; Tremblay, *dit* Picoté), VIII, 893

Gagnier, Geneviève (Touchet), II, 90

Gagnier, Jean-Josaphat, XII, 533

Gagnier, Marie-Marguerite (Labrie), VI, 381

Gagnier, Pierre-Rémi, VI, 381; VIII, 331

Gagnon, Adeline. *See* Pelletier

Gagnon, Antoine, VII, 27, **332–33**, 384; VIII, 227, 591; IX, 615, 616

Gagnon, Catherine. *See* Cartier

Gagnon*, Charles-Antoine-Ernest (1846–1901), XII, 890

Gagnon, Charles-Octave, III, 712; XII, 1023

Gagnon, Elizabeth. *See* Marchessault

Gagnon*, Ernest (1834–1915), VII, 592; X, 228; XI, 343, 873; XII, 533

Gagnon, Ferdinand, XI, **329–32**, 424; XII, 248

Gagnon, Françoise. *See* Goudeau

Gagnon, Françoise (Cotton), III, 144

Gagnon, Geneviève. *See* Bouin, *dit* Dufresne

Gagnon, Hilary, XII, 251

Gagnon, Jacques (Joseph), IV, 153, 154; VII, 204

Gagnon, Jean, I, 319

Gagnon, Jean-Baptiste (clergyman), VIII, 140

Gagnon, Jean-Baptiste (father of FERDINAND), XI, 329

Gagnon, Jeanne (Chapeleau), XII, 172

Gagnon, Joseph, III, 222, 443

Gagnon, Louise (Merle), VIII, 625

Gagnon, Lucien (Julien), VII, 210, 239, **333–35**, 513, 758; X, 545, 546

Gagnon, Madeleine-Renée. *See* Roger

Gagnon, Malvina. *See* Lalime

Gagnon, Marie-Anne. *See* Longtin

Gagnon, Marie-Josephte (Paquet), IX, 615

Gagnon, Marie-Madeleine (Lepage de Sainte-Claire), III, 390

Gagnon, Mathurin, I, **319–20**

Gagnon*, Philéas (1854–1915), IV, 424; VII, 775; X, 19

Gagnon, Pierre (brother of LUCIEN), VII, 333

Gagnon, Pierre (brother of MATHURIN), I, 319

Gagnon, Pierre (father of MATHURIN), I, 319

Gagnon, Sophie. *See* Régnier

Gagnon, Thérèse (Demers), V, 244

Gagnon, Zacharie, VII, 332

Gahickdodon, III, 614

Gaiachoton. *See* Kayahsota?

Gaignard, Philippe, I, 277

Gaignier, Marguerite (Pinard), I, 550

Gaignon. *See* Gagnon

Gaillard. *See also* Rey

Gaillard, Catherine. *See* Leduc

Gaillard, Guillaume, II, 43, **234–35**, 409, 448, 487; III, 45, 153

Gaillard, Hilaire, II, 234

Gaillard, Jean-Baptiste, III, 647

Gaillard, Joseph-Ambroise, IV, 430

Gaillard, Louise-Catherine. *See* Denys de Saint-Simon

Gaillard, Marie-Catherine. *See* Neveu

Gaillard, Marie-Louise, named de la Sainte-Vierge, IV, 535

Gaillard, Mathieu, I, **320**; II, 618

Gaillard, Périnne-Louise (Labillois), IX, 438

Gaillardet, Théodore-Frédéric, XI, 178, 273

Gailliard, Françoise (Moreau de Brésoles), I, 512

Gaines, Edmund Pendleton, VIII, 238

Gaingnon. *See* Gagnon

Gainsborough, Earl of. *See* Noel

Gainsborough, Thomas, IV, 26

Gairdner, Meredith, XI, 885

Gairdner, Robert Hunter, IX, 15, 274; XII, 1000

Galan (Galand). *See* Haché-Gallant

Galard. *See also* Gaillard

Galard, Marie-Joseph de, VI, 667

Galarneau, Thérèse (Juneau, *dit* Latulippe), VIII, 446

Galaup, Jean-François de, Comte de Lapérouse, IV, 157, 244, **282–83**, 341, 366, 383, 518, 519, 584, 684, 741, 743; V, 80, 103, 105, 194, 363, 500; VI, 271, 320, 775; IX, 702

Galaup, Louise-Éléonore de, Comtesse de Lapérouse. *See* Broudou

Galaup, Marguerite de. *See* Rességuier

Galaup, Victor-Joseph de, IV, 282

Galbraith, Robert Leslie Thomas, XII, 466

Galbraith, William, XII, 843

Gale, Alexander, VII, 910; VIII, 68, 77, 273, **310–11**, 545; IX, 742

Gale, Anna. *See* Noyes

Gale, Anna Rebecca (Hunt), XII, 457

Gale, Elizabeth (Fowler), XII, 326

Gale, Georgianna M. (Perley), XI, 681
Gale, Jean. *See* Esson
Gale, John, VIII, 310
Gale, Margaret. *See* Scarth
Gale, Mary Ann (Needham), X, 543
Gale, Rebecca. *See* Wells
Gale, Robert Leake, XII, 326, 327
Gale, Samuel, V, 184, 834; VI, 223, **268–70**, 338, 427, 560, 688, 816; VII, 614, 817; IX, 296; XII, 457
Gale, Samuel, V, 268, 697; VI, 167, 270; VII, 667, 731, 907, 914; VIII, 22, 207, 575, 719, 726, 727; IX, 242, **296–97**, 728; XI, 237
Galen, Christoph Bernhard von, I, 142
Galhet, Monsieur (soldier), III, 310
Galiano. *See* Alcalá-Galiano
Galiffet de Caffin, Catherine de. *See* Aubert de La Chesnaye
Galiffet de Caffin, François de, I, 524; II, 402, 523, 527; III, **233**
Galiffet d'Honon, Joseph de, III, 233
Galiffet d'Honon, Marguerite de. *See* Bonfils
Galiffet d'Honon, Pierre de, III, 233
Galilei, Galileo, XII, 255
Galinée. *See also* Bréhant
Galinée, Monsieur de (ancestor of René BRÉHANT de Galinée), I, 126
Galinier, Dominique, I, 220, 612, 644
Gallant. *See also* Haché-Gallant
Gallant, Anne. *See* Chiasson
Gallant, Fidèle, V, 335
Gallant, Jean-Baptiste, V, 335
Gallant, L'Ange, V, 335
Gallant, Louis, V, 335
Gallant, Madeleine. *See* Doucet
Gallant, Victor, V, 335
Gallant, Xavier, known as Pinquin, V, **335–36**
Gallard, Charlotte, II, **235–36**, 466, 606; III, 220, 238, 369
Gallard, Claude. *See* Faye
Gallard, René, II, 235
Gallatin, Abraham Alfonse Albert, XII, 401, 402
Galléan, Cornélie-Henriette-Sophie-Louise-Hortense-Gabrielle, Princesse de Galléan (Forbin-Janson, Comtesse de Forbin-Janson), VII, 304
Galleran, Guillaume, I, **320**, 417
Galliay, Marie (Serres), V, 752
Galliford, John, XI, 652
Galliot, Jacques, I, 313
Gallishan, Elizabeth (Burpe), VII, 120
Gallop, Esther (Burpee), VIII, 118
Gallop, William, V, **336–37**, 646; VI, 362, 562
Galloway, Countess of. *See* Dashwood
Galloway, Earl of. *See* Stewart
Galloway, Agnes (Munn), V, 616, 617
Galloway, Joseph, V, 438
Galochau, Jean, III, 621
Galphin (Gaulfin, Gaulphin), George, V, 340
Galt, Sir Alexander Tilloch, VII, 335, 338; VIII, 543; IX, 588, 727, 777, 792, 793; X, 10, 45, 46, 99, 100, 128, 131, 144, 145, 147, 231, 282, 326, 327, 355, 466, 548, 591, 631, 632, 641, 642, 643, 645, 674, 679, 684, 708, 717, 722, 725; XI, 124, 156, 157, 161, 166, 246, 287, 288, 412, 438, 439, 557, 572, 706, 768, 770, 832, 833, 902; XII, 7, 90, 149, 174, 248, 261, 262, 279, **348–56**,
385, 391, 392, 393, 394, 395, 487, 596, 598, 654, 683, 687, 737, 902, 905, 1040, 1055, 1056, 1059
Galt, Amy Gordon, Lady Galt. *See* Torrance
Galt, Elizabeth. *See* Tilloch
Galt, Elliott. *See* Torrance
Galt*, Elliott Torrance (1850–1928), XII, 354, 355
Galt, Evelyn Cartier (Springett), XII, 356
Galt, Jean. *See* Thomson
Galt, John (father of JOHN), VII, 335
Galt, John (grandson of JOHN), XII, 355
Galt, John (son of JOHN), VII, 338; XII, 348
Galt, John, VI, 286, 481, 761; VII, 261, 262, **335–40**, 538, 539, 547, 754, 874, 882; VIII, xxvi, 9, 327, 410, 598; IX, 416, 671, 717, 757, 768, 837; X, 706; XII, 348, 356
Galt, Sir Thomas, VII, 335, 338; VIII, 473; X, 632; XII, 348, 683
Galton, Ann (Peyton), VI, 580
Galvão, António, I, 154, 235
Gálvez, José de, IV, 622
Galway, Viscount. *See* Monckton
Galway, Viscountess. *See* Manners
Gamache, Catherine. *See* Lots
Gamache, Christine, VIII, 312
Gamache, Françoise. *See* Bacelet, *dit* Casirtan
Gamache, Louis, VIII, **311–13**; IX, 255
Gamache, Marie-Reine. *See* Després, *dit* Disséré
Gamache, Michel-Arsène, VIII, 311
Gamache, Nicolas, II, 155
Gamache, Pierre-Louis, VIII, 312
Gamard, Monsieur (ship's pilot), I, 256
Gamarre, Josephte (Madran), VIII, 590
Gambier, Deborah. *See* Stiles
Gambier, James, IV, 161; VI, 271
Gambier, James, 1st Baron Gambier, V, 360; VI, 71, **270–71**, 323, 708, 784
Gambier, John, VI, 270
Gambier, Louisa, Baroness Gambier. *See* Matthew
Gamble. *See also* Gammill
Gamble, Elizabeth Bowles. *See* Brenchley
Gamble, Isabella Elizabeth. *See* Clarke
Gamble, Isabella Leah (Horne), VII, 417, 418
Gamble, John, VIII, 392, 511; X, 299; XI, 332
Gamble, John William, VI, 416; VII, 417; VIII, 5; IX, 109, 166, 313; X, 121, 262, **299–300**; XI, 332, 713, 714
Gamble, Joseph Clarke, VIII, 523, 524; IX, 662; X, 610; XI, 143, 332
Gamble, Leah Tyrer (Allan), VIII, 4, 5
Gamble, Mary. *See* Macaulay
Gamble, Matilda. *See* Atkinson
Gamble, Minerva Anne. *See* Niles
Gamble, Nancy. *See* Henson
Gamble, Rachel Crookshank (Macaulay, Lady Macaulay), VIII, 511
Gamble, Raynald D'Arcy, XII, 107
Gamble, William, VII, 417; VIII, 5, 371; X, 290, 299; XI, 311, **332–33**
Gamelain, Françoise. *See* Bellanger
Gamelain, Françoise (Pinard), I, 321
Gamelain, Michel, I, 321
Gamelain de La Fontaine, Marguerite. *See* Crevier
Gamelain de La Fontaine, Michel, I, **320–21**, 418, 468, 550; II, 236, 584, 616; III, 311; VIII, 313
Gamelin, Mlle (of Montreal), VII, 688

Gamelin, Angélique. *See* Giasson
Gamelin, Angélique (Hervieux), III, 290
Gamelin, Charlotte (Malhiot), III, 422; V, 571
Gamelin, Élisabeth (Malhiot), V, 572; VIII, 605
Gamelin, Émilie. *See* Tavernier
Gamelin, Ignace, II, **236**, 457; III, 234, 422; IV, 283, 287; V, 571
Gamelin, Ignace, II, 236, 530; III, 146, 153, 234, 249, 485, 503, 592, 617; IV, 11, 46, 235, **283–85**, 287, 362, 590; V, 572
Gamelin, Jacques-Alexis, II, 236
Gamelin, Jane Sophia. *See* Walker
Gamelin, Jean-Baptiste, VIII, 864
Gamelin, Joseph, IV, 285
Gamelin, Joseph-Jacques, III, 290
Gamelin, Marguerite. *See* Lemoine
Gamelin, Marguerite (Loedel), VI, 402
Gamelin, Marianne. *See* Lemaître-Lamorille
Gamelin, Marie-Élisabeth. *See* Spagniolini
Gamelin, Marie-Jeanne. *See* Maugras
Gamelin, Marie-Louise. *See* Dufrost de La Gemerais
Gamelin, Marie-Louise. *See* Lorimier
Gamelin, Michel-Joseph, III, 598
Gamelin, Pierre (father of PIERRE), VIII, 313
Gamelin, Pierre (father of Pierre GAMELIN Maugras), II, 236; III, 233
Gamelin, Pierre, VIII, **313–14**
Gamelin, Pierre-Joseph, IV, **285–87**; VI, 383, 402
Gamelin, *dit* Châteauvieux, Antoine, IV, 294
Gamelin, *dit* Châteauvieux, Laurent-Eustache, II, 239; III, 249; IV, 77
Gamelin, *dit* Châteauvieux, Suzanne (Gill), IV, 294
Gamelin, *dit* Gaucher, Louise-Archange (Testard de Montigny), IX, 782
Gamelin Maugras, Marie-Clémence. *See* Dufrost de La Gemerais
Gamelin Maugras, Pierre, III, **233–34**, 242; IV, 235, 287
Gammill (Gemmell, Gamble), James, VII, 56
Gammon, Rebecca (Barss; M'Alpine), VI, 411
Gancleau, Jean, II, 441
Gand. *See* Derré
Gandeacteua (Gandeacteüa, Gandeaktena, Gandeakteoua, Gandiaktua), I, **321–22**, 651; II, 107
Ganet, François, II, 220, 292, 649, 650; III, 20, **234–35**, 456, 478, 479, 636, 644
Gangnon. *See* Gagnon
Ganiodaio (Handsome Lake), IV, lvi
Ganishe. *See* Gonish
Gannassatiron, II, 255
Ganneaktena. *See* Gandeacteua
Gannenrontié. *See* Lauzon, Pierre de
Gannensagouas (Marie-Thérèse), I, 118
Gannenstenhawi. *See* Williams, Eunice
Gannes de Falaise, Anne de (Rousseau de Villejouin), IV, 688, 689
Gannes de Falaise, Barbe de. *See* Denys de La Trinité
Gannes de Falaise, Bernardin de (Louis-Joseph), IV, 81
Gannes de Falaise, Élisabeth de. *See* Catalogne
Gannes de Falaise, François de, II, 236; III, 384
Gannes de Falaise, Françoise de. *See* Le Bloy
Gannes de Falaise, Jean-Baptiste de, IV, 391
Gannes de Falaise, Louis de, II, 236
Gannes de Falaise, Louis de, II, **236**, 579; III, 235; IV, 688

Gannes de Falaise, Louise de. *See* Legardeur de Tilly
Gannes de Falaise, Louis-François de, III, 236
Gannes de Falaise, Marguerite de. *See* Leneuf de La Vallière et de Beaubassin
Gannes de Falaise, Marguerite-Madeleine de (Couagne), II, 154; IV, 174
Gannes de Falaise, Michel de, III, 6, 175, **235–36**; IV, 15, 254, 443, 678, 688, 783
Gannes de Falaise, Pierre de, III, 223
Gannes de Falaise, Thérèse de. *See* Bouat
Gannett, Caleb, IV, 258
Ganong*, William Francis (1864–1941), III, 416; V, 136, 137; VI, 112, 561; X, 704; XII, 460
Ganson, Joseph, XII, 1090, 1091
Gantès, Jean-François de, III, 188
Gape, John. *See* Gowan, Robert
Gapper, Mary Sophia (O'Brien), X, 554; XII, 525, 792
Garakontié, I, 445
Garakontié (Garakonké), I, **322–23**, 462, 464, 525, 555; II, 194, 237, 342
Garat, Pierre, I, 476
Garaud, Monsieur (merchant), IV, 66
Garault, Anne de (Garnier), I, 324
Garaut. *See* Garreau
García. *See also* Juárez
García, Diego, I, 156
Garde (Gardes), Élisabeth (Estèbe), IV, 263
Garden, Euphemia. *See* Forbes
Garden, George, VI, 19, **271–73**, 285, 644; VII, 28, 381; VIII, 186, 321
Garden, Jane (Thompson), VIII, 884
Gardiner, Anna. *See* Lane
Gardiner, Anna Matilda (Bagnall), VIII, 35
Gardiner, Charles John, 1st Earl of Blessington, VII, 337
Gardiner, Henry Lynedoch, X, 406
Gardiner, John, VIII, 872
Gardiner, Marguerite, Countess of Blessington. *See* Power
Gardiner, Sarah Sophia (Haszard), X, 339
Gardiner, Singleton, VI, 612; VII, 40
Gardiner, Sylvester, V, 5
Gardiner, William, VII, 428
Gardner, Alan, 1st Baron Gardner, IV, 744, 745; VII, 50
Gardner, Ann. *See* Booker
Gardner, Dorothea (Barrie), VII, 50
Gardner, George, VIII, 395
Gardner, Mary (Foreman), VIII, 299; X, 292
Gardner, Mary Ann (Bouchette), X, 77
Gardner, Sarah (Townsend), X, 685
Gardner, Thomas, IX, 399
Gardner, William, V, 127
Gareman, Florence (Boucher), II, 140
Garennes, Louis, V, 269
Garfield, A. B. E. F., VIII, 266
Gargas, Sieur de (writer), I, 577; II, 182, 184
Gargot. *See also* Lorit
Gargot, Anne. *See* Lardeau
Gargot, Hilaire, I, 323
Gargot, Jean, I, 323
Gargot de La Rochette, Nicolas, I, 296, **323–24**, 594
Garhio (Garhi), Marie, I, 522
Garibaldi, Giuseppe, X, 304; XI, 548, 892; XII, 57, 925
Gariépy, Geneviève (Corbin), III, 138

Gariépy, Henriette (Pâquet), XII, 818
Gariépy, Marie (Renaud), X, 613, XI, 727
Gariépy, Marie (Renaud, *dit* Cannard), IV, 659
Garin, André-Marie, IX, 343
Garland. *See also* Lester
Garland, Amy. *See* Lester
Garland, Augustus Lester, VI, 274
Garland, Charles, V, **337–38**
Garland, Francis Penton, VI, 274
Garland, George (father of CHARLES), V, 337
Garland, George (father of GEORGE), V, 492, 624, 725, 784, 838, 839; VI, 273, 274, 275, 311
Garland, George, V, 492; VI, **273–75**; VII, 590
Garland, John, V, 337
Garland, John Bingley, V, 492; VI, 273, 274, 275, 311, 312; IX, 694; X, 50
Garland, Joseph, V, 838
Garland, Joseph Bingley, IX, 84
Garland, Joseph Gulston, VI, 274
Garland, Katherine (wife of THOMAS), I, 324
Garland, Lester, VI, 274
Garland, Maria, VI, 275
Garland, Mary Sloat (Hunt), VII, 425
Garland, Merwyn Ainsley, XI, 63
Garland, Thomas, I, **324**
Garnault, Louis, IX, 297
Garneau, Alfred, IX, 303, 304, 305, 306; X, 203; XI, 186; XII, 271
Garneau, David, IX, 297
Garneau, François-Xavier, IX, 297
Garneau, François-Xavier, I, 112; III, 254; IV, xxxiii, 232, 320; VI, 40; VII, 61, 73, 504, 523, 592; VIII, 96, 420, 496, 503, 834, 912; IX, 41, 42, 113, 143, 250, 255, 261, **297–306**, 450, 464, 573, 811; X, 13, 21, 132, 165, 203, 218, 583, 635; XI, 36, 83, 177, 185, 186, 342, 343, 489, 490, 851, 873, 905; XII, 385, 558, 570, 737
Garneau, Georgiana (Brousseau), XI, 115
Garneau, Gertrude. *See* Amiot-Villeneuve
Garneau, Hector, IX, 305, 306
Garneau, Honoré, IX, 298
Garneau, Jacques, IX, 298
Garneau, Jean, V, 463
Garneau, Marie-Émélie (Routier), IX, 298
Garneau, Marie-Esther. *See* Bilodeau
Garneau*, Pierre (1823–1905), XI, 115, 190, 331, 774; XII, 271, 724, 1065
Garnett, Mr (Methodist leader), IV, 437
Garnier. *See also* Grenier
Garnier, Anne. *See* Garault
Garnier, Antoine, VI, 669; VII, 489; VIII, 490
Garnier, Charles, I, 41, 125, 203, **324–25**, 388, 461, 562, 652
Garnier, Constant, XII, **356–57**
Garnier, Guillemette (Bourgeoys), I, 115
Garnier, Jean, I, 324
Garnier, Jean-Baptiste, III, 621
Garnier, John Hutchison, XII, **357–58**
Garnier, Julien, I, 322; II, 107, **237–38**, 473, 540, 643; III, 330, 335, 336, 337, 360
Garnier, Marie. *See* Christe
Garnier, Mary Letitia (wife of CONSTANT), XII, 356
Garnier, *dit* Nadeau, Jean, II, 16
Garnier de Chapouin, Jacques, I, 590

Garnkirk. *See* Dunlop
Garnom, Marie-Anne (Poitevin d'Anglebert), V, 294
Garnot, Pierre, X, 153
Garo. *See* Garreau
Garohiaé (Garonhiagué). *See* Ogenheratarihiens
Garon, Marie-Claire (Cimon), XI, 191
Garon, Pierre, XI, 191, 519
Garraty, Emmaline (Emanaline, Emeline) (Glasier), XII, 376
Garreau. *See also* Maugue-Garreau
Garreau, Élisabeth (Lalande; Guy), III, 271
Garreau, François, III, 598
Garreau, Léonard, I, 282, 307, 308, **325**, 651
Garreau, Marguerite (Payne), II, 513
Garreau, Pierre, II, 513
Garreau, *dit* Saint-Onge, Marie-Anne. *See* Maugue
Garreau, *dit* Saint-Onge, Pierre, IV, 287, 529
Garreau, *dit* Saint-Onge, Pierre, IV, **287–88**, 510; V, 570, 582, 737
Garrett, Alexander Charles, XII, 441
Garrett, Dorcas, VIII, 472
Garrettson, Catharine. *See* Livingston
Garrettson, Freeborn, V, 468, 573; VI, 64, 65, **275–77**; VII, 52, 587
Garrettson, John, VI, 275
Garrettson, Sarah. *See* Hanson
Garrick, David, IV, 114
Garrigues de Saint-Fauste, Marie-Josèphe-Jeanne (Belvèze), X, 48
Garrioch, Alfred Campbell, IX, 137
Garrioch, Peter, VII, 207, 450; VIII, 819
Garrish, Sarah, II, 303
Garrison, William Lloyd, IX, 704; XII, 925, 927
Garry, Francis N. A., VIII, 315
Garry, Isabella, VIII, 314
Garry, Nicholas, VI, 100; VII, 269, 567, 736, 901, 902, 913; VIII, 85, 91, **314–15**, 813
Garry, Phoebe. *See* Vesey
Garstin, Cordelia Anne (Colborne), IX, 137
Garth. *See* McDonald; Macdonald
Garthbeg. *See* McTavish
Gartly. *See* Simpson
Gartshore, John, VIII, 279; XI, 651
Garven, Mary Anne. *See* Merry
Garvie, John, X, 300
Garvie, William, X, **300–1**, 460; XII, 436, 766
Garvin, Amelia Beers. *See* Warnock
Garvin*, John William (1859–1935), XI, 212, 213
Gary, Jemimah (Washburn), VI, 804
Gasche, Cécile (Adhémar), II, 11
Gaschet, Françoise. *See* Phélypeaux
Gaschet, Hélène. *See* Bourgina
Gaschet, Pierre, III, 237
Gaschet, René, I, 81, 583; III, **236–37**
Gascoin, Léocadie, named Marie des Sept-Douleurs, XII, **358–60**
Gascoin, Michel-Jean, XII, 359
Gascoin, Rosalie-Renée. *See* Chardon
Gascoing, Marguerite (Guillouet d'Orvilliers), II, 270
Gaskin, Mr (gunner), VII, 303
Gasnier, Anne (Clément Du Vuault de Monceaux; Bourdon), I, 113, 585; II, 585
Gaspar, Marguerite (Schindler), IV, 702

Gaspar Soiaga. *See* Kondiaronk
Gaspé. *See also* Aubert
Gaspé, Catherine (Boisseau), VII, 89, 502
Gass, George Wright, X, 719
Gassin, Françoise (Natte), V, 622
Gastaignol, Marie (Daccarrette), III, 156
Gastaldo, Giacomo, I, 659
Gastineau, Julien-Pierre, XII, 546
Gastineau, Marie-Anne (Joubin-Boisvert), XII, 507
Gastineau de Sainte-Marie, Louis, IV, 11
Gastineau Duplessis, Charlotte. *See* Le Boulanger
Gastineau Duplessis, Jean-Baptiste, III, **237–38**; IV, 360, 591
Gastineau Duplessis, Louis, III, 237
Gastineau Duplessis, Marguerite. *See* Duplessis
Gastineau Duplessis, Marie. *See* Crevier
Gastineau Duplessis, Marie-Joseph (Olivier de Vézin), III, 237; IV, 591
Gastineau Duplessis, Nicolas (father), I, 231; III, 237
Gastineau Duplessis, Nicolas, II, 283
Gaston III, *dit* Phébus, Comte de Foix, II, 4
Gaston, Jean, V, 497
Gastonguay, Angélique (Dénéchaud), V, 248; VII, 241
Gastonguay, Jean-Baptiste, V, 248
Gastonguay, Marie-Josephte-Félix (Lemaire), X, 437
Gatchell, Dorothy (Pote), III, 531
Gatchell, Nathan B., XII, 1069
Gaté, Marie-Josephte (Cherrier), XI, 187
Gates, Benjamin, VI, 277
Gates, Clarissa. *See* Adams
Gates, Frederick W., IX, 512
Gates, Horatio, IV, 110, 114; V, 33
Gates, Horatio, VI, 238, **277–80**, 602, 815; VII, 26, 28, 594, 619, 620, 717; VIII, 542; IX, 396; X, 440, 518; XI, 533
Gathercole, John Cyrus A., IX, 469
Gatien, Félix, VI, 206, 486; VII, **340–41**; VIII, 212; IX, 117
Gatien, Jean-Baptiste (clergyman), VIII, 330, 331
Gatien, Jean-Baptiste (father of FÉLIX), VII, 340
Gatien, Marie-Françoise. *See* Aubin-Delisle
Gatin, Élisabeth (Martel de Belleville), III, 433
Gatin, Geneviève (Nouchet), III, 490, 491
Gatin, Jean, III, 490
Gatineau, Monsieur (fur trader), V, 835
Gatrowani. *See* Ottrowana
Gatty, Alfred, XI, 333
Gatty, Horatia Katharine Frances (Eden), XI, 333
Gatty, Juliana Horatia (Ewing), XI, **333–34**
Gatty, Margaret. *See* Scott
Gaubert, Mme. *See* Briand
Gaubert, Mathurin, IV, 95
Gaubil, Antoine, III, 336
Gaucher. *See* Gamelin
Gauchet, Marie (Dupont), II, 204
Gauchet de Belleville, Catherine (Migeon de Branssat), I, 508; III, 450; IV, 535
Gaudais, Jeanne (Dupont), II, 205, 365
Gaudais Du Chartran, Nicolas, I, 326
Gaudais-Dupont, Louis, I, 79, 248, 323, **325–26**, 428, 512, 538, 629; II, xvii, 205, 365
Gaudar, Marie (Lauson), I, 428, 429, 431
Gaudarville. *See* Peuvret
Gaudaur*, Jacob Gill (1858–1937), XII, 408, 797

Gaudé, Dominique, III, 145
Gaudé, Françoise, III, **238–39**, 369
Gaudé, Françoise (Jourdain, *dit* Labrosse), III, 316
Gaudé, Marguerite. *See* Picard
Gaudé, Marguerite (Jarry; Durocher), III, 210
Gaudé, Marie (Couagne; Derivon de Budemon), II, 153, 154, 529; III, 145, 146
Gaudé, Nicolas, III, 238
Gaudet. *See also* Godet
Gaudet, Agnès. *See* Chiasson
Gaudet, Anne (Cormier), V, 203, 204
Gaudet, Athanase, XI, 334
Gaudet, Augustin, V, 203
Gaudet, Charles-Dominique, IX, 561
Gaudet, Deneige. *See* Levasseur
Gaudet, G.-F., XI, 441
Gaudet, Gertrude. *See* Le Blanc
Gaudet, Gertrude (Arsenault), XII, 40
Gaudet, Joseph, V, 261
Gaudet, Joseph, XI, **334–35**
Gaudet, Joseph-F., XII, 40
Gaudet, Marguerite (Bastarache, *dit* Basque), V, 57
Gaudet, Marie-Blanche (Poirier), XII, 836
Gaudet, Marie-Gertrude (Doucet), V, 261
Gaudet*, Placide (1850–1930), IV, 470; V, 58, 203; VI, 228; VII, 805; XI, 40, 350
Gaudin. *See also* Godin
Gaudin, James, X, 112
Gaudin, *dit* La Poterie, Louis-Nicolas, V, 727
Gaudion, Pierre-Nicolas, III, 61, 549, 567
Gaudot, Salomé (Montmollin), V, 600
Gaudreau, Catherine (Basset), I, 79
Gaudreau, Joséphine. *See* Cauchon
Gaudron, Marie. *See* Gohel
Gaudron, Nicolas, III, 239
Gaudron de Chevremont, Charles-René, III, **239–40**
Gaudron de Chevremont, Marie-Bénigne. *See* Derome
Gaudry, Angélique (Bruce), XII, 132
Gaudry, *dit* Bourbonnière, Nicolas, I, 45
Gaufin, Jean-Philippe, III, 240
Gaufin, Marie-Joseph. *See* Moreau
Gaufin, Valérien (Jean-Philippe), III, **240–41**, 295
Gaugräbe (Gaugreben). *See* DeGaugreben
Gaukel, Dorothea. *See* Weikmillar
Gaukel, Friedrich, VIII, 265, **315–16**
Gaukel, Maria. *See* Roschang
Gaukel, Polly. *See* Kaufman
Gaul, Ellen (Power), XI, 709
Gauldrée-Boilleau, Charles-Henri-Philippe, Baron Gauldrée-Boilleau, XI, 515
Gaulfin. *See* Galphin
Gaulin, Antoine, II, 22, 106, 187, 199, **238**; VIII, 317
Gaulin, François (father of ANTOINE), II, 238
Gaulin, François (father of RÉMI), VIII, 316
Gaulin, Françoise. *See* Amiot
Gaulin, Marie. *See* Rocheron
Gaulin, Rémi, VI, 394; VII, 423, 431, 543, 549, 551, 705, 762; VIII, 141, 241, **316–19**, 615, 703, 704, 713; IX, 206, 207, 254, 781, 798; X, 322; XI, 95, 96, 714; XII, 594
Gaulphin. *See* Galphin
Gault*, Andrew Frederick (1833–1903), XI, 335; XII, 131, 136, 456, 631
Gault, Elizabeth J. *See* Bourne

Gault, Leslie, XI, 335

Gault, Mary. *See* Hamilton

Gault, Mathew Hamilton, XI, 233, **335–36**, 557, 774, 936, 937; XII, 136

Gault, Robert Leslie, XII, 631

Gaulthier, Hélène (Chicoisneau), V, 186

Gaultier, Françoise. *See* Colin

Gaultier, Jean-Baptiste, III, 98, 173

Gaultier, Jean-François, II, 596, 597; III, 29, 30, 31, 154, 180, 315, 334, 648, **675–81**; IV, 45, 91, 407, 729

Gaultier, Madeleine-Marie-Anne. *See* Tarieu de La Pérade

Gaultier, Marie. *See* Guyon Desprez

Gaultier, Marie (Quintal), IV, 649

Gaultier, Marie-Anne (Soupiran), III, 596

Gaultier, Marie-Charlotte (Delort), III, 173

Gaultier (Gauthier), Marie-Thérèse (Carrerot; Hertel de Rouville), III, 98; IV, 14

Gaultier, René, III, 675

Gaultier de Bruslon, Jean, II, 429, 515

Gaultier de Comporté, Angélique (Riverin), I, 326; II, 187, 576

Gaultier de Comporté, Marie. *See* Bazire

Gaultier de Comporté, Marie-Anne (Peuvret de Gaudarville; Dutisné), I, 326; II, 42, 215, 525

Gaultier de Comporté, Philippe, I, 84, 105, 106, **326**; II, xxiv, 29, 251, 275, 375, 525, 576

Gaultier de La Vérenderie, Adam-Pierre, I, 327

Gaultier de La Vérenderie, Bertrande. *See* Gourdeau

Gaultier de La Vérendyre, François. *See* Gaultier du Tremblay, François

Gaultier de La Vérendrye, Jean-Baptiste, II, 40, 202, **238–40**; III, 46, 241, 244, 245, 249, 250, 251; IV, 77, 288, 289

Gaultier de La Vérendrye, Louis, III, 245, 247

Gaultier de La Vérendrye, Louise-Antoinette. *See* Mézières de Lépervanche

Gaultier de La Vérendrye, Louis-Joseph, III, 171, 234, **241–44**, 245, 251, 252, 375; IV, 288, 289, 425, 427, 513; IX, 455

Gaultier de La Vérendrye, Marie-Amable. *See* Testard de Montigny

Gaultier de La Vérendrye de Boumois, Pierre, III, 241, **244–45**, 249, 252, 375; IV, 284, 288, 289

Gaultier de Rinault, Gillette. *See* Vernon

Gaultier de Rinault, Philippe, I, 326

Gaultier de Varennes, Charlotte-Louise-Angélique. *See* Sarrazin

Gaultier de Varennes, Jacques-René, II, 578; III, **245–46**, 247, 604

Gaultier de Varennes, Jean-Baptiste, II, 19, 109, **240–41**; IV, 439

Gaultier de Varennes, Jean-Hippolyte, II, 598; III, 246

Gaultier de Varennes, Marie. *See* Boucher

Gaultier de Varennes, Marie-Jeanne. *See* Le Moyne de Sainte-Hélène

Gaultier de Varennes, Marie-Renée (Dufrost de La Gemerais; Sullivan), II, 201, 202; III, 234, 246, 247, 603, 604; IV, 234, 235

Gaultier de Varennes, René, III, 246, 603

Gaultier de Varennes, René, I, **326–28**, 468; II, 32, 85, 202, 240, 523, 545; III, 245, 246, 247, 603; IV, 234

Gaultier de Varennes et de La Vérendrye, Marie-Anne. *See* Dandonneau Du Sablé

Gaultier de Varennes et de La Vérendrye, Pierre, I, 11, 37; II, xxix, xxxii, xxxv, 10, 35, 40, 168, 201, 202, 239, 240; III, xxxiv, xxxvii, 46, 47, 82, 107, 121, 137, 158, 234, 241, 242, 244, **246–54**, 285, 301, 331, 341, 375, 376, 432, 444, 485, 492, 580, 595, 603, 604; IV, 77, 178, 234, 283, 284, 288, 289, 359; V, 498, 563; VIII, 342; IX, 329; XII, 1002

Gaultier Du Tremblay, François, III, 241, 243, 249, 252; IV, **288–89**

Gaultier Du Tremblay, Madeleine (Petit de Levilliers), II, 523

Gaume, Jean-Joseph, IX, 19, 63; XI, 836; XII, 819, 1018

Gauron, Marguerite (Lozeau), III, 410

Gaustrax, III, 452; IV, 138

Gauthier. *See also* Gaultier; Gautier

Gauthier, Monsieur (attorney), XII, 745

Gauthier, Agapit, X, 301

Gauthier, Amable, IX, 552; X, **301**

Gauthier, Antoine, X, 301

Gauthier, Augustin (carpenter), III, 316

Gauthier, Augustin (father of FÉLIX-ODILON), X, 301

Gauthier, Catherine (Duquet), I, 298

Gauthier, Euphrosine. *See* Gendron

Gauthier, Félix-Odilon, X, **301–2**

Gauthier, Gosephte. *See* Girardin

Gauthier, Guillaume, I, 479

Gauthier, Louis-Onésime, VIII, 409

Gauthier, Louis-Pascal, XII, 360

Gauthier, Louis-Zéphirin, X, 301

Gauthier, Marie. *See* Trudelle

Gauthier, Marie-Angèle, named Sister Marie-Angèle, XII, **360–61**

Gauthier, Marie-Charles. *See* Chôlet

Gauthier, Marie-Jeanne (Masson), VII, 592

Gauthier, Marie-Sophie. *See* Lapane

Gauthier, Pierre, VIII, 917

Gauthier, *dit* Saint-Germain, Louise (Krieghoff), X, 408, 409, 410

Gauthier, *dit* Saint-Germain, Marguerite (Cicot), XI, 821

Gauthier de La Chenaye, Marie. *See* Pichon

Gauthier de La Chenaye, Philippe, I, 606

Gautier. *See also* Gaultier

Gautier, Mme (pauper), V, 769

Gautier, Abel-Frédéric, XI, 339

Gautier, Anne. *See* Leblanc, *dit* Le Maigre

Gautier, Antoine, IV, 320

Gautier, Catherine (Lozeau), III, 410

Gautier, Gabriel, I, 89, 90, 258

Gautier, Jean-Baptiste, V, 339

Gautier, Jean-Jacques, IV, 124

Gautier, Joseph, III, 254; V, 339

Gautier, Luce (Roussel Ciquard), VI, 145

Gautier, Madeleine (Campion), IV, 132

Gautier, Marie-Renée (Varin, *dit* La Pistole), IV, 748

Gautier, Nicolas, III, 255; V, **338–40**

Gautier, Nicolas-Gabriel, III, 254

Gautier (Gauthier), Pierre, III, 254, 255; V, 339

Gautier, *dit* Bellair, Anne-Marie (Bergeaux; Mercure), V, 589

Gautier, *dit* Bellair, Joseph-Nicolas, III, **254–55**, 366; IV, xxv, 79, 252; V, 338, 339, 589

Gautier, *dit* Bellair, Marguerite (Bourdon de Dombourg), IV, 79; V, 339

Gautier, *dit* Bellair, Marie. *See* Allain
Gautier, *dit* Bellair, Marie-Josephe (Du Pont Duvivier), IV, 252
Gautier de Verville, Charles, IV, 302, 564; V, 8, 230, 836
Gautron, Marie-Louise. *See* Bolduc
Gautron, Michel, VIII, 319
Gautron, *dit* Larochelle, Henriette. *See* Proulx
Gautron, *dit* Larochelle, Siméon, VIII, **319–20**; XI, 491; XII, 1025
Gautron, *dit* Larochelle, Sophie. *See* Vachon, *dit* Pomerleau
Gauvin, Élisabeth-Éléonore (Ostell), XII, 810
Gauvin, Étienne, VII, 892
Gauvin, François, III, 569
Gauvin, Henri-Alphonse, VIII, 616, 617; XI, 117; XII, 810
Gauvin, Luce-Monique. *See* Pinguet
Gauvin, Marie-Sophie (Perrault), IX, 632
Gauvreau, Adélaïde (Dénéchau), VI, 280, 281; VII, 241, 242
Gauvreau, Alexis, VI, 280
Gauvreau, Angèle. *See* Ouvrard, *dit* Laperrière
Gauvreau*, Antoine-Adolphe (1841–1911), XII, 1050, 1051
Gauvreau, Charles-Arthur, XII, 252
Gauvreau, Édouard, VI, 280
Gauvreau, Félicité. *See* Le Maître-Bellenoix
Gauvreau, Ferdinand-Edmond, IX, 439; X, 302
Gauvreau, Josette. *See* Vanfelson
Gauvreau, Louis (father of FERDINAND-EDMOND), X, 302
Gauvreau, Louis (husband of Félicité Le Maître-Bellenoix), X, 503
Gauvreau, Louis, VI, 95, **280–82**, 424; VII, 241; VIII, 359; XII, 86
Gauvreau, Louis-Petrus, XI, 337
Gauvreau, Marguerite (Roy-Audy), VII, 761
Gauvreau, Marie (Martel de Saint-Antoine), IV, 148
Gauvreau, Marie-Anne. *See* Barbeau
Gauvreau, Marie-Anne. *See* Hamel
Gauvreau, Marie-Geneviève (Rageot de Saint-Luc), II, 540
Gauvreau, Marie-Louise. *See* Beleau
Gauvreau, Marie-Luce. *See* Simard
Gauvreau, Marie-Reine-Josephte (Belleau, Lady Belleau), VI, 280; IX, 362; XII, 86
Gauvreau, Pierre (artisan), II, 430; III, 498
Gauvreau, Pierre (father of PIERRE), XI, 336
Gauvreau, Pierre, XI, **336–37**
Gauvreau, Théophile-Alfred, XI, 337
Gauvreau, Théophile-Elzéar, XI, 337
Gavarni, Paul. *See* Chevalier, Sulpice-Guillaume
Gavazzi, Alessandro, VIII, 171; IX, 194, 243; X, 164, 487, 715; XI, 283, 924; XII, 210, 473
Gaverocke, Alice (Hayman), I, 365
Gawèhe (Gawickie), III, xxxviii, **255–56**
Gawler, George, IX, 471
Ga'wu (George Cowhoe), XII, 289, 290
Ga'wu aw, XII, 289
Gay, Antoinette (Regnaud), X, 611
Gay, Bunker, V, 741
Gay, Elizabeth. *See* Stanlake
Gay, James, XII, **361–62**
Gay, Mary (Black), VI, 62; IX, 52
Gay, Robert-Michel, II, **241**; III, 268, 542, 543
Gayahgwaahdoh. *See* Kaieñ?kwaahtoñ

Gay Desenclaves, Jean-Baptiste de, III, 120, 166, **256–57**, 343, 438; IV, xxv, 254
Gayon. *See* Lalande; La Lande
Gayot, Jean-Baptiste, II, 575; III, 352
Gayot (Goy), Nicolas, II, 33, 464, 465, 508, 509
Gazan, François, IV, 125
Gazel, Pierre, VI, 201
Geale, Benjamin, IX, 265
Geanneau. *See* Jeanneau
Geddes, Andrew, VIII, 328
Geddes, Anne Catherine (Macaulay), X, 453
Geddes, David, IV, 399
Geddes, James (doctor), VIII, 392
Geddes, James (engineer), VII, 49
Geddes, John, XII, 21
Geddes, John Gamble, IX, 165; X, 607; XI, 327; XII, 681
Geddes, Leah Allan (Henry), VIII, 391
Geddes, Margaret (Gilkison; Derry), VIII, 327
Geddie, Charlotte Lenora Harrington. *See* MacDonald
Geddie, John, X, 302
Geddie, John, VII, **341–42**; XII, 829
Geddie, John, VII, 342; VIII, 452, 453; IX, 325, 326; X, **302–3**, 308
Geddie, Mary. *See* Menzies
Gédouin, Madeleine de (Le Picard de Norrey), II, 415
Gee, Sarah (Smyth), VI, 723
Geest, Catherine (Cavelier), I, 172; II, 123
Geezhigo-w-ininih. *See* Kezhegowinninne
Geffrard, Fabre-Nicolas, XI, 3
Gehman, Catherine (Weber), XI, 913
Geikie, Archibald Constable, VIII, 68
Geikie*, Walter Bayne (1830–1917), XI, 329; XII, 1123
Gélinas, Aimé, XI, 729
Gélinas, Amable (Gérin, *dit* Lajoie), XI, 338, 340
Gélinas, Évariste, X, **303–5**, 580; XI, 716
Gélinas, Jean, X, 304; XI, 342
Gélinas, Joseph, X, 304
Gélinas, Louis-Aimé, XII, 1026
Gélinas, Mathilde-Sabine. *See* Parent
Gélinas, Théotise. *See* Hudon-Beaulieu
Gélineau, Étienne, X, 304
Gell, Eleanor Isabella. *See* Franklin
Gell, Joseph, VI, 282
Gell, Molly Ann (Thomas), VI, **282–83**; VII, 902
Gellée, Pierre, I, 277
Gemmel, Hugh, XII, 543
Gemmel, Mary, VIII, 646
Gemmell. *See also* Gammill
Gemmell, Robert, X, 124
Gemmill, John Robert, X, 127
Genaple, Catherine. *See* Coursier
Genaple, Claude, II, 241
Genaple de Bellefonds, François, I, 203, 561, 565, 664; II, xxii, xxiii, xxiv, **241–43**, 286, 418, 451, 514, 576
Genaple de Bellefonds, Jean-François, II, 243
Genaple de Bellefonds, Joseph, II, 243
Genaple de Bellefonds, Marie-Anne. *See* La Porte
Gendron. *See also* Deshaies-Gendron
Gendron, Éloi, I, 328
Gendron, Euphrosine (Gauthier), X, 301
Gendron, François, I, **328**, 550
Gendron, Gillette. *See* Doussineau
Gendron, Louise. *See* Fournier

Gendron, Marie-Louise. *See* Dion
Gendron, Marie-Madeleine (Devau, *dit* Retor), IV, 216
Gendron, Pierre, II, 582
Gendron, Pierre-Samuel, XI, **337–38**, 480, 624
Gendron, Simon, XI, 337
Généreux, Esprit-Anaclet, XII, 1036, 1037
Genest, André, IV, 376
Genêt, Edmond-Charles, V, 152, 591, 592
Genevay, Charlotte Magenty. *See* Mount
Geneviève de l'Enfant-Jésus. *See* Regnard Duplessis
Geneviève de Saint-Augustin. *See* Juchereau Duchesnay
Geneviève de Sainte-Madeleine. *See* Gosselin
Geneviève de Saint-Pierre. *See* Boucher
Geneviève-Agnès de Tous-Les-Saints. *See* Skanudharoua
Genlis, Comte de, IV, 448
Genner, Samuel, II, 378
Genoude, Antoine-Eugène de, IX, 18
Gensanne, Monsieur de (pupil of Claude-Thomas DUPUY), II, 212
Gensfleisch zur Laden (Gutenberg), Johannes, XII, 250
Gentle, Margaret (Drummond), VI, 220
Gently (Gentilly), Josephine (Lavallée), XII, 532
Geoffrion, Aimé, XII, 362
Geoffrion, Almaïde. *See* Dansereau
Geoffrion, Catherine. *See* Brodeur
Geoffrion, Christophe-Alphonse, X, 316; XII, 260, 264, **362–63**
Geoffrion, Eulalie. *See* Dorion
Geoffrion, Félix, XII, 362, 363
Geoffrion, Félix, XII, 362, **363**, 506, 651
Geoffroy, Catherine (Paillard), II, 506
Geoffroy, Louis, II, **243–44**, 522
George, Prince of Denmark, II, 286
George I, King of Great Britain and Ireland, II, 123, 198, 287, 443, 498, 652, 661, 668; III, 295, 405; IV, xxi
George II, King of Great Britain and Ireland, II, 93, 670; III, 283, 363, 405, 447, 508, 586, 623, 642, 654, 663, 669, 673; IV, xxii, 21, 109, 455, 503, 676; V, 141, 767; VI, 494, 557
George III, King of Great Britain and Ireland, III, 108, 143, 213, 367, 704; IV, xxvii, xl, xlvi, xlviii, 25, 38, 41, 97, 106, 146, 161, 179, 280, 304, 323, 434, 452, 543, 686, 763; V, 55, 142, 212, 222, 241, 297, 313, 397, 408, 432, 434, 465, 488, 583, 630, 765, 791, 805, 851; VI, 16, 55, 202, 256, 333, 345, 352, 393, 516, 583, 585, 679, 723, 724; VII, 53, 94, 349, 363, 416, 474, 481, 523, 684, 783; VIII, 286, 494, 710, 755, 857, 927; IX, 266, 759, 780; X, 142, 503; XII, 724
George IV, King of Great Britain and Ireland, III, 650; IV, 195, 230; V, 114, 213, 268, 336, 400, 449, 536, 559, 674, 697, 851; VI, 43, 98, 167, 190, 420, 425, 544, 596, 618; VII, 31, 58, 139, 151, 178, 216, 422, 434, 439, 510, 512, 641, 732, 769, 780, 807, 889, 890; VIII, 5, 47, 494, 514, 585, 597, 603, 649, 733, 843, 844; IX, 138, 140, 189, 333, 334, 411, 498, 730, 759; X, 19, 189, 503; XI, 352
George, Barbara. *See* Ross
George, David, IV, 515, 627; V, **340–42**, 469; VI, 89, 129, 313, 799; VII, 123; VIII, 360
George, Elizabeth (mother of JAMES), IX, 306
George, Enoch, VI, 673, 674
George, F. W., XII, 881
George, Henry (economist), VIII, 438; XII, 143, 707

George, Henry (son-in-law of William COCKRAN), IX, 137
George, James (father of JAMES), IX, 306
George, James (merchant), IX, 202
George, James, VIII, 72; IX, **306–8**, 462, 496
George, Janet. *See* Kerr
George, Margaret (wife of JAMES), IX, 306
George, Phillis (wife of DAVID), V, 340
George, Sir Rupert Dennis, VII, 24, 435; VIII, 382, 757; IX, 179
George, Susan (Susannah) (Le Breton), VII, 493
Georgemé, Séraphin, II, **244–45**
Georges, Pierre, I, 476
Georges, Samuel, I, 98, 101, 293, 476, 565
Georges, Suzanne (Lomeron), I, 476
George William Frederick Charles, Duke of Cambridge, IX, 845; X, 291, 292, 695; XI, 932, 933; XII, 245, 450, 576, 734, 736
Géramb, Ferdinand de, Baron de Géramb, named Father Marie-Joseph, VIII, 330
Gerard, Alexander, V, 768
Gérard, Conrad-Alexandre, V, 893
Gérard, Louis-Bertrand, III, 204
Gerbet, Philippe-Olympe, VII, 487
Gère, *dit* Larose, Thérèse de (Franks), VII, 329
Gergy. *See* Languet
Géricault, Théodore, X, 392
Gérin. *See also* Jarin
Gérin, Abbé, IV, 75
Gérin, Denis, XI, 340
Gérin, Elzéar, X, 148; XI, 289, **338–40**; XII, 599
Gérin, Henri, XI, 342
Gérin*, Léon (1863–1951), XI, 342
Gérin (Guérin), Marguerite (Boisseau), IV, 75
Gérin, Marie-Agathe-Élodie. *See* Dufresne
Gérin, *dit* Lajoie, Amable. *See* Gélinas
Gérin, *dit* Lajoie, Antoine, XI, 338, 340
Gérin-Lajoie, André, VIII, 129
Gérin-Lajoie, Antoine, VII, 449, 880, 881; VIII, 259, 260, 420; IX, 214, 255, 614; X, 133, 203, 267, 304, 432, 580, 584; XI, 83, 338, **340–44**, 495, 883; XII, 323, 1014
Gérin-Lajoie, Charles, VIII, 129; XII, 556
Gérin-Lajoie, Joséphine-Henriette. *See* Parent
Gérin-Lajoie, Ursule. *See* Rivard-Laglanderie
Gérin-Lajoie, Victoire. *See* Caron
Germain. *See also* Langlois
Germain, Anna-Séphora (Fafard; Paradis), XI, 306
Germain, Antoine, III, 478
Germain, Césaire, X, **305**
Germain, Césaire-Ernest, X, 305
Germain, Charles, III, 163, 417, 425; IV, 79, 214, **289–90**, 423, 633, 783; VI, 573
Germain, Édouard-Pépin, X, 305
Germain, François, III, 478
Germain (Sackville), George, 1st Viscount Sackville, IV, 5, 22, 23, 281, 350, 428, 452, 571, 726, 792; V, 142, 146, 147, 148, 225, 238, 433, 482, 767, 805, 891, 893, 894, 896; VI, 295, 394, 511, 788, 790; VII, 87; VIII, 823
Germain, Jean-Baptiste, X, 305
Germain, Joseph-Gérasime, X, 305
Germain, Joseph-Louis, II, 40, 41, 161, **245–46**, 341, 474, 608; III, 359
Germain, Louis, VII, 468
Germain, Marguerite (Davanne), V, 223

Germain, Marguerite (Moreau), III, 472
Germain, Marie. *See* Dusablé
Germain, Zoé. *See* Pépin
Germaine, Queen of Aragon and Sicily. *See* Foix, Germaine de
Germon, Barthélemi, II, 455
Gérôme, Jean-Léon, XII, 287, 288, 830, 831
Gerrald, Elizabeth (Jackson), VII, 438
Gerrard, Ann. *See* Grant
Gerrard, Richard, VIII, 322
Gerrard, Samuel, IV, 311; V, 260, 377, 635; VI, 180, 238, 254, 255, 260, 273, 472, 531, 533, 602, 644; VII, 225, 310, 311, 342, 566, 611, 879; VIII, **320–22**, 542, 631; IX, 316; X, 524
Gerrard, Sir Thomas, I, 333
Gerrish, Benjamin, III, 174; IV, 52, 116, 266, 273, 274, **290–91**, 292, 414, 528, 704; V, 121; VIII, 344
Gerrish, Elizabeth (Green), IV, 312
Gerrish, Enoch, VI, 283
Gerrish, John, IV, 290, 291
Gerrish, Joseph, III, 174, 365; IV, 52, 94, 273, 290, **291–92**, 414; V, 109, 240; VIII, 344
Gerrish, Mary. *See* Brenton
Gerrish, Mary. *See* Cradock
Gerrish, Mary. *See* Moody
Gerrish, Mary (Gray), VIII, 344
Gerrish, Moses, VI, 283
Gerrish, Moses, VI, **283–84**, 363
Gerrish, Rebecca. *See* Dudley
Gerrish, Ruth. *See* Ingalls
Gerrish, Sarah. *See* Hobbes
Gertrude, Mother. *See* Fleming
Gervais. *See also* Talbot
Gervais, Catherine. *See* Tellier
Gervais, Gualbert, XI, **344**
Gervais, Jean, I, 508
Gervais, Nicolas, XI, 344
Gervais, Oscar, XI, 344
Gervaise, Cécile (Cartier), V, 164
Gervaise, Charles, III, 257
Gervaise, Louis, III, **257–58**
Gervaise, Marie. *See* Boyer
Gervaise, Marie-Joseph (Besnard, *dit* Carignant), IV, 58
Gervaise, Marie-Madeleine. *See* Langlois
Gervaise, Michel, V, 164, 165, 185
Gesner, Abraham, IX, 308
Gesner, Abraham, VII, 291; VIII, 378, 957; IX, **308–12**, 665, 666, 667, 825, 850; XI, 91, 727, 929; XII, 193, 230, 1051
Gesner, David Henry, XII, 513, 514
Gesner, Elizabeth (Chipman), XII, 193
Gesner, George Weltden, IX, 310, 311
Gesner, Harriet. *See* Webster
Gesner, Henry (father), IX, 308
Gesner, Henry, IX, 312
Gesner, Nicholas, IX, 308
Gesner, Sarah. *See* Pineo
Gesner, Sarah. *See* Stewart
Gesner, Susannah Charlotte (Lampman), XII, 513, 514
Gethings, Charlotte Holt (Macpherson), VIII, 18
Geyer, George, I, 39, 301, **328–29**, 509, 606, 657; II, 50, 265, 266, 309, 310
Geyer, Karl Andreas, VIII, 528

Geyer, Mary Ann (Belcher), VII, 62; X, 42
Geyesutha. *See* Kayahsota?
Ghernish. *See* MacDonald
Ghezo, King of Dahomey, VII, 918
Giard, Antoine, III, 258
Giard, Antoine, III, **258**, 443; V, 174
Giard, Catherine (Cerré), V, 174
Giard, Claude. *See* Prat
Giard, François, XI, 345
Giard, Gabriel, III, 258
Giard, Louis, VI, 507; XI, 290, **345–46**; XII, 736
Giard, Lucille. *See* Drolet
Giard, Marianne. *See* Lafontaine
Giard, Marie-Charles. *See* Daigle
Giard, Nicolas, III, 258
Giasson, Angélique (Gamelin), IV, 285
Giasson, Jacques (agent), VI, 665
Giasson, Jacques (partner of Joseph FLEURY Deschambault), IV, 268
Gibault, Marie-Joseph. *See* Saint-Jean
Gibault, Pierre, V, 342
Gibault, Pierre, IV, 171, 303; V, **342–43**, 433
Gibb, Benaiah, VI, 284, 285
Gibb, Benaiah, VI, **284–85**; VII, 611
Gibb, Catherine. *See* Campbell
Gibb, Duncan, VIII, 647, 648; IX, 181
Gibb, Eleanor. *See* Pastorius
Gibb, Eleanor Catherine (Millar), VII, 611, 612
Gibb, Elizabeth (Orkney), VI, 285
Gibb, Harriet Ann. *See* Valentine
Gibb, Isaac Jones, VII, 621; X, 523
Gibb, Isabella (Torrance), VIII, 322
Gibb, James (financier), VIII, 647
Gibb, James (merchant), XII, 928
Gibb, James, VII, 71, 565; VIII, **322–24**, 894; IX, 538, 640; XI, 773
Gibb, James Duncan, VI, 284
Gibb, Marion. *See* Torrance
Gibb, Thomas (brother of JAMES), VIII, 322, 323
Gibb, Thomas (son of BENAIAH), VI, 284
Gibb, Thomas (uncle of James Gibb ROSS), XI, 773
Gibbard, William, IX, 408
Gibbon, Edward, IV, xlvi; V, 182; VII, 603
Gibbon, Jane (Allan), VII, 14
Gibbons, Edward, I, 223, 241, 594, 636
Gibbons, Frances Eliza. *See* DuVernet
Gibbons, James, XII, 1020, 1023
Gibbons, Margaret (wife of Edward), I, 241
Gibbons, Richard, IV, 292
Gibbons, Richard, IV, 266, 274, **292–93**, 522, 562; V, 108, 510, 766, 767; VI, 194, 195, 213, 790; VII, 87
Gibbons, Richard Collier Bernard Des Barres Marshall, IV, 293; VI, 114, 118, 203, 213, 214, 538, 792; VII, 10, 839
Gibbons, Simon Thomas, XII, **363–65**
Gibbons, Susannah (mother of RICHARD), IV, 292
Gibbons, Susannah (Dodd), VI, 213; X, 232
Gibbons, Suzanna. *See* Sheperd
Gibbons, Thomas, XII, 363
Gibbons, William, I, 20, 74, 144, 145, **329**
Gibbs, Almira. *See* Ash
Gibbs, Caroline. *See* Tate
Gibbs, Fred, XII, 154
Gibbs, James, VI, 27; VIII, 39, 761; XII, 809

Gibbs, Temperance (Gildersleeve), VIII, 325
Gibbs, Thomas, XI, 346
Gibbs, Thomas Nicholson, X, 128; XI, 145, 312, **346–47**, 825
Gibbs, William Henry, XI, 346
Gibotte. *See* Guiboche
Gibson, Abraham, VII, 381
Gibson*, Alexander (1819–1913), XI, 688; XII, 775
Gibson, Anne Margaret (Egan), VIII, 268
Gibson, Clara (Shorey), XII, 969
Gibson, David, VII, 519, 794; VIII, 550; IX, 266, **312–14**, 503, 689; X, 91, 344; XI, 714, 914
Gibson, Edmund, II, 663
Gibson, Eliza. *See* Milne
Gibson, James (father of DAVID), IX, 313
Gibson, James (merchant), V, 127
Gibson, James (son of DAVID), IX, 313
Gibson, James Alexander, XII, 69
Gibson, Janet (Young), X, 722
Gibson, John, XI, 321; XII, 569, 570
Gibson*, Sir John Morison (1842–1929), XI, 223; XII, 1113
Gibson, Margaret. *See* Watson
Gibson, Margaret (McGill), V, 527
Gibson, William, IX, 313
Gibson, William Milnor, XII, 69
Gibsone, Sir John, II, **246**, 274, 293, 395, 564, 580, 666; III, 488
Gidley, Richard M., XI, 566
Gidney, Angus Morrison, VII, 576, 815; VIII, 656; XI, **347–48**; XII, 538
Gidney, Experience. *See* Beals
Gidney, Frances (Morrison; Crosskill), VI, 173
Gidney, Ingraham, XI, 348
Gidney, Joshua, XI, 347
Gidney, Phoebe. *See* Morrison
Gié, Sire de. *See* Rohan
Gien, Comte de. *See* Séguier
Giengwahtoh. *See* Kaienʔkwaahtoñ
Giffard, Denise. *See* Peiras
Giffard, Jeanne. *See* Poignant
Giffard, Joseph, I, 326, 331, 428; II, 30, 307, 514, 639; VI, 367
Giffard, Louise (Lauson de Charny), I, 331, 428, 431
Giffard, Marc, I, 330
Giffard, Marie. *See* Regnouard
Giffard, Marie (Juchereau de La Ferté), I, 331, 400; II, 33, 302, 303, 304
Giffard, Marie-Françoise, named Marie de Saint-Ignace, I, **329–30**, 348; II, 303
Giffard, Marie-Thérèse (Juchereau de Saint-Denis), I, 331, 402, 550; II, 305, 307, 427; III, 317
Giffard, Michèle-Thérèse. *See* Nau de La Boissière et de Fossambault
Giffard de Moncel, Robert, I, 30, 218, 232, 281, 297, 319, 326, 329, **330–31**, 344, 359, 401, 417, 428, 431, 447, 584; II, xvi, 82, 514; V, 288; X, 18, 579; XI, 272
Gifford, Algernon, XII, 364, 365
Gigault, Bernardin, Marquis de Bellefonds, II, 343
Gigault, George-Auguste, XI, 488
Gigeon, Faustin, VI, 487; V, 436
Gigot, Abbé, VIII, 212
Gigot, Edward Francis, XI, 151

Gigou, Anne (Guyart), III, 272
Giguère, Henriette (Darveau), X, 214
Gijben, Johannes Arnoldus, VII, 882
Gijben, Maria. *See* Bloem
Gil, Jerónimo Antonio, VI, 742
Gilbert, Adrian, I, 251, 336
Gilbert, Anne. *See* Aucher
Gilbert, Belinda (Patrick), XI, 676
Gilbert, Effie. *See* Patrick
Gilbert, Elisha Benjamin, XI, 448
Gilbert, François-Xavier, VIII, 202
Gilbert, Geneviève (Bureau), VII, 119
Gilbert, George A., XII, 327, 328
Gilbert, Grove Sheldon, VII, 320
Gilbert, Henry, VIII, 805
Gilbert, Sir Humphrey, I, 19, 23, 154, 228, 229, 251, 278, **331–36**, 362, 363, 364, 380, 531, 532, 668, 677
Gilbert, Sir John, I, 279, 333, 335, 336
Gilbert, Joseph, V, 274
Gilbert, Katherine. *See* Champernowne
Gilbert, Moses, X, 354, 357
Gilbert, Otho, I, 331
Gilbert, Sir William Schwenck, XI, 142; XII, 623, 660
Gilchrist, Belle (mother of FREDERICK CHARLES), XII, 365
Gilchrist, Charles, XII, 365
Gilchrist, Frederick Charles, XII, **365–66**
Gilchrist, Harriet Marian. *See* Newbegin
Gilchrist, Hiram, VIII, 325
Gilchrist, James Aiken, VIII, 325
Gilchrist, John, VIII, 324
Gilchrist, John, VII, 75, 713; VIII, 92, **324–25**; IX, 149, 483
Gilchrist, Lucretia. *See* Gove
Gilchrist, Margaret (Williamson), XII, 1101
Gilchrist, Samuel (grandfather), VIII, 324
Gilchrist, Samuel, VIII, 325
Gilchrist, Sarah. *See* Aiken
Gilchrist, William, XI, 306
Gildemeester, Marie Louise (Tuyll van Serooskerken, Baroness van Tuyll van Serooskerken), VIII, 899
Gilder, Helena. *See* De Kay
Gilder, Richard Watson, XII, 288
Gilder, William Henry, XII, 955
Gildersleeve, Charles Fuller, VIII, 326; IX, 315; XII, 151
Gildersleeve, Henry, VI, 405, 470; VIII, **325–27**, 760; IX, 314; XI, 378
Gildersleeve, Henry Herchmer, VIII, 326
Gildersleeve, Louisa Anne. *See* Draper
Gildersleeve, Obadiah, VIII, 325
Gildersleeve, Overton Smith, VIII, 326; IX, **314–15**
Gildersleeve, Philip, VIII, 325
Gildersleeve, Sarah. *See* Finkle
Gildersleeve, Temperance. *See* Gibbs
Gilderslieve. *See* Gildersleeve
Gilkison, Archibald, XI, 934
Gilkison, David, VI, 285
Gilkison, David, VI, 286; VII, 337; VIII, **327–28**
Gilkison, Isabella. *See* Grant
Gilkison, Jasper Tough, VI, 286; VIII, 293, 327; XI, 452, 453
Gilkison, Margaret. *See* Geddes
Gilkison, Mary. *See* Walker
Gilkison, William, VI, **285–86**; VII, 336; VIII, 327

Gill. *See also* Gell
Gill, Alfred, VIII, 394
Gill, Antoine, IV, 294
Gill, Augustin, VII, 19
Gill, Catherine. *See* Bazin
Gill, Charles-Ignace, IX, 315; XI, 31, 809, 811
Gill*, Charles-Ignace-Adélard (1871–1918), IX, 315
Gill, Delphire. *See* Senécal
Gill, Elizabeth. *See* McDougald
Gill, Ignace, IV, 294; IX, **315**; XI, 808
Gill, Jane (Morehouse), VI, 518
Gill, Jane Henrietta. *See* Robins
Gill, Joseph-Louis, known as Magouaouidombaouit, IV, 290, **293–94**
Gill, Joseph Solo, VI, 282
Gill, Louisa Emma (Angwin), XII, 28
Gill, Marie-Jeanne. *See* Nanamaghemet
Gill, Mary Colley (Bentley), V, 67
Gill, Michael, II, 246; III, 68, 324; VI, 311
Gill, Michael, II, **246–47**, 388
Gill, Moses, II, 246
Gill, Nicholas (merchant), IX, 436
Gill, Nicholas (son or grandson of MICHAEL), II, 246
Gill, Relief. *See* Dowse
Gill, Rosalie. *See* James
Gill, Samuel, IV, 293; IX, 315
Gill, Suzanne. *See* Gamelin, *dit* Châteauvieux
Gill, Thomas, IX, 315
Gill, William, V, 67
Gill, Xavier, IV, 294
Gillam, Mr. *See* Kelly, James
Gillam, Abigail (daughter of BENJAMIN), II, 247
Gillam, Abigail (wife of BENJAMIN), II, 247
Gillam, Ann, II, 247
Gillam, Benjamin (grandfather of BENJAMIN), I, 337
Gillam, Benjamin (uncle of BENJAMIN), I, 337; II, 537
Gillam, Benjamin, I, 39, 129, 130, 227, 338, 528, 601; II, **247**, 538
Gillam, Hannah (grandmother of BENJAMIN), I, 337
Gillam, Hannah (Sharpe), I, 338
Gillam, Martha, I, 338
Gillam, Phoebe. *See* Phillips
Gillam (Williams), Thomas, II, 478
Gillam, Zachariah, I, 338
Gillam, Zachariah, I, 82, 83, 129, 226, 227, **336–38**, 385, 519, 601, 607; II, 247, 537
Gillespie, Alexander (brother of GEORGE), XI, 553, 671
Gillespie, Alexander (father of GEORGE), VII, 342
Gillespie, Alexander (political opponent of Charles Edward Poulett THOMSON), VII, 860
Gillespie, Alexander (son of GEORGE), VII, 342; X, 394
Gillespie, Caroline Matilda. *See* Arnoldi
Gillespie, Catherine. *See* Cameron
Gillespie, George, V, 635, 636; VI, 531, 665; VII, **342–43**, 702; VIII, 287, 321; IX, 315, 316
Gillespie, Grizzel. *See* Paterson
Gillespie, Helen. *See* Hamilton
Gillespie, John, V, 817; VI, 254, 531; VII, 342; VIII, 321
Gillespie, Robert, VI, 531; VII, 27, 342, 835; VIII, 254, 321; IX, **315–17**, 553; X, 394; XII, 744
Gillespie, Sir Robert, IX, 316
Gillespie, Sir Robert Rollo, IX, 857
Gillespie, Thomas, VI, 204

Gillet, Monsieur (valet), II, 116
Gillet, Marguerite (Bernard de La Rivière), II, 58
Gilley, Isabella (Baldwin; Dinning), XI, 264; XII, 51
Gilley, Jane (Black), VIII, 92
Gilley, Walter, XII, 51
Gillies, David, XII, 136
Gillies, John, X, 176
Gilliland, Susan (Macaulay), IV, 494
Gilliland, William, IV, 494
Gillmor*, Arthur Hill (1824–1903), XI, 830; XII, 18, 28
Gillmore, Ann. *See* Allen
Gillmore, George, V, **343–45**; VI, 294
Gillray, James, IV, 578
Gilly, William Stephen, IX, 37
Gilman, Arthur Delavan, XII, 345, 535
Gilman, Elizabeth (Hale), III, 274
Gilman, Francis Edward, XI, 913
Gilman, Joseph D., IX, 257
Gilmor, Charles Todd, X, 74
Gilmor, Janet Anne (Morrison), XI, 615
Gilmore, Elvira (Edson), XI, 296
Gilmore, Mary. *See* Lillicoe
Gilmore, Thomas, IV, 105, 106, **294–95**, 392, 393, 423, 424, 533; V, 224; VII, 650
Gilmour, Agnes. *See* Strang
Gilmour, Allan (father of ALLAN, 1775–1849), VII, 343
Gilmour, Allan (uncle of ALLAN, 1805–84), VIII, 753, 754; IX, 652, 653; X, 305, 306; XI, 348, 349
Gilmour, Allan (son of JOHN), XII, 367
Gilmour, Allan, VII, **343–44**; XII, 366
Gilmour, Allan, VI, 255; VII, 344; VIII, 753; IX, 653, 773; X, 305, 306; XI, **348–50**; XII, 366
Gilmour, Allan, VIII, 268; X, 306; XII, 322, **366–68**, 900
Gilmour, Barbara (Ritchie), VIII, 753
Gilmour, Betty (mother of ALLAN, 1816–95), XII, 366
Gilmour, Boyd, XI, 291, 627
Gilmour, Caroline. *See* White
Gilmour, David (brother of JOHN), VIII, 93; X, 305, 306
Gilmour, David (father of ALLAN, 1816–95), XII, 366
Gilmour, David (lumberman), XII, 367
Gilmour, Elizabeth. *See* Pollok
Gilmour, J. D., XII, 367
Gilmour, James, VII, 343, 344; VIII, 268, 736, 737; X, 306; XII, 366, 367
Gilmour, John (clergyman), X, 295
Gilmour, John (father of ALLAN, 1805–84), XI, 348
Gilmour, John (father of JOHN), X, 305
Gilmour, John (son of JOHN), XII, 367
Gilmour, John, VIII, 93; X, **305–6**; XI, 349; XII, 367
Gilmour, Margaret. *See* Urie
Gilmour, Margaret (Rubidge), X, 635
Gilmour, Marion (Manuel), XII, 367
Gilmour, Matilda. *See* White
Gilpin, Alfred, XII, 368
Gilpin, Bernard, XII, 368
Gilpin, Charlotte. *See* Smith
Gilpin, Edwin, XII, 368
Gilpin, John Bernard, XII, 368
Gilpin, John Bernard, X, 362; XII, **368–69**
Gilpin, Mary Elizabeth. *See* Miller
Gilpin, William, VIII, 64; XII, 525
Gilzean, Ann (Johnston), VI, 354; VII, 444
Gimbal, Madeleine. *See* Morisseau

Gingell, William Bruce, XII, 343, 344
Gingras, Charles, IX, 317
Gingras, Cyrille, XI, 515
Gingras, Édouard (musician), IX, 855
Gingras, Édouard (son of ÉDOUARD), VIII, 329
Gingras, Édouard, VIII, **328–29**
Gingras, Jean-Élie, VIII, 649
Gingras, Léon, VIII, 328, **329–30**; IX, 118; X, 87
Gingras, Louis, VII, 28; VIII, 682; IX, 117, 118, **317**
Gingras, Louise. *See* Contremine, *dit* Jolicœur
Gingras, Marguerite. *See* Gaboury
Gingras, Marie-Charlotte. *See* Blanchard, *dit* Raynaud
Gingras, Pierre, VIII, 328, 329
Giniès, Thérèse-Catherine-Rose (Grollier), IX, 342
Ginkel, Godert, 1st Earl of Athlone, II, 279
Ginty, John, XII, 699
Gioux, Françoise (Raudot), II, 555
Giovio, Giulio, I, 660
Giovio, Paolo, I, 660
Gipps, Sir George, VII, 6; X, 706; XII, 762
Gipson, Lawrence Henry, III, 149
Girard. *See also* Giard; Miot; Miot-Girard
Girard, Monsieur (politician), XII, 263
Girard, Amable, XII, 369
Girard, Jacques, III, 257, 343, 425, 426; IV, **295–97**, 453, 457; V, 719
Girard, Jean, III, 612, 613
Girard, Jeanne-Élisabeth (Legardeur de La Mothe-Tilly), III, 376
Girard, Josephte. *See* Daunais
Girard, Madeleine (Tantouin de La Touche), II, 618
Girard, Marc-Amable, XI, 193, 611, 612, 644, 742; XII, 33, **369–73**, 1008
Girard, Marie-Aurélie. *See* La Mothe
Girard, Stephen, VII, 257
Girard de La Place, Simon. *See* La Place, Simon-Gérard de
Girardin, Charles-François, VI, 635
Girardin, Gosephte (Gauthier), X, 301
Girardin, Jeanne (Barbe), II, 276
Girardin, Marie-Clotilde (Raymond; Henry), VI, 635; VII, 394, 395, 739
Giraud, Elizabeth (Bunting), XII, 139
Giraud, Jeanne de (Saurel), I, 602
Giraudin, Jeanne (Bertrand), II, 411
Girault Du Poyet, Marguerite (Le Prévost Duquesnel), III, 392
Girod, Amury, VII, 173, **344–47**, 513, 586, 679, 689; VIII, 245, 259, 279, 332, 792; IX, 811, 827; X, 307, 574
Girod, Jhuan, VII, 347
Girod, Zoé. *See* Ainsse
Girot, Jehan, I, 421
Girouard, Angèle, VIII, 330
Girouard, Anselme, XI, 350
Girouard, Antoine, VI, 286
Girouard, Antoine, IV, 81; VI, 207, **286–88**, 589, 598, 651, 680; VII, 488; VIII, 174, 175, 456, 592; XI, 725; XII, 252
Girouard*, Désiré (1836–1911), X, 600; XII, 506, 1026
Girouard, Émélie. *See* Berthelot
Girouard, Félicité (Dumouchel), VIII, 330
Girouard, François, VIII, 330
Girouard, Gilbert-Anselme, XI, **350–51**; XII, 802
Girouard, Jean-Joseph, V, 49, 50; VI, 382, 680; VII, 172,

173, 174, 248, 258, 345, 346, 422, 515; VIII, 40, **330–34**, 471, 479, 791, 916; IX, 441, 458, 775, 818; X, 306, 499, 574, 655
Girouard, Joseph (father), VIII, 330
Girouard, Joseph, VIII, 40, 330
Girouard, Marguerite. *See* Chaperon
Girouard, Marie-Anne. *See* Baillairgé
Girouard, Marie-Louise. *See* Félix
Girouard, Mathilde. *See* Prat
Girouard, Sophia. *See* Baker
Girouard, Suzanne. *See* Jaillet
Giroux, Adélaïde. *See* Michaud
Giroux, Alfred, IX, 318
Giroux, André-Raphaël, VIII, 40; IX, **317–19**
Giroux, Eugène, IX, 318
Giroux, Joseph, IX, 318
Giroux, Louis, IV, 484
Giroux, Louise (Jacquet), IV, 386
Giroux, Marie-Anne. *See* Pageot
Giroux, Marie-Anne (Besserer), IX, 48
Giroux, Marie-Louise (Rodier), VII, 757
Giroux, Marie-Louise-Alphonsine (Normand), XI, 814
Giroux, Michel, IX, 317
Giroux, Pierre, VI, 28
Giroux, Pierre-O., XII, 133
Giroux, Sélina. *See* Bédard
Giroux, Thomas, II, 82
Girroir, Angélique. *See* Le Blanc
Girroir, Hubert, XI, **351–52**
Girroir, Joseph, XI, 351
Girtin, Thomas, VII, 401; XII, 526
Girty, Catharine. *See* Malott
Girty, George, V, 345
Girty, James (brother of SIMON), IV, 777, 778, 779; V, 345; VI, 611
Girty, James (witness), IV, 778
Girty, Mary. *See* Newton
Girty, Simon, V, 345
Girty, Simon, IV, 410, 499, 777, 778; V, 301, **345–46**
Gisborne, Alida Ellen. *See* Starr
Gisborne, Frederic Newton, XII, **373–76**, 383
Gisborne, Hartley (uncle), XII, 373
Gisborne, Hartley, XII, 376
Gisborne, Hartley P., XII, 373
Gisborne, Henrietta. *See* Hernaman
Giscaro, Marquis de. *See* Rivière
Giscaro, Marquise de. *See* Pastour de Costebelle
Gittens, Elizabeth (Colston), I, 233
Gittens, William, I, 233
Gitton, Jean, II, 28, 275, 464, 465
Givins, Angelique. *See* Andrews
Givins, Caroline Ann (Hillier), VII, 409
Givins, James, V, 120; VII, 200, 314, **347–48**, 409, 466, 917; VIII, 431, 432
Givins, Saltern, VII, 159
Glackemeyer, Anna Sabina. *See* Queren
Glackemeyer, Frederick, VII, **348–50**, 573, 762; VIII, 634, 635; XI, 352
Glackemeyer, Johann Wilhelm, VII, 348
Glackemeyer, Josephte. *See* Just
Glackemeyer, Marie-Anne. *See* O'Neil
Glackmeyer, Charles, VIII, 262
Glackmeyer, Edward, VII, 709

Glackmeyer, Félix, IX, 250
Glackmeyer, Frederick, VII, 762
Glackmeyer, Henriette (Molt), VII, 348; VIII, 634; XI, 353
Glackmeyer, Louis-Édouard, VII, 348, 790; IX, 300, 301; X, 105, 132; XI, 203, **352–53**, 499
Glackmeyer, Marie-Henriette. *See* Lagueux
Glackmeyer, Marie-Reine-Joséphine. *See* Duvernay
Glackmeyer, Sophie. *See* Roy Portelance
Gladman, George, V, 526, 712; IX, 319; X, 481
Gladman, George, VI, 795; VIII, 590; IX, **319–20**; X, 273; XI, 384, 441, 662
Gladman, Harriet. *See* Vincent
Gladman, Henry, IX, 319
Gladstone, Sir John, VIII, 166
Gladstone, William Ewart, VI, 399; VIII, xxvii, xxviii, 842; IX, 290, 349; X, 58, 368, 443; XI, 74, 255, 769; 328, 437, 600, 663, 713, 715, 716, 717, 856, 927, 1047, 1053, 1085
Gladu, Marguerite (McKay), XII, 640
Gladu, Sarah (MacKintosh), VII, 567
Gladwin, Dorothy (Jebb), IX, 412
Gladwin, Frances. *See* Beridge
Gladwin, Henry, IV, 297
Gladwin, Henry, III, 95, 306, 527, 528, 529, 558, 652; IV, 241, **297**, 337, 552, 587, 722, 762, 768
Gladwin, Mary. *See* Dakeyne
Glandelet, Charles de, I, 117, 506; II, 19, 44, 45, 90, 132, **247–49**, 259, 329, 332, 372, 629; III, 168, 545, 684
Glandons. *See* Desdevens
Glanville. *See* Evelyn-Glanville
Glapion, Augustin-Louis de, III, 142, 580; IV, 134, 135, **297–99**, 372; V, 146
Glasgow, George, V, **346–47**; VII, 66
Glasgow, Margaret. *See* Green
Glasier, Ann (Stevens; wife of BEAMSLEY PERKINS), IV, 299
Glasier, Beamsley Perkins, IV, **299–301**; V, 413, 415; VI, 718; VII, 198; XII, 376
Glasier, Benjamin (father), IV, 300; XII, 376
Glasier, Benjamin, XII, 376
Glasier, Duncan D., XII, 376
Glasier, Emmaline. *See* Garraty
Glasier, John, VII, 289; XII, **376–78**
Glasier, Martha (mother of JOHN), XII, 376
Glasier, Sarah. *See* Eveleth
Glasier, Stephen (brother of JOHN), XII, 376, 377
Glasier, Stephen (father of BEAMSLEY PERKINS), IV, 299
Glass, Alexander, VIII, 541
Glass, Henry, X, 124
Glass, Jannet (Siveright), VIII, 820
Glass, John (businessman), X, 724; XI, 556
Glass, John (clergyman), XI, 304
Glass, Lawrence, VIII, 541
Glaude. *See* Claude
Glazier. *See* Glasier
Gleason, John, XII, 324
Gledhill, Bathsheba Placentia, II, 250
Gledhill, Grace America, II, 250
Gledhill, Isabella. *See* Atkinson
Gledhill, Isabella. *See* Richmond
Gledhill, Joseph, II, 250, 251
Gledhill, Margaret Carolina, II, 250
Gledhill, Robert, II, 249

Gledhill, Samuel, II, **249–51**; III, 324, 516, 517
Gledstanes, Anne (Palliser), XI, 661
Glegg, John Baskerville, V, 522; VI, 375; VII, 311; VIII, 161
Gleig, George, VIII, 832
Glemet, Pierre, IV, 125, 271, 565, 566, 754
Glen. *See also* Glenn
Glen, Alexander, XI, 353
Glen, Jane. *See* Reed
Glen, Jane Elizabeth (Jannetie) (Cuyler), V, 222
Glen, John Sanders, III, 587
Glen, Marie-Anne-Julie. *See* Hertel de Rouville
Glen, Thomas, IX, 29, 393; XI, **353–54**
Glenaladale. *See* MacDonald; M'Donald
Glencairn, Lord. *See* Gordon, Lord Gordon
Glendenning, Janet (McLeay), XII, 668
Glendonwyn, Henriette. *See* Chauveau
Glene, Elizabeth (Ramsay, Countess of Dalhousie), VII, 722
Glenelg, Baron. *See* Grant
Glengarry. *See* Macdonald; Macdonell
Glenie, James, IV, 329; V, 94, 136, 158, 159, 160, 162, 258, **347–58**, 506, 646; VI, 7, 99, 246, 356, 474, 504, 562, 563, 654, 719, 740, 755, 788; VII, 121, 198, 331, 806
Glenie, Mary Anne. *See* Locke
Glenie, Melville, V, 356
Glenn, Adélaïde. *See* Belcourt
Glenn, John, XI, **354–55**; XII, 568
Glenn, Margaret Emma (Marshall d'Avray), X, 497
Glennie, Professor, V, 357
Glikhikan (Glickhican), IV, **301–2**; V, 301, 345, 882; VI, 189
Glin, Knight of. *See* FitzGerald
Gloade. *See* Glode
Globensky, Auguste-France, IX, 320; X, 306
Globensky, Charles-Auguste-Maximilien, VII, 173; IX, 320, 321
Globensky, Élisabeth. *See* Lemaire Saint-Germain
Globensky, Frédéric-Eugène, VIII, 331, 791; IX, 458; X, 306
Globensky, Hortense (Prévost), IX, 320; X, **306–7**
Globensky, Marie-Anne. *See* Panet
Globensky, Marie-Françoise. *See* Brousseau, *dit* Lafleur de Verchères
Globensky, Maximilien, VII, 173, 761; VIII, 791; IX, **320–21**; X, 307; XII, 535
Globensky, Octavie (Laviolette), XII, 535
Glode, Charles, VII, 609; VIII, **334–35**
Glode, Francis, VIII, 334
Glode, Gabriel, VIII, **335–36**
Glode, Jack, VII, 609; VIII, 335
Glode, John, VIII, 334
Glöckner, Catharina (Philips), VII, 694
Gloria, Jean, I, **339**; II, xvi
Gloria, Marie. *See* Bourdon
Gloria, Perrette. *See* Vaulthier
Gloria, Pierre, I, 339
Glory, Laurent, II, 302
Gloucester, Duke of. *See* William
Gloucester and Edinburgh, Duchess of. *See* Mary
Gloux, Olivier, known as Gustave Aimard, X, 166
Glover, Amelia (Jarvis), IX, 411; X, 379

Glover, Elizabeth Rosetta, Lady Glover. *See* Scott
Glover, Frederick Augustus, XI, 355
Glover, Sir John Hawley, XI, **355–57**, 433, 632; XII, 165, 860
Glover, Mary. *See* Broughton
Glover, Sarah (Cooper), IX, 155, 157
Glover, Thomas, XII, 280
Glower. *See* Glode
Glyn. *See also* Glenn
Glyn, George Carr, 1st Baron Wolverton, XI, 166
Glyn, Thomas C., VIII, 427
Glynn, Hannah (McClure), X, 455
Glynn, John, V, 145
Gobeil, Jeanne-Angélique (Prat), II, 531
Gobert, Catherine (Liénard de Beaujeu), III, 402
Gobin, Gabrielle. *See* Bécasseau
Gobin, Jean, II, 32, 217, **251–52**, 273, 276, 522
Gobin, Jeanne (Petit), II, 522
Godard, Hannah (Caddy), XI, 137
Godard (Goddard), James Mason, V, 495, 879
Godard, Marie (Hudon), XII, 455
Godard (Godart), Marie-Louise (Boschenry, Baronne de Drucourt), III, 71
Godard, Philomène (Hudon), XII, 455
Godbold, Mary Ann (Jeffery), XII, 469
Godbout*, Archange (1886–1960), III, 94, 690, 722; IX, 903
Godbout, Élisabeth (Dorval), IX, 216
Goddard, James Stanley, V, 322, 368, 760; VI, 317
Goddard, William, V, 743
Godé. *See also* Gaudé
Godé, Françoise. *See* Gadoys
Godé, Mathurine (Saint-Père; Le Moyne de Sainte-Marie), I, 598; II, 386, 405; III, 385, 580
Godé, Nicolas, I, 319, 598; III, 580
Godeau, Antoine, I, 644
Godefroy, Barbe, I, 340
Godefroy, Charlotte, I, 340
Godefroy, Jean-Amador, II, 190
Godefroy, Jean-Paul, I, 45, 112, 145, **339–40**, 341, 344, 447, 623; II, xvi, 83
Godefroy, Marie. *See* Marteau
Godefroy, Marie-Madeleine. *See* Legardeur de Repentigny
Godefroy, Marie-Thérèse. *See* Bondy
Godefroy, Perrette. *See* Cavelier
Godefroy, Pierre, I, 340
Godefroy, Robert, I, 339
Godefroy, Thérèse (Renaud Dubuisson), III, 551
Godefroy de Linctot, Catherine-Apolline. *See* Blondeau
Godefroy de Linctot, Daniel-Maurice, IV, **302–3**, 564
Godefroy de Linctot, Hyacinthe, IV, 302
Godefroy de Linctot, Louis-René, IV, 302
Godefroy de Linctot, Marie-Charlotte (Ailleboust de La Madeleine), IV, 11
Godefroy de Linctot, Maurice-Régis, IV, 302
Godefroy de Linctot, René, III, 269
Godefroy de Lintot, Jean, I, 121, 223, **340–41**, 369, 467; II, 168, 252, 253
Godefroy de Lintot, Marie. *See* Leneuf
Godefroy de Lintot, Marie-Charlotte (Hertel de La Fresnière), III, 288
Godefroy de Lintot, Michel, II, 70, **252**; III, 288
Godefroy de Lintot, Perrinne. *See* Picoté de Belestre

Godefroy de Lintot, René, II, 252
Godefroy de Normanville, Louis, II, 252; VI, 288
Godefroy de Normanville, Marguerite. *See* Seigneuret
Godefroy de Normanville, Thomas, I, 340, **341**, 489, 490
Godefroy de Saint-Paul, Françoise. *See* Lepellé
Godefroy de Saint-Paul, Françoise (Boucher de Montbrun), III, 82
Godefroy de Saint-Paul, Jean-Amador, II, **252**; III, 82, 224
Godefroy de Saint-Paul, Madeleine (Boucher de Montbrun), III, 82
Godefroy de Saint-Paul, Marguerite. *See* Jutrat
Godefroy de Tonnancour, Charles-Antoine, II, 253; III, **258–59**
Godefroy de Tonnancour, Charles-Antoine, IV, **303–4**, 332; V, 216, 217; VI, 288
Godefroy de Tonnancour, Joseph-Marie, VI, **288–89**; IX, 321
Godefroy de Tonnancour, Léonard, VI, 288; IX, **321–22**
Godefroy de Tonnancour, Louise. *See* Carrerot
Godefroy de Tonnancour, Louise (Ramezay), IV, 650
Godefroy de Tonnancour, Louis-Joseph, II, 253; III, 430, 539; IV, 185, 303, **304–5**, 316, 547; V, 143, 570, 687, 736, 737; VI, 132, 288; VII, 200
Godefroy de Tonnancour, Louis-René-Labadie, V, 737
Godefroy de Tonnancour, Marguerite. *See* Ameau
Godefroy de Tonnancour, Marguerite. *See* Cherrier
Godefroy de Tonnancour, Marguerite (Coffin), VII, 200
Godefroy de Tonnancour, Marguerite-Renée, named de la Croix, IV, 319
Godefroy de Tonnancour, Marie-Catherine. *See* Pélissier
Godefroy de Tonnancour, Marie-Geneviève, named de Sainte-Hélène, IV, 319
Godefroy de Tonnancour, Marie-Joseph, IX, 321
Godefroy de Tonnancour, Mary. *See* Scamen
Godefroy de Tonnancour, Pierre-Joseph, VII, 739; VIII, 18
Godefroy de Tonnancour, Reine. *See* Frémont
Godefroy de Tonnancour, René, II, 204, **252–53**, 529; III, 110, 258, 539, 551; IV, 304, 319, 650; VI, 288
Godefroy de Tonnancour, Ursule (Charly Saint-Ange), III, 110
Godefroy de Vieuxpont, Catherine. *See* Poulin de La Fontaine
Godefroy de Vieuxpont, Jacques, I, 274, **341**
Godefroy de Vieuxpont, Joseph, I, 553; II, **253–54**
Godefus. *See* Boucault
Goderich, Viscount. *See* Robinson
Godet. *See also* Gaudet
Godet, Charles, XI, 334
Godet, Gédéon, II, 538, 539
Godet, Margaret Charlotte (Radisson), II, 539
Godet, Marguerite. *See* Panneton
Godet, Rolland, I, 245, **341–42**; II, xvi
Godet Des Maretz, Christine de, I, 342
Godet Des Maretz, Claude de, I, 190, **342**, 346
Godet Des Maretz, Cléophas de, I, 342
Godet Des Maretz, François de, I, 342
Godet Des Maretz, Jeanne de. *See* Gravé Du Pont
Godet Des Maretz, Marie de. *See* La Marck
Godet Des Maretz, Paul de, I, 342
Godet Du Parc, Jean de, I, 190, 342
Godfrey, Arabella. *See* Churchill
Godfrey, Charlotte (Boscawen), III, 70
Godfrey, Elizabeth Anne (Need), XII, 781

Godfrey, Philip, VIII, 257
Godfrey, Sophia Ann. *See* Minns
Godfroy, Jacques, III, 528, 529
Godin, Antoine, XII, 110
Godin, Jean-Baptiste, VIII, 290
Godin (Gaudin), Louise (Vézina), III, 648
Godin, Marie-Louise-Florence-Eudoxie (Valois), IX, 802
Godin, Sophia (Morse), V, 609
Godin, *dit* Bellefontaine, *dit* Beauséjour, Joseph, IV, **305–6**; V, 412
Godin, *dit* Bellefontaine, *dit* Beauséjour, Marie-Anne. *See* Bergeron d'Amboise
Godin, *dit* Chatillon, *dit* Bellefontaine, Gabriel, IV, 305
Godin, *dit* Chatillon, *dit* Bellefontaine, Marie-Angélique. *See* Robert Jasne
Godinot, Nicolas, VII, 170, 171
Godley, Dennis, XII, 750
Godon, Marthe (Testard de Montigny), IX, 782
Godsman, John. *See* Davidson, William
Godsman, William, IV, 195
Godson. *See* Gotson
Godwin, Mary. *See* Wollstonecraft
Goes, Damien de, I, 234, 235
Goesbriand, Louis de, IX, 549
Goessman, John, VII, **350–51**, 641
Goessman, John Gerhard, VII, 351
Goethe, Johann Wolfgang von, VIII, 651
Goethe, Ottilie von. *See* Pogwisch
Goff, Anna. *See* Neville
Goff, Fade, V, 336; VI, 566; VII, **351–52**
Goff, Mary Somaindyke. *See* Ryan
Goff, Richard, VII, 351
Goff, Sarah Matilda (Wright), XI, 940
Goffar, Anne-Jeanne (Dosquet), IV, 220
Goffe. *See* Trowbridge
Goffe, Edmund, II, 254
Goffe, Elijah, III, 213
Goffe, Hannah. *See* Bernard
Goffe, Hannah. *See* Lynde
Goffe, Mary. *See* Norden
Goffe, Samuel, II, 254
Goforth, William, IV, 320
Gofton, Ingram, II, 493, 663
Goggins, Sarah (Blanchard), VII, 81; X, 70
Goguen. *See* Gueguen
Goguet, Denis, IV, 306
Goguet, Denis, III, 145, 485, 608, 643; IV, 35, 66, 69, 123, 126, 128, 182, **306–7**, 362, 422, 624, 632; V, 395, 396
Goguet, Louise-Élisabeth. *See* Feré Duburon
Goguet, Marguerite-Thérèse-Sibylle (mother of DENIS), IV, 306
Gohel, Marie (Gaudron), III, 239
Gohiet, François, XII, 1020
Gohin, Pierre-André, Comte de Montreuil, III, 186; IV, **307–8**, 651, 672
Gohin de Montreuil, Monique-Françoise. *See* Petit
Gohin de Montreuil, Nicolas, IV, 307
Gohn. *See* John
Gohsmann, Catharina Maria. *See* Schulte
Gohsmann, Johann. *See* Goessman, John
Gohsmann, Johann Henrich, VII, 350
Goigni. *See* Richard
Going, Clemena. *See* Murray

Golard, Françoise (Petit de Levilliers de Coulanges), II, 523
Gold. *See also* Gould
Gold, Jonathan, XI, 365
Gold, Rachel. *See* Lee
Goldfrap, James, IV, 570; V, 142
Goldie, Emma Jane. *See* Mitchell
Goldie, Frances. *See* Owen
Goldie, James, XII, 378
Goldie, John (grandfather), VII, 312; XII, 378
Goldie, John, XII, 378
Goldie, Thomas, XII, **378–79**
Goldie, Thomas Leigh, VIII, 394, 619; X, 326
Golding, John, VI, 246
Goldsbury, Elizabeth (Cutler), VII, 223
Goldschmidt, Johanna Maria. *See* Lind
Goldsmith, Elizabeth (Small), IV, 766, 767; VI, 608, 721; VII, 638; VIII, 336; IX, 724
Goldsmith, Henry, IX, 322
Goldsmith, Mary. *See* Mason
Goldsmith, Oliver, IX, 322
Goldsmith, Oliver, VI, 171; VII, 180; IX, **322–23**
Goldthwait, Benjamin, III, **259–60**, 484; IV, 651
Goldthwait, Charity. *See* Edwards
Goldthwait, John, III, 259
Goldthwait, Sarah. *See* Hopkins
Golkowsky, George, III, 212
Golpin, Mary (Hunt), X, 372
Gómara, López de, I, 154
Gombert, Sieur (partner of Louis-Simon LE POUPET de La Boularderie), II, 418
Gomes, Estevão, I, 21, **342–43**
Gonʔaongote. *See* Williams, Eunice
Gonçalves. *See* Gonsales
Góngora. *See* Lújan
Gonillon, Catherine de (Duplaix; Daccarrette), III, 157; IV, 245
Gonillon, Jeanne (Daccarrette), III, 156
Gonish, Étienne, VII, 352
Gonish, John, VII, 352
Gonish, Peter, VII, **352–53**
Gonsales, João, I, 153, 302, 304, **343**
Gonwatsijayenni. *See* Koñwatsiʔtsiaiéñni
González, Gertrudis (Martínez), IV, 519
Gooch, Sir Daniel, X, 331
Gooch, Elizabeth (Austin), II, 287
Good, Mr (publisher), VIII, 266
Good, Alice. *See* Douglas
Good, Allen, VIII, 44
Good, Charles, X, 247; XII, 523
Good, Eleanor. *See* Bull
Good, James, X, 331
Good, James, XI, **357–58**
Good, John Booth, XII, 441
Goodall, Lydia, III, 295
Gooderham, Alfred Lee, XI, 360
Gooderham, Charles Horace, XI, 360
Gooderham, Elizabeth (Worts), XI, 937
Gooderham*, George (1820–1905), XI, 360, 481, 938
Gooderham, Harriet Tovell. *See* Herring
Gooderham, Henry, X, 331; XI, 360
Gooderham, James (grandfather), XI, 358
Gooderham, James, XI, 360
Gooderham, Margaret. *See* Bright

Gooderham, Sarah (mother of WILLIAM, 1790–1881), XI, 358

Gooderham, William (1790–1881), XI, 347, **358–60**, 937, 938

Gooderham, William (1824–89), XI, 359, **360–61**; XII, 993

Goodfellow, Barbara (MacKinlay), IX, 510

Goodfellow, James, XII, **379–82**, 754, 755

Goodfellow, Margaret. *See* Dodds

Goodfellow, Rosina. *See* Whiteford

Goodfellow, William, XII, 379

Goodhue, Charles Frederick Henry, VII, 281; IX, 323

Goodhue, George Jervis, VIII, 856; IX, **323–24**, 603, 618; X, 206, 403; XI, 63, 501

Goodhue, Josiah, IX, 323

Goodhue, Josiah Cosmore, VI, 399; IX, 323

Goodhue, Louisa. *See* Matthews

Goodhue, Maria. *See* Fullerton

Goodhue, Mary G. (Cronyn), X, 206

Goodhue, Rachel. *See* Burr

Goodrich, Samuel Griswold, X, 527

Goodridge, Augustus Frederick, XII, 311, 381, 757, 956

Good Stream. *See* Ohnaweio

Goodwin, Caroline (Hodgson), VI, 321

Goodwin, Robert, V, 886; VI, 321

Goold (Gould), Arthur, V, 666

Goold, Edward L., XII, 1117

Goold, Franklin P., XII, 157, 1090, 1091

Goold, Nathan, V, 135

Goold, Ralph W., XII, 1090, 1091

Goossens, Pierre-François, IV, 565

Gordan, Antoine, IV, 375

Gordon. *See also* Hamilton-Gordon; Watson-Gordon

Gordon, Mr (justice of the peace), V, 432

Gordon, Adam, V, 697; VIII, xxxii

Gordon, Lord Adam, V, 214; VI, 412

Gordon, Alexander, 4th Duke of Gordon, V, 488, 795; VIII, 295

Gordon, Andrew Robertson, XII, **382–83**, 981

Gordon*, Arthur Hamilton, 1st Baron Stanmore (1829–1912), IX, 414, 620; X, 101, 140, 160, 192, 265, 288, 289, 332, 340, 495, 713; XI, 278, 688, 828, 829, 830, 831, 833, 897, 933; XII, 18, 26, 49, 116, 338, 536, 741, 750, 910, 1053, 1054, 1105

Gordon, Charles George, XI, 326, 472, 929; XII, 117, 244, 245

Gordon*, Charles William (1860–1937), XII, 490, 906

Gordon, Charlotte, Lady Haddo. *See* Baird

Gordon, Lady Charlotte (Lennox, Duchess of Richmond and Lennox), V, 488, 489; VIII, 295

Gordon, Daniel, XII, 905

Gordon*, Daniel Miner (1845–1925), XII, 618

Gordon, Edward John, VII, 543; VIII, 299; IX, 103, **324–25**

Gordon, Elizabeth Amelia. *See* Macdonald

Gordon, Ellen Catherine. *See* Powell

Gordon, Francis, IX, 324

Gordon, George (George Herbert). *See* Gordon, Lord Gordon

Gordon, Lord George, VI, 475

Gordon, George, Lord Haddo, IX, 326

Gordon, George Nicol, IX, **325–26**; X, 303, 308; XII, 839

Gordon, Lord Gordon, X, **307–8**; XI, 194

Gordon, Lady Harriet, IX, 752

Gordon, Helen (Taylor), V, 795

Gordon, Helen Skinner. *See* King

Gordon, James, V, 349

Gordon, James A., XII, 902

Gordon, James Douglas, IX, 326; X, 303, **308**; XII, 839

Gordon, Janet. *See* MacGregor

Gordon, John (father of GEORGE NICOL), IX, 325; XII, 839

Gordon, John (father of JAMES DOUGLAS), X, 308

Gordon, John (merchant), X, 33

Gordon, John, IX, **326–27**, 806; XII, 318, 642

Gordon, John, XI, **361–63**, 481

Gordon, John Herbert Charles. *See* Gordon, Lord Gordon

Gordon, John William, X, 406

Gordon, Julia Charlotte Sophia, Lady Gordon. *See* Mackenzie-Stewart

Gordon, Leslie, XII, 383

Gordon, M. G. H., XI, 285

Gordon, Margaret. *See* MacDonell of Scothouse

Gordon, Margaret. *See* McKernan

Gordon, Margaret (Bannerman, Lady Bannerman), IX, 27, 28

Gordon, Mary. *See* Ramsey

Gordon, Mary. *See* Robertson

Gordon, Mary Elizabeth. *See* Parker

Gordon, Mary Elizabeth (Leith), VII, 498

Gordon, Peter, VI, 457; VIII, 451, 452

Gordon, Robert, IX, 439

Gordon, Thomas, X, 33

Gordon, William (brother of JOHN, 1792–1869), IX, 327

Gordon, William (office holder), IV, 398; V, 507

Gordon, William (of Fredericton), V, 349, 350

Gordon of Wardhouse, Isabella (MacDonald of Glenaladale), V, 515

Gore, Annabella. *See* Wentworth

Gore, Arthur Saunders, 2nd Earl of Arran, IX, 327

Gore, Caroline. *See* Beresford

Gore, Caroline Maria (Daly, Lady Daly), IX, 190, 192

Gore, Sir Charles Stephen, VIII, 18, 465, 712; IX, 143, **327–29**, 595, 596, 597, 826, 827; X, 236; XII, 89

Gore, Desiah (Starr), XI, 846

Gore, Elizabeth, Countess of Arran. *See* Underwood

Gore, Francis, VIII, 336

Gore, Francis, V, 65, 111, 171, 189, 366, 441, 521, 550, 551, 734, 750, 765, 772, 796, 797, 841, 842, 845, 856; VI, 4, 5, 8, 79, 80, 114, 117, 152, 215, 216, 264, 406, 441, 540, 542, 543, 544, 551, 608, 609, 610, 612, 613, 624, 647, 656, 657, 698, 723, 747, 804; VII, 36, 37, 58, 161, 162, 175, 285, 286, 318, 366, 419, 438, 439, 440, 462, 546, 638, 835, 848, 864, 865, 919, 929; VIII, 4, 161, **336–41**, 387, 596, 597, 598, 607, 749, 750, 858, 885, 945; IX, 332, 647, 661, 755, 756

Gore, Graham, X, 28

Gore, Ralph, IX, 190

Gore, Sarah Rachel, Lady Gore. *See* Fraser

Goreham. *See also* Gorham

Goreham, Anne. *See* Spry

Goreham, Elizabeth (Hunter; wife of JOSEPH), IV, 308

Goreham, Joseph, III, xxix, 129, 257, 664; IV, 111, 161, 193, **308–10**; V, 58, 63, 204, 240, 258, 295, 296; VI, 193, 242, 739; VII, 274

Gorel, Hélène (Marin), II, 458

Gorges, Sir Ferdinando, I, 51, 262, 497

Gorham, Elizabeth. *See* Allyn

Gorham, Eville, VII, 815
Gorham, John, III, **260–61**, 438, 483, 532, 583, 653; IV, 169, 308, 679
Gorham, Lucy (Morton), XI, 620
Gorham, Mary. *See* Thacter
Gorham, Nathaniel, V, 781
Gorham, Shobal (Shubael), III, 260; IV, 308
Gorham, Walter, VIII, 687
Goring, Francis, V, 781, 841
Gorrell, James, III, **261–62**, 410, 528; V, 835
Gorribon, Pierre de, I, 400
Gorry, Jean, I, 216
Gorst, Thomas, I, 47, 49, 50, 83, 226, 337, **343**, 477; II, 537
Gosford, Countess of. *See* Pole; Sparrow
Gosford, Earl of. *See* Acheson
Goslin, James Pratt, VI, 265, 266
Gosline, Ann (Shaw), V, 752
Gosling*, William Gilbert (1863–1930), V, 221
Gosnold, Bartholomew, I, 189, 364
Goss, Charlotte Augusta (Fry), XII, 342
Gossage, Brookes Wright, IX, 550
Gosse, Eliza. *See* Brightwen
Gosse, Elizabeth, XI, 363
Gosse, Emily. *See* Bowes
Gosse, Hannah. *See* Best
Gosse, John, VIII, 673, 674
Gosse, Philip Henry, VII, 590; XI, **363–64**; XII, 1060
Gosse, Thomas, XI, 363
Gosselin*, Amédée-Edmond (1863–1941), III, 691; IV, 755, 801; IX, 863; X, 735; XI, 486
Gosselin, Antoine, VIII, 302; X, 690
Gosselin*, Auguste-Honoré (1843–1918), III, 11, 553, 560; IV, 637; X, 611
Gosselin, Catherine. *See* Monty
Gosselin, Cécile (Douaire de Bondy; Feltz), IV, 265
Gosselin, Charlotte. *See* Ouimet
Gosselin, Clément, V, 146, **358–59**
Gosselin, Gabriel (father of CLÉMENT), V, 358
Gosselin, Gabriel (husband of Louise Guillet), II, 273
Gosselin, Geneviève. *See* Crépeaux
Gosselin, Geneviève, named de Sainte-Madeleine, II, 93
Gosselin, Jean-Baptiste, III, 193, 223, **262–64**, 315
Gosselin, Joseph (father of LÉON), VII, 353
Gosselin, Joseph (father of SCHOLASTIQUE), X, 308
Gosselin, Josephte. *See* Pageot
Gosselin, Léon, IX, 458, 696
Gosselin, Léon, VII, **353–55**; VIII, 260, 536; XI, 341; XII, 569
Gosselin, Louis (adopted son of Pierre HAIMARD), II, 273
Gosselin, Louis (brother of CLÉMENT), V, 359
Gosselin, Louis (coureur de bois), III, 493
Gosselin, Louise. *See* Guillot
Gosselin, Louise (Amyot), XII, 20
Gosselin, Marie. *See* Dionne
Gosselin, Mary. *See* Graddon
Gosselin, Scholastique, X, **308–9**
Gosselin, Thérèse. *See* Viger
Gosset, William Driscoll, IX, 82; X, 246; XI, 604
Gossin, Jules, VIII, 676
Gossip, Anne Catherine. *See* Coade
Gossip, Mary Ann (mother of WILLIAM), XI, 364
Gossip, William, VIII, 193; XI, **364–65**, 848
Gossip, William G., XI, 364

Gother, Elizabeth (Mann), VI, 484
Gotson, Christiana. *See* Veyssière
Gotteville de Belile, Robert-David, II, **254–55**; III, 178, 191
Gottschalk, Louis Moreau, XI, 671
Gouault, Gaspard, I, 108
Goubert, Charlotte-Élisabeth (Foucher), III, 227
Goudeau, Françoise (Gagnon), I, 320
Goudge, Henry, VIII, 417
Goudge, Maria Louisa (Burnyeat; Archibald), XI, 29
Goudie (Gowdie), Catharine (Workman), X, 717; XI, 936; XII, 1122
Goudie, Elizabeth. *See* Greenwood
Goudie, James, VI, 291; IX, 823; XII, 800
Goudie, Jane. *See* Black
Goudie, John, VI, 289, 292
Goudie, John, V, 67; VI, **289–92**, 423, 424, 532; VII, 134, 484, 619, 744, 873, 879; VIII, 558, 648
Goudon. *See* Gowding
Goudreau, Monsieur (trapper), VIII, 313
Goudreau, Félix, XII, 920
Gouentagrandi, I, 634; II, xxxvi, **255–56**
Gougé, Dominique, VII, 386
Gougeon, Antoine, II, 71
Gougeon, Huguette (Blanchard), II, 71
Gougeon, Jeanne. *See* Chabrat
Gouger, Rebecca (Cramp), XI, 209
Gough, Françoise-Renée. *See* Pommereau
Gough, Isabella. *See* Carvell
Gough, James, XII, 740
Gough, John, III, 525
Gough, Patrick, IX, 710
Gough, Thomas Barnes, V, 857
Gouin. *See also* Guernon
Gouin, Charles, XI, 306, 460
Gouin, Élisa. *See* Mercier
Gouin, Georges-Alexandre, X, 33
Gouin, Josephte (Méthotte), VIII, 628
Gouin*, Sir Lomer (1861–1929), XII, 725, 727
Gouin, Louis, V, 792
Gouin, Marguerite (Bonami, *dit* L'Espérance), XI, 88
Gouin, Pierre-Trefflé, IX, 215
Goulaine de Laudonnière, René de, I, 469
Goulburn, Henry, V, 882; VI, 214; VIII, xxviii, xxix, 351; IX, 182
Gould. *See also* Goold
Gould, Augustus Addison, IX, 144
Gould, Sir Charles, IV, 83, 84, 85
Gould, Ira, VIII, 220; IX, 367, 823; X, 591, 717, 723; XII, 809
Gould, Jason, VIII, 268
Gould, Jay, X, 307; XII, 150
Gould, John, V, 501; VI, 258
Gould, Joseph, XI, 144, 233, 347, **365–66**; XII, 43
Gould, Julia Elizabeth. *See* Bramley
Gould, King, II, 591; III, 9; IV, 83
Gould, Mary. *See* James
Gould, Nathaniel, VIII, 541, 542, 543; IX, 639, 640; XII, 863
Gouldrup, Charlotte (Lord), XI, 532
Goulet, Alexis, VIII, 821; IX, 329
Goulet, Elzéar, VIII, 821; IX, **329–30**, 708; XI, 192, 540, 740; XII, 33
Goulet, Hélène. *See* Jérôme, *dit* Saint-Matte

Goulet, Josephte. *See* Siveright
Goulet*, Maxime (1855–1932), VIII, 821
Goulet, Thomas, III, 396
Goumard, Claire (Du Gua), I, 291
Gounod, Charles, XII, 317, 471, 533
Goupil, Joseph, VII, 167; VIII, 218
Goupil, René, I, 42, 124, **343–44**, 388, 389, 523; II, 157
Goupy (Goupil), Marie (Aubert), II, 26
Gourdan, Claude-Madeleine (Le Normant), III, 386
Gourdau. *See* Gourdeau
Gourdeau, Bertrande (Gaultier de La Vérenderie), I, 327
Gourdeau, François, XII, 280
Gourdeau de Beaulieu, Antoine, I, 345; II, 256
Gourdeau de Beaulieu, Éléonore. *See* Grandmaison
Gourdeau de Beaulieu, Jacques, I, 344, 345; II, 256, 449
Gourdeau de Beaulieu, Jeanne-Renée (Macard), I, 345; II, 449
Gourdeau de Beaulieu et de La Grossardière, Jacques, I, 345; II, **256–57**, 296
Gourdeau de Beaulieu et de La Grossardière, Marie. *See* Bissot
Gourdeau de Beaulieu et de La Grossardière, Pierre-Jacques, II, 256
Gourdon, Monsieur (officer), II, 146
Gourges, Dominique de, I, 381, 469
Gourlay, Janet. *See* Fleming
Gourlay, Jean. *See* Henderson
Gourlay, Mary. *See* Reenan
Gourlay, Oliver, IX, 330
Gourlay, Robert Fleming, V, 551, 661, 674, 853; VI, 56, 103, 115, 116, 149, 154, 160, 199, 230, 247, 248, 420, 421, 436, 503, 543, 544, 609, 612, 613, 631, 657, 723, 747, 772, 805; VII, 37, 38, 58, 124, 162, 178, 182, 230, 244, 251, 262, 318, 367, 375, 378, 417, 420, 439, 456, 457, 466, 472, 497, 584, 780, 781, 795, 835; VIII, 54, 69, 186, 305, 325, 337, 340, 409, 410, 450, 514, 515, 596, 597, 600, 604, 694, 945; IX, **330–36**, 498, 546, 551, 670, 672, 684, 755, 756, 817; X, 705, 706; XI, 248
Gournay, Marie de (Rousseau), I, 484
Gourville. *See* Du Pont; Hérauld
Goussé, Monsieur (office holder), II, 149, 151
Goussé, Charles-Gaspard de, Chevalier de La Rochalar, III, 633
Goutin, Abraham (Alexandre) de, II, 257
Goutin, Anne de (Du Pont de Renon; Hertel de Cournoyer), II, 205, 257
Goutin, Antoine de, II, 257
Goutin, François-Marie de, II, 219, 257, 258; III, 79, 184, **264–65**, 389, 533, 567; IV, 41, 56, 455
Goutin, Jacques de, II, 257
Goutin, Jeanne de. *See* Tibaudeau
Goutin, Jeanne de, II, 257
Goutin, Joseph de, II, 257
Goutin, Louise de, II, 257
Goutin, Magdelaine de, II, 257
Goutin, Marguerite de, II, 257
Goutin, Marguerite-Madeleine de (Boucher), III, 79
Goutin, Marie-Angélique de. *See* Aubert de La Chesnaye
Goutin, Marie-Angélique de. *See* Puyperoux de La Fosse
Goutin, Marie-Anne de (Bailly de Messein), IV, 41
Goutin, Marie-Joseph de, II, 257
Goutin, Mathieu de, II, 257
Goutin, Mathieu de, I, 577; II, 37, 45, 182, 183, 205,

**257–58**, 352, 462, 480, 481, 579, 625, 630, 654; III, 79, 264, 681, 682
Gouyé, Thomas, II, 270
Gouze, Guillaume, IV, 624
Gouze, Marie-Anne. *See* Chasle
Gove, Jonathan, VIII, 324
Gove, Lucretia (Gilchrist), VIII, 324
Gover (Grover), Mary Ann (Holman), XII, 443
Governor Blacksnake. *See* Thaonawyuthe
Governor Tomah. *See* Tomah, Pierre (d. in or after 1827)
Gow, Agnes. *See* Ferguson
Gow, Alley (Dorland), VI, 214
Gow, John, XI, 366
Gow, Mary Maxwell. *See* Smith
Gow, Niel, XI, 366
Gow, Peter, XI, **366–67**
Gowan, Alice. *See* Hitchcock
Gowan, Aliza Amelia (Peck), X, 313
Gowan, Emily (Ferguson), X, 314
Gowan, Frances Jane (Ferguson), X, 282, 313
Gowan, Francis Anne. *See* Turner
Gowan, Harcourt, X, 313
Gowan*, Sir James Robert (1815–1909), IX, 725; X, 314; XII, 583, 598, 609, 610, 611, 612, 1048
Gowan, John Hunter, X, 309
Gowan, Margaret. *See* Hogan
Gowan, Nassau C., X, 313
Gowan, Ogle Robert, VII, 116, 117, 260, 453, 458, 459, 695; VIII, 305, 426, 535, 797, 822; IX, 45, 46, 99, 166, 345, 521, 644, 858; X, 80, 109, 110, 118, 121, 255, 282, 299, **309–14**, 325, 360, 554; XI, 347, 366, 730, 877; XII, 594
Gowan, Robert, VII, 658; VIII, 157; IX, 22; X, **314–15**
Gowanlock, John, XI, 306
Gowanlock, John Alexander, XII, 478
Gowanlock, Theresa Mary. See Johnson
Gowdie. *See* Goudie
Gowding (Goudon), Elizabeth (Kirke), I, 404
Goweaaey (Goweah). *See* Gawèhe
Gowen, Hammond (brother-in-law of Sir Henri-Gustave Joly* de Lotbinière), XII, 694
Gowen, Hammond (partner of William HALL), VIII, 353
Gowen, Helenore (Hall), VIII, 353
Gower. *See also* Leveson-Gower
Gower, Abel, V, 359
Gower, Elizabeth. *See* Logan
Gower, Lady Elizabeth (Waldegrave, Countess Waldegrave), VI, 795
Gower, Sir Erasmus, V, **359–61**, 633; VI, 271, 323; VII, 764; VIII, 264
Gower, Letitia. *See* Lewes
Gowler, Mary (Cochrane), XII, 200
Goy. *See* Gayot
Goyau, Magdeleine (Dumouchelle), VII, 258
Goyer, Olivier, II, 106, 176, 249, **258–59**, 268
Goyette, Odilon, XII, 100
Gozon, Marthe de (Montcalm), III, 458
Grabot, Barthelemie (Lahaille), V, 471
Graburn, Marmaduke, XI, 478, 479
Grace, Elizabeth. *See* O'Neil
Grace, James, III, 136, 137
Grace, John, VII, 854, 855

Grace, Mary. *See* Toler
Grace, Richard, VI, 293
Grace, Thomas, named Father James, V, 458; VI, **292–93**;
  VII, 801
Graddon, Mary (Gosselin), VII, 353
Gradis, Abraham, IV, 67, 69, 92, 209, 632
Gradis, David, IV, 66, 657
Gradwell, Robert, VI, 596
Grady. *See also* O'Grady
Grady, Standish, VII, 659
Graeme, Anne (Hamond, Lady Hamond), VI, 310
Grafton, Duke of. *See* Fitzroy
Graham, Miss (McDowall), VII, 557
Graham, Aaron, V, **361–62**, 596, 641; VI, 636
Graham, Agnes. *See* Allan
Graham, Andrew, II, 310; III, 285, 287, 304; IV, 156, 157,
  160, 340, 377, 378, 518, 524, 647, 742, 743, 758, 761;
  V, **362–63**, 450; VI, 775
Graham, Ann. *See* Brown
Graham, Ann (Anderson), XII, 21
Graham, Ann (Swan), XI, 865
Graham, Barbara. *See* Bowie
Graham, Catherine, Lady Graham. *See* Stewart
Graham, Donald, VI, 409
Graham, Elizabeth. *See* Grant
Graham, Elizabeth. *See* Whidden
Graham, Elizabeth (wife of HUGH), VI, 293
Graham, Elizabeth (Forbes), III, 218
Graham, Felix, V, 681, 682
Graham, Franklin (Thomas), XII, 306
Graham, Hugh, VI, 293
Graham, Hugh, V, 344; VI, 87, **293–94**
Graham, J. C., XII, 783
Graham, James, 3rd Duke of Montrose, VII, 33
Graham, James Elliot, XII, **383–84**
Graham, James R., XII, 747
Graham, Jane (McBeath), V, 512
Graham, Janet (Dunlop), VII, 259, 260
Graham, John Hamilton, XII, **384–86**
Graham, John Wellington, XII, 469
Graham, Joseph, XII, 383
Graham, Ketchum, X, 230
Graham, Margaret (Edmundson), VIII, 266
Graham, Margaret (Nisbet), VII, 653
Graham, Mary (Oxenden), XII, 812
Graham, Mary Jane. *See* Aikins
Graham, Patricia. *See* Sherer
Graham, Peter, XI, 140
Graham, Richard, Viscount Preston, II, 538
Graham, Thomas, VIII, 127
Graham*, Sir Wallace (1848–1917), XI, 210, 755; XII,
  1042
Grahame*, James Allan (1825–1905), IX, 853; X, 486; XI,
  383; XII, 641
Grais. *See* Le Gouès
Gramont, Antoine-Charles, Duc de Gramont, II, 434
Gramont, Armand de, Comte de Guiche, II, 440
Gramont, Marguerite-Louise-Suzanne de, Comtesse de
  Guiche. *See* Béthune
Granby, Marquess of. *See* Manners
Grand, Nanette (Ann) (Prévost), V, 693
Grand Agnier, Le. *See* Togouiroui
Grandbois, Paul-Étienne, XI, 814

Grandchamp. *See* Allenou; Corneillier
Grand Condé, Le. *See* Condé, Louis II
Grande Armée, La. *See* La Grande Armée
Grande Gueule, La. *See* Otreouti
Grandet, Joseph, II, 196
Grande Terre, La. *See* Ohonsiowanne
Grandfontaine. *See* Andigné
Grandin*, Vital-Justin (1829–1902), X, 556, 614; XI, 305,
  310, 746; XII, 22, 1005, 1006, 1007, 1008, 1010
Grandison, Viscount. *See* St John
Grand Maison. *See* Malepart
Grandmaison. *See also* Borry
Grandmaison, Éléonore de (Boudier de Beauregard;
  Chavigny de Berchereau; Gourdeau de Beaulieu; Cail-
  hault de La Tesserie), I, 56, **344–45**, 418, 537; II, 141,
  223, 256, 449
Grandmesnil. *See* Véron
Grandmont, Sieur de (governor), I, 507
Grandpré. *See also* Boucher; Duteau; La Court
Grandpré, Alexandre, IX, 344
Grand Sauteux, Le. *See* Minweweh
Grandval. *See* Morthon
Grandville. *See* Bécart
Granet, Dominique, XI, 42; XII, 697
Grange, Captain, II, 266
Grange, Geneviève (Levasseur), I, 473, 474
Grange, John Thomas, XI, 853
Granger, Eli, V, 597
Granger, Élisabeth (Hébert), VI, 314
Grangula (Grangular). *See* Otreouti
Grannis, John, VIII, 147, 221; IX, 144
Granpré. *See* La Court
Grant. *See also* Forsyth; Ogilvie-Grant
Grant, Miss (Colebrooke), IX, 145
Grant, Mr (merchant), VII, 735
Grant, Mrs. *See* Bennett
Grant, Alexander, IV, 52, 291
Grant, Alexander, IV, 777; V, 17, 39, 189, **363–67**, 441,
  443, 536, 718, 732, 855, 856; VI, 21, 115, 211, 215, 285,
  309, 473, 698, 804; VII, 36, 439, 864; VIII, 4, 34, 336,
  339; XII, 675
Grant, Amelia Sophia (Forbes, Lady Forbes), VII, 301
Grant, Ann. *See* Lynd
Grant, Ann (Gerrard), V, 260; VIII, 320
Grant, Ann (Smith), XI, 834
Grant, Anne. *See* Freeman
Grant, Anne Randall Scott (Ballantyne), XII, 53
Grant, Archange (Dickson), VI, 211
Grant, Barbara (Mitchell), XII, 740
Grant, Catharine (Fraser), VIII, 302
Grant, Catherine. *See* McDonald
Grant, Catherine (Jordan), V, 260
Grant, Charles (father), IV, 385; V, 85, 86, 144, 364; VII,
  165, 311
Grant, Charles, VI, 765
Grant, Charles, 1st Baron Glenelg, VII, 6, 7, 8, 141, 180,
  294, 295, 296, 370, 547, 549, 550, 682, 894, 922; VIII,
  xxv, xxvii, xxxi, xxxiv, xxxvi, 29, 183, 207, 233, 251,
  253, 254, 376, 377, 407, 419, 441, 523, 640, 641, 742,
  808, 859, 956; IX, 23, 71, 142, 168, 178, 226, 230, 399,
  400, 501, 554, 675, 687, 709, 794; X, 62, 63, 189, 342,
  343, 344, 345, 600, 601, 619, 710, 711, 712; XI, 28, 914,
  945

Grant, Charles James Irwin, Baron de Longueuil, XI, 808
Grant, Charles William, Baron de Longueuil, V, 373, 375; VII, 394, 500, 667; VIII, 760; IX, 700; X, 428, 429; XI, 533
Grant, Christina Theresa (Keefer), X, 394
Grant, Colin P., VII, **355–56**, 551, 552, 560
Grant, Colquhoun, IX, 336
Grant, Cuthbert (Quebec merchant), IV, 310
Grant, Cuthbert (Trois-Rivières merchant), IV, 310
Grant, Cuthbert, IV, **310**; VIII, 341, 500; X, 276
Grant, Cuthbert, IV, 310; V, 268, 751; VI, 100, 167, 251, 445; VII, 78, 249, 250, 671, 795, 845; VIII, 5, **341–44**, 349, 482, 527, 537, 766, 767, 821; IX, 95, 780; X, 276; XI, 539, 875; XII, 124, 125
Grant, Daniel, VII, 483
Grant, David (brother of WILLIAM, 1744–1805), V, 370
Grant, David (father of CUTHBERT, d. 1799), IV, 310
Grant, David (partner of Peter GRANT), V, 531; VII, 356; VIII, 121
Grant, David Alexander, IV, 269; V, 64, 246, 370, 371, 372, 373, 374, 603; VI, 700; VII, 500, 523
Grant, Duncan, VII, 355
Grant, Elizabeth. See MacKay
Grant, Elizabeth (Finlay), V, 260
Grant, Elizabeth (McKenzie; Graham), X, 476
Grant, Elizabeth McIntosh (Macgeorge), XI, 557
Grant, Francis, VI, 110
Grant, Frederika (Ross), XII, 924
Grant, Geneviève. See Forbes
Grant*, George Monro (1835–1902), VII, 558; IX, 495; X, 44, 193, 369; XI, 609, 611, 724, 764, 772; XII, 447, 617, 618, 663, 767
Grant, Grace (Cameron), VI, 110
Grant, Helen. See McDonald
Grant, Helena. See Chisholm
Grant, Helena (Dallas), XI, 230
Grant, Henry C., VII, 364
Grant, Isabella (Fraser), IX, 282
Grant, Isabella (Frobisher), VI, 267
Grant, Isabella (Gilkison), VI, 285; VIII, 327
Grant, Isabella (Sellar), IX, 711
Grant, Isobel (Grant), V, 363
Grant, James (father of Sir WILLIAM), VI, 294
Grant, James (officer), III, 219, 378
Grant, James (physician), X, 462
Grant, James (relative of John COFFIN, 1729–1808), V, 214
Grant, James (son of CUTHBERT, d. 1799), IV, 310; VIII, 341
Grant, James, IV, 133, **311**; V, 259, 512, 715; VI, 111, 446, 743
Grant, Sir James, VII, 400
Grant, Sir James Alexander, X, 128; XII, 153, 601, 938
Grant, James Charles, VII, 667; XI, 874
Grant, Jane. See Holmes
Grant, Jane (Chandler), VII, 165
Grant, Jane (Christie), XII, 195
Grant, Jane (Langford), VII, 483
Grant, Jane Dickson (Ballantyne), XII, 53
Grant, Jane Elizabeth (Maitland), V, 372
Grant, Janet (Powell), VI, 605
Grant, Janet (Stuart), VII, 837
Grant, Jean. See Tyrie
Grant, John (father of WILLIAM, 1743–1810), V, 376

Grant, John (fur trader), IV, 171; V, 90, 259, 260, 376; VI, 111; VIII, 320
Grant, John (Jamaican planter), VI, 110
Grant, John (of Lachine, Quebec), VII, 79, 356
Grant, John (politician), XII, 917
Grant, John (son of ALEXANDER), V, 367
Grant, John (supply contractor), V, 368, 373
Grant, John Marshall, XI, 604, 606
Grant, Sir Lewis, IX, 337
Grant, Lucy Chandler (Haliburton), VI, 307; IX, 348
Grant, Sir Ludovic, VIII, 538
Grant, Madelaine. See Desmarais
Grant, Margaret. See Brodie
Grant, Margaret (Blackwood), VII, 79
Grant, Margaret (Forsyth), VII, 311
Grant, Margaret (Grant), IV, 310
Grant, Margaret (Schank), VI, 694
Grant, Marguerite. See Fafard, dit Laframboise
Grant, Marguerite, V, 509
Grant, Maria. See Pollard
Grant, Maria (Breland), XII, 124
Grant, Marie. See McGillis
Grant, Marie-Anne-Catherine. See Fleury Deschambault
Grant, Marie-Charles-Joseph. See Le Moyne de Longueuil
Grant, Marie-Élisabeth (Montenach), VII, 500; VIII, 108
Grant, Marjory (Macdonell), VIII, 538
Grant, Mary. See Jenckes
Grant, Mary, VII, 356
Grant, Mary (Brown), VI, 87
Grant, Mary (Falcon), IV, 310; X, 276
Grant, Naomi (Macpherson), XII, 682
Grant, Patrick (father of ALEXANDER), V, 363
Grant, Patrick (publisher), XII, 762
Grant, Peter (fur trader), V, 531; VIII, 121
Grant, Peter (son or nephew of PETER), VII, 356
Grant, Peter, V, 534; VII, **356–57**
Grant, Richard, V, 260
Grant, Robert (businessman), VIII, 465, 466
Grant, Robert (fur trader), IV, 365, 366; V, 561, 603, 656; VIII, 341
Grant, Robert (merchant), III, 130, 365; V, 368, 369, 817; VI, 89
Grant, Sarah Ann (Richardson), VI, 639
Grant, Sophia (McLean), IX, 514; XI, 568
Grant, Susannah. See Coffin
Grant, Thérèse. See Barthe
Grant, Thomas (distiller), V, 878, 879
Grant, Thomas (son-in-law of David LYND), V, 460, 509
Grant, Ulysses S., X, 316, 328, 485, 556, 559; XI, 768; XII, 701, 742
Grant, Walter Colquhoun, IX, **336–38**; XI, 627; XII, 833
Grant, William (carpenter), VI, 384
Grant, William (father of WILLIAM, 1744–1805), V, 367
Grant, William (1744–1805), III, 111; IV, 127, 197, 315, 324, 477, 492, 538, 571, 686, 716, 725, 755, 794; V, 21, 22, 43, 44, 45, 67, 87, 91, 108, 132, 142, 191, 233, 277, 288, 289, 290, 291, 317, 318, **367–76**, 385, 427, 460, 483, 493, 509, 527, 576, 603, 699, 745, 746, 793, 794, 816, 843, 880; VI, 49, 254, 346, 384, 416, 424, 532, 587, 615, 627, 639, 699, 819; VII, 311, 357, 500, 504, 523, 524; VIII, 952
Grant, William (1743–1810), IV, 133, 304, 311, 754; V, 259, 260, **376–77**, 563; VI, 110, 111, 516; VIII, 320

Grant, Sir William, V, 87, 142, 148, 149; VI, 267, **294–96**, 511, 606, 694
Grant, William Henry, XII, 574
Grant*, William Lawson (1872–1935), X, 369
Grant, William R., XI, 633
Grantham, Baron. *See* Robinson
Grantley, Baron. *See* Norton
Granton, Lord. *See* Hope
Granville. *See also* Bécart
Granville, Earl. *See* Carteret
Granville, Earl of. *See* Leveson-Gower
Grape, The. *See* Chomina
Grasett, Ann Bligh. *See* Stevenson
Grasett, Anne Elizabeth (Hagarty), XII, 399
Grasett, Henry, XI, 367
Grasett, Henry James, IX, 719; X, 54, 55; XI, **367–69**; XII, 399
Grasett*, Henry James (1847–1930), XII, 274
Grasett, Sarah Maria. *See* Stewart
Grass, Margaret. *See* Swartz
Grass, Mary Ann (wife of MICHAEL), V, 377
Grass, Michael, IV, 683; V, **377–79**; VI, 146, 214
Grasse, François-Joseph-Paul de, Comte de Grasse, V, 62, 105, 176
Grasse, Marie-Reine (Lanoullier), III, 350
Grasset de Saint-Sauveur, André, IV, 312
Grasset de Saint-Sauveur, André, III, 611; IV, **311–12**
Grasset de Saint-Sauveur, Jacques, IV, 312
Grasset de Saint-Sauveur, Jean, IV, 311
Grasset de Saint-Sauveur, Louise. *See* Roussel
Grasset de Saint-Sauveur, Marie-Anne. *See* Nolan Lamarque
Grasset de Saint-Sauveur, Marie-Joseph. *See* Quesnel Fonblanche
Grassett, George, XI, 559
Grassie, George, VIII, 300, 929; X, 293
Gratry, Auguste-Joseph-Alphonse, IX, 466
Gratton, Martin, VIII, 481
Grautoff, Theresa Jane Despard (Pemberton), XII, 832
Gravé. *See* Gravé Du Pont
Gravé de La Rive, Charles-Yves, V, 379
Gravé de La Rive, Henri-François, IV, 7, 42, 43, 49, 50, 74, 100, 370, 371, 373, 424, 510, 511, 642; V, **379–80**, 459, 492, 523, 524, 580; VI, 586, 587; VIII, 201
Gravé de La Rive, Louise-Jeanne-Marguerite. *See* Mercier
Gravé Du Pont, Christine. *See* Martin
Gravé Du Pont, François, I, 28, 61, 64, 86, 98, 160, 188, 189, 190, 191, 194, 208, 209, 210, 265, 292, 293, 300, 342, **345–46**, 347, 386, 422, 432, 433, 470, 473, 601, 602, 638
Gravé Du Pont, Jeanne (Godet Des Maretz), I, 342, 346
Gravé Du Pont, Robert, I, 95, 98, **346–47**
Gravel*, Elphège (1838–1904), XI, 253, 494; XII, 509, 821
Gravel, Jean-Adolphe, III, 283; X, 236
Gravel, Julie-Adèle (Barsalou), XII, 62
Gravel, Ludger, IX, 565
Gravel, Sophie. *See* Fabre
Gravelet, Jean-François (Charles Blondin), VII, 313; XII, **386–87**
Graveline, Sieur de (expedition member), III, 83
Gravelle, Marguerite. *See* Prieur
Gravelle, Pierre, II, 648
Gravenor, Elizabeth (Stourton), I, 614

Graves, Alfred Perceval, VII, 866
Graves, Algernon, V, 679; XII, 102
Graves, Booty, IV, 160, 365; V, 512, 602, 656, 683
Graves, Charles Patrick Ranke, VII, 866
Graves, Elizabeth. *See* Budgell
Graves, Elizabeth, Baroness Graves. *See* Williams
Graves, Jane (MacDonnell), XI, 555
Graves, Margaret. *See* Spinkes
Graves, Robert James, X, 83; XI, 428
Graves, Robert von Ranke, VII, 866
Graves, Samuel, IV, 790; V, 754; VI, 562; VII, 361
Graves, Thomas, V, 380
Graves, Thomas, 1st Baron Graves, III, 132; IV, 163, 598, 599; V, 62, 176, **380–82**, 491; VI, 323, 638
Graves, William, VI, 719
Gravier, Charles, Comte de Vergennes, IV, 144, 312; V, 433, 893
Gravier, Jacques, II, 110, 197, **259–60**, 347, 454, 455, 468, 469, 543, 653; III, 380
Gravois, Joseph, IV, 222
Gray, Alexander, IV, 37, 492, 716; V, 8, 150, 747; VI, 296, 512
Gray, Andrew, V, 366; VIII, 794
Gray, Ann (wife of Alexander), IV, 37
Gray, Archibald, VI, 294
Gray, Asa, IX, 200; X, 82, 106; XII, 401, 542, 869
Gray, Avis Phillips. *See* Easson
Gray, Benjamin Gerrish, IX, 338
Gray, Benjamin Gerrish, IV, 291; VI, 54; VIII, 172, **344–47**; IX, 338
Gray, Charlotte (Wood), VII, 922
Gray, Edward William, IV, 59, 263, 385, 386, 442, 533, 549, 703; V, 218, 298, 373, **382–84**, 391, 614, 652, 716; VI, 237, 238, 296, 297; VIII, 389
Gray, Elizabeth. *See* Chipman
Gray, Elizabeth. *See* Low
Gray, Elizabeth. *See* Ormond
Gray, Elizabeth (mother of ROBERT, 1755–1806), V, 387
Gray, Elizabeth (Ainslie, Lady Ainslie), VII, 9
Gray, Elizabeth (Ballenden), VIII, 59
Gray, Elizabeth (Jarvis), VIII, 428, 430
Gray, Frost Ralph, V, 386
Gray, George, V, 723
Gray, Hugh, V, 210, 495, 817
Gray, I. W. D. *See* Gray, John William Dering
Gray, Isabella (McMillan), VI, 475
Gray, James (father of ROBERT ISAAC DEY), V, 388
Gray, James (rival of Jonas JONES), VII, 459
Gray, James F., VII, 22
Gray, John (deacon), III, 471
Gray, John (father of EDWARD WILLIAM and JOHN), V, 382, 383; VI, 296
Gray, John (merchant), V, 142, 288
Gray, John (printer), IV, 532, 534
Gray, John, IV, 37; V, 71, 384, 420, 581, 718; VI, **296–97**, 472, 744, 745; VII, 584
Gray, John, 11th Lord Gray, VII, 9
Gray, John Edward, IX, 658, 660; XI, 543
Gray, John H., XI, 752
Gray, John Hamilton (1811–87), VI, 298; VIII, 810; X, 594, 595, 596, 597, 679; XI, **369–72**, 667, 668, 669, 700, 701; XII, 319
Gray, John Hamilton (1814–89), IX, 87, 382, 409, 410,

413, 414, 565; X, 287, 289, 543; XI, 224, **372–76**, 578, 754, 828, 829, 897; XII, 18, 79, 232, 536, 684, 897, 1051, 1052, 1054, 1105
Gray, John William Dering, VIII, 345; IX, 35, 187, **338–40**; XII, 714
Gray, Jonathan Abraham, V, 218, 383, 384, 614; VI, 285, 297; VII, 617, 621
Gray, Joseph (father of BENJAMIN GERRISH), IV, 290; VIII, 344
Gray, Joseph (grandfather of JOHN HAMILTON, 1814–89), XI, 372
Gray, Margaret. *See* Oakes
Gray, Martha. *See* Atkins
Gray, Mary. *See* Burns
Gray, Mary. *See* Gerrish
Gray, Mary. *See* Pullman
Gray, Mary. *See* Thomas
Gray, Mary (Bidwell), VI, 54; X, 60
Gray, Mary Ann. *See* Scott
Gray, Phoebe. *See* Wallen
Gray, Ralph, V, 83, 369, **384–87**, 509; VI, 49
Gray, Robert, IV, 73, 218, 411, 412, 419, 519; V, **387–88**, 410, 411
Gray, Robert, IV, 551; V, 220, 309, 310, 311, 335; VI, 108, 162, **297–98**, 566, 663, 736, 785; VIII, 36, 428; XI, 369
Gray, Robert Don Quadra, IV, 73; V, 388
Gray, Robert Isaac Dey, V, 17, 326, **388–89**, 518, 520; VI, 79
Gray, Sarah Caroline. *See* Cambridge
Gray, Susan. *See* Pennefather
Gray, Thomas (partner of Michael FRANCKLIN), IV, 273
Gray, Thomas (poet), X, 537
Gray, William (brother-in-law of Ward CHIPMAN, 1754–1824), VI, 142
Gray, William (father of JOHN HAMILTON, 1814–89), XI, 372
Gray, William (father of ROBERT, 1755–1806), V, 387
Gray, William (interpreter), VII, 911
Gray, William (newspaper owner), VII, 182, 183
Graydon, John, II, 36, **260–61**, 274, 348, 373, 486, 565, 583, 659, 666
Graydon, Newenham P., XII, 1028
Gray Lock, II, 665; III, **265–67**
Great Mohawk. *See* Togouriroui
Great Sun, II, 110
Great World. *See* Ohonsiowanne
Grece, Charles Frederick, V, 138, 373; VII, **357–58**
Grece, John William, VII, 357
Greeley, Aaron, VIII, 116
Greeley, Ebenezer, VIII, 378, 803
Greeley, Horace, IX, 505, 509; X, **315–16**; XII, 925
Greeley, Mary. *See* Woodburn
Greeley, Mary Youngs. *See* Cheney
Greeley, Zaccheus, X, 315
Greely, Adolphus Washington, VIII, 449
Greely, Jonathan, X, 624
Green, Amelia (mother of GEORGE EVERITT), XII, 387
Green, Ann (Merrick), VI, 500
Green, Anna (Winslow), V, 486, 869
Green, Anson, VI, 675; VIII, 442; IX, 635, 737, 750; X, **316–18**, 358, 638; XI, 640, 734
Green, Bartholomew, III, 267
Green, Bartholomew, III, 90, **267**

Green, Benjamin, IV, 193, 313, 764; V, 390
Green, Benjamin, III, 130; IV, 51, 169, 199, 274, **312–13**, 560; V, 389, 430; VI, 511; VIII, 928
Green, Caroline Anne (Fuller), XII, 343
Green, Charles (father of GEORGE EVERITT), XII, 387
Green, Charles (son of FRANCIS), V, 390
Green, Columbus H., X, 318
Green, Eliza, X, 318
Green, Eliza Maria (Stewart), VIII, 837; XI, 854
Green, Elizabeth. *See* Gerrish
Green, Elizabeth. *See* Irwin
Green, Ernest, VIII, 208, 209
Green, Francis, V, **389–90**; VI, 129; VII, 831
Green, George Everitt, XII, **387–88**
Green, Hannah. *See* Hammond
Green, Hannah (Hopkins), X, 358
Green, Harriet. *See* Mathews
Green, Isabella. *See* Ross
Green, Jacob, X, 65
Green, James (fur trader), VIII, 767
Green, James (runner), XII, 29
Green, James, V, 440; VI, **298–300**; VII, 15, 225, 242; VIII, 793, 837
Green, John (brother of BENJAMIN), IV, 312
Green, John (father-in-law of Caleb HOPKINS), X, 358
Green, John Cleveland, VIII, 895, 896, 897, 898; XI, 407
Green, Joseph (brother of BENJAMIN), IV, 312
Green, Joseph (father of ANSON), X, 316
Green, Joseph (father of BENJAMIN), IV, 312
Green, Lydia. *See* Vorce
Green, Margaret. *See* Pierce
Green, Margaret, XII, 387
Green, Margaret (Draper), VI, 332
Green, Margaret (Glasgow), V, 347
Green, Margaret Ann (Howe), V, 430
Green, Margaretta (Davers, Lady Davers), III, 166
Green, Maria. *See* Mather
Green, Maria (wife of JAMES), VI, 299, 300
Green, Norvin, XII, 168
Green, Rachel. *See* Hopkins
Green, Sarah. *See* Cronk
Green, Susan (Baddeley), X, 29
Green, Susanna. *See* Wenman
Green, Susanna (Green), V, 389
Green, Thomas Hill, XI, 943
Green, Timothy, V, 72
Green, Valentine, V, 844
Green, Walter, XII, 387
Green, Warren, VII, 779, 780
Green, William (1787–1832), VI, 299, **300**
Green, William (fl. 1783–1833), VI, **300–2**
Green, William Saunders Sebright, X, 587
Greene, Anne (Mason), I, 496
Greene, Daniel Joseph, XII, 957
Greene, Edward, I, 496
Greene, Elizabeth, III, 133
Greene, Harriet (Doutre), XI, 277
Greene, Henry, I, 145, 374, 375, 376, 377, 378
Greene, Lucy Huntington (Atwater), X, 18
Greenfield. *See* Macdonell
Greenhow, Robert, V, 388
Greenlaw, Anne (Semple), V, 750

Greenly, Elizabeth Browne (Coffin), VII, 196
Greenock, Baron. *See* Cathcart
Greenshields, J., XII, 632
Greenshields, James Blackwood, IX, 316; XI, 5
Greenshields, James Naismith, XI, 748
Greenshields, John, VI, 534
Greenshields, John Blackwood, VIII, 734
Greenstockings, VI, 328, 329
Greenway, Richard, I, 476, 666
Greenway*, Thomas (1838–1908), XI, 645, 646, 647; XII, 129, 148, 294, 372, 373, 510, 511, 582, 953, 1010, 1087
Greenwood, Deborah. *See* Bootman
Greenwood, Elizabeth (Goudie), VI, 289
Greenwood, Grace. *See* Smith
Greenwood, Margaret (Barker), XI, 48
Greenwood, William, VI, 302
Greenwood, William, VI, **302–3**
Greer, Archibald, XI, 575
Greer, Mary Ann (Shibley), XI, 819
Greese, Margaret. *See* Miller
Greffière, Renée (Couagne), II, 153
Gregg, William, XII, 492
Gregory XVI, VI, 748; VII, 296, 305, 307, 423, 487, 489, 656, 887; VIII, 259, 290, 291, 307, 490, 722; IX, 465, 698, 797; X, 53; XI, 42, 94, 95, 97, 100, 275
Gregory, Anne. *See* Skaꙗennetsi
Gregory, Anne (Procter), VI, 616
Gregory, George (merchant), VIII, 952
Gregory, George (son of JOHN, d. 1817), V, 391
Gregory, George (son of JOHN, 1806–61), IX, 341
Gregory, Isabella. *See* Ferguson
Gregory, Jane Prescott. *See* Forsyth
Gregory, John, IV, 366, 506; V, 332, 333, **390–92**, 512, 537, 561, 562, 564, 565, 566, 603, 656, 820; VI, 72, 454, 455, 509; VII, 311, 566; VIII, 500
Gregory, John, IX, 87, **340–41**; X, 497
Gregory, Louise (Boucherville), XII, 118
Gregory, Maria (Mitchell), V, 391; VI, 509
Gregory, Mary. *See* Grosvenor
Gregory, Mary (Milly) (Allan), V, 15
Gregory, William, IV, 350, 570, 724, 725; V, 605
Greig, Margaret Elizabeth (Fenwick), XII, 314
Greig, William, XI, 452
Greive, Edward, VII, 67, 68; X, 32
Grelleau, Sieur (partner of François MOUNIER), III, 477
Grenet, Jacques, VII, 28
Grenet, Marie-Thérèse (Bouchette; Rollet), V, 100
Grenet, Simon, I, 267
Grenete, Marie-Louise (Chenneque), VI, 134; VII, 176
Grenew, William, XII, 422
Grenier (Garnier), Françoise (Langlois), I, 417
Grenier, Gabriel, X, 580
Grenier, Joseph, XI, 186; XII, 510
Grenier, Louis-Philippe, VIII, 492
Grenier, Marie-Angélique (Paré), IX, 616; X, 578
Grenier, Marie-Mathilde-Henriette (Parent), X, 580
Grenier, Pierre, VII, 148
Grennew. *See* Grunow
Grenolle, Monsieur (explorer), I, 132
Grenon. *See* Guernon
Grenouille, La. *See* Oumasasikweie
Grenville, Anne, Baroness Grenville. *See* Pitt
Grenville, George, IV, xxxiv, 571, 788

Grenville, George Nugent Temple, 1st Marquess of Buckingham, V, 542; VIII, 857
Grenville (Greynvile), Sir Richard, I, 278; IV, 744
Grenville, Richard, 2nd Earl Temple, V, 54
Grenville, Richard Plantagenet Campbell Temple Nugent Brydges Chandos, 3rd Duke of Buckingham and Chandos, IX, 714, 715; XI, 634
Grenville, Richard Temple Nugent Brydges Chandos, 1st Duke of Buckingham, VII, 46
Grenville, William Wyndham, 1st Baron Grenville, IV, 346, 698, 717; V, 22, 149, 151, 152, 586, 820, 874; VI, 150, 594; VII, 524
Greslon Laviolette, Jeanne (Dasilva), III, 165
Greville, Charles Cavendish Fulke, VII, 855
Grey. *See also* Gray
Grey, Earl of. *See* Robinson
Grey, Charles, VII, 478; VIII, 164
Grey, Charles, 1st Earl Grey, V, 35, 691; VI, 257; VIII, xxvi; IX, 24, 234
Grey, Charles, 2nd Earl Grey, VI, 594; VII, 84, 151, 477, 478; VIII, xxvii, 465; IX, 236
Grey, Sir Charles Edward, VII, 6, 7
Grey, Frances Elizabeth. *See* Ellis
Grey, Sir George, VII, 296; IX, 70, 195, 695; X, 116, 494; XI, 44, 432
Grey, Lady Hannah Althea (Bettesworth; Ellice), IX, 234, 236
Grey, Harriet. *See* White
Grey, Harry, X, 318
Grey, Henry George, Viscount Howick and 3rd Earl Grey, VII, 6, 7, 145, 146, 856, 906; VIII, xxvii, xxviii, xxix, xxx, xxxi, xxxii, xxxiv, xxxv, 136, 297, 382, 383, 464, 475, 604, 782, 827, 850, 957, 958; IX, 24, 28, 56, 83, 89, 90, 92, 147, 191, 237, 376, 382, 383, 401, 485, 547; X, 158, 179, 184, 257, 285, 342, 434, 712; XI, 74, 138, 220, 308, 412, 445; XII, 113, 856, 896
Grey, Lady Louisa Elizabeth (Lambton, Countess of Durham), VII, 476; XII, 525
Grey, William, X, 280, **318–19**
Grey, William, 9th Earl of Stamford, X, 318
Grey, William de, 1st Baron Walsingham, IV, xxxiii, xli, xlvii; V, 605
Grey Cloud. *See* Mar-pi-ya-ro-to-win
Greynvile. *See* Grenville
Greysac, Gabriel, III, 642
Greysolon de La Tourette, Claude, II, 31, **261**, 263, 264, 633
Greysolon Dulhut, Daniel, I, 132, 227, 228, 289, 290, 400; II, xxxiii, 13, 31, 105, **261–64**, 279, 302, 317, 440, 471, 488, 633, 635; III, 237, 373, 493
Gribond, Jeanne (Trotain), II, 637
Gridley, Hannah. *See* Deming
Gridley, Rebecca (mother of RICHARD), IV, 313
Gridley, Richard, IV, 313
Gridley, Richard, IV, **313–14**
Gridley, Samuel, IV, 314
Gridley, Sarah. *See* Blake
Griebel, Alice, VIII, 347
Griebel, Ferdinand (Frederick), VIII, **347–48**
Griebel, Heinrich, VIII, 347
Griebel, Johanna (wife of FERDINAND), VIII, 347
Griebel, Johann Heinrich, VIII, 347
Griebel, Julius, VIII, 347

Grier*, Sir Edmund Wyly (1862–1957), XII, 102, 529
Grieve, Desire. *See* Parker
Grieve, Edward, VIII, 368
Grieve, Elizabeth (Oliver), XI, 651
Grieve, James Johnston, XI, 376
Grieve, Jane. *See* Richardson
Grieve, John Thomas, IX, 436
Grieve, Margaret. *See* Johnston
Grieve, Robert (grandfather), XI, 376
Grieve, Robert, XI, 376
Grieve, Walter, VII, 99; XI, 67, 354, **376**, 432; XII, 543
Grieve*, Walter Baine (1850–1921), XII, 756
Griffen, Eliza Margaret. *See* Bird
Griffen, Mary (Ryerson), X, 640
Griffin, Frederick, VII, 67
Griffin, George, XII, 388
Griffin, Henry, VI, 279; VII, 620, 621; X, 519, 520
Griffin, Jane (Franklin, Lady Franklin), VI, 437; VII, 325, 326, 327; VIII, 79, 80; IX, 12, 199, 389; X, 247, **319–20**, 407, 478, 562, 563, 748; XI, 200, 470, 471; XII, 123, 835, 836, 878
Griffin, John, X, 319
Griffin*, Martin Joseph (1847–1921), XII, 137
Griffin, Mary. *See* Guillemard
Griffin, Mary (Simpkinson), X, 320
Griffin, Robert (fur trader), V, 259, 260
Griffin, Robert (partner of Daniel SUTHERLAND), VI, 279, 433, 744, 745
Griffin, S. P., VIII, 448
Griffin, William Henry, VIII, 84; XI, 855; XII, **388–89**, 599
Griffith. *See* App-Griffith
Griffith, Benjamin Peck, VIII, 509
Griffith, Sir John, I, 477
Griffith, John, VII, **358–59**
Griffith, Richard, III, 296
Griffith, Sarah. *See* McGinnis
Griffith, William, VII, 359
Griffiths, Ellen (Barker), XI, 48
Griffiths, Thomas, XI, 220
Griffyn, Owen, I, 316, 317
Grigg, George C., VII, 364
Grignon, Jean, II, 28, 275
Grignon, Pierre, IV, 171
Grigor, Catherine Louisa. *See* Foreman
Grigor, William, VII, 16, 875; VIII, **348–49**, 905
Grihaut, *dit* Larivière, Angèle (Cannon), VI, 120
Grillot de Poilly, Claude-Victor, III, 267
Grillot de Poilly, François-Claude-Victor, III, 229, 230, **267–68**, 440, 700
Grimaldi, Françoise de (Crisafy), II, 162
Grimère, Richarde (Lory), II, 446
Grimes, John, IV, 158, 159, 713
Grimington, Anne (wife of MICHAEL, d. 1710), II, 267
Grimington, Michael (d. 1710), I, 308; II, 42, 50, 171, 231, 232, **264–67**, 311, 319, 395, 644
Grimington, Michael (fl. 1698–1719), II, **267**
Grimmer, Mary Ann (Murchie), XII, 773, 774
Grinnell, Henry, VII, 326; VIII, 448; IX, 199; X, 27, 319, 327, 328; XI, 393, 470
Gripenberg, Johanna Henrica (Schoultz), VII, 779
Gripière de Moncroc, Joseph de, Marquis de Laval, IV, 208
Grisé, Antoine, IV, 315
Grisé, Antoine, IV, 270, **315**

Grisé, Catherine. *See* Lévesque
Grisé, Françoise. *See* Marcoux
Grisé, Françoise. *See* Poyer
Grisé, Jean-Baptiste, IV, 315; VII, 622
Griswold, Deborah (Denison), III, 174
Griswold, Alexander Viets, XII, 574
Groad, Cableal. *See* Glode, Gabriel
Grob, Anna (Knaut), IV, 414
Gröen, Élisabeth (Mariauchau d'Esgly), II, 456
Groff, Andrew, VI, 235
Grogan, Elizabeth Van Rensselaer. *See* Powell
Grogan, John, VII, 639
Grohman. *See* Baillie-Grohman
Groisard, Jeanne (Dupuy), I, 297
Grollier, Jean-Jacques, IX, 342
Grollier, Pierre-Henri, IX, **342**; XI, 310; XII, 1005
Grollier, Thérèse-Catherine-Rose. *See* Giniès
Grondin. *See also* Pardaillan
Grondin, Élisabeth (Proulx), X, 602
Grondin, Jeanne (Chartier), III, 112
Groot, Hugo de, known as Hugo Grotius, IV, 230
Gros Blanc, VIII, 3
Grosbois. *See* Boucher
Gros-Louis, Christine. *See* Vincent
Gros Ours. *See* Mistahimaskwa
Grosse, Renée (Claparède), III, 123
Grosset. *See* DuVernet
Grosset Muirhead, Miriam (DuVernet), VII, 268
Grossin, Élisabeth-Marguerite. *See* Veau, *dit* Sylvain
Groston, Jean, II, 267
Groston, Marie. *See* Rebourceau
Groston de Saint-Ange, Élisabeth. *See* Chorel de Saint-Romain, *dit* d'Orvilliers
Groston de Saint-Ange, Élisabeth (Coulon de Villiers), II, 267; IV, 177
Groston de Saint-Ange, Louis, IV, 316
Groston de Saint-Ange, Louis-Daniel, IV, 316
Groston de Saint-Ange, Marguerite. *See* Crevier
Groston de Saint-Ange, Marie-Rose, II, 267
Groston de Saint-Ange, Pierre (father), II, 67, 216, 267
Groston de Saint-Ange, Pierre, II, 267
Groston de Saint-Ange, Robert, II, 156, **267–68**; III, 105, 491; IV, 315
Groston de Saint-Ange et de Bellerive, Louis, II, 267; III, 530; IV, **315–16**, 683
Grosvenor, Florence. *See* Townsend, Florence
Grosvenor, Mary (Gregory), IX, 340
Grosvenor, Sarah. *See* Mitchell, Sarah
Grothé, André-Zéphirin, VI, 487, 488
Grothé, Christian, V, 36, 436; VI, 487, 664
Grotius, Hugo. *See* Groot, Hugo de
Grotton. *See* Groston
Grouard*, Émile-Jean-Baptiste-Marie (1840–1931), XI, 311
Grougnard, Marie-Anne (Suzor), V, 788
Groulx*, Lionel (1878–1967), III, 722; IV, 232, 376; IX, 143, 903; X, 569
Grouvel, Marguerite. *See* Auber
Grouvel, Martin, I, 305
Grove*, Frederick Philip (1872–1948), IV, 555
Grove, Hannah (Moulton), IV, 564
Grover. *See also* Gover
Grover, William, III, 287, 304

Groves, Margaret Sophia (Cameron), XI, 142, 143
Grubbe, Anne Elizabeth (Haviland), XII, 415
Grubbe, John, XII, 415
Gruel de La Peltrie, Chevalier de, I, 207
Gruel de La Peltrie, Marie-Madeleine de. *See* Chauvigny
Grundy, Joseph, XII, 754
Grunewalt, Caspar Frederic, V, 727
Grunow (Grunno, Grennew), Matilda Louisa (Heintzman), XII, 421
Grymington (Gryminton). *See* Grimington
Gschwind, Anna. *See* Fletcher
Gschwind, Anna (Simpson), VI, 303
Gschwind, John Frederick Traugott, VI, **303–4**
Guay. *See also* Gay
Guay, Isabelle (Cooke), IX, 152
Guay, Marguerite (Levasseur), II, 430
Guay, Pierre-Malcolm, XII, 1121
Gubbins, Elizabeth Catherine (Beauclerk, Duchess of St Albans; Cary, Viscountess Falkland), XI, 155
Gubbins, Joseph, V, 356; VI, 396, 474, 685, 724
Gudridr (Thorsteinn; wife of THORFINNR *karlsefni* Thordarson), I, 612, 642
Gueguen, Anne. *See* Arsenault
Gueguen, Anne. *See* Hamonez
Gueguen, Jacques, VI, 304
Gueguen, Joseph, VI, **304–5**, 651
Gueguen, Mary. *See* Quessy
Gueguen, Nanette. *See* Surette
Guémenée, Prince de. *See* Rohan
Güemes Pacheco Horcasitas Padilla, Juan Vicente de, 2nd Count of Revilla Gigedo, IV, 520; V, 10, 11, 198, 615; VI, 233, 234, 742, 743
Guen, Hamon, III, **268–69**, 542; IV, 507, 636
Guénet. *See also* Quenet
Guenet, Anne. *See* Desloges
Guenet, Marie, named de Saint-Ignace, I, 310, **347–49**, 353
Guénet, Marie-Clémence, III, 369
Guenet, Roger, I, 347
Guénet, Toussaint, I, 575; II, 27
Guénin, Hilarion, I, 55, 420, 438; II, 344, 345
Guer. *See* Kirke
Guéranger, Prosper, XI, 96, 99, 725; XII, 1016
Guercheville, Marquise de. *See* Pons
Guérin. *See also* Gérin
Guérin, Jean, I, 282
Guérin, Jean-Baptiste, known as Paulin-Guérin, XII, 845, 850
Guérin, Jeanne (Lom d'Arce), II, 440
Guérin, Louis, III, 304
Guérin, Madeleine (La Joue), II, 337
Guérin, Marie-Anne (Jacquin, *dit* Philibert; Cardeneau), III, 96, 304; IV, 66
Guérin, Marthe (Chaverlange), I, 474
Guerne. *See* Le Guerne
Guernier, *dit* Laviolette, Charlotte. *See* Lenoir
Guernier, *dit* Laviolette, Jean-Pierre, VIII, 492
Guernish. *See* MacDonald
Guernon, François, V, 392
Guernon, Jeanne (Saint-Georges), II, 381
Guernon (Gouin, Grenon), Marguerite (Bonami, *dit* Lespérance), XI, 88
Guernon, Marie. *See* Coulon

Guernon, *dit* Belleville, François, IV, 151, 201, 507; V, **392–93**
Guernon, *dit* Belleville, Jean-Baptiste, V, 392
Guernon, *dit* Belleville, Marie. *See* Dalpech, *dit* Bélair
Guernon, *dit* Belleville, Marie (Martin; wife of FRANÇOIS), V, 392
Guerout, Jacques, VI, 305
Guerout, Josephte Maria. *See* Woolsey
Guerout, Judith. *See* Lévesque
Guerout, Julie (LeMesurier), VI, 306; IX, 462
Guerout, Louis, VI, 306
Guerout, Marie-Anne-Magdeleine. *See* Mayer
Guerout, Narcisse, VI, 306
Guerout, Pierre, IV, 477; VI, **305–6**, 383; VII, 673; IX, 462
Guerout, Sophie (Juchereau Duchesnay), VI, 306
Guerry, Lewis, IV, 738; V, 747
Guertin, Catherine (Foureur, *dit* Champagne), IV, 272
Guesdron, Julien, II, **268**
Gueslis. *See* Vaillant
Guettard, Jean-Étienne, III, 675, 676, 679, 680
Gueudeville, Nicolas, II, 443
Guevel, Annette (André), XII, 22
Guévremont, Jean-Baptiste, X, 657; XI, 811
Gugi, Hans George, IV, 316
Gugi, Thérèse. *See* Reis
Gugy, Barthélemy, IV, 317; VII, 359
Gugy, Bartholomew Conrad Augustus, VI, 368; VII, 283, 359, 465; VIII, 249; IX, 258, 597, 776, 795, 826; X, **320–22**, 326, 337; XI, 41, 725, 927
Gugy, Conrad, IV, **316–17**, 320; V, 214, 277, 484, 736, 887; VII, 359; VIII, 128
Gugy, Jeanne-Élisabeth. *See* Teissier
Gugy, Julia (Willan), XI, 927
Gugy, Juliana. *See* O'Connor
Gugy, Louis, IV, 317; VI, 239, 390, 634; VII, 119, **359–60**; VIII, 260; X, 320, 502
Gugy, Louise. *See* Duchesnay
Gugy, Louise-Sophie. *See* Juchereau Duchesnay
Gugy, Mary. *See* McGrath
Guiberge, Jeanne (Cabazié), II, 111
Guibert, François-Apollini, Comte de Guibert, IX, 772
Guibert, Jacques-Antoine-Hippolyte de, III, 468
Guibert, Michel-Claude, II, 181
Guiboche, Louis, VIII, 349
Guiboche, Louis, VIII, **349**, 482, 766
Guibord, Henriette. *See* Brown
Guibord, Joseph, IX, **342–43**; X, 154, 527, 689; XI, 218, 276, 277, 439, 507, 777, 893; XII, 255, 256, 505, 721
Guibord, *dit* Archambault, Marie-Anne. *See* Célerier, *dit* Roch
Guibord, *dit* Archambault, Paul, IX, 343
Guichard, Charlotte (Sabrevois de Bleury), IV, 690
Guichard, Jean, IV, 690
Guichard, Simon, V, 680
Guichard, *dit* Bourguignon, Marie-Céleste (Koenig, Baroness von Koenig), VI, 378
Guichart, Françoise-Marie. *See* Cozer
Guichart, Sylvestre, IV, 317
Guichart (Guichart de Kersident), Vincent-Fleuri, IV, **317–18**; V, 480
Guichaud, Henriette (Fargues; Dunn), V, 287, 290, 492; VII, 280

Guichaud, Jacques, V, 290
Guiche, Comte de. *See* Gramont
Guiche, Comtesse de. *See* Béthune
Guichen, Comte de. *See* Du Bouëxic
Guignard, Gilles, I, 505
Guignas, Michel, III, 44, 81, **269**
Guignecourt (Guignicourt), Monsieur (companion of LA ROCQUE de Roberval), I, 423, 425
Guigues, Bruno, X, 322
Guigues, Joseph-Bruno, VIII, 318, 572, 703; IX, 34, 96, 398; X, 107, 108, **322–24**, 429, 609, 662; XI, 33, 34, 97, 169, 170, 243, 450, 694, 867, 868; XII, 190, 1003
Guigues, Thérèse. *See* Richier
Guilbaut, Jeanne (Lorimier), II, 445
Guild, William (father), XI, 126
Guild, William, XI, 126
Guilford, Earl of. *See* North
Guilhermy, Hélène (Martin), III, 435
Guillaume, V, 241
Guillebaut, Suzanne (Fézeret), II, 221
Guillebert, *dit* Laframboise, Jean, II, 507
Guillemard, Mary (Griffin), X, 319
Guillemin, Étienne, III, 613
Guillemot, Anne, I, 349
Guillemot, Étiennette. *See* Després
Guillemot, Eugène, X, 568
Guillemot, François, I, 349
Guillemot, *dit* Du Plessis-Kerbodot, Guillaume, I, 297, **349**, 428, 430, 431, 574; II, 83, 84
Guillemote, Catherine (Jacquiés, *dit* Leblond), II, 294
Guillet*, Edwin Clarence (1898–1975), VII, 406; VIII, 30, 473, 474
Guillet, Jean-Baptiste, IX, 343
Guillet, Louis, VIII, 617; IX, **343–44**, 796
Guillet, Louise. *See* Leclerc
Guillet, Marguerite. *See* Langlois
Guillet, Marie-Élisabeth, named Sainte-Barbe, III, 630
Guillet, Paul, III, 217
Guillet, Valère, VIII, 128, 618
Guillet, *dit* Tourangeau. *See also* Tourangeau
Guillet, *dit* Tourangeau, Adélaïde. *See* Bernier
Guillet, *dit* Tourangeau, Jean, XII, 1064
Guillet de Chaumont, Antoine, III, 269
Guillet de Chaumont, Félicité. *See* Ailleboust Des Muceaux
Guillet de Chaumont, Marie-Catherine. *See* Legras
Guillet de Chaumont, Marie-Louise. *See* Esprit
Guillet de Chaumont, Nicolas-Auguste, III, 88, 210, **269–70**; IV, 46
Guillier, Marie (Couturier), II, 159
Guillimen. *See* Guillimin
Guillimin, Angélique-Jeanne (Latouche MacCarthy), III, 357
Guillimin, Charles, II, 269
Guillimin, Charles, II, **268–69**, 447; III, 153, 357, 376, 549, 558; IV, 318, 319
Guillimin, Charlotte (Trottier Desrivières; McGill), V, 526, 529, 705, 819; VI, 204
Guillimin, Françoise. *See* Lemaître-Lamorille
Guillimin, Geneviève-Élisabeth (Regnard Duplessis de Morampont), III, 549
Guillimin, Guillaume, II, 268
Guillimin, Guillaume, II, 269; III, 75, 226, 596, 647; IV, **318–19**; V, 478; VI, 204

Guillimin, Marie-Charlotte (Riverin; Badelard), III, 558; V, 46, 47, 648
Guillimin, Marie-Claude-Geneviève. *See* Foucault
Guillimin, Marie-Françoise, named de Saint-Antoine, IV, **319–20**
Guillimin, Marie-Joseph (Legardeur de Saint-Pierre; La Corne), III, 376; IV, 426
Guillon, Augustine-Marie (Reboul), X, 609
Guillon, Jean, I, 296, 323
Guillon (Guyon), Jean-Baptiste, IV, 461
Guillon, Louis, V, 737
Guillon (Guyon), Marguerite (Lemoine Despins), IV, 461
Guillon-Duplessis, Archange (Larocque), IX, 457
Guillory, Simon, III, 178, 179
Guillot, Gefroy, I, 392, 554
Guillot, Jacques, IV, 320
Guillot, Louise (Gosselin; Haimard), II, 273
Guillot, Marguerite. *See* Loiseleur
Guillot, Marie. *See* Abancourt
Guillot, *dit* Larose, François, IV, 316, **320–21**; V, 99
Guillot, *dit* Larose, Marie. *See* Rateau
Guillot de La Forest, Sieur (duellist), II, 450
Guillouet, Louis, Comte d'Orvilliers, V, 62
Guillouet d'Orvilliers, Anne-Marie. *See* Le Febvre de La Barre
Guillouet d'Orvilliers, Claude, II, 270
Guillouet d'Orvilliers, Claude, II, 186, **269–70**, 603; III, 190
Guillouet d'Orvilliers, Gilbert, II, 270
Guillouet d'Orvilliers, Jean, II, 270
Guillouet d'Orvilliers, Louis, II, 270
Guillouet d'Orvilliers, Marguerite. *See* Gascoing
Guillouet d'Orvilliers, Marie-Claude. *See* Vicq de Pontgibaud
Guillouet d'Orvilliers, Paul, II, 270
Guillouet d'Orvilliers, Rémy, I, 664; II, 269, **270–71**
Guimont, Jean-Baptiste, VI, 487
Guinaud, Henry, V, 42
Guines, Duc de, V, 752
Guinet, Sieur de (merchant), I, 538
Guío, José, V, 140
Guion, Denis, II, 271, 352
Guion, Élisabeth. *See* Boucher
Guion, François, II, **271**, 352
Guion, Joseph, II, 271
Guion, Marie-Anne. *See* Roberge
Guion, Marie-Thérèse (Laumet, *dit* de Lamothe Cadillac), I, 416; II, 271, 352
Guion Desprez, Geneviève (Chavigny Lachevrotière), II, 142
Guise, Duc de. *See* Lorraine
Guité. *See* Guitet; Guitté
Guitet, Claude, V, **393–94**
Guitet, Élisabeth. *See* Peyrot
Guitet, Joseph, V, 393
Guitet, Modeste. *See* Landry
Guitet, René, V, 393
Guiton de Monrepos, Jacques-Joseph, III, 140, 228, 246, **270–71**, 279, 340, 445, 450, 604
Guitté, Pierre-Joseph, IX, **344–45**; XI, 810
Guittel. *See* Quittel
Guitton, Madeleine (Hamelin de Bourgchemin), I, 360
Guiyahgwaahdoh. *See* Kaien?kwaahton

Guizot, François, X, 611; XII, 250
Gullen, Augusta. *See* Stowe
Gun, Isabella. *See* Gunn, Isabel
Gundlack, Frederick, VII, 620
Gundry, Thomas, VIII, 874; XI, 392
Gunn, Alexander, IV, 534
Gunn, Christian (McBeath), XI, 539
Gunn, Donald, VII, 207; IX, 137; X, **324–25**; XI, 19, 643
Gunn, George, II, 62
Gunn, Isabel, V, **394**
Gunn, Jean (Manson), X, 495
Gunn, Margaret. *See* Swain
Gunn, Mary E. (Evans), XII, 297
Gunn, Robert, XII, 297
Gunn, Samuel, XI, 582
Gunn, T. C., XII, 368
Gunn, William (father of DONALD), X, 324
Gunn, William (schoolmaster), IV, 534
Gunnbjörn Ulfsson, I, 676
Gunning, James A., IX, 6
Gurnett, Anne (mother of GEORGE), IX, 345
Gurnett, Catherine. *See* Darby
Gurnett, George, IX, 345
Gurnett, George, VI, 200, 248, 399, 422, 467, 468, 728, 742; VII, 320; VIII, 106, 125, 178, 253, 358, 700; IX, **345–47**, 497, 509, 657, 741; X, 310, 528; XII, 200
Gurney, Anne (Hawkins), IX, 378
Gurney, Byrem, XI, 376
Gurney, Charles, XI, 376, 377
Gurney, Daniel, IX, 436
Gurney, Edward, XI, 377
Gurney, Edward, VI, 253; XI, **376–77**, 608; XII, 1088
Gurney, Elizabeth (Fry), VII, 609; IX, 167
Gurney, George, XI, 377
Gurney, Joseph John, VII, 609
Gurney, Nancy (wife of EDWARD), XI, 376
Gurney, Samuel, VIII, 334
Gush, William, VIII, 16; XI, 679
Gustin, Elisha, VIII, 147
Gutenberg, Johannes. *See* Gensfleisch
Guthrie, George James, X, 660
Gutiérrez, Diego, I, 157
Guy, Anne (wife of JOHN), I, 351
Guy, Catherine. *See* Vallée
Guy, Charlotte (Berthelet), X, 53
Guy, Élisabeth. *See* Garreau
Guy, Élisabeth. *See* Leduc
Guy, Étienne, V, **394–95**, 398, 399; VII, 360
Guy, Hippolyte, VIII, 504
Guy, Jeanne. *See* Truillier, *dit* Lacombe
Guy, John, I, 23, 233, 240, 241, 243, 300, **349–51**, 365, 496, 534, 584, 655, 656, 668, 670; VI, 707
Guy, Joseph, V, 398, 399; VIII, 831
Guy, Josette. *See* Curot
Guy, Louis, VII, 361; IX, 858
Guy, Louis, V, 398, 399, 829; VI, 49, 285; VII, **360–61**, 666, 717; VIII, 910; IX, 699; X, 53
Guy, Marie (Bénard), III, 63
Guy, Marie (Claparède), III, 123
Guy, Marie-Émilie (Salaberry), IX, 699
Guy, Marie-Josephte. *See* Hervieux
Guy, Nicholas, I, **351**, 656

Guy, Nicolas, III, 271; VII, 360
Guy, Philip, I, 233, 350
Guy, Pierre, III, **271–72**, 290; IV, 204; V, 97, 395
Guy, Pierre, III, 271; IV, 34, 35, 59; V, 42, 43, 44, 241, 243, 278, 394, **395–99**, 663; VII, 360
Guyar. *See* Geyer
Guyart, Anne. *See* Gigou
Guyart, Florent, I, 351
Guyart, Jean-Baptiste, III, 272
Guyart, Jeanne. *See* Michelet
Guyart, Marie, named de l'Incarnation (Martin), I, 8, 30, 31, 32, 41, 55, 65, 108, 113, 198, 205, 208, 223, 225, 226, 231, 268, 269, 274, 325, **351–59**, 414, 430, 446, 455, 457, 511, 512, 516, 523, 536, 551, 552, 555, 556, 603, 604, 610, 618, 624, 632, 647, 665; II, 84, 91, 361, 365, 536, 537, 657; III, 106; IX, 256; XII, 820
Guyart de Fleury, Élisabeth. *See* Jobin
Guyart de Fleury, Jean-Baptiste, III, **272**
Guyasuta. *See* Kayahsotaʔ
Guyer. *See* Geyer
Guyon. *See also* Guillon; Guion
Guyon, Barbe (Paradis), II, 508
Guyon, Denis, I, 396; II, 158, 161, 347
Guyon, Françoise-Charlotte, Marquise de Diziers. *See* Alavoine
Guyon, Jacques, I, 359
Guyon, Jean, I, **359**
Guyon*, Louis (1853–1928), IX, 563, 565
Guyon, Louise. *See* Racine
Guyon, Louise (Thibault; Damours de Freneuse), I, 246; II, 166, 177, 257, 481; III, 207, 499, 552, **681–82**
Guyon, Marguerite (Damours de Chauffours), II, 166; III, 474, 681
Guyon, Marie (mother of Jean GUYON Du Buisson, d. 1663), I, 359
Guyon, Marie-Anne (Tétreau), X, 674
Guyon, Simon, I, 359; II, 166; III, 681
Guyon Després, Angélique (Margane de Lavaltrie), II, 456; III, 429
Guyon Després, Joseph, III, 473, 523
Guyon Desprez, Élisabeth (Périnault), V, 662
Guyon Desprez, Marie (Gaultier), III, 98, 173
Guyon Desprez, Marie-Joseph (Marin de La Malgue), III, 431; IV, 512
Guyon Du Buisson, Élisabeth. *See* Couillard de Lespinay
Guyon Du Buisson, Jean (d. 1663), I, 232, 281, 330, **359**
Guyon Du Buisson, Jean (1619–94), I, 238, **359–60**
Guyon Du Buisson, Mathurine. *See* Robin
Guyon Durouvray, Jean, III, 134
Guyon Durouvray, Marguerite-Suzanne (Constantin), III, 134
Guyon Durouvray, Marie-Élisabeth (Le Moyne de Martigny et de La Trinité), II, 405
Guyon Fresnay, Marie-Thérèse (Baudoin), III, 35
Guyot de Lamirande, Marie-Claire-Françoise (Rigaud de Vaudreuil), III, 556
Guyotte, Étienne, I, 78; II, **271–72**, 412, 594
Guytard, Jean, II, 517
Gwai-Gu-unlthin. *See* Eda'nsa
Gwillim, Elizabeth. *See* Spinkes
Gwillim, Elizabeth Posthuma (Simcoe), IV, 418; V, 405, 428, 754, 759; VI, 256, 257, 388, 415, 558, 582, 583, 587; VII, 57, **361–63**, 693; VIII, 191, 857; XII, 525

Gwillim, Thomas, VII, 361
Gwilt, Louisa (Leach), XI, 502
Gwyn, Christiana (Collier, Lady Collier), IV, 160
Gwynne, Anne Murray. *See* Powell
Gwynne, Eliza. *See* Nelson
Gwynne*, John Wellington (1814–1902), VIII, 10; X, 325; XI, 399; XII, 899
Gwynne, Margaret Robinson. *See* Barr
Gwynne, William, X, 325
Gwynne, William Charles, VIII, 282, 933; IX, 79; X, **325–26**; XI, 219
Gyard. *See* Girard
Gylberte. *See* Gilbert
Gyles, Hannah. *See* Heath
Gyles, John, II, 26, 167, 476, 665, 669; III, 265, **272–73**
Gyles, Ruth. *See* True
Gyles, Thomas, III, 273
Gyrard. *See* Girard
Gzowski, Casimir Stanislaus (first son of Sir CASIMIR STANISLAUS), XII, 391
Gzowski, Casimir Stanislaus (second son of Sir CASIMIR STANISLAUS), XII, 391
Gzowski, Sir Casimir Stanislaus, VII, 223; VIII, 931; IX, 424; X, 258, 355, 356, 404; XI, 140, 226, 360, 368, 592; XII, 72, 189, 213, 350, **389–96**, 454, 576, 592, 683, 684, 907, 962, 965, 1107
Gzowski, Helena, Countess Gzowski. *See* Pacewicz
Gzowski, Maria M., Lady Gzowski. *See* Beebe
Gzowski, Stanislaw, Count Gzowski, XII, 389

HAANEL*, Eugene Emil Felix Richard (1841–1927), XI, 641
Habberton, John, XII, 316
Haberkorn, Emil, XII, 316, 317
Haberkorn, Margaret. *See* Finlayson
Haché, Juste, XII, **397–98**
Haché, Suzanne. *See* Cormier
Haché, Vénérande. *See* Pinet
Haché, *dit* Gallant, François, XII, 397
Haché, *dit* Gallant, Nathalie. *See* Thibodeau
Haché-Gallant, Anne. *See* Cormier
Haché-Gallant, Michel, II, **272**
Hachin, *dit* Baron, Marie-Angélique (Archambault), VIII, 19
Hackenwelder (Heckewelder), John Gottlieb Ernestus, IV, 301, 302; VI, 375; VIII, 411
Hacker, Frederick, VIII, 39; XI, 118, 336; XII, 320
Hacket, William, V, 83; VI, 326; X, 697
Hackett, Nelson, VII, **363–65**; VIII, 106
Hackett, Thomas, VIII, 171; XI, 61
Hackstaff, George Heyworth, IX, 618
Hadden, Mr (lieutenant), X, 691
Haddo, Lady. *See* Baird
Haddo, Lord. *See* Gordon
Haddon, Mr (painter), XII, 318
Haddon, John, XI, 465
Hadfield, Joseph, V, 318; VII, 523
Hadley, Hannah (Campbell, Lady Campbell), VI, 113
Hadley, Mary (Pattee), VIII, 688
Hadrill, George, XI, 678
Hänke, Elias Georg Thomas, V, 399
Hänke, Rosalia (mother of Tadeo HAENKE), V, 399
Haenke, Tadeo, V, **399–400**, 571; VI, 743

Hagaman, Benjamin, VIII, 310
Hagaman, Worthington Ely, VIII, 310
Hagan, Michael, XII, **398–99**, 699
Hagarty, Anne Elizabeth. *See* Grasett
Hagarty, Sir John Hawkins, IX, 324, 566; X, 561; XI, 144; XII, **399–400**
Hagarty, Matthew, XII, 399
Ha-ga-sa-do-ni (Deerfoot), XII, 29
Hagerman, Anne. *See* Fisher
Hagerman, Anne Elizabeth (Joseph), VII, 371; VIII, 444
Hagerman, Anne Louise (Newbigging; Stanton; Magrath), VII, 652; IX, 740
Hagerman, Caroline. *See* Tysen
Hagerman, Christopher Alexander, VI, 32, 92, 118, 165, 182, 266, 416, 613, 631, 633, 706, 773; VII, 38, 229, 230, 231, **365–72**, 410, 445, 456, 457, 458, 459, 460, 461, 471, 549, 580, 652, 662, 664, 772, 773, 833, 857, 858; VIII, 8, 28, 377, 444, 512, 514, 515, 518, 519, 520, 521, 587, 623, 786, 846, 848, 855, 871, 946; IX, 49, 69, 108, 333, 431, 499, 500, 501, 523, 534, 551, 686, 700, 725, 740, 803; X, 62, 63, 119, 253, 254, 257, 259, 310, 311, 668, 705, 706; XII, 907
Hagerman, Daniel, VI, 56; VII, 366; IX, 330, 551; X, 60
Hagerman, Elizabeth. *See* Macaulay
Hagerman, Elizabeth Emily. *See* Merry
Hagerman, Frank, VII, 372
Hagerman, Joseph N., VII, 445
Hagerman, Maria (Stoughton), VII, 366
Hagerman, Mary Jane (Robinson), X, 371
Hagerman, Nicholas, VII, 365
Haggart, John Graham, X, 294; XII, 152, 610, 1046, 1120
Haggarty, Patrick, VI, 421
Hague*, George (1825–1915), XI, 9, 233, 359, 380, 575; XII, 486
Haguenier, Marguerite (Malepart de Grand Maison, *dit* Beaucour; Lasselin), III, 422; IV, 507
Haguenier, Paul, II, 14
Hahnemann, Christian Friedrich Samuel, IX, 32
Haies. *See* Hayes
Hailer, Catharine (Breithaupt), XII, 123
Hailes, Grace (Holbrook), VII, 413
Hailes, Harris William, V, 795; VII, 187, 413
Haimard, Étienne, II, 273
Haimard, Louise. *See* Guillot
Haimard, Martine. *See* Hurault
Haimard, Pierre, II, 43, **272–73**
Haine, Mercy (Coles), X, 183
Haines, Grace (Rolph), IX, 685
Haines, Nancy (Duncombe), IX, 228
Haines, Thomas, VIII, 99
Hains. *See also* Ainsse; Hainse
Hains, Joseph, V, 599
Hains, Marie-Françoise (Mondelet), V, 599; VII, 621
Hainse (Hains), Marie-Magdeleine (Larue), VIII, 491
Haire, Alexander, VII, 765; VIII, 947
Haitor (Hayter), Martha (Slade), IV, 711
Hake, Samuel, IV, 327
Hakluyt, Richard (father), I, 332, 333, 530, 531
Hakluyt, Richard, I, 88, 89, 151, 158, 170, 333, 336, 363, 364, 371, 380, 409, 531, 532, 586, 659, 660, 672, 678
Halcro, Joshua, X, 720
Haldane, George, VIII, 350

Haldane, James Alexander, VI, 172; XI, 78

Haldane, John, VI, 321, 387, 465; VII, 498; VIII, **350–51**, 527, 556, 820; X, 477

Haldane, Josette. *See* Latour

Haldane, Katharine. *See* Murray

Haldane, Robert, VI, 172; IX, 608; XI, 78

Haldimand, Anthony Francis, V, 901, 902

Haldimand, François-Louis, IV, 793; V, 887

Haldimand, Sir Frederick, III, 89, 274, 332, 409, 620; IV, xlviii, liv, lvii, 3, 5, 6, 7, 8, 39, 40, 49, 109, 118, 119, 120, 121, 130, 147, 155, 162, 179, 181, 185, 190, 197, 205, 229, 230, 231, 232, 276, 277, 279, 280, 281, 289, 290, 294, 299, 303, 305, 316, 317, 321, 322, 323, 324, 330, 331, 336, 337, 347, 352, 367, 369, 370, 371, 385, 391, 394, 398, 418, 428, 442, 446, 476, 485, 492, 493, 506, 532, 537, 538, 543, 544, 549, 566, 613, 623, 635, 658, 682, 683, 687, 694, 723, 735, 757, 778, 787, 791, 792, **793–94**; V, 3, 8, 9, 14, 21, 43, 44, 57, 64, 91, 95, 96, 131, 132, 147, 148, 150, 156, 158, 173, 182, 204, 214, 224, 229, 231, 238, 240, 241, 252, 254, 255, 256, 259, 262, 273, 277, 284, 290, 298, 313, 316, 317, 332, 334, 343, 347, 348, 359, 364, 370, 371, 378, 384, 398, 425, 427, 433, 434, 454, 455, 470, 482, 492, 517, 537, 552, 576, 583, 584, 585, 589, 599, 602, 621, 637, 649, 654, 687, 700, 703, 710, 715, 737, 747, 752, 760, 788, 789, 790, 805, 806, 811, 836, 843, 863, 864, 870, **887–904**; VI, 30, 101, 102, 133, 145, 146, 152, 179, 184, 189, 194, 258, 338, 353, 363, 403, 427, 445, 494, 502, 511, 512, 606, 609, 615, 658, 679, 688, 695, 718, 760, 769, 788, 789; VII, 413, 665; VIII, 690

Haldimand, Gaspard, V, 887

Haldimand, Jean-Abraham, III, 273

Haldimand, Marie-Madeleine. *See* Treytorrens

Haldimand, Peter Frederick, III, **273–74**; V, 426, 902

Hale, Bernard, VI, 585

Hale, David, XII, 400

Hale, Edward, VI, 166; X, 326

Hale, Edward, VI, 9; VII, 372; VIII, 221; IX, 347; X, 321, **326–27**; XII, 348, 349

Hale, Edward John, X, 326

Hale, Elizabeth. *See* Clark

Hale, Elizabeth. *See* Gilman

Hale, Elizabeth Frances. *See* Amherst

Hale, Eliza Cecilia. *See* Bowen

Hale, Horatio Emmons, XI, 452, 453; XII, **400–3**

Hale, Jeffery, VI, 9; VII, 372; IX, **347–48**; X, 326

Hale, John (father of JOHN), VI, 257; VII, 372

Hale, John (partner of Joshua MAUGER), IV, 527

Hale, John, V, 193; VI, 9, 50, 120, 257, 549, 585; VII, **372–73**, 825; IX, 347; X, 326

Hale, Katherine. *See* Warnock, Amelia Beers

Hale, Margaret. *See* Pugh

Hale, Mary. *See* Chaloner

Hale, Sir Matthew, XII, 610

Hale, Robert, III, 274

Hale, Robert, III, **274–75**

Hale, Sarah Josepha. *See* Buell

Hale, William, V, 557

Halevear. *See* Olivier

Haley, Augusta Ann (Jeffery), XII, 469

Haley, Mary (FitzGibbon), IX, 264

Half King. *See* Pomoacan; Tanaghrisson

Halhead, Edward, III, **275–76**, 635

Haliburton, Arthur Lawrence, 1st Baron Haliburton, IX, 350

Haliburton, Louisa. *See* Neville

Haliburton, Lucy Chandler. *See* Grant

Haliburton*, Robert Grant (1831–1901), IX, 350; X, 362; XI, 322, 323, 324

Haliburton, Sarah Harriet. *See* Owen

Haliburton, Susanna. *See* Francklin

Haliburton, Susanna. *See* Otis

Haliburton, Susanna Lucy Anne (Weldon), XII, **403–4**

Haliburton, Thomas Chandler, VI, 88, 173, 294, 307, 308; VII, 22, 107, 270, 291, 339, 536, 537, 792, 803, 804, 875; VIII, 64, 193, 334, 355, 516; IX, 40, 225, **348–57**, 550, 620, 828; X, 72, 363, 364, 539; XI, 308, 925, 926; XII, 13, 15, 403, 570, 966

Haliburton, William, VI, 306, 307; IX, 348

Haliburton, William Hersey Otis, VI, **306–8**, 781; VII, 22, 933; VIII, 752; IX, 348

Halifax, Earl of. *See* Dunk; Montagu

Halkett, Alexander, VIII, 802

Halkett, Anna. *See* Todd

Halkett, James B., XI, 468

Halkett (Wedderburn), John, V, 266; VI, 441, 547, 814; VII, 900, 902; VIII, 250, **351–53**, 720, 721

Halkett (Wedderburn), Sir John, VIII, 351

Halkett, Katherine. *See* Douglas

Halkett, Mary. *See* Hamilton

Halkett, Sir Peter, VIII, 351

Hall, Abraham Oakey, X, 555

Hall, Agnes. *See* Burgess

Hall, Amelia Margaret (Peel), XII, 830

Hall, Angelique. *See* Fortier

Hall, Ann (Bowes), IX, 76

Hall, Archibald, VII, 25, 810; VIII, 404; IX, 16, **357–58**

Hall, Basil, V, 861; VII, 830

Hall, Benedicta Maria Theresa (Gage, Viscountess Gage), IV, 278

Hall, Caroline (Parkman), XII, 823

Hall, Charles Francis, I, 94, 318; VII, 271, 326; VIII, 449; X, 320, **327–29**; XI, 382, 394; XII, 954, 955

Hall, Charles Henry, VIII, 353, 354

Hall, Charlotte. *See* Simpson

Hall, Christopher, I, 316, 317, 318, 375

Hall, Diana. *See* Cobbie

Hall, Elisha, IX, 230

Hall, Elizabeth (Baillie), IX, 21

Hall, Francis (author), VI, 373

Hall, Francis (engineer), VI, 742; VII, 278

Hall, Frederick, X, 504

Hall, George Barker, IX, 149

Hall, George Benson, V, 366; VI, **308–10**; VIII, 794; X, 329

Hall, George Benson, VI, 308; VIII, 692; IX, 487; X, 33, **329–30**; XI, 813, 814; XII, 145, 531, 620, 758, 890

Hall, Helen, Lady Hall. *See* Douglas

Hall, Helenore. *See* Gowen

Hall, Henry, VIII, 353

Hall, Jacob, IX, 357

Hall, James (paleontologist), VII, 761; X, 65, 445, 446; XII, 233

Hall, James (politician), VIII, 92

Hall, James, I, 5, 20, 74, 243, **360**, 408

Hall, John (Peterborough businessman), IX, 205

Hall, John (Toronto businessman), IX, 76
Hall, John B., XII, 993
Hall*, John Smythe (1853–1909), XII, 197, 696
Hall, Joseph, XII, 701
Hall, Lucille H. (Fairweather), XII, 306
Hall, Martha (Binney), V, 81
Hall, Mary (Fenerty), XII, 313
Hall, Mary (Roche; mother of Sir ROBERT), V, 400, 401
Hall, Mary Jane. *See* Patterson
Hall, Parker L., XII, 390
Hall, Peter Patterson, X, 329; XII, 280
Hall, Phoebe Eliza (Stevenson), XI, 852
Hall, Prince, IV, 515
Hall, Rebecca. *See* Ferguson
Hall, Robert, V, 401
Hall, Sir Robert, V, **400–1**
Hall, Sherman, IX, 420
Hall, Stephen, V, 81
Hall, Stephen Sneden, XII, 306
Hall, William, XII, 886
Hall, William, VIII, 34, **353–54**
Hall, William Augustin, XI, 271
Hall, Sir William King, XII, 39
Hallam, John, XII, 993
Hallam, Lewis, IV, 556; V, 66
Hallé, Marie-Joseph, named de Saint-François d'Assise, IV, 472
Halliburton, Sir Brenton, V, 109; VI, 568, 731; VII, 23, 88, 104, 144, 433, 530, 531, 532, 534, 535, 875; VIII, **354–57**, 417, 603, 756, 827; IX, 37; X, 140, 189, 387; XI, 74, 946, 947, 948
Halliburton, John (father), V, 24, 109, 187, 297; VI, 310; VIII, 354
Halliburton, John, VIII, 354
Halliburton, John Croke, VIII, 417; X, 364
Halliburton, Margaret. *See* Inglis
Halliburton, Margaret (Collins), X, 189
Halliburton, Mary (Polly) (Beckwith), IX, 37
Halliburton, Susannah. *See* Brenton
Halliday, Margaret (Black), XI, 79
Hallock, Charles, XII, 269
Hallot, Marie-Scholastique (Desandrouins), IV, 211
Hallowell. *See also* Carew
Hallowell, Benjamin, V, 303
Hallowell, Edith (Ross), VIII, 768
Hallowell, Elizabeth (Bethune), VIII, 768; X, 58
Hallowell, James, V, 333, 562, 565, 566; VI, 455; VII, 566
Hallowell, Margaret Mary (Wood), IX, 848
Hallowell, Maria. *See* Sutherland
Hallowell, Mary (Elmsley), V, 303; IX, 239
Hallowell, William (doctor), XII, 106
Hallowell, William (fur trader), V, 565; VI, 318, 455, 665; VII, 566
Halpen, Helen (Sexton), X, 646
Halstead, John, IV, 403
Halton, William, V, 765, 841; VI, 543, 624; VIII, 339
Haly, Aylmer, X, 330
Haly, Harriett. *See* Hebden
Haly, Richard O'Grady, X, 330
Haly, William, VI, 419
Haly, Sir William O'Grady, X, **330**; XI, 296; XII, 576
Ham, Cynthia (Hooper), XI, 421
Ham, George Henry, XII, 778

Ham, John, VIII, 695
Ham, Mary Polly (Perry), VIII, 694
Hamare, Gratiane. *See* Moreau
Hamare, Julien, II, 273
Hamare de La Borde, Geneviève. *See* Lambert
Hamare de La Borde, Geneviève-Louise, II, 273
Hamare de La Borde, Jean-Baptiste-Julien, II, **273–74**; III, 74, 291
Hambly, William, VI, 406; VII, 92
Hamel, Monsieur (apparently landowner), VIII, 312
Hamel, Abraham, IX, 360; XI, 309, 902
Hamel, André-Rémi, VI, 585; VII, **373–74**; X, 131; XI, 177; XII, 86
Hamel, Anne-Félicité. *See* Levasseur, *dit* Lavigne
Hamel, Antoine, V, 827
Hamel, Charles (father of ANDRÉ-RÉMI), VII, 373
Hamel, Charles (merchant), X, 21
Hamel, Ernest, IX, 360
Hamel, Félicité (Bonhomme, *dit* Beaupré), III, 69
Hamel, Félixine (Cassegrain), IX, 122
Hamel, François-Xavier, IX, 358
Hamel, Georgina-Mathilde. *See* Faribault
Hamel, Hortense (Chabot), VIII, 137
Hamel, Jean, I, 473
Hamel, Joseph, VIII, 385; X, 30
Hamel*, Joseph-Arthur-Eugène (1845–1932), IX, 364
Hamel, Julie-Hermine, IX, 359
Hamel, Marie. *See* Bedouin
Hamel, Marie (Bertrand), IX, 487
Hamel, Marie (Plamondon), XII, 845, 848
Hamel, Marie-Adélaïde. *See* Roy
Hamel, Marie-Anne (Gauvreau), VI, 280
Hamel, Marie-Françoise. *See* Routhier
Hamel, Marie-Renée (Belleau), XII, 86
Hamel, Odilon-Zéphirin, IX, 66
Hamel, Pierre, III, 135
Hamel, Théophile (François-Xavier), I, 170; V, 72; VII, 227, 881; VIII, 496, 582; IX, 121, 249, **358–64**; X, 715; XI, 309; XII, 101, 190, 846, 847, 848, 850
Hamel, Théophile-Gustave, IX, 359
Hamel*, Thomas-Étienne (1830–1913), III, 691; IV, 801; IX, 118, 119, 120, 863; X, 135, 432, 589, 735; XI, 64, 65, 83, 258, 485, 486, 491, 496, 513; XII, 304, 820, 913
Hamelin, Angélique (Pollet), III, 524
Hamelin, Joseph, XI, 193, 744
Hamelin, Louis, III, 249, 250, 432
Hamelin, Nicolas, IV, 678
Hamelin, Salomon, IX, 330; XII, 125
Hamelin de Bourgchemin, François, I, 360
Hamelin de Bourgchemin, Madeleine. *See* Guitton
Hamelin de Bourgchemin et de L'Hermitière, Anne-Marie, I, 361
Hamelin de Bourgchemin et de L'Hermitière, Élisabeth. *See* Dizy, *dit* Montplaisir
Hamelin de Bourgchemin et de L'Hermitière, François, I, 361
Hamelin de Bourgchemin et de L'Hermitière, Jacques-François, I, **360–61**; II, 190
Hamelin de Bourgchemin et de L'Hermitière, Marguerite, I, 361
Hamilton. *See also* Baillie
Hamilton, Captain, V, 776
Hamilton, Alexander (politician), V, 553

Hamilton, Alexander (servant), VIII, 437
Hamilton, Alexander, V, 406, 453; VII, **374–76**, 378, 497, 693
Hamilton, Alicia (Killaly), X, 402
Hamilton, Andrew, I, 107, **361**, 493, 657
Hamilton, Ann (Caldwell), V, 130; VII, 133
Hamilton, Ann (Fenerty), XII, 311, 312
Hamilton, Anne. *See* Kilgallen
Hamilton, Annie. *See* Brown
Hamilton, Annie Isabel, XII, 29
Hamilton, Archibald James, VIII, 437, 438
Hamilton, Cassandra Agnes, Lady Hamilton. *See* Chamberlayne
Hamilton, Catherine. *See* Askin
Hamilton, Charles (father of GEORGE, 1781–1839), VII, 379
Hamilton, Charles (office holder), XII, 312
Hamilton, Sir Charles, V, 243, 672; VI, 274, 373, 410, 580, 692, 707; VII, 115, 153, 301, 302, 303, **376–77**, 628, 629; VIII, 94, 165, 403; IX, 159
Hamilton*, Charles (1834–1919), XII, 425
Hamilton, Clarence, VIII, 493; XII, 913
Hamilton, Eliza. *See* Hill
Hamilton, Eliza (Macdonald), XI, 551
Hamilton, Elizabeth. *See* Chetwood
Hamilton, Elizabeth. *See* Lee
Hamilton, Elizabeth (Montgomery), IX, 565
Hamilton, Elizabeth Ann (Anderson), V, 672, 673, 674; VI, 510; X, 12
Hamilton, Ellen Marion. *See* Wood
Hamilton, Frances Pasia. *See* Macpherson
Hamilton, Gavin Major, VI, 50
Hamilton, George (son of GEORGE, 1781–1839), VII, 383; XI, 379
Hamilton, George (1788–1836), V, 406, 453; VI, 229, 230; VII, 375, **377–79**, 466, 734; VIII, 600, 945
Hamilton, George (1781–1839), VII, 70, 71, **379–83**, 401, 796, 797; VIII, 688, 689, 691; IX, 13; XI, 379, 589; XII, 366
Hamilton, George, Earl of Orkney, II, 104
Hamilton, Georgiana (Caddy), XI, 137
Hamilton, Grizel (daughter of OTHO), III, 276
Hamilton, Grizel (mother of OTHO), III, 276
Hamilton, H. J., XII, 384
Hamilton, Hannah Owen. *See* Jarvis
Hamilton, Hariot Georgiana (Blackwood, Lady Dufferin and Ava), X, 292; XII, 75, 367, 525
Hamilton, Helen (Gillespie), VII, 342
Hamilton, Helen (Hamilton Douglas, Countess of Selkirk), V, 264
Hamilton, Henrietta Martha, Lady Hamilton. *See* Drummond
Hamilton, Henry (father of HENRY), IV, 321
Hamilton, Henry (merchant), XI, 332
Hamilton, Henry, IV, 37, 49, 82, 197, 198, 260, **321–25**, 337, 367, 371, 399, 493, 496, 499, 506, 564, 702, 722, 792; V, 3, 8, 21, 26, 43, 44, 74, 100, 132, 148, 150, 238, 242, 253, 271, 273, 283, 289, 290, 298, 301, 317, 343, 344, 371, 427, 433, 637, 647, 649, 684, 802, 819, 836, 843, 895; VI, 189, 699; VII, 347
Hamilton, Herbert. *See* Gordon, Lord Gordon
Hamilton, Hugh, V, 130
Hamilton, Isaac, IV, 768

Hamilton, Isabella. *See* Torrance
Hamilton, Isabella (French), XI, 326
Hamilton, James (governor), III, 502
Hamilton, James (merchant), VII, 93
Hamilton, James (painter), XII, 122
Hamilton, James (partner of Francis Jones BARNARD), XI, 51
Hamilton, James (partner of Martin Gay BLACK), IX, 40, 52
Hamilton, James (Quebec merchant), XII, 88
Hamilton, James (Queenston merchant), XII, 675
Hamilton, James (son of ROBERT), XI, 501
Hamilton, James, XII, **404–5**
Hamilton, James, 1st Duke of Hamilton and 2nd Earl of Cambridge, I, 369, 405, 613
Hamilton, James Matthew, X, 12; XII, 404
Hamilton, Jane (Campbell), VIII, 123
Hamilton, Jean. *See* Cambie
Hamilton, Jean. *See* McLachlan
Hamilton, Jean. *See* Wight
Hamilton, Jessie (Douglas), X, 238
Hamilton, John (brother of GEORGE, 1781–1839), VII, 380, 381
Hamilton, John (deacon), VIII, 968
Hamilton, John (father of ROBERT), V, 402
Hamilton, John (father of ROBERT DOUGLAS), VIII, 357
Hamilton, John (office holder), III, 587
Hamilton, John (officer), IV, 791
Hamilton, John (son of OTHO), III, 276, 277
Hamilton, John (1802–82), V, 406; VI, 470; VII, 375, 383; VIII, 326, 534; IX, 49, 241, 314; XI, 114, **377–79**; XII, 682
Hamilton, John (1827–88), XI, 7, 9, **379–81**; XII, 153
Hamilton, Sir John, VII, 376
Hamilton, John Macaulay, XII, 81
Hamilton, John Robinson (lawyer), VIII, 196, 206, 207
Hamilton, John Robinson (politician), XII, 521
Hamilton, Joseph, VIII, 869
Hamilton, Katherine Glenn Macaulay Rae (Begg), XII, 81
Hamilton, Louisa. *See* Jupp
Hamilton, Maria Lavinia. *See* Jarvis
Hamilton, Mary. *See* Dawson
Hamilton, Mary. *See* Handfield
Hamilton, Mary. *See* Herkimer
Hamilton, Mary. *See* Robinson
Hamilton, Mary (Gault), XI, 335
Hamilton, Mary (Halkett), VIII, 351
Hamilton, Mary (Merritt), VII, 602; IX, 544
Hamilton, Mary (Taylor), X, 673
Hamilton, Otho, III, 276
Hamilton, Otho, II, 670; III, 10, **276–77**, 514
Hamilton, Peter Hunter, VI, 230
Hamilton, Peter Stevens, XII, 218, **405–7**
Hamilton, Rebecca. *See* Lewis
Hamilton, Richard, XI, 137
Hamilton, Richard Vesey, VIII, 624
Hamilton, Robert (brother of GEORGE, 1781–1839), VII, 380, 381
Hamilton, Robert (father of PETER STEVENS), XII, 405
Hamilton, Robert (HBC factor), XI, 612
Hamilton, Robert (son of GEORGE, 1781–1839), VII, 383; XI, 379, 380
Hamilton, Robert (son of ROBERT), VI, 470; XI, 377, 378

Hamilton, Robert, IV, 494, 505, 777; V, 38, 39, 168, 280, **402–6**, 439, 442, 453, 492, 548, 549, 639, 660, 661, 669, 718, 719, 724, 734, 757, 781, 782, 814, 815, 819, 841, 842, 846, 856; VI, 5, 93, 147, 148, 149, 154, 178, 209, 211, 254, 296, 406, 488, 539, 544, 559, 607, 624, 629, 638, 746; VII, 57, 250, 251, 309, 310, 312, 375, 378, 693, 697, 920; VIII, 33, 185, 208; IX, 331, 332; XI, 377
Hamilton, Robert Douglas, VIII, **357–59**
Hamilton, Sarah (Stewart), V, 776, 778
Hamilton, Sophia. *See* Stevens
Hamilton, Lady Susannah (Cochrane, Countess of Dundonald; Hay, Marchioness of Tweeddale), III, 283
Hamilton, Susannah Christiana. *See* Craigie
Hamilton, Thomas, III, 276
Hamilton, William (brother of GEORGE, 1781–1839), VII, 380, 381; VIII, 688
Hamilton, William (merchant), VI, 166
Hamilton, William (son of WILLIAM), X, 331
Hamilton, William, X, **330–31**
Hamilton, Sir William, XI, 534
Hamilton Douglas, Dunbar, 4th Earl of Selkirk, V, 264
Hamilton Douglas, Helen, Countess of Selkirk. *See* Hamilton
Hamilton-Gordon, George, 4th Earl of Aberdeen, VIII, xxvii, xxxi, 274, 275, 465; IX, 235, 327, 806; X, 55
Hamilton-Gordon, Ishbel Maria, Marchioness of Aberdeen and Temair. *See* Marjoribanks
Hamilton-Gordon*, John Campbell, 7th Earl of Aberdeen and 1st Marquess of Aberdeen and Temair (1847–1934), XII, 341, 450, 586, 610, 630, 1047, 1048
Hamlin, Laura (Miller), X, 514
Hamlyn, Richard Julian, VIII, 889
Hamm, Albert, XII, **407–8**
Hammersley, Diana (Hills), XII, 440
Hammill, Mariah (Prescott), VIII, 709
Hammond, Archelaus, VII, 120
Hammond, George, VIII, 857
Hammond, Hannah (Green), III, 267
Hammond, Lillian Ann (Seely), XI, 804
Hammond, Maximilian Montague, VIII, 902
Hammond, Melvin Ormond, XII, 743
Hammond, S. T., XII, 924
Hammond, Theodosia Elizabeth (Back), X, 29
Hamon, Madelaine (Faribault), V, 312
Hamond, Sir Andrew Snape, IV, 111; V, 94, 148, 434; VI, **310–11**
Hamond, Anne, Lady Hamond. *See* Graeme
Hamond, Cecilia. *See* Sutherland
Hamond, Marie (Hantraye), IV, 326
Hamond, Robert, VI, 310
Hamond, Susannah. *See* Snape
Hamonez, Anne (Gueguen), VI, 304
Hampden. *See* Hart, Adolphus Mordecai
Hampshire, Sir Thomas, I, 229
Hampson, John, I, 611
Hampton, Baron. *See* Pakington
Hampton, Wade, VI, 342, 343, 388, 520, 521; IX, 484, 485
Hamtramck, John Francis, V, 553
Hanbury. *See* Bateman-Hanbury
Hancock, John (HBC employee), II, 313, 315
Hancock, John (politician), IV, 144
Hancock, Thomas, III, 33, 403; IV, 560; V, 554
Hand, Mr (engineer), IX, 577

Handasyde, Roger, II, 274
Handasyde, Thomas, II, 246, **274**, 564
Handcock, Richard Butler, VIII, 17
Handel, George Frideric, VIII, 347; XII, 708
Handfield, Elizabeth. *See* Winniett
Handfield, John, III, 277
Handfield, John, III, **277–78**, 421, 665; IV, xxvi, 676
Handfield, Mary (Hamilton) III, 277
Handfield, Thomas, III, 277
Handford, Mary (Ellis), VIII, 270
Hands. *See also* Ainse
Hands, William, IV, 778; V, 722; VI, 600, 601; VIII, 34, 337; XI, 268
Handsome Lake. *See* Ganiodaio; Skanyadariyoh
Handsome Man, IX, 623
Handsome Woman, XII, 717
Handy, Henry S., VIII, 852
Handy, Martha Jane (Killaly), X, 402
Handyside (Lawson), Elizabeth (Lawson), VII, 491
Haney, Mary Jane. *See* Todd
Haney, Michael John, XII, 933
Hanford, Alice Caroline (Carvell), XII, 166
Hanford, Julia Ann (Tilley), XII, 1051, 1052
Hangard, Catherine de. *See* La Roque
Hangard, Robert de, I, 425
Hanington, Daniel, VII, 384
Hanington, Daniel Lionel, VII, 384; XI, 298; XII, 339, 340
Hanington, Mary. *See* Derby
Hanington, William, VII, 384
Hanington, William, VII, **383–85**
Hankey, Robert, V, 42
Hankin, Philip James, IX, 715; XI, 635, 950
Hankinson, Catherine Edwards (Hoare; Parry, Lady Parry), VIII, 683
Hankinson, Reuben, XI, 146
Hanlan*, Edward (1855–1908), XI, 616; XII, 407, 408, 647, 796, 797
Hanna, Elizabeth. *See* Saul
Hanna, James, IV, **325–26**, 411, 498, 568; VI, 350; VII, 830
Hanna, James G., V, 329, **406–7**; VI, 432, 556, 557; VIII, 359
Hanna, James Godfrey, V, 407, 461; VIII, **359–60**
Hanna, Jane (Orkney), V, 406; VI, 556
Hanna, Margaret Nelson (Aylwin), X, 24
Hanna, Margaret Roberts. *See* Eckart
Hanna, Mary (Macnider), V, 406
Hanna, William, VI, 433
Hannah. *See* Tookolito
Hannah (fl.1800–4), IV, 777, 778, 779
Hannah (niece of Richard CARTWRIGHT), V, 168
Hannah, John, XII, 472
Hannam, John, I, 584
Hannam, William, I, 584
Hannan, James, XI, 381
Hannan, Mary. *See* Carroll
Hannan, Michael, XI, **381–82**, 709; XII, 411, 880, 1040, 1041
Hannay*, James (1842–1910), III, 439; IV, xxi; V, 162, 353, 646; VI, 141, 356, 684, 686, 687; VII, 141, 142; VIII, 377, 378; IX, 619, 621; X, 140, 271, 543, 714; XI, 298, 375, 833; XII, 17, 20, 537, 1059, 1106
Hannay, Margaret (Sproat), IX, 738

Hanover, Elector of. *See* George I
Hanrahan, Edmund, VIII, 199; X, **331–32**; XII, 862
Hanrahan, Mary (wife of EDMUND), X, 332
Hans, III, 322
Hansard, Eleanor (Coster), VIII, 171, 173, 941
Hanse. *See* Hince
Hans Hendrik, VIII, 448, 449; XI, **382–83**, 393
Hanson, John Halloway, VIII, 940
Hanson, Richard Davies, VII, 118
Hanson, Sarah (Merriarter; Garrettson), VI, 275
Hanson, Sarah (Ogden), VIII, 660; IX, 610
Hansteen, Christopher, XI, 799
Hantraye, Claude, IV, **326**
Hantraye, Marie. *See* Hamond
Hantraye, Marie-Françoise. *See* Viger
Hantraye, Marie-Marguerite. *See* Debuire
Hantraye, Noël, IV, 326
Haouilamek. *See* Ouenemek
Happy, Jesse, VII, 363; VIII, 106
Harakontie. *See* Garakontié
Harbidge, Elizabeth. *See* Bowden
Harbidge, George, VII, 901, 902; X, 108
Harboard, William, IV, 55
Harborne, William, I, 85
Harcourt, Comte d'. *See* Lorraine
Harcourt, Margaret Irene. *See* Sarney
Harcourt*, Richard (1849–1932), XII, 1113
Harcourt, Robert, I, 366
Harcourt, Simon, 1st Earl Harcourt, VIII, 204
Hardee, William Joseph, X, 648
Hardi, Gabrielle (Chabert de Joncaire), II, 125
Harding, C. A., IX, 413
Harding, Ebenezer Fitch, VIII, 32
Harding, Elizabeth (Miles), VI, 504, 505; VII, 610
Harding, Francis Pym, X, **332**
Harding, George (brother of THOMAS), VIII, 361
Harding, George (father-in-law of Elijah MILES), VI, 505
Harding, George Johnstone, VII, 203
Harding, Harris, VI, 276, 574; VII, 123, 252, 272; VIII, 179, **360–61**, 611; X, 214
Harding, Israel, VIII, 360
Harding, James Duffield, VIII, 833; XII, 326, 327
Harding, Leah (mother of THOMAS), VIII, 361
Harding, Mary. *See* Johnson
Harding, Mehitable. *See* Harrington
Harding, Sarah. *See* Harris
Harding, Theodore Seth, VI, 276; VII, 252; VIII, 179; XI, 895
Harding, Thomas, VIII, 361
Harding, Thomas, VIII, 98, 224, **361–62**
Harding, William, VIII, 361
Harding, William Stenning, VII, 203
Hardinge, Henry, 1st Viscount Hardinge, VIII, 30
Hardison, Benjamin, VIII, 466
Hardison, George, XII, 529
Hardisty, Eliza. *See* McDougall
Hardisty, Margaret. *See* Sutherland
Hardisty, Mary. *See* Allen
Hardisty, Richard, XI, 383, 384
Hardisty, Richard Charles, XI, **383–84**, 442, 443, 739, 900; XII, 641, 671, 672
Hardisty, William Lucas, XI, 383, **384–85**; XII, 936

Hardouineau, Renée (Beauharnois de Beaumont et de Villechauve), II, 52
Hardouineau de Landianière, Pierre, III, 42
Hardouineau de Landianière, Renée. *See* Pays
Hardwicke, Earl of. *See* Yorke
Hardy*, Arthur Sturgis (1837–1901), XII, 53, 332, 333, 1095
Hardy, Campbell, X, 362; XII, 268, 269
Hardy, Catherine, Lady Hardy. *See* Stanyan
Hardy, Sir Charles, IV, 326
Hardy, Sir Charles, III, 132, 668; IV, 84, **326–27**; V, 382; VI, 134
Hardy, Elias, IV, 196, **327–29**; V, 35, 157, 352, 353, 504, 867, 868; VI, 141, 395, 811; VIII, 361
Hardy, Elizabeth, Lady Hardy. *See* Burchett
Hardy, George, V, **407–8**, 777
Hardy (Ardie), Jeanne (Trotain, *dit* Saint-Seürin), II, 637
Hardy, Jessie W. (Chipman), XII, 193
Hardy, Marguerite (Macard), II, 448
Hardy, Martha. *See* Huggeford
Hardy, Mary, Lady Hardy. *See* Tate
Hardy, Mary (Nelles), XI, 640
Hardy, Sir Thomas Masterman, VI, 561
Hardy, William, V, 737
Hare, Alexander, XI, 568, 757
Hare, Elizabeth (Clark), V, 188
Hare, John James, XII, 10
Hare, Mary Teresa (Mullock), IX, 581
Hare, Nicholas, XI, 568
Harel, Marie-Élizabeth (Périnault), V, 662
Harewood, Countess of. *See* Thynne
Harewood, Earl of. *See* Lascelles
Harffy, William, V, 449
Hargon, Jeanne de (Martel de Berhouague), II, 458
Hargrave, Dugald John, VIII, 590
Hargrave, James, VI, 648, 795; VII, 3, 4, 205, 526; VIII, 59, 61, 561, 562, 573, 589, 590, 821; IX, 130, 169, 170, **364–66**, 529, 530; X, 485; XI, 52, 53, 554, 824; XII, 53, 194, 408, 877
Hargrave, Jane. *See* Melrose
Hargrave, Joseph, IX, 364
Hargrave, Joseph James, VIII, 574, 590; IX, 365, 602, 603; XI, 554; XII, 84, **408–9**, 954
Hargrave, Letitia. *See* Mactavish
Hargrave, Letitia Lockhart (Schofield), VIII, 590
Hargrave, Margaret. *See* Alcock
Hargrave, Mary Jane (Ogston), VIII, 590
Hargrave, Rachel (Frobisher), IV, 276; V, 331
Harismendy, Jean, IV, 66
Harkin, Peter Henry, VII, 574
Harkness, James, VI, 534; VII, 233
Harkness, John, V, 287; VII, 224
Harkness, John Graham, VII, 545
Harkness, Peter, VI, 204; VII, 79
Harlay de Champvallon, François de, I, 646, 647; II, 361, 362, 363, 368
Harley, Ada A. (DesBrisay), XII, 250
Harley, Ann. *See* Coughlan
Harley, John, VII, 4; VIII, 783, 784; X, **332–33**
Harley, Mary Ann, X, 333
Harley, Robert, 1st Earl of Oxford, II, 659, 660
Harley, William, X, 332, 333
Harlow, Elizabeth (White), XI, 918

Harlow, George Henry, XI, 918
Harman, Dorothy Bruce. *See* Murray
Harman, Georgiana. *See* Huson
Harman, Georgina Mary, XII, 409
Harman, John, I, 443
Harman, Lloyd Cusack Athill Murray, XII, 410
Harman, Mary (Harrison), IX, 372
Harman, Samuel, XII, 409
Harman, Samuel Bickerton, XII, **409–10**
Harman, Samuel Bruce, XII, 409, 410
Harmar, Josiah, V, 3, 594, 807, 852; VII, 847
Harmon, Calvin, VII, 386
Harmon, Daniel, VII, 385
Harmon, Daniel Williams, V, 543; VII, **385–86**, 475; VIII, 158, 556, 575; IX, 150
Harmon, Johnson, II, 544; III, 476, 477
Harmon, Lizette. *See* Duval
Harmon, Lucretia. *See* Dewey
Harney, William Selby, IX, 36
Harnois, Augustin, VIII, 262
Harnois, Reine (Duvernay), VIII, 262
Harot, Marie (La Salle), II, 348
Harper, Anne (Ward), IX, 820
Harper, Charles, VI, 206; VII, 502; VIII, **363**, 938; XII, 507
Harper, Charlotte. *See* Bleau
Harper, Hannah Elizabeth (Read), VIII, 743
Harper, Isabel (Shortt), IX, 719
Harper, Jacques, VIII, 363
Harper, Jean, VIII, 363, 720; IX, 94; XII, 507
Harper, Jerome, X, **333–34**
Harper, Joseph, V, 689
Harper, Lewis, VIII, 363
Harper, Thaddeus, X, 333, 334
Harper, William (merchant), V, 817
Harper, William (schoolmaster), V, 394
Harral, Francis, XII, 996
Harries, John, IV, 402; V, 123, **408**, 473, 633; VI, 10
Harries, Phoebe (wife of JOHN), V, 408
Harrington, Anna Lois. *See* Dawson
Harrington*, Bernard James (1848–1907), XII, 236
Harrington, Charles Fortnum, IX, 293, 294
Harrington, Elizabeth. *See* O'Keefe
Harrington, Harriet Amelia (Van Cortlandt), X, 691
Harrington, Hester E. (Ross), XII, 924
Harrington, Joanna, named Sister Mary Benedicta, XII, **410–12**
Harrington, John, XII, 410
Harrington, Maria (McLachlin), X, 480
Harrington, Mehitable (Harding), VIII, 360
Harriott, Anne. *See* Rowand
Harriott, Clara. *See* Morris
Harriott, Elizabeth. *See* Pruden
Harriott, Frances. *See* Bunn
Harriott, John Edward, VIII, 780; IX, 130, **366–67**, 722; X, 391; XII, 194, 932
Harriott, Margaret (Rowand), IX, 367
Harriott, Nancy. *See* Rowand
Harriott, Rachel (Bunn), X, 111
Harris, Alanson, XI, 386, 387; XII, 701, 705, 706
Harris, Alexander, X, **334–35**
Harris, Amelia. *See* Ryerse
Harris, Ann (Patterson), XII, 828
Harris, Benjamin, XI, 385

Harris, Charlotte Ann (wife of JOSEPH HEMINGTON), XI, 388
Harris, Christopher Prince (grandfather), IX, 367
Harris, Christopher Prince, IX, 368; XII, 412, 479
Harris, Cordelia Anne (mother of JOSEPH HEMINGTON), XI, 387
Harris, Critchlow, XI, 857
Harris, Dennis, X, 247
Harris, Elijah, X, 124
Harris, Eliza (Muir), IX, 369
Harris, Elizabeth. *See* Atkinson
Harris, Elizabeth. *See* Scott
Harris, Elizabeth. *See* Spurr
Harris, Elizabeth, I, 81
Harris, Elizabeth (Blaiklock), VII, 80
Harris, Eliza Locke. *See* Walker
Harris, Emery, IX, 367
Harris, Fanny (Deas), X, 216
Harris, Frederick Warren, IX, **367**
Harris, George Poulett, XII, 364
Harris, Harriet (Stevenson), XII, 988
Harris, Henry, XII, 745
Harris, Henry William, XI, 234
Harris, James (cheese maker), XII, 171
Harris, James (clergyman), VII, 467
Harris, James Stanley, XI, **385–86**
Harris, Jane. *See* Andrew
Harris, Jane. *See* Tufford
Harris, Jane. *See* Yonge
Harris, Johanna Evered (Worsley), VI, 817
Harris, John (commandant), III, 614
Harris, John (husband of Amelia RYERSE), VIII, 670, 672; XI, 782
Harris, John (office holder), VII, 833, 834
Harris, John (son of Amelia RYERSE), XI, 782
Harris, John, V, **408–9**, 660; VI, 562
Harris, John, XI, **386–87**; XII, 703, 1117
Harris, John J., XI, 112, 113, 590
Harris, John Leonard, IX, 368; XII, **412–13**, 479
Harris, John Leonard Whitney, XII, 413
Harris, Jonathan, IV, 351
Harris, Joseph, XI, 387
Harris, Joseph, XII, **413–14**
Harris, Joseph Hemington, IX, 141; XI, **387–88**, 540
Harris*, Lloyd (1867–1925), XI, 387
Harris, Louisa Ann. *See* Wilson
Harris, Lucy. *See* Charles
Harris, Martha. *See* Douglas
Harris, Mary. *See* Cowie
Harris, Mary. *See* McKinney
Harris, Mary. *See* Morgan
Harris, Mary. *See* Redford
Harris, Matthew, V, 409; XII, 828
Harris, Michael, VIII, 733; XII, 988
Harris, Michael Spurr, IX, **367–68**; XII, 412
Harris, Rachel. *See* Bolscomb
Harris, Rachel (Smith), XI, 834
Harris, Rebecca. *See* Cummer
Harris, Robert, V, 409
Harris*, Robert (1849–1919), VII, 751; VIII, 405; XI, 429; XII, 102, 288, 315, 337, 789, 793, 830
Harris, Robert William, VIII, 110; IX, **368–69**, 512; XI, 126, 128, 129, 423, 608

Harris, Sally. *See* Wilder

Harris, Samuel, IX, 367

Harris, Sarah (Harding), VIII, 360

Harris, Sarah Ann. *See* Troop

Harris, Sophia Howard. *See* Ryerson

Harris, Thomas (brother of JOHN, 1841–87), XI, 387

Harris, Thomas (father of JOHN, 1739–1802), V, 408, 409

Harris, Thomas Dennie, VIII, 930; X, **335–36**; XI, 676; XII, 675

Harris, Ursula Sarah. *See* Carr

Harris, William (clergyman), X, 511

Harris, William (father of ALEXANDER), X, 334

Harris*, William Critchlow (1854–1913), XI, 856, 857; XII, 638

Harris, William Robert, X, 335

Harrison, Anna E. *See* Muckle

Harrison, Anne. *See* Bellmore

Harrison, Audrey (Townshend, Viscountess Townshend), V, 822

Harrison, Benjamin, VII, 900

Harrison, Charles (clergyman), VII, 444

Harrison, Charles (politician), XII, 290

Harrison*, David Howard (1843–1905), XI, 646

Harrison, Dorothy (Russell), VI, 669

Harrison, Edmund Thomas, VIII, xxxiii

Harrison, Edward, IV, **329–31**, 477, 571; V, 164, 460, 745, 817; VI, 615

Harrison, Ellen. *See* Humphreys

Harrison, Frances. *See* Butler

Harrison, Gilbert Henry, X, 617

Harrison, James (father, partner of John BURSTALL), XII, 145

Harrison, James (partner of Thomas RIDLEY), X, 617

Harrison, James (son, partner of John BURSTALL), XII, 145

Harrison, John, IX, 369

Harrison, John, II, **274–75**; III, 421

Harrison, John P., XII, 414

Harrison, Kennithina Johana. *See* Mackay

Harrison, Margaret (Jones), V, 460, 461

Harrison, Marguerite (Bruneau), IX, 94

Harrison, Mark Robert, XII, **414–15**

Harrison, Mary. *See* Harman

Harrison, Mary (mother of SAMUEL BEALEY), IX, 369

Harrison, Mary (Lobley), XI, 523

Harrison, Mary (Medcalf), X, 504

Harrison, Richard, X, 336

Harrison, Robert Alexander, X, 123, **336–37**; XI, 621; XII, 98, 593, 1108

Harrison, Robert Launcelot, XII, 414

Harrison, Samuel Bealey, VII, 32, 364, 409, 580, 606, 859; VIII, 29, 30, 49, 50, 84, 652; IX, **369–73**, 523; X, 254, 255, 404

Harrison, Sarah (Hatheway), IX, 374; X, 339

Harrison, Sophia Soltau (Pim), XI, 691

Harrison, Susie Frances. *See* Riley

Harrison, Thomas (partner of John BURSTALL), XII, 145

Harrison, Thomas (partner of Thomas RIDLEY), X, 617

Harrison, Thomas C., XII, 414

Harrison, William (bailiff), VIII, 170

Harrison, William (clergyman), XII, 1051

Harrison, William Henry, V, 594, 619, 775, 796, 797, 798, 799; VI, 601, 617; VII, 132, 848, 849; VIII, 287; IX, 415; X, 483

Harrower, David, V, 879

Harry, Marguerite (Pollet), III, 523

Hart, Mr (jeweller), XI, 440

Hart, Aaron, IV, 40, **331–33**, 384, 754; V, 194, 484, 494; VI, 365, 366; VII, 386, 387; VIII, 365, 367; X, 337; XI, 234, 388, 455

Hart, Aaron Ezekiel, VII, 388; VIII, **363–65**

Hart, Aaron Philip, VII, 149, 150, 264, 514; VIII, 363, 364, 365; X, 337

Hart, Adolphus Mordecai, VII, 388; VIII, 363, 364, 365; X, **337–38**

Hart, Alexander (Asher), IV, 332; V, 194; VII, 386, 387; VIII, 365, 366

Hart, Alexander Thomas, VIII, 369

Hart, Amelia (Hyman), XI, 440

Hart, Areli Blake, VIII, 368

Hart, Arthur Wellington, VIII, 367

Hart, Benjamin, IV, 332, 754; V, 194; VI, 390, 717; VII, 69, 386, 387, 611; VIII, 363, 364, **365–67**; IX, 380; X, 337; XI, 388

Hart, Caroline Athalia, VII, 388

Hart, Catherine, IV, 332

Hart, Charlotte, IV, 332

Hart, Constance Hatton (Hart), X, 337

Hart, Dorothea. *See* Judah

Hart, Elizabeth. *See* Richardson

Hart, Elizabeth, IV, 332

Hart, Ephraim, VII, 386; VIII, 365

Hart, Esther Eliza, VII, 388, 880

Hart, Ezekiel, IV, 332, 333, 754; V, 27, 194, 207, 208, 210, 235, 828; VI, 22, 47, 338, 533, 717; VII, 66, 201, **386–89**, 784, 880; VIII, 363, 365, 366, 368, 369, 655; X, 337

Hart, Ezekiel Moses, XII, 451

Hart, Frances. *See* Lazarus

Hart, Frances. *See* Noah

Hart, Frances Michael. *See* David

Hart, George E., VII, 109

Hart, George Henry, IX, 38

Hart*, Gerald Ephraim (1849–1936), X, 337

Hart, Hannah (Clinch), V, 189

Hart, Harriet, VII, 388

Hart, Harriot Judith (Hart), VIII, 365; XI, 388

Hart, Henry (editor), XII, 451

Hart, Henry (uncle of EZEKIEL and MOSES), IV, 331; VII, 386; VIII, 367

Hart, Ira Craig, VII, 388; VIII, 364, 365, 369

Hart, Joseph, V, 190

Hart, Julia Catherine. *See* Beckwith

Hart, Lemon, IV, 331

Hart, Levi, IX, 839

Hart, Louisa Howard, VIII, 368

Hart, Marmaduke, VI, **311–12**; VIII, 165

Hart, Mary Kent. *See* Bradbury

Hart, Moses (brother of AARON), IV, 331, 332

Hart, Moses (brother of SAMUEL), V, 410

Hart, Moses, IV, 332; V, 64; VI, 22, 174, 365, 366; VII, 136, 386, 387, 388, 468, 879; VIII, 289, 364, 365, 366, **367–70**

Hart, Moses E., IX, 487

Hart, Orobio, VIII, 368

Hart, Phoebe. *See* David

Hart, Rebecca. *See* Byrne

Hart, Rebecca (Howe), VI, 332
Hart, Reuben Ingriam, IX, 839
Hart, Samuel, V, **409–10**
Hart, Samuel Becancour, VII, 388; VIII, 364, 365, 366
Hart, Samuel Peters, VIII, 391, 502
Hart, Sarah. *See* Judah
Hart, Sarah, IV, 332
Hart, Sarah (David), VIII, 363; XI, 234
Hart, Stephen, VII, 56
Hart, Susanna. *See* Winter
Hart, Susannah (Tulk), VI, 312
Hart, Theodore, VIII, 367; X, 724; XI, **388–89**, 409, 410, 455; XII, 214
Harte, Walter Blackburn, XII, 138, 499
Hartley, Edward, X, 445
Hartley, Thomas, IV, 405
Hartman, John, VIII, 370
Hartman, Joseph, VI, 12; VIII, 57, **370–71**, 550, 790; X, 725; XI, 939; XII, 594
Hartman, Mary. *See* Webb
Hartman, Mary Ann. *See* Cosford
Hartman, William, VI, 12
Hartney, Henry Jervis, XII, 922
Hartog, Alphonse, XII, 93
Hartshorne, Abigail. *See* Tremain
Hartshorne, Elizabeth. *See* Ustick
Hartshorne, Hugh, VI, 314
Hartshorne, John (grandfather), VI, 312
Hartshorne, John, VI, 314
Hartshorne, Lawrence, VI, 314; IX, 175
Hartshorne, Lawrence, V, 850; VI, **312–14**; VIII, 891
Hartshorne, Lucy. *See* Saltar
Hartshorne, Lucy (Shortt), IX, 719
Hartshorne, Robert, VI, 313; VIII, 891
Hartt, Charles Frederick, X, **338**; XI, 210
Hartt, Jarvis William, X, 338; XII, 139
Hartt, Lucy. *See* Lynde
Hartt, Prudence. *See* Brown
Hartt, Samuel, IX, 515
Hartwell, Joseph K., VII, 458
Harvard, Elizabeth. *See* Parks
Harvard, William Martin, VIII, **371–74**
Harvey. *See also* Hervey
Harvey, Agnes (Northup), X, 551
Harvey, Alexander, XII, 858
Harvey, Alexander, XI, **389–90**
Harvey, André, VIII, 893
Harvey, Ann. *See* Charleton
Harvey, Augustus, V, 464
Harvey*, Augustus William (1839–1903), XII, 755
Harvey, Caroline. *See* Marks
Harvey*, Daniel Cobb (1886–1966), V, 429; VIII, 193, 506, 752; IX, 828, 834; X, 363; XI, 527, 944
Harvey, Elizabeth, Lady Harvey. *See* Lake
Harvey, Eugenius, XI, 353
Harvey, Harriet (Bowring), XI, 108
Harvey, John, XI, 389, 390
Harvey, Sir John, V, 82; VI, 541, 821; VII, 48, 49, 99, 141, 143, 144, 156, 297, 442, 444, 445, 508, 518, 637, 658, 692, 694, 743, 772, 858, 859, 868, 869, 888, 899, 925; VIII, xxiv, 104, 151, 153, 161, 173, 184, 193, 233, 234, 295, 296, 309, 348, 362, **374–84**, 399, 400, 470, 487, 488, 511, 739, 757, 802, 806, 808, 841, 842, 868, 904,

905, 922, 923, 949, 950, 958; IX, 23, 37, 145, 169, 263, 394, 400, 418, 455, 605, 619, 721; X, 50, 278, 365, 385, 386, 433, 438, 551, 553, 601, 710, 712; XI, 66, 308, 376, 567, 673, 761, 799, 862, 926; XII, 574, 797, 896
Harvey, Margaret. *See* Stuart
Harvey, Martha (Cornish), XII, 215
Harvey, Mary (Paton), XII, 827
Harvey*, Moses (1820–1901), XI, 356; XII, 379, 753
Harvey, Pierre, VIII, 893
Harvey, Thomas, I, 574
Harvicker, J., VII, 790
Harvie, Elizabeth (Armour), VIII, 21
Harvie, John A., XI, 834
Harvie, Nicholas, IX, 403
Harvie, Susanna (Hutchinson), IX, 403
Harwick, Abraham van, I, 450
Harwick, Stephen van, I, 391, 450
Harwood. *See also* Lotbinière
Harwood, Elizabeth. *See* Unwin
Harwood, John, IX, 373
Harwood, Marie-Louise-Josephte. *See* Chartier de Lotbinière
Harwood, Robert Unwin, VI, 133; VIII, 20; IX, **373–74**, 541
Hase, Ann (Pope), XII, 855
Haskel, Daniel, VII, 386
Haskins, Mrs. *See* Kelly
Haskins, Charles, VII, 389
Haskins, James, VII, **389–90**
Haskins, Mary Ann. *See* Everitt
Haslam, Sarah, VIII, 668
Haslett, John James, X, 45
Hassall, Elizabeth (wife of THOMAS), VII, 390
Hassall, Margaret, VII, 390
Hassall, Mary Emily (Middleton), XII, 733
Hassall, Thomas, VII, 390
Hassall, Thomas, VII, 276, **390**
Hassard. *See* Haszard
Hasse, Gertrude (Holland), V, 425, 426
Hasseltine, Nancy Judson (Sanborn), X, 643
Hassler, Ferdinand Rudolph, VII, 866
Hastie, Elizabeth (Cowan), XII, 217
Hastings, Marquess of. *See* Rawdon-Hastings
Hastings, Horace Lorenzo, XI, 804
Hastings, Selina, Countess of Huntingdon. *See* Shirley
Hastings, Susanna. *See* Willard
Hastings, Warren, IV, 115; V, 754; VII, 523
Haswell, Amelia Mary (Pullen), XI, 718
Haswell, Mary. *See* Cordis
Haswell, Mary (Montresor), IV, 552
Haswell, Robert, IV, 419; V, 388, **410–11**, 586
Haswell, William, V, 410
Haszard, George, X, 339
Haszard, James Douglas, VI, 172, 568; VII, 437, 734, 742, 903, 904; VIII, 36, 37, 505, 506, 563, 827; IX, 830; X, **339**; XI, 201
Haszard, Jane (mother of JAMES DOUGLAS), X, 339
Haszard, Sarah Sophia. *See* Gardiner
Haszard, Susanna Jane. *See* Nelmes
Haszard, Thomas Rhodes, X, 339
Haszard (Hassard), Waitsill (Douglas), V, 262
Haszard, William B., VI, 161, 162, 566
Hatch, Harris, IX, 263

Hatch*, Harry C. (1884–1946), XII, 1081

Hatch, Jane (Parker), IX, 619, 620

Hateouati. *See* Otreouti

Hatfield, Amelia (Fisher), X, 285, 287

Hatfield, David, VI, 756

Hatfield, Nancy (Fortune; Taylor), VIII, 867

Hatfield, Sally (Taylor), VI, 756, 757

Hatherton, Baron. *See* Littleton

Hatheway, Calvin Luther, IX, **374–75**; X, 339

Hatheway, Ebenezer, IX, 374

Hatheway, George Luther, IX, 374; X, **339–41**; XI, 298, 545, 688, 830, 897; XII, 338, 881, 1034, 1070, 1098, 1105

Hatheway, Julia (Chandler), IX, 123

Hatheway, Julia Caroline (Turnbull), XII, 1070

Hatheway, Martha. *See* Slason

Hatheway, Sarah. *See* Harrison

Hathorne, John, I, 26, 246; II, 145, 167, 450, 579, 654

Hatsell, John, V, 292

Hatt, John Ogilvie, VII, 909; IX, 745

Hatt, Mary. *See* Cooley

Hatt, Mary (mother of RICHARD), V, 411

Hatt, Richard, V, 411

Hatt, Richard, V, 280, 405, **411–12**, 643, 765, 856; VI, 159, 160, 198, 199, 488, 539; VII, 57, 58; VIII, 279, 945; X, 436

Hatt, Samuel, V, 280, 411, 412, 643; VI, 344; VII, 682; VIII, 471; IX, 455

Hatt, Susan (Leeming), X, 436

Hattanville, Antoine, II, 234

Hattanville, Jeanne-Françoise. *See* Gadois

Hatton, Sir Christopher, I, 93, 94

Hatton, Sarah (Johnston), X, 382

Haubichon, Jean, I, 270

Hauchecorne, Abbé, VIII, 212

Haudebourg. *See* Volant

Haultain*, Sir Frederick William (1857–1942), XII, 1048

Haun, Sarah (Burwell), VII, 125

Haun, William, VII, 833

Hauser, Frederick, V, 94

Hausman, *dit* Ménager, Thérèse-Esther (Florence; Perrault), V, 668

Haussonville, Comte d'. *See* Cléron

Hautefort de Montignac, Marie-Aimée de (Estourmel, Marquise d'Estourmel), III, 213

Hauteville. *See* Bourgonnière; Le Vieux

Hautmesnil (Hautmesnyl). *See* Philippe

Hautraye. *See* Hantraye

Havard de Beaufort, François-Charles, known as L'Avocat, III, **278–79**, 625

Havelock-Allan, Sir Henry Marshman, XII, 733

Haven, Jens, III, 213, 411; IV, liii, 225, **333–34**, 536, 537, 599; V, 54, 829, 830; VII, 474; VIII, 477

Haven, Mary. *See* Butterworth

Haven, Miranda (Arms), VIII, 23

Haviland, Amelia Janetta. *See* Boyd

Haviland, Anne Elizabeth. *See* Grubbe

Haviland, Caroline. *See* Lee

Haviland, Jane (Wetmore), VI, 810

Haviland, Jane Rebecca. *See* Brecken

Haviland, Peter, IV, 334

Haviland, Salusbury. *See* Aston

Haviland, Sarah Frances (DeBlois), XI, 241

Haviland, Thomas Heath, VI, 821; VII, 104, 145; VIII, 198, 297, 376, 565, 825; IX, 28, 155, 156, **375–77**, 395, 401, 404; X, 161; XI, 241; XII, 415

Haviland, Thomas Heath, IX, 376; X, 597; XI, 701, 702, 703; XII, 166, **415–18**, 840, 857

Haviland, William, III, 86; IV, 23, 24, 143, **334–36**, 481, 495, 545, 569, 679, 680, 769; V, 104

Havy, Mme. *See* François

Havy, François, III, 38, 210, 216, 224, 271, **280–83**, 305, 370, 371, 501; IV, 45, 126, 357, 476; V, 41, 276

Hawawes (Awanwest), Nicholas, VI, 678

Hawe, Ellen (O'Callaghan), X, 555

Hawe, King Hans, VI, 117

Hawes, Sir Benjamin, XI, 881

Hawke, Anthony Bewden, VI, 522; VII, 580, 755; IX, 98, **377–78**, 405

Hawke, Edward, 1st Baron Hawke, III, 71, 209, 557, 657; IV, 126, 282, 327, 699

Hawke, Eliza (wife of ANTHONY BEWDEN), IX, 377

Hawke*, John Thomas (1845–1922), XII, 340, 341

Hawkeridge, William, I, 144, **362**

Hawkesbury, Baron. *See* Jenkinson

Hawkey, Margaret Gordon. *See* Milligan

Hawkins, Alfred, III, 305; VII, 81, 287, 823, 837; VIII, **384–86**; X, 627

Hawkins, Alfred George, VIII, 385

Hawkins, Anna (Thompson), XI, 877

Hawkins, Anne. *See* Gurney

Hawkins, Ann Eliza (Rawlinson; Austin), IX, 11

Hawkins, Elizabeth. *See* Ellery

Hawkins, Ernest, V, 475, 476; VIII, 94, 172; IX, 209, 289, 292, **378–79**; X, 40; XI, 654

Hawkins, Frances Hume (Simpson), VIII, 811; XI, 824

Hawkins, George, VIII, 385

Hawkins, Harriett (Molesworth), X, 516

Hawkins, Henry, IX, 378

Hawkins, Sir John, I, 228, 316, 331, 380, 381, 530

Hawkins, John Summerfield, X, 449; XI, 20, 21

Hawkins, Lydia (Chandler), IX, 124

Hawkins, Martha. *See* Paterson

Hawkins, Sophia Anna. *See* Lefroy

Hawkins, Walter, XII, 259

Hawkins, William (pirate), I, 228

Hawkins, William (surveyor), VII, 747; VIII, 92

Hawkridge. *See* Hawkeridge

Hawks, Joseph, XI, 603

Hawks, Mary Susannah (Moody), XI, 603, 605

Hawksett, Samuel, VII, 398

Hawley, Henry, III, 666

Hawley, Joseph-Adolphe, IX, 193

Hawley, Margaret Waugh. *See* Buckham

Hawley, Pamelia (Roblin), IX, 679

Hawley, William Fitz, VIII, **386**

Hawn, Mathias, V, 842

Haws, Calista. *See* Calvert

Haws, John, VIII, 387; XII, 740

Haws, John, VII, 612, 654; VIII, **386–87**; X, 349

Haws, Richard Calvert, VIII, 387

Hawthorne, Margaret (Taylor), X, 671

Hawthorne, Nathaniel, IX, 351; X, 347; XII, 570

Hay, Agathe (Testard Louvigny de Montigny), V, 802

Hay, Alexander, VII, 600

Hay, Agnes Dunlop (Browne), XII, 131

Hay, Arthur, 9th Marquess of Tweeddale, XI, 771
Hay, Bettrice. *See* Henderson
Hay, Charles, IV, **336**; V, 737, 893
Hay, Lord Charles, III, 218, **283–84**, 662; IV, 3
Hay, Charles, 3rd Marquis of Tweeddale, III, 283
Hay, Edward Henry George Gunter, XII, 370, 371
Hay, Frances. *See* Berkeley
Hay, George, IV, 496; V, 523
Hay, Janet. *See* Reid
Hay, Jean. *See* Alexander
Hay, Jehu (John), IV, 322, **336–37**, 762; V, 710, 802
Hay, Jemima. *See* Huddleston
Hay, John, V, 284
Hay, John Dunlop, XI, 391
Hay, John James, VII, 543
Hay, Julia Charlotte Sophia, Marchioness of Tweeddale.
  *See* Mackenzie-Stewart
Hay, Julie-Marie. *See* Réaume
Hay, Margaret (Bayne), VIII, 67
Hay, Margaret (Bruce), IV, 107
Hay, Mary. *See* Dunlop
Hay, Mary (wife of CHARLES), IV, 336
Hay, Robert, XI, 390
Hay, Robert, IX, 391; XI, **390–91**, 448, 449, 551; XII, 292
Hay, Robert William, VII, 742; VIII, xxix, xxx, xxxi, 356,
  671
Hay, Susannah, Marchioness of Tweeddale. *See* Hamilton
Hay, Thomas, 9th Earl of Kinnoull, V, 347
Hay, Udney, IV, 336
Hay, William (father of WILLIAM), XI, 391
Hay, William (merchant), V, 284
Hay, William, VIII, 486, 876, 961; XI, 119, **391–93**, 856
Hayden, Fade, VIII, 533
Hayden, John, VIII, 533
Haydn, Franz Joseph, XII, 222, 223, 708
Hay-Drummond, Robert Auriol, 10th Earl of Kinnoull,
  VIII, xxx
Hayenwatha. *See* Hiawatha
Hayes. *See also* Hay; Hays
Hayes, Abigail. *See* David
Hayes, Abigail. *See* Levy
Hayes, Andrew, IX, 379
Hayes, Ann. *See* Barton
Hayes, Benjamin, XI, 393
Hayes, Catherine, VIII, 347
Hayes, Charles, VII, 579
Hayes, Edward, I, 334, 335, 336, **362–65**, 531, 532
Hayes, Isaac Israel, VIII, 449; XI, 382, **393–94**; XII, 123,
  955
Hayes, Mary (Lawrence), XI, 501
Hayes, Melita (Miller), XI, 594
Hayes, Moses Judah, VIII, 364, 366, 543; IX, **379–81**, 655;
  X, 405; XI, 254
Hayes, Robert, VII, 579
Hayes, Rutherford Birchard, XII, 701
Hayes, Thomas, I, 365
Hayet, Madeleine. *See* Hénaut
Hayet, Marguerite (Véron de Grandmesnil; Chouart Des
  Groseilliers), I, 223, 228; II, 535, 647
Hayet, Sébastien, I, 223; II, 535
Hayman, Alice. *See* Gaverocke
Hayman, Grace. *See* Spicer
Hayman, Henry, II, 291

Hayman, Nicholas, I, 365
Hayman, Robert, I, **365–66**, 584, 656, 669
Hayne, Thomas, II, 610
Haynes, Charlotte. *See* Moresby
Haynes, Emily Josephine. *See* Pittendrigh
Haynes, Hester. *See* Carmichael
Haynes, John Carmichael, IX, 81; XI, **394–95**
Haynes, Jonas, XI, 394
Hayot, Angélique, named de Saint-Joseph, III, 318
Hayot, Louise (Normandin), II, 499
Hays. *See also* Hay; Hayes
Hays (Hayes), Andrew, IV, 332
Hays, Catherine. *See* Trestler
Hays, Eleazar, IX, 213
Hays, John, VI, 666
Hays, Joseph Eleazar, V, 828
Hays, Josephte. *See* Trestler
Hays, Marie Abby Victoria (Dorion), IX, 213
Hayt, Monson, V, 35
Hayter. *See also* Haitor
Hayter, Elizabeth Tuck (Macaulay), VI, 415; VIII, 511, 522
Hayter, Sir George, IX, 656
Hayter, John, IV, 711
Haythorne, Edward Curtis (uncle), XII, 418
Haythorne, Edward Curtis, XII, 418, 419
Haythorne, Elizabeth Radcliffe. *See* Scott
Haythorne, John, XII, 418
Haythorne, Joseph, XII, 418
Haythorne, Mary. *See* Curtis
Haythorne, Robert Poore, X, 597; XI, 532, 668, 701; XII,
  40, 417, **418–19**, 426, 452, 512, 639, 837, 910
Haythorne, Thomas Joseph, XII, 418, 419
Hayward, John, VIII, 942, 943
Hayward, Nicholas, I, 226
Hazard, Ann (Tredwell), VIII, 890
Hazen, Charlotte. *See* La Saussaye
Hazen, Deborah. *See* Murray
Hazen, Elizabeth (Chipman), VI, 135, 140; VIII, 149
Hazen*, Sir John Douglas (1860–1937), XI, 448
Hazen, John, VI, 756
Hazen, Moses, IV, 150, 230, 269, 271, 305, 320, 548, 691;
  V, 31, 34, 146, 358, 359, **412–15**, 415, 416
Hazen, Robert Fraser, VIII, 362
Hazen, Robert Leonard, V, 416; VII, 445; VIII, 809, 810;
  IX, 35, 146, 147, 381, 623; X, 285, **341–42**, 711, 712;
  XII, 536, 896
Hazen, Sarah. *See* Le Baron
Hazen, Sarah (Simonds), VI, 717
Hazen, Sarah Ann. *See* Botsford
Hazen, Sarah Lowell (Murray; Botsford), IX, 62; XI, 90;
  XII, 115
Hazen, William, VI, 655; X, 341
Hazen, William, IV, 196, 389; V, 16, 94, 413, **415–17**, 504,
  506, 630, 867; VI, 138, 140, 141, 718, 719; VIII, 149,
  150, 805; X, 341; XI, 90
Hazeur, Anne. *See* Soumande
Hazeur, Catherine. *See* Martin de Lino
Hazeur, Élisabeth. *See* Barbe
Hazeur, François (father of FRANÇOIS), II, 275
Hazeur, François (grandson of FRANÇOIS), IV, 339, 357
Hazeur, François, II, 180, **275–77**, 300, 484, 526, 575, 576,
  598; III, 134, 284; IV, 337
Hazeur, François-Marie-Joseph, II, 277

Hazeur, Jean-François, II, 234, 275
Hazeur, Jean-François, II, 276, **277**, 465, 598
Hazeur, Jeanne-Louise, II, 275
Hazeur, Joseph-Thierry, II, 276, 277, 598; III, 114, 223, **284–85**, 354, 616; IV, 142, 286, 337, 338, 339; V, 196
Hazeur, Louis-Ignace, II, 277
Hazeur, Madeleine, II, 275
Hazeur, Marie. *See* Proust
Hazeur, Marie-Anne (Sébille), II, 275
Hazeur, Marie-Anne-Ursule (Sarrazin), II, 276, 597, 598; III, 675
Hazeur de L'Orme, Pierre, II, 60, 249, 276, 277, 598, 640; III, 50, 62, 63, 108, 115, 192, 193, 223, 239, 284, 285, 344, 354, 390, 481, 616, 675; IV, 142, 220, **337–39**, 429, 430, 440, 539, 661
Hazeur Des Ormeaux, Charles, II, 129
Hazeur Des Ormeaux, Léonard, II, 129, 275
Hazeur Des Ormeaux, Marie-Anne. *See* Pinguet
Hazlett, Margaret (Armour), XII, 36, 37
Hazlewood, Samuel, X, **342**
Hazlitt, T. G., IX, 206
Hazzen, Abigail. *See* White
Hazzen, Moses, V, 412, 415
Hea, Joseph R., XI, 447
Heacock, Susannah (Lloyd), VII, 508
Head, Anna Gabriella (Mendes; Roper), X, 342
Head, Anna Maria, Lady Head. *See* Yorke
Head, Charles Franklin, VII, 118
Head, Sir Edmund Walker, VII, 445; VIII, 66, 70, 161, 247, 361, 383, 435, 739, 810, 867, 868; IX, 23, 59, 147, 341, **381–86**, 409, 413, 526, 565, 573, 623, 627, 628, 629, 665, 767, 777; X, 97, 131, 140, 158, 181, 258, 285, 286, 342, 356, 464, 494, 543, 644, 647, 666, 712, 713; XI, 181, 226, 372, 447, 609; XII, 116, 232, 262, 351, 561, 594, 672, 717, 749, 896, 897, 931, 1052, 1089
Head, Frances Anne. *See* Burges
Head, Sir Francis Bond, VII, 6, 11, 42, 43, 91, 102, 183, 200, 214, 215, 222, 234, 260, 317, 370, 406, 451, 460, 509, 549, 550, 704, 720, 756, 843, 846, 917; VIII, xxiv, xxxiv, 11, 12, 27, 28, 30, 47, 48, 84, 205, 253, 254, 419, 431, 441, 444, 445, 512, 520, 523, 524, 585, 640, 643, 696, 697, 698, 733, 743, 798, 846, 847, 852, 853, 859, 926, 927, 932, 933; IX, 9, 13, 24, 68, 99, 230, 241, 265, 266, 313, 336, 346, 351, 399, 400, 407, 423, 501, 502, 522, 589, 593, 657, 674, 675, 685, 686, 687, 724, 750, 751, 760, 788; X, 62, 63, 124, 233, 253, 254, 310, 311, 317, **342–45**, 484, 530, 607, 618, 619, 622, 641, 646, 693; XI, 150, 407, 517, 713, 714, 778, 787, 914; XII, 102, 681, 906, 988
Head, James Roper Mendes, X, 342
Head, Jane, Lady Head. *See* Walker
Head, Sir John, IX, 381
Head, Julia Valenza, Lady Head. *See* Somerville
Head, Michael, VII, 390
Head, Samuel, VII, **390–92**; VIII, 398
Head, Sophia Augusta. *See* Eagleson
Headley, Elizabeth. *See* Young
Headley, John, V, 664
Healey, John R., X, 203, 213
Healy (Healey), Elvira (Hilton), IX, 390
Heaney, Martin, IX, 179; XII, 839
Heard, Elizabeth (Lunn), XI, 533
Heard, Ellen (Whale), XI, 915

Hearn. *See also* Herron
Hearn, Catherine. *See* Power
Hearn, John, XII, **420–21**
Hearn, John Gabriel, XII, 421
Hearn, Mary. *See* Doran
Hearn, Matthew Aylward, XII, 324
Hearn, Thomas, XII, 420
Hearne, Diana (mother of SAMUEL), IV, 339
Hearne, Eliza (McKeagney), X, 475
Hearne, Samuel, IV, 339
Hearne, Samuel, I, 378; II, xxviii, 232, 320, 615; III, xxxiii, 303; IV, 47, 157, 165, 166, 245, 283, **339–42**, 384, 518, 519, 523, 524, 583, 584, 647, 684, 727, 741, 742, 743, 758, 760; V, 363, 450, 500, 656, 683; VI, 20, 249, 481, 753; VII, 324; VIII, 878
Heartz, Jane Lambert (Bell), XII, 29
Heath, Elizabeth. *See* Allen
Heath, Elizabeth (Pettit), V, 669
Heath, Émilie. *See* Reeves
Heath, Emily (Boulton), XII, 119
Heath, Hannah (Gyles), III, 273
Heath, James William Adhémar, X, 346
Heath, John, VIII, 871; X, **345–46**
Heath, William, X, 345
Heaviside, Ann Maria (Willis), IX, 387, 841
Heaviside, Elizabeth (mother of MARY), IX, 386
Heaviside, Jane (Wedderburn), VII, 899; IX, 387
Heaviside, Mary (Love, Lady Love), VII, 899; IX, **386–87**
Heaviside, Thomas, VII, 899; VIII, 102; IX, 386
Heavy. *See* Le Pesant
Heavysege, Charles, IX, 390; X, **346–48**; XII, 460, 558, 946
Heavysege, Harriet (Pettigrew), X, 346
Heavysege, Mary Ann. *See* Oddy
Hebbard, Jedidiah. *See* Hibbard, Jedediah
Hebbard, John, V, 422
Hebbard, Martha. *See* Durkee
Hebden, Harriett (Haly), X, 330
Hébécourt. *See* Le Dossu
Hébert, Adrienne. *See* Duvivier
Hébert, Anne (Bourg), IV, 80
Hébert, Anne (Jonquet), I, 264, 368, 437, 578
Hébert, Anne (Niquet), VI, 315
Hébert, Casimir, IX, 464; XI, 424
Hébert, Élisabeth. *See* Granger
Hébert, Étienne, VI, **314–15**
Hébert, François, VI, 315
Hébert, Françoise (Fournier), I, 264
Hébert, Françoise (Le Blanc), VI, 314
Hébert, Geneviève (Provancher), XII, 868
Hébert, Guillaume, I, 264, 367, 368, 578; II, 489
Hébert, Guillemette (Couillard de Lespinay), I, 109, 145, 236, 237, 264, **366–67**, 368, 386, 517, 578; II, 33; VII, 213
Hébert, Hélène. *See* Desportes
Hébert, Honoré, VI, 315
Hébert, Jacques, I, 367
Hébert, Jean-Baptiste (brother of ÉTIENNE), VI, 314
Hébert, Jean-Baptiste (father of ÉTIENNE), VI, 314, 315
Hébert, Jean-Baptiste (son of ÉTIENNE), VI, 315; VIII, 717; IX, 552, 795; XI, 395
Hébert, Jean-François, VI, **315–16**
Hébert, Joseph (brother of ÉTIENNE), VI, 315

Hébert, Joseph (son of JOSEPH), I, 367
Hébert, Joseph, I, 264, **367**
Hébert, Judith. *See* Lemire
Hébert, Julie (Leblanc), XI, 505
Hébert, Louis, I, 367
Hébert, Louis, I, 29, 96, 101, 108, 189, 195, 236, 237, 238,
    264, 347, 366, **367–68**, 437, 578; II, 33, 148, 213; III,
    678, 680; VII, 213; VIII, 174
Hébert*, Louis-Philippe (1850–1917), I, 221, 232; IX, 285;
    XI, 105, 259; XII, 549
Hébert, Marguerite (Désilets), XI, 251
Hébert, Marguerite (Le Blanc), VI, 314
Hébert, Marie. *See* Rollet
Hébert, Marie (Le Blanc), VI, 314
Hébert, Marie (Milette), IX, 552
Hébert, Marie (Richard), X, 615
Hébert, Marie-Charlotte. *See* Poytiers
Hébert, Marie-Joseph. *See* Côté
Hébert, Marie-Joseph (Brassard Deschenaux), IV, 88
Hébert, Marie-Josephte. *See* Babin
Hébert, Maurice, X, 413
Hébert, Médard, VIII, 210
Hébert, Nicolas, I, 367
Hébert, Nicolas-Tolentin, VI, 315; XI, **395–97**, 690; XII,
    758
Hébert, Noël, X, 615
Hébert, Simon, VII, 243
Hébert, Vital, XII, 1034, 1035
Hébert, *dit* Larivière, Roland, I, 267
Héchon. *See* Chaumonot, Pierre-Joseph-Marie
Hecht, Jules, IX, 600
Heck, Barbara. *See* Ruckle
Heck, Lois. *See* Wright
Heck, Paul, V, 728, 729; VII, 392
Heck, Samuel, V, 729; VII, **392–93**
Heckedorn, Anna Maria (Denke), VII, 243, 244
Heckewelder. *See also* Hackenwelder
Heckewelder, John, VII, 244
Hecquet de La Cloche, Marie-Catherine. *See* Homasset
Hector, Sir James, VIII, 3; X, 81; XI, 662, 663; XII, 540
Hedden (Heddon), Isaac, V, 136, 355
Hedding, Elijah, VI, 670, 674
Hedge, Lucy (Wilkes), XI, 923
Hedge, Samuel, X, 450
Hedges, Phoebe (Benedict), VIII, 81
Hedouin, Madeleine-Ursule. *See* Rancin
Heer, Frédérique-Louise. *See* Ouvrier
Heer, Jean-Tobie, V, 417
Heer, Louis-Chrétien, IV, 442; V, **417**; VII, 255, 774
Heer, Marie-Angélique de. *See* Badel
Heer, Marie-Louise de (De Lisle), V, 417
Hefele, Johanna Josepha Walpurga (Moll), V, 70
Hegan, Ann (Parks), IX, 621
Hegan, John, IX, 621
Hegan, Sampson, II, 25
Hegel, Georg Wilhelm Friedrich, XII, 458
Heine, William, III, 624
Heineman, Pines (Phineas), IV, 332
Heinrich, Anton. *See* Henry, Anthony
Heintzman, Anna Matilda Louisa (Bender), XII, 422
Heintzman, Charles, XII, 422
Heintzman, Charles Theodore, XII, 423
Heintzman*, George Charles (1860–1944), XII, 423

Heintzman, Herman, XII, 423
Heintzman, Johann Gerhard, XII, 423
Heintzman, Matilda Louisa. *See* Grunow
Heintzmann, Theodor August, VIII, 347; XII, **421–24**
Heintzmann, William Francis, XII, 423
Heire. *See* Heer
Heister, Leopold Philipp von, V, 427
Heke Pokai, Hone Wiremu, XII, 733
Helbronner*, Jules (d. 1921), XI, 32, 802
Hélène, III, 266
Hélène de Saint-Augustin. *See* Boullé
Hélie (Élie) Du Tillet, Madeleine (Mius d'Entremont,
    Baronne de Pobomcoup), I, 510
Helliwell, Ann. *See* Ashworth
Helliwell, John, IX, 387
Helliwell, Joseph, IX, 387, 388
Helliwell, Louisa. *See* Neelon
Helliwell, Mary. *See* Wilson
Helliwell, Sally. *See* Lord
Helliwell, Sarah (Clarkson), X, 174
Helliwell, Thomas, IX, 387
Helliwell, Thomas, IX, **387–88**
Helliwell, William, IX, 387, 388
Hellmuth, Catherine Maria. *See* Evans
Hellmuth*, Isaac (1817–1901), IX, 246, 292; X, 208, 209;
    XI, 89, 90, 221, 314, 570, 640; XII, 736
Helluin, Geneviève-Adélaïde-Albertine (Devisme), XII,
    257
Hellyer, Thomas, XII, 534
Helm, John, VII, 893
Helmcken, Cecilia. *See* Douglas
Helmcken*, John Sebastian (1824–1920), VIII, 590, 646,
    836; IX, 115, 338, 714; X, 247; XI, 32, 33, 635, 636;
    XII, 113, 240, 241, 642, 915, 929
Helmer, Andrew, VII, 882
Helvétius, Claude-Adrien, VII, 645
Hely-Hutchinson, John, 1st Baron Hutchinson, VIII, 458
Hemans, Felicia Dorothea. *See* Browne
Hemans, Williby, X, 516
Hémard de Denonville, Charles de, II, 98
Hémard de Denonville, Marie de (Brisay), II, 98
Hemming, Martha (Dunkin), XI, 286
Hénault, Gabriel, IV, 463
Hénault, Geneviève. *See* Fauteux
Hénault, Norbert, VIII, 288
Hénault, Pierre, IV, 463
Hénault, *dit* Delorme, François, VI, 665
Hénaut. *See also* Énault
Hénaut, Madeleine (Hayet; Radisson), I, 223; II, 535
Henday, Anthony, II, 309; III, xxxii, 171, **285–87**, 303,
    304, 332, 342, 595; IV, 740, 761; V, 363
Henderson, Alexander, XI, **397–98**
Henderson, Andrew, VIII, 335; IX, **388–89**
Henderson, Archibald, VI, 233
Henderson, Bettrice (Hay), XI, 390
Henderson, Catherine. *See* Udny
Henderson, Daniel J., XI, 561
Henderson, Edward, X, 112
Henderson, Eliza, IX, 388
Henderson, George (architect), XI, 392
Henderson, George (son of ANDREW), IX, 388
Henderson, Harriet Kirkpatrick (Ansley), VII, 20
Henderson, Helen (Waugh), VI, 806

Henderson, Isabella (Carvell), XII, 166
Henderson, James (Montreal merchant), X, 354
Henderson, James (Quebec merchant), VI, 532; VIII, 690
Henderson, James (Scottish merchant), VI, 418, 419
Henderson, Jean (Gourlay), IX, 330
Henderson, John (architect), XI, 391
Henderson, John (brother of ALEXANDER), XI, 397
Henderson, John (father of ALEXANDER), XI, 397
Henderson, John (mason), V, 424
Henderson, John (partner of George Richard RENFREW), XII, 889
Henderson, John Lanceley Hodge, IX, 763
Henderson, Letitia Grace, XI, 121
Henderson, Louise E. See Ewart
Henderson, Margaret (wife of ALEXANDER), XI, 397
Henderson, Margaret (Campbell), VIII, 122
Henderson, Mary (Drew), X, 259
Henderson, Mary (McMaster), XI, 577
Henderson, Mary Ann Jane (Renfrew), XII, 889
Henderson, Susannah. See Slack
Henderson, William (acquaintance of James McGILL), V, 530
Henderson, William (clergyman), XI, 523
Henderson, William (landowner), VII, 426
Henderson, William Simpson, XII, 889
Hendery, Robert, XII, **424–25**
Hendery, Sarah. See Maysenhoelder
Hendey. See Henday
Hendon, Jane (Campbell, Lady Campbell), VII, 142
Hendrick. See Tekarihogen (d. 1830)
Hendrick (Hendrick Peters). See Theyanoguin
Hendricken, Margaret (Forrestall; Henry), XI, 398
Hendricken, Thomas Francis, XI, 331
Hendrickson, Hannah Ann (Peterson), VIII, 700
Hendrie*, William (1831–1906), X, 650, 651
Hendrik, Prince of the Netherlands, VIII, 901
Hendry. See also Henday
Hendry, William, VI, 15; X, 284
Hendry, William A., IX, 787
Héneau, Sophie (Mayrand), X, 502
Heneker*, Richard William (1823–1912), XI, 706; XII, 827, 828, 902
Henessey, Mary (O'Sullivan), XII, 811
Heney, Hugh, VI, 442
Heney, Hugue, VII, 226, 227, 393, 622
Heney, Hugues, V, 323; VII, **393–94**, 666, 667, 905; VIII, 914
Heney, Marie-Léocadie. See Foucher
Heney, Thérèse. See Fortier
Heney, Thérèse (Mayrand), X, 503
Henke, Hone. See Heke Pokai, Hone Wiremu
Henley, Robert, 1st Earl of Northington, IV, xli, 571
Hennepin, Gaspard, II, 277
Hennepin, Jeanne, II, 278
Hennepin, Louis (Antoine), I, 175, 176, 226, 379, 415, 420, 438, 439, 440; II, xxxiii, 197, 262, **277–81**, 419, 443; III, 325; V, 821
Hennepin, Norbertine. See Leleu
Henniker, John, V, 413
Henning, Thomas, IX, 7, 470, 820; X, 291
Henri. See also Membertou
Henri (Patriote sympathizer), VII, 411
Henri (servant), I, 302, 366, 509

Henri II, King of France, I, 372, 421, 424; II, 328
Henri III, King of France, I, 261, 324, 421, 520
Henri IV, King of France, I, 23, 42, 96, 97, 99, 100, 134, 187, 188, 190, 209, 210, 214, 291, 299, 307, 323, 421, 422, 453, 471, 498, 501, 521, 601; III, 41; IV, xvii
Henrich, Anton. See Henry, Anthony
Henrietta Maria, Princess of France (Henrietta Maria, Queen Consort of England, Scotland, and Ireland), I, 81, 534, 596
Henry. See also Tekarihogen (d. 1830)
Henry VII, King of England, I, 120, 148, 149, 153, 164, 239, 302, 304, 343, 641
Henry VIII, King of England and Ireland, I, 155, 157, 565, 566, 585, 586, 643, 660
Henry Frederick, Prince of Wales, I, 144
Henry Prince. See Mis-koo-kee-new
Henry, Mme. See Duché
Henry, Alexander (merchant), VI, 316
Henry, Alexander (son of ALEXANDER, 1739–1824), VI, 318
Henry, Alexander, V, 177, 236, 237, 394, **418–19**, 501, 526, 560, 656; VI, 318; VII, 356; VIII, 85, 158, 412, 413, 454, 537, 556, 882; X, 297
Henry, Alexander, I, 225; III, 167, 452, 659, 660; IV, 132, 277, 365, 366, 389, 403, 496, 564, 675; V, 38, 39, 129, 260, 377, 418, 495, 496, 500, 529, 536, 553, 562, 592, 682, 684, 820, 821, 822; VI, **316–19**, 375, 547, 600, 822; VIII, 390; XI, 476
Henry, Anne. See Murdoch
Henry, Anthony, III, 91; IV, 19, 112, 267, **342–43**; VI, 321, 333, 508
Henry, Barbara (Spring; wife of ANTHONY), IV, 343
Henry, Charlotte. See Todd
Henry, Christianna. See McDonald
Henry, Christine. See Bethune
Henry, Edme, VII, 394
Henry, Edme, VI, 635; VII, **394–96**, 739
Henry, Eliza (McKeagney), X, 475
Henry, Elizabeth (wife of Alexander, merchant), VI, 316
Henry, Eunice. See Parker
Henry, Geneviève. See Fournier
Henry, George (clergyman), V, 509, 600, 768, 769
Henry, George (translator), VII, 277
Henry, Jane (Lynd), V, 509; VI, 326
Henry, John (father of WALTER), VIII, 391
Henry, John (son of ALEXANDER, 1739–1824), VI, 318
Henry, John, V, 209, 532; VI, 642; VII, 768; VIII, **387–90**
Henry, Joseph, XI, 509, 799
Henry, Julia, VI, 318
Henry, Julia (Ketson; wife of ALEXANDER), VI, 318
Henry, Julia (Bérard, dit Lépine), X, 439; XII, 554
Henry, Leah Allan. See Geddes
Henry, Margaret. See Hendricken
Henry, Margaret. See Miller
Henry, Margaret (Chabrand Delisle), IV, 138
Henry, Marie-Clotilde. See Girardin
Henry, Robert (brother of ALEXANDER, d. 1814), V, 418
Henry, Robert (father of ROBERT), VIII, 390
Henry, Robert (son of ALEXANDER, 1739–1824), VI, 318
Henry, Robert, V, 418; VI, 17; VII, 214; VIII, **390–91**, 502
Henry, Robert Nesbit, XI, 398
Henry, Sarah. See Tuhbenahneequay
Henry, Sophia Caroline. See McDonald

Henry, Walter, VIII, **391–93**
Henry, William (abolitionist), IX, 820
Henry, William (assistant of Sir John Henry LEFROY), XI, 508
Henry, William (fur trader), V, 418; VI, 318; VIII, 882
Henry, William Alexander, XI, 149, **398–400**, 731, 755; XII, 598, 899, 1043
Henshaw, Mary, VI, 666
Hensley, Charles, XII, 425
Hensley, Frances Anne Dover. *See* Hodgson
Hensley, Joseph, X, 187; XI, 528, 532, 668; XII, 418, **425–27**, 512
Hensley, Louisa Margaretta (mother of JOSEPH), XII, 425
Henson, Charlotte (wife of JOSIAH), XI, 400
Henson, Josiah, VIII, 89; IX, 705; XI, **400–1**; XII, 492, 960
Henson, Nancy (Gamble; wife of JOSIAH), XI, 400
Henty, George Alfred, VII, 415; XII, 824
Héon, Marie (Le Blanc), VI, 390
Hepburn, Isabel (Johnston), VI, 354
Hepburn, John, VI, 328; VII, 324; IX, **389–90**, 658; X, 26, 27
Hepburn*, Mitchell Frederick (1896–1953), XI, 584
Hepburn, William, VIII, 432, 512
Hepel, Ferdinand, XI, 836
Heracouansit. *See* Mog
Herald, James, XII, 670
Herald, Mary, VI, 417
Hérauld de Gourville, Marie (Du Pont Duvivier), II, 205; IV, 246
Hérault, Mme. *See* Moreau de Séchelles
Herbault. *See* Phélipeaux
Herbe Odoriférante. *See* Wikaskokiseyin, Abraham
Herbert, Ann. *See* Bates
Herbert, Catherine. *See* Eagan
Herbert, Gabriel, VII, 28
Herbert, Henry Howard Molyneux, 4th Earl of Carnarvon, IX, 214, 713, 714, 716; X, 192, 330, 357; XI, 300, 767; XII, 121, 242, 264, 430, 602, 650, 653
Herbert, Mary Eliza, VII, 396, 397; X, **348**
Herbert, Nicholas M., VII, 396
Herbert, Nicholas Michael, VII, 396; X, 348
Herbert, Philip, 4th Earl of Pembroke, I, 369, 405
Herbert, Sir Robert George Wyndham, XI, 770
Herbert, Sarah, VII, **396–97**, 576; X, 348
Herbert, Sir Thomas, I, 678
Herbin, Frédéric-Louis, III, 450
Herbin, Louis, IV, 733
Herbomez, Louis d', XI, 401
Herbomez, Louis-Joseph d', X, 222; XI, **401–3**; XII, 282, 283, 284, 817
Herbomez, Marie-Alexandrine d'. *See* Bricquet
Herchmer (Herkimer), Catherine (Markland), VII, 583; IX, 534
Herchmer, Eliza H. *See* Rose
Herchmer, Frances. *See* Turner
Herchmer (Herkimer), Jacob, VIII, 440
Herchmer (Herkimer), Lawrence, V, 169; VIII, 440, 441; IX, 534
Herchmer*, Lawrence William (1840–1915), XII, 427, 498, 499
Herchmer (Herkimer), William, VIII, 440, 441; XI, 317
Herchmer, William Macaulay, IX, 771; XII, 427

Herchmer, William Macauley, XII, **427–28**
Hérigault, Émilie (Peltier), VIII, 693; X, 588
Herincx, Guillaume, II, 278
Heriot, Anne Susanne. *See* Nugent
Heriot, Frederick George, VI, 343; VII, 281, **397–400**, 401; VIII, 769
Heriot, George, V, 228, 319; VI, 257, 552, 744; VII, 380, 397, 399, **400–3**, 818; VIII, 64, 605, 921; XI, 137
Heriot, J. C. A., VII, 398, 399
Heriot, John (father), VII, 400
Heriot, John, VII, 401
Heriot, Marjory (Heriot), VII, 400
Heriot, Roger, VII, 397
Herjólfr Bárdarson, I, 103
Herkimer. *See also* Herchmer
Herkimer, Johan Jost, XII, 427
Herkimer, Margaret Hickman. *See* England
Herkimer, Mary (McLean; Hamilton), IV, 505; V, 402; XI, 377
Herkimer, Nicholas, IV, 405, 694
Herlin, Claude, II, 84
Hermeindel, Joseph, VII, 890
Hernaman, Henrietta (Gisborne), XII, 373
Hernández. *See* Pérez
Heron, Andrew (brother of SAMUEL), V, 279, 419; VI, 420, 421; VIII, 69
Heron, Andrew (businessman), IX, 49
Héron, Antoine, I, 90
Heron, Francis, VI, 547; X, 495
Heron, Lucy (wife of SAMUEL), V, 420
Héron, Marie-Élisabeth (Le Moyne de Serigny et de Loire), II, 406; III, 557
Heron, Patrick, III, 9, **287–88**, 392; IV, 62, 253; V, 430
Heron, Robert, VII, 843
Heron, Samuel, V, 17, 65, 71, **419–21**, 453, 519, 597; VI, 52, 296
Heron, Sarah. *See* Ashbridge
Heron, Sarah. *See* Conott
Héroux, Georges, IX, 552; XI, 506
Héroux, Joseph, IX, 552; XI, 506
Héroux, Marie (wife of Onésime), IX, 488
Héroux, Onésime, IX, 487, 488
Herovin. *See* Irwin
Herrera y Tordesillas, Antonio de, I, 342
Herrett, Bertha C. (Mowat), XII, 768
Herries, Elizabeth (Marrant), IV, 515
Herring, Charlotte (Blake), IX, 60
Herring, Cynthia. *See* Buck
Herring, Harriet Tovell (Gooderham), XI, 358, 360
Herring, James Emerson, XII, 428
Herring, John, XII, **428–29**
Herring, Pamelia. *See* Fowler
Herring, William, XII, 428
Herrington, M. Eleanor, V, 256
Herriot. *See* Heriot
Herron, Martin, VII, 403
Herron, Mary (Herron), VII, 403
Herron, William, V, 473; VI, 691; VII, **403–4**
Herschel, Sir John Frederick William, XI, 800
Herschell, Farrer, 1st Baron Herschell, XII, 799
Herschi, Maria (Schneider), VII, 778
Herse, Jacques-Clément, IV, 532, 534; V, 243, 701; VII, 255

Hertel, Chevalier. *See* Hertel de Saint-François, Joseph-Hippolyte

Hertel, Eliza Charlotte de (Fenwick), XII, 314

Hertel, Jeanne. *See* Miriot

Hertel, Nicolas, I, 368

Hertel de Beaubassin, Catherine. *See* Jarret de Verchères

Hertel de Beaubassin, Pierre-Joseph, IV, 347

Hertel de Beaulac, Claude, II, 284

Hertel de Chambly, Charles, III, 551, 592

Hertel de Chambly, Geneviève. *See* Boucher de Grandpré

Hertel de Chambly, Michel, II, 284

Hertel de Chambly, René, II, 284, 285

Hertel de Cournoyer, Anne. *See* Goutin

Hertel de Cournoyer, Jacques, II, 284; III, 105, 233

Hertel de Cournoyer, Lambert, II, 284

Hertel de Cournoyer, Marie-Josephte (Lefebvre de Belle-feuille), IV, 445

Hertel de Cournoyer, Michel, II, 205

Hertel de Cournoyer, Thérèse (Saint-Ours), III, 577

Hertel de La Fresnière, Jacques, I, 238, **368–69**, 550; II, 282, 648

Hertel de La Fresnière, Joseph-François, I, 185, 239, 368, 369; II, **282–84,** 603, 628; III, 7, 83, 288, 289, 642; IV, 343

Hertel de La Fresnière, Madeleine (Véron de Grandmesnil), III, 642

Hertel de La Fresnière, Marguerite. *See* Thavenet

Hertel de La Fresnière, Marguerite (Crevier de Saint-François), I, 238, 369

Hertel de La Fresnière, Marguerite-Thérèse (Boucher de Niverville), III, 83; V, 97

Hertel de La Fresnière, Marie. *See* Marguerie

Hertel de La Fresnière, Marie-Charlotte. *See* Godefroy de Lintot

Hertel de La Fresnière, Marie-Madeleine (Pinard), I, 369, 550

Hertel de La Fresnière, Zacharie-François, II, 54, 283, 284, 632; III, 83, **288–89**

Hertel de Moncours, Pierre, II, 284

Hertel de Moncours, Pierre, II, **284**; III, 7

Hertel de Moncours, Thérèse. *See* Ailleboust de Périgny

Hertel de Rouville, Charlotte. *See* Labroquerie

Hertel de Rouville, Charlotte-Gabrielle. *See* Jarret de Verchères

Hertel de Rouville, Jean-Baptiste, II, 38, 54, 154, **284–86,** 296, 411, 437, 456, 495, 579, 606, 667; III, 35, 81, 104, 247, 324, 450, 493, 579; IV, 343, 770; V, 703; VIII, 939

Hertel de Rouville, Jean-Baptiste-François, II, 286; IV, 343, 653, 654

Hertel de Rouville, Jean-Baptiste-Melchior, III, 14; IV, 344; V, 236, **421–22**; VI, 341, 343, 344; VIII, 393; IX, 698

Hertel de Rouville, Jean-Baptiste-René, V, 421; VI, 342; VII, 643; VIII, **393–94**, 844

Hertel de Rouville, Jean-Baptiste-René-Jacques, VIII, 394

Hertel de Rouville, Jeanne. *See* Dubois

Hertel de Rouville, Louis-Antoine, III, 98

Hertel de Rouville, Louise-Catherine. *See* André de Leigne

Hertel de Rouville, Marie-Anne. *See* Legras

Hertel de Rouville, Marie-Anne. *See* Baudouin

Hertel de Rouville, Marie-Anne. *See* Hervieux

Hertel de Rouville, Marie-Anne-Charlotte (Brousseau), VIII, 394

Hertel de Rouville, Marie-Anne-Julie (Irumberry de Salaberry; Glen), V, 421; VI, 341; X, 698; XI, 441

Hertel de Rouville, Marie-Thérèse. *See* Gaultier

Hertel de Rouville, René-Ovide, II, 286; III, 14, 15, 285, 430, 433, 648; IV, 168, 229, 304, 316, **343–47**, 391, 492, 493, 532, 549, 602; V, 96, 146, 216, 225, 232, 383, 421, 599, 652, 737, 839, 892

Hertel de Saint-François, Elizabeth. *See* Robertson

Hertel de Saint-François, Étienne, III, **289–90**

Hertel de Saint-François, Françoise-Catherine (Irumberry de Salaberry), V, 449; VI, 341, 345

Hertel de Saint-François, Joseph (father), II, 284; III, 289; IV, 347

Hertel de Saint-François, Joseph, III, 289

Hertel de Saint-François, Joseph-Hippolyte, IV, **347–48**; V, 716

Hertel de Saint-François, Louis-Hippolyte, IV, 347; V, 716

Hertel de Saint-François, Marie-Anne. *See* Le Comte Dupré

Hertel de Saint-François, Pierre-Antoine, IV, 348

Hertel de Saint-François, Suzanne. *See* Blondeau

Hertel de Saint-Louis, Louis, II, 284

Hertford, Earl of. *See* Seymour

Hertford, Marquis of. *See* Seymour

Hervé, Édouard, XI, 339

Hervé, Marie. *See* Le Ber

Hervé (Hervet), Renée (Tibierge), III, 625

Hervé, Zacharie, V, 201

Hervey (Harvey), Alexander, XI, 389

Hervey, Ann. *See* Charleton

Hervey, John, 1st Earl of Bristol, V, 767

Hervey, Lord John Augustus, VI, 695

Hervey, Lady Louisa Carolina Isabelle (Smythe, Lady Smythe), V, 767

Hervey, Robert, X, 64

Hervey, William Jaffray, IX, 84

Hervieux, Angélique. *See* Gamelin

Hervieux, Catherine. *See* Magnan

Hervieux, Jacques (merchant), III, 290; IV, 268

Hervieux, Jacques (militia officer), VIII, 693

Hervieux, Jean-Baptiste, V, 421

Hervieux, Léonard-Jean-Baptiste, III, 290

Hervieux, Louise. *See* Quesnel Fonblanche

Hervieux, Louis-François, III, **290**, 367; IV, 268; V, 395

Hervieux, Marie-Anne (Hertel de Rouville), V, 236, 421; VI, 344; VIII, 393

Hervieux, Marie-Anne (La Corne), IV, 426; V, 791

Hervieux, Marie-Anne (Le Comte Dupré), III, 367; IV, 347, 442; V, 320, 481

Hervieux, Marie-Geneviève, named Sainte-Gertrude, III, 630

Hervieux, Marie-Jeanne (Sanguinet), IV, 698

Hervieux, Marie-Josephte (Guy), V, 394, 395; VII, 360

Hervieux, Michelle (La Corne Dubreuil), III, 333

Hervieux, Paul, VI, 664

Hervilly, Louis-Charles d', Comte d'Hervilly, VI, 619

Hesketh, Harriet Anne (Despard), VI, 202

Hespeler*, Wilhelm (1830–1921), XII, 1099

Hess, William, VI, 374

Hesse, Christina (Mills), X, 515

Hesse, Emmanuel, V, 836

Hessin, William, XII, 196

Hester, James, V, 526

Hester, John, V, 526

Hesther, Nancy, V, 526
Het, Mary (Smith), IV, 714
Hetherington, James, VIII, 541
Hett, Francis Paget, IX, 543
Hett, John Roland, XI, 374
Hétu, Leonard-Ovide, X, 600; XI, 70
Heu, *dit* Millet, Joseph, III, 541
Heuback, George, XII, 258
Heurter, Frederick Damien, VI, 100; VII, 671; VIII, 714
Heustis, Daniel D., VII, **404–6**, 924; VIII, 30, 534
Heustis, Julia Ann (Fulton), IX, 294
Heustis, Simon, VII, 404
Heward, Catherine. *See* Crookshank
Heward, Francis Harris, VII, 862
Heward, Stephen (father), VIII, 431
Heward, Stephen, VIII, 192
Hewett, Catherine Mary. *See* Biscoe
Hewett, Edward Osborne, XII, **429–31**
Hewett, Frances. *See* Thornewell
Hewett, John, XII, 429
Hewett, Sir William, XII, 429
Hewit, John, VII, 569
Hewit, Margaret (McLaren), VII, 569
Hewlett, Julia (Marling), XI, 587
Hey, Mrs. *See* Paplay
Hey, Elizabeth (Markham; Palmer; mother of WILLIAM), IV, 348
Hey, Thomas, IV, 348
Hey, William, IV, xlii, xliv, xlv, 104, 183, 229, 321, **348–50**, 725, 749, 790; V, 20, 142, 144, 145, 146, 606, 863; VI, 295, 491, 493, 615
Heyden, Lawrence, VIII, 52, 58, 849
Heylyn, Peter, I, 678
Heywood, Peter, X, 42
Hezeta, Bruno de, IV, 72, 623
Hianveu. *See also* Lafrance
Hianveu, Mathieu, III, 580
Hianveu, *dit* Lafrance. *See* Lafrance
Hianveu (Hyanveux), *dit* Lafrance, Louis-Charles, IX, 451
Hianveu (Hyanveux), *dit* Lafrance, Marie-Angélique-Émilie. *See* McDonell
Hiarse. *See* Dhiarse
Hiawatha, I, 7, 253, 254; II, xxix; III, xli; IV, lvii
Hibbard, Ashley, XI, **403–4**; XII, 62
Hibbard, Francis A., XI, 403
Hibbard, Hannah. *See* Labaree
Hibbard, Jedediah, V, **422–23**
Hibbard, Martha. *See* Porter
Hibbard, Mary (Dunn), XII, 277
Hibbard, Pliny V., XI, 403
Hibbard, Sarah Ann. *See* Lane
Hibernicus. *See* O'Reilly, Hugh
Hiché, Bernard, III, 290
Hiché, Charlotte. *See* Soupiran
Hiché, François-Gaspard, III, 292
Hiché, Henry, II, 234; III, 44, 78, **290–92**, 398, 434, 511, 596; V, 368
Hiché, Marguerite. *See* Legardeur de Saint-Pierre
Hiché, Marguerite-Françoise, named de Saint-Henri, III, 292
Hiché, Marie-Catherine. *See* Masson
Hiché, Marie-Josephte-Madeleine (Perthuis), III, 291, 292, 511; V, 368

Hick, Jannet. *See* Fisher
Hick, John, V, 320; VIII, 215
Hickey, Anna Eliza (Devlin), X, 230
Hickman, Margaret (Shaw), V, 752
Hicks, Ann. *See* Clarke
Hicks, Ann (mother of WILLIAM HENRY), XII, 431
Hicks, Elizabeth. *See* Russell
Hicks, Étienne-Hippolyte, X, 689; XI, 250
Hicks, Francis, XII, 431
Hicks, Hannah (Niles), X, 548
Hicks, Isabella. *See* Barrow
Hicks, Jane (Orr), XII, 806
Hicks, John, IV, **350–51**; V, 554; VII, 252
Hicks, M. C. (Kendall), VII, 463
Hicks, Thomas, IV, 350
Hicks, William, XII, 431
Hicks, William Henry, IX, 291; XII, 235, **431–32**
Hickson, Catherine, Lady Hickson. *See* Dow
Hickson, Sir Joseph, IX, 540; XII, **432–35**, 579
Hickson, Thomas, IV, 537; VIII, 477
Hierlihy, Timothy, VII, 714
Higginbottom, Thomas, V, 107
Higgins, Cornelius, V, 477
Higgins, David, IV, **352–53**, 551; V, 219, 263, 477, 478, 777; XI, 922
Higgins, David William, IX, 479, 480; XI, 300; XII, 241, 915
Higgins, Elizabeth. *See* Prince
Higgins, Emma Mary Philamena (O'Sullivan), XII, 811
Higgins, John, XI, 942
Higgins, Moore A., IX, 26
Higgins, William (chief constable), XI, 863
Higgins, William (merchant), XII, 126
Higginson, James, XI, 404
Higginson, Sir James Macaulay, VII, 607; VIII, 432, 632; XI, **404–5**
Higginson, Louisa. *See* Shakespeare
Higginson, Mary. *See* Macaulay
Higginson, Olivia. *See* Dobbs
Higgs, Mrs. *See* Hoerner
Highmore, Joseph, III, 674
Hil (Isle), Marie-Anne (Quirouet), VII, 718
Hilaire. *See also* Hillaire
Hilaire, Antoinette (Lombard), III, 406
Hildreth, Richard, VI, 58; IX, 351
Hildrith, Ann. *See* Wood
Hildrith, Isaac, V, **423–24**, 658; VI, 313, 319; VII, 278
Hildsley, Francis, II, 265
Hill, Aaron. *See* Kanonraron
Hill, Abigail (Masham, Baroness Masham), II, 286, 659
Hill, Alice, II, 286
Hill, Amos, XII, 1068
Hill, Angélique (Drolet), X, 260
Hill, Anne. *See* Fairbrother
Hill, Charles, VI, **319–20**, 622, 792; VIII, 704
Hill, Charles John (grand-nephew of CHARLES), VI, 319
Hill, Charles John (husband of Anne FAIRBROTHER), XII, 305, 306
Hill, Charles John Barton, XII, 306
Hill, Charles Samuel, VI, 319
Hill, Christian (Leake), II, 372
Hill, Christiana. *See* Brant
Hill, Clarissa (Todd), X, 681

Hill, David. *See* Karonghyontye
Hill, Eliza (Hamilton), XII, 404
Hill, Elizabeth. *See* Austin
Hill, Elizabeth. *See* Summerhill
Hill, Elizabeth (Lespérance), XI, 514
Hill, Elizabeth Adams (Poor), X, 590
Hill, George Stillman, IX, 147
Hill, George William, VIII, 357; XI, 75
Hill, Hannah Harriet. *See* Binney
Hill, Henry, XI, 405
Hill, Henry Aaron. *See* Kenwendeshon
Hill, Henry George, XI, **405–6**
Hill, Hester Maria (wife of HENRY GEORGE), XI, 405
Hill, Isaac. *See* Anoghsoktea
Hill, Isabella. *See* Allan
Hill, J. M., XII, 316
Hill*, James Jerome (1838–1916), XI, 476, 477, 539, 764; XII, 1031, 1058, 1095
Hill, John (brother of SAMUEL), II, 287
Hill, John (Moravian), IV, 225
Hill, John, II, 122, **286–87**, 437, 643, 651, 659, 661, 667
Hill, John, V, 27, 219, 310, 516, 568, 721, 775, 778, 825, 826, 848; VI, 108, 161, 162, 565, 566, 567, 662, 785, 786; VII, 351, **406–9**; IX, 179
Hill, Joseph, VI, 51, 52
Hill, Louisa Gordon. *See* Sheil
Hill, Margaret (Ferguson; wife of JOHN, d. 1841), VII, 406
Hill, Margaret (Morris), V, 629
Hill, Margaretta Rhoda. *See* Collins
Hill, Mary. *See* Brant
Hill, Mary Ann (Uniacke), VI, 319, 792
Hill, Nicholas Thomas, XII, 435, 436
Hill, Olivia. *See* Crook
Hill, Patrick, VI, 319
Hill, Peter (grandfather of SAMUEL), II, 287
Hill, Peter (merchant), I, 306, 450
Hill, Philip Carteret, X, 177, 395; XI, 25, 147, 620; XII, **435–39**, 1041, 1092
Hill, Priam B., XI, 583
Hill, Ralph, I, 450, 451
Hill, Rebecca (wife of CHARLES), VI, 319
Hill, Richard, II, 372
Hill, Robert (brother of CHARLES), VI, 319
Hill, Robert (father of CHARLES), VI, 319
Hill, Robert (nephew of CHARLES), VI, 319, 320
Hill, Robert Herbert, XII, 306
Hill, Roger, II, 287
Hill, Rosalie (Bridges), XII, 306
Hill, Samuel (father of JOHN, d. 1841), VII, 406
Hill, Samuel (ship's captain), VI, 351
Hill, Samuel, II, **287**
Hill, Samuel Smith, VII, 408
Hill, Sarah (mother of HENRY GEORGE), XI, 405
Hill, Sarah (mother of Sir STEPHEN JOHN), XII, 439
Hill, Sarah Ann. *See* Munnings
Hill, Sarah Mary. *See* Cross
Hill, Solomon, V, 856
Hill, Sir Stephen John, XI, 615, 635, 762; XII, 164, **439–40**, 600
Hill, Thomas, VIII, **394–96**, 803; IX, 392; X, 140
Hill, Sir Thomas Noel, VII, 317
Hill, William, XII, 439

Hill, William, I, 163, **369**, 405
Hill, William Maddox, VII, 408
Hill, Wills, 1st Earl of Hillsborough, III, 411; IV, xxxv, xxxvii, xxxviii, xlii, xliii, xliv, xlv, xlvi, 104, 202, 228, 309, 352, 428, 606, 607, 618, 634, 676, 725, 739, 788, 789; V, 142, 143, 145, 606; VI, 511
Hillaire de La Rochette, Alexandre-Robert (d'), III, 97, 300; IV, 57, 91, **353–54**
Hillaire de La Rochette, Barbe-Madeleine (Martin), IV, 354
Hillaire de La Rochette, Marie-Anne. *See* Levasseur
Hillaire de Moissacq et de La Rochette, Élisabeth. *See* Martin
Hillaire de Moissacq et de La Rochette, Charles-Robert, IV, 353
Hillerman, J. H., XII, 705
Hillier, Caroline Ann. *See* Givins
Hillier, George, V, 661; VI, 116, 497, 612, 770; VII, 315, 338, 368, 369, **409–11**, 439, 458, 494; VIII, 180, 202, 203, 515, 517, 518, 521, 597
Hillier, William, VI, 441, 442; VII, 206
Hillock, John, XII, 1119
Hills, Diana. *See* Hammersley
Hills, George, XII, 440
Hills, George, XII, 56, 79, 81, **440–43**, 552
Hills, Maria Philadelphia Louisa. *See* King
Hills, Sarah. *See* Caverly
Hills, William Henry, XII, 290
Hillsborough, Earl of. *See* Hill
Hillyer, Phoebe (Cossitt), V, 204
Hiltne, Sigmund, VI, 664
Hilton, Ann. *See* Dudley
Hilton, Ann. *See* Wilson
Hilton, Edward, II, 287
Hilton, Elvira. *See* Healy
Hilton, Henry, IX, 390
Hilton, James Henry, IX, 390
Hilton, John, VII, 359; VIII, 41, 42; IX, **390–91**; XI, 30, 499
Hilton, John Fisher, IX, 390
Hilton, William, VIII, 41; IX, 390; XI, 499
Hilton, Winthrop, II, 288
Hilton, Winthrop, II, **287–88**, 452, 543
Hilyard, Henry, X, 349
Hilyard, Margaret. *See* Miles
Hilyard, Matilda. *See* Dyer
Hilyard, Thomas, X, 349
Hilyard, Thomas, X, **349**
Hilyard, Thomas K., X, 349
Himsworth, Louisa. *See* Morrison
Himsworth, William Alfred, X, 436; XI, 204
Hince (Hanse), Joseph, VIII, 287
Hince (Hanse), Pelagie (Faribault), VIII, 287
Hinchelwood, Archibald, IV, 631
Hincks, Anne. *See* Boult
Hincks, Ellen (Ready), XI, 415
Hincks, Emily Louisa, Lady Hincks. *See* Delatre
Hincks, Sir Francis, VII, 32, 42, 43, 158, 164, 227, 231, 372, 860, 861, 894; VIII, 27, 43, 48, 49, 50, 51, 53, 54, 56, 57, 138, 205, 206, 230, 255, 256, 269, 371, 401, 540, 587, 629, 698, 707, 745, 789, 798, 799, 815, 822, 823, 849, 896, 932, 933, 964, 965; IX, 55, 56, 71, 76, 77, 83, 90, 91, 108, 212, 259, 344, 346, 371, 372, 400, 405, 442, 443, 444, 445, 446, 447, 448, 449, 464, 471, 506, 507,

524, 525, 526, 529, 569, 570, 575, 576, 618, 680, 685, 688, 689, 690, 701, 706, 735, 741, 776, 788, 844; X, 24, 55, 92, 93, 94, 95, 96, 97, 119, 125, 126, 127, 129, 134, 143, 144, 159, 169, 170, 224, 311, 314, 321, 325, 350, 355, 359, 441, 463, 464, 468, 508, 512, 536, 548, 620, 632, 642, 645, 654, 656, 708, 715, 724, 725, 727; XI, 7, 11, 12, 41, 127, 160, 166, 180, 227, 232, 247, 281, 282, 366, **406–16**, 517, 518, 542, 576, 616, 617, 618, 677, 698, 712, 713, 714, 730, 768, 781, 788, 789, 791, 822, 851, 852, 871, 883, 927, 939, 946; XII, 71, 72, 73, 89, 146, 171, 184, 214, 248, 261, 349, 350, 392, 393, 432, 487, 488, 604, 614, 615, 676, 683, 967, 1056, 1057, 1123

Hincks, Maria Ann. *See* Yandell
Hincks, Martha Anne, Lady Hincks. *See* Stewart
Hincks, Sarah Maria (wife of WILLIAM), X, 350
Hincks, Thomas, X, 536
Hincks, Thomas Dix, X, 349; XI, 406
Hincks, William, X, **349–50**; XI, 406, 541; XII, 540
Hind*, Henry Youle (1823–1908), VIII, 790; IX, 319, 804; X, 291; XI, 416, 417, 441, 553, 662, 712; XII, 15, 1110, 1111
Hind, Sarah. *See* Youle
Hind, Thomas, XI, 416
Hind, William George Richardson, XI, **416–18**
Hindenlang, Charles, VII, **411–12**, 514; X, 420, 546; XII, 761
Hine, John, V, 675
Hingston, Margaret Josephine. *See* Macdonald
Hingston*, Sir William Hales (1829–1907), X, 138; XII, 555, 615
Hingue de Puygibault, Marguerite-Barbe (Rocbert de La Morandière; Pécaudy de Contrecœur), IV, 618
Hinman, Benjamin, V, 29
Hins. *See* Ainsse
Hinton, Ann (Mott), V, 613; VI, 408
Hinton, Margaret. *See* Merritt
Hinton, Sir Thomas, I, 369
Hinton, William, I, 369, 370
Hinton, William, I, 93, **369–70**
Hinxman, Helen Harriet Gordon (Osborn), X, 562
Hiou, Anne, I, 116
Hipps, George, V, 385
Hiraque, Angélique (Pambrun), VII, 671
Hiriart, Jean, IV, 69
Hiriberry, Joannis de, II, **288**, 610
Hirouin. *See* Irwin
Hirst, Mary (Pepperrell, Lady Pepperrell), III, 505
Hispanioli. *See* Spagniolini
Hitchcock, Alice (Gowan), X, 313
Hitsman, John Mackay, V, 798; VI, 618; VIII, 465
Hixon, Ann. *See* Brodie
Hixon, Thomas, XII, 432
Hiyoua. *See* Wikinanish
Hoare, Catherine Edwards. *See* Hankinson
Hoare, Mary Jane (Kinnaird), IX, 820
Hobart, George Vere, VIII, 741
Hobart, Janet. *See* Maclean of Coll
Hobart, John Henry, IX, 759; XI, 388
Hobart, Robert, 4th Baron Hobart and 4th Earl of Buckinghamshire, V, 319, 542; VI, 271, 485, 641; VIII, xxvii
Hobbé, Françoise (Roy, *dit* Châtellerault), II, 584

Hobbes (Hobbs), Sarah (Gerrish), IV, 290, 291
Hobbes, Thomas, V, 486
Hobby, Ann (mother of Sir CHARLES), II, 288
Hobby, Sir Charles, II, 122, 238, **288–90**, 651; III, 3, 682
Hobby, John, II, 289
Hobby, Sir William, II, 288
Hobhouse, John Cam, 1st Baron Broughton, VIII, 603
Hobkirk, William Hamilton, XII, 600
Hobson, Benjamin, VI, **320**
Hobson, Mary Ann (Swabey), X, 669
Hobson, William Robert, XII, 954, 955
Hoby, Elizabeth, Lady Hoby. *See* Cooke
Hochstetter, J. G., IV, 580
Hocquart, Anne-Catherine. *See* La Lande
Hocquart, Gilles, II, 60, 66, 71, 95, 96, 97, 210, 235, 253, 269, 317, 373, 374, 380, 413, 447, 530, 531, 541, 542, 606, 617; III, 7, 14, 15, 26, 27, 38, 48, 50, 55, 56, 63, 64, 67, 74, 75, 76, 77, 78, 83, 99, 107, 115, 118, 135, 137, 139, 140, 145, 146, 153, 154, 159, 161, 164, 168, 178, 179, 180, 194, 202, 203, 205, 224, 225, 226, 227, 228, 237, 238, 239, 246, 249, 263, 270, 281, 284, 291, 299, 307, 315, 334, 339, 340, 344, 349, 350, 351, 352, 353, 354, 359, 377, 390, 399, 412, 433, 434, 444, 445, 456, 473, 482, 486, 490, 519, 520, 524, 525, 539, 540, 541, 550, 555, 557, 579, 580, 592, 593, 602, 603, 604, 608, 612, 617, 621, 631, 632, 637, 643, 647, 679; IV, 45, 61, 63, 64, 75, 76, 88, 95, 124, 167, 200, 209, 221, 236, 253, 264, 265, 284, 289, 318, 319, 344, **354–65**, 376, 432, 463, 464, 465, 473, 474, 488, 517, 539, 590, 601, 624, 636, 651, 690, 709, 720, 749, 750; V, 90; VIII, 258; XI, 175
Hocquart, Jean-Hyacinthe (father), IV, 354
Hocquart, Jean-Hyacinthe, IV, 354, 355
Hocquart, Jean-Hyacinthe-Louis-Emmanuel, IV, 354
Hocquart, Marie-Françoise. *See* Michelet Du Cosnier
Hodder, Edward, X, 350
Hodder, Edward Mulberry, IX, 707; X, 39, 84, **350–51**; XI, 855, 917; XII, 11, 106
Hodder, Frances. *See* Tench
Hodder, Geraldine M. L. (Stewart), XI, 855
Hodder, Mary (mother of EDWARD MULBERRY), X, 350
Hodge, Archibald, XI, 846
Hodge, Charles, XII, 202, 660
Hodge, Thomas, XI, 423
Hodges, Charles Howard, IV, 30
Hodges, James, X, **351–52**; XI, 510, 557; XII, 963
Hodgins*, John George (1821–1912), IX, 164; XI, 222, 223, 368, 587, 794
Hodgins, Thomas, X, 336
Hodgkin, Thomas, VIII, 441; IX, 162
Hodgkins, Mary (Bailey), V, 47
Hodgkinson, Mr (daguerreotypist), VII, 900
Hodgson, Caroline. *See* Goodwin
Hodgson, Edward Jarvis, XI, 76
Hodgson, Fanny. *See* McDonell
Hodgson, Frances Anne Dover (Hensley), XII, 425
Hodgson, George Wright, XI, 76
Hodgson, J. E., XI, 297
Hodgson, John, VIII, 922
Hodgson, John, V, 394, 712; VI, **320–21**, 794
Hodgson, Mary (Wade), VII, 892
Hodgson, Rebecca. *See* Robinson
Hodgson, Robert, X, 352

Hodgson, Robert, V, 28, **424–25**, 516, 720; VII, 76, 414, 511
Hodgson, Sir Robert, V, 425, 721; VII, 202; VIII, 297, 376, 430, 531, 563, 564; IX, 474; X, 186, 265, **352–53**, 461; XI, 528, 704; XII, 166, 417, 425, 841, 856, 910
Hodgson, Thomas, V, 679
Hodiau, Urbaine (Brossard), II, 105
Hodiau, *dit* Lafosse, Sébastien, II, 105
Hodiesne, Gervais, III, **292**; IV, 200
Hodiesne, Julien, III, 292
Hodiesne, Marguerite. *See* Lareau
Hodiesne, Renée. *See* Hubert
Hoek, Sander van, VIII, 925
Hoeootoerock (Junius), VI, 753, 754; VII, 324
Hoerner, Miss (Higgs), VIII, 396, 397
Hoerner, David-Balthazar, VIII, 397
Hoerner, Marguerite. *See* Chanel
Hoerner, Olympe (Tanner), VIII, **396–98**
Hoffman, John William, III, 513; IV, 780
Hoffmann, Charlotte. *See* Mansfield
Hoffmann, Matthias Francis, VI, 303; VII, 22, 391; VIII, **398–401**
Hogan, Hugh, V, 139
Hogan, John, VI, 694
Hogan, John Sheridan, VIII, **401–2**, 871; XI, 618, 939
Hogan, Madeline Wharton. *See* Metcalf
Hogan, Margaret (Gowan), X, 309
Hogan, Maria Julia (Wells), XI, 914
Hogan, Patrick, XI, 465
Hogan, Timothy, VII, 293, 294, 631
Hogarth, Catherine (Dickens), XI, 261
Hogarth, William, VIII, 14; X, 413
Hogg, James, VII, 335; IX, 391, 429
Hogg, James, VII, 14; VIII, 157, 394, 395; IX, 39, **391–93**
Hogg, Simon Jackson, XI, **418–19**
Hogg, Thomas, IX, 392
Hogsett, Aaron, VIII, **402–3**; IX, 393
Hogsett, George James, VIII, 403; IX, **393–94**, 820, 846; XI, 243, 433; XII, 956
Hogue, Marguerite (Charron), VII, 167
Hogue, Simon, VII, 60, 167; VIII, 763
Hoit, Albert Gallatin, VII, 684; VIII, 357, 833; IX, 850
Holbrook, D. B., XII, 374
Holbrook, Grace. *See* Hailes
Holbrook, James, VII, **412–13**
Holbrook, Sally (Knowlton), IX, 433
Holburne, Francis, III, xxv, 72, 93, 132, 209, 293; IV, 326, 327, 597; V, 280
Holcroft, Thomas, VI, 240
Holden, James, XII, 43, 44
Holden, Martha (Lyon), IV, 490
Holden, Thomas, X, 632
Holderness, Earl of. *See* D'Arcy
Holdright, Mary Jane (Little), XII, 563
Holdsworth, Ann (Newman), V, 625
Holdsworth, Arthur (father of ARTHUR), II, 290
Holdsworth, Arthur (son of ARTHUR), II, 291
Holdsworth, Arthur, II, **290–91**, 348, 439, 564
Holdsworth, Elizabeth. *See* Lane
Holdsworth, Mary (Newman), V, 625
Holdsworth, Mathew, XII, 121
Holdsworth, Robert, II, 290, 291
Holiday, Henry, XII, 490

Holl, Ann. *See* Lewis
Holl, Ann. *See* Smart
Holl, John M., IX, 394
Holl, John Myrie, VIII, 531; IX, 28, 191, 376, **394–96**; XI, 369, 527, 665, 940; XII, 925
Hollahan, James, VI, 409
Holland, Baron. *See* Fox
Holland, Earl of. *See* Rich
Holland, Anthony Henry, IV, 343; V, 612, 853, 854; VI, **321–23**, 508; VII, 22; VIII, 705, 922; IX, 54; XII, 312
Holland, Augustus Edward Crevier, XII, 417, 452
Holland, Eliza. *See* Merkel
Holland, Frederick Braham, VII, 414
Holland, Gertrude. *See* Hasse
Holland, Henry, V, 426
Holland, John, IX, 278
Holland, John Frederick, V, 335, 426, 428, 541; VI, 162, 414, 448, 566, 567, 663; VII, 96, **413–16**; VIII, 825
Holland, Margaret. *See* Appledore
Holland, Marie-Joseph. *See* Rollet
Holland, Mary. *See* Mortimer
Holland, Mary Emily. *See* Tissable
Holland, Matthias (Matthew), VI, 321
Holland, Philip John, VI, 322; VIII, 922; IX, 54, 186; X, 539
Holland, Samuel Johannes, III, 274, 673; IV, 79, 161, 162, 163, 552, 561, 570, 613, 716; V, 101, 149, 183, 222, 255, 378, **425–29**, 457, 499, 552, 589, 773, 834, 873, 874, 887, 892, 899; VI, 134, 193, 223, 269; VII, 95, 96, 413, 414, 811; XI, 55
Holland, Samuel John, VII, 415
Holland, Samuel Lester, V, 428
Holland, Theana (Fowell), IX, 278
Holles. *See* Pelham-Holles
Holloway, Mrs. *See* Waldron
Holloway, John, V, 360; VI, 176, **323–24**, 784; VII, 764, 765
Holloway, Robert, VI, 323
Holloway, William Cuthbert Elphinstone, VIII, 101; X, 404
Hollows, Catherine. *See* Tutty
Holly, Elizabeth (Coy), VII, 215
Holly, James Theodore, VIII, 90
Holly, Jesse, VI, 611
Hollywood, Ruth (Almon; Nash), V, 23
Holman, Alfred, XI, 419
Holman, Benjamin Phillips, XI, 419
Holman, Blanche. *See* Bradshaw
Holman, George W., XI, 419
Holman, Harriet. *See* Jacobs
Holman, Horatio, XII, 444
Holman, James, XII, 443
Holman, James Henry, XII, 413, **443–44**
Holman, Julia, XI, 419
Holman, Mary Ann. *See* Gover
Holman, Samuel, XII, 443
Holman, Sarah (Dalton), XI, **419–20**
Holman, William, II, 590
Holmes, Andrew Fernando, VI, 111; VII, 25, 26, 751, 809, 824, 914; VIII, 62, **403–5**; IX, 396; XI, 148, 271; XII, 232
Holmes, Anna. *See* Bugbee
Holmes, Arabella (Larue; Bellingham), XII, 88
Holmes, Benjamin, VI, 111; VII, 26; VIII, 403, 542; IX,

**396–97**; X, 321, 625, 722; XI, 61, 237, 850, 851; XII, 214, 988

Holmes, Charles, III, 55, 209, **293–94**, 669; IV, 699, 701

Holmes, Christina. *See* Fraser

Holmes, Christy. *See* Monroe

Holmes, Delia (Montferrand), VIII, 406

Holmes, Élisabeth. *See* Arnoldi

Holmes, Elkanah, VI, **324–25**

Holmes, George (half brother of JOHN, 1799–1852), VIII, 409, 457; XII, 297

Holmes, George (uncle of Malachy SALTER), IV, 695

Holmes, Harriett Nice (King), IX, 428

Holmes, Helen (McKay), XII, 641

Holmes, Henry, III, 293

Holmes, James, VII, 894

Holmes, Jane (Grant; Blackwood), V, 85, 86

Holmes, John (father of JOHN, 1799–1852), VIII, 405, 457

Holmes, John (father of JOHN, 1789–1876), X, 353

Holmes, John (rebaptized Jean), V, 295; VII, 502, 527; VIII, 212, 214, 215, **405–9**, 681, 682, 911; IX, 101, 117, 250; X, 202, 504, 611; XI, 177; XII, 297, 731, 1016, 1065

Holmes, John, X, **353–54**

Holmes, Juliet. *See* Wadsworth

Holmes, Marcus, XI, 929

Holmes, Margaret. *See* Macnider

Holmes, Maria Margaret (Day), XI, 237

Holmes, Mary (Holmes), III, 293

Holmes, Mary Ann (wife of WILLIAM, d. 1834), VI, 325

Holmes, Nathaniel, IV, 695

Holmes, Oliver Wendell, XII, 288

Holmes, Robert, III, 527

Holmes, Samuel, VII, 213

Holmes, Sarah (Etter), VI, 242

Holmes, Sarah (Salter), IV, 695

Holmes*, Simon Hugh (1831–1919), X, 353, 383; XI, 620; XII, 218, 437, 765, 1041, 1092

Holmes, Susan, named Mother Sainte-Croix, VIII, 406

Holmes, Susan (McDonell; Wilkes), XI, 923

Holmes, Susanna. *See* Scott

Holmes, Thomas, VI, 111; VIII, 403; IX, 396

Holmes, William, IV, **365–66**; V, 451, 561, 603, 656; VI, 775; VIII, 341

Holmes, William, V, 502; VI, **325–27**; VIII, 682; X, 564; XII, 88

Holroyd, George Sowley, VIII, 150

Holroyd, John Baker, 1st Earl of Sheffield, V, 21, 149, 491

Holstein. *See* Staël-Holstein

Holt, Charles A., VIII, 675; IX, 15

Holt, Charles Gates, XII, 464

Holt*, Sir Herbert Samuel (1856–1941), XII, 828

Holt, John, IV, 483

Holt, John Henderson, XII, 889, 890

Holtby, Mary (Jones) (Pamekezhegooqua), VII, 455

Holton, Anner. *See* Phillips

Holton, Aurora (Mills), X, 516

Holton, Charles P., XII, 322

Holton, Eliza. *See* Forbes

Holton, Ezra, X, 354

Holton, Luther Hamilton, VIII, 965, 966; IX, 268, 274, 397, 422, 492; X, 101, **354–58**, 466, 708, 723, 724, 725; XI, 5, 41, 157, 192, 211, 233, 389, 411, 439, 521, 557, 624, 677, 680, 722, 781; XII, 214, 254, 261, 262, 263,

279, 350, 351, 391, 392, 393, 394, 420, 649, 650, 651, 658, 683, 693

Holyland, Mary (Smyth), VII, 819

Holyoke, Edward Augustus, VI, 564

Holyoke, Mary (Arnold), II, 25

Homasset, Marie-Catherine (Hecquet de La Cloche), III, 548

Home, Alexander, 9th Earl of Home, XI, 43

Home, Alexandrina (Weld), VIII, 924

Home, Lady Charlotte (Baillie Hamilton), XI, 43

Home, David, VIII, 226

Home, Everard, VII, 600

Home, Sir George, I, 54, 311

Home, William, XII, 279, 280

Homem, Lopo, I, 304

Homer, XII, 250, 515, 961

Homer, Elizabeth (Strickland), IX, 767; XI, 857; XII, 995

Homer, Elizabeth B. *See* White

Homer, John, IV, 593

Homer, John, VII, **416–17**

Homer, Joseph, VII, 416

Homer, Joshua Attwood Reynolds, X, 530

Homer, Margaret (Coffin), XI, 197

Homer, Mary. *See* Atwood

Homer, Nancy (Crocker; wife of JOHN), VII, 416

Homfray, Emily Hettie Sabine (Pinsent), XII, 843

Homier, Sophie (Papin; David), IX, 615; XI, 235

Hommé, Eugène d', XII, 411

Honarreennha (Louis), I, 185

Honatteniate, I, **370–71**, 404, 548

Hone*, Jules (1833–1913), XII, 471

Honey, Christopher, VII, 121

Honey, Elizabeth. *See* Burrows

Honey, John Burrows. *See* Burrows, John

Honeyman, David, VIII, 895; XI, **420–21**

Honeyman, James, II, 663

Honeyman, Mary. *See* Donaldson

Honon. *See* Galiffet

Honorat, Jacques-Christophe, IX, 397

Honorat, Jean-Baptiste, VII, 799; VIII, 66, 572; IX, **397–98**; XI, 169, 396

Honorat, Marie-Thérèse. *See* Bremond

Hood, Andrew William, XII, 1118

Hood, Catherine. *See* Roe

Hood, Mary (Douglas), XII, 265

Hood, Richard, VI, 327

Hood, Robert, VI, **327–29**; VII, 324; IX, 389, 658; X, 26, 27

Hood, Samuel, 1st Viscount Hood, IV, 339; VII, 196

Hook, Hannah (Sanborn), X, 641

Hook, Theodore Edward, IX, 350, 353

Hook, Walter Farquhar, XII, 440

Hooke, Delia (Berton; Fitzgerald), VII, 73

Hooker, Alfred, X, 354

Hooker, Sir Joseph Dalton, IX, 660; XI, 544; XII, 541, 542

Hooker, Philip, V, 678

Hooker, Sir William Jackson, VI, 218, 219, 220, 222; VII, 599; IX, 162, 660, 665, 742; X, 81, 82; XI, 662, 885; XII, 539, 540, 541

Hoolson. *See* Œhulhtzœn

Hooper, Augustus Frederick Garland, IX, 680; XI, 421, 422, 853

Hooper, Catherine (Butcher), XI, 136

Hooper, Cavalier, XI, 421
Hooper, Cynthia. *See* Ham
Hooper, Edmund John Glyn, XI, **421–22**
Hooper, Isabel. *See* Richmond
Hooper, John, IX, **399**
Hooper, John G., XI, 421
Hooper, Sarah, XI, 421
Hooper, William, IV, 714
Hooper, William Henry, XI, 421
Hoops, Adam, VI, 30
Hoore. *See* Hore
Hoosiens, III, 355
Hope, Adam, VIII, 748; X, 68; XI, 128, 130, **422–24**
Hope, Charles, 1st Earl of Hopetoun, IV, 366
Hope, Charles, Lord Granton, VII, 245
Hope, Charles James, XI, 423
Hope, Christian. *See* Bogue
Hope, George, XI, 422; XII, 103
Hope, Sir George, VIII, 771; IX, 691
Hope, Hannah. *See* White
Hope, Henry, IV, 323, 324, 330, **366–68**, 694, 716; V, 56, 96, 148, 149, 156, 214, 283, 343, 523, 576, 760, 901; VI, 150
Hope, Isabella (Beers), XII, 75
Hope, Sir James, XI, 592
Hope, John, VII, 599
Hope, Mary E. (Beers), XII, 75
Hope, Peter, VII, 76
Hope, Robert, XI, 422
Hope, Sarah. *See* Jones
Hope, Thomas, VIII, 63
Hope, Thomas Charles, X, 444
Hopetoun, Earl of. *See* Hope
Hope Weir, Anne. *See* Vane
Hope Weir, Charles, IV, 366
Hopkins, Mrs (of Liverpool, N.S.), VIII, 63
Hopkins, Caleb, VIII, 55, 854; IX, 718; X, 126, 169, 316, **358–60**
Hopkins, Edward Martin, VIII, 816, 818; X, 486; XI, 556
Hopkins, Elizabeth (Eastman), IX, 232
Hopkins, Frances. *See* Davis
Hopkins, Frances Anne. *See* Beechey
Hopkins, Hannah. *See* Green
Hopkins*, John Castell (1864–1923), XII, 203
Hopkins, Mark, XI, 292
Hopkins, Mary. *See* Swayze
Hopkins, Mary (Storm), XII, 991
Hopkins, Rachel (Green), X, 316, 358
Hopkins, Samuel, V, 519
Hopkins, Samuel, II, **291–92**
Hopkins, Sarah (Goldthwait), III, 259
Hopkins, Silas, X, 358
Hopkins, W. R., VII, 160
Hopkins, Warwick M., XII, 631
Hopkirk, James, VII, 859; VIII, 652
Hopper, Albert, VII, 823
Hopper, Anna. *See* Sparling
Hopper, Arthur, X, 360
Hopper, Arthur, X, **360**
Hopper, Emma. *See* Smith
Hopper, Jane (Sproule; Didsbury), VII, 823
Hopper, John Elisha Peck, XII, **444–45**
Hopper, Martha (Crandall), VIII, 179

Hopper, Mary (Miles), XII, 736
Hopper, Robert, XII, 444
Hopper, Sara (mother of ARTHUR), X, 360
Hopper, Sarah. *See* Peck
Hoppner, Henry Parkyns, VI, **329–30**; VIII, 771, 772; IX, 692
Hoppner, John, VI, 329
Hoppner, Phoebe. *See* Wright
Hopson, Anne (Bennett), III, 295
Hopson, Grace, III, 295
Hopson, Peregrine Thomas, III, 136, 166, 183, 212, 283, **294–95**, 362, 363, 364, 405, 417, 513, 583, 586, 604; IV, xxv, 50, 110, 169, 170, 313, 512, 526, 560, 562, 581, 780
Hopsonn, Sir Thomas, III, 294
Hopton, Ralph, Lord Hopton, I, 653
Horace, VI, 84; VIII, 88; XII, 16, 961
Horan, Edward John, VIII, 704; IX, 118, 201, 207; X, 105, **360–61**, 488, 542, 561; XI, 170, 171, 694; XII, 153, 519, 594, 599, 1017, 1018
Horan, Eleanore. *See* Cannon
Horan, Frances Agnes (Maguire), X, 488
Horan, Gordian, VIII, 581; X, 360
Horan, Henrietta (Murray), X, 541
Horcasitas. *See* Güemes
Horden, Elizabeth. *See* Oke
Horden, Ellen Hudson, XII, 446
Horden, John, VII, 277; XII, **445–47**
Horden, Sarah. *See* Seward
Horden, William, XII, 445
Hore, Richard, I, 5, 19, **371–72**, 565, 566
Horehouasse. *See* Ourehouare
Horetzky, Charles George, XII, **447–48**
Horetzky, Felix, XII, 447
Horetzky, Mary Julia. *See* Ryan
Horetzky, Sophia. *See* Robertson
Horn, Kate M. (Buckland), XII, **448–49**
Horn, Philipina Maria (Phébé) (Arnoldi), V, 36; VI, 14; VII, 25
Hornby, Geoffrey Thomas Phipps, IX, 36
Horné, Catherine de. *See* Duval
Horne, Isabella Leah. *See* Gamble
Horné, Jacques de, II, 292
Horne, Robert Charles, VI, 164, 265; VII, 318, **417–18**, 462, 519; VIII, 642; IX, 662
Horné, *dit* Laneuville, Jacques de, II, **292**
Horné, *dit* Laneuville, Marie de. *See* Sivadier
Horner. *See also* Hornor
Horner, Samuel, IV, 483
Horning, Hannah (Land), IX, 454
Horning, Josephine (Rymal), XII, 934
Hornor, Isaac, VI, 330
Hornor, Mary (mother of THOMAS), VI, 330
Hornor, Olive. *See* Baker
Hornor, Thomas, V, 733; VI, 11, **330–31**, 632
Horsey, Edward, VIII, 761; IX, 164
Horsey, Edwin Ernest, VIII, 326
Horsford, Eben Norton, V, 885
Hort, Fenton John Anthony, XII, 660
Horton. *See also* Wilmot-Horton
Horton, Amos, VI, 253; VIII, 120
Horton, William, VI, 706; X, 644
Horwood, Olivia (Pack), VIII, 673

Hosier, Mary (Knight), VIII, 477
Hoskin, Alfred, XI, 144
Hoskin, John, XII, 586
Hoskin, Maria Elizabeth. *See* Blake
Hoskins, John Box, IV, 568; V, 388, 411, 586
Hosmer*, Charles Rudolph (1851–1927), XI, 814; XII, 801
Hosmer, George, XII, 408, 797
Hossack, Agnes Simpson (Cassils), XII, 167
Hosta (Dosta), Monsieur d' (soldier), II, 603
Hoste, Sir William, XI, 912
Hosterman, Thomas, VI, 243
Hostler, Mary. *See* McRae
Hot Ash. *See* Ogenheratarihiens
Hotchig, III, 406
Hoteouate. *See* Otreouti
Hôtesse. *See* Otis
Hotesse, Marie-Anne. *See* Caron
Hotham, William, 1st Baron Hotham, IV, 160
Hotman, François, I, 42, 43
Hotman, Suzanne (Manthet d'Argentenay; Ailleboust), I, 42, 43
Hot Powder. *See* Ogenheratarihiens
Hotrehouati. *See* Otreouti
Hotsinoñhyahta?, IV, **368**, 596, 735
Houde, Angèle. *See* Descoteaux
Houde, Antoine, XI, 424
Houde, Catherine. *See* Dougherty
Houde, Célestin, IX, 795
Houde, Frédéric, XI, 330, **424–25**; XII, 304
Houdet, Antoine, VI, 331
Houdet, Antoine-Jacques, VI, 84, **331–32**; VII, 495, 655, 759; VIII, 240, 242, 406, 728
Houdet, Jacquine (Houdet), VI, 331
Houdin, Antoine-Pierre, IV, 127
Houdin, Catherine. *See* Thunay, *dit* Dufresne
Houdin, Elizabeth, III, 296
Houdin, Jean-Michel, named Father Potentien, III, 240, **295–97**; IV, 103
Houdin, John, III, 296
Houdin, Kitty, III, 296
Houdon, Madeleine (Le Verrier), II, 433
Houel, Louis, I, 192, 386, 590
Hough, Charles, VIII, 329
Hough, Franklin Benjamin, V, 40, 41; XI, 522
Hough, William, VI, 373
Houghton, Charles Frederick, XII, **449–51**
Houghton, Marie (Brent), XII, 450
Houghton, Marion. *See* Dunsmuir
Houghton, Richard, VII, 911
Houliston, Agnes. *See* Mercer
Houliston, George Baillie, X, 34; XII, **451–52**
Houliston, Isabella. *See* Baptist
Houliston, John, IX, 487; XII, 451
Houliston, Thomas, XII, 451
Hounsfield, Mary (Bettridge), X, 59
Hounsom, John, V, 373
House, Abigail (Doggett), IV, 219
Household (Cameron), Elizabeth (Wood), VII, 921
Houssart, Hubert, II, 371, 372
Houston*, William (1844–1931), XII, 1113
Houstoun, Mary Neilson (Cochrane), XII, 201
Houstoun, Wallace, XII, 290
Houtreaouti. *See* Outreouti

Hovey, Ebenezer, VI, 174
Hovey, Mary (Huntington), XI, 437
Hovey, Percilla (Dimock), IV, 217
How, David, III, 297
How, Deborah (Cottnam), V, **429–30**; VI, 777
How, Edward, III, 8, 34, 136, **297–98**, 326, 416, 417, 421, 514, 583, 665; IV, 455; V, 429, 430; VI, 778
How, Elizabeth. *See* D'Eath
How, Henry, X, **361–62**; XI, 420
How, Louisa Mary. *See* Watkins
How, Marie-Madeleine. *See* Winniett
How, Thomas, X, 361
Howard, Dr. *See* Beach, Thomas Billis
Howard, Alan Campbell Palmer, XI, 429
Howard, Benjamin, VI, 166
Howard, Beulah (Stephens), XI, 850
Howard, Charles, 2nd Baron Howard and 1st Earl of Nottingham, I, 668
Howard, Emily. *See* Severs
Howard, George William Frederick, 7th Earl of Carlisle, VIII, 831
Howard, Henry, XI, 420, **425–26**, 744, 750
Howard, James Scott, VI, 474, 728; VIII, 28, 84; IX, **399–400**
Howard, Jemima Frances. *See* Meikle
Howard, John (father of JAMES SCOTT), IX, 399
Howard, John (son of JOSEPH), IV, 369, 403; V, 684
Howard, John George, VII, 223, 495; VIII, 10, 178, 281, 432, 486, 872, 876, 959, 960; X, 270; XI, 225, **426–28**; XII, 404, 792, 1123
Howard, Joseph, IV, 348, **369–70**, 403, 759; V, 20, 21, 142, 727, 741
Howard, Margaret. *See* Kent
Howard, Margaret (Seaman; wife of PETER), VII, 419
Howard, Marguerite. *See* Réaume
Howard, Lady Maria (Carleton, Baroness Dorchester), V, 141
Howard, Mary. *See* Scott
Howard, Mary Frances. *See* Chipman
Howard, Matthew, VII, 419
Howard, Matthew Munsel, VII, 420, 459, 695; VIII, 305, 426; IX, 99
Howard, Nannie. *See* Melville
Howard, Peter, V, 857; VI, 215, 656; VII, **418–20**, 439, 453, 795; VIII, 340
Howard (Bagot), Richard, VII, 31
Howard, Robert, XI, 428
Howard, Robert Jared Bliss, XI, 429
Howard, Robert Palmer, XI, 149, **428–29**; XII, 314
Howard, Salome. *See* McLean
Howard, Sarah. *See* Munsel
Howard*, Thomas (1845–1903), XI, 194; XII, 33
Howard, Thomas, 2nd Earl of Arundel, I, 241
Howard, Thomas, 2nd Earl of Effingham, V, 140, 145
Howard, Thomas, Earl of Surrey and 3rd Duke of Norfolk, I, 566
Howard, Thomas, 4th Duke of Norfolk, XI, 427
Howard, Thomas S., XI, 474
Howard, William, IV, 78; V, 129; VI, 317
Howatt, Cornelius, XII, 417, **452–53**
Howatt, Ellen. *See* Miller
Howatt, Helen (Bell), XII, 453
Howatt, James, XII, 452

Howatt, Jane. *See* Bell

Howatt, Nelson, XII, 453

Howe, Alexander, IV, 627; V, **430–31**; VI, 33, 34, 129

Howe, Caleb (father), V, 740

Howe, Caleb, V, 740

Howe, Catherine Susan Ann. *See* McNab

Howe, Elias, XII, 1088

Howe, Elizabeth (Sedgwick), I, 604

Howe, George Augustus, 3rd Viscount Howe, III, 462; IV, 4, 5, 85, 278

Howe, Helen McKellar. *See* Bontein

Howe, Jemima. *See* Sawtelle

Howe, John (son of JOHN), VI, 322, 334, 335; X, 362

Howe, John (spy), VI, 332

Howe, John, IV, 343; VI, 157, 242, 301, 322, **332–35**, 508, 782; VII, 763, 875; IX, 54; X, 362

Howe, Joseph, VI, 332

Howe, Joseph, V, 692, 854; VI, 171, 332, 333, 334, 335, 508, 777, 778, 782; VII, 14, 21, 22, 23, 24, 25, 82, 83, 84, 85, 107, 143, 144, 269, 270, 308, 392, 437, 441, 492, 537, 540, 609, 610, 685, 803, 804, 811, 815, 858, 875, 876, 934; VIII, 74, 75, 160, 168, 169, 193, 194, 222, 300, 334, 335, 348, 356, 383, 392, 415, 416, 417, 460, 569, 603, 656, 657, 658, 732, 756, 891, 892, 903, 904, 905, 906, 929, 956, 957, 958; IX, 7, 37, 40, 54, 130, 154, 176, 177, 184, 225, 226, 227, 244, 281, 294, 295, 349, 350, 352, 353, 355, 382, 388, 426, 427, 531, 567, 601, 602, 723, 724, 731, 739, 747, 748, 786, 787, 791, 822, 828, 830, 839; X, 7, 13, 36, 71, 85, 158, 159, 160, 172, 189, 232, 285, 287, 353, **362–70**, 384, 385, 386, 387, 438, 441, 456, 457, 458, 460, 468, 476, 497, 539, 540, 551, 591, 592, 652, 664, 679, 685, 714; XI, 22, 23, 24, 30, 46, 74, 106, 147, 148, 155, 156, 197, 215, 278, 279, 280, 308, 309, 347, 373, 398, 399, 412, 442, 462, 502, 525, 572, 573, 620, 621, 700, 709, 710, 717, 741, 754, 768, 772, 831, 835, 847, 848, 925, 926, 927, 945, 946, 947; XII, 13, 31, 32, 34, 193, 218, 229, 231, 238, 239, 313, 350, 354, 368, 374, 406, 438, 481, 562, 564, 600, 603, 683, 712, 729, 741, 858, 871, 963, 966, 1039, 1040, 1053, 1054, 1056, 1059

Howe, Margaret Ann. *See* Green

Howe, Martha. *See* Minns

Howe, Mary. *See* Ede

Howe, Moses, V, 740, 741

Howe, Rebecca. *See* Hart

Howe, Richard, 1st Earl Howe, VII, 196

Howe, Richard, 4th Viscount Howe, IV, 708; V, 221, 274, 280, 281, 382, 435, 595

Howe, Squire, V, 740

Howe, Sydenham, VI, 335

Howe, William, 5th Viscount Howe, III, xxvii, 172, 173, 672; IV, 3, 94, 114, 115, 160, 394, 706, 708, 790; V, 23, 115, 147, 222, 227, 505, 629, 657, 865, 890

Howell, Ann (Bemister), XII, 91

Howell, Ann (Tocque), XII, 1060

Howell, Dollie (Wisner), XII, 1116

Howell, Elizabeth (Copway), IX, 420

Howell, John, IV, 411, 412

Howell, Thomas Bayley, IV, 502

Howells, Eliza Beulah (Elliot), X, 270; XI, 452

Howells, Emily Susanna (Johnson), X, 270; XI, 452

Howells, William C., XI, 880

Howells, William Dean, X, 44; XI, 452

Howes (Howse), Henry, VIII, 414

Howick, Viscount. *See* Grey

Howison, Janet. *See* Bogle

Howison, John, VIII, **409–11**; XII, 996

Howison, William, VIII, 409

Howitt, Samuel, VII, 317

Howlan*, George William (1835–1901), X, 194, 596, 597, 613; XI, 701, 702, 703; XII, 40, 166, 167, 417, 419, 639, 640, 837

Howland, Elizabeth (Little), III, 403

Howland*, Henry Stark (1824–1902), XI, 575

Howland, Joanna (White), VI, 813

Howland, Laura Edith. *See* Chipman

Howland, Mary Ann. *See* Blyth

Howland, Oliver Aiken, XII, 104

Howland, Peleg, XII, 43

Howland, Thomas F., VI, 435, 436

Howland, William Holmes, XII, 43, 45, 274, 336, **453–55**, 703, 992

Howland*, Sir William Pearce (1811–1907), IX, 253, 788, 804; X, 101, 299, 668; XI, 245, 554, 938; XII, 154, 296, 453, 1054, 1056

Howley, Eliza. *See* Burke

Howley*, James Patrick (1847–1918), IX, 160; XI, 429, 632; XII, 379

Howley, Katherine (Morris), XI, 615

Howley, Mary. *See* Saint John

Howley*, Michael Francis (1843–1914), VI, 694; VII, 220; IX, 72; X, 688; XI, 429; XII, 357, 861

Howley, Richard, XI, 429

Howley, Richard Vincent, XI, 429

Howley, Thomas, XI, **429–30**

Howley, William, X, 60, 278, 453, 663

Howorth, William, XI, 356, **430–31**

Howse. *See also* Howes

Howse, Ann (mother of JOSEPH), VIII, 411

Howse, Jane Mary (Livingston), XII, 567

Howse, Jenny, VIII, 414

Howse, Joseph, VI, 253; VII, 748; VIII, 90, **411–14**, 583, 881; XII, 567

Howse, Thomas, VIII, 411

Howting, John, I, 565

Hoyle, Elizabeth B. *See* Nye

Hoyle, Henry, VIII, 415

Hoyle, Pamela. *See* Wright

Hoyle, Robert, XI, 691

Hoyle, Robert, IV, 395, 484; VIII, **414–15**

Hoyles, Anne. *See* Wright

Hoyles, Sir Hugh William, VII, 421; VIII, 863; IX, 29, 30, 196, 393, 394, 469, 584, 606, 695, 846; X, 141, 332, 400, 716; XI, 29, 44, 66, **431–34**, 634, 674, 881, 910, 918; XII, 91, 92, 161, 162, 163, 482

Hoyles, Jean, Lady Hoyles. *See* Liddle

Hoyles, Lucretia. *See* Brown

Hoyles, Newman Wright, XII, 887

Hoyles, Newman Wright, VII, **420–21**; IX, 694; XI, 431

Hoyles, William, VII, 420

Hoyt, Azor, VI, 373

Hoyt, Caroline. *See* Scales

Hoyt, Charles Hale, XII, 948, 949

Hoyt, Flora. *See* Walsh

Hoyt, Jesse, IX, 505

Hoyt, Munson, IV, 329

Hoyt, William K., VII, 625
Hsüen-yeh. *See* K'ang-hsi
Huard, Marie-Angélique (Dussaus), V, 293
Huard, Thérèse (Lambert), III, 346
Huard, *dit* Désilets, Marie-Joseph (Drapeau), V, 269
Huart Dormicourt, Marc-Antoine, III, 205
Huault, Jacques, I, 372
Huault de Montmagny, Charles, I, 43, 44, 45, 111, 121, 124, 127, 128, 186, 197, 203, 205, 215, 216, 217, 218, 237, 250, 324, 344, 348, 354, 370, **372–74**, 389, 401, 403, 404, 414, 446, 454, 472, 481, 482, 485, 523, 548, 567, 574, 595, 596, 602, 663, 665; II, xv, 82, 83, 158, 253, 307, 540
Hubbald. *See* Hubbud
Hubbard, Benjamin F., VI, 174
Hubbard, George, VIII, 886
Hubbard, Hester Ann (Case), VI, **335–36**; VIII, 132, 133
Hubbard, Jane Isabella (Street), IX, 766
Hubbard, John Gellibrand, 1st Baron Addington, VIII, 275
Hubbard, Maria (Adams), XII, 9
Hubbard, W. D. W., XII, 1070
Hubbard, Mary (Pond), V, 681
Hubbard, William, V, 353; VI, 504; IX, 766
Hubbard, William Peyton, X, 3
Hubbell, Mary (Dorwin), XI, 267
Hubbs, Flora Amelia. *See* Ross
Hubbs, Paul Kinsey. *See also* Ross, Charles
Hubbs, Paul Kinsey, XII, 929
Hubbud (Hubbald), James, II, 314
Hubert, Angélique-Jeanne (Lajus), IV, 432
Hubert, Auguste-David, VI, 379
Hubert, Catherine (Baron; Foretier), V, 322; VIII, 301
Hubert, Cécile. *See* Cartier
Hubert, Élisabeth (Boulduc), II, 88, 89
Hubert, Elizabeth (Du Val), VIII, 257
Hubert, Jacques-François, IV, 370
Hubert, Jean-François, IV, 7, 42, 43, 72, 82, 90, 102, 136, 190, 234, 288, 318, 367, **370–75**, 432, 436, 445, 453, 469, 470, 511, 534, 698, 779, 799; V, 12, 13, 77, 92, 124, 125, 150, 179, 180, 186, 202, 245, 246, 247, 294, 343, 380, 434, 480, 493, 509, 523, 524, 570, 587, 633, 663, 667, 687, 688, 691, 701, 704; VI, 145, 170, 201, 304, 315, 391, 397, 447, 450, 471, 486, 587, 596, 669; VII, 201, 246, 422, 591, 644, 720; VIII, 201; XI, 87
Hubert, Josephte. *See* Kanhopitsa
Hubert, Louis-Édouard, VII, **421–23**
Hubert, Marc-Antoine, II, 425; III, 381
Hubert, Marie (Thirement), II, 514
Hubert, Marie-Anne. *See* La Porte
Hubert, Marie-Josephte. *See* Chartier
Hubert, Marie-Louise. *See* Maranda
Hubert, Marie-Ursule (Neilson), VII, 644, 649
Hubert, Petrus, X, 33
Hubert, Pierre, VII, 421
Hubert, René, II, xxiv, 201, 243, 485; III, 372
Hubert, René-Auguste-Richard, VIII, 617, 668; X, 415
Hubert, Renée (Hodiesne), III, 292
Hubert de Lacroix, Marie-Anne (Couagne; La Corne), III, 331
Hubou (Huboust, Hubout), Guillaume, I, 554, 578
Hubou, Marie. *See* Rollet
Huck-Saunders, Jane. *See* Kinsey
Huddleston, Jemima (Hay), XI, 392

Hudon, Alexandre, XII, 455
Hudon, Atala. *See* Aubert de Gaspé
Hudon, Ephrem, X, 417, 524; XII, 456
Hudon, Hyacinthe, VII, **423–24**, 799; VIII, 317, 554, 627, 712; X, 689
Hudon, J.-Eusèbe, X, 20
Hudon, Jérémie, VII, 423
Hudon, Julie. *See* Chapais
Hudon, Marie. *See* Bergereau
Hudon, Marie. *See* Godard
Hudon, Pantaléon, VIII, 245
Hudon, Philomène. *See* Godard
Hudon, Victor, XI, 774, 808; XII, **455–57**
Hudon-Beaulieu, Théotiste (Gélinas), X, 304
Hudson, Mr (naval officer), IV, 420
Hudson, Ann (Naper; Fraser), V, 330
Hudson, Christine (Brauneis), VI, 85; X, 88
Hudson, George (capitalist), IX, 525
Hudson, George (HBC employee), VIII, 878
Hudson, Hannah (Leverett), I, 475
Hudson, Henry, I, 20, 74, 83, 144, 145, 190, 252, 312, 318, 329, **374–79**, 384, 385, 668, 679
Hudson, James, XII, 715
Hudson, John, I, 377, **379**
Hudson, Margaret (Medley), XII, 713, 716
Hudson, Thomas (captain), VI, 234
Hudson, Thomas (painter), V, 824
Huestis. *See also* Heustis
Huestis*, George Oxley (1821–1905), VIII, 941
Huet, Monsieur. *See* Le Loutre, Jean-Louis
Huet, Catherine (Le Loutre Després), IV, 453
Huet, Paul, I, 296, **379**, 552; II, 278
Huet de La Valinière, Charles, V, 431
Huet de La Valinière, Olive. *See* Arnaud
Huet de La Valinière, Pierre, IV, 511, 544; V, **431–34**
Huet Dulude, Josephte (Massue), IX, 538
Hugessen. *See* Weston-Hugessen
Huggan, Margaret (Murray), XI, 633
Huggeford, Martha (Hardy), IV, 327, 329
Huggeford, Peter, IV, 329
Huggins, Edward, IX, 853
Hughes, Colonel, IX, 523
Hughes, Miss (McDonell), VI, 444
Hughes, Clifton. *See* Gidney, Angus Morrison
Hughes, David John, IX, 725, 843
Hughes, Elizabeth (Archibald), XI, 29
Hughes, Frances (Beatty), XII, 69
Hughes, Grace Dorothea (Kennedy), XI, 468
Hughes, Isabella (Collins), VII, 203
Hughes, James, IV, 115; V, 531; VIII, 412, 619, 866, 881
Hughes, Jane, Lady Hughes. *See* Sloane
Hughes, Jane (Brown), XI, 116
Hughes, Joanna (Wilson), IX, 843
Hughes, Joanne, Lady Hughes. *See* Collyer
Hughes, John, IX, 18, 582; X, 191
Hughes, John Joseph, VII, 171
Hughes, John Taylor, VIII, 818
Hughes, Mary (Osborn), IV, 594
Hughes, Mary Major (Whelan), IX, 833
Hughes, Philadelphia (Lount), VII, 518
Hughes, Sir Richard, V, 434
Hughes, Sir Richard, IV, 30, 111, 196; V, **434–35**; VI, 310
Hughes, William, V, 872

Hughson, Maria (Earle), XI, 295
Hughson, Nathaniel, VI, 229; VII, 378
Hugo, Victor-Marie, X, 164, 166
Hugo of Ireland, I, 678
Hugot, Anne (Desgrez), III, 51
Huguet, Charlotte. *See* LaMotte
Huguet, Claude, V, 435
Huguet, Jean, IV, 375
Huguet, Joseph, IV, **375–76**, 544; V, 432
Huguet, Magdeleine (Dupéré, *dit* Champlain), V, 436; VI, 231
Huguet, Scholastique-Geneviève. *See* Verhoune
Huguet, *dit* Latour, Agathe-Henriette (McDonell), V, 436, 437; VII, 488, 625; VIII, 864
Huguet, *dit* Latour, Charlotte. *See* Desève
Huguet, *dit* Latour, Claire. *See* Trudeau
Huguet, *dit* Latour, Josette. *See* Valois
Huguet, *dit* Latour, Louis (uncle), IV, 702; V, 435, 436, 437, 727; VI, 230, 663
Huguet, *dit* Latour, Louis, V, 435, 436, 437
Huguet, *dit* Latour, Louis-Maximilien-Théodore, V, 436
Huguet, *dit* Latour, Magdelaine. *See* You
Huguet, *dit* Latour, Marie-Louise. *See* Dalciat
Huguet, *dit* Latour, Pierre, V, 435, 436, 437; VIII, 637
Huguet, *dit* Latour, Pierre, III, 346; IV, 629, 702; V, 218, 219, **435–38**, 708, 727, 728; VI, 230, 487; VII, 17; VIII, 637, 638
Huguet, *dit* Latour, Scholastique, V, 436
Huikill, Amelia (Schwatka), XII, 954
Huillé. *See* Brisay
Huiquinanichi. *See* Wikinanish
Huish, Robert, VIII, 773
Hulbert, Jerome B., XI, 184, 191, 491
Hull, Mary. *See* Spencer
Hull, Mary Margaret. *See* Anglin
Hull, Philomela (Cook), IX, 151
Hull, Sally (Westbrook), VI, 808
Hull, William, V, 14, 112, 522, 543, 643, 714, 798; VI, 56, 463, 609, 808; VIII, 34; IX, 8, 245, 668
Hullah, John Pyke, XII, 959
Hullett, William, V, 495
Hullmandel, Charles Joseph, VII, 823; XI, 106; XII, 326
Hulot, Philippe, II, 338
Hulsman, Lewis (Ludovic), VII, 483
Humberston, Charles, VII, 595
Humberstone, William, XII, 672
Humbert, Elizabeth (mother of STEPHEN), VII, 424
Humbert, François-Joseph-Michel, V, 481
Humbert, John, VII, 424
Humbert, Martha (wife of STEPHEN), VII, 424
Humbert, Martha (Fairweather), XII, 306
Humbert, Mary. *See* Wyer
Humbert, Stephen, VII, 424
Humbert, Stephen, VI, 356; VII, **424–25**
Humboldt, Friedrich Wilhelm Karl Heinrich Alexander von, V, 400; XI, 799
Hume, Andrew, X, 558
Hume, Anne Margaret (Blake), VIII, 95; IX, 55; X, 206
Hume, Catherine Honoria (Blake), IX, 55, 56, 59, 151; XI, **434**
Hume, David, III, 601; IV, 4; V, 182, 486; VI, 774; VIII, 957
Hume, Edward, I, 611

Hume, Eliza (Connor), IX, 151
Hume, James Deacon, VIII, 548, 549
Hume, John James, VII, 715
Hume, Joseph, VI, 633; VII, 5, 40, 42, 82, 315, 377, 855, 865; VIII, xxvi, 602, 866; IX, 157, 230, 441, 498, 500, 501; X, 514, 626; XI, 44, 786; XII, 1079
Hume, Joseph Samuel, XI, 434
Hume, William, IX, 55; XI, 434
Humfrey, Laurence, I, 531
Humières, Duc d'. *See* Crevant
Humpherville, John, XI, 436
Humphraville, Lamira (Chamberlain), VI, 128
Humphraville (Ompherville), Lisette (Louise) (Rowand), VIII, 779
Humphrey, Mr (hangman), VII, 265
Humphrey, John Albert, IX, 368; XII, 412, 479
Humphrey, Lois (Black), XI, 78
Humphreys, Caroline. *See* Watkins
Humphreys, Caroline Amelia. *See* Ridout
Humphreys, David, V, 741
Humphreys, Ellen (Foster; Harrison), VII, 316; IX, 372
Humphreys, Francis, VIII, 749; X, 370
Humphreys, James, V, 438
Humphreys, James, V, **438–39**
Humphreys, James Dodsley, VIII, 347, 750; X, **370–71**
Humphreys, John Basil, XI, 434
Humphreys, Mary. *See* Yorke
Humphreys, Mary Elizabeth. *See* Morgan
Humphreys, Mary Hardwick. *See* Unwin
Humphreys, Susanna. *See* Assheton
Humphreys, Thomas Basil, XI, 300, **434–36**, 840
Humphries, Matilda (Edmonds), XII, 294
Hund, Frederick, VIII, 634
Hunkajuka, X, **371–72**; XII, 125
Hunsdon, Baron. *See* Cary
Hunt, Mr (sailmaker), VII, 426
Hunt, Mrs (friend of Elizabeth Posthuma GWILLIM), VII, 363
Hunt, Abram Spurr, XII, 881
Hunt, Anna Rebecca. *See* Gale
Hunt, Charles, X, **372**; XI, 269
Hunt, Charles Brewer, X, 372
Hunt, Emma. *See* Brewer
Hunt, Henry, V, 675
Hunt, Henry Holdsworth, V, 626
Hunt, James, VII, **425–27**, 879; XII, 1072
Hunt, James Henry Leigh, VII, 82
Hunt, Jane Elizabeth. *See* Sterry
Hunt, John, X, 372
Hunt, John Inkerman Alexander, X, 372
Hunt, Mary. *See* Golpin
Hunt, Mary (Moore), XI, 607
Hunt, Mary Sloat. *See* Garland
Hunt, Peleg, XII, 457
Hunt, Robert, XI, 436, 571
Hunt, Sarah (Sabine), XI, 798
Hunt, Susan (Phillips), XII, 842
Hunt, Thomas (captain), I, 262, 650
Hunt, Thomas (brother of JAMES), VII, 426
Hunt, Thomas (father of JAMES), VII, 425
Hunt, Thomas Sterry, VIII, 775; X, 105, 445, 446, 448; XI, 53, 495, 899; XII, 233, 234, 235, 236, **457–58**
Hunt, Weston, VII, 426; IX, 274

Hunt, William, VII, 426
Hunt, William Henry, XII, 326
Hunt, William Holman, XII, 751, 752, 793
Hunt, Wilson Price, VIII, 190, 557, 766
Hunter, Agnes. *See* Strickland
Hunter, Alexander, XI, 497
Hunter, Ann (wife of JAMES), XI, 436
Hunter, Ann Agnes (Russell), VIII, 783
Hunter, Anne. *See* Nixon
Hunter, Charles, VII, 427
Hunter, Charles, VII, **427–28**, 879; X, 77
Hunter, Charles D., V, 344
Hunter, Charlotte (Taylor), XII, 1028
Hunter, Cuthbert, VII, 428
Hunter, Elizabeth. *See* Goreham
Hunter, Elizabeth. *See* Tough
Hunter, Euphemia. *See* Jack
Hunter, Hamilton, XII, 922
Hunter, Isabella (Todd), XII, 1062
Hunter, James (associate of James PEACHEY), IV, 613
Hunter, James (partner of William FORSYTH, d. 1814), V, 327; VI, 262
Hunter, James, VII, 277; X, 109, 275; XI, **436–37**
Hunter, Jean. *See* Ross
Hunter, Jean, Lady Hunter. *See* Dickson
Hunter, Jeffrey, VIII, 860
Hunter, John. *See also* Hunter-Duvar, John
Hunter, John, V, 189
Hunter*, John Edwin (1856–1919), XII, 707
Hunter, John MacKenzie, XII, 458
Hunter, Sir Martin, VI, 408, 518, 685, 724, 726, 727, 811; VII, **428–30**, 658; XII, 797
Hunter, Peter (Patrick), IV, 778, 779; V, 17, 18, 101, 265, 280, 303, 304, 365, 366, 405, 420, **439–43**, 453, 470, 495, 502, 548, 549, 732, 749, 753, 844, 845, 855, 856; VI, 177, 215, 299, 452, 485, 600, 608, 609, 610, 613, 656, 698, 721, 804; VII, 35, 36, 38, 175, 251, 401, 419, 438, 439, 544, 554, 812, 813, 864, 929; VIII, 191, 336, 337, 338, 339, 482, 639; IX, 752
Hunter, Robert. *See* Carundawana
Hunter, Robert (accountant), XII, 922, 923
Hunter, Robert (associate of Samuel THOMPSON), XI, 877
Hunter, Robert (doctor), XII, 534
Hunter, Robert (governor), II, 112, 498, 547
Hunter, Robert (Greenock, Scotland, merchant), V, 617; VIII, 647
Hunter, Robert (London merchant), VI, 400, 471; VII, 522, 523
Hunter, Robert (son of Robert, London merchant), VI, 179, 471; VII, 523
Hunter, Sarah (Douglas), VIII, 233
Hunter, William, VI, 548
Hunter-Duvar, Anne. *See* Carter
Hunter-Duvar, John, XII, **458–60**
Hunter of Knap, John, V, 439
Huntingdon, Countess of. *See* Shirley
Huntingdon, Jabez, V, 664
Huntingford, Edward, XI, 313
Huntington, Mrs (Marsh; wife of LUCIUS SETH), XI, 439
Huntington, Collis Potter, XI, 293, 840
Huntington, Herbert, VII, 143, 144; VIII, **415–18**; IX, 226, 426, 747; X, 232, 365; XI, 925, 945
Huntington, Jedediah Vincent, IX, 279

Huntington, Lucius Seth, IX, 435; X, 123, 150, 293, 294; XI, 7, 238, **437–39**; XII, 6, 603, 628, 649, 651, 652, 653, 654, 987, 1057
Huntington, Lydia (Cogswell), VIII, 167
Huntington, Martha. *See* Walker
Huntington, Mary. *See* Hovey
Huntington, Miner, VIII, 415
Huntington, Miriam Jane. *See* Wood
Huntington, Rebecca. *See* Pinkney
Huntington, Richard, XII, 538
Huntington, Russell, XI, 439
Huntington, Seth, XI, 437
Huntington, Tryphena (Church), VII, 186
Huntley, Mrs, Lady Huntley. *See* Drury
Huntley, Ann. *See* Webster
Huntley, Anne, Lady Huntley. *See* Skinner
Huntley, Sir Henry Vere, VII, 145, 202; VIII, 297, 430, 485, 563, 564, 566; IX, **400–2**, 403, 829; X, 184, 339, 352, 461, 669; XI, 567, 665, 699, 940; XII, 425, 839, 840, 856, 857
Huntley, Richard, IX, 400
Huntly, Hannah (Doel), X, 233
Huot, Catherine. *See* Plante
Huot, Charles, VIII, 313
Huot*, Charles (1855–1930), VI, 132; XII, 849
Huot, François (father of FRANÇOIS), VI, 50, 168
Huot, François (notary), XI, 500
Huot, François, V, 580; VI, **336–37**, 585; VII, 188, 430; VIII, 491, 937
Huot, Françoise. *See* Villers
Huot, Hector-Simon, VI, 337, 658; VII, 7, 61, 373, **430–31**, 870; IX, 190, 261, 262; X, 580; XII, 1032
Huot, Jacques, IX, 402
Huot, Josephte. *See* Clouet
Huot, Louise-Jeanne-Eugénie (Évanturel), XII, 298
Huot, Marie. *See* Maheu
Huot, Marie-Catherine, named Sainte-Madeleine, VII, 54, 431; IX, **402–3**
Huot, Marie-Charles. *See* Leblond
Huot, Marie-Françoise (Huot), VII, 431
Huot, Marie-Françoise, named Sainte-Gertrude, VII, **431–32**; VIII, 317; XI, 96
Huot, Marie-Louise. *See* Robitaille
Huot, Philippe, XII, 627
Huot*, Pierre-Gabriel (1831–1913), X, 262; XII, 324, 853
Huot, Pierre-Michel, VII, 431
Huot Saint-Laurent, Josephte (Tessier), VI, 762
Huppé, *dit* Lagroix, Antoine, IV, 142
Huppé, *dit* Lagroix, Charlotte. *See* Jérémie, *dit* Lamontagne, *dit* Douville
Huppé, *dit* Lagroix, Jacques, IV, 376
Huppé, *dit* Lagroix, Joseph, IV, 172, **376–77**
Huppé, *dit* Lagroix, Marie-Françoise (Brassard), IV, 87
Huppé, *dit* Lagroix, Michel, IV, 376
Huppé, *dit* Lagroix, Suzanne. *See* Le Normand
Hurault, Henri-Emmanuel, Marquis de Vibraye, III, 116
Hurault, Marie (Rousselot; Testu de La Richardière), III, 620
Hurault, Martine (Haimard), II, 273
Hurd, Master (son of SAMUEL PROUDFOOT), VII, 846
Hurd, Anne Mary. *See* Pratt
Hurd, Elizabeth. *See* Proudfoot
Hurd, Frederica. *See* Wynyard

291

Hurd, Samuel Proudfoot, VII, 175, 846; VIII, **418–19**, 523
Hurd, Thomas, VIII, 418
Hurd, Thomas Gladwin, VIII, 419
Huret, Grégoire, I, 551
Hurlbert, Jesse Beaufort, XII, 1057
Hurlburt, Betsy Almira. *See* Adams
Hurlburt, Eliza Jane (Rosebrugh), VI, 336
Hurlburt, Hannah. *See* Mosier
Hurlburt, Heman, X, 372
Hurlburt, Sylvester, VI, 336
Hurlburt, Thomas, VII, 276; X, **372–73**
Hurley, Mary (Nugent), VIII, 656
Hurt, Mary (Keats, Lady Keats), VI, 371
Hurteau, Cordélie (Dansereau), X, 374
Hurteau, Françoise. *See* Lamarre
Hurteau, Gabriel, X, 373
Hurteau, Isidore, X, **373–74**
Hurteau, Louise. *See* Duhamel
Hurtebise (Hurtubise), Marin, IV, 178
Hurtin, William, V, 613
Hus, Jan, II, 9
Husbands, Hermon, V, 309
Huse, Sarah (Merrill), XI, 589
Huskisson, William, VI, 421, 610; VII, 226, 731, 741, 742;
    VIII, xxvii, xxxi, 437, 461, 462, 601, 603; IX, 221, 810
Huson, George, XII, 409
Huson, Georgiana (Harman), XII, 409
Huss, John. *See* Hus, Jan
Hussey, John, III, 358; IV, 630
Hussey, Thomas, IV, 6, 511
Hustice, Charlotte. *See* Wiggins
Huston, Andrew, V, 843
Huston, James, V, 702; VII, 515; VIII, 16, **419–21**, 504,
    692, 702; IX, 33, 302, 305, 439; XI, 37, 178, 343; XII,
    270, 324, 570
Huston, John, V, 869; VI, 30
Huston, Théotiste. *See* Audette, *dit* Lapointe
Huston, William, VIII, 419
Hutchings, Anne (Carter), X, 141
Hutchings, Charles, V, 444
Hutchings, Hannah. *See* Sparke
Hutchings, Henry, V, 444
Hutchings, Richard, V, **443–44**, 596; VI, 636
Hutchings, Robert, V, 443
Hutchins, Catherine (Cushing), X, 212
Hutchins, Hannah May (McArthur), XI, 538
Hutchins, Margaret (wife of THOMAS), IV, 377
Hutchins, Thomas, IV, **377–78**, 390, 524, 525, 726, 741,
    758; V, 362
Hutchinson, Baron. *See* Hely-Hutchinson
Hutchinson, Mr (clergyman), XII, 364
Hutchinson, Agnes (Fife), X, 283
Hutchinson, Anne, I, 601
Hutchinson, Anne, named Mother Ignatia, XI, 240
Hutchinson, Bridget (Sanford; Phillips), I, 337, 601
Hutchinson, Charles, XII, 1086, 1087
Hutchinson, Elizabeth. *See* Wilder
Hutchinson, Faith (Savage), II, 601
Hutchinson, Foster, VI, 676
Hutchinson, John (doctor), XI, 263
Hutchinson, John (father-in-law of Joshua BELL), IX, 43
Hutchinson, Margaret (Allison), VIII, 15
Hutchinson, Margaret (Sabatier), VI, 676

Hutchinson, Margaret (Wiswall), V, 870, 871
Hutchinson, Mary (Sullivan), XII, 1000
Hutchinson, Robert, IX, **403–4**
Hutchinson, Samuel, IX, 403
Hutchinson, Susanna. *See* Harvie
Hutchinson, Thomas (governor), II, 496, 544; III, 200, 477;
    IV, 300, 769; V, 831, 865; VI, 74, 75, 136, 682, 718;
    VII, 86
Hutchinson, Thomas (storeowner), VIII, 876
Hutchison, Ann Frederica (Esten), IX, 244
Hutchison, Henry, XI, 778, 779
Hutchison, John, XII, 997
Hutchison, Margaret. *See* Fisher
Hutchison, Margaret (Campbell), XI, 148, 533
Hutchison, William, V, 320; XI, 533
Hutton, Mrs. *See* Belyea
Hutton, Ann. *See* Scott
Hutton, Frances. *See* McCrea
Hutton, George, XII, 460, 461
Hutton, James (captain), V, 68
Hutton, James (geologist), XI, 72
Hutton, James B., XI, 880
Hutton, James Scott, XII, **460–61**
Hutton, Joseph, IX, 404
Hutton, Margaret. *See* Bentley
Hutton, Mary. *See* Burton
Hutton, Mary. *See* Swanwick
Hutton, Samuel, XII, 407, **461–62**
Hutton, William, VII, 389; IX, 98, 377, **404–5**
Huxley, Thomas Henry, IX, 419, 660; X, 349, 350
Huyghue, Isabella Clarke. *See* Totten
Huyghue, Samuel, XII, 462
Huyghue, Samuel Douglas Smith, VIII, 193; XII, **462–63**
Hwistesmetxē´qEn, VIII, **421–22**, 527, 654
Hyanveux. *See also* Hianveu
Hyatt, Abraham, VI, 337
Hyatt, Anna. *See* Canfield
Hyatt, Charles (uncle), VI, 339
Hyatt, Charles, VI, 339
Hyatt, Cornelius, VI, 337
Hyatt, Elizabeth (Schurman), V, 743
Hyatt, Galen, VI, 339
Hyatt, Gilbert, VI, 270, **337–39**, 575, 816
Hyde, Baron. *See* Villiers
Hyde, Edward, 3rd Earl of Clarendon, II, 546
Hyde, Emily (Blanshard), XII, 113
Hyde, George, XII, 136
Hyde, Margaret, IX, 27
Hyde, Thomas, V, 784
Hyde, William, 566
Hyman, Amelia. *See* Hart
Hyman, Annie Maria. *See* Niles
Hyman*, Charles Smith (1854–1926), X, 68, 374, 375
Hyman, Elizabeth. *See* Birrell
Hyman, Ellis Walton, IX, 789; X, 68, **374–75**, 549
Hyman, Frances L. *See* Kingsley
Hyman, Isaac Elias, XI, 440, 441
Hyman, Jacob, X, 374
Hyman, Jesse Willett, X, 375
Hyman, Percy, XI, 441
Hyman, Sarah (mother of ELLIS WALTON), X, 374
Hyman, William, XI, **440–41**
Hynes, Ann (Clarke), XI, 193

IBERVILLE. *See* Le Moyne
Iddings, Charles W., XI, 662
Idinsaw. *See* Eda'nsa; Tahaygen
Idle, Christopher, VI, 532; IX, 638, 639
Idle, Jonathan, VI, 532
Idotliazee, IV, 339, 584
Iffland, Anthony von, VI, 68, 259, 576, 681; IX, 218, 572; X, **375–76**; XI, 272
Iffland, Elizabeth von. *See* Allen
Iffland, John (Johann), X, 375
Iffland, Marie-Madeleine. *See* Bideau, *dit* Portugal
Ignace, IV, 375
Ignace de Paris, I, **379–80**
Ignatia, Mother. *See* Hutchinson
Ignatius of Loyola, XII, 698
Ignon Ouaconisen, II, 646
Ikaenikiakew, Frances. *See* Singing Before
Ilanos, Matheo, III, 157
Imasees. *See* Āyimisīs
Imbault, Maurice (Jean-Jacques), III, 94, **298–99**
Imbert, Agathe. *See* Trefflé, *dit* Rottot
Imbert, Anne-Louise. *See* Lagrange
Imbert, Bertrand, III, 350; IV, **378–79**
Imbert, Catherine-Agathe, IV, 128
Imbert, Edmée. *See* Chambrois
Imbert, Jacques, III, **299–300**, 491, 648; IV, 67, 88, 91, 127, 128, 187, 205, 353, 629
Imbert, Jean, III, 299
Imbert, Jean-Simon, IV, 187
Imbert, Marie-Anne. *See* Maisonnat, *dit* Baptiste
Imbert, Pierre, IV, 378
Imbert, Saubade. *See* Castera
Imbert, Simon, I, 95, 98, 100, 299, 470
Imoda, Jean B., X, 560
Inchiquin, Baron. *See* O'Brien
Ingall, Frederick Lennox, X, 32
Ingalls, Ruth (Gerrish), VI, 283, 284
Ingalls, Sarah Elizabeth (Fisher), IX, 262
Ingersoll, Charles (businessman), IX, 544
Ingersoll, Charles (politician), VI, 331; IX, 229
Ingersoll, Elizabeth. *See* Dewey
Ingersoll, Jared, V, 94
Ingersoll, Laura (Secord), V, 83, 168, 800; VII, 780; VIII, 208, 245; IX, 264, **405–7**; X, 181; XII, 1075
Ingersoll, Robert Green, XII, 867
Ingersoll, Thomas, IX, 405
Ingham, Sarah. *See* Logan
Ingilby, Sir John, VII, 50
Ingilby, Julia Wharton (Barrie, Lady Barrie), VII, 50
Inglefield, Sir Edward Augustus, VIII, 80; IX, 167
Inglis, Archibald, V, 444
Inglis, Charles, VII, 435
Inglis, Charles, IV, 94, 139, 244, 259, 327, 604, 626, 738, 753, 769; V, 25, 59, 60, 109, 124, 128, 135, 204, 205, 219, 314, 318, 344, **444–48**, 475, 476, 573, 601, 602, 605, 637, 657, 694, 785, 787, 832, 850, 871, 872; VI, 13, 87, 156, 157, 198, 208, 209, 297, 301, 396, 405, 523, 525, 714, 731, 732, 799; VII, 52, 88, 218, 272, 432, 529, 530, 540, 816, 832; VIII, 354, 355, 459; IX, 379, 637, 770; XI, 75
Inglis, David, XI, 467
Inglis, Elizabeth. *See* Cochran
Inglis, John, V, 86, 820; VI, 644

Inglis, John, V, 446, 872; VI, 53, 54, 157, 461, 692, 714, 732; VII, 84, 144, 272, **432–36**, 531, 533, 724, 732; VIII, xxv, 172, 173, 345, 346, 355, 359, 460, 724, 756, 783, 901, 902, 968; IX, 161, 177, 379, 408, 601, 638, 801, 841, 847; X, 110, 383, 453, 539, 663; XI, 74; XII, 872
Inglis, Sir John, VII, 436
Inglis, John Bellingham, V, 86
Inglis, Margaret. *See* Crooke
Inglis, Margaret (Halliburton), VIII, 354
Inglis, Mary. *See* Vining
Inglis, Mary (Denoon), VII, 245
Inglis, Sir Robert Harry, IX, 676
Ingraham, Joseph, IV, 420; V, 387
Ingram, David, I, 333, **380–81**
Ingres, Jean-Auguste-Dominique, IX, 362
Ings, John, VIII, 563, 564, 565; X, 339, 594, 596; XI, 202
Inkster*, Colin (1843–1934), IX, 626; X, 377, 631; XII, 954
Inkster, James, III, 124; V, 712
Inkster, John, X, 377
Inkster, John, X, **376–77**
Inkster, Mary. *See* Sinclair
Inman, Elizabeth. *See* Murray
Inman, Henry, XII, 414
Innes, Alexander, IV, 744
Innes, George Mignon, XII, 823
Innis, Caroline I. *See* Monro
Innis*, Harold Adams (1894–1952), V, 528, 683, 685
Innis, James, VII, 691
Innis, Mary Emma. *See* Quayle
Innocent XI, II, 329
Iovhanné, Johannes. *See* Proulx, *dit* Clement, Jean-Baptiste
Ipilkvik (Joe Ebierbing), X, 327, 328; XI, 382; XII, 955
Iredell, Abraham, V, **448–49**, 553, 774; VI, 330
Iredell, Hannah. *See* Luckens
Iredell, Hester. *See* Marsh
Iredell, Robert, V, 448
Ireland, Joseph Norton, XII, 306
Ireland, Moses, X, 530
Irelande, Bazile, V, 564
Irish, Charles, V, 218
Iron Body. *See* Nabpace
Ironside, Frances Symington (Cotter), XI, 204
Ironside, George, IV, 778; VI, 153, **340–41**, 706; IX, 407
Ironside, George, VI, 340; IX, 10, **407–8**; XI, 204
Ironside, Isabella. *See* Vocemassussia
Ironside, McGregor, IX, 408
Iroquet, I, 70, 131, 190, **381–82**, 603
Irumberry de Salaberry. *See also* Salaberry
Irumberry de Salaberry, Charles-Michel d', V, 297, 421, 449, 450, 696; VI, 170, 180, **341–45**, 346, 368, 377, 388, 584, 634, 680, 681, 689; VII, 235, 349, 360, 388, 397, 461, 666, 671, 682, 897, 898; VIII, 245, 393, 677, 693, 909; IX, 320, 485, 553, 698; X, 13, 181; XI, 441
Irumberry de Salaberry, Charles-René-Léonidas d', IX, 361, 772; X, 677; XI, **441–42**, 739; XII, 601, 1007
Irumberry de Salaberry, Charlotte-Hermine-Louise-Catherine d' (Juchereau Duchesnay), VI, 346; VII, 461
Irumberry de Salaberry, Édouard-Alphonse d', IV, 43; V, 297, **449–50**; VI, 341, 345, 346, 517
Irumberry de Salaberry, Françoise-Catherine d'. *See* Hertel de Saint-François

Irumberry de Salaberry, François-Louis d', V, 449, 450; VI, 341, 346

Irumberry de Salaberry, Ignace-Michel-Louis-Antoine d', IV, 43; V, 75, 174, 297, 449, 461, 508, 702, 794, 827; VI, 291, 341, **345–46**, 368, 517; VII, 461, 622

Irumberry de Salaberry, Louise-Joséphine. *See* Allard

Irumberry de Salaberry, Marie-Anne-Julie d'. *See* Hertel de Rouville

Irumberry de Salaberry, Marie-Louise. *See* Baby

Irumberry de Salaberry, Marie-Victorine-Cordélia. *See* Franchère

Irumberry de Salaberry, Maurice-Roch d', V, 449, 450; VI, 341, 346

Irvin, Samuel M., VIII, 853

Irvine*, Acheson Gosford (1837–1916), XI, 195, 598, 870; XII, 673, 780, 803

Irvine, Adam, VI, 346

Irvine, Ann. *See* Bell

Irvine, Ann. *See* Pyke

Irvine, Annie Routh. *See* LeMesurier

Irvine, Elizabeth (Irvine), VI, 346

Irvine, George, XII, 29

Irvine, George, IX, 274; XI, 27, 184, 191; XII, 251, **464–65**, 628, 903, 904

Irvine, James, V, 461, 769; VI, 61, **346–47**, 516, 528, 531, 533, 622; VII, 134, 920; VIII, 838; XII, 464

Irvine, John George, VI, 347; XII, 464

Irvine, Margaret (Penny), XII, 835

Irvine, Robert, VIII, 68; IX, 621

Irving*, Sir Æmilius (1823–1913), XI, 583

Irving, Edward, VII, 124; XI, 797; XII, 1130

Irving, Elizabeth Jane. *See* Dixon

Irving, George Clerk, XI, 916

Irving, Sir Henry, known as John Henry Brodribb, XII, 669

Irving, James, VIII, 922

Irving, John, XII, 955

Irving*, John (1854–1936), X, 217, 378; XII, 804

Irving, Judith. *See* Westfield

Irving, Paulus Æmilius, III, 542; IV, **379–80**, 491, 538, 570, 579; V, 142

Irving, Sir Paulus Æmilius, IV, 380

Irving, Thomas, XII, 785

Irving, Washington, V, 472, 814; IX, 278, 420

Irving, William, IV, 379

Irving, William, X, **377–78**; XI, 866

Irwin, Elizabeth (Green), VI, 300

Irwin, Marie, named de la Conception, I, 382

Irwin, Thomas, VII, **436–38**, 542, 609; VIII, 297; IX, 157; XII, 319

Isaac. *See* Glikhikan

Isaac of Onoquaga, V, 804

Isaacs, Benjamin, V, 832

Isaacs, Mary. *See* Pickett

Isabeau, Antoinette (Planton), II, 292; III, 234, 235

Isabeau, Arnoud, II, 292; III, 234

Isabeau, Marie-Anne (Bolvin), III, 67

Isabeau, Michel-Philippe, II, 120, **292**, 648, 649, 650; III, 234, 235, 636, 644

Isabel, Guillaume, I, 468

Isadore, XII, **465–66**

Isambart, Joseph, II, 153; IV, 147, 148

Isambart, Périnne, IV, 147

Isapo-muxika, VIII, 4; XI, 261, **442–45**, 596, 598, 599, 600, 695, 697; XII, 29, 30, 673, 674, 718, 779, 858

Isbister, Adam, IV, 380

Isbister, Alexander Kennedy, VII, 455; VIII, 819; X, 47; XI, 220, **445–46**

Isbister, George, IV, 32

Isbister, Helen. *See* MacKinlay

Isbister, Joseph, II, 232; III, 127, 301, 341, 654; IV, 33, **380–81**, 383

Isbister, Judith. *See* Middleton

Isbister, Mary. *See* Kennedy

Isbister, Thomas, XI, 445

Isbister, William, III, 300

Isbister, William, III, **300–1**; IV, 380

Isham, Ann. *See* Skrimshire

Isham, Catherine. *See* Mindham

Isham, Charles Thomas, III, 304; IV, 33, 47, 157; V, 194, **450–51**, 500; VII, 138

Isham, James, V, 451

Isham, James, II, 310; III, 285, 286, 287, **301–4**, 448, 472, 482, 483, 490, 520, 593, 594, 595, 661, 662; IV, 46, 47, 383, 517, 518, 523; V, 362, 450

Isham, Jane, V, 451

Isham, Mary, V, 451

Isham, Price, V, 451

Isham, Thomas (great-uncle), V, 450

Isham, Thomas, V, 451

Isham, Whitby, III, 301

Ishquaketa, III, 13

Isle. *See* Hil

Isle-Dieu, Abbé de L'. *See* La Rue

Isnard, Danty d', II, 595, 596

Issaurel, Béatrice. *See* La Palme

Istowun-eh'pata. *See also* Isapo-muxika

Istowun-eh'pata, XI, 442

Istre, Élisabeth. *See* Forestier

Istre, Joseph, III, 220

Itarey, I, 451

Itine, XII, 289

Itouralde. *See* Artaguiette

Ivar Bárdarson, I, 679

Ives, Artemissa. *See* Bullock

Ives, Eli, XII, 466

Ives, Elizabeth Emma. *See* Pope

Ives, William Bullock, XI, 708; XII, **466–67**, 1120, 1121

Iyokaki (Sleeping Woman), XII, 970

Izard, George, VIII, 238

Izard, Sarah (Campbell), IV, 131

JACAU, Anne. *See* Melanson, *dit* La Verdure

Jacau, Jeanne (Allard de Sainte-Marie), IV, 14

Jacau, Jeanne-Françoise (Rodrigue), IV, 678

Jacau (Jacault, Jacob), Thomas, IV, 382

Jacau de Fiedmont, Louis-Thomas, III, xxii, 87; IV, 14, 36, 250, **382–83**, 459, 631, 641, 652, 678; V, 104

Jachée, Françoise (Chartier de Lotbinière), II, 138

Jack, IV, 779; V, 239

Jack, Caroline Amelia. *See* Disbrow

Jack*, David Russell (1864–1913), XII, 537

Jack, Euphemia (Hunter), V, 439

Jack, Janet. *See* Bryden

Jack, Marian Ellen. *See* Peters

Jack, Peter, XI, 446

Jack, William, IX, 619
Jack, William Brydone, VIII, 224; IX, 666; XI, 373, **446–48**, 828
Jackman*, Arthur (1843–1907), X, 378
Jackman, Bridget. *See* Burbage
Jackman, Charles, I, 317
Jackman, Thomas, X, 378
Jackman, William, X, **378–79**
Jackson. *See also* Jacobs
Jackson, Mr (merchant), VI, 208
Jackson, Alfred, IX, 119
Jackson, Amelia (Kielley), VIII, 467
Jackson, Andrew, VIII, 446; IX, 220, 498, 537; XII, 471
Jackson, Artemas, XI, 547
Jackson, Augusta Mary Melissa (Baldwin), IX, 24
Jackson, Charles Thomas, IX, 308
Jackson, Christopher, VII, 440
Jackson, Edward, X, **379**; XI, 584, 607, 608; XII, 939
Jackson, Eleanor Bowers (Ward), VIII, 922
Jackson, Elizabeth. *See* Gerrald
Jackson, Elizabeth (Macgeorge), XI, 557
Jackson, Emmeline (Sanford), X, 379; XII, 939
Jackson, Francis, VIII, 6
Jackson, Francis James, V, 533
Jackson, George, VII, 272
Jackson, Hannah (Loring), IV, 486
Jackson, Henry, VIII, 970
Jackson, Henry Beecroft, X, 274
Jackson, James (Quebec teacher), V, 330
Jackson, James (Scottish teacher), IX, 652
Jackson, James, VI, 92, 675; VIII, **422–23**, 715; IX, 80
Jackson, John (businessman), VII, 617, 618; VIII, 630; X, 517
Jackson, John (clergyman), V, 496; VI, 537; X, 18
Jackson, John (engineer), X, 404
Jackson, John, II, **293–94**, 350, 351, 438, 486, 487, 564, 583
Jackson, John Mills, V, 170, 171, 842, 856, 857; VI, 579, 610; VII, 419, **438–40**; VIII, 339; IX, 24
Jackson, Josiah, VII, 438
Jackson, Lydia Ann. *See* Sanford
Jackson, M. C. (Williams), XI, 929
Jackson, Margaret, II, 486
Jackson, Mary. *See* Bissett
Jackson, Mary Amelia (Vincent), XII, 1075
Jackson, Milldred (Bibb), VIII, 89
Jackson, Phoebe (Willcocks), V, 859
Jackson, Richard. *See* Richards, Jackson John
Jackson, Sir Richard Downes, VII, 31, 32, 364, **440–41**; VIII, 101, 102, 135, 164; IX, 741, 806, 858
Jackson, Robert Edwin, XI, 236
Jackson, Sarah (Stephens), XI, 850
Jackson, Sarah (Stewart), VIII, 837
Jackson, Thomas C., XII, 924
Jackson*, William Henry (1861–1952), XI, 745, 746, 748, 750; XII, 608, 723
Jackson, William Mather, X, 386, 591, 725; XI, 412; XII, 350, 392
Jackson, William Walrond, X, 84
Jacob. *See also* Jacau
Jacob, Charlotte (Thomson), VII, 855
Jacob, Edwin, VIII, 172, 173; IX, 339, **408–9**; XI, 446, 447; XII, 232

Jacob, Étienne, II, 294
Jacob, Étienne, II, **294**, 648
Jacob, Jeanne. *See* Bellejambe
Jacob, Jeanne. *See* Fressel
Jacob, John, IX, 408
Jacob, Mary Jane. *See* Patterson
Jacob, Namaria (mother of EDWIN), IX, 408
Jacobi*, Otto Reinhold (1812–1901), XI, 296; XII, 327, 328, 789
Jacobs, Abraham, IV, 386
Jacobs, Angélique, IV, 385
Jacobs, Baptist Samuel, IV, 385
Jacobs, Elizabeth. *See* Anderson
Jacobs, Ferdinand, III, 595; IV, 47, 157, 377, **383–84**, 518, 523, 583, 647; V, 450, 656
Jacobs (Jackson), Harriet (Phillips; Holman), XI, 419
Jacobs, John Baptist, IV, 385; VI, 665
Jacobs, John Levy, IV, 385
Jacobs, Marie-Josette. *See* Audette, *dit* Lapointe
Jacobs, Mary (wife of PAHTAHSEGA), XI, 660
Jacobs, Mary Geneviève, IV, 385
Jacobs, Mary Marianne, IV, 385
Jacobs, Peter. *See also* Pahtahsega
Jacobs, Peter, X, 4; XI, 653, 654, 661
Jacobs, Samuel (seigneur), VI, 344
Jacobs, Samuel (son of FERDINAND), IV, 384
Jacobs, Samuel (son of SAMUEL), IV, 385
Jacobs, Samuel, IV, 37, 330, 331, 332, **384–86**; V, 20, 164, 368, 369, 385, 713; VI, 95; VIII, 368
Jacobs, Thomas, IV, 385
Jacobus, Rachael. *See* Lydekker
Jacquelin, Françoise-Marie (Saint-Étienne de La Tour), I, **383–84**, 505, 594, 595; IV, xxiii
Jacquelin, Jean-François, III, 282
Jacquemart, Marie-Christine (Delezenne), IV, 204
Jacquerault (Jacquero). *See* Jacrau
Jacquereau, Anne (Mercier), III, 442, 443
Jacques (fl. 1694), II, 375
Jacques (fl. 1829), VII, 289
Jacques, John, IX, 391; XI, 390, **448–49**
Jacques, Mary. *See* Quinton
Jacques, Thomas, XI, 448
Jacquet, Élisabeth. *See* Bourget
Jacquet, François, II, 467
Jacquet, François, IV, 45, **386–87**
Jacquet, Joseph, IV, 386
Jacquet, Louise. *See* Giroux
Jacquier, Anne (Lestringant), II, 426
Jacquies, Adélaïde. *See* Prahm
Jacquies, Adolphe, VIII, **423–24**, 962; XII, 269
Jacquiés, Barbe. *See* Segris
Jacquies, Catherine. *See* Ponsy
Jacquies, Hilaire-Jacob, VIII, 423
Jacquiés, Luc, II, 294
Jacquiés, *dit* Leblond, Catherine. *See* Guillemote
Jacquiés, *dit* Leblond, Jean, II, **294–95**
Jacquin, Anne. *See* Perrot
Jacquin, Jean-Claude, III, 304
Jacquin, Nikolaus Josef, V, 399
Jacquin, *dit* Philibert, Marie-Anne. *See* Guérin
Jacquin, *dit* Philibert, Nicolas, III, 96, **304–5**; IV, 66, 449
Jacquin, *dit* Philibert, Pierre-Nicolas, III, 304
Jacquinot, Barthélemy, I, 455, 539

Jacrau, Joseph-André-Mathurin, III, 194, 399; IV, 74, 100, 183, **387–88**, 642, 643, 719; V, 144, 379; VI, 493
Jacson, Antoine, V, 49, **451–52**; VI, 24; VIII, 38
Jacson, Antoine-Joseph, V, 451
Jacson, Louis (grandfather), V, 451
Jacson, Louis, V, 452
Jacson, Madeleine. *See* Fleury
Jacson, Marie-Marguerite. *See* Chamberland
Jadis, Charles Newland Godfrey, IV, **388–89**
Jadis, Elizabeth. *See* Newland
Jadis, John Godfrey Maximilian, Count d'Adié, IV, 388
Jadis, Margaret (wife of CHARLES NEWLAND GODFREY), IV, 388
Jaffray, Christiana (Robertson), IX, 667
Jager, Claude, I, 205
Jago, George, II, 295
Jago, John, II, **295**
Jaillet, Suzanne (Girouard), XI, 350
Jalbert, François, VIII, 726; X, 527
Jallais, Marie (Leclerc), II, 380
Jallot (Jalleau), Jeanne (Terrier de Francheville et de Repentigny; Poulin de La Fontaine), I, 553; II, 227, 254, 529
Jalobert, Alizon. *See* Des Granches
Jalobert, Bertrand, I, 384
Jalobert, Jehanne. *See* Maingard
Jalobert, Macé, I, 167, 169, **384**, 520
Jalot, Marie-Antoinette. *See* Chouart Des Groseilliers
Jamay. *See* Jamet
Jambe de Bois. *See* Gargot de La Rochette, Nicolas
James, Father. *See* Grace, Thomas
James (fl. 1800), IV, 778
James (fl. 1804), IV, 779
James I, King of England, Scotland, and Ireland (James VI of Scotland), I, 23, 50, 51, 52, 67, 69, 144, 243, 369, 481, 496, 597, 667, 668; IV, xvii, xix
James II, King of England, Scotland, and Ireland, I, 92, 227, 329, 544, 605, 631; II, 100, 101, 496, 497, 539, 636, 643; III, 176, 428, 602
James III, King of Scotland, VII, 538
James, the Old Pretender, III, 116; VII, 830
James, Abigail (Jessup), V, 454
James, Alexander, XII, 250, 1092
James, Catherine (Neilson), VII, 649
James, Edwin, VII, 845
James, Ezekiel, XI, 366
James, George Payne Rainsford, IX, 543
James, Henry, XI, 333
James, Sir Henry, XII, 815
James, Jane (Palmer), XII, 815
James, John, VII, 121
James, Mary (Gould), XI, 365
James, Mary Ann (Moschell), VII, 636
James, Mary Ann (Stewart), VI, 735
James, Philip, VIII, 200, **424–25**, 908; X, 511
James, Reginald, VI, 103; VII, 133, 821
James, Richard, I, 229
James, Robert, IX, 136
James, Rosalie (Gill), IV, 293
James, Thomas, I, 349, 384
James, Thomas, I, 20, 83, 144, 311, 329, 349, 362, 376, 377, **384–85**, 408
James, William (author), VI, 803

James, William (of Bristol, England), I, 306
Jameson, Anna Brownell. *See* Murphy
Jameson, Anna Maria (Browne), XI, 119; XII, 131
Jameson, Ann Elizabeth. *See* Thurman
Jameson, Sir George Inglis, XII, 468
Jameson, Mary. *See* Sympson
Jameson, Richard Willis, XII, **468**
Jameson, Robert, IX, 158, 160, 161, 658
Jameson, Robert Sympson, VII, 370, 459, 605, 695; VIII, 29, 282, **426–28**, 432, 512, 586, 649, 650, 651; IX, 58, 99, 163, 245; X, 109, 132, 310, 610
Jameson, Thomas, VIII, 426
Jamet, Denis, I, 192, 265, 296, **385**, 437, 590
Jamet, John, III, **305–6**, 452; V, 129; VI, 317
Jamieson, Janet (Jeanette) (Russell), XI, 779
Jamieson, John, IX, 316
Jamieson, Neil, V, 646
Jamin, Gilles, I, 265
Jamin, Pierre, I, 503, 504
Jamot, Gilbert, XI, 449
Jamot, Jean-François, XI, **449–51**, 537, 939; XII, 103
Jamot, Jeanne. *See* Cornabat
Jandet, Marguerite, III, 94
Janes, John, I, 375
Janes, Joseph S., XI, 583
Janes, William D. B., XII, 62
Jangouessy. *See* Chingouessi
Jannasch*, Hermann Theodor (1849–1931), X, 513
Jannasch, Marie. *See* Miertsching
Jannière, Jeanne (Bourdon de Dombourg; Denys de Bonaventure), I, 114; II, 176; III, 175, 552, 682
Janot. *See* Jeanneau
Janot, *dit* Bourguignon, Henri, III, 171
Jansac, Jeanne-Beatrix de. *See* Mongenet
Janson. *See also* Forbin-Janson
Janson, Paul, I, 213
Janson, *dit* Lapalme, Charles, III, 306, 307
Janson, *dit* Lapalme, Christophe, II, 530; III, 306
Janson, *dit* Lapalme, Dominique, II, 160; III, 165, **306–8**; IV, 204, 732
Janson, *dit* Lapalme, Jeanne-Charlotte. *See* Couturier, *dit* Le Bourguignon
Janson, *dit* Lapalme, Louis, II, 160; III, 306, 307
Janson, *dit* Lapalme, Madeleine. *See* Trefflé, *dit* Rottot
Janson, *dit* Lapalme, Madeleine-Ursule. *See* Rancin
Janson, *dit* Lapalme, Marie-Catherine (Delezenne), IV, 204; VI, 183, 184
Janson, *dit* Lapalme, Marie-Geneviève. *See* Pelletier
Janson, *dit* Lapalme, Marie-Joseph. *See* Couturier, *dit* Le Bourguignon
Janson, *dit* Lapalme, Philippe, III, 306, 307
Janson, *dit* Lapalme, Pierre, II, 111, 200, 338, 418; III, 304, 306, 307
Jantot. *See* Jeantot
Janvrin, Brelade, VI, 347
Janvrin, Elizabeth. *See* Lecq
Janvrin, Esther Elizabeth. *See* Filleul
Janvrin, Francis, VI, 348, 653; VIII, 257
Janvrin, Frederick, VI, 348; XI, 440
Janvrin, John, VI, 348
Janvrin, John, VI, **347–49**, 370; VIII, 257
Janvrin, Philip, VI, 348; VIII, 257
Jaques, George Edward, XI, 363

Jaques, Richard, III, 477
Jardine, Alexander (father), IX, 409
Jardine, Alexander, IX, 410, 411
Jardine, Euphemia. *See* Reid
Jardine, Helen. *See* Davidson
Jardine, James, VII, 71
Jardine, Robert, IX, **409–11**; XI, 224; XII, 444
Jarin (Jarrin, Gérin), Jean, XI, 340
Jarlais (Desjarlais), Hélène (Picotte), VI, 581
Jarret, Claudine. *See* Pécaudy
Jarret, Jean, II, 295
Jarret, *dit* Beauregard, Marie-Joseph (Josephte) (Lagimonière), VIII, 481
Jarret, *dit* Beauregard, Pierre, XI, 249
Jarret de Verchères, Alexandre, II, 295; III, 310
Jarret de Verchères, Angélique (Coulon de Villiers), II, 156; III, 148, 150; IV, 177
Jarret de Verchères, Antoine, III, 308
Jarret de Verchères, Catherine (Hertel de Beaubassin), IV, 347
Jarret de Verchères, Charlotte-Gabrielle (Raimbault de Saint-Blaint; Hertel de Rouville), IV, 344
Jarret de Verchères, François, II, 295; III, 308
Jarret de Verchères, François-Michel, III, 308
Jarret de Verchères, Jean, III, 399
Jarret de Verchères, Jean-Baptiste, II, 367
Jarret de Verchères, Louis, II, 285
Jarret de Verchères, Madeleine. *See* Ailleboust de Manthet
Jarret de Verchères, Marguerite-Gabrielle (Levrault de Langis), III, 399
Jarret de Verchères, Marie. *See* Perrot
Jarret de Verchères, Marie-Jeanne (Douhet de Larivière, *dit* de L'Étang; Du Verger d'Aubusson), III, 308
Jarret de Verchères, Marie-Madeleine (Tarieu de La Pérade), I, 239, 418; II, 156, 224, 295; III, **308–13**, 676; IV, 728
Jarret de Verchères, Pierre, II, 285, **295–96**; III, 310
Jarrin. *See* Jarin
Jarry, Émery, II, 163
Jarry, Jean-Baptiste, III, 210
Jarry, Marguerite. *See* Gaudé
Jartoux, Pierre, III, 336
Jarvie, Agnes (Buchanan), XI, 125, 127
Jarvie, William, VIII, 4
Jarvis, Abraham, V, 25
Jarvis, Amelia. *See* Glover
Jarvis, Anna Maria. *See* Boyd
Jarvis, Anna Maria. *See* Mountain
Jarvis, Anne (Ellis), X, 270
Jarvis, Anne Frances (Meredith), XII, 728, 729, 730, 731
Jarvis, Arthur, XII, 867
Jarvis, Edward, IV, 32, **389–90**, 743; V, 712; VI, 766
Jarvis, Edward James, VI, 350, 727, 821; VII, 742, 904; VIII, 102, **428–30**, 484, 531, 564; IX, 62, 63; XII, 840
Jarvis, Edward Lutwyche, XII, 895
Jarvis, Elizabeth. *See* Gray
Jarvis, Elizabeth Ann (Robinson), X, 622
Jarvis, Frederick William, IX, 411
Jarvis, George Stephen Benjamin, V, 113; IX, 803; X, 164, **379–80**
Jarvis, Hannah. *See* Peters
Jarvis, Hannah Owen (Hamilton), VII, 375, 693, 694

Jarvis, John C., X, 723
Jarvis, Julia. *See* Sherwood
Jarvis, Leonard, V, 413, 415, 416; VI, 718
Jarvis, Maria (Mary) Lavinia (Hamilton), VII, 378
Jarvis, Martha. *See* Seymour
Jarvis, Mary. *See* Arnold
Jarvis, Mary Boyles (wife of SAMUEL PETERS). *See* Powell
Jarvis, Mary Boyles (wife of WILLIAM BOTSFORD). *See* Powell
Jarvis, Munson, V, 647; VI, **349–50**; VIII, 428
Jarvis, Polly (Patty) Marvin (Peters), VI, 578
Jarvis, Ralph Munson, VI, 350
Jarvis, Samuel (agent), VI, 718
Jarvis, Samuel (brother of MUNSON), VI, 350
Jarvis, Samuel (father of MUNSON), VI, 349
Jarvis, Samuel (father of WILLIAM), V, 452
Jarvis, Samuel (political candidate), V, 94
Jarvis, Samuel Peters, VIII, 432
Jarvis, Samuel Peters, V, 453; VI, 164, 265, 560, 604, 608, 612, 772; VII, 55, 375, 418, 693, 917; VIII, 47, 125, 163, **430–33**, 512, 521, 602, 709, 750, 831, 853, 934; IX, 411, 497, 521, 647, 661, 674, 700, 724; X, 12, 618; XI, 405, 427, 521
Jarvis, Stephen, VIII, 750, 884; IX, 411; X, 379
Jarvis, William, VI, 350
Jarvis, William, V, 65, 420, 441, 449, **452–53**, 597, 815, 816, 854; VI, 349, 350, 374, 415, 578, 579, 608, 624; VII, 285, 375, 378, 518, 554, 693, 694, 812; VIII, 337, 430, 750, 885; IX, 411; X, 618, 622
Jarvis, William Botsford, VII, 519, 704; VIII, 47, 282, 523, 524, 643, 750; IX, 265, **411–12**, 503, 662, 724, 744; X, 618; XI, 713; XII, 729
Jarvis, William Munson, VI, 426; IX, 165, 519; XI, 552
Jasne. *See* Robert
Jauge, Simon, V, 42
Jautard, Thérèse. *See* Bouat
Jautard, Valentin, IV, 36, 229, 336, **390–92**, 532, 533, 534, 547, 697; V, 621, 737, 892, 894
Jay, John (merchant), I, 386
Jay, John (politician), V, 629; VI, 33
Jay, John (tucker), I, 386
Jay, John, I, 19, 21, 147, 239, 240, **386–87**
Jaynes, Maurice, VIII, 391
Jean, Caroline Susan (LeVesconte), X, 440
Jean, Catherine (Bossu), V, 93
Jean, Jacqueline (Véniard de Bourgmond), II, 645
Jean, Marie-Louise (Koenig, Baroness von Koenig), VI, 378
Jean-Armand. *See* Andehoua
Jean-Baptiste. *See also* Atironta (d. 1650)
Jean Baptiste. *See* Kitchi-manito-waya
Jean-Baptiste (brother of STAYEGHTHA), V, 775
Jean-Baptiste (son of GRAY LOCK), III, 266
Jean-Baptiste, Brother. *See* Dufresne
Jeançonne. *See* Jeanson
Jean L'Ancien. *See* Boispineau, Jean-Jard
Jeanneau, Catherine. *See* Perrot
Jeanneau, Étienne, III, 313
Jeanneau, Étienne, III, 299, **313–14**; IV, 71
Jeanneau, Jacquette. *See* Clément
Jeanne de Sainte-Marie, I, 348
Jeanne-Françoise de Sainte-Hélène. *See* Bermen de La Martinière

Jeanne-Françoise de Saint-Ignace. *See* Juchereau de la Ferté
Jeannin, Pierre, known as Président Jeannin, I, 470
Jeanson. *See also* Janson
Jeanson, Guillaume, IV, xxix, **392**
Jeanson, Jean-Baptiste, IV, 392
Jeanson, Marie-Josette. *See* Aucoin
Jeantot, Jean, III, **314**
Jebb, Amelia Rose, Lady Jebb. *See* Pelham
Jebb, Dorothy. *See* Gladwin
Jebb, John, VI, 240
Jebb, Joshua, IX, 412
Jebb, Sir Joshua, VII, 129; IX, **412–13**
Jebb, Mary Legh. *See* Thomas
Jecob, Captain. *See* Winninnewaycappo
Jefferey, John, V, 106
Jefferey, Sarah (Bradford), V, 106
Jeffers, Elizabeth (Diamond), X, 230
Jeffers, Jane. *See* Frith
Jeffers, Jane Eleanor. *See* Dougall
Jeffers, Nancy. *See* Maurice
Jeffers, Robert, XII, 468
Jeffers, Wellington, IX, 736, 737; XII, **468–69**
Jefferson, Robert, XI, 695
Jefferson, Thomas, IV, 303, 322, 337, 412; V, 313, 583, 693, 848; VI, 55, 333, 772; VII, 429, 912; VIII, 387, 388; X, 569
Jeffery, Albert Oscar, XII, 470
Jeffery, Alexander Haley, XII, 470
Jeffery, Augusta Ann. *See* Haley
Jeffery, Charles Llewellyn, XII, 470
Jeffery, Elizabeth (mother of THOMAS NICKLESON), VII, 441
Jeffery, James, VIII, 93
Jeffery, James Edgar, XII, 470
Jeffery, John (father of THOMAS NICKLESON), VII, 441
Jeffery, John (shipbuilder), VIII, 93; XII, 1072
Jeffery, Joseph (father of JOSEPH), XII, 469
Jeffery, Joseph (grandson of JOSEPH), XII, 470
Jeffery, Joseph, XII, **469–70**
Jeffery, Martha Maria. *See* Uniacke
Jeffery, Mary Ann. *See* Godbold
Jeffery, Thomas Nickleson, VII, 24, 84, 88, 142, **441–42**, 531, 533; VIII, 356, 603
Jeffery, William Henry, IX, 598, 599
Jefferys*, Charles William (1869–1951), IV, 120
Jefferys, Thomas, III, 108; V, 767
Jeffrey, Andrew, XII, 994
Jeffrey, John, V, 491, 641, 764, 783, 784, 785, 838; VI, 274
Jeffrey, Joseph W., V, 784
Jehin, Jules-Antoine, XII, 470
Jehin, Marie-Joséphine-Pétronille. *See* Prume
Jehin-Prume, Érasme, XII, 472
Jehin-Prume, Frantz, XII, **470–72**, 532, 533
Jehin-Prume, Hortense. *See* Leduc
Jehin-Prume, Jules, XII, 471
Jehin-Prume, Rosita. *See* Del Vecchio
Jékimbert, Geneviève. *See* Allard
Jékimbert (Kimber), Joseph-Antoine, VII, 468; VIII, 470
Jelly, Geneviève (Saint-Hilaire; Couture), XI, 208
Jemison, Mary, IV, 405; V, 14
Jenčič, Maria Katharina Josefa (Baraga), IX, 31

Jenckes, Joseph, XII, 925
Jenckes, Mary (Grant), XII, 925
Jendon, Pierre, III, 141
Jendon, Victoire. *See* Coron
Jenison, Jean, V, 599
Jenkins, Ann, II, 664
Jenkins, Elizabeth (Deblois), VI, 181
Jenkins, George, V, 614; VI, 505
Jenkins, Harriet. *See* Shepstone
Jenkins, James Mairs, VII, 443
Jenkins, Jane. *See* Forrest
Jenkins, John, XII, 472
Jenkins, John, XII, **472–74**
Jenkins, John Edward, X, 231; XII, 473
Jenkins, Louisa Mary. *See* MacLennan
Jenkins, Louis Charles, VII, 434, 435; XII, 319
Jenkins, Mary. *See* Evans
Jenkins, Mary (Beardsley), VIII, 69
Jenkins, Mary Hatfield. *See* Stockton
Jenkins, Penelope. *See* Winslow
Jenkins, Rebecca (Elder), VII, 271
Jenkins, William, VII, **442–43**; VIII, 72
Jenkinson, Anthony, I, 331
Jenkinson, Charles, 1st Earl of Liverpool, IV, 571; VI, 357
Jenkinson, Elizabeth (Story), XII, 994
Jenkinson, Robert Banks, 2nd Earl of Liverpool, V, 213, 521, 522, 655, 842; VI, 566; VII, 768, 872; VIII, xxvii, 165, 389; IX, 21, 220, 306
Jenks, David Harris, XII, 365
Jenner, Abraham, VII, 896
Jenner, Edward, V, 189, 190; VIII, 483; X, 497
Jenner, George Charles, V, 190
Jenner, Magdalena (Élisabeth) (Watteville), VII, 896
Jennings, Amelia Clotilda, XII, **474–75**
Jennings, Ann. *See* Leighton
Jennings*, Emily Howard (Stowe) (1831–1903), XII, 1075, 1113
Jennings, Harriet, XII, 474
Jennings, John, X, 380
Jennings, John, VII, 192; VIII, 874; X, **380–81**; XI, 397
Jennings, Joseph, XII, 474
Jennings, Margaret. *See* Cumming
Jennings, Sarah (Churchill, Duchess of Marlborough), II, 286, 659
Jennison, John, III, 620
Jennison, Susan (Spencer), X, 663
Jenny, VI, 417
Jensen, Stephen, IV, 334
Jérémie, Claude, I, 387
Jérémie, Hélène. *See* Macart
Jérémie, *dit* Lamontagne, Catherine (Aubuchon; Lepallieur de Laferté), II, 296, 413; III, **314–15**, 408
Jérémie, *dit* Lamontagne, Françoise. *See* Bourot
Jérémie, *dit* Lamontagne, Françoise, II, 296
Jérémie, *dit* Lamontagne, Jeanne. *See* Pelletier
Jérémie, *dit* Lamontagne, Marie-Madeleine. *See* Tetesigaguoy
Jérémie, *dit* Lamontagne, Marie-Madeleine (Mallet), II, 451
Jérémie, *dit* Lamontagne, Nicolas, II, 256, **296–300**, 319, 406, 614; III, 498
Jérémie, *dit* Lamontagne, Noël, I, 60, **387**; II, 159, 256, 296, 451; III, 314

Jérémie, *dit* Lamontagne, *dit* Douville, Charlotte (Huppé, *dit* Lagroix), IV, 376
Jérôme. *See also* Atecouando (fl. 1749–57)
Jérôme, V, 261
Jérôme, King of Westphalia. *See* Bonaparte, Jérôme
Jérôme, Angélique. *See* Letendre, *dit* Batoche
Jérôme, Angélique (Rolette), X, 628
Jérôme, *dit* Latour, François (Franceway), IV, 365
Jérôme, *dit* Latour, Marie-Joseph (Roy), V, 727
Jérôme, *dit* Saint-Matte, Hélène (Goulet), IX, 329
Jersey, Earl of. *See* Villiers
Jervis, John, 1st Earl of St Vincent, III, 132; V, 759; VI, 796; VII, 196; VIII, 70; X, 178
Jervois, Elizabeth. *See* Maitland
Jervois, Lucy. *See* Norsworthy
Jervois (Jervoise), William, XII, 475
Jervois, Sir William Francis Drummond, XII, **475–76**, 910
Jeryan, Dorothy, named de Saint-Joseph, III, 24
Jeskakake, III, 320, 614
Jessen, Dettlieb Christopher, V, **453–54**
Jessen, Francisca Barbara. *See* Rudolf
Jessie Joyful. *See* Mamenawatum
Jessop*, John (1829–1901), XI, 757
Jessop, Mary (Barry), VII, 52; X, 35
Jessopp, Henry Bate, IX, 205
Jessup, Abigail. *See* Dibble
Jessup, Abigail. *See* James
Jessup, Ebenezer, V, 454
Jessup, Edward, V, 455; VI, 427
Jessup, Edward, IV, 710; V, 307, **454–55**, 457; VI, 146, 264, 502, 804; VII, 92; VIII, 304; IX, 414
Jessup, Hamilton Dribble, XI, 677
Jessup, Joseph, V, 454
Jessup, Phyllis Ann (Beechey, Lady Beechey), VIII, 70
Jetté, Jean-Marie, IX, 111
Jetté*, Sir Louis-Amable (1836–1920), VIII, 479; X, 148, 149, 155, 423; XI, 71, 480, 624, 893; XII, 362, 692, 720
Jetté, Marie-Rosalie. *See* Cadron
Jewer, John, II, 10, 62, 563
Jewett. *See also* Jouett
Jewett, Dorothy (Caleff), V, 134
Jewett, Jedediah, V, 47
Jewitt, Edward, VI, 350
Jewitt, Hester. *See* Jones
Jewitt, John Rodgers, V, 618, 619; VI, **350–51**; XII, 130
Jilbert. *See* Gilbert
Jillard, Anne (MacGregor), VIII, 547
Joannès, Armand de, IV, 652
Joannès, François-Augustin de, Baron de Chacornacle, II, 300
Joannès de Chacornacle, II, 220, **300**
Joannès de Chacornacle, Balthazar de, II, 300
Joannès de Chacornacle, Catherine de. *See* Mortier
Job, Jessy. *See* Carson
Job, John (father), V, 119, 120; X, 381; XII, 888
Job, John, X, 381
Job, Robert, X, 381; XII, 888
Job, Samuel, X, 381; XII, 889
Job, Sarah. *See* Bulley
Job, Thomas Bulley, X, **381**; XII, 888, 889
Job, Thomas Raffles, X, 381; XII, 889
Jobert, Charlotte. *See* Larchevêque
Jobert, Charlotte (Frobisher), V, 332, 333; VI, 267

Jobert, Jean-Baptiste, IV, 82; V, 333; VI, 699
Jobin, André, VII, 666; VIII, **433–35**; IX, 459; X, 500
Jobin, Angélique. *See* Sarrère, *dit* La Victoire
Jobin, Élisabeth (Guyart de Fleury), III, 272
Jobin, Émilie. *See* Masson
Jobin, François (blacksmith), II, 516
Jobin, François (father of ANDRÉ), VIII, 433
Jobin, Françoise (Dandonneau, *dit* Lajeunesse), II, 168
Jobin, Joseph-Hilarion, VIII, 618
Jobin*, Louis (1845–1928), XII, 46
Jobin, Marie. *See* Archambault
Jobin, Marie-Élize. *See* Dorval
Jobin, Marie-Joseph. *See* Baudry
Jobin, Virginie (Masson), X, 500
Jobson, Margaret Yelloby (Côté), VII, 209
Jobson, Thomas, VII, 209
Jobson, Thomas-Robert, XII, 692
Jock, Jimmy. *See* Bird, James
Jodrell, Anne (Clitherow), VIII, 163
Joe, IV, 295, **392–93**
Joe, Sylvester, VI, **351–52**
Joe Beef. *See* McKiernan, Charles
Joe Ebierbing. *See* Ipilkvik
Joel, George, VIII, 369
Jogues, Isaac, I, 11, 41, 42, 112, 124, 125, 203, 344, 370, 371, 373, **387–90**, 403, 404, 410, 411, 414, 454, 457, 459, 461, 462, 523, 524, 566; II, 157, 158; VII, 171; XI, 94
Johannes, Bishop. *See* Watteville
John, Captain. *See* Deserontyon, John; Nagiscoig; Ogimauh-binaessih
John (father of David GEORGE), V, 340
John, Catharine. *See* Brant
John, James, VI, 352; IX, 160
John, Noel, VII, **443–44**
John August, V, 784; VI, 70
John Chrysostom, XII, 713
Johnny Appleseed. *See* Chapman, John
Johnson, Miss (Welch), V, 845
Johnson, Mr (teacher), X, 282
Johnson, Alexander Smith, XI, 767
Johnson, Ann (Claus), IV, 155; VI, 151
Johnson, Anne. *See* Warren
Johnson, Anne (Dease), V, 228
Johnson, Arthur Jukes, X, 382
Johnson, Benjamin, VI, 565
Johnson, Bethiah. *See* Barker
Johnson, Catherine. *See* Weissenberg
Johnson, Charles Christopher, VII, 112
Johnson, Christopher, IV, 394
Johnson, Dederika. *See* Memlingh
Johnson, Edwin, X, 587
Johnson, Elizabeth (Clench), VI, 153; VIII, 161
Johnson, Elizabeth (Kerr), VI, 374; VII, 466
Johnson, Ellen (mother of JOHN MERCER), IX, 413
Johnson, Emily Susanna. *See* Howells
Johnson, Emma (Waterhouse; Tripp), XII, 1090
Johnson, Evelyn Helen Charlotte, VIII, 620
Johnson, Francis, I, 390, 391, 392, 450, 451
Johnson, Sir Francis Godschall, VIII, 110; IX, 530; XI, 139, 286, 722; XII, **476–78**, 951
Johnson, George (businessman), XI, 147
Johnson, George (friend of Joseph HOWE), X, 368

Johnson, George (son of GEORGE HENRY MARTIN), XI, 453

Johnson, George (son of Sir WILLIAM), IV, 418

Johnson, George, I, **390–92**, 450, 451

Johnson, George Henry Martin, VI, 759; VIII, 620; X, 270; XI, **451–53**, 639; XII, 401

Johnson, Godschall, XII, 476

Johnson, Guy, IV, 117, 118, 119, 120, 130, 149, 155, 308, 368, **393–94**, 397, 405, 409, 410, 730, 731, 735; V, 147, 229, 254, 262, 804, 806, 811, 843, 895, 896; VI, 353

Johnson, Helen. *See* Martin

Johnson, Henrietta. *See* Shirreff

Johnson, Henry, XII, 478

Johnson, Isabella (Barnes), V, 57

Johnson, Isabelle. *See* Corporon

Johnson, Jacob. *See* Tekahionwake

Johnson, James, XII, 1057

Johnson, James Bovell, X, 382

Johnson, Jeanet (Brauneis), X, 88

Johnson, John. *See* Enmegahbowh

Johnson, John (father of WILLIAM ARTHUR), X, 381

Johnson, John (professor), XI, 773

Johnson, Sir John, IV, 119, 130, 149, 330, 393, 394, 397, 406, 417, 494, 566, 710, 735; V, 149, 179, 229, 230, 254, 255, 282, 291, 302, 320, 365, 388, 405, 454, 517, 518, 519, 537, 552, 660, 669, 718, 757, 760, 772, 781, 786, 787, 806, 807, 841, 852, 894, 895, 896, 898, 899; VI, 8, 152, 179, **352–54**, 357, 374, 377, 387, 388, 404, 428, 435, 436, 439, 575, 607, 689, 739, 772, 816; VII, 413, 496, 517, 583, 618, 911; VIII, 161, 194; IX, 683; XI, 655

Johnson, John, V, 803; VI, 759; VIII, 620; XI, 451, **453–54**; XII, 402

Johnson, John Mercer, IX, 413

Johnson, John Mercer, IX, **413–14**; X, 286; XI, 466, 578, 828; XII, 740

Johnson, Laura Eliza. *See* Jukes

Johnson, Louisa (Miles), IX, 550

Johnson, Lucy. *See* Bisshopp

Johnson, Martha A. *See* Upper

Johnson, Martin, II, 265

Johnson, Mary, Lady Johnson. *See* Watts

Johnson, Mary (Harding), VIII, 361

Johnson, Mary (Polly) (Johnson), IV, 393

Johnson, Mary (Lefferty), VII, 496

Johnson, Mary Gates. *See* Jones

Johnson, Mary Louisa, Lady Johnson. *See* Mills

Johnson, Mathew, IV, 321

Johnson*, Pauline (1861–1913), X, 270; XI, 452; XII, 213

Johnson, Peter Warren, IV, 417, 418

Johnson, Samuel (college president), V, 58

Johnson, Samuel (writer), III, 583; IV, 554, 555; V, 56, 166; VIII, 426, 427, 741

Johnson, Sarah (Duckworth), V, 273

Johnson, Smoke. *See* Johnson, John (1792–1886)

Johnson, Susanna. *See* Willard

Johnson, Theresa Mary (Gowanlock), XI, 460; XII, **478**

Johnson, Thomas, IX, 209

Johnson, Thomas Hall, XI, 497, 672, 780

Johnson*, Urbain (1824–1918), IV, 392

Johnson, William. *See also* Jeanson, Guillaume; Teka-wiroñte

Johnson, William (father of Guillaume JEANSON), IV, 392

Johnson, William (soldier), IV, 731

Johnson, Sir William, III, xxxvii, xxxviii, xli, 49, 95, 101, 126, 158, 159, 174, 185, 186, 214, 255, 256, 262, 320, 321, 322, 409, 410, 452, 495, 526, 527, 530, 536, 561, 588, 607, 614, 623, 624, 651, 652, 655; IV, xxxvi, xxxvii, xxxviii, lvii, 23, 24, 26, 27, 57, 84, 86, 117, 119, 130, 137, 138, 149, 154, 155, 173, 174, 241, 279, 280, 282, 297, 299, 307, 309, 314, 337, 347, 368, 375, 393, **394–98**, 404, 408, 409, 417, 418, 489, 506, 582, 586, 587, 595, 596, 668, 669, 675, 676, 679, 681, 691, 692, 730, 731, 733, 734, 735, 762; V, 129, 228, 229, 253, 299, 454, 517, 519, 523, 567, 681, 706, 716, 786, 803, 804, 888; VI, 152, 153, 264, 317, 352, 353, 374, 440, 444; VII, 466, 496, 554, 651; VIII, 161; XI, 453

Johnson, William Arthur, IX, 550; X, 55, 84, **381–82**

Johnson, William Samuel, VI, 156

Johnston, Mr (councillor), IV, 398

Johnston, Agnes (Weld), XII, 1092

Johnston, Alexander, IV, 398

Johnston, Alexander, IV, **398–99**; V, 507

Johnston, Amelia Elizabeth. *See* Almon

Johnston, Ann. *See* Gilzean

Johnston, Ann, IV, 400

Johnston, Anna. *See* Randolph

Johnston, Charlotte (Oge-Buno-Quay) (McMurray), XII, 680

Johnston, David, XI, 454

Johnston, Elizabeth. *See* Lichtenstein

Johnston, Elizabeth. *See* McNeil

Johnston, Elizabeth (Colvill, Baroness Colvill), III, 131

Johnston, Elizabeth (Crawley), XI, 214

Johnston, Elizabeth Murray. *See* Bliss

Johnston, Elizabeth Wildman (Ritchie), VII, 506; VIII, 751; X, 383; XI, 754; XII, 895

Johnston, Francis, VI, 553

Johnston, George (brother of GEORGE MOIR), X, 382

Johnston, George (father of WILLIAM, d. 1828), VI, 359

Johnston, George (son of JOHN), VI, 357; VIII, 651

Johnston, George Moir, X, **382–83**

Johnston, Harriet Maria. *See* Millidge

Johnston, Helen (Ogilvie), XII, 800

Johnston, Hugh, XI, 608; XII, 266

Johnston, Hugh, V, 647; VI, **354–56**, 726, 756; VII, 444, 895; XII, 139

Johnston, Hugh, VI, 354; VII, 424, **444–45**, 658; VIII, 803, 808, 809, 810; IX, 146, 147; X, 711

Johnston, Isabel. *See* Hepburn

Johnston, James (father of WILLIAM, 1782–1870), IX, 414

Johnston, James, IV, 37, 295, **399–400**, 571, 618, 645, 646; V, 19, 142, 289, 509, 699; VI, 326; VII, 575

Johnston, James, VII, 184, **445–46**; VIII, 135, 839; IX, 13, 14

Johnston, James Finlay Weir, VIII, **435–36**; IX, 87, 383, 630, 666, 767

Johnston, James William, XII, 882, 966

Johnston, James William, VII, 16, 123, 202, 507, 911, 932; VIII, 118, 168, 193, 357, 383, 416, 417, 613, 657, 752, 902, 904, 905, 968; IX, 177, 226, 295, 426, 427, 536, 601, 602, 748, 841; X, 7, 73, 232, 352, 353, 364, 365, **383–88**, 440, 457; XI, 22, 106, 155, 214, 308, 398, 525, 619, 686, 754, 755, 925, 926, 944, 945, 946, 947, 948, 949; XII, 30, 31, 32, 35, 406, 481, 765, 791, 870, 872, 879

Johnston, Jane (wife of JAMES, d. 1849), VII, 446
Johnston, Jane (Obah-dahm-wawn-gezzhago-quay)
    (Schoolcraft), VI, 357, 358
Johnston, John (brother of JAMES, d. 1800), IV, 399
Johnston, John (brother of WILLIAM, 1782–1870), IX, 415
Johnston, John (shipbuilder), VIII, 126
Johnston, John (son of Elizabeth LICHTENSTEIN), VII, 507
Johnston, John (teacher), VI, 484
Johnston, John (uncle of John William RITCHIE), XI, 754
Johnston, John, VI, 100, 101, **356–59**, 547; XII, 680
Johnston, John Purss, IV, 400
Johnston, Joseph, XII, 800
Johnston, Laleah (Burpee), VIII, 118
Johnston, Laleah Peyton (Almon), VII, 16
Johnston, Lewis (grandfather), X, 383
Johnston, Lewis, VII, 491; VIII, 567
Johnston, Lewis Saurin, VI, 357
Johnston, Louisa. See Pryor
Johnston, Margaret. See Macnider
Johnston, Margaret. See Thurburn
Johnston, Margaret (Grieve), XI, 376
Johnston, Margaret (Whittemore), VIII, 930
Johnston, Marguerite (Solomon), VIII, 831
Johnston, Mary Geddie (Matheson), XII, 829
Johnston, Richard, IV, 482
Johnston, Samuel Fulton, XII, 829
Johnston, Sarah. See Hatton
Johnston, Sarah, V, 192
Johnston, Sarah Elizabeth (wife of WILLIAM, d. 1828), VI,
    359
Johnston, Sarah Mortimer. See Smith
Johnston, Susan. See Oshaguscodawaqua
Johnston, Susan (Lang), XI, 486
Johnston, Thomas W., XI, 819
Johnston, William (father of HUGH, 1756–1829), VI, 354
Johnston, William (father of JOHN), VI, 356
Johnston, William (uncle of Walter GRIEVE), XI, 376
Johnston, William, V, 862; VI, 122, **359–61**, 567, 568, 785;
    VII, 408, 415; VIII, 36, 443, 824, 825, 827; X, 352
Johnston, William, VII, 29, 405; VIII, 305, 788; IX,
    **414–15**; X, 652; XII, 644
Johnston, William, XI, **454**
Johnston, William F., XII, 703, 705
Johnston, William Martin, VII, 16, 506; X, 383; XII, 895
Johnston Blair, Jemima (Ferguson), IX, 251, 253
Johnston-Brown, Martha (Sefton), XII, 959
Johnstone. See also Johnston
Johnstone, Bridget (Bonnycastle), VII, 90
Johnstone, Frances (Bonnycastle, Lady Bonnycastle), VII,
    90
Johnstone, George, V, 136; VI, 811
Johnstone, James, IV, 400
Johnstone, James, known as Chevalier de Johnstone, III,
    136, 137; IV, **400–1**, 455
Johnstone, John, V, 681
Johnstone, Thomas Cooke, XI, 748
Johnstone, Walter, VI, **361–62**; VIII, 452
Johnstone, William, V, 482
Johonerissa. See Tanaghrisson
Joibert. See Joybert
Joinville, Prince de. See Orléans
Joinville, Gabriel de, I, 434
Jolicœur. See Contremine

Jolicœur, Monsieur (soldier), II, 645
Jolicœur, Philippe-Jacques, XII, 86
Joliette. See also Jolliet
Joliette, Barthélemy, VI, 786, 787; VII, **446–50**, 757, 851;
    VIII, 60, 288; IX, 533, 703; XI, 173, 208
Joliette, Charles Barthélemy, VII, 446
Joliette, Charlotte. See Lanaudière
Jolliet. See also Aux
Jolliet, Adrien, I, 173, 225, 227, 248, 393, 536, 626; II, 192,
    347
Jolliet (Joliette), Antoine, VII, 446
Jolliet, Catherine. See Faribault
Jolliet, Charles, II, 66
Jolliet, Claire (Fleury de La Gorgendière), II, 224; III, 216;
    IV, 268, 661
Jolliet, Claire-Françoise. See Bissot
Jolliet, Jean-Pierre, known as Chevalier d'Au, III, 7
Jolliet, Louis, I, 11, 15, 35, 76, 84, 104, 105, 146, 173, 174,
    175, 178, 225, 226, 227, 289, 345, **392–98**, 400, 452,
    480, 491, 492, 565, 572, 625, 657, 665; II, xxxi, xxxviii,
    8, 66, 68, 141, 148, 192, 227, 228, 230, 256, 273, 296,
    300, 302, 347, 413, 422, 489, 607, 634; III, xxxv, 216,
    339, 380, 609, 616, 620; IV, 268; V, 288; VII, 446; IX,
    774; XII, 1002
Jolliet, Marie. See Viel
Jolliet, Zacharie, I, 394, 396, 606, 657; II, 231
Jolliet d'Abancourt, François, II, 300
Jolliet d'Anticosti, Charles, II, 301; III, 281
Jolliet de Mingan, Jean-Baptiste, II, **300–1**; III, 609
Jolliet de Mingan, Jean-Joseph, II, 301
Jolliet de Mingan, Marie. See Mars
Jolliet de Mingan, Marie-Anne (L'Archevêque; Taché), III,
    608, 609; VI, 749; IX, 774
Jolliette, Claire (Volant de Chamblain; Boisseau), V, 91;
    VII, 89
Jolliffe, Diana (Belcher), X, 42
Jolliffe, James Hare, VI, 532; VII, 873
Jolliffe, Peter, V, 491
Jollivet, Louis, III, 199; IV, 109, 286
Jollyet, Jean, I, 392, 554
Jollyet, Marie. See Abancourt
Joly, Angélique. See Marchand
Joly, Jean, II, 32
Joly, Julie-Christine. See Chartier de Lotbinière
Joly, Julien, III, 622
Joly, Pierre-Gustave, VI, 133
Joly-Cœur. See Perrot
Joly* de Lotbinière, Sir Henri-Gustave (1829–1908), IX,
    612; X, 25, 26, 36, 602, 615; XI, 27, 184, 192, 480, 520,
    521, 522, 531, 812; XII, 20, 90, 176, 177, 211, 251, 299,
    324, 657, 693, 694, 721, 722, 913, 928, 987, 1065, 1121
Jomini, Antoine-Henri, Baron de Jomini, IX, 772; XII, 621
Joncaire. See Chabert
Jonckau, Jean-J., XI, 805
Jones. See also Owen-Jones
Jones, Mr (father of SOLOMON), VI, 363
Jones, Mr (surgeon), VII, 247
Jones, Mr (surveyor), V, 183
Jones, A., X, 647
Jones, Abner, XII, 479
Jones, Alfred Augustus (Misquahke), VII, 455
Jones*, Alfred Gilpin (1824–1906), XI, 710; XII, 436, 437,
    651

Jones, Alpheus, V, 458; VII, 452; VIII, 181, 602; XII, 258

Jones, Anne (Williams), V, 862

Jones, Annie E. (Boyd), XII, 121

Jones, Augustus, IV, 12, 756; VI, 406, 759, 760; VII, 251, **450–52**, 455; VIII, 309, 439, 440, 620; IX, 592, 593

Jones, C. J., XII, 259

Jones, Caleb, V, 137, **456**, 506; VI, 7, 75, 139, 474, 740; VII, 692

Jones, Catharine, VII, 451

Jones, Catherine (Evans), X, 274

Jones, Catherine (Marshall), X, 496

Jones, Catherine Garden. *See* Simpson

Jones, Charles, V, 458, 748, 787; VI, 364; VII, 38, 419, 420, **452–54**, 457, 458; VIII, 305

Jones, Charles Mercer, IX, 417

Jones, Charlotte. *See* Coursol

Jones, Charlotte (Benett), XII, 479

Jones, Charlotte (Sherwood), V, 457; VII, 795; VIII, 796

Jones, Chilion, XI, 464; XII, 344, 345, 534, 930

Jones, Christiana. *See* Kayatontye

Jones, Daniel, VI, 90, 127, 363, 364; VII, 782

Jones, David (lawyer), X, 109

Jones, David (missionary), V, 852

Jones, David (politician), VIII, 797

Jones*, David Allanson (1836–1910), XII, 865

Jones, David Thomas, VII, 390, **454–55**, 526, 568, 571, 901, 902; VIII, 91, 721, 767, 811; IX, 134, 135, 784; X, 108; XII, 612

Jones, Dunham, VI, 364

Jones, Ebenezar (father), VII, 450

Jones, Ebenezar, VII, 451

Jones, Edwin, XI, 190

Jones, Elisha (father), V, 456

Jones, Elisha, V, 457

Jones, Eliza (Boulton), V, 457; VII, 294; IX, 69; XII, 101

Jones, Eliza (Juchereau Duchesnay), VI, 368

Jones, Elizabeth. *See* Field

Jones, Elizabeth. *See* Steeves

Jones, Elizabeth (wife of CALEB), V, 456

Jones, Elizabeth (wife of HENRY, 1776–1852), VIII, 437

Jones, Elizabeth (Larkin), VIII, 489

Jones, Elizabeth Jane. *See* Beer

Jones, Elizabeth Mary. *See* Strachan

Jones, Elizabeth Vaughan (Ross), V, 461

Jones, Emily (McCaul), XI, 540

Jones, Emily (Shortland), XI, 820

Jones, Emmeline Sedate (Bell), XII, 85

Jones, Ephraim, V, 455, **456–58**; VII, 452, 456, 795; VIII, 796, 797; IX, 69, 99; X, 310

Jones, Fanny (Shorey), XII, 968

Jones, Florella. *See* Smith

Jones, Frances Amelia (Brouse), XI, 114

Jones, Frederick, VII, 454

Jones, Hannah. *See* Corey

Jones, Hannah. *See* Simpson

Jones, Harold, VII, 563

Jones, Henry, VII, 453

Jones, Henry, III, **315–16**, 327, 504

Jones, Henry, VIII, **436–39**

Jones, Henry John, VIII, 437, 438

Jones, Herbert Chilion, XII, 5

Jones, Hester (Jewitt), VI, 350

Jones, Inigo, V, 678

Jones, Jacob, XII, 479

Jones, James, V, 647

Jones, James, IV, 81, 511; V, 12, 123, 125, **458–59**, 524, 671; VI, 292, 293, 393, 447, 450; VII, 801, 802

Jones, John (grand jury member), V, 462

Jones, John (landowner), VII, 136

Jones, John (nephew of JOHN, d. 1818), V, 462; VI, 277

Jones, John (newspaper owner), VII, 625, 626; IX, 460

Jones, John (notary), V, 462

Jones, John (politician), V, 462

Jones, John (printer), VIII, 259, 729, 735

Jones, John (soldier), IX, 276

Jones, John (teacher), V, 462

Jones, John, IV, **401–2**, 437; V, 408, 633

Jones, John, V, 67, 373, **459–62**, 494, 699, 713, 816, 834; VI, 95, 347, 533, 556; VIII, 115, 124

Jones, John, VI, 283, **362–63**

Jones, John, VI, 555; VII, 451, **455–56**, 828; VIII, 439, 440, 441, 443; XI, 473, 474

Jones, John Collier, VIII, 437

Jones, John Matthew, X, 362

Jones, John Paul, V, 264; VI, 652

Jones, John Philpott, VII, 297

Jones, John W., XII, 194

Jones*, John Walter (1878–1954), VIII, 444

Jones, Jonas, VIII, 58, 511

Jones, Jonas, V, 457, 458, 558; VI, 57, 118, 771; VII, 38, 102, 215, 365, 367, 371, 372, 452, 453, **456–61**, 695; VIII, 514, 516, 519, 521, 534, 535, 587, 796, 797, 798; IX, 49, 333; X, 310, 379, 483; XI, 540

Jones, Jonathan (uncle), V, 222; VI, 363

Jones, Jonathan, VI, 364

Jones, Joseph (auctioneer), V, 462

Jones, Joseph (coroner), IX, 699; XI, 206

Jones, Josiah, V, 457

Jones, Julia Maria. *See* Collier

Jones, Louisa (Blake), VIII, 95

Jones*, Sir Lyman Melvin (1843–1917), XI, 387; XII, 705

Jones, Margaret. *See* Harrison

Jones, Margaret. *See* Locke

Jones, Margaret (Nepean), VI, 537

Jones, Margaret S. *See* Beke

Jones, Martha Anne (Bridgland), X, 91

Jones, Mary. *See* Allen

Jones, Mary. *See* Holtby

Jones, Mary. *See* Lloyd

Jones, Mary. *See* Stuart

Jones, Mary. *See* Tunnicliffe

Jones, Mary (Gage), VIII, 309

Jones, Mary (Ross), VIII, 770

Jones, Mary (Ruttan), X, 637

Jones, Mary (Sefton), XII, 959

Jones, Mary Elizabeth. *See* Ford

Jones, Mary Gates (Johnson), XII, 476

Jones, Mary-Jane. *See* Ross

Jones, Matilda, VIII, 443

Jones, Millicent (Palmer), VI, 565; XI, 664

Jones, Nathaniel, VI, 277, 279

Jones, Oliver, XII, **478–80**

Jones, Owen, X, 649

Jones, Peter, VI, 283

Jones, Peter, V, 467; VI, 336, 555, 758; VII, 55, 276, 277,

348, 451, 455, 456, 828; VIII, 133, 162, 438, **439–43**, 620, 898; IX, 9, 420, 590, 593; X, 640, 648; XI, 316, 317, 473, 474, 655, 660, 796; XII, 186
Jones, Peter Edmund (Kahkewaquonaby), VIII, 442
Jones, Phylina. *See* Foote
Jones, Polly, VIII, 440
Jones, Rice, I, 671
Jones, Richard, VIII, 437
Jones, Richard W., V, 139
Jones, Robert (author), IX, 162
Jones, Robert (physician), IV, 82; V, 502
Jones, Robert (politician), XII, 255
Jones, Robert, VIII, **443–44**, 569
Jones, Ruth. *See* Lee
Jones, Samuel, VI, 136
Jones, Samuel I., IX, 735
Jones, Sarah. *See* Dunham
Jones, Sarah. *See* Tekarihogen
Jones, Sarah (Charland), V, 183
Jones, Sarah (Hope), IV, 366
Jones, Sarah Elizabeth. *See* Disney
Jones, Sidney, VII, 453
Jones, Simeon, V, 457
Jones, Solomon, V, 455; VI, **363–65**; VII, 452; VIII, 797; IX, 99; X, 310
Jones, Stephen (brother of EPHRAIM), V, 457
Jones, Stephen (of Machias, Mass.), IV, 490
Jones, Stephen James, XI, 934
Jones, Strachan, XII, 936
Jones, Strachan Graham, IX, 417
Jones, Stuart, VII, 454
Jones, Susan (wife of HENRY, 1776–1852), VIII, 437
Jones, Thomas Mercer, VII, 261, 262, 338, 882; VIII, 9, 900; IX, **415–17**, 751, 753, 768, 836, 837, 838; X, 459
Jones, W. H., X, 534
Jones, William (father of ROBERT), VIII, 443
Jones, William (son of EPHRAIM), V, 458; VII, 452
Jonquet, Anne. *See* Hébert
Jonquet, Étienne, I, 437, 578
Jonquières, Catherine de (Latour), IV, 439
Jopp, Charles, XII, 619
Joram Chappuis, *dit* Comtois, Jean, IV, 748
Joram Chappuis, *dit* Comtois, Marie-Louise. *See* Varin, *dit* La Pistole
Jordan, Alex, X, 81
Jordan, Ann. *See* Livingston
Jordan, Annie. *See* Walters
Jordan, Caroline Matilda (Knox; Lawson), XII, 539
Jordan, Catherine. *See* Grant
Jordan, Catherine (Claus), VI, 151
Jordan, Daniel, XII, 226
Jordan, Edward, VI, 319; VII, 88; VIII, 36
Jordan, George Clifford, XII, 448
Jordan, Jacob, V, 260, 566
Jordan, Jacob, IV, 58, 59, 243, 286, 399, **402–4**; V, 164, 191, 656, 684, 821; VI, 151, 285, 432; VII, 200; VIII, 236
Jordan, Louisa Sophia (Daniel), XII, 226
Jordan, Margaret (wife of Edward), VIII, 36
Jordan, Marie-Anne. *See* Raby
Jordan, Patrick, IX, 846
Jordan*, William George (1852–1939), XII, 767
Jordy, Élisabeth de. *See* Pradines

Jordy, Louise de. *See* Rathery
Jordy, Pierre de, II, 185
Jordy, Pierre-François de, II, 185, 186
Joseph. *See also* Chihwatenha; Manitougatche; Teondechoren; Teouatiron; Togouiroui
Joseph (potter), IV, 386
Joseph, Bishop. *See* Spangenberg, Augustus Gottlieb
Joseph, Captain. *See* Wowurna
Joseph, Father. *See* Du Tremblay
Joseph, King of Naples; Joseph, King of Spain. *See* Bonaparte, Joseph
Joseph, Abraham, VI, 365
Joseph, Abraham, VI, 366; VIII, 41; XI, 234, 388, **454–56**
Joseph, Andrew Cohen, XI, 456
Joseph, Anne Elizabeth. *See* Hagerman
Joseph, Benjamin, I, 74
Joseph, Catharine (David), VI, 366
Joseph, Céline. *See* Lyons
Joseph, Esther (de Sola), VI, 366; XI, 254
Joseph, Fanny (Françoise) (Lola), VIII, 509
Joseph, Fanny David, XI, 234
Joseph, Frank John, VIII, 445
Joseph, George, VIII, 446
Joseph, Gershom, VI, 366
Joseph, Henry, V, 194; VI, **365–66**; VII, 30, 329; XI, 254, 454, 455
Joseph*, Jacob Henry (1814–1907), VI, 366; XI, 455
Joseph, Jesse (partner of Benjamin HART), VIII, 366
Joseph, Jesse (son of HENRY), VI, 366; XI, 254, 455; XII, 131
Joseph, John, VII, 127, 370, 460; VIII, 28, **444–45**, 520
Joseph, Judah, VI, 365; VIII, 369
Joseph, Judah George, VIII, 113, 114, **445–46**; IX, 601
Joseph, Montefiore, XI, 456
Joseph, Naphtali, V, 193; VI, 365
Joseph, Rachel. *See* Solomons
Joseph, Rebecca (wife of JUDAH GEORGE), VIII, 445
Joseph, Samuel (sculptor), VIII, 444
Joseph, Samuel (son of HENRY), VI, 366
Joseph, Simeon Alfred, VIII, 445
Joseph, Sophia. *See* David
Josephte (wife of Jean-Baptiste LETENDRE, *dit* Batoche), VI, 398
Josephte-Antoinette de Sainte-Marie. *See* Chaussegros de Léry
Jossard, Élisabeth (Poitiers Du Buisson), III, 532
Josselin, Nicolas, I, 267
Jost, Edward, XI, 406
Joubert, Monsieur (captain), I, 263
Joubin-Boisvert, Augustin, XII, 506
Joubin-Boisvert, Marie-Anne. *See* Gastineau
Joubin-Boisvert, Marie-Anne (Richer-Laflèche), XII, 506, 507
Jouenne de Lorière, Louise-Françoise (Beaussier de Lisle), III, 54
Jouet, Louis, IV, 252
Jouett (Jewett), Ann (Beckwith), X, 41
Jouin, Bernardine (Lafontaine), III, 339
Joulin, Étienne, II, 28
Jourdain, Anne (Perrot de Rizy), II, 520
Jourdain, Augustin, VI, 366
Jourdain, Charles, V, 140, 495; VI, **366–67**
Jourdain, Henriette, VI, 366

Jourdain (Jourdon), Madeleine (Magdalene) (Williams), VIII, 939
Jourdain, Michel, III, 170; VI, 366
Jourdain, Michel-Augustin, V, 305
Jourdain, Victoire-Adélaïde (Tourangeau), XII, 1064
Jourdain, *dit* Bellerose, Marie-Françoise (Deguise, *dit* Flamand), IV, 203
Jourdain, *dit* Bellerose, Pierre, IV, 203
Jourdain, *dit* Labrosse, Charles, VI, 366
Jourdain, *dit* Labrosse, Denis (father), III, 316
Jourdain, *dit* Labrosse, Denis, III, 316
Jourdain, *dit* Labrosse, Dominique, III, 316
Jourdain, *dit* Labrosse, Françoise. *See* Gaudé
Jourdain, *dit* Labrosse, Marie-Joseph. *See* Aubuchon, *dit* L'Espérance
Jourdain, *dit* Labrosse, Marie-Madeleine. *See* Fagot
Jourdain, *dit* Labrosse, Paul, III, 316
Jourdain, *dit* Labrosse, Paul-Raymond, III, **316–17**; IV, 472; V, 497; VI, 366
Jourdan. *See also* Launé-Jourdan
Jourdan, Monsieur (secretary to the king), II, 587
Jourdan, Françoise (Simon de Longpré), I, 607
Jousserand, Nicole de (Menou), I, 502
Jousset, Louise (Maugue; La Sague), I, 498
Joutel, Henri, I, 79, 180, 182; II, 124, 197, 441; III, 106
Jouve, Odoric-Marie, III, 690; IV, 142
Jouvency, Joseph, III, 23
Jouy, Comte de. *See* Berthelot; Rouillé
Jovenazo, Duke of, II, 443
Joy, James Frederick, XI, 10
Joybert, Jacques, I, 399
Joybert, Pierre-Jacques, I, 399
Joybert de Soulanges, Marie-Geneviève (Le Moyne de Longueuil), IV, 463; V, 486
Joybert de Soulanges et de Marson, Louise-Élisabeth de (Rigaud de Vaudreuil, Marquise de Vaudreuil), I, 399; II, 202, **301–2**, 547, 558, 567, 570, 580; III, 7, 118, 176, 247, 372, 555, 556, 603; IV, 660, 662
Joybert de Soulanges et de Marson, Marie-Françoise de. *See* Chartier de Lotbinière
Joybert de Soulanges et de Marson, Pierre de, I, 25, 40, 62, 63, 185, 203, **398–400**, 667; II, 5, 166, 301, 409, 477
Joyce, John, VI, 348
Joyer, René-Pierre, IV, 137; VII, 246, 752
Joyeuse. *See also* Villaret
Joyeuse, Anne, Duc de Joyeuse, I, 87, 88, 89, 421
Joyeuse, François de, I, 386
Juan Chou, I, 263
Juana, Queen of Castile, I, 41
Juarez, Benito Pablo, XII, 308
Jubé, Jacques, III, 639
Juchault de Lamoricière, Christophe-Louis-Léon, X, 542
Juchereau, Françoise (Bermen de La Martinière), II, 56
Juchereau, Jean, I, 401, 402
Juchereau, Jeanne. *See* Creste
Juchereau de La Ferté, Charlotte, I, 400
Juchereau de La Ferté, Denis-Joseph, I, 400; II, **302–3**, 304, 388, 441
Juchereau de La Ferté, Jean, I, 108, 202, 331, **400**, 401, 402, 580, 584, 587, 588, 589; II, 33, 228, 302, 303, 304
Juchereau de La Ferté, Jeanne-Françoise, named de Saint-Ignace, I, 111, 231, 310, 329, 359, 400, 487, 631;

II, 44, 80, 93, 116, 130, 132, 161, **303–4**, 528; III, 369, 547, 711; IV, 440
Juchereau de La Ferté, Marie. *See* Giffard
Juchereau de La Ferté, Marie, named de Sainte-Thérèse, I, 400
Juchereau de La Ferté, Marie-Louise (Aubert de La Chesnaye), I, 400; II, 33, 34; III, 22
Juchereau de La Ferté, Noël, I, 108, 400; II, 304
Juchereau de Maur, Geneviève (Legardeur de Tilly), I, 448, 602; II, 236, 387; III, 373
Juchereau de Maur, Jean, I, 60, 330, 400, **401**, 402, 448; II, 35; XI, 456
Juchereau de Maur, Marie. *See* Langlois
Juchereau de Maur, Paul-Augustin, I, 400; II, 35, **304–5**; III, 22
Juchereau de Saint-Denis, Charlotte-Françoise, known as Comtesse de Saint-Laurent (Viennay-Pachot; Dauphin de La Forest), I, 661; II, 69, 170, 256, **305**, 306, 557, 587
Juchereau de Saint-Denis, Emanuela. *See* Ramón de Navarro
Juchereau de Saint-Denis, Joseph, I, 402
Juchereau de Saint-Denis, Louis, II, 306, 307, 355; III, **317–18**, 383, 423
Juchereau de Saint-Denis, Louise-Madeleine (Lestringant de Saint-Martin), II, 426
Juchereau de Saint-Denis, Marie-Anne (Pollet de La Combe-Pocatière; Ruette d'Auteuil), I, 550, 551; II, 391, 586
Juchereau de Saint-Denis, Marie-Catherine (Legardeur de Repentigny), IV, 447, 448
Juchereau de Saint-Denis, Marie-Thérèse. *See* Giffard
Juchereau de Saint-Denis, Nicolas, I, 48, 146, 331, **401–2**, 448, 550, 661; II, 56, 305, 307, 426; III, 317; V, 463; VI, 367
Juchereau de Saint-Denys, Charles, I, 508; II, 180, 224, **305–7**, 468, 508, 525, 645; III, 317, 402
Juchereau de Saint-Denys, Joseph-Charles, II, 307
Juchereau de Saint-Denys, Thérèse-Denise. *See* Migeon de Branssat
Juchereau Des Chatelets, Noël, I, 319, 401, **402–3**, 447, 448; II, xv
Juchereau de Vaulezar, François, II, 525
Juchereau Duchesnay, Antoine, III, 115, 549; V, 462
Juchereau Duchesnay, Antoine, IV, 344, 702; V, 231, **462–64**, 470, 482, 793, 879, 881; VI, 68, 289, 367, 368, 531; VII, 461
Juchereau Duchesnay, Antoine-Louis, V, 464; VI, 306, **367–68**, 423, 585; VII, 170, 462; X, 388
Juchereau Duchesnay, Antoine-Narcisse, VI, 306, 368
Juchereau Duchesnay, Caroline. *See* Têtu
Juchereau Duchesnay, Caroline-Élisa (Ermatinger), IX, 242
Juchereau Duchesnay, Catherine. *See* Le Comte Dupré
Juchereau Duchesnay, Catherine-Henriette (Blanchet), V, 464; VI, 68
Juchereau Duchesnay, Charles-Edmond, X, 389
Juchereau Duchesnay, Charles-Maurice, VI, 368
Juchereau Duchesnay, Charlotte-Hermine-Louise-Catherine. *See* Irumberry de Salaberry
Juchereau Duchesnay, Édouard-Louis-Antoine-Alphonse, VII, 462
Juchereau Duchesnay, Édouard-Louis-Antoine-Charles, IX, 858; X, 236; XII, 862
Juchereau Duchesnay, Élisabeth-Suzanne. *See* Taschereau

Juchereau Duchesnay, Eliza. *See* Jones

Juchereau Duchesnay, Elzéar-Henri, VI, 368, 751; IX, 463; X, 163, **388–89**, 603; XI, 456

Juchereau Duchesnay, Geneviève, named de Saint-Augustin, II, 91; III, 318, 349, 543

Juchereau Duchesnay, Henriette-Julie (Campbell), X, 131

Juchereau Duchesnay, Henri-Jules, XI, **456–57**

Juchereau Duchesnay, Henri-Théodore, X, 152

Juchereau Duchesnay, Ignace, I, 402, 543; II, 42, **307**, 448, 540; III, 318; VI, 367

Juchereau Duchesnay, Jean-Baptiste, V, 464; VI, 367, **368–69**, 681; VII, 461; VIII, 18

Juchereau Duchesnay, Julie. *See* Perrault

Juchereau Duchesnay, Julie-Louise. *See* Liénard de Beaujeu de Villemonde

Juchereau Duchesnay, Julie-Marguerite, named de Saint-Antoine, V, 464

Juchereau Duchesnay, Louise-Élizabeth (Prévost), XII, 862

Juchereau Duchesnay, Louise-Françoise (Taschereau), V, 464, 793

Juchereau Duchesnay, Louise-Sophie (Gugy), VI, 368

Juchereau Duchesnay, Marie-Anne, VI, 368

Juchereau Duchesnay, Marie-Catherine. *See* Peuvret Demesnu

Juchereau Duchesnay, Marie-Catherine, named de Saint-Ignace, V, 462

Juchereau Duchesnay, Marie-Eustache, V, 462

Juchereau Duchesnay, Marie-Françoise. *See* Chartier de Lotbinière

Juchereau Duchesnay, Marie-Joseph, named de l'Enfant-Jésus, III, **318–19**, 349, 543, 544

Juchereau Duchesnay, Marie-Louise. *See* Fleury de La Gorgendière

Juchereau Duchesnay, Marie-Thérèse (Denys de Vitré; Ailleboust), VI, 345

Juchereau Duchesnay, Michel-Louis, V, 464; VI, 346, 368, 750; VII, **461–62**, 890; VIII, 154

Juchereau Duchesnay, Sophie. *See* Guerout

Juchereau Duchesnay, Sophie-Louise (Dunn), VIII, 251

Juchereau Duchesnay de Saint-Denis, Madeleine-Louise (Sallaberry), III, 582; VI, 345

Judah, Abraham, V, 193

Judah, Adolphus H., X, 3

Judah, Dorothea (Hart), IV, 331; VII, 386; VIII, 365, 367

Judah, Henry Hague, VIII, 363; X, 219, 220

Judah, Isaac, IV, 332

Judah, Jane. *See* Toyer

Judah, Joseph, IV, 332

Judah, Samuel, IV, 331, 332, 385

Judah, Sarah (Hart), VIII, 368

Judah, Thomas Storrs, VIII, 363

Judah, Uriah, IV, 331, 332; VIII, 368

Judith (mother of David GEORGE), V, 340

Judkins, Fanny Cooper (Murray), XI, 630

Judson, William Lees, XII, 830

Juet, Robert, I, 374, 375, 376, 377, 378

Jugier, Jérôme, IV, 286

Jugon. *See* Lemaître

Juhan, John James, VI, 573

Juillet, Blaise, I, 271

Juillet, Marie-Louise-Catherine (Durocher), III, 210

Jukes, Augustus, XI, 559, 749, 750

Jukes, Georgina Augusta. *See* Meredith

Jukes, John, IX, 417

Jukes, Joseph Beete, IX, 160, **417–19**; XI, 632; XII, 589

Jukes, Laura Eliza (Johnson), X, 381

Jukes, Sophia. *See* Beete

Julian, Étiennette (Saint-Père), I, 598

Julie-Marguerite de Saint-Antoine. *See* Juchereau Duchesnay

Julien, Monsieur (sculptor), VI, 24

Julien, Francis, V, 465

Julien, John, V, **464–65**; VI, 678; VII, 658

Julien, Simon, VI, 24

Julienne-Angélique de Jésus Pâtissant. *See* Dollier de Casson

Jullien, Louis, IV, 566

Jumeau, Emmanuel, I, 438

Jumonville. *See* Coulon

Juncken, Henry, VIII, 353

June, Martha (Waterous), XII, 1090

June, Tom. *See* Tom June

Juneau, Félix-Emmanuel, XI, **457–58**; XII, 431, 1066

Juneau, Josephte. *See* Villers

Juneau, Josette. *See* Vieau

Juneau, Laurent-Salomon, VIII, **446–47**; X, 533

Juneau, Nicholas, XI, 457

Juneau, Pierre, VIII, 446

Juneau, *dit* Latulippe, François, VIII, 446

Juneau, *dit* Latulippe, Thérèse. *See* Galarneau

Jung, Jean, III, 501

Junius. *See* Hoeootoerock

Jupiter, Robert, VII, 698

Jupp, Louisa (Hamilton), XII, 404

Jurie, Robert, I, 267

Jury*, Alfred F. (d. 1916), XII, 388, 866, 1113

Juson, Richard, VII, 909; IX, 512; XII, 886

Jussaume, *dit* Saint-Pierre, Marie-Louise (Du Calvet), IV, 231

Jussaume, *dit* Saint-Pierre, Pierre, IV, 228, 231

Jussieu, Antoine de, II, 595, 596, 597, 600; III, 675

Jussieu, Antoine-Laurent de, II, 596

Jussieu, Bernard de, III, 30, 675, 678; V, 592

Just, Dorothée-Magleine (Vanfelson), VIII, 906

Just, John Conrad, VIII, 906

Just, Josephte (Glackemeyer), VII, 348

Just, Madeleine (Le Gay de Beaulieu; You de La Découverte), II, 127, 673; IV, 235

Juste, Angélique (Levasseur), IV, 473

Jutra*, Claude (1930–87), XII, 297

Jutra, Marie (Poulin), II, 529; III, 537

Jutras, Claire (Bolvin), III, 68

Jutras, *dit* Desrosiers, Jean-Baptiste, III, 24

Jutrat, Marguerite (Godefroy de Saint-Paul), II, 252

KACHENOOTING, Bigwind, XI, 848

Kachenooting, George. *See* Steinhauer, Henry Bird

Kachenooting, Mary, XI, 848

Kadnèche. *See* Annance

Kaghswaghtaniunt (Kachshwuchdanionty), III, **319–20**, 614

Kaghswoughdioony, III, 321

Kaghswoughtioony (Kaghswughtioni). *See* Kakouenthiony

Kahgegagahbowh (Kahkakakahbowh), IX, **419–21**; XII, 186

Kahikohan, I, 48
Kahkewaquonaby. *See* Jones, Peter; Jones, Peter Edmund
Kahn, Johanetta (Oppenheimer), XII, 803
Kah-pah-yak-as-to-cum. *See* Kāpeyakwāskonam
Kaieñ²kwaahtoñ, IV, lvi, 118, 396, **404–6**, 417, 730; V, 254, 805, 896; VI, 353, 703
Kaigwiaidosa. *See* Madjeckewiss
Kain, William, V, 640; VI, **369–70**
Kains, George, XII, 89
Kaiser, Johann Baptist, named Father François-Xavier, VIII, 627
Kaiūtwah²kū (Cornplanter), IV, lvi, 118, 405, 410; V, 805, 896
Kajnquiratiton. *See* Cagenquarichten
Kakee-manitou-waya. *See* Kitchi-manito-waya
Kakikekapo. *See* Kahgegagahbowh
Kā-kīwistāhāw* (d. 1906), XII, 779
Kakouenthiony, III, **320–21**, 451, 494
Kallihirua, VIII, **447–48**
Kalliou. *See* Callihoo
Kalm, Anna Magaretha. *See* Sjöman
Kalm, Catherine. *See* Ross
Kalm, Gabriel, IV, 406
Kalm, Pehr, II, 595, 596, 597; III, 145, 169, 315, 675, 676, 679, 680; IV, **406–8**; V, 228; XI, 586
Kalogg. *See* Kellogg
Kamantowiwew. *See* Kitchi-manito-waya
Kamehameha I, King of Hawaii, IV, 746
Kamehameha III, King of Hawaii, VIII, 817
Kamiakin, XII, 817
Kaminska, Rosalie de (Rottermund, Countess de Rottermund), VIII, 774
Kamīyistowesit, XI, **458–59**, 461
Kanadqua, X, 104
Kanaghgwasea. *See* Canaghquiesa
Kanaghkwase. *See* Karaghtadie
Kanaharighton (Kanakarighton). *See* Cagenquarichten
Kanakonme. *See* Anatoha
Kane, Elisha Kent, VII, 326; VIII, **448–50**; IX, 200; XI, 382, 393, 394, 470; XII, 122
Kane, Frances. *See* Loach
Kane, Harriet. *See* Clench
Kane, Jane Duval. *See* Leiper
Kane, John Kintzing, VIII, 448
Kane, Michael, X, 389
Kane, Paul, VI, 649; VII, 100, 846; VIII, 86; IX, 149, 360, 366, 537; X, 166, 227, **389–94**, 427; XII, 101, 793, 932, 1110
K'ang-hsi (Hsüen-yeh), Emperor of China, III, 470
Kanhopitsa, Josephte (Clarke; Boucher; Hubert), VIII, 158
Kanon, Jacques, III, **321–22**; IV, 125, 601, 616, 729
Kanonraron (Aaron, Aaron Hill), IV, 692, 730; V, 255, 807, 809; VIII, 620
Kanouse, Henry Alfred, XII, 778
Kan tuck ee gun, III, 525
Kant, Immanuel, XII, 458
Kapapamahchakwew, XI, 261, 306, **459–60**, 599, 600, 747; XII, 478
Kāpeyakwāskonam, XI, 459, **461–62**; XII, 497
Kapula, XII, 466
Karaghiagigo, IV, 735
Karaghtadie (Karaghiagdatie), III, **322–23**, 331, 623; VI, 759; VII, 665

Karekowa. *See* Tarbell, John
Karhiio, Louis, VII, 137
Karighwaycagh (Catherine), VI, 552, 553
Karikohe. *See* Tarbell, John
Karl Wilhelm Ferdinand, Duke of Brunswick, IV, 589; V, 582
Karonghyontye (David Hill), IV, 692; VI, 373
Karpik, IV, 225, 536
Karrahogle. *See* Tekarihogen (d. 1830)
Karrer, Louis-Ignaz, III, 93, 94
Kaské. *See* Charlot
Katalouibois. *See* Koutaoiliboe
Katem, Michael, V, 337
Kateri. *See* Tekakwitha
Katzmann, Christian Conrad Gaspar, XI, 462
Katzmann, Martha. *See* Prescott
Katzmann, Martha Elizabeth (Morton), XII, 764
Katzmann, Mary Jane (Lawson), VII, 14; XI, **462–63**; XII, 474, 764
Kaufman, Polly (Gaukel), VIII, 315
Kaulback, Henry Adolphus Newman, X, 172
Kavanagh, Félicité. *See* LeJeune
Kavanagh, James, VI, 370
Kavanagh, John, X, 8
Kavanagh, Laurence, VI, 370
Kavanagh, Laurence, VI, 217, 308, **370–71**, 792; VII, 177, 433; VIII, 227
Kavanagh, Margaret. *See* Farrell
Kavanaugh, Benjamin T., XII, 186
Ka-we-zauce. *See* Kiwisānce
Kāwīcitwemot, XI, 599, 600
Kawiti, XII, 733
Kay, Ann. *See* Cruickshank
Kay, John, V, 512
Kay, Mary Anne (Kendall), VII, 463
Kay, Mary Lucy (wife of THOMAS), IX, 421
Kay, Mungo, VI, 701
Kay, Thomas, IX, **421–22**; X, 724
Kay, William (school director), XII, 61
Kay, William (trader), V, 512
Kayahsota² (Kayashoton), III, 95, 652; IV, **408–10**; V, 253
Kayatontye (Christiana Brant) (Jones), VII, 455; VIII, 440
Kaye, Sir John Lister, XII, 991
Kaye, Sir John William, VIII, 848; IX, 370
Kayenquaraghton. *See* Kaieñ²kwaahtoñ
Kaygill, Thomas, V, 678
Kaylus. *See* Thubières
Kean. *See also* Kane
Kean, Edmund, VII, 110; XII, 1067
Kearney, Lawrence Cunningham, VIII, 860, 861
Keating, John William, VII, 55; XII, 854
Keating, William, VI, 409, 411
Keats, Elizabeth (mother of Sir RICHARD GOODWIN), VI, 371
Keats, John, XII, 516
Keats, Mary, Lady Keats. *See* Hurt
Keats, Richard, VI, 371
Keats, Sir Richard Goodwin, V, 473, 474, 671; VI, 163, **371–73**, 614, 708, 802; VII, 152, 765; VIII, 264, 403, 658
Kebeshkamokwe, Theresa Catherine (Assiginack), IX, 9, 10
Keble, John, X, 84; XII, 440, 681

Kecheahgahmequa. *See* Field, Elizabeth
Keefer, Anne E. *See* Crawford
Keefer, Annie. *See* McKay
Keefer, Catherine. *See* Lampman
Keefer, Christina Theresa. *See* Grant
Keefer, Elizabeth (Coltrin; Chadwick), VIII, 450
Keefer, Esther Magdalen. *See* Secord
Keefer, George, VIII, 451
Keefer, George, VIII, **450–51**; X, 394; XI, 463
Keefer, George Alexander, XI, 819
Keefer, Jacob, VIII, 450
Keefer, Jacob, VIII, 451, 966; IX, 792; X, **394–95**
Keefer, James, X, 200
Keefer, Jane. *See* McBride
Keefer, Mary. *See* Swaize
Keefer, Mary, VIII, 450
Keefer, Rosalie E. *See* Pocock
Keefer, Samuel, VIII, 450
Keefer, Samuel, VI, 481; VII, 50; VIII, 451; X, 200, 404, 405; XI, **463–65**, 510; XII, 496, 561, 627, 930
Keefer*, Thomas Coltrin (1821–1915), VIII, 297, 451, 553, 965, 967; XI, 120, 464, 465, 510, 589, 682; XII, 494, 619, 962
Keele, William Conway, VII, 843
Keeler, Rebecca (Bangs), IX, 26
Keen, William, III, 91, 324
Keen, William, II, 152, 153, 609; III, 10, 68, **323–24**, 506
Keene, Laura, IX, 60
Keeshick (Kezicks), Charles, XI, 474
Kegedonce, Peter Jones, XI, 474
Keighley, William Walker, XII, 976
Keir, Christian. *See* Wood
Keir, John, VIII, 451
Keir, John, VIII, **451–53**; XII, 829
Keir, Mary. *See* Burnet
Keirnan, Jane (Baird; Vallières de Saint-Réal), VII, 880
Keissis. *See* Caissy
Keith, Viscount. *See* Elphinstone
Keith, Alexander, VII, 875; X, **395–96**; XI, 392, 486, 856
Keith, Anne Jane. *See* Finlayson
Keith, Betsey (Swanston), VIII, 454
Keith, Christina. *See* Brims
Keith, Donald, X, 39
Keith, Donald George, X, 395
Keith, Eliza (Keith), X, 395
Keith, George, VIII, 86, 158, 159, 350, **453–54**, 538, 547
Keith, Helen (Pillon), VIII, 454
Keith, Isabella. *See* Bruce
Keith, J. C., XII, 318
Keith, James, VIII, 453, 454
Keith, James, VII, 808; VIII, 85, 159, 176, 453, **454–55**, 540, 766, 821; IX, 150, 199; XI, 169
Keith, Jean (Connon), XII, 207
Keith, John, XII, 207
Keith, Mary (Taylor), VIII, 454
Keith, Nanette. *See* Sutherland
Keith, Ruel, VI, 733
Keith, Sarah Ann. *See* Stalcup
Keith, Susan. *See* Angus
Keith, Sir William, III, 66
Kell, Eliza (Labatt), IX, 436
Keller, Friedrich Gottlob, XII, 136, 312
Keller, Joseph-Benjamin, VII, 642

Kellett, Sir Henry, VIII, 624; IX, 167; X, 42, 43, 89, **396–97**, 454, 455, 562; XI, 199, 200, 691, 692, 718; XII, 38, 892
Kellett, John Dalton, X, 396
Kelley, Arthur Reading, IV, 811
Kelley, Rebecca (Massey), VIII, 621
Kellie, Earl of. *See* Erskine
Kellogg, Edward, XI, 850
Kellogg, Ensign H., XI, 832; XII, 1040
Kellogg, Joanna, III, 324, 325
Kellogg, Jonathan, III, 324
Kellogg, Joseph, III, **324–26**; IV, 770
Kellogg, Martin (father), III, 324
Kellogg, Martin, III, 324, 325
Kellogg, Rachel. *See* Devotion
Kellogg, Rebecca, III, 324
Kellogg, Sarah. *See* Dickinson
Kelly, Mrs Andrew, XII, 93
Kelly, Miss (Haskins), VII, 389
Kelly, Bridget. *See* Doohan
Kelly, Catherine. *See* Lennon
Kelly, Edward, VIII, 637
Kelly, Eliza Ann. *See* Long
Kelly, Elizabeth. *See* Molyneux
Kelly, Francis, X, **397–98**
Kelly, Gilbert, XI, 465
Kelly, J. M., XI, 466
Kelly, James, XI, 568
Kelly, James (Gillam, Sampson Marshall), I, 301
Kelly*, James Butler Knill (1832–1907), X, 73; XII, 797
Kelly, Jean-Baptiste, V, 186; VI, 593; VII, 730; VIII, **455–58**, 595; XII, 297
Kelly, John, VIII, 455
Kelly, Joseph, V, 413
Kelly, Louisa. *See* Bliss
Kelly, Margaret. *See* Fraser
Kelly, Margaret. *See* Knee
Kelly, Marguerite. *See* Migneron
Kelly, Marguerite-Adèle (Tessier), XII, 1032
Kelly, Michael, VI, 409, 410
Kelly, Michael John, XI, **465–66**; XII, 311, 862
Kelly, Owen, VI, 372
Kelly, Richard, VIII, 170
Kelly, Thomas, VIII, 798
Kelly, William, XI, 55
Kelly, William Moore, VII, 580
Kelly, William Moore, XI, **466–67**
Kelly, Winifred (McMahon), VIII, 581
Kelsey, Elizabeth. *See* Dix
Kelsey, Elizabeth, II, 313
Kelsey, Henry, I, 227, 329, 529, 611; II, xxviii, 10, 42, 50, 51, 267, 298, 319, **307–15**, 320, 394, 395, 454, 616, 617; III, xxxiii, 285, 414, 415, 489, 599
Kelsey, John (grandfather), II, 308
Kelsey, John (uncle), II, 308
Kelsey, John, II, 314
Kelsey, Mary, II, 313
Kelsey, Thomas (goldsmith), II, 308
Kelsey, Thomas (officer), II, 308
Kelso*, John Joseph (1864–1935), XII, 388
Kelson, William, VI, 274
Kélus. *See* Thubières
Kelynge, Martha (Osborn, Lady Osborn), IV, 594

Kemble, Charles, VII, 110
Kemble, Francis, VII, 462
Kemble, Gertrude. *See* Bayard
Kemble, John Philip, VII, 110
Kemble, Margaret (Gage), IV, 279
Kemble, Maria Theresa. *See* de Camp
Kemble, Peter, IV, 279
Kemble, Rebecca. *See* Franks
Kemble, Sarah (Siddons), VII, 110, 782
Kemble, William, VII, 287, **462–63**
Kemeneur. *See* Timineur
Kemp, Alexander Ferrie, XI, **467–68**; XII, 192
Kemp, George, V, 838; VIII, 673
Kemp, Grace. *See* Ferrie
Kemp, James, VIII, 673
Kemp, Jane Fortune (Edmonds), XII, 294
Kemp, Joseph, XI, 504, 505
Kemp, Mary. *See* Leahey
Kemp, Simon, XI, 467
Kempt, Mrs. *See* Walker
Kempt, Gavin, VIII, 458
Kempt, Sir James, VI, 98, 214, 371, 481, 642, 645, 727,
    748; VII, 10, 68, 81, 129, 190, 283, 300, 361, 393, 433,
    441, 465, 482, 532, 548, 549, 609, 623, 640, 650, 703,
    724, 726, 730, 731, 770, 771, 789, 837, 879, 884, 905,
    933; VIII, 142, 221, 297, 298, 334, 355, 428, **458–65**,
    583, 603, 627, 755, 758, 827, 866; IX, 174, 175, 237,
    328, 810, 812
Kempthorne, Sir John, II, 315
Kempthorne, Thomas, II, 25, 226, **315–16**, 580, 637
Kempton, Hannah (Bradford), XII, 122
Kendall, Charles, IX, 550, 551
Kendall, Edward, VII, 463
Kendall, Edward Nicholas, VI, 218, 754; VII, 325, **463–64**;
    VIII, 663; X, 27, 38
Kendall, Franklin Richardson, VII, 464
Kendall, M. C. *See* Hicks
Kendall, Mary Anne. *See* Kay
Kendall, Rebecca S. (Fyfe), X, 296
Kendrick, Alder W., IX, 727
Kendrick, Dianna Harriet (Smith), IX, 727
Kendrick, Huldah. *See* Pease
Kendrick, John, IV, 411
Kendrick, John, IV, **410–12**, 419, 420, 519; V, 387, 410,
    411
Kennedy, Miss (Ramsay), XI, 721
Kennedy, Aeneas, VIII, 875
Kennedy, Alexander, VI, 436; VII, 138; VIII, 576; X, 284;
    XI, 445, 470
Kennedy, Sir Arthur Edward, IX, 115, 479, 712, 713, 716;
    X, 117; XI, **468–70**, 950; XII, 129, 240
Kennedy, Catharine. *See* Lambert
Kennedy, Eleanor Eliza. *See* Cripps
Kennedy, Elizabeth (Finlayson), X, 284
Kennedy, Elspeth (Elspy) (McKay), V, 532; VI, 464
Kennedy, George, XI, 471
Kennedy*, George Allan (1858–1913), XII, 858
Kennedy, Georgina Mildred. *See* Macartney
Kennedy, Grace Dorothea. *See* Hughes
Kennedy, Hugh, XI, 468
Kennedy, Hugh Alexander, V, 676
Kennedy, John (father of WILLIAM NASSAU), XI, 471
Kennedy, John (of Lucan, Ont.), X, 234

Kennedy*, Sir John (1838–1921), XII, 619
Kennedy, John Frederick, XII, 551
Kennedy, Mary (Isbister), XI, 445
Kennedy, Mary Ann (Delaney), X, 218
Kennedy, Mary Anne. *See* Chambers
Kennedy, Norah (Donnelly), X, 234
Kennedy, Patrick, X, 234
Kennedy, William, VII, 118; VIII, 910; XI, 874
Kennedy, William, VIII, 80; IX, 199, 389, 390; X, 89, 407;
    XI, 19, **470–71**, 554
Kennedy, William Nassau, XI, **471–73**, 562; XII, 245
Kennelly, David Thomas, IV, 109; VII, 667
Kennelly, Jeanne-Marie-Catherine. *See* Bruyères
Kenney, Delina (Baker), XII, 50
Kennicott, Robert, XI, 385
Kenny, Ann, Lady Kenny. *See* Forrestall
Kenny, David, IX, 820
Kenny, Sir Edward, X, 66; XII, **480–82**
Kenny, Jeremiah, XII, 480
Kenny, Johanna. *See* Crean
Kenny, Thomas, XII, 480, 481
Kenny*, Thomas Edward (1833–1908), XII, 1044
Kenougé. *See* Kinongé
Kenrich, Phebe S. (Rogers), XI, 763
Kensey (MacKenzie), William, III, 129
Kent, Ann Sophia (Power), XII, 859
Kent, Ann Susanna (Willis), X, 706
Kent, Benjamin, VII, 86
Kent, Ellen F. *See* Donnelly
Kent, James, VII, 627; XII, 482
Kent, John, VI, 728; X, 53
Kent, John, VII, 99, 113, 114, 153, 154, 155, 220, 293, 627,
    630, 631, 632, 633, 634, 793; VIII, 104, 381, 468, 469,
    948, 949, 950; IX, 28, 29, 30, 70, 71, 393, 435, 583, 584,
    585, 605, 606, 682, 694, 820, 846; X, 8, 141, 180, 331,
    **398–401**, 601, 687, 716; XI, 66, 354, 432, 433, 615, 673,
    674, 760, 761, 863, 910; XII, 91, 161, 162, 482, 563,
    564, 565
Kent, Margaret (Howard), XI, 428
Kent, Mary. *See* Carigan
Kent, Mary Ann (Anne) (Wallace), XI, 906
Kent, Robert, VII, 627
Kent, Robert John, XII, **482–83**, 956
Kent, Sarah (Blowers), VII, 86, 87
Kent, Susanna (Smithers), VI, 620
Kent, William, VI, 620
Kent and Strathearn, Duchess of. *See* Victoria Mary
    Louisa
Kent and Strathearn, Duke of. *See* Edward Augustus
Kentish, Elizabeth Mildred Wale (Mountain), VI, 523, 528;
    IX, 578
Kenwendeshon, VI, **373–74**, 552, 758; VII, 520; XI, 640
Kenwick (Kenwrick). *See* Kendrick
Kenwrick, Elizabeth. *See* Atkins
Kenwrick, Solomon, IV, 410
Keogh, Mary, XI, 318
Kephart, Horace, VIII, 449
Kepitanal (Kepitenat). *See* Capitanal
Kepler, Johannes, VIII, 214
Keppel, Lady Anne Amelia (Coke, Countess of Leicester;
    Ellice), IX, 234
Keppel, Augustus, 1st Viscount Keppel, IV, 259, 327, 600,
    701

Keppel, Frederick, V, 746
Keppel, George, 3rd Earl of Albemarle, IV, 501; V, 141
Keppel, Sophia, Countess of Albemarle and Viscountess Bury. *See* MacNab
Keppel, William Anne, 2nd Earl of Albemarle, IV, 278
Keppel, William Charles, 4th Earl of Albemarle, IX, 234
Keppel, William Coutts, Viscount Bury and 7th Earl of Albemarle, IX, 527; XI, 474
Ker. *See also* Kerr
Ker, James, X, 401
Ker, Janet (Ker), X, 401
Ker, Jessie. *See* Russell
Ker, Robert, X, **401**
Kerbodot. *See* Guillemot
Kerby, Alison. *See* Donaldson
Kerby, James, VIII, **465–67**
Kerby, Jane. *See* Lambert
Kerby, John, VIII, 465
Kerby, Mary (Wallace), VI, 798
Kerdement, Mr (captain), I, 421
Kerdisien. *See* Pichot
Keredern, Philippe-Régis-Denis de, Baron de Trobriand, XI, 36
Kerfily, Marquis de. *See* Castel
Kerfily, Marquise de. *See* Kerven
Kerlérec. *See* Billouart
Kermode, William, VII, 924
Kernighan, Robert Kirkland, VII, 475; XI, 307
Kérouac, Charles de, X, 401
Kérouac, Éléonore. *See* Létourneau
Kérouac, Josette. *See* Blanchette
Kérouac, Léon, X, **401–2**
Kerr, Archibald, VIII, 875
Kerr, Charles, IV, 37
Kerr, David Shank, XII, 17
Kerr, Elizabeth. *See* Brant
Kerr, Elizabeth. *See* Johnson
Kerr, Elizabeth (Leston; Spike), X, 664
Kerr, Elizabeth (Weld), VIII, 924
Kerr, George (merchant), VI, 582
Kerr, George (politician), XII, 740, 741
Kerr, Isabella (wife of JAMES), VII, 464
Kerr, James, V, 234; VI, 578, 584; VII, 61, 190, **464–66**, 872; VIII, 154; X, 68
Kerr, James Hooper, X, **402**
Kerr, James Kirkpatrick, XI, 497, 917
Kerr, Janet (George), IX, 307
Kerr, Jean. *See* Murray
Kerr, John, I, 544
Kerr, John Blaine, XII, 768, 833
Kerr, Lady Louisa (Lennox), V, 488
Kerr, Magdalen (Cochran), 190
Kerr, Margaret (wife of JAMES), VII, 464
Kerr, Mary (Young), VI, 822
Kerr, Mary J. *See* Bull
Kerr, Mary Margaret (Clark), V, 673; VI, 147, 375
Kerr, Robert (businessman), XII, 379
Kerr, Robert (father of JAMES), VII, 464
Kerr, Robert, V, 279, 639, 841; VI, 93, 147, **374–75**; VII, 466
Kerr, Robert Johnson, VI, 760, 761
Kerr, Wilfred Brenton, VII, 883
Kerr, William, XI, 3, 5

Kerr, William Henry, 4th Marquess of Lothian, V, 488
Kerr, William Johnson, V, 673; VI, 375, 632; VII, 378, **466–67**, 516; VIII, 245, 709; IX, 264, 406, 499
Kerr, William Simcoe, VII, 467
Kerr, William Warren Hastings, XII, 5
Kerrill, Elizabeth (Amherst), IV, 20
Kerrivan, Peter, IV, **784–85**
Kerry, Anthony, XII, 483
Kerry, John, XII, **483–84**, 745
Kerry, Laura Gilson. *See* Parmenter
Kerry, Mary Margaret. *See* Smyth
Kerry, William, XII, 483
Kerry (Cary), William, VII, 715
Kerry, William Simons, XII, 483
Kersaint. *See* Coëtnempren
Kershaw, John, X, 717
Kersident. *See* Guichart
Kersteman, William, XII, 73
Kertk. *See* Kirke
Kertland, Sarah Georgina (Molesworth), X, 516
Kervan, Thomas, IV, 784
Kerven, Françoise-Jeanne de (Castel, Comtesse de Saint-Pierre, Marquise de Crèvecœur et de Kerfily), II, 306
Kerwan (Kerwin). *See* Kirwan
Kerwin, Patrick, XI, 32
Kesterman, Mary. *See* Brewse
Kesterman, William, IV, 93
Ketchum, Ann. *See* Mercer
Ketchum, Ann (Love; wife of JESSE), VII, 467
Ketchum, Henry George Clopper, VII, 188; XII, **484–85**
Ketchum, Isobel (Isabella) (Clark), VI, 146, 147
Ketchum, Jane (Perley), IX, 628
Ketchum, Jesse (father of JESSE), VII, 467; IX, 422
Ketchum, Jesse (son of JESSE), VII, 468
Ketchum, Jesse, VI, 11, 12, 632, 633; VII, 163, 442, 467, 794, 822; VIII, 46, 642, 932; IX, **422–24**, 498, 499, 500, 508, 724, 788; XI, 153, 517, 712, 796
Ketchum, Joseph, VII, 467
Ketchum, Mary. *See* Robbins
Ketchum, Mary (Thomson), IX, 788
Ketchum, Mary Ann. *See* Rubergall
Ketchum, Mary Ann (mother of HENRY GEORGE CLOPPER), XII, 484
Ketchum, Mary Ann (Clopper), VII, 186
Ketchum, Mary Ann (Leavitt), VII, 493
Ketchum, Mollie. *See* Robbins
Ketchum, Richard, XII, 484
Ketchum, Sarah E. *See* Milner
Ketchum, Seneca, VII, 351, **467–68**; IX, 422
Ketchum, William, VIII, 896; IX, 423
Ketchum, William Quintard, VIII, 173
Ketelby, Thomas, I, 522
Ketson, Julia. *See* Henry
Ketura (Pahellau), VIII, 477
Keveny, Owen, V, 267, **465–66**; VI, 100, 442, 446; VIII, 343
Keys, David Reid, XII, 668
Keys, Lolitia (McDonnell; Sexton), X, 647
Kezhegowinninne (Kezigkoenene), VIII, 440; IX, 591, 593; X, 692; XI, **473–75**; XII, 186
Kezicks. *See* Keeshick
Khisipikiwam, Agatha, I, 481

Kiala, II, xxx, **316–17**, 503; III, xxxiv, 46; IV, lii
Kiashuta. *See* Kayahsota?
Kidd, Adam, VI, **375–77**; VII, 828
Kidd, Alexander, VI, 375
Kidd, Mary (Morgan), XII, 760
Kidd*, Thomas (d. 1950), IX, 216
Kidston, Catherine Glen (McKnight), XII, 659
Kidston, William, IX, 738, 739; XI, 619, 633
Kieffer. *See also* Keefer
Kieffer, Ann. *See* Waldruff
Kieffer, George, VIII, 450
Kieffer, Mary. *See* Cooke
Kieffer, Samuel, VIII, 450
Kielley, Amelia. *See* Jackson
Kielley, Edward, VII, 154, 155, 507, 508, 793; VIII, **467–70**; X, 601; XI, 673, 760
Kier, Archibald Renfrew, XI, 840
Kier, Martha (Smithe), XI, 840
Kierzkowski, Alexandre-Édouard, VII, 236; IX, **424–25**; XII, 390
Kierzkowski, Caroline-Virginie. *See* Saint-Ours
Kierzkowski, Filip Jakub, IX, 424
Kierzkowski, Louise. *See* Debartzch
Kierzkowski, Maryanna Ludwika. *See* Liebermann
Kil-a-ko-tah (Marguerite Clatsoppe) (wife of James Mc-
    MILLAN; wife of Louis Labonté), VIII, 584
Kilborn, Charles, VI, **377–78**
Kilborn, John, VII, 458
Kilborn, Joseph, VI, 338, 574
Kilborn, Margaret. *See* Young
Kilborn, Mary (Sangster), XII, 944, 946
Kilborn, Thomas, VI, 377
Kilby, Christopher (uncle), III, 326
Kilby, Christopher, III, 10, 326, 586
Kilby, Sarah. *See* Ellis
Kilby, Sarah. *See* Sempkins
Kilby, Thomas, III, **326–27**; IV, 312
Kildalloig. *See* Campbell
Kildare, Earl of. *See* Fitzgerald
Kilgallen, Anne (Erlan; Hamilton), X, 331
Kilgour, Agnes (Cotter), XI, 204
Kilgour, Jeanie (Wilson), XII, 1114
Killaly, Alicia. *See* Hamilton
Killaly, Hamilton Hartley, VII, 32, 33, 34, 605, 861; VIII, 101; IX, 370; X, 164, **402–6**, 648, 708; XI, 463, 464, 501, 817; XII, 391, 561, 886, 930, 961
Killaly, Jack, XI, 817
Killaly, John A., X, 402
Killaly, Martha Jane. *See* Handy
Killam, Elizabeth Gale. *See* Dudman
Killam, Frank, IX, 428
Killam, George, IX, 425
Killam*, Izaak Walton (1885–1955), XII, 773
Killam, John, IX, 425
Killam, Sarah. *See* Allen
Killam, Sophia. *See* Corning
Killam, Thomas, VIII, 127; IX, **425–28**; X, 551; XI, 197, 398
Killed Twice, XII, 970
Killmaster, Henry John, XI, 907
Kilnar, Emma (McKeand), XI, 562
Kilpatrick, Robert, III, 315, **327**
Kimball, R. H., XI, 813

Kimber. *See also* Jékimbert
Kimber, Emmélie. *See* Boileau
Kimber, Hector, VIII, 471
Kimber, Joseph (father of TIMOTHÉE), VIII, 470
Kimber, Joseph (relative of James G. HANNA), V, 406
Kimber, Josette. *See* Dabin
Kimber, Marie-Euphrosine (Doucet), VIII, 231
Kimber, Marie-Josette. *See* Robitaille
Kimber, René, VII, **468–69**; VIII, 231
Kimber, René-Joseph, VII, 172, 213, 468, 880; VIII, 231, 332, 364, 365, 471, 838; XI, 889, 890; XII, 66
Kimber, Timothée, VII, 25, 248; VIII, **470–72**, 616, 915
Kimberley, Earl of. *See* Wodehouse
Kimble, Colby, XII, 414
Kincardine, Countess of. *See* Cumming-Bruce
Kincardine, Countess of. *See* Lambton
Kincardine, Earl of. *See* Bruce
Kineubenae, V, **466–67**; VII, 250, 929; VIII, 440
King, Mrs. *See* Fisher
King, Agnes Elizabeth. *See* Budden
King, Amelia. *See* Sherwood
King, Andrew, VIII, 851; XII, 659
King, Anne. *See* Robinson
King, Boston, IV, 515; V, 341, **468–69**
King, Charles, XI, 813
King, Charles (brother of JAMES, 1848–1900), XII, 488
King, Charles (father of JAMES, 1848–1900), XII, 488
King, Charles (father of Marie-Louise), XII, 175
King, Edmund Alexander, XII, 488
King, Edward Hammond, IX, **428–29**, 478, 479; XII, 523
King, Edwin Henry, V, 320; X, 10, 684; XI, 157, 575, 768; XII, 107, **485–88**, 988
King, Elizabeth. *See* Lumley
King, Elizabeth. *See* Torrence
King, Elizabeth (Dearin), XI, 239
King, Frederic, XII, 488
King, Frederick, IX, 429
King, George (father of WILLIAM HENRY), VIII, 472
King, George (Montreal merchant), V, 821; VI, 432, 433
King, George (Quebec merchant), V, 406
King, George, IX, **429**
King*, George Edwin (1839–1901), IX, 429; X, 340; XI, 298, 897; XII, 338, 339, 341, 775, 881, 1098, 1103
King, Hannah. *See* Waterman
King, Harriett (Wells), VIII, 925, 927
King, Harriett Nice. *See* Holmes
King, Helen (Winer; Bethune), XII, 106
King, Helen Skinner (Gordon), XII, 490
King, Henrietta (mother of WILLIAM HENRY), VIII, 472
King, Henry, XII, 488
King, James (clerk), VII, 735
King, James (newspaperman), VI, 165; VII, 662, 663
King, James, IV, 156, **412–13**; V, 55; VII, 830
King, James, XII, **488–89**
King, Janet Mcpherson. *See* Skinner
King, Jemima Nicolina. *See* Baxter
King, John (brother of JAMES, 1848–1900), XII, 488
King, John (educator), IX, 509; XI, 248; XII, 888
King, John (physician), VI, 773; VIII, 933
King, John (sailor), I, 376, 377
King, John (under-secretary of state), VI, 558
King, John Mark, XI, 467; XII, **489–91**, 617
King, John William, IX, 428

King, Maria Philadelphia Louisa (Hills), XII, 440
King, Marie-Louise (Chapleau), XII, 172, 175
King, Mary. *See* Scott
King, Mary Ann. *See* Fowler
King, Mary Mourning. *See* Phares
King, Ralph, XII, 489
King, Richard, X, 406
King, Richard, X, 319, **406–8**; XII, 878
King, Sir Richard, XII, 440
King, Robert, XII, 752
King, Sally (Burley), VI, 91
King, Sarah. *See* Murray
King, Sarah Ann. *See* Lawson
King, Violet (wife of BOSTON), V, 468, 469
King, Walter B., XII, 745
King, Warden, VIII, 632
King, William. *See* Peguis
King, William (clergyman), VIII, 170, 171
King, William (father of WILLIAM), XII, 491
King, William (geologist), XII, 234
King, William (shipbuilder), IV, 48; V, 83
King, William (soldier), V, 750
King, William, IX, 107, 820; X, 707; XII, **491–93**, 960
King, William Henry, VIII, **472–74**
King*, William Lyon Mackenzie (1874–1950), IX, 508; XI, 804; XII, 921
King, Willobe, known as Olive Le Roy (Castaing), IV, 136
Kingdon, Hollingworth Tully, XII, 716
Kinglake, Alexander William, VIII, 275, 921
Kingminguse, IV, **413**
King Newcomer. *See* Netawatwees
King of Kanadesaga. *See* Kaieñʔkwaahtoñ
King Philip. *See* Pometacom
Kingsford, Elizabeth (mother of WILLIAM), XII, 493
Kingsford, Maria Margaret. *See* Lindsay
Kingsford, William, XII, 493
Kingsford, William, IV, xlviii, 502; VIII, 155, 341; IX, 576; XI, 427, 884; XII, **493–96**, 619
Kingsley, Charles, XII, 570
Kingsley, Frances L. (Hyman), X, 375
Kingsmill, George Roden, XI, 323
Kingston, Francis Sophia. *See* Rooke
Kingston, George Templeman, XI, 226, 243, **475–76**; XII, 160
Kingston, Henrietta. *See* Malone
Kingston, Lucy Henry, XI, 475
Kingston, William Henry Giles, XI, 475
Kinloch, Anne (Maclean), IV, 504
Kinnaird, Mary Jane. *See* Hoare
Kinnear, Andrew, IX, 430
Kinnear, David, VIII, 22; IX, **429–30**; XI, 680; XII, 279, 351
Kinnear, Janet. *See* Muir
Kinnear, Letitia. *See* Boyd
Kinnear, Mary (wife of DAVID), IX, 430
Kinnear, Thomas, XI, 150
Kinnear, William Boyd, VII, 610, 692, 915; VIII, 362, 377, 807; IX, 123, 263, 381, **430–31**; X, 286, 712; XI, 135
Kinnoull, Earl of. *See* Hay; Hay-Drummond
Kinonchamek, III, 529
Kinongé, II, xxxvii, **317–18**, 415, 505
Kinousaki, III, xxxix, **328**, 451

Kinsey, Jane (Ferrie), VII, 284
Kinsey, Jane (Huck-Saunders), IV, 701
Kinton, Julie-Élisabeth-Geneviève. *See* Morrison
Kinton, Thomas, IX, 450
Kinzie, John, VII, 132
Kinzie, Juliette Augusta. *See* Magill
Kiotseaeton (Kioutsaeton), I, 7, 65, 112, 186, 371, 373, 389, **403–4**, 548, 665; II, 82, 158
Kiouet, I, 204
Kipling, John, IV, 727, 743, 744; V, 885; VI, 321
Kipling, Rudyard, XI, 333
Kipp, Joseph, X, 560
Kirby. *See also* Kerby
Kirby, Ann (mother of ANN and JOHN), VII, 469
Kirby, Ann (Macaulay), IV, 494; VII, **469**, 470, 472; VIII, 513, 514; X, 452
Kirby, Cecilia. *See* Bethune
Kirby, John, VII, 469, 470
Kirby, John, IV, 494; V, 79, 168, 327; VI, 215, 470, 772; VII, 229, 368, **469–73**, 559, 584; VIII, 513
Kirby, Mary. *See* Macaulay
Kirby, Sarah (Trimmer), VII, 481; XII, 996
Kirby, William (author), IX, 659
Kirby, William (brother of ANN and JOHN), VII, 469
Kirby*, William (1817–1906), III, 143, 304, 677; IV, 449, 660; VIII, 204; X, 538, 656; XII, 572, 995, 1076
Kirchoffer, Nesbitt, XI, 928
Kirk, Abdiel, VII, 44
Kirk, Abigail (Bamford), VII, 44, 45
Kirk, James, VII, 915
Kirk, John Angus, IX, 537; XI, 149
Kirkbride, Thomas Story, XII, 985
Kirkby, Richard, II, 666
Kirkby, William, XI, 437
Kirkby, William West, XII, 936
Kirkconnell*, Watson (1895–1977), VII, 561
Kirke, Mrs, Lady Kirke (wife of Sir DAVID), I, 406
Kirke, David, I, 406
Kirke, Sir David, I, 24, 25, 29, 53, 54, 59, 76, 110, 122, 133, 159, 160, 161, 162, 163, 196, 199, 200, 237, 243, 278, 287, 303, 311, 313, 330, 340, 342, 366, 368, 369, **404–7**, 411, 428, 452, 453, 489, 494, 495, 498, 511, 521, 533, 561, 567, 579, 613, 652, 653, 665
Kirke, Elizabeth. *See* Gowding
Kirke, George, I, 406, 567
Kirke, Gervase (Jarvis), I, 404; II, 538
Kirke, James (Jarvis), I, 405, 406, 407, 652
Kirke, Sir John, I, 405, 406, 407; II, 538
Kirke, Sir Lewis, I, 199, 242, 405, 406, **407**, 408, 473, 487, 495, 636
Kirke, Mary, II, 538
Kirke, Philip, I, 406
Kirke, Thomas, I, 408
Kirke, Thomas, I, 405, 406, **407–8**, 487
Kirkland, James, X, 612
Kirkland, Jean (Doak), VIII, 224, 225
Kirkland, Margaret (Nairn), XII, 777
Kirkland, Marion (Reid), X, 612
Kirkland, Samuel, III, xxxviii; IV, 117, 368, 731; V, 803, 804, 811
Kirkpatrick, Alexander, IX, 431; XII, 496
Kirkpatrick, Barbara Isabella (Buller), VII, 117; IX, 100
Kirkpatrick, Elizabeth (Foster), VII, 316

Kirkpatrick, Frances Jane. *See* Macaulay

Kirkpatrick, Sir George Airey, IX, 432; XII, **496–97**, 604, 686, 688

Kirkpatrick, Sir George Macaulay, XII, 497

Kirkpatrick, Helen. *See* Fisher

Kirkpatrick, Isabel Louise, Lady Kirkpatrick. *See* Macpherson

Kirkpatrick, Marianne. *See* Sutton

Kirkpatrick, Stafford Frederick, VII, 159

Kirkpatrick, Thomas, VIII, 518; IX, **431–32**, 577, 725; XII, 496

Kirouac. *See also* Kérouac

Kirouac*, Conrad, named Brother Marie-Victorin (1885–1944), V, 593; XII, 769, 869

Kirouac, Germain, VIII, 536

Kirouet. *See* Quirouet

Kirshung-oak. *See* Qissunguaq

Kirwan, Ann (mother of Miss KIRWIN), VIII, 474

Kirwan, James, VIII, 474

Kirwan, Miss, named Sister Mary Bernard, VII, 631; VIII, **474–76**; IX, 556; XII, 974

Kirwan, Thaddeus T., XI, 693, 694

Kirwan, Thomas, IX, 832, 834

Kirwin. *See* Irwin

Kisensik, III, xxxvii, **328**

Kishigowininy. *See* Kezhegowinninne

Kissock, Helen (Browne), XI, 119

Kitchen, Ellen (Fenelon), XII, 310

Kitchi-manito-waya, XII, **497–99**, 970

Kitchin, Eusebius Bacchus, IV, 32, 726

Kit Fox, XII, 718

Kittier, William, IV, 711

Kittimakegin (Miserable Man), XI, 460

Kittson, Élise. *See* Marion

Kittson, George (adoptive father of WILLIAM), VII, 473

Kittson, George (father of NORMAN WOLFRED), XI, 476

Kittson, Helen. *See* McDonald

Kittson, Nancy. *See* Tucker

Kittson, Norman Wolfred, VII, 777; VIII, 819; IX, 261; X, 46, 47, 168, 628; XI, **476–77**; XII, 206, 207

Kittson, William, VII, **473**; IX, 851

Kiwisānce, XI, **477–78**

Kiyasuta. *See* Kayahsotaˀ

Klatsassin (Klatsassan, Klattasine), IX, **432–33**; X, 104, 697

Klein. *See* Cline

Klingancourt. *See* Damours de Clignancour

Klingensmith, Fisjary (High Flyer), VIII, 477

Klingensmith, Molly Ann (wife of PETER), VIII, 476

Klingensmith, Peter, known as White Peter, VIII, **476–77**

Klingersmith, Peter. *See* Peter, John

Klock, George, IV, 692; VII, 651

Kluck, William, V, 602; V, 507

Klutschak, Heinrich Wenzl, XII, 955

Klyne, Jane (McDonald), VIII, 527; XII, 612

Kmoch, George, VII, 474; X, 284

Knap. *See* Hunter

Knaplund, Paul, VIII, xxix

Knapp, Joseph, X, 723

Knaut, Anna. *See* Grob

Knaut, Benjamin, IV, 414

Knaut, Catherine (Newton), IV, 414

Knaut, Jane. *See* Brimner

Knaut, Lewis, IX, 710

Knaut, Philip Augustus, IV, 52, 291, **414**

Knee, Margaret (Kelly), XI, 465

Kneeland, John, IV, 695

Kneeshaw, Richard, X, 450

Kneller, Sir Godfrey, XII, 405

Kneller, Henry, IV, 398, **414–15**, 726; V, 224, 863; VI, 295

Knight, Ann Cuthbert. *See* Rae

Knight, Charles, XII, 997

Knight, Charles Edward, XII, 145

Knight, Elizabeth (wife of JAMES), II, 320

Knight, Elizabeth (Livingston), II, 436

Knight, Gabriel, I, 408

Knight, Gilpin, II, 320

Knight, James, I, 385; II, 20, 42, 50, 51, 56, 171, 231, 232, 266, 267, 291, 311, 312, 313, 314, **318–20**, 394, 406, 407, 604, 614, 615, 616, 617, 627, 628, 644, 658, 663; III, 414, 446, 489, 599; IV, 339

Knight, James Innes, VIII, 734

Knight, Jessie, VIII, 734

Knight, John, I, 5, 20, 243, 360, 375, 397, **408**

Knight, Joseph Philip, IX, 600; X, 371

Knight, Mary. *See* Hosier

Knight, Richard, II, 318

Knight, Richard, VI, 66; VII, 220; VIII, 75, **477–79**

Knight, Richard Payne, VIII, 759

Knight, Robert, VIII, 734

Knight, Thomas Andrew, VI, 219

Knight, William, X, 372

Knight, William Henry, XII, 145

Knockleith. *See* Ellice

Knollys, Henry, I, 332

Knorr, Hannah (Sower), IV, 721

Knower, Sarah (Merry), VI, 501

Knowles, Ann (West), VII, 900

Knowles, Betsy. *See* Dimock

Knowles, Sir Charles, III, 276, 293, 294, 572, 628, 656; IV, 83, 93, 169, 737

Knowles, Martha (Parker), VII, 680

Knowles, Mary (Moore), IV, 553

Knowling, Sarah (Fowell), IX, 277

Knowlton, Laura. *See* Moss

Knowlton, Lucinda (Willard), VI, 816

Knowlton, Luke (grandfather), VIII, 757; IX, 433

Knowlton, Luke, IX, 433

Knowlton, Paul Holland, IX, 276, **433–35**; X, 531; XI, 438

Knowlton, Sally. *See* Holbrook

Knowlton, Sarah, IX, 434

Knowlton, Sarah (Masters; Dimock), IV, 217

Knowlton, Selucia (Robinson), VIII, 757

Knowlton, Silas, IX, 433

Knowlton, T. A., XI, 297

Knox, Andrew, I, 496

Knox, Caroline Matilda. *See* Jordan

Knox, Henry, V, 40, 415, 808; VI, 607

Knox, Jane. *See* Carre

Knox, John (father of JOHN), IV, 415

Knox, John (founder of Church of Scotland), VI, 459

Knox, John, III, 89, 305, 360, 421; IV, **415–16**, 487, 773

Knox, Mary (Boomer), XI, 89

Knox, Thomas (customs collector), V, 4

Knox, Thomas (muster master), V, 630

Knox, Thomas (politician), VI, 356

Knox, William, IV, xl, xlvi, xlviii; V, 149, 351, 353; VI, 356, 395

Koberger, Anton, XII, 16

Koch (Cook), Elizabeth (Rudolf), VIII, 782

Koé. *See* Gawèhe

Koenig, Edmond-Victor de, Baron von Koenig, VI, **378–79**

König, Edmund von, Baron von König, VI, 378

König, Louise-Émilie von, Baroness von König. *See* Rudolfi

Koenig, Marie-Céleste de, Baroness von Koenig. *See* Guichard, *dit* Bourguignon

Koenig, Marie-Louise de, Baroness von Koenig. *See* Jean

Kohl, Johann Georg, XII, 809

Kohler, Auguste, IX, 31, 408

Kohlmeister, Anna Elizabeth. *See* Reimann

Kohlmeister, Benjamin Gottlieb, VII, **473–74**; X, 284

Kointaguettez. *See* Ohquandageghte

Kolno. *See* Scolvus

Konantewenteta. *See* Konwatewenteta

Kondiaronk, II, xxx, 20, 102, 103, 108, 119, **320–23**, 344, 423, 441, 444, 593, 643; III, xxxv; IV, liii

Konieschguanokee (Captain Pipe), IV, 302; V, 345

Konwatewenteta, VII, 912; VIII, 939

Koñwatsi?tsiaiéñni, IV, 119, 397, 405, 410, **416–19**; V, 786, 803, 804; VI, 374; VII, 466

Koopman, Judith. *See* Diutz

Koopman, Levi. *See* Marchand, Louis

Koopman, Solomon, XI, 585

Kościuszko, Tadeusz, VI, 660

Koska, Stanislas (Aharathanha), VII, 889

Kossuth, Lajos, VIII, 853; X, 670

Kotsinoghyâtà. *See* Hotsinoñhyahta?

Kotte (Koth, Cotté), Lewis, IV, 613

Kouategeté. *See* Ohquandageghte

Kouée. *See* Gawèhe

Kough, Mary (wife of PATRICK), IX, 436

Kough, Patrick, VII, 154, 220, 293, 294, 590; VIII, 725, 726; IX, **435–36**

Koutaoiliboe (Koutaouileone), II, xxxvii, 317, **323–24**, 415, 453, 503; III, 576

Koweahe. *See* Gawèhe

Koyah (Kower, Kouyer), IV, 218, 411, **419–20**

Koželuh, Leopold Antonín, VI, 499

Krabbé, Frederick J., VIII, 624

Krainguille, Monsieur (emissary), I, 593

Krausler. *See* Crysler

Krepper, John, VII, 468

Kribs, Elizabeth. *See* Pannebecker

Kribs, Louis P., XII, **499–500**, 580

Kribs, Ludwig, IX, 467

Kribs, Ludwig (Lewis), XII, 499

Kribs, Millie. *See* Cliff

Krieghoff, Cornelius, VII, 100; VIII, 82, 833; IX, 359, 792; X, 264, **408–14**; XI, 285, 286, 417, 802, 803; XII, 367, 789, 928

Krieghoff, Emily (Burnett; Wendt), X, 409, 413

Krieghoff, Ernst, X, 409

Krieghoff, Isabella Ludivica. *See* Wauters

Krieghoff, Johann Ernst, X, 408

Krieghoff, Louise. *See* Gauthier, *dit* Saint-Germain

Kruger (Cruger), Polly (Meyers), VI, 502

Krum, John Christian, III, 212

Kruzenshtern, Ivan Fedorovich, V, 80

Kryn. *See* Togouiroui

Kukatosi-poka (Kucka-toosinah), XI, **478–79**

Kunz, Matthew, III, 212

Kuper, Sir Augustus Leopold, XII, 290

Kupreianov, Ivan Antonovich, VII, 572

Kurczyn, Sarah (Lovell), XII, 569, 573

Kuriahtaaty. *See* Karaghtadie

Kur-king, VII, 271

Kurz, Rudolf Friedrich, XII, 778

?Kwah, VII, **474–75**

Kwaku Dua I, King of Ashanti, VII, 918

Kwolī′la, VIII, 421

Kwulu, Joseph, XII, 936

Kyen-da-nent (Sally) (wife of Ebenezer ALLAN), V, 15

Kyi-i-staah. *See also* Isapo-muxika

Kyi-i-staah (Bear Ghost), XI, 444

Kyiyo-siksinum (Black Bear), IX, 624; XII, 717

Kynynmound. *See* Elliot-Murray-Kynynmound

Kyte, Ernest Cockburn, VIII, 642

Ky-yo-kosi. *See* Potts, Jerry

LAAH CEIL MANATOI ELAAH (wife of Okah TUBBEE), VIII, 898, 899

Labadie, Évariste-Odilon, X, 691

Labadie, Guillaume-Louis, VIII, 702

Labadie, Louis, V, 688; VI, **379–81**; VII, 646; VIII, 258

Labadie, Louise-Zéphyrine. *See* Quintal

Labadie, Marie-Archange. *See* Charron

Labadie, Marie-Josephte. *See* Privée

Labadie, Marie-Louise. *See* Paquet

Labadie, Pierre, VI, 379

Labadie, Théotiste (Derome), X, 226

Labadie, *dit* Saint-Pierre, Angélique, IX, 813

Labaig, Jean de, II, 4, 7

Labaig, Marie de. *See* Abbadie de Saint-Castin

La Balluë. *See* Magon

La Balme. *See* Mottin

La Barbotière, Monsieur (ship's captain), I, 499

Labaree, Hannah (Hibbard), XI, 403

La Baronnière. *See* Froyer

La Barre. *See also* Charon; Charron; Le Febvre

La Barre, Anne de. *See* Adhémar de Lantagnac

La Barre, Augustin-Antoine de, III, 5

La Barthe, Jeanne (Claverie), III, 124; IV, 125

La Barthe, Jean-Pierre, IV, 66, 126

Labat, Monsieur (engineer), II, 480

Labat (Labatt), Jane (wife of Valentine Knightley Chetwode), IX, 436

Labat (Labatt), Valentine Knightley Chetwode, IX, 436

Labatt, Eliza. *See* Kell

Labatt, Ephraim, IX, 437

Labatt, Hugh Francis, IX, 437

Labatt, John, IX, 437

Labatt*, John (1838–1915), XII, 470

Labatt, John Kinder, IX, **436–37**; X, 372

Labatt, John Sackville, IX, 437

Labatt, Robert, IX, 437

Labatut, Baron de. *See* Navailles

Labatut, Baronne de. *See* Mius d'Entremont de Pobomcoup

La Baume, Gustave, VII, 483

Labauve, François, VII, 204, 579; VIII, 65

La Bazanière, Louise de. *See* Briet

La Bazanière, Marie-Suzanne de (Lorant; Le Roy Desmarest), II, 424; III, 396
La Bazanière, Pierre de, II, 424
L'Abbé, Monsieur (ship's captain), I, 100, 101
Labbé, Charles, V, 116
La Beaume. *See* Tailhandier
Labelle, Angélique. *See* Maher
Labelle, Antoine, XII, 501
Labelle, Éloïse. *See* Leclaire
Labelle, Elzéar, IX, 438; XII, 504
Labelle, François, VII, 680; VIII, 136, 137; X, 266, 505
Labelle, François-Xavier-Antoine, IX, 782; X, 723; XI, 7, 13, 184; XII, 59, 90, 302, 303, **500–3**, 722, 725, 727, 1026
Labelle, Jean-Baptiste (clergyman), VII, 148
Labelle, Jean-Baptiste (father of JEAN-BAPTISTE), XII, 503
Labelle, Jean-Baptiste, XI, 3; XII, **503–4**, 570
Labelle, Jean-Baptiste-Napoléon, IX, 437
Labelle, Ludger, IX, **437–38**; X, 148; XI, 71, 623; XII, 173
Labelle, Marie. *See* Alain
Labelle, Marie-Charlotte (Chartrand), IX, 126
Labelle, Marie-Eugénie-Henriette. *See* Morin
Laberee, Sophia (Pope), XI, 705
Labelle, Sophie. *See* Porlier
Laberge, Ambroise, X, 414
Laberge, Charles, X, **414–17**; XI, 480; XII, 260, 505, 692, 693, 694, 723, 1013
Laberge, Denis-Aristide, XI, 187
Laberge, Édouard, XII, 693
Laberge, François, III, 346
Laberge, Hélène-Olive. *See* Turgeon
Laberge, Jean, XII, 762
Laberge, Joseph, VIII, 202
Laberge, Marie-Françoise (Lambert, *dit* Saint-Paul), III, 346
Laberge, Rose. *See* Franchère
Labillois, Charles-Marie, IX, **438–39**
Labillois, Émilie. *See* Meagher
Labillois, Jean-Pierre, IX, 438
Labillois, Périnne-Louise. *See* Gaillard
La Blanchetière. *See* Renardin
La Boische. *See* Beauharnois
La Boissière. *See* Nau
Labonté. *See also* Campion
Labonté, Monsieur (soldier), III, 310
Labonté, Marguerite. *See* Kil-a-ko-tah
La Borde. *See also* Delaborde; Hamare; Mullois
Laborde, Catherine. *See* Dechart
Laborde, Catherine (Soupiran), II, 613
La Borde, Jean, III, 157, 158, 172, 452, 567; IV, 126, **420–23**, 558, 644, 645, 646, 678
La Borde, Jean de, III, 172
Laborde, Louise. *See* Dupuy
La Borde, Marguerite (Daccarrette), III, 157
Laborde, Sébastien-Charles, IV, 422
Laborde (Borda) d'Aloperca, Martin, IV, 420
Labossière, Thérèse (Millier), XI, 594
Labouchere, Henry, 1st Baron Taunton, VII, 144; VIII, 416; IX, 177, 196, 384; X, 258, 439; XI, 308, 662
La Bouille. *See* Fromont
La Boularderie. *See* Le Poupet
La Boulardière. *See* Dugué
La Boulasserie. *See* Ailleboust

La Boulaye. *See* Duret
La Bouteiller de La Bouteillerie, Suzanne, II, 181
La Bouteillerie. *See* Deschamps
Labrador. *See* Foucher
Labrador, The. *See* Fernandes, João
La Branche, Jacques-O., XI, 325
Labrèche. *See also* Dalgueuil; Déziel
La Brèche, Sieur (assistant to François POULIN de Francheville), II, 530
Labrèche, Louis, X, 417
Labrèche, Marguerite-Julie. *See* Viger
Labrèche-Viger, Caroline. *See* Laflamme
Labrèche-Viger, Louis, IX, 193, 614; X, 154, **417**, 524, 533; XI, 496; XII, 173, 254, 260, 262, 506
Labrecque, Michel-Thomas, XII, 1023
La Brède, Baron de. *See* Secondat
La Bretonnière. *See also* Neveu
La Bretonnière, Jacques-Quintin de, III, **329**, 480
Labrie, Jacques, V, 211; VI, 326, **381–82**, 386; VII, 25, 172, 690; VIII, 87, 331, 456, 471, 791; IX, 300, 568; XI, 489
Labrie, Marie-Marguerite. *See* Gagnier
Labrie, Zéphirine (Chénier; Desrochers), VI, 381, 382; VII, 172
La Broquerie. *See also* Boucher; Chartier
Labroquerie (Boucher de La Broquerie), Charlotte de (Hertel de Rouville), VIII, 393
Labroquerie (Boucher de La Broquerie), Joseph-Antoine, XII, 1002
Labroquerie (Boucher de La Broquerie), Josephte (Labruère), VIII, 606
Labroquerie (Boucher de La Broquerie), Louise-Henriette de (Taché), XII, 1002, 1012
La Broquerie, Marie-Hippolyte de (Boucher de La Bruère), X, 76
Labrosse. *See also* Jourdain
La Brosse, Monsieur (ship's commander), I, 423
Labrosse, Geneviève (Coutlée, *dit* Marcheterre), VI, 169
La Brosse, Jean-Baptiste de, II, 296; IV, 106, 294, 295, **423–25**; V, 201
La Brosse, Jean de, IV, 423
La Brosse, Louise de. *See* Duboiscuvier
Labruère (La Bruère). *See also* Boucher
Labruère (Boucher de La Bruère), Catherine de (Lacoste), VIII, 479; X, 418
Labruère (Boucher de La Bruère), Charles, VIII, 606
Labruère, Josephte. *See* Labroquerie
Labruère (Boucher de La Bruère), Sophie (Malhiot), VIII, 606
Labrunie, Gérard (Gérard de Nerval), VIII, 503
La Bruyère. *See also* Boucher; Court; Fabry
La Bruyère, Jean de, VII, 90
Labry. *See* Nau
La Burgue, Alexis-Théodore de, VII, 28
Labutte. *See* Chesne
La Caille, Nicolas-Louis de, III, 31; VIII, 212
La Cailleterie. *See* de Lisle
La Cardonnière. *See* Rouer
Lacasse, Lucie-Parmélie (Lesperance), XII, 557
Lacasse, Napoléon, VIII, 291; XI, 458
Lacasta. *See* Sessé
Lacelle, Agathe de (Réaume), V, 710
Lacelle, Jacques, V, 852

Lacelle, Mary. *See* Blue Jacket

Lacerte, Élie, XI, 340

La Cetière, Anne de. *See* Bier

La Cetière, Florent de, II, 43, 170, 273, **325**, 576, 577; III, 398, 647

La Cetière, Jean de, II, 325

Lacey, Elizabeth (Lane), VIII, 485

La Chaise. *See also* Aix; Andigné

La Chaise, Jacques de, II, 204; III, 40

Lachance. *See also* Pepin; Pépin

Lachance, P., XI, 207

La Chapelle. *See also* Renou

La Chapelle, Sieur (captain), II, 95

Lachapelle*, Emmanuel-Persillier (1845–1918), XI, 744, 777

La Chassaigne (La Chassagne). *See* Bouillet

La Chasse, Edmée. *See* Roussol

La Chasse, Joseph de, III, 329

La Chasse, Pierre de, II, xxxvii, 333, 475, 543, 544, 664, 665, 669; III, xxxix, 23, 24, **329–31**, 359, 477, 580

La Chaussaye; La Chaussée. *See* Beauharnois

La Chauvignerie. *See* Maray

La Chenaye. *See* Gauthier

La Chenette, Mme. *See* Couc, Elizabeth

La Chenette, Monsieur (husband of Elizabeth COUC), II, 645

La Chesnardière. *See* Ruis-Embito

La Chesnaye. *See* Aubert; Duquet

Lachevrotière; La Chevrotière. *See* Chavigny

Lach-Szyrma, Krystyn, IX, 299

Laciseraye. *See* Lefebvre

La Citière. *See* Lauson

Laclède Liguest, Pierre de, V, 272; XII, 558

La Cloche. *See* Hecquet

Laclos. *See* Choderlos

La Colle, III, **331**

La Colombière. *See also* Céré; La Corne

La Colombière, Bertrand de, II, 326

La Colombière, Claude de, II, 326

La Colombière, Joseph de, I, 78, 506; II, 134, 240, **325–27**, 360, 376, 528, 594, 597; IV, 535

La Colombière, Marguerite de. *See* Coindat

Lacombe. *See also* Truillier; Trullier

Lacombe*, Albert (1827–1916), VII, 137; VIII, 318; IX, 32; X, 46, 47, 82, 471, 661, 702; XI, 305, 442, 443, 444, 598; XII, 952, 1004, 1005, 1009

Lacombe, Catherine. *See* Quevillon

Lacombe, Jacques-Joseph, IV, 216

Lacombe, Léocadie. *See* Boucher

Lacombe, Patrice, IX, **439–40**

La Combe-Pocatière. *See* Pollet

Lacordaire, Henri, VII, 307; VIII, 408, 490; X, 580; XI, 96, 494, 725, 726

La Corne, Antoinette de. *See* Allemagne

La Corne, Charlotte de (Douglas), IV, 224

La Corne, Élisabeth de. *See* Ramezay

La Corne, François-Josué de, VI, 201

La Corne, Geneviève-Élisabeth de (Tarieu de Lanaudière), V, 791

La Corne, Jean-Marie de, II, 249

La Corne, Louis de, known as Chevalier de La Corne, III, 183, 285, 322, **331–32**, 333, 361, 375, 623; IV, 54, 169, 425, 426, 427, 434, 461, 633, 637, 651, 793; V, 98, 888

La Corne, Louis de, known as La Corne *l'aîné*, III, 390; IV, 224; V, 578

La Corne, Luc de, II, 327

La Corne, Luc de, known as Chaptes de La Corne or La Corne Saint-Luc, III, 48, 243, 332, 333, 376, 600, 652; IV, xliii, 41, 59, 129, 149, 155, 289, **425–29**, 442, 513, 543, 564, 633, 634, 759, 794; V, 96, 143, 724, 791; VI, 317; XI, 87

La Corne, Marie-Angélique de (Margane de Lavaltrie), V, 578

La Corne, Marie-Anne de. *See* Hervieux

La Corne, Marie-Anne de. *See* Hubert de La Croix

La Corne, Marie-Anne de (Campbell), IV, 129, 427

La Corne, Marie-Joseph de. *See* Guillimin

La Corne, Marie-Louise-Charlotte de (Le Comte Dupré), IV, 427, 442

La Corne, Marie-Marguerite de. *See* Boucher de Boucherville

La Corne, Marie-Marguerite de (Lennox; Viger), IV, 427; VIII, 909

La Corne, Maurice de (Jean-Louis), IV, 454

La Corne de Chaptes, Jean-Louis de, II, **327–28**, 456; III, 331, 332, 333; IV, 425, 429

La Corne de Chaptes, Joseph-Marie de, IV, 96, 338, **429–31**, 571; VI, 317

La Corne de Chaptes, Marie de. *See* Pécaudy de Contrecœur

La Corne de Chaptes, Marie-Madeleine de, named du Saint-Sacrement, III, **332–33**

La Corne de La Colombière, Pierre-Antoine de, III, 76

La Corne Dubreuil, François-Josué de, III, **333**; IV, 425, 633

La Corne Dubreuil, François-Michel de, III, 333

La Corne Dubreuil, Michelle de. *See* Hervieux

La Corne Saint-Luc. *See* La Corne, Luc de

La Corriveau. *See* Corriveau, Marie-Josephte

La Corruble. *See* Bouge, Ange

La Coste. *See also* Courault; Courreaud

Lacoste, Alexandre, X, 418

Lacoste*, Sir Alexandre (1843–1923), X, 154, 418, 435; XI, 729; XII, 179, 903, 1026

Lacoste, Catherine. *See* Labruère

Lacoste, Charlotte Magenty. *See* Mount

Lacoste, Élisabeth (Peltier), VIII, 693

Lacoste, Joséphine. *See* Dubois

Lacoste, Louis, X, 417

Lacoste, Louis, VIII, 471, 479, 914, 915; IX, 650; X, **417–19**; XI, 698, 822; XII, 369

Lacoste, Louis-René, VIII, **479–80**; X, 418; XII, 363

Lacoste, Marie-Antoinette-Thaïs. *See* Proulx

La Côte. *See* Courreaud

La Coudrelle, Marquis de. *See* Puisaye

La Coudrelle, Marquise de. *See* Bibron de Corméry

La Couèche. *See* Le Blanc, Madeleine

La Cour. *See* Bégon; DesBrisay

La Court de Pré-Ravillon et de Granpré, I, 306, **408–9**, 450, 671

Lacouture. *See* Cochy

La Cressonière. *See* Couture

Lacroix. *See also* Hubert

La Croix. *See also* Milly; Prevost; Réaume

La Croix, Monsieur (drowning victim), III, 493

Lacroix, Anne-Madeleine. *See* Dontaille

315

La Croix, Catherine de. *See* Clément
La Croix, Charles-Eugène-Gabriel de, Marquis de Castries, IV, 471, 646
La Croix, Dominique de, III, 334
Lacroix, Françoise-Pélagie. *See* Poncy
Lacroix, Hubert, V, 233; VI, 382
Lacroix, Hubert-Joseph, III, 334; VI, **382–84**, 385; VIII, 480
Lacroix, Hubert-Joseph de, III, 315, **334**, 675; VI, 382; VIII, 480
Lacroix, Jacques-Hubert, V, 827
Lacroix, Janvier-Domptail, VI, 383; VIII, 242, **480–81**
La Croix, Jean, II, 507
La Croix, Jean de, II, 328; III, 113
Lacroix, Louise. *See* Launière
Lacroix, Marie-Anne. *See* Bouate
Lacroix, Marie-Henriette (Pangman), VIII, 481
Lacroix, Marie-Louise (Rodier), X, 625
Lacroix, Michel, VI, 665, 666
Lacroix, Paul (brother of HUBERT-JOSEPH), VI, 382, 383
Lacroix, Paul (father-in-law of Charles-Séraphin RODIER, 1797–1876), X, 625
Lacroix, Paul-Joseph, VI, 665, 666
Lacroix, Peter Paul, VIII, 130
Lacroix, Pierre-Paul, VIII, 482
La Croix de Chevrières de Saint-Vallier, Jean-Baptiste de, I, 56, 76, 77, 80, 92, 117, 141, 175, 286, 291, 338, 361, 439, 506, 507, 536, 540, 635, 649; II, 14, 19, 40, 44, 55, 58, 60, 76, 90, 92, 93, 95, 99, 109, 110, 117, 124, 128, 132, 133, 134, 135, 137, 140, 151, 160, 171, 174, 175, 176, 186, 189, 194, 199, 200, 207, 210, 222, 227, 235, 240, 244, 245, 247, 248, 258, 259, 272, 304, 326, **328–34**, 336, 337, 341, 346, 350, 357, 366, 371, 372, 377, 379, 381, 429, 431, 449, 456, 462, 466, 478, 491, 492, 506, 522, 528, 533, 545, 571, 586, 594, 597, 608, 613, 628, 629, 638, 640, 641; III, 5, 23, 40, 44, 51, 62, 63, 78, 113, 114, 168, 180, 193, 194, 195, 199, 201, 202, 204, 222, 223, 227, 233, 240, 259, 284, 306, 318, 319, 330, 333, 348, 349, 352, 369, 386, 390, 413, 419, 443, 469, 487, 512, 522, 523, 564, 574, 575, 616, 629, 632, 633, 640, 681, 683, 684; IV, 180, 220, 222, 338, 387, 509, 535, 649, 708, 765; V, 245; VII, 165; VIII, 481; IX, 217; XI, 87, 103
La Croix de Chevrières de Saint-Vallier, Jean de, II, 328
La Croix de Chevrières de Saint-Vallier, Marie de. *See* Sayve
Lacroix-Mézière, Suzanne (De Lisle), V, 241, 591; IX, 200
La Croix-Nord. *See* Trunel
Ladan, Adrien, II, **334–35**, 370, 419, 421
La Dauversière. *See* Le Royer
Ladde, Harriot Conway (Willson), X, 709
La Découverte. *See* You
La Demoiselle. *See* Memeskia
La Doussinière. *See* Duchesneau
La Durantaye. *See* Morel
La Duye. *See* Lafon
La Fare, Marquis de, III, 458
La Fargue, Jacques. *See* Brandeau, Esther
Lafatigue. *See* Billeron
La Faye, Louis-François de, II, **335–36**
La Fayette, Marquis de. *See* Motier
Lafayette, John, XII, 330
Lafayette, Mary Ann (Fraser), XII, 329

La Ferre, Marie de, I, 478, 512
La Ferrière. *See* Erouachy
La Ferrière, Comte de. *See* Berryer
La Ferté. *See* Juchereau
Laferté. *See also* Lepallieur
Laferté, Antoine, XI, 812
La Ferté de La Madeleine, Abbé de, I, 494
La Feuille. *See* Wahpasha
La Feuillée, Alixe de (Des Granges de Mauprée; La Motte de Lucière), I, 415
Lafever, Minard, XI, 92
Lafferty. *See also* Lefferty
Lafferty, Sarah (Spencer), IX, 736
Laffont, Jean-Baptiste, V, 342
Laffriquain. *See* Tribaut
Lafitau, Catherine. *See* Berchenbos
Lafitau, Jean, III, 334
Lafitau, Joseph-François, II, 237, 596; III, 106, 184, 315, **334–38**
Lafitau, Pierre-François, III, 334, 336
Lafite, Marguerite (Denys), I, 258, 259
Laflamme. *See also* Lebœuf
Laflamme, Caroline (Labrèche-Viger), X, 417
Laflamme, Godefroy, XII, 505
Laflamme*, Joseph-Clovis-Kemner (1849–1910), X, 106; XII, 46
Laflamme, Toussaint-Antoine-Rodolphe, VIII, 420; IX, 614; X, 252, 415, 417; XI, 273, 276, 277, 480, 737, 755; 5, 247, 260, 362, 363, **505–6**, 651, 695, 721
Laflèche. *See also* Richer-Laflèche
Laflèche, Monsieur (coureur de bois), I, 225
Laflèche, Louise (Suzor), V, 788
Laflèche, Louis-François, VII, 502; VIII, 562, 722, 723; IX, 20, 66, 95, 153, 154, 215, 466; X, 137, 161, 192, 193, 304; XI, 13, 34, 87, 88, 104, 109, 110, 171, 185, 250, 251, 252, 253, 310, 338, 339, 496, 726, 876, 892, 893, 894; XII, 177, 304, 464, **506–12**, 520, 731, 820, 821, 875, 1003, 1004, 1009, 1010, 1011, 1021, 1022, 1023
Lafleur. *See also* Bailly; Couc; Petitpas; Pinsonneau; Richard
Lafleur, Eugène, XII, 5
Lafleur, Louis-Hercule, XI, 811
Lafleur, Théodore, IX, 610; X, 675
Lafleur, *dit* Plamondon, Ignace, IV, 141
Lafleur de Verchères. *See* Brousseau
Lafond. *See also* Richard
Lafond, Antoine, IX, 66
Lafond, Éliza (Boucher de Niverville), IX, 66
La Fond, Étienne de, II, 83; III, 629
La Fond, Geneviève de (Trottier), III, 629
La Fond, Marie de. *See* Boucher
Lafon de La Duye, Catherine de. *See* Bégon
Lafont, Jeanne (Pécholier; Bedout), V, 62
Lafontaine. *See also* Bellot
La Fontaine. *See also* Gamelain; Marion; Ménard; Poulin
La Fontaine, Adèle, Lady La Fontaine. *See* Berthelot
Lafontaine, Aimé, XII, 197
Lafontaine, Bernardine de. *See* Jouin
Lafontaine, Catherine (Mercier), III, 442
Lafontaine, François, VIII, 655
Lafontaine, Jean-Baptiste de, III, 339
La Fontaine, Julie-Élisabeth-Geneviève, Lady La Fontaine. *See* Morrison

Lafontaine, Laurent-David, XI, 425

La Fontaine, Louis-Hippolyte, IX, 450

La Fontaine, Sir Louis-Hippolyte, VI, 783; VII, 26, 32, 62, 73, 148, 158, 208, 227, 354, 478, 604, 605, 606, 607, 643, 757, 858, 880; VIII, 17, 22, 34, 49, 50, 51, 52, 53, 54, 55, 56, 57, 58, 136, 138, 146, 148, 164, 219, 230, 256, 261, 262, 285, 332, 333, 368, 392, 424, 434, 479, 553, 629, 668, 679, 698, 786, 792, 799, 822, 848, 849, 850, 865, 912, 913, 915, 916, 919, 932; IX, 55, 56, 57, 71, 73, 74, 83, 90, 91, 92, 109, 190, 191, 211, 212, 238, 244, 250, 257, 259, 287, 323, 344, 371, 372, 373, 396, 397, 437, **440–51**, 458, 463, 469, 485, 486, 490, 505, 524, 525, 547, 560, 569, 570, 571, 575, 595, 596, 611, 614, 635, 644, 645, 650, 687, 690, 702, 725, 728, 762, 775, 776, 777, 779, 795, 796, 804, 811, 815, 816, 818, 819; X, 24, 37, 92, 93, 94, 95, 119, 125, 126, 127, 132, 133, 134, 135, 143, 151, 219, 255, 256, 257, 261, 311, 312, 321, 359, 431, 440, 462, 463, 466, 487, 512, 515, 526, 527, 564, 567, 568, 570, 576, 577, 579, 583, 584, 622, 642, 714, 715, 722, 724; XI, 35, 41, 58, 60, 98, 127, 150, 160, 169, 170, 178, 179, 180, 188, 206, 238, 249, 273, 281, 282, 286, 341, 405, 408, 409, 410, 411, 415, 498, 518, 519, 618, 640, 657, 680, 698, 713, 821, 822, 850, 890, 914, 927; XII, 66, 67, 181, 249, 253, 260, 308, 349, 369, 473, 593, 1013, 1014, 1025, 1130

Lafontaine, Marianne (Martin; Giard; Dornon), III, 258, 443

Lafontaine de Belcour, Antoine de, IV, 315

Lafontaine de Belcour, Charlotte de. *See* Bissot

Lafontaine de Belcour, Geneviève de. *See* Lambert

Lafontaine de Belcour, Gilles de, III, 602

Lafontaine de Belcour, Jacques de, II, 66; III, 47, 48, 75, 154, 217, 270, **338–41**, 422, 509, 602, 608, 647; IV, 183, 381, 571, 602; V, 426

Lafontaine de Belcour, Marie-Josephte de (Cugnet), IV, 182, 315

Lafontaine de Belcour, Nicolas-Joseph de, V, 43, 794

La Fontanelle. *See* Eder

Laforce. *See also* Pepin; Pépin

Laforce, Madeleine. *See* Corbin

Laforce, Madeleine (Lusignan), VIII, 781

Laforce (Pépin, *dit* Laforce), Marie-Josephte (Langlois, *dit* Germain), VIII, 488

Laforce, René-Hippolyte, IV, 613; V, 462, **470–71**

Laforce, Sophie (Langevin), XI, 487; XII, 519

La Forest. *See also* Dauphin; Guillot; Tavernier; Testard

La Forest, Gabriel de, II, 169

La Forest, Jeanne de. *See* Noreau

La Forest, Marc-Antoine de, II, **336**; III, 98

La Forest, Marie-Anne de. *See* Courthiau

La Forest, Pierre de, III, 158

La Forest de La Gemerais, Marguerite de (Dufrost de Boissemances), II, 202

Laforey, John, III, 71

Laforge. *See also* Sageot

Laforge, Monsieur (manufacturer), V, 259

Laforme, Monsieur (innkeeper), III, 139

Lafosse. *See* Hodiau

La Fosse. *See also* Puyperoux

La Fosse, Antoine de, II, 156

La Fosse, Jean-Charles de, VI, 27

La Fosse, Louise de (Coulon de Villiers), II, 156

La Fourche. *See* Nissowaquet

La Fourière (La Foyrière). *See* Erouachy

Laframboise. *See also* Fafard; Guillebert

La Framboise. *See also* Fafard

Laframboise, Alexis, XI, 479

Laframboise, Claude, V, 377

La Framboise, Joseph (father), VII, 582

La Framboise, Joseph, VII, 582

Laframboise, Josette (Lamothe), VI, 388

La Framboise, Josette (Pierce), VII, 582

Laframboise, Jules, XI, 480

Laframboise, Lucie-Angélique. *See* Cotté

La Framboise, Marguerite-Magdelaine. *See* Marcot

Laframboise, Maurice, IV, 172; VI, 208; XI, 338, **479–81**; XII, 253, 254, 324, 693, 719, 720, 721

Laframboise, Michel, IX, 851

Laframboise, Rosalie. *See* Dessaulles

Lafrance. *See also* Hianveu; Lévesque

Lafrance*, Ambroise (1847–1905), IX, 702; XI, 515, 516

Lafrance, Charles-Édouard-François, XII, 397

Lafrance, François-Xavier-Stanislas, VIII, 591; IX, 438, 439, **451–52**; XII, 397, 547, 549

Lafrance, Jean-Baptiste, V, 418; IX, 455

La France, Joseph, III, **341–42**

Lafrance, Louis, X, 614, 615

Lafrance, Pierre, VII, 643

Lafrance, Placide (Villebrun, *dit* Provencher), XI, 716

Lafranchise. *See* Contant

Lafrenaye. *See also* Leclère

La Frenaye, François de (Pierre-Antoine), II, 125, **336–37**

La Frenaye, Geneviève de. *See* Lepage

La Frenaye, Martin de, I, 409

Lafrenaye, Pierre-Richard, X, 219, 249; XI, 529

La Frenaye de Brucy, Antoine de, I, **409–10**, 547, 600; II, 336

La Frenaye de Brucy, Hélène de. *See* Picoté de Belestre

Lafrenière, Sophie (Olivier; Marion; Reeves), VI, 487, 488

La Frésillière. *See* Loppinot

La Fresnière. *See* Hertel

Lagacé, Monsieur (fur trader), VIII, 421

Lagacé, Pierre-Minier, X, 228

La Galissonière. *See* Barrin

La Galissonière, Marquis de. *See* Barrin

La Galissonière, Marquise de. *See* Lauson

La Garaye. *See also* Marot

La Garaye, Comte de, III, 192

Lagarde, André-Toussaint, VIII, 79

La Garde, Pierre de, II, 637

Lagarde, Pierre-Paul-François de, IV, 318, **431–32**, 521, 636

La Garenne. *See also* Durand

La Garenne, Marie (Peuvret), I, 542

La Gauchetière. *See* Migeon

La Gemerais. *See* Dufrost; La Forest

Lagemodière. *See* Lagimonière

La Gesse. *See* Ramezay

Lagier, André, X, 419

Lagier, Jean-Marie, X, 419

Lagier, Lucien-Antoine, VIII, 66; IX, 96, 397; X, **419**

Lagier, Marie-Madeleine. *See* David

Lagimodière. *See also* Lagimonière

Lagimodière, Elzéar, IX, 330; XII, 175, 1008

Lagimonière, Jean-Baptiste, VIII, 481

Lagimonière, Jean-Baptiste, V, 267; VI, 398; VIII, **481–82**; IX, 663; X, 296, 297; XI, 736

Lagimonière, Julie (Riel), VIII, 482; IX, 663; X, 297; XI, 736

Lagimonière, Marie-Anne. *See* Gaboury

Lagimonière, Marie-Joseph. *See* Jarret, *dit* Beauregard

Lagimonière, Reine (Lamère), VIII, 481; X, 297

La Giraudais. *See* Chenard

La Giraudière (La Girodière). *See* Baye

Laglanderie. *See* Rivard-Laglanderie

Lagny, Jean-Baptiste de, II, 74, 76, 182

Lagoanere, Blaise, IV, 245

Lagoanere, Catherine. *See* Daccarrette

La Gondalie. *See* La Goudalie

Lagorce, Charles, IX, 452

Lagorce, Charles-Irénée, IX, **452–53**; X, 297, 298; XI, 99; XII, 1133

Lagorce, Marie-Angèle. *See* Morin

La Gorgendière. *See* Fleury

La Goudalie, Charles de, III, 120, **342–43**, 438

La Grande Armée, II, 469

La Grande Gueule. *See* Otreouti

La Grande Terre. *See* Ohonsiowanne

Lagrandeur. *See* Dumontet

La Grandrive. *See* Dupuy

La Grange. *See also* Léger

La Grange, Sieur de. *See* Varlet

La Grange, Anne de (Buade, Comtesse de Frontenac et de Palluau), I, 134, 135, 142; II, 483

Lagrange, Anne-Louise (Imbert), IV, 378

Lagrange, Gabrielle. *See* Anneville

Lagrange, Jean-Baptiste, III, 222; IV, 390

Lagrange, Jean-Baptiste-Martin, IV, 378

Lagrange, Mathieu, II, 59

Lagrave, Augustin, V, 436

Lagrave, Eulalie, IX, 802

La Grave, Louis de, V, 752

Lagrené, Pierre de, II, **337**

La Grenouille. *See* Oumasasikweie

La Grive Des Assises, Monsieur (quartermaster), IV, 645

Lagroix (Lagrouais, La Groy, Lagroye). *See* Huppé

La Grossardière. *See* Gourdeau

La Groye, Marquis de. *See* Aloigny

La Groye, Marquise de. *See* Chasteigner; Macard

Laguer de Morville, Claude-Dorothée, II, 337; III, 191

Laguer de Morville, Marie-Thérèse. *See* Lajoüe

Lagueux, Cécile-Adélaïde (Brunet), X, 105; XII, 133

Lagueux, Étienne-Claude, VI, 532, 546, 681; XI, 353

Lagueux, Joseph, XI, 698

Lagueux, Josephte-Aurélie. *See* Mignault

Lagueux, Louis, VI, 384, 585; VIII, 141

Lagueux, Louis, VI, **384–85**, 750, 763; VII, 373, 430, 877, 879; VIII, 141, 206

Lagueux, Louise. *See* Bégin

Lagueux, Marie-Henriette (Glackmeyer), XI, 353

Lagueux, Rose-Louise. *See* Bergevin, *dit* Langevin

Laguide Meynier, Madeleine (Perrot), I, 117, 540

La Hailandière, Célestin de, VIII, 145

Lahaille, Barthelemie. *See* Grabot

Lahaille, Jean-Baptiste, IV, 234; V, 146, **471–72**; VI, 24, 526, 549

Lahaille, Joseph, V, 471

La Halle. *See* Delhalle

Lahaye. *See also* Le Pellé

La Haye. *See also* Marguerie

La Haye, Monsieur de (clergyman), I, 356

La Haye, Clare Elizabeth de (Berthon), XII, 100

Lahaye, Thérèse, XI, 173

La Héronnière, Sieur de (intendant), I, 582

Lahontan, Baron de. *See* Lom

La Houlière. *See* Marchant

Laidlaw, Ann. *See* Middleton

Laidlaw, George, XI, 453

Laidlaw, George, X, 651; XI, 227, 359, 362, **481–83**, 616, 617

Laidlaw, James, VI, 453

Laidlaw, John, VI, 294

Laidlaw, Robert, IX, 124

Laidlaw, William, VI, 438

Laigne, Julien, II, 58

Laigu, *dit* Lanoue, René-Charles, III, 278, 279

Lain, Elizabeth (Bell), VIII, 73

Laîné. *See* Lebon

Laing. *See also* Lang

Laing, Mrs (wife of William), IV, 432

Laing, James, VII, 65

Laing, Murdoch, XII, 670

Laing, Robert, VIII, 110

Laing, William, IV, 105, 432

Lair, Mr (chaplain), II, 8, 9

Laird, Alexander, X, 419

Laird, Alexander, X, **419–20**; XII, 512

Laird, Alexander, XI, 417, **512–13**

Laird, Ann. *See* Carruthers

Laird*, David (1833–1914), IX, 831; X, 211, 308, 419, 595, 597, 612; XI, 371, 443, 458, 548, 549, 595, 598, 613, 668, 701, 702; XII, 23, 48, 419, 512, 513, 639, 651, 729

Laird (Lord), Huldah (Ryan), VI, 670

Laird, Janet. *See* Orr

Laird, Rebecca P. *See* Read

Laisné, Élisabeth (Dasilva, *dit* Portugais), III, 165

Laisné, *dit* Laliberté, Marie-Élisabeth (Deguise, *dit* Flamand), IV, 203

La Janière. *See* Fleury

La Jannaye. *See* Chaton

La Jemerais; Lajemmerais. *See* Dufrost

Lajeunesse. *See* Dandonneau

Lajimonière. *See* Lagimonière

Lajoie. *See also* Gérin; Gerin-Lajoie

Lajoie, Étienne, IX, 701

Lajoie, Pascal, XI, 173

Lajoie, Thècle (Mailloux), 488

La Jonquière. *See* Taffanel

La Jonquière, Marquis de. *See* Taffanel

La Jonquière, Marquise de. *See* La Valette

La Joubardière. *See* Berthé

Lajoüe, François de, II, 58, **337–39**, 451, 467; III, 398

La Joue, Jacques de, II, 337

La Joue, Madeleine de. *See* Guérin

Lajoüe, Marie-Agnès de (Levasseur), II, 337; III, 398

Lajoüe, Marie-Anne de. *See* Ménage

Lajoüe, Marie-Madeleine de (Frontigny; Boucault de Godefus), III, 77, 78

Lajoüe, Marie-Thérèse de (Laguer de Morville), II, 337

Lajus, Angélique-Jeanne. *See* Hubert

Lajus, Anne. *See* Vigneau

Lajus, Élisabeth-Simone (Almain; Couillard), III, 345

Lajus, François, III, 345; IV, **432**; VI, 41; VII, 61

Lajus, François-Marie-Olivier-Hubert, IV, 432

Lajus, François-Michel, III, 345

Lajus, Jean, III, 344

Lajus, Jean-Baptiste (Jean-François), III, 345

Lajus, Jean-Baptiste-Isidore-Hospice, IV, 432

Lajus, Jordain, III, **344–45**, 519; IV, 432

Lajus, Louise-Élisabeth. *See* Moreau, *dit* Lataupine

Lajus, Luce (Bédard), IV, 432; VI, 40, 41; VII, 61

Lajus, Marguerite. *See* Audet de Piercotte de Bailleul

Lajus, Marguerite-Ursule (Vaillant; Noël), III, 345

Lajus, Marie-Louise. *See* Roger

Lajus, René-Flavien, IV, 432

Lake, Sir Bibye, III, 302, 447

Lake, Lady Elizabeth (Harvey, Lady Harvey), VIII, 373; X, 278

Lake, Gerard, 1st Viscount Lake, VII, 603; VIII, 374

Lalancette. *See* Landriaux; Lebreton

Lalande. *See also* Lefrançois

La Lande, Anne-Catherine de (Hocquart), IV, 354

Lalande, Anne de (Chesneau), I, 287

Lalande, Élisabeth. *See* Garreau

Lalande, Étienne, III, 258

Lalande, Jean, III, 271

La Lande, Jean de, I, 390, **410–11**, 414; II, 158

Lalande, Louis, X, 418

La Lande, Robert de, I, 288

Lalande de Gayon, Jacques de, I, 104, 105, 146, 289, 395, 396, 397; III, 339

Lalande de Gayon, Marie de. *See* Couillard

La Lande Gayon, Marie-Thérèse de (Aubert de La Chesnaye), II, 34

Lalane, Christophe de, III, 194; IV, 387, 642, 719

Lalanne. *See also* Laporte

Lalanne, Pierre, IV, 270

Lalawethika. *See* Tenskwatawa

Lalemand. *See* Allemand

Lalemant, Charles, I, 43, 111, 121, 125, 160, 197, 213, 214, 217, 246, 329, **411–12**, 413, 428, 447, 453, 456, 484, 493, 494, 498, 521, 561

Lalemant, Gabriel, I, 9, 31, 64, 124, 126, 219, **412–13**, 414, 459, 483, 561, 562

Lalemant, Jérôme, I, 91, 123, 246, 268, 284, 354, 355, 357, 374, 388, 389, 404, 410, 411, 412, **413–15**, 428, 430, 431, 456, 459, 461, 473, 477, 498, 561, 562, 640, 662, 665; II, xvi, 84, 158, 237, 460

Laliberté. *See also* Laisné; Senet

Laliberté*, Alfred (1878–1953), III, 143; IV, 424; XII, 889

Laliberté, Rose (Rochette), XII, 920

Lalime. *See also* Lépine

Lalime, Alfred-G., XI, 330

Lalime, Malvina (Gagnon), XI, 330

Lalime, Marie-Josephte (Clouet), VII, 188

Lallemant, Louis, I, 126, 387, 563

Lally, Agnes Elizabeth (Bernard; McCarthy), XII, 578

Lally, Emma Catherine (McCarthy), XII, 578

Lally, Thomas-Arthur, Baron de Tollendal, Comte de Lally, IV, 126

La Lochetière. *See* Tavernier

Lalonde, Agathe (Valois), X, 690

Lalonde, Louis, named Father Louis-Marie, XII, 869

La Londe, Marc, II, 524

Lalonde, *dit* L'Espérance, Jean, II, 350

La Londette (Lalonde), Louis, III, 242

La Madeleine. *See* Ailleboust; La Ferté

La Maisonfort Du Boisdecourt, Alexandre de, Marquis de La Maisonfort, III, 209, **345–46**, 636

La Maisonfort Du Boisdecourt, Catherine de, Marquise de La Maisonfort. *See* Chicoyneau

La Majour, Sieur de. *See* Arrigrand

Lamaletie, Jean-André, III, 226; IV, 67, 126, **433–34**, 615, 750

Lamaletie, Louis, IV, 433

Lamaletie, Marie-Anne. *See* Benet

Lamaletie, Marie-Thérèse. *See* Foucault

La Malgue. *See* Marin

La Malotière. *See* Ruette

La Marche; Lamarche. *See also* Baudry; Danguel; Marin; Périnneau

La Marche, Dominique de (François), II, **339**; IV, xxi

Lamarche, Godefroy, XI, 103

La Marche, Jacques de, I, 477

La Marche, Jean-François de, IV, 136, 374; V, 180, 671; VI, 201, 391; VII, 720

Lamarck, Chevalier de. *See* Monet

La Marck, Marie de (Godet Des Maretz), I, 342

La Marck, Robert IV de, Duc de Bouillon, I, 424

La Margue; La Marque. *See also* Marin

Lamarque. *See also* Nolan

La Marque, Monsieur (student), I, 246

La Marque, Jacques de, II, 421, 626

La Marque, Marie de. *See* Pournin

La Marque, Marie-Anne de (Nolan; Frenel; Tonty), II, 632; III, 485

Lamarque, Marie-Marguerite (Bolvin), III, 68

La Marre. *See also* Varin

La Marre, Sieur de (locksmith), I, 473

Lamarre, Anne (Duquet de La Chesnaye), I, 298

Lamarre, Antoine, II, 339

Lamarre, Françoise (Hurteau), X, 374

Lamarre, Marguerite. *See* Levasseur

Lamarre, *dit* Bélisle, Catherine. *See* Demosny

Lamarre, *dit* Bélisle, Henri, II, **339–40**

Lamarre, *dit* Bélisle, Jeanne. *See* Archambault

Lamarre, *dit* Bélisle, Marie-Catherine (Sicard), II, 340

Lamarre, *dit* Bélisle, Périnne. *See* Dandonneau

Lamartine. *See* Hindenlang, Charles

Lamartine, Alphonse de, VIII, 330, 503; IX, 193, 465

La Martinière. *See* Bermen; Lomeron

Lamb, Mr (of Upper Canada), VI, 91

Lamb, Freelove (Collver), V, 196

Lamb, Henry, VI, 91; VII, **475–76**

Lamb, Reuben W., VII, 923

Lamb, William, III, 654; IV, 381

Lamb, William, 2nd Viscount Melbourne, VII, 118, 478, 479, 480, 894; VIII, xxxiv, 464, 745; IX, 89, 235, 237, 676; X, 345

Lambert, Catharine (Kennedy), XI, 471

Lambert, David Rogers, VIII, 192

Lambert, Eustache, I, 146, 396, **415**

Lambert, Gabriel, II, 274

Lambert, Geneviève (Hamare de La Borde), II, 273

Lambert, Geneviève (Lafontaine de Belcour), III, 339

Lambert, Jane (Kerby), VIII, 465

Lambert, John, IV, 753; V, 138, **472–73**, 792; VI, 223, 591, 593; VII, 349, 358, 387
Lambert, Joseph-Honoré-Octavien, XI, 306
Lambert, Julia Maria, VIII, 192
Lambert, Louis, II, 273
Lambert, Marguerite (Montminy), XII, 758
Lambert, Marie. *See* Laurence
Lambert, Marie-Madeleine (Chartier de Lotbinière), II, 138, 457; III, 112
Lambert, Marie-Renée. *See* Roussel
Lambert, Patrick, V, **473–74**, 633; VI, 372, 613, 614, 690, 691, 711; VII, 293, 403, 404; VIII, 107; XII, 860
Lambert, Paul, III, 346
Lambert, Pierre, VII, 134
Lambert, Radegonde (Blanchard), II, 71
Lambert, Richard Stanton, XII, 751
Lambert, Samuel F., VIII, 192
Lambert, Sarah Susanna (Crookshank), VIII, 191
Lambert, Thérèse. *See* Huard
Lambert, Thérèse, named Sainte-Marie-Médiatrice, III, 719
Lambert, Ursule (Pâquet), XII, 818
Lambert, *dit* Saint-Paul, Marguerite. *See* Maillou, *dit* Desmoulins
Lambert, *dit* Saint-Paul, Marie-Françoise. *See* Laberge
Lambert, *dit* Saint-Paul, Paul, III, **346–47**; IV, 535; V, 709
Lambert de Baussy, Marie-Catherine (Philippe de Haut-mesnil de Marigny), II, 525
Lambert Dumont, Charles-Louis, VIII, 492
Lambert Dumont, Charlotte-Louise (Poulin de Courval Cressé), III, 540; V, 216; VI, 385
Lambert Dumont, Eustache (father), II, 82
Lambert Dumont, Eustache, III, 374, 540
Lambert Dumont, Eustache-Louis, V, 481; VI, 385; VII, 495
Lambert Dumont, Louise-Angélique (Lefebvre de Bellefeuille), VI, 385; VII, 495
Lambert Dumont, Madeleine (Bouat), II, 82
Lambert Dumont, Marguerite-Angélique. *See* Boisseau
Lambert Dumont, Marie (Bissot), II, 66
Lambert Dumont, Marie-Narcisse. *See* Lemaire Saint-Germain
Lambert Dumont, Nicolas-Eustache, VI, 381, **385–87**, 478; VII, 172; VIII, 492, 791; XII, 535
Lambert Dumont, Sophie. *See* Ménéclier de Montrochon
Lambert Dumont, Sophie. *See* Vanneck
Lamberville, Jacques de, I, 635; II, xx, xxxiv, xxxvi, **340–42**, 343, 473, 643; III, 428
Lamberville, Jean de, I, 322, 323, 443, 445, 465, 525, 526, 633; II, xx, xxxvi, 62, 101, 340, 341, **342–44**, 474, 585; III, 335
Lambly, Ann. *See* Mackie
Lambly, Elizabeth Pierce. *See* Bailey
Lambly, Frances. *See* Richardson
Lambly, James Bankier, IX, 454
Lambly, John, V, 96; VIII, 101; IX, 453
Lambly, John Robert, IX, **453–54**
Lambly, Osborn Richardson, IX, 454
Lambly, William Harvard, IX, 454
Lambourg, Mary. *See* Quessy
Lambton, Anne Barbara Frances. *See* Villiers
Lambton, Charles William, VII, 478
Lambton, Harriet. *See* Cholmondeley
Lambton, John George, 1st Earl of Durham, IV, 655, 656;

V, 759; VI, 646, 791; VII, 9, 31, 43, 56, 117, 118, 143, 144, 149, 158, 180, 204, 227, 231, 248, 264, 282, 354, 371, 398, 444, 472, **476–81**, 490, 504, 550, 579, 580, 604, 638, 648, 703, 710, 758, 771, 789, 799, 815, 816, 856, 857, 859, 861, 862, 880, 925; VIII, xxv, xxxvi, 27, 29, 48, 54, 116, 163, 164, 188, 198, 210, 288, 296, 321, 332, 379, 383, 416, 471, 539, 617, 668, 678, 691, 700, 730, 745, 747, 769, 778, 786, 839, 845, 847, 853, 855, 860, 910; IX, 89, 93, 100, 142, 190, 192, 201, 237, 238, 239, 273, 275, 349, 351, 352, 374, 383, 415, 441, 442, 524, 554, 579, 595, 664, 675, 676, 683, 744, 760, 798, 814, 818; X, 78, 142, 254, 257, 260, 345, 364, 384, 491, 500, 505, 506, 527, 582, 623, 655; XI, 35, 60, 178, 365, 366, 407, 408, 480, 517, 585, 609, 657, 787, 825, 874, 875, 905, 925, 945; XII, 89, 346, 495, 503, 582, 856, 1079
Lambton, Louisa Elizabeth, Countess of Durham. *See* Grey
Lambton, Lady Mary Louisa (Bruce, Countess of Elgin and of Kincardine), IX, 89
Lambton, Robert de, VII, 476
Lambton, William Henry (father), VII, 476
Lambton, William Henry, VII, 477
La Meilleraye, Sieur de (merchant), I, 434
La Mennais, Félicité-Robert de, VI, 106; VII, 487, 655, 656, 678, 700, 886; VIII, 212, 259, 291, 490, 503, 711; IX, 465, 466; X, 569, 580, 585; XI, 94, 95, 493, 725, 726, 891; XII, 252, 253
Lamer, Marie de (Nicollet), I, 516
Lamère, Louise. *See* Panet
Lamère, Reine. *See* Lagimonière
La Mer Monte. *See* Chomina
La Meslée. *See* Crevier
La Milletière. *See* Dubois
Laminière. *See* Lamy
La Minotière. *See* Niort
Lamirande. *See also* Guyot
Lamirande, Monsieur (bank cashier), XI, 276
Lamoignon, Guillaume de, I, 220; II, 656, 657
La Mollerie. *See* Maleray
La Monnerie, Monsieur de (commander), III, 310
Lamont, Mr (businessman), XI, 898
Lamontagne. *See also* Baquette; Jérémie
Lamontagne, Gabriel, VI, 554
Lamontagne, Marie-Anne (Fabre), VIII, 282
Lamontagne, Marie-Euphradine (Perrault), IX, 633
La Morandière. *See* Rocbert
Lamoreaux, Hester (Burr), IX, 109
Lamorel Le Pippre de Nœufville, Simon, II, 566
La Morénerie. *See* Lamorinie
Lamoricière. *See* Juchault
Lamorille. *See* Lemaître; Lemaître-Lamorille
Lamorinie, Jean-Baptiste de, III, **347**; IV, 241
La Mothe. *See also* Ango
Lamothe. *See also* Aigron; Bigot; Dagneau
Lamothe, Catherine. *See* Blondeau
La Mothe, Charlemagne, VI, 231
Lamothe, Guillaume (Jean-Baptiste-Guillaume-Alexis), IX, 438
Lamothe, Gustave, XI, 891
Lamothe, Joseph, VI, 387, 664
Lamothe, Joseph-Maurice, VI, **387–88**, 666; VII, 716, 735
Lamothe, Josette. *See* Laframboise

La Mothe, Marie-Aurélie (Versailles; Girard), XII, 369, 371

La Mothe, Nicolas de, I, 441

Lamothe Cadillac. *See* Laumet

La Mothe-Fénelon. *See* Salignac

La Mothe-Tilly. *See* Legardeur

La Motte. *See also* Aigron; Cahideuc; Langan; La Rue

La Motte (La Motte-Picquet). *See* Picquet

LaMotte, Charlotte (Huguet), V, 435

La Motte, Clémence. *See* Badon

La Motte, Jean de, I, 415

Lamotte, Marie de (Lepallieur), II, 413

La Motte de Lucière, Alixe de. *See* La Feuillée

La Motte de Lucière, Dominique, I, 175, **415–16**; II, 278

Lamotte de Saint-Paul, Pierre, I, 415, **416**

La Motte-le-Vilin, Monsieur (prisoner), I, 68

Lamouline. *See* Landrière

Lamouraux-Rochefort, Madeleine (Morin), IV, 558

Lamoureux, Françoise (Duprac), II, 206

Lamoureux, Pierre, XII, 571

Lamoureux, *dit* Saint-Germain, Joseph, IV, 585

La Moye. *See* Pipon

Lampen, William, V, 52, 53

Lamphier, Betsy (Clark), XII, 198

Lamphier, Thomas, XII, 198

Lampman, Agnes Ann. *See* McNeal

Lampman, Archibald, XII, 513, 514

Lampman, Archibald, XI, 142; XII, 204, 205, 460, **513–18**, 947, 1076

Lampman, Archibald Otto, XII, 515

Lampman, Arnold Gesner, XII, 515

Lampman, Catherine (Keefer), VIII, 450; X, 394; XI, 463

Lampman, Maud Emma. *See* Playter

Lampman, Natalie Charlotte (MacInnes), XII, 515

Lampman, Peter, XII, 513

Lampman, Susannah Charlotte. *See* Gesner

Lampson, William, VIII, 570, 844

Lamy (Laminière), Adélaïde-Marie-Joséphine (Routh), VIII, 778

Lamy, Joseph, II, 458

Lamy, Louise (Marin de La Malgue; Legardeur de Beauvais), II, 458; III, 374, 432

Lamy, Marie. *See* Decheuraineville

Lamy, Marie (Dagneau Douville), III, 158; IV, 191

Lamyma, II, 562

La Nanette (wife of Billy CALDWELL), VII, 132

La Nasse. *See* Manitougatche

Lanaudière; La Naudière. *See also* Tarieu

Lanaudière (Tarieu Taillant de Lanaudière), Charlotte (Joliette), VII, 446, 447

La Nauraye. *See* Niort

Lancaster, Elizabeth. *See* Bonner

Lancaster, Hannah Maria (Daniel), XII, 226

Lancaster, Sir James, I, 499

Lancaster, Joseph, VI, 106, 206; VII, 322, **481–83**, 689; VIII, 665, 936; IX, 298, 770; XI, 533

Lancaster, Mary (Robinson; wife of JOSEPH), VII, 481

Lancaster, Richard, VII, 481

Lancaster, Sarah. *See* Foulkes

L'Ancien (violinist), XI, 671

Lancto, Marianne (Bauvais), VII, 60

Lanctôt, Agnès. *See* Boire

Lanctot, Agnès. *See* Doutre

Lanctôt, Alexis, X, 420

Lanctôt, Angélique. *See* Raymond

Lanctot, Edmond, X, 420

Lanctot*, Gustave (1883–1975), IV, 232; V, 359; IX, 306; XI, 709

Lanctot, Hippolyte, X, 420

Lanctôt, Magloire, VII, 740; X, 25, **420**; XI, 273, 821

Lanctot, Mary. *See* Miller

Lanctot, Médéric, IX, 194, 344, 437, 438, 564, 615; X, 148, 249, 304, **420–26**; XI, 275, 329, 330, 480, 709; XII, 173, 262

Lanctot, Philéas, X, 425

Lanctôt, Pierre, VIII, 209; X, 420

Land, Hannah. *See* Horning

Land, Isabella (Chisholm), X, 167

Land, Phebe. *See* Scott

Land, Robert, IX, 454; X, 167

Land, Robert, IX, **454–55**

Landeau, Marie-Noëlle (Tétro), II, 627

Landen. *See also* Landers

Landen, Herman, V, 748

Landergan. *See* Lonergan; Lundrigan

Landers (Landen), Ellen (Desbrisay), V, 249; VI, 197

Landianière. *See* Hardouineau

Landmann, George Thomas, V, 366, 391, 486, 502, 692, 821, 840; VI, 77, 532; VIII, **482–84**

Landmann, Isaac, VIII, 482

Landon, Fred, VIII, 267, 716; IX, 881; X, 746; XII, 587

Landon, Letitia Elizabeth (Maclean), XII, 776

Landon, Lydia (Read), VIII, 743

Landon, Simple, I, 55, 420; II, **344–45**

Landriaux, Louis, IV, 434

Landriaux, Louis-Nicolas, IV, 265, **434–35**; V, 201; VI, 699

Landriaux, Marie-Anne. *See* Prud'homme

Landriaux, Marie-Louise. *See* Bourond

Landrican, Michael, V, 338

Landrière. *See also* Des Bordes

Landrière, Marie-Anne-Angélique (Mechtler), VI, 499

Landrière Des Bordes, Antoine-Gilles, IV, 435

Landrière Des Bordes, Jean-Marie, IV, 148, **435–36**, 580

Landrière Des Bordes, Marie-Gilles. *See* Chaussegros de Léry

Landrière Des Bordes, Pierre-Paul, IV, 436

Landrière Lamouline, Pierre, III, 401, 441, 442; IV, 125

Landrigan. *See* Lundrigan

Landrio. *See* Landriaux

Landron, Monsieur (militia officer), IV, 320

Landron, Élisabeth. *See* Chavigny

Landron, Étienne, I, 56, 664; II, 32; III, 347

Landron, François-Xavier, III, 348

Landron, Jean-François, III, 181, 182, 346, **347–48**

Landron, Marie-Anne. *See* Bergeron

Landry, Alexis, IV, xxviii, 78, 240, **436–37**; VI, 304; VII, 85

Landry, Allain, X, 426

Landry, Amand, X, **426**; XII, 1035

Landry, Anastasie. *See* Dupuis

Landry, Antoinette (Bourg), II, 93

Landry, Caroline-Eulalie. *See* Lelièvre

Landry, Cécile (Terriot), II, 625

Landry, Charles, II, 93

Landry, Claire. *See* Le Blanc

Landry, Claude, V, 393
Landry, Émerence. *See* Painchaud
Landry, Jean, IV, 436; V, 393
Landry, Jean-Étienne, X, 36; IX, 119; XI, 162, 272, **483–86**; XII, 732, 1022
Landry, Marie. *See* Bernard
Landry, Marie. *See* Terriot
Landry, Marie-Anne (Trahan), V, 826
Landry, Marie-Josephe (Boudrot), V, 102
Landry, Modeste (Guitet), V, 393
Landry, Pélagie. *See* Caissie
Landry*, Philippe (1846–1919), XI, 207, 484, 485, 486; 726, 758, 1009, 1043
Landry*, Sir Pierre-Amand (1846–1916), X, 426; XI, 298, 351; XII, 40, 339, 340, 837, 1035
Landry, René, II, 625
Landry, Sébastien-Étienne, VIII, 675; XI, 483
Lane, Ambrose, VI, 122, 821; VII, 146, 415; VIII, 444, **484–85**, 531, 742, 825, 827, 828; IX, 474
Lane, Anna (Gardiner; wife of RICHARD), X, 427
Lane, Daniel, I, **416–17**
Lane, Elisha, VIII, 322, 323; XI, 773
Lane, Elizabeth. *See* Lacey
Lane, Elizabeth (Vavasor; Holdsworth), II, 291
Lane, Henry, II, 291
Lane, Henry Bowyer, VIII, 485
Lane, Henry Bowyer Joseph, VIII, 178, 281, 282, **485–87**, 875, 960, 961
Lane, James, VIII, 259
Lane, John, II, 476
Lane, John Hamilton, VIII, 484
Lane, Lucy Anne. *See* Sharpe
Lane, Maria (Logan), XII, 568
Lane, Mary. *See* McDermot
Lane, Mary. *See* Smith
Lane, Michael, V, 274
Lane, Richard, IX, 624; X, **426–27**, 486
Lane, Sarah. *See* Dickinson
Lane, Sarah Ann (Hibbard), XI, 404
Lanergan. *See also* Lundrigan
Lanergan, Edward, VI, 409
La Neuville. *See* Buache
Laneuville. *See* Horné
Lang, George, VIII, 928; XI, **486–87**, 856
Lang, James, VII, 922
Lang, Janet (Morris), VIII, 638; IX, 574
Lang, Susan. *See* Johnston
Langan, Gilonne-Charlotte de (Cahideuc, Comtesse Dubois de La Motte), III, 92
Langan, Julia (Leslie), X, 440
Langan, Patrick, VI, 95, 433, 471, 635; X, 440
Langdell, Christopher Columbus, XII, 887
Langdon, John E., V, 728; XI, 515
Langdon, Olive (Danforth), VI, 176
Lange, André de, IV, 125
Langelier. *See also* Largillier
Langelier*, Charles (1851–1920), XI, 192; XII, 853, 854, 1038, 1065
Langelier*, Sir François (1838–1915), XI, 338, 484, 496; XII, 1023, 1037, 1038, 1046
Langelier*, Jean-Chrysostome (1845–1910), VI, 175; XI, 903
Langevin; L'Angevin. *See also* Bergevin; Cartier

Langevin*, Adélard (1855–1915), XII, 199, 500, 510, 1087
Langevin, Antoine, VIII, 487
Langevin, Antoine, VIII, **487–88**; IX, 361, 362
Langevin, Catherine. *See* Leclaire
Langevin, Charles, VI, 168; VII, 594, 595; IX, 274; XII, 1036
Langevin, Edmond, IV, 75; XI, **487–88**, 836; XII, 520, 521
Langevin*, Sir Hector-Louis (1826–1906), VIII, 262; IX, 211, 274, 783; X, 45, 147, 192, 226, 677, 686; XI, 3, 12, 27, 115, 161, 171, 176, 183, 184, 185, 245, 252, 287, 339, 487, 491, 492, 493, 626, 721, 750, 822, 902, 920, 921; XII, 8, 87, 174, 175, 176, 178, 179, 180, 258, 270, 280, 293, 324, 495, 520, 521, 556, 600, 602, 603, 605, 606, 608, 610, 627, 628, 629, 630, 687, 721, 722, 723, 726, 737, 899, 1006, 1010, 1019, 1022, 1043, 1045, 1055, 1065, 1068
Langevin, Jean, VII, 595; XI, 487; XII, 519, 875
Langevin, Jean, X, 194, 218, 226, 430, 488; XI, 250, 274, 487, 488, 836; XII, **518–22**, 820, 868, 913, 1022
Langevin, Julie (Trudel), XI, 891
Langevin, Justine. *See* Têtu
Langevin, Malvina (Derome), X, 226
Langevin, Sophie. *See* Laforce
Langford, Chloe Sweeting (Taylor), XII, 1029
Langford, Edward Edwards, IX, 428; X, 116, 117, 196, 243, 246, 478; XII, 113, **522–23**, 642, 837
Langford, Flora. *See* Phillips
Langford, Grace. *See* Nordbeck
Langford, James J., VII, **483–84**; IX, 599
Langford, Jane. *See* Grant
Langford, John (father of JAMES J.), VII, 483
Langford, John (Halifax silversmith), IX, 599
Langford, John (London silversmith), VII, 483
Langford, John (pewterer, 1719–1757), VII, 483
Langford, John (pewterer, 1780), VII, 483
Langford, Nathaniel Pitt, XI, 742
Langford, Thomas (pewterer), VII, 483
Langford, Thomas (silversmith), VII, 483
Langford, William Payne, VII, 483
Langhorn, John, IV, 710; V, **474–77**, 787; VI, 3, 525, 601; VII, 366, 557
Langhorne, William, VII, 182
Langis. *See* Levrault
Langlade. *See* Mouet
Langlais, Geneviève (Duberger), VI, 223
Langlais, Guillaume, III, 398
Langlais, Joseph-Alfred, XI, 484; XII, 727
Langley. *See also* Longley
Langley*, Henry (1836–1907), VIII, 874; XI, 392; XII, 992
Langley, Nicholas, VIII, 314
Langley, Sarah. *See* Scott
Langley, Sarah (wife of Thomas), VIII, 314
Langley, Thomas, VIII, 314
Langley, William, VII, 510
Langlois, Adrienne (Larché), II, 272
Langlois, Françoise. *See* Grenier
Langlois, Françoise (Desportes), I, 264, 495
Langlois, Guillaume, I, 417
Langlois, Jacques, III, 348
Langlois, Jean, II, 158
Langlois, Jeanne. *See* Millet
Langlois, Marguerite (Guillet), IX, 343
Langlois, Marguerite (Martin), I, 495; II, 460

Langlois, Marguerite (Vachon), II, 639, 640
Langlois, Marie. *See* Crevet
Langlois, Marie (Caën), I, 159
Langlois, Marie (Juchereau de Maur), I, 400, 401
Langlois, Marie-Madeleine (Gervaise), III, 257
Langlois, Marie-Thérèse. *See* Lessard
Langlois, Marie-Thérèse, named de Saint-Jean-Baptiste, III, 318, 319, **348–49**, 543
Langlois, Mary (Metherall), X, 511
Langlois, Michel, V, 418
Langlois, Noël, II, 32
Langlois, Noël, I, 330, **417**
Langlois, Pierre (businessman), IX, 274
Langlois, Pierre (politician), V, 87; VII, 133
Langlois, *dit* Germain, Augustin-Hyppolite, VIII, 489
Langlois, *dit* Germain, Augustin-René, VIII, **488–89**
Langlois, *dit* Germain, Catherine. *See* Sauvageau
Langlois, *dit* Germain, Charles, VIII, 489
Langlois, *dit* Germain, Louis, IV, 44, 295; VIII, 488
Langlois, *dit* Germain, Marie-Josephte. *See* Laforce
Langlois, *dit* Germain, Pierre-Olivier, VIII, 489
Langlois, *dit* Saint-Jean, Marie-Louise (Baillargeon), IX, 17
Langloiserie; L'Angloiserie. *See* Piot
Langman, Edward, IV, 194, 402, **437–38**, 771
Langman, John, IV, 437
Langmuir*, John Woodburn (1835–1915), X, 467; XI, 591; XII, 1125, 1126
Langoissieux, Charles (Pierre), I, 320, **417**
Langon. *See* Trégu
Langrishe, Elizabeth (Robinson), XI, 760
Langrishe, Fanny Harriet (Loftus; Le Gallais), IX, 460
Langristain. *See* L'Estobec
Langton, Anne, XII, **523–27**, 782, 997
Langton, Ellen. *See* Currer
Langton*, Hugh Hornby (1862–1953), VI, 112; XII, 525, 527, 1114
Langton, John, VII, 75, 712; VIII, 57, 92; IX, 59, 149; X, 406; XI, 541, 792; XII, 72, 524, 525, 526, **527–29**, 595, 599, 730, 782, 963, 1111, 1112
Langton, Lydia. *See* Dunsford
Langton, Thomas, XII, 523, 524, 527
Langton, William, XII, 524, 525, 526, 528
Langtry, C. J., XII, 863
Langtry, John, X, 56
Langtry, Joseph Millar, VIII, 578
Languedoc, Angélique. *See* Samson
Languedoc, Anna Maria. *See* Philipps
Languedoc, François, V, 117; VI, 290; VII, 134, **484–85**, 762, 877
Languedoc, Jacques, VII, 484
Languedoc, Louise (Roy Portelance), VII, 762, 763
Languet de Gergy, Jean-Joseph, IV, 295
Langy. *See* Levrault
Lanigan, Eleanor (Tobin), VII, 867; XI, 880
Lanigan, Margaret (Fuller), IX, 293
Lanigan, Patrick, VII, 867
Lanman, Charles, X, 346, 347
Lanne, Jean, IV, 421
Lannelongue, Anne. *See* Richard
Lannelongue, Armand, III, 349
Lannelongue, Jean-Baptiste, III, **349–50**; IV, 253, 378, 379
Lannelongue, Marie. *See* Barrière

Lannelongue, Pierre, III, 350
Lannion, Félicité-Sophie de (La Rochefoucauld, Duchesse de La Rochefoucauld-Liancourt, Duchesse d'Estissac), VI, 388
Lanogenu, Monsieur (agent), IV, 126
Lanois. *See* Enouille
La Noraye. *See* Niort
Lanoue. *See* Laigu
La Noue. *See* Legu; Robutel
Lanouette. *See* Rivard
Lanouguère, Jean de, I, 417
Lanouguère, Jeanne de. *See* Samalins
Lanouguère, Louis de, III, 311
Lanouguère, Louise-Rose de, named de Sainte- Catherine, III, 311
Lanouguère, Marguerite-Renée de. *See* Denys de La Ronde
Lanouguère, Thomas de, I, 321, **417–18**, 600; II, 224, 616; III, 311
Lanoullier, Jean, III, 350, 352
Lanoullier, Marie. *See* Tollet
Lanoullier, Marie-Reine. *See* Grasse
Lanoullier de Boisclerc, Jean-Eustache, III, 74, 145, 159, **350–52**, 353, 374; IV, 203, 304, 359, 360, 590, 658, 749
Lanoullier de Boisclerc, Jeanne. *See* André de Leigne
Lanoullier de Boisclerc, Marie-Germaine-Eustache (Bénard), III, 63, 352
Lanoullier de Boisclerc, Marie-Jeanne. *See* Bocquet
Lanoullier de Boisclerc, Marie-Marguerite. *See* Duroy
Lanoullier de Boisclerc, Nicolas, II, 152; III, 14, 15, 48, 61, 62, 64, 77, 153, 170, 350, **352–54**, 616; IV, 88, 356
Lanoullier Des Granges, Paul-Antoine-François, III, 172, 353
Lansdowne, Marquess of. *See* Petty-Fitzmaurice
Lansdowne, Louisa Elizabeth (Wetmore), XII, 1096
Lansing, Gysbertje (Roseboom), III, 568
Lantagnac. *See* Adhémar
La Oja. *See* Wahpasha
Lapalice, Joseph-Hengard, IX, 552
Lapalice, Ovide-Michel-Hengard, IV, 655; IX, 538, 539
Lapalme. *See* Janson
La Palme (de Palme), Monsieur (office holder), I, 89, 418
La Palme*, Béatrice (Issaurel) (1878–1921), XII, 472
Lapane, Marie-Sophie (Gauthier), X, 301
Laparé, Charles, VII, 707
Laparre, Élie, V, 248
Lapause. *See* Plantavit
Lapeire, Joseph-Guillaume, IV, 135
La Pelouze. *See* Carrefour
La Peltrie. *See* Gruel
La Pérade. *See* Tarieu
Lapérade, Marie-Louise (Roy), IV, 689
La Pérelle. *See* Eury
Lapérière. *See also* Desjardins
Lapérière (Boucher de La Perrière), François, VIII, 606
Lapérière (Boucher de La Perrière), Julie (Malhiot), VIII, 606
Lapérière, Marie-Charlotte. *See* Pécaudy de Contrecœur
La Périne. *See* Maleray
Lapérouse, Comte de. *See* Galaup
Lapérouse, Comtesse de. *See* Broudou
La Perrière. *See* Boucher; Marin
Laperrière. *See* Fabre; Ouvrard
Lapeyre, Jean-Pierre, III, 608

Lapham, Increase Allen, X, 484
La Picanier. *See* Dagneau
La Picardière. *See* Bégon
La Pierre. *See* Chauvin
Lapierre. *See also* Lebourdais; Meunier
Lapierre, André, XI, 763
Lapierre, Eugène, IX, 633; XII, 534
La Pinaudière. *See* Bourdon
La Pistole. *See* Varin
La Place, Eustache de, II, 345
La Place, Jacques de, I, 215, 485
La Place, Louis-Hyacinthe de (Jean-Claude), I, 339; II, **345**
La Place, Marie de. *See* Le Couteux
La Place, Pierre de, I, 338; II, 345
La Place, Simon-Gérard de (Jean), I, **338–39**; II, 345, 579; III, 163, 273
La Plagne. *See* Espiet
La Plante. *See* Leriger
Laplante, *dit* Champagne, Charles, XII, 173
La Pocatière. *See* Pollet
Lapointe. *See also* Audette; Desherbert
Lapointe, Jean-Baptiste, V, 727
Lapointe, Louis-Eugène-Hercule, XII, 127
La Poippe, Sieur de, I, **418–19**, 530
Lapommeraie. *See* Robert
La Pommeraye, Charles de, I, 167
Laporte, Arnaud de, III, 355
La Porte, Françoise de. *See* Faucrolle
La Porte, Jean de, II, 345
La Porte, Marie-Anne de (Genaple de Bellefonds; Hubert), II, 241
Laporte, Pierre-Arnaud de, III, 354, 355; IV, 358, 517, 644, 645, 655, 656, 668
Laporte de Lalanne, Jean (Armand) de, III, 226, **354–55**
La Porte de Louvigny, Louis de, II, xxi, 15, 70, 115, 218, 220, 223, 300, 316, 318, **345–47**, 386, 389, 433, 475, 488, 502, 515, 518, 547, 567, 571, 588; III, 81
La Porte de Louvigny, Marie de. *See* Nolan
La Porte de Louvigny, Marie-Anne de (Testard de Montigny), II, 627; III, 278; IV, 733
La Potardière, Sieur de (ironmaster), I, 626
La Poterie. *See* Gaudin; Leneuf
La Potherie. *See* Le Roy
Lappare, Henry, VIII, 479
La Prade. *See* Pelletier
La Promenade. *See* Larchevêque
Lapum, James Noxon, XI, 819
La Ralde, Raymond de, I, 162, 411, **419**, 521, 579
La Ralière (La Ratière). *See* Des Herbiers
Laramée. *See* Mathieu
La Ramée, Sieur de. *See* Melanson, Charles
Larché, Adrienne. *See* Langlois
Larche, Charles, IV, 58
Larché, Pierre, II, 272
Larcher, Henri-Michel, IV, 438
Larcher, Jean-Baptiste-Adolphe, IX, 63; XII, 719
Larcher, Marie-Anne. *See* Marinier
Larcher, Nicolas, IV, 421, **438–39**, 558, 644, 678
Larchevêque, Charlotte (Jobert), V, 333
L'Archevêque, Jean, III, 523
Larchevêque, Josette (Marie-Joseph) (Dejean), V, 237
Larchevêque, Marguerite (Chaboillez), V, 177, 178

L'Archevêque, Marie-Anne. *See* Jolliet de Mingan
L'Archevêque, Marie-Thérèse (Tisserant de Moncharvaux), III, 626
Larchevêque, *dit* La Promenade, Jacques, V, 178
Larchevesque, Marie-Madeleine. *See* Réaume
Larcum, Elizabeth (Townsend), III, 628
Lardeau, Anne (Gargot), I, 323
Lardeau, Jacques, I, 323
Lareau, Edmond (Pierre-Bénoni-Evremond), VIII, 330, 420; IX, 193; X, 166; XI, 343, 458, **488–91**; XII, 580
Lareau, Marguerite. *See* Robillard
Lareau, Marguerite (Campagna; Hodiesne), III, 292
Lareau, Odile. *See* Sylvestre
Lareau, Pierre-Bénoni, XI, 488
La Renaudière, Monsieur (engineer), II, 646
Large, Mary (Stevenson), XI, 852
Largillier, Jacques, known as Le Castor, I, 394, 491; II, 144, **347**
La Ribourde, Gabriel de, I, 55, 176, 177, 265, **420**, 438, 499, 501; II, 278, 280, 344, 345
La Richardie, Armand de, III, 47, 102, **355–56**, 650; IV, 612, 640
La Richardière. *See* Testu
La Rigaudière. *See* Martaud
Larissy, Mary (Skerry), VII, 810
La Rivaudais. *See* Quesnel
La Rive. *See* Gravé
Larivée, Charles, IV, 748
Larivée, Eustache, IV, 748
La Rivière. *See also* Bernard; Byssot; Le Mercier; Lorimier; Poncet
Larivière. *See* Douhet; Grihaut; Hébert
La Rivière, Monsieur (soldier), II, 414
La Rivière*, Alphonse-Alfred-Clément (1842–1925), XI, 646, 716; XII, 129, 370, 372, 1008
Larkin, Ann (mother of PATRICK JOSEPH), XII, 529
Larkin, Charles Fox, VIII, 489
Larkin, Elizabeth. *See* Jones
Larkin, Elizabeth (Entremont), XI, 303
Larkin, Ellen. *See* Maguire
Larkin, George, II, 260, 290, **348**
Larkin, John, VIII, 489
Larkin, John, VIII, 317, **489–91**; XII, 183
Larkin, Patrick Joseph, XII, **529–30**, 629, 782, 783
Larkin, Thomas, XII, 529
La Rochalar, Chevalier de. *See* Goussé
Laroche, Monsieur (clergyman), VIII, 677
La Roche, Monsieur (servant), II, 264
Laroche, Arline (Voyer), X, 695
La Roche, Marie-Gabrielle (Dasilva, *dit* Portugais), III, 165
La Roche, Marie-Joseph (Requiem; Dumas), V, 276
La Roche Daillon, Jacques de, I, 420
La Roche Daillon, Jeanne de. *See* Froyer de La Baronnière
La Roche Daillon, Joseph de, I, 132, **420–21**, 533
La Roche de Mesgouez, Troilus de, Marquis de La Roche-Mesgouez, I, 23, 27, 88, 209, 210, 345, **421–22**
La Rochefoucauld, Félicité-Sophie de, Duchesse de La Rochefoucauld-Liancourt, Duchesse d'Estissac. *See* Lannion
La Rochefoucauld, François de, Duc de La Rochefoucauld, VII, 90
La Rochefoucauld, François-Alexandre-Frédéric de, Duc de

La Rochefoucauld-Liancourt, Duc d'Estissac, V, 101, 639, 755; VI, **388–89**; VII, 813; VIII, 925

La Rochefoucauld, Louis de, Marquise de Roye, III, 356

La Rochefoucauld, Marie de, known as Mlle de La Roche-Guyon (La Rochefoucauld de Roye, Duchesse d'Estissac), VI, 388

La Rochefoucauld, Marie-Louise-Nicole de (La Roche-foucauld de Roye, Marquise de Roucy, Duchesse d'Anville), III, 356

La Rochefoucauld, Marthe de, Marquise de Roye. *See* Ducasse

La Rochefoucauld de Roye, Jean-Baptiste-Louis-Frédéric de, Marquis de Roucy, Duc d'Anville, III, 27, 49, 50, 54, 98, 213, 214, **356**, 357, 367, 417, 438, 498, 610, 657; IV, 33, 62, 79, 421, 454, 459, 558, 588, 644, 651; V, 97, 498

La Rochefoucauld de Roye, Louis-François-Armand de, Duc d'Estissac, VI, 388

La Rochefoucauld de Roye, Marie-Louise-Nicole de, Mar-quise de Roucy, Duchesse d'Anville. *See* La Rochefoucauld

La Rochefoucauld-Liancourt, Duc de. *See* La Roche-foucauld

La Rochefoucauld-Liancourt, Duchesse de. *See* Lannion

La Rochefoucauld-Roye, Éléonore-Christine (Phélypeaux, Comtesse de Pontchartrain et de Maurepas), II, 296; III, 309, 310

La Roche-Guyon, Duchesse de. *See* Schomberg

Larochelle. *See also* Gautron

Larochelle, Anselme-Hyppolite, VIII, 320

Larochelle, Georgiana. *See* Plante

Larochelle, Louis-Napoléon, VIII, 320; X, 163; XI, **491–93**; XII, 277

Larochelle, Marie-Louise (Vaillancourt), VIII, 320

La Rochette. *See* Gargot; Hillaire

Larocque. *See also* Rochbrune

Larocque, Alfred, X, 52

Larocque, Amélia. *See* Berthelet

Larocque, Angélique. *See* Leroux

Larocque, Archange. *See* Guillon-Duplessis

La Rocque, Charles, VII, 485; VIII, 210; IX, 20, 78, 193, 466; X, 266, 416, **427–31**; XI, 99, 104, 493, 494, 595; XII, 1021

Larocque, François-Alfred-Chartier, IX, 456; X, 53

La Rocque, François-Antoine, V, 512; VII, 672; IX, 455, 456

La Rocque, François-Antoine, IV, 172; V, 177; VI, 795; VII, 594, 595, 716, 718, 737; VIII, 500, 556; IX, 288, **455–56**

La Rocque, Henri, X, 428

Larocque, Henry, VIII, 210

Larocque, Joseph, VIII, 176, 500; IX, **456–57**

La Rocque, Joseph, VIII, 333, 711, 712; IX, 465; X, 175, 428, 429; XI, 171, 174, **493–95**, 693; XII, 1003, 1018

Larocque, Louis-Isaac, X, 694

La Rocque, Marie-Angèle. *See* Paré

Larocque, Marie-Catherine-Émilie. *See* Cotté

La Rocque, Pierre-Dominique, VIII, 284

La Rocque, Sophie. *See* Robert

La Rocque, Timothée-Amable, XI, 493

La Rocque de Roberval, Jean-François de, I, 27, 159, 169, 301, 309, 384, **422–25**, 469; III, 109; XII, 459

Larocque de Rochbrune, Alphonse-Barnabé, XII, **530–31**

Larocque de Rochbrune, Marie-Julie. *See* Beauchemin

La Rodde. *See* Senezergues

Laron. *See* Sauguaaram

La Ronde. *See* Bourassa; Denys

La Roque, Catherine de (Hangard), I, 425

La Roque, Charlotte de (Madaillan), I, 424

La Roque, Jean (Pierre) de, I, 424

La Roque, Marguerite de, I, 423, 424, **425–26**

La Roque, *dit* Couillaud, Bernard de, I, 422

La Roque, *dit* Couillaud, Isabeau de. *See* Poitiers

La Roque* de Roquebrune, Robert (1889–1978), IV, 269

La Rose. *See* Belleau

Larose. *See also* Daveluy; Gère; Guillot; Pichon; Rousseau

Larose, Ludger, XII, 171

La Rouvillière. *See* Michel

La Rozière. *See* Carlet

Larrante (Rende), Marie (Sagean), II, 589

Larré, Sauveur-Romain, VII, 59, 774

Larrey, Dominique-Jean, Baron Larrey, VIII, 96

Larrivé, Charles, VI, 635

Larsher, Monsieur (agent), III, 676

Larsonneur, François, V, 436, 727; VI, 230

Larthigue, Jacques, VII, 485, 674

Larthigue, Marie-Charlotte. *See* Cherrier

Lartigue. *See also* Bidoux

Lartigue, François, II, 381

Lartigue, Jean-Jacques, IV, 148

Lartigue, Jean-Jacques, IV, 148; V, 93, 186; VI, 39, 125, 126, 287, 288, 332, 397, 398, 570, 571, 589, 591, 592, 595, 596, 597, 658, 668, 669, 748, 828; VII, 8, 9, 19, 171, 209, 423, 447, **485–91**, 496, 543, 547, 574, 623, 624, 625, 626, 642, 643, 656, 657, 667, 678, 680, 689, 699, 700, 705, 718, 727, 746, 759, 760, 774, 798, 799, 851, 852, 858, 877, 879, 886, 887, 940; VIII, 20, 137, 141, 143, 144, 145, 213, 240, 259, 317, 457, 490, 592, 593, 594, 595, 616, 666, 703, 711, 712, 720, 722, 728, 729, 730, 777, 864, 909, 912, 939, 974; IX, 17, 18, 100, 206, 228, 465, 533, 681, 698, 797, 798, 799, 800, 807, 809, 817, 861; X, 163, 428, 429, 505, 532, 570, 578, 689, 733; XI, 84, 94, 95, 168, 249, 251, 493, 585, 714, 725, 955; XII, 1018

Lartigue, Jeanne. *See* Dhiarse

Lartigue, Joseph, II, 220, 381; III, 216, **356–57**, 387, 454

Lartigue, Marie-Madeleine (Fautoux), III, 216

Lartigue, Pierre-Jérôme, IV, 558, 644, 645

Larue, Achille, XII, 324

Larue, Adélaïde. *See* Roy

Larue, Arabella. *See* Holmes

Larue, Auguste, IX, 487; XII, **531–32**

Larue, Augustin, VIII, 491

Larue, Édouard-Wilbrod, VIII, 492

Larue, Étienne de, II, 348

Larue, Félicité (Thibaudeau), X, 676

La Rue, François-Alexandre-Hubert, IX, 286; X, 106, 203; XI, 342, **495–97**

Larue, François-Xavier, IV, 42, 43; VI, 119, 120; VII, 430; VIII, **491–92**

La Rue, Georges, XII, 1038

Larue, Georges-Antoine, XI, 484

Larue, Guillaume de, II, 348

Larue, Guillaume de, II, 282, **348**, 517

Larue, Julie (Taché), VI, 749

Larue, Maria Jane. *See* McClaren

La Rue, Marie-Alphonsine. *See* Panet

Larue, Marie-Anne (Suzor), V, 788

Larue, Marie de. *See* Pepin
Larue, Marie de. *See* Pouilliot
Larue, Marie-Desanges (Angers), VIII, 16
Larue, Marie-Magdeleine. *See* Hainse
Larue, Marie-Marguerite. *See* Robichaux
Larue, Nazaire, XI, 495
Larue, Olivier, XII, 531
Larue, Omer, XI, 329
La Rue, Pierre de, Abbé de L'Isle-Dieu, III, 17, 18, 120, 121, 165, 166, 192, 194, 196, 198, 199, 223, 257, 343, 415, 416, 425, 426, 575; IV, 80, 95, 96, 97, 235, 237, 238, 289, 296, 452, 453, 454, 456, 529, 645; V, 172, 471
La Rue, Roger, XII, 1038
Larue, Rose Délima (St Jean), XII, 937
Larue, Thérèse. *See* Delisle
Larue, William, XII, 88
La Rue de La Motte, Louis de, I, 416
Larwill, Edwin, XII, 492, 644
La Sablonnière. *See* Brunet; Varin
La Sague, Jean de, I, 498
La Sague, Louise de. *See* Jousset
La Salle. *See also* Cavelier; Perthuis
La Salle, Charles de, II, 348
La Salle, François de, II, 349
La Salle, Jean de, I, 425
La Salle, Jean-Baptiste de, II, 335; III, 221, 613; IX, 681
La Salle, Jeanne-Catherine de. *See* Berenhardt
La Salle, Madeleine de. *See* Chartroux
La Salle, Marie de. *See* Harot
La Salle, Nicolas de (father of NICOLAS), II, 348
La Salle, Nicolas de (son of NICOLAS), II, 349
La Salle, Nicolas de, II, 260, **348–49**, 399; III, 380, 381
La Salle, Rose de (Marquette), I, 490
La Salle, Simon de, II, 349
La Salle de Sertrouville, Marie-Anne de. *See* Carrerot
La Salle de Sertrouville, Quentin de, II, 119
La Saudrais, Girard de, IV, 247
La Saussaye. *See also* Dagneau; Le Coq
La Saussaye, Charlotte de (Hazen), V, 412
Lascaris. *See* also Savoie-Lascaris
Lascaris, Charles-Emmanuel, Marquis d'Urfé et de Baugé, II, 349
Lascaris, Joseph-Marie, Marquis d'Urfé et de Baugé, Comte de Sommerive, II, 12
Lascaris, Marguerite, Marquise d'Urfé et de Baugé. *See* Allègre
Lascaris d'Urfé, François-Saturnin, I, 599, 600, 647; II, **349–50**
Las Casas, Bartolomé de, XII, 250
Lascelles, Henry, 3rd Earl of Harewood, IX, 457
Lascelles, Horace Douglas, IX, **457–58**; XI, 291
Lascelles, Lady Louisa, Countess of Harewood. *See* Thynne
Lascoret, Anne. *See* Richard
Lascoret, Jean-Baptiste, III, 350; IV, 253
Laserre, Peter, VIII, 527
Lash, John Bean, XI, 461, 675, 746
Lash*, Zebulon Aiton (1846–1920), XII, 203, 1108
Lasher, Henry, XI, 852
Lasher, John, XI, 852
Laskin*, Bora (1912–84), XII, 898
La Source. *See* Thaumur
Lassaigne, Anne (Chapoton), III, 102

Lassare, Ignace, V, 676
Lassay, Marquis de. *See* Madaillan
Lasselin, Marguerite. *See* Haguenier
Lasselin, Romain, IV, 507
Lasson, Georges de, III, 455
Latard, Joséphine. *See* Legris
Lataupine; La Taupine. *See* Moreau
Lately Gone. *See* Mékaisto
Laterreur. *See* Ducros
Laterrière. *See also* Sales
Laterrière, Jean (Jean-Baptiste, Jean-Pierre). *See* Sales
Laterrière, Pierre de
La Tesserie. *See* Cailhault
La Tête Blanche. *See* Gray Lock
Latham, John, IV, 377; V, 227, 362
Latham, Robert, II, 37, 118, 274, 293, **350–51**, 487, 583, 643
Lathern*, John (1831–1905), X, 714; XI, 734
La Thibaudière. *See* Denys
Lathrop, Holester, XII, 1090, 1091
Latimer, Charles, VII, 844; X, 548
Latimer, Hugh, VIII, 521
Latimer, James, VIII, 852
La Tortue. *See* Mikinak
La Touche. *See* Aulneau; Tantouin; Texier
Latouche MacCarthy, Angélique-Jeanne. *See* Guillimin
Latouche MacCarthy, Charles, III, **357–58**; IV, 10
Latouche MacCarthy, Hélène. *See* Shee
Latouche MacCarthy, Timothée, III, 357
Latour. *See also* Dézéry; Dufour; Huguet; Jérôme; Leblanc; Leblond
La Tour. *See* Saint-Étienne
Latour, Bertrand de, I, 291, 551, 630; II, 259, 365, 420, 628, 629; III, 115, 223, 318, 349, 543, 549, 638, 711; IV, 338, **439–41**, 539; XI, 185
Latour, Catherine de. *See* Jonquières
Latour, Félicité (Lenoir, *dit* Rolland), IX, 464
Latour, Isabella (McKenzie; McBean), VI, 466
Latour, Jean-Baptiste, IV, 178
Latour, Jean de, II, 627; IV, 141, 601
Latour, Josette (McKay; Haldane), VI, 465; VIII, 350
Latour, Marguerite. *See* Prud'homme
Latour, Pierre, IV, 178
Latour, Pierre de, IV, 439
La Tourasse, Catherine. *See* Bugaret
La Tourasse, Charles, known as Chevalier, I, 361, **426–27**, 544, 576; II, 183
La Tour d'Auvergne, Henri de, Vicomte de Turenne, I, 283, 615; II, 182, 191, 433
Latour-Dézéry, François-Xavier, V, 233, 243, 701; VI, 397; VII, 255
La Tourette. *See* Greysolon
Latour-Maubourg, Marquis de. *See* Fay
La Tousche. *See also* Pézard
La Tousche, Jacques de, II, 347
La Trinité. *See* Denys; Le Moyne
Latrobe, Benjamin Henry, XI, 92
La Troche. *See* Savonnières
Latter, Augusta (Boulton), XII, 119
Lattie, Alexander, IX, 624
Latuilière, Jean, IV, 433
La Tuillerie. *See* Moufle
Latulippe. *See* Juneau; Leheup

Laubara (Laubaras). *See* Olabaratz
Lauberivière. *See* Pourroy
Laubia. *See* Loubias
Laubret, Catherine (Dugay), II, 202
Laubrière. *See* Lefebvre
Laud, William, I, 406; XII, 1122
Lauder, Abram William, X, 632; XI, **497–98**; XII, 644
Lauder, Maria Elise. *See* Toof
Lauder, Thomas D., XI, 497
Lauder, William Waugh, X, 371; XI, 497
Lauderdale, Earl of. *See* Maitland
Laudonnière. *See* Goulaine
Laughead, W. B., IX, 564
Laughton, Ann (Roe), V, 721
Laughton, Sir John Knox, IV, 123
Laulne, Louise de (Chambly), I, 185
Laumet, Jean, II, 351
Laumet, Jeanne. *See* Péchagut
Laumet, *dit* de Lamothe Cadillac, Antoine, I, 141, 201, 582; II, xxxvii, 12, 41, 48, 77, 115, 116, 119, 134, 142, 144, 163, 170, 173, 181, 183, 187, 215, 218, 229, 271, 300, 317, 318, 324, 327, 339, **351–57**, 386, 414, 415, 425, 453, 468, 475, 501, 505, 508, 515, 546, 547, 558, 562, 568, 569, 571, 618, 631, 635, 643, 645, 646, 647, 655; III, xxxix, 51, 66, 80, 96, 147, 258, 317, 355, 379, 381, 446, 451, 640, 643; IV, lvi
Laumet, *dit* de Lamothe Cadillac, Marie-Thérèse. *See* Guion
Laumet de Lamothe Cadillac, Antoine, II, 356
Laumet de Lamothe Cadillac, Marie-Madeleine, II, 355
Laumet de Lamothe Cadillac, Marie-Thérèse, II, 173
Launay, Alain de, III, 444, 580
Launay-Rasilly, Claude de, I, 503, 504, 567, 569, 593, 594
Launé-Jourdan, Monsieur de (grandfather of Marie-Catherine de SIMON de Longpré, named de Saint-Augustin), I, 607
Launière, Joseph, VII, 911
Launière, Louise (Lacroix), VI, 383
Laurason. *See* Lawrason
Laure, Pierre-Michel, II, xxxiv, 296, **357–58**; III, 330; IV, 424
Laurence, Marie (Lambert), I, 396, 415
Laurens, Elizabeth (Fisher), VI, 256
Laurens, Henry, V, 630
Laurent. *See also* Lola
Laurent, Adélaïde-Estelle (Bellot), VIII, 79
Laurent, Angélique (Trullier, *dit* Lacombe), VI, 786
Laurent, Anne (Saillant), IV, 692
Laurent, Elizabeth. *See* O'Brien
Laurent, Eugénie-Eliza (Letellier de Saint-Just), XI, 519
Laurent, François, IX, 783
Laurent, Françoise (Corolère), III, 140
Laurent, Guillaume-Antoine, III, 140
Laurent, Michel, XI, 235, 755
Laurent, Nicolas, III, 222, 443
Laurent, Paul, III, **358–59**
Laurent, *dit* Bérichon, Silvain, VI, 786
Laurie, Mrs (of Toronto), VIII, 402
Laurie, John Wimburn, XII, 577, 734
Laurier*, Sir Wilfrid (1841–1919), IX, 345, 464, 563, 564, 565; X, 423; XI, 112, 163, 188, 192, 229, 275, 290, 424, 488, 500, 521, 657, 658, 659, 711, 750, 810, 812, 815, 921; XII, 5, 53, 91, 97, 103, 114, 115, 141, 148, 181,

182, 246, 260, 264, 292, 293, 294, 303, 324, 333, 362, 388, 422, 457, 465, 500, 506, 511, 554, 555, 586, 630, 651, 652, 669, 695, 696, 721, 726, 743, 744, 791, 837, 854, 865, 987, 991, 1011, 1027, 1037, 1038, 1046, 1065, 1085, 1087, 1120, 1121, 1130
Laurin, Catherine. *See* Fluet
Laurin, Joseph, XI, 498
Laurin, Joseph, VIII, 479; XI, **498–99**
Laurin, Marie-Louise. *See* Dalaire
Lauriot, François, V, 51
Lauris de Castellane, Marie-Thérèse-Charlotte de (Montcalm), III, 458
Lauson, Anne. *See* Boivin
Lauson, Anne de. *See* Després
Lauson, Charles-Joseph de, II, 57
Lauson, François de, I, 427, 428
Lauson, Gilles, I, **427**
Lauson, Jean de (d. 1666), I, 45, 112, 145, 146, 200, 202, 203, 214, 232, 237, 245, 340, 349, 372, 401, 412, **427–29**, 431, 473, 475, 542, 574, 579, 580, 606; II, xvi, 84, 85, 136, 158, 639; III, 26
Lauson, Jean de (d. 1661), I, 274, 428, **429–31**, 432, 574, 665; II, xvi, 56, 92; IX, 463; XI, 851
Lauson, Marie. *See* Archambault
Lauson, Marie de. *See* Gaudar
Lauson, Marie-Catherine-Antoinette (Barrin de La Galissonière, Marquise de La Galissonière), III, 26
Lauson, Pierre, I, 427
Lauson de Charny, Charles de, I, 46, 91, 92, 146, 331, 400, 428, 429, **431–32**, 537, 579, 580, 589; II, 639
Lauson de Charny, Louise de. *See* Giffard
Lauson de La Citière, Catherine de. *See* Nau de La Boissière et de Fossambault
Lauson de La Citière, Louis de, I, 428, 542
Lauson de Lirec, François de, I, 427
Lauson de Lirec, Isabelle de. *See* Lottin
L'Autheur. *See* Descayrac
Lauverjat, Étienne, III, **359–60**, 584
Lauvrière, Émile, IV, xxi, xxvi, xxxi
Lauzer, Anne-Armèle (Martin), XI, 587
Lauzières, Pons de, Marquis de Thémines, I, 193
Lauzon, Marguerite de. *See* Riot
Lauzon, Pierre de, III, 360
Lauzon, Pierre de, III, 47, 269, 329, **360–61**, 480, 481, 580; IV, 488
La Vaivre, Jacques de, IV, 137
Laval, Marquis de. *See* Gripière
Laval, Anne-Charlotte de, II, 359
Laval, Emme de (Montmorency, Duchesse de Montmorency), II, 359
Laval, François de, II, 359
Laval, François de, I, 31, 32, 33, 42, 46, 55, 57, 72, 76, 77, 78, 80, 85, 86, 91, 92, 111, 112, 116, 117, 120, 137, 198, 202, 203, 237, 245, 249, 264, 265, 283, 284, 286, 289, 290, 291, 310, 313, 315, 321, 322, 323, 325, 326, 331, 354, 355, 356, 359, 366, 393, 414, 431, 432, 438, 466, 472, 479, 507, 534, 536, 539, 542, 554, 555, 556, 563, 580, 587, 588, 589, 590, 599, 606, 609, 610, 629, 630, 644, 646, 647, 648, 649, 651, 665; II, xvii, xix, 5, 18, 19, 27, 29, 30, 31, 55, 72, 79, 91, 106, 108, 134, 194, 207, 227, 234, 237, 240, 244, 248, 271, 278, 294, 303, 304, 305, 326, 328, 329, 330, 332, 335, 337, **358–72**, 378, 379, 383, 390, 419, 420, 421, 426, 429, 448, 460, 471,

489, 501, 521, 522, 531, 541, 561, 586, 612, 627, 637, 638, 639, 640, 642, 643, 648, 655, 657; III, 11, 47, 104, 193, 199, 201, 202, 284, 522, 546, 648, 683, 684; IV, 338, 440, 649; VIII, 214, 215, 290, 407; IX, 117, 255, 301; XI, 87, 103, 488, 490
Laval, Gabriel de, II, 359
Laval, Guy de, II, 359
Laval, Henri de, II, 359
Laval, Hugues de (father), II, 358, 359
Laval, Hugues de, II, 360
Laval, Isabelle de, II, 359
Laval, Jean-Louis de, II, 360
Laval, Michelle de. *See* Péricard
La Valette. *See also* Nogaret
La Valette, Marie-Angélique de (Taffanel de La Jonquière, Marquise de La Jonquière), III, 609
La Valinière. *See* Huet
La Valle, Catherine (Stuart), VII, 838
Lavallée. *See also* Bouchard; Cotentin; Paquet
Lavallée, Monsieur (merchant), IV, 425
Lavallée, Augustin, X, 153
Lavallée* (Paquet, *dit* Lavallée), Augustin (1816–1903), XII, 532
Lavallée, Calixa, IX, 855; X, 153; XII, 471, 472, **532–34**, 913
Lavallée, Charlotte-Caroline. *See* Valentine
Lavallée, Josephine. *See* Gently
Lavallée, Josephte (Lépine), XII, 554
Lavallée, Louis, III, 541
Lavallée, Louise (Macdonald), VIII, 536
Lavallée, Marie-Charlotte (Chauveau), XI, 177
Lavallée Constantin. *See* Constantin
La Vallière. *See* Leneuf
Lavaltrie. *See* Margane
La Varenne. *See* Bonneau
Lavau, Monsieur (engraver), IV, 507
La Vau, Catherine de (Barbier), II, 44
Lavaud, Jean, III, 184
Lavell*, Michael (1825–1901), XI, 750
Lavender, Jane. *See* Young
La Vente. *See* Roulleaux
Laver, Augustus, XI, 464
Laver, Augustus, XII, 344, 345, **534–35**, 930
Laver, Elizabeth. *See* Fox
Laver, George, XII, 534
Laver, Mary Ann (mother of AUGUSTUS), XII, 534
Laverdière. *See also* Cauchon
Laverdière, Charles-Honoré, IX, 203, 250; X, **432–33**; XI, 115, 588; XII, 247, 271
La Verdure. *See* Doucet; Du Tartre; Melanson
Laverdure. *See also* Potier
Laverdure, Marie (Basset), II, 46
La Vérenderie; La Vérendrye. *See* Gaultier
La Verge, Marguerite (Daumont de Saint-Lusson), I, 249
Lavergne. *See also* Roux-Lavergne
Lavergne, Anne. *See* Bernon
La Vergne*, Armand (1880–1935), XII, 65
Lavergne, Émilie. *See* Barthe
Lavergne, Françoise (Petitpas), II, 524
Lavergne, Joseph, XII, 854
Lavergne, Pierre (defendant), V, 77; VII, 486
Lavergne, Pierre (father-in-law of Claude PETITPAS), II, 524

Laverlochère, Nicolas, VII, 496; XI, 244
La Vernède de Saint-Poncy, Claude de, III, 120, 438; IV, 453
La Viazère. *See* Senau
La Victoire. *See* Sarrère
La Vieuville, Charles, Duc de La Vieuville, I, 521
Lavigne. *See also* Levasseur; Poutré-Lavigne; Rivard; Tessier
Lavigne, Arthur, XI, 671; XII, 746
Lavigne, Azarie, XI, **499–500**
Lavigne, Hippolyte, XI, 499
Lavigne, Lucie. *See* Brodeur
Lavigne, Marie-Angélique (Odelin), VII, 655
Lavignon, Monsieur (teacher), VIII, 140
Lavigueur. *See also* Delage
Lavigueur, Célestin, XI, **500**
Lavigueur, Émile, XI, 500
Lavigueur*, Henri-Edgar (1867–1943), XI, 500
Lavigueur, Mary. *See* Childs
Lavillangevin. *See* Allenou
La Ville. *See* Rocquant
La Ville, Pierre-Éléonor, Marquis de Férolles, II, 270
Lavimaudier (Lavimodière). *See* Lagimonière
Lavine, V, 389
La Violette. *See also* Bétourné
Laviolette. *See also* Greslon; Guernier; Mousseaux
Laviolette, Monsieur (servant), III, 310
La Violette, Monsieur (trafficker in spirits), I, 666
Laviolette, Monsieur, I, 121, 127, 143, **432**
Laviolette, Alfred, VIII, 492
Laviolette, Angélique. *See* Drouin
Laviolette, Arthur, VIII, 492
Laviolette, Elmire. *See* Dumont
Laviolette, Gabriel Atina, VII, 138
Laviolette, Godefroy, VIII, 492; X, 533; XII, 74, **535–36**
Laviolette, Josephte (Boucher de Niverville), IX, 66
Laviolette, Marie-Jessie-Béatrice. *See* Lévesque
Laviolette, Octavie. *See* Globensky
Laviolette, Pierre, VIII, 675
Laviolette, Pierre, VIII, **492–93**; XII, 535
Laviolette, Sévère, XII, 535
Laviolette, Virginie (Desjardins), IX, 204
L'Avocat. *See* Havard
Lavoie, Marie (Bourgeault), XI, 91
Lavoisier, Antoine-Laurent de, V, 187; VII, 930; VIII, 866
La Vrillière, Marquis de. *See* Phélypeaux
Law, Ewan, X, 175
Law, George Henry, X, 110, 516
Law, Henry, IV, 328
Law, James, X, 721; XI, 126, 128
Law, John (educator), VI, 425; XI, 784
Law, John (speculator), II, 425; III, 20, 152, 381; IV, 665
Law, Marie (Clerk), X, 174, 175
Law, Robert, X, **433–34**
Law, Thomas, XI, 271
Law, William, IV, 19
Lawder, Hester (Skinner), V, 762
Lawe, George, V, 621
Lawe, John, VII, 328, 329
Lawe, Rachel. *See* Franks
Lawler, Stephen, VIII, 234
Lawless, Nicholas, 1st Baron Cloncurry, VI, 97
Lawless, Valentina Letitia (Burton), VI, 97

Lawlor. *See also* Lola
Lawlor, Elizabeth (Wallis), XII, 1081
Lawlor, Patrick, VIII, 582
Lawlor, Simon, VI, 120
Lawlor, Stephen, VI, 711
Lawlor, Susanna (Reid; Byles), V, 128
Lawrason, Abigail. *See* Lee
Lawrason, Lawrence (father of LAWRENCE), XI, 501
Lawrason, Lawrence (merchant), V, 670
Lawrason, Lawrence, VIII, 748, 749, 856, 875; IX, 323; X, 533; XI, **500–1**
Lawrason, Louisa (Ridout), VIII, 748
Lawrason, Rachel. *See* Pettit
Lawrear, Elizabeth (Chase; Brookes; Veyssière), IV, 752
Lawrence, Alexander, VII, **491**; XII, 536
Lawrence, Alma (Farrar), XI, 312
Lawrence, Anna C. *See* Bloomfield
Lawrence, Charles, III, 70, 71, 87, 120, 129, 130, 174, 212, 277, 293, 295, 298, 332, **361–66**, 418, 457, 479, 514, 573, 583, 586, 604, 662, 663, 666, 667; IV, xxv, xxvi, xxvii, 16, 21, 51, 52, 53, 93, 94, 110, 169, 170, 216, 217, 219, 290, 291, 292, 351, 414, 527, 540, 560, 581, 631, 695, 703, 704, 724, 764, 774, 776; V, 240, 554, 869; VI, 88, 268, 717; VII, 275; VIII, 805, 929; XI, 303; XII, 14
Lawrence, Clarissa Goss (Doolittle), IX, 209, 210
Lawrence, George Hunter, VII, 491; XII, 536
Lawrence, Herbert, III, 361
Lawrence, James (brother of WILLIAM DAWSON), XI, 502
Lawrence, James (ship's captain), VII, 106
Lawrence, John (uncle), XI, 502
Lawrence, John, XI, 502
Lawrence, Joseph Wilson, VI, 74; VII, 491; X, 285; XII, 19, 37, **536–38**, 895, 1052
Lawrence, Lockhart, XI, 502
Lawrence, Margaret. *See* Barr
Lawrence, Mary. *See* Hayes
Lawrence, Mary. *See* Wilson
Lawrence, Mary Jane. *See* Lockhart
Lawrence, Samuel, XII, 149
Lawrence, Sir Thomas, V, 543, 706; VII, 100, 875; VIII, 18; XII, 100
Lawrence, William Dawson, XI, 501
Lawrence, William Dawson, XI, **501–2**
Lawson, Alexander, XII, 539
Lawson, Alexander, VII, 417; XI, 348; XII, **538–39**
Lawson, Ann. *See* Atkinson
Lawson, Caroline Matilda. *See* Jordan
Lawson, Catherine (mother of ALEXANDER), XII, 538
Lawson, Daniel, XII, 538
Lawson, David, IV, 353, 551; V, 219, 262, 263, 310, **477–78**, 720; VI, 130
Lawson, Elizabeth. *See* Handyside
Lawson, Elizabeth (Curtis), V, 219
Lawson, Elizabeth (Fenerty), XII, 311
Lawson, Ellen (wife of DAVID), V, 477
Lawson, Frances. *See* Bell
Lawson, Frances Campbell. *See* Ring
Lawson, George, VIII, 894
Lawson, George, IX, 461, 462; X, 534; XI, 773; XII, 236, **539–42**, 990
Lawson, Henry, X, 211
Lawson, John (father of WILLIAM, 1772–1848), VII, 491; VIII, 704

Lawson, John (lawyer), X, 352
Lawson, Lucy. *See* Stapley
Lawson, Margaret. *See* McEwan
Lawson, Margaret (Wilkie), VIII, 936
Lawson, Mary Jane. *See* Katzmann
Lawson, Peter, XI, 907
Lawson, Sarah. *See* Shatford
Lawson, Sarah Ann (King), VIII, 472
Lawson, Sarah Elizabeth (Fairbanks), VII, 278
Lawson, William (father of WILLIAM, 1793–1875), X, 434
Lawson, William (husband of Mary Jane KATZMANN), XI, 462
Lawson, William, VI, 781; VII, 278, **491–93**, 933; VIII, 710; IX, 178; X, 7, 73, 293
Lawson, William, X, **434**
Lawton, George, VI, 399
Lawton, Sarah (Rogers), XI, 763
Lay, Robert W., XI, 321
Layssard. *See* Marafret
Lazare, Martin, IX, 600
Lazarus, Abraham, XII, 93
Lazarus, David, IV, 332
Lazarus, Frances (Hart), VII, 386, 388; VIII, 363; X, 337
Lazenby*, Emma (Spencer) (1834–1934), XII, 764
Lazenby, Mary (Shenston), XII, 967
Lazy Young Man. *See* Si'k-okskitsis
Lea, Annie (Lord), XI, 532
Lea, Clara Richmond (Stirling), XI, 856
Lea, John, XI, 532
Lea, Margaret (MacDonnell), X, 470
Leach, Elizabeth. *See* Turnbull
Leach, Eliza Margaret. *See* Easton
Leach, Jessie. *See* Skirving
Leach, Louisa. *See* Gwilt
Leach, Mary (Mountain), V, 613
Leach, Robert, XI, 502
Leach, William Turnbull, VIII, 67, 751; X, 607; XI, **502–4**
Leacock, Edward Philip, XI, 646
Leacock*, Stephen Butler (1869–1944), VII, 536; VIII, 59; IX, 357; XII, 232
Lead, William, III, 37
Leaden, William, VIII, 327
Leader, John Temple, X, 260
Leahey, Julia. *See* Doyle
Leahey, Mary (Kemp; wife of Robert), XI, 504
Leahey, Richard Henry, XI, **504–5**
Leahey, Robert, XI, 504
Leak, Elizabeth (Tuckett), XII, 1069
Leake, Andrew, II, 373
Leake, Christian. *See* Hill
Leake, Sir John, II, 226, 315, **372–73**, 637, 659
Leake, Richard (grandfather), II, 372
Leake, Richard, II, 373
Lean, Alexander, IV, 525
Lear, Edward, XII, 327
Learmont, William, XII, 62
Leatham, Elizabeth (Foulis), IX, 277
Leatherlips, V, 775
Leau. *See* Le Moyne
Leavens, Lydia (Chandler), X, 156
Leavenworth, Anne Fleming (Cameron), XII, 149
Leavenworth, Henry, VIII, 287
Leavis, Mr (assistant to Michael RICHARDS), II, 564

Leavitt, Daniel, VII, 683
Leavitt, Francis, VII, 683
Leavitt, Hephzibah. *See* Peabody
Leavitt, Jonathan, VII, 493, 683
Leavitt, Mary Ann. *See* Ketchum
Leavitt, Thomas, VII, 493
Le Baillif, Georges, I, 160, 194, 320, **433**, 437
Le Baillif, Olivier, I, 366, 452
Le Barbier, Marie (Marsolet de Saint-Aignan; Le Maistre), I, 494
Le Baron. *See also* Auger
Le Baron, II, 321; III, 446
Le Baron, Sarah (Hazen), V, 415
Le Barroys, Claude, I, 400, 617, 628, 629
Le Basque. *See* Bastarache
Lebasque. *See* Debigaré
Le Baudy, Catherine (Tour; Le Gouès de Sourdeval), II, 389
Lebé, Françoise. *See* Lemaître-Lamorille
Lebé, Marie-Bernadine (Foucher), III, 227
Lebeau, Dr, III, 676
Lebeau, Claude, II, **373–74**
Lebeau, Madeleine (Pépin), VII, 685
Lebel, Eugénie (Thériault), XII, 1034
Lebel, Félicité (Bouchard), XII, 117
Lebel, Guillaume, I, 66
Le Ber (Leber). *See also* Le Bret
Le Ber, Colette. *See* Cavelier
Le Ber, François, II, 374
Le Ber, Jacques, I, 105, 178, 284, 289, 295, 410, 416, 444, 464, 508; II, 29, 178, 272, 275, **374–76**, 377; III, 407; XII, 6
Le Ber, Jeanne. *See* Le Moyne
Le Ber, Jeanne, I, 117; II, 375, **376–77**; III, 407; IV, 530; IX, 248
Le Ber, Marie (Bourassa, *dit* La Ronde; Hervé), IV, 77
Le Ber, Marie, named de l'Annonciation, II, 374, 376
Le Ber, Pierre, I, 416; II, 127, 133, 134, 375, **377–78**; III, 407
Le Ber, Robert, II, 374
Le Ber de Saint-Paul, Louis, II, 375
Le Ber de Senneville, Jacques, II, 375, 377; III, 579; IV, 54
Le Ber de Senneville, Jean, IV, 265
Le Ber de Senneville, Marie-Louise (Benoist), IV, 54
Le Ber Du Chesne, Jean-Vincent, II, 133, 375, 376, 603
Le Berger. *See* Honatteniate
Le Berre, Charles-Joseph, IV, 387
Lebert, Michelle (Pépin, *dit* Laforce), III, 571; V, 470
Lebeuf, Calixte, XI, 488
Le Bey, Jean, II, 366
Le Blais, Charlotte (Le Courtois), IV, 443
LeBlanc*, Édouard-Alfred (1870–1935), XII, 548
Le Blanc, Angélique (Girroir), XI, 351
Leblanc, Anne (Ménage), II, 467
Leblanc, Antoine, III, 366; IV, 441
Leblanc, Augustin, XI, 506
Leblanc, Augustin, IX, 552; XI, **505–6**
Leblanc, Benjamin, IV, 78
Leblanc, Charles, X, 434
Leblanc, Charles-André, X, 153, 154, 249, **434–35**; XI, 7, 289, 891
Le Blanc, Claire (Landry), IV, 436
Le Blanc, Claire (Robichaux, *dit* Cadet), V, 719

Leblanc, Daniel, IV, xx
LeBlanc, Édouard (Nede), VII, 752
Le Blanc, Élisabeth. *See* Boudrot
Leblanc, Elmire (Desnoyers), X, 435
Leblanc, Emilie (wife of ÉTIENNE, 1839–97), XII, 543
Leblanc, Esther (Bourdages), IV, 78, 79; VI, 80
Leblanc, Étienne, XI, 505
Le Blanc, Étienne, V, 27; VI, **390**
Leblanc, Étienne, XII, **543**
Le Blanc, Félicité (Comeau), IX, 148
Le Blanc, Françoise. *See* Hébert
Le Blanc, Gertrude (Gaudet), V, 261
Le Blanc, Jacques, IV, 441
Le Blanc, Jean. *See* Outoutagan
Leblanc, Jean-Baptiste, IV, 78
Leblanc, Jean-Jacques, VI, 390
Leblanc, Jean-Olivier, VII, 448
Le Blanc, Joseph (brother of ÉTIENNE, d. 1831), VI, 390
Le Blanc, Joseph (son of PIERRE), IV, 441
Leblanc, Joseph, X, 422
Le Blanc, Josette. *See* Richerville
Leblanc, Judith (Milette), IX, 551
Leblanc, Julie. *See* Dumont
Leblanc, Julie. *See* Hébert
Leblanc, Louise. *See* Brien-Desrochers
Le Blanc, Madeleine. *See* Bourg
Le Blanc, Madeleine, known as La Couèche, IV, 441
Le Blanc, Marguerite. *See* Hébert
Leblanc, Marguerite. *See* Wilson
Leblanc, Marguerite (Dugas), IV, 239
Le Blanc, Marie. *See* Bourgeois
Le Blanc, Marie. *See* Hébert
Le Blanc, Marie. *See* Héon
Leblanc, Marie. *See* Tessier
Le Blanc, Marie-Anne (Paris), III, 501
Leblanc, Marie-Christine. *See* Delvecchio
Le Blanc, Marie-Madeleine. *See* Babin
Le Blanc, Marie-Marguerite (Doucet), IV, 222
Leblanc, Marie-Mathilde (Dunn), X, 435; XI, 288
Le Blanc, Melina (wife of ÉTIENNE, 1839–97), XII, 543
Le Blanc, Nancy. *See* McKenzie
Le Blanc, Nathalie (Babineau), XI, 39
Le Blanc, Noël, II, 608
Le Blanc, Pierre (brother-in-law of Alexander BOURG, *dit* Belle-Humeur), III, 421
Le Blanc, Pierre (husband of Nancy McKENZIE), VIII, 561
Le Blanc, Pierre, IV, xxix, 222, **441**; V, 261; VI, 228
Leblanc, Pierre-Cajetan, VI, 186
Leblanc*, Pierre-Évariste (1853–1918), XII, 88
Leblanc, René, IV, xx, 78
Leblanc, Thérèse (Bruneau), VIII, 108
Leblanc, *dit* Latour, François, V, 656
Leblanc, *dit* Le Maigre, Anne. *See* Bourg, *dit* Belle-Humeur
Leblanc, *dit* Le Maigre, Anne (Gautier), V, 339
Leblanc, *dit* Le Maigre, Joseph, III, 84, 255, **366–67**; IV, xxv, 239, 240, **441**; V, 339
Leblanc de Marconnay, Hyacinthe-Poirier, VII, 353, 354, 412, 427; VIII, 260; IX, 100, **458–59**, 697
Le Bland, Jean. *See* Outoutagan
Le Bléis, Loetitia-Constance-Marie (Bray), X, 89
Leblond. *See also* Jacquiés
Leblond, Jacques (lawyer), VII, 876

Leblond, Jacques (merchant), VI, 50; VII, 119
Leblond, Joseph (father-in-law of Guillaume-Eugène CHINIC), XI, 190
Leblond, Joseph (freemason), VII, 689
Leblond, Joseph (husband of Julie Perrault), VIII, 864
Leblond, Joseph (merchant), VII, 119
Leblond, Julie. *See* Perrault
Leblond, Marie-Anne-Claire (Chinic), XI, 190
Leblond, Marie-Charles (Huot), VI, 336
Leblond de Latour, Antoine, II, 378
Leblond de Latour, Jacques, II, 338, **378–80**, 451; III, 648
Leblond de Latour, Marc-Antoine, II, 378
Leblond de Latour, Pierre, II, 378
Le Bloy, Françoise (Gannes de Falaise), II, 236
Lebœuf, Monsieur (landowner), II, 338
Lebœuf, *dit* Laflamme, Toussaint, XII, 505
Lebon, Pierre, I, 114
Lebon, *dit* Laîné, Damase, XI, 152
Le Borgne, Chevalier, III, 232
Le Borgne, Emmanuel, I, 62, 90, 129, 234, 257, 258, 259, 379, 380, **433–35**, 468, 469, 504, 505, 514, 595, 604
Le Borgne, Jeanne. *See* François
Le Borgne, Jeanne (Bazire), I, 84
Le Borgne de Belle-Isle, Alexandre, II, 3, 7; III, 567
Le Borgne de Belle-Isle, Alexandre, I, 62, 426, 433, 434, **435–36**, 513, 514, 636; II, 581
Le Borgne de Belle-Isle, Anne (Rodrigue; Duperié), II, 581, 582; IV, 678
Le Borgne de Belle-Isle, Marie. *See* Saint-Étienne de La Tour
Le Borgne de Belle-Isle, Marie-Josephe. *See* Abbadie de Saint-Castin
Le Borgne de Belle-Isle, Marie-Josephe (Rondeau; Du Pont Duvivier), III, 567; IV, 783
Le Borgne de l'Île. *See* Tessouat
Le Borgne Du Coudray, André, I, 436
Le Borgne Du Coudray, Emmanuel, I, 434, 435
Le Boucher, Marie (Auber), I, 72
Le Boulanger, Charlotte (Gastineau Duplessis), III, 237
Le Boulanger, Madeleine-Louise (Poulin), III, 537
Le Boulanger, Marie-Anne, III, 233
Le Boulanger, Marie-Renée (Lemoine, *dit* Despins), IV, 461, 462
Le Boulanger (Boulanger), Pierre, II, 16
Le Boullenger, Jean-Antoine, II, 455, 469
Lebourdais, A., X, 653
Lebourdais, *dit* Lapierre, Jacques, V, 77; XI, 86
Le Bourguignon. *See* Couturier
Le Boutillier, Amy, VIII, 493
Le Boutillier, Anne. *See* Amy
Le Boutillier, David, VIII, **493–94**; XII, 310
Le Boutillier, Edward, VIII, 493
Le Boutillier, Elizabeth. *See* Robin
Le Boutillier, Henriette-Marie (Fauvel), XII, 309
Le Boutillier, John, VIII, 155, 156, 196, 257; X, **435**; XI, 320; XII, 309
Le Boutillier, Josué, VIII, 493
Leboux, Guillaume, II, 419
Le Bovier de Fontenelle, Bernard, II, 422, 595
Le Bret (Leber, Le Ber), Élisabeth (Moyen Des Granges), I, 231, 295
Le Breton, Guillaume, I, 167
Le Breton, Jane (wife of John), VII, 493

Lebreton, Jeanne (Villieu), II, 653
Le Breton, John, VII, 493
Le Breton, John, VI, 630, 631; VII, **493–95**, 795; VIII, 69
Le Breton, Madeleine (Bernières, Baronne d'Acqueville), I, 91
Lebreton, Marie-Anne-Rosalie (Leroy), XI, 512
Le Breton, Susan. *See* George
Lebreton, *dit* Lalancette, Pierre-Henri, V, 248
Le Breton-Bastille, Guillaume, I, 167
Le Brochet. *See* Kinongé
LeBrun. *See* Brown
Le Brun, Monsieur (company director), II, 417, 418
Le Brun, François, III, 360
Lebrun, Isidore-Frédéric-Thomas, VI, 40; VIII, 593; IX, 298, 299, 300, 301
Le Brun, Jean, III, 550
Lebrun de Duplessis, Élizabeth (Ferland), IX, 254
Lebrun de Duplessis, Jean-Baptiste, V, 478
Lebrun de Duplessis, Jean-Baptiste, V, **478–80**; IX, 254
Lebrun de Duplessis, Julie-Louise (Beckwith), IX, 38; X, 41
Lebrun de Duplessis, Marie. *See* Champigny
Lebrun de Duplessis, Marie-Catherine. *See* Mettot
Le Cadet. *See* Chomina
Le Cain (Le Quesne), Alicia Maria (Ritchie), IV, 675; VIII, 751
Le Cain (Le Quesne), Francis Barclay, IV, 675
Le Camus. *See also* Camus
Le Camus, Étienne, II, 328
Le Caron, Henri. *See* Beach, Thomas Billis
Le Caron, Joseph, I, 58, 193, 222, 223, 265, 385, 386, 433, **436–38**, 511, 546, 590, 591, 612, 661
Le Caron, Nannie. *See* Melville
Lecarulier. *See* Sareillier
Le Castor. *See* Largillier
Le Cavelier, Adrienne. *See* Duvivier
Le Cavelier, Marie-Madeleine (Forestier), II, 68, 226; III, 220
Lecavelier, Toussaint, IV, 58
Le Cavelier, *dit* Deslauriers, Robert, II, 226
Lechasseur, Jean, I, 286; II, 252, **380**, 518, 529
Le Chasseur, Roger-Chrétien, III, 553; IV, 539
Lechassier, François, II, 96, 567; III, 221, 342, 486
Le Chauvreulx. *See* Chauvreulx
Le Chevalier, Jeanne-Marguerite (Lévesque; Deschamps de La Bouteillerie), II, 181
Le Chevalier Roome, John, IV, 329
Lechtier (Lechter) de Chalus, Monsieur (ship's captain), II, 304
Leckie, Robert, XI, 130
Leclair, François, V, 727
Le Clair, Jean-Baptiste, II, 380
Leclair, Pierre, II, 528
Leclaire, Catherine (Langevin), VIII, 487
Leclaire, Éloïse (Labelle), IX, 437
Leclaire, R., I, 77
Leclerc. *See also* Leclère
Leclerc, Alix, I, 115
Leclerc, Anastasie. *See* Perrault
Leclerc, Georges-Louis, Comte de Buffon, III, 263, 334, 679; VI, 85; V, 182
Leclerc, Hilaire, I, 447
Leclerc, Ignace (merchant), IV, 90; V, 242

Leclerc, Ignace (professor), XII, 159
Le Clerc, Jacques, II, 509; III, 352
Leclerc, Jacques-Sébastien, VI, 24
Leclerc, Jean-Baptiste, II, **380–81**
Leclerc, Jean-Benoît, XI, 506
Leclerc, Louise (Guillet), IX, 344
Leclerc, Marguerite. *See* Bétourné
Leclerc, Marguerite. *See* Pepin
Leclerc, Marie. *See* Jallais
Leclerc, Michel, V, 480
Leclerc, Michel, IV, 318; V, 92, **480–81**; VIII, 777
Leclerc, Nazaire, XI, **506–8**; XII, 869
Leclerc, Robert, II, 380
Le Clercq, Chrestien, I, 14, 211, 222, 223, 265, 411, 433, 437, **438–41**, 509, 552, 661; II, xxxiii, 174, 197, 217, 230, 278, 396, 419, 477; III, xxxvi, 416
Le Clercq, Maxime, I, 438; II, 421
Leclère, Josephte. *See* Castonguay
Leclère, Marie-Anne. *See* Bourg
Leclère, Pierre-Édouard, VI, 783; VII, 411, 625, 626, 717, 758; VIII, 729, 735; IX, **459–60**, 814; XI, 586, 708
Leclère, *dit* Lafrenaye, Pierre, IX, 459
Le Cocq. *See* Le Coq
Le Cointre, Anne, named de Saint-Bernard, I, 310, 347, 353
Le Collier Pendu. *See* Kaghswaghtaniunt
Lecompte. *See* Le Conte Dupré
Lecompte, Jean, I, 267
Le Comte. *See* Lenoir
Le Comte Dupré, Catherine. *See* Martel de Brouague
Le Comte Dupré, Catherine (Juchereau Duchesnay), V, 231, 463, 464, 482, 881; VI, 368; VII, 461, 785
Le Comte Dupré, Françoise (Le Moine), V, 482
Le Comte Dupré, Georges-Hippolyte, known as Saint-Georges Dupré, III, 367; IV, 427, **441–43**, 549; V, 43, 383, 481, 482, 652
Le Comte Dupré, Jean-Baptiste (son of JEAN-BAPTISTE, 1731–1820), V, 482
Le Comte Dupré, Jean-Baptiste, III, **367**; IV, 347, 442; V, 320, 481
Le Comte Dupré, Jean-Baptiste, III, 367; IV, 442; V, 95, 231, 463, **481–82**
Le Comte Dupré, Louise-Charlotte, V, 482
Le Comte Dupré, Marie-Angélique (Cugnet), V, 482
Le Comte Dupré, Marie-Anne. *See* Hervieux
Le Comte Dupré, Marie-Anne (Hertel de Saint- François), IV, 347, 348
Le Comte Dupré, Marie-Charlotte. *See* Liénard de Beaujeu
Le Comte Dupré, Marie-Louise-Charlotte. *See* La Corne
Le Comte Dupré, Pierre-Hippolyte, IV, 442
Le Comte Dupré, Thérèse (Baby), IV, 38; V, 41
Le Conte, Anne. *See* Defosse
Le Conte, Charles, II, 381
LeConte, John Lawrence, XI, 108
Le Conte Dupré, Louis, II, 81, 131, **381**; III, 367, 390; V, 481
Le Conte Dupré, Marie-Catherine. *See* Saint-Georges
Le Conte Dupré, Marie-Charlotte (Charly Saint-Ange), II, 131; III, 110
Le Coq, Robert, I, **441**
Le Coq de La Saussaye, René, I, 67, 68, 69, 95, 98, 101, 299, 367, **441–42**
L'Écossais. *See* Martin, Abraham

Lecourt, Alexandrine-Victorine-Georgiana (Tassé), XII, 1025
Lecourt, Charles, III, 524
Lecourt, Joseph-Pierre-Michel, VII, 680
Le Courtois, Charlotte. *See* Le Blais
Le Courtois, François-Gabriel, IV, 136; VI, **390–91**; VII, 246; VIII, 201
Le Courtois, Thomas, IV, 443
Le Courtois de Surlaville, Michel, III, 498; IV, **443–44**, 644, 645, 655, 656, 657, 688
Lecoustre, Claude, I, 91
Le Couteulx, Monsieur (suspected spy), VIII, 605
Le Couteur, Sarah (Mauger), IV, 525
Le Couteux, Marie (La Place), I, 338; II, 345
Le Coutre de Bourville, Élisabeth. *See* Faustin
Le Coutre de Bourville, François, III, 367
Le Coutre de Bourville, François, II, 226, 412; III, 98, **367–69**; IV, 15, 247, 466
Le Coutre de Bourville, Marie-Anne. *See* Rousseau de Villejouin
Lecq, Elizabeth de (Janvrin), VI, 347
Le Creux Du Breuil, Anne. *See* Motin
Le Creux Du Breuil, Nicolas, I, **442**, 503, 514, 568, 642
Le Crochet. *See* Kiotseaeton
Lecron. *See* Lekron
L'Écuyer, Eugène, IX, 440
Lécuyer, François, VI, 557
Lecuyer, Joseph, VI, 664
L'Écuyer, Mathilde (Plamondon), XII, 853
Le Cygne. *See* Onasakenrat, Joseph
Le Derniers. *See* Delesdernier
Ledesma, Jacques, I, 125
Le Despencer, Baron. *See* Dashwood
Lediard, Thomas, II, 662
Ledieu, Léon, XI, 716
Ledingham, Agnes. *See* Allan
Ledingham, Anna Maria Brown. *See* Rogers
Ledingham, John, XII, 543
Ledingham, John, XII, **543–44**
Le Dorz, Bénin, II, **381–82**
Le Dossu d'Hébécourt, Louis-Philippe, III, 85
Ledoux, Claude-Nicolas, VIII, 761
Ledoux, Marie-Josephte (Mignault), IX, 548
Ledroit, *dit* Perche, Anne (Audivert, *dit* Romain), VI, 658
Ledroit, *dit* Perche, Louise (Lefrançois), VI, 391
Ledru, Jean-Antoine, IV, **444–45**; V, 124, 306; VII, 801
Le Dru, Pierre, V, 800
Leduc, Anne-Françoise, named Saint-Joseph, III, 238, **369**
Leduc, Catherine (Gaillard), II, 234
Leduc, Clovis, VIII, 328
Leduc, Élisabeth (Guy), III, 271
Leduc, Geneviève (Cheval; Migneron), III, 121
Leduc, Hippolyte, XII, 23
Leduc, Hortense (Jehin-Prume), XII, 472
Leduc, Jean, III, 369
Leduc, Jean-Baptiste, VI, 316
Leduc, Marie. *See* Soulignié
Leduc, Marie, III, 369
Leduc, Philippe, III, 234
Leduc Des Fontaines, Jessé, II, 149, 151, 448
Le Duff, Michel-Ange, II, 382
Ledyard, John, V, 80
Lee, Abigail (Lawrason), XI, 501

Lee, Ann (Street), VI, 739
Lee, Annie Jane (Baldwin), XII, 51
Lee, Arthur Brindley, XII, 994
Lee, Caroline (Haviland), IV, 334
Lee, Catherine (Dumas), V, 278
Lee, Charles, IV, 606; V, 147
Lee, Charlotte, Countess of Lichfield. See Fitzroy
Lee, Dorothy (Temple), I, 636
Lee, Edmund, I, 636
Lee, Edward, I, 643
Lee, Edward Henry, 1st Earl of Lichfield, III, 369
Lee, Elizabeth (Hamilton), IV, 321
Lee, Fitzroy Henry, III, 324, **369–70**
Lee, Sir Francis, XI, 294
Lee, Harriet. See Lockwood
Lee, Harriet Louisa. See Smith
Lee, Helena (Durie), XI, 294
Lee, Jason, VIII, 578
Lee, John (partner of François MOUNIER), III, 477
Lee, John (uncle of Louis RIEL, 1844–85), XI, 744
Lee, Joseph, V, 482
Lee, Lucy (mother of SAMUEL), V, 482
Lee, Mary. See Neilson
Lee, Rachel (Gold), XI, 365
Lee, Robert, VII, 765; X, 456
Lee, Robert Edward, X, 334
Lee, Ruth (Jones), VI, 363
Lee, Samuel, V, **482–83**, 795; VI, 263; VIII, 292
Lee, Sarah (wife of SAMUEL), V, 482
Lee, Selina (Chisholm; Thomson), IX, 788
Lee, Thomas (merchant), III, 477; IV, 187; V, 278
Lee, Thomas (notary), V, 84; VI, 40, 50, 95, 281, 591, 763;
    VIII, 491
Lee, Thomas (road supervisor), VI, 518
Lee, Thomas Conrad, XII, 51, 52
Lee, Thomas Hawkins, VIII, 446
Lee*, Walter Sutherland (1836–1902), XII, 43
Lee, William, X, 435
Lee, William Henry, X, **435–36**; XI, 203, 204
Leech, Mary. See Macdonald
Leech, Peter, XII, 544
Leech, Peter John, XII, 130, **544–45**
Leech, Susan (mother of PETER JOHN), XII, 544
Leech, Susan (Colclough), VI, 160
Leeds, Duke of. See Osborne
Leeds, John, V, 614
Leek. See Macdonell; MacDonell
Leeming, Margaret Hickman. See England
Leeming, Ralph, VI, 3, 373, 528, 758; VII, 520; X, **436–37**
Leeming, Susan. See Hatt
Leeming, Thomas, XII, 47
Leeming, William, VI, 528; X, 437; XI, 326
Lees, Sir Harcourt, X, 309
Lees, Jane, V, 485
Lees, John (brother of JOHN), V, 483
Lees, John (mechanic), VII, 505
Lees, John, IV, 317, 320; V, 181, 182, 277, 283, **483–85**;
    VI, 296, 515; VII, 64, 65, 66, 387
Lees, Mary (Steven), IX, 745
Lees, Nancy, V, 485
Lees, Sarah, V, 485
Leeser, Isaac, XI, 254
Leeves, Elizabeth Juliana (Sabine, Lady Sabine), XI, 798

Lefaivre, Robert-Alexis, X, 690
Lefaivre, dit Despins, Marie-Philie (Marchildon), VIII, 617
Le Fascheux de Couttes, Françoise (Lom d'Arce), II, 440
Le Faucheur, Monsieur (defendant), I, 161
Lefebvre, Anne. See Anjoult
Lefebvre, Apolline. See Abraham
Lefebvre, Camille, IX, 452; XI, 350; **545–50**, 891, 1035
Lefebvre, François, III, 346
Lefebvre, Geneviève. See Pelletier
Lefebvre, Gervais, III, 312
Lefebvre, Hyacinthe, II, 278
Lefebvre, Jacques, II, 382, 529
Lefebvre, Jean, III, 38, 210, 224, 271, 280, 281, 282, 305,
    **370–71**; IV, 45, 476; V, 41, 276
Lefebvre, Jean-Baptiste (father-in-law of Jean-Baptiste
    RENAUD), X, 613
Lefebvre, Jean-Baptiste (politician), VI, 381, 386; VII, 172;
    VIII, 791
Lefebvre, Jeanne. See Aunois
Lefebvre, Jeanne (Descaris; Tessier, dit Lavigne), IV, 732
Lefebvre, Louis, XII, 546
Lefebvre, Madeleine (Serres), V, 752
Lefebvre, Marie (Rochbrune, dit Larocque), XII, 530
Lefebvre, Marie-Anne (Poulin de Courval Cressé), III, 539
Lefebvre, Marie-Catherine (Valois), IX, 802
Lefebvre*, Marie-Elmina, named Marie de l'Eucharistie
    (1862–1946), IX, 364
Lefebvre, Marie-Hélène (Aide-Créquy), IV, 8
Lefebvre, Marie-Madeleine (Minet; Simon; Olivier), III,
    494
Lefebvre, Marie-Sophie (Renaud), IX, 363; X, 613; XI, 727
Lefebvre, Marie-Soulange (Bardy), IX, 32
Lefebvre, Pierre, II, 382
Lefebvre, Thomas, II, 382
Lefebvre, Thomas, II, **382**; III, 371
Lefebvre, Timothée, II, 382
Lefebvre, Véronique. See Bouthillier
Lefebvre, dit Boulanger, Anastasie (Couture), XI, 207
Lefebvre, dit Duchouquet, Angélique (Sanguinet), IV, 697
Lefebvre, dit Laciseraye, Catherine. See Trottier
Lefebvre, dit Laciseraye, Marie-Anne (Alavoine), III, 7
Lefebvre, dit Laciseraye, Michel, II, **382–83**
Lefebvre Angers, Geneviève-Françoise. See Faucher
Lefebvre Angers, Jean-Baptiste, III, 371
Lefebvre Angers, Marie-Angélique, named Saint-Simon,
    III, **371**; IV, 638; V, 703
Lefebvre Angers, Simon, III, 371
Lefebvre Belle-Isle, Marie-Josephte, named Saint-Benoît,
    III, 630
Lefebvre de Bellefeuille, Anne. See Baudry
Lefebvre de Bellefeuille, Antoine, IV, 446; V, 217; VI,
    385; VII, 495
Lefebvre de Bellefeuille, Eustache-Antoine, VIII, 791
Lefebvre de Bellefeuille, François, III, 372; IV, 29, **445–46**;
    V, 902
Lefebvre de Bellefeuille, Geneviève (Angeac), IV, 29
Lefebvre de Bellefeuille, Georges, III, 372; IV, 445, 446
Lefebvre de Bellefeuille, Jean-François, III, **371–72**; IV,
    445
Lefebvre* de Bellefeuille, Joseph-Édouard (1840–1926),
    IX, 63, 64, 65; X, 252, 537; XI, 13
Lefebvre de Bellefeuille, Louis-Charles, VII, **495–96**; X,
    532

Lefebvre de Bellefeuille, Louise-Angélique. *See* Lambert Dumont

Lefebvre de Bellefeuille, Marie-Josephte. *See* Hertel de Cournoyer

Lefebvre de Bellefeuille, Pierre (uncle), III, 372

Lefebvre de Bellefeuille, Pierre, IV, 445, 446

Lefebvre de Cheverus, Jean-Louis, X, 688

Le Febvre de La Barre, Monsieur, known as Chevalier de La Barre (grandson of Joseph-Antoine LE FEBVRE de La Barre), I, 446

Le Febvre de La Barre, Anne-Marie (Guillouet d'Orvilliers), II, 269, 270

Le Febvre de La Barre, Antoine, I, 442

Le Febvre de La Barre, Joseph-Antoine, I, 103, 105, 114, 130, 137, 178, 179, 180, 227, 295, 338, **442–46**, 464, 465, 488, 523, 525, 526, 541, 554, 576, 650; II, 31, 32, 48, 49, 60, 61, 63, 98, 99, 101, 112, 120, 137, 162, 169, 194, 195, 205, 214, 217, 222, 223, 228, 237, 247, 252, 253, 261, 263, 270, 282, 302, 307, 341, 343, 375, 380, 390, 401, 440, 470, 471, 472, 473, 488, 517, 518, 532, 538, 575, 576, 586, 617, 620, 624, 634, 635, 641; III, 82, 373

Le Febvre de La Barre, Madeleine. *See* Belin

Le Febvre de La Barre, Marie. *See* Mandat

Lefebvre de Laubrière, Louise (Arsac, Marquise de Ternay), IV, 31

Lefebvre-Duchouquet, Charles, IV, 639

Lefebvre-Duchouquet, Charles-Joseph, V, 164

Lefebvre Du Guesclin, Dominique, I, 409

Lefebvre Duplessis Faber, Catherine-Geneviève. *See* Pelletier

Lefebvre Duplessis Faber, François, II, 69, 70, 578; III, 372

Lefebvre Duplessis Faber, François, III, 205, **372–73**, 375, 505, 611, 637; IV, 77

Lefebvre Duplessis Faber, François-Hippolyte, III, 373

Lefebvre Duplessis Faber, Joseph-Alphonse, III, 373

Lefebvre Duplessis Faber, Madeleine. *See* Chorel de Saint-Romain, *dit* d'Orvilliers

Lefebvre Duplessis Faber, Pierre, III, 372

Le Fène. *See* Phlem

Lefevre. *See also* Shaw-Lefevre

Le Fevre, François, II, 271, **383**

Lefevre, Marie (De La Vigne; Bailly), VI, 29

Lefèvre d'Albon, Paul, II, 270

Lefferty, Bryan, VII, 496

Lefferty, John Johnston, VI, 632; VII, 314, **496–98**; VIII, 69

Lefferty, Mary. *See* Johnson

Le Flot, Michelle (Perrot, *dit* Vildaigre), II, 520

Le Fourreur. *See* Foureur

Lefouyn, Marie-Madeleine (Dupuy), II, 207

Lefranc, Marie-Catherine (Baveux), IX, 34

Le Franc, Marin-Louis (Marie-Louis), IV, 241; VI, 751

Lefrançois, Alexis (clergyman), V, 13

Lefrançois, Alexis (relative of Pierre PERROT de Rizy), II, 520

Lefrançois, Charles, V, 211; VI, 47, **391–92**, 750; VII, 504

Lefrançois, Joseph-Philippe, VI, 287

Lefrançois, Louise. *See* Ledroit, *dit* Perche

Lefrançois, Marie. *See* Vézina

Lefrançois, Nicolas (father of CHARLES), VI, 391

Lefrançois, Nicolas (relative of Pierre PERROT de Rizy), II, 520

Lefrançois, Pierre, II, 520

Lefrançois de Lalande, Joseph-Jérôme, IV, 636, 637; VIII, 212

Lefroy, Charlotte Anna, Lady Lefroy. *See* Dundas

Lefroy, Emily Mary. *See* Robinson

Lefroy, Sir John Henry, VII, 499; XI, 475, **508–10**, 569, 799; XII, 101, 876, 1110

Lefroy, John Henry George, XI, 508

Lefroy, Sophia. *See* Cottrell

Lefroy, Sophia Anna (Hawkins), IX, 378

Left Hand, XII, 970

Legacé, Monsieur (teacher), VIII, 250

Legacé, Josette (Work), IX, 853; XII, 317, **550–51**

Legacé, Pierre, XII, 550

Le Gagneur, Monsieur (ship's captain), II, 61

Legaic (probably great-uncle of PAUL), XII, 551

Legaic (uncle of PAUL), XII, 551

Legaic, Paul, XII, **551–52**

Le Gall, Jacques, I, 425

Le Gallais, Fanny Harriet. *See* Langrishe

Le Gallais, Richard, IX, 460

Le Gallais, Susan. *See* Mason

Le Gallais, Wellmein William, IX, **460**

Le Gallois de Beaujeu, Taneguy, I, 180, 181, 182

Legardeur, Marguerite (Dubreuil), II, 201

Legardeur, Marie-Madeleine. *See* Blondeau

Legardeur de Beauvais, Louise. *See* Lamy

Legardeur de Beauvais, Madeleine. *See* Marchand

Legardeur de Beauvais, Marie-Barbe. *See* Saint-Ours

Legardeur de Beauvais, Marie-Renée (Chaussegros de Léry), III, 116; IV, 145

Legardeur de Beauvais, René, III, 357

Legardeur de Beauvais, René, I, 650; III, 116, 119, **373–74**; IV, 463

Le Gardeur de Courtemanche, Augustin, II, 7, 8, 9, 13, 17, 114, 172, 185, 218, 287, **383–84**, 437, 458, 459, 523, 533, 567, 575, 603, 651; III, 134, 135, 228, 429, 433

Legardeur de Courtemanche, Jacques-François, IV, 192

Legardeur de Courtemanche, Marie, IV, 192

Le Gardeur de Courtemanche, Marie-Charlotte. *See* Charest

Le Gardeur de Courtemanche, Marie-Joseph (Foucher), III, 228

Legardeur de Croisille, Charles, II, 669; III, 367, **374**; IV, 446

Legardeur de Croisille, Marie-Anne-Geneviève. *See* Robinau de Bécancour

Legardeur de Croisille et de Montesson, Claire-Françoise. *See* Boucher de Boucherville

Legardeur de Croisille et de Montesson, Joseph-Michel, III, 525; IV, 109, 213, **446–47**, 512, 651; V, 97

Legardeur de La Mothe-Tilly, Jean-Baptiste, III, 376

Legardeur de La Mothe-Tilly, Jeanne-Élisabeth. *See* Girard

Legardeur de Moncarville et de Tilly. *See* Legardeur de Tilly

Legardeur de Repentigny, Agathe. *See* Saint-Père

Legardeur de Repentigny, Agathe (Bouat), II, 82

Legardeur de Repentigny, Catherine (Ailleboust Des Muceaux), I, 47, 447; II, 12, 13, 14, 421; III, 7

Legardeur de Repentigny, Catherine-Angélique. *See* Payen de Noyan et de Chavoy

Le Gardeur de Repentigny, Ignace, II, 386

Legardeur de Repentigny, Jean-Baptiste, I, 517; II, 27, 383, **384–85**, 386; III, 374

Legardeur de Repentigny, Jean-Baptiste-René, II, 156, 385; IV, 447, 448

Legardeur de Repentigny, Louis, III, 69, 119; IV, **447–48**, 449, 733; V, 128, 129, 231; VI, 547

Legardeur de Repentigny, Louis-Gaspard, IV, 448

Legardeur de Repentigny, Marguerite. *See* Nicollet de Belleborne

Legardeur de Repentigny, Marguerite (Leneuf de La Poterie), I, 446, 467, 468, 575; II, 409

Legardeur de Repentigny, Marguerite (Saint-Ours Deschaillons), III, 578

Legardeur de Repentigny, Marguerite-Jeanne. *See* Mignon

Legardeur de Repentigny, Marie. *See* Favery

Legardeur de Repentigny, Marie-Catherine. *See* Juchereau de Saint-Denis

Legardeur de Repentigny, Marie-Jeanne-Madeleine, named de Sainte-Agathe, II, **385**; III, 581

Legardeur de Repentigny, Marie-Joseph, named de la Visitation, III, 319, 544, 581

Legardeur de Repentigny, Marie-Madeleine (Godefroy), I, 340, 447

Legardeur de Repentigny, Marie-Madeleine-Régis. *See* Chaussegros de Léry

Legardeur de Repentigny, Pierre, I, 216, 287, 330, 339, 353, 402, **446–47**, 467, 495; II, 105, 385

Legardeur de Repentigny, Pierre, II, 306, **385–86**, 459, 655; III, 579, 581

Legardeur de Repentigny, Pierre-Jean-Baptiste-François-Xavier, III, 289, 304; IV, **448–49**, 576, 612

Legardeur de Saint-Pierre, Jacques, II, 387; III, 46, 48, 151, 158, 162, 178, 243, 245, 322, 331, 332, 347, **374–76**, 611, 623; IV, 66, 256, 363, 426, 512, 514, 617, 618; V, 98

Legardeur de Saint-Pierre, Jean-Paul, II, 12, 317, 324, **386–87**, 415; III, 105, 291, 374

Legardeur de Saint-Pierre, Marguerite (Hiché), III, 291, 292

Legardeur de Saint-Pierre, Marie-Anne (Nolan Lamarque), III, 485

Legardeur de Saint-Pierre, Marie-Joseph. *See* Guillimin

Legardeur de Saint-Pierre, Marie-Josette. *See* Leneuf de La Vallière

Legardeur de Tilly, Monsieur (officer), III, 377

Legardeur de Tilly, Anne-Geneviève. *See* Rocbert de La Morandière

Legardeur de Tilly, Armand, III, 377

Legardeur de Tilly, Catherine. *See* Cordé

Legardeur de Tilly, Catherine (Saurel), I, 602; II, 59, 593

Legardeur de Tilly, Charles, I, 145, 288, 402, 446, **447–48**, 467, 468, 581, 582, 587, 588, 602; II, 32, 125, 167, 236, 387, 584, 593; III, 373; IV, 33

Legardeur de Tilly, Françoise-Charlotte (Damours de Clignancour), II, 167

Legardeur de Tilly, Geneviève. *See* Juchereau de Maur

Legardeur de Tilly, Geneviève-Gertrude (Céloron de Blainville), II, 125

Legardeur de Tilly, Jean-Baptiste, III, **376–77**, 582

Legardeur de Tilly, Louise (Gannes de Falaise), II, 236

Legardeur de Tilly, Madeleine. *See* Boucher

Legardeur de Tilly, Madeleine-Angélique (Aubert de Gaspé), IV, 33

Legardeur de Tilly, Marguerite. *See* Volant

Legardeur de Tilly, Marguerite (Le Gouès de Grais; Saint-Ours; Le Moyne de Longueuil, Baronne de Longueuil), II, 403, 593; III, 385

Legardeur de Tilly, Marie (Berthier), II, 59

Legardeur de Tilly, Marie-Anne, III, 377

Legardeur de Tilly, Marie-Louise (Rouer de Villeray et de La Cardonnière), II, 584; III, 570

Legardeur de Tilly, Pierre-Noël, I, 448; II, 32, **387**

Legardeur de Tilly, René, I, 446, 447

Legardeur de Villiers, Charles-Pierre, II, 517

Legardeur de Villiers, Marie-Charlotte (Robinau de Bécancour, Baronne de Portneuf), II, 577; III, 374

Légaré, Antoine, X, **437**; XI, 457

Légaré, Cyrille-Étienne, IX, 120, 800; XII, 269; XII, 1123

Légaré, Geneviève. *See* Damien

Légaré, Ignace, X, 437

Légaré*, Jean-Louis (1841–1918), XI, 870

Légaré, Joseph, VIII, 289, 494

Légaré, Joseph, V, 72; VI, 28, 300, 763; VII, 194, 246, 427, 744, 789, 790, 870; VIII, 138, **494–98**, 629; IX, 33, 361; X, 410; XI, 15, 928; 321, 845, 846, 847

Légaré, Louise. *See* Routier

Légaré, Marie. *See* Parant

Le Gaudier, Antoine, I, 411

Le Gauffre, Thomas, II, 361

Le Gay de Beaulieu, Jean-Jérôme, II, 127, 673

Le Gay de Beaulieu, Madeleine. *See* Just

Le Gay de Beaulieu, Marie (Migeon de La Gauchetière), III, 450

Le Gay de Beaulieu, Marie-Madeleine (Chabert de Joncaire), II, 126; III, 101; IV, 137

Legendre, François, VII, 711

Legendre, Jean-Baptiste, VII, 166

Legendre, Lucas, I, 293

Legendre, Marie-Anne. *See* Proulx

Legendre*, Napoléon (1841–1907), IX, 65; XI, 290, 513; XII, 271, 308

Léger, César, I, 557

Léger, Élie, II, 387

Léger, Jeanne. *See* Félix

Léger, Louise. *See* Fauvel

Léger, Marie. *See* Des Reaux

Léger, Marie-Jeanne (Picard), IV, 628

Léger de La Grange, Jean, II, 17, 138, 205, 246, **387–88**, 531

Legex. *See* Legaic

Legge, Charles, XI, **510–11**

Legge, Francis, IV, 29, 53, 111, 116, 132, 209, 266, 267, 274, 275, 292, 309, 389, **449–52**, 529, 562, 581, 603, 705, 706, 737, 764; V, 81, 82, 216, 545, 548, 607, 608, 660, 670; VI, 310, 511

Legge, George, 1st Baron Dartmouth, I, 92

Legge, William, 1st Earl of Dartmouth, II, 583, 637

Legge, William, 2nd Earl of Dartmouth, III, 111; IV, xxxviii, xxxix, xlv, xlvi, xlvii, 175, 275, 281, 309, 321, 349, 449, 450, 451, 452, 484, 571, 607, 676, 686, 726, 737, 759, 789, 790; V, 142, 143, 145, 146, 147, 220, 843; VI, 511, 615

Leggett, Elizabeth Bond (Morris), V, 607; VI, 519

Leggett, Sibylla Amelia Maria Sophia (Morris), X, 534

Leggo, William, X, 359

Leggo, William Augustus, XII, 247

Leggo*, William Augustus (1830–1915), XII, 247, 248, 249

Legion. *See* Sullivan, Robert Baldwin
Le Gouès de Grais, Catherine-Charlotte (Le Moyne de Longueuil, Baronne de Longueuil), III, 385
Le Gouès de Grais, Louis-Joseph, II, 403; III, 385
Le Gouès de Grais, Marguerite. *See* Legardeur de Tilly
Le Gouès de Merville, Claude-Charles, I, 465; II, 125
Le Gouès de Sourdeval, Catherine. *See* Le Baudy
Le Gouès de Sourdeval, Sébastien, II, **388–89**, 511
Legrand, Alexandre, XII, 848
Legrand, François, II, 374
Legrand, Jean-Baptiste, V, 322, 323, 324
Legrand, Marie, Dame Du Faradon (Normant), III, 486
Legrand, Thérèse (Foretier), V, 322, 323, 324, 325; VIII, 301
Le Grand Agnier. *See* Togouiroui
Legrand de Sintré, Gabriel-Christophe, III, 102
Le Grand Sauteux. *See* Minweweh
Legras, Françoise-Élisabeth (Neveu), III, 482; IV, 709
Legras, Jean, II, 221; IV, 46
Legras, Jean-Baptiste, III, 251, 485
Legras, Marie. *See* Philippe
Legras, Marie-Anne (Delaunay), II, 173
Legras, Marie-Anne (Hertel de Rouville), IV, 653
Legras, Marie-Catherine (Barsalou; Guillet de Chaumont), III, 270; IV, 46
Le Gresley, Philip, VIII, 257
Legris, Joseph-Hormidas, XII, 160
Legris, Joséphine (Solomon; Latard), VIII, 831
Legris, Marguerite (Bourdon), II, 92
Legris, Marie-Angélique (Martineau), V, 579
Legris, *dit* Lépine. *See* Lépine
Le Gros, Marie-Thérèse (Lorit, *dit* Gargot), II, 447
Legu, *dit* La Noue, Jean-Baptiste, IV, 748
Leguay, François, IV, 534
Le Guay, François, VI, 383
Le Guerne, François, III, 425; IV, **452–53**; V, 102; VI, 315
Le Guerne, Yves, IV, 452
Le Guet (Du Guay), Monsieur (clergyman), IV, 452
Le Guettier, Jean-Charles, III, 410
Le Héricy, Guillaume, I, 89
Le Herron, Christine (Conroy), X, 194
Leheup, *dit* Latulippe, Charlotte. *See* Desève
Leheup, *dit* Latulippe, Jean, V, 435
Leheup, *dit* Latulippe, Marguerite, V, 436
Le Hir, Arthur, XI, 776; XII, 223
Lehouillier, Dorothée. *See* Sales Laterrière
Lehouillier, François-Xavier, V, 738
Le Hour, Marie (Chaboulié), II, 127
Lehoux, Anne (Robidoux), III, 279
Leibniz, Gottfried Wilhelm, II, 443, 444
Leicester, Countess of. *See* Keppel
Leichhardt, Friedrich Wilhelm Ludwig, X, 558
Leifr *heppni* Eiriksson (Leif the Lucky), I, 17, 104, **448–49**, 612, 642, 643, 676
Leigh, Charles, I, 391, 392, 409, **449–52**
Leigh, Joan. *See* Oliph
Leigh, John, I, 449
Leigh, John, V, 244; VI, 175, **392–93**, 409, 410, 411; VII, 115, 152, 303, 507, 628
Leigh, Maria (mother of JOHN), VI, 392
Leigh, Oyph, I, 452
Leigh, Robert, VI, 392
Leighton, Ann (Jennings), XII, 474

Leigne. *See* André
Leiningen, Prince of. *See* Emich Charles
Leiningen, Princess of. *See* Victoria Mary Louisa
Leiper, Jane Duval (Kane), VIII, 448
Leir, Henrietta Anne. *See* Carleton
Leisler, Jacob, I, 586
Leitch, Euphemia. *See* Paterson
Leitch, John, IX, 460
Leitch, Margaret. *See* Sharp
Leitch, William, IX, 307, **460–62**; XI, 263, 609; XII, 540, 541, 767, 990, 1102
Leith, Alexander, VII, 498
Leith, Sir Alexander, VII, 498
Leith, George, VI, 340; VII, 498
Leith, James, V, 635; VI, 531; VII, 78, **498–99**; VIII, 350; IX, 732; XI, 18
Leith, Mary (Black), VII, 78
Leith, Mary Elizabeth. *See* Gordon
Leith, William Hay, VII, 499
LeJacq, Jean-Marie, XII, 285
Lejamtel, François, V, 12, 13, 181, 458, 671; VI, **393–94**; VII, 551; VIII, 227, 316, 626
Le Jardinier. *See* Voyer
Le Jeune; Lejeune. *See also* Young
LeJeune, Felicité (Kavanagh), VI, 370
Le Jeune, Jean-Marie, XII, 283, 285
Lejeune, Joseph, VIII, 498
Le Jeune, Julie-Catherine (Rodier), X, 624
Le Jeune*, Louis-Marie (1857–1935), IX, 864; X, 737
LeJeune, Marie-Henriette (Comeau; Lejeune, *dit* Briard; Ross), VIII, **498–99**
Lejeune, Martine. *See* Roy
Le Jeune, Olivier, I, 366, **452**
Le Jeune, Paul, I, 70, 120, 122, 123, 124, 126, 143, 159, 164, 186, 197, 203, 205, 207, 214, 215, 287, 310, 341, 348, 404, 412, 432, 452, **453–58**, 473, 481, 482, 487, 494, 516, 517, 518, 527, 533, 549, 563, 633, 637, 661, 665, 673; II, 85
Lejeune, *dit* Briard, Bernard, VIII, 498
Lejeune, *dit* Briard, Marie-Henriette. *See* LeJeune
Le Jumeau, Renée, II, 490
Lekron (Lecron), Susanna (Susan) (Zeisberger), V, 883
LeLacheur, John Windsor, VIII, 376; XI, 567; XII, 856
Leleu, Norbertine (Hennepin), II, 277
Lelièvre, Caroline-Eulalie (Landry), XI, 483
Lelièvre, Francis Tito, IX, 233
Lelièvre, Jane (Eccles), IX, 233
Lelièvre, Roger, V, 834; VI, 123, 191, 223, 391; VII, 502, 709; XI, 352, 483; XII, 846
Le Loutre, Jean-Louis, III, 29, 34, 120, 128, 136, 165, 183, 196, 295, 298, 332, 358, 362, 363, 415, 417, 425, 438; IV, xxiv, 36, 62, 93, 169, 170, 253, 256, 257, 289, 290, 452, **453–58**, 630, 636, 637; V, 172, 203; VI, 304
Le Loutre Després, Catherine. *See* Huet
Le Loutre Després, Jean-Maurice, IV, 453
Lely, Sir Peter, VIII, 649
Le Maigre. *See* Leblanc
Lemaire. *See also* Lemer
Lemaire, Abbé, III, 120, 166
Lemaire, Antoine-Hyacinthe, X, 437
Lemaire, Félix-Hyacinthe, X, **437–38**
Le Maire, François, III, 639
Lemaire, Ignace, VII, 499

Lemaire, Luce. *See* Barcelo
Le Maire, Madeleine (Philippe de Hautmesnil de Mandeville), II, 525
Lemaire, Marie-Josephte-Félix. *See* Gastonguay
Lemaire, Marie-Louise. *See* Castonguay
Lemaire, Marie-Marguerite, VII, 59, **499–500**
Lemaire, *dit* Saint-Germain, Venance, IV, 277; V, 259; VI, 547
Lemaire de Saint-Germain, Charles-François, V, 432
Lemaire Saint-Germain, Angélique (Bouthillier), VI, 84
Lemaire Saint-Germain, Élisabeth (Globensky), IX, 320
Lemaire Saint-Germain, Hyacinthe, VI, 84
Lemaire Saint-Germain, Marie-Narcisse (Lambert Dumont), VI, 385
Le Maistre, Denis, I, 495
Le Maistre, Élisabeth. *See* Théodore
Le Maistre, Francis, IV, 180; V, 132, **485–86**, 553, 584; VI, 173, 653
Le Maistre, François-Guillaume, V, 485
Lemaistre, Isaac, *dit* Lemaistre de Sacy, IX, 18
Le Maistre, Jacques, I, **458**, 525, 612, 662
Le Maistre, Margaret. *See* Stuart
Le Maistre, Marie. *See* Le Barbier
Lemaître, Bertrane. *See* Michelle
Lemaître, François (father of François LEMAÎTRE, *dit* Jugon), III, 377
Lemaître, François (printer), VI, 392; VIII, 261; IX, 459, 814
Lemaître, François (seigneur), III, 263
Lemaître, Marie (Perrault), VII, 686
Lemaître, Michel, IX, 315
Lemaître, *dit* Jugon, François, III, **377–78**
Lemaître, *dit* Jugon, Jean, III, 377
Lemaître, *dit* Jugon, Marie. *See* Collet
Lemaître, *dit* Lottinville, Geneviève-Sophie (Bellerose), XII, 87
Lemaître-Augé, Marie-Louise (Caron), XII, 159
Le Maître-Bellenoix, Félicité (Gauvreau; Mayrand), X, 503
Le Maître Duaime, François, IV, 317
Lemaître-Lamorille, François, I, 553; V, 478
Lemaître-Lamorille, Françoise (Lebé; Guillimin), II, 268; IV, 318, 319
Lemaître-Lamorille, Marguerite. *See* Poulin de La Fontaine
Lemaître-Lamorille, Marianne (Gamelin), IV, 286; VIII, 313
Lemaître Lottinville, Jean, VI, 231
Lemaître Lottinville, Sophie, VI, 231
Le Marchand de Lignery, Anne. *See* Robutel de La Noue
Le Marchand de Lignery, Constant, II, 216, 316, 386, **389–90**, 475, 503, 529, 547, 563, 569; III, 43, 80, 81, 103, 245, 329, 378, 402; IV, 180, 463, 651, 663, 732
Le Marchand de Lignery, François-Marie, II, 39; III, 158, 219, **378–79**, 535, 536; IV, 396, 513, 670, 733
Le Marchand de Lignery, Joseph, II, 389
Le Marchand de Lignery, Marguerite. *See* Du Sillar
Le Marchand de Lignery, Marie-Thérèse. *See* Migeon de La Gauchetière
Le Marchand de Lignery, Marie-Ursule. *See* Aubert de La Chesnaye
Le Marchant, Sir Denis, X, 438
Le Marchant, Jeanne (Leneuf), I, 340, 467
Le Marchant, John Gaspard, X, 438

Le Marchant, Sir John Gaspard, VII, 633; VIII, 233, 950; IX, 294, 583, 721; X, 399, 433, **438–39**, 534, 551, 590; XI, 43, 686, 835, 863, 881, 947; XII, 564, 834
Le Marchant, Margaret Anne. *See* Taylor
Le Marchant, Mary. *See* Carey
Le Marié, Guillaume, I, 167
Lemarinier, Catherine (Dubreuil), II, 201
Le May*, Léon-Pamphile (1837–1918), IX, 121; X, 203, 690; XI, 83, 500, 852; XII, 271
Lemay, Tertullier, XII, 543
Le Meilleur, Jacques, II, 241
Lemelin, Jeanne (Moore), II, 487
Leménager, Élizabeth. *See* Bourgeois
Leménager, Jean, VII, 28
Le Ménager, Marguerite (Courtois), VI, 390
Lemer (Lemaire), Nicole (Boucher), II, 82, 83
Le Mercier, Andrew, III, 135
Le Mercier, Charlotte. *See* Le Rebours
Le Mercier, Françoise. *See* Boucher de La Bruère
Le Mercier, François-Joseph, I, 108, 125, 212, 244, 255, **458–60**, 461, 552, 562, 563; II, 139
Le Mercier, François-Marc-Antoine, III, xix, 537; IV, 211, 227, 382, **458–61**, 616, 641; V, 677
Le Mercier, Marie. *See* Du Jardin
Le Mercier, Nicolas-François, IV, 458
Le Mercier, Paul, I, 458
Le Mercier de La Rivière de Saint-Médard, Pierre-Paul, IV, 65
LeMesurier, Annie Routh (Irvine), XII, 464
LeMesurier, Edward, IX, 462
LeMesurier, Havilland, IX, 462
LeMesurier, Henry, IX, 462
LeMesurier, Henry, VI, 306, 816; VII, 71; VIII, 268, 691, 952; IX, **462–63**; XII, 464
Le Mesurier, John, X, 454
Lemesurier, John, XI, 162
LeMesurier, Julie. *See* Guerout
Lemesurier, Peter, V, 107
Lemieux, Élisabeth. *See* Franquelin
Lemieux, François, XII, 922
Lemieux, François-Xavier, IX, **463–64**; X, 632; XI, 822
Lemieux*, Sir François-Xavier (1851–1933), XI, 626, 710, 748; XII, 178, 310, 854
Lemieux, Gabriel (farmer), IX, 463
Lemieux, Gabriel (father of FRANÇOIS-XAVIER), IX, 463
Lemieux, Joseph, II, 230
Lemieux, Judith. *See* Bonneville
Lemieux, Julie (Cauchon), XI, 164
Lemieux, Pierre, IX, 463
Lemieux*, Rodolphe (1866–1937), XII, 695, 727
Le Minime. *See* Barbier
Lemire, Flore (Proulx), VIII, 717
Lemire, Jean, I, **460**, 589; II, 120, 506
Lemire, Josephte (Bellecourt), X, 46
Lemire, Judith (Hébert), XI, 395
Lemire, L.-A., VIII, 290
Lemire, Louise. *See* Marsolet
Lemire, Marie-Anne (Catalogne), II, 120, 122
Lemire-Marsolet, Darie-Aurélie, named Sainte-Henriette, III, 719; IV, 830; IX, 899
Lemire Marsolet, Isidore (Charles-Antoine), V, 569
Lemire Marsolet, Jean, IV, 732
Lemoine, Alexandre, IX, 538

Lemoine, Ann (Cotton), VII, 211

Lemoine, Benjamin, VIII, 952

Lemoine, Emma (Cauchon), XI, 164

Le Moine, Françoise. *See* Le Comte Dupré

Le Moine, Gaspard, XI, 728

Le Moine*, Sir James MacPherson (1825–1912), III, 143, 305; IX, 719; X, 13; XI, 87, 88; XII, 36, 271, 308, 558, 737, 928, 1076

Lemoine, Jean, II, 236; III, 379

Le Moine, John Francis, V, 482

Lemoine, Joseph, VI, 665

Lemoine, Julie (Woolsey), VIII, 952

Lemoine, Madeleine. *See* Chavigny de Berchereau

Lemoine, Marguerite (Gamelin), II, 236; IV, 283

Lemoine, Marie-Louise. *See* Zemballe

Lemoine, *dit* Despins, Marie-Renée. *See* Le Boulanger

Lemoine, *dit* Despins, René-Alexandre, III, 379; IV, 5, 461, 462

Lemoine, *dit* Monière, Alexis, III, 379, 233, 477; IV, 11, 461, 621

Lemoine, *dit* Monière, Marie-Josephte. *See* Couagne

Lemoine, *dit* Monière, Marie-Marguerite (Pennisseaut; Fresnoy; Fontanille), IV, 621, 622

Lemoine, *dit* Monière, Pierre-Alexis, III, 379, 477

Lemoine Despins, Jacques-Alexis, IV, 461

Lemoine Despins, Jacques-Joseph, IV, 5, 67, 125, 148, 435, **461–62**, 592, 750

Lemoine Despins, Jean-Baptiste (uncle), IV, 7, 125

Lemoine Despins, Jean-Baptiste, IV, 461

Lemoine Despins, Marguerite. *See* Guillon

Lemoine Despins, Marguerite (Adhémar), IV, 5

Lemoine Despins, Marguerite-Charlotte. *See* Rocbert de La Morandière

Lemoine Despins, Marguerite-Thérèse, IV, 238, **462–63**, 508; VI, 169

Lemoisin, Louis, III, 65

Lemonier, François, V, 592, 622

Lemonnier, Louis-Guillaume, III, 30; V, 592

Le Monnier, Pierre-Charles, III, 30

Lemort, Anne. *See* Dubois

Lemort, Jacques, I, 535

Le Mouton, Magdelainne (Le Saulnier), VI, 396

Le Moyne, Anne (Messier), II, 469

Le Moyne, Élisabeth (Rémy), II, 561

Le Moyne, Guillaume, XII, 749

Le Moyne, Jeanne (Le Ber), II, 375, 376, 377

Le Moyne, Judith. *See* Du Chesne

Le Moyne, Pierre, I, 463

Le Moyne, Simon, I, 10, 66, 70, 130, 206, 244, 295, 307, 315, 322, 414, 429, 458, **460–62**, 502, 523, 525, 563; II, xxxiv, 282, 624, 625

Le Moyne d'Assigny, Nicolas, IV, 765

Le Moyne de Bienville, François, I, **463**; II, 392; III, 379

Le Moyne de Bienville, Jean-Baptiste, I, 463; II, xxviii, 67, 203, 204, 215, 259, 260, 267, 306, 349, 355, 396, 408, 425, 428, 455, 457, 513, 525, 636, 646, 653; III, xxxiii, 36, 40, 99, 148, 150, 317, **379–84**, 423, 424, 503, 626; IV, li, 54, 137, 315, 633, 663, 664; V, 487; XII, 825

Le Moyne de Châteauguay, Antoine, II, 408

Le Moyne de Châteauguay, Louis, I, **463**; II, 394, 407, 513

Le Moyne de Leau, Nicolas, III, 581

Le Moyne de Longueuil, Catherine-Charlotte, Baronne de Longueuil. *See* Le Gouès de Grais

Le Moyne de Longueuil, Charles, Baron de Longueuil, I, 464; II, xxxvi, 87, 112, 126, 389, **401–3**, 404, 503, 567, 573, 598; III, 42, 43, 76, 159, 217, 245, 328, 384, 385, 568, 649; IV, 41, 235, 463; XII, 749

Le Moyne de Longueuil, Charles, Baron de Longueuil, II, 403; III, 5, 21, 47, 378, 383, **384–85**, 612; IV, 148, 237, 256, 265, 268, 296, 407, 476, 633, 662, 692, 729; V, 97; VII, 500

Le Moyne de Longueuil, Charles-Jacques, Baron de Longueuil, IV, 268, 269; V, 369; VII, 500

Le Moyne de Longueuil, Claude-Élisabeth, Baronne de Longueuil. *See* Souart d'Adoucourt

Le Moyne de Longueuil, Geneviève (Liénard de Beaujeu de Villemonde), V, 49; VI, 689

Le Moyne de Longueuil, Joseph, II, 403

Le Moyne de Longueuil, Joseph-Dominique-Emmanuel, IV, 346, 347, 464, 634; V, 96, 231, 232, 233, **486–88**, 499; VI, 132, 368, 690; VIII, 890; IX, 703

Le Moyne de Longueuil, Louise. *See* Prud'homme

Le Moyne de Longueuil, Marguerite, Baronne de Longueuil. *See* Legardeur de Tilly

Le Moyne de Longueuil, Marie-Anne (Bouillet de La Chassaigne), II, 87

Le Moyne de Longueuil, Marie-Anne-Catherine, Baronne de Longueuil. *See* Fleury Deschambault

Le Moyne de Longueuil, Marie-Catherine (Tarieu de La Naudière), IV, 729; V, 792

Le Moyne de Longueuil, Marie-Catherine-Joseph, VII, 500

Le Moyne de Longueuil, Marie-Charles-Joseph, Baronne de Longueuil (Grant), IV, 269; VI, 699; VII, **500–1**; X, 374; XI, 780

Le Moyne de Longueuil, Marie-Geneviève. *See* Joybert de Soulanges

Le Moyne de Longueuil, Paul-Joseph, known as Chevalier de Longueuil, III, 49, 451, 495, 496, 600; IV, 146, 150, 368, **463–65**, 582, 651; V, 231, 486, 498; VII, 500

Le Moyne de Longueuil et de Châteauguay, Catherine. *See* Thierry

Le Moyne de Longueuil et de Châteauguay, Catherine-Jeanne (Payen de Noyan), II, 513; III, 502; IV, 611

Le Moyne de Longueuil et de Châteauguay, Charles, I, 103, 105, 225, 231, 271, 287, 289, 295, 319, 322, 444, 445, **463–65**, 507, 508, 555; II, xvii, 29, 253, 375, 390, 397, 401, 403, 405, 406, 469, 508, 536, 581, 624; III, 379, 580; XII, 825

Le Moyne de Maricourt, Françoise. *See* Aubert de La Chesnaye

Le Moyne de Maricourt, Marie-Madeleine. *See* Dupont de Neuville

Le Moyne de Maricourt, Paul, I, 465, 653; II, xxxvi, 20, 34, 107, 114, 126, 160, 205, 391, 394, 401, 402, **403–5**, 621, 622, 631; III, 192, 407

Le Moyne de Martigny, Félicité-Élisabeth. *See* Bailly de Messein

Le Moyne de Martigny, Jacques (brother-in-law of Charles-François BAILLY de Messein), IV, 43

Le Moyne de Martigny, Jacques (officer), VIII, 605

Le Moyne de Martigny et de La Trinité, Jacques, II, 405, 406

Le Moyne de Martigny et de La Trinité, Jean-Baptiste, II, 298, 302, **405–6**

Le Moyne de Martigny et de La Trinité, Marie-Élisabeth. *See* Guyon Durouvray

Le Moyne de Sainte-Hélène, Catherine (Robutel de La Noue), II, 581

Le Moyne de Sainte-Hélène, Jacques, I, 466

Le Moyne de Sainte-Hélène, Jacques, I, 463, **465–67**, 545, 653; II, 13, 391, 392, 401, 403, 482, 581, 608; III, 245, 586

Le Moyne de Sainte-Hélène, Jeanne. *See* Dufresnoy Carion

Le Moyne de Sainte-Hélène, Marie-Jeanne (Gaultier de Varennes), III, 245

Le Moyne de Sainte-Marie, Catherine (Robutel de La Noue) III, 581

Le Moyne de Sainte-Marie, Françoise, III, 385

Le Moyne de Sainte-Marie, Jacques, II, 405, 470; III, 385, 580

Le Moyne de Sainte-Marie, Marguerite, named du Saint-Esprit, III, **385–86**; IX, 217

Le Moyne de Sainte-Marie, Mathurine. *See* Godé

Le Moyne de Serigny, Monsieur, Chevalier de Loire (son of Joseph LE MOYNE de Serigny et de Loire), II, 408

Le Moyne de Serigny et de Loire, Élisabeth-Catherine (Rigaud de Vaudreuil, Marquise de Vaudreuil), III, 557

Le Moyne de Serigny et de Loire, Joseph, I, 463; II, 203, 298, 394, 395, 398, 403, **406–8**, 513; III, 557

Le Moyne de Serigny et de Loire, Marie-Élisabeth. *See* Héron

Le Moyne d'Iberville, François-Jean, II, 399

Le Moyne d'Iberville, Jean-Baptiste, II, 399

Le Moyne d'Iberville, Jean-Charles, II, 399

Le Moyne d'Iberville, Marie-Thérèse, II, 399

Le Moyne d'Iberville, Pierre-Joseph-Louis, II, 399

Le Moyne d'Iberville et d'Ardillières, Marie-Thérèse. *See* Pollet de La Combe-Pocatière

Le Moyne d'Iberville et d'Ardillières, Pierre, I, 26, 61, 80, 179, 227, 308, 339, 361, 400, 463, 465, 493, 529, 547, 551, 577, 582, 611, 641, 649, 653; II, 6, 36, 42, 50, 62, 65, 116, 140, 145, 167, 169, 177, 197, 203, 227, 228, 231, 232, 246, 257, 265, 266, 271, 298, 302, 303, 305, 306, 307, 311, 319, 349, 354, 355, 387, **390–401**, 403, 405, 406, 407, 408, 417, 421, 427, 428, 446, 449, 450, 454, 458, 479, 487, 495, 510, 513, 534, 581, 589, 590, 605, 608, 626, 635, 636, 654, 666; III, 42, 81, 176, 317, 380, 414, 450, 454, 469, 470, 488, 599; XII, 825

Lemprière, John, XII, 514

Lempriere, Thomas James, X, 514

Lendrum, Frances (Mack), XI, 559

Leneuf, Jeanne. *See* Le Marchant

Leneuf, Marie (Godefroy de Lintot), I, 340, 467; II, 252, 253

Leneuf, Mathieu, I, 340, 467

Leneuf de Beaubassin, Monsieur (ship's captain), IV, 588

Leneuf de Beaubassin, Marguerite (Poulin de Courval), III, 539

Leneuf de Beaubassin, Marie-Charlotte. *See* Daccarrette

Leneuf de Beaubassin, Philippe, II, 412; III, 157; IV, 28, 245, 246, 588

Leneuf de La Poterie, Catherine (Denys de La Ronde), I, 418; II, 33, 174, 176, 178, 224, 545; III, 176

Leneuf de La Poterie, Jacques, I, 60, 186, 446, **467**, 468, 575, 589; II, 16, 83, 84, 168, 174, 178, 272, 409

Leneuf de La Poterie, Marguerite. *See* Legardeur de Repentigny

Leneuf de La Poterie, Marie-Anne (Robinau de Bécancour, Baronne de Portneuf), I, 467, 575, 576; II, 577, 579

Leneuf de La Vallière, Jacques, II, 410

Leneuf de La Vallière, Judith (Villieu), II, 654

Leneuf de La Vallière, Louis, II, 412; III, 34; IV, 455

Leneuf de La Vallière, Marie-Josette (Legardeur de Saint-Pierre), II, 387; III, 374

Leneuf de La Vallière, Michel, IV, 252

Leneuf de La Vallière et de Beaubassin, Alexandre, I, 90; II, 180, 235, 287, 388, **408–9**, 410, 452, 495, 543; III, 596; IV, 764

Leneuf de La Vallière et de Beaubassin, Barbe (Aubert Duforillon), III, 22, 291

Leneuf de La Vallière et de Beaubassin, Barbe (Delort; Rousseau de Villejouin), IV, 689

Leneuf de La Vallière et de Beaubassin, Françoise. *See* Denys de La Trinité

Leneuf de La Vallière et de Beaubassin, Marguerite (Gannes de Falaise), II, 236; III, 235; IV, 688

Leneuf de La Vallière et de Beaubassin, Marie. *See* Denys

Leneuf de La Vallière et de Beaubassin, Michel (d. 1705), I, 90, 258, 260, 396, 399, 467; II, 32, 71, 94, 236, 272, 387, 408, **409–11**, 477, 629, 630, 654; III, 22

Leneuf de La Vallière et de Beaubassin, Michel (d. 1740), II, **411–12**; III, 454; IV, 689

Leneuf de La Vallière et de Beaubassin, Renée. *See* Bertrand

Leneuf Du Hérisson, Anne, known as Du Hérisson (Desrosiers), I, 468

Leneuf Du Hérisson, Michel, I, 340, **467–68**, 550; II, xvi, 85, 86, 252, 253

Leney, William Satchwell, VII, 823; XI, 106

Lenfestey, Hilary, XII, 928

Lennap, Cornelia van (Waldegrave, Baroness Radstock), VI, 795

Lennon, Catherine (Kelly), X, 397

Lennox, Charles, 2nd Duke of Richmond, Lennox, and Aubigny, III, 405

Lennox, Charles, 3rd Duke of Richmond and Lennox, V, 141, 142, 149, 348, 349, 350, 357, 425, 488

Lennox, Charles, 4th Duke of Richmond and Lennox, V, 72, **488–90**, 882; VI, 85, 368, 496, 497, 513, 596, 668, 716, 734, 745, 769; VII, 129, 189, 266, 268, 312, 486, 724, 728, 740, 770, 916; VIII, 295, 596, 618, 828, 940; IX, 133

Lennox, Charles Gordon, 5th Duke of Richmond, VIII, 464

Lennox, Charlotte, Duchess of Richmond and Lennox. *See* Gordon

Lennox*, Edward James (1855–1933), XII, 707, 783

Lennox, Emilia Charlotte (Berkeley, Lady Berkeley), V, 72

Lennox, Lord Fitzroy George Gordon, VIII, 831

Lennox, Lord George Henry, V, 488

Lennox, John, IV, 427; VIII, 909

Lennox, Lady Louisa. *See* Kerr

Lennox, Marie-Marguerite. *See* La Corne

Lennox, Lady Mary (Fitzroy, Lady Fitzroy), VI, 85, 745; VIII, 295

Lennox, Lady Sarah (Maitland, Lady Maitland), VI, 498; VII, 51; VIII, 596

Lennox and March, Countess of. *See* Stewart

Le Nobletz, Monsieur (uncle of Jean-Gabriel-Marie LE PAPE Du Lescoät), II, 414

Lenoir, Charlotte (Guernier, *dit* Laviolette), VIII, 492
Lenoir, Claudine (mother of François LENOIR, *dit* Rolland), II, 412
Lenoir, Françoise (Liébert), V, 497
Lenoir, Marie (Chartier), I, 202
Lenoir, Marie-Joseph (Cirier), IV, 151
Lenoir, Rolland, II, 412
Lenoir, Vincent, III, 316; IV, 151; V, 497
Lenoir, *dit* Le Comte, Gilles, III, 398
Lenoir, *dit* Rolland, Félicité. *See* Latour
Lenoir, *dit* Rolland, François, I, 47; II, 271, **412–13**
Lenoir, *dit* Rolland, Gabriel, II, 173
Lenoir, *dit* Rolland, Joseph, VIII, 493, 503; IX, **464–65**; XI, 275; XII, 504
Lenoir, *dit* Rolland, Marie-Angélique. *See* Cazelet
Lenoir, *dit* Rolland, Marie-Joseph. *See* Delaunay
Lenoir, *dit* Rolland, Marie-Madeleine. *See* Charbonner
Lenoir, *dit* Rolland, Nicolas, IX, 464
Lenoir de Rouvray, Laurent-François, IV, 187
Le Normand, Suzanne (Huppé, *dit* Lagroix), IV, 376
Le Normant, Ange, III, 386
Le Normant, Claude-Madeleine. *See* Gourdan
Le Normant de Mézy, Anne-Marie. *See* Debrier
Le Normant de Mézy, Élisabeth. *See* Lescoffier
Le Normant de Mézy, Jacques-Ange, II, 255, 292, 582, 612, 649; III, 98, 264, **386–89**, 396, 455, 456, 512, 532, 567, 574, 575, 576, 644; IV, 465
Le Normant de Mézy, Marie-Louise-Augustine. *See* Salignac
Le Normant de Mézy, Sébastien-François-Ange, III, 98, 264, 357, 387, 389, 455, 567, 576, 644; IV, 60, 61, 67, 252, 253, 254, 255, 420, **465–68**, 665, 668
Le Normant d'Étioles, Jeanne-Antoinette. *See* Poisson
Lens, Bernard, III, 624
Lent, Catherine (McCarty; McDougall), IV, 494
Leo XII, VII, 656; VIII, 306
Leo XIII, XI, 110, 259, 451, 805, 868; XII, 47, 185, 199, 302, 304, 411, 502, 581, 696, 724, 725, 732, 799, 1022, 1050, 1066, 1078
Leolo. *See* Lolo
León. *See* Ponce
Leon, Esther Serena Joseph (Clench), VIII, 161
Leonard, Charles Weston, XII, 553
Leonard, Daniel, VI, 136
Leonard, Delos, VIII, 499; XII, 553
Leonard, Elijah, VIII, **499–500**; XI, 898; XII, 552, 553
Leonard, Elijah, VII, 924; VIII, 499; X, 374, 375; XI, 63; XII, **552–54**
Leonard, Emeline. *See* Woodman
Leonard, Frank Elton, VII, 924; XII, 553, 554
Leonard, George, VI, 396
Leonard, George, IV, 328; V, 389, 867; VI, 13, 112, 143, **394–96**; VII, 198; VIII, 507; IX, 62
Leonard, Harriet Ann (Esson), IX, 243
Léonard, Hubert, XII, 471
Léonard, Jean-Claude. *See* Baveux, Jean-Claude-Léonard
Leonard, Jemima (Perkins), V, 665
Leonard, Lewis, VIII, 499
Leonard, Lyman, VIII, 499; XII, 553
Leonard, Mary. *See* Stone
Leonard, Nancy (Cunnabell), IX, 186
Leonard, Nathaniel, VI, 394
Leonard, Priscilla. *See* Rogers

Leonard, Richard, VII, 314
Leonard, Samuel, VIII, 499; XII, 966
Leonard, Sarah. *See* Thatcher
Leonard, Sarah. *See* Williams
Leonard, Sarah Evanson (Becher), XI, 62
Leonard, Thomas, VIII, 300
Léonard, *dit* Mondor, Marie-Anne (Martel), XII, 699
Léonard d'Auxerre, Monsieur (Capuchin), I, 129
Léonard de Chartres, I, 434, **468–69**
Leopold I, King of the Belgians (Leopold Georg Christian Friedrich, Prince of Saxe-Coburg-Saalfeld), VI, 517; VII, 478; XI, 851; XII, 471
Leopold Eberhard, Prince of Montbéliard, II, 424
Leopold George Duncan Albert, Duke of Albany, XII, 150
Lepage. *See also* Bastien-Lepage
LePage, Alice. *See* Foster
LePage, Andrew, XI, 511
Lepage, Archange (Bouc), VI, 78
Lepage, Charles-Olivier, V, 727
LePage, Charlotte. *See* McNeill
LePage, Elizabeth. *See* Mellish
Lepage, Françoise (Taché), XII, 1012
Lepage, Geneviève (La Frenaye), I, 409
Lepage, Geneviève (Marcoux), V, 575
LePage, John, VIII, 565; XI, **511–12**
Lepage, Marie-Rogère (Peuvret Demesnu), I, 543
Lepage, René, II, 305, 584; V, 270
Le Page, *dit* Chaudron, Monsieur (cook), I, 425
Lepage de Saint-Barnabé, Pierre, III, 99
Lepage de Sainte-Claire, Louis, II, 81, 153; III, 122, 285, **390–91**, 522, 593; IV, 11, 356, 358, 359, 361, 690, 779
Lepage de Sainte-Claire, Marie-Madeleine. *See* Gagnon
Lepage de Sainte-Claire, René, III, 390
Le Page Du Pratz (Duprat), Antoine-Simon, II, 598, 653
Lepailleur, François-Georges, VII, 147, 148
Lepailleur, François-Maurice, VII, 149, 150, 264; XII, 762
Lepallier, Jean, II, 413
Lepallier, Marie. *See* Lamotte
Lepallier de Laferté, Catherine. *See* Jérémie, *dit* Lamontagne
Lepallier de Laferté, Catherine (Adhémar), III, 4
Lepallieur de Laferté, François-Michel, II, 413; III, 500
Lepallieur de Laferté, Marie-Louise (Lorimier de La Rivière), III, 408; VI, 402
Lepallieur de Laferté, Michel, II, xxiv, 164, 297, **413–14**; III, 4, 314, 315, 347, 408, 473
Le Pape Du Lescöat, Jean-Gabriel-Marie, II, 414; III, 169; IV, 235
Lepellé, Antoine, II, 252
Lepellé, Françoise (Vauvril; Godefroy de Saint-Paul), II, 252
Le Pellé Lahaye, Marie-Josephe (Deslandes; Blondeau), V, 89, 700
Le Pers, Jean-Baptiste, III, 107
Lépervanche. *See* Mézières
Le Pesant, II, xxxiii, xxxvii, 12, 173, 317, 318, 324, 354, 386, **414–15**, 475, 505, 506; III, 576
Le Petit Chef. *See* Wikaskokiseyin
Le Piat. *See* Piat
Le Picard. *See also* Olivier
Le Picard, Anne (Oriol; Ailleboust Des Muceaux), II, 14; IV, 11

Le Picard, Jean, II, 276; III, 642
Le Picard, Joseph, III, 642, 643
Le Picard, Marie-Anne (Barbel), II, 42; III, 642; IV, 44
Le Picard, Marie-Catherine (Véron de Grandmesnil), III, 642
Le Picard de Letéland Du Mesnil, Louis, II, 417
Le Picard de Norrey, Auguste-Philippe, II, 415
Le Picard de Norrey, Louis, II, 416
Le Picard de Norrey, Madeleine. *See* Gédouin
Le Picard Du Guay. *See* Auguel
Le Picard Du Mesnil de Norrey, Jacques, II, **415–17**, 520
Le Picard Du Mesnil de Norrey, Marie-Renée. *See* Chorel de Saint-Romain, *dit* d'Orvilliers
Le Picart, Pierre, IV, 338
Lépinay (L'Épiné). *See* Couillard
Lépine. *See also* Bérard
Lépine*, Ambroise-Dydime (d. 1923), IX, 329, 708; X, 59, 198, 230, 439, 476, 556, 557; XI, 46, 151, 193, 194, 520, 624, 707, 738, 740, 741, 743, 744, 935; XII, 132, 175, 363, 371, 554, 652, 655, 1008
Lépine, Jean-Baptiste, IX, 330, 708; X, **439**; XI, 740; XII, 132
Lépine, Josephte. *See* Lavallée
Lépine, Maxime, XII, **554–55**
Lépine (Legris, *dit* Lépine), Sophie (Paquet, *dit* Lavallée), VIII, 680
Lépine, *dit* Lalime, Joseph, III, 142
Lépine, *dit* Lalime, Marie. *See* Roy
Lépine, *dit* Lalime, Michel, VII, 188
Le Pippre. *See* Lamorel
Le Poitevin. *See* Paillard
Le Pont. *See* Gravé Du Pont
Le Porc-épic. *See* Noro
Le Porz, Marie (Nédélec), XII, 780
Le Poupet de La Boularderie, Antoine, II, 417; III, 475; IV, **468–69**, 644, 645
Le Poupet de La Boularderie, Éléonore-Jeanne. *See* Beaugny
Le Poupet de La Boularderie, Louis-Simon, II, 38, **417–18**; III, 177; IV, 252, 468
Le Poupet de La Boularderie, Madeleine. *See* Melançon
Le Poupet de La Boularderie, Marie-Madeleine (Mazière), II, 417
Le Poupet de Saint-Aubin, Antoine, II, 417
Le Poupet de Saint-Aubin, Jacqueline. *See* Arnoulet
Le Prestre de Vauban, Sébastien, I, 664; II, 230, 337, 649; III, 117, 190, 645
Le Prêtre. *See* McDonell, John
Le Prévost, Jacques, III, 391
Le Prévost, Jeanne. *See* Fauvault
Le Prévost, Pierre-Gabriel, II, 379; III, **391–92**
Le Prévost Duquesnel, Jean-Baptiste-Louis, III, 18, 93, 94, 175, 182, 236, 288, 368, **392–93**, 416, 609, 645; IV, 56, 60, 61, 62, 83, 247, 253, 254, 588, 643
Le Prévost Duquesnel, Marguerite. *See* Girault Du Poyet
Leprince, Joseph, V, 813
Le Prince, Marie-Barbe (Beaumont), IV, 631
Leprohon, Alcibiade, XI, 93
Leprohon, Bernard-Henri, IX, 703; XI, 58
Leprohon, Édouard-Martial, XII, 66, 555
Leprohon, Jean-Lukin, X, 536; XII, **555–56**
Leprohon, Jean-Philippe, V, 243; VI, 787; VII, 255, 501
Leprohon, John Layton, XI, 62

Leprohon, Joseph-Onésime, VII, 255, **501–2**, 721; XI, 87, 689; XII, 507, 555
Leprohon, Louise-Émilie-Hermine (Smith), XII, 977
Leprohon, Louis-Xavier, VIII, 40; XII, 977
Leprohon, Marguerite. *See* Parent
Leprohon, Marie-Julie-Léocadie (Coté), XI, 203
Leprohon, Marie-Louise. *See* Lukin
Leprohon, Rosanna Eleanora. *See* Mullins
Le Proust, Jean, III, 430
Le Quesne. *See* Le Cain
Le Rageois de Bretonvilliers, Alexandre, I, 540, 600
Le Raisin. *See* Chomina
Le Rat. *See* Kondiaronk
Lerche, Jean-Henry, V, 218, 436
Lereau, Marie (Buisson), II, 108
Le Rebours, Charlotte (Le Mercier), IV, 458
Leriger de La Plante, Marie-Catherine (Bourassa, *dit* La Ronde), IV, 77
Lerned, Margarette (McQuesten), XI, 583
Lernoult, Richard Berrenger, V, 147
Lerole. *See* Canchy
Le Rond d'Alembert, Jean, V, 102
Le Rouge, Jean, I, 619, 664; II, 338, **418–19**; III, 306
Le Rouge, Jeanne. *See* Poitevin
Le Rouge, Jeanne (Couton), III, 144; IV, 172
Leroux, Angélique (Larocque), IX, 455, 456
Leroux, Germain, IX, 455
Leroux, Laurent, IV, 310; VI, 786; VII, 739; VIII, **500–1**; IX, 455, 456
Le Roux, Louise (Olivier), IV, 590
Leroux, Marie-Esther. *See* Loisel
Le Roux, Thomas-François, IV, 81, 444, **469–70**; V, 458; VI, 293
Leroux, Valentin, I, 439, 440; II, 174, 222, 335, **419**, 420, 421
Leroux d'Esneval, Angélique (Marie des Anges) (Raymond), VII, 739
Leroux d'Esneval, Germain, VIII, 500
Leroux d'Esneval, Marie-Catherine. *See* Vallée
Leroux-Duplessis. *See* Robreau
LeRoy. *See also* Roy
Le Roy, Catherin, II, 424
Le Roy, Henri, I, 265; II, **419–21**
Le Roy, Jacques, IV, 252
Le Roy, Jeanne-Marie. *See* Boyat
Le Roy, Marguerite (Champlain), I, 186
Le Roy, Marguerite (Durocher), III, 210
Le Roy, Marie (Paumart), I, 534
Le Roy, Marie (Regnard Duplessis), II, 561; III, 547, 549
Leroy, Marie-Anne-Rosalie. *See* Lebreton
Le Roy, Olive. *See* King, Willobe
Leroy, Pierre, XI, 512
Leroy, Pierre-Auguste, XI, **512–14**
Le Roy de La Potherie, Charles-Auguste, II, 422
Le Roy de La Potherie, Élisabeth. *See* Saint-Ours
Le Roy de La Potherie, Marc-René-Augustin, II, 422
Le Roy de La Potherie, Pierre-Denis, II, 422
Le Roy de La Potherie, *dit* Bacqueville de La Potherie, Claude-Charles, I, 40, 77, 112, 249, 522, 611; II, xxviii, 64, 87, 114, 127, 143, 162, 297, 322, 323, 379, **421–23**, 483, 486, 494, 499, 504, 517, 519, 533, 546, 593, 618, 624; III, xxxiii, 308, 309, 310, 311; VIII, 352

Le Roy de La Potherie de Bacqueville, Charles-Auguste, II, 421

Le Roy de La Potherie de Bacqueville, Françoise. *See* Du Sicquet d'Esmainville

Le Roy Desmarest, Claude-Joseph, II, **424**; III, 172, 396, 397; IV, 420

Le Roy Desmarest, Marie-Suzanne. *See* La Bazanière

Le Royer de La Dauversière, Jeanne. *See* Baugé

Le Royer de La Dauversière, Jérôme (father), I, 214

Le Royer de La Dauversière, Jérôme, I, 31, 109, 213, 214, 216, 218, 219, 220, 221, 412, 454, 457, 478, 480, 485, 487, 512, 648; II, 489, 490, 491; III, 395

Le Royer de La Dauversière, Joseph, I, 214

Le Royer de La Dauversière, Renée (Marie). *See* Oudin

Léry. *See also* Chaussegros

Léry, Vicomte de. *See* Chaussegros

Léry, Jean de, I, 469

Lesage, Alain-René, II, 142

Lesage, Charles-Alexandre, XI, 456

Lesage, Joseph, V, 77

Lesage, Pierre-Louis, named Brother Adelbertus, IX, 681

Lesage*, Siméon (1835–1909), XI, 26, 27, 331

Le Saulnier, Candide-Michel, IV, 90; V, 92; VI, **396–98**, 553, 669; VII, 746; VIII, 490

Le Saulnier, François, VI, 396

Le Saulnier, Magdelainne. *See* Le Mouton

Le Sauvage. *See* Normandin

Lescarbot, Claude, I, 471

Lescarbot, Françoise. *See* Valpergue

Lescarbot, Marc, I, 471

Lescarbot, Marc, I, 12, 28, 64, 67, 69, 72, 95, 96, 97, 98, 99, 170, 188, 189, 197, 198, 292, 293, 294, 300, 307, 346, 367, **469–72**, 500, 501, 526, 527, 564, 568, 591, 604; II, 429; III, 337

Lescöat (Lescouat). *See* Le Pape

Lescoffier, Élisabeth (Letellier; Le Normant de Mézy), IV, 467

Lescot (Lescault), Marie (Boutroue d'Aubigny), I, 120

Les Derniers. *See* Delesdernier

Lesdiguières, Duc de. *See* De Bonne

Lesdiguières, Duchesse de. *See* Rochechouart

Le Selle, Jeanne (Estienne Du Bourgué de Clérin), II, 221

Le Sesne, Louise (Puisaye, Marquise de Puisaye), VI, 618

Lesieur-Désaulniers, Charlotte. *See* Rivard-Dufresne

Lesieur-Désaulniers, François (father), IX, 465; XII, 556

Lesieur-Désaulniers, François, IX, 465; XI, 556

Lesieur-Désaulniers, François-Sévère, XII, 556

Lesieur-Désaulniers, Isaac-Stanislas, VIII, 240, 241, 711; IX, **465–67**; X, 430; XI, 493, 726; XII, 556, 1003

Lesieur-Désaulniers, Louis-Léon, XII, **556–57**

Lesieur-Désaulniers, Marie Flora Josephine. *See* Merrill

Leslie, Charlotte (Sprott), IX, 738

Leslie, Frank, XI, 213

Leslie, Hugh, VIII, 663

Leslie, James, X, 440

Leslie, James, VI, 232, 238, 346; VII, 82, 920; VIII, 21, 101, 542; IX, 441, 505; X, 219, **440**; XI, 206, 533; XII, 986, 987

Leslie, John, XII, 425

Leslie, Julia. *See* Langan

Leslie, Robert, XII, 368

Leslye, William, IV, 564

Lesparre. *See* Madaillan

Lespérance; L'Espérance. *See also* Aubuchon; Bonami; Compain; Lalonde; Levasseur; Magnan; Rocheleau

L'Espérance, Baronne de. *See* Curie

Lespérance, Monsieur (merchant), II, 492

L'Espérance, Monsieur (soldier), III, 308

L'Espérance, Anne-Claire de. *See* Du Pont de Renon

Lespérance, Catherine. *See* Bélanger

L'Espérance, Charles-Gabriel-Sébastien de, Baron de L'Espérance, II, 424; IV, 29, **470–71**, 679; V, 339

L'Espérance, Charles-Léopold-Ébérard de, II, **424–25**; IV, 470

Lespérance, Elizabeth. *See* Hill

Lespérance, Jean-Baptiste, XII, 557

L'Espérance, Jeanne-Françoise de. *See* Rodrigue

Lesperance, John, X, 44; XII, **557–59**

Lesperance, Lucie-Parmélie. *See* Lacasse

L'Espérance, Marguerite de. *See* Dangeac

Lespérance (Rocheleau, *dit* Lespérance), Pierre (Pierre-André), IX, 702

Lespérance, Pierre, VII, 18; XI, **514–16**

Lesperance, Rita, XII, 558

Lespérance, Rita-Élizabeth. *See* Duchanquette

Lespérance, Simon Talon, VII, 247; XI, 84

Lespinay (L'Espinay). *See also* Couillard

Lespinay, Hutin de, I, 425

Lespinay, Jean-Michel de, II, **425–26**; III, 381

Lespinay, Marie de. *See* Caulincourt

Lespinay, Nicolas de, I, 423, 425

Les Prairies. *See* Paskwāw

Lessard, Élisabeth (Caron), X, 131

Lessard, Étienne de, II, **426**

Lessard, Marguerite de. *See* Sevestre

Lessard, Marie (Normand), VIII, 655

Lessard, Marie-Thérèse de (Langlois), III, 348

Lessel, Arthur C., XII, **559–60**

Lessel, Caroline. *See* Dauphine

Lessel, Catherine (mother of ARTHUR C.), XII, 559

Lessel, James, XII, 559

Lesseps, Jean-Baptiste-Barthélemy de, Baron de Lesseps, IV, 283

Lesslie, Charles, XI, 516, 517

Lesslie, Edward (father), IX, 497; XI, 516

Lesslie, Edward, XI, 516

Lesslie, Grace. *See* Watson

Lesslie, Grace (Paterson), VIII, 687

Lesslie, Jacqueline (wife of JAMES), XI, 519

Lesslie, James, VII, 163; VIII, 50, 55, 687, 829, 932; IX, 423, 497, 505, 506, 507, 509, 576, 618; X, 126, 127, 233; XI, 127, 407, 408, **516–19**, 542, 712, 713, 714; XII, 296

Lesslie, John, IX, 399, 497; XI, 516, 517

Lesslie, Joseph, IX, 399; XI, 516, 517, 518

Lesslie, William, XI, 516, 517

Lestage, Esther de. *See* Sayward

Lestage, Jean de (father), III, 393

Lestage, Jean de, III, 393, 394

Lestage, Joseph-Alphonse, III, 426

Lestage, Marie de, III, 394

Lestage, Marie-Madeleine de. *See* Rivet

Lestage, Pierre de, III, 394

Lestage, Pierre de, II, 69, 463, 509, 602; III, 253, 307, 353, **393–94**, 491; IV, 356, 357, 360

Lestage, Saubade de. *See* Noliboise

Lestanc, Jean-Marie-Joseph, XI, 305, 598
L'Estang. *See* Brunet; Petit
Lester, Amy (Garland), VI, 273
Lester, Benjamin, IV, 159, 712; V, 166, 189, **490–92**, 725, 726, 784, 785, 838; VI, 273, 274, 275, 784
Lester (Garland), Benjamin Lester, VI, 274
Lester, Charles Edwards, IX, 88
Lester, Francis, V, 490
Lester, Isaac, IV, 159, 712, 713; V, 491
Lester, Sir John, V, 492; VI, 273
Lester, Louise, XI, 325
Lester, Margaret (Peters), VII, 690; VIII, 699
Lester, Rachel. *See* Taverner
Lester, Robert, V, 332, 460, **492–97**, 566, 794, 816, 877, 878; VI, 424; VII, 311; VIII, 581
Lester, Susannah. *See* Taverner
L'Estobec de Langristain, Marie-Gabrielle-Élisabeth (Prevost), IV, 643
Leston, Elizabeth. *See* Kerr
Leston, Francis, X, 664
L'Estrange, Monsieur (professor), X, 534
L'Estrange, Elizabeth (Cosby), III, 143
Lestrange, Henri-Louis de, named Father Augustin, VIII, 625, 626, 627
Lestringant, Anne de. *See* Jacquier
Lestringant, Nicolas de, II, 426
Lestringant de Saint-Martin, Alexandre-Joseph, II, **426–27**; III, 22
Lestringant de Saint-Martin, Louise-Madeleine. *See* Juchereau de Saint-Denis
Lestringant de Saint-Martin, Madeleine-Thérèse, II, 427
Lestringant de Saint-Martin, Marie-Anne-Josette (Montéléon; Aubert de La Chesnaye), II, 90, 427; III, 22
Le Sueur, Jacques-François, III, **394–95**
Le Sueur, Jean, known as Abbé de Saint-Sauveur, I, 111, 112, 310, 339, **472**; II, 82, 158, 366
Le Sueur, Jean-Paul, II, 428
Le Sueur, Marguerite. *See* Messier
Le Sueur, Pierre, II, 180, 230, **427–29**, 508, 589; III, 493
Le Sueur, Pierre, III, 369, **395–96**; IV, 201
Le Sueur*, William Dawson (1840–1917), IX, 509; XII, 191, 516, 826
Le Suisse. *See* Miville
Leszczyńska, Marie. *See* Marie Leszczyńska
Le Tac, Xiste, II, 175, 244, **429–30**
Le Talon, II, 504
Letancour, Sieur de. *See* Decoste, Jean-Baptiste
L'Étang (Létant). *See* Brunet
L'Étang. *See* Douhet
Letardif, Barbe. *See* Esmard
Letardif, Louise. *See* Couillard
Letardif, Olivier, I, 72, 163, 344, 452, **473**, 517, 518, 554; II, 27, 158
Letartre, Élisabeth (Pagé, *dit* Carcy), III, 498
Letéland Du Mesnil. *See* Le Picard
Letellier, Élisabeth. *See* Lescoffier
Letellier, François, XI, 519
Le Tellier, François-Michel, Marquis de Louvois, I, 535
Letellier, Mary (Bruff), V, 115
Letellier de Saint-Just, Eugénie-Eliza. *See* Laurent
Letellier de Saint-Just, François, VI, 125, 749; XI, 519
Letellier de Saint-Just, Luc, X, 26, 204, 213; XI, 176, 177, 180, 181, 480, **519–21**, 531, 625, 812, 884; XII, 8, 84,

105, 176, 178, 197, 464, 651, 655, 694, 721, 722, 913, 987, 1037
Letellier de Saint-Just, Marie-Sophie. *See* Casgrain
Letellier de Saint-Just, Michel, XI, 519
L'Étendard. *See* Dandane
Letendre, Arthur-Prisque, XI, 329
Letendre, Geneviève (Pelletier; Volant de Radisson), II, 655
Letendre, Jean-Baptiste, VI, 398
Letendre, Marie-Madeleine. *See* Cardin, *dit* Loiseau
Letendre, Oiseau, XI, 193
Letendre, Xavier, XI, 326
Letendre, *dit* Batoche, Angélique (Jérôme), VI, 398
Letendre*, *dit* Batoche, François-Xavier (d. 1901), VI, 398
Letendre, *dit* Batoche, Jean-Baptiste, VI, 398
Letendre, *dit* Batoche, Jean-Baptiste, VI, **398–99**
Letendre, *dit* Batoche, Josephte (Versailles), VI, 398
Letendre, *dit* Batoche, Louis (Louison), VI, 398
L'Étenduère, Marquis de. *See* Des Herbiers
Lethbridge, William, XII, 354
Letondal, Arthur (Joseph-Auguste), XII, 472
Letondal, Paul, XI, 671; XII, 504, 532
Le Tort, Jacques, III, 65
Le Tort, James, III, 65
Letourneau. *See* Siginakee
Létourneau, Catherine. *See* Boisseau
Létourneau, Éléonore (Kérouac), X, 401
Létourneau, Jean, IV, 172
Létourneau, Jean-Charles, VII, **502–3**
Létourneau, Joseph, XI, 872
Létourneau, Joseph-Marie, VII, 502
Létourneau, Lazard, VIII, 758
Létourneau, Marie. *See* Rateau
Létourneau, Marie-Françoise. *See* Cloutier
Létourneau, Marie-Geneviève (Deblois), VIII, 206
Létourneau, Michel, IV, 629; V, 436
Le Tourneux, Louis-Octave, XII, 270
Le Tourneux (Letourneux), Pierre-Louis, VII, 595
Lett, Benjamin, V, 114; VIII, 390, **501–2**, 853, 960
Lett, Elizabeth. *See* Warren
Lett, Samuel, VIII, 501
Lett*, Stephen (1847–1905), XII, 731
Lett, Thomas, VIII, 502
Lett, William Pittman, VIII, 840
Lettoré, Joseph, VII, 412; VIII, 261
Leuduger, Jean, III, 10; IV, 95
Leutze, Emanuel Gottlieb, XII, 287
Levack, Helen (Mowat), VIII, 644; XII, 767
Levadoux, Michel, VI, 145, 486
LeVallée, Elizabeth (Bott; Withall), XII, 1117
Le Valois, Monsieur (Jesuit), II, 328
Le Vasseur, Monsieur (explorer), I, 423, 425
Levasseur, Angélique. *See* Juste
Levasseur, Anne. *See* Ménage
Levasseur, Anne-Félicité (Hamel), I, 474
Levasseur, Anne-Thérèse (Fornel), III, 222, 224
Levasseur, Charles, III, 397, 398
Levasseur, Deneige (Gaudet), XI, 334
Levasseur, Élisabeth-Françoise (Ferrand), IV, 354
Levasseur, François-Noël, II, 431; III, 397; IV, **471–73**, 475; V, 49, 304
Levasseur, G., I, 188

Levasseur, Geneviève. *See* Grange
Levasseur, Geneviève, III, 238
Levasseur, Guillaume, IV, xvii
Levasseur, Jeanne (Rouillard), III, 572
Levasseur, Louis (father of LOUIS), III, 396
Levasseur, Louis (son of Jean LEVASSEUR, *dit* Lavigne), I, 473
Levasseur, Louis, III, 172, 389, **396–97**, 575
Levasseur, Louis-Armand, IV, 354, 473
Levasseur, Madeleine. *See* Chapeau
Levasseur, Madeleine. *See* Vilers
Levasseur, Madeleine (Maillot), VI, 482
Levasseur, Marguerite. *See* Bélanger
Levasseur, Marguerite. *See* Guay
Levasseur, Marguerite (Lamarre), II, 339
Levasseur, Marie-Agnès. *See* Lajoüe
Levasseur, Marie-Anne. *See* Lorant
Levasseur, Marie-Anne (Hillaire de La Rochette), IV, 353
Levasseur, Marie-Anne (Trullier, *dit* Lacombe), VI, 786
Levasseur, Marie-Claude (Cotté), IV, 171
Levasseur, Marie-Françoise-Renée (Martin), III, 435
Levasseur, Marie-Geneviève. *See* Côté
Levasseur, Marie-Madeleine. *See* Turpin
Levasseur, Michel, II, **430**; III, 498, 499
Levasseur*, Nazaire (1848–1927), VII, 349; VIII, 635; X, 229; XI, 83, 84
Levasseur, Noël, I, 473; II, 430
Levasseur, Noël, I, 473, 474; II, 127, **430–32**; III, 397, 648; IV, 471, 475, 535, 649
Levasseur, Pierre (father of PIERRE-NOËL), II, 467; III, 397
Levasseur, Pierre (son of RENÉ-NICOLAS), IV, 474, 475; V, 638
Levasseur, Pierre-Noël, III, 398
Levasseur, Pierre-Noël, I, 474; II, 200, 337, 431; III, **397–98**; IV, 471, 472
Levasseur, René-Nicolas, III, 139, 435, 539, 540, 612; IV, 354, 361, **473–75**, 620; V, 638
Levasseur, Stanislas, III, 398
Levasseur, Thérèse, III, 172
Levasseur, Ursule (Roger), II, 582
Levasseur, *dit* Borgia, Marguerite (Amiot), VII, 16, 18
Levasseur, *dit* Delor, Jean-Baptiste-Antoine, II, 431; III, 397; IV, 471, 472, **475–76**; V, 304
Levasseur, *dit* Delor, Marie-Régis. *See* Cartier
Levasseur, *dit* Lavigne, Jean, I, **473–74**, 645; II, xvi, 430; III, 397; IV, 471
Levasseur, *dit* Lavigne, Marguerite. *See* Richard
Levasseur, *dit* L'Éspérance, Jeanne. *See* Chaverlange
Levasseur, *dit* L'Éspérance, Pierre, I, 225, **474**; III, 397; IV, 471
Levasseur Borgia, Joseph, V, 208; VI, 47, 48, 50, 68, 386; VII, **503–5**, 878, 880
Le Vasseur Borgia, Louis, VII, 503
Le Vasseur Borgia, Marie-Anne. *See* Trudel
Le Vasseur Borgia, Narcisse-Charles, VII, 505
Levasseur de Neré, Jacques, II, 121, 229, 337, **432–33**, 553, 559, 569, 578; III, 190
Levasseur de Neré, Marie-Françoise. *See* Chavenault
Léveillé. *See also* Valier
Léveillé, Monsieur (merchant), IV, 592; V, 185
Léveillé, Lionel, XI, 424
Léveillé, Mathieu, III, 279, **398–99**
Levell, Emma (Bland), XII, 111

Leven, Earl of. *See* Melville
Le Veneur, Jean, I, 165
Lévêque, François, V, 256
Lévêque, Marie-Angélique (Sauvageau), VII, 774
Lévêque, Marie-Anne-Agathe (Eynard), X, 273
Lévêque, Véronique (Digé), V, 256
Lever, Charles James, IX, 353
Leverett, Anne. *See* Fisher
Leverett, Hannah. *See* Hudson
Leverett, John, I, **474–75**, 573, 595, 605, 636
Leverett, Sarah. *See* Sedgwick
Leverett, Thomas, I, 474
Le Verrier, Madeleine. *See* Houdon
Leverrier, Marie. *See* Deguire, *dit* Desrosiers
Leverrier, Pierre, IV, 202
Le Verrier de Boisguibert, Nicolas, II, 433
Le Verrier de Rousson, François, II, xxi, 224, **433**, 589; III, 579; IV, 476, 663
Le Verrier de Rousson, Jeanne-Charlotte. *See* Fleury Deschambault
Le Verrier de Rousson, Louis, II, 433; IV, **476**
LeVesconte, Caroline (MacDougall), X, 440
LeVesconte, Caroline Susan. *See* Jean
LeVesconte, Isaac, IX, 293, 294; X, 172, **440–41**; XI, 398
LeVesconte, Jane. *See* Malzard
LeVesconte, Peter, X, 440
Leveson-Gower, Granville George, 2nd Earl Granville, IX, 715, 845; XI, 635, 769, 770, 933
Lévesque, Catherine. *See* Trottier Desauniers Beaubien
Lévesque, Catherine (Grisé), IV, 477
Lévesque, Charles-François, VIII, **502–3**
Lévesque, Charlotte-Mélanie. *See* Panet
Levesque, François (father of FRANÇOIS), IV, 476
Lévesque, François (relative of John OGILVY), V, 635
Lévesque, François, III, 282, 370; IV, 229, **476–77**; V, 494, 601, 889; VI, 305, 615; VIII, 503
Lévesque, Guillaume, VII, 412, 737; VIII, 502, **503–5**; XII, 762
Lévesque, Jeanne-Marguerite. *See* Le Chevalier
Lévesque, Judith (Guerout), VI, 305
Lévesque, Marc-Antoine-Louis, VII, 235; VIII, 502, 503
Lévesque, Marie. *See* Pouchet
Lévesque, Marie-Jessie-Béatrice (Laviolette), VIII, 503
Lévesque, Mary Jessy. *See* Morrison
Lévesque, Robert, II, 181
Lévesque, *dit* Lafrance, Charles-Joseph, XI, 872
Levey, Charles E., VIII, 102; XI, 72
Levi, Blume (Mohr), XII, 745
Levi, Philip, XII, 745
Le Vieux, Pierre, III, 433
Le Vieux de Hauteville, Marguerite. *See* Lyonne
Le Vieux de Hauteville, Marie. *See* Renardin de La Blanchetière
Le Vieux de Hauteville, Nicolas, I, 475
Le Vieux de Hauteville, Nicolas, I, 431, **475**; II, xvi
Levilliers. *See* Petit
Levingston. *See* Livingston
Lévis, François de, Duc de Lévis, III, xxi, xxii, xxv, xxvii, 12, 84, 85, 86, 89, 132, 211, 332, 400, 441, 459, 461, 462, 463, 467, 468, 469, 510, 535, 552, 555, 578, 591; IV, 14, 24, 34, 58, 64, 137, 144, 183, 214, 307, 401, 448, 449, 460, 476, **477–82**, 517, 531, 563, 621, 637, 641, 642, 652, 670, 671, 672, 673, 674, 701, 739, 751; V, 40,

41, 96, 104, 164, 498, 638, 677, 739, 888; IX, 360, 562; XII, 46

Lévis, Gabrielle-Augustine de, Duchesse de Lévis. *See* Michel de Danton

Lévis (Lévy), Henri de, Duc de Ventadour, I, 58, 186, 195, 521

Lévis, Jean de, Baron d'Ajac, IV, 477

Lévis, Jeanne-Marie de, Baronne d'Ajac. *See* Maguelonne

Lévis, Pierre-Marc-Gaston de, Duc de Lévis, IV, 482

Lévis-Mirepoix, Gaston-Charles-Pierre de, Duc de Lévis-Mirepoix, IV, 477, 482; V, 103

Leviston, Hugh, XII, 567

Leviston, Mary Ann. *See* Fitzsimmins

Levrard, Charles, IV, 729

Levrault de Langis, Alexis, III, 399, 400

Levrault de Langis, Léon-Joseph, III, 399

Levrault de Langis, Marguerite-Gabrielle. *See* Jarret de Verchères

Levrault de Langis Montegron, Jean-Baptiste, III, **399–400**

Levrault de Langis Montegron, Madeleine. *See* Ailleboust de Manthet

Levreau, Charles, III, 509

Levreau (L'Heureux), Marie (Phlem, *dit* Yvon), III, 518

Levret, Suzanne (Arnoux), III, 18

Levy. *See also* Solomons; Thubières

Lévy. *See* Lévis

Levy, Mr (owner of an assembly room), IV, 556

Levy, Abigail (Hayes), IX, 380

Levy, Eleazar, IV, 331, 332, 384, 571; VIII, 365

Levy, George Edward, VII, 611

Levy, Gershom, IV, 332, 385, 718, 719

Levy, Hayman, IV, 718

Levy, Isaac, IV, 332, 385

Levy, Rosetta (Benjamin), XII, 93

Levy, Simon, IV, 332

Lewellin, John Lewellin, VIII, **505–6**

Lewellin, Mary. *See* Woodley

Lewen. *See* Ross

Lewes, John Lee, VIII, 813

Lewes, Letitia (Gower), V, 359

Lewin, James Davies, XII, **560**, 1071

Lewin, Mary. *See* Furmage

Lewin, Samuel, XII, 560

Lewin, Sarah Ann. *See* Clarke

Lewis, Alma Hopkins. *See* Freeman

Lewis, Amy. *See* Bradley

Lewis, Andrew, V, 554

Lewis, Ann (Holl), IX, 394

Lewis, Ann (Wilcocke), VI, 815

Lewis, Anna. *See* Eccles

Lewis, Asahel Bradley, VI, **399–400**, 422; VII, 127; VIII, 608, 860

Lewis, Barnabas, VI, 399

Lewis, Edward (grandfather of Sir Thomas BUTTON), I, 144

Lewis, Edward (landowner), VII, 406

Lewis, Elizabeth (wife of WILLIAM), IV, 482

Lewis, Elizabeth (Rowsell), XI, 778

Lewis, Elizabeth Susan. *See* Wilson

Lewis, Felix, XII, 560

Lewis, Gaius, IX, 747

Lewis, Sir George Cornewall, X, 406; XI, 6

Lewis, Helen. *See* Street

Lewis, Ichabod, XII, 560

Lewis*, Ida (Cheney), known as Julia Arthur (1869–1950), XII, 623, 1067

Lewis, James, XI, 638

Lewis, John Bower, VII, 446; VIII, 510; X, 441

Lewis, John Bower, VIII, 840; X, **441**

Lewis, John Frederick, XII, 793

Lewis, John Pitt, XII, 454

Lewis*, John Travers (1825–1901), IX, 378, 763, 771; X, 55, 536; XI, 628

Lewis, John W., XI, 497

Lewis, Margaret (Button), I, 144

Lewis, Maria Sophia (Evans), VIII, 276

Lewis, Martha Hamm (Peters), XII, **560–61**

Lewis, Martha Maria. *See* Shaw

Lewis, Mary (Ryerson), X, 638

Lewis, Meriwether, V, 9, 418, 419; VIII, 3, 556, 661, 881; IX, 455

Lewis, Rebecca (Hamilton), XI, 379, 381

Lewis, Sir Thomas Frankland, XI, 874

Lewis, William, IV, **482–84**, 721; V, 506, 717; VII, 763, 764

Lewthwaite, Frances (MacColl), XII, 588

Lexington, Baroness. *See* St Leger

Leys, Francis, VII, 506

Leys, John, VII, **505–6**

Leys, William, VII, 506

Lhalle. *See* Delhalle

L'Hérault, *dit* L'Heureux, Élise (Benoît, *dit* Livernois), IX, 47

L'Héritier de Brutelles, Charles-Louis, V, 593

L'Hermitière. *See* Hamelin

L'Hermitte, Jacques, II, 435

L'Hermitte, Jacques, II, 36, 154, 339, **433–35**, 479, 482

L'Hermitte, Marie. *See* Chevalier

L'Hermitte, Marie. *See* Preaux

L'Heureux. *See also* Levreau; L'Hérault

L'Heureux, Jacques, II, 578

L'Huillier, Alexandre, II, 428

L'Huissier, Christophe, IV, 202

Liancourt. *See* Du Plessis; La Rochefoucauld-Liancourt

Liancourt, Duc de. *See* Du Plessis

Liancourt, Marquise de. *See* Schomberg

Liard, V, 419

Liard, Suzanne (Mounier), IV, 565

Libert, Nicolas, I, 248

Lichfield, Countess of. *See* Fitzroy

Lichfield, Earl of. *See* Lee

Lichtenstein, Elizabeth (Johnston), VII, 16, **506–7**; VIII, 752; X, 383; XII, 895

Lickford, Charles John. *See* Warner, Charles

Liddall. *See* Lydall

Liddel, Elizabeth (Ramage), V, 705

Liddell, Andrew, V, 611

Liddell, Henry Thomas, 1st Earl of Ravensworth, VII, 477; XI, 686

Liddell, Janet. *See* Martin

Liddell, John (father of THOMAS), X, 441

Liddell, John (merchant), V, 611

Liddell, Maria (Phipps), XI, 686

Liddell, Susan Anne Jane. *See* Stewart

Liddell, Thomas, VIII, 68, 641; IX, 496; X, **441–43**; XI, 503; XII, 767, 1102

Liddell, William, V, 611

Liddle, Jean (Hoyles, Lady Hoyles), XI, 431
Liddon, Henry Parry, XII, 490
Lidius. *See* Lӱdius
Lieberkühn, Samuel, V, 885
Liebermann, Maryanna Ludwika (Kierzkowski), IX, 424
Liébert, Anne. *See* Des Porques
Liébert, Françoise. *See* Lenoir
Liébert, Philippe (father of PHILIPPE), V, 497
Liébert, Philippe (rebel), V, 146
Liébert, Philippe, IV, 151, 201; V, 392, 393, **497–98**; VI, 626; VII, 685
Liebrich, Anna Justina. *See* Schwartz
Liégeois, Jean, I, **475–76**
Liele, George, V, 340
Liénard, Bonaventure, II, 173, 174
Liénard, Geneviève (Mallet), II, 451
Liénard de Beaujeu, Catherine. *See* Gobert
Liénard de Beaujeu, Charles-François, IX, 702
Liénard de Beaujeu, Charlotte (Varin de La Marre), III, 402; IV, 749
Liénard de Beaujeu, Daniel-Hyacinthe-Marie, III, 31, **400–2**, 403, 524; IV, 207, 242, 442, 447, 617, 733; V, 41, 498; VI, 689; IX, 703
Liénard de Beaujeu, Louis, II, 390, 529; III, 384, 400, **402–3**, 422; IV, 749; V, 498; VI, 689
Liénard de Beaujeu, Louis-Joseph, III, 403
Liénard de Beaujeu, Marie-Charlotte (Le Comte Dupré), IV, 442
Liénard de Beaujeu, Michelle-Élisabeth. *See* Foucault
Liénard de Beaujeu, Philippe, III, 402
Liénard de Beaujeu, Thérèse-Denise. *See* Migeon de Branssat
Liénard de Beaujeu de Villemonde, Adèle (Filion), VI, 690
Liénard de Beaujeu de Villemonde, Charles-François, V, 499; VI, 690
Liénard de Beaujeu de Villemonde, Élisabeth-Geneviève, VI, 690
Liénard de Beaujeu de Villemonde, Geneviève. *See* Le Moyne de Longueuil
Liénard de Beaujeu de Villemonde, Julie-Louise (Juchereau Duchesnay), V, 462, 498; VI, 367
Liénard de Beaujeu de Villemonde, Louis, III, 403, 529; IV, 41, 72, 639; V, 6, 358, 462, **498–99**; VI, 689
Liénard de Beaujeu de Villemonde, Louise-Charlotte. *See* Cugnet
Liette. *See also* Tonty
Liette, Isabelle de (Tonty), II, 631, 633
Liette, Pierre-Charles de, II, 128, **435–36**, 569, 631, 636; III, 627
Light, Alexander, II, 493; III, 302
Light, Alexander Luders, XII, 484, **561–63**
Light, Alexander Whalley, XII, 561
Light, Jane. *See* Smart
Light, Mary Jane. *See* Torrens
Light, William (officer), XI, 718
Light, William (steward), VIII, 773
Lightenstone. *See also* Lichtenstein
Lightenstone, Catherine. *See* Delegal
Lightenstone, John G., VII, 506
Lighthall*, William Douw (1857–1954), XII, 558, 944, 945, 947, 948, 1075
Lignères. *See* Desportes
Lignery. *See* Le Marchand

Lignières. *See* Darles
Ligny, François de, IX, 18
Ligondès (Ligondez) de Linars, Jean de, III, 368
Ligonier, John (Jean-Louis), 1st Earl Ligonier, III, 218, 668, 669; IV, 3, 20, 21, 22, 84, 773; V, 141, 823
Liguest. *See* Laclède
Liguori, Alfonso Maria de', VII, 886
Lilburne, William, II, 290, 564
Lilford, Baron. *See* Powys
Lilia, Marie-Anne (Douglas, Comtesse de Douglas), IV, 224
Lillicoe, Mary (Gilmore), IV, 295
Lillie, Adam, IX, **467–68**; XI, 923, 924; XII, 667
Lillie, Elizabeth (wife of ADAM), IX, 467
Lilliot, Richard, VII, 134
Lillo, George, V, 689; VII, 110
Lilly, Elizabeth (Badgley), VII, 30; IX, 16; XI, 40
Lilly, Emma Gaden (Noad), X, 551
Lilly, George, VII, 105, 155, **507–8**, 793; VIII, 469; XI, 28, 760
Lilly, John, VII, 30
Lilly, Mary Ann. *See* Roberts
Lilly, William, VII, 507
Lily of the Mohawks. *See* Tekakwitha
Limoges, Joseph de, II, 55
Limoges, Joseph-Magloire, XI, 595
Limoges, Marguerite-Hortense (Dugal), VI, 227
Limoges, Marie-Rose (Sureau, *dit* Blondin), XI, 864
Limousin, Valère (Depéret), III, 180
Linars. *See* Ligondès
Linch, Thomas, V, 396
Lincoln, Earl of. *See* Clinton
Lincoln, Abraham, X, 514; XII, 354, 449, 469, 751, 885, 925
Lincourt. *See* Amiot
Linctot. *See* Godefroy
Lind, Henry, IX, **468–69**; XI, 432
Lind, Johanna Maria (Jenny) (Goldschmidt), VIII, 347
Lindenow, Godske, I, 243
Lindley, Harry, XI, 419
Lindo, Elizabeth (O'Brien), IX, 607
Lindsay, Clara (Bouchette), X, 78
Lindsay, Henrietta Amelia (Fletcher), XII, 320
Lindsay, James, 7th Earl of Balcarres and 24th Earl of Crawford, X, 443
Lindsay, Sir James Alexander, IX, 845; X, **443–44**; XI, 759, 838
Lindsay, John, IX, 550
Lindsay, Lionel, VI, 598; VII, 17; XI, 905
Lindsay, Maria Margaret (Kingsford), XII, 493
Lindsay, Maria Margaret Frances. *See* Pennington
Lindsay, Marianne. *See* Melvin
Lindsay, Lady Sarah Elizabeth. *See* Savile
Lindsay, William (father of WILLIAM), VI, 400, 401
Lindsay, William (merchant), VI, 318
Lindsay, William, V, 287, 509; VI, **400–2**, 658
Lindsay, William Burns (father), VI, 401; XII, 320
Lindsay, William Burns, VI, 401
Lindsey*, Charles (1820–1908), V, 685; VI, 266; VII, 365; VIII, 30, 267, 643; IX, 496, 497, 507, 508, 509, 576, 788; X, 43; XI, 518; XII, 72, 73
Lindsey, George Goldwin Smith, IX, 509; XII, 147
Linfoot, John, X, 529

Lingard, John, VIII, 489

Linière. *See* Perrault

Linklater, Thomas, VIII, 546

Linklater, William, VI, 17; VII, 748

Linnaeus (Linné, von Linné), Carl (Carolus), II, 596; III, 108, 676, 678; IV, 406, 407; V, 581; VII, 645; X, 138

Lino. *See* Martin

Linthorne, Benjamin, VI, 532

Linton, John James Edmonstoune, IX, **469–70**, 837

Linton, Margaret. *See* Dallas

Linton, Margaret. *See* McDougall

Linton, Robert, IX, 489; XI, 757

Lintot. *See* Godefroy

Lionne. *See* Lyonne

Lippincott, Esther Borden (Denison), X, 224

Lirec. *See* Lauson

L'Irlande. *See* Riel

Lisgar, Baron. *See* Young

Lisle. *See* Beaussier

L'Isle-Dieu, Abbé de. *See* La Rue

Lisloye. *See* Dupuy

Listenois, Prince de. *See* Bauffremont

Lister, Joseph, 1st Baron Lister, XII, 12, 315

Lister, Sarah (Robinson), IV, 677

Liston, Janet. *See* Scougall

Liston, Robert (husband of Janet SCOUGALL), VII, 914

Liston, Robert (surgeon), XI, 271

Liston, Sir Robert, V, 809, 810

Litchfield, John Charles, IX, 470

Litchfield, John Palmer, IX, **470–71**; XI, 591

Litchfield, Louisa. *See* Maddock

Litchfield, William, XII, 635

Little, Mr (lumberman), XII, 665

Little, Mr (tailor), XII, 893

Little, Anne. *See* Youell

Little, Brigid. *See* Costin

Little, Cornelius, XII, 563

Little, Eleanor Margaret (Scott), XII, 955

Little, Elizabeth. *See* Howland

Little, Isaac, III, 403

Little, James, XI, **521–23**; XII, 135

Little, John, XII, 161, 563, 564, 956

Little*, Sir Joseph Ignatius (1835–1902), XI, 68; XII, 158, 381, 482, 565, 955

Little, Margaret (Elliot), X, 269

Little, Mary. *See* Otis

Little, Mary (Winslow), IV, 774

Little, Mary Jane. *See* Holdright

Little, Michael McLean, VII, 220, 294

Little, Otis, III, 90, **403–5**; IV, 581

Little, Philip Francis, VIII, 234, 862, 950; IX, 29, 169, 189, 196, 393, 583, 606, 682, 721, 820, 846; X, 331, 399; XI, 29, 43, 44, 66, 354, 376, 432, 615, 674, 881, 910; XII, 161, 163, 482, **563–66**, 955

Little, William, XI, 522; XII, 665

Little Abraham. *See* Teiorhéñhsere?

Little Bear. *See* Apaschiskoos

Little Beard. *See* Sequidonquee

Little Chief. *See* Hunkajuka

Little Child. *See* Kiwisãnce

Little Chip. *See* Peguis

Little Crow. *See* Taoyateduta

Littlefield, Hannah (Moulton), III, 476

Littlefield, Josiah, II, 664

Littlehales. *See* Baker

Little Pigeon. *See* Guiboche, Louis

Little Pine. *See* Minahikosis

Little Plume, XII, 29

Little Saulteaux, XII, 499

Little Soldier. *See* Hunkajuka

Littleton, Edward John, 1st Baron Hatherton, VIII, 649

Little Turtle. *See* Michikinakoua

Livaudais. *See* Énault

Livaudière. *See* Péan

Livernois. *See also* Benoît

Livernois, Gilles, II, 379

Livernois, Jules, IX, 48

Livernois*, Jules-Ernest (1858–1933), IX, 48

Liverpool, Earl of. *See* Jenkinson

Livingston, Alida. *See* Schuyler

Livingston, Ann (Jordan), IV, 402

Livingston, Anna Maria B. *See* Armstrong

Livingston, Catharine (Garrettson), VI, 275

Livingston, Catherine (De Peyster), IV, 210

Livingston, Elizabeth. *See* Knight

Livingston, Henry, XII, 566

Livingston, Hugh, XII, 567

Livingston, Isabella. *See* Wheten

Livingston, James, IV, 142, 546; V, 146, 413, 414, 826

Livingston, Jane Mary. *See* Howse

Livingston, Janet (Montgomery), IV, 545

Livingston, Janet (Smith), IV, 714, 718; VII, 816

Livingston, John (fur trader), IV, 402

Livingston, John (publisher), XI, 298

Livingston, John, II, 4, **436–38**, 650; III, 8

Livingston, John, XII, **566–67**

Livingston, Margaret (Vetch), II, 650, 652

Livingston, Mary. *See* Winthrop

Livingston, Philip John, IV, 300

Livingston, Robert, II, 112, 436, 650

Livingston, Robert R., X, 403

Livingston, Samuel Henry Harkwood, XI, 355; XII, **567–68**

Livingston, Walter Ross, XI, 526, 527; XII, 856

Livingston, William, IV, 714, 715

Livingstone, David, XII, 668

Livingstone, Hester (Brown), XI, 116

Livingstone, Mary (Stewart), I, 613

Livingstone, Sydney (Carter), XII, 161

Livius, Anna Elizabeth. *See* Tufton Mason

Livius, Peter, IV, 484

Livius, Peter, IV, 58, 230, 232, 350, 398, **484–86**, 492, 791; V, 21, 142, 146, 148, 260, 843, 849, 863; VI, 494, 511

Lizars, Daniel Horne, VII, 262

Lizars*, Kathleen Macfarlane (d. 1931), VII, 262, 883

Lizars, Robina (Smith), VII, 262, 883

Lizeiras. *See* Delicérasse

Lizot, Joseph, IV, 71

Lizot, Marie-Françoise (Blais), IV, 71

Llanas. *See* Bodega

Lliebb. *See* Lublé

Lloyd, Mr (explorer), I, 239

Lloyd (Loyd), Mr (ship's captain), I, 308; II, 266

Lloyd, Clara (Felton), X, 282

Lloyd, David (brother of THOMAS), II, 439

Lloyd, David (lawyer), IV, 526

Lloyd, Elizabeth (Loring), VII, 517
Lloyd, Hoyes, X, 296
Lloyd, Humphrey, XI, 508, 509, 799, 800
Lloyd, James, I, 545
Lloyd, Jesse, VII, **508–10**; IX, 502, 813, 814
Lloyd, John, I, 19, 386
Lloyd, Mary (Jones), VII, 454
Lloyd, Nathaniel, V, 373; VI, 422
Lloyd, Philip, V, 373; VI, 422
Lloyd, Phoebe. *See* Crossley
Lloyd, Prudence (Sproule), V, 773
Lloyd, Susannah. *See* Heacock
Lloyd, Thomas, X, 282
Lloyd, Thomas, II, 97, 98, 118, 152, 218, 261, 291, 293,
    350, 351, **438–39**, 486, 487, 565, 582, 583, 610, 619,
    643; III, 177, 454, 618
Lloyd, Thomas George Biddle, VI, 393
Lloyd, William, VII, 508, 510
Llwyd, Humphrey, I, 677
Loach, Frances (Kane), X, 389
Lobley, Benjamin, XI, 523
Lobley, Elizabeth Ann. *See* Mais
Lobley, Joseph Albert, XI, 368, **523–24**, 917; XII, 813
Lobley, Mary. *See* Harrison
Locie. *See* Losee
Lock, Angélique (Trudeau), XII, 1068
Lock, Susan (McKay), XI, 560
Locke, John (philosopher), I, 519; IV, 230; V, 372; VI, 46;
    VII, 675; X, 572
Locke, John (politician), X, 457
Locke, Margaret (Jones), VIII, 443
Locke, Mary Anne (Glenie), V, 347, 349, 356
Lockerby, Elizabeth Newell (Bacon), XI, **524–25**
Lockerby, John, XI, 524
Lockerby, Margaret. *See* Forbes
Lockhart, Grace Annie (Dawson), XII, 10
Lockhart, James, IX, 657
Lockhart, John Gibson, IX, 429
Lockhart, Letitia (Mactavish), VIII, 589; IX, 529; X, 485
Lockhart, Mary Jane (Lawrence), XI, 501
Lockhart, Miriam (Lowe; Tupper), XI, 895
Lockman, Carolina, III, 405
Lockman, Christopher, XII, 1088
Lockman, John, III, 405
Lockman, Leonard, III, 212, **405**
Lockman, Tanalia (wife of LEONARD), III, 405
Lockwood, Anthony, VIII, 506
Lockwood, Anthony, VI, 143; VIII, **506–8**
Lockwood, Harriet (Lee; wife of ANTHONY), VIII, 506
Lockwood, Mary. *See* McCall
Locock, Susanna (Pim), XI, 691
Loedel, Charles Peter, IX, 703
Loedel, Henry Nicholas Christopher, V, 88, 89; VI, **402**
Loedel, Henry-Pierre, VI, 402; VII, 824
Loedel, Marguerite. *See* Gamelin
Loedel, Marie-Antoinette. *See* Tarieu Taillant de
    Lanaudière
Loedel, Peter Charles, VI, 402; VII, 447, 448, 449
Loewe, Louis, XI, 254
Loewendahl. *See* Lowendahl
Lofthouse, Joseph, XII, 383
Loftus, Fanny Harriet. *See* Langrishe
Logan, Alexander, XI, 547

Logan, Alexander, XII, **568–69**
Logan, Ann, IX, 472
Logan, Benjamin, V, 852
Logan, Elizabeth (Gower), X, 448
Logan, George, VIII, 862
Logan, Hart (uncle), V, 286; VI, 259, 260; VII, 618; X, 444
Logan, Hart, X, 444
Logan, Isaac, VII, 24
Logan, James (businessman), VI, 259
Logan, James (secretary), III, 66
Logan, Janet. *See* Edmond
Logan, John, XI, 547
Logan, Margaret (McDonald), XI, 547
Logan, Margaret (White), VI, 812
Logan, Maria. *See* Lane
Logan, Mary (wife of ROBERT), IX, 472
Logan, Robert, VI, 438; VII, 749; VIII, 91, 766, 767; IX,
    **472–73**; XII, 568
Logan, Sarah (Ingham; mother of ALEXANDER and wife of
    ROBERT), IX, 472; XII, 568
Logan, William, VI, 259; X, 444
Logan, Sir William Edmond, VII, 761, 810; VIII, 62, 73,
    88, 774, 775; IX, 160, 309, 390, 419; X, 30, 65, 137,
    **444–49**; XI, 49, 73, 255, 420, 631, 632, 731, 732, 803,
    899; XII, 41, 233, 234, 235, 457, 458, 540, 736, 737
Logie, Rebecca (Dunn), XII, 277
Loid (Loyd), Thomas, VII, 616, 617; X, 517
Loignon, Geneviève (Demers), VIII, 210
Loir, Guillaume, V, 709
Loire. *See* Le Moyne
Loiseau. *See also* Cardin; Lozeau
Loiseau, Antoine, IV, 148
Loiseau, Jean, III, 410
Loisel, Marie-Esther (Leroux), VIII, 500
Loiseleur, Marguerite (Guillot), IV, 320
Loiselle, Amable, XI, 585
Loisy, Catherine (Badeaux), IV, 40
Lok, Michael, I, 316, 317, 318, 332, 659, 676, 677
Lola, Fanny. *See* Joseph
Lola, Noel, VIII, 508
Lola, Noel, VIII, **508–9**
Lola, Peter, VIII, **509**
L'Ollivier de Tronjoly, François-Jean-Baptiste, IV, 77, 598
Lolo, Jean-Baptiste, known as St Paul, IX, **473**; XI, 882
Lolo, Sophia (Tod), IX, 473; XI, 882
Lomas, Adam, XII, 349
Lomas, Robert, XII, 864
Lombard, Antoinette de. *See* Hilaire
Lombard, Ephraim H., VIII, 868
Lombard, Jean-Adrian de, III, 406
Lombard, Marguerite (Bigot), IV, 59, 60
Lombard de Combles, Jean-Claude-Henri de, III, **405–6**;
    IV, 211
Lombard de Combles, Marie-Rose de. *See* Périn
Lom d'Arce, Françoise de. *See* Le Fascheux de Couttes
Lom d'Arce, Isaac de, Baron de Lahontan, II, 440
Lom d'Arce, Jeanne de. *See* Guérin
Lom d'Arce, Louis-Armand de, Baron de Lahontan, I, 526;
    II, 72, 142, 322, 328, **439–45**, 478, 510; III, 456; V, 684;
    XI, 490
Lomeron, David, I, 101, 248, **476**, 592
Lomeron, Jeanne. *See* Duquerny
Lomeron, Suzanne. *See* Georges

Lomeron de La Martinière, Daniel, I, 476
London, Bartholomew, V, 639, 640
London, Catherine (Rictenburgh), V, 640
London, Mary. *See* Osborn
London, Sarah, VI, 246
Londonderry, Marquess of. *See* Stewart
Lonergan, Anne (Power), XII, 859
Lonergan (Landergan), Patrick, V, 122, 632
Long. *See also* Fraisses
Long, Eliza Ann (Kelly), XI, 466
Long, John, IV, **486**; V, 567, 707, 836
Long, John Joseph, XII, 70
Long, Peter Ball, XI, 934
Long, Robert James, VIII, 923
Long, Stephen Harriman, VI, 720
Long, Thomas, XII, 70
Long, Victor Albert, XII, 1031
Longchamps-Montendre, Marie-Joséphine de
     (Bougainville), V, 102
Long Coat. *See* Anandamoakin
Longee, Joseph, XII, 901, 902
Longfellow, Henry Wadsworth, IV, xx, xxiii; VIII, 503; IX,
     351, 420, 421; XI, 512, 654; XII, 288, 361, 414, 474,
     549, 788, 925, 945, 948, 1077
Longland, John, III, 127, **406–7**, 453, 454
Longley, Asaph, XI, 525
Longley, Avard, XI, **525–26**; XII, 437, 1092
Longley, Betty, III, 407
Longley, Charlotte Augusta. *See* Troop
Longley, Delivrance. *See* Crisp
Longley, Dorcas. *See* Poole
Longley, George, VII, **510–11**; VIII, 690
Longley, Hannah Maria. *See* Whitman
Longley, Israel, XI, 525
Longley*, James Wilberforce (1849–1922), XII, 407
Longley, John, III, 407
Longley, Lydia (rebaptized Lydia-Madeleine), named
     Sainte-Madeleine, III, **407–8**
Longley, Ruth. *See* Wells
Longley, William (father), III, 407
Longley, William, III, 407
Longman, Thomas, XII, 572
Longmoor. *See also* Longmore
Longmoor, Robert, V, 501
Longmoor, Robert, IV, 157, 366, 518, 684, 760; V, 450,
     **500–1**, 682; VI, 317, 775
Longmoor, William, V, 500
Longmoore, Margaret (Armstrong), XI, 30
Longmore, Alexander, V, 501
Longmore, Christiana Lætitia. *See* Cox
Longmore, George, V, 799, 800; VII, 180
Longmore, George, IV, 589; V, 201, 202, **501–3**; VI, 258,
     325, 416, 549, 556, 586; VIII, 483
Longmuir, Catharine Mary (Simonds), VIII, 805
Longmuir, Eleanor. *See* Pickard
Longmuir, Richard White, XII, 1117
Longpré. *See also* Simon
Longpré, Marie (Bissot de Vinsenne), II, 67
Longsdon, William, VIII, 964
Longtin, Marie-Anne (Gagnon), VII, 333
Longueuil. *See* Le Moyne
Longueuil, Baron de. *See* Grant; Le Moyne
Longueuil, Baronne de. *See* Fleury Deschambault; Grant;

Legardeur de Tilly; Le Gouès de Grais; Le Moyne de
     Longueuil; Souart d'Adoucourt
Longueval, Robert de, I, 423, 425
Longueville, Duc de. *See* Orléans
Longueville, Henri, Duc de Longueville, I, 58
Longworth, Agnes. *See* Auld
Longworth, Elizabeth White. *See* Tremaine
Longworth, Francis (father of FRANCIS, d. 1843), VII,
     511
Longworth, Francis, VII, **511–12**; XI, 526, 528
Longworth, Francis, VII, 511; XI, **526–28**, 665
Longworth, Israel, VI, 307; VII, 23, 25; VIII, 123
Longworth, John, IX, 416
Longworth, John, VII, 511; XI, 527, **528–29**
Longworth, Mary. *See* Fitzgerald
Longworth, Nicholas, X, 264
Longworth, Robert, XI, 526
Longworth, Sarah Parker. *See* Watts
Longworth, Susan (Robson), XII, 914
Loomis, Abigail (Post), VII, 701
Loosey. *See* Losee
Loosley, Charles, IV, 483
Loppinot, Jean-Chrysostome, II, 445
Loppinot, Jean-Chrysostome, II, **445**, 654
Loppinot, Jeanne. *See* Doucet
Loppinot, Jeanne (Couagne), IV, 174
Loppinot, Louis, II, 445
Loppinot de La Frésillière, Marie-Josephe. *See* Seigneur
Loran, François, VI, 487
Loranger. *See also* Rivard
Loranger, Jean-Marie, XI, 529
Loranger, Louis-Onésime, XI, 480, 529
Loranger, Sarah-Angélique. *See* Truteau
Loranger, Thomas-Jean-Jacques, VIII, 17, 262, 668; IX,
     320; XI, 170, **529–31**, 822, 823; XII, 723
Loranger, Zélie-Angélique. *See* Borne
Lorans, Angélique (Pressart), IV, 642
Lorant, Jean-François, II, 424; III, 396
Lorant, Marie-Anne (Levasseur), III, 396
Lorant, Marie-Suzanne. *See* La Bazanière
Lord. *See also* Delort; Laird
Lord, Annie. *See* Lea
Lord, Artemus, XI, 532
Lord, Charlotte. *See* Gouldrup
Lord, Jeanne (Marié), II, 534
Lord, John, XI, 531
Lord, John Keast, X, **449–50**
Lord, Lucy Chandler (Russell), XI, 779
Lord, Mary. *See* Moulton
Lord, Sally (Helliwell), IX, 387
Lord, William, VIII, 372
Lord, William Warren, XI, **531–33**, 700; XII, 419
Loreau, Angélique (Saint-Étienne de La Tour), II, 592
Lorgeril, Jeanne-Élisabeth de. *See* Bégon
Lori. *See* Lorit
Lorière. *See* Jouenne
Lorimer, John G., VIII, 868, 869
Lorimier. *See* Chamilly
Lorimier, Agathe de (Ducharme), VIII, 245
Lorimier, Anne de. *See* Skaouennetsi
Lorimier*, Charles-Chamilly de (1842–1919), IX, 65
Lorimier, Chevalier de, VI, 404; VII, 105, 210, 264, 346,
     412, **512–16**; VIII, 583

Lorimier, Claude-Nicolas-Guillaume de, IV, 375; VI, **402–4**; VII, 516; VIII, 245
Lorimier, François-Chevalier de, VII, 512
Lorimier, Guillaume de, II, 445
Lorimier, Guillaume-François de, VI, 404
Lorimier, Guillaume-Verneuil de, VII, 512
Lorimier, Henriette de. *See* Cadieux
Lorimier, Jean-Baptiste-Chamilly de, VII, 105
Lorimier, Jean-Baptiste de, VI, 404; VII, **516–17**
Lorimier, Jean-Claude-Chamilly, VI, 403
Lorimier, Jeanne de. *See* Guilbaut
Lorimier, Louise de. *See* Schuyler
Lorimier, Marguerite de. *See* Rousseau
Lorimier, Marguerite-Adélaïde de. *See* Perrault
Lorimier, Marie-Louise de (Gamelin), IV, 285; VI, 402
Lorimier, Marie-Madeleine-Claire de. *See* Brassard Descheneaux
Lorimier de La Rivière, Claude-Nicolas de, II, 446; III, **408–9**; IV, 54, 636, 637; VI, 402
Lorimier de La Rivière, Guillaume de, I, 109; II, **445–46**, 513; III, 408
Lorimier de La Rivière, Marie-Louise de. *See* Lepallieur de Laferté
Lorimier de La Rivière, Marie-Marguerite de. *See* Chorel de Saint-Romain, *dit* d'Orvilliers
Lorimier de Verneuil, Marguerite. *See* Sabrevois de Bleury
Lorin, Françoise (Nau), III, 480
Lorin, Henri, I, 142
Loring. *See also* Sauguaaram
Loring, Ann. *See* Smith
Loring, Elizabeth. *See* Lloyd
Loring, Hannah. *See* Jackson
Loring, Joshua, IV, 486; VII, 517
Loring, Joshua, III, xxv; IV, 3, 23, 24, **486–88**, 588; V, 363; VII, 517
Loring, Mary. *See* Curtis
Loring, Mary Ann. *See* Campbell
Loring, Robert Roberts, IV, 487; VI, 113; VII, **517–18**
Loring, Thomas L., IV, 486
Lorit, *dit* Gargot, François, II, **446–47**
Lorit, *dit* Gargot, Marie-Thérèse. *See* Le Gros
Lorit, *dit* Gargot, Perrette. *See* Parement
L'Orme. *See* Hazeur
Lormel, Monsieur (ship's captain), II, 82
Lormier. *See* Lorimier
Lorne, Marchioness of. *See* Louise Caroline Alberta
Lorne, Marquess of. *See* Campbell
Loron. *See* Sauguaaram
Lorraine, Charles de, Duc d'Aumale, I, 96
Lorraine, Charles de, Duc de Guise, I, 214
Lorraine, Henri de, Comte d'Harcourt, I, 248
Lorrimier. *See* Lorimier
Lorris (Lorry). *See* Lorit
Lorson, Catherine (Marcol), III, 427
Lort. *See* Delort
Lory, César, II, 446
Lory, Richarde. *See* Grimère
Losada. *See also* Mollineda; Moziño
Losada, Manuela (Mosiño), V, 615
Losee, Elenor (mother of WILLIAM), VI, 404
Losee, John, VI, 404
Losee, Mary. *See* Carman
Losee, William, IV, 495; VI, 147, **404–6**

Lossing, Benson John, VI, 406; IX, 407
Lossing, Catherine. *See* Delong
Lossing, Christina. *See* Woolweaver
Lossing, Hannah. *See* Brill
Lossing, Nicholas, VI, 406
Lossing, Peter, VIII, 708; VI, **406–7**
Lossing, Solomon, VI, 407; VIII, 293
Lotbinière. *See* Chartier; Joly
Lotbinière, Marquis de. *See* Chartier
Lotbinière, Marquise de. *See* Chaussegros de Léry
Lotbinière* Harwood, Louis de (1866–1934), X, 89
Loteridge. *See* Lottridge
Lothain, Ann (Williamson), XII, 1101
Lothian, Marquess of. *See* Kerr
Lothman de Barrois, Marie (Navarre), IV, 579
Lots, Catherine (Gamache), VIII, 312
Lott, Herman, VIII, 949
Lottin, Isabelle (Lauson de Lirec), I, 427
Lottinville. *See* Lemaître
Lottridge, John, III, **409–10**
Lottridge, Richard, III, 409
Lottridge, Thomas, III, 409
Loubert, Pierre, V, 393
Loubert (Loubère), Pierre, VI, 651; VII, 752
Loubias (Laubia), Arnoult de, I, 327
Loubier, Louise, III, 620
Loubier, Louise (Solomons), VI, 434
Loubinois de Tourneuve, Jean, II, 125
Loucks, Nancy (Crysler), VIII, 194
Loudon*, James (1841–1916), X, 350
Loudon, John Claudius, VIII, 710
Loudoun, Earl of. *See* Campbell
Louet, Anne. *See* Morin
Louet, Catherine. *See* Thierry
Louet, Claude, II, 447; III, 421, 620
Louet, Jean, II, 447
Louet, Jean-Claude, II, xxiv, 151, **447**
Loughborough, Baron. *See* Wedderburn
Lougheed*, Sir James Alexander (1854–1925), XII, 30, 154
Loughnan, Clementina (Beckwith, Lady Beckwith), VI, 38
Loughnan, John, VI, 293; VIII, 307, 308, 656, 664, 920
Louis. *See also* Honarreennha; Ogenheratarihiens; Taondechoren
Louis, Captain. *See* Wahawanulet, Louis
Louis, Colonel. *See* Atiatoharongwen
Louis (French youth), I, 603
Louis (Montagnais), I, 511
Louis (son of MEMBERTOU), I, 500, 501
Louis IX (St Louis), King of France, I, 121, 126; III, 169
Louis XIII, King of France, I, 100, 102, 133, 134, 160, 191, 194, 196, 217, 405, 433, 437, 501, 502, 584, 592, 593, 594; II, 87, 98, 136; IV, xix
Louis XIV, King of France, I, 32, 35, 40, 55, 60, 62, 74, 76, 92, 104, 108, 109, 117, 119, 134, 135, 136, 137, 138, 139, 141, 174, 180, 202, 216, 220, 227, 238, 249, 261, 284, 288, 290, 330, 429, 443, 446, 467, 487, 510, 511, 513, 528, 535, 541, 542, 556, 561, 570, 571, 572, 576, 585, 587, 615, 616, 624, 631, 636, 646, 647, 648, 664; II, xvii, xviii, xix, 4, 26, 29, 32, 71, 72, 73, 76, 77, 85, 87, 88, 89, 90, 95, 98, 99, 100, 101, 103, 104, 112, 113, 114, 115, 129, 133, 134, 137, 141, 146, 155, 162, 175, 186, 205, 213, 229, 235, 262, 278, 280, 295, 302, 307, 325,

327, 328, 329, 330, 332, 333, 335, 353, 361, 363, 364, 365, 366, 367, 368, 369, 370, 375, 396, 397, 401, 420, 424, 431, 444, 448, 470, 471, 472, 483, 495, 496, 511, 518, 527, 538, 547, 554, 567, 570, 577, 578, 591, 595, 605, 620, 628, 633, 635, 641, 649; III, xvi, xvii, xx, 42, 57, 59, 60, 67, 248, 328, 356, 381, 552, 554, 557; IV, xx, 355, 465; VI, 491; VII, 213, 360;

Louis XV, King of France, II, xx, 52, 87, 476, 530, 570, 605; III, xvi, 8, 19, 140, 192, 240, 242, 248, 270, 291, 338, 350, 353, 384, 467, 486, 491, 566; IV, 65, 227, 355, 401, 439, 469, 472, 636, 637, 664, 673, 750; XI, 655

Louis XVI, King of France, III, 115; IV, 750; V, 671; VI, 388, 640, 679; VIII, 618, 778; XI, 31

Louis XVIII, King of France, VI, 517, 596, 620; VII, 27, 72

Louis, Jean, III, 382

Louis de France, II, 98, 104

Louis de Sainte-Foi. *See* Amantacha

Louise Caroline Alberta, Duchess of Saxony (Campbell, Marchioness of Lorne and Duchess of Argyll), XI, 6, 9, 297, 500, 515, 905; XII, 533

Louise de Saint-Augustin. *See* Soumande

Louise de Saint-Eustache. *See* Chartier de Lotbinière

Louise de Sainte-Marie. *See* Chomedey

Louise-Olive de Saint-Paul. *See* Roy

Louise-Rose de Sainte-Catherine. *See* Lanouguère

Louis-Marie, Father. *See* Lalonde

Louis-Philippe, King of the French, V, 449; VI, 517, 518; VII, 305, 307; VIII, 291, 619; X, 260, 497; XI, 96, 847

Lount, Elizabeth. *See* Soules

Lount, Gabriel, VII, 518

Lount, George, VII, 519

Lount, Philadelphia. *See* Hughes

Lount, Samuel, VII, **518–19**, 596; VIII, 27, 30, 520, 643, 855; IX, 412, 503, 675, 686, 687, 689; X, 622, 639, 641

Lount, William, XII, 103

L'Ours. *See* Le Pesant

Loustelneau, Catherine de (Denys de Vitré), II, 179

Loustelneau, Charles de, II, 179

Loustelneau, Charlotte de. *See* Buday Fleury

Louthood, Alexandre, XI, 814

Louvières. *See* Damours

Louvigny. *See also* Bernières; La Porte; Testard

Louvigny d'Orgemont, Paul, II, 147

Louvois, Marquis de. *See* Le Tellier

Lovaine, Baron. *See* Percy

Lovat, Lady. *See* Stewart

Love, Ann. *See* Ketchum

Love, Catherine (Vincent), VII, 888

Love, Sir James Frederick, IX, 386, 387

Love, Mary, Lady Love. *See* Heaviside

Love, Timolean, IX, 518

Lovelace, Francis, II, 107

Lovell, Catherine-Louise (Dorion), X, 235, 236

Lovell, Jane. *See* Beasly

Lovell, John, VII, 354, 660; VIII, 160, 232, 536, 551; IX, 41, 84, 343, 667; X, 537; XI, 12, 59, 147, 216, 254, 321, 859; XII, 89, 90, 231, 408, **569–74**, 753, 946, 998, 1076

Lovell, John Wurtele, XII, 572

Lovell, Patience (Wright), VI, 329

Lovell, Robert, XII, 569

Lovell, Robert Kurczyn, XII, 572, 573

Lovell, Sarah. *See* Kurczyn

Løvendal. *See* Lowendahl

Lovett, Abigail. *See* Thayer

Lovett, Beulah. *See* Morse

Lovett, Phineas, VI, 407

Lovett, Phineas, VI, **407–8**

Lovingheart, Dr. *See* Campbell, Andrew

Low, Charles Adamson, VII, 382; VIII, 691; IX, 13

Low, Elizabeth (Gray), V, 388

Low, Mary (Spark), V, 768

Low, Will Hickock, XII, 288

Lowden, William, VI, 806

Lowe, Bridget. *See* Eastman

Lowe, Frederick C., VIII, 14, 266; XII, 667

Lowe, James, X, 479

Lowe, John, IX, 258

Lowe, Miriam. *See* Lockhart

Lowe, Robert, IX, 384

Lowe, Thomas, IX, 624; X, 486

Lowe, William Hamilton, XI, 394

Lowell, Charles, XII, 574

Lowell, Charles Russell, XII, 574

Lowell, Harriet Brackett. *See* Spence

Lowell, James Russell, XII, 574

Lowell, Mary Ann. *See* Duane

Lowell, Robert Traill Spence, XII, 574

Lowell, Robert Traill Spence, VIII, 199; XII, **574–75**

Lowendahl (Løvendal, Loewendahl), Ulrich-Frédéric-Valdemar (Ulrik Frederick Woldemar), Comte de Lowendahl, IV, 504

Lower*, Arthur Reginald Marsden (1889–1988), VI, 226; XII, 665

Lowman, Mary. *See* Bird

Lowman, Mary (Bird), X, 67

Lowth, Robert, V, 747

Lowther, Katherine (Powlett, Duchess of Bolton), III, 669

Lowther, Robert, III, 669

Loy, George di Madeiros, XII, 136

Loyard, Jean-Baptiste, II, 198, **447–48**; III, 23, 163

Loyd. *See* Lloyd; Loid

Loyseau, Charles, II, 211

Lozana, Feliciana (Suria), VI, 742

Lozeau, Catherine. *See* Gautier

Lozeau, Catherine Hedwige (Futvoye), XII, 346

Lozeau, François, III, 410

Lozeau, Jean-Baptiste, III, **410–11**

Lozeau, Marguerite. *See* Gauron

Lozeau, Marguerite. *See* Mercier

Lozeau, Pierre-Louis, III, 410

Luard, Elizabeth. *See* Scott

Luard, Hannah. *See* Chamberlin

Luard, Henry Reynolds, XI, 604, 606, 607

Luard, John, XII, 575

Luard, Richard George Amherst, XI, 929; XII, 244, **575–77**, 733, 734

Lubet, Antoinette (Dénéchaud), V, 248

Lublé (Lliebb), Catharina (Mayerhoffer), VIII, 622

Luc, Brother. *See* François, Claude

Lucas, Francis, III, **411–12**; IV, 158, 334, 536, 537; V, 166

Lucas, Jacqueline (Auber), I, 72

Lucas, Jean, named Brother Rombaud, IX, 681

Lucas, Joseph, IV, 702; V, 329, 436; VI, 230

Lucas, Louis, X, 260

Lucas, Marie-Adéline, named Mother Séraphine du Divin Cœur de Jésus, XI, 110

Lucas, Richard, I, 315, 417, **476–77**, 606, 666; II, 318
Lucas Dontigny, François, III, 187
Lucas Dontigny, Marie-Madeleine. *See* Baudouin
Lucault (Lucau). *See* Barbeau
Lucchesi-Palli, Caroline, Princess of Campofranco. *See* Caroline
Luce, Bethia (Swayze), VI, 746
Lucier, Félicité (Manson), X, 496
Lucière. *See* La Motte
Luckens, Hannah (Iredell), V, 448
Luckman, Mr (officer), V, 674
Lucky Man. *See* Papewes
Lucy, VI, 350
Ludlow, Ann. *See* Ver Planck
Ludlow, Daniel, V, 505
Ludlow, Elizabeth (Robinson), VI, 654
Ludlow, Frances (mother of GABRIEL GEORGE and GEORGE DUNCAN). *See* Duncan
Ludlow, Frances (wife of GEORGE DUNCAN). *See* Duncan
Ludlow, Gabriel (father), V, 505
Ludlow, Gabriel, V, 503, 505
Ludlow, Gabriel George, IV, 329; V, 156, 157, 161, **503–5**, 506; VI, 356, 502, 518; IX, 62
Ludlow, Gabriel Ver Planck, V, 504
Ludlow, George, VII, 330
Ludlow, George Duncan, IV, 55; V, 349, 456, 503, **505–7**, 630, 867; VI, 75, 138, 142, 247, 395, 518, 654, 684, 811; VII, 73, 88, 198; VIII, 150; XII, 537
Lugger, Elizabeth (mother of ROBERT), VII, 519
Lugger, Joseph, VII, 519
Lugger, Robert, VII, **519–21**; VIII, 276; X, 270, 437; XI, 639
Lugrin, Charles Henry, VI, 409
Lugrin, Charles S., VI, 409
Lugrin, Deborah Ann. *See* Smiler
Lugrin, George Kilman, V, 613; VI, **408–9**; VIII, 156
Lugrin, Jane (Chubb), VI, 409; VIII, 156
Lugrin, Peter, VI, 408
Lugrin, Simeon Lee, VII, 612
Luján Silva y Góngora, Pedro Francisco, Duke of Almodóvar del Río, I, 676; IV, 687
Lukens, John, V, 448
Lukin, Jean-Baptiste, VII, 238
Lukin, Marie-Louise (Leprohon), XII, 555
Lukin, Pierre, VIII, 433
Lukin, Windham William, IX, 844
Lumisden, Isabella (Strange, Lady Strange), VII, 830, 831
Lumley, Elizabeth (King), X, 406
Lumley, Sir William, X, 663
Lumsden, John, V, 218
Lumsden, John M., XI, 312
Luna, Pedro de, I, 342
Lundie. *See* MacDonell
Lundrigan, James, VI, 393, **409–11**, 711; VII, 115, 152, 303, 507, 628, 629; VIII, 234
Lundrigan, Sarah. *See* Morgan
Lundy, Benjamin, X, 206
Lundy, Francis James, X, 58; XII, 464
Lundy, Thomas, VII, 835
Lunette, Françoise (Ménage), II, 467
Lunn, Alexander Hutchison, XI, 533
Lunn, Elizabeth. *See* Heard
Lunn, Margaret. *See* Fisher

Lunn, Rachel (Wyatt), VII, 929
Lunn, William, XI, 533
Lunn, William, V, 320; VII, 725; XI, 148, **533–34**
Lupien, *dit* Baron, Angélique. *See* Courault, *dit* La Coste
Lupien, *dit* Baron, Antoine, III, 412
Lupien, *dit* Baron, Jean-Marie, III, 412
Lupien, *dit* Baron, Marie-Marthe. *See* Chauvin
Lupien, *dit* Baron, Nicolas, III, 412
Lupien, *dit* Baron, Pierre, III, 139, **412–13**; IV, 362, 690
Luria, Rebecca (Cohen), V, 193
Lush, William, VIII, 246, 247
Lusher, Esther (wife of ROBERT LANGHAM), VII, 521
Lusher, Robert Langham, VI, 67; VII, **521–22**; VIII, 666
Lushington, Henrietta, Lady Lushington. *See* Prescott
Lusignan. *See also* Dazemard
Lusignan, Adeline de. *See* Roy
Lusignan, Alexandre de, X, 635
Lusignan, Alphonse, IX, 121, 195; X, 425, 430; XI, 186; XII, 308, 325
Lusignan, Charles, IV, 7, 8, 534; VIII, 781
Lusignan, Madeleine. *See* Laforce
Lusignany, Émilie L. (Roy), VIII, 781
Lussier, Camille, XI, 289
Lussigny, Monsieur (brother-in-law of Daniel GREYSOLON Dulhut), II, 262, 345
Luteau, Apollinaire, II, 130, 223
Lutwyche, Edward Goldstone, V, 94, 161, 162
Luxembourg. *See* Raphaël
Luxton*, William Fisher (1844–1907), XI, 46; XII, 129
Luzançay. *See* Carré
Lyall*, Peter (1841–1912), XII, 131
Lyall, William, XI, 534
Lyall, William, XI, **534**, 773
Lydall, Sir Richard, I, 477
Lydall, William, I, 83, 343, **477**
Lyde, Sarah (Byles), V, 128
Lydekker, Rachael (Aycrigg; Jacobus), VII, 918
Lydia, XII, 551
Lÿdius, Geneviève. *See* Massé
Lÿdius, Isabella (mother of JOHN HENDRICKS; Staats), IV, 488
Lÿdius, Johannes, IV, 488
Lÿdius, John Hendricks, III, 322, 623; IV, 173, **488–90**
Lyell, Sir Charles, VII, 760, 761; IX, 383, 660, 666; X, 84, 445; XI, 544, 631; XII, 230, 231, 232, 233
Lyle, Alexander, IX, 174, 182; XI, 501
Lyman, Benjamin, X, **450–51**; XII, 296
Lyman, Charles, X, 450
Lyman, Daniel, V, 350, 353
Lyman, Delia Almira. *See* Wells
Lyman, Elisha, X, 450
Lyman, Hannah. *See* Stiles
Lyman, Henry, X, 450, 451
Lyman, Lewis, X, 450
Lyman, Richard, X, 450
Lyman, Roswell Corse, X, 450
Lyman, William, VIII, 631; IX, 288; X, 450
Lymburner, Adam, IV, 58, 399, 557; V, 150, 151, 232, 270, 283, 370, 373, 493, 566, 576, 647, 650, 769, 816, 843; VI, 19, 123, 166, 254, 400, 424, 471, 472, 494; VII, **522–25**, 575
Lymburner, John, V, 843; VII, 522

Lymburner, Mathew, V, 370, 746, 816; VI, 95, 305; VII, 523, 524
Lymburner, Mathew, VIII, 489
Lynch, Miss, named Sister Mary Xavier, VIII, 475
Lynch, Ann. See Connolly
Lynch, Anna. See McCormick
Lynch, David (father of JOHN), XI, 534
Lynch, David (shipbuilder), XI, 888
Lynch, Isidore, IV, 35
Lynch, James, XI, 535
Lynch, James Spencer, XII, 641
Lynch, John, XI, 534–35
Lynch, John Joseph, IX, 492; X, 192, 510, 662; XI, 222, 257, 450, 535–38, 649, 694, 715, 864, 880, 904; XII, 28, 185, 199, 330, 331, 332, 333, 334, 689, 690, 811, 867, 1078, 1084, 1085, 1086, 1087
Lynch, Peter, VII, 21, 22; VIII, 354; IX, 184; XII, 765
Lynch, Susan. See Monger
Lynd, Ann (Grant), V, 509
Lynd, David, V, 75, 91, 192, 385, 507–10; VI, 326
Lynd, Hutchinson, V, 509
Lynd, Jane. See Henry
Lynd, Jane (Dodd), V, 509
Lynd, John, V, 508
Lynde, Hannah (Goffe), II, 254
Lynde, Lucy (Hartt), X, 338
Lynde, Samuel, II, 254
Lyndhurst, Baron. See Copley
Lynds, David B., X, 696
Lynds, Susan (Waddell), X, 696
Lynn, Margaret E. (Boyd), XII, 121
Lynn, Martha (Dennis), VI, 187
Lynn, Samuel George, IX, 241; XII, 183
Lynne, Marrianne (White), IV, 766; VI, 721
Lynson, Jane. See Robinson
Lyon. See also Bowes-Lyon; Fellowes
Lyon, Abigail (Bates), VII, 53
Lyon, Barbara (Day), XI, 237
Lyon (Lyons), Benjamin, IV, 332, 718, 719
Lyon, Catharine (Ward; Cameron), XII, 146
Lyon, Catherine. See Radenhurst
Lyon, Electa Ann (Wanzer), XII, 1088
Lyon, Elizabeth. See Philips
Lyon, Frances Clayton, VII, 52
Lyon, George, VIII, 509
Lyon, George, VII, 446; VIII, 509–11, 553, 707, 733
Lyon, George Francis, VII, 463; VIII, 684; IX, 387
Lyon, James, V, 626
Lyon*, James Walter (d. 1933), XII, 39
Lyon, Jean (Brown), IX, 88
Lyon, Martha. See Holden
Lyon, Mary (mother of JAMES), IV, 490
Lyon, Robert (uncle), VIII, 510; XI, 827
Lyon, Robert, VIII, 510, 733; IX, 843
Lyon, Sarah. See Skillen
Lyon, Thomas, VIII, 510
Lyon, William Radenhurst Richmond, VIII, 510
Lyon, Zopher, IV, 490
Lyon de Saint-Ferréol, Jean, II, 577; III, 223, 413–14, 522
Lyonnais. See also Bossu
Lyonnais, Joseph, VII, 775
Lyonne, Marguerite (Le Vieux de Hauteville), I, 475

Lyonne, Martin de, I, 477–78, 558
Lyons. See also Lyon
Lyons, Mr (preacher), VI, 405
Lyons, Mr (teacher), IV, 495
Lyons, Ann. See McLachlan
Lyons, Barnett, IV, 332; V, 194
Lyons, Bernard, VI, 666
Lyons, Céline (Joseph), VI, 366
Lyons, Charles, V, 478; VI, 736
Lyons, Denis, VI, 691
Lyons, Elijah, VII, 368
Lyons, Isabella (Bill), XII, 108
Lyons, Jacques Judah, V, 194; XI, 254, 256
Lyons, James (engineer), X, 404
Lyons, James (merchant), XII, 480
Lyons, James (politician), VI, 638
Lyons, John, V, 419; VII, 712
Lyons, Louis, VI, 666
Lyons, Louisa Rose (Murray), XII, 775
Lyons, Richard Bickerton Pemell, 1st Earl Lyons, XII, 750
Lyons, William, VI, 416
Lysaght, Averil M., V, 221
Lyschander, Claus C., I, 675
Lysons, Sir Daniel, X, 131
Lyttleton, Sir Richard, IV, 84, 85
Lytton, Baron. See Bulwer-Lytton

MABANE, Mrs. See Wedel
Mabane, Adam, III, 541, 542; IV, 6, 104, 278, 323, 324, 345, 367, 379, 380, 491–94, 547, 554, 574, 579, 602, 658, 716, 791, 794; V, 44, 91, 142, 145, 146, 149, 150, 181, 215, 277, 278, 284, 317, 371, 583, 745, 839, 863, 892, 901, 902; VI, 258, 511, 512, 513, 606, 615; VII, 523; IX, 718; XI, 87
Mabane, Isabell, IV, 493; V, 215; VII, 64
Mabey, George, IX, 473
Mabey, Mary (mother of PAUL), IX, 473
Mabey, Paul, VIII, 444, 484, 548, 826; IX, 473–74
Mably. See Bonnot
McAdam, Elizabeth (Burns), XII, 142
McAdam, John, XII, 774, 1097
MacAilein, Iain. See MacGhillEathain, Iain
Macain, Jean, I, 98, 101, 293, 476, 565
McAllister, James, XII, 479
McAllister, Jennie Elizabeth (McMichael), VII, 871
Macallum, Archibald, X, 451–52
Macallum, Donald, X, 451
Macallum, Elizabeth. See Charles
Macallum, John, VII, 455, 526–27, 902; VIII, 590; IX, 136, 784; XI, 19
Macallum, Margaret (Charles), VII, 526
Macallum, Maria. See Adams
Macallum, Mary. See Biggar
Macallum, Mary Macalpine. See Barramollach
McAlpin, Daniel, V, 585
McAlpine, Charles L., VIII, 81
M'Alpine, Christian (mother of JOHN), VI, 411
M'Alpine, Jane (wife of JOHN), VI, 411
M'Alpine, John, VI, 411–12
M'Alpine, Peter, VI, 411
M'Alpine, Rebecca. See Gammon
M'Alpine, Sarah. See Caverly
M'Alpine, Sarah. See Walker

Macara, John, XI, 542

Macara, William, XII, 764

Macard, Catherine-Gertrude (Deschamps de La Bouteillerie), II, 180, 181

Macard, Charles, I, 345; II, 149, 276, **448–49**; III, 493

Macard, Geneviève (Bazire; Provost; Aloigny, Marquise de
La Groye), I, 84, 85; II, 16, 533

Macard, Jeanne-Renée. *See* Gourdeau de Beaulieu

Macard, Marguerite. *See* Couillard de Lespinay

Macard, Marguerite. *See* Hardy

Macard, Marie-Anne (Bécart de Granville), II, 53, 213; III,
55

Macard, Marie-Thérèse (Alavoine), III, 7

Macard, Thomas, II, 448

Macard, *dit* Champagne, Nicolas, I, 84; II, 16, 181, 448

Macarmick, Catherine. *See* Buller

Macarmick, James, V, 510

Macarmick, Philippa (mother of WILLIAM), V, 510

Macarmick, William, IV, 293, 522; V, 53, 204, 223,
**510–11**, 546, 634, 766, 780; VI, 195, 213, 348, 393, 535;
VII, 10

Macart, Hélène (Jérémie), I, 387

MacArthur, Miss (MacColl), XII, 588

McArthur, Alexander, XI, **538–39**

McArthur, Alexander, XII, **577–78**

McArthur, Archibald, XII, 578

McArthur, Duncan (historian), V, 232

McArthur, Duncan (officer), VII, 821

McArthur, Hannah May. *See* Hutchins

McArthur, John (brother of ALEXANDER, 1839–95), XII,
577

Macarthur, John (father of Alexander MCARTHUR,
1843–87), XI, 538

McArthur, John (father of ALEXANDER, 1839–95), XII, 577

McArthur, Margaret. *See* McMartin

McArthur, Mary Jane (wife of ALEXANDER, 1839–95), XII,
577

McArthur, Peter (brother of ALEXANDER, 1843–87), XI,
538

McArthur, Peter (brother of ALEXANDER, 1839–95), XII,
577, 578

Macarthur, Sarah. *See* Dallas

McArthur, Walter James, XII, 578

Macartney, George, 1st Earl Macartney, V, 359

Macartney, Georgina Mildred (Kennedy), XI, 468

Macarty, Ursule (Perrault), IV, 496; VI, 576; VII, 687, 688

Macarty Mactigue, Barthélemy de, II, 523

McAskill, Angus, IX, **474–75**

McAskill, Christina. *See* Campbell

McAskill, Norman, IX, 474

Macátepilesis. *See* Mécatépilésis

Macaulay, Æneas, VI, 412

Macaulay, Angus, V, 547, 860, 862; VI, 122, 161, 162,
**412–15**, 566; VIII, 37, 570, 741, 824

Macaulay, Ann. *See* Kirby

Macaulay, Anne Catherine. *See* Geddes

Macaulay, Anne Gee. *See* Elmsley

Macaulay, Ann Elizabeth, VIII, 521

Macaulay, Charlotte Sarah. *See* Vesconte

Macaulay, Donald, XII, 523

Macaulay, Elizabeth (Hagerman), VII, 365, 366

Macaulay, Elizabeth Tuck. *See* Hayter

Macaulay, Frances Jane (Kirkpatrick), XII, 496

Macaulay, Genevieve. *See* Burrow

Macaulay, George, VII, 366

Macaulay, Helen. *See* Macpherson

Macaulay, Henry, VI, 417

Macaulay, James, VII, 845

Macaulay, James, V, 502; VI, 325, **415–16**; VII, 156, 207,
365, 920; VIII, 191, 341, 511, 522; X, 299

Macaulay, Sir James Buchanan, VI, 91, 118, 266, 369, 416,
425, 426, 497, 729; VII, 42, 314, 367, 369, 371; VIII, 29,
46, 205, 432, **511–13**, 523; IX, 513; X, 257; XI, 845

Macaulay, John, IV, 494; VI, 32, 215, 216, 470, 544, 772,
773; VII, 75, 157, 229, 365, 366, 367, 368, 370, 371,
372, 409, 410, 411, 453, 456, 457, 458, 459, 461, 469,
470, 472, 558, 559, 580, 584, 857, 893, 894; VIII, 6, 7, 8,
10, 11, 28, 29, 255, 419, 445, **513–22**, 523, 534, 760,
761, 847; IX, 49, 333, 551, 670, 672, 700, 753, 755, 761,
763, 857; X, 30, 453, 622; XI, 378; XII, 496, 682

Macaulay, John Simcoe, VI, 416; VIII, 29, 187, 188, 419,
511, **522–24**, 799; IX, 535, 724, 725

Macaulay, Mary. *See* Macdonald

Macaulay, Mary. *See* Macleod

Macaulay, Mary (Gamble), X, 299

Macaulay, Mary (Higginson), XI, 404

Macaulay, Mary (Nixon; Kirby), VII, 469

Macaulay, Naomi Helen McIntosh, VIII, 521

Macaulay, Rachel, Lady Macaulay. *See* Crookshank

Macaulay, Rachel Crookshank, Lady Macaulay. *See* Gamble

Macaulay, Robert, VII, 469, 472; VIII, 513

Macaulay, Robert, IV, **494**; V, 326, 492; VII, 469, 470,
583; VIII, 513; X, 452

Macaulay*, Robertson (1833–1915), XI, 335

Macaulay, Sarah Hayter (Cartwright), VII, 156

Macaulay, Sarah Phillis. *See* Young

Macaulay, Susan. *See* Gilliland

Macaulay, Thomas Babington, 1st Baron Macaulay, XI,
248; XII, 112

Macaulay, William, IV, 494

Macaulay, William, IV, 494; VI, 32; VII, 469, 472; VIII,
513, 837; IX, 753; X, **452–53**

Macaulay, Zachary, V, 68

Macaulay, Zachary, IV, 759; V, 146; VI, **416–17**

McAuley, Catherine Elizabeth, named Sister Mary Catherine, VIII, 184

M'Auslane, Peter, V, 776

McBean, Isabella. *See* Latour

McBean, John, VI, 466; VIII, 86

MacBean, Mary (Fraser), VI, 263; VIII, 304

McBeath, Alexander, XI, 539

McBeath, Christian. *See* Gunn

McBeath, Christina (McVicar), IX, 532; XII, 690

McBeath, Erie. *See* Smyth

McBeath, George, IV, 311; V, 299, 300, 333, **511–13**, 561,
603, 682, 683, 715, 818; VI, 285

McBeath, Jane. *See* Graham

McBeath, Margaret, V, 715

McBeath, Mary. *See* McLean

McBeath, Robert, IX, 330; X, 549; XI, **539–40**

McBeth, Adam, X, 550

Macbeth, Anne Gilbert. *See* Sanders

Macbeth, Catherine. *See* Sutherland

Macbeth, George, IX, 475

Macbeth, George, VIII, 860; IX, **475–76**; XI, 62

MacBeth, Mary (Nisbet), X, 549, 550
Macbeth, Thomas Talbot, IX, 476
Macbraire, Mr (ironmonger), VI, 418
MacBraire, Elizabeth. *See* Bower
MacBraire, James, VI, 323, **417–20**, 710; VII, 598, 634
MacBraire, John Joseph, VI, 419, 420
MacBrayne, Elizabeth Stevenson (Macgeorge), XI, 557
McBride, Edward, VI, 420
McBride, Edward William, VI, 248, **420–21**
McBride, Hannah. *See* Washburn
McBride, James (businessman), XII, 379
McBride, James (of Niagara, Upper Canada), VI, 420
McBride, Jane (Emory; Keefer), VIII, 450
McBride, Mary. *See* Bradshaw
McBride, Peter (father of EDWARD WILLIAM), VI, 420
McBride, Peter (merchant), VIII, 862; XII, 378
McBride, Peter (of Niagara, Upper Canada), VI, 420
McBride*, Sir Richard (1870–1917), XII, 626
McBride, Robert Kerr, XII, 379
McBride, Thomas James, XII, 702, 705, 706, 707
McCabe, Annie, named Sister Mary Stanislaus, XII, 209
MacCabe, Cornelius, X, 193
McCabe, Mary (Decoigne), VII, 238
McCall, Daniel, VI, 331
McCall (McColl), Donald (Donell), VI, 421, 422
McCall, Duncan, V, 734; VI, **421–22**; VII, 40
McCall, Elsie. *See* Simpson
McCall, Jemima. *See* Fairchild
McCall, John, VI, 421, 422
McCall, Mary (Lockwood; wife of DUNCAN), VI, 421
McCallum, Archibald, VI, 423
McCallum, Bertie, XI, 704
McCallum, Colin, VII, 707, 708
McCallum, Daniel, VII, 880; XI, 901
McCallum, Duncan, VI, 423
McCallum, Ellen (Barrett), XI, 53
MacCallum, George, XII, 879
McCallum, James, VI, 423
McCallum, James, V, 648, 879, 881; VI, 124, 125, **422–25**; VII, 877; VIII, 962
McCallum, Janet (wife of JAMES), VI, 422
McCallum, John (merchant), VI, 125, 423
McCallum, John (son of JAMES), VI, 423
McCallum, John William, VII, 739
McCallum, Peter Duncan, XII, 333
MacCallum, Stephen, XI, 699
McCandless, Henry, XI, 454
McCann, Rosanna, named Sister Mary Basilia, VIII, 920; IX, **476–77**; XII, 410
McCardle, Mary (McConville), VII, 527
McCarey, William. *See* Tubbee, Okah
McCarney, Catherine (McKeagney), VIII, 554
MacCarthy. *See also* Latouche
McCarthy, Agnes Elizabeth. *See* Lally
McCarthy, Ann (Hannah) (wife of JAMES OWEN), VI, 425
McCarthy, Calahan, VI, 426
McCarthy, Catherine. *See* O'Brian
McCarthy, Charles, XII, 208
McCarthy, Charlesina Hope. *See* Manners
McCarthy, D'Alton, X, 78; XII, 578
McCarthy, D'Alton, XI, 418; XII, 27, 138, 246, 293, 372, **578–88**, 609, 610, 617, 807, 887, 1011, 1108, 1130
McCarthy, Eleanor (Conway), XII, 208

McCarthy, Emma Catherine. *See* Lally
McCarthy, James, XII, 208
McCarthy, James Owen, VI, **425–26**; VIII, 512
McCarthy, Jeffery A., XII, 585
McCarthy, Jeremiah, VI, 428
McCarthy, Jeremiah, V, 217, 278; VI, **426–29**; VIII, 211, 212
McCarthy, Justin, VII, 645
McCarthy, Marie-Magdelaine. *See* Dubergès
McCarthy, Mary (Brown), VII, 387; VIII, 368
McCarthy, Mary (Cronan), XII, 221
MacCarthy, Mary Elizabeth (Sullivan), III, 602
MacCarthy, Robert, Viscount Muskerry, II, 251; III, 619
McCartney, Jane (Chadwick), XII, 171
McCarty, Catherine. *See* Lent
Maccarty, Charles, IV, 247
McCarty, Charles Justin (James), IV, **494–95**; VI, 147, 405
McCarty, John, IV, 495
McCarty, Richard, IV, **495–96**
McCarty, Ursule. *See* Benoît
McCaul, Emily. *See* Jones
McCaul, Emily Augusta (Macdougall), XII, 619
McCaul, John, VIII, 959; X, 172, 173, 270; XI, **540–42**, 778; XII, 399, 619, 1111
McCaulay, Frances (Rollo), V, 723
McCauley. *See* Macaulay
McCausland, Harriet (Shortt), IX, 719
MacCaw, Thomas, XII, 350
McCawley, Anne. *See* Odell
McCawley, George, VI, 54; VII, 413; IX, 638; X, 110, **453–54**
McClaren, Maria Jane (Larue), XII, 531
McClean, Arthur, X, 310
McClearn, Matthew, IX, **477–78**
McClearn, Robert, IX, 477
McClearn, Sarah. *See* West
McClearn, Sophia. *See* Darrow
McClelan, Abner Reid, XI, 578
McClellan, George Brinton, X, 291; XII, 430
McClellan, Mary (McMicking), IX, 517
McClellan (McLellan), Robert, V, 526; VIII, 190
McClelland. *See* McLelan
McClement, Patrick, V, 330
McClement, Susanna (Smith), IX, 728
Macclesfield, Earl of. *See* Parker
McCliesh, Elizabeth (Norton), III, 489; IV, 583
McCliesh, Mary (wife of THOMAS), III, 415
McCliesh, Mary (Coats), III, 127
McCliesh, Thomas, III, 414
McCliesh, Thomas, II, 10, 51, 56, 65, 291, 313, 492; III, 127, **414–15**, 489, 599, 662
McClintock*, Sir Francis Leopold (1819–1907), VII, 327; VIII, 624, 625; IX, 693; X, 89, 319, 327, 396, 397, 407, 408, 563; XI, 543, 544, 691; XII, 878, 954
McClure, Adam, IX, 478
McClure, Constance Ada. *See* Tudor
McClure (Maclure), George, VI, 230, 231
McClure, Hannah. *See* Glynn
McClure, James, XII, 444
McClure, Jane. *See* Elgee
McClure, John, X, 455
McClure, Leonard, IX, 428, **478–80**; XI, 469; XII, 240, 914
McClure, Margaret. *See* Bussell

McClure, Margaret. *See* Wilson
McClure, Robert, X, 454
McClure, Sir Robert John Le Mesurier, VII, 327; VIII, 624; IX, 167, 693; X, 28, 42, 396, 397, **454–55**, 513, 562, 563; XI, 199, 200, 201, 691, 692; XII, 38
McClure, Sarah. *See* Trelford
McClure, William, X, **455–56**
McColl. *See also* McCall
MacColl, Mrs. *See* MacArthur
MacColl, Dugald, XII, 588
M'Coll, Duncan, V, 25, 573; VI, 65, **429–32**; XI, 733
M'Coll, Elizabeth. *See* Channal
MacColl, Evan, XII, **588–89**, 1116
MacColl, Frances. *See* Lewthwaite
M'Coll, Hugh, VI, 429
McColl, John, IX, 742
McColl, Louisa (Dunlop), VII, 259, 263
McColl, Margaret (McDonald), X, 459
MacColl, Mary. *See* Cameron
MacColl, Mary Jemima (Schulte), XII, 588
McConnachay, Barbara (Richardson), XI, 731
McConnell, George, VIII, 821
McConnell, Gilbert S., XII, 805
McConnell, John, VIII, 148; IX, 727; X, 642, 674
McConnell, William, XII, 195
McConville, Arthur, VII, 527
McConville, Henri-Jean, IX, 330
McConville, John, VII, **527**
McConville, Joseph Norbet Alfred, VII, 527
McConville, Mary. *See* McCardle
McConville, Mary Magdalen. *See* Mackie
McConville, Meredith, VII, 527
McCord, Andrew, XI, 542
McCord, Andrew Taylor, XI, **542–43**, 616; XII, 410
McCord, Aurelia Felicite. *See* Arnoldi
McCord, Aurelia Sophia (Polette), XI, 698
McCord, Charlotte. *See* Taylor
McCord, David Ross, IX, 870; X, 738; XII, 737
McCord, Della, VI, 628
McCord, Jane (Fraser), IV, 276; V, 224
McCord, John (father), V, 142, 331, 406, 508, 637; VI, 432
McCord, John, V, 723; VI, 432
McCord, John Samuel, VI, 434; VIII, 232, 524, 525
McCord, Margaret (mother of ANDREW TAYLOR), XI, 542
McCord, Margaret (Bleakley), VI, 72
McCord, Margery. *See* Ellis
McCord, Robert, X, 306
McCord, Sarah. *See* Solomons
McCord, Thomas, VIII, 525; X, 135, 488; XI, 721
McCord, Thomas, V, 723, 820; VI, 72, **432–34**, 640, 744; VII, 235, 622, 623; VIII, 524, 914
McCord, William King, VI, 120, 434; VII, 27, 682; VIII, **524–25**; X, 587; XI, 698
MacCormick. *See* Macarmick
McCormick. *See also* Macarmick
McCormick, Alexander, VII, 527
McCormick, Andrew, XII, 73
McCormick, Anna (Lynch), XI, 535
McCormick, Cæsar, IV, 228
McCormick, Charles, V, 602, 656
McCormick, Elizabeth. *See* Turner
McCormick, Martha (O'Hara), V, 637; VI, 556
McCormick, Mary. *See* Cornwall

McCormick, Robert, XI, 543
McCormick, Robert, XI, **543–44**
McCormick, Sheppard, VIII, 391, 502
McCormick, William, VII, **527–29**
McCorquadale, Sarah. *See* McDougall
McCoubrey, John Williams, VII, 154, 155, 631, 632, 634, 793; X, **456**
McCourt, Peter, IX, 828, 834
McCowen*, John Roche (1844–1908), XII, 157
McCoy. *See* Coy
McCrae, David, V, 512
McCrae, Erie. *See* Smyth
McCrae, Thomas, XII, 384, 446
McCrea, Frances (Hutton), IX, 404
McCrea, Robert Barlow, IX, 582; X, 280; XII, **589–90**
McCreight*, John Foster (1827–1913), XI, 435, 757, 839; XII, 241, 916
McCrossan, Thomas, XII, 43
McCuaig, Dorothy (Ridout), X, 619
McCuaig, James Simeon, XII, 602, 603
McCuen, Charles, IV, 756
MacCullagh, William, X, 303; XI, 772, 773
McCulloch, Elizabeth. *See* Neilson
McCulloch, Ferdinand, XI, 556
McCulloch, Isabella. *See* Walker
McCulloch, James Maitland, VI, 629, 630
McCulloch, John, XII, 786
McCulloch, Michael (father of THOMAS), VII, 529
McCulloch, Michael (politician), IX, 444
McCulloch, Thomas, VII, 540
McCulloch, Thomas, V, 124, 612; VI, 158, 322, 460, 461, 659, 660, 791, 800; VII, 22, 81, 82, 83, 84, 85, 107, 330, 341, **529–41**, 867, 933, 934; VIII, 222, 355, 452, 460, 613, 755, 756, 955; IX, 7, 281, 352, 738, 828; X, 302, 303, 353, 539; XI, 28, 215, 772, 926, 944; XII, 30, 230, 268, 828, 895, 900
McCully, Clarence, X, 457
McCully, Eliza. *See* Creed
McCully, Esther. *See* Pipes
McCully, Jonathan, X, 71, 300, **456–59**; XI, 23, 754, 755; XII, 31, 32, 598, 1055
McCully, Samuel, X, 456
McCurdy, Isaac, XI, 544
McCurdy, James Frederick, XII, 618
McCurdy, James MacGregor, XI, **544–45**
McCurdy, John (clergyman), XI, 879
McCurdy, John (doctor), V, 190
McCurdy, John (officer), V, 412
McCutcheon. *See also* McGill
McCutcheon, Hugh, XII, 398
McCutcheon, John (father of Peter McGILL), VIII, 540
McCutcheon, John (officer), IX, 699
McCutcheon, Mary. *See* McGill
McDavitt, Catherine (McNiff), V, 551
McDermot, Andrew, VII, 207; VIII, 344, 766, 819; IX, 261, 530; X, 47, 168, 427; XI, 45, 47, 219, 476, **545–46**, 562; XII, 568
McDermot, Annabella. *See* Ross
McDermot, Annie (Bannatyne), XI, 44, 45, 842
MacDermot, Catherine. *See* O'Connor
McDermot, Charles Edward, X, 67
McDermot, Henry, XI, 546
McDermot, Mary (Lane), X, 427

McDermot, Mary Sarah (Mactavish), IX, 530
MacDermot, Miles, XI, 545
McDermot, Sarah. *See* McNab
McDermott, James, XI, 150, 618
MacDhòmhnaill, Eilidh. *See* MacDonald of Glenaladale, Helen
MacDhòmhnaill, Iain. *See* MacDonald of Glenaladale, John
MacDhòmhnaill, Seumas. *See* MacDonald, James
MacDhòmhnaill 'Ic Iain, Iain, VII, 560; VIII, **525–26**
MacDhòmhnuill, Alasdair. *See* MacDonell of Scothouse, Alexander
McDonagh, Patrick, IX, 240
MacDonald; McDonald. *See also* MacDonell; Macdonell; McDonell
MacDonald, Miss (MacDonell), VIII, 537
Macdonald, Alexander (bishop), V, 523; VI, 447
MacDonald, Alexander (clergyman), VII, 551
McDonald, Alexander (father of DONALD, d. 1879), X, 459
MacDonald, Alexander (father of John Sandfield MACDONALD), X, 462
MacDonald, Alexander (poet), VI, 459
McDonald, Alexander, VI, **434–35**
Macdonald, Alexander, 1st Baron Macdonald of Sleat, VI, 412
MacDonald, Alexander Francis, X, 463
MacDonald, Allan, XII, 613
MacDonald*, Allan (1832–1901), XI, 477, 478
McDonald, Amelia. *See* Cameron
Macdonald*, Andrew Archibald (1829–1912), XII, 166, 416, 419, 639
MacDonald, Angus (brother of Iain MACDHÒMHNAILL 'IC IAIN), VIII, 526
McDonald, Angus (father of ANGUS, 1830–89), XI, 548
McDonald, Angus (father of ARCHIBALD), VIII, 526
McDonald, Angus (father of Bernard Donald MACDONALD), VIII, 528
McDonald, Angus (d. 1887), VII, 15; XI, **546–48**
McDonald, Angus (1830–89), VIII, 529; IX, 824, 831; X, 186, 264, 265, 595, 596, 612; XI, 529, **548–50**, 667; XII, 639
McDonald, Angus Ban, VI, 436
MacDonald, Ann. *See* Watt
MacDonald, Ann (Boyd), X, 85
McDonald, Anna Matilda. *See* Brecken
Macdonald, Anne MacIan (Steele), IX, 743
Macdonald, Annie Elizabeth. *See* Alcorn
McDonald, Archibald, V, 466; VI, 443; VIII, 61, 413, **526–28**, 577; IX, 513; X, 239, 720; XII, 612, 613
MacDonald, Augustine (Austin), V, 516; VI, 447
MacDonald, Augustine Ralph, VIII, 532
MacDonald, Benjamin, XII, 613
Macdonald, Bernard Donald, VI, 449, 450; VII, 332, 333; VIII, 227, 228, 487, **528–30**, 531, 535; IX, 451; X, 47, 186, 194, 461; XI, 548, 567, 684, 685; XII, 319, 416, 548, 591, 637, 638
McDonald, Catherina, VII, 541
Macdonald, Catherine. *See* Fraser
McDonald, Catherine (Conroy), X, 194
McDonald, Catherine (Grant), VI, 437
Macdonald*, Charles (1828–1901), XI, 773
McDonald, Charles, VI, **435–36**, 739; VIII, 533, 534
MacDonald, Charlotte Lenora Harrington (Geddie), X, 303
McDonald, Christan. *See* Stewart
McDonald, Christianna (Henry), XI, 398
MacDonald, Christie, VIII, 526
MacDonald, Christina, XII, 613
MacDonald, Christine (Montgomery), XI, 601
McDonald, Collin, VI, 436; VIII, 534, 535
McDonald, Daniel, VIII, 961
McDonald, De Bellefeuille, IX, 482
MacDonald, Donald (brother of HELEN and JOHN Mac-Donald of Glenaladale), IV, 496, 607; V, 513, 514, 515
MacDonald, Donald (cousin of Ranald MACDONALD), XII, 613
McDonald, Donald (father-in-law of John Small MACDONALD), VII, 541
McDonald (McKay), Donald (father of DONALD, 1783–1867), IX, 480
MacDonald, Donald (father of Iain MACDHÒMHNAILL 'IC IAIN), VIII, 525
McDonald, Donald (nephew of Donald MACKAY), VI, 464
McDonald, Donald (partner of James LOVELL), XII, 569
Macdonald, Donald (servant), IV, 43
MacDonald, Donald (surveyor), VI, 301
MacDonald, Donald, V, 516; VI, 122, 737; VII, 104, 542; VIII, 444, 484, 529, **530–33**, 547, 826
McDonald, Donald, IX, **480–81**
McDonald, Donald, X, **459–60**; XII, 976
MacDonald*, Donald (1909–86), XII, 356
Macdonald, Duncan (brother of EDWARD C.), XI, 550
McDonald, Duncan (landowner), VI, 428
McDonald, Edmund Mortimer, X, 300, 383, **460**
Macdonald, Edward C., XI, 313, **550–51**
Macdonald, Eliza. *See* Hamilton
Macdonald, Elizabeth. *See* Nielson
Macdonald, Elizabeth Amelia (Gordon; Carrall), X, 139
Macdonald, Ellen (Walsh), XII, 1083
McDonald, Emma (Mowat), XII, 767
McDonald, Finan, VI, 253, 437; VII, 473; VIII, 176, 421, 766, 881; IX, 851
MacDonald, Flora Anna Maria (Macdonell), V, 516
McDonald, Frances. *See* Mitchell
McDonald, Francis John, XII, **590–91**
McDonald, George, X, 460
McDonald, Grace. *See* McLean
Macdonald, Grant Stuart (Robertson), XI, 757
McDonald, Harriet (Skinner; Macdonell (Greenfield)), V, 762
MacDonald, Helen. *See* MacDonald of Glenaladale
Macdonald, Helen. *See* Shaw
McDonald, Helen (Kittson; Grant), VII, 473
McDonald, Helen Jane, VIII, 532
McDonald, Henrietta Maria. *See* Mallory
McDonald, Herbert Stone, XII, 331
MacDonald, Hugh (bishop), VI, 447
Macdonald, Hugh (father of Sir JOHN ALEXANDER), VI, 480; XII, 591
McDonald, Hugh (politician), XI, 399
Macdonald*, Sir Hugh John (1850–1929), XII, 450, 592, 605, 611, 712
Macdonald, Isabella. *See* Clark
McDonald, Isabella (Macdonald), VII, 541
McDonald, James (brother of JOHN, 1770–1828), VI, 437
McDonald, James (son of ALEXANDER), VI, 435
MacDonald, James, IV, 444, **496–97**; V, 514, 524; VI, 447

McDonald*, James (1828–1912), X, 71, 383, 395, 441; XI, 573

MacDonald, James Charles, XII, 639, 640

Macdonald, James Simon, VI, 90

McDonald, Jane. *See* Klyne

McDonald, Jean (mother of ANGUS, d. 1887; Smith), XI, 546

MacDonald, John. *See also* MacDhòmhnaill 'Ic Iain, Iain

MacDonald, John (bishop), IV, 496, 497

McDonald, John (father of CHARLES), VI, 435

McDonald, John (father of FRANCIS JOHN), XII, 590

McDonald, John (father of George Richard John MAC-DONELL), IX, 484

McDonald, John (father of JOHN, 1787–1860), VIII, 533

Macdonald, John (father of JOHN, 1824–90), XI, 551

McDonald, John (father of John MCDONALD of Garth), IX, 482

MacDonald, John (father of John Small MACDONALD), VII, 541

Macdonald, John (father of RONALD), VIII, 535

Macdonald, John (surveyor), X, 459

McDonald, John, VI, **436–37**, 466; VIII, 350

McDonald, John, VI, 436; VII, 460, 510; VIII, 188, **533–35**, 552; XII, 767

McDonald, John, V, 516; VIII, 529, 530, 532; IX, 400; X, 397, **460–62**; XI, 567, 699; XII, 591, 839

Macdonald, John, XI, 362, 391, **551–52**, 575; XII, 43, 706, 707, 976, 1119

Macdonald, John Alexander, XII, 592

Macdonald, Sir John Alexander, VI, 468, 480; VII, 102, 159, 472, 580, 780; VIII, 57, 171, 230, 231, 402, 513, 540, 552, 641, 645, 800, 837, 840; IX, 45, 57, 59, 83, 84, 130, 163, 253, 258, 267, 268, 293, 315, 383, 384, 427, 463, 492, 493, 507, 526, 531, 576, 577, 578, 588, 646, 680, 690, 705, 706, 708, 715, 725, 726, 734, 737, 777, 778, 804, 835, 845; X, 10, 23, 31, 44, 79, 97, 98, 99, 100, 101, 102, 118, 119, 120, 121, 122, 123, 128, 131, 136, 139, 144, 145, 146, 147, 148, 149, 150, 151, 157, 160, 170, 171, 191, 192, 201, 210, 247, 257, 258, 277, 282, 288, 289, 293, 294, 311, 312, 314, 332, 336, 340, 356, 361, 364, 369, 387, 422, 441, 458, 460, 464, 465, 466, 467, 468, 469, 476, 481, 499, 515, 533, 561, 591, 593, 597, 598, 632, 643, 645, 650, 651, 656, 668, 674, 677, 685, 698, 713, 717, 725, 727, 729; XI, 7, 8, 12, 13, 16, 24, 27, 30, 32, 45, 47, 51, 63, 69, 81, 82, 111, 123, 124, 129, 134, 140, 141, 144, 145, 146, 149, 151, 157, 160, 161, 164, 166, 167, 170, 176, 183, 192, 193, 196, 197, 198, 204, 206, 207, 211, 216, 224, 227, 230, 232, 233, 238, 245, 246, 263, 279, 280, 283, 287, 288, 293, 298, 301, 307, 312, 324, 325, 336, 346, 347, 348, 350, 351, 374, 377, 378, 379, 381, 399, 415, 416, 422, 438, 442, 444, 451, 456, 464, 489, 505, 520, 521, 525, 530, 537, 551, 552, 555, 573, 574, 579, 592, 593, 598, 609, 610, 611, 612, 613, 618, 622, 625, 626, 634, 644, 645, 646, 647, 648, 649, 650, 659, 675, 677, 681, 682, 689, 697, 698, 702, 703, 704, 706, 707, 708, 710, 731, 737, 738, 739, 741, 743, 744, 746, 747, 750, 753, 758, 759, 767, 768, 769, 770, 771, 775, 783, 791, 792, 803, 815, 818, 819, 820, 822, 827, 831, 832, 837, 838, 840, 846, 853, 855, 877, 884, 907, 908, 909, 910, 921, 927, 928, 929, 932, 934; XII, 3, 6, 7, 8, 26, 28, 32, 34, 35, 36, 63, 73, 83, 85, 86, 89, 90, 91, 98, 116, 126, 129, 132, 137, 138, 140, 141, 144, 148, 149, 150, 151, 152, 153,

154, 162, 166, 167, 173, 176, 178, 179, 180, 181, 184, 202, 204, 205, 215, 221, 240, 241, 242, 244, 246, 247, 258, 262, 263, 264, 266, 292, 293, 325, 334, 345, 351, 352, 353, 354, 355, 370, 393, 395, 406, 412, 417, 419, 427, 429, 433, 434, 435, 436, 447, 450, 451, 453, 457, 466, 475, 481, 487, 494, 497, 499, 500, 528, 540, 566, 567, 573, 576, 578, 579, 580, 581, 582, 583, 584, 588, **591–612**, 614, 620, 623, 628, 629, 630, 633, 634, 636, 644, 649, 652, 653, 654, 655, 658, 663, 664, 673, 676, 677, 678, 679, 684, 685, 686, 687, 688, 689, 703, 704, 706, 712, 718, 720, 721, 722, 723, 724, 725, 726, 729, 731, 735, 736, 741, 742, 743, 744, 750, 751, 752, 775, 784, 788, 801, 818, 822, 881, 884, 885, 894, 898, 907, 908, 913, 915, 916, 923, 934, 937, 940, 951, 952, 953, 964, 965, 983, 987, 990, 1007, 1008, 1010, 1023, 1025, 1027, 1040, 1041, 1042, 1043, 1044, 1045, 1054, 1055, 1056, 1057, 1058, 1059, 1063, 1065, 1085, 1091, 1102, 1103, 1106, 1108, 1114, 1120, 1130

McDonald, John Archibald, VIII, 532, 533

Macdonald, John Cameron, XII, 334

Macdonald, John Sandfield, VIII, 52, 56, 57, 303, 304, 583, 822, 840; IX, 75, 84, 253, 267, 268, 397, 492, 493, 494, 513, 576, 705, 726, 778; X, 98, 99, 101, 102, 126, 128, 144, 145, 146, 213, 219, 356, 420, **462–69**, 642, 667, 668, 676, 693, 725; XI, 49, 81, 82, 144, 145, 146, 157, 196, 229, 283, 347, 367, 379, 411, 414, 438, 464, 480, 497, 520, 530, 652, 677, 681, 792, 822, 823, 878, 883, 908, 920, 928, 934; XII, 7, 69, 151, 254, 263, 299, 330, 331, 352, 487, 596, 599, 614, 615, 644, 650, 684, 720, 922, 1032, 1037, 1054, 1108

Macdonald, John Small, VII, **541–42**

McDonald, John T., VII, 871

Macdonald, Louisa, XII, 607, 611, 1102

Macdonald, Louise. *See* Lavallée

McDonald, Magdalen (McGillivray), VI, 454; IX, 482

McDonald, Margaret. *See* Logan

McDonald, Margaret. *See* McColl

MacDonald, Margaret. *See* MacDonald of Glenaladale

Macdonald, Margaret. *See* MacKinnon

McDonald, Margaret (MacKintosh), XI, 566

McDonald, Margaret (Patterson), XII, 828

McDonald (Macdonald), Margaret (Wightman), XI, 922

Macdonald, Margaret (Williamson), XII, 1102

Macdonald, Margaret Josephine. *See* MacDonell

Macdonald, Margaret Josephine (Hingston), XII, 615

Macdonald, Margaret Mary Theodora, XII, 98, 604, 611, 990, 1044

McDonald, Maria Anne (Marianne) (Barnston), VIII, 61

McDonald, Marie. *See* Poitras

Macdonald, Marie Christine. *See* Waggaman

McDonald, Mary. *See* Campbell

MacDonald, Mary. *See* Forbes

McDonald, Mary. *See* Rankin

McDonald, Mary. *See* Stone

MacDonald, Mary (Boyd), X, 85

McDonald, Mary (Dowd), XII, 267

Macdonald, Mary (Leech), XII, 544

Macdonald, Mary (Macaulay), VI, 412

MacDonald, Mary (MacDonald), VIII, 525

McDonald, Mary (McDonald), XII, 590

McDonald, Mary (MacEachern), VI, 447

Macdonald, Nancy (Macdonald), X, 462; XII, 613

McDonald, Nelly. *See* McDonell

MacDonald, Penelope (MacDonald), VIII, 528
Macdonald, Ranald, VIII, 526; XII, **612–13**
Macdonald, Ranald Sandfield, XII, 614
McDonald, Robert XII, 936
MacDonald, Roderick Charles, V, 516; X, 461
MacDonald, Rolland, X, 164
MacDonald, Ronald (husband of Helen MACDONALD of Glenaladale), V, 514
McDonald, Ronald (son of ALEXANDER), VI, 435
Macdonald, Ronald, VI, 595; VII, 354; VIII, 528, **535–37**; IX, 453; X, 226, 512
MacDonald, Ronald Bernard, IX, 832
McDonald, Sophia Caroline (Henry), XI, 398
Macdonald, Stuart, X, 198
Macdonald, Susan Agnes, Baroness Macdonald. *See* Bernard
MacDonald, Thomas, VII, 542
Macdonald, William (father of EDWARD C.), XI, 550
MacDonald, William (son of John MACDONALD of Glenaladale), V, 516
MacDonald*, Sir William Christopher (1831–1917), V, 516; VIII, 532; XII, 288, 495
Macdonald, William John, IX, 656
MacDonald, William Peter, VII, 230, **542–44**, 705; VIII, 318; IX, 240, 325, 604
McDonald, William Stone, VI, 436; VIII, 535
MacDonald (Ridge), Allan, VIII, 526
Macdonald (Sandfield), Alexander, XII, 613
Macdonald (Sandfield), Alexander Francis, XII, 95
Macdonald (Sandfield), Donald Alexander, VIII, 304; X, 463, 464; XII, 95, **613–15**
McDonald le Borgne. *See* McDonald, John
MacDonald of Boisdale, Colin, IV, 497; V, 514
Macdonald of Garth, Helen (Campbell, Lady Campbell), VII, 139
McDonald of Garth, John, IV, 310; V, 236, 266, 559, 560, 635; VI, 436, 547, 705; VII, 564, 577, 735, 748; VIII, 158, 413, 734, 881, 882; IX, **481–83**
McDonald of Garth, Nancy. *See* Small
MacDonald of Ghernish (Guernish), Margaret (MacDonald of Glenaladale), V, 514, 515, 516; VIII, 530; X, 460
M'Donald of Glenaladale, Alexander, V, 513, 514
MacDonald of Glenaladale, Helen (MacDonald), V, **513–14**, 515; VI, 121
MacDonald of Glenaladale, Isabella. *See* Gordon of Wardhouse
MacDonald of Glenaladale, John, IV, 129, 152, 496, 497, 607, 608, 610; V, 28, 219, 220, 263, 311, 424, 425, 513, **514–17**, 569, 721, 779, 848, 861, 862, 873; VI, 109, 121, 161, 196, 298, 413, 414, 415, 447, 662, 736, 737, 806; VII, 407, 542; VIII, 528, 530, 954; X, 460
MacDonald of Glenaladale, Margaret. *See* MacDonald of Ghernish
M'Donald of Glenaladale, Margaret. *See* MacDonell of Scothouse
MacDonald of Glenaladale, Margaret, V, 513
MacDonald of Glenaladale, Margaret (MacDonald), VII, 541
Macdonald of Sleat, Baron. *See* Macdonald
McDonell, Mrs. *See* Hughes
McDonell, Mrs. *See* MacDonald
McDonell, Mrs. *See* Ulich
Macdonell, Captain, VI, 439

Mcdonell, Mr (merchant), VII, 735
Macdonell, Aeneas, VI, 321; VIII, 350
McDonell, Agathe-Henriette. *See* Huguet, *dit* Latour
Macdonell, Alexander (fur trader), X, 475
McDonell, Alexander (politician), VIII, 741
McDonell, Alexander (secretary), VIII, 161, 162
MacDonell, Alexander, V, 751; VI, **437–39**, 547; VIII, 344, 719; IX, 472
McDonell, Alexander, V, 78, 440, 518, 521, 525, 695; VI, 165, 221, 440, 448, 449, 476, 482, 532, 589, 595, 596, 627, 628; VII, 230, 337, 355, 543, **544–51**, 553, 555, 661, 662, 663, 664, 705; VIII, xxv, 34, 316, 317, 490, 539, 547, 593, 594, 764; IX, 9, 26, 69, 206, 240, 324, 483, 484, 499, 533, 604, 760; X, 310; XI, 864; XII, 199
MacDonell, Alexander, VII, 355, **551–52**; VIII, 303, 316; IX, 360
McDonell, Alexander, VI, 522; VII, 75, 712, 755; VIII, 324, 586; IX, 149, **483**
McDonell, Alexander Ranaldson, 15th Chief of Clan Macdonald of Glengarry, VIII, 539
Macdonell, Allan (brother of ARCHIBALD), VI, 439
Macdonell, Allan (father-in-law of Simon FRASER), IX, 285
Macdonell, Allan (grandfather of ALLAN), XI, 552
McDonell, Allan, VI, 111; VIII, **537–38**, 821
Macdonell, Allan, VII, 554; VIII, 401; XI, **552–55**; XII, 198, 1108
MacDonell, Angus (clergyman), VII, 661, 705; VIII, 34
MacDonell, Angus (Ignace) (father of JEAN-FRANÇOIS-MARIE-JOSEPH), IX, 485
MacDonell, Angus (son of Allan McDONELL), VIII, 538
Macdonell, Angus Duncan, XI, 553
Macdonell, Ann, V, 523
McDonell, Ann (Fraser), VIII, 302
McDonell, Anne. *See* Smith
McDonell (MacDonell), Archibald (office holder), V, 772
McDonell, Archibald (shipowner), VIII, 326
Macdonell, Archibald, IV, 495; V, 92; VI, **439–40**
Macdonell, Sir Archibald Cameron, XII, 499
Macdonell, Archibald John, XII, 562, 604
McDonell, Catherine. *See* McDonell of Collachie
MacDonell, Catherine. *See* MacLeod of Bernera
MacDonell, Catherine (Fraser), IX, 285
MacDonell, Catherine (Thomson), X, 680
McDonell, Donald, V, 550
MacDonell, Donald Aeneas, VI, 440; VII, 553; VIII, 303; X, **469–70**; XII, 731
Macdonell, Duncan, IX, 483, 484
Macdonell, Duncan, 14th Chief of Clan Macdonell of Glengarry, VIII, 538
McDonell, Duncan Cameron, V, 437; VIII, 864
McDonell, Elizabeth. *See* Pickell
Macdonell, Elizabeth (Macdonell), IX, 483
McDonell, Fanny (Hodgson), X, 352
Macdonell, Flora Anna Maria. *See* MacDonald
Macdonell, George Richard John, V, 79, 762; VI, 182, 183, 264, 343, 344; VII, 129, 456, 666; VIII, 511, 639; IX, 99, **484–85**
McDonell, Helen. *See* Yates
MacDonell, Hugh, VII, 551
Macdonell, Isabella (Chewett), VII, 175; IX, 128
McDonell, Isabella (Macdonell), VI, 440; X, 469
MacDonell, James, V, 718

Macdonell, Sir James, VII, 478; VIII, 163, 164, **538–39**, 712

Macdonell, Janet (Macdonell), IX, 483

MacDonell, Jean-François-Marie-Joseph, VII, 758; VIII, 260; IX, **485–86**

McDonell, John (François-Marie-Joseph), X, 545

McDonell, John (husband of Susan Holmes), XI, 923

McDonell, John (son of Allan MCDONELL), VIII, 538

McDonell, John, IV, 310; V, 656; VI, 436, 440; VII, 356, **552–54**

Macdonell, Laura. *See* Arundel

McDonell, Magdeleine. *See* Poitras

McDonell, Margaret. *See* Cameron

McDonell, Margaret (Cameron), VII, 137

MacDonell, Margaret Josephine (Macdonald), XII, 613

McDonell (McDonald), Marie-Angélique-Émilie (Hianveu (Hyanveux), *dit* Lafrance), IX, 451

MacDonell, Marie-Anne. *See* Picoté de Bélestre

Macdonell, Marjory. *See* Grant

MacDonell, Mary. *See* Chisholm

MacDonell, Mary (wife of ALEXANDER, fl. 1813–28), VI, 437

MacDonell, Mary (Fraser), VI, 263

McDonell, Mary (Fraser), VIII, 304

McDonell, Mary (MacDonell), X, 469

Macdonell, Miles, V, 266, 267, 268, 451, 466, 523, 525, 751; VI, 100, 116, 251, 267, **440–44**, 445, 456, 466, 748, 767; VII, 138, 139, 206, 552, 553, 570, 749; VIII, 342, 413, 482, 527, 557, 714, 719, 779; IX, 285; X, 469; XI, 553

Macdonell, Nancy. *See* Macdonell of Greenfield

McDonell, Nelly (McDonald), VI, 436

Macdonell, Ranald, IX, 484

MacDonell, Roderic, V, 40, 524; VIII, 776

Macdonell*, Samuel Smith (1823–1907), XI, 756

McDonell, Susan. *See* Holmes

McDonell (Aberchalder), Hugh, V, 518, 753, 772; VI, **444–45**

Macdonell (Aberchalder), Janet (Macdonell of Greenfield), V, 520; VI, 445

McDonell (Aberchalder), John, IV, 683; V, 282, **517–18**, 519, 520, 772, 782; VI, 444, 475; IX, 483

McDonell (Collachie), Alexander, V, 126, 265, 266, 519, 520, 521, 522; VI, 148, 264, 440, 441, 759; VII, **554–56**; VIII, 303; XI, 552

Macdonell (Collachie), Angus, V, 188, 189, 388, 389, 420, **518–20**, 845, 854, 855; VI, 440, 721; VII, 175, 554

McDonell (Collachie), James (brother of Angus MACDONELL (Collachie)), V, 519

Macdonell (Collachie), James (cousin of John MACDONELL (Greenfield)), V, 523

Macdonell (Greenfield), Alexander, IX, 483

Macdonell (Greenfield), Alexander, V, 268, 520, 544; VI, 440, 442, **445–46**; VII, 78, 138; VIII, 342, 343, 351, 454, 689, 714; IX, 484

Macdonell (Greenfield), Donald, V, 522, 523; VI, 446; VIII, 303, 583; IX, **483–84**, 858

Macdonell (Greenfield), Duncan, VIII, 303

Macdonell (Greenfield), Harriet. *See* McDonald

Macdonell (Greenfield), John, V, 83, 113, 114, **520–23**, 857, 858; VI, 440, 446, 540, 609; VII, 36; VIII, 431, 583; IX, 484, 668; X, 618

McDonell (Leek), Archibald, VIII, 302

Macdonell (Leek), Isabella (McLean), VI, 475; IX, 512

MacDonell-Bélestre, John. *See* MacDonell, Jean-François-Marie-Joseph

McDonell of Aberchalder, Alexander, V, 517; VI, 444

McDonell of Collachie, Allan, V, 517, 518, 519; VI, 444; VII, 554

McDonell of Collachie, Catherine (Macdonell), VI, 440

McDonell of Collachie, Helen. *See* MacNab

Macdonell of Glengarry, Alexander Ranaldson, VII, 544

Macdonell of Greenfield, Alexander, V, 520; VI, 445

Macdonell of Greenfield, Janet. *See* Macdonell (Aberchalder)

Macdonell of Greenfield, Nancy (Anne) (Macdonell), VI, 440

MacDonell of Leek, Archibald, X, 469

Macdonell of Leek, John, V, 517; VI, 444, 475

MacDonell of Lundie, Donald, VIII, 537

MacDonell of Scothouse, Alexander, V, **523–25**; XII, 613

MacDonell of Scothouse, Angus (Æneas), V, 523

McDonell of Scothouse, John, VI, 440; VII, 552

MacDonell of Scothouse (Scotus), Margaret (M'Donald of Glenaladale; Gordon), V, 513, 514

MacDonnell, Blanche Anne. *See* Skurray

Macdonnell, Daniel James, XII, 202, 578, **615–19**, 660, 707, 767, 867

Macdonnell, Eleanor. *See* Milnes

McDonnell, Elizabeth (McNiff), V, 551

Macdonnell, Elizabeth Logie. *See* Smellie

McDonnell, Francis, X, 647

Macdonnell, George (clergyman), XII, 615

Macdonnell, George (officer), IX, 857

MacDonnell, George (rector), X, 470

MacDonnell, Jane. *See* Graves

McDonnell, Lolitia. *See* Keys

MacDonnell, Margaret. *See* Croates

MacDonnell, Margaret. *See* Lea

McDonnell, Mary Louisa (Richardson), VI, 638

MacDonnell, Richard, X, 470; XI, 555

MacDonnell, Sir Richard Graves, IX, 192; XI, **555–56**, 932, 933

MacDonnell, Robert, X, 470

MacDonnell, Robert Lea, IX, 16, 358; X, **470–71**; XI, 272

Macdonough, Thomas, VII, 710

McDouall, James, VI, 291; VII, 619

McDouall, John, VII, 556

McDouall, Robert, VI, 29, 100, 358, 465, 643, 817, 818; VII, **556–57**; VIII, 112, 831; X, 12

McDougal, Isabella (Cameron), XI, 142

McDougal, Janet. *See* Wilson

McDougal, John, IX, 486

McDougald, Allen, IX, 315

McDougald, Elizabeth (Gill), IX, 315

McDougald, Marie. *See* McPherson

McDougall, Mrs. *See* MacLean

McDougall, Abigail. *See* Steinhauer

Macdougall, Alan, XII, **619–20**

McDougall, Alexander (businessman), XII, 379, 381

MacDougall, Alexander (shipowner), XI, 502

McDougall, Alexander (solicitor general), XI, 398

McDougall, Alexander, V, 525, 526; VI, 111, **446–47**; X, 114

McDougall, Alexander Mills, IX, 486, 488, 489

MacDougall, Anne. *See* Smelt

McDougall, Anne, V, 526
McDougall, Anne (Paterson), IX, 489
MacDougall, Caroline. *See* LeVesconte
McDougall, Catharine. *See* Cameron
McDougall, Catherine. *See* Lent
McDougall, David (son of GEORGE MILLWARD), X, 471, 472
McDougall, David (son of JOHN, 1805–70), IX, 488
McDougall, Donald, VI, 446, 447
MacDougall, Dugald (Donald) Lorn, XI, **556–57**
Macdougall, Duncan (adjutant general), X, 557
McDougall, Duncan (father of ALEXANDER and DUNCAN) V, 525; VI, 446, 447
MacDougall, Sir Duncan, XII, 621
McDougall, Duncan, V, **525–27**, 533; VI, 447; VIII, 85, 158, 176, 190, 557, 766, 882; IX, 279
McDougall, Edgar Mill, XII, 621
McDougall, Eliza (Hardisty), XI, 383
McDougall, Elizabeth. *See* Chantler
MacDougall, Elizabeth (Baldwin), VIII, 58
Macdougall, Emily Augusta. *See* McCaul
McDougall, George (businessman), IX, 486, 489
McDougall, George (officer), III, 95, 528
McDougall, George (sailor), IX, 12
McDougall, George (son of DUNCAN), V, 526, 527; VI, 447, 705
McDougall, George (son of JOHN, 1805–70), IX, 488
MacDougall, George Campbell, XI, 556
McDougall, George Millward, X, **471–72**; XI, 383, 598, 849, 900
MacDougall, Hartland Brydges, XI, 556
MacDougall, Hartland St Clair, XI, 556
McDougall, Helen Oliver. *See* Baptist
MacDougall, Isaac Duncan, X, 441
McDougall, James (fur trader), VII, 475; IX, 283
McDougall, James (son of JOHN, 1805–70), IX, 488
McDougall, Janet Wilson (Nilson), IX, 489
McDougall, John (brother of William*), XII, 950
Macdougall, John (father of ALAN), XII, 619
McDougall, John (husband of Catherine Lent), IV, 495
McDougall, John (son of JOHN, 1805–70), IX, 488, 489; XI, 814
McDougall, John, IX, **486–89**; XII, 620, 1000
McDougall, John, XII, **620–21**
McDougall*, John Chantler (1842–1917), IX, 602, 603; X, 471, 472; XI, 443, 849, 900
McDougall, John Lorn, VIII, **539–40**
McDougall*, John Lorn (1838–1909), VIII, 540; X, 128; XII, 656
MacDougall, Joseph Easton, XII, 455
McDougall, Louis, VI, 447
MacDougall, Louisa Augusta. *See* Napier
McDougall, Lucy. *See* Boston
McDougall, Margaret. *See* Purvis
McDougall, Margaret (Linton), IX, 489
MacDougall, Marianne Adelaide, Lady MacDougall. *See* Miles
McDougall, Marion. *See* Shaw
McDougall, Mary. *See* Cowans
McDougall, Mary Charlotte (Belisle), VI, 447
MacDougall, Sir Patrick Leonard, IX, 772; X, 292; XII, 347, **621–22**
MacDougall, Peter, XI, 556

McDougall, Robert, IX, 488, 489
McDougall, Samuel, VIII, 539
McDougall, Sarah (McCorquadale), VI, 447
McDougall, Thomas, IX, 488; X, 34
McDougall, William, IX, 488; XI, 716; XII, 451
McDougall*, William (1822–1905), VIII, 267; IX, 10, 252, 253, 267, 407, 507, 531, 576, 736; X, 70, 94, 95, 96, 98, 100, 101, 125, 126, 149, 169, 276, 368, 465, 468, 630, 677; XI, 133, 144, 245, 411, 422, 518, 677, 716, 737, 738, 739, 841, 842, 884; XII, 72, 82, 85, 132, 154, 600, 601, 655, 729, 950, 1108
McDowal, Jane (wife of John), VIII, 395
McDowal, John, VIII, 395
McDowall, Mrs. *See* Graham
McDowall, Hannah. *See* Washburn
Macdowall, James, VII, 134
McDowall, John, VII, 557
Macdowall, Margaret (Stewart), I, 613
McDowall, Robert, V, 308, 476; VI, 216, 805; VII, **557–58**; VIII, 696; IX, 232; X, 660
Macdowall, Uchtred, I, 613
McDowell, Claire, XII, 623
McDowell, Eugene Addison, XII, **622–24**
McDowell, Harriet Frances. *See* Reeves
McDowell, Samuel, VII, 273
McDuff, Thomas, X, 306
Macé. *See also* Druillon; Massé
Macé, Catherine, I, 220, 458, **478**, 480, 487, 512; X, 156
Macé, Guillé, I, 478
Mace, Lida (Lydia) (Crandall), VIII, 180
Macé, Philippe. *See* Martineau
Macé, René, I, 478
McEachen, Emanuel, X, **472–73**
MacEachern, Angus Bernard, IV, 497; V, 125, 458, 516, 671; VI, 106, **447–51**, 589, 595, 596, 738; VII, 27, 332, 546, 547, 551, 552; VIII, 227, 306, 316, 487, 528, 529, 535, 554; IX, 154, 155, 616; XI, 684; XII, 548, 590, 637
MacEachern, Hugh Bàn, VI, 447
MacEachern, Mary. *See* MacDonald
McEnes, Ellen. *See* Bédard, Hélène
McEwan, Margaret (Lawson), XII, 539
MacFadyen, Margaret (MacLean), VII, 559
McFarland, Margaret (Pettit), V, 669
MacFarlane, Alexander, IX, 295
Macfarlane, Elizabeth. *See* Erskine
McFarlane, Elizabeth (Nugent), VIII, 656
Macfarlane, Isura. *See* Carrington
Macfarlane, James, VI, 772, 773; VII, 90, **558–59**
McFarlane, Malcolm, XI, 587
McFarlane, Peter, VI, 284
MacFarlane, Roderick, IX, 6; X, 276
MacFarlane*, Thomas (1834–1907), X, 445
Macfarlane, Walter (husband of Lady Elizabeth Erskine), III, 131
Macfarlane, Walter (merchant), XI, 551
MacFarlane, William Godsoe, VIII, 395; IX, 392
McGarrigle, Paddy, XII, 377
McGarvey, Bridget. *See* Murray
McGarvey, Francis, XII, 624
McGarvey, John, XII, 625
McGarvey, Margaret. *See* Cooper
McGarvey, Owen, XI, 499; XII, **624–25**
McGary, James, VIII, 449

McGaw, Samuel A., XII, 413
McGee, Dorcas Catherine. *See* Morgan
McGee, James, IX, 489
McGee, John, XI, 377
McGee, Mary Theresa. *See* Caffrey
McGee, Thomas D'Arcy, VII, 544; VIII, 402; IX, 5, 97, 98, 377, **489–94**, 835; X, 123, 154, 193, 229, 231, 277, 347, 466, 561, 625, 725; XI, 42, 145, 152, 192, 283, 322, 323, 379, 565, 649, 731, 774, 782, 822, 843, 871, 884; XII, 26, 89, 98, 247, 254, 262, 398, 406, 573, 595, 598, 599, 662, 677, 1054, 1108
Macgeorge, Andrew, XI, 557
Macgeorge, Elizabeth. *See* Jackson
Macgeorge, Elizabeth McIntosh. *See* Grant
Macgeorge, Elizabeth Stevenson. *See* MacBrayne
McGeorge, John, VI, 61
McGeorge, Mary. *See* Black
Macgeorge, Robert Jackson, VIII, 899; X, 172; XI, **557–58**; XII, 667
McGhee, Thomas, VIII, 671
MacGhillEathain, Iain, VII, 355, **559–61**
MacGhillEathain, Isabella. *See* Black
MacGibbon, Christian (Rintoul), VIII, 750
McGill, Andrew, V, 179, 286, 436, 529, 655, 821; VI, 472; IX, 753
McGill, Ann. *See* Wood
McGill, Catherine. *See* Crookshank
McGill, Catherine. *See* McLimont
McGill, Charlotte. *See* Guillimin
McGill, Isobel, V, 529
McGill, James, V, 527
McGill, James, IV, 5, 59, 277, 278, 319, 547, 698, 703, 757; V, 8, 38, 90, 134, 168, 179, 180, 183, 211, 218, 233, 285, 286, 287, 299, 300, 319, 320, 332, 333, 372, 384, 402, 436, 460, 484, 485, 489, 496, **527–30**, 561, 564, 566, 572, 581, 614, 663, 681, 705, 706, 722, 818, 819, 820, 821, 822; VI, 72, 204, 205, 210, 254, 318, 433, 471, 472, 476, 507, 527, 531, 642, 643, 645, 665, 702, 743; VII, 79, 224, 343, 622, 824, 825, 827; VIII, 404; IX, 580, 754, 755; X, 58; XI, 503; XII, 233
McGill, Janet (Mowat), XII, 767
McGill, John, IV, 48; V, 527, 529, 819
McGill, John, V, 326, 365, 440, 441, 442, 548, 549, 753, 756, 856; VI, **451–54**, 608, 629, 630, 698, 723; VII, 438, 812, 813; VIII, 4, 191, 337, 540, 541, 795
McGill, John Shuter Davenport, VIII, 543
McGill, Margaret. *See* Gibson
McGill, Mary (McCutcheon), VIII, 540
McGill (McCutcheon), Peter, VI, 59, 238, 278, 453; VII, 9, 26, 71, 77, 160, 453, 579, 580, 594, 612, 620, 703, 824; VIII, 7, 10, 298, 321, **540–44**, 631, 785, 800; IX, 274, 316, 373, 390, 554, 639, 640, 641; X, 10, 132, 134, 326, 519, 520, 591, 715; XI, 121, 268, 557, 781, 850, 874, 898; XII, 349, 863
McGill, Robert, VI, 94; VIII, **544–46**, 560, 640, 750; XII, 767
McGill, Sarah Elizabeth Shuter. *See* Wilkins
McGill, Sydenham Clitherow, VIII, 543
McGill, William (father of ROBERT), VIII, 544
McGill, William (Ontario politician), XI, 312
McGill, William (P.E.I. politician), X, 264, 472
McGillicuddy, Daniel, XII, 148
McGillis, Duncan, VII, 592, 593

McGillis, Hugh, IX, 482
McGillis, Marie (Grant), VIII, 341
McGillivray, Alexander, IX, **494–95**
MacGillivray, Angus, X, 85
McGillivray, Ann. *See* Easthope
McGillivray, Anne. *See* McTavish
McGillivray, Anne, VI, 456
McGillivray, Christina. *See* McRae
McGillivray, Donald, V, 530; VI, 454; VII, 561
McGillivray, Donald, XII, **625–26**
McGillivray, Duncan, IV, 310; V, **530–32**, 561, 565, 742; VI, 29, 454, 455, 664, 665, 667, 704; VII, 561, 566, 825; VIII, 3, 390, 881
McGillivray, Edward, XII, 672
McGillivray, Elizabeth McCormick. *See* Skinner
McGillivray, Isabella. *See* McLean
McGillivray, Joseph, VI, 457; VIII, 85
McGillivray, Magdalen. *See* McDonald
McGillivray, Magdalen, VI, 456
McGillivray, Magdalene, V, 532
McGillivray, Marjory (Shaw), VI, 704, 705
McGillivray, Neil, XII, 626
McGillivray, Sarah Douglas. *See* Parker
McGillivray, Simon (nephew of SIMON), IX, 722
McGillivray, Simon (son of WILLIAM), VI, 456; IX, 532
McGillivray, Simon, V, 544, 822; VI, 260, 441, 442, 455, 456, 602, 704, 765, 815; VII, 310, **561–62**, 619, 737, 913; VIII, 85, 314, 315, 321, 342, 351, 576; IX, 229, 234
McGillivray, Susan (wife of WILLIAM), VI, 454
McGillivray, William, V, 532
McGillivray, William, V, 134, 265, 266, 267, 333, 391, 530, 532, 542, 544, 559, 561, 564, 565, 566, 684; VI, 167, 204, 210, 236, 285, 296, 437, 440, 443, **454–57**, 469, 477, 643, 665, 704, 705, 765, 766; VII, 78, 556, 561, 566, 578, 619, 736, 825; VIII, 85, 303, 314, 341, 342, 351, 389, 390, 455, 483, 527, 546, 575, 576, 719; IX, 234, 482, 532; X, 114
McGillivray (Dalcrombie), John, VIII, 158, 303, **546–47**; X, 462
MacGillivray of Dalcrombie, Elizabeth. *See* Shaw of Dores
MacGillivray of Dalcrombie, Farquhar, VIII, 546
McGinn, Thomas, IX, 61
McGinnis, Alexander, VII, 184
McGinnis, Elizabeth (Plenderleath), VII, 184
MacGinnis, Richard, IX, 609
McGinnis, Sarah (Griffith), VII, 358
McGinnis, William, VII, 185
McGoey, Thomas, IX, 13
McGovern, Annie, X, 49
McGovock (McGovack), George, IV, 759
McGowan. *See also* Magowan
McGowan, Edward, IX, 81; XI, 605; XII, 78
Macgowan, Peter, VIII, 506
McGrath, Mary (Gugy), X, 322
McGray, Asa, VII, **562–63**
McGray, Susanna. *See* Stoddard
McGray, William, VII, 562
McGreevy, Bridget Caroline. *See* Nowlan
McGreevy, Mary Ann. *See* Rourke
McGreevy, Mary Georgina. *See* Woolsey
McGreevy, Robert (father), XII, 626
McGreevy, Robert, XII, 627, 628, 629, 630
McGreevy, Rose. *See* Smith

McGreevy, Thomas, XI, 170, 464, 728, 774, 813; XII, 293, 421, 464, 500, 610, **626–31**, 726, 913, 931
MacGregor, Ann. *See* McKay
MacGregor, Anne. *See* Jillard
MacGregor, Christiana Ann (Patterson), XII, 828
McGregor, Christina (Cameron), X, 124
McGregor, Coll, V, 285
MacGregor, David, VIII, 547
McGregor, Euphemia (Cameron), X, 124
MacGregor, Frances (Mitcheson), X, 32
McGregor*, Gordon Morton (1873–1922), XII, 1080
McGregor, Gregor, IV, 506; VI, 462
McGregor, James (cousin of JOHN), VI, 462
MacGregor, James (son-in-law of James CARMICHAEL), VIII, 126, 127
MacGregor, James Drummond, V, 660; VI, 87, 131, 294, 370, **457–62**, 659, 660; VII, 529, 531, 533, 538, 539, 540, 560; VIII, 127, 452, 569, 769, 770; IX, 281; X, 476; XII, 230, 828, 829
MacGregor*, James Gordon (1852–1913), XII, 772
MacGregor, Janet. *See* Dochert
MacGregor, Janet. *See* Ross
MacGregor, Janet (Gordon; wife of JAMES DRUMMOND), VI, 457
McGregor, John (cousin of Andrew MUIR), VIII, 646; XI, 627
McGregor, John (officer), VIII, 741
McGregor, John, VI, **462–63**
MacGregor, John, VI, 737; VIII, 444, 484, **547–49**, 826; IX, 161, 162, 299, 300, 474
McGregor, Margaret (Mann), XII, 691
McGregor, Margaret (Rogers), VI, 655
McGregor, Martha. *See* Scott
MacGregor, Mary Helena. *See* Thompson
McGregor, Sarah (McKenzie), X, 476
MacGregor, William, VIII, 452
McGregor of Clober, James, V, 284
McGuckian, Lawrence, VI, 375
McGuirk, Rosanna (McPhelim), IX, 527
McGulpin, Angelique. *See* Bead-way-way
McGulpin, Patrick, VI, 29
Machar*, Agnes Maule (1837–1927), IX, 496; XII, 776
Machar, John, IX, 496
Machar, John, VI, 467; VIII, 645; IX, 306, **495–96**; X, 442; XII, 767
McHardy, Charles, VI, 259
McHardy, Margaret (Fleming), VI, 259
Machault d'Arnouville, Jean-Baptiste de, III, 18, 55, 72, 171, 230, 300, 461; IV, 88, 242, 250, 257, 258, 307, 467, 615, 617, 750
McHeffey, Richard A., XI, 279
McHenry, James, V, 810
Machiavelli, Niccolò, IX, 772
Machin, Henry Turner, XII, 903
Machiquawish. *See* Madjeckewiss
Machir. *See also* Machar
Machir, David, IX, 495
Machir, Jean. *See* Walker
Macho, B., V, 321
Machray*, Robert (1831–1904), X, 673; XI, 437, 570, 571, 572, 611, 647, 738, 917; XII, 1006
McIllree, John Henry, XII, 499
MacIlraith, John, IX, 661

McIlworth, Thomas, IV, 397
McIlwraith*, Jean Newton (1859–1938), IV, 401
McIlwraith*, Thomas (1824–1903), XII, 358
McInerney*, George Valentine (1857–1908), XI, 350
McInnes, Alexander, XII, 631, 939
McInnes, Donald, XII, **631–34**, 939, 963
McInnes, Duncan, XII, 631
McInnes, Hugh, XII, 631
McInnes, Johanna. *See* Stuart
McInnes, Mary Amelia. *See* Robinson
MacInnes, Natalie Charlotte. *See* Lampman
Macintosh. *See also* MacKintosh
McIntosh, Alexander, VII, 563
MacIntosh, Alexander Fisher, VI, 702, 783; VIII, 781
MacIntosh, Allan, VII, 563
McIntosh, Ann. *See* Ferguson
McIntosh, Catherine Oswald. *See* Stewart
McIntosh, Charles, VIII, 550
McIntosh, David, VIII, 550
McIntosh, Donald, V, 534
McIntosh, Elsie (Dent), XI, 246
MacIntosh, Emilia (Simpson), VI, 720
McIntosh, Hannah. *See* Doran
McIntosh, Helen. *See* Baxter
McIntosh, James, VIII, 550
McIntosh, Sir James, VII, 647
McIntosh, Janet (Christie), VIII, 154
McIntosh, Janet (Fraser), V, 330
MacIntosh, John, VIII, 549
McIntosh, John, VII, **563–64**
McIntosh, John, VIII, **549–50**
McIntosh, John G., VIII, 839
McIntosh, Juliet (mother of JOHN, 1777–1846), VII, 563
McIntosh, Robert, VIII, 550
McIntosh, Sarah Ann (Crosskill), VIII, 192
McIntosh, William, VIII, 550
McIntyre, Alexander, XII, **634–35**
McIntyre, Angus, XII, 637
McIntyre, Archibald, IX, 475
McIntyre, Daniel Eugene, VIII, 53, 304
McIntyre, Duncan, XII, 6, **635–37**
MacIntyre, Duncan Ban, VI, 459
McIntyre, James (merchant), XII, 886
McIntyre, James (stonemason), XII, 974
McIntyre, Jane Allan. *See* Cassils
McIntyre, John Malcolm, XII, 637
McIntyre, Joseph, XII, 634
McIntyre, Margaret (McMartin), VIII, 582
McIntyre, Margaret Malissa. *See* Falconer
McIntyre, Peter, VIII, 247, 530; IX, 831, 832, 833; X, 186, 194, 195, 594, 595, 597; XI, 548, 549, 684, 701, 702, 703; XII, 40, 319, 416, 419, **637–40**, 837
McIntyre, Robert, XII, 635
McIntyre, Sarah. *See* MacKinnon
McIntyre, William Cassils, XII, 637
MacIsaac, Angus, XII, 1042
MacIver, Charles, IX, 180, 182
MacIver, David, IX, 180, 181, 182, 185
Maciver, Isabella (Mackenzie), V, 537
McIver, Murdo, XII, 493
McIvor, Mr (businessman), XII, 634
Mack, Catherine Jane. *See* Adams
Mack, Desiah (Davison), XII, 229

Mack, Frances. *See* Lendrum
Mack, Frederick, XI, 559
Mack, Theophilus, IX, 745; XI, **558–59**; XII, 783
McKay. *See also* McDonald
McKay, Agnes (Moore), IV, 556
McKay, Alexander (landowner), VIII, 126
McKay, Alexander (postmaster), V, 385
MacKay, Alexander, IV, 757; V, 526, **532–34**, 540, 814; VI, 465, 665; VII, 138; VIII, 190, 557, 558, 580, 766; IX, 722
McKay, Alexander Ross, V, 532
McKay, Angus, XI, 675; XII, **640–41**
McKay, Ann. *See* Crichton
McKay, Ann. *See* Marsters
McKay, Ann. *See* Matheson
McKay, Ann (MacGregor), VI, 457
McKay, Annie (MacKinnon; Keefer), VIII, 552
MacKay, Archibald, XII, 479
McKay, Augusta, X, 473
McKay, Catherine. *See* White
McKay, Catherine (Clarke), XI, 194
McKay, Catherine (Fraser), IX, 280
McKay, Catherine (Thomson), XI, 878
MacKay, Christiana (Fraser), IX, 280
McKay, Christina (mother of THOMAS), VIII, 552
Mackay, Christina (wife of ROBERT WALTER STUART), VIII, 551; XII, 571
McKay, Deborah (Bentley), V, 67
McKay, Donald (father of Alexander MACKAY and WILLIAM), V, 532; VI, 464
Mackay, Donald (father of ROBERT WALTER STUART), VIII, 551
MacKay, Donald (HBC employee), IV, 310; V, 534
McKay, Donald (NWC employee), VI, 321
McKay, Donald (shipbuilder), XII, 342
Mackay, Donald (son of DONALD), VI, 464
Mackay, Donald (uncle of John GORDON), XI, 361, 362
Mackay, Donald, V, 534; VI, **463–64**
Mackay, Edward, XI, 361, 362, 559, 560
McKay, Eliza. *See* Davidson
MacKay, Elizabeth (Grant), VIII, 341
McKay, Elizabeth (Thomson), VI, 772; IX, 788
McKay, Elspeth. *See* Kennedy
McKay, Flora (Ross), VIII, 769
Mackay, Francis, V, 315
McKay, George, XI, 571
McKay, Harriet. *See* Ballenden
MacKay, Hector S., VI, 623
McKay, Helen. *See* Holmes
Mackay, Hugh (nephew of JOSEPH), XI, 559, 560
McKay, Hugh (office holder), IV, 557; V, 67
McKay, James (father of ANGUS and JAMES), X, 473; XII, 640
Mackay, James (nephew of JOSEPH), XI, 560
McKay, James (sergeant), XI, 591
McKay, James, VIII, 780; X, **473–75**; XI, 21, 194, 662; XII, 33, 370, 371, 640, 641
Mackay, Jane. *See* Baptist
McKay, John (brother-in-law of James NISBET), X, 549, 550
McKay, John (father of THOMAS), VIII, 552
McKay, John (father of JOHN RICHARDS), X, 475
MacKay, John (merchant), V, 280, 411, 845; VI, 198

McKay, John (oarsman), XII, 408
Mackay, John, IV, **498–99**; VI, 36, 351, 797, 798; VII, 831
McKay, John, V, **534–35**, 886; VI, 464, 795; VIII, 714; XII, 641
McKay, John Richards, V, 535; X, **475**; XII, 641
Mackay, Joseph, XI, 361, **559–60**; XII, 7
McKay, Joseph William, X, 6; XII, 523, **641–43**, 834
McKay, Josette. *See* Latour
Mackay, Kennithina Johana (Harrison), X, 336
McKay, Lauchlan, XII, 342
MacKay, Louise. *See* Chartier de Lotbinière
Mackay, Margaret (Wilson), XII, 1109
McKay, Marguerite. *See* Gladu
McKay, Marguerite. *See* Rowand
MacKay, Marguerite. *See* Waddens
Mackay, Marie-Anne (Quinson de Saint-Ours), V, 752
McKay, Mary. *See* Bunn
McKay, Mary. *See* Favell
Mackay, Mary. *See* McKenzie
MacKay, Mary (McKenzie; Sinclair), VIII, 556, 558; IX, 722
Mackay, Robert, VIII, 553; X, 37, 249; XI, 187
Mackay*, Robert (1840–1916), X, 34; XI, 560
Mackay, Robert Walter Stuart, VIII, 385, **551**; XII, 571
McKay, Roderick, IX, 280
McKay, Samuel, III, 542; V, 231, 315, 413
McKay, Smith, XI, 67, 68, **560–62**
Mackay, Stephen, VIII, 331
McKay, Susan. *See* Lock
McKay, Thomas, V, 532, 533, 534; IX, 513
McKay, Thomas, VI, 220, 481, 812; VII, 130, 927; VIII, 188, 269, **551–54**; IX, 654; XI, 229; XII, 258, 664, 750, 931
McKay, Virginie. *See* Rolette
Mackay, William (clergyman), VIII, 828, 829
McKay, William (father of Joseph MACKAY), XI, 559
McKay, William (father of JOSEPH WILLIAM), XII, 641
McKay, William (HBC postmaster), XII, 832
McKay, William (HBC trader), XI, 597
MacKay, William (son of John MCKAY), V, 535
Mackay, William (son of William MCKAY), VI, 464
McKay, William, V, 532; VI, 236, **464–66**; VII, 138, 206, 556, 557; VIII, 78, 112, 244, 287, 350, 831; X, 12
McKay, William J., VI, 369
McKeagney, Catherine. *See* McCarney
McKeagney, Eliza. *See* Hearne
McKeagney, Eliza. *See* Henry
McKeagney, Henry, VIII, **554–55**
McKeagney, James Charles, X, 59, **475–76**
McKeagney, Patrick, VIII, 554
McKeand, Mrs. *See* Cochrane
McKeand, Alfred, XI, **562**
McKeand, Emma. *See* Kilnar
McKeand, James, XI, 562
McKechin (Mackechnie), Margaret (Weller), IX, 826
Mackechnie, Andrew, VIII, 555
Mackechnie, Anna Maria Barbara. *See* Poore
Mackechnie, Henry, VIII, 555
Mackechnie, Stuart Easton, VIII, **555–56**
McKee, Alexander (brother-in-law of Arthur RANKIN), XII, 884
McKee, Alexander (landowner), VII, 528
McKee, Alexander, IV, 119, 260, 337, **499–500**, 777, 778;

V, 39, 229, 301, 302, 306, 345, 365, 535, 536, 552, 707, 721, 749, 758, 807, 852; VI, 8, 101, 152, 189, 340, 607; VII, 55; VIII, 33, 857
McKee, Mary (Rankin), XII, 884
McKee, Thérèse. *See* Askin
McKee, Thomas, IV, 499
McKee, Thomas, IV, 499, 778, 779; V, 39, 302, 365, **535–36**; VI, 21
McKeen, John, VI, 741
McKeen, Rachel. *See* Todd
McKeen, William, VIII, 782
McKeever, Maria (De Haven), IX, 199
McKellar, Archibald, XI, 146, 497; XII, 492, **643–45**, 646, 648
McKellar, Donald, XII, 646
McKellar, Duncan, XII, 645, 690
Mackellar, Elizabeth. *See* Basaline
McKellar, Flora. *See* McNab
Mackellar, John, IV, 501
McKellar, John, XII, **645–47**
McKellar, Lucy. *See* McNab
McKellar, Margaret. *See* Brodie
McKellar, Mary, XII, 646
McKellar, Mary Catherine. *See* Powell
Mackellar, Patrick, III, 33, 89, 667; IV, 93, **500–1**; V, 425
McKellar, Peter (brother of JOHN), XII, 645, 646
McKellar, Peter (father of ARCHIBALD), XII, 643
McKelsey, Ann (Chandler), IX, 124
McKendree, William, VI, 673; VII, 44
McKenna, Harriet (Burns), XII, 143
McKenna, John, IV, 271
McKenney, Amos, VI, 159, 247
McKenney, Elizabeth. *See* Reily
McKenney, Henry, XI, 562; XII, 949
McKenney, Henry, X, 645; XI, 45, **562–63**; XII, 949, 950
McKenney, Lucy. *See* Stockwell
McKenney, Matilda. *See* Schultz
McKenney, Thomas Loraine, VI, 358
MacKenzie. *See also* Kensey
McKenzie, Mr (fur trader), V, 538
Mackenzie, A. K., VIII, 229, 401
McKenzie, Adelgonde Humbert. *See* Droz
McKenzie, Agnes. *See* Russell
Mackenzie, Alexander (brewer), IV, 384
McKenzie, Alexander (clergyman), VI, 660
Mackenzie, Alexander (father of ALEXANDER, 1822–92), XII, 647
Mackenzie, Alexander (father of DONALD, HENRY, and JAMES, d. 1849, McKenzie and RODERICK, d. 1844), VI, 468; VII, 564, 565; VIII, 557
Mackenzie, Alexander (merchant), IV, 571; V, 277
Mackenzie, Alexander (son of RODERICK, d. 1844) VII, 567
McKenzie, Alexander, V, 533, 544; VI, 436, **466–67**; VII, 735
Mackenzie, Alexander, IX, 125, 150, 507; X, 95, 101, 102, 123, 126, 127, 128, 157, 171, 191, 211, 219, 283, 292, 294, 330, 357, 359, 599, 727; XI, 7, 24, 25, 69, 123, 130, 134, 163, 164, 196, 198, 207, 224, 233, 261, 298, 300, 324, 336, 347, 374, 399, 422, 439, 465, 480, 520, 521, 622, 624, 625, 652, 668, 681, 689, 707, 710, 711, 731, 744, 770, 820, 832, 833, 853, 897, 907, 934; XII, 6, 8, 26, 28, 35, 83, 95, 98, 140, 148, 151, 220, 241, 264, 291,

292, 325, 353, 363, 371, 406, 430, 432, 437, 438, 448, 494, 495, 506, 536, 560, 568, 579, 588, 602, 603, 604, 606, 614, 633, 636, 644, **647–59**, 674, 685, 721, 729, 733, 738, 742, 837, 854, 857, 881, 898, 916, 935, 937, 952, 979, 1037, 1041, 1057, 1068, 1092
Mackenzie, Sir Alexander, I, 378; II, xxviii; III, xxxiii; IV, 310, 506, 741, 746, 757; V, 266, 391, 512, 532, 533, **537–43**, 562, 563, 564, 565, 581, 603, 635, 636, 656, 683, 684, 685, 822; VI, 20, 236, 296, 375, 436, 454, 455, 466, 468, 469, 531, 533, 635, 641; VII, 78, 309, 324, 342, 414, 565, 566, 567; VIII, 100, 321, 483, 500, 546, 818; IX, 282, 283, 285, 553; X, 38
Mackenzie, Alexander John, XII, 357, 358
M'Kenzie, Angus, X, 620
McKenzie, Ann. *See* Bethune
MacKenzie, Ann (Bell), VI, 516; VII, 66
Mackenzie, Lady Augusta (Murray, Lady Murray), VII, 639
McKenzie, Barbara (Chisholm), VII, 178
McKenzie, Benjamin, VII, 526
McKenzie, Catharine. *See* Milton
MacKenzie, Catherine (Monro), VI, 516
MacKenzie, Catherine (Quirouet), VII, 718
Mackenzie, Catherine (mother of DONALD, HENRY, and JAMES, d. 1849, McKenzie and RODERICK, d. 1844), VI, 468; VII, 564, 565; VIII, 557
MacKenzie, Catherine Eliza. *See* Crombie
Mackenzie, Catherine Elizabeth (Mathieson), IX, 540
Mackenzie, Charles (brother of ALEXANDER, 1822–92), XII, 656
McKenzie, Charles (son of JAMES, 1788–1859), VIII, 559
McKenzie, Charles, V, 177; VIII, 350, **556–57**; IX, 455
Mackenzie, Charles Roderick, VII, 567
McKenzie, Christian (Carmichael), VIII, 126
MacKenzie, Colin, V, 543
Mackenzie, Daniel (father of WILLIAM LYON), IX, 496
McKenzie, Daniel (fur trader), V, 267, 544; VI, 444
McKenzie, Donald, V, 526, 533; VI, 253, 468; VII, 473, 565, 578; VIII, 158, 190, **557–58**, 561, 766, 779, 811, 889; IX, 260, 366, 722; X, 495; XI, 882
McKenzie, Elizabeth. *See* Cameron
McKenzie, Elizabeth. *See* Grant
McKenzie, Elizabeth (Chalmers; Mackenzie), IX, 496, 497
McKenzie, Ellen. *See* Fitzsimons
Mackenzie, Frederick, XI, 937
Mackenzie, Geddes (Mackenzie, Lady Mackenzie), V, 537, 542
Mackenzie, George (father-in-law of Sir ALEXANDER), V, 542
Mackenzie, George (grandfather of George BROWN), X, 91
Mackenzie, George (lawyer), XII, 592, 593
Mackenzie, George, VI, **467–68**
Mackenzie, George, 3rd Earl of Cromarty, VII, 639
McKenzie, George Rogers, VIII, 126, 127; X, **476–77**
McKenzie, Hector Æneas, VIII, 556
Mackenzie, Helen. *See* Neil
McKenzie, Henry, VI, 72, **468–69**, 664, 765; VII, 381, 564, 565, 566; VIII, 557, 719
McKenzie, Holt, V, 101
Mackenzie, Hope Fleming, X, 128; XII, 647, 648
Mackenzie, Isabel. *See* Baxter
McKenzie, Isabella. *See* Latour

Mackenzie, Isabella. *See* Maciver
Mackenzie, James (merchant), IV, 304; V, 377; VI, 516; VII, 66
McKenzie, James (son of JAMES, 1788–1859), VIII, 559
Mackenzie, James (son of WILLIAM LYON), IX, 497
McKenzie, James, VI, **469–71**; VII, 506
McKenzie, James, IV, 424; VI, 468, 705; VII, **564–65**, 566; VIII, 350, 557
McKenzie, James, VIII, **558–60**
Mackenzie, Jane. *See* Sym
McKenzie, Janet. *See* Blair
McKenzie, Janet. *See* Fraser
McKenzie, John (brother-in-law of James CARMICHAEL), VIII, 126, 303
Mackenzie, John (businessman), V, 320; IX, 540
McKenzie, John (father of GEORGE ROGERS), X, 476
Mackenzie, John (hospital administrator), XI, 533
MacKenzie, John (soldier), X, 477
Mackenzie, John (uncle of Sir ALEXANDER), V, 537
McKenzie, John, VIII, 303, **560–61**, 640; IX, 495; X, 606
MacKenzie, John George, VII, 249, 250
MacKenzie, John George Delhoste, VIII, 927; X, 382, **477**
MacKenzie, John Gordon (merchant), IX, 555
McKenzie, John Gordon (investor), XI, 5
Mackenzie, John I., XI, 130
McKenzie, Julia (Carpmael), XII, 160
MacKenzie, Kenneth (doctor), XII, 217
Mackenzie, Kenneth (father of Sir ALEXANDER), V, 537
McKenzie, Kenneth (father of KENNETH, 1811–74) X, 477
MacKenzie, Kenneth, V, **543–44**; VII, 517, 736
McKenzie, Kenneth, X, 242, **477–79**; XII, 61, 523
McKenzie, Kenneth John, VII, 532, 533, 534, 535, 540; VIII, 222
MacKenzie, Lachlan, VIII, 569
MacKenzie, Louisa (wife of KENNETH, d. 1816), V, 544
McKenzie, Louisa (Bethune), VII, 566; VIII, 85; XII, 106
McKenzie, Margaret. *See* Badden
McKenzie, Margaret (Anderson), IX, 6
McKenzie, Margaret (Auldjo), VI, 18
Mackenzie, Margaret (Cuthbert), IV, 190
MacKenzie, Margaret (daughter of KENNETH, d. 1816), V, 544
MacKenzie, Margaret (mother of KENNETH, d. 1816), V, 543
Mackenzie, Marianne (Brown), IX, 88; X, 91
McKenzie, Mary. *See* MacKay
McKenzie, Mary (Mackay), VI, 464
Mackenzie, Mary (Scott), XII, 957, 958
Mackenzie, Mary (Thompson), XII, 658
Mackenzie, Mary Stewart. *See* Fleming
Mackenzie, Murdoch, V, 537
Mackenzie, Nancy. *See* Fisher
McKenzie, Nancy (McTavish; Le Blanc), VII, 566, 578; VIII, 226, 558, **561**
Mackenzie, Rachel. *See* Chaboillez
Mackenzie, Robert (brother of ALEXANDER, 1822–92), XII, 647
Mackenzie, Robert (half-brother of Thomas MARKLAND), X, 12
MacKenzie, Roderick (officer), IV, 153, 240, 436; V, 339
McKenzie, Roderick (son of RODERICK, d. 1859), VI, 101; VIII, 821; IX, 6
Mackenzie, Roderick, V, 177, 179, 391, 537, 538, 539, 541, 542, 544, 565, 684; VI, 383, 454, 468, 469, 665, 704; VII, 190, 191, 356, 564, **565–67**, 578, 595, 837; VIII, 85, 453, 483, 556, 557, 561
McKenzie, Roderick, VI, 444; VII, 526; VIII, 350, **562–63**, 821; XII, 1004
McKenzie, Samuel, VIII, 562
McKenzie, Sarah. *See* McGregor
Mackenzie, Sarah (Mackenzie), VI, 467
Mackenzie, Thomas H., VII, 284
McKenzie, William (father of JOHN), VIII, 560
Mackenzie, William (trader), IV, 571
Mackenzie*, Sir William (1849–1923), XI, 293; XII, 626, 699
Mackenzie, William James, X, 651
Mackenzie, William Lyon, VI, 12, 78, 80, 116, 118, 149, 164, 165, 199, 200, 248, 265, 266, 331, 399, 421, 422, 467, 468, 498, 542, 543, 545, 609, 612, 632, 633, 657, 741, 772, 773; VII, 40, 43, 56, 58, 84, 100, 124, 126, 127, 158, 164, 178, 180, 183, 230, 234, 253, 261, 313, 315, 317, 318, 319, 365, 367, 369, 370, 376, 379, 404, 405, 418, 420, 439, 442, 456, 457, 458, 460, 466, 467, 497, 506, 509, 519, 548, 549, 550, 559, 596, 601, 638, 662, 663, 664, 665, 695, 712, 715, 756, 773, 794, 863, 883, 896, 904, 923; VIII, xxiii, xxvii, 5, 6, 7, 8, 12, 46, 47, 48, 51, 54, 56, 57, 69, 105, 119, 120, 125, 178, 186, 187, 208, 229, 255, 256, 276, 305, 325, 340, 401, 431, 445, 466, 493, 501, 512, 523, 550, 598, 602, 603, 609, 622, 623, 642, 643, 696, 697, 707, 785, 797, 798, 852, 853, 854, 855, 871, 885, 896, 897, 932, 945, 946; IX, 8, 25, 68, 69, 100, 109, 124, 131, 139, 140, 141, 149, 163, 201, 229, 230, 231, 265, 299, 306, 313, 336, 345, 387, 400, 411, 412, 415, 416, 423, **496–510**, 520, 522, 523, 546, 589, 596, 643, 662, 672, 674, 683, 685, 686, 687, 689, 724, 744, 746, 758, 788, 813, 814, 815, 842; X, 61, 62, 95, 109, 118, 160, 170, 225, 233, 254, 259, 262, 309, 310, 314, 343, 344, 358, 359, 395, 398, 482, 484, 489, 529, 530, 533, 546, 555, 557, 559, 573, 618, 622, 623, 639, 641, 642, 671; XI, 166, 248, 312, 366, 407, 411, 516, 517, 518, 542, 712, 713, 714, 786, 797, 863, 914; XII, 42, 262, 525, 528, 934, 1078
Mackenzie, William S., XII, 957
Mackenzie-Stewart, Julia Charlotte Sophia (Hay, Marchioness of Tweeddale; Rose, Lady Rose; Gordon, Lady Gordon), XI, 771
McKerlie, Daniel, X, 169, 170
McKernan, Margaret (Gordon), IX, 324
MacKey, Rosena (Skead), XI, 826
MacKey, William, XI, 826
Mackie, Ann (Lambly), IX, 454
McKie, Charlotte (Pryor), XII, 870
Mackie, John, XII, 921
Mackie, Mary Magdalen (McConville), VII, 527
McKiernan, Charles, known as Joe Beef, XI, **563–65**
McKiernan, Margaret. *See* McRae
McKiernan, Mary. *See* McRae
Mackieson, John, XI, **565–66**
Mackieson, Matilda. *See* Brecken
McKim, Andrew, IX, 294, 747
McKim*, Anson (1855–1917), XII, 286
Mackin, Denis, VIII, 475
McKindlay, John, IV, 757; VI, 297, **471–73**, 476, 635; VII, 523
McKindlay, Peter, VI, 471

MacKinlay, Andrew, VII, 875; VIII, 400; IX, **510–11**; XI, 420
McKinlay, Archibald, VIII, 421
MacKinlay, Barbara. *See* Goodfellow
MacKinlay, Helen (Isbister), IV, 380
MacKinlay, John, IX, 510
MacKinlay, Margaret. *See* Alardyce
MacKinlay, William, IX, 510
McKinley, Eleanor (McMillan), VIII, 584
McKinney, Mary (Harris), V, 408
McKinnon, Mrs. *See* Crane
McKinnon, Mrs (wife of WILLIAM), V, 546
Mackinnon, Alexander, VII, 560
MacKinnon, Annie. *See* McKay
MacKinnon, Colin Francis, VIII, 247, 308; IX, 217; X, 475, **479–80**; XI, 351; XII, 548
MacKinnon, Donald Alexander, XII, 48
MacKinnon, Helen (Stewart), V, 775, 776, 825; VI, 735
MacKinnon, John (businessman), VIII, 552, 553; XI, 229; XII, 258
MacKinnon, John (father of COLIN FRANCIS), X, 479
MacKinnon, John (father of William Charles MCKINNON), IX, 511
McKinnon, John (son of RANALD), V, 544
McKinnon, Letitia. *See* Piggott
MacKinnon, Margaret (Macdonald), VIII, 535
McKinnon, Ranald, V, **544–45**; VI, 77
MacKinnon, Sarah (McIntyre), XII, 637
MacKinnon, Una. *See* MacLeod
McKinnon, W. A., IX, 475
McKinnon, William, IV, 523; V, 204, **545–46**, 634, 780; VI, 213, 535; IX, 511
McKinnon, William Charles, V, 545; IX, **511**
Mackintosh, Agnes. *See* Dallas of Cantray
Mackintosh*, Charles Herbert (1843–1931), XI, 683, 708, 920; XII, 971
Mackintosh, Duncan, V, 543
Mackintosh, J. C., X, 293
Mackintosh, Sir James, VIII, 602
MacKintosh, John, VIII, 376, 529, 530; IX, 158; X, 90, 419, 461; XI, **566–68**, 666; XII, 856
Mackintosh, Margaret. *See* MacDonald
Mackintosh, Mary Archange. *See* Baudry, *dit* Desbuttes, *dit* Saint-Martin
MacKintosh, Robert James, XI, 634
MacKintosh, Sarah. *See* Gladu
MacKintosh, William, VII, 568
MacKintosh, William, VII, **567–68**; VIII, 158
Mackintosh of Castle Leathers, Duncan, VI, 473
Mackintosh of Mackintosh, Angus, 26th Chief of Clan Chattan and 25th Chief of Clan Mackintosh, V, 722; VI, 8, **473**
Macklem, Caroline. *See* Street
Macklem, Hannah (Nelles), XI, 639
Macklem, Julia Abigail (Denison), XII, 243
Macklem, Sarah (Nelles), XI, 639
Macklin, J. P., VIII, 804
Macklin(?), Sarah (Noble), III, 483
Macklish. *See* McCliesh
McKnight, Alexander, XII, 617, **659–60**
McKnight, Catherine Glen. *See* Kidston
McKnight, Mary. *See* Murdoch
McKnight, Samuel, XII, 659

McKown, John, IV, 769
McKown, Mary. *See* Willard
Mackworth, Agnes (Watts; Crowne), I, 241, 242
Mackworth, Humphrey, I, 241
McLachlan, Alexander, XII, 663
McLachlan, Alexander, XII, 570, **660–64**, 922
McLachlan, Ann (Lyons), XII, 660, 661
McLachlan, Charles (uncle), XII, 661
McLachlan, Charles, XII, 660, 661
McLachlan, Clamina (McLachlan), XII, 660, 661, 663
McLachlan, Daniel (great-uncle), XII, 660, 661
McLachlan, Daniel, XII, 663
McLachlan, Elizabeth (Merrall), XII, 660, 661
McLachlan, Jean. *See* Sutherland
McLachlan, Jean (Hamilton), XII, 660, 661
McLachlan, John (clergyman), XII, 614
McLachlan, John (partner of John GALT), VII, 336
McLachlan, John (son of ALEXANDER), XII, 663
McLachlan, Malcolm (uncle), XII, 661
McLachlan, Malcolm, XII, 663
McLachlan, Mary, XII, 663
McLachlin, Claude, XI, 682
McLachlin, Daniel, X, 481
McLachlin, Daniel, VIII, 268, 840; X, **480–81**
McLachlin, Hugh (grandfather), X, 480
McLachlin, Hugh (uncle), X, 480
McLachlin, Hugh, X, 481
McLachlin, John, X, 481
McLachlin, Maria. *See* Harrington
McLachlin, William, X, 480
MacLaggan, Alexander, VIII, 224
Maclaine, Margaret (Rankin), VIII, 741
McLane, David, IV, **501–3**; V, 84, 87, 462, 486, 691, 878; VI, 174, 186, 347, 515, 549, 557, 560, 574, 641, 701; VII, 199, 783, 784, 911
McLaney, Martha. *See* Dennis
MacLaomuinn, Eoghan, V, 547
Maclaren, Albert, XII, 665
Maclaren, Alexander, XII, 665
Maclaren, Ann. *See* Sully
Maclaren, David (brother of JAMES), XII, 664
MacLaren, David (father of James MACLAREN), XII, 664
Maclaren, David (son of JAMES), XII, 664, 665
McLaren, Donald, VII, 568
MacLaren, Elizabeth. *See* Barnet
McLaren, Isabella (Buntin), XII, 135
Maclaren, James, VIII, 553; XII, 197, **664–66**
Maclaren, James Barnet, XII, 665
McLaren, Jane. *See* Evatt
Maclaren, Jane (Crawford), VI, 172
Maclaren, John (uncle), VIII, 553; XII, 664, 665, 1130
Maclaren, John, XII, 665
McLaren, Margaret. *See* Hewit
McLaren, Neil, VII, **568–69**
McLaren, Peter, XI, 846
Maclaren, William, XII, 665
McLaren, William Paterson, VIII, 44; IX, **511–12**; XII, 886
McLarn. *See* McClearn
MacLauchlan, James Augustus, XII, 17, 20
Mclea, Frances (Brooking), IX, 84
McLean. *See also* McLane
MacLean, Miss (McDougall), VIII, 539

McLean, Alexander (brother of ARCHIBALD, 1791–1865), IX, 513; X, 462, 463
McLean, Alexander (clergyman), IX, 495
MacLean, Alexander (laird), VII, 560
Maclean, Alexander (politician), IX, 223
McLean, Alexander D., XI, 756
MacLean, Allan (father of Iain MACGHILLEATHAIN), VII, 559
MacLean, Allan (father of Malcolm Alexander MACLEAN), XII, 666
MacLean, Allan (of Kingston), IV, 505; V, 169, 765; VI, 215; VII, 559; VIII, 252; IX, 485
Maclean, Allan, IV, 229, 309, 336, **503–4**, 548, 606, 791; V, 30, 78, 131, 191, 282, 515, 517, 584, 893, 894, 899; VI, 475
McLean, Allan, IX, 514; XI, **568–69**, 757
McLean, Allen (son of ARCHIBALD, d. 1830), VI, 474
Maclean, Ann. See Smith
Maclean, Anne. See Kinloch
McLean, Anne Margaret (Wilson), V, 864
MacLean, Annie. See Warren
McLean, Annie, XI, 568
McLean, Archibald, XI, 568
McLean, Archibald, V, 135; VI, 7, **473–75**; VII, 331; IX, 399
McLean, Archibald, IV, 505; V, 521, 522, 558, 748; VI, 475; VII, 179, 365, 371, 456, 458, 459, 460, 545; VIII, 195, 511, 514, 521, 608; IX, 499, **512–13**; X, 257, 462, 693; XI, 581
McLean, Archie, IX, 514
MacLean, Bessie Emma Mathilda. See Dyas
McLean, Catherine (Pritchard), VIII, 713
Maclean, Catherine (Rankin), VIII, 741
Maclean, Catherine Isabella (Fraser), VII, 329
McLean, Charles (father of JOHN, 1828–86), XI, 570
McLean, Charles (outlaw), XI, 568
MacLean, Charles (son of DONALD), IX, 514
MacLean, Christian (Rose), XII, 921
Maclean, Donald, IV, 503
McLean, Donald, IX, **513–14**; XI, 568
MacLean, Donald Charles, X, **481–82**
Maclean, Duncan, VII, 203; VIII, **563–66**; IX, 400; X, 594; XII, 840
McLean, Elizabeth (mother of NEIL, 1759–1832), VI, 475
McLean, Eugenia Clarissa. See Evans
McLean, Flora Campbell. See Stalwart
McLean, Francis, IV, 161, 503, **504–5**, 606; V, 16, 134, 336, 434, 557; VI, 283, 362, 429, 740
McLean, George, XI, 569
McLean, Grace (McDonald), VI, 434
McLean, Harriet (McLean; Walker), IV, 505
McLean, Hector, V, 536, 710, 772; VI, 340
MacLean*, Hugh Cameron (1866–1949), XII, 287
McLean, Isabella. See Macdonell (Leek)
Maclean, Isabella (Fraser), VII, 329
McLean, Isabella (McGillivray), VIII, 546, 547
McLean, Jane (mother of Malcolm Alexander MACLEAN), XII, 666
McLean, Jane (Clindinning), XII, 200
Maclean, Janet (Maclean), IV, 503
MacLean, Jannet. See Watson
McLean, Jessie H. See Cameron
McLean, Jessie H. (Cameron), XII, 147

McLean, Joan. See McPherson
MacLean, John. See MacGhillEathain, Iain
Maclean, John (author), XII, 1057
McLean, John (father of NEIL, 1759–1832), VI, 475
McLean, John (litigant), VIII, 479
McLean, John (1828–86), X, 209; XI, 195, **570–72**
Maclean, John (d. 1890), VI, 765; VII, 277; VIII, 309, 539; X, 272, 273, 284; XI, 470, 508, **569–70**
Maclean*, John Bayne (1862–1950), VIII, 68; XII, 286, 287
Maclean, John Brown, VI, 462
McLean, John Jenkin, V, 864
McLean, Joseph C., XII, 591
McLean, Julia (McLean of Torren), VI, 473
Maclean, Kathleen Wilhelmina. See Flood
Maclean, Lauchlan, VI, 299
Maclean, Letitia Elizabeth. See Landon
MacLean, Malcolm Alexander, XII, **666–67**
McLean, Margaret. See Charles
McLean, Margaret. See MacFadyen
MacLean, Margaret Anne. See Cattanach
Maclean, Mary. See Campbell
McLean, Mary. See Herkimer
McLean, Mary (McBeath), XI, 539
MacLean, Mary Elizabeth (Nutting), IX, 601
McLean, Neil, IV, 495, **505**, 683; V, 402; VI, 475; XI, 377
McLean, Neil, VI, **475**; VII, 251; VIII, 303, 546, 583; IX, 512
MacLean, Peter, IX, **514–15**
McLean, Prudence. See French
MacLean, Salome (Howard), VI, 474; IX, 399
MacLean, Sarah (Smith), V, 766
Maclean, Sophia. See Grant
McLean, Susan. See Drummond
Maclean, William (father of Francis McLEAN), IV, 504
McLean, William (son of ARCHIBALD, d. 1830), VI, 474
Maclean*, William Findlay (1854–1929), XI, 307; XII, 704, 705
McLean*, William John (1841–1929), XI, 599, 600
Maclean of Coll, Alexander, VIII, 741
Maclean of Coll, Janet (Hobart), VIII, 741
McLean of Torren (Torranbeg), Hector, VI, 473
McLean of Torren, Julia. See McLean
Maclear, Isabel. See Arbuckle
Maclear, Thomas, VIII, 14, 188, 189, 790; XI, 558, 724; XII, 188, 212, **667–68**, 998
Maclear, Thomas A., XII, 667
Maclear, William H., XII, 667
McLearn. See also McClearn
McLearn, Elizabeth. See Fenton
McLearn, Harriet. See Stout
McLearn, James, VIII, 566
McLearn, Richard, VIII, **566–68**
McLeay, Grace. See Warner
McLeay, James Franklin, XII, **668–69**
McLeay, Janet. See Glendenning
McLeay, John, XII, 668
McLeay, Murdo, XII, 668
McLelan, Archibald Woodbury, VIII, 568, 569; X, 368; XI, 24, **572–74**, 768, 927; XII, 36, 383, 389, 607, 611, 979, 1042, 1043
McLelan, Caroline. See Metzler
McLelan, David, VIII, 568

McLelan, Gloud Wilson, VIII, 416, **568–69**; XI, 572, 574
McLelan, Martha. *See* Spencer
McLelan, Mary. *See* Durling
McLelan, Peter, VIII, 568
McLellan. *See also* McClellan
McLellan, Alexander James, XII, 430, 763
McLellan, Archibald, V, 466; VI, 100; VIII, 343
McLellan, Catharine. *See* Morton
MacLellan, Malcolm, X, 479
MacLennan, Catherine. *See* MacNab
MacLennan, Donald Ban, X, 468
McLennan, Hugh, XII, **669–70**
McLennan, Isabella. *See* Stewart
McLennan, John (brother of HUGH), XII, 670
McLennan, John (father of HUGH), XII, 669
MacLennan, John (lawyer), X, 468
MacLennan, John, VIII, 444, **569–70**, 742, 770
McLennan*, John Stewart (1853–1939), III, 73, 229; XII, 670
MacLennan, Louisa Mary (Jenkins), XII, 473
McLennan, Margaret, VI, 720
McLennan*, William (1856–1904), IV, 401; XII, 670
MacLeod, Mr (merchant), X, 722
McLeod, Alexander, IX, 544
McLeod, Alexander, VII, 859; VIII, 401; IX, 505; X, **482–83**, 546
McLeod, Alexander Roderick, VII, 570
McLeod, Alexander Roderick, VII, **569–70**, 572; VIII, 59, 573; IX, 851
McLeod, Angus Jonas, XII, **670–71**
McLeod, Archibald Norman, V, 268, 466, 559; VI, 664; VII, 138, 498; VIII, 158, 453, 482, 546; X, 720
McLeod, Bélonie. *See* Siméon
McLeod, Benjamin, XII, 48
MacLeod, Cécile. *See* Robert
McLeod, Charlotte. *See* Pruden
McLeod*, Clement Henry (1851–1917), X, 659; XII, 161
M'Leod, Donald, VII, 404; VIII, 305, 853; IX, 230, 231, 551; X, **483–84**, 514
McLeod, Donald, XII, **671–72**
McLeod, Duncan, VI, 474; VII, 330, 331
McLeod, Ellen Norman. *See* Morrison
McLeod, Emma Grace (Pringle), XII, 864
McLeod, Ezekiel, IX, **515–16**
MacLeod, Flora (Buchanan), V, 546
McLeod, François, VIII, 573
McLeod, George, XI, 350
MacLeod, Hugh, VIII, 569
McLeod, Isabel (Bontine), XII, 135
McLeod, Isabella (Stewart), VIII, 839
Macleod, James Farquharson, XI, 112, 443, 478, 870; XII, **672–75**, 718, 858
McLeod, James W., IX, 293; XI, 947
Macleod, Jane. *See* Fry
McLeod, John (businessman), VIII, 966; XII, 884
MacLeod, John (inn owner), VI, 168
McLeod, John (posse member), XI, 568
McLeod, John (son of PETER), VIII, 571, 573
McLeod, John, VII, **570–71**, 572; VIII, 421; IX, 513
McLeod, John M., VII, **571–73**; XII, 155
McLeod, Joseph, IX, 516
McLeod, Josephte. *See* Atikuapi
McLeod, Justina (Scobie), VIII, 789; XII, 212

MacLeod, Kenneth, VII, 572
McLeod, Magloire, XI, 339, 893
McLeod, Malcolm, VII, 571; XII, 613
MacLeod, Margaret. *See* Arnett
McLeod, Margaret (Cameron), VII, 139; XII, 149
McLeod, Margaret B. (Des Brisay), VIII, 215
McLeod, Martin, VII, 249, 250
Macleod, Martin Donald, XII, 672
Macleod, Mary, VII, 560
MacLeod, Mary (Macaulay), VI, 412
MacLeod, Mary (McLeod), IX, 516
Macleod, Mary Isabella. *See* Drever
McLeod, Neil, XI, 210; XII, 40
MacLeod, Norman, VI, 660; IX, 475, **516–17**
MacLeod, Normand, IV, **505–6**; V, 390, 391, 537, 562, 603, 656; VI, 454; VII, 565; VIII, 500
McLeod, Peter, VIII, 570
McLeod, Peter, VII, 569; VIII, 139, 140, **570–73**, 893; IX, 398, 640, 642; X, 635; XI, 396; XII, 864
Macleod, Roderick, VIII, 839
McLeod, Sarah (Ballenden), VII, 570; VIII, 59, **573–75**; XI, 139, 875, 876; XII, 206
MacLeod, Sarah (Swift), XII, 1001
MacLeod, Tormad, X, 85
MacLeod, Una (Eunice) (MacKinnon), X, 479
McLeod, William, XI, 304
MacLeod, William Bernard, VII, 355; X, 479
MacLeod of Bernera, Catherine (MacDonell), V, 523
McLimont, Catherine (McGill), VIII, 544
McLoughlin, Angélique. *See* Fraser
McLoughlin, David (uncle), VII, 573; VIII, 575, 576
McLoughlin, David, VIII, 580; X, 486
McLoughlin, John (father of JOHN and MARIE-LOUISE), VII, 573; VIII, 575
McLoughlin, John (son of JOHN), VIII, 226, 579, 817; IX, 852; X, 496
McLoughlin, John, IV, 757; V, 534, 544; VI, 259, 436, 466, 721; VII, 78, 205, 569, 572, 573, 672, 808, 838, 845; VIII, 85, 121, 226, 314, 352, 454, **575–81**, 584, 661, 662, 813, 816, 817; IX, 260, 327, 553, 806, 851, 852, 853, 854; X, 239, 240, 241, 247, 484, 485, 486, 495, 496; XI, 885, 886, 887, 888; XII, 317
McLoughlin, Joseph, VIII, 584
McLoughlin, Marguerite. *See* Waddens
McLoughlin, Marie-Louise, named de Saint-Henri, VII, 100, **573**, 870; VIII, 594
McLoughlin, Victoire. *See* McMillan
Maclure. *See* McClure
McLure, George, VI, 94
Maclure*, Samuel (1860–1929), XII, 1049
McMackin, Thomas, XI, 804
McMahon, Hugh, XI, 78
McMahon, John Baptist, VII, **573–75**
McMahon, Mary. *See* Malone
McMahon, Michael, VII, 574
McMahon, Patrick, VIII, 581
McMahon, Patrick, VI, 120; VIII, **581–82**; IX, 361; X, 175
McMahon, Winifred. *See* Kelly
McMartin, Alexander, V, 522; VII, 549; VIII, 303, **582–83**
McMartin, Daniel, XII, 85
McMartin, Malcolm, VIII, 582
McMartin, Margaret. *See* McIntyre
McMartin, Margaret (McArthur), XII, 577

McMartin, Mary. *See* Carlyle
McMaster, Arthur Robinson, XI, 574
McMaster, James, V, 646
McMaster, James Alphonsus, X, 542
McMaster, James Short, XI, 574, 575
McMaster, Mary. *See* Henderson
McMaster, Susan. *See* Moulton
McMaster, William (father of WILLIAM), XI, 574
McMaster, William (store owner), XII, 972
McMaster, William, VIII, 934; IX, 804; XI, 10, 158, 167, 415, 553, 554, **574–78**; XII, 43, 45, 151, 225, 296, 486, 882
MacMechan*, Archibald McKellar (1862–1933), IV, 169, 170; VI, 500; IX, 185; X, 223; XII, 15, 16
McMechan, John, X, 68
MacMhannain, Calum Bàn, V, **546–48**
McMichael, Christina (Christian) (Ansley), VII, 20
McMichael, Daniel, XI, 144, 166
McMichael, Jennie Elizabeth. *See* McAllister
McMicken, Ann Theresa. *See* Duff
McMicken, Gilbert, VIII, 966; IX, 588; X, 559; XI, 611, 613, 614, 645; XII, 68, 597, 602, **675–80**, 951
McMicking, Laura. *See* Chubbock
McMicking, Mary. *See* McClellan
McMicking*, Robert Burns (1843–1915), IX, 517, 519
McMicking, Thomas, IX, **517–19**; X, 656; XI, 417; XII, 642
McMicking, William, IX, 517
McMicking, William Francis, IX, 518
MacMillan, Alexander (clergyman), XII, 618
McMillan, Alexander (duellist), VII, 852
McMillan, Alexander (grandfather of ARCHIBALD), VI, 475
McMillan, Alexander (son of ARCHIBALD), VI, 477, 478
McMillan, Allan, VIII, 583
MacMillan*, Angus (1817–1906), XI, 701
McMillan, Archibald, VI, **475–79**
McMillan, Daniel, XII, 662
McMillan, Donald, XII, 615
MacMillan, Donald Baxter, VIII, 449
McMillan, Eleanor. *See* McKinley
McMillan, Elizabeth (Cull), VI, 175
McMillan, Isabella. *See* Gray
McMillan, James, VI, 720; VII, 571; VIII, 158, 176, 412, 413, 527, 576, **583–84**, 813, 814; IX, 851; X, 495, 720; XI, 52; XII, 155
McMillan, James Eliphalet, IX, 479
McMillan, John, XI, **578–79**
Macmillan*, John C. (1862–1926), IX, 832; X, 461
McMillan, Joseph C., XI, **579–80**
McMillan, Margaret. *See* Cameron
McMillan, Mary (wife of JOSEPH C.), XI, 579
McMillan, Mary (Cochrane), XII, 201
McMillan, Mary Stewart. *See* McNutt
McMillan, Victoire (McLoughlin), VIII, 584
MacMillan, Wilhemina (Black), VII, 77
McMonagle, John, VI, 779
McMullen, Daniel, IX, 419
McMullen, Élisabeth, V, 293
McMullen, George William, X, 293, 294, 698; XI, 7; XII, 73, 987
McMullen, James, XII, 195
McMullen, John Mercier, X, 627

McMullen, Mary Jane (Christie), XII, 195
McMun, Jane (Black), V, 83
MacMurchy, Archibald, XI, 367; XII, 662, 1077, 1095
McMurdo, Jessie Gordon (Monroe), XII, 753
McMurdo, Thomas, VIII, 233; XI, 429; XII, 754
McMurray, Amelia. *See* Baxter
McMurray, Anne Christie. *See* Ballenden
McMurray, Bradshaw, XII, 680
McMurray, Charlotte. *See* Johnston
McMurray, Elizabeth (wife of THOMAS), XI, 580
McMurray, Jane. *See* Baxter
McMurray, Jane (Cumming), IX, 170
McMurray, Mary (mother of WILLIAM), XII, 680
McMurray, Thomas, VIII, 100; IX, 170
McMurray, Thomas, XI, **580–81**; XII, 69
McMurray, William, VIII, 60
McMurray, William, VIII, 86; XI, 653; XII, **680–82**, 808
McMurrich, George, XI, 582
McMurrich*, James Playfair (1859–1939), XI, 582
McMurrich, Janet. *See* Dixon
McMurrich, John, VIII, 875; IX, 804; XI, **581–82**; XII, 73, 684
McMurrich, William Barclay, XI, 582
McNab, A. B., VIII, 899
McNab, Alexander, X, 317
MacNab, Allan, IX, 519
MacNab, Sir Allan Napier, VI, 159, 230, 248, 425, 468; VII, 39, 56, 59, 100, 116, 157, 158, 178, 234, 253, 379, 453, 459, 460, 466, 497, 606, 909; VIII, 10, 43, 44, 49, 57, 96, 99, 106, 120, 138, 170, 171, 195, 230, 276, 280, 293, 401, 402, 486, 502, 585, 587, 588, 679, 687, 708, 798, 800, 822, 823, 896, 946, 964, 965; IX, 9, 11, 49, 57, 59, 91, 92, 104, 165, 230, 266, 313, 323, 329, 345, 360, 362, 369, 370, 383, 463, 471, 499, 503, 507, **519–27**, 570, 571, 576, 611, 645, 690, 697, 707, 726, 727, 735, 745, 746, 776, 777, 844, 858; X, 35, 96, 97, 119, 120, 124, 127, 131, 144, 170, 225, 256, 257, 259, 277, 311, 321, 462, 464, 591, 607, 623, 632, 637, 642, 676, 715, 716, 721; XI, 122, 123, 128, 160, 166, 180, 181, 206, 232, 282, 366, 410, 414, 498, 536, 552, 554, 581, 608, 618, 649, 677, 822, 837, 853, 915; XII, 72, 73, 89, 101, 184, 262, 410, 593, 594, 630, 631, 681, 745, 886, 962, 1013
MacNab, Anne. *See* Maule
MacNab, Anne. *See* Napier
McNab, Archibald, 17th Chief of Clan Macnab, VIII, 50, **584–89**, 733, 799
MacNab, Catherine (MacLennan), VIII, 569
McNab, Catherine Susan Ann (Howe), VI, 335; X, 363
MacNab, David Archibald, VIII, 585; IX, 521, 745
MacNab, Dugald, VIII, 585
McNab, Dugald C., VIII, 586
McNab, Duncan, VIII, 586, 587
MacNab, Elizabeth. *See* Brooke
McNab, Flora (McKellar), XII, 643
MacNab, Francis, 16th Chief of Clan Macnab, VIII, 584
McNab, Helen (McDonell of Collachie), V, 519; VII, 554
McNab, James, VII, 144; VIII, 160, 416, 417, 904, 905; IX, 226; X, 385; XI, 157
McNab, John (attorney), X, 630
McNab, John (fur trader), VI, 320
McNab, John (HBC chief trader), VII, 206; IX, 102
MacNab, John (merchant), XII, 43

McNab, Lucy (McKellar), XII, 643
McNab, Margaret. *See* Robertson
MacNab, Mary. *See* Stuart
MacNab, Mary Gibbens (Cassels), XI, 157
MacNab, Robert (father of Sir ALLAN NAPIER), IX, 527
MacNab, Robert (father of Archibald MCNAB), VIII, 584
McNab, Sarah (Bunn), IX, 102
McNab, Sarah (McDermot), XI, 545
MacNab, Sophia (Keppel, Countess of Albemarle and
    Viscountess Bury), IX, 527
McNabb, Alexander (brother of COLIN), V, 549, 550
McNabb, Alexander (magistrate), XI, 648
McNabb, Colin, V, **548–50**; VI, 211
McNabb, Colin A., V, 549
McNabb, Elizabeth (wife of COLIN), V, 548
McNabb, James, V, 548, 550
McNabb, James, V, 548, 549, **550–51**; VI, 503; VII, 439
MacNabb, John, V, 841
McNabb, Mary Ann. *See* Fraser
McNabb, Simon, V, 549, 550
McNair, Andrew, V, 287
McNally, Charles, XII, 860
McNally, Walter, X, 44
Macnamara, Miss (Bourchier), IX, 72
Macnamara, John (merchant), IV, 506
McNamara, John (schoolteacher), VII, 918
McNaught, John, VI, 346
McNaughton, Archibald, IX, 518
Macnaughton, John (clergyman), IX, 270
McNaughton, John (crown lands agent), VII, 755
Macnaughton, Joseph, VIII, 729
McNaughton, William, X, 657; XI, 557; XII, 664
McNeal. *See also* McNeill
McNeal, Agnes Ann (Lampman), XII, 513
McNeall, Richard, V, 818
MacNee, Sir Daniel, VI, 222
McNeil, Elizabeth (Johnston), VI, 356
McNeil, John, XII, 221
McNeil, Marie (Bilodeau), IX, 359
McNeil, Neil, XII, 647
McNeill, Charlotte (LePage), XI, 512
McNeill, Edward, XII, 970
MacNeill, Sir John Benjamin, XI, 685
McNeill, Martha (wife of WILLIAM HENRY), X, 485
McNeill, Mathilda (wife of WILLIAM HENRY), X, 485
McNeill, Rebecca (mother of WILLIAM HENRY), X, 484
McNeill, Rebecca (Elwyn), XI, 302
McNeill (McNeal), Sarah (Pringle), XII, 864
McNeill, William Henry, X, 484
McNeill, William Henry, VIII, 646; IX, 260, 852; X,
    **484–85**, 535; XI, 302
McNeilly, Isaac Robert, XII, 380
McNeily, Alexander James Whiteford, XII, 164
McNicol, Magdalen. *See* Nairne
McNicol, Peter, V, 621
McNider, Mrs (merchant), VII, 593
Macnider, Adam Lymburner, V, 287; VII, **575–76**
Macnider, John, IV, 400; V, 372, 406; VII, 575; VIII, 286,
    614
Macnider, Margaret (Johnston; Holmes), IV, 400; V, 699,
    700; VI, 325; VII, 575
Macnider, Mary. *See* Hanna
Macnider, Mary (Marchand), VIII, 614; XII, 692

Macnider, Mathew, IV, 400; V, 372, 699; VI, 166; VII,
    575; VIII, 286
Macnider, Rosina. *See* Aird
McNider, William, VI, 400
McNiff, Catherine. *See* McDavitt
McNiff, Elizabeth. *See* McDonnell
McNiff, Patrick, V, 38, 306, 448, **551–53**; VI, 318
McNult, Grace (Corrigan), VIII, 169
McNutt, Alexander, V, 553
McNutt, Alexander, III, 664; IV, 527, 529, 781; V, 409,
    **553–57**; VI, 319; VIII, 568; IX, 838
McNutt, Benjamin, V, 556, 557
McNutt, Jane (wife of ALEXANDER), V, 553
McNutt, Jane Elizabeth (Rand), XI, 722
McNutt, Mary Stewart (McMillan), XI, 578
MacNutt*, William Stewart (1908–76), V, 157, 356, 605;
    VI, 561; VII, 141, 657, 658; VIII, 377, 378, 803, 808,
    842; IX, 401, 409; XI, 375, 526; XII, 896
Macomb, Alexander, V, 299, 512; VI, 102
Macomb, William, V, 3, 299, 511, 512; VI, 8, 102; VIII, 33
Maçon, Elizabeth. *See* O'Neill
Macormick. *See* Macarmick
Macoun*, John (1831–1920), XII, 447, 448, 541, 542,
    926
Macoun*, William Tyrrell (1869–1933), VII, 563
Macphail*, Sir Andrew (1864–1938), XII, 841
McPhail, Daniel, X, 295
McPhail, Mary Isabella (Montgomery), XI, 602
McPhail*, William (1830–1905), XI, 601, 602
McPharlane, Mary (Cassidy), X, 153
McPhee, Janet (Redpath), IX, 655
McPhelim, Catherine (mother of FRANCIS), IX, 527
McPhelim, Francis, IX, **527–28**
McPhelim, Peter, IX, 527
McPhelim, Rosanna. *See* McGuirk
MacPherson, Mr (shoemaker), XII, 983
MacPherson, Alexander, XI, 39
Macpherson, Allan, VI, 479; VII, 470
Macpherson, Ann. *See* Shaw
Macpherson, Annie, XII, 323
Macpherson, Charlotte Holt. *See* Gethings
Macpherson, Christina, XII, 682
Macpherson, Daniel, V, 499
Macpherson, David, XII, 682
Macpherson, David Hamilton, XII, 688
Macpherson, Sir David Lewis, VIII, 182, 513; X, 355, 467,
    522, 632, 651, 668, 725; XI, 7, 12, 13, 156, 378, 746,
    938; XII, 73, 140, 350, 391, 392, 393, 394, 496, 603,
    604, 606, 607, 608, **682–89**, 1042
McPherson, Donald, VII, 576
Macpherson, Donald, VI, **479–80**; XII, 591
McPherson, Elizabeth (Sayer), V, 742
Macpherson, Elizabeth Sarah Badgley, Lady Macpherson.
    *See* Molson
Macpherson, Elspeth (Macpherson), VI, 479
Macpherson, Frances Pasia (Hamilton), XI, 378; XII, 682
Macpherson, Gerardine. *See* Bate
Macpherson, Helen (Macaulay), VIII, 513; XII, 682
McPherson, Irene (McPherson), VII, 576
Macpherson, Isabel Louise (Kirkpatrick, Lady Kirkpatrick),
    XII, 496
McPherson, James, VII, 576
McPherson, Joan (McLean), IX, 512

Macpherson, John (brother of Sir DAVID LEWIS), VIII, 181, 182; XII, 682
McPherson, John (partner of Ellis Walton HYMAN), X, 374
McPherson, John, VII, 396, **576–77**; VIII, 193; IX, 787
McPherson, Josiah, XI, 400
Macpherson, Laughlan Thomas, VIII, 139, 571
Macpherson, Lowther Pennington, XII, 592
McPherson, Marie (McDougald), IX, 315
McPherson, Murdoch, X, 541; XI, 570; XII, 156
Macpherson, Naomi. *See* Grant
Macpherson, William Molson, XII, 688
McQuarters, Hugh, VI, 487
McQueen, Mary, V, 673
McQueen, Thomas, IX, **528–29**
McQuesten, Calvin, XI, 377, **582–84**, 608
McQuesten, David, XI, 582
McQuesten, Elizabeth. *See* Fuller
McQuesten, Esther. *See* Baldwin
McQuesten, Isaac Baldwin, XI, 584
McQuesten, Margaret. *See* Fisher
McQuesten, Margarette. *See* Lerned
McQuesten, Thomas Baker, XI, 584
McQuesten, William W., XI, 583
Macquin. *See* Macain
McRae, Christina (McGillivray), XII, 626
Macrae, Flora (Matheson), X, 501
McRae (Rae), Margaret (McKiernan), XI, 565
McRae (Rae), Mary (Hostler; McKiernan), XI, 565
MacRae, Sophia (Moffatt), IX, 553
MacRaing, Con-duiligh. *See* Rankin, Coun Douly
MacRobie, Dorothy (Roger), X, 627
McSkimming, Margaret (Neilson), VII, 649
McSpiritt, Francis, XII, **689–90**
MacSwain, Angus, VIII, 570
MacSwain, John, XII, 48
MacSween, Alexander, VIII, 664
McSweeney, Mr (newspaperman), VIII, 229
McSweeny, Edward, VI, 792
McSwiney, Edward, V, **557–59**; VI, 115
McTaggart, Mr (foundry owner), XII, 543
McTaggart, John, XI, 685
Mactaggart, John, VI, 127, **480–82**, 760; VII, 33, 122, 262, 927; VIII, 410, 552, 585
McTavey, Patrick, VIII, 229
McTavish, Alexander (father of DONALD), V, 559
McTavish, Alexander (fur trader), VIII, 85
McTavish, Anne (McGillivray), V, 530; VI, 454; VII, 561
McTavish, Catherine A. *See* Turner
McTavish, Charlotte. *See* Thomas
Mactavish, Donald, VIII, 818
McTavish, Donald, V, 419, **559–60**; VI, 704; VIII, 350, 390, 546; IX, 482
Mactavish, Dugald, VIII, 589; IX, 529; X, 485
Mactavish, Dugald, VIII, 589; IX, 365, 529, 853; X, 199, 426, 427, **485–87**
McTavish, Elizabeth. *See* Cameron
McTavish, Ellen (Anglin), XII, 23
McTavish, George Simpson, XI, 204
McTavish, Grace (Dodd), VIII, 226, 561
Mactavish, Hector, VIII, 589
McTavish, John, VI, 764
McTavish, John George, V, 526; VII, 566, 567, **577–78**, 808, 838, 913; VIII, 85, 159, 176, 226, 350, 453, 454, 558, 561, 589, 811; IX, 169, 170, 365, 456, 529, 530; X, 485
McTavish, John H., VIII, 780; XII, 600, 607
Mactavish, Lachlan, Chief of Clan Tavish, VII, 577; IX, 529
Mactavish, Letitia. *See* Lockhart
Mactavish, Letitia (Hargrave), VI, 768; VII, 327, 526; VIII, 574, **589–90**; IX, 198, 365, 529, 530, 648; X, 485, 486; XI, 824, 886; XII, 53, 408
Mactavish, Maria. *See* Simpson
McTavish, Marie-Marguerite. *See* Chaboillez
Mactavish, Mary Sarah. *See* McDermot
McTavish, Nancy. *See* McKenzie
MacTavish*, Newton McFaul (1877–1941), X, 413; XII, 288
McTavish, Simon, IV, 48, 262, 277, 311; V, 177, 179, 260, 284, 287, 299, 300, 332, 333, 377, 384, 391, 511, 512, 525, 530, 531, 532, 541, 542, 559, **560–67**, 603, 682, 683, 715, 819, 820, 821, 822, 878; VI, 111, 285, 454, 455, 456, 468, 469, 476, 664, 700, 704, 743, 744; VII, 561, 565, 566, 577, 595; VIII, 538, 575, 589; IX, 282, 283, 529; XI, 13
McTavish, Sophia. *See* Rowand
Mactavish, William, VIII, 589, 663; IX, 131, 365, 366, **529–32**, 780; X, 70, 485; XI, 245, 738, 740, 841, 842; XII, 156, 408, 951, 1006, 1007
McTavish of Garthbeg, John, V, 560
MacTier, Grace (Pangman), V, 656
Mactigue. *See* Macarty
Macuina. *See* Muquinna
MacVane, Margaret (Mann), XII, 691
McVicar, Christina. *See* McBeath
McVicar, Christina, XII, 690
MacVicar*, Donald Harvey (1831–1902), XII, 617, 618
McVicar, George A., XII, 690
McVicar, Kate, XI, **584–85**
MacVicar, Malcolm, XI, 158, 577; XII, 882
McVicar, Robert, VIII, 660; IX, 170, **532–33**; XII, 690
McVicar, Victoria, XII, **690–91**
McWilliams, William G., XII, 454
Madaillan, Charlotte de. *See* La Roque
Madaillan, Louis de, I, 424
Madaillan de Lesparre, Armand de, Marquis de Lassay, II, 262
Madden, Mary Anne (Sadlier), IX, 494; X, 536
Madden, Thomas, VI, 674; IX, 27
Maddock, Louisa (Litchfield), IX, 470
Maddock, Luke, VII, 626, 627, 630
Madeleine (housekeeper), IV, 233
Madeleine (wife of TOTIRI), I, 651
Madeleine (wife of Nicolas VINCENT), VII, 889
Madeleine de la Résurrection. *See* Bâcon
Madeleine du Sacré-Cœur. *See* Desjardins
Madeline. *See* Qua-hail-ya
Madgshon, John, III, 213
Madison, James, V, 113, 695; VI, 55, 56, 333; VIII, 34, 389
Madjeckewiss, V, 568
Madjeckewiss, III, 660; IV, 241, 486, 564; V, 129, 130, **567–68**, 715, 760, 836; VI, 188, 317
Madoc (Madog ab Owain Gwynedd), I, **677–78**
Madokawando, II, 5, 6
Madran, Jean-Baptiste, VIII, 590
Madran, Jean-Marie, VII, 333; VIII, **590–91**

Madran, Josephte. *See* Gamarre
Madrid, Duke of. *See* Carlos
Madry, Françoise. *See* Duquet
Madry, Jean, I, 47, 80, 109, 255, **478–79**; II, 488
Maera. *See* Myeerah
Magdelaine, I, 640
Magee, Johannah (Donnelly), X, 234
Magellan, Ferdinand, I, 155, 342, 658
Magendie, François, VI, 764
Magesse. *See* Martel
Maggiolo (Maiollo), Viscount of, I, 304, 659
Magill, Juliette Augusta (Kinzie), VII, 582
Magill, Maxwell Leroy, VII, 228; IX, 509
Maginn, William, VII, 262
Magnan, Catherine (Hervieux), III, 290
Magnan\*, Charles-Joseph (1865–1942), XI, 458, 873
Magnan, Jean-Baptiste, IV, 658
Magnan, Jean-Charles, XI, 182
Magnan, Marie-Louise. *See* Decharnay
Magnan, Péronelle de (Dubois Berthelot), III, 189
Magnan, Pierre, I, 211, 303, **479**, 509
Magnan, *dit* L'Espérance, Marie-Anne (Picoté de Belestre), IV, 634
Magné (Magnié, Manié), Marie (Chartier), III, 111
Magnien, François, II, 642
Magnus, Olaus, I, 680
Magon de La Balluë, Luc, IV, 506
Magon de La Balluë, Pélagie. *See* Porrée
Magon de Terlaye, François-Auguste, IV, 431, **506–7**, 521; V, 118, 392; XI, 655
Magos. *See* Martel
Magouaouidombaouit. *See* Gill, Joseph-Louis
Magowan, Peter, V, **568–69**, 721, 776, 847, 848; VI, 161, 195, 413, 565, 566, 662; VII, 864
Magrath, Anne Louise. *See* Hagerman
Magrath, Charles, XI, 916
Magrath, E., VIII, 341
Magregory, Patrick, III, 568
Maguelonne, Jeanne-Marie de (Lévis, Baronne d'Ajac), IV, 477
Maguire, Catherine. *See* O'Hara
Maguire, Charles Butler, VI, 125; XI, 57
Maguire, Ellen (Larkin), XII, 529
Maguire, Frances Agnes. *See* Horan
Maguire, John, VIII, 591
Maguire, John, X, **487–88**
Maguire, Margaret. *See* Swite
Maguire, Marie-Justine. *See* Casgrain
Maguire\*, Mary Ann, named Sister Mary Francis (1837–1905), XII, 411
Maguire, Matthew, X, 487
Maguire, Thomas, VI, 126, 288, 593, 598, 748; VII, 573, 798, 818, 851, 892; VIII, 317, 458, **591–96**; IX, 568, 797; X, 428
Magures (Majurs), John, XII, 785
Mahan, Alfred Thayer, IV, 123; VI, 803
Mahdī. *See* Muḥammad Aḥmad ibn 'Abd Allāh
Maher, Angélique (Labelle), XII, 501
Maheu, Monsieur (of Île d'Orléans), I, 645
Maheu, Anne. *See* Convent
Maheu, Marie (Huot), VI, 336
Maheu, René, I, 494
Maheut, Geneviève. *See* Bissot

Maheut, Jean, I, 480
Maheut, Louis, I, 479, 480
Maheut, Louis, I, **479–80**; II, 168
Maheut, Marguerite. *See* Corrivault
Maheut, René, I, 479
Maheux\*, Arthur (1884–1967), IX, 642
Mahiet, Michel, IV, 124
Mahigan Aticq Ouche. *See* Miristou
Mahkesīs (Mahkaysis), XI, 674, 675
Mahyet, Madeleine (Riverin), II, 574
Mai, Angelo, VIII, 593
Mailhet. *See* Mallet
Mailhiot. *See* Malhiot
Mailhot, Alfred, IX, 360
Mailhot, Charles-Édouard, XI, 658
Mailhot, Marie-Marguerite. *See* Roussel
Mailhot, Modeste, VI, 483
Mailhot, Nicolas-François, VI, 119, **482–83**; VII, 790
Mailhot, Robert-Léonard, VI, 483
Maillard, Pierre, II, 412; III, 34, 183, 358, **415–19**, 425, 497, 498; IV, 41, 74, 79, 214, 290, 296, 453, 454, 455, 644, 676, 776; V, 172, 379, 393; VI, 304; VII, 436; VIII, 78, 79
Maillé. *See* Mallet
Maillebois, Marquis de. *See* Desmarest
Maillet. *See also* Mallet
Maillet, Charles-Louis, VI, 184
Maillet, Gilbert, II, 159
Maillet, Jean, I, 480
Maillet, Marguerite, XI, 40
Maillet, Marie. *See* Rivard
Maillet, Marie, I, 220, 458, 478, **480**, 487, 512; X, 156
Maillet, Marie-Josephte (Campion), IV, 132
Maillot. *See also* Mailhot
Maillot, Joseph, VI, 482
Maillot, Madeleine. *See* Levasseur
Maillou, Amable, IV, 205, 629
Maillou, Angélique. *See* Marchand
Maillou, Antoine, V, 245
Maillou, Benjamin, V, 569
Maillou, Benjamin-Nicolas, IV, 288; V, **569–70**; VI, 85
Maillou, Joseph, VIII, 331
Maillou, *dit* Desmoulins, Anne. *See* Delaunay
Maillou, *dit* Desmoulins, Jean-Baptiste, II, 120; III, 165, 170, 234, 307, **419–21**, 637; IV, 202, 659
Maillou, *dit* Desmoulins, Joseph (uncle), III, 419, 420
Maillou, *dit* Desmoulins, Joseph, III, 346, 420
Maillou, *dit* Desmoulins, Louise. *See* Phélippeaux
Maillou, *dit* Desmoulins, Louis-Marie, III, 420
Maillou, *dit* Desmoulins, Marguerite. *See* Caron
Maillou, *dit* Desmoulins, Marguerite (Lambert, *dit* Saint-Paul), III, 346
Maillou, *dit* Desmoulins, Marguerite (Vallette de Chévigny), III, 637
Maillou, *dit* Desmoulins, Marie-Catherine. *See* Amiot, *dit* Villeneuve
Maillou, *dit* Desmoulins, Marie-Joseph, named de Saint-André, III, 420
Maillou, *dit* Desmoulins, Pierre (father), III, 419
Maillou, *dit* Desmoulins, Pierre, III, 346, 420
Maillou, *dit* Desmoulins, Vital, III, 420
Mailloux, Alexis, VI, 226; VII, 670, 671, 800; X, **488–89**, 605; XI, 168, 689; XII, 189

Mailloux, Amable, VI, 226; X, 488
Mailloux, Élie, IV, 9
Mailloux, Thècle. *See* Lajoie
Mailly, Abbé, XI, 169
Mainfold, Miss (Tracey), VI, 783
Maingard, Jehanne (Jalobert), I, 384
Maingart, Jacques, I, 167
Maintenon, Marquise de. *See* Aubigné
Mainville, Monsieur (NWC employee), V, 466; VI, 100, 446
Mainville, Damien, XII, 1133
Mainville (Melville), Élizabeth (Starnes), XII, 986
Mainville, Isabella (Ross), XII, 929
Mainwaring, Sir George, I, 481
Mainwaring, Sir Henry, I, 24, **481**, 668
Maiollo. *See* Maggiolo
Mair*, Charles (1838–1927), V, 800; IX, 617, 707; XI, 45, 322, 323, 324, 737, 740, 741, 743, 841, 842; XII, 82, 119, 459, 460, 558, 950, 951, 1076
Mair, Martha (Stephenson), VII, 824
Mais, Elizabeth Ann (Lobley), XI, 523
Maisaninnine* (d. 1907), XII, 832
Maisonbasse. *See* Deschevery
Maisonnat, Hélie, II, 449
Maisonnat, Jeanne. *See* Ségure
Maisonnat, Judith. *See* Soubiron
Maisonnat, Madeleine. *See* Bourg
Maisonnat, Marguerite. *See* Bourgeois
Maisonnat, Marie-Madeleine (Winniett), III, 277, 297, **421–22**, 665
Maisonnat, *dit* Baptiste, Marie-Anne (Cahouet; Imbert), IV, 378
Maisonnat, *dit* Baptiste, Pierre, I, 577; II, 3, 46, 167, 271, 394, **449–50**, 459, 667; III, 421, 596, 665; IV, 378
Maisonneuve. *See also* Chomedey; Puybarau
Maisonneuve, Augustin, XI, 310
Maisonneuve, Charles-Augustin, XII, 1005
Maistre, Joseph de, Comte de Maistre, VII, 487; IX, 466; XI, 94, 891; XII, 501
Maitland, Sir Alexander, IV, 610; V, 515
Maitland, Elizabeth (Jervois), XII, 475
Maitland, James, 8th Earl of Lauderdale, V, 35
Maitland, Jane. *See* Mathew
Maitland, Jane Elizabeth. *See* Grant
Maitland, John, VIII, 162; IX, 827
Maitland, Louisa. *See* Crofton
Maitland, Peregrine, VIII, 596
Maitland, Sir Peregrine, V, 489; VI, 11, 12, 31, 32, 80, 115, 116, 117, 149, 164, 165, 230, 247, 266, 334, 467, 470, 496, 497, 498, 513, 527, 543, 545, 610, 611, 612, 613, 632, 633, 706, 723, 729, 760, 770, 773; VII, 23, 39, 40, 42, 51, 58, 63, 88, 162, 163, 178, 200, 230, 308, 313, 314, 315, 318, 319, 338, 350, 365, 368, 369, 372, 378, 391, 409, 410, 411, 417, 418, 439, 441, 456, 458, 466, 494, 497, 520, 535, 546, 547, 548, 641, 682, 698, 725, 753, 754, 755, 822, 843; VIII, xxiv, 6, 46, 47, 162, 180, 252, 337, 355, 356, 384, 398, 431, 440, 441, 511, 515, 517, 518, 519, 522, 585, **596–605**, 642, 694, 724, 750, 854, 856, 926, 945, 946; IX, 139, 141, 265, 313, 334, 423, 498, 545, 670, 671, 672, 673, 674, 740, 755, 757, 759, 769; X, 233, 557, 705, 706; XI, 796
Maitland, Sarah, Lady Maitland. *See* Lennox
Maitland, Thomas, VIII, 596

Maitland, William, V, 259, 372; VI, 18, 19, 271, 285; VII, 28
Maître Abraham. *See* Martin
Maitwaywayninnee. *See* Matayawenenne
Major, Hannah. *See* Matthews
Major, Jean. *See* Cambie
Major Cope. *See* Cope, Jean-Baptiste
Majurs. *See* Magures
Makatachinga, III, 530
Makheabichtichiou, I, **481–82**, 527
Makin, Dennis, VI, 244
Makisabi, II, 128, 515; III, 576
Makoyi-koh-kin (Wolf Thin Legs). *See* Pītikwahanapi-wīyin
Makoyi-ksiksinum. *See* Sotai-na
Makoyi-Opistoki* (d. 1913), XII, 718, 719
Malalamet, III, 266
Malapart, André, I, **482**, 613
Malard, Anthelme, V, 480; VII, 495
Malartic. *See* Maurès
Malaspina, Marchioness of. *See* Melilupi
Malaspina, Marquis of. *See* Morello
Malaspina, Alejandro, I, 676; IV, 568; V, 11, 140, 399, 400, **570–71**; VI, 742, 743
Malbeque, Étiennette-Louise (Petit de Levilliers), II, 523
Malchelosse*, Gérard (1896–1969), V, 530; IX, 564
Malcolm, Eliakim, VII, 56, 127; VIII, 276; X, **489–90**
Malcolm, Finlay, X, 489
Malcolm, Samantha. *See* Sexton
Malcolm, Tryphena (mother of ELIAKIM), X, 489
Malcolmson, Margaret (Wingfield), XII, 1115
Malcouronne, Adelle (Brisebois), XI, 111, 112
Maldonado. *See* Ferrer; Flórez
Malen (Mallen), Marie (Bernier), IV, 57
Malepart de Beaucourt, Benoîte. *See* Camagne
Malepart de Beaucourt, François, III, 422; IV, **507–8**; V, 417, 497; VII, 255
Malepart de Grand Maison, *dit* Beaucour, Marguerite. *See* Haguenier
Malepart de Grand Maison, *dit* Beaucour, Paul, III, **422–23**; IV, 507
Maleray de La Mollerie, Jacques, II, 451
Maleray de La Mollerie, Louis-Hector, II, 451
Maleray de La Périne, Isaac, II, 450
Maleray de La Périne, Marie. *See* Tessier
Maleray de Noiré de La Mollerie, Françoise. *See* Picoté de Belestre
Maleray de Noiré de La Mollerie, Jacques, II, **450–51**
Malet. *See* Mallet
Malherbe, Father, I, 607
Malherbe, François, I, **483**
Malherbe, François, VI, **483–84**
Malherbe, François de, I, 470
Malherbe, Marie. *See* Chennequy
Malherbe, Marie-Louise. *See* Thomas, *dit* Bigaouet
Malherbe, *dit* Champagne, François, VI, 483
Malherbe, *dit* Champagne, Marie-Anne. *See* Margane de Lavaltrie
Malhiot. *See also* Mailhot
Malhiot, Adolphe, X, 491
Malhiot, Charles-Christophe, V, 603; X, **490–91**, 544; XII, 818
Malhiot, Charlotte. *See* Gamelin

Malhiot, Édouard-Élisée, VII, 210, 239, 514; VIII, 145; X, 77, 78, **491–92**, 545, 546; XI, 659
Malhiot, Élisabeth. *See* Gamelin
Malhiot, François, V, **571–73**; VIII, 605
Malhiot, Françoise (Boucher de La Perrière), III, 81
Malhiot, François-Victor, V, 572; VIII, 605
Malhiot, François-Xavier, V, 572; VII, 239; VIII, **605–6**; X, 490
Malhiot, Guillaume, IV, 178
Malhiot, Henri-Gédéon, XI, 191
Malhiot, Jean, III, 374, 422; V, 571
Malhiot, Jean-François, III, 81, 270, **422**; IV, 284; V, 571
Malhiot, Julie. *See* Boucher de La Perrière
Malhiot, Julie-Éliza. *See* Marchand
Malhiot, Madeleine. *See* Marchand
Malhiot, Marguerite (Trottier Desrivières Beaubien), IV, 508; V, 828
Malhiot, Marie-Anne. *See* Massé
Malhiot, Pierre-Édouard, XI, 807
Malhiot, Pierre-Ignace, V, 572; VIII, 605
Malhiot, Sophie. *See* Labruère
Malie, Joseph, VII, 204, **578–79**; VIII, 65
Maling, Thomas, XI, 198
Malins, Elizabeth (Cary), IX, 114
Malins, Sir Richard, IX, 114
Malisson. *See* Manisson
Mallemouche, Jeanne de (Chauvin de Tonnetuit), I, 209
Mallen. *See* Malen
Mallepart. *See* Malepart
Mallet, Catherine (Roy, *dit* Portelance), VII, 762
Mallet, Denis, II, 200, 338, 379, **451–52**
Mallet, Ellen (Cameron), X, 118
Mallet, Geneviève. *See* Liénard
Mallet, Louisa. *See* Deupet
Mallet, Louis-Denis, II, 451
Mallet, Madeleine. *See* Thunay, *dit* Dufresne
Mallet, Madeleine (Couture), II, 157
Mallet, Marguerite. *See* Sarrazin
Mallet, Marie-Anne-Marcelle, VIII, 582; IX, 799; X, **492–93**, 603; XI, 109
Mallet, Marie-Madeleine. *See* Jérémie, *dit* Lamontagne
Mallet, Paul, III, 423, 424
Mallet, Pierre, III, 423
Mallet, Pierre-Antoine, III, **423–24**
Mallet, Renée. *See* Padouillet
Mallet, Vital, X, 492
Malli. *See* Malie
Mallinson, Harriet (Barr), XII, 60
Malloch, Edward, VII, 446
Malloch, George, XI, 730
Malloch, John Glass, VIII, 552
Mallory, Abia. *See* Dayton
Mallory, Benajah, V, 734, 846, 857, 858; VI, 331, 399, 422, 489, 490, 543, 804; VII, 419; VIII, 533, **606–10**, 860
Mallory*, Caleb Alvord (1841–1926), XII, 584
Mallory, Henrietta Maria (McDonald), VIII, 533
Mallory, Ogden, VIII, 606
Mallory, Sally. *See* Bush
Mallory, Sarah (Baker; Bush; Smart), X, 659
Mally. *See* Malie
Malmros, Oscar, XI, 740
Malo, Isidore, VIII, 489

Malo, Louis-Stanislas, VIII, 196, 206
Malone, Henrietta (Kingston), XI, 475
Malone, Mary (McMahon), VII, 574
Maloney, Catherine (wife of Francis), IX, 556
Maloney, Francis, IX, 556
Maloney, Margaret, VI, 256
Maloney, Patrick, XI, 591
Malott, Catharine (Girty), V, 345
Malouin. *See also* Cormier; Rinfret
Malouin, Jacques, XI, 775
Malqueneck, Baron de, II, 279
Maltby, Elizabeth (Pretyman Tomline), VI, 528
Malte-Brun, Conrad, VIII, 330
Malthus, Thomas Robert, VI, 42; VII, 645; IX, 330, 331
Maltot, Sieur de (commandant), II, 203
Malzard, Jane (LeVesconte), X, 440
Mamenawatum (Seeseeb, Jessie Joyful) (wife of Henry Bird STEINHAUER), XI, 848
Man, James, V, **573–74**; VI, 65, 276; VII, 52, 424
Man (Mann), John, V, 573
Man, Thomas, II, 319
Manach, Jean (Jacques), III, 358, 417, **424–26**; IV, 79, 214, 239, 296, 456, 457; VI, 304
Manachoos (Bad Arrow), XI, 460
Manahan, Anthony, VII, 368, **579–81**; VIII, 543
Manahan, Patrick, VII, 579
Manahan, Sarah Phebe. *See* Nugent
Manby, Thomas, IV, 747; VII, 51
Mance, Sœur. *See* Céré
Mance, Catherine. *See* Émonnot
Mance, Charles, I, 483
Mance, Jeanne, I, 31, 43, 78, 208, 215, 216, 217, 219, 220, 230, 231, 310, 344, 412, 453, 457, 478, 480, **483–87**, 512, 547, 640, 648; II, 194, 376, 489, 490; IX, 247; X, 156
Mancelin, Élisabeth de (Thavenet), II, 628
Manchester, Duke of. *See* Montagu
Manchot, II, 255
Mancini-Mazarini, Louis-Jules, Duc de Nivernais, VI, 86
Mandat, Galiot, I, 446
Mandat, Marie (Le Febvre de La Barre), I, 446
Manderston, Margaret (Walker), VI, 797
Mandet, Marie (Allemand), I, 56
Mandeville. *See* Philippe
Manet, Anne (Fond), II, 581
Manette (Monette), V, 39; VIII, 744; IX, 8
Mangan, James Clarence, IX, 494
Mangeant, Anne. *See* Deschamps
Mangeant, Louis, III, 426
Mangeant, Marguerite. *See* Caissy
Mangeant, *dit* Saint-Germain, François, II, 23; III, 84, **426–27**
Manié. *See* Magné
Mani-kap-ina. *See* Maskepetoon
Manisson (Malisson), *dit* Philibert, Marie-Catherine (Bélanger), VIII, 77
Manisto'kos. *See* Onista'poka
Manitou, III, 530
Manitouabeouich (Marie-Olivier-Sylvestre) (Prévost), I, 554
Manitougatche, I, **487–88**, 533
Manitu-potis. *See* Hunkajunka
Mann. *See also* Man

Mann, Anne. *See* Wade
Mann, Cornelius, VI, 484
Mann*, Sir Donald (1853–1934), XI, 293; XII, 626, 699
Mann, Edward Isaac, IV, 153; V, 637; VII, 204
Mann, Elizabeth. *See* Gother
Mann, Gother, IV, 108; V, 118, 441, 442; VI, 182, 183, 223, 482, **484–85**, 789; VII, 129; VIII, 483
Mann, Horace, XII, 880
Mann, Horatio, XII, 855
Mann, Jane Sophia (Durnford), VII, 266
Mann, John (father of JOHN), XII, 691
Mann, John (oarsman), XII, 407
Mann, John, XII, **691–92**
Mann, Margaret. *See* McGregor
Mann, Margaret. *See* MacVane
Mannary, William, XII, 622
Mannereuil. *See* Dugey
Manners, Charles, 4th Duke of Rutland, V, 120
Manners, Charlesina Hope (McCarthy), XII, 578
Manners, Lady Elizabeth (Monckton, Viscountess Galway), IV, 540
Manners, John, Marquess of Granby, IV, 773; V, 166, 610
Manners-Sutton, Charles, VIII, 460; IX, 637; X, 494, 663
Manners-Sutton, Charles, 1st Viscount Canterbury, X, 494
Manners-Sutton, Georgiana. *See* Tompson
Manners-Sutton, John Henry Thomas, 3rd Viscount Canterbury, VIII, 810; IX, 409, 410, 413, 527, 623, 631; X, 140, 159, 271, 286, 287, 289, **493–95**, 666; XI, 373, 828, 833; XII, 536, 897, 1052, 1053, 1105
Manners-Sutton, Lucy Maria Charlotte, Viscountess Canterbury. *See* Denison
Manners-Sutton, Thomas, X, 494
Manning*, Alexander Henderson (1819–1903), IX, 728; XII, 245, 454, 976, 1119
Manning, Edward, VI, 276; VII, 123, 177, 252, 272, 531, 562; VIII, 148, 149, 179, 361, 566, 567, 568, **610–14**; XI, 214, 895; XII, 108, 109
Manning, Henry Edward, XII, 712, 812
Manning, Isaac, XII, 902
Manning, James, VI, 276; VIII, 360, 611
Manning, James William, XII, 882
Manning, Joseph, III, 274
Manning, Margaret (O'Brien), IX, 604
Manning, Nancy. *See* Carroll
Manning, Peter, VIII, 610
Manning, Rebecca. *See* Skinner
Manning, Susan Selina. *See* Smith
Manning, Walter Carroll, IX, 40
Mannock, John, VII, 94, 95
Mannucci-Benincasa, Caterina (Falardeau), XI, 309
Mannucci-Benincasa Capponi, Francesco, Marquis Mannucci-Benincasa Capponi, XI, 309
Manoel (Manuel) I, King of Portugal, I, 234, 236, 303, 304, 305
Manraize, René, XI, 813
Manseau, Angélique (Fortier), IV, 271
Manseau, Antoine, IX, 533
Manseau, Antoine, V, 181, 671; VII, 423, 449; VIII, 241, 316, 317, 712; IX, **533–34**; XI, 173
Manseau, Élizabeth (Beaubien), X, 36
Manseau, Joseph-Amable, X, 31
Manseau, Marie. *See* Côté
Manseau, Marie-Jeanne (Beaubien), XI, 57

Manseau, Marie-Josephte (Brassard), X, 86
Mansel, Lady. *See* Bayly
Mansel, Sir Edward, IV, 694
Mansel, Sir Robert, I, 144
Mansfield, Earl of. *See* Murray
Mansfield, Charlotte (Hoffmann), VIII, 398
Mansfield, Charlotte Henrietta (Tuyll van Serooskerken, Baroness van Tuyll van Serooskerken), VIII, 899, 901
Mansfield, Margaret (Arnold), V, 28
Manson, Donald, X, 495
Manson, Donald, VIII, 226, 579; IX, 514; X, **495–96**
Manson, Félicité. *See* Lucier
Manson, Jean. *See* Gunn
Manson, Margaret Catherine Johan Levack (Rose), XII, 921, 922, 923
Manson, William, XII, 667
Mant, Richard, VI, 734
Mantell, Robert Bruce, XII, 949
Mantes. *See also* Côme
Mantes, Monsieur de (associate of Clerbaud BERGIER), I, 89
Manthet. *See* Ailleboust
Manthet d'Argentenay, Dorothée de (Ailleboust), I, 45, 47
Manthet d'Argentenay, Jean de, I, 42
Manthet d'Argentenay, Suzanne de. *See* Hotman
Manuel. *See also* Manoel
Manuel, Dolly, V, 99
Manuel, Emmanuel, IV, 332
Manuel, John, XII, 367
Manuel, Marion. *See* Gilmour
Manwaring. *See* Mainwaring
Many Names. *See* Akay-nehka-simi
Many Spotted Horses. *See* Aka-kitsipimi-otas
Mao Tse-tung, XII, 107
Maquay, John Leland, VIII, 385
Maquet, Alexis, IV, 134, 298
Maquilla (Maquinna). *See* Muquinna
Mar, Earl of. *See* Erskine
Mara, Alice. *See* Barnard
Mara, John Andrew, XI, 50, 568; XII, 399, 916
Marafret Layssard, Pierre-Étienne, III, 222
Marais. *See* Marest
Marakle. *See* Markle
Maranda, Charles, VII, 581
Maranda, Geneviève (Schindler), IV, 702
Maranda, Jean-Baptiste, VII, **581–82**; VIII, 627
Maranda, Marie-Angèle. *See* Beaudoin
Maranda, Marie-Louise (Hubert), IV, 370
Maray de La Chauvignerie, Michel, II, 126, 625; III, 101, 320, 401, 614
Marcel, Monsieur (aide-de-camp), III, 467
Marcellin, Marie-Anne (Bréard), IV, 91
March. *See also* Marsh
March, Esther (By), VII, 128
March, Hugh, II, 452
March, Jemina. *See* True
March, John, II, 17, 37, 38, 177, 206, 238, 288, 409, 417, **452–53**, 495; III, 22, 25, 177, 200, 273, 470, 474, 552, 596
March, Judith (mother of JOHN), II, 452
March, Maria (Duncan), V, 281
March, Mary. *See* Demasduwit
March, Peter, XII, 101

Marchand, Amanda. *See* Bingham
Marchand, Angélique (Joly; Maillou), V, 569
Marchand, Charles-Jubilé, XII, 694
Marchand, Charlotte. *See* Céré
Marchand, Étienne (father of ÉTIENNE), IV, 509
Marchand, Étienne (silversmith), IV, 205
Marchand, Étienne, III, 193; IV, 99, 101, **509–10**, 543, 574; V, 185, 245; VI, 485
Marchand, Félix-Gabriel, VIII, 615; X, 16, 25, 415; XI, 480; XII, 91, 121, 181, **692–97**, 725, 727, 854
Marchand, Félix-Marie, XI, 305, 306
Marchand, François, VIII, 209, 614
Marchand, Françoise. *See* Roussel
Marchand, Gabriel, VII, 500; VIII, 209, **614–15**; XII, 692
Marchand, Geneviève (Marcoux), V, 575
Marchand, Hersélie. *See* Turgeon
Marchand, Jean (carpenter), I, 77
Marchand, Jean (settler), VIII, 614
Marchand, Jean-Baptiste, IV, 90, 188; V, 92, 186, 242; VI, 332, **485–87**; VII, 340, 850
Marchand, Joseph, VI, 485
Marchand, Louis (broker), X, 25
Marchand, Louis (brother of GABRIEL), VIII, 209, 210, 614
Marchand, Louis (father of GABRIEL), VIII, 614
Marchand, Louis (father of JEAN-BAPTISTE), VI, 485
Marchand, Louis (innkeeper), III, 493
Marchand, Louis (merchant), V, 575, 576, 577; VI, 305
Marchand, Louis (son of Louis, merchant), V, 576
Marchand, Louis, XI, **585–87**
Marchand, Louis-François-Wilfrid, X, 533; XI, 586; XII, 173
Marchand, Madeleine (Malhiot; Legardeur de Beauvais), III, 374, 422; V, 571
Marchand, Marguerite, named de Sainte-Ursule, V, 224
Marchand, Marie-Anne. *See* Durand
Marchand, Marie-Anne (Charest), X, 161
Marchand, Marie-Geneviève. *See* Marcoux
Marchand, Marie-Louise (Bachand), X, 25
Marchand, Marie-Luce-Eugénie. *See* Patry
Marchand, Marie-Marguerite. *See* Boucher de Niverville
Marchand, Marie-Renée (Decoste), IV, 200
Marchand, Mary. *See* Macnider
Marchand, Nicolas (militia officer), VI, 485; VIII, 614
Marchand, Nicolas (tailor), IV, 200
Marchand, Octave, XII, 1034
Marchant de La Houlière, Mathieu-Henri, III, 230, 440
Marchessault, Monsieur (politician), XI, 811
Marchessault, Élizabeth (Gagnon), XI, 329
Marchessaut, Abraham-François, VIII, 615
Marchessaut, Christophe, VIII, 616
Marchessaut, Émélie. *See* Cormier
Marchesseau, Jean, VIII, 616
Marchesseault, Judith. *See* Morin
Marchesseault, Siméon, VII, 247, 248, 478; VIII, 471, 605, **615–17**; X, 75; XI, 84
Marcheterre. *See* Coutlée; Dandurand
Marchildon, Louis, VIII, 617
Marchildon, Marguerite (Turcot), IX, 795
Marchildon, Marie-Philie. *See* Lefaivre, *dit* Despins
Marchildon, Thomas, VIII, **617–18**; IX, 212, 344
Marchildon, Victoire. *See* Alexandre
Marchin, I, 507
Marchinton, Elizabeth (wife of PHILIP), V, 575

Marchinton, Joseph, V, 575
Marchinton, Mary (Welsford), V, 575; VIII, 927
Marchinton, Philip, V, **574–75**; VI, 276, 429; VII, 122; VIII, 927
Marcle. *See* Markle
Marcol, Catherine. *See* Lorson
Marcol, Gabriel, III, **427–28**, 580, 628
Marcol, Pascal, III, 427
Marconnay. *See also* Leblanc
Marconnay, Angélique-Renée-Françoise. *See* Péan
Marconnay, Louis-Michel de, known as Marquis de Marconnay, IV, 616, 660
Marcot, Jean-Baptiste, VII, 582
Marcot, Marguerite (Paquin), VII, 677
Marcot, Marguerite-Magdelaine (La Framboise), VII, **582–83**
Marcot, Marie. *See* Neskech
Marcotte, Marie-Josephte (Saincennes), X, 656
Marcotte, Nathalie (Desroches), VI, 206
Marcou, V. H., XII, 889
Marcoux, André, V, 231
Marcoux, Françoise (Grisé), IV, 315
Marcoux, François-Xavier, V, 77; VIII, 939; X, 163
Marcoux, Geneviève. *See* Alliés
Marcoux, Geneviève. *See* Lepage
Marcoux, Geneviève. *See* Marchand
Marcoux, Germain, V, 575
Marcoux, Jean-Baptiste, V, 576, 577
Marcoux, Joseph, VIII, 618
Marcoux, Joseph, VII, 148, 828, 866; VIII, **618–19**, 636, 666, 776, 777, 939; XII, 223, 224, 570
Marcoux, Louis (clergyman), VII, 642
Marcoux, Louis (Patriote), VIII, 457, 616; IX, 594
Marcoux, Louise. *See* Bélanger
Marcoux, Louise-Élizabeth (De Bonne), V, 231
Marcoux, Marie. *See* Vallière
Marcoux, Marie-Anne. *See* Dunière
Marcoux, Marie-Geneviève (Marchand), V, 576
Marcoux, Marthe (Baudoin), III, 35
Marcoux, Pierre (father of PIERRE), V, 231, 575, 576, 577
Marcoux, Pierre (political candidate), VII, 61
Marcoux, Pierre, V, 283, **575–78**; VI, 239, 305, 367; VII, 673
Marcus, Thérèse-Élisabeth (Yung), XII, 1133
Marcy, William Learned, VIII, 28; X, 14, 63
Maréchal. *See also* Dière; Marshall
Maréchal, Louis-Delphis-Adolphe, VIII, 21; XI, 865; XII, **697–98**
Maréchal, Marie-Joseph (Élie), II, 216
Mareschal, Georges, III, 344
Marest, Joseph-Jacques, II, 317, 318, 324, 353, 415, **453–54**, 455, 503, 505; III, 103, 105, 269, 451, 577, 580
Marest, Pierre-Gabriel, I, 61; II, 55, 140, 306, 347, 453, **454–55**, 468, 469, 645; III, 103
Maret, Guillaume, II, 526
Maret, Henri, XI, 101
Marett, Elizabeth Anne (Massue), IX, 539
Marett, Henriette. *See* Boone
Marett, James Lamprière, VII, 61; IX, 539
Marett, Julie-Henriette (Bédard), VII, 61
Mareuil, Jacques de, I, 139, **488–89**; II, 130, 586
Mareuil, Pierre de, III, **428–29**
Margane de Batilly, François-Marie, II, **455–56**; III, 429

Margane de Lavaltrie, Angélique. *See* Guyon Després

Margane de Lavaltrie, François, II, 384, 456; III, **429–30**, 524; IV, 91

Margane de Lavaltrie, Louise. *See* Bissot

Margane de Lavaltrie, Louise-Charlotte. *See* Ailleboust d'Argenteuil

Margane de Lavaltrie, Louis-François, III, 429

Margane de Lavaltrie, Madeleine-Louise (Ailleboust de Périgny), III, 7

Margane de Lavaltrie, Marguerite (Dutisné), II, 215

Margane de Lavaltrie, Marie-Angélique. *See* La Corne

Margane de Lavaltrie, Marie-Anne (Malherbe, *dit* Champagne), VI, 483

Margane de Lavaltrie, Pierre-Paul, IV, 476; V, 578

Margane de Lavaltrie, Pierre-Paul, IV, 191, 402; V, **578–79**, 687; VIII, 890

Margane de Lavaltrie, Séraphin, II, 455; III, 7, 429; V, 578

Margane de Lavaltrie, Suzanne-Antoinette (Tarieu Taillant de Lanaudière), V, 579; VII, 447

Margaret. *See also* Nahovway

Margaret (wife of John THOMAS), VI, 766

Margarett. *See* Williams, Eunice

Margetson, Anne (Caulfeild), II, 122

Margetson, James, II, 122

Margon. *See* Plantavit

Margry, Pierre, III, 254; VIII, 911; IX, 250, 448, 450, 451; XII, 66, 824

Marguerie, François, I, 489

Marguerie, Jean, IV, 421

Marguerie, Louise. *See* Cloutier

Marguerie, Marie (Hertel de La Fresnière; Moral de Saint-Quentin), I, 238, 369, 550; II, 282, 648

Marguerie, Marthe. *See* Romain

Marguerie de La Haye, François, I, 60, 186, 341, 369, **489–90**, 639; II, 282

Marguerite. *See also* Williams, Eunice

Marguerite, IV, 35

Marguerite d'Angoulême (Marguerite, Queen of Navarre), I, 424, 425, 426

Marguerite de Sainte-Ursule. *See* Marchand

Marguerite de Saint-Jean-Baptiste. *See* Bourdon

Marguerite de Saint-Louis de Gonzague. *See* Davanne

Marguerite de Saint-Pierre. *See* Blais; Dizy de Montplaisir

Marguerite de Valois, known as La Reine Margot (Marguerite, Queen of Navarre), I, 549

Marguerite-Françoise de Saint-Henri. *See* Hiché

Marguerite-Renée de la Croix. *See* Godefroy de Tonnancour

Maria. *See* Williams, Eunice

Maria Carolina, Princess of Austria (Maria Carolina, Queen of the Two Sicilies), X, 497

Marianne (wife of William TODD, d. 1851), VIII, 888

Mariauchau d'Esgly, Élisabeth. *See* Gröen

Mariauchau d'Esgly, François, II, 186, **456–57**, 558; III, 112, 434; IV, 299, 510

Mariauchau d'Esgly, François-Louis, II, **457**

Mariauchau d'Esgly, Louise (Martel de Brouague), III, 434; V, 481

Mariauchau d'Esgly, Louise-Philippe. *See* Chartier de Lotbinière

Mariauchau d'Esgly, Louis-Philippe, III, 112, 434; IV, 42, 81, 87, 101, 102, 142, 371, 372, 430, 444, **510–12**, 543,

789, 799; V, 76, 143, 150, 202, 380, 433, 434, 458, 480, 481, 524; VI, 86, 286, 485, 587, 650; XI, 87

Mariauchau d'Esgly, Pierre, II, 456

Maricourt. *See* Le Moyne

Marie. *See also* Aonetta; Williams, Eunice

Marie, Sieur. *See* François-Marie de Paris

Marie (Pawnee), III, 482

Marie (sister of Joseph MALIE), VII, 579

Marie (wife of MEMBERTOU), I, 501

Marie (wife of NEGABAMAT), I, 516

Marie, III, 8, **430–31**; V, 98

Marié, Charles, VI, 119

Marié, Denise (Quesneville), II, 534

Marié, Jeanne. *See* Lord

Marie, Louis, VIII, 397

Marié, Pierre, II, 534

Marie-Adélaïde de Sainte-Clotilde. *See* Pinsonaut

Marie-Agnès, Mother. *See* Dufresne

Marie-Andrée de Sainte-Hélène. *See* Regnard Duplessis

Marie-Angèle, Sister. *See* Gauthier

Marie-Angélique de Saint-Martin. *See* Viger

Marie-Anne, Mother. *See* Sureau, *dit* Blondin

Marie-Anne-Archange de Saint-Bernard. *See* Panet

Marie-Anne de la Nativité. *See* Migeon de Branssat

Marie-Anne de Saint-Benoît. *See* Davis

Marie-Anne de Sainte-Cécile. *See* Davis

Marie-Anne de Saint-Olivier. *See* Paquet

Marie-Anne-Louise de Saint-François-Xavier. *See* Taschereau

Marie-Antoinette, Princess of Austria (Marie-Antoinette, Queen of France), VI, 317

Marie-Catherine de Saint-Alexis. *See* Payen de Noyan

Marie-Catherine de Saint-Augustin. *See* Simon de Longpré

Marie-Catherine de Saint-Ignace. *See* Juchereau Duchesnay

Marie-Catherine de Saint-Joachim. *See* Tibierge

Marie-Catherine du Saint-Sacrement. *See* Charly Saint-Ange

Marie-Charlotte (wife of ATIATOHARONGWEN), V, 40

Marie-Charlotte (wife of Joseph-Victor Couvret), VI, 547

Marie-Charlotte de Saint-Claude de la Croix. *See* Ramezay

Marie-Charlotte de Saint-Michel. *See* Aubert de La Chesnaye

Marie de Bonsecours. *See* Gadbois

Marie de la Conception. *See* Irwin

Marie de l'Annonciation. *See* Le Ber

Marie de l'Assomption. *See* Barbier

Marie de l'Eucharistie. *See* Lefebvre

Marie de l'Incarnation. *See* Guyart; Raizenne

Marie de Médicis, Queen of France, I, 98, 99, 100

Marie de Saint-Basile. *See* Bertrand

Marie de Saint-Bernard. *See* Savonnières

Marie de Saint-Bonaventure-de-Jésus. *See* Forestier

Marie de Sainte-Euphrasie. *See* Pelletier

Marie de Sainte-Thérèse. *See* Juchereau de La Ferté

Marie de Sainte-Thérèse-de-Jésus. *See* Bourdon

Marie de Saint-Ignace. *See* Giffard; Guenet

Marie de Saint-Joseph. *See* Bourdon; Savonnières

Marie de Saint-Vincent de Paul. *See* Angers

Marie des Anges. *See* Sayward

Marie des Sept-Douleurs. *See* Gascoin

Marie du Sacré-Cœur. *See* Fisbach

Marie du Sacré-Cœur, Mother. *See* Valois

Marie-Élisabeth, Sister. *See* Turgeon

Marie-Esther de Saint-Joseph. *See* Chaloux
Marie-Félix (Dubocq), I, 286
Marie-Françoise de Saint-Antoine. *See* Guillimin
Marie-Françoise de Saint-Charles. *See* Caron
Marie-Françoise de Saint-Jacques. *See* Panet
Marie-Françoise de Saint-Pierre. *See* Buisson de Saint-Cosme
Marie-Gabrielle de l'Annonciation. *See* Denis
Marie-Geneviève de Sainte-Hélène. *See* Godefroy de Tonnancour
Marie-Geneviève de Saint-François d'Assise. *See* Parent
Marie-Jeanne-Madeleine de Sainte-Agathe. *See* Legardeur de Repentigny
Marie-Joseph, Father. *See* Géramb
Marie-Joseph (wife of Pierre TOMAH), VI, 774
Marie-Joseph-Angélique, II, **457–58**
Marie-Joseph de la Visitation. *See* Legardeur de Repentigny
Marie-Joseph de l'Enfant-Jésus. *See* Juchereau Duchesnay; Wheelright
Marie-Joseph de Saint-André. *See* Maillou, *dit* Desmoulins
Marie-Joseph de Saint-François d'Assise. *See* Hallé
Marie-Joseph de Saint-Michel. *See* Blais
Marie-Josephte de la Nativité. *See* Paquet
Marie-Léonie, Sister. *See* Paradis
Marie Leszczyńska (Marie, Queen of France), III, 24
Marie-Louise de la Sainte-Vierge. *See* Gaillard
Marie-Louise de Saint-Augustin. *See* Painchaud
Marie-Louise de Saint-Henri. *See* McLoughlin
Marie-Louise de Saint-Martin. *See* Curot
Marie-Madeleine, Mother. *See* Céré
Marie-Madeleine de Saint-Louis. *See* Maufils
Marie-Olivier-Sylvestre. *See* Manitouabeouich
Marier, Bénoni, VIII, 482
Marie-Renée de la Nativité. *See* Boulic
Marie-Rosalie de la Nativité. *See* Cadron
Marie-Rose, Mother. *See* Durocher
Mariet, Joseph, II, 130, 241
Marie-Thérèse. *See* Gannensagouas
Marie-Thérèse de Saint-Jean-Baptiste. *See* Langlois
Marie-Thérèse of Austria, Infanta of Spain (Marie-Thérèse, Queen of France), I, 499
Marie-Ursule des Anges. *See* Chéron
Marie-Vénérande de Sainte-Claire. *See* Melançon
Marie-Victorin, Brother. *See* Kirouac
Marigny. *See also* Philippe
Marigny, Sieur de (supporter of Jacques RAUDOT), II, 558, 559
Marillac. *See also* Auger
Marillac, Louise de, I, 484
Marin. *See also* Morin
Marin, Hélène. *See* Gorel
Marin, Jacques, II, 458
Marin, Lancelot, I, 121
Marin, Louis, III, 491
Marin, Marie-Madeleine (Coulon de Villiers), IV, 177
Marin de La Malgue, Catherine. *See* Niquet
Marin de La Malgue, Charles-Paul, II, **458**; III, 374, 431, 432
Marin de La Malgue, Charlotte. *See* Fleury de La Gorgendière
Marin de La Malgue, Joseph, II, 458; III, 171, 243, 244, 400, 431; IV, 449, **512–14**, 680, 733

Marin de La Malgue, Louise. *See* Lamy
Marin de La Malgue, Marie-Joseph. *See* Guyon Desprez
Marin de La Malgue, Paul, II, 458, 581; III, xl, 46, 47, 48, 49, 101, 162, 255, 319, 367, 375, 378, **431–32**, 438, 532, 578, 611, 614; IV, lvi, 54, 63, 213, 239, 248, 256, 268, 432, 458, 489, 512, 513, 617, 618, 733; V, 40, 835
Marin de La Perrière, Claude, III, 158, **432**
Marin de La Perrière, Marie-Madeleine. *See* Coulon de Villiers
Marinier, Marie-Anne (Larcher), IV, 438
Marion, Amable, X, 143
Marion, Denise (Peiras), II, 514
Marion, Élise (Kittson), XI, 476
Marion, Louis, VIII, 218
Marion, Marie-Charlotte. *See* Foisy
Marion, Michel, VI, 487
Marion, Nicolas, III, 519
Marion, Rosalie (Bélanger), XII, 84
Marion, Salomon, V, 436, 437; VI, **487–88**, 666; VIII, 637, 638
Marion, Sophie. *See* Lafrenière
Marion, *dit* La Fontaine, Abel, II, 440; III, 568
Marjoribanks*, Ishbel Maria (Hamilton-Gordon, Marchioness of Aberdeen and Temair) (1857–1939), XII, 586, 610, 943, 953, 973, 1047
Mark. *See* March
Markham, Sir Clements Robert, IX, 12; XII, 878
Markham, Elizabeth. *See* Hey
Markland, Anna (wife of GEORGE HERCHMER), IX, 534
Markland, Catherine. *See* Herchmer
Markland, George Herchmer, VI, 22, 771; VII, 229, 367, 368, 370, 456, 470, 472, 583, 756; VIII, 11, 47, 48, 162, 253, 514, 515, 520, 521, 926; IX, 502, **534–36**; X, 343
Markland, Thomas, IV, 494; V, 326, 492; VI, 215, 297, 470; VII, 367, 368, 471, **583–85**; VIII, 6; IX, 534, 557; X, 12
Markle, Mrs (Vrooman; wife of ABRAHAM), VI, 488
Markle, Abraham, V, 643, 724, 725, 733, 749, 857, 858; VI, 22, 229, **488–91**, 542, 698; VIII, 608, 609
Markle, Catharine (wife of ABRAHAM), VI, 488
Marks, Agnes Jane. *See* Buchanan
Marks, Caroline (Harvey), IX, 457
Marks, Frederick, IX, 457
Marks, George, XII, 698
Marks*, George Thomas (d. 1907), XII, 699
Marks, Grace, XI, 150, 618
Marks, Mary (mother of THOMAS), XII, 698
Marks, Mary Norah, XII, 698
Marks, Samuel, XII, 698
Marks, Thomas, XII, 646, **698–99**
Marlborough, Duchess of. *See* Jennings
Marlborough, Duke of. *See* Churchill
Marleau, Gabrielle (Serres), V, 752
Marler, George Carlyle, V, 602
Marling, Alexander, XI, **587**
Marling, John F., XI, 587
Marling, Julia. *See* Hewlett
Marlowe, Julia (Sothern), XII, 316
Marlowe, Owen, IX, 597, 598
Marlowe, Virginia. *See* Nickinson
Marmet, Alphonse, IX, 120
Marmette, Joseph, XII, 911
Marmette, Joseph-Étienne-Eugène, XI, 83; XII, 308, 325

Marmier, Xavier, VI, 224; IX, 302; XI, 182

Marmont. *See* Viesse

Marmontel, Antoine-François, XI, 671; XII, 532

Marmontel, Jean-François, V, 233

Maroist, Guillaume, II, 648

Marot, Bernard, I, 442, **490**, 505, 593, 642

Marot, Clément, I, 423, 424

Marot de La Garaye, Angélique-Sylvie (Dubreil, Comtesse de Pontbriand), III, 161, 192

Marotte, Claude, VII, 885

Mar-pi-ya-ro-to-win (Grey Cloud), V, 10, 835

Marples, John, XII, 866

Marquet. *See* Benoît

Marquette, Benoît, XI, 457

Marquette, Jacques, I, 15, 35, 58, 174, 175, 178, 244, 248, 282, 394, 395, 453, 460, **490–93**; II, xxxi, xxxvi, xxxvii, xxxviii, 128, 144, 259, 347, 501, 634; III, xxxv, 380; XII, 1002, 1003

Marquette, Rose. *See* La Salle

Marquette de Tombelles, Nicolas, I, 490

Marquis. *See also* Canac

Marquis*, Calixte (1821–1904), XI, 253; XII, 508, 509, 820, 1022

Marquis, Marc, XII, 549

Marquis*, Thomas Guthrie (1864–1936), XI, 141

Marr, John, IV, 108; VI, 768, 788

Marrant, Elizabeth. *See* Herries

Marrant, John, IV, **514–16**; V, 469

Marriott, Elizabeth Hester (Morrison), VI, 520

Marriott, Sir James, IV, xlvi; V, 145

Marriott, Randolph, VI, 520

Marryat, Catherine. *See* Shairp

Marryat, Charlotte. *See* Von Geyer

Marryat, Frederick, VII, **585–86**; VIII, 830; XI, 333, 585

Marryat, Joseph, VII, 585

Mars, Anne. *See* Faye

Mars, Anne (Couagne), II, 153

Mars, Jean, II, 105

Mars, Marie (Jolliet de Mingan; Volant d'Haudebourg), II, 301

Mars, Marie (Rivière; Berry), III, 168

Mars, Michelle (Dubocq; Riverin), III, 557

Mars, Simon, II, 301; III, 557

Marsain, Anne (Bailly de Messein), IV, 41

Marsan*, Isidore-Joseph-Amédée (1844–1924), X, 15

Marsden, Miss (Anderson), XI, 18

Marsden, George, VII, 587

Marsden, Joshua, VI, 65; VII, 424, **586–88**, 854; VIII, 82; XII, 692

Marsden, Mary. *See* Seabury

Marsden, William, IX, 218; X, 36

Marseille. *See* Natte; Sicard

Marsh. *See also* March

Marsh, Mr (settler), V, 335

Marsh, Mrs. *See* Huntington

Marsh, Abraham, V, 857; VII, 545

Marsh, David O., X, 374

Marsh, Edward, IX, 232

Marsh, Elizabeth, I, 493

Marsh, Eunice (Dimock), IV, 217

Marsh, Hester (Hetty) (Iredell), V, 448

Marsh, Jane (Richardson), VIII, 743

Marsh, John, I, 39, 107, 361, **493**, 529, 657, 672; II, 50, 231, 265

Marsh, Thomas (Liverpool, England, merchant), VII, 748, 749

Marsh, Thomas (P.E.I. merchant), V, 335; VI, 566

Marsh, William, V, 422

Marshall, Ann (mother of JOHN JOSEPH), IX, 536

Marshall, Catherine. *See* Jones

Marshall, Charles, VI, 513; IX, 671; X, 526

Marshall, Elias, VII, 197

Marshall, Elisabeth Golding. *See* Elrington

Marshall, Elizabeth, VIII, 588

Marshall, Esther Maria. *See* Ballaine

Marshall, John George, VII, 88, 589, 910; VIII, 222, 755; IX, 187, 536; X, **496–97**; XI, 106

Marshall, John Joseph, IX, **536–37**; XI, 106

Marshall, Joseph, VII, 588; X, 496

Marshall, Joseph, VII, **588–89**; IX, 536; XI, 14

Marshall, Joseph H., IX, 536

Marshall, Joseph Head, Baron d'Avray, X, 497

Marshall, Margaret (wife of JOSEPH), VII, 588; X, 496

Marshall, Margaret Jane (Bourinot), XI, 105, 106

Marshall, Mary (mother of JOSEPH), VII, 588

Marshall, Sampson. *See* Kelly, James

Marshall, William (agronomist), VIII, 278

Marshall, William (settler), VII, 754

Marshall d'Avray, Laurestine Marie, X, 497

Marshall d'Avray, Margaret Emma. *See* Glenn

Marshall de Brett Maréchal, Joseph, Baron d'Avray, VII, 291; IX, 341, 666; X, **497–98**; XI, 447, 828

Marsham, Charles, 2nd Earl of Romney, X, 291

Marsham, Charles, 3rd Earl of Romney, X, 292

Marsham, Lady Frances (Fletcher), X, 291

Marsham, Lady Harriet (Fletcher), X, 292

Marshe, Witham, III, 147

Marsil, David, VII, 173, 174

Marsolet. *See also* Lemire; Lemire-Marsolet

Marsolet, François. *See* Sasousmat

Marsolet, Jean, II, 159

Marsolet, Louise (Lemire), I, 460; II, 120

Marsolet, Marguerite. *See* Couture

Marsolet de Saint-Aignan, Marie. *See* Le Barbier

Marsolet de Saint-Aignan, Marie (Damours de Chauffours), I, 201, 245; II, 166, 167, 653

Marsolet de Saint-Aignan, Nicolas, I, 133, 196, 199, 200, 245, 452, **493–95**, 516, 574; II, 16, 121, 159

Marsollet, Nicolas, I, 473

Marson. *See* Joybert

Marsters. *See also* Masters

Marsters, Ann (McKay; wife of RICHARD UPHAM), VII, 589

Marsters, Deborah (Brown), VII, 589

Marsters, Mary. *See* Upham

Marsters, Nathaniel, VII, 589

Marsters, Richard Upham, VII, 483, **589–90**; XI, 116

Marsters, Ruth, VII, 590

Marsters, William, VII, 589

Marston, Benjamin, IV, 516

Marston, Benjamin, IV, 197, **516–17**; V, 162, 465, 468, 506; VI, 6, 564

Marston, Elizabeth. *See* Winslow

Marston, Margaret (Philipse; Ogilvie), IV, 586

Marston, Sarah. *See* Swett

Martaud La Rigaudière, Agathe (Pélissier), IV, 618
Martch. *See* March
Marteau, Marie (Godefroy), I, 339
Marteau, Renée (Robinau de Bécancour), I, 574
Marteilhe, John (Jean), III, 478; IV, 602; V, 146, 369
Martel, Élisée, XII, 700
Martel, Étienne, VIII, 196
Martel, François, II, 460
Martel, Isaac, I, 209
Martel, Joseph-Nicolas, II, 460; IV, 517
Martel, Lévi, XII, 699
Martel, Louise-Catherine, II, 459
Martel, Marie-Agathe. *See* Baudoin
Martel, Marie-Anne. *See* Léonard, *dit* Mondor
Martel, Marie-Anne. *See* Trottier Des Ruisseaux
Martel, Marie-Anne (Boucher), V, 95
Martel, Marie-Darie. *See* Beaupré
Martel, Nicolas, II, 459
Martel*, Oscar (1848–1924), XII, 472, 700
Martel, Pierre (brother hospitaller), III, 314
Martel, Pierre (son of RAYMOND), II, 459
Martel, Pierre, XII, **699–700**
Martel, Pierre-Michel (Philippe-Michel), II, 460; IV, **517**, 632
Martel, Raymond, II, 383, **458–59**, 533; III, 433
Martel, Zébédée, XII, 700
Martel de Belleville, Élisabeth. *See* Gatin
Martel de Belleville, Jean-Urbain, II, 460; III, **432–33**; IV, 344, 517
Martel de Berhouague, Jeanne. *See* Hargon
Martel de Berhouague, Pierre, II, 458
Martel de Brouague, Anne-Marie. *See* Favry Du Ponceau
Martel de Brouague, Catherine (Le Comte Dupré), V, 481
Martel de Brouague, François, II, 7, 8, 9, 384; III, 75, 228, 354, 429, **433–35**, 631, 632; IV, 145, 271, 650, 754; V, 481
Martel de Brouague, Louise. *See* Mariauchau d'Esgly
Martel de Brouague, Louise (Chaussegros de Léry), III, 434; IV, 145; VI, 133; VII, 169, 213
Martel de Brouague, Marie-Charlotte. *See* Charest
Martel de Brouague, Pierre-Gratien, II, 383, 458; III, 433
Martel de Magos, Jean, I, 577; II, 450, **459–60**; III, 433; IV, 517
Martel de Magos, Marie-Anne. *See* Robinau
Martel de Saint-Antoine, Jean-Baptiste-Grégoire, II, 460; IV, 148, 461, 517, 750
Martel de Saint-Antoine, Marie. *See* Gauvreau
Martell, Henry, IX, 226, 293
Marten, Humphrey, III, 304; IV, 33, 47, 157, 390, **517–19**, 684, 740, 742, 743, 760, 761; V, 194, 450, 500, 711, 712; VIII, 878, 879
Marten, John America, IV, 518
Marter, Jane Augusta (Wood), XI, 934
Martignon. *See* Aprendestiguy
Martigny. *See* Le Moyne
Martin. *See also* Marten; Mécabou
Martin, Abraham, known as L'Écossais or Maître Abraham, I, 223, 233, 263, 264, 287, 379, 417, **495–96**; II, 460
Martin, Anne (Côté), I, 495
Martin, Anne (Dumas), IV, 242
Martin, Anne-Armèle. *See* Lauzer
Martin, Arthur, XI, 587, 588

Martin, Barbe-Madeleine. *See* Hillaire de La Rochette
Martin, Barthélemy, III, **435**; IV, 124, 126, 353, 354
Martin, Brigitte (Bréaux; Bourg), VI, 86
Martin, Catherine. *See* Rollston
Martin, Catherine. *See* Vigneau
Martin, Charles-Amador, I, 495; II, 227, **460–61**
Martin, Charles-Bruno, IV, 353
Martin*, Chester (1882–1958), VIII, 382; X, 364, 365, 369
Martin, Christine (Gravé Du Pont), I, 346, 347
Martin, Christopher, I, **496**
Martin, Claude (father), I, 351
Martin, Claude, I, 351, 352, 355, 356, 357, 358, 552; III, 106
Martin, Edward, XII, 887
Martin, Élisabeth (Hillaire de Moissacq et de La Rochette), IV, 353
Martin, Elizabeth. *See* Newell
Martin, Elizabeth (Ainslie), V, 4, 745
Martin, Elizabeth (Forrester), VII, 307
Martin, Ellen (Cary), IX, 114
Martin, Énarde (Pécody), I, 535
Martin, Eustache, I, 109, 264, 386, 495
Martin, Félix, II, 237; III, 689; IV, 797; VII, 171; VIII, 619, 792; IX, 63, 67, 250, 861; X, 734; XI, 70, **587–89**
Martin, Gabrielle (Sabrevois de Sermonville), II, 588
Martin, George, X, 347
Martin, George, II, 274, **461**, 497
Martin, George, VI, 760; VIII, **619–21**; XI, 453
Martin, Helen (Johnson), VIII, 620; XI, 451, 452, 453
Martin, Hélène. *See* Guilhermy
Martin, Hélène (Étienne; Chouart Des Groseilliers), I, 223, 495
Martin, Henri, IX, 303
Martin, Henry, XI, 452
Martin, J. A., XI, 599
Martin, Jacques-Augustin, XI, 587
Martin, James, X, 331
Martin, Janet (Liddell), X, 441
Martin, Jean-Baptiste-Tropez, III, 435; IV, 124, 126, 127, 353, 354
Martin, John, VII, 533; VIII, 569
Martin, John Wills, VII, **590–91**; VIII, 246
Martin*, Joseph (1852–1923), XI, 646; XII, 582, 953, 1010, 1011
Martin (Martine), Judith (Delesdernier), V, 239
Martin, Louis, I, 267
Martin, Louise (Vincent), VII, 889
Martin, Lucy. *See* Bates
Martin, Marguerite. *See* Langlois
Martin, Marguerite (Daniel), I, 247
Martin, Marguerite (Racine), I, 263, 379, 495
Martin, Marianne. *See* Lafontaine
Martin, Marie. *See* Guernon, *dit* Belleville
Martin, Marie. *See* Guyart
Martin, Marie (Boucher, *dit* Belleville), VII, 93
Martin, Marie-Françoise-Renée. *See* Levasseur
Martin, Marie-Françoise-Thérèse, known as Theresa of the Child Jesus, XII, 816
Martin, Martha. *See* Taylor
Martin, Mathieu, II, **462**
Martin, Morgan Lewis, VIII, 446
Martin, Nicolas, IV, 69
Martin, Peter. *See also* Oronhyatekha

Martin, Peter, XI, 374
Martin, Phoebe. *See* Cooper
Martin, Pierre, II, 462
Martin, S. W., VIII, 886
Martin, Sarah (Cawdell), VII, 161
Martin, Thomas, I, 496
Martin*, Thomas Mower (1838–1934), XII, 327
Martin, Vincent, III, 435; IV, 353
Martin, *dit* Barnabé, Evelina, XI, 745
Martin, *dit* Barnabé, Fabien, XI, 743, 744
Martin de Lino, Angélique. *See* Chartier de Lotbinière
Martin de Lino, Antoine (Guillaume), II, 204, **462**, 465
Martin de Lino, Antoinette. *See* Chalmette
Martin de Lino, Catherine. *See* Nolan
Martin de Lino, Catherine (Hazeur), II, 277, 465
Martin de Lino, Charles, II, 462, 465
Martin de Lino, Claude, II, 464
Martin de Lino, Geneviève-Françoise (Adhémar de Lantagnac), II, 465; III, 5
Martin de Lino, Ignace-François-Pierre, II, 464; III, 134
Martin de Lino, Jean-François, II, 46, **462–64**; III, 352, 393, 550
Martin de Lino, Jean-Marie, II, 462, 465
Martin de Lino, Marie-Anne. *See* Peyrant
Martin de Lino, Marie-Anne, II, 465
Martin de Lino, Mathieu-François, I, 56; II, 33, 150, 161, 462, 463, **464–65**, 514, 526, 575; III, 5
Martin de Lino de Chalmette, Louis-Xavier, III, 424
Martineau, Augustin, V, 579
Martineau, Françoise. *See* Mercier
Martineau, Harriet, VIII, 651; XI, 861; XII, 328, 525
Martineau, Jérôme, V, 271, **579–80**; VII, 90
Martineau (Martineaut), Marie (Rousseaux St John), V, 724
Martineau, Marie-Angélique. *See* Legris
Martineau, Paul, XII, 722
Martineau, Philippe (Macé), I, 478
Martinet, Catherine. *See* Ducas
Martinet, Henri, VII, 591
Martinet, Marie-Joseph. *See* Descaris
Martinet, Paul, II, 465
Martinet, *dit* Bonami, Louis, VII, **591–92**; XII, 46
Martinet de Fonblanche, Jean, I, 109; II, 226, **465–66**
Martinet de Fonblanche, Marguerite. *See* Prud'homme
Martínez. *See also* Flórez
Martínez, Gertrudis González de. *See* González
Martínez Fernández y Martínez de la Sierra, Esteban José, IV, 73, 283, 325, 411, **519–21**, 568, 622, 623, 744; V, 10, 197, 387, 571, 586; VI, 233, 350
Martino, Mr (artist), XII, 849
Martins, João, I, 234
Martire d'Anghiera, Pietro (Peter Martyr), I, 151, 152, 153, 154, 155
Martissans, Pierre, IV, 253
Maruffo, Raphael, I, 586
Marvin, Edgar, XII, 1132
Marx, Karl Heinrich, X, 670
Mary (daughter of Atiatoharongwen), V, 41
Mary (mother of James Bird), XII, 110
Mary (wife of John Dugald Cameron), VIII, 121
Mary (wife of Peter Fidler), VI, 249, 251
Mary, Duchess of Gloucester, IX, 289
Mary, Queen of Scotland, I, 96, 382
Mary I, Queen of England and Ireland, I, 157; VIII, 521

Mary II, Queen of Great Britain and Ireland, I, 329, 426, 544, 545, 611; II, 50, 103, 231; IV, xxiv
Mary Ann (wife of George Nelson), VIII, 653
Mary Basilia, Sister. *See* McCann
Mary Benedicta, Sister. *See* Harrington
Mary Bernard, Sister. *See* Kirwan
Mary Catherine, Sister. *See* McAuley
Mary Elizabeth, Sister. *See* O'Neill
Mary Francis, Mother. *See* Creedon
Mary Francis, Sister. *See* Maguire
Mary John, Sister. *See* Power
Mary Joseph, Sister. *See* Nugent
Mary Josephine, Sister. *See* Carroll
Mary Magdalen, Sister. *See* O'Shaughnessy
Mary March. *See* Demasduwit
Mary Martha, Sister. *See* Bunning
Mary of St John of God, Mother. *See* Nagle
Mary Stanislaus, Sister. *See* McCabe
Mary Vincent, Mother. *See* Conway
Mary Vincent, Sister. *See* Nugent
Mary Vincentia, Sister. *See* Donnelly
Mary Xavier, Sister. *See* Lynch; Molony
Mascarene, Elizabeth. *See* Perry
Mascarene, Jean, III, 435
Mascarene, Margaret. *See* Salavy
Mascarene, Paul, II, 24; III, 4, 9, 84, 120, 128, 143, 144, 236, 256, 260, 261, 276, 277, 297, 421, 427, **435–40**, 483, 517, 518, 583, 597, 665, 682; IV, xxii, xxv, 169, 239, 254, 295, 539, 559, 676, 783; VI, 88
Mascle, Jean, III, 440
Mascle, Suzanne. *See* Courtade
Mascle de Saint-Julhien, Jean, III, 72, 230, 231, 268, **440–41**, 667
Maseres, Francis, I, xlii, xliv, xlv, xlviii, 7, 37, 104, 139, 150, 183, 184, 229, 230, 232, 295, 348, 349, 388, 398, 415, 554, 618, 642, 725, 753, 788, 789; V, 42, 49, 142, 144, 145, 151, 224, 317, 348, 357, 369, 479, 600, 605, 606, 862; VI, **491–96**, 512; VII, 524, 525; VIII, xxv; IX, 254
Maseres, Magdalene. *See* Pratt du Clareau
Maseres, Peter Abraham, VI, 491
Masham, Abigail, Baroness Masham. *See* Hill
Masham, Samuel, 2nd Baron Masham, II, 287
Mash-i-pi-nash-i-wish. *See* Madjeckewiss
Maskawpistam (Muscowpetung), XI, 675
Maskelyne, Nevil, X, 874
Maskepetoon, VIII, 819; IX, **537–38**; XII, 110, 932
Mason. *See also* Tufton
Mason, Anne. *See* Greene
Mason, Charles Kemble, XII, 306
Mason, Elizabeth (wife of John, ironmaster), XI, 898
Mason, Hannah (Waldo), III, 652
Mason, Isabella. *See* Steed
Mason, Jane (Berthelot), XII, 98
Mason, Jemima (Clark), V, 188
Mason, John (clergyman), VI, 232
Mason, John (father of John), I, 496
Mason, John (ironmaster), XI, 897, 898
Mason, John, I, 51, 243, 262, 350, **496–97**, 650, 655
Mason, John Herbert, XI, 676, 736
Mason, Louise (Delagrave), X, 218
Mason, Margaret (Young), X, 720
Mason, Mary (Goldsmith), IX, 322

Mason, Sophia. *See* Thomas
Mason, Susan (Le Gallais), IX, 460
Mason, William (merchant), VI, 600
Mason, William (missionary), VII, 4, 276, 277; IX, 784; XI, 849; XII, 931
Mason, William (rioter), IX, 448, 776
Massard, Leopold, I, 170
Massasoit, II, xxxv
Masse, Adeline (Roy), X, 635
Masse, Denis, II, 517
Massé, Énemond, I, 67, 68, 94, 95, 97, 98, 100, 101, 121, 142, 214, 299, 307, 338, 387, 411, 441, 442, 453, 470, **497–98**, 501, 560
Massé, François, I, 497
Massé, Geneviève (Lÿdius), IV, 488
Masse, Jeanne (Constantin), III, 134
Massé (Macé), Marie-Anne (Malhiot; Courreaud de La Coste), IV, 178
Masse, Marie-Louise-Flore (Chauveau), XI, 177
Masse, Michel, VI, 484; IX, 110
Massé, Philippe. *See* Bica
Massé, Samuel, IX, 363
Masséna, André, Duc de Rivoli, Prince d'Essling, IX, 37
Masseras, Eugène, X, 164
Massey, Ann. *See* Moreton
Massey, Charles Albert, XII, 701, 702, 703, 704, 705, 707, 708
Massey*, Charles Vincent (1887–1967), XII, 709
Massey*, Chester Daniel (1850–1926), XII, 701, 702, 703, 708, 709
Massey, Daniel, VIII, 621
Massey, Daniel, VIII, **621–22**; XII, 700
Massey, Eliza Ann. *See* Phelps
Massey, Eyre, 1st Baron Clarina, IV, 504, 706, 707
Massey, Frederick Isaiah, XII, 703, 705, 706
Massey, Frederick Victor, XII, 705, 707
Massey, Hart Almerrin, VIII, 621; XI, 583; XII, 428, 454, 633, **700–9**, 843, 1119
Massey, Juliana (Wallis), XII, 1081
Massey*, Lillian Frances (Treble) (1854–1915), XII, 701, 709
Massey, Lucina. *See* Bradley
Massey, Mary. *See* Fryer
Massey, Rebecca. *See* Kelley
Massey, Samuel, XII, 709
Massey, Samuel, XII, **709–11**
Massey*, Walter Edward Hart (1864–1901), XII, 703, 704, 706, 708
Massiac, Claude-Louis de, known as Marquis de Massiac, III, 18, 73; IV, 467, 616; V, 738
Massicotte*, Édouard-Zotique (1867–1947), III, 232; IV, 269, 655; VI, 667; VII, 619; VIII, 736, 919; IX, 438; X, 502; XI, 343, 851; XII, 100
Massillon, Jean-Baptiste, I, 488
Massinger, Philip, VI, 815
Massiot, Gamaliel, V, 226
Masso, Imbert de, I, 498
Masson, Adolphe, X, 501
Masson, Alfred, X, 501
Masson, Alphonsine (Duhamel), XII, 277
Masson, Antoine, VII, 592
Masson, Catherine, VII, 592
Masson, Cécile (Masson), X, 500

Masson, Damase, X, 501
Masson, Damien, VIII, 332; X, 500
Masson, Émilie (Jobin), VIII, 433, 434
Masson, Eustache, X, 500
Masson, Francis, V, **580–81**; VI, 297
Masson, François, I, 439
Masson, Gilles, VII, 592; X, 498
Masson, Isidore-Édouard-Candide, X, **498–99**
Masson, Joseph, VII, 592
Masson, Joseph, VI, 635, 666; VII, 26, 225, 226, 395, **592–96**, 717, 737, 739; VIII, 332, 479, 629; IX, 63, 379, 456; X, 10, 498; XI, 208, 315, 692; XII, 173, 928, 1036
Masson, Louis, X, 499
Masson*, Louis-François-Rodrigue (1833–1903), VII, 356, 565, 566; IX, 466; X, 498; XI, 112, 624, 815, 920; XII, 173, 174, 179, 180, 746, 1000
Masson, Luc-Hyacinthe, VII, 172, 173; VIII, 331, 332; X, **499–500**, 544
Masson (Musson), Lucresse (Arnoux), III, 18
Masson, Marc-Damase, VIII, 433, 692; IX, 204; X, **500–1**
Masson, Marie (Pézard de La Tousche), I, 543
Masson, Marie-Catherine (Hiché), III, 290
Masson, Marie-Geneviève-Sophie. *See* Raymond
Masson, Marie-Jeanne. *See* Gauthier
Masson, Marie-Josephte-Caroline. *See* Dumas
Masson, Marie-Louise. *See* Beaupré
Masson, Marie-Louise. *See* Choquet
Masson, Marie-Scholastique (Peltier), VIII, 692
Masson, Odile. *See* Watier
Masson, Pierre, X, 500
Masson, Pierre-Marc, X, 500
Masson, Scholastique. *See* Pfeiffer
Masson, Suzanne. *See* Pfeiffer
Masson, Virginie. *See* Jobin
Masson, Wilfrid, X, 498; XII, 1036
Masson, Wilfrid-Antoine, X, 220
Masson de Montbrac, Jacques-Joseph, IV, 521
Massot, Joseph, IV, 125
Massot, Nicolas, IV, 124
Massow, Mrs. *See* Crausee
Massow, Friederike Charlotte Louise von (Riedesel, Frelin zu Eisenbach), V, **582–84**
Massow, Hans Jürgen Detloff von, V, 582
Massue, Aignan-Aimé, VIII, 605
Massue, Elizabeth Anne. *See* Marett
Massue, Gaspard, IX, 538
Massue, Josephte. *See* Huet Dulude
Massue, L.-H., X, 144
Massue, Louis-Huet, XII, 65
Massue, Louis-Joseph, VIII, 116, 323, 691; IX, **538–39**; XI, 180, 901; XII, 1037
Massue, Pélagie (Morand), VIII, 637
Massy. *See also* Massey
Massy, Geoffrey, VIII, 621
Mast, Magdalena (Troyer), VII, 870
Masta, Pierre-Paul. *See* Osunkhirhine
Master, Legh, V, 846
Masters (Marsters), Abraham, IV, 217
Masters, John, III, 618; V, 491
Masters, Margaret (Byng, Viscountess Torrington), III, 91
Masters, Ruth (Storer), II, 54
Masters, Sarah. *See* Knowlton
Masterton, Ann (Derbishire), IX, 201

Matahachitoux (Soulier Rouge), IV, 664, 665
Mataut, Jean-Pierre, I, 490
Mataut, Louise. *See* Cloutier
Matayawenenne (Maitwaywayninnee), V, 185
Matchekewis. *See* Madjeckewiss
Mathé, Hugues, II, 29
Mather, Ann (Finlayson), XII, 316
Mather, Cotton, I, 544, 545; III, 25; XII, 823
Mather, Eleazar, II, 667
Mather, Eunice (Williams), II, 667; IV, 770
Mather, Henrietta (Cathcart, Countess Cathcart), VIII, 135
Mather, Increase, I, 544, 545; V, 127
Mather*, John (1832–1907), XII, 367, 1130
Mather, John B., XII, **711–12**
Mather, Margaret. *See* Finlayson, Margaret
Mather, Margaret (mother of JOHN B.), XII, 711
Mather, Maria (Mary) (Green), III, 267
Mather, William (father of JOHN B.), XII, 711
Mather, William (merchant), XI, 397
Mathers, Alexander, XII, 195
Matheson, Ann (McKay), XI, 559
Matheson, Annabella. *See* Russel
Matheson, Arthur James, X, 501
Matheson, Flora. *See* Macrae
Matheson, Isabella (Ross), XI, 772
Matheson, John, X, 501
Matheson, John William, XII, 829
Matheson, Mary Fraser. *See* Robertson
Matheson, Mary Geddie. *See* Johnston
Matheson, Robert, XII, 52
Matheson, Roderick, VII, 69; X, **501–2**, 650
Matheson*, Samuel Pritchard (1852–1942), XI, 471
Matheson, William, XI, 772
Mathevet, Blanche. *See* Ranc
Mathevet, Claude, IV, 521
Mathevet, Jean-Claude, IV, 431, 507, **521–22**
Mathew. *See also* Matthew
Mathew, George, VI, 169
Mathew, Jane (Maitland), VIII, 596
Mathew, Theobald, IX, 489, 490, 494, 820; X, 191
Mathews. *See also* Matthews
Mathews (Matthews), Ann (Coffin), VII, 198
Mathews, Catalina. *See* Abeel
Mathews, David, IV, 523
Mathews, David, IV, 293, **522–23**; V, 53, 204, 205, 222, 223, 389, 510, 511, 546, 634, 766, 767, 780; VI, 113, 194, 195, 213, 535, 536
Mathews, Edmond, III, 409
Mathews, Edward, IX, 705
Mathews, Harriet (Green), V, 389
Mathews, Mary. *See* Simpson
Mathews, Robert, V, 14, 378, **584–85**, 840, 901, 902; VI, 102, 445, 769
Mathews, Sarah. *See* Seymour
Mathews, Thomas, III, 131, 557, 610
Mathews, Vincent, IV, 522
Mathews, William, IX, 6
Mathews, William Tryon, IV, 523
Mathewson, Henry, XI, 80
Mathewson, James, IX, 555
Mathieson, Alexander, V, 320; VIII, 560; IX, **539–40**
Mathieson, Catherine Elizabeth. *See* Mackenzie
Mathieson, George, IX, 539

Mathieson, Janet. *See* Ewing
Mathieson, Mary (Munro), XII, 771
Mathieu, I, 71
Mathieu*, Michel (1838–1911), XI, 811; XII, 64, 65
Mathieu, *dit* Laramée, Élisabeth (Boyer), IX, 77
Mathieu, *dit* Laramée, Joseph, IX, 77
Mathison, Harriet. *See* Vandenburgh
Mathison, John Augustus, IX, 203, **540–41**
Mathon, Marie-Thérèse (Desdevens de Glandons), IV, 215
Mathusson, Françoise (Plessy, *dit* Bélair), III, 523
Matlack, Lucius D., VIII, 90
Matokinajin, IX, 780
Maton, Adolphe, XII, 532
Matonabbee, IV, 47, 339, 340, 341, 383, **523–24**, 584; V, 683; VI, 20
Matooskie. *See* McKenzie, Nancy
Matrine. *See* Qua-hail-ya
Matte, François, XII, 846
Matthew*, George Frederick (1837–1923), IX, 309; X, 338
Matthew (Mathew), Louisa (Gambier, Baroness Gambier), VI, 271
Matthews. *See also* Mathews
Matthews, Cecilia Eliza (Sullivan), VIII, 846
Matthews, Ellen (Barnston), VIII, 61; XI, 52
Matthews, F. B., XI, 130
Matthews, George, XII, 921
Matthews, Hannah (Major; wife of PETER), VII, 596
Matthews, James Skitt, XII, 666
Matthews, Jane Hamlin (Partelow), IX, 622
Matthews, John, I, 567
Matthews, John, VI, 11, 266, 420, **496–99**; VII, 126, 127, 178, 314; VIII, 846; IX, 323, 684
Matthews, Keith, VI, 349, 420, 637
Matthews, Louisa (Goodhue), IX, 323, 324; XI, 63
Matthews, Mary. *See* Ruttan
Matthews, Mary Elizabeth (Downs), XII, 268
Matthews, Peter, VII, 519, **596–97**; VIII, 27, 30, 61, 520, 643, 855; IX, 412, 675; X, 639, 641
Matthews, Thomas Elmes, VII, 596, 597
Matthey, Frederick, VI, 438
Matthieu, Guillaume, II, 95
Mattice, Mary Magdalen (Brass), VII, 102
Maturin, Edmund, XI, 75; XII, **712–13**
Maturin, Henry, XII, 712
Maubourg. *See* Latour-Maubourg
Maudave, Comte de. *See* Féderbe
Maude, John, V, 636
Maudon, Grâce (Plantavit de Lapause de Margon), V, 678
Maudoux, Abel, I, 578; II, 45, 223, 445, 480; III, 207, 499
Maufet, Ursule (Fiset), IX, 261
Maufils, Françoise (Picard), IV, 629
Maufils, Madeleine. *See* Poulain
Maufils, Marie-Madeleine, named de Saint-Louis, II, **466**
Maufils, Pierre, II, 466
Maugean. *See* Mangeant
Maugenest, François, IV, 524
Maugenest, Germain, IV, **524–25**, 726; V, 840
Maugenest, Louise. *See* Descary
Maugenest, Marie-Anne. *See* Saint-Horan
Maugenest, Rosalie. *See* Barrère
Maugenet, Frances-Desirée (Berthon), XII, 100
Mauger. *See also* Gadois
Mauger, Elizabeth (Mauger), IV, 525

Mauger, J., IV, 529
Mauger, Joshua, III, 364, 457, 583; IV, 52, 53, 116, 131, 266, 273, 274, 275, 291, 450, 452, **525–29**, 561, 695, 696, 780; V, 81, 250, 556, 607, 666, 843; VI, 98, 99; VIII, xxv, 709
Mauger, Josué, IV, 525
Mauger, Louise (Gadoys), I, 319, 557; III, 232
Mauger, Sarah. *See* Le Couteur
Mauger, Sarah, IV, 525
Maugis, Charlotte (Miville), I, 511
Maugras. *See also* Gamelin
Maugras, Jacques, II, 283
Maugras, Marguerite (Véronneau), III, 643
Maugras, Marie-Jeanne (Gamelin), III, 233
Maugue, Antoine, I, 498
Maugue, Claude, I, **498**; II, 226, 421, 440; IV, 529
Maugue, Françoise. *See* Rigaud
Maugue, Louise. *See* Jousset
Maugue, Louise (Brunet, *dit* La Sablonnière), III, 88
Maugue, Marie-Anne (Garreau, *dit* Saint-Onge), IV, 287, 529
Maugue-Garreau, Marie-Josèphe, named de l'Assomption, IV, **529–30**, 638; V, 117, 143
Maule, Anne (MacNab), VIII, 584
Maule Ramsay, Fox, 11th Earl of Dalhousie, XII, 1079
Maulibock, "Cockney Bill," VIII, 968
Maulibock, Mary. *See* Preston
Maumousseau, Françoise, II, 235, **466–67**
Maumousseau, Jean, II, 466
Maumousseau, Renée. *See* Verron
Maupas. *See* Pouchot
Maupassant, Eustache, I, **498–99**
Maupeou, Guillaume de, II, 442
Mauprée. *See* Des Granges
Maur. *See* Juchereau
Maurault, Cyriac, IX, 541
Maurault, Émilie. *See* Sirois, *dit* Duplessis
Maurault, Jean-Élie, IX, 541
Maurault, Joseph-Pierre-Anselme, IV, 294; IX, **541–42**
Maurault*, Olivier (1886–1968), VI, 554; XI, 92
Maurault, Thomas, IX, 541
Maurel, Marie (Dessane), X, 228
Maurepas, Comte de. *See* Phélypeaux
Maurepas, Comtesse de. *See* La Rochefoucauld-Roye
Maurès de Malartic, Anne-Joseph-Hippolyte de, Comte de Malartic, IV, **530–31**; V, 104, 677
Maurès de Malartic, Antoinette-Charlotte de, Comtesse de Montricoux. *See* Savignac
Maurès de Malartic, Pierre-Hippolyte-Joseph de, Comte de Montricoux, IV, 530
Maurice, Mrs (companion of the wife of Henry SERGEANT), I, 605, 657
Maurice (Vignau), Jacques, III, 358
Maurice, Jean-Baptiste, III, 103, 137
Maurice, Marie-Josephte (Tavernier), VIII, 863
Maurice, Mary (Switzer), VIII, 854, 855
Maurice, Nancy (Jeffers), XII, 468
Maurin, Archange. *See* Dagneau Douville de Quindre
Maurin, François, III, **441–42**; IV, 125, 127, 435, 461, 517, 565, 621
Maurin, Jean, IV, 559
Maurin, Marguerite-Geneviève. *See* Mounier
Maurin, Philippe, III, 441

Maury, Alexandre, V, 200
Maury, Jean-Louis, IV, 529; V, 200, 704
Maury, Matthew Fontaine, IX, 199
Mause. *See* Meuse
Mauvide, Jean, III, 518
Maver, George, XII, 195
Mavit, Aymare, IV, 286
Mavor, William, VIII, 925
Mawson, Catherine (Dent), XI, 246
Maxfield, Sarai (Sheppard), IX, 718
Maximilian, Archduke of Austria (Maximilian I, Emperor of Mexico), XII, 308, 471
Maximilian, Prince of Wied-Neuwied, IX, 537
Maximilian II Emanuel, Elector of Bavaria, II, 279, 643
Maxse, Sir Henry Berkeley FitzHardinge, XI, 356
Maxwell, Agnes (Fraser), V, 330
Maxwell, Anne (Colvile), XII, 206
Maxwell, Charles William, VII, 865
Maxwell, Elizabeth, VI, 117
Maxwell, Isabella (Allan), V, 15
Maxwell, Margaret (Pagan), V, 645; VI, 561
Maxwell, Sir Murray, VII, 742
Maxwell, Sarah. *See* Ainse
Maxwell, William (cabinet-maker), XI, 390, 448
Maxwell, William (trader), VI, 8
May, Emmiley (Penny), XI, 680
May, Henry, I, **499**
May, Rudolph von, VI, 648
May, Samuel, IX, 288
May, Samuel Joseph, IX, 705, 820
May, Sir Thomas Erskine, XI, 884
Mayar. *See* Myeerah
Mayar; Mayard. *See* Maillard
Mayawassino. *See* Musquakie
Mayberry, Nancy (Strobridge), VI, 741, 742
Mayer, André, I, 88
Mayer, Jean, VI, 305
Mayer, Johann Michael, V, 37
Mayer, Marie-Anne-Magdeleine (Guerout), VI, 305
Mayerhoffer, Caroline. *See* Stahl
Mayerhoffer, Catharina. *See* Lublé
Mayerhoffer, Michael, VIII, 622
Mayerhoffer, Vincent Philip, VII, 351; VIII, **622–23**, 700
Mayers. *See* Meyers
Mayhew, Jonathan, V, 870
Maynard, Abbé, XII, 819
Maynard, Amelia Ann (Robertson-Ross), XI, 758
Maynard, Emma (wife of George), VIII, 427
Maynard, George, VIII, 427
Maynard, Hannah (Thompson), VII, 853
Mayne, John, VI, 372
Mayne, Leonora (Daly), X, 213; XI, 231
Mayne, Richard Charles, IX, 473, 514
Maynwaringe. *See* Mainwaring
Mayrac. *See* Meyracq
Mayrand, Sister, I, 117
Mayrand, Agathe. *See* Roy
Mayrand (Mérand), Anne, II, 44
Mayrand, Étienne, X, **502–3**
Mayrand, Félicité. *See* Le Maître-Bellenoix
Mayrand, Jean-Baptiste, X, 502
Mayrand, Joseph-Arsène, VIII, 722
Mayrand, Sophie. *See* Héneau

Mayrand, Thérèse. *See* Heney
Mayrant, Antoine, VI, 50
Maysenhoelder, John, XII, 424
Maysenhoelder, Sarah (Hendery), XII, 424
Mazarin, Jules, I, 44, 389, 442, 615; II, 48, 362, 363, 631, 656
Mazarini. *See* Mancini-Mazarini
Mazas, Alexandre, II, 52
Mazé. *See* Peronne
Mazel. *See also* Agrain
Mazel, Mr (engraver), V, 687
Mazenod, Charles-Fortuné de, X, 322
Mazenod, Charles-Joseph-Eugène de, VII, 267, 304; VIII, 66, 722; IX, 19, 342, 397, 398; X, 275, 419, 609; XI, 33, 34, 96, 310, 401; XII, 190, 282, 1003, 1004, 1005, 1006
Mazière, Marie-Madeleine. *See* Le Poupet de La Boularderie
Mead, Joseph Hooper, XII, 43
Meade, George Gordon, XI, 592
Meade, Margaret Irene, Countess Clanwilliam. *See* Sarney
Meagher, Émilie (Labillois), IX, 438
Meagher, Henrietta Charlotte (Sangster), XII, 944, 946
Meagher, Henry, VII, 597
Meagher, John, VIII, 196; IX, 438
Meagher, Maria (Skerry), VII, 810
Meagher, Mary (Crotty; wife of THOMAS), VII, 597
Meagher*, Nicholas Hogan (1842–1932), X, 71; XI, 947
Meagher, Thomas, VII, 597, 598
Meagher, Thomas, VII, **597–98**
Meagher, Thomas Francis, VII, 598
Meahan, James, X, 271
Mea ire. *See* Myeerah
Méan, Jean-Ferdinand, Baron de Méan, II, 332
Meares, John, IV, 218, 244, 325, 520, 568, 746, 768; V, 197, 198, 387, 541, **585–87**, 686; VI, 36
Meares, Sarah (Burnaby), X, 111
Mearns, Duncan, VIII, 272, 640
Mears, Charlotte (Miles), VII, 610, 611
Mears, Thomas, VI, 478; VII, 380, 381, 553; VIII, 688, 890
Measam, Dorothée (Méthot), VIII, 628
Measam, Joseph, VII, 176
Measam, Julie (Chinic), XI, 189
Measam, Julie (Simard), X, 654
Measam, William, VIII, 628
Mécabou (Martin), I, 199
Mécatépilésis (Macatapilésis), III, 527; IV, 408
Mecham, George Frederick, VIII, **623–25**; X, 396, 397; XI, 691
Mechin, Jeanne (Baudry), III, 451
Mechtler, Mr (musician), VI, 499
Mechtler, Mrs (singer), VI, 499
Mechtler, Guillaume-Joseph, VI, **499–500**
Mechtler, Marie-Anne-Angélique. *See* Landrière
Mechtler, Marie-Madeleine. *See* Moreau
Mechtler, Pierre-Paul, VI, 499
Meckinac. *See* Mikinak
Medcalf, Alfred, X, 504
Medcalf, Francis Henry, IX, 77, 588; X, **503–4**; XI, 542, 616; XII, 976
Medcalf, Martha (mother of FRANCIS HENRY), X, 503
Medcalf, Mary. *See* Harrison
Medcalf, William, X, 503
Medicine Calf. *See* Natose-Onista; Natose-Onistors

Medicine Fire. *See* Natowes-tsitsi
Medicine Pipe Man Returning with a Crane War Whoop. *See* Nina'msko'taput-sikumi
Medicine Snake Woman. *See* Natawista
Medicine Snake Woman (Culbertson), IX, 623
Médicis. *See* Catherine de Médicis; Marie de Médicis
Medicraft, Henry, XII, 909
Medley, Charles Steinkopff, XII, 716
Medley, Christiana. *See* Bacon
Medley, Edward Shuttleworth, XII, 714
Medley, George, XII, 713
Medley, Henrietta (mother of JOHN), XII, 713
Medley, Henry, V, 380
Medley, John, VII, 434, 435; VIII, 172, 173, 174, 228, 942, 943, 951; IX, 35, 338, 339, 341, 378, 379, 392, 408; X, 495; XI, 333; XII, 18, 446, **713–17**, 798, 814, 1052
Medley, Margaret. *See* Hudson
Medlicott, Jane (Scriven), XI, 803
Medoux, Jean, IV, 252
Medoux, Louis, IV, 252
Medrano, Catalina de (Cabot), I, 158
Mee-may. *See* Mīmīy
Meenish (wife of John THOMAS; wife of Richard Stevens), VI, 766
Meesinkeeshick, III, 595
Megapolensis, Jan, I, 462
Megginch. *See* Drummond
Meignot, Marie-Françoise. *See* Fornel
Meigs, Carlos Darius, XI, 808, 809, 810
Meikle, Jemima Frances (Howard), XI, 426
Meiklejohn, William, V, 880
Meilleur, Jean, X, 504
Meilleur, Jean-Baptiste, IV, 801; VII, 25, 32, 168, 254; VIII, 87, 136, 137, 240, 241, 288, 426, 458, 912; IX, 100, 200, 449, 862; X, 15, 75, 76, 266, 326, 401, 418, **504–9**, 527, 583, 603; XI, 87, 88, 115, 181, 182, 345; XII, 64, 271, 1066
Meilleur, Joséphine. *See* Éno, *dit* Deschamps
Meilleur, Joséphine-Charlotte (Barthe), X, 505; XII, 64
Meilleur, Marie-Suzanne. *See* Blaignier
Mein, Margaret. *See* Ellis
Mein, Susan (Sibbald), IX, **542–43**
Mein, Thomas, IX, 542
Mékaisto, IX, 624; X, 662; XI, 445; XII, 673, 674, **717–19**, 778, 779, 802, 803, 858, 970
Mekaoua, II, 474
Melançon, Jean-Baptiste, V, 587
Melançon, Madeleine (Le Poupet de La Boularderie), II, 417; IV, 468
Melançon, Marie-Anne. *See* Robichaud
Melançon, Marie-Vénérande, named de Sainte-Claire, V, **587–88**, 659
Melanson, Anne (Saint-Étienne de La Tour), I, 514; II, 590; IV, xix
Melanson, Charles, I, **499–500**; II, 625; IV, xix
Melanson, Marguerite (Comeau), IX, 148
Melanson, Marie. *See* Dugas
Melanson, Nanette. *See* Surette
Melanson, *dit* La Verdure, Anne (Jacau), IV, 382
Melanson, *dit* La Verdure, Marguerite. *See* Mius d'Entremont
Melanson, *dit* La Verdure, Marguerite (Bourg, *dit* Belle-Humeur), III, 83, 366; IV, 441

Melanson, *dit* La Verdure, Pierre, I, 436, 499, 500, 510; II, 46, 625; III, 83
Melbourne, Viscount. *See* Lamb
Meldola, Raphaël, XI, 254
Meldola, Rebecca (de Sola), XI, 254
Meldrum, Helen (Abercromby), IV, 4
Melfort. *See* Campbell
Melgund, Viscount. *See* Elliot
Melilupi, Catalina (Morello, Marchioness of Malaspina), V, 570
Méline, Jules, XII, 59
Mellan, Claude, VI, 27
Mellanson, Peter, II, 198
Mellany, Catherine (Devlin), X, 229
Mellis, Mary (Douglas), IX, 217; XI, 271
Mellish, Elizabeth (LePage), XI, 511
Mellish, Thomas, V, 745
Melms, Frank F., XII, 955
Melo. *See* Rivera
Meloche, Françoise (Berthelet), VI, 52
Melrose, Jane (Hargrave), IX, 364
Melun. *See* Arbalestre
Melvill, Sir James Cosmo, IX, 180
Melville. *See also* Mainville
Melville, Viscount. *See* Dundas; Saunders Dundas
Melville, David, 8th Earl of Leven, IX, 461
Melville, Henry, XII, 106
Melville, Nannie (Le Caron), XII, 68
Melvin, John, VI, 95
Melvin, Louisa (Caldwell), V, 133
Melvin, Marianne (Lindsay), VI, 400
Melvin, Robert, VI, 95; VII, 134; VIII, 353, 838
Membertou, I, 69, 97, 100, 307, 367, **500–1**, 526, 529, 604
Membré, Zénobe, I, 176, 178, 179, 180, 420, 438, 440, **501–2**; II, 278, 419, 634
Memeskia (La Demoiselle, Old Britain), III, xlii, 100, 525; IV, liv, 563, 633, 666
Memlingh, Dederika (Johnson), X, 381
Ménage, Anne. *See* Leblanc
Ménage, Anne (Levasseur), II, 467
Ménage, Dorothée. *See* Brassard
Ménage, François (grandfather), II, 467
Ménage, François, II, 467
Ménage, Françoise. *See* Lunette
Ménage, Jean-Baptiste, II, 467
Ménage, Marie-Anne (Lajoüe), II, 337, 467
Ménage, Pierre, I, 572; II, 337, 338, **467**
Ménager. *See* Hausman
Ménard, Marie (Bourdon), II, 92
Ménard, Maurice, III, 147
Ménard, René, I, 65, 206, 225, 251, 461, **502**, 566; II, 157, 317
Ménard, *dit* La Fontaine. *See also* La Fontaine
Ménard, *dit* La Fontaine, Antoine, IX, 440
Ménard, *dit* La Fontaine, Marie-Josephte. *See* Fontaine, *dit* Bienvenue
Ménars, Marquis de. *See* Charron
Mendelssohn-Bartholdy, Jakob Ludwig Felix, XII, 471
Mendes, Anna Gabriella. *See* Head
Mendes, Fernando, X, 342
Mendes, Moses, X, 342
Méndez, Martin, I, 156
Mendip, Baron. *See* Ellis

Mendoza. *See also* Dominguez
Mendoza, Pedro de, I, 342
Ménéclier de Montrochon, Sophie (Lambert Dumont), VI, 385
Menehwehna. *See* Minweweh
Menendez, Mr (seaman), I, 310
Menescardi, Giustino, I, 152
Meneux, *dit* Châteauneuf, Jacques, I, 550
Meneval. *See* Des Friches
Méneveau, Anne (Mondelet), V, 599
Ménilles, Marquis de, VI, 618
Mennander, Carl Fredrik, IV, 406
Mennard, Marie-Louise (Plessy, *dit* Bélair), VI, 586
Menneval. *See* Des Friches
Menneville. *See* Duquesne
Menou, Nicole de. *See* Jousserand
Menou d'Aulnay, Charles de, I, 25, 32, 62, 63, 66, 90, 129, 234, 256, 257, 258, 259, 261, 323, 379, 380, 383, 433, 435, 442, 468, 469, 490, **502–6**, 514, 569, 593, 595, 596, 604; II, 94, 625
Menou d'Aulnay, Jeanne de. *See* Motin
Menou d'Aulnay, Marie de, I, 436
Menou de Charnisay, René de, I, 433, 502, 505
Menspéré, II, 646
Mentor, Dominique-François, IV, 204, 205
Menut, Alexandre, V, 75, **588–89**
Menut, Marie. *See* Deland
Mény, Marie-Madeleine. *See* Péan
Menzies, Dr, V, 46
Menzies, Ann (mother of ARCHIBALD), VII, 599
Menzies, Archibald, IV, 747; V, 56, 540; VI, 222; VII, **599–600**
Menzies, Barbara (Shirreff), VII, 796
Menzies, George, VII, **600–1**; X, 656
Menzies, Harriet. *See* Burton
Menzies, James, VII, 599
Menzies, Janet (wife of ARCHIBALD), VII, 599
Menzies, John H., XII, 410
Menzies, Mary (Geddie), VII, 341; X, 302
Menzies, Mary (Scales), XII, 948
Menzies, William, VII, 599
Menzies of Menzies, Sir Robert, Chief of Clan Menzies, VII, 599
Mequinac. *See* Mikinak
Mérand. *See* Mayrand
Merçan, Jean, I, 260
Merçan, Marie-Anne. *See* Denys de Fronsac
Mercator, Gerard, I, 678, 680
Mercer, Mrs. *See* Dickson
Mercer, Agnes (Houliston), XII, 451
Mercer, Alexander, IX, 543
Mercer, Alexander Cavalié, IX, **543–44**, 850
Mercer, Andrew, VIII, 749; IX, 661; X, **509–10**; XII, 325
Mercer, Andrew Francis, X, 509, 510
Mercer, Ann (Ketchum), VII, 467
Mercer, Frasquita. *See* Rice
Mercer, Graeme, X, 715
Mercer, James, III, 588
Mercer, John, VII, 364
Mercer, Lawrence W. (defendant), IX, 151
Mercer, Lawrence William (husband of Mary Catherine Powell), XII, 643

Mercer, Margaret Ann Young (Dawson, Lady Dawson), XII, 230, 237
Mercer, Mary, X, 509
Mercer, Mary Catherine. *See* Powell
Mercer, Robert, VII, 364
Mercer, Sarah. *See* Day
Mercer, Thomas, VII, 467
Mercereau, Pierre, II, 506
Mercier. *See also* Le Mercier
Mercier, Mme (sister-in-law of Jean-Eustache LANOULLIER de Boisclerc), III, 350, 353
Mercier, Anne. *See* Jacquereau
Mercier, Antoine, X, 510
Mercier, Antoine, X, **510–11**; XI, 655
Mercier, Augustin, VI, 681; VIII, 682; X, 375
Mercier, Catherine. *See* Lafontaine
Mercier, Catherine-Henriette (Faucher), XII, 308
Mercier, Élisa (Gouin), XII, 720
Mercier, Élisabeth. *See* Chirat
Mercier, Eliza J. (Barry), X, 36
Mercier, Françoise (Martineau), V, 579
Mercier, François-Xavier-Romuald, VIII, 487
Mercier, Héva (Fauteux), XII, 721
Mercier, Honoré, XII, 721
Mercier, Honoré, VII, 174; IX, 65; X, 16, 25; XI, 26, 110, 192, 211, 277, 289, 329, 488, 489, 493, 560, 624, 646, 658, 659, 743, 750, 894, 912; XII, 8, 20, 21, 59, 65, 88, 99, 126, 176, 177, 179, 180, 197, 252, 266, 272, 276, 277, 303, 310, 362, 363, 372, 465, 489, 502, 503, 510, 554, 580, 581, 582, 609, 629, 630, 693, 694, 695, **719–28**, 799, 904, 913, 917, 928, 987, 1011, 1022, 1026, 1044, 1046, 1065, 1130
Mercier, Iberville, XII, 721
Mercier, Jean-Auguste, III, 443
Mercier, Jean-Baptiste, XII, 719
Mercier, Jean-François, III, 258, **442–43**
Mercier, Jean-Pierre, II, 117, 628; III, 105, 442, **443–44**, 640
Mercier, John Dyer, IV, 791
Mercier, Joseph-Marie, III, 443
Mercier, Josephte (Poutré-Lavigne), XI, 708
Mercier, Julie (Beaupré), VII, 757
Mercier, Julien, XII, 719
Mercier, Léopoldine. *See* Boivin
Mercier, Louis (father), III, 410, 442, 443
Mercier, Louis, III, 443
Mercier, Louise-Jeanne-Marguerite (Gravé de La Rive), V, 379
Mercier, Louis-Sébastien, V, 233
Mercier, Marguerite (Des Bordes Landrièvé), IV, 435
Mercier, Marguerite (Lozeau), III, 410
Mercier, Marie-Catherine. *See* Timineur
Mercier, Sophie (Bruguier), X, 107
Mercier, Virginie. *See* Saint-Denis
Mercil (Mercille), Marie (Bétournay), X, 59
Mercœur, Duc de. *See* Vandémont
Mercure, Monsieur (creditor of François-Pierre CHERRIER), IV, 148
Mercure, Anne-Marie. *See* Gautier, *dit* Bellair
Mercure, François, V, 589
Mercure, Joseph (father of LOUIS), V, 589
Mercure, Joseph (settler), VII, 711
Mercure, Louis, V, **589–90**

Mercure, Louis-Michel, V, 589
Mercure, Madeleine. *See* Thibodeau
Mercure, Michel, V, 589
Meredith, Anne Frances. *See* Jarvis
Meredith, Colborne Powell, XII, 730
Meredith, Edmund Allen, X, 584; XII, 98, 367, 599, 603, **728–31**, 900
Meredith, Georgina Augusta (Jukes), IX, 417
Meredith, Mary Webb (Bernard), X, 51
Meredith*, Richard Martin (1847–1934), XII, 1028
Meredith, Thomas, XII, 728
Meredith, Sir William Collis, XI, 286, 721; XII, 4, 7, 728
Meredith*, Sir William Ralph (1840–1923), X, 645; XI, 537, 614; XII, 138, 199, 333, 334, 580, 581, 582, 583
Meredudd ap Rhys, I, 677
Meriel (Meriel de Meulan), Henri-Antoine, II, **467–68**, 606; IV, 765
Mérieu. *See* Pastour
Mérieux. *See* Saint-Germain
Mérimée, Prosper, X, 150
Merivale, Herman, VIII, xxxiv, xxxv; X, 245; XI, 604, 605
Merkel, Eliza (Holland; Sherlock), VI, 321
Merkel, James W., VII, 237
Merkut, XI, 382
Merlac, André-Louis de, I, **506–7**; II, 249, 304, 326, 330
Merle, Charles, VIII, 625
Merle, Jacques, named Father Vincent de Paul, V, 125; VI, 217; VII, 54, 552; VIII, 307, **625–28**; XII, 640
Merle, Louise. *See* Gagnon
Merlet, Monsieur (rebel), V, 687
Mermande. *See* Sagean
Mermet, Jean, II, 306, 455, **468–69**, 501, 653
Mermet, Joseph-D., VIII, 909
Mérode, Xavier de, X, 542
Merrall, Elizabeth. *See* McLachlan
Merrett. *See* Merritt
Merriarter, Sarah. *See* Hanson
Merrick, Ann. *See* Green
Merrick, Barbara (Button), I, 144
Merrick, John, V, 872; VI, **500–1**; VIII, 755
Merrick, Rhys, I, 144
Merrick, Sarah. *See* Boyer
Merrick, William, VI, 500
Merrick, William Parsons, VI, 500
Merrill, Adaline. *See* Church
Merrill, Horace, XI, 229, **589–90**; XII, 258
Merrill, Horace B., XI, 590
Merrill, Marie Flora Josephine (Lesieur-Désaulniers), XII, 556
Merrill, Mary (Poor), X, 590
Merrill, Milton W., XI, 590
Merrill, Nathaniel, XI, 589
Merrill, Sarah. *See* Huse
Merriman, Anne (Chamberlain), VI, 128
Merritt, Amy. *See* Purdy
Merritt (Merrett), Caroline Matilda (Wood), XI, 936
Merritt, Catharine Rodman. *See* Prendergast
Merritt, E. D., XI, 5
Merritt, Gabriel Wetmore, XII, 1070
Merritt, Isabella. *See* Milby
Merritt, Janet. *See* Morris
Merritt, Jedediah Prendergast, IX, 547
Merritt, Joseph Flewelling, XII, 1070

Merritt, Margaret. *See* Simpson
Merritt, Margaret (Hinton; Eastman), IX, 232
Merritt, Mary. *See* Hamilton
Merritt, Nehemiah, VII, **601–2**, 612, 654; IX, 544
Merritt, Thomas, VII, 601, 602
Merritt, Thomas, VII, 375, 378, 601, **602–3**; IX, 544
Merritt, William Hamilton, IX, 575
Merritt, William Hamilton, V, 522, 673, 858; VI, 93, 159,
    255, 489, 730, 747; VII, 34, 49, 375, 466, 518, 602, 606,
    745, 833, 834, 917; VIII, xxvi, 8, 9, 12, 52, 53, 56, 70,
    208, 252, 253, 409, 450, 451, 523, 785, 786, 787, 798,
    875, 885; IX, 164, 498, 520, 525, **544–48**, 575, 643, 645,
    744, 745, 837; X, 127, 255, 403, 708; XI, 463, 521, 789;
    XII, 149, 391, 783, 1013
Merry, Anthony, V, 20
Merry, Benjamin, VI, 501
Merry, Elizabeth Emily (Hagerman), VII, 365, 370
Merry, John S., VI, 501
Merry, Jonathan, VI, 501
Merry, Mary Anne (Garven), XII, 809
Merry, Ralph (father of RALPH), VI, 501
Merry, Ralph (grandfather of RALPH), VI, 501
Merry, Ralph (son of RALPH), VI, 501, 502
Merry, Ralph, VI, **501–2**
Merry, Sarah. *See* Knower
Merry, Sarah. *See* Sylvester
Merry, William, IX, 669
Merry del Val, Rafaelo, XII, 511
Merton, Thomas, VIII, 628
Merveille, Captain, I, 347
Merveilleux, Louis-François de, II, 424
Merven, Tanguay, IV, 678
Merville, *See* Le Gouès
Mervin, Bridget (Nooth), VI, 548
Mésaiger, Charles-Michel, III, 108, 249, 251, **444**, 580; IV,
    289
Meschecunnaqua. *See* Michikinakoua
Meschin, Jérémie de, III, 392
Mesgouez. *See* La Roche
Meshecunnaqua (Me-She-Kin-No-Quah). *See* Michikina-
    koua
Mesnu. *See* Peuvret
Meson Basse. *See* Deschevery
Mesplet, Antoinette. *See* Capeau
Mesplet, Fleury, IV, 107, 229, 336, 346, 373, 391, **532–34**,
    689, 697, 698; V, 173, 298, 383, 590, 591, 621, 737,
    892, 894; VI, 392
Mesplet, Jean-Baptiste, IV, 532
Mesplet, Marie. *See* Mirabeau
Mesplet, Marie-Anne. *See* Tison
Messamouet, I, 96, **507**, 604
Messayé, Gabriel, IV, 386
Messein. *See* Bailly
Messer, Robert C., XII, 344
Messier, Anne. *See* Le Moyne
Messier, David, II, 469
Messier, Élisabeth (Thierry), II, 469
Messier, Jacques, II, 469
Messier, Marguerite. *See* Bar
Messier, Marguerite (Le Sueur), II, 427
Messier, Martine (Primot), I, 465, **507–8**; II, 193, 469
Messier, *dit* Saint-Michel, Michel, II, 164, 427, **469–70**
Messiter, Charles Alston, XI, 597

Mestigoït, I, 164, 533
Mésy. *See* Saffray
Metacomet. *See* Pometacom
Metaminens. *See* Perrot, Nicolas
Metawiss, IV, 774
Metayer, Catherine (Déat), III, 169
Métayer-Descombes, Marie-Reine (Rombau), VIII, 735
Metcalf, Alice Elizabeth. *See* Bustin
Metcalf, Emma. *See* Clarke
Metcalf, George, XI, 590
Metcalf, Jane. *See* Morphet
Metcalf, Jane (Seaman), IX, 709
Metcalf, Madeline Wharton (Hogan), VIII, 402
Metcalf, William George, XI, **590–91**
Metcalfe, Charles Theophilus, 1st Baron Metcalfe, VII, 32,
    159, 227, **603–8**, 914; VIII, xxv, 18, 51, 52, 135, 137,
    148, 205, 229, 256, 368, 379, 445, 571, 632, 641, 652,
    679, 735, 745, 746, 799, 830, 840, 848, 849; IX, 56,
    90, 146, 177, 190, 191, 238, 266, 344, 372, 445, 446,
    524, 628, 635, 677, 690, 697, 700, 725, 728, 775, 795,
    796, 815, 816, 819, 837, 838; X, 24, 69, 92, 93, 118,
    119, 132, 133, 143, 219, 233, 255, 256, 257, 263, 311,
    359, 404, 462, 502, 512, 522, 619; XI, 35, 127, 178, 179,
    203, 272, 281, 404, 405, 409, 713, 787, 788; XII, 89,
    206, 493
Metcalfe, Isabel (Corby), XI, 203
Metcalfe, James, XI, 939
Metcalfe, Susanna Selina Sophia, Lady Metcalfe. *See* De-
    bonnaire
Metcalfe, Sir Theophilus John, VII, 603, 604
Metcalfe, Sir Thomas Theophilus, VII, 603
Metherall, Francis, VIII, 424, 425, 908; X, **511–12**; XI, 304
Metherall, Mary. *See* Langlois
Metherall, Mary. *See* Nelson
Methoataske, VII, 847
Méthot. *See also* Méthotte
Méthot, Antoine-Prospère, VIII, 368, 628
Méthot, Dorothée. *See* Measam
Méthot, Elzéar, XII, 731
Méthot, François-Xavier, VII, 426; VIII, 497, **628–30**; XI,
    189
Méthot, Joseph, XII, 731
Méthot, Louis, VIII, 628
Méthot, Marie-Xavier. *See* Desrochers
Méthot, Michel-Édouard, IX, 120; XI, 496; XII, **731–32**,
    799
Méthot, Philéas, VIII, 629
Méthot, Winceslas, XI, 190
Méthotte. *See also* Méthot
Méthotte, Joseph, VIII, 628
Méthotte, Josephte. *See* Gouin
Metigonèque. *See* Metiwemig
Métivier, Marc-Anselme de, III, 612
Métivier, Marguerite (Ducharme), IV, 233
Métivier, Marie-Anselme de, II, 96
Métivier, Marie-Josette (Conefroy), V, 202
Metiwemig (Metigonèque, Mitewemeg), I, 65; II, 625
Métru, Nicolas, II, 159
Metternich, Clemens Lothar Wenzel, Prince von Metter-
    nich, VII, 296, 297
Mettot, Marie-Catherine (Lebrun de Duplessis), V, 478,
    479
Metzler, Caroline (McLelan), XI, 572, 573

Metzler, Mary Elizabeth (Spike), X, 664
Meudell, W. F., IX, 741
Meulan. *See* Meriel
Meulles, Mme de. *See* Bégon de La Picardière
Meulles, Jacques de, I, 90, 178, 238, 265, 298, 327, 340, 443, 444, 445, 446, 508, 526, 578, 664; II, xxii, 31, 32, 63, 72, 75, 89, 99, 100, 177, 205, 228, 242, 263, 380, 409, 421, **470–73**, 524, 533, 576, 578, 583; III, 57, 648; IV, xvii
Meulles, Pierre de, II, 470
Meunier, Jean. *See* Lenoir, *dit* Rolland, Joseph
Meunier, Josephte (Vanfelson), VIII, 906
Meunier, *dit* Lapierre, Angélique (Rodier), XI, 763
Meur, Jeanne de (Duparc), III, 204
Meurin, Sébastien-Louis, III, 36, 442; IV, 271, 390; V, 342
Meuse, Andrew James, VII, **608–10**
Meuse, Louis Noel, VII, 610
Meuse, Magdalen. *See* Tony
Meusnier, Anne (Richard), I, 573
Mexborough, Earl of. *See* Savile
Meyer, Franz F., VII, 483
Meyer, Hoppner Francis, VII, 176; VIII, 791; XII, 101
Meyer, Jeann (?) George, IV, 702
Meyer, Leopold von, XII, 503
Meyer, Minna (Carpenter), X, 138
Meyerbeer, Giacomo. *See* Beer, Jakob Liebmann Meyer
Meyers, Dorothy (Crysler), VIII, 194
Meyers, Jacob, VI, 503
Meyers, John Walden, V, 550; VI, **502–4**
Meyers, Polly. *See* Kruger
Meyers, Sophia. *See* Davy
Meynardie, Monsieur (businessman), V, 395
Meynier. *See* Laguide
Meyracq. *See also* Domingué
Meyracq (Mayrac), Marie (Fautoux), III, 216
Mézière. *See also* Lacroix-Mézière
Mézière, Charlotte-Archange (Berthelot), V, 591
Mézière, Henry-Antoine, IV, 534; V, 241, **590–91**; VI, 591, 680
Mézière, Marie-Eugénie. *See* Passy
Mézière, Michel-Archange. *See* Campeau
Mézière, Pierre, V, 590
Mézière, Pierre-François, IV, 5, 270, 534; V, 590, 652; VI, 145
Mézière, Simon-André, V, 590
Mézières, Pierre, VII, 688
Mézières de Lépervanche, Louise-Antoinette de (Gaultier de La Vérendrye), III, 243; IV, 289
Mézillac. *See* Du Pont
Mézy. *See* Le Normant; Saffray
Miall, Edward, XI, 346
Miatt. *See* Myatt
Miçel (Witzel), Gabriel, I, 157
Michaels, Myer, VI, 179
Michaud, Adélaïde (Giroux), IX, 318
Michaud, Alexandre, VII, 147
Michaud, Christophe, VI, 81
Michaud, Élisabeth. *See* Ouellet
Michaud*, François-Xavier-Joseph (1841–1903), XII, 339, 881
Michaud*, Joseph (1823–1902), XI, 93
Michaud, Louis, IV, 124
Michaud, Magdelaine (Dionne), VIII, 222

Michaud, Marie-Salomé (Canac, *dit* Marquis), VII, 147
Michaud, Suzanne (Deschênes), XII, 251
Michaux, André, V, 592
Michaux, André, V, 581, **592–93**; VI, 549; X, 105
Michaux, Cécile. *See* Claye
Michaux, François-André, V, 592, 593
Michaux, Marie-Charlotte. *See* Barbet
Michel, Anne. *See* Fane
Michel, Barbe. *See* Esmard
Michel, Gilles, I, 473
Michel, Jacques, I, 405
Michel, John, XI, 591
Michel, Sir John, IX, 845; X, 74; XI, **591–93**; XII, 750
Michel, Louise Anne. *See* Churchill
Michelance, Marie de (Sallaberry), III, 582
Michelborne, Sir Edward, I, 252
Michel de Danton, Gabriel, IV, 481
Michel de Danton, Gabrielle-Augustine (Lévis, Duchesse de Lévis), IV, 481
Michel de Villebois, Anne. *See* Rostan
Michel de Villebois, Jean-Baptiste, III, 444
Michel de Villebois de La Rouvillière, Honoré, III, 30, 56, 240, 270, 295, **444–46**, 563, 564, 626; IV, 359, 665, 668, 709, 749, 750
Michel de Villebois de La Rouvillière, Honoré-Henri-Michel-Étienne, III, 445
Michel de Villebois de La Rouvillière, Marie-Catherine-Élisabeth. *See* Bégon de La Cour
Michel de Villebois de La Rouvillière, Marie-Catherine-Élisabeth, III, 240, 445
Michelet, Jeanne (Guyart), I, 351
Michelet, Jules, XI, 276; XII, 826
Michelet Du Cosnier, Marie-Françoise (Hocquart), IV, 354
Michelle, Bertrane (Lemaître), III, 377
Michiconiss (Michiguiss). *See* Madjeckewiss
Michie, James, XII, 44
Michikinakoua (Michikiniqua), V, 3, **593–95**, 796, 808, 852; VI, 189, 325; VII, 347, 847
Michipichy, II, 505; III, xxxv, **446**, 495; IV, liii
Michon, Abel, II, 156; III, 237
Michon, Geneviève (Taché), IX, 774
Mickle, Sara, V, 114
Micoc. *See* Mikak
Middleton, Ann (Laidlaw), XI, 481
Middleton, Charles, XII, 733
Middleton, Charles, 1st Baron Barham, V, 281
Middleton, Christopher, II, 10, 314, 493, 604; III, 302, 303, 415, **446–50**, 471, 472, 490, 520, 544, 599, 624, 625, 662, 663; IV, 218, 339, 377, 380
Middleton, Eugénie, Lady Middleton. *See* Doucet
Middleton, Fanny. *See* Wheatley
Middleton, Sir Frederick Dobson, XI, 326, 459, 562, 600, 697, 747, 749, 929; XII, 74, 75, 84, 96, 119, 450, 554, 577, **732–36**
Middleton, Jane, III, 449
Middleton, Judith (Isbister), III, 449; IV, 380
Middleton, Mary Emily. *See* Hassall
Middleton, Robert, X, **512–13**
Middleton, Roger, I, 300
Middleton, Sarah Louisa (Broke, Lady Broke), VII, 106
Mieray. *See* Myeerah
Miertsching, C. A. *See* Erxleben
Miertsching, Erdmuth. *See* Naacké

Miertsching, Johann, X, 513
Miertsching, Johann August, X, **513–14**; XII, 38
Miertsching, Marie (Jannasch), X, 513
Migeon, Jean, I, 508
Migeon, Marie. *See* Desbordes
Migeon de Branssat, Catherine. *See* Gauchet de Belleville
Migeon de Branssat, Jean-Baptiste, I, 47, 79, 105, **508**, 541;
    II, 193, 205, 223, 305; III, 402, 450; IV, 535
Migeon de Branssat, Marie-Anne, named de la Nativité, IV,
    **535–36**; V, 224
Migeon de Branssat, Thérèse-Denise (Juchereau de
    Saint-Denys; Liénard de Beaujeu), II, 305; III, 400, 402;
    V, 498
Migeon de La Gauchetière, Daniel, II, 224; III, 378, **450**,
    520
Migeon de La Gauchetière, Marie. *See* Le Gay de Beaulieu
Migeon de La Gauchetière, Marie-Thérèse (Le Marchand
    de Lignery), III, 378; IV, 178
Mighells. *See* Miles
Mignac (Mignaque). *See* Miniac
Mignault, Basile, IX, 548
Mignault, Josephte-Aurélie (Lagueux), VI, 384
Mignault, Marie-Aurélie (Boyer), IX, 78
Mignault, Marie-Josephte. *See* Ledoux
Mignault, Pierre-Marie, V, 186; VI, 589, 593; VIII, 626;
    IX, 78, 193, **548–49**; X, 428
Mignault, Roch-Moïse-Samuel, IX, 315
Migneau, Louis, IV, 629
Migner, Octave, XII, 126
Migneron, Geneviève. *See* Leduc
Migneron, Marguerite (Kelly), VIII, 455
Migneron, Thérèse (Serres), V, 752
Mignon, Marguerite-Jeanne (Legardeur de Repentigny),
    IV, 449
Mignon, Philippe-Jean-Baptiste, IV, 449
Mignot, Marie-Cécile (Raymond), III, 617
Mignot, *dit* Chatillon, Jean, I, 490
Mignot, *dit* Chatillon, Louise. *See* Cloutier
Mignowitz, Henry, VII, 483; IX, 599
Mikahestow, John. *See* Mékaisto
Mikak, III, 411; IV, **536–37**, 740
Mikinak, III, xxxix, 328, **450–51**, 496; IV, 464
Milan, Duke of. *See* Sforza
Milan, William, V, 465
Milard, Fanny (Doan; Doan), VII, 253
Milbanke, Ann, Lady Milbanke. *See* Delavall
Milbanke, Mark, V, 361, 408, **595–96**, 632; VI, 244, 323,
    636
Milbanke, Mary. *See* Webber
Milbanke, Sir Ralph, V, 595
Milbourne, Ann (Pozer), XI, 710
Milburn, Thomas, VIII, 856
Milby, Isabella (Merritt), VII, 601
Mildmay, William, III, 30
Miles. *See also* Henry, Walter
Miles, Abner, V, 419, 420, **596–98**; VII, 207
Miles, Anna (mother of EDWARD MADAN), IX, 549
Miles, Charles Falconer, IX, 549
Miles, Charlotte. *See* Mears
Miles, Edward Madan, IX, **549–50**
Miles, Elijah, IX, 551; X, 230
Miles, Elijah, V, 355; VI, **504–5**, 740, 755; VII, 610
Miles, Eliza. *See* Moore

Miles, Elizabeth. *See* Harding
Miles, Elizabeth. *See* Wilson
Miles, Ephraim, IX, 550
Miles, Frances. *See* Cornwell
Miles, Frederick William, VI, 504; VII, 216, **610–11**, 916;
    VIII, 118; XII, 445
Miles, George, VI, 504
Miles, Hannah. *See* Olmstead
Miles, Henry Hopper, XI, 345; XII, **736–38**
Miles, James, V, 597
Miles, Justus, VI, 504
Miles, L. Richard, XII, 736
Miles, Laura. *See* Spafford
Miles, Lawford Edward, IX, 549
Miles, Louisa. *See* Johnson
Miles, Lucinda. *See* Daniels
Miles, Margaret (Hilyard), X, 349
Miles, Marianne Adelaide (MacDougall, Lady Mac-
    Dougall), XII, 621
Miles, Mary. *See* Hopper
Miles, Mary Elizabeth (Bibb), VIII, 89
Miles, Mercy (wife of ABNER), V, 596
Miles, Nelson Appleton, XI, 869
Miles, Richard, XI, 924
Miles, Robert Seaborn, VIII, 813; XII, 446
Miles, Samuel (brother of ELIJAH), VI, 504
Miles, Samuel (clergyman), II, 663
Miles, Stephen, V, 169; VI, 722; VII, 471; VIII, 514; IX,
    333, **550–51**
Milette, Alexis, IX, **551–52**; X, 301; XI, 505, 506
Milette, Bénoni, IX, 552
Milette, Joseph, IX, 551, 552; XI, 505
Milette, Joseph-Octave-Norbert, IX, 552
Milette, Judith. *See* Leblanc
Milette, Marie. *See* Hébert
Milette, Michel, IX, 552
Milette, Pierre, IX, 552
Mill, James, IX, 817
Mill, John Stuart, IX, 817; X, 607, 608; XII, 148, 243
Millage. *See* Millidge
Millais, John Guille, IX, 160
Millar, Eleanor Catherine. *See* Gibb
Millar, James, VII, 612
Millar, James, VII, **611–12**; XI, 5; XII, 809
Millar, James Morton, VII, 612
Millar, John, VIII, 122
Millar*, John (1842–1905), XI, 587
Millard, Jessie (Secord), VII, 780
Millard, Lucy (Duncombe), IX, 228
Mille, Claire-Sophie. *See* Bonnet
Mille, Hypolite, VIII, 291
Mille, Hypolite-Joseph. *See* Fenouillet, Émile de
Milledge. *See also* Millidge
Milledge, John, V, 598
Miller, Adelaide Augusta. *See* Chamberlain
Miller, Alexander, VI, 751
Miller, Andrew, V, 608
Miller, Ann (Read), VIII, 743
Miller, Anne Jeanette. *See* Curtis
Miller, Annie (Muir), VIII, 646; XI, 626
Miller, Benjamin, X, 514
Miller, Ellen (Howatt), XII, 452
Miller, Garret Trafalgar Nelson, X, 534

391

Miller, George, V, 373; VI, 367
Miller, George Martell, XII, 708
Miller, Helen. *See* Dow
Miller, Henrietta. *See* Ranney
Miller, Henry, IV, 714; VI, 175, 580
Miller, Hugh, XII, **738–39**
Miller, James, V, 204, 546, 634, 780; VI, 113, 535, 536
Miller, James Andrews, XI, **593–94**
Miller, Jane, VI, 113, 536
Miller, John (clergyman), XII, 681
Miller, John (father of JAMES ANDREWS), XI, 593
Miller, John (member of the Patrons of Industry), XII, 708
Miller, John (shipowner), VIII, 369
Miller, John Bellamy, XI, 594
Miller, John Classon, XI, **594**; XII, 70
Miller, Kenneth A., XII, 738
Miller, L., XII, 96
Miller, Laura. *See* Hamlin
Miller, Lewis, XII, 701, 702
Miller, Linus Wilson, VII, 56, 405, 924; VIII, 419; IX, 124; X, 483, **514**; XII, 1079
Miller, Margaret (Binney), V, 81
Miller(?), Margaret (Greese; Henry), IV, 343
Miller, Maria (Bell), VII, 69
Miller, Maria Frances Ann. *See* Morris
Miller, Mary (Lanctot), X, 420
Miller, Mary (Tupper), XI, 895
Miller, Mary Ann Elizabeth (Carter), X, 140
Miller, Mary Elizabeth (Gilpin), XII, 368
Miller, Melita. *See* Hayes
Miller, Michael, IV, 194
Miller, Penelope (Clopper), VII, 187
Miller, Peter, XI, 547
Miller, Priscilla Victoria (Orr), XII, 806
Miller, Richard, XI, 593
Miller, Samuel, XI, 594
Miller, Thomas, I, 519
Miller, William (adventist), VIII, 106, 271, 747
Miller, William (engraver), XII, 1109
Miller, William (merchant), XI, 406
Miller, William (official), V, 608
Miller, William (paper manufacturer), XI, 547; XII, 135
Miller, William (politician), XI, 698, 933
Miller, William (son of HUGH), XII, 738
Miller, William T., XI, 547
Millet. *See also* Heu
Millet, Jean-François, X, 410; XII, 288, 328
Millet, Jeanne (Langlois), I, 417
Millet, Pierre, I, 322, 634; II, xxxvi, 107, 237, 255, **473–74**; III, 104
Millette. *See also* Milette
Millette, Mme (houseowner), VI, 488
Millidge, Harriet Maria (Johnston), VII, 444
Millidge, John, V, 598
Millidge, Mercy. *See* Berker
Millidge, Phoebe (Chandler), X, 157
Millidge, Sarah. *See* Simonds
Millidge, Thomas, IV, 626; V, 94, **598–99**; VII, 612
Millidge, Thomas, V, 598, 647; VI, 655; VII, 444, **612–13**; VIII, 224, 806; X, 620
Millidge, Thomas Edward, VII, 613; XII, 560, 785
Millier, Hilaire, XI, **594–95**
Millier, Jean-Baptiste, XI, 594

Millier, Thérèse. *See* Labossière
Milligan, Margaret Gordon (Hawkey; FitzRoy, Lady Fitzroy), VIII, 295, 297
Millington, Mary Ann (Prince), IX, 643, 644, 645, 646
Millman, William, XII, 426
Milloy, Alexander, X, 515
Milloy, Donald, X, 515
Milloy, Duncan, VIII, 966; X, **515**
Milloy, Euphemia. *See* Thompson
Milloy, William, X, 515
Mills, Anna Cecilia. *See* Craigie
Mills, Aurora. *See* Holton
Mills, Christina. *See* Hesse
Mills*, David (1831–1903), X, 294; XII, 140, 204, 607, 729, 822
Mills, Edward, I, 672
Mills, Frederick W., X, 228
Mills, George, VII, 922
Mills, Harriet Ann (Roche; Boomer), XI, 89
Mills, Isabella (Monk), VII, 624
Mills, James, X, 515
Mills, James A., XII, 887
Mills, John, IX, 164
Mills, John B., X, 404
Mills, John Easton, IX, 276, 288
Mills, Joseph Langley, V, 489; VI, 206, 320, **505–8**, 527, 537, 581, 734, 735; VII, 15, 190, 488, 527, 614, 646, 675, 682, 727, 767, 809, 826, 878; VIII, 937; IX, 110; XII, 1000
Mills, Mary Louisa (Johnson, Lady Johnson), XII, 476
Mills, Moses, VI, 505
Mills, Samuel Sylvester, IX, 611; X, **515–16**; XI, 414
Mills, Sarah (mother of JOSEPH LANGLEY), VI, 505
Mills, Sir Thomas, IV, 198, **537–38**, 579, 792; V, 142, 191, 289, 370
Mills, William, XII, 139
Mills, William Neilson, XII, 786
Millward, Joseph Henry, XI, 418
Milly, Catherine. *See* Baudry
Milly, François, III, 452; IV, 645
Milly, François, III, **451–52**; IV, 253
Milly, Gaspard, III, 451
Milly, Jean, III, 451
Milly, Louise. *See* Dupuy
Milly, Marie. *See* Aubert
Milly, Thomas (brother of FRANÇOIS), III, 451
Milly, Thomas (nephew of FRANÇOIS), IV, 422
Milly, *dit* La Croix, Jean, III, 451; IV, 239
Milmine, Alexander, V, 259
Milne, Alexander, IX, 313
Milne, Eliza (Gibson), IX, 313
Milne, James, VI, 53
Milne*, John C. (1838–1922), VI, 253
Milne, William H., VII, 81
Milner, Christopher, X, **516**
Milner, Isaac, VII, 825
Milner, Sarah E. (Ketchum), XII, 484
Milnes, Charlotte Frances, Lady Milnes. *See* Bentinck
Milnes, Eleanor (Macdonnell), XII, 615
Milnes, John, VII, 613
Milnes, Mary. *See* Shore
Milnes, Sir Robert Shore, IV, 135; V, 18, 45, 95, 106, 121, 206, 209, 212, 213, 214, 215, 218, 226, 234, 246, 247,

291, 292, 319, 374, 384, 398, 439, 449, 470, 486, 494, 577, 579, 648, 649, 651, 655, 659, 692, 792, 794, 880, 881; VI, 106, 201, 338, 346, 483, 513, 524, 537, 559, 560, 581, 588, 593, 594, 641, 642; VII, 96, 357, 402, 486, **613–16**, 668, 767, 771, 784, 873; VIII, 675, 842; X, 77
Milot, Jean, II, 105
Milton, Lady. *See* Beauclerk
Milton, Viscount. *See* Wentworth-Fitzwilliam
Milton, Catharine (McKenzie), VI, 469
Milton, Frances (Trollope), XI, 861
Milton, John, V, 630; VIII, 744; XII, 516, 945
Mīmīy, XI, **595–96**, 712
Minahikosis, XI, 459, **596–97**, 598, 599; XII, 780
Minavavana. *See* Minweweh
Minchilay, II, 503
Minchin, William, XII, 21
Mindham, Catherine (Isham), III, 301
Mine, Jean de, II, 593
Mine, Marie-Anne de. *See* Saint-Ours
Minet, Monsieur (engineer), I, 180
Minet, Anne. *See* Bonhomme
Minet, Anne (Perthuis), II, 520
Minet, Marie-Madeleine. *See* Lefebvre
Minet, Marie-Madeleine, III, 494
Mingan. *See* Jolliet
Miniac, Jean-Pierre de, III, 120, 196, 203, 285, 343; IV, 295, 387, 430, **538–40**
Minissis. *See* Guiboche, Louis
Minixi. *See* Onistah-sokaksin
Minnitt, Anne (Fitzgerald), XII, 318
Minns, Martha (Howe), VI, 332, 508
Minns, Sarah (mother of WILLIAM), 508
Minns, Sophia. *See* Brown
Minns, Sophia Ann (Godfrey), VI, 508
Minns, William, VI, 508
Minns, William, VI, 322, 333, **508**; VIII, 922; X, 664
Minor, Keturah (Denison), VI, 186
Minot, Mercy (Wiswall), V, 870
Minto, Earl of. *See* Elliot; Elliot-Murray-Kynynmound
Minweweh, III, xxxviii, 262, **452–53**, 530, 660; IV, lv, 78, 233, 241, 582; V, 129, 567; VI, 317; VIII, 744
Miot, *dit* Girard, Angélique (Cuvillier), VII, 224
Miot-Girard, Hilaire, XI, 698
Mirabeau, Marie (Mesplet), IV, 532, 533, 534
Miramion. *See* Beauharnais
Miramont, Monsieur de (officer), II, 182, 184
Mirande, Marguerite. *See* Bourgeois
Mirau, Magdeleine (Doucet), VI, 216; VIII, 231
Miray, Louis, V, 463
Mirepoix. *See* Lévis-Mirepoix
Mires. *See* Meyers
Mireux, Marie-Madeleine (Daulé), VIII, 201
Miriot, Jeanne (Hertel), I, 368
Miristou, I, 61, 195, 479, **508–9**
Miron. *See* Morin
Miscomote (Miscamote), II, **474**
Miscouaky (Misconky, Miscoualzy), II, xxxvii, 414, 453, **474–75**, 505; III, 446
Misèle. *See* Bonne
Miserable Man. *See* Kittimakegin
Miskel, Caroline. *See* Scales, Caroline
Mis-koo-kee-new (Red Eagle, Henry Prince), IX, 626

Miskouaky. *See* Miscouaky
Miskouensa, II, 499
Mis-kwa-bun-o-kwa, VII, 845
Misquahke. *See* Jones, Alfred Augustus
Missègle. *See* Bonne
Missenden, Samuel, I, **509–10**
Missilier, Françoise (Bourgeaux), X, 81
Mistahimaskwa, XI, 112, 261, 306, 444, 459, 460, 461, 596, **597–601**, 613, 675, 696, 745, 747; XII, 120, 478, 735, 780, 855, 858
Mistawāsis (Big Child), XI, 695
Mistigoose (wife of Robert Goodwin), VI, 321
Mitchell, Miss (Roubaud), IV, 686
Mitchell, Alexander, XII, 827
Mitchell, Andrew (grandfather), VI, 508
Mitchell, Andrew, VI, 510
Mitchell, Ann. *See* Dobie
Mitchell, Barbara. *See* Grant
Mitchell, Daniel, VI, 509, 510
Mitchell, David, V, 391; VI, 509, 665
Mitchell, David, V, 715; VI, **508–11**; VII, 582; VIII, 831
Mitchell, Elizabeth. *See* Anderson
Mitchell, Elizabeth. *See* Bertrand
Mitchell, Elizabeth (Radcliff), VII, 719
Mitchell, Emma Jane (Goldie), XII, 378
Mitchell, Frances (McDonald), X, 459
Mitchell, George, VI, 510
Mitchell, George, III, **453**
Mitchell, Harriet. *See* Ussher
Mitchell, Isabella. *See* Carvell
Mitchell, James (businessman), XI, 150
Mitchell, James (clergyman), VII, 531, 535, 536, 537, 538, 539, 540
Mitchell, James (judge), VI, 92; X, 459; XI, 784
Mitchell, James (son of James, clergyman) VII, 540
Mitchell, James, XI, 448; XII, **739–40**
Mitchell, Jessie (Crawford), VI, 509
Mitchell, John (commodore), II, 439
Mitchell, John (mapmaker), VI, 142
Mitchell, John (Methodist missionary), V, 68
Mitchell, John (Presbyterian clergyman), VI, 807
Mitchell, Maria. *See* Gregory
Mitchell, Mary (Polly) (Welch), V, 845
Mitchell, Mary Anne. *See* Ryder
Mitchell, Peter, XII, 740
Mitchell, Peter, IX, 413; X, 288; XI, 466, 475, 578, 579, 833; XII, **740–44**, 978, 979, 1056, 1105, 1107, 1130
Mitchell, Ross, XII, 953
Mitchell, Samuel, VII, 237
Mitchell, Samuel Alfred, XII, 1102
Mitchell, Sarah. *See* Taylor
Mitchell, Sarah (Townsend), known as Sarah Grosvenor, XII, 1067
Mitchell, Thomas, III, 123, 127, 406, **453–54**, 533
Mitchell, W., IX, 479
Mitchell, William (father of JAMES), XII, 739
Mitchell, William (partner of Joseph FORSYTH), V, 327
Mitchell, William (son of DAVID), VI, 510
Mitchell, William (theatre owner), IX, 597
Mitchell, William Roland, XI, 663
Mitcheson, Catherine (Bagg), X, 32
Mitcheson, Frances. *See* MacGregor
Mitcheson, Robert, X, 32

Mitchikiweese. *See* Madjeckewiss
Mite8ameg8k8 (Marie Couc, *dit* Lafleur), III, 147
Mitewemeg. *See* Metiwemig
Mitford, James, III, 287
Mitford, Mary Russell, XI, 858
Mith-coo-coo-man E'Squaw (Agathas, Mary) (wife of
    William Hemmings COOK), VII, 206, 207
Mitigoukwe (Jeanne), I, 640
Mitscherlich, Eilhard, XI, 218
Mit'tee'na'pew. *See* Matonabbee
Mittleberger, Ann Maria (Rykert), VIII, 785
Mittleberger, Charles, VIII, 785, 786
Mittleberger, John, VIII, 785, 786
Mitton, Elizabeth (Clarke), I, 654
Mius. *See also* Meuse
Mius, Francis, III, 358, 359, 418
Mius d'Entremont, Anne, Baronne de Pobomcoup. *See*
    Saint-Étienne de La Tour
Mius d'Entremont, Jacques, Baron de Pobomcoup (father),
    I, 510, 514; II, 205, 512
Mius d'Entremont, Jacques, Baron de Pobomcoup, VII,
    275
Mius d'Entremont, Madeleine, I, 510
Mius d'Entremont, Madeleine, Baronne de Pobomcoup.
    *See* Hélie Du Tillet
Mius d'Entremont, Marguerite, Baronne de Pobomcoup.
    *See* Amirault
Mius d'Entremont, Marguerite (Melanson, *dit* La Verdure),
    I, 500, 510; III, 83
Mius d'Entremont, Philippe, I, 510; II, 3, 7
Mius d'Entremont, Philippe, Baron de Pobomcoup, I, **510**,
    595; IV, 247; VII, 275; XI, 303
Mius d'Entremont, Thérèse. *See* Abbadie de Saint-Castin
Mius d'Entremont de Pobomcoup, Anne (Saillans; Pastour
    de Costebelle; Navailles, Baronne de Labatut), II, 512
Mius d'Entremont de Pobomcoup, Jeanne (Du Pont
    Duchambon), IV, 247, 249
Mius d'Entremont de Pobomcoup, Marie (Du Pont
    Duvivier), II, 205; III, 499, 552; IV, 250, 783
Mius de Plemazais, Abraham, I, 510, 514
Mius de Plemazais, Marguerite. *See* Saint-Étienne de La
    Tour
Miville, Charlotte. *See* Maugis
Miville, François, I, 511
Miville, Jacques, I, 511ʹ
Miville, Marie (Amiot, *dit* Villeneuve), I, 60
Miville, Marie-Anne (Crémazie), X, 201, 202
Miville, Pierre, known as Le Suisse, I, **511**
Miville Dechêne, François-Gilbert, XII, 695
Mixter, Charles Whitney, X, 608, 609
Mkedepenase (Blackbird), VII, 821
Moberly, Frank, XII, 447
Moberly, Henry John, VIII, 3
Moberly, Walter, X, 112; XI, 764
Mociño. *See* Moziño
Modjeska, Helena; Modrzejewska, Jadwiga. *See* Opid,
    Jadwiga
Moffat, George, XII, 752
Moffatt. *See also* Johnstone
Moffatt, Caroline. *See* Covert
Moffatt, George, V, 544, 636; VI, 238, 254, 255, 260, 273,
    602, 644; VII, 342, 453, 478, 611, 612, 620, 682, 717;
    VIII, 21, 321, 542, 543, 631, 836; IX, 166, 290, 316,

373, 396, **553–56**, 650, 696, 697; X, 440, 520, 524, 591,
    708; XI, 41, 58, 188, 874; XII, 349, 744
Moffatt, John Ogilvy, X, 524
Moffatt, Kenneth MacKenzie, XII, 745
Moffatt, Lewis, IX, 553; XI, 582; XII, **744–45**
Moffatt, Lewis Henry, XII, 745
Moffatt, Sophia. *See* MacRae
Mog, II, 475
Mog, II, xxxvi, **475–77**, 645; III, xxxvii, 477, 584
Mogé. *See* Gadois
Mogford, John, XII, 793
Mohier, Gervais, I, **511**
Mohr, Mme (merchant), XII, 745
Mohr, Amelia, XII, 745
Mohr, Blume. *See* Levi
Mohr, Clara, XII, 745
Mohr, E. P., XII, 745
Mohr, Eugene Phillip, XII, 745, 747
Mohr, Fanny, XII, 745
Mohr, Henry Ralph, XII, 745
Mohr, Herman, XII, 745
Mohr, Lenorah, XII, 745
Mohr, Philippine, XII, 745
Mohr, Sigismund, XII, **745–47**
Moile, Nicholas Thirning. *See* Bliss, Henry
Moir, Alexander, XI, 906
Moir, Benjamin, XII, 747
Moir, Isabella (Paton), XII, 827
Moir, James William, XII, 747
Moir, Maria. *See* Ward
Moir, Mary Isabella. *See* Church
Moir, William Church, XI, 906; XII, **747–48**
Moira, Earl of. *See* Rawdon-Hastings
Moireau, Claude, I, 264; II, **477–78**
Moisan, Cécile (Petit-Clair), VIII, 701
Moisan, Claire (Vézina), XI, 901
Moisan, Marie-Denis (Robitaille), XII, 911
Moissacq. *See* Hillaire
Molé, Marie-Louise (Talon, Marquise de Boulay), III, 458
Molesby (Mosely), Solomon, VII, 363, 364
Molesworth, Arthur Nepean, X, 516
Molesworth, Balfour Nepean, X, 517
Molesworth, Harriett. *See* Hawkins
Molesworth, Sarah Georgina. *See* Kertland
Molesworth, Thomas Nepean, X, **516–17**
Molesworth, Sir William, VIII, xxxiv
Molière. *See* Poquelin, Jean-Baptiste
Molin, Antoine-Alexis, VII, 256
Molin, Laurent, I, 63
Molin, Marie (Bermen de La Martinière), II, 57
Molina, Count of. *See* Carlos
Moll. *See also* Berczy
Moll, Albrecht Theodor, V, 70
Moll, Johanna Josepha Walpurga. *See* Hefele
Moll, Johann Albrecht Ulrich (Wilhelm Albert Ulrich von).
    *See* Berczy, William
Moll, Joseph, IX, 210; XII, 506
Molleur, Jacques-Emery, XII, 695
Molleur*, Louis (1828–1904), XII, 693, 694
Mollineda y Losada, Francisca de (Bodega), IV, 72
Molloy, Jane (Devine), XI, 256
Molloy, John William, IX, 720, 794; X, 178
Molony, Belinda, named Sister Mary Xavier, IX, **556–57**

Molson, Alexander, VIII, 633

Molson, Anne (Molson), X, 519, 522; XII, 235, **748–49**

Molson, Edith, XII, 749

Molson, Elizabeth. *See* Badgley

Molson, Elizabeth Sarah Badgley (Macpherson, Lady Macpherson), X, 522; XII, 682, 748

Molson, George Elsdale, VIII, 633

Molson, Harriet Bousfield (Clerk), IX, 558

Molson, John (grandfather of JOHN, 1763–1836), VII, 616

Molson, John (son of JOHN, 1787–1860), VIII, 633; X, 522, 525; XII, 748

Molson, John, VI, 104, 238, 259, 469; VII, 110, **616– 21**; VIII, 325, 369, 542, 630, 781; IX, 557, 597; X, 517, 518, 519, 520; XI, 533

Molson, John, VI, 238, 260; VII, 594, 617, 618, 619, 620; VIII, 268, 543, 544, **630–34**; IX, 280, 373, 554, 557, 558; X, 23, 517, 518, 519, 520, 521, 522, 524, 525; XII, 748

Molson, John Henry Robinson, VIII, 632; IX, 289, 558; X, 520, 521, 523, 524

Molson, John Thomas, IX, 558, 559; XII, 5

Molson, Joseph Dinham, VIII, 633

Molson, Louisa Goddard. *See* Frothingham

Molson, Martha (Molson), VIII, 630; IX, 557, 558; X, 520

Molson, Martha Ann (Spragge), IX, 558

Molson, Mary. *See* Elsdale

Molson, Mary Ann Elizabeth (Barrett), IX, 558

Molson, Mary Ann Elizabeth (Molson), VIII, 630

Molson, Samuel Elsdale, VIII, 633

Molson, Sarah Insley. *See* Vaughan

Molson, Sophia. *See* Stevenson

Molson, Thomas, VII, 229, 617, 618, 619, 620; VIII, 630, 631, 632, 633; IX, **557–59**, 577; X, 517, 518, 519, 520, 521, 522, 523, 524

Molson, William, X, 522

Molson, William, VI, 291, 602; VII, 30, 606, 617, 618, 619, 620; VIII, 630, 631, 632, 633, 815; IX, 224, 557, 558, 559, 792; X, 219, **517–26**; XI, 40, 281, 315, 533, 803; XII, 232, 262, 682, 748, 810

Molson, William Markland, IX, 558; X, 524; XI, 496

Molt, Adolphe-Alphonse, VIII, 635

Molt, Frédéric-Félix, VIII, 635

Molt, Harriett. *See* Cowan

Molt, Henriette. *See* Glackmeyer

Molt, Théodore-Frédéric, VI, 40; VII, 348, 775; VIII, **634–36**; X, 229

Molyneux, Elizabeth (Kelly; Shuldham; Butler), IV, 707

Molyneux, Émery, I, 252

Mompesson, Anne (Porteous), VII, 700

Monbeton de Brouillan, Charlotte de. *See* Des Roches Duplesy

Monbeton de Brouillan, Georgette de. *See* Pouy

Monbeton de Brouillan, Jacques de, II, 478

Monbeton de Brouillan, Jacques-François de, I, 246, 530; II, 3, 6, 36, 37, 45, 64, 167, 169, 177, 246, 257, 258, 382, 395, 411, 434, 442, 445, **478–82**, 510, 579, 590, 605, 626, 654, 666; III, 177, 207, 454, 681, 682

Monbeton de Brouillan, *dit* Saint-Ovide, Joseph de, II, 12, 22, 23, 122, 152, 198, 218, 219, 220, 225, 255, 336, 339, 411, 412, 417, 439, 479, 482, 510, 511, 512, 524, 610, 611, 619, 643, 649; III, 6, 20, 22, 79, 93, 116, 120, 157, 173, 177, 178, 191, 208, 222, 264, 357, 368, 386, 387, 388, 389, 396, **454–57**, 475, 500, 512, 532, 566, 567,

574, 575, 576, 597, 630, 644; IV, 15, 247, 252, 360, 466

Moncarville. *See* Legardeur

Monceaux. *See* Clément; Ruette

Moncel. *See* Giffard

Moncharvaux. *See* Tisserant

Monchy. *See* Mouchy

Monck, Bridget, Viscountess Monck. *See* Willington

Monck, Charles Joseph Kelly, 3rd Viscount Monck, XII, 749

Monck, Charles Stanley, 4th Viscount Monck, IX, 33, 253, 268, 385, 714, 777, 778; X, 103, 122, 146, 148, 405, 465, 466, 467; XI, 82, 280, 592, 634, 905, 932, 933; XII, 151, 597, 598, **749–51**, 983, 1053, 1054

Monck, Lady Elizabeth Louise Mary (Monck, Viscountess Monck), XI, 84; XII, 749, 751

Monck, Henry Stanley, 1st Earl of Rathdowne, XII, 749

Monckton, Elizabeth, Viscountess Galway. *See* Manners

Monckton, John, 1st Viscount Galway, IV, 540

Monckton, Robert, III, xxvi, 87, 129, 362, 363, 364, 365, 425, 479, 513, 570, 589, 590, 601, 605, 667, 668, 669, 670, 672; IV, xxv, xxviii, 22, 36, 93, 141, l93, 213, 250, 289, 335, 382, 436, 452, 453, 501, **540–42**, 570, 631, 668, 680, 700, 714, 769, 773, 774, 780; V, 58, 203, 227, 412, 823, 843; VII, 854

Moncoq, Guillaume, VIII, 636

Moncoq, Marie-Anne. *See* Desmottes

Moncoq, Michel, VIII, **636–37**; XII, 183

Moncours. *See* Hertel

Moncrieff, James, IV, 501

Moncroc. *See* Gripière

Mondelé. *See* Mondelet

Mondelet, Anne. *See* Méneveau

Mondelet, Charles-Elzéar, V, 600; VII, 227, 623, 667; VIII, 248, 259, 667; IX, 101, 441, 458, 560; X, 37, 154, 219, 506, **526–28**, 579, 689; XI, 187, 277

Mondelet, Charlotte. *See* Boucher de Grosbois

Mondelet, Didier, V, 599

Mondelet, Dominique, V, **599–600**; VII, 621

Mondelet, Dominique, V, 600; VII, 226, 227, 393, 623, 667, 763, 905, 906; VIII, 259, 284, 667; IX, 441, **559–61**, 650, 696; X, 526, 527, 653; XI, 187, 821

Mondelet, Harriet. *See* Munro

Mondelet, Jean-Marie, V, 183, 591, 600; VI, 59, 238, 433, 434, 584, 634, 787; VII, 227, **621–24**; VIII, 259, 914; IX, 459, 559; X, 526

Mondelet, Juliana. *See* Walker

Mondelet, Marie-Françoise. *See* Hains

Mondelet, Mary. *See* Woolrich

Mondelet, Mary Elizabeth Henrietta. *See* Carter

Mondelet, *dit* Bellefleur. *See* Mondelet

Mondion, Scholastique-Aimée (Plamondon), XII, 853

Mondor. *See* Léonard

Mon-e-guh-ba-now. *See* Maskepetoon

Monet, Jean-Baptiste-Pierre-Antoine de, Chevalier de Lamarck, X, 65

Monet, *dit* Bellehumeur, Marguerite (Riel), XI, 736, 745

Monette. *See* Manette

Money, Miss (nurse), XI, 559

Monfort. *See* Demers

Monforton, Monsieur (merchant), IV, 702

Mongan, Charles, V, 600

Mongenais, Jean-Baptiste-Amédée, XI, 814

Mongenet. *See also* Montgenet
Mongenet, Charles-Benjamin, VI, 517
Mongenet, Charles-Jean, VI, 517
Mongenet, Édouard, VI, 517
Mongenet, Jean-Claude (father), VI, 516
Mongenet, Jean-Claude, VI, 517
Mongenet, Jeanne-Beatrix (Jansac), VI, 517
Mongenet, Jeanne-Claude. *See* Pussot
Mongeon, Marguerite (Cartier, *dit* L'Angevin), V, 164; X, 142
Monger, Susan (Lynch), XI, 535
Monic, Jean de, II, 482
Monic, Jeanne de. *See* Dufresnoy Carion
Monic, Joseph de, II, 36, 45, 214, 434, 479, **482–83**, 510; III, 454, 499
Monic, Marguerite de. *See* Comet
Monière. *See* Lemoine
Monjeau, Marie-Justine (Robitaille), XII, 912
Monk, Ann. *See* Dering
Monk, Caroline. *See* Debartzch
Monk (Monck), Christopher, 2nd Duke of Albemarle, I, 544
Monk, Eliza Ann. *See* Fitzgerald
Monk, Elizabeth. *See* Adams
Monk, Elizabeth Ann (Aubrey), VI, 514
Monk, George Henry, III, 457; VI, 512, 514; VIII, 481
Monk, Henry Wentworth, XII, **751–52**
Monk, Isabella. *See* Mills
Monk, James, III, **457–58**; IV, 526, 560; VI, 511
Monk, Sir James, III, 457; IV, 185, 229, 274, 313, 345, 400, 451, 581, 716; V, 77, 81, 84, 149, 150, 151, 152, 192, 226, 370, 373, 492, 508, 697, 705, 843, 863; VI, 86, 295, 494, **511–15**, 524, 578, 606, 607, 643, 714; VII, 25, 225, 523, 769, 783, 785, 786, 788, 872; VIII, 239, 492, 726, 843; IX, 809
Monk, John Benning, XII, 751
Monk, Maria, VII, **624–26**; VIII, 703
Monk, Samuel Cornwallis, VII, 236; X, 37, 424, 624; XI, 415, 766
Monk, Samuel Wentworth, VIII, 502
Monk, William, VII, 624
Monnier, Henry, VIII, 13
Monnoir. *See* Ramezay
Monplaisir. *See* Dizy
Monrepos. *See* Guiton
Monro. *See also* Munro
Monro, Alexander, XII, **752–53**
Monro, Caroline I. (Innis; wife of ALEXANDER), XII, 753
Monro, Catherine. *See* MacKenzie
Monro, Christine. *See* Fisher
Monro, David, IV, 198; V, 182, 484, 566; VI, 417, **515–16**; VII, 64, 65, 66, 67, 68; VIII, 837, 838
Monro, David Arthur, VII, 68
Monro, George, III, 460; IV, 426
Monro, George, VII, 418; VIII, 255, 523, 524, 798; IX, 346, 725; X, **528–29**; XI, 542, 864
Monro, John (brother of GEORGE), X, 528
Monro, John (father of ALEXANDER), XII, 752
Monro, Mary. *See* Chappell
Monro, Thomas, VI, 526; IX, 578
Monroe, Christy (Holmes), X, 353
Monroe, James, VI, 803; VII, 31; VIII, 389
Monroe, James H., XII, 754, 757

Monroe, Jessie Gordon. *See* McMurdo
Monroe, John (father), XII, 753
Monroe, John, XII, 756
Monroe, Moses, XII, 379, 380, **753–58**, 956
Mons. *See* Monts
Monseignat, Charles de, II, 276, 283, 352, 448, **483–86**, 576; III, 58, 60
Monseignat, Claude de. *See* Sainte
Monseignat, Hélène de. *See* Perchot
Monseignat, Jean de, II, 483
Monseignat, Louis-Denis de, II, 485
Monseignat, Marguerite de. *See* Delesnerac
Monson, Lewis, 1st Baron Sondes, IV, 348
Montagu, Anne (Wilmot), III, 663
Montagu, Basil, VIII, 427
Montagu, Lord Charles Greville, VII, 714
Montagu, Edward, III, 663
Montagu, George, 1st Earl of Halifax, III, 663
Montagu, John, IV, 159, 259, 402, 437, 470; VI, 371
Montagu, John, 4th Earl of Sandwich, IV, 164, 600, 763
Montagu, Mary (Osborn), III, 496
Montagu, William, 5th Duke of Manchester, VII, 316
Montague, Eliza (Thom), VII, 852
Montague, Walter Humphries, XII, 585, 1120
Montaigne. *See also* Eyquem
Montaigne, Michel de, I, 471
Montalan, Éléonore (Berger), II, 54
Montalembert, Comte de. *See* Forbes
Montaño. *See* Rivera
Montarville. *See* Boucher
Montbazillac, Vicomte de. *See* Brisay
Montbeillard. *See* Potot
Montbéliard, Prince of. *See* Leopold Eberhard
Montbrac. *See* Masson
Montbrun. *See also* Boucher
Montbrun, Pierre, V, 258
Montcalm, Angélique-Louise de, Marquise de Montcalm. *See* Talon de Boulay
Montcalm, Louis de, III, 458
Montcalm, Louis-Daniel de, III, 458
Montcalm, Louis-Joseph de, Marquis de Montcalm, II, 43; III, xviii, xix, xx, xxi, xxvi, 12, 19, 55, 84, 85, 86, 99, 102, 161, 171, 188, 198, 289, 293, 328, 400, 406, 408, 441, **458–69**, 510, 526, 534, 535, 537, 554, 555, 570, 588, 669, 670, 671, 672, 673, 676; IV, 5, 14, 23, 34, 54, 63, 68, 84, 88, 96, 143, 146, 183, 211, 214, 224, 242, 257, 307, 308, 312, 347, 353, 382, 395, 401, 426, 449, 459, 460, 478, 479, 480, 481, 482, 487, 495, 500, 503, 514, 521, 530, 531, 563, 582, 589, 612, 616, 620, 633, 636, 637, 641, 642, 651, 660, 662, 669, 670, 671, 672, 673, 674, 687, 729, 733, 739, 773; V, 47, 103, 104, 163, 164, 191, 196, 369, 487, 677, 738, 739, 767, 823, 888; VI, 128, 505, 645, 769, 774; VII, 190, 242, 287, 310, 731, 789, 905; VIII, 18; IX, 75, 250, 360; XI, 588; XII, 424, 502, 825
Montcalm, Marie-Thérèse-Charlotte de. *See* Lauris de Castellane
Montcalm, Marthe de. *See* Gozon
Montchervaux. *See* Tisserant
Montcoq. *See* Moncoq
Monteagle, Baron. *See* Parker; Spring-Rice
Montecalunya. *See* Cabot, John
Montefiore, Sir Moses, XI, 254

Montegron. *See* Levrault

Monteil. *See* Vassal

Montéléon, Louis de, II, 90, 427

Montéléon, Marie-Anne-Josette de. *See* Lestringant de Saint-Martin

Montenach, Marie-Élisabeth de. *See* Grant

Montenach, Wilhelmine-Dudding de (Perrault de Linière; Ryan), XI, 780

Montendre. *See* Longchamps-Montendre

Montespan, Marquise de. *See* Rochechouart de Mortemart

Montesquieu, Baron de. *See* Secondat

Montesson. *See* Legardeur

Montet, Marie (David), II, 170

Montezuma II. *See* Dickson, James

Montferrand. *See also* Favre

Montferrand, Delia. *See* Holmes

Montferrand, *dit* Favre, Esther. *See* Bertrand

Montferrand, *dit* Favre, Hélène, IX, 562

Montferrand, *dit* Favre, Joseph, VIII, 918, 919; IX, **561–65**; XII, 728

Montferrand, *dit* Favre, Joseph-Louis, IX, 563

Montferrand, *dit* Favre, Marie-Anne. *See* Trépanier

Montfort. *See also* Demers

Montfort, François, III, 220

Montgenet, Thérèse-Bernardine, Comtesse de Montgenet, known as Mme de Saint-Laurent, V, 297, 298, 449, 849; VI, 173, 341, 345, **516–18**, 535, 723; VII, 923; XI, 931

Montgolfier, Étienne, II, 414; III, 199, 296, 487; IV, 6, 89, 90, 98, 188, 201, 236, 238, 270, 286, 318, 371, 391, 430, 463, 509, 510, 532, **542–45**, 572, 639; V, 92, 146, 241, 245, 294, 396, 432, 480, 498, 680, 687, 703, 892; VI, 145, 586

Montgolfier, Jacques-Étienne, IV, 542

Montgolfier, Joseph-Michel, IV, 542

Montgolfier, Raymond, IV, 542

Montgomerie, Hugh E., XI, 614

Montgomery, Earl of. *See* Herbert

Montgomery, Alexander, X, 529

Montgomery, Anne (Townshend, Viscountess and Marchioness Townshend), V, 824

Montgomery, Barbara (Walker), VI, 797

Montgomery, Christiana (Cuthbert), VIII, 195, 196

Montgomery, Christine. *See* MacDonald

Montgomery, Donald, VIII, 196; IX, 565

Montgomery, Donald, XI, **601–3**; XII, 48

Montgomery, Elizabeth. *See* Hamilton

Montgomery, Frances (Morrison), XI, 615, 617

Montgomery, Henry, XII, 213

Montgomery, Hugh, VIII, 196; IX, 565

Montgomery, Sir James, IV, 551; V, 268; VI, 565; VII, 408; VIII, 547; XI, 922

Montgomery, Sir James William, IV, 352, 353, 497, 550, 551, 607, 608; V, 219, 220, 262, 263, 310, 311, 477, 478, 514, 720, 777, 778, 779, 824, 826, 848; VII, 407

Montgomery, Janet. *See* Livingston

Montgomery, John, VIII, 196, 809; IX, 146, **565–66**

Montgomery, John, VII, 794; IX, 266, 503, 504, 744; X, 344, 459, 482, 510, **529–30**, 641; XI, 615, 617

Montgomery, Malcolm, XI, 601

Montgomery, Margaret, Lady Montgomery. *See* Scott

Montgomery, Mary. *See* Franklyn

Montgomery, Mary. *See* Ross

Montgomery, Mary. *See* Wilmot

Montgomery, Mary Isabella. *See* McPhail

Montgomery, Nancy. *See* Penman

Montgomery, Richard, IV, 40, 215, 230, 262, 271, 336, 345, 347, 390, 427, 503, 532, **545–50**, 629, 791; V, 5, 30, 31, 36, 40, 64, 98, 131, 147, 164, 191, 254, 272, 331, 358, 383, 396, 414, 492, 572, 575, 652, 802, 812; VI, 16, 202, 403, 695, 769; VII, 89; X, 13

Montgomery, Robert, VI, 162, 401

Montgomery, Thomas, IV, 545

Montgomery, William, IX, 565

Montgomery, William, IV, **550–52**; V, 262, 477, 824, 848

Montgomery, William Scott, IX, 565

Monthelet. *See* Mondelet

Montignac. *See* Hautefort

Montigny. *See also* Papineau; Testard

Montigny, Monsieur de (printer), X, 422

Montigny, François de, II, 110, 134, 171, 331; III, 263, **469–70**, 640, 684, 685

Montigny, Marie-Avine de (Trottier Desrivières), VI, 557

Montigny, Ovide, VIII, 421

Montijo, Eugénie de, Countess of Teba (Eugénie, Empress of the French), VIII, 619

Montisambert; Montizambert. *See* Boucher

Montmagny. *See* Huault

Montmainier, Marie de (Dumas), II, 42

Montminy, Joseph, XII, 758

Montminy, Marguerite. *See* Lambert

Montminy, Théophile, XII, 58, **758–59**

Montmollin, David-François de, IV, 104, 139, 140, 657, 698, 738, 753, 754; V, 146, **600–2**, 613; VI, 305; VII, 644, 673

Montmollin, Élyse de, V, 602

Montmollin, Francis Godot de, V, 601

Montmollin, Jane de. *See* Bell

Montmollin, John Frederick de, V, 601

Montmollin, John Samuel de, V, 601; VI, 179

Montmollin, Louis de, V, 600

Montmollin, Salomé de. *See* Gaudot

Montmorency, Monsieur de (employer of Pierre PERROT de Rizy), II, 520

Montmorency, Charlotte-Marguerite de (Princesse de Condé), I, 484

Montmorency, Emme de, Duchesse de Montmorency. *See* Laval

Montmorency, Henri II de, Duc de Montmorency, I, 159, 186, 187, 194, 195, 427, 433

Montmorency, Mathieu II de, Duc de Montmorency, known as Le Grand, II, 359

Montorgueil. *See* Dauphin

Montortier, Monsieur de (cousin of René GAULTIER de Varennes), I, 327

Montoson, Sieur de (officer), II, 532

Montour, Mme. *See* Couc, Elizabeth

Montour, Monsieur (agent), II, 126

Montour, Andrew (Henry), III, 147, 502; V, 602; VI, 7

Montour, Catherine, III, 147

Montour, Geneviève. *See* Wills

Montour, Henry Isaac Horatio, V, 603

Montour, Julie-Éliza (Malhiot), X, 490

Montour, Louis, III, 147

Montour, Nicholas, V, 373, 494, 561, 562, **602–4**, 738, 821; VI, 7, 432; VII, 200; IX, 152; X, 490

Montour, Nicolas (Nicholas), V, 604; VIII, 342

Montour, Sarah. *See* Ainse
Montpensier, Duc de. *See* Bourbon
Montpensier, Duchesse de. *See* Bourbon; Orléans
Montpetit, André-Napoléon, IX, 437, 438, 563, 564, 565; X, 218, 695; XI, 623; XII, 325
Montpetit*, Édouard (1882–1954), X, 586
Montplaisir. *See* Dizy
Montresor, Frances. *See* Tucker
Montrésor, Frank Montrésor, IV, 553
Montresor, James Gabriel, IV, 552
Montresor, John, IV, **552–53**; V, 657
Montresor, Mary. *See* Haswell
Montreuil. *See* Gohin; Sedillot
Montricoux, Comte de. *See* Maurès
Montricoux, Comtesse de. *See* Savignac
Montrochon. *See* Ménéclier
Montrose, Duke of. *See* Graham
Monts. *See also* Du Gua
Monts, Sieur de, I, 325, **511–12**, 615
Montsaulnin, Adrienne de (Renaud d'Avène de Des Méloizes et de Berges), I, 572
Montviel (Monviel). *See* Vassal
Monty, Catherine (Gosselin), V, 358
Monvoisin, Catherine. *See* Deshayes
Moodey, Samuel, II, 664
Moodie, Agnes Dunbar (FitzGibbon; Chamberlin), XII, 998, 999, 1131
Moodie, Benjamin, IX, 566
Moodie, Donald, IX, 566
Moodie, James, IX, 566
Moodie, John Wedderburn Dunbar, IX, **566–67**; XI, 858, 859, 860; XII, 524, 573, 996
Moodie, Robert (colonel), VII, 519, 635
Moodie, Robert (son of JOHN WEDDERBURN DUNBAR), XI, 860
Moodie, Susanna. *See* Strickland
Moodie, William, XII, 62
Moody, Ann (wife of JOHN), II, 487
Moody, Caleb, III, 470
Moody, Dwight Lyman, XII, 169, 707, 708
Moody, Edward A., VI, 322; IX, 829
Moody, Hampden Clement Blamire, VIII, 101
Moody, Hannah. *See* Sewall
Moody, James, IV, 222; V, **604–5**; IX, 175
Moody, Jane. *See* Robinson
Moody, Janet McAuslyn. *See* Watson
Moody, John (auctioneer), IX, 746
Moody, John (father of JAMES), V, 604
Moody, John, II, 37, 97, 98, 117, 118, 165, 250, 293, 350, 351, 438, 439, **486–87**, 583, 619, 643; III, 618, 619
Moody, Joseph, III, 471
Moody, Joshua, X, 530
Moody, Judith. *See* Bradbury
Moody, Mary, III, 471
Moody, Mary (Gerrish), VI, 283
Moody, Mary Susannah. *See* Hawks
Moody, Phebe, VI, 181
Moody, Richard Clement, IX, 81, 82, 132, 712; X, 112, 245, 246, 701; XI, 394, **603–7**; XII, 78, 544, 815, 833, 1132
Moody, Ruth. *See* Plummer
Moody, Samuel, III, **470–71**
Moody, Sewell Prescott, X, **530–31**; XII, 784

Moody, Thankful (Street), VII, 832
Moody, Thomas, XI, 603
Moody, William, III, 470
Mooers (Moores), Elizabeth (Perley), V, 665
Moon, Henry Frederick. *See* Smith, Henry More
Moon, Henry J., VIII, 391, 502
Moon, Susanna (Bartlett), VIII, 63
Mooney, Mr (lawyer), XII, 330
Mooney, Edward L., IV, 397
Mooney, Sophia M. (Pond), V, 685
Moor, Mary. *See* Bradley
Moor, Mary (Donkin), XI, 266
Moor, Thomas, XI, 648
Moor, William, III, 39, 303, 448, 449, **471–72**, 594, 625, 663
Moore, Miss or Mrs (wife of WEYAPIERSENWAH), V, 852
Moore, Mr (boxer), IX, 562
Moore, Agnes. *See* McKay
Moore, Ann (Collins), VI, 164
Moore, Catherine. *See* Streit
Moore, Catherine (Waller, Lady Waller), VI, 801
Moore, Cécile. *See* Richardson
Moore, Dennis, X, 379; XI, **607–8**
Moore, Edward (master gunner), II, 487
Moore, Edward (son of JOHN WARREN), XII, 759
Moore, Eleanor (Motton), XII, 765
Moore, Elias, VI, 400; IX, 618
Moore, Eliza (Billings; Miles; Cushman), VII, 610, 611
Moore, Elizabeth (Nelles), VII, 650, 651; XI, 639
Moore, Frances (Brooke), IV, 103, 104, **553–56**; V, 130, 228, 582
Moore, George (loyalist), VI, 370
Moore, George (partner of JOHN WARREN), XII, 759
Moore, Harriet A. *See* Stone
Moore, Harris, XII, 759
Moore, J. H., XII, 440
Moore, James, IX, 78
Moore, Jeanne. *See* Lemelin
Moore, John, V, 69; IX, 637
Moore, Sir John, IV, 504; V, 110; VI, 661; VII, 139, 268, 819; VIII, 926; IX, 37, 137; X, 433
Moore, John Warren, XII, **759**
Moore, Joseph, IX, 562
Moore, Leah (Stone), VI, 738
Moore, Mary. *See* Hunt
Moore, Mary. *See* Knowles
Moore, Mary (Roblin), IX, 679
Moore, Mary Louisa. *See* DeWolfe
Moore, Nicholas, X, 531
Moore, Philip Henry, IX, 434, 435; X, **531–32**; XI, 438
Moore, Pierre, II, 487
Moore, Sarah (Digby), IV, 553, 554
Moore, Solomon, VI, 4
Moore, Stephen, V, 314, 315
Moore, Susan. *See* Tyson
Moore, Thankful. *See* Foster
Moore, Thomas (father of FRANCES), IV, 553
Moore, Thomas (poet), VI, 375, 376, 728; VIII, 346, 386; IX, 559
Moore, Thomas (Quaker), V, 642, 643
Moore, Thomas (ship's captain), IV, 32
Moore, Thomas, II, 235, 409, **487–88**
Moore, Thomas Edward Laws, X, 396; XI, 691, 718

Moore, Tristram, XII, 759
Moore, Wilhelmina (Webster), IX, 824
Moore, William (clergyman), X, 550
Moore, William (grandfather of JOHN WARREN), XII, 759
Moore, William, IV, 107, **556–58**, 580; V, 66, 460, 790, 834
Moores. *See also* Mooers
Moores, Elizabeth (Mowat), XII, 768
Moorsom, Eleanor (mother of WILLIAM SCARTH), IX, 567
Moorsom, Isabella. *See* Wilkins
Moorsom, Sir Robert, IX, 567
Moorsom, William Scarth, VII, 803; VIII, 732, 957; IX, **567–68**
Moquet, Denis, II, 278
Moquin, Jean-Baptiste, XII, 546
Moquin, Louis, VII, 161, 349; VIII, 214; X, 24
Moquin, Véronique. *See* Bouthillier
Mora. *See* Mouet
Moral de Saint-Quentin, Marie. *See* Marguerie
Moral de Saint-Quentin, Marie-Thérèse (Véron de Grand-mesnil), II, 648; III, 642
Moral de Saint-Quentin, Quentin, I, 369; II, 16, 63, 648
Morampont. *See* Regnard
Moran, James, VII, 895
Moran, Robert Greer, XII, 785
Moran, Thomas, XI, 683
Morand, Laurent, VIII, 637
Morand, Marie-Anne. *See* Dufresne
Morand, Paul (Hypolithe), V, 436, 437; VI, 487; VIII, **637–38**; XII, 424
Morand, Pélagie. *See* Massue
Moranget. *See* Crevel
Morant, Joseph, VII, 255
Moras. *See* Peirenc
Morasse (Perenne de Moras), Marie (Désilets), VIII, 217
Moray, Elizabeth (Rollo, Baroness Rollo), III, 565
Mordaunt, Charles, 3rd Earl of Peterborough, II, 274
Mordaunt, Sir John, III, 666; IV, 171
Morden, Melinda Burgess (Butler), VI, 98
More, Elizabeth (Rastell), I, 565
More, Hannah, VII, 266
More, Sir Thomas, I, 565, 566
Moreau. *See also* Desjordy; Moireau
Moreau, Monsieur (attorney general), IV, 755
Moreau, Basile, XII, 359
Moreau, Catherine (Adhémar), III, 4; IV, 5; V, 3
Moreau, Charles, XII, 547
Moreau, Edme, III, **472–73**
Moreau, François, III, 300
Moreau, Françoise. *See* Fortier
Moreau, François-Urbain, III, 473
Moreau, Georges, III, 473
Moreau, Gratiane (Hamare), II, 273
Moreau, Hippolyte, VIII, 703; X, **532**
Moreau, Jacques, III, 472
Moreau, Jean, VIII, 559
Moreau, Jean-Baptiste, III, **473–74**, 635, 650; IV, 775; V, 199
Moreau, Louis-Edmond, XI, 344; XII, 57
Moreau, Louis-Ignace, IX, 302
Moreau*, Louis-Zéphirin (1824–1901), X, 430; XI, 485, 488, 595; XII, 304, 1022
Moreau, Marguerite. *See* Germain

Moreau, Marguerite. *See* Tremblay
Moreau, Marie-Joseph (Gaufin), III, 240
Moreau, Marie-Madeleine (Bazil), III, 38
Moreau, Marie-Madeleine (Mechtler), VI, 499
Moreau, Marie-Madeleine (Roma), III, 566
Moreau, Pierre, VII, 149, 264; X, 153, 154, 434, 435
Moreau, Pierre-Moïse, VIII, 210
Moreau, Raphaël, X, 532
Moreau, *dit* Lataupine, Louise-Élisabeth (Lajus), III, 344; IV, 432
Moreau, *dit* La Taupine, Pierre, I, 394; II, 532
Moreau de Brésoles, François, I, 512
Moreau de Brésoles, Françoise. *See* Gailliard
Moreau de Brésoles, Judith, I, 220, 458, 478, 480, 487, **512–13**; II, 164; X, 156
Moreau de Saint-Méry, Médéric-Louis-Élie, III, 556, 634
Moreau de Séchelles, Mlle (Hérault), IV, 76, 755
Morehouse, Daniel, VI, **518–19**; VII, 777
Morehouse, Elizabeth. *See* Sullivan
Morehouse, Jane. *See* Gill
Morehouse, Joseph, VI, 518
Morel, Monsieur (merchant), III, 396
Morel, Captain, I, 292
Morel, Cécile (Chénier), VII, 172
Morel, Claude, I, 469
Morel, François, VI, 582; VIII, 175
Morel, Fréderic, I, 469
Morel, Thomas, I, 108, **513**; II, 19
Morel de La Durantaye, Alliette. *See* Du Houssaye
Morel de La Durantaye, Françoise. *See* Duquet
Morel de La Durantaye, Joseph-François, II, 489
Morel de La Durantaye, Louis-Joseph, III, 291
Morel de La Durantaye, Olivier, I, 444, 479; II, 43, 48, 49, 217, 218, 235, 263, 303, 346, 388, **488–89**, 518, 635; III, 237, 373, 568
Morel de La Durantaye, Thomas, II, 488
Morello, Carlo, Marquis of Malaspina, V, 570
Morello, Catalina Melilupi de, Marchioness of Malaspina. *See* Melilupi
Morency. *See* Baucher; Beauché
Moreri, Louis, II, 208
Moresby, Charlotte (Haynes), XI, 394
Moresby, Sir Fairfax, X, 196, 243
Moreton. *See also* Mortin
Moreton, Ann (Massey), XII, 709
Moreton, Julian, XII, **759–60**
Morgan, Colin, XII, 760
Morgan, Colin Daniel, XII, 761
Morgan, Daniel, V, 31
Morgan, Dorcas Catherine (McGee), IX, 489
Morgan, H. R., VIII, 268
Morgan, Henry, XI, 851; XII, **760–61**
Morgan*, Henry James (1842–1913), V, 18; VIII, 160, 161, 386, 536, 967; IX, 66, 72, 251, 287, 387, 893; X, 680; XI, 129, 152, 204, 298, 322, 323, 324, 558, 680, 838, 871; XII, 76, 249, 316, 662, 922
Morgan, J. H., XI, 522
Morgan, James (father), XII, 761
Morgan, James, XI, 851; XII, 761
Morgan, John Pierpont, XI, 770
Morgan, Lewis Henry, III, 335, 337; IX, 420; XII, 402
Morgan, Mary. *See* Kidd
Morgan, Mary (Harris), XI, 386

Morgan, Mary Elizabeth (Humphreys), XI, 434
Morgan, Sarah (Lundrigan), VI, 409
Morgan, Sarah (Tassie), XI, 868
Morgan, Sydney, Lady Morgan. *See* Owenson
Morgan, William (brother of HENRY), XII, 761
Morgan, William (captain), VI, 421
Morgann, Maurice, IV, xlv, 348, 349; V, 144, 148, **605–7**; VI, 493
Morhouse, Abraham, IV, 37
Morice*, Adrien-Gabriel (1859–1938), XI, 402; XII, 213, 283, 284, 285
Morice, James, IX, 391
Morice, William, V, 204, 476
Morillon, Suzanne (Danré de Blanzy), III, 163
Morillon Du Bourg, I, 435, 436, **513–14**, 636
Morillonnet, *dit* Berry, Claude, III, 633
Morimé. *See* Lamorinie
Morin. *See also* Roberol
Morin, Achille, VIII, 504; XII, **761–63**
Morin, Adèle. *See* Raymond
Morin, Agnès (Bonhomme, *dit* Beaupré), III, 69
Morin, Anne (Louet; Deneau), II, 447
Morin, Antoine (brother of Jean-Baptiste MORIN de Fonfay), IV, 28, 421, 558, 559
Morin, Antoine (fisherman), IV, 124
Morin, Antoinette. *See* Caldwell
Morin, Augustin, IX, 568
Morin, Augustin-Norbert, VI, 382, 802; VII, 7, 32, 61, 148, 353, 427, 606, 739, 757, 789, 856; VIII, 57, 96, 138, 141, 147, 197, 223, 230, 259, 260, 284, 331, 371, 592, 629, 679, 834, 907, 916, 933; IX, 74, 75, 83, 90, 119, 212, 261, 262, 299, 302, 344, 440, 441, 444, 448, 449, 464, 471, 506, 507, 525, **568–72**, 575, 576, 645, 688, 689, 690, 707, 726, 735, 775, 776, 795, 796, 811, 812, 844; X, 37, 95, 96, 119, 126, 133, 134, 135, 143, 144, 151, 169, 170, 201, 226, 256, 321, 462, 464, 508, 512, 526, 533, 548, 574, 580, 581, 591, 632, 642, 654, 722, 724, 725; XI, 70, 160, 166, 170, 176, 178, 180, 232, 238, 273, 282, 341, 366, 408, 411, 413, 414, 416, 519, 616, 618, 677, 698, 721, 730, 822, 837, 852, 853, 939; XII, 72, 184, 261, 262, 501, 593, 614, 1013, 1024, 1032, 1123
Morin, Claude, IV, 558
Morin, Claude-Marie-François, IV, 205
Morin, Félicité. *See* Peltier
Morin (Marin, Miron), Félicité (Franchère), IX, 279
Morin, Germain, I, 264, 392; II, **489**
Morin, Hélène. *See* Desportes
Morin, Jean-Baptiste (clergyman), VII, 669
Morin, Jean-Baptiste (official), I, 264
Morin, Joseph (father of LOUIS-SIMÉON), X, 533
Morin, Joseph (mason), IV, 203
Morin, Joseph-Marie, XII, 507
Morin, Judith (Marchesseault), VIII, 616
Morin, Louis-Siméon, IX, 614; X, 135, 219, 417, **533**; XI, 721; XII, 87, 173
Morin, Madeleine. *See* Lamouraux-Rochefort
Morin, Marianne. *See* Cottin, *dit* Dugal
Morin, Marie, I, 78, 216, 221, 230, 231, 478, 480, 512; II, 133, 466, **489–92**; III, 155, 369
Morin, Marie-Angèle (Lagorce), IX, 452
Morin, Marie-Anne (Deguise, *dit* Flamand), III, 170; IV, 202

Morin, Marie-Anne (Pinguet de Vaucour), III, 521
Morin, Marie-Archange (Fournier), XII, 323
Morin, Marie-Esther. *See* Routier
Morin, Marie-Eugénie-Henriette (Labelle), XII, 503
Morin, Marie-Françoise (Poireaux; Raby), IV, 650
Morin, Marie-Madeleine (Rageot), I, 561; II, 540, 541
Morin, Noël, I, 264; II, 489
Morin, Octave, VIII, 479
Morin, Paul, VII, 18
Morin, Pierre-Hector, XII, 761, 762
Morin, Pierre-Louis, VI, 554; XI, 588
Morin, Samuel, V, 816
Morin, Victoire. *See* Côté
Morin*, Victor (1865–1960), IX, 438
Morin, William, V, 117
Morin, *dit* Chêneverd, Marie-Élizabeth (Bruneau), V, 116
Morin de Fonfay, Jean-Baptiste, IV, 421, **558–59**, 644, 645
Morin de Fonfay, Marie-Charlotte. *See* Boschet de Saint-Martin
Morine*, Sir Alfred Bishop (1857–1944), XII, 755, 756, 757
Morison, Elizabeth (Cameron), X, 115
Morison, Flora (Rankin), VIII, 741
Morison, Samuel Eliot, VIII, 390; XII, 825
Morisseau, Madeleine (Gimbal; Dumas Saint-Martin), IV, 243, 244
Morisseau, Marie-Josephte (Strouds), III, 602
Morisseaux, Jean-Baptiste-Laurent, IV, 571
Morisset*, Gérard (1898–1970), III, 67, 68, 346, 422, 645, 648, 695; IV, 206, 805, 806; V, 49, 710; VIII, 218, 637, 638; IX, 870; X, 301, 413; XI, 92; XII, 850
Morisson, Donald George, XII, 253
Moriyama, Enosuke, XII, 612
Morland, George, XII, 405
Morley, Baron. *See* Parker
Morley, Earl of. *See* Parker
Morley, Elizabeth (Punshon), XI, 719
Morley, John, 1st Viscount Morley, XI, 771
Mornay. *See* Duplessis
Mornington, Earl of. *See* Wellesley; Wellesley-Pole
Morosini, Francesco, I, 135
Morpain, Jacques, III, 474
Morpain, Marguerite. *See* Audoire
Morpain, Marie-Joseph. *See* Damours de Chauffours
Morpain, Pierre, II, 3, 38, 142; III, 6, **474–76**, 507; IV, 248, 253, 588, 589
Morpeth, Lord. *See* Howard, George William Frederick
Morpeth, H. D., IX, 223
Morphet, Jane (Metcalf), XI, 590
Morreau, James, VII, 56, 376; VIII, 27; IX, 124; X, 514
Morrell, Sarah (Seely), XI, 804
Morrice*, David (1829–1914), XII, 456
Morrill, Eleanor. *See* Beach
Morrill, Margaret. *See* Andrews
Morrill, Simeon, X, **533–34**; XI, 501
Morrin, Catherine. *See* Evans
Morrin, Joseph, V, 249; VI, 401, 576, 577, 681; VIII, 938; IX, 32, 286, 360, **572–73**; X, 376; XI, 271, 272, 484, 721; XII, 211, 911, 912, 1032
Morris, Miss (Robertson), XII, 900
Morris, Mr (schoolmaster), VI, 783
Morris, Alexander (father), VIII, 638; IX, 574
Morris, Alexander (son), VIII, 639; IX, 575

Morris, Alexander, VIII, 641; IX, 461; X, 472, 474, 650; XI, 46, 151, 193, 194, 248, 249, 458, 595, 598, **608–15**, 695, 706, 716, 935, 942; XII, 152, 187, 370, 371, 605, 612, 641, 679
Morris, Alexander Cline, XI, 614
Morris, Catherine M., X, 534
Morris, Charles (father of CHARLES, 1711–81), IV, 559
Morris, Charles, III, 128, 130, 174, 364, 365, 457, 583; IV, 53, 92, 110, 273, 300, 313, 351, 451, **559–63**, 581; V, 108, 426, 607, 608, 874; VI, 89, 511, 519, 737; X, 534
Morris, Charles, IV, 300, 562, 603, 626; V, 94, 407, 598, **607–8**; VI, 30, 519
Morris, Charles, V, 109, 607, 612; VI, 34, 319, 362, **519–20**, 780; VIII, 159, 355, 506, 756; IX, 173, 573
Morris, Charlotte. See Pernette
Morris, Charlotte, XI, 679
Morris, Clara (Harriott), XII, 622
Morris, Craig, IX, 210; XII, 507
Morris, David, VIII, 176, 177
Morris, Edmund, VIII, 930
Morris*, Edmund Montague (1871–1913), XI, 614
Morris, Edward, VII, 627, 633; XI, **615**
Morris*, Edward Patrick, 1st Baron Morris (1859–1935), IX, 460; XII, 755, 756, 757, 956, 957
Morris, Elizabeth. See Cochran
Morris, Elizabeth Bond. See Leggett
Morris, Eliza Hoosse (Barlow), VII, 47
Morris, Emily Rosamond. See Murney
Morris, Esther. See Rainsthorpe
Morris, Eunice Alice (Barnes), VII, 48
Morris, Felix, XII, 623
Morris, Frances. See Bullen
Morris, Frank J., XII, 158
Morris, Frederick William, VI, 519; IX, **573–74**, 586
Morris, Geoffrey, VI, 709, 710
Morris, Gouverneur, V, 630
Morris, Guy, X, 534
Morris, Isabella (Webb), XI, 912
Morris, Isabella (Wilkins), VII, 910
Morris, James, VII, 627
Morris, James, VIII, 639, 789, 797; IX, 99, 253, **574–76**, 736; X, 127, 650; XI, 414; XII, 388
Morris, James Rainstorpe, V, **608–9**; VI, 799
Morris, Janet. See Lang
Morris, Janet (Merritt), IX, 575
Morris, Janet Maria. See Solomon
Morris, Joe, XI, 679
Morris, John Lang, VIII, 642
Morris, John Spry, VI, 520; VIII, 906
Morris, Katherine. See Howley
Morris, Lewis (grandfather), III, 587, 658
Morris, Lewis, VII, 910
Morris, Margaret. See Cline
Morris, Margaret. See Hill
Morris, Maria, VI, 777, 778
Morris, Maria (Weeks), XII, 1092
Morris, Maria Frances Ann (Miller), V, 608; VII, 815; IX, 40; X, **534–35**; XII, 542, 786, 1131
Morris, Mary. See Coy
Morris, Mary. See Foley
Morris, Mary. See Read
Morris, Mary (Blaiklock), VII, 80
Morris, Mary (Danks), IV, 193

Morris, Mary (Smith), IX, 730
Morris, Mary Christianne. See Paul
Morris, Maud, XII, 865
Morris, Patrick, VI, 71, 410, 692, 693, 710, 711; VII, 113, 114, 152, 153, 154, 155, 156, 220, 296, 421, 590, 598, **626–34**, 842; VIII, 234, 235, 381, 403, 468, 947, 950; IX, 70, 71, 85, 168, 436, 605, 682; X, 179, 398, 553, 601, 687; XI, 242, 615, 673; XII, 482
Morris, Rachel. See Butler
Morris, Robert (politician), V, 629
Morris, Robert (ship's captain), I, 601
Morris, Roger, III, 142
Morris, Rutton, VII, 48
Morris, Sibylla Amelia Maria Sophia. See Leggett
Morris, Simon, VII, 627, 633; XI, 615
Morris, Susannah (wife of JAMES RAINSTORPE), V, 608
Morris, Thomas, IV, 762
Morris, Tom, XI, 679
Morris, William (army officer), XI, 912
Morris, William (clergyman), VII, 685
Morris, William (settler), IV, 40
Morris, William, VI, 33; VII, 69, 606, 852; VIII, 187, 188, 545, 583, 601, **638–42**, 645, 733, 750, 800; IX, 191, 539, 575; X, 119, 255, 257, 502, 650; XI, 378, 608
Morris, William Selwyn Hierliehy, XII, 364
Morrison, Alexander, V, 313
Morrison, Angus, VIII, 371; IX, 680; XI, 167, 228, 542, **615–17**, 853; XII, 983
Morrison, Charles-François-Calixte, IX, 450
Morrison, Charlotte. See Nickinson
Morrison, Christiana. See Wright
Morrison, Daniel, IX, **576–77**, 597; XI, 518, 877
Morrison, Donald, X, 303
Morrison, Effie. See Patrick
Morrison, Elizabeth. See Bloor
Morrison, Elizabeth Hester. See Marriott
Morrison, Ellen Norman (McLeod), X, 482
Morrison, Frances. See Gidney
Morrison, Frances. See Montgomery
Morrison, Hannah. See Faulkner
Morrison, Hugh, XI, 615, 617
Morrison, Isabella. See Fletcher
Morrison, Jacob L., VII, 928
Morrison, James, IV, 330
Morrison, Janet Anne. See Gilmor
Morrison, John (father of JOSEPH WANTON), VI, 520
Morrison, John (grandfather of THOMAS FLETCHER), XI, 619
Morrison, John (surveyor), VI, 228
Morrison, Joseph A., XI, 619
Morrison, Joseph Curran, VII, 896; VIII, 114, 964, 965, 966; IX, 55, 151; X, 656; XI, 167, 615, 616, **617–19**; XII, 72, 594, 595
Morrison, Joseph Wanton, V, 696, 762; VI, 286, **520–21**, 661; VII, 366; VIII, 194
Morrison, Julie-Élisabeth-Geneviève (Jane) (Kinton; La Fontaine, Lady La Fontaine), IX, 450
Morrison, Kezia (Keziah) (Durand), VI, 228
Morrison, Louisa (Himsworth), X, 436
Morrison, Margaret Brown. See Fletcher
Morrison, Mary. See Curran
Morrison, Mary. See Wanton
Morrison, Mary (Finlayson), XII, 317

Morrison, Mary (Foster), XI, 322
Morrison, Mary Jessy (Lévesque), VIII, 503
Morrison, Phoebe (Gidney), XI, 347
Morrison, Thomas David, VI, 11; VII, 163, 319, 369, 409, 665; VIII, 48, 358, **642–44**, 846, 933; IX, 229, 502, 687, 724; XII, 71
Morrison, Thomas Fletcher, XI, **619–20**
Morrison, William, VIII, 642
Morrogh, Francis, V, 493
Morrogh, Robert, V, 332, 492, 493, 494, 495, 566, 746
Morrogh, Robert Lester, V, 746; VIII, 502
Morrow, James Bain, IX, 182
Morrow, Robert, IX, 182, 739
Morse, Beulah (Lovett), VI, 407
Morse, H. D., XII, 786
Morse, Harriet (Smyth, Lady Smyth), V, 609; VII, 819
Morse, James, IX, 62
Morse, James Shannon, IX, 746
Morse, Joseph, III, 588
Morse, Lucy (End), X, 271
Morse, Robert, V, **609–11**; VII, 819
Morse, Samuel Finley Breese, XII, 373, 375, 1090
Morse, Sarah (Stewart), IX, 746
Morse, Silas Livingston, VIII, 657
Morse, Sophia. See Godin
Morse, Thomas, V, 609
Morson, Jane (Smith), VIII, 828
Mortemart. See Rochechouart
Morthon de Grandval, Pierre de, II, 270
Mortier, Catherine (Joannès de Chacornacle), II, 300
Mortimer, Alexander, V, 611
Mortimer, Arthur, VII, 635
Mortimer, Edward, V, **611–12**, 660; VI, 268, 322, 460, 461, 780, 781, 800; VII, 530, 531, 532; VIII, 122, 222, 355
Mortimer, George, VII, **634–36**; VIII, 95
Mortimer, Harvey Walklate, VII, 634
Mortimer, Herbert, VII, 635
Mortimer, Jane. See Wallace
Mortimer, Jane (Clark; Topp), X, 683
Mortimer, Mary. See Barford
Mortimer, Mary. See Smith
Mortimer, Mary (Holland), VII, 635
Mortimer, Sarah. See Patterson
Mortimer, Thomas, VII, 635
Mortimer, William, VIII, 122
Mortin (Moreton), Catherine (Corrigan), VIII, 169
Morton, Mrs Alice, XII, 154
Morton, Ann. See Cogswell
Morton*, Arthur Silver (1870–1945), III, 254; V, 531, 532, 683
Morton, Catharine (McLellan), XII, **763–64**
Morton, Charles, XI, 621
Morton, Ezelia. See Ford
Morton, George Augustus, XII, 763
Morton, George Elkana, X, 593; XII, **764–65**
Morton, Ida, XII, 154
Morton, James (businessman), IX, 822
Morton, James (father of SILVANUS), XI, 620
Morton, James, VI, 221; IX, 431, **577–78**, 726; XI, 157
Morton, John (father of GEORGE ELKANA), XII, 764
Morton, John (son of SILVANUS), XI, 621
Morton, Lemuel James, XII, 764
Morton, Levi Parsons, XI, 770

Morton, Lucy. See Gorham
Morton, Martha Elizabeth. See Katzmann
Morton, Mary. See Sipperal
Morton, Samuel George, XII, 1110
Morton, Silvanus, XI, **620–21**
Morton, William, VIII, 449; XI, 382
Morton*, William Lewis (1908–80), XI, 742; XII, 408
Morville. See Laguer
Morville, Comte de. See Fleuriau
Moschel, Johann Friedrich, VII, 636
Moschel, Maria Elisabetha. See Windenheimer
Moscheles, Ignaz, VIII, 634
Moschell, Johann Adam, V, 199; VII, 330, **636**
Moschell, Mary Ann. See James
Moseley, Ebenezer Tilton, XII, 438
Mosely. See also Molesby
Mosely, Eliza Jane (Willis), X, 704
Moses, Katy, IV, 416; V, 803
Mosher, James, XI, 834
Mosier, Hannah (Hurlburt), X, 372
Mosiño. See also Moziño
Mosiño, Juan Antonio, V, 615
Mosiño, Manuela Losada de. See Losada
Mosley. See Mozely
Moss, Amy. See Sullivan
Moss, Ann. See Quigley
Moss*, Sir Charles (1840–1912), XI, 621; XII, 887
Moss, Jacob, XII, 228
Moss, John, XI, 621
Moss, Laura (Knowlton), IX, 433
Moss, Thomas, X, 336; XI, 322, 324, **621–22**, 846; XII, 908
Mossion, Robert, I, 474
Mostyn, John, IV, 577
Mostyn, Savage, III, 70, 363; IV, xxvi
Motier, Marie-Joseph-Paul-Yves-Roch-Gilbert, Marquis de La Fayette, IV, 229, 230; V, 238, 414, 583, 788, 893; IX, 771, 805
Motin, Anne (Le Creux Du Breuil), I, 442
Motin, Jeanne (Menou d'Aulnay; Saint-Étienne de La Tour), I, 114, 129, 257, 261, 433, 434, 436, 442, 469, 503, 505, 510, **514**, 595; II, 591
Motin de Corcelles (Courcelles), Louis, I, 442, 503, 514
Mott, Mrs (mother of JACOB S.), V, 613
Mott, Amelia (Ryan), V, 612; VII, 763, 766
Mott, Andrew Cook, X, 535
Mott, Ann. See Hinton
Mott, Eliza, VII, 460
Mott, Gabriel F., V, 613
Mott, Henry Youmans, XII, 770
Mott, Jacob S., V, **612–13**; VI, 408; VII, 764; VIII, 156
Mott, John, V, 612; VII, 763
Mott, Nelson, VII, 239
Mott, Valentine, XII, 925
Mott, William Hinton, V, 613
Mottin. See Motin
Mottin de La Balme, Augustin, V, 3, 594; VI, 189
Motton, Eleanor. See Moore
Motton, Maggie. See Coleman
Motton, Rachel. See Flemming
Motton, Robert, XII, 765
Motton, Robert, XII, **765–67**, 871
Motz, James, VIII, 559

Mouat, Mary Ann. *See* Ainsley
Mouat, William, X, 535
Mouat, William Alexander, X, **535–36**
Mouchy, Nicolas de, I, **514**; II, 514
Mouet, Marie (Cadot), V, 130
Mouet de Langlade, Augustin, IV, 563
Mouet de Langlade, Charles (emissary), V, 715
Mouet de Langlade, Charles (son of CHARLES-MICHEL), IV, 563
Mouet de Langlade, Charles-Michel, III, xlii, 496, 526; IV, liv, 78, 303, 486, **563–64**, 582, 666, 718; V, 8, 499, 567, 568, 760; VI, 188, 317
Mouet de Langlade, Charlotte-Ambroisine. *See* Bourassa, *dit* La Ronde
Mouet de Langlade, Domitilde. *See* Domitilde
Mouet de Mora, Catherine (Amiot), III, 13
Moufle de La Tuillerie, Barthélemy, III, 398
Mouisset, David, IV, 387
Mouïsset, François, III, 398, 399
Moule, Frances Barbara (Wells; Wallace), XII, 1094
Moulton, Dana D., XII, 50
Moulton, Ebenezer, IV, **564–65**; V, 744
Moulton, Hannah. *See* Ballard
Moulton, Hannah. *See* Grove
Moulton, Hannah(?). *See* Littlefield
Moulton, Jeremiah, II, 477, 544; III, **476–77**
Moulton, Joseph, III, 476
Moulton, Mary (Lord; wife of JEREMIAH), III, 477
Moulton, Robert, IV, 564
Moulton, Susan (Fraser; McMaster), XI, 158, 577; XII, 948
Mounier, Adam, IV, 565
Mounier, François, III, **477–78**, 541; IV, 125, 187, 379, 565, 574, 579, 788; V, 142, 276, 369
Mounier, Henry, III, 477; IV, 565
Mounier, Jean (uncle), IV, 566
Mounier, Jean, IV, 565, 625
Mounier, Jean-Mathieu, IV, 125, 128, **565–66**; V, 276
Mounier, Marguerite-Geneviève (Maurin), III, 441
Mounier, Michel, IV, 566
Mounier, Suzanne. *See* Liard
Mount, Charlotte Magenty (Genevay; Lacoste), X, 418
Mount, Jane. *See* Burtch
Mount, Moses, VI, 521
Mount, Roswell, VI, 399, 496, **521–23**; VII, 126, 755; VIII, 438
Mountain, Ann. *See* Postle
Mountain, Anna Maria (Jarvis), X, 380
Mountain, Charlotte Anna. *See* Dundas
Mountain, Eliza (Arabin), VI, 526
Mountain, Elizabeth Mildred Wale. *See* Kentish
Mountain, Frances Mingay. *See* Brooke
Mountain, George Jehoshaphat, V, 602, 769, 787; VI, 375, 505, 526, 527, 528, 717, 735; VII, 526, 828; VIII, 25, 644, 743, 769, 866, 937; IX, 209, 275, 276, 289, 378, 379, 541, **578–81**, 719, 732, 760, 848; X, 58, 547, 548; XI, 208, 503, 653, 872; XII, 573, 681, 1100
Mountain, George Robert, VI, 526
Mountain, Harriet Mary (Nicolls), X, 548
Mountain, Jacob, V, 613; VI, 523
Mountain, Jacob, IV, 102, 372, 738, 753; V, 18, 68, 69, 106, 212, 246, 292, 330, 334, 445, 476, 489, 494, 579, 601, 613, 614, 692, 696, 756, 769, 770, 787, 808, 880; VI, 47, 53, 297, 375, 423, 506, 507, **523–29**, 558, 559, 560, 587, 588, 592, 593, 594, 600, 715, 716, 717, 734; VII, 124, 211, 212, 280, 310, 379, 486, 614, 615, 682, 767, 768, 769, 771, 784, 788, 825, 826, 828; VIII, 25, 94, 644, 665, 937; IX, 3, 110, 115, 209, 578, 752, 754, 757, 759, 770, 848; X, 53, 57, 452, 570; XI, 784
Mountain, Jacob George, IX, 460
Mountain, Jacob George, VIII, **644**; IX, 578; X, 278; XII, 364
Mountain, Jacob Henry Brooke, V, 787; VI, 526; VIII, 644
Mountain, Jehosaphat, IV, 753; V, 106, 134, 601, **613–15**; VI, 523, 525, 528, 717, 822; IX, 578
Mountain, Mary. *See* Leach
Mountain, Mary Hume. *See* Thomson
Mountain, Salter Jehosaphat, V, 614, 747; VI, 505, 523, 528; IX, 578, 579; X, 5, 380
Mountain, Sophia. *See* Bevan
Mount Stephen, Baron. *See* Stephen
Mourongeau, Catherine. *See* Frontigny
Mourongeau, Jacques, III, 78
Mouroy, Mlle de (fiancée of Marc LESCARBOT), I, 470
Mousseau (Mousset), Domitille (Domethilda) (Duhamel), XII, 277
Mousseau, Hersélie. *See* Desrosiers
Mousseau, Joseph-Alfred, VII, 148, 150; IX, 437; XI, 340, 521, **622–26**; XII, 88, 173, 176, 178, 248, 451, 465, 722, 987
Mousseau, Louis, XI, 622
Mousseau, Sophie. *See* Duteau, *dit* Grandpré
Mousseaux, Louise de (Pélerin de Saint-Amant), I, 256; II, 515
Mousseaux, Marguerite. *See* Sauriot
Mousseaux, *dit* Laviolette, Jacques, XI, 622
Moussette, Antoine, XI, 424
Mouthe, Marie-Ursule (Feltz), IV, 264, 265
Mouton, Romain, XII, 387
Mowat*, Angus McGill (1892–1977), XII, 767
Mowat, Bertha C. *See* Herrett
Mowat, Blanche (Simpson), XII, 768
Mowat, Elizabeth. *See* Moores
Mowat, Emma. *See* McDonald
Mowat, George, VIII, 645
Mowat, Helen. *See* Levack
Mowat, Henry, VI, 562
Mowat, James Gordon, XII, 383
Mowat, Jane, Lady Mowat. *See* Ewart
Mowat, Janet. *See* Bower
Mowat, Janet. *See* McGill
Mowat, John, VIII, **644–45**; IX, 162; XII, 767
Mowat, John Bower, VIII, 645; XII, 617, **767–68**
Mowat, John L., XII, 768
Mowat, Margaret (Stewart), XI, 854
Mowat, Oliver, VIII, 644
Mowat*, Sir Oliver (1820–1903), VII, 558; VIII, 282, 402, 644, 645, 849; IX, 108, 268, 315, 324, 804; X, 99, 100, 101, 102, 118, 171, 193, 359, 466, 509, 510, 530, 707; XI, 145, 146, 221, 222, 223, 312, 347, 367, 450, 497, 536, 537, 593, 609, 614, 618, 648, 672, 682, 792, 793, 846, 934; XII, 27, 53, 137, 138, 150, 151, 153, 196, 199, 294, 331, 332, 333, 334, 395, 453, 489, 497, 579, 582, 583, 606, 607, 644, 649, 658, 723, 724, 725, 767, 822, 908, 922, 973, 975, 1044, 1085, 1108, 1113
Mowat, Susannah (Susan) Elizabeth (Wilmot), XII, 1104
Mowat, Thomas, XII, **768**

Mowatt, Margaret (Allan), VIII, 4
Mower, Nahum, V, 298; VI, 815; VII, 111; VIII, 221; IX, 550; X, 717; XI, 936
Moxley, Thomas, V, 511, 780
Moxus, II, 475, 543, 666
Moyen, Denis, XII, 769
Moyen, Jean, X, 106; XII, **769–70**, 868
Moyen, Marguerite. *See* Bachelerie
Moyen Des Granges, Élisabeth. *See* Le Bret
Moyen Des Granges, Élisabeth (Closse), I, 231
Moyen Des Granges, Jean-Baptiste, I, 231, 295
Moyen Des Granges, Marie (Dugué de Boisbriand), I, 231, 295; II, 203
Moyer. *See* Mohier
Moylan*, James George (1826–1902), XI, 216; XII, 153
Moyne, Alayne, I, 371
Moysant, François, VII, 94
Mozart, Wolfgang Amadeus, XII, 223
Mozely (Mosley), Nancy, V, 506
Moziño, María Rita Rivera de. *See* Rivera y Melo Montaño
Moziño Losada Suárez de Figueroa, José Mariano, V, 11, 198, **615–16**
Muckle, Anna E. (Harrison), X, 336
Mudge, Zacariah, VII, 127
Mudjeckewiss (Mudjekewiss). *See* Madjeckewiss
Mühlenberg, Gotthilf Henry Ernest, VII, 244
Müller, Georg, XI, 723
Müller, Johannes von, VIII, 291
Müller, Julius, XII, 489
Müller, Max, X, 608; XII, 112, 401, 582
Münster, Bishop of. *See* Galen
Muerel, Anne (Bonnécamps), IV, 76
Muhammad Aḥmad ibn ʿAbd Allāh, known as the Mahdī, XII, 117, 245
Muhlenberg, William Augustus, VIII, 747
Muhlig, Mathilda E. (Downs), XII, 268
Muir, Adam Charles, V, 302, 775; VI, **529–31**, 617; VII, 821
Muir, Andrew, VIII, **646**; XI, 627; XII, 113
Muir, Annie. *See* Miller
Muir, Archibald, VIII, 646; XI, 627
Muir, Charles F., XII, 974
Muir, Eliza. *See* Harris
Muir, George Manly, VI, 530; XI, 208, 318
Muir, Isabella. *See* Weir
Muir, Isabella Ellen, VIII, 646
Muir, James Landers, XI, 284
Muir, Janet (Kinnear), IX, 430
Muir, John, VIII, 646, 836; IX, 337; XI, 291, **626–27**
Muir, Mary (Dick), XI, 259
Muir, Mary Elizabeth Alexowina. *See* Bender
Muir, Michael, VIII, 646
Muir, William, IX, 369
Muirhead. *See also* DuVernet; Grosset
Muirhead, Deborah Catherine (Richards), XI, 730
Muirhead, James, VI, 374
Muiron, Claudine. *See* Seroin
Muiron, David-Bernard, III, 20, 235, **478–79**, 644
Muiron, François, III, 478
Muiron, Marie. *See* Champion
Muis. *See* Mius
Mulberry, Susanna (Salter), IV, 695
Mulcaster, Sir William Howe, VI, 521; VII, 46

Mulgrave, Earl of. *See* Phipps
Mulkins, Hannibal, X, 536
Mulkins, Jane Gray. *See* Dennis
Mullen, Eldon, X, 498
Mullens, Priscilla (Alden), II, 14
Mullett, James, X, 514
Mullins, Francis, X, 536
Mullins, Jane (Clarke), VI, 150
Mullins, Rosanna. *See* Connelly
Mullins, Rosanna Eleanora (Leprohon), IX, 855; X, **536–38**; XI, 322; XII, 555, 570, 573
Mullock, John Thomas, VII, 299; VIII, 475, 950; IX, 29, 30, 39, 189, 557, **581–86**, 606, 682, 819, 846; X, 279, 399, 400; XI, 43, 432, 433, 615, 881; XII, 162, 563, 564, 565, 590, 860
Mullock, Mary Teresa. *See* Hare
Mullock, Thomas J., IX, 581
Mullois, Marie (Saint-Ours), II, 592, 593; III, 505, 578
Mullois, Thomas, II, 592
Mullois de La Borde, Madeleine (Pézard de La Tousche Champlain), I, 543
Mulock*, Sir William (1844–1944), XII, 246, 941, 993
Mulvany, Charles Pelham, XI, **627–28**
Mulvany, Mrs Elizabeth, XI, 627
Mulvany, Frances Elizabeth (Shanly), X, 648; XI, 817; XII, 961
Mulvany, Henry William, XI, 627
Mulvey*, Stewart (1834–1908), XI, 611, 645; XII, 952
Mumford, John, XI, 405
Muncaster, Baron. *See* Pennington
Munck. *See* Munk
Muncoq. *See* Moncoq
Munday, Marguerite. *See* Corneillier, *dit* Grandchamp
Munday, William, V, 783
Mundell, Anne (Richardson), IX, 658
Mundell, James, IX, 658
Munden, Elizabeth (Munn), XII, 770
Munden, Elizabeth (Norman), XI, 642
Munden, Naomi (Munn), X, 538
Mundy, Frances (FitzRoy), VIII, 295
Munk, Erik Nielsen, I, 514
Munk, Jens Eriksen, I, 20, **514–15**; II, 265, 297
Munk, Katherine. *See* Adriansdatter
Munn, Agnes. *See* Galloway
Munn, Alexander, IV, 49; V, **616–18**, 699; VI, 532; VIII, 647
Munn, Catherine. *See* Edward
Munn, David, V, 617; VIII, 647, 649; X, 518
Munn, Dugald, XII, 770
Munn, Elizabeth. *See* Munden
Munn, Elizabeth. *See* Stewart
Munn, Isabella. *See* Fisher
Munn, James (brother of ALEXANDER), V, 617; VIII, 647
Munn, James (shipbuilder), V, 617
Munn, John (brother of ALEXANDER), V, 617; VIII, 646, 647, 648
Munn (McMunn), John (father of ALEXANDER), V, 616; VIII, 647
Munn, John (father of JOHN, 1788–1859), VIII, 646
Munn, John (nephew of ALEXANDER), VIII, 649
Munn, John, V, 617; VI, 289; VII, 233, 877, 923; VIII, 93, **646–49**; IX, 795

Munn, John, VIII, 199; X, 331, **538–39**, 600, 618; XI, 284; XII, 770
Munn, Naomi. *See* Munden
Munn, Robert Stewart, X, 538; XII, **770–71**
Munn, Stewart, X, 538
Munn, William Punton, X, 538; XII, 770
Munnings, Sarah Ann (Hill), XII, 439
Munro. *See also* Monro
Munro, Alexander, IX, 474
Munro, Catherine. *See* Forrest
Munro, Cornelia (Paterson; Fraser), VI, 263
Munro, Duncan, V, 385
Munro, Ebenezer F., XII, 405
Munro, F., XII, 153
Munro, George, XI, 364, 773, 948; XII, **771–73**
Munro, George William, XII, 772
Munro, Harriet (Mondelet), IX, 559
Munro, Harry, V, 785
Munro, Hector, XI, **628–29**
Munro, Henry (doctor), V, 543; VII, 25; VIII, 575
Munro, Henry (politician), IV, 351
Munro, Hugh (father of JOHN), IV, 566
Munro, Hugh (loyalist), XI, 69
Munro, Hugh, VII, 258, **636–38**; VIII, 292; X, 271
Munro, Jane. *See* Barnet
Munro, John (father of GEORGE), XII, 771
Munro, John (merchant), V, 285, 460, 461, 700; VI, 346, 476, 477, 478
Munro, John (publisher), IX, 54
Munro, John (son of GEORGE), XII, 772
Munro, John, IV, **566–67**; V, 282, 518, 519, 772; VI, 132, 263, 264
Munro, Laurence John, XI, 900
Munro, Martha (wife of HUGH), VII, 636
Munro, Mary. *See* Brower
Munro, Mary. *See* Mathieson
Munro, Mary Charlotte (Dennis; Chartier de Lotbinière), VI, 132
Munro, Pierre-Antoine-Conefroy, IX, 16; XI, 303
Munro, Rachael. *See* Warren
Munro, Thomas, X, 174
Munroe. *See also* Monro
Munroe, James, VI, 172; VIII, 894
Munse, Jane (Crawford), IX, 166
Munsel (Munsall), Sarah (Howard), VII, 419
Munson, Lamira Juliana (Randal), VII, 733
Munson, Mrs Letitia, XI, **629–30**
Muquinna, IV, lv, 73, 325, 411, 498, 519, 520, **567–69**, 767, 768; V, 11, 12, 411, 571, 586, 615, 618; VI, 234, 743
Muquinna, V, **618–19**; VI, 350, 351
Murav'ev, Nikolai Nikolaevich, XI, 932
Murcé, Marquis de. *See* Valois-Villette
Murchie, Andrew, XII, 773
Murchie, Daniel, XII, 773
Murchie, James, XII, **773–75**
Murchie, Janet. *See* Campbell
Murchie, John G., XII, 775
Murchie, Margaret Jane. *See* Thorpe
Murchie, Mary Ann. *See* Grimmer
Murchison, Duncan, XI, 332
Murchison, Sir Roderick Impey, X, 65, 408; XI, 662
Murderer. *See* Cherououny

Murdoch, Andrew, X, 539
Murdoch, Anne (Henry), VI, 169
Murdoch, Beamish, III, 34, 439, 498, 573; V, 690; VI, 88, 90, 173, 307, 622; VII, 12, 177, 237, 308, 589; VIII, 732, 752; X, 363, **539–40**; XI, 147, 847; XII, 13
Murdoch, Charles, IX, 586, 587
Murdoch, Elizabeth. *See* Beamish
Murdoch*, George (1850–1910), XI, 418
Murdoch, James (brother of WILLIAM), IX, 586
Murdoch, James (clergyman), IV, 490; V, 199, 344, 871; X, 539
Murdoch, James Edward, XII, 668
Murdoch, Mary (McKnight), XII, 659
Murdoch, Sir Thomas William Clinton, VII, 31, 32, 858, 859, 860, 861; VIII, xxxii, xxxiii, 709; IX, 818
Murdoch, William, IX, 586
Murdoch, William, IX, 574, **586–87**; X, 73
Mure, Charlotte (Pinguet), VI, 534
Mure, Hutcheson, IV, 352
Mure, James, VI, 534
Mure, John, V, 84, 319, 461, 635, 636, 769, 817, 827, 835; VI, 50, 254, 255, 367, 385, 424, **531–35**, 641; VII, 65, 342, 372, 833, 873; VIII, 321, 690, 838
Mure, Margaret. *See* Porteous
Mure, William, VI, 534
Murillo, Bartolomé Esteban, XII, 849
Murison, Alexander, IX, 181
Murney, Edmund, IX, 45
Murney, Emily Rosamond (Morris), IX, 574
Murney, Henry, VII, 470; IX, 557, 574
Murphy, Captain, X, 264
Murphy, Anna Brownell (Jameson), VIII, 177, 426, 427, 596, **649–51**, 831, 860, 861; XI, 778; XII, 525, 680
Murphy, Arthur, IV, 556
Murphy, Catherine Hannah (Tobin), VII, 867
Murphy, Denis Brownell, VIII, 649
Murphy, Edward, VII, 292
Murphy, Francis, XI, 752
Murphy, Gertrude Anna (Collins), XII, 204
Murphy, Harriet Courtland (Vail), XI, 896
Murphy, Helena (Cannon), V, 139; VI, 119
Murphy, James (clergyman), VIII, 475
Murphy, James (of Kingston, Ont.), XII, 811
Murphy, John, XI, 862
Murphy, Margaret (Cunard), IX, 170, 172
Murphy, Martin, XII, 368
Murphy, Mary (Carey), XI, 151
Murphy, Michael, VI, 418, 419
Murphy, Michael, IX, **587–89**; XII, 258, 420, 597, 655, 675
Murphy, Owen Eugene, XII, 629, 630
Murphy, Peter Sarsfield, XII, 62
Murphy, Robert, X, 587
Murphy, Sarah (O'Meara), XI, 653
Murray. *See also* Elliot-Murray-Kynynmound
Murray, Alexander (clerk), VII, 208, 652; XII, 744, 745
Murray, Alexander (father of ALEXANDER, d. 1762), III, 479
Murray, Alexander, III, 363, **479–80**; IV, xxv
Murray, Alexander, IX, 160; X, 445, 446, 447, 448; XI, 356, **630–33**, 732; XII, 164, 440, 562
Murray, Alexander, 4th Baron Elibank, IV, 569
Murray, Alexander Hunter, X, **540–41**; XI, 384; XII, 74, 935

Murray, Anne. *See* Campbell
Murray, Anne. *See* Witham
Murray, Anne (Powell), V, 189, 521, 522; VI, 540, 603, 604, 605, 607, 608; VII, **638–39**, 693, 704, 920; VIII, 11
Murray, Anthony (father), XI, 630
Murray, Anthony, XI, 630, 631
Murray, Augusta, Lady Murray. *See* Mackenzie
Murray, Bridget (McGarvey), XII, 624
Murray, Catharine (Rollo, Baroness Rollo), III, 565
Murray, Sir Charles Augustus, VI, 709
Murray, Christina (Bertram), XII, 103
Murray, Clemena (Going), XII, 776
Murray, Cordelia. *See* Collier
Murray, Daniel (archbishop), VIII, 307, 665
Murray, Daniel (loyalist), V, 354, 831
Murray, David, XI, 633
Murray, David, 2nd Earl of Mansfield, VII, 831
Murray, Davidson Munro, XII, 409
Murray, Deborah (Hazen), X, 341
Murray, Dorothy Bruce (Harman), XII, 409
Murray, Edward, XII, 775
Murray, Elizabeth. *See* Cummins
Murray, Elizabeth (Campbell; Smith; Inman), VII, 638, 639
Murray, Elizabeth (Robertson), XII, 901, 904
Murray, Elizabeth (Upham), V, 831
Murray, Elizabeth, Baroness Murray. *See* Stirling
Murray, Fanny Cooper. *See* Judkins
Murray, George, VI, 608; VII, 639
Murray, George, XI, 619, **633–34**; XII, 250
Murray, Lord George, IV, 400
Murray, Sir George, VI, 609; VII, 163, 190, 314, **639–41**, 731, 905, 906; VIII, xxvii, xxxi, xxxv, 462, 463, 583, 602; IX, 161, 669; XI, 630, 631
Murray, Helen Fletcher. *See* Bower
Murray, Henrietta. *See* Horan
Murray, Hugh (father of HUGH), X, 541
Murray, Hugh (ship chandler), XII, 420
Murray, Hugh, X, **541–43**
Murray, Huson William Munro, XII, 409
Murray, Isabella (Isabel) (Bliss), VI, 73
Murray, James (businessman), XII, 529, 782, 783
Murray, James (seigneur), VII, 111
Murray, James (uncle of ANNE), VII, 638
Murray, James, III, xxi, 26, 37, 64, 85, 86, 89, 90, 132, 138, 143, 197, 198, 199, 212, 272, 274, 289, 290, 293, 296, 340, 341, 365, 418, 477, 478, 541, 549, 606, 608, 668, 669, 670, 671; IV, xxxiii, xxxv, xxxvii, xl, xli, xliii, xlix, 23, 24, 37, 71, 74, 97, 98, 103, 104, 105, 106, 109, 129, 134, 137, 138, 139, 141, 146, 150, 162, 182, 183, 189, 190, 211, 228, 243, 265, 276, 279, 280, 290, 298, 299, 319, 324, 335, 344, 347, 348, 370, 379, 380, 381, 384, 399, 415, 430, 447, 464, 480, 481, 482, 491, 492, 493, 500, 509, 531, 535, 536, 537, 538, 541, 543, 552, 554, **569–78**, 579, 602, 618, 623, 641, 642, 643, 650, 672, 686, 692, 694, 700, 719, 725, 729, 752, 758, 759, 779, 787, 788; V, 4, 19, 20, 91, 98, 130, 131, 132, 141, 142, 143, 144, 153, 181, 224, 225, 272, 277, 288, 289, 315, 330, 331, 368, 369, 379, 384, 389, 412, 413, 425, 426, 427, 462, 478, 479, 494, 507, 511, 578, 588, 620, 658, 699, 711, 745, 819, 823, 824, 864, 889; VI, 491, 492, 523, 712; VII, 133, 235, 591; IX, 360, 774; XII, 46
Murray, James Wolfe, III, 479
Murray, Jean (Kerr), VII, 464

Murray, Jemima Alexandrina (Bedson), XII, 74, 75
Murray, Jessie. *See* Dickson
Murray, John (artist), XI, 515
Murray, John (brother of ANNE), VII, 638
Murray, John (father of ANNE), VII, 638
Murray, John (father of ROBERT), VIII, 651
Murray, John (lawyer), V, 831; VI, 73; X, 341
Murray, John (merchant), VIII, 642
Murray, John (son of JOHN), VI, 782
Murray, John, IV, 523; V, 53, 205, 546, 634, 766, 780; VI, 113, 202, 203, 213, **535–36**
Murray, John, 2nd Earl of Dunmore, V, 822
Murray, John, 4th Earl of Dunmore, IV, xxxviii, 626, 790; V, 301, 340, 423, 852; VI, 101, 297, 683
Murray, John Clark, XII, 216
Murray*, John Wilson (1824–1906), XI, 78
Murray, Josette (Saint-Ours), VI, 680; VII, 235
Murray, Katharine (Haldane), VIII, 350
Murray, Lionel William John, 8th Earl of Dysart, VII, 396
Murray, Louisa, Lady Murray. *See* Paget
Murray, Louisa Annie, XII, 328, 329, **775–77**
Murray, Louisa Rose. *See* Lyons
Murray, Margaret. *See* Huggan
Murray, Margaret. *See* Robertson
Murray, Margaret (Cassils), XII, 167
Murray, Marian (O'Hara), X, 557
Murray, Marianne (wife of ALEXANDER, d. 1762), III, 479
Murray, Mary. *See* Pasco
Murray, Mary, VII, 638
Murray, Mary Ann. *See* Patterson
Murray, Patrick, 5th Baron Elibank, IV, 577
Murray, Richard, IV, 579
Murray, Robert, VIII, 426, **651–52**; X, 506
Murray*, Robert (1832–1910), IX, 326
Murray, Sarah (King), XII, 488
Murray, Sarah Lowell. *See* Hazen
Murray, Walter, XI, 633
Murray, Walter, IV, 379, **579**; V, 142
Murray*, Walter Charles (1866–1945), XI, 448
Murray, William (brother of ALEXANDER, 1810–84), XI, 632
Murray, William (financier), XII, 136
Murray, William, 1st Earl of Mansfield, IV, xli, 537, 571; V, 145
Murray, William, 3rd Earl of Mansfield, VI, 218
Murray, Sir William, VII, 639; XI, 631
Mursay, Marquis de. *See* Valois-Villette
Murtagh, James, XII, 367
Muscowpetung. *See* Maskawpistam
Muse. *See* Meuse
Musgrave, Anthony, XI, 634
Musgrave, Sir Anthony, IX, 585, 606, 715, 716; X, 139; XI, 395, 433, **634–37**, 757; XII, 240, 241, 295, 439, 601, 910, 915
Musgrave, Christiana Elizabeth. *See* Byam
Musgrave, Jeanie Lucinda, Lady Musgrave. *See* Field
Musgrave, Mary Harris. *See* Sheriff
Musgrave, Sir Thomas, V, 156
Muskerry, Viscount. *See* MacCarthy
Musquakie, VII, 11, 747; IX, **589–90**; X, 12, 622
Musson. *See also* Masson
Musson, Eliza (Spencer), X, 663
Musson, John, IX, 572

Mutigny de Vassan, Jean-Baptiste, III, 535; IV, 540
Muttlebury, Frederick Creighton, IX, 535
Muy. *See* Daneau
Muzzarelli, Alfonso, VII, 886
Myarwikishigoqua (Mary Crane) (Sonego), IX, 590
Myatt, Joseph, II, 10, 291, 292, **492–93**, 602; III, 599, 661
Mychell, William, I, 158
Myeerah (Myecruh), V, **619–20**, 775, 798; VII, 821
Myer, Joseph, IV, 228
Myers, Christopher, VII, 888; VIII, 161, 794
Myers, Hyam, IV, 332, 384; V, 193
Myers, Mary (Wood), IV, 775, 776
Myers, Samuel H., XI, **637–39**; XII, 666
Mykok. *See* Mikak
Mynne, Anne (Calvert, Baroness Baltimore), I, 162
Mynne, George, I, 162
Myres. *See also* Meyers
Myres, Sir John, III, 338
Myrick, Elizabeth. *See* Osborn
Myrick, William, IV, 593
Mytton, Elizabeth (Wetherall), IX, 826

NAACKÉ, Erdmuth (Miertsching), X, 513
Nabpace (Iron Body), XI, 460
Nadeau. *See also* Garnier
Nadeau, Louis, V, 277
Nadeau, Marie-Geneviève (Fisbacht), XI, 318
Nafrechoux, Catherine (Chaumier; Foucault), III, 227
Nafrechoux, Françoise (Pommereau), III, 524
Nafrechoux, Isaac, II, 517
Nafrechoux, Louise (Raimbault), II, 542
Nafziger, Christian, VII, 351, **641–42**
Nafziger, Maria (wife of CHRISTIAN), VII, 641
Nafziger, Peter, VII, 641
Nageant, Hadelin, XII, 60
Nagel, Mr (violinist), VII, 775
Nagiscoig (Captain John), II, 476, 668
Nagle, Honoria (Nano), named Mother Mary of St John of God, VIII, 474
Nagot, François-Charles, V, 186
Nahnebahwequay, VIII, 440; IX, **590–91**; XI, 317, 474
Nahovway (Margaret) (mother of JAMES and WILLIAM Sinclair), VIII, 819; IX, 722
Naingishkung, Joseph Benson, IX, 590
Nairn, Alexander, XII, 777
Nairn, Elizabeth. *See* Watt
Nairn, James, XII, 777
Nairn, John, XII, 777
Nairn, Margaret. *See* Kirkland
Nairn, Stephen, XII, **777–78**
Nairne, Christiana. *See* Emery
Nairne, Christine, V, 621
Nairne, John, V, 621
Nairne, John, IV, 276, 548, 570, 574; V, 31, 330, 585, **620–22**; VI, 769; VII, 401, 569
Nairne, Magdalen (McNicol), V, 621
Nairne, Mary (Blackburn), V, 621
Nairne, Thomas, V, 621
Nameur, Louis de, I, 313
Namier, Sir Lewis Bernstein, IV, 528
Namo-pisi (Crooked Back), XII, 858
Nanamaghemet, Marie-Jeanne (Gill), IV, 293
Nancy. *See also* Shawnadithit

Nancy (daughter-in-law of TANAGHRISSON), III, 614
Nancy (Ann) (fugitive), V, 456; VI, 75, 138, 139
Nancy (wife of John Peter PRUDEN), IX, 648
Naneogauchit, I, 222, 578
Nannary, William, XII, 622
Nanoo, James, VII, 4
Nantel, Antonin, XI, 513
Nantel*, Guillaume-Alphonse (1852–1909), XII, 180, 696
Nanton, Georgina Rosalie (Taylor), XI, 871
Napagabiscou, I, 511
Naper, Ann. *See* Hudson
Napheys, George Henry, XII, 668
Napier, Anne (MacNab), IX, 519
Napier, Catherine (Christie), IV, 150
Napier, Sir Charles, X, 332
Napier, Sir Charles James, VI, 38
Napier, Duncan Campbell, IV, 154; VII, 496; VIII, 245, 619; IX, **591–92**, 627
Napier, George, X, 74
Napier, Sir George Thomas, IX, 742
Napier, Louisa Augusta (MacDougall), XII, 621
Napier, Peter, V, 95, 334
Napier, Robert, IX, 180, 181, 185
Napier, Samuel Hawkins, XII, 398
Naples, Queen of. *See* Foix, Germaine de
Napoleon I, Emperor of the French, III, xvi, xxii; V, 68, 69, 131, 242, 347, 489, 655, 660, 696, 861; VI, 16, 47, 94, 201, 380, 395, 402, 526, 536, 624, 680, 701, 713, 803; VII, 46, 51, 94, 217, 228, 304, 336, 343, 380, 543, 585, 865, 882; VIII, 135, 214, 238, 391, 392, 418, 459, 596, 622, 625, 634, 689, 732, 744, 823; IX, 21, 34, 37, 138, 444, 450, 543, 652, 849; X, 190, 305, 334, 497, 634; XI, 585; XII, 100, 102, 298, 390, 524, 621, 977
Napoleon III, Emperor of the French, VIII, 80, 619, 775; IX, 855; X, 48, 164, 165, 166, 448; XI, 339; XII, 820, 1013, 1077
Napper, James, II, **493**; III, 302
Narbonne, Pierre-Rémi, VII, 412, 484, 485, 514
Narcis, Joseph-Philippe, III, 566
Nardini, Antonio, XII, 356
Nares, Sir George Strong, VIII, 449, 624, 685; X, 29, 320, 563; XI, 382; XII, 878
Nase, Henry, VII, 198
Nash, John, VIII, 760, 873
Nash, Ruth. *See* Hollywood
Nasmyth, James, X, 231
Nasse, La. *See* Manitougatche
Natawista (Natawista Iksana), XII, **778–79**
Natchookoneck (Calf of Many Colours, Spotted Calf), XII, 497
Natel, Antoine, I, 300
Nathal, Louis. *See* Frasse de Plainval, Louis
Nathan, Esther (Nordheimer), IX, 600
Nathan, Henry, XII, 152
Nathan, Simon, IV, 385
Nathaniel, II, 668
Nathorst, Alfred Gabriel, XI, 382
Natos-api (Old Sun, Crockery Old Man), VIII, 3, 4; XII, 779
Natos-api, VIII, 4; XI, 443; XII, **779**
Natose-Onista (Medicine Calf, Button Chief), XII, 718
Natose-Onistors (Medicine Calf), XII, 802
Natoukwabekwe (Cecilia), I, 527

Natowes-tsitsi (Medicine Fire), XII, 29
Natoyist-siksina. *See* Natawista
Natsape, VI, 743
Natte, Françoise. *See* Gassin
Natte, Jean-Noël, V, 622
Natte, *dit* Marseille, Jean-Sébastien, V, **622–23**
Natte, *dit* Marseille, Marguerite. *See* Ducheneau, *dit* Sanregret
Natte, *dit* Marseille, Marie-Louise. *See* Fluette
Nau, Charles, VII, 642
Nau, François, II, 40
Nau, Françoise. *See* Lorin
Nau, Louis, VII, **642–44**; VIII, 393
Nau, Louise. *See* Pagé
Nau, Lucas, III, 480
Nau, Luc-François, III, 361, **480–81**, 627
Nau, *dit* Labry, Jacques, VI, 381
Nau, *dit* Labry, Marie-Louise. *See* Brousseau
Naud, Jean, XII, 1032
Naud, Mariane. *See* Perrault
Nau de La Boissière et de Fossambault, Catherine (Lauson de La Citière; Peuvret Demesnu), I, 428, 542, 543; II, 524
Nau de La Boissière et de Fossambault, Jacques, I, 542; II, 525
Nau de La Boissière et de Fossambault, Michèle- Thérèse (Giffard), I, 326
Naughton (Norton), Martha (Buell), VI, 90; IX, 99; X, 109
Nault*, André (1829–1924), IX, 330, 708; X, 439, 476; XI, 245, 740; XII, 132, 175, 1008
Nault, Jean-Zéphirin, IX, 119
Nault, Napoléon, XI, 748
Navailles, Anne de, Baronne de Labatut. *See* Mius d'Entremont de Pobomcoup
Navailles, Laurent de, Baron de Labatut, II, 512
Navarre, Queen of. *See* Marguerite d'Angoulême; Marguerite de Valois
Navarre, Antoine-Marie-François de, IV, 579
Navarre, Françoise (Émond), V, 304
Navarre, Jeanne de. *See* Plugette
Navarre, Marie. *See* Lothman de Barrois
Navarre, Pierre, IV, 260
Navarre, Robert, III, 525; IV, 435, **579–80**
Navarro. *See also* Ramón
Navarro, Don Juan de, III, 610
Navarro, Mary de. *See* Anderson
Navières, Jean, III, 481
Navières, Joseph, III, **481–82**
Navières, Madeleine. *See* Sicot
Nawahjegezhegwabe (Nawachjkekezhegwabe), VII, 456; VIII, 440; IX, **592–93**; XI, 473
Naywash (Neywash), V, 799
Nazette. *See* Noguet
Nazrey, Willis, XII, 259
Neal, Dorothy (Davison), IV, 197
Nealon, Frances Maria (Babbitt), XI, 39
Neatby*, Hilda Marion (1904–75), IV, 59, 279, 350; VI, 495
Neave, George, V, 838
Nebourvele. *See* Boucher
Ne-can-nete, XII, **779–80**
Necker, Germaine, Baronne de Staël-Holstein, known as Madame de Staël, VIII, 650; XI, 178; XII, 525, 776

Necker, Jacques, V, 486
Neckère, Léo-Raymond de, VII, 170
Necushin (mother of George ATKINSON, 1777–1830), IV, 33; VI, 15
Nédélec, Jean-Marie, XII, **780–81**
Nédélec, Louis, XII, 780
Nédélec, Marie. *See* Le Porz
Neé, Luis, V, 399
Need, Elizabeth Anne. *See* Godfrey
Need, John, XII, 781
Need, Mary. *See* Welfitt
Need, Thomas, XII, 525, **781–82**
Needham, Sir Joseph, IX, 82; X, 117; XI, 236; XII, 79
Needham, Mark D., X, 543
Needham, Mrs Mark D. *See* Fraser
Needham, Mary Ann. *See* Gale
Needham, William Hayden, VII, 74; VIII, 810, 842; X, 14, **543–44**; XI, 372; XII, 338, 897
Neele, J. S., IV, 578
Neelon, Augusta (Benson), XII, 783
Neelon, Cinderella. *See* Read
Neelon, George Mortimer, XII, 783
Neelon, James William, XII, 783
Neelon, Louisa (Helliwell), XII, 783
Neelon, Louisa Latham. *See* Chisholm
Neelon, Sylvester, XI, 650; XII, 529, **782–84**
Negabamat, I, 222, 282, **516**, 640
Negaskoumat, I, 516
Nègre, Marquèze (Rouffio), III, 571
Negushwa. *See* Egushwa
Nehemiah, XII, 638
Neil, Helen (Mackenzie), XII, 647
Neill, Patrick, VII, 540
Neilson, Adelaide, XII, 316
Neilson, Agnes Janet, VII, 644
Neilson, Catherine. *See* James
Neilson, Elizabeth, VII, 644
Neilson, Elizabeth (McCulloch), VII, 529
Neilson, Francis, VII, 644
Neilson, Isabel. *See* Brown
Neilson, Isabel (aunt), VII, 649
Neilson, Isabel, VII, 644
Neilson, J., VII, 366
Neilson, Jane (Sprott), IX, 738
Neilson, Janet (aunt), VII, 649
Neilson, Janet, VII, 644
Neilson, John (businessman), VIII, 748
Neilson, John (son of JOHN), VII, 644; X, 512
Neilson, John, IV, 43, 502, 581, 689, 690; V, 67, 84, 298, 702, 768, 769; VI, 42, 43, 48, 84, 98, 120, 123, 124, 191, 279, 381, 423, 424, 645; VII, 18, 72, 94, 111, 119, 168, 180, 188, 225, 226, 227, 286, 361, 373, 393, 462, 489, 503, 525, 623, **644–49**, 650, 717, 718, 739, 740, 744, 817, 818, 836, 856, 878, 880, 892, 894, 905; VIII, xxvii, 154, 155, 156, 213, 214, 284, 433, 489, 536, 711, 907, 937, 938; IX, 83, 190, 250, 261, 262, 300, 336, 360, 443, 444, 458, 498, 560, 561, 649, 650, 696, 699, 798, 808, 809, 810, 811, 812, 815; X, 61, 69, 132, 134, 219, 512, 567, 580; XI, 59, 179, 713; XII, 89, 249
Neilson, Margaret. *See* McSkimming
Neilson, Margaret, VII, 644
Neilson, Marie-Ursule. *See* Hubert
Neilson, Mary, VII, 644

Neilson, Mary (Cordner), XII, 213
Neilson, Mary (Lee), VI, 95
Neilson, Samuel, IV, 43, 107, 393, **580–81**, 689; V, 768, 834; VI, 380; VII, 644; XII, 249
Neilson, Samuel, VI, 255, 256; VII, 286, 644, 645, 646, **649–50**; VIII, 408, 938; X, 512; XII, 249
Neilson, William (grandfather), IV, 580; VII, 644
Neilson, William (uncle), VII, 644, 649
Neilson, William, VII, 644, 646, 648, 650; X, 512
Ne-kah-nea (Ne-kah-new). *See* Ne-can-nete
Nelles, Abraham, V, 857
Nelles, Abram, VI, 286; VII, 520, 652; X, 270; XI, 451, 452, **639–40**
Nelles, Elizabeth. *See* Moore
Nelles, Elizabeth (Stevens), VI, 734
Nelles, Emilia (Alexander), X, 5
Nelles, Hannah. *See* Macklem
Nelles (Nellis), Hendrick William (Henry), VII, 650, 651
Nelles (Nellis), Henry, VII, 651
Nelles, Maria Jane. *See* Waddell
Nelles, Mary. *See* Hardy
Nelles, Mary Bakewell. *See* Wood
Nelles, Robert, V, 520, 639, 643, 673, 845; VII, 57, **650–52**; X, 5; XI, 639
Nelles, Samuel Sobieski, IX, 461; X, 317; XI, **640–42**, 729, 734, 936; XII, 142
Nelles, Sarah. *See* Macklem
Nelles (Nellis), Warner, VII, 651
Nelles (Nellis), William (grandfather), VII, 650
Nelles (Nellis), William, VII, 652
Nelles, William, XI, 640
Nelligan*, Émile (1879–1941), IX, 465
Nelmes, Susanna Jane (Haszard), X, 339
Nelson, Alfred, VIII, 792
Nelson, Amelia (Robertson), IX, 667
Nelson, Anne (Brown), X, 99
Nelson, Belle (Ridout), X, 619
Nelson, Caroline. *See* Scott
Nelson, Charlotte-Josephte. *See* Noyelle de Fleurimont
Nelson, David, IV, 55
Nelson, Eliza (Gwynne), X, 325
Nelson, Elizabeth. *See* Tailer
Nelson, Emily. *See* Stanton
Nelson, Eugène, X, 547
Nelson, Frances. *See* Quinn
Nelson, George, VI, 536
Nelson, George, VI, 436, 537; VII, 138; VIII, **652–54**
Nelson, Horace Henry, IX, 16, 17, 596
Nelson, Horatio, 1st Viscount Nelson, IV, 49; V, 110, 435, 585, 631, 636; VI, 323, 371, 587, 645; VII, 45; VIII, 669, 783; IX, 485; X, 700, 701
Nelson, Horatio Admiral, XI, 62
Nelson, Hugh, X, 530; XI, 50, 237; XII, **784–85**
Nelson, Jane. *See* Dies
Nelson, Jane, VIII, 653
Nelson, John, V, 636
Nelson, John, I, 576, 637, 654; II, 14, 94, 177, 184, 442, 459, 464, **493–94**; III, 653
Nelson, John Dies, IX, 32, 439
Nelson, Léocadie. *See* Boucher
Nelson, Mary. *See* Temple
Nelson, Mary (Metherall), X, 511
Nelson, Robert (father of HUGH), XII, 784

Nelson, Robert (ship's captain), I, 144; II, 494
Nelson, Robert, VI, 180, 537; VII, 25, 105, 149, 210, 264, 334, 411, 412, 513, 514, 515, 620, 757, 758, 894; VIII, 144, 145, 146, 285, 313, 471, 539, 653; IX, 32, 73, 144, 811, 814; X, 143, 261, 490, 491, 492, 499, **544–47**, 569, 576; XI, 60, 585; XII, 118, 761
Nelson, Thomas, X, 99; XII, 54
Nelson, Uriah, XII, 1131
Nelson, William (father of ROBERT), X, 544
Nelson, William (publisher), X, 99; XII, 54, 1113
Nelson, William, VI, **536–37**; VIII, 652; IX, 553, 575, 593
Nelson, Wolfred, VI, 537; VII, 25, 174, 241, 248, 346, 478, 757; VIII, 49, 286, 392, 457, 471, 539, 616, 617, 653, 711, 791, 792, 844; IX, 16, 32, 61, 328, 434, 572, 575, **593–97**, 614, 811, 814, 826; X, 76, 78, 376, 544, 545, 574, 575, 577, 715; XI, 60, 187, 272, 353, 586; XII, 253, 261, 730
Nemiers (Nemire), George, V, 639, 640
Nemisses. *See* Guiboche, Louis
Nenangoussikou, II, 495
Neogaouachit. *See* Naneogauchit
Neolin, III, 527
Nepean, Sir Evan, IV, 197, 218, 231, 324, 604, 687, 753, 766; V, 21, 317, 350, 351, 371, 427; VI, 537, 538; VII, 524
Nepean, Johanna Francisca Carolina. *See* Wedikind
Nepean, Margaret. *See* Jones
Nepean, Nicholas, VI, 537
Nepean, Nicholas, VI, 114, 213, 214, 370, **537–39**; VII, 839
Nepomoit (Joseph), II, 199, 670
Nepveu. *See* Neveu
Nerbonne, Louis, VIII, 218
Neré. *See* Levasseur
Néret, Jean-Baptiste, II, 465, 509, 575; III, 352
Nerkingoak, IV, 536
Néron, Jean, V, 271
Nerval, Gérard de. *See* Labrunie, Gérard
Nesbitt, John James, VIII, 93, 559; XII, 52
Nesbitt, Rebecca (Phelan; wife of WILLIAM), IV, 581
Nesbitt, William, III, 418; IV, 209, 451, **581–82**, 724; V, 108, 556; VI, 551
Nescambiouit, II, xxxviii, 25, **494–96**, 626, 627; III, 505
Neskech, Marie (Marcot), VII, 582
Nesle, Sieur de (ship's captain), II, 82
Nesmond, André de, Marquis de Nesmond, I, 309; II, 246, 452; III, 454
Ness, May (Craigie), IX, 165
Nessegombewit. *See* Nescambiouit
Nestichio, IV, 48
Netawatwees (King Newcomer), III, xxxiv; IV, lii; V, 883
Net-no-kwa, VII, 844
Nettle, Richard, XII, 1107
Neufeld, Gerhard, XII, 1099
Neuman, Gottlob, III, 651
Neuman, Henry, VI, 389; VII, 813
Neuville. *See also* Dupont
Neuville, Jean-Baptiste de, IV, 375
Neuvillette. *See* Robinau
Nève, Gilette (Cheval), III, 121
Névellet, Marguerite de (Bouat), II, 81, 509
Nevers, Duchesse de, I, 425
Nevers, Phineas, IV, 195; V, 556

Nevers, Sarah (Davidson), IV, 195
Never Ties His Shoes (Oral Talker), XII, 803
Nevet, Comte de, III, 192, 199; IV, 319
Neveu, Françoise-Élisabeth. *See* Legras
Neveu, Jacques, III, 482
Neveu (Neveu de La Bretonnière), Jean-Baptiste, III, **482**; IV, 46, 709
Neveu, Marguerite (Simonnet), IV, 709
Neveu, Marie-Catherine (Gaillard), II, 234
Neveu, Marie-Denise. *See* Sevestre
Neveu, Marie-Jeanne. *See* Passard
Neveu, Philippe, III, 482
Neveu de La Bretonnière. *See* Neveu
Nevile, Sophia Charlotte (Ainslie), VII, 9
Neville, Anna (Goff), VII, 351
Neville, Louisa (Haliburton), IX, 350; XII, 403
Nevins, Archibald, V, 623
Nevins, Archibald, V, **623–25**
Nevins, Charlotte (Fothergill), VII, 317
Nevins, Grace. *See* Penrose
Nevins, James, XII, **785–86**
Nevins, Jane (wife of ARCHIBALD), V, 623
Nevins, Jane (Wright), X, 718; XII, 785
Nevins, Jane Wright, XII, 785
Nevins, Penrose, V, 623
Nevins, Pim, V, 623
Nevins, Robert, V, 624
Nevins, Susannah. *See* Richardson
Nevins, Thomas, V, 623, 624
Nevitt, Richard Barrington, XII, 778
New, Chester William, VII, 477; IX, 143
Newaukeshickwab, IV, 774
Newbegin, Harriet Marian (Gilchrist), XII, 365
Newberry, John Strong, XII, 233
Newberry, William, IV, 778; VI, 611
Newbigging, Anne Louise. *See* Hagerman
Newbigging, James, VII, 208, **652–53**; XII, 744
Newcastle-under-Lyme, Duke of. *See* Clinton
Newcastle-upon-Tyne, Duke of. *See* Pelham-Holles
Newcombe, Henry A., XII, 922
Newcomer, King. *See* Netawatwees
Newechekeshequeby. *See* Nawahjegezhegwabe
Newell, Elizabeth (Alexander; Martin), XI, 4
Newell, Elizabeth (Odell), VII, 657; XII, 797
Newell, Susanna (Pond), V, 681
Newhouse, Seth, VI, 760
Newland, Elizabeth (Jadis), IV, 388
Newland, Robert, I, 82, 666; II, 537
Newlands, Barbara (Cunningham), X, 210
Newman, Amelia (wife of WILLIAM HERMAN), XII, 786
Newman, Ann. *See* Holdsworth
Newman, Catherine (mother of WILLIAM HERMAN), XII, 786
Newman, Charlotte Louisa. *See* Cromartie
Newman, Henry, II, 348
Newman, Holdsworth, V, 625
Newman, J. W., XII, 786
Newman, John (brother of ROBERT), V, 625, 626
Newman, John (merchant), V, 625
Newman, John Henry, IX, 289, 762; X, 54, 548; XII, 490, 712, 713, 715
Newman, Lydston, V, 625, 626
Newman, Mary. *See* Holdsworth

Newman, Richard (uncle), V, 625
Newman, Richard, V, 625, 626
Newman, Robert, V, 625
Newman, Robert, V, **625–27**, 641
Newman, Sir Robert William, V, 626
Newman, Ruth. *See* Plummer
Newman, Thomas (father), V, 625, 626
Newman, Thomas, V, 626
Newman, William. *See also* Smith, Henry More
Newman, William, V, 641, 785, 838; VI, 637
Newman, William Herman, XII, **786–87**
Newman, William P., VII, 181; XI, 400; XII, 960
Newnham, Jervois Arthur, XI, 523; XII, 446
News Carrier. *See* Carrihogo
Newsom, George, V, 623
Newton, Ensign, III, 343; IV, 539
Newton, Catherine. *See* Knaut
Newton, Charlotte Ann (Fairbanks), XI, 308
Newton, Eliza (Uniacke), VI, 789
Newton, Emmeline. *See* Tod
Newton, Hannah Adams (Binney), V, 81
Newton, Henry (brother-in-law of Jonathan BINNEY), IV, 561; V, 81
Newton, Henry (son of Hibbert), VII, 257
Newton, Hibbert, VII, 257
Newton, Sir Isaac, II, 595; VIII, 214, 240
Newton, Jean (Drummond), VI, 220
Newton, John (office holder), IV, 199, 414, 450, 451, 581, 695; V, 81
Newton, John (officer), VII, 806
Newton, John (son of JOHN), III, 482, 483
Newton, John, III, 303, **482–83**, 593
Newton, Louisa W. (Dumaresq), VII, 257
Newton, Margaret. *See* Walker
Newton, Mary (Girty; Turner), V, 345
Newton, Thomasina (wife of JOHN), III, 482
Newton, William, XI, 571
Newton, William Henry, XI, 882
Newton, Sir William John, VIII, 604
Neyeswamak, XII, 551
Neyon de Villiers, Pierre-Joseph, III, 528, 529
Neywash. *See* Naywash
Nias, George Elmes, IX, 428
Nicanapé. *See* Chachagouesse
Nichiwa. *See* Maskepetoon
Nichol, John Pringle, IX, 461
Nichol, Robert, V, 403, 522, 643, 782; VI, 4, 5, 148, 149, 212, 230, 248, 489, 490, **539–46**, 610, 630, 631, 657, 809; VII, 37, 38, 41, 58, 251, 313, 370, 457, 919, 920; VIII, 340, 476, 515, 517, 518, 597, 608, 858; IX, 332
Nichol, Theresa. *See* Wright
Nichol, Thomas W., VIII, 836
Nichol, Walter, XII, 1102
Nicholas. *See also* Karaghtadie
Nicholas I, Emperor of Russia, VIII, 756
Nicholas of Lynne, I, **678–79**
Nicholas, Hiran, VII, 134
Nicholls, Charlotte. *See* Brontë
Nichols, Katharine (Upham), V, 830
Nichols (Nicolls), Louisa (Sellar), IX, 711
Nichols, Louisa Matilda (Richey), XI, 733
Nichols, Moses, VII, 282
Nichols, Zoé. *See* Ainsse

Nicholson, Amy. *See* Vernon
Nicholson, Donald, XII, 886
Nicholson, Edith (Francklin), IV, 272
Nicholson, Elizabeth Luttrell (Winton), VIII, 947; IX, 846
Nicholson, Francis, II, 3, 38, 39, 122, 123, 152, 165, 167, 177, 186, 198, 205, 206, 254, 258, 272, 274, 289, 437, 445, 461, 487, **496–99**, 547, 582, 588, 591, 603, 627, 644, 651, 652, 661, 668; III, 6, 177, 200, 207, 208, 264, 276, 421, 436, 500, 516, 579, 596, 622, 623, 665; IV, xxi, 251
Nicholson, Grace Vernon (Ritchie, Lady Ritchie), XII, 895, 900
Nicholson, Thomas, II, 496
Nicholson, Thomas L., XII, 895
Nickalls, James, VIII, 760
Nick'a'thu'tin. *See* Primeau, Louis
Nickinson*, Charlotte (Morrison) (1832–1910), IX, 576, 597, 598
Nickinson, Eliza (Peters), IX, 597
Nickinson, Isabella (Walcot), IX, 597, 598
Nickinson, John, IX, 576, **597–98**; XII, 306
Nickinson, Mary Ann. *See* Talbot
Nickinson, Virginia (Marlowe), IX, 597
Nickle*, William Folger (1869–1957), XII, 496
Nickus. *See* Karaghtadie
Nicol, George, IV, 763
Nicola. *See* Hwistesmetxē′qEn
Nicolas. *See also* Orontony
Nicolas (clerk), I, 90, 238
Nicolas (Pawnee), II, 216
Nicolas (sailor), II, 9
Nicolas, Auguste, XII, 501
Nicolas, François, VII, 412, 514; X, 527
Nicolas, Louis, II, 53
Nicolas de Chamfort. *See* Chamfort, Sébastien-Roch-Nicolas
Nicolle, Charles-Dominique, VI, 201
Nicollet, Marie. *See* Lamer
Nicollet, Thomas, I, 516
Nicollet de Belleborne, Jean, I, 35, 186, 197, 367, 369, 410, 473, 489, **516–18**, 639; II, xli, 383, 385, 448; III, 374
Nicollet de Belleborne, Marguerite. *See* Couillard de Lespinay
Nicollet de Belleborne, Marguerite (Legardeur de Repentigny), I, 517; II, 383, 385, 386; III, 374
Nicolls. *See also* Nichols
Nicolls, Gustavus, X, 547
Nicolls, Harriet Mary. *See* Mountain
Nicolls, Heriot Frances. *See* Thomson
Nicolls, Jasper Hume, IX, 580; X, **547–48**; XI, 523; XII, 385, 736, 813, 1100
Nicolls, Richard, I, 308
Nicolson, Janet Ann (Bethune), XII, 106
Nicou-Choron, Stéphane-Louis, IX, 632
Niedermeyer, Louis, X, 228
Nielson, Elizabeth (Macdonald), XI, 551
Niepce, Nicéphore, XII, 787
Nieto. *See* Alenzo
Nightingale, Florence, IX, 660, 733; XI, 559; XII, 217
Nij-Kwenatc-anibic. *See* Cuoq, Jean-André
Nika, I, 183; II, 197
Nikonha, XII, 402
Niles, Annie Maria (Hyman), X, 375, 549

Niles, Gertrude. *See* Dykert
Niles, Hannah. *See* Hicks
Niles, Henry, X, 548
Niles, Minerva Anne (Wenham; Gamble), X, 299
Niles, Stephen, X, 548
Niles, W. H., X, 65
Niles, William E., VII, 844; X, 375, **548–49**
Nilson, Janet Wilson. *See* McDougall
Nilson, Robert, IX, 489
Nimimitt (Nimquid). *See* Wenemouet
Nimmo, Alexander, VIII, 541
Nims, Abigail (Towatogowash, rebaptized Élisabeth) (Raizenne), V, 703; VI, 627
Nina, Lorenzo, X, 251
Nina-kisoom (Chief Moon), XII, 718, 778
Ninākon. *See* Minweweh
Nina'msko'taput-sikumi (Medicine Pipe Man Returning with a Crane War Whoop), XII, 970, 971
Ninasinlahelawas, XII, 289
Nind, Philip Henry, IX, 296; XI, 301, 302
Ningausim, IV, 756
Ninivois, III, 527
Ninsotin, V, 835
Ninstints, IV, 420
Niort de La Minotière, Pierre de, III, 569
Niort de La Noraye, Louis de, I, 63; II, 426
Nipimoit. *See* Nepomoit
Niquet, Anne. *See* Hébert
Niquet, Catherine (Marin de La Malgue), II, 458; III, 431
Nisbet, James, X, **549–50**; XI, 80; XII, 54
Nisbet, Margaret. *See* Graham
Nisbet, Mary. *See* MacBeth
Nisbet, Robert, VII, 654
Nisbet, Thomas (father of JAMES), X, 549
Nisbet, Thomas (son of THOMAS), VII, 654
Nisbet, Thomas, VII, **653–55**
Nisbett, William, IV, 608
Nish, Damaris (Smith), VII, 814
Nissowaquet, IV, 300, 563, **582–83**; V, 8, 229; VI, 188
Nitachinon. *See* Chabert de Joncaire, Philippe-Thomas
Nitschmann, David, V, 883
Nivard Saint-Dizier, Étienne, V, 286; VI, 666
Nivard Saint-Dizier, Marie-Anne (Picoté de Belestre), IV, 633
Nivernais, Duc de. *See* Mancini-Mazarini
Niverville. *See* Boucher
Niverville, Chevalier. *See* Boucher de Niverville, Joseph
Nixon, Ann, I, 520
Nixon, Anne (Hunter), VII, 428
Nixon, Em, I, 520
Nixon, John, VIII, 859
Nixon, John, I, 39, 84, 232, 281, 324, 328, 416, 477, **518–20**, 543, 553, 605, 666; II, 49, 231, 318
Nixon, Joseph, VIII, 281
Nixon, Mary. *See* Macaulay
N'Kuala. *See* Hwistesmetxē′qEn
N'Kwala, Sophie, XII, 450
Nngkwigetklals. *See* Tahaygen
Noad, Emma Gaden. *See* Lilly
Noad, Henry John, IX, **598–99**
Noad, James Street, IX, 598, 599
Noad, John Batson, IX, 598
Noad, Joseph, VII, 269; IX, 195; X, **550–51**

Noad, Rachel. *See* Street
Noah, II, 474
Noah, Frances (Hart), VII, 386
Noailles, Adrien-Maurice de, Comte d'Ayen, Duc de Noailles, III, 231, 556; IV, 750
Noailles, Anne-Jules de, Duc de Noailles, II, 567
Noailles, Louis de, Duc d'Ayen, III, 556
Noailles, Louis-Antoine de, II, 567
Noailles, Lucie-Félicité de (Estrées, Duchesse d'Estrées), III, 15
Nobili, Domenico, VIII, 654
Nobili, John, VIII, **654–55**; X, 221
Nobili, Rosa. *See* Eutizi
Noble, Anna Maria (Browne), X, 104
Noble, Arthur, III, 128, 150, 260, 261, 331, **483–84**, 514, 653; IV, 213, 291, 459, 559, 651; V, 498
Noble, Francis, III, 483, 484
Noble, George C., XI, 682
Noble, Hannah. *See* Barker
Noble, James, III, 483
Noble, John, IV, 712; V, 675
Noble, John Hatt, V, 675
Noble, Maria (Beasley), VII, 56
Noble, Mary (Margaret) (Riddle; wife of SETH), V, 627
Noble, Ruhama. *See* Rich
Noble, Sarah. *See* Macklin
Noble, Seth, V, 296, **627–28**, 666; VI, 718
Noble, Thomas, V, 627
Noble Du Revest, Joseph-François de, III, 93; IV, 699
Nodogawerrimet, III, xxxviii, **484–85**, 585
Nodowance, IV, 260
Noegabinat. *See* Ouagabemat
Noel, Bernard. *See* Bernard, Noël
Noel, Charles Noel, Baron Barham and 1st Earl of Gainsborough, VIII, 396
Noël, Étienne, I, 167, 169, 384, 520
Noel, Frances (Philipps), III, 515
Noël, Geneviève. *See* Dussaut
Noel (Edwards), Sir Gerard Noel, VIII, 650
Noel, Henry, 4th Earl of Gainsborough, VII, 9
Noël, Jacques, I, 598
Noël, Jacques, I, 23, 170, 384, 409, **520**
Noël, Jean (father of Étienne), I, 520
Noël, Jean (son of JACQUES), I, 520
Noël, Jean-Baptiste (clergyman), IV, 134, 298
Noël, Jean-Baptiste (father of MARIE-GENEVIÈVE), V, 165, 269; VI, 546; VII, 170
Noël, Jeanne. *See* Cartier
Noel, John, XII, 834
Noel, Louis, XII, 834
Noël, Marguerite (Toussaint), XII, 1065
Noël, Marguerite (Trestler), V, 827
Noël, Marguerite-Ursule. *See* Lajus
Noël, Marie-Geneviève (Drapeau), V, 269; VI, **546**; XII, 296
Noel, Mary. *See* Peminuit Paul
Noël, Michel, I, 520
Nœufville. *See* Lamorel
Nogaret de La Valette, Jean-Louis, Duc d'Épernon, I, 427
Noguet (Nazette), Marie-Anne (Payzant; Caigin), VI, 573
Noinville, Noël-Alexandre de, III, 342
Noiré. *See* Maleray
Noirefontaine, Monsieur (explorer), I, 423, 425

Noirmont. *See* Pipon
Noiseux, François-Xavier, III, 122; IV, 142, 754; V, 77, 253, 295; VI, 14, 207, 572; VIII, 366
Nolan, Anne (Desjordy Moreau de Cabanac), II, 186
Nolan, Catherine (Martin de Lino), II, 462, 463, 464, 465
Nolan, Jean-Baptiste, III, 485
Nolan, Jean-Marie, III, 251, 485
Nolan, Marie (La Porte de Louvigny), II, 346
Nolan, Marie-Anne. *See* La Marque
Nolan, Marie-Louise (Cauchon), XI, 164
Nolan, Pierre, II, 186, 464
Nolan Lamarque, Charles, III, 251, 450, **485–86**, 520; IV, 46, 283, 284, 311
Nolan Lamarque, Jacques-Marie, III, 243; VI, 383
Nolan Lamarque, Marie-Anne. *See* Legardeur de Saint-Pierre
Nolan Lamarque, Marie-Anne (Grasset de Saint-Sauveur), IV, 311
Nolan Lamarque, Marie-Anne-Thérèse. *See* Céloron de Blainville
Nolet, Mme (sorceress), X, 20
Noliboise, Saubade de (Lestage), III, 393
Nolin, Angélique, VI, 547; VIII, 720
Nolin, Augustin, VI, 547
Nolin*, Charles (d. 1907), VI, 548; XI, 738, 745, 746; XII, 554, 555, 608
Nolin, Jean-Baptiste, VI, 236, 317, **546–48**; VIII, 720
Nolin, Louis, VI, 100, 547; VII, 517
Nolin, Louise (Couillard de Lespinay), II, 156
Nolin, Marguerite, VI, 547; VIII, 720
Nolin, Marie-Angélique. *See* Couvret
Nonosbawsut, V, 243, 244; VI, 706
Nonosecash (Assakis), V, 885
Noodogawirramet. *See* Nodogawerrimet
Noogoonik, VII, 270
No-okska-stumik (Three Bulls), XI, 444, 445
No-okskatos (Three Suns), VIII, 3; XI, 442; XII, 779
Noonan, James L., XI, 4
Nooth, Bridget. *See* Mervin
Nooth, Elizabeth (wife of JOHN MERVIN), VI, 548
Nooth, Henry, VI, 548
Nooth, John Mervin, IV, 589; V, 202, 471, 501, 502, 503, 592, 684; VI, 68, 258, 325, **548–50**
Norbury, Earl of. *See* Toler
Nordbeck, Caroline (wife of PETER), IX, 599
Nordbeck, Grace (Langford; wife of PETER), VII, 483; IX, 599
Nordbeck, Peter, VII, 483, 875, 876; IX, **599–600**; XI, 116; XII, 786
Norden, Mary (Goffe), II, 254
Norden, Nathaniel, II, 254
Nordheimer, Abraham, VIII, 347, 445; IX, **600–1**; X, 371; XII, 188, 222, 959
Nordheimer, Esther. *See* Nathan
Nordheimer, Fanny. *See* Rosenthal
Nordheimer, Isaac, IX, 600
Nordheimer, Meier, IX, 600
Nordheimer, Samuel, IX, 600; X, 371; XII, 43, 188, 222, 223, 959
Noreau, Jeanne (La Forest), II, 169
Noremberguer (Cromberger), Lazaro (Lazaro Aleman), I, 157
Norfolk, Duke of. *See* Howard

Norman, Ann (Truscott), VIII, 895
Norman, Elizabeth. *See* Munden
Norman, Georgina (Southcott), XII, 981
Norman, Nathan, XI, **642**
Normanby, Marquess of. *See* Phipps
Normand, Anne-Françoise (Boutillier), IX, 73
Normand, Augustin-Nicolas, VIII, 655
Normand, Charles, IV, 203
Normand, Claire. *See* Dufresne
Normand, François (brother-in-law of ALEXIS and
    CHARLES-FRANÇOIS Painchaud), VIII, 675
Normand, François (nephew of ALEXIS and CHARLES-
    FRANÇOIS Painchaud), VIII, 675
Normand, François (son of FRANÇOIS), VIII, 655
Normand, François, VIII, **655–56**
Normand, Hercule, VIII, 655
Normand, Marie. *See* Lessard
Normand, Marie-Louise-Alphonsine. *See* Giroux
Normand, Télesphore-Eusèbe, XI, 340, 814
Normand, Victoire. *See* Painchaud
Normandeau, Joseph, IV, 703; V, 436; VI, 487, 488
Normandeau*, Louis (1812–91), IX, 610; X, 428, 429
Normandeau, *dit* Deslauriers, Marie-Madeleine. *See*
    Sasseville
Normandin, Daniel, II, 170, **499**
Normandin, Étienne, X, 153
Normandin, Jacob, II, 499
Normandin, Louise. *See* Hayot
Normandin, Madeleine (Billy), II, 499
Normandin, Marie. *See* Briant
Normandin, Pierre, II, 276
Normandin, *dit* Le Sauvage, Laurent, II, 170
Normandin, *dit* Le Sauvage, Marie-Louise (David), II, 170
Normant, Charles, III, 486
Normant, Marie. *See* Legrand
Normant Du Faradon, Louis, II, 143, 492; III, 164, 165,
    193, 195, **486–88**; IV, 201, 235, 236, 237, 542; V, 498
Normanville. *See* Godefroy
Noro, II, xxx, **499–500**, 504
Noroy, Sieur de. *See* Bochart
Norquay, Mrs. *See* Spence
Norquay, Elizabeth. *See* Setter
Norquay, Isabella. *See* Truthwaite
Norquay, John (cousin of JOHN), XI, 643
Norquay, John (father of JOHN), XI, 642
Norquay, John, XI, 47, 194, 593, 613, **642–47**, 909; XII,
    83, 128, 129, 370, 372, 658, 941, 983
Norrey. *See* Le Picard
Norris, Catharine (Rendell), XII, 888
Norris, Catherine (Crookshank), VIII, 191
Norris, Elizabeth. *See* Aylmer
Norris, George, XII, 6
Norris, James, XI, 650; XII, 529, 782, 783, 971
Norris, John, XII, 671
Norris, Sir John, II, 246, 293, 395, 564, 666; III, **488–89**,
    655
Norris Da Costa, Mary (De Haven), IX, 199
Norsworthy, Lucy (Jervois), XII, 475
North, Brownlow, X, 516
North, Christopher. *See* Wilson, John
North, Edward, XI, 286
North, Frederick, Lord North and 2nd Earl of Guilford, IV,
    xlii, xliii, xlvi, xlvii, 6, 25, 129, 230, 260, 280, 349, 538,

571, 609, 726, 792; V, 134, 148, 152, 241, 479, 849,
    890, 898, 899; VI, 75, 89, 137
North, J. B., XI, 834
Northcote, James, V, 382
Northington, Earl of. *See* Henley
Northumberland, Duchess of. *See* Burrell
Northumberland, Duke of. *See* Percy
Northup, Agnes. *See* Harvey
Northup, Emily. *See* Cochran
Northup, Jeremiah, X, 172, **551–52**; XI, 280
Northup, John, X, 551
Northup, Joseph, X, 551
Northwick, Baroness. *See* Bateman-Hanbury
Norton. *See also* Naughton
Norton, Mr (father of JOHN), VI, 550
Norton, Mrs. *See* Anderson
Norton, Amos, XI, 357
Norton, Caroline Elizabeth Sarah. *See* Sheridan
Norton, Catherine. *See* Karighwaycagh
Norton, Elizabeth. *See* McCliesh
Norton, Fletcher, 1st Baron Grantley, IV, xli
Norton, Hiram, VII, 458; VIII, 743; IX, 825; XII, 258
Norton, John (clergyman), III, 162
Norton, John (Tehonakaraa) (son of JOHN), VI, 552
Norton, John, IV, 416; V, 114, 255, 412, 803, 804, 810; VI,
    3, 102, 103, 152, 153, 331, 373, 542, **550–53**, 760; VII,
    369, 466, 520, 849; VIII, 409, 744; XI, 453
Norton, John Pitkin, VIII, 436
Norton, Joseph, VII, 562
Norton, Margaret. *See* Nahovway
Norton, Mary (Polly), IV, 584
Norton, Moses, III, 490, 534; IV, 33, 339, 340, 523,
    **583–85**, 727; V, 451; IX, 722
Norton, Sir Reginald, VIII, 744
Norton, Richard, II, xxvii, 51, 65, 308, 310, 313, 493, 604,
    616; III, xxxiii, 415, 447, **489–90**, 520, 599, 661; IV,
    383, 523, 583
Norton, Sarah (mother of RICHARD), III, 489
Norton, Sarah (wife of MOSES), IV, 584
Norton, Thomas, IX, 721
Nosawaguet. *See* Nissowaquet
Notman, Alice Merry. *See* Woodwark
Notman, Charles Frederick, XII, 790
Notman, Elizabeth (Bell), VIII, 72
Notman, James, XII, 444
Notman, Janet. *See* Sloan
Notman, William, XII, 787
Notman, William, IX, 736; X, 263; XI, 683, 871, 872, 899;
    XII, 207, 247, 248, 287, 335, 336, 444, **787–91**
Notman*, William McFarlane (1857–1913), XII, 790
Nottingham, Earl of. *See* Howard
Nouchet, Barbe. *See* Barrat
Nouchet, Geneviève. *See* Gatin
Nouchet, Joseph, III, 226, **490–91**
Nouchet, Joseph-Étienne, III, 226, 490, **491**; IV, 624
Nouchet, Julien, III, 490
Nouchet, Louise-Catherine. *See* Foucault
Nouë, Anne de, I, **52**, 121, 410, 453, 527; II, 83
Nouel. *See* Noël
Nouette, Jacques, III, 205
Nourse, William, VII, 249, 250; VIII, 391
Nouvel, Henri, I, 50, 59, 282; II, 159, 347, **500–2**; III, 103
Nov dogg aw wer imet. *See* Nodogawerrimet

Novello, Vincent, XII, 504
Noverre, Augustin, VIII, 347
Nowlan, Agathe. *See* Perrault
Nowlan, Bridget Caroline (McGreevy), XII, 626
Nowlan, Edward, VI, 265, 266
Nowlan, Maurice, VIII, 863
Nowlan, Patrick, IX, 393
Nowlan, Pelagius, VII, 292, 404
Noxon, James, XI, 652
Noyan. *See* Payen
Noyelle de Fleurimont, Charlotte-Josephte (Nelson), IX, 593, 595, 597
Noyelles, Marie de. *See* Bridou
Noyelles, Pierre-Philippe de, Baron de Fleurimont, III, 491
Noyelles de Fleurimont, Charles-Joseph de, III, 242, 245, 492
Noyelles de Fleurimont, Marie-Charlotte de. *See* Petit de Levilliers
Noyelles de Fleurimont, Nicolas-Joseph de, II, 156; III, 16, 46, 47, 242, 245, 253, 378, 430, **491–93**; IV, 34, 288; V, 97
Noyelles de Fleurimont, Pierre-Philippe de, III, 492
Noyes, Sieur de (officer), II, 578
Noyes, Anna (Gale; Byles), V, 127
Noyes, C., VIII, 675
Noyes, Elizabeth L. (Abbott), XII, 3
Noyes, Eliza Heath Ellen (Wurtele; Cary), IX, 115
Noyes, Thomas, VI, 477
Noyon (Danio), Jacques-René de, III, 493
Noyon, Abigail de. *See* Stebbins
Noyon, Catherine de. *See* Chevalier
Noyon, Dorothée de, IV, 765
Noyon, Édouard de, I, 250
Noyon, Jacques de, III, 248, **493–94**; IV, 173
Noyon, Jean de, III, 493
Noyon, Marie de. *See* Chauvin
Noyon, Marie de (Renaud), III, 494
Noyon, Suzanne de (David), I, 250
Noyrot, Philibert, I, 160, 411, 412, **521–22**, 579, 596, 665
Nugent, Agnes, named Sister Mary Vincent, VIII, 185
Nugent, Anne (Dease), XI, 240
Nugent, Anne Susanne (Heriot), VII, 397
Nugent, Elizabeth. *See* McFarlane
Nugent, Ellen Maria. *See* Creedon
Nugent, Frank Staynor, XII, 468
Nugent, John, VII, 579
Nugent, John, X, **552**
Nugent, John Valentine, VII, 113, 155, 156, 296; VIII, 184, 381, 468, 949, 951; IX, 71; X, **552–53**, 687; XI, 28, 429, 673
Nugent, Maria, named Sister Mary Joseph, VIII, 184
Nugent, Mary. *See* Hurley
Nugent, Mary, XII, 157, 158
Nugent, Patrick, VIII, 656
Nugent, Richard, VII, 815; VIII, **656–58**, 958; XII, 753
Nugent, Sarah Phebe (Manahan), VII, 579
Nunns, J. F., X, 371
Nurse, Joshua Billings, IX, 195
Nursey, Walter R., XII, 83, 84
Nutimus, IV, 27
Nutt, George Washington Morrison, XI, 865
Nutt, John, I, **522**
Nutt, Robert, I, 522

Nuttall, Reginald, XI, 638
Nutter, David, VII, 272, 610
Nutter, Valentine, V, 438
Nutting, James Walton, VII, 123; VIII, 656, 968; IX, **601–2**; XI, 214
Nutting, John, IX, 601
Nutting, Mary. *See* Walton
Nutting, Mary Elizabeth. *See* MacLean
Nye, Elizabeth B. (Hoyle), VIII, 415

OAGIMONT. *See* Ouagimou
Oakes, Forrest, IV, 262, 263, **585–86**; V, 368, 382, 656, 683; X, 273
Oakes, Georgiana (Vavasour), IX, 806
Oakes*, Sir Harry (1874–1943), VI, 149
Oakes, Jemima (Ermatinger), IV, 263; VI, 236, 237
Oakes, John, IV, 205, 206, 585; V, 36, 37, 436, 736, 737; VI, 231, 664
Oakes, John Meticamish, IV, 585
Oakes, Margaret (Gray), V, 382
Oakley, Alfred, XI, **647–49**
Oakley, Elizabeth (Southack), III, 596
Oakley, Emily (wife of ALFRED), XI, 647
Oakley, George, V, 495
Oakley, Mary (Fuller), IX, 293
Obah-dahm-wawn-gezzhago-quay. *See* Johnston, Jane
Obalski*, Joseph (1852–1915), XI, 456
O Bask. *See* Bastarache
O'Beirne, Claire (mother of EUGENE FRANCIS), IX, 602
O'Beirne, Eugene Francis, IX, 518, **602–3**; X, 700
O'Beirne, John, IX, 602
Obemau-unoqua (Nancy?), V, 742; VII, 776
Oberholser. *See* Overholser
Obiniguaro. *See* Oubignaro
Obomsawin, Simon, VIII, 78
O'Brian, Catherine (McCarthy), VI, 426
O'Brian, Sarah (Shuler), VIII, 476, 477
O'Brien, Anne (England), V, 306
O'Brien*, Cornelius (1843–1906), XII, 36, 166, 638
O'Brien, Daniel, XII, 791
O'Brien, Dennis, IX, 323, **603–4**, 618
O'Brien, Edward George, VII, 231; VIII, 804; IX, 607; X, **554**; XI, 877; XII, 792
O'Brien, Eliza (de Blaquière), VIII, 204
O'Brien, Elizabeth. *See* Lindo
O'Brien, Elizabeth (Laurent; Têtu), IX, 362, 783
O'Brien, Henry, XII, 454
O'Brien, James, V, 306
O'Brien, James (Bronterre), X, 313
O'Brien, Jane. *See* Shotwell
O'Brien, Jane. *See* Smith
O'Brien, John, X, 361; XII, 199, 332
O'Brien, John, VIII, **658–60**
O'Brien, John Daniel O'Connell, XII, **791–92**
O'Brien, Katherine Jane. *See* Brough
O'Brien, Laurence, VII, 156, 296, 633; VIII, 233, 234, 381, 863; IX, 30, 70, 584, **604–6**, 682; XI, 432, 433, 673, 881
O'Brien, Lucius, IX, 606; X, 554
O'Brien, Lucius, 13th Baron Inchiquin, XII, 792, 795
O'Brien, Lucius James, VIII, 804; IX, **606–7**; X, 554
O'Brien, Lucius Richard, X, 393, 554; XI, 919; XII, 327, 328, 336, 525, **792–96**
O'Brien, Margaret. *See* Manning

O'Brien, Margaret. *See* St John
O'Brien, Margaret (Cleary), XII, 198
O'Brien, Mary. *See* Callender-Campbell
O'Brien, Mary. *See* Darcy
O'Brien, Mary Sophia. *See* Gapper
O'Brien, Rachel-Charlotte. *See* Frobisher
O'Brien, Richard Baptist, VIII, 307, 664, 665, 920; IX, 828
O'Brien, Rosalie. *See* Roche
O'Brien, William, XII, 455, 811
O'Brien*, William Edward (1831–1914), XI, 594; XII, 581, 584, 609, 617
O'Bryan, William, VIII, 200; X, 511
Obwandiyag. *See* Pontiac
O'Callaghan, Father, VII, 347
O'Callaghan, Charlotte Augustina. *See* Crampe
O'Callaghan, Edmund Bailey, VI, 784; VII, 173, 346, 347, 503, 513, 527, 758; VIII, 147, 261, 284, 285, 703, 730, 915; IX, 73, 201, 301, 302, 458, 485, 594, 650, 695, 811, 814; X, 20, 361, 545, **554–56**, 575; XI, 117, 172
O'Callaghan, Ellen. *See* Hawe
Ocard, Pierrette (Satin), VII, 773
Ochagach (Ochakah). *See* Auchagah
Ochiltree, Lord. *See* Stewart
Ochterloney, David, III, 544
Ocken (Ockenfuss), Lorenz, XII, 458
Ocnort, Monsieur (architect), VI, 27
O'Connell, Daniel, VI, 783; VII, 5, 8, 9, 114, 154, 221, 293, 294, 295, 298, 547, 598, 631, 664, 842; VIII, xxv, 199, 229, 470, 947; IX, 25, 70, 71, 154, 155, 226, 299, 485, 489, 490, 582, 829; X, 313, 559, 580; XII, 89, 357, 791, 1083
O'Connell, Daniel (Charles), Count O'Connell, IX, 25
O'Connell, Mary (Baldwin), IX, 25, 26
O'Connor, Bridget (Doyle), IX, 225
O'Connor, Catherine (MacDermot), XI, 545
O'Connor, Daniel, VII, 445, 446; IX, 287
O'Connor*, Dennis (1841–1911), XI, 904; XII, 1085
O'Connor, Ellen (mother of WILLIAM JOSEPH), XII, 796
O'Connor, Feargus, X, 313
O'Connor, J., IX, 393
O'Connor, John, XI, 649
O'Connor, John, X, 561; XI, **649–50**; XII, 330, 885
O'Connor, John J., XII, 797
O'Connor, Juliana (Gugy), VII, 359; X, 320
O'Connor, Mary. *See* Barrett
O'Connor, Mary (O'Connor), XI, 649
O'Connor, Mary Anne (Friel), IX, 287, 288
O'Connor, Michael, XII, 796
O'Connor, Richard Alphonsus, XII, 199
O'Connor, Roderick, IX, 288
O'Connor, William Joseph, XII, 407, **796–97**
Odatsighta, II, 474, 502
Oddy, Mary Ann (Heavysege), X, 346
Odelin, Jacques, VII, 655
Odelin, Jacques, VII, **655–57**; IX, 465; XII, 252
Odelin, Marie-Angélique. *See* Lavigne
Odell, Anne. *See* de Cou
Odell, Anne (McCawley), X, 453
Odell, Elizabeth. *See* Newell
Odell, Elizabeth (Baillie), VII, 658, 659; IX, 23
Odell, Elizabeth Ann. *See* Bliss
Odell, George Clinton Densmore, XII, 316, 317, 949
Odell, John, V, 628

Odell, Jonathan, V, 34, 155, 156, 157, 162, 355, 589, **628–31**, 868; VI, 140, 171, 246; VII, 657, 658, 659; XII, 797, 798
Odell, Temperance. *See* Dickinson
Odell, William, V, 628
Odell, William Franklin, V, 465, 630; VI, 54, 138; VII, 97, 140, 187, 291, 443, 445, **657–59**, 865; VIII, 274, 378, 809, 841; IX, 23, 146; X, 315, 453, 644, 711; XII, 691, 797
Odell, William Hunter, VII, 74, 659; X, 73; XII, 18, **797–98**
Odeserundiye. *See* Deserontyon, John
Odet d'Orsonnens, Louise-Sophie d'. *See* Rocher
Odet d'Orsonnens, Marie-Louise-Adeline d'. *See* Dorval
Odet d'Orsonnens, Marie-Salomée d'. *See* Poirier
Odet d'Orsonnens, Protais d', XII, 798
Odet d'Orsonnens, Thomas-Edmond d', VIII, 136; XII, 304, **798–99**
Odin, Henriette (Feller), VII, 185, 210; VIII, 396; IX, **607–10**; X, 428, 633, 675; XI, 209, 924; XII, 225
Odivert. *See* Romain
O'Donel, Ann. *See* Crosby
O'Donel, Eleonora (O'Sullivan), VII, 666
O'Donel, James Louis, V, 122, 123, 360, 408, 473, 494, 595, **631–34**; VI, 243, 244, 711; VII, 630; XII, 860
O'Donel, Michael (father), V, 631
O'Donel, Michael, V, 631
O'Donnell, James, VI, **553–55**; VII, 667, 696, 697; VIII, 763; XI, 92; XII, 809
O'Donnell*, John Harrison (1838–1912), XI, 46, 64, 193
O'Donoghue*, Daniel John (1844–1907), XI, 505, 580, 638, 648; XII, 703
O'Donoghue, William Bernard, X, 439, **556–57**, 559; XI, 472, 624, 740, 742, 743; XII, 34, 68, 132, 363, 370, 602, 678, 1008
O'Donohoe, John, XII, 330, 331, 333
O'Donovan, Margaret (Alleyn), XI, 15
O'Dwyer, C. P., VIII, 229
O'Dwyer, Esther (Dixon), X, 231
Œhulhtzœn (Hoolson), VII, 474
O'Farrell, John, XI, 498
Offenbach, Jacques, X, 228
Ogden, Ann. *See* Richardson
Ogden, Charles Richard, VI, 717; VII, 72, 105, 150, 264, 300, 667, 810, 878, 879, 880, 893, 906; VIII, 109, 155, 248, 617, 662, 729, 844, 848; IX, 459, **610–11**; X, 181, 337, 526; XII, 88
Ogden, Charles S., XI, 880
Ogden, David, X, 10
Ogden, Harriet Lawrence (Evans), VIII, 662; IX, 246
Ogden, Isaac, V, 211, 226, 388, 538, 614, 684; VI, 86, 377, 512; VII, 119, 788, 872; VIII, 109, 660, 726; IX, 246, 610
Ogden, John Cosens, VI, 528
Ogden, Jonathan (judge), V, 726; VI, 784
Ogden, Jonathan (owner of stage-coach line), IX, 825
Ogden, Julia. *See* Rivet
Ogden, Mary Aston Augusta. *See* Coffin
Ogden, Peter Skene, VI, 251, 254, 720; VII, 78, 473, 569; VIII, 350, 577, 580, **660–63**, 766, 814, 818; IX, 197, 456, 625, 850, 851, 852, 854; X, 241, 242, 391, 426, 486; XI, 16, 17, 885, 886; XII, 110
Ogden, Sarah. *See* Hanson

Ogden, Susan. *See* Clarke
Ogden*, Uzziel (1828–1910), XII, 10, 11
Oge-Buno-Quay. *See* Johnston, Charlotte
Ogenheratarihiens (Ogeratarihen), I, **522–23**
Ogilvie, Captain, I, 305
Ogilvie, Alexander, IX, 822, 823; XII, 800
Ogilvie*, Alexander Walker (1829–1902), IX, 823; XI, 335, 645, 755, 758; XII, 620, 800, 801
Ogilvie, Helen. *See* Johnston
Ogilvie, Helen. *See* Watson
Ogilvie, James, IV, 523; V, 53, 205, 339, 546, **634–35**, 766; VI, 213, 535, 536; VII, 394
Ogilvie, John (brother of ALEXANDER WALKER and WILLIAM WATSON), IX, 823; XII, 800, 801
Ogilvie, John (officer), V, 636
Ogilvie, John, IV, liv, 139, **586–87**, 691; V, 785
Ogilvie, Margaret. *See* Marston
Ogilvie, Mary (Pearson; Brown), VI, 87
Ogilvie, Penelope (wife of JAMES), V, 634
Ogilvie, Susanna Catharine. *See* Symes
Ogilvie, William, IV, 586
Ogilvie, William Watson, XII, **800–1**
Ogilvie-Grant, Francis William, 6th Earl of Seafield, VIII, 251
Ogilvie-Grant, Mary Ann. *See* Dunn
Ogilvy, Jane. *See* Dunlop
Ogilvy, John, V, 286, 564, **635–37**, 718; VI, 236, 254, 285, 531, 533, 641, 665, 701, 702; VII, 342; VIII, 320, 321, 366, 882; IX, 553
Ogimauh-binaessih, VI, **555–56**; VIII, 440
Ogle, Sir Charles, VIII, 101
Ogle, George, X, 309
Ogletree, Francis, XII, 370, 371
O'Grady, John, VII, 661
O'Grady, John Caulfield, VIII, 170
O'Grady, Margaret. *See* Thompson
O'Grady, Standish, VII, **659–61**; XII, 570
O'Grady, William John, VI, 165, 426; VII, 42, 320, 369, 548, 549, 555, **661–65**; VIII, 34, 229, 317; IX, 25, 69, 240, 324, 501, 509
Ogston, Mary Jane. *See* Hargrave
O'Halloran, Henry Dunn, VII, 352, 353, 579; VIII, 65
O'Hara, Catherine (Maguire), X, 487
O'Hara, Charles, VI, 160, 161
O'Hara, Edward, V, 637; VI, **556**, 653
O'Hara, Elizabeth. *See* Cameron
O'Hara, Fanny. *See* Taylor
O'Hara, Felix, V, **637–38**, 864, 902; VI, 556; VIII, 25
O'Hara, Henry, V, 637
O'Hara, Hugh, V, 637
O'Hara, Maria Charlotte (Arnold), VIII, 25
O'Hara, Marian. *See* Murray
O'Hara, Martha. *See* McCormick
O'Hara, Mary (Chaussegros de Léry), IX, 128
O'Hara, Oliver, V, 637
O'Hara, Robert, X, 557
O'Hara, Walter, VII, 200; X, **557**
O'Hare, Catherine (Schubert), IX, 518
O'Hea, Timothy, X, **558**
Ohkipiksew (Water Bird), XII, 718
Ohnaweio (Good Stream), VII, 911
Ohonsiowanne (Ohoengewaene), II, xxxvi, 20, **502**, 631
Ohquandageghte, IV, **587–88**

Ohrante. *See* Oteroughyanento
Ohtowaˀkéhson, V, 804; VI, 759, 760; VII, 467, **665–66**; VIII, 309
Oille, Elizabeth. *See* Decker
Oille, George Nicholas, XI, 650
Oille, George Nicholas, XI, **650–51**; XII, 783, 971
Oille, Lucius Sterne, XI, 651; XII, 529
Oionhaton, I, 42, 212, 344, **523–24**
Oja, La. *See* Wahpasha
Ojeda, Alonso de, I, 151
Oke, Elizabeth (Horden), XII, 445
O'Keefe, Elizabeth (Harrington), XII, 410
O'Keefe*, Eugene (1827–1913), XII, 1086
Okemapenesse. *See* Ogimauh-binaessih
Okill, Jane (Stuart), V, 785, 786; VII, 835; VIII, 842; IX, 770
Okill, John Leigh, VIII, 761
Okimawaskawikinam. *See* Letendre, *dit* Batoche, Jean-Baptiste
Oklomsky, Mr (officer), VII, 411
Olabaratz, Catherine d'. *See* Despiaube
Olabaratz, Jean d', IV, 23, 487, 589; V, 363, **638–39**
Olabaratz, Joannis-Galand d', III, 635; IV, 61, 247, 253, **588–89**, 657; V, 638
Olabaratz, Marguerite-Angélique d'. *See* Collas
Olaf I Tryggvesson, King of Norway, I, 448
Old Abraham, IV, 730
Old Belt. *See* Kaghswaghtaniunt
Old Britain. *See* Memeskia
Old Crooked Neck, V, 803
Oldham, Jacob, VI, 469
Oldham, William, IV, 369, 403
Olding, Nicholas Purdue, V, 660
Old King (Old Smoke). *See* Kaieñˀkwaahtoñ
Oldmixon, John, I, 50
Old Sun. *See* Natos-api
Old Swan. *See* A-ca-oo-mah-ca-ye
O'Leary, Ellen. *See* Power
O'Leary, Frederick, XII, 802
O'Leary, Henry, XI, 466; XII, **801–2**
O'Leary*, Henry Joseph (1879–1938), XII, 802
O'Leary, Louis James, XII, 802
O'Leary, Mary (O'Leary), XII, 801
O'Leary, Mary Ann. *See* Brittain
O'Leary, Richard, XII, 802
O'Leary, Theophilus, XII, 801
Olier, Jean-Jacques, I, 45, 57, 111, 115, 213, 214, 215, 219, 220, 480, 486, 612, 644, 648; II, 414; IX, 247
Oliph, Joan (Leigh), I, 450
Oliphant, Laurence, VIII, 163; X, 164
Oliphant, Mary (Elliot), XII, 296
Oliphant of Rossie, Catherine (Drummond of Megginch), VIII, 236
Oliva, Catherine. *See* Couillard Des Islets
Oliva, Frédéric-Godlip, IV, 589
Oliva, Frédéric-Guillaume, IV, **589–90**; V, 501; VI, 258
Oliva, Jean-Paul (Giovanni Paolo), I, 460; II, 161
Olive, Gregory, IV, 592; V, 843
Oliver, Adam, XI, 221, 497, **651–53**; XII, 657
Oliver, Elizabeth. *See* Grieve
Oliver, Ellen. *See* Rintoul
Oliver* (Bowsfield), Frank (1853–1933), XII, 991
Oliver, Jane (Cary), VI, 123

Oliver, Jeanett. *See* Armstrong
Oliver, John, XI, 651
Oliver, Sarah Maria (Dennis), XI, 244
Oliver, Thomas Hamilton, VIII, 93, 649; XII, 1072
Oliver, William Sanford, VI, 141
Olivera, Mr (violinist), XII, 532
Oliver Julian, Brother. *See* Thibault
Olivier. *See also* Le Jeune
Olivier, Captain, V, 313
Olivier, Mrs (wife of Henri), IX, 608
Olivier, Abel, III, 281, **494**; IV, 203
Olivier, Antoine, III, 639
Olivier, François, III, 494
Olivier, Françoise. *See* Dardaine
Olivier, Henri, IX, 608; X, 633
Olivier, Hugues, IV, 590
Olivier, Louis-Auguste, VIII, 420; XI, 623; XII, 818
Olivier, Louise. *See* Le Roux
Olivier, Marie. *See* Castille
Olivier, Marie-Anne. *See* Varlet
Olivier, Marie-Anne-Charlotte (Armstrong), XI, 31
Olivier, Marie-Madeleine. *See* Lefebvre
Olivier, Nicolas-Joseph-Godefroy, IV, 591
Olivier, Simon, I, 524
Olivier, Sophie. *See* Lafrenière
Olivier, Tersile (Alexine) (Fafard), XI, 305
Olivier, *dit* Le Picard, Marc-Antoine, I, **524**
Olivier Darmeville, Sieur (brother of Pierre-François
    OLIVIER de Vézin), IV, 590
Olivier de Saint-Maurice, Charles-Honoré, IV, 591
Olivier de Vézin, Marie-Joseph. *See* Gastineau Duplessis
Olivier de Vézin, Pierre-Darmeville, IV, 591
Olivier de Vézin, Pierre-François, III, 153, 154, 237, 351,
    592, 593, 617; IV, 167, 284, 362, **590–91**
Ollerhead, Mr (magistrate), IX, 468, 469; XI, 432
Ollivier, Jacques-David, IV, 690
Olmechin. *See* Onemechin
Olmstead, Hannah (Miles), VI, 504
Olmstead, Mary. *See* Street
Olmstead, Sarah (Wright; Sparks), IX, 734; XII, 1129
O'Lone, Hugh F., X, 645
Olry, Joseph-Antoine, V, 478
O'Mahony, John, IX, 588; X, 559
O'Mahony, Timothy, XI, 538
Oman, Mitchell, VIII, 878
Omand, Frances (Beddome), XI, 63
O'Meara, Charles P., XI, 653
O'Meara, Frederick Augustus, IX, 11, 379; X, 12; XI,
    **653–55**, 714
O'Meara, John Patrick, VIII, 582
O'Meara, Margaret Johnston. *See* Dallas
O'Meara, Sarah. *See* Murphy
O'Meara*, Thomas Robert (1864–1930), XI, 653
Ommanney, Erasmus, VIII, 447, 448, 623, 624; IX, 12, 199
Omoxesisixany (Big Snake, Black Snake Man), X, 392
Ompherville. *See* Humphraville
Omukaiee (Big Swan), VIII, 4
Onanguicé (Onanguisset). *See* Ounanguissé
Onasakenrat, Joseph, V, 480; XI, **655–56**
Onaské, II, 324
Oñate, Juan de, II, xxxii
Ondaaiondiont, I, 65, 66, 71, **524–25**
Ondakion (Pierre), I, 610

Onderdonk*, Andrew (1848–1905), XII, 398, 626, 804
Ondessonk. *See* Jogues, Isaac; Le Moyne, Simon
One Arrow. *See* Kāpeyakwāskonam
Onedahauet, II, 665; III, 266
O'Neil. *See also* O'Neill
O'Neil, Elizabeth (Grace), VI, 292
O'Neil, Jean-Baptiste, XI, 352
O'Neil, Marie-Anne (Glackemeyer), VII, 348; XI, 352
O'Neill, Anne (wife of TERENCE JOSEPH), X, 560
O'Neill, Catherine, named Sister Mary Elizabeth, XII,
    411
O'Neill, Elizabeth (Maçon; Dougall), XI, 268
O'Neill, James, XII, 622
O'Neill, John, X, 74, 282, 556, **558–59**; XI, 193, 245, 472,
    743, 839; XII, 68, 677, 678
O'Neill, Mary. *See* Crow
O'Neill, Patrick A., VIII, 229
O'Neill, Terence Joseph, VIII, 934; X, 80, **559–60**
O'Neill, William John, XII, 552
Onemechin, I, 69, 507, 529
Onesakenarat. *See* Onasakenrat
Onistah-sokaksin, IX, 623; X, **560–61**; XII, 717
Onista'poka, XII, 718, **802–3**
Onis tay say nah que im. *See* Peenaquim
Onkiswathetami. *See* Swatana
Onondamokin. *See* Anandamoakin
Onontio. *See* Huault de Montmagny, Charles
Ononwarogo, III, 320, **494–95**
Onoquaga. *See* Isaac
Onorotandi, I, 73
Onslow, George, IV, 226
Onslow, Georges, X, 228
Ontaniendo. *See* Atecouando
Onughranorum, IV, 734
Onwanonsyshon. *See* Johnson, George Henry Martin
Onwarenhiiaki. *See* Williams, Eleazer
Ooligbuck (Oolibuck), VI, 754; VIII, **663–64**; XII, 876
Ooligbuck (Ouligbuck), William, VIII, 663; XII, 876
Oominewahjeween. *See* Herchmer, William
Oonchiarey, I, 590
Opee-o'wun. *See* Si'k-okskitsis
Opid, Jadwiga (Helena) (Modrzejewska; Chlapowski),
    known as Helena Modjeska, XII, 622
Opie, John, VI, 803
Oppenheimer, Charles, XII, 803, 804
Oppenheimer, Christine (Sarah) (wife of DAVID), XII, 803
Oppenheimer, David, XII, 295, 666, **803–6**
Oppenheimer, Isaac, XII, 803, 804
Oppenheimer, Johanetta. *See* Kahn
Oppenheimer, Julia. *See* Walters
Oppenheimer, Salomon, XII, 803
Orakwanen-takon. *See* Cuoq, Jean-André
Oral Talker. *See* Never Ties His Shoes
Orange, Prince of. *See* William II
Orban, Alexis-Jules, XII, 769
Orbigny, Claude d' (Potot de Montbeillard), IV, 641
Ord, John, III, 608
O'Regan, Anthony, X, 419; IX, 96; XII, 191
O'Regan, Margaret (Anglin), XII, 23
Orehaoue. *See* Ourehouare
Oreil. *See* Doreil
O'Reiley, Eleanor (Collins), XII, 204
O'Reilley, Edward, XII, 894

O'Reilly, Anne (Smith), VII, 811
O'Reilly, Bernard, IX, 211
O'Reilly, Bridget, X, 509, 510
O'Reilly, Gerald, IX, 611
O'Reilly, Gerald, IX, **611–12**
O'Reilly, Henrietta. *See* Waters
O'Reilly, Hugh, VIII, 307, **664–65**
O'Reilly, James, IX, 73, 835; X, **561**; XII, 599, 893
O'Reilly, Margaret (Talbot, Baroness Talbot), VIII, 857
O'Reilly, Mary Jane. *See* Redmond
O'Reilly, Michael McCartin, XI, 864
O'Reilly, Miles, VIII, 708, 709
O'Reilly, Peter, X, 561
O'Reilly*, Peter (1825–1905), IX, 296; XI, 841; XII, 466, 1049
Orelli, Johann Ulrich von, VI, 660
Orelli, Juliana Wilhelmina Carolina von (Rottenburg, Baroness de Rottenburg), VI, 660
Orford, Earl of. *See* Walpole
Orfroy, Urbain, IX, 152
Orgemont. *See* Louvigny
Orgeville. *See* Pannier
O'Riley. *See* O'Reilly
Orillat, Jean, IV, 591
Orillat, Jean, IV, 58, 403, **591–93**; V, 178, 185, 277, 322, 654, 662
Orillat, Marie. *See* Dupuy
Orillat, Marie-Amable. *See* Filiau, *dit* Dubois
Orillat, Marie-Luce-Amable (Réaume), IV, 593
Orillat, Thérèse-Amable. *See* Viger
Oriol, Anne. *See* Le Picard
Oriol, Vital, II, 14
Orkney, Earl of. *See* Hamilton; Sinclair
Orkney, Alexander, VI, 557
Orkney, Elizabeth. *See* Gibb
Orkney, James, VI, 285
Orkney, James, V, 329, 406; VI, **556–57**; VII, 17
Orkney, Jane. *See* Hanna
Orkney, Mary (Somerville), XI, 843
Orléans, Duc d'. *See also* Louis-Philippe
Orléans, Duc d', I, 436
Orléans, Anne-Marie-Louise d', Duchesse de Montpensier, I, 134, 135
Orléans, Charles d', Duc d'Orléans, Comte de Clermont, I, 425
Orléans, Charles-Paris d', Comte de Saint-Pol, Duc de Longueville, II, 112
Orléans, Claude d', II, 98
Orléans, François-Ferdinand-Philippe-Louis-Marie d', Prince de Joinville, X, 625
Orléans, Jacqueline d' (Brisay de Denonville), II, 98
Orléans, Jean-Baptiste-Gaston d', I, 134
Orléans, Louise-Élisabeth d', Queen of Spain, III, 106
Orléans, Louis-Philippe d', Comte de Paris, XII, 362
Orléans, Louis-Philippe-Joseph d', Duc d'Orléans (Philippe Égalité), X, 582
Orléans, Marie-Louise d', Duchesse de Montpensier. *See* Bourbon
Orléans, Philippe d', Duc d'Orléans, XII, 362
Orléans, Philippe d', Duc d'Orléans, Regent of France, I, 328; II, 338, 570; III, 104, 118, 248, 330, 336, 566; IV, 124, 468
Orlebar, John, XI, 55

Ormé (Ormeaux). *See* Hazeur
Orme, Robert, IV, 281
Ormond, Elizabeth (Eliza) (Gray), XI, 372, 375
Ormond, Harry Smith, XI, 372
Ormond (Ermon), Marie-Bernardine (Vuadens), IV, 757
Ormsby, William George, VII, 608
Orne, Lois (Paine), VI, 563
Ornelin, Marie-Magdelaine. *See* Dubergès
Oronhyatekha* (1841–1907), XII, 187
Orontony, II, xxx; III, xxxv, xxxvi, xxxix, xli, 46, 158, 328, 355, 451, **495–96**, 525, 607, 613; IV, liii, liv, 464, 640, 728
Orpheus Junior. *See* Vaughan, Sir William
Orr, Elizabeth (Poor), X, 590
Orr, James, IX, 105
Orr, Jane. *See* Hicks
Orr, Janet (Burns), IX, 104
Orr, Janet (Laird), X, 419; XII, 512
Orr, Priscilla Victoria. *See* Miller
Orr, Robert, IX, 558
Orr, Samuel G. P., XII, 806
Orr, Wesley Fletcher, XII, **806–7**
Orsborn, Ann (Yeo), IX, 855
Orsonnens. *See* Odet
Ortelius, Abraham, I, 280, 680
Orval. *See* Bouchard
Orville, Sieur d' (settler), I, 189, 293
Orvilliers. *See* Chorel; Guillouet
Osborn, Ann (Chipman), VII, 177; XII, 193
Osborn, Sir Danvers, III, 126, **496–97**
Osborn, Edward, X, 561
Osborn, Eliza. *See* Todington
Osborn, Elizabeth (Myrick; Paine; Doane), IV, **593–94**
Osborn, Helen Harriet Gordon. *See* Hinxman
Osborn, Henry, II, 251; III, 126, 219, 315, 324, 517; IV, 257, **594–95**, 699; V, 596
Osborn, Jedidah. *See* Smith
Osborn, John, III, 496
Osborn, Sir John, III, 496; IV, 594
Osborn, Martha, Lady Osborn. *See* Kelynge
Osborn, Mary. *See* Hughes; Montagu
Osborn, Mary (London), V, **639–40**; VII, 251
Osborn, Noel, X, 562
Osborn, Samuel, IV, 593
Osborn, Sarah. *See* Byng
Osborn, Sherard, IX, 12, 168; X, 42, 43, 455, **561–63**; XII, 38
Osborne, Mr (publisher), VII, 222
Osborne, Mr (sawmill owner), VII, 873
Osborne, Charles, XII, 949
Osborne, Sir Edward, XII, 429
Osborne, James, XI, 608
Osborne, James Kerr, XII, 705
Osborne, Nicholas, VIII, 366
Osborne, Thomas, 1st Duke of Leeds, II, 152
Osgood, Josiah, VIII, 665
Osgood, Samuel, XII, 259
Osgood, Sarah. *See* Stevens
Osgood, Thaddeus, V, 770; VI, 50, 533; VII, 481, 482, 826; VIII, **665–67**
Osgood, William, VI, 557
Osgoode, William, IV, 502, 766; V, 18, 71, 84, 152, 234, 285, 291, 304, 602, 691, 692, 730, 731, 757; VI, 134,

269, 270, 512, 513, **557–60**, 587, 588, 607, 609, 670; VII, 614, 783, 812, 813; VIII, 281
Oshaguscodawaqua (Susan Johnston, wife of JOHN), VI, 357, 358
O'Shaughnessy, Miss, named Sister Mary Magdalen, VIII, 475
Osler*, Britton Bath (1839–1901), XI, 78, 748; XII, 580, 586, 807, 887
Osler*, Sir Edmund Boyd (1845–1924), X, 393; XII, 44, 103, 807
Osler, Edward, XII, 807
Osler, Ellen Free. See Pickton
Osler*, Featherston (1838–1924), X, 336; XI, 322, 621
Osler, Featherstone Lake, X, 54; XI, 653; XII, **807–8**
Osler, Mary. See Paddy
Osler*, Sir William (1849–1919), X, 39, 84, 382; XI, 149, 429, 591, 748; XII, 232, 315, 383, 384, 573, 807
O'Soup*, Louis (d. c. 1920), XI, 477, 478
Ossaye, Frédéric-M.-F., IX, **612–13**
Ossoli, Sarah Margaret, Marchioness Ossoli. See Fuller
Ostell, Charlotte (mother of JOHN), XII, 808
Ostell, Élisabeth-Éléonore. See Gauvin
Ostell, Isaac, XII, 808
Ostell, John, VI, 554; VIII, 911; XI, 92; XII, 131, **808–11**
Ostilly (Ostigny), Théotiste (Duhamel), XII, 276
Ostryge, Henry, I, 157, 158
O'Sullivan, Cécile. See Berthelet
O'Sullivan, Daniel Tim-Daniel. See Sullivan, Daniel
O'Sullivan, Dennis Ambrose, XII, **811–12**
O'Sullivan, Eleonora. See O'Donel
O'Sullivan, Emma Mary Philamena. See Higgins
O'Sullivan, Jeanne-Marie-Catherine. See Bruyères
O'Sullivan, John (doctor), XII, 333
O'Sullivan, John (father of MICHAEL), VII, 666
O'Sullivan, Mary. See Henessey
O'Sullivan, Michael, XII, 811
O'Sullivan, Michael, IV, 109; VI, 59, 104, 126; VII, 300, **666–68**, 880, 893; IX, 559; X, 526
Osunkhirhine (Pierre-Paul Masta), VII, 19; VIII, 78; IX, 541
Oswald, Elizabeth (Bruce), IX, 89
Oswald, James, VIII, 81, 964, 966; X, 394
Oteroughyanento (Ohrante), V, 805, 811
Otetiani. See Shakóye:wa:thaˀ
Otheman, Edward, VII, 854
Otis, James, III, 403
Otis, Joseph, IV, 351
Otis (Otisse, Hôtesse), Marie (Vincent), XI, 905
Otis, Mary (Little), III, 403
Otis, Susanna (Lusanna) (Haliburton), VI, 306, 307
Otkwande. See Ohquandageghte
O'Toole, Lawrence, I, 560
Otoutagon. See Outoutagan
Otqueandageghte. See Ohquandageghte
Otreouti, I, 7, 322, 445, 458, **525–26**; II, 344, 440, 518, 620, 624
Otridge, Mr (bookseller), VII, 634
Otsinnonannhont (Barnabé), I, 652
Otsinughyada. See Hotsinoñhyahtaˀ
Otter, William, XI, 663
Otter*, Sir William Dillon (1843–1929), XI, 696, 747; XII, 427, 576, 734
Ottoutagan. See Outoutagan

Ottrowana, IV, **595–96**
Otty, Catherine McGill (Earle), XI, 295
Ouabachas. See Wahpasha
Ouabangué, II, 500
Ouachala (Ouachalard), II, xxx, 316, **502–3**, 504
Ouaconisen. See Ignon
Ouagabemat (Noegabinat), I, 222
Ouagimou, I, 69, **526–27**, 529
Ouane. See Le Moyne, Simon
Ouangote. See Williams, Eunice
Ouaouënouroué, Nicolas, III, 266
Ouaourené. See Wowurna
Ouary, Françoise (Renardin de La Blanchetière), I, 475
Ouashala (Ouashalas). See Ouachala
Ouasson. See Wasson
Oubee, VI, 70
Oudiette, Jean, II, 29, 30, 574, 575
Oudin, Renée (Marie) (Le Royer de La Dauversière), I, 214
Ouebadinskoue (Marie-Madeleine Chrestienne) (Boucher), I, 200, 354; II, 86
Ouechala. See Ouachala
Ouellet*, David (1844–1915), VIII, 40
Ouellet, Élisabeth (Michaud), VII, 147
Ouellet, Fabien, XI, 498
Ouenanguenet. See Wenemouet
Ouenemek, II, xxxviii, 324, 502, **503–4**
Ouenouadahronhé. See Vincent, Gabriel
Oughtred, Henry, I, 228, 229
Ougier, Benedict, V, 641
Ougier, Peter, V, 641
Ougier, Peter, V, **640–42**, 785, 838; VI, 637
Ouhensiouan. See Ohonsiowanne
Ouibignaro, II, 7, 8, 9
Ouikouiroumenit, II, 476
Ouilameg (Ouilamek). See Ouenemek
Ouimet, Adolphe, IX, 63, 64; XI, 623; XII, 1027
Ouimet, André, VII, 758; VIII, 284, **667–68**; XI, 302; XII, 118
Ouimet, Benjamin, X, 492; XI, 302
Ouimet, Charlotte. See Roy
Ouimet, Charlotte (Gosselin), V, 358
Ouimet*, Gédéon (1823–1905), VIII, 668; IX, 194; X, 204, 305, 533; XI, 26, 27, 235, 287, 320, 344, 345, 513; XII, 173, 174, 175, 257, 464, 738, 903, 1006
Ouimet, Jean, VIII, 667
Ouimet*, Joseph-Aldéric (1848–1916), XI, 813; XII, 1074
Ouimet, Marie. See Bautron
Ouligbuck (Oullibuck, Oulybuck). See Ooligbuck
Oumasasikweie (Joseph), I, 548, 640
Oumasasikweie, I, 10, **527–28**
Ounanguissé, II, xxxviii, 503, **504**
Ouracha. See Garnier, Charles
Ourehouare, I, **528**, 537
Oureouhat. See Otreouti
Ours, L'. See Le Pesant
Oussaye, Élisabeth (Roger), II, 582
Ousson. See Wasson
Outaouliboy. See Koutaoiliboe
Outchetaguin, I, 381, 603
Outchiouanish (Marie) (Pelletier), II, 357
Outetoucos, I, 603
Outlan. See Outlaw
Outlaw, Françoise. See Denis

Outlaw, John, I, 39, 107, 130, **528–29**; II, 308
Outlaw, Mary. *See* Saille
Outoutagan, II, xxxvii, 173, 317, 414, 475, **504–6**; III, 147
Outram, Sir James, IX, 5
Outreouhati. *See* Otreouti
Outsitsony, I, 574
Ouvard, *dit* Laperrière, Angèle (Gauvreau), XI, 336
Ouvrier, Frédérique-Louise (Heer), V, 417
Ouwoorana. *See* Wowurna
Overholser, Barbara (wife of JACOB), V, 642
Overholser, Jacob, V, **642–45**; VI, 212, 611, 698; VII, 36, 244, 602; VIII, 69, 186
Oviatt, William, IX, 639
Owain Gwynedd, King of Gwynedd, I, 677
Owasser. *See* Wasson
Owen. *See also* Robinson-Owen
Owen, Amy. *See* Vernon
Owen, Anne. *See* Davies
Owen, Sir Arthur Davies, VI, 560
Owen, David, IV, 596
Owen, David, VI, 301, **560–61**; VIII, 671
Owen, Edward, VI, 560
Owen, Sir Edward Campbell Rich, IV, 597; V, 401, 876; VI, 560; VIII, 669; XI, 355, 782
Owen, Frances (Goldie), XII, 378
Owen, Hannah (Peters), VII, 693
Owen, James. *See* McCarthy, James Owen
Owen, John (clergyman), VI, 551, 552, 553
Owen, John (trader), III, 614
Owen, John (writer), I, 365
Owen*, Lemuel Cambridge (1822–1912), XI, 703
Owen, Martha. *See* Evans
Owen, Owen, VI, 560
Owen, Polly (Eastman), IX, 232
Owen, Sir Richard, IX, 660
Owen, Robert, V, 297; VI, 42; VIII, 437, 438
Owen, Sarah Harriet (Williams; Haliburton), IX, 350
Owen, William (brother of DAVID), VI, 560
Owen, William (judge), V, 146
Owen, William (painter), IX, 543
Owen, William, IV, **596–97**; VI, 560; VIII, 668
Owen, William Fitz William, IV, 597; VI, 560; VIII, **668–73**; IX, 263; X, 396; XI, 54, 56, 57, 718, 782, 820; XII, 444, 895
Owen-Jones, Percy, XII, 900
Owens, James. *See* McCarthy, James Owen
Owenson, Sydney (Morgan, Lady Morgan), VIII, 921
Oxenden, Anne Charlotte (Alston), X, 9
Oxenden, Ashton, X, 58, 548; XI, 314, 523; XII, 716, **812–14**
Oxenden, Sir Henry, XII, 812
Oxenden, Mary. *See* Graham
Oxenden, Sarah. *See* Bradshaw
Oxford, Earl of. *See* Harley
Oxford, James, V, 465
Oxford, Thomas, I, 24, 278, 370
Oxnard, Thomas, VI, 283
Oxner, Anna Matilda (Rudolf), VIII, 782
Ozanam, Antoine-Frédéric, VIII, 676
Ozon, Potentien, II, 174, 419, **506**

PABST, Gustav, XII, 316, 317
Pabst, Margaret. *See* Finlayson

Pacaud, Alida (Dumoulin), VIII, 247
Pacaud, Angélique. *See* Brown
Pacaud, Anne-Hermine. *See* Dumoulin
Pacaud, Charles-Adrien, X, 77; XI, 657, 659
Pacaud, Clarice. *See* Duval
Pacaud, Édouard-Louis, VII, 880; XI, 170, **656–58**, 659, 808; XII, 66
Pacaud*, Ernest (1850–1904), XI, 659; XII, 362, 724, 725, 726, 890
Pacaud, Françoise. *See* Dumoulin
Pacaud, Georges-Jérémie, XI, 658, 659
Pacaud, Jean-Baptiste-Napoléon-Gaspard, XI, 659
Pacaud, Joseph, XI, 656, 658
Pacaud, Joseph-Narcisse, XI, 657
Pacaud, Julie-Aurélie. *See* Boucher de La Bruère
Pacaud, Louise-Adélaïde (Barthe), XII, 65
Pacaud, Philippe-Napoléon, VIII, 247; XI, 657, **658–60**; XII, 66, 252
Pace, Grace (Cook), IV, 163
Pacewicz, Helena (Gzowski, Countess Gzowski), XII, 389
Pacheco. *See* Güemes
Pachirini, I, 485
Pachot. *See* Viennay-Pachot
Pacifique, Brother. *See* Caron; Duplessis
Pacifique de Provins, I, 129
Pack, Anna. *See* Ash
Pack, Olivia. *See* Horwood
Pack, Robert, VII, 112, 113; VIII, 199, 235, **673–75**
Pack, Stephen Olive, VIII, 673
Packard, Alpheus Spring, XI, 65
Packnake, IV, 301
Packs a Knife. *See* Isapo-muxika; Istowun-eh'pata
Padanuques, Jacques, III, **497–98**
Paddock, Anna (Thurgar), X, 681
Paddock, Thomas, VIII, 507
Paddy, Mary (Osler), XII, 807
Padilla. *See* Güemes
Padouillet, Renée (Mallet), II, 451
Pagan, David, V, 645
Pagan, George, V, 645
Pagan, John (uncle), V, 645
Pagan, John, V, 284, 645, 646; VI, 562
Pagan, Margaret. *See* Maxwell
Pagan, Miriam. *See* Pote
Pagan, Robert, V, 134, 161, 336, 337, 351, 355, 645, 646, 874; VI, 35, 356, 362, **561–63**, 726
Pagan, Thomas (uncle), V, 645
Pagan, Thomas, V, 645, 646; VI, 60, 562
Pagan, William, V, 645; VI, 561
Pagan, William, V, 94, 337, **645–47**; VI, 60, 355, 356, 562, 563, 719, 725; VII, 777
Paganini, Niccolò, VIII, 347
Page, Mr (author of a report), I, 93
Pagé, Angélique (Daine), III, 159
Page, David, VII, 589
Pagé, Éléonore (Derome), X, 225
Pagé, Élizabeth (Triaud), VII, 869
Page, John, XII, 1068
Pagé, Joseph, VI, 582
Pagé, Louise (Nau), VII, 642
Page, Mary (Dunn; Secord), VII, 780
Page, Mary Eliza (Rogers), XII, 921
Page, Mrs Susanna, IV, 767

Page, Thomas Otway, VI, 159
Pagé, *dit* Carcy, Élisabeth. *See* Letartre
Pagé, *dit* Carcy, Guillaume, II, 347; III, 498
Pagé, *dit* Carcy, Jacques, II, 430; III, 182, 348, **498–99**, 509
Pagé, *dit* Carcy, Marie-Anne (Boisseau), IV, 75; V, 90
Pagé, *dit* Carcy, Marie-Louise. *See* Roussel
Pagé, *dit* Carcy, Raymond, I, 473, 495; II, 347
Pagé, *dit* Carcy, Suzanne (Perrault), III, 509; IV, 623
Pageot, Josephte (Gosselin), X, 308
Pageot, Marie-Anne (Giroux), IX, 317
Pagès, Monsieur (businessman), II, 654
Paget, Sir Charles, VII, 478
Paget, Henry William, 1st Marquess of Anglesey, VIII, 374, 375, 377, 379
Paget, Sir James, X, 38; XI, 559
Paget, Lady Louisa (Erskine, Lady Erskine; Murray, Lady Murray), VII, 639, 640
Pagnuelo*, Siméon (1840–1915), XI, 71, 103, 250, 424, 891, 893; XII, 277
Pagnuelo, Wilbrod, XII, 105
Pahellau. *See* Ketura
Pahtahsega, VI, 335; VII, 276; VIII, 133, 440; XI, 653, **660–61**; XII, 186
Paillard. *See also* Paillé
Paillard, André, II, 506
Paillard, Catherine. *See* Geoffroy
Paillard, Charles, II, 507
Paillard, Gabriel, II, 507
Paillard, Léonard, known as Le Poitevin, II, **506–7**
Paillard, Louise-Marie. *See* Vachon
Paillé (Paillard), Louise (Prat), X, 599
Paillet, Monsieur (businessman), V, 395
Pain, Félix, II, 198, 206, 219, 238, 512; III, **499–500**, 522, 681; IV, xxi
Painchaud, Alexis, VII, 668; VIII, **675–76**
Painchaud, Angélique. *See* Drouin
Painchaud, Charles-François, VI, 126, 589, 590, 593, 597; VII, 204, **668–71**; VIII, 142, 213, 214, 458, 595, 675; X, 488, 602, 604; XI, 168, 483
Painchaud, Émerence (Landry), XI, 483
Painchaud, François, VII, 668; VIII, 675; X, 563
Painchaud, Jean-Baptiste-Félix, VIII, 675, 676
Painchaud, Joseph, VIII, **676–77**; IX, 798
Painchaud, Joseph, V, 202; VI, 259, 326, 327, 576, 680, 681; VIII, 675, 676, 682; IX, 32, 286, 572; X, 18, **563–64**; XI, 271, 483, 484; XII, 1128
Painchaud, Joseph-Alexis, VIII, 675, 676
Painchaud, Marguerite. *See* Arseneaux
Painchaud, Marie-Angélique. *See* Drouin
Painchaud, Marie-Geneviève. *See* Parant
Painchaud, Marie-Louise, named de Saint-Augustin, VIII, 675
Painchaud, Victoire (Normand; Ahier), VIII, 675
Paine, Elizabeth. *See* Osborn
Paine, Lois. *See* Orne
Paine, Sarah. *See* Chandler
Paine, Thomas, IV, 327; VI, 10; VIII, 890
Paine, Timothy, VI, 563
Paine, William (husband of Elizabeth OSBORN), IV, 593
Paine, William (son of Elizabeth OSBORN), IV, 593
Paine, William, VII, **563–65**
Painter, Elizabeth, V, 648
Painter, John, V, 284, **647–48**; VI, 423, 424

Painter, Margaret. *See* Stuart
Paisley, Hugh, VIII, 581
Paizs (Paizsos), István. *See* Parmenius, Stephanus
Pajet. *See* Pagé
Pajot, Claude (Biencourt de Poutrincourt), I, 96, 98, 99
Pajot, Isaac, I, 96
Pakakis, IX, 592
Paka'panikapi. *See* Si'k-okskitsis
Pakenham, William, XI, 223
Pakington, John Somerset, 1st Baron Hampton, IX, 118, 583; XI, 412
Pako, III, 248
Palairet, Jean, XI, 458
Palate. *See* Si'k-okskitsis
Palatine, Count. *See* Rupert
Palatine, Princess. *See* Elizabeth Charlotte
Paley, Isaac, VII, 683
Paley, William, VII, 785; VIII, 866; XI, 784, 786; XII, 112
Palladio, Andrea, VII, 130
Palli. *See* Lucchesi-Palli
Palliser. *See also* Tootac
Palliser, Anne. *See* Gledstanes
Palliser, Frederick Hugh, XI, 664
Palliser, Hugh, IV, 597
Palliser, Sir Hugh, III, 37, 38, 411, 412; IV, 28, 29, 122, 158, 159, 163, 194, 225, 333, 334, 412, 437, 536, **597–601**, 701, 712; V, 54, 55, 73, 166, 220, 274, 338, 369, 381, 641, 675; VI, 323, 694, 707
Palliser, John, VIII, 3, 820; IX, 537; X, 81, 473; XI, 553, **661–64**; XII, 194, 540, 815
Palliser, Mary. *See* Robinson
Palliser, William, XI, 661
Palliser, Wray, XI, 661
Palliser Walters, Sir Hugh, IV, 600
Pallu, François, II, 360
Palluau, Comte de. *See* Buade
Palluau, Comtesse de. *See* La Grange; Phélypeaux de Pontchartrain
Palme. *See* La Palme
Palmer, Mr (preacher), V, 340
Palmer, Mrs (boarding-school owner), VII, 638
Palmer, Abijah, VI, 755
Palmer, Acalus Lockwood, XI, 298; XII, 19
Palmer, Barbara. *See* Villiers
Palmer, Charles, XI, 668
Palmer, Edward, I, 306
Palmer, Edward, VI, 568; VII, 145, 146; VIII, 529, 531, 564, 565; IX, 28, 157, 183, 395, 401; X, 184, 186, 187, 194, 264, 420, 461, 593, 594, 595, 596, 597, 598; XI, 202, 369, 370, 371, 512, 526, 528, 532, 567, **664–70**, 700, 701, 702, 940; XII, 415, 416, 425, 638, 839, 857
Palmer, Elizabeth. *See* Hey
Palmer, Ester (Esten), IX, 244
Palmer, Hannah (Yates), XI, 940
Palmer, Henry, VI, 568
Palmer, Henry Spencer, XI, 606, 663; XII, **815–16**
Palmer*, Herbert James (1851–1939), XI, 669
Palmer, Isabella Phoebe. *See* Tremain
Palmer, James Bardin, V, 127, 220, 335, 569, 776, 826, 862; VI, 161, 162, 163, 195, 196, 298, 359, 360, 361, 413, 414, **565–69**, 662, 785, 786, 818; VII, 76, 103, 352, 407, 408, 414, 415, 511, 903, 904, 925; VIII, 36, 37, 505, 741, 824, 825, 827; XI, 664

Palmer, Jane. *See* James
Palmer, John, II, 6
Palmer, John Freke, XII, 815
Palmer, Joseph, VI, 565
Palmer, Mary (Connell), X, 191
Palmer, Mary Jane Pearson. *See* Wright
Palmer, Millicent. *See* Jones
Palmer, Noble, XI, 940
Palmer, Phoebe, XII, 169
Palmer, Susanna. *See* Bardin
Palmer, Wait, V, 340
Palmer, Walter, XII, 169
Palmer, William, XI, 568
Palmerston, Viscount. *See* Temple
Palsgrave, Charles Theodore, XII, 571
Paltry. *See* Patry
Paludy, Baron de. *See* Tonty
Pambrun, André-Dominique, VII, 671
Pambrun, Angélique. *See* Hiraque
Pambrun, Catherine. *See* Umfreville
Pambrun, Pierre-Chrysologue, VII, **671–72**; VIII, 343, 714
Pamekezhegooqua. *See* Holtby, Mary
Pampalon, Alfred, XII, **816–17**
Pampalon, Antoine, XII, 816
Pampalon, Joséphine. *See* Dorion
Pampalon, Pierre, XII, 816
Pandosy, Charles, XII, 282, 284, **817–18**
Pandosy, Esprit-Étienne-Charles-Henri, XII, 817
Pandosy, Marguerite-Joséphine-Marie. *See* Dallest
Panet, Bernard-Antoine, V, 648, 649
Panet, Bernard-Claude, IV, 602; V, 77, 292, 649, 668, 676;
    VI, 120, 125, 126, 316, 332, 379, 448, 449, 483, 506,
    507, 528, **569–71**, 588, 589, 597, 624, 669, 691, 693,
    748; VII, 19, 148, 322, 341, 423, 486, 489, 581, 642,
    656, 662, 669, 670, 679, 680, 746, 759, 767, 784, 798,
    823, 828, 851, 879, 886, 887; VIII, 78, 129, 142, 214,
    240, 302, 317, 406, 456, 457, 554, 591, 592, 593, 728,
    729; IX, 17, 117, 152, 361, 634, 797, 862; X, 46, 604,
    675; XI, 87, 167, 168, 956; XII, 1016
Panet, Bonaventure, V, 653; VII, **672–73**
Panet, Cécile (Frémont), IX, 286
Panet, Charles, V, 648; VII, 427; IX, 779; X, 236, 604
Panet, Charlotte-Mélanie (Lévesque), VIII, 502, 503
Panet, Harriet. *See* Antill
Panet, Jacques, IV, 602; V, 648; VI, 569, **571–72**
Panet, Jean-Antoine, VIII, 170
Panet, Jean-Antoine, IV, 89, 603; V, 45, 46, 87, 182, 208,
    226, 233, 235, 257, 283, 292, 372, 373, 421, 484, 493,
    578, 588, 603, **648–52**, 653, 654, 695, 828, 878, 881; VI,
    47, 132, 151, 226, 305, 346, 368, 383, 401, 569, 585,
    641, 701, 712, 751; VII, 72, 200, 235, 242, 300, 673,
    689, 767, 783; VIII, 488, 677, 906; IX, 249, 360, 807
Panet, Jean-Baptiste, IV, 603
Panet, Jean-Claude, III, 26, 555, 608; IV, 75, 124, 127, 243,
    344, 492, **601–3**; V, 91, 146, 149, 150, 648, 652, 653;
    VI, 569, 571
Panet, Jean-Nicolas, IV, 601; V, 652
Panet, Léon, V, 654
Panet, Louis, V, 648; VII, 709; IX, 774; XI, 658; XII, 270,
    1064
Panet, Louise (Angers; Lamère), VIII, 16
Panet, Louise-Amélie (Berczy), V, 654; VII, 13, 836; X, 50
Panet, Louise-Clorinthe. *See* Bouthillier

Panet, Louise-Philippe. *See* Badelard
Panet, Luce. *See* Casgrain
Panet, Marguerite. *See* Dunière
Panet, Marie (Dorion), X, 235
Panet, Marie (Taschereau), V, 648, 649; VI, 751; VIII, 778;
    XII, 1016, 1024
Panet, Marie-Alphonsine (La Rue), XI, 495
Panet, Marie-Anne. *See* Cerré
Panet, Marie-Anne. *See* Trefflé, *dit* Rottot
Panet, Marie-Anne (Panet; Globensky), IX, 320
Panet, Marie-Anne-Archange, named de Saint-Bernard, V,
    649
Panet, Marie-Françoise, named de Saint-Jacques, V, 649
Panet, Marie-Louise. *See* Barolet
Panet, Marie-Madeleine-Françoise. *See* Foucher
Panet, Nicolas-Gabriel, IV, 601
Panet, Philippe, V, 648, 649; VI, 125, 681; VII, 9, 61, 62,
    191, 504, 880, 905; VIII, 503, 504, **677–78**; IX, 286,
    560, 682, 683; X, 134, 582; XI, 495, 519; XII, 45
Panet, Pierre, III, 146, 367, 441; IV, 185, 547, 601, 602,
    716; V, 277, 288, **652–53**, 654, 839; VII, 672
Panet, Pierre-Louis, V, 106, 175, 234, 257, 290, 373, 508,
    650, **653–55**, 663, 701; VI, 86, 237, 305, 383; VII, 13,
    30, 673, 872; VIII, 480, 502, 503, 890; IX, 613; X, 50
Panet, Pierre-Louis, IX, **613–14**
Pangman, Bastonnais (Joseph?), V, 656
Pangman, Grace. *See* MacTier
Pangman, John, V, 656; VIII, 481
Pangman, Marie-Henriette. *See* Lacroix
Pangman, Peter, VIII, 342
Pangman, Peter, IV, 160, 366, 585; V, 391, 537, 562, 566,
    602, 603, **656–57**, 682, 684; VI, 469; VIII, 500
Pannebecker, Elizabeth (Kribs), XII, 499
Panneton, Charles-Heliodore, XI, 671
Panneton, Charles-Marie, XI, **670–71**
Panneton, Françoise-Élisabeth (Duval), VI, 230
Panneton, Louis-Edmond, XII, 904
Panneton, Marguerite (Godet), XI, 334
Panneton, Philippe-Élisée, XI, 814
Panneton, Théodore (father), III, 430
Panneton, Théodore, IV, 331
Panneton, Zoë. *See* Durondu
Pannier d'Orgeville, Jacques, III, 398
Panounias (Panoniac), I, 69, 293, 500, 526, **529–30**
Panther, V, 774
Panton, George, V, **657–58**
Panton, James Hoyes, XI, 454
Panton, T. C., XI, 919
Paoli, Pasquale, V, 421; VIII, 105
Papamahchakwayo. *See* Kapapamahchakwew
Papelard, Constance Laure (Eaton), XII, 287
Papewes* (Papaway) (d. 1901), XI, 461
Papin, Basile, IX, 614
Papin, Gilles, III, 493
Papin, Hélène (Verrier), III, 643
Papin, Joseph, IX, 194, **614–15**; X, 282, 415, 422, 533; XI,
    26, 99, 235; XII, 261, 262, 505, 853
Papin, Marie-Louise (Archambault), IX, 615
Papin, Marie-Rose. *See* Pelletier
Papin, Marie-Sophie. *See* Homier
Papin, *dit* Barolette, Catherine, V, 293
Papineau, André-Augustin, VI, 207; VII, 676, 880; IX, 74;
    XI, 657

Papineau, Angélique-Louise. *See* Cornud

Papineau, Antoine, V, 165

Papineau, Augustin-Cyrille, X, 429; XI, 479; XII, 254, 719, 720

Papineau, Azélie (Bourassa), X, 577

Papineau, Denis-Benjamin, VI, 478; VII, 606, 607, 676; VIII, 269, 543, **678–80**, 800; IX, 191, 445, 463, 555, 642, 697, 728, 776, 816; X, 134, 255, 256, 566; XI, 41, 281, 341, 479; XII, 253

Papineau, Denis-Emery, VIII, 678; XII, 505

Papineau, Eugénie (Boutillier), IX, 73

Papineau, Ezilda, X, 321, 577; XII, 846

Papineau, Gustave, IX, 212; X, 321

Papineau, Joseph, VII, 673; X, 565

Papineau, Joseph, IV, 148; V, 233, 241, 373, 572, 833; VI, 42, 49, 207, 226, 287, 383, 386, 512, 640, 641, 669, 701; VII, 185, 353, 360, 381, 485, 618, 622, 667, **673–77**, 783; VIII, 186, 491, 678, 912, 914; X, 564, 565; XI, 187, 624

Papineau, Julie. *See* Bruneau

Papineau, Lactance, VIII, 404, 711; X, 575

Papineau, Louis-Joseph, II, 193; IV, 148; V, 117, 186, 208, 489, 651, 695; VI, 40, 42, 47, 48, 50, 82, 83, 98, 120, 205, 207, 241, 272, 279, 281, 382, 384, 386, 387, 585, 590, 591, 594, 597, 634, 645, 646, 680, 715, 716, 763, 764, 783, 802; VII, 6, 7, 8, 26, 61, 62, 72, 84, 119, 147, 148, 158, 161, 169, 172, 173, 180, 190, 208, 209, 210, 211, 225, 226, 227, 235, 236, 247, 254, 282, 332, 345, 346, 353, 354, 361, 374, 393, 412, 430, 449, 465, 478, 482, 484, 489, 503, 504, 512, 513, 525, 547, 605, 606, 623, 645, 647, 648, 660, 667, 670, 676, 677, 719, 727, 728, 729, 730, 731, 737, 739, 740, 751, 757, 758, 763, 769, 786, 787, 788, 789, 818, 823, 836, 872, 878, 880, 881, 887, 894, 905, 906, 922; VIII, 22, 51, 55, 56, 108, 138, 141, 144, 145, 146, 147, 155, 156, 212, 213, 214, 219, 221, 223, 248, 253, 261, 262, 284, 285, 286, 290, 301, 320, 322, 331, 392, 415, 420, 433, 456, 462, 463, 471, 479, 492, 493, 497, 501, 563, 592, 616, 629, 648, 667, 678, 679, 693, 694, 711, 712, 717, 730, 735, 778, 781, 791, 792, 798, 843, 844, 907, 909, 910, 911, 914, 915, 916, 962; IX, 32, 48, 73, 74, 91, 94, 100, 142, 210, 211, 212, 250, 299, 300, 301, 328, 441, 442, 443, 450, 458, 464, 485, 486, 504, 560, 561, 563, 569, 571, 594, 595, 596, 614, 649, 650, 651, 696, 697, 775, 795, 796, 808, 809, 810, 811, 812, 813, 814, 815, 818, 826; X, 13, 18, 61, 62, 75, 76, 77, 132, 142, 143, 160, 213, 236, 237, 260, 321, 337, 355, 415, 418, 429, 491, 505, 512, 526, 527, 544, 545, 546, 554, 555, **564–78**, 579, 580, 581, 584, 585, 626, 642, 655, 694; XI, 35, 36, 37, 60, 72, 84, 95, 98, 106, 117, 160, 179, 180, 187, 237, 273, 275, 341, 353, 455, 479, 488, 499, 533, 624, 657, 659, 850, 886, 889; XII, 66, 86, 88, 89, 118, 249, 252, 253, 260, 261, 300, 719, 788, 846, 853, 1014, 1025

Papineau, Louis-Joseph-Amédée, VII, 26, 106, 248; VIII, 261, 667, 909; IX, 816; X, 545, 547

Papineau, Marie. *See* Delain

Papineau, Marie-Agnès (Viger), VIII, 913, 914

Papineau, Marie-Josephte. *See* Beaudry

Papineau, Marie-Louise (Truteau), X, 688

Papineau, Marie-Rosalie (Dessaulles), VI, 207, 428; VII, 256, 676; IX, 74; XI, 479; XII, 252

Papineau, Rosalie. *See* Cherrier

Papineau, Samuel, II, 507

Papineau, Toussaint-Victor, VII, 676

Papineau, *dit* Montigny, Catherine. *See* Quevillon

Papineau, *dit* Montigny, Samuel, II, **507**; VII, 673

Paplay, Miss (Hey), IV, 348

Pâquet, Anselme-Homère, XII, **818**

Pâquet, Benjamin, XII, 818, 821

Pâquet, Benjamin, IX, 120, 800; X, 686; XI, 104, 250, 251, 290, 726; XII, 304, 507, 508, 509, 510, **818–22**, 1022, 1023

Paquet, Élisabeth. *See* Choret

Pâquet, Étienne, XII, 818

Pâquet, Étienne-Théodore, XI, 86; XII, 903

Pâquet, Françoise. *See* Robillard

Pâquet, Henriette. *See* Gariépy

Paquet, Jean-Baptiste (contractor), XI, 336

Paquet, Jean-Baptiste (father of MARIE-ANNE), VI, 572

Paquet, Joseph, IX, 615

Paquet, Joséphine, I, 487

Paquet, Joséphine (Josephte) (Paquet, *dit* Lavallée), VIII, 680

Paquet, Joseph-Marie, VII, 333; IX, **615–16**; XII, 397

Paquet, Joseph-Michel, VIII, 140

Pâquet, Louis, XI, 104

Paquet*, Louis-Adolphe (1859–1942), VII, 94; XII, 821, 1027

Pâquet, Louis-Honoré, XII, 46, 819, 820, 821

Paquet, Marie (Robert, *dit* Lapommeraie), VI, 650

Paquet, Marie (Forgues; Drouin), VIII, 235

Paquet, Marie-Anne, named de Saint-Olivier, VI, **572–73**

Paquet, Marie-Josephe. *See* Gagnon

Paquet, Marie-Josephte, named de la Nativité, IV, 319, 320

Paquet, Marie-Louise (Labadie), VI, 379

Paquet, Marie-Marguerite-Maurice (Scott), VIII, 792

Pâquet, Marie-Thérèse (Têtu), IX, 783

Paquet, René, III, 165

Pâquet, Timothée, XII, 818

Pâquet, Ursule. *See* Lambert

Paquet, *dit* Lavallée. *See also* Lavallée

Paquet, *dit* Lavallée, André, I, 77; VIII, 40, **680–81**; XI, 506

Paquet, *dit* Lavallée, Jean, VIII, 681

Paquet, *dit* Lavallée, Jean-Baptiste, VIII, 680

Paquet, *dit* Lavallée, Joséphine. *See* Paquet

Paquet, *dit* Lavallée, Marie. *See* Baquette, *dit* Lamontagne

Paquet, *dit* Lavallée, Marie-Hermine. *See* Turgeon

Paquet, *dit* Lavallée, Sophie. *See* Lépine

Paquin, Jacques, VI, 146; VII, 19, 26, 173, 174, 346, **677–79**; VIII, 792; X, 532

Paquin, Jean-Baptiste, VII, 678

Paquin, Marguerite. *See* Marcot

Paquin, Marie (Duchaîne), VIII, 239

Paquin, Marie-Madeleine (Perrault), III, 510

Paquin, Paul, VII, 677

Paquine. *See* Pasquine

Parabego (Partarabego), Anne (Denys de Fronsac), I, 260; II, 477

Paradis, Anna-Séphora. *See* Germain

Paradis, Augustin, V, 139

Paradis, Barbe. *See* Guyon

Paradis, Catherine. *See* Batailler

Paradis, Claude, III, 500

Paradis*, Élodie, named Sister Marie-Léonie (1840–1912), XII, 549

Paradis, François-Xavier, IX, 361
Paradis, Geneviève. *See* Cussy
Paradis, Jean, II, 508
Paradis, Jean, II, **508**, 660
Paradis, Marguerite (Cadier), X, 142
Paradis, Marie-Angélique. *See* Boivin
Paradis, Pierre, II, 508
Paradis, Roland, III, **500–1**; IV, 204, 748
Paradis, Thérèse (Bourget), XI, 94
Parant, Antoine (father of ANTOINE), VIII, 681
Parant, Antoine (father of JOSEPH), VIII, 682
Parant, Antoine, VI, 650; VII, 280; VIII, 242, 329, **681–82**, 937; XI, 94
Parant, Geneviève. *See* Bois
Parant, Gilbert, I, 573
Parant, Joseph, VI, 259, 577, 762; VIII, **682–83**
Parant, Marie (Légaré), X, 437
Parant, Marie-Antoinette. *See* Doucet
Parant, Marie-Geneviève (Painchaud), VIII, 676; X, 563
Parant, Pierre, X, 579
Parant, Suzanne. *See* Richard
Parat, Antoine, I, 26, 419, **530**; II, 46, 429
Parcot, Jane (Schureman), V, 742
Pardaillan de Grondin, Antoine-François, Marquis d'Antin, III, 610
Pardee, Aaron B., XI, 671
Pardee, Emma Kirby. *See* Forsyth
Pardee, Jane. *See* Elliott
Pardee, Timothy Blair, XI, 367, 450, **671–73**; XII, 333
Paré, Alfred, XI, 353
Paré, Ambroise, IV, 434
Paré, Catherine, named Saint-Louis-des-Anges, III, 630
Paré, Hubert, VIII, 675; IX, **616–17**; XI, 763
Paré, Jacques, V, 322
Paré, Jean-Romuald, VII, 642; XII, 698
Paré, Joseph-Octave, VII, 705; IX, 617; X, 250, **578**; XI, 105
Paré, Justine. *See* Vinet
Paré, Léon, IX, 616; X, 578
Paré, Marie-Angèle (La Rocque), XI, 493
Paré, Marie-Angélique. *See* Grenier
Paré, Marie-Anne. *See* Caron
Pareja. *See* Alcalá-Galiano
Parement, Perrette (Lorit, *dit* Gargot), II, 447
Parent. *See also* Parant
Parent, Charles, VII, 679
Parent, Charlotte-Cécile. *See* Rouillard
Parent, Claire (Deblois; Bouthillier), VI, 84
Parent, Édouard, VIII, 408
Parent, Étienne, III, 617
Parent, Étienne, VII, 8, 61, 72, 188, 430, 650, 879; VIII, 263, 332, 407, 408, 420, 497, 536, 629, 682, 962; IX, 118, 249, 261, 262, 299, 300, 444, 445, 446, 568, 813; X, 32, 132, 203, 304, **579–87**; XI, 35, 37, 83, 159, 160, 178, 342, 690; XII, 269, 1032, 1033
Parent, Étienne-François, X, 579
Parent, Hélène (Roy), X, 635
Parent, Jean-Louis-Laurent, III, 560; VI, 569
Parent, Joseph, V, 658
Parent, Joséphine-Henriette (Gérin-Lajoie), X, 580; XI, 342
Parent, Josephte. *See* Clouet
Parent, Léandre, VIII, 40
Parent, Louis-François, VII, **679–80**

Parent, Marguerite (Leprohon), VII, 501
Parent, Marie (Corbin), III, 138
Parent, Marie-Anne. *See* Chaboillez
Parent, Marie-Anne. *See* Chatellereaux
Parent, Marie-Augustine (Sulte), X, 580
Parent, Marie-Geneviève, named de Saint-François d'Assise, V, 587, **658–59**
Parent, Marie-Josephte (Caron), VIII, 128
Parent, Marie-Louise (Baillairgé), V, 49, 51; VI, 24
Parent, Marie-Madeleine. *See* Sasseville
Parent, Marie-Mathilde-Henriette. *See* Grenier
Parent, Mathilde-Sabine (Gélinas; Bonald), X, 304, 580
Parent, Pierre, V, 436
Parepoint. *See* Pierpoint
Pargellis, Stanley McCrory, III, xxix
Paris, Comte de. *See* Orléans
Paris, Antoine, III, 501
Paris, Bernard, III, **501**
Paris, Felix Louis, XII, 424, 425
Paris, Ferdinando John, IV, 695
Paris, John, VIII, 588
Paris, Marie-Anne. *See* Le Blanc
Paris, Marie-Gervaise (Berbudeau), IV, 56
Paris, Renée. *See* Boucher
Parisel, Jean-François, I, 108
Parisette, Anne (Pillard), III, 521
Parisien, Norbert, IX, **617–18**; XII, 951
Parisis, Pierre-Louis, X, 87
Park, George Hamilton, VIII, 850, 870; IX, 688; XII, 1123
Park, James, VII, 335, 336
Park, Mungo, V, 55
Park, Theoda (Williams), II, 667
Park, Thomas Fletcher, VIII, 120
Park, William, IV, 722
Parke, Edward Deane, XII, 822
Parke, Ephraim Jones, X, 645; XII, **822–23**
Parke, George Holmes, XII, 1072
Parke, Harriet Rose (Wilkes; wife of THOMAS), IX, 619
Parke, Henry W., IX, 327; XII, 641
Parke, Mary Helen. *See* Southwick
Parke, Philip, XII, 613
Parke, Robert, IX, 603, 618
Parke, Sarah (mother of EPHRAIM JONES), IX, 619; XII, 822
Parke, Thomas, VI, 400; VIII, 281; IX, 603, **618–19**; XI, 407, 517; XII, 822
Parker, Albert Edmund, 3rd Earl of Morley, XI, 21
Parker, Benjamin (father), VII, 680
Parker, Benjamin, VII, 681
Parker*, Daniel McNeill (1822–1907), VII, 16; IX, 281; XII, 1128
Parker, Desire (Grieve; Seely), IX, 710
Parker, Elizabeth Margaret Sheddon. *See* Wyer
Parker, Eunice (Henry), VII, 394
Parker, Henry, 12th Baron Morley, I, 407
Parker*, Sir Horatio Gilbert (1862–1932), X, 538; XII, 213
Parker, Sir Hyde, V, 110
Parker, James, V, 716; IX, 243
Parker, Jane. *See* Hatch
Parker, John G., VIII, 326
Parker, John Stewart, XI, 888
Parker, Katherine Jane. *See* Brough
Parker, Lydia (Sawtelle), V, 740

Parker, Martha. *See* Knowles
Parker, Mary. *See* Snow
Parker, Mary Elizabeth (Gordon), XII, 382
Parker, Sir Melville, XII, 382
Parker, Neville, VIII, 152; IX, **619–20**
Parker, Octavius, XI, 806
Parker, Rebecca (Bushel), III, 90
Parker, Robert, IX, 619, 620
Parker, Robert, VI, 811; VII, 424, 691; VIII, 151, 152; IX, 35, 339, 619, **620–21**, 766; X, 288, 341; XII, 20, 897
Parker, Samuel, XII, 626
Parker, Sarah Douglas (McGillivray), XII, 626
Parker, Snow, VII, **680–81**; VIII, 63
Parker, Susan. *See* Robinson
Parker, Thomas, 3rd Earl of Macclesfield, VI, 778
Parker, Thomas Sutherland, XI, 920
Parker, William, V, 635; VI, 254, 471, 531; VII, 523; VIII, 320, 321, 322
Parker, Sir William, VII, 197
Parker, William Buck Carthew Augustus, VIII, 928; XI, 486
Parkhurst, Anthony, I, 332, 334, 363, **530–31**
Parkhurst, John, I, 530
Parkin, Annie Connell, Lady Parkin. *See* Fisher
Parkin, Edward, VII, **681–83**; X, 587; XII, 1000
Parkin, Edward Bradley, X, 587
Parkin, Edward Cullen, VII, 683
Parkin*, Sir George Robert (1846–1922), VII, 291; X, 498; XI, 448; XII, 586, 714
Parkin, John Buckworth, VII, 683; X, **587**
Parkin, Katherine. *See* Bradley
Parkin, Sarah. *See* Cullen
Parkins, Susanna (Finlay), V, 314
Parkinson, Barton, V, 729
Parkinson, Ellinor (Addison), VI, 3
Parkinson, Lazarus, XI, 79
Parkman, Caroline. *See* Hall
Parkman, Caroline Hall (Cordner), XII, 214
Parkman, Catherine Scollay. *See* Bigelow
Parkman, Elias, XII, 823
Parkman, Eliza W. S., XII, 825
Parkman, Francis, XII, 823
Parkman, Francis, I, 142; III, 34, 149, 256, 707; IV, xxi, 24, 580, 681; V, 412; VIII, 35, 155, 911; IX, 420; X, 13; XI, 87, 172; XII, 14, 15, 17, 37, 112, 214, 215, 590, **823–27**
Parkman, Samuel, XII, 823
Parks, Ann. *See* Hegan
Parks, Cornelius, XII, 322
Parks, Elizabeth (Harvard), VIII, 371
Parks*, John Hegan (1836–1903), IX, 621
Parks, Samuel, IX, 621
Parks, William, IX, **621–22**
Parkyn, William, VIII, 632
Parkyns, John, V, 664
Parlane, Alexander, VII, 611
Parley, Peter. *See* Goodrich, Samuel Griswold
Parlow, Nancy (Brouse), XI, 114
Parma, Duke of. *See* Charles III
Parmenius, Stephanus, I, 5, 333, 334, 335, 363, **531–32**
Parmenter, Laura Gilson (Kerry), XII, 483
Parmentier, Charles, II, 27
Parmentier, Jean, I, **532–33**
Parmentier, Raoul, I, 532

Parmouth, Jane Christie (Simpson), XII, 972
Parnel, Elizabeth. *See* Southack
Parnell, Charles Stewart, XII, 68, 69, 1087
Parnell, Harriet (Shadd), XII, 960
Parr, Eleanor. *See* Clements
Parr, Harriet (Dobson; Brymer), VI, 89
Parr, John, IV, 603
Parr, John, IV, 57, 111, 112, 223, 292, 293, 328, 389, 444, 452, 516, 522, 556, **603–5**, 625, 626, 627, 723; V, 25, 94, 109, 128, 136, 148, 156, 158, 222, 251, 281, 309, 310, 344, 431, 435, 445, 465, 589, 605, 610, 634, 657, 658, 866, 867; VI, 34, 90, 137, 194, 195, 276, 283, 310, 395, 562, 676, 731, 740, 790, 799, 813; VII, 87, 832
Parr, Sara. *See* Walmesley
Parry, Caleb Hillier, VIII, 683
Parry, Catherine Edwards, Lady Parry. *See* Hankinson
Parry, Edward St John, XI, 916
Parry, Isabella Louisa, Lady Parry. *See* Stanley
Parry, Sarah. *See* Rigby
Parry, Sir William Edward, I, 75, 312, 375, 378; III, 128, 449; V, 56; VI, 329, 330, 648; VII, 324, 325, 326, 911; VIII, 70, **683–86**, 771, 772; IX, 11, 167, 180, 387, 658, 659, 691, 692; X, 42, 454; XI, 543, 798; XII, 38
Pars, Marie (Picoté de Belestre), I, 547
Parsons, Eliza. *See* Flood
Parsons, Eliza (Ridout), VIII, 749
Parsons, Hannah (rebaptized Catherine) (Bermen de La Martinière), III, 64
Parsons, Philip, II, 454
Parsons, Robert John, XI, 239, 673
Parsons, Robert John, VII, 48, 49, 113, 114, 153, 154, 155, 156, 220, 632, 634, 765; VIII, 233, 403, 470, 659, 948, 950, 951; IX, 70, 436, 606; X, 8, 553, 687; XI, 44, 239, **673–74**, 760; XII, 563, 564, 565
Parsons, Robert Mann, XI, 604; XII, 815
Parsons, William, VII, 712, 862, 863
Partarabego. *See* Parabego
Partelow, Jane Hamlin. *See* Matthews
Partelow, Jehiel, IX, 622
Partelow, John Richard, VI, 355; VIII, 739; IX, 146, 381, **622–23**, 767; X, 159, 285, 712
Particelli d'Émery, Michel, I, 198
Partridge, Frances, known as Sister St Frances Patrick, VII, 625
Partridge, Mary (Belcher), IV, 50
Pas, Isaac de, Marquis de Feuquières, I, 296
Pascal, Blaise, IV, 92; VIII, 291
Pascal d'Auxerre, Father, I, 129
Pascal de Troyes, Father, I, 468, 504
Pascaud, Anne. *See* Puyperouse
Pascaud, Antoine (son of ANTOINE, d. 1717), II, 509; III, 290, 485, 486
Pascaud, Antoine, I, 400; II, 81, 269, 304, 387, 463, 464, **508–9**; III, 52, 352, 393; IV, 357, 605
Pascaud, Antoine, IV, 306, **605**, 750
Pascaud, Catherine. *See* Berteau
Pascaud, Élisabeth. *See* Cournoyer
Pascaud, Guillaume (father of ANTOINE, d. 1717), II, 508
Pascaud, Guillaume (father of ANTOINE, 1729–86), IV, 605
Pascaud, Jean (grandfather), IV, 605
Pascaud, Jean (uncle), IV, 605
Pascaud, Jean, IV, 605; V, 395
Pascaud, Joseph-Marie, II, 509; III, 290

Pascaud, Marguerite. *See* Bouat
Pascaud, Marie-Anne. *See* Baulos
Pascaud, Pierre, IV, 605
Pasco, Mary (Murray), VI, 535
Pascoe, Charles Frederick, V, 107
Paskwāw (Pasquah), XI, 596, **674–75**, 712; XII, 125
Pasqualigo, Lorenzo, I, 148, 149, 150
Pasqualigo, Pietro, I, 235
Pasqualoni, Vincenzo, XII, 849
Pasquier, Jean, II, 33, 464, 465, 508
Pasquine, I, **533**, 586; II, 182
Passard, Marie-Jeanne (Neveu), III, 482
Passenger, William, II, 152, 487
Passmore, Maria (Beach), XII, 68
Passy, Marie-Eugénie de (Mézière), V, 591
Pastedechouan, I, 164, 265, 488, **533–34**
Pasteur, Monsieur (wood-carver), VIII, 781
Pasteur, Charles-Bernard, V, 591; VIII, 87, 258
Pasteur, Louis, XI, 217
Pastorius, Abraham, VI, 284
Pastorius, Eleanor (Gibb), VI, 284
Pastour de Costebelle, Anne. *See* Mius d'Entremont de Pobomcoup
Pastour de Costebelle, Anne. *See* Tour
Pastour de Costebelle, Anne-Catherine de (Bertaut), II, 512
Pastour de Costebelle, Barthélemy, II, 509, 510
Pastour de Costebelle, François-Barthélemy, II, 509
Pastour de Costebelle, Françoise, II, 509
Pastour de Costebelle, Louis, II, 478, 509, 510
Pastour de Costebelle, Marie. *See* Du Plessis
Pastour de Costebelle, Marie-Josèphe (Rivière, Marquise de Giscaro), II, 512
Pastour de Costebelle, Philippe, I, 530; II, 15, 36, 152, 205, 214, 254, 285, 339, 388, 389, 411, 417, 442, 479, 482, 487, **509–13**, 611, 637; III, 177, 357, 455, 499, 618; IV, xxi
Pastour de Mérieu, Joseph, II, 509, 510
Patch, Sam, VII, 313
Patenaude, Geneviève (Bourassa), XII, 120
Patenaude, Josephte (Callihoo), VII, 137
Patenaude, Marie (Callihoo), VII, 137
Patenotre, Marie (Plante), III, 522
Paterson. *See also* Patterson
Paterson, Alexander Thomas, XII, 632
Paterson, Anne. *See* McDougall
Paterson, Charles, IV, 277, 365; V, 8, 9, 39, 229, 561, 656, 682
Paterson, Cornelia. *See* Munro
Paterson, David, VIII, 687; XI, 675, 676
Paterson, Elizabeth (Robb), IX, 665
Paterson, Euphemia (Leitch), IX, 460
Paterson, Grace. *See* Lesslie
Paterson, Grizzel (Gillespie), VII, 342
Paterson, Hannah. *See* Wilson
Paterson, James, X, 336
Paterson, Jean. *See* Frazer
Paterson, John (Newfoundland merchant), XII, 770
Paterson, John (Quebec merchant), VI, 531
Paterson, John (son-in-law of John MCDOUGALL, 1805–70), IX, 489
Paterson, John, VIII, 280, **686–88**; XI, 675; XII, 391
Paterson, Marion (Vennor), XI, 898
Paterson, Martha (Hawkins), VIII, 385

Paterson, Peter (father of JOHN and PETER), VIII, 686; IX, 497; XI, 675, 676
Paterson, Peter (nephew of JOHN and PETER), XI, 676
Paterson, Peter, VIII, 687, 930; IX, 657; XI, **675–76**
Paterson, William, XII, 43
Patés. *See* Du Paty
Patetchoanen. *See* Pastedechouan
Patin, Guy, I, 80
Patiner, Henry, I, 156
Patmore, Coventry, X, 347
Paton, Andrew, XI, 706; XII, **827–28**
Paton, Elizabeth (Cochrane), VII, 192
Paton, Isabella. *See* Moir
Paton, James, XII, 827
Paton, John, IX, 461
Paton, Mary. *See* Harvey
Patoulet, Jean-Baptiste, I, 63, 120, **534**, 581, 621, 627; II, 146, 147
Patriarch. *See* Fléché
Patrick, Abigail Ann. *See* Brouse
Patrick, Asa, XI, 676
Patrick, Belinda. *See* Gilbert
Patrick, Effie (Gilbert; Morrison), VIII, 642
Patrick, William, VIII, 105; XI, **676–77**; XII, 963
Patrick, William Poyntz, VIII, 642; XI, 676
Patrie, Louise (Démarest), VIII, 209
Patrizi, Constantin, X, 193
Patron, Jean-Jacques, II, 262
Patry, Jean, XI, 336
Patry (Paltry), Marie-Luce-Eugénie (Bell; Marchand; Thériault), XII, 1034
Pattee, Clarissa. *See* Thomas
Pattee, David, VII, 380, 381; VIII, **688–89**, 890
Pattee, Gordon B., XI, 681
Pattee, John, VIII, 688
Pattee, Mary. *See* Hadley
Pattee, Moses, VIII, 688
Patten, Amanda Jane. *See* Darling
Patterson, Abraham, XII, 828
Patterson, Andrew Dickson, VI, 105; VII, 825
Patterson, Ann. *See* Harris
Patterson, Anna. *See* Sovereene
Patterson, Christiana Ann. *See* MacGregor
Patterson, Edith. *See* Bridges
Patterson, Elizabeth. *See* Todd
Patterson, Elizabeth (Amherst), VI, 9
Patterson, Elizabeth (Bonaparte), V, 660
Patterson, Elizabeth (Willard), VI, 816
Patterson, George, V, 660
Patterson, George, I, 335; VI, 462; VII, 636; XII, 250, **828–30**
Patterson, George Geddie, VII, 22, 81, 83; XII, 830
Patterson, Georgiana. *See* Sparrow
Patterson, Hester. *See* Warren
Patterson, Isabella (Bowles), XI, 107
Patterson, Isabella Susan (Cockburn), XI, 195
Patterson*, James Colebrooke (1839–1929), XII, 148
Patterson, Joan (Farrell), X, 277
Patterson, John (brother of WALTER), IV, 606, 609; V, 309, 310
Patterson, John (deacon), V, 660; XII, 828
Patterson, Leslie, VI, 612
Patterson, Margaret. *See* McDonald

Patterson, Mary (mother of PETER), VIII, 689
Patterson, Mary Ann (Murray), XI, 633
Patterson, Mary Jane (Hall), VIII, 692; X, 329
Patterson, Mary Jane (Jacob), IX, 408
Patterson, Peter (businessman), XII, 701, 703
Patterson, Peter (father of PETER), VIII, 689
Patterson, Peter, VI, 290, 532; VII, 70, 71, 510, 873, 874;
    VIII, xxv, **689–92**; IX, 773; X, 32, 329; XII, 279
Patterson, Robert, IX, 316
Patterson, Robert, V, 409, 611, **659–60**
Patterson, Robert J., XI, **677–78**
Patterson, Robert S., VIII, 452
Patterson, Sarah (Mortimer), V, 611, 660
Patterson, Sarah Ann (Dickson), VIII, 222
Patterson, W. J. Ballantyne, XI, 679
Patterson, Walter, IV, 128, 129, 152, 352, 551, **605–11**; V,
    27, 219, 249, 250, 309, 310, 477, 513, 515, 775, 777,
    778, 825, 826, 873; VI, 107, 108, 130, 131, 197, 198,
    736; VII, 406, 407; IX, 27
Patterson, William, IV, 606
Patterson, William Albert, XI, 262
Patterson, William Jeffrey, IX, 44; XI, **678–79**
Patteshall, Jane (Cope), III, 136
Patteson, Thomas Charles, X, 469, 632; XI, 697; XII, 98,
    189, 604, 605, 606, 607, 611, 612, 685, 689
Patti, Adelina, IX, 855
Pattin, John, III, 496, **501–2**
Pattinson, Richard, VI, 8
Pattle, Eliza Susan (Wakefield), IX, 817
Patton, Horatio, IX, 779
Patton, Horatio Nelson, VIII, 559
Patton, James, XI, 582, 621; XII, 73, 97, 604, 605
Patton, Mary (Allan), V, 15
Patton, Robert, VIII, 443
Patton, William Randall, VII, 213
Pattulo, George Robson, XII, 657
Pauger, Adrien de, III, 105
Paugus, II, 26
Paul. *See also* Peminuit
Paul (brother of TOTIRI), I, 652
Paul (saint), XII, 250
Paul V, I, 97
Paul, Aurélie (Trudeau), XI, 889
Paul, Hobblewest, XI, 679
Paul, Malti, VIII, 334
Paul, Mary Christianne (Morris), XI, **679–80**
Paul, Samuel. *See* Peminuit Paul, Louis-Benjamin
Paulet. *See also* Polette
Paulet, Antoine (father of Antoine POLETTE), XI, 698
Paulet, Antoine (settler), XI, 698
Paulet (Powlett), Charles, Baron St John, 6th Marquis of
    Winchester and 1st Duke of Bolton, II, 496, 497
Paulet, Charles Ingoldsby, 13th Marquis of Winchester,
    VIII, 649
Paulet, Marie-Josephe. *See* Bertrand
Paulian, Aimé-Henri, VIII, 212
Paulin-Guérin. *See* Guérin, Jean-Baptiste
Paulmy d'Argenson, Marquis de. *See* Voyer
Paulo, Catherine (Campot), III, 96
Paulus. *See also* Powlis; Sahonwagy
Paulus, IV, 692
Paulus Petrus, IV, 691
Paumart, Guillaume, I, 534

Paumart, Jean, I, **534**
Paumart, Marie. *See* Le Roy
Paumereau. *See* Pommereau
Pauperet, Claude, II, 17, 388
Pautaussigae. *See* Pahtahsega
Pavie, Théodore, IX, 302
Pawling, Benjamin, V, **660–61**, 669, 782, 841; VI, 247
Pawling, Jesse, V, 660
Pawling, Peter Ten Broeck, V, 661
Pawling, Susan (wife of BENJAMIN), V, 660
Pawpine. *See* Pierpoint
Pawpitch, IV, 518
Paxinosa, IV, 27
Payen de Chavoy, Pierre, II, 513
Payen de Noyan, Catherine-Jeanne. *See* Le Moyne de
    Longueuil et de Châteauguay
Payen de Noyan, Gilles-Augustin, III, 382, 503
Payen de Noyan, Louise-Catherine. *See* Ailleboust de
    Manthet
Payen de Noyan, Marie. *See* Faucon Dumanoir
Payen de Noyan, Marie-Catherine, named de Saint-Alexis,
    V, **661–62**
Payen de Noyan, Pierre, II, 131, 446, **513**; III, 502; IV, 611
Payen de Noyan, Pierre-Benoît, III, **502–3**
Payen de Noyan et de Chavoy, Catherine-Angélique
    (Legardeur de Repentigny), IV, 449, 612
Payen de Noyan et de Chavoy, Louise-Catherine. *See* Aille-
    boust de Manthet
Payen de Noyan et de Chavoy, Pierre-Jacques, II, 131, 180;
    III, 110, 373, 450, 492, 503, 588; IV, 85, 449, **611–12**;
    V, 661
Payet, Marguerite (Couturier, *dit* Le Bourguignon), II, 160
Payet, Marie-Joseph (Pouget), V, 687
Payet, *dit* Saint-Amour, Pierre, I, 633; II, 141
Payfer. *See* Pfeiffer
Payipwat* (d. 1902), XI, 477, 478, 675; XII, 780, 802, 858
Payne, Benjamin Charnock, IV, 758
Payne, François-Amable, II, 513
Payne, Hiram, V, 204
Payne, Humphrey, II, 513
Payne, John, II, 513
Payne, John Howard, IV, 594
Payne, Lawrence, II, 513
Payne, Marguerite. *See* Garreau
Payne, Mary. *See* Rivers
Payne, Samuel, II, **513–14**; III, 346
Payne, Thomas, VI, 119
Paypamakeesit (Round the Sky), XI, 460
Pays, Renée (Hardouineau de Landianière; Beauharnois de
    La Boische, Marquise de Beauharnois), III, 42
Payzant, John, IV, 19; VI, 276, 293, **573–74**; VII, 252;
    VIII, 360, 610, 611
Payzant, Louis, VI, 573
Payzant, Marie-Anne. *See* Noguet
Payzant, Mary. *See* Alline
Pazhekezhikquashkum. *See* Bauzhi-geezhig-waeshikum
Peabody, Mrs. *See* Perley
Peabody, Francis, VI, 717, 718; VII, 493, 683
Peabody, Francis, VI, 651; VII, 4, **683–84**, 806; VIII, 783
Peabody, George, VIII, 448
Peabody, Hannah (Simonds), VI, 717, 718; VII, 806; VIII,
    805
Peabody, Hephzibah (Leavitt), VII, 493

Peabody, John G., VII, 714
Peabody, Lydia (Brooker; wife of FRANCIS), VII, 683
Peabody, Mary. *See* Brown
Peabody, Stephen, VII, 683
Peache, Alfred, X, 208
Peachey, James, IV, **612–14**; V, 228, 428; VII, 95
Peachy*, Joseph-Ferdinand (1830–1903), VIII, 40
Peacock, William, XI, 31
Peacocke, George John, X, 74; XI, 245
Peake, James Ellis, VII, 104
Peale, Charles Willson, V, 313, 811; VI, 186
Péan, Angélique. *See* Renaud d'Avène Des Méloizes
Péan, Angélique-Renée-Françoise (Marconnay), IV, 616, 660
Péan, Anne. *See* Corbarboineau
Péan, Jean-Pierre, III, 503
Péan, Marie-Madeleine (Mény), IV, 99
Péan, Michel-Jean-Hugues, III, 19, 124, 160, 300, 441, 464, 504, 525, 537, 551; IV, 65, 66, 67, 69, 70, 88, 91, 124, 125, 459, 517, **614–17**, 621, 642, 659, 670, 680, 750; V, 104, 164, 191, 711
Péan, René-Pierre, IV, 615
Péan de Livaudière, Jacques-Hugues, II, 339; III, 69, 102, 340, **503–4**, 505; IV, 315, 614, 654
Péan de Livaudière, Marie-Françoise. *See* Pécaudy de Contrecœur
Pearce, Patrick, VIII, 532
Pearce, Stephen, XI, 544; XII, 879
Pearce*, William (1848–1930), XI, 921; XII, 672, 688
Pearkes, George, X, **587**
Pearkes, Mary Elizabeth. *See* Dorman
Pearley. *See* Perley
Pearse*, Benjamin William (1832–1902), XII, 833, 834
Pearson, Bartholomew, I, 350, **534–35**
Pearson, Elizabeth. *See* Baguleughe
Pearson, Maria Bolton (Douglas), XII, 265
Pearson, Mary. *See* Ogilvie
Pearson, Thomas, VIII, 304
Peary, Robert Edwin, VIII, 449; XI, 394
Pease, Captain, I, 567
Pease, Huldah (Kendrick), IV, 410
Peaseley, William, III, **504**; IV, 437
Peasley, Mr (businessman), VIII, 758
Peaslie, Robert, V, 415; VI, 718
Pécaudy, Charles, I, 535
Pécaudy, Claudine (Jarret), II, 295
Pécaudy de Contrecœur, Anne. *See* Dubois
Pécaudy de Contrecœur, Antoine, III, 505
Pécaudy de Contrecœur, Antoine, I, **535–36**; II, 295, 592; III, 308, 505
Pécaudy de Contrecœur, Barbe. *See* Denys de La Trinité
Pécaudy de Contrecœur, Claude-François, IV, 617
Pécaudy de Contrecœur, Claude-Pierre, I, 536; III, 81, 94, 148, 149, 150, 373, 401, 505, 526, 600, 614; IV, xliii, 257, 459, 464, **617–18**, 634; V, 98, 143, 185, 272
Pécaudy de Contrecœur, François, III, 525
Pécaudy de Contrecœur, François-Antoine, I, 535; II, 495, 593; III, 55, 159, 160, 503, **505**, 637; IV, 614, 617
Pécaudy de Contrecœur, Jeanne. *See* Saint-Ours
Pécaudy de Contrecœur, Louise (Daine), III, 159, 505; IV, 66, 614
Pécaudy de Contrecœur, Marguerite-Barbe. *See* Hingue de Puygibault

Pécaudy de Contrecœur, Marie (La Corne de Chaptes), II, 327; III, 331, 332, 333; IV, 425, 429
Pécaudy de Contrecœur, Marie-Charlotte (Laperière), VIII, 606
Pécaudy de Contrecœur, Marie-Françoise (Péan de Livaudière), III, 503, 405; IV, 614
Pécaudy de Contrecœur, Marie-Madeleine. *See* Boucher de La Perrière
Péchagut, Jeanne (Laumet), II, 351
Péché (Peshe), Monsieur (*engagé*), V, 684
Pechegechequistqum. *See* Bauzhi-geezhig-waeshikum
Pécholier, Jeanne. *See* Lafont
Pecholier, Thomas, V, 42
Peck, Aliza Amelia. *See* Gowan
Peck, Ebenezer, X, 653
Peck, Kendrick, IV, 295
Peck, Sarah (Hopper), XII, 444
Peck, William, X, 313
Peckham, Sir George, I, 333, 334, 336, 363, 380, 531, 677
Pécody, Benoît de, I, 535
Pécody, Énarde de. *See* Martin
Pedley, Alice. *See* Curtain
Pedley, Charles, IV, 785; X, **587–88**; XII, 589
Pedley, James, X, 587
Pedley, Sarah. *See* Stowell
Pedro I, Emperor of Brazil, IX, 25
Peek, Rhoda (Collins), X, 188
Peel, Amelia Margaret. *See* Hall
Peel, Émilie Marguerite, XII, 831
Peel, Isaure Fanchette. *See* Verdier
Peel, John Robert, XII, 830
Peel, Mildred (Ross, Lady Ross), XII, 830, 831
Peel, Paul, XII, 288, 337, 405, **830–32**
Peel, Sir Robert, VI, 114, 706; VII, 31, 32, 286, 604, 605, 607, 608, 640, 859; VIII, xxviii; IX, 89, 354, 355, 430, 445, 675, 676, 806; X, 257, 345, 394, 443, 494, 705, 728; XI, 155; XII, 100, 101, 292
Peel, Robert André, XII, 831
Peel, Sir William, IX, 327, 806; XII, 641
Peemeecheekag, XII, **832**
Peenaquim, IX, **623–24**; X, 661; XII, 717, 718, 778, 970
Peers, Augustus Richard, XI, 384
Peers, Eliza. *See* Yale
Peers, H., IX, 624
Peers, Henry Newsham, IX, **624–26**; X, 486
Peet, Rebecca (Selee), VII, 782
Peguis (Pegeois, Pegouisse, Pegowis, Pegqas), VII, 517, 901; VIII, 352; IX, 135, **626–27**, 732
Peguy, Marie-Anne (Fournier), VII, 321
Peiras, Anne de. *See* Thirement
Peiras, Catherine de, II, 514
Peiras, Denise de. *See* Marion
Peiras, Denise de (Giffard), II, 514
Peiras, Élisabeth de (Pinguet de Targis), II, 514
Peiras, Jean de, II, 514
Peiras, Jean-Baptiste de, I, 581; II, 179, 369, **514**
Peiras, Louis de, II, 514
Peiras, Marie-Madeleine de (Denys de Saint-Simon), II, 60, 178, 514; III, 180
Peirce (Pierce), Sarah (Winslow), V, 869
Peire, Philippe, II, 180
Peire (Peré), Pierre, II, 180, 214, 276, 526
Peirenc de Moras, François-Marie de, IV, 467

Peirese, Nicolas de, I, 294
Pelegrin. *See* Pellegrin
Pélerin, Ambroise (Pierre), II, 244, **514–15**
Pelerin, Élizabeth (Chenneque), VI, 134
Pélerin, Ignace, I, 256
Pélerin (Pelerin), Marie (Charron), VII, 168
Pelerin, Marie-Vénérande (Ranvoyzé), V, 707; VI, 633;
    VII, 752
Pélerin, Philippe, I, 91
Pélerin de Saint-Amant, Louise. *See* Mousseaux
Pélerin de Saint-Amant, Pierre, I, 256; II, 474, 515
Pelham, Lady Amelia Rose (Jebb, Lady Jebb), IX, 412
Pelham, George, X, 110
Pelham, Henry, III, 658
Pelham-Holles, Thomas, 4th Duke of Newcastle-upon-
    Tyne, II, 22, 251; III, 9, 10, 33, 126, 127, 183, 261, 276,
    293, 294, 362, 426, 517, 585, 587, 642, 653, 658; IV, 21,
    57, 395, 571
Pélissier, Agathe. *See* Martaud La Rigaudière
Pélissier, Catherine. *See* Delzenne
Pélissier, Christophe, IV, 205, 243, 288, 399, **618–19**, 629;
    V, 21, 277, 289, 735, 736, 843; VI, 183, 184
Pélissier, François-Christophe, IV, 618
Pélissier, Marie-Catherine. *See* Delezenne
Pélissier, Marie-Catherine (Godefroy de Tonnancour), VI,
    288; IX, 321
Pélissier, Marthe. *See* Baudoin
Pélissier de Féligonde, Jean-François, V, 680
Pᴇlkamū'lôx, VIII, 421
Pell, Augustus J., XI, 296, 297
Pell, James (father), VII, 616, 617; X, 517
Pell, James, VII, 616
Pellegrin, François, IV, 619
Pellegrin, Gabriel, III, 464, 621, 622; IV, 10, 271, **619–21**;
    V, 103
Pellegrin, Madeleine. *See* Boissy
Pellegrin, Marie-Anne. *See* Bonnegrâce
Pellerin, Cécile. *See* Boudreau
Pellerin, Marie (Becquet), I, 86
Pellerin, Pierre, V, 102
Pellet. *See* Plet
Pelletier. *See also* Peltier
Pelletier, Adeline (Gagnon), XII, 251
Pelletier*, Alexis (1837–1910), IX, 19, 64; XI, 104, 109,
    175; XII, 819, 1018
Pelletier, Antoinette (Daine), III, 159
Pelletier, Catherine. *See* Vannier
Pelletier, Catherine, I, 439
Pelletier, Catherine-Geneviève (Lefebvre Duplessis Faber),
    III, 372, 373
Pelletier*, Sir Charles-Alphonse-Pantaléon (1837–1911),
    XI, 520; XII, 45
Pelletier, Didace (Claude), I, 439, **536**; II, 174, 176, 203,
    248, 258, 268, 419, 506, 515, 528; III, 259, 344
Pelletier, François, I, 387; II, 158
Pelletier, Frédéric, XII, 472
Pelletier, Geneviève. *See* Digé
Pelletier, Geneviève. *See* Letendre
Pelletier (Peltier), Geneviève (Lefebvre), II, 382; III,
    371
Pelletier, Georges, I, 536
Pelletier, Honoré-Cyrias, XI, 456
Pelletier, Jean-François-Xavier, II, 655; III, 372

Pelletier, Jeanne (Jérémie, *dit* Lamontagne), I, 387; II, 296;
    III, 314
Pelletier, Joseph (clergyman), XII, 397
Pelletier, Joseph (son-in-law of Jean Dɪɢé), V, 257
Pelletier, Joseph-Ferréol, IX, 614, 615
Pelletier*, Louis-Philippe (1857–1921), XII, 20, 251
Pelletier, Madeleine. *See* Thunay, *dit* Dufresne
Pelletier, Marie. *See* Outchiouanish
Pelletier, Marie-Adèle-Victorine. *See* Duvernay
Pelletier, Marie-Geneviève (Janson, *dit* Lapalme), III, 304
Pelletier, Marie-Rose (Papin), IX, 614
Pelletier (Peltier), Nicolas, II, 357
Pelletier, Ovide, VIII, 262
Pelletier, Pierre, V, 599
Pelletier, René, II, 382
Pelletier*, Romain-Octave (1843–1927), VIII, 692, 693;
    XI, 671; XII, 472, 504
Pelletier, Rose-Virginie, named Marie de Sainte-
    Euphrasie, X, 17
Pelletier (Peltier) de La Prade, Michel, I, 251, 494; II, 637
Pellew, Edward, 1st Viscount Exmouth, IV, 784; V, 444;
    VI, 212, 214; VIII, 886; X, 110
Pelling, Mr (apothecary), I, 578
Pellisier; Pellissier. *See* Pélissier
Pelly, Anne Rose. *See* Clouston
Pelly, Augustus Edward, VIII, 574; XI, 139, 875; XII, 206
Pelly, Douglas Raymond, XI, 77, 78
Pelly, George, VII, 808; VIII, 816; X, 486
Pelly, Sir John Henry, VIII, 580, 816; IX, 649; XII, 113
Pelly, Robert Parker, VI, 438, 648
Pelouse, Léon-Germain, XI, 296
Peltier. *See also* Pelletier
Peltier, Élisabeth. *See* Lacoste
Peltier, Émilie. *See* Hérigault
Peltier, Émilie (Peltier), VIII, 694
Peltier, Félicité (Morin), X, 533
Peltier, Guillaume, VIII, 693
Peltier, Hector, VIII, 694; X, 470, **588–89**; XI, 58, 102,
    303; XII, 798, 1017
Peltier, Henriette (Bourret), VIII, 694
Peltier, Jean-Baptiste-Généreux, VIII, 692
Peltier, Joseph-Féréol, VIII, 694
Peltier, Marie-Scholastique. *See* Masson
Peltier, Orphir, VIII, **692–93**
Peltier, Romain-Octave, VIII, 692
Peltier, Suzanne Ellen. *See* Van Felson
Peltier, Toussaint, VIII, 693
Peltier, Toussaint, VIII, 479, **693–94**; IX, 682; X, 588; XI,
    70
Pemberton, Augustus Frederick, XII, 523, 833
Pemberton, Edward H., XII, 464
Pemberton, Frederick Bernard, XII, 834
Pemberton, George, VI, 192; VII, 836; VIII, 691, 962; IX,
    83, 274
Pemberton, Hélène. *See* Desbarats
Pemberton, Henry, VI, 192
Pemberton, Jeremy, V, 251
Pemberton, Joseph, XII, 832
Pemberton, Joseph Despard, XI, 605; XII, 130, 240, 642,
    **832–34**, 1049
Pemberton, Margaret. *See* Stephens
Pemberton, Sophia Theresa (Beanlands; Deane-
    Drummond), XII, 832

Pemberton, Sophie. *See* Desbarats
Pemberton, Susan Frances, XII, 833
Pemberton, Theresa Jane Despard. *See* Grautoff
Pembroke, Earl of. *See* Herbert
Pemecka. *See* Peemeecheekag
Peminuit, Paul, VII, 684; XII, 834
Peminuit Paul, François, VII, 684, 685; XII, 834
Peminuit Paul, Jacques-Pierre, VII, 685; XII, **834–35**
Peminuit Paul, Jean-Lucien, VII, 684
Peminuit Paul, Louis-Benjamin, VII, **684–85**; XII, 834
Peminuit Paul, Madeleine (mother of JACQUES-PIERRE), VII, 684; XII, 834
Peminuit Paul, Mary (Noel; wife of JACQUES-PIERRE), XII, 834
Peminuit Paul, Pierre, VII, 684
Peminuit Paul, Sally (wife of JACQUES-PIERRE), XII, 834
Pemmeenauweet, Paussamigh. *See* Peminuit Paul, Louis-Benjamin
Pemoussa, II, 502, **515–16**, 562; III, 577
Pemucheka. *See* Peemeecheekag
Penagashea (Changing Feathers), VII, 847
Pe-na-koam. *See* Peenaquim
Peñalossa, Diego, Count of Peñalossa, I, 179
Peña Saravia, Tomás de la, IV, 623
Pender, Daniel, XII, 892
Pendergast, John G., XI, 898
Pendleton, John B., IX, 386, 387
Pengelly, Robert Lamport, XI, 803, 804
Penhallow, Samuel, II, 452, 495, 544
Pénigaut (Pénicaut), André-Joseph, II, 428, 455
Pénissault (Penisseau). *See* Pennisseaut
Penman, George, V, 407
Penman, Nancy (Montgomery), IX, 565
Penn, Anna (Carpenter), X, 137
Penn, Turton, VII, 227, 894
Penn, William, III, 65
Penn, Sir William, I, 605; II, 667
Pennant, Thomas, IV, 341, 377, 378; V, 54, 167, 221, 362
Pennasca (Sébastien), I, 396
Pennée, Marguerite-Alice-Gertrude (Amyot), XII, 20
Pennefather, Edward, IX, 627
Pennefather, Sir John Lysaght, X, 332
Pennefather, Lavina (St Leger, Lady St Leger), IV, 694
Pennefather, Richard Theodore, IX, 381, 591, **627–28**; XII, 596
Pennefather, Susan (Gray), XI, 369, 371
Pennefather, Suzan. *See* Darby
Penney, George W., XII, 761
Penney, John, X, 306
Penney, William Archibald, XII, 765
Pennington, John, 1st Baron Muncaster, X, 443
Pennington, Maria Margaret Frances (Lindsay), X, 443
Pennisseaut, Catherine. *See* Bry
Pennisseaut, Charles, IV, 621
Pennisseaut, Louis, III, 441, 442; IV, 66, 125, 127, 461, 517, 615, 616, **621–22**
Pennisseaut, Marie-Marguerite. *See* Lemoine, *dit* Monière
Penniston, Susan (Clinton), III, 126
Pennoyer, Jesse, VII, 186, 199; VI, 338, 377, **574–76**, 816
Pennoyer, John, VI, 575
Pennoyer, Joseph, VI, 574
Pennoyer, Lucy. *See* Crippen
Pennoyer, Martha. *See* Ferguson

Penny, Edward Goff, XI, 680
Penny, Edward Goff, IX, 166, 430; X, 355; XI, 438, **680–81**; XII, 248
Penny, Eleanor Elizabeth. *See* Smith
Penny, Emmiley. *See* May
Penny, Helen. *See* Robertson
Penny, John, XI, 680
Penny, Margaret. *See* Irvine
Penny, Susan (Benning), IX, 46
Penny, William, XII, 835
Penny, William, VII, 271, 327; VIII, 448, 624, 773; IX, 12, 199, 200; X, 29, 561, 562; XII, **835–36**, 878
Penrose, Grace (Nevins), V, 623
Penrose, Richard, V, 623
Penrose, Thomas, V, 623
Penrose, William, V, 623
Pense, Edward John Barker, XI, 49; XII, 497
Pensens. *See* Espiet
Penthièvre, Duc de. *See* Bourbon
Pentland, Margaret. *See* Baptist
Pentland, William Charles, IX, 640; X, 34
Penukwiim. *See* Peenaquim
Pepin, Angélique (Deguire, *dit* Desrosiers), IV, 201, 202
Pepin (Pepin, *dit* Lachance), Angélique (Judith) (Canac), VII, 146
Pepin, Charlotte. *See* Stubinger
Pepin, Charlotte (Campion, *dit* Labonté), IV, 132
Pépin, Jacqueline (Cusson), II, 166
Pépin, Jean-Baptiste, VII, 685
Pépin, Joseph, V, 497; VI, 625, 626; VII, 60, **685–86**; VIII, 763
Pepin, Louise (Racine), IX, 360; XI, 720; XII, 874
Pépin, Madeleine. *See* Lebeau
Pepin, Marguerite (Leclerc), II, 380
Pepin, Marie (Larue), II, 348
Pépin, Marie-Ursule (Pinard), I, 550
Pépin, Zéphyrin, VII, 686
Pépin, Zoé (Germain), X, 305
Pépin, *dit* Lachance. *See also* Pepin
Pépin, *dit* Lachance, Marie-Françoise (Chabot), IX, 122
Pépin, *dit* Laforce. *See also* Laforce
Pépin, *dit* Laforce, Marie-Joseph (Rouer de Villeray), III, 571
Pépin, *dit* Laforce, Michelle. *See* Lebert
Pépin, *dit* Laforce, Pierre, III, 239, 571; IV, 692; V, 470
Pépin, *dit* Laforce, Véronique (Saillant), IV, 692
Pepperrell, Andrew (great-grandfather), II, 516
Pepperrell, Andrew, III, 508
Pepperrell, Joan (mother of WILLIAM) II, 516
Pepperrell, Margery. *See* Bray
Pepperrell, Mary, Lady Pepperrell. *See* Hirst
Pepperrell, William, II, **516**; III, 505
Pepperrell (Sparhawk), Sir William, VI, 75, 137; VII, 87
Pepperrell, Sir William, II, 516; III, xxiv, 6, 10, 33, 49, 98, 116, 175, 209, 260, 264, 267, 274, 294, 345, 350, 356, 396, 452, 457, 470, 471, 475, **505–9**, 566, 615, 641, 642, 644, 653, 655, 656, 657; IV, 15, 62, 83, 84, 168, 213, 239, 248, 254, 299, 312, 314, 363, 420, 454, 688, 783; V, 134, 869; VI, 188
Pepys, Samuel, I, 226; II, 308, 659
Perceval, John, 2nd Earl of Egmont, III, 658; IV, 606; V, 315
Perche. *See* Ledroit

Perchot, Hélène (Monseignat), II, 483
Percival, Michael Henry, V, 746
Percy, Algernon, 2nd Baron Lovaine, IV, 197
Percy, Frances Julia, Duchess of Northumberland. *See* Burrell
Percy, Francis, II, 153
Percy, Hugh, 2nd Duke of Northumberland, V, 811, 865, 868; VI, 394, 551, 552, 553; VII, 64, 813; VIII, 793
Percy, Hugh Smithson, 1st Duke of Northumberland, IV, 197, 198
Percy, Marcella (Ashe), XII, 41
Perdita. *See* Darby, Mary
Perdrigean, Françoise (Vienne), IV, 754
Péré. *See* Peire
Peré, Arnaud, I, 226, 537
Peré, Jean, I, 226, 393, 528, **536–37**, 572, 626, 627; II, 347
Père Joseph, I, 222
Perenne de Moras. *See* Morasse
Pérez Hernández, Juan Josef, IV, lv, 72, 165, 519, 567, **622–23**
Péricard, François de, II, 359
Péricard, Michelle de (Laval), II, 358, 359
Perichon, Noël-Mathurin-Étienne, IV, 353
Périer, Étienne de, III, 40, 382
Perier de Salvert, Antoine-Alexis, IV, 247, 254, 588
Périgny. *See* Ailleboust
Périgord. *See* Talleyrand-Périgord
Périn, Marie-Rose (Lombard de Combles), III, 406
Périnau, Jacques, V, 662
Périnau, Marie-Joseph. *See* Cusson
Périnau, Toussaint, V, 662
Périnault, Élisabeth. *See* Guyon Desprez
Périnault, Joseph, IV, 140; V, 241, 322, 323, **662–63**; VI, 385, 635
Périnault, Marie-Élisabeth. *See* Harel
Périnault, Marie-Josephte (Varin, *dit* La Pistole; Roy Portelance), IV, 748; VII, 762
Périnault, Pierre-Joseph, V, 663
Périnneau, *dit* Lamarche, François, IV, 272
Peritsol, R. Abram, XI, 254
Perkins, Abigail. *See* Backus
Perkins, Elizabeth. *See* Young
Perkins, Hutton, XI, 409
Perkins, Jacob, V, 663
Perkins, Jemima. *See* Leonard
Perkins, Simeon, IV, 116, 219, 222; V, 63, 116, 410, 573, 608, **663–65**; VI, 37, 77, 90, 412, 574, 682, 813; VII, 52, 587, 681; VIII, 62, 63, 82, 360; IX, 710; XI, 308
Perkins, Thomas, III, 411; IV, 158; V, 166
Perkins, Zebulon, V, 116
Perley, Miss (Peabody), VII, 683
Perley, Amos (Patriot), VII, 254
Perley, Amos (politician), VI, 755
Perley, Elizabeth. *See* Mooers
Perley, Eunice. *See* Putnam
Perley*, Sir George Halsey (1857–1938), XI, 682
Perley, Georgianna M. *See* Gale
Perley, Israel, V, 555, 627, **665–67**, 774; VI, 718; VII, 120
Perley, Jane. *See* Ketchum
Perley, John, XI, 681
Perley, Mabel E. Ticknor. *See* Stevens
Perley, Mary (Perley), IX, 628
Perley, Moses, IX, 628

Perley, Moses Henry, VI, 687; VII, 47, 243, 291, 352, 437, 443, 654, 899; VIII, 65, 66, 435, 809; IX, **628–32**, 767; X, 14, 338, 653; XI, 373; XII, 463
Perley, Susanna (mother of WILLIAM GOODHUE), XI, 681
Perley, Thomas, V, 665
Perley, William Goodhue, XI, 113, **681–83**, 826
Permangle, Marquis de. *See* Chouly
Pernette, Charlotte (Morris), VI, 519; IX, 573
Pernette, Joseph, III, 212; VI, 519
Pernette, Sophia (Barry), X, 36
Pernette, Sophia Augusta (Eagleson; Collins), IV, 258
Perny, Nicolas, IV, 124
Péroine, Marguerite (Phlem), III, 518
Perone, Giovanni, IX, 466
Peronne de Mazé, Louis, I, 468, **537**, 589
Peronne Des Touches, Michel, I, 537, 538; II, 385
Peronne Dumesnil, Jean, I, 112, 326, 401, **537–39**, 580, 606; II, 385
Perosse, Valeron, I, 88
Pérot, Gilles, I, **539**
Perras, Monsieur (of Quebec), IV, 619
Perrault. *See also* Perrot
Perrault, Monsieur (of Montreal), IV, 148
Perrault, Agathe (Nowlan), VIII, 863, 864
Perrault, Anastasie (Leclerc), XI, 506
Perrault, Charles (author), IX, 563; XII, 546
Perrault, Charles (son of JACQUES, known as Perrault *l'aîné*), IV, 624
Perrault, Charles-François, IV, 624; V, 570; VI, 85
Perrault, Charles-Norbert, X, 375; VI, 192, **576–77**, 681, 763
Perrault, Charles-Ovide, VII, 236, 757; VIII, 284, 285, 364, 667, 668, 693; IX, 540, 633, 696; X, 577, 600; XI, 821; XII, 300
Perrault, Charlotte. *See* Boucher de Boucherville
Perrault, Charlotte-Louise. *See* Desbarats
Perrault, Chrysostôme, VII, 167
Perrault, Corinne (Trudeau), XII, 1068
Perrault, Delphine-Denise (Bourgeau; Sincennes), X, 657
Perrault, Éléonore (Dufresne), XII, 275
Perrault, François, VI, 124
Perrault, François, III, 501, **509–10**; IV, 623; V, 283; VII, 687
Perrault, Françoise-Charlotte (Voyer), VII, 891
Perrault, Guillaume-Michel, IV, 623; V, 667
Perrault, Henri-Maurice, XII, 810
Perrault, Jacques (brother of FRANÇOIS), III, 509
Perrault, Jacques (father of FRANÇOIS), III, 509
Perrault, Jacques (father of PAUL), III, 510
Perrault, Jacques (son of JACQUES-NICOLAS), V, 667
Perrault, Jacques, known as Perrault *l'aîné*, III, 13, 509, 510; IV, 148, 306, 461, 462, 591, **623–24**, 692; V, 6, 368, 481, 499, 667; VI, 577; VII, 686, 687, 883
Perrault, Jacques-Nicolas, III, 13; IV, 624; V, 283, 576, **667–69**; VI, 305; VII, 686, 687; XII, 222
Perrault, Jean-Baptiste, IV, 304, 316, 623; VII, 686
Perrault, Jean-Baptiste, V, 533, 635, 741; VII, **686–87**, 736
Perrault, Joseph (father), VIII, 863
Perrault, Joseph, VIII, 863
Perrault, Joseph-Adolphe, XII, 300
Perrault, Joseph-François (clergyman), III, 510; IV, 287, 509, 574, 623; VII, 686, 687
Perrault, Joseph-François (politician), XI, 480

Perrault, Joseph-François, III, 510; IV, 496, 698; V, 225, 233, 241, 243, 386, 508, 651, 701, 880; VI, 27, 42, 49, 86, 120, 192, 241, 300, 392, 546, 576, 577, 586, 635, 658; VII, 72, 242, 255, 345, 430, 482, 503, 504, 686, **687–90**, 818, 877, 880, 892; VIII, 109, 290, 592, 594, 701, 726, 937; IX, 250, 261, 298, 300, 347; XII, 86
Perrault, Joseph-François-Xavier, VII, 689; VIII, 202
Perrault, Joseph-Julien, VIII, 318; IX, **632–33**
Perrault, Josephte. *See* Baby
Perrault*, Joseph-Xavier (1838–1905), IX, 612; XII, 57
Perrault, Julie (Juchereau Duchesnay), X, 388
Perrault, Julie (Leblond), VIII, 863
Perrault, Julien (father-in-law of Édouard-Raymond FABRE), VIII, 283
Perrault, Julien (father of JOSEPH-JULIEN), IX, 632
Perrault, Julien (father of LOUIS), IX, 633
Perrault, Julien, I, **539**
Perrault, Louis, VII, 687, 688
Perrault, Louis, VIII, 261, 283, 635; IX, 343, 458, **633**; X, 555; XI, 117; XII, 300, 1068
Perrault, Louise (Vassal de Monviel), VII, 883
Perrault, Louis-François, IV, 623
Perrault, Luce (Fabre), VIII, 283, 286; XII, 300, 301
Perrault, Marguerite. *See* Caché
Perrault, Marguerite. *See* Roy
Perrault, Marguerite-Adélaïde (Lorimier), VII, 512
Perrault, Mariane (Naud; Tessier), XII, 1032
Perrault, Marie. *See* Lemaître
Perrault, Marie-Anne. *See* Amiot
Perrault, Marie-Anne. *See* Tavernier
Perrault, Marie-Claire (Cuvillier), VII, 224
Perrault, Marie-Euphradine. *See* Lamontagne
Perrault, Marie-Joseph. *See also* Rivard, *dit* Lanouette
Perrault, Marie-Joseph (Deschenaux), V, 252
Perrault, Marie-Louise. *See* Taschereau
Perrault, Marie-Madeleine. *See* Paquin
Perrault, Marie-Reine (Cheniquy), XII, 189
Perrault, Marie-Sophie. *See* Gauvin
Perrault, Mathilde. *See* Roy
Perrault, Michel, V, 668; VI, 125; VIII, 223
Perrault, Olivier, IV, 624; V, 234, 668, 794; X, 18, 388; VI, 125, **577–78**, 581, 585, 751, 752; VII, 686, 877, 879, 880; VIII, 726
Perrault, Pacôme, II, 419
Perrault, Paul, III, **510–11**
Perrault, Pierre, V, 668; VI, 125
Perrault, Suzanne. *See* Pagé, *dit* Carcy
Perrault, Thérèse-Esther. *See* Hausman, *dit* Ménager
Perrault, Ursule. *See* Macarty
Perrault, Zéphirin, XI, 272
Perrault de Linière, Wilhelmine-Dudding. *See* Montenach
Perrault *l'aîné*. *See* Perrault, Jacques; Perrault, Jacques-Nicolas
Perré, Henri, XI, **683–84**
Perreault, Catherine (Dionne), VIII, 222, 223; IX, 362
Perreault, Hyacinthe, I, **539–40**; II, 222
Perrée, John, VIII, 257
Perrey, Sylvain-Éphrem, VIII, 529; XI, **684–85**; XII, 637, 837
Perrier, Sir Anthony, IX, 196
Perrier, Philippe, I, 43
Perrigo, James, VII, 514
Perrin, Antoine, II, **516**

Perrin, Catherine. *See* Boissières
Perrin, Jacques, II, 516
Perrin, Marie-Anne. *See* Chotard
Perrin, Nicolas, VII, 60
Perrinault. *See* Périnault
Perron, Pélagie-Victoire (Rieutord), V, 713
Perrot. *See also* Perrault
Perrot, Anne (Jacquin), III, 304
Perrot, Bertrand, II, 43
Perrot, Catherine (Jeanneau), III, 313
Perrot, François, II, 517
Perrot, François-Marie, I, 66, 84, 102, 105, 117, 136, 175, 204, 287, 288, 295, 409, 410, 418, 436, 464, 465, 508, **540–42**, 576, 581, 584, 600, 631; II, 6, 56, 112, 182, 184, 193, 194, 410, 412, 514, 522, 532, 616; IV, xviii
Perrot, John, I, 81
Perrot, Sir John, I, 228
Perrot, Joseph, II, 43
Perrot, Madeleine. *See* Laguide Meynier
Perrot, Madeleine. *See* Raclot
Perrot, Marie. *See* Sivot
Perrot, Marie (Jarret de Verchères), II, 295; III, 308, 311
Perrot, Nicolas, I, 40, 132, 174, 248, 249, 308, 547, 548, 625, 640; II, 129, 263, 380, 422, 423, 427, 453, 484, 488, 500, 504, **516–20**; III, 493
Perrot, *dit* Joly-Cœur, Nicolas, II, 517
Perrot, *dit* Vildaigre, Jacques, II, 518
Perrot, *dit* Vildaigre, Michelle. *See* Le Flot
Perrot de Fercourt, Monsieur (brother of François-Marie PERROT), I, 541
Perrot de Rizy, Anne. *See* Jourdain
Perrot de Rizy, Marie. *See* Willis
Perrot de Rizy, Pierre, II, 520; III, 631
Perry, Anthony, VIII, 694
Perry, Charles, IV, 149
Perry, Elizabeth (Mascarene), III, 435
Perry, George Hugo, IX, 288; XI, **685–86**
Perry, James, VIII, 476
Perry, Jemima Gary. *See* Washburn
Perry, Jersua (Jerusha) (Dumaresq), VII, 257
Perry, Margaret. *See* Carroll
Perry, Mary Polly. *See* Ham
Perry, Matthew Calbraith, XII, 612
Perry, Oliver Hazard, V, 875; VII, 46
Perry, Peter, VI, 467; VII, 158, 379, 497; VIII, 8, 48, 54, 55, 253, **694–99**, 946; IX, 618, 680, 685; X, 60, 62, 94, 343, 624; XI, 407, 517, 518
Perry, Robert, VIII, 694
Perry, Stanislaus Francis, XII, 40, 452, **836–38**
Persico, Ignazio, XI, 104
Perth, Earl of. *See* Drummond
Perthuis, Anne. *See* Minet
Perthuis, Charles, II, 520
Perthuis, Charles, II, **520–21**, 526; III, 511, 558; IV, 624
Perthuis, Charles-Régis, IV, 625
Perthuis, Jean-Baptiste-Ignace, III, 291, **511–12**; IV, 602, 625
Perthuis, Joseph, IV, 625
Perthuis, Joseph, II, 520; III, 140, 478, 491; IV, **624–25**
Perthuis, Marie (Rouer de Villeray), I, 579
Perthuis, Marie-Anne. *See* Chasle
Perthuis, Marie-Joseph (Riverin), III, 588
Perthuis, Marie-Josephte-Madeleine. *See* Hiché

Perthuis, Marie-Madeleine. *See* Roberge
Pérusse Des Cars, Marquis de, IV, 56, 457
Pesant, Le. *See* Le Pesant
Peschart, Mme, Baronne de Bossac. *See* Dollier de Casson
Peschart, Gabriel, Baron de Bossac, II, 191
Pesequan (Joseph Fiddler), XII, 832
Peshe. *See* Péché
Pestalozzi, Johann Heinrich, IX, 271; X, 497; XII, 524, 527
Pestel, Ekaterina von (Billings), V, 79
Pétau, Denis, I, 203
Petch, Robert, VIII, 281
Peter. *See also* Kingminguse
Peter (schoolmaster), V, 255
Peter, John (Peter Clensmith), VIII, 477
Peterborough, Earl of. *See* Mordaunt
Peters, Abigail. *See* Thompson
Peters, Alexander Nevers, XII, 560, 561
Peters, Alfred Edward, XI, 727
Peters*, Arthur (1854–1908), XII, 841
Peters, Benjamin Lester, VII, 691; VIII, 700
Peters, Benjamin Lester, VII, 691; VIII, **699–700**
Peters, Charles (actor), IX, 597
Peters, Charles (brother of BENJAMIN LESTER and CHARLES JEFFERY), VII, 691
Peters, Charles Jeffery, V, 456; VI, 138, 139, 246, 740; VII, 74, 274, 658, **690–93**; VIII, 699, 803, 841; IX, 147, 399, 430, 620; XI, 446
Peters, Eliza. *See* Nickinson
Peters, Elizabeth. *See* Baker
Peters, Frederick, XII, 513, 841
Peters, George P., VII, 274
Peters, George R., VII, 203
Peters, Hannah. *See* Chenery
Peters, Hannah. *See* Owen
Peters, Hannah (Jarvis), V, 452, 453; VI, 578, 579; VII, 362, 378, **693–94**; VIII, 430
Peters, Harry, VII, 691; VIII, 699
Peters, Hendrick. *See* Theyanoguin
Peters, James (great-uncle), VI, 811; VII, 690, 691; VIII, 699
Peters, James, VII, 691
Peters, James Horsfield, VII, 202, 691; VIII, 563; IX, 179, 400; XI, 664, 665, 668; XII, 415, **838–42**
Peters, John, IV, 393
Peters, Joseph, X, 590
Peters, Joseph, IV, **625–26**, 705; V, 318, 833
Peters*, Mabel (d. 1914), XII, 561
Peters, Margaret. *See* Lester
Peters, Marian Ellen (Jack), XI, 446
Peters, Marianne Elizabeth. *See* Forbes
Peters, Martha Hamm. *See* Lewis
Peters, Mary. *See* Birdseye
Peters, Mary. *See* Cunard
Peters, Mary (Cunard), VII, 691; IX, 170; XII, 838
Peters, Mary Ann. *See* Sharmen
Peters, Mary Ann. *See* Winnett
Peters, Mercy (Buell), VI, 90
Peters, Pauly. *See* Sahonwagy
Peters, Polly Marvin. *See* Jarvis
Peters, Sally (wife of THOMAS), IV, 626
Peters, Samuel Andrew, IV, 625, 626; V, 344, 832; VI, 523, 578, 579; VII, 693
Peters, Samuel Jarvis, VI, 579

Peters, Sarah (Wetmore), VI, 810, 811; VII, 691
Peters, Susan Ann (Tilley), XII, 1051
Peters, Thomas, IV, 604, **626–28**; V, 341, 469; VI, 89, 129, 313, 799
Peters, Thomas Horsfield, VII, 691; XII, 838
Peters, Thomas W., XII, 1051
Peters, Valentine H., VIII, 699
Peters, William (cousin of BENJAMIN LESTER and CHARLES JEFFREY), VII, 691
Peters, William (father of JOSEPH), IV, 625
Peters, William Birdseye, VI, **578–80**; VII, 694; VIII, 69
Peters, William Tyng, VII, 691; VIII, 699
Petersen, Johan Carl Christian, VIII, 448, 449
Petersen, Paulus. *See* Sahonwagy
Peterson, Hannah Ann. *See* Hendrickson
Peterson, Harriet Middleton. *See* Clayton
Peterson, Heinrich Wilhelm, VII, 778; VIII, 265, 271, 316, **700–1**
Peterson, Henry, XII, 797
Peterson, Johann Dietrich, VII, 351; VIII, 700
Peterson, Julianna Sophia Amelia. *See* Borck
Pethick, Eliza (Pope), XI, 704
Petit. *See also* Pettit
Petit, Sieur (ship's captain), II, 630
Petit, Adrien, II, 521
Petit, Anne (Piot de Langloiserie), II, 526
Petit, Catherine. *See* Du Bellineau
Petit, Catherine. *See* Dufloc
Petit, Charlotte. *See* Dugué de Boisbriand
Petit, Claude, IX, 344
Petit, Eliza (Bayfield), XI, 54
Petit, Émilion, IV, 67
Petit, François, II, 522
Petit, Gédéon, III, 65
Petit, Jean, I, 295; II, **521**, 527; III, 352
Petit, Jeanne. *See* Gobin
Petit, Louis, I, 544, 649; II, 183, 184, 477, **521–22**, 638
Petit, Louise (Corbin), IV, 167
Petit, Marguerite. *See* Véron de Grandmesnil
Petit, Monique-Françoise (Gohin de Montreuil), IV, 307
Petit, Pierre, II, 521
Petit, Pierre, II, **522–23**; III, 67, 540; IV, 167
Petit, Suzanne. *See also* Dupuy
Petit, Suzanne (Caën), I, 161
Petit Boismorel, Jean, II, 521
Petit Boismorel, Marie-Anne (Plessy, *dit* Bélair), III, 523; VI, 586
Petit Chef, Le. *See* Wikaskokiseyin
Petitchouan. *See* Chomina
Petit-Clair, Cécile. *See* Moisan
Petit-Clair, Pierre, VIII, 701
Petitclair, Pierre, VII, 776; VIII, 420, **701–2**; IX, 113, 298
Petit-Claire, Claude-Joseph, V, 437
Petit-Claire, Marie-Louise. *See* Dalciat
Petit de L'Estang, Marie (Troyes), I, 653
Petit de Levilliers, Charles, II, 523
Petit de Levilliers, Charles, II, **523–24**; III, 491
Petit de Levilliers, Élisabeth. *See* Berruyer
Petit de Levilliers, Étiennette-Louise. *See* Malbeque
Petit de Levilliers, Madeleine. *See* Gaultier Du Tremblay
Petit de Levilliers, Marie-Charlotte (Noyelles de Fleurimont), III, 491, 492
Petit de Levilliers, Robert, II, 523

Petit de Levilliers de Coulanges, Françoise. *See* Golard
Petit de Levilliers de Coulanges, Pierre-Louis, II, 523
Petit de Thoizy, Marie-Anne (Druillon de Macé), IV, 226
Petit de Verneuil, Jacques, II, 521
Petit de Verneuil, Marie. *See* Viel
Petit-Étienne, Véronique (Vincent), VII, 889
Petitot, *dit* Saint-Sceine (Sincennes), Marguerite (Doucet), IV, 222; V, 261
Petitpas, Barthélemy, III, 34, **512–13**
Petitpas, Catherine. *See* Bugaret
Petitpas, Claude, II, **524**; III, 512
Petitpas, Françoise. *See* Lavergne
Petitpas, Henriette (Robichaux), IV, 676
Petitpas, Jacques, II, 6, 605
Petitpas, Louis, III, 418
Petitpas, Madeleine. *See* Coste
Petitpas, Marguerite (Sevestre), I, 606
Petitpas, Marie-Thérèse (wife of CLAUDE), II, 524; III, 512
Petitpas de Lafleur, Claude, II, 524
Petit Pigeon. *See* Guiboche, Louis
Petit Pin. *See* Minahikosis
Petiver, James, I, 677
Petley, Robert, VII, 270; IX, 850
Peto, Sir Samuel Morton, X, 351, 591; XI, 413
Petrequin. *See* Pettrequin
Petrie, Margaret (Simpson), XI, 824
Petrie, Mary (Reid), IX, 656
Pétrimoulx, Catherine. *See* Faribault
Pétrimoulx, François, VII, 446
Petrimoulx, Médard, IV, 653
Petrimoulx, Michel, III, 420, 429
Pétrimoulx, Zoé (Rollin), VIII, 762
Petry, William, VII, 923
Pett, Phineas, I, 144, 362
Petters. *See* Peters
Pettigrew, Harriet. *See* Heavysege
Pettis, Drusilla (Cotton), VII, 211
Pettit, Deborah, VI, 628
Pettit, Elizabeth. *See* Heath
Pettit, Margaret. *See* McFarland
Pettit, Nathaniel, V, 669
Pettit, Nathaniel, V, 639, 660, 661, **669–70**, 841
Pettit, Rachel (Lawrason), XI, 501
Pettrequin, Jean, III, **513**; IV, 780; V, 250
Petty, Frances (Rolph), IX, 683
Petty, William, 2nd Earl of Shelburne, III, 296, 478; IV, xxxv, xl, xlii, 183, 298, 336, 399, 430, 571, 577, 603, 686, 753, 788, 792; V, 142, 143, 144, 148, 149, 155, 156, 158, 162, 606, 607, 610, 897, 898; VI, 310
Petty-Fitzmaurice, Henry, 3rd Marquess of Lansdowne, VII, 23, 631
Petty-Fitzmaurice*, Henry Charles Keith, 5th Marquess of Lansdowne (1845–1927), XI, 444, 509, 646; XII, 337, 576, 610, 611, 666, 703, 723, 733, 735, 803, 811, 899, 1023
Peugnet, Monsieur (newspaper owner), VIII, 735
Peuvret, Jacques, I, 542
Peuvret, Marie. *See* La Garenne
Peuvret de Gaudarville, Alexandre, I, 326, 543; II, 42, 215, 485, **524–25**
Peuvret de Gaudarville, Alexandre-Joseph, II, 525
Peuvret de Gaudarville, Geneviève. *See* Bouteville

Peuvret de Gaudarville, Marie-Anne. *See* Gaultier de Comporté
Peuvret de Gaudarville, Marie-Anne, II, 525
Peuvret Demesnu, Catherine. *See* Nau de La Boissière et de Fossambault
Peuvret Demesnu, François, I, 542
Peuvret Demesnu, Jean-Baptiste, I, **542–43**, 587; II, xvii, xix, 307, 524, 582
Peuvret Demesnu, Marie-Catherine (Juchereau Duchesnay), I, 543; II, 307; III, 318
Peuvret Demesnu, Marie-Rogère. *See* Lepage
Peyrant, Antoine, II, 465
Peyrant, Marie-Anne (Martin de Lino), II, 465
Peyrot, Élisabeth (Guitet), V, 393
Peyton, Ann. *See* Galton
Peyton, John, V, 243, 244; VI, 176, 392, 393, 580, 581, 706, 707, 708; VII, 115, 377; IX, 159, 418
Peyton, John, IV, 714; V, 243; VI, 70, 71, 175, **580–81**; VIII, 924
Pezard de Champlain, Louise (Vallières de Saint-Réal), VII, 876, 880
Pezard de Champlain, Pierre-Melchior, VII, 876
Pézard de La Tousche, Claude, I, 543
Pézard de La Tousche, Étienne, II, 186, 528
Pézard de La Tousche, Madeleine (Desjordy de Cabanac), II, 185
Pézard de La Tousche, Marie. *See* Masson
Pézard de La Tousche Champlain, Étienne, I, **543**; II, 168, 185
Pézard de La Tousche Champlain, Madeleine. *See* Mullois de La Borde
Pfeiffer (Payfer), Scholastique (Masson), X, 500
Pfeiffer (Payfer), Suzanne (Masson), VII, 592
Pfozer, Johann Georg. *See* Pozer, George
Phares, Mary Mourning (King), XII, 491
Phébus. *See* Gaston III
Phelan, Catharine. *See* Brennan
Phelan, James Julien Theodore, VIII, 260, 261, 493; X, 219
Phelan, Joseph, VIII, 702
Phelan, Patrick, V, 122, 632
Phelan, Patrick, VII, 625; VIII, 318, 319, **702–4**; IX, 48, 207; X, 107, 361, 463; XI, 96; XII, 189, 614
Phelan, Rebecca. *See* Nesbitt
Phelan, William (Nova Scotia clergyman), IV, 470; V, 458, 459; VI, 292, 293, 393; VII, 801
Phelan, William (P.E.I. clergyman), IX, 832
Phélipeaux d'Herbault, Georges-Louis, IV, 55
Phélippeaux, Catherine. *See* Boutet
Phélippeaux (Philipeaux, Philippeau), Charles, I, 201; II, 612
Phélippeaux, Louise (Maillou, *dit* Desmoulins), III, 420
Phelps, Benajah, IV, 490; V, 199; VI, 293
Phelps, Davenport, V, 808, 809; VIII, 887
Phelps, David, V, 412
Phelps, Elijah, V, 781; VI, 629, 630, 631
Phelps, Eliza Ann (Massey), XII, 700
Phelps, Lois (Viets), V, 832
Phelps, Noah, XII, 783
Phelps, Oliver (canal builder), XII, 783
Phelps, Oliver (land speculator), V, 781
Phelps, Richard, VI, 761, 762
Phélypeaux, Éléonore-Christine, Comtesse de Pontchartrain et de Maurepas. *See* La Rochefoucauld-Roye

Phélypeaux, Françoise (Senat; Gaschet), III, 237
Phélypeaux, Jean-Frédéric, Comte de Maurepas, II, 53, 66, 210, 225, 226, 239, 269, 284, 302, 374, 390, 457, 520, 530, 571, 573, 650; III, 13, 16, 17, 27, 29, 38, 40, 41, 42, 44, 45, 48, 49, 55, 61, 74, 75, 76, 78, 79, 80, 93, 107, 110, 117, 118, 119, 120, 135, 145, 153, 154, 175, 178, 179, 180, 182, 200, 203, 223, 224, 226, 228, 234, 239, 240, 246, 249, 250, 251, 252, 253, 255, 256, 259, 263, 264, 270, 284, 291, 292, 312, 319, 334, 339, 340, 343, 344, 353, 354, 361, 368, 382, 383, 389, 390, 398, 399, 416, 433, 434, 445, 455, 456, 492, 532, 539, 541, 545, 550, 558, 566, 575, 592, 593, 604, 627, 630, 631, 637, 644, 645, 646, 647, 675; IV, 56, 60, 62, 63, 76, 123, 167, 239, 284, 318, 339, 355, 358, 359, 361, 363, 364, 376, 435, 440, 465, 466, 467, 473, 539, 590, 611, 612, 624, 636, 663, 665, 666, 667, 749, 750
Phélypeaux, Jérôme, Comte de Pontchartrain et de Maure- pas, II, 7, 39, 64, 68, 114, 115, 116, 121, 132, 134, 147, 230, 238, 270, 299, 301, 302, 304, 326, 349, 353, 354, 355, 384, 388, 422, 428, 453, 456, 457, 465, 466, 482, 495, 511, 531, 532, 543, 546, 547, 550, 551, 552, 554, 556, 557, 558, 559, 567, 568, 569, 570, 587, 589, 632, 672; III, 51, 53, 58, 59, 60, 61, 83, 96, 177, 200, 233, 368, 372, 380, 381, 429, 474, 498, 552, 557, 681; IV, xxi, 661
Phélypeaux, Louis, Comte de Pontchartrain, I, 138, 510, 534; II, 57, 73, 74, 79, 93, 167, 184, 197, 280, 305, 353, 421, 442, 443, 449, 483, 532, 549, 555, 575, 586; III, 41, 42
Phélypeaux, Louis, Comte de Saint-Florentin et Marquis de La Vrillière, II, 426
Phélypeaux, Marie-Suzanne. *See* Talon
Phélypeaux de Pontchartrain, Anne. *See* Beauharnois
Phélypeaux de Pontchartrain, Anne (Buade, Comtesse de Frontenac et de Palluau), I, 133
Phélypeaux de Pontchartrain, Paul, III, 51
Phélypeaux de Villesavin, Isabelle. *See* Blondeau
Phélypeaux de Villesavin, Jean, I, 484
Philibert. *See* Jacquin; Manisson
Philip II, King of Spain, I, 187, 316
Philip III, King of Spain, I, 676
Philip V, King of Spain, II, 98, 104, 115, 397; III, 609
Philipeaux. *See* Phélippeaux
Philipot, Michel, I, 167
Philippe VI, King of France, III, 554
Philippe, Marie (Legras, Fézeret), II, 221
Philippeau. *See* Phélippeaux
Philippe (Philippes) de Hautmesnil de Mandeville, Antoine, II, 525
Philippe de Hautmesnil de Mandeville, François, II, 306, **525–26**
Philippe (Philippes) de Hautmesnil de Mandeville, Madeleine. *See* Le Maire
Philippe de Hautmesnil (Hautmesnyl) de Marigny, Jean- Vincent, I, 508; II, 17, 105, 133, 525
Philippe de Hautmesnil (Hautmesnyl) de Marigny, Marie-Catherine. *See* Lambert de Baussy
Philippe de Hautmesnil de Marigny, Marie-Gabrielle (Amiot de Vincelotte), II, 17
Philippe de Saint-Lambert, Gabriel, II, 525
Philippe Égalité. *See* Orléans, Louis-Philippe-Joseph d'
Philippine-Gertrude de Sainte-Dominique. *See* Boullongne
Philippon, Claire. *See* Taschereau

Philippon, Joseph-Antoine, VI, **581**; XII, 1016
Philippon, Marie-Louise. *See* Faucher
Philippon, *dit* Picard, Yves, VI, 581
Philipps, Ann. *See* Dyson
Philipps, Anna Maria (Languedoc), VII, 484
Philipps, Catherina. *See* Stratham
Philipps, Charles, XII, 349
Philipps, Elizabeth. *See* Cosby
Philipps, Erasmus, III, 514
Philipps, Erasmus James, III, 276, 298, 453, **514–15**, 665
Philipps, Frances. *See* Noel
Philipps, John, V, 670
Philipps, John, IV, 776; V, **670**
Philipps, Judith. *See* Wood
Philipps, Richard, III, 515
Philipps, Richard, II, 22, 23, 24, 93, 96, 97, 152, 198, 199, 250, 274, 590, 591, 601, 652, 663, 664, 668, 670; III, 9, 83, 135, 136, 143, 208, 276, 277, 287, 326, 342, 363, 426, 427, 436, 437, 439, 514, **515–18**, 597; IV, xxii, xxv, 83, 170, 539, 774
Philips, Catharina. *See* Glöckner
Philips, Elizabeth (Lyon), VIII, 509
Philips, Henricus Philippus, VII, 694
Philips, Henry Joseph, VII, **694–95**
Philips, James, VII, **695–96**
Philips, John B., VII, 694
Philips, Louisa Carolina. *See* Schmidt
Philips, Nathaniel, VI, 709; VII, 507
Philips, Philip, VII, 695
Philips, Salome. *See* Brown
Philips, Susanna (Wilkes), XI, 923
Philipse, Margaret. *See* Marston
Philipse, Philip, IV, 586
Philipse, Susanna (Robinson), VI, 654
Phillipps, John, V, 670
Phillips, Alfred Moore, XII, **842–43**
Phillips, Anner (Holton), X, 354
Phillips, Benjamin Jonas, VIII, 365
Phillips, Bridget. *See* Hutchinson
Phillips, Charles, V, 377
Phillips, Elizabeth (Barker), XI, 48
Phillips, Elizabeth (Everill; Alden), II, 15
Phillips, Flora (Langford), XII, 522
Phillips, Frederick, XII, 413
Phillips, Harriet. *See* Jacobs
Phillips, Jane (Scott), V, 745, 746
Phillips, Jehiel, VII, 510
Phillips, John (geologist), X, 445
Phillips, John (mason), VI, 191
Phillips, John (surgeon), III, 212, 405
Phillips, John Arthur, XII, 248
Phillips, John Smith, XII, 842
Phillips, Margaret Jane. *See* Coyne
Phillips, Nettie (Walt), XII, 843
Phillips, Mary (wife of William, major), I, 337
Phillips, Mary (Finlay), V, 314, 318, 745
Phillips, Nettie (Walt), XII, 843
Phillips, Phoebe (Gillam), I, 337, 338, 601; II, 247
Phillips, Sir Richard. *See* Galt, John
Phillips, Samuel (father-in-law of Hugh FINLAY), V, 333
Phillips, Samuel (office holder), VI, 84, 400
Phillips, Sarah. *See* Bacon
Phillips, Susan. *See* Hunt

Phillips, Thomas (artist), VI, 553

Phillips, Thomas (clergyman), VI, 266; X, 34, 35

Phillips, Thomas (contractor), VI, 220, 812; VII, 130; VIII, 552; IX, 654

Phillips, Thomas (nephew of Thomas LLOYD), II, 439

Phillips, Wendell, XII, 925, 927

Phillips, William (colonel), IV, 442; VI, 788

Phillips, William (major), I, 337, 601; II, 15

Phillips, William (nephew of Thomas SCOTT, d. 1810), V, 746

Phillips, William (office holder), VI, 84

Phillips, William (partner of John Christopher REIFFEN- STEIN), VII, 743

Phillips, William (partner of Joseph-Rémi VALLIÈRES de Saint-Real), VII, 877

Phillips, Ziba, VII, 510

Philliskirk, Harrison, XII, 995

Phillpotts, George, VII, 314, 315; IX, 138

Phillpotts, Henry, IX, 138, 143, 676

Philpin de Rivières, Jean-Baptiste-Elizé, VI, 146

Phipps, Catherine Anne (Prevost), V, 693

Phipps, Constantine Henry, 2nd Earl of Mulgrave and 1st Marquess of Normanby, VII, 144, 405; VIII, xxvii; IX, 5; X, 601; XI, 686, 945

Phipps, Constantine John, 2nd Baron Mulgrave, V, 54, 55

Phipps, George Augustus Constantine, 3rd Earl of Mul- grave and 2nd Marquess of Normanby, XI, 278, 555, **686–87**, 947, 948; XII, 14, 436

Phipps, Jemima. See Sawtelle

Phipps, Laura. See Russell

Phipps, Maria. See Liddell

Phipps, Mary, V, 740, 741

Phipps, Submit (Willard), V, 740, 741

Phipps, Thomas, I, 543

Phipps, Thomas, I, 39, **543–44**; II, 265

Phipps, William, V, 740

Phips, James, I, 544

Phips, Mary. See Spencer

Phips, Mary (mother of Sir WILLIAM), I, 544

Phips, Spencer, III, 128, 508

Phips, Sir William, I, 26, 76, 90, 139, 146, 250, 260, 397, 402, 426, 436, 466, 542, **544–46**, 576, 577, 586, 649; II, 6, 14, 19, 36, 46, 80, 94, 109, 120, 137, 159, 160, 168, 172, 177, 183, 184, 185, 186, 222, 227, 229, 244, 257, 268, 283, 284, 326, 338, 352, 383, 401, 404, 410, 441, 452, 482, 483, 494, 522, 532, 591, 593, 601, 605, 638, 660, 662; III, 109, 155, 245, 586, 596, 669; IV, xix

Phlem, Guillaume, III, 518

Phlem, Marguerite. See Péroine

Phlem, dit Yvon, Marie. See Levreau

Phlem, dit Yvon, Yves, III, **518–20**

Phokus Valerianos (Valerianatos). See Fuca, Juan de

Phyn, George, VI, 639

Phyn, James, IV, 261; V, 282, 299, 646; VI, 639; VII, 309

Phyn, Jean (Forsyth), V, 325; VII, 309

Pian, Jean-Marie, XI, 244

Pianovi. See Pienovi

Piapot. See Payipwat

Piat, Irénée, I, **546–47**

Pica, Henry. See Kribs, Louis P.

Picard. See also Philippon

Picard, Françoise. See Maufils

Picard, Jacques, XI, 912

Picard, Louis-Alexandre, III, 620; IV, 205, 206, 548, **628–30**; V, 37, 329, 436

Picard, Louise, VI, 534

Picard, Marguerite (Gaudé), III, 238

Picard, Marie (Ducharme), IV, 233

Picard, Marie-Jèanne. See Léger

Picard, Marie-Madeleine (Serré), V, 174

Picard, Pierre (clergyman), VI, 286, 287

Picard, Pierre (son of LOUIS-ALEXANDRE), IV, 629

Picard, Pierre-François, IV, 628

Picard, dit Destroismaisons, Zoé-Henriette (Crevier), XI, 217

Picard Destroismaisons, Marie-Geneviève (Chartier), VIII, 140

Picard Destroismaisons, Philippe, IX, 633

Picard Destroismaisons, Rosalie. See Fournier

Picard Destroismaisons, Thomas-Ferruce, VII, 901; VIII, 720; IX, **633–34**

Picart, dit Beauchemin, Antoine, XI, 58

Picart, dit Beauchemin, Marguerite. See Fontaine

Picault, Pierre-Étienne, VIII, 918

Piccolomini, Monsignor, II, 362, 363

Pichard, Amable, V, 458, **670–71**; VI, 106, 448

Piché, Aristide, XII, 559

Piché, Basile, VIII, 242

Piché, Pierre, VIII, 242

Pichery, Anne de, I, 265

Pichon. See also Pichot

Pichon, Jean, IV, 630

Pichon, Marie. See Esnault

Pichon, Marie (Gauthier de La Chenaye; Sevestre), I, 583, 606

Pichon, Thomas, III, 73, 166, 498, 589; IV, 249, 250, 443, **630–32**, 645, 656, 657, 661

Pichon, dit Larose, Monsieur (fur trader), II, 645

Pichot de Querdisien Trémais, Charles-François, IV, 68, 517, 616, **632–33**

Pickard, Charles Frederick Allison, VII, 854

Pickard, David, XI, 688

Pickard, Edward Dwight, VII, 854

Pickard, Eleanor (Longmuir; Withall), XII, 1117

Pickard, Hannah Maynard. See Thompson

Pickard, Hephziba. See Burpee

Pickard, Humphrey, VII, 853, 854; VIII, 15, 216; XI, **687–88**; XII, 9, 16, 298

Pickard, John, X, 288; XI, **688–89**, 830; XII, 26

Pickard, Mary. See Burpee

Pickard, Mary. See Yerxa

Pickard, Mary Rowe. See Carr

Pickard, Thomas, XI, 687

Pickell, Elizabeth (MacDonell), IX, 486

Pickell, John, IX, 486

Pickering, John, XII, 401

Pickersgill, Richard, IV, 165

Pickett, Mary (Isaacs; Viets), V, 832

Pickmore, Francis, V, **671–72**; VI, 373, 692; VII, 152, 220, 301; VIII, 264

Pickton, Ellen Free (Osler), XII, 807, 808

Picot, Jeanne de (Brethous), IV, 245

Picoté. See Tremblay

Picoté de Belestre, François, I, 547; II, 411, 626

Picoté de Belestre, Françoise (Maleray de Noiré de La Mollerie), II, 450, 451

Picoté de Belestre, Françoise-Marie-Anne (Dagneau Douville de Quindre), III, 158
Picoté de Belestre, François-Louis, IV, 634
Picoté de Belestre, François-Marie, IV, 633
Picoté de Belestre, François-Marie, III, 527, 611; IV, xliii, 346, 347, 442, 546, **633–36**, 680; V, 96, 98, 143, 232, 487, 802; VI, 132; VIII, 313
Picoté de Belestre, Hélène (La Frenaye de Brucy; Céloron de Blainville), I, 410, 547; II, 125, 336; III, 99
Picoté de Belestre, Jeanne-Geneviève, I, 547; II, 390, 391, 447, 450
Picoté de Belestre, Marie. See Pars
Picoté de Belestre, Marie-Anne. See Magnan, dit L'Espérance
Picoté de Belestre, Marie-Anne. See Nivard Saint-Dizier
Picoté de Bélestre, Marie-Anne (MacDonell), IX, 485
Picoté de Belestre, Marie-Anne (Tonty), I, 547; II, 631; III, 627
Picoté de Belestre, Marie-Catherine. See Trottier Desruisseaux
Picoté de Belestre, Perrinne (Godefroy de Lintot), I, 547; II, 252
Picoté de Belestre, Pierre, I, 266, 271, 273, 410, 508, **547**; II, 631
Picotte, Archange. See Déjarlais
Picotte, Hélène. See Jarlais
Picotte, Jean-Baptiste, VI, 581
Picotte, Louis, VI, **581–82**; VII, 119
Picq, Marie (Charpentier; Carrerot), II, 119; III, 97, 98, 173
Picq, Thomas, II, 119
Picques, Bernard, II, 360
Picquet, André, IV, 636
Picquet, François, III, xxxvii, xxxviii, 28, 30, 47, 181, 256, 268, 269, 408, 494; IV, 36, 431, 506, 507, 521, 587, **636–38**
Picquet, Marie-Philippe. See Berthet
Picquet de La Motte, Toussaint-Guillaume, Comte Picquet de La Motte, known as La Motte-Picquet, IV, 282
Picton, Sir Thomas, IX, 25, 37
Piddington, Thomas Angelo, XII, 1118
Pidgeon, George, VII, 288; IX, 841
Pidgeon, Thomas C., XII, 893
Pidianske (Pidiwamiska) (Marie-Mathilde) (Abbadie de Saint-Castin, Baronne de Saint-Castin), II, 3, 5; III, 3
Pidou de Saint-Olon, Louis-Marie, III, 640
Pieahpot. See Payipwat
Pied de Corbeau. See Isapo-muxika
Piedmont. See Raimbault
Piel (Pierre), IX, 433
Pienovi, Angelo, XI, 92; VII, **696–97**
Pier. See Saint-Aubin
Pierce. See also Peirce
Pierce, Benjamin Kendrick, VII, 582
Pierce, Editha Eliza (Bronson), XI, 112
Pierce, Elizabeth (Welch), V, 845
Pierce, Franklin, IX, 385
Pierce, Jason C., VII, 160; X, 519
Pierce, John, XI, 39
Pierce, John A., X, 710
Pierce, Josette. See La Framboise
Pierce, Margaret (Green), IV, 312; V, 389
Pierce, Moses, VIII, 494
Piercotte. See Audet

Pierdeney, VII, 243
Pierdeney, Joseph, VII, 243
Pierdon, Mr (engraver), XII, 67
Piernas, Pedro Josef, IV, 316
Pierpoint, Richard, VI, 262; VII, **697–98**
Pierre. See also Basquet, Pierre; Gawèhe
Pierre (Iroquois), IV, 375
Pierre (servant), II, 639
Pierre, III, xxxiv, 205, 450, **520**
Pierre, Toma. See Tomah, Pierre, known as Governor Tomah
Pierre-Antoine. See Pastedechouan
Pierre-Benoit. See Benoit
Pierre-Jean, dit La Tête Blanche. See Gray Lock
Pierriche. See Falcon, Pierre
Pierron, Jean, I, 108, 315, **547**, 635; II, 61, 140
Piers, Elizabeth. See Thomas
Piers, Harry, V, 635; VII, 342, 694, 876; XI, 463; XII, 17, 368
Piers, Henry, X, 77
Piers, Lewis Edward, VIII, 704; X, 176
Piers, Mercy. See Foster
Piers, Temple Foster, VI, 319; VIII, **704–6**; X, 176
Piers, Temple Stanyan, VI, 319; VIII, 704
Piers, William Bevil Thomas, VIII, 705
Pierson, Charles, VIII, 82
Pierson, Philippe, I, 321
Piersons, Nicholas, V, 871
Pieskaret, I, 71, 370, 403, **547–48**
Piet. See Picq
Piette, Henriette (Brisebois), XI, 111
Pigarouich, I, 6, **548–49**, 640
Pigeon. See also Mīmīy
Pigeon, A.-P., XII, 100
Pigeon, Barthelemy, VII, 698
Pigeon, Félix, X, 613
Pigeon, François-Xavier, VI, 126; VII, 488, **698–700**, 728; IX, 698
Pigeon, Marie. See Delorme
Pigeon, Marie-Anne (Renaud), X, 613
Pigeon, Véronique-Aimée. See Trudelle
Pigewis. See Peguis
Pigeyre, Marie (Soulerin), X, 662
Piggott, Letitia (McKinnon), V, 544
Pigot, Hugh, IV, 223
Pigott-Carleton, Henrietta Anne. See Carleton
Pigwys. See Peguis
Pihew-kamihkosit (Red Pheasant), XI, 695, 696
Pijart, Claude, I, 549
Pijart, Claude, I, 231, 459, **549**, 566, 645; II, 234
Pijart, Geneviève. See Charon
Pijart, Gilette (Boulduc), II, 88
Pijart, Pierre, I, 125, 203, 328, 459, **549–50**
Pike. See Kinongé
Pike, Warburton Mayer, X, 38
Pike, Zebulon Montgomery, V, 9, 836; VI, 72
Pilate, II, 646
Piles, Roger de, I, 313
Pilgrim, Robert, III, 123, 214, **520–21**, 561, 562, 661, 662; IV, 33, 381, 383
Pilkington, Grace (mother of ROBERT), VI, 582
Pilkington, Hannah. See Tylee
Pilkington, Robert, VI, 582

Pilkington, Robert, VI, **582–83**; VIII, 10, 483
Pillard, Anne. *See* Parisette
Pillard, Louis, III, 521; IV, 331
Pillard, Louis, III, 67, **521**
Pillard, Marguerite. *See* Beaudry
Pillard, Marie-Angélique. *See* Dubuc
Pillard, Pierre, III, 521
Pillet, Antoine, IV, 59
Pillet, Charles, I, 211
Pillet, Félicité (Besnard, *dit* Carignant), IV, 58
Pillet, François-Benjamin, VI, 666
Pillet, Henriette (Trottier Des Rivières Beaubien), VII, 247
Pillet, Ignace, IV, 58
Pillet, Pascal, IV, 58, 592
Pilling, James Constantine, XII, 285
Pillon, Boyer, IV, 229; V, 893
Pillon, Helen. *See* Keith
Pilon, Jean, II, 166
Pilon, Venant, IX, 64, 65
Pilote. *See also* Crusson
Pilote, Ambroise, XI, 689
Pilote, François, XI, 396, 397, 496, **689–91**; XII, 1019
Pilote, Marguerite. *See* Coulombe
Pilotte, Angelique, V, **672–74**; VI, 115, 770, 771; VIII, 708
Pim, Bedford Clapperton Trevelyan, VIII, 624; X, 396, 397, 407, 455; XI, **691–92**; XII, 38
Pim, Edward Bedford, XI, 691
Pim, Sophia Soltau. *See* Harrison
Pim, Susanna. *See* Locock
Pinard. *See also* Pyvart
Pinard, Claude, I, 321, 550
Pinard, Françoise. *See* Gamelain
Pinard, Jean, I, 550
Pinard, Louis, I, 321, 328, 369, **550**
Pinard, Marguerite. *See* Gaignier
Pinard, Marguerite (Resche), III, 553
Pinard, Marie. *See* Rivard
Pinard, Marie-Madeleine. *See* Hertel de La Fresnière
Pinard, Marie-Magdeleine (Proulx), VII, 710
Pinard, Marie-Ursule. *See* Pépin
Pinart, Alphonse-Louis, VII, 438
Pinaud, Françoise. *See* Daret
Pinaud, Jean, II, 526
Pinaud, Louise. *See* Douaire de Bondy
Pinaud, Nicolas, I, 56; II, 520, **526**; III, 569
Pindar, Peter. *See* Wolcot, John
Pineda, Antonio, V, 399
Pinel, Philippe, VI, 326, 763; XII, 1125
Pineo, Henry Gesner, X, 71
Pineo, Sarah (Gesner), IX, 308
Pinessie. *See* Binessie
Pinet, Alexis, V, 51
Pinet (Desmarest), Gabrielle (Renaud Dubuisson), II, 563; III, 551
Pinet, Pierre-François, II, 55, 468, 501
Pinet, Vénérande (Haché), XII, 397
Pinguet, Charles, II, 66; III, 522
Pinguet, Charlotte. *See* Mure
Pinguet, Françoise (Delaunay), II, 173
Pinguet, François-Xavier, VI, 534
Pinguet, Jean, III, 284, 522
Pinguet, Joseph-Régis, III, 522
Pinguet, Luce-Monique (Voyer), VII, 891, 892

Pinguet, Marie-Anne (Chambalon; Hazeur Des Ormeaux), II, 129
Pinguet de Bellevue, Nicolas-Charles, III, 522
Pinguet de Targis, Élisabeth. *See* Peiras
Pinguet de Vaucour, Jacques, III, 521
Pinguet de Vaucour, Jacques-Nicolas, III, 35, 499, **521–22**
Pinguet de Vaucour, Marie-Anne. *See* Morin
Pinhey, Hamnett Kirkes, VII, 183, 184; VIII, 510, 585, **706–7**
Pinhey, Mary. *See* Townley
Pinhey, Mary Anne. *See* Tasker
Pinhey, William, VIII, 706
Pining, Mr (explorer), I, 679
Pinkham*, William Cyprian (1844–1928), X, 209
Pinkney, Rebecca (Russell; Huntington), VIII, 415
Pinn. *See* Pynne
Pinolt. *See* Pinaud
Pinquin (Pinquaing). *See* Gallant, Xavier
Pinsent, Anna Brown. *See* Cooke
Pinsent, Emily Hettie Sabine. *See* Homfray
Pinsent, Louisa. *See* Broom
Pinsent, Robert John, VIII, 94; X, **589–90**; XI, 762, 881; XII, 843
Pinsent, Sir Robert John, X, 589; XII, **843–45**
Pinson, Andrew (father of ANDREW), V, 675
Pinson, Andrew (grandson of ANDREW), V, 675
Pinson, Andrew, IV, 599, 712; V, 576, **674–76**
Pinson, Ann. *See* Dodd
Pinson, William, V, 675
Pinsonaut, Clotilde. *See* Raymond
Pinsonaut, Marie-Adélaïde, named de Sainte-Clotilde, VI, 584
Pinsonaut, Marie-Honorine-Euphémie, VI, 584
Pinsonaut, Paul-Théophile, VI, **583–84**, 635; VII, 395, 622, 739; XI, 692
Pinsoneault, Alfred, VI, 584; VII, 395; IX, 612; XI, 275
Pinsoneault, Pierre-Adolphe, VI, 584; VII, 706; IX, 16, 20, 216; X, 190, 430, 662; XI, **692–95**; XII, 183, 1077, 1078, 1084, 1085
Pinsoneaut, Clothilde (Baby), IX, 16
Pinsonnault, Euphrasie. *See* Artaud
Pinsonnault, Gédéon, X, 527
Pinsonnault, Joseph, X, 527
Pinsonnault, Thomas, VI, 583
Pinsonneau, *dit* Lafleur, Ignace, IV, 585
Pinteado, Captain, I, 316
Piol Zusup (Pierre-Joseph?), VI, 678
Piot de Langloiserie, Anne. *See* Petit
Piot de Langloiserie, Charles-Gaspard, I, 295; II, 521, **526–27**; IV, 638
Piot de Langloiserie, Charlotte-Angélique, named Sainte-Rosalie, IV, 638
Piot de Langloiserie, Louis, II, 527
Piot de Langloiserie, Marie-Charlotte (Ruette d'Auteuil de La Malotière), II, 527
Piot de Langloiserie, Marie-Marguerite, named Saint-Hippolyte, IV, 529, **638**
Piot de Langloiserie, Marie-Thérèse. *See* Dugué de Boisbriand
Piot de Langloiserie, Martin, II, 526
Piot de Langloiserie, Suzanne (Céloron de Blainville), II, 527
Piozzi, Hester Lynch. *See* Salusbury

Pipe, Captain. *See* Konieschguanokee
Piper, G. A., IX, 107
Piper, Hiram, XII, 10
Piper, Louisa Adelia (Aikins), XII, 10
Piper, Lydia Ann (Aikins), XII, 10
Piper, Robert S., IX, 554
Pipes, Esther (McCully), X, 456
Pipes*, William Thomas (1850–1909), XII, 1092
Pipon de La Moye, Thomas, VI, 652
Pipon de Noirmont, James, VI, 652
Piraube, Martial, I, 372, 374, 554
Pirie*, Alexander Fraser (1849–1909), XI, 307
Piron, Pierre, I, 109
Piscator. *See* Henry, Walter
Piscot, Étienne, III, 240
Pisqua. *See* Paskwāw
Pitantouin. *See* Tantouin
Pitchy. *See* Peachey
Pither, Robert, XII, 187
Pithou, Pierre, I, 629
Pītikwahanapiwīyin, XI, 443, 444, 445, 459, 460, 596, 599, 600, **695–97**, 745, 747; XII, 734, 735
Piton, Marie (Du Val), VIII, 257
Pitre, Cécile. *See* Boudreau
Pitre, François, V, 102
Pitre, Jean, V, 102
Pitre, Jean-Baptiste, V, 102
Pitt. *See also* Picq
Pitt, Anne (Grenville, Baroness Grenville), IV, 747
Pitt, John, 2nd Earl of Chatham, IV, 747; V, 155, 356; VI, 661
Pitt, Sarah (Carpmael), XII, 160
Pitt, Thomas, 1st Baron Camelford, IV, 747
Pitt, Thomas, 2nd Baron Camelford, IV, 747; VII, 50, 51
Pitt, William, IV, 73, 115, 485, 715; V, 21, 148, 149, 156, 488, 492, 566, 758, 759, 844; VI, 137, 295, 310, 523, 526, 557; VII, 401, 441, 523; VIII, 336, 374
Pitt, William, 1st Earl of Chatham, III, xxviii, xxix, 33, 71, 209, 588, 601, 654, 668; IV, xxxiii, 3, 21, 22, 23, 25, 84, 85, 106, 481, 571, 699, 700, 701; V, 130, 141, 145, 155, 767, 823
Pittendrigh, Emily Josephine (Haynes), XI, 394
Pittendrigh, George, XII, 768
Pitton de Tournefort, Joseph, II, 188, 594, 595, 596, 600; III, 675
Pitts, Daniel H., XII, 221
Pitts*, Herman Henry (1858–1923), XII, 341
Pius VI, IV, 637; V, 242, 246, 632
Pius VII, VI, 596; VII, 304
Pius VIII, VII, 292
Pius IX, I, 354; VII, 298; VIII, 318, 491, 713; IX, 18, 117, 118, 211, 287, 325, 448, 450, 491, 549; X, 95, 148, 193, 250, 315, 429, 430, 431, 493, 542, 715; XI, 96, 97, 98, 102, 105, 171, 172, 276, 289, 311, 339, 344, 450, 494, 507, 693, 694, 710, 726, 755, 777, 805; XII, 57, 177, 183, 267, 301, 359, 520, 799, 819, 834, 912, 1004, 1007, 1022, 1050, 1077, 1084
Pius XI, I, 121, 184, 246, 324, 343, 410, 412
Pius XII, I, 121
Piuze, Édouard-Ferdinand, V, 676
Piuze, J.-R., V, 676
Piuze, Liveright, V, **676**
Piuze, Marie-Anne. *See* Aubut

Piuze, Rémi, V, 676
Pivert, Nicolas, I, 233, 311
Piza, David, V, 194
Place, Francis, IX, 817
Place, Thomas, V, 193
Placide, Caroline (Waring; Blake), IX, 60
Placide, Thomas, IX, 60
Plain. *See* Paskwāw
Plaines. *See* Damours
Plainval. *See* Frasse
Plamondon. *See also* Lafleur
Plamondon, Antoine, IV, 9; V, 72; VII, 100, 246, 341, 592, 869, 870; VIII, 213, 214, 494, 496; IX, 33, 358, 359, 361, 362, 363; XI, 309, 905; XII, **845–53**
Plamondon, Étienne, XII, 848, 849
Plamondon, François-Pierre, XII, 853
Plamondon, Ignace, XII, 845
Plamondon, Joseph, VI, 584
Plamondon, Louis, V, 702; VI, **584–85**; VII, 373, 876, 877; IX, 208
Plamondon, Louise. *See* Robitaille
Plamondon, Marc-Aurèle, VIII, 834; IX, 33; XI, 160; XII, 270, 324, **853–54**
Plamondon, Marguerite. *See* Clément
Plamondon, Marie. *See* Hamel
Plamondon, Mathilde. *See* L'Écuyer
Plamondon, Philippe, XII, 853
Plamondon, Pierre (farmer), XII, 848
Plamondon, Pierre (father of ANTOINE), XII, 845
Plamondon, Rosalie. *See* Amiot
Plamondon, Rosalie-Louise-Geneviève (Donegani), VI, 585; IX, 208
Plamondon, Scholastique-Aimée. *See* Mondion
Planché, James Robinson, XII, 449
Plantavit de Lapause de Margon, Grâce. *See* Maudon
Plantavit de Lapause de Margon, Henri, V, 678
Plantavit de Lapause de Margon, Jean-Guillaume, III, 510; IV, 308, 460, 531; V, **676–78**
Planté, Bernard, V, 788
Plante, Catherine (Huot), IX, 402
Plante, Charles, III, 194, 263, 390, **522–23**, 546, 553; IV, 387
Plante, Claude, III, 522
Planté, Dominique-Bernard, VI, 68, 585
Plante, Édouard-Gabriel, IX, 800; X, 432; XI, 588
Plante, George, V, 576
Plante, Georgiana (Larochelle), XI, 491
Plante, Jean-Baptiste, IV, 748
Planté, Joseph-Bernard, V, 580; VI, 280, 337, 516, 577, **585–86**; VII, 66, 468, 709; VIII, 313; IX, 249
Plante, Marie. *See* Patenotre
Planté, Marie-Josephte. *See* Faucher
Planté, Marie-Julie (Faribault), IX, 249, 362
Planté, Marie-Louise. *See* Berthelot
Planton, Antoinette. *See* Isabeau
Plato, XII, 250
Platt, Ann (Wilson; Theller), VIII, 870
Platt, George, VII, 617
Platt, John, V, 614
Platt, Margaret (Tredwell), VIII, 890
Platt, Prudence (Roblin), X, 624
Plattier, Jean, I, 394
Plaw, John, V, 678

Plaw, John, V, **678–80**; VI, 195; VIII, 444
Plaw, Mary (mother of JOHN), V, 678
Plaw, Mary (wife of JOHN), V, 678
Playfair, Andrew William, X, 650
Playfair, John Speirs, XI, 582; XII, 103
Playfair, Lyon, 1st Baron Playfair, X, 362
Playter*, Edward (1834–1909), XII, 515
Playter, Elizabeth (Rogers), VI, 655
Playter, Ely, V, 597; VIII, 885
Playter, George, IX, 825
Playter, George Frederick, VI, 405; IX, **634–36**
Playter, James, V, 597
Playter, Maud Emma (Lampman), XII, 515
Playter, Sarah (Rogers), VI, 655
Plemazais (Plemarch). *See* Mius
Plenderleath. *See also* Christie
Plenderleath, Amelia Martha. *See* Bowman
Plenderleath, Elizabeth. *See* McGinnis
Plenderleath, Marie-Marguerite. *See* Chaboillez
Plenderleath, Rachel, IV, 151; VII, 184
Plenderleath, William Smith, VII, 595
Plessis, Joseph-Octave, III, 524; IV, 42, 97, 98, 100, 101,
102, 137, 147, 445, 799; V, 13, 45, 123, 125, 181, 186,
200, 203, 207, 209, 211, 213, 217, 236, 246, 247, 248,
271, 290, 292, 374, 380, 459, 471, 473, 489, 493, 494,
495, 588, 633, 651, 659, 662, 671, 678, 688, 691, 695,
738, 745, 770; VI, 14, 28, 39, 85, 97, 98, 106, 120, 125,
126, 145, 146, 167, 170, 202, 205, 216, 217, 286, 287,
293, 316, 332, 368, 370, 386, 391, 394, 448, 449, 450,
486, 499, 506, 507, 524, 526, 527, 528, 547, 569, 570,
571, 572, **586–99**, 650, 668, 669, 691, 714, 715, 716,
748; VII, 19, 27, 61, 94, 95, 131, 132, 168, 201, 246,
280, 321, 322, 332, 341, 349, 355, 398, 403, 404, 422,
423, 431, 486, 487, 488, 489, 495, 501, 524, 525, 545,
546, 547, 551, 574, 591, 615, 655, 656, 657, 667, 668,
669, 678, 679, 684, 689, 699, 700, 720, 721, 727, 728,
729, 736, 746, 759, 767, 769, 770, 771, 784, 787, 788,
798, 801, 802, 803, 869, 876, 877, 878, 879, 885, 886,
901; VIII, 19, 78, 214, 227, 231, 241, 242, 243, 249,
250, 302, 316, 317, 406, 455, 456, 457, 458, 528, 535,
536, 554, 591, 592, 595, 618, 626, 627, 665, 681, 682,
718, 719, 720, 776, 777; IX, 18, 32, 152, 227, 254, 317,
533, 548, 549, 615, 633, 698, 797, 798, 800, 862; X,
162, 488, 578, 604; XI, 87, 94, 96, 167, 168, 684; XII,
424, 1018, 1023
Plessis, Louis-Joseph, IX, 440
Plessis-Bélair, François, V, 77
Plessy, *dit* Bélair, Charles, III, 524; IV, 654
Plessy, *dit* Belair, Françoise. *See* Mathusson
Plessy, *dit* Bélair, Jean, III, 523
Plessy, *dit* Bélair, Jean-Louis, III, **523–24**; IV, 654; VI, 586
Plessy, *dit* Bélair, Joseph-Amable, III, 524; VI, 586
Plessy, *dit* Bélair, Marie-Anne. *See* Petit Boismorel
Plessy, *dit* Bélair, Marie-Louise. *See* Mennard
Plet, François, I, 177; II, 169
Pleyel, Ignaz, VII, 349
Pleynet, Marie-Françoise (Fontbonne), VIII, 298
Plichon, *dit* Saint-Louis, Louis, III, 258
Plimsoll, Miss (educator), VIII, 833; X, 409
Plinguet, Jacques-Alexis, VIII, 285, 712; IX, 65, 193, 194;
X, 237; XI, 766
Plomer, Caroline Eliza (Campbell), VII, 145
Plomer, Sir William, VII, 145

Ploumelle, Jeanne (Poulin), I, 553
Pluche, Noël-Antoine, IV, 640
Plugette (Pluiette), Jeanne (Navarre), IV, 579
Plum, Elizabeth (Downs), XII, 268
Plumb, Elijah Griswold, XI, 697
Plumb, Elizabeth. *See* Street
Plumb, Grace Hubbard. *See* Burr
Plumb, Josiah Burr, VII, 835; XI, **697–98**
Plumby, Mary (Duberger), VI, 224
Plumier, Monsieur (botanist), II, 188
Plummer, Rebecca (Addison), VI, 3
Plummer, Ruth (Newman, Moody), III, 471
Plunket, Lady Catherine. *See* Aylmer
Plunkett, Edmund W., XII, 964
Pobomcoup, Baron de. *See* Mius
Pobomcoup, Baronne de. *See* Amirault; Hélie Du Tillet;
Saint-Étienne de La Tour
Pocahontas, I, 67
Pocatière. *See* Pollet
Pochard, Alexandre, IV, 532, 534
Pocklington, William, XII, 802, 803
Pocock, Rosalie E. (Keefer), XI, 463
Pocquet, Pierre, II, 629
Pogwisch, Ottilie von (Goethe), VIII, 650
Poignant, Jeanne (Giffard), I, 330
Poilly. *See* Grillot
Poincet, Martin, I, 460
Poinsu, François, IV, 239
Point, François, IX, 636
Point, Marie-Nicole. *See* Boursois
Point, Nicolas, IX, **636–37**
Point, Pierre, VII, 171, 706; VIII, 34; IX, 636, 637; X, 190
Pointis. *See* Desjean
Pointon, Philip, XI, 550
Poireaux, Marie-Françoise. *See* Morin
Poirel, Madeleine (Bourdon de Dombourg et de La
Pinaudière), IV, 79
Poirier. *See also* Perrey; Perry
Poirier, Bibienne (Arsenault), XII, 39
Poirier, Marie. *See* Chiasson
Poirier, Marie (Chouart), I, 223
Poirier, Marie-Blanche. *See* Gaudet
Poirier, Marie-Salomée (Odet d'Orsonnens), XII, 798
Poirier, Pascal, IX, 616
Poirier*, Pascal (1852–1933), XI, 350; XII, 40, 144, 546,
548, 549, 550, 837
Poirier, Pierre (father), XI, 684
Poirier, Pierre, XII, 836
Poisset, Françoise, III, 348
Poisset, Louise-Françoise (Barthe), XII, 64, 65
Poisson, Barbe (Barbeau, *dit* Lucault; Celles Duclos), I,
464; II, 164, 221
Poisson, Édouard-Modeste, VIII, 248
Poisson, François, I, 635
Poisson, Jeanne-Antoinette, Marquise de Pompadour (Le
Normant d'Étioles), IV, 354, 467
Poisson, Jules-Adolphe, XII, 854
Poisson, Médéric, XII, 854
Poitevin, Le. *See* Paillard, Léonard
Poitevin, Alphonse, XII, 247
Poitevin, Jeanne (Le Rouge), II, 418
Poitevin d'Anglebert, Joseph, V, 294
Poitevin d'Anglebert, Marie-Anne. *See* Garnom

Poitiers, Diane de, II, 328
Poitiers, Isabeau de (La Roque, *dit* Couillaud), I, 422
Poitiers Du Buisson, Élisabeth. *See* Jossard
Poitiers Du Buisson, Jean-Baptiste, III, 532
Poitras, Cécile (David), XI, 235
Poitras, Jeanne (Ranvoizé), V, 707
Poitras, Magdeleine (McDonell), VII, 553
Poitras, Marie (McDonald), VI, 436
Poitras, Pierre, XII, 132
Poivre, Pierre, IV, 243, 752
Polding, John Bede, XII, 762
Pole. *See also* Wellesley-Pole
Pole, Sir Charles Morice, V, 190, 360; VI, 271, 797
Pole, Millicent (Acheson, Countess of Gosford), VII, 5
Pole, Millicent (Clitherow), VIII, 164
Pole Carew, Caroline (Estcourt), VIII, 273, 274, 275
Polemond, Jean-Baptiste, III, 18
Polette. *See also* Paulet
Polette, Anne. *See* Duval
Polette, Antoine, VIII, 249; IX, 66; X, 418; XI, 529, 657, **698–99**
Polette, Aurelia Sophia. *See* McCord
Polette, Henriette. *See* Dubuc
Polk, James Knox, IX, 235
Pollard, Mrs Ann, VI, 601
Pollard, Edward, IV, 118; VI, 599
Pollard*, Maria (Grant) (d. 1937), XII, 764
Pollard, Richard, IV, 779; V, 787; VI, 525, **599–602**; VII, 528
Pollet, Angélique. *See* Hamelin
Pollet, Arnould-Balthazar, III, 519, **524**
Pollet, Germain, III, 524
Pollet, Marguerite. *See* Harry
Pollet de La Combe de La Pocatière, Catherine. *See* Rossin
Pollet de La Combe de La Pocatière, François, I, 550
Pollet de La Combe-Pocatière, François, I, **550–51**; II, 391, 584, 586
Pollet de La Combe-Pocatière, Marie-Anne. *See* Juchereau de Saint-Denis
Pollet de La Combe-Pocatière, Marie-Louise (Rouer de Villeray et de La Cardonnière), I, 551; II, 584
Pollet de La Combe-Pocatière, Marie-Thérèse (Le Moyne d'Iberville et d'Ardillières; Béthune, Comtesse de Béthune), I, 551; II, 391, 399
Pollexfen, Henry, III, 151
Pollock, George, VII, 607
Pollock, Guy. *See* Hamilton, Robert Douglas
Pollock, Robert, VII, 192
Pollock, William, V, 507
Pollok, Allan, IX, 495
Pollok, Arthur, VII, 343; VIII, 753; IX, 652; X, 305; XI, 349; XII, 366
Pollok, Elizabeth (Gilmour), VII, 343
Pollok, John, VII, 343; VIII, 753; IX, 652; X, 305; XI, 349; XII, 366
Polo, Marco, I, 147, 150
Polonceaux, Henry, IV, 206; VI, 664; VIII, 638
Pomerleau. *See* Vachon
Pomeroy, Robert, XII, 394, 684
Pomeroy, Theodore, XII, 394, 684
Pomeroy, Timothy Conklin, VI, 91, 92
Pometacom (King Philip), II, xxxv, 6, 145; III, 265
Pominouet. *See* Peminuit Paul

Pominville, François-Pierre, X, 59, 143; XI, 529; XII, 99
Pommereau, Catherine-Élisabeth (Bruyères), III, 525; IV, 109; V, 118
Pommereau, Claire-Françoise. *See* Boucher de Boucherville
Pommereau, Françoise. *See* Nafrechoux
Pommereau, Françoise-Renée (Gough), III, 525
Pommereau, Gilles-François, III, 525
Pommereau, Jean-Baptiste, III, 339, 429, **524–25**; IV, 91, 109, 263, 447
Pommereau, Jean-François, III, 525
Pommereau, Pierre-Jacques, III, 524
Pommier, Hugues, I, 314, 359, **551**; II, 19
Pomoacan (Half-King), IV, 302
Pompadour, Marquise de. *See* Poisson
Pomroy, Benjamin, XII, 827
Ponce de León, Rodrigo, Duke of Arcos, II, 633
Poncet, Joseph-Antoine, I, 551
Poncet de La Rivière, Joseph-Antoine, I, 205, 208, 216, 217, 352, **551–52**, 563, 610, 645, 665; II, 535, 624
Poncet de La Rivière et de Brétigny, Jean, I, 551
Poncet de La Rivière et de Brétigny, Marguerite. *See* Thiersault
Poncin, Claude, IV, 508; V, 187, **680–81**; VI, 39
Poncin, Jean, V, 680
Poncin, Marie. *See* Clameron
Poncy, Françoise-Pélagie (Lacroix), VI, 382, 383; VIII, 480
Poncy, François-Philippe, VI, 382
Pond, Charles Hobby, V, 685
Pond, Mary. *See* Hubbard
Pond, Nathan Gillette, V, 685
Pond, Peter, V, 681
Pond, Peter, II, xxviii; III, xxxiii; IV, 245, 262, 310, 365, 403, 585, 741, 757; V, 129, 300, 391, 512, 537, 538, 539, 561, 592, 602, 603, 656, **681–86**, 818; VI, 188, 249, 317, 454; VIII, 500, 546
Pond, Sophia M. *See* Mooney
Pond, Susanna. *See* Newell
Pondiac (Pondiak, Pondiag). *See* Pontiac
Ponekeosh, XII, **854–55**
Pons, Antoinette de, Marquise de Guercheville (Du Plessis de Liancourt), I, 67, 68, 69, 94, 95, 98, 100, 101, 294, 299, 367, 441, 521, 560
Ponsonby, John William, 4th Earl of Bessborough, VII, 902
Ponsy, Catherine (Jacquies), VIII, 423
Pontarion. *See* Castagnac
Pontbriand. *See also* Dubreil
Pontbriand, Comte de. *See* Dubreil
Pontbriand, Comtesse de. *See* Marot de La Garaye
Pontbriand, Claude de, I, 167
Pontchartrain. *See also* Phélypeaux
Pontchartrain, Comte de. *See* Phélypeaux
Pontchartrain, Comtesse de. *See* La Rochefoucauld-Roye
Ponteack. *See* Pontiac
Pontevès, Elzéar de, Marquis de Pontevès, III, 188
Pontevès, Marguerite-Charlotte-Baptistine de (Doreil), III, 188
Pontgibaud. *See* Vicq
Pont-Gravé. *See* Gravé Du Pont
Pontiac (Pontiague, Pontiak), II, 316; III, xxxiv, xxxvi, xxxvii, xxxviii, xxxix, 13, 95, 159, 167, 256, 262, 306, 410, 451, 452, 495, **525–31**, 559, 652; IV, xxxv, xxxvi,

xlix, lii, liv, lv, lvi, lvii, 24, 39, 85, 150, 174, 241, 260, 294, 297, 301, 316, 337, 347, 384, 396, 397, 408, 427, 487, 506, 552, 573, 575, 576, 580, 587, 634, 675, 680, 722, 734, 761, 762, 768; V, 38, 89, 129, 253, 300, 462, 511, 567, 714, 796, 804, 883, 889; VI, 317, 352; VIII, 35, 258, 744; XII, 823, 824, 825

Pontif, Jeanne. *See* Saint-Étienne de La Tour

Pontleroy. *See* Sarrebource

Pontois, Édouard de, VII, 412

Pontonnier, Marie (Gadois), II, 234

Pool, John, IX, 699

Poole, Charles, IX, 217

Poole, Dorcas (Longley), XI, 525

Poole, Mary Ann (Chaffey), VI, 127

Poole, Samuel, IX, 836

Poole, Samuel Sheldon, VI, 77

Poole, Susannah (Campbell), VI, 113

Poole, Thomas Wesley, X, 636

Poole, Sir William, I, 93

Pooley, Charles Edward, XI, 236

Pooley, H., IX, 850

Pooley, Sophia. *See* Burthen

Poor, Elizabeth. *See* Orr

Poor, Elizabeth Adams. *See* Hill

Poor, John Alfred, VIII, 543; IX, 792, 793; X, **590–93**, 722; XII, 349

Poor, Laura Elizabeth, X, 592, 593

Poor, Margaret Robinson. *See* Barr

Poor, Mary. *See* Merrill

Poor, Silvanus, X, 590

Poore, Anna Maria Barbara (Mackechnie), VIII, 555

Poore, Sir Edward, VIII, 555; X, 391

Pooter, Frédéric de, VIII, 308

Pope, A. M., VIII, 628

Pope, Alexander, IV, 554; V, 629

Pope, Ann. *See* Hase

Pope, Eliza. *See* Campbell

Pope, Eliza. *See* Pethick

Pope, Elizabeth Emma (Ives), XI, 708; XII, 466

Pope, Eliza M. *See* Cooke

Pope, George F., IX, 380

Pope, Helen. *See* DesBrisay

Pope, James Colledge, IX, 831; X, 187, 195, 211, 397, 398, 473, 594, 596, 597, 598, 613; XI, 241, 242, 371, 532, 549, 667, 668, **699–705**; XII, 40, 166, 417, 418, 419, 452, 639, 837, 855, 857, 910

Pope, John (father of JOHN HENRY), XI, 705

Pope, John (half-brother of JOSEPH), XII, 855

Pope, John Henry, IX, 727; X, 642; XI, 288, 610, **705–8**; XII, 466, 607, 610, 827

Pope, Joseph, VII, 145, 202; VIII, 135, 198, 531, 564; IX, 157, 401, 857; X, 184, 188, 593; XI, 526, 532, 664, 665, 667, 699, 702; XII, 416, 839, **855–58**

Pope*, Sir Joseph (1854–1926), X, 593; XI, 703, 771; XII, 153, 599, 606, 611, 612, 687

Pope, Lucy. *See* Colledge

Pope, Mary Ann (Fowler), XII, 326

Pope, Percis Maria. *See* Bailey

Pope, Percy, XI, 704

Pope*, Rufus Henry (1857–1944), XI, 707; XII, 467

Pope, Sophia. *See* Laberee

Pope, Thomas (canon), XII, 860

Pope, Thomas (father of JOSEPH), XII, 855

Pope, Thomas (mayor), IX, 360; XII, 1064

Pope, William (artist), VII, 93

Pope, William (brother of JOSEPH), XII, 855, 857

Pope, William Henry, VIII, 532, 954; IX, 181, 183, 184, 376, 404, 831, 832; X, 186, 187, 194, 264, 265, 419, **593–99**, 612, 679; XI, 529, 548, 549, 666, 667, 668, 669, 699, 700, 701, 702, 704; XII, 166, 374, 639, 765, 840, 855, 857

Popham, Sir John, I, 69

Popincourt de Roberval, Alix de, I, 422

Popple, Alured, II, 591

Poquelin, Jean-Baptiste (Molière), I, 139, 141, 607; II, 76; III, 639; V, 233, 248, 702; VIII, 407, 702

Porc-épic, Le. *See* Noro

Porcheron. *See* Descombes-Porcheron

Porcupine. *See* Peemeecheekag

Porden, Eleanor Anne (Franklin), VII, 325; X, 319

Porlier, Angélique. *See* Cuillerier

Porlier, Catherine, III, 167

Porlier, Claude, II, 256

Porlier, Claude-Cyprien-Jacques, IV, 270, 638

Porlier, Jacques, VI, 72; X, 76

Porlier, Marguerite (Boucher-Belleville), X, 76

Porlier, Marie. *See* Bissot

Porlier, Pierre-Antoine, IV, 100, **638–39**

Porlier, Sophie (Labelle), XII, 503

Porrée, Pélagie (Magon de La Balluë), IV, 506

Portanier, Claire (Beaussier), III, 54

Portelance. *See* Roy

Porten, Robert, I, 107

Porteous, Andrew, V, 284, 286

Porteous, Andrew, VI, 665; VII, **700–1**; VIII, 541

Porteous, Anne. *See* Mompesson

Porteous, James, VII, 701; VIII, 242

Porteous, Jane, VIII, 734

Porteous, John (father), IV, 58, 261, 311, 592, 722, 732; V, 282, 284, 286, 299, 326; VI, 179, 531, 639; VII, 700

Porteous, John (son), V, 566; VI, 285

Porteous, John (partner of Thomas PORTEOUS), VI, 602

Porteous, Josepha. *See* Carqueville

Porteous, Margaret (Mure), VI, 531

Porteous, Olivia. *See* Everest

Porteous, Thomas, V, 566; VI, 296, **602–3**, 668, 812; VIII, 242; IX, 379

Porteous, William, V, 566; VI, 285, 665; VII, 700

Porter, Aaron, III, 125

Porter, Agnes. *See* Dryden

Porter, Asa, V, 509

Porter, Charles, VI, 157, 158, 799; VII, 723; VIII, 459; IX, **637–38**; X, 453

Porter, Eleanor. *See* Wallace

Porter, James, X, **599**

Porter, Jane. *See* Brown

Porter, John (businessman), XII, 1000

Porter, John (lumberman), X, 124; XII, 366

Porter, John R., IX, 487

Porter, Martha (Hibbard), V, 422

Porter, Nathaniel, V, 422

Porter, Susannah (Cleveland), III, 125

Porter, Thomas, IX, 637

Porteret, Pierre, I, 491; II, 144

Portland, Duke of. *See* Cavendish

Portland, Earl of. *See* Bentinck

Portlock, Joseph Ellison, V, 686
Portlock, Nathaniel, IV, 166, 218, 244, 744; V, 587, **686–87**
Portman, Maurice Berkeley, XI, 63
Portneuf. *See* Robinau
Portneuf, Baronne de. *See* Legardeur de Villiers; Leneuf de La Poterie
Portugais. *See* Dasilva
Portugal. *See* Bideau
Portugal, Princess of. *See* Catherine
Possel, Ursule-Thérèse (Duquesne), IV, 255
Post, Abigail. *See* Loomis
Post, Christian Frederick, III, 212
Post, Jordan, VII, 701
Post, Jordan, VI, 11; VII, **701–2**
Post, Melinda. *See* Woodruff
Post, Sarah (Belcher), V, 63
Postle, Ann (Mountain), V, 613; VI, 523
Pote, Dorothy. *See* Gatchell
Pote, Jeremiah, V, 337; VI, 561, 562
Pote, Miriam (Pagan), VI, 561
Pote, William, III, 531
Pote, William, III, **531–32**, 650
Potel, Jacqueline (Bourdon), I, 113, 114, 430, 480; II, 91, 92
Potentien, Father. *See* Houdin, Jean-Michel
Poterat, Marquis de, X, 275
Potevin, François, III, 144
Pothier. *See also* Potier
Pothier, Mgr, I, 534
Pothier, Anne-Françoise. *See* Bruyeres
Pothier, Anne-Marguerite (Entremont), VII, 275; XI, 303
Pothier, Aram J., XI, 330
Pothier, Claude, II, 105
Pothier, Jessé-Louise (Jessy Louise) (Desbarats), VII, 703; IX, 203
Pothier, Louise. *See* Courraud Lacoste
Pothier, Louise (Couagne), III, 145; IV, 173
Pothier, Louis-Toussaint, VII, 702
Pothier, Marie (Rocbert), III, 562
Pothier, Robert-Joseph, XI, 109
Pothier, Toussaint, II, 376
Pothier, Toussaint, IV, 109; V, 324, 727; VI, 72, 285, 383, 664, 665; VII, 342, 667, **702–4**, 836, 879; VIII, 301, 321; IX, 203, 807
Pothorst, Hans, I, 679
Potier. *See also* Poitiers
Potier, Jacques, IV, 640
Potier, Marie. *See* Duchatelet
Potier, Marie (Devau), IV, 216
Potier, Pierre-Philippe, III, 355, 528; IV, 370, **640–41**; V, 710
Potier, *dit* Laverdure, Étienne, VII, 702
Potier de Courcy, Madeleine (Callières), II, 112
Potier de Saint-Denis, Jacques, I, 25, 63
Potier Dubuisson, Marie-Charlotte. *See* Arnaud
Potier Dubuisson, Robert, II, 35, 220; III, **532–33**
Potot de Montbeillard, Claude. *See* Orbigny
Potot de Montbeillard, Fiacre-François, III, 672; IV, 243, 382, 460, 620, **641–42**
Potot de Montbeillard, François-Augustin, IV, 640
Potot de Montbeillard, Jean, IV, 641
Potot de Montbeillard, Louise, IV, 641

Potot de Montbeillard, Marie-Claude. *See* Carlet de La Rozière
Potter, Alonzo, XII, 574
Potter, John, XII, 971
Potter, Mercy (Spencer), V, 772
Potter, Nathaniel, IV, 675, 680, 681
Potter, Richard, XI, 123; XII, 432, 433
Potter, Robert, VI, 523
Potter, William W., V, 238
Pottié (Pottier). *See* Potier
Pottier, Étiennette. *See* Beauvais
Pottier, Jean, II, 527
Pottier, Jean-Baptiste, II, xxiv, 16, 163, **527–28**, 562; III, 537
Pottier, Marguerite. *See* Sainctes
Pottinger, Charlotte (Thompson), IX, 785; XII, 1039
Pottle, Thomas, IV, 177
Potts, Andrew R., XII, 858
Potts, Elizabeth (wife of JOHN), III, 534
Potts, George, III, 304; IV, 46
Potts, James (judge), IV, 398; V, 4
Potts, James (printer), IX, 429; XI, 680
Potts, Jerry, XI, 112, 597; XII, 673, 803, **858–59**
Potts, John (clergyman), XII, 355, 704
Potts, John (son of JOHN), III, 534
Potts, John, III, 151, **533–34**
Potts, Mary (Ainslie), V, 4
Potts, Samuel, VII, 395
Potvin*, Damase (1879–1964), IX, 440
Potvin, Jean-Baptiste, VII, 581
Pouchet, Marie (Lévesque), IV, 476
Pouchot (Pouchot de Maupas), Pierre, III, 378, **534–37**; IV, 24, 27, 54, 211, 396, 487, 587, 637, 773
Poudre Chaude. *See* Ogenheratarihiens
Poudret, Antoine, VIII, 288
Poudret, François, III, 598
Poudret, Marie-Anne-Élisabeth (Faribault), VIII, 288
Poudret, Marie-Apolline. *See* Spagniolini
Poudrette, Jean-Baptiste, IX, 699
Pouget, Jean-Baptiste-Noël, IV, 190; V, 313, **687–88**; VI, 379, 380
Pouget, Marie-Joseph. *See* Payet
Pouget, Paul, V, 687
Pouget, Susanne (Sabatier), VI, 676
Pouget Duclaux, Antoine de, VI, 668; VII, 487
Pouilliot, Marie (Larue), II, 348
Poujoulat, Jean-Joseph-François, VIII, 330
Poulain, Guillaume, I, 379, **552**
Poulain, Madeleine (Maufils), II, 466
Poulard, Louis, III, 377
Poulet, Captain, I, 626
Poulet, Georges-François, known as Monsieur Dupont, II, **528–29**, 629; III, 223
Poulin, Guillot, IV, 386
Poulin, Jeanne. *See* Ploumelle
Poulin, Louis (politician), VIII, 175
Poulin, Louis (seigneur), V, 331
Poulin, Louise (Archambault), X, 16
Poulin, Madeleine-Louise. *See* Le Boulanger
Poulin, Marie. *See* Jutra
Poulin, Marie (Charland), V, 183
Poulin, Marie (Fortier), VIII, 302
Poulin, Michel, I, 553; II, 529; III, 537

Poulin, Pierre, I, 552
Poulin, Pierre, II, 530; III, 146, 153, **537–38**; IV, 284
Poulin de Courval, Angélique. *See* Dumoulin
Poulin de Courval, François, IV, 618
Poulin de Courval, Françoise. *See* Foucault
Poulin de Courval, François-Louis, III, **538–39**; IV, 31, 729, 733
Poulin de Courval, Jean-Baptiste, I, 553; II, **529**; III, 539
Poulin de Courval, Louise. *See* Cressé
Poulin de Courval, Louis-Jean, II, 529; III, 63, 538, **539**; IV, 263, 391
Poulin de Courval, Marguerite. *See* Leneuf de Beaubassin
Poulin de Courval, Marie-Madeleine. *See* Forestier
Poulin de Courval, Michel, III, 537
Poulin de Courval, Thérèse. *See* Bouat
Poulin de Courval Cressé. *See also* Cressé
Poulin de Courval Cressé, Charlotte-Louise. *See* Lambert Dumont
Poulin de Courval Cressé, Claude, III, 433, 538, 539; V, 216
Poulin de Courval-Cressé, Jean-Baptiste, IV, 332
Poulin de Courval Cressé, Louis-Pierre, III, **539–40**; IV, 474; V, 216; VI, 385; VIII, 249
Poulin de Courval Cressé, Marie-Anne. *See* Lefebvre
Poulin de Francheville, François, I, 553; II, 153, 236, 457, **529–30**; III, 146, 153, 154, 239, 402, 537; IV, 167, 284, 358, 590
Poulin de Francheville, Marie-Angélique, II, 529
Poulin de Francheville, Thérèse. *See* Couagne
Poulin de La Fontaine, Catherine (Godefroy de Vieuxpont), I, 553; II, 254
Poulin de La Fontaine, Jeanne. *See* Jallot
Poulin de La Fontaine, Marguerite (Lemaître Lamorille), I, 553
Poulin de La Fontaine, Maurice, I, **552–53**; II, xvi, xvii, 16, 254, 529
Pouliot, Léon, XI, 105
Pouliot, Paschal, IX, 854
Poulliot, Marguerite (Salgé), VI, 712
Poulous. *See* Sahonwagy
Pound, Arthur, IV, 86
Poundmaker. *See* Pītikwahanapiwīyin
Poupart, Pierre, II, 517
Pourchaut. *See* Pouchot
Pournin, Marie (Testard de La Forest; La Marque), I, 641; II, 421, 626
Pourroy de Lauberivière, Claude-Joseph de, II, 530
Pourroy de Lauberivière, François-Louis de, II, 60, **530–31**; III, 193, 223, 263, 285, 344, 422, 481, 487, 545; IV, 221, 509, 521, 539, 601; XI, 87, 259
Pourroy de Lauberivière, Marie-Anne de. *See* Saint-Germain
Poursin-Escande, Monsieur (agent), XI, 814
Poussans, Antoinette de (Chavigny Lachevrotière), II, 142
Poussin, Nicolas, I, 313; XII, 848, 850
Pouteret de Bellecourt, *dit* Colombier, Jean-François, I, 225
Poutré, Félix, IX, 459; XI, **708–9**
Poutré, Rose. *See* Bénac
Poutré-Lavigne, Josephte. *See* Mercier
Poutré-Lavigne, Pierre, XI, 708
Poutrincourt. *See* Biencourt
Pouy, Georgette (Monbeton de Brouillan), II, 478

Powderly, Terence Vincent, XI, 638
Powel, David, I, 678
Powell, Andrew, VIII, 268
Powell, Anne. *See* Murray
Powell, Anne, VI, 608
Powell, Anne, VI, 540, **603–5**, 610, 624; VII, 638, 639; IX, 668, 671
Powell, Anne (Clarke), VI, 606, 607, 608
Powell, Anne Murray (Gwynne), VI, 610; X, 325
Powell, Charles Stuart, V, **688–90**; VI, 508
Powell, Cordelia, V, 688, 690
Powell, Daniel, I, 162, 672
Powell, Elizabeth. *See* Bleeker
Powell, Elizabeth, VII, 639
Powell, Elizabeth Van Rensselaer (Stuart; Grogan), VII, 639
Powell, Ellen Catherine (Gordon), IX, 325, 326; X, 308
Powell, Fidelia, V, 688
Powell, Francis, VII, 605
Powell, Grant, XII, 729
Powell, Grant, VI, 416, 604, 609; VII, 418, **704–5**; VIII, 642, 933; XII, 643
Powell, Henry Watson, IV, 48
Powell*, Israel Wood (1836–1915), XII, 806
Powell, Jane (Willcocks), V, 854
Powell, Janet. *See* Grant
Powell, Jeremiah (great-uncle), VI, 606
Powell, Jeremiah, VI, 608
Powell, John (father of WILLIAM DUMMER), VI, 605
Powell, John (grandfather of WILLIAM DUMMER), VI, 605
Powell, John (grandson of WILLIAM DUMMER), V, 189; VI, 610; IX, 346, 503; X, 529
Powell, John (officer), II, 293
Powell, John (son of WILLIAM DUMMER), VI, 609; VIII, 431
Powell, John Ambrose Hume, VII, 852
Powell, Mrs Margaret, IX, 535
Powell, Mary. *See* Boyles
Powell, Mary Ann (wife of CHARLES STUART), V, 688
Powell, Mary Boyles (Jarvis) (aunt), V, 522; VI, 540, 608; VIII, 430
Powell, Mary Boyles (Jarvis), IX, 412
Powell, Mary Catherine (Mercer; McKellar), XII, 643
Powell, S., V, 688
Powell, Snelling, V, 689
Powell, Thomas William, VI, 608
Powell*, Walker (1828–1915), XI, 759; XII, 430, 576
Powell, William (associate of Ralph MERRY), VI, 501
Powell, William (grandson of WILLIAM DUMMER), V, 523
Powell, William (uncle of WILLIAM DUMMER), VI, 605
Powell, William Dummer (son of GRANT), VII, 704
Powell, William Dummer (son of WILLIAM DUMMER), VI, 608
Powell, William Dummer, IV, 6, 7, 162, 229, 777, 778, 779; V, 17, 18, 65, 172, 268, 366, 440, 521, 522, 523, 643, 644, 718, 721, 748, 750, 842, 856; VI, 79, 80, 94, 114, 116, 117, 118, 199, 247, 364, 494, 512, 558, 559, 560, 603, 604, **605–13**, 631, 656, 661, 698, 706, 723, 745, 770, 771; VII, 124, 285, 318, 368, 410, 439, 638, 639, 704, 795, 920, 921; VIII, 5, 48, 251, 337, 430, 596, 597, 598, 602, 604, 608, 793, 795, 859; IX, 333, 412, 484, 668, 669, 670; X, 325, 618
Powell, William Frederick, IX, 576; X, 481

Power, Miss (Skinner), V, 762
Power, Miss, named Sister Mary John, VIII, 474
Power, Anna Mathilda (Cochran), X, 177
Power, Anne. *See* Lonergan
Power, Ann Sophia. *See* Kent
Power, Caroline Benedict (Duncan), XI, 284
Power, Catherine. *See* Sutton
Power, Catherine (Hearn), XII, 420
Power, Ellen. *See* Gaul
Power, Ellen (O'Leary), XII, 801
Power, James, VII, 112, 113; VIII, 199
Power, John, VI, 613
Power, John, V, 474; VI, **613–14**, 691
Power, Katherine (mother of PATRICK), XI, 709
Power, Lawrence, XI, 709
Power*, Lawrence Geoffrey (1841–1921), XI, 710; XII,
    860, 1040
Power, Marguerite (Farmer; Gardiner, Countess of
    Blessington), VII, 337
Power, Martin, XII, 860
Power, Mary. *See* Roach
Power, Michael, XII, 859
Power, Michael, VII, 19, 171, 192, 543, **705–6**; VIII, 317,
    318, 703, 712, 713, 874; IX, 26, 67, 372; X, 578; XI,
    240, 715; XII, 183
Power, Michael Joseph, XII, **859–60**
Power, Patrick, V, 632; VI, 243, 244
Power, Patrick, XI, **709–10**
Power, Richard, I, 324, 476, **553**
Power, Samuel, VIII, 746
Power, Susanne. *See* Aubert de Gaspé
Power, Thomas, IV, 470; VI, 145; VII, 801
Power, Thomas Joseph, XI, 68; XII, 164, **860–61**
Power, William (father of MICHAEL), VII, 705
Power, William (judge), IX, 779; X, 20, 487
Powers, Mary (Fiset), IX, 261
Powhatan, I, 67
Powles. *See* Powlis
Powless. *See* Sahonwagy
Powless, Margaret. *See* Brant
Powlett. *See also* Paulet
Powlett, Katherine, Duchess of Bolton. *See* Lowther
Powlis, George, VI, 706; VIII, **707–9**
Powlis, Joseph, VIII, 708
Powlis, Margaret. *See* Brant
Powlis, Noah, VII, 460
Powlis (Paulus), Paul (Paulus), VIII, 707, 708
Powlis, Susannah. *See* Davis
Pownall, Sir George, IV, 477; V, 21, 224, 225, 318; VI,
    **614–16**; VII, 771
Pownall, John (father of Sir GEORGE), IV, 452; VI, 614
Pownall, John (landowner), V, 407
Pownall, Thomas, III, 509, 654; VI, 615
Powys, Thomas, 1st Baron Lilford, V, 21; VII, 524
Poyer, Françoise (Grisé), IV, 315
Poynter, William, VII, 486
Poyntz, Mary E. A. (Smith), XI, 835
Poyntz, Newdigate, VI, 817
Poytiers, Marie-Charlotte (Hébert), I, 367
Pozer, Ann. *See* Milbourne
Pozer, Christian Henry, XI, 491, **710–11**
Pozer, Elizabeth (Southeron), VII, 708
Pozer, George (grandson of GEORGE), VII, 708

Pozer, George (son of GEORGE), VII, 708
Pozer, George, VI, 424; VII, 136, **706–9**, 892; XI, 710
Pozer, Hannah (Alford), VII, 708
Pozer, Jacob, V, 881; VII, 708
Pozer, John, VII, 708
Pozer, Magdalen. *See* Sneider
Pozer, William, VII, 708; XI, 710
Pozer, William Milbourne, XI, 710
Pradel, Jean-Charles de, III, 36
Pradier, Marie-Claudine de (Charbonnel, Comtesse de
    Charbonnel), XII, 182
Pradines, Élisabeth de (Jordy), II, 186
Prag, Martin, X, 216
Prahm, Adélaïde (Jacquies), VIII, 423
Praslin. *See* Choiseul-Chevigny
Prat, Charles-Ferdinand, X, 599
Prat, Claude (Giard), III, 258
Prat, Jean-Baptiste, X, 599
Prat, Jean-Baptiste, IX, 651; X, **599–600**; XII, 62, 170, 171
Prat, Jeanne-Angélique. *See* Gobeil
Prat, Louis, II, xxiv, 387, 430, **531–32**; III, 180, 621
Prat, Louise. *See* Paillé
Prat, Marie-Joseph (Denys de Saint-Simon), III, 180; IV,
    207
Prat, Mathilde. *See* Roy
Prat, Mathilde (Girouard), X, 600
Prato, Albertus de, I, 586
Pratt, Ann (Savage), VI, 688
Pratt, Anne Mary (Hurd), VIII, 418
Pratt, Catherine. *See* Stevenson
Pratt, Charles, VII, 901; XI, **711–12**
Pratt, Charles, 1st Earl of Camden, IV, 571
Pratt (Pratte), François, VI, 486
Pratt, Grace Agnes (Pringle), XII, 864
Pratt, James, I, 369
Pratt, John. *See* Prat, Jean-Baptiste
Pratt, John Jeffreys, 2nd Earl and 1st Marquess Camden, V,
    366; VI, 160, 723, 724; VII, 767; VIII, xxvii, 336
Pratt, Matthew, IV, 397
Pratt, Sarah (Dalton), VII, 228
Pratt du Clareau, Magdalene du (Maseres), VI, 491
Pratte. *See also* Pratt
Pratte, François-Xavier, X, 615
Pratte, Marguerite (Badeaux), IV, 40
Pratte, Marianne Pelagie Emilie (Crooks), VIII, 190
Preaux, Marie (L'Hermitte), II, 435
Preble, Jedediah, III, 129, 257
Précourt, Luc, IX, 487
Préfontaine. *See also* Fournier
Préfontaine, Christophe, X, 144
Preissac, Anne de. *See* Dupré
Preissac, Lambert de, IV, 642
Preissac, Paul de, IV, 642
Preissac d'Arlens, Jean-Gérard de, IV, 642
Preissac d'Arlens, Paul de, IV, 642
Preissac de Bonneau, Louis de, IV, **642**
Prendergast, Catharine Rodman (Merritt), IX, 544
Prendergast, James, XII, 861
Prendergast*, James-Émile-Pierre (1858–1943), XII, 1010
Prendergast, James Luke, IV, 465; XII, **861–62**
Prendergast, Margaret. *See* Bransfield
Prentice, Anna (Willard), IV, 769
Prenties, Miles, IV, 556; V, 508

Prentiss, Guy R., XII, 631
Pré-Ravillon. *See* La Court
Prescott, Anne. *See* Blagden
Prescott, Anne (Fairbanks), VII, 278; XI, 308
Prescott, Charles Ramage, VII, 491, 533; VIII, **709–11**
Prescott, Elizabeth (Willard), IV, 769
Prescott, Hannah. *See* Whidden
Prescott, Harriet. *See* Skinner
Prescott, Henrietta (Lushington, Lady Lushington), X, 600
Prescott, Sir Henry, VII, 98, 114, 155, 294, 295, 296, 297, 298, 507, 508, 632; VIII, 107, 199, 233, 235, 246, 380, 382, 469, 949, 950; IX, 168, 418, 694; X, 180, 398, 433, **600–1**, 687; XI, 28, 673, 880; XII, 862
Prescott, Isaac, X, 600
Prescott, Jonathan, IV, 696; VIII, 709
Prescott, Mariah. *See* Hammill
Prescott, Martha (Katzmann), XI, 462
Prescott, Mary Anne Charlotte. *See* Auvergne
Prescott, Richard, V, 690
Prescott, Robert, V, 71, 84, 87, 140, 152, 236, 246, 253, 319, 439, 455, 536, 649, **690–93**, 749, 758, 879, 881; VI, 123, 134, 186, 269, 270, 338, 452, 524, 549, 559, 574, 575, 587, 620, 641, 688, 816; VII, 65, 199, 201, 241, 468, 613, 646, 767, 783, 889; VIII, xxiv; IX, 219, 296
Prescott, William George, IX, 181
Presland, Plowden, VIII, 953
Pressart, Angélique. *See* Lorans
Pressart, Colomban-Sébastien, III, 203; IV, 74, 183, 370, 387, 388, **642–43**, 755; V, 144, 379; VI, 493
Pressart, François, IV, 642
Pressé, Hyacinthe-Olivier, II, 523; III, 67, **540–41**
Preston, Viscount. *See* Graham
Preston, Amias (Amyas), I, 278, 279
Preston, Charles, IV, 546; V, 413, 802
Preston, Mary (Maulibock; wife of RICHARD), VIII, 968
Preston, Mary (Boulton), VI, 78
Preston, Richard, V, 342; VII, 123; VIII, 160, **968–70**
Preston, Sir Robert, VI, 218
Preston*, William Thomas Rochester (1851–1942), VII, 122
Pretsche, Paul, XII, 247
Pretty Wolverine Woman. *See* Anu'tsis-tsis-aki
Pretyman Tomline, Elizabeth. *See* Maltby
Pretyman Tomline, Sir George, VI, 523, 524; VII, 211, 825
Prévert. *See* Sarcel
Prévost. *See also* Provost
Prévost, Amable, IX, 488; XII, 62, 862
Prévost, Amaranthe (Viger), VIII, 909
Prévost, Augustin, V, 693, 887
Prevost, Catherine Anne. *See* Phipps
Prévost, Charlotte. *See* Vien
Prévost, Gédéon-Mélasippe, IX, 571
Prevost, Sir George, V, 45, 87, 112, 113, 119, 138, 140, 213, 292, 314, 346, 401, 424, 489, 529, 558, 643, 651, 668, **693–98**, 714, 748, 829, 851, 875, 876, 881; VI, 38, 47, 48, 68, 82, 158, 188, 210, 216, 240, 258, 261, 277, 290, 309, 326, 333, 341, 342, 343, 368, 388, 390, 402, 416, 448, 472, 513, 519, 521, 527, 533, 538, 541, 551, 552, 581, 592, 594, 609, 617, 642, 643, 644, 661, 662, 668, 701, 712, 714, 715, 724, 777, 781, 782, 790, 803, 816; VII, 66, 87, 96, 104, 162, 189, 201, 217, 218, 280, 316, 366, 373, 394, 397, 402, 428, 429, 462, 504, 529, 545, 556, 640, 676, 710, 727, 744, 761, 768, 769, 770, 786, 787, 833, 872, 888, 897, 898; VIII, xxiv, xxxii, 100, 155, 236, 237, 238, 239, 287, 304, 366, 389, 755, 777, 793, 794, 795, 796, 843, 909; IX, 48, 75, 187, 188, 245, 296, 297, 360, 412, 484, 485, 594, 639, 754, 808; X, 566
Prévost, Guillaume (father), X, 306
Prévost, Guillaume, X, 306
Prévost, Hortense. *See* Globensky
Prévost, Jacques, V, 887
Prevost, James Charles, X, 243; XII, 290, 982
Prévost, Josephte. *See* Quévillon
Prévost, Josephte (Chabot), VIII, 137
Prevost, Louis-Amable, VII, 698
Prévost, Louise-Élizabeth. *See* Juchereau Duchesnay
Prevost, Marie. *See* Abancourt
Prevost, Marie-Gabrielle-Élisabeth. *See* L'Estobec de Langristain
Prévost, Marie-Josephte (Desjardins), IX, 203
Prévost, Marie-Olivier-Sylvestre. *See* Manitouabeouich
Prévost, Martin, I, 392, **553–54**
Prévost, Michel, VI, 787
Prévost, Nanette. *See* Grand
Prévost, Oscar, XII, **862–63**
Prevost, Philippe, IV, 643
Prévost, Pierre, I, 553
Prevost, Robert, IV, 643
Prévost, Rosalie-Victoire. *See* Bernard
Prévost, *dit* Tremblay, Aurélie, XII, 297
Prévost de Fontenay, Monsieur (engineer), II, 154
Prevost de La Croix, Charles-Auguste, IV, 646
Prevost de La Croix, Jacques, III, 18, 72, 73, 79, 184, 185, 188, 230, 231, 367, 389, 440; IV, 56, 60, 61, 401, 421, 422, 438, 443, 455, 558, 605, 630, 631, **643–47**, 656
Prevost de La Croix, Jacques-Marie-André, IV, 646
Prevost de La Croix, Louis-Anne, IV, 646
Prevost de La Croix, Marguerite-Thérèse. *See* Carrerot
Prevost de La Croix, Pierre-François, IV, 644
Prévot, Nicolas, V, 813
Priat, Yves, II, 142; III, 612
Price, Mr (merchant), V, 322
Price, Benjamin, III, **541–42**; IV, 243, 570, 576, 618; V, 289, 413, 714
Price, Caroline Cecilia (Blaiklock), VII, 80
Price, Charles. *See also* Isham, Charles Thomas
Price, Charles, VII, 101
Price, Charlotte (Bowring), VII, 101
Price, David, IX, 638, 641
Price, David Edward, IX, 642; X, 602; XI, 774, 775; XII, 863, 864
Price, Edward George, IX, 642; XII, 864
Price, Elizabeth Anne. *See* Rubergall
Price, Evan John, IX, 642; X, 602; XII, 280, **863–64**
Price, George, XII, 461, 462
Price, Henry Ferrier, IX, 642; XII, 864
Price, Herbert Molesworth, XII, 280
Price, James (merchant), III, 541
Price, James (office holder), VIII, 961
Price, James Hervey, VIII, 55, 370, 641; IX, 415, 688; X, 94, 125, 127, 299; XI, 127, 407, 408, 518, **712–14**; XII, 72
Price, Jane. *See* Stewart
Price, Joseph, XII, 1116
Price, Lewis Albert, XII, 864
Price, Mary. *See* Evans

Price, Mary, XII, 863
Price, Mary (Dickerson), VIII, 221
Price, Richard (grandfather), IX, 638
Price, Richard (uncle), XII, 864
Price, Richard, XII, 864
Price, Samuel, IX, 638
Price, Walter (clergyman), IV, 438; V, 633
Price, Walter (politician), VII, 331
Price, William, VI, 546; VII, 71, 426, 448, 564; VIII, 124,
    139, 323, 541, 542, 544, 571, 572, 573, 691, 893, 894;
    IX, 179, 274, 398, 486, **638–43**, 774; X, 601, 635; XI,
    396, 720; XII, 104, 863, 864
Price*, Sir William (1867–1924), IX, 642; XII, 864
Price, William Evan, IX, 642; X, **601–2**; XII, 864
Pricket, Abacuk, I, 144, 145, 374, 375, 376, 377, 378
Priddis, Harriet, VIII, 716
Prideaux, John, IV, 23, 396, 586, 733; V, 681, 888
Priest, Elizabeth (Pushee), VII, 714
Priestley, James, VII, 45; XI, 733
Priestley, Joseph, V, 182; VI, 548; VIII, 866
Priestman, Matthew, VIII, 281
Prieur, François-Xavier, VII, 514
Prieur, Marguerite (Verreau; Gravelle), II, 648
Prieur, Marie (Chambalon), II, 129
Prieur, Perrette (François), I, 312
Primault, Joachim, III, 547
Primeau, Jean-Baptiste, XI, 330
Primeau, Joseph, IV, 647
Primeau, Louis, IV, 47, 160, **647**
Primot, Antoine, I, 465, 507; II, 469
Primot, Catherine. See Thierry
Primot, Martine. See Messier
Prince, VII, 475
Prince, Albert, IX, 646; XI, 756
Prince, Charlotte. See Franchère
Prince*, Edward Ernest (1858–1936), XII, 979
Prince, Elizabeth (Higgins), IV, 352
Prince, Hermine (Richard), X, 615
Prince, Jean, VIII, 711
Prince, Jean-Charles, VII, 423, 431, 488, 656, 747; VIII,
    318, **711–13**, 865; IX, 465; XI, 95, 96, 249, 493, 494,
    693
Prince, Job, IV, 352
Prince, John, VII, 235, 253, 364, 365, 715; VIII, 27, 34,
    120, 852; IX, 469, 524, **643–47**; X, 642; XI, 269, 410,
    649; XII, 884
Prince, Mary (mother of JOHN), IX, 643
Prince, Mary Ann. See Millington
Prince, Richard, IX, 643
Prince, Rosalie. See Bourg
Prince, Septimus Rudyerd, IX, 646
Prince, William Stratton, XII, 273, 274
Prince Consort of Great Britain and Ireland. See Albert
Prince Regent. See George IV
Pring, Anne (wife of DANIEL), VII, 709
Pring, Daniel, VI, 803, 817; VII, **709–10**
Pring, Martin, I, 75
Pringle, Alexander, VI, 772; VII, 558; VIII, 514, 645
Pringle, Elizabeth Susanna. See Wenman
Pringle, Emma Grace. See McLeod
Pringle, Grace, XII, 864
Pringle, Grace Agnes. See Pratt
Pringle, Jane. See Balneavis

Pringle, John Alexander, IX, 551
Pringle, Lockwood, XII, 864
Pringle, Robert, IV, 259, 402, **647–48**, 707; V, 762
Pringle, Sarah. See McNeill
Pringle, Thomas (officer), VI, 695
Pringle, Thomas (poet), IX, 566; XI, 858
Pringle, William, IV, 764
Pringle, William Allen, XII, **864–68**
Printemps. See Dupont
Prior, Charles, IX, 768
Prior, Thomas, VI, 284
Pritchard, Azariah, VI, 616
Pritchard, Azariah, VI, **616**
Pritchard, Catherine. See McLean
Pritchard, Charles, XII, 160
Pritchard, Edward W., V, 347
Pritchard, Eleanor (Bonner; Delesdernier), V, 240
Pritchard, James, VI, 616
Pritchard, John, VIII, 713
Pritchard, John, V, 535; VI, 438; VII, 671; VIII, 342,
    **713–15**
Pritzel, Georg August, X, 105
Privée, Marie-Josephte (Dancereau; Labadie), VI, 380, 381
Procter, Anne. See Gregory
Procter, Elizabeth. See Cockburn
Procter, Henry, V, 302, 346, 748, 775, 799, 876; VI, 21,
    102, 103, 210, 340, 343, 463, 486, 521, 530, 541,
    **616–18**, 661, 662, 706; VII, 58, 494, 743, 821, 849, 898;
    VIII, 33, 100, 119, 794, 795; IX, 8
Procter, Richard, VI, 616
Prophet. See Tenskwatawa
Proteau, Marie-Josephe (Cadot), V, 128
Prou. See also Proulx
Prou, Françoise (Tabeau), VI, 747
Proctor, John, XII, 631
Proudfoot, Caroline Brooks. See Stow
Proudfoot, Elizabeth (Hurd), VIII, 418
Proudfoot, Isobel. See Aitchison
Proudfoot, John James Aitchison, VIII, 716
Proudfoot, William, VII, 234, 442, 520; VIII, 68, 72,
    **715–16**
Proudfoot, William, VII, 652; VIII, 8, 9, 519, 523; IX,
    **647–48**, 745; XI, 156, 166, 167
Proulx, Basile, IV, 556; V, 497
Proulx, Élisabeth. See Grondin
Proulx, Élisabeth (Provencher), VIII, 718
Proulx, Flore. See Lemire
Proulx, Geneviève. See Crevier Descheneaux
Proulx, Henriette (Gautron, dit Larochelle), VIII, 319
Proulx, Jean-Baptiste (father of LOUIS, 1751–1838), VII,
    710
Proulx, Jean-Baptiste, VII, 166; VIII, **716–18**
Proulx, Jean-Baptiste, VII, 705; VIII, 308, 317; XI,
    **714–16**; XII, 1084
Proulx, Joseph, VII, 711; VIII, 716
Proulx, Joséphine (Boucher de Boucherville), VIII, 100
Proulx, Louis (father of LOUIS, 1804–71), X, 602
Proulx, Louis, VII, **710–12**
Proulx, Louis, IX, 361; X, 389, **602–3**; XI, 37, 274, 483,
    493
Proulx, Louis-Basile (bourgeois), VIII, 100
Proulx, Louis-Basile (father of JEAN-BAPTISTE, 1808–81),
    XI, 714

Proulx, Marie-Anne. *See* Brassard
Proulx, Marie-Anne (Legendre), VII, 711
Proulx, Marie-Antoinette-Thaïs (Lacoste), X, 418
Proulx, Marie-Magdeleine. *See* Pinard
Proulx, Marie-Thaïs. *See* Foisy
Proulx*, *dit* Clément, Jean-Baptiste, known as Johannes Iovhanné (1846–1904), XII, 799
Proust. *See also* Proulx
Proust, Marie (Hazeur), II, 275
Prouvereau, Sébastien, I, 60, 387; II, 159
Prouville, Alexandre de, Marquis de Tracy, I, 11, 33, 40, 41, 47, 48, 62, 74, 108, 113, 185, 202, 221, 245, 277, 308, 322, 353, 355, 393, 398, 400, 401, 402, 409, 416, 418, 442, 464, 511, 516, 547, **554–57**, 570, 571, 580, 584, 589, 602, 616, 617, 624, 627, 630, 635, 550; II, xix, 5, 59, 61, 85, 106, 107, 141, 191, 252, 282, 367, 385, 488, 540, 592; III, 201
Prouville, Louise de, Marquise de Tracy. *See* Fouilleuse
Prouville, Marie de. *See* Bochart de Champigny
Prouville, Pierre de, I, 554
Prouville de Tracy, Charles-Henri de, I, 557
Provancher, Geneviève. *See* Hébert
Provancher, Joseph-Étienne, XII, 868
Provancher, Léon, IX, 200, 201; X, 105, 106, 508, 635; XI, 64, 65, 108, 217; XII, 541, 542, 769, 848, **868–70**
Provencher. *See also* Villebrun
Provencher, Élisabeth. *See* Proulx
Provencher, Jean-Baptiste, VIII, 718
Provencher, Joseph-Alfred-Norbert, XI, 339, 612, **716–17**; XII, 1025, 1026
Provencher, Joseph-Norbert, VI, 547, 595, 596; VII, 232, 431, 489, 517, 547, 571, 736, 799, 901; VIII, 19, 241, 248, 249, 250, 352, 363, **718–24**; IX, 94, 95, 633, 634, 802; X, 221, 308, 676, 677; XI, 34, 168, 169, 310, 311, 716; XII, 507, 1003, 1004, 1011
Provencher, Louise. *See* Delagrave
Provencher, Sébastien, I, 49
Provost. *See also* Prévost
Provost, Catherine (Barbel), II, 42
Provost, Charles, II, 532
Provost, François, I, 85, 664; II, 16, 162, 163, 458, **532–33**
Provost, Geneviève. *See* Macard
Provost, Henri, VIII, 396
Provost, Jeanne. *See* Gousset
Provost*, Théophile-Stanislas (1835–1904), X, 86
Prowse*, Daniel Woodley (1834–1914), IV, 599, 600, 771, 785; V, 382; VI, 163; VIII, 104; IX, 72; X, 180, 279, 400, 433, 600; XI, 44, 354, 357, 433; XII, 161, 756, 888, 1061
Prowse, Robert, XI, 674
Pruden, Ann. *See* Armstrong
Pruden, Charlotte (McLeod), VII, 571
Pruden, Elizabeth (Harriott), IX, 366
Pruden, John Peter, VII, 571; IX, 366, **648–49**
Pruden, Margaret. *See* Smith
Pruden, Nancy. *See* Nancy
Pruden, Peter, IX, 648
Prud'homme, Claude, I, 557
Prud'homme, Eustache, XII, 504
Prud'homme, Firmin, VII, 412
Prud'homme, François, I, 557
Prud'homme, Isabelle. *See* Aliomet
Prud'homme, Louis, I, 557

Prud'homme, Louis, I, 177, 230, 319, **557**; II, 466
Prud'homme, Louise (Bonne de Missègle; Le Moyne de Longueuil), III, 70; V, 230, 487
Prud'homme, Marguerite (Martinet de Fonblanche; Latour), II, 466
Prud'homme, Marie-Amable (Coulon de Villiers), III, 148
Prud'homme, Marie-Anne (Landriaux), IV, 434
Prud'homme, Marie-Françoise (Roy), V, 727
Prud'homme, Paul, II, 466
Prud'homme, Pierre, I, 177, 557
Prud'homme, Roberte. *See* Gadoys
Prume. *See also* Jehin-Prume
Prume, François-Hubert, XII, 471
Prume, Marie-Joséphine-Pétronille (Jehin), XII, 470
Pruneau, Pierre, II, 273
Prunier, Honorade (Vachon de Belmont), II, 641
Pryor, Charlotte. *See* McKie
Pryor, Edward, VIII, 724
Pryor, Elizabeth Ann (De Mille), X, 223
Pryor, Elizabeth Mary. *See* Boggs
Pryor, Eliza Phoebe. *See* Pyke
Pryor, Emily (Binney), X, 66
Pryor, Henry, XII, 765, 791, **870–71**, 966, 1039
Pryor, Jane. *See* Vermilye
Pryor, Johanna. *See* Schwartz
Pryor, John, VIII, 724; X, 6; XII, 870, 871
Pryor, John, VIII, 612, 613; X, 223; XI, 209, 215; XII, 109, 870, **871–73**
Pryor, Louisa (Wentworth; Johnston), X, 386; XII, 870
Pryor, Mary Barbara. *See* Voss
Pryor, Sarah. *See* Stevens
Pryor, Sophia (Almon), X, 6
Pryor, William, VIII, 168, **724–25**; XI, 717
Pryor, William, VIII, 724; X, 189; XI, **717–18**
Puckeshinwa, V, 796; VII, 847
Puebla, Gonsalez de, I, 148
Pufendorf, Samuel, Baron von Pufendorf, IV, 230; VII, 645
Puget, Peter, IV, 768
Pugh, Margaret (Hale), XII, 400
Pugh, William, XII, 401
Pugin, Augustus Welby Northmore, VIII, 942, 943; XI, 392; XII, 343
Puibusque, Adolphe de, IX, 250, 805; XI, 179
Puisaye, André-Louis-Charles de, Marquis de La Coudrelle, VI, 618
Puisaye, Joseph-Geneviève de, Comte de Puisaye, V, 86, 440, 519, 731; VI, **618–21**, 623, 624; VII, 79, 876; VIII, 337
Puisaye, Joséphine de, VI, 620
Puisaye, Louise de, Marquise de Puisaye. *See* Le Sesne
Puisaye, Marthe-Françoise de, Marquise de La Coudrelle. *See* Bibron de Corméry
Puiseaux, Pierre de, I, 215, 216, 217, 401, 485, **557–58**, 640
Pullen, Abigail Louisa. *See* Berton
Pullen, Amelia Mary. *See* Haswell
Pullen, William, XI, 718
Pullen, William John Samuel, VIII, 624; XI, 384, 543, 692, **718–19**; XII, 877
Pulling, George Christopher, VI, 176, 580
Pullman (Pulman), John, V, 321; XI, 533
Pullman, Mary (Gray), VI, 296
Punderson, Ebenezer, V, 59

Punderson, Sylvia (Beardsley), V, 59, 60
Punshon, Elizabeth. *See* Morley
Punshon, Fanny. *See* Vickers
Punshon, John, XI, 719
Punshon, Maria. *See* Vickers
Punshon, Mary. *See* Foster
Punshon, William Morley, XI, 640, **719–20**; XII, 266, 701
Punton, William, X, 538
Purcell, Ann (Scott), VI, 424
Purcell, James, VII, 220; VIII, **725–26**
Purcell, Martin, II, 250, 487
Purcell, Patrick, XII, 699, 933
Purcell, Thomas, V, 108
Purchas, Samuel, I, 74, 75, 101, 158, 329, 349, 360, 379, 471, 586, 677, 678
Purdom, Alexander, XII, 822
Purdom, Thomas Hunter, XII, 822
Purdon, Alicia (Uniacke), VI, 789
Purdon, Charity Christina (Fitzgerald), XII, 318
Purdy, Amy (Merritt), VII, 601, 602
Purdy, Elizabeth. *See* Brundage
Purdy, Hazzard Wilcox, VII, 713
Purdy, Hulda. *See* Yates
Purdy, Jesse, VII, 712
Purdy, Jesse Thomas, VII, 713
Purdy, Sabia. *See* Wilcox
Purdy, William, VII, **712–13**, 862
Purington, H. E., XII, 759
Purse, Alexander, V, 699
Purse, Isabel. *See* Blenshel
Purser, William, VII, 195
Purss, John, IV, 399, 618; V, 493, 509, **699–700**
Purvis, George, XII, **873–74**
Purvis, Hannah (wife of GEORGE), XII, 873
Purvis, James, VII, 713
Purvis, Mrs Janet (Campbell), IX, 489
Purvis, Margaret (McDougall), IX, 486, 489
Purvis, Nancy, VII, **713–14**
Pusey, Edward Bouverie, VIII, 866; IX, 289; X, 84; XII, 681, 714
Pushee, Elizabeth. *See* Priest
Pushee, Henry, VII, 714
Pushee, Jane. *See* Brown
Pushee, Nathan, VII, 714
Pushee, Nathan, VII, **714–15**
Pussot, Jeanne-Claude (Claudine) (Mongenet), VI, 516
Puthuff, William Henry, VI, 510
Putman, Clarissa, VI, 352
Putman, John Harold, XI, 794
Putnam, Charles Simonds, X, 709
Putnam, Eleanor. *See* Dygart
Putnam, Elizabeth (Rice), XI, 729
Putnam, Ellen (Dickie), XI, 262
Putnam, Eunice (Perley), V, 665
Putnam, Israel, V, 666
Putnam, Seth, VII, 715
Putnam, Warner Herkimer, VII, 716
Putnam, William, VII, 253, **715–16**; X, 548, 549
Puybareau, Pierre, III, 220
Puybarau de Maisonneuve, Jean, II, 617
Puybarau de Maisonneuve, Madeleine. *See* Baudry
Puygibault. *See* Hingue
Puyperouse, Anne (Pascaud), IV, 605

Puyperoux de La Fosse, Marie-Angélique (Goutin), III, 264
Puysieux, Marquis de. *See* Bruslart
Pyke, Captain, XII, 1065
Pyke, Ann. *See* Scroope
Pyke, Ann (Irvine), VI, 346, 622
Pyke, Eliza. *See* Tremain
Pyke, Elizabeth. *See* Allan
Pyke, Eliza Phoebe (Pryor), XII, 870
Pyke, George, IV, 502; V, 27, 90, 769; VI, 622; VII, 67, 643, 892; VIII, **726–27**, 906; XII, 870
Pyke, John, VI, 621
Pyke, John George, IV, 763; VI, 346, **621–22**; VIII, 726; XII, 870
Pyle, Joseph, VI, 91
Pyle, William, I, 652
Pyndar, Katherine (Katherina) (Sherbrooke, Lady Sherbrooke), VI, 712
Pyne. *See also* Pynne
Pyne, Thomas, IV, 784
Pynne, John, II, 533
Pynne, Robert, II, 533, 534
Pynne, William, II, 534
Pynne, William, II, 395, **533–34**
Pyper, James, XII, 225
Pytheas of Massilia, I, 17
Pyvart (Pinard) de Chastullé, Marguerite-Françoise (Beauharnois de La Boische), II, 52; III, 41, 51
Pyvart de Chastullé, Marie-Anne (Beauharnois de La Boische et de La Chaussée), III, 50

QALASIRSSUAQ. *See* Kallihirua
Qinousaki. *See* Kinousaki
Qissunguaq (Kirshung-oak), VIII, 447
Quadra. *See* Bodega
Qua-hail-ya, X, 217
Quaife, Milo Milton, IV, 322; V, 553
Quain, Mrs Mary, V, 59, 60
Quant, Mary. *See* Webber
Quarante Sols. *See* Michipichy
Quary, Robert, III, 65
Quâs. *See* ?Kwah
Quayle, Mary Emma (Innis), V, 759; VII, 363
Quéan (Quen), Eustache (Boullongue), I, 43, 110
Quélen, Hyacinthe-Louis de, Comte de Quélen, VI, 201
Quélus. *See* Thubières
Quémar, Jacquette, IV, 95
Quémar, Jacquette (Burel), IV, 95
Quen. *See also* Quéan
Quen, Jean de, I, 48, 341, 404, 459, 552, **558–59**, 645, 646
Quénault, Charles. *See* Savary, Charles
Quénault, Charlotte-Éliane (Savary), XI, 801
Quenebenaw. *See* Kineubenae
Quenet (Guénet), Jean-Baptiste, II, 215
Quenneville. *See* Quesneville
Quentin, Claude, I, 214, **560**
Quentin, Jacques, I, 68, 95, 299, **560**
Quer. *See* Kirke
Querbes, Louis, XI, 174
Querbonyer, Monsieur (commandant), I, 210, 422
Querdisien. *See* Pichot
Quéré de Tréguron, Maurice, II, 241; III, 268, 269, **542–43**; XI, 655
Queren, Anna Sabina (Glackemeyer), VII, 348

Querno, Camillo. *See* Odell, Jonathan
Querque. *See* Kirke
Quertier, Édouard, IX, 779; X, **604–5**; XII, 189
Quertier, Hélier, X, 604
Quertier, Marie-Anne. *See* Ariail
Quesnel, Auguste, XII, 911
Quesnel, Charlotte. *See* Verchères de Boucherville
Quesnel, Emma (Robitaille), XII, 912
Quesnel, Frédéric-Auguste, V, 702; VII, 227, 606, 716, 717, 739; VIII, 332, 914; IX, 486, 560, 561, **649–51**, 655, 811; X, 405; XI, 160, 206; XII, 912
Quesnel, Jacques, II, 230; III, 290
Quesnel, Joseph, V, 233, 243, **700–3**; VI, 499; VII, 255, 645, 716; VIII, 420; IX, 649
Quesnel, Joseph-Timoléon, V, 702; IX, 649, 650
Quesnel, Josette. *See* Cotté
Quesnel, Jules-Maurice, IV, 172; V, 702; VI, 624; VII, **716–18**; IX, 284, 554, 649, 745
Quesnel, Louis-Auguste, V, 700
Quesnel, Marguerite. *See* Denaut
Quesnel, Marie-Anne. *See* Franquelin
Quesnel, Marie-Josephte. *See* Cotté
Quesnel, Marie-Josephte. *See* Deslandes
Quesnel, Mélanie (Coursol; Cherrier), V, 702; IX, 649; XI, 187, 206
Quesnel, Pasquier, II, 528
Quesnel, Pélagie-Jeanne-Marguerite. *See* Duguen
Quesnel, Pierre, V, 701
Quesnel, Timoléon, VII, 239
Quesnel de La Rivaudais, Isaac, V, 700
Quesnel Fonblanche, Jacques, IV, 312
Quesnel Fonblanche, Louise (Hervieux), III, 290; V, 395
Quesnel Fonblanche, Marie-Joseph (Grasset de Saint-Sauveur), IV, 312
Quesneville, Denise. *See* Marié
Quesneville, Jean, II, **534**
Quesneville, Jeanne. *See* Saye
Quesneville, Pierre, II, 534
Quessy, Mary (Lambourg; Gueguen), VI, 304, 305
Questach (Cockeye), IV, 389, 518
Quet, Catherine (mother of Laurent QUETTON St George), VI, 622
Quet, Étienne, VI, 623
Quet, Jean, VI, 622
Quetton de St Georges, Adèle. *See* Barbeyrac
Quetton St George, Henry, VI, 625
Quetton St George, Laurent, VI, 51, 604, 608, 619, 620, **622–25**, 772; VII, 36, 37, 638, 716, 717, 919, 920; VIII, 4, 5, 100; IX, 24
Quevillon, Catherine (Lacombe; Papineau, *dit* Montigny; Daniel; Verac), II, 507
Quévillon, Jean-Baptiste (father), VI, 625
Quévillon, Jean-Baptiste, VI, 625
Quévillon, Josephte (Prévost), X, 306
Quévillon, Louis, VI, 226, 227, 315, 570, **625–26**; VII, 60, 167, 685, 686; VIII, 38, 218, 655, 763; IX, 126, 127, 552; X, 301
Quévillon, Marie-Anne. *See* Cadieux
Queylus. *See* Thubières
Quiala. *See* Kiala
Quiasutha. *See* Kayahsota?
Quiblier, Catherine (Quiblier), VIII, 727
Quiblier, Jean, VIII, 727

Quiblier, Joseph-Vincent, VI, 669; VII, 100, 118, 171, 412, 423, 489, 760, 774, 799; VIII, 317, 490, 539, 703, **727–31**, 777; IX, 50, 228, 246, 460, 681; X, 17, 89; XI, 42; XII, 846
Quider. *See* Schuyler, Peter
Quigg, Dr, III, 504
Quigley, Ann (Moss), XI, 621
Quigley, Michael, VI, 119; VIII, 581, 582
Quignon, François, I, 314
Quimby, Alfred Campbell, XII, 1069
Quimper, Manuel, IV, 568; VI, 233
Quin (Quinn), Edmond, VII, 203
Quin (Quinn), James, VII, 203
Quin (Quinn), Mary (Collins), VII, 203
Quinan, James, VIII, 554
Quinan, John, VII, 581; IX, 651
Quinan, John Joseph, IX, **651**
Quinan, Joseph W., IX, 651
Quincy, Esther (Sewell), VI, 700; VII, 782
Quincy, Josiah, VII, 86
Quindre. *See* Dagneau
Quiniard, Antoine, II, 534
Quiniard, Jeanne. *See* Branquais
Quiniard, *dit* Duplessis, Antoine-Olivier, II, xxiii, **534–35**
Quiniard, *dit* Duplessis, Marie-Louise. *See* Bolper
Quinipeno. *See* Kineubenae
Quinn. *See also* Quin
Quinn, Frances (Nelson), XII, 784
Quinn, Thomas Trueman, XI, 306, 459, 460, 599; XII, 478
Quinousaquy. *See* Kinousaki
Quinson de Saint-Ours, Charles-Roch, V, 231, 752
Quinson de Saint-Ours, Marie-Anne. *See* Mackay
Quintal. *See also* Boyer; Quittel
Quintal, Augustin (baptized Joseph), I, 312; II, 200; III, 67; IV, **649–50**
Quintal, François, IV, 649
Quintal, Louise-Zéphyrine (Labadie), VI, 381
Quintal, Marie. *See* Gaultier
Quinton, Mary (Jacques), XI, 448
Quiquinanis. *See* Wikinanish
Quiring, Walter, XII, 1099
Quirk, Eliza. *See* Chipman
Quirk, John, VIII, 731
Quirk, John, VII, 713; VIII, **731–32**
Quirk, Matthias, VIII, 732
Quirk, Phebe. *See* Tupper
Quirk, Sarah. *See* Cowin
Quirouet, Catherine. *See* MacKenzie
Quirouet, François, VII, 718
Quirouet, François, V, 260; VII, 176, **718–19**, 879; X, 260
Quirouet, Marguerite (Drolet), X, 260
Quirouet, Marie-Anne. *See* Hil
Quirouet, Olivier, VII, 176, 718
Quirouet, Rémi, VI, 546
Quisence, Jeanne (Barrat), II, 45, 481
Quitawape. *See* Atiatoharongwen
Quittel (Guittel, Quitter, Quintal), Marthe (Verreau), II, 648

RABELAIS, François, I, 170, 365, 424; IV, xxiii; VI, 764; VIII, 438
Rabut, Benoît, named Brother Facile, IX, 681
Rabutin-Chantal, Marie de, Marquise de Sévigné, I, 117; IV, 656; VIII, 291

Raby, Augustin, IV, 210, **650**, 700; V, 95; VI, 134, 626
Raby, Augustin-Jérôme, V, 373, 493; VI, **626–27**
Raby, Catherine. *See* Chauveaux
Raby, Françoise. *See* Delisle
Raby, Marie-Anne (Jordan), IV, 402
Raby, Marie-Françoise. *See* Morin
Raby, Marie-Gillette. *See* Turgeon
Raby, Mathieu, IV, 650
Racey, Charlotte (Elliot), X, 270
Racine, Antoine, X, 685; XI, 38, 488, 720; XII, 303, 304, 521, 868, **874–76**
Racine, Dominique, X, 685; XI, 38, 513, 514, **720–21**, 873; XII, 874, 1023
Racine, Étienne, I, 495
Racine, Jean, V, 248; VI, 84; VIII, 407
Racine, Louise. *See* Pepin
Racine, Louise (Guyon), I, 359; III, 681
Racine, Marguerite. *See* Martin
Racine, Marie-Anne. *See* Atkin
Racine, Michel (father), XI, 720; XII, 874
Racine, Michel, XI, 720
Racine, Pierre, VII, 774
Rackham, Katherine (Strickland), IX, 768
Raclot, Ildebon, II, 517
Raclot, Madeleine (Perrot), II, 517
Raclot, Marie. *See* Viennot
Racsenagate, IV, 368
Racy, John, V, 291
Radcliff, Elizabeth. *See* Mitchell
Radcliff, John Smyth, IX, 526; XI, 128, 129
Radcliff, Sarah Ann. *See* Armstrong
Radcliff, Thomas, VII, 719
Radcliff, Thomas, VII, 234, **719–20**; VIII, 870
Radcliff, William, VII, 719
Radcliffe-Brown, Alfred Reginald, III, 338
Raddish (Reddish), Thomas, V, 303
Radenhurst, Ann. *See* Campbell
Radenhurst, Catherine (Lyon), VIII, 509
Radenhurst, John, VII, 834; VIII, 419, 523
Radenhurst, Lucy Edith. *See* Ridout
Radenhurst, Thomas, VIII, 732
Radenhurst, Thomas Mabon, VIII, 510, **732–34**; XII, 85
Radisson. *See also* Volant
Radisson, Elizabeth (wife of PIERRE-ESPRIT), II, 539
Radisson, Françoise (Volant de Saint-Claude), II, 655
Radisson, Madeleine. *See* Hénaut
Radisson, Margaret Charlotte. *See* Godet
Radisson, Pierre-Esprit, II, 535
Radisson, Pierre-Esprit, I, 16, 20, 35, 39, 42, 48, 49, 56, 82, 83, 129, 130, 223, 226, 227, 228, 270, 271, 273, 274, 282, 337, 338, 377, 397, 406, 464, 509, 518, 528, 529, 578, 602, 625, 653; II, 31, 247, 298, 391, **535–40**, 647
Radisson, *dit* Duplessis, Marguerite. *See* Duplessis
Radstock, Baron. *See* Waldegrave
Radstock, Baroness. *See* Lennap
Rae. *See also* McRae; Rea
Rae, Alexander, VIII, 564
Rae, Ann Cuthbert (Knight; Fleming), VII, 714; VIII, **734–35**; X, 606
Rae, Catherine Jane Alicia. *See* Thompson
Rae, Eliza (wife of JOHN, 1796–1892), X, 606
Rae, Jackson, XI, 8, 380

Rae, John (father of ANN CUTHBERT and JOHN, 1796–1872), VIII, 734; X, 605
Rae, John (father of JOHN, 1813–93), XII, 876
Rae, John, VII, 733; VIII, 734; X, **605–9**, 708, 709; XI, 868; XII, 149
Rae, John, VII, 327; VIII, 663; IX, 6, 43, 659; X, 319, 407, 541; XI, 200, 436, 718, 854; XII, 642, 833, **876–79**
Rae, Margaret. *See* Cuthbert
Rae, Margaret Glen. *See* Campbell
Rae, Richard Bempede Johnstone Honeyman, XII, 878
Rae, Robert, XI, 671
Rae, Thomas, XII, 878
Rae, William Glen, X, 486
Raeburn, Henry, V, 314
Raffeix, Pierre, I, 48, 108, 321, 651; II, 19, **540**; III, 104, 335, 649
Raffetot. *See* Deschamps
Rafinesque, Constantine Samuel, X, 65
Rageot, François, I, 561; II, 58, 325, 541, 576
Rageot, Gilles, I, 394, 474, 550, **560–61**; II, xix, 129, 133, 242, 325, 347, 540, 541, 576
Rageot, Isaac, I, 560
Rageot, Jean-Baptiste, I, 561
Rageot, Louise. *See* Duret
Rageot, Marie-Madeleine. *See* Morin
Rageot, Marie-Madeleine (Rivet Cavelier), II, 576
Rageot, Philippe, I, 561; II, 238
Rageot de Beaurivage, Gilles, I, 561
Rageot de Saint-Luc, Charles, I, 561; II, 138, **540–41**, 576
Rageot de Saint-Luc, Marie-Geneviève. *See* Gauvreau
Rageot de Saint-Luc, Marie-Madeleine-Geneviève, II, 541
Rageot de Saint-Luc, Nicolas, I, 561; II, **541**, 576
Raglan, Baron. *See* Somerset
Ragueneau, François, I, 214, 453, 561
Ragueneau, Paul, I, 44, 64, 71, 123, 125, 128, 143, 184, 185, 186, 205, 206, 214, 225, 296, 328, 412, 414, 455, 459, 460, 461, 489, **561–64**, 607, 608, 609, 610, 637, 640; II, xvi, 85, 536, 537
Raguet, Gilles-Bernard, III, 40
Raguse, Duc de. *See* Viesse
Raikes, Hariet (Cayley), XI, 165
Raikes, Robert, V, 189
Raimbault, Charlotte. *See* Damours
Raimbault, Claude, II, 541
Raimbault, Étienne, VII, 720
Raimbault, Françoise. *See* Doucet
Raimbault, Jean, VI, 202, 589, 597, 598, 599; VII, 131, 166, 255, 321, 322, 340, 501, 502, 591, 655, 668, **720–21**; VIII, 19, 259, 595, 681, 718, 720; X, 602; XI, 87
Raimbault, Jean-André, VI, 201
Raimbault, Jeanne-Françoise. *See* Simblin
Raimbault, Louise. *See* Nafrechoux
Raimbault, Marguerite (Boucher de Boucherville), II, 542; III, 80; V, 96
Raimbault, Marie-Thérèse. *See* Sallé
Raimbault, Pierre, IV, 647
Raimbault, Pierre, II, 111, **541–42**, 617, 618; III, 44, 80, 205, 270, 340, 422, 450, 520
Raimbault de Piedmont, Joseph-Charles, II, **542**, 627; III, 164
Raimbault de Saint-Blaint, Charlotte-Gabrielle. *See* Jarret de Verchères

Raimbault de Saint-Blaint, Madeleine (Boucher de Boucherville), V, 96; VIII, 100
Raimbault de Saint-Blaint (Simblin), Paul-François, II, 542
Raimbault de Saint-Blaint, Pierre-Marie-Joseph, III, 611; IV, 344
Raimond. *See also* Raymond
Raimond, Joseph, XI, 725
Raimond, Louise. *See* Cartier
Raimondvert, Catherine (Archambault), XI, 25
Rain, Mary (Stewart), VI, 736
Rainer, Dr, I, 553
Rains, Gabriel James, XII, 817
Rainsborough, William, I, 407
Rainsford, Harriet (Wetmore), VI, 810; XII, 1096
Rainsford, William Stephen, XII, 453
Rainsthorpe, Esther (Morris), IV, 559
Rainville, Charlotte (Corbin), IV, 167
Rainville, François, VIII, 260
Rainville, Henri-Benjamin, XII, 7
Rainville, Henri-Félix, XII, 277
Rainy Chief. *See* Sotai-na
Raisin, Anne. *See* Collet
Raisin, Edmé, I, 564
Raisin, Marie, I, 116, **564**
Raisin, Nicolas, I, 564
Raizenne, Amable-Simon, IV, 188; V, 703
Raizenne, Élisabeth. *See* Nims, Abigail
Raizenne, Ignace. *See also* Rising, Josiah
Raizenne, Ignace, VIII, 791
Raizenne, Jean-Baptiste-Jérôme, VI, 627
Raizenne, Marie, named Saint-Ignace, V, 118, **703–4**; VI, 627
Raizenne, Marie-Charlotte. *See* Sabourin
Raizenne, Marie-Clotilde, named Marie de l'Incarnation, VI, **627–28**; VIII, 34
Raizenne, Marie-Madeleine, named Saint-Herman, V, 703
Rale, Sébastien, II, xxxvi, 64, 287, 476, 477, **542–45**, 668, 669; III, xxxvii, 104, 330, 476, 477, 584
Raleigh, Sir Carew, I, 279, 331
Raleigh, Sir Walter, I, 251, 278, 331, 332, 333, 335, 363, 364, 668, 669
Ralfe, James, V, 276
Ralluau, Jean, I, 292, 293, **564–65**
Ralston, Elizabeth (Tiffany), V, 814
Ramage, Mrs (Taylor; wife of JOHN), V, 705
Ramage, Catharine. *See* Collins
Ramage, Elizabeth. *See* Liddel
Ramage, John, V, **704–6**; VII, 255
Ramage, Victoria. *See* Ball
Rambau, Alfred-Xavier, VII, 236, 412, 625; VIII, **735–36**; X, 75; XI, 851; XII, 66
Rambau, Marie-Antoinette. *See* Allard
Rameau de Saint-Père, François-Edme, IV, xviii, xx, 239; IX, 65, 302; X, 47; XI, 182, 183, 186; XII, 501, 548, 549
Ramezay, Catherine de. *See* Tribouillard
Ramezay, Charlotte-Marguerite de (Bellot), IV, 652
Ramezay, Claude de, II, 548
Ramezay, Claude de, I, 602; II, xxi, 25, 33, 47, 81, 87, 162, 181, 186, 354, 389, 402, 409, 436, 497, 533, **545–49**, 569, 571, 589, 606, 626, 645; III, 22, 81, 146, 190, 247, 543, 563, 579; IV, 41, 235, 650, 653, 690
Ramezay, Élisabeth de (La Corne), IV, 224; V, 578
Ramezay, Jean-Baptiste-Nicolas-Roch de, II, 548; III, xxii,

xxv, 49, 110, 255, 256, 378, 417, 438, 467, 483, 484, 511, 538, 578, 608, 650; IV, 10, 33, 34, 63, 143, 213, 296, 319, 361, 382, 446, 454, 459, 480, 602, 633, **650–53**, 672, 728, 783; V, 97, 108, 128, 498; X, 13
Ramezay, Louise de. *See* Godefroy de Tonnancour
Ramezay, Louise de, II, 548; IV, 650, **653–55**
Ramezay, Louise-Geneviève de (Deschamps de Boishébert), II, 181; IV, 212, 654
Ramezay, Marie-Charlotte de. *See* Denys de La Ronde
Ramezay, Marie-Charlotte de, named de Saint-Claude de la Croix, III, 319, **543–44**; IV, 650, 653
Ramezay, Timothé de, II, 545
Ramezay de La Gesse, Charles-Hector de, II, 547, 548; IV, 650
Ramezay de Monnoir, Louis de, II, 548
Ramón, Diego, III, 317
Ramón de Navarro, Emanuela (Juchereau de Saint- Denis), III, 317
Ramondine, Marie-Josèphe (Rodrigue), IV, 679
Ramsay. *See also* Maule Ramsay
Ramsay, Mrs. *See* Kennedy
Ramsay, Alexander Gillespie, VIII, 44
Ramsay, Christian, Countess of Dalhousie. *See* Broun
Ramsay, David (associate of James YEO), IX, 857
Ramsay, David (father of THOMAS KENNEDY), XI, 721
Ramsay, David (landowner), VI, 629, 630
Ramsay, David, V, **706–7**; VI, 112, 555
Ramsay, Donald, V, 407
Ramsay, Eleonor (Wurtele), VI, 819, 820
Ramsay, Elizabeth, Countess of Dalhousie. *See* Glene
Ramsay, George, V, 706
Ramsay, George (Jack), V, 814
Ramsay, George, 8th Earl of Dalhousie, VII, 722
Ramsay, George, 9th Earl of Dalhousie, V, 698, 850; VI, 82, 97, 98, 104, 126, 135, 158, 241, 287, 300, 307, 319, 326, 353, 354, 368, 381, 386, 434, 477, 478, 497, 498, 507, 513, 520, 528, 529, 530, 543, 554, 596, 597, 631, 642, 645, 676, 701, 702, 714, 716, 724, 727, 744, 769, 793, 799, 802; VII, 22, 25, 33, 51, 68, 69, 80, 88, 97, 109, 129, 135, 166, 168, 172, 179, 180, 183, 189, 190, 191, 197, 204, 225, 226, 233, 242, 258, 259, 266, 282, 286, 287, 310, 312, 314, 317, 326, 348, 372, 393, 433, 465, 494, 512, 518, 532, 537, 547, 553, 566, 623, 645, 646, 647, 649, 650, 689, 701, 703, 719, **722–33**, 740, 742, 743, 770, 771, 787, 788, 789, 790, 798, 811, 818, 824, 872, 877, 878, 879, 884, 889, 905, 907, 908, 911, 922, 931, 932, 933; VIII, xxiv, xxvii, xxxiv, 18, 125, 128, 141, 154, 155, 159, 207, 331, 354, 355, 374, 375, 384, 385, 393, 404, 457, 459, 460, 461, 462, 463, 501, 506, 596, 598, 599, 603, 605, 665, 706, 717, 755, 777, 791, 838, 844, 901, 907, 914, 938, 962; IX, 113, 133, 174, 189, 219, 246, 276, 302, 313, 560, 594, 596, 610, 613, 637, 718, 797, 801, 810, 849; X, 516, 526, 528, 544, 655; XI, 72, 187, 889
Ramsay, George, 12th Earl of Dalhousie, X, 590; XI, 881
Ramsay, Hew, VIII, 22; IX, 429
Ramsay, James, XII, 314
Ramsay, Margaret (Crooks), VIII, 185, 190
Ramsay, Thomas Kennedy, X, 135; XI, 234, 623, **721–22**
Ramsey, Alexander, XI, 764; XII, 1030
Ramsey, Martha. *See* Burch
Ramsey, Mary (Gordon), IX, 325; X, 308

Ramusio, Giovanni Battista, I, 151, 153, 154, 170, 235, 658, 660
Ranc, Blanche (Mathevet), IV, 521
Rancin, Madeleine-Ursule (Hedouin; Janson, *dit* Lapalme), III, 306
Rancour, Joseph, III, 138
Rand, Deborah. *See* Tupper
Rand, Eliza Irene. *See* Barnaby
Rand, Emeline Augusta. *See* Eaton
Rand, Jane Elizabeth. *See* McNutt
Rand, Mary (Bill), XII, 108
Rand, Silas, XI, 722
Rand, Silas Tertius, VII, 437, 610; XI, **722–24**; XII, 319, 764
Rand, Theodore Harding, IX, 272; XI, 158, 210, 381, 577; XII, **879–84**
Rand, Thomas Woodworth, XII, 879
Randal, Benjamin, VII, 733
Randal, Lamira Juliana. *See* Munson
Randal, Robert, VI, 11, 116, 229, 248, 266, 543, 611, **628–33**, 747; VII, 312, 314, 319, 494, 794, 833; VIII, 69, 599, 602, 689; IX, 497, 498, 673, 684; XII, 1078
Randal, Roxana. *See* Case
Randal, Stephen, VII, **733–34**, 810
Randall, Benjamin, IV, 20
Randall, James, V, 783
Randall, Joseph, V, 783
Randall, Lydia, VIII, 611
Randin, Hugues, I, **565**; II, 59, 262
Randolph, Anna (Johnston), IX, 414
Randolph, Edward, II, 247
Randolph of Roanoke, John, VI, 55
Ranger, François, VII, 239
Ranjit Singh, VII, 603
Rankin, Alexander, VIII, 738
Rankin, Alexander, VI, 757; VII, 4, 5, 343, 344; VIII, xxv, **736–40**, 753; IX, 147, 171, 177, 452, 652, 653, 766, 767; X, 271, 712; XII, 741
Rankin, Ann. *See* Strang
Rankin, Arthur, VIII, 966; IX, 646, 726; X, 126; XI, 649; XII, 146, 648, **884–85**
Rankin, Catherine. *See* Maclean
Rankin, Charles Stuart, VIII, 437; X, 259; XI, 244; XII, 884
Rankin, Coun Douly, VII, 734, 735; VIII, 484, **740–42**
Rankin, Flora. *See* Morison
Rankin, George (father of ARTHUR), XII, 884
Rankin, George (son of COUN DOULY), VII, 734
Rankin, Helen. *See* Ferguson
Rankin, James (father of ALEXANDER and ROBERT), VIII, 736; IX, 652
Rankin, James (son of ROBERT), IX, 653
Rankin, James (surveyor), IV, 162
Rankin, John (businessman), XI, 362
Rankin, John (nephew of ROBERT), VII, 343, 344; IX, 652, 653; XI, 349, 350
Rankin, John, III, 449, **544**, 663
Rankin, Margaret. *See* Maclaine
Rankin, Mary. *See* Collins
Rankin, Mary. *See* McKee
Rankin, Mary. *See* Stuart
Rankin, Mary (McDonald), VIII, 526
Rankin, Neil, VIII, 741

Rankin, Robert, VII, 344; VIII, 738, 753; IX, **652–54**; X, 306, 314, 315; XI, 349; XII, 376
Rankin, William, VII, **734–35**
Rankine, Mary (Dawson), XII, 230
Ranney, Henrietta (Miller), XI, 593
Ranney, Maria Susan (Chewett), XII, 188
Ransom, Abigail Hyde (Street), VII, 832; X, 668
Ransonnet, Sylvestre-François-Michel, III, **544–45**, 630
Ranuyer, Mathieu, II, 130
Ranville. *See* Baby
Ranvoizé, Étienne, V, 707
Ranvoizé, Jeanne. *See* Poitras
Ranvoyzé, Étienne, IV, 332; V, 708, 709; VI, **633–34**; VII, 119, 622; IX, 533
Ranvoyzé, François, III, 346; IV, 205, 206; V, 51, 218, 329, 437, **707–10**; VI, 183, 488, 572, 633; VII, 17, 752
Ranvoyzé, Françoise. *See* Fillion
Ranvoyzé, François-Ignace, V, 709; VI, 634
Ranvoyzé, Louis (uncle), V, 709
Ranvoyzé, Louis, V, 708; VI, 634
Ranvoyzé, Marie-Vénérande. *See* Pelerin
Ranvoyzé, Marie-Vénérande (Deblois), X, 136
Raoul, Jeanne (Savonnières de La Troche), I, 603
Raoûx, Claire (Faillon), IX, 246
Rapelje, Abraham A., V, 734
Raphaël. *See* Santi
Raphael*, William (1833–1914), XII, 789
Raphaël de Luxembourg, Father, II, 41; III, 40, 41
Rapine de Boisvert, Charles, I, 219, 484, 485
Rapp, John George, VIII, 316
Rashleigh, Robert, IV, 58; V, 173, 396, 416, 494, 789, 843
Rashley, Richard Ernest, VIII, 386
Rasilly. *See* Launay-Rasilly; Razilly
Rasle (Rasles). *See* Rale
Rastel de Rocheblave, Anne-Elmire de. *See* Bouthillier
Rastel de Rocheblave, Louise-Elmire de, VII, 738
Rastel de Rocheblave, Marie-Michelle de. *See* Dufresne
Rastel de Rocheblave, Philippe-François de, IV, 322; V, 175, 243; VI, 586; VII, 688, 735, 737
Rastel de Rocheblave, Pierre de, V, 544; VI, 30, 387; VII, 227, 688, 717, **735–39**; VIII, 350, 504
Rastell, Elizabeth. *See* More
Rastell, John, I, 565, 566
Rastell, John, I, 371, **565–66**
Rastoulle, François, VI, 664
Rastrick, Anna Mary. *See* Stephens
Rastrick, Edward Lewellyn, XII, 886
Rastrick, Francis Reginald, XII, 886
Rastrick, Frederick James, XII, **885–87**
Rastrick, John Urpeth (grandfather), XII, 885
Rastrick, John Urpeth, XII, 886
Rastrick, Sarah (mother of FREDERICK JAMES), XII, 885
Rat, Le. *See* Kondiaronk
Ratchford, James, VIII, 15
Ratchford, Maria Sophia (Starr), XI, 846
Rateau, Marie (Létourneau; Guillot, *dit* Larose; Sicard), IV, 320
Rathbun*, Edward Wilkes (1842–1903), XII, 70, 322
Rathbun, Hugo Burghardt, XI, 852, 853; XII, 70, 322
Rathdowne, Earl of. *See* Monck
Rathery, Louise de (Jordy), II, 185
Rattan. *See* Ruttan

453

Ratté, François, VIII, 328
Rattenbury*, Francis Mawson (1867–1935), XII, 1049
Rattier, Catherine. *See* Rousseau
Rattier, Jean, II, xxiv, **549**
Rattier, Marie. *See* Rivière
Rattier, Pierre, II, 549; III, 398
Rattray, Alexander, XI, 724
Rattray, William Jordan, XI, **724–25**; XII, 668
Raudin. *See* Randin
Raudot, Antoine-Denis, II, 7, 9, 48, 120, 121, 125, 242, 270, 286, 301, **549–54**, 555, 556, 559, 560, 570, 587, 608, 632; III, 57, 88, 104, 112, 563
Raudot, Françoise. *See* Gioux
Raudot, Jacques, I, 452; II, 13, 41, 42, 52, 57, 58, 111, 120, 121, 131, 132, 139, 147, 155, 173, 201, 223, 224, 234, 252, 276, 277, 283, 286, 301, 305, 325, 327, 372, 375, 381, 384, 402, 406, 413, 430, 432, 448, 465, 484, 508, 526, 535, 541, 550, 551, 552, **554–61**, 562, 566, 569, 574, 576, 587, 597, 604, 632, 672; III, 53, 57, 81, 83, 104, 112, 190, 191, 205, 220, 233, 234, 498, 520, 523, 563, 570
Raudot, Jean, II, 549, 555
Raudot, Jean-Baptiste, II, 555
Raudot, Louis-François, II, 555
Raudot, Marguerite. *See* Talon
Raudot, Marguerite-Françoise, II, 555
Raudot de Chalus, Jacques-Denis, II, 555, 558, 560; III, 104
Raux, Joseph-Alexandre, V, 271
Rauzan, David de, VII, 305
Ravel, Jean-Baptiste, V, 680
Raven (Sunday) (mother of Ranald MACDONALD), VIII, 526; XII, 612
Ravensberg. *See* Brasseur de Bourbourg, Charles-Étienne
Ravensworth, Earl of. *See* Liddell
Ravillon. *See* La Court
Rawdon-Hastings, Francis, 1st Marquess of Hastings, V, 811; VII, 439
Rawlings, Elizabeth (Fisher), VI, 256
Rawlinson, Ann Eliza. *See* Hawkins
Rawson, Jane (Black), V, 84
Rawson, Rawson William, VIII, 432
Rawson, Sentlow, V, 84
Ray, James H., IX, 625
Ray, Walter John, XII, 864
Raybould, William, XI, 638
Raye, Pierre, I, 493
Rayleigh, Baron. *See* Strutt
Raymbaut, Charles, I, 388, 549, **566–67**; II, 157
Raymo (Raymond), John Edward, VII, 247
Raymond. *See also* Raimond
Raymond, Adèle (Morin), IX, 568
Raymond, Angélique. *See* Leroux d'Esneval
Raymond, Angélique (Lanctôt), X, 420
Raymond, Archange. *See* Denaut
Raymond, Clotilde (Pinsonaut), VI, 584, 635; XI, 692
Raymond, Étienne, III, 617
Raymond, George, I, 279, 499
Raymond, Hermine (Varin), XI, 277
Raymond, Jean-Baptiste, XII, 105
Raymond, Jean-Baptiste, VI, 383, 471, 584, **634–36**; VII, 395, 593, 739; XI, 692
Raymond, Jean-Louis de, Comte de Raymond, III, 6, 50,

136, 183, 229, 231, 417, 498, 616; IV, 28, 401, 438, 439, 443, 444, 630, 631, 644, 645, **655–57**
Raymond, Jean-Moïse, VI, 635; VII, 148, 666, 667, **739–40**; VIII, 501; X, 420; XI, 692
Raymond, Joseph, IX, 568
Raymond, Joseph-Marie, III, 617
Raymond, Joseph-Sabin, VI, 288; VII, 656; VIII, 457, 593, 711, 712, 713; IX, 465, 466, 568; X, 429, 430; XI, 289, 290, 493, 494, **725–26**; XII, 255, 720, 820, 1003
Raymond, Maria (Wright), XI, 938
Raymond, Marie-Cécile. *See* Mignot
Raymond, Marie-Clotilde. *See* Girardin
Raymond, Marie-Françoise. *See* Damours de Louvières
Raymond, Marie-Geneviève-Sophie (Masson), VI, 635; VII, 593, 595; X, 498; XII, 173
Raymond, Rémi, X, 429; XII, 720
Raymond, William, IX, 170
Raymond*, William Odber (1853–1923), IV, 723; V, 60, 155, 590, 869; VII, 288, 291; VIII, 509; XI, 448; XII, 537, 717
Raymond Des Rivières, Charles de, IV, 655, 657
Raynal, Guillaume, V, 165, 202, 233, 248, 486; VII, 677; XI, 490
Raynaud. *See* Blanchard
Rayncer, Joseph, XII, 451
Rayner, John, I, **567**
Raynsforde, Thomas, I, 279
Razilly. *See also* Launay-Rasilly
Razilly, Catherine de. *See* Valliers
Razilly, François de (father), I, 567
Razilly, François de, I, 209, 567
Razilly, Gabriel de, I, 567
Razilly, Isaac de, I, 25, 32, 54, 63, 196, 234, 247, 256, 258, 311, 442, 471, 482, 490, 502, 503, **567–69**, 593, 594, 642; II, 480
Ré. *See* Derré
Rea (Rae), Alexander (merchant), VI, 565
Rea (Rae), Alexander (politician), VIII, 564; IX, 157, 830; X, 184
Rea (Rae), Alice (Askin), V, 37
Read, Ann. *See* Miller
Read, Cinderella (Neelon), XII, 782
Read*, David Breakenridge (1823–1904), VI, 118; VIII, 341, 513, 596, 743; IX, 109, 677; XI, 143, 146; XII, 496
Read, Hannah Elizabeth. *See* Harper
Read, James, VIII, 743
Read, Jennet. *See* Breakenridge
Read, John, IV, 559
Read, John Landon, VIII, **743**
Read, Lydia. *See* Landon
Read, Mary (Morris), IV, 559; V, 607, 608
Read, Moses, VIII, 743
Read, Obediah, VIII, 743
Read, Rebecca P. (Laird), XII, 512, 513
Read, Robert, X, 294
Read, William Case, VIII, 743
Reade, Alfred, VII, 352, 353, 445; VIII, 809, 842; IX, 146, 147, 622, 767; X, 271, 644, 711
Reade, Charles, XII, 572, 922
Reade, Frances Elizabeth. *See* Colebrooke
Reade, George Hume, VII, 754
Reade*, John (1837–1919), IX, 390; X, 346, 347
Reade, Sarah (Cutler), VII, 223

Reade, Sarah (De Peyster), IV, 210
Reader, Joseph, XI, 712
Reader, Robert, XII, 92
Ready, Ellen. *See* Hincks
Ready, John, VI, 122, 360, 568, 737, 819; VII, 189, 415,
    511, **740–43**, 925; VIII, 37, 444, 484, 505, 506, 548,
    570, 827, 886
Ready, Sarah. *See* Tobin
Ready, Susanna. *See* Bromley
Real. *See* Corte-Real
Réaume, Sieur (trader), III, 145
Réaume, Agathe. *See* Lacelle
Réaume, Alexis, IV, 592, 593
Réaume, Angélique. *See* Beauchamp
Réaume, Charles, IV, 697
Réaume, Charles, V, **710–11**
Réaume, Hyacinthe, V, 710
Réaume, Julie-Marie (Hay), IV, 336
Reaume (Eaume), Louis, VIII, 446
Réaume, Marguerite (Howard), IV, 369
Réaume, Marguerite (Welles), IV, 697
Réaume, Marie-Anne (Gadiou; Bellet), VI, 49
Réaume, Marie-Louise (Fournerie de Vézon; Robertson),
    V, 714
Réaume, Marie-Luce-Amable. *See* Orillat
Réaume, Marie-Madeleine (Larchevesque; Chevallier), III,
    122
Réaume, Marie-Renée (Renaud, *dit* Cannard), IV, 658
Réaume, Mary Frances (Baby; Caldwell), VIII, 119
Réaume, Thérèse (Sanguinet), IV, 697
Réaume (Rhéaume), *dit* La Croix, Susanne (Baby, *dit*
    Dupéront), IV, 38; VI, 21; VIII, 33
Réaumur. *See* Ferchault
Reboul, Augustine-Marie. *See* Guillon
Reboul, Louis-Antoine, X, 609
Reboul, Louis-Étienne-Delille, X, **609–10**; XI, 244; XII,
    197, 780
Rebourceau, Marie (Groston), II, 267
Rebow, John Gurdon, XII, 68
Récamier, Joseph-Claude, XI, 57
Receveur, Marguerite (Boulanger), IX, 67
Rêche. *See* Resche
Récher, Jean-Félix, III, 11, 194, 198, 199, 259, **545–47**,
    554; IV, 100, 387; V, 379
Reconciled. *See* Cherououny
Record, Charles B., XI, **726–27**
Record, Charlotte. *See* Bennett
Record, Edwin Albert, XI, 727
Red Cloud, XI, 869
Red Crow. *See* Mékaisto
Red Crow, Frank. *See* Astohkimi
Reddish. *See* Raddish
Reddy, Thomas, V, 139
Red Eagle. *See* Mis-koo-kee-new
Redford, Mary (Harris), X, 334
Redgrave, Stephen, IX, 518
Red Head. *See* Kakšenthiony; Ononwarogo
Red Jacket. *See* Shakóye:wa:thaʔ
Redmond, Mary Jane (O'Reilly), X, 561
Redon, Louis, X, 260
Redouté, Pierre-Joseph, V, 592
Redpath, Elizabeth (Dougall), XI, 270
Redpath, Jane. *See* Drummond

Redpath, Janet. *See* McPhee
Redpath, John, VI, 220, 481, 554, 812; VII, 34, 129, 927;
    VIII, 543, 544, 552, 583; IX, 105, 430, **654–55**; X, 405,
    525; XI, 12, 269, 270, 557; XII, 808, 809, 846
Redpath, John James, IX, 655
Redpath, Peter, IX, 654, 655; XI, 10, 69, 557; XII, 236
Red Pheasant. *See* Pihew-kamihkosit
Red Plume, XII, 970
Redwood, Nicholas, I, 652
Reece, William Sheldon, XII, 442
Reed, Hayter, XI, 598, 599
Reed, J., VIII, 56
Reed, Jane (Glen), XI, 353
Reed, John Langham, XI, 492
Reed, Salyer, XI, 203
Reed, Solomon, V, 744
Reekie, Robert James, XI, 11
Reenan, Mary (Gourlay), IX, 330, 336
Rees, Evans, X, 610
Rees, William, VII, 319; VIII, 869, 870; IX, 706; X,
    **610–11**; XII, 1123
Reesor, David, XI, 312
Reeve, John, XII, 887
Reeve, Richard Andrews, XII, 887
Reeve, Sarah. *See* Bielby
Reeve, Sarah Theresa. *See* Bielby
Reeve, William, XII, 887
Reeve, William Albert, XII, **887–88**
Reeves, Mr (teaching assistant), IX, 452
Reeves, Émilie (Heath), X, 346
Reeves, Harriet Frances (Fanny) (McDowell), XII, 623
Reeves, James Augustus, XII, 945
Reeves, John, VI, 636
Reeves, John, IV, 713; V, 53, 361, 444, 596, 632, 726; VI,
    244, **636–37**, 796; VII, 152; X, 588; XII, 589
Reeves, Sophie. *See* Lafrenière
Régemortes, Noël de, III, 229, 230, 700
Regnard, Jean-François, V, 233; VIII, 702
Regnard Duplessis, François, II, 156
Regnard Duplessis, François-Xavier, II, 561; III, 549
Regnard Duplessis, Geneviève, named de l'Enfant-Jésus,
    III, 547
Regnard Duplessis, Georges, II, 14, 138, 214, 485, **561**; III,
    547, 549
Regnard Duplessis, Marie. *See* Le Roy
Regnard Duplessis, Marie-Andrée, named de Sainte-
    Hélène, II, 304, 333, 460, 561; III, **547–49**, 625, 690,
    711; IV, 189
Regnard Duplessis, Marie-Madeleine. *See* Coulon de
    Villiers
Regnard Duplessis de Morampont, Charles-Denis, III, 64,
    **549**
Regnard Duplessis de Morampont, Geneviève-Élisabeth.
    *See* Guillimin
Regnaud, Antoinette. *See* Gay
Regnaud, François-Joseph-Victor, VIII, 408; X, **611**
Regnault, Christophe, I, 124, 562
Régnier, Sophie (Gagnon), VII, 333
Regnouard, Marie (Giffard), I, 329, 330
Reiche. *See* Resche
Reickert, Catharine (mother of George RYKERT), VIII, 785
Reickert (Reichert, Rikert), Zacherius, VIII, 785
Reid, Mr (officer), VI, 411

Reid, Mr (schoolmaster), V, 768
Reid, Anne (Cobbett), VI, 154, 155
Reid, Christian. *See* Arnot
Reid, Euphemia (Jardine), IX, 409
Reid, Sir George, XII, 1114
Reid\*, George Agnew (1860–1947), XI, 683; XII, 288, 336, 830, 831
Reid, Hugo, IX, 510; X, **611–12**
Reid, Isabel, IX, 497
Reid, James (clergyman), VI, 528; VII, 212, 826
Reid, James (judge), V, 655; VI, 433; VII, 643, 872; IX, 568, 682
Reid, James Murray, IX, **655–56**
Reid, Janet (Hay), XI, 391
Reid, John, IV, 385; VIII, 842
Reid, Sir John Watt, XII, 1047
Reid, John Young, XII, 136
Reid, Marion. *See* Kirkland
Reid, Mary. *See* Petrie
Reid, Mary (Strickland), IX, 768
Reid, Peter, X, 611
Reid, Robert, VII, 829; IX, 768; X, 104
Reid\*, Sir Robert Gillespie (1842–1908), XII, 756
Reid, Robert Haley, XII, 470
Reid, Susanna. *See* Lawlor
Reid, Thomas (philosopher), XI, 534
Reid, Thomas (politician), XI, 391
Reid, Thomas (sergeant), VI, 155
Reiffenstein, John Christian, VII, 744
Reiffenstein, John Christopher, VI, 617; VII, **743–44**; VIII, 495
Reiffenstein, John Edward, VII, 743
Reiffenstein, Miriam. *See* Carr
Reigen, Frederick, X, 137
Reilly. *See also* O'Reilly
Reilly, Edward, IX, 824, 831, 832; X, 264, **612–13**; XI, 202, 549; XII, 369
Reilly, Hannah (wife of EDWARD), X, 613
Reilly, James, XII, 672
Reily, Elizabeth (McKenney; Schultz), XI, 562; XII, 949
Reimann, Anna Elizabeth (Kohlmeister), VII, 473
Reinel, Pedro, I, 235, 303, 304
Reinhard, Charles de, V, 466; VI, 100, 446
Reinhart, John, VIII, 359
Reis, Thérèse (Gugi), IV, 316
Reische. *See* Resche
Rembaud, François-Joseph, III, 8
Rémillard, Édouard, XI, 710
Remington, Simon J., XII, 556
Remington, Stephen, VII, 211
Remmington, John, VII, 273
Remogis, Françoise (Ameau), II, 16
Rémond, Jean-Baptiste-Moyse de, VI, 634
Rémus. *See* Romieux
Rémy, Élisabeth. *See* Le Moyne
Rémy, Marie (Céloron), II, 125
Rémy, Michel, II, 561
Rémy (Rémy de Saint-Rémy), Pierre, II, 125, 195, 528, **561–62**
Rémy de Courcelle, Daniel de, I, 33, 40, 48, 55, 62, 80, 108, 111, 120, 135, 174, 204, 308, 322, 327, 355, 393, 400, 402, 416, 452, 464, 539, 540, 543, 555, 556,

**569–72**, 581, 599, 615, 616, 617, 624, 625, 627, 629, 630; II, xix, 85, 106, 136, 141, 192, 195, 282, 385, 540, 579; III, 201
Renan, Ernest, XI, 776; XII, 223, 224
Renard, Baptiste, XII, 599
Renard, Marie (Bigot), IV, 59
Renardin de La Blanchetière, Françoise. *See* Ouary
Renardin de La Blanchetière, Marie (Le Vieux de Hauteville), I, 475
Renardin de La Blanchetière, Vincent, I, 475
Renau d'Éliçagaray, Bernard, III, 117
Renaud. *See also* Desferières
Renaud, Auguste, XI, 350
Renaud, Frances Mary (Sullivan), XII, 1000
Renaud, Hélène-Flavie. *See* Chicoux-Duvert
Renaud, Jean, IV, **657–58**; V, 601, 794; VI, 531
Renaud, Jean-Baptiste, X, 613; XI, 727
Renaud, Jean-Baptiste, X, 613; XI, 397, 586, **727–29**, 774, 814; XII, 1026
Renaud, Jean-Louis, XI, 728
Renaud, John Lewis, IV, 658
Renaud, Louis, III, 494
Renaud, Louis, X, **613–14**; XI, 275, 380, 556, 557, 586, 727, 893, 895
Renaud, Louise. *See* Bizard
Renaud, Marie. *See* Gariépy
Renaud, Marie. *See* Noyon
Renaud, Marie-Anne. *See* Pigeon
Renaud, Marie-Sophie. *See* Lefebvre
Renaud, Martha. *See* Sheldon
Renaud, Napoléon, X, 614
Renaud, Paul-Émile, IV, 376
Renaud, Pierre-Simon, V, 691; VI, 379
Renaud, Zoé-Aimée (Trudel), X, 614; XI, 894
Renaud, *dit* Cannard, Marie. *See* Gariépy
Renaud, *dit* Cannard, Marie-Renée. *See* Réaume
Renaud, *dit* Cannard, Michel, IV, 658
Renaud, *dit* Cannard, Pierre, IV, 202, **658–59**
Renaud d'Avène de Desmeloizes, François-Marie, I, **572–73**; II, 205; III, 112, 549
Renaud d'Avène de Desmeloizes, Françoise-Thérèse. *See* Dupont de Neuville
Renaud d'Avène de Desmeloizes, Marie-Françoise (Chartier de Lotbinière), III, 112; IV, 141, 143
Renaud d'Avène de Des Méloizes et de Berges, Adrienne. *See* Montsaulnin
Renaud d'Avène de Des Méloizes et de Berges, Edmé (Aimé), I, 572
Renaud d'Avène Des Méloizes, Agathe-Louise. *See* Fresnoy
Renaud d'Avène Des Méloizes, Angélique. *See* Chartier de Lotbinière
Renaud d'Avène Des Méloizes, Angélique (Péan), III, 551; IV, 66, 459, 614, 615, 616, 621, 642, **659–60**
Renaud d'Avène Des Méloizes, Catherine-Madeleine, II, 129
Renaud d'Avène Des Méloizes, Louis-François, V, 711
Renaud d'Avène Des Méloizes, Marie-Jeanne, II, 463
Renaud d'Avène Des Méloizes, Nicolas, III, 550; IV, 88; V, **711**
Renaud d'Avène Des Méloizes, Nicolas-Marie, I, 572; II, 463; III, 5, 112, **549–51**; IV, 173, 358, 659; V, 711
Renaud Dubuisson, Gabrielle. *See* Pinet

Renaud Dubuisson, Jacques-Charles, II, 68, 122, 128, 515, **562–63**, 627, 645; III, 491, 551, 576, 577
Renaud Dubuisson, Louise (Tonty de Liette), III, 627
Renaud Dubuisson, Louis-Jacques-Charles, III, **551–52**
Renaud Dubuisson, Madeleine (Chabert de Joncaire), III, 101
Renaud Dubuisson, Marie-Charlotte (Catalogne), II, 122
Renaud Dubuisson, Thérèse. *See* Godefroy
Renaudot, Eusèbe, I, 174, 175, 179; II, 517
Rende. *See* Larrante
Rendell, Catharine. *See* Norris
Rendell, Elias, V, 119, 120
Rendell, Herbert, XII, 158
Rendell, John, XII, 888
Rendell, Stephen, X, 381; XII, **888–89**
Renden (Rendin). *See* Randin
Render, Thomas, II, 10, 62, **563–64**
René, Patrice, III, **552**, 681, 682
Renforth, James, XII, 462
Renfrew, Allan Edmund, XII, 890
Renfrew, Eliza Jane. *See* Tweddle
Renfrew, George Richard, XII, **889–91**
Renfrew, Mary Ann Jane. *See* Henderson
Renfrew, Thomas, XII, 889
Reni, Guido, XI, 309, 310
Rennie, Adam, VII, 15
Rennie, David, IX, 159
Rennie, John, VI, 481
Renny, Agnes (Young), VII, 930; VIII, 955; XI, 943
Renny, William, XI, 944
Renon. *See* Du Pont
Renou, *dit* La Chapelle, François, I, 321, 578
Renou, *dit* La Chapelle, Marguerite. *See* Crevier
Renouard, Henri, VII, 28
Renswore, Dame (widow), II, 279
Renton, James, VIII, 762
Renton, Jane (Vincent), VI, 795
Renty, Gaston, Baron de Renty, I, 214, 219
Réopelle, Dominique, VI, 666
Repentigny. *See also* Legardeur; Terrier
Repentigny, Mme de (of Montreal), II, 187
Requiem, Marie-Joseph. *See* La Roche
Resche, François, III, 553
Resche, Marguerite. *See* Pinard
Resche, Pierre-Joseph, III, 223, **553–54**; IV, 535; V, 196
Rességuier, Marguerite de (Galaup), IV, 282
Retor. *See* Devau
Retz, François, III, 360
Réveillaud, Eugène, IX, 256
Reventa. *See* Eliza
Revilla Gigedo, Count of. *See* Güemes
Révol, Hélène. *See* Bastard
Révol, Jacques, III, 554
Révol, Marie-Charlotte. *See* Roy
Révol, Pierre, III, **554–55**; IV, 243, 386, 729; V, 276
Rexford*, Elson Irving (1850–1936), XI, 523
Rey Gaillard, Françoise. *See* Gailleteau
Rey Gaillard, Pierre, I, 261; II, 106, 129, 256; III, 509
Reymer, Nicholas, II, 264
Reynard, Alexis, X, **614–15**; XI, 310
Reynard, Alexis-Joseph, X, 614
Reynard, Victoire. *See* Dugas
Reyner. *See also* Rayner

Reyner, William, I, 567
Reynolds, Miss (Ward), IX, 820
Reynolds, Dorothy (Coates), IX, 131
Reynolds, Edmund John, XII, 330
Reynolds, Elizabeth Winslow (Comingo), VI, 168, 169
Reynolds, Frederic, VII, 110
Reynolds, James, XII, 963
Reynolds, John (bishop), IX, 729
Reynolds, John (publisher), VII, 664; VIII, 228
Reynolds, Sir Joshua, IV, 26, 122, 702; V, 824; XI, 915; XII, 100
Reynolds, Michael, VIII, 228
Reynolds, Thomas, XI, 556, 557
Reynolds*, William Kilby (1848–1902), XII, 20
Rézé, Joseph-Pierre, XII, **891–92**
Rézé, Louise. *See* Chevalier
Rézé, Michel, XII, 891
Rézine. *See* Raizenne
Rhéaume (Rheaume). *See also* Réaume
Rhéaume, Angèle (Besserer), IX, 48
Rhéaume, Charlotte-Euphémie (Blain de Saint-Aubin), XI, 82
Rhéaume, Jacques-Philippe, IX, 33; XI, 82
Rhéaume, Joseph, VII, 138
Rhoades, John, I, 39, 40, 185, **573**
Rhodes, Alexandre de, II, 360
Rhodes, Elizabeth (Williams), XI, 930
Rhodes, James, XII, 788
Rhodes, William, IX, 274; XI, 774; XII, 864
Riall, Catherine. *See* Caldwell
Riall, Elizabeth, Lady Riall. *See* Scarlett
Riall, Phineas, VII, 744
Riall, Sir Phineas, V, 642; VI, 182, 212, 541, 661; VII, 312, **744–46**, 889; VIII, 236, 237
Ribaut (Ribault), Jean, I, 333, 469
Ribbel. *See* Ribble
Ribble, Anthony, VI, 92
Ribble, David, VI, 92
Ribble (Ribbel), Henry, VI, 91, 92
Ribble, William, VI, 91
Ribenzki, Catherine (Bigault d'Aubreville), VI, 59
Ribero, Pedro, I, 342
Riberpré, Monsieur de (patron), I, 88
Ricard, Françoise (Forestier), II, 226
Ricard, Narcisse-Édouard, IX, 247
Ricard, Pascal, X, 322; XI, 401; XII, 282, 817
Ricardo, David, VII, 645
Ricci, Lorenzo, III, 580
Riccoboni, Marie-Jeanne, IV, 553
Rice. *See also* Spring-Rice
Rice, Elizabeth. *See* Putnam
Rice, Elizabeth (Chandler), VIII, 138; X, 157
Rice, Fanny Lavinia. *See* Starr
Rice, Francis William, 5th Baron Dynevor, XI, 208
Rice, Frasquita (Fanny) (Mercer), IX, 543
Rice, Henry, III, 615
Rice, Henry Mower, XII, 1029
Rice, Jacob, II, 163, 291, 534, **564**, 636; III, 219
Rice, Mary (Button), I, 144
Rice, Mary Ann. *See* Konwatewenteta
Rice, Samuel, XI, 729
Rice, Samuel Dwight, VII, 854; VIII, 134; XI, **729–30**, 931; XII, 10, 142

457

Rice, Sarah (Sally) (Cushing), X, 211
Rice, Susannah (Baker), VI, 30
Rice, Thomas, II, 564
Rice, Sir Walter, I, 144
Rich, Edwin Ernest, V, 683, 685; VII, 567; VIII, 413
Rich, Henry, Earl of Holland, I, 369, 405
Rich, Robert, 1st Earl of Warwick, I, 67, 69
Rich, Ruhama (Emery; Noble), V, 627
Rich, Sir Thomas, VIII, 669
Rich, William Bennett, VII, 260
Richard III, King of England, I, 120, 239
Richard, André, I, 266, 477, 539
Richard, Anne. *See* Meusnier
Richard, Anne (Lascoret; Lannelongue), III, 350
Richard, Catherine (Brossard), II, 105; III, 87
Richard, Charles-Auguste, X, 615
Richard*, Édouard-Émery (1844–1904), III, 34; X, 615
Richard, Euphrasie (Dupuis), X, 265
Richard, Françoise (Dupuy), X, 266
Richard, Gabriel, VI, 486
Richard, Hermine. *See* Prince
Richard, Jean. *See also* Richards, Jackson John
Richard, Jean (father of Guillaume RICHARD, *dit* Lafleur), I, 573
Richard, Jean (interpreter), I, 573
Richard, Jean-Baptiste, I, 573; II, 673
Richard, Jeanne. *See* Bonnet
Richard, Louis, VI, 315
Richard, Louis-Claude, V, 593
Richard, Louis-Eusèbe, X, **615**
Richard, Madeleine. *See* Blanchard
Richard*, Marcel-François (1847–1915), XII, 40, 548
Richard, Marguerite (Dugas), IV, 239
Richard, Marguerite (Levasseur, *dit* Lavigne), I, 473
Richard, Marie. *See* Hébert
Richard, Marie (Robichaud), VI, 228
Richard, Marie-Anne. *See* You de La Découverte
Richard, Michel, II, 105
Richard, Pierre, XII, 282, 284, 817
Richard, Suzanne (Parant), I, 573
Richard, *dit* Lafleur, Guillaume, I, **573–74**
Richard, *dit* Lafond, Michel, III, 173
Richard de Goigni, Anne (Blaise Des Bergères de Rigauville), II, 68, 69
Richardie. *See* La Richardie
Richards, Albert Elswood, XII, 330
Richards, Albert Norton, IX, 100; X, 201; XI, 730; XII, 330
Richards, Alice Mary. *See* Tabor
Richards, Anna (mother of JACKSON JOHN), VII, 746
Richards, Calcina (Buell), X, 110
Richards, Deborah Catherine. *See* Muirhead
Richards, Eleanor. *See* Thomas
Richards, Elizabeth (Rogers), XII, 921
Richards, Emma Jane (mother of Sir GEORGE HENRY), XII, 892
Richards, Francis, II, 93
Richards, Sir George Henry, VIII, 97; IX, 36; X, 562, 563; XI, 201; XII, **892–93**
Richards, George Spencer, XII, 892
Richards, Jackson John, VI, 592, 668, 669; VII, **746–47**; VIII, 490
Richards, Jacob, II, 564

Richards, John (ancestor of Guillaume RICHARD, *dit* Lafleur), I, 573
Richards, John (father of WILLIAM), IV, 727; V, 711, 712
Richards, John (loyalist), V, 772
Richards, John (shipbuilder), IX, 425
Richards, Margaret (Spencer), V, 772
Richards, Mary. *See* Young
Richards, Michael, II, 260, 261, 274, 290, 293, 373, 438, 486, 534, **564–65**, 582; III, 488
Richards, Phoebe. *See* Buell
Richards, Stephen (father), XI, 730
Richards, Stephen, X, 467; XI, 203, 652, 730, 780; XII, 146, 887
Richards, Thomas (father of JACKSON JOHN), VII, 746
Richards, Thomas (uncle of WILLIAM), V, 711, 712
Richards, William, III, 124; V, 711
Richards, William, IV, 33; V, **711–12**
Richards, Sir William Buell, VIII, 305; IX, 100, 835; X, 312, 463; XI, 399, 671, **730–31**; XII, 146, 184, 400, 898
Richardson, Mr (merchant), VI, 243
Richardson, Ann (Ogden; Anderson), X, 10
Richardson, Anne. *See* Mundell
Richardson, Barbara. *See* McConnachay
Richardson, Cécile (Cecilia) (Moore), II, 487
Richardson, Charles, VI, 498
Richardson, Daniel, XII, 893
Richardson, Edward, IX, 656
Richardson, Edward Mallcott, IX, **656–57**
Richardson, Eliza. *See* Austen
Richardson, Eliza (Fothergill), VII, 317
Richardson, Elizabeth (Hart), XII, 893
Richardson, Euphemia (Robson), XII, 914
Richardson, Eweretta Jane (Auldjo), VI, 19
Richardson, Frances (wife of HUGH), IX, 657
Richardson, Frances (Lambly), IX, 453
Richardson, Gabriel, IX, 658
Richardson, George Armstrong, XII, 893, 894
Richardson, Georgina McIntosh (Campbell), XI, 149
Richardson, Helen (Auldjo), VII, 28
Richardson, Henry Hobson, XII, 131, 345, 993
Richardson, Henry Wartman, XII, 893, 894
Richardson, Hugh, VII, 178, 506, 833; IX, 49, 128, 241, 346, **657–58**; XI, 378
Richardson*, Hugh (1826–1913), XI, 600, 748, 749; XII, 152, 674
Richardson, James, X, 615
Richardson, James, VI, **638–39**
Richardson, James, VI, 638, 675; VIII, 133, 440; IX, 27, 730, 749; X, **615–17**; XI, 796; XII, 297
Richardson, James, IX, 419; X, 445; XI, 49, 50, 632, **731–32**
Richardson, James, XII, **893–95**
Richardson*, James Armstrong (1885–1939), XII, 894
Richardson, James Henry, VIII, 58, 935
Richardson, Jane. *See* Marsh
Richardson, Jane (Grieve), XI, 376
Richardson, Janet. *See* Armstrong
Richardson, John, VI, 639
Richardson, John, IV, 39, 261; V, 183, 212, 233, 300, 320, 326, 327, 333, 372, 374, 384, 485, 512, 566, 572, 636, 691, 697, 816, 820, 864, 882; VI, 18, 19, 95, 96, 97, 204, 210, 226, 272, 297, 433, 456, 471, 532, 533, 602, **639–47**, 702, 764, 765; VII, 28, 225, 309, 310, 311, 614,

619, 620, 622, 719, 728, 730, 736, 768, 770, 783, 786, 818, 825, 878; VIII, 194, 321, 322, 388, 663, 690; IX, 554, 811; X, 10; XI, 272
Richardson, John, V, 800; VI, 530, 618, 809; VII, 732, 792, 855; VIII, 22, 366, **743–48**, 921; X, 536; XII, 570
Richardson, Sir John, VI, 218, 221, 222, 328, 754; VII, 324, 325, 326, 327, 463, 599; VIII, 686; IX, 6, 43, 389, 390, **658–61**; X, 26, 27, 28, 38; XI, 436, 509, 543, 662, 799, 885; XII, 876, 877
Richardson, Katherine Elizabeth (Archibald), XI, 28
Richardson, Lucy (Buchanan), VIII, 109
Richardson, Madelaine. See Askin
Richardson, Margaret Ann (Foreman), X, 293
Richardson, Maria Caroline. See Drayson
Richardson, Mary. See Booth
Richardson, Mary. See Fletcher
Richardson, Mary. See Stiven
Richardson, Mary Louisa. See McDonnell
Richardson, Matthew, IV, 111
Richardson, Patience (Wright), VII, 926
Richardson, Prudence. See Caldwell
Richardson, Rebecca. See Dennis
Richardson, Robert (father-in-law of James NEVINS), XII, 785
Richardson, Robert (father of JOHN, 1796–1852), VIII, 743
Richardson, Robert (son of JAMES, d. 1832), VI, 638
Richardson, Roxanna. See Day
Richardson, Samuel, IV, 553
Richardson, Samuel, VII, **747–48**
Richardson, Sarah. See Ashmore
Richardson, Sarah Ann. See Grant
Richardson, Susannah. See Wartman
Richardson, Susannah (Nevins), XII, 785
Richardson, Thomas, IX, 657
Richaume, Marie-Madeleine (Brunet, dit La Sablonnière), III, 87
Richebourg, Chavagne de, II, 203
Richelieu. See Vignerot
Richelieu, Cardinal de. See Du Plessis
Richer. See also Dagron-Richer
Richer, Edmond, I, 629
Richer, Jean, I, 225
Richer, Pierre-Daniel, III, 360
Richer-Laflèche. See also Laflèche
Richer-Laflèche, Louis-Modeste, XII, 506
Richer-Laflèche, Marie-Anne. See Joubin-Boisvert
Richer-Laflèche, Modeste, XII, 506
Richerville. See also Drouet
Richerville, Monsieur (scout), III, 399
Richerville, Josette (Le Blanc), VI, 390
Richery, Joseph de, V, 675
Richeterre. See Dessailliant
Richey, Louisa Matilda. See Nichols
Richey, Matthew, VIII, 83, 373, 478; IX, 187, 635; XI, **733–35**
Richey, Matthew Henry, XI, 734
Richey, Wellesley, VII, 755
Richier, Thérèse (Guigues), X, 322
Richmond, Duke of. See Lennox
Richmond, Isabel (Hooper), XI, 421
Richmond, Isabella (Gledhill), II, 250
Richmond, Lennox and Aubigny, Duke of. See Lennox

Richmond, Silvester, II, 671
Richmond and Lennox, Duchess of. See Gordon
Richmond and Lennox, Duke of. See Lennox
Richomme, Françoise (Sarcel de Prévert), I, 602
Richter, Adrian Ludwig, VIII, 13
Rickard, Elizabeth (Doggett), IV, 219
Ricker, Lois (Wright), XII, 1129
Rickman, Julia Agnes (Shaw), VI, 704
Rictenburgh, Catherine. See London
Riday-Beauceron. See Ridé
Ridday, dit Beauceron, Jean, III, 472, 473
Riddell, Archibald Alexander, IX, 507
Riddell, Sir Charles James Buchanan, XI, 799
Riddell, Sir John, VI, 698
Riddell, Robert, XI, 409
Riddell*, William Renwick (1852–1945), IV, 230; VI, 118, 389, 560, 613; VII, 865; IX, 58; XII, 782
Riddle, Mary. See Noble
Ridé (Riday-Beauceron), Marie-Louise (Viger), V, 833
Rideout, Molly (Carroll), XI, 153
Rider, Elizabeth (Cobb), III, 128
Rider, Lydia (Cobb), III, 128
Ridge. See MacDonald
Ridley, George Neville, VII, 580
Ridley, Nicholas, VIII, 521
Ridley, Thomas, VIII, 435
Ridley, Thomas, VII, 112; VIII, 199; X, 538, **617–18**; XII, 770
Ridley, Thomas Harrison, X, 617, 618
Ridley, William, X, 617
Ridley, William, XII, 290, 443, 552
Ridout, Anna Maria Louisa. See Sullivan
Ridout, Belle. See Nelson
Ridout, Caroline. See Cumberland
Ridout, Caroline Amelia (Humphreys), VIII, 750; X, 371
Ridout, Dorothy. See McCuaig
Ridout, E. H., XII, 291
Ridout, Eliza. See Parsons
Ridout, Frances Elizabeth (Small), IX, 724
Ridout, George (father of GEORGE PERCIVAL and JOSEPH DAVIS), X, 619; XI, 735
Ridout, George (father of THOMAS), VI, 647
Ridout, George, V, 522; VI, 647, 648, 770; VIII, 7, 28, 427, 733, 750, 855, 932; IX, 724; X, 62, 344, 345, **618–19**; XI, 864
Ridout, George Charmbury, VIII, 748
Ridout, George Percival, VIII, 748, 749, 801; X, 80, 119, **619–20**; XI, 501, 676, 735, 736
Ridout, George Samuel, VIII, 750
Ridout, Isabella (mother of SAMUEL SMITH, wife of THOMAS), VI, 647; VIII, 749
Ridout, John (uncle), VI, 164; VII, 418; VIII, 431; IX, 771, 674, 724; X, 618
Ridout, John, VIII, 750
Ridout, Joseph Davis, VII, 652; VIII, 748; X, 619, 620; XI, 225, 501, 676, **735–36**
Ridout, Julia Elizabeth. See Bramley
Ridout, Lionel Augustus Clark, VIII, **748–49**; XI, 501
Ridout, Louisa. See Lawrason
Ridout, Lucy Edith (Radenhurst), VIII, 732
Ridout, Mary. See Campbell
Ridout, Mary Ann. See Wright
Ridout, Mary Hardwick. See Unwin

Ridout*, Matilda (Edgar, Lady Edgar) (1844–1910), XII, 291

Ridout, Matilda Ann. *See* Bramley

Ridout, Samuel Smith, VI, 647; VIII, **749–50**; X, 371, 509, 619

Ridout, Septimus Adolphus, VIII, 748

Ridout, Thomas, IX, 662; XI, 225, 226

Ridout, Thomas, V, 65, 66, 846; VI, 52, 406, 416, **647–48**, 657; VII, 175, 207, 319, 350, 794, 822; VIII, 6, 418, 431, 523, 642, 732, 749, 858; IX, 661, 724; X, 618, 619

Ridout, Thomas Gibbs, VI, 647, 648; VII, 418, 929; VIII, 6, 7, 517, 750, 897; IX, 647, **661–63**, 746; X, 619; XI, 156, 225, 226, 427, 618, 736; XII, 291

Ridsdale, Francis, VI, 166

Riedesel, America von (Bernstorff, Countess von Bernstorff), V, 583

Riedesel, Friederike Charlotte Louise von, Frelin zu Eisenbach. *See* Massow

Riedesel, Friedrich Adolph von, Freiherr zu Eisenbach, IV, 589; V, 457, 582, 583, 747, 896; VI, 378, 788; VII, 348

Riedesel, Georg Karl von, Freiherr zu Eisenbach, V, 583

Riedesel, Louisa Augusta Elizabeth Canada von, V, 583

Riel, Julie. *See* Lagimonière

Riel, Louis, VII, 777; VIII, 344, 482; IX, 95, **663**, 802; X, 47; XI, 139, 736, 737, 875, 876; XII, 125

Riel, Louis, VI, 548; VII, 173; VIII, 171, 344, 482; IX, 329, 330, 531, 617, 618, 626, 663, 707, 708; X, 59, 67, 70, 111, 148, 149, 198, 210, 230, 296, 297, 357, 377, 439, 468, 472, 476, 556, 557, 559, 628, 630, 631, 646, 669, 677, 729, 756; XI, 27, 45, 46, 47, 62, 64, 80, 112, 145, 151, 163, 192, 193, 194, 207, 245, 250, 267, 306, 322, 330, 331, 383, 424, 441, 442, 444, 456, 459, 461, 478, 488, 493, 507, 520, 538, 540, 546, 563, 571, 599, 600, 610, 611, 624, 628, 643, 644, 655, 696, 697, 707, 716, **736–52**, 763, 776, 777, 842, 844, 870, 935; XII, 20, 23, 33, 34, 35, 36, 37, 65, 82, 88, 96, 119, 125, 132, 148, 152, 171, 175, 176, 179, 180, 201, 203, 292, 303, 347, 363, 369, 370, 371, 372, 373, 510, 554, 580, 600, 601, 602, 608, 609, 641, 649, 652, 653, 678, 688, 690, 691, 723, 734, 735, 743, 950, 951, 952, 954, 983, 1007, 1008, 1009, 1026, 1030, 1031, 1042, 1043, 1120

Riel, Marguerite. *See* Monet, *dit* Bellehumeur

Riel, *dit* L'Irlande, Jean-Baptiste, IX, 663

Riel, *dit* L'Irlande, Marguerite. *See* Boucher

Riely. *See* O'Reilly

Rieutord, François, V, 713; VIII, 248

Rieutord, Françoise. *See* Deray

Rieutord, Hermine (Dumoulin), VIII, 247, 248

Rieutord, Jacques, V, 712

Rieutord, Jean-Baptiste, V, 713

Rieutord, Jean-Baptiste, IV, 385; V, 315, **712–13**

Rieutord, Louis, V, 713

Rieutord, Marie-Josette. *See* Audette, *dit* Lapointe

Rieutord, Pélagie-Victoire. *See* Perron

Rifos, Miguel, I, 156

Rigaud, Françoise (Maugue), I, 498

Rigaud, John Francis, V, 811

Rigaud de Vaudreuil, Anne de (Adhémar de Lantagnac), II, 565; III, 5

Rigaud de Vaudreuil, Antoine de, II, 565

Rigaud de Vaudreuil, Antoinette de. *See* Colombet

Rigaud de Vaudreuil, Arnaud de, Baron de Vaudreuil, II, 566, 571

Rigaud de Vaudreuil, Élisabeth-Catherine de, Marquise de Vaudreuil. *See* Le Moyne de Serigny et de Loire

Rigaud de Vaudreuil, François-Aimé de, II, 565

Rigaud de Vaudreuil, François-Pierre de, II, 301, 574; III, 48, 162, 181, 215, 217, 459, 461, 557, 578; IV, 54, 145, 146, 242, 256, 265, 363, 459, 464, 478, 512, 517, **660–62**, 663, 667, 686; V, 487

Rigaud de Vaudreuil, Jean de, Vicomte de Vaudreuil, II, 573; IV, 243, 669, 673

Rigaud de Vaudreuil, Jean-Louis de, III, 557

Rigaud de Vaudreuil, Jean-Louis de, Baron de Vaudreuil, II, 565

Rigaud de Vaudreuil, Joseph-Hyacinthe de, II, 574; III, **555–56**

Rigaud de Vaudreuil, Joseph-Hyacinthe-François de Paulede, III, 556

Rigaud de Vaudreuil, Louise de. *See* Fleury de La Gorgendière

Rigaud de Vaudreuil, Louise-Élisabeth de, II, 574

Rigaud de Vaudreuil, Louise-Élisabeth de, Marquise de Vaudreuil. *See* Joybert de Soulanges et de Marson

Rigaud de Vaudreuil, Louis-Philippe de, Marquis de Vaudreuil, III, 557; IV, 303

Rigaud de Vaudreuil, Louis-Philippe de, Marquis de Vaudreuil, II, 374, 573; III, 104, **556–57**, 621; IV, 256, 673

Rigaud de Vaudreuil, Marie de, Baronne de Vaudreuil. *See* Chateauverdun

Rigaud de Vaudreuil, Marie-Claire-Françoise de. *See* Guyot de Lamirande

Rigaud de Vaudreuil, Marie-Josèphe de, II, 574

Rigaud de Vaudreuil, Marie-Louise de (Villeneuve), II, 574

Rigaud de Vaudreuil, Philippe de, II, 566

Rigaud de Vaudreuil, Philippe de, Marquis de Vaudreuil, I, 138, 139, 140, 239, 399, 463, 634; II, 4, 12, 13, 17, 26, 36, 37, 39, 41, 42, 48, 68, 70, 74, 77, 79, 81, 87, 96, 103, 110, 111, 113, 114, 126, 128, 132, 139, 143, 147, 150, 162, 163, 167, 169, 173, 180, 186, 198, 203, 223, 224, 252, 256, 264, 268, 276, 283, 285, 286, 287, 301, 302, 303, 304, 316, 317, 318, 323, 324, 327, 333, 338, 346, 353, 354, 383, 384, 386, 387, 389, 401, 402, 403, 404, 405, 406, 409, 410, 414, 415, 428, 432, 433, 435, 437, 441, 446, 447, 448, 449, 453, 456, 457, 464, 475, 476, 477, 480, 484, 492, 495, 497, 502, 503, 504, 505, 509, 515, 516, 519, 523, 527, 528, 543, 544, 546, 547, 548, 552, 553, 555, 558, 559, 560, 561, 562, 563, **565–74**, 576, 580, 581, 585, 587, 588, 589, 597, 606, 622, 623, 626, 627, 632, 651, 653, 667, 668, 669, 672; III, xli, 3, 5, 15, 23, 42, 44, 50, 51, 53, 56, 57, 58, 59, 60, 61, 62, 81, 83, 86, 87, 89, 104, 112, 113, 118, 159, 176, 178, 190, 191, 200, 217, 224, 233, 245, 248, 289, 299, 330, 360, 402, 410, 428, 429, 431, 486, 503, 512, 550, 555, 556, 563, 564, 576, 603, 632, 682; IV, 235, 510, 660, 662, 663

Rigaud de Vaudreuil, Philippe-Antoine de, Baron de Vaudreuil, II, 573

Rigaud de Vaudreuil de Cavagnial, Jeanne-Charlotte de, Marquise de Vaudreuil. *See* Fleury Deschambault

Rigaud de Vaudreuil de Cavagnial, Pierre de, Marquis de Vaudreuil, I, 345, 399; II, 224, 301, 433, 573, 574; III, xix, xx, xxi, xxii, 8, 12, 21, 22, 47, 85, 101, 149, 161, 185, 188, 198, 215, 255, 256, 259, 289, 300, 332, 361, 373, 376, 383, 402, 408, 418, 424, 425, 445, 459, 460, 461, 462, 463, 464, 465, 466, 467, 468, 469, 510, 534,

535, 536, 540, 549, 555, 557, 560, 570, 578, 579, 588, 591, 601, 617, 626; IV, xxxiii, 3, 23, 24, 27, 28, 54, 57, 63, 76, 79, 88, 125, 138, 143, 146, 147, 183, 201, 207, 221, 227, 242, 250, 256, 257, 265, 268, 286, 289, 307, 311, 312, 368, 382, 408, 426, 435, 448, 449, 453, 460, 464, 465, 467, 476, 478, 479, 480, 481, 482, 512, 514, 517, 563, 587, 588, 595, 612, 614, 616, 617, 620, 633, 634, 636, 637, 641, 651, 652, 660, 661, **662–74**, 685, 729, 734, 739, 751, 764, 765, 770; V, 41, 58, 103, 104, 164, 368, 470, 498, 499, 677, 711, 738, 739, 740, 741, 888; XII, 825

Rigault, Geneviève (Testu Du Tilly), III, 620
Rigault, Georges, IX, 681
Rigault, Pierre-François, III, 541
Rigauville. *See* Blaise; Des Bergères
Rigby, Elizabeth (Eastlake, Lady Eastlake), VIII, 651
Rigby, Sarah (Parry), VIII, 683
Rigney, Thomas, VIII, 930
Rikert. *See* Reickert
Riley, Amos, XI, 400
Riley, Isaac (slave owner), XI, 400
Riley, Isaac (settler), XII, 492
Riley, Robert Thomas, XII, 941
Riley*, Susie Frances (Harrison) (1859–1935), XII, 776
Rimmer, Thomas, XII, 670
Rinault. *See* Gaultier
Rind, William Alexander, V, 717; VIII, 35, 36
Rindge, Elizabeth (Wentworth), V, 848
Rindisbacher, Barbara Ann. *See* Wyss
Rindisbacher, Peter, VI, **648–50**
Rindisbacher, Pierre, VI, 648, 649
Rine, David Isaac Kirwin, XI, **752–53**
Rinfret*, Thibaudeau (1879–1962), XII, 324, 325
Rinfret, *dit* Malouin, Éléonore (Vézina), XI, 901
Rinfret, *dit* Malouin, Rémi, XI, 901
Rinfret, *dit* Malouin, Thérèse (Deguise, *dit* Flamand), IV, 203
Ring, Frances Campbell (Lawson), XII, 538
Ring, Lucy (Scott), V, 744
Ring, Zebedee, XII, 785
Ringuet, Julie (Thériault), XII, 1034
Rintoul, Christian. *See* MacGibbon
Rintoul, Ellen (Oliver), XI, 651
Rintoul, John, IX, 667
Rintoul, Robert, VIII, 750
Rintoul, Sophia. *See* Aitken
Rintoul, William, VIII, 67, 72, 281, 641, **750–51**, 767; X, 92; XII, 210
Rió. *See* Almodóvar
Riopel, Louis-Joseph, XII, 310, 913
Riordan, Amelia. *See* Ames
Riordon*, Charles (1847–1931), XI, 753; XII, 138
Riordon, Jeremiah, XI, 753
Riordon, John, XI, 753
Riordon, John, XI, **753–54**; XII, 137
Riot, Marguerite (Lauzon), III, 360
Rioux, Jean, II, 179
Rioux, Nicolas, II, 528; III, 572
Ripley, Eleazar Wheelock, VIII, 238
Ripon, Earl of. *See* Robinson
Ripon, Marquess of. *See* Robinson
Risbé, Jean-François, IV, 205, 629
Rischmuller, William, IX, 837

Rishworth, Mary (Sayward), II, 601
Rising, John, IV, 30
Rising, Josiah (Shoentakwanni, Ignace Raizenne), V, 703; VI, 627
Rising Sun, VII, 132
Riss, François, I, 170; IX, 360
Ritchey, John, VIII, 178, 960
Ritchie, Miss (possibly mistress of Sir James DOUGLAS), X, 238
Ritchie, Alexander J., VIII, 657, 658
Ritchie, Alicia Maria. *See* Le Cain
Ritchie, Amelia Rebecca. *See* Almon
Ritchie, Andrew, IV, 674
Ritchie, Ann (Zouch), V, 385, 386
Ritchie, Anne. *See* Bond
Ritchie, Arthur, VIII, 753
Ritchie, Barbara. *See* Gilmour
Ritchie, Benjamin, V, 385
Ritchie, Caroline Maria (Dodd), X, 232
Ritchie, David, VIII, 753
Ritchie, Edmund, VII, 909; IX, 746
Ritchie, Elizabeth. *See* Best
Ritchie, Elizabeth Wildman. *See* Johnston
Ritchie, Grace Vernon, Lady Ritchie. *See* Nicholson
Ritchie, Hugh, V, 385
Ritchie, Jennet (Janet) (wife of JOHN), IV, 674
Ritchie, John, XII, 126
Ritchie, John, IV, **674–75**; VI, 310; VIII, 751
Ritchie, John Almon, XII, 515, 516
Ritchie, John Corbett, VI, 114, 203, 538
Ritchie, John William, VIII, 752; X, 679; XI, 373, **754–55**; XII, 871, 895
Ritchie, Leitch, XI, 858
Ritchie, Martha. *See* Strang
Ritchie, Mary. *See* Strang
Ritchie, Robert, VIII, 753
Ritchie, Thomas, VI, 77, 307; VII, 506; VIII, 334, **751–53**; X, 383; XI, 754; XII, 895
Ritchie, Thomas Weston, X, 249; XI, 766
Ritchie, William (notary), VI, 174
Ritchie, William (son of WILLIAM), VIII, 754
Ritchie, William, VII, 344; VIII, 631, **753–54**; IX, 288, 539; X, 720; XI, 349; XII, 366
Ritchie, Sir William Johnston, IV, 675; VIII, 810; IX, 413, 623; X, 286, 543, 712, 713; XI, 372, 755, 828; XII, 18, 19, 20, 313, **895–900**, 1051, 1052, 1053, 1104, 1105
Ritchot, Janvier, IX, 330
Ritchot*, Joseph-Noël (1825–1905), X, 70, 645, 646; XI, 46, 442, 738, 740, 741, 742, 743, 744; XII, 82, 601, 1007, 1030
Ritchot, Pierre, VII, 512
Ritchot, Ursule (Valois), X, 690, 691
Rivard (Rivard-Dufresne), Augustin, VIII, 128; XII, 556
Rivard, Delphine. *See* Choquette
Rivard (Pinard), Marie (Maillet), I, 480
Rivard, Marie-Françoise (Caron), VIII, 128
Rivard, Nicolas, II, 446
Rivard, Sévère, XI, 61, 235, **755–56**
Rivard, *dit* Lanouette, Marie-Joseph (Perrault), III, 510
Rivard, *dit* Lavigne, Nicolas, XI, 755
Rivard, *dit* Loranger, Joseph, XI, 529
Rivard, *dit* Loranger, Marie-Louise. *See* Dugal
Rivard, *dit* Loranger, Robert, II, 584

Rivard-Dufresne. *See also* Rivard
Rivard-Dufresne, Charlotte (Lesieur-Désaulniers), IX, 465;
    XII, 556
Rivard-Dufresne, Marguerite (Rivard-Laglanderie), XI, 755
Rivard-Laglanderie, Augustin, XI, 755
Rivard-Laglanderie, Marguerite. *See* Rivard-Dufresne
Rivard-Laglanderie, Ursule (Gérin-Lajoie), XI, 342
Rivarol, Antoine, known as Comte de Rivarol, VII, 90
Rive, Marguerite (Brien, *dit* Dérocher), VIII, 218
Rivera y Melo Montaño, María Rita (Moziño), V, 615
Riverin, Angélique. *See* Gaultier de Comporté
Riverin, Denis, I, 326, 402; II, 32, 179, 214, 275, 276, 302,
    338, 526, 556, **574–76**; III, 15, 52, 153, 557, 681
Riverin, Joseph, II, 235; III, 22, 557
Riverin, Joseph, III, **557–58**; IV, 248, 249; V, 46
Riverin, Madeleine. *See* Mahyet
Riverin, Marie-Charlotte. *See* Guillimin
Riverin, Marie-Joseph. *See* Perthuis
Riverin, Marie-Joseph (Du Pont Duchambon de Vergor),
    IV, 248, 249
Riverin, Michelle. *See* Mars
Riverin, Pierre, II, 574
Riverin, Pierre-Sévère, XI, 152
Rivers, Mary (Payne), II, 513
Rivet, Julia (Ogden), VIII, 660, 662
Rivet, Marie-Madeleine (Lestage), III, 394
Rivet, Xavier, XI, 655
Rivet Cavelier, Marie-Madeleine. *See* Rageot
Rivet Cavelier, Pierre, II, xxiv, 485, **576–77**; III, 35
Rivière, Claude, VI, 332; VII, 495, 759; VIII, 239, 242
Rivière, François, III, 168
Rivière, François de, Marquis de Giscaro, II, 513
Rivière, Marie. *See* Mars
Rivière, Marie (Rattier), II, 549
Rivière, Marie-Josèphe de, Marquise de Giscaro. *See*
    Pastour de Costebelle
Rivières. *See* Philpin
Rivington, James, IV, 105
Rivoli, Duke of. *See* Masséna
Rivrain, Monsieur (character witness), VII, 707
Rizy. *See* Perrot
Roach, Eliza Catherine, XI, 803, 804
Roach, Mary (Power), VII, 705
Roach, William Henry, VII, 82, 84
Roachford. *See* Rochfort
Roaf, John, XI, 322
Roaf, John, IX, **663–65**, 705, 706, 707; XII, 1123
Roan, Charles, VIII, 969
Roanoke. *See* Randolph
Robaille, Jean, IV, 205
Robaud, Jacques, II, 161
Robaut, Louis-Aloysius, XI, 806
Robb, Mr (slave-owner), XI, 400
Robb, Charles (father), IX, 665
Robb, Charles, X, 445
Robb, Donald, XII, 436
Robb, Elizabeth. *See* Paterson
Robb, Ellen. *See* Coster
Robb, James, VII, 413, 464; VIII, 173, 435, 436; IX, 87,
    **665–67**; XI, 447
Robbins, Mary (Mollie) (Ketchum), VII, 467; IX, 422
Robe, Sir William, V, 61; VI, 308
Robereau, *dit* Duplessis, Pierre, IV, 654

Roberge, Denis, II, 19, 520, 639
Roberge, Geneviève. *See* Auber
Roberge, Marie-Anne (Guion), II, 271
Roberge, Marie-Madeleine (Perthuis), II, 520; III, 511; IV,
    624
Roberol, *dit* Morin, Pierre, II, 637
Robert, Antoine, IV, 505
Robert, Antoine-Bernardin, V, 93, 659; VI, 202, 216,
    **650–51**
Robert, Auguste, XI, 756
Robert, Cécile (MacLeod), IV, 505
Robert, Clément, II, **577**; III, 413
Robert, David ap, I, 655
Robert, Edme-Nicolas, II, 208; III, 62, 427
Robert, Elizabeth (Vaughan), I, 655
Robert, Guillemette (Bizard), I, 102
Robert, Jean-de-Dieu-François, V, 432
Robert, Marguerite (Sigogne), VII, 800
Robert, Nicolas-François, IV, 200
Robert, Sophie (La Rocque), X, 428
Robert, Victor, XII, 693
Robert, *dit* Lapommeraie, Marie. *See* Paquet
Robert, *dit* Lapommeraie, Pierre, VI, 650
Robert de Fortel, Louis, I, 32, 615; II, xvii
Robert Jasne, Marie-Angélique (Godin, *dit* Chatillon, *dit*
    Bellefontaine), IV, 305
Roberts, Ann (mother of Lewis), I, 574
Roberts, Ann (wife of Lewis), I, 574
Roberts, Benjamin, IV, 582, **675–76**, 681; V, 8
Roberts, Charles, XI, 454
Roberts, Charles, V, 112, 695, **713–14**; VI, 29, 210, 236,
    358, 465, 509, 547, 643; VII, 552, 703; VIII, 831; IX, 8
Roberts*, Sir Charles George Douglas (1860–1943), VII,
    14; X, 498; XI, 75, 142, 448; XII, 204, 205, 206, 213,
    460, 513, 515, 517, 518, 558, 714, 947
Roberts, Charlotte (Dunn), VIII, 251, 253
Roberts, David, XI, 358
Roberts, Emma Champion. *See* Armstrong
Roberts, Frederick Sleigh, 1st Earl Roberts, XII, 115
Roberts, Gabriel, I, 574
Roberts, George, IX, 341
Roberts*, George Goodridge (1832–1905), X, 498; XII, 18,
    714
Roberts, Henry, IV, 218, 744, 745
Roberts, Hugh, IV, 176
Roberts, Jessie. *See* Alexander
Roberts, Kenneth Lewis, III, xxix; IV, 683
Roberts, Lewis, I, **574**
Roberts, Mary Ann (Lilly), VII, 507
Roberts, Robert, VII, 71
Roberts, William Milnor, XII, 390, 391
Roberts, William Randall, IX, 588; X, 558, 559; XII, 68
Robertson, Mrs. *See* Morris
Robertson, Agnes. *See* Bow
Robertson, Alexander (brother of James, 1747–1816) V,
    716, 717
Robertson, Alexander (father of Andrew, 1827–90) XI,
    757
Robertson, Alexander (merchant), VII, 356
Robertson, Alexander (son of James, 1831–1900), XII, 901
Robertson, Alexander Rocke, XI, 756
Robertson, Alexander Rocke, XI, **756–57**
Robertson, Amelia. *See* Nelson

Robertson, Amy (wife of JAMES), V, 717
Robertson, Andrew, X, **620**, 641; XII, 64, 901, 905
Robertson, Andrew, XI, 362, **757–58**
Robertson, Caroline. *See* Street
Robertson, Catherine. *See* Askin
Robertson, Catherine. *See* Christie
Robertson, Catherine. *See* Sharp
Robertson, Charles, IX, 667
Robertson, Charles, III, 95, 167, 306, 528, **558–59**; IV, 761
Robertson, Charlotte (Farries), V, 715, 716
Robertson, Christiana. *See* Jaffray
Robertson, Colin, VII, 750
Robertson, Colin, V, 237, 266, 267, 751; VI, 251, 252, 267,
   321, 437, 438, 443, 456, 534, 705, 765, 767, 768; VII,
   78, 139, 498, 561, 567, 570, 571, 578, 671, 736, **748–50**,
   913; VIII, 91, 158, 159, 176, 314, 343, 414, 453, 454,
   482, 527, 557, 714, 812, 813, 820, 888, 889; IX, 197,
   260, 456, 472, 553; X, 297
Robertson, Cornelia Eleanor. *See* Brooks
Robertson, Daniel, III, 542; V, 106, 129, 413, 512, 568,
   **714–16**; VI, 477, 743, 744
Robertson, David, V, 168, 404, 718; VI, 296
Robertson, Effie. *See* Eberts
Robertson, Elizabeth. *See* Murray
Robertson, Elizabeth (Hertel de Saint-François; Davis), V,
   715, 716
Robertson, Elizabeth (Stuart, Lady Stuart), VIII, 842
Robertson, Elizabeth Amelia. *See* Campbell
Robertson, Frances Catherine (Bayard), IX, 35
Robertson, George (officer), VIII, 17
Robertson, George (partner of William FORSYTH, d. 1814)
   V, 327; VI, 262
Robertson, George R., X, 620, 641; XII, 64, 901, 905
Robertson, Grant Stuart. *See* Macdonald
Robertson, Helen (Penny), XII, 835
Robertson, Henrietta (Burpee), XI, 133
Robertson, Hugh, VI, 635; VII, 593, 594, 595; XII, 1036
Robertson, James (father of ANDREW, 1815–80) X, 620
Robertson, James (father of JOSEPH GIBB and MARGARET
   MURRAY), XII, 901, 904, 905
Robertson, James (father of WILLIAM, 1784–1844), VII,
   750
Robertson, James (fur-trade supplier), VII, 356
Robertson, James (merchant), XII, 972
Robertson, James (officer), IV, 686; V, 505
Robertson, James (son of JAMES, 1831–1900), XII, 901
Robertson, James, IV, 482; V, 27, 438, **716–17**; VIII, 36
Robertson, James, XII, **900–1**
Robertson*, James (1839–1902), XII, 202
Robertson, James C., XI, 386
Robertson*, James Wilson (1857–1930), XII, 1093
Robertson, Jane. *See* Dunlop
Robertson, Jean. *See* Stewart
Robertson, Jean (Faerrie), IX, 258
Robertson, John (son of DANIEL), V, 716
Robertson, John (son of JAMES, 1831–1900), XII, 901
Robertson, John (settlement leader), VIII, 856
Robertson, John, VIII, 98, 362, 810; X, 159, 287, **620–22**;
   XI, 223; XII, 560, 1051
Robertson*, John Ross (1841–1918), V, 375, 759; VI, 266;
   VII, 363, 367; IX, 346, 577, 838; XI, 247; XII, 500, 572,
   1119
Robertson, Joseph Gibb, X, 620; XII, 464, **901–4**, 905

Robertson, Margaret (McNab), VIII, 584, 588
Robertson, Margaret (Sutherland), V, 716; VI, 743, 745
Robertson, Margaret Bruce. *See* Eberts
Robertson, Margaret Murray, X, 620; XII, 901, **904–6**
Robertson, Margaret R. (Fairweather), XII, 306
Robertson, Marie-Louise. *See* Réaume
Robertson, Mary (wife of JAMES, 1747–1816), V, 717
Robertson, Mary (Gordon), XII, 905
Robertson, Mary Cameron. *See* Ross
Robertson, Mary Fraser (Matheson), X, 501
Robertson, Mary Jane. *See* Woodward
Robertson, Patrick, Lord Robertson, XII, 758
Robertson, Rachel Cuthbert (Chisholme), VII, 180
Robertson, Robert, X, 620
Robertson, Samuel (brother of COLIN), VII, 748
Robertson, Samuel (brother of WILLIAM, d. 1806) V, 402,
   718
Robertson, Sarah (Ferres), IX, 257
Robertson, Sophia. *See* Dobie
Robertson, Sophia (Horetzky), XII, 447
Robertson, Theresa. *See* Chalifoux
Robertson*, Thomas (1852–1902), XI, 198
Robertson, Thomas Jaffray, IX, **667–68**
Robertson, William (father of COLIN), VII, 748
Robertson, William (historian), VI, 87, 88
Robertson, William (minister), VIII, 715
Robertson, William (partner of Joseph MASSON), VII, 593,
   595; XII, 1036
Robertson, William, V, 38, 168, 365, 403, 404, 449,
   **718–19**, 722, 723, 821; VI, 473, 607, 628
Robertson, William, VI, 104, 113, 296; VII, 25, 26,
   **750–52**, 824; VIII, 404; IX, 16, 32, 357
Robertson, William Wilcox, X, 620; XII, 901, 905
Robertson-Ross, Amelia Ann. *See* Maynard
Robertson-Ross, Patrick, X, 729; XI, **758–60**; XII, 347, 622
Roberval. *See* La Rocque
Roberval, Dame de. *See* Popincourt
Robeshaw; Robichau; Robichaud. *See* Robichaux
Robespierre, Maximilien de, V, 105, 702
Robichaud, Euphrosine (Aumon), X, 23
Robichaud, Louis, V, 813
Robichaud, Marie. *See* Richard
Robichaud, Marie, named Saint-Vincent-de-Paul, III, 18;
   IV, 638
Robichaud, Marie-Anne (Melançon), V, 587
Robichaud, Marie-Françoise (Couillard-Després), VIII, 174
Robichaud, Marie-Josèphe (Doucet), V, 261
Robichaud, Marie-Josephte (Dugas), VI, 227, 228
Robichaud, Prudent, VI, 228
Robichaux, Charles, V, 720
Robichaux, Félicité. *See* Cyr
Robichaux, Florent, VII, 752
Robichaux, Frédéric, VII, 752
Robichaux, Henriette. *See* Petitpas
Robichaux, Isidore, V, 720
Robichaux, Jean-Baptiste, V, 719; VII, 752
Robichaux, Jean-Baptiste, V, **719–20**; VI, 652; VII, 85, 752
Robichaux, Jeanne. *See* Bourgeois
Robichaux, Joseph, V, 720
Robichaux, Louis, VII, 752
Robichaux, Louis, III, 418; IV, **676–77**; V, 393; VI, 651;
   VII, 752
Robichaux, Marie-Louise. *See* Thibodeau

Robichaux, Marie-Marguerite (Larue), XII, 531
Robichaux, Marie-Modeste (Blanchard), VII, 85
Robichaux, Michel, V, 720
Robichaux, Otho, IV, 677; VI, 262, 304, **651–52**; VII, 752
Robichaux, Pierre, V, 720
Robichaux, Prudent, II, 23; III, 418; IV, 676; V, 261
Robichaux, Vénérande, IV, 677; VI, 651; VII, **752**
Robichaux, *dit* Cadet, Claire. *See* Le Blanc
Robichaux, *dit* Cadet, Joseph, V, 719
Robicheau, Frederick Armand, VII, 804; IX, 418; XI, 303
Robicheaux. *See* Robichaux
Robidoux, Anne. *See* Lehoux
Robidoux, Charles, III, 278, 279
Robidoux*, Ferdinand (1849–1931), XII, 340
Robie, Elizabeth. *See* Creighton
Robie, Mary. *See* Bradstreet
Robie, Simon Bradstreet, V, 832; VI, 307; VII, 21, 22, 23, 25, 278, 531, 532, 724; VIII, 300, 355, 356, 459, 752, **754–57**, 782; X, 352, 383
Robie, Thomas, VIII, 754
Robillard, Françoise (Pâquet), XII, 818
Robillard, Honoré, XII, 938
Robillard, J.-C., VIII, 781
Robillard, Joseph, VII, 173
Robillard, Marguerite (Lareau), XI, 488
Robin, Anne. *See* Dauvergne
Robin, Charles, IV, 79, 180; V, 637, 719, 720; VI, 556, 595, 651, **652–54**; VII, 85; VIII, 257; XII, 309
Robin, Claude (Fredin), III, 14
Robin, Elizabeth (Le Boutillier), X, 435
Robin, Isabeau (Babie), I, 74
Robin, Jacques, IV, xxvii
Robin, James, VI, 654
Robin, John, VI, 652
Robin, Mathurine (Guyon Du Buisson), I, 359
Robin, Philip (father), VI, 652, 653
Robin, Philip, VI, 654
Robin, Philippe (applicant), VII, 357
Robin, Philippe (father of CHARLES), VI, 652
Robin, *dit* Des Forges, Étienne, I, 267
Robin de Coulogne, Thomas, I, 97, 100
Robinau, Marie-Anne (Martel de Magos), I, 577; II, 459; III, 433; IV, 517
Robinau de Bécancour, François-Alexandre, II, 578
Robinau de Bécancour, Louise-Catherine (Desjordy Moreau de Cabanac), II, 186; III, 171
Robinau de Bécancour, Marie-Anne, Baronne de Portneuf. *See* Leneuf de La Poterie
Robinau de Bécancour, Marie-Anne-Geneviève (Legardeur de Croisille), II, 577; III, 374; IV, 446
Robinau de Bécancour, Marie-Charlotte, Baronne de Portneuf. *See* Legardeur de Villiers
Robinau de Bécancour, Marie-Marguerite-Renée, II, 577; III, 245
Robinau de Bécancour, Pierre, I, 349, 574
Robinau de Bécancour, Pierre, Baron de Portneuf, I, 575; II, xxiii, 242, **577–79**; III, 74, 105, 245, 350, 374, 420
Robinau de Bécancour, René, Baron de Portneuf, I, **574–76**, 582; II, 27, 48, 186, 577, 578, 579
Robinau de Bécancour, Renée. *See* Marteau
Robinau de Fortelle, François, I, 575
Robinau de Neuvillette, Daniel, II, 3, 145, 578, **579**

Robinau de Portneuf, Jacques, II, 577, 578
Robinau de Portneuf, Marguerite. *See* Daneau de Muy
Robinau de Portneuf, Marie-Louise. *See* Dandonneau Du Sablé
Robinau de Portneuf, Philippe-René, III, **559–60**; IV, 74
Robinau de Portneuf, Pierre, III, **560–61**
Robinau de Portneuf, René, II, 6, 172, 283, 383, 578, **579–80**; III, 168, 559, 560
Robinau de Villebon, Joseph, I, 26, 80, 246, 250, 338, 426, 427, 436, 510, 529, 542, 575, **576–78**, 586, 649, 654; II, 14, 46, 47, 109, 145, 166, 167, 177, 183, 257, 271, 394, 449, 450, 459, 464, 479, 578, 579, 605, 626, 630, 654; III, 7, 170, 273, 476, 596, 681; IV, xxiv, 305
Robins, Alice (Forsyth), V, 325; IX, 273
Robins, Ann. *See* Vickery
Robins, James, V, 326
Robins, Jane Henrietta (Gill), IX, 315
Robins, Margaret. *See* Anderson
Robins, Paul, VIII, 425, 908
Robins, William, IX, 315
Robinson. *See also* Robertson; Robison
Robinson, Alexander, XII, 248
Robinson, Anne (Baird), VIII, 41
Robinson, Anne (King), IX, 428
Robinson, Augusta Anne (Strachan), IX, 751; XII, 101
Robinson, Beverley (grandfather), VI, 654
Robinson, Beverley (uncle), V, 59, 349, 646; VI, 654
Robinson, Beverley, VI, 655
Robinson, Sir Bryan, VII, 99, 507, 508; VIII, 380, 384; IX, 469; XI, 66, **760–63**; XII, 161, 565, 844
Robinson, Catharine (Williams), XI, 930
Robinson, Christopher, XI, 760
Robinson, Christopher, IV, **677–78**, 777; V, 307, 388, 518, 782; VI, 51, 264, 656; VII, 57, 175, 752, 753, 778; VIII, 890; IX, 668; X, 622
Robinson*, Christopher (1828–1905), XI, 748, 749; XII, 586, 733, 907
Robinson, Christopher Blackett, XII, 286, 923
Robinson, Daniel Ludlow, VI, 655
Robinson, Elizabeth. *See* Langrishe
Robinson, Elizabeth. *See* Ludlow
Robinson, Elizabeth Ann. *See* Jarvis
Robinson, Emily Mary (Lefroy), XI, 508; XII, 101
Robinson, Emma, Lady Robinson. *See* Walker
Robinson, Esther. *See* Sayre
Robinson, Frances Elizabeth. *See* Wood
Robinson, Frederick, VII, 756
Robinson, Frederick John, 1st Viscount Goderich and 1st Earl of Ripon, VI, 12, 632, 791, 820, 821; VII, 23, 83, 88, 370, 463, 465, 535, 549, 623, 755, 865, 906, 907; VIII, xxvii, xxx, xxxii, 155, 292, 356, 418, 844, 845; IX, 69, 143, 498, 500, 673, 674, 811, 812; X, 180, 206; XI, 352
Robinson, Sir Frederick Philipse, VI, 38; VII, 366; XII, 102
Robinson, Frederick Phillips, IX, 623
Robinson, George, X, 179
Robinson, George Duncan, VI, 655
Robinson, George Frederick Samuel, 2nd Earl of Grey and 1st Marquess of Ripon, XII, 601, 602
Robinson, George Richard, VI, 311, 312; VIII, xxvi; IX, 84, 85, 86; X, 179
Robinson, Heaton Bowstead, VIII, 671, 672
Robinson, Hercules, VI, 393; VII, 303; XI, 760; XII, 910

Robinson, Hercules George Robert, 1st Baron Rosmead, XII, 910
Robinson, Hezekiah, VIII, **757–58**
Robinson, Hezekiah Luke, VIII, 758
Robinson, Isabella (Dickson), XI, 263
Robinson, Isabella (Sibbald), VII, 756
Robinson, J. H., X, 166
Robinson, James, VII, 743
Robinson, Sir James Lukin, X, 336
Robinson, Jane. *See* Scholey
Robinson, Jane (Lynson; Moody), V, 604
Robinson, John (apparently uncle of CHRISTOPHER), IV, 677
Robinson, John (father of JOSEPH HIRAM), XII, 909
Robinson, John (grandfather of JOHN), VI, 654
Robinson, John, V, 646; VI, 563, **654–55**, 697; VII, 330, 612, 806; IX, 620
Robinson, Sir John, I, 82
Robinson, Sir John Beverley, IV, 677; V, 65, 66, 113, 114, 457, 520, 521, 522, 558, 559, 643, 644, 787; VI, 21, 31, 52, 56, 79, 80, 92, 94, 115, 118, 164, 165, 199, 216, 247, 248, 265, 266, 420, 425, 426, 497, 498, 513, 542, 544, 545, 579, 604, 605, 610, 612, 613, 631, 632, 698, 742, 770, 771, 773, 791; VII, 38, 39, 40, 42, 157, 158, 162, 229, 314, 319, 337, 365, 366, 367, 369, 370, 371, 372, 378, 409, 410, 453, 456, 457, 458, 460, 461, 497, 546, 547, 548, 638, 639, 664, 692, 704, 752, 753, 756, 788, 796, 822, 860, 920; VIII, xxiii, xxv, 6, 9, 11, 12, 27, 28, 29, 47, 48, 180, 187, 195, 251, 252, 337, 341, 365, 444, 445, 511, 512, 513, 514, 515, 516, 517, 518, 519, 520, 521, 597, 598, 599, 600, 602, 639, 643, 689, 695, 709, 794, 798, 844, 846, 847, 871, 885, 927, 945; IX, 7, 69, 139, 333, 335, 387, 422, 513, 520, 523, 534, 535, 542, 545, 657, **668–79**, 684, 751, 753, 757, 758, 764; X, 78, 79, 121, 253, 343, 344, 530, 622, 705; XI, 248, 387, 508, 509; XII, 101, 633, 672, 906
Robinson, John Beverley, VIII, 445; IX, 677; X, 510; XI, 227, 509, 551; XII, 102, 151, **906–9**, 976, 1108
Robinson, John Morris, VI, 655; IX, 766
Robinson, Jonathan (grandfather), VIII, 757
Robinson, Jonathan, VIII, 758
Robinson, Joseph, V, 28, 127, 263, 309, 310, 311, 424, 425, 478, 515, **720–21**; VI, 245, 565; VII, 103
Robinson, Joseph Hiram, XII, **909–10**
Robinson, Lelia (wife of JOSEPH), V, 720
Robinson, Louisa Matilda (Allan), XII, 101
Robinson, Mary. *See* Darby
Robinson, Mary. *See* Lancaster
Robinson, Mary (Delisle), X, 219
Robinson, Mary (Hamilton; Bellet), VI, 50
Robinson, Mary (Palliser), IV, 597
Robinson, Mary Amelia (McInnes), XII, 631, 633
Robinson, Mary Jane. *See* Hagerman
Robinson, Matilda (Brecken), V, 720; VII, 103
Robinson, Nicholas, IV, 597
Robinson, Olivia Edith Dean, Lady Robinson. *See* Townshend
Robinson, Peter, IV, 677
Robinson, Peter, IV, 677; V, 65; VI, 51, 52, 266, 416, 522, 647, 773; VII, 37, 42, 382, 410, 476, 641, 726, **752–57**, 829; VIII, 9, 47, 253, 598, 885, 926; IX, 483, 502, 521, 535, 668, 671, 672, 677, 758; X, 104, 343, 618, 622, 636
Robinson, Rebecca (Hodgson), V, 424, 720; X, 352

Robinson, Richmond, IX, 178
Robinson, Sir Robert, I, 93, 370; II, **580–81**
Robinson, Roxilana (Van Norman), XI, 897
Robinson, Sarah. *See* Lister
Robinson, Sarah. *See* Taylor
Robinson, Sarah (mother of JOSEPH HIRAM), XII, 909
Robinson, Sarah Ann (Boulton), X, 79
Robinson, Selina. *See* Brooking
Robinson, Selucia. *See* Knowlton
Robinson, Simon, IX, 843
Robinson, Susan (Parker), IX, 620
Robinson, Susanna. *See* Philipse
Robinson, Thomas (merchant), IV, 118
Robinson, Thomas (painter), XI, 803
Robinson, Thomas, 1st Baron Grantham, III, 362
Robinson, Webb, VI, 50
Robinson, William (doctor), VII, 105
Robinson, William (soldier), VIII, 466
Robinson, William (son-in-law of Robert DOAK), VIII, 225
Robinson, William (surveyor), VIII, 960; XII, 286
Robinson, William Benjamin, IV, 677; V, 453; VI, 604; VII, 519, 607, 752, 753; VIII, 309; IX, 9, 10, 56, 151, 407, 744; X, 256, 257, 283, 405, **622–24**; XI, 166, 553, 612; XII, 187, 854, 907
Robinson, Sir William Cleaver Francis, X, 352; XI, 702, 705; XII, 417, 419, 452, 476, **910–11**
Robinson, William Henry (merchant), XII, 145
Robinson, William Henry (politician), IX, 23
Robinson-Owen, John James, VIII, 672
Robison (Robinson), Ann Ellice (Stuart), IX, 771
Robison, Elizabeth. *See* Cartwright
Robison, Martha Smith (Chewett), IX, 129; XII, 188
Robison, Thomas Weeks, VIII, 24
Robitaille, Albertine, XII, 912
Robitaille, Amédée, XII, 912
Robitaille, Charlotte. *See* Verchères de Boucherville
Robitaille, Emma. *See* Quesnel
Robitaille, Étienne, XII, 911
Robitaille, François, V, 285
Robitaille, Geneviève-Luce (Bélanger; Séguin), VII, 781
Robitaille, Joseph, VII, 763
Robitaille, Louis (brother of THÉODORE), XII, 913
Robitaille, Louis (silversmith), VI, 557; VII, 17
Robitaille, Louis-Adolphe, VII, 239; XII, 912
Robitaille, Louise (Plamondon), VI, 584
Robitaille, Marie-Anne (Bruneau), V, 116
Robitaille, Marie-Denis. *See* Moisan
Robitaille, Marie-Josette (Kimber), VII, 468
Robitaille, Marie-Justine. *See* Monjeau
Robitaille, Marie-Louise (Huot), VI, 336
Robitaille, Olivier, VI, 577; XI, 901, 902; XII, **911–12**
Robitaille, Philippe, III, 424
Robitaille, Romain, V, 285
Robitaille, Théodore, XI, 177, 521; XII, 721, 726, **912–14**
Robitaille, Zoé-Louise. *See* Dénéchaud
Roblet. *See* Roblot
Roblin, David, IX, **679–80**; X, 624; XI, 819, 852, 853
Roblin, John, V, 857; VI, 805; IX, 679
Roblin, John Philip, IX, 680; X, **624**
Roblin, Mary. *See* Moore
Roblin, Pamelia. *See* Hawley
Roblin, Philip, X, 624
Roblin, Prudence. *See* Platt

465

Roblin*, Sir Rodmond Palen (1853–1937), XII, 413
Roblot, Claude, IX, 680
Roblot, Louis, named Brother Aidant, VIII, 730; IX, **680–81**
Roblot, Madeleine. *See* Dadavant
Robreau, *dit* Leroux-Duplessis, Pierre, III, 88
Robson, Ann (Selby), VI, 699
Robson, Ebenezer, X, 701; XII, 914
Robson, Euphemia. *See* Richardson
Robson, Frederick William, XII, 919
Robson, Hubert, VII, 574
Robson, John, XII, 914
Robson, John, IX, 479, 518, 715; X, 245, 246; XI, 33, 237, 606; XII, 78, 227, 240, 241, 242, **914–19**
Robson, Joseph, II, 309, 310, 312, 314; III, 214, 490, 521, **561–62**; IV, 740
Robson, Robert, XII, 914
Robson, Susan. *See* Longworth
Robutel de La Noue, Anne (Le Marchand de Lignery), II, 390; III, 378
Robutel de La Noue, Catherine. *See* Le Moyne de Sainte-Hélène
Robutel de La Noue, Catherine. *See* Le Moyne de Sainte-Marie
Robutel de La Noue, Claude, II, 581
Robutel de La Noue, Marie-Anne, IV, 238
Robutel de La Noue, Suzanne. *See* Gabrielle
Robutel de La Noue, Thomas, III, 561
Robutel de La Noue, Zacharie, II, 13, 523, **581**, 603; III, 105, 248, 414
Rocan, *dit* Bastien, Marie-Josephte (Desrochers), VIII, 218
Rocbert, Abel, III, 562
Rocbert, Marie. *See* Pothier
Rocbert de La Morandière, Anne-Geneviève (Legardeur de Tilly), III, 376
Rocbert de La Morandière, Élisabeth. *See* Duverger
Rocbert de La Morandière, Étienne, III, 563; IV, 618
Rocbert de La Morandière, Étienne, II, 47, 160, 672; III, 56, 445, **562–63**, 564; VIII, 258
Rocbert de La Morandière, François-Abel-Étienne, VIII, 258
Rocbert de La Morandière, Jacques-Urbain, II, 47; III, 563
Rocbert de La Morandière, Louis-Joseph, III, 445, 563; IV, 41, 359, 461
Rocbert de La Morandière, Marguerite-Barbe. *See* Hingue de Puygibault
Rocbert de La Morandière, Marguerite-Charlotte (Lemoine Despins), IV, 461
Rocbert de La Morandière, Marguerite-Élisabeth-Ursule (Chabert de Joncaire de Clausonne), IV, 137
Rocbert de La Morandière, Marie-Anne-Julie (Crevier Duvernay), VIII, 258
Rocbert de La Morandière, Marie-Élisabeth (Bégon de La Cour), III, 16, 30, 56, 158, 170, 240, 295, 296, 316, 376, 377, 445, **563–65**; IV, 250, 265, 268, 461
Roch. *See* Célerier
Rochambeau, Comte de. *See* Vimeur
Rochbrune. *See* Larocque
Rochbrune, *dit* Larocque, Charles, XII, 530
Rochbrune, *dit* Larocque, Marie. *See* Lefebvre
Roche, Annie Elizabeth (wife of JOHN KNATCHBULL), VIII, 758
Roche, David, VIII, 759

Roche, George Molyneux, VIII, 759
Roche, Harriet Ann. *See* Mills
Roche, John, VIII, 758
Roche, John Knatchbull, VIII, **758–59**; XII, 320
Roche, Mary. *See* Hall
Roche, Rosalie (O'Brien), IX, 607
Rocheblave. *See* Rastel
Rocheblave, Chevalier de. *See* Rastel de Rocheblave, Philippe-François de
Rochechouart de Mortemart, Françoise-Athénaïs de, Marquise de Montespan, II, 328; III, 106
Rochechouart de Mortemart, Gabrielle-Victor de, Duchesse de Lesdiguières, III, 106
Rochechouart de Mortemart, Louis-Victor de, Duc de Vivonne, II, 162; III, 106
Rochefort. *See* Lamouraux-Rochefort
Rocheleau, Louise (Crevier, *dit* Bellerive), XI, 217
Rocheleau, Marie (Bresse), XII, 126
Rocheleau, *dit* Lespérance. *See also* Lespérance
Rocheleau, *dit* Lespérance, André, XI, 514
Rocheleau, *dit* Lespérance, Charlotte. *See* Sasseville
Rochemonteix, Camille de, II, 161, 259, 607, 608; III, 689
Rochemore, Vincent de, IV, 65
Rocher, Barthélémy, IX, 697
Rocher, Louise-Sophie (Odet d'Orsonnens), XII, 798
Rocher, Marie-Élisabeth-Alix (Sabrevois de Bleury), IX, 697
Rocheron, Marie (Gaulin), II, 238
Rochette, Cléophas, XII, **920**
Rochette, Gaspard, XII, 920
Rochette, John, XII, 920
Rochette, Malvina. *See* Brulotte
Rochette, Olivier (father), XII, 920
Rochette, Olivier, XII, 920
Rochette, Pierre, VI, 819
Rochette, Rose. *See* Laliberté
Rochfort, Elizabeth. *See* Cane
Rochfort, John, VIII, 468; IX, **681–82**
Rochon, Jérémie, XII, 762
Rochon, Toussaint, VII, 105
Rockefeller, John Davison, XII, 1095
Rockingham, Marquess of. *See* Watson-Wentworth
Rocquant, *dit* La Ville, Pierre, III, 96
Rocques de Carbouere, Jeanne de (Dejean), V, 237
Rodas, Miguel de, I, 156
Roddam, Lucy Mary. *See* Clinton
Roddam, Robert, III, 127
Roddick, John Irvine, XII, 844
Roddick*, Sir Thomas George (1846–1923), XI, 429; XII, 96, 315, 844, 1044
Rodgers. *See also* Rogers
Rodgers, David, V, 301, 345
Rodier, Angélique. *See* Meunier, *dit* Lapierre
Rodier, Barthélémy, VII, 757
Rodier, Charles-Séraphin, VIII, 919; IX, 208, 397, 811; X, **624–26**; XI, 61, 586, 763
Rodier, Charles-Séraphin, X, 625; XI, **763**
Rodier, Édouard-Étienne, VII, 208, 334, 479, 513, **757–59**; VIII, 504, 694, 711, 915; IX, 73; X, 142, 505, 545, 574, 624
Rodier, Élise. *See* Beaupré
Rodier, Jean-Baptiste (father of CHARLES-SÉRAPHIN, 1797–1876), X, 624

Rodier, Jean-Baptiste (father of CHARLES-SÉRAPHIN, 1818–90), XI, 763
Rodier, Julie-Catherine. *See* Le Jeune
Rodier, Julie-Victoire. *See* Dumont
Rodier, Marie-Desanges. *See* Sedillot, *dit* Montreuil
Rodier, Marie-Louise. *See* Giroux
Rodier, Marie-Louise. *See* Lacroix
Rodier, Pierre, X, 624
Rodney, George Brydges, 1st Baron Rodney, III, 283; IV, 223, 226, 282; V, 274; VII, 196
Rodrigue, Anne. *See* Le Borgne de Belle-Isle
Rodrigue, Antoine, IV, 678, 679
Rodrigue, Antoine, III, 236; IV, 28, 245, 246, 439, 470, **678–79**
Rodrigue, Claude, IV, 679
Rodrigue, Jean-Baptiste, II, **581–82**; IV, 678
Rodrigue, Jeanne-Françoise. *See* Jacau
Rodrigue, Jeanne-Françoise (L'Espérance), IV, 470, 679
Rodrigue, Joseph-Baptiste, IV, 678
Rodrigue, Marguerite-Josephte (Du Pont Duchambon), IV, 249
Rodrigue, Marie-Josèphe. *See* Ramondine
Rodrigue, Michel (uncle), II, 582; III, 236, 357; IV, 128, 249, 422, 678
Rodrigue, Michel, IV, 679
Rodrigue, Pierre (merchant), IV, 421
Rodrigue, Pierre (son of JEAN-BAPTISTE), II, 582; IV, 136, 678
Rodrigue, Rose. *See* Castaing
Roe, Alexander Hall, XII, 428, 429
Roe, Ann. *See* Laughton
Roe, Catherine (Hood), VI, 327
Roe*, Henry (1829–1909), XI, 917
Roe, Sir Thomas, I, 144, 312
Roe, Walter, V, 449, **721–22**; VI, 559
Roebling, John Augustus, VIII, 964
Roebuck, Ebenezer, X, 626
Roebuck, Henrietta. *See* Falconer
Roebuck, John Arthur, VI, 681; VII, 8, 82, 412, 478; VIII, xxvi, 781; IX, 299, 500, 812; X, 514, **626–27**, 655; XI, 786; XII, 1079
Roebuck, Zipporah. *See* Tickell
Rogan, Elizabeth (Ross), X, 629
Rogan, Frank, X, 629
Roger. *See also* Caissy
Roger, Father, XII, 46
Roger, Monsieur (merchant), II, 187
Roger, Ann. *See* Cruikshank
Roger, Charles, X, 627
Roger, Charles, X, **627–28**
Roger, Dorothy. *See* MacRobie
Roger, Élisabeth. *See* Oussaye
Roger, Guillaume, II, 582
Roger, Guillaume, II, **582**; III, 344
Roger, Madeleine-Renée (Gagnon), I, 319
Roger, Marie-Louise (Lajus), III, 344
Roger, Ursule. *See* Levasseur
Rogers, Albert Bowman, XI, **763–65**
Rogers, Albert L., XI, 764
Rogers, Anna Maria Brown (Ledingham), XII, 543, 544
Rogers, Arthur, IV, 682
Rogers, Charles (historian), X, 627
Rogers, Charles (partner of Robert HAY), XI, 390

Rogers, Charles (soldier), X, 627
Rogers, David, XII, 921
Rogers, David McGregor, V, 388, 520, 549, 842, 857; VI, 215, 503, 540, 608, **655–58**, 804, 805; VII, 38, 285, 367, 419, 439; VIII, 194, 337, 339
Rogers, Elias, XII, 455
Rogers, Elizabeth. *See* Browne
Rogers, Elizabeth. *See* Playter
Rogers, Elizabeth. *See* Richards
Rogers, Elizabeth (Wiswall), V, 870
Rogers, Frederic, 1st Baron Blachford, VIII, xxxiv
Rogers, George, VIII, 632
Rogers, Hannah (Ward), VIII, 922
Rogers, J., XII, 791
Rogers, James (father), IV, 679
Rogers, James (son), IV, 682; VI, 655; X, 16
Rogers*, James (1826–1903), IX, 616; X, 193; XI, 171, 578; XII, 26, 27, 28, 144, 209, 411, 548, 637, 638, 1055
Rogers, Jonathan, IV, 675
Rogers, Joseph, XII, 796
Rogers, Margaret. *See* McGregor
Rogers, Margaret (Caleff), V, 134
Rogers, Mary (mother of ROBERT), IV, 679
Rogers, Mary (Armstrong), X, 16
Rogers, Mary (Wyatt), VII, 929
Rogers, Mary Eliza. *See* Page
Rogers, Nellie. *See* Brush
Rogers*, Norman McLeod (1894–1940), XII, 921
Rogers, Phebe S. *See* Kenrich
Rogers, Priscilla (Leonard), VI, 394
Rogers, Richard, IV, 679
Rogers, Robert, III, xxix, 95, 452, 525, 526; IV, li, 3, 174, 241, 278, 294, 297, 309, 335, 423, 513, 563, 582, 583, 606, 634, 675, 676, **679–83**, 685; V, 7, 8, 38, 129, 412, 585, 589, 888; VI, 90, 188, 317, 362, 503, 574, 655, 656
Rogers, Robert Vashon (father), VII, 159; X, 536
Rogers, Robert Vashon, XII, 496
Rogers, Samuel (of Maugerville, N.B.), V, 556
Rogers, Samuel (poet), VIII, 759
Rogers, Sarah. *See* Lawton
Rogers, Sarah. *See* Playter
Rogers, Thomas (architect), VIII, 759
Rogers, Thomas (son of THOMAS), VIII, 759
Rogers, Thomas, VII, 159; VIII, 281, **759–62**
Rogers, William Henry, XII, **920–21**
Rogers, Zoar, XI, 763
Rogerson*, James Johnstone (1820–1907), XI, 432; XII, 311, 379, 754
Rogerson, Richard, IX, 598
Rogerson, William, XI, 826
Rohan, Charles, IX, 536; XI, 948
Rohan, Charles de, Prince de Soubise, IV, 481
Rohan, Louis de, Prince de Guémenée, I, 533
Rohan, Pierre de, Sire de Gié, I, 423
Rohrbacher, René-François, IX, 247; XII, 507
Roi. *See also* Roy Portelance
Roi (Roy), Charles, VI, 392
Roi, *dit* Audi, Marguerite-Marie (Darveau), VII, 231
Rojas, Francisco de, I, 156
Roland, Angélique-Françoise (Coron), III, 140, 141
Roland, Euphrasine. *See* Donay
Roland, Pierre, XI, 765
Rolette, Angélique. *See* Jérôme

Rolette, Charles-Frédéric, V, 101
Rolette, Jean-Joseph, VII, 328; X, 628
Rolette, Joseph, IX, 329; X, **628**, 669
Rolette, Luce. *See* Bouchette
Rolette, Marguerite. *See* Dubois
Rolette, Virginie (McKay), 640
Rolfe, Benjamin, II, 285
Roll, Louis de, Baron de Roll, VII, 543
Rolland. *See also* Lenoir
Rolland, Angélique. *See* Boisseau
Rolland, Charles-Octave, IX, 683
Rolland, Esther. *See* Boin
Rolland, François, V, 243, 701; VII, 255
Rolland, François-Roch, IX, 682
Rolland, Henri-Auguste, IX, 683
Rolland, Jean-Baptiste, VI, 84; XI, **765–66**, 813; XII, 502, 1115
Rolland, Jean-Damien, XI, 765, 766
Rolland, Jean-Roch, VII, 643, 718; VIII, 288, 504, 726, 727; IX, 360, 363, **682–83**; XI, 657
Rolland, Marguerite. *See* Estimauville
Rolland, Stanislas-Jean-Baptiste, XI, 765
Rolles, Samuel, VI, 70
Rollet, Marie (Hébert; Hubou), I, 110, 222, 302, 366, 367, 368, 509, **578**
Rollet, Marie-Joseph (Holland), V, 426, 428; VII, 413
Rollet, Marie-Thérèse. *See* Grenet
Rollete, Susanne (Chenneque), VI, 134
Rollette. *See* Rolette
Rollin, Charles, III, 26; V, 486; VI, 650; VIII, 242
Rollin, Dominique, VIII, 762
Rollin, Dominique-Benjamin, VII, 757
Rollin, Magdeleine. *See* Bouthellier
Rollin, Paul, VI, 626; VII, 60, 685, 686; VIII, **762–64**
Rollin, Zoé. *See* Pétrimoulx
Rollo, Andrew, 5th Baron Rollo, III, **565**, 668; IV, 22, 688; V, 172, 719; VI, 227
Rollo, Catharine, Baroness Rollo. *See* Murray
Rollo, Cecilia. *See* Johnstone
Rollo, Elizabeth, Baroness Rollo. *See* Moray
Rollo, Frances. *See* McCaulay
Rollo, James, V, **723**
Rollo, John, III, 565
Rollo, Mary (Rollo, Baroness Rollo), III, 565
Rollo, Robert, 4th Baron Rollo, III, 565
Rollston, Catherine (Martin), VIII, 619; XI, 453
Rolph, Frances. *See* Petty
Rolph, Frances (wife of THOMAS), VIII, 764
Rolph, George, VI, 266; VII, 39, 40, 379; VIII, 946; IX, 520, 525, 683, 685; XI, 712
Rolph, Grace. *See* Haines
Rolph, John, VI, 11, 165, 422, 497, 543, 545, 612, 631, 632, 633, 773; VII, 40, 41, 42, 92, 126, 163, 178, 314, 319, 338, 369, 378, 379, 404, 457, 497, 509, 519, 664, 756; VIII, 46, 47, 48, 57, 253, 254, 340, 598, 599, 600, 603, 604, 642, 643, 846, 850, 852, 870, 926, 932, 933, 934, 935, 946; IX, 8, 139, 201, 228, 313, 500, 501, 502, 503, 504, 506, 673, **683–90**, 707; X, 60, 61, 62, 95, 126, 127, 169, 325, 343, 484, 705; XI, 54, 114, 248, 328, 407, 411, 517, 518, 712, 713, 795; XII, 10, 11, 12, 106, 1123
Rolph, Joseph T., X, 270
Rolph, Romaine, VI, 601; IX, 683
Rolph, Sarah (Ryerson), XI, 795
Rolph, Thomas (father of JOHN), IX, 683
Rolph, Thomas (son of JOHN), IX, 683
Rolph, Thomas, VII, 181; VIII, 303, 427, **764–65**; IX, 377
Roma, Jean-Pierre, II, 219; III, 533, **566–67**; IV, 249
Roma, Jean-Pierre-Michel, IV, 248
Roma, Marie-Anne (Du Pont Duchambon), IV, 249
Roma, Marie-Madeleine. *See* Moreau
Romagnac, François, III, 571
Romain. *See also* Audivert
Romain, Agathe. *See* Debigaré, *dit* Lebasque
Romain, André, VII, 889
Romain, François, VI, 658, 659
Romain, François, VI, 240, 584, **658–59**
Romain, Marthe (Marguerie), I, 489
Romain, Robert, XI, 920
Romainville. *See* Bourdon
Romanes, George, X, 442; XII, 767
Romanet de Briderie, Monsieur (correspondent of Joseph NAVIÈRES), III, 481
Romans, Alexander, VII, 536
Rombau. *See also* Rambau
Rombau, Claude-Joseph, VIII, 735
Rombau, Marie-Reine. *See* Métayer-Descombes
Rombaud, Brother. *See* Lucas
Romby, Marie-Marguerite de (Franquet), III, 228
Romero, Antonia (Cardero), V, 140
Romeyer, Jeanne (Deléage), XI, 243
Romieux, Pierre, I, **578–79**
Romilly, Samuel, VI, 183
Romilly, Sir Samuel, VI, 296
Romney, Earl of. *See* Marsham
Romney, George, V, 706, 811; XII, 100
Rompré, Marquis de. *See* Fleutelot
Romulus. *See* Romieux
Ronceray, Andrée de, II, 490
Roncetti, Cesare, XI, 250
Rondeau, Étienne, II, 273
Rondeau, Françoise. *See* Baudry
Rondeau, Jacques, III, 567, 568
Rondeau, Jacques-Philippe-Urbain, III, 389, **567–68**; IV, 60, 421, 783
Rondeau, Marie-Josephe. *See* Le Borgne de Belle-Isle
Rondoenie. *See* Orontony
Rondort, Jacques, II, 516
Ronsard, Pierre, I, 425
Ronsard, Pierre de, V, 702
Roode, Hannah (Clounter), IX, 162
Rooke, Francis Sophia (Kingston), XI, 475
Rooke, Sir George, II, 226, 260, 373, 659
Roome. *See* Le Chevalier
Rooney, John, VI, 425, 426; VIII, 512
Rooney, Matthew, XII, 290
Roope, John, II, 117, **582–83**
Rooseboom. *See* Roseboom
Roothaan, Jean, VII, 171; IX, 67
Roots, Peter Philanthropos, VI, 733
Roper, Anna Gabriella. *See* Head
Roper, Eliza (de Blaquière), VIII, 204
Roque, Catherine. *See* Durand
Roque, Guillaume, VII, 759
Roque, Jacques-Guillaume, V, 187; VI, 332; VII, 489, 495, **759–60**, 762, 799; VIII, 141, 317, 728, 729; XI, 57, 58
Roquebrune. *See* La Roque

Roquefeuil, Camille de, V, 618
Roquefeuil, Jacques, Comte de Roquefeuil, III, 27
Roquemont de Brison, Claude, I, 59, 263, 330, 402, 405, 411, 521, 561, **578**, 593, 596
Rorke, John, X, 332
Rosa, Narcisse, XI, 505
Rosamond*, Bennett (1833–1910), X, 650; XII, 631, 941
Rosamond, James, VII, 69; X, 650
Rosanvern, Monsieur. *See* Le Loutre, Jean-Louis
Roschang, Maria (Gaukel), VIII, 315
Roscoe, Francis James, XII, 242
Rosé, Sieur de (merchant), I, 538
Rose, Charles Day, XI, 770
Rose, Charlotte, Lady Rose. *See* Temple
Rose, Christian. *See* Maclean
Rose, Christian Ludwig, V, 830
Rose, Christina Henrietta (Brewer), XII, 924
Rose, Daniel, XII, 921, 923
Rose, Daniel Alexander, XII, 923, 924
Rose, David, XII, 1069
Rose, Donald, XII, 921
Rose, Elizabeth. *See* Fyfe
Rose, Eliza H. (Herchmer), XII, 427
Rose, George Maclean, XII, 924
Rose, George Maclean, X, 44; XI, 752, 877; XII, 140, 212, 663, **921–24**, 969, 1101
Rose, Henry, XII, 921, 922
Rose, Hugh James, XII, 440
Rose, Isabella Gair (Smith), VIII, 828
Rose, Jean (Fraser), VII, 330
Rose, Sir John, IX, 492; X, 150, 368, 405, 684; XI, 6, 12, 124, 157, 288, 415, 464, 573, 575, **766–72**, 927; XII, 261, 279, 406, 486, 487, 571, 601, 602, 627, 636, 685, 986, 1007, 1056, 1058, 1068
Rose, John Edward, XI, 608
Rose, Julia Charlotte Sophia, Lady Rose. *See* Mackenzie-Stewart
Rose, Malcolm Cameron, XII, 921, 923
Rose, Margaret Catherine Johan Levack. *See* Manson
Rose, Nicolas, III, 580
Rose, Samuel, IX, 589
Rose, Toussaint, II, 112
Rose, William, XI, 766
Rose, William Andrew, XII, 436
Rose, William Manson, XII, 923
Roseboom, Gerritje. *See* Coster
Roseboom, Gysbertje. *See* Lansing
Roseboom, Hendrick, III, 568
Roseboom, Johannes, III, **568–69**
Rosebrugh, Eliza Jane. *See* Hurlburt
Roseharp. *See* Cawdell, James Martin
Roselli, Francesco, I, 148
Rosenthal, Fanny (Nordheimer), IX, 600
Rosier, James, I, 667
Rosmead, Baron. *See* Robinson
Rosny, Baron de. *See* Béthune
Ross. *See also* Robertson-Ross
Ross, Aaron, XII, 43
Ross, Alexander, XI, 326
Ross, Alexander, V, 419, 533, 534; VI, 438; VII, 454, 473; VIII, 131, 344, 574, 661, **765–68**, 882; IX, 137, 261, 279, 663; X, 324, 629; XI, 79, 139, 220, 775, 776, 875; XII, 206

Ross, Alexander McKenzie, XI, 464, 510
Ross, Alexander Milton, XII, **924–28**
Ross, Andrew, VIII, 770
Ross, Ann, Lady Ross. *See* Coulman
Ross, Ann (Sangster), XII, 944
Ross, Annabella (McDermot; Bird), X, 67
Ross*, Arthur Wellington (1846–1901), XII, 666
Ross, Augusta Elizabeth. *See* Baldwin
Ross, Barbara (George), IX, 307
Ross, Bernard Rogan, X, **629**; XI, 385
Ross, Catherine (Kalm), IV, 406
Ross, Charles (brother of MALCHOM), IV, 685
Ross, Charles (trader), VII, 205; XII, 318, 929
Ross, Charles (Paul Kinsey Hubbs), XII, 929, 930
Ross, Christian. *See* Adair
Ross, Christian. *See* Clark
Ross, Christina (Ross), X, 629
Ross, David, V, 614; IX, 61
Ross, David Alexander, XII, **928–29**, 1000
Ross, Donald (chief factor), VII, 276; IX, 529; X, 67, 390, 629; XI, 52, 436
Ross, Donald (clergyman), IX, 306
Ross, Donald (professor), XII, 767
Ross, Dunbar, IX, **690–91**; XI, 657; XII, 1025
Ross, Duncan, VI, 172, 294, 458, 459, 460, **659–60**; VII, 272, 529; VIII, 452; XI, 772
Ross, Edith. *See* Hallowell
Ross, Elijah, XII, 461
Ross, Elizabeth. *See* Corsane
Ross, Elizabeth. *See* Rogan
Ross, Elizabeth Vaughan. *See* Jones
Ross, Flora. *See* McKay
Ross, Flora Amelia (Hubbs), XII, **929–30**
Ross, Frances (Bird), X, 67
Ross, Frank, XI, 775
Ross, Frederika. *See* Grant
Ross, G., VIII, 675
Ross, George (father of Sir JAMES CLARK), IX, 691
Ross, George (son of MALCHOM), IV, 685
Ross, George McLeod, VIII, **768–69**
Ross*, Sir George William (1841–1914), XI, 222, 223, 537, 587, 697; XII, 332, 333, 659, 934, 1026, 1113
Ross, Harriet Ann. *See* Valentine
Ross, Henrietta (Black), VIII, 768; X, 549; XI, 79, 776
Ross, Hester E. *See* Harrington
Ross, Hugh (grandfather of Charles SANGSTER), XII, 944
Ross, Hugh (officer), XI, 759
Ross, Hugh, VIII, 123, **769–70**
Ross, Isabella. *See* Creelman
Ross, Isabella. *See* Mainville
Ross, Isabella. *See* Matheson
Ross, Isabella (Green), VIII, 767
Ross, James (father of BERNARD ROGAN), X, 629
Ross, James (husband of Marie-Henriette LEJEUNE), VIII, 498
Ross, James (merchant), V, 461; VI, 478
Ross, James, VIII, 768; X, **629–31**; XI, 19, 46, 563, 738, 740, 776; XII, 82, 950, 983
Ross, James, VI, 660; VIII, 452; XI, **772–73**; XII, 35, 217
Ross*, James (1848–1913), XI, 482; XII, 4
Ross, Sir James Clark, VII, 271, 326; VIII, 685, 686, 771, 772, 773; IX, 12, 167, 659, **691–94**; X, 29, 454, 561; XI, 199, 543, 544, 798, 799; XII, 835

Ross, James Gibb, VIII, 323; XI, 162, 163, 492, **773–75**; XII, 665, 1072, 1118
Ross, Jane. *See* Davidson
Ross, Janet (MacGregor), VIII, 547
Ross, Jean (Jane) (Hunter), XI, 436, 437
Ross, Jemima (Coldwell), VIII, 768
Ross, John (brother of JAMES GIBB), VIII, 323; XI, 773; XII, 280, 1118
Ross, John (father of DAVID ALEXANDER), XII, 928
Ross, John (fur trader), V, 391, 537, 538, 562, 656, 683, 684; VI, 454, 463; VII, 565; VIII, 500
Ross, John (lawyer), IX, 261
Ross, John (politician), VIII, 222
Ross, John, IV, 121, 505, **683–84**, 710; V, 40, 378, 806; VI, 146, 147
Ross, Sir John, I, 75; VI, 329, 330, 754; VII, 323; VIII, 71, 447, 448, 623, 624, 683, **770–74**; IX, 12, 691, 692, 693; X, 26, 28, 406, 407, 561; XI, 798; XII, 835, 876
Ross, John, VIII, 57, 58, 815; IX, 98, 166, 526, 575, 680; X, 144, 200, 336, 561, **631–33**; XI, 11, 226, 414, 497, 781, 853; XII, 43, 351, 595
Ross*, John Jones (1831–1901), XI, 26, 426, 493, 626; XII, 179, 451, 464, 465, 722, 724, 904
Ross*, John Theodore (1862–1954), XII, 280, 665
Ross, Malchom, IV, 157, **684–85**, 741, 742; V, 451, 500; VI, 249, 776; VIII, 879, 880
Ross, Margaret. *See* Crawford
Ross, Margaret. *See* Smith
Ross, Margaret (mother of DAVID ALEXANDER; Strang), XII, 928
Ross, Marie-Henriette. *See* LeJeune
Ross, Mary. *See* Jones
Ross, Mary (Flett), VIII, 768; XI, 776
Ross, Mary (Spark; Montgomery), V, 768
Ross, Mary Cameron (Robertson), XI, 758
Ross, Mary-Jane (Jones), VIII, 51
Ross, Mathilda (Cochrane), X, 178
Ross, Mildred, Lady Ross. *See* Peel
Ross*, Philip Dansken (1858–1949), XII, 137
Ross, Robert B., VIII, 852, 872
Ross, Sally, VIII, 766, 767; X, 629; XI, 79, **775–76**
Ross, Thomas, VI, 283
Ross, Wallace, XII, 797
Ross, Walter, XII, 602
Ross, William (accountant), XII, 286
Ross, William (father of ALEXANDER MILTON), XII, 924
Ross, William (landowner), VI, 301
Ross, William (merchant), IV, 71
Ross, William (politician), XI, 198
Ross, William (son of ALEXANDER), VIII, 768; X, 629
Ross, William Gerrard, XII, 628
Ross, William Moray, VIII, 769
Rossa, O'Donovan, XII, 273
Rossay, Angélique. *See* Cadet
Rossay, Jérôme, IV, 124
Rosse, Leon, VIII, 886
Rossell, Bridget (Warren), VI, 802
Rossie. *See* Oliphant
Rossignol, Jean, I, 292
Rossin, Catherine (Pollet de La Combe de La Pocatière), I, 550
Rossini, Gioacchino Antonio, XI, 671; XII, 223
Ross Lewen, Archange. *See* Baby

Ross Lewen, Ralph, VI, 120
Rosslyn, Earl of. *See* Wedderburn
Rostan, Anne de (Michel de Villebois), III, 444
Rostan, Henri de, III, 444
Rottenburg, Anne-Marie. *See* Brunatti
Rottenburg, Francis de, Baron de Rottenburg, V, 65, 66, 558, 643, 748, 749; VI, 182, 183, 341, 342, 344, 416, 552, 617, **660–62**; VII, 46, 366, 397, 466, 516, 743; VIII, 236, 237, 239, 795; IX, 669, 755
Rottenburg, Franz Gottfried, VI, 660
Rottenburg, George Frederick de, Baron de Rottenburg, VI, 660
Rottenburg, Juliana Wilhelmina Carolina de, Baroness de Rottenburg. *See* Orelli
Rottermund, Cordelia de, Comtesse de Rottermund. *See* Debartzch
Rottermund, Édouard-Sylvestre de, Comte de Rottermund, VII, 236; VIII, **774–76**; IX, 424; X, 445
Rottermund, François de, Count de Rottermund, VIII, 774
Rottermund, Rosalie de, Countess de Rottermund. *See* Kaminska
Rottot. *See also* Trefflé
Rottot*, Jean-Philippe (1825–1910), XI, 218; XII, 1129
Roubaud, Marguerite. *See* Tressol
Roubaud, Pierre-Joseph-Antoine, III, 296; IV, 7, 98, 231, 294, 298, 299, 423, 574, **685–87**, 788; V, 143; VI, 492, 494
Roubaud, Pierre-Pascal, IV, 685
Roubel, P., VI, 662
Roubel, William, V, 220, 862; VI, 161, 162, 163, 298, 414, 566, 567, **662–63**
Roubillac, Louis-François, III, 658
Roucy, Marquis de. *See* La Rochefoucauld
Roucy, Marquise de. *See* La Rochefoucauld
Rouer d'Artigny, Louis, I, 583; II, 152, 235, 583; III, 45, **569–70**; IV, 624; V, 76
Rouer de Villeray, Benjamin, III, **570–71**; IV, 250, 541, 631
Rouer de Villeray, Catherine. *See* Sevestre
Rouer de Villeray, Charles, I, 583
Rouer de Villeray, Jacques, I, 579
Rouer de Villeray, Louis, I, 91, 112, 202, 288, 448, 538, **579–83**, 584, 587, 588, 589, 606; II, xvi, xvii, 137, 138, 508, 583; III, 569
Rouer de Villeray, Marie. *See* Perthuis
Rouer de Villeray, Marie-Anne. *See* Du Saussay de Béniont
Rouer de Villeray, Marie-Catherine (Sallaberry), III, 582
Rouer de Villeray, Marie-Joseph. *See* Pépin, *dit* Laforce
Rouer de Villeray et de La Cardonnière, Augustin, I, 551, 583; II, 277, **583–84**; III, 569, 570
Rouer de Villeray et de La Cardonnière, Marie-Louise. *See* Legardeur de Tilly
Rouer de Villeray et de La Cardonnière, Marie-Louise. *See* Pollet de La Combe-Pocatière
Rouffio, Dominique, III, 571
Rouffio, Étienne, III, 571
Rouffio, François, III, 571
Rouffio, Jean, III, 571
Rouffio, Jean-Jacques, III, 571
Rouffio, Joseph, III, **571–72**; IV, 123; V, 276
Rouffio, Louise. *See* Cadet
Rouffio, Marquèze. *See* Nègre
Rouffio, Pierre, III, 571

Rouffray, Pierre, I, 479
Rougemont, Philippe, I, 168
Rough, Julius, XII, 413
Rouillard, Ambroise (baptized Louis-Joseph), III, 99, **572**
Rouillard, Charlotte-Cécile (Parent), VII, 679
Rouillard, Jean, III, 572
Rouillard, Jean-Baptiste, IV, 203
Rouillard, Jeanne. *See* Levasseur
Rouillard, Marie-Anne (Deguise, *dit* Flamand), III, 170
Rouillard, Marie-Charlotte. *See* Trotain, *dit* Saint-Seürin
Rouillard, *dit* Fondville, Joseph, II, 637
Rouillé, Antoine-Louis, Comte de Jouy, III, 31, 117, 124, 184, 245, 246, 253, 385, 435, 486, 540, 556, 561, 578, 608, 616; IV, 64, 67, 146, 249, 254, 256, 258, 438, 443, 456, 467, 615, 655, 656, 657, 665, 666, 667; V, 172, 638
Rouillé, Mathurin, II, 335
Rouleau*, Charles-Borromée (1840–1901), XI, 460
Rouleau, Thomas-Grégoire, XII, 1066
Roullaud, Henri, XII, 100
Roulleaux de La Vente, Henri, II, 260, 349; III, 380, 381
Roundhead. *See* Stayeghtha
Round the Sky. *See* Paypamaskeesit
Roupe, Jean-Baptiste, V, 481; VII, 774; VIII, 240, 618, 729, **776–77**
Roupe, Marie-Joseph. *See* Clocher
Roupe, Samuel, VIII, 776
Rourke, Mary Ann (McGreevy), XII, 626
Rous, John, III, 70, 128, 209, 293, 362, 363, **572–74**, 628; IV, 110, 213, 242, 249, 700
Rous, Joseph, III, 573
Rous, Mary (Bulkeley), IV, 109
Rous, Rachel (wife of JOHN), III, 573
Rousse, Jacques, VI, 642
Rousseau, Antoine, XII, 105
Rousseau, Catherine (Rattier), II, 549
Rousseau, Célestin-Zéphirin, IX, 634
Rousseau, Charlotte. *See* Foureur
Rousseau, Dominique, VI, 666
Rousseau, Dominique, IV, 206, 272, 629; V, 36, 436, 727; VI, 29, 230, 487, **663–67**; VII, 700
Rousseau, Édouard, IX, 32
Rousseau, François, VI, 664
Rousseau, François-Dominique, IV, 71
Rousseau, Jacques, VI, 550
Rousseau*, Jacques (1905–70), III, 677, 678, 679; X, 106
Rousseau, Jean-Jacques, II, 444; IV, 44, 92; V, 233, 248, 701; VI, 85, 764; VII, 209, 430, 603, 645, 675, 677; X, 573, 585
Rousseau, Léon, XII, 66
Rousseau, Marguerite (Lorimier), VII, 516
Rousseau, Marie. *See* Gournay
Rousseau, Marie-Anne (De Lisle), VI, 666
Rousseau, Pierre (Sulpician), IV, 637
Rousseau, Pierre (watchmaker), III, 410
Rousseau, *dit* Beausoleil, Louis-Alexandre, VI, 663
Rousseau, *dit* Beausoleil, Marie-Joseph. *See* Chabot
Rousseau, *dit* Larose, Laurent, II, 127
Rousseau, *dit* Saint-Jean, Jean-Bonaventure, V, 723
Rousseau, *dit* Saint-Jean, Marie-Reine. *See* Brunet
Rousseau de Souvigny, Jeanne. *See* Saint-Étienne de La Tour
Rousseau de Souvigny, Marie-Josephte (Chassin de Thierry), III, 115

Rousseau de Souvigny, Pierre, III, 115
Rousseau de Villejouin, Anne. *See* Gannes de Falaise
Rousseau de Villejouin, Barbe. *See* Leneuf de La Vallière et de Beaubassin
Rousseau de Villejouin, Gabriel, III, 6, 368; IV, 688
Rousseau de Villejouin, Gabriel, III, 176, 615; IV, **688–89**
Rousseau de Villejouin, Marguerite (Tarride Duhaget), III, 615
Rousseau de Villejouin, Marie-Anne (Le Coutre de Bourville), III, 368
Rousseau de Villejouin, Marie-Josephte. *See* Bertrand
Rousseau de Villejouin, Michel, IV, 688
Rousseaux, Joseph Brant, V, 724
Rousseaux St John, John Baptist, V, **723–25**; VI, 159, 488; VII, 57; VIII, 86, 87
Rousseaux St John, Margaret. *See* Clyne
Rousseaux St John, Marie. *See* Martineau
Roussel, Catherine. *See* Fournier
Roussel, Catherine, I, 583
Roussel, Étienne, I, 583
Roussel, Françoise (Marchand), VIII, 614
Roussel, Françoise (Villedonné), II, 653
Roussel, Geneviève (Chambalon), I, 583; II, 129, 130
Roussel, Jeanne. *See* Bouette
Roussel, Louise, I, 583
Roussel, Louise (Grasset de Saint-Sauveur), IV, 311
Roussel, Louise-Catherine (Saillant), IV, 692
Roussel, Madeleine. *See* Du Mortier
Roussel, Marguerite (Chabrand), IV, 138
Roussel, Marie-Anne (Baudouin; Dusautoy), III, 35
Roussel, Marie-Louise (Pagé, *dit* Carcy), III, 498
Roussel, Marie-Marguerite (Mailhot), VI, 482, 483
Roussel, Marie-Renée (Lambert), II, 274
Roussel, Pierre, IX, 120; XI, 485; XII, 820
Roussel, Thérèse (Berthelot), V, 74; VII, 72
Roussel, Timothée, I, **583**; II, 653; III, 237, 305; V, 74; VII, 72
Roussel Ciquard, François, VI, 145
Roussel Ciquard, Luce. *See* Gautier
Rousselot, Benjamin-Victor, X, 689; XI, **776–78**
Rousselot, Jean, XI, 776
Rousselot, Marie. *See* Allion
Rousselot, Marie. *See* Hurault
Roussol, Edmée (La Chasse), III, 329
Rousson. *See* Le Verrier
Roussy, Louis, VII, 210; VIII, 396; IX, 608, 609; X, 428, **633–34**, 675; XI, 924
Routh, Abigail. *See* Eppes
Routh, Adélaïde-Marie-Joséphine. *See* Lamy
Routh, Elsie. *See* Draper
Routh, Havilland LeMesurier, VIII, 268; IX, 462
Routh, Henry, XII, 273
Routh, Henry Lloyd, VI, 274
Routh, Marie-Louise, Lady Routh. *See* Taschereau
Routh, Randolph, VIII, 778
Routh, Sir Randolph Isham, V, 725; VI, 751; VII, 478; VIII, **777–79**
Routh, Richard, V, 190, 492, **725–27**, 839; VI, 274, 784, 797; VIII, 777
Routhier*, Sir Adolphe-Basile (1839–1920), VIII, 421; XI, 115, 893; XII, 197, 533, 1024
Routhier, Félix, XI, 380
Routhier, François, VIII, 655

Routhier, Joseph-Honoré, XI, 258
Routhier, Marie-Françoise (Hamel), IX, 358
Routhier, Sophie (Franchère), IX, 279, 280
Routier, Charles, IX, 298
Routier, Louise (Légaré), VIII, 494
Routier, Marie-Émélie. *See* Garneau
Routier, Marie-Esther (Morin), XII, 762
Routier, Marie-Jeanne (Voyer, *dit* Le Jardinier; Dubreuil), II, 201
Rouvier, Sophronie (Chevalier), X, 165
Rouville. *See* Hertel
Rouvray. *See* Lenoir
Rouvroy, Claude-Henri de, Comte de Saint-Simon, VIII, 745; X, 585
Rouvroy, Louis de, Duc de Saint-Simon, I, 135; II, 57; III, 64
Roux, Françoise-Élizabeth. *See* Durand
Roux, Jean-Baptiste, VI, 667
Roux, Jean-Henry-Auguste, IV, 90; V, 93, 187, 200, 247, 295, 494, 680, 691; VI, 39, 126, 146, 397, 398, 486, 570, 587, 588, 589, 594, **667–69**, 748; VII, 486, 487, 488, 667, 746, 759, 774; VIII, 490, 626, 728, 729, 730; X, 17
Roux, Joseph-Philibert, VII, 824
Roux, Pierre-Jean-Louis-François, VIII, 66; IX, 397
Roux-Lavergne, Pierre-Célestin, IX, 466
Row. *See also* Roe
Row, Betty (mother of WILLIAM BICKFORD), IX, 694
Row, John (father), IX, 694
Row, John, IX, 694
Row, Thomas, VII, 302
Row, Thomas R., IX, 605
Row, William Bickford, VII, 507; IX, 393, **694–95**; XI, 29, 44
Rowan, Charles, X, 634
Rowan, Sir Charles, X, 634
Rowan, Martha. *See* Sprong
Rowan, Mary. *See* Wilson
Rowan, Robert (brother of WILLIAM), X, 634
Rowan, Robert (father of WILLIAM), X, 634
Rowan, Sir William, VIII, 24; IX, 69; X, **634–35**
Rowand, Alexander, VIII, 780, 818
Rowand, John (father of JOHN), VII, 25; VIII, 779
Rowand, John (son of JOHN), VIII, 780; IX, 367
Rowand, John, VI, 218; VIII, 557, 562, **779–81**, 815; IX, 366, 367, 623; X, 391; XII, 932
Rowand, Lisette. *See* Humphraville
Rowand, Margaret. *See* Harriott
Rowand, Marguerite (McKay), VIII, 780; X, 473
Rowand, Nancy (Harriott), VIII, 780; IX, 367
Rowand, Sophia (McTavish), VIII, 780
Rowe. *See also* Roe
Rowe, Christian (Street), V, 784
Rowe, Edward, V, 784
Rowe, James, V, 784
Rowe, John, VII, 406
Rowell*, Newton Wesley (1867–1941), XI, 804
Rowland, David, VII, 220
Rowland, John, XI, 397
Rowland, John Hamilton, V, 658
Rowland, William, XII, 932
Rowley, Roger, I, 584
Rowley, Thomas, I, 241, 350, 497, **584**
Rowney, Thomas H., XII, 234

Rowsell, Clara (Dixon), X, 231
Rowsell, Elizabeth. *See* Lewis
Rowsell, Henry, VIII, 203, 829; XI, 205, **778–79**, 877, 878
Rowsell, Samuel, XI, 778
Rowsell, Sarah (mother of HENRY), XI, 778
Rowsell, William, XI, 778, 779, 877
Rowswell, John, VI, 127
Roy. *See also* Roi; Roy Portelance
Roy, Adélaïde (Larue), XI, 495
Roy, Adeline. *See* Masse
Roy, Adeline (Lusignan), X, 635
Roy, Adolphe, XI, 807, 808, 810, 811
Roy, Adolphe V., XII, 62
Roy, Agathe (Mayrand; Auger), X, 502
Roy*, Alfred-Valère (1850–1934), XII, 549
Roy, Angélique (Batailler), II, 508
Roy*, Camille (1870–1943), VIII, 88; IX, 119
Roy, Catherine. *See* Ducharme
Roy, Catherine (Delorme), VII, 239
Roy, Charles (brother of LOUIS), IV, 690
Roy, Charles (father of JOSEPH), VIII, 781
Roy, Charles-Fleury, IX, 633
Roy, Charlotte (Brosseau; Ouimet), VIII, 667
Roy, Clovis-Joseph, XII, 1025
Roy, David, VIII, 127
Roy, Élizabeth. *See* Beauchamp
Roy, Éloïse (Élise) (Archambeault), XI, 25
Roy, Émilie L. *See* Lusignany
Roy, Étienne-Féréol, VI, 787
Roy, Félicité (Boucher), IX, 63
Roy, François (father of LOUIS), IV, 689
Roy, François (furniture-maker), VIII, 236
Roy, François (lawyer), IX, 440
Roy, François-Elzéar, XI, 162, 163, 272, 744, 748
Roy, François-Xavier, XI, 318
Roy, Geneviève (Sasseville), IX, 701
Roy, Guillaume-Ernest, X, 422
Roy, Hélène. *See* Parent
Roy, Jacques (father of NARSISE), V, 727
Roy, Jacques (brother of Louis ROY PORTELANCE), VII, 762
Roy, James Alexander, X, 363, 367, 369
Roy, Jean, IV, 702
Roy, Jean-Joseph, IV, 424
Roy, Joseph (father of LOUIS-DAVID), X, 635
Roy, Joseph (grandfather of Pierre-Joseph-Olivier CHAUVEAU), XI, 177, 178
Roy, Joseph (merchant), III, 142, 554
Roy, Joseph, VIII, 284, 433, 489, 667, **781–82**; XII, 88
Roy*, Joseph-Edmond (1858–1913), VII, 233, 485; VIII, 232, 480, 682; XII, 732
Roy, Joseph-Marie, IV, 689, 690; V, 298
Roy*, Joseph-Rouer (1821–1905), VIII, 480; XII, 1025
Roy, Louis, IV, **689–90**; V, 298, 814; VIII, 887
Roy, Louis-David, VIII, 834; IX, 201, 261, 300; X, **635**; XI, 177, 178
Roy, Louise. *See* Chevalier
Roy, Louise-Olive, named de Saint-Paul, IV, 690
Roy, Marguerite, named de la Conception, III, 17, 191, **574–75**, 630
Roy, Marguerite (Perrault), IX, 633
Roy, Marie. *See* Brunet

Roy, Marie. *See* Fisbach
Roy, Marie (Couture), XI, 208
Roy, Marie (Lépine, *dit* Lalime; Corpron), III, 142
Roy, Marie-Adélaïde (Hamel), VII, 373
Roy, Marie-Charlotte (Révol), III, 554; V, 276
Roy, Marie-Françoise. *See* Prud'homme
Roy, Marie-Joseph. *See* Jérôme, *dit* Latour
Roy, Marie-Louise. *See* Lapérade
Roy, Marie-Louise (Chauveau), XI, 177
Roy (LeRoy), Martine (Lejeune), VIII, 498
Roy, Mathilde (Perrault; Prat), X, 600
Roy, Mathurin, II, 639
Roy, Michel (father of Michel ROY, *dit* Châtellerault), II, 584
Roy, Michel (silversmith), IV, 206; V, 218, 436, 727
Roy, Narsise, V, 436, **727–28**
Roy, Pierre (brother of NARSISE), V, 727
Roy, Pierre (clergyman), XI, 659
Roy, Pierre (farmer), XI, 208
Roy, Pierre (father of MARGUERITE), III, 574
Roy*, Pierre-Georges (1870–1953), III, 19, 143, 312, 434, 616, 721; IV, 461, 509, 517, 755; VI, 401, 483; VII, 287, 348, 349; VIII, 628; IX, 123, 902; X, 205, 413, 763; XI, 88, 189, 343, 903
Roy, Robert, XII, 149
Roy, Thomas, VII, 760
Roy, Thomas, VII, **760–61**
Roy, William, V, 55, 348
Roy, *dit* Châtellerault, Françoise. *See* Hobbé
Roy, *dit* Châtellerault, Michel, II, **584**
Roy, *dit* Desjardins, Antoine, II, 466
Roy, *dit* Desjardins, Rosalie (Cadron, *dit* Saint-Pierre), IX, 111
Roy, *dit* Portelance, Catherine. *See* Mallet
Roy, *dit* Portelance, Joseph, VII, 762
Roy, *dit* Portelance, Marie-Angélique (Ducharme), V, 272; VIII, 244
Royal*, Joseph (1837–1902), VIII, 301; IX, 63, 64, 65, 816; XI, 151, 193, 194, 339, 611, 643, 644, 716, 744, 755, 935; XII, 204, 369, 370, 371, 372, 1008, 1010, 1026
Roy-Audy, Jean-Baptiste, VII, 761
Roy-Audy, Jean-Baptiste, VII, **761–62**, 869, 870, 877; VIII, 263, 496; XI, 336
Roy-Audy, Julie. *See* Vézina
Roy-Audy, Marguerite. *See* Gauvreau
Roybon d'Allonne, Jacques de, II, 584
Roybon d'Allonne, Madeleine de, II, **584–85**
Roy-Desjardins, Agathe (Cotté), IV, 171
Roye. *See* La Rochefoucauld; La Rochefoucauld-Roye
Roye, Marquis de. *See* La Rochefoucauld
Roye, Marquise de. *See* Ducasse
Royer, Joseph-Marie, IX, 215
Roy Portelance, Louis, VII, **762–63**
Roy Portelance, Louise. *See* Languedoc
Roy Portelance, Marie-Josephte. *See* Périnault
Roy Portelance, Sophie (Glackmeyer), VII, 762
Rozinoghyata. *See* Hotsinoñhyahta?
Rozoy. *See* Dugey
Ruau (Bau), Perrine (Terriot), II, 625
Rubelles. *See* Bonneau
Rubens, Peter Paul, VI, 25; IX, 361, 363
Rubergall, Elizabeth Anne (Price), XI, 712
Rubergall, Mary Anne (Ketchum), IX, 422; XI, 712

Rubidge, Charles, VI, 730; VIII, 117; X, **635–36**; XII, 527, 930
Rubidge, Eleanor (mother of FREDERICK PRESTON), XII, 930
Rubidge, Frederick Preston, VII, 33; X, 164, 635; XI, 337; XII, 534, 809, 886, **930–31**
Rubidge, Jane Georgina. *See* Boswell
Rubidge, Margaret. *See* Clarke
Rubidge, Margaret. *See* Gilmour
Rubidge, Robert, X, 635; XII, 930
Rubin, V, 878
Ruckle, Barbara (Heck), V, **728–29**; VI, 405; VII, 392
Ruckle, Bastian (Sebastian), V, 728
Ruckle, Margaret. *See* Embury
Rudd, James Sutherland, V, 27, 68, 106; VII, 622
Rudd, Juliana. *See* Walker
Ruddock, Francis, IX, 621
Ruddock, Joseph, IX, 621
Rudduck, Sarah (Cleveland; Fillis), IV, 267
Rudmose, Kristiane Augusta Maria Eleonora (Brown), XII, 129
Rudolf, Anna Matilda. *See* Oxner
Rudolf, Catherine. *See* Stevens
Rudolf, Elizabeth. *See* Koch
Rudolf, Francisca Barbara (Jessen), V, 453
Rudolf, John Christopher, VIII, 782
Rudolf, Leonard Christopher, III, 212; VIII, 782
Rudolf, William, VIII, **782–83**
Rudolfi, Louise-Émilie (König, Baroness von König), VI, 378
Rudolph, John Charles, X, 587
Rueff, Jules, X, 260
Ruehegan, III, 520
Ruelland, Ludger, IX, 364
Ruette d'Auteuil, Claire-Françoise. *See* Clément Du Vuault de Monceaux
Ruette d'Auteuil, Denis-Joseph, I, 136, 202, 288, 289, 580, 581, 582, **584–85**, 587, 588, 589; II, 137, 585
Ruette d'Auteuil, Louise-Geneviève (Daneau de Muy), III, 162
Ruette d'Auteuil, Marie-Anne. *See* Juchereau de Saint-Denis
Ruette d'Auteuil, Marie-Claire (Crisafy, Marquise de Crisafy), II, 163
Ruette d'Auteuil de La Malotière, Marie-Charlotte. *See* Piot de Langloiserie
Ruette d'Auteuil de La Malotière, Pierre, II, 527
Ruette d'Auteuil de Monceaux, François-Madeleine-Fortuné, I, 289, 551, 585; II, 42, 90, 134, 149, 163, 302, 303, 305, 325, 354, 448, 527, 546, 547, 557, 558, 569, 571, 575, **585–88**; III, 51, 52, 58, 104, 201, 202, 410
Ruggles, Philo T., IX, 311
Ruggles, Sarah, VIII, 709
Ruggles, Seraph Cutler (Weeks), XII, 1092
Ruggles, Timothy, IV, 769
Ruis-Embito de La Chesnardière, Charles-Claude de, IV, 91
Ruiter, Henry, VII, 186
Ruiter, Jacob, VII, 186
Ruiter, John. *See* Ruyter, Johannes
Rumsey, Benjamin, V, 181
Runchey, Robert, VII, 698
Rundle, Grace. *See* Carvosso

Rundle, Mary. *See* Wolverson
Rundle, Robert, XII, 931
Rundle, Robert Terrill, VII, 137, 276, 390; VIII, 780; IX, 537; X, 4, 391, 471, 472; XII, 110, **931–32**
Running Crane. *See* Onista'poka
Rupert, Count Palatine, I, 281, 406, 604, 642
Rusconi, Carlo, VI, 185
Rush, Benjamin, VI, 87, 155, 764
Rush, Emily (Cuthbert), IX, 187
Rush, Richard, VII, 31; X, 403
Rushmore, Mary. *See* Carman
Rushout, Elizabeth Augusta, Baroness Northwick. *See* Bateman-Hanbury
Rushworth, Bryan, II, 610
Rushworth, George, III, 123
Ruskin, John, XI, 226; XII, 344, 714, 715, 751, 752, 794
Russel, Alexander Jamieson, VII, 823
Russel, Annabella (Matheson), X, 501
Russell, Mr (of Newfoundland), I, 567
Russell, Captain, I, 93
Russell, Agnes (McKenzie), X, 477
Russell, Alexander, XI, 779
Russell, Alexander Jamieson, X, 446; XI, 779
Russell, Alicia Fenton (Samson; Benson), VII, 772
Russell, Andrew, X, 45; XI, 256, **779–80**
Russell, Ann (Anne) (Ellice), V, 299; IX, 234
Russell, Ann Agnes. *See* Hunter
Russell, Anne (Dudley, Countess of Warwick), I, 318
Russell, Dennis, VII, 795
Russell, Dorothy. *See* Harrison
Russell, Elizabeth. *See* Warnar
Russell, Elizabeth, Lady Russell. *See* Cooke
Russell, Elizabeth (Brenton), V, 108
Russell, Elizabeth (Hicks), IV, 350
Russell, Elizabeth, V, 766; V, 189, 730, 732, 854; VI, **669–70**, 721; VII, 35, 36, 37; VIII, 185; IX, 24
Russell, Henry, X, 370
Russell, Jane (Annand), XI, 22
Russell, Janet. *See* Jamieson
Russell, Jannett (mother of JOSEPH), VIII, 783
Russell, Jeremy Condy, IV, 414
Russell, Jessie (Ker), X, 401
Russell, John, IV, 536
Russell, John, 1st Earl Russell, VII, 7, 43, 118, 144, 148, 172, 296, 297, 345, 354, 427, 477, 512, 857, 858, 859, 861; VIII, xxvii, xxviii, xxxii, xxxiv, 48, 49, 135, 254, 296, 356, 364, 378, 379, 416, 465, 471, 616, 641, 667, 764, 904, 907, 915, 957; IX, 89, 90, 92, 146, 157, 169, 226, 237, 238, 315, 501, 523, 555, 594, 605, 676; X, 76, 77, 254, 345, 364, 367, 438, 553, 574, 581, 626, 640; XI, 308, 659
Russell, John, 4th Duke of Bedford, III, 261, 362, 659; IV, 168, 169, 559, 571; V, 729
Russell, John, 6th Duke of Bedford, VII, 481
Russell, John Scott, VII, 922
Russell, Joseph, VII, 5, 683; VIII, 737, **783–84**; X, 333
Russell, Laura (Phipps), XI, 686
Russell, Lindsay Alexander, XI, 21, 841; XII, 140, 688
Russell, Lucy Chandler. *See* Lord
Russell, Margaret (Drummond, Lady Drummond), VIII, 236
Russell, Margaret (Willcocks), V, 859
Russell, Peter, IV, 12, 756, 766, 767; V, 35, 71, 189, 303,

304, 307, 326, 365, 440, 453, 519, 536, 548, 719, 724, **729–32**, 749, 753, 782, 808, 810, 814, 815, 854, 859, 860; VI, 51, 152, 159, 177, 330, 406, 452, 453, 558, 560, 600, 608, 619, 669, 670, 721, 746; VII, 35, 36, 175, 207, 250, 312, 347, 348, 410, 451, 693, 812, 864; VIII, 185, 337, 483, 606, 890; IX, 24
Russell, Rebecca. *See* Pinkney
Russell, Richard, V, 729; VI, 669
Russell, Robert, VI, 380
Russell, Thomas, VIII, 783
Russell, William, VIII, 236
Russell, William Howard, IX, 844, 845
Russell, Willis, X, 627; XI, 774
Rust, Rebecca (Danks), IV, 193
Rustan, Pascal. *See* Fabre, *dit* Laperrière, Henri-Marie-Paschal
Rut, John, I, 19, 301, **585–86**
Rutgers, Mary (Barclay), VI, 33
Ruther, Mr (painter), XII, 977
Rutherford, Christian (Ainslie), V, 4
Rutherford, Edward Henderson, VIII, 930; XII, 44
Rutherford, John, III, 167; IV, 761
Rutherford, Peter, VIII, 552
Rutherford, Walter, III, 537
Ruthven, John, V, 381
Rutland, Duke of. *See* Manners
Ruttan, Elizabeth (Thomson; Townley), VI, 772, 773
Ruttan, Henry, VIII, 117; X, **636–37**
Ruttan, Henry Jones, VIII, 555; X, 637; XI, 825
Ruttan, Margaret. *See* Steele
Ruttan, Mary. *See* Jones
Ruttan (Rutan, Rattan), Mary (Matthews), VII, 596, 597
Ruttan, William, X, 636
Ruysch, Johannes, I, 148, 678
Ruyter, Johannes, known as John Ruiter, V, 839
Ruyter, Michiel Adriaanszoon de, I, 25, 443, 496
Ruzé. *See* Coiffier
Ryall, George, IV, 83
Ryan, Amelia. *See* Mott
Ryan, Ann (Burns), XII, 143
Ryan, Anne (Switzer), VIII, 854
Ryan, Carroll, XI, 685
Ryan, Deborah (wife of JOHN B.) IX, 695
Ryan, Edward, X, 48; XI, 780, 781
Ryan, Eleanor (Shea), VI, 709; VII, 793
Ryan, Henry, VI, **670–76**; VII, 521; VIII, 132, 180, 422, 946; IX, 80; X, 638; XI, 154
Ryan, Hugh, XII, 699, **932–34**, 964
Ryan, Huldah. *See* Laird
Ryan, James A., X, **637–38**; XI, 307; XII, **934**
Ryan, John (brother of HUGH), XII, 933
Ryan, John (merchant), VI, 710; VII, 228
Ryan, John (son of JOHN B.), IX, 695
Ryan, John (tailor), VII, 152, 598
Ryan, John, IV, 483, 721; V, 506, 612, 613; VI, 301, 323, 408; VII, 351, **763–66**; XI, 673
Ryan, John B., VIII, 147; IX, **695**; XI, 780, 781
Ryan, Joseph, VI, 709, 710
Ryan, Joseph O'Connell, XI, 613
Ryan, Lewis Kelly, VI, 410; VII, 765, 766
Ryan, Margaret. *See* Conway
Ryan, Margaret. *See* Walsh
Ryan, Martin, XII, 932

Ryan, Mary Julia (Horetzky), XII, 447
Ryan, Mary Somaindyke (Goff), VII, 351
Ryan, Matthew, XII, 674, 675
Ryan, Michael, VII, 764, 765, 766
Ryan, Michael Patrick, X, 230
Ryan, Patrick, VI, 709, 710, 711
Ryan, Roderick, XII, 447
Ryan, Thomas, X, 684; XI, 5, 42, 557, **780–82**
Ryan, Timothy, VI, 709, 710
Ryan, Wilhelmine-Dudding. *See* Montenach
Rybot, Francis, III, 620
Ryckman, Edward Baird, VIII, 42
Ryckman, Edward Bradshaw, VIII, 42
Ryckman, Emmaline Edmond. *See* Baird
Ryder, John, XI, 304
Ryder, Mary Anne (Mitchell), XII, 739
Ryerse, Amelia (Harris), VII, 46, 870; VIII, 670, 672; XI, **782–83**
Ryerse, Elizabeth. *See* Colwell
Ryerse, Johanna. *See* Van der Hoff
Ryerse (Ryerson), Luke (Luyckes), V, 732
Ryerse, Samuel, V, 59, 196, **732–35**, 846, 847; VI, 331, 421, 422; VIII, 607; XI, 782, 783, 795
Ryerse, Sarah. *See* Underhill
Ryerson, Charles Egerton, XI, 791
Ryerson, Edway (Edwy) Marcus, X, 638; XI, 784, 795
Ryerson, Egerton, V, 721; VI, 11, 32, 165, 248, 675; VII, 230, 366, 442, 522, 543, 606, 858, 859, 860, 861; VIII, xxiv, 28, 29, 55, 134, 188, 203, 230, 372, 373, 440, 442, 652, 697, 790, 791, 849; IX, 27, 87, 139, 140, 141, 164, 230, 372, 383, 409, 423, 498, 500, 501, 509, 540, 551, 635, 664, 736, 737, 750; X, 4, 16, 45, 54, 63, 125, 253, 255, 256, 262, 317, 323, 442, 459, 466, 467, 616, 638, 639, 640, 641, 646; XI, 222, 223, 228, 247, 317, 327, 367, 475, 497, 536, 541, 576, 587, 617, 640, 719, 730, 733, 734, **783–95**, 796, 797, 798, 849, 942, 943; XII, 184, 232, 297, 298, 385, 469, 528, 571, 594, 880, 959, 1086, 1112
Ryerson, George, VIII, 28, 133, 441; IX, 500, 683; X, 638, 639; XI, 784, **795–98**
Ryerson*, George Ansel Sterling (1854–1925), XI, 309, 795; XII, 97, 497
Ryerson, Hannah. *See* Aikman
Ryerson, Isabella Dorcas. *See* Sterling
Ryerson, John, VI, 675; VII, 665; VIII, 29, 133, 372, 373, 643; IX, 27, 729; X, 4, 317, 373, 616, **638–40**, 641; XI, 640, 660, 733, 784, 785, 795, 796, 797, 849; XII, 127, 297
Ryerson, Joseph, V, 733, 846; VI, 331; VII, 92; X, 638, 640; XI, 783, 795
Ryerson, Mary. *See* Armstrong
Ryerson, Mary. *See* Griffen
Ryerson, Mary. *See* Lewis
Ryerson, Mary (Bostwick), VII, 92
Ryerson, Mehetable. *See* Stickney
Ryerson, Samuel, XI, 795, 797
Ryerson, Sarah. *See* Rolph
Ryerson, Sophia. *See* Symes
Ryerson, Sophia Howard (Harris), XI, 222, 783, 785, 791
Ryerson, William, VI, 266; VIII, 29, 310, 442; IX, 27, 420; X, 4, 638, 639, **640–41**; XI, 640, 733, 784, 787, 795, 796; XII, 297
Rykert, Ann Maria. *See* Mittleberger

Rykert, George, VII, 376; VIII, **785–87**
Rykert, John Charles, XI, 497; XII, 935
Ryland, Charlotte. *See* Warwick
Ryland, Elizabeth. *See* Frith
Ryland, George Herman, VII, 771
Ryland, Herman Witsius, V, 18, 45, 84, 207, 208, 212, 213, 246, 292, 651, 655, 696; VI, 47, 97, 174, 380, 524, 587, 588, 594, 595, 642, 716; VII, 80, 104, 380, 401, 486, 614, 615, 624, 646, 727, 729, **766–72**, 784, 790, 817, 825, 872; VIII, 388, 389, 462; IX, 115
Ryland, John Collett, VII, 766
Ryland, William Deane, VII, 770
Rymal, Jacob, XII, 934
Rymal, Joseph, XI, 907; XII, 658, **934–35**
Rymal, Josephine. *See* Horning
Rymal, Lydia Ann. *See* Terryberry

SAAROM. *See* Atecouando (fl. 1701–26)
Saattoq (Sa-too), VIII, 447
Sabatier, Antoine, III, 98, 387, 396, **575–76**; IV, 60, 420, 644
Sabatier, Charles. *See* Wugk, Charles-Désiré-Joseph
Sabatier, François, I, 514
Sabatier, François de Paule, III, 576
Sabatier, Jean, VI, 676
Sabatier, Joseph, III, 575
Sabatier, Madeleine. *See* Arnauld
Sabatier, Margaret. *See* Hutchinson
Sabatier, Susanne. *See* Pouget
Sabatier, William, VI, **676–78**; VII, 63; VIII, 866
Sabatis. *See* Gill, Antoine
Sabin, Joseph, V, 765
Sabine, Sir Edward, VIII, 71, 771, 772; IX, 691; XI, 508, 509, 662, **798–800**
Sabine, Elizabeth Juliana, Lady Sabine. *See* Leeves
Sabine, James, VII, 220
Sabine, Joseph, XI, 798
Sabine, Sarah. *See* Hunt
Sabourin, Marie-Charlotte (Raizenne), VI, 627
Sabourin, Marie-Madeleine (Tonty de Liette), III, 627
Sabourin, Sara. *See* Enneson
Sabourin, *dit* Chauniers, Catherine (Foucault), III, 226
Sabrevois, Charles de, II, 589; III, 258; IV, 690, 691
Sabrevois, Jacques-Charles de, II, 563, 580, **588–89**; III, 105; IV, 690
Sabrevois, Jeanne de. *See* Boucher
Sabrevois de Bleury, Amelia. *See* Bowers
Sabrevois de Bleury, Charlotte de. *See* Guichard
Sabrevois de Bleury, Clément, IX, 696
Sabrevois de Bleury, Clément-Charles, VII, 345, 354, 757; VIII, 260, 364, 745; IX, 458, 485, 486, 650, **696–97**
Sabrevois de Bleury, Clément de, II, 548, 589; III, 412; IV, 362, 653, **690–91**
Sabrevois de Bleury, Jean-Clément de, IV, 691
Sabrevois de Bleury, Marguerite de (Dandonneau Du Sablé; Lorimier de Verneuil), IV, 691
Sabrevois de Bleury, Marie-Élisabeth-Alix. *See* Rocher
Sabrevois de Sermonville, Christophe de, II, 589; IV, 690
Sabrevois de Sermonville, Gabrielle de. *See* Martin
Sabrevois de Sermonville, Henri de, II, 588
Saccardy, Vincent, I, 533, 576, **586–87**; II, 183
Sacépée (Saccapee), Joachim de, V, 740

Saché, Louis-Césaire, VIII, 243
Sacheuse (Saccheous), John, VIII, 771
Sack, Isaac, XII, 835
Sackville, Viscount. *See* Germain
Sackville, James, XI, 803, 804
Sackville, Lionel Cranfield, 1st Duke of Dorset, IV, 20
Sacy. *See* Lemaistre
Sadlier, James, X, 175
Sadlier, Mary Anne. *See* Madden
Saenredam, Pieter Jansz, VII, 193
Saffray de Mézy, Augustin de, I, 32, 47, 113, 146, 202, 203, 221, 245, 323, 325, 400, 448, 467, 537, 542, 543, 549, 556, 570, 580, 584, **587–90**, 592; II, xvii, xix, 85, 365, 366, 367
Sagard, Gabriel (baptized Théodat), I, 70, 73, 121, 123, 125, 130, 132, 133, 160, 211, 222, 233, 263, 265, 346, 368, 382, 417, 419, 433, 437, 509, 511, 546, 578, **590–92**, 639, 663; II, 281, 429; X, 166; XI, 851
Sagaunash. *See* Caldwell, Billy
Sa Ga Yeath Qua Pieth Tow (Brant), V, 803
Sage, John, V, 35
Sagean, Jean, II, 589
Sagean, Marie. *See* Larrante
Sagean, Mathieu, II, **589–90**
Sageot. *See also* Sajos
Sageot, Geneviève (Adhémar de Saint-Martin), II, 11
Sageot, *dit* Laforge, Marie-Madeleine. *See* Sasseville
Sagouarrab (Sagouarrat, Saguaarum). *See* Sauguaaram
Sagoyewatha. *See* Shakóye:wa:tha?
Saguima, II, 324, 515; III, xxxix, **576–77**
Sahneu, XII, 935
Sahneuti (Sahnyateh), XII, **935–36**
Sahonwagy (Sahonwadi), IV, **691–92**; VIII, 708
Saillans, Anne de. *See* Mius d'Entremont de Pobomcoup
Saillans, Antoine de, II, 38, 512
Saillant, Anne. *See* Laurent
Saillant, Jacques, IV, 692
Saillant (Saillant de Collégien), Jean-Antoine, III, 142, 397; IV, **692–93**; V, 74, 288, 289, 478
Saillant, Louise-Catherine. *See* Roussel
Saillant, Véronique. *See* Pépin, *dit* Laforce
Saille, Mary (Outlaw), I, 529
Sailly, Anne-Françoise de. *See* Bourduceau
Sailly, Louis-Arthus de, I, 47, **592**
Sailly, Pierre. *See* Gagnon, Ernest
Sainbel. *See* Vial
Saincennes. *See also* Sincennes
Saincennes, Jacques, X, 656
Saincennes, Marie-Josephte. *See* Marcotte
Sainctar, Catherine (Baillif), I, 76
Sainctes, Marguerite de (Pottier), II, 527
Saindon, Apolline (Bertrand), XII, 104
Saindon, Louis, VII, 164
Sainsbury, Arabella (Cowley), XI, 208
Saint-Aignan. *See* Marsolet
Saint-Aignan, Duc de. *See* Beauvillier
Saint-Aimé, George. *See* Pelletier, Alexis
St Albans, Duchess of. *See* Gubbins
St Albans, Duke of. *See* de Vere
St Albans, Viscount. *See* Bacon
Saint-Amant. *See also* Pélerin
Saint-Amant, Joseph-Charles, VII, 398
Saint-Amour. *See* Payet

Saint-André. *See* Besnard; Monbeton de Brouillan, Jacques-François de
Saint-Ange. *See* Charly; Groston
Saint-Antoine. *See* Martel
Saint-Arnaud, Damase, XI, 506
Saint-Arsène. *See* Arnaud
Saint-Aubin. *See also* Blain; Le Poupet; Serreau
Saint-Aubin, Ambroise, IV, 13, 30, **693**, 736; V, 16, 295; VI, 678, 679
Saint-Aubin, Joseph, VI, 678
Saint-Aubin, Joseph-Thomas, VI, **678–79**
Saint-Augustin. *See* Compain
Saint-Aulaire, Marquis de. *See* Beaupoil
Saint-Auron. *See* Maugenest
Saint-Barnabé. *See* Lepage
Saint-Benoît. *See* Lefebvre Belle-Isle
Saint-Bernard, Raymond de, I, 352, 357
Saint-Blaint. *See* Raimbault
Saint-Castin. *See* Abbadie
Saint-Castin, Baronne de. *See* Béarn-Bonasse; Damours de Chauffours; Pidianske
Saint-Chéran. *See* Saint-Thairau
St Cir, Monsieur (NWC employee), V, 564
St Clair, Arthur, V, 3, 553, 594, 807, 808, 852; VII, 847
Saint-Clair, Pierre de, II, 434, 479, **590**
Saint-Claude. *See* Volant
Saint-Columbe, Monsieur (engineer), II, 184
Saint-Cosme. *See also* Buisson
Saint-Cosme, II, 110
Saint-Cosme, Théotiste (Dejean), V, 237, 238
St Croix, Benjamin de, VII, 103
St Croix, Margaret de. *See* Desbrisay
St Croix, Margaret Leah de (Brecken), VII, 103
Saint-Cyrque (Saint-Sircq), Monsieur de (officer), II, 603
Saint-Denis. *See also* Potier
Saint-Denis; Saint Denys. *See also* Juchereau
Saint-Denis, Élisabeth (Boudria), VII, 149
Saint-Denis, Geneviève (Dière, *dit* Maréchal), XII, 697
Saint-Denis, Virginie (Mercier), XII, 719, 720
Saint-Dizier. *See* Nivard
Sainte, Claude de (Monseignat), II, 483
Sainte-Agnès. *See* Tibierge
Sainte-Angèle. *See* Arnoldi
Sainte-Barbe. *See* Guillet
Sainte-Beuve, Charles-Augustin, VIII, 291; XI, 83, 273
Sainte-Cécile. *See* Durocher
Sainte-Claire. *See* Lepage
Sainte-Croix. *See* Brice
Sainte-Croix, Mother. *See* Holmes
Sainte-Élisabeth. *See* Dorval
Sainte-Florine. *See* Chauveau
Sainte-Gertrude, Sister. *See* Hervieux; Huot
Sainte-Hélène. *See* Le Moyne
Sainte-Henriette. *See* Lemire-Marsolais
Sainte-James, Baron de. *See* Baudart
Sainte-Madeleine. *See* Huot; Longley
Sainte-Marie. *See also* Allard; Gastineau; Le Moyne
Sainte-Marie, Chevalier de. *See* Allard de Sainte-Marie
Sainte-Marie, Marie-Anne (Voyer), VIII, 918
Sainte-Marie-Médiatrice. *See* Lambert
Sainte-Rosalie. *See* Piot de Langloiserie
Sainte-Rose. *See* Brunet, *dit* L'Estang
Saint-Esprit. *See* Le Moyne de Sainte-Marie

Saint-Étienne. *See also* Dinan

Saint-Étienne de La Tour, Agathe de (Bradstreet; Campbell), II, **590–91**; IV, xix, 83

Saint-Étienne de La Tour, Angélique de. *See* Loreau

Saint-Étienne de La Tour, Anne de. *See* Melanson

Saint-Étienne de La Tour, Anne de (Mius d'Entremont, Baronne de Pobomcoup), I, 510, 514; II, 206, 512

Saint-Étienne de La Tour, Charles de, II, 592

Saint-Étienne de La Tour, Charles de, I, 25, 32, 51, 53, 54, 62, 66, 90, 97, 102, 223, 234, 241, 248, 257, 258, 311, 323, 383, 433, 434, 435, 436, 469, 471, 476, 490, 495, 503, 504, 510, 514, 567, 569, **592–96**, 597, 604, 605, 636; II, 206, 460, 590, 591; IV, xviii, xix, xxiii; VII, 275; X, 426; XI, 303

Saint-Étienne de La Tour, Charles de, I, 436, 514; II, 39, **591–92**; III, 503

Saint-Étienne de La Tour, Claude de, I, 25, 53, 54, 77, 503, 579, 592, 593, 594, **596–98**, 605; IV, xix

Saint-Étienne de La Tour, Françoise-Marie de. *See* Jacquelin

Saint-Étienne de La Tour, Jacques de, I, 514; II, 590; IV, xix

Saint-Étienne de La Tour, Jeanne de. *See* Motin

Saint-Étienne de La Tour, Jeanne de (Aprendestiguy), I, 66, 595

Saint-Étienne de La Tour, Jeanne de (Pontif; Rousseau de Souvigny), III, 115

Saint-Étienne de La Tour, Marguerite de (Mius de Plemazais), I, 510, 514

Saint-Étienne de La Tour, Marie de (Le Borgne de Belle-Isle), I, 436, 514; II, 581

Saint-Eugène, Sieur de (clerk), II, 135

Saint-Fauste. *See* Garrigues

Saint-Ferréol. *See* Lyon

Saint-Florentin, Comte de. *See* Phélypeaux

Saint-Flour, Chevalier de, II, 446

St Frances Patrick, Sister. *See* Partridge, Frances

Saint-François. *See* Crevier; François; Hertel; Trottier

Saint-François, Sieur de. *See* Bourdon

Saint-Front. *See* Duclos

Saint-Gaudens, Augustus, XII, 288

St George. *See* Quetton

Saint-Georges, Adélaïde de. *See* Allsopp

Saint-Georges, Adrien de, II, 381

Saint-Georges, Jeanne de. *See* Guernon

Saint-Georges, Laure de. *See* Thibaudeau

Saint-Georges, Marie-Catherine de (Le Conte Dupré), II, 81, 381; III, 367

Saint-Georges Dupré. *See also* Le Comte Dupré, Georges-Hippolyte

Saint-Georges Dupré, Hippolyte, VII, 757

Saint-Germain. *See also* Audouart; Cureux; Diverny; Gauthier; Lamoureux; Lemaire; Mangeant

Saint-Germain, Amable. *See* Sénécalle

Saint-Germain, Sieur (apparently of Martinique), III, 377

Saint-Germain, Bernard, VII, 148

Saint-Germain, Eugénie (Cardinal), VII, 148, 150

Saint-Germain, Jean-Baptiste, IX, 697

Saint-Germain, Jean-Baptiste, VI, 126; VII, 488; VIII, 593, 712, 728; IX, **697–98**, 797; XI, 94; XII, 891

Saint-Germain-Beaupré. *See* Foucault

Saint-Germain de Mérieux, Marie-Anne de (Pourroy de Lauberivière), II, 530

Saint-Henri, Mother. *See* McLoughlin

Saint-Herman. *See* Raizenne

Saint-Hilaire. *See also* Hillaire

Saint-Hilaire, Élie, XI, 191

Saint-Hilaire, Geneviève. *See* Jelly

Saint-Hilaire, Pierre, XI, 208

Saint-Hippolyte. *See* Piot de Langloiserie

Saint-Horan. *See also* Maugenest

Saint-Horan (Saint-Jorand), Marie-Anne (Maugenest), IV, 524

Saint-Ignace. *See* Raizenne

Saint-Jacques. *See* Cheval

Saint-Jacques, Henriette. *See* Dessaulles

Saint-James. *See* Beauvais

Saint-Jean. *See also* Bourdon; Langlois; Rousseau; Serre

Saint-Jean, Mother. *See* Fontbonne

St Jean, Élizabeth. *See* Causabon, *dit* Didier

Saint-Jean, Marie-Joseph (Gibault), V, 342

St Jean, Marie-Louise. *See* Fréchette

St Jean, Pierre, XII, **936–38**

St Jean, Rose Délima. *See* Larue

St Jean, Sylvain (Silvas), XII, 937

Saint-Jérôme, Mother, I, 353

St John. *See also* Rousseaux

St John, Baron. *See* Paulet

St John, Elizabeth Louisa (Bagot, Baroness Bagot), VII, 30

St John, Henry, 1st Viscount Bolingbroke, II, 286, 497, 659, 660, 662; III, 200; V, 486; VI, 774; X, 314

St John, John, 2nd Viscount St John, VII, 30

St John, Margaret (O'Brien), XII, 792

Saint John, Mary (Howley), XI, 429

St John, Oliver, Viscount Grandison, I, 94

St John, Sarah Anne (Todd), XI, 883

St John, William Charles, XII, 1060

Saint-Jorand. *See* Maugenest

Saint-Joseph. *See* Leduc; Trottier

Saint-Julhien. *See* Mascle

Saint-Julien, Pierre, VI, 49

Saint-Jure, Jean-Baptiste de, I, 484, 485

Saint-Just. *See* Biencourt; Letellier

Saint-Lambert. *See* Philippe

Saint-Laurent. *See* Huot

Saint-Laurent, Comte de. *See* Berthelot

Saint-Laurent, Comtesse de. *See* Juchereau de Saint-Denis

Saint-Laurent, Mme de. *See* Montgenet, Thérèse-Bernardine

St Leger, Mrs. *See* Bayly

St Leger, Sir Anthony, I, 82

St Leger, Barrimore Matthew, IV, 114, 118, 120, 155, 323, 324, 367, 405, 410, 417, **694–95**, 710, 731; V, 33, 57, 88, 254, 347, 584, 746, 747, 805; VI, 264

St Leger, Sir John, IV, 694

St Leger, Lavina, Lady St Leger. *See* Pennefather

St Leger, Mary (Sutton, Baroness Lexington), I, 82

St Lo, George, II, 659

St Lo, John, II, 89

Saint-Louis. *See also* Hertel; Plichon

Saint-Louis, Augustin, VIII, 632

Saint-Louis-des-Anges. *See* Paré

Saint-Lubin, Léon de, VIII, 347

Saint-Luc. *See* La Corne; Rageot

Saint-Luc, Marquis de. *See* Espinay

Saint-Lusson. *See* Daumont

Saint-Mars (Saint-Marc), Jean-Baptiste, II, 513
Saint-Martin. *See also* Adhémar; Baudry; Boschet; Boutet; Dumas; Hindenlang, Charles; Lestringant
Saint-Martin, Joannis (Jean) de, III, 157
Saint-Mas, Monsieur (agent), I, 433
Saint-Matte. *See* Jérôme
Saint-Maur. *See* Dupré
Saint-Maurice. *See* Dubois; Faucher; Olivier
Saint-Médard. *See* Le Mercier
Saint-Méry. *See* Moreau
Saint-Michel. *See also* Messier
Saint-Michel, Charles, X, 512
Saint-Nectaire. *See* Senneterre
Saint-Olive, Claude de, II, 54
Saint-Olon. *See* Pidou
Saint-Onge. *See also* Garreau
Saint-Onge, Alphonsine (Dupuis), X, 266
Saint-Ours. *See also* Quinson; Roch
Saint-Ours, Aurélie. *See* Faribault
Saint-Ours, Caroline-Virginie de (Kierzkowski), IX, 424
Saint-Ours, Charles, VIII, 288, 916
Saint-Ours, Charles de, VI, 287, 316, **679–80**; VII, 235; VIII, 332, 605; X, 236, 428
Saint-Ours, Charles-Pierre de, VI, 680
Saint-Ours, Charles-Quinson de, VI, 679
Saint-Ours, Charlotte de. *See* Deschamps de Boishébert
Saint-Ours, Élisabeth de (Le Roy de La Potherie), II, 422, 593
Saint-Ours, François-Roch de, VI, 679, 680; VII, 360; VIII, 504; IX, 424, 696; X, 236
Saint-Ours, François-Xavier de, III, 34, **577–78**
Saint-Ours, Hélène de. *See* Céloron de Blainville
Saint-Ours, Henri de, II, 592
Saint-Ours, Henriette-Amélie de (Dorion), X, 236
Saint-Ours, Jacques-Philippe de, VI, 679
Saint-Ours, Jeanne de. *See* Calignon
Saint-Ours, Jeanne de (Pécaudy de Contrecœur), I, 535; II, 593; III, 503, 505; IV, 617
Saint-Ours, Jeanne-Geneviève de, VI, 679
Saint-Ours, Josette de. *See* Murray
Saint-Ours, Josette de (Debartzch), VI, 680; VII, 235
Saint-Ours, Marguerite de. *See* Legardeur de Tilly
Saint-Ours, Marie de. *See* Mullois
Saint-Ours, Marie-Anne de (Mine), II, 593
Saint-Ours, Marie-Barbe de (Legardeur de Beauvais), III, 374
Saint-Ours, Paul-Roch, IV, 716; V, 149, 150, 208, 877; VI, 679, 680; VIII, 288
Saint-Ours, Pierre de, II, 125, 593; III, 577
Saint-Ours, Pierre de, I, 418; II, 105, 203, 323, 403, **592–93**, 616; III, 233, 374, 385, 505, 577, 578
Saint-Ours, Roch de, VII, 360
Saint-Ours, Thérèse de. *See* Hertel de Cournoyer
Saint-Ours Deschaillons, Jean-Baptiste de, II, 285, 296, 495, 593; III, 104, 450, **578–79**
Saint-Ours Deschaillons, Marguerite de. *See* Legardeur de Repentigny
Saint-Ours Deschaillons, Pierre-Roch de, III, 183, 332, 579; IV, xliii, 455, 634; V, 98; VI, 679
Saint-Ovide. *See* Monbeton
St Paul. *See* Lolo, Jean-Baptiste
Saint-Paul. *See also* Godefroy; Lambert; Lamotte; Le Ber
Saint-Paul, Claude de, I, 313

Saint-Pé, Jean-Baptiste de, II, 40; III, 204, 361, 428, **579–80**; IV, 240, 298, 685
Saint-Père. *See also* Rameau
Saint-Père, Agathe de (Legardeur de Repentigny), II, 385, 386, 552, 597; III, 579, **580–81**
Saint-Père, Étienne de, I, 598
Saint-Père, Étiennette de. *See* Julian
Saint-Père, Jean de, I, 79, 218, 230, 231, **598–99**; II, xvi, 386; III, 580
Saint-Père, Mathurine de. *See* Godé
Saint-Pierre. *See also* Bernardin; Bréguier-Saint-Pierre; Cadron; Denys; Du Pont; Jussaume; Labadie; Legardeur
Saint-Pierre, Comte de. *See* Castel
Saint-Pierre, Comtesse de. *See* Kerven
St Pierre (Sappier), Louise, VIII, 508
Saint-Pierre, Paul de, V, 433
Saint-Placide. *See* Boucher de Montbrun
Saint-Pol, Comte de. *See* Orléans
Saint-Poncy. *See* La Vernède
Saint-Quentin. *See* Moral
Saint-Réal. *See* Vallières
Saint-Rémy. *See* Rémy
Saint-Romain. *See* Chorel
Saint-Sacrement. *See* Bourgeoys; La Corne de Chaptes
Saint-Saëns, Camille, XI, 671
Saint-Sauveur. *See* Grasset
Saint-Sauveur, Abbé de. *See* Le Sueur
Saint-Sceine. *See* Petitot
Saint-Seürin. *See* Trotain
Saint-Séverin. *See* Ameau
Saint-Simon. *See also* Denis; Denys; Lefebvre Angers; Rouvroy
Saint-Simon, Claude-Anne de, Duc de Saint-Simon, IV, 208
Saint-Sircq. *See* Saint-Cyrque
Saint-Terone. *See* Maugenest
Saint-Thairau (Saint-Turine, Saint-Chéran), Antoinette de (Tarride Duhaget), III, 615
Saint-Vallier. *See* La Croix
Saint-Victor. *See* Coster
Saint-Vilmé. *See* Ailleboust
St Vincent, Earl of. *See* Jervis
Saint-Vincent, Abbé de, III, 415; IV, 453
Saint-Vincent, Henri-Albert de, IV, 263
Saint-Vincent-de-Paul. *See* Robichaud
Saito, Uta, XII, 815
Sajan. *See* Sagean
Sajos (Sageot), Marie-Charlotte (Darris; Digé), V, 257
Sakayengwaraton. *See* Johnson, John (1792–1886)
Sakima. *See* Saguima
Sakonentsiask, III, 615
Sakumow Sagma. *See* Segipt
Salaberry. *See also* Irumberry; Sallaberry
Salaberry, Marie-Émilie. *See* Guy
Salaberry, Melchior-Alphonse de, VII, 858; VIII, 693; IX, 362, 363, **698–99**, 771; X, 404; XI, 82
Saladin, Simon, II, 283
Salavy, Margaret de (Mascarene), III, 435
Salazar, Jeanne de (Biencourt), I, 96
Sales, Jean-Pierre de, V, 735
Sales Laterrière, Dorothée de (Lehouillier), IV, 619; V, 736, 737, 738; VI, 183, 184
Sales Laterrière, Edmond de, VI, 185

Sales Laterrière, Eulalie-Antoinette. *See* Dénéchaud
Sales Laterrière, Marc-Pascal de, V, 737, 738; VI, 184, 680, 681; VII, 879; IX, 360; X, **431–32**
Sales Laterrière, Marie-Catherine de. *See* Delezenne
Sales Laterrière, Mary Ann. *See* Bulmer
Sales Laterrière, Pierre de, IV, 205, 206, 288, 336, 589, 618, 619; V, 100, 277, **735–38**, 893; VI, 120, 183, 184, 185, 300, 680; VII, 65; IX, 774; X, 431
Sales Laterrière, Pierre-Jean de, V, 737, 738; VI, 184, 261, **680–82**; X, 18, 375
Salgé, Marguerite. *See* Poulliot
Salières, Marquis de. *See* Chastelard
Salignac de La Mothe-Fénelon, François de, I, 599; II, 330; IV, 467; VIII, 283
Salignac de La Mothe-Fénelon, François de, I, 127, 136, 175, 270, 287, 297, 410, 539, 584, **599–601**, 613, 647; II, 45, 130, 193, 194, 195, 227, 349, 350, 514, 561, 582, 637
Salignac de La Mothe-Fénelon, Marie-Louise-Augustine de (Le Normant de Mézy), IV, 467
Salisbury. *See* Salusbury
Salisbury, Earl of. *See* Cecil
Sall, IV, 779
Sallaberry, Angélique de, III, 582
Sallaberry, Madeleine-Louise de. *See* Juchereau Duchesnay de Saint-Denis
Sallaberry, Marie de. *See* Michelance
Sallaberry, Marie-Catherine de. *See* Rouer de Villeray
Sallaberry, Marsans de, III, 582
Sallaberry, Michel de, III, 377, **582–83**; VI, 345
Sallé, Marie-Thérèse (Raimbault), II, 541
Salleneuve, Jean-Baptiste de, III, 347; IV, 640
Sally. *See* Kyen-da-nent
Salmon, Edme-Gatien, III, 40, 382
Salmon, George C., VIII, 476
Salmon, John, XII, 454
Salmon, Thomas, II, 251
Salomon. *See also* Allemewi
Salomon, Elias, IV, 332, 385
Saltar, Lucy (Hartshorne), VI, 312
Salter, Elizabeth Isabella Caroline (Darling, Lady Darling), IX, 195
Salter, John, V, 618; VI, 350
Salter, Joseph, IX, 368; XI, 91, 544, 727
Salter, Malachy, IV, 695
Salter, Malachy, IV, 29, 52, 110, 116, 273, 291, 313, 562, **695–97**; VII, 492
Salter, Sampson, VII, 86
Salter, Sarah. *See* Holmes
Salter, Sarah (Blowers), VII, 86
Salter, Susanna. *See* Mulberry
Saltonstall, Dudley, IV, 504
Saltonstall, Gurdon, II, 498
Salusbury, Sir Henry, I, 656
Salusbury, Hester. *See* Cotton
Salusbury, Hester Lynch (Thrale; Piozzi), III, 583
Salusbury, John, III, **583–84**
Salusbury, Lucy (mother of JOHN), III, 583
Salusbury, Thomas (father), III, 583
Salusbury, Thomas, III, 583
Salvaye, (Pierre?) de, III, 65
Salvert. *See* Perier
Samalins, Jeanne de (Lanouguère), I, 417

Sampson, Alicia. *See* Brush
Sampson, Eliza Chipman. *See* Winslow
Sampson, James, VII, 410, 418; VIII, 761; IX, **699–701**; XI, 263, 266, 940
Sampson, Richard, II, 118
Sampson, William, IX, 699
Samson, Alicia Fenton. *See* Russell
Samson, Angélique (Languedoc), VII, 484
Samson, James (doctor), XII, 1073, 1074
Samson, James (father of JAMES HUNTER), VII, 772
Samson, James Hunter, VI, 773; VII, 497, **772–73**; VIII, 45; IX, 41, 45
Samuel, Emmanuel, XI, 801
Samuel, Joseph, IX, 177
Samuel, Kate. *See* Seckelman
Samuel, Lewis, VIII, 445; XI, **800–1**; XII, 93
Samuel, Mark, XI, 800, 801
Samuel, Phebe (David), V, 193; VI, 179
Samuel*, Sigmund (1867–1962), XI, 800
Sanborn, David Edwin, X, 641
Sanborn, Edwin David, X, 641
Sanborn, Eleanor Hall. *See* Brooks
Sanborn, Hannah. *See* Hook
Sanborn, John Sewell, IX, 727; X, 418, **641–43**, 654; XI, 437, 706; XII, 351
Sanborn, Nancy Judson. *See* Hasseltine
Sancé, Michel de, I, 229
Sánchez de Arévalo, Rodrigo, XII, 16
Sancton, Jane (Seely), IX, 710
Sand, George. *See* Dupin, Aurore
Sandby, Paul, V, 227; VI, 256; VII, 193, 194, 400; IX, 849
Sandeman, Catherine Edith. *See* Brown
Sandeman, Robert, VI, 128; VII, 814
Sanders, Anne Gilbert (Macbeth), IX, 475
Sanders, Edward Howard, XI, 394
Sanders, John, IX, 475
Sandersleben, Henriette-Edwige. *See* Curie
Sanderson*, Charles Rupert (1887–1956), VIII, 30
Sanderson, David, VII, 138
Sanderson, Ellen (Withrow), XII, 1118
Sanderson, George R., IX, 736
Sanderson, John, VII, 138
Sanderson, Margaret (Stirling), XI, 856
Sanderson, Robert, IV, 313
Sanderson, William (associate of James RICHARDSON, 1819–92), XII, 893
Sanderson, William (merchant), I, 251, 252
Sandfield. *See* Macdonald
Sandford. *See* Sanford
Sandham*, Henry (1842–1910), XII, 248, 336, 337, 789, 790, 793
Sandin, Anna Magaretha. *See* Sjöman
Sandom, Jane Gabrielle. *See* Constables
Sandom, Williams, VII, 34, 779; VIII, **787–89**; IX, 278; X, 259, 404, 454
Sandray, Monsieur de (secretary), IV, 686
Sandrier. *See* Imbert
Sands, Edward, VI, 349, 356
Sandwell*, Bernard Keble (1876–1954), X, 517
Sandwich, Earl of. *See* Montagu
Sandwith, Georgina Frederica Locke (Campbell, Lady Campbell), XII, 150
Sandys, Alicia (Cockburn, Lady Cockburn), IX, 132

479

Sandys, Sir Edwin, I, 69
Sandys, Francis, V, 678
Sanford, Bridget. *See* Hutchinson
Sanford, Eli, XII, 939
Sanford, Emmeline. *See* Argall
Sanford, Emmeline. *See* Jackson
Sanford, Esbon, I, 129, 337, 338, **601**
Sanford, Harriet Sophia. *See* Vaux
Sanford, John, I, 601
Sanford, Lydia Ann (Jackson), X, 379; XII, 939
Sanford, Sarah (wife of ESBON), I, 601
Sanford, William Eli, X, 379; XII, 631, **938–44**, 1047
Sangouessy. *See* Chingouessi
Sangster, Alexander, XII, 529
Sangster, Amos W., XII, 947
Sangster, Ann. *See* Ross
Sangster, Charles, X, 536; XI, 216; XII, 460, 558, 570, 573, 662, 667, **944–48**
Sangster, Charlotte Mary, XII, 946
Sangster, Florence, XII, 946
Sangster, Gertrude, XII, 946
Sangster, Henrietta Charlotte. *See* Meagher
Sangster, James, XII, 944
Sangster, John Herbert, IX, 667; X, 452; XII, 571
Sangster, Mary. *See* Kilborn
Sangster, Roderick, XII, 946
Sanguinet, Angélique. *See* Lefebvre, *dit* Duchouquet
Sanguinet, Christophe, IV, 592, 697, 698
Sanguinet, Joseph, IV, 592, 697, 698; V, 322
Sanguinet, Marie-Jeanne. *See* Hervieux
Sanguinet, Simon, III, 522; IV, 204, 697
Sanguinet, Simon, IV, 72, 373, 547, 549, **697–98**; V, 242, 289; VII, 394
Sanguinet, Thérèse. *See* Réaume
San Jaime, Duke of. *See* Alfonso
Sankey, Ira David, XI, 804
Sanlerg, Gabrielle. *See* Senler
Sanregret. *See* Ducheneau
Sanschagrin. *See* Duberger
Sanson, Alexander, XI, 360
Sanson, Moullart, II, 121
Santa Cruz, Alonso de, I, 156, 157, 304, 342
Santi (Sanzio), Raffaello, known as Raphael, XII, 845, 848, 849, 850
Santoni, Jacques-Philippe, X, 322
Sanytyi. *See* Sahneuti
Saossarinon, I, 634
Sapaillé. *See* Taschereau
Sapir*, Edward (1884–1939), XII, 402
Sappier. *See* St Pierre
Saquima (Saquin). *See* Saguima
Sarah. *See also* Shawnadithit; Susewik; Tekarihogen
Sarah (wife of James BIRD), XII, 110, 111
Sarah (wife of KARAGHTADIE), III, 322; VI, 759; VII, 665
Sarah (wife of Thomas THOMAS), VI, 767, 768
Sarasin Depelteau, Angélique (Cartier), IV, 709
Saravia. *See* Peña
Sarcel de Prévert, Françoise. *See* Richomme
Sarcel de (Du) Prévert, Jean, I, 188, 189, 292, 507, **601–2**
Sareau, Catherine. *See* Brossard
Sareau, Jean, II, 105
Sareillier (Sarcelié, Lecarulier), Isabau (Élisabeth) (Castaing), IV, 135

Sargeant, Winthrop, V, 574
Sargent, Catherine. *See* Winthrop
Sargent, Charles Sprague, V, 593; X, 106
Sargent, Damaris (Yeo), IX, 855, 856
Sargent, Epes, VI, 682
Sargent, John (evangelical), VIII, 179
Sargent, John (son of JOHN), VI, 682
Sargent, John, VI, **682–83**, 813; VII, 416
Sargent, Margaret. *See* Whitney
Sargent, Sophia (Bennett), VIII, 82
Sargent, William Browne, VI, 682
Sargent, Winthrop (editor), V, 629
Sargent, Winthrop (governor), V, 4
Sargent, Winthrop (son of JOHN), VI, 682
Sargison, George Andrew, XI, 51
Sarney, Margaret Irene (Harcourt; Shuldham, Baroness Shuldham; Meade, Countess Clanwilliam), IV, 707
Sarraute-Marjolet, Jacques de, II, 4
Sarrazin, Charlotte-Louise-Angélique (Gaultier de Varennes), II, 598; III, 246
Sarrazin, Claude (father), II, 593
Sarrazin, Claude, II, 598
Sarrazin, Claude-Michel, II, 598; III, 184; IV, 338, 339
Sarrazin, Joseph-Michel, II, 598; III, 675; IV, 339
Sarrazin, Madeleine. *See* Bonnefoy
Sarrazin, Marguerite (Mallet), X, 492
Sarrazin, Marie-Anne-Ursule. *See* Hazeur
Sarrazin, Marie-Jeanne, II, 598
Sarrazin, Michel, I, 107; II, 44, 47, 48, 60, 212, 276, 307, 533, **593–600**; III, 67, 285, 315, 334, 344, 353, 369, 410, 603, 675, 677, 678, 679, 680; IV, 338, 357; IX, 201
Sarrazin, Nicolas, II, 239; IV, 77
Sarreau. *See also* Serreau
Sarreau, Sieur (of Martinique), III, 398
Sarrebource de Pontleroy, Élisabeth. *See* Arbalestre de Melun
Sarrebource de Pontleroy, Nicolas, III, xix, 229, 464; IV, 143, 144, 146, 211, 672; V, **738–40**
Sarrebource Pontleroy de Beaulieu, Jacques, V, 738
Sarrebource Pontleroy de Beaulieu, Madeleine. *See* Coustan
Sarrère, *dit* La Victoire, Angélique (Jobin), VIII, 433
Sartine, Antoine de, Comte d'Alby, III, 141, 441, 442; IV, 69, 243, 422, 646
Sarychev, Gavriil Andreevich, V, 80
Sasoonan. *See* Allumapees
Sasousmat (François Marsolet), I, 164, 533
Sass, Henry, XI, 919
Sasseville, Charlotte (Rocheleau, *dit* Lespérance), XI, 514
Sasseville, François, V, 218; VII, 18; VIII, 582, 638; IX, **701–2**; XI, 515
Sasseville, Geneviève. *See* Roy
Sasseville, Joseph (father), IX, 701
Sasseville, Joseph, IV, 702; VI, 557; IX, 701
Sasseville, Louise-Charlotte (Côté), XI, 203
Sasseville, Marie-Madeleine (Normandeau, *dit* Deslauriers; Sageot, *dit* Laforge; Parent), IV, 204
Sastaretsi. *See* Kondiaronk
Saswaypew (Cut Nose), XI, 461
Saswee. *See* Leblanc, *dit* Latour, François
Satin, Joseph, VII, 773
Satin, Pierrette. *See* Ocard
Sa-too. *See* Saattoq

Satouta, I, 637
Sattin, Abbé, II, 378
Sattin, Antoine, VII, **773–74**
Saucier*, Joseph (1869–1941), XI, 671
Saucier, Moïse, XII, 504
Sauer. *See also* Sower
Sauer, Martin, V, 80
Sauguaaram, II, 665, 669; III, xxxix, 136, **584–85**
Saul, Elizabeth (Hanna; Allen), V, 406; VIII, 359
Saul, George, III, 586
Saul, Thomas, III, 365, **585–86**; IV, 695, 696; VI, 89
Saulcier, Charles, II, 201
Saulnier, Étienne, I, 264
Saulnier, Joseph, V, 58
Saumarez, James, 1st Baron Saumarez, VIII, 770, 771
Saumarez, Madeline (Durell), III, 208
Saumarez, Sir Thomas, VI, 431; IX, 138
Saunders. *See also* Huck-Saunders
Saunders, Lady. *See* Buck
Saunders, Mr (of Scarborough, England) I, 370
Saunders, Arianna Margaretta Jekyll. *See* Chalmers
Saunders, Ariana Margaretta Jekyll (Shore), VI, 685, 727;
    VIII, 801
Saunders, Sir Charles, III, xxv, 132, 209, 210, 293, 465,
    573, 592, 606, 669, 671; IV, 163, 210, 223, 250, 460,
    597, 600, 601, 650, 652, **698–702**, 751; V, 141, 142,
    145, 823, 824; VI, 134
Saunders*, Edward Manning (1829–1916), X, 369; XI, 210
Saunders, Eliza (Flood), VI, 684
Saunders, Elizabeth (mother of JOHN), VI, 683
Saunders, Elizabeth Sophia. *See* Storie
Saunders, James, IV, 698
Saunders, John, V, 456; VI, 73, 76, 518, **683–88**, 810, 811;
    VII, 692; VIII, 428, 803, 832; IX, 620; X, 643
Saunders, John Simcoe, VI, 409, 684, 685, 686, 687; VIII,
    428, 809, 841; IX, 23, 87, 409; X, **643–44**, 712; XII, 17,
    232
Saunders, Jonathan, VI, 683
Saunders, Louisa (Shanly), XI, 817
Saunders, Maria (Eagar), VII, 269
Saunders, Mary (Burpe), VII, 120
Saunders, Mary (Ellegood), VI, 683
Saunders, Thomas (merchant), V, 838; VII, 840, 841
Saunders, Thomas (militia officer), XI, 817
Saunders, William, VII, 840, 841
Saunders*, William (1836–1914), XI, 108; XII, 1093
Saunders Dundas, Robert, 2nd Viscount Melville, VI, 61,
    359, 567, 803
Saur. *See* Sower
Saurel, Catherine de. *See* Legardeur de Tilly
Saurel, Jeanne de. *See* Giraud
Saurel, Mathieu de, I, 602
Saurel, Pierre de, I, 308, 418, 555, **602–3**; II, 11, 59, 60,
    592
Sauri. *See* Saury
Saurin, Joseph, VIII, 328, 329
Sauriot (Sauviot), Marguerite (Mousseaux), XI, 623
Saury (Sauri), Jean, VI, 84; VIII, 212
Sauvage de Chatillonnet, Jean-Louis-Melchior, V, 480
Sauvageau, Catherine (Langlois, *dit* Germain), VIII, 488
Sauvageau, Charles, VI, 86; VII, **774–76**; XII, 570
Sauvageau, Flavien, VII, 775
Sauvageau, Marie-Angélique. *See* Corbin

Sauvageau, Marie-Angélique. *See* Lévêque
Sauvageau, Marie-Anne. *See* Atkin
Sauvageau, Marie-Luce-Émilie (Aubin), XI, 37
Sauvageau, Michel, VI, 336; VII, 774
Sauvageau, Michel-Flavien, XI, 37
Sauvageau, Tancrède, XI, 810, 811
Sauvaget, Jean, I, 553
Sauveterre. *See* Aussillon
Sauviot. *See* Sauriot
Sauvole, Ensign, III, 380
Savaète, Arthur, XI, 105; XII, 511, 512
Savage, Alfred, X, 450
Savage, Ann. *See* Pratt
Savage, Arthur, II, **600–1**; III, 518
Savage, Elizabeth. *See* Scottow
Savage, Faith. *See* Hutchinson
Savage, James, VI, 688
Savage, John (Fenian), X, 559
Savage, John (son of JOHN), VI, 688
Savage, John, VI, 270, **688–89**, 819; VII, 186
Savage, Perez, II, 601
Savage, Thomas, II, 601
Savage, Thomas, I, 545; II, 532, **601**
Savageau. *See* Sauvageau
Savard, Monsieur (pilot), IV, 650
Savard (Savarre), Isabelle (Élizabeth) (Falardeau), XI, 309
Savari. *See* Du Plessis-Savari
Savary, Charles, XI, **801–2**
Savary, Charlotte-Éliane. *See* Quénault
Savary, Pierre-François-Théodore, XI, 801
Saveeah. *See* Sahneuti
Saveraine, Ann. *See* Waldruff
Saveraine, Frederick, VIII, 450
Saveuse de Beaujeu, Adélaïde. *See* Aubert de Gaspé
Saveuse de Beaujeu, Catherine. *See* Chaussegros de Léry
Saveuse de Beaujeu, Catherine-Charlotte (Barron;
    Bisaillon), VI, 690
Saveuse de Beaujeu, Georges-René, Comte de Beaujeu, VI,
    690; IX, **702–3**; X, 20
Saveuse de Beaujeu, Jacques-Philippe, V, 488; VI, 285,
    **689–90**; IX, 702
Saveuse de Beaujeu, Philippe-Arthur-Quiquerand, IX, 703
Saveuse de Beaujeu, Raoul, IX, 703
Savignac, Antoinette-Charlotte de (Maurès de Malartic,
    Comtesse de Montricoux), IV, 530
Savigny, Marie-Anne de. *See* Aubert de Courserac
Savile, Henry, I, 82
Savile, John, 3rd Earl of Mexborough, X, 443
Savile, Lady Sarah Elizabeth (Lindsay), X, 443
Savoie-Lascaris, Renée de, II, 349
Savonnières de La Troche, Jeanne de. *See* Raoul
Savonnières de La Troche, Marie de, named de Saint-
    Joseph (de Saint-Bernard), I, 108, 352, **603–4**
Savonnières de La Troche, Simon de, I, 603
Savoy, Duke of. *See* Charles Emmanuel
Savoy, Marquis of. *See* Easton, Peter
Savoye, Marie, IV, 8l
Sawantanan. *See* Vincent, Louis (father); Vincent, Louis
Sawers, Alexander Frater, VIII, 74
Sawers, William Q., VI, 335; VII, 22; VIII, 657
Sawiya. *See* Sahneuti
Sawtelle, Jemima (Phipps; Howe; Tute), V, **740–41**

Sawtelle, Jonathan, V, 740
Sawtelle, Josiah, V, 740
Sawtelle, Lydia. *See* Parker
Sawyer, Agnes. *See* Brown
Sawyer, Anna. *See* Springer
Sawyer*, Artemas Wyman (1827–1907), 882
Sawyer, David. *See* Kezhegowinninne
Sawyer, Eliza. *See* Tobin
Sawyer, Eliza Jane. *See* Baxter
Sawyer, Sir Herbert, VII, 106, 217, 709
Sawyer, Jane. *See* Wetosy
Sawyer, John, XI, 802
Sawyer, John James, VII, 867
Sawyer, Joseph. *See also* Nawahjegezhegwabe
Sawyer, Joseph, VIII, 309; IX, 26, 592
Sawyer, Josiah, VI, 338
Sawyer, Luther Demock, XI, 583; XII, 701
Sawyer, P. T., XII, 701
Sawyer, Stephen Payson, XI, 583
Sawyer, William, XI, **802–3**
Sax, Pierre-Télesphore, X, 686; XII, 1020
Saxe, Maurice de, Comte de Saxe, known as Maréchal de
    Saxe, III, xv, xvi, 185, 186, 458, 466, 535; IV, 443
Saxe-Coburg and Gotha, Duke of. *See* Alfred Ernest Albert
Saxe-Coburg-Saalfeld, Prince of. *See* Leopold I
Saxe-Coburg-Saalfeld, Princess of. *See* Charlotte Augusta
Saxony, Duchess of. *See* Louise Caroline Alberta
Saxton, Charlotte (Campbell), VIII, 123; IX, 113
Say, Jean-Baptiste, X, 571
Sayde Pasha, III, 62
Saye, Jeanne (Quesneville), II, 534
Saye and Sele, Viscount of. *See* Fiennes
Sayenqueraghta. *See* Kaieñʔkwaahtoñ
Sayer. *See also* Sayward
Sayer, Mrs. *See* Obemau-unoqua
Sayer, Anne Maria (Fraser), XII, 335
Sayer, Elizabeth. *See* McPherson
Sayer, Henry (son of JOHN and Obemau-unoqua), V, 742
Sayer, Henry (son of JOHN and possibly Obemau- unoqua),
    V, 742
Sayer, James, V, 742
Sayer, John, IV, 369; V, 533, **741–42**; VII, 776
Sayer, John Charles, V, 742
Sayer, Josette. *See* Frobisher
Sayer, Margaret, V, 742
Sayer, Pierre-Guillaume, V, 742; VI, 398; VII, **776–77**;
    VIII, 59, 344, 817, 819; IX, 95, 663; X, 47, 168, 324; XI,
    45, 138, 139, 546, 736, 875; XII, 125, 206
Saymond, Daniel, I, 590
Sayre, Esther (Robinson; Beman), IV, 677; VI, 51; VII,
    752, 753, 778; IX, 668; X, 622
Sayre, James, V, 59
Sayre, James, VII, **777–78**
Sayre, John, V, 59; VII, 777
Sayre, John S., XI, 544
Sayre, Mary. *See* Bowes
Sayre, Polly. *See* Smith
Sayre, William Pagan, VII, 777
Sayve, Marie de (La Croix de Chevrières de Saint-Vallier),
    II, 328
Sayward (Sayer), Esther (rebaptized Marie-Joseph)
    (Lestage), II, 601, 602; III, 253, 393, 394; IV, 765
Sayward, Mary. *See* Rishworth

Sayward, Mary (rebaptized Marie-Geneviève), named
    Marie des Anges, II, **601–2**; III, 394, 407
Sayward, William, II, 601
Scadding, Charles, VII, 652
Scadding*, Henry (1813–1901), VI, 80, 702; VII, 506, 652,
    702, 822; VIII, 125, 358, 427, 585, 596, 623, 830, 934;
    IX, 131, 132, 657; X, 54, 610, 671; XI, 240, 248, 249,
    392
Scales, Caroline (Hoyt), known as Caroline Miskel and
    Caroline Miskel-Hoyt, XII, **948–49**
Scales, Christopher Colombus, XII, 948
Scales, George W., XI, 727
Scales, Joab, XII, 948
Scales, Mary. *See* Menzies
Scales, Sarah, XII, 948
Scallan, Thomas, VI, 690
Scallan, Thomas, V, 474; VI, 614, **690–94**, 711; VII, 292,
    294, 403, 404, 630; VIII, 107; XII, 860
Scallon, Edward, VII, 448, 449; IX, **703–4**
Scallon, Hermine, IX, 704
Scallon, Mathew, IX, 703
Scallon, Mathilde. *See* Ducondu
Scamen (Scammon), Mary (rebaptized Marie) (Godefroy
    de Tonnancour), IV, 305
Scarborough, James, X, 535
Scarff, Thomas H., XII, 39
Scarlett, Elizabeth (Riall, Lady Riall), VII, 744
Scarroyady, III, xl, 320, 607, 613, 614; IV, lvi
Scarth, John, V, 394
Scarth, Margaret (Gale), VIII, 310
Scarth*, William Bain (1837–1902), XI, 645; XII, 129,
    609, 612
Scatchamisse, II, 492, **602**
Scatcherd, Anne. *See* Farley
Scatcherd, Isabella. *See* Sprague
Scatcherd, John, X, 644
Scatcherd, Lavinia (Campbell), XII, 150
Scatcherd, Robert Colin, X, 645
Scatcherd, Thomas, X, 45, **644–45**; XII, 822
Scatts Eye. *See* Scorch Eye
Schadow von Godenhaus, Friedrich Wilhelm von, X,
    408
Schank, Mrs (Fitzgerald; wife of JOHN), VI, 694
Schank, Alexander, VI, 694
Schank, John, IV, 231; V, 364; VI, **694–96**, 788
Schank, Margaret. *See* Grant
Schank, Margaret (Wight), VI, 695
Schank, Mary. *See* Burnet
Scherch, Maria (Erb), VI, 235
Scheuer, Edmund, XII, 93
Schieffelin, Jacob, VI, 101
Schieffelin, Thomas, VI, 296
Schiller, Charles Edward, X, 219
Schiller, Johann Christoph Friedrich von, VIII, 744
Schimmelpinck, Lydia (Douglas), IV, 223
Schindler, Frédéric, IV, 702
Schindler, Geneviève. *See* Maranda
Schindler, Joseph, IV, 702
Schindler, Joseph (Jonas), IV, **702–3**; V, 329, 436, 727; VI,
    230, 663
Schindler, Marguerite. *See* Gaspar
Schinotti, J. F., VII, 869
Schlegel, August Wilhelm von, VIII, 650

Schleiger, Marie-Magdelaine, V, 509
Schloezer, Christian Andrew, III, 411
Schmid, Luc, III, 307
Schmid, Luke, IV, 294
Schmid, Madeleine. *See* Trefflé, *dit* Rottot
Schmidt, Mr (architect), VII, 297
Schmidt, Louis, XI, 737; XII, 554
Schmidt, Louisa Carolina (Philips), VII, 694
Schnall, John, VII, 244
Schneider, Barbara. *See* Eby
Schneider, Christian, VII, 778
Schneider, Jacob, VII, 778
Schneider, Jacob B., VII, 778
Schneider, Joseph, VII, **778–79**; VIII, 316
Schneider, Joseph E., VII, 778
Schneider, Maria. *See* Herschi
Schnetz, Victor, IX, 359
Schörg, Joseph, VIII, 86, 87
Schofield, Ira, VII, 843
Schofield, Letitia Lockhart. *See* Hargrave
Schofield, Sarah (Watson), V, 843
Schofield, William, VIII, 177
Scholes, Francis, XII, 62
Scholey, Jane (Robinson), XII, 909
Schomberg, Sir Alexander, III, 606
Schomberg, Henry (Sir Alexander?), III, 417, 418, 425
Schomberg, Jeanne de (Du Plessis, Marquise de Liancourt, Duchesse de La Roche-Guyon), I, 484
Schoolcraft, Henry Rowe, III, 660; VI, 357, 358; VII, 687, 845; VIII, 411, 651; IX, 420; XI, 654
Schoolcraft, James, VII, 845
Schoolcraft, Jane. *See* Johnston
Schott, Charles Anthony, VIII, 449
Schoultz, Ann Cordelia von. *See* Campbell
Schoultz, Johanna Henrica von. *See* Gripenberg
Schoultz, Nils von, VII, 158, 405, 472, **779–80**; VIII, 27, 788; IX, 278, 415, 701, 857; XII, 592
Schoultz, Nils Fredrik von, VII, 779
Schrader, J. A. M., VII, 694
Schreiber*, Sir Collingwood (1831–1918), XII, 419, 610, 611
Schreiber, Mary S., XII, 807
Schrimshire. *See* Skrimsher
Schubert, Augustus, IX, 518
Schubert, Catherine. *See* O'Hare
Schubert, Franz, VIII, 634
Schubert, Rose, IX, 518
Schulte, Catharina Maria (Gohsmann), VII, 350
Schulte, Mary Jemima. *See* MacColl
Schultz, Agnes Campbell, Lady Schultz. *See* Farquharson
Schultz, Elizabeth. *See* Reily
Schultz, Sir John Christian, IX, 330, 531, 617, 707; X, 67, 324, 630, 631; XI, 45, 64, 245, 323, 324, 538, 540, 553, 562, 563, 643, 644, 645, 737, 738, 739, 740, 741, 742, 743, 744, 841, 842, 935; XII, 33, 82, 119, 132, 244, 370, 540, 641, 941, **949–54**, 982, 1010
Schultz, Matilda (McKenney; step-mother of Sir JOHN CHRISTIAN), XII, 953
Schultz, William Ludwig, XII, 949
Schumacher, Jacob, VII, 778
Schureman, Jacob, V, 742
Schureman, Jane. *See* Parcot
Schurman, Elizabeth. *See* Hyatt

Schurman*, Jacob Gould (1854–1942), V, 743; XII, 772, 773
Schurman, Jane. *See* Bonnet
Schurman, William, V, **742–43**
Schussele, Christian, XII, 830
Schuyler, Abraham, II, 341, 402; III, 428
Schuyler, Alida (Van Rensselaer; Livingston), II, 436
Schuyler, Arent, III, 587
Schuyler, Catalyntje (Cuyler), V, 222
Schuyler, Cornelia (Catherine?) (DePeyster), VI, 188
Schuyler, Elizabeth. *See* Staats
Schuyler, Engeltie. *See* Van Schaick
Schuyler, Hester. *See* Walter
Schuyler, Hon Yost, V, 33
Schuyler, Johannes, III, 265, **586–87**; IV, 770
Schuyler, Louise (Lorimier), VI, 403, 404; VII, 516
Schuyler, Margarita. *See* Van Slichtenhorst
Schuyler, Maria. *See* Van Rensselaer
Schuyler, Mary (wife of PETER, d. 1762), III, 587
Schuyler, Peter, I, 239; II, 21, 112, 148, 168, 237, 474, 502, 523, **602–4**, 624; III, 428, 568, 586, 622, 623
Schuyler, Peter, III, **587–89**; IV, 612; V, 740; VI, 188
Schuyler, Philip John, III, 587; IV, 545, 546, 694, 730; V, 29, 30, 33, 40, 413, 519, 826; VI, 403, 444, 502
Schuyler, Philip Pieterse, II, 602; III, 586
Schuyler, Swantie. *See* Dyckhuyse
Schwartz, Anna Justina (Liebrich; wife of OTTO WILLIAM), IV, 703
Schwartz, Johanna von (Pryor), XI, 717
Schwartz, Otto William, IV, 110, **703–4**
Schwatka, Ada Josephine. *See* Brackett
Schwatka, Amelia. *See* Huikill
Schwatka, Frederick, XI, 393; XII, 936, **954–55**
Schwatka, Frederick G., XII, 954
Schwindt. *See* Gschwind
Scobie, Hugh, VII, 847; VIII, 14, 52, 370, **789–91**, 961; X, 656; XI, 127, 877; XII, 101, 188, 212, 213, 667
Scobie, James, VIII, 789
Scobie, Justina. *See* McLeod
Scoble, Sir Andrew Richard, IX, 706
Scoble, John, IX, 475, **704–6**, 769; XI, 400, 401; XII, 492, 960
Scoble, Mary Anne. *See* Stainburn
Scoble, Thomas Clarkson, IX, 706
Scofield. *See* Scovill
Scollen, Constantine Michael, X, 661
Scolvus, John, I, **679**
Scorch Eye, IV, 420
Scoresby, William, V, 55
Scot, Dominique, I, 495
Scot, Sir John, I, 496
Scothouse. *See* MacDonell; McDonell
Scott, Mrs (friend of Henrietta Thompson (Wolfe)), III, 589
Scott, Captain, III, 663
Scott, Abigail (wife of GEORGE), III, 590
Scott, Alexander Stewart, VII, 879
Scott, Ann. *See* Purcell
Scott, Ann, VIII, 792
Scott, Ann (Hutton), XII, 460
Scott, Benjamin Alexander, XI, 774
Scott, Caroline (Nelson), VIII, 792
Scott, Alfred Henry, X, 70, **645–46**; XI, 563, 740, 741; XII, 82, 601, 1007, 1030

Scott, Catherine. *See* Ferguson
Scott, Charles Armstrong, XI, 491, 492, 493
Scott, Christopher, VI, 61, 563, **696–98**
Scott, David, VII, 830
Scott*, David Lynch (1845–1924), XI, 748
Scott*, Duncan Campbell (1862–1947), XII, 188, 513, 514, 515, 516, 517, 518, 947
Scott, Eleanor Margaret. *See* Little
Scott, Elizabeth (Harris), V, 408
Scott, Elizabeth (Luard), XII, 575
Scott, Elizabeth Radcliffe (Haythorne), XII, 418
Scott, Elizabeth Rosetta (Glover, Lady Glover), XI, 355, 356, 632
Scott, Erskine, XII, 576
Scott, Frances (Barrett), XI, 53
Scott, Frances (Becher), XI, 62
Scott, George, III, 589
Scott, George, III, xxvi, xxvii, xxviii, 87, **589–90**, 667, 671; IV, 21, 193, 308, 630, 631, 705
Scott, Sir George Gilbert, VIII, 725, 942; X, 281; XI, 391
Scott, George L., XII, 55
Scott, Gilbert, IX, 224
Scott, Harriet Sophia (VanKoughnet), IX, 803; X, 693
Scott, Helen (Burn), VIII, 113
Scott, Henri-Arthur, X, 413, 736
Scott, Hugh (brother of THOMAS, d. 1870), IX, 708
Scott, Hugh (insuranceman), XII, 43
Scott, Isabella (Chanter), X, 161
Scott, James (associate of Duncan MACLEAN), VIII, 563, 564
Scott, James (lawyer), XI, 928
Scott, James (partner of Adam Lymburner MACNIDER), VII, 575
Scott, Jane. *See* Phillips
Scott, Janet (Armstrong), XII, 39
Scott, John (Baptist lay exhorter), VI, 172
Scott, John (brother-in-law of John LYNCH), XI, 534
Scott, John (father of JONATHAN, 1744–1819), V, 743
Scott, John (of London), VI, 95
Scott, John (seaman), V, 166
Scott, John, VIII, 934; IX, 664, **706–7**; XII, 1123
Scott, John, 1st Earl of Eldon, V, 18
Scott, John Morin, IV, 715
Scott, Jonathan, IV, 18, 19, 565; V, **743–45**
Scott, Jonathan, X, **646**
Scott, Jonathan Holten, XII, 1131
Scott, Joseph, III, 590; IV, 199, **704–5**; VI, 676
Scott, Julia. *See* Scovill
Scott, Lucy. *See* Ring
Scott, Lydia. *See* Thwing
Scott, Margaret (Gatty), XI, 333
Scott, Margaret (Montgomery, Lady Montgomery), IV, 550
Scott, Margaret Ramsey. *See* Cottnam
Scott, Marie-Marguerite-Maurice. *See* Paquet
Scott, Martha (McGregor), VI, 462, 463
Scott, Mary. *See* Mackenzie
Scott, Mary (Argall; Washington), I, 67
Scott, Mary (Howard), IX, 399
Scott, Mary (King), XII, 489
Scott, Mary Ann (Gray), V, 384
Scott, Moses, V, 743
Scott, Neil, VIII, 792
Scott, Patrick J., XII, 755, 756, **955–57**

Scott, Phebe (Land), IX, 454
Scott, Rebecca (Brenton), V, 108; VII, 104
Scott, Sir Reginald, I, 67
Scott, Richard, VI, 500, 501
Scott*, Sir Richard William (1825–1913), IX, 287, 492, 725; X, 45, 122, 201, 277, 323, 361, 441, 465, 466, 468, 641, 668; XI, 193, 229, 379, 520, 536, 672, 677, 823, 908; XII, 323, 331, 333, 370, 656, 664
Scott, Robert, V, 166
Scott, Robert Falcon, VII, 327; X, 748
Scott, Sarah (Langley), VII, 510
Scott, Susanna (Holmes), VIII, 403; IX, 396
Scott, Sydney (Crawford), XI, 212
Scott, Thomas (army officer), V, 8, 229
Scott, Thomas (farmer), XI, 750; XII, 723
Scott, Thomas (father-in-law of Robert Poore HAY-THORNE), XII, 418
Scott, Thomas (father of THOMAS, 1746–1824), VI, 698
Scott, Thomas (golfer), XII, 108
Scott, Thomas (landowner), VII, 136
Scott, Thomas (naval officer), II, 153; III, 323
Scott, Thomas (politician), XI, 644, 645, 839, 942; XII, 372
Scott, Thomas, IV, 89; V, 6, 182, 332, 495, **745–46**
Scott, Thomas, V, 17, 66, 304, 365, 389, 440, 443, 521, 549, 639, 643, 644, 734, 750, 782, 856; VI, 80, 114, 116, 422, 452, 540, 608, 609, 610, 611, 656, **698–99**, 723; VII, 37, 285, 366, 438, 813, 814; VIII, 10, 337, 795, 890; IX, 669; X, 509
Scott, Thomas, VIII, 171; IX, 329, 330, 618, **707–9**; X, 59, 198, 439, 476, 556, 646; XI, 46, 145, 151, 192, 193, 323, 737, 740, 741, 743, 744, 747, 842; XII, 33, 119, 132, 148, 175, 371, 578, 601, 602, 652, 951, 1007, 1008
Scott, Thomas Charles Heslop, V, 56, **746–47**
Scott, Thomas Seaton, VIII, 944; XII, 345, 346, **957–59**
Scott, Walter, XII, 957
Scott, Sir Walter, V, 264; VI, 483; VII, 336, 337, 339, 417, 538, 539; VIII, 356, 791; IX, 348, 392, 429, 543; X, 5, 21, 175; XI, 222, 424, 537; XII, 53, 823, 945, 1109
Scott, William (brother of THOMAS, 1764–1824), VI, 698
Scott, William (clergman), XII, 759
Scott, William (father of WILLIAM HENRY), VIII, 791
Scott, William (reputed illegitimate son of CHRISTOPHER), VI, 697
Scott, William (shipbuilder), VI, 696
Scott, William (son of JOHN), IX, 707
Scott, William Henry, VI, 386; VII, 172, 173, 346; VIII, 331, 471, **791–92**; IX, 458, 614; X, 306
Scott, Winfield, VII, 745; VIII, 375, 379
Scottee, Joshua, I, 242
Scottow, Elizabeth (Savage), II, 601
Scotus. *See* MacDonell
Scougall, Janet (Cassels), XI, 156
Scougall, Janet (Liston; Willoughby), VII, 914
Scouler, John, VII, 599; XI, 885, 886
Scovil, Elias, VI, 13
Scovil, James, V, 25
Scovill, Judith (Smith), XII, 55
Scovill, Julia (Scott), XII, 55
Scovill, Polly. *See* Barber
Scovill, Smith, XII, 55
Scovill (Scofield), Stephen, XII, 55
Scratchemisse. *See* Scatchamisse
Scribble, Sam, XII, 449

Scribe, Eugène, VIII, 702
Scrimshire. *See* Skrimsher
Scriven, James, XI, 803
Scriven, Jane. *See* Medlicott
Scriven, Joseph Medlicott, XI, **803–4**
Scroggs, John, II, 313, 320, 493, 658; III, 447, 448, 489, 599, **604**
Scroope, Ann (Pyke; Wenman), IV, 763, 764; VI, 621
Scrope (Thomson), George Julius Poulett, VII, 855
Scrutator. *See* Henry, Walter
Scudder, Samuel Hubbard, XI, 108; XII, 233
Scull, Gideon Delaplaine, IV, 553
Seabury, David, V, 431; VI, 33, 34
Seabury, Mary (Marsden), VII, 586
Seabury, Samuel, IV, 327; V, 94
Seafield, Earl of. *See* Ogilvie-Grant
Sealey. *See also* Seelye
Sealey, Rebecca H. (Wait), XII, 1078
Sealgair, Iain. *See* MacDhòmhnaill 'Ic Iain, Iain
Seaman, Amos Peck, IX, **709–10**
Seaman, Caleb, VII, 782
Seaman, Jane. *See* Metcalf
Seaman, Job, IX, 709
Seaman, Margaret. *See* Howard
Seaman, Nathan, IX, 709
Seaman, Zena. *See* Thomas
Seargeant, Lewis James, XII, 433, 435
Searle, Henry Ernest, XII, 797
Sears, James, VII, 289; VIII, 157
Sears, James H., VIII, 786
Sears, Robert, VIII, 157
Sears, Thomas, VII, 404
Seaton, Baron. *See* Colborne
Seaton, Baroness. *See* Yonge
Sébastien. *See* Pennasca
Sébille, Jean, II, 275
Sébille, Marie-Anne. *See* Hazeur
Seccomb, Hannah. *See* Willis
Seccomb, Peter, IV, 705
Seccombe, John, IV, 490, **705–6**; V, 199; VII, 252
Seccombe, Mercy. *See* Williams
Seccombe, Thomas, V, 258
Séchelles. *See* Moreau
Seckelman, Kate (Samuel), XI, 800
Secondat, Charles de, Baron de La Brède et de Montesquieu, III, 334; V, 372; VI, 10; VII, 430, 645, 675; X, 586
Secondon. *See* Secoudon
Secord, Catharine. *See* Smith
Secord, Charles B., IX, 407
Secord, David, V, 857; VII, **780–81**
Secord, Elizabeth, IX, 406
Secord, Esther Magdalen (Keefer), VIII, 450
Secord, James (father), VII, 780
Secord, James, VII, 780; IX, 405, 406
Secord, Jessie. *See* Millard
Secord, Laura. *See* Ingersoll
Secord, Madelaine. *See* Badeau
Secord, Magdalen (Cartwright), V, 167, 168; VII, 156
Secord, Mary. *See* Page
Secord, Peter, VII, 780
Secord, Sarah (Swayze), VI, 746
Secoudon, I, 96, 507, 526, 529, 564, **604**

Sedgewick*, Robert (1848–1906), XII, 1042, 1043, 1045
Sedgwick, Adam, IX, 418
Sedgwick, Catherine Maria, VII, 396
Sedgwick, Elizabeth. *See* Howe
Sedgwick, Robert, I, 25, 39, 241, 259, 434, 435, 469, 474, 595, **604–5**; II, 94
Sedgwick, Sarah (Leverett), I, 475
Sedgwick, Theodore, VI, 55
Sedgwick, William, I, 604
Sedillot, *dit* Montreuil, Marie-Desanges (Rodier), XI, 763
Sédilot, Marie (Blanchet; Adhémar de Saint-Martin), II, 11
Seebach, Andrew, VII, 882
Seeds, Samuel, VIII, 156, 157
Seein, Molly (Crandall), VIII, 180
Seeley. *See also* Selee
Seeley, Elisabeth (Wood), XII, 1121
Seely, Alexander McLeod, XI, **804–5**
Seely, Caleb, V, 747; IX, **710**
Seely, Desire. *See* Parker
Seely, Ebenezer, IX, 710
Seely, Mrs Ellen, VIII, 809
Seely, Hipzabeth (mother of CALEB), IX, 710
Seely, Jane. *See* Sancton
Seely, Joseph, V, **747–49**; VI, 215
Seely, Lillian Ann. *See* Hammond
Seely, Phoebe. *See* Collins
Seely, Phoebe Ann (Campbell), XI, 146
Seely, Sarah. *See* Morrell
Seely, Seth, XI, 804
Seelye (Sealey), Augustus, V, 747
Seelye, Henry E., XII, 915
Seen from Afar. *See* Peenaquim
Seeseeb. *See* Mamenawatum
Sefton, Henry, XII, 959
Sefton, Henry Francis, XII, **959–60**
Sefton, Martha. *See* Johnston-Brown
Sefton, Mary. *See* Jones
Seghers, Charles-François, XI, 805
Seghers, Charles John, X, 222; XI, **805–6**
Seghers, Paulina (Seghers), XI, 805
Segipt, I, 53, **605**
Segris, Barbe (Jacquiés), II, 294
Seguaron. *See* Sauguaaram
Seguenot, François, II, 376
Séguier, Pierre, Comte de Gien, Duc de Villemor, I, 214, 484, 505
Séguin, Monsieur (controller), IV, 558, 644, 645
Séguin, Charlotte. *See* Clément
Séguin, Félicité-Zoë (Dugal), VI, 227
Séguin, François, VII, 781
Séguin, François-Hyacinthe, VII, **781–82**
Séguin, Geneviève-Luce. *See* Robitaille
Seguin, Hilaire, VI, 487
Séguin, Marie-Josephte. *See* Augé
Séguin, Pierre, VI, 227
Séguin, Robert-Lionel, VII, 173
Ségure (Chignac), Jeanne (Maisonnat), II, 449
Seignelay, Marquis de. *See* Colbert
Seigneur, Marie-Josephe (Loppinot de La Frésillière; Claparède), III, 123
Seigneuret, Étienne, II, 647
Seigneuret, Marguerite (Godefroy de Normanville; Boudor), II, 252, 253

Seigsworth, Julius, XII, 428
Seixas, Gershom Mendas, V, 194
Selby, Ann. *See* Robson
Selby, Charlotte (Desbarats), IX, 203
Selby, Elizabeth (wife of PRIDEAUX), V, 749
Selby, Elizabeth (Derenzy), V, 750
Selby, George (father of GEORGE), VI, 699
Selby, George (father of PRIDEAUX), V, 749
Selby, George, IV, 82, 434; V, 566, 752; VI, **699–700**; VII, 666, 667
Selby, Marguerite. *See* Baby
Selby, Marie-Josèphe. *See* Dunbar
Selby, Mary (Selby), V, 749
Selby, Prideaux, V, 120, 121, 449, 536, **749–50**; VI, 115; VIII, 337
Selby, William Dunbar, VI, 700; IX, 203
Selee, Hannah (Whooley (Woolley); wife of PEET), VII, 782
Selee, Peet, V, 747; VII, 419, **782**
Selee, Rebecca. *See* Peet
Selee, Truman, VII, 782
Selkirk, Countess of. *See* Hamilton; Wedderburn
Selkirk, Earl of. *See* Douglas; Hamilton Douglas
Selkirk, Mary (Skead), XI, 826
Sellar, Alexander, IX, 711
Sellar, Isabella. *See* Grant
Sellar, Louisa. *See* Nichols
Sellar*, Robert (1841–1919), IX, 711
Sellar, Thomas, IX, **710–11**
Seller, John, I, 337
Sellers, Harry, XII, 646
Sellon, Sarah Ann (Valentine), VII, 875
Sells, John, XII, 553
Selwyn*, Alfred Richard Cecil (1824–1902), X, 66, 448; XI, 49, 218, 732, 899; XII, 140, 236
Semlin*, Charles Augustus (1836–1927), XI, 568; XII, 613
Sempé, Édouard, IX, 121, 854, 855; XI, 851
Sempkins, Sarah (Kilby), III, 326
Semple, Anne. *See* Greenlaw
Semple, Robert, V, 750
Semple, Robert, V, 267, 466, 544, **750–52**; VI, 167, 236, 251, 437, 443, 446, 456, 466, 748, 768; VII, 498, 570, 671, 749, 795; VIII, 5, 91, 343, 414, 537, 714, 719, 821; IX, 285; X, 276; XI, 539
Sénat, Antoine, II, 67
Senat, Françoise. *See* Phélypeaux
Senati. *See* Sahneuti
Senau, *dit* La Viazère, Michel, I, 524
Seneca King. *See* Kaieñ?kwaahtoñ
Senécal, Adolphe, XI, 807, 808
Sénécal, Adrien, XI, 806
Sénécal, Ambroise, XI, 806, 807
Sénécal, Ambroise, XI, 809
Senécal, Delphine. *See* Dansereau
Senécal, Delphire (Gill), XI, 809, 810
Sénécal, Louis-Adélard, IX, 315, 345; X, 220; XI, 8, 27, 625, 626, 657, 755, 766, 774, 781, **806–17**; XII, 126, 176, 178, 179, 180, 464, 465, 620, 621, 629, 722, 903, 904
Sénécal, Marie-Anne. *See* Brodeur
Sénécal, Michel, XI, 249
Senécal, Michel, XI, 806, 807
Senécal, Octavie (Blumhart), XI, 809

Sénécalle, Amable (Saint-Germain), IX, 697
Senet, Gertrude. *See* Daunet
Senet, Pierre, II, 604
Senet, Suzanne. *See* Vanier
Senet, *dit* Laliberté, Nicolas, II, **604**
Senex, John, III, 325
Senezergues, Louis de, III, 590
Senezergues de La Rodde, Étienne-Guillaume de, III, xx, **590–91**
Senilh, Joseph, V, 276
Senior, Nassau William, X, 608
Senler, Gabrielle (Fillion), I, 305
Senneterre (Saint-Nectaire), Jean-Charles de, III, xxii
Senneville. *See* Le Ber
Sentenne, Léon-Alfred, X, 250, 252
Sentner, Caleb, V, 335
Seppings, Sir Robert, VI, 696
Sequaresera, III, 321
Sequidonquee (Little Beard), IV, 121
Séraphine du Divin Cœur de Jésus, Mère. *See* Lucas
Séré. *See* Cerré
Sergeant, Mrs (wife of HENRY), I, 657
Sergeant, Henry, I, 130, 315, 329, 519, **605–6**, 657, 666; II, 49, 231, 265, 318
Sergeant, Thomas, I, 606
Serigny. *See* Le Moyne
Sérindac, Antoine, III, 637
Seringe, Nicolas-Charles, X, 81
Serkoak, IV, 536
Serles, Ephraim, VI, 729
Sermonville. *See* Sabrevois
Serna. *See* Alcalá-Galiano
Seroin, Claudine (Muiron), III, 478
Serooskerken. *See* Tuyll
Serquigny. *See* Aché
Serré. *See also* Cerré
Serré, Jean-Baptiste, III, 144
Serré, Joseph, V, 174
Serre, Madeleine (Cadieux), VII, 131
Serré, Marie-Madeleine. *See* Picard
Serre, *dit* Saint-Jean, Fleury-Théodore, IX, 78
Serreau de Saint-Aubin, Jean, II, 6, **604–5**; III, 111
Serreau de Saint-Aubin, Marguerite. *See* Boileau
Serres, Alexandre, V, **752**
Serres, Dominique, III, 592
Serres, Gabrielle. *See* Marleau
Serres, Jean-Baptiste, V, 752
Serres, Madeleine. *See* Lefebvre
Serres, Marie. *See* Galliay
Serres, Thérèse. *See* Migneron
Sertrouville. *See* La Salle
Servian. *See* Alquier
Servien, Bishop, II, 360
Sessé y Lacasta, Martín de, V, 615, 616
Sessions, J. D., XI, 837
Seton, Alexander, IX, 5
Seton, Elizabeth Ann. *See* Bayley
Seton*, Ernest Thompson (1860–1946), XII, 336
Settee*, James (1816–1902), IX, 732; XI, 436; XII, 201
Setter, Elizabeth (Norquay), XI, 642, 643
Settle, Dionise, I, 670
Seurat, Georges, VIII, 290
Severance, Frank H., VIII, 796

Severs, Emily (Howard), XI, 428
Sevestre, Catherine (Rouer de Villeray), I, 580, 583; II, 583; III, 569
Sevestre, Charles, I, 606
Sevestre, Charles, I, 145, 429, 580, 583, **606**; II, xvi, 426
Sevestre, Étienne, I, 606
Sevestre, Ignace, I, 606
Sevestre, Louis, I, 606
Sevestre, Marguerite. *See* Petitpas
Sevestre, Marguerite (Lessard), II, 426
Sevestre, Marie. *See* Pichon
Sevestre, Marie-Denise (Neveu), III, 482
Sevestre, Thomas, I, 606
Sévigné, Marquise de. *See* Rabutin-Chantal
Sewall. *See also* Sewell
Sewall, Hannah (Moody), III, 470, 471
Sewall, Samuel, III, 470, 505
Sewall, Stephen, IV, 51
Seward, Sarah (Horden), XII, 445
Seward, William Henry, X, 15, 483, 514; XI, 278, 880; XII, 925
Sewel, William, I, 81
Sewell, Edmund Willoughby, VII, 788
Sewell, Eliza Jannet, VI, 96
Sewell, Esther. *See* Quincy
Sewell, G. W., XII, 537
Sewell, Henrietta. *See* Smith
Sewell, James Arthur, IX, 119; XI, 309, 484
Sewell, Jane. *See* Caldwell
Sewell, John St Alban, VII, 783
Sewell (Sewall), Jonathan, IV, 292; VI, 136, 605, 700; VII, 782
Sewell, Jonathan, IV, 502, 718; V, 18, 45, 60, 69, 77, 84, 193, 208, 212, 225, 231, 234, 246, 247, 292, 373, 374, 494, 691, 697, 769, 794, 863, 881; VI, 16, 73, 96, 98, 138, 300, 483, 504, 512, 513, 524, 578, 587, 588, 593, 594, 641, 643, 685, 700, 701, 702, 714, 715, 750, 791; VII, 25, 80, 169, 189, 225, 285, 286, 387, 464, 465, 486, 614, 615, 729, 730, 767, 769, 770, 771, **782–92**, 817, 818, 825, 872, 905; VIII, xxiii, xxv, xxxii, 150, 260, 289, 462, 492, 842, 843, 844, 845, 937; IX, 75, 115, 188, 297, 678, 809; X, 18, 326, 570; XI, 353
Sewell, Robert Shore Milnes, VII, 787
Sewell, Stephen, V, 133, 218, 614, 697; VI, 86, 138, 205, 296, 644, **700–3**; VII, 666, 667, 782, 786; VIII, 150, 239, 843; IX, 649
Sewell, Thomas, IX, 785
Sewell, William Smith, VII, 787; VIII, 962
Sewengisik. *See* Steinhauer, Henry Bird
Sexton, Helen. *See* Halpen
Sexton, James Ponsonby, X, 647
Sexton, Jane Elizabeth. *See* Carswell
Sexton, John, X, 646, 647
Sexton, John Ponsonby, VIII, 694, 703; X, **646–47**
Sexton, Levi, VIII, 181
Sexton, Lolitia. *See* Keys
Sexton, Samantha (Malcolm), X, 489
Seygris. *See* Segris
Seymour, Benjamin, IX, 680; XI, 928
Seymour, Edward, VII, 56
Seymour, Edward Adolphus, 11th Duke of Somerset, IX, 330, 331

Seymour, Edward Adolphus, 12th Duke of Somerset, IX, 36
Seymour, Eliza Maria (Brush), XI, 120
Seymour, Elizabeth (Stapleton; Conger), IX, 149
Seymour, Emily W. (Williams), XI, 928
Seymour, Florence Maria. *See* Stapleton
Seymour, Francis, 1st Earl and 1st Marquess of Hertford, IV, 146
Seymour, Francis, 2nd Marquess of Hertford, IX, 711
Seymour, Francis Charles, 3rd Marquess of Hertford, IX, 711
Seymour, Frederick, IX, 82, 296, 433, 457, **711–17**; X, 117, 198, 199, 697; XI, 299, 300, 395, 468, 469, 634, 635, 950, 951; XII, 240, 450, 914, 915
Seymour, Sir George Francis, IX, 327, 375, 376, 856; XII, 474
Seymour, George Franklin, XII, 1001
Seymour, Georgiana Mary, Lady Seymour. *See* Berkeley
Seymour, Henry Augustus, IX, 711
Seymour, Horatio, X, 337
Seymour, Margaret. *See* Williams
Seymour, Martha (Jarvis), V, 452; VI, 349
Seymour, Sarah (Mathews), IV, 522
Seymour, Uriah, XI, 898
Seynes, Jules de, XII, 769
Sforza, Gian Galeazzo, Duke of Milan, I, 164
Sforza, Ludovico (il Moro), Duke of Milan, I, 22, 148, 150, 164
Shackleton, Sir Ernest Henry, XI, 918
Shadd, Abraham Doras, XII, 960
Shadd, Harriet. *See* Parnell
Shadd, Mary Ann Camberton (Cary), VIII, 89, 90; IX, 821; XII, 492, **960–61**
Shade, Mrs (Andrews; wife of ABSALOM), IX, 717
Shade, Absalom, VII, 251, 467, 909; VIII, 187; IX, **717–18**, 745; X, 622; XI, 89
Shade, Isabella Jemima. *See* Davidson
Shadgett, William H., VI, 392
Shafer, Joseph, VIII, 818
Shaftesbury, Earl of. *See* Cooper
Shah-wun-dais, VIII, 133, 440; X, **647–48**; XII, 127, 186
Shairp, Catherine (Marryat), VII, 585
Shakespear, Louisa (Higginson), XI, 404
Shakespeare*, Noah (1839–1921), XII, 242, 243
Shakespeare, William, V, 607, 689; VI, 334, 483; VIII, 173, 650, 702; XII, 316, 317, 328, 449, 662, 668, 669, 945, 949, 1111, 1113
Shakoyen'kwaráhton. *See* Johnson, John (1792–1886)
Shakóye:wa:tha?, V, 121, 724; VI, 324, 376, 552, **703–4**, 760; VIII, 620
Shanap, III, 654
Shand, William, VI, 812
Shank; Shanks. *See also* Schank
Shank, David, VI, 578, 579
Shanly, Charles Dawson, X, **648–49**; XI, 817; XII, 961
Shanly, Ellen (Villiers), XII, 965
Shanly, Frances Elizabeth. *See* Mulvany
Shanly, Francis, VIII, 81; X, 648, 703; XI, 617, **817–19**; XII, 395, 961, 962, 963, 964, 965
Shanly, James (father), X, 648; XI, 817; XII, 961
Shanly, James, XI, 817
Shanly, Louisa. *See* Saunders

Shanly, Walter, VIII, 81, 269; X, 648; XI, 69, 114, 557, 677, 817, 818, 819; XII, 350, 392, 393, 395, 396, 683, **961–66**
Shanly, William, X, 648
Shannon, Viscount. *See* Boyle
Shannon, Annie Starr. *See* Fellows
Shannon, James, XII, 604
Shannon, James Noble, XII, 966
Shannon, Nancy. *See* Allison
Shannon, Richard Cutts, XII, 966
Shannon, Samuel Leonard, VI, 67; XII, **966–67**
Shannon, Steven, XI, 710
Shannon, William, XII, 668
Shanson, Gilliom. *See* Jeanson, Guillaume
Shantz*, Jacob Yost (1822–1909), XII, 1099
Shapleigh, Alexander, I, 652
Shapleigh, Catherine (Treworgie), I, 652
Sharkee, Monsieur. *See* Chartier, Michel
Sharman, Ambrose, VI, 741
Sharman, Ann (Carman), VI, 741
Sharman, Sarah (Brown), IX, 86
Sharmen, Mary Ann (Peters), XII, 838
Sharp, Catherine (Robertson), VII, 748
Sharp, Granville, IV, 627
Sharp, James (archbishop), VII, 539
Sharp, James (of Quebec), VI, 119
Sharp, Margaret (Leitch), IX, 460
Sharpe, Cogswell A., VII, 855
Sharpe, E. A., XII, 929
Sharpe, Hannah, I, 338
Sharpe, Lucy Anne (Lane), VIII, 485
Sharples, Charles, X, 649; XII, 279
Sharples, Henry, X, 649
Sharples, James, V, 114, 543
Sharples, John, X, **649–50**; XI, 901; XII, 421
Sharples*, John (1847–1913), X, 649
Sharples, William (great-uncle), X, 480, 649
Sharples, William, X, 649
Sharpless, Mary (Blackadar), IX, 54
Sharpnack, Catharine (Sower), IV, 721
Shash. *See* Leblanc, *dit* Latour, François
Shatford, Sarah (Lawson), VII, 491
Shaver, Peter, VIII, 105
Shaw, Mr (school proprietor), VIII, 354
Shaw, Dr, V, 126
Shaw, Æneas, V, 303, 365, 440, **752–54**, 842; VI, 451, 452, 473, 518; VII, 175; XII, 297
Shaw, Alexander, V, 376, 534; VI, 464; VII, 137
Shaw, Alice Theodosia (Shaw Chipman), VIII, 149
Shaw, Andrew, X, 717
Shaw, Angus (fur trader), V, 534
Shaw, Angus (Métis), VIII, 342
Shaw, Angus, IV, 727; V, 525, 530, 531, 559; VI, 446, 455, **704–5**; VII, 566, 567, 913; IX, 482
Shaw, Angus, Chief of Clan Ay, V, 752
Shaw, Ann. *See* Gosline
Shaw, Ann (Macpherson), VI, 479, 480
Shaw, Anna, VI, 704
Shaw, Anne. *See* Dallas of Cantray
Shaw, Anne. *See* Downsley
Shaw, Bela, VI, 399
Shaw, Charles Æneas, XI, 764
Shaw, Charlotte (Evans), XII, 297

Shaw, David, IX, 73
Shaw, Duncan, X, 665
Shaw, Emily Elizabeth (Beavan), VII, **792–93**
Shaw, Sir Frederick, VI, 425
Shaw, Helen. *See* Forgie
Shaw, Helen (Macdonald), VI, 480; XII, 591
Shaw, Hopestill (Tillson), IX, 789
Shaw, Isabella, VI, 704
Shaw, Isaiah, V, 598
Shaw, James, VIII, 733; X, **650**
Shaw, Jane. *See* Wood
Shaw, Jean (Armour), VIII, 21
Shaw, Julia Agnes. *See* Rickman
Shaw, Margaret. *See* Hickman
Shaw, Margaret (Bell), VIII, 76
Shaw, Margaret Hickman. *See* England
Shaw, Maria (Wheate; Cochrane), X, 178
Shaw, Marion (McDougall), V, 525; VI, 704, 705
Shaw, Marjory. *See* McGillivray
Shaw, Martha Maria (Lewis), XII, 560
Shaw, Mary (Croft), XI, 218
Shaw, Phineas, V, 350
Shaw, Richard, X, 650
Shaw, Robert, VIII, 322; X, 519
Shaw, Samuel, VII, 792
Shaw, Samuel William, XI, 355
Shaw, Susan Catherine (Cooney), IX, 154
Shaw, William (manager), XI, 190
Shaw, William (securities dealer), X, 708
Shaw, William (son of ANGUS), VI, 704
Shaw, William, IV, 674, **706–7**, 776; V, 390
Shawanakiskie, VI, 118, 611, **705–6**; VIII, 708
Shaw Chipman, Alice Theodosia. *See* Shaw
Shaw-Lefevre, Sir John George, VIII, 113
Shawnadithit, II, 8; V, 240; VI, 176, 580, **706–9**; VII, 115, 377; IX, 161
Shawnee Prophet. *See* Tenskwatawa
Shaw of Dores, Elizabeth (MacGillivray of Dalcrombie), VIII, 546
Shaw-shaw-wa-ne-ba-se. *See* Tanner, John
Shea*, Sir Ambrose (d. 1905), VI, 711; VII, 49, 793; IX, 393, 394, 583, 584, 585, 606, 846; X, 8, 398, 400, 716; XI, 239, 243, 432, 433, 634, 674; XII, 91, 162, 163, 164, 165, 311, 482, 564, 754, 844, 956
Shea, Bridget (Skerry), VII, 810
Shea*, Sir Edward Dalton (1820–1913), VI, 711; VII, 793; X, 8; XI, 354
Shea, Eleanor. *See* Ryan
Shea, Mrs Eleanor Ann, VIII, 467
Shea, Henry, VI, 711
Shea, Henry, VI, **709–12**; VII, 598, 793
Shea, John, VI, 710, 711; VII, 154, 793; X, 456
Shea, John Dawson Gilmary, VIII, 79; IX, 256; XII, 737
Shea, Joseph, VI, 711; VII, 294; VIII, 468
Shea, Richard, VI, 410
Shea, Sarah Ann (Baird), XII, 49
Shea, William Richard, VI, 711; VII, **793–94**
Sheaffe, Margaret, Lady Sheaffe. *See* Coffin
Sheaffe, Sir Roger Hale, V, 82, 110, 111, 114, 191, 215, 522, 748, 750, 765; VI, 388, 489, 541, 551, 552, 661; VII, 175, 199, 348, 375, 517, 518, 602, 888; VIII, 5, 186, 236, 239, **793–96**; IX, 245, 754
Sheaffe, Susannah. *See* Child

Sheaffe, William, VIII, 793
Sheard, Joseph, X, 155; XII, 410
Sheawaquanep. *See* Zheewegonab
Shedden, Jean. *See* Wyllie
Shedden, John, X, 650
Shedden, John, X, **650–51**; XI, 359, 362, 560; XII, 152, 602
Shedden, Robert, V, 646
Shedden, William, V, 646
Shee, Sir George, V, 18
Shee, Hélène (Latouche MacCarthy), III, 357
Sheed, George, VIII, 545
Sheed, Robert, VII, 491
Sheehan, Walter Butler, IV, 119
Sheepscot Jo. *See* Wowurna
Sheepshanks, John, XII, 443
Sheffield, Earl of. *See* Holroyd
Sheffield, Mary T., XII, 707
Shehyn*, Joseph (1829–1918), XII, 1065, 1072
Sheil, Louisa Gordon (Hill), XII, 439
Shelburne, Earl of. *See* Petty
Sheldon, Martha (Renaud), IV, 657, 658
Sheldon, Mary (Wisner), XII, 1116
Shelley, Percy Bysshe, XII, 515, 516, 517, 945
Shelton, Hannah Ann (Andrews), V, 24
Shendoreth. *See* Demasduwit
Shenston, Benjamin, XII, 967
Shenston, Mary. *See* Lazenby
Shenston, Mary. *See* Strahan
Shenston, Thomas Strahan, XI, 410, 411; XII, **967–68**, 1117
Shepard, Catherine. *See* Fisher
Shepard, John D., XII, 1090
Shepard, Joseph, VII, 794
Shepard, Joseph, VI, 647; VII, **794**
Shepard, Marie. *See* Tomlin
Shepard, Thomas, I, 343, **607**, 642
Sheperd, Suzanna (Gibbons), IV, 292
Shepherd, Elizabeth. *See* White
Shepherd, Francis John, XII, 315
Shepherd, James, VI, 584, **712**
Shepherd, Sir Samuel, IV, 766, 767; VI, 583
Shepherd, Thomas William, IX, 436
Sheppard*, Edmund Ernest (1855–1924), XI, 753; XII, 137, 245, 499, 500
Sheppard, George, IX, 84, 576, 577; X, 98, 464; XI, 81, 117, 877; XII, 72
Sheppard, Harriet. *See* Campbell
Sheppard, Isabella (Bennett), XI, 65
Sheppard, Peter, V, 107; IX, 15
Sheppard, Sarai. *See* Maxfield
Sheppard, Thérèse. *See* Bellenoy
Sheppard, William, IX, 718
Sheppard, William, VII, 64, 168; VIII, 123, 769; IX, 114, **718–19**; XI, 336
Sheppard, William Grant, V, 107, 108
Shepstone, Harriet (Jenkins), XII, 473
Sherard, William, II, 596
Sheraton*, James Paterson (1841–1906), XI, 368; XII, 395, 453, 993
Sherbrooke, Sir John Coape, V, 267, 268, 314, 489, 698, 882; VI, 37, 38, 158, 167, 233, 239, 267, 326, 343, 456, 516, 519, 594, 657, 701, 702, **712–16**, 724, 725, 732,

792, 801; VII, 186, 189, 217, 218, 225, 428, 457, 486, 684, 722, 724, 727, 728, 769, 770, 787, 817; VIII, xxiv, 355, 575, 626, 719, 824, 843, 955; IX, 36, 173, 548
Sherbrooke, Katherine, Lady Sherbrooke. *See* Pyndar
Sherbrooke, Sarah (Coape (Sherbrooke)), VI, 712
Sherbrooke (Coape), William, VI, 712
Sherburne, Henry, V, 802; VI, 403
Sherer, Patricia (Graham), V, 363
Sheridan, Caroline Elizabeth Sarah (Norton; Stirling-Maxwell, Lady Stirling-Maxwell), IX, 181
Sheridan, Richard Brinsley Butler, V, 438, 689; VI, 483; VII, 783, 869; XII, 305, 449, 642, 833
Sheriff, Mary Harris (Musgrave), XI, 634
Sherlock, Eliza. *See* Merkel
Sherlock, Thomas, IV, 775
Sherman, Jaimy, VIII, 179
Sherman, Prudence (Denison), III, 174
Sherrick, John, VIII, 402
Sherwood, Adiel, V, 748; VI, 262; IX, 166; X, 310, 380, **651–52**; XII, 322
Sherwood, Amelia (King), XI, 110
Sherwood, Anna. *See* Brownson
Sherwood, Caroline (Crawford), IX, 166
Sherwood, Charlotte. *See* Jones
Sherwood, Charlotte (Elmsley), IX, 239, 240; XI, 110
Sherwood, George, IX, 166, 655; X, 200, 405, 631, 650; XI, 166
Sherwood, Helen (Crawford), X, 200
Sherwood, Henry, VII, 32, 253, 459, 606, 924; VIII, 29, 43, 56, 86, 109, 162, 255, 512, 523, 524, 543, 587, 679, **796–801**, 822; IX, 99, 166, 371, 372, 463, 523, 524, 525, 725, 796; X, 79, 80, 118, 119, 200, 256, 257, 310, 311, 528, 619; XI, 41, 341, 927; XII, 593
Sherwood, Julia (Jarvis), X, 380
Sherwood, Justus, IV, 153; V, 637; VI, 90; VII, 795
Sherwood, Levius Peters, V, 457; VI, 118, 165, 265, 266, 421, 630, 631, 772; VII, 40, 100, 371, 419, 420, 456, 457, 458, **794–96**, 896; VIII, 188, 708, 709, 796; IX, 99, 166, 240, 360; X, 200, 631, 705
Sherwood, Mary. *See* Baldwin
Sherwood, Mary Graham. *See* Smith
Sherwood, Reuben, V, 557; VI, 183
Sherwood, Samuel, VIII, 419, 504
Sherwood, Sarah. *See* Bottum
Sherwood, Thomas, X, 651
Shewaquonap (Shewequenap). *See* Zheewegonab
Shewescome, III, 151
Shibley, Henry, XI, 819
Shibley, Kate, XI, 819
Shibley, Mary Ann. *See* Greer
Shibley, Schuyler, XI, **819–20**
Shickluna, Joseph, XII, 783
Shickluna, Louis, X, 515; XI, 650, 651; XII, 529, 783, 971
Shiels, Andrew, VII, 396; VIII, 903; X, **652–53**
Shiels, Ellen (wife of ANDREW), X, 652
Shiels, Isabella. *See* Blair
Shiheileedza, X, 104
Shikellimy. *See also* Swatana
Shikellimy, John, III, 607
Shilling, Andrew, I, 75
Shinguacouse, X, 623
Shingwauk, XII, 680, 681

Shippen, Margaret (Peggy) (Arnold), V, 28, 34, 35, 36
Shirlaw, Walter, XII, 288
Shirley, Selina (Hastings, Countess of Huntingdon), V, 135; VII, 122; VIII, 177
Shirley, William, II, 524; III, xxiv, xxv, xxix, xxx, 9, 10, 30, 32, 33, 87, 101, 126, 255, 260, 261, 274, 275, 288, 322, 325, 326, 362, 363, 365, 403, 404, 438, 439, 483, 507, 512, 572, 585, 588, 628, 641, 653, 654, 655, 657; IV, 52, 83, 84, 281, 314, 395, 487, 489, 540, 559, 560, 588, 679, 769, 774, 775; VI, 188; VII, 275
Shirreff, Adam Dixon, IX, 413
Shirreff, Alexander, VII, 797
Shirreff, Barbara. See Menzies
Shirreff, Charles, VII, 382, 383, **796–98**; VIII, 839
Shirreff, Henrietta (Johnson), IX, 413
Shirreff, Jane. See Coxon
Shirreff, Jane. See Wilson
Shirreff, Robert (grandfather), VII, 796
Shirreff, Robert, VII, 184, 796, 797; VIII, 839
Shirreff, William, III, 143, 276, 518
Shives, Martha. See Wiggins
Shives, Robert, X, 653
Shives, Robert, VII, 792; VIII, 157; IX, 631; X, **653**
Shiwelean. See Hwistesmetxē′qEn
Shoemaker, Jacob S., VI, 235
Shoentakwanni. See Rising, Josiah
Shononhsé:se¹. See Martin, George (1767–1853)
Shoolbred, John, V, 483
Shore, Ariana Margaretta Jekyll. See Saunders
Shore, Ellen Mary (Fletcher), X, 291
Shore, George, VI, 74, 663, 678, 685, 686, 687, 727; VII, 807; VIII, 152, 506, 507, **801–4**; IX, 147; X, 71
Shore, John, 1st Baron Teignmouth, X, 291
Shore, Mary (Milnes), VII, 613
Shorey, Clara. See Gibson
Shorey, Fanny. See Jones
Shorey, Fanny. See Wheeler
Shorey, Hollis, XII, **968–70**
Shorey, Samuel E., XII, 968
Short, Ann. See Brown
Short, Charles John, X, 654
Short, Edward, X, 641, **653–54**; XII, 351
Short, John (great-grandfather), VI, 716
Short, John, X, 653
Short, John Quirk, X, 653
Short, Mary. See Wood
Short, Richard, I, 546
Short, Richard, I, 76; II, 200, 452; III, **591–92**; V, 50, 228, 767
Short, Robert, X, 654
Short, Robert Quirk, VI, **716–17**; VII, 211, 825; VIII, 276, 366; X, 653
Short, Thomas, IX, 149
Shortiss, Lucinda (Barber), X, 34
Shortland, Elizabeth. See Tonkin
Shortland, Emily. See Jones
Shortland, Peter Frederick, VI, 193; VIII, 672; XI, 718, **820–21**
Shortland, Thomas George, XI, 820
Shortridge, Samuel, IX, 658
Shortt*, Adam (1859–1931), IV, xlv, 128; VI, 277, 278; VII, 861; VIII, xxviii
Shortt, Harriet. See McCausland

Shortt, Isabel. See Harper
Shortt, John, IX, 719
Shortt, Jonathan, IX, **719–20**; XI, 654
Shortt, Lucy. See Hartshorne
Shot Close. See Astohkomi; Isapo-muxika
Shotwell, Jane (O'Brien), IX, 603
Shovell, Sir Cloudesley, II, 636; III, 488
Shreve, Thomas, V, 446
Shufelt, Catherine. See Church
Shufelt, Elizabeth (Church), VII, 186
Shufelt, William, VII, 186
Shuldham, Elizabeth. See Molyneux
Shuldham, Lemuel, IV, 707
Shuldham, Margaret Irene, Baroness Shuldham. See Sarney
Shuldham, Molyneux, 1st Baron Shuldham, IV, 122, 176, **707–8**; V, 220, 221, 369, 595
Shuler, John, VIII, 477
Shuler, Sarah. See O'Brian
Shumway, Amni, XI, 568
Shute, Samuel, II, 476, 543, 544, 609, 610, 668
Shuter, John, VIII, 688
Shuttleworth*, Edward Buckingham (1842–1934), XII, 296
Shuwescome, V, 885
Sibbald, Archibald, IX, 542
Sibbald, Charles, IX, 542
Sibbald, Isabella. See Robinson
Sibbald, Susan. See Mein
Sibbald, Thomas, IX, 542
Sibbald, William (father), IX, 542
Sibbald, William, VI, 728; IX, 542
Sibley, Ezekiel, IX, 720
Sibley, Henry Hastings, IX, 780; X, 168, 628; XI, 476; XII, 1029
Sibley, Isaac, IX, 720
Sibley, Jane. See Woodworth
Sibley, Joseph, IX, **720**
Sibley, Mary. See West
Sibley, Michael, IX, 720
Sicard. See also Cucurron
Sicard, Augustin, IV, 320
Sicard, Barthélemi, II, 340
Sicard, Marie. See Rateau
Sicard, Marie-Catherine. See Lamarre, dit Bélisle
Sicard, dit Marseille, Barthélemy, IV, 618
Sicard de Carufel, Marie-Olive (Casavant), X, 153
Sicot, Madeleine (Navières), III, 481
Sicotte. See also Chicot; Cicot
Sicotte, Eugène, XI, 823
Sicotte, Louis-Victor, VII, 737; VIII, 260, 668; IX, 74, 75, 94, 253, 267, 268, 463, 576, 776; X, 25, 144, 145, 219, 405, 418, 420, 464, 465, 466, 507, 725; XI, 81, 144, 157, 160, 176, 180, 181, 196, 283, 345, 464, 530, 677, 698, **821–24**, 878; XII, 7, 254, 262, 263, 299, 596, 720, 986, 1032, 1054, 1108
Sicotte, Louis-Wilfrid, XI, 346, 623; XII, 173
Sicotte, Marguerite-Émélie. See Starnes
Sicotte, Victor-Benjamin, XI, 823
Siddons, Sarah. See Kemble
Sidmouth, Viscount. See Addington
Sidney, Sir Henry, I, 331
Sierra. See Martínez

Sieyès, Emmanuel-Joseph, VI, 781
Sifert, Monsieur (husband of Sébastienne Curie), II, 424
Sifert, Sébastienne. *See* Curie
Sifton*, Sir Clifford (1861–1929), IX, 837; XI, 646; XII, 141, 585, 586, 983
Sifton, Henry, XII, 1028
Siginakee (Blackbird, Letourneau), IV, 233
Signaÿ, François, VII, 798
Signay, Joseph, III, 99; V, 769; VI, 126, 192, 449, 571, 748; VII, 131, 132, 148, 231, 332, 341, 423, 424, 489, 501, 574, 581, 626, 643, 657, 669, 671, 679, 680, 705, **798–800**, 851, 887, 892; VIII, 20, 78, 79, 108, 129, 130, 142, 143, 250, 290, 302, 363, 457, 487, 488, 529, 582, 593, 594, 676, 711, 712, 722, 728, 729; IX, 17, 18, 39, 302, 317, 441, 541, 797, 798, 799, 862; X, 46, 47, 221, 488, 604, 675, 733; XI, 84, 96, 99, 168, 257, 336, 956; XII, 189, 190, 732, 846
Signay, Marguerite. *See* Vallée
Sigogne, Jean-Mandé, IV, xxix, 81; V, 458; VI, 217; VII, 275, 609, 610, 684, **800–6**; VIII, 334, 626; IX, 350; X, 83
Sigogne, Mandé, VII, 800
Sigogne, Marguerite. *See* Robert
Sigouin, Zoé (Chapleau), XII, 172
Sīkākwayān (Skunk Skin), XI, 695
Sikes, Walter, I, 652
Siki'muka. *See* Onista'poka
Si'k-okskitsis, XII, 498, **970–71**
Silcox, Joseph, XI, 924
Silhouette, Étienne de, III, 30
Sillery. *See* Brulart
Silliman, Benjamin (father), VIII, 324; X, 361; XI, 72; XII, 457
Silliman, Benjamin, X, 361; XII, 457
Sillitoe, Acton Windeyer, XII, 283, 443
Sills, Jonathan, V, 99
Sills, Joseph, V, 99
Silly, Jean-Baptiste de, II, **605–6**; III, 444
Silva. *See* Luján
Silvain. *See* Dupleix
Silvain, Timothée. *See* Sullivan, Timothy
Silver, Catherine. *See* Zouberbuhler
Silver, Mary. *See* Williams
Silver, Mary (rebaptized Adélaïde), II, **606–7**; IV, 765
Silver, Thomas, II, 606
Silver Heels. *See* Aroas
Silverman, Lyon, XII, 228
Silverthorn, Rebecca (Chisholm), VII, 178; X, 167
Silvester, Joseph. *See* Joe, Sylvester
Silvia (servant), V, 216
Silvy, Antoine, I, 56, 244, 653; II, 94, **607–9**; III, 104, 204; IV, 424
Simard, Alfred, IX, 287
Simard, Angèle (Simon), XI, 191
Simard, Arthur, XII, 696
Simard, Constance (Chaperon), VIII, 139
Simard, Georges-Honoré, VII, 188; VIII, 629; X, **654–55**; XI, 774; XII, 1037
Simard, Julie. *See* Measam
Simard, Louise. *See* Clouet
Simard, Marie-Luce (Gauvreau), XI, 336
Simard, Pierre, X, 654
Simard, Thomas, VIII, 893, 894

Simblin. *See also* Raimbault
Simblin, Jeanne-Françoise (Raimbault), II, 541, 542
Simcoe, Elizabeth Posthuma. *See* Gwillim
Simcoe, Francis Gwillim, VII, 362
Simcoe, John, III, 210; IV, 163; V, 754
Simcoe, John Graves, IV, 12, 119, 198, 260, 418, 445, 499, 567, 677, 682, 689, 766; V, 15, 35, 71, 78, 93, 101, 120, 121, 124, 151, 152, 170, 188, 196, 255, 279, 282, 297, 303, 306, 326, 365, 388, 404, 405, 428, 439, 448, 452, 453, 455, 518, 519, 541, 552, 553, 594, 596, 597, 661, 669, 707, 718, 722, 724, 730, 731, 732, 733, 734, 749, 752, 753, **754–59**, 772, 773, 781, 787, 802, 808, 809, 814, 815, 820, 821, 859, 860, 868, 884; VI, 8, 21, 159, 177, 187, 201, 256, 264, 296, 353, 388, 389, 415, 444, 451, 452, 453, 518, 523, 548, 549, 558, 559, 560, 578, 582, 583, 600, 607, 608, 609, 628, 647, 650, 683, 684, 695, 721, 722, 733, 746, 808; VII, 39, 42, 56, 175, 250, 347, 361, 362, 554, 602, 665, 691, 693, 697, 811, 812, 813; VIII, 4, 10, 33, 116, 191, 340, 430, 511, 516, 522, 524, 540, 606, 793, 857, 858, 860; IX, 519, 544, 756; X, 644, 706
Simcoe, Katherine. *See* Stamford
Sime, Alexander, XI, 804
Siméon, Bélonie (McLeod), VIII, 570
Simeoni, Giovanni, XI, 424; XII, 799
Simmonet, Philippe, IV, 708
Simms, Henry, VII, 297
Simms, James, VI, 693, 708; VII, 99, 294, 631; VIII, 246, 804; IX, 70, 168, 694, **720–21**, 794
Simms, Joseph, IX, 720
Simms, Mary (mother of JAMES and SOPHIA), VIII, 804; IX, 720
Simms, Pamela (Fitzgerald), IV, 159
Simms, Sophia (Dalton), VII, 228; VIII, **804–5**
Simms, William, VIII, 804; IX, 720
Simon. *See also* Cimon; Pieskaret
Simon, Angèle. *See* Simard
Simon, Hubert, XI, 191
Simon, Marie-Madeleine. *See* Lefebvre
Simon, Pierre-Antoine. *See* Maillard, Pierre
Simon, *dit* Delorme, Hyacinthe-Marie, VI, 207, 287; VII, 235
Simon, *dit* Delorme, Jacques-Hyacinthe, VI, 207
Simon, *dit* Delorme, Marie-Anne. *See* Crevier Décheneaux
Simon, *dit* Delorme, Marie-Josephte (Debartzch), VII, 235, 711
Simon de Longpré, Françoise de. *See* Jourdan
Simon de Longpré, Jacques de, I, 607
Simon de Longpré, Marie-Catherine de, named de Saint-Augustin, I, 31, 204, 310, 314, 457, 472, 551, 563, **607–10**; II, 84, 161
Simonds, Ann. *See* Charters
Simonds, Catharine Mary. *See* Longmuir
Simonds, Charles, VI, 717, 720; VII, 47, 48, 140, 141, 187, 444, 658, 806, 807; VIII, 346, 377, 738, 803, **805–11**, 841; IX, 22, 23, 35, 146, 622; X, 157, 315, 543; XI, 372; XII, 897, 1052, 1104
Simonds, Edward, VII, 683
Simonds, Hannah. *See* Peabody
Simonds, James, IV, 329, 389, 723; V, 16, 415, 416, 608; VI, 655, **717–20**; VII, 493, 612, 683, 806; VIII, 805
Simonds, Lucy Anne. *See* Clopper
Simonds, Margaret. *See* Walker

Simonds, Nathan, VI, 717
Simonds, Richard, V, 415; VI, 717, 718
Simonds, Richard, VI, 651, 717; VII, 5, 140, 683, **806–8**; VIII, 805, 806, 807; IX, 221
Simonds, Sarah. *See* Hazen
Simonds, Sarah (Millidge), VI, 655; VII, 612
Simonet, Élisabeth. *See* Bériault
Simonet, Jean-Baptiste, III, 592
Simonet, Marguerite-Victoire (Braun), XI, 109
Simonet d'Abergemont, Geneviève. *See* Boucher de Grandpré
Simonet d'Abergemont, Jacques, III, 153, 351, **592–93**, 617; IV, 284, 362, 590
Simonet d'Abergemont, Jean-Baptiste, III, 593
Simonet d'Abergemont, Marie. *See* Foissey
Simonin, Maurice, III, 350; IV, 124
Simonnet, François, IV, 148, 270, **708–10**; V, 436
Simonnet, Marguerite. *See* Bougret Dufort
Simonnet, Marguerite. *See* Neveu
Simonnet, Marie. *See* Boismenay
Simonnet, Marie-Louise, IV, 709
Simonnet, Philippe, IV, 708
Simons, Levy, IV, 332
Simons, Peter, VIII, 648
Simons, Titus Geer, V, 814, 815; VIII, 5, 887
Simons, William (apprentice to John MUNN), VIII, 648
Simons, William (shipbuilder), VI, 291
Simpkinson, Mary. *See* Griffin
Simpson, Æmilius, VI, **720–21**; VII, 808; XI, 52
Simpson, Albert Benjamin, XII, 454
Simpson, Alexander (cashier), XII, 988
Simpson, Alexander (father of ÆMILIUS and ALEXANDER), VI, 720; VII, 808
Simpson, Alexander, VI, 720; VII, **808–9**; VIII, 816
Simpson, Anna. *See* Gschwind
Simpson, Annie. *See* Burke
Simpson, Blanche. *See* Mowat
Simpson, Caleb P., X, 230
Simpson, Catherine Garden (Jones), XII, 479
Simpson, Charles Alexander, VI, 303
Simpson, Charlotte (Hall; Armstrong), XII, 37
Simpson, Eliza Charlotte (Anderson), IX, 5; XI, 16
Simpson, Elsie (McCall), VI, 421
Simpson, Emilia. *See* MacIntosh
Simpson, Esther Louisa. *See* Terry
Simpson, Frances Hume. *See* Hawkins
Simpson, Frances Ramsay (Simpson, Lady Simpson), VII, 454; VIII, 121, 561, 574, 589, **811–12**, 814, 815, 817, 889; XI, 824; XII, 53, 155
Simpson, Geddes Mackenzie, VIII, 811, 812, 814; XI, 824
Simpson, George, VIII, 812
Simpson, Sir George, V, 532; VI, 20, 254, 437, 438, 648, 720, 721, 754, 768; VII, 4, 78, 160, 205, 206, 207, 232, 249, 250, 276, 277, 325, 454, 455, 473, 526, 565, 568, 569, 570, 571, 572, 578, 672, 737, 748, 749, 750, 808, 838, 902, 913; VIII, 59, 85, 91, 113, 121, 122, 131, 159, 226, 315, 343, 349, 350, 413, 454, 455, 527, 537, 538, 540, 556, 557, 558, 561, 562, 571, 573, 574, 575, 576, 577, 578, 579, 580, 584, 589, 660, 661, 662, 663, 714, 721, 766, 767, 779, 780, 811, **812–19**, 820, 821, 889; 893; IX, 6, 42, 95, 135, 136, 150, 169, 197, 198, 199, 260, 261, 337, 365, 366, 456, 457, 472, 513, 529, 530, 625, 626, 634, 722, 773, 806, 851, 852, 853, 854; X, 6, 27, 28, 47, 114, 115, 239, 240, 241, 242, 244, 272, 273, 284, 390, 392, 393, 426, 473, 486, 496, 541, 629, 720, 724; XI, 5, 17, 19, 52, 53, 88, 169, 204, 219, 220, 231, 383, 384, 445, 476, 509, 545, 546, 569, 570, 662, 663, 767, 775, 824, 854, 855, 875, 876, 882, 886, 887; XII, 53, 113, 114, 155, 156, 206, 207, 477, 507, 680, 681, 682, 876, 877, 931, 932, 1004
Simpson, George Geddes, VIII, 811
Simpson, George Stewart, VIII, 814
Simpson, Hannah (Jones), VIII, 443
Simpson, Harriet A. (wife of MELANCTHON), XII, 971
Simpson, Horatio Nelson, VI, 720
Simpson, Isobel Graham (Finlayson), VIII, 589, 811; IX, 260; XI, **824**; XII, 53
Simpson, James (businessman), VIII, 785
Simpson, James (cousin of ROBERT), XII, 972
Simpson, James Kay, XI, 599
Simpson, James Keith, VIII, 814
Simpson, Sir James Young, IX, 281; XI, 559, 824
Simpson, Jane Christie. *See* Parmouth
Simpson, John (brother of MELANCTHON), XII, 971
Simpson, John (father of JOHN, 1812–85), XI, 824
Simpson, John (ship's captain), I, 107, 361, 493, 673
Simpson, John (1788–1873), VI, 381, 386, 478; VII, 118, 172; VIII, 332, 434; IX, 533; X, 626, **655–56**
Simpson, John (1807–78), VII, 600; VIII, 790; IX, 517, 551; X, **656**
Simpson, John, XI, 346, **824–26**
Simpson, Mrs John. *See* Baker
Simpson, John Henry Pelly, VIII, 811, 818
Simpson, John McKenzie, VIII, 814
Simpson, Lucy. *See* Stanynought
Simpson, Margaret. *See* Petrie
Simpson, Margaret (Merritt), XII, 973
Simpson, Maria, XII, 923
Simpson, Maria (Mactavish), VIII, 814, 818
Simpson, Maria (Wallace), VIII, 814
Simpson, Marie (Darveau), X, 213
Simpson, Mary (Mathews), V, 584
Simpson, Mary (Simpson), VI, 720; VII, 808; VIII, 812
Simpson, Mary Anne. *See* Botsford
Simpson, Melancthon, XI, 651; XII, 69, 529, **971**
Simpson, Peter, XII, 972
Simpson, Robert, XII, **971–73**
Simpson, Sarah. *See* Burke
Simpson, Thomas, VII, 206, 326, 808, 809; VIII, 455, 562, 663, 815; IX, 42, 197, 198, 199, 648; X, 28, 407; XI, 882; XII, 876, 877, 878
Simpson, Wemyss McKenzie, XII, 34, 194
Simpson, William B., X, 655
Simpson, Zipporah. *See* Tickell
Simpson of Gartly, Mary (Ellice of Knockleith), IV, 261; V, 299
Sims, Henry Augustus, XII, 345
Sims, Jabez W., XI, 654
Sims, James Marion, XI, 559
Sims, John, VII, 555
Sinate. *See* Sahneuti
Sincennes. *See also* Petitot
Sincennes, Clotilde-Héloise. *See* Douaire Bondy
Sincennes, Delphine-Denise. *See* Perrault
Sincennes, Jacques-Félix, X, **656–58**; XI, 586; XII, 664

Sinclair, Aemilia (Sinclair), V, 759
Sinclair, Alexander, V, 759
Sinclair*, Alexander Maclean (1840–1924), V, 547; VI, 462; VII, 560; VIII, 526
Sinclair, Andrew, I, 243
Sinclair, Arthur, VI, 817
Sinclair, Benjamin, VII, 390; XI, 849; XII, 932
Sinclair, Catherine M. S. *See* Stewart
Sinclair, Colin, IX, 722
Sinclair, Donald Maclean, VI, 462
Sinclair, Dugald, XI, 78
Sinclair, Elizabeth. *See* Bird
Sinclair, Harriette (Cowan), VIII, 819, 820
Sinclair, Henry, 1st Earl of Orkney, I, 680
Sinclair, James, VII, 777; VIII, 344, 767, **819–20**; IX, 260, 261, 537, 722; X, 168, 377; XI, 219, 476, 546; XII, 110
Sinclair, John (businessman), VII, 155
Sinclair, John (trader), XI, 597
Sinclair, John (translator), VII, 277; IX, 784
Sinclair, Sir John, VII, 930; IX, 332
Sinclair, Margaret. *See* Nahovway
Sinclair, Margaret (wife of Benjamin), VII, 390
Sinclair, Margaret (Clare; Allan), IX, 130
Sinclair, Maria, VIII, 819
Sinclair, Maria Merrick. *See* Clarke
Sinclair, Mary. *See* Campbell
Sinclair, Mary. *See* MacKay
Sinclair, Mary (Christie), XI, 663; XII, 194
Sinclair, Mary (Inkster), X, 377
Sinclair, Patrick, V, 8, 38, 129, 260, 273, 567, 715, **759–61**, 836; VI, 189, 509
Sinclair, Peter, VIII, 408
Sinclair, Phoebe (Bunn), IX, 102
Sinclair, Stephen, II, 231
Sinclair, Thomas (brother of WILLIAM), VI, 721; IX, 722; X, 484
Sinclair, Thomas (magistrate), XII, 132
Sinclair, Thomas (merchant), IX, 130
Sinclair, Wilhelmina Matilda (Stuart), XI, 862
Sinclair, William, VIII, 819; IX, 722; X, 377
Sinclair, William, VIII, 663; IX, **722–23**; XII, 194
Singing Before (Frances Ikaenikiakew), XII, 718
Singleton, George, IV, **710–11**
Singleton, Henry, IV, 223
Singleton, John, IV, 710
Singleton, Mary. *See* Moore, Frances
Singleton, Nancy. *See* Ferguson
Sinnookeesick (Sounding Sky), XII, 497, 498
Sinnott, James, V, 473; VI, 693
Sinotte, Jérémie, X, 424
Sintez, V, 835
Sintré. *See* Legrand
Siongorochti. *See* Kaieñ?kwaahtoñ
Sipperal, Mary (Morton), XII, 763
Sire. *See* Cyr
Sirier. *See* Cirier
Sirois, Lavery, VI, 185
Sirois, Pierre, VII, 164
Sirois, *dit* Duplessis, Émilie (Maurault), IX, 541
Sirois, *dit* Duplessis, Hypolite, VII, 147
Sirois-Duplessis, Joseph, X, 686
Sirois-Duplessis, Pascal, V, 588; VI, 749
Sismonde de Sismondi, Jean-Charles-Léonard, VI, 42

Sisoyaki (Cutting Woman), XI, 444
Sissons*, Charles Bruce (1879–1965), VIII, 791; X, 639; XI, 729, 783, 785, 795, 796
Sitting Bull. *See* Ta-tanka I-yotank
Sitting on an Eagle Tail. *See* Sotai-na
Sitting White Buffalo. *See* Mékaisto
Sivadier, Marie (Horné, *dit* Laneuville), II, 292
Siveright, Jannet. *See* Glass
Siveright, John, VIII, 820
Siveright, John, VI, 236, 466, 765; VIII, 815, **820–22**; IX, 169, 329
Siveright, Josephte (Goulet), VIII, 821; IX, 329
Sivert. *See* L'Espérance
Sivot, Marie (Perrot), II, 517
Sjöman, Anna Magaretha (Sandin; Kalm), IV, 406
Skaⴈennetsi (Anne Gregory) (wife of Claude-Nicolas-Guillaume de LORIMIER), VI, 404
Skakel, Alexander, VII, 809
Skakel, Alexander, VI, 260; VII, 733, 751, **809–10**; VIII, 403, 404, 734; IX, 357, 610; X, 444, 606; XI, 40
Skakel, Christian. *See* Dalrymple
Skakel, Isabella (Skakel), VII, 809
Skanawati (John Buck), XI, 453
Skanudharoua (Skannud-Haroï) (Geneviève-Agnès de Tous les-Saints), I, **610–11**
Skanyadariyoh (Handsome Lake), VI, 704, 758; VII, 520
Skatzi. *See* Scorch Eye
Skead, James, VIII, 268; XI, 113, 682, **826–27**
Skead, Mary. *See* Selkirk
Skead, Rosena. *See* MacKey
Skead, William, XI, 826
Skeels, Anna (Mary) (Wood), XII, 1121
Skeet, Ann (Cooper; Cullen), XI, 201
Skeffington, George, II, 89, **609**, 626
Skelton, Miss (teacher), VI, 336
Skelton, Catherine. *See* Ball
Skelton*, Oscar Douglas (1878–1941), XII, 485
Skelton, Thomas, V, 141
Skene, William, III, 143, 276, 514
Skerrett, John, V, 633, **761–62**, 763; VI, 271, 781
Skerrett, John Byrne, V, 761
Skerry, Bridget. *See* Shea
Skerry, John, VII, **810–11**
Skerry, Luke, VII, 810
Skerry, Maria. *See* Meagher
Skerry, Mary. *See* Larissy
Skey, Miss (Durell), III, 208
Skey, James, X, 691
Skidegate, IV, 420
Skillen, Sarah (Lyon), IV, 490
Skinner, Mrs. *See* Power
Skinner, Anne (Huntley, Lady Huntley), IX, 401
Skinner, Constance Langford (Davie), XI, 236
Skinner, Elizabeth McCormick (McGillivray), IX, 494
Skinner, Harriet. *See* McDonald
Skinner, Harriet (Prescott), V, 763
Skinner, Hester. *See* Lawder
Skinner, James, VIII, 715
Skinner, James Atchison, X, 74
Skinner, Janet Mcpherson (King), XII, 489
Skinner, John, IX, 753
Skinner, Otis, XII, 316, 317
Skinner, Rebecca (Manning), VIII, 610, 613

Skinner, Robert Pringle, V, **762**, 763
Skinner, Thomas, XII, 523
Skinner, Thomas, V, 633, 761, **762–63**; VI, 418; VII, 628; VIII, 264
Skinner, Thomas James, X, 116, 242
Skinner, William (father), V, 762
Skinner, William, V, 762
Skirving, Catherine Seaton (Ewart), XII, **973–74**
Skirving, Jessie (Leach), XI, 502
Skirving, John, XII, 973
Skirving, Margaret. *See* Wardlaw
Skolvsson. *See* Scolvus
Skrimsher, Samuel, III, 593
Skrimsher, Samuel, III, 483, **593–94**
Skrimshire, Ann (Isham), III, 301
Skroeder, John, X, 33
Skulkinanse, IV, 419, 420
Skunk Skin. *See* Sīkākwayān
Skurray, Blanche Anne (MacDonnell), XI, 555
Skyring, Miss (Capreol), XI, 150
Slack, Susannah (Henderson), IX, 388
Slacum, William A., VIII, 578
Slade, Ann (mother of JOHN), IV, 711
Slade, David, IV, 713; V, 764
Slade, Elizabeth (mother of THOMAS), V, 764
Slade, John (grandfather of JOHN), IV, 711
Slade, John (son of JOHN), IV, 713; V, 764
Slade, John, IV, **711–14**; V, 491, 675, 764, 785
Slade, John Haitor, IV, 713
Slade, Martha. *See* Haitor
Slade, Robert (brother of THOMAS), IV, 711, 713; V, 764, 785; VI, 274, 275
Slade, Robert (cousin of THOMAS), V, 764
Slade, Robert (father of THOMAS), IV, 713; V, 764
Slade, Robert (nephew of THOMAS), V, 764
Slade, Thomas (brother of JOHN), IV, 711
Slade, Thomas (cousin of THOMAS), V, 764
Slade, Thomas (nephew of THOMAS), V, 764
Slade, Thomas, IV, 713; V, **764–65**; VI, 274
Slany (Slaney), John, I, 233, 349, 350, 650
Slason, Martha (Hatheway), X, 339
Slater, Edward Beda, VIII, 490
Slater, Esther. *See* Sparks
Slater, James Dyson, IX, 735
Slater, James Gibson, XII, 246
Slater, John, III, 277
Slattery*, John Luke (1847–1907), XII, 861
Slave Woman. *See* Thanadelthur
Slayter, Joseph, V, 843
Sleat. *See* Macdonald
Sleeman*, George (1841–1926), XII, 378
Sleeping Woman. *See* Iyokaki
Sleeth, David, XI, 579, 580
Sleigh, Mrs. *See* Franklin
Sleigh, Burrows Willcocks Arthur, IX, **723–24**
Sleigh, Sarah. *See* Campbell
Sleigh, William Willcocks, IX, 723
Slevin, Édouard, IX, 640
Slichtenhorst. *See* Van Slichtenhorst
Slingsby, William, VIII, 687
Sloan, Janet (Notman), XII, 787
Sloane, Sir Hans, I, 669; II, 444
Sloane, Jane (Hughes, Lady Hughes), V, 434

Slocum, John Jay, VII, 625, 626
Slodtz, René-Michel (Michel-Ange), VI, 26, 27
Small, Charles Coxwell, VI, 721, 722
Small, Charlotte (Thompson), VIII, 881, 882
Small, Edward A., XII, 969
Small, Elizabeth. *See* Goldsmith
Small, Frances Elizabeth. *See* Ridout
Small, James Edward, VI, 164, 721; VII, 32, 37; VIII, 47, 431, 523, 698, 849, 932; IX, 151, 346, 411, 412, 498, 674, **724–25**; X, 253, 528; XI, 864
Small, John (officer), V, 515
Small, John (uncle of JOHN), VI, 722
Small, John, IV, 766; V, 17, 420, 441, 453, 519, 855; VI, 583, **721–22**; VII, 36, 554, 813; VIII, 336; IX, 724
Small, Joseph, VI, 721
Small, Margaret (Campbell), VII, 139
Small, Mary. *See* Atwell
Small, Nancy (McDonald of Garth), VIII, 881
Small, Patrick, IV, 366, 741; V, 561, 562, 603; VI, 454; VIII, 881
Small Eyes. *See* Abishabis
Smallwood, Charles, VII, 105; X, **658–59**; XI, 799; XII, 788
Smart, Alexander, X, 659
Smart, Ann (Holl), IX, 394
Smart, James Allan, XII, 141
Smart, Jane (Light), XII, 561
Smart, Margaret (mother of WILLIAM), X, 659
Smart, Phylina. *See* Foote
Smart, Sarah. *See* Mallory
Smart, Thomas, II, 15, 22, 198, 288, 524, **609–10**; III, 182, 456, 512, 597
Smart, William (silk manufacturer), IX, 394
Smart, William (son of WILLIAM), X, 659
Smart, William, VI, 232, 262, 436; VIII, 77; X, **659–60**
Smeaton, Dorothea (White), XI, 919
Smellie, Elizabeth Logie (Macdonnell), XII, 615
Smellie, George, VIII, 68; XII, 616
Smelt, Anne (MacDougall), XII, 621
Smeulders, Joseph-Gauthier-Henri, XI, 485, 514; XII, 88, 304, 509, 510
Smiler, Christopher, XI, 135
Smiler, Deborah Ann (Lugrin), VI, 408
Smiles, Samuel, XII, 61
Smiley, Agnes (mother of ROBERT REID), VIII, 822
Smiley, Hugh Creighton, VIII, 822
Smiley, John Gibson, VIII, 822
Smiley, Margaret. *See* Switzer
Smiley, Robert Reid, VI, 248; VII, 117; VIII, **822–23**; XI, 608, 920
Smiley, Samuel, VIII, 822
Smillie, William Cumming, VIII, 385; XII, 248
Smirke, Sir Robert, XII, 809
Smith. *See also* Bell-Smith; Smithe; Vernon-Smith
Smith, Miss (educator), X, 661
Smith, Mrs (educator), X, 661
Smith, Abram N., XII, 55
Smith, Adam, VI, 646; VII, 24, 417, 645; VIII, 278, 417; X, 91, 571, 607, 680, 708; XI, 923; XII, 243
Smith, Albert, VIII, 274
Smith, Sir Albert James, IX, 409, 414, 620; X, 140, 160, 286, 287, 288, 340, 426, 498, 544, 713; XI, 91, 224, 278, 298, 350, 374, 447, 578, 579, 688, **827–34**, 888,

897, 933; XII, 18, 25, 116, 338, 484, 536, 649, 654, 741, 743, 798, 898, 979, 1052, 1053, 1054, 1055, 1056, 1057, 1097, 1105
Smith, Alcibiado, XII, 976
Smith, Alexander, XII, **974–75**
Smith, Alexander Mortimer, XI, 836, 837, 938; XII, **975–76**
Smith, Amélie. *See* Eméric
Smith*, Andrew (1834–1910), IX, 252; X, 84; XI, 133
Smith, Ann. *See* Cook
Smith, Ann. *See* Grant
Smith, Ann (Loring), VII, 517
Smith, Ann (Maclean), VIII, 563, 565
Smith, Anne. *See* O'Reilly
Smith, Anne. *See* Waylen
Smith, Anne (McDonell), VI, 723; VII, 554; XI, 552
Smith, Augusta Louisa (mother of SIDNEY), XI, 837
Smith, Barbara Leigh (Bodichon), VIII, 651
Smith, Benjamin Walker, VII, 747
Smith, Bennett, XI, **834–35**
Smith, Bernard, X, 193
Smith, Bowen, XI, 827
Smith, Caroline. *See* Dauphine
Smith, Catharine (Secord), VII, 780
Smith, Charles (butcher), VI, 582
Smith, Charles (son of BENNETT), XI, 834
Smith, Charles Douglass, V, 250, 336, 679, 826; VI, 109, 122, 123, 359, 360, 361, 362, 414, 415, 447, 448, 567, 568, 737, 785, 786, 818, 819; VII, 76, 352, 408, 414, 415, 511, 740, 741, 925; VIII, xxiv, 36, 37, 444, 484, 531, 533, 547, 548, 741, **823–28**, 954; IX, 474; X, 339; XII, 462
Smith, Charles Farquharson, XII, 989
Smith, Charles-Gustave, X, 89, 228, 229; XII, 504, **976–78**
Smith, Charles Jeffry, V, 804
Smith, Charles McKeivers, XII, 237
Smith, Charles Mather, X, 698; XI, 7; XII, 73
Smith, Charlotte. *See* Brant
Smith, Charlotte (Gilpin), XII, 368
Smith, Charlotte Esther. *See* Weems
Smith, Cordelia. *See* Wigley
Smith, Damaris. *See* Nish
Smith, David (associate of Henry MORGAN), XII, 760, 761
Smith, David (clergyman), V, 344; VI, 294, 458
Smith, Sir David William, IV, 766, 767; V, 120, 279, 282, 302, 326, 388, 405, 448, 518, 519, 552, 597, 730, 734, 749, 755, 782, 814, 815, 841, 842, 846; VI, 21, 159, 211, 389, 452, 473, 578, 600, 608, 721; VII, 57, 175, **811–14**, 929; VIII, 10, 33, 185, 606, 607
Smith, Dianna Harriet. *See* Kendrick
Smith*, Donald Alexander, 1st Baron Strathcona and Mount Royal (1820–1914), VII, 838; IX, 708; X, 70, 111, 487, 631, 677; XI, 45, 46, 47, 53, 124, 125, 383, 385, 442, 477, 540, 546, 613, 614, 642, 646, 707, 739, 740, 742, 743, 942; XII, 6, 8, 33, 83, 152, 153, 194, 235, 248, 288, 363, 370, 409, 455, 601, 603, 631, 636, 641, 679, 749, 777, 788, 951, 1008, 1058
Smith, Edward (biographer), V, 56
Smith, Edward (chief factor), VII, 568, 572; VIII, 454
Smith, Edward Osborne, XI, 839
Smith, Eleanor Elizabeth (Finley; Penny), XI, 680
Smith, Elias, XI, 837
Smith, Elizabeth. *See* Fereday

Smith, Elizabeth. *See* Murray
Smith, Elizabeth (Street; Benedict), V, 781
Smith, Elizabeth Orde Usher (Arthur, Lady Arthur), VIII, 26
Smith, Emma (Hopper), XII, 444
Smith, Erastus W., IX, 311
Smith, Mrs Erminnie A., XI, 453
Smith*, Ernest D'Israeli (1853–1948), VII, 563
Smith, Flavie. *See* Fournier
Smith, Florella (Jones), VII, 452
Smith, Frances. *See* Woodcock
Smith, Frances (Black), IX, 52
Smith, Frances Louisa (Worthington), IX, 728; XII, 1129
Smith, Francis, III, 303, 472, **594**
Smith, François-Xavier-Louis-Théodule, XI, 836
Smith, Frank (brother of Sir HENRY), IX, 700
Smith, Frank (furniture manufacturer), IX, 391
Smith*, Sir Frank (1822–1901), IX, 475; XI, 227, 803; XII, 42, 43, 330, 333, 454, 585, 586, 711, 1086
Smith, Fraser, V, 559, 560
Smith, Frederica Ubrica Charletta Catherina (Carmichael), VI, 122
Smith, Frederick, VIII, 387
Smith, George (clergyman), V, 190
Smith, George (merchant), V, 611, 612; VII, 532; VIII, 122; X, 382
Smith, George Sidney, VIII, 825
Smith*, Goldwin (1823–1910), X, 79, 102; XI, 247, 248, 324, 724; XII, 147, 204, 236, 453, 515, 586, 657, 688, 753, 867, 1094, 1114
Smith, Grace, VII, 460
Smith, Grace (Greenwood), VI, 302
Smith, Hannah (Fanning), V, 308
Smith, Harriet (Cadman; wife of PHILANDER), IX, 728
Smith, Harriet Louisa (Lee), X, 436
Smith, Harriette Elizabeth. *See* Dixon
Smith, Sir Harry George Wakelyn, XII, 966
Smith, Henrietta (Harriet) (Sewell), IV, 718; V, 769; VII, 785, 790
Smith, Henrietta Jane Cater. *See* Busby
Smith, Henry (builder), V, 679
Smith, Henry (warden), IX, 83, 164, 252, 700, 725, 726; X, 94, 97, 470
Smith, Sir Henry, VII, 102, 103; VIII, 837; IX, 164, 578, **725–27**; X, 591; XI, 140
Smith, Henry Bowyer, VIII, 824, 825
Smith, Henry Hall, XII, 608, 612
Smith, Henry More, VII, 53, 691
Smith, Henry Stanley, XII, 145
Smith, Henry William, XI, **835**
Smith, Hollis, VIII, 221; IX, **727–28**; X, 642; XI, 706; XII, 1129
Smith, Horace, XI, 469
Smith, Isaac, V, 679
Smith, Isaac B., VIII, 422
Smith, Isabella (wife of ALEXANDER), XII, 974
Smith, Isabella (Coates), IX, 131
Smith, Isabella Gair. *See* Rose
Smith, James (architect), XII, 131
Smith, James (father of JAMES, 1806–68), IX, 728
Smith, James (father of SAMUEL), VI, 722
Smith, James (Newfoundland resident), II, 611
Smith, James (politician), X, 263

Smith, James, II, **610–11**
Smith, James, VII, 606; IX, 191, 257, **728**, 779; XII, 5
Smith, James, XI, **836**
Smith, James Edward, XII, 410
Smith, James Royer, XI, 835
Smith, Jane. *See* Morson
Smith (Smyth), Jane (O'Brien), XII, 791
Smith, Jane (Stuart), VII, 835
Smith, Jane Isabella. *See* Clarke
Smith, Janet. *See* Colquhoun
Smith, Janet. *See* Livingston
Smith, Janet (Jennet) (Bethune), IX, 49
Smith, Jean. *See* McDonald
Smith, Jedediah Strong, VII, 570
Smith, Jedidah (Osborn), IV, 593
Smith, Jesse, XII, 237
Smith, John (army officer), VII, 603
Smith, John (assistant to John HORDEN), XII, 446
Smith, John (associate of Wellwood WAUGH), VI, 806
Smith, John (brother of BENNETT), XI, 834
Smith, John (captain), I, 67, 101, 132, 262, 650
Smith, John (clergyman), VI, 58
Smith, John (father of BENNETT), XI, 834
Smith, John (father of CHARLES DOUGLASS), VIII, 823
Smith, John (father of Sir DAVID WILLIAM), V, 749; VII, 811
Smith, John (paper manufacturer), XI, 546
Smith, John (son of BENNETT), XI, 834
Smith, John, VIII, **828–29**
Smith, John, XI, **836–37**; XII, 975
Smith, Sir John. *See* Smyth, John
Smith, John B., XI, 837
Smith, John C., XI, 837
Smith, John David, IX, 49; XI, 837
Smith, Sir John Frederick Sigismund, VIII, 26
Smith, John Shuter, IX, 804; XI, 837
Smith, John Spencer (uncle), VIII, 823
Smith, John Spencer, VIII, 825
Smith, John Wilson Young, XI, 832
Smith, Joseph, IX, 731
Smith, Joseph, III, 171, 287, 304, **594–95**; IV, 47
Smith, Judith. *See* Scovill
Smith, Judson Newman, XII, 927
Smith, Julia (Beemer; Crandall), VIII, 180
Smith, Kitty (wife of FRANCIS), III, 594
Smith, Larratt William Violett, VII, 372
Smith, Laura Louise, IX, 407
Smith, Levi, IX, 727
Smith, Lewis, XI, 948
Smith, Sir Lionel, IX, 195
Smith, Louise-Émilie-Hermine. *See* Leprohon
Smith, Lucy. *See* Bates
Smith, Marcus, XI, 764; XII, 280, 448
Smith, Margaret (Pruden), IX, 648
Smith, Margaret (Ross), X, 629, 630
Smith, Maria (Wait), XII, 1078, 1079
Smith, Mary. *See* Het
Smith, Mary. *See* Morris
Smith, Mary. *See* Talbot
Smith, Mary. *See* Tyler
Smith, Mary. *See* Wilkinson
Smith, Mary (wife of JOHN, d. 1881), XI, 836
Smith, Mary (Eaton), XII, 287

Smith, Mary (Lane), VIII, 484
Smith, Mary (Mortimer), V, 611
Smith, Mary (Willis), X, 704
Smith, Mary Ann. *See* Barnes
Smith, Mary Ann. *See* Bennett
Smith, Mary Blithe (Evans), VII, 275
Smith, Mary E. A. *See* Poyntz
Smith, Mary Graham (Sherwood), VIII, 796
Smith, Mary Maxwell (Gow), XI, 366
Smith, Mary Spafford. *See* Barker
Smith, Matilda Caroline (Allan, Lady Allan), XI, 5
Smith, Michael, V, 65, **765–66**; VIII, 608
Smith, Nathan (doctor), VII, 777
Smith, Nathan (educator), VIII, 324
Smith, Nelly (Campbel), X, 129
Smith, Nicholas, XII, 770
Smith, Patrick Henry, 877
Smith, Peter, XI, 547
Smith, Peter, IV, 494; V, 168, 169; VI, **722**; VII, 57, 471; VIII, 796; IX, 49
Smith, Philander, IX, 27, **728–30**; X, 616
Smith, Phœbe (Talbot), VII, 842
Smith, Polly (Sayre), VII, 777
Smith, Rachel. *See* Harris
Smith, Ralph, VII, 842
Smith, Rebecca. *See* Beckwith
Smith, Rebecca (Couche), VI, 369
Smith, Richard, VIII, 416, 459; IX, 178, 225, **730–32**; XI, 944
Smith, Robert, VIII, 828
Smith, Robert Thompson, XI, 50
Smith, Robina. *See* Lizars
Smith, Rose (McGreevy), XII, 626
Smith, Ruth Roach (Chandler), VIII, 138
Smith, Sally. *See* Wright
Smith, Samuel, XI, 834
Smith, Samuel, V, 673, 674; VI, 230, 612, 721, **722–23**; VII, 457, 554; VIII, 5, 431; IX, 332, 333, 670, 756; X, 436
Smith, Sarah. *See* MacLean
Smith, Sarah. *See* Wisdom
Smith, Sarah (Blackburn), XI, 80
Smith, Sarah Marie. *See* Young
Smith, Sarah Mortimer (Johnston), X, 382
Smith, Seba, IX, 352
Smith, Sidney, IX, 680; XI, 196, **837–38**, 920; XII, 323, 596
Smith, Solomon, VI, 302
Smith, Susanna. *See* McClement
Smith, Susanna. *See* Webber
Smith, Susanna Selina Sophia. *See* Debonnaire
Smith, Susannah Elizabeth (Valentine), VII, 875
Smith, Susan Selina (Manning), IX, 728
Smith, Thomas (accountant), VII, 338
Smith, Thomas (father of RICHARD), IX, 730
Smith, Thomas (governor), V, 595
Smith, Thomas (partner of Charles James Fox BENNETT), XI, 68
Smith, Sir Thomas, I, 331, 335, 374
Smith, Thomas B., VII, 216
Smith, Thomas Edward, XI, 827
Smith, Thomas Watson, VI, 170; VII, 272
Smith, Tim, IX, 432

Smith, Titus, VII, 814
Smith, Titus, VII, **814–16**; X, 534; XI, 348; XII, 312
Smith, W. H., XI, 838
Smith, W. R., X, 111
Smith, Walter H., XI, 899
Smith, Warren, XII, 407
Smith, William (agent), VI, 652
Smith, William (brother of BENNETT), XI, 834
Smith, William (brother of TITUS), VII, 814
Smith, William (clergyman), III, 125; V, 785
Smith, William (father of WILLIAM, 1728–93), IV, 714
Smith, William (geologist), V, 55; X, 445
Smith, William (Halifax merchant), IV, 266
Smith, William (HBC member), VIII, 85
Smith, William (newspaper publisher), VII, 734
Smith, William (partner of William FORSYTH, d. 1814), V, 328; VI, 313
Smith, William (Quebec merchant), VI, 96
Smith, William (transporter), VII, 375
Smith, William, IV, 37, 42, 299, 324, 345, 367, 372, 373, 400, 485, 493, 537, 576, 698, **714–18**; V, 21, 45, 90, 132, 148, 149, 150, 153, 192, 232, 242, 300, 317, 371, 372, 373, 427, 479, 505, 816, 839, 843, 844, 862, 863, 901; VI, 269, 295, 338, 380, 494, 512, 558, 615; VII, 197, 783, 816, 817
Smith, William, V, 53, **766–67**, 780; VI, 213, 536
Smith, William, III, 254; IV, 718; V, 696; VII, 788, **816–19**; VIII, 88, 155, 592; IX, 250, 255, 300
Smith, William, XII, **978–81**, 1107
Smith, William Alexander. See De Cosmos, Amor
Smith, William Henry, XII, 354
Smith, William Henry, VI, 253; VIII, 14, 762, 873, 875; X, **660–61**; XII, 667
Smith, William Osborne, XI, 64, **838–39**
Smith, William S., XI, 855
Smith, Sir William Sidney, V, 875; VIII, 823, 824, 827
Smithe, Martha. See Kier
Smithe, William, XI, 236, 237, **839–41**; XII, 227, 916
Smithers, Benson, VIII, 968, 970
Smithers, Susanna. See Kent
Smithsend, John, I, 612
Smithsend, Nicholas, I, 308, **611**; II, 266
Smithsend, Richard, I, **611–12**; II, 487
Smiths John. See Flemish Bastard
Smithson, William, VIII, 15
Smithurst, Christiana (mother of JOHN), IX, 732
Smithurst, John, IX, 136, 626, **732–33**; X, 108; XI, 19, 875
Smithurst, William, IX, 732
Smits Jan. See Flemish Bastard
Smollett, Tobias George, III, 370, 601; IV, 416; V, 486; IX, 351, 354
Smyth. See also Smith; Smithe; Smythe
Smyth, Amelia Anne (wife of GEORGE STRACEY), VI, 723
Smyth, Sir Edward Selby, X, 330; XI, 326, 760; XII, 347, 576
Smyth, Erie (McCrae; McBeath), V, 512
Smyth, George Brunswick, VI, 725
Smyth, George Stracey, V, 162; VI, 7, 73, 143, 209, 396, 505, 655, 685, **723–28**, 741, 756, 811; VII, 27, 187, 331, 429, 658; VIII, 42, 102, 103, 150, 428, 506, 507, 802, 803, 806, 832, 842, 951; IX, 53, 62, 219, 622; X, 71
Smyth, Harriet, Lady Smyth. See Morse
Smyth, James Carmichael, VII, 819

Smyth, Sir James Carmichael, V, 609; VII, 129, 725, **819–20**
Smyth, John, VI, 723
Smyth, John, VIII, **829–30**
Smyth, John Gee, VI, 724
Smyth, Mary. See Holyland
Smyth, Mary Margaret (Kerry), XII, 483
Smyth, Peter, X, 172, 475
Smyth, Samuel, XII, 893
Smyth, Sarah. See Gee
Smyth, Wyllys, VI, **728–29**
Smythe. See also Smithe
Smythe, Betsy (Thom), VII, 852
Smythe, Harriet E. (Thom), VII, 852
Smythe, Sir Hervey, III, 592; V, 228, **767–68**
Smythe, Lady Louisa Carolina Isabelle. See Hervey
Smythe, Sir Robert, V, 767
Snake, William, VII, 11; IX, 589; X, 12
Snape, Susannah (Hamond), VI, 310
Sneider, Magdalen (Pozer), VII, 706
Snell, Mary (Wheelwright), IV, 764
Snelling, Richard, XII, 604
Sneppy. See Atkinson, George (1777–1830)
Snider, George, XII, 684
Snider, Jacob C., VI, 235
Snipe. See Norton, John
Snodgrass*, William (1827–1905), XII, 618, 1102
Snorri Thorfinnsson, I, 5, **612**, 643
Snow, Emma Catherine. See Bradley
Snow, John, XI, 841
Snow, John Allan, IX, 707; XI, 737, **841–43**; XII, 203, 950
Snow, Mary (Parker), VII, 680
Snow, Stephen, V, 573
Snowball*, Jabez Bunting (1837–1907), XI, 466; XII, 742
Snow Tail. See Waxaway
Snuff the Blanket, III, 654
Snyder, George E., XI, 223
Snyder, William H., XI, 75
Soane, Sir John, VIII, 281, 552; XI, 118
Sohon, Gustavus, X, 391
Soiaga, Gaspard. See Kondiaronk
Soines, I, 66
Soissons, Comte de. See Bourbon
Sola. See de Sola
Solander, Daniel Carl, IV, 762; V, 55, 167
Solís. See Díaz
Solo, Henri, III, 410
Solomon, IV, 57
Solomon, Elizabeth. See Dubois
Solomon, Esther (Benjamin), XII, 93
Solomon, Ezekiel, VIII, 830
Solomon, Janet Maria (Jessie) (Morris), IX, 573
Solomon, Joséphine. See Legris
Solomon, Lewis, VIII, 831
Solomon, Marguerite. See Johnston
Solomon, Moses, X, 371
Solomon, William, VIII, **830–32**
Solomon, William Lemon, XI, 243
Solomons (Solomon), Benjamin Samuel, VI, 365, 366
Solomons, Ezekiel, IV, 332, 524, 525, 718, 719, 726; V, 376; VI, 317
Solomons, Levy, IV, 332, **718–19**, 725; V, 194; VI, 365, 434; VII, 329; XI, 455

Solomons, Louise. *See* Loubier
Solomons (Levy), Mary (Franks), VII, 329
Solomons (Solomon), Rachel (Joseph), V, 194; VI, 365, 366; XI, 254, 454
Solomons, Rebecca. *See* Franks
Solomons (Solomon), Sarah (McCord), VI, 434; VIII, 524
Sombrun, Jean-Baptiste, III, 13
Somers, Charlotte (White), IX, 836
Somerset, Duke of. *See* Seymour
Somerset, Lady. *See* Stevenson, Florence
Somerset, Lord Fitzroy James Henry, 1st Baron Raglan, VIII, 275; IX, 79
Somerset, Lord Frederick A. *See* Birchall, Reginald
Somerville, Alexander, VIII, 762
Somerville, Alexander, X, 74; XI, **843–44**
Somerville, Alexander Carnegie, VIII, 832
Somerville, Charlotte. *See* Blaney
Somerville, Emma. *See* Binks
Somerville, James (editor), XI, 307; XII, 941
Somerville, James (father of ALEXANDER), XI, 843
Somerville, James (father of JAMES, 1775–1837), VII, 820
Somerville, James, V, 320, 770; VI, 232, 447, 472, 823; VII, 77, 809, **820–21**; VIII, 272, 936, 937
Somerville, James, VI, 726; VII, 413; VIII, **832–33**; XI, 446
Somerville, John Southey, 15th Baron Somerville, VII, 481
Somerville, Julia Valenza (Head, Lady Head), IX, 657; X, 342
Somerville, Marianne. *See* Veitch
Somerville, Martin, VIII, **833–34**
Somerville, Mary. *See* Orkney
Somerville, Pattison. *See* Brown
Somerville, Robert Brown, XI, 722
Somerville, William, V, 746; VI, 416
Sommerive, Comte de. *See* Lascaris
Sommillard, Catherine, I, 116
Sommillard, Louise (Fortin), I, 116
Sommillard, Marguerite, I, 116, 117
Soncino, Raimondo de, I, 22, 148, 149, 150, 164
Sondes, Baron. *See* Monson
Sonego, Bunch. *See* Tyatiquob
Sonego, Catherine Bunch. *See* Nahnebahwequay
Sonego, Mary. *See* Myarwikishigoqua
Sonneck, Oscar George Theodore, V, 68
Sonntag, August, XI, 393
Sonntag, William, X, 263
Sononchiez. *See* Chabert de Joncaire, Louis-Thomas
Sophog Velligul. *See* Ouimet, Adolphe
Soranhes, I, 58, 59
Sorbier de Villars, François, IV, 189, 234, 510, 642, **719–20**; V, 380; VII, 17
Sorel. *See* Saurel
Sores (Soré, Sors), Marie (Caën), I, 159
Sorester. *See* Forrester
Sosawaket. *See* Nissowaquet
Sosé. *See* Onasakenrat, Joseph
Sotai-na (Sotenah), IX, 623; X, **661–62**
Sothern, Julia. *See* Marlowe
Soto, Hernando de, I, 171
Souart, Gabriel, I, 108, 206, 220, 273, 508, 539, 592, **612–13**, 644, 647, 648; II, 46, 194, 335, 376, 401, 490; III, 612

Souart d'Adoucourt, Claude-Élisabeth (Le Moyne de Longueuil, Baronne de Longueuil), II, 401; III, 384; IV, 463
Soubiran, Monsieur (swindler), VIII, 389, 390
Soubiron, Judith (Maisonnat), II, 449; III, 421
Soubise, Prince de. *See* Rohan
Soubras, Pierre-Auguste de, II, 106, 219, 336, 339, **611–12**; III, 264, 389, 396, 475, 512, 576
Soufflot, Germain, VI, 24
Souhet, Marthe. *See* Bélanger
Soulage, Catherine (Boutet de Saint-Martin), I, 119
Soulanges. *See* Joybert
Soulard. *See also* Baudry
Soulard, Auguste, VIII, **834–35**; XII, 324
Soulard, Eugène, XII, 849
Soulard, François, XI, 901
Soulard, François-Marie, VIII, 834
Soulard, Mathurin, I, 271
Soulard, Pascal, IV, 241; V, 708
Soulard, Théotiste. *See* Voisine
Soulègre, Monsieur de (officer), II, 182, 352
Soulerin, Jean-Mathieu, VIII, 636; X, **662–63**; XI, 536, 903, 904; XII, 183
Soulerin, Marie. *See* Pigeyre
Soulerin, Mathieu, X, 662
Soules, Elizabeth (Lount), VII, 518, 519
Soulier Rouge. *See* Matahachitoux
Soulignié (Souligny), Marie (Leduc), III, 369
Souligny, Félix, VIII, 675; IX, 616
Soullard, Catherine. *See* Boutet
Soullard, Jean, II, 612
Soullard, Jean, II, **612**
Soullard, Jean-Baptiste, II, 612
Soullard, Jeanne. *See* Couvreur
Soullard, Jeanne (Baudry, *dit* Des Butes), II, 48; III, 37
Soumande, Anne (Hazeur), II, 275, 277; III, 284; IV, 337
Soumande, Jean, II, 111, 598
Soumande, Louis, II, **612–13**; III, 397
Soumande, Louise, named de Saint-Augustin, II, 93, 612, **613**; III, 330
Soumande, Marie-Anne-Marguerite (Coulon de Villiers de Jumonville), III, 150
Soumande, Pierre, II, 275, 612, 613; III, 153
Soumande, Simone. *See* Coté
Sounding Sky. *See* Sinnookeesick
Sou-neh-hoo-way, V, 798; VI, 530; VII, **821**
Souoias. *See* Kondiaronk
Soupiran, Antoine, II, 613
Soupiran, Catherine. *See* Laborde
Soupiran, Charles-Simon, II, 614; III, 596
Soupiran, Charlotte (Hiché; Arnoux), III, 292
Soupiran, Louis-François, III, 553; IV, 539
Soupiran, Louise-Catherine (Bourdages), VI, 81
Soupiran, Marie-Anne. *See* Gaultier
Soupiran, Marie-Jeanne. *See* Avisse
Soupiran, Marthe. *See* Bélanger
Soupiran, Simon, II, **613–14**; III, 595; IV, 178
Soupiran, Simon, II, 614; III, **595–96**
Soupras, Eustache, XI, 585
Sourdeval. *See* Le Gouès
Sourdy. *See* Desjordy
Souste, Sieur (manufacturer), II, 134
Souste, André, III, 633; IV, **720–21**
Souste, Jean-Marie, IV, 720

Souste, Marguerite. *See* Vulliermet
Souste, Marie-Louise. *See* Estienne Du Bourgué de Clérin
Souter, John. *See* Galt, John
Southack, Cyprian, III, 596
Southack, Cyprian, I, 90, 250, 299; II, 14, 46, 409; III, **596–97**, 635
Southack, Elizabeth. *See* Foy
Southack, Elizabeth. *See* Oakley
Southack, Elizabeth (Parnel; Tyng), III, 635
Southam*, William (1843–1932), XI, 753
Southampton, Earl of. *See* Wriothesley
Southcott, Georgina. *See* Norman
Southcott, James Thomas, XII, **981–82**
Southcott, John (father), XII, 981
Southcott, John, XII, 981
Southcott, John Thomas, XII, 981, 982
Southcott, Mary (mother of JAMES THOMAS), XII, 981
Southeron, Elizabeth. *See* Pozer
Southeron, John, VII, 708
Southesk, Earl of. *See* Carnegie
Southey, Robert, V, 166; VIII, 427
Southgate, Horatio, XII, 1061
Southgate, James Johnson, IX, 457
Southmayd, Allen, II, 152
Southouse, Edward, IV, 229, 345, 391; V, 216, 225, 232, 863
Southwell, Harriet Anne (Bisshopp, Baroness Zouche), V, 82
Southwick, Mary Helen (Parke), XII, 822
Southworth, Alice (Church), II, 145, 146
Southworth, Constant, II, 145
Southworth, Elizabeth. *See* Collier
Souvigny. *See* Rousseau
Sovereen, Anne. *See* Culver
Sovereen (Sovereign), David, VI, 729
Sovereene, Anna (Patterson), VI, 729
Sovereene, Henry, VI, **729–30**
Sovereene, Mary. *See* Beemer
Sovereign, Philip, V, 857
Sowatsi-tapitowpi. *See* Sotai-na
Sowengisik. *See* Steinhauer, Henry Bird
Sower, Catharine. *See* Sharpnack
Sower, Christopher, IV, 721
Sower, Christopher, IV, 483, 626, **721–22**; V, 318, 613; VI, 301, 395; VII, 764
Sower, Hannah. *See* Knorr
Sowerby, James de Carle, X, 65
Sozap (Suzack), II, 26
Spada, Cardinal, II, 280
Spada, Pietro, VIII, 925
Spafford, Elizabeth (Thomson), VI, 772
Spafford, Frances D. (Stanton), IX, 740
Spafford, Laura (Miles), IX, 550
Spagniolini, Catherine. *See* Bénard, *dit* Carignan
Spagniolini, Charlotte. *See* Bourleton
Spagniolini, Domenico, III, 597
Spagniolini, Françoise. *See* Boucher de Niverville
Spagniolini, Jean-Baptiste, III, 598
Spagniolini, Jean-Fernand, III, **597–98**
Spagniolini, Margherita. *See* Tussichi
Spagniolini, Marie-Apolline (Poudret), III, 598; VIII, 288
Spagniolini, Marie-Élisabeth (Gamelin), III, 598
Spangenberg, Augustus Gottlieb (Bishop Joseph), III, 607

Spain, Infanta of. *See* Marie-Thérèse
Sparhawk. *See* Pepperrell
Sparhawk, Edward Vernon, XII, 569
Spark, Alexander, IV, 580, 581; V, 69, 320, 330, 700, **768–71**; VI, 531, 534, 592, 822; VII, 133, 644, 820; VIII, 937
Spark, John, V, 768
Spark, Mary. *See* Low
Spark, Mary. *See* Ross
Spark, Robert, VIII, 582
Sparke, Hannah (Hutchings), V, 443
Sparke, Henry, V, 443, 444
Sparks, Esther (Slater), IX, 735
Sparks, Jared, XII, 823
Sparks, Mary (Wright), IX, 735; XII, 1129
Sparks, Nicholas, IX, 735
Sparks, Nicholas, VII, 122, 382, 494; VIII, 840; IX, **733–35**; XII, 1129
Sparks, Sarah. *See* Olmstead
Sparling, Anna (Hopper), X, 360
Sparling, Joseph Walter, XII, 491
Sparrow, Georgiana (Patterson), XI, 677
Sparrow*, John B. (d. 1913), XII, 449
Sparrow, Mary (Acheson, Countess of Gosford), VII, 5
Sparrow, Mary (Thompson), IX, 785
Spaulding, Ira, VIII, 81, 82, 965, 966
Spearman, James Morton, VII, 793
Spears, Margaret. *See* Blanchard
Spedon, Andrew Learmont, VIII, 161
Spelman, Thomas, XII, 408
Spelman, William, XII, 407
Spence, Mrs (Norquay; grandmother of JOHN), XI, 643
Spence, Andrew, XI, 745, 746; XII, 608
Spence, Charlotte. *See* Cook
Spence, Charlotte. *See* Thomas
Spence, George, III, 600, 654
Spence, Harriet Brackett (Lowell), XII, 574
Spence, James, IV, 48; V, 194; VII, 206
Spence, John, III, 123, 124
Spence, Joseph, VIII, 158
Spence, Peter (father of THOMAS, 1832–1900), XII, 982
Spence, Peter (son-in-law of John THOMAS), VI, 766
Spence, Robert, IX, 576, **735–36**; XI, 414; XII, 594, 595
Spence, Sophia (Sapphira) Jacobina (Clarke), VIII, 158
Spence, Thomas, XI, **844–45**; XII, 1132
Spence, Thomas, XII, **982–84**
Spence, William, VII, 335, 336
Spencer, Miss (Treworgie), I, 652
Spencer, Abel, V, 772
Spencer, Ambrose, VIII, 853
Spencer, Aubrey George, VII, 434, 914; VIII, 94, 103, 104, 380, 725; IX, 468, 847; X, 279, 280, 281, 318, **663–64**; XI, 431; XII, 574, 575
Spencer, Benjamin, V, 772
Spencer, Sir Brent, VII, 268
Spencer, Eliza. *See* Musson
Spencer, Emma. *See* Lazenby
Spencer, George John, 2nd Earl Spencer, VII, 767, 768
Spencer, Hazelton, V, 92, 170, **771–73**; VI, 439
Spencer, James, IX, **736–38**; XII, 469
Spencer, John, VI, 437, 443; VII, 138
Spencer, John Charles, 3rd Earl Spencer, VII, 855
Spencer, Margaret. *See* Richards

Spencer, Martha (McLelan), VIII, 568; XI, 572
Spencer, Mary (Hull; Phips), I, 544
Spencer, Mercy. *See* Potter
Spencer, Robert, 1st Baron Spencer, I, 632
Spencer, Sarah. *See* Lafferty
Spencer, Susan. *See* Jennison
Spencer, William (father of AUBREY GEORGE), X, 663
Spencer, William (merchant), I, 239, 240
Spencer-Churchill, Lord Edward, VIII, 921
Spert, Sir Thomas, I, 155, 371, 565
Spicer, Grace (Hayman), I, 365
Spicer, Richard, I, 565
Spier, William, IX, 555
Spiers, Anne (Wallace), XI, 906
Spiesmacher, Frederick Christopher, V, 7, 8
Spike, Daniel, X, 664
Spike, Elizabeth. *See* Kerr
Spike, Grace. *See* Cullimore
Spike, James, VI, 508; X, 362, **664**
Spike, Mary Elizabeth. *See* Metzler
Spilsbury, Fanny. *See* Bayly
Spilsbury, Francis Brockell, VI, 730
Spilsbury, Francis Brockell, VI, **730–31**; VII, 214; VIII, 856
Spilsbury, Maria. *See* Taylor
Spinkes, Elizabeth (Gwillim), VII, 361
Spinkes, Margaret (Graves), VII, 361
Spinula, Agostino de, I, 150, 164
Spittal, John, V, 127
Splitlog, Thomas. *See* Sou-neh-hoo-way
Spöring, Herman Diedrich, IV, 406
Spohr, Louis, VII, 193, 194
Spontini, Gaspare Luigi Pacifico, XII, 471
Spooner, Charles, V, 767
Spooner, James, XII, 327
Sport, Prince William, VIII, 968
Spotted Calf. *See* Natchookoneck
Spragg, Frances (wife of JOSEPH), VII, 821
Spragg, John, VII, 611
Spragg, Joseph, VII, 822
Spragg, Joseph, VI, 11; VII, **821–23**; VIII, 926; IX, 423; XI, 845
Spragg, Sarah. *See* Bitterman
Spragge, Catherine Rosamund. *See* Thom
Spragge, George Warburton, VII, 822
Spragge, John Godfrey, VII, 822; IX, 245, 324; X, 118; XI, **845–46**; XII, 607
Spragge, Joseph Bitterman, VII, 822, 833, 834
Spragge, Martha Ann. *See* Molson
Spragge, William Prosperous, IV, 154; VII, 822; IX, 407
Spraggon, William, V, 861, 862; VII, 408
Sprague, Isabella (Scatcherd), X, 645
Sprague, Mary (Baldwin), IX, 25
Sprague, Otis, XII, 1132
Spratt, John, VIII, 474
Spread, Barbara (Baldwin), VII, 35; IX, 24
Spring, Barbara. *See* Henry
Springer, Anna (Sawyer), XI, 473
Springer, Benjamin, VII, 126
Springer, Daniel, V, 14; VI, 496, 497, 498, 808, 809
Springer, Henrietta (Beasley), VII, 56
Springer, Lewis, XII, 935
Springett, Evelyn Cartier. *See* Galt

Spring-Rice, Thomas, 1st Baron Monteagle, VII, 283, 293, 907, 908; VIII, xxvii, xxxi, 845; IX, 297; X, 140, 180
Sproat. *See also* Sprott
Sproat, Catherine Anne. *See* Wigham
Sproat*, Gilbert Malcolm (1834–1913), IX, 457; XI, 231; XII, 239, 243, 334, 335
Sproat, James, IX, 738
Sproat, Margaret. *See* Hannay
Sprong, Martha (Rowan), X, 634
Sprott, Charlotte. *See* Leslie
Sprott, G. W., IX, 495
Sprott, Jane. *See* Neilson
Sprott, John, VI, 823; VII, 536; IX, **738**
Sprott, Sarah. *See* Clarke
Sproule, Adam, V, 773
Sproule, Alicia (wife of GEORGE), V, 773
Sproule, George, IV, 81; V, 356, 448, 589, 590, 667, **773–74**; VII, 384, 854
Sproule, Jane. *See* Hopper
Sproule, Marianne. *See* Ardesoif
Sproule, Prudence. *See* Lloyd
Sproule, Robert (defendant), XII, 227
Sproule, Robert (student), VII, 823
Sproule, Robert Auchmuty, VII, **823–24**; VIII, 385; XI, 106
Sproule, Thomas, VII, 823
Spry, Anne (Goreham), IV, 308
Spry, Sir Richard, III, 293; VI, 193
Spry, William, IV, 108, 552, 561
Spurr, Elizabeth (Harris), IX, 367
Spurr, John W., XII, 1067
Spurrell, George, II, 10; III, 483, 490, 593, **598–99**; IV, 583
Spurrell, Joseph, III, 598
Spurrier, William, V, 838; IX, 46
Squair*, John (1850–1928), XII, 1107
Squando (Squanto), I, 650
Squanto (Squantum). *See* Tisquantum
Squash Cutter. *See* Yaghkaposin
Squire, Peter, VI, 549
Staats, Barent, III, 428
Staats, Elizabeth (Schuyler), III, 587
Staats, Isabella. *See* Lÿdius
Stabb, Ewen, XII, 984
Stabb, Fanny Elizabeth (wife of HENRY HUNT), XII, 984
Stabb, Frederick A., XII, 985
Stabb, Henry Hunt, XII, **984–86**, 1124
Stabb, Nicholas, XI, 433; XII, 984
Stabb, Thomas (father), XII, 984
Stabb, Thomas, XII, 984
Stacey, Margaret Black (Stuart), XI, 861
Stach, Matthew, III, 212
Staël, Mme de; Staël-Holstein, Baronne de. *See* Necker, Germaine
Staffe, Philip, I, 375, 376, 378
Stafford, Michael, XI, 241
Stahl, Caroline (Mayerhoffer), VIII, 622
Stainburn, Mary Anne (Scoble), IX, 704
Staines, Emma Frances. *See* Tahourdin
Staines, John Collins, VIII, 835
Staines, Mary (mother of ROBERT JOHN), VIII, 835
Staines, Robert John, VIII, **835–36**; IX, 337, 853; X, 116, 196, 242; XII, 113, 441, 523, 550, 833

Stairs, Joanna. *See* Stayner
Stairs, Joanna (Bessonett; Brown), XI, 116
Stairs, John (grandfather), V, 390; IX, 738
Stairs, John, IX, 739
Stairs*, John Fitzwilliam (1848–1904), XII, 705
Stairs, Margaret. *See* Wiseman
Stairs*, William James (1819–1906), IX, 184, 739; X, 177
Stairs, William Machin, VIII, 705; IX, 226, **738–40**
Stalcup, Sarah Ann (Keith), X, 395
Stalwart, Flora Campbell (MacLean), IX, 514
Stamaty, Camille, XI, 671
Stamford, Earl of. *See* Grey
Stamford, Katherine (Simcoe), V, 754
Stamp, Edward, X, 216, 217, **664–65**; XII, 240
Stamp, Maria (wife of EDWARD), X, 665
Stanbury, James, XII, 797
Standing Buffalo. *See* Tatanka-najin
Stanfield, George, VIII, 543
Stanford, Leland, XI, 292, 840
Stanhope, James, 1st Earl Stanhope, II, 250, 286
Stanhope, Philip Dormer, 4th Earl of Chesterfield, V, 182, 486
Staniford, Margaret (Calef), V, 134
Stanlake, Elizabeth (Gay), XII, 361
Stanley, Lady Charlotte (Burgoyne), IV, 113
Stanley, Edward, 11th Earl of Derby, III, 425; IV, 113
Stanley, Edward George Geoffrey Smith, Baron Stanley and 14th Earl of Derby, VI, 425; VII, 49, 98, 99, 141, 283, 306, 326, 370, 549, 579, 604, 605, 607, 608, 682, 755, 880, 906, 907; VIII, xxvii, xxviii, xxix, xxxi, xxxiii, xxxiv, 65, 297, 564, 738, 764, 808, 844, 845; IX, 22, 146, 147, 169, 189, 266, 371, 445, 500, 524, 716, 741, 812, 815; X, 180, 257, 345, 402, 404, 606; XI, 225, 409, 848
Stanley, Edward Henry, 15th Earl of Derby, XII, 742
Stanley, Edward Smith, 13th Earl of Derby, VII, 540
Stanley*, Frederick Arthur, Baron Stanley and 16th Earl of Derby (1841–1908), XII, 75, 610, 611, 1045, 1048
Stanley, Gilbert, VIII, 408
Stanley, Isabella Louisa (Parry, Lady Parry), VIII, 683
Stanley, James, known as Lord Strange, IV, 113
Stanley, John Mix, VI, 649; X, 391, 392
Stanmore, Baron. *See* Gordon
Stannard, William, I, 343
Stansbury, Joseph, V, 34, 629, 631
Stanser, Elizabeth (Best), VI, 53
Stanser, Mary (wife of ROBERT), VI, 731
Stanser, Robert, VI, 731
Stanser, Robert, IV, 94; V, 124, 872; VI, 13, 53, 158, 393, **731–32**; VII, 432, 434; VIII, 94, 398, 460; IX, 801, 841; X, 516
Stanser, Sarah (mother of ROBERT), VI, 731
Stansfeld, Robert Walker, VII, 280, 281
Stanton, Anne Louise. *See* Hagerman
Stanton, Emily (Nelson), XII, 784
Stanton, Frances D. *See* Spafford
Stanton, Isaac Brock, XII, 784
Stanton, Joanna (Denison), III, 174
Stanton, Margaret (mother of ROBERT), IX, 740
Stanton, Robert, VI, 32, 728, 773; VII, 40, 369, 370, 458, 498; VIII, 515, 519, 602, 829, 885; IX, 346, **740–41**; XII, 680
Stanton, William, IV, 115; IX, 740

Stanyan, Catherine (Hardy, Lady Hardy), IV, 326
Stanynought, Lucy (Simpson), XII, 235
Stapeldon, Hannah (Tremlett), VI, 784
Stapleton, Charlotte (Beechey), VIII, 70
Stapleton, Elizabeth. *See* Seymour
Stapleton, Florence Maria (Seymour), IX, 713
Stapley, Lucy (Lawson), XII, 539, 540
Starchild. *See* Kukatosi-poka
Stark, Agatha Georgiana. *See* Street
Stark, Elizabeth. *See* Young
Stark, John, VII, 113; IX, 71
Stark, John M., X, 186
Stark, Mark Young, VIII, 68, 73; IX, **741–42**; XII, 211
Stark, Mary. *See* Bannatyne
Stark, Robert, IX, 741
Starke, Mariana, XII, 524
Starnes. *See also* Sterns
Starnes, Benjamin, XII, 986
Starnes, Eleanore. *See* Stuart
Starnes, Élizabeth. *See* Mainville
Starnes, Henry, IX, 492, 651; X, 625; XI, 61, 586, 767, 823, 825; XII, **986–88**
Starnes, John, XI, 311
Starnes, Marguerite-Émélie (Sicotte), XI, 823; XII, 986
Starns, Nathan, V, 218, 436, 727; VI, 487, 664
Starr, Alida Ellen (Gisborne), XII, 373
Starr, Cartland, VIII, 394
Starr, Desiah. *See* Gore
Starr, Fanny Lavinia (Rice), XI, 729
Starr, Frances. *See* Throckmorton
Starr, George H., X, 176
Starr, John, VII, 108; IX, 174; XI, 846, 847
Starr, John Leander, XI, **846–48**
Starr, Joseph, IX, 181
Starr, Maria Sophia. *See* Ratchford
Starr, Mary Jane (Belcher), IX, 40
Starr, Rebecca. *See* Crane
Starr, Sarah (Belcher), IX, 40
Starr, William Joseph, XI, 847, 848
Staunton, Richard, II, 51, 62, 65, 312, 319, 492; III, 414, 489, **599–600**, 624
Staveley, Edward, VIII, 944
Stayeghtha, V, 619, **774–75**, 798, 799; VII, 821
Stayner, Charles St Clair, VI, 333
Stayner, Joanna (Stairs), IX, 738
Stayner, John, IX, 738, 742
Stayner, Louisa. *See* Sutherland
Stayner, Mary. *See* Allen
Stayner, Thomas, IV, 685; VI, 17
Stayner, Thomas Allen, VI, 745; VII, 701, 861; VIII, 84, 148; IX, 399, 739, 740, **742–43**; XI, 286, 855; XII, 489
Stealing, John, V, 123
Stebbins, Abigail (rebaptized Marguerite) (Noyon), III, 493; IV, 765
Stebenne, Elizabeth. *See* Nims, Abigail
Stedman, Anne Sarah (Bushby), X, 112
Steed, Isabella (Mason), I, 496
Steedman, William, V, 684
Steel, Elizabeth (Campbell), X, 130
Steel, John, V, 101; VI, 296
Steel, Thomas, II, 497
Steel, William, VI, 534
Steele. *See also* Still

Steele, Anne MacIan. *See* Macdonald
Steele, Elizabeth Seeley. *See* Coucher
Steele, Elmes, IX, 743
Steele, Elmes Yelverton, VIII, 790; IX, **743–44**; X, 622
Steele, Howard D., XII, 250
Steele, Jane Emily. *See* Ewart
Steele, John (father of ELMES YELVERTON), IX, 743
Steele, John (surgeon), III, 405
Steele, Margaret (Ruttan), X, 636
Steele, Mary. *See* Benfield
Steele, Richard, IV, 553
Steele, Samuel, IX, 743
Steele*, Sir Samuel Benfield (1849–1919), IX, 744; XI, 600, 870; XII, 465, 466, 859, 970
Steele, William, IV, 526, 527
Steenoven, Cornelius, III, 640
Steenwijck, Cornelis van, I, 573
Steer, Elizabeth (Story), XII, 994
Steer, John, XI, 910; XII, 981, 995
Steeves, Elizabeth (Jones), XII, 479
Steeves, Gilbert Martin, X, 666
Steeves, Henry. *See* Stief, Heinrich
Steeves, James Abel, X, 666
Steeves, James Thomas, X, 666
Steeves, Joseph, X, 665
Steeves, Martha. *See* Cross
Steeves, Mary (Steeves), X, 666
Steeves, William Henry, IX, 414; X, 286, **665–67**; XI, 828
Stefansson*, Vilhjalmur (1879–1962), VII, 327; X, 328, 454; XII, 879, 955
Stegmann, Mary (Wilmot), XII, 1106
Stein, Adolphus, VIII, 248
Steiner, Maria (Denke), VII, 243
Steinhauer, Abigail (McDougall), XI, 849
Steinhauer, Henry Bird, IV, 276, 277, 390; IX, 784; X, 471; XI, 660, **848–50**; XII, 128, 186
Steinhauer, Jessie. *See* Mamenawatum
Steinmeyer, Ferdinand, known as Ferdinand Farmer, IV, 270
Steinner, Jacob, IV, 386
Steinweg, Heinrich Engelhardt, XII, 422
Stent, Frederick Warburton, XI, 464
Stent, Thomas, XII, 344, 534, 535, 930
Stephen, Alexander, IX, 243
Stephen, Francis, XI, 757
Stephen*, George, 1st Baron Mount Stephen (1829–1921), X, 684; XI, 10, 124, 439, 477, 481, 482, 645, 646, 706, 707, 757, 767, 770; XII, 6, 8, 434, 455, 608, 612, 631, 632, 633, 636, 653, 827, 828, 1058
Stephen, Sir James, VII, 99, 144, 153, 314, 377; VIII, xxix, xxx, xxxi, xxxii, xxxiii, xxxiv, xxxv, xxxvi, 297, 380, 384, 444, 604, 827; IX, 21, 147, 221, 794; X, 179, 180, 345
Stephens, Anna Mary (Rastrick), XII, 885
Stephens, Beulah. *See* Howard
Stephens, Charles Henry, XI, 722
Stephens*, George Washington (1832–1904), X, 249; XII, 7, 425
Stephens, Harrison, IX, 555; X, 722, 723; XI, 315, **850–51**; XII, 214, 761, 809
Stephens, Jane (Evans), VIII, 277
Stephens, John Lloyd, XI, 137
Stephens, Margaret (Pemberton), XII, 832
Stephens, Samuel, XI, 850
Stephens, Sarah. *See* Jackson
Stephens, Sheldon, XI, 850
Stephenson, Clarissa. *See* Chapin
Stephenson, Eleazer Williams, IX, **744–45**; XI, 559
Stephenson, Henry Frederick, XI, 382
Stephenson, Isabella. *See* Torrance
Stephenson, John, VII, 824
Stephenson, John, VII, 25, 751, **824–25**; VIII, 404; IX, 286; XI, 271; XII, 1122
Stephenson, Martha. *See* Mair
Stephenson, Robert, XI, 510; XII, 963
Stephenson, Rufus, IX, 745
Stephenson, Thomas Bowman, XII, 942
Stephenson, William, XI, 925
Sterling. *See also* Stirling
Sterling, Angélique. *See* Cuillerier, *dit* Beaubien
Sterling, Ansel, XI, 795
Sterling, Isabella Dorcas (Ryerson), XI, 795
Sterling, James, IV, **722**; V, 282, 364
Sterling, Robert Nicholson, XI, 389
Sterling (Stirling), Thomas, IV, 316
Sterne, Laurence, V, 438
Sterns, Jonathan, IV, 604; V, 109, 251; VI, 34, 307, 519, 790; VII, 87, 831; VIII, 754
Sterns (Starnes), Truman, VIII, 136
Sterry, Jane Elizabeth (Hunt), XII, 457
Steuben, Friedrich Wilhelm von, V, 899
Steven, Andrew, VIII, 293; IX, **745–46**
Steven, James, IX, 745
Steven, Laura (wife of ANDREW), IX, 745
Steven, Mary. *See* Lees
Stevens, Abel, V, 728
Stevens, Abel, V, 65; VI, 51, **732–34**; VII, 453; VIII, 180
Stevens, Adélaïde-Rosa-Josephe. *See* Wautier
Stevens, Ann. *See* Glasier
Stevens, Ann Jane (Wood), XII, 1121
Stevens, Brooke Bridges, VI, **734–35**; VII, 682, 827
Stevens, Catherine (Rudolf), VIII, 782
Stevens, Elizabeth. *See* Nelles
Stevens, Eunice. *See* Buck
Stevens, Henry Thaddeus, XII, 566
Stevens, Isaac Ingalls, IX, 625; XII, 817
Stevens, Jacques-Joseph, XI, 851
Stevens*, James Gray (1822–1906), XII, 17, 739
Stevens, John Frank, XI, 764
Stevens, Mabel E. Ticknor (Perley), XI, 681
Stevens, Marie. *See* Valier, *dit* Léveillé
Stevens, Mary. *See* Doolittle
Stevens, Paul, IX, 703, 854; XI, **851–52**
Stevens, Phineas, III, 21
Stevens, Roger (father), VI, 732
Stevens, Roger, VI, 732, 733
Stevens, Sarah (mother of BROOKE BRIDGES), VI, 734
Stevens, Sarah (Osgood), VI, 665
Stevens, Sarah (Pryor), XII, 870, 871
Stevens, Sophia (Hamilton), XII, 405
Stevens, Thomas, VI, 734
Stevens, William, VIII, 321
Stevenson, Agnes Rebecca. *See* Dougall
Stevenson, Ann Bligh (Grasett), XI, 367
Stevenson, Catherine (Pratt), XI, 712
Stevenson, David, XI, 77

Stevenson, David Barker, VIII, **836–37**; X, 624
Stevenson, Edward, XI, 852
Stevenson, Florence (Birchall), XI, 77
Stevenson, Harriet. *See* Harris
Stevenson, James (brewer), IX, 557
Stevenson, James (father of JAMES), XII, 988
Stevenson, James (publisher), IX, 399
Stevenson, James, VII, 797; XII, 107, **988–89**
Stevenson, John, XI, 422, **852–54**
Stevenson, Jonathan Drake, VIII, 853
Stevenson, Maggie, XII, 154
Stevenson, Mary. *See* Large
Stevenson, Phoebe. *See* Barker
Stevenson, Phoebe Eliza. *See* Hall
Stevenson, Robert, XI, 142, 143
Stevenson, Sarah (Christie), IV, 151
Stevenson, Sophia (Molson), IX, 559
Stevenson, Thomas H., XII, 414
Stevenson, Timothy, VIII, 836
Stevenson, William, VII, 462
Stewart. *See also* Mackenzie-Stewart; Stuart
Stewart, Miss (Campbell), XI, 149
Stewart, Alexander (attorney), VI, 630; IX, 498, 724
Stewart, Alexander (clergyman), VIII, 550; IX, 112
Stewart, Alexander (constable), VIII, 474
Stewart, Alexander (fur trader), V, 418, 532; VII, 838;
    VIII, 176, 454
Stewart, Alexander, VII, 25, 82, 84, 142, 144; VIII, 416,
    657; IX, 176, 225, 226, **746–48**; X, 232, 456; XI, 925,
    947
Stewart, Alica Murray. *See* Drysdale
Stewart, Anne, Countess of Galloway. *See* Dashwood
Stewart, Bonaventure, V, 473
Stewart, Catherine (mother of DONALD ALEXANDER), XII,
    989
Stewart, Catherine (Graham, Lady Graham), VII, 825
Stewart, Catherine (Stewart), VIII, 839
Stewart, Catherine M. S. (Sinclair), V, 759
Stewart, Catherine Oswald (McIntosh), VIII, 549
Stewart, Charles (customs officer), V, 4
Stewart, Charles (lawyer), VII, 364
Stewart, Charles (notary), V, 252, 289, 385, 509
Stewart, Charles, V, 250, 309, 311, 335, 425, 569, **775–76**,
    779, 847, 848, 862; VI, 161, 162, 163, 195, 196, 359,
    414, 565, 566, 567, 568, 662, 663, 736, 738; VIII, 36,
    824
Stewart, Charles Coles, VII, 654
Stewart, Charles Grey, IX, 641
Stewart, Charles James, V, 422; VI, 3, 507, 526, 528, 689;
    VII, 20, 124, 212, 635, 682, 733, **825–29**; VIII, 25, 95,
    162, 276, 620, 622, 706, 768; IX, 209, 276, 289, 291,
    579, 580, 581, 719, 759, 760, 771, 848; X, 5, 53, 57,
    206, 269; XI, 367, 368, 427, 639; XII, 680
Stewart, Christan (McDonald), IX, 480
Stewart, David (administrator), V, 781; VI, 821
Stewart, David (merchant), VIII, 375, 956
Stewart, Donald Alexander, XII, **989–90**
Stewart, Dugald, IX, 742, 755; XI, 534
Stewart, Elizabeth. *See* Bremner
Stewart, Lady Elizabeth (Fraser, Lady Lovat; Stewart,
    Countess of Lennox and March; Stewart, Countess of
    Arran) I, 613
Stewart, Elizabeth (Munn), XII, 770

Stewart, Elizabeth (Williams), V, 860
Stewart, Eliza Maria. *See* Green
Stewart, Flora (Townshend), V, 825
Stewart, Frances. *See* Browne
Stewart*, George (1848–1906), VIII, 157; XII, 900, 946
Stewart, Geraldine M. L. *See* Hodder
Stewart, Hannah. *See* Turner
Stewart, Harriet. *See* Vincent
Stewart, Helen. *See* MacKinnon
Stewart, Hope James, X, 390
Stewart, Hugh Alexander, XII, 1120
Stewart, Isabella. *See* McLeod
Stewart, Isabella (Boston), IX, 61
Stewart, Isabella (McLennan), XII, 669
Stewart, James (brother of ALEXANDER), IX, 746
Stewart, James (contractor), XII, 647
Stewart, James (father of ALEXANDER), IX, 746
Stewart, James (judge), V, 861; VII, 23, 531, 911; VIII,
    354, 355, 756
Stewart, James (merchant), XI, 4
Stewart, James (newspaper owner), XI, 680
Stewart, James (partner of Thomas NISBET), VII, 654
Stewart*, James (1826–1911), XI, 900
Stewart, James, Earl of Arran, I, 613
Stewart, James, 4th Lord Ochiltree, I, 25, 53, 54, 248, 305,
    482, **613–14**
Stewart, James Green, IX, 6; XI, **854–55**
Stewart, Jane. *See* Douglas
Stewart, Jane (Price), IX, 641; X, 601; XII, 863
Stewart, Jean (Robertson), VII, 750
Stewart, John (doctor), XII, 989
Stewart, John (editor), VIII, 733
Stewart, John (father of JOHN, 1773–1858), VIII, 837
Stewart, John (HBC employee), VII, 737
Stewart, John (nephew of JOHN, d. 1834), VI, 738
Stewart, John (newspaper owner), IX, 429
Stewart, John (officer), IV, 401
Stewart, John (professor), IX, 462
Stewart, John (shipbuilder), XI, 834
Stewart, John, IV, 129, 609, 610; V, 309, 516, 775, 776,
    777, 778, 779, 848; VI, 122, 298, 360, 415, 568,
    **735–38**, 786; VII, 351, 408, 415, 740, 741; VIII, 37,
    444, 484, 531, 547, 825, 826, 827; IX, 223, 474
Stewart, John, VI, 299, 516; VII, 67, 68; VIII, **837–39**; XI,
    56, 367, 854
Stewart, John, X, **667**
Stewart, John, XI, 48, 263; XII, 541, **990**
Stewart, John, 4th Earl of Atholl, I, 613
Stewart, John, 7th Earl of Galloway, VII, 825
Stewart, John Cunningham, XI, **855–56**
Stewart*, John James (1844–1907), III, 91; XII, 1042
Stewart, Margaret. *See* Macdowall
Stewart, Margaret. *See* Mowat
Stewart, Margaret (Desbrisay), V, 775; VI, 197; VIII, 215
Stewart, Martha Anne (Hincks, Lady Hincks), XI, 406
Stewart, Mary. *See* Desbrisay
Stewart, Mary. *See* Livingstone
Stewart, Mary. *See* Rain
Stewart, Mary (Campbell), XI, 147
Stewart, Mary (Cockrell), VI, 159
Stewart, Mary (Dumaresq), VII, 257
Stewart, Mary (Edson), XI, 296
Stewart, Mary (Tassie), XI, 868

Stewart, Mary Ann. *See* James
Stewart, McLeod, VIII, 840
Stewart, Murdoch, XII, 989
Stewart, Nancy. *See* Blue Jacket
Stewart, Patrick Maxwell, VIII, xxvi
Stewart, Peter, VII, 258
Stewart, Peter, IV, 129, 551, 608, 609, 610; V, 27, 28, 219,
    220, 250, 263, 309, 310, 311, 424, 516, 568, 720, 775,
    **776–79**, 825, 826, 847, 848, 861, 873; VI, 108, 161,
    197, 565, 735, 736; VII, 407
Stewart, Peter DesBrisay, X, 264
Stewart, R. D., IX, 319
Stewart, Ranald, VIII, 839
Stewart, Robert (brother of PETER), V, 777
Stewart, Robert (merchant), VIII, 375, 956; IX, 179
Stewart, Robert, 1st Viscount Castlereagh and 2nd
    Marquess of Londonderry, V, 18, 85, 94, 161, 210, 292,
    365, 504, 542; VI, 114, 164, 347, 577, 594, 737, 781,
    790; VII, 65, 388, 438, 439, 872, 910; VIII, xxvii, 202,
    387, 388, 389
Stewart, Sarah. *See* Hamilton
Stewart, Sarah. *See* Jackson
Stewart, Sarah. *See* Morse
Stewart, Sarah (Gesner), XII, 514
Stewart, Sarah Maria (Grasett), XI, 367
Stewart, Susan Anne Jane (Liddell), X, 441
Stewart, Thomas Alexander, VII, **829–30**; VIII, 92; IX,
    768; X, 104; XII, 524, 527, 997
Stewart, William (Baptist clergyman), IX, 113
Stewart, William (father of THOMAS ALEXANDER), VII,
    829
Stewart, William (merchant), XI, 4
Stewart, William (Presbyterian clergyman), VIII, 67
Stewart, William (surgeon), VI, 258
Stewart, William, VIII, **839–40**
Stewart, William, 5th Lord Ochiltree, I, 613
Stewart, Sir William, V, 110
Stiahta. *See* Stayeghtha
Stickney, Mehetable (Ryerson), X, 638, 640; XI, 783, 795
Stief, Heinrich (Henry Steeves), X, 665, 666
Stieglitz, Christian Ludwig, V, 678
Stikeman, Alfred W., IX, 269
Stiles, Deborah (Gambier), VI, 270
Stiles, Ezra, V, 684
Stiles, Hannah (Lyman), X, 450
Still (Steele), Murphy, IV, 626
Stillman, Ellen (Barnard), XI, 50
Stimson, Elam, IX, **748–49**
Stimson, Elam Rush, IX, 749
Stimson, Mary Anne Frances. *See* Bolles
Stimson, Susan. *See* Bolles
Stinson, John, V, 857
Stinson, Joseph, VII, 276; VIII, 133; IX, 635, **749–51**; X,
    317; XI, 733; XII, 298
Stinson, Mary. *See* Cheatle
Stinson, Thomas, VIII, 687
Stinson, William, IX, 749
Stirling. *See also* Sterling
Stirling, Countess of. *See* Erskine
Stirling, Earl of. *See* Alexander
Stirling, Clara Richmond. *See* Lea
Stirling, David, XI, 392, 405, 486, **856–57**; XII, 982
Stirling, Elizabeth (Murray, Baroness Murray), IV, 569

Stirling, Elleonora C. (Campbell), XII, 155
Stirling, James, XI, 856
Stirling, Jane. *See* Fullerton
Stirling, John, VII, 391; VIII, 348, 398
Stirling, Margaret. *See* Sanderson
Stirling-Maxwell, Caroline Elizabeth Sarah, Lady
    Stirling-Maxwell. *See* Sheridan
Stirton, David, XII, 934
Stisted, Charles, X, 667
Stisted, Eliza. *See* Burn
Stisted, Sir Henry William, X, 467, **667–68**
Stisted, Maria. *See* Burton
Stiven (Stivens), Mary (Richardson), IX, 658
Stobo, Robert, III, 149, 588, **600–2**; IV, 425, 709; V, 470
Stobo, William, III, 600
Stocken, Harry William Gibbon, XII, 779
Stocking, Abner, V, 29
Stocks, Elizabeth (Black), VI, 62
Stockton*, Alfred Augustus (1842–1907), XII, 537
Stockton, Mary Hatfield (Jenkins), VII, 442
Stockton, Rebecca (Cuthbert), IV, 190
Stockwell, Lucy (McKenney), XI, 562
Stoddard, Elizabeth (Fillis), IV, 267
Stoddard, John, II, 667
Stoddard, Susanna (McGray), VII, 562
Stoesz, David, XII, 1099
Stokes, J. W., XII, 29
Stofflemire. *See* Tufflemier
Stokes, Jane, I, 81
Stokes, William, X, 83; XI, 428
Stone, Mrs (wife of Thomas, merchant), VI, 70
Stone, Abigail. *See* Cogswell
Stone, Alfred, IX, 558
Stone, Caroline (Farewell), XI, 311
Stone, Constance Emily. *See* Wainewright
Stone, F. W., XII, 644
Stone, Harriet A. (Moore), X, 531
Stone, Joel, V, 552; VI, 435, 436, 532, **738–39**; VII, 380,
    419, 452; VIII, 534, 609
Stone, Leah. *See* Moore
Stone, Mary (mother of THOMAS), XII, 991
Stone, Mary (McDonald), VI, 435
Stone, Mary (Polly) (Leonard), VIII, 499; XII, 552, 991
Stone, Rebecca. *See* Bishop
Stone, Stephen, VI, 738
Stone, Thomas (father of THOMAS), XII, 991
Stone, Thomas (merchant), V, 784; VI, 70
Stone, Thomas, XII, **991**
Stone, William Leete, V, 256, 584, 803, 811, 812; VI, 325,
    762; VII, 625, 626
Stoney, Edmund, VI, 758
Stoó-kya-tosi (Two Suns, Sun Old Man, Father of Many
    Children), IX, 623; XII, 717, 778
Storer, Jeremiah, II, 54
Storer, Mary, II, 54
Storer, Priscilla, II, 54
Storer, Rachel (rebaptized Marie-Françoise) (Berger), II,
    54
Storer, Ruth. *See* Masters
Storie, Elizabeth Sophia (Saunders), X, 644
Storm, Agnes. *See* Cotterill
Storm, John, IX, 429
Storm, Mary. *See* Hopkins

Storm, Thomas, VIII, 282; XII, 991
Storm, William George, VIII, 486, 761, 876; XI, 225, 226, 228; XII, 344, **991–94**
Storrow, Thomas, XI, 116
Story, Elizabeth. *See* Jenkinson
Story, Elizabeth. *See* Steer
Story, George, XII, 994
Story, George Philliskirk, XII, **994–95**
Story, Mary-Ann Angelica (Buell), IX, 99
Story, William, XII, 994
Stouf, Jean-Baptiste, VI, 24
Stoughton, Maria. *See* Hagerman
Stoughton, Mary (Dennis), XI, 244
Stoughton, William, II, 452, 494
Stourton, Edward, I, 614
Stourton, Elizabeth. *See* Gravenor
Stourton, Erasmus, I, 163, **614**
Stourton, Mary (mother of ERASMUS), I, 614
Stout, Abigail (Tremain), VIII, 891
Stout, Elizabeth Sarah. *See* Crowdy
Stout, Harriet (Bown; McLearn), VIII, 566
Stout, Henrietta Amelia (Binney), XI, 73
Stout, Martha Wingate. *See* Weeks
Stout, Richard, IV, 523; V, 511, **779–81**; VI, 113, 370, 535, 536; VII, 10, 839; VIII, 566
Stovin, Richard, VII, 897
Stow, Caroline Brooks (Proudfoot), IX, 647
Stow, David, IX, 271
Stow, John, I, 151
Stowe*, Augusta (Gullen) (d. 1943), XI, 54
Stowe, Emily Howard. *See* Jennings
Stowe, Harriet Elizabeth. *See* Beecher
Stowell, Sarah (Pedley), X, 588
Stoyell, Thomas, V, 597
Strachan, Agnes, IX, 753
Strachan, Alexander Wood, IX, 753
Strachan, Ann. *See* Wood
Strachan, Augusta Anne. *See* Robinson
Strachan, Elizabeth. *See* Findlayson
Strachan, Elizabeth, IX, 753
Strachan, Elizabeth Mary (Jones), IX, 416, 753
Strachan, George Cartwright, IX, 753; X, 224
Strachan, James (brother of JOHN), IX, 755
Strachan, James (merchant), IV, 330
Strachan, James McGill, VII, 262, 371; VIII, 798; IX, 416, **751**, 753; X, 120; XI, 150; XII, 101, 593, 907
Strachan, John (father of JOHN), IX, 752
Strachan, John (son of JOHN), IX, 753
Strachan, John, V, 65, 68, 79, 83, 170, 457, 520, 529, 557, 695, 697, 750, 787; VI, 5, 6, 11, 12, 21, 22, 32, 55, 56, 94, 118, 159, 160, 199, 229, 266, 364, 426, 453, 456, 467, 470, 522, 525, 526, 527, 528, 529, 543, 545, 604, 609, 610, 611, 612, 613, 648, 698, 721, 723, 762, 771, 791, 801; VII, 42, 58, 74, 75, 80, 100, 124, 125, 159, 163, 208, 212, 230, 261, 319, 337, 338, 366, 367, 368, 369, 372, 375, 409, 410, 417, 443, 453, 456, 458, 467, 469, 481, 543, 545, 546, 547, 548, 549, 550, 638, 640, 652, 662, 704, 733, 795, 822, 827, 828, 833, 836, 852, 857, 858, 896, 920, 921; VIII, xxv, xxvii, xxxiv, 5, 6, 8, 10, 11, 28, 45, 46, 48, 55, 84, 95, 116, 117, 120, 187, 195, 205, 206, 272, 276, 304, 336, 337, 340, 410, 431, 441, 511, 512, 514, 515, 516, 517, 518, 519, 521, 522, 523, 524, 527, 528, 585, 587, 596, 597, 600, 601, 602,

622, 623, 640, 641, 706, 733, 734, 760, 795, 796, 798, 799, 859, 885, 926, 927, 933, 945; IX, 49, 55, 59, 68, 69, 129, 139, 140, 141, 204, 205, 240, 290, 291, 292, 332, 333, 334, 335, 378, 379, 411, 416, 417, 423, 484, 498, 499, 508, 512, 528, 534, 535, 540, 542, 545, 550, 579, 657, 661, 668, 669, 670, 672, 674, 677, 678, 683, 684, 719, 724, 733, 737, 740, **751–66**, 770, 771, 836, 838; X, 35, 40, 53, 54, 55, 56, 57, 60, 61, 80, 84, 119, 120, 121, 206, 207, 224, 253, 256, 269, 270, 274, 321, 350, 381, 382, 442, 452, 453, 469, 536, 607, 618, 622, 693; XI, 89, 219, 248, 313, 326, 327, 367, 387, 388, 503, 540, 541, 558, 570, 639, 653, 654, 676, 784, 785, 793, 796, 845, 868, 872, 914, 916, 917; XII, 101, 106, 410, 680, 681, 808
Strachan, Robert, VIII, 321
Strahan, Gregory. *See* Trahan, Grégoire
Strahan, Mary (Shenston), XII, 967
Strang, Agnes (Gilmour), XI, 348
Strang, Andrew, VII, 595
Strang, Ann (Rankin), IX, 653
Strang, John (Quebec businessman), VII, 594, 595; XII, 928, 1036
Strang, John (St Andrews, N.B., merchant), VIII, 753; IX, 653; XII, 895
Strang, Margaret. *See* Ross
Strang, Martha (Ritchie), XII, 895
Strang, Mary (Ritchie), VIII, 753
Strang, Struthers, VII, 594, 595
Strange, Lord. *See* Stanley
Strange, Anne. *See* Dundas
Strange, Elizabeth (Ward) (mother of JOHN), VII, 894
Strange, Elizabeth (Ward) (wife of JOHN), VII, 894
Strange, Isabella, Lady Strange. *See* Lumisden
Strange, James Charles Stuart, IV, 325, 498; V, 618; VI, 36, 797; VII, **830–31**
Strange, Jane, Lady Strange. *See* Anstruther
Strange, Sir John, IX, 69
Strange, Louisa, Lady Strange. *See* Burroughs
Strange, Margaret. *See* Durham
Strange, Maxwell William, IX, 73; XII, 990
Strange, Orlando Sampson, XI, 263; XII, 1074
Strange, Sir Robert, VII, 830, 831
Strange, Sir Thomas Andrew Lumisden, IV, 112; VI, 34, 790; VII, 87, 88, 104, 830, **831–32**
Strange*, Thomas Bland (1831–1925), XI, 460, 600, 747, 839; XII, 478, 734
Strapp, Patrick, IX, 393, 820
Stratham, Catherina (Bagshawe; Philipps), III, 518
Strathcona and Mount Royal, Baron. *See* Smith
Strathmore, Earl of. *See* Bowes-Lyon
Strathy, George William, IX, 600
Stratton (Straton), Frances Maria (Street), VIII, 840
Straunge, Robert, I, 239, 240
Street, Abigail. *See* Freeman
Street, Abigail. *See* Ransom
Street, Abigail Hyde. *See* Ransom
Street, Agatha Georgiana (Stark), IX, 741
Street, Alfred Locke, VII, 73
Street, Ann. *See* Lee
Street, Ann Frances (Berton), VI, 741; VII, 73
Street, Caroline (Cummings; Macklem; Robertson; Becher), XI, 62
Street, Christian. *See* Rowe

Street, Cynthia (Fuller), XI, 326
Street, Elizabeth. *See* Smith
Street, Elizabeth (Plumb), XI, 697
Street, Elizabeth (Wilmot), VII, 915
Street, Frances Maria. *See* Stratton
Street, George, XI, 919
Street, George Frederick, VI, 687, 741, 757, 810; VII, 73, 74, 140, 141, 188, 658, 691; VIII, 183, 378, 783, 807, 808, 833, **840–42**; IX, 766; X, 284, 543; XII, 17, 895
Street, Helen (Lewis), X, 441
Street, Jane Isabella. *See* Hubbard
Street, John (grandfather), V, 783
Street, John, V, 785
Street, John Ambrose Sharman, VI, 741; VII, 73; VIII, 739, 840, 841, 842; IX, 171, 413, **766–67**; X, 494; XI, 828; XII, 338, 838, 1104, 1105
Street, Mark, V, 785
Street, Mary (mother of THOMAS), V, 783
Street, Mary (Bird), V, 785
Street, Mary (Darling; Olmstead), VI, 178
Street, Mary (Ussher), V, 673, 782
Street, Nehemiah, VII, 832
Street, Peter (uncle), V, 783
Street, Peter, V, 784, 785
Street, Phoebe. *See* Van Camp
Street, Rachel (Noad), IX, 598
Street, Richard Porter, VIII, 44
Street, Robert, I, 652
Street, Samuel, V, 781
Street, Samuel, IV, 113, 119; V, 70, 71, 388, 518, 661, **781–83**, 841, 842, 857; VI, 178, 540, 746; VII, 250, 251, 832, 915; VIII, 185
Street, Samuel, V, 548, 549, 643, 672, 782; VI, 147, 148, 149, 211, 229, 539, 629, 630, 631, 632, 633; VII, 314, 315, **832–35**; VIII, 10, 252, 279, 281, 438; IX, 332; X, 668; XI, 326, 697
Street, Samuel Denny, V, 136, 137, 161, 353, 355, 356, 456; VI, 7, 73, 75, 139, 140, 142, 356, 474, 504, **739–41**, 755, 810; VII, 73, 121; VIII, 840, 841, 842; IX, 766
Street, Samuel Denny Lee, VI, 741
Street, Thankful. *See* Moody
Street, Thomas, VI, 739
Street, Thomas, V, 491, 641, **783–85**; VI, 274
Street, Thomas Clark, VII, 834; VIII, 10; IX, 745; X, 122, **668–69**; XI, 583, 697; XII, 151
Street, Timothy, VI, 498, 747
Street, William Augustus, XII, 149
Street, William Henry, VI, 741
Street, William Purvis Rochfort, XII, 1073, 1074
Streit, Catherine (Moore), X, 531
Stremler, Jacques-Michel, IX, 19; XII, 1018
Stretton, John, IV, 176, 177
Strickland, Agnes, IX, 768; XI, 857, 858; XII, 996, 997, 998
Strickland, Agnes (Hunter), XII, 458
Strickland, Catharine Parr (Traill), VIII, 64, 651; IX, 768; X, 172, 536; XI, 212, 857, 858, 859, 861; XII, 514, 525, 570, 667, 781, 926, **995–99**, 1131
Strickland, Elizabeth. *See* Homer
Strickland, Elizabeth, XI, 857, 858; XII, 996
Strickland, Emma. *See* Black
Strickland, Jane Margaret, XII, 996

Strickland, Katherine. *See* Rackham
Strickland, Mary. *See* Reid
Strickland, Roland, XII, 119
Strickland, Samuel, VII, 262, 263, 337, 882; VIII, 440; IX, **767–69**; XI, 138, 212, 857, 858, 859; XII, 524, 782, 996, 997, 998
Strickland, Sara, XII, 996
Strickland, Susanna (Moodie), VII, 263, 389, 792; VIII, 358, 651; IX, 355, 566, 768; X, 536; XI, 212, 322, **857–61**; XII, 514, 525, 558, 570, 573, 662, 776, 782, 922, 945, 948, 996, 997, 998, 999
Strickland, Thomas, IX, 767, 768; XI, 857, 858; XII, 995, 996
Strickland, Walter George, V, 705
Stricklar, Oliver, II, 233
Stritch, Mary (Truscott), VIII, 895
Strobridge, James Gordon, VI, 420, **741–42**; VII, 379, 466; VIII, 186, 946
Strobridge, Nancy. *See* Mayberry
Stroh, Jacob, VIII, 316
Strong, Charles Edward, X, 63
Strong, George Templeton, X, 63, 64
Strong, George Washington, X, 63
Strong, John Bass, VI, 671; VIII, 15, 941
Strong, Lemira (Colby), IX, 144
Strong, Richard, I, 306
Strong*, Sir Samuel Henry (1825–1909), XI, 399; XII, 291, 889, 899
Strong, T. W., XII, 1115
Strouds, Gilles William (rebaptized Louis-Claude-Joseph), III, 340, **602**
Strouds, Marie-Josephte. *See* Morisseau
Strouds, Pierre, III, 602
Strouds, Rachel Relind. *See* Baionas
Strouds, William, III, 602
Strouss, Carl, XII, 804
Strowbridge, Elizabeth (Bushell), III, 90
Strozzi, Philippe, I, 87
Struckhoff, Caroline, named Sister Teresa, XI, 111
Strutt, John James, 2nd Baron Rayleigh, VIII, 94
Stuart. *See also* Stewart
Stuart, Andrew, V, 785
Stuart, Andrew, V, 329, 787; VI, 42, 43, 48, 50, 584, 585; VII, 42, 43, 48, 50, 264, 646, **835–37**, 877, 878, 879, 880; VIII, 109, 155, 214, 681, 845, 907; IX, 83, 360, 808, 810, 811; X, 30, 68, 77, 282, 567; XI, 238; XII, 999
Stuart, Sir Andrew, VII, 835; IX, 487; X, 20; XI, 927; XII, 928, **999–1000**
Stuart, Annabella. *See* Campbell
Stuart, Ann Ellice. *See* Robison
Stuart, Catherine. *See* La Valle
Stuart, Charles. *See also* Charles, the Young Pretender
Stuart, Charles, V, 776
Stuart, Charles, VIII, 409, 410; IX, **769–70**
Stuart, Sir Charles, VI, 299
Stuart, Charles Beebe, VIII, 81; IX, 526; XI, 817
Stuart, Charles Edward. *See* Charles, the Young Pretender
Stuart, Charlotte-Elmire. *See* Aubert de Gaspé
Stuart, David (commissioner), VII, 837; VIII, 421, 766, 882
Stuart, David (fur trader), V, 533
Stuart, Donald (grandfather), VII, 837

Stuart, Donald, VII, 838
Stuart, Eleanore (Starnes), XII, 986
Stuart, Elizabeth, Lady Stuart. *See* Robertson
Stuart, Elizabeth Van Rensselaer. *See* Powell
Stuart, Francis Harris, VIII, 115
Stuart, George Okill, V, 17, 401, 786, 787; VI, 3, 31, 32, 370, 416, 525, 526, 527, 528; VII, 920; VIII, 760, 762; IX, 68, 411, 519, 520, 579, 724, 754, **770–71**; X, 60, 155; XI, 265, 861
Stuart, George Okill, VIII, 645, 834; IX, 771; XI, 177, **861–62**
Stuart, Gilbert, V, 314, 594, 706, 811
Stuart, Gustavus George, XII, 928
Stuart, Henry (brother of Sir ANDREW), XII, 197, 1000
Stuart, Henry (forge owner), VII, 68
Stuart, Henry Coleridge, IV, 811; IX, 880
Stuart, Isabel, VII, 838
Stuart, James. *See also* James, the Old Pretender
Stuart, James, XI, 862
Stuart, Sir James, V, 787; VI, 43, 47, 48, 50, 205, 513, 701, 802; VII, 9, 622, 667, 730, 769, 785, 786, 789, 836, 837, 857, 879, 880, 906; VIII, 109, 154, 491, 559, 781, **842–45**; IX, 297, 299, 363, 450, 485, 594, 672, 808, 809, 848; X, 567; XI, 187, 352, 861; XII, 1000
Stuart, Jane. *See* Okill
Stuart, Jane. *See* Smith
Stuart, Janet. *See* Grant
Stuart, Johanna (McInnes), XII, 631
Stuart, John (clergyman), VIII, 272
Stuart, John (grocer), XI, 389, 907
Stuart, John (politician), VII, 224
Stuart, John (sheriff), VIII, 195; IX, 520
Stuart, John (son of JOHN, 1740/41–1811), V, 786
Stuart, John (son of JOHN, 1780–1847), VII, 838
Stuart, John (superintendent), IV, xxxviii, 450
Stuart, John, IV, 418, 495, 692, 710, 730; V, 17, 255, 321, 445, 475, 476, 524, **785–88**, 804; VI, 3, 405, 525, 526, 528, 600, 638, 716, 717; VII, 452, 583, 835; VIII, 842, 937; IX, 534, 668, 752, 753, 754, 770; XII, 999
Stuart, John, VI, 437; VII, 385, 498, 570, 578, **837–39**; VIII, 454, 558, 561, 573; IX, 283, 284, 285, 722; XI, 882
Stuart, John, XI, **862–63**
Stuart, John, 3rd Earl of Bute, IV, 571; V, 315
Stuart, Sir John, VI, 713
Stuart, Louisa Anna. *See* Bindon
Stuart, Lucy. *See* Brooks
Stuart, Margaret (Harvey), XI, 389
Stuart, Margaret (Le Maistre), V, 486, 647
Stuart, Margaret (Painter), V, 647
Stuart, Margaret Black. *See* Stacey
Stuart, Marguerite. *See* Dumoulin
Stuart, Mary. *See* Mary, Queen of Scotland
Stuart, Mary. *See* Dinwiddie
Stuart, Mary. *See* Taylor
Stuart, Mary (Jones), V, 787; VII, 452
Stuart, Mary (MacNab), IX, 520
Stuart, Mary (Rankin), XII, 884
Stuart, Peter, IV, 107, 324; V, 43, 289, 368, 369, 372, 373, 374, 494, 509, 699, 816, 879, 881; VII, 65
Stuart, Robert, V, 533; VIII, 766
Stuart, Sophia, IX, 527
Stuart, Wilhelmina Matilda. *See* Sinclair

Stuart, William, II, xxvii, xxviii, 171, 310, 319, **614–16**, 627, 628, 658; III, xxxii, 285
Stubbs, William, XII, 585, 586
Stubinger, Charlotte (Pépin), VII, 685; IX, 127
Studholme, Gilfred, IV, 80, 161, **723–24**; V, 16, 296, 416, 589, 867; VI, 739, 740; VII, 215
Studley, Daniel, I, 390, 392, 450
Stüwitz, Dr, IX, 418
Sturge, Joseph, IX, 704
Stutsman, Enos, X, 628, **669**; XI, 740; XII, 82
Stutsman, Jacob, X, 669
Stutsman, Nicholas, X, 669
Suárez. *See* Moziño
Subercase. *See* Auger
Sublet de Noyers, François, I, 313
Suckling, Frances. *See* Duport
Suckling, George, III, 130; IV, 37, 399, 415, 570, **724–26**; V, 426, 605; VI, 491, 492
Sue, Eugène, X, 165; XI, 82, 273, 276
Sue, Jean-Joseph, VI, 24
Süe, Pierre, VIII, 212
Suève, Edmond de, I, 321, 418; II, **616–17**; III, 311, 312
Suisse, Le. *See* Miville, Pierre
Sulivan, Charlotte, XI, 242
Sulivan, Laurence, VIII, 505; IX, 241
Sulleon, IX, 418
Sullivan, Amy (Moss), XI, 621
Sullivan, Anna Maria Louisa (Ridout), IX, 661
Sullivan, Sir Arthur Seymour, XI, 142; XII, 623, 660
Sullivan, Augusta Elizabeth (Baldwin), VIII, 45, 46, 47, 48, 58, 59
Sullivan, Augustus Baldwin, VIII, 846
Sullivan, Barbara. *See* Baldwin
Sullivan, Cecilia Eliza. *See* Matthews
Sullivan, Daniel (father of ROBERT BALDWIN), VIII, 845, 846
Sullivan, Daniel (father of TIMOTHY), III, 602
Sullivan, Daniel (nephew of William Warren BALDWIN), VII, 37; VIII, 846
Sullivan, Daniel (undersecretary), VII, 768
Sullivan, Daniel, XI, **863–64**
Sullivan, Edward, X, 207; XI, 314, 917; XII, **1000–1**
Sullivan*, Edward Alan (1868–1947), XII, 1000
Sullivan, Elizabeth (Morehouse), VI, 518
Sullivan, Emily Louisa. *See* Delatre
Sullivan, Frances Mary. *See* Renaud
Sullivan, Henry, VIII, 846
Sullivan, James (agent), VI, 142
Sullivan, James (apprentice), V, 329
Sullivan, Jeremiah, XI, 863
Sullivan, John (officer), IV, 118, 405, 484, 549, 735; V, 32, 147, 414, 895
Sullivan, John (police superintendent), XII, 157
Sullivan, John William, XI, 662, 663
Sullivan, Marie-Renée. *See* Gaultier de Varennes
Sullivan, Mary. *See* Hutchinson
Sullivan, Mary (Whelan), IX, 835
Sullivan, Mary Elizabeth. *See* MacCarthy
Sullivan, Michael, XII, 96
Sullivan, Patrick, XI, 863, 864
Sullivan, Robert, XII, 571
Sullivan, Robert Baldwin, VI, 425, 468; VII, 32, 37, 42, 315, 370, 638, 665, 756; VIII, 11, 29, 46, 49, 52, 53, 57,

426, 520, 696, 709, **845–50**, 959; IX, 56, 57, 68, 400, 513, 535, 661, 662, 700; X, 255, 618; XI, 406, 621, 863, 883; XII, 1107
Sullivan, Timothy, known as Timothée Silvain, III, 246, 271, 373, **602–4**, 675; IV, 235
Sullivan\*, Sir William Wilfred (1843–1920), X, 195, 473; XI, 242, 601, 922; XII, 40
Sully, Duc de. *See* Béthune
Sully, Ann (Maclaren), XII, 664
Sully, Thomas, VIII, 495
Sulte\*, Benjamin (1841–1923), III, 305, 629; IV, 168, 232; V, 702; VI, 582, 717; VII, 387, 388, 503, 743; IX, 256, 562, 563, 564, 565, 796; X, 150, 304, 433, 579, 580, 584; XI, 82, 84, 330, 332, 343, 489, 490, 671, 709; XII, 271, 308, 325, 504
Sulte, Marie-Augustine. *See* Parent
Summerhill, Elizabeth (Hill), VII, 406
Sumner, Charles, IX, 845; X, 263; XI, 769
Sumner, John Bird, IX, 290, 719; XI, 18
Sumner, William Henry Tyler, XII, 479
Sunday. *See* Raven
Sunday, John. *See* Shah-wun-dais
Sunderland, Mary (Blake), V, 88
Sunderlin, Wallis, VI, 733
Sunley, Maria Louisa (Birrell), X, 68
Sun Old Man. *See* Natos-api; Stoó-kya-tosi
Sureau, *dit* Blondin, Esther, named Mother Marie-Anne, VIII, 20; XI, **864–65**; XII, 360, 697, 698
Sureau, *dit* Blondin, Jean-Baptiste, XI, 864
Sureau, *dit* Blondin, Marie-Rose. *See* Limoges
Surette, Nanette (Melanson; Gueguen), VI, 305
Suria, Feliciana Lozana de. *See* Lozana
Suria, Francisco, VI, 742
Suria, Maria Josefa Dominguez de Mendoza de. *See* Dominguez de Mendoza
Suria, Tomás de, V, 140; VI, **742–43**
Surlaville. *See* Le Courtois
Surrey, Earl of. *See* Howard
Surveyor. *See* Fabre
Susewisk, IX, 537
Sussex, Duke of. *See* Augustus Frederick
Suter, James K., XII, 919
Sutherland, Alexander, XII, 660
Sutherland\*, Alexander (1833–1910), XI, 608; XII, 1119
Sutherland, Alexander Macbeth, VII, 593
Sutherland, Catherine (Macbeth), IX, 475
Sutherland, Cecilia (Hamond), VI, 310
Sutherland, Daniel, IV, 311; V, 106, 284, 564, 715, 716; VI, 296, 297, 433, 664, **743–46**; VII, 718; IX, 742
Sutherland, Donald, VI, 464
Sutherland, George (clergyman), X, 612; XI, 202
Sutherland, George (HBC employee), IV, 727
Sutherland, George, IV, 524, **726–27**; V, 531; VI, 776; XI, 458
Sutherland, Hugh John, IX, 618; XII, 951
Sutherland\*, Hugh McKay (1843–1926), XI, 652
Sutherland, Isabella. *See* Campbell
Sutherland, James (HBC clerk), VII, 671; VIII, 343; X, 475
Sutherland, James (landowner), XI, 197
Sutherland, James (NWC clerk), VIII, 454
Sutherland, James, IV, **727–28**; V, 535, 885; VI, 464, 795; VII, 138

Sutherland, Jane (Vincent), VI, 795
Sutherland, Jean (McLachlan), XII, 660
Sutherland, Jessie (Cameron), XI, 141
Sutherland, John (HBC employee), VI, 321
Sutherland, John (militia officer), IX, 73
Sutherland, John (political candidate), IX, 618; XI, 540
Sutherland, John (son of GEORGE), IV, 727
Sutherland, Laura (wife of THOMAS JEFFERSON), VIII, 851
Sutherland, Louisa, V, 716
Sutherland, Louisa (Stayner), IX, 742
Sutherland, Margaret. *See* Robertson
Sutherland, Margaret (Hardisty), XI, 383, 384
Sutherland, Maria (Hallowell), V, 716
Sutherland, Murdoch, VIII, **850–51**
Sutherland, Nanette (Keith), VIII, 454
Sutherland, Patrick, III, 295, 513, **604–5**; IV, 780
Sutherland, Thomas Jefferson, VII, 405; VIII, 431, **851–54**; IX, 643
Sutherland, Viola, VIII, 853
Sutherland, William (doctor), IX, 16, 17, 358; XI, 58
Sutherland, William (lawyer), XII, 30
Sutherland, William (newspaperman), XI, 80
Sutton. *See also* Manners-Sutton
Sutton, Catherine (Power), XII, 860
Sutton, Catherine Bunch. *See* Nahnebahwequay
Sutton, Eleanor (Estcourt), VIII, 273
Sutton, Julia Anna (Wright), XII, 1131
Sutton, Marianne (Kirkpatrick), IX, 431
Sutton, Mary, Baroness Lexington. *See* St Leger
Sutton, William (lay missionary), IX, 590
Sutton, William (newspaper owner), IX, 100
Suzack. *See* Sozap
Suzanne. *See* Connolly; Gouentagrandi
Suzor, Anne-Marie-Angélique. *See* Defoy
Suzor, François, V, 788
Suzor, François-Michel, V, **788–89**
Suzor, François-Timothée, IX, 771
Suzor, Hippolyte, IX, 771
Suzor, Louis-Timothée, IX, **771–72**; XII, 99
Suzor, Louise. *See* Laflèche
Suzor, Marie-Anne. *See* Grougnard
Suzor, Marie-Anne. *See* Larue
Suzor, Sophie. *See* Évanturel
Suzor-Coté\*, Marc-Aurèle de Foy (1869–1937), XII, 171
Swabey, Catherine. *See* Bird
Swabey, Mary Ann. *See* Hobson
Swabey, Maurice, X, 669
Swabey, William, VII, 146; IX, 830; X, **669–70**; XI, 940
Swain, James, V, 185; VII, 138; X, 324
Swain, Margaret (Gunn), X, 324
Swain, Thomas, VI, 250; VII, 205
Swaine, Charles, III, 502
Swaine, Francis, V, 767
Swainson, William, IX, 659
Swaize, Mary (Keefer), VIII, 450
Swan, II, **617**
Swan, Alexander, XI, 865
Swan, Ann. *See* Graham
Swan, Anna Haining (Bates), XI, **865–66**
Swan, Isaac, VI, 107
Swan, James Gilchrist, XII, 290
Swanley, Robert, I, 567
Swanston, Betsey. *See* Keith

Swanston, John, VIII, 454
Swanton, Emma (wife of ROBERT), III, 606
Swanton, Robert, III, xxv, 132, **605–6**; IV, 210; V, 203
Swanwick, Mary (Hutton), IX, 404
Swart, Claudius Clavus, I, 18, 680
Swartz, Margaret (Grass), V, 377
Swatana, III, xxxviii, xl, **606–8**; IV, lvi
Swayne, Hugh, V, 780; VI, 213, 214, 538, 792; VII, 10, **839–40**
Swayne, John, VII, 839
Swayze, Bethia. See Luce
Swayze, Caleb, VI, 746
Swayze, Isaac, V, 405, 661, 782, 842, 845, 856; VI, 154, 631, **746–47**; VII, 251; IX, 334
Swayze, Lena (Ferris; wife of ISAAC), VI, 746
Swayze, Mary (Hopkins), X, 358
Swayze, Miriam. See Drake
Swayze, Sarah. See Secord
Sweatman*, Arthur (1843–1909), XI, 368, 654, 917
Swedenborg, Emanuel, VIII, 271
Swediaur, François-Xavier, V, 46
Sweeney, Campbell, VII, 893
Sweeney, Charlotte. See Temple
Sweeney, James, VI, 372
Sweeney*, John (1821–1901), X, 193, 230; XI, 40; XII, 26, 28, 122, 209, 339, 547, 548, 721, 881
Sweeney, Robert, XI, 771
Sweeny, Jane Douglass (Caldwell), VI, 104
Sweeny, Maria (Esson), VIII, 272
Sweeny, Thomas William, XII, 68
Sweet, Nathaniel, XII, 759
Sweet Grass. See Wikaskokiseyin
Sweetland, David, VII, 406
Sweetland, Henry, IV, 784
Sweetman, Juliet. See Forstall
Sweetman, Michael, VII, 841
Sweetman, Nicholas, VII, 842
Sweetman, Pierce, VII, **840–42**
Sweetman, Roger, VII, 840
Sweetman, Roger F., VII, 841, 842
Sweezey. See Swayze
Swett, Sarah (Marston), IV, 516
Swift, Alice. See Culshaw
Swift, Edward, XII, 1001
Swift, Henry, XII, **1001–2**
Swift, Jonathan, II, 444; V, 486; VI, 155; VII, 539; XII, 1100
Swift, Sarah. See McLeod
Swiggett, Howard, IV, 121
Swinburne, Algernon Charles, XII, 516
Swinyard, Thomas, XI, 226
Swite, Margaret (Maguire), VIII, 591
Switzer, Anne. See Ryan
Switzer, Edmund, XII, 865
Switzer, John, VIII, 854
Switzer, Margaret (Smiley), VIII, 822
Switzer, Martin, VII, 253; VIII, **854–55**
Switzer, Mary. See Maurice
Sydenham, Baron. See Thomson
Sydenham, Thomas, III, 677
Sydney, Viscount. See Townshend
Sykes, Grace Valentine (Waddington), X, 696
Sykes, Sarah (Fisher), X, 290

Sylvain. See also Dupleix; Veau
Sylvain, Isabelle. See Veau, dit Sylvain, Élisabeth-Marguerite
Sylvain, Mathurine (Talbot), III, 612
Sylvester, Joseph. See Joe, Sylvester
Sylvester, Sarah (Merry), VI, 501
Sylvestre, Odile (Lareau), XI, 488
Sym, Jane (Mackenzie), XII, 647, 658
Sym, Robert, IV, 82; VI, 699; VII, 25
Syme, James, XI, **866–67**
Syme, Janet (wife of JAMES), XI, 866
Symes, Angélique-G. See Cuvillier
Symes, George, V, 374; IX, 772
Symes, George Burns, IX, **772–74**; XI, 5, 12, 547; XII, 279
Symes, Henry Richard, VII, 224
Symes, Robert, VII, 169, 427; IX, 773; XI, 36
Symes, Sophia (Ryerson), XI, 795
Symes, Susanna Catharine (Ogilvie), IV, 586
Symington, Dr, IX, 518
Symmes, Charles, VII, 928
Symonds, Mary (Winslow), V, 865
Sympson, Mary (Jameson), VIII, 426
Syrier. See Cirier
Szalatnay, Márk, X, **670–71**
Szesdrakowski, Mr (officer), VII, 411
Szkolny. See Scolvus
Szyrma. See Lach-Szyrma

TABARET, Adélaïde. See Forêt
Tabaret, Antoine, XI, 867
Tabaret, Joseph-Henri, X, 322, 323; XI, **867–68**; XII, 977
Tabeau, Antoine, V, 177
Tabeau, Françoise. See Prou
Tabeau, Jean-Baptiste (father of PIERRE-ANTOINE), VI, 664, 747
Tabeau, Jean-Baptiste (partner of Étienne-Charles CAMPION), V, 259
Tabeau, Pierre-Antoine, VI, 593, **747–49**; VII, 349, 489, 736, 887; VIII, 592, 593, 594, 719
Tabor, Alice Mary (Richards), XII, 892
Taché, Alexandre-Antonin, III, 609; VIII, 562, 722, 723; IX, 95, 617, 802; X, 38, 70, 148, 149, 322, 474, 578; XI, 34, 46, 47, 124, 152, 164, 170, 192, 249, 310, 311, 442, 461, 546, 611, 613, 736, 738, 741, 742, 743, 746, 842; XII, 23, 132, 181, 204, 304, 369, 507, 508, 510, 554, 600, 601, 641, 652, 678, 680, **1002–12**, 1046
Taché, Charles (father), IX, 774
Taché, Charles, VI, 369; XII, 1002, 1012
Taché, Émilie-Hélène-Henriette (Coursol), XI, 206
Taché, Étienne, III, 608
Taché, Sir Étienne-Paschal, III, 609; VII, 503; VIII, 138, 170, 171, 230, 231, 332, 371; IX, 253, 268, 383, 448, 463, 645, 690, 772, **774–79**, 796, 804, 858; X, 96, 99, 100, 122, 131, 144, 146, 147, 405, 465, 466, 623, 656, 674, 695; XI, 83, 129, 160, 161, 170, 176, 180, 181, 196, 206, 283, 287, 412, 464, 536, 581, 610, 618, 822, 908, 932; XII, 86, 89, 151, 184, 263, 352, 594, 596, 684, 750, 818, 1012, 1013, 1108
Taché, Eugène-Étienne, XI, 337
Taché, Françoise. See Lepage
Taché, Geneviève. See Michon
Taché, Jacques-Vinceslas, VI, 749

Taché, Jean, III, 76, 160, 340, **608–9**; IV, 67, 306, 362; V, 277; VI, 749; IX, 774
Taché, Jean-Baptiste (agent), VII, 569
Taché, Jean-Baptiste (politician), III, 609; VI, 369, 749; VII, 763; XII, 1012
Taché, Joseph-Charles, III, 609; IX, 63, 65, 97, 121, 194, 213; X, 21, 78, 152, 203, 231, 415; XI, 115, 160, 178, 186, 342, 495; XII, 270, 271, 324, 597, 599, 848, 1002, **1012–16**
Taché, Joséphine-Éléonore. See Estimauville
Taché, Julie. See Larue
Taché, Louis, XI, 338; XII, 254, 255
Taché, Louise-Henriette. See Labroquerie
Taché, Louis-Paschal-Achille, VI, 750; VIII, 457; XII, 296, 297
Taché, Marguerite. See Dauzet
Taché, Marie-Anne. See Jolliet de Mingan
Taché, Marie-Louise. See Decharnay
Taché, Pascal, V, 75; VI, **749–50**; IX, 774
Taché, Paschal, VI, 749
Taché, Sophie. See Baucher, dit Morency
Taffanel de La Jonquière, Catherine de. See Bonnes
Taffanel de La Jonquière, Jacques-Pierre de, Marquis de La Jonquière, III, 6, 22, 27, 29, 30, 69, 100, 148, 169, 183, 204, 214, 243, 246, 255, 289, 320, 329, 356, 357, 375, 378, 385, 400, 428, 435, 451, 484, 486, 496, 502, 561, 570, **609–12**, 628, 629; IV, 15, 35, 45, 63, 66, 79, 91, 145, 173, 174, 202, 213, 236, 237, 254, 256, 271, 289, 311, 382, 407, 449, 454, 455, 459, 470, 512, 514, 614, 615, 623, 633, 651, 666, 667, 688, 692, 728; V, 98, 176
Taffanel de La Jonquière, Jean de, III, 609
Taffanel de La Jonquière, Marie-Angélique de, Marquise de La Jonquière. See La Valette
Tagancout. See Tekanoet
Tagaskouïta. See Tekakwitha
Tagawirunte. See Tekawiroñte
Tahahaiadoris, III, 95, 652; IV, 408
Tahaygen* (d. 1920), XII, 290
Tahourdin, Emma Frances (Staines), VIII, 835, 836; IX, 853
Tahourdin, Horace Foster, VIII, 835
Tahpit, IX, 433
Taiearonk, I, 354
Taignoagny, I, 11, 166, 167, 275, 276
Tailer, Elizabeth (Nelson), II, 494
Tailhan, Jules, IX, 120
Tailhandier, Antoine, II, 617
Tailhandier, Jeanne (Tétro), II, 627
Tailhandier, dit La Beaume, Madeleine. See Baudry
Tailhandier, dit La Beaume, Marien, II, 470, **617–18**, 627; III, 397, 598
Taillant. See Tarieu
Taillon, Georgine. See Archambault
Taillon*, Sir Louis-Olivier (1840–1923), X, 16; XI, 626; XII, 65, 277, 303, 362, 696, 723, 724, 987, 1046
Tait, James Sinclair, XII, 158
Tait, John, XI, 437
Taite, Mary. See Auld
Také, III, 527, 529
Talbot, Baroness. See O'Reilly
Talbot, Edward, VIII, 855
Talbot, Edward Allen, VII, 214, **842–44**; VIII, 410, 855, 856; IX, 618, 769; X, 548, 671

Talbot, Esther. See Allen
Talbot, Freeman, VII, 843; VIII, 856; X, 404, 671
Talbot, Jacques, III, 612
Talbot, Jacques, III, 221, **612–13**
Talbot, James, V, 632
Talbot, John, VII, 716, 842, 844; VIII, 855; IX, 9; X, 548, **671**
Talbot, Lydia. See Baird
Talbot, Marcus, XI, 81; XII, 922
Talbot, Margaret, Baroness Talbot. See O'Reilly
Talbot, Marie-Marthe (Bélanger), IX, 39
Talbot, Mary (Smith), IX, 725
Talbot, Mary Ann (Nickinson), IX, 597
Talbot, Mary Jane. See Blake
Talbot, Mathurine. See Sylvain
Talbot, Phoebe. See Smith
Talbot, Richard, VIII, 857
Talbot, Richard, VI, 730; VII, 842; VIII, **855–57**; X, 671
Talbot, Thomas, V, 14, 112, 440, 753; VI, 22, 399, 400, 496, 497, 498, 541, 612, 808, 809; VII, 92, 124, 125, 126, 127, 128, 733; VIII, 9, 10, 337, 476, 598, 608, 651, 856, **857–62**, 967; IX, 8, 140, 436, 475, 476, 683; X, 273, 345, 462, 503; XI, 62, 138, 795; XII, 643
Talbot, dit Gervais, Marie-Angélique (Valin), XII, 1071
Talfourd, Field, VIII, 438
Talleyrand-Périgord, Charles-Maurice de, XII, 611
Tally, Sarah (Coles), X, 182
Talon. See Lespérance
Talon, Le. See Le Talon
Talon, Anne. See Bury
Talon, Artus, I, 614
Talon, Denis, I, 629
Talon, Jean, II, 555
Talon, Jean, I, 29, 32, 34, 35, 36, 47, 48, 55, 60, 62, 63, 85, 86, 111, 116, 119, 120, 127, 135, 146, 174, 175, 185, 193, 198, 203, 226, 237, 238, 248, 260, 261, 287, 297, 313, 315, 326, 327, 340, 345, 355, 393, 394, 399, 400, 416, 418, 464, 494, 534, 535, 536, 539, 540, 550, 553, 555, 556, 560, 565, 570, 571, 580, 581, 582, 592, 600, 602, **614–32**, 648; II, xviii, xix, 17, 28, 59, 85, 86, 141, 179, 181, 242, 295, 338, 344, 347, 367, 368, 369, 378, 380, 418, 467, 488, 508, 517, 531, 533, 559, 592, 653; III, 60, 62, 201, 202, 247, 308, 311, 548, 581, 648; IV, 356, 360; XI, 185; XII, 558
Talon, Marguerite (Raudot), II, 555
Talon, Marie-Louise, Marquise de Boulay. See Molé
Talon, Marie-Suzanne (Phélypeaux), II, 555
Talon, Omer, I, 629
Talon, Omer, Marquis de Boulay, III, 458
Talon, Phillippe, I, 614
Talon de Boulay, Angélique-Louise (Montcalm, Marquise de Montcalm), III, 458, 467
Talon Du Quesnoy, Jean. See Talon, Jean
Talon-Lesperance. See Lesperance
Taloot. See Telloot
Talus, dit Vendamont, Julien, II, 465
Tambareau, Damien-Henri, X, 510
Tamburini, Michelangelo, III, 335, 336
Tanaghrisson, III, xxxvi, 101, 148, 150, 319, 320, **613–15**
Tancré, Antoine, II, 374
Tancré, Jean, II, 374
Tandihetsi, I, 71, 404; II, 83
Tanfield, Anne (wife of Clement), I, 632

Tanfield, Clement, I, 632
Tanfield, Elizabeth, I, 632
Tanfield, Sir Francis, I, **632**, 669
Tanfield, Sir Lawrence, I, 632
Tangeux. *See* Courtin
Tanguay\*, Cyprien (1819–1902), III, 122, 125, 140, 141, 391, 410, 602, 629; VII, 592; X, 433; XII, 271
Tanner, Charles Augustus, VIII, 396
Tanner, Jean-Emmanuel, VIII, 396, 397
Tanner, John, VII, 844
Tanner, John, VII, **844–45**
Tanner, Olympe. *See* Hoerner
Tanswell, Ann. *See* Blacklock
Tanswell, Charles, V, 790
Tanswell, James, V, 330, 373, **789–91**
Tanswell, Marie-Joseph. *See* Coutant
Tanswell, Stephen Joseph, V, 790
Tanswell, Thomas, V, 789
Tantia Topi, XI, 592
Tantouin de La Touche, Louis, II, 36, 114, 147, 353, 574, **618–19**; III, 563
Tantouin de La Touche, Madeleine. *See* Girard
Taondechoren, I, 11, **632–33**
Taouestaouis. *See* Le Moyne de Maricourt, Paul
Taoyateduta (Little Crow), IX, 780
Tapin, Étienne, XII, 66
Tapin, Marie-Louise-Esther (Barthe), XII, 64, 65
Tappan, Lewis, IX, 470, 704, 769, 820
Taranto, Émile, XII, 472
Taratouan (Taratwane), I, **633**, 637, 639
Tarbell, Elizabeth. *See* Wood
Tarbell, John, III, **615**
Tarbell, Sarah (rebaptized Marguerite), III, 615
Tarbell, Thomas (father), III, 615
Tarbell, Thomas, III, 615
Tarbell, Zachariah, III, 615
Tarbotton, Elizabeth Wilkinson (Barr), XII, 60
Tarbox, John Neil, XII, 1088
Tard. *See* Du Tartre
Tardivel\*, Jules-Paul (1851–1905), IX, 862; XI, 186, 484; XII, 100, 510, 825, 1026, 1027
Tardy, François, II, 466
Tardy, Marie, II, 326
Tareha, I, **633–34**; II, 255
Targis. *See* Pinguet
Tarhe (Crane), V, 797; VII, 821
Tarieu de Lanaudière, Catherine (Aubert de Gaspé), IV, 34; VI, 16; X, 18, 20
Tarieu de La Naudière, Charles-François, III, 312; IV, xliii, 91, **728–30**; V, 43, 143, 791, 792; VI, 132
Tarieu de Lanaudière, Charles-Louis, IV, 43, 50, 427, 547, 716, 729; V, 44, 99, 100, 372, 380, 687, **791–92**, 793; VI, 16, 679; VII, 119, 254, 357
Tarieu de Lanaudière, Geneviève-Élisabeth. *See* La Corne
Tarieu de Lanaudière, Louise, X, 20
Tarieu de La Naudière, Louise-Geneviève. *See* Deschamps de Boishébert
Tarieu de Lanaudière, Marie-Anne (Baby), V, 43, 45; VII, 373; IX, 14
Tarieu de La Naudière, Marie-Catherine. *See* Le Moyne de Longueuil
Tarieu de Lanaudière, Xavier-Roch, IV, 729; V, **792–93**; VI, 750

Tarieu de La Pérade, Madeleine-Marie-Anne (Testu de La Richardière; Coulon de Villiers; Gaultier), III, 150, 620, 676
Tarieu de La Pérade, Marie-Madeleine. *See* Jarret de Verchères
Tarieu de La Pérade, Pierre-Thomas, I, 418; II, 547; III, 311, 312, 313, 519, 676; IV, 216, 728; XII, 725
Tarieu Taillant de Lanaudière, Charles-Gaspard, V, 578; VII, 447
Tarieu Taillant de Lanaudière, Gaspard, VII, 449; IX, 703
Tarieu Taillant de Lanaudière, Marie-Antoinette (Loedel), VII, 447
Tarieu Taillant de Lanaudière, Marie-Charlotte (Joliette), IX, 703
Tarieu Taillant de Lanaudière, Pierre-Paul, VII, 447, 448
Tarieu Taillant de Lanaudière, Suzanne-Antoinette. *See* Margane de Lavaltrie
Tarihia (Christine), I, 652
Tarride Duhaget, Antoinette. *See* Saint-Thairau
Tarride Duhaget, Charles, III, 615
Tarride Duhaget, Marguerite. *See* Rousseau de Villejouin
Tarride Duhaget, Robert, II, 220; III, 533, **615–16**; IV, 15, 444, 644, 688
Tarrigha (Tarsha). *See* Tareha
Tarte\*, Joseph-Israël (1848–1907), X, 193; XI, 27, 484; XII, 178, 179, 180, 292, 309, 610, 611, 629, 630, 723, 726, 727, 1011, 1045
Tascher, Hélène-Marguerite-Barbe (Chabert de Cogolin, Marquise de Chabert), V, 176
Taschereau, Agnès, VI, 751
Taschereau, Antoine-Charles, V, 794; IX, 779
Taschereau, Charles-Antoine, VI, 752
Taschereau, Claire (Philippon), VI, 581
Taschereau, Claire-Caroline, VI, 751
Taschereau, Élisabeth-Suzanne (Juchereau Duchesnay), VI, 751; X, 388; XI, 456
Taschereau, Elzéar-Alexandre, III, 617; VI, 751; VII, 800; VIII, 215, 407, 408, 778; IX, 19, 20, 119, 120, 121; X, 388, 430, 589, 603, 686; XI, 38, 42, 43, 103, 104, 171, 172, 177, 185, 250, 251, 253, 258, 259, 274, 303, 424, 485, 488, 507, 513, 720, 726; XII, 46, 117, 301, 302, 303, 304, 508, 509, 510, 511, 519, 521, 522, 724, 732, 758, 799, 811, 819, 820, 821, 849, 874, 875, 888, 913, **1016–24**, 1050
Taschereau, Françoise. *See* Boucher de La Bruère de Montarville
Taschereau, Gabriel-Elzéar, V, 794; VI, 753
Taschereau, Gabriel-Elzéar, III, 617; IV, 72, 549; V, 43, 45, 61, 146, 182, 370, 577, 650, **793–95**, 863; VI, 225, 346, 577, 750, 751, 752; VII, 188, 402; X, 567
Taschereau, George-Louis, V, 794
Taschereau, Henri, XII, 308
Taschereau\*, Sir Henri-Elzéar (1836–1911), XI, 711; XII, 899
Taschereau\*, Sir Henri-Thomas (1841–1909), XI, 624
Taschereau, Jean-Thomas, V, 87, 208, 211, 212, 235, 649, 794; VI, 42, 43, 47, 48, 68, 82, 225, 384, 392, 581, **750–51**, 753; VII, 72, 133, 462, 504, 785, 836, 878; VIII, 154, 223, 388, 778; X, 388; XI, 456; XII, 1016, 1024
Taschereau, Jean-Thomas, VII, 751; VIII, 223, 678; IX, 119; X, 136; XI, 731; XII, 247, 521, 912, **1024–25**
Taschereau, Joseph-André, VI, 753; IX, 728, **779–80**; XI, 183; XII, 1024

Taschereau, Julie-Louise (Fortier), V, 794
Taschereau*, Louis-Alexandre (1867–1952), X, 136
Taschereau, Louise-Adèle. *See* Dionne
Taschereau, Louise-Adèle (Angers), VIII, 16
Taschereau, Louise-Françoise. *See* Juchereau Duchesnay
Taschereau, Marie. *See* Panet
Taschereau, Marie, V, 793
Taschereau, Marie-Anne-Louise, named de Saint-
  François-Xavier, III, 617; VI, **751–52**
Taschereau, Marie-Claire. *See* Fleury de La Gorgendière
Taschereau, Marie-Joséphine. *See* Caron
Taschereau, Marie-Louise (Perrault), V, 794; VI, 577
Taschereau, Marie-Louise (Routh, Lady Routh), VI, 751;
  VIII, 778
Taschereau, Marie-Louise-Élizabeth. *See* Bazin
Taschereau, Pierre-Elzéar, VI, 753; VIII, 223, 319; IX,
  779
Taschereau, Thomas-Jacques, III, 69, 154, 179, 217, 300,
  353, 592, **616–17**; IV, 284, 359, 361, 362, 363, 421, 590;
  V, 793; VI, 751
Taschereau, Thomas-Pierre-Joseph, V, 794; VI, 240, 581,
  751, **752–53**; VIII, 18; IX, 779
Taschereau de Sapaillé, Christophe, III, 616
Taschereau de Sapaillé, Renée. *See* Boutin
Tasker, Anne (Wentworth; Bellew), V, 847
Tasker, James, VIII, 862
Tasker, Mary Anne (Pinhey), VIII, 706
Tasker, Patrick, VIII, **862–63**
Tasquantum. *See* Tisquantum
Tassé, Adélina. *See* Daoust
Tassé, Alexandrine-Victorine-Georgiana. *See* Lecourt
Tassé, Joseph, XII, 1025
Tassé, Joseph, IV, 637; XI, 230, 625, 683, 716, 729, 743;
  XII, 938, **1025–28**
Tassie, James, XI, 868
Tassie, Mary. *See* Stewart
Tassie, Sarah. *See* Morgan
Tassie, William, XI, **868–69**; XII, 616
Tassy, Félix de, I, 81; III, 237
Tatamy, Tunda (Moses), IV, 27
Ta-tanka I-yotank (Ta-tanka Yotanka), IX, 780; X, 227; XI,
  443, 598, **869–71**; XII, 674, 788
Tatanka-najin, IX, **780–81**; XI, 19, 869; XII, 22
Tate, Caroline (Gibbs), XI, 346
Tate, James (HBC officer), VIII, 878
Tate, James (schoolmaster), IX, 848
Tate, Mary (Hardy, Lady Hardy), IV, 326
Tatham, Charles Heathcote, VIII, 959
Tatnam, James, I, 553, 666
Taton, *dit* Brind'amour, Judith (Voyer), VIII, 918
Tattannoeuck, VI, 328, **753–55**; VII, 324; VIII, 663
Taudet. *See* Tollet
Taunchey, John, IX, 419
Taunton, Baron. *See* Labouchere
Tau-yau-ro-too-yau (Between the Logs), VII, 821
Tavel, Sophie de (Watteville), VII, 896, 898
Taverner, Abraham, III, 618
Taverner, Jacob, V, 491
Taverner, Rachel (wife of WILLIAM), III, 618
Taverner, Rachel (Lester), V, 491
Taverner, Susannah (Lester), V, 491
Taverner, William (father of WILLIAM), III, 618
Taverner, William (son of WILLIAM), III, 619

Taverner, William, II, 118, 439, 487, 583, 611; III, **617–20**;
  V, 491
Tavernier, Antoine, VIII, 863
Tavernier, Émilie (Gamelin), VII, 488; VIII, 301, 713,
  **863–66**; X, 297; XI, 96; XII, 1033
Tavernier, François, VIII, 863
Tavernier, Marie-Anne (Perrault), VIII, 863
Tavernier, Marie-Josephte. *See* Maurice
Tavernier de La Forest, *dit* La Lochetière, Jean, I, 267, 269;
  II, 234
Tawmaugh, IV, 57
Taxous, II, 475
Tayler, Henry, I, 228, 229
Taylor, Mrs. *See* Durell
Taylor, Mrs. *See* Ramage
Taylor, Colonel, V, 605
Taylor, Mr (father of ALEXANDER), V, 795
Taylor, Alexander, V, 483, **795**
Taylor, Ann. *See* Cameron
Taylor, Ann. *See* Urquhart
Taylor, Anne (mother of HENRY), VIII, 866
Taylor, Anne Eliza (wife of JOHN), X, 672
Taylor, Anne Flora (Burns), IX, 109
Taylor, Benjamin, VI, 756
Taylor, Catherine (Brenton), VII, 104
Taylor, Charles, VII, 357
Taylor, Charlotte. *See* Hunter
Taylor, Charlotte (McCord), XI, 542
Taylor, Chloe Sweeting. *See* Langford
Taylor, Daniel, XII, 1028
Taylor, David, VIII, 101
Taylor, Edward C., VIII, 900
Taylor, Eliza. *See* Wilkinson
Taylor, Elizabeth. *See* Archibald
Taylor, Elizabeth, XII, 1031
Taylor, Elizabeth (Taylor), VII, 233
Taylor, Elizabeth Johnson (Davie), VII, 233; VIII, 559
Taylor, Elizabeth Wallace (Badgley), XI, 40
Taylor, Ernest Manly, XII, 55
Taylor, Ervin J., X, 199
Taylor, Fanny (O'Hara), X, 557
Taylor, Gain Bartlett, VI, 756
Taylor, George (brother of JOHN), X, 671, 672
Taylor, George (father of JOHN FENNINGS), XI, 871
Taylor, George (Quebec shipbuilder), VII, 233
Taylor, George (surveyor), XII, 876
Taylor, George (Weymouth, N.S., shipbuilder), XI, 146
Taylor, Georgina Rosalie. *See* Nanton
Taylor, Helen. *See* Gordon
Taylor, Henry (brother-in-law of James JOHNSTON), IV,
  399; V, 699
Taylor, Henry (father of HENRY), VIII, 866
Taylor, Henry (nephew of James JOHNSTON), IV, 400
Taylor, Sir Henry, VIII, xxxii, xxxiii
Taylor, Henry, VIII, **866–67**
Taylor, Henry, XII, **1028–29**
Taylor, Sir Herbert, VIII, 26
Taylor, Isaac Boulton, X, 46
Taylor, James (father of JAMES, d. 1856), VIII, 867
Taylor, James (father of JAMES WICKES), XII, 1029
Taylor, James (father of WILLIAM, d. 1834), VI, 755, 756;
  XII, 691
Taylor, James (of Taylortown, N.B.), VI, 755

Taylor, James (politician), VII, 681
Taylor, James (shipbuilder), II, 56
Taylor, James (son of JAMES, 1761–1834), VI, 755
Taylor, James (uncle of JOHN), X, 671
Taylor, James, VI, 504, 741, **755–56**
Taylor, James, VI, 757; VII, 188; VIII, **867–69**
Taylor, James Wickes, X, 646; XII, **1029–31**
Taylor, Jane (mother of JAMES, d. 1856), VIII, 867
Taylor, Jane (mother of WILLIAM, d. 1834), VI, 756
Taylor, Jane (Bemister), XII, 91
Taylor, John (father of JOHN), X, 671
Taylor, John (nephew of James JOHNSTON), IV, 400
Taylor, John (partner of John ESSON), IX, 243
Taylor, John (political candidate), XI, 46
Taylor, John (politician), XII, 766
Taylor, John (writer), VII, 357
Taylor, John, X, **671–72**; XI, 575
Taylor, John F., VI, 757; VIII, 868
Taylor, John Fennings, XI, 871
Taylor, John Fennings, IX, 646; XI, 206, 734, **871–72**, 911;
  XII, 789, 791
Taylor, John M., V, 826
Taylor, John W., VIII, 852
Taylor, Joseph Fenwick, VIII, 657
Taylor, Margaret. *See* Bartlett
Taylor, Margaret. *See* Hawthorne
Taylor, Margaret Anne (Le Marchant), X, 438
Taylor, Maria. *See* Wickes
Taylor, Maria (Campbell), XI, 146
Taylor, Maria (Spilsbury), VI, 730
Taylor, Martha (Martin), VII, 590
Taylor, Mary. *See* Hamilton
Taylor, Mary. *See* Keith
Taylor, Mary (Stuart), VII, 838
Taylor, Mary Elizabeth. *See* Denison
Taylor, Matthew, VI, 755
Taylor, Nancy. *See* Hatfield
Taylor, Nathaniel, IV, 89; V, 509
Taylor, Richard, VI, 755
Taylor, Sally. *See* Hatfield
Taylor, Samuel E., IX, 76
Taylor, Sarah (mother of HENRY), XII, 1028
Taylor, Sarah (Mitchell), III, 453
Taylor, Sarah (Robinson), VIII, 757
Taylor, Thomas (brother of JOHN), X, 671, 672
Taylor, Thomas (clergyman), VII, 272
Taylor, Thomas (lawyer), VI, 247; VIII, 125
Taylor, Tom, XII, 449
Taylor, William (clergyman), VI, 232; VIII, 77
Taylor, William (lawyer), IV, 604; V, 109, 251; VI, 34
Taylor, William (merchant), V, 262
Taylor, William, VI, 741, 755, **756–57**, 810; VIII, 868
Taylor, William, VIII, 396, 666; X, 41, **672–73**
Taylor, William Henry, X, **673–74**
Taylor, Wittewronge, III, 208
Taylour, Joseph, II, 152, 291, 439, **619**
Taylour, Thomas, II, 619
Tayorheasere. *See* Teiorhéñhsere?
Tazewell, Master (son of SAMUEL OLIVER), VII, 846
Tazewell, Mary Ann (wife of SAMUEL OLIVER), VII, 847
Tazewell, Samuel Oliver, VI, 773; VII, **845–47**; VIII, 419
Teabout, Henry, VIII, 325
Téata, III, 528, 529

Teba, Countess of. *See* Montijo
Tebbets, Horace, XII, 374
Tecarihoga. *See* Tekarihogen (Henry)
Techenet, Mme. *See* Couc, Elizabeth
Tecumpease, VII, 847
Tecumseh (Tech-kum-thai), II, 316; V, 113, 114, 302, 594,
  619, 748, 774, 775, **795–801**, 811, 852; VI, 210, 617;
  VII, 133, 743, 821, 847, 848, 849, 850; VIII, 45, 338,
  744; X, 181; XII, 855
Teed, John, VII, 62; VIII, 582, 678; IX, 695
Teedyuscung, III, 323; IV, 27
Teefy, John Read, X, 174; XI, 904; XII, 811
Teefy, Matthew, VIII, 804, 830
Teel, Susan (Baird), VIII, 42
Teemer, John, XII, 408, 797
Teeter, Mary. *See* Cooke
Tee Yee Geen Ho Ga Row. *See* Theyanoguin
Tegakwitha. *See* Tekakwitha
Tegancourt (Tegancout, Tegancouti, Teganeout,
  Tegannehout). *See* Tekanoet
Teganissorens, I, 445, 634; II, xxx, xxxi, xxxvi, 169, 321,
  401, 502, **619–23**, 631; III, 321, 622
Tegarihogen (Tegariouguen). *See* Tekarihoken
Tegaskouïta. *See* Tekakwitha
Tegonhatsiongo (Anastasie), I, 635
Teharihogen. *See* Tekarihoken
Teharonhiagannra, I, 460
Tehastakout. *See* Tonatakout
Téhatsiendahé. *See* Tsiewei, Michel
Tehkummeh (Tetekumah), Francis, IX, 408
Teholagwanegen (Tehoragwanegen, Tehora Kwanekeu).
  *See* Williams, Thomas
Tehonakaraa. *See* Norton, John
Tehorenhaegnon, I, **634–35**
Tehowagherengaraghkwen (Tehonwawenkaragwen), VI,
  555, **758–59**; VII, 455, 520; VIII, 440, 620
Tehowaghwengaraghkwin, V, 803
Teichmann, Emil, XII, 552
Teignmouth, Baron. *See* Shore
Teiorhéñhsere?, IV, **730–31**; V, 786
Teissier, Jean, IV, 386
Teissier, Jeanne-Élisabeth (Gugy), VII, 359
Teiyoquande. *See* Teyohaqueande
Tekahionwake. *See also* Johnson, Pauline
Tekahionwake (Jacob Johnson), XI, 453
Tekakwitha, Kateri, I, 522, **635–36**; II, 139, 144, 341; VIII,
  619
Tekanoet, II, xxxix, 256, **623–24**; III, xl
Tekarihogen (Tekarihogea, Tekarihó:ken) (Henry), V, 804,
  808; VI, **759–60**, 761; VII, 251, 451, 665, 666; VIII, 133,
  439, 620
Tekarihogen (John Brant), V, 804; VI, 153, 159, 373, 481,
  551, 758, 759, **760–62**; VII, 466, 467, 520, 666, 917;
  VIII, 162, 620
Tekarihogen (Tekerehogen), Sarah (Jones), VI, 759, 760;
  VII, 451; VIII, 439
Tekarihoken, II, xxxiv, **624–25**
Tekawiroñte, IV, **731**
Tekonwakwehinni, Marie-Anne, VII, 137
Tekouerimat. *See* Negabamat
Telari-o-lin. *See* Vincent, Zacharie
Telfer, Catherine (Barnard), XI, 50
Telfer, Euphemia. *See* Denham

Telfer, Margaret (Christie), X, 171
Telfer, Mary (White), VI, 812
Telfer, Walter, VIII, 850, **869–70**; IX, 688; X, 610; XII, 1123
Telfer, William, VIII, 869
Telford, Thomas, VI, 19; VII, 33
Telgmann, Oscar F., XI, 142
Tellier, Catherine (Gervais), XI, 344
Tellier, Josephte (Barbier), VIII, 60
Tellier, Louis, XII, 719
Tellier, Rémi-Joseph, IX, **781–82**
Tello. *See* Espinosa
Telloot (Taloot, Tellot), IX, 432, 433
Telmon, Adrien, VII, 267; VIII, 66; IX, 397; X, 86, 107
Temme, Ferdinand Conrad, VII, 636
Tempest, Sir Henry, V, 361
Templar, Annie (Buller), IX, 100
Temple, Earl. *See* Grenville
Temple, Charlotte (Sweeney; Rose, Lady Rose), XI, 771
Temple, Dorothy. *See* Lee
Temple, Henry, VI, 702; VIII, 781
Temple, Henry John, 3rd Viscount Palmerston, VIII, 379; IX, 93, 235, 349; X, 258, 482, 483; XI, 767; XII, 750
Temple, Isaac, VIII, 901; IX, 601, 801
Temple, Sir John (father of Sir THOMAS), I, 636
Temple, Sir John (office holder), VI, 35
Temple, Mary (Nelson), II, 494
Temple, Robert, III, 123, 662
Temple, Thomas, XI, 688
Temple, Sir Thomas, I, 636
Temple, Sir Thomas, I, 25, 62, 63, 241, 399, 407, 434, 435, 436, 475, 500, 513, 595, 605, **636–37**, 654, 666, 667; II, 459, 494; III, 653; IV, xvii, xxiv
Templer, Dudley, V, 652
Templeton, William, XII, 805
Tenanguer. *See* Duparc
Ten Broeck, John, V, 643; VIII, 69
Ten Broeck, Peter, V, 669, 841
Tench, Frances (Hodder), X, 350
Ten Eyck, James, XII, 408
Tennant, George, XI, 594
Tennyson, Alfred, 1st Baron Tennyson, IX, 355; XI, 142; XII, 123, 188, 361, 490, 516, 945, 1077
Tenskwatawa, V, 302, 594, 774, 775, 796, 797, 798, 800, 852; VI, 340, 552; VII, 821, **847–50**; XII, 123, 188, 361, 490, 516, 945, 1077
Teondechoren (Joseph), I, 42, 212, 344, 523
Teoniahigarawe. *See* Theyanoguin
Teouatiron, I, 633, **637–38**
Teresa, Mother. *See* Dease
Teresa, Sister. *See* Brennan; Struckhoff
Terlaye. *See* Magon
Terme, Jean, II, 604, 605
Termont. *See* Demay
Ternay. *See* Arsac
Ternay, Marquise de. *See* Lefebvre de Laubrière
Terohaute, Michel, VI, 328
Terriau (Terriault). *See* Terriot
Terrick, Richard, IV, 104; V, 600, 747
Terrier de Francheville et de Repentigny, Jeanne. *See* Jallot
Terrier de Francheville et de Repentigny, Marin, I, 553; II, 227
Terrill, Frederick William, XII, 573

Terrill, Harriet (wife of TIMOTHY LEE), X, 674
Terrill, Hazard Bailey, VIII, 148; X, 674
Terrill, Joseph Hazard, X, 674
Terrill, Timothy Lee, IX, 727; X, 548, 642, **674**; XII, 385
Terriot, Cécile. *See* Landry
Terriot, Jeanne (Tibaudeau), II, 257, 629
Terriot, Jehan, II, 625
Terriot, Marie (Cormier; Landry), IV, 436
Terriot, Perrine. *See* Ruau
Terriot, Pierre, II, **625**
Terron. *See* Colbert
Terroux, François, III, 620; IV, 731
Terroux, Jacques, VI, 432, 434
Terroux, Jacques, III, **620**; IV, 629, **731**; V, 889; VI, 434, 652
Terry, Alfred Howe, XI, 870
Terry, Esther Louisa (Simpson), XII, 971
Terry, Sarah Maria (Thomson), IX, 788
Terryberry, Lydia Ann (Rymal), XII, 934
Tessier*, Albert (1895–1976), IX, 864
Tessier, Auguste, XII, 695
Tessier, Cyrille, IX, 862
Tessier, Élisabeth (Damours), I, 245
Tessier, François-Xavier, VI, 68, 576, **762–64**; VIII, 682; IX, 358, 572
Tessier, Jacques, II, 11
Tessier, Jean-Marie, VIII, 490
Tessier, Josephte. *See* Huot Saint-Laurent
Tessier, Jules, XII, 695
Tessier, Laurent, I, 452
Tessier, Lewis, XII, 956
Tessier, Marguerite-Adèle. *See* Kelly
Tessier, Mariane. *See* Perrault
Tessier, Marie (Leblanc), XI, 505
Tessier, Marie (Maleray de La Périne), II, 450
Tessier, Marie-Anne (Gaboury), X, 296
Tessier, Michel (father of FRANÇOIS-XAVIER), VI, 762
Tessier, Michel (father of ULRIC-JOSEPH), XII, 1032
Tessier, Michel (notary), VIII, 207
Tessier, Ulric, XII, 1032
Tessier, Ulric-Joseph, VIII, 101; IX, 119; XI, 190, 902; XII, 308, 848, 912, **1032–33**, 1036
Tessier, *dit* Chaumine, Paul, IV, 732
Tessier, *dit* Lavigne, Jacques, IV, 732
Tessier (Texier), *dit* Lavigne, Jacques, IV, 732
Tessier, *dit* Lavigne, Jean, II, 133
Tessier, *dit* Lavigne, Jeanne. *See* Lefebvre
Tessier, *dit* Lavigne, Marie. *See* Adhémar, *dit* Saint-Martin
Tessier, *dit* Lavigne, Paul, IV, **731–33**
Tessier, *dit* Lavigne, Urbain, I, 427; II, 164
Tessouat (fl. 1603–13), I, 6, 192, 662, **638–39**
Tessouat (d. 1636), I, 10, 222, 489, 516, 633, **639**
Tessouat (Tesswehas), I, 548, 558, **640–41**
Test, Sara (Dencke), VII, 243
Testard de La Forest, Gabriel, I, 180, **641**; II, 298, 394, 406, 626
Testard de La Forest, Jacques, I, 641; II, 626
Testard de La Forest, Marie. *See* Pournin
Testard de Montigny, Benjamin-Antoine, IX, 782, 783; X, 420, 542; XI, 755, 893, 894
Testard de Montigny, Casimir-Amable, VI, 385; IX, **782–83**
Testard de Montigny, Jacques, II, 36, 37, 118, 252, 395,

495, 534, 563, 609, **625–27**, 653; III, 81, 105, 238, 243, 278, 488, 505; IV, 733; IX, 782

Testard de Montigny, Jean-Baptiste-Jérémie, V, 32, 802

Testard de Montigny, Jean-Baptiste-Philippe, IV, 449, **733–34**; V, 801

Testard de Montigny, Louise-Archange. *See* Gamelin, *dit* Gaucher

Testard de Montigny, Louis-Étienne, IX, 782

Testard de Montigny, Marguerite. *See* Damours de Chauffours

Testard de Montigny, Marie-Amable (Gaultier de La Vérendrye), III, 243

Testard de Montigny, Marie-Anne. *See* La Porte de Louvigny

Testard de Montigny, Marie-Charlotte. *See* Trottier Desrivières

Testard de Montigny, Marie-Louise. *See* Allaire

Testard de Montigny, Marthe. *See* Godon

Testard de Montigny, Pierre-Benjamin, V, 802

Testard Louvigny de Montigny, Agathe. *See* Hay

Testard Louvigny de Montigny, Charlotte. *See* Trottier Desrivières

Testard Louvigny de Montigny, Jean-Baptiste-Pierre, V, 306, 552, **801–3**; VI, 8

Testu, Captain, I, 300

Testu, Guillaume, I, 679

Testu de La Richardière, Madeleine-Marie-Anne. *See* Tarieu de La Pérade

Testu de La Richardière, Marie. *See* Hurault

Testu de La Richardière, Richard, II, 520; III, 22, 150, **620–22**, 676; IV, 10, 360, 619

Testu Du Tilly, Geneviève. *See* Rigault

Testu Du Tilly, Pierre, III, 620

Tête Blanche, La. *See* Gray Lock

Tetekumah. *See* Tehkummeh

Tetesigaguoy (Marie-Madeleine) (Jérémie, *dit* Lamontagne), II, 256, 296

Tetrault (Tetrau). *See* Tétreau

Tétreau, Auguste-Pascal, VIII, 201

Tétreau, François, XI, 289; XII, 719, 720

Tétreau, Harriet (wife of HUBERT-JOSEPH), X, 675

Tétreau, Hubert-Joseph, IX, 610; X, **674–75**

Tétreau, Jean-Baptiste, X, 674

Tétreau, Marie-Anne. *See* Guyon

Tétreault. *See* Tétreau

Tétro, Jean-Baptiste, II, 617, **627**

Tétro, Jeanne. *See* Tailhandier

Tétro, Louis, II, 627

Tétro, Marie-Noëlle. *See* Landeau

Tett, Benjamin, VI, 127

Têtu, Caroline. *See* Dionne

Têtu, Caroline (Juchereau Duchesnay), XI, 457

Têtu, Cécile. *See* Chabot

Têtu, Charles, VII, 643

Têtu, Charles-Hilaire, IX, 360, **783–84**

Têtu, Charlotte. *See* Bonenfant

Têtu, Cirice, VIII, 223; IX, 360; XI, 457, 902

Têtu, Cléophée, named Thérèse de Jésus, XII, **1033–34**

Têtu, David, IX, 783

Têtu, David-Henri, IX, 359; X, 161

Têtu, Elizabeth. *See* O'Brien

Têtu, Eugène, IX, 362

Têtu, Félix (merchant), IX, 640

Têtu, Félix (notary), V, 231, 253; VI, 50, 424; IX, 48

Têtu, François, IX, 783

Têtu*, Henri (1849–1915), III, 546, 712; IV, 95; V, 248; VI, 569, 571, 598, 599; IX, 800; XI, 87, 519; XII, 117, 472, 1034

Têtu, Horace, VIII, 628

Têtu, Jean-François, XII, 1033

Têtu, Justine (Langevin), IX, 783

Têtu, Ludger, VIII, 223

Têtu, Marie-Thérèse. *See* Pâquet

Têtu, Nazaire, IX, 640

Têtu, Vital, VII, 858; IX, 798; X, 132

Teuleron, Pierre, I, 401

Tewathiron. *See* Teouatiron

Tewennihata. *See* Thewanihattha

Texier. *See also* Tessier

Texier de La Touche, Marie-Reine. *See* Berbudeau

Texier de La Touche, Pierre-Alexis, IV, 56

Teyarhasere. *See* Teiorhéñhsere⁷

Teyohaqueande, IV, 596, **734–35**; V, 895

Teyoninhokarawen. *See* Norton, John

Teyonnhehkewea, VIII, 619

Tey-yagh-taw. *See* Stayeghtha

Thackeray, William Makepeace, VIII, 173; XII, 570

Thacter, Mary (Gorham), III, 260; IV, 308

Thain, Alexander, VII, 309

Thain, Thomas, V, 635; VI, 73, 665, **764–66**, 815; VII, 29, 736, 737; VIII, 719, 883

Thalberg, Sigismund, XII, 503

Thanadelthur, II, xxvii, 319, 614, 615, **627–28**; III, xxxii

Thanayieson. *See* Tanaghrisson

Thaonawyuthe, IV, 404, 406

Tharbell. *See* Tarbell

Tharca. *See* Tareha

Tharoniakanere. *See* Marcoux, Joseph

Thatcher, Sarah (Leonard), VI, 394

Thaumur de La Source, Dominique, II, 628

Thaumur de La Source, Dominique-Antoine-René, II, 117, **628**; III, 105, 443, 640

Thaumur de La Source, Jeanne. *See* Bonhomme

Thaumur de La Source, Marie-Louise, IV, 235

Thavenet, Élisabeth de. *See* Mancelin

Thavenet, Jean-Baptiste, VI, 668, 669; VII, 54, 59, 487, 499, 798, **850–52**; VIII, 408, 457, 593, 594, 728; IX, 698, 797, 798; XII, 224

Thavenet, Marguerite de (Hertel de La Fresnière), I, 185; II, 284, **628–29**; III, 7, 83, 288

Thavenet, Marie-Françoise de, I, 185; II, 628, 629

Thavenet, Raymond de, II, 628

Thaxter, Samuel, III, 200

Thayendanegea. *See also* Jones, John

Thayendanegea (Thayeadanegea, Thayendanegen, Joseph Thayendanegea), III, xxxvii, 323; IV, liv, lv, lvi, lvii, 119, 121, 130, 149, 155, 405, 406, 416, 613, 692, 710, 731, 756; V, 40, 72, 121, 229, 254, 255, 256, 440, 517, 549, 707, 724, 731, 758, 786, **803–12**, 843, 896, 898, 899, 900; VI, 3, 4, 8, 112, 152, 154, 177, 324, 373, 375, 550, 551, 552, 583, 608, 620, 703, 758, 759, 760, 761, 762, 772, 808; VII, 192, 250, 348, 450, 451, 455, 466, 467, 520, 651, 665, 666, 917; VIII, 310, 606, 620, 708, 709, 744; XI, 317, 453; XII, 401

Thayer, Abigail (Lovett), VI, 407

Thayer, Nathaniel, XI, 10

Thayer, Simeon, IV, 550
Thearihogen. *See* Tekarihoken
Théberge. *See also* Thiberge
Théberge, Adrien, IX, 63
Thebo. *See* Thibault
Theller, Ann. *See* Platt
Theller, Edward Alexander, VII, 234, 235, 426, 720; VIII, 27, 120, 401, 502, 616, 852, 853, **870–72**; IX, 643; X, 260, 346; XI, 269
Thellusson, Ann (Windham), IX, 844
Thémines, Marquis de. *See* Lauzières
Thémines, Alexandre de, VII, 869
Théodore, Élisabeth (Le Maistre), V, 485
Théoragwanegon, Thomas. *See* Williams, Thomas
Theresa of the Child Jesus. *See* Martin
Thérèse. *See* Oionhaton
Thérèse de Jésus. *See* Têtu
Thériaud (Thériault). *See* Terriot
Thériault, Élisabeth (Entremont), XI, 303
Thériault, Eugénie. *See* Lebel
Thériault, François-Régis, XII, 1034
Thériault, Julie. *See* Ringuet
Thériault, Lévite, XII, **1034–36**
Thériault, Marie-Luce-Eugénie. *See* Patry
Thériault, Prosper, XII, 1133
Thério. *See* Terriot
Théry, Antoine, II, 161
Théry, Marguerite (Crespieul), II, 161
Thésié. *See* Tessier
Thesiger, Frederic, 1st Baron Chelmsford, XI, 919
Thesiger, George, V, 390
Thevet, André, I, 88, 170, 276, 423, 424, 425, 426, **679–80**; III, 337
Thévin, Judith (Champion de Cicé), II, 130
Thew, William, IX, 473
Thewanihattha (Tewennihata), Marguerite (Monique) (wife of ATIATOHARONGWEN), V, 40
Thewathiron. *See* Teouatiron
Theyanoguin, III, 185, 186, 322, 331, **622–24**; IV, lvii, 154, 395, 416, 691; V, 803
Thiathoharongouan. *See* Atiatoharongwen
Thibaud. *See* Thibault
Thibaudeau. *See also* Tibaudeau
Thibaudeau, Alfred, XII, 1036, 1037, 1038
Thibaudeau, Alfred-Arthur, XII, 1037, 1038
Thibaudeau, Charles-François, XII, 1038
Thibaudeau, Édouard, VIII, 206
Thibaudeau, Émilie. *See* Delisle
Thibaudeau, Félicité. *See* Larue
Thibaudeau, Isidore, VIII, 629; X, 615, 676; XI, 190, 774, 902; XII, 912, **1036–38**
Thibaudeau, Joseph-Élie, X, **675–76**; XII, 1036, 1037
Thibaudeau, Joseph-Rosaire, X, 676; XI, 62, 755; XII, 722, 1036, 1037, 1038
Thibaudeau, Laure. *See* Drolet
Thibaudeau, Laure (Saint-Georges), XII, 1037
Thibaudeau, Pierre-Chrisologue, X, 675; XII, 1036
Thibaudeau, Urbain, XII, 1037, 1038
Thibaudier, Antoine, XI, 173
Thibault (Tibault), Charles, I, 246; III, 681
Thibault*, Charles (1840–1905), XI, 330; XII, 99, 269, 272
Thibault, Charlotte. *See* Carrier
Thibault, Claude, II, 457

Thibault, Georges, VIII, 243
Thibault, Jean-Baptiste, X, 676
Thibault, Jean-Baptiste, VII, 232, 276, 390; VIII, 562, 722, 780; X, **676–78**; XI, 305, 441, 442, 739; XII, 601, 932, 1003, 1004, 1007
Thibault, Joseph Nick, XII, 765, 1041
Thibault, Louise. *See* Guyon
Thibault, Marie-Josephte (Bédard), VI, 39, 41
Thibault, Marie-Madeleine (Verrier), III, 646
Thibault, Norbert, named Brother Oliver Julian, XI, **872–74**
Thibeault, Carmelle. *See* Tremblay
Thibeault, Olivier, XI, 872
Thiberge (Théberge), Jean, I, 394
Thibierge, Élisabeth-Cécile (Estèbe), IV, 263
Thibierge, Étienne, IV, 263
Thibierge, Jacques, III, 523
Thibodeau. *See also* Tibaudeau
Thibodeau, Agnès. *See* Dugas
Thibodeau, Agnès (Brossard, *dit* Beausoleil), III, 87
Thibodeau, Alexis (father-in-law of Otho ROBICHAUX), VI, 651
Thibodeau, Alexis (father of SIMON), V, 812
Thibodeau (Thibaudeau), Cécile (Cormier), V, 203
Thibodeau, Joseph, V, 813
Thibodeau, Madeleine (Mercure), V, 589
Thibodeau, Marguerite. *See* Dupuis
Thibodeau, Marguerite-Suzanne (Laflamme), XII, 505
Thibodeau, Marie-Anne. *See* Blanchard
Thibodeau, Marie-Anne. *See* Drolet
Thibodeau (Thibaudeau), Marie-Louise (Robichaux), VI, 651
Thibodeau, Michel, III, 87
Thibodeau, Nathalie (Haché, *dit* Gallant), XII, 397
Thibodeau, Simon, V, **812–13**
Thiboult, Thomas, II, 90, 528, **629**
Thiboutot, Mr (defendant), X, 635
Thielcke, Henry Daniel, VII, 890; VIII, 495; XI, 905; XII, 845, 846
Thielen. *See* Tielen
Thier, *dit* Du Mont, Henry de, IX, 632
Thierry. *See also* Chassin
Thierry, Sieur (attorney), II, 155
Thierry, Augustin, IX, 304
Thierry, Catherine (Louet), II, 447
Thierry (Primot), Catherine (Le Moyne de Longueuil et de Châteauguay), I, 463, 465, 507; II, 133, 390, 401, 403, 406, 469, 508; III, 379; XI, 851
Thierry, Élisabeth. *See* Messier
Thierry, Guillaume, II, 469
Thiersant, François-Gabriel de, II, 221
Thiersant, François-Henri de, II, 221
Thiersant, Marie-Joseph de. *See* Fézeret
Thiersant, Pierre-François de, II, 221
Thiersault, Marguerite (Poncet de La Rivière et de Brétigny), I, 551
Thiollière, Simon-Pierre, IV, 306
Thirel. *See* Pichon
Thirement, Anne (Peiras), II, 514
Thirement, Jacques, II, 514
Thirement, Marie. *See* Hubert
Thirkill, Lancelot, I, 120, 150, 164, **641**
Thirtle, John, VII, 193
Thistlethwaite, Isabel (Wetherald), XII, 1095

Thodatowan. *See* Martin, Louise

Thoizy. *See* Petit

Tholuck, Friedrich August Gottreu, XII, 489

Thom, Mrs. *See* Bisset

Thom, Adam, VII, 6, 118, 777; VIII, 385, 574, 766, 767, 818, 910; IX, 95, 136, 257, 260, 554, 732; X, 47, 69; XI, 139, 208, 546, 680, 766, **874–77**; XII, 125, 206, 477

Thom, Adam Bisset, XI, 876

Thom, Alexander, VII, 852

Thom, Alexander, VII, **852–53**, 920; XI, 845

Thom, Andrew, XI, 874

Thom, Anne. *See* Blachford

Thom, Betsy. *See* Smythe

Thom, Catherine Rosamund (Spragge), XI, 845

Thom, Eliza. *See* Montague

Thom, Elizabeth. *See* Bisset

Thom, Harriet E. *See* Smythe

Thom, James (partner of James FRASER), VI, 262, 263

Thom, James (Presbyterian), VIII, 938

Thoma. *See* Tomah

Thomas Aquinas, VII, 95, 656

Thomas, Ann (mother of WILLIAM), VIII, 872

Thomas, Ann (Christie), VI, 766; VIII, 454; X, 167; XII, 194

Thomas, Ann (Evans), X, 274

Thomas, Arnold William, XII, 213

Thomas, Caroline Ann (Copp), XII, 212

Thomas, Catherine (Bunn), IX, 102; X, 111

Thomas, Charles (official), VI, 289, 390; VII, 876

Thomas, Charles (son of JOHN), VI, 766

Thomas, Charlotte. *See* Vassal de Monviel

Thomas, Charlotte (McTavish; Spence), VI, 766; VII, 577

Thomas, Clarissa (Pattee), VIII, 688

Thomas, Cyrus Pole, VIII, 876

Thomas, David, VII, 49

Thomas, Edward Cartwright, VIII, 44

Thomas, Eleanor (Richards), V, 712

Thomas, Elizabeth (Piers), VIII, 704

Thomas, Francis Wolferstan, IX, 323

Thomas, François-Marie (Pierre-Marie), XII, 285

Thomas, George (merchant), V, 281

Thomas, George (son of Sir Hugh PALLISER), IV, 600

Thomas, George Elliot, XII, 188, 212

Thomas, Henry, XII, 1036, 1037

Thomas, Isaiah, III, 91, 267; IV, 342, 343

Thomas, James, VIII, 969

Thomas, Jean, I, 442, 490, 569, **642**

Thomas, Jennie (Belford), X, 43

Thomas, John (bishop), III, 634

Thomas, John (brother of WILLIAM), VIII, 872, 876

Thomas, John (merchant), I, 343

Thomas, John (officer), IV, 548, 549; V, 31

Thomas, John, IV, 525; V, 712; VI, **766–67**; VII, 577; X, 167

Thomas, John Morgan, XII, 422

Thomas, Louis-Aubert, VII, 883

Thomas, Martha. *See* Tutin

Thomas, Mary (Gray), VIII, 344

Thomas, Mary Legh (Jebb), IX, 412

Thomas, Merrick, VII, 179

Thomas, Molly Ann. *See* Gell

Thomas, Peter, VI, 282

Thomas, Pierre. *See* Tomah, Pierre, known as Governor Tomah

Thomas, Pierre-Jacques, VII, 889

Thomas, Sarah Rachel (Wilkins), XI, 925

Thomas, Sophia (Mason), VI, 768; VII, 277; IX, **784**; XII, 931

Thomas, Thomas, VI, 767

Thomas, Thomas, VI, 15, 766, **767–68**, 795; VII, 749; VIII, 91, 158, 414; IX, 102, 784

Thomas, William (father of WILLIAM), VIII, 872

Thomas, William (HBC employee), V, 185

Thomas, William (politician), VII, 293; VIII, 381, 948; IX, 85, 435; X, 600; XI, 44

Thomas, William, VII, 192, 706; VIII, 178, 282, 467, 486, **872–78**, 944, 960, 961; IX, 346; XI, 225, 405, 486; XII, 344, 626, 885, 991, 1086

Thomas, William Bevil, VIII, 704

Thomas, William Tutin, VIII, 874, 876

Thomas, Zena (Zeniah) (Seaman), IX, 709

Thomas, *dit* Bigaouet, Marie-Louise (Malhebe), VI, 483

Thomassin, Marguerite (Chabert), XII, 170

Thomé, Antoinette (Collet), II, 149

Thomelin, Ambroise de. *See* Aulquoy

Thomelin, Jean de, I, 213

Thomelin, Marie de (Chomedey), I, 213

Thomey, Arthur, IV, 177

Thomey, John, V, 338

Thompson. *See also* Thomson

Thompson, Abigail (Peters), IV, 625

Thompson, Alfred Andrew, VIII, 885

Thompson, Alfred Burke, VIII, 885

Thompson, Alice. *See* Charters

Thompson, Ann (mother of DAVID), VIII, 878

Thompson, Anna. *See* Hawkins

Thompson, Annie Emma, Lady Thompson. *See* Affleck

Thompson, Austin Seton, XII, 45

Thompson, Catherine Jane Alicia (Rae), XII, 876

Thompson, Catherine-Zéphirine (Dessaulles), XII, 252, 253

Thompson, Charlotte. *See* Pottinger

Thompson, Charlotte. *See* Small

Thompson, Cornelius, VIII, 884, 885

Thompson, David (father of DAVID, 1770–1857), VIII, 878

Thompson, David (politician), VII, 909, 917

Thompson, David, IV, 647, 685, 741; V, 177, 236, 418, 500, 526, 531, 541, 559, 563, 656, 685, 741; VI, 249, 253, 398, 455, 466, 776; VII, 139, 204, 577, 716; VIII, 85, 412, 413, 421, 546, 583, 766, **878–84**; IX, 482, 648; X, 30; XI, 72

Thompson, David, V, 800; IX, **784–85**

Thompson, Ebenezer, VII, 853

Thompson, Edward, III, 449, 544, **624–25**, 663

Thompson, Eliza (Birrell), X, 68

Thompson, Elizabeth. *See* Cooper

Thompson, Euphemia (Milloy), X, 515

Thompson, Frances. *See* Cooper

Thompson, Frances Alice, XII, 1044, 1045

Thompson, Frederick, VIII, 885

Thompson, Frederick William, XII, 801

Thompson, G. W., VIII, 125

Thompson, George, VI, 769

Thompson, George Ash, XII, 876

Thompson, Hannah. *See* Maynard

Thompson, Hannah Maynard (Pickard), VII, **853–54**; XI, 687

Thompson, Henrietta (Wolfe), III, 666

Thompson, Henry (businessman), VII, 863

Thompson, Henry (son of DAVID, 1770–1857), VIII, 883

Thompson, Sir Henry, XII, 1058

Thompson, Henry Horace, VIII, 885

Thompson, Henry Leggatt, XII, 213

Thompson, James (carpenter), XI, 487

Thompson, James (clergyman), XI, 924

Thompson, James (father of JAMES), VI, 768

Thompson, James (office holder), X, 21

Thompson, James (son of JAMES), VI, 769

Thompson, James, VI, 223, **768–70**

Thompson, Jane. *See* Garden

Thompson, John (brother of DAVID, 1770–1857), VIII, 878

Thompson, John (father of TOLER), VII, 854, 855

Thompson, John (lumberman), X, 32

Thompson, John (partner of Jean-Baptiste ROLLAND), XI, 765

Thompson, John (partner of William Eppes CORMACK), IX, 161

Thompson, John (sailmaker), V, 618, 619; VI, 350, 351

Thompson, John G., XII, 36, 37

Thompson, John Gawler, VI, 769; VIII, 207; X, 217

Thompson, John Sparrow, VII, 576, 577, 875; VIII, 193, 656; IX, 186, 270, **785–87**; XII, 237, 1039

Thompson, Sir John Sparrow David, IX, 787; XI, 237, 460, 573, 620, 948; XII, 8, 28, 181, 246, 266, 340, 411, 438, 467, 582, 583, 584, 585, 607, 609, 610, 611, 612, 707, 765, 860, 941, 953, 1010, 1011, **1039–48**, 1059, 1120

Thompson, John Thomas Connolly, XII, 1044

Thompson, Joseph (brother of Sir JOHN SPARROW DAVID), XII, 1039

Thompson, Joseph (son of Sir JOHN SPARROW DAVID), XII, 1044

Thompson, Joseph (uncle of Sir JOHN SPARROW DAVID), IX, 786

Thompson, Joseph, I, 232, 281, 607, **642**, 666

Thompson, Joshua Spencer, X, **678–79**

Thompson, Lewis, X, 558

Thompson, Maggie, X, 234

Thompson, Margaret (O'Grady), VII, 659

Thompson, Mary. *See* Mackenzie

Thompson, Mary. *See* Sparrow

Thompson, Mary. *See* Toler

Thompson, Mary, V, 673; VI, 611, **770–72**

Thompson, Mary Aloysia (Wragge), XII, 1044

Thompson, Mary Helena (MacGregor), XII, 1044, 1047

Thompson, Mary S. *See* Thomson

Thompson, Rebecca. *See* Boyce

Thompson, Rebecca (mother of WILLIAM), VIII, 884

Thompson, Rebecca Agatha. *See* Armour

Thompson, Samuel (merchant), VI, 4

Thompson, Samuel (son of DAVID, 1770–1857), VIII, 883

Thompson, Samuel, VII, 261, 320; VIII, 401, 790, 804; IX, 77, 576, 607; X, 80, 119, 120, 172, 554; XI, 778, **877–78**, 880; XII, 1044, 1047

Thompson, Thomas (alderman), IX, 788

Thompson, Thomas (father of THOMAS), IX, 787

Thompson, Thomas (son of THOMAS), IX, 788

Thompson, Thomas, IX, **787–88**

Thompson*, Thomas Phillips (1843–1933), XII, 500, 865, 866

Thompson, Toler, VII, **854–55**

Thompson, Toussaint, X, 422

Thompson, William (brother of Sir JOHN SPARROW DAVID), XII, 1039

Thompson, William (father of SAMUEL), XI, 877

Thompson, William (office holder), IX, 601

Thompson, William (officer), IV, 320, 549; V, 99, 147

Thompson, William, VIII, **884–85**

Thompson, William Alexander, VI, 769

Thomson. *See also* Scrope

Thomson, Alexander (businessman), X, 721

Thomson, Alexander (father of MARY), VI, 770

Thomson*, Andrew (1830–1907), XI, 379, 774; XII, 280

Thomson, Andrew Henry, VII, 855

Thomson, Archibald, IV, 494; VI, 772; IX, 788

Thomson, Catherine. *See* McDonell

Thomson, Catherine. *See* McKay

Thomson, Charles Edward Poulett, 1st Baron Sydenham, VII, 31, 32, 34, 43, 62, 98, 144, 158, 184, 231, 308, 354, 364, 371, 394, 423, 440, 441, 460, 551, 580, 604, 608, 638, 703, 717, 732, 799, **855–62**, 880, 894, 914; VIII, xxv, xxviii, xxxii, 11, 29, 30, 48, 49, 50, 101, 125, 164, 255, 261, 303, 379, 383, 416, 424, 445, 502, 513, 521, 523, 535, 619, 640, 709, 733, 745, 764, 788, 798, 839, 840, 845, 848, 927, 935; IX, 5, 55, 101, 143, 146, 190, 201, 202, 238, 257, 259, 301, 370, 371, 372, 416, 442, 444, 445, 523, 524, 541, 555, 575, 618, 622, 644, 650, 676, 681, 697, 699, 700, 726, 741, 744, 747, 761, 775, 795, 796, 805, 818, 825, 837; X, 35, 125, 130, 131, 132, 219, 220, 254, 255, 257, 262, 263, 325, 326, 358, 364, 384, 403, 521, 527, 583, 619, 625, 655; XI, 35, 41, 118, 127, 155, 238, 281, 408, 713, 733, 787, 788, 945; XII, 89

Thomson, Charlotte. *See* Jacob

Thomson, Daniel Edmund, XI, 576

Thomson, Edward William, VI, 773; IX, 501, **788–89**; X, 290; XI, 939

Thomson*, Edward William (1849–1924), XII, 515, 516, 517

Thomson, Eleanor (Aylen), IX, 13

Thomson, Eliza (Bell), VIII, 72

Thomson, Elizabeth. *See* McKay

Thomson, Elizabeth. *See* Ruttan

Thomson, Elizabeth. *See* Spafford

Thomson, George (lawyer), X, 679

Thomson, George (shipbuilder), X, 718

Thomson, Heriot Frances (Nicolls), X, 547

Thomson, Houstoun (Cochran), VII, 190

Thomson, Hugh Christopher, VI, 57, 164, 470, 623, **772–74**; VII, 229, 559, 846; IX, 38, 551, 740; XII, 731

Thomson, J., IV, 295

Thomson, James (editor), VIII, 356

Thomson, James (father of JOHN), XI, 878

Thomson, James (merchant), XII, 21

Thomson, James (poet), IV, 491, 554; VI, 123

Thomson, Jane (Fyfe), X, 295

Thomson, Jean (Galt), VII, 335

Thomson, John (artist), VI, 168

Thomson, John (brother-in-law of Peter AYLEN), IX, 13, 734

Thomson, John (businessman), XI, 379

Thomson, John (father of John, businessman), XI, 379

Thomson, John, VII, 5, 891; XI, **878–79**
Thomson, John Poulett, VII, 855
Thomson, Johnson, X, 524
Thomson, Mary. *See* Ketchum
Thomson, Mary Ann. *See* Abrams
Thomson, Mary Hume (Mountain), IX, 579, 581
Thomson, Mary S. (Thompson), XI, 877
Thomson, Nellie (Easton), VI, 231
Thomson, Samuel, XI, 260
Thomson, Samuel Robert, X, **679–80**; XI, 888; XII, 354, 426
Thomson, Sarah Maria. *See* Terry
Thomson, Sarah Maria (Fisher), X, 290
Thomson, Selina. *See* Lee
Thomson, Skeffington, X, 679
Thomson, Thomas, VIII, 404, 405; IX, 665
Thomson, William (brother-in-law of Peter AYLEN), IX, 13, 734
Thomson, William (father-in-law of Andrew William COCHRAN), VII, 190
Thomson, William (shipowner), XII, 785
Thomson, William Alexander, X, **680–81**; XI, 129, 907
Thorbjörn, I, 612
Thorburn, Alexander Gillan, XII, **1048–49**
Thorburn, David, VII, 497, 917; VIII, 162, 208
Thorburn, Elizabeth. *See* Davis
Thorburn*, Sir Robert (1836–1906), XI, 108, 376; XII, 311, 380, 482, 754, 755, 770, 956
Thorfinnr *karlsefni* Thordarson, I, 5, 448, 449, 612, **642–43**
Thorfinnsson. *See* Snorri
Thorgerdr, I, 103
Thorn, Helena. *See* Van Slyck
Thorn, Jonathan, V, 526, 533, 534, **813–14**; VIII, 766; IX, 279
Thorn, Nancy (Westbrook), VI, 808
Thorn, Samuel, V, 813
Thornbarrow, Elizabeth (Coventry), IX, 163
Thorne, Anna Maria. *See* Wilcocks
Thorne, Benjamin, VII, 862
Thorne, Benjamin, VII, 635, 712, **862–64**
Thorne, Heneritta (mother of BENJAMIN), VII, 862
Thorne, James, X, 511
Thorne, Robert (d. 1519), I, 302, **643–44**
Thorne, Robert (1492–1532), I, 21, 148, 302, **643–44**
Thorne, William (brother of BENJAMIN), VII, 862
Thorne, William (forebear of Jonathan THORN), V, 813
Thorne, William (shipowner), I, 302
Thornewell, Frances (Hewett), XII, 429
Thornton, Mr (merchant), XII, 296
Thornton, Ann. *See* Cuthbert
Thornton, Sir Edward, X, 102; XI, 255, 769
Thornton, Joshua, IV, 487
Thornton, Patrick, VIII, 99
Thorold, William James, XII, 949
Thorp, Ann Eliza (Buell), X, 110
Thorp, Bonna. *See* Debrisay
Thorp, John, XII, 361
Thorp, Robert T., VII, 864
Thorpe, Margaret (Cox), VIII, 175
Thorpe, Margaret Jane (Murchie), XII, 773, 774
Thorpe, Robert, V, 18, 65, 171, 365, 366, 405, 441, 442, 443, 453, 643, 734, 782, 810, 842, 845, 855, 856, 857, 858, 860; VI, 4, 5, 57, 79, 114, 154, 160, 215, 452, 543,

609, 610, 656, 698, 804, 805; VII, 36, 38, 41, 163, 251, 286, 438, 439, 638, 794, **864–65**, 919, 929; VIII, 4, 194, 338, 339, 340, 341, 387; IX, 498; X, 705
Thorsteinn, I, 448, 449, 612, 642
Thorvaldr, I, 449, 612, 643
Thorvaldr Asvaldsson, I, 676
Thorvaldsen, Bertel, VII, 100
Thouin, Mathilde (Benoît), XII, 94
Thoureault. *See* Toureault
Thowaghwenkarakwen. *See* Tehowagherengaraghkwen
Thrale, Hester Lynch. *See* Salusbury
Three Bulls. *See* No-okska-stumik
Three Suns. *See* No-okskatos
Thresher, Eliza Wilson. *See* Brooks
Thresher, George Godsell, VIII, **885–87**
Thresher, Rachel (mother of GEORGE GODSELL), VIII, 886
Thresher, Thomas, VIII, 886
Throckmorton, Frances (Starr), XI, 846
Thu a higon. *See* Ruehegan
Thubières de Levy de Queylus, Gabriel, I, 46, 56, 57, 78, 126, 220, 310, 486, 552, 559, 599, 612, **644–49**, 662; II, 45, 191, 192, 194, 247, 360, 361, 364, 370, 637; V, 658
Thunay, *dit* Dufresne, Catherine (Demers Monfort; Houdin), III, 295, 296
Thunay, *dit* Dufresne, Madeleine (Pelletier; Mallet), III, 423
Thuot, Marie-Michel-Archange, XI, 95
Thuot Duval, Pierre, III, 581
Thurburn, Margaret (Johnston), VI, 354
Thurgar, Anna. *See* Paddock
Thurgar, John Venner, X, 681
Thurgar, John Venner, X, **681**
Thurlow, Edward, 1st Baron Thurlow, IV, xlvi; V, 145
Thurman, Ann Elizabeth (Jameson), XII, 468
Thurseau, Monsieur (merchant), VIII, 286
Thurston, David, XI, **879–80**
Thurston, John, VII, 317
Thurston, Samuel R., VIII, 580
Thury, Louis-Pierre, I, 309, 577, **649**; II, 238, 630; III, 476
Thwing, Lydia (Scott), V, 743
Thyerry, Charlotte (Chassin), III, 115
Thynne. *See also* Carteret
Thynne, Lady Louisa (Lascelles, Countess of Harewood), IX, 457
Tiahogwando. *See* Teyohaqueande
Tiarks, Auguste Antoinette Sophie. *See* Toel
Tiarks, Christine Dorothea. *See* Ehrentraut
Tiarks, Johann Gerhard, VII, 865
Tiarks, Johann Ludwig, VII, 658, **865–67**
Tibaudeau. *See also* Thibodeau
Tibaudeau, Agnès (Brossard), II, 105
Tibaudeau, Jeanne. *See* Territot
Tibaudeau, Jeanne (Goutin), II, 205, 257, 630; III, 264
Tibaudeau, Marguerite (Brossard), II, 105
Tibaudeau, Pierre, II, 71, 105, 257, 410, **629–30**, 654
Tibault. *See* Thibault
Tibbetts, Benjamin Franklin, VIII, 951; IX, 123; XII, 377
Tibbits, James, VIII, 559; IX, 123, 598; XI, 208
Tibierge, Monsieur, II, **630**
Tibierge, Angélique, named de Sainte-Agnès, III, 625
Tibierge, Hippolyte, III, 625
Tibierge, Marie-Catherine, named de Saint-Joachim, III, **625–26**

Tibierge, Renée. *See* Hervé
Tiblemont, Nicolas, I, 267
Tice, Gilbert, V, 805
Tichborne, Elizabeth Anne (Dormer, Lady Dormer), IX, 215
Tickell, Zipporah (Roebuck; Simpson), X, 626, 655
Tidmarsh, James, VI, 242
Tidmarsh, Margaret Elizabeth (Etter), VI, 242
Tieck, Johann Ludwig, VIII, 650
Tiedemann, Hermann Otto, XII, **1049–50**
Tiedemann, Mary. *See* Bissett
Tielen, Jean, XII, 816, **1050–51**
Tierney, Mrs Mary Adelaide, VII, 682
Tiffany, Elizabeth. *See* Ralston
Tiffany, Frances. *See* Davis
Tiffany, George, VII, 58
Tiffany, George Sylvester, VIII, 708
Tiffany, Gideon, V, 814; VIII, 887
Tiffany, Gideon, V, 14, 814, 815; VIII, **887–88**
Tiffany, Oliver, V, 639, 814; VIII, 888
Tiffany, Ruth. *See* Tomlinson
Tiffany, Sarah. *See* Dean
Tiffany, Silvester, V, 639, 640, **814–16**; VI, 177, 746; VIII, 887
Tigoransera. *See* Teiorhéñhsere˞
Tilden, Bryant, VII, 845
Tilden, John H., XI, 377
Tiley, Mary (Fuller), XII, 343
Till, Mary Barbra (Fisher), VII, 288
Tilley, Alice Starr, Lady Tilley. *See* Chipman
Tilley, Amelia Jane (Young), X, 726
Tilley, Julia Ann. *See* Hanford
Tilley, Sir Samuel Leonard, VIII, 157, 810; IX, 123, 392, 410, 411, 414, 515, 516, 714; X, 100, 101, 160, 191, 286, 287, 288, 289, 340, 494, 543, 621, 666, 713, 719; XI, 171, 224, 296, 298, 372, 373, 374, 375, 573, 578, 579, 688, 689, 700, 828, 829, 831, 832, 888, 897; XII, 25, 28, 116, 122, 148, 166, 226, 313, 353, 419, 429, 453, 536, 537, 561, 566, 567, 598, 599, 602, 607, 610, 612, 623, 633, 636, 658, 741, 743, 897, 1042, 1043, **1051–60**, 1096, 1097, 1103, 1104, 1105, 1106
Tilley, Susan Ann. *See* Peters
Tilley, Thomas Morgan, XII, 1051
Tilley, William Harrison, XII, 1057
Tilliard, Henry, I, 369
Tilloch (Tulloch), Alexander, XII, 348
Tilloch, Elizabeth (Galt), VII, 335, 336, 339; XII, 348
Tillson*, Edwin D. (1825–1902), IX, 790
Tillson, George, VI, 407; IX, **789–90**; XI, 898
Tillson, George Barker, IX, 790
Tillson, Harvey, IX, 790
Tillson, Hopestill. *See* Shaw
Tillson, Mary Ann. *See* Van Norman
Tillson, Nancy. *See* Barker
Tillson, Stephen, IX, 789
Tilly. *See* La Mothe-Tilly; Legardeur
Tilstone, William Henry, VIII, 268; IX, 462
Tilton, Barnabas, IX, 410
Tilton, John, XII, 979
Timineur (Kemeneur), Marie-Catherine (Mercier), XII, 719
Timm, Sarah H., XII, 448
Timothée, Captain, I, 292
Timpany, A. V., X, 215

Timpany, Mrs A. V., X, 215
Tims, John Edward, VIII, 642; XI, 864
Tims, John William, XII, 779
Tin, Antoinette (Chaudillon), II, 140
Tindal, John, X, 380
Ting. *See* Tyng
Tingley, Stephen, XI, 51
Tinker, Sarah (Bronson), XI, 112
Tinkham, Joseph, VI, 813
Tinling, William, IV, 684; VI, 146
Tinnewabano (Tinpot), V, 184, 185
Tinon-Desroches, Ignace, VI, 85
Tinsley, Joseph, XII, 935
Tinsley, William, VII, 159
Tionnotoguen. *See* Togouiroui
Tipperary, Earl of. *See* George William Frederick Charles
Tippett (Tippetts), Martha (DeLancey), V, 239
Tipping, William, V, 586
Tipton, John, I, 85
Tipu Sahib, Sultan of Mysore, VI, 797; VII, 428
Tirel. *See* Pichon
Tisdale, David, XII, 941
Tisnet. *See* Dutisné
Tison, Jean-Baptiste, IV, 533
Tison, Marie-Anne (Mesplet), IV, 533
Tisquantum, I, 262, **649–50**
Tissable, Mary Emily (Holland), VII, 413
Tissenay. *See* Dutisné
Tisserant de Moncharvaux, François, III, 626
Tisserant de Moncharvaux, Jean-Baptiste, III, 626
Tisserant de Moncharvaux, Jean-Baptiste-François, III, **626–27**
Tisserant de Moncharvaux, Marie-Agnès. *See* Chassin
Tisserant de Moncharvaux, Marie-Louise. *See* Vienne
Tisserant de Moncharvaux, Marie-Thérèse. *See* L'Archevêque
Tissot, Jean, XI, 310; XII, 1005
Titailt. *See* Blarye
Titameg (wife of John Favell), V, 534
Titian. *See* Vecellio
Titus, Ama (Coy), VII, 215; VIII, 176
Titus, Phebe (Phoebe) (Willson), IX, 841
Tiwatacout. *See* Tonatakout
Tiyanoga. *See* Theyanoguin
Tiyerhasere. *See* Teiorhéñhsere˞
Tkobeitch. *See* Malie
Tlelh, IX, 514
Tlupananulg, VI, 743
Tobacco's Son, V, 343
Tobin, Anne (Young), XI, 944
Tobin, Catherine. *See* Walsh
Tobin, Catherine Hannah. *See* Murphy
Tobin, Eleanor. *See* Lanigan
Tobin, Eliza (Sawyer), VII, 867
Tobin, Emily Cecilia. *See* Bullen
Tobin, James, VII, **867–68**; X, 189; XI, 880; XII, 436
Tobin, James William, VII, 633, 867; VIII, 223; IX, 29, 583, 604; X, 590; XI, 432, **880–81**
Tobin, John, XII, 1062, 1067
Tobin, John, IX, **790–91**
Tobin, Sir John, VII, 740
Tobin, John Michael, VIII, 703; X, 521
Tobin, Michael (grandfather), VII, 867

Tobin, Michael (uncle), VII, 867; XI, 944
Tobin, Michael, VII, 867; VIII, 782; IX, 174; XI, 947
Tobin, Sarah (Ready), VII, 740
Tobin, Stephen, XI, 710
Toby, Maurice, I, 148, 149
Tocque, Ann. *See* Howell
Tocque, Annie S. W., XII, 1062
Tocque, Eliza Touzou. *See* Chauncey
Tocque, Philip, XII, 1060
Tocque, Philip, VII, 274; VIII, 76; XI, 363; XII, **1060–62**
Tocqueville. *See* Clérel
Tod, Ann (Burns), VI, 93
Tod, Charlotte, V, 818
Tod, Eliza. *See* Waugh
Tod, Emmeline (Newton), XI, 882
Tod, James, XI, 882
Tod, James, V, 116, 117, 182, 270, 278, 329, 459, 493, 667, **816–18**; VI, 336, 531
Tod, John, VII, 568; VIII, 422, 836; IX, 337, 473, 625, 853, 854; X, 196, 239, 241, 242, 248, 495; XI, **881–83**; XII, 61, 114
Tod, Sophia. *See* Lolo
Todd, Albert Edward, XII, 1063
Todd, Alice. *See* Clow
Todd, Alpheus, VI, 45; IX, 5; XI, **883–85**
Todd, Andrew, V, 820; VI, 357
Todd, Anna (Halkett), VIII, 351
Todd, Anne. *See* Fox
Todd, Arthur Hamlyn, XI, 884, 885
Todd, Charles Fox, XII, 1063
Todd, Charlotte (Henry), VIII, 391
Todd, Clarissa. *See* Hill
Todd, Elizabeth. *See* Dennett
Todd, Elizabeth (Patterson), IV, 606
Todd, Freeman H., X, 682
Todd, George, VIII, 868
Todd, Hannah. *See* Worthley
Todd, Henry Cooke, XI, 883
Todd, Isaac, IV, 184, 277, 703; V, 14, 38, 90, 168, 180, 287, 298, 299, 319, 332, 333, 371, 402, 404, 440, 492, 494, 495, 496, 511, 527, 528, 529, 561, 564, 580, 603, 681, 718, 722, **818–22**; VI, 81, 204, 318, 357, 531, 543, 600, 642, 822; VII, 251, 524, 768, 825; VIII, xxvi
Todd, Isabella. *See* Hunter
Todd, Jacob Hunter, XII, **1062–64**
Todd, John (father of Jacob Hunter), XII, 1062
Todd, John (father of Robert Clow), IX, 791
Todd, Mary (Ferrier), XI, 315
Todd, Mary Anne. *See* Boyle
Todd, Mary Jane (Haney; wife of William, 1803–73), X, 681
Todd, Rachel (Archibald; McKeen), VII, 21
Todd, Robert Clow, IX, **791–92**; X, 306; XI, 309
Todd, Rosanna. *See* Wigley
Todd, Sarah Anne. *See* St John
Todd, Sarah Holmes (Davie), XII, 1063
Todd, Valent Ellison, IX, 792
Todd, William, X, 681
Todd, William, VIII, 811, **888–90**
Todd, William, X, **681–82**; XII, 377
Todevin, Marie (Brehaut), V, 107
Todington, Eliza (Osborn), X, 561
Toel, Auguste Antoinette Sophie (Tiarks), VII, 865

Tofflemire. *See* Tufflemier
Togouiroui (Togoniron), I, 322, **650–51**; II, 107
Tohaswuchdoniunty. *See* Kaghswaghtaniunt
Tohonsiowanne. *See* Ohonsiowanne
Tokarihogea. *See* Tekarihogen
Tokhrahenehiaron, I, 370, 403
Toldervy, J. B., XI, 447, 448
Toler, John, 1st Earl of Norbury, VII, 855
Toler, John George, VII, 868
Toler, Joseph, VII, **868**
Toler, Mary (Grace; Thompson), VII, 854, 855
Tolfrey, Frederic, V, 490
Tollendal, Baron de. *See* Lally
Tollet (Taudet), Marie (Lanoullier), III, 352
Tolmie, Alexander, XI, 885
Tolmie, Jane. *See* Work
Tolmie, Marjory. *See* Fraser
Tolmie*, Simon Fraser (1867–1937), XI, 885, 887
Tolmie, William Fraser, VII, 808; VIII, 97, 590, 836; IX, 530, 853; X, 242, 486, 535; XI, 882, **885–88**
Tom, V, 816
Toma, Joseph. *See* Saint-Aubin, Joseph-Thomas
Toma, Pierre. *See* Tomah, Pierre, known as Governor Tomah
Tomah, Captain, VI, 678
Tomah, Governor. *See* Tomah, Pierre
Tomah, Francis, VI, 774; VII, **868–69**
Tomah, Joseph. *See also* Saint-Aubin, Joseph-Thomas
Tomah, Joseph, VI, 678
Tomah, Pierre, VI, 774
Tomah (Tomas), Pierre, IV, 13, 30, 196, 389, 693, **735–36**; V, 17; VI, 678, 774
Tomah, Pierre, known as Governor Tomah, VI, **774–75**
Tombelles. *See* Marquette
Tombyll, Rasmus, XI, 500
Tomer. *See* Tomah
Tomer, Joseph. *See* Saint-Aubin, Joseph-Thomas
Tomison, William, IV, 47, 366, 518, 684, 726, 727, 742, 743, 760; V, 194, 195, 450, 451, 500, 531, 566, 656; VI, 251, 704, **775–77**; VIII, 90, 878, 879
Tom June, VI, 70
Tomkins, Frederick, XII, 215
Tomlin, Marie (Shepard; Burton), IX, 6
Tomline. *See* Pretyman
Tomlinson, Ruth (Tiffany), VIII, 887
Tomma. *See* Tomah
Tomma, Joseph. *See* Saint-Aubin, Joseph-Thomas
Tompson, Georgiana (Manners-Sutton, Viscountess Canterbury), X, 494
Tonatakout, II, xxxix, 20, 323, 502, **631**; III, xl
Tonge, Bonnell, VI, 782
Tonge, Elizabeth. *See* Bonnell
Tonge, Grizelda Elizabeth Cottnam, VI, **777–78**, 782; VII, 576
Tonge, Martha Grace. *See* Cottnam
Tonge, Richard Peter, V, 334
Tonge, William Cottnam, IV, 737; V, 410, 612, 693, 694, 850, 851; VI, 113, 118, 268, 313, 333, 777, **778–83**, 800; VII, 21, 589, 910; VIII, 754, 755
Tonge, Winckworth, IV, 93, 451, **736–38**; V, 430, 850; VI, 89, 90, 778
Tonkin, Elizabeth (Shortland), XI, 820
Tonnancour. *See also* Godefroy

Tonnancour, Josette (Chartier de Lotbinière), VI, 132
Tonnetuit. *See* Chauvin
Tonsahoten, I, 321, **651**; II, 107
Tonty, Alphonse, II, 219, 632; III, 627
Tonty, Alphonse (de), Baron de Paludy, I, 416, 547; II, 48,
    81, 300, 306, 353, 355, 435, 508, **631–33**, 645; III, 45,
    96, 105, 288, 289, 485, 493, 627; IV, 634
Tonty, Claude-Joseph, III, 627
Tonty, Henri (de), I, 79, 114, 175, 176, 177, 178, 444; II,
    xxxii, 49, 76, 110, 124, 169, 170, 171, 173, 181, 306,
    320, 397, 435, 443, 450, 488, 508, 589, 624, 631,
    **633–36**, 672; III, 65, 380, 469
Tonty, Isabelle de. *See* Liette
Tonty, Laurent (Lorenzo) de, Baron de Paludy, II, 631, 633
Tonty, Marie-Anne. *See* La Marque
Tonty, Marie-Anne. *See* Picoté de Belestre
Tonty, Marie-Françoise, II, 632
Tonty, Marie-Josette (Damours de Louvières), II, 633
Tonty, Pierre-Antoine, II, 632; III, 627
Tonty, Thérèse (Desjordy), II, 633
Tonty de Liette, Charles-Henri-Joseph de, II, 436, 632; III,
    **627**
Tonty de Liette, Louise de. *See* Renaud Dubuisson
Tonty de Liette, Marie-Madeleine de. *See* Sabourin
Tony, Magdalen (Meuse), VII, 610
Toof, Maria (Marie) Elise (Lauder), XI, 497
Tooker, Joseph, VI, 169
Tooker, Mary (wife of Joseph), VI, 169
Tookolito (Hannah), VII, 271; X, 327, 328
To-oo-troon-too-ra. *See* Sou-neh-hoo-way
Toosey, James, IV, 738
Toosey, John, IV, 738
Toosey, Philip, IV, **738–39**; V, 57, 182, 601, 613, 614; VI,
    523
Toosey, Sarah. *See* Denton
Tootac (Palliser), IV, 536, 537
Topean, XII, 499
Topley*, William James (1845–1930), XII, 789
Topp, Alexander, X, **682–83**; XII, 617
Topp, Jane. *See* Mortimer
Topping, Thomas, VI, 17
Torakaron. *See* Tarbell, Zachariah
Torcapel, Monsieur (engraver), XI, 515
Torcapel, Jean, I, 91
Tordesillas. *See* Herrera
Torranbeg. *See* McLean
Torrance, Amy Gordon (Galt, Lady Galt), XII, 355
Torrance, Andrew, VIII, 633
Torrance, Daniel, IX, 793
Torrance, David, XI, 211
Torrance, David, VIII, 559; IX, 792, 793; X, 657, **683–85**,
    717, 722; XI, 211, 316, 923
Torrance, Edward Fraser, X, 684
Torrance, Elizabeth. *See* Fisher
Torrance, Elizabeth Kissock (mother of DAVID), X, 683
Torrance, Elliott (Galt), XII, 355
Torrance, Frederick William, IX, 793; XI, 206, 609
Torrance, George William, X, 683; XI, 211
Torrance, Isabella. *See* Gibb
Torrance, Isabella (Hamilton), VIII, 357
Torrance, Isabella (Stephenson), VII, 824
Torrance, James (uncle), IX, 792; X, 683
Torrance, James, IX, 792

Torrance, Jane (Torrance), X, 683
Torrance, John, X, 683; XI, 211, 316
Torrance, John, V, 320; VI, 477, 478; VII, 619; VIII, 322,
    630; IX, 208, 430, **792–94**; X, 394, 591, 683, 684, 722;
    XI, 211, 316, 850, 923; XII, 355, 683, 809
Torrance, Margaret Watson. *See* Ferrier
Torrance, Marion (Gibb), VIII, 322
Torrance, Robert Lindsay, XII, 39
Torrance, Thomas (father), IX, 792; X, 683, 684
Torrance, Thomas, VI, 477; VII, 619; VIII, 322; IX, 792,
    793; X, 440, 518, 683, 684, 722
Torrance, William, VIII, 322
Torren. *See* McLean
Torrence, Elizabeth (King), XII, 491
Torrens, Mary Jane (Light), XII, 561
Torrie, William S., XII, 479
Torriehouse. *See* Erskine
Torrington, Viscount. *See* Byng
Torrington, Viscountess. *See* Masters
Torrington*, Frederic Herbert (1837–1917), X, 173, 371;
    XII, 708
Torry, Alvin, VI, 758; VIII, 440, 620; XI, 473
Tosi, Pascal, XI, 806
Totiri (Totihri), I, 42, 523, **651–52**
Totocatapik, VII, 271
To-to-win (Helen) (wife of Robert DICKSON), VI, 209
Totten, Isabella Clarke (Huyghue), XII, 462
Totten, Mary (Winniett), VII, 917
Tottenham, Synge, IV, 388
Touaniscou, I, 69
Touchet, Geneviève. *See* Gagnier
Touchet, Simon, III, 377
Touchet, Thomas, II, 90
Tough, Elizabeth (Hunter), VII, 427
Tough, Jasper, VIII, 321; IX, 316
Toulouse, Comte de. *See* Bourbon
Toupin, François, VI, 666
Toupin, Joseph, XII, 267
Toupin, Louise-Renée (Barbel), II, 42
Toupin, Marguerite. *See* Boucher
Toupin, Marie-Anne (Bédard), V, 60
Toupin, Toussaint, I, 404; II, 82
Toupin, *dit* Dussault, Françoise. *See* Delisle
Tour, Anne de (Pastour de Costebelle), II, 389, 511
Tour, Catherine de. *See* Le Baudy
Tour, Germain de, II, 389, 511
Tour, Marie-Anne de (Allard de Sainte-Marie), II, 15; IV,
    14
Tourangeau. *See also* Guillet
Tourangeau, Adolphe, XII, **1064–65**, 1072
Tourangeau, Victoire-Adélaïde. *See* Jourdain
Tourblanche. *See* Martinet de Fonblanche
Toureault (Thoureault), Françoise (Archambault), I, 427;
    X, 15
Tournefort. *See* Pitton
Tourneuve. *See* Loubinois
Tournois, Jean-Baptiste, III, 329, 361, 428, 481, 611,
    **627–28**; IV, 36; V, 40
Tourond, Baptiste, X, 439
Tourville. *See also* Duteau
Tourville, Louis, XI, 808, 809
Tousley, Sikes, VI, 809
Toussaint, François-Xavier, VIII, 302; XII, **1065–67**

Toussaint, Jeanne (Carpentier), II, 528
Toussaint, Justine. *See* Fortier
Toussaint, Marguerite. *See* Noël
Toussaint, Pierre, XII, 1065
Toussiqui. *See* Tussichi
Touvrey, Philippe, VII, 334, 411; X, 546
Towatogowash. *See* Nims, Abigail
Tower, Jessie (Fergusson), IX, 251
Towne, Benjamin, V, 438
Towne, Francis, VI, 257
Towner, Enoch, V, 832, 833
Townley, Adam, VII, 635; IX, 205; X, 208
Townley, Elizabeth. *See* Ruttan
Townley, Mary (Pinhey), VIII, 706
Townsend, Elizabeth. *See* Larcum
Townsend, Florence (Allen), known as Florence Grosvenor, XII, 1067
Townsend, Gregory, VI, 89, 90
Townsend, Harry, XII, 1067
Townsend, Isaac, III, **628–29**
Townsend, Sir Isaac, III, 628
Townsend, John, XII, 1067
Townsend, John, XII, **1067–68**
Townsend, Lucinda, X, 685
Townsend, Mary (mother of JOHN), XII, 1067
Townsend, Micah, VI, 270
Townsend, Micajah, VII, 212
Townsend, Sarah. *See* Gardner
Townsend, Sarah. *See* Mitchell
Townsend, William, X, 685
Townsend, William H., X, **685**; XII, 50
Townshend, Anne, Viscountess and Marchioness Townshend. *See* Montgomery
Townshend, Audrey, Viscountess Townshend. *See* Harrison
Townshend, Cecil Wray, VIII, 741
Townshend, Charles, IV, 84, 147, 571
Townshend, Charles, 2nd Viscount Townshend, IV, 168
Townshend, Charles, 3rd Viscount Townshend, III, 669; V, 822
Townshend*, Sir Charles James (1844–1924), VIII, 357, 756; X, 71
Townshend, Sir Charles Vere Ferrers, V, 824
Townshend, Charlotte, Viscountess Townshend. *See* Compton
Townshend, Lady Charlotte Barbara (Bisshopp), V, 82
Townshend, Flora. *See* Stewart
Townshend, George, 4th Viscount and 1st Marquess Townshend, III, xxvi, 172, 365, 466, 669, 670, 672, 674; IV, 109, 147, 308, 541, 570, 608, 609, 610, 652, 700, 701; V, 82, 141, 310, 311, 347, 348, 477, **822–25**; VI, 133, 788
Townshend, Henry Dives, IX, 269
Townshend, Lord James Nugent Boyle Bernardo, IX, 155, 156, 157, 375, 376
Townshend, Mary (Cornwallis), IV, 168
Townshend, Olivia Edith Dean (Robinson, Lady Robinson), XII, 910
Townshend, Richard, V, 825
Townshend, Thomas, 1st Viscount Sydney, IV, 6, 230, 293, 367, 371, 485, 687, 707; V, 145, 148, 149, 150, 151, 156, 157, 158, 241, 309, 585, 807, 819, 863, 897, 898, 899, 900; VI, 194, 195

Townshend, William, V, 27, 250, 262, 263, 310, 425, 516, 779, **825–26**; VI, 107, 108, 109, 163, 359, 567, 818; VII, 352, 407, 414; VIII, 36, 824, 954
Toyer, Ellen (Abbott), X, 3
Toyer, Jane (Judah), X, 3
Toyer, Mary, X, 3
Tracey, Mrs. *See* Mainfold
Tracey, Ann (Wilson), VI, 783, 784; X, 715
Tracey, Daniel, VI, **783–84**, 802; VII, 26, 226, 482, 512, 751, 771, 781, 789; VIII, 260, 433, 781, 870, 918, 919; IX, 441, 554, 560; X, 526, 581, 715; XI, 117
Tracey, Denis, VI, 783
Tracey, John, VI, 783, 784
Tracey, Mary, XII, 157
Tracy. *See* Prouville
Tracy, Marquise de. *See* Fouilleuse
Trahan, Charles (grandfather), V, 826
Trahan, Charles, V, 827
Trahan, Édouard, XII, 342
Trahan, Grégoire, known as Gregory Strahan, V, **826–27**
Trahan, Guillaume, II, 94
Trahan, Jeanne (Bourgeois), II, 94
Trahan, Joseph, V, 827
Trahan, Madeleine, V, 826
Trahan, Marguerite. *See* Bourque
Trahan, Marie-Anne. *See* Landry
Trahan, Mary, V, 827
Trahan, Paul, V, 827
Trahan, Sophie (Bourassa), XII, 120
Traill, Anne Traill Fotheringhame (Atwood), XII, 999
Traill, Catharine Parr. *See* Strickland
Traill, Katharine Agnes Strickland, XI, 212; XII, 998
Traill, Katharine Parr, XII, 998
Traill, Thomas, XII, 524, 996, 997, 998
Traill, Walter John Strickland, XII, 999
Traill, William Edward, XII, 999
Trall, Russell Thacher, XII, 925, 927
Tranchant, Antoine, III, 398
Tranchant, Élisabeth. *See* Contant
Tranchemontagne, Joseph-Guillaume, XI, 809
Tranclar. *See* Trustler
Tranquille, VII, 79
Traquair, Ramsay, III, 118, 346
Travers*, Mary, known as La Bolduc (Bolduc) (1894–1941), IX, 563, 564
Traversy, Captain de, I, 40, 308
Travis, Esther (Barnard), III, 25
Travis, Jeremiah, XI, 578
Travis*, Jeremiah (d. 1911), XII, 19, 675, 1098
Treadwell. *See also* Tredwell
Treadwell, Charles Platt, VIII, 890
Treble, Lillian Frances. *See* Massey
Tredwell, Ann. *See* Hazard
Tredwell, Margaret. *See* Platt
Tredwell, Nathaniel Hazard, VIII, 688, **890–91**
Tredwell, Thomas, VIII, 890
Tree, Sir Herbert Beerbohm, XII, 669
Trefflé, *dit* Rottot, Agathe (Imbert), III, 299
Trefflé, *dit* Rottot, Élisabeth (Dunière), V, 283; VII, 673
Trefflé, *dit* Rottot, François, III, 135, 596
Trefflé, *dit* Rottot, Madeleine (Schmid; Janson, *dit* Lapalme), III, 307

Trefflé, *dit* Rottot, Marie-Anne (Panet), V, 652, 654; VII, 672
Trefflé, *dit* Rottot, Marie-Jeanne. *See* Avisse
Trefflé, *dit* Rottot, Marie-Joseph (Woolsey), VIII, 952
Trefflé, *dit* Rottot, Pierre, III, 135, 348; VIII, 952
Trefry, Elizabeth (Churchill; Faulkner), X, 171
Tregent, A. E., XI, 764
Tregouaroti, I, 603
Trégu de Langon, Madeleine-Angélique (Verville), II, 648
Tréguron. *See* Quéré
Trelawny, Edward, III, 316
Trelford, Sarah (McClure), X, 455
Tremain, Abigail. *See* Stout
Tremain, Abigail (Hartshorne), VI, 312
Tremain, Benjamin, VI, 505, 546
Tremain, Eliza (Pyke), VIII, 726
Tremain, Isabella Phoebe (Palmer), XI, 668
Tremain, James, VIII, 891
Tremain, John (brother of RICHARD), VIII, 892
Tremain, John (merchant), VI, 538
Tremain, Jonathan, V, 511, 779, 780; VI, 113, 313, 535, 536, 538; VIII, 891
Tremain, Mary. *See* Boggs
Tremain, Richard, VIII, 300, **891–92**
Tremaine, Elizabeth White (Longworth), XI, 528
Trémais. *See* Pichot
Tremblay. *See also* Prévost
Tremblay, Adolphe-Louis, XI, 329
Tremblay, Alexis, X, 685
Tremblay, Carmelle (Thibeault), XI, 872
Tremblay, Charlotte (Dufour, *dit* Bona), VI, 224
Tremblay, Élisabeth (Dufour, *dit* Bona), VI, 224
Tremblay, François, VIII, 892
Tremblay, Henri-Jean, II, 79, 80, 109, 117, 134, 171, 207, 227, 341; III, 51, 52, 413, 470, 636, **683–85**
Tremblay, Josephte. *See* Duguay
Tremblay, Magdeleine. *See* Beauché, *dit* Morency
Tremblay, Marguerite (Moreau), X, 532
Tremblay, Marie (Valin), XII, 1071
Tremblay, Marie-Joseph (Boucher), V, 95
Tremblay, Mary Ellen. *See* Connolly
Tremblay, Montague, VI, 8
Tremblay, Pierre, VI, 546
Tremblay, Pierre-Alexis, X, 36, 602, **685–87**; XI, 115, 185, 192; XII, 521, 899
Tremblay, Rémi, XI, 490; XII, 1026
Tremblay, *dit* Picoté, Alexis, VIII, 893
Tremblay, *dit* Picoté, Alexis, VII, 569; VIII, 323, **892–94**; IX, 640; XII, 864
Tremblay, *dit* Picoté, Augustin, VIII, 894
Tremblay, *dit* Picoté, François, VIII, 893
Tremblay, *dit* Picoté, Isaïe, VIII, 893
Tremblay, *dit* Picoté, Modeste. *See* Bouliane
Tremblay, *dit* Picoté, Olive. *See* Gagné
Tremlett, Hannah. *See* Stapeldon
Tremlett, Robert, VI, 784
Tremlett, Thomas, VI, 784
Tremlett, Thomas, V, 127, 837; VI, 71, 298, 567, 710, **784–86**; VII, 152; VIII, 429, 824
Trench, Sir Robert, VIII, 42
Trent, Agnes. *See* Colquhoun
Trent, William, XII, 972
Trépanier, Léon, IX, 438

Trépanier, Marie-Anne (Montferrand, *dit* Favre), IX, 563
Tress, William, XI, 225
Tressol, Marguerite (Roubaud), IV, 685
Tressonville. *See* Chardon
Trestler, Miss (Dorion), X, 238
Trestler, Catherine (Hays), V, 828
Trestler, Henry-Daniel, V, 828
Trestler, Iphigénie (Dorion), V, 828; XII, 260
Trestler, Jean-Baptiste, V, 827, 828; VII, 105; IX, 210; XI, 58; XII, 260
Trestler, Jean-Joseph, V, **827–28**; VI, 385
Trestler, Josephte (Hays), IX, 213
Trestler, Marguerite. *See* Noël
Trestler, Marie-Anne-Joseph. *See* Curtius
Trestler, Marie-Josephte, V, 828
Trestler, Marie-Madeleine (Adhémar), V, 828
Trestler, Marie-Marguerite, V, 828
Trestler, Michel-Joseph, V, 828
Trevanion, Sir Nicholas, II, 152, 164, 564, **636–37**
Trevanion, Richard, II, 636
Trevannion, Sophia (Byron), IV, 121
Trevenen, James, IV, 413
Trevet, Françoise de (Benoist), IV, 54
Trevor, Frances Hornby (Barkley), IV, 498; VI, 36, 37
Trevor, Sir John, I, 144
Trevor, Richard, III, 275
Trewerghy. *See* Treworgie
Treworgie, Mrs. *See* Spencer
Treworgie, Catherine. *See* Shapleigh
Treworgie, James, I, 652
Treworgie, John, I, 652
Treworgie, John, I, 24, 406, **652–53**
Treytorrens, Marie-Madeleine de (Haldimand), IV, 793; V, 887
Triaud, Élizabeth. *See* Pagé
Triaud, Louis-Hubert, VII, **869–70**
Tribaut, *dit* Laffriquain, Louis, V, 727
Tribouillard, Catherine (Ramezay), II, 545
Tribouillard, Hilaire, II, 545
Trickett, Edward, XII, 408
Trigge, Arthur St Lawrence, X, 735
Trigge, Elizabeth Mary (Dickinson), XII, 257
Trigge, Thomas, VII, 166
Trigholon, Sarah (Abrams), VII, 4
Trimlett. *See* Tremlett
Trimmer, Sarah. *See* Kirby
Tripp, Charles Nelson, XI, 930
Tripp, Denson, XII, 1090
Tripp, Emma. *See* Johnson
Tripp, Henry, XI, 930
Trites, Jacob, XI, 90
Trites, John Starr, XII, 479
Trobriand, Baron de. *See* Keredern
Tröstler. *See also* Trestler
Tröstler, Henry, V, 827
Tröstler, Magdeleine. *See* Feitten
Trollope, Anthony, IX, 293; X, 44; XII, 344, 922
Trollope, Frances. *See* Milton
Tronjoly. *See* L'Ollivier
Tronquet, Guillaume, I, 557, 558; II, 82
Tronson, Louis, I, 80, 117, 134, 180, 244; II, 44, 124, 128, 175, 191, 194, 195, 196, 241, 245, 272, 326, 336, 467, 594, 638, 641; III, 542

Troop, Catherine. *See* Fellows
Troop, Charlotte Augusta (Longley), XI, 525
Troop*, Howard Douglas (d. 1912), XI, 133, 888, 889
Troop, Jacob V., XI, 888
Troop, Jacob Valentine, XI, **888–89**; XII, 1097
Troop, Jared Chipman, XI, 835
Troop, Sarah Ann (Harris), IX, 367; XII, 412
Troop, Tamar. *See* Bath
Troop, Valentine, XI, 888
Troop, William Henry, XI, 525
Trotain, François, II, 637
Trotain, Jeanne. *See* Gribond
Trotain, *dit* Saint-Seürin, François, II, **637**
Trotain, *dit* Saint-Seürin, Jeanne. *See* Hardy
Trotain, *dit* Saint-Seürin, Marie-Charlotte (Rouillard), II, 637
Trotter, Alexander, VI, 482
Trotter, Elizabeth. *See* Eadie
Trotter, James, XI, 864
Trotter*, Reginald George (1888–1951), X, 369
Trotter, Thomas, XI, 158; XII, 879
Trotter, Thomas, VII, 536; VIII, 769, **894–95**; XI, 398; XII, 230
Trottier, Dom, III, 161
Trottier, Catherine (Lefebvre, *dit* Laciseraye), II, 382
Trottier, Catherine, named Saint-François, III, 629
Trottier, Geneviève. *See* La Fond
Trottier, Jean-Baptiste, III, 629
Trottier, Jules, III, 629; X, 36
Trottier, Marguerite, named Saint-Joseph, III, 17, 574, 575, **629–30**
Trottier, Thérèse (Ducharme), V, 272
Trottier, *dit* Beaubien, Michel, II, 380
Trottier Desauniers, Catherine. *See* Charest
Trottier Desauniers, Jacques, III, 632
Trottier Desauniers, Marguerite. *See* Chéron
Trottier Desauniers, Marguerite (Charest), IV, 141
Trottier Desauniers, Marie-Catherine (Charest), IV, 141
Trottier Desauniers, Pierre, III, 631; IV, 739
Trottier Desauniers, Pierre, II, 43, 66, 125; III, 111, 434, 509, **631–32**; IV, 10, 141, 362, 650, 739
Trottier Desauniers, Pierre-François, III, 632
Trottier Desauniers Beaubien, Catherine (Lévesque), IV, 476; V, 494
Trottier Desrivières. *See also* Desrivières
Trottier Desrivières, Amable, VI, 204
Trottier Desrivières, Catherine (Dejordy de Villebon), III, 171
Trottier Desrivières, Charlotte. *See* Guillimin
Trottier Desrivières, Charlotte (Testard Louvigny de Montigny), V, 801
Trottier Desrivières, Julien, IV, 178
Trottier Desrivières, Marie-Avine. *See* Montigny
Trottier Desrivières, Marie-Charlotte (Testard de Montigny), IV, 733; V, 801
Trottier Desrivières, Pierre, VI, 557
Trottier-Desrivières, Pierre-Julien, IV, 284
Trottier Desrivières, Thomas-Hippolyte, V, 527
Trottier Des Rivières Beaubien. *See also* Des Rivières
Trottier Desrivières-Beaubien, Basile-Benjamin, IX, 696
Trottier Desrivières Beaubien, Charlotte. *See* Boucher de La Bruère
Trottier Desrivières Beaubien, Eustache, V, 480, 828

Trottier Desrivières Beaubien, Eustache-Ignace, IV, 318, 508; V, **828–29**; VII, 247, 688
Trottier Des Rivières Beaubien, Henriette. *See* Pillet
Trottier Desrivières Beaubien, Marguerite. *See* Malhiot
Trottier Desrivières Beaubien, Marguerite-Thérèse (Desrivières), VI, 204
Trottier Desrivières Beaubien, Marie-Appolline. *See* Bailly de Messein
Trottier Des Rivières Beaubien, Pierre-Charles-Robert, VII, 247
Trottier Des Ruisseaux, Antoine, II, 533
Trottier Des Ruisseaux, Marie-Anne (Martel), II, 459
Trottier Desruisseaux, Marie-Catherine (Cuillerier, *dit* Beaubien; Picoté de Belestre), IV, 632
Trottier Dufy Desauniers, Marie-Thomas. *See* Fleury de La Gorgendière
Trottier Dufy Desauniers, Thomas-Ignace, IV, 549, **739–40**; V, 143, 383
Trouin. *See* Duguay-Trouin
Troup, Alexander, VII, 483
Troup, Robert, VI, 611
Trout, Nehemiah, I, 496
Trouvé, Claude, I, 82, 544, 599, 647; II, 45, 130, 184, 410, 522, **637–39**
Trowbridge (Goffe), Edmund, VI, 74
Troy, Edward, VII, 292, 294, 295, 296, 299, 631; VIII, 107, 198, 468; IX, 71, 72; X, 180, 553, 600, **687–88**; XI, 242
Troy, Elizabeth (Delaney), XI, 242
Troy, John Thomas, V, 473
Troyer, David Michael, VII, 870
Troyer, John, VII, **870–71**
Troyer, Magdalena. *See* Mast
Troyer, Michael, VII, 870
Troyer, Sophrona, VII, 870
Troyes, Madeleine de. *See* Alard
Troyes, Marie de. *See* Petit de L'Estang
Troyes, Michel de, I, 653
Troyes, Pierre de, known as Chevalier de Troyes, I, 39, 56, 107, 130, 315, 324, 329, 361, 417, 465, 509, 529, 537, 606, 611, **653–54**, 657, 672; II, 49, 62, 69, 101, 102, 120, 231, 267, 284, 307, 319, 390, 391, 392, 393, 405, 412, 445, 563, 581, 607, 608
Truchi (Truchy), Jeanne-Antoinette de (Adhémar de Lantagnac), III, 5
Trudeau, Mme (boarding-school mistress), VI, 584
Trudeau, André, XII, 808
Trudeau, Angélique. *See* Lock
Trudeau, Aurélie. *See* Paul
Trudeau, Claire (Huguet, *dit* Latour), V, 436
Trudeau, Corinne. *See* Perrault
Trudeau, Eugène, XI, 890
Trudeau, François (father of ROMUALD), XI, 889
Trudeau, François (father of TOUSSAINT), XII, 1068
Trudeau, Jean-Baptiste, XI, 302
Trudeau (Truteau), Jean-Baptiste, VII, 172
Trudeau, Lactance, XI, 890, 891
Trudeau, Marguerite. *See* Weilbrenner
Trudeau, Romuald, VIII, 262; IX, 78; XI, 763, **889–91**
Trudeau, Toussaint, XII, 599, 933, **1068**
Trudel. *See also* Trudelle
Trudel, Augustin, V, 271; VI, 546
Trudel, Eudoxie (Viger), X, 694
Trudel, Eugène-Hercule, XI, 58

Trudel, Ferdinand, XI, 493; XII, 277

Trudel, François-Xavier, XI, 891

Trudel, François-Xavier-Anselme, VIII, 713; X, 193, 614; XI, 71, 252, 626, 802, **891–95**; XII, 88, 99, 100, 178, 304, 372, 510, 722, 723

Trudel, Henriette (De Lisle), IX, 200

Trudel, Henri-Louis-François-Xavier-Édouard, XI, 895

Trudel, Josephte. *See* Fabre

Trudel, Julie. *See* Langevin

Trudel, Marguerite. *See* Chaperon

Trudel, Marie. *See* Charbonneau

Trudel, Marie-Anne (Le Vasseur Borgia), VII, 503

Trudel, Olivier, XI, 891

Trudel, Pascal, IX, 200

Trudel, Zoé-Aimée. *See* Renaud

Trudelle, Barbe (Dorion), VII, 254

Trudelle, Charles, IV, 9; VII, 592; IX, 117

Trudelle, Marie (Gauthier), X, 301

Trudelle, Véronique-Aimée (Pigeon), X, 613

True, Jemima (March), II, 452

True, Ruth (Gyles), III, 273

Trueman, Milcah (Allison), VIII, 15

Truillier, *dit* Lacombe. *See also* Lacombe

Truillier, *dit* Lacombe, François-Xavier, IX, 439

Truillier, *dit* Lacombe, Geneviève. *See* Adhémar

Truillier, *dit* Lacombe, Jeanne (Guy), III, 271; V, 395

Trullier, *dit* Lacombe, Angélique. *See* Laurent

Trullier, *dit* Lacombe, Jacques, VI, 786

Trullier, *dit* Lacombe, Jacques, VI, **786–87**; VII, 447; VIII, 500

Trullier, *dit* Lacombe, Marie-Anne. *See* Levasseur

Trumbull, John (painter), V, 41

Trumbull, John (printer), V, 717

Trumbull, Jonathan, IV, 527

Trunel de la Croix-Nord, Irma (Dessane), IX, 362; X, 228

Truscott, Ann. *See* Norman

Truscott, George, VIII, 8, 797, **895–98**; IX, 241; XI, 407

Truscott, Mary. *See* Croucher

Truscott, Mary. *See* Stritch

Truscott, William, VIII, 895

Trustler (Tranclar, Trutter), Marianne (Clarke), VIII, 158

Trutault, Joseph-Amable, VI, 379

Trutch*, Sir Joseph William (1826–1904), IX, 715, 716; XI, 300, 435, 635, 636, 844, 845; XII, 241, 601, 915, 1132

Truteau. *See also* Trudeau

Truteau, Alexis-Frédéric, VII, 424; IX, 450; X, 154, 176, 250, 251, 532, **688–90**; XI, 170, 250, 531, 777; XII, 505

Truteau, Élisabeth (Baudry), VII, 54

Truteau, Marie (Armand), III, 17

Truteau, Marie-Louise. *See* Papineau

Truteau, Sarah-Angélique (Loranger), XI, 531

Truteau, Toussaint (defendant), V, 165

Truteau, Toussaint (father of ALEXIS-FRÉDÉRIC), X, 688

Truthwaite, Isabella (Norquay), XI, 642

Trutter. *See* Trustler

Try, John, VI, 603; XI, 586

Trye, James, IV, 262

Tryggvesson. *See* Olaf I

Tryon, William, IV, 427, 613; V, 94, 239, 308, 657, 890; VII, 777

Tsalekulhyé, VII, 474

Tsaouenhohi; Tsawouenhouhi. *See* Vincent, Nicolas

Tsiewei, Michel, VII, 889, 890

Tsinonwanhonte, V, 810

Tsohahissen. *See* Romain, André

Tsondatsaa (Charles), I, 42, 523

Tsondoutannen (Thomas), I, 143

Tubbee, Mosholeh, VIII, 898

Tubbee, Okah, VIII, **898–99**

Tubinaniqua. *See* Tuhbenahneequay

Tuck, Samuel, VIII, 23

Tuck*, William Henry (1831–1913), XII, 17, 19

Tucker, Frances. *See* Bruere

Tucker, Frances (Montresor), IV, 552

Tucker, Hannah, VI, 311

Tucker, Henry, IX, 794

Tucker, Joseph, V, 8

Tucker, Lewis, V, 27

Tucker*, Louis Norman (1852–1934), XI, 523

Tucker, Mary (Forbes), VII, 503

Tucker, Mary Todd. *See* Bruere

Tucker, Nancy (Kittson), XI, 476

Tucker, Relief Ann (Turnbull), XII, 1070

Tucker, Richard Alexander, VI, 693; VII, 99, 104, 153, 629; VIII, 11, 28, 29, 135, 431, 432, 468, 512, 586, 848; IX, 70, 168, 721, **794–95**; X, 178; XI, 28

Tucker, Robert, V, 431

Tucker, Sarah, IX, 137

Tuckerman, Henry Theodore, XII, 123

Tuckett, Elias, XII, 1069

Tuckett, Elizabeth. *See* Leak

Tuckett, George Elias, XII, 940, **1068–70**

Tuckett, George Thomas, XII, 1069

Tuckett, John Elias, XII, 1069

Tuckett, Mary (mother of GEORGE ELIAS), XII, 1069

Tuckey, Jack, II, 233

Tudor, Constance Ada (McClure), X, 455

Tudor, William, VI, 375

Tuffet, Jean, I, 248, 490, 593

Tufflemier (Stofflemire, Tofflemire, Tufflemear), Jacob, IV, 778

Tufflemier (Stofflemire), Ruth (wife of Jacob), IV, 777, 778

Tufford, Jane (Harris), XI, 386

Tufton Mason, Anna Elizabeth (Livius), IV, 484

Tufton Mason, John, IV, 484

Tuglavina (Tuglawina, Tukelavinia), IV, 536, 537, **740**; V, 830

Tuhbenahneequay (Sarah Henry), VII, 451, 455; VIII, 439, 440; IX, 593

Tuke, Daniel Hack, XI, 591; XII, 1126

Tuke, James Hack, XII, 1123

Tuke, William, XII, 1125

Tulk, Charles Augustus, VI, 312

Tulk, Susannah. *See* Hart

Tullis, Janet (Barclay), VIII, 61

Tulloch. *See* Tilloch

Tullok, James, V, 700

Tully*, Kivas (1820–1905), VIII, 14, 485, 555, 877; IX, 657; X, 405; XI, 228, 591; XII, 907

Tunnicliffe, Mary (Jones), VI, 363

Tunstall, James Marmaduke, IV, 139, 151; V, 298, 614; VI, 822; VII, 211, 825

Tunstall, Sarah. *See* Christie

Tupper, Betsy. *See* Dimock

Tupper, Charles, XI, 895
Tupper, Charles, VI, 31; VII, 611; VIII, 613, 895; XI, 214, 722, 805, **895–96**
Tupper*, Sir Charles (1821–1915), VII, 611; IX, 130, 271, 272, 295, 427, 574, 709, 791, 840; X, 7, 71, 100, 172, 192, 300, 353, 366, 367, 368, 369, 387, 395, 440, 457, 458, 476, 688; XI, 8, 12, 23, 24, 106, 123, 124, 147, 215, 248, 279, 280, 351, 381, 398, 399, 420, 525, 555, 573, 667, 668, 697, 704, 707, 709, 717, 754, 755, 758, 770, 772, 803, 813, 814, 835, 856, 896, 921, 933, 947, 948; XII, 32, 116, 151, 163, 181, 246, 353, 354, 406, 430, 447, 467, 485, 498, 539, 568, 579, 585, 586, 600, 601, 602, 605, 607, 610, 612, 633, 636, 687, 704, 751, 765, 865, 879, 880, 881, 908, 966, 1040, 1042, 1043, 1054, 1055, 1056, 1058, 1059, 1068, 1120, 1121, 1128
Tupper*, Sir Charles Hibbert (1855–1927), XII, 610, 611, 979, 980, 1120, 1121
Tupper, Deborah (Rand), XI, 722
Tupper, Edith, V, 114
Tupper, Elizabeth. See West
Tupper, Ferdinand Brock, V, 114
Tupper, Hannah (Creelman), XII, 217
Tupper, Martha (Annand), XI, 22
Tupper, Mary. See Miller
Tupper, Miriam. See Lockhart
Tupper, Nathan, VII, 681
Tupper, Phebe (FitzRandolph; Quirk), VIII, 731
Turc de Castelveyre, Claude, III, 632
Turc de Castelveyre, Louis, named Brother Chrétien, II, 135, 378; III, 76, 292, **632–34**; IV, 237, 720
Turc de Castelveyre, Marie. See Bonnel
Turcot. See also Turcotte
Turcot, Abel, IX, 795
Turcot, Augustin, IX, 795
Turcot, Joseph, IX, 795
Turcot, Marguerite. See Marchildon
Turcot, Marie-Renée (You de La Découverte), II, 672
Turcot, Philippe, IX, 78
Turcotte*, Arthur (1845–1905), IX, 796; XII, 721
Turcotte, Flore. See Buteau
Turcotte, François-Magloire, VII, 173, 333
Turcotte, Gustave-Adolphe-Narcisse, IX, 796
Turcotte, Jean-Baptiste (father of LOUIS-PHILIPPE), X, 690
Turcotte, Jean-Baptiste (fur trader), VII, 138
Turcotte, Joseph-Édouard, VIII, 217, 332, 493, 618, 800; IX, 66, 344, 487, **795–97**; X, 321, 418; XI, 341, 908; XII, 531
Turcotte, Louis-Philippe, VIII, 679; X, 136, 433, **690**; XI, 247, 343, 490, 530; XII, 262, 271
Turcotte, Marie-Josephte. See Fortier
Turenne, Vicomte de. See La Tour
Turgeon, Adélard, XII, 695
Turgeon, Élisabeth, named Sister Marie-Élisabeth, XII, 520
Turgeon, Geneviève, VI, 788
Turgeon, Geneviève (Turgeon), VI, 787
Turgeon, Hélène-Olive (Laberge), X, 415
Turgeon, Hersélie (Marchand), XII, 692
Turgeon, Hubert, VI, 788
Turgeon, Jean, IV, 64
Turgeon, Joseph (notary), VII, 781
Turgeon, Joseph (surveyor), V, 580
Turgeon, Joseph-Balzara, XII, 937
Turgeon, Joseph-Ovide, X, 415

Turgeon, Louis (father of LOUIS), VI, 787; IX, 797
Turgeon, Louis (son of LOUIS), VI, 788
Turgeon, Louis, VI, **787–88**; VIII, 914; IX, 797
Turgeon, Louise-Élisabeth. See Dumont
Turgeon, Marie (Bilodeau), III, 519
Turgeon, Marie-Ermine (Viger), VI, 788; VIII, 914
Turgeon, Marie-Françoise. See Couillard
Turgeon, Marie-Gillette (Raby), VI, 626
Turgeon, Marie-Hermine (Paquet, dit Lavallée), VIII, 680
Turgeon*, Onésiphore (1849–1944), XII, 27
Turgeon, Pierre-Flavien, VI, 126, 588, 593, 597, 598, 787; VII, 204, 332, 486, 573, 705, 798, 799, 879; VIII, 228, 318, 572, 593, 594, 595, 703, 713, 728, 729, 914; IX, 18, 19, 20, 117, 118, 254, 317, 533, 541, **797–800**, 862; X, 87, 603; XI, 38, 95, 97, 99, 168, 169, 170, 208, 257, 258, 689, 956; XII, 184, 190, 590, 637, 846, 1016, 1017
Turgis. See Saint-Étienne de La Tour
Turin, Marie (André), III, 14
Turmenys, Philippe de, I, 221
Turnbull, Elizabeth (Leach), XI, 502
Turnbull, George, V, 8, 129, 237
Turnbull, Isabella (Christie), X, 171
Turnbull, John, XII, 828
Turnbull, John Duplessis, VII, 110
Turnbull, Julia Caroline. See Hatheway
Turnbull, Margaret (Babbitt), XI, 39
Turnbull, Relief Ann. See Tucker
Turnbull, Sarah (Cockburn), 195, 196
Turnbull*, Wallace Rupert (1870–1954), XII, 1071
Turnbull, William Baxter, XII, 1070
Turnbull, William Wallace, XII, **1070–71**
Turner, Lieutenant, I, 68
Turner, Bardin, VIII, 15, 183
Turner, Catherine A. (McTavish), VII, 578; VIII, 811
Turner, Charles Barker, IX, 803
Turner, Dawson, VII, 599
Turner, Edwin R., XI, 802
Turner, Elizabeth (McCormick), VII, 527
Turner, Elizabeth (VanKoughnet), IX, 803
Turner, Ellen (Wakefield), IX, 817, 818
Turner, Ephraim, I, 337
Turner, Frances (Herchmer), XII, 427
Turner, Francis Anne (Gowan), X, 313
Turner, Gaius, XI, 834
Turner, Hannah (Stewart), VI, 735
Turner, James (father), XI, 562
Turner, James, XI, 562
Turner, Jane (Christie), VII, 182
Turner, John (coach driver), VIII, 509
Turner, John (Hamilton merchant), XI, 562
Turner, John (HBC employee), XII, 446
Turner, John (Toronto businessman), XI, 648, 837
Turner*, John Herbert (1834–1923), XII, 805
Turner, Joseph Mallord William, VII, 401; VIII, 63; XII, 287, 326, 328, 794, 1109
Turner, Margaret (Dunn), XII, 277
Turner, Mary. See Newton
Turner, Nicholas, V, 382, 383
Turner, Orasmus, VIII, 606
Turner, Robert, VIII, 269
Turner, Samuel, V, 68
Turner, Sarah (Duval), X, 268
Turner, Susanna (Wright), V, 873; VI, 818; VII, 924

Turner, Sybilla Maria. *See* Willin

Turner, Thomas Andrew, VI, 180, 815; VII, 112, 179, 182; VIII, 22

Turner, W. S., X, 726

Turner, William, V, **829–30**

Turnor, Elizabeth (wife of PHILIP), IV, 742

Turnor, Philip, IV, 310, 365, 366, 389, 525, 684, **740–42**, 758; V, 450, 500, 539; VI, 249, 320, 775, 776; VIII, 349, 879

Turnpenny, Mary (Cawthra), VII, 163; X, 155

Turpin, Alexandre, II, 134

Turpin, Marie-Madeleine (Levasseur), II, 430, 431; IV, 471, 475

Turquand, Bernard, VIII, 256

Turtle. *See* Mikinak

Turton, Sir Thomas Edward Michell, VII, 118, 478; IX, 237

Tussichi (Toussiqui), Margherita (Spagniolini), III, 597

Tute, Amos, V, 741

Tute, James, III, 452; IV, 681

Tute, Jemima. *See* Sawtelle

Tutin, Martha (Thomas), VIII, 872

Tutin, Richard, VIII, 872

Tuttle, Charles Richard, IX, 137

Tutty, Catherine (Hollows; wife of WILLIAM), III, 635

Tutty, Gruzzel. *See* Drew

Tutty, William, III, 634

Tutty, William, III, 125, 275, 473, **634–35**; IV, 94, 775

Tuvache, Captain, I, 208

Tüyaguande. *See* Teyohaqueande

Tuyll van Serooskerken, Carel Lodewijk van, Baron van Tuyll van Serooskerken, VIII, 899, 900

Tuyll van Serooskerken, Charlotte Henriette van, Baroness van Tuyll van Serooskerken. *See* Mansfield

Tuyll van Serooskerken, Marie Louise van, Baroness van Tuyll van Serooskerken. *See* Gildemeester

Tuyll van Serooskerken, Sophie Mathilde Henriette Bilitonia Wilhelmine van, VIII, 901

Tuyll van Serooskerken, Vincent Gildemeester van, Baron van Tuyll van Serooskerken, VIII, **899–901**; X, 127

Tuzo, Anna Maria (Alston), X, 9

Twain, Mark. *See* Clemens, Samuel Langhorne

Twatt, Magnus, IV, 366

Tweddle, Eliza Jane (Renfrew), XII, 889

Tweeddale, Marchioness of. *See* Hamilton; Mackenzie-Stewart

Tweeddale, Marquess of. *See* Hay

Tweedie*, Lemuel John (1849–1917), XII, 740

Twenhofel, W. H., X, 65

Twide, Richard, I, 380

Twining, E. C., XII, 747

Twining, John Thomas, VI, 732; VII, 12, 434, 435; VIII, **901–2**, 968; IX, 601, 841; X, 383, 384; XII, 872

Twining, Sarah. *See* Weeks

Twining, Susan Mary. *See* Winnett

Twining, William, V, 446; VIII, 901

Twisden, Isabella. *See* Duncan

Twisden, Thomas, V, 281

Twiss, William, V, 347, 348; VI, 146, 484, 769, **788–89**

Twite, Catherine (Boyle), IX, 835

Two Sicilies, Princess of. *See* Caroline

Two Suns. *See* Stoó-kya-tosi

Tyantenagen. *See* Jones, John

Tyatiquob (Bunch Sonego), IX, 590

Tye, George, IX, 711

Tyhorihoga. *See* Tekarihogen (Henry)

Tylee, Hannah (Pilkington), VI, 582

Tylee, John, VI, 582

Tyler, Abigail (Andrews), V, 24

Tyler, Sir Henry Whatley, XII, 433, 434

Tyler, Mary (Smith), VII, 811

Tyler, Moses Coit, V, 629, 631

Tyng, Anne. *See* Waldo

Tyng, Edward, I, 654

Tyng, Edward, I, 426, 576, **654**; II, 14, 25, 177, 494; III, 635

Tyng, Edward, I, 654; III, **635–36**; IV, 588

Tyng, Elizabeth. *See* Clarke

Tyng, Elizabeth. *See* Southack

Tyng, Rebecca (Dudley), III, 200

Tyorhansera. *See* Teiorhéñhsere?

Tyrell, Thomas. *See* Pichon

Tyrie, Jean (Grant), V, 367

Tyrkir, I, 449

Tyrrell*, Joseph Burr (1858–1957), IV, 342; V, 539; VIII, 883

Tyrrell, Rhoda (Duncombe), IX, 228

Tyrrell, William, IX, 110

Tyrwhitt-Drake, Montague William, XI, 236; XII, 240

Tysen, Caroline (Hagerman), VII, 365, 372

Tyson, George Emory, X, 328; XI, 382

Tyson, James, XII, 384

Tyson, Susan (Moore), XI, 607

Tytler, Patrick Fraser, XII, 54

UBALDINI, Roberto, I, 97, 307

Udny, Catherine (Henderson), XI, 397

Ulich, Miss (McDonell), VI, 444

Ullebuck. *See* Ooligbuck

Ulpius, Euphrosynus, I, 659

Umfreville, Catherine (Pambrun), VII, 671

Umfreville, Edward, IV, 277, 518, 684, **742–43**; V, 362, 450; VI, 464; VIII, 779

Umfreville, Thomas, VII, 671

Underdown, John, II, 152, 439

Underhill*, Frank Hawkins (1889–1971), VI, 45; XII, 659

Underhill, Isaac D., VIII, 338

Underhill, Sarah (Davenport; Ryerse), V, 732; XI, 782

Underwood, Benjamin Franklin, XII, 866, 867

Underwood, Elizabeth (Gore, Countess of Arran), IX, 328

Une Flèche. *See* Kāpeyakwāskonam

Ungquaterughiathe. *See* Swatana

Uniacke, Alicia. *See* Purdon

Uniacke, Andrew Mitchell, VIII, 657; IX, 226

Uniacke, Eliza. *See* Newton

Uniacke, Elizabeth Gould. *See* Francklin

Uniacke, James Boyle, VI, 61, 789, 791; VII, 83, 144, 492, 804; VIII, 74, 382, 400, 416, 417, 757, 782, **903–6**, 957, 958; IX, 181, 225, 226, 295, 748, 786; X, 7, 73, 365, 385, 438; XI, 76, 398, 709, 926, 945, 946

Uniacke, Martha Maria. *See* Delesdernier

Uniacke, Martha Maria (Jeffery), VII, 441

Uniacke, Mary Ann. *See* Hill

Uniacke, Norman, VI, 789

Uniacke, Norman Fitzgerald, VI, 789; VII, **872**; IX, 75, 297

Uniacke, Richard John (1753–1830), V, 124, 239, 240,

832, 868; VI, 121, 319, 780, **789–92**; VII, 22, 23, 87, 441, 530, 531, 533, 681, 831, 872; VIII, 167, 355, 704, 726, 756, 903; IX, 225, 801
Uniacke, Richard John (1789–1834), VI, 319, 371, 789, **792**, 810; VII, 22, 82, 237, 804, 839; X, 73
Uniacke, Robert Fitzgerald, VI, 789; VII, 435; VIII, 902; IX, 37, 40, **801**, 841
Uniacke, Rosina Jane. *See* Black
Uniacke, Sophie. *See* Delesdernier
Unton, Henry, I, 531
Unwin, Charles, IX, 550
Unwin, Elizabeth (Harwood), IX, 373
Unwin, Mary Hardwick (Humphreys; Ridout), VIII, 749; X, 370
Upham, Charles Wentworth, V, 831
Upham, Elizabeth. *See* Murray
Upham, Frances Chandler (Weldon), XII, 403
Upham, Jabez, V, 830
Upham, Joshua, V, 35, 456, 506, **830–32**; VI, 73, 142, 394; VII, 783; VIII, 139, 150; X, 157
Upham, Katharine. *See* Nichols
Upham, Mary. *See* Chandler
Upham, Mary (Marsters), VII, 589
Upham, Sarah Green (Bliss), VI, 73
Upjohn, Richard, VIII, 942
Upper, Martha A. (Johnson), XII, 478
Upton, John, II, 672
Upton, Leslie Francis Stokes, VI, 707; XII, 1015
Upton, Mary (Yonge), II, 672
Urcudoy, Marie d' (Echenic), VI, 134
Ure, George P., VIII, 877; XI, 312
Ure, Robert, IX, 307; XII, 202
Urfé. *See* Lascaris
Urfé, Marquis de. *See* Lascaris
Urfé, Marquise d'. *See* Allègre
Uriah Heap. *See* O'Donoghue, William Bernard
Urie, Margaret (Gilmour), X, 305; XI, 348
Urquhart, Ann (Taylor), V, 795
Urquhart, Hugh, VIII, 272; IX, 803; X, 462
Urquhart, May (Begg), XII, 81
Ursúa. *See* Bucareli
Urtebise, Élisabeth (Barsalou), IV, 46
Urville. *See* Dumont
Usakechack, V, 184
Usborne, George William, VII, 874; VIII, 690
Usborne, Henry, VI, 289, 290, 424, 532; VII, 70, 380, **872–75**; VIII, 689, 690
Usborne, Phœbe Ann. *See* Birch
Usborne, Thomas, VII, 873, 874
Ussher, Edgeworth, VIII, 501
Ussher, Harriet (Mitchell), VI, 510
Ussher (Usher), John, V, 672, 673
Ussher, John Tannatt, XI, 568
Ussher, Mary. *See* Street
Ussher, Samuel, VIII, 525
Ustaiechta. *See* Stayeghtha
Ustick, Elizabeth (Hartshorne), VI, 312
Ustick, William, VI, 312

VACHER, Françoise (Compain, *dit* L'Espérance), V, 200, 201
Vachon, Louise-Marie (Paillard), II, 506
Vachon, Marguerite. *See* Langlois

Vachon, Marguerite (Duprac), II, 206, 639
Vachon, Paul (d. 1703), II, xxiii, 206, **639–40**
Vachon, Paul (d. 1729), II, **640–41**
Vachon, Sapience. *See* Vateau
Vachon, Vincent, II, 639
Vachon de Belmont, François, I, 116, 273, 274, 445, 598; II, 134, 241, 562, **641–42**; III, 180, 486, 649
Vachon de Belmont, Jean-Baptiste, II, 641
Vachon de Belmont, Jean-François, II, 641
Vachon de Belmont et de Crapanoz, Ennemond, II, 641
Vachon de Belmont et de Crapanoz, Honorade. *See* Prunier
Vachon, *dit* Pomerleau, Sophie (Gautron, *dit* Larochelle), VIII, 319; XI, 491
Vail, Albert Smith, XII, 939, 941
Vail, Charlotte Hannah. *See* Arnold
Vail, Edwin Arnold, XI, **896–97**
Vail, Frances Charlotte. *See* Cougle
Vail, Harriet Courtland. *See* Murphy
Vail, John Cougle, XI, 896
Vail, William, XI, 897
Vail*, William Berrian (1823–1904), XI, 198, 633, 897; XII, 436, 651, 655
Vaillancourt, Cyrille, VIII, 320
Vaillancourt, Cyrille-Émile, VIII, 320
Vaillancourt*, Émile (1889–1968), VIII, 38; IX, 552
Vaillancourt, Marie-Louise. *See* Larochelle
Vaillant, Edwidge (Bourgeau), XI, 92
Vaillant, Marguerite-Ursule. *See* Lajus
Vaillant, Marie-Ursule-Antoinette (Vienne), IV, 754
Vaillant, Sébastien, II, 188, 595, 596, 597, 599, 600; III, 675, 678
Vaillant de Gueslis, François, II, 237, 502, 585, **642–43**
Valade, François (carpenter), VII, 256, 682
Valade, François (father of MARIE-LOUISE), IX, 802
Valade, François-Xavier, XI, 750
Valade, Marie-Charlotte. *See* Cadotte
Valade, Marie-Louise, named Mother Valade, VII, 432; VIII, 722; IX, **802**; XI, 96, 306; XII, 1003
Valbelle, Chevalier de, I, 443
Valbringue, Robert. *See* La Rocque de Roberval, Jean-François de
Valdés y Flores Bazán, Cayetano, V, 11, 140, 571; VI, 234
Valée, Marguerite (Cauchon), XI, 159
Valentine, Charlotte-Caroline (Lavallée), XII, 532
Valentine, Harriet Ann (Gibb; Ross), XII, 928
Valentine, Isaac, IX, 379
Valentine, Mary. *See* Fisher
Valentine, Sarah Ann. *See* Sellon
Valentine, Susannah Elizabeth. *See* Smith
Valentine, Thomas, IV, 162
Valentine, William, IX, 787; VI, 335; VII, 253, 270, **875–76**; VIII, 886; XI, 679; XII, 791
Valera. *See* Alcalá-Galiano
Valerianos, Apostolos (Valerianatos, Phokus). *See* Fuca, Juan de
Valets, Jean, I, 201, 267, 269, 270, 273
Valier, *dit* Léveillé, Marie (Stevens), XI, 851
Valière, Julie (Dumont), X, 435
Valin, Marie. *See* Tremblay
Valin, Marie, V, 479
Valin, Marie-Angélique. *See* Talbot, *dit* Gervais
Valin, Marie-Virginie-Célina. *See* Bardy

529

Valin, Pierre-Vincent, VIII, 649; IX, 32; XII, 1065, **1071–73**
Valin, Thomas-Henri, VII, 100
Valin, Toussaint, XII, 1071
Vallance, William, IX, 694
Valle, Anne Susanne Caroline (Beckwith), IX, 38
Vallée, Catherine (Berthelette; Guy), V, 394
Vallée, Charles (landowner), III, 478
Vallée, Charles (printer), VI, 392
Vallée, François-Madeleine, III, **636–37**
Vallée, Joseph, IX, 78, 288; XI, 59
Vallée, Laurence. See Casselle
Vallée, Louis-Félix, III, 637
Vallée*, Louis-Prudent (1837–1905), IX, 47
Vallée, Madeleine (Brassard Deschenaux), IV, 89; V, 252; VI, 84
Vallée, Marguerite (Cazeau), V, 173
Vallée, Marguerite (Signaÿ), VII, 798
Vallée, Marie (Varlet), III, 639
Vallée, Marie-Catherine (Beaudin; Leroux d'Esneval), VIII, 500
Vallée, Pierre-Stanislas, X, 694
Vallée, Roch-Pamphile, XI, 115, 484
Vallée, Thérèse (Beaudry), XI, 59
Vallely. See Aylen
Vallerand, Flavien, VI, 392; X, 580
Vallerand, Louis de Gonzague, XII, 1072
Vallet Des Barres, Anne-Catherine. See Cuvier
Vallet Des Barres, Joseph-Léonard, VI, 192
Vallette de Chévigny, Charles, III, 637
Vallette de Chévigny, Marguerite. See Maillou, dit Desmoulins
Vallette de Chévigny, Marie-Anne. See Deschamps de Fellière
Vallette de Chévigny, Médard-Gabriel, III, 373, **637–38**; IV, 473
Vallier, François-Elzéar, III, 11, 192, 194, 413, 545, **638–39**; IV, 387, 429, 719
Vallière, Louis-Florent de, Marquis de Vallière, IV, 208
Vallière, Marguerite, VI, 622
Vallière, Marie (Marcoux), VIII, 618
Vallières, Jean-Baptiste, VII, 876
Vallières, Marguerite. See Corneillier, dit Grandchamp
Vallières de Saint-Réal, Jane. See Keirnan
Vallières de Saint-Réal, Joseph-Rémi, VI, 83, 168, 384, 390, 582, 585, 681; VII, 9, 67, 191, 227, 373, 427, 504, 728, 818, 836, **876–82**, 892; VIII, 214, 907; IX, 360, 561, 682, 683, 795, 810; X, 567, 580, 582; XI, 657
Vallières de Saint-Réal, Louise. See Pezard de Champlain
Valliers, Catherine de (Razilly), I, 567
Vallin, Mr (tailor), IX, 835
Valls, Anna Maria (Felton), VII, 281; X, 282
Valmur. See Bricault
Valois, Agathe. See Lalonde
Valois, Joseph-Moïse, XI, 59
Valois, Josette (Huguet, dit Latour), V, 436
Valois, Jude, X, 691
Valois, Louise (Beauchemin), XI, 59
Valois, Marie-Catherine. See Lefebvre
Valois, Marie-Louise-Florence-Eudoxie. See Godin
Valois, Michel-François, IX, **802–3**
Valois, Narcisse, X, 690
Valois, Narcisse, X, 423, **690–91**

Valois, Pierre, IX, 802
Valois*, Salomé, named Marie du Sacré-Cœur (1830–1906), X, 222; XII, 360
Valois, Simon, X, 691
Valois, Ursule. See Ritchot
Valois-Villette, Philippe de, Comte de Murcé (Mursay), II, 98
Valpergue, Françoise de (Lescarbot), I, 471
Valrennes. See Clément
Vanacott, Hatty (Darby), IV, 194
Van Allen, Elisa (Elizabeth) (Askin), IX, 8
Van Alstine, Peter, V, 92, 378, 552, 772; VI, 214; VII, 557
Van Beest, Albert, XII, 122
Van Blacklandt. See Blacklandt
Van Braam, Jacob, III, 149, 600, 601; IV, 227
Van Bramer, James, X, 530
Van Brocklin, Philip Cady, VIII, 499; XII, 553, 1090
Vanbrugh, Sir John, V, 689
Vanbrugh, Philip, IV, 226
Van Buren, Martin, IX, 415, 504, 505
Van Buskirk, Abraham, VI, 793
Van Buskirk, Jacob, VI, **793–94**
Van Buskirk, Sarah. See Breen
Van Buskirk, Sophia. See Van Dam
Van Camp, Phoebe (Street), V, 781
Van Cortlandt, Edward, X, 108, **691–92**
Van Cortlandt, Gertrude, X, 691
Van Cortlandt, Harriet Amelia. See Harrington
Van Cortlandt, Philip, X, 691
Vancouver, Bridget. See Berners
Vancouver, George, IV, 73, 166, 218, 244, 325, 411, 568, **743–48**, 768; V, 12, 80, 387, 540, 541, 615; VI, 234; VII, 50, 51, 327, 599; XII, 833, 893
Vancouver, John, IV, 747
Vancouver, John Jasper, IV, 743
Van Curler. See Curler
Van Dam, Sophia (Van Buskirk), VI, 793
Vandandaigue, dit Gadbois, Angélique. See Daignault
Vandandaigue, dit Gadbois, Victor, X, 297
Vandémont, Philippe-Emmanuel de, Duc de Mercœur et de Penthièvre, I, 421
Vandenburgh, Harriet (Mathison), IX, 540
Vandeput, George, IV, 112
Vanderbilt, Cornelius, IX, 793
Vanderburg, Catherine. See Delong
Vanderburgh, William Henry, XII, 110
Van der Donck. See Donck
Van der Dostyne. See Dostyne
Vandergrift, Elizabeth Margaret (Albro), VII, 12
Van der Hoff, Johanna (Ryerse), V, 732
Vandersluys, Jasper, VIII, 352
Vandervoort, Melinda Freeland, VIII, 473
Van de Velde, James Oliver, XII, 190
Vandry, Marie (Couillard de Lespinay), II, 156
Vandusen, Conrad, X, 692
Vandusen, Conrad, IX, 591, 593; X, **692–93**; XI, 474
Van Dyke, Sir Anthony, V, 496
Vane, Lady Anne (Hope Weir), IV, 366
Vane, George, II, 22, 351, 439, **643–44**, 651, 652
Van Egmond, Anthony Jacob William Gysbert, VII, 260, **882–83**; IX, 323, 502, 503
Van Egmond, Marie Susanne Elizabeth. See Dietz
Vaner (Vannier), Hans, I, 383

Vanfelson, Antoine (Anthony), VIII, 906
Vanfelson, Dorothée-Magleine. *See* Just
Vanfelson, George, V, 649; VI, 585; VII, 61, 189, 374, 878, 879, 880; VIII, 232, **906–7**; IX, 779; X, 589
Vanfelson, Josephte. *See* Meunier
Vanfelson, Josette (Gauvreau), VI, 280
Van Felson, Suzanne Ellen (Peltier), X, 589
Van Felson, William, IV, 79
Van Gennep, Arnold, III, 337
Van Harwick. *See* Harwick
Van Horn, Hannah (Foy; Carleton), V, 155
VanHorne, Gregory, VII, 47, 601; VIII, 362
Van Horne*, Sir William Cornelius (1843–1915), XI, 707, 764, 840; XII, 8, 168, 288, 337, 433, 434, 608, 636, 666, 704, 705, 795, 800, 965, 1010
Vanier, Suzanne (Senet), II, 604
Van Kemper, Martha Maria Iqualin (DuVernet Grosset Muirhead), VII, 268
Van Keugh. *See* Cook
VanKoughnet, Elizabeth. *See* Turner
VanKoughnet, Eve. *See* Empey
VanKoughnet, Harriet Sophia. *See* Scott
Vankoughnet, Lawrence, XI, 598, 599, 748; XII, 718
Vankoughnet, Margaret Ann (Chesley), X, 163
VanKoughnet, Michael, X, 693
VanKoughnet, Philip, VII, 459; VIII, 534, 583; IX, 333, 803; X, 632, **693–94**; XI, 609
VanKoughnet, Philip Michael Matthew Scott, VIII, 799; IX, 98, 108, 319, 377, **803–4**; X, 231, 693; XI, 144, 838, 845; XII, 908
Vannasse, François, II, 166
Vanneck, Sophie (Lambert Dumont), II, 82
Vannier, Catherine (Pelletier), I, 536
Van Norman, Benjamin, IX, 789, 790; XI, 898
Van Norman, Daniel C., XII, 219
Van Norman, John, XI, 897
Van Norman, Joseph, VI, 252; VIII, 499, 543; IX, 789; XI, **897–98**; XII, 552
Van Norman, Mary Ann (Tillson), XI, 898
Van Norman, Roxilana. *See* Robinson
Van Norman, Sarah. *See* de Pue
Van Nostrand, May Susee (Frasse de Plainval), XI, 325
Vannovous, Frederick, XII, 1000
Vanpatten, John, VII, 698
Van Rensselaer, Alida. *See* Schuyler
Van Rensselaer, Jeremiah, II, 342, 602
Van Rensselaer, Kiliaen, I, 527
Van Rensselaer, Maria (Schuyler), II, 602
Van Rensselaer, Nicholas, II, 436
Van Rensselaer, Rensselaer, VIII, 852; IX, 415, 503, 504; X, 483; XI, 914
Van Rensselaer, Stephen, VIII, 794
Van Schaick, Engeltie (Schuyler), II, 602
Van Schaick, Goose, IV, lv
Van Serooskerken. *See* Tuyll
Vansittart, Elizabeth Johanna (Cockburn), VII, 193
Vansittart, Henry, VIII, 205; X, 59, 259
Van Slichtenhorst (Van Slichtarhorst), Margarita (Schuyler), II, 602; III, 586
Van Slyck, Cornelius A., VIII, 181
Van Slyck, Helena (Thorn), V, 813
Van Steenwijck. *See* Steenwijck
Vantelon. *See* Esprit

Van Tuyll. *See* Tuyll
Van Wittel, Gaspar, VII, 193
Van Zandt, John, IX, 422
Var. *See* Saint-Aubin
Vardon, George, VIII, 432; X, 164
Varennes. *See* Gaultier
Varin, Angéline (Doutre), XI, 277
Varin, Hermine. *See* Raymond
Varin, Jacques, VI, 749; VII, 762, 763; VIII, 223; XII, 190
Varin, Jean-Baptiste, XI, 277
Varin, *dit* La Pistole, Jacques, IV, 748
Varin, *dit* La Pistole, Jacques, IV, **748–49**; V, 218, 727; VII, 762
Varin, *dit* La Pistole, Louis-Joseph, IV, 748
Varin, *dit* La Pistole, Marie-Josephte. *See* Périnault
Varin, *dit* La Pistole, Marie-Louise (Joram Chappuis, *dit* Comtois), IV, 748
Varin, *dit* La Pistole, Marie-Renée. *See* Gautier
Varin, *dit* La Pistole, Nicolas (father), IV, 748
Varin, *dit* La Pistole, Nicolas, IV, 748
Varin de La Marre, Charlotte. *See* Liénard de Beaujeu
Varin de La Marre, Jean-Baptiste-François-Marie, IV, 750
Varin de La Marre, Jean-Victor, II, 95; III, 64, 74, 124, 225, 300, 402, 647; IV, 66, 67, 68, 91, 187, 216, 265, 356, 359, 461, 517, 615, 616, 644, 728, **749–51**; V, 652
Varin de La Sablonnière, Jean, IV, 749
Varlet, Achille, Sieur de Verneuil, III, 639
Varlet, Charles, Sieur de La Grange, III, 639
Varlet, Dominique-Marie, III, **639–41**
Varlet, Jean-Achille, III, 639
Varlet, Marie. *See* Vallée
Varlet, Marie-Anne (Olivier), III, 639
Varley, John, VII, 401
Varnham, Sophia (Booker), VIII, 98
Varnum, Phineas, VII, 778
Vassal, Guillaume, XI, 341
Vassal, Henri, XI, 808, 809, 810, 811
Vassal de Monviel, Charlotte. *See* Boucher de La Perrière
Vassal de Monviel, Charlotte (Thomas), VII, 883
Vassal de Monviel, François, V, 45, 270, 793; VI, 368, 385; VII, **883–85**, 892
Vassal de Monviel, François-Germain, VII, 883
Vassal de Monviel, Louise. *See* Perrault
Vassall, John, IV, 677
Vassall, William, IV, 677
Vassan. *See* Mutigny
Vasse, Anne (Becquet), I, 86
Vasseur. *See* Levasseur
Vateau, Sapience (Vachon), II, 639
Vattemare, Nicolas-Marie-Alexandre, VIII, 495; IX, 250, 300, **804–6**; XII, 847
Vauban. *See* Le Prestre
Vaubougon. *See* Chauvigny
Vaucour. *See* Pinguet
Vaudésir. *See* Baudart
Vaudive, Nicolas-Félix, IV, 69
Vaudreuil. *See* Rigaud
Vaudreuil, Baron de. *See* Rigaud
Vaudreuil, Baronne de. *See* Chateauverdun
Vaudreuil, Marquise de. *See* Fleury Deschambault; Joybert de Soulanges et de Marson; Le Moyne de Sérigny et de Loire
Vaudreuil, Vicomte. *See* Rigaud

Vaughan, Anne. *See* Christmas
Vaughan, David, VIII, 632
Vaughan, David, II, 56, 267, 319, 320, **644**
Vaughan, Elizabeth. *See* Elliot
Vaughan, Elizabeth. *See* Robert
Vaughan, Francis, I, 655
Vaughan, George, II, **644–45**; III, 641
Vaughan, Herbert Alfred, XII, 117
Vaughan, John, 1st Earl of Carbery, I, 655
Vaughan, Sir John, V, 730
Vaughan, Mrs Katherine (wife of Walter), I, 654
Vaughan, Margaret. *See* Cutt
Vaughan, Mary. *See* Belcher
Vaughan, Mercy (Crandall), VIII, 179
Vaughan, Richard F., VIII, 621
Vaughan, Samuel, VIII, 210
Vaughan, Sarah Insley (Molson), VII, 616, 617; VIII, 630;
    IX, 557; X, 517
Vaughan, Walter, I, 654
Vaughan, William, II, 644
Vaughan, William, II, 644; III, 116, 507, 508, **641–42**, 653;
    IV, 83
Vaughan, Sir William, I, 162, 365, 496, 632, **654–57**, 668,
    672
Vaulezar. *See* Juchereau
Vault. *See* Clement
Vaulthier, Perrette (Gloria), I, 339
Vaultier, Monsieur (servant), I, 105
Vaulx, Jacques de, I, 88, 89
Vauquelin, Jean, III, 73, 321, 322, 606, 667; IV, 22, 589,
    **751–52**; V, 203; IX, 298
Vause, Edward, IV, 199
Vautrollier, Thomas, I, 531
Vauvilliers, Jeanne de (Basset Des Lauriers), I, 79
Vauvril, Françoise. *See* Lepellé
Vauvril de Blason, Marguerite (Boucher de Grandpré;
    Blaise Des Bergères de Rigauville), I, 109; II, 70
Vaux, Calvert, XII, 958
Vaux, Harriet Sophia (Sanford), XII, 939, 943
Vaux, William Sandys Wright, XI, 662
Vavasor, Elizabeth. *See* Lane
Vavasor, Henry, II, 291
Vavasor, Roger, II, 291
Vavasour, Frances Elizabeth Hartwell. *See* Dickson
Vavasour, Georgiana. *See* Oakes
Vavasour, Henry William, V, 673; VIII, **907–8**; IX, 806
Vavasour, Louisa. *See* Dunbar
Vavasour, Mervin, VII, 440; VIII, 662, 907; IX, 327,
    **806–7**; X, 426
Vavasour, William, VIII, 907
Vaz Dourado, Fernan, I, 304
Veal, Sarah (Burwell), VII, 124, 125
Veau, *dit* Sylvain, Élisabeth-Marguerite (Isabelle)
    (Grossin), III, 142, 143
Veaux. *See* Devau
Vecellio (Vecelli), Tiziano, known as Titian, IX, 363; XII,
    846
Vega, Gregoria Rosalia de la (Cardero), V, 140
Végreville, Valentin, XII, 23
Veitch. *See also* Vetch
Veitch, Marianne (Somerville), VII, 820
Veitch, Marion. *See* Fairly
Veitch, William (father), II, 650

Veitch, William, II, 650
Veith. *See also* Vieth
Veith, William, IX, 599
Veith, William James, VII, 483
Vélez Cachupín, Tomás, III, 424
Venables, Robert, I, 605
Vence, Henri-François de, IX, 18
Vendamont. *See* Talus
Vendôme, Duc de. *See* Bourbon
Veney, Anderson, XII, **1073–74**
Veney, Levi, XII, 1073
Veney, Mrs Mattie, XII, 1073
Véniard de Bourgmond, Étienne de, II, xxix, xxxi, xxxiv,
    267, 414, 475, 632, **645–47**; III, xxxiv, 147; IV, 315
Véniard de Bourgmond, Jacqueline de. *See* Jean
Véniard Du Vergier, Charles de, II, 645
Veniot*, Peter John (1863–1936), XII, 341
Venner, John Lawder (Lauder), X, 681
Vennor, Henry, XI, 898
Vennor, Henry George, X, 445; XI, **898–900**; XII, 789
Vennor, Marion. *See* Paterson
Ventadour, Duc de. *See* Lévis
Verac, Catherine de. *See* Quevillon
Vercambre, Sophie-Joseph (Wugk), IX, 854
Verchères. *See* Jarret; Lafleur
Verchères de Boucherville, Charlotte (Quesnel; Robitaille),
    XII, 911
Verdier, Isaure Franchette (Peel), XII, 830, 831
Verdon, Vincent, II, 382
Verdun, Sieur de. *See* Dupuy
Vere, Baron. *See* Beauclerk
Verelst, John, III, 624
Verey, Edward G., XI, 900
Verey, George, XI, **900–1**
Verey, Sarah Ann. *See* Coulson
Vergennes, Comte de. *See* Gravier
Vergese d'Aubussargues, Magdalen de (DesBrisay), V,
    249
Vergil, Polydore, I, 151
Vergor. *See* Du Pont
Verhoune, Scholastique-Geneviève (Huguet), IV, 375
Verier. *See* Verrier
Verity, William Henry, XII, 701
Vermilye, Jane (Pryor), VIII, 724
Vernas, Gabrielle-Marie (Carrefour de La Pelouze), V, 163
Verne, Jules, X, 90
Verner, Mrs Elinor (wife of HUGH), I, 657
Verner*, Frederick Arthur (1836–1928), X, 393; XII, 336,
    789
Verner, Hugh, I, **657**; II, 231
Verneuil. *See* Bochart; Chaspoux; Lorimier; Petit
Verneuil, Sieur de. *See* Varlet
Verney, Sir Harry, X, 698
Vernhes, Jeanne-Marie (Aleyrac), IV, 14
Vernon, Amy (Nicholson; Owen), VIII, 669, 672
Vernon, Charles Albert, XII, 449, 450
Vernon, Edward, III, 136, 628, 655, 662
Vernon, Forbes George, XII, 449, 450
Vernon, Gillette de (Gaultier de Rinault), I, 326
Vernon, Hannah (Clench), VI, 153
Vernon-Smith, T. T., IX, 277
Véron de Grandmesnil, Catherine (Fleury Deschambault),
    IV, 268

Véron de Grandmesnil, Étienne, I, 223; II, 522, 523, **647–48**; III, 642, 643
Véron de Grandmesnil, Étienne, II, 648; III, **642–43**; IV, 268
Véron de Grandmesnil, Guillaume, I, 223; II, 647
Véron de Grandmesnil, Jean, I, 223; II, 535, 647
Véron de Grandmesnil, Madeleine. *See* Hertel de La Fresnière
Véron de Grandmesnil, Marguerite. *See* Hayet
Véron de Grandmesnil, Marguerite (Petit), II, 522; IV, 167
Véron de Grandmesnil, Marie-Catherine. *See* Le Picard
Véron de Grandmesnil, Marie-Thérèse. *See* Moral de Saint-Quentin
Véronneau, Agathe, III, **643**
Véronneau, Catherine-Antoine (Faribault), V, 312; VIII, 286, 287
Véronneau, Louis, III, 643
Véronneau, Marguerite. *See* Maugras
Ver Planck, Ann (Ludlow), V, 503, 504
Verrault, François, VII, 564
Verrazzano, Bernardo da, I, 657
Verrazzano, Fiametta da. *See* Capelli
Verrazzano, Gerolamo da, I, 657, 659, 660
Verrazzano, Giovanni da, I, 19, 21, 27, 72, 165, 187, 188, 332, 333, 342, 374, 469, 585, 586, **657–60**; III, 248; VII, 169
Verrazzano, Nicolo da, I, 657
Verrazzano, Piero da, I, 657
Verrazzano, Piero Andrea da, I, 657
Verreau, Barthélemy, II, **648**
Verreau*, Hospice-Anthelme-Jean-Baptiste (1828–1901), III, 691, 695; IV, 41, 698, 801; VIII, 912; IX, 863, 873; X, 218, 736, 741; XI, 27, 180, 181, 182, 185, 344, 345; XII, 820
Verreau, Marguerite. *See* Prieur
Verreau, Marthe. *See* Quittel
Verreau, *dit* Le Bourguignon, Barthélemy, II, 648
Verrier, Christophe, III, 643
Verrier, Claude-Étienne, III, 79, 646
Verrier, Étienne, II, 154, 648, 649, 650; III, 79, 80, 116, 118, 191, 235, 389, 455, 478, **643–46**; IV, 15, 62, 248, 253
Verrier, Guillaume, III, 646
Verrier, Hélène. *See* Papin
Verrier, Louis-Guillaume, II, 150, 152; III, 4, 64, 74, 164, 203, 225, 228, 491, 511, **646–48**, 675; IV, 182, 186, 318, 343, 359, 624
Verrier, Marguerite. *See* Ferrant
Verrier, Marie-Madeleine. *See* Thibault
Verrier, Pierre, I, 557
Verrier, Roberte. *See* Gadoys
Verrill, Addison Emery, X, 65
Verron, Renée (Maumousseau), II, 466
Versailles, Alfred (father), XII, 369
Versailles, Alfred, XII, 373
Versailles, Josephte. *See* Letendre, *dit* Batoche
Versailles, Marie-Aurélie. *See* La Mothe
Vertefeuille. *See* Bachand
Verville. *See also* Gautier
Verville, Guillaume de, II, 648
Verville, Jean-François de, II, 154, 292, 611, **648–50**; III, 79, 80, 117, 118, 191, 234, 389, 455, 575, 644
Verville, Louis de, II, 648

Vesconte, Charlotte Sarah (Macaulay), X, 453
Vesey, Phoebe (Garry), VIII, 314
Vésin. *See* Olivier
Vesins, Élisabeth de (Couillard), I, 236
Vespucci, Amerigo, I, 151, 155, 658
Vetch, Alida, II, 652
Vetch, Margaret. *See* Livingston
Vetch, Samuel, II, 21, 22, 38, 39, 122, 123, 167, 238, 287, 289, 436, 437, 461, 497, 498, 508, 546, 643, 644, **650–52**, 660; III, 200, 207, 208, 276, 436, 515
Vetch, William, II, 652
Veuillot, Louis, VIII, 291; IX, 63, 65, 247; X, 87, 166, 430; XI, 96, 100, 101, 273, 289, 891; XII, 177, 849
Veulle, Adelaide Anne Amelia de (Ash), XI, 33
Veulle, Sir John de, XI, 33
Veyrac. *See* Chabrand
Veysey, John, IV, 700
Veyssière, Monsieur (friend of Joseph NAVIÈRES), III, 481
Veyssière, Christiana (Gotson; wife of LEGER-JEAN-BAPTISTE-NOËL), IV, 752
Veyssière, Elizabeth. *See* Lawrear
Veyssière, Jean, IV, 565
Veyssière, Leger-Jean-Baptiste-Noël, named Father Emmanuel, III, 296; IV, 104, 139, 140, **752–54**; V, 146, 600, 602, 614; VI, 492; VIII, 276
Veyssière, Pierre, IV, 565
Veyssières, Étienne, IV, 752
Veyssières, Françoise. *See* Fraysse
Vézier, François, II, 159
Vézier, Marie. *See* Couture
Vézin (Vézain). *See* Olivier
Vézina, Adolphe, XI, 903
Vézina, Alexandre-Augustin, VII, 176
Vézina, Charles, II, 378, 379; III, **648–49**
Vézina, Claire. *See* Moisan
Vézina, Éléonore. *See* Rinfret, *dit* Malouin
Vézina, François (father of CHARLES), III, 648
Vézina, François (father of FRANÇOIS), XI, 901
Vézina, François, XI, 190, **901–3**; XII, 912, 1036
Vézina, Joseph (builder), XI, 336
Vézina, Joseph (musician), XII, 533
Vézina, Julie (Roy-Audy), VII, 761
Vézina, Louise. *See* Godin
Vézina, Ludger, XI, 903
Vézina, Marie. *See* Clément
Vézina, Marie (Lefrançois), VI, 391
Vézina, Olivier-Désiré, XII, 1018
Vézina, Pierre, V, 226; VII, 387, 388; VIII, 248
Vézina, Toussaint, XI, 336
Vezins, Marie (Villedonné), II, 652
Vézon. *See* Fournerie
Viabon. *See* Lestringant de Saint-Martin
Vial de Sainbel, Anna Louisa. *See* Walker
Vial de Sainbel, Charles, V, 839
Vialar, Anthony, V, 492
Vialars, Antoine, IV, 35, 461; V, 396
Vialars, Daniel, IV, 35, 286, 461; V, 395, 396
Vianney, Jean-Baptiste-Marie, VII, 170
Viau, Charles-Théodore, XII, **1074–75**
Viau, Delphine (Bourgeau), XI, 93
Viau, Marie-Émilie. *See* Deguise
Viau, Marie-Josephte. *See* Barrette
Viau, Pierre, VII, 885

Viau, Pierre, VII, **885–88**; IX, 17
Viau, *dit* Cinq-Mars, Florence. *See* Deniger
Viau, *dit* Cinq-Mars, Marc, XII, 1074
Vibraye, Marquis de. *See* Hurault
Vicars, Johnstone, VIII, 94
Vickers, Fanny (Punshon), XI, 719
Vickers, Maria (Punshon), XI, 719
Vickery, Ann (Robins), VIII, 200, 425, **908–9**
Vicq de Pontgibaud, Marie-Claude de (Guillouet d'Orvilliers), II, 269
Victor Emmanuel II, King of Italy, X, 542; XI, 548; XII, 268
Victoria, Queen of Great Britain and Ireland, IV, 628; V, 298; VI, 517; VII, 269, 279, 362, 412, 579, 607, 685, 859; VIII, 27, 65, 357, 438, 441, 494, 495, 745, 830, 901; IX, 117, 168, 198, 317, 390, 475, 492, 591, 726; X, 43, 48, 66, 73, 74, 116, 132, 145, 148, 191, 207, 320, 327, 345, 397, 443, 448, 503, 529, 623, 625, 632, 648, 663; XI, 14, 150, 155, 297, 319, 414, 433, 443, 578, 605, 632, 686, 769, 847, 866, 932; XII, 114, 115, 120, 123, 338, 353, 358, 364, 395, 412, 423, 458, 495, 669, 729, 788, 884, 907, 933, 967, 983, 1023, 1032, 1055, 1082, 1083, 1121, 1131
Victoria King (wife of PEGUIS), IX, 626
Victoria Mary Louisa (Princess of Leiningen; Duchess of Kent and Strathearn), V, 298
Vidal, Alexander, X, 138, 623
Vidal, Alexander Thomas Emeric, VIII, 669
Vidal, Aymerick, VIII, 648
Vidal, Charles, XI, 725
Vidal, Jean, III, 596
Vidal, Michel, XII, 324
Vidalle, Anne (Chaussegros), III, 116
Vieau, Jacques, VIII, 446
Vieau, Josette (Juneau), VIII, 446
Vieille Robe de Castor. *See* Chomina
Viel, Marie (Jolliet; Petit de Verneuil; Des Forges), II, 521
Viel, Nicolas, I, 58, 263, 420, 437, 440, 590, 639, **661**
Viele, Aernout Cornelissen, I, 526
Vien, Charlotte (Prévost), I, 553
Viennay-Pachot, Charlotte-Françoise. *See* Juchereau de Saint-Denis
Viennay-Pachot, François, I, 56, 397, **661**; II, 69, 276, 305
Viennay-Pachot, Jean-Daniel-Marie, III, 105
Viennay-Pachot, Jeanne. *See* Avamy
Viennay-Pachot, Marie-Françoise (Berthier; Blaise Des Bergères de Rigauville), II, 60, 69
Vienne, Françoise de. *See* Perdrigean
Vienne, François-Joseph de, IV, 263, 271, **754–55**; V, 369
Vienne, Jean, V, 396
Vienne, Jean de, IV, 754
Vienne, Marguerite, I, 233
Vienne, Marie-Louise de (Tisserant de Moncharvaux), III, 626
Vienne, Marie-Ursule-Antoinette de. *See* Vaillant
Viennot, Marie (Raclot), II, 517
Viesse de Marmont, Auguste-Frédéric-Louis, Duc de Raguse, IX, 772
Vieth, Adolphus Christoph, VI, **794**
Vieth, Anna Christina. *See* Vormitter
Vieth, Anna Dorothea. *See* Brehm
Vieth, Johann Ludwig, VI, 794
Viets, Hester. *See* Botsford

Viets, John, V, 832
Viets, Lois. *See* Phelps
Viets, Mary. *See* Pickett
Viets, Roger, V, **832–33**
Viets, Roger Moore, V, 833; IX, 620
Vieux Crapaud,˙III, 248
Vieuxpont (Vieux-Pont). *See also* Godefroy
Vieuxpont, Alexandre de, I, 453, 665
Vieuxtemps, Henri, XII, 471
Viger. *See also* Labrèche-Viger
Viger, Amaranthe. *See* Prévost
Viger, Aurélie. *See* Faribault
Viger, Bonaventure, X, 694
Viger, Bonaventure, VII, 264; VIII, 209, 471; X, **694**; XII, 88
Viger, Denis, IV, 148; V, **833–34**; VII, 485, 674; VIII, 241; IX, 807; XI, 187
Viger, Denis-Benjamin, IV, 148; V, 186, 208, 209, 235, 322, 324, 649, 651, 834; VI, 40, 42, 47, 48, 82, 84, 98, 381, 433, 597, 802; VII, 148, 225, 226, 227, 235, 242, 262, 353, 361, 393, 485, 489, 504, 605, 606, 607, 618, 622, 623, 647, 650, 666, 667, 703, 719, 728, 729, 739, 746, 762, 836, 856, 858, 878, 879, 880; VIII, xxvii, 52, 137, 141, 258, 259, 262, 284, 285, 301, 433, 434, 592, 667, 679, 681, 730, 781, 844, 909, 910, 914, 915; IX, 64, 65, 74, 188, 191, 201, 250, 262, 298, 299, 300, 372, 441, 443, 444, 445, 447, 500, 560, 568, 569, 649, 650, 697, 728, 779, 805, **807–17**, 818, 819; X, 93, 133, 255, 256, 417, 436, 566, 575, 694; XI, 59, 60, 106, 179, 187, 188, 281, 282, 409, 851; XII, 66, 253, 847
Viger, Eudoxie. *See* Trudel
Viger, Jacques (father of DENIS), V, 833
Viger, Jacques (father of JACQUES), V, 75; VIII, 909
Viger, Jacques (shoemaker), III, 473
Viger, Jacques, II, 259, 378; III, 691; IV, 427, 509, 510, 801; V, 184, 702, 834; VI, 52, 84, 279, 342, 344, 382, 680; VII, 240, 361, 622, 623, 624, 667, 836, 887; VIII, 87, 260, 458, 542, 594, 595, **909–13**, 914, 919, 939, 940; IX, 208, 249, 250, 300, 450, 485, 800, 807, 812, 863; X, 51, 577, 736; XI, 172, 182, 285, 821
Viger, Louis, VIII, 913
Viger, Louise. *See* Carmel-Levasseur
Viger, Louis-Michel, V, 834; VI, 278, 788; VII, 226, 240, 353, 482; VIII, 108, 219, 284, 288, 332, 369, 471, **913–17**; IX, 649, 682, 807, 814; X, 337, 575; XI, 187; XII, 87
Viger, Marguerite (Berthelet), VI, 52; VII, 666; X, 52
Viger, Marguerite-Julie (Labrèche), X, 417
Viger, Marie-Agnès. *See* Papineau
Viger, Marie-Amable. *See* Foretier
Viger, Marie-Angélique, named de Saint-Martin, IV, 190; V, 659
Viger, Marie-Ermine. *See* Turgeon
Viger, Marie-Françoise (Hantraye), IV, 326
Viger, Marie-Louise. *See* Ridé
Viger, Marie-Marguerite. *See* La Corne
Viger, Périne, IX, 807
Viger, Périne-Charles. *See* Cherrier
Viger, Thérèse (Gosselin), VII, 353
Viger, Thérèse-Amable (Orillat), IV, 591; V, 654
Vignal, Guillaume, I, 46, 130, 458, 612, **661–62**; II, 164, 426
Vignau. *See also* Maurice

Vignau, Jean-Raymond, IV, 123
Vignau, Marie-Joseph. *See* Cadet
Vignau, Nicolas de, I, 191, 192, 638, **662–63**
Vigneau, Anne (Lajus), III, 344
Vigneau, Catherine (Martin), II, 462
Vigneau, Charlotte (Ainsse), IX, 200
Vigneault, Stanislas, IV, 385
Vignerot, Marie-Madeleine de, Duchesse d'Aiguillon (Beauvoir Du Roure de Combalet), I, 203, 297, 347, 348, 373, 483, 484; VII, 869
Vignerot Du Plessis, Armand-Jean, Duc de Richelieu, I, 483
Vignerot Du Plessis, Louis-François-Armand de, Duc de Richelieu, III, 31; IV, 468, 469
Vignerot Du Plessis de Richelieu, Emmanuel-Armand de, Duc d'Aiguillon, III, 111; IV, 739
Vignola, Giacomo da, VI, 26; VII, 697; VIII, 213
Vignon, Firmin, IX, 66; XI, 276
Vigny, Alfred de, X, 22
Vilain, Jeanne (Chevalier), II, 142
Vilbon. *See* Dejordy
Vildaigre. *See* Perrot
Vilermaula, Louis-Michel de, II, 164, 562; III, **649**
Vilers, Madeleine (Levasseur), II, 430
Villade, Antoine, VI, 581
Villain, Jean (jeweller), I, 663
Villain, Jean (uncle of JEAN-BAPTISTE), I, 663
Villain, Jean-Baptiste, I, **663**
Villain, Jeanne. *See* Barbé
Villain, Jeanne (Bernier), I, 663
Villaine, Louis de, I, 425
Villaret de Joyeuse, Louis-Thomas, Comte de Villaret de Joyeuse, V, 62
Villars. *See also* Sorbier
Villars, Mme de (godmother of AMANTACHA), I, 58
Villazur, Pedro de, II, xxxvii, 646
Ville. *See also* Villes
Ville, Sieur de (ship's captain), II, 82
Villebois. *See also* Michel
Villebois, Monsieur de (proposed intendant), III, 51
Villebon. *See* Dejordy; Robinau
Villebrun, *dit* Provencher. *See also* Provencher
Villebrun, *dit* Provencher, Godfroi, XI, 716
Villebrun, *dit* Provencher, Placide. *See* Lafrance
Villechauve. *See* Beauharnois
Villedonné, Étienne de, II, 652
Villedonné, Étienne de, II, 626, **652–53**
Villedonné, Françoise de. *See* Roussel
Villedonné, Marie de. *See* Damours de Chaffours
Villedonné, Marie de. *See* Vezins
Villefranche. *See* Grisé
Villegaignon. *See* Durand
Villehardouin, Geoffroi de, XI, 489
Villejouin (Villejoin, Villejoint). *See* Rousseau
Villemain, Abel-François, XI, 178
Villemenon, Sieur (adviser to Samuel de CHAMPLAIN), I, 433
Villemonde. *See* Liénard
Villemor, Duc de. *See* Séguier
Villeneuve. *See also* Amiot; Amiot-Villeneuve
Villeneuve, Marquis de. *See* Duret
Villeneuve, Alphonse, XI, 171
Villeneuve, Domitilde. *See* Domitilde

Villeneuve, Gaspard de, II, 574
Villeneuve*, Jean-Marie-Rodrigue (1883–1947), IX, 864; X, 737
Villeneuve, Marie de (Bonne de Missègle), III, 69
Villeneuve, Marie-Louise de. *See* Rigaud de Vaudreuil
Villeneuve, Robert de, I, **663–64**; II, 229, 432, 532; III, 190
Villeray. *See* Rouer
Villermaula (Villermola). *See* Vilermaula
Villermont. *See* Cabart
Villers, Françoise (Huot), VI, 336; VII, 430
Villers, Jean de, IV, 124
Villers, Josephte de (Juneau), XI, 457
Villes, Jean-Marie de, II, 455, 645, **653**; III, 66
Villesavin. *See* Phélypeaux
Villette. *See* Valois
Villiers. *See also* Coulon; Legardeur; Neyon
Villiers, Lady Anne Barbara Frances (Lambton; Wyndham), VII, 476
Villiers, Barbara, Countess of Castlemaine and Duchess of Cleveland (Palmer), III, 369
Villiers, Christopher, 1st Earl of Anglesey, I, 614
Villiers, Ellen. *See* Shanly
Villiers, Frank, XI, 325
Villiers, George, 1st Duke of Buckingham, I, 365, 419, 669
Villiers, George, 4th Earl of Jersey, VII, 476
Villiers, George William Frederick, 4th Earl of Clarendon, IX, 8
Villieu, Claude-Sébastien de, II, 653
Villieu, Claude-Sébastien de, I, 426, 427, 578; II, 47, 71, 185, 257, 410, 626, 629, **653–54**, 664; III, 190
Villieu, Jeanne de. *See* Lebreton
Villieu, Judith de. *See* Leneuf de La Vallière
Villieu, Sébastien de, II, 238, **654–55**
Vimeur, Jean-Baptiste de, Comte de Rochambeau, IV, 32, 212; VII, 254, 255
Vimont, Barthélemy, I, 124, 205, 215, 216, 248, 348, 382, 389, 404, 430, 453, 516, **665**; III, 310
Vincelette, Clément, XI, 484
Vincelotte. *See* Amiot
Vincenne (Vincennes). *See* Bissot
Vincennes. *See* Chartrand, Vincent
Vincent. *See also* Clément
Vincent, III, **650**
Vincent, Mr (teacher), V, 255
Vincent, Ann (Cobbett), VI, 154
Vincent, Archange (Bétournay), X, 59
Vincent, Catherine. *See* Love
Vincent, Charles, XI, **903–4**
Vincent, Christine (Gros-Louis), VII, 889
Vincent, Elizabeth, XI, 643
Vincent, Gabriel, XI, 905
Vincent, George Philips, XII, 1075
Vincent, Harriet (Stewart; Gladman), VI, 795; VIII, 590; IX, 319
Vincent, Jane. *See* Renton
Vincent, Jane. *See* Sutherland
Vincent, John (father of JOHN), VII, 888
Vincent, John (son of THOMAS), VI, 795
Vincent, John, V, 82, 643, 696, 765, 875; VI, 489, 541, 617, 661; VII, 556, 698, 743, **888–89**; VIII, 161, 186, 374, 466, 795; IX, 544
Vincent, John Heyl, XII, 701
Vincent, José, VII, 890

Vincent, Joseph, III, 650
Vincent, Joseph-Victor, XI, 903
Vincent, Louis (brother of NICOLAS), VII, 890
Vincent, Louis (father of NICOLAS), VII, 889
Vincent, Louis (schoolteacher), VII, 646
Vincent, Louise. *See* Martin
Vincent, Marie. *See* Otis
Vincent, Marie (Falardeau; wife of ZACHARIE), XI, 905
Vincent, Marie-Thérèse-Augustine. *See* Charrière
Vincent, Mary Amelia. *See* Jackson
Vincent, Matthew, IV, 527
Vincent, Michael, VI, 266; VII, 369; VIII, 946
Vincent, Nicolas, III, 650; VII, **889–90**
Vincent, Pierre, V, 812, 813
Vincent, Prosper, III, 650
Vincent, Robert, III, 474, **650–51**
Vincent, Sarah Anne (Curzon), XII, **1075–76**
Vincent, Stanislas, III, 650
Vincent, Thomas, VI, 795
Vincent, Thomas, VI, 321, **794–95**; VII, 913; IX, 319
Vincent*, Thomas (1835–1907), XII, 446
Vincent, Véronique. *See* Petit-Étienne
Vincent, Zacharie, III, 650; VII, 890; XI, **905**; XII, 846
Vincent de Paul, I, 91, 208
Vincent de Paul, Father. *See* Merle
Vine, Esther (White), XI, 919
Vinet, Alexandre-Rodolphe, XII, 490
Vinet, Hippolyte, IX, 616
Vinet, Justine (Paré), IX, 616, 617
Vinet, Marie-Anne. *See* Beaudry
Vining, Daniel, XII, 1076
Vining, Lydia (mother of PAMELIA SARAH), XII, 1076
Vining, Mary (Inglis), V, 444
Vining, Pamelia Sarah (Yule), XII, 570, **1076–77**
Vinsenne. *See* Bissot
Virazel. *See* Belrieux
Virgil, XII, 250
Virot, Claude-François-Louis, III, 21
Virtue, George, VIII, 63, 64
Visitation. *See* Ailleboust de La Madeleine
Visscher, Frederick, VII, 911
Visscher, N. J., I, 525
Visseri. *See* Dutisné
Vitally, Antoine, IV, 286
Vitré. *See* Denys
Vitry, Jean, I, 108
Vivant, Laurent, VIII, **917–18**
Vivian, Mary Carne (Campbell), VIII, 123
Vivonne, Duc de. *See* Rochechouart
Vocemassussia (Isabella Ironside, wife of GEORGE), VI, 340
Voelter, Heinrich, XII, 136
Vogel, Sir Julius, XII, 476
Vogeli, Félix, IX, 612
Voisin, Father, XII, 46
Voisine, Théotiste (Soulard), VIII, 834
Volant, Anne-Marie (Cailly), III, 93
Volant, François, II, 529
Volant, Marguerite (Legardeur de Tilly), II, 387
Volant, Nicolas, II, 43
Volant de Chamblain, Claire. *See* Jolliette
Volant de Chamblain, François, V, 91
Volant de Radisson, Étienne, II, 505, **655**; III, 205, 372

Volant de Radisson, Geneviève. *See* Letendre
Volant de Saint-Claude, Claude, II, 655
Volant de Saint-Claude, Claude, II, **655–56**
Volant de Saint-Claude, Françoise. *See* Radisson
Volant de Saint-Claude, Pierre, II, **655–56**
Volant d'Haudebourg, Jean-Louis, II, 66, 301; III, 579; IV, 181
Volant d'Haudebourg, Marie. *See* Mars
Volney, Comte de. *See* Chassebœuf
Voltaire. *See* Arouet, François-Marie
Vondenvelden, Isaac, V, 834
Vondenvelden, Marie. *See* Young
Vondenvelden, Marie-Suzanne. *See* Voyer
Vondenvelden, William, V, 835
Vondenvelden, William, IV, 154, 502; V, 67, 139, 183, 184, 428, 460, **834–35**; VI, 174, 191, 223, 391, 532; VII, 199, 579; X, 527
Vondy, Janet (mother of JOHN), VII, 890
Vondy, John, VII, **890–91**; XI, 879
Vondy, Thomas, VII, 890
Von Geyer, Charlotte (Marryat), VII, 585
Von Kreuz, Paul. *See* Lacroix, Paul
Von Linné. *See* Linnaeus
Vorce, Lydia (Green), X, 316
Vormitter, Anna Christina (Vieth), VI, 794
Vosburgh, Mr (loyalist), X, 694
Voss, Mary Barbara (Pryor), VIII, 724; XI, 717
Vossnack, Emil, XI, **906**
Vossnack, Ida. *See* Cassoni
Vouet, Simon, I, 214, 313
Vowell, Arthur Wellesley, XII, 642
Vox. *See* Devau
Voyer, Antoine, VIII, **918–19**; IX, 562
Voyer, Antoine-René de, Marquis de Paulmy d'Argenson, IV, 655
Voyer, Arline. *See* Laroche
Voyer, Charles, VI, 191; VII, 891
Voyer, Charlotte (Frémont), IX, 286
Voyer, Françoise-Charlotte. *See* Perrault
Voyer, Jacques, VIII, 918
Voyer, Jacques, V, 165, 270; VII, 709, **891–92**; VIII, 359; IX, 113
Voyer, Joseph, III, 312, 518
Voyer, Josette (Desbarats), VI, 191; VII, 462; IX, 202
Voyer, Judith. *See* Taton, *dit* Brind'amour
Voyer, Louis, X, 694
Voyer, Luce-Monique. *See* Pinguet
Voyer, Ludger-Napoléon, X, **694–95**
Voyer, Marc-Pierre de, Comte d'Argenson, III, 458, 459; IV, 175, 478; V, 102
Voyer, Marie-Anne. *See* Sainte-Marie
Voyer, Marie-Madeleine (Bernard de La Rivière), II, 59
Voyer, Marie-Suzanne (Vondenvelden), V, 834
Voyer, Michel, IV, 125
Voyer, *dit* Le Jardinier, Jacques, II, 201
Voyer, *dit* Le Jardinier, Marie-Jeanne. *See* Routier
Voyer d'Argenson, Marc de, II, 656
Voyer d'Argenson, Pierre de, I, 46, 48, 206, 224, 225, 269, 270, 283, 288, 330, 431, 538, 563, 580, 588, 645, 646, 665; II, 136, 158, 363, 364, 536, **656–58**
Voyer d'Argenson, René de, II, 656
Vroom, Fenwick William, VIII, 346
Vrooman, Mrs. *See* Markle

Vuadens. *See also* Waddens
Vuadens, Adam Samuel, IV, 757
Vuadens, Marie-Bernardine. *See* Ormond
Vuil, Daniel, I, 284, **665–66**
Vulliermet, Marguerite (Souste), IV, 720
Vuyart, Nicolas, III, 221
Vyner, Sir Robert, I, 83

WABACUMAGA. *See* Wabbicommicot
Wabakinine (Wabacoming), IV, **755–56**; V, 707; VII, 451
Wabasha (Wabashar). *See* Wahpasha
Wabbicommicot, III, xxxvii, 215, **651–52**; IV, 174; V, 467
Wabenose. *See* Wahbanosay
Waber, Marie-Élisabeth, II, 526
Wabicanine. *See* Wabakinine
Wabojeeg (Waub Ojeeg), VI, 357
Wabunmashue. *See* Wapinesiw
Wachiouess. *See* Madjeckewiss
Waddell, James, X, 303
Waddell, Jane Walker. *See* Blanchard
Waddell, John (father of JOHN), X, 695
Waddell, John (uncle of Alexander Rocke ROBERTSON), XI, 756
Waddell, John, X, 666, **695–96**
Waddell, Katherine, XII, 516
Waddell, Maria Jane (Bingle; Nelles), VII, 650
Waddell, Nancy. *See* Blanchard
Waddell, Susan. *See* Lynds
Wadden, Mary Ann (Wood), XII, 1120
Waddens, Jean-Étienne, IV, 592, **757**; V, 77, 259, 532, 538, 683, 684; VI, 207, 471; VII, 523; VIII, 85, 349, 580
Waddens, Marguerite (MacKay; McLoughlin), IV, 757; V, 532, 534; VIII, 580
Waddens, Marguerite-Anne (Dessaulles), VI, 207
Waddens, Marie-Josephte. *See* Deguire
Waddens, Véronique (Bethune), IV, 757; V, 77, 78; VII, 74; VIII, 85; IX, 48; X, 53, 57
Waddilove, William James Darley, VII, 828; X, 269
Waddington, Alfred Penderell, IX, 432, 514, 712; X, 104, 198, **696–98**; XI, 301; XII, 1049
Waddington, Frederick, X, 696
Waddington, Grace Valentine. *See* Sykes
Waddington, Thomas, X, 696
Waddington, William, X, 696
Wade, Anne (Mann), VI, 484
Wade, Cooper, II, 666
Wade, Henry, VII, 893
Wade, John, VII, 893
Wade, John Chipman, XI, 398
Wade, Mary. *See* Hodgson
Wade, Mason, VII, 412; XII, 827
Wade, Ralph, VII, 893
Wade, Robert, VII, **892–93**
Wadins. *See* Waddens
Wadsworth, Benjamin, II, 25
Wadsworth, George, X, 450
Wadsworth, James, VIII, 268
Wadsworth, Juliet (Holmes), VIII, 403
Wäber. *See also* Webber
Wäber, Rosina, IV, 762
Wageezhegome. *See* Ogimauh-binaessih
Wager, Sir Charles, III, 447, 448, 659
Waggaman, Camille. *See* Armault

Waggaman, George Augustus, X, 462
Waggaman, Marie Christine (Macdonald), X, 462
Waggoner, Joseph, III, 304, 595; IV, 47
Waggoner, Rowland, II, 65, **658**; III, 595; IV, 380
Wagner, Mr (of Hamburg), VII, 694
Wagner, Christine. *See* Diemert
Wagner, Dominique, XII, 1077
Wagner, James Theodore, XII, **1077–78**, 1085
Wagner, Richard, XI, 671
Wagner*, William (1820–1901), XI, 645, 675
Wahawanulet, Louis (Captain Louis), III, 266
Wahbanosay, VII, 451; VIII, 439; IX, 592
Wahbuneeb, Samuel, VIII, 440
Wahpasha, V, 835, 836; VI, 189
Wahpasha, IV, 486; V, 10, 760, **835–37**; VI, 189
Wainewright, Constance Emily (Stone), XII, 991
Wainwright, Francis, II, 38, 452
Wainwright, Lucy (Waldo), III, 652
Wainwright, Mary. *See* Williams
Wainwright, Simon, II, 606
Waipykanine. *See* Wabakinine
Waisowindebay. *See* Musquakie
Wait, Benjamin, VII, 56, 460; VIII, 27; IX, 124, 125; XII, **1078–79**
Wait, Maria. *See* Smith
Wait, Oliver, VI, 812; XI, 267
Wait, Rebecca H. *See* Sealey
Waite, Annette (Watson), X, 699
Wakefield, Edward, IX, 817
Wakefield, Edward Gibbon, VII, 118, 478, 606; VIII, xxiii, 764; IX, 190, 191, 192, 236, 237, 335, 441, **817–19**; XII, 206, 833
Wakefield, Eliza Susan. *See* Pattle
Wakefield, Ellen. *See* Turner
Wakefield, Susanna. *See* Crash
Wakefield, William Hayward, IX, 817
Wakeham, Robert Roberts, VII, 629
Wakeshogomy. *See* Ogimauh-binaessih
Waks, Elizabeth Eleanor (Weld), XII, 1093
Walbank, Thomas, III, 504
Walbran*, John Thomas (1848–1913), IX, 36
Walcot, Charles Melton, IX, 597
Walcot, Henry Talbot, XII, 145
Walcot, Isabella. *See* Nickinson
Waldegrave, Cornelia, Baroness Radstock. *See* Lennap
Waldegrave, Elizabeth, Countess Waldegrave. *See* Gower
Waldegrave, John, 3rd Earl Waldegrave, VI, 795
Waldegrave, William, 1st Baron Radstock, V, 360, 408, 726, 763; VI, 9, **795–97**
Waldie, John, XII, 577
Waldo, Ann (Tyng), III, 635
Waldo, Hannah. *See* Mason
Waldo, Jonathan, III, 652
Waldo, Lucy. *See* Wainwright
Waldo, Samuel, II, 494; III, 6, 128, 259, 483, 635, 642, 645, **652–54**; IV, 780
Waldorf, Ann (Clarke), VIII, 158
Waldren, Ann Maria (Williams), XII, 1100
Waldron (Walrond), Miss (Holloway), VI, 323
Waldron, Anne Collard (Davie), XI, 236; XII, 227
Waldron, John, V, 839
Waldron, John, V, 641, 785, **837–39**
Waldron, Joseph, V, 837

Waldron, Martha (mother of JOHN), V, 837
Waldron, Mary. *See* Young
Waldron, Solomon, XII, 186
Waldruff, Ann (Kieffer; Saveraine), VIII, 450
Wales, Prince of. *See* Edward VII; Edward VIII; Frederick Louis; George IV
Wales, Princess of. *See* Alexandra; Augusta; Caroline Amelia Elizabeth; Charlotte Augusta
Wales, William, IV, 339, 341, 377, 740, 741, 744, **757–58**
Walford, Miss E. (Wix), IX, 846
Walkem*, George Anthony (1834–1908), X, 139; XI, 33, 51, 236, 300, 301, 374, 435, 756, 757, 840; XII, 79, 80, 240, 292, 295, 653, 916
Walker, Miss (Kempt), VIII, 458
Walker, Alexander, VIII, 458
Walker, Alexander, IV, 498, 499; V, 618; VI, **797–98**; VII, 830, 831
Walker, Anna Louisa (Vial de Sainbel; wife of THOMAS), V, 839
Walker, Anne (wife of Nehemiah, mariner), I, 666
Walker, Barbara. *See* Montgomery
Walker, Bridget (Archibald), IX, 7
Walker, David, VII, 529
Walker, Edward, V, 748
Walker, Edward Chandler, XII, 1081
Walker, Elizabeth. *See* Chamberlen
Walker, Elizabeth (Barbier), VIII, 60
Walker, Eliza Locke (Harris; David), XI, 234
Walker, Emma (Robinson, Lady Robinson), VI, 604; IX, 669; XII, 101, 906
Walker, Fowler, IV, 574; VI, 491
Walker, Franklin Hiram, XII, 1081
Walker, George, IV, 436
Walker, Hannah (mother of WILLIAM), IV, 760
Walker, Harriet. *See* McLean
Walker, Helen (Watson), IX, 822
Walker, Hiram, XII, 147, **1079–81**
Walker, Hiram Alexis, XII, 1081
Walker*, Horatio (1858–1938), XII, 336, 789
Walker, Sir Hovenden, I, 36, 76; II, 21, 52, 80, 122, 246, 250, 254, 286, 287, 289, 304, 384, 437, 485, 490, 497, 508, 511, 569, 643, 651, **658–62**, 667; III, 177, 178, 200, 429, 596, 662
Walker, Isabella (McCulloch), VII, 529
Walker, James (brother of NEHEMIAH), I, 666
Walker, James (doctor), VIII, 60
Walker, James (politician), V, 572, 840
Walker, James Harrington, XII, 1081
Walker, Jane. *See* Finlay
Walker, Jane (Head, Lady Head), IX, 381
Walker, Jane Sophia (Gamelin), VIII, 313
Walker, Jean (Machir), IX, 495
Walker, John (author), VIII, 427
Walker, John (lawyer), VIII, 525
Walker, John (merchant), IV, 682
Walker, John (shipowner), IV, 163
Walker, John (traveller), I, 333
Walker, Juliana (Rudd; Mondelet), VII, 622
Walker, Louisa Nash, V, 839
Walker, Margaret. *See* Manderston
Walker, Margaret, XI, 632
Walker, Margaret (Boston), IX, 61
Walker, Margaret (Newton; Simonds), VII, 806

Walker, Maria (Williams), XI, 931
Walker, Martha (Huntington), VIII, 415
Walker, Mary (Gilkison), VI, 285
Walker, Mary Abigail. *See* Williams
Walker, Myles, IX, 7
Walker, Nehemiah, I, 666
Walker, Nehemiah, I, 39, 84, 232, 324, 417, 476, 518, 519, 528, 543, 605, 606, 657, **666**; II, 231, 264
Walker, Obediah, I, 667
Walker, Patrick, XI, 137
Walker, Rebecca (Durnford), VII, 265
Walker, Richard, I, 62, 399, 637, **666–67**
Walker, Robert, VIII, 876; X, 434
Walker, Ruth. *See* Buffum
Walker, Sarah (wife of RICHARD), I, 667
Walker, Sarah (M'Alpine), VI, 411
Walker, Thomas, VIII, 755
Walker, Thomas, IV, 130, 184, 270, 295, 345, 348, 369, 379, 380, 546, 576, 634, **758–60**; V, 20, 64, 98, 142, 146, 382, 413, 432, 517, 527, 818; VI, 417, 492
Walker, Thomas, V, **839–40**
Walker, William (brother of NEHEMIAH), I, 666
Walker, William (businessman), VI, 255; VII, 311, 894; IX, 179, 273, 274, 275
Walker, William (father-in-law of John BOSTON), IX, 61
Walker, William (father of ALEXANDER), VI, 797
Walker, William (father of Sir HOVENDEN), II, 658
Walker, William (father of NEHEMIAH), I, 84, 666
Walker, William (father of WILLIAM, 1797–1844), VII, 893
Walker, William (son of WILLIAM, d. 1792), IV, 760
Walker, William, IV, 157, 740, **760–61**; V, 451, 683; VIII, 90
Walker, William, VII, 648, 667, **893–94**; VIII, 525, 694, 915; IX, 699; XI, 187; XII, 88, 89
Walker, William P., VI, 58
Walker, Willis, XII, 1079
Walk-in-the-Water. *See* Myeerah
Wall, Rachel. *See* Butler
Wallace, Miss (Fenety), XII, 313
Wallace, Alfred, VII, 363, 364, 365
Wallace, Anne. *See* Spiers
Wallace, Catherine (Bell), X, 45
Wallace, Charles Wentworth, VI, 799, 801; VII, 16; VIII, 348
Wallace, Edward, VI, 799
Wallace, Eleanor (Porter), VI, 799; IX, 637
Wallace, Frances Barbara. *See* Moule
Wallace, James, XI, 749
Wallace, Sir James, V, 763
Wallace, James Nevin, VII, 569
Wallace, Jane (Mortimer; Wilkins), XI, 926
Wallace, John (father of WILLIAM), XI, 906
Wallace, John (son of MICHAEL), VI, 799
Wallace, John Sinclair, VIII, 555
Wallace, Maria. *See* Simpson
Wallace, Mary. *See* Kerby
Wallace, Mary Ann. *See* Kent
Wallace, Michael, V, 608, 612, 850; VI, 313, 520, 780, **798–801**; VII, 63, 531, 533; VIII, 300, 345, 603; IX, 637
Wallace*, Nathaniel Clarke (1844–1901), XII, 584, 585, 586, 1120
Wallace, Robert, XI, 834
Wallace, Thomas, IX, 810

Wallace, Thomas J., XI, 948

Wallace, William (professor), XII, 1102

Wallace, William (Scottish national hero), V, 287

Wallace, William (shipbuilder), XI, 834

Wallace, William (son of MICHAEL), VI, 799

Wallace, William, XI, **906–8**; XII, 500

Wallace*, William Stewart (1884–1970), V, 331; VI, 495, 496, 815; VIII, 101, 580; IX, 406, 535; X, 627

Wallack, James William (father), IX, 598

Wallack, James William, IX, 598

Wallack, Lester, XII, 449

Wallbridge, Lewis, XI, 422, 593, 646, 853, **908–9**; XII, 606

Wallbridge, Mary. *See* Everett

Wallbridge, Thomas Campbell, XI, 909

Wallbridge, William, XI, 908

Wallen, Phoebe (Phebe) (Frost; Gray), V, 334, 386

Waller, Alvan F., VIII, 579

Waller, Catherine, Lady Waller. *See* Moore

Waller, Sir Edmund, VI, 802

Waller, Elizabeth. *See* Willis

Waller, Jocelyn, VI, 783, **801–2**; VIII, 259, 260; IX, 810; XI, 187

Waller, Sir Robert, VI, 801

Waller, William, VIII, 375

Walley, John, I, 466, 545; II, 601, **662**

Walling, Henry Francis, XII, 249

Wallis, Anne (Duckworth), V, 273

Wallis, Arthur Frederick, XII, 138

Wallis, Benjamin, II, 265

Wallis, Elizabeth. *See* Lawlor

Wallis, James (merchant), XII, 88

Wallis, James (settler), XII, 527

Wallis, Jemima Mary Gwynne, Lady Wallis. *See* Wilson

Wallis, John, V, 273

Wallis, Juliana. *See* Massey

Wallis, Provo, XII, 1082

Wallis, Provo Featherstone, XII, 1081, 1082

Wallis, Sir Provo William Parry, XII, **1081–83**

Wallis, Samuel, XII, 1082

Wallmoden, Amalie Sophie Marianne von. *See* Wendt

Walls, Elizabeth (Bellingham, Lady Bellingham), XII, 88

Wallscourt, Baron. *See* Blake

Walmesley, Sara (Parr), IV, 603

Walpole, Horatio (Horace), 4th Earl of Orford, III, 92, 150, 166; IV, 114, 571; V, 822

Walpole, Robert, 1st Earl of Oxford, II, 24; III, 283, 447

Walpole, Sir Spencer, XI, 884

Walrond. *See* Waldron

Walsh. *See also* Welch

Walsh, Ann (Young), VIII, 962

Walsh, Aquila, XI, 907, **909–10**

Walsh, Catherine (Cochran), X, 176

Walsh, Catherine (Tobin), IX, 790

Walsh, David, VIII, 469

Walsh, Edward, VI, 9

Walsh, Ellen. *See* Macdonald

Walsh, Flora (Hoyt), XII, 949

Walsh, Francis Legh (Leigh), V, 846, 847; XI, 909

Walsh, James, XII, 1083

Walsh*, James Morrow (1843–1905), XI, 326, 477, 870; XII, 673, 674

Walsh, Jane Wilson. *See* Adams

Walsh, John, XI, 536, 537, 695, 715, 904; XII, 183, 294, 332, 333, 811, 934, 1078, **1083–88**

Walsh, Joseph, VIII, 919

Walsh, Joseph-Alexis, Vicomte Walsh, VII, 805

Walsh, Kyran, VIII, 247; IX, 393, 584, **819–20**

Walsh, Margaret (Ryan), XII, 932

Walsh, Mary (Donlevy), VIII, 228

Walsh, Michael A. J., XI, 32

Walsh, Raphael, VI, 565

Walsh, Robert, XII, 862

Walsh, Sarah (Adamson), IX, 4

Walsh, Thomas, I, 329; II, 42, 177, 311, 393, 394, 407, 454

Walsh, Thomas Leigh (Legh), XI, 909

Walsh, William, VII, 298, 805; VIII, 193, 307, 554, 627, 656, 664, 665, **919–21**; IX, 476, 477, 651; X, 191, 480; XI, 381; XII, 834, 1083

Walsingham, Baron. *See* Grey

Walsingham, Sir Francis, I, 251, 252, 332, 333, 363, 380

Walt, Nettie. *See* Phillips

Walter, Hester (Schuyler), III, 587

Walter, John, V, 881

Walter, Rebecca (Byles), V, 128

Walter, William, V, 657, 658

Waltermeyer, Hans (Waltermyer, Johannes). *See* Meyers, John Walden

Walters. *See also* Palliser

Walters, Annie (Jordan), XII, 448

Walters, Julia (Oppenheimer), XII, 803

Walters, William, III, 320

Walton, Anna Maria (Berk; Boulton), IX, 68

Walton, Charles, IX, 181

Walton, Charles Albert, XII, 992

Walton, Izaak, IX, 5; XII, 995

Walton, Joseph Soper, XII, 351, 902

Walton, Mary (Nutting), IX, 601

Walton, Matthew, XI, 542

Wandagan, V, 706

Wandering Spirit. *See* Kapapamahchakwew

Wands, William, V, 814

Wanduny. *See* Orontony

Wanostrocht, Nicholas, XII, 493

Wan-o-wen-re-teh. *See* Rollston, Catherine

Wanton, Mary (Morrison), VI, 520

Wanton, William, IV, 769

Wanungonet. *See* Wenemouet

Wanzer, Electa Ann. *See* Lyon

Wanzer, Richard Mott, XII, **1088–89**

Wapackcamigat (Wapaumagen). *See* Wabbicommicot

Wapasha. *See* Wahpasha

Wapinesiw (Wappenessew), IV, 47, **761**

Wappisis, III, 123, **654–55**; IV, 381, 518

Warburton, Anna. *See* Acton

Warburton, Augustus, VII, 743

Warburton, Bartholomew Elliott George, VIII, 921

Warburton, Elizabeth Augusta. *See* Bateman-Hanbury

Warburton, George, VIII, 921

Warburton, George Drought, VIII, **921–22**; XII, 692

Warburton, James, VII, 145, 146; VIII, 564, 566; IX, 856; XI, 532; XII, 426

Ward, Mrs. *See* Reynolds

Ward, Anne. *See* Harper

Ward, Arthur Clitheroe, XI, 21

Ward, Caleb, VII, 895

Ward, Catharine. *See* Lyon
Ward, Eber, XII, 147
Ward, Edmund (father of EDMUND), VIII, 922
Ward, Edmund (father of JOHN), VII, 894
Ward, Edmund, VI, 322, 508; VII, 12, 22; VIII, **922–23**
Ward, Edward, IV, 617
Ward, Eleanor Bowers. *See* Jackson
Ward, Elizabeth (mother of JOHN). *See* Strange
Ward, Elizabeth (wife of JOHN). *See* Strange
Ward, Felix, VI, 338
Ward, Hannah. *See* Rogers
Ward, James, XII, **1089–90**
Ward*, James Kewley (1819–1910), XI, 522
Ward, Jane, VIII, 402
Ward, John, VII, 894, 895
Ward, John, VI, 356; VII, **894–95**
Ward, John Dod, VII, 29; XI, 121
Ward, Lebbeus B., XI, 121
Ward, Lucretia (Willard), VI, 816
Ward, Maria (Moir), XII, 747
Ward, Mary, XI, 240
Ward, Richard, II, 51, 65, 267, 493, **662–63**
Ward, Robert, VIII, 923
Ward, Samuel, XI, 121
Ward, Samuel Ringgold, VIII, 89; IX, **820–21**; XII, 492, 960
Ward, Sarah (Williams), XI, 928
Ward, Thomas (brother-in-law of Ward CHIPMAN, 1754–1824), VI, 142
Ward, Thomas (judge), XI, 928
Ward, Thomas (theatre lessee), IX, 597
Ward, William (clergyman), V, 190
Ward, William (father of SAMUEL RINGGOLD), IX, 820
Ward, William George, X, 548; XII, 440
Ward, William H., X, 394
Ward, William James, X, 716
Warde, Richard, I, 343
Warden, Matthew, III, 151
Wardhouse. *See* Gordon
Wardlaw, Margaret (Skirving), XII, 973
Wardlaw, Ralph, IX, 467
Ware, Elijah W., XI, 377
Ware, Mary (Eddy), V, 295
Ware, Walter, VII, 111
Waring, Caroline. *See* Placide
Waring, Richard, V, 468
Wark. *See also* Work
Wark, Henry, IX, 850
Warmow, Mathias, XII, 836
Warnar, Elizabeth (Russell), V, 729
Warner, Charles, known as Charles John Lickford, XII, 669
Warner, Grace (McLeay), XII, 668, 669
Warner, Henry, XII, 342
Warner, John, II, 265
Warnock, Amelia Beers (Garvin) (Katherine Hale), XI, 212, 213
Warracansit (Warracunsit, Warrawcuset). *See* Mog
Warre, Sir Henry James, VII, 440, 441; VIII, 662; IX, 327, 806; X, 391, 426
Warren, Anne (Johnson), IV, 394
Warren, Annie (MacLean), X, 482
Warren, Bridget. *See* Rossell
Warren, Caroline, Lady Warren. *See* Clavering

Warren, Catherine. *See* Aylmer
Warren, Elizabeth (Church), II, 145
Warren, Elizabeth (Lett), VIII, 501
Warren, Ellen (Dyas), XII, 286
Warren, Henry, V, 842
Warren, Hester (Patterson), IV, 606
Warren, Isabella (Fraser), XII, 335
Warren, Joanna (Anglin), XII, 23
Warren, John (doctor), V, 737
Warren, John (merchant), XI, 501
Warren, John (son of JOHN), V, 642, 644, 842; VI, 761
Warren, John, V, 405, 548, 642, 643, 644, 660, 661, 669, **840–42**, 846, 856; VI, 211; VIII, 185
Warren, John B., XI, 346
Warren, John Borlase, VI, 802
Warren, Sir John Borlase, V, 69, 82; VI, 38, **802–4**; VII, 709
Warren, John Henry, XI, 108, 433, **910–11**
Warren, Laura (Bowring), XI, 108
Warren, Mary (wife of JOHN), V, 840
Warren, Michael, III, 655
Warren, Sir Peter, III, 6, 49, 91, 209, 294, 345, 356, 507, 508, 572, 610, 628, 636, 642, 644, 653, 654, **655–59**; IV, 62, 83, 168, 239, 248, 363, 394, 417, 420, 454, 783; V, 134; IX, 196
Warren, Rachael (Rachel) (Munro), XII, 771
Warren, Sir Robert, VII, 35
Warren, Susannah. *See* de Lancey
Warren, W. H., VII, 776
Warren, William (father of JOHN HENRY), XI, 910
Warren, William (officer), X, 561
Warrow, VII, 821
Warsong. *See* Wasson
Wartman, Susannah (Richardson), XII, 893
Warton, Britannia (Burns), IX, 109
Warwick, Countess of. *See* Russell
Warwick, Earl of. *See* Dudley; Rich
Warwick, Charlotte (Ryland), VII, 766
Warwick, John, XII, 631
Warwick, William (potter), IX, 836
Warwick, William (printer), XII, 923
Washburn, Daniel, VI, 56, 805; X, 60
Washburn, Ebenezer, V, 521, 550, 772, 841; VI, 215, **804–6**; VII, 419, 557, 896; VIII, 694
Washburn, Hannah (McBride; wife of EBENEZER), VI, 804
Washburn, Hannah (McDowall), VII, 557
Washburn, Jemima Gary (Perry), VIII, 694
Washburn, Jemimah. *See* Gary
Washburn, Margaret. *See* FitzGibbon
Washburn, Sarah. *See* de Forest
Washburn, Simeon, VI, 804
Washburn, Simon Ebenezer, V, 521; VI, 265, 805; VII, 37, 40, **896**; IX, 55; X, 262; XI, 617
Wash-e-soo E'Squaw (Agathas, Aggathas), VII, 206
Washiabitt, III, 595
Washington, George, III, 148, 149, 150, 151, 320, 375, 376, 587, 600, 601, 614; IV, 34, 177, 178, 227, 229, 256, 257, 322, 408, 459, 490, 522, 547, 617, 667, 681, 736; V, 16, 24, 28, 29, 30, 33, 34, 36, 40, 96, 148, 227, 239, 295, 313, 343, 414, 604, 627, 629, 705, 706, 808, 810, 873, 893, 895, 896, 899; VI, 647, 793; VII, 523, 714
Washington, John, VIII, 447
Washington, John, II, 601, **663**; III, 277

Washington, Martha. *See* Dandridge
Washington, Mary. *See* Scott
Washington, William, VII, 714
Wasiteck, VII, 3
Wasnidge, Elizabeth (Workman), XII, 1122
Wasson, IV, 762
Wasson (Wassong), III, 95, 96; IV, lv, **761–62**; V, 567
Water Bird. *See* Ohkipiksew
Waterbury, Rebecca (Cudlip), XI, 223
Waterhouse. *See also* Waterous
Waterhouse, Benjamin, V, 737
Waterhouse, Eleazer, XII, 1090
Waterhouse, Emma. *See* Johnson
Waterman, Eunice. *See* Dean
Waterman, Experience. *See* Freeman
Waterman, Hannah (King; Arnold), V, 28
Waterman, Patience. *See* Freeman
Waterman, Richard, V, 491
Waterman, Zenas, IX, 821
Waterman, Zenas, IX, **821–22**
Waterous, Charles Horatio, XII, **1090–92**
Waterous, Frank, XII, 1091
Waterous, Frederick, XII, 1091
Waterous, Martha. *See* June
Waters, Abigail (Cleveland), III, 125
Waters, Charles, VIII, 689
Waters, Edmund, VIII, 443
Waters, Henrietta (O'Reilly), IX, 611
Waters, Henry Harcourt, IX, 611
Waters, William, VIII, 5, 887
Waterton, Charles, XII, 268
Watier, Joachim, X, 500
Watier, Odile (Élodie) (Masson), X, 500
Watkin, Sir Edward William, IX, 235, 385, 411; X, 633; XI, 53, 123, 933; XII, 263, 432, 434, 435, 595, 1055
Watkins, Caroline (Humphreys), XI, 434
Watkins, Edwin Arthur, XII, 446
Watkins, John, X, 335; XI, 6
Watkins, Kathleen. *See* Blake
Watkins, Louisa Mary (How), X, 361
Watson, Annette. *See* Waite
Watson, Sir Brook, IV, 53, 57, 58, 112, 244, 273, 313, 369, 528, 592, 618, 696, 717, 721; V, 20, 22, 23, 173, 192, 277, 289, 371, 396, 416, 494, 789, **842–44**, 869, 870; VI, 87, 99, 357; VII, 522, 523, 817; VIII, xxv, 300
Watson, Caroline, III, 592
Watson, Charles, III, **659**
Watson, David, XII, 483, 745
Watson, Grace (Lesslie), XI, 516
Watson, Helen. *See* Walker
Watson, Helen, Lady Watson. *See* Campbell
Watson, Helen (Ogilvie), IX, 822; XII, 800
Watson*, Homer Ransford (1855–1936), XI, 683; XII, 207, 328, 336, 789
Watson, Isaac, XI, 911
Watson, Isabella (Cooper), VII, 207, 208
Watson, J. M., XI, 911
Watson, James Craig, X, **698–99**
Watson, Janet McAuslyn (Moody), X, 530
Watson, Jannet (McLean), XI, 570
Watson, John (clergyman), IX, 467
Watson, John (father of Sir BROOK), V, 843
Watson, John (father of CHARLES), III, 659

Watson, John (father of WILLIAM), IX, 822; XII, 800
Watson, John M., XI, 911
Watson, Jonas, VII, 450
Watson, Joseph, VIII, 84
Watson, Lawrence White, XII, 48
Watson, Margaret (Gibson), IX, 313
Watson, Margaret Janet (wife of SAMUEL JAMES), XI, 911
Watson, Rebecca. *See* Bacon
Watson, Rebecca. *See* Buller
Watson, Rebecca (Dalton), VII, 228
Watson, Richard, XI, 785, 786
Watson, Robert (brother of WILLIAM), IX, 823
Watson, Robert (newspaperman), IX, 740, 741
Watson, Samuel James, XI, 872, **911–12**
Watson, Sarah. *See* Schofield
Watson, Sereno, X, 82
Watson, Simon Zelotes, V, 14; VI, 477, 808; VIII, 337
Watson, Stewart, X, 390
Watson, Susan (Chandler), IX, 123
Watson, Thomas (father), VI, 330
Watson, Thomas, VI, 330
Watson, Thomas Hart, XII, 52
Watson, William, X, 698
Watson, William, IX, **822–24**; XII, 800
Watson-Gordon, Sir John, VIII, 405
Watson-Wentworth, Charles, 2nd Marquess of Rockingham, IV, xli, 348, 571; V, 149, 848, 851; VI, 491
Watt, Ann (MacDonald), VII, 542
Watt, Elizabeth (Nairn), XII, 777
Watt, James, VIII, 630
Watteau, Jean-Antoine, XII, 102
Wattenwyl. *See* Watteville
Watters, Charles, XI, 888
Watteville, David de, VII, 896
Watteville, Frédéric de, VII, 897
Watteville, John de (Bishop Johannes), III, 212
Watteville, Louis de, VI, 343, 344; VII, 312, **896–99**
Watteville, Magdalena de. *See* Jenner
Watteville, Rodolphe de, VII, 898
Watteville, Sophie de. *See* Tavel
Watts, Agnes. *See* Mackworth
Watts, Anne (Firth), VII, 285
Watts, Charles, XII, 843, 866
Watts, Isaac, VI, 457, 461
Watts, John, I, 241
Watts*, John William Hurrell (1850–1917), XI, 919; XII, 329
Watts, Margaret (wife of RICHARD), II, 663
Watts, Mary (Johnson, Lady Johnson), VI, 352
Watts, Richard, I, 241
Watts, Richard, II, 275, **663–64**
Watts, Robert Nugent, VII, 398; VIII, 769
Watts, Sarah Parker (Longworth), XI, 526
Waub Ojeeg. *See* Wabojeeg
Waugh, Alexander (clergyman), X, 659
Waugh, Alexander (father of WELLWOOD), VI, 806
Waugh, Catherine. *See* Colven
Waugh, Eliza (Tod), XI, 882, 883
Waugh, Helen. *See* Henderson
Waugh, Samuel Bell, X, 390
Waugh, Wellwood, VI, 121, **806–7**; VIII, 122
Waugh-we-ya-pe-yis-sin-ious. *See* Weyapiersenwah
Waunathoake. *See* Demasduwit

Wauters, Isabella Ludivica (Krieghoff), X, 408
Wautier, Adélaïde-Rose-Josephe (Stevens), XI, 851
Wawanosh, William, XII, 187
Wawanolewat. *See* Gray Lock
Wawapessenwa. *See* Weyapiersenwah
Wawatam, III, **659–60**; V, 129; VI, 317
Wawenesse, IV, 133
Wawenorrawot. *See* Gray Lock
Waxaway, II, **664**
Way*, Charles Jones (1835–1919), XII, 789
Waylen, Anne (Smith), VII, 811
Waymouth, George, I, 20, 189, 318, 375, 397, 650, **667–68**
Wayne, Anthony, IV, 260, 410, 499; V, 121, 535, 553, 556, 594, 802, 808, 852; VI, 8, 102, 550, 628
Weah, XII, 290
Weal, Margaret (Chadwick), XII, 171
Weals, John, X, 412
Weatherald, Thomas, X, 517
Weatherbe*, Sir Robert Linton (1836–1915), XI, 210
Webb, Daniel, III, 460
Webb, David, XII, 453
Webb, Edward, XI, 912
Webb, Grace (wife of JAMES), III, 661
Webb, Harriet (Calvin), XI, 139
Webb, Isabella. *See* Morris
Webb, James, III, **660–61**; IV, 259; V, 381
Webb, Mary (Hartman), VIII, 370
Webb, Mary Ann. *See* Blyth
Webb, Philip Barker, X, 81, 82
Webb, Sarah Ann. *See* Whitcomb
Webb, Sophia Elizabeth (Cox), X, 198
Webb, William Hoste, IX, 122, 727; XI, **912–13**
Webber (Wäber), Abraham, IV, 762
Webber, George, VI, 709; VIII, **923–24**
Webber, Hannah (Whitman), VIII, 929
Webber, John, IV, **762–63**
Webber, Mary (Milbanke), V, 595
Webber, Mary (Quant; mother of JOHN), IV, 762
Webber, Samuel, V, 874
Webber, Susanna (Smith), VII, 817
Weber, Anna, XI, **913**
Weber, Catherine. *See* Gehman
Weber, John, XI, 913
Webster, Ann (Huntley), IX, 400
Webster, Arthur (Montreal merchant), V, 218; VIII, 283
Webster, Arthur (Sherbrooke, Que., businessman), XII, 348
Webster, Daniel, X, 483, 591
Webster, Eliza (Dalrymple), VIII, 197
Webster, Elizabeth. *See* Cruickshank
Webster, Hannah (Foster), XI, 321
Webster, Harriet (Gesner), IX, 308, 312
Webster, Hugh, VI, 407
Webster, Isaac, IX, 308, 824
Webster, James (land purchaser), XII, 683
Webster, James (partner of Adam FERGUSSON), IX, 252, 253
Webster, John, VIII, 197
Webster*, John Clarence (1863–1950), III, 667; IV, 458
Webster, Joseph Harding, IX, **824**; X, 612; XI, 549
Webster, Prudence. *See* Bentley
Webster, Wilhelmina. *See* Moore
Webster, William Bennett, IX, 308, **824–25**

Wechikiwekapawiqua (Catharine Cameron), VI, 555; VIII, 440
Wedd, Charlotte Ross (Cameron), XI, 143
Wedderburn. *See also* Colvile; Halkett
Wedderburn, Alexander, VII, 289, **899**; IX, 387, 629; XII, 692
Wedderburn, Alexander, 1st Earl of Rosslyn, IV, xlv, xlvi, xlvii, xlviii, 349; V, 145; VIII, 351
Wedderburn, Jane. *See* Heaviside
Wedderburn, Jean (Douglas, Baroness Daer and Short-cleuch, Countess of Selkirk), V, 264, 265, 266, 269; VI, 167; VIII, 527, 575, 720
Wedderburn, Mary Louisa. *See* Eden
Wedderburn, William, XI, 298
Wedel, Miss (Mabane), IV, 491
Wedikind, Johanna Francisca Carolina (Nepean), VI, 537
Weedon, Edwin, XII, 791
Wee-kas-koo-kee-say-yin. *See* Wikaskokiseyin
Weekes, George, VIII, 479
Weekes, Hannah (Franklin), VII, 323
Weekes, William, V, 17, 171, 366, 405, 420, 441, 443, 519, 643, 782, 810, 842, **844–45**, 854, 855, 856; VI, 4, 5, 177, 215, 656, 804; VII, 13, 251, 438, 864, 865, 929; VIII, 607
Weeks, Catherine Charlotte (Crosskill), VIII, 192
Weeks, Joshua Wingate, V, 48, 128; VIII, 901; XII, 1092
Weeks, Maria. *See* Morris
Weeks, Martha Wingate (Stout), V, 779
Weeks, Mary Ann Sarah (Dodd), X, 232
Weeks, Otto Richard Schwartz, XII, 1092
Weeks, Otto Schwartz, XII, 437, 438, 859, **1092–93**
Weeks, Sally (Bailey), V, 47
Weeks, Sarah (Twining), VIII, 901
Weeks, Seraph Cutler. *See* Ruggles
Weems (Wemyss), Charlotte Esther (Smith), XII, 237
Wegg, George Samuel, IV, 758
Weggishgomin. *See* Ogimauh-binaessih
Weh-yah-pih-ehr-sehn-waw. *See* Weyapiersenwah
Weibel, Jakob Samuel, VI, 648
Weikmillar, Dorothea (Gaukel), VIII, 315
Weilbrenner, Joseph, VII, 500
Weilbrenner, Marguerite (Trudeau), XI, 889
Weilbrenner, Marie-Julie (Boucher de La Bruère), X, 76
Weingardner, Ellen, XI, 629, 630
Weir. *See also* Hope
Weir, Miss (sister of George, clergyman), IX, 307
Weir, Anne (White), XI, 918
Weir, G. J., VII, 335
Weir, George (clergyman), IX, 306, 307, 462
Weir, George (soldier), VII, 479; VIII, 471, 726; IX, 143, 328, 329, 827; X, 527
Weir, Isabella (Muir), VIII, 646
Weir, Robert (merchant), XII, 135
Weir, Robert (newspaper owner, d. 1843), IX, 257, 429; XI, 680
Weir, Robert (newspaper owner, d. 1846), IX, 208, 429; XI, 680
Weir*, William (1823–1905), VIII, 160, 161
Weis, George, V, 248
Weiser, Johann Conrad, III, 496, 606, 607, 613, 614; IV, 154
Weiss, Jean-Jacques, XI, 289, 339

Weissenberg (Wisenberg, Wysenberk), Catherine (Johnson), IV, 155, 397, 417; VI, 352
Welch, Mrs. *See* Johnson
Welch, Elizabeth. *See* Pierce
Welch, Francis, V, 845
Welch, L. A., XII, 585
Welch, Mary. *See* Mitchell
Welch, Thomas, V, 405, 733, 734, 842, **845–47**; VI, 160, 211, 331, 421, 422; VIII, 607
Weld, Agnes. *See* Johnston
Weld, Alexandrina. *See* Home
Weld, Charles Richard, VIII, 925; IX, 768
Weld, Elizabeth. *See* Kerr
Weld, Elizabeth Eleanor. *See* Waks
Weld, Isaac, VIII, 924
Weld, Isaac, IV, 738; V, 228, 302, 472; VIII, **924–25**; XII, 524
Weld, Joseph (grandfather), XII, 1093
Weld, Joseph, XII, 1093
Weld, Theodore Dwight, IX, 769
Weld, Thomas, VII, 663; VIII, 317
Weld, Thomas Saxon, XII, 1093
Weld, William, XI, 133; XII, **1093–94**
Weld, William Stephen, XII, 1093
Welding, William Erastus, XII, 157
Weldon, Frances Chandler. *See* Upham
Weldon, Haliburton, XII, 403
Weldon, John Wesley, V, 831; VIII, 395; IX, 146; XII, 403
Weldon*, Richard Chapman (1849–1925), XII, 888
Weldon, Susanna Lucy Anne. *See* Haliburton
Welfitt, Mary (Need), XII, 781
Well, Bernard, II, 337; IV, 135, 299; V, 432
Wellbeloved, Emma (Carter), X, 140
Weller*, John Laing (1862–1932), IX, 826
Weller, Mrs Madelein Marcia, IX, 826
Weller, Margaret. *See* McKechin
Weller, Mercy. *See* Willcox
Weller, William, IX, **825–26**
Welles, John, IV, 140, 277, 697; V, 20, 21
Welles, Marguerite. *See* Réaume
Wellesley, Arthur, 1st Duke of Wellington, IV, 26; V, 489, 695, 696, 697, 698, 761; VI, 38, 99, 183, 257, 402, 713, 734; VII, 30, 31, 42, 129, 130, 142, 266, 268, 336, 398, 440, 640, 641, 722, 731, 740, 819, 820, 904, 905; VIII, xxvii, 135, 375, 459, 461, 462, 465, 538, 596, 602, 604, 827, 857; IX, 37, 63, 72, 79, 137, 138, 139, 221, 336, 462, 543, 595, 675, 858; X, 334, 403, 404, 438, 439, 634
Wellesley, Richard, 2nd Earl of Mornington and 1st Marquess Wellesley, VII, 142
Wellesley, Richard Colley, 1st Marquis of Wellesley, X, 309
Wellesley-Pole, Mary Charlotte Anne (Bagot, Lady Bagot), VII, 30; VIII, 588
Wellesley-Pole, William, 3rd Earl of Mornington, VII, 30
Wellington, Duke of. *See* Wellesley
Wells, Alphonso, IX, 276
Wells, Amanda (mother of JAMES EDWARD), XII, 1094
Wells, Delia Almira (Lyman), X, 451
Wells, Frances Augusta (Wisner), XII, 1116
Wells, Frances Barbara. *See* Moule
Wells, Harriett. *See* King
Wells, Horace Clough, XI, 914
Wells, Isaac Brock, XI, 915

Wells, James Edward, XII, 1094
Wells, James Edward, XII, 225, **1094–95**
Wells, John (architect), VI, 554; VII, 80; XI, 92
Wells, John (politician), VIII, 710
Wells, Joseph, VIII, 925
Wells, Joseph, VII, 756, 822; VIII, 29, 47, 48, 253, 427, **925–27**; IX, 79, 535, 761; X, 35, 343
Wells, Maria Julia. *See* Hogan
Wells, Mary (mother of JOSEPH), VIII, 925
Wells, Phoebe (Flint), XII, 321
Wells, Rebecca (Gale), VI, 269; IX, 296
Wells, Rebecca M. *See* Chase
Wells, Ruth (Longley), VII, 510
Wells, Samuel, VI, 269
Wells, Sarah. *See* Clough
Wells, Thomas, XI, 652
Wells, William (businessman), VII, 510
Wells, William (father of WILLIAM BENJAMIN), XI, 914
Wells, William (Indian agent), V, 796
Wells, William Benjamin, VIII, 743; XI, **913–15**
Welsford, Augustus Frederick, V, 575; VIII, **927–28**; XI, 486
Welsford, John, V, 575; VIII, 927
Welsford, Mary. *See* Marchinton
Welsh. *See also* Welch
Welsh, David, XII, 659
Welsh, Jane Baillie (Carlyle), XII, 776
Welsh, Richard, VII, 840, 841
Welton*, Daniel Morse (1831–1904), XII, 882
Wemyss. *See also* Weems
Wemyss, Robert, XI, 130, 423
Wendell, Jacob, II, 26
Wendt, Count de, X, 413
Wendt, Amalie Sophie Marianne von, Countess of Yarmouth (Wallmoden), IV, 21
Wendt, Emily de. *See* Krieghoff
Wenemouet (Wenemowet, Wenemuit), II, xxxvii, 495, **664–66**, 669; III, 584
Wenger, Christian, VI, 807
Wenger, Elizabeth. *See* Eschlemann
Wenger, Johannes, VI, **807–8**
Wenham, Minerva Anne. *See* Niles
Wenman, Amos, IV, 763
Wenman, Ann. *See* Scroope
Wenman, Elizabeth Susanna (Pringle), IV, 764
Wenman, Richard, IV, 451, **763–64**; V, 670; VI, 621, 622
Wenman, Susanna (Green), IV, 764
Wenongonet (Wenoggenet). *See* Wenemouet
Wensley, Sarah (Winslow), IV, 774
Wentworth. *See also* Watson-Wentworth
Wentworth, Annabella (Gore), VIII, 336
Wentworth, Anne. *See* Tasker
Wentworth, Benning (uncle), III, 453; V, 848, 871
Wentworth, Benning, IV, 112; V, 850
Wentworth, Sir Charles Mary, V, 850
Wentworth, Edward Lowe, VI, 129
Wentworth, Elizabeth. *See* Rindge
Wentworth, Frances Deering (Atkinson; Wentworth, Lady Wentworth), V, 848, 849, 851
Wentworth, Henry, IX, 850
Wentworth, John, V, 311, 569, 775, 779, 780, **847–48**
Wentworth, Sir John, IV, 111, 112, 484, 485, 516, 605; V, 48, 124, 188, 240, 281, 297, 310, 314, 316, 328, 349,

350, 351, 354, 355, 356, 410, 423, 424, 431, 445, 608, 609, 634, 635, 646, 689, 693, 698, 763, 766, 847, **848–52**, 872; VI, 35, 89, 90, 99, 113, 129, 136, 157, 160, 173, 202, 203, 268, 313, 319, 333, 461, 517, 520, 535, 536, 564, 676, 726, 731, 756, 778, 779, 780, 781, 782, 790, 793, 799, 800, 807, 813; VII, 21, 63, 87, 104, 217, 589, 801, 814, 815, 832, 910; VIII, 336, 344, 345, 346, 354, 754, 891

Wentworth, Louisa. *See* Pryor
Wentworth, Mark Hunking, V, 848
Wentworth, Martha (Wentworth), V, 848
Wentworth, Paul, V, 851
Wentworth, Thomas, V, 847
Wentworth, Thomas Hanford, VII, **899–900**
Wentworth, William Henry, VII, 900
Wentworth-Fitzwilliam, Charles William, X, 196, 242
Wentworth-Fitzwilliam, Frances Harriet. *See* Douglas
Wentworth-Fitzwilliam, Laura Maria Theresa. *See* Beauclerk
Wentworth-Fitzwilliam, William, Viscount Milton, IX, 94, 602, 603; X, **699–700**; XII, 642
Wentworth-Fitzwilliam, William Thomas Spencer, 6th Earl Fitzwilliam, X, 699
Wentzel, Willard Ferdinand, VII, 324, 567
Wenungenit. *See* Wenemouet
Wesbrook, Frank Fairchild, XII, 918
Wesley, Charles, XI, 363; XII, 995
Wesley, John, IV, 19, 175, 176, 776; V, 258, 468, 573, 574, 575, 728, 729; VI, 62, 63, 64, 65, 67, 130, 131, 275, 276, 430, 557; VII, 45, 52, 164, 392, 587; VIII, 177, 373; IX, 56, 785; X, 615, 616; XI, 363, 641, 660, 719, 785, 786; XII, 995
Wesson, Francis L., XII, 572
West, Ann. *See* Knowles
West, Benjamin, III, 670; IV, 394; V, 768, 811; VII, 217, 336
West, Elizabeth. *See* Brechin
West, Elizabeth (Tupper), XI, 895
West, George, VII, 900
West, Hannah Rachel. *See* Foseler
West, Harriet. *See* Atkinson
West, Jacob Bailey, VIII, 928
West, James Thomas, VIII, 928
West, John, VI, 14, 282, 649, 754; VII, 390, 454, 455, **900–3**; VIII, xxx, 250, 721, 767; IX, 134, 135, 626; X, 108; XI, 711, 712
West, John Conrad, VIII, 928
West, John Conrade, VIII, **928–29**
West, John Wendel, VIII, 928
West, Mary (Sibley), IX, 720
West, Nathaniel Levy, VIII, 928
West, Sarah (McClearn), IX, 477
West, Thomas, 3rd Baron de La Warr, I, 67
West, William, VI, 483
West, William Pryor, VIII, 928
Westbrook, Andrew, V, 14, 749; VI, 406, **808–10**; VIII, 34, 608, 746
Westbrook, Anthony, VI, 808
Westbrook, Margaret Ann. *See* Crawford
Westbrook, Nancy. *See* Thorn
Westbrook, Sally. *See* Hull
Westbrook, Sarah. *See* Decker
Westbrook, Thomas, II, 544; III, 359

Westcott, Brooke Foss, XII, 660
Westfield, Judith (Irving), IV, 379
Westfield, William, IV, 379
Westmorland, Earl of. *See* Fane
Weston, Abijah, XI, 113
Weston, Anne (Carter), X, 141
Weston-Hugessen, Dorothea (Banks, Lady Banks), V, 54
Westphal, Alicia (Chambers; wife of Sir GEORGE AUGUSTUS ALEXANDER), X, 700
Westphal, Anna (mother of Sir GEORGE AUGUSTUS ALEXANDER), X, 700
Westphal, Sir George Augustus Alexander, X, **700–1**
Westphal, George Frederick, X, 700
Westphal, Philip, X, 701
Wetenhall, John, VIII, 55, 927; IX, 109; X, 126, 359
Wetherald*, Agnes Ethelwyn (1857–1940), XII, 776, 1095
Wetherald, Isabel. *See* Thistlethwaite
Wetherald, Jemima Harris. *See* Balls
Wetherald, John, XII, 1095
Wetherald, William, XII, **1095–96**
Wetherall, Edward R., X, 406
Wetherall, Sir Edward Robert, IX, 827
Wetherall, Elizabeth. *See* Mytton
Wetherall, Frances Diana. *See* Denton
Wetherall, Sir Frederick Augustus, V, 449; VI, 517; IX, 826
Wetherall, Sir George Augustus, VII, 248, 585; VIII, 616, 915; IX, 143, 328, 595, 682, **826–28**; X, 491; XI, 117; XII, 88, 89
Wetherall, T. A., VI, 428
Wetherell*, James Elgin (1851–1940), XI, 142
Wetherell, Robert Charles, VIII, 874
Wetmore, Abraham K. Smedus, VII, 692
Wetmore, Andrew Rainsford, VI, 810; X, 41; XI, 466, 830, 888; XII, 19, 1055, **1096–98**
Wetmore, Edward Ludlow, XII, 338
Wetmore, George, VI, 810
Wetmore, George Ludlow, VI, 741, 757, **810**, 811; VII, 74; VIII, 428, 841; XII, 895, 1096
Wetmore, Harriet. *See* Rainsford
Wetmore, Jane. *See* Haviland
Wetmore, Louisa Elizabeth. *See* Lansdowne
Wetmore, Sarah. *See* Peters
Wetmore, Sarah (Bliss), VI, 810
Wetmore, Thomas, V, 456, 647; VI, 73, 138, 139, 246, 740, **810–11**; VII, 691, 692, 868; VIII, 699, 841, 842; IX, 620; XII, 1096
Wetmore, Timothy, VI, 810, 811
Wetosy (Jane Sawyer), IX, 592; XI, 473
Wewonorawed. *See* Gray Lock
Wexar. *See* Waxaway
Wexler, Augustin, VII, 670
Weyapiersenwah (Wey-a-pic-e-sen-waw), V, 594, 774, 797, **852–53**; VI, 325
Weymouth. *See* Waymouth
Weymouth, Mary. *See* Whelan
Whale, Christopher, XI, 915
Whale, Ellen. *See* Heard
Whale, Grace (mother of ROBERT), XI, 915
Whale, John Claude, XI, 915
Whale, John Hicks, XI, 915
Whale, Mary (Whale), XI, 915
Whale, Robert (Reginald), XI, **915–16**; XII, 101

Whale, Robert Heard, XI, 915
Whaley, John, XI, 900
Whalley. *See* Walley
Wharton, John, IV, 634
Wharton, Joshua, VI, 281
Whately, Richard, IX, 719
Wheate, Jacob, X, 178
Wheate, Maria. *See* Shaw
Wheatley, Fanny (Middleton), XII, 733
Wheatley, William, XI, 910
Wheeler, Abel D., XII, 1132
Wheeler, Fanny (Shorey), XII, 968
Wheeler, Hannah (Danforth), VI, 176
Wheeler, Keziah (Beardsley), V, 58
Wheeler, Michael Francis, VIII, 490
Wheeler, Zalmon, VIII, 102; IX, 176
Wheelock, Eleazar, IV, 416, 731; V, 803, 804, 808; VI, 128; VII, 911
Wheelwright, Esther (rebaptized Marie-Joseph), named de l'Enfant-Jésus, II, 65; IV, 536, 554, **764–66**; V, 224, 741
Wheelwright, John (grandfather), IV, 764
Wheelwright, John, IV, 764
Wheelwright, Mary. *See* Snell
Wheelwright, Samuel, IV, 764
Whelan, Bridget. *See* Boyle
Whelan, Edward, IX, 833
Whelan, Edward, VII, 202; VIII, 563, 564, 565, 566, 954; IX, 223, 375, 376, 401, 404, **828–35**; X, 185, 187, 264, 339, 594, 595, 598, 612, 613; XI, 202, 371, 526, 532, 548, 665, 667, 669, 670, 700, 701, 704; XII, 319, 426, 639, 840
Whelan, John, XII, 974
Whelan, Mary. *See* Sullivan
Whelan, Mary (Weymouth; wife of EDWARD), IX, 833
Whelan, Mary Major. *See* Hughes
Whelan, Patrick James, IX, 493, **835**; X, 123, 561; XI, 145, 731; XII, 98, 599, 1108
Whelan, William, IX, 835
Wheler, Sir Francis, I, 546; II, 478, 510
Wherry, John L., XI, 504
Wheten, Isabella (Livingston), XII, 566
Whetstone, John, II, 666
Whetstone, Maria (wife of Sir WILLIAM), II, 666
Whetstone, Sir William, II, 260, **666**
Whewell, William, IX, 418
Whidden, Elizabeth (Graham), VI, 293
Whidden, Hannah (Prescott), VIII, 709
Whidden, Joseph, XI, 754, 755
Whiffen, Elzeard H., VIII, 889
Whistler, James Abbott McNeill, XII, 287
Whiston, David Hudson, XI, 116; XII, 787
Whitaker, Anne. *See* Andrews
Whitaker, Arundel Charlotte. *See* Burton
Whitaker, George, IX, 205; X, 55, 56, 208; XI, 368, 523, **916–18**; XII, 681
Whitaker, Philip, XI, 916
Whitbourne, Sir Richard, I, 229, 278, 279, 300, 362, 632, 655, 656, **668–69**
Whitbread, Samuel, VIII, 124
Whitcher, Charles, VII, 281, 282; VIII, 147
Whitcher, William, VII, 281
Whitcher, William Frederick, XII, 978, 979, 1107
Whitcomb, Benjamin, IV, 294

Whitcomb, Sarah Ann (Webb), XI, 912
White, Aaron, V, 423, 658
White, Abigail (Hazzen), V, 412, 415
White, Alexander, V, 57
White, Andrew, VI, 813
White, Andrew, VI, 220, **811–13**; VII, 33, 130; VIII, 552; IX, 654
White, Anne. *See* Weir
White, Augusta (Draper), XII, 273
White, Caroline (Gilmour), X, 305
White, Catherine (McKay), X, 475
White, Charlotte. *See* Somers
White, Cornelius, VI, 814
White, Deborah. *See* Whitworth
White, Dorothea. *See* Smeaton
White, Editha (Chamberlain), VI, 128
White, Edward, X, **701–2**; XII, 298
White, Edward, XI, **918**
White, Elijah P., X, 241
White, Elizabeth. *See* Harlow
White, Elizabeth. *See* Wilkey
White, Elizabeth (Shepherd), IV, 766
White, Elizabeth B. (Homer), VII, 416
White, Esther. *See* Vine
White, Frederick, XII, 140, 611
White, Frederick James, IX, 836
White, George Harlow, XI, **918–19**
White, Gideon (father of GIDEON), VI, 813
White, Gideon (loyalist), VI, 813
White, Gideon, VI, 138, **813–14**; VII, 714
White, Hannah (mother of EDWARD), X, 701
White, Hannah (Hope), XI, 422
White, Harriet (Grey), X, 318
White, Henry, V, 364
White, Isaac D., VI, 92
White, James (brother of JOSEPH), IX, 836
White, James (partner of William HAZEN), IV, 196, 389, 736; V, 16, 415, 416; VI, 718, 719, 720; VII, 493, 683
White, James Alfred, IX, 836
White, Joanna. *See* Howland
White, Joan Olive (Dunsmuir), XI, 290
White, John (father of JOHN, d. 1800), IV, 766
White, John (merchant), VII, 134, 484
White, John, I, 5, **669–70**
White, John, IV, **766–67**; V, 17, 307, 389, 453, 639, 722, 730, 815; VI, 558, 559, 583, 607, 670, 721; VII, 554, 812
White, John Henry, VII, 734, **903–4**
White, Joseph (father of JOSEPH), IX, 836
White, Joseph (merchant), IV, 711; V, 491, 783
White, Joseph, IX, **836**
White, Joseph Augustus, IX, 836
White, Margaret. *See* Logan
White, Marrianne. *See* Lynne
White, Mary. *See* Telfer
White, Mary (mother of EDWARD), XI, 918
White, Mary (Baird), VI, 813; VII, 33
White, Mary (Draper), X, 258
White, Matilda (Gilmour), X, 305
White, Nathaniel Whitworth (uncle), VI, 814; VII, 82; VIII, 752
White, Nathaniel Whitworth, XII, 438
White, Peter (lay preacher), X, 471

White, Peter (timberer), IX, 13, 734
White*, Peter (1838–1906), XI, 522
White, Richard, XI, 12, 920
White, Richard, III, **661**
White*, Robert Smeaton (1856–1944), XI, 919
White, Samuel, V, 491, 783; VI, 70, 274
White, Sarah Jane. *See* Woodman
White, Susannah (Bowring), VII, 101
White, Thomas, XI, 919
White, Thomas, III, 301, 302, 342, 521, 593, 654, **661–62**
White, Thomas, XI, 7, 12, 207, **919–21**, 937; XII, 610, 687
White, William (bishop), V, 786, 787
White, William (father of EDWARD, 1822–72), X, 701
White, William (father of EDWARD, 1811–86), XI, 918
White, William Kepple, IX, 469
White Antelope. *See* Apawakaasi
Whiteaves*, Joseph Frederick (1835–1909), XI, 218
White Calf. *See* Onista'poka
White Eyes, IV, 301
Whitefield, George, III, 125; IV, 402, 494, 514; V, 135, 729; VII, 825; VIII, 806
Whitefield, Mrs Martha, IV, 208
Whiteford, Rosina (Goodfellow), XII, 379
Whiteford, William, VIII, 22
Whitehead. *See* Gray Lock
White Head. *See* Theyanoguin
Whitehouse, Elizabeth (Bagnall), VIII, 35
Whitelaw, Francis M., VIII, 203
Whitelocke, John, IX, 543
White Mingo, III, 320
White Peter. *See* Klingensmith, Peter
White Thunder. *See* Kaghswaghtaniunt
Whiteway*, Sir William Vallance (1828–1908), XI, 239, 284, 355, 356, 561, 642, 910, 911, 918; XII, 164, 165, 311, 379, 380, 381, 482, 754, 755, 756, 757, 770, 889, 956
White Wolf. *See* Sotai-na
Whitford, James Peter, VII, 138
Whitham. *See* Witham
Whiting, Algernon Sidney, XI, 346
Whiting, W. L., VIII, 181
Whitlaw, Mrs Elizabeth, V, 287
Whitlock, William, IX, 203, 541
Whitman, Abraham, VIII, **929–30**
Whitman, Hannah. *See* Webber
Whitman, Hannah Maria (Longley), XI, 525
Whitman, John, VIII, 929
Whitman, Marcus, VII, 672
Whitman, Mary. *See* Foster
Whitman, Walt, XII, 517
Whitmore, Arthur, III, 662
Whitmore, Edward, III, 663
Whitmore, Edward, III, 601, **662–63**, 666, 667; IV, 21, 22
Whitney, Benjamin, VII, 229
Whitney, Margaret (Barnard; Sargent), VI, 682
Whitney, Parkhurst, VII, 313
Whitney, Reuben Miles, VI, 277
Whittemore, Ezekiel Francis, VIII, **930–31**; XI, 150, 676
Whittemore, Margaret. *See* Johnston
Whittemore, Priscilla. *See* Belding
Whittemore, Thomas, VIII, 930
Whittier, John Greenleaf, XII, 925, 927, 945
Whittingham, Bernard, X, 405

Whittington, George, I, 350
Whitwill, Mark, XII, 342
Whitworth, Catherine (Aylmer, Baroness Aylmer), VII, 904
Whitworth, Charles, 1st Earl Whitworth, VII, 905
Whitworth, Deborah (White), VI, 813
Whitworth, Miles, VI, 813
Whitworth-Aylmer, Louisa Anne, Baroness Aylmer. *See* Call
Whitworth-Aylmer, Matthew, 5th Baron Aylmer, VI, 120, 207, 537, 702, 815; VII, 6, 51, 61, 68, 100, 136, 148, 226, 283, 311, 361, 374, 382, 383, 393, 465, 482, 620, 667, 737, 763, 770, 771, 789, 824, **904–8**; VIII, 18, 78, 124, 433, 463, 495, 615, 678, 711, 844, 939; IX, 217, 297, 695, 699, 811; X, 163, 512, 555; XI, 352
Whooley, Hannah. *See* Selee
Whymper*, Frederick (1838–1901), IX, 432; XII, 130
Whyte, Elizabeth (Esson), IX, 243
Whyte, James, VII, 908
Whyte, James Matthew, VII, **908–10**; VIII, 293; IX, 745, 746
Whyte, John, VII, 910
Whyte, John Lionel, VII, 910
Wickananish. *See* Wikinanish
Wickes, Maria (Taylor), XII, 1029
Wicksteed, Gustavus William, VII, 394; XII, 729
Widder, Charles, IX, 838
Widder, Charles Ignatius, IX, 836
Widder, Elizabeth Jane (wife of FREDERICK), IX, 838
Widder, Frederick, VII, 338; VIII, 9, 427, 900; IX, 416, 417, 644, **836–38**; X, 623
Widenham, Mary (FitzGibbon), IX, 264
Widmer, Annie, VIII, 935
Widmer, Christopher, VI, 416; VIII, 642, 869, **931–36**; X, 39, 325, 351, 610; XII, 1123
Widmer, Christopher Rolph, VIII, 935
Widmer, Emily Sarah. *See* Bignell
Widmer, Hannah (wife of CHRISTOPHER), VIII, 931
Widmerpole, Dorothy. *See* Frobisher
Widmerpole, Sir William, I, 318
Wiebe, Agatha. *See* Dyck
Wiebe, Elizabeth. *See* Dyck
Wiebe, Gerhard, XII, 1098
Wiebe, Gerhard, XII, **1098–1100**
Wiederhold, Alice de. *See* Douglas
Wied-Neuwied, Prince of. *See* Maximilian
Wieniawski, Henryk, XII, 471
Wier, Benjamin, IX, 838
Wier, Benjamin, IX, **838–41**; X, 176
Wier, John, VIII, 568
Wier, Phebe (mother of BENJAMIN), IX, 838
Wier, Phoebe (Wier), IX, 838
Wigand, Georg, VIII, 13
Wigate, John, III, 449, 544, 594, **663**
Wiggins, Charlotte (Hustice; Arnold), VI, 13
Wiggins, Martha (Shives), X, 653
Wiggins, Richard Berrian, IX, 339
Wiggins, Samuel, VII, 915
Wiggins, Susanna (Susan) Harriet (Wilmot), VII, 915; XII, 1104
Wigham, Catherine Anne (Sproat), IX, 457
Wight, Helen (Dickson), VII, 250
Wight, Jean (Hamilton), V, 402

Wight, John, VI, 695
Wight, Margaret. *See* Schank
Wightman, John (father of JOSEPH), XI, 922
Wightman, John (minister), VI, 361
Wightman, Joseph, XI, **922–23**
Wightman, Margaret. *See* McDonald
Wightman, Margaret Ray. *See* Armstrong
Wightman, Sir William, X, 72
Wigley, Cordelia (Smith), XI, 835
Wigley, Rosanna (Todd), XII, 1062
Wikaskokiseyin, X, **702**; XI, 598
Wikinanish, IV, 767
Wikinanish, IV, lv, 244, 568, 569, **767–68**; V, 387, 618, 619; VI, 234
Wilamak. *See* Ouenemek
Wilberforce, Samuel, IX, 292
Wilberforce, William, IV, 413; V, 68, 531, 575; VII, 520, 634, 822, 825; VIII, xxix, 444, 968
Wilbrenner, Corine, IX, 445
Wilby, Julia Amelia (Crawley), XI, 214
Wilcocke, Ann. *See* Lewis
Wilcocke, Samuel, VI, 814
Wilcocke, Samuel Hull, VI, 241, 267, 446, 765, **814–16**; VII, 183; VIII, 351
Wilcocks, Anna Maria (Thorne), VII, 862
Wilcocks, Horace S. L., VII, 863
Wilcox. *See also* Willcocks; Willcox
Wilcox, Sabia (Purdy), VII, 712
Wilde, Jane Francisca, Lady Wilde. *See* Elgee
Wilde, Oscar O'Flahertie Wills, IX, 494
Wilde, William Brock, XII, 970, 971
Wilder, Elizabeth (Hutchinson), IX, 403
Wilder, Sally (Harris), IX, 367
Wild Person. *See* Onistah-sokaksin
Wilds, George, V, 47
Wilhelm I, German Emperor (Wilhelm I of Prussia), IX, 36
Wilkes, Charles, IX, 199; XI, 17; XII, 401
Wilkes, George H., XII, 1091
Wilkes, Harriet Rose. *See* Parke
Wilkes, Henry, VIII, 666; IX, 467, 468; X, 599, 683; XI, **923–24**
Wilkes, John, IV, 571, 619; V, 82; VIII, 155
Wilkes, John Aston (father), XI, 923
Wilkes, John Aston, VI, 374
Wilkes, Lucy. *See* Hedge
Wilkes, Martha. *See* Cooke
Wilkes, Robert, X, **702–3**; XI, 616, 818; XII, 151
Wilkes, Susan. *See* Holmes
Wilkes, Susanna. *See* Philips
Wilkey, Elizabeth (White), IX, 836
Wilkie, A., VIII, 454
Wilkie, Daniel, VIII, 938
Wilkie, Daniel, V, 330, 770, 790; VI, 260, 505; VII, 649, 809; VIII, 109, 363, 495, **936–39**; IX, 202, 572; X, 24, 68, 77, 691; XI, 176; XII, 320, 845, 928
Wilkie, James, VIII, 936
Wilkie, James Charles William, V, 853
Wilkie, John, VII, 579
Wilkie, Margaret. *See* Lawson
Wilkie, Walter Coltheart, V, 853
Wilkie, William, V, **853–54**; VI, 322; VII, 88
Wilkings, Patty (Foster), IX, 276
Wilkins, Harriett Annie, XI, **925**

Wilkins, Isaac, VI, 34; VII, 87, 910; XI, 926
Wilkins, Isabella. *See* Morris
Wilkins, Isabella (Moorsom), IX, 567
Wilkins, Jane. *See* Wallace
Wilkins, John, XI, 925
Wilkins, John, III, 262, 530; IV, **768–69**
Wilkins, Lewis Morris, V, 216; VI, 780; VII, 22, 279, 492, **910–11**; VIII, 355, 757; IX, 567; X, 496; XI, 925, 926
Wilkins, Lewis Morris, VII, 144, 910; VIII, 416; IX, 295, 426; XI, **925–26**
Wilkins, Martin Isaac, VII, 910; IX, 281; XI, 24, 279, 280, 633, **926–27**
Wilkins, Martin S., VII, 910
Wilkins, Robert Charles, VIII, 542
Wilkins, Sarah. *See* Creighton
Wilkins, Sarah Elizabeth Shuter (McGill), VIII, 540, 542, 543
Wilkins, Sarah Rachel. *See* Thomas
Wilkinson, Catherine (Calvin), XI, 139
Wilkinson, Cecilia. *See* Bethune
Wilkinson, Eliza (Taylor; Dickson), VI, 211
Wilkinson, Elizabeth, IV, 317; VIII, 128
Wilkinson, James, V, 9, 32, 171; VI, 342, 343, 520, 521, 661; VIII, 105
Wilkinson, Jemima, VIII, 606
Wilkinson, John, VIII, 274; IX, 630, 767; X, **703–4**
Wilkinson, John A., XII, 53
Wilkinson, John Alexander, VIII, 120
Wilkinson, John Miles, XII, 705
Wilkinson, Mary (Smith), VIII, 823
Wilkinson, Mary Rebecca. *See* Curry
Wilkinson, Moses, IV, 515; V, 468
Wilkinson, Robert Mortimer, XII, 592
Wilkinson, Walter Butler, VII, 469
Wilkinson, William, IX, 413
Wilkison, William Henry, XII, 887
Willan, John Henry, VIII, 424; XI, **927–28**
Willan, Julia. *See* Gugy
Willan, Thomas William, XI, 927
Willard, Abel (nephew of ABIJAH), IV, 769
Willard, Abel (prisoner), IV, 432
Willard, Abijah, IV, **769–70**; VI, 394; VII, 691, 777
Willard, Anna. *See* Prentice
Willard, Elizabeth. *See* Patterson
Willard, Elizabeth. *See* Prescott
Willard, Frances Elizabeth Caroline, XII, 220, 221, 763
Willard, George Busby, VIII, 219
Willard, Henry E., IX, 60
Willard, Joshua, VI, 816
Willard, Lucinda. *See* Knowlton
Willard, Lucretia. *See* Ward
Willard, Mary (McKown; wife of ABIJAH) IV, 769
Willard, Samuel, IV, 769
Willard, Samuel, VI, 575, 688, **816–17**; VII, 199; VIII, 406
Willard, Submit. *See* Phipps
Willard, Susanna (Johnson; Hastings), IV, 294
Willcocks, Charles (grandfather), V, 859
Willcocks, Charles, V, 859
Willcocks, Jane. *See* Powell
Willcocks, Joseph, V, 66, 171, 405, 412, 443, 643, 782, **854–59**, 860; VI, 4, 5, 52, 154, 215, 406, 489, 490, 540, 542, 543, 579, 609, 647, 656, 657, 670, 721, 723, 747,

804; VII, 35, 36, 37, 38, 162, 285, 419, 438, 439, 602, 651, 929; VIII, 47, 339, 607, 608, 609, 620, 945; IX, 669
Willcocks, Margaret. *See* Russell
Willcocks, Margaret Phœbe (Baldwin), V, 860; VI, 624, 670; VII, 35, 36, 37, 42, 43; VIII, 45
Willcocks, Maria, VI, 407, 670; VII, 37; IX, 789
Willcocks, Phoebe. *See* Jackson
Willcocks, Robert, V, 854
Willcocks, William, IV, 677; V, 65, 71, 420, 597, 729, 731, 732, 854, **859–60**; VI, 406, 670; VII, 13, 35, 36, 37; VIII, 4, 339, 885
Willcox, Clara (Bidwell), X, 60
Willcox (Wilcox), Mercy (Weller), IX, 826; X, 390
Wille, Johann Georg, IV, 762
Willem I, King of the United Netherlands, VII, 31; VIII, 274, 899
Willem II, King of the United Netherlands, IX, 138
Willes, Richard, I, 154
Willet, Marinus, V, 40
William. *See* Tuglavina
William I, King of England, I, 121
William III, King of Great Britain and Ireland (William of Orange), I, 92, 329, 426, 544, 545; II, 103, 183, 246, 262, 279, 280, 497, 601, 650; III, 515; IV, xxiv
William IV, King of Great Britain and Ireland, IV, 556; V, 122, 123, 128, 408, 632, 849; VI, 23, 88, 679, 818; VII, 6, 23, 51, 89, 268, 482, 840, 842; VIII, 27, 295, 441, 773; IX, 693; X, 342, 503; XI, 155, 567
William, Duke of Gloucester, II, 286
William Augustus, Duke of Cumberland, III, 218, 362, 666; IV, 21; V, 141, 822, 823; VI, 192
William Henry, Prince. *See* William IV
William King. *See* Peguis
William of Canajoharie. *See* Tekawiroñte
William of Orange. *See* William III
Williams, Abigail. *See* Allen
Williams, Alma (Corby), XI, 202
Williams, Ann. *See* Fothersall
Williams, Anne. *See* Jones
Williams, Ann Maria. *See* Waldren
Williams, Arthur Trefusis Heneage, XI, 326, 747, **928–29**; XII, 576, 735
Williams, Bealing Stephen, VII, 288
Williams, Catharine. *See* Robinson
Williams, Charles Joseph, XI, 930
Williams, Commodore. *See* Gillam, Thomas
Williams, David, XII, 1100
Williams, Edward Hosier, IX, 350
Williams, Eleazer, VII, 911, 912; VIII, 618, **939–40**; X, 163
Williams, Eliezer, VII, 825
Williams, Elizabeth. *See* Rhodes
Williams, Elizabeth. *See* Stewart
Williams, Elizabeth (Graves, Baroness Graves), V, 380
Williams, Emily W. *See* Seymour
Williams, Ephraim, III, 186
Williams, Eunice. *See* Mather
Williams, Eunice (Marie, Marguerite), II, 667; IV, **770–71**; VII, 911, 912
Williams, Eunice (Denison), VI, 187
Williams, Griffith, IV, **771–72**
Williams, Hannah (Douglas), XI, 271
Williams, Henry Rogers, X, 156

Williams, James, V, **860–62**; VI, 413, 414; VII, 555
Williams, James Miller, XI, 631, **929–30**
Williams*, James Samuel (1838–1929), XI, 579, 580; XII, 153
Williams, James William, IX, 209, 292; XII, 211, 813, **1100–1**
Williams, Jenkin, IV, 72, 549; V, 8, 18, 43, 45, 224, 226, 234, 493, 794, **862–65**, 881, 902; VI, 511, 615; VII, 767, 872
Williams, John (brother of ELEAZER), VIII, 939
Williams, John (brother of GRIFFITH), IV, 771
Williams, John (clergyman), XII, 1061
Williams, John (gunner), I, 376
Williams, John (missionary), IX, 325
Williams, John (1664–1729), II, 80, 285, 437, 450, **667**; III, 200, 493; IV, 770; VII, 911; VIII, 939
Williams, John (fl. 1711–18), II, **667–68**
Williams, John Æthuruld, XI, **930–31**
Williams, John David, XI, 930
Williams, John James, VII, 894
Williams, John Tucker, IX, 68; XI, 928
Williams, Joseph, VII, 384
Williams, Julia (Blackman), VIII, 94
Williams, Lennox, XII, 1101
Williams, Lewis, IX, 232
Williams, M. C. *See* Jackson
Williams, Madeleine. *See* Jourdain
Williams, Margaret (Seymour), IX, 711
Williams, Maria. *See* Walker
Williams, Martha, VI, 192, 196
Williams, Mrs Mary, XI, 428
Williams, Mary (Silver; Wainwright), II, 606
Williams, Mary Abigail (Walker), XII, 1079
Williams, Mary Ann. *See* Konwatewenteta
Williams, Matilda (Corby), XI, 203
Williams, Mercy (Seccombe), IV, 705
Williams, Miles, IX, 557
Williams, Reason, XI, 357
Williams, Rebecca. *See* Clarke
Williams, Richard, VI, 672; VIII, **940–41**
Williams, Robert, II, 667
Williams, Roger, XII, 925
Williams, Sally. *See* Fidler
Williams, Samuel, II, 667
Williams, Sarah. *See* Ward
Williams, Sarah, VII, 911
Williams, Sarah (Leonard), VIII, 499
Williams, Sarah Eliza (mother of JAMES WILLIAM), XII, 1100
Williams, Sarah Harriet. *See* Owen
Williams, Stephen, IV, 770
Williams, Susannah Stephens (Fisher), VII, 288; X, 284
Williams, Theoda. *See* Park
Williams, Thomas. *See also* Tehoragwanegen
Williams, Thomas (brother of WILLIAM FENWICK), XI, 932
Williams, Thomas (commissary general), XI, 931
Williams, Thomas (merchant), V, 511, 682
Williams, Thomas (of Annapolis Royal, N.S.) IV, 674
Williams, Thomas, IV, 770; V, 40; VII, **911–12**; VIII, 939, 940
Williams, Victor Arthur Seymour, XI, 928
Williams, Warham, III, 581; IV, 770
Williams, William (clergyman), XII, 909

Williams, William (father-in-law of John SECCOMBE), IV, 705

Williams, William (sailor), VII, 912

Williams, William, VI, 267, 705; VII, 205, 567, 578, 901, **912–14**; VIII, 85, 91, 158, 315, 350, 812, 813, 814

Williams, Sir William Fenwick, V, 298; X, 291, 405, 534; XI, 279, 555, 592, 755, **931–34**, 948; XII, 750

Williams, William Peere, V, 380

Williamson, Sir Adam, IV, 768, 772

Williamson, Ann. See Lothain

Williamson, Charles, V, 70, 71; VII, 13; VIII, 793

Williamson, David, IV, 302; V, 345

Williamson, Elizabeth (Ainslie), V, 4

Williamson, George, III, xxv; IV, 22, 24, **772–73**

Williamson, Isabella (Dorwin), XI, 267

Williamson, James, VIII, 645; XII, **1101–3**

Williamson, James Gilchrist, XII, 1102

Williamson, Margaret. See Gilchrist

Williamson, Margaret. See Macdonald

Williamson, William, XII, 1101

Williamson, William Crawford, XII, 233

Willin, Sybilla Maria (Turner), V, 830

Willington, Bridget (Monck, Viscountess Monck), XII, 749

Willis, Ann Maria. See Heaviside

Willis, Ann Susanna. See Kent

Willis, Edward, XII, 313, **1103–4**

Willis, Elizabeth (Cullen; Waller), VI, 801

Willis, Eliza Jane. See Mosely

Willis, Hannah (Seccomb), IV, 705

Willis, John (father of EDWARD), XII, 1103

Willis, John (father of JOHN ROBERT), X, 704

Willis, John (father of ROBERT), IX, 841

Willis, John Robert, X, 362, **704**; XI, 420; XII, 1103

Willis, John Walpole, VI, 115, 118, 164, 165, 266, 631, 632, 773, 802; VII, 39, 40, 163, 338, 369, 497, 794, 795, 896; VIII, 46, 69, 125, 512, 519, 602, 642, 643, 733, 797, 801, 847; IX, 139, 673, 674, 684, 724; X, 233, **704–7**

Willis, Kathleen. See Blake

Willis, Marie (Arnaud; Perrot de Rizy; Cotton), II, 520; IV, 173

Willis, Mary. See Billopp

Willis, Mary. See Smith

Willis, Mary (mother of ROBERT), IX, 841

Willis, Mary Ann. See Artz

Willis, Mary Isabella. See Bowes-Lyon

Willis, Michael, VIII, 68, 273; IX, 107, 820; X, 3, 455, **707–8**; XII, 492

Willis, Nathaniel Parker, VIII, 64

Willis, Robert, VII, 16, 434; VIII, 345, 968; IX, 339, 387, **841**; XII, 872

Willis, Sarah. See Adams

Willis, William (clergyman), X, 707

Willis, William (father of JOHN WALPOLE), X, 704

Williscroft, John, XI, 306

Willison*, Sir John Stephen (1856–1927), XII, 104, 138, 331, 500, 582

Williston, John Thomas, VIII, 739; IX, 171, 766

Willoughby, Bridget (mother of THOMAS), I, 670

Willoughby, Edward, I, 670

Willoughby, Sir Hugh, I, 158

Willoughby, Janet. See Scougall

Willoughby, Mark, VII, 185, **914–15**; XII, 573

Willoughby, Mary (mother of MARK), VII, 914

Willoughby, Sir Percival, I, 240, 351, 534, 535, 584, 670

Willoughby, Thomas, I, 240, 584, **670–71**

Willoughby, William, I, 443

Willoughby, William, 3rd Earl of Enniskillen, X, 313

Willoughby, William Hall, VII, 914

Wills, Charles, VIII, 941

Wills, Elizabeth. See Bolt

Wills, Emily. See Coster

Wills, Frank, VIII, 174, **941–45**; IX, 291; XII, 714, 957

Wills, Geneviève. See Dunière

Wills, Geneviève (Montour), V, 603

Wills, John, IX, 482

Wills, Meredith, V, 283, 603; VI, 95

Willson, Ann (mother of JOHN), VIII, 945

Willson, Beckles, III, 589

Willson, Catherine (mother of DAVID; Willson), IX, 841

Willson, Crowell, VII, 439

Willson, David, VIII, 52; IX, 131, **841–43**

Willson, Elizabeth. See Bowlby

Willson, Harriot Conway. See Ladde

Willson, Hugh Bowlby, VIII, 106; IX, 166, 655; X, 607, **708–9**

Willson, John (father of DAVID), IX, 841

Willson, John (trader), VI, 8

Willson, John, V, 857; VI, 199, 229, 230, 247, 248, 489, 542; VII, 38, 57, 58, 222, 262, 378, 379, 419, 439, 497, 909; VIII, 337, 523, 600, 608, 708, 847, **945–47**; IX, 520; X, 708

Willson, Phebe. See Titus

Willson, Sarah. See Ainse

Willson*, Thomas Leopold (1860–1915), X, 708

Wilmot, Allen C., V, 9; VI, 210; VII, 328

Wilmot, Anne. See Montagu

Wilmot, Christopher, III, 663

Wilmot, Elizabeth. See Black

Wilmot, Elizabeth. See Street

Wilmot, Hannah. See Bliss

Wilmot, Helen Matilda. See Clark

Wilmot, Jane. See Ballock

Wilmot, John McNeil, VII, 610, **915–16**; VIII, 98, 387; XII, 1104, 1106

Wilmot, Lemuel, VII, 915

Wilmot, Lemuel Allan, VI, 409, 757; VII, 74, 141, 916; VIII, 183, 377, 394, 700, 739, 808, 809; IX, 23, 86, 146, 147, 310, 381, 382, 392, 623, 767; X, 41, 140, 158, 159, 285, 286, 288, 341, **709–14**; XII, 537, 896, 897, 1104, 1105, 1106

Wilmot, Mary. See Stegmann

Wilmot, Mary (Montgomery), X, 530

Wilmot, Montagu, III, 365, **663–65**; IV, xxvii, 51, 110, 131, 193, 274, 291, 292, 308, 313, 528, 562, 695, 781; V, 261, 409, 415, 555, 556

Wilmot, Robert Duncan, VII, 915, 916; VIII, 810; IX, 382, 410, 413; X, 191, 287, 543, 666, 713; XI, 372, 578, 803, 830; XII, 25, 741, 897, 898, 1051, 1052, 1055, **1104–6**

Wilmot, Samuel, XII, 768, **1106–7**

Wilmot, Samuel Street, V, 550; VII, 319, 641; XII, 930, 1106

Wilmot, Susanna Harriet. See Wiggins

Wilmot, Susannah Elizabeth. See Mowat

Wilmot, William, VI, 504, 755; VII, 915, 916; X, 709

Wilmot-Horton, Sir Robert John, VI, 632, 681; VII, 282,

549

629, 647, 729, 753, 754, 755, 756, 788; VIII, xxvii, xxviii, xxix, xxx, xxxi, xxxii, 764; IX, 175, 637, 671, 672, 757, 758; X, 636
Wilson. *See also* Willson
Wilson, Adam, VI, 553
Wilson, Sir Adam, VIII, 52, 587; IX, 76, 566; X, 79, 258; XI, 322, 553, 554; XII, 907, **1107–9**
Wilson, Alexander (father of CHARLES), X, 715
Wilson, Alexander (merchant), V, 499
Wilson, Andrew (father of Sir ADAM), XII, 1107
Wilson, Andrew (HBC employee), XI, 882
Wilson, Andrew (Montreal publisher), IX, 429, 430, 540; XI, 680
Wilson, Andrew (Ottawa publisher), VIII, 553
Wilson, Ann. *See* Platt
Wilson, Ann. *See* Tracey
Wilson, Ann (Hilton), II, 287
Wilson, Anne Margaret. *See* McLean
Wilson, Archibald, XII, 1109
Wilson, Catherine-Angélique. *See* Ailleboust de Manthet
Wilson, Charles, VII, 833
Wilson, Charles, VI, 784; IX, 243, 360, 362, 363, 651; X, 130, **715**; XI, 117
Wilson, Sir Charles William, XI, 20, 21; XII, 817
Wilson, Christina (Currier), XI, 229
Wilson, Sir Daniel, IX, 11; X, 40, 258, 393; XI, 219, 368, 541; XII, 213, 236, 402, 528, **1109–14**
Wilson, Ebenezer, IX, 843
Wilson, Edward (partner of William NOTMAN), XII, 789
Wilson, Edward (surgeon), I, 374, 375, 378
Wilson*, Edward Francis (1844–1915), XI, 314; XII, 1001
Wilson, Elizabeth. *See* Crocket
Wilson, Elizabeth (Miles), XII, 736
Wilson, Elizabeth Susan (Lewis), X, 441
Wilson, Emma, Lady Wilson. *See* Dalton
Wilson, George (brother of Sir DANIEL), XII, 1112
Wilson, George (businessman), XII, 147
Wilson, Hannah (Paterson), XI, 675
Wilson, Helen (Benson), XI, 69
Wilson, Helen Walker (Billings), X, 64
Wilson, Henry Maitland, 1st Baron Wilson, X, 558
Wilson, Hiram, IX, 705; XI, 400, 401
Wilson, Hugh, XII, 136
Wilson, Humphrey, II, 287
Wilson, James (alleged Methodist preacher), VI, 805
Wilson, James (apparent artist), VI, 358
Wilson, James (architect), XII, 343
Wilson, James (Indian agent), XII, 718, 719, 803
Wilson, James (miller), V, 724; VII, 57; VIII, 86, 87
Wilson, James (politician), VI, 11
Wilson, James (zoologist), VI, 218
Wilson, James Crocket, XII, **1114–15**
Wilson, Jane. *See* Brown
Wilson, Jane. *See* Chalmers
Wilson, Jane (Ewart), VIII, 280
Wilson, Jane (Shirreff), VII, 796
Wilson, Jane Sybil, XII, 1113
Wilson, Janet. *See* Aitken
Wilson, Janet (McDougal), IX, 486
Wilson, Jean. *See* Adam
Wilson, Jean (Caldwell), VI, 104
Wilson, Jeanie. *See* Kilgour

Wilson, Jemima Mary Gwynne (Wallis, Lady Wallis), XII, 1081
Wilson, Joanna. *See* Hughes
Wilson, John (author), VII, 792; IX, 162, 429
Wilson, John (businessman), VIII, 648
Wilson, John (clergyman), VIII, 25
Wilson, John (colonial administrator), VIII, 239
Wilson, John (Glasgow merchant), IX, 652
Wilson, John (HBC clerk), XII, 936
Wilson, John (Montreal merchant), VI, 417
Wilson, John, VIII, 510, 733, 800; IX, **843–44**; XI, 62; XII, 822
Wilson, Joseph, XI, 859
Wilson, Louisa Ann (Harris), XI, 385
Wilson, Margaret. *See* Mackay
Wilson, Margaret (McClure), IX, 478
Wilson, Marguerite (Couillard; Leblanc), X, 435
Wilson, Marie-Angélique-Flore (Couillard), VII, 213
Wilson, Marion (Cook), XII, 210
Wilson, Mary (Helliwell), IX, 387
Wilson, Mary (Lawrence), VII, 491; XII, 536
Wilson, Mary (Rowan), X, 634
Wilson, Mary Elizabeth. *See* Dixon
Wilson, Robert, XI, 135
Wilson, Sir Robert Thomas, XII, 1081
Wilson, Samuel, XII, 1114
Wilson, Susan Grace. *See* Codner
Wilson, Thomas (father-in-law of Antoine-Gaspard COUILLARD), VII, 213
Wilson, Thomas (merchant), IX, 555; XI, 810, 811
Wilson, Thomas (partner of James TOD), V, 817
Wilson, Thomas C., VIII, 77, 829
Wilson*, Thomas Edmond (1859–1933), XI, 764
Wilson, Washington L., VII, 364
Wilson, William (clergyman), VII, 274
Wilson, William (merchant), VI, 102
Wilson, William (seaman), I, 374, 376, 377
Wilson, William Mercer, X, **715–16**
Wily, Daniel Berkely, XII, 886
Wiman*, Erastus (1834–1904), XI, 879; XII, 292
Winans, Edward Sheldon, VIII, 555
Winans, George E. A., X, 692
Winans, James, VII, 617
Winans, John, VII, 617
Winans, William Henry, X, 692
Winchelsea, Earl of. *See* Finch
Winchester, Marquis of. *See* Paulet
Winchester, Charles, IV, 401
Winchester, Mary (Cambridge), VI, 107, 110, 818
Winchester, William, VI, 107, 108
Windenheimer, Maria Elisabetha (Moschel), VII, 636
Winder, W., XI, 883
Winder, William, IX, 266
Windham, Ann. *See* Thellusson
Windham, Sir Charles Ash, IX, **844–46**; X, 443; XI, 592
Windham, Charlotte Jane, Lady Windham. *See* Des Voeux
Windham, Marianne Catherine Emily. *See* Beresford
Windham, William. *See* Lukin, William
Windham, William, VI, 195, 619; VII, 285, 929; VIII, xxvii, 339
Windson, John, VI, 505
Winer, Dr, XII, 106
Winer, Helen. *See* King

Winger, John. *See* Wenger, Johannes
Wingfield, Alexander Hamilton, XII, **1115–16**
Wingfield, Margaret. *See* Malcolmson
Winman. *See* Wenman
Winn, Joseph, V, 65; VIII, 180
Winne. *See* Wynne
Winnenimmit. *See* Wenemouet
Winnett, Mary Ann (Peters), VIII, 699
Winnett (Winniett), Susan Mary (Twining), VIII, 901
Winniett, Anne (Cosby), III, 143, 421, 665
Winniett, Augusta Julia, Lady Winniett. *See* Fenwick
Winniett, Elizabeth (Handfield), III, 277, 421, 665
Winniett, James, VII, **916–17**
Winniett, Joseph, III, 277, 665
Winniett, Marie-Madeleine. *See* Maisonnat
Winniett, Marie-Madeleine (How), III, 297, 421, 665; V, 430
Winniett, Mary. *See* Totten
Winniett, William, VII, 917
Winniett, William, II, 22; III, 3, 143, 277, 297, 421, **665–66**; VII, 918
Winniett, Sir William Robert Wolseley, VII, **917–18**
Winninnewaycappo, IV, **773–74**
Winser, Peter, X, 332; XI, 354
Winslow, Anna. *See* Green
Winslow, Anna, V, 869, 870
Winslow, Bethiah. *See* Barker
Winslow, Edward (father of EDWARD), V, 865
Winslow, Edward (great-great-grandfather of EDWARD), V, 865
Winslow, Edward, IV, xxviii, 55, 328, 516, 677, 723; V, 35, 155, 156, 157, 161, 162, 354, 356, 390, 504, 505, 590, 613, 630, 774, 795, **865–69**, 874; VI, 73, 76, 136, 137, 140, 141, 142, 394, 395, 474, 651, 685, 725, 813; VII, 121, 187, 198, 330, 331, 401, 429, 691, 783; VIII, xxiv; IX, 699; XII, 537
Winslow, Edward Byron, XII, 338
Winslow, Elizabeth (Marston), IV, 516
Winslow, Eliza Chipman (Sampson), IX, 699
Winslow, Hannah. *See* Dyer
Winslow, Isaac, IV, 774
Winslow, John, V, 869
Winslow, John, III, xxviii, xxix, 129, 260, 275, 277, 362, 363, 572, 589; IV, xxviii, 314, 540, 679, **774–75**; V, 295; XII, 14
Winslow, John Francis Wentworth, VI, 810
Winslow, Joshua, V, 6, 132, 485, 486, 843, **869–70**
Winslow, Mary. *See* Little
Winslow, Mary. *See* Symonds
Winslow, Penelope, V, 390
Winslow, Penelope (Jenkins; Winterbottom), VI, 725, 727
Winslow, Sarah. *See* Peirce
Winslow, Sarah. *See* Wensley
Winslow, Sophia Adams (Farrar), XI, 312
Winter, Mr (Roman Catholic), VIII, 201
Winter, James, VI, 311
Winter, Susanna (Hart), VI, 311
Winter, Thomas, XII, 1090
Winter, William, I, 229, 333, 532
Winterbottom, Penelope. *See* Winslow
Winterlake, Sir James, IX, 648
Winthrop, Catherine (Browne; Sargent), VI, 682
Winthrop, Fitz-John, II, 436, 603; III, 586, 587

Winthrop, John (forebear of John SARGENT), VI, 682
Winthrop, John (great-grandfather of Winthrop HILTON), II, 287
Winthrop, Mary (Livingston), II, 436
Winton, Ebenezer, VIII, 950; X, 716
Winton, Elizabeth Brown (wife of HENRY), IX, 846
Winton, Elizabeth Luttrell. *See* Nicholson
Winton, Francis, VIII, 950; IX, 846; XI, 4
Winton, Henry, VIII, 950; IX, 584, **846**
Winton, Henry David, VII, 99, 154, 293, 294, 299, 631, 632, 793; VIII, 107, 199, 468, 469, **947–51**; IX, 47, 846; X, 180, 398, 687; XI, 673
Winton, Robert (grandfather), VIII, 947
Winton, Robert, VIII, 950; IX, 846
Winton, Teresa Maria (mother of HENRY DAVID), VIII, 947
Wisdom, Sarah (Smith), VII, 814
Wise, H., XII, 408
Wiseman, Margaret (Stairs), IX, 738
Wiseman, Nicholas Patrick Stephen, VI, 748; VIII, 489, 731; X, 176; XII, 712
Wisenberg. *See* Weissenberg
Wisewood, Solomon. *See* Ross, Duncan
Wisner, Charles Harrison, XII, 1116
Wisner, Dollie. *See* Howell
Wisner, Frances Augusta. *See* Wells
Wisner, Jesse Oldfield, XII, **1116–17**
Wisner, Mary. *See* Sheldon
Wisner, Moses, XII, 1116
Wisner, Wareham Sheldon, XII, 1116
Wiswall, Elizabeth. *See* Rogers
Wiswall, John, V, 48, 122, 833, **870–72**; VII, 432
Wiswall, Margaret. *See* Hutchinson
Wiswall, Mercy. *See* Minot
Wiswall, Peleg (grandfather), V, 870
Wiswall, Peleg, V, 872; VII, 22, 87, 609, 803, 804; VIII, 354, 756, 757
Withall, Eleanor. *See* Pickard
Withall, Elizabeth. *See* LeVallée
Withall, William John, XII, **1117–18**
Witham (Whitham), Anne (Murray), IV, 569
Witham, Charles D., VII, 483
Witham, George, VII, 483; IX, 599
Witham, Jane Catherine (Deblois), VII, 237
Withers, John Collier, VII, 765, 766
Witherspoon, John, V, 646; VI, 562
Withewacapo, X, 108
Withipoll, John, I, 386
Withrow, Ellen. *See* Sanderson
Withrow, James, XII, 1118
Withrow, John Jacob, XI, 648; XII, 708, **1118–20**
Withrow, Margaret. *See* Foster
Withrow*, William Henry (1839–1908), XI, 730
Witzel. *See* Miçel
Wiwurna. *See* Wowurna
Wix, Mrs. *See* Browne
Wix, Mrs E. *See* Walford
Wix, Edward, VI, 303; VII, 153, 294; IX, **846–48**; X, 278
Wix, Samuel, IX, 846
Wobenosay. *See* Wahbanosay
Wodehouse, John, 1st Earl of Kimberley, X, 444; XII, 243, 910
Wolcot, John (Peter Pindar), IX, 543
Wolcott, Roger, III, 645

Wolfall, Robert, I, 85
Wolfe, Edward, III, 666
Wolfe, Henrietta. *See* Thompson
Wolfe, James, I, 76; III, xvii, xviii, xx, xxi, xxv, xxvi,
    xxvii, xxix, xxx, 33, 71, 72, 85, 89, 129, 172, 173, 209,
    210, 289, 293, 296, 364, 372, 440, 464, 465, 466, 468,
    480, 509, 544, 559, 589, 590, 592, 601, 662, 663,
    **666–74**; IV, 3, 14, 21, 22, 23, 34, 37, 93, 109, 112, 134,
    163, 168, 193, 224, 250, 278, 279, 308, 314, 316, 327,
    332, 379, 415, 446, 448, 476, 479, 500, 503, 531, 541,
    552, 563, 569, 570, 579, 603, 641, 651, 671, 674, 680,
    694, 697, 700, 737, 772, 773; V, 104, 130, 141, 164,
    412, 425, 428, 739, 767, 823, 824; VI, 135, 192, 223,
    475, 505, 645, 769; VII, 190, 242, 287, 310, 372, 660,
    731, 789; VIII, 18, 92; IX, 41, 42, 75, 282, 360; X, 440;
    XI, 550; XII, 581, 825, 863, 925
Wolfe, Walter, III, 668
Wolff, Augustus, VII, 527
Wolf Thin Legs. *See* Pītikwahanapiwīyin
Wolhaupter, Benjamin, VII, 919; VIII, **951–52**
Wolhaupter, Catharine Phoebe. *See* Brannan
Wolhaupter, Charles, VIII, 951
Wolhaupter, Charles John, VIII, 951
Wolhaupter, Gottfried, VII, 918
Wolhaupter, John, VII, **918–19**; VIII, 951; XII, 139
Wolhaupter, Mary Payne. *See* Aycrigg
Wollaston, John, IV, 397
Wollstonecraft, Mary (Godwin), VIII, 734; XII, 525
Wolseley*, Garnet Joseph, 1st Viscount Wolseley
    (1833–1913), IX, 330; X, 111, 152, 443, 556, 631; XI,
    192, 325, 355, 472, 592, 742, 759, 933; XII, 33, 74, 117,
    132, 244, 245, 369, 427, 633, 673, 951, 1007
Wolsey, Thomas, I, 155
Wolstenholme, Sir John, I, 362, 374
Wolverson, Mary (Rundle), XII, 931
Wolverton, Baron. *See* Glyn
Wood, Alexander, XII, 701
Wood, Alexander, V, 65, 285, 326; VI, 611, 613, 623; VII,
    37, 702, **919–21**; VIII, 4, 5, 6, 192
Wood, Ann (Hildrith), V, 423
Wood, Ann (McGill; Strachan), V, 529; IX, 751, 753,
    764
Wood, Anna. *See* Skeels
Wood, Ann Jane. *See* Stevens
Wood, Caroline Matilda. *See* Merritt
Wood, Charles, VII, **921–22**; VIII, 647; XI, 502
Wood, Charlotte. *See* Gray
Wood, Charlotte (mother of EDMUND BURKE), XI, 934
Wood, Christian (Keir), VIII, 451
Wood, Christina Adelaide (Cameron), XI, 142, 143
Wood*, Edmund (1830–1909), XII, 813
Wood, Edmund Burke, X, 468, 641; XI, 145, 146, 246,
    593, 744, **934–35**; XII, 432
Wood, Elisabeth. *See* Seeley
Wood, Eliza (Crane), VIII, 183
Wood, Elizabeth. *See* Household
Wood, Elizabeth (Chappell), IX, 125
Wood, Elizabeth (Duval), X, 268
Wood, Elizabeth (Tarbell), III, 615
Wood, Ellen Marion (Hamilton), XI, 381
Wood, Enoch, VIII, 15, 177, 216, 442; IX, 737; X, 646,
    710; XI, 640, 729, 734, **935–36**
Wood, Frances Elizabeth (Robinson), XII, 910

Wood, George, VII, 923
Wood, Henry, V, 477
Wood, Sir Henry Evelyn, XI, 593
Wood, James (brother of ALEXANDER), VII, 919
Wood, James (father of ALEXANDER), VII, 919
Wood, James (manufacturer), XI, 385
Wood, Jane (Shaw), IV, 706
Wood, Jane Augusta. *See* Marter
Wood, Joanna (Bulley), V, 119
Wood, John (brother of CHARLES), VII, 921, 922
Wood, John (father of CHARLES), VII, 921
Wood, John (father of JOHN FISHER), XII, 1120
Wood, John (silversmith), V, 727
Wood, John Fisher, XII, 582, **1120–21**
Wood, John O., XI, 936
Wood*, Josiah (1843–1927), XI, 833; XII, 116, 340
Wood, Judith (Philipps), V, 670
Wood, Margaret. *See* Barclay
Wood, Margaret, XII, 1121
Wood, Margaret Mary. *See* Hallowell
Wood, Marie. *See* Dupuis, *dit* Caton
Wood, Mary. *See* Myers
Wood, Mary (Short), VI, 716
Wood, Mary Ann. *See* Wadden
Wood, Mary Bakewell (Nelles), XI, 640, 936
Wood, Miriam Jane (Huntington), XI, 437
Wood, Robert (father of ROBERT), VII, 923
Wood, Robert (of Quebec), V, 881
Wood, Robert (of Saint John), VI, 301
Wood, Robert, VII, **922–23**
Wood, Robert A., XI, 936
Wood, Samuel (father of EDMUND BURKE), XI, 934
Wood, Samuel (father of SAMUEL SIMPSON), IX, 848
Wood, Samuel Simpson, VI, 528, 717, 735; VIII, 276, 768;
    IX, **848–49**
Wood, Sarah (mother of ENOCH), XI, 935
Wood, Sarah (Douglas, Lady Douglas), IV, 223; IX, 218
Wood, Selina (Evans), VIII, 277
Wood, Thomas (brother of ALEXANDER), VII, 921
Wood, Thomas (father of THOMAS, 1711–78), IV, 775
Wood, Thomas (father of THOMAS, 1815–98), XII, 1121
Wood, Thomas, III, 418; IV, 94, 674, 706, **775–76**; V, 670
Wood, Thomas, XII, **1121–22**
Wood, Thomas Frank, XII, 1121
Wood, Thomas Lett, XI, 469
Wood, Walter Abbott, XII, 701
Wood, William, XI, 935
Wood, William Charles Henry, V, 152
Woodbee. *See* Wappisis
Woodburn*, James Ramsay (1838–1912), XII, 444
Woodburn, Mary (Greeley), X, 315
Woodbury (Woodberry), Anna (Barnard), III, 25
Woodcock, Frances (Smith), VIII, 823
Woodcock*, Percy Franklin (1855–1936), XII, 337
Woodfall, William, VI, 114, 213; IX, 369
Woodford, Sir Ralph James, VI, 820; VII, 579
Woodhouse. *See* Wydowse
Woodill, James, VI, 243
Woodin, William, V, 239
Woodley, James E., XII, 126
Woodley, Mary (Lewellin), VIII, 505
Woodman, Apphia. *See* Elden
Woodman, Edmund, VII, 923

Woodman, Elijah Crocker, VII, 56, 405, **923–24**; VIII, 162; XII, 552
Woodman, Emeline (Leonard), VII, 924; XII, 552
Woodman, Emily (Cunningham), X, 701
Woodman, Lydia. *See* Crocker
Woodman, Sarah Jane (White), X, 701
Woodruff, Margaret Ann (Zimmerman), VIII, 963
Woodruff, Melinda (Post), VII, 701
Woodruff, Richard, VIII, 964
Woodruff, Samuel, XII, 783
Woodruff, Wilford, VIII, 784
Woodruff, William, VIII, 785
Woods, John, X, 716
Woods, Joseph (father of JOSEPH), X, 716
Woods, Joseph (politician), VIII, 84
Woods, Joseph, X, **716–17**; XI, 432
Woods, Mary (mother of JOSEPH), X, 717
Woodward, Albert Gallatin, XII, 902
Woodward, Bernard Bolingbroke, VIII, 64, 65
Woodward, James Robertson, XI, 492
Woodward, Lucretia Bourdette (DesBrisay), XII, 250
Woodward, Mary Jane (Robertson), XII, 901
Woodwark, Alice Merry (Notman), XII, 787
Woodworth, Douglas Benjamin, XII, 437, 438, 439, 1092
Woodworth, Jane (Sibley), IX, 720
Woodworth, John Bowles, IX, 838, 839
Wool, John Ellis, V, 113
Woolford, John Elliott, VI, 54, 757; VII, 722, 725, 733; IX, **849–50**
Woolford, Margaret. *See* Erskine
Woolrich, James, V, 294
Woolrich, Julia (Connolly), VII, 205, 206; IX, 150
Woolrich, Mary (Mondelet), IX, 561
Woolsey, George, VIII, 952
Woolsey, John Bryan, VIII, 952
Woolsey, John William, VIII, 952
Woolsey, John William, V, 566; VI, 95, 96, 305; VII, 426; VIII, 838, **952–53**
Woolsey, Josephte Maria (Guerout), VI, 305, 306
Woolsey, Julie. *See* Lemoine
Woolsey, Marie-Joseph. *See* Trefflé, *dit* Rottot
Woolsey, Mary Georgina (McGreevy), XII, 626
Woolsey, Robert, VI, 556; VIII, 952
Woolsey, Thomas, IX, 537, 602; X, 471; XI, 849
Woolsey, William Darly, VIII, 952
Woolweaver, Christina (Lossing), VI, 406
Wooster, David, IV, 345, 390, 427, 442, 547, 548, 549, 697; V, 31, 32, 64, 383, 414, 652; VI, 403
Wooster, Edward, IV, 776
Wooster, Hezekiah Calvin, IV, **776–77**
Worcester, William, I, 386
Wordsworth, Christopher, XII, 812, 813
Wordsworth, Dorothy, XII, 776
Wordsworth, William, XII, 516, 945
Work, Betsy (Budd), X, 108
Work, Jane (Tolmie), XI, 885
Work, John, VIII, 528, 579, 662, 816; IX, **850–54**; X, 108, 239, 241, 273, 486, 495; XI, 885; XII, 290, 317, 550, 552
Work, Josette. *See* Legacé
Work, Sarah (Finlayson), XII, 317
Workman, Alexander, X, 717
Workman, Annie. *See* Eadie

Workman, Benjamin, IX, 725; X, 717; XI, 908, 936; XII, 214, 1122
Workman, Catharine. *See* Goudie
Workman, Elizabeth. *See* Wasnidge
Workman, Joseph, X, 717; XI, 936; XII, 1122
Workman, Joseph, VII, 825; VIII, 875, 927, 933, 934; IX, 109, 689; XI, 329, 590, 591, 899; XII, 71, **1122–27**
Workman, Matthew, X, 717
Workman, Samuel, X, 717; XII, 1122
Workman, Thomas, X, 717; XI, 557, 851, 920, **936–37**; XII, 214, 1122
Workman, William (clergyman), XII, 1122
Workman, William (son of William, clergyman), XII, 1122
Workman, William, IX, 78, 288, 289, 650; X, 138, 219, 220, **717–18**, 727; XI, 61, 69, 557, 803, 936; XII, 214, 530, 1122
Worrell, Catherine (mother of CHARLES), VIII, 953
Worrell, Charles, VI, 109, 566; VIII, 563, **953–55**; IX, 394, 395; X, 593, 594; XII, 415, 765
Worrell, Edward, VIII, 953
Worrell, Jonathan (father), VIII, 953
Worrell, Jonathan, VIII, 953
Worrell, William Bryant, VIII, 953
Worsley, Henry (father of MILLER), VI, 817
Worsley, Henry (governor), III, 405
Worsley, Johanna Evered. *See* Harris
Worsley, Mary. *See* Dickonson
Worsley, Miller, VI, 210, **817–18**; VII, 557; VIII, 112; IX, 699, 700
Worth, William Jenkins, VIII, 788
Worthington, Arthur Norreys, XII, 1129
Worthington, Edward Dagge, IX, 728; XII, **1127–29**
Worthington, Frances Louisa. *See* Smith
Worthington, George, VI, 262
Worthington, James, XII, 993
Worthington, John (contractor), XII, 963
Worthington, John (father of EDWARD DAGGE), XII, 1128
Worthington, John (father-in-law of Jonathan BLISS), VI, 75; X, 73
Worthington, Mary. *See* Dagge
Worthington, Mary (Bliss), VI, 74, 75, 76; X, 71, 72
Worthington, Richard, IX, 42
Worthington, Thomas, VIII, 163
Worthington, William, I, 158
Worthley, Hannah (Todd), X, 681
Worts, Elizabeth. *See* Gooderham
Worts, George, XII, 486
Worts, James, XI, 358, 937
Worts, James Gooderham, XI, 938
Worts, James Gooderham, X, 651; XI, 311, 346, 358, 359, 360, 362, 481, **937–38**
Worts, Sarah. *See* Bright
Worts, Thomas Frederick, XI, 938
Woudby. *See* Wappisis
Wowurna, II, xxxvi, 476, 477, 543, **668–70**; III, xxxvii
Wragge, Mary Aloysia. *See* Thompson
Wrangel, Ferdinand Petrovitch, Baron von Wrangel, VIII, 816
Wraxall, Sir Nathaniel William, IV, 26
Wray, Sir Cecil, V, 825
Wren, Sir Christopher, VIII, 444
Wright, Mr (fur trader), V, 512
Wright, Abigail. *See* Wyman

Wright, Abigail (Brigham), VII, 928
Wright, Abraham, XI, 938
Wright, Alexander, VII, 63
Wright*, Alexander Whyte (d. 1919), XI, 307, 648; XII, 500
Wright, Alonzo, IX, 735; XI, 229, 230, 244, 589; XII, **1129–30**
Wright, Amos, VIII, 401; IX, 788; XI, **938–39**
Wright, Anne (Hoyles), VII, 420
Wright, Archibald, XI, 942
Wright, Benjamin (canal builder), VII, 459
Wright, Benjamin (officer), III, 266
Wright, Carroll Davidson, XI, 331
Wright*, Cecil Augustus (1904–67), XII, 887
Wright, Charles (father-in-law of Henry Wolsey BAY-FIELD), XI, 54; XII, 1130
Wright, Charles (son of CHARLES), VII, 146
Wright, Charles, V, 874; VI, **818–19**; VII, 924, 925; XI, 940
Wright, Christiana (Morrison), VII, 928
Wright, Christopher Columbus, VII, 928; IX, 13; XII, 1129
Wright, Edward, I, 144, 252
Wright, Edward Graves Simcoe, XI, 151, 864
Wright, Elizabeth. See Chandler
Wright, Elizabeth (Chipman), VIII, 149, 150
Wright, Fanny Amelia (Bayfield), VIII, 886; XI, 54; XII, **1130–31**
Wright, Francis H., XII, 822
Wright, George, V, **872–73**; VI, 157, 732; VIII, 901
Wright, George, V, 874; VI, 109, 785, 818, 819; VII, 741, **924–26**; VIII, 295, 297, 824; XI, 939, 940; XII, 856
Wright, George, V, 874; VII, 925; VIII, 564; XI, **939–40**
Wright, George J., VI, 392
Wright, George Newenham, VII, 195
Wright, Gustavus Blinn, XI, 844, 845; XII, **1131–33**
Wright, Hannah (Currier), XI, 229
Wright, Henry, VIII, 150, 807
Wright, Henry Hover, VIII, 934; XII, 10, 11, 12
Wright, Henry Press, XII, 815
Wright, Sir James, VII, 506
Wright, Jane. See Nevins
Wright, Joseph, X, 721
Wright, Joshua R., VIII, 691
Wright, Julia Anna. See Sutton
Wright, Lois. See Ricker
Wright, Lois (Heck), VII, 392
Wright, Lydia. See Cambridge
Wright, Maria. See Raymond
Wright, Mark, XI, 137
Wright, Martha. See Bisse
Wright, Mary. See Cochran
Wright, Mary. See Sparks
Wright, Mary (Duncan), V, 281
Wright, Mary Ann (Ridout), VIII, 748; X, 619; XI, 735
Wright, Mary Jane Pearson (Palmer), XII, 815
Wright, Pamela (Hoyle), VIII, 415
Wright, Patience. See Richardson
Wright, Patience. See Lovell
Wright, Phebe. See Cambridge
Wright, Philemon, VII, 927, 928; IX, 734; XII, 1129
Wright, Philemon, VI, 221, 386, 481; VII, 20, 70, 269, 357, 383, 494, 553, **926–29**; IX, 733; X, 691; XI, 237; XII, 1129

Wright, Phoebe (Hoppner), VI, 329
Wright, Richard, X, 718, 719; XI, 502; XII, 785
Wright, Robert, V, 823
Wright, Ruggles (father), VI, 478; VII, 927, 928; VIII, 268, 269; IX, 13; X, 23, 691; XI, 229, 237, 238; XII, 1129
Wright, Ruggles, VIII, 691
Wright, Sally (Smith), IX, 727
Wright, Sarah. See Olmstead
Wright, Sarah Matilda. See Goff
Wright, Silas, VIII, 502
Wright, Susanna. See Turner
Wright, Theresa (Nichol), VI, 539, 540
Wright, Thomas (father of THOMAS), V, 873
Wright, Thomas (father of PHILEMON), VII, 926
Wright, Thomas (politician), V, 873
Wright, Thomas, IV, 128, 607, 610; V, 426, 678, 773, 774, 777, **873–74**; VI, 109, 197, 563, 736, 818; VII, 924; XI, 940
Wright, Tiberius, VII, 927, 928; IX, 13; XII, 1129
Wright, William (father of GEORGE, 1752–1819), V, 872
Wright, William (lawyer), IX, 339
Wright, William (son of GEORGE, 1752–1819), V, 872
Wright, William, IX, 766; X, **718–19**; XI, 502; XII, 785
Wrigley*, George Weston (1847–1907), XII, 584
Wriothesley, Henry, 3rd Earl of Southampton, I, 667
Wrong*, George MacKinnon (1860–1948), XII, 495, 826
Wroth, Robert, II, 23, **670**; III, 276, 517
Württemberg, Duke of. See Friedrich I
Wugk, Charles-Désiré-Joseph, known as Charles Sabatier, VIII, 347; IX, **854–55**; XI, 851; XII, 532
Wugk, Charles-Théophile, IX, 854
Wugk, Sophie-Joseph. See Vercambre
Wulff, George, V, 182
Wurtele, Catherine. See Andrews
Wurtele, Edward Campbell, XI, 808, 809
Wurtele, Eleonor. See Ramsay
Wurtele, Elisabetha (mother of JOSIAS), VI, 819
Wurtele, Eliza Heath Ellen. See Noyes
Wurtele, Jacob, VI, 819
Wurtele, John, VI, 819
Wurtele, Jonathan, VI, 819, 820
Wurtele*, Jonathan Saxton Campbell (1828–1904), XI, 808; XII, 903, 904
Wurtele, Josias, IX, 115
Wurtele, Josias, V, 6, 708; VI, **819–20**
Wyatt. See also Wyet
Wyatt, Charles Burton, V, 855, 856; VI, 5, 647; VII, 36, 37, 175, 286, 438, 439, 865, **929–30**; VIII, 339, 340, 749
Wyatt, Emma (Baker), VIII, 43
Wyatt, Frederick Joseph, IX, 84
Wyatt, James, VII, 929; VIII, 281
Wyatt, Mary. See Rogers
Wyatt, Rachel. See Lunn
Wyatt, Sir Thomas, I, 157
Wydowse (Woodhouse), Thomas, I, 374, 377, 378
Wyer, Elizabeth Margaret Sheddon (Parker), IX, 619
Wyer, Mary (Adams; Humbert), VII, 424
Wyer, Thomas, V, 336, 337; VI, 562; IX, 263
Wyet, Sylvester, I, 5, 306, 364, 451, **671–72**
Wyeth, Nathaniel Jarvis, VIII, 578
Wyld, James, VIII, 385
Wylde, Charles James, IX, 839
Wylde, John Thomas, IX, 839

Wylie, David, IX, 100; XII, 330
Wylie, James, XII, 85
Wyllie, Jean (Shedden), X, 650
Wyllie, Robert Crichton, X, 608
Wyman, Abigail (Wright), VII, 926
Wyndham, Anne Barbara Frances. *See* Villiers
Wyndham, Charles, 2nd Earl of Egremont, IV, xxxiii, xxxv, xxxviii, 571, 572; V, 4
Wyndham, Charles William, VII, 477
Wyndham, George Francis, 4th Earl of Egremont, X, 636
Wyndham, Thomas, I, 316
Wynne, Edward, I, 162, 614, **672**
Wynne, Peter, VIII, 489
Wynne, William, VIII, 489
Wynyard, Frederica (Hurd), VIII, 418
Wynyard, George, VI, 713
Wysenberk. *See* Weissenberg
Wyss, Barbara (Barbe) Ann (Rindisbacher), VI, 648
Wythes, George, VIII, 965
Wzôkhilain. *See* Osunkirhine

XAVIER, François, IV, 13

YAGHKAPOSIN (Squash Cutter), IV, 27
Yale, Eliza (Peers), IX, 625
Yale, James Murray, VII, 568; IX, 625; X, 6, **719–20**; XI, 882
Yandell, Maria Ann (Hincks), X, 350
Yarker, George Wheatley, VII, 472
Yarmouth, Countess of. *See* Wendt
Yates, Albert Hinde, XI, 526
Yates, Hannah. *See* Palmer
Yates, Helen (McDonell), V, 517
Yates, Horatio, XI, 263, **940–41**; XII, 990
Yates, Hulda (Purdy), VII, 712
Yates, James, VIII, 836; IX, 337
Yates, Jane. *See* Bower
Yates, John Barentse, IX, 545, 546
Yates, Mary Ann, IV, 555
Yates, William, XI, 940
Yatza, XII, 289
Yell, Archibald, VII, 364
Yellowhead, IX, 589
Yellowhead, Elizabeth (wife of MUSQUAKIE), IX, 590
Yellowhead, Isaac, IX, 590
Yellowhead, Jane, IX, 590
Yellowhead, William. *See* Musquakie
Yeo, Ann. *See* Orsborn
Yeo, Damaris. *See* Sargent
Yeo, George Cosby, V, 8, 877
Yeo, James (father of JAMES), IX, 855
Yeo, James (father of Sir JAMES LUCAS), V, 874
Yeo, James, VI, 109; VIII, 270; IX, **855–57**; X, 183, 184; XI, 665; XII, 838
Yeo*, James (1832–1916), IX, 856
Yeo, Sir James Lucas, V, 83, 400, 401, 696, 697, **874–77**; VI, 309, 469, 541, 638, 730, 803, 818; VII, 46, 494, 709, 710, 888; VIII, 237, 238, 239, 795
Yeo*, John (1837–1924), IX, 856, 857
Yeo, Mary. *See* Francis
Yeo, William, IX, 856, 857
Yeomans. *See also* Youmans
Yeomans, Lené (Chasley), X, 163

Yeoward, Thomas, V, 635; VI, 531; VIII, 321
Yerxa, Mary (Pickard), XI, 688
Yockney, Samuel, V, 679
Yong (Yonge). *See* Young
Yonge, Charlotte Mary, XI, 333
Yonge, Elizabeth (Colborne, Baroness Seaton), VII, 150; VIII, 437; IX, 138
Yonge, Sir George, V, 755
Yonge, James (clergyman), IX, 138
Yonge, James (son of JAMES), II, 672
Yonge, James, II, **670–72**
Yonge, Jane. *See* Crampporn
Yonge, Jane (Harris), XI, 388
Yonge, Joanna. *See* Blackaller
Yonge, John, II, 670
Yonge, Mary. *See* Upton
Yool (Yuil), Margaret (Dougall), XI, 268, 270
Yore. *See also* Ewer
Yore (Ewer), William, VI, 243
York, Duke of. *See* Edward IV; Frederick Augustus; James II
York, Erasmus. *See* Kallihirua
York, Jack, IV, **777–79**; V, 639; VI, 262, 611; VII, 697
York, Sir John, I, 316
Yorke, Anna Maria (Head, Lady Head), IX, 381, 383
Yorke, Charles, IV, xxxiii, xli, xlii, xlvii, 348; V, 605; VI, 491
Yorke, Gilbert, I, 85, 317
Yorke, John (colonel), IX, 177
Yorke, John (lieutenant-colonel), IV, 293, 522; V, 223, 766; VI, 194
Yorke, Joseph, 1st Baron Dover, IV, 686
Yorke, Mary (Humphreys), V, 438
Yorke, Mary Alice (Davie), XII, 227
Yorke, Philip, 1st Earl of Hardwicke, IV, 50, 348
You, Magdelaine (Huguet, *dit* Latour; Duval), VI, 230
You, Marie-Renée. *See* Turcot
You, Pierre, II, 672
You de La Découverte, Madeleine. *See* Just
You de La Découverte, Marie-Anne (Richard), I, 573; II, 673
You de La Découverte, Philippe, II, 673; III, 450, 520
You de La Découverte, Pierre, I, 573; II, 125, 160, **672–73**; IV, 235
Youden, Captain, XI, 642
Youell, Anne (Little), XI, 521
Youle, Sarah (Hind), XI, 416
Youmans, Arthur, XII, 219, 220
Youmans, David, X, 640
Youmans (Yeomans), Horace, XII, 322
Youmans, Letitia. *See* Creighton
Young, Abraham, XI, 888
Young, Adelaide Annabella. *See* Dalton
Young, Agnes. *See* Renny
Young, Alexander, V, 460, 879
Young*, Sir Allen William (1827–1915), X, 320; XII, 955
Young, Amelia Jane. *See* Tilley
Young, Andrew, VI, 377
Young, Ann. *See* Walsh
Young, Anne. *See* Coleman
Young, Anne. *See* Tobin
Young, Archibald, X, 128
Young, Archibald Hope, V, 476

Young, Sir Aretas William, VI, **820–22**; VII, 103, 352, 742, 925; XI, 940

Young, Arthur, IV, 738; IX, 330

Young, Brigham, VIII, 784; X, 320

Young, Catherine Ainslie, V, 879

Young, Cecilia Eliza Cowan. *See* Cameron

Young, Charles, VIII, 296, 531, 564, 956; IX, 179; XII, 563

Young, Charles Bedford, XII, 240

Young, Christian. *See* Ainslie

Young, David, XI, 941

Young, David, XI, **941–42**

Young, David Douglas, IX, 773

Young, Edward, XII, 1057, 1058

Young*, Egerton Ryerson (1840–1909), IX, 537

Young, Elizabeth (Headley; Perkins), V, 664

Young, Elizabeth (Stark), IX, 741

Young, Elizabeth Ainslie, V, 879

Young, Esther (Douse), IX, 222

Young*, George (1821–1910), X, 471; XI, 571, 936

Young, George Edme, V, 179, 564

Young, George H., XII, 983

Young, George Paxton, XI, **942–43**

Young, George Renny, VI, 322; VII, 930, 934; VIII, 193, 657, 904, 905, 922, **955–59**; IX, 178, 179, 426, 567; X, 7, 363; XI, 944, 945, 946; XII, 231, 829

Young, Gilbert Ainslie, V, 879

Young, James (brother of JOHN, 1808–73), X, 720

Young, James (chemist), IX, 311, 312; XI, 929

Young, James (father of JOHN, d. 1825) VI, 822

Young, James (father of JOHN, 1808–73), X, 720

Young, James, I, **672–73**; II, 266, 308

Young*, James (1835–1913), XII, 644

Young, Jane. *See* Brooking

Young, Jane (Lavender; Barker), XII, 55

Young, Janet. *See* Gibson

Young, Janet (mother of JOHN, 1773–1837), VII, 930

Young, John, XII, 50

Young, John, V, 6, 83, 84, 100, 101, 133, 212, 234, 270, 278, 317, 373, 464, 484, 489, 493, 494, 495, 603, 648, 650, 691, 692, 695, 696, 713, 746, 816, **877–83**; VI, 18, 225, 367, 392, 423, 424, 476, 524, 532, 533, 556, 642, 712; VII, 614, 767, 769, 771, 784, 785, 786; VIII, 961

Young, John, V, 78, 279, 320, 321, 770; VI, 93, 472, **822–23**; VII, 820

Young, John, V, 612, 853; VI, 61, 315, 322, 461, 801; VII, 12, 22, 24, 108, 224, 270, 278, 279, 492, 537, 723, 816, 875, **930–35**; VIII, 222, 416, 710, 903, 922, 955; IX, 40, 550; XI, 943, 944, 945; XII, 841, 1040

Young, John (1808–73), VII, 909; VIII, 43, 44, 294, 875; IX, 368, 512; X, **720–22**; XI, 126, 128, 423; XII, 886

Young, John (1811–78), VIII, 138, 220; IX, 83, 224, 274, 367, 397, 422, 823; X, 522, 591, 613, 683, **722–28**; XI, 12, 13, 41, 211, 238, 412, 510, 511, 557, 586, 758, 850, 851; XII, 214, 261, 262, 350, 391, 809, 963

Young, John, 1st Baron Lisgar, IX, 845; X, **728–29**; XI, 280, 636, 741, 760, 769; XII, 33, 186, 602, 1007

Young, John Wilson, XI, 832

Young, Joseph-Marie, IX, 453; XII, **1133–34**

Young, Lucy. *See* Frederick

Young, Lydia Marion. *See* Brown

Young, Margaret. *See* Mason

Young, Margaret (Kilborn), VI, 377

Young, Marie (Vondenvelden), V, 834

Young, Mary. *See* Kerr

Young, Mary (Creighton), XI, 216

Young, Mary (Richards), XII, 892

Young, Mary (Waldron), V, 837

Young, Mary Cordelia (wife of THOMAS, d. 1860), VIII, 959

Young, Monique-Ursule. *See* Baby

Young, Plomer, VII, 696, 779; VIII, 521, 788; IX, 72, 278, **857–58**

Young, Robert (father-in-law of John WALDRON), V, 837

Young, Robert (officer), VII, 743

Young, Robert (superintendent), VI, 627

Young, Robert (uncle of DAVID), XI, 941

Young*, Robert (1834–1904), XI, 466; XII, 398

Young, Samuel, V, 837

Young, Sarah, Lady Young. *See* Cox

Young, Sarah Marie (Smith), XI, 827, 832

Young, Sarah Phillis (Macaulay), VIII, 513

Young, Thomas, VIII, 959

Young, Thomas, I, **673**

Young, Thomas, VIII, 14, 485, **959–61**; XI, 427

Young, Thomas Ainslie, V, 879, 882; VI, 421; VIII, 423, **961–63**; XI, 36

Young, Walter, IV, 165

Young, William (author), XII, 316

Young, William (father of JOHN, 1773–1837), VII, 930

Young, William (father of JOHN, 1811–78), X, 192, 722

Young, William (father of Sir WILLIAM ALEXANDER GEORGE), XI, 949

Young, Sir William, VII, 143, 144, 576, 875, 904, 930, 932, 933; VIII, 193, 357, 416, 417, 569, 657, 904, 955, 956, 957, 958; IX, 177, 178, 225, 293, 294, 427, 567, 731, 747, 791, 839, 840; X, 71, 73, 85, 352, 367, 387, 438, 457, 685, 728; XI, 30, 149, 398, 525, 686, 717, 754, 755, 773, 925, **943–49**; XII, 31, 34, 35, 229

Young, Sir William Alexander George, X, 117; XI, **949–51**

Young Man Chief. *See* Maskepetoon

Youville, Charles-Marie-Madeleine d', II, 673; IV, 235, **779–80**; V, 202, 293

Youville, François-Madeleine d', II, 673; IV, 235, 779

Youville, Joseph-François d', II, 673; IV, 235, 779

Youville, Marie-Marguerite d'. *See* Dufrost de Lajemmerais

Yroquet. *See* Iroquet

Yuil. *See* Yool

Yule, James Colton, XII, 225, 1076

Yule, John, VIII, 916

Yule, Pamelia Sarah. *See* Vining

Yule, William, VI, 344

Yung. *See also* Young

Yung, Nicolas, XII, 1133

Yung, Thérèse-Élisabeth. *See* Marcus

Yung, *dit* Lejeune. *See* Young

Yvon. *See* Phlem

ZAINER, Günther, XII, 16

Zamet, Sébastien, I, 483

Zeisberger, David, V, 883

Zeisberger, David, III, 319, 607; IV, 260, 301, 302; V, 346, 799, **883–85**; VI, 189; VII, 244; VIII, 411

Zeisberger, Rosina (Anna) (mother of DAVID), V, 883

Zeisberger, Susanna. *See* Lekron

Zemballe, Marie-Louise (Lemoine), III, 379
Zeno, Antonio, I, 316, **680–81**
Zeno, Nicolò, I, 316, **680–81**
Zheewegonab, V, **885–86**
Zichmni (potentate), I, 680
Zimmerman, Emmeline. *See* Dunn
Zimmerman, Margaret Ann. *See* Woodruff
Zimmerman, Samuel, VI, 200; VIII, 81, 82, **963–67**; IX, 577, 647; X, 394, 515; XI, 128, 416, 464, 618; XII, 72, 676, 884
Zimmermann, Pierre-Joseph-Guillaume, XII, 977

Zinzendorf, Nikolaus Ludwig, Count von Zinzendorf, III, 147, 607; V, 883
Zitelli, Zepherino, XII, 509, 510, 820
Zoëgal, Joseph, XI, 694
Zorn, Jacques, IV, 618
Zouberbuhler, Catherine (Silver), IV, 781
Zouberbuhler, Sebastian, III, 513; IV, 526, **780–81**; V, 250
Zouch, Ann. *See* Ritchie
Zouch, John Thomas, V, 386
Zouche, Baron. *See* Bisshopp
Zouche, Baroness. *See* Southwell